P9-CME-791

ENCYCLOPEDIA
OF
AMERICAN QUAKER GENEALOGY

WILLIAM WADE HINSHAW, Washington, D.C.
Author and Publisher

THOMAS WORTH MARSHALL, Washington, D. C.
Editor and Compiler

DR. HARLOW LINDLEY, Columbus, Ohio
(Collaborator and Historian for Ohio)

THE OHIO QUAKER GENEALOGICAL RECORDS
(Now to be Published)

LISTING: Marriages, Births, Deaths, Certificates, Disownments, etc., and Much Collateral Information of Interest to Genealogy, History, Biology, and Social Conditions.

VOLUME V

(NOTE: This book is one of a two-vol-set, designated as Volumes IV & V, and contains about one-half of the Ohio Quaker Genealogical Records; the other half will be found in Volume IV.)

CONTENTS: Volume V contains the genealogical records found in all original books (known to exist) of the 21 Monthly Meetings listed below and now belonging to and under the jurisdiction of The Wilmington Yearly Meeting, Clinton Co., Ohio, and/or The Indiana Yearly Meeting, Richmond, Indiana. All of the 21 Monthly Meetings are located in south central, western and southwestern Ohio. (See Volume IV for the records of 25 Monthly Meetings in eastern and northern Ohio, 4 Monthly Meetings in western Pa., and one Monthly Meeting in Michigan.)

N. B.: All Branches are included, viz: Orthodox, Hicksite, Wilbur and Guerney Friends. The Genealogical Records of Meetings of all Types are kept by Monthly Meetings. (The Monthly Meeting is the executive body of the Quaker organization. It is attended by delegates from the several Meetings for Worship which belong to and are governed by it. It is a business meeting which administers the affairs of its subordinate meetings, viz: Meetings for Worship and their Preparative Meetings. Although hundreds of Meetings for Worship have been established in Ohio, their genealogical records are found in the books of the Monthly Meetings which govern them.)

Names of the 21 Mo. Mtgs., whose records are contained in this book, and dates of organization:

1. Miami, Warren Co., O. 1803
2. Fairfield, Highland Co., O. 1807
3. West Branch, Miami Co., O. 1807
4. Center, Clinton Co., O. 1807
5. Elk, Preble Co., O. 1809
6. Caesar's Creek, Clinton Co., O. 1810
7. Fall Creek, Highland Co., O. 1811
8. Mill Creek, Miami Co., O. 1811
9. Clear Creek, Clinton Co., O. 1812
10. Union, Miami Co., O. 1813
11. Cincinnati, Hamilton Co., O. 1815
12. Newberry, Clinton Co., O. 1816
13. Lees Creek, Highland Co., O. 1817
14. Springfield, Clinton Co., O. 1818
15. Westfield, Preble Co., O. 1821
16. Green Plain, Clark Co., O. 1821
17. Springborough, Warren Co., O. 1824
18. Dover, Clinton Co., O. 1824
19. Hopewell, Clinton Co., O.
20. Wilmington, Clinton Co., O. 1868
21. Van Wert, Van Wert Co., O. 1875

Data extracted from original Books of Minutes and Records by:
Cleo F. Thornburgh, Dorothy H. (THORNBURGH) Fausey,
Mrs. J. E. McMullan and Margaret S. Norris,
under the personal direction of
Dr. Harlow Lindley, of Columbus, Ohio

Data edited, compiled and tabulated by
Thomas Worth Marshall, of Washington, D. C.

Mrs. J. E. McMullan, of Huntington, Indiana,
Special Assistant Compiler

All work under the personal supervision of
William Wade Hinshaw, Washington, D. C.

Originally published: Ann Arbor, Michigan, 1946
Reprinted: Genealogical Publishing Co., Inc.
Baltimore, 1973, 1994
Library of Congress Catalogue Card Number 68-31728
International Standard Book Number 0-8063-0549-5
Made in the United States of America

AFFECTIONATELY AND FILIALLY
DEDICATED TO
THE MEMORY OF ALL OUR QUAKER ANCESTORS
WHOSE METICULOUSLY KEPT RECORDS
FURNISH THE DATA FOR THIS
ENCYCLOPEDIA OF AMERICAN QUAKER GENEALOGY

F O R E W O R D

Before starting to search these records, the ancestor-seeker should give careful study to the Introductions (to Volumes IV & V) by Thomas W. Marshall; also, to the Historical sketches by Dr. Harlow Lindley. To save much time and possible confusion, the list of abbreviations should be memorized. They are all simple and easy to understand. Each abbreviation "stands for" several words, and, sometimes, for an entire sentence. Had we not made use of them, the bulk of the material would have filled double, or triple, the space now occupied. From the beginning, almost 300 years ago, Clerks and Recorders have, in the writing up of minutes and records, followed certain forms which were set out for their guidance by those who worked directly under the instructions of George Fox, the founder of The Society of Friends. Our abbreviations, covering many such forms, have been made up primarily to save space and time; and, secondarily, to save costs.

The searcher should clearly understand that all data included in these books are condensed transcriptions from actual minutes and records found in original books of Monthly Meetings; and, therefore, are SOURCE MATERIAL. Beyond making occasional notes, where they could be helpful to the searcher, and arranging the data into alphabetical and chronological order, all entries are intended to convey the full information necessary to genealogical research, as found in original books; and nothing more. The original data is furnished in these books in such form that the searcher should find it easily possible to trace out family lines, if directions are followed, insofar as these records permit.

In tracing family lineages through these records, the searcher should keep several points in mind, as outlined below:-

(a) The genealogical records of all members of Meetings of all types are kept by Monthly (Business) Meetings, which are attended by delegates sent by their sub-ordinate meetings:-Meetings for Worship and their Preparative Meetings. The Monthly Meeting is the executive body of the Quaker Organization. It is a business meeting which administers the affairs of its sub-ordinate Meetings, of which there are usually several under control of each Monthly Meeting.

The Monthly Meeting, as stated, keeps all records, such as births, deaths, burials, marriages, disownments, certificates of removal, members received and released, etc., for all Meetings for Worship which it controls; and, since these are the records which are of interest to genealogy, it is usually only necessary to search the Monthly Meeting books for genealogical purposes.

(b) "The Meeting for Worship is the core and center of all Quaker organizations. For, without the frequent gathering for Divine Light and Leading, none of the other Quaker activities would be possible."(John Cox Jr.) Here Quakers meet, in their meeting houses, or in private homes; their meeting begins in Silence, and often no word is spoken throughout the entire time of the meeting, although any member may speak if spiritually moved to do so. Many men and women of recognized high spiritual "leading" have been made Ministers; but for almost two centuries, Ministers were not paid salaries, although their traveling expenses were usually paid when making Religious Visits to other meetings than their own. At present (1946) Quaker Ministers usually receive small allowances from their meetings, although not enough to be called salaries. They are expected to make their living by outside activities.

(c) Every member of The Society of Friends is registered as a member of a Meeting for Worship and of the Monthly Meeting to which it belongs. An established Meeting for Worship is usually allowed its own Preparative Meeting, made up of its overseers, which attends to the general care of the affairs of the Meeting.

(d) The YEARLY MEETING is the law-giving body governing all other bodies, and is attended by delegates from all lower branches, although only delegates from the Quarterly Meetings are allowed to vote. The entire Quaker organization is purely Democratic in nature and form. For example:- when a question comes up among the Overseers of the Meeting for Worship, it is taken to the Monthly Meeting for decision; unless there is serious objection the decision of the Monthly Meeting is final. When some member has been disowned, and the disowned member feels he was wronged, he can carry the matter to the Quarterly Meeting; and if not satisfied with that Meeting's decision, he can carry the matter on to the Yearly Meeting for a final decision. It works out like a lawsuit which is carried from court to higher court, until it reaches the United States Supreme Court.

(e) MEMBERSHIP: Members are received into membership in one of the following ways:- (1) by certificate from another Monthly Meeting; (2) by their own request; (3) by birthright; (4) by Letter of Transfer from a church of another denomination; (5) by convincement; and (6) by being transferred without a certificate from a "mother" Monthly Meeting to a newly organized Monthly Meeting which has been set-off from the "mother" Monthly Meeting, in which case the member is called a Charter Member of the new Meeting.

FOREWORD

(f) MEETING HOUSES are usually owned by the Meeting for Worship. Monthly Meetings are often held at the different meeting houses under their control, rotating between or among them. Sometimes a Monthly Meeting is always held at the same meeting house, month after month. The name of the Monthly Meeting may be the same name as a Meeting for Worship, or it may have an entirely different name. The Monthly Meeting is a separate ENTITY from any Meeting for Worship under its control.

(g) CERTIFICATES OF REMOVAL:- When a member wishes to remove to a locality which is within the verge, or boundaries of another Monthly Meeting, regardless of the distance away, he is required by the Discipline to ask for and receive a certificate of removal, transferring his membership to the other Monthly Meeting. When a request for such a certificate is made, a committee is appointed to examine into his conversation, business affairs, etc.; if nothing be found to obstruct, the certificate is issued. Such a certificate is regarded as a guaranty that he is a member in good standing, has paid his just debts, and fulfilled all other obligations. If an obstruction be found, the certificate is withheld until the obstruction shall have been removed.

(h) CERTIFICATES TO MARRY:- When a man wishes to marry a woman who is a member of another Monthly Meeting, he requests a certificate to that meeting in order to marry there, usually, though not always, giving the name of the woman he intends to marry. Such a certificate is NOT a transfer of membership, but is a certificate of good character and shows that he is free of all other marriage engagements. Without such a certificate, he will not be "liberated" to marry the woman, by the meeting to which she belongs. If allowed to marry, the Meeting carefully supervises the marriage to see that it is "orderly accomplished", according to the Rules of Discipline. Until within the past sixty years, members were strictly forbidden to marry non-members, on pain of disownment.

(i) BIBLE RECORDS:- The Family Bible record may show that the parents were married at a certain meeting house. But that does not signify that the record of their marriage certificate will be found in the books of a Monthly Meeting of that name. The Meeting House belongs to a Meeting for Worship. If at that time, the Meeting for Worship did not have a Monthly Meeting of its own, but belonged to a Monthly Meeting of another name, the record of the marriage certificate will be found in the Marriage Register of that Monthly Meeting. When new Monthly Meetings were organized in rapid succession, as was the case in Ohio, this must be taken into consideration by searchers.

(j) BIRTHS;- Only the births of children born while a family belongs to a certain Monthly Meeting are, usually, recorded in the books of that Monthly Meeting; to locate the births of all children of any family, searchers should examine the birth records of each Monthly Meeting to which that family ever belonged. Also, when a certificate is issued to a man & his wife & children, transferring their memberships to another Monthly Meeting, the certificate lists only the children which are not adults; separate certificates are issued to the adult children.

(k) Members often live in one State, near the border, and belong to a Meeting for Worship in that neighborhood, and at the same time belong to a Monthly Meeting located across the State line in another State. For: when certificates of removal are issued, they are addressed to the Monthly Meeting located nearest to the members' new residences; and, this Monthly Meeting may be across the State border in an adjoining State. For example: Until 1808, when White Water Monthly Meeting was established in Wayne Co., Ind., Friends who removed to and settled in Indiana, were members of Miami Monthly Meeting, Ohio and/or West Branch Monthly Meeting, Ohio. Then, when White Water Monthly Meeting was organized (1808) these Friends' memberships were transferred to that Monthly Meeting; also, a Meeting for Worship was established at White Water in 1806, to which these Friends living in Indiana belonged, although their genealogical records were kept (until 1808) in one or another Monthly Meeting in Ohio. So, until 1808, Friends living in Indiana, and wishing to marry each other, had to travel to their Monthly Meeting in Ohio in order to gain permission to marry, making two such trips; then, if liberated to marry, they could be married in their own Indiana homes, or, after 1806, in White Water Meeting House; or they could be married in one or another Ohio Meeting House, as they may have chosen to do. Men often traveled, on horse back, hundreds of miles to marry the girls of their choice, who belonged to some other Monthly Meeting in a distant State. This was a common occurrence during the early days of Ohio, when young men who had migrated with their parents to Ohio, journeyed back to their former homes to marry their childhood sweethearts. On such a journey, a young man would likely take along an extra horse, in order to bring his young wife home with him. Quakers were ever romantic. Their romances abound in the records of all Monthly Meetings. Until now, these precious books, so full of romance, have been hidden away and have seldom been read by any persons other than the clerks and recorders who copied them originally.

WILLIAM WADE HINSHAW

The Mayflower
Washington, D. C.
(1946 A.D.)

I N T R O D U C T I O N

When the Quakers began settlements in Ohio and Indiana, their meetings were established by and attached to Redstone, (Pa.) Quarterly Meeting in Baltimore Yearly Meeting. This condition continued until 1813, when Ohio Yearly Meeting was established by Baltimore Yearly Meeting and took jurisdiction over all meetings in Ohio, western Pennsylvania and Indiana. Indiana Yearly Meeting was established in 1821 and took jurisdiction over western Ohio and all of Indiana. With the Hicksite separation, separate Yearly Meetings were established to serve the Hicksite Monthly Meetings in the territory of Ohio Yearly Meeting and those in the territory of Indiana Yearly Meeting. About 1854 Ohio Yearly Meeting was divided into the Gurney and Wilbur branches. The Gurney branch holds its Yearly Meeting at Damascus--the Wilbur branch at Stillwater, near Barnesville. About 1892, Wilmington Yearly Meeting was organized and took jurisdiction over the meetings in south-central Ohio which had previously belonged to Indiana Yearly Meeting. Indiana Yearly Meeting still has jurisdiction over meetings in west-central and south-western Ohio.

The Monthly Meetings whose records are abstracted in this volume are those in the areas of Wilmington Yearly Meeting and Indiana Yearly Meeting. Records of meetings formerly held in these areas, but now laid down (including Hicksite) are included. Attempt has been made to designate all Hicksite records by the letter H.

Records of Monthly Meetings in the areas of the two Ohio Yearly Meetings may be found in Volume IV of this Encyclopedia.

The first Friends migrating to Ohio became members of Hopewell Monthly Meeting, Virginia, and a little later of Westland or Redstone Monthly Meetings, Pennsylvania until they could establish meetings of their own. As Monthly Meetings were established in Ohio these Friends automatically became members of the new meetings within whose territories they happened to reside. No certificates of transfer were issued and no list of names was entered in the records of either meeting. Similarly, when an Ohio Meeting was divided to set up a new Monthly Meeting, the membership was divided according to place of residence and no list of members of the new meeting was entered in the records of either meeting. The names of persons who became members of new meetings in this way will disappear from the records of the parent meeting but may be followed to the records of any new meeting in which they may appear by reference to the family name index at the end of the book.

Washington, D. C. THOMAS WORTH MARSHALL

C O N T E N T S

ABBREVIATIONS

b	born
bur	buried
cert	certificate
ch	child, children
co	chosen overseer (s)
com	complained, complained of
con	condemned
d	died
dec	deceased
dis	disowned, disowned for
dt	daughter, daughters
fam	family
form	formerly
gc	granted certificate
gct	granted certificate to
gl	granted letter
h	husband
jas	joined another society
ltm	liberated to marry, left at liberty to marry
m	marry, married, marrying, marriage
mbr	member
mbrp	membership
mcd	married contrary to discipline
MH	meeting house
MM	monthly meeting
mos	married out of society
mou	married out of unity
mtg	meeting
prc	produced a certificate
prcf	produced a certificate from
QM	quarterly meeting
rec	receive, received
recrq	received by request
relfc	released from care for
relrq	released by request
rem	remove, removed
rm	reported married
rmt	reported married to
roc	received on certificate
rocf	received on certificate from
rol	received on letter
rolf	received on letter from
rpd	reported
rq	request, requests, requested
rqc	requested certificate
rqct	requested certificate to
rqcuc	requested to come under care (of mtg)
rst	reinstate, reinstated
s	son, sons
uc	under care (of mtg)
w	wife
YM	yearly meeting

MIAMI MONTHLY MEETING

Miami Monthly Meeting, located on the Little Miami River in Warren County, was the first to be established in southwestern Ohio. It was the center from which Quakerism spread over western Ohio and throughout Indiana - the territory now embraced in Wilmington, Indiana and Western Yearly Meetings. The settlement of Friends in the section about the present site of Waynesville began in the closing years of the eighteenth century. A meeting for worship was established about 1801. Miami Monthly Meeting was opened 10 Mo. 13, 1803, by permission of Redstone Quarterly Meeting, held at Westland, Pa., 9 Mo. 5, 1803. The parent monthly meeting was Westland.

Prior to the establishment of Miami Monthly Meeting, the Friends moving into this section left their certificates of membership at Westland Monthly Meeting, Washington County, Pa., or at Concord Monthly Meeting, Belmont County, Ohio. The former meeting had been in existence since 1785; the latter was not set up until about the end of 1801. Usually the records of certificates received do not mention the place of settlement of the new members, but one exception to this rule has been noted. Under date of 12 Mo. 25, 1802, Westland minutes record the receipt of nine certificates from Bush River Monthly Meeting, S. C., with the statement that the persons named were settled at little Miami. These certificates were dated 9 Mo. 25, 1802, and were for the following named persons: Samuel Kelly, wife, Hannah, and six children; Abijah O'Neal, wife, Anna, and seven children; James Mills, wife, Lydia, and nine children; Robert Kelly, wife, Sarah, and two children; Alexander Mills, wife, Eunice, and four children; Layton Jay, wife, Elizabeth, and six children; Ellis Pugh and wife, Rachel; Mary Paty, wife of Charles; Ann Horner, wife of Thomas. There are indications that some of the men mentioned above, including Abijah O'Neal, Samuel Kelly and James Mills, had been settled on the Little Miami for two or three years previous to the date of their certificates.

There is no complete list of the names of those who constituted the original membership of Miami Monthly Meeting. A few of them, in addition to those already mentioned above were, Abigail Cleaver (wife of Ezekiel), Amos Cook, Elizabeth Cook, David Falkner, Judith Faulkner, Robert Furnas, David Holloway, Andrew Hoover, Edward Kinley, Margaret Kinley, Samuel Linton, Bathsheba Lupton, Martha Painter, Isaac Perkins, Thomas Perkins, Phiniah Perkins, Rowland Richards, Lydia Richards, John Smith, Samuel Spray, Mary Spray, William Walker, Jehu Wilson, Dinah Wilson and Jemima Wright. Abigail Cleaver, Abijah O'Neal, Jehu Wilson and Dinah Wilson were chosen as elders; Abigail Cleaver, Hannah Kelly, Isaac Perkins and William Walker, overseers; Samuel Linton and Judith Faulkner, clerks; Anna O'Neal, assistant clerk; Samuel Spray and Samuel Kelly, representatives to the quarterly meeting at Redstone; Robert Furnas, recorder of births and deaths.

The new meeting had a phenominal growth from the beginning. The migration from the south to the Northwest, which disrupted so many meetings in North Carolina, South Carolina and Georgia, was in full tide and for several years Miami was the principal objective point of the home seekers. In the first five years of its existence, Miami Monthly Meeting received about 550 certificates of membership from other monthly meetings. Of these certificates about 170 were from South Carolina, 150 from North Carolina, 75 from Virginia, 50 from Tennessee and 35 from Georgia. Others were from New Jersey, Pennsylvania and Maryland. The total number of memberships received on the basis of these certificates was about 2200.

The first meeting house, a log structure, was built in 1805, according to account. Previous to that time meetings were held in private houses. In 1811, a brick meeting house was constructed. In 1828 the meeting was divided into two branches. The followers of the doctrines of Elias Hicks constituted one branch, called Hicksite after the name of their leader. Those who rejected Hicks's teachings formed the other branch, called Orthodox. The Orthodox branch, being in the minority, withdrew to the old log meeting house, while the Hicksites remained in possession of the brick house.

Some of the inferior meetings set up under Miami Meeting were: Lees Creek, Todsfork, West Branch, Elk Creek, Caesar's Creek, Clear Creek, Fall Creek, Union, Center, Fairfield, Hopewell, Darby Creek.

At the time of the separation the Hicksites retained and continued to use all the record books except the men's minute book. This latter book appears to have fallen into Orthodox hands as it is now at the Yearly Meeting House (Orthodox) at Richmond, Indiana.

RECORDS

AARONS
1817, 2, 26. Samuel rocf Chester MM, N. J., dtd 1817,11,7

ADAMS
----, --, --. Ezra b 1794, 3, 1 d 1865,11,23; m Sarah ----- b 1796,5,23 d 1883,5,16

Ch:		
Isaac	b 1817, 1, 1	d 1844, 3, 5
Charles	" 1818, 9, 3	" 1903, --,--
Savory	" 1820, 12, 28	" 1900, 4,12
David	" 1822, 10, 4	" 1824, 2,23
Jason	" 1825, 1, 29	" 1827, 8,13
Rachel	" 1827, 8, 9	" 1860, 1,27
Charity	" 1829, 5, 15	
Maryann	" 1830, 11, 27	" 1892, 1,10
Amos P.	" 1833, 8, 19	" 1886, 6, 8
Lydia	" 1835, 7, 14	" 1850, 3,21
Sarah B.	" 1839, 3, 6	" 1843, 8,16
Abi	" 1842, 4, 2	

1805, 11, 14. William & w, Millicent, rocf Deep Creek MM, N. C., dtd 1805,4,6
1817, 4, 30. Thomas [Addams] & w, Ann, & dt, Ruth, rocf Short Creek MM, dtd 1816,11,19
1819, 6, 30. Thomas & fam gct Elk MM
1820, 2, 23. John & w, Ruth, & s, Jesse, rocf Byberry MM, Pa., dtd 1819,12,28
1820, 5, 31. Benjamin rocf Wrightstown MM, Pa., dtd 1820,2,9
1821, 7, 25. Rebecca recrq
1821, 7, 25. Sarah recrq
1822, 12, 25. Ezra recrq with permission of Byburry MM
1824, 1, 28. Benjamin & fam gct Middletown MM, Pa.
1824, 6, 30. Sarah recrq
1824, 9, 29. Isaac, Charles & Savory recrq
1828, 8, 27. Jeddiah recf Westfield MM, dtd 1828,5,28
1829, 1, 28. Ezra dis jH
1829, 7, 29. Ruth dis jH
1829, 8, 26. Sarah dis jH
1838, 8, 22. Mary M. rocf Fairfield MM, dtd 1838,4,26
1840, 5, 27. Jesse dis mou
1840, 7, 22. Jesse dis mou (H)
1842, 3, 23. Isaac dis mou
1846, 8, 26. Rachel dis jas (H)
1847, 6, 23. Savory dis jas (H)
1847, 10, 27. Charity Manington (form Adams) dis mou (H)
1854, 1, 25. Amos dis disunity (H)
1854, 2, 22. Mary Ann dis jas (H)
1859, 12, 21. Abi dis jas (H)
1887, 2, 23. Mary L. (form Cadwallader) relrq
1889, 7, 24. Charles dropped from mbrp (H)
1907, 2, 20. Stella & Prudence recrq
1914, 5, 27. Stella & Prudence dropped from mbrp

ADDINGTON
1807, 6, 11. John & ch, Sarah, Elizabeth & James, roc dtd 1806,9,20

ALBERTSON
1830, 2, 24. Josiah & w, Hannah, rocf Caesars Creek MM, dtd 1829,12,31
1830, 9, 29. Josiah & w, Hannah, gct Caesars Creek MM

ALCOR
1919, 3, 30. Ruth Palmer recrq (H)

ALLEN
----, --, --. Francis H. b 1823,3,31 d 1902, 11,3 bur Milford, O.; m Malinda WAY b 1827,7,11 d 1912,6,24 bur Milford, O. (H)
Ch: William F. b 1858, 4, 1
Phebe H. " 1860, 12, 20 d 1896, 9,10

1808, 9, 10. Mary [Allan] rocf Hopewell MM, dtd 1808,5,2
1811, 5, 29. Jackson & w, Sarah, & ch, Edward, Mary, Joseph, Solomon, Rebecca, Alex, Sarah, Anna, Harmony & Wesley, rocf Hopewell MM
1811, 5, 29. Cert rec for Ruth from Hopewell MM, Va., dtd 1811,5,9, endorsed to Cesar's Creek
1811, 5, 29. Mary Butcher (form Allen) con mou
1811, 6, 26. Mary rocf Hopewell MM, dtd 1810, 10,31
1812, 2, 26. Cert rec for Mary, minor, from Hopewell MM, dtd 1811,12,5, endorsed to Caesars Creek MM
1835, 12, 23. Rebecca E. (form Crispin) con mou (H)
1836, 4, 20. Rebecca C. gct Pilesgrove MM, N. J. (H)
1846, 9, 23. Mary (form Evans) dis mou (H)
1847, 7, 21. Mary (form Evans) dis mou
1894, 11, 24. Phebe Michener (form Allen), w Richard, & infant dt, Anna, acepted as mbr after cert miscarried (H)
1914, 3, 29. Wm. T. relrq (H)

ALLISON
1806, 4, 10. Amelia & ch, Gulielma Sanders, John Sanders, Samuel Sanders & Martha Sanders, rocf Westfield MM, N. C., dtd 1805,8,24

ANDERSON
----, --, --. Martha, w Wm. H., b 1806,3,4 d 1895,3,24 bur Miami (H)

1806, 7, 10. Hannah (form Painter) con mou
1808, 1, 14. Cert rec for Susannah from Lost Creek MM, Tenn., dtd 1807,10,31, endorsed to Fairfield MM
1832, 6, 27. Martha (form Smith) con mou (H)
1833, 5, 22. Martha gct Springborough MM (H)

ANDERSON, continued
1833, 9, 25. Jane (form Cadwallader) dis jH
1834, 8, 27. Jane (form Cadwalader) con mou (H)
1851, 8, 27. Martha rocf Springborough MM, dtd 1851,7,24 (H)
1879, 3, 26. Mary gct Kokomo MM, Ind.; returned 1879,6,25
1883, 8, 22. Mary M. gct Penn MM, Mich.
1910, 10, 26. Charles W. recrq (H)

ANDREW
1806, 12, 11. Robert [Andrews] rocf Spring MM, N. C., dtd 1806,7,26
1808, 4, 14. Robert & w, Mary, & ch, John, William, Ruth, Abigail & Mary, rocf Center MM, N. C., dtd 1807,8,15
1809, 2, 11. Robert & w, Mary, & ch, Ruth, John, Abigail, Mary & William, gct West Branch MM

ANSON
1891, 3, 25. Marion Lewis con mou (H)
1893, 3, 22. Margaret Ruth recrq
1894, 11, 24. Marion L. gct Gwynedd MM, Pa.(H)
1897, 2, 24. Jesse recrq
1910, 7, 27. Margaret gct Dayton MM, O.

ANTHONY
1813, 6, 30. Christopher & w, Mary, & ch, Penelope, Rachel & Charlotte, roc
1814, 8, 31. Charlotte Morgan (form Anthony) con mou
1817, 7, 30. Charles & w, Elizabeth, & ch, Elija, Judith, Henrietta, Sally & Joseph, rocf Clear Creek MM, dtd 1817,1,12
1821, 9, 26. Charles & w, Elizabeth, & dt, Susan Evans, rocf Cincinnati MM
1826, 6, 28. Eliza Snider (form Anthony) con mou
1827, 7, 25. Charles & fam gct Newberry MM
1827, 7, 25. Judith gct Newberry MM
1866, 1, 24. Rhoda [Antony] dropped from mbrp; form mbr Fall Creek or Centre MM which had been laid down (H)

ANTRAM
1768, 6, 29. David [Antrim] b
1829, 4, 1. Aaron L. [Antrim], s John & Ann, Warren Co., O.; m at residence of Jonathan Harvey, Martha HARVEY, dt Isaac & Lydia, Warren Co., O., b 1809,5,24
Ch: Anslem b 1830, 1, 1
Micajah T. " 1834, 12, 27
Isaac H. " 1837, 10, 13

1831, 9, 7. Edward, s John & Ann, Warren Co., O., b 1809,2,20 d 1848,12,17; m at Grove, Zalinda MACY, dt David & Sarah, Warren Co., O., b 1811,8,11 d 1894,1,26(H)
Ch: Sarah Ann b 1832, 6, 13 d 1890, 6, 5
Martha D. " 1839, 10, 13 " 1865, 12,17
Laura E. " 1847, 8, 17 " 1870, 7, 6

1844, 3, 14. Daniel d bur Waynesville
1848, 12, 16. Ann d ae 79 (H)
1855, 5, 5. Martha, w Aaron, d bur Waynesville
1807, 4, 9. Thomas [Antrim] recrq
1810, 1, 31. David [Antrim] rocf Hopewell MM, dtd 1809,11,6
1825, 8, 31. Ann & ch, Aaron L., Edmund & Charity, rocf Springfield MM, dtd 1825,6, 25
1829, 5, 27. Ann [Antrum] dis jH
1829, 5, 27. Charity Ann [Antrum] dis jH
1830, 12, 29. Edmund dis jH
1837, 4, 26. Charity Ann Scrogg (form Antrim) dis mou (H)
1852, 5, 26. Anslum con mou
1855, 12, 26. Sarah Ann Varner (form Antram) con mcd (H)
1857, 1, 21. Micajah T. [Antrim] dis mou
1860, 2, 22. Isaac H. con mou
1871, 12, 27. Barbara N. [Antrim] recrq
1871, 12, 27. Charity Ann & ch (s: William & Aaron) recrq
1872, 1, 24. Aaron L. con mou
1872, 1, 24. William Henry, Aaron L. Jr. & Lydia Martha [Antrim] recrq
1883, 4, 25. Ida M. [Antrum] & dt, Marie, recrq
1899, 2, 22. W. H., I. H. & I. M. dropped from mbrp on rq
1899, 2, 22. Mary H. & Brightie L. dropped from mbrp on rq

ARCHDEACON
1884, 5, 28. Ellen R. recrq
1886, 3, 24. Mary recrq
1887, 4, 20. Rachel, George Jr. & Joanna recrq
1906, 7, 25. George & Rachel dropped from mbrp

ARMITAGE
1810, 3, 6. Mark b

1821, 11, 28. Mark & Grace, ch Eleanor, rocf Gorge St. MM, Upper Canada, dtd 1820,8,30
1822, 1, 30. Eleanor recrq after dis by Yonge St. MM, Upper Canada
1823, 5, 28. Eleanor & dt, Grace, gct Elk MM
1829, 9, 30. Mark con mou

ARNETT
----, --, --. Thomas b 1791,6,30; m Rachel FORTNER
Dt: Hannah b 1814, 12, 2
1853, 11, 2. Thomas, s Vanentine & Sarah, Warren Co., O.; m at Miami, Hannah HUDSON, dt Samuel & Dinah, Warren Co., O.

1847, 5, 26. Thomas & w, Rachel, rocf Center MM, dtd 1847,5,12
1878, 10, 23. Hannah gct Phila. MM, Pa.

ARNOLD
1804, 12, 13. Rachel & her ancient mother, Mary Jay, rocf Bush River MM, S. C., dtd 1804,8,25
1811, 1, 30. Anderson & Thomas rocf Springfield MM, N. C., dtd 1804,2,4
1811, 1, 30. Cert rec for Susanna from Springfield MM, dtd 1809,2,4, endorsed to Stillwater MM
1838, 12, 26. Lydia (form Mills) dis mou

ATKINSON
1874, 9, 23. Joseph recrq
1875, 5, 26. Ann, Mary & Martha recrq
1875, 7, 21. Nellie recrq
1878, 10, 23. Mary relrq
1881, 5, 25. Joseph relrq
1884, 6, 25. Nellie recrq

AUSTIN
1809, 9, 9. Rachel Clutch (form Austin) con mou
1814, 11, 30. Prudence rocf Eavesham MM, N.J., dtd 1814,9,9
1839, 1, 23. Joshua & w, Priscilla, & ch, Rachel, Isaac D., Rebecca, Lucy Ann & Joshua, rocf Evesham MM, N. J., dtd 1838, 12,4 (H)
1839, 2, 20. Isaac, Rebecca & Lucy Ann C., ch Joshua & Priscilla, rocf Evesham MM, N. J., dtd 1839,1,11
1843, 8, 23. Isaac dis mou & training with the militia (H)
1844, 3, 27. Isaac dis mou
1844, 5, 22. Rachel Haines (form Austin) con mou (H)
1855, 11, 21. Joshua dis disunity (H)
1886, 12, 22. Rebecca Dinwiddie (form Austin) relrq (H)

AYERS
1857, 8, 26. Sarah Jane (form Cadwalader) dis mcd (H)

BABCOCK
1840, 10, 29. Rachel [Babock] m David CADWALLADER (H)
1872, 2, 22. Julia A. m John UNDERWOOD (H)

1838, 4, 25. Rachel recrq (H)
1871, 11, 22. Juliann rocf White Water MM, Ind., dtd 1871,10,25 (H)

BACON
1832, 11, 21. Hannah (form Hopkins) dis mou (H)

BAILEY
----, --, --. Josiah m Susanna BALLARD (H)
Ch: Josiah b 1814, 12, 12 d 1815, 7,17
Susannah " 1815, 9, 9 ae 2 yr.
1820, 12, 7. Hiram [Baily], s John & Rebecca, Clinton Co., O.; m at Hopewell, Rachel THOMAS, dt Edward & Mary, Warren Co., O.
1840, 12, 2. Emmor b 1809,6,27 d 1879,2,24; m Mary SATTERTHWAITE, dt John & Elizabeth, Warren Co., O., b 1817,6,29 d 1907,5,30 (H)(Emmor, s Emmor & Elizabeth, Warren Co., O.)
Ch: Elizabeth b 1841, 8, 22
Ann " 1844, 3, 1 d 1847, 7,12
Susan " 1846, 3, 19 d 1892,10,15
Phebe " 1849, 9, 8 " 1915, 3,24
Emmor S. " 1853, 8, 16
George L. " 1858, 3, 5
1878, 3, 18. Phebe m Thomas SHERWOOD (H)

1805, 12, 12. David & w, Ruth, & ch, Henry, Stanton, John, Bathsheba & Elizabeth, rocf Mount-pleasant MM, Va., dtd 1805,8,31
1806, 3, 13. Daniel rocf Upper MM, dtd 1805, 3,16
1808, 3, 22. Henry dis training with militia
1809, 4, 8. David rocf Back Creek MM, N.C., dtd 1807,3,28
1809, 4, 8. Cert rec for Catherine [Bayly] & dt, Caroline, from Back Creek MM, N. C., dtd 1807,3,18, endorsed to West Branch MM
1810, 9, 26. David & w, Ruth, & ch, Stanton, John, Barsheba & Elizabeth, gct White Water MM
1815, 1, 25. Josiah & w, Susanna, & ch, Almeda, Robert Barclay, Judith, Daniel, James Edwin, Mary Byrum & Susanna, rocf South River MM, Va., dtd 1814,12,10
1816, 9, 25. Susannah [Bayley] & six ch gct Center MM
1817, 2, 26. White Water MM was given permission to rst Henry [Baily]
1820, 11, 29. Hiram rocf Center MM, dtd 1820, 11,18
1821, 7, 25. Rachel gct Center MM
1836, 7, 27. Abijah Johnson gct Dover MM, to m Elizabeth Bailey
1842, 10, 26. Mary (form Satterthwaite) dis mou
1866, 1, 24. Thos. & fam dropped from mbrp; form mbr of Fall Creek or Centre MM which had been laid down (H)
1889, 7, 24. George S. gct Cincinnati MM (H)
1917, 9, 30. Emmor D. recrq (H)
1921, 4, 24. Pearl M. recrq

BAIRD
1863, 11, 25. Lydia Ann (form Brown) dis mou

BAKER
1812, 6, 24. Thomas & w, Sarah, & ch, Nayl, Phebe, Thomas, Branton & William H., rocf London Grove MM, dtd 1812,4,8
1812, 6, 24. Rachel rocf London Grove MM, Pa., dtd 1812,4,8
1812, 7, 29. Joshua rocf London Grove MM, dtd 1812,4,8
1817, 2, 26. Richard rocf Nottingham MM, Md., dtd 1816,7,5

BAKER, continued
1818, 8, 26. Rachel Jones (form Baker) con mou
1822, 2, 27. Sarah & ch gct Green Plain MM
1822, 2, 27. Richard, Joshua & Neil gct Green Plain MM
1824, 4, 28. Phebe Kenton (form Baker) dis mou
1845, 3, 26. Benjamin Johnson gct Fall Creek MM, to m Susanna Baker (H)
1868, 10, 21. Elcy H. A. rocf Easton MM, N.Y., dtd 1868,9,17 (H)

BALDWIN
1804, 10, 11. Jesse & w, Hannah, & ch, Enos, William, Uriah, Walter, David, Richard, Sarah & Sophia, rocf Mount Pleasant MM, Va., dtd 1803,11,26
1806, 6, 12. Jess & w, Ann, rocf New Garden MM, N. C., dtd 1805,8,31
1807, 8, 3. William dis mcd
1807, 8, 3. Anna (form Crews) dis mcd

BALLARD
----, --, --. Nathan m Martha ----- d 1811,10, 30 (H)
Ch: Elizabeth b 1810, 6, 2
----, --, --. Thomas m Sarah LEWIS (H)
Ch: Rachel b 1821, 10, 31 d 1828,11,11
Sarah Jane " 1828, 12, 1
Elizabeth " 1815, 6, 28 d 1839, 6,--
Barkley " 1817, 1, 26
Achilles " 1819, 8, 31
Addison " 1823, 11, 31
Micajah " 1826, 8, 7
Rachel " 1832, 3, 30
Hannah Ann " 1835, 11, 21
----, --, --. Frederick b 1812,1,19; m Hannah TAYLOR b 1816,1,30 d 1883,12,8 (H)
Ch: Mary T. b 1840, 4, 24 d 1870, 1, 8
Susan Maria" 1846, 9, 9
Caroline " 1849, 9, 20
Sarah T. " 1853, 11, 8 d 1881, 6,12
Hellen L. " 1856, 10, 14

1804, 12, 13. Moorman & w, Minerva, & ch, David, Ruth & Simeon, rocf New Hope MM, Tenn., dtd 1804,7,21
1804, 12, 13. Spencer & w, Rebecca, & ch, Amos, Benejah, Lydia & Ideteth, rocf New Hope MM, Tenn., dtd 1804,7,21
1806, 4, 10. Elizabeth rocf Westfield MM, N. C., dtd 1805,8,24
1806, 8, 14. Ruth Galladay (form Ballard) con mou
1810, 1, 31. John rocf Mt. Pleasant MM, Va., dtd 1809,9,30
1810, 5, 30. Nathan & w, Martha, & ch, Ahira, Sarah, Rhoda, David & Samuel, rocf Mt. Pleasant MM, Va., dtd 1809,9,30
1813, 1, 27. Nathan gct Elk MM, to m
1817, 8, 27. Nancy & ch, Grandison Butterworth, Samuel Moorman, William Fredrick & Elizabeth Ann, rocf South River MM, dtd 1817,7, 12
1818, 6, 24. Nathan gct New Garden MM, Ind.
1819, 3, 31. Thomas & w, Sarah, & ch, Elizabeth & Barclay, rocf Clear Creek MM, dtd 1819,3,13
1820, 12, 27. Rhoda, minor, gct New Garden MM, Ind.
1823, 10, 29. Nathan & w, Catherine, gct Chester MM, Ind.
1824, 2, 25. Thomas & w, Sarah, & ch, Elizabeth, Barclay, Achilles, Rachel & Addison, gct Clear Creek MM
1825, 11, 30. Thomas & w, Sarah, & ch, Elizabeth, Barclay, Achillas, Rachel & Addison B., rocf Clear Creek MM, dtd 1825,8,13
1829, 8, 26. Granderson B. dis jH
1829, 8, 26. Nancy dis jH
1829, 8, 26. Sarah dis jH
1829, 8, 26. Thomas dis jH
1832, 4, 25. Jonathan rocf Springfield MM, dtd 1832,3,13
1833, 3, 27. Samuel M. dis disunity (H)
1833, 10, 23. William F. dis jH
1833, 10, 23. Elizabeth Ann dis jH
1834, 4, 23. Grandison dis disunity (H)
1834, 8, 27. Elizabeth Plummer (form Ballard) con mou (H)
1836, 7, 27. E. Ann Harris (form Ballard) con mou (H)
1837, 12, 27. Elizabeth Plummer (form Ballard) dis mou & jH (men's minutes: for joining Methodists)
1838, 10, 24. William F. gct Centre MM, to m Hannah Taylor (H)
1841, 2, 24. Hannah rocf Center MM, dtd 1840, 10,15 (H)
1841, 3, 24. Barclay dis mou (H)
1842, 2, 23. Jonathan gct Bloomfield MM
1846, 11, 25. Thomas & w, Sarah, & ch, Rachel Mourning & Hannah Ann, gct White Water MM (H)
1888, 1, 25. Elizabeth dropped from mbrp (H)
1889, 7, 24. William F. dropped from mbrp (H)
1889, 7, 24. Helen L. dropped from mbrp (H)
1889, 7, 24. Caroline Gregory (form Ballard) dropped from mbrp (H)
1889, 7, 24. Susan M. Hill (form Ballard) dropped from mbrp (H)
1889, 10, 23. Micajah rpd mcd many years before (H)
1889, 11, 20. Micajah gct White Water MM,Ind. (H)

BALLINGER
1804, 12, 13. Mary, w Jonathan, & ch, Mary Ann, rocf New Hope MM, Tenn., dtd 1804,7, 21
1805, 12, 12. Jesse rocf New Hope MM, dtd 1805,9,21
1806, 8, 14. Jonathan [Ballenger] rocf Lost Creek MM, dtd 1805,5,25, endorsed by New Hope MM, 1805,8,24
1808, 4, 14. Joshua [Ballenger] & w, Sarah,

BALLINGER, continued
rocf Evesham MM, N. J., dtd 1808,1,14
1819, 6, 30. Isaac & w, Hannah, & ch, Mary Ann, Abraham, Isaac, Hannah & Samuel, rocf Burlington MM, dtd 1819,5,3
1820, 1, 26. Isaac & fam gct Elk MM

BANES
1854, 3, 22. Isaac & w, Hannah, rocf Center MM, dtd 1854,2,16 (H)
1866, 1, 24. Nancy [Baines] dropped from mbrp; form mbr Fall Creek or Centre MM which had been laid down

BARCUS
1835, 3, 25. Beulah (form Hopkins) con mou (H)
1841, 9, 22. Beulah gct Whitewater MM (H)

BARNARD
1814, 8, 31. Ruth rocf Nantucket MM, dtd 1814, 4,28

BARNETT
1805, 9, 12. Jane rocf Deep Creek MM, dtd 1805,4,6
1806, 8, 14. Thomas [Barnet] & w, Theodate, & ch, Jesse, James & William, rocf Deep Creek MM, N. C., dtd 1805,4,6

BARNES
1821, 6, 9. William, s Isaac & Sarah, b

BARRETT
----, --, --. George b 1796,12,6 d 1875,7,24; m Mahala ----- b 1805,8,15 d 1870,1,30 (H)
----, --, --. Isaac M. m Rebecca S. ----- b 1829,12,12 d 1854,1,31 (H)
Ch: Thomas S. b 1851, 9, 1
George " 1853, 5, 26 d 1854, 1,23
1865, 12, 29. Mariell d (H)

1805, 12, 12. Jonathan & w, Rachel, & ch, Jesse, Benjamin, Ellis, Levi & Lydia, rocf Hopewell MM, dtd 1805,9,2
1807, 8, 13. Richard & w, Sarah, & ch, Lydia, Sarah, Sydney, Amy & Richard, rocf Hopewell MM, dtd 1807,3,2
1807, 8, 13. Eleanor [Barret] rocf Hopewell MM, Va., dtd 1807,3,2
1844, 3, 27. George & w, Mahala, & ch, Maria, Isaac, Slocumb, Mahala M., John, Calista & Mary L., rocf Allum Creek MM, dtd 1843, 9,21 (H)
1851, 8, 27. Rebecca S. rocf Green Plain MM, dtd 1851,7,16 (H)
1851, 10, 22. Maria Butler (form Barrett) dis mcd (H)
1856, 11, 26. Isaac M. dis mcd (H)
1858, 10, 27. Mahala M. Swayne (form Barrett) con mcd (H)
1864, 7, 27. John R. [Barret] dis mcd (H)
1868, 9, 23. Calista dis jas (H)
1868, 9, 23. Rosa dis jas (H)
1889, 1, 23. Thos. Swayne relrq (H)

BARTLETT
1881, 2, 23. J. Henry Sherwood gct Baltimore MM, Md., to m Sarah A. Bartlett (H)

BARTON
1810, 7, 25. Samuel, Ann & Patience, ch William, rocf Upper Evesham MM, N. J., dtd 1810,5,12
1821, 4, 25. Anna Montgomery (form Barton) con mou
1821, 9, 26. Samuel dis mcd [dis mou
1824, 4, 28. Patience Kendrick (form Barton)
1830, 1, 27. Sarah dis jH
1835, 5, 27. Jacob & w, Sydney, & ch, Mary & Edward, rocf Cincinnati MM, dtd 1835,2, 26 (H)
1884, 7, 23. Alice C. gct White Water MM,Ind.

BATEMAN [(H)
----, --, --. John m Hannah ----- d 1821,10,13
Ch: Hannah b 1815, 12, 19
William " 1818, 5, 19 d 1819,11,--
John T. " 1821, 1, 18
1815, 11, 15. Rachel m Isaac JONES
1817, 1, 2. Ann m Joel WRIGHT

1814, 10, 26. William & w, Elizabeth, rocf Monallen MM, Pa., dtd 1814,8,18
1814, 10, 26. Rachel Elizabeth rocf Monallan MM, Pa., dtd 1814,8,18
1814, 12, 28. John & w, Hannah, & ch, Lydia, Mary Ann, Joel Mahlon & Rachel, rocf Dennings Creek MM, dtd 1814,8,10
1815, 9, 27. Ann rocf Manallinnan MM, Pa., dtd 1815,8,24
1816, 10, 30. Jacob recrq
1817, 6, 25. Jacob denied mbrp on objection of Monallen MM, Pa.
1817, 12, 31. Rachel [Baterman] (form Mullen) con mou
1819, 8, 25. Elizabeth B. Leeds (form Bateman) dis mou
1824, 2, 25. John gct Fairfield MM, to m Deborah Ingham
1824, 8, 25. Deborah rocf Fairfield MM, dtd 1824,6,26
1838, 11, 21. Mahlon rocf Springborough MM, dtd 1838,11,20
1841, 9, 22. Mary Ann rocf Springboro MM, dtd 1841,8,24
1844, 5, 22. Mary Ann gct Springborough MM
1853, 7, 27. Mahlon rqct Goshen MM
1917, 7, 29. Ellwood transferred to this mtg from Springboro (H)

BATTEN
1807, 8, 3. Richard Jr. & w, Ann, rocf Bush River MM, S. C., dtd 1807,4,24

BAUER
1817, 11, 26. Isaac & w, Sarah, & ch, Jonothan & Lydia, rocf Maures River MM, N. J., dtd 1817,2,10

BAXTER
1806, 10, 9. Mary rocf Warrington MM, Pa., dtd 1806,6,7

BAYLIES
1887, 11, 23. Rachel B. (form Butterworth & later Henry) rpd mcd (H)
1887, 11, 23. Carrie Corinne, dt Rachel B., recrq (H)
1903, 3, 25. Rachel M. B. & Caroline Corinne relrq (H)

BAYNES [(H)
----, --, --. John H. b 1837,8,21 d 1904,7,24

BEALS
1807, 9, 16. Jacob, s Daniel & Susanna, Hiland Co., O.; m at a public mtg held in Fairfield Twp., Mary THORNBURGH, dt Edward & Phebe, Hiland Co., O.
1827, 12, 5. Jesse, s John & Mary, Clinton Co., O.; m at Grove, Dinah MOON, dt Richard & Vashti, Warren Co., O.

1804, 10, 11. Jacob rocf Mount Pleasant MM, Va., dtd 1803,12,31
1804, 10, 11. Hannah [Bales], dt Evan Evans, rocf Southland MM, Va., dtd 1804,2,1
1804, 11, 8. John & ch, Nathan, Thomas, Ann & Daniel, also his aged mother, Sarah Beals, her gr dt, Tabitha Beals, & gr s, Abel Thornburgh, rocf Mount Pleasant MM, Va., dtd 1803,11,26
1804, 11, 8. Mary & s, Asaph Hiatt, rocf Mount Pleasant MM, Va., dtd 1803,11,26
1804, 11, 8. Susannah [Bails] & ch, Curtis, Jacob, Elizabeth Ann, Catron, Rachel & Susannah, rocf Mount Pleasant MM, Va.
1804, 12, 13. John Boater [Bails] & w, Lois, & ch, Eunice, Isaac, Mary, Jonothan, Jane, Sarah & Nathan, rocf New Hope MM, Tenn., dtd 1804,7,21
1806, 4, 10. Abraham [Bales] & w, Mahetabel, & ch, Abijeh & Elizabeth, rocf Lost Creek MM, Tenn., dtd 1805,11,30
1806, 5, 8. Unice Templin (form Beales) dis mou
1806, 9, 11. Hannah [Beales] con mou
1806, 9, 11. Tabitha George (form Beals) con mou
1807, 4, 9. Curtis rpd mcd
1807, 4, 9. Daniel [Bales] rocf New Hope MM, dtd 1807,1,24
1807, 9, 10. Ann dis
1808, 9, 10. Cert rec for Priscilla, & dt, Rachel, Priscilla & Lydia, from Lost Creek MM, Tenn., dtd 1806,5,31, endorsed to Fairfield MM
1828, 3, 26. Dinah gct Newberry MM

BEAMISH
1820, 11, 29. William rocf Bury MM, Suffolk Co., Eng., dtd 1819,4,1
1823, 9, 24. William gct Silver Creek MM, Ind.

BEAR
1890, 9, 24. Rachel Minerva (form Davis) relrq (H)

BECKETT
1898, 1, 26. Clara M. (form McKinney) released from mbrp (H)

BEESON
1893, 6, 21. Edward [Beason] & w, Sadie, & ch, Paul & Percy, gct Wilmington MM

BELL
1810, 5, 30. Lydia (form Smith) dis mou

BENBOW
1809, 5, 12. Elizabeth, dt Edward & Mary, b (H)

1806, 8, 14. Edward & w, Mary, & ch, Barclay, Mary, Evan, Edward, Benjamin & Parshall, rocf Bush River MM, dtd 1806,4,26
1807, 9, 10. Bartly dis
1809, 9, 9. Mary (form McClure) dis mou
1815, 2, 22. Edward & fam gct White Water MM
1815, 2, 22. Mary gct White Water MM [to m
1819, 10, 27. Evan prcf West Grove MM, Ind.,
1820, 3, 29. Maria gct West Grove MM, Ind.
1831, 4, 27. Rachel (form Venable) dis jH.

BENHAM
1891, 4, 22. Mary gct Wilmington MM

BENSON
1805, 11, 14. James & w, Elizabeth, & ch, William, Mary, Henry, Jonothan, James, Thomas, Samuel, Clark & Hester, rocf Cane Creek MM, S. C.

BERGER
1905, 2, 22. James recrq

BEYER
1821, 11, 28. Jacob & w, Margaret, rocf Shrewsbury MM, dtd 1820,7,8

BICKET
1877, 4, 25. Clara (form McKinney) rpd mcd (H)

BIGGS
1900, 11, 21. Ralph recrq
1914, 4, 22. Emmerine recrq

BIGONY
1895, 5, 22. I. F. [Bigoney] & w recrq
1900, 10, 24. Ira F. & w relrq
1911, 1, 25. Howard relrq

BIRDSALL
----, --, --. Martha, dt Andrew, b about 1822 d 1889,3,30 bur Oakland, O. (H)
1838, 11, 28. William, s Whitson & Rachel, Clinton Co., O.; m at Grove, Ruth WALES, dt Samuel & Chloe Welch, Warren Co., O. (H)

1835, 5, 27. Zady & ch, Sarah, Lidia, Phebe, Priscilla & Thomas, rocf Cincinnati MM, dtd 1834,11,20
1839, 2, 20. Ruth gct Center MM (H)
1846, 7, 22. R. [Birdsal] rocf Centre MM, dtd 1846,6,18 (H)
1865, 6, 21. Hannah G. [Birdsal] gct Sandy Spring MM, Md. (H)
1866, 1, 24. Edward [Burdsal] rec; form mbr of Fall Creek or Centre MM which had been laid down (H)
1866, 1, 24. Rachel [Burdsal] rec in mbrp; form mbr Fall Creek or Centre MM which had been laid down (H)
1866, 1, 24. Samuel [Burdsal] rpd mcd (H)
1866, 1, 24. Mary Ann [Burdsal] rpd mcd (H)
1866, 1, 24. William H. [Burdsal] rpd mcd (H)
1866, 1, 24. Rachel Sabin (form Burdsal) rpd mcd (H)
1866, 4, 25. Samuel [Birdsal] & w, Mary Ann, gct White Water MM (H)
1870, 10, 26. William & w, Rachel (or Ruth) dis jas (H)
1875, 11, 24. Mary Ann [Birdsal] rocf White Water MM, dtd 1875,5,26 (H)
1885, 1, 21. Edward [Birdsal] dropped from mbrp. (H)

BISHOP
1806, 2, 13. Robert recrq
1809, 6, 10. Ann (form Hawkins) con mou

BISPHAM
----, --, --. Jerusha d 1844,10,7 bur Waynesville; m Abigail ----- d 1844,10,8

1815, 8, 30. Josiah & w, Jerusha, & dt, Hannah, rocf Chester MM, dtd 1815,5,4
1815, 8, 30. Thomas & w, Hannah, rocf Chester MM, N. J., dtd 1815,5,4
1829, 2, 25. Jonah dis jH
1830, 3, 31. Hannah Mills (form Bispham) dis mou & jH
1830, 3, 31. Hannah Mills (form Bispham) con mou (H)
1830, 5, 26. Jerusha dis jH
1832, 11, 21. Joseph dis disunity (H)
1841, 4, 21. Elizabeth Rogers (form Bispham) dis mou (H)
1842, 1, 26. Elizabeth Rogers (form Bispham) dis mou
1843, 9, 20. Jerusha rst
1843, 12, 1. William dis mou (H)
1844, 3, 27. William [Bisphim] dis mou
1844, 3, 27. Elizabeth (form Ward) dis mou (H)
1845, 12, 24. Elizabeth (form Ward) dis mou

BLACK
1822, 11, 27. Betsy recrq
1825, 6, 29. Betsy Dougherty (form Black) dis mou & jas

BLACKBURN
----, --, --. Washington m Mary Ann GOOD b 1839,4,11 (H)
Ch: Charles b 1863, 1, 15
Anna " 1860, 2, 25
1880, 5, 5. Elias, s Hiram & Mary Ann, Bedford Co., Pa.; m at residence of David Furnas, Ann D. FURNAS, dt David & Jane, Warren Co., O. (H)
1894, 12, 20. Charles G. Blackburn, s Washington & Mary Ann, Highland Co., O.; m at residence of Ellis Good, Bertha HOLLOWELL, dt Elwood & Mary D., Highland Co., O. (H)

1866, 8, 22. Mary Ann (form Good) con mcd (H)
1880, 8, 25. Anna D. gct Dunnings Creek MM, Pa. (H)
1894, 11, 24. Charles G. & Anna recrq (H)
1895, 5, 22. Mary Ann, Anna, Charles G. & Bertha H. set off as mbr of Executive Mtg at Clear Creek (H)
1926, 6, 27. Charles G. relrq (H)

BLANCHARD
1784, 8, 24. Stephen b (H)

1825, 4, 27. Stephen recrq
1829, 6, 24. Stephen dis jH

BLANTON
1907, 2, 20. Marvin recrq
1909, 2, 24. Marvin & w, Fannie, relrq

BLOOMER
1906, 8, 14. Sarah (form Overman) dis mou

BLOXOM
1819, 6, 30. Elizabeth rocf Ceasars Creek MM
1822, 9, 25. Elizabeth [Bloxsom] gct Green Plain MM

BOGAN
1872, 6, 26. Ella J. & Mary E. recrq
1903, 10, 21. Edward & w recrq
1911, 2, 22. Rolla, Evan & Lelia recrq
1911, 2, 22. Edgar & w, Mary O., & ch, Raleigh L., Evan O. & Lelia N., gct Caesars Creek MM, O.
1913, 12, 24. Willard recrq

BOGARDUS
1884, 1, 24. Joseph A., s James N. & Elizabeth, New York Co., N. Y.; m at residence of David Furnas, Elizabeth FURNAS, dt Davis & Jane S., Warren Co., O. (H)

1884, 4, 23. Elizabeth F., w Joseph, gct New York MM (H)

BOLTZ
1887, 4, 20. Anna & Ella recrq
1890, 10, 22. Anna B. Wright (form Boltz) relrq

BOND
1807, 11, 12. William & w, Charlotte, & ch, Mary, Sarah, Lydia, Jesse & Charlotte, rocf Deep Creek MM, N. C., dtd 1807,9,5
1809, 2, 11. William & w, Charlotte, & ch, Mary, Sarah, Lydia, Jesse & Charlotte, gct West Branch MM
1809, 11, 4. Benjamin & w, Susannah, & ch, Joseph, Edward, Mary, Ruth, Elizabeth, Hannah & Moses, rocf Mt. Pleasant MM, dtd 1809,8,26
1810, 7, 25. Cert rec for Benjamin, endorsed to Cesar's Creek MM
1810, 10, 31. Hannah rocf Hopewell MM, Va., dtd 1810,4,2
1812, 2, 26. Joseph & w, Rachel, & ch, Dairus, Eunice, John, Mordicai & Joseph, rocf Westfield MM, dtd 1811,10,12
1845, 8, 27. Zimri Hollingsworth gct White Water MM, to m Sarah Bond

BOON
----, --, --. Arnold d 1857,7,1; m Hannah ----- d 1858,12,29 (H)
Dt: Ellen
1850, 3, 6. Ellen [Boone] m Levi COOK (H)

1847, 9, 22. Isaac Evans gct Springboro MM, to m Anna S. Boon
1848, 8, 23. Arnold & w, Hannah, & ch, Ellen, rocf Springborough MM, dtd 1848,7,27

BORDEN
1811, 3, 27. Elizabeth & s, Archibald & Peter, rocf Redstnne MM, dtd 1810,12,28
1811, 9, 25. Elizabeth Hewlings (form Burdin) rpd mcd
1816, 1, 31. Mary rocf Redstone MM, dtd 1815,9,29
1818, 3, 25. Archibald gct Cincinnati MM
1822, 2, 27. Mary Ward (form Burdin) dis mou
1827, 6, 26. Peter gct Center MM

BORTON
1825, 12, 7. Rebecca m John BROWN

1823, 10, 29. Edward [Borten] & w, Mary, & ch, Rebecca, Job, Emmeline, James, Mary Ann & Edward, rocf Woodbury MM, N. J., dtd 1823,8,23
1825, 2, 23. Sarah & ch, Hannahann, Beulah & Miriam, rocf Woodbury MM, N. J., dtd 1824, 9,27
1827, 5, 30. Edward & fam gct Springborough MM
1827, 8, 29. Job [Borten] rocf Springboro MM, dtd 1827,8,28
1829, 2, 25. Job [Barton] dis jH
1829, 6, 24. Sarah & ch, Hanah Ann, Beulah, Marian, William W. & Elizabeth, gct Springborough MM

1830, 11, 24. Job gct Whitewater MM, to m Ann Moore; cert returned because Job failed to appear (H)
1831, 8, 31. Job con mou (H)
1832, 4, 25. Job gct Springborough MM
1835, 5, 27. Jacob & w, Sydney, & ch, Mary & Edward, rocf Cincinnati MM, dtd 1835,2,26 (H)
1841, 5, 26. Jacob dis disunity (H)
1849, 2, 21. Sidney, w Jacob, & ch, Mary, Edward, Elizabeth & William, gct Cincinnati MM

BOSWELL
1817, 10, 29. Ezra & fam gct White Water MM

BOWMAN
1831, 11, 30. Ann [Boman] (form Grey) dis mou
1883, 7, 23. John & w, Phebe, recrq
1892, 7, 27. John H. relrq

BOYER
1832, 8, 22. Jacob dis jH

BRADBURY
1907, 2, 20. Anna C. recrq
1910, 9, 21. Anna C. relrq

BRADDOCK
1843, 5, 24. Priscilla & Amanda recrq (H)
1844, 9, 25. Priscilla (or Rachel) & Amanda dis jas (H)
1906, 1, 21. Frank & w, Jennie, & ch, Fred Dewayne & Warren K., recrq
1928, 3, 25. Raymon [Braddoc] recrq (H)

BRADLEY
1873, 2, 18. Milton recrq
1874, 6, 24. Anna (form Terrill) con mou
1881, 3, 23. Annie & ch, Zella & Thomas Edward, gct Oskaloosa MM
1883, 3, 21. Milton dis disunity

BRADSTREET
1897, 11, 24. Eliza relrq

BRADWAY
1809, 10, 14. John & w, Abigail, & ch, Jono-

BRADWAY, continued
than, Josiah, Dorcas, Elizabeth, John, Abigail, William & Thomas, rocf Greenwich MM, N. J., dtd 1804,8,29
1809, 10, 14. Beulah rocf Lower Greenwich MM, N. J., dtd 1804,8,27
1811, 6, 26. Beulah Ward (form Bradway) dis mou
1812, 1, 29. Josiah dis
1816, 5, 29. John & fam gct White Water MM
1819, 5, 25. Josiah [Broadway] recrq

BRANDA
1895, 5, 22. Alice D. (Jones) set off as mbr of Executive Mtg at Clear Creek (H)
1909, 6, 23. Alice D. dropped from mbrp (H)

BRANNON
1900, 1, 24. Thomas Benjamin recrq

BRANSON
1804, 12, 13. Jane & ch, Thomas, Jacob & Elizabeth, rocf New Hope MM, Tenn., dtd 1804,7,21
1812, 2, 26. Cert rec for Ann & ch, Ruth, Rebecca, Elizabeth, Abraham & Rachel, from Hopewell MM, dtd 1811,11,7, endorsed to Darby Creek MM
1866, 1, 24. Ruth dropped from mbrp; form mbr of Fall Creek or Centre MM which had been laid down (H)

BRATTON
1808, 7, 14. Jonathan & w, Ann, rocf Deep River MM, N. C., dtd 1807,11,2

BRAY
1807, 2, 12. Henry & w, Keziah, & ch, Edward, Richard, Joseph, Abijah, Mary & Keziah, rocf Deep Creek MM, N. C., dtd 1805,12,7
1807, 2, 12. Sarah rocf Deep Creek MM, N. C., dtd 1805,12,7
1811, 6, 26. Joseph dis mcd
1811, 8, 28. Mary Chamness (form Bray) dis mcd
1811, 9, 25. Henry & w, Keziah, & ch, Edward, Richard, Abigail, (Abijah) Heziah & Maccy, gct Ceasars Creek MM
1811, 10, 30. Sarah Sutton (form Bray) dis mcd

BRAZILTON
1812, 2, 26. Cert rec for Sarah from Deep River MM, N. C., dtd 1808,9,5, endorsed to White Water MM

BREED
1871, 6, 21. Margaret (form Whitacre) rpd mcd (H)
1871, 11, 22. Margaret gct Wapsinonoc MM (H)

BRELSFORD
----, --, --. James d 1866,1,30 ae 92; m Jane ----- d 1860,9,9 (H)

1819, 11, 24. Rebecca (form Simmons) dis mcd; living at Falls MM, Pa.
1827, 6, 27. Jane (form Trogmorton) con mou
1829, 6, 24. Jane dis jH
1838, 9, 26. James recrq (H)

BREVITT
1820, 9, 27. John Webster [Brevet] rocf Baltimore MM, dtd 1820,8,11
1822, 7, 31. John Webster gct Green Plain MM

BRIDGES
1804, 7, 12. Charles & w, Eddy, & ch, Jesse & Jemima, rocf Bush River MM, S. C., dtd 1804,3,31

BRIGGS
1909, 10, 27. Ralph dropped from mbrp

BROADWICK
1812, 11, 25. Beulah [Bradrick] rocf Plainfield MM, dtd 1812,8,22
1829, 3, 25. Beulah gct Arba MM, Ind.
1830, 11, 24. Beulah rocf Arba MM, Ind.
1833, 9, 25. Beulah [Broadrick] gct Goshen MM

BROOKS
1804, 10, 11. Nimrod & Mary, ch James, rocf Bush River MM, S. C., dtd 1804,4,28
1806, 5, 8. John rocf Bush River MM, S. C., dtd 1805,11,30
1807, 4, 9. Charity [Brook] & ch, Elizah, Ruth, Susanah, Keturah & Lucinda, rocf Bush River MM, S. C., dtd 1806,9,27
1807, 4, 9. Hannah rocf Bush River MM, dtd 1806,3,29
1808, 4, 14. Mary dis
1808, 5, 12. Nimrod rpd mcd
1813, 12, 29. John dis military service
1816, 9, 25. Hannah gct White Water MM
1816, 12, 25. Nimrod & fam gct West Branch MM
1855, 9, 26. Johnson & w, Mary P., & ch, John Edward & Lucy B., rocf Springboro MM, dtd 1855,7,24
1883, 4, 25. William T. (or L.) & w, Ella J., & s, Ralph Edward, recrq

BROWN
----, --, --. Asher Sr. d 1832,3,2 ae 71; m Mary ----- d 1851,5,4 (H)

Ch:		
Samuel	b 1788, 6, 27	d 1812, 8,16
Ann	" 1792, 9, 8	" 1825, 9,29

----, --, --. Asher m Mary WARD (H)

John	b 1804, 7, 17	
Asher	" 1806, 6, 12	d 1887, 3,12
Allen	" 1808, 10, 14	" 1888, 2,14

----, --, --. David b 1784,9,26 d 1862,10,5; m Mary WILKINS b 1769,10,27 d 1857,10,15 (H)

Ch:		
Elizabeth Wilkins	b 1809, 12, 26	d 1888, 5,20
Sarah	" 1813, 5, 11	" 1849,10,12

1809, 3, 16. Mercer, s Mercer & Sarah, Preble

BROWN, continued
Co., O.; m at Elk, Mary SMITH, dt Joseph & Hannah
1812, 5, 7. Samuel, s Asher & Mary, Warren Co., O.; m at Turtle Creek, Rebecca EVANS, dt John & Elizabeth, Warren Co., O.
1813, 12, 1. Elizabeth m James MILLS
1814, 9, 8. Rebecca m David MORGAN
----, --, --. Sarah, w Allen, b 1816,12,13 d 1885,8,9 (H)
1818, 9, 2. Samuel, s Clayton & Elizabeth, Warren Co., O.; m at Waynesville, Ruth GAUSE, dt Solomon & Ruth, Greens Co., O.
1821, 11, 7. Benjamin, s Asher & Mary, Warren Co., O., b 1798,4,24 d 1873,9,22; m at Waynesville, Sarah CHAPMAN, dt Benjamin & Mary, b 1800,1,13 d 1873,1,26 (H)
Ch: Esther Ann b 1822, 7, 30 d 1906, 5,25
Charles F. " 1824, 12, 19 " 1854, 10,30
Mary " 1827, 1, 7 " 1894, 9,20
Benjamin Chapman " 1830, 11, 7 " 1842, 9, 7
Sarah " 1830, 11, 7 " 1912, 4,12
----, --, --. Catherine b 1823,9,20 d 1901,7, 16 (H)
1822, 2, 13. Hannah m Joseph LEWKINS
1824, 1, 7. Mary C. m James SMITH
1825, 12, 7. John, s Asher & Mary, Warren Co., O.; m at Miami, Rebecca BORTON, dt Edward & Mary, Warren Co., O.
1827, 5, 2. Asher, s Asher & Mary, Warren Co., O., b 1806,6,12; m at Miami, Esther JONES, dt Daniel & Elizabeth, Warren Co., O., b 1809,3,3
Ch: Samuel b 1828, 2, 2
Seth " 1830, 7, 23
Mary Ann " 1835, 11, 16
Caroline Elizabeth " 1843, 11, 15
Joseph " 1846, 5, 8
1827, 10, 3. Benjamin, s Clayton & Elizabeth, Preble Co., O.; m at Miami, Maryann CRAIG, dt Samuel & Martha, Warren Co., O.
1832, 10, 3. Elizabeth m Thomas BURNET
1836, 4, 30. Elmira (form Lownes), w Allen K., b (H)
1842, 8, 31. John, s Asher & Mary, Clinton Co., O.; m at Miami, Elizabeth R. JONES, dt Daniel & Elizabeth, Warren Co., O.
----, --, --. John b 1810,5,16; m Newel ----- b 1815,1,5
Ch: Lydia Ann b 1843, 7, 8
Mary E. " 1840, 3, 1
Joseph John" 1852, 9, 22
1847, 12, 23. Sarah m Samuel B. MOORE (H)
----, --, --. Samuel b 1828,2,2; m Hannah EVANS b 1827,11,12
Ch: Mary Ann b 1852, 9, 8
1853, 5, 8. Hannah (form Evans) d bur Waynesville
1854, 1, 26. Aaron W., s John & Mary W., Wayne Co., Ind.; m at Miami, Hannah BURNET dt John & Elizabeth, Warren Co., O., b 1836,7,5
Ch: Oliver W. b 1855, 8, 5
1854, 3, 1. Ruth m Richard MATHER
1855, 5, 6. John d
1855, 10, 19. Aaron W. d bur Waynesville
----, --, --. Seth b 1830,7,23; m Marthann HILL b 1836,1,24
Ch: Emma E. b 1856, 10, 20
Annie M. " 1857, 9, 17
----, --, --. Ethan A. m Hannah Ann CHANDLER b 1830,8,2 d 1906,11,18 (H)
Ch: Charles A. b 1863, 4, 3
Annetta " 1866, 3, 18
1862, 10, 1. Mary Ann m Joseph MATHER
1863, 9, 30. Mary Elizabeth m William JANNEY
----, --, --. Ner b 1839,2,12; m Ellen Jane SNOWDEN b 1832,8,18
Ch: Mary Lydia b 1865, 12, 2
1865, 5, 3. Caroline E. m Joseph R. EVANS
1868, 8, 23. Israel, s Asher, Sr. d ae 72 (H)
1887, 12, 22. Annetta m J. Emerson DODDS (H)

1804, 7, 12. Asher & w, Mary, & ch, David, Samuel, Ann, Israel, Benjamin & Mary, rocf Woodberry MM, N. J., dtd 1804,4,10
1805, 4, 11. Richard & w, Mary, & ch, Sarah, Lydia, Mercer, John, William, Richard & Jonathan, rocf Wrightsboro MM
1805, 8, 8. Mercer rocf Wrightsboro MM, dtd 1805,6,2
1805, 9, 12. Sarah rocf Wrightsborough MM, Ga., dtd 1804,6,2
1806, 3, 13. Thomas rocf Deep Creek MM, N.C., dtd 1805,10,5
1806, 9, 11. Isaac rocf Jack Swamp MM, N.C., dtd 1806,2,1
1806, 12, 11. Joel & w, Rachel, & ch, Elgar & William, rocf Crooked Run MM, dtd 1806,8,2
1808, 3, 10. David rpd mcd
1808, 4, 14. Phebe rocf Pilesgrove MM, N. J., dtd 1807,8,27
1808, 12, 10. Mary recrq
1808, 12, 10. Elizabeth recrq
1809, 7, 8. Catherine, Susanna, Mary & Hampton, ch Joseph & Mary, recrq
1810, 1, 31. Mary, w David, recrq
1810, 8, 29. Dinah (form Cook) dis mou
1811, 3, 27. Merriam & ch, Sarah, Jane, Mary, Aaron & Elizabeth, rocf Plymouth MM, dtd 1810,10,20
1812, 9, 30. Cert rec for Merriam & ch, Sarah, Jane, Mary, Elizabeth, Ruth & Aron, from Plymouth MM, dtd 1810,10,20, endorsed to Darby Creek MM
1813, 8, 25. Elizabeth recrq of parents, David & Mary
1815, 11, 29. John & w, Sarah, & ch, Elizabeth, Nathaniel, Joseph & Bathsheba, rocf Evesham MM, N. J., dtd 1815,9,9
1815, 11, 29. Beulah rocf Upper Eavesham MM, N. J., dtd 1815,9,9
1815, 11, 29. Virgin rocf Upper Eavesham MM,

BROWN, continued
N. J., dtd 1815,9,9
1815, 12, 27. Abraham rocf Upper Evesham MM, N. J., dtd 1815,10,7
1815, 12, 27. Clayton rocf Upper Evesham MM, N. J., dtd 1815,9,9
1816, 7, 31. Mahlon & w, Alice, & ch, Clayton, Virgin, Ann, Mary, Mahlon & Alice, rocf Upper Evesham MM, dtd 1816,5,11
1816, 7, 31. William rocf Upper Evesham MM, N. J., dtd 1816,5,11
1816, 7, 31. Samuel rocf Upper Evesham MM, N. J., dtd 1816,10,7(?)
1816, 12, 25. Samuel rocf Mouris River MM, N. J., dtd 1816,10,4
1818, 5, 27. Hampton rpd mcd
1818, 5, 27. Susanna Mills (form Brown) dis mou
1818, 6, 24. Clayton gct Elk MM
1819, 2, 24. William gct Elk MM
1819, 4, 28. Samuel & w, Ruth, gct Elk MM
1819, 6, 30. Moses rocf Rich Square & Jack Swamp MM, N. C., dtd 1818,2,21
1819, 8, 25. Catherine dis
1819, 12, 29. Thomas con mcd
1820, 3, 29. Beulah gct Elk MM
1820, 3, 29. Virtin gct Elk MM
1820, 3, 29. Mahlon & fam gct Elk MM
1820, 7, 26. Abraham gct Elk MM
1820, 8, 30. Samuel gct Elk MM
1821, 12, 26. Hannah rocf Mount Holly MM, N.J., dtd 1821,11,8
1823, 8, 27. Hampton rqct New Garden MM, Ind.
1823, 9, 24. Chester MM, Ind. was granted permission to rst Catherine
1824, 4, 28. Hampton dis
1827, 10, 31. John gct Center MM, to m Mary Carpenter
1827, 11, 28. Mary Ann gct Westfield MM
1828, 1, 30. Mary W. rocf Centre MM, dtd 1828,1,19
1829, 1, 28. Asher dis jH
1829, 2, 25. David dis jH
1829, 3, 25. Israel dis jH
1829, 4, 29. Mary W. dis jH
1829, 11, 25. Elizabeth dis jH
1829, 11, 25. Sarah dis jH
1830, 4, 28. John recrq
1830, 8, 25. Benjamin dis jH
1830, 8, 25. Sarah dis jH
1830, 12, 29. John & w, Mary, & s, Aaron W., gct Whitewater MM, Ind.
1831, 1, 26. Elizabeth recrq
1832, 1, 25. John & w, Mary W., & s, Aaron W. rocf White Water MM, dtd 1831,12,28
1833, 8, 21. Allen dis jH
1834, 5, 21. John Jr. con mou
1836, 12, 21. John & w, Mary, & ch gct Center MM
1837, 6, 21. Allen dis mou (H)
1837, 11, 22. Newel recrq
1838, 1, 24. Israel con mou (H)
1839, 9, 25. Cert for Abia W. from Upper Springfield MM, dtd 1838,12,22, endorsed to Short Creek MM
1843, 6, 21. John & ch, Aaron W. & Ann Eliza, rocf Center MM, dtd 1843,4,12
1846, 12, 26. Mary C. & Ruth B. recrq
1850, 12, 25. Samuel gct White Water MM, to m Hannah Evans
1851, 11, 26. Hannah rocf White Water MM, dtd 1851,7,23
1852, 8, 25. Rachel (form Ward) con mcd (H)
1853, 3, 23. Mary (form Dutton) dis mcd (H)
1853, 5, 25. John A. & w, Elizabeth, & dt, Mary Emily, gct White Water MM, Ind.
1853, 5, 25. Ann Eliza gct White Water MM
1853, 8, 24. Mary dis mcd (H)
1855, 3, 21. Seth gct White Water MM, to m Mary Ann Hill
1855, 7, 25. Martha Ann rocf White Water MM, dtd 1855,6,27
1856, 4, 23. Hannah J. & s, Oliver, gct East Grove MM, Ia.
1856, 5, 23. Esther Ann Taylor (form Brown) dis mou
1856, 10, 22. Seth & w, Martha Ann, & dt, Emma E., gct White Water MM, Ind.
1857, 1, 21. Esther Ann Taylor (form Brown) dis mcd (H)
1858, 3, 24. Samuel gct Springfield MM, to m Elizabeth W. Hadley
1858, 8, 25. Seth & w, Martha Ann, & ch, Emma E. & Annie Mary, rocf White Water MM, dtd 1858,4,28
1858, 12, 22. Elizabeth H. rocf Springfield MM, dtd 1858,12,18
1861, 3, 27. Elmira L. rocf Clear Creek MM, dtd 1861,3,1 (H)
1861, 7, 24. Cert rec for Catharine from [ed Plainfield MM, O., dtd 1860,6,14 (H) return
1861, 7, 24. Hannah Ann (form Chandler) con mcd (H)
1863, 9, 23. Sarah L. (form West) rocf Sandy Spring MM, Md., dtd 1863,8,5 (H)
1863, 10, 21. Ann Baird (form Brown) dis mou
1863, 11, 25. Lydia Ann Baird (form Brown) dis mou
1864, 10, 26. Samuel & w, Elisabeth, & ch, Mary Anna & Evan, gct Springboro MM
1865, 5, 24. Rachel Caroline dis mcd (H)
1866, 7, 25. Jane (form Snowden) dis mcd (H)
1867, 7, 24. Joseph J. con mou
1867, 8, 21. Rosanna E. rocf Plainfield MM, dtd 1867,7,3
1867, 9, 25. Seth & w, Martha Ann, & ch, Emma E. & Anna M., gct Newgarden MM, Ind.
1869, 8, 25. Joseph J. & w, Rosa E., & ch, Viola Mary & Clara Esther, gct Spring Creek MM, Ia.
1871, 2, 22. Samuel & w, Elizabeth H., & ch, Mary Anna, Evan Henry & John Franklin, rocf Springborough MM, dtd 1871,1,24
1871, 3, 22. Ner & w, Ellen Jane, & dt, Mary Lydia, recrq
1874, 6, 24. Charles A. & Annetta H., ch

BROWN, continued
Hannah Ann, recrq
1877, 4, 25. Samuel & w, Elizabeth H., & ch, Evan H. & John Franklin, gct Westfield MM, Ind.
1882, 3, 23. Catharine rocf Plainfield MM, O., dtd 1882,1,19 (H)
1887, 6, 22. Marianna gct Poplar Ridge MM, Ind.
1890, 7, 23. Margaretta K. rocf White Water MM, Ind., dtd 1890,6,28
1893, 11, 22. Charles A. relrq (H)
1899, 2, 22. Charles A. recrq (H)
1914, 8, 30. Elmira L. relrq (H)
1920, 7, 25. Charles A. dropped from mbrp (H)

BRUCE
1876, 3, 22. Eunice (or Brice) (form Mosher) rpd mcd (H)

BURDIN
1811, 9, 25. Elizabeth Hewlings (form Burdin) [rpd mcd
1822, 2, 27. Mary Ward (form Burdin) dis mou

BURGESS
1769, 11, 4. Betty b
1807, 4, 28. Moses b
1811, 9, 5. Tacy b
----, --, --. John b 1813,10,13; m Elizabeth HARVEY b 1816,4,11
Ch: Elisha H. b 1838, 3, 20 d 1838, 9,21
Mary " 1840, 9, 17
Sarah Harvey " 1844, 2, 26
John " 1847, 8, 18
Jesse Harvey " 1851, 11, 1
----, --, --. Jesse m Elizabeth HARVEY
Ch: Mary Emily b 1830, 1, 10
Thomas H. " 1833, 7, 17
Martha Ann " 1836, 1, 12
Mahala L. " 1839, 3, 16
William H. " 1842, 3, 8
1831, 9, 1. Isaac b
1846, 2, 19. Tacy m Job HADLEY
1854, 12, 20. Mary E. d bur Harveysburgh
1859, 3, 3. Martha Ann m Enos DOAN

1830, 11, 24. Mary (form Wales) con mou (H)
1832, 1, 25. Joseph H. rocf Clear Creek MM, dtd 1832,12,19
1834, 5, 21. Isaac, minor s Joseph H., recrq
1835, 8, 26. Thomas & w, Betty, rocf Fairfield MM, dtd 1835,7,23
1835, 8, 26. Tacy rocf Fairfield MM, dtd 1835,7,23
1835, 8, 26. Martha rocf Fairfield MM, dtd 1835,7,23
1835, 12, 23. John Tompkins rocf Fairfield MM, dtd 1835,9,24
1836, 1, 27. Jesse & w, Elizabeth, & ch, Mary Emily & Thomas H., rocf Fairfield MM, dtd 1836,1,21
1836, 2, 21. Letitia rocf Fairfield MM, dtd 1835,12,24
1837, 4, 26. John T. gct Springfield MM, to m Elizabeth Harvey
1837, 12, 27. Elizabeth rocf Springfield MM, dtd 1837,10,17
1838, 7, 25. Moses rocf Springfield MM, dtd 1838,7,17
1838, 11, 21. Martha Ham (form Burgess) dis mou
1842, 7, 27. Joseph H. gct Fairfield MM
1848, 2, 23. Joseph H. & w, Juliet, & ch, Aaron B. & Valena, rocf Fairfield MM, dtd 1847,11,20
1849, 2, 21. Joseph H. & w, Juliet, & ch, Isaac W., Aaron & Valena, gct Pleasant Plain MM, Ia.
1851, 10, 22. Moses dis
1853, 2, 23. Betty gct White Lick MM, Ind.
1857, 6, 24. John T. & w, Elizabeth, & ch, Mary, Sarah, John & Jesse H., gct Mill Creek MM, Ind.
1863, 9, 23. Thomas H. gct Marlborough MM, N. Y., to m Mary G. Heaton
1865, 5, 24. Thomas H. gct Marlboro MM, N.Y.
1866, 1, 24. William H. gct Rich Square MM, N. C.
1866, 6, 20. Kansas MM was given permission to rst Moses

BURGURNAL
1906, 5, 23. Alma M. (form Elsay Oliver) relrq

BURKHARD
1891, 1, 21. Phebe & s, Edgar, recrq

BURNET
----, --, --. Robert b 1776,6,29; m Anna ----- b 1779,2,15
Ch: Rebecca b 1805, 1, 23
Rachel " 1808, 2, 21
Thomas " 1811, 10, 4
Lydia " 1813, 10, 22
William " 1818, 10, 22 d 1849, 8,28 bur Waynesville
Smith b 1820, 5, 2 " 1851, 3,12 bur Waynesville
Eliza b 1818, 11, 30
----, --, --. Daniel [Burnett] b 1781,11,31 d 1859,2,5; m Ann GAUSE b 1780,9,15 d 1856,11,29
Ch: Ruth b 1806, 7, 7 d 1810, 5,21
Anabel M. " 1808, 3, 21 " 1880, 8,29
Mary " 1811, 7, 25 " 1812, 9,19
Stephen " 1813, 7, 30 " 1894, 2,13
Joseph " 1816, 8, 17 " 1818, 8,13
William " 1819, 6, 25 " 1884, 5,19
Jesse " 1822, 2, 17 " 1822, 3,17
1813, 6, 2. Rachel m David EVANS
1822, 2, 6. John, s Robert & Anna, Warren Co., O., b 1800,3,25; m Elizabeth HAWKINS, dt Isaac & Mary, Warren Co., O., b 1803, 12,18

BURNET, John & Elizabeth, continued
Ch: Mary Ann b 1823, 11, 11
Amos " 1826, 1, 2
Seth " 1829, 4, 17
Rebecca " 1832, 10, 16
Hannah " 1836, 7, 5
----, --,---. David b 1803,2,4; m Hannah WILSON b 1805,7,8
Ch: Christopher
Seth
1832, 10, 3. Thomas, s Robert & Ann, Warren Co., O.; m at Miami, Elizabeth BROWN, dt Joseph & Dinah, Warren Co., O., b 1812,3,7
Ch: Sarah b 1833, 10, 6
Jemima " 1836, 7, 28
Abraham " 1844, 2, 13
Mary Emma " 1850, 12, 14
1833, 10, 30. Stephen, s Samuel & Ann, Warren Co., O., b 1813,7,30 d 1894,2,13; m at Miami, Hannah JONES, dt Jesse & Lydia, Warren Co., O., b 1811,12,5 d 1893,9,12 (H)
Ch: Lydiaann b 1835, 6, 5 d 1915,12, 9
Joseph H. " 1838, 12, 1 " 1891, 4,16
Owen J. " 1843, 4, 15 " 1924,12, 5
Jesse " 1845, 1, 4 " 1848, 3,17
Jonathan Y." 1847, 3, 26 " 1909, 7, 8
Sarah E. " 1849, 4, 4
Franklin C." 1851, 10, 18
Emma Matilda " 1853, 7, 25
1837, 10, 8. Robert d
1839, 2, 27. Anabel M. m Isaac L. MILLS (H)
1840, 8, 5. William b 1819,6,25 d 1884,5,19; m Elizabeth SINCLAIR, dt John & Rachel, b 1818,6,25 d 1902,7,2 (H)(William was s of Daniel & Ann, Warren Co., O.)
Ch: Charles b 1841, 11, 27 d 1864,10,18
Rachel Ann " 1843, 5, 4 " 1910, 2,11
Matilda P. " 1845, 6, 12
Eli D. " 1848, 1, 12 " 1912, 1, 4
Martha R. " 1850, 12, 13
Mary L. " 1852, 9, 14 " 1909, 9, 6
Sarah Ellen" 1855, 9, 12
1845, 4, 30. Mary Ann m John PYLE
1846, 4, 1. Rebecca m Jesse SPRAY
1854, 1, 26. Hannah J. m Aaron W. BROWN
1873, 10, 23. Sarah E. m Samuel BUTTERWORTH (H)

1845, 12, 24. Smith con mou
1846, 6, 24. Sarah recrq
1847, 12, 22. David & w, Eliza, gct Spiceland MM
1848, 4, 26. Anna gct Caesars Creek MM
1850, 8, 21. Amos dis disunity
1851, 12, 24. Seth dis disunity
1855, 4, 25. Lydiann Gorden (form Burnet) con mcd (H)
1855, 12, 26. Rebecca Satterthwaite (form Burnet) con mou
1856, 4, 23. John & w, Elizabeth, gct East Grove MM, Ia.
1862, 11, 26. Joseph H. [Burnett] rpd mcd (H)
1864, 6, 22. Sarah B. Smith (form Burnet) con mou
1866, 11, 21. Jemima Misseldine (form Burnett) con mou
1868, 11, 26. Owen J. [Burnett] con mcd (H)
1869, 6, 23. Matilda Slack (form Burnett) rpd mcd (H)
1870, 10, 26. Eli [Burnett] con mcd (H)
1870, 10, 26. Jonathan [Burnett] con mcd (H)
1871, 1, 25. Emma Retallic (form Burnet) con mou
1873, 4, 23. Charles S. dis mou
1874, 6, 24. Lydia dis disunity
1877, 3, 21. Emma M. Keys (form Burnett) rpd mcd (H)
1885, 3, --. Mary J. Hollowell (form Burnett) rpd mcd (H)
1895, 2, 20. Sarah Ellen Meredith (form Burnett) con mou (H)
1906, 6, 20. Louisa G. recrq (H)
1928, 3, 25. Charles recrq (H)

BURNSTEIN
1917, 7, 29. Eliza dropped from mbrp (H)

BURRIS
1806, 4, 10. John & w, Esther, rocf Westfield MM, N. C., dtd 1805,10,19
1806, 8, 14. John Jr. & w, Francis, & ch, Milly, Daniel, Betsy & Rebecca, rocf Westfield MM, N. C., dtd 1806,3,22

BURSON
1838, 8, 1. David, s Edward & Jemima, Monroe Co., Pa. m at Waynesville, Margaret EVANS, dt Thomas & Hannah, Warren Co., O., b 1818,8,26
Ch: Edward Thomas b 1839, 5, 22
Ann Elizabeth " 1841, 3, 29
Lydia Ann " 1843, 10, 22

1837, 8, 23. David S. rocf Goshen MM, dtd 1837,8,3
1842, 8, 24. Brooks Johnson gct Center MM, to m Lydia Burson
1852, 9, 22. Edward & w, Jemima, rocf Center MM, dtd 1852,5,12; Edward d before cert arrived
1853, 9, 20. Jemima gct White Water MM
1853, 12, 21. David L. & w, Margaret, & ch, Hannah Wells & Rachel Haskett, gct White Water MM, Ind.

BUTCHER
1811, 5, 29. Mary (form Allen) con mou

BUTLER
1840, 2, 6. William E., s Micajah & Ann, Warren Co., O.; m at Miami, Rhoda JOHNSON, dt Micajah & Rebecca, Warren Co., O.
1843, 5, 26. Rhoda T. d
1852, 6, 2. William E., s Micajah & Ann, Warren Co., O.; m at Miami, Rhoda Ann

BUTLER, continued
MOFFITT, dt James & Elizabeth Johnson, Warren Co., O.

1806, 6, 12. Samuel & w, Ursula, & ch, Mourning, Nathan, Lucy, Lydia, Tabitha, Simmons F. & Sarah Ann, rocf Upper MM, dtd 1806,2, 15
1806, 11, 13. William & w, Mary, & ch, David, Jonothan, Michael & Elizabeth, rocf Upper MM, dtd 1806,8,16
1809, 11, 4. Amos rocf Bradford MM, Pa., dtd 1808,2,3
1812, 5, 27. Daniel & w, Sarah, & ch, James, Mary, Susannah, Nancy, Benjamin & Martha, rocf Fairfield MM, dtd 1810,8,25
1814, 11, 30. William & w, Nancy, rocf South River MM, Va., dtd 1814,9,10
1831, 8, 31. Judith dis jH
1841, 3, 4. Rhoda J. gct Springboro MM
1851, 10, 22. Maria (form Barrett) dis mcd (H)
1852, 8, 25. Rhoda A. gct Springboro MM

BUTTERWORTH
----, --, --. Benjamin, s Isaac & Averilla (Gilbert), b 1766,2,11 d 1833,1,20; m Rachel MOORMAN b 1765,1,26 d 1848,3,10 (H)
Ch: Polly b 1787, 6, 15 d 1863, 1,26
Betsy " 1788, 9, 3 " 1843,11, 9
Milly " 1789, 9, 15 " 1830, 8,31
Nancy " 1791, 5, 21 " 1844, 7, 5
Moorman " 1793, 3, 5 " 1841,11,11
Benjamin " 1794, 10, 24 " 1869, 9,24
Isaac " 1796, 5, 7 " 1801,12, 2
Samuel " 1798, 6, 30 " 1872, 2,21
Rachel M. " 1800, 11, 7 " 1872, 2, 3
William " 1802, 9, 27 " 1884, 8,27
Henry T. " 1809, 6, 4 " 1893, 11,5
----, --, --. Benjamin Jr. b 1794,10,24 d 1869 9,24; m Judith WELCH b 1799,10,20 d 1885, 9,4 (H)
Ch: Mary M. b 1818, 11, 25
Samuel G. " 1820, 2, 18 d 1825, 5,23
Amos H. " 1821, 10, 23 " 1824, 9,22
William W. " 1823, 6, 15
Rachel " 1824, 11, 22 " 1825, 1,22
Isaac " 1825, 11, 29
Ruth C. " 1827, 8, 27
Moses E. " 1829, 2, 14 " 1901, 3, 5
Sarah E. " 1831, 5, 3
Benjamin T." 1833, 11, 6
Turner W. " 1837, 10, 9
----, --, --. Samuel b 1798,6,30 d 1872,2,21; m Hannah TAYLOR d 1850,9,5 (H)
Ch: Jesse T. b 1823, 5, 11 d 1882, 9,26
Naomi " 1825, 8, 8 " 1825,11,24
Edward B. " 1827, 7, 14 " 1890,10, 1
Israel " 1829, 7, 19 " 1853, 6,10
Rachel " 1831, 10, 17 " 1831,12,11
Sarah " 1832, 12, 1 " 1851, 9,18
1825, 9, 7. Moorman, s Benjamin & Rachel, Warren Co., O., b 1793,3,5 d 1841,10,11; m at Miami, Fanny SMITH, dt Joseph & Rachel Warren Co., O., b 1801,3,26 d 1889,4,16 (H)
Ch: Thomas b 1826, 10, 17 d 1830, 9, 6
Clarkson " 1828, 12, 29
Edith " 1831, 3, 24 " 1909, 7,20
Martha " 1833, 11, 28
Paulina " 1838, 5, 19 " 1915, 7, 1
Ruthanna " 1841, 3, 9 " 1900,11,16
----, --, --. William b 1802,9,27 d 1884,8,27; m Elizabeth LINTON b 1807,7,29 d 1884,2,23 (H)
Ch: Louisa b 1828, 1, 5 d 1830, 7,26
Kalista " 1829, 11, 29
Nathan " 1831, 12, 11 " 1850, 7,24
Rachel " 1833, 1, 7 " 1910, 9, 8
Susan " 1835, 6, 13 " 1909, 9,16
Benjamin " 1837, 10, 22 " 1898, 1,16
Elizabeth " 1840, 4, 12 " 1884, 9,25
1830, 11, 3. Henry T., s Benjamin & Rachel, Warren Co., O., b 1809,6,4 d 1893,11,5; m at Grove, Nancy WALES, dt Isaac & Ruth, Warren Co., O., b 1809,11,20 d 1909,12,6 (H)
Ch: Jane b 1831, 8, 23
Benjamin " 1833, 7, 13 d 1834, 8,17
Mary " 1834, 10, 18 " 1910, 7,30
Isaac W. " 1836, 9, 26 " 1904,10,31
Ann " 1838, 9, 13
Emma " 1841, 4, 12
Rachel M. " 1844, 6, 19
Moorman " 1846, 11, 16 d 1853, 4, 1
Henry Thomas " 1849, 1, 6 " 1853, 2, 8
Caroline " 1852, 2, 6
1831, 12, 1. Rachel M. m John SANDERS (H)
1849, 3, 28. Edward B., s Samuel & Hannah, Warren Co., O., b 1827,7,14 d 1890,10,1; m at Miami, Hannah ROGERS, dt Josiah & Abigail, Warren Co., O., b 1825,4,30 d 1873,5,1 (H)
Ch: Abigale b 1850, 4, 25 d 1851, 4,26
Samuel " 1852, 12, 12
Sarah Jane " 1854, 2, 14 " 1873, 6, 4
Ellen " 1856, 3, 6
Mary " 1858, 9, 11
Josiah " 1861, 10, 3
Edward B. m 2nd Priscilla A. -----
----, --, --. Jesse T. b 1823,5,11 d 1882,9, 26; m Ruth E. OGBORN b 1826,1,27 d 1893, 12,7 (H)
Ch: John Ogborn b 1860, 6, 29 d 1860, 8,10
Mary Eliza " 1862, 5, 15
----, --, --. Benjamin b 1837,10,22 d 1898,1, 16; m Mary SEILER b 1841,3,11 (H)
Ch: Mary E. b 1866, 11, 1
1873, 10, 23. Samuel, s Edward & Hannah, Warren Co., O., b 1852,12,12; m Sarah BURNET, dt Stephen & Hannah, Warren Co., O. (H) (m at residence of Stephen Burnet)
Ch: Stella H. b 1874, 11, 6 d 1910, 1,27
Ernest " 1876, 11, 21

1813, 3, 31. Benjamin & Rachel & ch, Moorman,

BUTTERWORTH, continued
Benjamin, Samuel, Rachel, William & Henry Thomas, rocf South Run MM, Va., dtd 1812, 10,10
1818, 10, 28. Benjamin Jr. rpd mcd
1819, 2, 24. Judith (form Welch) con mou
1822, 2, 27. Samuel gct Center MM
1822, 8, 28. Hannah rocf Center MM, dtd 1822, 7,20
1826, 4, 26. William gct Center MM, to m
1826, 12, 27. Elizabeth rocf Centre MM, dtd 1826,10,21
1829, 6, 24. Benjamin dis jH
1829, 6, 24. Morman dis jH
1829, 6, 24. Samuel dis jH
1829, 6, 24. William dis jH
1829, 8, 26. Fanny dis jH
1829, 8, 26. Rachel dis jH
1829, 8, 26. Rachel Jr. dis jH
1829, 10, 28. Henry T. dis jH
1831, 8, 31. Judith dis jH
1831, 9, 28. Elizabeth & Hannah dis jH
1836, 6, 22. Benjamin & w, Judith, & ch, Mary M., William H., Isaac, Ruth Caroline, Moses Elwood, Sarah E. & Benjamin T., gct White Water MM (H)
1842, 5, 25. Jesse & Isaac Townsend recrq of William Butterworth (H)
1849, 9, 26. Edith Girten (form Butterworth) dis mou (H)
1849, 11, 21. Fanny dis disunity (H)
1851, 5, 21. Jesse T. gct White Water MM, to m Ruth E. Ogburn (H)
1851, 9, 24. Ruth E. rocf White Water MM, dtd 1851,8,27 (H)
1853, 1, 26. Henry T. dis disunity (H)
1853, 1, 26. Clarkson dis disunity (H)
1853, 1, 26. Nancy dis disunity (H)
1853, 1, 26. Martha dis disunity (H)
1855, 1, 24. Jane Foster (form Butterworth) con mcd (H)
1857, 10, 21. William dis disunity (H)
1858, 6, 23. Rachel Hadley (form Butterworth) dis mcd (H)
1858, 10, 27. Susan Murdock (form Butterworth) rpd mcd (H)
1869, 2, 22. Emma B. Danforth (form Butterworth) con mcd (H)
1872, 11, 20. William B. recrq (H)
1873, 9, 24. Benjamin con mcd (H)
1876, 2, 23. Benjamin gct Cincinnati MM (H)
1876, 8, 23. Fanny & Priscilla recrq (H)
1877, 7, 25. Rachel B. Henry (form Butterworth) con mcd (H)
1878, 10, 25. Clarkson rst (H)
1885, 10, 21. Ruthanna Witham (form Butterworth) relrq (H)
1886, 11, 24. Ellen Chandler (form Butterworth) rpd mcd (H)
1887, 7, 27. Ann Thatcher (form Butterworth) dis jas (H)
1887, 11, 23. Rachel B. Baylies (form Butterworth & later Henry) rpd mcd (H)
1888, 11, 21. Mary Eliza Frazee (form Butterworth) dis (H)
1889, 3, 27. Isaac W. rpd mcd (H)
1889, 6, 26. Isaac W. gct Cincinnati MM (H)
1896, 4, 22. Mary B. (form Butterworth) con mcd (Mary B. Linton) (H)
1911, 10, 25. Edith P. rst (H)

CADWALADER
1813, 12, 1. Jonah, s Thos. & Jane, Hamilton Co., O., b 1789,8,14 d 1879,7,21; m at Hopewell, Priscilla WHITACRE, dt Robert & Patience, Warren Co., O., b 1795,7,21 d 1870,4,28 (H)
Ch: Jane b 1815, 5, 3 d 1899, 4,26
Robert " 1817, 3, 9 " 1895, 1, 7
Patience " 1818, 5, 24
Thomas " 1820, 3, 5 " 1849, 3,21
Aquilla " 1823, 1, 24 " 1850, 7,20
Noah " 1824, 11, 19
Rachel " 1827, 5, 26 " 1848, 2,25
Andrew " 1828, 8, 20 " 1904, 4, 6
Enos " 1830, 6, 29 " 1908, 2,14
Clarkson " 1833, 1, 1
Leah " 1835, 12, 28
Jonas " 1822, 7,27
when a ch
----, --, --. Mahlon & Elizabeth
Ch: Deborah b 1815, 8, 18
John T. " 1820, 5, 15
Achilles D." 1822, 8, 14
Elizabeth Ann " 1824, 12, 22
Mildred I. " 1827, 12, 27
Charles T. " 1830, 4, 15
1817, 12, 4. Esther m James HOLLINGSWORTH
1817, 12, 4. Naomi m Elijah THOMAS
1818, 6, 4. Thomas, s Thos. & Jane, Warren Co., O., b 1795,5,3; m at Hopewell, Vashti THOMAS, dt Edward & Mary, Warren Co., O. b 1797,9,10
Ch: Ezra b 1819, 3, 4
Eli " 1825, 3, 20
1834, 5, 28. William [Cadwallader], s Mahlon & Elizabeth, Warren Co., O.; m at Miami Mary STAUNTON, dt Frederick & Hannah, Warren Co., O., b 1812,11,20 (William was b 1810,3,21)
Ch: Charles Edward b 1835, 3, 17
Ann Eliza " 1836, 8, 26
Hannah S. " 1839, 9, 13
Mary Margaret " 1843, 7, 13
1843, 9, 21. Patience W. m Hiram GREGG (H)
1840, 10, 29. David, s Thomas & Jane, Warren Co., O., b 1807,7,22 d 1888,9,8; m at Rochester, Rachel BABCOCK, dt Benjamin & Sarah, d 1885,7,19 (H)
Ch: Benjamin b 1846, 10, 3 d 1901, 4,19
Aaron " 1851, 9, 13 " 1904, 9,11
1848, 3, 2. Thomas, s Jonah & Priscilla, Warren Co., O.; m at Harveysburgh, Phebe

CADWALADER, Thomas, continued
FALLIS, dt Richard & Phebe, Warren Co., O.
1850, 3, 5. Aquilla, s Jonah & Priscilla, Warren Co., O.; m at dwelling house of Turner Welch in Ind., Martha WELCH, dt Turner & Esther, Tippencanoe Co., Ind. (H)
----, --, --. Andrew b 1828,8,20 d 1904,4,6; m Esther PEIRCE b 1830,6,30 d 1913,12,10 (H)
Ch: Pierce J. b 1853, 12, 27
Dorah
Priscilla " 1855, 10, 6
Clinton H. " 1858, 5, 8 d 1868, 9,21
Andrew W. " 1863, 3, 24
Mary " 1865, 6, 30
1855, 3, 22. Leah m Isaiah F. WELCH (H)
----, --, --. Clarkson b 1833,1,1 d 1908,2,14; m Mary E. WILLIAMSON b 1840,10,1 (H)
Ch: Frank W. b 1861, 9, 23
Ada B. " 1864, 3, 10
Jonah C. " 1866, 6, 21
Miriam " 1873, 7, 16
Hallie A. " 1876, 12, 18
1882, 4, 27. Dora P. m John D. GALLAGHER (H)
1896, 11, 26. Mary m Lewis DONNALLY (H)

1813, 9, 29. Jona [Cadwallader] rocf Goose Creek MM, Va., dtd 1813,6,13
1815, 3, 29. Joseph & Judah [Cadwallader] rocf Center MM, dtd 1815,2,4
1815, 3, 29. Betsy & Birone [Cadwallader] rocf Center MM, dtd 1815,2,4
1815, 3, 29. Elizabeth [Cadwallader] gct Cesar's Creek MM
1816, 11, 27. Thomas [Cadwallader] Jr. rocf South River MM, dtd 1816,10,12
1816, 11, 27. Jane [Cadwallader] & ch, Naomi, Esther, Abner, Joseph & David, rocf South River MM, dtd 1816,9,14
1819, 11, 24. Judith gct Cesars Creek MM
1823, 1, 29. Joseph [Cadwallader] gct Clear Creek MM, to m Catherine Cox
1824, 5, 26. Joseph [Cadwallader] gct Clear Creek MM
1826, 3, 29. Mary (form Thomas) con mou
1826, 6, 28. Abner [Cadwallader] dis mcd
1829, 5, 27. Jane [Cadwallader] dis
1829, 5, 27. Priscilla [Cadwallader] dis
1829, 5, 27. Jonah [Cadwallader] dis jH
1829, 5, 27. Thomas [Cadwallader] dis jH
1829, 11, 25. David [Cadwallader] dis jH
1830, 5, 26. Joseph [Cadwallader] dis mou
1830, 9, 29. Mary gct Arba MM, Ind.
1831, 4, 27. Thomas & w, Vashti, & ch, Ezra & Eli, gct Arba MM, Ind.
1833, 5, 22. Thomas dis disunity (H)
1833, 9, 25. Jane Anderson (form Cadwallader) dis jH
1834, 8, 27. Jane Anderson (form Cadwalader) con mou (H)
1835, 5, 27. William rocf Springborough MM, dtd 1835,4,21
1837, 10, 25. Deborah [Cadwallader] rocf Springborough MM, dtd 1837,9,19
1837, 10, 25. Elizabeth [Cadwallader] & ch, Judith, John T., Achilles, Elizabeth, Mildred & Charles, rocf Springborough MM, dtd 1837,9,19
1838, 11, 21. Judith Haines (form Cadwalader) con mou
1839, 4, 24. Thomas recrq (H)
1845, 3, 26. Malon [Cadwallader] rst with permission of South River MM
1845, 5, 21. Joseph gct Center MM, to m Rachel Farquhar
1845, 12, 24. Achilles [Cadwallader] con mou
1848, 1, 26. Deborah Fallis (form Cadwalader) con mou
1848, 4, 26. Jane rocf Center MM, dtd 1846,7,15
1848, 10, 25. Elizabeth A. dis joining Methodists
1848, 11, 22. Rachel rocf Center MM, dtd 1848,9,13
1851, 8, 27. William con mou
1851, 8, 27. Lena (form Trahern) con mou
1852, 1, 21. William gct Goshen MM
1852, 3, 24. Lina gct Goshen MM
1852, 8, 25. Andrew W. gct Center MM, to m Esther W. Pierce (H)
1853, 11, 23. Noah gct White Water MM, to m Elizabeth Gause (H)
1854, 4, 26. Elizabeth rocf White Water MM dtd 1854,3,22 (H)
1854, 9, 20. Mildred T. Westhermer (form Cadwalader) rpd mou
1854, 10, 25. John & w, Rachel, & ch, Albert D., Isaac H. & John F., gct Center MM
1855, 4, 25. Hester rocf Center MM, dtd 1854,12,14 (H)
1855, 4, 25. Jonah dis disunity (H)
1856, 1, 23. Charles dis mou
1857, 2, 18. Noah & w, Elizabeth G., gct White Water MM, Ind. (H)
1857, 8, 26. Sarah Jane Ayers (form Cadwalader) dis mcd (H)
1858, 8, 25. Achilles D. dis disunity
1860, 1, 25. Clarkson dis mcd (H)
1860, 10, 24. Enos dis mcd (H)
1871, 1, 25. Jonah [Cadwallader] recrq
1872, 1, 24. Achilles [Cadwallader] recrq
1872, 8, 21. Clarkson & w, Mary E., & ch, Frank W., Adah B. & Jonah C., recrq
1873, 4, 23. Achilles D. con mou
1873, 4, 23. Horace con mou
1881, 1, 26. John F. [Cadwallader] relrq
1881, 9, 21. Pierce J. [Cadwallader] gct Cincinnati MM (H)
1882, 9, 20. Achilles gct Union MM
1887, 2, 23. Mary L. Adams (form Cadwallader) relrq
1889, 3, 27. Phebe [Cadwallader] gct Kansas City MM, Mo.
1891, 12, 23. Achilles rocf Union MM, dtd 1891,12,5
1899, 6, 21. Miriam [Cadwallader] relrq (H)

CADWALADER, continued
1920, 7, 25. Dr. Jonah C. [Cadwallader] dropped from mbrp (H)
1921, 11, 27. Andrew W. gct Orange Grove MM, Calif. (H)
1930, 3, 30. Dorothy Cheyney recrq (H)

CALDHOUN
1828, 7, 30. Elizabeth & ch, William & Mary, rocf Stillwater MM, dtd 1828,2,23

CAMMACK
1812, 4, 1. John, s James & Joann, Montgomery Co., O.; m at Hopewell, Jane HOLLINGSWORTH, dt John & Rachel, Warren Co., O.
1819, 7, 8. Samuel, s James & Rachel, Wayne Co., Ind.; m at Hopewell, Hannah HOLLINGSWORTH, dt John & Rachel, Warren Co., O.

1805, 7, 11. James [Commack] & w, Rachel, & ch, John, Samuel, William, Amos & Elizabeth, rocf Bush River MM, dtd 1805,2,23
1815, 4, 26. James & fam gct White Water MM
1816, 4, 24. John [Cammac] & fam gct New Garden MM, Ind.
1820, 2, 23. Hannah gct White Water MM
1850, 8, 21. Henry Steddom Jr. gct Chester MM, to m Sallie Cammack

CAMPBELL
1856, 9, 24. Malinda rocf Springfield MM, dtd 1856,9,20
1867, 3, 27. Malinda Sherwood (form Campbel) con mou
1872, 6, 26. Martha Jane recrq
1872, 12, 25. Martha Jane gct Kokomo MM, Ind.
1876, 12, 27. Martha rocf Kokomo MM, dtd 1876,6,12

CANBY
1808, 1, 20. Joseph, s Samuel & Ann, Warren Co., O.; m at Miami, Lydia PEDRICK, dt Isaac & Hannah, Warren Co., O. (H)
Ch: Richard
Sprigg b 1808, 9, 30
Ann " 1810, 10, 31

1807, 11, 12. Joseph rocf Goose Creek MM, Va., dtd 1807,2,3
1808, 9, 10. Israel rocf Goose Creek MM, Va., dtd 1807,10,20
1812, 12, 30. Joseph dis disunity & military service
1818, 12, 30. Israel dis holding slaves & mcd
1835, 4, 22. Joshua & w, Esther, & ch, Susan D., Elizabeth M., Andrew E. & Evan T., rocf Springborough MM, dtd 1835,2,19 (H)
1835, 12, 23. William, minor, rocf Alexandria MM, D. C., dtd 1835,9,24 (H)
1839, 2, 20. Richard S. dis mou
1839, 5, 22. Ann Kitchen (form Canby) rpd mou
1841, 4, 21. Hannah Evans (form Canby) dis mou
1845, 10, 22. Joseph dis disunity (H)
1846, 3, 25. Susan Hackney (form Canby) con mou (H)
1846, 9, 23. William gct Baltimore MM for Western District (H)
1854, 4, 26. Elizabeth Heston (form Canby) dis mcd (H)
1860, 4, 25. Hester & ch, William H. & Hester B., gct Prairie Grove MM, Ia. (H)
1860, 4, 25. Letitia H. gct Prairie MM, Ia. (H)
1860, 4, 25. Mary gct Prairie Grove MM, Ia. (H)
1860, 9, 26. Andrew E. gct Prairie Grove MM, Ia. (H)
1860, 9, 26. Evan T. gct Prairie Grove MM, Ia. (H)
1888, 1, 25. Richard Sprigg & Ann dropped from mbrp (H)

CANADY
1807, 8, 3. Walter & w, Nancy, & ch, Mary, John, Nathan & Henry, rocf Lost Creek MM

CAPPS
1804, 6, 13. Sarah rocf Back Creek MM, N.C., dtd 1804,10,27

CARDER
1887, 9, 21. Elizabeth recrq
1888, 4, 22. Clarence & Anna recrq

CAREY
1866, 12, 26. Almira (form Connard) dis mcd (H)

CARMON
1860, 4, 2. Ruth d (H)

1854, 7, 26. Ruth [Carman] rocf Center MM, dtd 1854,6,15 (H)

CARPENTER
1827, 10, 31. John Brown gct Center MM, to m Mary Carpenter
1844, 8, 21. David F. Johnson gct Cincinnati MM, to m Catherine Carpenter

CARR
1806, 9, 7. Job, s Job & Catherine, Warren Co., O.; m at Miamie, Ruth MASON, dt James & Rebeckah, Warren Co., O.
1807, 4, 15. Elizabeth m Daniel MILLS

1804, 12, 13. Benjamin & w, Patience, & ch, Elizabeth, Thomas, Benjamin & Hezekiah, rocf Westfield MM, N. C., dtd 1804,9,22
1806, 1, 9. Job rocf Mount Holly MM, dtd 1805,9,5
1813, 5, 26. Ruth & ch, John Mason, Mary Ann & Hannah, gct Great Eggharbor MM, N. J.
1816, 6, 26. Ruth, w Job, & ch, John, Mer-

CARR, continued
riam, Hannah & Job, rocf Great Egg Harbor MM, N. J., dtd 1815,11,6
1819, 7, 28. Job dis
1821, 10, 31. Job dis
1822, 5, 29. Job rst by order of QM
1823, 3, 26. Job dis
1868, 7, 22. Mary Ann (form Edwards) dis mou & jas
1905, 2, 22. La Rue recrq
1905, 4, 26. Reba recrq
1906, 5, 23. Guy C. recrq

CARRINGTON
1871, 6, 21. Alice recrq
1888, 12, 26. Fannie relrq

CARROLL
----, --, --. Dr. Thomas b 1794,4,15 d 1871,3,13; m Anne LYNCH b 1797,11,14 d 1871,5,19 (H)
Ch: Foster b 1823, 8, 18 d 1851, 7,14
Robert W. " 1826, 7, 28 " 1897,12,17
Laura " 1832, 6, 1 " 1906, 1,31
----, --, --. Joseph b 1780,--,-- d 1843,12,9; m Elizabeth ----- b 1797,1,12 d 1869,8,28 (H)
Ch: Rebecca b 1831, 6, 10
Eliza A. " 1829, 6, 5
Joseph " 1833, 5, 1
Sarah " 1837, 1, 12
Solon " 1839, 5, 25
----, --, --. Enos b 1818,8,22 d 1850,4,26; m Mary Ann SMITH b 1819,11,14 d 1859,2,28 (H)
Ch: Marean b 1841, 3, 20
Abi " 1843, 1, 4 d 1903, 2, 6
Elizabeth " 1844, 7, 25
Marry " 1847, 3, 29
Eli " 1849, 6, 23 " 1910, 4,--
1868, 4, 1. Abi m Aaron CHANDLER (H)

1844, 2, 21. Enos & w, Mary Ann, & ch, Marian & Aby, rocf Fall Creek MM, dtd 1844,7,22 (H)
1866, 1, 24. Joseph dis mcd (H)
1866, 1, 24. Eliza A. Ireland (form Carroll) rpd mcd (H)
1866, 1, 24. Rebecca H. Murry (form Carroll) rpd mcd (H)
1866, 1, 24. Albert & Solon rec in mbrp; form mbr of Fall Creek or Center MM, which had been laid down (H)
1866, 1, 24. John dropped from mbrp; form mbr of Fall Creek or Centre MM, which had been laid down (H)
1866, 11, 21. Solon dis mcd (H)
1869, 3, 24. Mary C. Griffin (form Carroll) dis mcd (H)
1871, 2, 22. Hannah Mary & ch, George E. & John Q., rocf Dover MM, dtd 1870,12,15
1871, 7, 26. Eli S. dis mcd (H)
1873, 5, 21. Joseph C. & ch, Anna B. & Rosa L., recrq
1884, 10, 22. Albert relrq (H)
1886, 3, 24. John Quincy relrq
1887, 9, 21. Cammie rocf Newberry MM, O., dtd 1887,7,19
1889, 7, 24. Eliza A. Ireland (form Carroll) dropped from mbrp (H)
1894, 1, 24. George E. & w, Cammie, & ch, Inea & Ester, gct Newberry MM
1903, 12, 23. Solon rocf Ceasars Creek MM, dtd 1903,11,26
1907, 4, 24. Emma Mae Clement recrq
1907, 11, 30. Solon & w, Emma C., gct Ceasars Creek MM

CARTER
1805, 9, 12. James dis mcd
1805, 12, 12. Mordecai rocf Cane Creek MM, N. C., dtd 1805,9,7
1815, 6, 28. Mordecai gct Elk MM
1883, 4, 25. Edna recrq
1887, 4, 20. Zephaniah recrq
1901, 6, 26. Lucile H. gct Ceasars Creek MM

CARTWRIGHT
----, --, --. Sarah b 1804,1,11 d 1873,11,10

1837, 12, 27. Sarah rocf Alexandria MM, dtd 1837,8,24 (H)
1917, 5, 27. Seth Levering recrq (H)

CARVER
----, --, --. George b 1808,8,14 d 1899,4,12; m Ann ----- b 1810,1,19 d 1880,12,11 (H)
Ch: Mary H. b 1834, 12, 16 d 1880,12,11
Martha J. " 1837, 4, 21
Jacob M. " 1840, 11, 5
Charles R. " 1843, 5, 5
Agnes " 1847, 1, 3
Wilmer " 1849, 10, 6 d 1897, 2,14
Edwin " 1852, 4, 30

1844, 5, 22. George & w, Ann, & ch, Mary Hannah, Martha Jane, Jacob M. & Charles R., rocf Center MM, dtd 1843,11,30 (H)
1844, 6, 26. Eli rocf Center MM, dtd 1843,11,30 (H)
1847, 12, 22. Ruth Ann (form Jessop) con mou (H)
1848, 8, 23. Ruth Ann (form Jessop) dis mou
1889, 12, 25. Ruth Anna (form Jessop) dropped from mbrp; jas (H)
1889, 2, 20. Eli dropped from mbrp; jas (H)
1890, 1, 23. Ruth Anna dropped from mbrp (H)
1890, 3, 26. Wilmer rec or released by rq (H)
1890, 11, 26. Charles R. dropped from mbrp (H)
1909, 4, 21. Edwin dropped from mbrp (H)

CAST
1913, 4, 23. Walter recrq

CHADWICK
1813, 3, 24. Hepsibah & ch, Eunice & Eliza,

CHADWICK, continued
rocf Nantucket MM, dtd 1812,12,31
1813, 4, 28. Timothy Folger & w, Hepsibah, & Phebe Chadwick, rocf Nantucket MM, dtd 1812,12,31

CHAFFANT
1866, 1, 24. Abner & fam dropped from mbrp; form mbr of Fall Creek or Centre MM which had been laid down (H)

CHAMNESS
1811, 8, 28. Mary (form Bray) dis mcd

CHANDLER
----, --, --. Aaron, s David & Miriam, Warren Co., O.; b 1794,9,30 d 1875,1,27; m Hannah WARD b 1796,9,16 d 1838,9,22 (H)
Ch: Isaac b 1817, 5, 13
David " 1818, 12, 9 d 1901, 9,23
Asahel " 1820, 9, 26 " 1894, 7,29
Ann " 1822, 8, 10 " 182[illegible], 1,15
Miriam " 1824, 9, 8
Lydia " 1826, 7, 9
Elwood " 1828, 7, 27 " 1857, 9,12
Hannah Ann " 1830, 8, 2
Aaron " 1332, 2, 2 " 1832,12,31
Eli " 1833, 10, 3
Mary " 1835, 12, 23 " 1856, 6,28
Aaron m 2nd 1840,10,28, Maria WARD, dt Isaac & Ann
Ch: Asa b 1842, 7, 19
Martha " 1844, 1, 5
Esther " 1845, 1, 23
Joseph " 1846, 3, 15
1820, 3, 23. Miriam, w David, d ae 67 (H)
1841, 9, 23. Benjamin [Chandlee], s Goldsmith & Phebe, Jay Co., O., b 1820,10,11 d 1853, 5,27; m at Rochester, Rebecca WHITACRE, dt Aquilla & Ruthanna, Warren Co., O., b 1821,10,13 (H)
Ch: Aquilla G. b 1842, 6, 25
Ruthanna " 1846, 5, 3
Phebe N. " 1847, 8, 10
Ellen Jane " 1849, 3, 26
Marietta " 1851, 7, 29
Benj. Lewis" 1853, 10, 30
1843, 5, 23. Miriam [Chandles] m Jacob PIERCE (H)
----, --, --. David b 1818,12,9 d 1901,9,23; m Lydia Ann MULLIN b 1821,12,10 d 1858,5, 30 (H)
Ch: Aaron B. b 1844, 1, 13 d 1915, 9,19
John T. " 1846, 1, 27
Edwin " 1849, 10, 3
Milton " 1852, 8, 7 d 1853, 5, 1
William F. " 1855, 6, 5 " 1863, 2, 6
Mary Ann " 1855, 6, 5 " 1864, 3, 6
1847, 11, 4. Phebe N. [Chandlee] m Silas WHARTON (H)
1861, 2, 28. David, s Aaron & Hannah, Warren Co., O.; m at Hopewell, Sarah Jane GREGG, dt Benjamin & Sidney Daniel, Warren Co., O. (H)
1868, 4, 1. Aaron B., s David & Lydia Ann, Warren Co., O., b 1844,1,13 d 1919,9,19; m at Waynesville, Abi CARROLL, dt Enos & Mary Ann, Warren Co., O., b 1843,1,4 d 1903,2,6 (H)
Ch: Marianna b 1872, 10, 1 d 1908, 6,21
Walter D. " 1876, 8, 31
----, --, --. Edwin b 1849,10,3; m Sidney J. PETIT b 1850,7,16 (H)
Ch: Lewis W. b 1874, 3, 4
Alfred E. " 1880, 3, 14 d 1882, 5,16
Ruthanna " 1884, 2, 10
Elizabeth " 1886, 10, 29

1814, 4, 27. Merriam & s, Aaron, rocf Redstone MM, dtd 1814,3,4
1817, 2, 26. David recrq
1817, 8, 27. Aaron rpd mcd
1817, 8, 27. Hannah (form Ward) con mou
1817, 10, 29. David rst with permission of Kennett MM
1818, 3, 25. Goldsmith Jr. & w, Phebe, & ch, Mary Elizabeth & Jonathan Goldsmith, rocf Hopewell MM, Va., dtd 1818,2,5
1829, 2, 25. Aaron dis jH
1829, 5, 27. Hannah dis jH
1841, 5, 26. Isaac con mou (H)
1842, 7, 27. Rebecca P. gct Camden MM, Ind. (H)
1843, 12, 1. David con mou (H)
1844, 3, 27. David dis mou
1845, 6, 25. Lydia Ann rocf Springborough MM, dtd 1845,4,22 (H)
1847, 3, 24. Benjamin L. [Chandlee] & w, Rebecca P., & ch, Aquilla & Ruthanna, rocf White Water MM, dtd 1846,9,23 (H)
1847, 4, 21. Phebe N. [Chandlee] rocf White Water MM, dtd 1847,2,24 (H)
1848, 2, 23. Miriam Pierce (form Chandler) dis mou
1849, 6, 20. Lydia Whitacre (form Chandler) rpd mou; d before action was taken (H)
1850, 10, 23. Isaac dis mcd (H)
1855, 3, 21. Eli dis mcd (H)
1860, 10, 24. Rebecca P. & ch, Aquilla Goldssmith, Phebe N., Benjamin Lewis & Margaretta, gct Prairie Grove MM, Ia. (H)
1861, 7, 24. Hannah Ann Brown (form Chandler) con mcd (H)
1867, 11, 20. Asahel con mcd (H)
1867, 11, 20. Martha Engle (form Chandler) dis mcd (H)
1870, 1, 26. Asa con mcd (H)
1871, 8, 23. David & w, Sarah Jane, gct Springboro MM (H)
1876, 8, 23. Sidney Jane & ch, Lewis W., recrq (H)
1876, 9, 20. David Chandler & w, Sarah Jane, & niece, Rachel Alma Daniel, rocf Springboro MM, dtd 1876,8,24 (H)
1881, 6, 22. Ellwood recrq
1884, 7, 23. Asahel gct Camden MM, Ind. (H)

CHANDLER, continued
1885, 6, 24. Elwood gct Kansas City MM, Mo.
1886, 11, 24. Ellen (form Butterworth) rpd mcd (H)
1889, 11, 20. Joseph & Asa dropped from mbrp (H)
1890, 3, 26. Joseph rec (or released) by rq (H)
1904, 4, 20. Ella B. relrq (H)
1917, 7, 29. John F. dropped from mbrp (H)

CHAPLIN
1897, 1, 27. George recrq

CHAPMAN
1821, 11, 7. Sarah m Benjamin BROWN
----, --, --. Joseph B., s Benjamin & Mercy, Warren Co., O.; m at Miami, ----- -----
Dt: Ann b 1827, 9, 19 d 1845, 3, 4
Joseph B. m 2nd 1832,6,13, Charlotte HAINES, dt Noah & Anna, Warren Co., O., b 1811,1,14 d 1844,4,13
Ch: Mary b 1833, 7, 10 d 1851, 1,18
Noah H. " 1835, 1, 24
Joseph B. " 1837, 2, 24 " 1904, 4, 6
Charles F. " 1840, 7, 6
Margaretta " 1841, 12, 29 " 1856, 7,18
James H. " 1843, 12, 10 " 1844, 4,10
Joseph B. d 1847,8,31
1874, 6, 3. Charles F., s Joseph B. & Charlotte H., Warren Co., O.; m at residence of Joseph Stanton, Elizabeth M. STANTON, dt Joseph & Catherine Ann, Warren Co., O. (H)

1819, 7, 28. Joseph rocf Phila. MM, dtd 1819, 6,22 (ND MM)
1819, 7, 28. Sarah rocf Phila. MM for the Northern Dist., dtd 1819,5,25
1829, 2, 25. Joseph B. dis jH
1860, 2, 22. Noah H. gct Cincinnati MM (H)
1882, 5, 24. Elizabeth M. recrq (H)
1883, 5, 23. George recrq
1886, 3, 24. Elizabeth M. relrq (H)
1886, 4, 21. Charles F. relrq (H)
1886, 4, 21. Charles F. & w, Elizabeth M., & ch, Margaret C., Joseph B. & James Albert, recrq
1892, 4, 20. Joseph B. relrq (H)
1923, 8, 26. Mary B., Charles B. & Robert D. recrq (H)
1926, 7, 25. Joseph B. rocf Miami MM

CHENOWETH
1909, 1, 27. Caroline & Howard recrq

CHEW
----, --, -- Reuben & Rebecca
Ch: Malinda b 1827, 1, 29
Emily " 1828, 3, 10
Angeline " 1830, 8, 5
Ann " 1832, 8, 22
Mary " 1835, 3, 30
Ruth b 1837, 3, 30

1850, 11, 20. Emily & Angeline rocf Rush Creek MM, dtd 1850,10,17
1850, 11, 20. Reuben & ch, Mary & Ruth, rocf Rush Creek MM, dtd 1850,10,17
1851, 8, 27. Reuben & dt, Mary & Ruth, rocf Springfield MM, dtd 1851,6,21
1851, 8, 27. Emily & Angeline rocf Springfield MM, dtd 1851,6,21
1867, 4, 24. Mary Edwards (form Chew) con mou

CLARK
1805, 6, 13. Mary & ch, Mary, Jonothan & Rebecca, rocf Cane Creek MM, S. C., dtd 1805,2,16
1806, 4, 10. Mary Little (form Clerk) dis mou
1818, 2, 25. Maria rocf Phila. MM, dtd 1817, 11,29
1819, 10, 27. Maria [Clerk] gct Mulberry St. MM, Phila.
1825, 8, 31. Mary & Hannah recrq of father, Robert
1828, 5, 28. Mary gct Green Plain MM
1840, 4, 22. Hannah Williams (form Clark) con mou (H)
1854, 8, 22. Jane rocf Cincinnati MM, dtd 1854,8,17
1866, 1, 24. Martha dropped from mbrp; form mbrp of Fall Creek or Centre MM which had been laid down (H)
1883, 4, 25. George M. recrq
1885, 12, 23. George E. & w, Emma G. (form Slack) & s, Henry Neal, relrq
1899, 3, 22. Anna Brace rocf Ceasars Creek MM, dtd 1899,2,23
1920, 7, 25. Marianna W. dropped from mbrp (H)
1921, 3, 27. Maria B. rocf Darlington MM, Eng. (H)

CLAWSON
1842, 9, 1. William, s Josiah & Rebeccah, Wayne Co., O.; m at Harveysburgh, Rebecca POOL, dt Caleb & Sarah Harvey

1842, 11, 23. Rebecca & ch gct White Water MM

CLEAVER
----, --, --. Ezekiel & Abigail (H)
Ch: Mary b 1789, 6, 19
Abigail " 1792, 5, 12
Ezekiel " 1794, 7, 1
Peter " 1796, 10, 10
David " 1799, 5, 11
Lydia " 1801, 10, 29
Nathan " 1804, 12, 30
Ezekiel, the father, d 1832,9,22; Abigail, the mother, d 1833,2,2
1806, 7, 16. Martha m John DUTTON
1808, 12, 14. Mary m William GRAY
1816, 4, 3. Abigail m Josiah ROGERS
1819, 5, 5. Peter, s Ezekiel & Abigail, Warren Co., O., b 1796,10,18; m at Miami, Sa-

CLEAVER, Peter, continued
rah CREW, dt Hiram & Hannah, Warren Co., O., b 1801,1,21
Ch: John b 1820, 2, 12
Levi L. " 1823, 9, 26
Nathan " 1828, 2, 16
William H. " 1830, 8, 19
Anna " 1821, 11, 11
Jesse A. " 1826, 1, 31
1820, 5, 3. Lydia m Nathan DAVIS
1822, 11, 11. Anna d
1824, 4, 8. Ezekiel L., s Peter & Alice, Warren Co., O.; m at Springborough, Mary TAYLOR, dt Mordecai & Frances, Warren Co., O.
1828, 2, 24. Jesse d

1806, 6, 12. Martha rocf Crooked Run MM, Va., dtd 1805,11,2
1808, 3, 10. Ezekiel recrq
1823, 2, 26. Ezekiel L. rocf Pipe Creek MM, Md., dtd 1822,6,15
1823, 9, 24. Ezekiel Jr. dis
1828, 3, 26. David dis attending a mcd
1828, 8, 27. Nathan dis mcd
1829, 1, 28. Ezekiel [Clever] dis jH
1829, 8, 26. Abigail dis jH
1829, 5, 27. Ezekiel L. dis jH
1829, 5, 27. Mary dis jH
1831, 1, 26. Ezekiel & w, Mary, gct Springborough MM (H)
1844, 12, 25. John dis mou
1846, 9, 23. Levi dis disunity
1851, 6, 25. Nathan dis mou
1855, 4, 25. William dis mou

CLEVENGER
1886, 2, 24. Hannah recrq

CLIFTON
----, --, --. Sarah C. b 1811,7,9 d 1908,6,29 (H)

1891, 7, 22. Sarah L. rocf Plainfield MM,N.J. (H)

CLOUD
1806, 10, 15. Joseph, Warren Co., O.; m at Miami, Jane McCOY, Warren Co., O.
----, --, --. Joel b 1785,3,7; m Hannah ----- b 1786,1,25
Ch: Tamar b 1812, 6, 7
Joseph " 1813, 12, 12
Thomas " 1815, 6, 21
Mary Earl " 1817, 3, 8
Anna " 1818, 12, 18
Cynthia M. " 1820, 12, 20
Cornelius H. b 1822, 9, 2
Jonathan Milton " 1824, 8, 12

1805, 11, 14. Joseph & ch, Joel & Abigail, rocf Cane Creek MM, N. C., dtd 1805,5,10
1806, 7, 10. Jonothan & w, Elizabeth, & ch, Ann, Joel, Elizabeth & William, rocf Cane Creek MM, N. C., dtd 1805,9,7
1807, 10, 8. Mary Hussey (form Cloud) con mou
1808, 1, 14. Mary rpd mcd
1809, 12, 27. Mary rocf Lost Creek MM, Tenn., dtd 1808,5,26
1810, 5, 30. Joseph gct Center MM, to m
1811, 3, 27. Mary rocf Cesar's Creek MM, dtd 1810,9,29
1811, 6, 26. Joel gct Cesars Creek MM, to m
1812, 6, 24. Hannah rocf Cesars Creek MM, dtd 1812,4,25
1814, 9, 28. Jonathan & fam gct White Water MM
1817, 2, 26. Mary gct Ceasars Creek MM
1817, 2, 26. Abigail gct Ceasars Creek MM
1832, 3, 21. Joel & w, Hannah, & ch, Joseph, Mary Earl, Anna, Thomas, Cynthia Marlissa, Cornelius & Jonathan, rocf Springfield MM, dtd 1832,3,13
1832, 3, 21. Joel & w, Hannah, & ch gct Sugar River MM

CLUTCH
----, --, --. ----- m Rachel ----- b 1774,2,24
Ch: Elizabeth b 1810, 8, 8
Lydia E. " 1814, 5, 20
Rachel A. " 1817, 12, 17

1809, 9, 9. Rachel (form Austin) con mou
1815, 7, 26. Rachel rpd mcd
1817, 4, 30. Elizabeth & Lydia, ch Rachel, recrq
1824, 5, 26. Rachel, dt Rachel, recrq
1831, 1, 26. Rachel dis jH
1833, 9, 25. Elizabeth dis disunity
1835, 6, 24. Lydia Henry (form Clutch) dis mou

CLUXTON
1885, 6, 24. Evelyn (form Hiatt) relrq to jas (H)

COATE
1815, 10, 4. Henry, s Marmaduke & Mary, Warren Co., O.; m at Miami, Rebekah WILSON, dt Robert & Mercy

1804, 10, 11. Henry [Coat] & w, Mary, & ch, Lydia, Isaac, Mary, Samuel & Rhoda, rocf Bush River MM, S. C., dtd 1804,7,23
1804, 11, 8. Marmaduke & w, Mary, & ch, John & Jesse, rocf Bush River MM, dtd 1804,8,25
1804, 11, 8. Samuel & w, Margaret, & ch, James & Joseph, rocf Bush River MM, S. C., dtd 1804,2,25
1805, 7, 11. Moses & w, Elizabeth, & ch, Jane, Mary, Thomas, Esther & Joseph, rocf Bush River MM, dtd 1804,2,25
1806, 5, 8. James [Coats] rocf Bush River

COATE, continued
MM, S. C., dtd 1805,8,31
1806, 7, 10. William & w, Elizabeth, rocf Bush River MM, S. C., dtd 1805,7,27
1808, 9, 10. Mary [Coats], w William, roci Bush River MM
1812, 7, 29. Henry [Coates] & ch, Isaac, Mary, Samuel, Rhoda, Rachel & Hester, rocf West Branch MM, dtd 1812,7,23
1816, 6, 26. Henry & fam gct Union MM
1841, 7, 21. William Longstreet gct Center MM, to m Martha Coate

CO CA
1852, 2, 25. Co Ca (Shawnee Indian) recrq

COFFEE
----, --, --. Isaac & Elizabeth
Ch: Rachel Ann b 1828, 7, 2
Charles
William " 1832, 7, 2

1838, 1, 24. Isaac & w, Betsy, & ch, Rachel Ann & Charles W., rocf Plainfield MM, dtd 1837,11,22
1848, 6, 21. Isaac & w, Betsey, & s, Charles W., gct Salem MM, O.
1848, 6, 21. Rachel Ann gct Salem MM, O.

COFFIN
1847, 3, 25. Charles F., s Elijah & Naomi, Wayne Co., Ind.; m at Miami, Rhoda M. JOHNSON, dt John & Judith, Warren Co., O.

1805, 12, 12. Samuel rocf Deep River MM, N.C., dtd 1805,9,2
1814, 8, 31. Benjamin & w, Hepzibah, & ch, Sarah, Henry & Joseph Paddock Jr., rocf Nantucket MM, dtd 1814,4,28
1814, 8, 31. Sarah & ch, Reuben, Eliza & Christopher Colger Coffin, rocf Nantucket MM, dtd 1814,4,28
1814, 8, 31. Sarah & dt, Elizabeth & Sarah Barnard Coffin, rocf Nantucket MM, dtd 1814,4,28
1847, 5, 26. Rhoda M. gct White Water MM,Ind.
1852, 2, 25. Eli Johnson gct White Water MM, to m Mary Coffin

COFFMAN
1914, 4, 22. Abie recrq

COIL
1808, 6, 9. Ann (form Smith) dis mou

COLDWELL
1807, 12, 10. James, s Joseph & Mary, Montgomery Co., O.; m at Elk Creek, Martha TOWNSEND, dt Isaac & Mary Cook, Butlar Co., O.

1806, 2, 13. James [Colwell] recrq
1806, 9, 11. Joseph & ch, Margaret, John & James, recrq
1806, 9, 11. Miriam & ch recrq

COLLINS
1901, 12, 25. Thomas recrq

COLLYER
1808, 6, 9. Rachel [Coller] (form Smith) dis mou
1812, 5, 27. John & w, Rhoda, & ch, Mary, Benejah, Elizabeth & Jonothan, rocf Stillwater MM, O., dtd 1811,10,29

COMBS
1834, 3, 26. Almyra (form Starbuck) dis mou

COMER
1805, 8, 8. Elizabeth rocf Cane Creek MM, S. C., dtd 1805,2,16
1806, 7, 10. Joseph rocf Cane Creek MM, S. C., dtd 1806,2,15
1806, 8, 14. Robert & w, Martha, & ch, Mary, Amos & Anna, rocf Cane Creek MM, S. C., dtd 1806,3,22
1808, 11, 12. Rebeccah rocf Cane Creek MM, S. C., dtd 1806,11,22
1809, 8, 5. Elizabeth gct West Branch MM
1848, 7, 26. Anna (form Jessop) dis mou
1884, 5, 21. Clara recrq

COMPTON
1805, 11, 27. Joseph [Comton], s Samuel & Elizabeth, Warren Co., O.; m at Miami, Christianna STEDDOM, dt Henry & Martha, Warren Co., O.
1806, 5, 15. Elizabeth [Compton] m John HORNER
1806, 12, 18. Rebekah [Comton] m Willis WHITSON
1807, 3, 18. John [Comton], s Samuel & Elizabeth, Montgomery Co., O.; m at Miami, Ann PEDDRICK, dt Isaac, Warren Co., O.
1810, 12, 1. Isaac Pedrick, s John & Ann, b
1833, 10, 31. John, s Amos & Rebecca, Green Co., O.; m at Turtle Creek, Rebecca STEDDOM, dt John & Alice, Warren Co., O.
1840, 9, 26. Isaac P. d bur near residence in Warren Co., O.

1804, 5, 10. Matthew rocf Cane Creek MM, S. C., dtd 1804,3,24
1804, 5, 10. Samuel & w, Elizabeth, & ch, Joseph & Elizabeth, rocf Bush River MM, S. C., dtd 1804,2,25
1805, 4, 11. Samuel rocf Cane Creek MM, S. C., dtd 1803,12,24
1805, 6, 13. Amos & w, Rebecca, & ch, Betty, Samuel, Mary, Rebecca, Lydia & Sally, rocf Cane Creek MM, S. C., dtd 1805,3,23
1805, 6, 13. Stephen & w, Dinah, & ch, Henry, Sally & Amos, rocf Cane Creek MM, S. C., dtd 1805,3,23
1806, 4, 10. Rebecca & ch, Nathan & Joshua,

COMPTON, continued
rocf Cane Creek MM, dtd 1805,8,24
1807, 8, 3. John rocf Bush River MM, S. C., dtd 1807,4,24
1809, 5, 6. John & w, Ann, & dt, Lydia, gct Center MM
1834, 2, 19. Isaac P. rocf Cesars Creek MM, dtd 1834,1,23
1834, 2, 19. Rebecca gct Caesars Creek MM
1840, 4, 22. John F. Steddom gct Cesars Creek MM, to m Mary Ann Compton
1869, 1, 27. Susannah E. (form Dakin) con mou
1869, 3, 24. Susannah gct Cesars Creek MM
1883, 4, 25. Daniel recrq
1884, 7, 23. Elijah & ch, Forest D., Albert E., Charles & Martha F., rocf Cesars Creek MM, dtd 1884,5,22
1886, 3, 24. Daniel relrq
1887, 4, 20. Ada, minor, recrq
1887, 4, 20. Priscilla S. recrq
1887, 5, 25. Jesse M. rocf Cesars Creek MM, dtd 1887,4,21
1905, 5, 24. Jesse & w, Priscilla S., & dt, Mary Anna, gct Ceasars Creek MM
1909, 12, 22. Martha & Mabel relrq
1916, 5, 24. E. & w gct Dayton MM

CONARD
1810, 9, 14. Benjamin b
----, --, --. Joseph b 1805,9,22 d 1854,4,6;
-- m Rebecca GOOD b 1809,1,20 d 1885,1,2 (H)
Ch: Lewis b 1829, 7, 27
Esther " 1831, 11, 27 d 1832,10,17
Charles " 1834, 7, 19 " 1861, 10,29
Evans " 1837, 1, 14 " 1839, 4,11
Franklin " 1839, 8, 19 " 1898, 2,14
Susannah " 1842, 3, 10 " 1865, 9,15
Sarah " 1846, 6, 17 " 1877, 7, 8
Martha " 1847, 5, 21 " 1868, 6,10
Lydia Ann " 1850, 9, 16
----, --, --. Benjamin b 1810,9,14; m ----- ----- (H)
Ch: Almira b 1836, 12, 29
Cornelius " 1838, 8, 13
Alice R. " 1840, 1, 22
George R. " 1842, 1, 5
William " 1844, 11, 23
Elwood H. " 1849, 1, 24
Mary " 1852, 4, 23
----, --, --. George R. b 1842,1,5; m Martha GOOD b 1842,3,27 d 1877,5,2 (H)
Ch: Helen G. b 1867, 4, 27
Harvey E. " 1869, 3, 26
Elma E. " 1872, 11, 25 d 1884, 11,5
Robert R. " 1877, 4, 11
William W. " 1877, 4, 11 " 1877, 6,27

1866, 1, 24. Rebecca rpd mcd (H)
1866, 1, 24. Franklin [Connard] rpd mcd (H)
1866, 1, 24. Martha [Connard] rpd mcd (H)
1866, 1, 24. George B. rpd mcd (H)
1866, 1, 24. William rpd mcd (H)
1866, 1, 24. Elwood, Maris & Lydia [Connard] rec in mbrp; form mbr of Fall Creek or Center MM which had been laid down (H)
1866, 1, 24. Sarah [Connard] minor, rec in mbrp; form mbr of Fall Creek or Center MM which had been laid down (H)
1866, 8, 22. Alice Johnson (form Conard) con mcd (H)
1866, 8, 22. Benjamin rpd mcd; dropped from mbrp (H)
1866, 8, 22. Carnelius rpd mcd; dropped from mbrp (H)
1866, 12, 26. Almira Carey (form Connard) dis mcd (H)
1877, 9, 26. Elwood H. gct Chesterfield MM, Pa. (H)
1889, 1, 23. William dis disunity (H)
1889, 10, 23. Lewis relrq (H)
1895, 5, 22. George R., Helen G., Harvey E., Robert R. & Lydia Ann set off as mbr of Executive Mtg at Clear Creek (H)
1909, 6, 23. Harvey E. dropped from mbrp (H)
1920, 7, 25. George R., Helen G. & Dr. Robert dropped from mbrp (H)

CONNER
1806, 8, 14. John & w, Rachel, & ch, William, Catherine, Jesse, John, Thomas & Mary, rocf Bush River MM, dtd 1805,11,30
1809, 9, 9. Joseph gct West Branch MM
1815, 7, 26. John [Connor] & ch, Catherine, Rachel & Isaac, rocf Cesars Creek MM, dtd 1815,6,26
1816, 10, 30. John dis mcd
1820, 7, 26. Catherine Meloy (form Connor) dis mou
1839, 6, 26. Isaac [Connor] gct White Water MM (H)
1839, 7, 24. Isaac dis jH
1884, 5, 28. Clara recrq
1892, 7, 27. Annie relrq
1917, 10, 24. Ellen Sherwood relrq

CONOVER
1817, 7, 30. Mary rocf Shrewsburg MM, dtd 1817,3,3
1855, 9, 26. Hannah (form Evans) con mcd (H)
1865, 2, 22. Hannah dis jas (H)

CONWAY
1814, 2, 23. Elizabeth [Conoway] & ch, James, Lydia & Samuel, rocf Cesar's Creek MM, dtd 1814,1,29
1819, 3, 31. Elizabeth & ch, James, Joseph & Lydia, gct Mill Creek MM

COODER
1889, 7, 24. Clarissa (form Dingee) dropped from mbrp (H)

COOK
1812, 9, 2. Stephen, s Amos & Elizabeth, Warren Co., O.; m at Miami, Elizabeth EVANS, dt Benjamin & Hannah, Warren Co.,O.

COOK, continued
----, --, --. Amos b 1785,10,13 d 1866,3,5; m Susanna PERKINS b 1783,12,26 d 1843,5,11 (H)
Amos m 2nd Mary SMITH d 1846,6,26
Amos m 3rd Mary THOMAS b 1803,5,27 d 1877, 1,23
1805, 11, 27. John, s Amos & Elizabeth, Warren Co., O.; m at Waynesville, Dinah SPRAY, dt Samuel & Mary, Warren Co., O.
1806, 11, 20. Phebe m Francis MADOR
1807, 11, 26. James, s Eli & Martha, Butlar Co., O.; m at Elk Creek, Elenor MADDOCK, dt Samuel & Rachel, Butlar Co., O.
----, --, --. Abraham b 1792,4,19 d 1862,7,9; m Ruth HAWKINS b 1793,3,14 d 1863,2,21 (H)

Ch:			
	Ann	b 1813, 8, 14	
	Saaah	" 1815, 12, 12	
	Mahlon	" 1817, 10, 23	d 1824, 9, 5
	Levi	" 1819, 12, 4	" 1887, 10,8
	Stephen	" 1822, 3, 8	" 1898, 8, 4
	Noah	" 1824, 7, 12	" 1827, 9, 2
	Dinah	" 1826, 10, 16	
	Elisha	" 1829, 5, 28	" 1886, 4,18
	Lydia	" 1831, 12, 1	" 1915, 4,9
	Elizabeth	" 1835, 9, 22	

1818, 3, 4. Seth, s Isaac & Sarah, Warren Co., O.; m at Miami, Ruth COOK, dt Amos & Elizabeth, Warren Co., O. (H)

Ch:		
	Amos	b 1819, 7, 29
	Isaac	" 1822, 3, 9
	Elijah	" 1822, 8, 11

1850, 3, 6. Levi, s Abraham & Ruth, Warren Co., O., b 1819,12,4 d 1887,10,8; m at Miami, Ellen BOONE. dt Arnold & Hannah. Warren Co., O., d 1887,4,14 (H)

Ch:			
	Samuel B.	b 1851, 1, 10	d 1912,10, 7
	Ruth	" 1854, 8, 8	
	Hannah B.	" 1861, 4, 13	

----, --, --. Stephen b 1822,3,8 d 1898,8,4; m Mary WALKER b 1832,3,23 d 1893,3,20 (H)

Ch:		
	Phineas W.	b 1862, 11, 8
	Abraham	" 1865, 1, 18
	Ruth Hannah	" 1867, 9, 20

1864, 4, 7. Lydia m Abel SATTHERTHWAITE (H)
1874, 2, 25. Ruth m J. Franklin SMEDLEY

1805, 5, 9. Benjamin Hawkins & w, Olive, & ch, Amos, Levi, James & Hannah, & w's ch, Mary & Charity Cook, rocf Cane Creek MM, S. C., dtd 1805,2,16
1805, 5, 9. Isaac rocf Bush River MM, S. C., dtd 1805,2,23
1805, 7, 11. Eli & w, Martha, & ch, Isaac, James, Phebe, Nathan & Eli, rocf Cane Creek MM, dtd 1805,3,23
1805, 11, 14. Thomas & w, Keziah, & ch, Zimri, Isaac, Nathaniel, Eli, Wright & Charity, rocf Bush River MM, S. C., dtd 1805,8,31
1806, 1, 9. Isaac & w, Charity, rocf Bush River MM, S. C., dtd 1805,10,26
1806, 5, 8. Wright & w, Rebecca, & ch, Charity, Thomas & Isaac, rocf Bush River MM, S. C., dtd 1806,1,25
1806, 6, 12. Jacob & w, Judith, & ch, Elizabeth & Rebecca, rocf Deep River MM, N.C., dtd 1806,4,7
1806, 9, 11. Isaac & w, Sarah, & ch, Seth, Rebecca, Robert & Mary, rocf Cane Creek MM, S. C., dtd 1805,4,20
1807, 8, 3. Joseph & ch, John, Joseph, Uriah, Mary & Peter, rocf Bush River MM, S. C., dtd 1807,5,30
1808, 9, 10. William & w, Sarah, rocf Cane Creek MM, S. C., dtd 1806,3,22
1810, 4, 25. Thomas & w, Keziah, & ch, Zimri, Isaac, Nathaniel, Eli, Wright, Charity & Rebekah, gct White Water MM
1810, 8, 29. Dinah Brown (form Cook) dis mou
1812, 7, 29. Abraham gct Cesars Creek MM, to m
1812, 8, 28. Hiram gc
1813, 8, 25. Ruth rocf Cesars Creek MM, dtd 1813,7,31
1813, 10, 27. Amos gct Center MM, to m
1814, 3, 30. Susanna rocf Centre MM, dtd 1814,3,5
1817, 10, 29. William & w, Sarah, rocf Cane Creek MM, S. C., dtd 1806,3,22
1818, 1, 28. William & fam gct White Water MM
1818, 2, 25. Seth rocf Cesars Creek MM, dtd 1818,1,30
1825, 6, 29. Levi & w, Ann, & ch, Isaac & John Cook, & Thomas, Ann & William Hasket, gct Milford MM, Ind.
1825, 7, 27. Seth & w, Ruth, & ch, Amos, Isaac & Elijah, gct White Water MM
1827, 11, 28. Betty gct Duck Creek MM
1829, 1, 28. Abraham dis jH
1829, 1, 28. Stephen dis jH
1829, 2, 25. Amos dis jH
1829, 3, 25. Ruth dis jH
1829, 3, 25. Susannah dis jH
1829, 3, 25. Elizabeth dis jH
1833, 8, 31. Hannah dis jH
1834, 2, 19. Ann dis jH
1841, 2, 24. Susannah Hill (form Cook) dis mou & jH
1841, 4, 21. Jason dis mou (H)
1842, 5, 20. Jason dis mou
1842, 6, 22. Noah rocf Windham MM, Maine, dtd 1841,11,26, endorsed by Cincinnati MM 1842,8,17(?)
1845, 1, 22. Marcellous rocf Cincinnati MM, dtd 1844,10,24 (H)
1846, 8, 26. Jesse W. & w, Elizabeth, & ch, Theodor, Jesse W., Andrew M., Joseph R., Thomas W. & Emma, rocf Cincinnati MM, dtd 1846,7,23 (H)
1847, 2, 24. Noah gct Unity MM, Maine
1847, 5, 26. Jess W. & w, Elizabeth, & ch, Theodore, Jesse W., Andrew M., Joseph R., Thomas W. & Anna, gct Green Plain MM (H)
1849, 1, 24. Mary rocf Center MM, dtd 1848, 12,14 (H)
1849, 12, 26. Marcellius S. & ch, Esther Jane

COOK, continued
& Harriett E., gct Green Plain MM
1852, 9, 22. Stephen & w, Elizabeth, gct Plainfield MM, Ill. (H)
1853, 1, 26. Benjamin dis mcd (H)
1861, 8, 21. Stephen gct Green Plain MM, to m Mary Walker
1862, 1, 22. Mary W. rocf Green Plain MM, dtd 1861,12,18
1873, 7, 23. Sarah & Dinah gct Wapsinonoch MM, Iowa
1881, 5, 25. Amos & w, Elma D., rocf Cesar's Creek MM, dtd 1881,4,21
1882, 6, 21. Seth & w, Hannah J., & ch, Mary L., Lillie M., Besse A. & William P., rocf Ceasars Creek MM, dtd 1882,5,25
1886, 3, 24. Hannah B. Davis (form Cook) rpd mcd (H)
1890, 9, 24. Samuel B. relrq (H)
1905, 4, 26. Amos gct Ceasars Creek MM
1907, 2, 20. Maurice recrq
1916, 10, 29. Amos recrq (H)
1916, 11, 26. Amos & w, Ella, & ch, Ruth Emma, Margaret Anna & Ernest E., recrq (H)
1917, 10, 24. Seth relrq
1918, 12, 26. Amos rocf Xenia MM, dtd 1918,11, 20
1917, 7, 29. Abraham dropped from mbrp (H)
1920, 7, 25. Phineas dropped from mbrp (H)

COOPER
1836, 6, 8. Joseph C., s Isaac & Elizabeth, Montgomery Co., O.; m at Miami, Lydia EVANS dt Thomas & Hannah, Warren Co., O.

1806, 12, 11. Mary Ann (form Oneall) con mou
1807, 7, 9. William & w, Mary, & ch, Jacob & Ralph, rocf Cane Creek MM, S. C., dtd 1807,3,29
1811, 2, 27. Isaac & w, Abigail, & ch, Welmet, rocf Lost Creek MM, dtd 1807,5,25
1831, 2, 23. Webster G. Welch gct Mill Creek MM, to m Mary Cooper
1831, 5, 25. Joseph recrq (H)
1831, 12, 28. Mary Ann recrq (H)
1853, 7, 27. Elizabeth W. (form Dicks) dis mou
1853, 8, 24. Elizabeth (form Dicks) dis mcd
1856, 12, 24. Lydia E. gct White Water MM
1866, 1, 24. John rpd mcd (H)
1866, 1, 24. Thomas rpd mcd (H)
1866, 1, 24. Margaret Ellen rpd mcd (H)
1866, 1, 24. Mary Jane rpd mcd (H)
1866, 1, 24. Amos dropped from mbrp; form mbr of Fall Creek or Centre MM which had been laid down (H)
1866, 1, 24. Elenor dropped from mbrp; form mbr of Fall Creek or Centre MM which had been laid down (H)
1866, 1, 24. Elma dropped from mbrp; form mbr Fall Creek or Centre MM which had been laid down (H)
1866, 1, 24. James W., Elwood, Alfred & Jesse D., minors, rec in mbrp; form mbr Fall Creek or Centre MM which had been laid down (H)
1867, 9, 25. John R. con mcd (H)
1867, 10, 23. Jesse & w, Mary E., & ch, Margaret E., James W., Elwood, Alfred, Jesse & Thomas, gct Prairie Grove MM, Ia. (H)
1868, 2, 19. John R. gct Prairie Grove MM,Ia. (H)
1885, 8, 26. Mary J. Hough (form Cooper) relrq (H)

COPPOCK
1805, 9, 12. John & w, Ann, & ch, Jesse, Eunice, Aaron, James, Isaac & John, rocf Wrightsboro MM, Ga. dtd 1805,3,30
1806, 7, 10. Jane & ch, William & Jesse, rocf Bush River MM, S. C., dtd 1805,4,27
1806, 12, 11. James & w, Hannah, & ch, Moses, Susannah & Martha, rocf Bush River MM, S. C., dtd 1806,8,30
1809, 11, 4. Moses gct West Branch MM
1811, 6, 26. Susanna Pugh (form Coppock) dis mcd to first cousin
1814, 1, 26. James & w, Hannah, & dt, Mariba, gct Mill Creek MM

CORDER
1889, 6, 26. Leola recrq

CORE
1877, 11, 21. Seth W. Furnas gct Maple Grove MM, Ind., to m Emily Core (H)

CORWIN
1823, 9, 24. Sarah (form Ross) dis mou
1859, 12, 21. Mahala C. (form Johnson) dis mcd (H)
1886, 3, 24. Mariana recrq
1894, 6, 20. Marianna relrq

COUGLE
1849, 5, 23. William Longstreet gct Springfield MM, to m Hannah Cougle

COWAN
1841, 2, 24. Maria M. rocf Center MM, dtd 1840,10,15 (H)

COWGILL
1807, 4, 9. John recrq

COX
----, --, --. John b 1772,5,9; m Sarah ----- b 1782,3,2 (H)

Ch:		
Mary	b	1798, 10, 2
Martha	"	1803, 3, 23
Hannah	"	1805, 2, 14
James	"	1807, 1, 1
Susannah	"	1810, 8, 13
Selah	"	1813, 1, 17
Ann	"	1815, 8, 15

1813, 9, 1. Jonathan Jr., s Jonathan & Mary,

COX, continued
Montgomery Co., O.; m at Hopewell, Charity HOLLINGSWORTH, dt John & Rachel, Warren Co., O.
1817, 2, 5. David, s Richard & Ann, Warren Co., O.; m at Miami, Mary COX, dt John & Sarah, Warren Co., O.
1817, 2, 5. Mary m David Cox
1823, 11, 6. Letitia m Thomas KERSEY

1805, 9, 12. Jonothan & w, Mary, & ch, John, Mary, Elizabeth, Catherine, Joseph & Susanna, rocf Bush River MM, dtd 1805,2,23
1806, 6, 12. David & w, Jane, & ch, Sarah, Elizabeth, Mary & Margaret, rocf Bush River MM, dtd 1804,7,28
1806, 7, 10. Jeremiah & w, Catharine, & ch, Mary, Jeremiah, Margery, Ruth, Emma, Hannah, Elijah & Enoch, rocf Cane Creek MM, N. C., dtd 1806,4,3
1806, 8, 14. Benjamin rocf Cane Creek MM, dtd 1805,10,6
1806, 8, 14. John & w, Patience, & ch, Joshua, Josiah, Simon, Margery, Patience & Hannah, rocf Cane Creek MM, N. C., dtd 1804,11,3
1807, 4, 9. William & w, Elizabeth, & ch, Jemima, John, Elizabeth & Sarah, rocf Bush River MM, dtd 1806,3,29
1808, 1, 14. Thomas Sr. & w, Sarah, rocf Cane Creek MM, N. C., dtd 1807,9,5
1808, 1, 14. Thomas Jr. & w, Sarah, & ch, Mary, Stephen, Martha, Thomas, Aaron, Joshua & Catherine, rocf Cane Creek MM, N. C., dtd 1806,10,23
1808, 4, 14. Enoch & w, Gertrude, & ch, Hannah, Phebe, Mary, Herman & Enoch, rocf Cane Creek MM, N. C., dtd 1807,10,3
1811, 12, 25. Phebe (form Somers) dis mcd
1814, 12, 28. John & w, Sarah, & ch, Mary, Martha, Hannah, James, Susannah & Selah, rocf Union MM, dtd 1814,9,3
1815, 6, 28. Charity gct West Branch MM
1820, 12, 27. David rocf Cesars Creek MM, dtd 1820,9,29
1821, 9, 26. David & fam gct Honey Creek MM, Ind.
1823, 1, 29. Joseph Cadwallader gct Clear Creek MM, to m Catherine Cox
1823, 10, 29. John & fam gct Cesars Creek MM
1824, 8, 25. Martha Spray (form Cox) dis mou
1826, 1, 25. David & fam (dt: Ruth & Mary) gct Honey Creek MM
1890, 11, 26. Alice & Agnes relrq (H)
1896, 1, 26. Martha Ann (nee Jessup) dropped from mbrp (H)

CRAFT
1807, 1, 8. Mary rocf Salem MM, N. J., dtd 1806,10,27
1811, 1, 30. Sarah (form Ward) con mou
1829, 6, 24. Sarah dis jH

CRAIG
1827, 10, 3. Maryann m Benjamin BROWN

1806, 7, 10. Martha & ch, Letitia & Jacob, rocf Salem MM, N. J., dtd 1806,4,28
1819, 5, 26. Martha Nutt (form Craig) dis mou
1825, 8, 31. Jacob gct White Water MM, Ind.
1832, 11, 21. Jacob gct White Water MM

CRAMPTON
----, --, --. Samuel b 1779,7,18; m Rachel ----- b 1781,8,1 d 1814,8,1 (H)
Ch: Jeremiah Cooper b 1800, 8, 1
Rachel Miller " 1802, 4, 25
Merrick Star " 1804, 3, 1
Mary Cooper" 1806, 2, 7
Joshua Johnson " 1807, 12, 29
Elizabeth Neil " 1809, 11, 27
Casandra M." 1812, 1, 5
Ruth Haines" 1813, 12, 9
1816, 2, 7. Samuel, s Samuel & Mary, Warren Co., O.; m at Miami, Mary HAMTON, dt Jacob & Eunice, Warren Co., O.
1817, 3, 6. Rachel m Andrew HAMPTON

1811, 12, 25. Samuel & w, Rachel, & ch, Jeremiah, Rachel, Merrick, Mary, Joshua & Elizabeth, rocf Hopewell MM, dtd 1811,10,7
1818, 1, 28. Samuel & fam gct White Water MM
1823, 9, 24. Jonothan recrq
1824, 3, 31. Jeremiah dis jas & mcd
1827, 3, 28. Jonathan [Cramton] dis
1888, 1, 25. Jeremiah Cooper, Rachel Miller, Merrick Starr, Mary Cooper, Joshua Johnson, Elizabeth Miller, Cassandra M. & Ruth Haines dropped from mbrp (H)

CRAWFORD
1848, 4, 26. Meribe (form Scott) dis mou (H)

CREW
----, --, --. Hiram & Hannah
Ch: Rebecca
Sarah b 1801, 1, 21
Lavina
1806, 7, 3. Rebecca, dt Hiram & Hannah, b
1819, 5, 5. Sarah m Peter CLEAVER

1806, 4, 10. John & w, Judith, & ch, Joshua, John Ellison, Martha, Sarah Ladd, Ann & Elizabeth, rocf Mt. Pleasant MM, Va., dtd 1804,8,25
1806, 8, 14. Martha Perkins (form Crew) rpd mou; d before question was settled
1807, 6, 11. Ann Baldwin (form Crews) dis mou

CREW, continued
1807, 9, 10. Elizabeth [Crews] (form Withy) dis mcd
1808, 3, 10. Phebe rocf Deep River MM, N. C., dtd 1807,9,7
1810, 1, 31. Phebe [Crews] gc
1819, 2, 24. Hannah rocf Centre MM, dtd 1818,11,21
1819, 3, 31. Sarah [Crews] rocf Center MM, dtd 1819,3,3
1828, 5, 28. Rebecca [Crews] rocf Springfield MM, dtd 1828,4,26
1830, 3, 31. Hannah rocf Springfield MM, dtd 1830,1,12
1832, 3, 21. Lavina recrq
1838, 7, 25. Lavina Lewis (form Crew) con mou
1843, 4, 26. Rebecca gct Bloomfield MM, Ind.
1871, 3, 22. Rachel [Croo] rocf Cherry Grove MM, dtd 1871,2,11
1883, 4, 25. John H. [Crews] recrq
1883, 5, 23. Josiah W. recrq
1904, 5, 25. Eli relrq

CRISPIN
----, --, --. Jonathan b 1775,7,20 d 1815,8,28; m Elizabeth WARD d 1814,1,5 (H)
Ch: Rowland
Owen b 1810, 7, 9
Joseph " 1812, 5, 11 d 1814, 8, 7
1827, 11, 7. Mary W. m Joseph HOPKINS

1807, 7, 9. Jonothan & w, Elizabeth, & ch, Rebecca, Mary Ward & Elizabeth, roc
1815, 12, 27. Rebecca, Mary Ward & Roland Owen, ch Jonathan, rocf Cincinnati MM, dtd 1815, 12,21
1817, 11, 26. Elizabeth rocf Cincinnati MM, dtd 1817,10,16
1829, 7, 29. Elizabeth [Crispen] dis jH
1829, 8, 26. Rebecca dis jH
1829, 12, 30. Rowland dis jH
1833, 4, 24. Rowland con mou (H)
1835, 12, 23. Rebecca E. Allen (form Crispin) con mou (H)
1845, 2, 19. Rowland dis jas (H)
1855, 4, 25. Mary [Crispen] (form Ward) con mcd (H)
1855, 10, 23. Mary gct Piles Grove MM (H)
1858, 1, 27. Elizabeth gct Cincinnati MM (H)
1867, 5, 22. Cert rec for Elizabeth from Cincinnati MM, O., endorsed to White Water MM [(H)

CROASDALE
1820, 11, 29. Joseph Jr. & w, Lydia, & ch, Charles Edward Amos T. & Joseph, rocf Byberry MM, Pa., dtd 1820,8,29
1821, 11, 28. Lydia & ch gct Byberry MM, Pa.

CROSS
1917, 7, 29. Abbie Willard transferred to this mtg from Springboro (H)

CURL
1810, 3, 28. Joseph & w, Sarah, rocf Salem MM, Ohio, dtd 1809,9,12
1813, 3, 31. James & w, Ruth, & ch, Joseph, Samuel, Ruth, James, Hannah, Enoch, Hadley & John, rocf Goose Creek MM, Va., dtd 1812,12,4
1931, 4, 26. Alonzo & w, Olive, rocf Springfield MM (H)

CURRAN
1887, 4, 20. Patrick Francis [Curn] recrq
1890, 3, 26. Patrick dis disunity

DAKIN
----, --, --. James m Nancy RICH b 1816,4,6 d 1899,10,17 (H)
Ch: Eva M. b 1851, 3, 16 d 1877, 4,28
Martha A. " 1853, 8, 25 " 1877, 6,21
Jehiel " 1855, 12, 25
Sarah J. " 1841, 6, 15 " 1885,11, 1
1874, 9, 23. Sarah Jane m John H. SAYER (H)

1839, 3, 27. Nancy Ann (form Rich) dis mou (H)
1842, 12, 21. Nancy (form Rich) dis mou
1864, 7, 27. Deborah (form Hatton) dis mcd (H)
1867, 7, 24. Susannah E. & Lydia E., recrq
1868, 1, 22. Lydia E. Jones (form Dakin) con mou
1869, 1, 27. Susannah E. Compton (form Dakin) con mou
1870, 4, 20. Nancy A. & ch, Eva M., Martha A. & Jehiel, recrq (H)
1870, 4, 20. Sarah Jane recrq (H)
1884, 5, 21. George W., Prudie, Ida May & George Jr. recrq
1886, 3, 24. Emma recrq
1887, 4, 20. Frank M. recrq
1891, 8, 26. Hamelton Dakin & w, Sarah A., & dt, Nellie Rebecca, rocf Ceasars Creek MM, dtd 1891,7,23
1892, 2, 24. Ada recrq
1909, 10, 27. George Dakin Sr. & George Dakin Jr. dropped from mbrp
1913, 4, 23. George Sr. recrq

DALSIN
1890, 3, 26. Frank dis disunity

DANFORTH
----, --, --. Horace P. b 1833,5,17 d 1907, 10,6; m Emma BUTTERWORTH b 1841,4,12 (H)d
Ch: Carrie b 1869, 4, 3 [1912,7,12
Effie " 1873, 10, 24
Robert Southgate " 1875, 12, 25
Henry Thomas b 1879, 5, 5

1869, 2, 22. Emma B. (form Butterworth) con mcd (H)

DANFORTH, continued
1887, 11, 23. Emma B. recrq (H)
1887, 11, 23. Effie, Robert & Henry, ch Emma B., recrq (H)
1907, 9, 25. Horace P. recrq (H)
1920, 7, 25. Henry T. dropped from mbrp (H)

DANIEL
----, --, --. Benjamin (nm) m Sidney ----- b 1781,4,2 (H)
Ch: Ruth b 1816, 9, 28
Sarah J. " 1818, 7, 31
John " 1820, 4, 25
Rachel " 1823, 11, 26
Sidney " d 1841, 4, 7
----, --, --. Robert b 1786,7,4 d 1859,5,13; m Martha HACKNEY b 1786,12,25 d 1869,4,11 (H)
Ch: William F. b 1820, 8, 18 d 1877, 8,14
Martha J. " 1824, 7, 9
Robert B.
Lydia E. " 1829, 11, 26 " 1905, 7,14
Rebecca A. " " 1911, 5, 1
----, --, --. John & ----- (H)
Ch: Mary Belle b 1857, 9, 25
R. Alma " 1862, 12, 14

1837, 3, 22. Sydney & dt, Ruth & Sarah Jane, rocf Hopewell MM, dtd 1836,10,8 (H)
1838, 10, 24. Sarah Jane Gregg (form Daniel) con mou (H)
1839, 7, 24. John [Daniels] recrq (H)
1843, 10, 25. Rachel recrq (H)
1849, 6, 20. Ruth Pettet (form Daniels) con mou (H)
1849, 6, 20. Rachel Fairchild (form Daniels) con mou (H)
1851, 10, 22. John F. [Daniels] dis mcd (H)
1866, 1, 24. Martha J. Howard (form Daniel) rpd mcd (H)
1866, 1, 24. Rachel rpd mcd (H)
1866, 1, 24. Martha, Lydia, Rebecca & William rec in mbrp; form mbr of Fall Creek or Centre MM, which had been laid down (H)
1876, 9, 20. David Chandler & w, Sarah Jane, & niece, Rachel Alma Daniel rocf Springboro MM, dtd 1876,8,24 (H)
1876, 9, 20. Mary Belle rocf Springboro MM, dtd 1876,8,24 (H)
1889, 7, 24. Martha J. Howard (form Daniel) gct Marietta MM, Ia. (H)

DANKIN
1807, 3, 12. Samuel & w, Mary, & ch, Amos, Sarah, Mary, Rachel & Isaac, rocf New Hope MM

DARLING
1882, 9, 20. Walter gct Muscatine MM

DAVIS
1807, 1, 15. Samuel, s Abiather & Lydia, Montgomery Co., O.; m at West Branch, Dorkis JONES, dt Samuel & Mary, Montgomery Co.,O.
1820, 5, 3. Nathan, s Elisha & Alce, Warren Co., O.; m at Miami, Lydia CLEAVER, dt Ezekiel & Abigail, Warren Co., O.
----, --, --. Elizabeth (Allen) b 1822,4,1 d 1903,2,26 bur Miami Cemetery (H)
1828, 6, 6. Elizabeth Ann b (H)
----, --, --. Spencer b 1834,2,1; m Lydia TOMPKINS b 1841,1,13 (H)
Ch: Armanis C. b 1862, 1, 4
Samuel V. " 1864, 7, 17
Rachel Minerva " 1866, 12, 22
Lydia Alice " 1872, 2, 25
Olive Ellen " 1877, 6, 24
----, --, --. Caleb m Martha STOUT b 1808,5,28 d 1878,10,11 (H)
Ch: Charles B. b 1850, 4, 16
Elizabeth Alice " 1848, 1, 14
----, --, --. Mark b 1842,5,11 d 1914,4,3 (H)
1889, 9, 20. Samuel V. d (H)

1804, 7, 12. Abiathar [Davies] & w, Rachel, & ch, Samuel, John, Mary, Sabilla, Benjamin, Sarah & Lydia, rocf Wrightsborough MM, dtd 1804,5,5
1805, 6, 13. Amos rocf Bush River MM, S. C., dtd 1805,3,30
1809, 12, 27. Amos gct Stillwater MM, to m
1815, 1, 25. John & w, Hannah, & ch, Anna Maria, Mary Jordan Samuel, Sarah & Charlotte, rocf South River MM, Va., dtd 1814,11,12
1819, 12, 29. Nathan rocf Center MM, Pa., dtd 1818,10,17
1821, 2, 28. Thomas rocf Chester MM, Pa., dtd 1820,12,16
1821, 4, 25. Caleb rocf Center MM, Pa., etd 1820,1,13
1822, 4, 24. Nathan & w, Lydia, & dt, Elizabeth, gct West Grove MM, Ind.
1842, 6, 22. Elizabeth Ann recrq (H)
1848, 11, 22. Elizabeth Ann Myres (form Davis) con mou (H)
1856, 8, 27. Martha (form Satterthwaite) dis mcd (H)
1863, 6, 24. Allen rocf Sugar River MM, Ind., dtd 1863,6,13
1866, 1, 24. Spenser con mcd (H)
1866, 1, 24. Martha, Charles B. & Elizabeth rec in mbrp; form mbr of Fall Creek or Center MM which had been laid down (H)
1866, 8, 22. Lydia (form Tompkins) con mcd (H)
1867, 5, 22. Allen gct Springfield MM, O.
1875, 5, 26. Lucinda recrq
1875, 8, 25. Elizabeth Alice James (form Davis) con mcd (H)
1876, 3, 22. William recrq
1880, 8, 25. Elizabeth A. rocf Chester MM, dtd 1880,7,8 (H)
1881, 3, 23. Mary Ann rocf Dover MM, O.

DAVIS, continued
1885, 1, 21. Charles B. relrq (H)
1886, 3, 24. Hannah B. (form Cook) rpd mcd (H)
1887, 2, 23. Silas & w, Ruth, & ch, Anna, Alice Jane & Leroy, rocf Dover MM
1888, 4, 25. Silas & w, Ruth, & ch, Martha Ann, Alice Jane & Leroy S., gct Springfield MM
1890, 9, 24. Rachel Minerva Bear (form Davis) relrq (H)
1891, 4, 22. Annanias C. dropped from mbrp
1891, 11, 25. Mark rocf Chester MM, N. J., dtd 1891,11,5 (H)
1893, 3, 22. Mary Ann gct Dover MM
1895, 5, 22. Spencer, Lydia, Lydia Alice & Olive Ellen set off as mbr of Executive Mtg at Clear Creek (H)
1900, 11, 21. Edith Mosher recrq
1907, 2, 20. Sue W. & Eva recrq
1908, 4, 22. Sue W. & dt Eva, relrq
1909, 10, 27. Ethith & Veo dropped from mbrp
1917, 7, 29. Lydia, Lydia A. & Olivia E. dropped from mbrp (H)

DEARDORF
1853, 3, 23. Lydia (form Dutton) dis mcd (H)

DEARTH
1821, 7, 25. Keturah (form Townsend) dis mou

DENLINGER
1854, 11, 29. Rebecca (form Haines) dis mcd (H)

DENNIS
1908, 7, 27. Edith S. gct South 8th St., Richmond MM, Ind.

DEVIT
1917, 10, 28. Angeline F. recrq (H)

DICKEY
1838, 5, 23. Jane (form Gray) dis mou (H)

DICKINSON
1900, 4, 25. Sophie G. relrq

DICKS
----, --, --. Achilles b 1795,2,4; m Hannah HARVEY b 1801,8,16
Ch: William b 1821, 3, 28
Calvin " 1822, 7, 11
Levi " 1824, 3, 9
Mary " 1825, 8, 28
Sally " 1828, 7, 9
Joshua " 1830, 5, 14
Agatha
----, --, --. Nathan b 1788,1,4 d 1848,5,10; m Sally JOHNSON b 1797,6,26 (H)
Ch: Martha I. b 1822, 1, 30 d 1839, 8,22
Elizabeth W. " 1824, 6, 22
Elijah J. b 1827, 10, 11
James B. " 1835, 5, 7
Sarah M. " 1838, 11, 23

1814, 10, 26. Agatha [Decks] & s, Achilles, rocf South River MM, Va., dtd 1814,9,10
1815, 7, 26. Nathan rocf South River MM, Va., dtd 1815,4,8
1819, 3, 31. Nathan [Dix] rocf Springfield MM, dtd 1819,3,27
1819, 8, 25. Sally rocf Fairfield MM, dtd 1819,6,26
1824, 10, 27. Achilles D. & w, Hannah, & ch, William, Calvin & Levi, rocf Springfield MM, dtd 1824,7,31
1829, 5, 27. Nathan dis jH
1829, 5, 27. Sally dis jH
1841, 8, 25. Achilles D. [Dix] & fam gct Bloomfield MM, Ind.
1842, 3, 23. Calvin [Dix] dis jas
1847, 6, 23. William [Dix] rocf Bloomfield MM, dtd 1847,2,10
1852, 9, 22. Sally & ch, James B. & Sarah M., gct Fall Creek MM, Ind. (H)
1853, 1, 26. Cert for Sally & ch to Fall Creek MM, Ind., granted 1852,9mo, returned with information they live too remote from mtg
1853, 3, 23. Elijah J. dis mcd (H)
1853, 7, 27. Elizabeth Cooper (form Dicks) dis mou
1853, 8, 24. Elizabeth Cooper (form Dicks) dis mcd (H)

DILL
1805, 9, 12. Phebe rocf Wrightsborough MM, Ga., dtd 1805,8,4

DILLON
1804, 7, 12. Mary (form Jay) dis mou

DINGEE
----, --, --. Charles b 1819,5,11 d 1887,7,3; m Hannah JACKSON b 1817,10,28 (H)
Ch: Marcus b 1856, 7, 21
Clarissa " 1843, 12, 18
Anna " 1849, 10, 27
Adaline " 1851, 6, 17
Lydia " 1858, 5, 11

1866, 1, 24. Hannah [Dingy] dropped from mbrp; form mbr of Fall Creek or Centre MM, which had been laid down (H)
1889, 7, 24. Hannah, Marcus & Lydia dropped from mbrp (H)
1889, 7, 24. Clarissa Cooder (form Dingee) dropped from mbrp (H)
1889, 7, 24. Adaline Dowles (form Dingee) dropped from mbrp (H)
1889, 7, 24. Anna Hanlin (form Dingee) dropped from mbrp (H)
1895, 5, 22. Ruth set off as mbr of Executive Mtg at Clear Creek (H)

DINWIDDIE
1886, 12, 22. Rebecca (form Austin) relrq (H)

DISBROUGH
1901, 12, 25. Joseph recrq
1901, 12, 25. Joseph gct Ceasars Creek MM

DISHAN
1832, 3, 21. Dinah rocf Lick Creek MM, Ind., dtd 1832,2,18
1832, 8, 22. Dinah [Dishon] gct Lick Creek MM, Ind.

DIXON
1806, 7, 10. Ann, w Sam, rocf Cane Creek MM, N. C., dtd 1805,12,7

DOAN
----, --, --. Wilson Spray b 1863,11,22; m Myra HOLBROOK b 1869,2,14 (H)
Ch: Florence
Holbrook b 1893, 4, 10
Marcia
Sibyl " 1894, 9, 15
Dorothy " 1896, 8, 30 d 1899, 3,18
----, --, --. Jesse b 1795,7,8 d 1880,12,5; m Lydia BALLARD (H)
Jesse m 2nd Rebecca SMITH b 1798,4,1 d 1894,1,2
1822, 7, 22. Jacob, s Joseph & Jemima, Clinton Co., O.; m at Hopewell, Hannah STUBBS, dt Isaac & Margaret, Warren Co., O.
1859, 3, 3. Enos, s John & Eunice, Hamilton Co., O., b 1834,5,21; m at Harveysburgh, Martha Ann BURGESS, dt Jesse & Elizabeth, Warren Co., O., b 1836,1,12
Ch: Mary
Emily b 1859, 12, 14
John " 1861, 3, 19
Esther Ann " 1863, 3, 8

1805, 4, 11. Joseph & w, Jemima, & ch, John, William, Joseph, Jesse, Jonathan, Jacob, Ruth, Elizabeth & Rachel, rocf Cane Creek MM, N. C., dtd 1804,9,1
1826, 12, 27. Jacob rocf Center MM, dtd 1826, 8,19
1829, 5, 27. Jacob dis jH
1829, 6, 24. Hannah dis jH
1837, 4, 26. Jacob dis (H)
1844, 10, 23. Mary Ann Nixon (form Doan) dis mou (H)
1859, 8, 24. Martha Ann [Doane] gct Westfield MM, Ind.
1864, 1, 27. Enos & w, Martha, & ch, Mary Emily, John & Esther Ann, rocf Greenwood MM dtd 1863,12,30
1865, 4, 26. Enos [Doane] & w, Martha Ann, & ch, Mary Emily, John & Esther, gct Clear Creek MM
1870, 7, 27. Martha & ch, John, Esther Ann, Enos & Albert, rocf Spring Creek MM, Ia., dtd 1870,7,2
1873, 7, 23. Martha [Done] & ch, John Enos, Albert & Esther Ann, gct Rich Square MM, N. C.
1898, 7, 27. Wilson & w, Myra Holebrook, & ch, Florence Holebrook, Marcia Sibyl & Dorothy, recrq (H)
1901, 2, 20. Wilson & w, Myra H., & dt, Florence H. & Marcia S., gct Fall Creek MM, Ind. (H)

DODDS
1887, 12, 22. J. Emerson, s Isaiah L. & Mary R., Adams Co., O.; m at residence of Ethan A. Brown, Annetta BROWN, dt Ethan A. & Hannah A., Warren Co., O. (H)

1891, 11, 25. Annetta B. relrq (H)
1908, 1, 22. Wm. C. & w, Josephine A., & ch, Goldie L. & Carl W., recrq
1912, 4, 24. Josephine & s, Carl, relrq
1914, 5, 27. Wm. C. dropped from mbrp

DONNALLY
1896, 11, 26. Lewis, s Augustus & Elizabeth, Kanawha Co., Va., b 1864,7,27; m at residence of Andrew Cadwallader in Chicago, Mary C. CADWALLADER, dt Andrew & Esther, b 1865,6,30 (H)
Ch: Cadwallader
b 1900, 3, 29 d 1907, 1,10

DORLAND
1878, 4, 24. Walter E. rocf Oskaloosa MM, Ia., dtd 1878,1,5
1882, 9, 20. Walter gct Muscatine MM, Ia.

DOUGHERTY
1810, 9, 26. Hannah [Dohety] (form Morman) con mou
1825, 6, 29. Betsy (form Black) dis mou & jas

DOUGHMAN
1839, 7, 24. Matilda S. recrq (H)
1844, 10, 23. Matilda Lode (form Doughtman) dis mou (H)
1844, 11, 20. Matilda Sothie (form Doughman) dis mou (H)

DOWLES
1889, 7, 24. Adaline (form Dingee) dropped from mbrp (H)

DOWNES
1865, 11, 22. Elizabeth con mcd (H)
1871, 4, 26. Elizabeth C. gct Wapsanonoch MM, Ia. (H)

DOWNING
----, --, --. Jacob b 1807,6,6 d 1862,6,9; m Jane W. UNDERWOOD b 1813,2,-- d 1907,1,23 (H)
Ch: Hannah M. b 1839, 8, 14
Maria M. " 1848, 10, 15

DOWNING, Jacob & Jane W., continued
Ch: Matilda J. b 1851, 4, 10
Joseph J. " 1858, 10, 20
1871, 12, 28. Matilda Jane m Zephaniah UNDERWOOD (H)
----, --, --. Joseph J. b 1858,10,20; m Almina J. SPENCER b 1859,1,12 (H)
Ch: Adella M. b 1884, 5, 2
Ada Irene " 1888, 12, 29

1868, 5, 27. Jane U. & ch, Maria M., Matilda J. & Joseph, rocf Center MM, Pa., dtd 1868,5,6 (H)
1868, 5, 27. Hannah M. rocf Center MM, Pa., dtd 1868,5,6 (H)
1871, 7, 26. Maria Romine (form Downing) rpd mcd (H)
1883, 4, 25. Joseph J. gct West Branch MM, Pa., to m Almina J. Spencer (H)
1883, 9, 26. Almina J. rocf West Branch MM, Pa., dtd 1883,9,23 (H)

DRAKE
1845, 1, 22. Ann (form Haines) con mou (H)

DUBOIS
1807, 8, 3. Hannah (form Mullin) dis mcd

DUDLEY
1839, 7, 24. Elton rocf Evesham MM, dtd 1839, 5,10
1841, 4, 21. Elton dis mou

DUKEMINEER
----, --, --. Isaac b 1762,10,30; m Anna ----- b 1764,9,28
Ch: Hannah b 1798, 11, 1
Ann " 1801, 5, 28
Isaac " 1809, 4, 24
1818, 12, 2. Elizabeth m Gershom PERDUE
1832, 2, 1. Hannah m Thomas WELLS

1806, 11, 13. Isaac & w, Anna, rocf Haddonfield MM, N. J., dtd 1806,9,8
1809, 3, 11. Isaac [Dukemanneer] & w, Ann, & ch recrq
1809, 3, 11. Elizabeth, Hannah & Ann (Dukminear), ch Isaac, recrq
1833, 1, 23. Isaac dis mou
1857, 4, 22. Ann gct White River MM

DUNCAN
1808, 8, 11. Cert rec for Elizabeth from Bush River MM, S. C., dtd 1807,8,29, endorsed to Center MM

DUNHAM
1904, 5, 25. David E. recrq

DUNKER
1806, 9, 11. Jesse rocf New Hope MM, Tenn., dtd 1806,3,24

DUTTON
1806, 7, 16. John, s James & Lydia, Warren Co., O., b 1781,7,29; m Martha CLEAVER, dt Ezekiel & Mary, b 1771,1,21 (H)
Ch: Mary b 1807, 12, 6
James V. " 1809, 9, 29
Lydia " 1811, 6, 15
Asa " 1813, 6, 14
Silus " 1815, 10, 2

1805, 5, 9. David & w, Phebe, & ch, Margaret & Thomas, rocf New Hope MM, Tenn., dtd 1804,11,7
1806, 2, 13. John recrq
1830, 1, 27. Martha dis jH
1830, 1, 27. Mary dis jH
1830, 1, 27. Lydia dis jH
1830, 1, 27. John dis jH
1853, 3, 23. James V. dis mcd (H)
1853, 3, 23. Asa dis mcd (H)
1853, 3, 23. Silas dis mcd (H)
1853, 3, 23. Mary Brown (form Dutton) dis mcd (H)
1853, 3, 23. Lydia Deardorf (form Dutton) dis mcd (H)

DYER
1830, 1, 27. Milly recrq without permission of South River MM (H)

EACHES
1804, 12, 13. Phebe & dt, Mary, rocf New Hope MM, Tenn., dtd 1804,8,25
1806, 4, 10. Mary Kirby (form Eachus) dis mou

EASTMAN
1856, 9, 27. Calista con mcd (H)

EASTLOCK
1866, 8, 22. Ruth McVey (form Eastlock) con mcd (H)

EASTON
1917, 7, 29. Sarah E. transferred to this mtg from Springboro (H)

ECKMAN
1889, 2, 20. Firman recrq
1894, 2, 21. Firman relrq

EDGERTON
1816, 3, 27. Samuel & w, Elizabeth, & ch, William, Sarah, Hannah, Prudence, Rachel & Tabitha, rocf Stillwater MM, dtd 1815, 11,28

EDWARDS
----, --, --. Nathaniel b 1774,9,2; m Mary ----- b 1775,10,15 (H)
Ch: Jane b 1801, 1, 11 d 1804, 4,22
William " 1802, 9, 5
Joshua " 1804, 3, 4
Ruth " 1808, 3, 18

EDWARDS, Nathaniel & Mary, continued
Ch: Ruth b 1808, 3, 18
Mary " 1809, 3, 29
John " 1811, 1, 24
Sarah " 1812, 11, 10
David " 1814, 10, 9
Jonathan " 1816, 11, 1
Hadley " 1818, 2, 17
----, --, --. Elizabeth b 1802,12,31 d 1888, 7,6 (H)
1805, 6, 26. William, s William & Jane, Warren Co., O.; m at Waynesville, Jemima BRIDGES, dt Charles & Edith, Warren Co.,O.
----, --, --. Archibald m Ann HARVEY b 1786,11, 5
Ch: Ruth
Jane
Lydia b 1808, 8, 26
Elizabeth " 1810, 4, 11
Mary " 1811, 7, 16
John D. " 1813, 7, 24
Isaac " 1815, 5, 26
Rebecca " 1817, 9, 12
Harlan H. " 1820, 3, 20
Eleanor C. " 1822, 6, 30
1822, 11, 6. William, s Nathaniel & Mary, Warren Co., O.; m at Miami, Elizabeth NEWMAN, dt Jonathan & Anny, Warren Co., O.
1829, 11, 27. Eliza d
----, --, --. Joshua b 1804,3,4; m Sarah HARVEY b 1807,11,23
Ch: William H. b 1830, 12, 13
Nathaniel " 1837, 6, 7
John " 1840, 11, 23
Martha H. " 1844, 3, 13
Eliza " 1827, 2, 19
Mary Jane " 1829, 3, 21
James B. " 1832, 12, 19
Elizabeth Ann " 1835, 7, 18
Isaac Fisher " 1847, 6, 23
1831, 11, 2. Sarah m Isaac HARVEY
1832, 1, 5. Mary m William NEWLIN
----, --, --. Isaac b 1815,5,26; m Nancy ----- b 1816,2,14
Ch: Joshua H. b 1836, 8, 30
Jane H. " 1838, 3, 11
Martha " 1841, 2, 18
Archibald " 1842, 9, 20
Mary Ann " 1845, 3, 27
Lydia " 1847, 7, 7
Jehu " 1849, 3, 5
1839, 7, 21. Joshua H. d bur Harveysburgh
----, --, --. John D. b 1813,7,24; m Eliza Jane ----- b 1822,1,26
Ch: Wm. Henry b 1841, 4, 29
David " 1843, 9, 8
Harlan " 1846, 2, 22
Edith Ann " 1848, 9, 30
Mary E. " 1851, 8, 11
Milton " 1854, 7, 3
1841, 10, 18. Ruth d
1842, 8, 31. Wm. Henry d
1852, 4, 3. Nancy d bur Harveysburgh
1853, 3, 27. Mary d bur Waynesville
1854, 7, 19. Milton T. b
1861, 11, 28. Jane H. m Obadiah MENDENHALL
1863, 4, 25. John D. d

1805, 2, 14. Nathaniel & w, Mary, & ch, William & Joshua, rocf Cane Creek MM, N. C., dtd 1804,8,4
1805, 2, 14. William [Edward] rocf Spring MM, dtd 1804,9,3
1806, 1, 9. Archibald & w, Ann, rocf Spring MM, N. C., dtd 1805,9,31
1808, 9, 10. John rocf Spring MM, N. C., dtd 1807,12,27
1826, 4, 26. Joshua gct Springfield MM, to m Sarah Harvey
1827, 1, 31. William & fam gct Duck Creek MM, Ind.
1828, 8, 27. Joshua & fam gct Springfield MM
1829, 2, 25. Mary Pugh (form Edwards) con mou
1829, 5, 27. Archibald & w, Ann, & ch, Mary, John, Isaac, Rebecca, Harlan H. & Eleanor C., rocf Springfield MM, dtd 1829,4,14
1829, 5, 27. Lydia rocf Springfield MM, dtd 1829,4,14
1829, 5, 27. Elizabeth rocf Springfield MM, dtd 1829,4,14
1830, 6, 30. Joshua & w, Sarah, & dt, Mary Jane, rocf Springfield MM, dtd 1830,6,15
1832, 1, 25. Elizabeth Hale (form Edwards) rpd mou
1835, 8, 26. Isaac gct Springfield MM, to m Nancy Harvey
1836, 2, 21. Nancy rocf Springfield MM, dtd 1835,12,15
1840, 6, 25. Rebecca Mills (form Edwards) dis mou
1842, 4, 20. Eleanor C. Turner (form Edwards) con mou
1842, 7, 27. Eliza Jane rocf Bloomfield MM, Ind., dtd 1842,4,6
1843, 7, 26. David & w, Susannah, & dt, Eliza Ann, rocf Spiceland MM, dtd 1843,6,21
1843, 7, 26. Jonathan dis mou
1844, 11, 21. David & w, Susannah, & fam gct Spiceland MM
1846, 12, 26. Isaac dis
1851, 3, 26. William dis disunity
1856, 5, 21. John D. gct West Union MM, Ind., to m Hannah Haddock
1856, 9, 24. Hannah Edwards & ch, William Daniel & Thomas T. Haddock, rocf West Union MM, dtd 1856,5,11
1857, 1, 21. John dis mou
1858, 7, 21. Joshua & w, Sarah, & ch, Nathan & John, gct Springfield MM
1863, 8, 26. Lydia Roberts (form Edwards) con mou
1863, 8, 26. Martha con mou
1866, 1, 24. Elizabeth rpd mcd (H)

EDWARDS, continued
1866, 5, 23. Hannah gct Clear Creek MM
1867, 4, 24. Mary (form Chew) con mou
1867, 5, 22. Harlan E. con mou
1867, 11, 20. David con mou
1868, 7, 22. Mary Ann Carr (form Edwards) dis mou & jas
1868, 7, 22. Edith Moris (form Edwards) con mou
1869, 3, 25. Lydia E. Johnson (form Edwards) dis mou & jas
1869, 7, 21. Harlan con mou
1870, 11, 23. John & w, Charlotte, & ch, Mary, Annie, Ellwood, Lydia, Athelia & Evalina, recrq
1870, 11, 23. David gct Cincinnati MM
1871, 6, 21. Isaac recrq
1872, 6, 26. Mary Ann & ch, Christianna, Margaret Erma & Edwin L., recrq
1876, 7, 26. Nettie gct Cincinnati MM
1907, 11, 20. Charles recrq

EHRHARDT
1808, 4, 14. Sarah [Airhart] (form Libole) dis mou

ELBON
1913, 4, 23. Frank S. & Emma recrq

ELCOCK
1882, 11, 21. Rebecca Ann relrq

ELLIMAN
1805, 11, 14. William & w, Jane, & ch, David, Isaac & Mary, rocf Bush River MM, S. C., dtd 1805,7,27
1805, 11, 14. Elizabeth & Hannah rocf Bush River MM, dtd 1805,7,27
1805, 12, 12. Susanna [Elleman] & ch, Drusilla, Elizabeth, Temperance, Enos & Susannah, rocf New Hope MM, Tenn., dtd 1805, 9,21, endorsed by Lost Creek MM

ELLIOTT
----, --, --. Hannah B. (Jones), b 1821,5,23 d 1899,2,8 (H)

1814, 6, 29. Hannah [Eliot] (form Stubbs) con mou
1815, 4, 26. Hannah [Elliot] gct Elk MM
1832, 1, 25. William rocf Green St. MM, Phila., dtd 1831,11,17 (H)
1839, 11, 20. Rebecca M., Sarah, William, Edwin & Esterianna, ch John, rocf Wilmington MM, Del., dtd 1839,4,1 (H)
1858, 11, 24. Rebecca Ann Ferris (form Elliott) con mcd (H)

ELLIS
1804, 12, 13. Mordecai & w, Sarah, & ch, Eleanor, Job, Samuel, Anna, Susannah & Isaac, rocf Hopewell MM, dtd 1804,9,3
1805, 7, 11. Rowland rocf Redstone MM, dtd 1805,3,1
1806, 2, 13. John & w, Tamar, & ch, Elijah & Thomas, rocf New Hope MM, dtd 1805,9,21
1806, 3, 13. Thomas & w, Lydia, & ch, Martha, Hannah, John, James, Rachel & Levi, rocf New Hope MM, Tenn., dtd 1805,9,21
1806, 9, 11. Jehu & w, Phebe, & ch, Mordecai, Hiram, Beulah & Nehemiah, rocf Lost Creek MM, dtd 1806,4,26
1868, 12, 23. Guli E. (form Harvey) con mou
1869, 1, 27. Gulielma gct Cesars Creek MM
1874, 4, 22. Mary Jane & dt, Sarah Amanda, recrq
1885, 7, 22. Elizabeth C. & ch, Edith U., Mary E. & Leonidas F., rocf Caesars Creek MM, dtd 1885,6,25
1888, 9, 26. Elizabeth C. & ch, Edith V., Mary E. & Leonidas F., gct West Grove MM
1894, 8, 29. S. H. recrq
1904, 4, 20. Mary Belle relrq (H)
1921, 7, 30. Anna C. recrq (H)

ELLZEY
1806, 6, 12. William & w, Agatha, & ch, Lemuel, Keziah, Garard, Esther & Priscilla, rocf Upper MM, dtd 1806,2,15
1903, 6, 24. Mauld Alma [Elzy] recrq

EMBREE
1804, 7, 12. John & Mary rocf Wrightsboro MM, dtd 1804,5,5
1804, 11, 8. Amos & w, Sarah, & ch, Mary, Rebeccah, John, Sarah, Joseph, Mercer & Amos, rocf Wrightsborough MM, Ga., dtd 1804,6,2
1806, 9, 11. Isaac & w, Hannah, & ch, James, Rebecca, Isaac & Moses, rocf New Hope MM, Tenn., dtd 1806,7,19
1806, 9, 11. Thomas & w, Esther, & ch, Elijah, Rachel & Sarah, rocf New Hope MM, Tenn., dtd 1806,7,19
1812, 6, 24. Davis rocf Phila. MM, dtd 1812, 4,28
1814, 1, 26. Jesse rocf Baltimore MM, dtd 1813,11,10
1814, 3, 30. Davis rpd mcd

EMLEY
1886, 3, 24. Mary L. recrq

EMMONS
1892, 3, 23. Cassina C. recrq

EMORY
1807, 5, 4. Rebecca Moore (form Emory) dis

ENGLE
1825, 11, 2. Isaac, s Robert & Jane, Warren Co., O.; m at Miami, Mary E. HAINES, dt Abraham & Hannah, Warren Co., O.
1856, 10, 6. Isaac d (H)

1812, 11, 25. Abraham rocf Plainfield MM, dtd

ENGLE, continued
1812,9,26
1816, 7, 31. Joshua & w, Hannah, & ch, Jane, Elizabeth, Joshua & Hannah Ann, rocf Evesham MM, N. J., dtd 1816,5,10
1817, 7, 30. Joshua & fam gct Cesars Creek MM
1825, 7, 27. Isaac rocf Evesham MM, N. J., dtd 1825,5,6
1831, 3, 30. Ann (form Wharton) con mou (H)
1836, 11, 23. Isaac gct Green Plane MM, to m Sarah MERRIT
1837, 7, 26. Sarah M. rocf Green Plain MM, dtd 1837,6,14 (H)
1858, 11, 24. Sarah M. gct Green Plain MM (H)
1859, 7, 27. Ann (form Hopkins) dis mcd (H)
1867, 11, 20. Martha (form Chandler) dis mcd (H)

ENLOSS
1917, 3, 25. Isabel recrq (H)

ENNIS
1858, 1, 6. Mary Elizabeth b (H)

1878, 5, 22. Mary Elizabeth [Enis] recrq (H)
1887, 4, 20. Mordecai E. recrq
1889, 7, 24. Mary E. McFaul (form Ennis) rpd mcd (H)
1892, 12, 21. Mordecai dis

ENSEY
1889, 6, 26. John recrq

EVANS
----, --, --. Benjamin b 1760,10,12; m Hannah SMITH b 1767,7,3 (H)
Ch: Thomas b 1791, 12, 12
David " 1793, 6, 30
Elizabeth " 1795, 2, 6
Owen " 1800, 3, 16
George " 1802, 2, 25
Sarah " 1804, 3, 6
Mary " 1806, 2, 2
Jason " 1807, 11, 25
1809, 8, 10. Mary m Levi HAWKINS
----, --, --. Jesse & Esther (H)
Ch: Juretee b 1812, 8, 21
Risdon " 1814, 6, 2
Rian " 1815, 11, 14
1812, 5, 7. Rebecca m Samuel BROWN
1812, 9, 2. Elizabeth m Stephen COOK
1813, 6, 2. David, s Benjamin & Hannah, Warren Co., O.; m at Miami, Rachel BURNETT, dt John & Rebecca (H)
Ch: John b 1814, 3, 9
Joel " 1816, 1, 23
Seth " 1817, 10, 21
Evan " 1820, 7, 1 d 1821,10,21
Owen " 1821, 8, 17 " 1823, 1,29
Rebecca " 1823, 8, 15
Benjamin " 1824, 12, 16
Mary " 1826, 7, 27
Hannah " 1829, 4, 3
Ch: Ann b 1831, 5, 1
Jason " 1833, 3, 13 d 1907, 8,23
----, --, --. Thomas & Hannah (H)
Ch: Benjamin b 1814, 11, 6
Lydia " 1816, 8, 13
Margaret " 1818, 8, 26
Isaac " 1821, 3, 1
Ann " 1823, 4, 18
Mary " 1825, 8, 5
Thomas m 2nd Elizabeth ROBINSON b 1802,1, 24
Ch: William R. b 1834, 12, 3
Owen " 1836, 12, 8
George L. " 1838, 9, 17
Joseph " 1840, 11, 16
1813, 10, 6. Thomas, s Benjamin & Hannah, Warren Co., O.; m at Miami, Hannah PEDRICK, dt Isaac & Hannah, Green Co., O.
1820, 6, 7. Hannah Ann m John WARD
1821, 2, 7. Hepsabah m Samuel STEVENSON
----, --, --. George b 1802,2,25; m Mary ----- b 1798,3,6 (H)
Dt: Asenath b 1822, 10, 14
1822, 2, 6. George, s Benjamin & Hannah, Warren Co., O.; m at Miami, Mary HASKIT, dt Thomas & Ann, Warren Co., O.
1822, 10, 3. Ruth m Benjamin SATTERTHWAITE
1822, 11, 6. Mary m Richard PEDRICK
1828, 1, 11. Hannah, w Thomas, d bur Turtle Creek
1829, 6, 3. Rachel m Henry Fletcher
----, --, --. Jason b 1807,11,25 d 1876,3,11; m Mary HAINES, b 1815,8,12 d 1889,4,25 (H)
Ch: Sarah b 1837, 6, 12 d 1916,10, 7
Susan " 1841, 1, 1 " 1898, 9,15
Benjamin " 1843, 4, 23 " 1913, 5,14
1830, 7, 10. Benjamin Sr. d bur Waynesville
1836, 6, 8. Lydia m Joseph C. COOPER
1837, 7, 23. Benjamin, s Thomas, d bur Miami Cemetery
1838, 8, 1. Margaret m David S. BURSON
1839, 11, 21. Owen, s Thomas, d bur Miami Cemetery
----, --, --. Joel b 1816,1,23 d 1907,9,17; m Elizabeth ----- b 1820,6,20 d 1872,12,4 (H)
Ch: Rachel
Caroline b 1845, 6, 6
John S. " 1849, 7, 31
David " 1851, 12, 4
1845, 4, 24. Ann m William G. KINSEY
1851, 6, 24. Sarah d bur Waynesville
1851, 10, 29. Mary P. m Jesse J. KENWORTHY
1852, 5, 11. Thomas d bur Miami Cemetery
1853, 9, 19. Hannah Sr. d bur Waynesville
----, --, --. William R. b 1834,12,3; m Margaret HADLEY b 1836,10,13
Ch: George
1865, 5, 3. Joseph R., s Thomas & Elizabeth M., Marion Co., Ind.; m at Waynesville, Caroline E. BROWN, dt Asher & Esther J., Warren Co., O.

EVANS, continued
1804, 5, 10. Benjamin & w, Hannah, & ch, Thomas, David, Elizabeth, Owen & George, roc dtd 1804,1,28
1804, 10, 11. Evan & w, Patience, & ch, Lydia, John, Rachel & Parmelia, rocf Southland MM, Va., dtd 1803,12,28
1804, 10, 11. Hannah Bales, dt Evan Evans, rocf Southland MM, Va., dtd 1804,2,1
1806, 6, 12. Joseph & w, Esther, & ch, Margaret, Robert, Mary, Aaron & Sarah, rocf Wrightsboro MM, Ga., dtd 1805,4,6
1807, 11, 12. Joseph & w, Lydia, & ch, William, Job, Samuel, Joseph, Ruth, Charles & Aaron, rocf Haddonfield MM, N. J., dtd 1807,3,2
1810, 11, 28. Keziah rocf Haddonfield MM, N.J., dtd 1810,9,10
1810, 11, 28. Owen rocf Haddonfield MM, dtd 1810,9,10
1810, 11, 28. Rebekah rocf Haddonfield MM, N. J., dtd 1810,9,10
1811, 3, 27. Sarah rocf Haddonfield MM, N. J., dtd 1810,11,30
1812, 8, 28. William dis mcd
1814, 1, 26. Samuel gct Chester MM, N. J.
1814, 3, 30. Joseph & w, Rachel, & ch, Nancy, Elizabeth, Robert, Rebecca & Susanna, rocf West Branch MM, dtd 1813,11,28
1815, 8, 30. Keziah Thomas (form Evans) dis mou
1815, 9, 27. Owen dis bearing arms
1815, 9, 27. Sarah Smith (form Evans) dis mou
1816, 11, 27. Jesse & w, Esther, & ch, Junitte, Risdon & Ryan, rocf New Garden MM, N. C., dtd 1816,8,31
1818, 4, 29. Cert rec for James from New Jersey, endorsed to New Garden MM, Ind.
1818, 9, 30. Job dis
1819, 6, 22. Rachel recrq
1819, 11, 24. Mary & ch, Beulah, Abel, Lydia, Martha, Charles, William & Henry, rocf Evesham MM, N. J., dtd 1819,8,6
1819, 11, 24. Hepsibah rocf Evesham MM, N. J., dtd 1819,8,6
1819, 11, 24. Hannah Ann rocf Evesham MM, N. J., dtd 1819,8,6
1819, 11, 24. Mary Jr. rocf Evesham MM, N.J., dtd 1819,8,6
1820, 3, 29. Joseph dis
1820, 5, 31. Asa dis
1820, 9, 27. Benjamin rocf Evesham MM, N.J., dtd 1820,8,11
1821, 1, 31. Jesse & fam gct White Water MM, Ind.
1822, 8, 28. Joseph Jr. dis
1823, 10, 29. Beulah Sairls (form Evans) dis mou
1824, 10, 27. Mary, w William, & ch, Abel, Lydia, Charles, Martha, William & Henry Emmor, gct West Grove MM, Ind.
1824, 10, 27. Mary Jr. gct West Grove MM, Ind.
1826, 2, 22. Owen gct White Water MM
1826, 3, 29. George & w, Mary, & ch gct Milford MM, Ind.
1827, 6, 27. Charles dis mcd
1827, 12, 26. Rachel Jr. dis attending a mcd
1828, 2, 27. Rachel dis disunity
1828, 11, 26. Jason gct Springborough MM, to m Amyrah Haines
1829, 2, 25. David dis jH
1829, 6, 24. Rachel dis jH
1829, 8, 26. Jason dis jH
1829, 11, 25. Amyrah rocf Springborough MM, dtd 1829,10,27 (H)
1829, 11, 25. Lydia dis jH
1831, 1, 26. Aaron dis jH
1832, 8, 29. Joseph & w, Rachel, & ch, Rebecca & Susannah, rocf Cincinnati MM, dtd 1832,5,31 (H)
1834, 1, 22. Thomas gct Springborough MM, to m Elizabeth Robinson
1834, 6, 25. Elizabeth M. rocf Springborough MM, dtd 1834,6,24
1835, 12, 23. Jacob gct Springborough MM, to m Mary Haines (H)
1836, 8, 24. Mary rocf Springborough MM (H)
1838, 7, 25. Rebecca E. Tate (form Evans) rpd mou; d before action was taken (H)
1838, 7, 25. Susan Patton (form Evans) rpd mou (H)
1839, 6, 26. Joel con mou (H)
1840, 5, 27. Joel dis mou & jH
1840, 5, 27. John rpd mou
1841, 4, 21. Hannah (form Canby) dis mou
1842, 7, 27. Noah S. Haines gct White Water MM, to m Elizabeth Evans (H)
1843, 1, 12. Jason & w, Mary, & ch, Sarah, Susanna & Benjamin, gct Cincinnati MM (H)
1846, 2, 18. Joel con mou (H)
1846, 2, 18. Eliza (form Satterthwaite) dis mou
1846, 3, 25. Elizabeth (form Satterthwaite) con mou (H)
1846, 9, 23. Mary Allen (form Evans) dis mou (H)
1847, 7, 21. Mary Allen (form Evans) dis mou
1847, 9, 22. Isaac gct Springboro MM, to m Anna S. Boon
1848, 5, 24. Ann S. rocf Springborough MM, dtd 1848,4,25
1850, 10, 23. Hannah gct White Water MM, Ind.
1850, 12, 25. Seth dis mcd (H)
1850, 12, 25. Samuel Brown gct White Water MM, to m Hannah Evans
1852, 10, 27. John dis mcd & jas (H)
1853, 3, 23. Ann C. Nutt (form Evans) dis mcd (H)
1853, 12, 21. Isaac P. gct White Water MM
1855, 4, 25. Benjamin gct Cincinnati MM (H)
1855, 4, 25. Jason dis mcd (H)
1855, 9, 26. Hannah Conover (form Evans) con mcd (H)
1859, 8, 24. William R. gct Springfield MM, to m Margaret Ann Hadley
1860, 2, 22. Margaret Ann rocf Springfield

EVANS, continued
MM, O., dtd 1860,2,18
1863, 6, 24. Christiana rocf Milford MM, Ind., dtd 1863,5,23
1865, 5, 24. Elizabeth M. gct Indianapolis MM
1865, 10, 25. Joseph R. & w, Caroline, gct Indianapolis MM
1865, 10, 25. William R. & w, Margaret Ann, & s, George H., gct Indianapolis MM, Ind.
1866, 3, 21. George dis mou
1868, 5, 27. Christianna gct Rich Square MM, N. C.
1888, 1, 25. Juretee, Risdon & Rian dropped from mbrp (H)
1899, 1, 25. David relrq (H)

EYLER
1905, 4, 26. Bessie recrq

FAIRCHILD
1849, 6, 20. Rachel (form Daniels) con mou (H)

FALLIS
----, --, --. John b 1809,9,14; m Deborah CADWALADER b 1815,8,18
Ch: Richard b 1847, 6, 1
John C. " 1850, 3, 25
1848, 3, 2. Phebe m Thomas CADWALLADER
1850, 11, 18. John d
1855, 5, 25. Elizabeth d (H)

1824, 10, 27. Amos Welch gct Springfield MM, to m Rachel Fallis
1837, 12, 27. Harriet rocf Center MM, dtd 1837,12,13
1840, 3, 23. Esther & John [Follis], ch Isaiah, rocf Green Plain MM, dtd 1840,1,15
1841, 8, 25. Harriett Wales (form Fallis) con mou
1842, 12, 21. Esther Smith (form Fallis) dis mou
1844, 7, 24. Thomas rocf Salem MM, dtd 1844, 2,14
1846, 4, 22. Phebe rocf Center MM, dtd 1845, 12,17
1848, 1, 26. Deborah (form Cadwalader) con mou
1849, 5, 23. John rocf Center MM, dtd 1849,1, 18
1850, 1, 23. John Jr. dis mou
1851, 11, 26. Elizabeth rocf Center MM, dtd 1851,8,14
1855, 8, 22. John dis mou
1878, 1, 23. Deborah & s, Richard & John, gct Oskaloosa MM, Ia.

FARMER
1808, 3, 10. William & w, Prudence, & ch, John & Matilda, rocf Bush River MM, S.C., dtd 1806,6,28

FARQUHAR
----, --, --. Jonah b 1778,3,13 d 1857,4,11; m Elizabeth ----- b 1790,1,4 d 1847,8,18 (H)
Ch: Mahlon b 1810, 11, 18
Andrew " 1812, 11, 27 " 1870, 3, 8
William " 1814, 8, 11 " 1814,10,22
William B. " 1815, 12, 15
Jacob " 1818, 4, 6
Allen " 1820, 2, 5 " 1826, 5,14
Benjamin " 1822, 2, 15
Amos " 1824, 9, 22 " 1872, 9,19
Sarah " 1826, 8, 7
Philip " 1828, 2, 16
Phebe " 1830, 5, 1
Isabella " 1836, 3, 13

1806, 6, 12. Benjamin & w, Rachel, & ch, Uriah, Cyrus, Allen, Jonathan, Josiah & Susannah, rocf Pipe Creek MM, dtd 1805,12, 14
1815, 8, 30. Uriah rocf Center MM, dtd 1815, 7,15
1820, 4, 26. Uriah dis mcd
1830, 11, 24. Jonah & s, Mahlon & Andrew, recrq (H)
1836, 2, 22. Andrew con mou (H)
1837, 7, 26. Mahlon dis mou (H)
1845, 5, 21. Joseph Cadwalader gct Center MM, to m Rachel Farquhar
1885, 10, 21. Benjamin relrq (H)
1885, 10, 21. Philip relrq (H)
1886, 2, 24. William B. relrq (H)
1886, 10, 27. Jacob dropped from mbrp (H)

FARR
1831, 3, 24. Tamar m Frederick HOOVER (H)
1836, 7, 2. Asenath N. m John L. WEST (H)

1830, 3, 31. Frederic Kindley gct Green Plain MM, to m Mary Farr Jr. (H)
1830, 10, 27. Tamar rocf Green Plain MM, dtd 1830,9,7 (H)
1841, 11, 24. Mary gct Camden MM, Ind. (H)

FAULKNER
1805, 11, 14. Jesse [Falkner] gct Virginia
1806, 10, 9. Hannah rpd mou
1806, 11, 13. Jesse [Falkner] dis mcd
1806, 12, 11. Martha rocf Hopewell MM, Va., dtd 1806,8,4
1806, 12, 11. Ellen rocf Hopewell MM, Va., dtd 1806,9,1
1807, 1, 8. Susanna rocf Hopewell MM, Va., dtd 1806,11,3
1807, 1, 8. Thomas, Hannah & Jane [Falkner] ch Jesse, also Thomas [Falkner], s Robert, rocf Hopewell MM, dtd 1806,11,3
1808, 1, 14. Hannah rocf Hopewell MM, Va., dtd 1807,7,6
1810, 6, 27. Susanna & Judith [Falkner], ch Jesse & Hannah, recrq
1814, 2, 23. Jesse [Falkner] & fam gct Center MM

FERGUSON
1808, 9, 10. Nimrod & w, Ann, & ch, Mary & Isaac, rocf South River MM, Va., dtd 1807, 10,20

FERRELL
1881, 3, 23. Cornelia gct Oskaloosa MM

FERRIS
1858, 11, 24. Rebecca Ann (form Elliott) con mcd (H)
1859, 6, 22. Rebecca Ann gct Maple Grove MM, Ind. (or Pa.)
1898, 2, 23. Marshie Hare relrq

FISHER
1836, '8, 31. Ruth m Eli HARVEY
1875, 1, 4. Anna C. m Abijah P. O'NEALL (H)
----, --, --. Isaac & Eunice
Ch: Cyrus W.
Lydia Ann
Hannah
Sinai
Mary
Horace

1804, 12, 13. James & w, Jane, & ch, Alice, Thomas, Mary, James, John, Hiram, Jane & Elizabeth, rocf New Hope MM, Tenn., dtd 1804,7,21
1813, 10, 27. Elias & w, Hannah, rocf South River MM, Va., dtd 1813,7,14
1826, 3, 29. Charles rocf South River MM, dtd 1825,12,10
1831, 11, 30. Isaac rocf Carmel MM, dtd 1831, 9,17
1833, 4, 24. Isaac gct White Water MM, to m Unice Street
1833, 11, 20. Eunice rocf White Water MM, Ind., dtd 1833,9,25
1835, 6, 24. Anna H. rocf Springfield MM, dtd 1835,5,12
1835, 6, 24. Ruth rocf Springfield MM, dtd 1835,5,12
1836, 10, 26. Letitia (form Haines) dis mou (H)
1837, 7, 26. Anna H. gct Springfield MM
1838, 8, 22. Isaac & w, Eunice, & ch, Cyrus & Lydia Ann, gct Salem MM, O.
1839, 6, 26. Isaac & w, Eunice, & ch, Cyrus W. & Lydia Ann, rocf Salem MM, dtd 1839,5, 22
1842, 9, 21. Isaac & fam gct Sugar River MM; returned because they joined Presbyterians
1848, 1, 26. Isaac dis jas
1852, 1, 21. Eunice dis jas
1854, 11, 22. Axhel E. rocf Springfield MM, dtd 1854,8,19
1857, 11, 25. Sarah F. (form Steddom) dis mou
1864, 10, 26. Lydia Ann & Hannah dis jas
1865, 2, 22. Lina Ann & Mary T. gct Spring Creek MM, Ia.
1865, 7, 26. Horace, minor, gct Spring Creek (or Salem) MM, Ia.
1867, 4, 24. Asael gct Salem MM, O.
1870, 9, 21. Anna C. recrq (H)
1873, 8, 27. Emily W. (form Ward) con mou
1883, 4, 25. Francis recrq
1883, 4, 25. Mary G. recrq
1888, 12, 26. Emma relrq

FITZPATRICK
1881, 9, 21. Ellen rocf Wilmington MM
1901, 8, 21. Ellen dropped from mbrp

FLETCHER
1829, 6, 3. Henry, s John & Sarah, Clinton Co., O.; m Rachel EVANS, dt James & Ann Still

1829, 9, 30. Rachel gct Caesars Creek MM
1866, 1, 24. Priscilla [Flecher] dropped from mbrp; form mbr Fall Creek or Centre MM which had been laid down

FOLGER
1813, 3, 24. Elizabeth [Folgar] & dt, Elizabeth & Mary, rocf Nantucket MM, dtd 1812, 11,26
1813, 3, 24. Margaret [Folgar] rocf Nantucket MM, dtd 1812,11,26
1813, 4, 28. Timothy Folger & w, Hepsibah, & Phebe Chadwick, rocf Nantucket MM, dtd 1812,12,31
1813, 7, 28. Tristram & w, Mary, & ch, Tristram, Eunice, Elijah, Mary, Sarah & Jared, rocf Nantucket MM, dtd 1812,5,27
1814, 5, 25. Elihu recrq
1814, 8, 31. Mary [Folgar] & dt, Sarah, Phebe & Mary, rocf Nantucket MM, dtd 1814, 4,28

FOLKERTH
1888, 4, 22. Jesse & Lucy recrq
1892, 3, 23. Jesse & Lucy [Follserth] gct Ceasars Creek MM
1896, 10, 21. Jesse & Lucy gct Ceasars Creek MM

FOLLIS
1895, 1, 23. Thomas recrq

FOSTER
----, --, --. John W. F. m Jane W. BUTTERWORTH b 1831,8,23
Ch: Mary E. F.
Wattles b 1869, 3, 1
Nina Irvin " 1882, 6, 6
The two ch recorded as protegees of John W. F. Foster & w

1855, 1, 24. Jane (form Butterworth) con mcd (H)
1876, 3, 22. Josiah (or Joshua) recrq
1882, 8, 23. Joseph relrq
1897, 5, 26. Nina Irwin recrq (H)

FOULKE
1808, 6, 15. Judah, s Joshua & Hannah, Warren Co., O.; m at Miami, Sarah RICHARDS, dt Rowland & Lydia, Warren Co., O.
1815, 2, 9. Margaret m George HATTON

1807, 2, 12. Judah [Faulke] recrq
1808, 3, 10. Margaret rocf Gwynedd MM, Pa., dtd 1807,10,27
1819, 2, 24. Judah [Faulk] & w, Sarah, & ch, Amelia, Cadwallader, Jesse Mary, Grace, Silas & John, rocf Richland MM, dtd 1818, 10,2
1819, 2, 24. Thomas [Faulk] rocf Richland MM, dtd 1818,10,2
1819, 10, 27. Cert rec for Ann from Richland MM, Pa., dtd 1818,10,2, endorsed to Plainfield MM, O.
1819, 10, 27. Cert rec for Elizabeth from Richland MM, Pa., dtd 1818,9,28, endorsed to Plainfield MM, O.
1917, 7, 29. Ann Rachel transferred to this mtg from Springboro (H)

FOX
1856, 6, 25. Caroline (form Harvey) con mou
1858, 7, 21. Caroline gct Pleasant Plain MM, Ia.

FRAME
----, --, --. Thomas L. b 1820,1,14 d 1902,10, 13; m Elizabeth THOMAS b 1821,5,27 d 1904,9,12 (H)
Ch: Georgianna b 1866, 3, 24
Phebe Alice" 1860, 9, 24
1879, 9, 10. William T., s Thomas L. & Elizabeth F., Warren Co., O.; m at Waynesville, Mary FURNAS, dt Robert F. & Bethiah M., Warren Co., O. (H)

1879, 3, 26. William H. rocf Stillwater MM, dtd 1879,3,15 (H)
1881, 12, 21. Thomas L. & w, Elizabeth S., & dt, Georgia Anna, rocf Stillwater MM, dtd 1881,7,16 (H)
1881, 12, 21. Phebe Alice rocf Stillwater MM, dtd 1881,7,16 (H)
1885, 11, 25. Mary F. relrq (H)
1886, 9, 22. William T. & w, Mary F., recrq
1887, 3, 23. Thomas L. & w, Elizabeth S., gct Stillwater MM, O. (H)
1887, 3, 23. Alace & Georgianna gct Stillwater MM (H)
1888, 7, 25. William T. & w, Mary, gct Haviland MM, Kans.
1890, 1, 22. Wm. T. & Mary F. rocf Lafayette MM, Kans., dtd 1889,12,28
1890, 9, 24. Thomas L. & w, Elizabeth, rocf Stillwater MM, dtd 1890,7,19 (H)
1890, 9, 24. Phebe Alice rocf Stillwater MM, dtd 1890,7,19 (H)
1890, 9, 24. Georgianna rocf Stillwater MM, dtd 1890,7,19 (H)
1895, 5, 22. Catherine W. recrq
1900, 10, 24. James Thomas recrq
1908, 3, 25. Wm. & w, Mary F., gct Pasadena MM, Calif.
1908, 3, 25. Katharyne W. gct Pasadena MM, Calif.
1909, 12, 22. Wm. T. & w, Mary F., rocf Pasadena MM, Calif.
1911, 5, 22. Eunice F. gct White Water MM, Ind. (H)

FRAVEL
----, --, --. ----- m Rebecca DOWNING
Ch: William J.
Owen W. b 1866, 7, 20
Myra J. " 1870, 12, 19
Mary E. " 1873, 1, 26

1869, 5, 26. Rebecca S. rocf Center MM, Pa., dtd 1869,5,5 (H)
1871, 4, 26. Rebeckah gct Center MM, Pa. (H)
1872, 9, 25. Rebecca rocf Center MM, Pa., dtd 1872,8,8 (H)
1874, 1, 21. William J., Owen W., Maria J. & Mary A., ch Rebecca, recrq (H)
1876, 2, 23. Rebecca S. & s, William J., gct Plainfield MM, O.
1876, 2, 23. Owen M., s Rebecca, gct Stillwater MM, O. (H)
1876, 10, 25. Owen M. 's cert returned from Stillwater since he had returned to this mtg (H)
1886, 7, 21. Myra J. gct Phila. MM (Race St.) Pa. (H)
1886, 8, 25. Owen W. gct Phila. MM (Race St.) Pa. (H)

FRAZEE
1875, 4, 21. Martin recrq
1888, 11, 21. Mary Eliza (form Butterworth) dis (H)

FRAZER
1885, 3, 25. George recrq
1892, 12, 21. Albert dis

FRED
1908, 5, 27. Mary W. dropped from mbrp

FREESTONE
1820, 5, 31. Martha (form Hollingsworth) con mou
1825, 1, 26. Martha gct Chester MM

FRENCH
1829, 11, 4. Mercy G. m John HAINES (H)

1819, 7, 28. Charles & w, Mercy G., & ch, James & William, rocf Phila. MM, dtd 1819,6,22 (ND MM)
1829, 3, 25. Mercy G. dis jH
1829, 12, 30. Mercy G. Haines & dt, Lydiaann French, gct Springborough MM (H)

FRENCH, continued
1845, 6, 25. William B. gct Cincinnati MM (H)
1871, 2, 22. Uriah recrq
1872, 7, 24. Uriah gct Springborough MM
1873, 7, 23. Elizabeth G. rocf White Water MM, dtd 1873,5,28
1874, 12, 23. Elizabeth F. gct Indianapolis MM

FRY
1887, 4, 20. Isaac L., Margaret E. & Charles W., recrq
1909, 10, 27. Isaac, Margaret & Charles W. dropped from mbrp

FRYBARGER
1888, 3, 21. Abraham & Grace B. recrq

FULTON
1850, 2, 20. Hannah rocf Cincinnati MM, dtd 1850,1,24

FUNDERBURG
1907, 4, 24. Jennie recrq

FUNKEY
1887, 3, 23. John A. & w, Clara W., & s, Pearl, rol
1893, 4, 26. John A. & Clara M. relrq

FURNAS
----, --, --. Robert & Hannah (H)
Ch: Mary b 1796, 11, 25
Esther " 1799, 1, 5
John " 1801, 3, 6
Seth " 1803, 3, 26
Joseph " 1805, 9, 9
1826, 3, 2. Joseph, s Joseph & Sarah, Miami Co., O.; m at Turtle Creek, Patience MILLS, dt Marmaduke & Patience, Warren Co., O.
1826, 11, 1. Seth, s Robert & Hannah; Warren Co., O., b 1803,3,26 d 1878,8,25; m at Miami, Dinah KINDLEY, dt Edward & Margaret, Warren Co., O., b 1804,7,30 d 1880,8,5 (H)
Ch: Davis b 1829, 1, 25 d 1906, 4, 7
Robert " 1830, 10, 10 " 1901, 9,18
Mary " 1832, 12, 30
A dt " 1834, 11, 13 d 1834,11,14
1847, 4, 29. Robert, s Robert & Hannah, Warren Co., O.; m at Turtle Creek, Anna HOLLINGSWORTH, dt Abraham & Eunice, Warren Co., O.
1852, 9, 1. Davis, s Seth & Dinah, Warren Co., O., b 1827,1,25 d 1906,4,7; m at Miami, Jane SATTERTHWAITE, dt John & Elizabeth, Warren Co., O., b 1828,4,23 (H) d [1868, 4, 19
Ch: Seth b 1853, 7, 1
Elizabeth " 1855, 8, 10
Anna Dinah " 1858, 1, 22
John Davis " 1861, 2, 15 d 1904,10,12
Frederick W. b 1866, 3, 30 " 1867, 3,20
Edwin S. " 1868, 4, 18
Davis m 2nd Sarah TRUMAN b 1829,8,14 d 1881,1,19
David m 3rd Sidney BLACKBURN b 1839,11,27 d 1912,12,21
----, --, --. Robert b 1830,10,10 d 1901,9,18; m Bethiah MOSHER b 1831,3,3 (H)
Ch: Mary b 1855, 4, 9
Seth W. " 1857, 8, 18
Calista " 1860, 2, 14 d 1862, 9,30
Eunice " 1862, 2, 8
Edith D. " 1864, 5, 1 " 1873,12,13
Phebe " 1868, 5, 20
Robert H. " 1870, 9, 23
1855, 11, 28. Mary m Jonathan MOSIER (H)
----, --, --. Seth b 1851,8,8; m Emily ----- [(H)
Ch: Oscar M. b 1878, 12, 30
Edith " 1880, 11, 1
Laura " 1885, 5, 28
William Frame " 1883, 6, 7
Charles C. " 1888, 5, 22
Alferd
Eugene
Horace
1879, 9, 10. Mary m William T. FRAME (H)
1880, 5, 5. Anna D. m Elias BLACKBURN (H)
1884, 1, 24. Elizabeth m Joseph A. BOGARDUS (H)
1888, 9, 27. Edwin S., s Davis & Jane S., Warren Co., O., b 1868,4,18; m at residence of Elihu Underwood, Harriet UNDERWOOD, dt Elihu & Hester, Clinton Co., O., b 1866,5,8 (H)
Ch: Seth Elisha b 1889, 12, 4
Lawrence Webber " 1891, 3, 31
Elihu " 1898, 7, 31
----, --, --. John D. b 1861,2,15 d 1904,10,12 m Ella CLIFFTON b 1857,10,30 (H)
Ch: Rachel Dakin b 1891, 9, 5
Mary Louisa" 1892, 12, 31
Sarah Jane " 1897, 2, 1

1804, 11, 8. John & w, Ruth, & ch, Christopher, Isaac, Mary & Joseph, rocf Bush River MM, S. C., dtd 1804,8,25
1806, 6, 12. Joseph & w, Sarah, & ch, Mary, John, Samuel, Joseph & Benjamin, rocf Bush River MM, dtd 1805,7,27
1809, 8, 5. Joseph & w, Sarah, & ch, Mary, John, Samuel, Joseph, Benjamin, William & Sarah, gct West Branch MM
1818, 3, 25. Isaac rocf Cesars Creek MM, dtd 1818,2,27
1819, 11, 24. Isaac [Furnace] gct Center MM, to m
1820, 2, 23. Esly [Furnes] rocf Centre MM, dtd 1820,2,19
1820, 10, 25. Isaac & fam gct Cesars Creek MM
1826, 4, 26. Patience N. gct Union MM
1826, 12, 27. Dinah gct Cesars Creek MM

FURNAS, continued
1829, 12, 30. Dinah recrq; had been dis by Cesars Creek MM for jH (H)
1830, 5, 26. Seth & s, Davis, recrq (H)
1847, 7, 21. Anna [Furnace] gct Caesars Creek MM
1854, 2, 22. Bethiah M. rocf Alum Creek MM, O., dtd 1854,1,25 (H)
1868, 5, 27. Calista recrq
1868, 6, 24. Isaac recf Cesar's Creek MM, dtd 1868,5,28
1868, 6, 24. Calista (form Mosher) dis mcd (H)
1870, 9, 21. Isaac & w, Calista, gct Gilead MM, O.
1870, 12, 21. Davis gct Phila. MM, to m Sarah S. Truman (H)
1871, 2, 22. Martha recrq
1871, 4, 26. Sarah L. rocf Phila. MM, Pa. (H)
1871, 7, 26. Adam rocf West Branch MM, dtd 1871,6,14
1877, 11, 21. Seth W. gct Maple Grove MM, Ind., to m Emily Core (H)
1878, 5, 22. Emily M. rocf Maple Grove MM (H)
1881, 8, 24. Adam & w, Martha, gct Muscatine MM, Ia.
1882, 12, 27. Robert F. [Furnace] & w, Bathiah M., & ch, Phebe & Robert H., gct White Water MM, Ind. (H)
1882, 12, 27. Eunice [Furnace] gct White Water MM, Ind. (H)
1883, 1, 24. Davis gct Baltimore MM, to m (H)
1884, 10, 22. Sidney [Furnace] rocf Baltimore MM, dtd 1884,9,10 (H)
1886, 11, 24. Phebe [Furnace] recrq
1886, 12, 22. Bethia [Furnace] recrq
1888, 7, 25. Bethia M. & Phebe gct Haviland MM, Kans.
1889, 2, 20. Seth M. & w, Emily M., & ch, Oscar M., Edith, William F., Laura & Charles C., relrq (H)
1889, 3, 27. Harriet E. recrq (H)
1891, 7, 22. Ella D. rocf Plainfield MM, N.J. (H)
1903, 8, 19. Bethiah M. recrq (H)
1908, 7, 22. Ella C. & ch, Rachel Dakin, Mary Louise & Sarah J., gct New York MM (H)
1911, 10, 25. Bethia M. gct White Water MM, Ind. (H)
1913, 5, 21. David & Ada recrq
1914, 8, 30. Harriet E. relrq (H)
1916, 10, 29. Rebecca, Roscoe & Anna recrq (H)
1918, 2, 20. Reba M. [Furnace] released from mbrp to Hicksite Friends
1918, 3, 31. Reba M. rocf Miami MM (H)
1920, 11, 28. Sara Hill recrq (H)
1930, 4, 27. Elizabeth rst by rq (H)
1931, 5, 31. Harriet recrq (H)

GALLADAY
1806, 8, 14. Ruth (form Ballard) con mou

GALLAGHER
1882, 4, 27. John D., s James & Rachel, Hamilton Co., O., d 1896,11,11; m at residence of Andrew Cadwallader, Dora CADWALADER, dt Andrew W. & Esther, Warren Co.,O., b 1855,10,6 (H)
Ch: Esther b 1883, 2, 15
James G. " 1884, 9, 20
Rachel Shaw" 1886, 8, 29
Andrew Cadwallader b 1888, 8, 7
John D. " 1892, 7, 15

1889, 3, 27. Dora P. & ch, Esther, James G., Rachel Shaw & Andrew Cadwallader gct Cincinnati MM (H)
1902, 6, --. James relrq (H)
1903, 6, 23. Esther C. & Rachel Shaw relrq (H)
1920, 7, 25. Dora C. & Andrew C. dropped from mbrp (H)

GALLEMORE
1868, 2, 26. Elisha, s William & Mary, Clinton Co., O.; m at Miami, Sarah Amanda SNODEN, dt Richard & Mary W., Clinton Co., O.
1886, 10, 27. Amanda [Galimore] (form Snowden) relrq (H)

GARDNER
1814, 8, 31. Robert Jr. & ch, Charles & Lydia, rocf Nantucket MM, dtd 1814,4,27

GARRETSON
----, --, --. John b 1770,4,27; m Rebecca ----- b 1774,3,7 (H)
Ch: Reuben T. b 1808, 5, 5
Ruthanna " 1810, 3, 3
Rhoda " 1811, 9, 9
Lydia " 1813, 4, 15
Phebe " 1816, 6, 1
1831, 5, 4. Reuben T., s John & Rebecca, Warren Co., O., b 1808,5,5; m at Miami, Sarah HAWKINS, dt Isaac & Mary, Warren Co., O., b 1810,4,11
Ch: John b 1833, 5, 31
Elizabeth " 1835, 4, 18
Charles F. " 1840, 2, 1
Rebecca " 1841, 10, 18
Isaac H. " 1838, 6, 27
Thomas " 1844, 4, 8
Joseph L. " 1848, 8, 26

1815, 10, 25. John & w, Rebecca, & ch, Reuben, Ruthanna, Rhoda & Lydia, rocf Monallen MM, Pa., dtd 1815,8,24
1819, 6, 30. Samuel Jr. rocf Warrington MM, dtd 1819,4,21
1831, 7, 27. Sarah gct Springborough MM
1833, 4, 24. Reuben T. & w, Sarah, rocf

GARRETSON, continued
Springborough MM, dtd 1833,4,23
1860, 12, 26. Isaac dis mou
1860, 12, 26. Margaret (form Rogers) dis mcd (H)
1864, 8, 24. Reuben L. & w, Sarah, & dt, Rebecca, & minor ch, Thomas & Joseph L., gct Spring Creek MM, Ia.
1865, 11, 22. John gct Spring Creek MM, Ia.
1866, 12, 26. Charles dis mou & jas
1881, 3, 23. Thomas & w, Rebecca Jane, rocf Dover MM, O.
1893, 3, 22. Thomas & w, Rebecca J., gct Dover MM

GARWOOD
1806, 2, 13. John & w, Esther, & ch, Deborah & Lot, rocf Crooked Run MM, dtd 1805,5,4
1806, 12, 11. Isiah rocf Crooked Run MM, Va., dtd 1806,5,3
1810, 1, 31. Thomas & w, Hannah, & ch, John, Robert & Abijah, rocf Crooked Run MM, dtd 1805,5,4
1810, 1, 31. Macy (form Heston) dis mou
1810, 2, 28. Daniel & ch, Joseph, John, Jonathan, Patience, Sarah & Daniel, rocf Crooked Run MM, dtd 1807,4,4
1810, 2, 28. Levi rocf Crooked Run MM, dtd 1807,4,4
1810, 8, 29. Mercy dis mcd
1810, 9, 26. John Jr. rpd mcd
1810, 9, 26. Daniel rpd mcd
1810, 9, 26. Deborah Stokes (form Garwood) con mou
1853, 10, 26. Sarah Ann (form Satterthwaite) dis mcd (H)

GASKELL
1823, 4, 30. Edward rocf Upper Springfield MM, N. J., dtd 1819,5,5
1873, 5, 21. Louisa gct Wilmington MM

GATES
1818, 6, 24. Susanna (form Gaunt) con mou
1818, 12, 30. Susanna rpd mcd; mbrp retained with consent of Cincinnati MM
1819, 11, 27. Susannah gct White Water MM

GAUNTT
----, --, --. Nebo & Judith
Ch: Ezekiel b 1803, 2, 2
Charles " 1807, 4, 18
Elias " 1809, 4, 11
Uriah " 1811, 3, 8
Jane " 1814, 6, 20
Jemima " 1816, 6, 20
Matilda " 1819, 7, 12

1806, 3, 13. Nebo & w, Judith, & ch, Beula, Sarah, Prudence, Susannah, Zimri & Ezekiel, rocf Bush River MM, S. C., dtd 1805, 3,30
1812, 2, 26. Sarah Wright (form Gaunt) dis mcd
1813, 1, 27. Beulah Ragan (form Gaunt) con mou
1814, 5, 25. Prudence Horsman (form Gaunt) con mou
1818, 6, 24. Susanna Gates (form Gaunt) con mou
1823, 4, 30. Jesse dis
1829, 2, 25. Charles dis jH
1829, 2, 25. Ezekiel dis jH
1829, 2, 25. Uriah dis jH
1831, 8, 31. Elias dis jH
1835, 3, 25. White River MM was granted permission to rst Ezekiel

GAUSE
----, --, --. Samuel b 1783,2,1 d 1865,4,4; m Mary PEIRCE b 1781,2,9 d 1866,12,1 (H)
Ch: Solomon b 1808, 11, 28 d 1880,5,22
Miriam " 1811, 1, 7 " 1864, 5,20
Ruthanna " 1812, 8, 27 " 1863, 9,13
Clarkson " 1814, 3, 11 " 1899, 9, 6
Mary P. " 1816, 7, 20 " 1818, 8,15
Maryann " 1818, 8, 20 " 1845, 2, 5
Martha " 1821, 5, 3 " 1906, 11,3
Richard " 1823, 9, 10 " 1912, 2, 1
1816, 3, 23. Ruth, dt Eli & Martha, b (H)
1818, 9, 2. Ruth m Samuel BROWN
----, --, --. Solomon b 1808,11,28 d 1880,5, 22; m Eliza VORE b 1814,12,15 (H)
Ch: Isaac V. b 1840, 6, 5
Ruthanna " 1845, 8, 26
1842, 8, 25. Clarkson, s Samuel & Mary, Warren ren Co., O.; b 1814,3,11 d 1899,9,6; m Sidney THOMAS, dt Camm & Elizabeth, d 1853, 8,7 (H)
Ch: Mary Elizabeth b 1843, 5, 31
Noah Albert " 1847, 6, 8 d 1872, 8,27
Clarkson m 2nd 1856,9,3, Elizabeth SHERWOOD, dt Eli & Mary SMITH, Warren Co., O., b 1822,9,19 d 1866,2,3
Dt: Anna Rebecca b 1858, 9, 27
Clarkson m 3rd Ruth RICHARDSON b 1826,6,6 d 1889,9,3
1842, 10, 27. Martha P. m Isaac MICHENER (H)
1843, 5, 3. Ruthanna m Samuel KELLY (H)
----, --, --. Richard P. b 1823,9,10 d 1912, 2,1; m Hannah RICHARDSON (H)
Ch: Samy b 1865, 6, 14
George R. " 1867, 9, 29
----, --, --. Samuel b 1820,5,18; m Mary J. ----- b 1836,8,22
Ch: Elkanah Beard b 1869, 8, 30
Esther Frame " 1871, 1, 9
1882, 2, 23. Mary E. m Franklin PACKER (H)
1884, 4, 29. Anna R. m Samuel JONES (H)

1814, 4, 27. Samuel & w, Mary, & ch, Solomon, Mary & Ruthannah, rocf Redstone MM, dtd 1814,3,4

GAUSE, continued
1814, 5, 25. Abram rocf Redstone MM, dtd 1814,3,4
1814, 5, 25. Eli & w, Martha, & ch, James P., Jesse & Anna, rocf Redstone MM, dtd 1814,3,4
1814, 5, 25. Solomon & w, Ruth, & dt, Ruth, rocf Redstone MM, dtd 1814,3,4
1816, 1, 31. Isaac & fam rocf Red Stone MM, dtd 1815,9,29
1817, 10, 29. Eli & fam gct Elk MM
1818, 11, 25. Abraham rpd mcd
1829, 1, 28. Samuel dis jH
1829, 3, 25. Mary dis jH
1829, 8, 26. Abraham dis jH
1829, 8, 26. Miriam dis jH
1831, 1, 26. Solomon dis jH
1833, 8, 21. Ruth Ann dis jH
1838, 7, 25. Solomon gct White Water MM, to m Jane Vore (H)
1838, 12, 26. Eliza rocf White Water MM, dtd 1838,11,28 (H)
1844, 6, 26. Clarkson dis jH
1848, 2, 23. Martha Michener (form Gause) dis mou
1853, 11, 23. Noah Cadwalader gct White Water MM, to m Elizabeth Gause (H)
1858, 3, 24. Richard P. gct Green Plain MM, to m Hannah Richardson (H)
1858, 10, 27. Hannah R. rocf Green Plain MM, dtd 1858,9,15 (H)
1863, 7, 23. Ruth Anna Shute (form Gause) con mcd (H)
1867, 6, 26. Isaac con mcd (H)
1869, 8, 25. Clarkson gct Green Plain MM, to m Ruth Richardson (H)
1870, 4, 20. Ruth rocf Green Plain MM, dtd 1870,3,16 (H)
1870, 5, 25. Samuel & w, Mary, & s, Elkanah B., rocf Duck Creek MM, dtd 1870,4,21
1872, 4, 24. Samuel & w, Mary J., & ch, Eleana B. & Hester F., gct Springfield MM
1880, 5, 26. Richard P. & w, Hannah R., & ch, Samuel C. & George R., gct White Water MM, Ind. (H)
1881, 10, 26. Eliza V. gct White Water MM,Ind. (H)
1883, 4, 25. Sophia recrq
1889, 10, 23. Isaac V. rpd mcd (H)
1889, 11, 20. Isaac V. gct White Water MM,Ind. (H)

GEORGE
1804, 12, 13. Jesse & w, Mary, & ch, Isaac, Enon, James, Phebe & Jesse, rocf Hopewell MM, dtd 1804,9,3
1806, 9, 11. Tabitha (form Beals) con mou

GEST
1807, 4, 9. Hannah & ch, Sarah, Mary, James, Baker & John, rocf Bush River MM, dtd 1806,10,25

GIBBS
1842, 10, 26. Hannah (form Ward) dis mou
1861, 5, 22. Ann (form Hains) dis mcd (H)

GIBSON
1881, 7, 27. Miller & w, Louisa M., rocf Columbus MM, O., dtd 1881,7,6
1890, 9, 2. Miller rec (or released) by rq
1896, 5, 27. Louisa M. relrq

GILLESPIE
1835, 3, 25. Penelope [Gillaspie] (form Johnson) con mou (H)
1836, 7, 27. Penelope gct White Water MM (H)

GILPIN
1835, 10, 29. Thomas, s John & Rebecca, Clinton Co., O.; m at Harveysburgh, Tacy PLUMMER, dt Asa & Grace, Warren Co., O.

1824, 6, 30. Elizabeth rocf London Grove MM, dtd 1824,5,5
1827, 7, 25. Rebeccah (form Van Horn) dis mou
1836, 5, 25. Tacy gct Caesars Creek MM
1840, 4, 22. Tacy rocf Caesars Creek MM, dtd 1840,2,20
1844, 3, 27. Tacy gct Cesars Creek MM
1886, 3, 24. Alfred & Lena recrq
1898, 6, 22. Alfred & w relrq

GIRTEN
1849, 9, 26. Edith (form Butterworth) dis mou (H)

GLOVER
1840, 4, 22. Clark rocf Evesham MM, dtd 1840, 2,7
1842, 3, 23. William, minor, rocf Redstone MM, dtd 1842,3,2
1843, 11, 22. Clark dis disunity
1844, 7, 24. Josiah rocf Haddonfield MM, N. J., dtd 1844,6,11 (H)
1848, 12, 27. Josiah gct Fall Creek MM, Ind. (H)
1848, 12, 27. William dis disunity

GODFREY
1878, 5, 22. William H. rocf Goshen MM, O., dtd 1878,2,16

GOOD
----, --, --. Charles b 1807,3,16 d 1895,3,30; m Betsy ----- b 1809,8,29 d 1899,11,5 (H)
Ch: Mary Ann b 1839, 4, 11
Elizabeth T. " 1840, 11, 30
Martha E. " 1842, 3, 27 d 1877, 5, 2
Ellis " 1845, 9, 25
Lydia C. " 1847, 11, 28
Evan " 1852, 8, 31
1886, 3, 3. Ellis, s Charles & Betsy, Highland Co., O.; m at residence of Elwood

GOOD, continued
Hollowell, Annie HOLLOWELL, dt Elwood & Mary D., Highland Co., O. (H)

1866, 1, 24. Ellis, Lydia, Evan & Rachel, minors, rec in mbrp; form mbr Fall Creek or Centre MM which had been laid down (H)
1866, 1, 24. Charles rpd mcd (H)
1866, 1, 24. Betsy rpd mcd (H)
1866, 1, 24. Lizzie rpd mcd (H)
1866, 1, 24. Martha rpd mcd (H)
1866, 8, 22. Mary Ann Blackburn (form Good) con mcd (H)
1887, 5, 25. Rachel M. Wright (form Good) relrq (H)
1895, 5, 22. Betsy, Lydia C., Ellen, Anna K. & Evan set off as mbr of Executive Mtg at Clear Creek (H)

GOODWIN
1807, 11, 12. Nathan & Richard rocf Piney Woods MM, N. C., dtd 1806,3,1
1903, 4, 22. Mary S. relrq

GOOLMAN
1849, 12, 26. Eunice (form Harvey) dis mou

GORDEN
1855, 4, 25. Lydiann (form Burnet) con mcd (H)
1905, 2, 22. Lester [Gordon] recrq

GRAHAM
1880, 7, 21. Mary relrq
1889, 2, 20. Charles H. & Jacob R. recrq
1889, 3, 27. John W. & Effie M. recrq
1889, 6, 26. William recrq
1892, 3, 23. Jacob & Nettie relrq
1907, 2, 20. Lydia recrq
1909, 10, 27. Lydia dropped from mbrp

GRAY
1808, 12, 14. William, s Nancy, Warren Co., O.; m at Miami, Mary CLEAVER, dt Ezekiel & Abigail, Warren Co., O. (H)

Ch:		
	Ann	b 1809, 9, 2
	Abigail	" 1811, 5, 14
	L. Jane	" 1813, 1, 20
	Rebecca	" 1814, 12, 16
	John	" 1816, 10, 31

1808, 3, 10. William recrq
1829, 5, 27. Mary dis jH
1829, 5, 27. Ann dis jH
1829, 6, 24. William dis jH
1831, 11, 30. Ann Boman (form Grey) dis mou (H)
1833, 4, 24. Asenath Moon (form Grey) dis mou (H)
1897, 12, 22. Walter recrq
1833, 4, 24. Abigail, Jane & Rebecca dis jH
1833, 9, 18. Abigzil dis (H)
1838, 5, 23. Jane Dickey (form Gray) dis mou (H)

1853, 4, 20. George dis mcd (H)
1853, 4, 20. John dis mcd (H)
1853, 4, 20. William dis mcd (H)

GREAVES
1809, 2, 11. William, Mary & Emma, ch John, rocf Cane Creek MM, dtd 1806,7,5

GREEN
----, --, --. Ann, wd John, b 1803,2,7 d 1873, 11,5 (H)
1826, 12, 6. David, s Reuben & Rhoda, Clinton Co., O., b 1800,6,2; m at Grove, Mary JESSOP, dt Thomas & Ann, Warren Co., O., b 1804,4,9

Ch:		
	Elijah	b 1831, 4, 24
	Thomas	" 1832, 11, 3
	Rhoda Ann	" 1834 , 5, 16
	Eli H.	" 1836, 12, 5
	Rebecca	" 1839, 10, 4
	Albert	" 1845, 2, 20
	Levi	" 1847, 5, 17
	William	" 1849, 8, 20

----, --, --. Jonathan b 1829,7,18; m Rachel WILLIAMS b 1832,1,13

Ch:		
	Asa Oscar	b 1853, 3, 5
	Mary Emily	" 1855, 2, 1
	Ann Louisa	" 1858, 12, 30

1854, 11, 30. Rhoda Ann m Caleb H. LEWIS
1856, 2, 28. Elijah, s David & Mary, Warren Co., O., b 1831,4,24; m at Harveysburgh, Emily HARVEY, dt John & Mahala, Warren Co., O. , b 1838,1,22

Ch:		
	Thomas	b 1857, 5, 25
	Caroline	" 1860, 10, 21

1856, 3, 6. Thomas d bur Harveysburgh
1861, 4, 6. Thomas Jr. d bur Harveysburgh

1806, 8, 14. Joseph rocf Upper Springfield MM, N. J., dtd 1805,4,3
1809, 12, 27. Cert rec for Esther from New Garden MM, N. C., dtd 1809,7,29, endorsed to Elk MM
1827, 1, 31. Mary gct Springfield MM
1853, 5, 25. David & w, Mary, & ch, Thomas, Eli, Rebecca, Albert, Levi & William, rocf Springfield MM, dtd 1853,4,16
1853, 6, 22. Rhoda Ann rocf Springfield MM, dtd 1853,4,16
1854, 8, 23. Elijah C. rocf Springfield MM, dtd 1854,7,15
1854, 10, 25. Cert rec for Asa B. & w, Susannah, & ch, William G. & John Riley, from Newberry MM, dtd 1854,7,17, endorsed back to Newberry MM
1855, 11, 21. Jonathan & w, Rachel, & ch, Asa Oscar & Mary Emily, rocf Goshen MM, dtd 1855,9,15
1860, 4, 25. Jonathan & w, Rachel B., & ch, Asa Oscar, Mary Emily & Anna Louisa, gct Springfield MM
1863, 6, 24. Polly rocf Sugar River MM, dtd 1863,6,13

GREEN, continued
1864, 4, 20. Elie con mou
1864, 5, 25. David & w, Mary, & ch, Albert, Levi & William, gct Plainfield MM, Ind.
1864, 5, 25. Elijah J. & w, Emily H., gct Plainfield MM, Ind.
1864, 5, 25. Rebecca gct Plainfield MM
1864, 9, 21. Eli gct Clear Creek MM
1866, 1, 24. Ann rec in mbrp; form mbr Fall Creek or Centre MM which had been laid down (H)
1867, 5, 22. Polly gct Springfield MM, O.

GREER
1827, 5, 30. Lydia [Grier] recrq
1828, 7, 30. Lydia rocf Bradford MM, dtd 1827,5,9
1837, 2, 27. Lydia gct Chester MM, Ind.

GREGG
1843, 9, 21. Hiram, s Samuel & Guli Elma, Jay Co., O.; m at Rochester, Patience W. CADWALADER, dt Jonah & Priscilla, Warren Co., O.(H)
1861, 2, 28. Sarah Jane m David CHANDLER (H)

1832, 10, 24. Eli & w, Martha, & ch, Rachel, Phebe, Ann, Alma A., William W., Ellis & Edgar, rocf Allum Creek MM, dtd 1832,8,23 (H)
1834, 6, 25. Rachel Redfern (form Gregg) dis mou (H)
1835, 2, 18. Rachel, Phebe, Ann, Almary & William, ch Eli & Martha, rocf Allum Creek MM, dtd 1834,10,23; cert for Rachel not accepted because of her mou & jH
1837, 6, 31. Eli & w, Martha, & ch, Ann, Alma A., William W., Eli, Edgar A. & Salathiel L., gct Milford MM, Ind. (H)
1837, 6, 31. Phebe H. gct Milford MM, Ind. (H)
1838, 10, 24. Sarah Jane (form Daniel) con mou (H)
1846, 2, 18. Patience gct White Water MM (H)
1898, 6, 22. Carrie D. recrq (H)
1907, 2, 20. Robert Danforth, s Frank B. & Carrie D., recrq (H)

GREGORY
1889, 7, 24. Caroline (form Ballard) dropped from mbrp (H)

GRIEST
----, --, --. Jane (Mullin) [Greist] b 1836, 5,21 d 1915,1,31(H)

1822, 2, 27. William rocf Monallen MM, Pa.
1823, 11, 26. Joseph [Grist] & w, Mary, & ch, Isaac, John, Amy, Mary & Micajah, rocf Monallen MM, Pa., dtd 1823,7,23
1823, 11, 26. Joseph W. [Grist] rocf Monallen MM, Pa., dtd 1823,7,23
1823, 11, 26. Anna rocf Monallen MM, Pa., dtd 1823,7,23
1824, 5, 26. Anna gct Center MM
1824, 5, 26. Joseph [Greist] & fam gct Cincinnati MM
1872, 8, 21. Mary (form Keiffer) dis mcd (H)
1894, 10, 24. Evalina Edwards gct Carthage MM, Ind.
1894, 10, 24. Athelina Edwards gct Indianapolis MM, Ind.

GRIFFIN
1806, 9, 11. Jacob [Griffen] & s, James & Samuel, rocf Back Creek MM, N. C., dtd 1805,2,23
1806, 9, 11. Mary rocf Back Creek MM, N. C., dtd 1805,2,23
1869, 3, 24. Mary C. (form Carroll) dis mcd (H)

GRIFFITH
1837, 5, 31. Lukens, s Isaac & Elizabeth; m at Miami, Elizabeth WHARTON, dt Silas & Mary, Warren Co., O. (H)

1833, 10, 24. Nancy Osborn rocf Center MM, dtd 1832,8,15
1836, 7, 27. Nancy Osborn gct Center MM
1837, 3, 22. Lukens rocf Horsham MM, Pa., dtd 1837,3,1 (H)
1846, 2, 18. Lukens dis mou (H)
1865, 3, 22. David L. rocf Hopewell MM, Va., dtd 1863,5,6

GRIMES
1839, 10, 30. George, s David & Elizabeth, Clinton Co., O.; m at Waynesville, Susanna SHEPHERD, dt Jesse & Elizabeth, Warren Co., O.

1840, 2, 19. Susannah gct Springfield MM

HACKNEY
----, --, --. William J. m Susan D. CANBY (H)
Ch: Evan
Lewis b 1845, 6, 13
Elmira B. " 1848, 10, 16
Canby H. " 1856, 7, 26

1832, 9, 26. Eleanor W. rocf Hopewell MM, dtd 1832,8,9 (H)
1832, 9, 26. Mary L. rocf Hopewell MM, dtd 1832,8,9 (H)
1832, 10, 24. Samuel B. prcf Hopewell MM, Va., dtd 1832,6,7; cert returned because of disunity (H)
1832, 10, 24. John Lewis prcf Hopewell MM, Va. cert returned because of disunity (H)
1832, 10, 24. Aaron, Edward Bond, Amos, William I. & Hugh, ch Aaron, rocf Hopewell MM, Va. (H)
1846, 3, 25. William con mou (H)
1846, 3, 25. Susan (form Canby) con mou (H)
1858, 11, 24. William J. & w, Susan D., & ch,

HACKNEY, continued
Evan L., Elmira B. & Canby H., gct Prairie Grove MM, Ia.
1868, 2, 19. Richard Snowden gct Hopewell MM, Va., to m Rachel Hackney (H)

HADLEY
----, --, --. Anna, wd Alfred, dt William & Martha Nixon, b 1825,3,27 d 1903,8,7 bur Clarksville, Clinton Co., O. (H)
1846, 2, 19. Job Hadley, s Joshua & Rebecca, Hendricks Co., Ind.; m at Harveysburgh, Tacy BURGESS, dt Thomas & Betty, Warren Co., O.
1846, 12, 4. Nathan, s Joshua & Rebecca, Hendricks Co., Ind.; m at Harveysburgh, Mary Ann HARVEY, dt John & Lydia, Warren Co., O.
1847, 6, 9. Samuel H., s Jacob & Mary, Clinton Co., O.; m at Miami, Emily JOHNSON, dt Micajah & Rebecca, Warren Co., O.
----, --, --. Edwin b 1826,5,16; m Jemima DOAN b 1830,9,28

Ch:			
	Eliza	b 1856, 10, 12	
	Olive	" 1858, 3, 22	d 1864, 9,30
	Ellen	" 1859, 5, 23	
	Ann	" 1861, 10, 9	
	Mary	" 1863, 3, 24	" 1864, 9,21
	Clarence Edwin	" 1864, 5, 1	

1863, 7, 29. Artemus N., s William L. & Mary N., Clinton Co., O.; m at Miami Elizabeth M. JONES, dt Samuel & Martha, Warren Co., O.
----, --, --. ----- & Elizabeth T.
Ch: Albert
Charles
Frances
Evaline
Calvin
Caroline
Jonathan

1846, 5, 27. Tacy gct Mill Creek MM, Ind.
1847, 4, 21. Mary Ann gct Mill Creek MM, Ind.
1847, 11, 24. Mary Ann gct Mill Creek MM, Ind.; one issued 1847,4mo not rec
1848, 1, 26. Emily J. gct Springfield MM
1851, 12, 24. Joseph C. Mather gct Springfield MM, to m Louisa Hadley
1858, 3, 24. Samuel Brown gct Springfield MM, to m Elizabeth W. Hadley
1858, 6, 23. Rachel (form Butterworth) dis mcd (H)
1859, 8, 24. William R. Evans gct Springfield MM, to m Margaret Ann Hadley
1861, 4, 24. Jonathan D. & w, Susanna W., & s, Evan H., rocf Springfield MM, dtd 1861, 4,20
1861, 6, 26. Edwin & w, Jemima D., & ch, Eliza, Olive & Ellen, rocf Springfield MM, dtd 1861,5,18
1864, 6, 22. Evan H. con mou
1865, 1, 25. Elizabeth N. & ch, Albert, Charles, Francis, Evaline, Calvin, Caroline & Jonathan, rocf Rocksylvania MM, Ia., dtd 1864,9,22
1865, 7, 26. Elizabeth M. gct Springfield MM
1865, 12, 27. Edwin & w, Jemima D., & ch, Eliza, Ellen, Annie & Clarence, gct White Water MM
1866, 1, 24. Anna rec in mbrp; form mbr Fall Creek or Centre MM which had been laid down (H)
1866, 2, 22. Jonathan D. & w, Susanna W., gct Springboro MM
1866, 3, 21. Evan H. gct Springboro MM
1866, 3, 21. Edwin & w, Jemima, & ch, Elisa, Ellen, Annie & Edwin C., gct White Water MM
1871, 4, 26. Elizabeth & ch, Charles, Francis, Evalina O., Calvin, Caroline & Johnathan, gct Wilmington MM
1871, 5, 24. Albert H. gct Wilmington MM
1874, 2, 18. Milton & w, Lucy M., & ch, Isaac H. & Otis, rocf Springfield MM, dtd 1874,1,17
1894, 2, 21. Sallie L. recrq
1895, 5, 22. Lizzie Ethel recrq
1898, 6, 22. Seth S. dropped from mbrp
1902, 6, 25. Simon rocf Dover MM, dtd 1902, 5,15
1905, 2, 22. Izma recrq
1905, 7, 26. Isaac & dt, Lizzie & Izma, relrq
1907, 8, 28. Otis M. & w, Florence, & ch, Robert M., Charles D., Mary E., Wilber S. & Bessie L., relrq
1892, 2, 24. Henry gct Chicago MM

HAINES
1808, 6, 22. Noah, s Robert & Margaret, Green Co., O., d 1834,7,19; m at Miami, Anna SILVER d 1849,9,13 (H)(dt Ann & Mary)

Ch:			
	Margaret	b 1809, 8, 13	d 1869, 4, 6
	Mary	" 1809, 8, 13	" 1812, 4,18
	Charlotte	" 1811, 1, 14	" 1844, 4,13
	Letitia	" 1814, 4, 4	" 1845, 4,12
	Amos	" 1813, 2, 23	" 1813, 3,31
	Noah S.	" 1816, 9, 18	" 1843, 8,14
	Ann	" 1818, 10, 29	" 1845, 5, 9
	James	" 1821, 11, 2	" 1841, 9,29
	Seth S.	" 1824, 2, 1	

1825, 11, 2. Mary E. m Isaac ENGLE
----, --, --. Jonathan [Hains] b 1786,4,5 d 1851,6,7; m Naomi STRATTON b 1786,3,18 d 1856,12,28
Dt: Mary C. b 1830, 2, 1
1829, 11, 4. John, s Isaac & Deborah, Montgomery Co., O.; m at Waynesville, Mercy G. FRENCH, dt Thomas & Sarah Gilpin, Warren Co., O. (H)
1832, 6, 13. Charlotte m Joseph B. CHAPMAN(H)
1834, 4, 30. Nathan B., s Bethuel & Rachel, Warren Co., O., b 1807,6,8 d 1846,8,17; m at Miami, Rebecca WHARTON, dt Silas & Mary, Warren Co., O., b 1812,12,12 (H)

HAINES, Nathan B. & Rebecca, continued
Ch: Silas W. b 1835, 9, 9
Ann E. " 1837, 2, 1
Freeman " 1838, 3, 21
Amos C. " 1840, 10, 7
Mary
Elizabeth " 1845, 4, 2
1835, 5, 9. Margaret d ae 81y (H)

1804, 10, 11. Enos & w, Mary, & ch, Esther, Joshua, Mahlon & Sarah, rocf Southland MM, Va., dtd 1803,12,28
1805, 7, 11. John & w, Betty, & ch, Hester, Stacey, Narcissa, Israel, Betty & Rheuben, rocf Crooked Run MM, dtd 1805,6,1
1806, 7, 10. Rebecca Collet (form Haines) rpd mou
1807, 2, 12. Noah rocf Crooked Run MM, dtd 1806,11,14
1809, 12, 27. Margaret & dt, Margaret, rocf Hopewell MM, Va., dtd 1809,9,4
1811, 6, 26. Amos rocf Hopewell MM, dtd 1811,3,7
1814, 3, 30. John [Hains] & w, Betty, & fam gct Ceasars Creek MM
1814, 3, 30. Esther [Hains] gct Ceasars Creek MM
1814, 10, 26. Amos rpd mcd
1815, 2, 22. Enos & fam gct Fairfield MM
1817, 7, 30. Margaret [Hains] rocf Cincinnati MM, dtd 1817,7,17
1819, 12, 29. John & w, Jemima, & ch, Amirah, Sarah, Susannah, Charles, Clark & Mary W., rocf Evesham MM, N. J., dtd 1819,9,10
1823, 11, 26. Naomi rst with permission of Upper Evesham MM, N. J.
1824, 6, 30. Susannah rocf Mount Holly MM, N. J., dtd 1824,5,6
1826, 2, 22. Hannah gct Westfield MM
1827, 7, 25. Rachel & dt, Bathsheba, rocf Evesham MM, dtd 1827,6,8
1827, 8, 29. Wilkins rocf Evesham MM, N. J., dtd 1827,6,8
1827, 9, 26. Nathan rocf Mt. Holly MM, N. J., dtd 1827,6,7
1827, 12, 26. Isaac Haskett gct Springborough MM, to m Rachel Haines
1828, 11, 26. Jason Evans gct Springborough MM to m Amyrah Haines
1829, 1, 28. Noah dis jH
1829, 3, 25. Anna dis jH
1829, 3, 25. Nathan [Hains] dis jH
1829, 3, 25. Rachel dis jH
1829, 5, 27. Wilkins dis jH
1829, 6, 24. Naomi dis jH
1829, 7, 29. Margaret dis jH
1829, 7, 29. Margaret Jr. dis jH
1829, 7, 29. Charlotte dis jH
1829, 8, 26. Bathsheba dis jH
1829, 12, 30. Rachel & Bathsheba gct Springborough MM (H)
1829, 12, 30. Mercy G. & dt, Lydiaann French, gct Springborough MM (H)
1830, 2, 24. Nathan B. gct Springborough MM(H)
1832, 11, 21. Martha [Hanes] rocf Springfield MM, dtd 1832,8,4
1833, 6, 26. Nathan B. rocf Springborough MM, dtd 1833,4,25 (H)
1833, 8, 21. Letitia dis jH
1833, 12, 25. Wilkins con mou (H)
1834, 12, 23. Jacob Evans gct Springborough MM, to m Mary Haines (H)
1836, 10, 26. Letitia Fisher (form Haines) dis mou (H)
1838, 11, 21. Judith (form Cadwalader) con mou
1839, 3, 27. Judith J. [Haynes] gct White Water MM, Ind.
1839, 9, 25. Mary E. recrq of mother, Naomi (H)
1839, 11, 20. Jonathan recrq (H)
1842, 7, 27. Noah S. gct White Water MM, to m Elizabeth Evans (H)
1842, 12, 21. Elizabeth rocf White Water MM, dtd 1842,11,28 (H)
1844, 5, 22. Rachel (form Austin) con mou (H)
1845, 1, 22. Ann Drake (form Haines) con mou (H)
1846, 2, 18. Elizabeth gct White Water MM (H)
1847, 11, 24. Seth dis mou (H)
1847, 11, 24. Eliza (form Hinchman) con mou (H)
1850, 3, 27. Seth D. dis mou
1854, 11, 29. Rebecca Denlinger (form Haines) dis mcd (H)
1855, 11, 21. Rachel dis jas (H)
1855, 11, 21. Mary L. (form Lukens) dis mou
1859, 6, 22. Silas M. dis disunity (H)
1859, 6, 22. Amos C. dis disunity (H)
1856, 10, 22. Mary [Haynes] (form Lukens) dis mcd (H)
1861, 5, 22. Ann Gibbs (form Hains) dis mcd (H)
1864, 7, 27. Mary Hawes (form Haines) dis mcd (H)
1865, 7, 26. Martha gct Pipe Creek MM, Ind.
1866, 7, 25. James H. recrq (H)
1883, 6, 20. Deborah rocf White River MM, dtd 1883,4,7
1884, 5, 21. Abi recrq
1885, 3, 25. James recrq
1886, 2, 24. James M. relrq (H)
1886, 2, 24. James W. recrq
1887, 3, 23. Amelia E. recrq
1887, 4, 20. John L. & Joseph recrq
1889, 2, 20. Robert H. [Hains] recrq
1890, 5, 21. Deborah W. gct Winchester MM, Ind.
1891, 6, 24. Anna M. Terrell (form Haines) gct Clear Creek MM
1892, 4, 20. James W. dis
1894, 2, 21. Amelia C. relrq
1896, 8, 26. Sadie recrq
1901, 4, 24. Naomi Almira [Haynes] relrq
1903, 10, 21. Abi recrq
1903, 12, 23. Abi recrq (H)

HAINES, continued
1905, 5, 24. Robert & Helen recrq
1905, 10, 25. Mary rst (H)
1914, 5, 27. Russell dropped from mbrp
1930, 2, 23. Elvin gct Chester MM (H)

HALE
----, --, --. Armoni, s Jacob & Martha (Harvey) b 1806,9,21 d 1900,9,6 (H)
----, --, --. William b 1790,9,27 d 1887,7,15; m Maria SABIN b 1797,3,3 d 1884,12,25 (H)
Dt: Martha b 1822, 8, 22 d 1902, 9,13
----, --, --. Elie & Ann
Ch: Mary b 1835, 2, 20
Alfred C. " 1837, 2, 18
Mary Ann " 1839, 4, 27
1855, 10, 31. Mary m Jonas JANNEY
1864, 11, 2. Sarah A. m David T. PRITCHARD

1832, 1, 25. Elizabeth (form Edwards) rpd mou
1833, 10, 24. Elizabeth gc
1850, 10, 23. Micajah Johnson gct Springfield MM, to m Ann Hale
1851, 3, 26. Ann Johnson & ch, Mary, Sarah Ann & Alfred C. Hale, rocf Springfield MM, dtd 1851,3,13
1854, 8, 23. William H. rocf Springfield MM, dtd 1854,7,15
1856, 7, 23. Miles M. [Hales] rocf Springfield MM, dtd 1856,5,17
1856, 11, 26. William H. dis mou
1860, 4, 25. Miles dis mou
1866, 1, 24. Ammonia rec in mbrp; form mbr Fall Creek or Centre MM which had been laid down (H)
1866, 1, 24. Maria rec in mbrp; form mbr Fall Creek or Centre MM which had been laid down (H)
1873, 4, 23. Alfred rpd mou
1878, 10, 25. William rst by rq (H)
1882, 9, 20. Lawrence gct Lawrence MM, Kans.
1882, 9, 20. Alfred gct Lawrence MM, Kans.
1889, 7, 24. Philip [Hole] recrq (H)
1889, 11, 20. Philip gct New York MM, N. Y.(H)

HALL
1813, 5, 26. Mary recrq
1814, 1, 26. Mary rocf Haddonfield MM, N. J., dtd 1813,11,8
1825, 1, 26. Mary dis non-attendance & jas
1870, 3, 23. Elizabeth (form Hunt) con mcd

HAM
1838, 11, 21. Martha (form Burgess) dis mou
1857, 1, 21. Tacy Ellen Ham, niece of Simon D. Harvey & w, Mary H., recrq
1870, 10, 25. Tacy Lukins (form Ham) dis mou
1872, 1, 24. William & w recrq
1873, 1, 22. Charles recrq
1876, 2, 23. Thomas rocf Springfield MM, Kans.
1883, 3, 21. Mary recrq
1883, 4, 25. Marion F. recrq

HAMILTON
----, --, --. John b 1810,2,18; m Mary Ann ----- b 1822,8,25
Dt: Maria
Louisa b 1857, 5, 11

1854, 5, 24. John & w, Mary Anne, rocf Nottingham MM, Eng., dtd 1854,1,26
1859, 5, 25. John & w, Mary Ann, & ch, Maria Louisa, gct Plymouth MM, Eng.
1874, 12, 23. Mary E. gct Kokomo MM, Ind.
1887, 4, 20. George R. & ch, Sarah Grace, Harry Blaine & Frank William, recrq
1887, 4, 20. Emma recrq
1887, 4, 20. Joseph & Corwin B. recrq

1891, 4, 22. George relrq
1900, 9, 26. Bessie [Hamelton] recrq
1902, 12, 24. Sarah Jane recrq
1909, 10, 27. Corwin dropped from mbrp
1914, 5, 27. Frank, Harry B., Lorina & Bessie dropped from mbrp
1925, 11, 29. Emma recrq (H)

HAMMER
1806, 6, 12. Charlotte & ch, Margaret, Rachel, David & Anna, rocf Bush River MM, S. C., dtd 1805,4,27

HAMMET
1806, 10, 9. Sarah rocf Westland MM, Pa., dtd 1806,8,23
1810, 11, 28. Sarah dis

HAMPTON
----, --, --. Sarah, w Andrew, b 1791,10,16 d 1814,4,27 (H)
1812, 1, 1. Andrew, s Jacob & Eunice, Warren Co., O.; m Sarah Mills, dt James & Lydia, Warren Co., O.
1816, 2, 7. Mary Hamton m Samuel Crampton
1817, 1, 2. Elizabeth m Jonathan VOTAW
1817, 3, 6. Andrew, s Jacob & Eunice, Warren Co., O.; m at Grove, Rachel CRAMPTON, dt Samuel & Rachel, Warren Co., O.
1818, 4, 2. David, s Jacob & Eunice, Warren Co., O.; m at Grove, Jane MOON, dt Simon & Judith, Warren Co., O.

1810, 3, 28. Jacob & w, Eunice, & ch, Anna, Jehiel, David, Elizabeth, Jacob, Elisha & Eleanor, recrq
1817, 3, 26. Jehiel dis mcd
1818, 1, 28. Andrew & fam gct White Water MM
1818, 6, 24. David & w, Jane, gct White Water MM
1819, 9, 29. Jacob Jr. gct Silver Creek MM, to m
1820, 12, 27. Jacob & fam gct Whitewater MM, Ind.

HANLIN
1889, 7, 24. Anna (form Dingee) dropped from

HANLIN, continued
mbrp

HANSELL
1883, 4, 25. Perry recrq

HARE
1831, 4, 27. Jemima rocf Cincinnati MM, O., dtd 1831,1,27
1831, 4, 27. Mary rocf Cincinnati MM, dtd 1831,1,27
1888, 3, 21. George & Nettie recrq
1892, 3, 23. George relrq
1898, 6, 22. Joseph dropped from mbrp
1905, 2, 22. Alice relrq

HARLAN
----, --, --. Harvey b 1801,5,9; m Ruth CHEW b 1800,11,18
Ch: Lydia b 1823, 8, 27
Milton " 1825, 4, 12
Nancy " 1826, 7, 28
Elwood " 1828, 5, 27

1805, 7, 11. George & w, Margery, & ch, Aaron, Samuel & Moses, rocf Redstone MM, dtd 1805,3,1
1807, 9, 10. Aaron dis mcd
1807, 10, 8. Cert rec for Edith from Springfield MM, N. C., endorsed to Center MM
1808, 1, 14. Samuel dis
1810, 7, 25. Moses [Harlen] dis
1810, 10, 31. Hannah [Harlen] (form Morrison) gct Center MM
1838, 9, 26. William recrq (H)
1840, 1, 22. Sarah rocf Springfield MM, dtd 1839,5,14
1840, 1, 22. Edith rocf Center MM, dtd 1839,2,13
1840, 6, 24. Elizabeth recrq (H)
1840, 8, 20. John [Harlen] rocf Springfield MM, dtd 1840,7,14
1850, 7, 24. John C. dis mou
1852, 2, 24. Sarah A. (form Hussey) dis mou
1853, 7, 27. Edith Rich (form Harlin) dis mou
1857, 11, 25. Mary (form Hussey) dis mou
1860, 1, 25. Carter B. & w, Maria, & dt, Mary Elizabeth, rocf Springfield MM, dtd 1859,10,15
1866, 1, 24. Enoch, Margaret A., Martha, Elizabeth, David R., Nathaniel E., Isaac S. & Emory B. dropped from mbrp; form mbr of Fall Creek or Centre MM which had been laid down
1866, 1, 24. Martha, minor, rec in mbrp; former mbr of Fall Creek or Centre MM which had been laid down
1869, 3, 25. Mary E. (form Harlan) con mou
1870, 4, 20. William dis mcd (H)
1882, 4, 26. Carter & w, Maria, gct Springfield MM, O.
1886, 4, 21. Nathaniel & w, Sarah, & s, Warren E., rocf Clear Creek MM, dtd 1886,4,10
1892, 1, 27. Warren gct Cincinnati MM, O.
1913, 4, 23. Josephine & Minerva recrq
1913, 6, 25. Viola & s, Everett, recrq

HARMELL
1887, 4, 20. Joseph recrq

HARPER
1831, 4, 22. Martha Ann & Sarah S., dt Daniel & Sarah, rocf Woodbury MM, N. J., dtd 1830,8,31
1874, 7, 22. Alice Sears (form Harper) recrq
1874, 7, 22. Emma Sayers (form Harper) recrq

HARPLIT
1887, 3, 23. Susan B. rol

HARRIS
1806, 12, 11. George & w, Hope, & ch, Esther, Martha, Deborah, Daniel & Isaiah, rocf Crooked Run MM, dtd 1806,8,2
1809, 12, 27. Benjamin & w, Margaret, & ch, Obidiah, Pleasant, James, Bersheba, John, Benjamin, Rebecca, David & Elvah, rocf Deep River MM, N. C., dtd 1807,5,4
1815, 4, 26. Elizabeth rocf Goose Creek MM, dtd 1814,8,14
1836, 7, 27. E. Ann (form Ballard) con mou (H)
1852, 9, 22. Elizabeth Ann, w William, gct Plainfield MM, Ill. (H)
1853, 9, 20. Red Cedar MM, Ia. was given permission to rst Elisabeth A.
1886, 3, 24. Anna Mary recrq
1897, 10, 22. Ernest rocf Center MM
1920, 12, 22. Ruth Ellen rocf Springfield MM, dtd 1920,12,18

HARRISON
----, --, --. William H. & Anna (H)
Ch: John A. b 1829, 1, 2
Stephen S. " 1831, 6, 15
Martha Ann " 1833, 10, 28
Ruthanna " 1836, 3, 25

1836, 3, 23. William H. & w, Ann, & ch, John A., Stephen L. & Marthaann, rocf Centre MM, dtd 1835,11,15
1849, 1, 24. John A. gct White Water MM (H)
1849, 1, 24. Stephen S., Martha Ann & Ruthanna, ch William, gct White Water MM (H)
1888, 1, 25. William H. & Anna & s, John A., dropped from mbrp (H)

HARROLD
1812, 2, 26. John rocf Westfield MM, dtd 1811,10,12

HART
1809, 5, 6. Isaac & w, Sarah, & ch, Esther, Rebecca, Elizabeth & Margaret, recrq
1809, 12, 27. Thomas rocf New Garden MM, N.C.,

HART, continued
dtd 1809,7,29
1809, 12, 27. Phineas rocf New Garden MM, N. C., dtd 1809,7,29

HARTLEY
1825, 4, 27. Elizabeth recrq
1835, 3, 25. Elizabeth gct White Water MM, Ind.

HARTSOCK
1887, 4, 20. Florence L. (or M.) recrq

1909, 1, 27. Lena B. recrq (H)
1916, 10, 29. Helen recrq (H)
1921, 4, 24. Ross recrq (H)
1931, 3, 29. Edna recrq (H)
1931, 4, 26. Wilton Heber, Owen Francis, Jean & Jane recrq (H)

HARVEY
1763, 12, 12. Isaac b
----, --, --. Isaac b 1763,5,5 d 1834,9,5; m Lydia -----
Ch: Ann b 1786, 11, 6
Ruth
Elizabeth
Rebecca
William " 1798, 12, 27
Harlan
Simon D. " 1804, 9, 18
Deborah " 1809, 5, 24
Martha " 1809, 5, 24
Isaac m 2nd Agatha ----
1807, 11, 18. William, s Caleb & Mary, Warren Co., O.; m at Miami, Rachel TOWNSEND, dt John & Elviry, Warren Co., O.
1810, 8, 1. Samuel, s Caleb & Mary, Clinton Co., O.; m at Miami, Rebekah KINDLEY, dt Edward & Margaret, Warren Co., O.
----, --, --. William b 1797,12,27; m Mary CREW b 1799,1,27
Ch: Joseph D. b 1819, 12, 11
Isaac " 1823, 12, 19
Jane " 1821, 11, 1
Maria " 1826, 5, 22
Hannah " 1828, 8, 5
Ruth " 1831, 12, 3 d 1856, 5,11 bur Harveysburg
Martha b 1833, 6, 12 " 1854, 9,19 bur Harveysburg
Lindly M. b 1835, 10, 17 " 1861, 1,14 bur Harveysburg
Deborah b 1838, 8, 26 " 1861, 1,14 bur Harveysburg
Aaron b 1844, 6, 7
----, --, --. John b 1800,7,16; m Lydia BALLARD b 1800,11,9
Ch: James b 1822, 7, 1
Mary Ann " 1823, 10, 18
Elias " 1825, 6, 10 d 1842, 9,16 bur Warren Co., O.
Martha b 1827, 1, 27
Eunice b 1829, 2, 2
John M. " 1831, 2, 22
John m 2nd Mahala PLUMMER b 1814,6,14
Ch: Lydia Ann b 1835, 8, 21
Emily " 1838, 1, 22
Caroline " 1839, 12, 5
Eli P. " 1842, 1, 1 d 1842, 2,16 bur Warren Co., O.
Abi b 1843, 1, 19 " 1844, 8, 4 bur Warren Co., O.
Alfred b 1845, 8, 14 " 1845,10,26 bur Warren Co., O.
Joseph b 1847, 3, 20 " 1853, 5,22 bur Warren Co., O.
Oliver b 1850, 3, 11
William A. " 1851, 7, 11 " 1853, 1, 6 bur Warren Co., O.
Charles b 1853, 2, 15 " 1853, 2,15 bur Warren Co., O.
----, --, --. Jesse b 1801,11,26; m Elizabeth BURGESS b 1801,9,22
Ch: William F. b 1825, 9, 20
Sarah F. " 1826, 9, 22
Thomas B. " 1827, 11, 29
Elisha B. " 1830, 9, 10
----, --, --. Simon D. b 1804,9,18; m Mary BURGESS b 1809,2,1
Ch: Wilson b 1828, 8, 26
Moses B. " 1830, 11, 20
Micajah M. " 1833, 8, 18
Thomas Clarkson " 1836, 8, 13
Gulielma " 1840, 8, 27
1829, 4, 1. Martha W. m Aaron ANTRIM
1831, 8, 29. Isaac d
1831, 11, 2. Isaac, s Caleb & Sarah, Clinton Co., O.; m at Miami, Sarah EDWARDS, dt Nathaniel & Mary, Warren Co., O.
1832, 11, 13. Lydia d bur Harveysburgh
1833, 11, 1. Deborah m Elisha HOBBS
1834, 2, 20. Rebecca m William POOL
1834, 5, 9. Isaac d ae 70y 5m (an elder)
1836, 4, 8. Elisha d bur Harveysburgh
1836, 8, 31. Eli, s William & Mary, Clinton Co., O.; m at Miami, Ruth FISHER, dt Joseph & Hannah, Columbiana Co., O.
----, --, --. Joseph D. b 1819,12,11; m Malinda CHEW b 1827,1,29
Ch: Rebecca Ann b 1845, 5, 30 d 1856, 3,13
Carter " 1847, 5, 25 " 1859, 8,26
Miles " 1849, 12, 13
Wilson " 1851, 11, 9
Martha Louise " 1853, 11, 28
Lindley M. " 1860, 11, 16
Charles " 1865, 9, 29 d 1858,10,26
Mary Alice " 1861, 11, 16
1846, 12, 4. Mary Ann m Nathan HADLEY
1854, 9, 9. Martha d
1856, 2, 28. Emilie P. m Elijah C. GREEN
1859, 4, 25. Lydia d bur Harveysburgh
1861, 1, 2. Lydia Ann m Kirk Linus MOTE

HARVEY, continued
1862, 8, 9. Mary H. d ae 83y

1806, 11, 13. Isaac rocf Spring MM, dtd 1806, 8,30
1806, 11, 13. Samuel rocf Spring MM, dtd 1806, 8,30
1807, 4, 9. Caleb & w, Sarah, & ch, Jesse, Joshua & Hannah, rocf Center MM, N. C., dtd 1806,9,20
1807, 4, 9. Eli & w, Mary, & ch, Lydia, William, Martha, Elizabeth, Ann & Mary, rocf Spring MM, N. C., dtd 1806,8,30
1807, 4, 9. Isaac & w, Lydia, & ch, Ruth, Elizabeth, Rebecca, William Harlan & Simon, rocf Spring MM, N. C., dtd 1806,8,30
1807, 4, 9. William rocf Spring MM, N. C., dtd 1806,8,30
1807, 7, 9. Joshua & w, Mary, & ch, Hannah, Caleb & Simon, rocf Cane Creek MM, S. C., dtd 1807,3,29
1807, 7, 9. Cert rec for Elizabeth from Springfield MM, N. C., dtd 1806,9,27, endorsed to Center MM
1810, 1, 31. Isaac gct Whitewater MM
1810, 1, 31. Rachel gct White Water MM
1810, 9, 26. Rebecca gct Center MM
1821, 8, 29. William & w, Mary, & s, Joseph, rocf Springfield MM, dtd 1821,7,28
1823, 9, 24. William & fam gct Springfield MM
1826, 4, 26. Joshua Edwards gct Springfield MM, to m Sarah Harvey
1828, 4, 30. Isaac & w, Agatha, rocf Springfield MM, dtd 1827,8,29
1828, 4, 30. Deborah rocf Springfield MM, dtd 1828,3,29
1828, 4, 30. Martha rocf Springfield MM, dtd 1828,3,29
1828, 11, 26. Simon D. rocf Springfield MM, dtd 1828,4,20
1828, 11, 26. Mary H., w Simon, rocf Fairfield MM, dtd 1828,4,26
1828, 12, 31. William & w, Mary, & ch, Joseph D., Jane, Isaac & Mariah, rocf Springfield MM, dtd 1828,3,29
1829, 1, 28. Harlan & w, Ruth, & ch, Lydia, Milton, Nancy & Ellwood, rocf Springfield MM, dtd 1829,1,13
1830, 5, 26. Jesse & w, Elizabeth, & ch, William Foster, Sarah T. & Thomas B., rocf Springfield MM, dtd 1830,5,11
1830, 6, 30. David rocf Springfield MM, dtd 1830,6,15
1831, 8, 31. William & w, Mary, rocf Springfield MM, dtd 1831,8,16
1831, 12, 28. Mary rocf Springfield MM, O., dtd 1831,12,13
1831, 12, 28. Sarah, Isaac & Davis, ch Samuel, dec, rocf Springfield MM, O., dtd 1831,12, 13
1832, 1, 25. Sarah gct Springfield MM
1832, 4, 25. John & w, Lydia, & ch, James, Mary Ann, Elias, Martha Eunice & John Medder, rocf Springfield MM, dtd 1832,3,13
1832, 6, 27. Rebecca Stratton & ch, Sarah, Isaac & Davis Harvey, Rebecca & Edward Stratton, recrq (H)
1833, 6, 26. David dis disunity
1833, 7, 24. Mary dis jH
1833, 7, 24. Sarah dis jH
1834, 8, 27. John [Harvy] gct Springfield MM, to m Mahala Plumer
1834, 10, 22. William & w, Mary, gct Springfield MM
1835, 1, 21. Mahala rocf Springfield MM, dtd 1834,12,16
1835, 8, 26. Isaac Edwards gct Springfield MM to m Nancy Harvey
1837, 1, 25. Caleb & w, Bathsheba, & ch, Asenath, Amos B., Silas, Mary & George, rocf Springfield MM, dtd 1836,11,15
1837, 2, 27. Ruth gct Springfield MM
1837, 4, 26. John T. Burgess gct Springfield MM, to m Elizabeth Harvey
1837, 7, 26. Harlin & w, Ruth, & ch gct Bloomfield MM, Ind.
1838, 12, 26. Caleb & w, Bathsheba, & ch gct Spiceland MM
1839, 12, 25. Rebecca Stratton & ch, Davis Harvey, Rebecca & Edward Stratton, gct Fall Creek MM, Ind. (H)
1839, 12, 25. Mary gct Fall Creek MM, Ind. (H)
1839, 12, 25. Sarah gct Fall Creek MM, Ind.
1840, 6, 24. William dis disunity
1840, 8, 26. Mary C. & ch gct Bloomfield MM, Ind.
1840, 8, 26. Jane gct Bloomfield MM, Ind.
1844, 7, 24. Isaac dis jH
1844, 7, 24. Davis dis mou
1847, 7, 21. James gct Fall Creek MM, to m Minerva Johnson
1848, 1, 26. Manerva rocf Fall Creek MM, dtd 1847,12,20
1849, 6, 20. Martha Stanley (form Harvey) dis mou
1849, 12, 26. Eunice Goolman (form Harvey) dis mou
1850, 12, 25. Joseph D. & w, Malinda, & ch, Rebecca Ann, Carter & Miles, rocf Rush Creek MM, dtd 1850,10,17
1850, 12, 25. Mary & ch, Ruth, Martha, Lindley M., Deborah & Aaron, rocf Rush Creek MM, dtd 1850,10,17
1851, 1, 22. James & w, Minerva, & s, Jervis, gct Pleasant Plain MM, Ia.
1851, 7, 23. William F. gct Mill Creek MM
1851, 10, 22. Thomas B. gct White Lick MM,Ind.
1851, 12, 25. Elizabeth gct White Lick MM
1851, 12, 25. Sarah gct White Lick MM
1852, 4, 21. Moses B. gct Mill Creek MM, Ind.
1853, 7, 27. William recrq
1856, 6, 25. Caroline Fox (form Harvey) con mou
1857, 1, 21. Tacy Ellen Ham, niece of Simon D. Harvey & w, Mary H., recrq
1858, 9, 22. Micajah dis mou

HARVEY, continued
1859, 2, 23. John & w, Mahala, & s, Oliver, gct Pleasant Plain MM, Ia.
1859, 2, 23. Lydia Ann gct Pleasant Plain MM, Ia.
1860, 4, 25. Wilson dis mou
1860, 6, 20. Sarah L. (form Lukins) dis mcd (H)
1860, 10, 24. Lydia Ann rocf Pleasant Plains MM, Ia., dtd 1860,9,8
1867, 11, 20. Aaron con mou
1868, 12, 23. Guli E. Ellis (form Harvey) con mou
1871, 2, 22. Simon D. gct Cesars Creek MM
1871, 12, 27. Micajah M. & s, Albert P., recrq
1872, 1, 24. Mary recrq
1878, 5, 22. Elizabeth R. recrq
1883, 4, 25. Nathan recrq
1886, 3, 24. Nathan relrq
1886, 6, 23. Miles & w, Elizabeth R., & dt, Lucile, gct Wilmington MM
1891, 1, 21. Lydia H. gct White Water MM,Ind.
1891, 2, 18. Miles & dt, Lucile, rocf Wilmington MM, dtd 1891,1,10
1894, 1, 24. Albert P. gct Marion MM, Ind.
1895, 7, 24. T. C. relrq
1898, 8, 31. Lydia rocf White Water MM, Ind., dtd 1898,7,28
1904, 2, 24. Micajah & dt, Anna B., gct Wilmington MM
1904, 7, 27. Winifred rocf Springfield MM, dtd 1904,7,16

HASKET
----, --, --. Thomas & Ann (H)

Ch:				
	Lydia	b 1796,	1,	14
	Mary	" 1798,	3,	6
	Isaac	" 1801,	8,	22
	Charity	" 1804,	12,	17
	Thomas	" 1807,	9,	21
	Ann	" 1810,	4,	2
	William	" 1813,	6,	20

1819, 2, 3. Lydia m Hugh MILLS
1819, 4, 7. Ann m Levi COOK
1822, 2, 6. Mary m George EVANS

1806, 5, 8. Ann & ch, Lydia, Mary, Isaac & Charity, rocf Bush River MM, S. C., dtd 1806,2,22
1807, 1, 8. Isaac [Haskett] & w, Rebecca, & dt, Lydia, rocf Bush River MM, S. C., dtd 1806,4,26
1811, 8, 28. Ann & ch, Lydia, Mary, Isaac & Charity, gct Ceasar's Creek MM
1815, 5, 31. Ann [Haskit] & ch, Lydia, Mary, Isaac & Charity, rocf Cesar's Creek MM, dtd 1815,5,26
1816, 8, 23. Thomas, Ann & William, ch Ann, recrq
1825, 6, 29. Levi Cook & w, Ann, & ch, Isaac & John Cook, & Thomas, Ann & William Hasket, gct Milford MM, Ind.
1825, 7, 27. Charity gct Milford MM, Ind.
1827, 12, 26. Isaac [Haskett] gct Springborough MM, to m Rachel Haines
1829, 11, 25. Isaac & s gct Springborough MM
1851, 11, 26. Isaac [Haskett] & w, Rachel, & ch, Joel, Ann, Susannah & Mary, rocf Springboro MM, dtd 1851,11,23
1856, 6, 25. Isaac & w, Rachel, & ch, Anna, Susan & Mary, gct Salem MM, Ia.
1884, 5, 28. William recrq

HASTINGS
1808, 8, 11. William rocf Back Creek MM, N. C., dtd 1807,3,28
1808, 8, 11. Cert rec for Sarah [Hastins] & ch, Ann, Catherine, Unice & Wellmet, from Back Creek MM, dtd 1807,3,28, endorsed to West Branch MM
1810, 8, 29. Joseph rocf Back Creek MM, N.C., dtd 1807,4,25
1819, 9, 29. Ann gct Ceasars Creek MM

HATHAWAY
1873, 2, 18. Abraham recrq
1900, 11, 21. Pearl & Phebe recrq
1914, 5, 27. Goldie dropped from mbrp

HATTON
1815, 2, 9. George, s Robert & Ann, Clinton Co., O.; m at Cincinnati, Margaret FOULKE, dt Joshua & Hannah, O.
1817, 3, 5. Edward, s Robert & Ann, b 1794, 9,27 d 1883,12,25; m at Miami, Rachel LUKENS, dt Levi & Elizabeth, Warren Co., O., b 1796,10,24 d 1879,5,25 (H)

Ch:					
	Lewis	b 1817,	12,	2	d 1822,10,24
	Ann	" 1819,	9,	4	" 1906, 5,26
	Levi	" 1821,	8,	6	
	George	" 1825,	3,	19	
	Jervis J.	" 1827,	10,	19	
	Susannah	" 1830,	2,	16	d 1868,11,27
	Elizabeth	" 1833,	8,	23	" 1854, 6, 3
	Mary E.	" 1836,	11,	14	
	Edward B.	" 1838,	10,	1	
	Rachel	" 1838,	10,	1	" 1841,10,17
	Deborah	" 1842,	7,	23	

----, --, --. Robert m Susanna EVANS (H)

Ch:				
	Joseph	b 1838,	3,	23
	Elizabeth	" 1839,	10,	2
	Sarah	" 1841,	7,	7
	Margaret	" 1843,	2,	22
	Eliza	" 1848,	1,	30
	Robert	" 1851,	6,	4
	Willits	" 1853,	4,	25
	Lorenzo M.	" 1857,	5,	19
	Edmond E.	" 1859,	10,	17

1850, 5, 1. Ann [Hatten] m Moses KELLY (H)
1872, 10, 9. George d (H)
1878, 12, 13. Hannah d (H)

1815, 1, 25. George rocf Center MM
1817, 1, 29. Edward rocf Cincinnati MM, dtd 1817,1,16
1817, 7, 30. Rachel rocf Center MM, Half Moon

HATTON, continued
Twp., Pa., dtd 1817,3,15
1829, 5, 27. Edward dis jH
1829, 5, 27. Rachel dis jH
1852, 8, 25. Ann Kelly (form Hatton) dis mou
1853, 11, 23. George & w, Hannah, rocf White Water MM, dtd 1853,11,23 (H)
1854, 4, 26. Robert & w, Susannah, & ch, Joseph, Elizabeth E., Sarah, Margaret, Eliza & Willits, rocf White Water MM, dtd 1854,3,22
1859, 5, 25. Jervis dis mcd (H)
1860, 5, 23. Edward B. dis disunity (H)
1863, 4, 22. Joseph gct Green Plain MM
1863, 4, 22. Elizabeth E., Sarah & Margaret gct Green Plain MM (H)
1863, 4, 22. Robert & w, Susannah E., & ch, Eliza, Robert, Willets, Lorenzo M. & Edmond E., gct Green Plain MM (H)
1864, 7, 27. Deborah Dakin (form Hatton) dis mcd (H)
1866, 9, 26. Levi L. con mou (H)

HAVENS
1820, 10, 25. Samuel rocf Upper Springfield MM, N. J., dtd 1820,9,6
1832, 7, 25. Samuel gct West Branch MM
1887, 4, 20. Cora recrq

HAWES
1864, 7, 27. Mary (form Haines) dis mcd (H)

HAWKE
1885, 11, 25. Sarah A. (form Sides) relrq

HAWKINS
----, --, --. Isaac b 1778,11,20; m Mary COOK b 1779,5,11 (H)
Ch: Elizabeth b 1803, 12, 18
Margaret " 1806, 2, 7
Abraham " 1808, 5, 20
Sally " 1810, 11, 4
Patty " 1813, 4, 24 d 1814, 7,10
Ruth " 1815, 4, 17
Isaac " 1818, 12, 11
Seth " 1821, 6, 21
1807, 11, 19. Amos, s Nathan & Ann, Butlar Co., O.; m at Elk Creek, Rachel JONES, dt Henry & Keziah, Butlar Co., O.
1807, 11, 26. Nathan, s Nathan & Ann, Butlar Co., O.; m at Elk Creek, Rebecca ROBARTS, dt Thomas & Ann, Butlar Co., O.
1809, 9, 8. Levi, s Benjamin & Martha, Butlar Co., O.; m Mary EVANS, dt Joseph & Esther, Butlar Co., O.
1821, 9, 8. John, s Nathan & Ann, Clinton Co., O.; m at Sugar Creek, Margery HORNER, dt Thomas & Ann, Montgomery Co., O.
1822, 2, 6. Elizabeth m John BURNET
1831, 5, 4. Sarah m Reuben T. GARRETSON
1831, 10, --. Isaac d bur Waynesville
1833, 8, 28. Ruth m Henry STEDDOM
1844, 12, 2. Mary d bur Waynesville
1864, 6, 2. Isaac E., s Abraham & Jane, Clinton Co., O.; m at Turtle Creek, Susan MATHER, dt David & Lurena, Warren Co., O.

1805, 5, 12. Amos rocf Cane Creek MM, S. C., dtd 1804,2,13
1805, 5, 9. Benjamin Hawkins & w, Olive, & ch, Amos, Levi, James & Hannah, & w's ch, Mary & Charity Cook, rocf Cane Creek MM, S. C., dtd 1805,2,16
1805, 6, 13. Isaac & w, Mary, & dt, Elizabeth, rocf Cane Creek MM, S. C., dtd 1805,2,16
1805, 6, 13. John & w, Sarah, & ch, Jesse, rocf Cane Creek MM, S. C., dtd 1805.2,16
1805, 7, 11. Isaac & w, Martha, rocf Cane Creek MM, dtd 1805,2,16
1806, 4, 10. Nathan & w, Ann, & ch, Nathan, Ann, James, Mary & Henry, rocf Cane Creek MM, S. C., dtd 1805,8,24
1806, 5, 8. Sarah, w James, & ch, Ruth, Dinah & Jehu, rocf Cane Creek MM, S. C., dtd 1806,2,15
1807, 6, 11. Amos & w, Phebe, & ch, Jonothan, Mary, Margaret & Christopher, rocf Cane Creek MM, S. C., dtd 1807,3,21
1807, 8, 3. Amos & w, Ann, & ch, Henry, Mary, Rebecca & Martha, rocf Cane Creek MM, S. C., dtd 1807,3,21
1809, 6, 10. Ann Bishop (form Hawkins) con mou
1821, 11, 28. Margery gct Ceasars Creek MM
1825, 3, 30. Margaret Jones (form Hawkins) con mou
1830, 9, 29. Abraham gct Springfield MM, to m Jane Hadley
1831, 3, 30. Jane rocf Springfield MM, dtd 1831,3,15
1834, 9, 24. Abraham & w, Jane, & s gct Springfield MM
1839, 4, 24. Isaac gct Springfield MM, to m Ruth Pyle
1840, 6, 24. Isaac gct Springfield MM
1842, 11, 23. Seth gct Springfield MM
1861, 2, 20. John Howard Johnson gct Springfield MM, to m Sarah H. Hawkins
1872, 2, 21. Susan Mather gct New Garden MM, Ind.
1905, 5, 24. Benjamin & w, Viola K., & dt, Helen Esther, rocf Ceasars Creek MM, dtd 1905,4,21
1910, 10, 26. Benjamin & w, Viola K., & dt, Helen E., gct Grassy Run MM, O.

HAWORTH
1804, 12, 13. George & w, Susannah, & ch, William, Mary, Sarah, Richard, Samuel & Dillon, rocf New Hope MM, Tenn., dtd 1804, 7,21
1804, 12, 13. James & w, Mary, & ch, William, James, George, Sarah, David, Jonathan & Charity, rocf New Hope MM, Tenn., dtd 1804,7,21

HAWORTH, continued
1804, 12, 13. John & w, Elizabeth, & ch, Moorman & Susannah, rocf New Hope MM, Tenn., dtd 1804,7,21
1805, 9, 12. Mahlon & w, Phebe, & ch, Rebecca, George, Ezekiel & Susanna, rocf New Hope MM, dtd 1805,1,19
1806, 4, 10. James & w, Rachel, rocf New Hope MM, Tenn., dtd 1805,9,21

HAY
1890, 10, 22. Florence (form Phillips) dis

HAYDOCK
1856, 5, 21. John D. Edwards gct West Union MM, Ind., to m Hannah [Haddock]
1856, 9, 24. Hannah Edwards & ch, William Daniel & Thomas T. [Haddock], rocf West Union MM, dtd 1856,8,11
1865, 1, 25. William con mou
1865, 5, 24. William gct Clear Creek MM, O.
1868, 7, 22. Daniel gct Cincinnati MM
1868, 7, 22. Thomas gct Cincinnati MM
1869, 7, 21. Daniel dis jas

HAYES
1900, 5, 23. John & w, Anna, & ch, Marie Pearl & infant s, rocf Springfield MM, dtd 1900,1,20; returned 1900,6,20 because of moving away

HAYNIE
1917, 7, 29. Nettie L. transferred to this mtg from Springboro (H)

HAYSLIT
1887, 3, 23. Susan B. recrq
1891, 11, 25. James R. [Hayslitt] recrq

HAZLETON
1917, 7, 29. Mary B. dropped from mbrp (H)

HEATON
1863, 9, 23. Thomas H. Burgess gct Marlborough MM, N. Y., to m Mary G. Heaton

HEDGER
1893, 4, 26. Claude recrq
1894, 3, 21. Claude relrq

HEIGHWAY
1849, 5, 23. Mary (form Rogers) dis mou (H)

HEINLEY
1907, 7, 24. Addie relrq

HELAR
1866, 1, 24. Martha dropped from mbrp; former mbr of Fall Creek or Centre MM which had been laid down (H)

HELMSTETHER
1909, 10, 27. Catherine dropped from mbrp

HENDERSON
1805, 11, 14. Rebekah & ch, Eli & Nathaniel, rocf Bush River MM, S. C., dtd 1805,8,31
1805, 11, 14. Richard & w, Rachel, & ch, Isaac, Susannah, Sarah & Keziah, rocf Bush River MM, S. C., dtd 1805,8,31
1805, 11, 14. Thomas rocf Bush River MM, S. C. dtd 1805,8,31
1807, 4, 9. Thomas rocf Bush River MM, dtd 1806,9,21
1809, 1, 14. Eli dis mcd
1809, 1, 14. Nathaniel dis
1809, 12, 27. Cert rec for Susannah from New Garden MM, N. C., dtd 1809,8,26, endorsed to White Water MM
1822, 8, 28. Silver Creek MM was granted permission to rst Eli

HENLEY
1806, 7, 10. Henry & s, Hezekiah, John & Joseph, rocf Back Creek MM, N. C., dtd 1805, 8,31
1806, 7, 10. Martha & dt, Mary & Rebecca, rocf Back Creek MM, dtd 1805,8,31
1806, 10, 9. Jesse & s, Stephen, Jacob & Noah, rocf Back Creek MM, N. C., dtd 1805,9,28

HENRY
----, --, --. ----- m Rachel M. B. ----- b 1844,6,19 (H)
Ch: Thomas B. b 1872, 8, 17
William E. " 1876, 10, 17
Carrie Corrinne Baylies b 1882,1,29, a ch by later m

1835, 6, 24. Lydia (form Clutch) dis mou
1877, 7, 25. Rachel B. (form Butterworth) con mcd (H)
1877, 10, 24. Thomas B. & William E., ch Rachel B., recrq (H)
1887, 11, 23. Rachel B. Baylies (form Butterworth & later Henry) rpd mcd (H)
1903, 3, 25. Thomas B. & William relrq (H)

HESTER
1806, 3, 13. Francis & w, Mary, & ch, Elizabeth, Thomas, Ruth, John, Robert & Mary, rocf New Garden MM, N. C., dtd 1805,9,28
1882, 9, 20. Joseph [Haster] relrq

HESTON
1809, 10, 14. William & w, Mercy, & dt, Mercy, rocf Redstone MM, dtd 1806,3,28
1810, 1, 31. Macy Garwood (form Heston) dis mou
1811, 3, 27. Ann rst
1819, 5, 25. William gct Cesars Creek MM
1854, 4, 26. Elizabeth (form Canby) dis mcd (H)
1917, 7, 29. Albert transferred to this mtg from Springboro (H)
1920, 5, 30. Charles Albert & Emma Jane, ch

HESTON, continued
Albert Heston, recrq (H)
1920, 7, 25. Edward W. dropped from mbrp (H)

HEWLINGS
1811, 9, 25. Elizabeth (form Burdin) rpd mcd

HIATT
----, --, --. Hezekiah b 1786,3,27 d 1872,7,2; m Ann PERKINS b 1785,4,21 d 1872,6,10 (H)

Ch:			
Sarah	b 1811, 4, 7	d 1899,12,20
Isaac P.	" 1813, 1, 4	" 1910, 12,30
Allen	" 1814, 12, 15	" 1888, 8, 1
Mary Ann	" 1816, 12, 3	" 1894, 9,13
Susannah	" 1819, 1, 4	
Lydia	" 1821, 3, 5	" 1849, 4, 1
Pheniah	" 1825, 4, 13	
Narcissa	" 1823, 5, 16	" 1853, 4,25
Amos C.	" 1827, 6, 28	" 1906, 3, 4

1842, 6, 2. Phebe m Sylvanus TALBERT
1847, 3, 4. Clarkson, s Christopher & Jemima, Clinton Co., O.; m at Hopewell, Jane HOLLINGSWORTH, dt James & Esther, Warren Co., O. (H)
1861, 10, 13. Warren, s Clarkson & Jane, b

1804, 11, 8. Mary Beals & s, Asaph Hiatt, rocf Mount Pleasant MM, Va., dtd 1803,11,26
1816, 8, 28. Silas & w, Ann, & ch, Jorden, Milla, Ascenith & Irene, rocf New Garden MM, N. C., dtd 1816,2,24
1818, 6, 24. Eleazer & w, Anna, & ch, Eliza, Jesse & Daniel, rocf Chester MM, dtd 1818,5,16
1819, 1, 27. Eliazer & fam gct White Water MM
1819, 2, 24. Sarah rocf Centre MM, dtd 1818, 11,21
1819, 3, 31. Jesse rocf Darby Creek MM, dtd 1819,1,19
1819, 4, 28. Silas & fam gct Ceasars Creek MM
1841, 8, 25. Isaac & w, Shanny D., & ch, Phebe T., Lydia, Martha Jane, Rebecca & Joseph P., rocf White Water MM, dtd 1841,6,23
1845, 8, 27. Isaac [Hiat] & fam gct Salem MM, Ia.
1845, 8, 27. Shanny & fam gct Salem MM, Ia.
1845, 8, 27. Lydia & Martha gct Salem MM, Ia.
1854, 11, 29. Martha (form Hollingsworth) dis mcd (H)
1866, 1, 24. Allen con mcd (H)
1866, 1, 24. Clarkson rpd mcd (H)
1866, 1, 24. Jane rpd mcd (H)
1866, 1, 24. Hezekiah, Ann, Isaac & Amos rec in mbrp; form mbr of Fall Creek or Centre MM which had been laid down (H)
1866, 1, 24. Lorenza, Francis, Evelyn, Albert, Lora & Warren, minors, rec in mbrp; form mbr of Fall Creek or Centre MM which had been laid down
1866, 1, 24. Elwood dropped from mbrp; former mbr of Fall Creek or Centre MM, which had been laid down (H)
1866, 1, 24. Mary Ann [Hiat] dropped from mbrp; former mbr Fall Creek or Centre MM, which had been laid down (H)
1885, 6, 24. Clarkson relrq to jas (H)
1885, 6, 24. Jane relrq to jas (H)
1885, 6, 24. Evelyn Cluxton (form Hiatt) relrq to jas (H)
1885, 6, 24. Francis T. relrq to jas (H)
1885, 7, 22. Albert P. relrq (H)
1885, 8, 26. Mary M. Lazenby (form Hiatt) relrq (H)
1885, 8, 26. Lora M. Roberts (form Hiatt) relrq (H)
1885, 10, 21. Lorenzo relrq (H)
1885, 10, 21. Edwin relrq (H)
1889, 3, 27. Warren relrq (H)
1904, 3, 23. Margaret Chapman gct South 8th St. Richmond MM, Ind.

HIBBARD
1827, 3, 28. Cert rec for James M. from Hopewell MM, dtd 1827,3,8, to m Mary Nixon, endorsed to Elk MM where she had rem

HIDAY
1792, 6, 17. Elizabeth b

1816, 7, 31. Elizabeth (form Pidgeon) con mou

HILL
1829, 11, 26. Robert, s William & Mary, Wayne Co., Ind.; m at Miami, Rebecca LATHROP, dt Jonathan & Susanna Wright, Warren Co., O. (H)
1838, 5, 9. Samuel, s Robert & Susanna, Wayne Co., Ind.; m at Miami, Susannah COOK, dt Stephen & Elizabeth, Warren Co., O. (H)

1804, 10, 11. Robert rocf Back Creek MM, N.C. dtd 1803,8,27
1804, 10, 11. Susanah & ch, Martha, rocf Back Creek MM, N. C., dtd 1803,8,27
1808, 8, 11. Benjamin & w, Mary, & ch, John, Jacob, William, Joseph & Sarah, roc, dtd 1806,8,30
1830, 3, 31. Rebecca Hill & dt, Emily Lathrop, gct White Water MM (H)
1839, 3, 27. Samuel rocf White Water MM, dtd 1839,3,13 (H)
1841, 2, 24. Susanna (form Cook) dis mou & jH
;852, 9, 22. Samuel & w, Susan, gct Plainfield MM, Ill. (H)
1855, 3, 21. Seth Brown gct White Water MM, to m Mary Ann Hill
1875, 10, 27. Samuel & w, Susan, gct Prairie Grove MM, Ia. (H)
1889, 7, 24. Susan M. (form Ballard) dropped

HILL, continued
from mbrp
1900, 5, 23. Enos W. & w, Dora, & s, Ralph J., rocf Ceasars Creek MM, dtd 1900,4,26
1909, 10, 27. Ralph relrq

HILLMAN
1873, 2, 18. Waldren recrq
1876, 3, 22. Aland M. recrq
1880, 11, 24. Walter gct White River MM, Ind.

HINCHMAN
----, --, --. Griffith b 1802,9,14 d 1879,1,26; m Mary B. ALLEN b 1802,5,26 d 1874,12,10 (H)
Dt: Eliza b 1829, 1, 17 d 1912, 4, 1

1845, 5, 21. Griffith & w, Mary, & dt, Eliza, rocf Springborough MM, dtd 1845,4,24 (H)
1847, 11, 24. Eliza Haines (form Hinchman) con mou (H)

HINSHAW
1855, 8, 22. Joseph C. Johnson gct Springfield MM, Ind., to m Elmina Hinshaw

HOAK
1931, 8, 30. Anna Louise, Benton Kellar, Monimia & Seth recrq (H)

HOBBS
1833, 11, 1. Elisha, s William & Priscilla, Henry Co., Ind.; m at Harveysburgh, Deborah HARVEY, dt Isaac & Lydia, Warren Co., O.
Ch: Jason d 1845, 6,26
bur Harveysburgh
Penina " 1848, 8, 8
bur Harveysburgh

1845, 2, 19. Elisha & w, Deborah, & ch, Martha, Louisa, Harvey, Anslem & Jason, rocf Walnut Ridge MM, dtd 1845,1,18
1851, 2, 19. Elisha & w, Deborah, & ch, Martha, Louisa, Harvey & Anslem, gct Spiceland MM

HOBSON
1808, 1, 14. William rocf Deep Creek MM, N. C., dtd 1807,10,3
1808, 10, 8. William gct Deep Creek MM, N. C.
1809, 2, 11. John & s, Hollowill & Joseph, rocf Contentney MM, dtd 1807,3,14
1809, 2, 11. Meriam rocf Great Contentney MM, N. C., dtd 1807,3,14

HODGSON
1806, 3, 13. Amos rocf New Garden MM, N. C., dtd 1803,8,27, endorsed by Concord MM, 1804,12,18
1806, 6, 12. Her & w, Acsah, & ch, Mary, Isaac, Jesse, Jonathan, Jehu & John, rocf New Garden MM, N. C., dtd 1805,11,2
1806, 9, 11. Solomon [Hodson] & w, Elizabeth, rocf Deep River MM, N. C., dtd 1805,12,2

HOFFMAN
1806, 7, 10. Lydia rocf Hopewell MM, Va., dtd 1806,5,5
1809, 12, 27. Sarah [Hoofman], dt Lydia Thomas, recrq
1893, 11, 22. Mary M. [Huffman] recrq

HOGE
1817, 4, 30. Elihu [Hoag] rocf Starksboro MM, Vt., dtd 1816,8,2
1850, 3, 27. Hannah rocf Hopewell MM, Va., dtd 1850,3,7
1853, 7, 27. Phebe rocf Sedar MM, Va., dtd 1853,3,9
1866, 11, 21. Phebe gct Hopewell MM, Va.
1867, 8, 21. Hannah gct Spring Creek MM, Ia.

HOGGATT
----, --, --. Jacob [Hockett] b 1804,5,3 d 1876,1,25; m Rhoda MOON b 1820,9,22 d 1901,10,27 (H)
Ch: Naomi T. b 1848, 2, 6
Orpha " 1852, 12, 9
Jared " 1857, 1, 13
Daniel H. " 1863, 12, 1
----, --, --. Daniel H., b 1863,2,1; m Alce JESSOP b 1866,3,27 (H)

1805, 4, 11. Joseph [Hockett] & w, Ruth, & ch, Ann, Elizabeth, Jesse & Jacob, rocf New Hope MM, Tenn., dtd 1804,11,17
1806, 2, 13. Moses & ch, Margaret, Mary, Sarah & Prudence, rocf New Hope MM, dtd 1805,9,21
1806, 6, 12. Stephen [Hockett] & w, Margaret, & ch, William, Joseph, Isaac, Ann, Hannah, Phebe, Stephen, Edward & Margaret, rocf New Garden MM, N. C., dtd 1805, 9,28
1807, 3, 12. David [Hockett] & w, Sarah, & ch, Phebe, rocf New Garden MM, dtd 1806, 9,27
1810, 1, 31. Moses & w, Deborah, & ch, Merriam, Rachel, Robert, Julia & Aaron, rocf Springfield MM. N. C.
1857, 8, 26. Joseph [Hoggat] & w, Elizabeth, rocf Salem MM, Ia., dtd 1857,6,17
1858, 9, 22. Joseph & w, Elizabeth, gct Springfield MM, N. C.
1866, 1, 24. Orpha, Jared & Daniel [Hockett], minors, rec in mbrp; form mbr of Fall Creek MM, which had been laid down

1866, 1, 24. Lucinda [Hockett] rpd mcd (H)
1866, 1, 24. Jacob [Hocket] rpd mcd (H)
1866, 1, 24. Rhoda [Hocket] rpd mcd (H)
1875, 5, 26. Naomi T. [Hocket] recrq (H)
1928, 3, 25. Elsie, Earl & Jean recrq (H)

HOGGATT, continued
1931, 8, 20. Ruth recrq (H)

HOLLINGSWORTH
----, --, --. Abraham, s Joseph, Warren Co., O., b 1769,3,4; m Eunice ----- b 1779,9,13
Ch: Martha b 1800, 8, 21[d 1814,5,29
Joseph " 1802, 5, 25
Henry " 1804, 1, 20
Anna " 1806, 7, 7
John " 1808, 8, 22
Jabez " 1811, 9, 3
Abraham m 2nd 1817,8,14 at Turtle Creek, Sarah PIDGEON, dt Samuel, Warren Co., O., b 1790,2,29
Ch: Elizabeth b 1818, 7, 12 d 1823, 9,27
Samuel " 1820, 3, 21
Margaret " 1822, 10, 16
Isaac " 1824, 9, 19
Zebulon " 1827, 3, 18
Mary " 1829, 8, 6
Eunice " 1831, 11, 18
1806, 5, 15. Susanna m Elisha JONES
1807, 1, 13. Susanna m Jonathan MOTE
1812, 4, 1. Jane m John CAMMACK
1813, 9, 1. Charity m John CAMMACK
1817, 12, 4. James Hollingsworth, s John & Rachel, Warren Co., O.; m at Hopewell, Esther CADWALADER, dt Thomas & Jane, Warren Co., O.
----, --, --. James b 1790,3,4 d 1864,10,10; m Hannah CADWALADER b 1800,1,25 d 1892,1, 8 (H)
Ch: Elias b 1820, 7, 16
Mahlon " 1822, 2, 24
Zimri " 1824, 2, 26
Jane " 1826, 8, 5
Rachel " 1828, 9, 26
Martha " 1830, 11, 16
Abner " 1832, 10, 14
Seth " 1834, 12, 21
Nathan " 1837, 4, 15
Emily " 1839, 4, 5 d 1861, 3,23
Rhoda " 1846, 6, 17 " 1864, 2,10
1819, 7, 8. Hannah m Samuel CAMMACK
1820, 12, 7. Joseph, s Jonah & Hannah, Warren Co., O., b 1786,3,17 d 1853,8,25; m Rhoda WHITACRE, dt Robert & Patience, Warren Co., O., b 1802,3,12 d 1884,2,25 (H)
Ch: Jonah
Robert b 1821, 11, 25 d 1846, 7, 3
Moses W. " 1823, 5, 17
Ruthanna " 1827, 6, 24
David " 1829, 9, 21 " 1849, 1,28
Patience " 1833, 11, 4 " 1839, 9, 5
----, --, --. Joseph b 1802,5,25; m Sally FURNAS b 1808,1,12
Ch: William b 1834, 1, 17
Elwood " 1836, 7, 26
Alice " 1838, 2,28
Abraham " 1840, 5, 28
Margaret
Ann " 1842, 5, 26
Ch: Joseph
Furnas b 1845, 2, 6
Jabez " 1847, 8, 26
Eunice F. " 1849, 11, 15
Mary I. " 1852, 8, 27
1842, 3, 30. Elias, s James & Esther, Warren Co., O., b 1820,7,16; m at Miami, Lidia SHERWOOD, dt Thomas & Dorcas, Warren Co., O., b 1821,10,3 d 1863,7,18 (H)
Ch: Thomas b 1843, 10, 7 d 1864,10,18
John " 1845, 10, 14 " 1865, 3,29
Ann " 1847, 11, 8
James " 1849, 10, 28
Franklin " 1853, 10, 15
Henry " 1863, 6, 7 " 1863, 9,13
1843, 3, 2. Mahlon, s James & Esther, Warren Co., O., b 1822,2,24; m at Hopewell, Mary WHITACRE, dt Acquilla & Ruthanna, Warren Co., O., b 1824,1,1 (H)
Ch: Edward b 1843, 12, 24
James " 1845, 2, 3
Rebecca C. " 1846, 7, 26
Charles M. " 1848, 1, 17
Rachel Ann
1843, 5, 31. Margaret d bur Turtle Creek
1845, 12, 14. Mary d bur Turtle Creek
1846, 12, 24. Ruthanna m Nathan HUNT (H)
1847, 3, 4. Jane m Clarkson HIATT (H)
1847, 4, 29. Anna m Robert FURNAS
1849, 1, 28. Susanna d bur Turtle Creek
1849, 11, 28. Abraham d bur Turtle Creek
----, --, --. Zimri b 1824,2,26; m Sarah BOND [(H)
Ch: Allen b 1851, 10, 3
Mary B. " 1853, 11, 1
Annie " 1860, 5, 27
1852, 11, 17. Mary I. d bur Turtle Creek
1856, 1, 3. Alice m Henry JAY
----, --, --. Abraham b 1840,5,28; m Celeste Susan MOTE b 1842,2,27
Ch: Albert
Rudolph b 1863, 2, 27
Charles E. " 1869, 1, 11 (?)
Clarence
Wildie " 1869, 6, 20 (?)
Maurice
Baxter " 1872, 12, 11
Joseph
Smith " 1874, 3, 23
Mary C. " 1879, 9, 10
----, --, --. Elwood b 1836,7,26; m Angeline PUCKET
Ch: John Gurney
b 1865, 5, 22
Alpheus D. " 1866, 11, 28
Douglas " 1869, 2, 5
Emma J. " 1872, 9, 9
Nathan Omor" 1875, 3, 8
Addie Mary " 1877, 11, 5
Florence N." 1879, 10, 18

1804, 11, 8. Abraham & w, Eunice, & ch, Martha, Joseph & Henry, rocf Bush River MM, S. C., dtd 1804,8,25

HOLLINGSWORTH, continued
1805, 11, 14. Isaac & w, Susanna, & ch, Susannah & John, rocf Bush River MM, S. C., dtd 1805,8,31
1805, 11, 14. Henry & w, Sarah & ch, Isaac, Eli, Catharine, Jane, Susannah, Mark & James, rocf Bush River MM, S. C., dtd 1805,8,31
1805, 12, 12. James & w, Sarah, & ch, Rachel, Joseph, Catherine, Mary, James, Keturah & Henry, rocf Bush River MM, dtd 1805,8,31
1806, 5, 8. Nathan rocf Bush River MM, S.C., dtd 1806,2,22
1806, 5, 8. Susanna rocf Bush River MM, S. C., dtd 1805,8,31
1806, 8, 14. Joel rocf Bush River MM, dtd 1806,5,31
1806, 9, 11. David & w, Catherine, & ch, Rebecca, Jonathan, Martha, Mary, Thomas & Joseph, rocf Bush River MM, S. C., dtd 1806,4,26
1806, 10, 9. John & w, Rachel, & ch, James, Henry, Jane, Charity, John, Nathan, George, Hannah & Joseph, rocf Bush River MM, S.C. dtd 1806,7,26
1807, 5, 4. Jacob & w, Martha, & ch, Anna & Rebecca, rocf Bush River MM, S. C., dtd 1806,9,27
1807, 8, 3. Jonothan rocf Bush River MM, S. C., dtd 1806,12,27
1808, 3, 10. Isaac & w, Hannah, & ch, John, Susannah, Gulielma & Phebe, rocf Deep River MM, N. C., dtd 1807,9,7
1809, 12, 27. Joseph rocf New Garden MM, N.C., dtd 1809,8,26
1809, 12, 27. William rocf New Garden MM, N. C., dtd 1809,8,26
1810, 9, 26. Isaac & w, Hannah, & ch, John, Susannah, Phebe & Gulielma, gct White Water MM
1810, 9, 26. Jonothan gct White Water MM
1812, 5, 27. James & w, Sarah, & ch, Rachel, Mary, James, Katurah, Henry & Ira, rocf West Branch MM, dtd 1812,4,23
1814, 2, 23. James & fam gct White Water MM
1816, 8, 24. Henry dis mcd
1817, 10, 29. John gct White Water MM, to m
1818, 5, 27. Solomon & w, Sarah, rocf Hopewell MM, Va., dtd 1817,4,13
1818, 11, 25. George dis
1819, 2, 24. Joseph rocf Baltimore MM, dtd 1818,12,11
1819, 11, 24. John & dt, Elizabeth, gct Center MM
1819, 11, 24. Cert rec for Mary from White Water MM, dtd 1818,12,26, endorsed to Center MM
1820, 5, 31. Martha Freestone (form Hollingsworth) con mou
1820, 10, 25. Rachel gct White Water MM
1820, 11, 29. Sarah gct Hopewell MM, Va.
1821, 7, 25. Martha Freestone (form Hollingsworth) rpd mcd
1822, 1, 30. Nathan gct White Water MM, Ind.
1827, 2, 27. Henry rpd mcd
1829, 5, 27. James dis jH
1829, 5, 27. Joseph dis jH
1829, 11, 25. Esther dis jH
1829, 11, 25. Rhoda dis jH
1830, 1, 27. Henry gct Springfield MM, Ind.
1833, 3, 27. Joseph gct Union MM, to m Sally Furnas
1833, 9, 25. Sally rocf Union MM, dtd 1833,9,18
1843, 8, 23. Elias dis mou
1843, 8, 23. Malon dis mou & jH
1843, 8, 23. Lydia (form Shearwood) dis mou
1845, 8, 27. Zimri gct White Water MM, to m Sarah Bond (H)
1847, 3, 24. Sarah rocf White Water MM, dtd 1846,8,26 (H)
1850, 7, 24. Mahlon C. & w, Mary, & ch, Edward W., James M., Rebecca C., Charles M. & Rachel Ann, gct Fall Creek MM, O. (H)
1852, 1, 21. Samuel dis mou
1854, 11, 29. Martha Hiatt (form Hollingsworth) dis mcd (H)
1855, 6, 20. Zebulon dis mou
1856, 8, 27. Rachel Townsend (form Hollingsworth) dis mcd (H)
1857, 4, 22. Isaac dis mou
1859, 9, 21. Rhoda gct Springborough MM (H)
1860, 2, 22. Nathan dis disunity (H)
1860, 2, 22. Zimri dis (H)
1863, 3, 25. Abraham con mou
1863, 6, 24. Angeline E. rocf Dover MM, Ind., dtd 1863,5,26
1863, 12, 23. Celeste S. rocf West Branch MM, dtd 1863,11,19
1866, 7, 25. Joseph con mou
1866, 12, 26. Margaret A. Sherwood (form Hollingsworth) con mou
1866, 12, 26. Sarah & ch, Allen, Mary B. & Anna, gct White Water MM, Ind. (H)
1866, 12, 26. Susannah P. rocf Union MM, dtd 1866,11,11
1867, 11, 20. Moses gct Springborough MM (H)
1873, 4, 23. Joseph Furnas & w, Susannah P., & ch gct Back Creek MM, Ind.
1875, 11, 24. Joseph F. & w, Susanna P., & ch, Idella, Clifford, Mary & Eber, rocf Back Creek MM, Ind.
1881, 3, 23. J. Furnace & w, Susanna, & ch, Idella, Clifford, Mary W. & Eber, gct Wilmington MM
1881, 10, 26. Jabez dis disunity
1882, 4, 26. J. Furnas & w, Susanna, & ch, Idella, Clifford, Mary L. W. & Eber, rocf Wilmington MM, O., dtd 1882,2,17
1886, 10, 27. Joseph F. & w, Susanna, & ch, Clifford, Mary W., Eber & Earl, gct Triumph MM, Neb.
1889, 1, 23. Abner relrq (H)
1889, 7, 24. James, s Elias, dropped from mbrp (H)
1889, 7, 24. Seth dropped from mbrp (H)

HOLLINGSWORTH, continued
1889, 7, 24. Ann Strate (form Hollingsworth) dropped from mbrp (H)
1889, 10, 23. Elias rpd mcd (several yr before) (H)
1889, 11, 29. Elias gct White Water MM, Ind. (H)
1893, 5, 24. Ellwood recrq
1894, 5, 24. Joseph Furnas & w, Susan P., & ch, Eber & Joseph Earl, rocf Fairview MM, Mo.
1895, 9, 25. Douglas & A. D. relrq
1895, 12, 25. Joseph Furnace & w, Susanna, & s, Joseph Earl, gct West Branch MM
1896, 1, 22. Eber gct West Branch MM
1896, 8, 26. Albert R. & w, Martha, & ch relrq
1897, 3, 24. Charles & Maurice A. relrq
1902, 6, --. Franklin dropped from mbrp (H)
1914, 4, 22. Glen & Wildie B. recrq

HOLLOWAY
----, --, --. David b 1771,6,23; m Hannah RICHARDS b 1774,1,30 (H)
Ch: Daton b 1795, 4, 27
Lydia " 1796, 12, 15
Margaret " 1799, 3, 7
John " 1801, 4, 10
Abigail " 1803, 6, 26
Hannah " 1807, 9, 25
David " 1809, 12, 6

HOLLOWELL
----, --, --. Elwood b 1824,5,3 d 1885,7,9; m Mary D. ----- b 1828,9,4 d 1881,4,3 (H)
Ch: Anna b 1854, 9, 5 d 1905,10,28
Edgar " 1861, 7, 31 " 1912,10, 6
Bertha " 1868, 5, 12
1886, 3, 3. Annie m Ellis GOOD (H)
1894, 12, 20. Bertha m Charles G. BLACKBURN (H)

1811, 2, 27. Robert & s, Smithson, Nathan & William, rocf Contentnea MM, N. C., dtd 1810,3,10
1811, 2, 27. Cert rec for Elizabeth (Hallowell] & dt, Michel, Peggy, Mary & Abby, from Contentney MM, N. C., dtd 1810,3,10, endorsed to White Water MM
1811, 12, 25. John & s, Jesse, Jonothan & John, rocf Contentnea MM, dtd 1807,3,14
1812, 2, 26. Miriam & dt, Mary & Sarah, rocf Contentney MM, N. C., dtd 1807,3,14
1878, 5, 22. Elwood & w, Mary, & ch, Edgar & Bertha, recrq (H)
1885, 2, 18. Anna recrq (H)
1885, 3, 18. Mary J. (form Burnett) rpd mcd (H)
1885, 4, 22. Mary J. gct Rush Creek MM, Ind. (or Maple Grove MM) (H)
1895, 5, 22. Edgar set off as mbr of Executive Mtg at Clear Creek (H)

HOLMES
1812, 6, 24. Jonothan & w, Mary, & s, David, rocf Haddonfield MM, N. J., dtd 1812,5,11
1823, 3, 26. Daniel dis mcd
1853, 3, 23. Hannah & s, Joseph, rocf Fairfax MM, Va., dtd 1853,2,16 (H)
1858, 8, 25. Hannah dis jas (H)
1860, 4, 25. Joseph dis jas (H)

HOLSCHOTH
1842, 10, 26. Lydia dis mou (H)

HOLWAY
1852, 8, 25. George N. & Maria A. rocf West Lake MM, Canada, dtd 1852,6,10
1854, 6, 21. George N. & w, Maria, & s, George Willet, gct Red Cedar MM, Ia.

HOOVER
1831, 3, 24. Frederick, s Andrew & Elizabeth, Wayne Co., Ind.; m at Miami, Tamar FARR, dt Edward & Mary (H)

1806, 4, 10. Catherine (form Yount) dis mou
1806, 6, 12. Susannah, dt Andrew, Warren Co., O., rmt Elijah Wright, at Waynesville
1806, 9, 11. David rocf Back Creek MM, N.C., dtd 1805,2,23
1807, 10, 8. Andrew & w, Elizabeth, & ch, Rebecca, Catherine & Sarah, gct West Branch MM
1831, 7, 27. Tamar gct White Water MM, Ind. (H)

HOPKINS
----, --, --. Priscilla b 1785,10,2 d 1873, 2,24 (H)
1827, 11, 7. Joseph, s Hezekiah & Martha, Warren Co., O.; m at Miami, Mary W. CRISPIN, dt Jonathan & Elizabeth, Warren Co., O.
1827, 12, 5. Richard, s Hezekiah & Martha, Warren Co., O., b 1804,12,4; m at Miami, Hannah WHARTON, dt Silas & Mary, Warren Co., O., b 1807,8,28 (H)
Ch: James W. b 1828, 10, 11
Martha " 1830, 9, 25 d 1831, 9, 8
Joseph " 1832, 7, 12
Mary " 1835, 8, 9 " 1839,12,19
Emily " 1838, 7, 23
Ann " 1840, 8, 12
Horace " 1845, 1, 8
1872, 9, 10. Jonathan d (H)

1806, 1, 9. Benjamin & w, Rebecca, & ch, Ann, Rebecca, Mary, Crisson, Lydia & Benjamin, rocf Haddonfield MM, N. J., dtd 1805,9,9
1814, 9, 28. Sarah rocf Phila. MM for Southern District, dtd 1814,5,25
1820, 10, 25. Hezekiah & ch, Mary, Ann, Richard, Hannah S., William, Beulah, Parker & Hezekiah, rocf Phila. MM, dtd 1820,6,28
1820, 12, 27. Joseph rocf Phila. MM, dtd 1820,

HOPKINS, continued
7,19
1825, 1, 26. Charles rocf Cincinnati MM, dtd 1824,11,25
1825, 8, 31. Charles dis
1829, 3, 25. Richard dis jH
1829, 5, 27. Joseph dis jH
1829, 5, 27. Hannah W. dis jH
1829, 6, 24. Mary W. dis jH
1829, 7, 29. Mary Ann dis jH
1829, 9, 30. Hannah dis jH
1831, 3, 30. William dis jH
1831, 5, 25. Mary Ann Shepherd (form Hopkins) con mou (H)
1832, 11, 21. Hannah Bacon (form Hopkins) dis mou (H)
1833, 4, 24. William con mou (H)
1835, 3, 25. Beulah Barcus (form Hopkins) con mou (H)
1837, 1, 25. Mary W. & ch, Jonathan C. & Mary W., gct Westfield MM (H)
1839, 12, 25. William gct White Water MM (H)
1845, 6, 25. Richard & w, Hannah, & ch, James, Joseph, Emily, Ann & Horace, gct Westfield MM
1850, 6, 26. Jonathan C. rocf Westfield MM, dtd 1850,4,24; returned with information that he had joined Mormon Society while a minor (H)
1851, 1, 22. Jonathan C. rocf Westfield MM, dtd 1850,11,27 (H)
1855, 5, 23. Jonathan con mcd (H)
1855, 7, 25. Jonathan gct Westfield MM (H)
1855, 9, 26. Cert rec for Prisilla from Baltimore MM, dtd 1855,8,9, endorsed to Center MM (H)
1855, 11, 21. Hannah L. & dt, Mary Catherine & Anne B., rocf Baltimore MM for Eastern & Western Districts, dtd 1855,8,9
1855, 11, 21. Hester B., Rachel H. & Sarah P. rocf Baltimore MM for Eastern & Western Dist., dtd 1855,8,9
1855, 12, 26. Hezekiah dis mcd (H)
1857, 8, 26. Elizabeth recrq
1857, 11, 25. Ann & Horace, ch Rickard, rocf White Water MM, dtd 1857,8,26 (H)
1858, 12, 22. Horace, s Richard, gct Westfield MM (H)
1859, 7, 27. Ann Engle (form Hopkins) dis mcd (H)
1859, 10, 26. Elizabeth B. rocf White Water MM, Ind., dtd 1859,9,21
1860, 6, 20. Jonathan C. rocf Westfield MM, dtd 1860,4,25 (H)
1860, 9,26. Horace L., minor, rocf Westfield MM, dtd 1860,7,25 (H)
1866, 1, 24. Pricilla rec in mbrp; former mbr of Fall Creek or Centre MM which had been laid down (H)
1867, 4, 24. Elizabeth B. gct White Water MM, Ind.

HORNADAY
1843, 3, 30. John, s Ezekiel & Elizabeth, Clinton Co., O.; m at Turtle Creek, Martha KERSEY, dt John & Anna, Warren Co.,O.

1808, 8, 11. Ruth rocf Cain Creek MM, dtd 1807,8,1
1843, 10, 25. Martha gct Springfield MM

HORNELL
1883, 4, 25. Meribah W. & Rosa M. recrq
1883, 5, 23. Hattie recrq

HORNER
1806, 5, 15. John, s Thomas & Ann, Montgomery Co., O., b 1780,6,13; m at Ceaser's Creek, Elizabeth COMPTON b 1779,12,19 (H)

Ch:		
Samuel	b	1807, 4, 14
Ann	"	1809, 1, 4
Joshua	"	1810, 2, 26
Rebecca	"	1811, 9, 4
Rachel	"	1812, 12, 19
Sally	"	1812, 12, 19
Elizabeth	"	1814, 9, 30

1807, 3, 18. David, s Thomas & Ann, Montgomery Co., O., b 1782,9,28; m at Miami, Sarah PARNELL, dt James & Esther, Warren Co., O., b 1784,6,18 (H)

Ch:		
Thomas	b	1808, 2, 27
James	"	1809, 10, 22
George	"	1811, 9, 1
Amos	"	1813, 5, 19
Levi	"	1815, 7, 21

1817, 8, 7. Sarah m Henry MILHOUS
1821, 9, 8. Margery m John HAWKINS

1805, 1, 10. Thomas recrq
1805, 8, 8. David recrq
1805, 11, 14. John recrq
1805, 12, 12. Jacob recrq
1807, 9, 10. Margery recrq
1813, 4, 28. Joseph recrq
1816, 11, 27. Elizabeth recrq
1817, 1, 29. Sarah recrq
1818, 1, 28. Joseph rpd mcd
1819, 2, 24. Merriam rocf Silver Creek MM, dtd 1818,12,12
1821, 12, 26. William recrq
1822, 8, 28. Jacob gct Cesars Creek MM, to m Lydia McDonald

1822, 11, 27. Lydia rocf Ceasars Creek MM, dtd 1822,10,31
1823, 3, 26. William gct Cesars Creek MM, to m Sally Compton
1823, 7, 30. Sally rocf Ceasars Creek MM, dtd 1823,6,26
1823, 11, 26. William & w, Sally, gct Silver Creek MM, Ind.

HORNEY
1844, 9, 26. David S., s Solomon & Elizabeth, Wayne Co., Ind.; m at Turtle Creek, Ann

HORNEY, continued
MATHER, dt Richard & Elizabeth, Warren Co., O.
1844, 9, 26. Jonathan, s Solomon & Elizabeth, Wayne Co., Ind.; m at Turtle Creek, Susanna L. MATHER, dt Richard & Elizabeth, Warren Co., O.
1852, 11, 4. Joel, s Solomon & Elizabeth, Wayne Co., Ind.; m at Turtle Creek, Sarah B. MATHER, dt Richard & Elizabeth

1845, 4, 23. Ann M. gct White Water MM, Ind.
1845, 4, 23. Susannah L. gct White Water MM
1850, 12, 25. Joseph D. & w, Malinda, & ch, Rebecca Ann, Carter H. & Miles, rocf Rush Creek MM, Ind., dtd 1850,10,17
1853, 2, 23. Sarah B. gct White Lick MM, Ind.

HORSMAN
1814, 5, 25. Prudence (form Gaunt) con mou

HOUGH
1806, 10, 9. Joseph rocf Redstone MM, dtd 1806,8,29
1885, 8, 26. Mary J. (form Cooper) relrq (H)

HOUGHTON
1838, 5, 23. William & w, Sally, & ch, Richard E. & Lucy, rocf Clear Creek MM, dtd 1838,5,22
1839, 11, 20. William & w, Sarah, & ch gct Salem MM, Ind.

HOUSEFELT
1900, 5, 23. Sarah relrq (H)

HOWARD
1866, 1, 24. Martha J. (form Daniel) rpd mcd (H)
1889, 7, 24. Martha J. (form Daniel) gct Marietta MM, Ia. (H)

HOWE
1873, 1, 22. Thomas G. recrq

HOWELL
1906, 2, 21. Benjamin S. & w, Florence, recrq
1907, 2, 20. Dean recrq

HOWETT
1889, 6, 26. Mary C. recrq

HOWLAND
1871, 12, 27. Harriett recrq
1886, 5, 26. George B. & w, Euphenia, & ch, Owen Clark & Benjamin, recrq
1892, 3, 23. George B. & w, Euphamia, & ch, Owen Clark & Benjamin, gct Cesars Creek MM

HOZER
1805, 10, 10. Elizabeth [Hozier] rocf Mount Pleasant MM, dtd 1804,10,27

1809, 4, 8. William & s, Nathan, rocf Back Creek MM, N. C., dtd 1807,3,28
1809, 4, 8. Cert rec for Millicent & dt, Mary, from Back Creek MM, N. C., dtd 1807,3,28, endorsed to West Branch MM
1810, 8, 29. Lewis rocf Back Creek MM, N.C., dtd 1807,4,25

HUDSON
1853, 11, 2. Hannah m Thomas ARNETT

1853, 8, 24. Hannah rocf Wexford MM, Ireland, dtd 1853,7,6
1871, 8, 23. Martha (form Jessop) dis mcd (H)

HUGHS
----, --, --. John & Susanna (H)
Ch: Elenor
Star b 1819, 11, 1
Charles " 1822, 1, 19

1819, 11, 24. John & w, Susanna, & ch, James, Phebe & John Pearson, rocf Exeter MM, Pa., dtd 1819,9,20

HULET
1811, 10, 30. Cert rec for Sarah from Shrewsbury MM, dtd 1807,7,6, endorsed to Fall Creek MM

HULTS
1841, 11, 24. Lydia (form Scott) dis mou

HUMPHREY
1914, 4, 22. Ora, Dora, Goldie, Roma & Raymond [Humphries] recrq
1916, 6, 22. Ora & w & ch gct New Berry MM

HUNT
1804, 11, 18. Sarah m Enos BALDWIN
----, --, --. Samuel b 1802,6,4 d 1884,11,--; m Elizabeth THOMAS d 1852,2,6 (H)
Ch: Joshua b 1832, 7, 15 d 1843, 2,16
Camm Thomas " 1834, 1, 22 " 1916, 1,18
John Eberlee " 1836, 1, 22
Mary " 1838, 2, 4 " 1843, 2, 9
Elizabeth " 1840, 7, 9 " 1904, 4,29
Martha Bye " 1843, 2, 20
Rachel " 1845, 5, 12 " 1915, 7, 8
Samuel " 1847, 8, 7 " 1905, 5,15

1804, 10, 11. Phineas rocf Back Creek MM, N.C., dtd 1804,8,25
1804, 10, 11. Elizabeth & ch, Sarah, Aaron, Catherine, Elizabeth, Eleazer, Mary, Margery & Phineas, rocf Back Creek MM, N. C., dtd 1804,2,25
1805, 8, 8. Samuel & w, Margaret, & ch, Mary, Rachel, Elizabeth, Christiana & Susannah, rocf Cane Creek MM, S. C., dtd 1805,2,16
1805, 12, 12. John & w, Mary, & ch, Uriah,

HUNT, continued
John, Grace, Rachel, Ann & Nathan, rocf Deep River MM, N. C., dtd 1805,9,2
1806, 1, 9. Mary rocf Cane Creek MM, S. C., dtd 1805,6,22
1806, 8, 14. Mary dis
1808, 1, 14. Asa rocf New Garden MM, dtd 1807,1,31
1808, 1, 14. Stephanus & w, Elizabeth, rocf Deep River MM, N. C., dtd 1805,1,7
1808, 1, 14. Jonothan & w, Phebe, & ch, Barnabas, Margaret & John, rocf Deep River MM, N. C., dtd 1805,9,2
1808, 1, 14. Cert rec for Merriam from New Garden MM, N. C., dtd 1806,8,30, endorsed to Fairfield MM
1809, 1, 14. Cert rec for Sarah & ch, Libni, Ezra, Hannah & Hamuel, dtd 1806,9,27, endorsed to Fairfield MM
1808, 3, 10. Samuel dis
1811, 7, 31. Margaret & dt, Elizabeth, Christiana, Susannah & Dinah, gct White Water MM
1811, 8, 28. Rachel Watkins (form Hunt) dis mcd
1829, 2, 25. Ann & ch, Esther W. & Benjamin, rocf Chesterfield MM, N. J., dtd 1828,11,4
1829, 2, 25. Joseph B. rocf Chesterfield MM, dtd 1828,11,4
1829, 2, 25. Clayton rocf Burlington MM, N. J., dtd 1828,11,3
1844, 8, 21. Samuel P. & w, Elizabeth, & ch, Thomas, John Eberly, Elizabeth & Martha, rocf Stillwater MM, dtd 1844,3,16 (H)
1853, 6, 22. Samuel P. dis disunity (H)
1857, 4, 22. J. Eberly dis mcd (H)
1859, 5, 25. Lydia S. (form Whitacre) con mcd (H)
1860, 2, 22. Ruth Anna dis jas (H)
1860, 10, 24. Lydia F. gct Prairie Grove MM, Ia. (H)
1870, 3, 23. Elizabeth Hall (form Hunt) con mcd (H)
1881, 5, 25. Ruth Ann recrq
1886, 2, 24. Ruth Anna gct White Water MM, Ind.
1889, 7, 24. Thomas Camm gct Cincinnati MM (H)
1889, 7, 24. Martha Bye gct Cincinnati MM (H)
1889, 7, 24. Rachel gct Cincinnati MM (H)

HURD
1835, 8, 25. Robert [Herd] recrq (H)
1836, 1, 27. Rosamond [Herd] recrq (H)
1851, 2, 19. Robert dis mcd (H)
1857, 11, 25. Robert rst by rq (H)
1868, 4, 22. Robert dis disunity (H)

HUSSEY
----, --, --. John b 1806,11,15; m Jane EDWARDS b 1807,6,4

Ch:				
Isaac	b 1828,	9,	27
Sarah Ann	" 1830,	1,	26
Elisha	" 1832,	10,	17
Elwood	b 1834,	10,	21
Mary	" 1837,	7,	22
Amos	" 1841,	1,	1
Lydia	" 1843,	8,	7
Christopher	" 1846,	4,	11

1806, 7, 10. Mary rocf Warrington MM, Pa., dtd 1805,11,9
1807, 1, 8. Lydia rocf Indian Spring MM, Md., dtd 1806,1,17
1807, 10, 8. Mary (form Cloud) con mou
1815, 1, 25. Lydia & ch gct Short Creek MM
1829, 11, 25. John & w, Jane, & s, Isaac, rocf Clear Creek MM, dtd 1829,10,15
1847, 2, 24. Christopher rocf Clear Creek MM, dtd 1846,12,12
1847, 9, 22. Christopher gct Clear Creek MM
1852, 2, 24. Sarah A. Harlan (form Hussey) dis mou
1852, 8, 25. Isaac dis disunity
1857, 11, 25. Mary Harlan (form Hussey) dis mou
1866, 8, 22. Mary Ann [Huzzey] (form Larkins) rpd mcd
1868, 12, 23. Elisha rpd mou & jas
1869, 6, 23. Amos con mou
1895, 5, 22. Mary Ann set off as mbr of Executive Mtg at Clear Creek (H)
1917, 7, 29. Mary Ann dropped from mbrp (H)

HUSTON
1824, 10, 27. Hannah [Husten] recrq
1829, 3, 25. Robert [Houston] dis jH
1829, 9, 30. Hannah dis jH

HUTCHENS
1819, 3, 31. Rachel (form Simmons) con mou
1820, 1, 26. Rachel gct Elk MM

HUTCHISSON
1856, 3, 26. Hannah (form Stokes) dis mcd (H)

HUTTON
1891, 4, 22. George relrq (H)

IDDINGS
1804, 12, 13. Benjamin & w, Phebe, & ch, Joseph, Benjamin, William, Phebe, Hannah & Mills, rocf New Hope MM, Tenn., dtd 1804, 7,21
1888, 1, 25. J. L. & w, Priscilla, recrq
1888, 3, 21. Johnettie recrq
1889, 3, 27. James L., Percilla & Jennetta gct West Branch MM, Ohio

INGHAM
1815, 10, 25. Deborah rocf Soleberry MM, Pa., dtd 1815,7,4
1815, 10, 25. Mary rocf Soleberry MM, Pa., dtd 1815,7,4
1824, 2, 25. John Bateman gct Fairfield MM, to m Deborah Ingham
1827, 1, 31. John Kelly O'Neal gct Spring-

INGHAM, continued
borough MM, to m Mary Ingham

INGLE
1829, 6, 24. Mary dis jH
1807, 6, 11. Amelia rocf New Hope MM, dtd 1805,9,21

INSCO
1806, 10, 9. Abel & w, Ann, rocf Bush River MM, S. C., dtd 1806,5,31

IRELAND
1866, 1, 24. Eliza A. (form Carroll) rpd mcd (H)
1889, 7, 24. Eliza A. (form Carroll) dropped from mbrp (H)

IRONS
1815, 9, 27. Rebecca rocf Haddinfield MM, N. J., dtd 1815,4,10
1824, 1, 28. Samuel [Iorns] recrq
1829, 1, 28. Samuel [Iarns] dis jH
1829, 4, 29. Rebecca [Iurns] dis jH
1880, 7, 21. Georgia [Irins] relrq
1885, 1, 21. Margaret S. relrq (H)
1907, 2, 20. Arthur recrq
1908, 8, 26. Lena rocf Ceasars Creek MM
1908, 9, 23. Ross Clayton, s Lena, recrq
1909, 10, 27. Arthur dropped from mbrp
1916, 5, 24. Lena & Ross gct Spring Valley MM

IRVIN
1861, 6, 13. Elizabeth (Adams) b (H)

1899, 2, 22. Elizabeth A. relrq (H)

JACKSON
----, --, --. Curtis b 1793,1,1 d 1850,4,3; m Lydia JACKSON b 1795,11,21 d 1876,1,21(H)
Ch: Lucinda b 1816, 7, 22 d 1875, 8, 3
Hannah " 1817, 10, 28
Phebe " 1819, 8, 21 " 1840, 8,22
John " 1821, 12, 29 " 1886, 2,25
Jury T. " 1824, 3, 18
Anna " 1827, 1, 28
Thomas S " 1830, 9, 17 " 1882,12,31
Jesse " 1833, 4, 24
Louisa " 1837, 8, 9
1888, 7, 13. Hannah d (H)

1805, 4, 11. Jacob & w, Ann, & ch, Jesse, Ann, Lydia, Curtis & Josiah, rocf New Hope MM, Tenn., dtd 1804,11,17
1805, 4, 11. Phebe & ch, Sarah, Charity, Uriah, Elizabeth, Keziah, William, Amon, Mary & Jesse, rocf New Hope MM, Tenn., dtd 1804,10,20
1807, 9, 10. Ann dis
1866, 1, 24. Lydia Sr. rpd mcd (H)
1866, 1, 24. Hannah rpd mcd (H)
1866, 1, 24. Lydia Jr. rpd mcd (H)
1866, 1, 24. Louisa rpd mcd (H)
1866, 1, 24. John rpd mcd (H)
1866, 1, 24. Thomas S. rpd mcd (H)
1866, 1, 24. Nancy rpd mcd (H)
1866, 1, 24. Malinda rpd mcd (H)
1885, 6, 24. Jury T. relrq to jas (H)
1885, 6, 24. Louisa Johnson (form Jackson) relrq to jas (H)
1885, 6, 24. Lydia relrq to jas (H)
1885, 6, 24. Anna Williams (form Jackson) relrq to jas (H)
1890, 11, 26. Jesse dropped from mbrp (H)
1891, 4, 22. Jesse rst by rq (H)
1895, 1, 23. Malinda relrq (H)
1895, 5, 22. Jesse set off asmbr of Executive Mtg at Clear Creek (H)

JAMES
1810, 8, 29. Thomas & w, Hannah, & ch, Isaac, Hannah, Thomas, Sarah & Phebe, rocf Middleton MM, dtd 1810,6,9
1875, 8, 25. Elizabeth Alice (form Davis) con mcd (H)
1875, 12, 22. Elizabeth Alice gct Maple Grove MM, Ind. (H)

JANNEY
----, --, --. James b 1804,8,29 d 1864,4,10; m Sarah Ann LUPTON b 1805,8,28 d 1891,10,31 (H)
Ch: Charles L. b 1831, 2, 22 d 1901,10,10
William P. " 1833, 6, 19
Edward " 1836, 11, 25 " 1918, 6,11
Samuel S. " 1839, 4, 24 " 1891,11, 6
Lewis " 1842, 2, 14
Mary " 1844, 9, 20
Louisa " 1847, 9, 3
----, --, --. Jonas Sr. d 1897,8,28; m Ruth DAVIS b 1817,--,-- d 1893,1,20 (H)
Ch: Elouisa b 1834, 9, 14
Oscar d in childhood
Ella " 1836, 9, 7
Nannie C. " 1841, 10, 1
J. Edwin " 1852, 10, 27
1855, 10, 31. Jonas, s Jonas & Pleasant, Louden Co., Va., b 1832,4,17; m at Miami, Mary HALE, dt Eli & Ann, Warren Co., O., b 1835,2,20
Ch: Anna P. b 1861, 11, 23
Eva " 1867, 7, 3
1863, 9, 30. William [Janny], s Jonas & Pleasant, Warren Co., O.; m at Waynesville, Mary E. BROWN, dt John & Newell, Warren Co., O., b 1840,3,1
Dt: Cosmelia
1871, 2, 23. Louis, s James & Sarah Ann, Warren Co., O., b 1842,2,14; m at residence of Clarkson Gause, Dorcas SHERWOOD, dt John & Elizabeth, b 1850,11,27 d 1875,10,13 (H)
Ch: Arthur b 1872, 1, 17 d 1892, 2,19
Ethel " 1874, 7, 4 " 1875, 1,27
1873, 4, 17. Mary H. d bur Miami Cemetery

JANNEY, continued
1838, 7, 25. Abel & w, Lydia, rocf Springborough MM, dtd 1838,6,21 (H)
1838, 12, 26. James M. [Janny] & w, Sarahann, & ch, Charles L., William P. & Edward, rocf Springborough MM, dtd 1838,11,22 (H)
1839, 3, 27. Abel & w, Lydia, gct Green Plain MM
1856, 8, 27. Joseph Sr. rocf Hopewell MM, dtd 1856,7,3
1862, 2, 19. William P. con mcd (H)
1863, 7, 22. William rec without his cert from Hopewell MM, Va., due to War conditions in the South
1865, 1, 25. Jonas & w, Ruth, & ch, Elouisa D., Mary E., Nancy C. & James E., rocf Springboro MM, dtd 1869,11,24 (H)
1869, 7, 21. William [Jenny] rocf Hopewell MM, Va.
1875, 4, 21. William & w, Mary E., & ch, Cosmelia N., Marianna & Ellen S., gct Maryville MM, Tenn.
1881, 1, 26. Louisa J. Zell (form Janney) rpd mcd (H)
1882, 4, 26. Anna Williams (form Janney) relrq
1882, 9, 20. Jonas & w, Ruth D., & dt, Nannie C., gct Fall Creek MM, Ind. (H)
1887, 2, 23. Eva L. relrq
1890, 5, 21. William P. relrq (H)
1917, 7, 29. Hannah transferred to this mtg from Springboro (H)
1919, 4, 27. Jeanette rec by rq (H)

JAY
----, --, --. John & Mary (H)
Ch: Martha b 1808, 9, 25
Henery " 1813, 8, 31
John " 1818, 1, 13
1806, 1, 15. Samuel, s John & Betty, Warren Co., O.; m at Miami, Bersheba PUGH, dt Rachel & David, Warren Co., O.
1807, 12, 3. John Jr., s John & Betty, Warren Co., O.; m at a public mtg in Turtle Creek Twp., Mary STEDDOM, dt Henry & Martha, Warren Co., O.
1856, 1, 3. Henry, s John & Mary, Wayne Co., Ind.; m at Turtle Creek, Alice Hollingsworth, dt Joseph & Sally, Warren Co., O.

1804, 5, 10. Jesse & w, Sarah, & ch, John & James, rocf Bush River MM, S. C., dtd 1803,12,31
1804, 5, 10. John & w, Betty, & ch, Marcy, John, Samuel, Walter, William, James, Lydia & Jane, rocf Bush River MM, S. C., dtd 1803,12,31
1804, 7, 12. Mary Dillon (form Jay) dis mou
1804, 12, 13. Rachel Arnold & her ancient mother, Mary Jay, rocf Bush River MM, S. C., dtd 1804,8,25
1806, 11, 13. Thomas & w, Mary, & ch, Rebecca, rocf Bush River MM, S. C., dtd 1806,5,31
1807, 6, 11. Lydia (form McMillan) con mou
1808, 8, 11. Jesse dis
1808, 10, 8. John & fam gct West Branch MM
1809, 6, 10. Lydia gct West Branch MM
1809, 10, 14. Samuel & w, Bershaba, & ch, Verlinda & David, gct West Branch MM
1809, 12, 27. David rocf New Garden MM, dtd 1807,1,31
1810, 5, 30. Rachel (form Mills) con mou
1810, 9, 26. Sarah, w Jesse, & ch, John, James, Thomas, Mary, Samuel & Denny, gct West Branch MM
1811, 4, 24. Walter Denny gct West Branch MM
1812, 9, 30. Mill Creek MM was granted permission to rst Jesse
1813, 6, 30. Samuel & w, Bathsheba, & ch, Nerlinda, David & Rachel, rocf Mill Creek MM, dtd 1813,4,24
1815, 6, 28. Samuel & fam gct Mill Creek MM
1820, 2, 28. David dis
1821, 8, 29. David rst by QM
1822, 1, 30. David dis
1822, 2, 27. Edith (form Mills) con mou
1822, 9, 25. Edith gct Cherry Grove MM
1822, 10, 30. Rachel gct Cherry Grove MM, Ind.
1824, 10, 27. John & w, Mary, & ch, Martha, Henry, John & Walter Denny, gct White Water MM
1827, 4, 25. Cherry Grove MM, Ind. was granted permission to rst David
1856, 1, 23. Alice H. gct Dover MM

JEFFRIES
1821, 10, 3. Catherine m Evan WARD

1805, 7, 11. Job [Jefferies] & ch, Darlington & Catherine, rocf Redstone MM, dtd 1805,3,1
1810, 3, 28. Job [Jeffers] rpd mcd
1810, 7, 25. Job [Jeffers] & s, Darlin, gct Center MM
1824, 10, 27. Hannah [Jefferis] rocf Center MM, dtd 1824,7,17
1826, 1, 25. Martha [Jefferis] rocf White Water MM, dtd 1825,12,17
1829, 8, 26. Martha dis jH
1830, 4, 28. Martha W. [Jefferis] gct White Water MM (H)
1837, 2, 27. Hannah [Jeffreys] gct Chester MM, Ind.
1895, 4, 24. Ella K. [Jeffer] relrq

JENKINS
1807, 2, 26. Ely [Jinkins], s Thomas & Maria, Montgomery Co., O.; m at West Branch, Ruth MENDINGHALL, dt Mordecai & Hannah, Montgomery Co., O.

JENKINS, continued
1805, 6, 13. Amos & w, Elizabeth, & ch, Samuel & David, rocf Bush River MM, S. C., dtd 1805,3,30
1805, 6, 13. Jesse & w, Hannah, & ch, Elizabeth, Rosanna, Phineas & Samuel, rocf Bush River MM, S. C., dtd 1805,3,30
1805, 7, 11. Thomas & ch, Zebulum, Issachar, Esther & Elizabeth, rocf Bush River MM, dtd 1805,3,30
1805, 11, 14. David & s, Enoch, rocf Bush River MM, S. C., dtd 1805,8,31
1805, 11, 14. Mary rocf Bush River MM, dtd 1805,8,31
1805, 11, 14. Harriet rocf Bush River MM, dtd 1805,8,31
1806, 10, 9. Eli rocf Bush River MM, S. C., dtd 1806,4,26
1806, 11, 13. David & w, Martha, & ch, Elizabeth, Rebecca, Robert, Mary, Sarah, Martha, Isaac & Ann, rocf Bush River MM, S., dtd 1806,4,22
1807, 2, 12. David, s Isaac, rocf Bush River MM, S. C., dtd 1806,5,31
1846, 6, 24. David, Jesse, Robert, Ann & Denny, ch Isaac, rocf Mississinewa MM, dtd 1846,5,13, endorsed by Mill Creek MM, 1846,6,16

JENNINGS
1817, 6, 25. Job rocf Woodbury MM, N. J., dtd 1816,10,10
1838, 11, 21. Deborah (form Mills) dis mou (H)
1839, 6, 26. Deborah (form Mills) dis mou
1859, 5, 25. Rachel rocf Maple Grove MM, Ind., dtd 1858,8,14 (H)
1861, 2, 20. Rachel gct Maple Grove MM, Ind. (H)

JESSOP
----, --, --. Thomas b 1775,8,3 d 1847, 2, 8; m Ann ----- b 1775,7,7 (H)
Ch: Jonathan b 1798, 12, 5 d 1829,11,18
Prudence " 1800, 10, 27 " 1824, 1,22
Richard W. " 1803, 10, 12 " 1888, 1,22
Mary " 1805, 4, 9
Thomas " 1807, 4, 12
Anna " 1809, 8, 2 " 1830, 3,18
Huldah " 1812, 8, 31 " 1840, 9,21
Rebecca " 1814, 12, 5
Elizabeth " 1816, 10, 18 " 1889, 9, 5
Jane " 1822, 10, 22 " 1823, 8,15
----, --, --. Richard b 1803,10,12 d 1888,1, 22; m Rebecca ----- b 1802,4,28 d 1868,1, 11(H)
Ch: Ruthanna b 1826, 8, 28
Cornely " 1829, 3, 5
Joseph " 1831, 1, 18
Mary " 1833, 8, 23 d 1838,11, 4
Micajah " 1836, 2, 12 " 1858,10,10
Huldah " 1838, 7, 29 " 1856, 6,20
Lydia Ann " 1840, 12, 8 " 1853, 3,28
Martha " 1844, 12, 10

1826, 12, 6. Mary [Jessup] m David GREEN
1829, 11, 4. Thomas Jr., s Thomas & Ann, Warren Co., O., b 1807,4,12; m at Grove Vashti MOON, dt Richard & Vashti, Warren Co., O., b 1810,3,3 (H)
Ch: Jesse b 1831, 9, 25
Johnathan " 1833, 5, 4
Martha Ann " 1834, 11, 4
Clark W. " 1836, 4, 21
Levi " 1838, 8, 24
Mary Jane " 1840, 10, 27
1846, 9, 2. Rebecca [Jessup] m James A. JOHNSON (H)
----, --, --. Joseph P. [Jessup] b 1831,1,18; m Mary B. LEWIS (H)
Ch: Alice b 1866, 3, 27

1810, 1, 31. Jonothan roc dtd 1809,2,--
1811, 2, 27. Isaac rocf Mount Pleasant MM, Va., dtd 1806,8,30
1811, 2, 27. Jacob & w, Rachel, & ch, Phebe, Rachel, Jacob, Sarah & Susanna, rocf Mount Pleasant MM, Va., dtd 1806,8,30
1817, 2, 26. Thomas [Jessup] & w, Ann, & ch, Jonothan, Prudence, Richard, Mary, Thomas, Anna, Huldah & Rebecca, rocf Clear Creek MM, dtd 1817,1,11
1821, 7, 26. Jonothan gct Cesars Creek MM
1821, 8, 29. Jontthan gct Cesars Creek MM, to m Patience Mills
1823, 7, 30. Jonathan [Jessup] gct Cesars Creek MM
1825, 3, 30. Richard gct Horsham MM, Pa.
1827, 10, 31. Richard W. & w, Rebecca, & dt, Ruth Ann, rocf Horsham MM, Pa., dtd 1827, 8,29
1829, 5, 27. Anna dis
1829, 5, 27. Ann dis jH
1829, 5, 27. Rebecca dis jH
1829, 5, 27. Richard dis jH
1829, 5, 27. Thomas dis jH
1829, 5, 27. Thomas Jr. dis jH
1830, 3, 31. Anna's d rpd
1831, 4, 27. Thomas Jr. & w, Vashti, gct White Water MM, Ind. (H)
1833, 5, 22. Huldah & Rebecca [Jesop] dis jH
1833, 8, 21. Thomas Jr. & w, Vashti, & ch, Jesse, rocf White Water MM, dtd 1833,7,24 (H)
1837, 10, 25. Elizabeth Moore (form Jessop) dis mou & jH
1847, 12, 22. Ruth Ann Carver (form Jessop) con mou (H)
1848, 7, 26. Anna Comer (form Jessop) dis mou
1848, 8, 23. Ruth Ann Carver (form Jessop) dis mou
1853, 7, 27. Daniel & w, Hannah Sophia, & s, Amos C., rocf Cesars Creek MM, dtd 1853,5, 26
1854, 6, 21. Jesse dis (H)
1854, 11, 29. Camby dis mcd (H)
1855, 2, 21. Daniel & w, Hannah Sophia, & s, Amos C., gct Fairfield MM, Ind.

JESSOP, continued
1855, 2, 21. Thomas & w, Vashti, & ch, Clark, Levi & Mary Jane, gct White Water MM (H)
1856, 9, 27. Martha Ann Whitsel (form Jessop) con mcd (H)
1863, 7, 22. Joseph P. gct Center MM, to m Mary B. Lewis (H)
1868, 4, 22. Joseph P. & w, Mary B., & ch, Alice, gct White Water MM, Ind. (H)
1870, 5, 25. Richard gct White Water MM (H)
1871, 8, 23. Martha Hudson (form Jessop) dis mcd (H)
1872, 4, 24. Richard W. [Jessup] rocf White Water MM, dtd 1872,3,27 (H)
1876, 3, 22. Joseph rocf White Water MM, dtd 1876,2,25 (H)
1878, 11, 20. Levi rocf White Water MM, dtd 1878,10,23 (H)
1887, 2, 23. Joseph relrq (H)
1889, 12, 25. Ruth Anna Carver (form Jessop) dropped from mbrp (H)
1896, 1, 26. Martha Ann Cox (nee Jessup) dropped from mbrp (H)
1908, 8, 19. Levi [Jessup] & w, Louisa, recrq (H)
1909, 8, 18. Mary B. rocf White Water MM, Ind., dtd 1909,6,23 (H)

JEWLIN
1811, 4, 24. Margery [Jeweland] (form Mc-Clure) con mou
1815, 11, 29. Margery gct Mill Creek MM

JOHN
1808, 1, 14. Ebenezer rocf Westfield MM, dtd 1806,12,13
1897, 1, 27. Anna [Johns] recrq

JOHNSON
1807, 8, 19. Penelope m John SEARS
----, --, --. Zachariah b 1786,2,8 d 1848,9,16; m Polly BUTTERWORTH b 1787,6,15 d 1863,1,26 (H)
Ch: Benjamin B. b 1811, 9, 19 d 1863, 2,23
James D. " 1811, 9, 19 " 1877, 5, 7
Mehala Jinnet " 1814, 10, 29 " 1886,11,26
----, --, --. Joseph b 1772,9,25 d 1838, 9,27; m Betsy BUTTERWORTH b 1788,9,3 d 1843,11,9 (H)
Ch: Rachel Ballard b 1813, 1, 3
James Anthony " 1814, 9, 25 d 1878, 5,26
Penelope " 1816, 11, 18 " 1899, 2, 4
Deborah " 1819, 2, 18 " 1844, 5,16
Joseph C. " 1828, 4, 25 " 1844, 7, 3
Benjamin " 1821, 5, 22
1813, 8, 4. Micajah, s John & Rhoda, Warren Co., O., b 1792,12,28; m at Miami, Rebecca O'NEAL, dt Abijah & Anna, Warren Co., O., b 1796,9,3
Ch: Abijah b 1815, 6, 17
Cynthiann b 1817, 4, 13
Edwin " 1818, 12, 22
Rhoda " 1820, 9, 12
Emily " 1822, 8, 1
Allen " 1825, 8, 1
John Kelly " 1828, 3, 29
Henry " 1830, 2, 15
Joseph C. " 1832, 5, 13
Martha Mary " 1836, 10, 1
John Howard " 1840, 4, 26
Micajah m 2nd Ann HALE, b 1802,8,30
1820, 12, 6. James B., s Elijah & Betsy, Ross Co., O.; m at Miami, Rhoda ONEALL, dt Abijah & Anna, Warren Co., O.
----, --, --. James b 1803,2,25; m Elizabeth ----- b 1800,5,2
Ch: Rhoda Ann b 1822, 6, 27
John G. " 1824, 1, 22
Alfred " 1825, 10, 28
Evan L. " 1827, 10, 21
Thatcher S. " 1829, 11, 4
Hannah M. " 1832, 1, 4
Mary B. " 1834, 3, 10
Rebecca N. " 1836, 5, 18
Amy " 1838, 5, 5
Sylvanus " 1831, 8, 30
James Brooks " 1843, 6, 30
1828, 7, 7. John K. d bur Miami Cemetery
1835, 9, 30. Ann m William B. SILVER (H)
----, --, --. James D. b 1811,9,19 d 1877,5,7; m Margaret SABIN b 1817,8,10 d 1890,2,19 (H)
Ch: Cyrus A. b 1837, 9, 23 d 1838, 2,13
Mahalah C. " 1838, 11, 17
Martha S. " 1843, 7, 29 " 1886, 8,17
James A. " 1845, 12, 18
1840, 2, 6. Rhoda m William E. BUTLER
1843, 5, 26. Rhoda (Butler) d
1845, 4, 1. Rebecca d bur Miami Cemetery
1846, 8, 27. Rhoda Ann m Nathan MOFFITT
1846, 9, 2. James A., s Joseph & Betsy; m at Grove, Rebecca JESSUP, dt Thomas & Ann, Warren Co., O. (H)
1847, 3, 25. Rhoda M. m Charles F. COFFIN
1847, 6, 9. Emily m Samuel H. HADLEY
1854, 3, 23. Alfred, s James & Elizabeth, Wabash, Ind.; m at Harveysburgh, Anna M. THORNE, dt John & Elizabeth, Warren Co., O.
1855, 10, 31. Martha M. m John E. KLEIN
1856, 11, 23. Allen d
1859, 8, 13. Micajah d bur Miami Cemetery
----, --, --. Joseph b 1832,5,13; m Elmina HINSHAW
1861, 10, 28. Tacy d (H)
----, --, --. John m Judith FORKNER
Ch: Brooks
Joel W.
David F.
Phebe
Rhoda M.
Eli
Rachel A.

JOHNSON, continued
1806, 7, 10. James & w, Sarah, & ch, Thomas, David & William, rocf New Garden MM, N.C., dtd 1805,11,30
1806, 8, 14. Ashley & w, Milly, & ch, Jonathan, Daniel, William, Nancy, Abner, Agatha, Martha, Ashley & Thomas, rocf South River MM, Va., dtd 1806,4,12
1806, 8, 14. Milly & ch, Micajah, Penelope & Elizabeth, rocf South River MM, Va., dtd 1806,2,8
1806, 8, 14. Pleasant & w, Nancy, & ch, Thomas, rocf South River MM, Va., dtd 1806,2,8
1806, 8, 14. Susannah rocf Southriver MM, Va., dtd 1806,2,8
1807, 2, 12. Jeptha rocf South River MM, Va., dtd 1806,10,11
1807, 9, 10. Ashley rocf Deep Creek MM, N.C., dtd 1807,4,4
1807, 9, 10. Charles & w, Susanah, & ch, David, Anna, Susannah, Polly Sally & Nancy, rocf South River MM, dtd 1806,9,13
1807, 9, 10. William & w, Agatha, & ch, Christopher, Moorman & Nancy, rocf South River MM, dtd 1806,9,13
1807, 10, 8. Edith rocf Deep Creek MM, N. C., dtd 1807,4,4
1807, 10, 8. Mary rocf Deep Creek MM, N. C., dtd 1807,7,4
1807, 10, 8. Cert rec for Rachel from Deep Creek MM, N. C., dtd 1807,4,4, endorsed to Center MM
1808, 7, 14. Jonothan & w, Hannah, & dt, Sithe, rocf Cane Creek MM, N. C., dtd 1807,10,3
1809, 9, 9. Cert rec for Nancy from Goos Creek MM, endorsed by South River MM, Va., 1807,4,11, endorsed by this mtg to Fairfield MM
1810, 11, 28. Jesse & w, Elizabeth, & ch, Jonothan, Silas, Joshua, Sarah & Eli, rocf Cane Creek MM, N. C., dtd 1810,8,4
1813, 3, 31. Anthony rocf Goose Creek MM, Va., dtd 1812,9,3
1813, 3, 31. James & w, Penelope, & ch, Elizabeth, Sarah, Judith, Mary, Penelope, Agnes & Rachel, rocf Goose Creek MM, Va., dtd 1812,9,3
1813, 3, 31. Jesse rocf Goose Creek MM, Va., dtd 1812,9,3
1813, 3, 31. Joseph & w, Betsy, rocf Goose Creek MM, Va., dtd 1812,9,3
1813, 6, 30. Micajah rocf Center MM, dtd 1813,5,1
1815, 1, 25. Christopher Anthony rocf South River MM, Va., dtd 1814,11,12
1816, 7, 31. Zachariah & w, Polly, & ch, Zachariah M., Benjamin B., James D. & Mahala, recrq
1817, 4, 30. Polly rst with permission of South River MM
1819, 11, 24. Thomas recrq
1820, 11, 29. James B. rocf Fairfield MM, dtd 1820,9,30
1823, 7, 30. James rocf Center MM, dtd 1823, 3,15
1824, 2, 25. Rhoda gct Fairfield MM
1829, 5, 27. Polly dis jH
1829, 6, 24. Joseph dis jH
1829, 7, 29. Zechariah M. dis jH
1829, 8, 26. Betsy dis jH
1829, 8, 26. Benjamin B. dis jH
1829, 8, 26. James D. dis jH
1830, 2, 24. James & w, Elizabeth, & ch, Rhoda Ann, John G., Evan L., Alfred & Thatcher, gct Center MM
1832, 4, 25. Benjamin B. con mou (H)
1832, 6, 27. Margaret rocf Wilmington MM, dtd 1832,6,1 (H)
1832, 6, 27. Ann rocf Wilmington MM, dtd 1832,6,1 (H)
1832, 7, 25. Robert & Joseph rocf Wilmington MM, dtd 1832,6,1 (H)
1832, 9, 26. Mahala I. J. (form Lindsey) con mou (H)
1834, 3, 26. Ann, minor, rocf Wilmington MM, dtd 1834,2,1
1835, 2, 18. John & w, Judith, & ch, Brooks, Joel W., David F., Phebe, Rhoda M., Eli & Rachel A., rocf Center MM, dtd 1834,11, 12
1835, 3, 25. Penelope Gillaspie (form Johnson) con mou (H)
1835, 7, 22. James A. con mou (H)
1836, 7, 27. Abijah gct Dover MM, to m Elizabeth Bailey
1836, 7, 27. James A. gct White Water MM (H)
1836, 7, 27. Joseph & w, Betsy, & ch, Deborah, Benjamin & Joseph C., gct White Water MM (H)
1837, 1, 25. Elizabeth rocf Dover MM, dtd 1836,12,15
1836, 7, 27. Rachel B. gct Whitewater MM (H)
1837, 2, 22. Robert dis mou (H)
1837, 2, 22. James & w, Elizabeth, & ch, Rhoda Ann, John G., Alfred, Evan L., Thatcher S., Hannah Maria, Mary B. & Rebecca, rocf Center MM, dtd 1837,1,18
1837, 11, 22. Ann Silver (form Johnson) dis mou & jH
1837, 12, 27. Abijah & w, Elizabeth, gct Springborough MM
1837, 12, 27. James D. con mou (H)
1839, 10, 23. Deborah rocf White Water MM, dtd 1839,6,26 (H)
1839, 10, 23. Betsey & ch, Benjamin & Joseph Clark Johnson, rocf White Water MM, dtd 1839,6,26 (H)
1840, 4, 22. Margaret & dt, Mahala C., recrq (H)
1841, 4, 21. Edwin gct Springboro MM, to m Eliza D. Stroud
1841, 11, 24. Edwin gct Springborough MM
1842, 8, 24. Brooks gct Center MM, to m Lydia Burson

JOHNSON, continued
1842, 11, 23. Brooks gct Springfield MM
1844, 8, 21. David F. gct Cincinnati MM, to m Catherine Carpenter
1844, 12, 25. Edwin & w, Eliza P., rocf Springboro MM, dtd 1844,10,22
1845, 3, 26. Benjamin gct Fall Creek MM, to m Susanna Baker (H)
1845, 7, 23. Susanna rocf Fall Creek MM, dtd 1845,6,21 (H)
1845, 11, 26. Catherine C. rocf Cincinnati MM, O., dtd 1845,7,17
1846, 2, 18. Zachariah M. dis setting up mtg contrary to discipline (H)
1846, 5, 27. Abijah & w, Elizabeth, & ch, Silviah B., John K. & Micajah D., rocf Dover MM, dtd 1846,4,16
1847, 1, 27. David F. & w, Catherine, & s, Albert C., gct Cincinnati MM
1847, 7, 21. James Harvey gct Fall Creek MM, to m Minerva Johnson
1848, 10, 25. Mahala Lindsey (form Johnson) dis mou
1849, 3, 21. John G. con mou
1849, 4, 25. Edwin & w, Eliza, gct Cincinnati MM, Ohio
1849, 9, 26. John G. gct West Branch MM
1850, 10, 23. Micajah gct Springfield MM, to m Ann Hale
1851, 2, 19. Rachel gct White Water MM, Ind.
1851, 3, 26. Evan Lewis gct Wabash MM
1851, 3, 26. Ann Johnson & ch, Mary, Sarah Ann & Alfred C. Hale, rocf Springfield MM, dtd 1851,3,13
1851, 4, 23. Thatcher S. gct Wabash MM, Ind.
1852, 2, 25. Eli gct White Water MM, to m Mary Coffin
1852, 2, 25. Isaac Jones gct West Union MM, to m Elizabeth B. Johnson
1852, 4, 21. Henry C. dis mou
1852, 6, 23. Mary C. rocf White Water MM, dtd 1852,5,26
1852, 9, 22. Polly & s, Benjamin B., gct Fall Creek MM, Ind. (H)
1852, 10, 27. Benjamin & w, Susannah, & ch, Amasa, Joseph, Deborah & Enos, gct Fall Creek MM, Ind. (H)
1852, 12, 22. Phebe gct White Water MM, Ind.
1853, 6, 22. James A. & w, Rebecca, gct Center MM (H)
1854, 3, 22. James & w, Elizabeth, & ch, Hannah M., Mary B., Rebecca N., Amy, Sylvanus & James Brooks, gct White Water MM, Ind.
1855, 6, 20. Anna M. gct White Lick MM, Ind.
1855, 7, 25. Abijah & w, Elizabeth, & ch, Sylvie B., John Kelly, Micajah D., Rebecca D., Overton A., Warren & Abijah H., gct Sugar River MM, Ind.
1855, 8, 22. Joseph C. gct Springfield MM, Ind., to m Elmina Hinshaw
1855, 9, 26. Brooks & w, Mary P., & ch, John Edward & Lucy B., rocf Springborough MM, dtd 1855,7,24
1856, 4, 23. David F. & w, Catharine C., & ch, Charles Albert, Calvin C., John, Joel W., Ida Caroline & Eli M., rocf Springfield MM, dtd 1856,3,15
1856, 8, 27. Elmina L. rocf Springfield MM, dtd 1856,6,21
1857, 2, 18. Brooks & w, Mary S., & ch, John Edward & Lucy B., gct Cincinnati MM; returned 1857,4,22
1857, 7, 22. James D. dis disunity (H)
1857, 11, 25. Brooks & w, Mary S., & ch, John Edward & Lucy B., gct Cincinnati MM
1858, 2, 24. Eli & w, Mary, gct White Water MM
1858, 3, 24. David F. & w, Catherine C., & ch, Charles Albert, John, Joel W., Ida Caroline & Eli M., gct White Water MM
1859, 12, 21. Mahala C. Corwin (form Johnson) dis mcd (H)
1861, 2, 20. John Howard gct Springfield MM, to m Sarah H. Hawkins
1862, 7, 23. John Howard gct Springfield MM
1863, 6, 24. Elmina L. gct Springfield MM,O.
1866, 8, 22. Alice (form Conard) con mcd (H)
1866, 8, 22. Deborah (form Jones) con mcd (H)
1866, 9, 26. Brooks & w, Mary S., & ch, Lucy B. & Charles, gct Cincinnati MM
1866, 9, 26. John Edward gct Cincinnati MM
1869, 3, 25. Lydia E. (form Edwards) dis mou & jas
1871, 1, 25. Lydia relrq
1874, 6, 24. James D. recrq (H)
1874, 9, 23. James A. gct Springboro MM (H)
1878, 3, 20. Atlanta recrq
1880, 4, 27. Martha Hale recrq (H)
1883, 4, 25. Bernice recrq
1885, 6, 24. Louisa (form Jackson) relrq to jas (H)
1895, 5, 22. Lizzie T., Alice R. & Deborah A. set off as mbr of Executive Mtg at Clear Creek (H)
1917, 7, 29. Denson S. transferred to this mtg from Springboro (H)
1917, 7, 29. Dorotha transferred to this mtg from Springboro (H)

JONES
----, --, --. Jesse O. b 1781,10,6 d 1864,1,4; m ----- ----- (H)
Ch: Owen
Hannah
Jesse m 2nd Mary WARD b 1787,3,30 d 1866,8,20

Ch:	b	d
Elizabeth	1818, 2, 25	1897, 6,26
Lydia	" 1819, 2, 18	" 1837, 5,19
Israel	" 1820, 10, 13	
Jonathan	" 1824, 2, 20	" 1846, 6,16
Rachel	" 1826, 2, 14	" 1837, 7,28
William	" 1828, 9, 14	" 1904, 8, 4
Jesse Jr.	" 1830, 2, 4	" 1830, 8,23
Isaac W.	" 1833, 12, 29	" 1834, 1, 3

----, --, --. Daniel b 1783,10,25; m Elizabeth ----- b 1786,2,14 (H)

JONES, continued
Ch: Samuel b 1807, 5, 10
Esther " 1809, 3, 3
Daniel " 1814, 8, 22
Elizabeth R. " 1817, 10, 8
Joseph R. " 1824, 6, 22
1806, 2, 7. Margaret (Hawkins), dt Isaac & Mary Hawkins, b
1806, 5, 15. Elisha, s John & Margaret, Warren Co., O.; m at Toddsfork, Susanna HOLLINGSWORTH, dt Isaac & Susanna, Warren Co., O.
1807, 1, 15. Dorkis m Samuel DAVIS
1807, 11, 19. Rachel m Amos HAWKINS
1815, 11, 15. Isaac, s Morgan & Hannah; m at Miami, Rachel BATEMAN, dt William & Elizabeth, Warren Co., O. (H)
Ch: Elizabeth b 1820, 6, 12 d 1820, 8,19
Hannah B. " 1821, 5, 23
----, --, --. John b 1796,11,2 d 1851,12,26; m Deborah B. ----- b 1802,10,13 d 1884,8,17 (H)
Ch: William b 1824, 2, 18
Joseph " 1826, 5, 31
Tacy B " 1828, 11, 2 d 1858, 1, 3
John A. " 1831, 7, 11
Thomas " 1834, 3, 9
Daniel B. " 1836, 2, 1
Deborah A. " 1838, 11, 13
Sarah E. " 1841, 2, 26
1827, 5, 2. Esther m Asher BROWN
1833, 8, 20. Daniel d bur Miami Cemetery
1833, 10, 30. Hannah T. m Stephen BURNET (H)
1834, 5, 1. Samuel, s Daniel & Elizabeth, Warren Co., O., b 1807,5,10; m at Turtle Creek, Martha MATHER, dt Richard & Elizabeth, Warren Co., O., b 1812,1,3
Ch: Susanna L. b 1835, 2, 12
Elizabeth " 1837, 2, 24
Daniel " 1839, 4, 9
Mary Price " 1840, 12, 21
Richard M. " 1843, 4, 29
Anna M. " 1845, 9, 21
Sarah B. " 1848, 2, 24
----, --, --. Daniel b 1814,8,22; m Hannah MABIE b 1815,10,29
Ch: Eliza M. b 1840, 9, 7
Charles W. " 1845, 4, 3
Daniel " 1847, 8, 19
1840, 3, 6. Daniel d
1844, 6, 29. Richard M. d
1846, 10, 1. Isaac, s Nathan & Margaret, Warren Co., O.; m at Turtle Creek, Rebecca KERSEY, dt John & Anna, Warren Co., O.
1849, 12, 3. Joseph R. d bur Miami Cemetery
1850, 10, 12. Elizabeth d bur Miami Cemetery
1856, 11, 22. Samuel d bur Miami Cemetery
----, --, --. Thomas b 1834,3,9; m ----- ----- (H)
Ch: Gertrude b 1860, 8, 19
Deborah Alice b 1867, 3, 24
1863, 7, 29. Elizabeth M. m Artemus N. HADLEY
1881, 1, 20. Charity d (H)
1884, 4, 29. Samuel, s Thomas R. & Mary A., Phila., Pa.; m at residence of Clarkson Gause, Anna R. GAUSE, dt Clarkson & Elizabeth, Warren Co., O. (H)
1888, 3, 2. Margaret d bur Miami
----, --, --. Isaac m Elizabeth JOHNSON

1805, 11, 14. David rocf Wrightsboro MM, dtd 1804,6,2
1805, 12, 12. Jonathan rocf Wrightsboro MM, dtd 1805,4,6
1805, 12, 12. Samuel & w, Mary, & ch, Dorcas, Samuel, Francis, Thomas, Sarah, Mary, Asa & Rachel, rocf Wrightsboro MM, dtd 1805,4,6
1806, 1, 25. John rocf "the MM in Ga." (Wrightsboro), dtd 1804,6,2
1806, 3, 13. Elisha rocf Bush River MM, dtd 1805,12,28
1806, 6, 12. Abijah & w, Rachel, & ch, Rebecca, Obidiah, Daniel, Jemima, David & Mary, rocf Deep Creek MM, N. C., dtd 1806,4,5
1806, 6, 12. Francis rocf Wrightsboro MM, dtd 1805,4,5
1806, 8, 14. Deborah rocf Wrightsborough MM, Ga., dtd 1805,4,6
1806, 8, 14. Henry rocf Wrightsboro MM, Ga., dtd 1805,4,6
1806, 8, 14. Newton & w, Ann, & ch, Henry, rocf Wrightsboro MM, dtd 1805,4,6
1806, 11, 13. George rocf Cane Creek MM, dtd 1805,8,3
1807, 3, 12. Henry & w, Prudence, & ch, Rachel Ann & John, rocf Cane Creek MM, N.C., dtd 1806,9,6
1808, 10, 8. Abijah & fam gc
1811, 3, 27. Elisha & w, Susannah, & ch, Sarah & Mary, gct West Branch MM
1811, 12, 25. Daniel & w, Elizabeth, & ch, Samuel & Esther, rocf Mt. Holly MM, dtd 1811,10,10
1814, 8, 31. Jonathan Wright Jr. gct Gunpowder MM, Md., to m Susannah B. Jones
1815, 2, 22. John rocf West Branch MM, dtd 1815,12,22(?)
1815, 3, 29. Hannah rocf Gunpowder MM, dtd 1815,1,25
1815, 8, 30. Isaac rocf Dimmings Creek MM, dtd 1815,6,14
1818, 7, 25. Rachel (form Baker) rpd mcd
1818, 10, 28. John gct West Branch MM
1818, 10, 28. Rachel gct Radnor MM, Pa.
1818, 11, 25. Hannah rocf Dunnings Creek MM, dtd 1818,8,12
1820, 2, 23. Hannah gct White Water MM
1820, 4, 26. John & w, Sarah, & dt, Mary, rocf West Branch MM, dtd 1820,3,18
1820, 9, 27. John & fam gct West Branch MM
1821, 2, 28. Harriet (form Pugh) con mou
1821, 10, 31. Morgan & ch, Robert, Susanna,

JONES, continued
Ruthanna & Morgan, rocf Dunnings Creek MM, dtd 1821,9,12
1825, 3, 30. Margaret (form Hawkins) con mou
1825, 10, 26. Mary rst in mbrp
1825, 12, 28. Jesse recrq
1827, 5, 30. Narcissa rocf Springfield MM, dtd 1827,3,31
1829, 2, 25. Jesse O. dis jH
1829, 3, 25. Mary dis jH
1829, 4, 29. Charity recrq
1833, 1, 23. Hannah J. recrq (H)
1833, 2, 20. Owen, Elizabeth, Lydia, Israel & Jonathan, recrq of parents, Jesse O. & Mary (H)
1839, 4, 24. Daniel rqct Center MM, to m Hannah H. Maybee
1839, 10, 23. Hannah rocf Center MM, dtd 1839, 10,16
1842, 5, 20. Isaac recrq
1843, 1, 25. Cynthia A. gct Upper Springfield MM, O.
1844, 3, 27. Elizabeth Mullen (form Jones) dis mou (H)
1848, 1, 26. Israel con mou (H)
1848, 11, 22. Israel gct Cincinnati MM (H)
1848, 12, 27. Owen gct Cherry Street MM, Phila.
1852, 2, 25. Isaac gct West Union MM, to m Elizabeth B. Johnson
1852, 6, 23. Isaac gct West Union MM, Ind.
1854, 3, 22. Isaac & w, Elizabeth B., rocf West Union MM, dtd 1854,3,13
1855, 5, 23. William dis disunity (H)
1855, 8, 22. Isaac & w, Elizabeth, gct West Union MM, Ind.
1855, 9, 26. Samuel gct Green Plain MM, to m Sarah Thorn
1856, 5, 21. Sarah T. rocf Green Plain MM, dtd 1856,3,12
1857, 3, 25. Sarah T. gct Green Plain MM
1860, 10, 24. Daniel & w, Hannah H., & ch, Eliza M., Charles W. & Daniel, gct Plainfield MM
1865, 3, 22. Annie M. gct White Water MM
1865, 5, 24. Isaac & w, Elizabeth B., rocf Wabash MM, Ind., dtd 1865,3,11
1865, 7, 26. Sarah gct Springfield MM
1866, 1, 24. Deborah rpd mcd (H)
1866, 1, 24. Sarah rpd mcd (H)
1866, 1, 24. Daniel rpd mcd (H)
1866, 8, 22. William dis mcd (H)
1866, 8, 22. John con mcd (H)
1866, 8, 22. Thomas con mcd (H)
1866, 8, 22. Deborah Johnson (form Jones) con mcd (H)
1866, 9, 26. Mary P. gct White Water MM
1867, 10, 23. Susan L. Morrow (form Jones) con mou
1868, 1, 22. Lydia E. (form Dakin) con mou
1869, 2, 24. Isaac & w, Elizabeth B., gct Poplar Ridge MM, Ind.
1871, 4, 26. Margaret gct White Lick MM, Ind.
1876, 10, 26. Margaret rocf Oskaloosa MM, Ia., dtd 1876,8,31
1882, 9, 20. Elizabeth Wharton (form Jones) rpd mcd (H)
1884, 12, 24. Anna Gause gct Green St. MM, Phila., Pa. (H)
1886, 1, 27. Gertrude recrq (H)
1887, 4, 20. Charles E. & ch, Abi M. & James B., recrq
1887, 5, 25. Rachel A. rocf Caesars Creek MM, dtd 1887,4,21
1890, 5, 21. Alice D. recrq (H)
1890, 5, 21. Sarah Alice recrq (H)
1895, 5, 22. Joseph T., Daniel B., John A., Thomas & Gertrude set off as mbr of Executive Mtg at Clear Creek (H)
1895, 5, 22. Alice D. (Jones) Branda set off as mbr of Executive Mtg at Clear Creek (H)
1898, 6, 22. Charles & s, James B., dropped from mbrp
1907, 2, 20. Celia recrq
1914, 3, 29. Della Downing relrq (H)

JOY
1887, 5, 25. Martha Elizabeth rocf Caesars Creek MM, dtd 1887,4,21
1913, 4, 23. S. Gordon & Sallie recrq

JUDKINS
1854, 8, 23. William N. & w, Mary, & ch, Charles P. & William, rocf Cincinnati MM, dtd 1854,8,17
1854, 8, 23. Rebecca E. rocf Cincinnati MM, dtd 1854,8,17
1856, 1, 23. William & w, Mary P., & ch, Charles P. & Edith, gct Cincinnati MM
1856, 1, 23. Rebecca E. gct Cincinnati MM

JUDY
1899, 2, 22. Lydia A. dropped from mbrp by rq

KEACH
1844, 8, 21. Rachel (form Burnett) con mou
1850, 6, 26. Rachel dis

KEEFER
1868, 11, 26. Jane M. & dt, Mary Sidney M., rocf Springborough MM, dtd 1868,10,22 (H)
1872, 8, 21. Mary Griest (form Keiffer) dis mcd (H)

KEESE
1895, 10, 23. Eunice M. gct Green Plain (H)

KEEVER
1917, 7, 29. Ida W., Edward & Wynne transferred to this mtg from Springboro (H)
1922, 5, 28. Stanley Wynne gct Duanesburg MM, to m Miriam Margaret Washburn (H)
1925, 8, 30. Jane, dt S. Wynne Keever, b 1924,10,20, recrq (H)
1925, 8, 30. S. Wynne gct Wakefield MM (H)

KELLY

----, --, --. Samuel b 1760,2,13 d 1851,2,4; m Hannah ----- b 1765,3,23 d 1839,7,26 (H)
Ch: Mary b 1789, 11, 22 d 1874, 7,18
Isaac " 1791, 10, 16 " 1822, 8,17
John " 1793, 11, 30
Thimothy " 1796, 3, 28
Samuel " 1798, 12, 17 d 1895,11,17
Moses " 1801, 4, 9 " 1803, 6,5
Moses " 1803, 9, 25 " 1878, 7,20
Anna " 1806, 5, 12 " 1835, 3,22

1814, 6, 1. Mary m Andrew WHITACRE

1824, 11, 3. Moses, s Samuel & Hannah, Warren Co., O., b 1803,9,25 d 1878,7,30; m at Miami, Abagale SATTERTHWAITE, dt Benjamin & Sarah, b 1805,10,10 d 1843,2,26 (H)
Ch: Ethan E. b 1825, 8, 9
Mary S. " 1831, 2, 5
John " 1834, 10, 18
Benjamin " 1837, 2, 9
Sarah L. " 1841, 6, 28
Moses m 2nd 1850,5,1 at Grove, Ann HATTON, dt Edward & Rachel, Warren Co., O., b 1819, 9,4 d 1906,5,26
Ch: Levi b 1853, 8, 27 d 1902, 4,26

----, --, --. Timothy b 1796,3,28; m Avis ----- b 1804,1,30 (H)
Dt: Jane S. b 1826, 2, 17

1829, 1, 8. Samuel, s Samuel & Hannah, Warren Co., O., b 1798,12,17 d 1895,11,17; m at Hopewell, Achsah STUBBS, dt Isaac & Margaret, Warren Co., O., b 1800,5,10 d 1840,10, 23 (H)
Ch: Margaret b 1831, 7, 27
Isaac " 1832, 9, 5
Anna " 1837, 3, 20
Hannah " 1840, 3, 16
Samuel m 2nd Ruthanna GAUSE d 1863,9,13 ae 51
Samuel m 3rd Sarah HAINES d 1877,4,27

1843, 5, 3. Samuel Jr., s Samuel & Hannah, Warren Co., O.; m at Miami, Ruthanna GAUSE, dt Samuel & Mary, Warren Co., O. (H)

----, --, --. Levi L. b 1853,8,27 d 1902,4,26; m Harriet SABIN b 1856,1,8 d 1906,2,19 (H)
Ch: Anna Mabel b 1877, 9, 14 d 1889,10,26
Alice Hortense " 1880, 1, 6 d 1892, 7, 7
Barton Hooper " 1884, 11, 22
Leona Christine " 1887, 1, 28
Ann Etta " 1889, 6, 20
Alicia " 1894, 4, 12

1805, 12, 12. Moses & w, Mary, & ch, Samuel & Anne, rocf Bush River MM, dtd 1805,8,31
1809, 12, 27. Cert rec for Charity from New Garden MM, N. C., dtd 1809,8,26, endorsed to White Water MM
1821, 10, 31. John dis mcd
1825, 1, 26. Timothy gct Green Plain MM, to m Avis Sleeper
1826, 2, 22. Avis rocf Green Plain MM, dtd 1826,1,2
1827, 12, 26. Timothy & w, Avis, & dt, Jane, gct Green Plain MM
1829, 2, 25. Samuel dis jH
1829, 3, 25. Moses dis jH
1829, 3, 25. Hannah dis jH
1829, 3, 25. Abigail dis jH
1829, 6, 24. Samuel Jr. dis jH
1829, 8, 26. Achsah dis jH
1829, 8, 26. Anna dis jH
1851, 5, 21. Ethan [Kelley] dis disunity (H)
1852, 10, 27. Anna (form Hatton) dis mou
1856, 11, 26. Ethen [Kelley] dis mou
1866, 11, 21. Sarah Roberts (form Kelley) dis mcd (H)
1868, 4, 22. Samuel [Kelley] gct Springborough MM, to m Sarah Pine (H)
1869, 3, 24. Sarah [Kelley] rocf Springborough MM, dtd 1869,1,28 (H)
1892, 9, 21. Harriet C. & ch, Barton Hoops, Christine Leona & Ann Etta, recrq; also dec dt, Alice Hortense, enrolled as mbr (H)
1895, 8, 28. Madora E. gct Londonderry MM
1920, 7, 25. Barton H. dropped from mbrp (H)

KELSEY

1870, 1, 26. Elizabeth (form Mather) con mou
1881, 1, 26. Elizabeth M. relrq

KEMP

1888, 4, 22. O. P. recrq

KENDALL

1808, 9, 10. William [Kenall] & w, Elizabeth, & ch, Joseph, William, Enion & Isaac, rocf Springfield MM, N. C., dtd 1806,9,6

KENDRICK

1824, 4, 28. Patience (form Barton) dis mou

KENTON

1824, 4, 28. Phebe (form Baker) dis mou

KENWORTHY

----, --, --. David & Dinah (H)
Ch: Sarah b 1796, 11, 6
Mary " 1800, 7, 25
Betty " 1805, 12, 12

1851, 10, 29. Jesse J., s William & Alice, Wayne Co., Ind.; m at Miami, Mary P. EVANS, dt Thomas & Hannah, Warren Co., O.

1804, 12, 13. David & w, Dinah, & ch, Sarah & Mary, rocf Cane Creek MM, S. C., dtd 1804, 10,20
1805, 6, 13. Jesse & w, Rachel, & ch, William & John, rocf Cane Creek MM, S. C., dtd 1805,2,16
1805, 8, 8. David & w, Tamar, & ch, Joshua, Isaac, William, Dinah & Mary, rocf Cane

KENWORTHY, continued
Creek MM, N. C., dtd 1805,5,4
1806, 6, 12. John & w, Rebecca, & ch, Olivar, William & Tamar, rocf Cane Creek MM, S. C., dtd 1806,2,15
1806, 6, 12. Ann rocf Cane Creek MM, S. C., dtd 1805,11,23
1808, 1, 14. Elisha & w, Mary, & ch, Sarah, Rachel, John, Tamar, Silas & Mary, rocf Cane Creek MM, dtd 1807,3,7
1821, 5, 30. Amos & w, Mary, & ch, William & Robert, rocf Westland MM
1852, 4, 21. Mary E. gct White Water MM

KERRICK
1906, 1, 21. James recrq
1906, 2, 21. Adra M. Beach rocf Ceasars Creek MM, dtd 1906,1,25

KERSEY
----, --, --. John b 1785,3,22; m Anna STEDDOM b 1788,12,15
Ch: Elizabeth b 1813, 11, 25
Henry " 1815, 2, 19
Martha " 1816, 11, 17
Thomas " 1818, 9, 8
Eleazar " 1820, 10, 7
John " 1823, 4, 8
Rebecca " 1825, 6, 21
Samuel " 1830, 6, 13
1823, 11, 6. Thomas, s Thomas & Rebekah, Clinton Co., O.; m at Turtle Creek, Letitia CRAIG, dt Samuel & Martha, Warren Co., O.
1832, 8, 24. Arena (Mote), dt Luke S. & Charity Mote, b
1843, 3, 30. Martha m John HORNADAY
1843, 11, 14. Elizabeth d bur Turtle Creek
1844, 11, 26. Anna d bur Turtle Creek
1846, 10, 1. Rebecca m Isaac JONES
----, --, --. Samuel & Arena Ellen
Ch: William
Rufus b 1865, 2, 18
Anna Mary " 1866, 8, 12
Madora
Elizabeth " 1868, 3, 14
Fanny Helen" 1869, 12, 25
1868, 9, 24. John d bur Turtle Creek

1805, 11, 14. Daniel rocf Springfield MM, N. C., dtd 1805,10,5
1807, 6, 11. Daniel gct Back Creek MM, N. C.
1813, 10, 27. Anna (form Steddom) rpd mcd
1815, 3, 29. John & dt, Elizabeth, rocf Center MM, dtd 1815,2,4
1824, 4, 28. Lettitia gct Springfield MM
1845, 4, 23. Thomas con mou
1855, 8, 22. Samuel gct Westfield MM, Ind.
1856, 6, 25. Samuel rocf Westfield MM, dtd 1856,5,1
1864, 2, 24. Samuel gct West Branch MM, to m Arena E. Mote
1865, 4, 26. Arena Ellen rocf West Branch MM, dtd 1865,4,13
1873, 4, 23. Thomas C. relrq
1908, 8, 26. Gertrude Von Hill rocf Chicago MM, Ill.

KEYS
1833, 6, 26. Stephen R. [Keese] gct Green Plain MM (H)
1877, 3, 21. Emma M. (form Burnett] rpd mcd (H)
1909, 1, 27. Warren recrq (H)
1919, 3, 30. J. Milton recrq (H)

KIGER
1840, 4, 22. Huldah con mou (H)

KIMBERLICK
1865, 4, 26. Amy gct Wapsinonoch MM, Ia. (H)

KIMBROUGH
1872, 6, 26. Caroline recrq
1872, 11, 30. Permelia & s, Ellsworth, rocf Springfield MM, dtd 1872,8,17

KINDLEY
----, --, --. Edward & Margaret (H)
Ch: Elizabeth b 1784, 5, 3
John " 1788, 4, 20
Rachel " 1786, 2, 22
Rebecca " 1790, 4, 4
Frederick " 1792, 5, 6
Isaac " 1794, 5, 8
Daniel " 1797, 9, 17
David " 1799, 12, 16
Mary " 1802, 3, 15
Dinah " 1804, 7, 30
Enoch " 1815, 11, 21
----, --, --. John b 1788,4,20; m Betty ----- b 1791,10,10 (H)
Ch: Jonathan b 1808, 9, 28
Joel " 1811, 1, 16
Sarah " 1813, 1, 7
Elizabeth " 1815, 4, 26
Ruth " 1817, 4, 30
1810, 8, 1. Rebekah m Samuel HARVEY
1822, 6, 12. Mary m Cornelius RATLIFF
1826, 11, 1. Dinah m Seth FURNACE
----, --, --. Frederick b 1792,5,6; m Mary ----- b 1803,4,23 (H)
Ch: Edward b 1831, 12, 29
Asa " 1833, 5, 7
Sarah " 1835, 3, 11
----, --, --. Enoch b 1815,11,21; m Susan ----
Ch: Daniel b 1839, 2, 23
Sarah E. " 1842, 10, 16
Margaret
Jane " 1844, 11, 22 d 1848, 7,30
Maryann " 1847, 6, 30 " 1850, 9,14
Davis " 1849, 8, 12
Emma " 1852, 8, 12
Susan " 1854, 11, 18
Davis " 1857, 6, 16
Cornelius " 1860, 5, 30

KINDLEY, continued
1809, 11, 4. Bette rocf Center MM, dtd 1809, 10,7
1813, 9, 29. Isaac gct Fall Creek MM, to m
1814, 3, 30. Ann rocf Fall Creek MM, dtd 1814,1,23
1817, 4, 30. Isaac [Kindly] & fam gct New Garden MM, Ind.
1820, 4, 26. John [Kenly] & fam gct Mill Creek MM
1829, 2, 25. Daniel [Kendley] dis jH
1829, 2, 25. Edward [Kendley] dis jH
1829, 2, 25. Frederick [Kendley] dis jH
1829, 3, 25. Margaret dis jH
1830, 3, 31. Frederic gct Green Plain MM, to m Mary Farr, Jr.
1836, 12, 21. Enoch dis mou & jH
1836, 12, 21. Enoch rpd mou (H)
1837, 3, 22. Edward & w, Margaret, gct Westfield MM (H)
1837, 4, 26. Daniel gct Westfield MM (H)
1837, 5, 24. Frederick & w, Mary, & ch, Edward, Asa, Sarah & Davis, gct Milford MM, Ind. (H)
1838, 7, 25. Enoch con mou (H)
1838, 12, 26. Enoch gct Westfield MM (H)
1856, 5, 21. Enoch & w, Susan, & ch, Daniel, Sarah, Eliza, Margaret Jane, Emily & Susan, rocf Westfield MM, dtd 1856,4,30
1859, 2, 23. Daniel dis mcd (H)
1861, 12, 25. Enoch & w, Susan, & ch, Margaret Jane, Emma, Susan, Davis & Cornelia, gct White Water MM, Ind. (H)
1861, 12, 25. Sarah gct White Water MM, Ind. (H)

KING
1823, 7, 30. Dean & w, Elizabeth, & dt, Rhoda Ann, rocf Cincinnati MM, dtd 1822,5,29
1823, 12, 31. Thomas recrq with permission of Stanford MM, N. Y.
1824, 7, 28. Dean gct White Water MM
1824, 8, 25. Sally recrq
1832, 2, 29. Thomas W. & w, Sally, & ch, Mary E., John T. & Henry D., gct White Water MM (H)
1856, 12, 24. Sarah (form Sabin) dis mcd (H)
1874, 3, 25. Quincy recrq
1874, 7, 22. Sarah recrq (H)
1875, 5, 26. Melissa A. recrq
1883, 4, 25. Abram L. & Charles E. recrq
1883, 4, 25. John A. recrq
1887, 3, 23. John A. relrq
1889, 12, 25. Martha E. rocf Ceasars Creek MM, dtd 1889,11,21
1897, 11, 24. Martha dropped from mbrp

KINSEY
1845, 4, 24. William G., s Nathaniel & Hannah, Hamilton Co., O.; m at Miami, Ann EVANS, dt Thomas & Hannah, Warren Co., O.
1850, 8, 13. Ann E. d bur Waynesville
----, --, --. Thomas W. b 1824,10,30 d 1894,3, 23; m Sarah E. ADAMS b 1836,7,13 (H)
Dt: Rachel C. b 1857, 3, 10

1845, 7, 23. Ann E. gct Cincinnati MM, endorsed back to this mtg 1845,10,25
1848, 6, --. William G. rocf Cincinnati MM, dtd 1848,7,18
1865, 7, 26. Thomas gct White Water MM
1917, 7, 29. Sarah E. & Rachel dropped from mbrp (H)

KIRBY
1805, 2, 14. Joseph recrq
1805, 6, 13. Sarah rocf Mount Holly MM, N. J., dtd 1805,2,7
1806, 4, 10. Mary (form Eachus) dis mou
1808, 3, 10. Sarah (form Mullen) con mou
1822, 7, 31. Sarah gct Green Plain MM
1830, 12, 29. Joseph dis jH
1831, 1, 26. Sarah dis jH
1835, 3, 25. Ann W. (form Strahl) dis mou (H)
1851, 1, 22. Eveline (form Scott) dis mcd (H)

KIRK
1875, 5, 26. Nora recrq

KITCHEN
1839, 5, 22. Ann (form Canby) rpd mou

KLEIN
1855, 10, 31. John E., s Madison & Hester, Warren Co., O.; m at Miami, Martha M. JOHNSON, dt Micajah & Rebecca, Warren Co., O.

1851, 3, 26. John Eberly [Klain] rocf Hopewell MM, Va., dtd 1851,3,6
1867, 8, 21. John E. & Martha M. gct Spring Creek MM

KLOPPER
1888, 3, 21. John recrq

KNIGHT
1866, 1, 24. Elizabeth C. rocf Dover MM, Ind.
1867, 7, 24. Elizabeth C. Steddom (form Knight) con mou
1870, 4, 20. Eliza Ann rocf Dover MM, dtd 1870,2,23
1871, 1, 25. Eliza Ann gct Dover MM

KOLWOORD
1920, 2, 25. Vera McMillan gct Muncie MM, Ind.

KOOGLER
1888, 3, 21. Wm. H. & Louisa recrq

KRESS
1888, 2, 22. Clara recrq

LACHEM
1884, 4, 23. Mary H. recrq

LACHEM, continued
1884, 5, 21. Martin Howard recrq
1886, 2, 24. Howard gct Hesper MM, Kans.

LACY
1898, 6, 22. Thomas rocf Wilmington MM, O.

LAFETRE
1825, 1, 26. Benjamin gct Shrewsbury MM, N.J.
1826, 7, 26. Robert dis mcd
1899, 7, 26. Mary [LaFetra] dropped from mbrp (H)

LAKE
1883, 5, 23. Park recrq

LAMB
1805, 12, 12. Josiah & w, Naomi, & ch, John, Esom, Hannah, Jonothan, Reuben & Ruth, rocf Piney Grove MM, S. C., dtd 1804,7,21, endorsed by Lost Creek MM, 1805,9,28
1807, 3, 12. Josiah & fam gct West Branch MM
1808, 7, 14. John rocf Piney Woods MM, dtd 1808,3,5
1809, 2, 11. Thomas rocf Piney Woods MM, dtd 1808,3,5

LANCASTER
1811, 10, 30. Rachel rocf West Branch MM, dtd 1811,10,24
1825, 2, 23. Rachel gct Springfield MM
1901, 4, 24. Phebe & s, Edgar Burkhart, gct Springfield MM

LANE
1809, 9, 9. Hannah rocf Deep River MM, N.C., dtd 1807,10,5

LARKIN
----, --, --. John S. b 1807,1,13 d 1867,2,5; m Sarah ----- b 1812,8,8 d before 1855 (H)
Ch: Isaac b 1833, 11, 23
Mary Ann " 1836, 2, 6
Elijah "
Margaret Edna " 1840, 12, 12 d 1888, 1,13
Rachel " 1842, 12, 5
Martha " 1845, 10, 5
John
William " 1850, 11, 2
----, --, --. Joseph b 1813,1,21 d 1852,10,24; m Margaret ----- b 1815,1,10 d 1866,5,30 (H)
Ch: Alonzo b 1841, 8, 13
Jesse F. " 1842, 11, 6
Martha Ann " 1844, 1, 23 d 1846,10,28
Salkeld " 1845, 11, 21
Mary F. " 1847, 10, 1
Nathan " 1849, 3, 9
Rachel S. " 1850, 11, 16
1866, 1, 24. Mary, Rachel, S. & Nathan, minors, rec in mbrp; form mbr of Fall Creek or Centre MM, which had been laid down (H)
1866, 1, 24. Martha rpd mcd (H)
1866, 1, 24. Rachel Sr. rpd mcd (H)
1866, 1, 24. Margaret rpd mcd (H)
1866, 1, 24. Alonsa rpd mcd (H)
1866, 1, 24. Jesse rpd mcd (H)
1866, 8, 22. Mary Ann Huzzey (form Larkins) rpd mcd (H)
1866, 8, 22. John rpd mcd (H)
1866, 8, 22. Isaac dis mcd (H)
1866, 8, 22. Elijah rpd mcd; dropped from mbrp (H)
1885, 6, 24. Alonzo relrq to jas (H)
1895, 5, 22. Jesse F., Salkeld, Mary F., Nathan & William set off as mbr of Executive Mtg at Clear Creek (H)
1911, 1, 25. Alonzo & Elizabeth rocf Clear Creek MM, O., dtd 1910,12,--
1912, 10, 24. Elizabeth & Alonzo gct Clear Creek MM, O.
1920, 7, 25. Jesse H., A. Claire & Mary F. dropped from mbrp (H)

LASHLEY
1884, 5, 28. Florence Emma, William & Robert B. recrq
1895, 3, 27. Alfred & Sarah J. recrq
1902, 6, 25. Alfred gct Springfield MM
1902, 11, 26. Robert Boon gct Springfield MM
1905, 10, 25. Alfred rocf Springfield MM
1905, 10, 25. Robert rocf Springfield MM
1916, 4, 21. Alfred gct La Harpe MM, Kans.

LATHROP
1829, 11, 26. Rebecca m Robert HILL (H)

1815, 12, 21. Rebecca (form Wright) dis mou
1819, 1, 27. Rebecca rst
1824, 6, 30. Emily, dt Rebekah, recrq
1829, 3, 25. Rebecca [Lothrop] dis jH
1830, 3, 31. Rebecca Hill & dt, Emily Lathrop, gct White Water MM (H)

LAWRENCE
1889, 4, 24. Caroline B. relrq (H)

LAZENBY
1866, 1, 24. Mary [Lasenbee] rpd mcd (H)
1885, 8, 26. Mary M. (form Hiatt) relrq (H)

LEEDS
----, --, --. Warner M. & Elizabeth (H)
Dt: Anna b 1820, 6, 17

1819, 8, 25. Elizabeth B. (form Bateman) dis mcd
1820, 4, 26. Warner M. rpd mcd
1821, 4, 25. Elizabeth B. recrq
1821, 7, 25. Warner M. rocf Stroudsburg MM, Pa., dtd 1821,6,21

LEEDS, continued
1821, 9, 26. Ann recrq of parents, Warner & Elizabeth B.
1822, 9, 25. Warner M. & w, Elizabeth, & dt, Anna, gct White Water MM, Ind.
1830, 12, 29. Ann & ch, Lettitia Craig, Vincent,Augustus, Ann E. & William C., rocf Springborough MM, dtd 1830,11,23 (H)
1831, 4, 27. Ann L. & ch, Letitia Craig, Vincent Augustus, Ann C. & William C., gct White Water MM, Ind. (H)

LEEKE
----, --, --. Hannah M. (Lupton) b 1814,10,1 d 1898,12,9 (H)
1892, 4, 20. C. Park [Leak] dis

LEGG
1871, 9, 20. Sarah J. recrq

LEONARD
1806, 10, 9. Ezekiel & w, Rebecca, & ch, Mary, Thomas & Hannah, rocf New Garden MM, N.C., dtd 1804,7,28
1807, 5, 4. John & w, Abigail, rocf Center MM, N. C., dtd 1807,2,21
1866, 1, 24. Susan rec in mbrp; form mbr of Fall Creek or Centre MM which had been laid down (H)
1867, 11, 20. Susan H. gct White Water MM, Ind. (H)

LEWIS
----, --, --. Jehu b 1792,7,13; m Eleanor ---- b 1794,12,22 (H)

Ch:				
	Betsey	b 1812,	9,	17
	Joel	" 1814,	3,	18
	Moses	" 1816,	4,	24

----, --, --. Jesse m Hannah HARVEY

Ch:				
	Sarah	b 1829,	12,	24
	Caleb	" 1832,	4,	10
	Nancy	" 1834,	8,	16
	Elizabeth	" 1836,	1,	30
	Phebe	" 1841,	1,	17
	Clark	" 1843,	4,	27
	Amos			

1842, 4, 27. Phebe d
1854, 11, 30. Caleb, s Jesse & Hannah, Warren Co., O., b 1832,4,10; m at Harveysburgh, Rhoda Ann GREEN, dt David & Mary, Warren Co., O., b 1834,5,16 (H)
----, --, --. Christopher b 1831,9,16; m Louisa HOLLOWELL b 1834,9,22 (H)

Ch:				
	Eugene C.	b 1860,	6,	20
	Walter H.	" 1862,	11,	17
	Marion (woman)	" 1866,	5,	25

1805, 4, 11. Sarah rocf Chesterfield MM, N.J., dtd 1804,10,2
1805, 5, 9. Thomas & w, Rachel, & ch, Charity, Zimri, William, Martha & Isaac, rocf Bush River MM, S. C., dtd 1805,2,23
1806, 10, 9. Caleb & w, Susannah, & ch, Isaac & Thomas, rocf Bush River MM, S.C., dtd 1806,7,26
1806, 10, 9. Thomas rocf Bush River MM, S.C., dtd 1806,7,26
1806, 10, 9. Martha & ch, Hester & Mary, rocf Bush River MM, dtd 1806,7,26
1808, 1, 14. William & w, Sarah, & dt, Elizabeth, rocf Hopewell MM, dtd 1807,4,6
1813, 9, 29. Nathan rocf Goose Creek MM, Va., dtd 1813,5,6
1813, 10, 27. Enoch & w rocf Goose Creek MM, dtd 1813,9,2
1815, 3, 29. John & w, Eleanor, & ch, Joel & Betsy, rocf Mt. Pleasant MM, Va., dtd 1814,5,28
1816, 1, 31. Joel & w, Sarah, & ch, Daniel, rocf South River MM, Va., dtd 1815,10,20
1819, 5, 25. Jehu & fam gct Clear Creek MM
1824, 1, 28. Daniel gct Cesars Creek MM
1824, 2, 25. Joel & fam gct Clear Creek MM
1836, 7, 27. Jesse & w, Hannah, & ch, Sarah, Caleb H., Nancy & Elizabeth, rocf Cesars Creek MM, dtd 1836,6,23
1838, 4, 23. Jonah rocf Clear Creek MM, dtd 1838,3,20
1838, 7, 25. Lavina (form Crew) con mou
1842, 11, 23. Jonah & fam gct Bloomfield MM
1863, 7, 22. Joseph P. Jessop gct Center MM, to m Mary B. Lewis (H)
1865, 4, 26. Enoch gct Wapsinonoch MM, Ia. (H)
1866, 1, 24. Enoch & fam dropped from mbrp; form mbr of Fall Creek or Centre MM which had been laid down (H)
1866, 8, 22. Christopher rpd mcd; dropped from mbrp (H)
1868, 4, 22. George H. gct White Water MM, Ind. (H)
1871, 5, 24. Caleb H. & w, Rhoda Ann & Martin Clarkson Young, a minor, gct Saline MM, Ill.
1871, 5, 24. Clark E., Elizabeth H. & Amos, brothers & sister, gct Saline MM, Ill.
1878, 9, 25. Christopher & w, Louisa, & ch, Eugene C., Walter C. & Marion, recrq (H)
1887, 4, 20. Lizzie L., Ulysses G. & Olive L. recrq
1887, 4, 20. Walter H. gct Birmingham MM, Pa. (H)
1888, 1, 25. Betsy, Joel & Moses dropped from mbrp (H)
1892, 10, 26. Lizzie & Olive relrq
1895, 5, 22. Christopher, Louisa K. & Eugene C. set off as mbr of Executive Mtg at Clear Creek (H)
1909, 9, 22. Olive Parshall relrq
1909, 10, 27. Grant dropped from mbrp

LIBOLE
1808, 4, 14. Sarah Airhart (Ehrhardt) (form Libole) dis mou

LIGHTFOOT
1811, 5, 29. Hannah & dt rocf Sadsbury MM, dtd 1810,12,4

LIMING
1889, 9, 25. Homer & Eliza recrq

LINDAMOOD
1889, 6, 26. Sarah E. & Alta recrq

LINDSEY
1832, 9, 26. Mahala I. J. Johnson (form Lindsey) con mou (H)
1848, 10, 25. Mahala (form Johnson)dis mou
1852, 9, 22. Mahala, w James, gct Fall Creek MM, Ind. (H)
1853, 1, 26. Cert granted Mahala to Fall Creek MM, Ind. 1852,9mo returned with information she lived too remote from mtg

LINTON
1806, 1, 22. David, s Samuel & Elizabeth, Warren Co., O.; m at Miami, Lettitia SILVER, dt Seth & Mary, Warren Co., O.
1806, 12, 31. Nathan, s Samuel & Elizabeth, Warren Co., O.; m at Lees Creek, Rachel SMITH, dt Seth & Elizabeth, Hiland Co.,O.

1828, 3, 26. Samuel dis
1830, 3, 31. Allen dis jH
1832, 9, 26. William dis jH
1836, 6, 22. Seth S. dis disunity
1846, 1, 21. Jonathan B. rocf Salem MM, dtd 1845,12,12
1846, 1, 21. Elizabeth & s, James William, rocf Center MM, dtd 1845,12,17
1846, 5, 27. Elizabeth & s, James William, gct Center MM
1882, 6, 21. Robert & w, Almira, & dt, Ethel, rocf Ceasars Creek MM, dtd 1882,5,25
1896, 4, 22. Mary B. (form Butterworth) con mcd (H)
1902, 10, 22. Mary Butterworth relrq (H)

LIPPENCOTT
1850, 6, 26. Pennington & w, Mary, & ch, Abigail B., John H. & Hannah B., rocf Springborough MM, dtd 1850,4,25 (H)
1851, 5, 21. Pennington & w, Mary G., & ch, Abigail B. & John H., gct Clear Creek MM, Ill. (H)
1878, 5, 22. Rebecca Ann recrq
1881, 4, 20. Oswell recrq
1883, 4, 25. Sadie recrq
1884, 3, 26. Oswell [Lippincott] gct Wilmington MM, O.
1884, 3, 26. William [Lippincott] gct Wilmington MM
1884, 8, 27. Charles rocf Cesars Creek MM, dtd 1884,6,26

LITTLE
1806, 4, 10. Mary (form Clerk) dis mou

LITTLER
1806, 5, 8. Mary (form Smith) dis mou

LIVINGSTON
1820, 7, 26. James rocf Center MM, Pa., dtd 1820,1,15
1822, 3, 27. James rpd mcd
1823, 3, 26. Tamar rocf Center MM, Pa., dtd 1819,12,18
1823, 4, 30. James gct New Garden MM, Ind.
1824, 10, 27. Tamar gct New Garden MM, Ind.

LLOYD
1862, 10, 29. Samuel, s Isaac & Ruth, Belmont Co., O.; m at Waynesville, Deborah J. STANTON, dt James & Ann, Warren Co.,O.

1863, 1, 21. Deborah J. gct Short Creek MM O.

LODE
1844, 10, 23. Matilda (form Doughtman) dis mou (H)

LODGE
1814, 11, 30. Jasabed & w, Sarah, & ch, William Johnson, Laban, Nelson, Celene & Caleb, rocf South River MM, Va., dtd 1814, 9,10

LONGACRE
1886, 8, 25. Edwin L. & w, Martha C., & ch, Isaac J., Lucy Ellen & Edwin B., recrq
1889, 9, 25. Martha E. & ch relrq
1892, 4, 20. Edwin relrq

LONGSTRETH
1842, 7, 17. Lambert, s William & Martha (Coate), b
1843, 12, 19. Martha d bur Turtle Creek
----, --, --. Lambert d bur Turtle Creek
----, --, --. Rachel P. b 1818,3,30 d 1887,2, 12 (H)

1817, 8, 27. Jacob rocf Phila. MM, dtd 1817, 5,29
1841, 4, 21. William recrq
1841, 7, 21. William gct Center MM, to m Martha Coate
1842, 6, 22. Martha rocf Center MM, dtd 1842, 2,16
1849, 5, 23. William gct Springfield MM, to m Hannah Cougle
1849, 12, 26. Hannah C. rocf Springfield MM, dtd 1849,10,20
1852, 4, 21. Rachel P. rocf Center MM, dtd 1852,2,19 (H)
1852, 9, 22. William & fam gct Mill Creek MM

LOTZ
1916, 3, 22. Erenst rocf Wilmington MM, dtd 1916,3,8

LOWNES
----, --, --. ----- [Lowndes] m Anna BIRDSALL b 1809,11,9 d 1887,9,6 (H)
Dt: Miriam b 1837, 4, 26

1867, 3, 27. Rebecca Whitacre (form Lownes) con mcd; mbr Springboro MM (H)
1870, 4, 20. Annie & Miriam [Lowdnes] rocf Springboro MM, dtd 1869,5,27 (H)
1877, 6, 20. Elizabeth A. Rust (form Lownes) con mcd (H)
1891, 10, 21. Miriam [Lowens] relrq (H)

LUKENS
----, --, --. Levi b 1767,6,24 d 1860,1,3; m Elizabeth CLEAVER b 1763,7,1 d 1831,2,2 (H)
Ch: Rachel b 1796, 10, 24 d 1879, 5,25
Joseph " 1797, 12, 28 " 1885, 3,23
Benjamin " 1799, 11, 4 " 1874,10, 6
John " 1801, 7, 9
Salathiel " 1803, 9, 12 " 1885, 9,30
Lewis " 1805, 12, 25 " 1807,10,12
Mary " 1810, 1, 1
----, --, --. Louisa b 1810,12,19 d 1880,2,7 (H)
1817, 3, 5. Rachel m Edward HATTON
1822, 2, 13. Joseph [Lewkins], s Levi & Elizabeth, Warren Co., O.; m at Waynesville, Hannah BROWN, dt Clayton & Elizabeth, Burlington Co., N. J.
1823, 3, 5. Benjamin, s Levi & Elizabeth, Warren Co., O.; m at Miami, Mary SATTERTHWAITE, dt Benjamin & Mary
----, --, --. Joseph [Lukins] b 1797,12,28; d 1885,3,23; m Hannah BROWN b 1795,6,20 d 1868,2,29 (H)
Ch: Elizabeth b 1824, 2, 15 d 1827, 2, 2
Levi " 1825, 12, 25 " 1912,10,29
Mary " 1828, 11, 29
Clayton " 1831, 3, 20
William " 1834, 8, 9
Joseph m 2nd Elcy HOWLAND
1832, 9, 12. Mary L. m Benjamin SATTERTHWAITE (H)
----, --, --. Rachel b 1843,4,4 d 1877,1,31
----, --, --. William m Sarah MACY b 1838,5,17 (H)
Ch: Charles E. b 1861, 12, 23

1808, 7, 14. Levi & w, Elizabeth, & ch, Rachel, Joseph, Benjamin, John & Salathiel, rocf Hopewell MM, dtd 1807,12,7
1825, 1, 26. John dis
1829, 5, 27. Benjamin dis jH
1829, 5, 27. Joseph dis jH
1829, 5, 27. Levi dis jH
1829, 5, 27. Elizabeth [Lukins] dis
1829, 5, 27. Mary [Lukins] dis
1829, 5, 27. Mary S. [Lukins] dis
1832, 8, 29. Salathiel dis mou (H)
1832, 11, 21. Salathiel dis mou
1834, 4, 23. Louisa recrq (H)
1852, 9, 22. Louisa, w Salathiel, gct Green Plain MM (H)
1855, 11, 21. Mary L. Haines (form Lukens) dis mou
1856, 10, 22. Mary Haynes (form Lukens) dis mcd (H)
1860, 6, 20. Sarah L. Harvey (form Lukins) dis mcd (H)
1862, 7, 23. William dis mcd (H)
1863, 4, 22. Clayton dis disunity (H)
1867, 6, 26. Louisa [Lukins] rocf Green Plain MM, dtd 1867,5,15 (H)
1867, 12, 25. Jane F. rocf Goshen MM, dtd 1867,11,23
1870, 4, 20. Rachel recrq (H)
1870, 10, 25. Tacy [Lukins] (form Ham) dis mou
1874, 7, 22. Mary Emma & s, John S., rocf Cesars Creek MM
1883, 3, 21. Charles E. recrq (H)
1885, 4, 22. Sarah recrq
1889, 7, 24. Levi [Lukins], s Joseph, dropped from mbrp (H)
1893, 3, 22. Hattie [Lukins] recrq
1893, 6, 21. Charles E. gct Chicago Executive MM, Ill. (H)
1895, 7, 24. Mary Emily & dt, Hattie, gct Wilmington MM, O.
1896, 1, 22. Tacy recrq
1904, 5, 25. Edward M. recrq (H)

LUNDY
1805, 4, 11. Nathan rocf Mount Pleasant MM, Va., dtd 1804,8,25

LUPTON
1805, 4, 17. Grace m William POPE
1807, 3, 18. Lydia m Jonathan SANDERS

1804, 4, 12. Solomon & w, Rachel, rocf Concord MM, O., dtd 1803,12,17
1804, 4, 12. William & w, Bathsheba, & ch, Lydia, Grace, Jonathan, Allen, Mary, Isaac, William, Davis & Mahlon, rocf Hopewell MM dtd 1803,10,3

LUTZ
1897, 4, 21. Laura (form Summers) relrq

LYNCH
----, --, --. Edward & Mary
Ch: Charles
Mary
Sally
Jonah
Lavina
Edwin
1856, 4, 23. Mary d bur Waynesville

1806, 8, 14. Charity rocf Bush River MM, dtd 1806,5,31
1817, 7, 30. Charity rocf Cincinnati MM, dtd 1817,6,19
1847, 11, 24. Edward & w, Mary, rocf Cincinnati MM, O., dtd 1847,11,18
1847, 11, 24. Sally & Mary rocf Cincinnati

LYNCH, continued
MM, O., dtd 1847,11,18; cert lost
1850, 9, 25. Charles E. rocf Cincinnati MM, dtd 1850,8,15
1866, 8, 22. Sally & Mary Jr. rocf Cincinnati MM, dtd 1847,11,18; cert had been lost

LYNDER
1875, 4, 21. William recrq

McAFEE
1907, 2, 20. Effie L. D. gct New York MM (H)

McCAULEY
1883, 6, 20. Carrie recrq
1884, 1, 23. Carrie relrq
1888, 10, 24. Caroline recrq

McCAY
1865, 9, 20. Martha N. con mcd (H)

McCLURE
1807, 1, 8. Robert & w, Margery, & ch, John, Mary, Margery, Robert & Rosanna, rocf Bush River MM, S. C., dtd 1806,7,26
1809, 9, 9. Mary Benbow (form McClure) dis mou
1811, 4, 24. Margery Jeweland (form McClure) con mou

McCOMAS
1883, 5, 23. Eliza recrq
1889, 4, 24. Maggie rocf Ceasars Creek MM
1891, 6, 24. Margaretta relrq
1911, 3, 22. Eliza relrq

McCOWAN
1841, 2, 24. Maria rocf Centre MM, dtd 1840, 10,15 (H)

McCOY
1806, 6, 12. Jane [McKoy] rocf Crooked Run MM, Va., dtd 1805,10,5
1824, 1, 28. Haines rocf Hopewell MM, dtd 1823,3,6
1832, 5, 23. Amos rocf Hopewell MM, Va., dtd 1832,4,4
1835, 6, 24. Amos dis mou

McDANIEL
1805, 6, 13. Jemima [McDanniel] & dt, Lydia, rocf Bush River MM, S. C., dtd 1805,2,23
1806, 12, 11. Sarah (form Stubbs) con mou

McDONALD
1805, 7, 11. Elizabeth [McDonnald] rocf Bush River MM, S. C., dtd 1804,11,24
1814, 11, 30. Sarah gct Elk MM
1822, 7, 31. Jacob Homer gct Cesars Creek MM, to m Lydia McDonald
1905, 2, 22. Sabin recrq

McFAUL
1889, 7, 24. Mary E. (form Ennis) rpd mcd (H)
1890, 3, 26. Mary Elizabeth gct Chicago Executive Mtg, Ill. (H)

McGLADE
1876, 3, 22. Robert recrq

McKAY
1921, 3, 23. E. Harold & w, Ila H., & ch, Allen H., rocf Dover MM, dtd 1920,2,17
1921, 3, 23. Howard F. & w, Edith S., & ch, Robert F. & Donald S., rocf Dover MM, dtd 1921,2,17

McKINNEY
----, --, --. William H. b 1827,3,31 d 1897, 7,25; m Mary Jane WHITACRE b 1824,8,29 (H)

Ch:		
Clara	b 1855, 12, 17	[d 1902,5,12
Corah	" 1859, 5, 12	
William H.	" 1862, 5, 3	d 1889, 9, 3
Mary	" 1866, 3, 1	
Adah	" 1869, 5, 7	

1856, 6, 25. Mary Jane (form Meredith) con mcd (H)
1872, 8, 21. William R., & ch, Clara, Corah, William, Mary & Adah, recrq (H)
1877, 4, 25. Clara Bicket (form McKinney) rpd mcd (H)
1898, 1, 26. Clara M. Beckett (form McKinney) released from mbrp (H)

McKINSEY
1816, 4, 24. Mary recrq
1900, 9, 26. Minnie & Laura Elizabeth recrq

McKNIGHT
1870, 4, 20. Eliza A. rocf Dover MM, Ind.

MacLAN
1805, 4, 11. Mary rocf New Hope MM, Tenn., dtd 1804,11,17

McMILLAN
1806, 7, 10. David & w, Hannah, & ch, Josiah, Eli, Deborah, Mary & David, rocf Newberry MM, dtd 1805,11,9
1806, 7, 10. Jonothan & ch, William, Jane & Newton, rocf Newberry MM, dtd 1806,4,12
1806, 7, 10. William rocf Newberry MM, dtd 1806,4,12
1806, 10, 9. Lydia rocf Warrington MM, Pa., dtd 1806,6,7
1807, 6, 11. Lydia Jay (form McMillan) con mou
1863, 12, 23. Eliza rocf Cincinnati MM, dtd 1863,11,19
1909, 2, 24. Charles rocf Dover MM
1911, 3, 22. Charles gl
1915, 1, 27. Joseph & w, Emma, & ch, Rebecca, Vera, Robert, Willis, Mark, Ruth, Dillon, Eva, Adelbert, Mabel & Herbert, rocf Cen-

McMILLAN, continued
ter MM, dtd 1914,12,16
1916, 4, 26. Robert gct Springfield MM
1916, 12, 7. John & w, Esther, rocf Leesburg MM, O., dtd 1916,11,16

McPHAIL
1903, 4, 22. Caroline gct Wilmington MM

McPHERSON
1807, 6, 11. Isaac & w, Betty, & dt, Ann, rocf Hopewell MM, dtd 1806,12,1

McVEY
1866, 8, 22. Ruth (form Eastlock) con mcd (H)
1885, 8, 26. Ruth (form Thornburg) relrq (H)

McWADE
1811, 4, 24. Achsah recrq

MACY
----, --, --. David b 1784,5,20 d 1863,11,14; m Sarah DICKS b 1790,6,9 d 1866,10,2 (H)
Ch: Micajah T. b 1808, 5, 15 d 1828,11,14
William D. " 1809, 11, 18 " 1883,--,--
Zalinda " 1811, 8, 11 " 1894, 1,26
Nathan D. " 1813, 7, 20 " 1899, 4, 7
Edward L. " 1816. 1. 9 " 1904.12.25
Milton T. b 1817, 11, 25
Abigail F. " 1824, 2, 24 " 1864,11, 1
1831, 9, 7. Zalinda m Edward ANTRAM (H)
1840, 2, 26. Milton T., s David & Sarah, Warren Co., O.; m at Salt-run, Caroline M. WALES, dt Isaac & Ruth, Warren Co., O. (H)

1814, 8, 31. George & w, Elizabeth, & ch, Margaret, Thomas, Barnard & Sarah, rocf Nantucket MM, dtd 1814,4,28
1816, 8, 28. David & w, Sarah, & ch, Micajah, Terrill, William, Zalinda & Nathan, rocf New Garden MM, dtd 1815,10,28
1829, 5, 27. David dis jH
1829, 5, 27. Sarah Mary dis jH
1829, 8, 26. William dis jH
1829, 8, 26. Zalinda dis jH
1837, 6, 21. Nathan con mou (H)
1837, 7, 26. Nathan D. dis mou & jH
1837, 12, 27. William con mou (H)
1840, 4, 22. Caroline M. (form Wales) dis mou & jH
1840, 11, 25. Milton dis mou & jH
1847, 6, 23. Nathan con mou (H)
1850, 10, 23. William dis disunity (H)
1851, 11, 26. Milton dis mcd (H)

MADDEN
----, --, --. Hiram m Hannah HARVEY b 1828,8,5
Ch: Arthur
Anna
Charles b 1844, 6, 18

1860, 1, 25. Hiram Jr. & w, Hannah C., & ch, Arthur & Anna Maria, rocf Springfield MM, dtd 1859,10,15
1900, 7, 25. Arthur W. gct Springfield MM
1902, 4, 23. Charles relrq

MADDOCK
1807, 11, 26. Elenor m James COOK

1805, 7, 11. Samuel & w, Rachel, & ch, Eleanor, rocf Wrightsboro MM, dtd 1805,4,5
1806, 6, 12. Francis rocf Wrightsboro MM, dtd 1805,4,6
1807, 4, 9. Nathan [Maddox] rocf Bush River MM, dtd 1806,10,25
1827, 4, 25. Martha [Mattack] rocf Evesham MM, N. J., dtd 1827,2,9

MADOR
1806, 11, 20. Francis, s Samuel, Butlar Co., O.; m at Elk Creek, Phebe COOK, dt Eli, Butler Co., O.

MANNINGTON
1847, 10, 27. Charity [Manington] (form Adams) dis mou (H)
1884, 5, 28. Lewis F. recrq
1885, 7, 22. Lewis F. relrq

MARSH
1917, 9, 30. Glenna & Hobart recrq (H)
1920, 7, 25. Hobart dropped from mbrp (H)

MART
1887, 4, 20. Sylvester E., Alice W., Edwin G., Carrie Earl, Harry Leroy & Frances Eugene, recrq
1898, 2, 23. Sylvester rocf Wilmington MM
1916, 5, 24. S. E., Alice & Elizabeth gct Dayton MM

MARTIN
1799, 7, 27. Abigail b

1825, 7, 27. Abigail (form Thomas) con mou
1886, 9, 22. Daniel C. & w, Margaret H., recrq
1888, 6, 20. Daniel C. & Margaret H. relrq
1914, 10, 21. Mary E. rocf Urbana MM
1917, 6, 20. Mary E. gct Pennville MM

MASON
1806, 9, 7. Ruth m Job CARR

1805, 6, 13. Ruth rocf Salem MM, N. J., dtd 1805,2,25

MASSIE
1805, 12, 12. Jane rocf Springfield MM,N.C., dtd 1805,9,28

MATHER
----, --, --. Richard b 1783,9,26; m Elizabeth LONGSTRETH b 1783,2,2
Ch: David b 1810, 1, 11

MATHER, Richard & Elizabeth, continued
Ch: Martha L. b 1812, 1, 3
Ann " 1814, 2, 8
Charles L. " 1816, 1, 30
Phineas R. " 1818, 2, 11
Susanna L. " 1820, 5, 29
Benjamin " 1822, 11, 5
Sarah B. " 1825, 3, 5
Joseph " 1827, 11, 29
1820, 7, 5. George, s Richard & Sarah, Warren Co., O.; m at Waynesville, Mary RICKETT, dt Thomas & Abigail, Warren Co., O.
1834, 5, 1. Martha L. m Samuel JONES
1838, 2, 1. David, s Richard & Elizabeth, Warren Co., O., b 1810,1,11; m at Turtle Creek, Lurana STEDDOM, dt Samuel & Susanna, Warren Co., O., b 1817,6,14
Ch: Susanna b 1838, 11, 9 d in infancy
Charles " 1840, 10, 11
Susanna " 1842, 9, 29
Elizabeth " 1844, 11, 20
Henry " 1847, 1, 4
Samuel " 1850, 1, 22
David Lindley " 1852, 6, 20
David m 2nd Louisa CARL
1842, 9, 14. Susanna d bur Turtle Creek
1844, 9, 26. Ann m David S. HORNEY
1844, 9, 26. Susanna L. m Jonathan HORNEY
1845, 2, 22. Elizabeth d ae 62 (an elder)
- --, --, --. Phineas B. m Ruth Ann POOLE
Ch: John P. b 1846, 3, 5
1852, 11, 4. Sarah B. m Joel HARVEY
1854, 3, 1. Richard, s Benjamin & Elizabeth, Warren Co., O.; m at Miami, Ruth BROWN, dt Joseph & Dinah, Warren Co., O.
1862, 10, 1. Joseph, s Richard & Elizabeth, Clinton Co., O.; m at Waynesville, Mary Ann BROWN, dt Asher & Esther J., Warren Co., O.
1864, 6, 2. Susan m Isaac E. HAWKINS
----, --, --. Charles bur Turtle Creek

1815, 5, 31. Richard & w, Elizabeth, & ch, David, Martha, Longstreth & Ann, rocf Darby MM, Pa., dtd 1815,3,16
1819, 10, 27. Richard & w, Sarah, & ch, George, Sarah & McIlvaine, rocf Phila. MM, dtd 1819,7,29
1820, 8, 20. Lydia rocf Abington MM, Pa., dtd 1820,4,24
1823, 11, 26. George dis
1826, 8, 30. Richard [Mathers] & fam gct Cincinnati MM
1826, 9, 27. Mary & ch gct Cincinnati MM
1838, 4, 23. Mary & ch, Rachel, Lucy, Sarah & Mary, rocf Mill Creek MM, dtd 1837,12,12
1842, 6, 22. Charles L. gct Upper Darby MM (cert returned for disunity)
1843, 11, 22. Mary dis jas
1843, 9, 20. Lucy Wharton (form Mather) dis mou
1844, 8, 21. Phineas R. gct White Water MM, to m Ruth Ann Pool
1844, 9, 25. Sarah dis jas
1845, 3, 26. Ruth Ann rocf White Water MM, dtd 1845,2,26
1849, 9, 26. Phineas R. & w, Ruth Ann, & ch, John R. & Elizabeth C., gct White Water MM
1851, 7, 23. Richard gct WD MM, Pa.
1851, 12, 24. Joseph C. gct Springfield MM, to m Louisa Hadley
1854, 5, 24. Joseph gct Springfield MM
1857, 10, 21. Richard rocf Burlington MM, N.J. dtd 1858,8,6
1863, 3, 25. Mary Ann gct Springfield MM
1863, 8, 26. David gct Goshen MM, to m Louisa A. Curl
1863, 12, 23. Louisa A. rocf Goshen MM, dtd 1863,11,21
1870, 1, 26. Elizabeth M. Kelsey (form Mather) con mou
1872, 1, 24. David & w, Louisa A., & s, David L., gct New Garden MM, Ind.
1872, 2, 21. Samuel gct New Garden MM, Ind.
1881, 3, 23. Henry gct White Water MM
1892, 7, 27. Charles, Ethan, Anna & Lillie relrq
1898, 6, 22. William relrq

MATHEWMAN
1887, 3, 23. Hannah J. & Rena rec by letter
1890, 3, 26. Hannah J. & dt, Rena, relrq

MATTHEWS
----, --, --. Oliver [Mathews] m Phebe WRIGHT
Ch: Joel b 1799, 11, 25
William " 1801, 9, 23
Ann " 1803, 10, 28
Jonathan " 1806, 6, 8
Susanna " 1808, 10, 30
Elizabeth " 1811, 9, 15
Aquila " 1818, 5, 30 d 1818, 9, 6

1806, 9, 11. Oliver & w, Phebe, & ch, Joel, William & Ann, rocf Gunpowder MM, Md., dtd 1805,12,14
1810, 9, 26. Oliver & w, Phebe, & ch, Joel, William, Ann, Jonothan & Susannah, rocf Center MM, dtd 1810,9,1
1811, 8, 28. Oliver [Mathews] & w, Phebe, & ch, Joel, William, Ann, Jonathan & Susannah, gct Center MM
1816, 1, 31. Oliver [Matthew] & w, Phebe, & ch, Joel, William, Ann, Jonothan, Susanna & Elizabeth, rocf Center MM, dtd 1815,12,16
1821, 2, 28. Ann Pennington (form Mathews) con mou
1821, 5, 30. Phebe dis consenting to her dt's mcd
1823, 11, 26. William dis
1824, 8, 25. Jonothan [Matthew] dis
1888, 1, 25. Joel, William, Ann, Jonathan, Susannah & Elizabeth dropped from mbrp (H)

MAXWELL
1805, 6, 13. Elizabeth rocf Salem MM, N. J., dtd 1805,3,25
1917, 12, 30. Max recrq (H)

MAYBEE
1839, 4, 24. Daniel Jones rqct Center MM, to m Hannah H. Maybee

MEEKS
1876, 3, 22. Elwood recrq

MELLFORD
1911, 10, 25. Minnie relrq

MELOY
1820, 7, 26. Catherine (form Connor) dis mou

MENDENHALL
1807, 2, 26. Ruth [Mendinghall] m Ely JINKINS
1861, 11, 28. Obadiah, s Obidiah & Rebecca, Hendricks Co., Ind.; m at Harveysburgh, Jane H. EDWARDS, dt Isaac & Nancy, Warren Co., O.
----, --, --. Lindley m Georgia FRAME b 1866, 3,24 (H)
Dt: Mary
Elizabeth b 1909, 7, 25 d same day

1804, 6, 14. Ellenor & ch, Ruth Mendenhall & Phebe Sumners, rocf Lost Creek MM, dtd 1804,3,31
1804, 10, 11. Joseph & w, Rachel, & ch, Mary, Tamer, Thaddeus & Lydia, rocf Deep River MM, N. C., dtd 1804,7,2
1804, 11, 8. John & w, Ruth, & ch, Richard, Joseph, Aaron, John, William, Margaret, Ruth & Catrin, rocf Springfield MM, N.C., dtd 1804,6,2
1805, 1, 10. Richard & w, Sarah, & ch, Benjamin, Gra, Obediah & Rebecca, rocf Deep Creek MM, N. C., dtd 1804,11,3
1805, 3, 14. William rocf Lost Creek MM, Tenn., dtd 1804,6,30
1805, 7, 11. Mordecai rocf Lost Creek MM, dtd 1805,1,25
1807, 8, 3. John, James & Marmaduke, ch Marmaduke, rocf Bush River MM, S. C., dtd 1807,5,30
1809, 12, 27. Elijah rocf New Garden MM, N. C., dtd 1809,7,29
1818, 4, 29. Mordecai & w gct White Water MM
1831, 4, 27. Caleb recrq (H)
1837, 11, 22. Caleb gct White Water MM (H)
1850, 6, 26. Lydia (form Ward) con mou
1855, 10, 24. Abijah Steddom gct Cesars Creek MM, to m Deborah Mendenhall
1862, 8, 27. Jane E. gct Plainfield MM, Ind.
1882, 6, 21. Lydia relrq
1884, 6, 25. Jane H. & dt, Abaetta, rocf Plainfield MM, Ind.
1887, 4, 20. Jason recrq
1908, 1, 22. J. Lindley rocf Still Water MM, O., dtd 1907,12,21 (H)
1921, 11, 27. Ethel recrq (H)

MENTEE
1890, 3, 26. Mary rec (or released) by rq (H)

MERCER
1859, 7, 27. Mary (form Sabin) dis mcd (H)
1897, 2, 24. Myrtle recrq

MEREDITH
1845, 2, 20. Seneca, s John & Rachel, Wayne Co., Ind.; m at Waynesville, Mary Jane WHITACRE, dt Andrew & Mary, Warren Co., O. (H)

1846, 4, 22. Senecca L. dis disunity (H)
1856, 6, 25. Mary Jane McKinney (form Meredith) con mcd (H)
1866, 1, 24. Elenor dropped from mbrp; form mbr of Fall Creek or Centre MM which had been laid down (H)
1895, 2, 20. Sarah Ellen (form Burnett) con mou (H)
1897, 9, 22. Ella B. gct Camden MM, Ind. (H)

MERRITT
----, --, --. Josiah Clement b 1828,8,31 d 1903,7,29; m Rebecca DOWNING b 1846,5,16 (H)

1836, 11, 23. Isaac Engle gct Green Plane MM, to m Sarah Merrit
1889, 1, 23. Edwin B. Michener gct Green Plain MM, to m S. Ellen Merritt
1902, 3, 26. Josiah Clement & w, Rebecca S., rocf Plainfield MM, O., dtd 1902,2,13 (H)

MESSENGER
----, --, --. ----- m Martha A. ----- b 1829,3, 24 (H)
Ch: Frank R. b 1870, 7, 28
Charles F. " 1873, 6, 30
Walter C. " 1874, 8, 10

1898, 3, 23. Walter C. gct Chicago Executive Mtg (H)
1898, 3, 23. Martha A. gct Chicago Executive Mtg (H)
1899, 2, 22. Charles F. & Frank R. relrq (H)

MESSICK
1818, 4, 29. Sarah (form Suffrins) dis mou

MEYERS
1848, 11, 22. Elizabeth Ann [Myres] (form Davis) con mou (H)
1885, 3, 25. Harry [Myres] recrq
1885, 3, 25. Mary recrq

MICHENER
1842, 10, 27. Isaac, s Benjamin & Abigail, Logan Co., O., b 1820,7,10 d 1869,6,22;

MICHENER, Isaac, continued
m at Miami, Martha GAUSE, dt Samuel & Mary, Warren Co., O., b 1821,5,3 d 1906,11, 3 (H)
Ch: Mary Ann b 1847, 6, 12
Edwin B. " 1851, 3, 11
Samuel Kelly " 1855, 6, 10
Richard Jehu " 1858, 9, 11
----, --, --. Edwin B. b 1851,3,11 d 1901,6,15; m Sarah E. MERRITT b 1854,1,23 (H)
Ch: Charles Edward b 1890, 2, 12
Ada " 1894, 11, 13
William Henry " 1896, 7, 31
----, --, --. Richard b 1858,9,11; m Phebe H. ALLEN b 1860,12,20 d 1896,9,10 (H)
Ch: Anna b 1894, 2, 20

1843, 3, 22. Martha [Mitchener] gct Goshen MM (H)
1848, 2, 23. Martha (form Gause) dis mou
1866, 3, 21. Isaac & w, Martha P., & ch, Mary Ann, Edwin, Samuel K. & Richard J., rocf Green Plain MM, dtd 1866,2,14 (H)
1886, 4, 21. Samuel R. rpd mcd (H)
1889, 1, 23. Edwin B. gct Green Plain MM, to m S. Ellen Merritt
1890, 5, 21. Sarah E. rocf Green Plain MM, dtd 1890,4,16
1894, 11, 24. Phebe (form Allen), w Richard, & infant dt, Anna, accepted as mbr after cert miscarried (H)
1901, 4, 24. Edwin B. & w, S. Ella M., & ch, Charles E., Ada & William H., relrq (H)
1911, 1, 25. Mary A. relrq (H)
1911, 2, 22. Anna relrq (H)

MIDDLETON
1827, 12, 26. Mary & ch, Phebe, Hannah, Richard & Rachel, rocf Stillwater MM, dtd 1827,11,24
1829, 5, 27. Mary dis jH
1829, 9, 30. Phebe dis jH
1831, 3, 30. Joseph dis jH
1832, 1, 25. Joseph dis mou (H)
1832, 2, 29. Mary Ann (form Moon) dis mou (H)
1834, 5, 21. Jehu & w, Mary, & ch, Hannah, Richard & Rachel, gct Milford MM, Ind. (H)
1834, 10, 22. Phebe gct Milford MM, Ind. (H)

MILLARD
1818, 7, 25. Catharine rocf Exeter MM, Pa., dtd 1818,5,27

MILLER
----, --, --. Solomon b 1780,7,21; m Ruth ----- (H)
Ch: Lydia b 1807, 4, 18
Ann " 1809, 6, 20
Robert " 1811, 1, 21
Thomas N. b 1812, 12, 8
Lewis N. " 1814, 6, 29
David H. " 1816, 6, 20

1816, 1, 31. Solomon & w, Ruth, & ch, Lydia, Ann, Robert, Thomas & Lewis, rocf Red Stone MM, dtd 1815,9,29
1819, 11, 24. Phebe rocf Cincinnati MM, dtd 1819,10,21
1821, 6, 27. David & w, Elizabeth, & ch, Mariah, Hannah & Eliza Jane, rocf Redstone MM, dtd 1821,4,4
1829, 3, 25. Lydia & three ch rocf Deerfield MM, dtd 1828,11,15 (H)
1832, 2, 29. Lydia & ch, Newton, Jesse, William, Reuben & Rachel, gct Green Plane MM (H)
1838, 4, 25. Phebe Ann recrq (H)
1854, 1, 25. Mary (form Sayre) dis mcd (H)
1874, 6, 24. Emma H. (form Steddom) con mou
1874, 8, 26. Emily gct Springboro MM
1876, 2, 22. Solomon W. & w, Emma, gct Spring Creek MM
1876, 2, 22. Samuel C. & w, Emma, & dt, Viola Zetta, gct Spring Creek MM, Ia.
1883, 1, 24. Joseph & w, Louisa, relrq
1883, 3, 21. David dis disunity
1891, 1, 21. Fannie (form Creighton) relrq
1892, 12, 21. Lewis & Caroline dis
1895, 5, 22. Martha set off as mbr of Executive Mtg at Clear Creek (H)
1917, 7, 29. Martha dropped from mbrp (H)

MILLHOUSE
1805, 11, 21. Henry [Milhous], s Robart & Elizabeth, Warren Co., O.; m at Cesars Creek, Anna STRAWN, dt George & Sarah, Warren Co., O.
1817, 8, 7. Henry [Milhous], s Robert & Sarah, Clinton Co., O.; m at Sugar Creek, Sarah HORNER, dt Thomas & Ann, Montgomery Co., O.

1805, 6, 13. Henry rocf Cane Creek MM, S. C., dtd 1805,3,23
1805, 7, 11. Robert & w, Sally, & ch, Henry, Samuel, John, Rebecca, Elizabeth & Ann, rocf Cane Creek MM, dtd 1805,3,23
1818, 2, 25. Sarah gct Cesars Creek MM

MILLICAN
1805, 2, 14. William & w, Hannah, & ch, Samuel, Jacob, John & Ann, rocf Springfield MM, dtd 1804,11,3
1805, 4, 11. William [Millikan] dis
1815, 12, 27. Samuel dis training in militia
1817, 9, 24. Hannah & ch, Jacob, John, Ann, Baptist, Betsy, Polly, Sally & Brazilton, gct Lick Creek MM, Ind.

MILLS
----, --, --. Marmaduke & Patience
Ch: Rachel b 1790, 11, 7

MILLS, Marmaduke & Patience, continued
Ch: Mary b 1792, 9, 15
Hugh " 1795, 2, 23
Joel " 1797, 4, 24
Ede " 1799, 6, 16
Anna " 1802, 4, 20
Patience " 1807, 8, 14
----, --, --. William d 1859,2,2; m Mary RICHARDS d 1837,3,6 (H)
Ch: Elizabeth b 1803, 4, 10
Rachel " 1805, 8, 1
Isaac " 1807, 9, 21 d 1862, 6, 2
Rowland R. " 1809, 11, 28
James " 1812, 2, 19
Lydia " 1814, 7, 11
Deborah " 1817, 1, 11
Franklin " 1819, 1, 20 d 1837, 2,20
Ruthanna " 1820, 11, 15
Ruth " 1820, 11, 15
1807, 11, 18. Isaac, s James & Lydia, Warren Co., O., d 1860,4,2; m Catherine RICHARDS, dt Rowland & Lydia, Warren Co., O., d 1860, 7,24 (H)
1807, 4, 15. Daniel, s Thomas & Jemima, Hiland Co., O.; m at Lees Creek, Elizabeth CARR, dt Benjamin & Patience, Hiland Co.,O.
1812, 1, 1. Sarah Mills m Andrew HAMPTON
1812, 3, 4. John, s James & Lydia, Warren Co., O.; m at Hopewell, Prudence THOMAS, dt Edward & Mary, Warren Co., O.
1812, 10, 3. Mary m Ruel RAGIN
1813, 12, 1. James, s James & Lydia, Warren Co., O., b 1789,9,9; m at Miami, Elizabeth BROWN, dt Joseph & Mary, Warren Co., O., b 1793,4,27
Ch: Sarah H. b 1814, 9, 1
Mary B. " 1815, 11, 11
Anna " 1817, 7, 25
Nathan " 1819, 5, 29
Joseph " 1821, 8, 22
Lydia " 1823, 5, 27
Susanna " 1825, 3, 22
Elisha " 1827, 10, 6
1819, 2, 3. Hugh, s Marmaduke & Patience, Warren Co., O.; m at Miami, Lydia HASKET, dt Thomas & Nancy Ann, Warren Co., O. (H)
Ch: Thomas H. b 1819, 10, 30
1819, 3, 4. Elisha, s James & Lydia, Warren Co., O.; m at Turtle Creek, Anna MILLS, dt Marmaduke & Patience, Warren Co., O.
1819, 3, 4. Anna m Elisha MILLS
1819, 5, 5. Elizabeth m David SAYRE
1826, 3, 2. Patience m Joseph FURNAS
----, --, --. Isaac, s William & Mary, Warren Co., O., b 1807,9,22 d 1862,6,2; m Hannah BISPHAM b 1812,12,13 d 1837,4,8 (H)
Ch: Mordica b 1831, 5, 1 d 1905, 8,20
Orlistus " 1833, 4, 12
Zillah " 1834, 9, 13 " 1838, 3, 1
Josiah " 1836, 1, 10
Isaac m 2nd 1839,2,27 Anable BURNET, dt Daniel & Ann, Warren Co., O., b 1808,3,21
Ch: William H. b 1840, 1, 12 d 1901, 6,10
Milton W. b 1844, 11, 12
Benjamin F." 1847, 1, 23
Henry C. " 1849, 5, 22 d 1852, 1,25
----, --, --. Mordicai b 1831,5,1 d 1905,8,20; m Mary HAINES b 1837,10,28 d 1908,11,20 (H)
---, --, --. Benjamin F. b 1847,1,23; m Sarah A. WOOD b 1847,12,26 (H)
Ch: Effie Anna b 1869, 12, 2
Wilbur Henry " 1871. 10, 28
Rachel Alice " 1874, 3, 15 d 1875, 5,17
Mary Belle " 1877, 9, 9
Ruth Hannah" 1880, 4, 18
Minnie May " 1882, 6, 13
Carrie " 1888, 12, 6

1804, 12, 13. Marmaduke & w, Patience, & ch rocf Bush River MM, dtd 1804,8,25
1804, 12, 13. William & w, Lydia, & ch, Charles, William, Thomas, Daniel & Patience, rocf Bush River MM, dtd 1804,8,25
1805, 5, 9. John & w, Mary, & ch, Enoch & Elijah Mills, & Ann Pearson, rocf Bush River MM, S. C., dtd 1805,2,23
1805, 5, 9. John Jr. & w, Phebe, & ch, William & Mark, rocf Bush River MM, S. C., dtd 1805,2,23
1806, 4, 10. Seth rocf Lost Creek MM, dtd 1806,1,25
1806, 11, 13. Strangman Stanley & w, Jemima, & her dt, Sarah Mills, also their ch, Strangeman, Jemima & Eliza, rocf New Garden MM, N. C., dtd 1806,8,30
1807, 2, 12. Daniel rocf Deep River MM, N.C., dtd 1806,9,1
1808, 3, 10. Richard rocf Deep Creek MM, N.C. dtd 1806,9,6
1810, 5, 30. Rachel Jay (form Mills) con mou
1818, 5, 27. Susanna (form Brown) dis mou
1818, 7, 25. David dis mcd
1820, 2, 23. Elisha & w gct New Garden MM,Ind.
1820, 4, 26. James & fam gct New Garden MM, Ind.
1821, 8, 29. Jonothan Jessop gct Cesars Creek MM, to m Patience Mills
1822, 2, 27. Edith Jay (form Mills) con mou
1822, 7, 31. Sarah rocf Ceasars Creek MM, dtd 1822,4,26
1822, 10, 30. Curtis dis mcd
1822, 11, 27. Joel gct Cherry Grove, Ind.
1823, 3, 26. Rachel Mullin (form Mills) dis mcd (paper sent to Green Plain MM for service)
1826, 4, 26. Patience gct Union MM
1826, 6, 28. Hugh & w. Lydia, & ch gct Milford MM, Ind.
1827, 7, 25. Sarah gct Fairfield MM
1829, 1, 28. William dis jH
1829, 3, 25. Mary dis jH
1829, 5, 27. Isaac dis jH
1830, 3, 31. Hannah (form Bispham) dis mou & [jH
1830, 3, 31. Isaac L. con mou (H)

MILLS, continued
1830, 3, 31. Hannah (form Bispham) con mou (H)
1831, 9, 28. James & w, Lydia, rocf Arba MM, dtd 1831,5,25
1835, 3, 25. Charles rocf Cesars Creek MM, dtd 1835,2,19
1835, 3, 25. Ann rocf Springfield MM, dtd 1835,2,17
1835, 5, 27. James & w, Elizabeth, & ch gct New Garden MM, Ind.
1835, 5, 27. Sarah H. & Mary gct New Garden MM, Ind.
1838, 11, 21. Deborah Jennings (form Mills) dis mou (H)
1838, 12, 26. Lydia Arnold (form Mills) dis mou
1839, 6, 26. Deborah Jennings (form Mills) dis mou
1840, 6, 25. Rebecca (form Edwards) dis mou
1842, 6, 22. Ruthanna Morford (form Mills) dis mou (H)
1843, 11, 22. Charles & w, Ann, gct Mill Creek MM
1844, 9, 25. Charles & w, Ann, rocf Mill Creek MM, dtd 1844,9,17
1845, 11, 26. Ruth Ann Morford (form Mills) dis mou
1855, 6, 25. Josiah B. dis mcd (H)
1855, 12, 26. Orlistus R. dis mcd (H)
1857, 5, 27. Mordecai con mcd
1858, 3, 24. Charles & w, Ann, gct Plainfield MM, Ind.
1861, 10, 23. William H. con mcd (H)
1867, 12, 25. Milton con mcd (H)
1869, 6, 23. Benjamin rpd mcd (H)
1870, 7, 27. Sarah A. & dt, Effia Anna, recrq (H)
1870, 12, 21. Anna E. recrq
1877, 3, 21. Anna relrq
1883, 5, 23. James J. recrq
1885, 8, 26. Milton W. relrq to jas (H)
1898, 5, 25. Mary M. recrq (H)
1899, 1, 25. Benjamin & w, Sarah, & ch, Minnie, May & Carry, relrq (H)
1900, 11, 21. Benjamin H. & w, Lydia J., & s, Roy J., rocf Ceasars Creek MM, dtd 1900,9,27
1904, 4, 20. Wilbur H. relrq (H)
1906, 4, 25. George D. & w, Luella, & s, Lindley, rocf Ceasars Creek MM, dtd 1906,3,22
1920, 7, 25. Carrie dropped from mbrp (H)

MILTENBERGER
1889, 3, 27. Emma relrq

MISSELDINE
1866, 9, 26. John recrq
1866, 11, 21. Jemima (form Burnett) con mou
1871, 8, 26. John F. con mou
1885, 3, 25. John F. relrq

MITCHEL
1821, 4, 25. Mary (form Wharton) con mou
1829, 9, 30. Mary dis jH

MOFFITT
1836, 8, 27. Nathan, s Charles & Elizabeth, Wayne Co., O.; m at Miami, Rhoda Ann JOHNSON, dt James & Elizabeth, Warren Co., O.
1852, 6, 2. Rhoda Ann m William E. BUTLER

1805, 7, 11. Hannah [Moffit] & dt, Mary & Hannah, rocf Cane Creek MM, N. C., dtd 1804,8,4

MONGER
1903, 3, 25. Alice M. relrq (H)

MONTGOMERY
1821, 4, 25. Anna (form Barton) con mou
1833, 8, 21. Anna dis jH
1847, 7, 21. Rebecca (form Ward) con mou (H)
1847, 12, 22. Elizabeth recrq
1850, 4, 24. Rebecca (form Ward) dis mou
1885, 1, 21. Sidney rocf Ceasars Creek MM, dtd 1884,11,27
1886, 3, 24. Owen recrq
1887, 4, 20. David & Sarah E. & ch, Lillie & Pearl, recrq
1898, 6, 22. Owen & w relrq

MOON
----, --, --. Richard b 1773,3,10; m Vashti ----- b 1768,6,17 d 1846,5,31 (H)
Ch: Dinah b 1805, 6, 15
Judith " 1806, 9, 24
Mary Ann " 1808, 6, 13
Vashti " 1810, 3, 4
Asenath " 1813, 8, 3
1818, 4, 2. Jane m David HAMPTON
1826, 2, 23. John, s Daniel & Ruth, Clinton Co., O.; m at Grove, Judith MOON, dt Richard & Vashti, O.
1826, 2, 23. Judith m John MOON
1827, 12, 5. Dinah m Jesse BEALS
1829, 11, 4. Vashti m Thomas JESSUP (H)

1806, 3, 13. Jane (form Mullen) dis mou
1806, 7, 10. James & w, Salina, rocf New Garden MM, N. C., dtd 1805,4,27
1816, 10, 30. Richard & w, Vashti, & ch, Dinah, Judith, Mary Ann, Vashti & Ascenith, rocf Center MM, dtd 1816,9,27
1816, 10, 30. Simon & w, Judith, rocf Center MM, dtd 1816,9,27
1817, 1, 29. Jane rocf Center MM, dtd 1816,11,16
1817, 2, 26. Simon & w, Lydia, rocf Centre MM, dtd 1816,8,15
1829, 5, 27. Mary Ann dis jH
1829, 5, 27. Vashti dis jH
1829, 5, 27. Vashti Jr. dis jH
1829, 7, 29. Richard dis jH

MOON, continued
1829, 10, 28. Lydia dis jH
1829, 10, 28. Mary rocf Falls MM, Pa., dtd 1829,8,8 (H)
1830, 1, 27. Simon dis jH
1830, 2, 24. Mary rocf Falls MM, Pa.; not accepted
1832, 2, 29. Mary Ann Middleton (form Moon) dis mou (H)
1833, 4, 24. Asenath (form Grey) dis mou (H)
1833, 6, 26. Simon & minor ch gct White Lick MM, Ind.
1838, 5, 23. Asenith dis mou
1888, 1, 25. Judith & Asenath dropped from mbrp (H)
1916, 1, 26. Wilkerson T. & w, Lydia, rocf Paoli MM, Ind., dtd 1915,10,6
1916, 4, 26. Wilkerson T. & w, Lydia, gct Paoli MM, Ind.

MOORE
1847, 12, 23. Samuel B. [More], s David & Mary, Preble Co., O.; m Sarah BROWN, dt David & Mary, Warren Co., O., b 1813,5,11 d 1849,10,12 (H)
Dt: Elizabeth B. b 1849, 9, 30

1804, 6, 14. Alice rocf Lost Creek MM, dtd 1804,3,31
1807, 5, 4. Rebecca (form Emory) dis
1809, 9, 9. Phebe & ch, Seborn, James, Benajah & Hannah Pleasant, recrq
1809, 12, 27. Dempsey rocf New Garden MM, N. C., dtd 1809,8,26
1809, 12, 27. Richard rocf New Garden MM, dtd 1809,8,26
1810, 11, 28. Alexander rocf New Garden MM, N. C., dtd 1810,5,26
1815, 11, 29. Mary rocf Upper Eavesham MM, N. J., dtd 1815,9,9
1817, 8, 27. Alice gct New Garden MM, Ind.
1820, 3, 29. Mary gct Elk MM
1830, 11, 24. Job Borton gct White Water MM, to m Ann Moore; cert returned because Job failed to appear (H)
1837, 8, 23. Elizabeth B. [More] con mou (H)
1837, 10, 25. Elizabeth (form Jessop) dis mou & jH
1848, 5, 24. Samuel B. & ch, Mary B. & David C., rocf Westfield MM, dtd 1848,4,26 (H)
1849, 1, 24. Sarah W., minor, rocf Westfield MM, dtd 1848,12,27 (H)
1849, 11, 21. Samuel B. & ch, Sarah W., Mary B. & David, gct Westfield MM, O. (H)
1864, 10, 26. Mary C. [More] rocf Blue River MM, dtd 1863,9,9 (H)
1866, 1, 24. Sarah, Lydia Ann, David R., Milton J., Samuel S., Edward G., Sarah E. & Elmira [Moor] dropped from mbrp; form mbr of Fall Creek or Centre MM which had been laid down
1873, 6, 25. Edith Ann gct Kokomo MM
1879, 1, 22. Mary Ann [More] rocf Fallowfield MM, Pa., dtd 1878,12,7 (H)
1885, 1, 21. Mary A. relrq (H)
1908, 9, 23. Idella H. gct Union MM

MOORMAN
1810, 11, 2. Peter [Marman], s David & Elizabeth, Champain Co., O.; m at Madriver, Dorothy MARMON, dt Robert & Margaret, Champain Co., O.
1810, 11, 2. Dorothy [Marman] m Peter MARMON

1807, 4, 9. David [Marmon] & w, Elizabeth, & ch, Martha, Elizabeth, Edmund, David & Pricilla, rocf Jack Swamp MM, N. C., dtd 1806,3,1
1807, 4, 9. Robert [Marmon] & w, Margaret, & ch, Rickman, Dorothy, Hannah, Obedience, Reames, Peter, Stephen & Joshua, rocf Jack Swamp MM, N. C., dtd 1806,3,1
1808, 3, 10. Africa & ch, Lehiles, Thomas, James & Charles, rocf South River MM, Va., dtd 1807,3,9
1808, 3, 10. Charles & w, Betsy, & ch, William, Nancy, Fanny, Robert, Betsy & Agatha rocf South River MM, Va., dtd 1807,3,9
1808, 3, 10. Micajah & w, Susannah, & ch, Africa & Thomas, rocf South River MM, Va.
1808, 9, 10. Martin [Marmon] & w, Susannah, & ch, James, Patsy, Anna, Robert & Sarah, rocf Short Creek MM, O., dtd 1808,3,22
1808, 9, 10. Obediance [Mourman] & dt, Elizabeth, rocf Short Creek MM, dtd 1808,3,22
1808, 10, 8. Raindy [Morman] & dt, Zilpha, rocf Jack Swamp MM, N. C., dtd 1807,3,7
1808, 11, 12. Samuel [Marmon] & w, Peggy, & ch, Rachel, Matilda, Martin, Lettice, Mary & Rebecca, rocf Short Creek MM, dtd 1808, 3,22
1810, 9, 26. Hannah Dohety (form Morman) con mou
1849, 11, 21. Thomas C. Jr. rocf Dover MM, dtd 1849,9,13
1852, 9, 22. Thomas C. [Morman] Jr. gct Dover MM
1866, 1, 24. Lydia (form Whinery) rpd mcd (H)

MORFORD
1842, 6, 22. Ruthanna (form Mills) dis mou (H)
1845, 11, 26. Ruth Ann (form Mills) dis mou
1883, 5, 23. Thomas recrq
1887, 6, 22. Thomas relrq

MORGAN
1814, 9, 8. David, s Jonathan & Elizabeth, Warren Co., O., b 1785,10,8; m at Turtle Creek, Rebecca BROWN, dt John & Elizabeth EVANS, Warren Co., O., b 1788,4,19 (H)
Ch: Samuel B. b 1817, 4, 1
John b 1819, 1, 23
Joseph " 1820, 11, 9
Elizabeth " 1822, 12, 22

MORGAN, David & Rebecca, continued
Ch: David Jr. b 1825, 5, 7
1846, 5, 30. Martha A., dt William & Matilda, b
----, --, --. James H. b 1844,12,24; m Anna L. SHERWOOD b 1867,1,24
Ch: Wm. Henry b 1891, 4, 2
Carl Sherwood " 1894, 1, 19

1813, 7, 28. David rocf Fairfield MM, dtd 1813,5,29
1814, 8, 31. Charlotte (form Anthony) con mou
1831, 1, 26. Rebecca dis jH
1841, 9, 22. Samuel B. dis disunity
1848, 11, 22. David dis disunity
1848, 11, 22. Joseph dis disunity
1848, 11, 22. John dis disunity
1849, 6, 20. David, Jr. gct Salem MM, Ia.
1850, 2, 20. Rebecca dis disunity
1850, 9, 25. Martha rocf Center MM, dtd 1850, 7,18 (H)
1881, 5, 25. James H. rocf Caesars Creek MM
1883, 6, 20. Mattie rocf Ceasar's Creek MM, dtd 1883,5,24
1890, 4, 23. Martha A. gct Ceasars Creek MM
1900, 2, 21. James H. & w & two ch gct Ceasars Creek MM
1913, 4, 23. Russell recrq

MORRIS
1833, 2, 20. Rebecca rocf Stillwater MM, dtd 1832,6,16 (H)
1835, 8, 26. Lydia rocf Stillwater MM, dtd 1835,4,25
1835, 8, 26. Lydia rocf Stillwater MM, dtd 1835,4,25
1868, 7, 22. Edith [Moris] (form Edwards) con mou
1871, 7, 26. John & w, Mary, rocf Center MM, dtd 1871,6,18
1873, 6, 25. Edith A. gct Kokomo MM, Ind.

MORRISON
1807, 10, 8. Hannah rocf Spring MM, dtd 1806, 8,30
1810, 10, 31. Hannah Harlen (form Morrison) gct Center MM

MORROW
1808, 3, 10. John & w, Mary, & ch, Andrew, Joseph, Hannah, Mary & Ruth, rocf Cane Creek MM, N. C., dtd 1807,5,9
1867, 10, 23. Susan L. (form Jones) con mou
1868, 3, 25. Susan L. gct White Water MM, Ind.
1868, 8, 26. Susan L. 's cert granted 3 mo returned & endorsed to Springfield MM, O.

MOSHER
1838, 12, 27. Eunice b
1855, 11, 28. Jonathan B., s Asa & Sarah, Warren Co., O.; m at Miami, Mary FURNAS, dt Seth & Dinah, Warren Co., O., b 1832,12, 30 (H)
Ch: Albert b 1856, 10, 6
Alice " 1859, 6, 10

1863, 5, 17. Beulah rocf Springboro MM, dtd 1863,4,23 (H)
1865, 5, 24. Beulah gct Blue River MM, Ind. (H)
1865, 11, 22. Calista rocf Green Plain MM, dtd 1865,11,15 (H)
1866, 4, 25. Eunice rocf Green Plain MM, dtd 1865,11,16 (H)
1868, 6, 24. Calista Furnas (form Mosher) dis mcd (H)
1876, 3, 22. Eunice Bruce (or Brice) (form Mosher) rpd mcd (H)
1890, 9, 24. Albert dropped from mbrp (H)

MOSS
1897, 11, 10. Frances Matilda (Walker) b 1817,5,24 d 1897,11,10

MOTE
1807, 1, 13. Jonathan, s David & Dorkis, Montgomery Co., O.; m Susanna HOLLINGSWORTH, dt George & Jane, Montgomery Co.,O.
----, --, --. Marcus b 1817,6,19; m Rhoda STEDDOM b 1821,8,10
Ch: Kirk Linus b 1840, 1, 28
Samuel Steddom " 1842, 9, 15
Henry Davis" 1847, 6, 24
Susanna Jane " 1850, 7, 9
Edwin L. " 1855, 12, 31
Edwin M. " 1857, 2, 18
1856, 3, 14. Edwin L. d bur Turtle Creek
1860, 11, 11. Edwin M. d bur Turtle Creek

1804, 7, 12. David & Dorcas rocf Wrightsborough MM, dtd 1804,3,3
1804, 7, 12. Jeremiah & w, Mary, & ch, William, David, Aaron, Jeremiah & Isaiah, rocf Wrightsborough MM, dtd 1804,3,12
1804, 7, 12. Jonathan & w, Ann, & ch, Timothy, David, Sarah, Jonothan, William, Elizabeth, Dorcas, Mary & Jeremiah, rocf Wrightsborough MM, dtd 1804,5,5
1805, 9, 12. John & w, Rachel, & ch, Elizabeth, David, John & Rachel, rocf Wrightsboro MM, Ga., dtd 1805,4,6
1806, 9, 11. William rocf Bush River MM, S. C., dtd 1806,1,25
1838, 5, 25. Rhoda (form Steddom) con mou
1838, 11, 21. Rhoda gct West Branch MM
1845, 8, 27. Marcus & w, Rhoda, & ch, Kirk L. & Samuel S., rocf West Branch MM, dtd 1845,6,19
1864, 2, 24. Samuel Kersey gct West Branch MM, to m Arena E. Mote
1867, 4, 24. Marcus & w, Rhoda L., & ch, Henry D. & Susannah J., gct White Water MM

MOTE, continued
1868, 2, 19. Samuel gct White Water MM
1882, 12, 27. Anna S. recrq
1884, 4, 23. Kirk L. & ch, Clarence Leslie & Minnie, gct White Water MM, Ind.
1885, 4, 22. Samuel Steddom & ch, Clara E., George H. & Jessie E., rocf White Water MM, dtd 1885,3,26
1885, 5, 27. Kirk L. rocf White Water MM, dtd 1885,4,23
1885, 12, 23. Kirk L. gct White Water MM, Ind.
1890, 2, 19. Kirk & dt, Minnie, rocf White Water MM, Ind., dtd 1890,1,25
1893, 1, 25. Lottie B. rocf West Branch MM, dtd 1893,1,14
1895, 8, 28. Samuel S., Bertie E., Jodie E. & George H. relrq
1897, 1, 27. Samuel S. & Emma recrq
1902, 7, 22. Emma V. relrq

MOTT
1842, 6, 22. Lydia P. rocf Scipio MM, N. Y., dtd 1840,12,17 (H)

MOUCE
1890, 8, 27. Ulysses L. & w, Clara, & ch, Howard & Vivian, rocf New Berry MM, dtd 1890,7,21
1903, 3, 25. Ulysses L. & w, Clara, & ch, Howard J., Vivien & Edwin W., gct Cincinnati MM

MULL
1903, 2, 18. Frances relrq

MULLEN
----, --, --. John [Mullin] m Lydia RICHARDS
Ch: Rebecca b 1802, 12, 20
Eli " 1806, 12, 19
Joseph " 1808, 11, 12
David " 1813, 4, 14
Elizabeth " 1815, 2, 22
Beulah " 1817, 12, 17
Mary Ann " 1819, 9, 10
Lydia Ann " 1821, 12, 11 d 1858,5,30

1806, 3, 13. Jane Moon (form Mullen) dis mou
1807, 8, 3. Hannah Dubois (form Mullin) dis mcd
1808, 3, 10. Sarah Kirby (form Mullen) con mou
1809, 11, 4. James [Mullin] rocf Hopewell MM, dtd 1809,4,3
1810, 6, 27. James dis mcd & attending musters
1811, 10, 30. Hannah rocf Chester MM, N. J., dtd 1811,5,9
1813, 1, 27. John [Mullin] dis
1813, 1, 27. John [Mullin] Jr. dis bearing arms in military service
1816, 5, 29. William [Mullin] recrq
1817, 12, 31. Rachel Baterman (form Mullen) con mou
1819, 4, 28. Christiana recrq
1819, 5, 26. Elizabeth rocf Upper Eavesham MM, N. J., dtd 1818,12,12
1821, 8, 29. Samuel [Mullin] gct Elk MM
1822, 9, 25. Isaiah [Mullin] dis mcd
1823, 3, 26. Rachel [Mullin] (form Mills) dis mcd(paper sent to Green Plain for service)
1823, 3, 26. Isaac recrq
1823, 3, 26. Noah, Job, Aaron, Ruth, Nathan, Seth, Ann, Maria & Jane, recrq of parents, Isaac & Elizabeth
1823, 4, 30. Rebecca dis [(H)
1844, 3, 27. Elizabeth (form Jones) dis mou
1877, 5, 23. Huldah Maria recrq
1882, 5, 24. Oella recrq
1882, 7, 26. Maria relrq
1897, 11, 24. Oella (form Scott) dropped from mbrp

MURDOCK
1858, 10, 27. Susan (form Butterworth) rpd mcd (H)
1879, 8, 27. Susan B. gct Race St. MM, Phila., Pa. (H)
1899, 7, 26. Susan B. rocf Phila. MM, dtd 1899,6,21 (H)

MURPHY
1810, 12, 26. Margaret rocf Cain Creek MM, N. C., dtd 1810,8,4
1814, 11, 30. Margaret gct White Water MM

MURRAY
1866, 1, 24. Rebecca H. [Murry] (form Carroll) rpd mcd (H)
1884, 5, 21. Anna recrq
1897, 11, 24. Mary Ellen, Emely & Kate [Murry] dropped from mbrp
1917, 7, 29. Elsie & Cora T. transferred to this mtg from Springboro (H)
1920, 5, 30. Donal Powell, Janet Helen & Natalie Eliza [Murry], ch Elsie J., recrq (H)
1925, 1, 25. Lowell Thomas recrq (H)

MYERS
1892, 12, 31. Elizabeth A. relrq (H)

NEAL
1805, 12, 12. William & w, Rachel, & ch, Mahlon, rocf New Hope MM, dtd 1805,10,19
1806, 6, 12. Henry & w, Rebecca, & ch, Benjamin, Phebe & William, rocf New Hope MM, dtd 1805,10,19
1817, 11, 26. Ann [Neill] rocf Hopewell MM, dtd 1817,8,9
1821, 2, 28. Mary [Neall] rocf Alexandria MM, Va., dtd 1820,9,21
1825, 12, 28. Ann gct Hopewell MM
1918, 6, 26. Wilhelmina & Margaret Louise rocf Cincinnati MM

NEAN
1824, 1, 28. Thompson & w, Elizabeth, & ch, Anna Elizabeth, Martin & Alexander, rocf Cincinnati MM, dtd 1823,11,27
1824, 4, 28. Thompson [Neane] & fam gct Cincinnati MM

NEDRY
1871, 12, 27. Eliza recrq

NEEDLES
1884, 5, 28. Anna recrq

NEELY
1854, 1, 25. Irena (form Sayre) dis mcd (H)

NELSON
1866, 9, 23. Alice (Hopkins) b (H)

1903, 12, 23 Alice dropped from mbrp

NEWBORN
1818, 1, 28. John rocf Redstone MM, dtd 1817,6,21
1818, 9, 30. David [Newburn] rocf Redstone MM, dtd 1817,10,22
1820, 3, 29. David [Newburn] gct Elk MM, O.

NEWLET
1811, 11, 27. Sarah, w Richard, rocf Shrewsbury MM, N. J., dtd 1811,7,6

NEWLIN
1808, 2, 17. John, s Eli & Sarah, Warren Co., O.; m at Miami, Esther STUBBS, dt John & Jane, Warren Co., O.

1832, 1, 5. William, s John & Esther, Clinton Co., O., b 1810,2,22; m at Harveysburgh, Mary EDWARDS, dt Archibald & Ann, Warren Co., O., b 1811,7,16
Ch: Eleanor C. b 1834, 1, 14
John D. " 1836, 10, 10
Henry " 1841, 9, 29
1840, 10, 16. John D. d

1807, 11, 12. John rocf Cane Creek MM, N. C., dtd 1806,10,4
1809, 5, 6. John & w, Hester, & s, Eli, gct Center MM
1832, 5, 23. Mary gct Springfield MM
1837, 1, 25. William & w, Mary, & ch, Eleanor & John D., rocf Springfield MM, dtd 1836, 12,13
1847, 12, 22. William & w, Mary, & fam gct White Lick MM, Ind.

NEWMAN
----, --, --. Jonathan b 1768,12,8; m Anna CLOUD b 1773,11,4 (H)
Ch: Mary Earl b 1797, 12, 3
Elizabeth " 1802, 9, 14
James M. C." 1807, 2, 27
Joseph " 1809, 12, 4
Joel " 1812, 7, 7
Jonathan
Thomas " 1815, 10, 5
1822, 11, 6. Elizabeth m William EDWARDS
1823, 3, 12. Mary Earl m Ellis WARD
1843, 12, 25. Anna (Cloud) d

1805, 8, 8. Jonathan & w, Ann, & ch, Mary Earl, John & Elizabeth, rocf Lost Creek MM, Tenn. dtd 1805,1,26
1809, 4, 8. Jonothan dis
1820, 10, 25. Jonothan recrq
1831, 1, 26. Joseph dis jH
1834, 8, 27. Joel dis jH
1852, 5, 26. Jonathan gct Spiceland MM; returned because of his rem back to Miami
1893, 4, 26. G. A. recrq
1895, 11, 20. Laura recrq
1912, 1, 24. G. A. gct Dayton MM, O.

NEWPORT
1848, 3, 22. Amanda Ann recrq (H)
1859, 8, 24. Amanda Wright (form Newport) con mcd (H)

NICHOLS
1807, 9, 10. James & w, Ann, & ch, Enoch, rocf Bush River MM, S. C., dtd 1805,4,27

NICHOLSON
1830, 11, 3. Valentine, s Daniel & Elizabeth, Clinton Co., O., b 1809,5,27; m at Grove, Jane S. WALES, dt Isaac & Ruth, Warren Co., O., b 1806,2,1 d 1906,9,9 (H)
Ch: Ruth W. b 1831, 10, 26 d 1846, 4,26
Elizabeth " 1833, 12, 10
Eden Finley" 1836, 1, 25 " 1838, 7, 7
Mary Ellen " 1839, 3, 29
Martha Jane" 1842, 6, 22
Louisa " 1844, 5, 20 " 1845, 8,--
Caroline M." 1846, 8, 12 " 1858, 8,12

1830, 6, 30. Daniel recrq (H)
1830, 6, 30. Elizabeth recrq (H)
1833, 7, 24. Daniel & w, Elizabeth, gct Milford MM, Ind. (H)
1839, 5, 22. Valentine & w, Jane, & ch, Ruth, Elizabeth & Mary Emily, gct Green Plain MM, dtd 1842,4,--
1842, 4, 20. Valentine & w, Jane, & ch, Ruth, Elizabeth & Mary Ellen, rocf Green Plain MM, dtd 1842,4,--
1844, 6, 26. Valentine dis disunity (H)
1884, 5, 21. Marian L. & Malissa recrq
1886, 11, 24. Marion L. & w, Malissa, gct Columbus MM, O.

NINDE
1816, 1, 3. Benjamin, s James & Miliorah, Warren Co., O.; m at Hopewell, Jane WHITACRE, dt Robert & Patience, Warren Co., O. (H) (Jane b 1799,9,21)
Ch: Priscilla b 1817, 1, 15 d 1818,5,3

NINDE, Benjamin & Jane, continued
Ch: Rhoda b 1818, 9, 22
James William " 1820, 3, 30
Margaret " 1822, 10, 14 d 1824, 9,21
Lindley " 1825, 3, 25
Henry P. " 1827, 8, 1
Rebecka " 1830, 5, 24

1814, 9, 28. Benjamin rocf Indian Spring MM, dtd 1814,7,16
1829, 5, 27. Benjamin dis jH
1829, 5, 27. Jane dis jH
1837, 12, 26. Benjamin & w, Jane, & ch, James William, Lindley, Henry, Rebecca, Rachel, Frederick & Martha, gct White Water MM (H)
1838, 12, 26. Rhoda gct White Water MM, Ind. (H)
1863, 12, 23. Henry P. con mou
1863, 12, 23. Henry P. gct Spring Creek MM, Ia.

NIXON
1804, 10, 11. Thomas rocf Back Creek MM, N.C., dtd 1803,8,27
1805, 6, 13. Mary rocf Springfield MM, N.C., dtd 1803,10,1, endorsed by Concord MM, O., dtd 1804,12,18
1807, 4, 9. Thomas dis
1807, 11, 12. Mary dis
1826, 6, 28. William & w, Martha, & ch, Mary, Susanna, Penina, Martha Ann, William & Ann, rocf Springbow MM, dtd 1826,5,26
1826, 11, 29. Samuel Jr. rocf Uwehlan MM, Pa., dtd 1826,5,4
1826, 11, 29. Sarah rocf Springborough MM, dtd 1826,10,24
1827, 3, 28. William & w, Martha, & seven minor ch gct Elk MM
1827, 3, 28. Cert rec for James M. Hibbard from Hopewell MM, dtd 1827,3,8, to m Mary Nixon, endorsed to Elk MM, where she had rem
----, --, --. Mary Ann (form Doan) dis mou (H)
1850, 2, 20. Oliver W. rocf New Garden MM, dtd 1849,11,17

NORODYKE
1825, 5, 5. Abraham, s Israel & Mary, Clinton Co., O.; m at Salem, Henrietta P. ANTHONY, dt Charles & Elizabeth, Warren Co., O.

1805, 4, 11. Abraham [Nordyke] & w, Mary, & ch, Hiram, rocf Lost Creek MM, Tenn., dtd 1804,8,25
1805, 6, 13. Israel & w, Mary, & ch, Elizabeth, Benejah, Hezekiah, Mary, Elijah & Abraham, rocf Lost Creek MM, dtd 1805,3,30
1806, 9, 11. Micajah & w, Charity, & ch, Phebe, Sarah, Isaac & Mary, rocf Lost Creek MM, dtd 1806,3,29
1825, 12, 28. Henrietta P. [Nordike] gct Clear Creek MM

NUTT
1817, 9, 23. Mary, w Aaron, d

1807, 9, 10. Mary recrq
1819, 5, 26. Martha (form Craig) dis mou
1853, 3, 23. Ann C. (form Evans) dis mcd (H)

OAKLEY
1819, 10, 27. George gct Fairfield MM, to m
1822, 9, 25. George dis mcd

O'BRIAN
1805, 4, 11. David & w, Elizabeth, & ch, Nancy, Mary, Jonothan, Esther, Elizabeth & Rebecca, rocf Wrightsboro MM, dtd 1804,7,28
1824, 3, 31. Thomas rocf Center MM, dtd 1824, 3,20
1830, 11, 24. Thomas [O'Brien] gct Silver Creek MM

OGBORN
----, --, --. Joseph Parker b 1785,10,3; m Elizabeth ----- b 1778,11,30 (H)
Ch: Hannah b 1808, 9, 5
Rebecca " 1810, 8, 27
Samuel F. " 1812, 11, 17
Isaac A. " 1815, 3, 14
Ann " 1817, 4, 9
Sarah B. " 1819, 12, 11
1871, 4, 28. Mary d (H)
1872, 10, 2. John d (H)

1822, 8, 28. Joseph P. w, Elizabeth, & ch, Hannah, Rebeccah, Samuel F., Isaac A., Ann & Sarah B., rocf Upper Evesham MM, N. J., dtd 1822,6,6
1824, 2, 25. Samuel [Ogburn] & w, Esther, & ch, Joseph, Mary, Allen, Edwin, Evan & Lydia, rocf Upper Evesham MM, N. J., dtd 1823,11,8
1825, 4, 27. Samuel & w, Esther, & ch, Joseph, Mary, Allen, Edwin, Evan, Lydia & Ezra, gct West Grove MM
1828, 10, 29. Caleb [Ogburn] Jr. rocf Phila. MM, dtd 1828,5,27
1831, 12, 28. Hannah & Rebecca gct Cincinnati MM, O.
1832, 1, 25. Joseph P. & w, Elizabeth, & ch, Samuel F., Isaac A., Ann & Sarah B., gct Cincinnati MM
1851, 5, 21. Jesse T. Butterworth gct White Water MM, to m Ruth E. Ogburn (H)
1854, 6, 21. John [Ogburn] & w, Mary, rocf White Water MM, dtd 1854,5,24 (H)

OGLESBEE
1899, 11, 22. Martha A. rocf Ceasars Creek MM, dtd 1899,10,26
1902, 9, 24. Alice Mae recrq
1905, 4, 26. George recrq

OGLESBEE, continued
1908, 4, 22. Martha M. & Alice M. gct Ceasars Creek MM
1914, 5, 27. George D. relrq

O'KEEFE
1862, 8, 14. Jesse (Hopkins) b

1903, 12, 23. Jesse dropped from mbrp (H)

OLIPHANT
1841, 7, 21. Harriet rocf Mount Holly MM, N. J., dtd 1841,4,18 (H)

OLIVER
1906, 5, 23. Alma M. Burgurnal (form Elsay Oliver) relrq

OLVIS
1881, 7, 27. William & w, Edna, & ch, Samuel William & Laverne, recrq
1884, 3, 26. William & w, Edna, & ch, Samuel William & Lavern, gct Springfield MM
1891, 10, 21. William P. & fam rocf Springfield MM, dtd 1891,7,18
1898, 4, 20. William & w & ch gct Ogden MM

O'NEALL
1758, 2, 23. Anna b
----, --, --. Abijah b 1762,1,21 d 1823,5,9; m Anna KELLY (H)

Ch:	b	d
Maryann	b 1785, 10, 3	d 1845, 9,19
Sarah	" 1787, 5, 31	" 1878, 9,28
J. Kelly	" 1789, 3, 23	" 1827, 9, 6
William	" 1791, 3, 10	" 1874, 7,18
Elisha	" 1793, 5, 1	" 1795, 9, 4
Rebecca	" 1796, 9, 23	" 1845, 4, 1
Abijah	" 1798, 12, 9	" 1874, 7, 9
Rhoda	" 1800, 8, 1	" 1841, 3, 3

1792, 1, 18. Mary b
1805, 7, 24. Sarah [Oneall] m Thomas PERKINS
1813, 8, 4. Rebecca [Oneall] m Micajah JOHNSON
1820, 12, 6. Rhoda [Oneall] m James B. JOHNSON
1875, 1, 4. Abijah P. [Oneall] s William & Martha, Warren Co., O.; m at residence of Charles F. Chapman, Anna FISHER, dt Elias & Letitia, Warren Co., O., b 1844,3,10 (H)

Ch:	b	d
Margaret H.	b 1877, 3, 28	d 1883, 8,16
William E.	" 1882, 11, 25	
Martha L.	" 1885, 6, 16	

1806, 12, 11. Mary Ann Cooper (form Oneall) con mou
1815, 5, 31. William dis
1818, 3, 25. Matthias [O'Neal] recrq
1827, 1, 31. John Kelly [O'Neal] gct Springborough MM, to m Mary Ingham
1827, 6, 27. Mary [O'Neal] & niece, Anna Swain, minor, rocf Springborough MM
1829, 3, 25. Abijah dis jH
1829, 6, 24. Anna (form Swain) dis mou
1832, 12, 26. Mary gct Springborough MM
1921, 7, 30. Irma, Albert E., Charles F., Anna M. & Hugh T. recrq (H)

OSBORN
1806, 6, 12. Elizabeth [Ozburn] rocf Cane Creek MM, N. C., dtd 1805,9,7
1813, 8, 25. Cert rec for Elizabeth [Ozborn] from Springfield MM, N. C., dtd 1812,9,5, endorsed to Clear Creek MM
1813, 9, 29. Isabel rocf Springfield MM, N.C.
1813, 9, 29. Jonothan rocf Center MM, N. C.
1816, 2, 28. William rocf Back Creek MM, N. C., dtd 1815,8,26
1829, 1, 28. Charles & w, Hannah, & ch, Narcissa, Cynthia, Gideon S., Charles N., Parker, Jordan, Benjamin & Sarah, rocf Springfield MM, O., dtd 1829,1,13
1830, 11, 24. Charles & w, Hannah, & ch, Narcissa, Cynthia, Gideon S., Charles N., Parker, Jordan, Benjamin, Sarah & Anna B., gct Springfield MM, Ind.
1909, 12, 22. Joseph & w, Elizabeth, & s, Harry, rocf Center MM, O., dtd 1909,11,17

OUTLAND
----, --, --. Josiah & Keziah (H)

Ch:	b
Jeremiah	b 1807, 5, 6
Robert	
Marmon	" 1808, 11, 27

1807, 4, 9. Josiah & w, Keziah, & ch, Patsy, rocf Rich Square MM, N. C., dtd 1806,3,15

OVERMAN
1864, 2, 3. David, s John & Ann, Grant Co., Ind.; m at Miami, Elizabeth Cooper WELCH, Warren Co., O.

1805, 12, 12. Mary & ch, Mary & Anna, rocf Back Creek MM, N. C., dtd 1805,4,27
1805, 12, 12. Miriam rocf Back Creek MM, N.C., dtd 1805,4,27
1806, 4, 10. Obadiah & w, Abigail, & ch, Isaac, Zadoc, Elisha, Sarah & Mary, rocf Mt. Pleasant MM, Va., dtd 1803,12,31
1806, 8, 14. Dempsey rocf Back Creek MM, N. C., dtd 1805,4,27
1806, 8, 14. Zebulum & s, Enoch, Elias, John & Nathan, rocf Back Creek MM, N. C., dtd 1805,4,27
1806, 8, 14. Sarah Bloomer (form Overman) dis mou
1866, 1, 24. Demsy dropped from mbrp; form mbr Fall Creek or Centre MM which had been laid down (H)
1866, 1, 24. Elias & fam, Enoch & fam & John & fam dropped from mbrp; form mbr Fall Creek or Centre MM which had been laid down (H)
1866, 1, 24. Milton dropped from mbrp; form mbr of Fall Creek or Centre MM which had been laid down (H)

OVERMAN, continued
1866, 3, 21. Elizabeth C. gct Mississinnewa MM

OWEN
1805, 6, 13. Ephraim & w, Sarah, & ch, John, Benjamin, Ephraim, Elizabeth, Sarah & Ruth, rocf Wrightsboro MM
1805, 6, 13. Samuel & w, Margery, & ch, Sarah, Ephraim, John, Mary & Benjamin, rocf Wrightsboro MM
1805, 6, 13. Mary rocf Wrightsborough MM, Ga., dtd 1805,3,23
1805, 6, 13. Deborah rocf Wrightsborough MM, Ga., dtd 1805,3,23
1805, 11, 14. Hannah rocf Wrightsborough MM, Ga., dtd 1805,5,25

PACKER
1882, 2, 23. Franklin, s Elisha & Asenath, Jefferson Co., O.; m at Waynesville, Mary E. GAUSE, dt Clarkson & Sidney, Jefferson Co., O., b 1843,5,31 (H)
Ch: Marianna b 1883, 2, 20
Margaretta " 1886, 11, 13

1805, 8, 8. Samuel & w, Sarah, & ch, Catherine, John, Samuel, Ann & William, rocf Woodberry MM, N. J., dtd 1805,5,14
1811, 9, 25. Samuel & w, Sarah, & ch, John, Samuel, Ann, William Paul, Richard & Joel, gct Woodberry MM
1811, 10, 30. Catherine gct Woodberry MM
1882, 12, 27. Franklin rocf Short Creek MM, O., dtd 1882,12,7 (H)
1908, 3, 25. Franklin & w, Mary Elizabeth G. & dt, Marianna & Margaretta, gct Wakefield MM, Pa. (H)

PADDOCK
1814, 8, 31. Samuel & w, Deborah, & dt, Lucretia, rocf Nantucket MM, dtd 1814,7,14
1814, 8, 31. Tristram rocf Nantucket MM, dtd 1814,5,26
1814, 8, 31. Alice, minor, rocf Nantucket MM, dtd 1814,4,28
1814, 9, 28. Benjamin & w, Jemima, & dt, Lydia, rocf Nantucket MM, dtd 1814,7,14
1814, 9, 28. Charles rocf Nantucket MM, dtd 1814,7,14
1814, 9, 28. William 2nd rocf Nantucket MM, dtd 1814,7,14
1815, 6, 28. Joseph & w, Ann, & ch, Phebe & Reuben, rocf Nantucket MM, dtd 1814,11,24

PAINTER
1806, 7, 10. Hannah Anderson (form Painter) con mou

PARDY
1819, 5, 26. Martha (form Welsh) con mou
1844, 8, 21. Ann recrq

PARHAM
1805, 4, 11. Rachel rocf Wrightsborough MM, dtd 1804,5,5
1809, 5, 6. Peter [Parram] & ch, Elizabeth, Zacheus, Delila & Benajah, recrq

PARKER
1897, 12, 22. Emmet N. relrq (H)

PARLETTE
1816, 7, 21. David recrq
1914, 5, 27. David, Rusell, Mary & Jesse [Parlett] dropped from mbrp

PARNELL
1807, 3, 18. Sarah m David HORNER

1809, 8, 5. Hester Pruet (form Parnel) dis mou
1813, 11, 24. George dis
1816, 10, 30. James gct Cesars Creek MM

PARRY
1891, 6, 24. George R. Thorpe gct White Water MM, Ind., to m Mary Parry Jr. (H)

PARSHALL
1898, 5, 25. Ida [Parshal] relrq
1900, 10, 24. M. L. & w, Ida, & ch, Helen & Olive, recrq

PATRICK
1887, 4, 20. Frances Curn recrq

PATTERSON
1808, 9, 10. Jacob rocf Jack Swamp MM, dtd 1807,12,5
1825, 5, 25. Beulah & ch, Samuel & Elwood, rocf Alexandria MM, dtd 1824,11,18
1830, 7, 28. Beulah & s, Samuel N. & Ellwood, gct Elk MM (H)

PATTON
1838, 7, 25. Susan (form Evans) rpd mou (H)

PATTY
1807, 2, 12. James [Peaty] & w, Ann, & ch, Samuel & Mark, roc dtd 1806,8,30
1813, 12, 29. James [Paty] & w, Anna, & ch, Mark, Samuel, Sarah, Nancy & Phebe, rocf West Branch MM, dtd 1813,11,25
1814, 10, 26. James & fam gct West Branch MM
1832, 8, 29. Mark recrq (H)
1835, 2, 18. Mark gct White Water MM, Ind. (H)
1861, 9, 25. Rebecca (form Steddom) con mou
1869, 1, 27. Margery (form Steddom) con mou
1869, 5, 26. Margaret gct Union MM

PAXTON
1806, 10, 15. Jacob [Paxson], s John & Mary, Warren Co., O.; m at Miami, Sitnah RICHARDS, dt Rolen & Lydia, Warren Co.,O.

PAXTON, continued
1806, 9, 11. Jacob rocf Mount Pleasant MM, Va., dtd 1806,6,28
1809, 7, 8. John & w, Mary, & ch, John, Nancy Susannah & William, rocf Mt. Pleasant MM, Va., dtd 1808,9,24
1811, 7, 31. Robert [Paxon] rocf Buckingham MM, Pa., dtd 1811,4,1

PEARSON
----, --, --. William & ----- (H)
Ch: Jesse b 1788, 11, 11
Samuel " 1791, 5, 25
Exile " 1793, 3, 7
Henry " 1796, 10, 5
Anna " 1799, 12, 19
1811, 1, 1. Mary d ae 77y (a minister)

1804, 5, 10. Samuel & w, Ann, & ch, Enoch & Mary, rocf Bush River MM, S. C., dtd 1803, 12,31
1805, 2, 14. Samuel & Henry [Pierson], s William, rocf Bush River MM, S. C., dtd 1804,8,25
1805, 5, 9. John Mills & w, Mary, & ch, Enoch & Elijah, & Ann Pearson, rocf Bush River MM, S. C., dtd 1805,2,23
1805, 9, 12. Thomas & w, Olive, & ch, Samuel, Elijah & Elisha, rocf Bush River MM, S. C., dtd 1805,3,30
1805, 10, 10. Samuel & w, Mary, & ch, Enoch, Henry, Hiram, Benjamin & Rachel, rocf Bush River MM, dtd 1805,3,30
1805, 11, 14. Benjamin & w, Esther, & ch, John, Furnas, Mary, Samuel, Moses, Joseph, Robert & Wilkinson, rocf Bush River MM, S. C., dtd 1805,7,27
1805, 11, 14. Mary rocf Bush River MM, dtd 1805,7,27
1805, 11, 14. Ruth rocf Bush River MM, dtd 1805,8,31
1806, 8, 14. Jesse rocf Bush River MM, dtd 1805,7,27
1806, 6, 14. Robert & w, Charity, & ch, Sarah, rocf Bush River MM, dtd 1806,4,26
1806, 9, 11. Enoch & w, Ann, & ch, Rebecca, Ann, Thomas & Isaac, rocf Bush River MM, S. C., dtd 1806,4,26
1806, 9, 11. Thomas [Pearsons] & w, Mary, rocf Bush River MM, S. C., dtd 1806,5,31
1809, 3, 11. Samuel dis
1809, 6, 10. Keziah rocf Bush River MM, S.C., dtd 1807,7,25
1809, 12, 27. Exile rocf New Garden MM, N. C., dtd 1809,8,26
1814, 2, 23. Samuel dis
1815, 12, 27. William & fam gct Cesar's Creek MM
1817, 2, 26. Henry gct White Water MM, to m
1817, 9, 24. Enoch, Mary, John & Ann, ch Samuel, gct Mill Creek MM
1819, 2, 24. Henry & fam gct Silver Creek MM
1853, 2, 23. Samuel T. Steddom gct Union MM, to m Esther Pearson

PECKOVER
1819, 2, 24. Edmund rocf Bristol MM, Eng., dtd 1818,7,29

PEDRICK
----, --, --. Isaac b 1754,3,3; m Hannah ---- b 1757,12,13
Ch: Hannah b 1790, 7, 15
Benjamin " 1814, 10, 6
Lydia " 1816, 8, 13
Margaret " 1818, 8, 26
Isaac " 1821, 3, 1
Ann " 1823, 4, 18
Mary P. " 1825, 8, 5
Hannah " 1827, 11, 12
1807, 3, 18. Ann m John COMTON
1808, 1, 20. Lydia m Joseph CANBY
1813, 10, 6. Hannah m Thomas EVANS
1822, 11, 6. Richard, s Isaac & Hannah, Green Co., O.; m at Miami, Mary EVANS, dt Benjamin & Hannah, Warren Co., O.
1835, 1, 9. Isaac d bur Caesars Creek
1846, 5, 19. Hannah d bur Caesars Creek

1806, 6, 12. Ann rocf Piles-grove MM, N.J., dtd 1806,4,24
1806, 6, 12. Isaac & w, Hannah, & ch, Lydia, Hannah, William, Richard, Elihu & Clayton, rocf Piles Grove MM, dtd 1806,4,24
1812, 1, 29. Phillip [Pednick] & w, Judith, & ch, Keturah, Jesse Townsend, Catherine & Elizabeth, rocf Salem MM, dtd 1811,12,17
1821, 7, 25. Judith [Pednick] dis
1821, 8, 29. Julia dis disunity
1822, 3, 27. Phillip & dt, Catharine & Elizabeth, gct White Water MM, Ind.
1824, 1, 28. Chester MM rq permission to rst Judith, but it was not granted
1824, 6, 30. Richard [Pednick] & w, Mary, gct White Water MM
1829, 6, 24. Chester MM, Ind. was given permission to rst Judith
1831, 2, 23. Richard rocf White Water MM, dtd 1831,1,26
1831, 12, 28. Rcchard gct White Water MM

PEEBLES
----, --, --. Elijah b 1783,2,12; m Christiana -----
Ch: Pleasant Dilworth b 1817, 9, 10
Catherine " 1819, 7, 3
Oliver Emlen " 1821, 9, 8
Deborah " 1825, 12, 3

1826, 3, 29. Samuel rocf Upper MM, Va., dtd 1826,10,19
1829, 8, 26. Elijah & w, Christiana, & ch, Pleasant Dilworth, Catharine, Oliver Emlin & Deborah, rocf Dover MM, dtd 1829,7,

PEEBLES, continued
16
1832, 1, 25. Deborah rocf White Water MM, dtd 1831,12,28
1833, 10, 24. Deborah gct Springborough MM
1835, 4, 22. Elijah's ch gct Dover MM
1835, 11, 25. Elijah dis
1842, 11, 23. Center MM was given permission to rst Elijah
1912, 2, 21. Charity [Peeble] gct Dayton MM,O.
1917, 7, 29. Jessie transferred to this mtg from Springboro (H)

PEITSMEYER
----, --, --. Charles m Gulielma SANDERS
Ch: Carrie S. b 1862, 5, 19
Eliza
Louiza " 1865, 1, 19

1861, 6, 26. Gulielma [Peitzmeyer] rocf Fairfield MM, dtd 1861,3,16
1866, 3, 21. Charles rocf Fairfield MM
1870, 4, 20. Charles [Petsmyre] & w, Gulielma, & ch, Carrie S., Elma L. & Sallie M., gct Chester MM

PEMBERTON
1806, 7, 10. Esther & ch, Robert, John, Isaiah, Mary & Elizabeth, rocf Bush River MM, S. C. dtd 1805,8,31

PENNINGTON
----, --, --. Eliza (Hatton) b 1786,2,26 d 1886, 2,15

1807, 4, 9. Josiah rocf Center MM, Penn., dtd 1807,1,17
1817, 5, 28. John & w, Eliza, & s, Robert Morris, rocf Center MM, Pa., dtd 1817,3,15
1821, 2, 28. Ann (form Mathews) con mou
1822, 3, 27. Josiah & w, Deborah, & ch, Levi Talbot, Mary, Susanna, John, Eliza & Rachel, rocf Stillwater MM, dtd 1822,3,23
1824, 7, 28. Josiah & fam gct White Water MM
1827, 4, 25. Paul rocf Center MM, Pa., dtd 1826,7,6
1844, 4, 24. David Burnet gct Spiceland MM, to m Eliza Pennington
1853, 11, 23. Eliza rocf White Water MM, dtd 1853,10,26 (H)

PENROSE
1811, 3, 27. Joseph & w, Mary, rocf Red Stone MM, dtd 1810,12,28

PERDUE
1818, 12, 2. Gershom, s Mentorpimm & Jemima, Hiland Co., O.; m at Miami, Elizabeth DUKEMINEER, dt Isaac & Ann, Warren Co.,O.

1818, 11, 25. Gershom rocf Fairfield MM
1819, 2, 24. Elizabeth gct Fairfield MM
1840, 3, 25. Hannah D. rocf Fairfield MM, dtd 1840,1,5

PERKINS
1805, 7, 24. Thomas, s Joseph & Ann, Warren Co., O., b 1774,2,18; m Sarah ONEALL, dt Abijah & Anna, Warren Co., O., b 1787,5, 31 d 1878,9,29 (H)
Ch: Joseph b 1806, 5, 5
Mary Ann " 1809, 1, 7
Pheniah " 1811, 9, 6
Isaac " 1814, 4, 1
Abijah " 1816, 12, 7
----, --, --. John b 1798,5,13; m Julia Ann EACHUS (H)
Dt: Priscilla b 1825, 11, 20
1821, 11, 1. Ann d ae 50 (H)

1804, 10, 11. Isaac & w, Peninah, & ch, Anne, Caleb, Abigail, Lydia, Salinah & John, rocf New Garden MM, N. C., dtd 1804,5,23
1804, 10, 11. Thomas rocf New Garden MM, N.C., dtd 1803,8,27
1806, 8, 14. Martha (form Crew) rpd mou; d before question was settled
1811, 1, 30. Ann rocf Salem MM, O., dtd 1810, 12,11
1812, 12, 30. Cert rec for Susanna from Deep Creek MM, N. C., dtd 1812,9,5, endorsed to Center MM
1821, 5, 30. Thomas gct Center MM
1866, 1, 24. Priscilla rec in mbrp; form mbr Fall Creek or Centre MM which had been laid down (H)
1885, 10, 21. Priscilla relrq (H)
1888, 1, 25. Abijah dropped from mbrp (H)

PETTET
1849, 6, 20. Ruth (form Daniels) con mou (H)

PFLUMER
1892, 9, 21. Sadie recrq

PHILLIPS
1806, 6, 12. George rocf Newberry MM, dtd 1806,4,12
1815, 4, 26. George dis mcd
1887, 4, 20. Pearlie & Florence recrq
1890, 10, 22. Florence Hay (form Phillips) dis
1892, 10, 26. Pearl [Philips] relrq

PICKEREL
1805, 1, 10. Henry & w, Achsah, & ch, Catherine & John, rocf Mount Pleasant MM, Va., dtd 1804,8,25

PICKERING
1866, 1, 24. Benjamin dropped from mbrp; former mbr of Fall Creek or Centre MM which had been laid down

PICKET
1808, 8, 11. Joshua [Piggott] & w, Sarah, & ch, Mary, Benjamin, Sarah & Joshua, rocf

PICKET, continued
Cane Creek MM, N. C., dtd 1807,9,5
1811, 2, 27. Joseph & w, Pricilla, & ch, Tamar, Anna, Lydia & Mary, rocf Deep River MM, N. C., dtd 1810,9,3
1812, 2, 26. Joseph [Pickett] & w, Pricilla, & ch, Tamar, Anna, Lydia, Mary & Sarah, gct Elk MM
1813, 2, 24. Abigail & ch, Elizabeth, Mary, Abigail, Ester & Ellen recrq

PIDGEON
----, --, --. Samuel & Mary (H)
Ch: Sarah b 1790, 2, 29
Elizabeth " 1792, 6, 17
Isaac " 1794, 9, 12
1817, 8, 14. Sarah m Abraham HOLLINGSWORTH (H)

1805, 9, 12. Samuel & ch, Sarah, Elizabeth & Isaac, rocf Springfield MM, N. C., dtd 1804,12,18
1816, 7, 31. Elizabeth Hiday (form Pidgeon) con mou
1822, 10, 30. Isaac [Pigeon] dis non-attendance

PIEPHO
1859, 2, 3. Sarah K. (Adams) b (H)

1803, 12, 23. Sarah K. dropped from mbrp (H)

PIERCE
----, --, --. Richard [Peirce] b 1783,5,13 d 1870,3,28; m Mary FALLIS b 1787,9,12 d 1872,4,3 (H)
Ch: Miriam b 1822, 5, 18 d 1888,10,15
John F. " 1824, 7, 18 " 1894,11,14
James " 1826, 3, 30 " 1892,12, 5
Martha " 1829, 7, 30 " 1905,11,19
Esther " 1830, 6, 24
1843, 5, 23. Jacob, s Jonathan & Hannah, Clark Co., O.; m at Miami, Miriam CHANDLES, dt Aaron & Hannah, Warren Co., O. (H)

1814, 10, 26. Thomas rocf Phila. MM, dtd 1814,5,23
1843, 7, 26. Miriam gct Green Plain MM (H)
1848, 2, 23. Miriam (form Chandler) dis mou
1852, 8, 25. Andrew W. Cadwalader gct Center MM, to m Esther W. Pierce (H)
1866, 1, 24. James rec in mbrp; form mbr Fall Creek or Centre MM which had been laid down (H)
1866, 1, 24. Richard & Mary rec in mbrp; form mbr of Fall Creek or Centre MM which had been laid down (H)
1866, 1, 24. Benjamin & fam dropped from mbrp; form mbr of Fall Creek or Centre MM which had been laid down (H)
1866, 1, 24. John L. dis mcd (H)
1866, 11, 21. James dis disunity (H)
1887, 4, 20. Mattie A. [Pears] recrq
1916, 10, 29. Howall recrq (H)
1917, 9, 30. Emma rocf Green Plain MM, O., dtd 1917,9,12 (H)

PIKE
1808, 8, 11. Cert rec for Rebeckah from Cain Creek MM, N. C., dtd 1808,4,2, endorsed to West Branch MM

PINE
1835, 3, 9. William H. b (H)
1843, 6, 16. Mary H., his sister, b (H)

1825, 6, 29. Simon rocf Haddonfield MM, N.J., dtd 1825,2,14
1868, 4, 22. Samuel Kelley gct Springborough MM, to m Sarah Pine (H)
1904, 4, 20. Ruth Hannah relrq (H)
1917, 7, 29. Mary Johnson transferred to this mtg from Springboro (H)
1920, 4, 25. James Arnold & Ruth Eleanor, ch Mary Johnson Pine, recrq (H)

PITMAN
1838, 1, 24. Anthony & w, Margaret, & ch, Rebecca, Esther, Elias, Eliza & Margaret, rocf Allum Creek MM, dtd 1837,12,25 (H)
1839, 7, 24. Anthony & w, Margaret, & ch, Rebecca, Esther, Elias, Eliza & Margaret, gct Whitewater MM (H)

PLEAS
1815, 8, 30. Jane & ch, William, Aaron, Lancaster, Isaac, Jane & Mariba Newby, rocf Symons Creek MM, N. C., dtd 1814,10,15, endorsed by Whitewater MM, 1815,7,29
1816, 10, 30. Jane [Plais] & ch, Aaron Lancaster, Isaac, Jane C. & Martha Newby, gct Short Creek MM
1819, 7, 28. William gct White Water MM
1828, 5, 28. Morris rocf Milford MM, Ind., dtd 1828,4,28
1828, 11, 26. Maurice [Place] gct Center MM (H)
1829, 3, 25. Morris [Plais] dis jH

PLUMMER
1835, 10, 29. Tacy m Thomas GILPIN
1856, 1, 24. Grace d bur Harveysburgh

1829, 5, 27. Ezra [Plumer] dis jH
1833, 10, 24. Jane M. rocf Short Creek MM, dtd 1839,9,18
1834, 8, 27. John Harvey gct Springfield MM, to m Mahala Plumer
1834, 8, 27. Elizabeth (form Ballard) con mou (H)
1835, 8, 26. Tacy rocf Fairfield MM, dtd 1835,7,23
1837, 12, 27. Elizabeth (form Ballard) dis mou & jH
1839, 2, 20. Elizabeth dis jas (H)
1840, 10, 21. Grace rocf Fairfield MM, dtd 1840,7,23

POLK
1895, 5, 22. Rachel set off as mbr of Executive Mtg at Clear Creek (H)

POOL
1834, 2, 20. William, s John & Elizabeth, Wayne Co., Ind.; m at Harveysburgh, Rebecca HARVEY, dt Caleb & Sarah, Warren Co.,O.
1842, 9, 1. Rebecca m William CLAWSON

1840, 1, 22. Rebecca H. & ch, Joseph & Elizabeth Ann, rocf White Water MM, Ind., dtd 1839,12,25
1844, 8, 21. Phineas R. Mather gct Whitewater MM, to m Ruth Ann Pool

POPE
1805, 4, 17. William, s Nathaniel & Martha, Hiland Co., O.; m at Lees Creek, Grace LUPTON, dt William & Bathsheba, Hiland Co., O.
1807, 3, 19. Betsy m Thomas SANDERS

1804, 10, 11. Martha rocf Mount Pleasant MM, Va., dtd 1803,11,25
1804, 12, 13. William & Elizabeth recrq
1807, 2, 12. Nathan rocf New Garden MM, N.C., dtd 1806,10,25

POTTORF
1872, 6, 26. Simeon L. recrq
1873, 1, 22. Margaret [Potterf] recrq
1873, 2, 19. Granville recrq
1880, 11, 24. Simeon relrq
1883, 3, 21. Granville dis disunity

POTTS
1820, 12, 27. Aquilla Whitacre gct White Water MM, Ind., to m Ruthanna Potts
1827, 6, 27. Samuel & w, Mary, & ch, Lindly & John, rocf Plainfield MM, dtd 1827,5,24

POWERS
1878, 3, 20. Sarah L. recrq

PRATHER
1861, 9, 25. Sidney (form Whittacre) con mcd (H)

PRESNALL
1902, 5, 21. Lydia Edwards gct Fairmount, Ind.

PRESTON
1839, 4, 19. Ann d

1829, 5, 27. Ann dis jH

PRINTS
1852, 8, 25. Asenath (form Ward) con mou
1863, 9, 23. Cynthia W. Pugh (form Printze) dis mou

PRITCHARD
1864, 11, 2. David T., s Samuel & Harriet, Henry Co., Ind.; m at Miami, Sarah A. HALE dt Eli & Anna, Warren Co., O.

1865, 3, 22. Sarah H. gct Raysville MM, Ind.
1884, 8, 27. Daniel & w, Emma, & ch, Alonzo B. & Nellie M., rocf Ceasars Creek MM, dtd 1884,6,26
1884, 11, 26. Clifford M. & Carlton C. rocf Chicago MM, Ill., dtd 1884,9,17
1885, 6, 24. Daniel & w & s gct Caesars Creek MM
1898, 6, 22. Clifford & Frances relrq
1906, 12, 20. Carlton relrq

PRICE
1809, 4, 8. Rice & s, James Rice & Robert, rocf Contentney MM, N. C., dtd 1807,3,14
1809, 4, 8. Cert rec for Catherine & dt, Mary, Catherine Ann & Zilpha, from Contentney MM, N. C., dtd 1807,3,14, endorsed to West Branch MM
1809, 4, 8. Cert rec for Sarah from Contentney MM, N. C., dtd 1807,3,14, endorsed to West Branch MM
1819, 11, 24. Samuel rocf Short Creek MM, dtd 1819,8,24
1822, 12, 25. Samuel gct Springfield MM
1851, 7, 23. Isaac K. Steddom gct Duck Creek MM, to m Narcissa Price

PRUET
1809, 8, 5. Hester (form Parnel) dis mou

PUCKETT
1865, 5, 24. Isaac P. C. Steddom gct Dover MM, Ind., to m Lucinda Puckett

PUGH
----, --, --. Ellis b 1749,1,21; m Phebe ----- b 1750,10,21
----, --, --. John b 1778,10,11; m Ruth JANNEY b 1788,6,17
1806, 1, 15. Bersheba m Samuel JAY
1814, 7, 7. Lot, s David & Rachel, Hamilton Co., O.; m at Cincinnati, Rachel ANTHONY, dt Christopher & Mary, Hamilton Co., O.
----, --, --. William, s Job & Sarah, b 1820, 9,10 d 1821,4,27 (H)
----, --, --. Achilles b 1805,3,10; m Anna Maria DAVIS b 1806,2,24

Ch:		
Esther	b 1834,	8, 31
John Davis	" 1838,	3, 14
Mary Taylor	" 1840,	9, 24
Rachel	" 1843,	4, 29
Achilles Henry	" 1846,	11, 24

1865, 11, 29. Mary T. m John WILDMAN

1804, 5, 10. David & w, Rachel, & ch, Belinda, Job, Bathsheba, Lot, Reu, William, Leah & Hannah, rocf Cane Creek MM, S. C.,

PUGH, continued
dtd 1804,3,24
1805, 1, 10. Azariah & w, Sophia, & ch, Harriet, Hiram, Ishmael, Thomas Joseph & William, rocf Bush River MM, dtd 1804,8,25
1806, 11, 13. Hannah rocf Bush River MM, dtd 1806,8,30
1807, 10, 8. Hannah rocf Wrightsborough MM, Ga., dtd 1804,8,4
1809, 8, 5. Verlinda Swift (form Pugh) con mou
1809, 10, 14. Job dis mcd
1809, 12, 27. Enoch rocf Hopewell MM, dtd 1809, 2,10
1811, 6, 26. Susanna (form Coppock) dis mcd to first cousin
1815, 10, 25. Caleb rocf Nottingham MM, Md., dtd 1815,9,6
1815, 12, 27. David & fam gct Cincinnati MM
1816, 10, 30. Hiram dis
1820, 8, 30. Ishmael rpd mcd
1820, 10, 25. Job & w, Sarah, & ch, David, Thomas, Rues, Rachel & William, rocf Cincinnati MM, dtd 1820,10,19
1821, 2, 28. Harriet Jones (form Pugh) con mou
1822, 6, 26. Job & fam gct Cincinnati MM
1824, 2, 25. Thomas dis mcd
1824, 12, 29. Joseph dis mcd
1829, 2, 25. Mary (form Edwards) con mou
1831, 11, 30. Ismael dis disunity
1832, 5, 23. Mary gct White River MM, Ind.
1840, 6, 24. Jesse recrq
1853, 9, 20. John & w, Ruth, rocf Hopewell MM, Va., dtd 1853,9,8
1855, 1, 24. Achilles & w, Anna Maria, & ch, John D., Mary T. & Achilles Henry, rocf Cincinnati MM, dtd 1854,12,21
1855, 1, 24. Esther rocf Cincinnati MM, dtd 1854,12,21
1863, 9, 23. Cynthia W. (form Printze) dis mou
1872, 5, 22. John D. gct Cincinnati MM
1875, 4, 21. Achiles & w, Annamaria, & dt, Esther, gct Cincinnati MM
1875, 6, 21. Henry E. gct Cincinnati MM
1904, 1, 27. Mary rocf Ceasars Creek MM, dtd 1903,12,24
1913, 4, 23. Mary relrq

PUSEY
1806, 12, 11. Mary & ch, Nathan, Mary, Joice, George & William, rocf Crooked Run MM, Va., dtd 1806,8,2
1806, 12, 11. Lydia rocf Crooked Run MM, Va., dtd 1806,8,2
1806, 12, 11. Margaret rocf Crooked Run MM, Va., dtd 1806,8,2
1820, 6, 28. Joel & w, Hannah, & dt, Martha, rocf Center MM, dtd 1820,5,20
1821, 5, 30. Joel & fam gct Center MM

PYLE
1845, 4, 30. John, s William & Mary, Clinton Co., O.; m at Miami, Mary Ann BURNET, dt John & Elizabeth, Warren Co., O.
1847, 3, 4. David, s William & Mary, Clinton Co., O.; m at Turtle Creek, Esther STEDDOM dt John & Alice

1839, 4, 24. Isaac Hawkins gct Springfield MM, to m Ruth Pyle
1845, 11, 26. Mary Ann gct Springfield MM
1847, 7, 21. Esther gct Springfield MM
1852, 7, 21. Moses Steddom gct Springfield MM, to m Sarah Pyle
1857, 1, 21. David & w, Esther S., & ch, Joseph S. & Abijah H., rocf Springfield MM, dtd 1856,12,20
1858, 3, 24. David & w, Esther, & ch, Joseph S. & Abijah, gct Springfield MM, O.
1889, 11, 20. Mary Ann rpd to have become mbr of Marietta MM, Ia. (H)

RANDLE
1805, 7, 11. Jonas & w, Sarah, & ch, John, Jehu, Jonathan, Mary & Jonas, rocf Cane Creek MM, dtd 1805,3,23
1806, 3, 13. Joseph & w, Ann, rocf Cane Creek MM, S. C., dtd 1805,8,24

RATCLIFF
1822, 6, 12. Cornelius [Ratliff], s Cornelius & Elizabeth, Wayne Co., Ind.; m at Miami, Mary KINDLEY, dt Edward & Margaret, Warren Co., O.

1805, 7, 11. Ann [Ratliff] & dt, Sarah, rocf Cane Creek MM, dtd 1804,8,4
1808, 4, 14. Amos & w, Eleanor, & ch, John, Margaret, Ann, Abner, Sarah, Eleanor, Elizabeth, Amos & Moses, rocf Cane Creek MM, N. C., dtd 1807,3,7
1822, 8, 28. Mary rqct White Water MM,Ind.

RAY
1811, 9, 5. Rebekah [Rea] m Joel STRATTON

1805, 6, 13. Elizabeth rocf Salem MM, N.J., dtd 1805,3,25
1810, 1, 31. Robert [Rhea] & w, Rebecca, rocf Crooked Run MM, dtd 1805,5,4
1810, 1, 31. Rebeckah, Jr. rocf Crooked Run MM, Va., dtd 1807,2,1

RAYBURN
1883, 4, 25. James N. & Margaret recrq

REAGAN
1812, 10, 3. Ruel [Ragin], s Reason & Mary, Warren Co., O.; m at Turtle Creek, Mary MILLS, dt Marmaduke & Patience, Warren.

REAGAN, continued
Co., O.

1804, 11, 8. Mary [Reagin] rocf Bush River MM, S. C., dtd 1804,8,25
1807, 10, 8. Leah [Ragan] recrq
1813, 1, 27. Beulah [Ragan] (form Gaunt) con mou
1824, 9, 29. Mary [Ragan] gct Ceasars Creek MM
1831, 5, 25. Reason & w, Mary, & ch, John, Dinah, Rachel & Mary, rocf Caesars Creek MM, dtd 1831,4,28
1838, 1, 24. Reason & w, Mary, & ch gct Caesars Creek MM

REASON
1879, 3, 26. Hannah E. recrq
1879, 6, 25. William H. recrq
1886, 4, 21. Edward recrq
1892, 6, 22. Margaret R. relrq
1893, 6, 21. Edward & fam gct Wilmington MM
1903, 3, 25. Edward & w, Sadie, & ch, Elsie, Paul & Percy, rocf Wilmington MM, O., dtd 1903,2,14

REAVE
1814, 6, 29. Elizabeth, w Jeremiah, & ch, Thompson, Elizabeth, Alexander, Hannah, Charles & Sarah, rocf Phila. MM, dtd 1814, 4,28

REDFERN
1834, 6, 25. Rachel (form Gregg) dis mou (H)

REED
1854, 2, 22. Emily (form Sayre) dis mcd (H)
1895, 2, 20. Naomi Almira recrq
1897, 2, 24. Raymond recrq
1930, 6, 29. Floramond recrq (H)

REESE
----, --, --. ----- m Thamizin M. LUPTON b 1818,--,-- d 1897,10,7 (H)
Ch: Samuel D. b 1847, 9, 22 d 1899, 9, 3
Martha A. " 1839, 3, 24

1806, 6, 12. Lewis [Reece] rocf Hopewell MM, Va., dtd 1806,3,3
1807, 8, 3. James [Reece] & w, Jane, & ch, Thomas & William, rocf Lost Creek MM, Tenn., dtd 1807,5,30
1814, 6, 29. Sally & ch recrq
1832, 8, 29. Stephen D. rocf Alum Creek MM, dtd 1832,7,26 (H)
1867, 10, 23. Ellen gct Prairie Grove MM, Ia. (H)

RETALLIC
1871, 1, 25. Emma (form Burnet) con mou
1876, 3, 22. Edmund recrq
1920, 5, 26. Emma [Retallick] relrq

REYNOLDS
1907, 2, 20. Fannie recrq

RHODES
1805, 11, 14. Ann rocf Cane Creek MM, dtd 1805,10,5
1806, 10, 9. Mary rocf Bush River MM, dtd 1806,7,26
1819, 1, 27. Moses & w, Susanna, & ch, Joseph & Martha, rocf Salem MM, O., dtd 1818,10,23
1821, 3, 28. Moses & fam gct New Garden MM, Ind.

RICH
----, --, --. Samuel d 1852,8,13; m Judith ----- d 1818,7,4 (H)
Ch: Nathan b 1801, 6, 6
John " 1802, 9, 9
Simon " 1804, 1, 21
Jacob " 1806, 10, 25
Susannah " 1808, 8, 20
Thomas " 1810, 5, 19
Isaac " 1812, 3, 29
Nancy " 1816, 4, 6 d 1899,10,17
Levi M. " 1817, 12, 12

1817, 8, 27. Samuel & w, Judith, & ch, Nathan, John, Simon, Jacob, Susanna, Thomas, Isaac & Nancy, rocf New Garden MM, N.C., dtd 1816,9,28
1820, 12, 27. Samuel gct Center MM, to m Lydia Thomas
1821, 6, 27. Lydia rocf Center MM, dtd 1821, 5,19
1822, 11, 27. Nathan gct White Water MM,Ind.
1826, 4, 26. John gct White Water MM
1829, 5, 27. Lydia dis jH
1829, 5, 27. Susannah dis jH
1829, 7, 29. Samuel dis jH
1829, 8, 26. Simon dis jH
1829, 9, 30. Thomas dis jH
1829, 9, 30. Nathan & w, Mary, & ch, Samuel, Rachel & Merrick, rocf New Garden MM, Ind., dtd 1829,4,23 (or from Dover MM)
1830, 10, 27. Jacob con mou
1832, 9, 26. Simon dis mou (H)
1833, 6, 26. Nathan & fam gct Chester MM,Ind.
1833, 9, 18. Thomas dis mou (H)
1833, 10, 23. Samuel & w, Lydia, & ch, Nancy Ann & Levi M., gct Springborough MM (H)
1833, 10, 23. Susanna gct Springborough MM (H)
1834, 7, 23. Isaac dis mou (H)
1835, 2, 18. Samuel & w, Lydia, & dt, Nancy Ann, rocf Springborough MM, dtd 1834,12, 25 (H)
1839, 3, 27. Nancy Ann Dakin (form Rich) dis mou (H)
1842, 8, 24. Levi dis mou
1842, 12, 21. Nancy Dakin (form Rich) dis mou
1853, 7, 27. Edith (form Harlin) dis mou

RICHARDS
1806, 10, 15. Sitnah m Jacob PAXSON
1807, 11, 18. Catherine m Isaac MILLS
1808, 6, 15. Sarah m Judah FOULKE

1865, 3, 22. Sarah H. gct Raysville MM

RICHARDSON
1869, 8, 25. Clarkson Gause gct Green Plain MM, to m Ruth Richardson

RICKETT
1820, 6, 5. Mary m George MATHER

1810, 4, 25. Thomas rocf Plainfield MM, dtd 1809,11,25
1813, 2, 24. Abigail [Rickets] & fam, Elizabeth, Mary, Abigail, Esther Fielding & Eleanor, recrq
1820, 4, 26. Thomas [Ricket] & w, Abigail, & ch, Mary, Abigail, Esther Ellen, Sarah & Thomas, rocf Cincinnati MM, dtd 1820,4,20
1826, 9, 27. Thomas & fam gct Cincinnati MM
1826, 9, 27. Abigail Jr. gct Cincinnati MM
1826, 9, 27. Esther F. gct Cincinnati MM

RIDGE
1820, 9, 27. Mahlon rocf Horseham MM, dtd 1820,5,31
1821, 6, 27. Jane recrq
1824, 6, 30. Hannah recrq
1829, 5, 27. Ann dis
1829, 5, 27. Hannah dis jH
1829, 6, 24. Mary dis jH

RIDGWAY
1866, 1, 24. Martha & Martha Jr. dropped from mbrp; form mbr of Fall Creek or Centre MM which had been laid down

RINEHART
1808, 1, 14. Adam & w, Catherine, & ch, Jeremiah, Barbara, George, Margaret, Solomon, Ann, Jacob, Lydia & Isaac, rocf Cane Creek MM, N. C., dtd 1807,9,5

ROACH
1818, 5, 27. George rpd mcd
1818, 12, 30. George dis by direction of Fairfax MM, Va.
1844, 10, 23. Hannah (form Whitacre) con mou (H)
1845, 7, 23. Mary Elizabeth, dt Hannah, recrq (H)

ROBERTS
1807, 11, 26. Rebecca [Robarts] m Nathan HAWKINS

1806, 3, 13. Jonathan & ch, Phebe, Rebecca & Bethulah, rocf Cane Creek MM, S. C., dtd 1805,4,20
1806, 4, 10. Mary & ch, John, Walter & Sarah, recrq
1806, 6, 12. Thomas [Robards] & w, Ann, & ch, Rebecca, Walter, David, Solomon, Whitson, Phebe, Sarah & Thomas, rocf Cane Creek MM, S. C., dtd 1806,3,22
1841, 6, 23. Charles H. rocf Cherry St. MM, Phila., dtd 1840,12,16
1844, 9, 25. Charles H. dis disunity (H)
1863, 8, 26. Lydia (form Edwards)con mou
1866, 11, 21. Sarah (form Kelley) dis mcd (H)
1885, 8, 26. Lora M. (form Hiatt) relrq (H)
1887, 6, 22. Carrie Annetta recrq
1897, 3, 24. Rachel R. recrq
1890, 3, 26. Caroline relrq
1917, 9, 30. Sarah K. rst (H)

ROBINS
1807, 9, 10. Bathsheba recrq

ROBINSON
1834, 1, 22. Thomas Evans gct Springborough MM, to m Elizabeth Robinson
1905, 2, 22. James recrq

ROCKHILL
----, --, --. Benjamin d 1862,4,7; m Ruth ----- (H)

1861, 7, 24. Benjamin & w, Ruth, recrq (H)
1884, 9, 24. Ruth relrq (H)

ROGERS
1816, 4, 3. Josiah, s Joseph & Esther, Warren Co., O., b 1792,3,31 d 1872,3,26; m Abigail CLEAVER, dt Ezekiel & Abigail, Warren Co., O., b 1792,5,12 d 1873,8,14 (H)

Ch:			
Elizabeth	b 1817, 5, 4	d 1820, 6,17
Empson	" 1819, 5, 26	
Esther	" 1822, 4, 14	" 1822, 6,28
Ezekiel	" 1822, 11, 22	" 1834, 8, 8
Hannah	" 1825, 4, 30	" 1873, 5, 1
Josiah	" 1826, 12, 7	
Mary	" 1829, 9, 20	
Abigail	" 1831, 11, 7	" 1844, 9, 4
Margaret	" 1838, 7, 16	

1849, 3, 28. Hannah m Edward W. BUTTERWORTH(H)

1813, 11, 24. Joseph & w, Esther, & s, Isaaih, rocf Mt. Holly MM, N. J., dtd 1813,8,5
1813, 11, 24. Samuel rocf Mt. Holly MM, N.J., dtd 1813,5,6
1814, 7, 27. Josiah rocf Piles Grove MM,N.J., dtd 1814,3,24
1815, 3, 29. Samuel dis
1816, 3, 27. Isiah dis mcd
1829, 1, 28. Josiah dis jH
1829, 8, 26. Abigail dis jH
1841, 4, 21. Elizabeth (form Bispham) dis mou (H)
1841, 10, 27. Empson con mou (H)
1842, 1, 26. Elizabeth (form Bispham) dis mou
1842, 1, 26. Empson dis mou

ROGERS, continued
1843, 5, 24. Martha recrq (H)
1845, 1, 22. Empson dis jas (H)
1845, 5, 21. Martha dis jas (H)
1849, 5, 23. Mary Heighway (form Rogers) dis mou (H)
1850, 2, 20. Isaiah Jr. dis (H)
1853, 11, 23. Elizabeth H. rst by rq
1860, 12, 26. Margaret Garretson (form Rogers) dis mcd (H)
1864, 8, 24. Abigail dis (H)
1887, 4, 20. William Jr. recrq
1890, 3, 26. William dis disunity
1919, 4, 23. Ruth relrq

ROMINE
1871, 7, 26. Maria (form Downing) rpd mcd (H)
1885, 12, 23. Maria M. relrq (H)
1886, 6, 23. Maria M. recrq

ROONEY
1895, 4, 24. Effie A. relrq (H)

ROP
1812, 9, 30. Thomas & Phineas rocf New Garden MM, Pa., dtd 1810,3,8
1812, 12, 30. Thomas dis mcd & accepting captain's commission in military service
1813, 2, 24. Phineas dis mcd

ROSHER
1895, 5, 22. Sarah set off as mbr of Executive Mtg at Clear Creek (H)

ROSS
1813, 2, 24. Phineas dis mcd
1819, 7, 28. Sarah rocf New Garden MM, Pa., dtd 1819,5,6
1819, 7, 28. Catherine rocf New Garden MM, Pa., dtd 1819,5,6
1823, 9, 24. Sarah Corwin (form Ross) dis mou

RUBEL
1806, 3, 13. Samuel & w, Rachel, & ch, Walter, Owen, Samuel, Henry, William, Rachel & Susannah, rocf Lost Creek MM, Tenn., dtd 1803,1,26

RUSSEL
1805, 6, 13. Rosanna & dt, Ann, rocf Bush River MM, S. C., dtd 1805,3,30
1805, 11, 14. Elizabeth & s, Isaac, rocf Bush River MM, dtd 1805,8,31
1810, 9, 26. James recrq
1815, 4, 26. James & w gct Cincinnati MM

RUST
1877, 6, 20. Elizabeth A. (form Lownes) con mcd (H)
1879, 7, 23. Elizabeth A. L. gct Cincinnati MM, O. (H)

RUTH
1805, 11, 14. Jane rocf Lost Creek MM, Tenn., dtd 1804,11,24

SABIN
----, --, --. William b 1803,2,27 d 1869,12,11; m Lydia ----- (H)
Ch: Matilda b 1830, 6, 3
Sarah " 1832, 6, 29
Mary " 1834, 8, 30
Paul " 1836, 6, 12
Elizabeth " 1838, 5, 27
Martha C. " 1840, 3, 31
Arnold T. " 1843, 10, 12
William H. " 1845, 11, 16

1839, 3, 27. William & w, Lydia, & ch, Matilda, Mary, Sarah, Paul & Elizabeth, rocf Center MM, dtd 1839,2,14 (H)
1856, 4, 23. Matilda Whitsel (form Sabin) rpd mcd (H)
1856, 12, 24. Sarah King (form Sabin) dis mcd (H)
1858, 9, 22. William dis disunity (H)
1859, 7, 27. Mary Mercer (form Sabin) dis mcd (H)
1866, 1, 24. Rachel (form Burdsal) rpd mcd (H)
1872, 2, 21. Louisa recrq
1875, 6, 23. George recrq
1875, 9, 22. Louisa Wright (form Sabin) gct Salem MM, Ia.
1884, 4, 23. George W. gct Wilmington MM
1890, 9, 24. William H. dropped from mbrp (H)

SAFETRA
1818, 12, 30. George W. & w, Elizabeth, & ch, James H. & Jane T., rocf Shrewsbury MM, N. J., dtd 1818,9,7
1818, 12, 30. Meribah & ch, Benjamin & Robert, rocf Shrewsbury MM, N. J., dtd 1818,9,7

SAINTMIRE
1830, 9, 29. Elizabeth recrq

SAIRLS
1823, 10, 29. Beulah (form Evans) dis mou

SAMS
1846, 8, 26. Mary rocf Byberry MM, Pa., dtd 1846,7,28 (H)

SAMUELS
1917, 6, 24. L. R. recrq (H)
1920, 7, 25. L. R. dropped from mbrp (H)

SANDERS
1807, 3, 18. Jonathan, s John & Milly, Hiland Co., O.; m at Lees Creek, Lydia LUPTON, dt William & Bathsheba, Hiland Co., O.
1807, 3, 19. Thomas, s John & Milly, Hiland Co., O.; m at Clear Creek, Betsy POPE, dt Nathaniel & Martha, Hiland Co., O.

SANDERS, continued
1831, 12, 1. John, s John & Milly, Hiland Co., O.; m at Salt Run, Rachel M. BUTTERWORTH, dt Benjamin & Rachel, Warren Co., O. (H)
1846, 9, 24. Richard B., s John C. & Eleanor, Highland Co., O.; m at Hopewell, Jane WHITACRE, dt Aquilla & Ruthann, Warren Co., O. (H)

1805, 6, 13. John & w, Mary, & ch, Benjamin, Mercy, Merriam, Sarah & Susannah, rocf dtd 1805,4,4
1806, 3, 13. Hezekiah rocf Deep River MM, N. C., dtd 1805,7,1
1806, 4, 10. Amelia Allison & ch, Gulielma Sanders, John Sanders, Samuel Sanders & Martha Sanders, rocf Westfield MM, N. C., dtd 1805,8,24
1806, 5, 8. Jonothan rocf Deep River MM, N. C., dtd 1805,7,1
1806, 6, 12. Jesse [Saunders] & w, Sarah, & ch, John, Jane, Susannah & Jesse, rocf Deep River MM, N. C., dtd 1806,2,3
1806, 6, 12. Thomas rocf Westfield MM, N. C., dtd 1805,8,24
1806, 9, 11. Miriam rocf Bush River MM, S.C., dtd 1806,5,31
1808, 1, 14. Hezekiah dis
1808, 6, 9. Anna [Saunders] & ch, Elizabeth, Isaac, Joseph, Sarah & Anna, rocf Redstone MM, dtd 1807,10,2
1808, 11, 12. Mary (form Suffrance) rpd mou
1809, 7, 8. Mary dis mcd
1813, 6, 30. Mary recrq
1832, 2, 29. Rachel M. gct Fall Creek MM, O. (H)
1842, 3, 23. Thomas & w, Emily, & ch, Deborah Ann & Daniel Webster, rocf Fairfield MM, dtd 1841,12,23
1844, 4, 24. Thomas & w, Emily, gct Center MM
1846, 12, 23. Jane gct Fall Creek MM (H)

SARBER
1900, 9, 26. Ida C. relrq

SATTERTHWAITE
----, --, --. John b 1786,6,22 d 1837,7,5; m Elizabeth LINTON b 1786,5,8 d 1871,12,25 (H)
Ch: Susan b 1812, 10, 2 d 1850, 8,22
Samuel " 1815, 4, 17 " 1840, 8, 5
Mary " 1817, 6, 29 " 1907, 5,30
Elizabeth " 1820, 6, 20 " 1872,12, 4
Giles " 1822, 10, 24 " 1871,10,28
Abel " 1824, 10, 21 " 1895, 12,4
Jane " 1828, 4, 23 " 1868, 4,19
1822, 10, 3. Benjamin L., s Benjamin & Sarah, Warren Co., O.; m at Turtle Creek, Ruth EVANS, dt Joseph & Lydia, Warren Co., O.
1823, 3, 5. Mary m Benjamin LUKENS
1824, 11, 3. Abigail m Moses KELLY
1832, 9, 12. Benjamin L., s Benjamin & Sarah, Warren Co., O.; m at Grove, Mary LUKENS, dt Levi & Elizabeth, Warren Co., O., b 1810,1,1 (H)
Ch: Elizabeth (by a form m)
Sarah Ann
Samuel
1840, 12, 2. Mary m Emmor BAILY (H)
----, --, --. ----- m Mary C. ----- b 1830,2, 1 d 1918,4,30 (H)
Dt: Naomi H. b 1851, 6, 12 d 1891, 2,21
1852, 9, 1. Jane m Davis FURNAS (H)
1864, 4, 7. Abel, s John & Elizabeth, Warren Co., O., b 1824,10,21 d 1895,12,4; m at Miami, Lydia COOK, dt Abraham & Ruth, Warren Co., O., b 1831,12,1 d 1912, 4, 9 (H)
Ch: Israel b 1868, 3, 3
Henry " 1870, 8, 29
Sarah " 1872, 8, 2 d 1880, 9,--
Willie " 1875, 1, 29

1811, 2, 27. John rocf Falls MM, Pa., dtd 1810,3,7
1811, 2, 27. Elizabeth rocf Center MM, dtd 1811,1,3
1815, 3, 29. John dis
1817, 6, 25. Sarah & ch, Caleb, Benjamin L., Mary & Abigail, rocf Upper Springfield MM, N. J., dtd 1817,5,7
1821, 2, 28. Rebecca (form Ward) con mou
1821, 9, 26. Caleb dis mcd
1823, 3, 26. Benjamin L., w, Ruth, gct West Grove MM, Ind.
1827, 1, 31. Benjamin & w, Ruth, & ch, Sarah Ann & Samuel, rocf West Grove MM, Ind. dtd 1827,1,13
1829, 2, 25. Benjamin L. dis jH
1829, 3, 25. Elizabeth dis jH
1829, 9, 30. Sarah dis jH
1829, 11, 25. Benjamin & w, Ruth, & ch, Sarah Ann & Samuel, gct Milford MM, Ind. (H)
1830, 1, 27. Ruth dis jH
1830, 8, 25. Rebecca dis jH
1830, 8, 25. Sarah dis jH
1832, 8, 29. Benjamin & ch, Sarahann & Samuel, rocf Milford MM, Ind., dtd 1832,7,19 (H)
1833, 7, 24. Susan dis jH
1836, 3, 23. Susan Wright (form Satterthwaite) con mou (H)
1837, 9, 20. Samuel dis disunity (H)
1838, 8, 22. Samuel dis disunity
1842, 10, 26. Mary Bailey (form Satterthwaite) dis mou
1846, 2, 18. Eliza Evans (form Satterthwaite) dis mou
1846, 3, 25. Elizabeth Evans (form Satterthwaite) con mou (H)
1851, 3, 26. Giles dis mcd (H)
1851, 4, 23. Mary C. con mcd (H)
1852, 9, 22. Samuel, s Benjamin L., gct Fall Creek MM, Ind. (H)
1852, 9, 22. Mary, w Benjamin L., & dt, Elizabeth, gct Fall Creek MM, Ind.
1853, 8, 24. Benjamin L. dis disunity (H)

SATTERTHWAITE, continued
1853, 10, 26. Sarah Ann Garwood (form Satterthwaite) dis mcd (H)
1855, 12, 26. Rebecca (form Burnet) con mou
1856, 1, 23. Joseph & w, Eliza, & ch, Martha A., Esther, Edith & Anna, rocf Wakefield MM, Pa., dtd 1855,12,6 (H)
1856, 4, 23. Rebecca B. gct East Grove MM, Ia.
1856, 8, 27. Martha Davis (form Satterthwaite) dis mcd (H)
1856, 11, 26. Joseph M. & w, Eliza, & ch, Esther, Edith & Anna, gct Fall Creek MM, Ind. (H)
1886, 7, 21. Naomi H. recrq (H)
1900, 7, 25. Frances Vance rocf Ceasars Creek MM, dtd 1900,6,21
1907, 3, 27. Fanny Vance gct Ceasars Creek MM
1917, 9, 30. Leslie J. & Sarah Cook recrq (H)
1917, 9, 30. Harry & Russell recrq (H)
1921, 11, 27. Anna & Ethel recrq (H)
1926, 2, 28. Ruth & Thelma recrq (H)
1926, 3, 28. Clement & George recrq (H)

SAWIN
1931, 12, 27. Horace recrq (H)

SAYRE
1819, 5, 5. David, s Silas & Sarah, Warren Co., O.; m at Miami, Elizabeth MILLS, dt William & Mary, Warren Co., O.
1874, 9, 23. John [Sayers], s Wm. & Mary, Green Co., O.; m Sarah J. DAKIN, dt James & Nancy, Warren Co., O., b 1841,6,15 d 1885,11,1 (H)
Ch: James
Wilbur b 1876, 10, 16
Artieneci " 1878, 10, 8

1818, 11, 25. David recrq
1821, 6, 27. David & w, Elizabeth, & dt, Minerva Noble, gct Blue River MM, Ind.
1831, 2, 23. David & w, Elizabeth, & ch, Minerva, Irena, Emily & Sarah, rocf Blue River MM, Ind., dtd 1829,11,7 (H)
1853, 5, 25. William dis jas (H)
1853, 6, 22. David dis jas (H)
1854, 1, 25. Minerva Thorp (form Sayre) dis mcd (H)
1854, 1, 25. Irena Neely (form Sayre) dis mcd (H)
1854, 1, 25. Mary Miller (form Sayre) dis mcd (H)
1854, 2, 22. Emily Reed (form Sayre) dis mcd (H)
1854, 2, 22. Elizabeth dis jas (H)
1854, 2, 22. Sarah dis jas (H)
1874, 7, 22. Emma [Sayers] (form Harper) recrq
1898, 2, 23. Arthenici [Sayrs] relrq (H)
1909, 4, 21. James Wilbur [Sayers] dropped from mbrp (H)

SCHOFIELD
1851, 10, 22. Elizabeth (form Scott) dis mcd (H)

SCHOOLEY
1805, 7, 11. Samuel & w, Cecilia, & ch, Israel, John, Ann, William & Betty, rocf Crooked Run MM, dtd 1805,6,1
1813, 5, 26. Samuel dis
1820, 8, 30. Israel dis mcd
1821, 9, 26. Cicily & ch, Samuel & Mahlon, gct Grumplain (Green Plain) MM
1821, 9, 26. Elizabeth gct Greenplain MM

SCOTT
1817, 7, 30. Thomas & w, Mary, & ch, Abner, Sarah, Daniel, Mary, Abigail, Ann & Amos, rocf Upper Springfield MM, N. J., dtd 1817,5,7
1833, 9, 25. Lydia, Martha, David, Aveline, Jasent & Elizabeth, minors, rocf Stillwater MM, dtd 1833,6,22
1834, 2, 19. Meribah & ch, Lydia Lee, Martha Williams, Evelyn, Jason & Elizabeth, rocf Goshen MM, dtd 1833,10,19
1836, 5, 25. David, minor, rocf Goshen MM, dtd 1836,4,16 (H)
1840, 5, 27. Martha Snider (form Scott) dis mou (H)
1841, 11, 24. Lydia Hults (form Scott) dis mou (H)
1848, 4, 26. Meribe Crawford (form Scott) dis mou (H)
1851, 1, 22. Eveline Kirby (form Scott) dis mcd (H)
1851, 10, 22. Elizabeth Schofield (form Scott) dis mcd (H)
1897, 11, 24. Oella Mullen (form Scott) dropped from mbrp

SCROGG
1837, 4, 26. Charity Ann (form Antrim) dis mou mou (H)

SEARS
1807, 8, 19. John, s John & Sarah, Hiland Co., O.; m at Lees Creek, Penelope JOHNSON, dt Christopher & Mildred, Hiland Co., O.

1807, 7, 9. John rocf Upper MM, dtd 1807,2,21
1832, 5, 23. Christopher & John, minors, rocf Dover MM, dtd 1831,7,14
1838, 3, 21. Jaohn dis mou
1838, 6, 21. Christopher con mou
1841, 8, 25. Christopher [Seers] gct Mississinewa MM
1847, 5, 26. David & w, Rachel, & ch, Rebecca & Tabitha, rocf Goshen MM, dtd 1847,4,17
1850, 3, 27. David & fam gct Springboro MM
1874, 7, 22. Alice (form Harper) recrq
1890, 6, 25. Wm. rocf Ceasars Creek MM, dtd 1890,4,24

SEARS, continued
1890, 9, 2. Ella recrq
1901, 5, 22. Ella relrq

SELLERS
1900, 10, 24. George Henry & w, Martha Emily, & ch, Dora Lena & Mary C., recrq
1914, 5, 27. George, Dora & Mary [Sellars] dropped from mbrp

SETTLES
1896, 6, 24. Minnie recrq
1897, 7, 21. Minnie gct Springfield MM

SEXTON
1814, 1, 26. Catherine rocf Plainfield MM, dtd 1813,9,25, endorsed by Center MM 1813,11,6
1814, 8, 31. Catherine [Saxton] gct Centre MM
1822, 2, 27. Hannah rocf Cincinnati MM, dtd 1822,1,--
1826, 8, 30. Hannah gct Milford MM, Ind.

SEYBOLD
1806, 7, 10. John & w, Sarah, & ch, Sarah, Rebecca, Alice, John, Joseph & Eleanor, rocf Wrightsboro MM, Ga., dtd 1805,4,6

SHAFFER
1875, 4, 21. Nathan recrq

SHANK
1877, 8, 22. George H. rocf Springfield MM, dtd 1877,7,21
1882, 3, 22. George Henry gct Springfield MM

SHARP
1807, 4, 9. Job recrq
1808, 5, 12. Phebe recrq
1809, 5, 6. Phebe rocf Eavesham MM, N. J., dtd 1809,4,7
1811, 11, 27. James rocf Evesham MM, N. J., dtd 1811,9,6
1819, 8, 25. Margaret rocf Evesham MM, N. J., dtd 1816,10,11
1866, 1, 24. Phebe dropped from mbrp; form mbr of Fall Creek or Centre MM which had been laid down (H)

SHAW
1814, 4, 7. John, s Samuel & Susannah, Hamilton Co., O., d 1851,4,9 ae 70; m at Cincinnati, Elizabeth WRIGHT, dt Jonathan & Susanna, Hamilton Co., O., d 1857,4,2 (H)
----, --, --. Edward m Peninnah HILL (H)
Ch: Robert H. b 1842, 11, 10
Rebecca " 1844, 9, 23
Elizabeth " 1841, 8, 1 d 1841, 8,24
John " 1849, 9, 6
Henry C. " 1852, 2, 27
Mary Elizabeth " 1847, 5, 8
William
Ch: Thomas b 1855, 7, 30
Susan Barnard " 1857, 11, 8

1810, 10, 31. John & w, Elizabeth, & ch, Joseph & John, rocf Short Creek MM, dtd 1810, 9,18
1810, 10, 31. Sarah rocf Short Creek MM, dtd 1810,9,18
1814, 2, 23. John rocf Westland MM, dtd 1813, 12,25
1818, 10, 28. John & fam gct Alum Creek MM
1830, 8, 25. Amos rocf Greenwich MM, N. J., dtd 1830,7,1 (H)
1849, 2, 21. Edward & w, Peninah, & ch, Robert Hill, Rebecca & Mary Elizabeth, rocf Green Plain MM, dtd 1849,1,17 (H)
1849, 2, 21. Elizabeth rocf Green Plain MM, dtd 1849,1,17 (H)
1849, 2, 21. Thomas rocf Green Plain MM, dtd 1849,1,17 (H)
1849, 4, 25. John recrq (H)
1860, 10, 24. Edward & w, Peninah, & ch, Robert H., Rebecca, Mary Elizabeth, John, Henry C., William T. & Susan B., gct White Water MM, Ind. (H)
1860, 10, 24. Thomas W. gct White Water MM, Ind. (H)

SHEETE
1906, 1, 21. Edith recrq

SHEHAN
1922, 7, 30. Anna E. recrq (H)

SHEPHERD
1839, 10, 30. Susanna m George GRIMES

1812, 7, 29. Susanna [Sheppard] & dt, Susanna, rocf Hopewell MM, dtd 1812,5,14
1814, 4, 27. Susanna & dt, Susanna, gct Centre MM
1814, 5, 25. Jesse [Sheppard] rocf Hopewell MM, dtd 1813,4,11
1831, 5, 25. Mary Ann (form Hopkins) con mou (H)
1836, 8, 24. Jesse & w, Elizabeth, & ch, Martha, Hannah, Jacob, Amaziah, Edith, Thomas & Allen, rocf Springfield MM, dtd 1836,8,16
1837, 1, 25. Susanna rocf Springfield MM, dtd 1836,11,15
1840, 7, 22. Hannah gct Mill Creek MM
1840, 11, 25. Jesse & w, Elizabeth, & fam gct Mill Creek MM
1843, 3, 22. Mary Ann gct Camden MM, Ind. (H)
1866, 1, 24. Mary dropped from mbrp; form mbr of Fall Creek or Centre MM which had been laid down
1887, 4, 20. Ella recrq

SHEREDAN
1806, 3, 13. Margaret rocf Orange County MM, N. C., dtd 1805,9,7 (Cane Creek MM)

SHERWOOD
----, --, --. Thomas d 1833,3,26; m Dorcas ----- b 1853,7,30 (H)
Ch: Henery b 1807, 7, 13 d 1898, 4,12
Sarah " 1811, 9, 1 " 1839, 3,14
Elizabeth " 1809, 9, 27 " 1872, 5, 3
John " 1814, 1, 6 " 1853, 5,24
Jonathan " 1815, 8, 25
Thomas " 1817, 11, 19 " 1843, 9,30
Lydia " 1821, 10, 3 " 1863, 7,18
Abigail " 1823, 10, 23 " 1843,11,24
Samuel " 1827, 10, 28 " 1847, 9,10
1838, 11, 28. Elizabeth m Isaac STUBBS (H)
1842, 3, 30. Lydia m Elias HOLLINGSWORTH (H)
1842, 11, 30. John, s Thomas & Dorcas, Warren Co., O.; m at Salt-run, Elizabeth C. SMITH, dt Eli & Mary, Warren Co., O. (H)
----, --, --. John b 1814,1,6 d 1853,5,24; m Elizabeth SMITH b 1822,9,19 d 1865,1,14(H)
Ch: Samuel B. b 1844, 2, 24 d 1865, 1,14
Hannah " 1846, 11, 16 " 1853, 5,15
Thomas " 1848, 3, 18
Darcus " 1850, 11, 27 " 1875,10,13
John Henry " 1853, 1, 6 " 1887,11, 5
1856, 9, 3. Elizabeth m Clarkson GAUSE (H)
----, --, --. Henry b 1807,7,13; m Malinda HALE b 1825,2,27
Dt: Anna L. b 1867, 1, 24
1871, 2, 23. Dorcas E. m Lewis JANNEY (H)
----, --, --. Isaac b 1848,3,18; m Phebe BAILY b 1849,9,8 d 1916,3,24 (H)
Ch: Fred B. b 1879, 12, 16
Laurence Thomas " 1886, 8, 15
1878, 3, 18. Thomas, s John & Elizabeth, Warren Co., O.; m at residence of Emmor Bailey Phebe BAILEY, dt Emmor & Mary, Warren Co., O. (H)
----, --, --. John Henry b 1853,1,6 d 1887,11,5 m Sattie BARTLETT b 1855,2,22 (H)
Ch: Elizabeth b 1882, 4, 25
William Henry " 1884, 1, 27
Albert Bartlett " 1866, 5, 5

1809, 12, 27. Dorcas con mou
1829, 1, 28. Thomas dis jH
1829, 9, 30. Henry dis jH
1829, 11, 25. Dorcas dis jH
1829, 11, 25. Elizabeth dis jH
1829, 11, 25. Sarah dis jH
1834, 5, 21. Henry dis mou (H)
1838, 5, 23. John dis jH
1838, 7, 25. Jonathan dis jH
1840, 4, 23. Jonathan dis mou (H)
1843, 8, 23. Lydia Hollingsworth (form Sherwood) dis mou
1866, 12, 26. Margaret A. (form Hollingsworth) con mou
1867, 3, 27. Malinda (form Campbel) con mou
1873, 11, 26. Henry recrq
1881, 2, 23. J. Henry gct Baltimore MM, Md., to m Sarah A. Bartlett
1885, 3, 25. Lydia M. relrq
1888, 4, 25. Elizabeth, William Henry & Albert Bartlett, ch J. Henry, gct Baltimore MM
1900, 6, 20. Malinda gct Ceasars Creek MM
1903, 1, 21. Charles H. & w, Lydia M., & ch, Edith Marie, Howard Brown, Ellen Edna & Mary Amanda, recrq
1907, 6, 26. Nellie recrq
1913, 4, 23. Helen recrq
1919, 3, 30. Alice Palmer rocf Center MM, Del. dtd 1919,3,2 (H)
1920, 4, 28. Charles & w, Lydia, relrq
1921, 2, 3. Howard relrq

SHIDAKER
1883, 4, 25. Charles H. & w, Louisa A., recrq
1883, 4, 25. Harter J. recrq
1900, 3, 27. Harter relrq

SHIELDS
1807, 10, 8. Cert rec for Hannah from Newhope MM, Tenn., endorsed to Center MM

SHINN
1825, 2, 16. Benjamin [Shin] d (H)

1815, 11, 29. Jane rocf Upper Eavesham MM, N. J., dtd 1815,9,9
1823, 8, 27. Benjamin rocf Haddonfield MM, N. J., dtd 1823,7,14

SHINAR
1758, 11, 6. Jane b

SHOEMAKER
1875, 4, 21. John recrq
1875, 5, 26. Mary & Georgiana recrq
1895, 1, 23. Mary R. relrq (H)

SHUTE
----, --, --. Robert b 1852,7,3; m Sarah LANE b 1852,4,23 (Robert's 2nd w) (H)
----, --, --. James b 1864,7,19 d 1906,8,17; m Eunice FURNAS b 1862,2,8 (H)
Ch: Edith Furnas b 1886, 10, 25

1863, 7, 23. Ruth Anna (form Gause) con mcd (H)
1864, 3, 23. Ruth Anna gct White Water MM (H)
1900, 4, 26. James H. & w, Eunice, & dt, Edith F., rocf White Water MM, Ind. (H)
1902, 7, 23. Robert H. rocf White Water MM, Ind. (H)
1905, 12, 27. Edith Furnas relrq (H)
1910, 4, 20. Robert H. gct White Water MM,

SHUTE, continued
Ind.
1920, 7, 25. Alice B. [Shutts] dropped from mbrp (H)

SIDENSTRICKER
1898, 6, 22. Abi M. [Siderstricker] dropped from mbrp
1905, 2, 22. Miriam & dt, Ivy & Lila, recrq
1906, 5, 23. Harry, s Ella, relrq

SIDES
1882, 1, 25. Sally A. recrq
1885, 11, 25. Sarah A. Hawke (form Sides) relrq

SILVER
1806, 1, 22. Lettitia m David LINTON
1808, 6, 22. Anna m Noah HAINS
1835, 9, 30. William B., s William & Rebekah, Warren Co., O.; m at Miami, Ann JOHNSON, dt Joshua & Margaret, Warren Co., O. (H)
1870, 9, 16. Samuel [Silvers] d (H)
1873, 8, 17. Tamson [Silvers] d ae 71(H)

1805, 2, 14. Seth & dt, Letitia, rocf Salem MM, N. J., dtd 1804,8,27
1805, 2, 14. Ann rocf Salem MM, N. J., dtd 1804,8,27
1819, 4, 28. Patience & ch recrq
1828, 5, 28. Samuel rocf Springboro MM, dtd 1828,5,27
1829, 2, 25. Samuel dis jH
1833, 5, 22. Tamson recrq (H)
1834, 12, 24. Samuel & w, Tamson, gct Westfield MM (H)
1835, 8, 25. William B. rocf Springborough MM, dtd 1835,7,23 (H)
1836, 8, 24. William B. & w, Ann, gct Westfield MM (H)
1837, 11, 22. Ann (form Johnson) dis mou & jH
1867, 1, 23. Samuel & w, Tamson, rocf Westfield MM, dtd 1866,12,26 (H)

SIMMONS
1807, 3, 12. Abigail rocf Newgarden MM, N.C., dtd 1806,8,30
1818, 6, 24. Rebecca [Simons] & ch, Rebecca Evaline & Thomas P., rocf Falls MM, Pa., dtd 1818,5,8
1818, 6, 24. Rachel rocf Falls MM, Pa., dtd 1818,5,8
1819, 3, 31. Rachel Hutchens (form Simmons) con mou
1819, 11, 24. Rebecca Brelsford (form Simmons) dis mcd; living at Falls MM, Pa.
1823, 6, 25. Rebecca & ch, Evalina & Thomas, gct Elk MM
1908, 10, 21. Louie [Simonds] recrq (H)

SIMS
1829, 8, 26. Stephen & w, Sarah, rocf Woodbury MM, N. J., dtd 1829,4,28
1898, 4, 20. Alice Underwood gct Ceasars Creek Creek MM

SIMPSON
1815, 10, 25. Anna rocf Abington MM, Pa., dtd 1815,5,29

SINCLAIR
----, --, --. John b 1772,10,14 d 1851,3,26; m Rachel ----- b 1775,4,13 d 1848,7,12 (H)
Ch: Keziah b 1799, 11, 8 d 1802, 3,23
Abraham " 1802, 2, 23 " 1866,12,15
Sarah " 1804, 1, 11 " 1873,11,10
Isaac Proctor " 1808, 4, 18 " 1878, 3,24
Rebecca Proctor " 1810, 3, 7 " 1892, 9,27
Jacob Lindley " 1812, 4, 15 " 1896, 3,20
John Musgrove " 1814, 12, 30 " 1868, 2,22
Elizabeth " 1818, 6, 25 " 1903, 7, 2
1840, 8, 5. Elizabeth m William BURNET (H)

1834, 11, 26. John & w, Rachel, & ch, John Musgrove & Elizabeth, rocf Indian Spring MM, Md., dtd 1834,10,8 (H)
1834, 11, 26. Rebecca P. rocf Indian Spring MM, dtd 1834,10,8 (H)
1837, 2, 22. Abraham rocf Indian Spring MM, Md., dtd 1837,2,8 (H)
1837, 8, 23. Isaac P. rocf Springborough MM, dtd 1837,5,25 (H)
1839, 10, 23. John Jr. con mou (H)
1840, 5, 27. John M. gct White Water MM (H)
1840, 10, 21. Isaac P. gct White Water MM (H)
1848, 12, 27. Abraham gct White Water MM (H)
1849, 12, 26. Abraham dis (H)

SISSON
1814, 3, 30. Elizabeth rocf Northern Dist. Nantucket MM, dtd 1813,8,25

SLACK
1869, 6, 23. Matilda (form Burnett] rpd mcd (H)
1879, 4, 23. Matilda P. gct Camden MM, Ind. (H)
1881, 3, 23. Emily Gertrude recrq
1885, 12, 23. George Clark & w, Emma (form Slack) relrq

SLEEPER
1830, 8, 26. Jacob, s Samuel & Patience, Clark Co., O.; m at Miami, Sarah WELCH, dt Samuel & Phebe, Warren Co., O.
1833, 1, 2. Buddell, s Samuel & Patience, Clark Co., O.; m at Miami, Elizabeth H. WELCH, dt Samuel & Chloe, Warren Co., O.

1825, 1, 26. Timothy Kelly gct Green Plain MM, to m Avis Sleeper
1825, 5, 25. Elizabeth & s, William, recrq

SLEEPER, continued
1827, 4, 25. Eliza & s, William, gct Cesars Creek MM
1830, 11, 24. Sarah gct Green Plain MM
1833, 9, 25. Elizabeth gct Green Plain MM
1835, 7, 22. Jonathan rocf Mount Holly MM, N. J., dtd 1835,6,6 (H)
1836, 9, 21. Jonathan con mou (H)
1837, 10, 25. Jonathan & ch, William, Ann & Mary, gct Green St. MM, Phila. (H)

SLOANE
1822, 4, 24. Elizabeth rocf Cincinnati MM, dtd 1822,2,28
1825, 2, 23. Elizabeth [Sloan] gct Cincinnati MM; returned

SMALL
1806, 8, 14. Gideon & w, Sarah, & ch, Obediah, Jonathan, Amos & Samuel, rocf Mt. Pleasant MM, Va., dtd 1805,1,26
1806, 8, 14. Joseph & w, Clarissa, & ch, Joshua, Joseph, Rachel & Anna, rocf Mt. Pleasant MM, Va., dtd 1805,1,26 (other records give w name as Clarkey)

SMEDLEY
1874, 2, 25. J. Franklin, s Ezra & Esther Ann, Chester Co., Pa.; m at Waynesville, Ruth COOK, dt Levi & Ellen, Warren Co., O. (H)

1874, 11, 25. Ruth C. gct Bradford MM, Pa. (H)

SMITH
1806, 12, 31. Rachel m Nathan LINTON
1807, 12, 16. Rosannah m James TOWNSEND
1809, 3, 16. Mary m Mercer BROWN
1824, 1, 7. James, s Chad & Elizabeth, Warren Co., O., b 1793,8,30; m at Miami, Mary C. BROWN, dt Asher & Mary, Warren Co., O., b 1802,4,27
Ch: Orlistus R. b 1824, 11, 30
Asher B. " 1827, 6, 22
Rachel A. " 1827, 6, 22
Mary Elizabeth " 1834, 8, 9
Charles " 1842, 4, 4
James m 2nd Lydia -----
Ch: Lydia
1825, 9, 7. Fanny m Moorman BUTTERWORTH
1833, 5, 2. Ruth m Moses TOMLINSON (H)
1842, 11, 30. Elizabeth C. m John SHERWOOD (H)
1842, 5, 5. Mary C. d bur Miami Mtg
1849, 8, 9. James d bur Miami
----, --, --. Asher B. b 1827,6,22; m Sarah BARNETT b 1833,6,10
Dt: Mary E. b 1872, 10, 24

1804, 10, 11. John & s, Nathan & John, rocf Back Creek MM, dtd 1803,8,27
1804, 10, 11. Tishe & ch, Rachel, Sarah, Elizabeth, Peninah & Gulielma, rocf Back Creek MM, N. C., dtd 1803,8,27
1805, 2, 14. Josiah & w, Letitia, & ch, Jordan Zadoc, rocf Springfield MM, N. C., dtd 1804,11,3
1805, 2, 14. Elizabeth & ch, Mary, Rachel, Ruth & Seth, rocf Newhope MM, Tenn., dtd 1804,8,18
1805, 4, 11. Rachel Trimble (form Smith) dis mou
1805, 9, 12. Joseph & w, Elizabeth, rocf Cane Creek MM, S. C., dtd 1805,2,18
1805, 9, 12. Robert & s, John, rocf Back Creek MM, N. C., dtd 1805,4,27
1805, 9, 12. Mary rocf Back Creek MM, N. C., dtd 1805,4,27
1805, 11, 14. Joseph & w, Lydia, & ch, Mordecai, Samuel, Elizabeth, Mary, Rebecca, William & Edmund, rocf Hopewell MM, dtd 1805,10,7
1806, 5, 8. Mary Littler (form Smith) dis mou
1806, 7, 10. Mary rocf Crooked Run MM, Va., dtd 1805,11,2
1807, 5, 14. Ann, Mary, Patience, Sarah & John, ch Joseph, recrq
1807, 7, 9. Rosanna recrq
1807, 8, 3. Daniel rocf Deep Creek MM, N.C., dtd 1807,5,2
1807, 8, 3. Jacob & ch, Rachel, John, Ann, Mary, Josiah, Jacob, Lydia, Sarah, Hannah, Isaac & Seth, rocf Hopewell MM, dtd 1807,2,2
1807, 10, 8. Catharine (form Veale) dis mou
1808, 3, 10. John dis mcd
1808, 3, 10. Catherine dis
1808, 6, 9. Ann Coil (form Smith) dis mou
1808, 6, 9. Rachel Coller (form Smith) dis mou
1808, 6, 9. Mary Taylor (form Smith) dis mou
1810, 3, 28. Josiah dis mcd
1810, 5, 30. Lydia Bell (form Smith) dis mou
1810, 7, 25. Hannah dis
1811, 5, 29. Daniel gct Mill Creek MM
1812, 2, 26. Mordicai roc dtd 1812,2,1
1815, 3, 29. Sally Snyder (form Smith) dis mcd
1815, 5, 31. Jacob W. & w, Ann, & ch, Elizabeth & Ann, rocf Darby MM, Pa., dtd 1815,3,16
1815, 9, 27. Sarah (form Evans) dis mou
1818, 5, 27. Thomas recrq
1818, 5, 27. Caleb Roper rocf Phila. MM, dtd 1818,2,18
1819, 5, 25. Eve recrq
1819, 7, 28. Caleb gct Burlington MM, N. J.
1819, 11, 24. Maria Ann, Henry, William, Margaret, John & Rachel, recrq of parents, Thomas & Eve
1820, 2, 23. Jacob Jr. dis mcd
1821, 1, 31. Thomas & fam gct Salem MM, Ind.
1821, 2, 28. Ruth rocf Wrightstown MM, Pa., dtd 1821,2,7
1822, 5, 29. James rocf Cesars Creek MM, dtd 1822,3,29
1822, 9, 25. Isaac dis mcd

SMITH, continued
1823, 12, 31. Fanny rocf Byberry MM, Pa., dtd 1823,7,1
1825, 10, 26. Thomas & w, Eve, & ch, Ann, Henry, William, Margaret, John, Rachel & Deborah, rocf Lick Creek MM, Ind.
1830, 2, 24. Ruth gct Wrightstown MM, Pa.(H)
1830, 12, 29. Martha rocf Wrightstown MM, Pa., dtd 1830,7,7 (H)
1830, 12, 29. Ruth rocf Wrightstown MM, Pa., dtd 1830,7,7 (H)
1830, 12, 29. Sarah rocf Smithfield MM, R.I., dtd 1830,9,30
1831, 6, 29. Ruth dis jH
1832, 6, 27. Martha Anderson (form Smith) con mou (H)
1833, 4, 24. Hugh H. rocf Cincinnati MM, dtd 1833,2,14
1833, 10, 23. Hugh H. gct Cincinnati MM
1835, 3, 25. Cert rec for Martha, w of Jonothan, & ch, Mary Ann, Charles, Eber U., Isaac, Jonathan, Cyrus, William, James & Sarah Emily, from Sadsbury MM, endorsed to White Water MM (H)
1841, 6, 23. Elizabeth recrq (H)
1842, 12, 21. Esther (form Fallis) dis mou
1845, 6, 25. Martha (form Steddom) dis mou
1846, 2, 18. Lydia rocf Springfield MM, dtd 1846,2,17
1846, 9, 23. Sarah con mou
1847, 2, 24. Sarah gct Center MM
1850, 6, 26. Lydia & dt, Lydia Ann, gct Springfield MM
1857, 2, 18. Orlistus R., Asher B., Rachel A. Mary Elizabeth & their minor brother, Charles G., gct Salem MM, Ia.
1861, 7, 24. Sarah A. rocf Shappagua MM, N.Y., dtd 1861,7,11 (H)
1863, 3, 25. Asher B. rocf Salem MM, Ia., dtd 1863,2,18
1864, 5, 25. Asher B. con mou
1864, 6, 22. Sarah B. (form Burnet) con mou
1872, 1, 24. Mary Ellen recrq
1872, 6, 26. Anna M. recrq
1876, 3, 22. Charles P. recrq
1878, 10, 23. Charles P. relrq
1879, 3, 26. Charles G. & w, Elvire P., & dt, Oriana, rocf White Water MM, dtd 1879,2,26
1881, 4, 25. Charles R. & w, Elvira P., & ch, Oreiania, gct White Water MM, Ind.
1907, 11, 20. Mary relrq
1916, 11, 26. Caroline rocf Chicago Executive Mtg, Ill., dtd 1916,11,12 (H)
1931, 5, 31. Elizabeth recrq (H)

SNEAD
1813, 11, 24. Cert rec for Sarah from South River MM, dtd 1813,9,11, endorsed to Clear Creek MM

SNIDER
1815, 3, 29. Sally [Snyder] (form Smith) dis mcd

1826, 6, 28. Eliza (form Anthony] con mou
1827, 5, 30. Eliza D. gct Cincinnati MM
1840, 5, 27. Martha (form Scott) dis mou (H)

SNOWDEN
----, --, --. Richard b 1800,3,19 d 1881,11,7; m Mary WEST b 1808,5,14 d 1863,5,12 (H)
Ch: Sarah
Amanda b 1830, 11, 18
Henry A. " 1834, 8, 8 d 1895,10,21
Charles E. " 1836, 10, 19 " 1892,11,27
Jane " 1832, 8, 19 " 1888, 4,18
Richard m 2nd Rachel G. HACKNEY b 1824,11, 2 d 1893,1,25
1868, 2, 26. Sarah Amanda m Elisha GALLIMORE

1866, 1, 24. Henry H. rpd mcd (H)
1866, 1, 24. Edward [Snowdon] rpd mcd (H)
1866, 1, 24. Amanda rpd mcd (H)
1866, 7, 25. Jane Brown (form Snowden) dis mcd (H)
1866, 11, 21. Charles E. dis mcd (H)
1867, 11, 20. Sarah Amanda rocf Center MM, dtd 1867,11,13
1868, 2, 19. Richard gct Hopewell MM, Va., to m Rachel Hackney (H)
1868, 5, 27. Rachel G. rocf Hopewell MM, Va., dtd 1868,5,7 (H)
1886, 10, 27. Amanda Galimore (form Snowden) relrq (H)

SOMERS
1898, 6, 22. Lewis relrq
1920, 7, 25. Edward O. dropped from mbrp (H)

SOTHIE
1844, 11, 20. Matilda (form Doughman) dis mou (H)

SOUTHGATE
1917, 7, 29. Esther P. dropped from mbrp (H)
1921, 12, 18. Esther Welch rst by rq (H)

SPENCER
----, --, --. John K. b 1831,6,26; m Priscilla RUSSELL b 1831,8,25 d 1876,11,26 bur Corwin
Ch: Mary Emma b 1855, 9, 29
Thomas R. " 1857, 4, 6
John K. " 1859, 4, 26
Sarah E. " 1861, 7, 7 d 1862, 8,13 bur Wilmington
Francis b 1863, 6, 29
Russell T. " 1865, 3, 4
Caroline " 1867, 9, 17
Charles A. " 1870, 12, 31
Albert Henry " 1876, 11, 26 d 1877, 7,26
Arthur Abram b 1876, 11, 26 " 1877, 8,27

1869, 8, 25. John K. & w, Priscilla, & ch, Mary E., Thomas R., John K., Frances, Rus-

SPENCER, continued
sell T. & Caroline, rocf Springfield MM, dtd 1869,7,17
1883, 4, 25. Joseph J. Downing gct West Branch MM, Pa., to m Almina J. Spencer
1887, 4, 20. Ada recrq
1892, 9, 21. Mary Emma gct White Water MM
1898, 12, 21. Russell L. gct Sabina MM

SPRAY
1805, 11, 27. Dinah m John COOK
1836, 9, 1. Jesse, s John & Sarah, Clinton Co., O.; m at Turtle Creek, Eunice STEDDOM, dt John & Alice, Warren Co., O.
1846, 4, 1. Jesse, s Samuel & Mary, Clinton Co., O.; m at Miami, Rebecca BURNET, dt Robert & Anna

1805, 6, 13. Mordecai & w, Sarah, & ch, Mary, Henry, William & Jesse, rocf Cane Creek MM, S. C., dtd 1805,2,16
1806, 3, 13. Mary rocf Bush River MM, N. C., dtd 1805,8,31
1811, 10, 30. Phebe rocf Elk MM, dtd 1811,10,5
1814, 2, 23. Phebe gct White Water MM
1824, 8, 25. Martha (form Cox) dis mou
1836, 2, 21. Samuel T. Steddom gct Cesars Creek MM, to m Margery Spray
1837, 1, 25. Eunice gct Ceasars Creek MM
1846, 5, 27. Rebecca gct Caesars Creek MM

STAFFORD
1805, 9, 12. Shadrack rocf Deep River MM, N. C., dtd 1805,6,3
1805, 10, 10. Jarvis & w, Rebecca, & ch, Tacy, James & John, rocf Piney Grove MM, S. C., dtd 1805,4,20

STALKER
1810, 1, 31. Rachel & ch, Elizabeth, George, Deborah & Eli, rocf Deep River MM, N. C., dtd 1808,9,5

STALL
1804, 8, 9. John & w, Francis, rocf Phila. MM, dtd 1803,12,13

STANFIELD
1805, 2, 14. William & w, Charity, & ch, John, Samuel, Jane & Mary, rocf Deep River MM, N. C., dtd 1804,7,2
1807, 2, 12. Thomas & w, Hannah, rocf New Hope MM, Tenn., dtd 1806,1,18

STANLEY
----, --, --. James & Prudence (H)
Ch: Eleazer b 1803, 12, 15
Mary " 1806, 4, 15
Ira " 1808, 10, 8
Rachel " 1811, 2, 16
Caleb " 1814, 4, 23
Rebecca " 1816, 4, 22
Achsah " 1819, 1, 6

1806, 11, 13. Strangman & w, Jemima, & her dt, Sarah Mills, also their ch, Strangeman, Jemima & Eliza, rocf New Garden MM, N. C., dtd 1806,8,30
1817, 2, 26. James & w, Prudence, & ch, Eleazer, Mary, Ira, Rachel, Caleb & Rebecca, rocf New Garden MM, N. C., dtd 1816,8,31
1819, 4, 28. James & fam gct Darby Creek MM
1849, 6, 20. Martha (form Harvey) dis mou
1850, 4, 24. Martha gct Mill Creek MM, Ind.
1888, 1, 25. Eleazar, Mary, Ira, Rachel, Caleb, Rebecca & Achsah dropped from mbrp (H)

STANTON
1810, 11, 7. Frederick, s James & Ann, Green Co., O., b 1784,2,7; m at Miami, Hannah SUFFRINS, dt David & Deborah, Warren Co., O., b 1790,10,5
Ch: Mary b 1812, 11, 20
Eliza " 1815, 8, 3 d 1838,11,10 bur Miami
James b 1818, 6, 9
David " 1822, 6, 11
John " 1825, 2, 16
Edward " 1828, 5, 11
Charles " 1831, 3, 11
----, --, --. Latham m Huldah ----- d 1813,3,27 (H)
Dt: Mary b 1813, 12, 28
Error in original record of Huldah's d, & b of dt, Mary
1834, 5, 28. Mary S. m William CADWALLADER
1862, 10, 29. Deborah J. m Samuel LLOYD
1874, 6, 3. Elizabeth M. m Charles F. CHAPMAN (H)

1805, 12, 12. Samuel rocf Center MM, N. C., dtd 1805,8,17
1805, 12, 12. Sarah rocf Bush River MM, dtd 1805,8,31
1806, 11, 13. William rocf Upper MM, dtd 1806,3,15
1811, 4, 24. Hannah gct Center MM
1811, 11, 27. James & w, Mary, & ch, Hannah, John, Susannah, Elijah & Amos, rocf Salem MM, O., dtd 1811,9,17
1811, 11, 27. Latham & w, Huldah, & ch, Hepsibah, Elizabeth, Hunnicut, Gulielma, Daniel, William & Stephen, rocf South Run MM, dtd 1810,9,8
1812, 8, 26. Fredrick & w, Hannah, rocf Center MM, dtd 1812,7,14
1814, 8, 31. Latham & ch gct Whitewater MM
1814, 8, 31. Catherine gct Center MM
1822, 7, 31. Joseph rocf Short Creek MM, dtd 1822,5,21
1823, 3, 26. Joseph gct Plainfield MM, to m Mary Townsend [1823,6,26
1823, 7, 30. Mary rocf Plainfield MM, dtd
1826, 1, 25. William rocf Western Branch MM, Va., dtd 1825,9,24 [1826,6,27
1826, 9, 27. Mary rocf Springborough MM, dtd

STANTON, continued
1829, 1, 28. Mary H. gct Springborough MM
1831, 6, 29. William F. gct Cincinnati MM
1838, 3, 21. James F. dis mou
1841, 3, 24. Frederick & w, Hannah, & ch gct Springboro MM
1858, 7, 21. Deborah Jane rocf Springboro MM, dtd 1858,7,20
1882, 7, 26. Mary Emma & Ellen J. relrq
1883, 3, 21. Joseph dis disunity
1883, 4, 25. Catherine Ann dis disunity
1888, 1, 25. Mary dropped from mbrp (H)
1912, 11, 20. Anna M. rocf White Water MM, Ind., dtd 1912,10,23 (H)

STARBUCK
1813, 9, 29. Alexander rocf Salem MM, dtd 1813,5,13
1816, 5, 29. Charles rocf Galloway MM, dtd 1815,8,23
1816, 5, 29. Uriah & w, Lydia, & ch, Rachel, Elizabeth, George, Thomas Hawes, John & Paul, rocf Galloway MM, dtd 1815,8,23
1817, 1, 29. Rachel Whitacre (form Starbuck) con mou
1817, 11, 26. Uriah & fam gct Silver Creek MM
1820, 9, 27. Dorcas rst with permission of Uxbridge MM, Mass.
1820, 11, 29. William, Almira, Eliza, Howland, Lelilah & Lydia, ch Charles & Dorcas, rec-rq
1833, 10, 23. Howland, Lydia, Benjamin F. & George, minor ch Charles, gct Silver Creek MM
1833, 11, 20. William dis mou
1834, 3, 26. Almyra Combs (form Starbuck) dis mou
1834, 4, 23. Delilah dis joining Methodists
1835, 7, 22. Dorcas dis disunity
1835, 8, 26. Charles dis
1906, 7, 25. Mary Edwards relrq

STARR
1809, 6, 10. Abner rocf Exeter MM, dtd 1808, 5,25

STEDDOM
----, --, --. Henry [Stedom] b 1754,4,15 d 1822,10,22; m Martha PEARSON b 1760,1,15(H)
Ch: Christianna b 1777, 5, 13
Eunice " 1779, 9, 13
John " 1782, 1, 26
Mary " 1784, 9, 12
Anna " 1788, 12, 15
Samuel " 1794, 7, 8
1805, 11, 27. Christianna m Joseph COMTON
1807, 12, 3. Mary m John JAY
----, --, --. John b 1782,1,26; m Alice TEAGUE b 1788,2,22
Ch: Henry b 1811, 10, 3
Rebecca " 1813, 2, 20
Eunice " 1815, 2, 11
Samuel b 1817, 6, 14
Martha " 1819, 9, 30
Abijah " 1822, 2, 14
Moses " 1824, 4, 28
Esther " 1827, 1, 10
Joseph " 1827, 1, 10
Anna T. " 1829, 2, 28
Sarah F. " 1829, 2, 28
1815, 11, 8. Samuel, s Henry & Martha, Warren Co., O., b 1794,7,8; m at Union, Susanna TEAGUE, dt Samuel & Rebekah, Miami Co., O. b 1798,6,13
Ch: Lurana b 1817, 6, 14
John Furnas " 1820, 5, 5
Rhoda " 1821, 8, 10
Henry " 1824, 3, 14
Isaac Kelly " 1827, 9, 18
Lydia " 1830, 9, 24
Rebecca T. " 1834, 8, 3
1822, 10, 27. Henry d bur Turtle Creek
1833, 8, 28. Henry, s John & Alice, Warren Co., O., b 1811,10,3; m at Miami, Ruth HAWKINS, dt Isaac & Mary, Warren Co.,O., b 1815,4,17
Ch: Mary H. b 1834, 11, 17
John H. " 1837, 1, 13
Alice C. " 1839, 5, 29
Seth " 1841, 6, 27
Eunice M. " 1844, 7, 7
Jason W. " 1846, 5, 24
Elizabeth Adaline " 1853, 8, 30 d 1854,10,12 bur Turtle Creek
Horace T. b 1856, 2, 3
Oscar F. " 1858, 3, 12
1833, 10, 31. Rebecca m John COMPTON
----, --, --. Samuel b 1817,6,14; m Margery SPRAY b 1817,8,16
Ch: Sarah Ann b 1837, 2, 14
John D. " 1838, 8, 31
Samuel m 2nd Esther PEARSON
Ch: Joseph J. b 1861, 2, 1
1836, 9, 1. Eunice m Jesse SPRAY
1838, 2, 1. Lurana m David MATHER
1847, 3, 4. Esther m David PYLE
1849, 11, 22. Seth d bur Turtle Creek
1851, 4, 3. Mary Ann (Compton) d bur Ceasars Creek
----, --, --. Isaac K. b 1827,9,18; m Narcissa PRICE b 1828,4,26
Ch: Martha b 1852, 8, 2 d 1853, 4,23 bur Turtle Creek
Francis W. b 1854, 4, 7
Laura " 1856, 5, 23
Alpheus " 1858, 1, 22 d 1863,10,20 bur Turtle Creek
Charity b 1860, 6, 20
Susanna " 1863, 1, 3
Rice
Myron
Isaac

STEDDOM, continued
----, --, --. Henry b 1824,3,14; m Sallie CAMMACK b 1825,2,10 d 1860,6,28 bur Turtle Creek
Ch: Emily b 1853, 8, 28
Albert " 1851, 7, 27 d 1851, 9,29 bur Randolph
Mary K. b 1851, 7, 27 " 1854, 8,29 bur Turtle Creek
Sylvan b 1855, 7, 29
Cornelia " 1856, 12, 11
Joseph " 1860, 6, 21 d 1860,11,13 bur Turtle Creek
Sallie b 1860, 6, 21 " 1860,10,31 bur Turtle Creek
Henry m 2nd Rhoda -----
Ch: Isaac
1852, 8, 26. Margery d bur Turtle Creek
1854, 2, 23. Lydia m Thomas TERRELL
1855, 7, 22. John d bur Turtle Creek
----, --, --. Moses b 1824,4,28; m Sarah PYLE b 1827,11,9
Ch: Albert W. b 1857, 8, 5 d 1858, 3,18 bur Turtle Creek
Maurice P. b 1860, 4, 27
1864, 1, 19. Eunice M. d bur Waynesville

1805, 2, 14. Henry & w, Martha, & ch, Christan John, Mary, Anna & Samuel, rocf Bush River MM, S. C., dtd 1804,8,25
1811, 1, 30. John gct West Branch MM, to m
1812, 8, 26. Alice rocf West Branch MM, dtd 1812,7,23
1813, 10, 7. Anna Kersey (form Steddom) rpd mcd
1815, 10, 25. Samuel gct Union MM, to m
1836, 2, 21. Samuel T. gct Cesars Creek MM, to m Margery Spray
1836, 7, 27. Margery rocf Cesars Creek MM, dtd 1836,6,23
1838, 5, 25. Rhoda Mote (form Steddom) con mou
1840, 4, 22. John F. gct Cesars Creek MM, to m Mary Ann Compton
1845, 4, 23. Abijah con mou
1845, 6, 25. Martha Smith (form Steddom) dis mou
1846, 4, 22. Mary Ann rocf Cesars Creek MM, dtd 1846,3,26
1850, 8, 21. Henry Jr. gct Chester MM, to m Sallie Cammack
1851, 7, 23. Isaac K. gct Duck Creek MM, to m Narcissa Price
1852, 5, 26. Narcissa rocf Duck Creek MM, dtd 1852,3,25
1852, 7, 21. Moses gct Springfield MM, to m Sarah Pyle
1853, 1, 26. Sarah P. rocf Springfield MM, dtd 1853,1,15
1853, 2, 23. Samuel T. gct Union MM, to m Esther Pearson
1853, 9, 20. Esther P. rocf Union MM, Pa., dtd 1853,9,14
1854, 5, 24. Sallie & ch, Mary & Emily, rocf Mill Creek MM, dtd 1854,4,11
1855, 10, 24. Abijah gct Cesars Creek MM, to m Deborah Mendenhall
1856, 5, 21. Deborah rocf Cesars Creek MM, dtd 1856,4,24
1856, 8, 27. Charles, Margery, Alice T. & Anna W., ch Abijah & Deborah, recrq
1856, 8, 27. John F. gct Short Creek MM, to m Sarah Terrill
1856, 8, 27. Anna T. White (form Steddom) dis mou
1857, 2, 18. Sarah J. rocf Short Creek MM, dtd 1857,1,21
1857, 11, 25. Sarah Fisher (form Steddom) dis mou
1860, 12, 26. Joseph dis mou
1861, 9, 25. Rebecca Patty (form Steddom) con mou
1863, 2, 18. John H. con mou
1863, 9, 23. Rhoda H. rocf West Branch MM, dtd 1863,8,15
1864, 11, 23. Henry & w, Ruth, & ch, Mary H., Alice C., Jason W., Horace T. & Oscar F., gct Spring Creek MM, Ia.
1864, 11, 23. John H. gct Spring Creek MM, Ia.
1865, 5, 24. Isaac P. C. gct Dover MM, Ind., to m Lucinda Puckett
1865, 7, 26. Alice gct Cesar's Creek MM
1865, 7, 26. Ann C. gct Cesar's Creek MM
1867, 7, 24. William C. con mou
1867, 7, 24. Elizabeth C. (form Knight) con mou
1868, 6, 24. William C. & w, Elizabeth C., & ch, Carrie E., gct Union MM
1869, 1, 27. Annie Williams (form Steddom) con mou
1869, 1, 27. Margery Patty (form Steddom) con mou
1869, 10, 27. Isaac P. C. gct Dover MM, Ind.
1873, 4, 23. John H. rocf Spring Creek MM, Ia., dtd 1873,3,1
1874, 5, 27. William C. & w, Elizabeth, & ch, Carrie C., Viola & Mary Ann, rocf Union MM
1874, 6, 24. Emma H. Miller (form Steddom) con mou
1875, 9, 22. Abijah & w, Deborah, & ch, Edward R., Martha L. & Ella C., gct White Water MM
1880, 7, 21. John H. relrq
1880, 11, 24. Sarah J. & ch, Mary T., Terrill, George, Charles, Newton, Rachel & Samuel, gct Oskaloosa MM, Ia.
1882, 5, 24. Henry & w, Rhoda, & s, Isaac H., gct Oskaloosa MM
1882, 5, 24. Sylvan gct Oskaloosa MM
1893, 7, 26. J. J. G. relrq

STEPHENS
1808, 1, 14. Gideon & w, Mary, & ch, Samuel & Mary, rocf Cane Creek MM, N. C., dtd 1806,10,23

STEPHENS, continued
1826, 12, 27. Barlow [Stevins] rocf Leeds MM, dtd 1825,2,17
1895, 9, 25. Alonzo & w, Ella, & ch, Alpha, rocf Cesars Creek MM
1905, 2, 22. Ella relrq
1906, 6, 20. Harry [Stevens] relrq
1917, 7, 29. Hallie A. [Stevens] dropped from mbrp (H)

STEVENSON
----, --, --. Samuel d 1852,1,28 ae 91; m Rebecca ----- (H)
Ch: Clayton b 1816, 7, 19
George " 1818, 7, 31
1821, 2, 7. Samuel, s Samuel & Catherine, Warren Co., O.; m at Miami, Hepsabah EVANS, dt William & Mary, Warren Co., O.
1836, 3, 2. Sarah m Thomas M. WALES (H)
1840, 12, 30. George, s Samuel & Rebecca, Warren Co., O.; m at Miami, Charlotte WARD, dt George & Deborah (H)

1815, 8, 30. Samuel & w, Rebecca, & ch, Samuel, William, Catherine, Mary Ann, James B., Joseph & Sarah, rocf Mount Holly MM, dtd 1815,4,6
1823, 2, 26. Samuel Jr. & w, Hepzibah,/gct West Grove MM, Ind. & s, Thomas Minor,
1829, 1, 28. Samuel dis jH
1829, 4, 29. Rebecca dis disunity
1831, 1, 26. Mary dis jH
1831, 2, 23. William dis jH
1838, 1, 24. James [Stevenson] dis mou (H)
1841, 3, 24. Joseph dis mou (H)
1842, 5, 20. Clayton [Stevenson] dis mou
1842, 6, 22. Joseph [Stevenson] dis mou
1842, 7, 27. George [Stevenson] dis jH
1856, 2, 20. George [Stevenson] dis disunity (H)
1876, 3, 22. Anna R. recrq
1891, 4, 22. Anna relrq

STINSON
1901, 8, 21. Edgar rocf Dover MM, dtd 1901,7, 18

STOCKTON
1814, 11, 30. Doughty rocf Upper Springfield MM, N. J., dtd 1813,9,8
1814, 11, 30. Job rocf Upper Springfield MM, N. J., dtd 1813,9,8
1814, 11, 30. Richard rocf Upper Springfield MM, N. J., dtd 1813,9,8

STOKES
1810, 9, 26. Deborah (form Garwood) con mou
1828, 1, 10. Ellis & w, Hannah, & ch, Hovan(?) M., Alfred E., Amanda, Mona & Ellis, rocf Chester MM, N. J., dtd 1827,3,26
1830, 10, 27. Horace M., Alfred E., Amanda, Maria, Ellis A. & Hannah M., ch Ellis & Hannah, rocf Chester MM, N. J., dtd 1830,9, 14
1834, 6, 25. Ellis dis (H)
1839, 12, 25. Horace M. dis mou (H)
1840, 11, 25. Horace M. dis mou
1843, 4, 26. Alfred E. dis disunity
1843, 12, 27. Amanda dis jH
1843, 12, 27. Maria dis jas
1844, 2, 21. Maria dis jas (H)
1856, 3, 26. Hannah Hutchisson (form Stokes) dis mcd (H)
1861, 3, 27. Alfred E. dis disunity (H)
1900, 10, 24. Helen C. recrq
1909, 1, 27. Helen relrq

STOUD
1888, 3, 21. Peter S., Mary C., Wm. & Sadie recrq
1926, 2, 28. Frederick D., Maybelle L. & Edna Mae recrq (H)

STOUT
1812, 9, 6. Jane b

1805, 2, 14. John & w, Ann, & ch, Margaret, George, Dinah, Mary, Sarah & Stephen, rocf Cane Creek MM, dtd 1804,9,1
1807, 8, 3. David rocf Cane Creek MM, N.C., dtd 1806,6,4
1808, 4, 14. Isaac & w, Susannah, & ch, Sarah, Jesse, Phebe, Rebecca, Lydia & Matilda, rocf Lost Creek MM, Tenn.,dtd 1807,10,31
1840, 1, 22. Jane rocf Springfield MM, dtd 1839,9,17
1840, 9, 23. Isaac rocf Center MM, dtd 1840, 7,16 (H)
1846, 11, 24. Jane gct Springfield MM
1854, 2, 22. Jane D. rocf Springfield MM, dtd 1854,2,18
1872, 4, 24. Deborah Ann & Mary L. recrq
1894, 2, 21. Isaac M. & w, Esther C., & ch, Nora Edna, Isaac M. Jr. & Maria, recrq
1894, 10, 24. Esther C. relrq (H)
1916, 3, 22. Isaac gct Pasadena MM, Calif.
1924, 8, 31. Esther C. rocf Miami MM (H)

STRAHL
1832, 9, 26. Philip & w, Sarah, & ch, Eli & Amos, rocf Stillwater MM, dtd 1832,7,21 (H)
1832, 9, 26. Ann W. rocf Stillwater MM, dtd 1832,7,21 (H)
1833, 3, 27. Eli & Amos [Strohl], minors, rocf Still Water MM, dtd 1833,1,26
1835, 3, 25. Ann W. Kirby (form Strahl) dis mou (H)
1840, 9, 23. Eli dis disunity (H)
1843, 3, 22. Amos dis jas & mou (H)

STRATE
1889, 7, 24. Ann (form Hollingsworth) dropped from mbrp (H)

STRATTON
1811, 9, 5. Joel, s Joseph & Naomi, Champain Co., O.; m at Darby Creek, Rebekah REA, dt Robert & Rebekah, Champain Co.,O.

1811, 1, 30. Jacob & w, Rebecca, & ch, Hannah & Sarah, rocf Middletown MM, dtd 1810,5,12
1811, 1, 30. Joel rocf Middleton MM, dtd 1810,5,12
1811, 1, 30. Joseph & w, Naomi, rocf Middletown MM, dtd 1810,3,12
1811, 1, 30. Hannah rocf Middleton MM, dtd 1810,5,12
1817, 7, 30. Eli & w, Eunice, & ch, Sarah, Jonothan, William & Joseph, rocf Green St. MM, Phila., dtd 1817,5,22
1817, 11, 26. Eli & fam gct Elk MM
1831, 12, 28. Rebecca & Edward, ch Joseph, rocf Springfield MM, O., dtd 1831,12,13
1832, 6, 27. Rebecca Stratton & ch, Sarah, Isaac & Davis Harvey, Rebecca & Edward Stratton, recrq (H)
1839, 12, 25. Rebecca & ch, Davis Harvey & Rebecca & Edward Stratton, gct Fall Creek MM, Ind.
1865, 2, 22. David [Strattan] & w, Harriet, & ch, Caroline O. & Edward L., gct Wapsinonoch MM, Ia.

STRAUSBURG
1888, 3, 21. Elias M. recrq

STRAWN
1805, 11, 21. Anna m Henry MILHOUS

1805, 6, 13. Anna rocf Cane Creek MM, S. C., dtd 1805,3,23

STREET
1805, 2, 14. Aaron & w, Mary, & ch, Samuel & Isaac, rocf Salem MM, N. J., dtd 1804,5,25
1807, 2, 12. Aaron dis attending musters
1808, 7, 14. Mary & ch, Samuel, Isaac, John & Lydia, gct Salem MM, O.
1815, 9, 27. Mary & dt, Eunice, rocf Salem MM, dtd 1815,9,12
1823, 4, 30. Samuel S. rocf Salem MM, O., dtd 1822,5,22
1831, 12, 28. Eunice gct White Water MM
1832, 1, 25. Samuel gct White Water MM
1833, 4, 24. Isaac Fisher gct White Water MM, to m Unice Street

STROUD
1841, 4, 21. Edwin Johnson gct Springboro MM, to m Eliza D. Stroud
1863, 5, 27. Charles & w, Susan B., rocf Goshen MM, dtd 1863,4,18
1863, 5, 27. Evalina B. rocf Goshen MM, dtd 1863,4,18
1869, 11, 24. Susan B. & dt, Eveline B., gct Cincinnati MM

STROUP
1883, 4, 25. Patience recrq

STROUSE
1909, 9, 22. Robert recrq

STUBBS
1808, 2, 17. Esther m John NEWLIN
1822, 7, 22. Hannah m Jacob DOAN
1829, 1, 8. Achsah m Samuel KELLY Jr. (H)

1838, 11, 28. Isaac, s Isaac & Margaret, Warren Co., O., b 1793,3,4 d 1874,4,18; m at Miami, Elizabeth SHERWOOD, dt Thomas & Dorcas, Warren Co., O., b 1809,9,27 d 1872,5,3 (H)

Ch:			
Margaret	b 1840, 10, 18		
Darcas	" 1842, 10, 11	d 1843, 8,12	
Albert	" 1844, 8, 12		
Isaac	" 1850, 4, 9	" 1882, 8,21	
Samuel	" 1847, 4, 12	" 1848,--,--	

1804, 12, 13. John & w, Jane, & ch, Esther, Sarah, Margaret, Hannah, John, Rachel, Joseph & Keziah, rocf Wrightsboro MM, Ga.
1805, 6, 13. Isaac & w, Margaret, & ch, John, Samuel, Isaac, Zimri, Achsah & Hannah, rocf Wrightsboro MM, dtd 1805,3,2
1805, 7, 11. Nathan & w, Elizabeth, & ch, William, Keziah, Hannah, Rebecca, Rachel, Joseph & Nathan, rocf Wrightsboro MM, dtd 1804,9,1
1805, 7, 11. Samuel & w, Mary, & ch, Rebecca, William, Tabitha, Newton, Martha, Sarah & Ann, rocf Wrightsboro MM, dtd 1805,3,2
1805, 7, 11. Joseph & w, Keziah, & ch, Amanda & John, rocf Wrightsboro MM, dtd 1804,9,1
1806, 12, 11. Sarah McDaniel (form Stubbs) con mou
1814, 6, 29. Hannah Eliot (form Stubbs) con mou
1814, 8, 31. John rpd mcd
1814, 11, 30. John & fam gct Elk MM
1814, 11, 30. Margaret gct Elk MM
1815, 6, 28. John gct Elk MM
1820, 6, 28. Samuel dis mcd
1828, 8, 27. Zimri dis mcd
1829, 5, 27. Isaac dis jH
1829, 5, 27. Isaac Jr. dis jH
1829, 5, 27. Margaret dis jH
1881, 3, 23. Eunice F. relrq

STUMP
1883, 4, 25. Daniel P. recrq
1883, 4, 25. Florence L. recrq
1894, 10, 24. Mary Emily [Stumps] recrq
1907, 8, 28. Mary relrq

SUFFRINS
----, --, --. David & Deborah (H)

Ch:		
Samuel	b 1807, 9, 7	
David	" 1801, 3, 29	

SUFFRINS, continued
1810, 11, 7. Hannah m Frederick STANTON

1806, 3, 13. David & w, Deborah, & ch, Mary, Hannah, John, Deborah, Sarah, Thomas & Jesse, rocf Mt. Pleasant MM, Va., dtd 1805,7,27
1808, 11, 12. Mary Sanders (form Suffrance) rpd mou
1818, 4, 29. Sarah Messick (form Suffrins) dis mou
1827, 2, 28. Thomas dis
1827, 9, 26. Harriet & ch, Samuel & Charles, rocf White Water MM, dtd 1827,8,22
1829, 3, 25. David dis jH
1829, 7, 29. Harriet dis jH
1831, 5, 25. David dis disunity
1833, 5, 22. David gct White Water MM (H)
1833, 7, 24. Harriett & ch, Samuel, Charles & Alfred, gct Whitewater MM (H)
1888, 1, 25. Samuel dropped from mbrp (H)

SUMMER (SUMNER)
1804, 6, 14. Ellenor Mendenhall & ch, Ruth Mendenhall & Phebe Sumners, rocf Lost Creek MM, dtd 1804,3,31
1806, 4, 10. Phebe rocf Westfield MM, dtd 1805,10,19
1806, 8, 14. Bowwater [Sumner] & w, Rebecca, & ch, John, Oliver, Isaac, Rebecca, Thomas, Allen & Mary, rocf Westfield MM, N.C., dtd 1806,3,22
1806, 8, 14. Esther rocf Westfield MM, N.C., dtd 1806,3,22
1811, 12, 25. Phebe Cox (form Somers) dis mcd
1897, 4, 21. Laura Lutz (form Summers) relrq
1897, 11, 24. John [Summers] & w, Ruth, & dt, Eunice V., relrq
1917, 7, 29. Edward O. [Summers] transferred to this mtg from Springboro (H)

SURFACE
1908, 3, 25. Charles & w, Mary, recrq
1910, 9, 21. Russell Daniel, Ida Marie & George Harold, ch Emma, recrq
1914, 5, 27. Charles dropped from mbrp

SUTTON
1811, 10, 30. Sarah (form Bray) dis mcd

SUYDAM
----, --, --. Gulielma (Taylor) b 1819,10,26 d 1897,3,16

1871, 8, 23. Gulielma rocf Springboro MM, dtd 1871,7,27 (H)

SWAIN
----, --, --. Elias H. [Swayne] m Mahala M. BARRETT (H)
Ch: George B. b 1858, 8, 26

1827, 6, 27. Mary O'Neal & niece, Anna Swain, minor, rocf Springborough MM
1829, 6, 24. Anna [O'Neal] (form Swain) dis mou
1858, 1, 27. Thomas [Swayne] rocf Green Plain MM, dtd 1857,12,16 (H)
1858, 10, 27. Mahala M. [Swayne] (form Barrett) con mcd (H)
1861, 1, 23. Mahala M. [Swayne] & ch, George B. & Samuel E., gct White Water MM, Ind.

SWALLOW
1805, 6, 13. John rocf Deep River MM, N. C., dtd 1804,11,5

SWARN
1815, 10, 25. David & w, Anna, & ch, Jonothan, Anna & Isarah, rocf Abington MM, Pa., dtd 1815,5,29

SWIFT
1809, 8, 5. Verlinda (form Pugh) con mou

SYMONDS
1911, 2, 17. Lonie d (H)

SYNNESTOEDT
1898, 10, 26. Mariah E. relrq (H)

TALBERT
1842, 6, 2. Sylvanus, s William & Miriam, Warrem Co., O.; m at Harveysburgh, Phebe HIATT, dt Isaac & Shannah, Warren Co., O.

1808, 7, 14. Thomas & w, Elizabeth, & ch, Job, Richard, William, Jonothan & Mary, rocf Deep River MM, N. C., dtd 1807,9,7
1808, 7, 14. William & w, Merriam, & dt, Anna, rocf Deep River MM, N. C., dtd 1807,9,7
1811, 11, 27. John [Talbot] & w, Mary, rocf Mt. Pleasant MM, Va., dtd 1811,8,31
1842, 3, 23. Sylvanus rocf Salem MM, Ind., dtd 1841,12,25
1845, 10, 22. Sylvanus & fam gct Salem MM, Ind.

TAMPSET
1851, 8, 27. Martha Ann (form Ward) dis mcd (H)

TATE
1838, 7, 25. Rebecca E. (form Evans) rpd mou; d before action was taken

TAYLOR
----, --, --. Abijah b 1781,3,3; m Mary ----- b 1794,1,8 (H)
Ch: Joseph Neill b 1813, 8, 23
John Ambrose " 1815, 8, 28
----, --, --. ----- m Mary SAXTON b 1789,9,29 d 1876,1,15 (H)
Ch: Sarah b 1816, 12. 9

TAYLOR, continued
----, --, --. Peter b 1785,12,14 d 1870,11,9; m Mary ----- b 1779,6,14 d 1863,4,11 (H)
Ch: Lydia Ann b 1820, 4, 15 d 1895, 3,16
1824, 4, 8. Mary m Ezekiel CLEAVER
1844, 8, 28. Mary m Amos COOK (H)

1808, 6, 9. Mary (form Smith) dis mou
1817, 11, 26. Abijah & w, Mary, & ch, Joseph Neill & John Ambrose, rocf Hopewell MM, dtd 1817,8,9
1822, 10, 30. Mordecai & w, Frances, & ch, Francis, Ambrose, Mordecai, Jaccob & Gulielma, rocf Hopewell MM, dtd 1822,1,10
1822, 10, 30. Mary rocf Hopewell MM, Va., dtd 1822,1,10
1822, 10, 30. Anna rocf Hopewell MM, Va., dtd 1822,1,10
1826, 12, 27. Mordecai Jr. rocf Springborough MM, dtd 1826,10,24
1827, 3, 28. John & w, Jane, & ch, Mary Jane, Anna & Joseph, rocf Cincinnati MM, dtd 1826,9,28
1829, 4, 29. Mordecai Jr. dis jH
1829, 5, 27. John & w, Jane, & ch, Anna & Joseph, gct Cincinnati MM, O.
1834, 3, 26. Mordecai gct Springborough MM (H)
1838, 6, 20. Peter & w, Mary, & ch, Lewis & Lydia Ann, rocf Springborough MM, dtd 1838,4,26 (H)
1838, 10, 24. William F. Ballard gct Centre MM to m Hannah Taylor (H)
1840, 1, 22. Mary & dt, Sarah & Susan, rocf Centre MM, dtd 1839,12,19 (H)
1841, 7, 21. Mary recrq (H)
1843, 12, 27. Sidewell dis disunity (H)
1844, 1, 24. John & w, Jane, & ch gct Cincinnati MM
1850, 1, 23. Peter & w, Mary, & dt, Lydia Ann, gct Springborough MM (H)
1852, 8, 25. Israel rocf Senter MM, dtd 1852, 6,16
1856, 5, 23. Esther Ann (form Brown) dis mou
1857, 1, 21. Esther Ann (form Brown) dis mcd
1859, 12, 21. Peter & w, Mary, & dt, Lydia[(H) Ann, rocf Springboro MM, dtd 1859,11,24 (H)
1875, 5, 26. Rachel & Rusha recrq
1882, 3, 22. Sarah dis (H)

TEAGUE
----, --, --. Samuel & Rebeccah (H)
Ch: Mary b 1783, 2, 10
Rebeccah " 1784, 9, 8
Lurannah " 1786, 9, 1
Alce " 1788, 2, 22
Esther " 1790, 2, 26
Joseph " 1792, 2, 26
Moses " 1794, 2, 6
Furnas " 1796, 7, 26 d 1796, 9,26
Susannah " 1796, 6, 13
Rhoda " 1801, 4, 2
Samuel b 1803, 8, 30
1815, 11, 8. Susanna m Samuel STEDDOM

1805, 12, 12. Samuel & w, Rebecca, & ch, Rebecca, Lurannah, Alice, Esther, Joseph, Moses, Susannah, Rhoda & Samuel, rocf Bush River MM, dtd 1805,8,31

TEMPLIN
1806, 5, 8. Unice (form Beales) dis mou

TERRILL
1854, 2, 23. Thomas, s Clark & Mary, Jefferson Co., O., b 1826,7,14; m at Turtle Creek, Lydia STEDDOM dt Samuel & Susanna, Warren Co., O., b 1830,9,24
Ch: Annie b 1855, 3, 30
Mary " 1857, 1, 2
Clark " 1858, 7, 5
Samuel " 1860, 7, 21
Lydia " 1862, 9, 6
Lurana " 1864, 11, 18

1807, 7, 9. Mary [Terrel] & ch, Pleasant, Christopher, David, Judith, Sarah, Joseph & Mary, rocf South River MM, Va., dtd 1806,10,11
1856, 6, 25. Thomas rocf Short Creek MM, dtd 1856,5,21
1856, 8, 27. John F. Steddom gct Short Creek MM, to m Sarah Terrill
1873, 11, 22. Thomas & w, Lydia, & ch, Mary S., Clark, Samuel S., Lydia & Lurana, gct Spring Creek MM, Ia.
1874, 6, 24. Anna Bradley (form Terrill) con mou
1881, 3, 23. Cornelia gct Oskaloosa MM, Ia.
1891, 6, 24. Anna M. (form Haines) gct Clear Creek MM
1893, 6, 21. Lurana M. [Terrill] rocf Oscaloosa MM, Ia.
1894, 12, 26. Lurana M. [Terrell] gct Springfield MM

TEST
1805, 6, 13. Samuel & w, Sarah, & ch, Elizabeth, Samuel, John & Rachel, rocf Salem MM, N. J., dtd 1805,3,25
1817, 7, 30. Samuel Jr. rocf Cincinnati MM, dtd 1817,7,17
1820, 10, 25. Samuel Jr. gct Silver Creek MM

THATCHER
1807, 1, 8. Thomas rocf Hopewell MM, dtd 1806,8,4
1807, 6, 11. Jesse rocf Hopewell MM, dtd 1806,12,1
1807, 6, 11. Thomas, Mary, David, Joseph & Ruth, minor ch Ruth, rocf Hopewell MM, Va., dtd 1806,12,1
1808, 1, 14. Ruth rocf Hopewell MM, Va., dtd 1807,3,2 [(H)
1887, 7, 27. Ann (form Butterworth) dis jas

THOMAS
1761, 7, 17. Edward b
1764, 2, 13. Mary b
1809, 1, 18. Isaac, s Edward & Mary, Warren Co., O.; m at Miami, Lydia HUFMAN, dt Merser & Susanna SHEPHERD, Warren Co.,O.
Ch: Levi L. b 1809, 11, 1
Edward L. " 1812, 2, 23
Sareptah " 1814, 1, 10
James H. " 1816, 1, 21
1812, 3, 4. Prudence m John MILLS
1817, 12, 4. Elijah, s Edward & Mary, Warren Co., O.; m at Hopewell, Naomi CADWALADER, dt Thomas & Jane, Warren Co., O.
1818, 6, 4. Charity m Nicholas TUCKET
1818, 6, 4. Vashti m Thomas CADWALADER
1820, 12, 7. Rachel m Hiram BAILY
1821, 6, 3. Abigail d ae 81
1842, 8, 25. Sidney m Clarkson GAUSE (H)

1805, 2, 14. Edward dis
1805, 2, 14. Thomas dis
1807, 4, 9. John & w, Ann, & ch, Isaah, Anna, John, George & William, rocf Bush River MM, dtd 1806,3,29
1807, 5, 4. Mary & ch, Evan, Nehemiah, Sarah & Phebe, rocf Bush River MM, S. C., dtd 1807,1,31
1807, 7, 9. Edward & w, Mary, & ch, Isaac, Charity, Prudence, Edward, Elijah, Elisha, Vashti, Abigail, Rachel, Mary & Elihu, rocf Bush River MM, S. C., dtd 1807,1,31
1809, 1, 14. Abigail rocf Bush River MM, S. C., dtd 1807,8,29, endorsed by West Branch MM, 1808,12,17
1809, 12, 27. Sarah Hoofman, dt Lydia Thomas, recrq
1811, 1, 30. David & w, Mary, & ch, Abel, rocf Middletown MM, dtd 1810,5,12
1813, 9, 29. Isaiah gct West Branch MM, to m
1815, 8, 30. Keziah (form Evans) dis mou
1816, 5, 29. Edward Jr. dis mcd
1816, 12, 25. Isaiah & fam gct West Branch MM
1816, 12, 25. John & fam gct West Branch MM
1817, 6, 25. John rocf Dunnings Creek MM, dtd 1817,4,16
1817, 6, 25. Lydia rocf Dunnings Creek MM, dtd 1817,4,16
1817, 6, 25. Jane & s, Robert, rocf Dunnings Creek MM,dtd 1817,4,16
1817, 6, 25. Ann & Jane Jr. rocf Dunnings Creek MM, dtd 1817,4,16
1818, 7, 25. Jacob Jr. rocf Exeter MM, dtd 1818,5,27
1818, 12, 30. Exeter MM, Pa. rq this mtg to deal with Jesse for mcd
1819, 8, 25. Ann rocf Centre MM, dtd 1819,7, 17
1819, 10, 27. Ann rst after dis by Salem MM, N. J.
1819, 10, 27. Elisha gct Clear Creek MM, to m
1819, 10, 27. Jesse rocf Exeter MM, Pa., dtd 1819,6,30
1819, 11, 24. Isaac recrq
1819, 11, 24. Isaac gct Center MM
1820, 5, 31. Isaac & fam gct West Grove MM, Ind.
1820, 12, 27. Edward dis
1820, 12, 27. Samuel Rich gct Center MM, to m Lydia Thomas
1820, 12, 27. Samuel Rich gct Center MM, to m Lydia Thomas
1821, 4, 25. Jacob gct Exeter MM, Pa.
1821, 8, 29. Edward rst by order of QM
1822, 3, 27. Elijah dis
1824, 5, 26. Ann & ch, Chalkley & Mary, gct Center MM
1824, 5, 26. Elihu dis
1825, 7, 27. Abigail Martin (form Thomas) con mou
1826, 3, 29. Mary Cadwalader (form Thomas) con mou
1826, 5, 25. Naomi dis attending a mcd
1827, 2, 28. Moses M. Whitacre gct Still Water MM, to m Pricilla Thomas
1830, 10, 27. Edward & w, Mary, gct Arba MM
1836, 4, 20. Abel & ch, Elmira, Charles W., Benjamin, Albert & Isaac H., rocf Springborough MM, dtd 1836,3,24 (H)
1836, 5, 25. Rebecca H. & ch, Almira, Charles W., Benjamin Franklin, Albert & Isaac H., rocf Springborough MM dtd 1836,5,24
1837, 7, 26. Rebecca & ch gct Springborough MM
1837, 9, 20. Abel J. & ch, Elmira, Charles, Benjamin, Alfred & Hays, gct Springborough MM
1842, 8, 24. Sidney rocf Stillwater MM, dtd 1842,6,18 (H)
1843, 5, 24. Elizabeth rocf Still Water MM, dtd 1843,2,18 (H)
1844, 2, 21. Rebecca H. & ch, Elmira, Charles W., Benjamin Franklin, Albert, Isaac Hays, Howard D. & Sarah Ellen, rocf Springborough MM, dtd 1844,1,23
1849, 6, 20. Elmira dis disunity
1851, 4, 23. Sarah Ellen gct London Grove, Pa.
1852, 1, 21. Charles W. gct Bermingham MM,Pa.
1856, 10, 22. Howard D. gct Phila. MM, Pa.
1872, 1, 24. Christopher M. & w & dt recrq
1888, 1, 25. Levi S., Edward S., Sareptah & James H. dropped from mbrp
1902, 6, 25. George & w, Eliza, rocf Springfield MM, dtd 1902,5,17
1903, 12, 23. Isaac rocf Dover MM, dtd 1903, 11,19
1913, 12 24. Louella recrq

THOMPSON
1821, 1, 4. Mary m Clarke WILLIAMS

1807, 6, 11. Joseph & w, Lydia, roc dtd 1806,9,20
1808, 3, 10. Joseph rocf Bush River MM, S. C., dtd 1806,5,31

THOMPSON
1807, 6, 11. Isaac rocf New Garden MM, N. C., dtd 1809,7,29
1809, 12, 27. Richard rocf New Garden MM, N. C., dtd 1809,7,29
1817, 6, 25. Mary, minor, rocf Half Moon Twp., Pa., dtd 1817,3,15
1846, 8, 26. Lydia B. rocf Springboro MM, dtd 1846,8,25
1849, 5, 23. Lydia B. [Thomson] gct Goshen MM
1876, 3, 22. Howard recrq
1881, 10, 26. Samuel recrq
1882, 6, 21. Eli & w, Hannah, rocf Ceasars Creek MM, dtd 1882,5,25
1885, 6, 24. Samuel B. gct Lawrence MM, Kans.
1900, 1, 24. Cora Amanda recrq
1909, 2, 24. Alfred & Decatur recrq
1914, 5, 27. Alfred & Decatur dropped from mbrp

THORN
----, --, --. Isaac b 1779,5,10; m Dorcas -----
Ch: John b 1799, 11, 25
----, --, --. John b 1799,11,25; m Elizabeth MOORE b 1804,3,27
Ch: Anna M. b 1827, 1, 19
Stephen M. " 1834, 9, 13
John Jr. " 1836, 9, 19
Alfred " 1838, 5, 19
Mary M. " 1842, 5, 15
1854, 3, 23. Anna M. m Alfred JOHNSON
1857, 12, 3. Isaac d ae 85 (a minister)
1862, 6, 30. John d bur Harveysburgh

1808, 6, 9. Catherine rocf Short Creek MM, O., dtd 1807,12,19
1831, 4, 27. Rachel rocf Chester MM, N. J., dtd 1831,4,9 (H)
1831, 8, 31. Ezra, Mary & Benjamin [Thorne] rocf Chester MM, N. J., dtd 1831,7,7 (H)
1832, 8, 29. Ruth & Mary gct White Water MM, Ind. (H)
1833, 5, 22. Benjamin [Thorne], s Benjamin, gct White Water MM (H)
1833, 5, 22. Ezra gct White Water MM (H)
1852, 5, 26. Isaac rocf Nine Partners MM, N. Y., dtd 1852,4,15
1852, 5, 26. Elizabeth & ch, Ann M., Stephen M., John Jr., Alfred M. & Mary M., roc
1853, 3, 23. John rst with permission of Nine Partners MM, N. Y.
1855, 9, 26. Samuel Jones gct Green Plain MM, to m Sarah Thorn
1856, 6, 25. Stephen M. gct White Lick MM
1863, 11, 25. Stephen M. rocf White Lick MM, Ind., dtd 1863,10,7
1870, 6, 22. Elizabeth & ch, Stephen, John, Alfred M. & Mary, gct Wilmington MM

THORNBURGH
1807, 9, 16. Mary m Jacob BEALS

1804, 11, 8. John Beals & ch, Nathan, Thomas, Ann & Daniel, also aged mother, Sarah Beals, her gr dt, Tabitha Beals, & gr s, Abel Thornburgh, rocf Mt. Pleasant MM, Va., dtd 1803,11,26
1805, 6, 13. Dinah rocf Lost Creek MM, Tenn., dtd 1804,6,30
1807, 3, 12. Edward [Thornbrough] & w, Keziah, & ch, Ann, Mary, Nathan, Joseph, Phebe, Jane, Edward, Jacob, Hannah & Keziah, rocf New Garden MM, N. C., dtd 1806,9,27
1809, 9, 9. Thomas rocf Lost Creek MM, dtd 1807,4,25
1816, 1, 31. Henry [Thornborough] & w, Rebecca, & ch, John, Elizabeth, Eunice, Milton & Hannah, rocf New Garden MM, N. C.
1817, 12, 31. Dinah gct Center MM
1820, 3, 29. Henry & fam gct White Water MM
1866, 1, 24. Joel [Thornburg] rpd mcd (H)
1866, 1, 24. Lydia [Thornburg] rpd mcd (H)
1866, 8, 22. Jacob [Thornburg] rpd mcd; dropped from mbrp (H)
1885, 8, 26. Ruth McVey (form Thornburg) relrq (H)

THORNTON
1866, 1, 24. Evan C. & w, Martha, rocf New Garden MM, Ind., dtd 1865,11,18
1870, 1, 26. Evan C. & w, Martha, gct Wilmington MM

THORP
----, --, --. George R. [Thorpe] b 1860,1,25; m Mary PARRY (H)
----, --, --. Jabes b 1817,3,22 d 1894,10,8; m Ann RICHARDSON b 1817,4,6 d 1886,3,2 (H)
Ch: George R. b 1860, 1, 25

1854, 1, 25. Minerva (form Sayre) dis mcd (H)
1864, 3, 23. Jabez & w, Anna R., & s, George, rocf Deerfield MM, O., dtd 1864,2,10 (H)
1864, 11, 23. Thomas & w, Maria, rocf Salem MM, O., dtd 1864,8,25 (H)
1865, 4, 26. Thomas & w, Maria, gct Green Plain MM (H)
1891, 6, 24. George R. [Thorpe] gct White Water MM, Ind., to m Mary Parry Jr. (H)
1891, 10, 21. Mary P. [Thorpe] rocf White Water MM, Ind., dtd 1891,9,23 (H)
1896, 11, 25. George R. [Thorpe] & w, Mary P., gct White Water MM, Ind. (H)

THROCKMORTON
1817, 7, 30. Job & w, Jane, rocf Shrewsbury MM, dtd 1817,5,5
1827, 6, 27. Jane Brelsford (form Throgmorton) con mou

THURSTON
1876, 6, 21. Amelia relrq

TICE
1892, 12, 21. Nathan Grant & Anna Jane recrq
1893, 4, 26. Wallace, minor, recrq

TIMBERLAKE
1811, 2, 11. Jonathan b

1829, 12,30. Jonathan rocf Clear Creek MM, dtd 1829,10,15
1832, 1, 25. Jonathan gct Clear Creek MM
1865, 4, 26. Amy gct Wapsinonoch MM, Ia. (H)
1866, 1, 24. John & fam dropped from mbrp; form mbr of Fall Creek or Centre MM which had been laid down (H)

TODHUNTER
1805, 8, 8. Isaac & w, Eleanor, & ch, Isaac, Abner, July, Jacob & Margaret, rocf New Hope MM, dtd 1804,11,17

TOMLINSON
1898, 6, 16. Alva Curtis, s Paul & Lydia, Randolph Co., Ind.; m at residence of Zephaniah Underwood, Ruth UNDERWOOD, dt Zephaniah & Matilda Jane, Clinton Co., O., b 1873,1,2 (H)
Ch: Ruth M.
Paul b 1906, 1, 30
Faith
Miriam
1833, 5, 2. Moses, s Josiah & Charity, Highland Co., O. b 1786,4,13 d 1867,10,14; m at Salt Run, Ruth SMITH, dt Joseph & Rachel Warren Co., O., b 1798,10,10 d 1862,10,7 (H)
Ch: Paul b 1834, 7, 26 d 1899, 9,27
Rachel " 1837, 4, 25 " 1877, 9,17

1806, 11, 13. Josiah & ch, Moses, Sarah, Mark, Dinah, Olive, Josiah, Charity, Jacob & William, rocf Springfield MM, N. C., dtd 1806,9,6
1833, 2, 20. Ruth gct Fall Creek MM, O. (H)
1866, 1, 24. Moses rpd mcd (H)
1866, 1, 24. Paul rpd mcd (H)
1868, 5, 27. Paul gct Green Plain MM (H)
1899, 7, 26. Ruthanna (form Underwood) gct White Water MM, Ind.
1905, 12, 27. Curtis & w, Ruthanna, & dt, Ruth Matilda, rocf White Water MM, Ind. dtd 1905,11,22 (H)
1905, 12, 27. Lydia A. rocf White Water MM, Ind., dtd 1905,11,22 (H)

TOMPKINS
----, --, --. Jacob b 1800,9,22 d 1886,7,9; m Rachel ----- b 1817,5,2 (H)
Ch: John b 1835, 10, 20
Joseph " 1837, 7, 27 d 1847, 9,15
Enoch " 1839, 2, 26 " 1883, 3,20
Lydia " 1841, 1, 13
Sarah " 1843, 6, 26 " 1856, 5,24
Mary " 1845, 9, 24 " 1872, 9, 8
Ch: William b 1847, 8, 3
Nancy " 1849, 11, 12 d 1881, 7, 8

1866, 1, 24. John rpd mcd (H)
1866, 1, 24. Enoch rpd mcd (H)
1866, 1, 24. Mary rpd mcd (H)
1866, 1, 24. William rpd mcd (H)
1866, 1, 24. Nancy rpd mcd (H)
1866, 1, 24. Sarah [Tomkins] dropped from mbrp; form mbr of Fall Creek or Centre MM which had been laid down (H)
1866, 8, 22. John [Tomkins] dis mcd (H)
1866, 8, 22. Lydia Davis (form Tomkins) con mcd (H)
1885, 10, 21. William relrq (H)
1895, 5, 22. Rachel Tompkins set off as mbr of Executive Mtg at Clear Creek (H)

TOMS
1871, 9, 20. Sarah E. recrq
1873, 6, 25. Sarah E. Worley (form Toms) con mou

TOWEL
1832, 1, 25. Henry & w, Ruth, & ch, Isaac, Jesse, Henry & Ruth, rocf Lick Creek MM, dtd 1831,11,19
1834, 5, 21. Henry & w, Ruth, & ch gct Lick Creek MM, Ind.

TOWNSEND
1807, 11, 18. Rachel m William HARVEY
1807, 12, 10. Martha m James COLDWELL
1807, 12, 16. James, s John & Elvy, Warren Co., O.; m at Miami, Rosannah SMITH, dt Hannah Evans, Warren Co., O.

1805, 1, 10. Martha & ch, John, Eli, Mary, Dinah & Ruth, rocf Cane Creek MM, S. C., dtd 1804,11,30
1808, 3, 10. John & w, Elvy, & ch, Jonathan, Mary, William, Hester, Sarah, Elizabeth, John & Barbara, gct West Branch MM
1808, 4, 14. Celia gct West Branch MM
1808, 5, 12. James & w, Rosannah, gct West Branch MM
1818, 6, 24. Josiah rocf Salem MM, N. J., dtd 1818,2,23
1820, 1, 26. Josiah con mcd
1820, 8, 30. Eli dis mcd
1821, 7, 25. Keturah Dearth (form Townsend) dis mou
1823, 3, 26. Joseph Stanton gct Plainfield MM, to m Mary Townsend
1823, 10, 29. Jesse dis non-attendance
1824, 5, 26. Thomas & w, Elizabeth, rocf Plainfield MM, dtd 1824,3,21
1824, 5, 26. Harriet rocf Plainfield MM, dtd 1824,4,22
1842, 5, 25. Jesse & Isaac Townsend recrq of William Butterworth (H)
1855, 3, 21. Isaac dis jas (H)
1856, 8, 27. Rachel (form Hollingsworth) dis

TOWNSEND, continued
mcd
1865, 10, 25. Sarah A. con mcd (H)
1866, 1, 24. Sarah A. gct White Water MM (H)

TRAHERN
1841, 1, 27. Asa & w, Elizabeth, rocf Short Creek MM, dtd 1840,9,22
1841, 1, 27. Linah rocf Short Creek MM, dtd 1840,9,22
1851, 8, 27. Lena Cadwalader (form Trahern) con mou
1854, 1, 25. Asa [Trayhorn] dis mou

TRIBBA
1764, 12, --. Ruth b

TRIBBY
1818, 8, 26. Ruth & ch, Sarah & Louisa, r cf Fairfax MM, Va., dtd 1817,10,29
1818, 8, 26. Elizabeth rocf Fairfax MM, Va., dtd 1817,10,29
1818, 12, 30. George rq mbrp; he was dis by Fairfax MM, Va.; rq not granted
1819, 3, 31. George recrq
1823, 6, 25. Sarah dis jas

TRIMBLE
----, --, --. Joseph b 1811,2,15 d 1898,11,18; m Sarah GILPIN b 1818,7,23 d 1902,1,16 (H)
Ch: William b 1847, 3, --
Joseph Gilpin " 1858, 9, 23
Eliza " 1856, 1, 15
Laura M. " 1861, 3, 4

1805, 4, 11. Rachel (form Smith) dis mou
1806, 7, 10. John & w, Rachel, & ch, William, John & Isaac, rocf Redstone MM, dtd 1806, 5,30
1807, 5, 4. James rocf Baltimore MM, dtd 1807,2,12
1917, 7, 29. Joseph G. & William dropped from mbrp (H)

TRUEBLOOD
1810, 8, 29. Josiah & ch, Peggy, William, Josiah & Lancaster, rocf Simonds Creek MM, dtd 1807,4,18
1810, 8, 29. Cert rec for Abigail from Symons Creek MM, N. C., dtd 1807,4,18, endorsed to White Water MM

TRUMAN
1820, 2, 23. Jeffery rocf Phila. MM, dtd 1819,12,28 (ND MM)
1824, 7, 28. Jeffery [Trueman] dis mcd
1870, 12, 21. Davis Furnas gct Phila. MM, to m Sarah S. Truman (H)

TUCKER
1818, 6, 4. Nicholas, s Abraham & Mary, Montgomery Co., O.; m at Hopewell, Charity THOMAS, dt Edward & Mary, Warren Co., O.
Ch: Mary B. b 1819, 4, 16
Sarah C. " 1820, 10, 6
Abigail G. " 1823, 1, 25 d 1823, 4,25
Naomi G. " 1824, 4, 10

1818, 5, 27. Nicholas rocf West Branch MM
1820, 4, 26. Nicholas rocf West Branch MM, dtd 1820,4,15
1826, 2, 22. Nicholas & w, Charity, & ch, gct New Garden MM, Ind.
1905, 2, 22. Eva recrq

TURNER
1842, 4, 20. Eleanor C. (form Edwards) con mou
1849, 2, 21. Elenor C. gct Bloomfield MM
1850, 12, 25. Eleanor C. rocf Rush Creek MM, dtd 1850,12,5
1883, 3, 21. Emma recrq

ULLUM
1887, 4, 20. Seymore [Ullom] recrq
1887, 4, 20. Lenore recrq
1905, 4, 26. Anna M. [Ulmun] relrq
1909, 3, 24. Helen relrq

UNDERHILL
----, --, --. Jacob & Sarah
Ch: Charles b 1833, 3, 23
Mary Amelia " 1836, 4, 29
William H. " 184-, 5, 17
1851, 10, 13. Charles d
1853, 8, 25. Mary A. m Richard WHITE

1835, 1, 21. Jacob & w, Sarah, & s, Charles, rocf Amewalk MM, N. Y., dtd 1835,1,9
1859, 8, 24. Jacob & w, Sarah, & s, William Henry, gct Amawalk MM, N. Y.

UNDERWOOD
----, --, --. Amos b 1786,8,18 d 1867,4,11; m Mary ----- b 1791,9,16 d 1847,12,13 (H)
Ch: Reuben b 1814, 10, 17
Isaac " 1816, 9, 30
John " 1818, 10, 26
Zephaniah " 1820, 11, 10 d 1900, 4,17
Amos " 1823, 3, 5 " 1850, 5,18
Lewis " 1825, 3, 16 " 1887, 2,27
Asenath " 1827, 4, 25
Thomas Elwood " 1829, 8, 22 " 1850, 3,11
Priscilla Jane " 1831, 12, 16 " 1854, 7,16
William " 1834, 6, 5 " 1893, 3, 4
Elihu " 1839, 2, 17
Amos m 2nd Priscilla LEWIS
----, --, --. Isaac b 1816,9,30 d 1878,11,13; m Catherine DAKIN (H)
Ch: Leona d 1887, 2,--
Warren
----, --, --. David W. b 1841,9,12; m Caroline

UNDERWOOD, continued
H. ----- b 1842,5,10 (H)
Ch: George T. b 1865, 9, 30
Alice W. " 1867, 8, 31
John G. " 1869, 4, 10
Charles " 1873, 8, 17
Toner M. " 1875, 3, 17
Walter B. " 1878, 6, 6
Annie M. " 1881, 6, 12
Laura B. " 1885, 4, 6
Hannah M. " 1868, 10, 22 d 1868,12, 6
----, --, --. Elihu b 1839,2,17; m Hester KIRK d 1899,9,6 (H)
Ch: Harriett E.b 1866, 5, 8
Daniel Baily " 1868, 3, 12
Elihu m 2nd Matilda DOWNING b 1851,4,10
1871, 12, 28. Zephaniah, s Amos & Mary, Clinton Co., O., b 1820,11,10 d 1900,4,17; m at home of John Underwood, Matilda DOWNING, dt Jacob & Jane, Warren Co., O., b 1851,4,10 (H)
Ch: Ruthanna b 1873, 2, 1
Zephaniah " 1875, 7, 5
Joseph " 1878, 5, 25
Olive " 1881, 3, 23 d 1882,10,27
Jane Eva " 1888, 2, 6
1872, 2, 22. John, s Zephaniah & Hannah, Warren Co., O., d 1883,12,10; m at home of Zephaniah Underwood, Julia BABCOCK, dt Benjamin & Sarah, b 1821,10,22 d 1912,8,29 (H)
1888, 9, 27. Harriet E. m Edwin S. FURNAS (H)
1898, 6, 16. R. Anna m J. Curtis TOMLINSON (H)

1814, 4, 27. Samuel recrq
1819, 10, 27. Samuel dis mcd
1854, 5, 24. Amos & w, Priscilla, & ch, William & Eli, rocf Center MM, dtd 1854,4,13 (H)
1854, 6, 21. Mary Ann rocf Carmel MM, dtd 1853,2,17, endorsed by Center MM, 1854,6, 15 (H)
1854, 6, 21. Rebecca Jane rocf Carmel MM, dtd 1853,2,17, endorsed by Center MM, 1854,6, 15 (H)
1858, 10, 27. Benjamin recrq
1859, 10, 26. William con mcd (H)
1861, 10, 23. Isaac rocf Center MM, dtd 1861, 9,19 (H)
1862, 11, 26. Elihu rpd mcd (H)
1868, 4, 22. Priscilla gct White Water MM, Ind. (H)
1871, 4, 26. John rocf Center MM, Pa. (H)
1880, 2, 25. David W. & w, Caroline H., & ch, George T., Alice M., John G., Charles O., Toner M. & Walter B., rocf Center MM, O., dtd 1880,2,5 (H)
1886, 5, 26. David & w, Caroline, & ch, Allis W., John G., Charles D., Toner M., Walter B., Anna M. & Laura G., relrq (H)
1886, 5, 26. David W. & w, Caroline H., & ch, Alice W., Chas. D., Laura J., Walter B., John G., Toner M. & Anna N., recrq
1897, 8, 24. George T. gct Center MM, Pa.(H)
1889, 7, 24. Catharine gct Fall Creek MM, Ind. (H)
1889, 11, 20. Rebecca Jane rpd to have become mbr of Marietta MM, Ia. (H)
1889, 12, 25. Warren relrq (H)
1897, 1, 27. David W., Caroline, Chas. O., Toner M., Walter B., Anna M. & Laura J., relrq
1898, 7, 27. Daniel B. recrq (H)
1899, 7, 26. Ruthanna Tomlinson (form Underwood) gct White Water MM, Ind. (H)
1910, 12, 21. Myrtle J. recrq (H)
1913, 2, 19. Wilhelmina & ch, Esther Ruth, Sarah Cecelia & Ada Grace, recrq (H)
1921, 7, 30. Irma recrq (H)
1925, 4, 25. Charles rst by rq (H)
1925, 5, 31. Myrtle relrq (H)

UPP
1907, 11, 20. Mary relrq

VAIL
1805, 7, 11. Stephen & w, Mary, & ch, Aaron, Randolph, Catherine & Hugh, rocf Redstone MM, dtd 1805,3,1
1815, 11, 29. Hugh dis mcd

VANDERBURG
1863, 4, 25. Mary B. recrq
1899, 2, 22. Mary B. dropped from mbrp by rq

VAN HORN
1805, 5, 9. Robert [Vanhorne] rocf Bush River MM, S. C., dtd 1804,7,28
1807, 8, 13. Cert rec for Joanna [Vanhorn] & dt endorsed to Center MM
1824, 3, 31. Rebecca, James & John, ch Robert, rocf Union MM, dtd 1824,2,7
1827, 6, 25. Rebeccah Gilpin (form Van Horn) dis mou
1831, 12, 28. James [Vanhorn] con mou
1833, 10, 23. John, minor, rocf Duck Creek MM, dtd 1833,7,25
1836, 8, 24. James gct Springfield MM; cert returned because of disunity
1837, 10, 25. James gct Springfield MM
1838, 2, 21. John dis mou

VARNER
1807, 4, 9. Nathaniel & w, Grace, & ch, Margaret, Lydia, Thomas, Samuel & Ann, rocf Bush River MM, S. C., dtd 1806,9,27
1837, 12, 27. Ann rocf Springfield MM, dtd 1837,10,17
1855, 12, 26. Sarah Ann (form Antram) con mcd (H)
1868, 3, 25. Nancy gct Minneapolis MM, Minn.

VAUGHN
1922, 4, 30. Anna rocf Orange Grove MM, Calif. (H)

VEAL
1806, 5, 8. Randal dis mcd
1807, 10, 8. Catharine Smith (form Veale) dis mou

VENABLE
1819, 11, 4. Maria m Evan BENBOW

1818, 4, 29. Joseph rocf Upper Evesham MM, N. J., dtd 1816,9,7
1818, 4, 29. Rachel & ch, Arthur, William, Maria, Thomas, Charles & Rachel, rocf Chester MM, N. J., dtd 1816,8,8
1819, 4, 28. Arthur dis training in militia
1819, 4, 28. Joseph dis training in militia
1819, 4, 28. William dis training in militia
1825, 8, 31. Charles dis
1827, 2, 28. Thomas dis non-attendance & training in militia
1831, 4, 27. Rachel Benbow (rorm Venable) dis jH
1875, 5, 26. Nancy S. recrq
1876, 3, 22. John recrq
1881, 3, 23. John relrq
1897, 1, 27. Della recrq

VESTAL
1805, 11, 14. Elizabeth rocf Cane Creek MM, N. C., dtd 1805,9,7
1806, 3, 13. Jemima, Samuel, Mary, Elizabeth & Rachel recrq of mother, Elizabeth

VICKERS
1806, 6, 12. Celia & ch, Joshua, William, John, Amelia & Joseph, rocf N. W. Fork MM, Md., dtd 1806,3,12
1884, 5, 21. Joseph recrq
1885, 7, 22. Joseph relrq
1886, 3, 24. Calvin C. recrq
1887, 12, 21. Calvin E. relrq

VORE
1838, 7, 25. Solomon Gause gct White Water MM, to m Jane Vore (H)

VOTAW
1917, 1, 2. Jonathan, s Sarah, Warren Co., O.; m at Sugar Creek, Elizabeth HAMPTON, dt Jacob & Eunice, Warren Co., O.

1811, 6, 26. Daniel rocf Salem MM, dtd 1811, 4,16
1813, 6, 30. Mary & ch, Eunice & Anna, recrq
1817, 4, 30. Daniel & fam gct Whitewater MM
1817, 4, 30. Jonothan & w gct White Water MM

WALES
----, --, --. Isaac b 1778,9,30 d 1824,9,29; m Ruth WELCH b 1784,7,7 d 1856,4,26 (H)

Ch:			
Mary	b 1803, 12, 2	d 1832, 1,25
Jane	" 1806, 2, 1	" 1906, 9, 9
Nancy	" 1809, 11, 20	
Thomas Montgomery	b 1812, 8, 17	d 1898, 9,15
Caroline	" 1818, 12, 1	" 1844, 8, 3

1830, 11, 3. Jane m Valentine NICHOLSON (H)
1830, 11, 3. Nancy m Henry T. BUTTERWORTH (H)
1836, 3, 2. Thomas M., s Isaac & Ruth, Warren Co., O.; m at Miami, Sarah STEVENSON, dt Samuel & Rebecca, Warren Co., O. (H)
1838, 11, 28. Ruth m William BIRDSALL (H)
1840, 2, 26. Caroline M. m Milton T. MACY (H)
----, --, --. Caroline (Sanders), w Richard F. b 1844,7,21 d 1895,11,16 (H)

1816, 3, 27. Isaac & w, Ruth, & ch, Mary, Jane, Nancy & Thomas Montgomery, rocf Fairfield MM, dtd 1815,9,30
1829, 9, 30. Jane dis jH
1829, 9, 30. Nancy dis jH
1829, 10, 28. Mary [Wailes] dis jH
1830, 1, 27. Ruth dis jH
1830, 11, 24. Mary Burgess (form Wales) con mou (H)
1833, 5, 22. Thomas dis jH
1840, 4, 22. Caroline M. Macy (form Wales) dis mou & jH
1841, 8, 25. Harriett (form Fallis) con mou
1842, 3, 23. Thomas M. dis mou (H)
1865, 12, 27. Caroline A. con mcd (H)
1878, 10, 25. Thomas M. rst by rq (H)
1888, 6, 20. Thomas M. relrq (H)

WALKER
----, --, --. Azel b 1774,4,21 d 1835,5,7; m Hannah JACKSON b 1782,2,1 d 1855,7,15 (H)

Ch:		
William	b 1803, 3, 17	d 1886, 8,31
Josiah Jackson	" 1805, 3, 16	" 1873, 8,16
Louis M.	" 1807, 10, 10	" 1872, 8,25
Joseph S.	" 1809, 7, 18	" 1887, 8,10
Rachel	" 1811, 7, 7	" 1875, 8,12
Ruth	" 1813, 8, 27	" 1875, 8,22
Elijah	" 1815, 3, 31	" 1843,10,15
Betsy Ann	" 1817, 5, 1	" 1886, 1,28
Abel	" 1819, 7, 28	" 1897, 2,20
Samuel	" 1821, 10, 6	" 1903, 8, 9

1804, 12, 13. Azel & w, Hannah, & s, William, rocf Hopewell MM, dtd 1804,9,3
1804, 12, 13. Mordecai & w, Rachel, rocf Hopewell MM, dtd 1804,9,3
1813, 3, 24. Mordecai & w, Rachel, gct Center MM
1819, 5, 25. Mordecai, Jr. rocf Center MM, dtd 1819,3,20
1820, 9, 27. Mordecai Jr. gct Center MM
1861, 8, 21. Stephen Cook gct Green Plain MM, to m Mary Walker
1866, 1, 24. Louis, Joseph, Rachel, Ruth, Betsy Ann, Abel & Samuel rec in mbrp; form mbr of Fall Creek or Centre MM, which had been laid down (H)
1886, 12, 22. Joseph S. rpd mcd (H)

WALKER, continued
1888, 3, 21. Will J. recrq

WALTERS
1807, 7, 9. Mary recrq

WALTON
1811, 12, 25. Edward & fam rocf Hopewell MM, dtd 1811,10,9

WANZER
1858, 3, 24. John & w, Melinda, & ch, George Henry & William Haviland, rocf Cincinnati MM, dtd 1858,3,18
1858, 11, 24. John & w, Malinda, & ch, George & William, gct Cincinnati MM

WARD
----, --, --. Isaac b 1742,3,22 d 1828,8,5; m Ann MASON b 1762,8,17 d 1845,5,5 (H)
Ch: Mary b 1787, 3, 30 d 1866, 8,20
Isaac " 1789, 2, 22 " 1858, 7,19
Mark " 1791, 2, 8
Ann " 1793, 1, 3
Josiah " 1794, 11, 3 " 1795,10,30
Hannah " 1796, 9, 16 " 1838, 9,22
Ellis " 1799, 2, 18
Evan " 1801, 6, 20 " 1849, 1,19
Maria Ohio " 1804, 5, 19 " 1869, 7, 2
----, --, --. George b 1767,3,26; m Deborah ----- b 1772,9,11 d 1818,8,17 (H)
Ch: Joshua b 1795, 12, 11
Rebecca " 1798, 3, 21
Eliza " 1800, 2, 1
Hannah " 1805, 12, 21
Sarah " 1807, 11, 17
Mary " 1809, 11, 8
Charlotte " 1812, 2, 8
----, --, --. Isaac Jr. b 1789,2,22 d 1858,7,19; m Mary ----- b 1797,6,12 d 1841,6,4(H)
Ch: Elizabeth b 1822, 5, 18
Mary B. " 1824, 7, 22 d 1858, 2, 7
Isaac H. " 1829, 5, 13 " 1830, 8,30
Allen " 1831, 8, 2 " 1846,10,29
1820, 6, 7. John, s John & Hannah, Warren Co., O.; m at Miami, Hannah Ann EVANS, dt Milliam & Mary, Warren Co., O.
1821, 10, 3. Evan, s Isaac & Ann, Warren Co., O., b 1801,6,20 d 1849,1,19; m at Miami, Catherine JEFFERIS, dt Job & Rebekah, Clinton Co., O., b 1801,9,29 (H)
Ch: Tailor V. b 1823, 2, 23
Rebecca J. " 1825, 1, 12
Martha Ann " 1827, 1, 18
Isaac " 1828, 11, 26 d 1829, 1,19
Owen " 1830, 1, 5
Rachel " 1832, 2, 22
Aaron " 1834, 1, 11 " 1834, 9,24
Josiah " 1835, 11, 15
Maria " 1837, 12, 9 " 1838, 9,29
Jason " 1839, 9, 14
Mary Ann " 1841, 6, 6 " 1843, 5, 4
Evan Moris " 1843, 10, 6
Ch: Colwell
Green b 1845, 6, 9 d 1845, 9, 5
1823, 3, 12. Ellis, s Isaac & Ann, Warren Co., O.; m at Miami, Mary Earl NEWMAN, dt Jonathan & Anna, Warren Co., O.
1840, 10, 28. Maria m Aaron CHANDLER (H)
1840, 12, 30. Charlotte m George STEVENSON (H)

1804, 8, 9. Isaac & w, Ann, & ch, Mary, Isaac, Mark, Ann, Hannah, Ellis, Evan & Maria, rocf Piles Grove MM, N. J., dtd 1804,3,22
1805, 1, 10. George & w, Deborah, & ch, Joshua, Rebecca, Eliza & Mary Ann, rocf Woodberry MM, N. J., dtd 1804,8,14
1806, 7, 10. Sarah rocf Haddonfield MM, N.J., dtd 1805,10,14
1810, 7, 25. Mary dis
1811, 1, 30. Sarah Craft (form Ward) con mou
1811, 6, 26. Beulah (form Bradway) dis mou
1817, 8, 27. Hannah Chandler (form Ward) con mou
1819, 11, 24. John Jr. rocf Haddonfield MM, N. J., dtd 1819,3,8
1821, 2, 28. John & w gct West Grove MM, Ind.
1821, 2, 28. Rebecca Satterthwaite (form Ward) con mou
1821, 8, 29. Isaac Jr. rpd mcd
1822, 2, 27. Mary (form Burdin) dis mou
1827, 7, 25. Mary con mou
1829, 1, 28. Evan dis jH
1829, 1, 28. Isaac dis jH
1829, 3, 25. Mary dis jH
1829, 5, 27. Ann dis jH
1829, 5, 27. Ann Jr. dis jH
1829, 5, 27. Catherine dis jH
1829, 5, 27. Maria Ohio dis jH
1829, 8, 26. George C. dis jH
1829, 12, 30. Ellis dis jH
1830, 1, 27. Mary Earl dis jH
1830, 3, 31. Mary dis jH
1830, 3, 31. Sarah dis jH
1830, 6, 30. Elizabeth & Mary recrq of parents, Isaac & Mary (H)
1830, 8, 25. Charlotte dis jH
1832, 8, 29. Sarah Watson (form Ward) dis mou (H)
1842, 10, 26. Hannah Gibbś (form Ward) dis mou
1844, 3, 27. Elizabeth Bispham (form Ward) dis mou
1845, 12, 24. Elizabeth Bispham (form Ward) dis mou
1847, 7, 21. Rebecca Montgomery (form Ward) con mou (H)
1847, 8, 25. Taylor dis disunity (H)
1849, 7, 25. Owen dis mou (H)
1850, 4, 24. Rebecca Montgomery (form Ward) dis mou
1850, 6, 26. Lydia Mendenhall (form Ward) con mou
1851, 8, 27. Martha Ann Tampset (form Ward) dis mcd (H)

WARD, continued
1852, 8, 25. Rachel Brown (form Ward) con mcd (H)
1852, 8, 25. Asenath Prints (form Ward) con mou
1855, 4, 25. Mary Crispen (form Ward) con mcd (H)
1856, 10, 22. Josiah dis disunity (H)
1858, 10, 27. Ann gct White Water MM, Ind. (H)
1858, 10, 27. Catharine & ch, Jason & Evan M. gct White Water MM, Ind. (H)
1871, 7, 26. Emma recrq
1873, 8, 27. Emily W. Fisher (form Ward) con mou
1876, 5, 24. Mary recrq
1884, 8, 27. Alpheus E. rocf Cesars Creek MM, dtd 1884,6,26

WARNER
----, --, --. Joshua Woodrow b 1823,10,24 d 1903,1,15; m Mahala HADLEY b 1827,2,25 d 1895,7,21 (H)

1807, 4, 9. John recrq
1822, 11, 27. Lydia rocf Ceasars Creek MM, dtd 1822,10,28
1866, 1, 24. Woodrow & Mahala rec in mbrp; form mbr of Fall Creek or Centre MM which had been laid down (H)
1891, 4, 22. J. Woodro & w, Mahala H., gct White Water MM, Ind. (H)
1901, 10, 23. J. Woodro rocf White Water MM, Ind. (H)

WASHBURN
1922, 5, 28. Stanley Wynne Keever gct Duanesburg MM, to m Miriam Margaret (H)

WATKINS
1811, 8, 28. Rachel (form Hunt) dis mcd

WATSON
1832, 8, 29. Sarah (form Ward) dis mou (H)

WATTLES
1892, 7, 27. Mary E. F. recrq (H)

WAY
----, --, --. Robert b 1788,7,17 d 1871,9,25; m Abigail WILLIAMS b 1802,1,21 d 1869,2,24 (H)
Ch: Phocion R. b 1826, 3, 14
Elias H. " 1828, 7, 18
Samuel C. " 1831, 3, 1
Jacob W. " 1836, 7, 5 d 1875, 3,21
David L. " 1838, 9, 8

1819, 3, 31. Robert rocf Center MM, dtd 1818, 12,19
1822, 12, 25. Robert gct Fairfield MM, to m Abigail Williams
1823, 7, 30. Abigail rocf Fairfield MM, dtd 1823,3,29
1852, 9, 22. Robert & w, Abigail, & s, David L., gct Green Plain MM (H)
1852, 9, 22. Phosian R. gct Cincinnati MM (H)
1857, 6, 24. Paschal rocf New Garden MM, Pa., dtd 1857,6,7 (H)
1858, 3, 24. Paschal gct Blue River MM (H)
1887, 2, 23. Dr. Samuel J. & w, Henriette, & dt, Fanny, recrq
1887, 10, 26. Fannie E. relrq
1891, 4, 22. Samuel C. dropped from mbrp (H)
1895, 3, 27. Frances Elizabeth recrq
1895, 5, 22. Elias H. set off as mbr of Executive Mtg at Clear Creek (H)
1920, 7, 25. Elias dropped from mbrp (H)

WEATHERHEAD
1908, 6, 24. Anna C. dropped from mbrp

WEBSTER
1805, 7, 11. Hannah & s, John, rocf Redstone MM, dtd 1805,3,1
1846, 11, 26. William R. rocf Center MM, dtd 1846,9,17 (H)
1847, 6, 23. Minerva G. recrq (H)
1849, 7, 25. William R. & w, Minerva, & dt, Florence, gct White Water MM, Ind. (H)
1866, 1, 24. Huth & William dropped from mbrp; form mbr of Fall Creek or Centre MM, which had been laid down (H)

WEEKS
1876, 3, 22. Elwood recrq

WELCH
----, --, --. Samuel b 1760,3,30; m Chloe ----- b 1763,3,5
Ch: Samuel Jr. b 1806, 12, 3
Webster G. " 1804, 10, 16
Elizabeth " 1802, 7, 23
Amos " 1796, 9, 23
----, --, --. Amos b 1796,9,23; m Rachel FALLIS b 1804,5,3
1830, 8, 26. Sarah m Jacob SLEEPER
----, --, --. Webster G. b 1804,10,16; m Mary COOPER
Ch: Turner b 1832, 12, 11
Elizabeth " 1836, 8, 30
1833, 1, 2. Elizabeth H. m Buddell SLEEPER
1850, 2, 21. John, s Turner & Esther, Tippecanoe Co., Ind.; m at Hopewell, Ann WHITACRE, dt Aquilla & Ruthann, Warren Co., O., b 1831,8,11 (H)
Ch: Savilla
Emma b 1851, 3, 17
Horace
Greeley " 1853, 5, 14
Addo Bell " 1856, 3, 13
Harriett
Lydia " 1862, 12, 3
1850, 3, 5. Martha m Aquilla CADWALADER (H)
1855, 3, 22. Josiah F., s Turner & Esther, Fountain Co., Ind., b 1830,8,1 d 1901,9, 15; m at Hopewell, Leah E. CADWALADER, dt

WELCH. continued
Jonah & Priscilla, Warren Co., O., b 1835, 12,28 d 1911,3,7 (H)
Ch: Warren T. b 1856, 5, 4
Francis J. " 1859, 1, 19
Thomas C. " 1861, 10, 23
Esther P. " 1866, 12, 2
Martha " 1868, 11, 29
----, --, --. Turner b 1832,12,11; m Ann M. HADLEY, b 1836,3,27 (Turner, s Webster & Mary)
1864, 2, 3. Elizabeth Cooper m David OVERMAN
----, --, --. Turner s Samuel & Chloe; m Mary Esther FALLIS
Ch: Martha
John
Isaiah
James
Robert Barclay
Amos

1816, 7, 31. Samuel [Welsh] & w, Chloe, & ch, Martha, Amos, Judith, Betsy, Sally Webster & Samuel, rocf Clear Creek MM, dtd 1816,8,6
1819, 2, 24. Judith Butterworth (form Welch) con mou
1819, 5, 26. Martha Pardy (form Welsh) con mou
1824, 10, 27. Amos gct Springfield MM, to m Rachel Fallis
1825, 3, 30. Samuel dis
1825, 11, 20. Rachel [Welsh] rocf Springfield MM, dtd 1825,2,26
1826, 11, 29. Samuel rst by YM
1831, 2, 23. Webster G. gct Mill Creek MM, to m Mary Cooper
1831, 5, 25. Mary rocf Mill Creek MM, dtd 1831,4,23
1832, 10, 24. Samuel gct West Grove MM, Ind., to m Rachel Williams
1833, 9, 25. Rachel rocf West Grove MM, Ind., dtd 1833,5,11
1836, 8, 24. Samuel & w, Rachel, gct Sugar River MM
1839, 2, 20. Samuel & w, Rachel, rocf Sugar River MM, Ind., dtd 1838,10,27
1839, 5, 22. Turner & ch, Mary, Martha, John, Isaac, James, Robert Barclay & Amos, rocf Sugar River MM, dtd 1838,12,29
1841, 7, 21. Rachel gct New Garden MM, Ind.
1843, 2, 22. Turner dis disunity
1843, 12, 27. Samuel con mou
1844, 6, 26. Amos dis mou
1850, 2, 20. Martha A. [Welsh] rocf Center MM, dtd 1850,2,14 (H)
1850, 6, 26. Webster G. con mou
1852, 10, 27. Oliver M., s Samuel, recrq of parent
1853, 7, 27. Mary Ann recrq
1858, 11, 24. Turner con mou
1859, 2, 25. Ann M. [Welsh] rocf Springfield MM, dtd 1859,2,19
1860, 4, 25. Leah dis disunity (H)
1869, 12, 22. Ann & ch, Horace G., Adda B. & Harriett L., gct Wapsinonoch MM, Ia.
1870, 1, 26. Oliver M. gct Wilmington MM
1870, 4, 20. James gct Benjaminville MM, Ill. (H)
1870, 6, 22. James con mcd (H)
1870, 6, 22. Eliza Whitacre (form Welch) con mcd (H)
1871, 2, 22. James gct Benjaminville MM,Ill. (H)
1872, 8, 21. Leah C. & ch, Esther & Martha, recrq (H)
1913, 2, 19. Gilbert M. & Thomas W. relrq
1917, 7, 29. Warren T., Frances J. & Thomas C. dropped from mbrp (H)

WELLS
1832, 2, 1. Thomas, s Robert & Elizabeth, Warren Co., O.; m at Miami, Hannah DUKEMINEER, dt Isaac & Ann, Warren Co., O.

1831, 9, 28. Thomas rocf Cincinnati MM, dtd 1831,8,28
1833, 12, 25. Thomas & w, Hannah, gct Newberry MM
1836, 5, 25. Thomas & w, Hannah, rocf Newberry MM, dtd 1836,4,18
1857, 4, 22. Thomas & w, Hannah, gct White River MM

WERNTZ
1907, 2, 20. Laura A. & Katherine M. recrq
1909, 10, 27. Laura dropped from mbrp

WEST
1836, 7, 2. John L., s Isaac & Letitia, Warren Co., O.; m at Miami, Asenath N. FARR, dt Edward & Mary, Warren Co., O. (H)
----, --, --. Charles b 1811,12,17 d 1881,4,16 m Maria DAKIN b 1816,8,3 d 1901,5,11 (H)

1809, 10, 14. Thomas rocf Monktown MM, dtd 1809,2,2
1835, 6, 24. John L. rocf Indian Spring MM, Md., dtd 1835,5,6 (H)
1841, 11, 24. John L. & w, Asenath, & ch, William Allen, Harvey & Mary, gct Camden MM, Ind. (H)
1855, 12, 26. Letitia rocf Center MM, dtd 1855,8,16 (H)
1863, 9, 23. Sarah L. Brown (form West) rocf Sandy Spring MM, Md. (H)
1866, 1, 24. Charles rec in mbrp; form mbr Fall Creek or Centre MM which had been laid down (H)
1866, 8, 22. David & s, Charles, rocf Cesars Creek MM, dtd 1866,7,26
1877, 3, 21. Robert K. gct Camden MM, Ind. (H)
1880, 8, 25. Maria recrq (H)

WESTHERMER
1854, 9, 20. Mildred T. (form Cadwalader) rpd mou

WHARTON
----, --, --. Silas d 1858,3,22 ae 84; m Mary DAVIS d 1845,5,9 ae 66 (H) (Silas was s Nehemiah & Elizabeth, Warren Co., O.)
Ch: Nehemiah b 1800, 1, 22 d 1856, 7,17
Mary " 1802, 11, 23 " 1843, 6,30
James " 1805, 1, 3 " 1814, 6,14
Hannah " 1807, 8, 28
Ann " 1809, 11, 28 " 1907, 2, 2
Rebecca " 1812, 12, 12
Elizabeth " 1816, 1, 10 " 1842, 10,29
Silas m 2nd 1847,11,4 at Hopewell, Phebe NEILL, dt John & Ann
1827, 12, 5. Hannah m Richard HOPKINS
1834, 4, 30. Rebecca m Nathan B. HAINES (H)
1837, 5, 31. Elizabeth m Lukens GRIFFITH (H)
----, --, --. Hannah (Satterthwaite), w Daniel, b 1816,10,10 d 1900,10,15 (H)

1821, 4, 25. Mary Mitchel (form Wharton) con mou
1829, 3, 25. Silas dis jH
1829, 5, 27. Mary dis jH
1829, 5, 27. Nehemiah dis jH
1829, 9, 30. Ann dis jH
1831, 1, 26. Rebecca dis jH
1831, 3, 30. Ann Engle (form Wharton) con mou (H)
1834, 2, 19. Nehemiah con mou (H)
1843, 9, 20. Lucy (form Mather) dis mou
1862, 7, 23. Phebe N. gct White Water MM, Ind. (H)
1864, 10, 26. Hannah B. rocf Phila. MM, dtd 1864,8,11 (H)
1875, 8, 25. Dixon & w, Sarah J., rocf Caesars Creek MM; returned because of removal back to Cesars Creek
1882, 9, 20. Elizabeth (form Jones) rpd mcd
1883, 5, 23. Jonathan recrq [(H)
1887, 4, 20. Sarah A. recrq
1889, 7, 24. Jonathan gct Friends Chapel Mtg, Ohio
1906, 5, 23. Albert relrq

WHINERY
----, --, --. Joseph b 1810,4,20 d 1892,6,9; m Sarah HIATT b 1811,4,7 d 1899,12,20 (H)
Ch: Thomas
Hiatt b 1835, 6, 23 d 1873, 6,28
Anna P. " 1837, 6, 7 " 1858, 2, 6
Ruth M. " 1839, 12, 4 " 1865, 3,14
Allen C. " 1846, 12, 14
Susan
Lydia " 1853, 7, 27 " 1882, 1,28

1866, 1, 24. Joseph & Sallie rec in mbrp; form mbr of Fall Creek or Centre MM which had been laid down
1866, 1, 24. Mark dropped from mbrp; form mbr Fall Creek or Centre MM which had been laid down (H)
1866, 1, 24. Thomas dis mcd (H)
1866, 1, 24. Lydia Moorman (form Whinery) rpd mcd (H)
1920, 7, 25. Allen C. dropped from mbrp (H)

WHITACRE
----, --, --. Robert b 1758,9,30 d 1828,9,18; m Patience McKAY b 1763,2,9 d 1836,4,21 (H)
Ch: Andrew b 1790, 8, 13 d 1864, 9,13
John " 1792, 1, 11
Priscilla " 1795, 7, 21 " 1870, 4,28
Aquilla " 1797, 9, 7
Jane " 1799, 9, 21
Rhoda " 1802, 3, 12 " 1884, 2,25
Moses " 1804, 6, 17 " 1842, 1, 8
1813, 12, 1. Priscilla m Jonah CADWALLADER
1814, 6, 1. Andrew, s Robert & Patience, Warren Co., O., b 1790,8,13 d 1864,9,13; m at Waynesville, Mary KELLY, dt Samuel & Hannah, Warren Co., O., b 1789,11,22 d 1874, 7,18 (H)
Ch: Hannah P. b 1815, 3, 13 d 1849, 5,14
Eliza Ann " 1818, 6, 5 " 1841, 9,10
Rhoda N. " 1820, 2, 29 " 1843, 5,11
Samuel
Kelly " 1822, 1, 29
Mary Jane " 1824, 8, 29 " 1902, 12,5
Emily S. " 1827, 5, 1 " 1849, 7,27
1816, 1, 3. Jane m Benjamin NINDE
1820, 12, 7. Rhoda m Joseph HOLLINGSWORTH
----, --, --. Aquilla, s Robert & Patience, Warren Co., O.; b 1797,9,7; m Ruthanna POTTS b 1797,12,4 d 1838,6,12 (H)
Ch: Rebecca
Potts b 1821, 10, 30
Mary Potts " 1824, 1, 1
Jane " 1825, 2, 25
Harriet " 1827, 6, 10 d 1848,10,23
Edward " 1829, 10, 11
Ann " 1831, 8, 11
Margaret " 1834, 6, 6
Lidia " 1836, 7, 31
Lindley " 1838, 6, 12 d 1838, 8,13
Aquilla m 2nd 1844,5,5 at Miami, Ann COOK, dt Abraham & Ruth, Warren Co., O.
Ch: Abraham b 1845, 3, 7 d 1845, 6,16
Ruthanna " 1846, 6, 11
Sarah C. " 1849, 1, 24
Albert " 1853, 3, 15
Maurice " 1855, 5, 25
Amos C. " 1857, 10, 5
----, --, --. Sarah B. (Vanskiver), w Aquilla, b 1833,4,1 d 1905,2,14 (H)
----, --, --. Moses M. b 1804,6,17 d 1842,1,8; m Priscilla THOMAS b 1803,12,7 d 1847,7,16 (H)
Ch: William T. b 1835, 1, 17 d 1907, 2, 8
Sidney T. " 1839, 6, 2 " 1901, 4, 2
1841, 9, 23. Rebecca G. m Benjamin CHANDLER (H)

WHITACRE, continued
1843, 3, 2. Mary P. m Mahlon HOLLINGSWORTH (H)
1845, 2, 20. Mary Jane m Seneca MEREDITH (H)
1845, 4, 3. Harriet B. m Marcellious COOK (H)
1846, 9, 24. Jane m Richard B. SANDERS (H)
1850, 2, 21. Ann m John WELCH (H)
----, --, --. William T. b 1835,1,17 d 1907,2,8 m Rebecca LOWNES b 1840,1,14 d 1911,10,24 (H)
Ch: Walter L. b 1867, 4, 30
Horace J. " 1869, 10, 10
Marion " 1871, 9, 8
Franklin T." 1874, 8, 26
William B. " 1878, 4, 12
Marianna " 1880, 10, 3

1806, 6, 12. Robert & w, Patience, & ch, Andrew, John, Priscilla, Aquilla, Jane, Rhoda & Moses, rocf Crooked Run MM, dtd 1805,1,5
1806, 11, 12. Jonas rocf Crooked Run MM, dtd 1806,8,30
1808, 7, 14. Jonas dis
1817, 1, 29. Rachel (form Starbuck) con mou
1817, 4, 30. John dis mcd
1820, 12, 27. Aquilla gct White Water MM, Ind., to m Ruthanna Potts
1821, 5, 30. Ruthanna rocf White Water MM, dtd 1821,3,21
1827, 2, 28. Moses M. gct Still Water MM, to m Prisilla Thomas
1827, 7, 25. Priscilla rocf Stillwater MM, dtd 1827,5,26
1829, 5, 27. Andrew dis jH
1829, 5, 27. Aquilla dis jH
1829, 5, 27. Patience dis jH
1829, 5, 27. Ruth Ann dis jH
1829, 11, 25. Mary dis jH
1830, 1, 27. Nancy recrq (H)
1833, 9, 25. Hannah dis jH
1833, 9, 25. Priscilla dis jH
1833, 11, 20. Moses dis jH
1834, 2, 19. Moses M. dis (H)
1843, 8, 23. Mary Hollingsworth (form Whitacre) dis mou
1844, 10, 23. Hannah Roach (form Whitacre) con mou (H)
1846, 10, 21. Samuel Kelly con mou (H)
1849, 6, 20. Lydia (form Chandler) rpd mou; d before action was taken (H)
1859, 5, 25. Lydia S. Hunt (form Whitacre) con mcd (H)
1861, 9, 25. Sidney Prather (form Whittacre) con mcd (H)
1865, 8, 22. Aquilla & w, Ann, & ch, Sarah C., Albert, Maurice & Amos C., gct Wapsinonoch MM, Ia. (H)
1865, 8, 22. Ruth Anna gct Wapsinonoch MM,Ia. (H)
1867, 3, 27. Rebecca (form Lownes) con mcd; mbr Springboro MM (H)
1867, 7, 24. William con mcd (H)
1869, 6, 24. Rebecca rocf Springboro MM, dtd 1867,11,21 (H)
1870, 3, 25. Edward P. con mcd (H)
1870, 4, 20. Eliza T. gct Wapsenonoch MM,Ia. (H)
1870, 6, 22. Eliza (form Welch) con mcd (H)
1870, 11, 23. Eliza gct Wapsanonoch MM, Ia.(H)
1870, 12, 21. Edward P. gct Wapsinonoch MM (H)
1871, 6, 21. Margaret Breed (form Whitacre) rpd mcd (H)
1873, 2, 19. Sarah B. rocf Westfield MM, dtd 1872,9,25 (H)
1881, 6, 22. Charles [Whitaker] & w, Sarah, & ch, Rosanna, Ida, Asa, John & Mary Ethel, recrq
1887, 4, 20. Ada L. recrq
1896, 3, 25. Asa relrq
1906, 2, 21. Charles & w, Addie, & dt, Loverna, relrq
1908, 1, 22. Walter H. relrq
1909, 1, 27. Joseph & s, Harold W., recrq

WHITE
1853, 8, 25. Richard, s Aaron & Margaret, Wayne Co., Ind.; m at Miami, Mary A. UNDERHILL, dt Jacob & Sarah, Warren Co., O.

1820, 2, 23. Joseph rocf Burlington MM, N.J., dtd 1819,11,1
1824, 9, 29. Tabitha rocf Burlington, N. J., dtd 1823,12,1
1854, 6, 21. Mary U. gct Red Cedar MM, Ia.
1856, 8, 27. Anna T. (form Steddom) dis mou
1895, 11, 20. Mary Neal recrq

WHITELY
1912, 11, 20. Elmira J. rocf White Water MM, Ind., dtd 1912,10,23 (H)

WHITSEL
1856, 4, 23. Matilda (form Sabin) rpd mcd (H)
1856, 6, 25. Emma M. con mcd (H)
1856, 9, 27. Martha Ann (form Jessop) con mcd (H)
1859, 6, 22. Susannah [Whitsal] rocf Springfield MM, dtd 1859,6,18
1861, 3, 27. Susannah [Whitsall] gct Springfield MM, O.

WHITSON
1806, 12, 18. Willis, s Solomon & Phebe, Butlar Co., O.; m at Elk Creek, Rebekah COMTON, dt Nathan & Ann Hawkins, Butler Co., O.

1804, 4, 12. Jordon rocf Cane Creek MM, S. C., dtd 1804,2,18
1804, 5, 10. Samuel rocf Cane Creek MM, S. C. dtd 1804,2,18
1804, 12, 13. Wyllis rocf Cane Creek MM, S.C., dtd 1804,11,17
1805, 4, 11. Solomon rocf Cane Creek MM, S. C.

WHITSON, continued
dtd 1804,12,22
1805, 5, 8. Jordon rpd mcd
1805, 6, 13. David & w, Mary, & ch, Phebe, rocf Cane Creek MM, S. C., dtd 1805,2,16
1805, 6, 13. John rocf Cane Creek MM, S. C., dtd 1805,3,23

WICKERSHAM
----, --, --. ----- m Rachel ----- b 1783,9,20 d 1867,5,23 (H)
Ch: David b 1806, 7, 14 d 1887,12, 8
Eliza " 1819, 3, 18 " 1888,10,11

1806, 12, 11. Enoch rocf Warrington MM, dtd 1806,10,11
1808, 4, 14. Margaret rocf Center MM, dtd 1808,3,5
1810, 10, 31. Enoch & fam gct Center MM
1812, 2, 26. Mary rocf Hopewell MM, dtd 1811, 11,7
1813, 6, 30. Isaac rocf Hopewell MM, dtd 1813,5,6
1866, 1, 24. Rachel, Eliza & David rec in mbrp; form mbr of Fall Creek or Centre MM which had been laid down (H)

WILDMAN
1865, 11, 29. John, s Edward & Hannah, Clark Co., O.; m at Waynesville, Mary T. PUGH, dt Achillas & Anna Maria, Warren Co., O.

1866, 7, 25. Mary T. gct Green Plain MM

WILKERSON
1817, 3, 26. Mahlon [Wilkinson] rocf Fairfax MM, dtd 1817,1,29
1818, 12, 30. Mahlon dis mcd
1825, 6, 29. Elizabeth & ch, Tacy, Aaron & Rachel, rocf Fairfax MM, Va., dtd 1823,10, 15
1879, 8, 27. Abiah recrq (H)

WILKINS
1839, 2, 20. Rachel rocf Green Plain MM, dtd 1839,1,16 (H)

WILLETS
1807, 1, 8. William rocf North West Fork MM, Md., dtd 1806,10,15
1813, 3, 31. Mahlon rocf Evesham MM, dtd 1813,2,5
1823, 3, 26. Mahlon dis mcd

WILLIAMS
1821, 1, 4. Clarke, s Enion & Martha, Warren Co., O.; m at Springborough, Mary THOMPSON, dt William & Sophia, Warren Co., O.

1805, 8, 8. Enion & s, Peter, Clark, Seth & Enion, rocf Back Creek MM, N. C., dtd 1805, 4,27
1806, 4, 10. John & w, Sarah, & ch, Benejah, Jonathan, Elizabeth, Matthew & John, rocf Mt. Pleasant MM, Va., dtd 1805,10,26
1806, 4, 10. Martha & dt, Abigail, rocf Back Creek MM, N. C., dtd 1805,4,27
1806, 7, 10. William & w, Phebe, & ch, Catherine, Mary, Josiah & Robert, rocf Deep River MM, N. C., dtd 1805,9,2
1809, 7, 8. Matthias rocf Mt. Pleasant MM, Va., dtd 1807,4,25
1809, 12, 27. Cert rec for Ann from New Garden MM, N. C., dtd 1809,8,26, endorsed to White Water MM
1814, 5, 25. Jesse & w, Sarah, & ch, Micajah Terrell, Achilles, Ann Lynch, Sarah, Robert, Elizabeth & Jesse Lynch, rocf Westfield MM, N. C., dtd 1814,4,9
1814, 11, 30. Ann dis joining Methodist Society
1815, 8, 30. Achilles gct New Garden MM, N.C. to m
1815, 12, 21. Jesse & fam gct Cincinnati MM
1816, 6, 26. Nathan & Zadoc rocf Newberry MM, Tenn., dtd 1814,3,5
1817, 4, 30. Jesse & w, Sarah, & ch, Anna L., Sarah, Elizabeth, Robert & Jesse, rocf Cincinnati MM, dtd 1817,2,20
1818, 7, 25. Beulah rocf New Garden MM, N.C., dtd 1818,2,28
1818, 9, 30. Achilles & fam gct White Water MM
1820, 2, 23. Robert gct White Water MM
1820, 5, 31. Jesse & fam gct White Water MM, Ind.
1820, 6, 28. Clark rocf Clear Creek MM, dtd 1820,4,8
1822, 11, 27. Robert Way gct Fairfield MM, to m Abigail Williams
1832, 10, 24. Samuel Welch gct West Grove MM, Ind., to m Rachel Williams
1840, 4, 22. Hannah (form Clark) con mou (H)
1869, 1, 27. Annie (form Steddom) con mou
1869, 5, 26. Anna gct Spiceland MM, Ind.
1881, 5, 25. George A. recrq
1883, 4, 25. Lucy C., David E. & Anna M. recrq
1885, 6, 24. Anna (form Jackson) relrq to jas (H)
1886, 2, 24. Stephen & w, Rachel, & s, Everette, recrq
1895, 5, 22. Rachel S. set off as mbr of Executive Mtg at Clear Creek (H)
1901, 2, 20. Geo., Anna & Lucy relrq
1908, 12, 23. Stephen & Rachel gct White Water MM, Ind.
1930, 2, 23. Stephen G. rocf Dayton MM (H)

WILLIAMSON
1850, 9, 20. Miriam rocf Center MM, dtd 1850,7,18 (H)
1855, 9, 26. Miriam dis disunity (H)
1868, 5, 27. Richard P. recrq
1872, 8, 21. Richard rpd mcd (H)
1882, 3, 22. Anna recrq

WILLIAMSON, continued
1882, 4, 26. Anna (form Janney) relrq

WILSON
----, --, --. Jesse b 1773,7,14; m Elizabeth ----- b 1781,6,22 (H)
Ch: George b 1801, 9, 30
Rachel " 1802, 12, 31
John " 1805, 10, 28 d 1808, 6, 9
Israel " 1808, 8, 27
Mary " 1810, 9, 23
Enoch " 1812, 9, 13
Aaron " 1815, 4, 17
Jesse " 1820, 12, 13 d 1821, 4,29
1815, 10, 4. Rebekah m Henry COATE

1804, 11, 8. Joseph & ch, Ann, Jane, Joseph, Mary, Elizabeth, Morgan & John, rocf Springfield MM, dtd 1804,6,2
1805, 6, 13. Jesse & w, Elizabeth, & ch, George & Rachel, rocf Salem MM, N. J., dtd 1805,3,25
1809, 9, 9. William & w, Ruth, & ch, Robert, John, Hannah, Darkin, William & Jane, rocf Duck Creek MM, dtd 1807,9,12
1811, 3, 27. Gabriel rocf Red Stone MM, dtd 1810,11,30
1811, 3, 27. Jeremiah & w, Joanna, & ch, Gabril, Elizabeth, Edith, Henry & William, rocf Redstone MM, dtd 1810,11,30
1811, 3, 27. Rebekah rocf Redstone MM, dtd 1810,11,30
1812, 8, 28. Gabriel dis training in militia & offering himself as a soldier
1814, 8, 31. Jeremiah dis mcd
1814, 9, 28. Jeremiah [Willson's] ch gct Darby Creek MM
1824, 6, 30. James rocf Nottingham MM, Pa., dtd 1824,3,12
1824, 6, 30. John & w, Catherine, & ch, Catherine & Hester Maria, rocf Nottingham MM, Pa., dtd 1824,3,12
1824, 5, 30. Nathan rocf Nottingham MM, Pa., dtd 1824,3,12
1829, 2, 25. David Burnet gct Cesars Creek MM, to m Hannah Wilson
1830, 3, 31. Thomas recrq (H)
1852, 11, 24. Thomas gct Fall Creek MM, Ind. (H)
1890, 1, 22. Sarah recrq
1892, 12, 21. Hattie, Myrtle & Pearl recrq
1901, 8, 21. Hattie, Pearl & Myrtle dropped from mbrp

WILTSEE
1817, 11, 26. Simeon & w, Elizabeth, & ch, Henry, Simeon, William, John & Martin, rocf Upper Evesham MM, dtd 1817,9,6
1818, 5, 27. Cert rec for Simeon & fam dtd 1818,4,11, endorsed to Elk MM

WINDER
1876, 1, 26. Rebecca H. rocf White Water MM, dtd 1875,12,22 (H)
1878, 2, 20. Rebecca H. gct White Water MM(H)

WINFIELD
1904, 6, 22. Charles & w, Jessie B., & s, Robert L., rocf Springfield MM

WISENER
1807, 5, 4. Jacob & w, Mary, & ch, Isaac, Sarah & Thomas, rocf Bush River MM, S.C., dtd 1807,1,31
1809, 4, 8. Jacob & w, Mary, & ch, Isaac, Sarah & Ruth, gct West Branch MM

WITHAM
1885, 10, 21. Ruthanna (form Butterworth) relrq (H)

WITHY
1806, 11, 13. James & w, Mary, & ch, Elizabeth, Jonathan & Jacob, rocf New Garden MM, N. C., dtd 1806,6,28
1807, 9, 10. Elizabeth Crews (form Withy) dis mcd

WOLF
1881, 6, 22. Emma recrq

WOLFRANN
1917, 8, 26. Wilhelm & w, Marion, recrq (H)
1918, 11, 8. William H. gl of standing (H)

WOOD
1823, 9, 24. Ruth rocf Westland MM, Pa., dtd 1823,4,24
1827, 1, 31. Jesse M. rocf Flushing MM, dtd 1826,6,23
1917, 7, 29. Lydia transferred to this mtg from Springboro (H)

WOODARD
----, --, --. Isaac & Jane [Woodward]
Ch: Abashai
Elizabeth
William
Mary Adaline

1838, 7, 25. Isaac M. & w, Jane, & ch, Abisha, Minerva, William & Mary, rocf Fairfield MM, dtd 1838,4,26
1842, 9, 21. Jane & ch gct Dover MM

WOOLARD
1876, 3, 22. Lewis recrq
1882, 6, 21. Lewis relrq

WOOLEY
1884, 4, 23. Anna recrq
1884, 5, 21. James & Leonidas recrq
1887, 4, 20. Curtis L. & Emmerson D. recrq
1892, 5, 25. Anna [Woolley] relrq
1892, 7, 27. James A. [Woolley] relrq
1897, 11, 24. Douglas & w, Florence, dis

WOOLEY, continued
1914, 5, 27. Curlis & Ella dropped from mbrp

WOOTEN
1902, 6, 25. Albert [Whoton] rocf Springfield MM, dtd 1902,5,17
1914, 1, 21. Abijah & fam rocf Gilead MM
1915, 9, 22. Abijah & w, Lucetta, & ch, Gurney, Dillon, Helen & Isom, gct Fairview MM, Kans.
1915, 9, 22. Nellie gct Wilmington MM

WORLEY
1807, 3, 12. Jacob & w, Phebe, & ch, Hiram, Rebecca, Milly, Katy, Patty, John & Jacob, rocf Westfield MM, N. C. dtd 1805,9,21
1873, 6, 25. Sarah E. (form Toms) con mou
1901, 8, 21. Sadie dropped from mbrp

WRIGHT
1814, 4, 7. Elizabeth m John SHAW
1817, 1, 2. Joel, s John & Elizabeth, Warren Co., O.; m near Springboro, Ann BATEMAN, dt William & Elizabeth, Warren Co., O.
1838, 10, 6. Amanda Ann (Newport) b

1803, 12, 8. Jemima & ch, Jane, Joshua, Jemima, Joab & Joel, rocf Bush River MM, S. C.
1805, 8, 8. Hannah & ch, Ann, Hannah, Mary, Sidney & Dillen, recrq
1805, 10, 10. Elijah rocf Springfield MM, N.C. dtd 1805,6,1
1805, 12, 12. Jonathan & w, Susannah, & ch, Joel, Susannah & Rebecca, rocf Gunpowder MM, Md., dtd 1805,9,25
1806, 1, 9. Jonothan rocf Gunpowder MM, Md., dtd 1805,9,25
1806, 3, 13. Joseph rocf New Hope MM, dtd 1805,10,19
1806, 3, 13. Elizabeth rocf Indian Spring MM, Md., dtd 1805,10,25
1806, 4, 10. Mary rocf Gunpowder MM, Md., dtd 1805,9,25
1806, 5, 8. Jonah rocf Bush River MM, S. C., dtd 1806,2,22
1806, 6, 12. Elijah, s Ralph, Warren Co., O., rmt Susannah Hoover, at Waynesville
1806, 6, 12. Israel rocf Pipe Creek MM, Md., dtd 1806,3,15
1806, 6, 12. Joel rocf Pipe Creek MM, Md., dtd 1806,3,15
1806, 9, 11. John & w, Vashti, rocf Bush River MM, S. C., dtd 1806,3,29
1806, 9, 11. Sarah (form Crews) dis mou
1806, 10, 9. Charity rocf Bush River MM, dtd 1806,4,26
1810, 1, 6. Israel dis mcd
1810, 1, 31. John & w, Margaret, & ch, James, Abraham, Isaac, Jacob, Ann, Solomon & Sarah, rocf New Hope MM, dtd 1805,1,19
1810, 3, 28. Jonothan Jr. rocf Center MM, dtd 1810,1,6
1810, 11, 28. John dis
1812, 2, 26. Sarah (form Gaunt) dis mcd
1812, 12, 30. Elizabeth [Write] rocf Fairfield MM, dtd 1812,10,30, endorsed by Ceasars Creek MM, 1812,12,5
1813, 4, 28. Joel rocf Center MM, dtd 1813, 3,6
1813, 11, 24. Jonothan & Susannah rocf Center MM, dtd 1813,11,6
1813, 11, 24. Susanna & Rebecca rocf Centre MM, dtd 1813,11,6
1814, 8, 31. Jonothan Jr. gct Gunpowder MM, Md., to m Susannah B. Jones
1814, 10, 26. Jonothan & w, Mary, & ch, Mahlon, Josiah, Aaron, Hannah & Jesse, rocf Monallen MM, Pa., dtd 1814,8,18
1815, 1, 25. Hannah B. rocf Gunpowder MM, dtd 1814,11,23
1815, 12, 21. Rebecca Lathrop (form Wright) dis mou
1816, 12, 25. Vashti & ch, James & William, gct White Water MM
1824, 6, 30. Gabriel recrq
1825, 12, 28. Gabriel dis disunity
1830, 10, 27. Charity gct Arba MM, Ind.
1836, 3, 23. Susan (form Satterthwaite) con mou (H)
1859, 8, 24. Amanda (form Newport) con mcd (H)
1859, 12, 21. Amanda gct Cincinnati MM (H)
1867, 4, 24. Amanda rocf Cincinnati MM, dtd 1866,12,20 (H)
1875, 9, 22. Louisa (form Sabin) gct Salem MM, Ia.
1876, 12, 27. Jonathan B. & w, Louiza, & dt, Grace L., rocf Salem MM, Ia.
1880, 3, 24. Jonathan & w, Louisa S., & ch, Grace L., gct Wilmington MM
1887, 5, 25. Rachel M. (form Good) relrq (H)
1890, 10, 22. Anna B. (form Boltz) relrq
1891, 1, 21. Isabella relrq (H)
1899, 10, 25. Jonathan B. & w, Louisa S., & dt, Grace L., & s, Paul, rocf Maryville MM, Tenn.
1901, 8, 21. Grace L. relrq
1908, 8, 19. Dr. Alfred recrq (H)
1910, 1, 26. Orpha P. recrq
1911, 2, 22. Paul H. & w, Opha E., & dt, Dorothy Evelyn, gct Short Creek MM, O.
1913, 3, 26. Ralph Elliott recrq (H)
1917, 7, 29. Jesse, Jane F. & Charles F. transferred to this mtg from Springboro (H)
1917, 7, 29. Lydia, Mary, Dr. Emily & Jonathan transferred to this mtg from Springboro (H)

WYSONG
1884, 5, 28. Alfred recrq
1908, 8, 26. Eva & s, Levi, rocf Ceasars Creek MM
1914, 5, 27. Levi dropped from mbrp
1916, 5, 24. Eva gct Spring Valley MM

YATES
1812, 10, 28. Mary [Yeates] & ch, Patrick, Clerky, Enoch & Elizabeth, rocf Lost Creek MM, dtd 1810,8,29
1814, 11, 30. Mary & ch gct White Water MM

YOUNG
----, --, --. William T. b 1832,2,19 d 1893,5, 12; m Mary E. MOON b 1838,2,6 (H)
Ch: Charles C. b 1864, 12, 12
Lelia Abi " 1867, 1, 29
Alice B. " 1869, 8, 28
Edward B. " 1874, 12, 30
Daisy J. " 1877, 4, 14 d 1906, 9, 1

1860, 6, 20. Martin Clarkson rocf Goshen MM, dtd 1860,5,19
1870, 5, 25. William T. & w, Mary E., & ch, Charles C., Lelia A. & Allice B., recrq (H)
1871, 5, 24. Caleb H. Lewis & w, Rhoda Ann, & Martin Clarkson Young, a minor, gct Saline MM, Ill.
1884, 5, 21. Alfred recrq
1891, 7, 22. Abi relrq (H)
1892, 10, 26. Charles H. [Younge] con mcd (H)
1893, 4, 26. Henry, Catherine & James recrq
1900, 5, 23. Charles H. relrq (H)
1901, 4, 24. James E. & sister, Sarah C., gct Ceasars Creek MM
1912, 8, 21. Edward B. relrq (H)
1914, 4, 22. James & Sarah Catherine recrq

YOUNT
1806, 4, 10. Catherine Hoover (form Yount) dis mou
1807, 4, 9. John rocf Back Creek MM, N. C., dtd 1804,10,27
1808, 1, 14. Eva [Yont] con mou
1808, 2, 11. Andrew rpd mcd
1808, 4, 14. Henry & w, Mary, & dt, Sarah, gct West Branch MM
1808, 4, 14. Andrew & w, Eve, & s, Dan, gct West Branch MM
1831, 3, 30. Frederick & w recrq (H)
1831, 4, 27. Mary recrq (H)

ZELL
----, --, --. Walter m Louisa J. ----- b 1847, 9,3(H)

1881, 1, 26. Louisa J. (form Janney) rpd mcd (H)
1900, 9, 26. Thomas & w, Lida T., & ch, Blanch Rachel, Edna Phoebe, Warren Truman & Elsie Rua, recrq
1902, 9, 24. Thomas & w, Lida, & dt, Blanch, dis
1902, 9, 24. Edna, Warren & Elsie relrq
1905, 11, 22. Walter recrq (H)
1920, 2, 1. Walter & w, Louiza J., gct Orange Grove MM, Calif. (H)

ZENTMEYER
1776, 11, 9. Elizabeth b
1836, 1, 16. Enos, s Samuel & Sophronia, b
1854, 2, 18. Elizabeth d bur Olive Branch

1856, 9, 24. Enos recrq
1866, 9, 26. Enos dis mou

ZIMMERMAN
1900, 9, 26. Thaddeus E. & ch, Charles M. & Ruth S., recrq

* * * * * * *

ANTHONY
1814, 7, 7. Rachel m Lot PUGH
1825, 5, 5. Henrietta P. m Abraham NORDYKE

BENBOW
1819, 11, 4. Evan, s Edward & Mary, Wayne Co., Ind.; m at Turtle Creek, Maria VENABLE dt Wm. & Rachel, Warren Co., O.

BURNET
1805, 7, 11. Rachel & Mary rocf Redstone MM, dtd 1805,3,1
1814, 5, 25. Daniel [Burnett] & w, Ann, & ch, Annabel & Stephen, rocf Redstone MM, dtd 1814,3,4
1816, 9, 25. John rocf Stillwater MM, dtd 1816,8,24
1826, 1, 31. Rebecca rocf Stillwater MM, dtd 1826,12,23
1826, 11, 26. David rocf Flushing MM, dtd 1827,7,27
1829, 1, 31. Rachel rocf Flushing MM, dtd 1828,3,1
1829, 2, 25. Daniel [Burnett] dis jH
1829, 2, 25. David gct Cesars Creek MM, to m Hannah Wilson
1829, 3, 25. Ann dis jH
1829, 7, 29. Annabel dis jH
1829, 12, 30. Hannah rocf Caesars Creek MM, dtd 1829,11,26
1830, 4, 28. Robert & w, Anna, & ch, Thomas, Lydia, William & Smith, rocf Flushing MM, dtd 1830,1,21
1842, 12, 21. William con mou
1843, 3, 22. William G. dis jH
1844, 4, 24. David gct Spiceland MM, to m Eliza Pennington
1844, 8, 21. Rachel Keach (form Burnett) con mou
1844, 11, 20. Eliza rocf Spiceland MM, dtd 1844,7,24

COLEMAN
1865, 9, 20. Martha [Colman] gct Plainfield MM, Ia.
1894, 3, 21. Martha gct Indianapolis MM, Ind.
1904, 4, 20. Minnie May relrq (H)
1915, 3, 24. Frank & w, Minnie, rocf Ceasars Creek MM, dtd 1915,2,25
1917, 7, 29. Anna transferred to this mtg from Springboro (H)

COLLET
1806, 7, 10. Rebecca (form Haines) rpd mou
1808, 1, 14. Cert rec for Rebecca from Hopewell MM, Va., dtd 1807,7,6; endorsed to Center MM
1813, 6, 30. Mary rocf Hopewell MM, dtd 1812, 10,5

COOK
----, --, --. Levi m Ann COOK (H)
Ch: Betty b 1800, 2, 12
Isaac " 1801, 12, 8
John " 1804, 12, 25

EDWARDS
1820, 2, 23. John recrq

FILSON
1897, 2, 24. Cornelia Ann & Cyntha Ellen recrq
1897, 3, 24. John C. recrq
1899, 6, 21. John & w, Cynthia E., & dt, Cornelia A., dropped from mbrp

HADLEY
1830, 9, 29. Abraham gct Springfield MM, to m Jane Hadley

HAINES
1834, 7, 20. Noah d ae 54 (an elder)

HOFFMAN
1809, 1, 18. Lidia [Hufman] m Isaac THOMAS

HOPKINS
1908, 2, 19. Horace relrq (H)
1917, 4, 29. Charles F. rocf Baltimore MM, dtd 1917,3,7 (H)

HORMAL
1891, 8, 26. Mehitable gct Chicago MM

JOHNSON
1841, 10, 28. Cynthia A. m Benjamin JONES

KERSEY
1846, 12, 17. Henry d bur Turtle Creek

LAFETRA
1818, 12, 30. Meribah & her two minor ch, Benjamin & Robert, rocf Shrewsbury MM, N. J., dtd 1818,9,7
1818, 12, 30. George W. & w, Elizabeth, & two minor ch, James H. & Jane T., rocf Shrews--bury MM, N. J., dtd 1818,9,7

LEWIS
1857, 1, 16. Hannah d ae 51

LUKENS
1884, 6, 22. Elcy H. A. d (a minister) (H)

MILLS
1819, 8, 25. Joel rpd mcd by Miami PM; con mcd 1819,11,24

OAKLEY
1819, 5, 26. George rocf Clear Creek MM, O., dtd 1819,4,10

SHERWOOD
----, --, --. Isaac, s Thomas & Dorcas, b 1830,3,7 d 1832,5,3

SWAIN
1858, 5, 6. Thomas d (h)

THOMAS
1820, 6, 28. Elisha gct Clear Creek MM, O.

WHEELER
1823, 7, --. Noah recrq
1829, 9, 30. Noah dis jH

CAESARS CREEK MONTHLY MEETING

Caesars Creek Monthly Meeting, in Clinton County, Ohio, six miles east of Waynesville, was set off from Center Monthly Meeting 5 Mo. 26, 1810, by order of Miami Quarterly Meeting.

Among the charter members were Robert Furnas, Clerk and elder; Ann Compton, clerk; John Mendenhall, Isaac Hawkins, Thomas Cox, Joseph Cook and Rachel Lewis, overseers; also appear the names of Spray, Wilson, Furnas, Milhouse, Arnold, Reagan, Mills, Whitson, Lewis, Cook, Cloud, Bridges, and Connor.

Many of the charter members of Caesars Creek Monthly Meeting were former members of Cane Creek Monthly Meeting, South Carolina. Their removal to Ohio took place in large numbers between 1803 and 1807.

RECORDS

ADAMS
1884, 3, 27. Azariah recrq
1884, 3, 27. Mary E. recrq
1896, 3, 26.. A. J. relrq
1898, 4, 21. Azariah J. recrq
1898, 5, 26. Mary E. & ch, Ethel & Lena, relrq
1901, 4, 25. Anna B. recrq
1905, 3, 23. Earl recrq
1905, 5, 25. Mary E. recrq
1901, 6, 22. Earl dropped from mbrp
1913, 6, 26. Azariah & Mary E. dropped from mbrp
1919, 6, 22. Azariah recrq

ADDINGTON
----, --, --. James & -----
Ch: Thomas b 1777, 2, 12
Mary " 1778, 9, 30
Sarah " 1781, 9, 6
Henry " 1784, 7, 2
Rebecca " 1787, 1, 10
Martha " 1789, 8, 28
James " 1792, 1, 15
Kerenhappuck " 1795, 3, 5
John " 1797, 5, 2

AGNEW
1908, 12, 24. Arthur recrq

AIRY
1875, 1, 28. Harmon recrq

ALBERTSON
1828, 9, 25. Josiah & w, Hannah, & her s, Harmon Kester, rocf Springfield MM, dtd 1828,6,28
1829, 12, 31. Josiah & w, Hannah gct Miami MM, O.
1830, 10, 28. Josiah & w, Hannah, rocf Miami MM, O., dtd 1830,9,27
1832, 3, 22. Josiah & w, Hannah, gct Newberry MM, O.

ALEXANDER
1862, 2, 20. Hannah (form Walton) con mcd
1876, 4, 27. Hannah relrq

ALLAMAN
1908, 12, 24. Missouri recrq
1909, 1, 28. Charles [Alliman] recrq

ALLEN
1815, 1, 5. Ruth m John COX
----, --, --. Joseph & Elizabeth
Ch: Mary b 1816, 10, 29
Amos " 1818, 5, 9
Solomon " 1820, 1, 30
----, --, --. Joseph b 1854,4,27 d 18-9,3,2 bur Caesars Creek
----, --, --. Jobe m Lydia COULTER
Ch: Josephine M. b 1861, 10, 21
Hannah L. " 1865, 11, 12

1810, 8, 25. Mary (form Benson) con mcd
1811, 7, 27. Ruth rocf Hopewell MM, dtd 1811, 5,9, endorsed by Miami MM, O.
1811, 7, 27. Jackson & w, Mary, & ch, Edward, Mary, Joseph, Solomon, Rebeckah, Alice, Sarah, Anna, Harmony & Wesley, rocf Hopewell MM, dtd 1811,5,9, endorsed by Miami MM, O., 1811,5,29
1812, 3, 28. Mary rocf Hopewell MM, Va., dtd 1811,12,5, endorsed by Miami MM, O., 1812, 2,26
1814, 5, 28. Joseph, Ruth & Deborah, ch Joseph, rocf Hopewell MM, Va., dtd 1813,11,4
1815, 6, 23. Joseph con mcd
1815, 8, 25. Edward dis disunity
1815, 9, 29. Elizabeth (form Cadwalader) con mcd
1815, 9, 29. Mary Moody (form Allen) con mcd
1818, 11, 27. Solomon dis mcd
1822, 1, 25. Joseph Jr. dis disunity
1822, 7, 26. Solomon rst at Greenplain MM, O. on consent of this mtg
1822, 7, 26. Alice Sanders (form Allen)con mcd
1824, 10, 28. Joseph & w, Elizabeth, & ch, Mary, Solomon, Preston & Eleanor, gct White Lick MM, Ind.
1825, 6, 30. Mary dis jas
1826, 6, 29. Mary Roberts (form Allen) dis mcd
1845, 8, 28. Margaret rocf Fairfield MM, Ind. dtd 1845,6,19
1850, 5, 23. Margaret gct Fairfield MM, Ind.
1906, 1, 25. Bessie & Ella recrq
1921, 4, 21. Charles W. & Fannie K. recrq

ANABE
----, --, --. D. W. [Anabee] b 1849,3,25; m Sarah A. ----- b 1858,7,8
Ch: Katie B. b 1885, 4, 3
Ollie V. " 1889, 5, 12
Anna M. " 1893, 3, 3
Lillian S. " 1896, 1, 18

1876, 6, 22. Sarah J. recrq
1896, 11, 26. Eunice relrq
1898, 5, 26. Katie recrq
1904, 4, 21. Katie & Olive V. dropped from mbrp
1913, 6, 26. Daniel W. & Sarah A. [Anabee] dropped from mbrp
1913, 6, 26. Lillian [Anabee] dropped from mbrp
1917, 4, 26. Daniel W. & w, Sarah A., recrq

ANDERSON
1793, 7, 29. Priscilla b d 1853,5,25 bur Caesars Creek

ANDERSON, continued
1836, 9, 16. John, s Wm. & Mary (Cosand), b
----, --, --. Phillip P. b 1844,7,9 d 1921,2,9 bur Caesars Creek
----, --, --. John W. b 1850,3,28 d 1921,5,31 bur Caesars Creek

1811, 8, 31. Elijah recrq
1870, 4, 21. Philip P. & John W. recrq
1870, 4, 21. Frank recrq
1888, 3, 22. J. W. relrq
1909, 1, 28. Harvey & w recrq
1909, 1, 28. Mabel recrq
1912, 1, 25. Neva Stanfield relrq

ANTHONY
1817, 1, 9. Thomas P., s Joseph & Rhoda, Clinton Co., O.; m in Old Town, Narcissa HAINS, dt John & Elizabeth, Green Co., O.

1817, 2, 21. Narcissa gct Cincinnati MM, O.

ANTRAM
1883, 12, 27. Mary C., dt Arthur & Margaret (Welch), b

1827, 9, 27. Elizabeth (form Clark) dis mcd
1881, 2, 24. Anna E. recrq
1881, 10, 27. Eliza relrq
1923, 12, 30. Mary rocf Dover MM

ANWYLER
1900, 7, 24. Elizabeth Moon dropped from mbrp

ARMENT
1908, 12, 24. Mary recrq
1925, 7, 23. A. E., John, Donald & Mary relrq

ARNETT
1833, 3, 4. Sarah b

ARMSTRONG
1925, 7, 23. W. C. & w relrq

ARNOLD
----, --, --. Mahala b 1800,4,9 d 1845,4,30 bur Caesars Creek
----, --, --. Jesse b 1785,9,15 d 1832,10,1; m Jane ----- b 1786,5,8 d 1863,8,4 bur Xenia

Ch:		
	John	b 1815, 12, 28
	Rachel	" 1817, 10, 11
	Mary	" 1823, 7, 24

1813, 11, 27. Jesse gct Center MM, O., to m there
1814, 5, 28. Jane rocf Center MM, O., dtd 1814,4,2
1832, 7, 26. Eleanor recrq
1833, 2, 21. John & Mahala recrq
1838, 1, 25. Rachel dis disunity
1828, 5, 24. John Jr. dis mcd
1841, 4, 22. Eleanor gct Sugar River MM, Ind.
1842, 6, 23. Mary dis disunity
1845, 10, 23. John dis joining Separatists
1870, 4, 21. John, Nancy & Emma recrq
1876, 4, 27. Nancy & dt, Emma, gct Newberry MM, O.
1893, 12, 28. Sarah Jane recrq
1915, 1, 28. Eber J. & w, Leona, recrq
1916, 9, 21. Eber J. & w, Lena, & s, Eugene, relrq

ARY
1909, 2, 25. Nannie recrq

ATKINSON
1816, 6, 28. Cephus & w, Abigail, rocf Center MM, dtd 1816,4,20
1822, 4, 26. Cephus & w, Abigail, & ch, Isaac & Levi, gct Green Plain MM, O.

AUSTIN
1885, 9, 24. James recrq
1887, 8, 25. James E. relrq

BABB
1878, 11, 13. Mary b

1905, 7, 27. Clinton, Anna, Vedith, Eva, Albert & Esther, rocf Wilmington MM, O.
1906, 2, 22. Nicholas D. & Allie rocf Center MM, O.
1913, 6, 26. May dropped from mbrp
1922, 2, 23. Ella E. recrq

BAGFORD
1921, 4, 21. Carrie Jenson recrq

BAILEY
1875, 8, 14. Mellie b

1913, 6, 26. Mellie dropped from mbrp

BAKER
1892, 11, 13. Anna b

1884, 3, 27. Walter J. recrq
1900, 7, 24. Brinton recrq

BALDWIN
----, --, --. J. W. b 1838,10,11; m Josephine ----- b 1843,5,12

1876, 1, 27. I. W. & Josephine recrq
1883, 3, 22. I. W. & w, Josephine, relrq

BALES
1885, 5, 1. Martha Ellen b

BALL
1874, 12, 24. James & w, Mary, recrq
1878, 2, 21. Rachel rècrq

BALLARD
1819, 11, 4. Sarah m Ira MENDENHALL
----, --, --. John b 1809,5,14; m Lydia ----- b 1816,1,17
Ch: Jordan W. b 1840, 8, 21
Rebecca J. " 1841, 9, 24
William A. " 1850, 11, 27
----, --, --. Jordon W. b 1840,8,21; m Martha F. ----- b 1846,3,8
Ch: Fred
Wayne b 1869, 4, 24
Thomas Elroy " 1870, 12, 20
Willa Elsie " 1872, 5, 26

1819, 2, 26. Joseph & w, Elizabeth, & ch, Alice, David, Susanna, Joel, Julianna, Almedia & Asa, rocf Center MM, O., dtd 1819,1,16
1819, 2, 26. Sarah rocf Center MM, O., dtd 1819,1,16
1820, 1, 28. Joseph & fam gct Elk MM
1830, 1, 28. Joshua Compton gct Center MM, O., to m Edith Ballard
1843, 9, 21. Enos Wilson gct Center MM, O., to m Rebecca Ballard
1865, 10, 26. John & w, Lydia, & s, Wm. Alpheus, rocf Center MM, O., dtd 1865,9,13
1865, 10, 26. Jordan W. rocf Center MM, O., dtd 1865,9,13
1865, 10, 26. Rebecca Jane rocf Center MM, O., dtd 1865,9,13
1873, 1, 23. Martha recrq
1873, 3, 27. Nina recrq
1878, 9, 26. John & w, Lydia, gct Center MM, O.
1884, 9, 25. Alpheus dis
1891, 11, 26. Fred W. & Willa relrq
1891, 11, 26. Martha F. & ch, Elroy & Edna Marie, rocf Wilmington MM, O.

BALLENGER
1821, 9, 28. Joshua [Ballinger] rocf Piles Grove MM, N. J., dtd 1821,7,26
1833, 6, 27. Joshua dis

BANGHAM
----, --, --. John C. b 1818,3,14; m Lydia M. ----- b 1839,1,11
Ch: Lovina b 1860, 9, 15
Anna " 1863, 3, 8
William J. " 1880, 1, 30

1889, 4, 25. John C. & w, Lydia M., & ch, Wm. J., rocf Wilmington MM, O.
1889, 4, 25. Lovina & Anna rocf Wilmington MM, O.
1898, 2, 24. Cyrus rocf Wilmington MM, O.
1906, 12, 27. John gct Long Beach MM, Calif.
1908, 4, 23. Wm. J. & w, Elizabeth C., & dt, Mabel E. gct Wilmington MM, O.

BARDY
1812, 1, 25. Mary recrq (she was a mbr at Bush River MM, S. C.; that mtg laid down before she got a cert)

BARNES
1901, 4, 25. Margaret recrq
1912, 4, 25. Lorenzo recrq
1925, 7, 23. Lorenzo relrq

BARNET
1813, 1, 30. Athanations [Barnett] rocf Center MM, O., dtd 1812,5,12
1826, 2, 23. Athenacions & fam gct Goshen MM
1829, 11, 26. Hannah [Bernet] gct Miami MM, O.

BARRETT
1813, 12, 19. Athanasious, s Athanasious & Jane, Green Co., O.; m in Mendinghalls Mtg, Margaret MENDENHALL, dt John & Ruth, Green Co., O.
----, --, --. Isaac M. b 1827,5,2 d 1891,1,2 bur Spring Valley; m Mary ----- b 1826,12,27
Ch: Don Carlos b 1868, 4, 22
Earnest Clifford " 1870, 12, 15
----, --, --. T. S. b 1851,9,1; m Carrie E. ----- b 1854,9,14
Ch: May Swayne b 1877, 9, 28 d 1883,12, 5
Frederick W. b 1879, 4, 13
M. Corrinn " 1887, 1, 31
1885, 6, 2. Clarabel m Thos. H. HARRISON
1886, 10, 12. Maryelle m R. H. DOLLIVER
----, --, --. John m Ella M. ----- b 1860,2,27
Ch: Lawrence b 1887, 8, 15
Mildred " 1890, 12, 13

1873, 12, 25. Isaac M. recrq
1875, 1, 28. Clara B. recrq
1875, 11, 13. Mary recrq
1877, 10, 25. Mary Ellen, Avanella, Don Carlos & Ernest Clifford, ch I. W., recrq
1878, 8, 22. R. E. recrq
1880, 3, 25. T. Swayne recrq
1884, 7, 27. Freddie, s Swayne, recrq
1885, 7, 23. Ella M. rocf Springfield MM, O.
1887, 5, 26. Jennie M. recrq
1892, 7, 28. R. E. & w relrq
1895, 10, 24. Ella & ch, Lawrence H. & Milford, recrq
1900, 1, 25. John R. recrq
1902, 2, 20. John R. & w, Ella, & ch, Lawrence & Mildred, gct Indianapolis MM, Ind.
1902, 4, 24. Ernest Clifford gct Indianapolis MM, Ind.
1905, 2, 23. Don C. gct Haverford MM, Pa.
1906, 10, 25. M. Corrine relrq
1913, 6, 26. Thomas Swayne & w, Caroline E., gct Dayton MM, O.; returned at her

BARRETT, continued
rq 1913,8,28
1913, 6, 26. Frederick Weller dropped from mbrp

BARWISE
1908, 10, 22. Margaret recrq

BATH
1909, 4, 22. Russell recrq

BATTEN
1818, 4, 24. Richard & fam gct Silver Creek MM

BAUSER
1893, 4, 27. Frank recrq

BEACH
----, --, --. Sarah E. b 1849,10,16 d 1873,1,1 bur Caesars Creek
----, --, --. Harrison b 1825,5,10; m Mary Ann ----- b 1830,4,1
Ch: Addra Maria b 1869, 7, 20
Samuel Foster " 1871, 9, 25
Elta Lorena " 1873, 11, 7

1870, 5, 26. Sarah Ellen, Martha Jane & Rachel Ann, recrq
1876, 9, 21. Harrison & w, Mary Ann, & ch, Adda Maria, Samuel Foster & Elta Lorena, recrq
1883, 4, 26. George & Luella recrq
1889, 2, 21. Harrison relrq
1894, 3, 22. Mattie recrq
1902, 5, 22. Charles A. recrq
1911, 7, 27. Samuel dropped from mbrp
1926, 11, 28. Charles dropped from mbrp

BEACHAM
1816, 3, 29. William & w & ch, Anna, Willis, Asa, Noah & Wesley, rocf Darby Creek MM, O., dtd 1816,3,16
1908, 3, 26. Rachel M. Charlton relrq

BEAMER
1824, 8, 26. Betty (form Hains) dis mcd

BEAR
1917, 3, 22. Samuel & Gladdis recrq

BEARD
1908, 3, 26. Hazel recrq
1910, 2, 24. Hazel relrq

BEEDLE
1885, 4, 23. Drusilla recrq
1885, 4, 23. Minnie, dt Drusilla, recrq
1897, 7, 22. Drusilla & Minnie dropped from mbrp

BEERS
1887, 12, 22. Louisa recrq

BEASON
1817, 4, 25. Igal [Beson] gct New Garden MM, Ind.
1817, 12, 26. Darius dis mcd
1818, 1, 30. Igal & w, Margaret, rocf New Garden MM, Ind., dtd 1817,10,18
1820, 2, 25. Igal & fam gct New Garden MM, Ind.

BEET
1885, 4, 23. Albert recrq

BELL
1875, 6, 24. Ella recrq

BELLER
1884, 4, 24. Adaline recrq
1897, 10, 28. Adaline relrq

BELT
1905, 3, 23. W. E. recrq
1905, 3, 23. Anna recrq
1905, 4, 27. Catherine recrq
1905, 5, 25. Forest J. recrq
1911, 6, 22. Forrest J. gct Xenia MM, O.
1917, 7, 26. Edward & Rosella Riley dropped from mbrp

BENDER
1913, 5, 22. Ida A. Harmon dropped from mbrp

BENEDICT
1863, 5, 28. Amy & s, Cyrus S., rocf Springborough MM, O.
1863, 5, 28. Malisse rocf Springboro MM, O.
1864, 12, 22. Amy & dt, Melisse, gct Grove MM, Ind.
1865, 3, 23. Israel & w, Sarah, & ch, Elwood, Phebe & Leonard, rocf Alum Creek MM, O.
1866, 8, 23. Israel & w, Sarah, & ch, Elwood, Phebe Ellen & Leonard, gct Springdale MM, Iowa

BENNETT
----, --, --. Geo. Wilson, s Edgar & Clara, b 1886,4,11; m Etta MOLER, dt Albert & Emma L., b 1889,6,1
Ch: Russell Leonard b 1909, 1, 2
Veda Alice " 1910, 6, 2
Velma May " 1910, 6, 2
Mildred Gertrude " 1911, 9, 12
Helen Elizabeth " 1914, 11, 11
Albert L. " 1913, 4, 14
Mary Lucile " 1918, 7, 13
James Craw-

BENNETT, Geo. Wilson & Etta, continued
Ch: ford b 1925, 5, 1
Sarah
Catherine " 1926, 7, 27

1906, 2, 22. George W. recrq
1926, 11, 28. Etta & ch, Russell, Veda, Velma, Mildred, Albert, Lucile, Hellen, James Crawford & Sarah Catherine, rocf Miami MM, O.

BENNINGTON
1917, 5, 24. Jesse & w, Camilla, recrq

BENSON
1812, 1, 30. Henry, s James & Elizabeth, Green Co., O.; m in Caesars Creek MH, Margaret HAMMER, dt David & Charlotte, Clinton Co., O.
1813, 12, 2. Jonathan, s James & Elizabeth, Green Co., O.; m in Caesars Creek MH, Ruth BROCK, dt George & Charity, Clinton Co.,O.
1816, 8, 1. Thomas, s James & Elizabeth, Green Co., O.; m in Caesars Creek MH, Mary KELLY, dt Robert & Sarah, Clinton Co., O.
----, --, --. George b 1847,10,31; m Sarah ----- b 1849,5,5
Ch: Harvey C. b 1876, 11, 16
----, --, --. Robert b 1870,1,18; m Martha KERN b 1869,10,25
Ch: Catherine b 1892, 6, 10
William " 1896, 11, 23
1902, 2, 13. Mary b

1810, 8, 25. Mary Allen (form Benson) con mcd
1817, 10, 24. Henry dis disunity
1822, 5, 24. Samuel dis mcd
1822, 7, 26. James Jr. dis disunity
1823, 4, 24. Jonathan dis disunity
1824, 12, 30. Margaret & ch gct Cherry Grove MM, Ind.
1824, 12, 30. Clark dis mcd
1825, 6, 30. Esther dis jas
1829, 4, 30. John dis mcd
1829, 7, 30. Thomas dis disunity
1830, 3, 25. Mary & ch, Jonathan, Mary Ann, Samuel, Sarah & Robert, gct Cherry Grove MM, Ind.
1831, 1, 27. Elizabeth gct Cherry Grove MM, Ind.
1831, 10, 27. Henry rst at Cherry Grove MM, Ind., on consent of this mtg
1834, 1, 23. John rst at Cherry Grove MM, Ind., on consent of this mtg
1835, 8, 27. Elijah dis disunity
1835, 8, 27. Ruth & ch, James, Isaac, Charity, Clark, Henry, Lucinda, Samuel & Jonathan, gct Cherry Grove MM, Ind.
1886, 4, 22. George & w, Sarah E., & s, Harvey C., recrq
1913, 6, 26. Harvey C. dropped from mbrp
1921, 4, 21. Vesper Marguerite recrq

BENTLEY
1879, 6, 19. Mabel M., dt Isaiah, b

1905, 7, 27. Mabel & Jeanette recrq
1926, 11, 28. Mable dropped from mbrp

BERGER
1908, 3, 26. Ruth recrq

BINGAMAN
1876, 1, 27. David recrq
1878, 12, 26. David [Bingamon] relrq

BIRCH
1906, 5, 24. George A. & w, Florence, rocf Center MM, O.
1906, 10, 25. George A. & w, Florence, relrq

BLAIR
----, --, --. Charlotte b 1820,3,26 d 1891,12, 20 bur Jenkins Burial Ground
----, --, --. ----- m Emma ----- b 1855,2,23
Ch: Wm. Ervin b 1895, 11, 28

1870, 4, 21. Charlotte recrq
1885, 4, 23. Emma J. recrq
1892, 4, 21. Alva recrq
1898, 3, 24. Wm. Ervin, s Emma, recrq
1901, 10, 24. Alva C. dropped from mbrp
1920, 6, 24. Marie Hall recrq

BLESSING
1903, 3, 26. Anna Hawkins b

1883, 3, 22. John recrq
1883, 3, 22. Francis A. recrq
1926, 11, 28. Anna Hawkins dropped from mbrp

BLOXOM
1814, 4, 30. William [Blocksom] & w, Mary, & ch, James, Nancy, Elizabeth, Maria, Priscilla, Sarah & William, rocf Fairfield MM, dtd 1814,3,26
1814, 4, 30. Anna rocf Fairfield MM, O., dtd 1814,3,26
1814, 4, 30. Charles rocf Fairfield MM, O., dtd 1814,3,26
1814, 4, 30. Richard & gr s, Gideon Johnson, rocf Fairfield MM, O., dtd 1814,1,29
1816, 11, 29. Ann Morgan (form Bloxom) con mcd
1817, 10, 24. Gregory dis disunity
1818, 9, 25. Wm. dis disunity
1819, 6, 25. Elizabeth gct Miami MM, O.

BLUNT
1909, 4, 22. Lulu recrq

BOCOCK
1814, 4, 30. Mary rocf Fairfield MM, O., dtd 1814,3,26

BOGAN
1914, 10, 7. Raleigh Leon m Marianne COMPTON
----, --, --. Evan, s W. E. & Mary, b 1895,5,3; m Ina May COMPTON, dt Horace & Lucy, b 1898,3,27
Ch: Marjorie C.b 1920, 12, 20
Robert Compton " 1924, 12, 27
----, --, --. Raleigh L., s W. E. & Mary, b 1893,10,5; m Marianna COMPTON, dt Horace & Lucy, b 1892,11,27
Ch: Dorothy Louise b 1918, 8, 3

1906, 12, 27. Elizabeth recrq
1911, 2, 23. Edgar & w, Mary O., & ch, Raleigh L., Evan V. & Leila N., rocf Miami MM, O.
1917, 3, 22. Lucile recrq
1927, 4, 24. Evan O. & w, Iva May, & ch, Marjory C. & Robert C., gct Xenia MM, O.

BOND
1810, 8, 25. Benjamin & w, Susannah, & ch, Joseph, Mary, Edward, Ruth, Elizabeth, Hannah & Moses, rocf Mt. Pleasant MM, Va., dtd 1809,8,26, endorsed by Miami MM, O., 1810,7,25
1814, 12, 30. Edward & w, Mary, rocf Fairfield MM, O., dtd 1814,10,29
1818, 4, 24. Ruth Woolman (form Bond) con mcd
1818, 4, 24. Joseph dis mcd
1818, 6, 26. Mary dis disunity
1819, 9, 24. Edward & w, Mary, gct Lees Creek MM, O.
1821, 6, 27. Edward Jr. dis disunity
1821, 10, 26. Edward & w, Mary, rocf Lees Creek MM, endorsed to Green Plain MM, O.

BONE
1917, 3, 22. Ruth, Earl, Herman, Allen & Glenna, recrq
1917, 3, 22. Raymond recrq
1918, 9, 26. Herman & Ruth, ch Wm., relrq
1925, 7, 23. Allen, Earl & Glenna relrq

BONNER
1884, 5, 23. Ragan b

1850, 12, 26. Hanah (form Reagan) dis mcd
1909, 2, 25. Ragan E. recrq
1911, 7, 27. Ragan E. relrq

BOOK
1901, 4, 25. William recrq

BOOKWALTER
1878, 9, 27. Evaline gct Elk MM, O.

BOOTS
----, --, --. Jemima b 1828,5,11 d 1922,1,21 bur New Burlington
1904, 1, 11. Thelma Rose b
1870, 4, 21. Jemima [Boot] recrq
1901, 4, 25. Bessie May recrq
1911, 9, 21. Wm. dropped from mbrp
1913, 6, 26. Cert for Estella & ch, Thelma Rose & Leroy Cline, granted to Dayton MM, O., returned at her rq 1913,8,28
1917, 7, 26. Estella Olive & ch, Thelma Rose, Leroy Cline & Pearl Cline dropped from mbrp

BOSTON
1876, 4, 1. Maud b

1896, 3, 26. Maud recrq

BOWERMASTER
1911, 6, 22. Mary Holly dropped from mbrp

BOWERS
1905, 7, 27. Lester & Nellie recrq
1905, 7, 27. Austie E. recrq
1925, 7, 23. L. A., Nellie & Austin relrq

BOWSER
1870, 8, 8. Frank b

1907, 4, 25. Frank recrq

BRACE
1890, 4, 24. Anna recrq

BRADFORD
1885, 10, 20. Sarah b
1905, 2, 23. Willis b

1841, 5, 27. Susanna (form Spray) dis mcd
1850, 1, 24. Sarah gct Fairfield MM, Ind.
1850, 2, 21. Sarah gct Fairfield MM, Ind.
1904, 1, 28. Sarah E. recrq
1905, 2, 3. Della & Willis recrq
1910, 10, 27. Cleora Della relrq
1926, 11, 28. Willis dropped from mbrp

BRADOCK
1885, 4, 23. Theodore E. recrq

BRADSTREET
1897, 7, 22. Arbie Mills relrq

BRADY
1820, 6, 23. Mary gct West Grove MM, Ind.

BRAGG
1884, 5, 22. Ann gct Dover MM, O.

BRANDENBURG
1909, 12, 23. W. L. & Margaret V. recrq

BRAY
----, --, --. Henry b 1755,8,29; m Keziah ----- b 1761,3,19
Ch: Jemima b 1778, 11, 30
John " 1780, 5, 8

BRAY, Henry & Keziah, continued
Ch: Henry b 1782, 2, 18
Sarah " 1784, 1, 26
Edward " 1786, 1, 18
Mary " 1788, 5, 25
Richard " 1790, 5, 22
Joseph " 1892, 6, 15

1812, 3, 28. Henry & w, Keziah, & ch, Edward, Richard, Abijah, Keziah & Massey, rocf Miami MM, O., dtd 1811,9,25
1812, 9, 26. Richard dis disunity
1818, 9, 25. Henry & fam gct Lick Creek MM, Ind.

BREWER
1817, 11, 26. Peter b

1898, 9, 22. Peter J. recrq

BRIDGMAN
1893, 4, 27. John C. & Mary E. recrq

BROCK
1813, 12, 2. Ruth m Jonathan BENSON
1821, 5, 21. Keturah m Layton JAY
1824, 9, 2. Malona m David MILLS
1835, 5, 12. Charity d bur Caesars Creek

1812, 5, 30. Elijah gct White Water MM, Ind.
1817, 9, 26. Susanna Hawkins (form Brock) con mcd
1823, 1, 30. Lucinda Jay (form Brock) con mcd

BROWN
----, --, --. Mahlon b 1779,9,26 d 1848,8,7 bur Caesars Creek; m Alice ----- b 1785,1, 16 d 1854,5,1 bur Wards
Ch: Clayton b 1803, 9, 26
1826, 10, 12. Clayton, s Mahlon & Alice, Preble Co., O., b 1803,9,26; m in Caesars Creek MH, Lydia COMPTON, dt John & Ann, Warren Co., O., d 1829,7,23
Ch: Richard b 1829, 6, 22 d 1829, 7,20
Clayton m 2nd Sarah COMPTON, dt Samuel & Phebe, Green Co., O. (m 1831,1,6)
Ch: Samuel C. b 1833, 3, 20
1849, 5, 19. Lydia b
----, --, --. Eli b 1844,6,9; m Phebe W. ----- b 1846,4,5
Ch: Louisa b 1870, 9, 30
Sarah " 1874, 2, 8

1827, 5, 31. Clayton rocf Westfield MM, dtd 1827,3,28
1832, 4, 26. Clayton & w, Sarah, gct Westfield MM
1847, 4, 22. Clayton & w, Sarah, & s, Samuel C. rocf Elk MM, O., dtd 1847,2,20
1847, 4, 22. Mahlon & w, Alice, rocf Elk MM, O., dtd 1847,2,20
1856, 5, 22. Clayton & w, Sarah, gct White Water MM, Ind.
1856, 5, 22. Samuel C. gct White Water MM, [Ind.
1870, 1, 27. Phebe W. con mcd
1870, 2, 24. Phebe W. gct West Elkton MM
1871, 4, 23. Eli & w, Phebe W., & dt, Louisa, rocf Elk MM, O.
1880, 4, 22. Eli & w, Phebe, & ch, Sarah, gct West Grove MM, Ind.
1885, 4, 23. Lenora recrq
1887, 1, 27. Lydia E. recrq
1892, 4, 21. Burn recrq
1905, 7, 27. Albert & Mary recrq
1923, 4, 29. Reva dropped from mbrp

BUFFKIN
1831, 2, 24. Thomas & w, Ruth, & ch, John, Bathsheba, Warner, Guli Elma, Sarah & Ruth, rocf Flushing MM, O., dtd 1830,10, 21, endorsed by Springboro MM, O., 1831, 2,22
1831, 7, 28. Thomas & w, Ruth, & ch, John, Warner, Gulielma, Sarah & Ruth, gct Green Plain MM, O.
1831, 7, 28. Bathsheba gct Green Plain MM, O.

BUHRMAN
1915, 1, 28. Wm. Wilbur d

1915, 1, 28. Lucille recrq
1915, 1, 28. Wm. Wilbur recrq
1926, 11, 28. Wilbur dropped from mbrp

BUNDY
1884, 10, 23. Henry C. & w, Mary, & ch, William, Ella, Alva & Mattie, rocf Goshen MM, O., dtd 1884,9,13
1885, 12, 24. Henry C. & w, Mary E., & ch, Wm. H., Mellie D., Alsie B. & Mertie L., gct Walnut Ridge MM, Ind.
1893, 7, 27. Hiram & w, Louisa C., & ch, Waller A., Adella May & Elmer A., rocf Grove MM, Ind.

BUNNELL
1923, 12, 30. Nellie Bogan b

BURDG
----, --, --. Hiram b 1837,12,21; m -----
Ch: Walter A. b 1875, 12, 21
Hiram m 2nd Louisa C. ----- b 1848,6,6
Ch: Adella May b 1882, 6, 14
Elmer A. " 1884, 7, 26

BURNET
----, --, --. Anna b 1779,2,15 d 1859,3,13 bur Caesars Creek
1829, 4, 2. David, s Robert & Anna, Warren Co., O.; m in Caesars Creek MH, Hannah WILSON, dt Christopher & Mary, Warren Co., O.
1843, 6, 2. George b
----, --, --. Francis Marion b 1846,8,21; m Margaret ----- b 1844,8,16
Ch: Effie R. b 1875, 11, 16

BURNET, Francis Marion & Margaret, continued
Ch: Roy W. b 1880, 5, 28 d 1880, 7,12
bur Caesars Creek

1824, 1, 29. Elizabeth (form Compton) con mcd
1827, 10, 25. Elizabeth [Burnett] gct Fairfield MM, Ind.
1846, 2, 19. Jesse Spray gct Miami MM, O., to m Rebecca Burnett
1848, 6, 22. Anna rocf Miami MM, O., dtd 1848, 4,26
1852, 8, 26. George & Francis Marion recrq of guardian

BURRIS
1814, 4, 30. Daniel rocf Fairfield MM, O., dtd 1814,2,26
1820, 3, 24. Daniel gct Fall Creek MM

BURTON
1875, 2, 25. Joshua recrq
1884, 4, 24. John W. [Burdon] recrq

BUTLER
1866, 9, 25. Charles b
1873, 11, 14. Ella b

1881, 4, 21. May recrq
1885, 4, 23. Elizabeth recrq
1896, 3, 26. Chas. H. & Ella recrq

BUTCHER
1915, 8, 26. Wm. M. & w, Adella, recrq

BYRD
1885, 4, 23. George recrq
1897, 7, 22. George dropped from mbrp

CACY
1813, 6, 26. Levina rocf West Branch MM, dtd 1813,2,25
1818, 11, 27. Levina [Casey] gct West Branch MM, O.

CADWALADER
1822, 2, 23. Judith m Isaac LEWIS

1815, 6, 23. Cert rec for Elizabeth from Miami MM, O., dtd 1815,3,29, returned because she mcd
1815, 9, 29. Elizabeth Allen (form Cadwalader) con mcd
1819, 12, 27. Judith rocf Miami MM, O., dtd 1819,11,24

CALHOON
1828, 7, 21. Elizabeth & ch, William & Mary, rocf Stillwater MM, O., dtd 1828,2,27, endorsed by Miami MM, O., 1828,7,30
1837, 3, 23. Wm. & Elizabeth, ch John, gct Springborough MM

CAMERON
1908, 12, 24. Emma, Grace & Daisy recrq

CANBY
1839, 3, 29. Susan D., Elizabeth & Andrew, ch Joshua & Esther, rocf Baltimore MM for E. & W. Dist., dtd 1839,9,6
1839, 3, 28. Evan, Maryann & Latitia, minor ch Joshua & Esther, rocf Baltimore MM for E. & W. Dist., dtd 1839,9,6
1845, 5, 22. Susan Hackney (form Canby) con mcd
1854, 10, 21. Elizabeth Heston (form Canby) con mcd

CANDILL
1910, 2, 24. Mark & Anna recrq

CANE
1889, 9, 26. Josie recrq
1897, 7, 22. Josie dropped from mbrp

CARBACK
----, --, --. ----- m Emma J. ----- b 1847, 11,24
Ch: Mary C. b 1869, 5, 30
Laura A. " 1871, 1, 2
Elizabeth A. " 1873, 7, 25

1876, 11, 23. Emma Jane & ch, Mary Catharine, Laura Alice & Elizabeth Ann, recrq
1881, 2, 24. Thomas recrq
1881, 2, 24. Martha Jane & Samuel recrq
1914, 3, 26. Samuel & ch, James Thomas & Mary Elizabeth, recrq
1925, 7, 23. Samuel, James & Elizabeth relrq

CARL
1880, 1, 22. Solon & w, Deborah, & ch, Warren, Clarence & William, rocf Dover MM, O.
1890, 1, 23. Deborah & ch, Warren, Alva, Clarence Walton & Willie Hayes, relrq

CARR
1854, 10, 27. Louisa b
1891, 8, 18. Elsie b
1886, 1, 24. Mary Esther, dt John & Louisa, b

1901, 4, 25. Roy recrq
1905, 2, 3. Harrison M. recrq
1906, 1, 25. Louise & Elsie recrq
1926, 11, 28. Harrison dropped from mbrp

CARROLL
1901, 6, 27. Solon recrq
1903, 11, 26. Solon gct Miami MM, O.
1907, 11, 21. Solon & w, Emma, rocf Miami MM, O.
1915, 3, 25. Emma relrq
1917, 7, 26. Solon dropped from mbrp
1920, 3, 25. Solon recrq

CARROTHERS
1888, 5, 24. Alice gct White Water MM, Ind.

CARTER
1838, 2, 6. George L. b
1860, 2, 29. Thomas C., s Jesse & Malinda, Clinton Co., O., b 1840,10,12; m in Richland MH, Rachel M. ELLIS, dt Elijah & Rebecca, Green Co., O., b 1840,4,30
Ch: Lydia Ann b 1861, 5, 17
Charles Foster " 1877, 10, 6
----, --, --. Thomas C. b 1840,10,12; m Almina H. ----- b 1857,7,3
Ch: Ruth E. b 1897, 3, 11
1881, 7, 27. Chester b
----, --, --. Charles b 1879,10,6; m Lucile HARVEY, b 1875,2,19
Ch: Lena May b 1901, 2, 28
Rachel E. " 1904, 5, 4
Harvey T. " 1909, 1, 16

1860, 6, 21. Thomas C. rocf Dover MM, dtd 1860,5,17
1887, 3, 24. Almina recrq
1893, 4, 27. George L. recrq
1901, 7, 25. Lucile H. rocf Miami MM, O.
1908, 2, 20. Thomas C. & w, Almina H., & dt, Ruth E., gct Hopewell MM, O.
1908, 12, 24. Fannie recrq
1920, 4, 22. Lucile & dt, Lena, relrq

CARY
1817, 4, 25. Thomas & w, Rhoda, & dt, Elizabeth, rocf Center MM, O., dtd 1817,4,19
1820, 2, 25. Thomas [Cairy] & fam gct Elk MM, O.

CHAMBLES
1856, 3, 8. Alie [Chamblis] b
----, --, --. Frank [Chambless] b 1830,5,12; m Sarah Ellen ----- b 1850,1,29
Ch: Jettie b 1883, 9, 15

1876, 2, 24. Alia recrq
1885, 4, 23. B. D. recrq
1885, 4, 23. Sarah E. recrq
1885, 4, 23. Flora recrq
1885, 4, 23. Elsie recrq

CHANCE
1905, 6, 22. Harry & Maude recrq

CHARLTON
----, --, --. ----- m Lydia A. ----- b 1861,5,17
Ch: Chester Carter b 1881, 7, 29
Rachel M. " 1885, 5, 12
Charles L. " 1893, 10, 9

1908, 3, 26. Charles L. relrq
1919, 8, 28. Lydia A. Carter relrq

1874, 1, 22. Susannah C. [Chineworth) recrq
1875, 9, 23. Susan B. relrq
1879, 4, 24. John [Chenaworth] recrq
1883, 3, 22. Wilson [Chenaworth] recrq
1884, 9, 25. John [Cheneworth] dis
1901, 4, 25. Clara recrq
1905, 2, 3. Elmer recrq
1908, 11, 26. Nellie R. recrq

1911, 7, 27. Elmer dropped from mbrp
1914, 12, 24. Alice recrq
1915, 1, 28. Elvin recrq
1916, 10, 26. Mary Elizabeth recrq
1917, 3, 22. Fred & Elvan recrq
1926, 11, 28. Elvin & Fred dropped from mbrp

CHITTUM
1925, 7, 23. Benjamin & Cora relrq

CLARK
1838, 12, 29. John A. b

1812, 4, 25. Elizabeth & ch, Jonathan, Henry, Cornelius & Elizabeth, recrq
1817, 11, 28. Jonathan dis disunity
1827, 5, 31. Henry Jr. dis disunity
1827, 8, 30. Cornelius dis disunity
1827, 9, 27. Elizabeth Antrim (form Clark) dis mcd
1880, 3, 25. John recrq
1899, 2, 23. Anna Brace gct Miami MM, O.
1912, 5, 23. Oscar recrq
1923, 4, 29. Oscar dropped from mbrp

CLEMER
1881, 3, 24. David & Osker recrq
1907, 4, 25. Oscar & David H. [Clemmer] recrq

CLEVENGER
1821, 7, 27. Massa (form Heston) con mcd

CLINE
1888, 11, 13. Pearl b

1879, 4, 24. Laura recrq
1901, 4, 25. Estella & Mellie recrq
1902, 4, 24. Victoria recrq
1908, 1, 23. Maggie M. recrq
1908, 2, 20. Pearl recrq

CLOUD
1811, 7, 4. Joel, s Joseph & Mary, Warren Co., O.; m in Caesars Creek MH, Hannah COX, dt Thomas & Tamar, Warren Co., O.
1824, 10, 4. Mary d bur Caesars Creek

1810, 9, 29. Mary gct Miami MM, O.
1812, 4, 25. Hannah gct Miami MM, O.
1817, 4, 25. Mary & Abigail rocf Miami MM, O., dtd 1817,2,26
1818, 8, 28. Abigail Moody (form Cloud) con mcd

COATS
1818, 2, 27. Charlotte [Coat] (form Wright)

COATS, continued
dis mcd
1836, 8, 25. Elijah & w, Rebecca, & ch, Hiram, rocf Center MM, O., dtd 1836,5,18
1837, 10, 26. Elijah & w, Rebecca, & ch, Hiram, gct Union MM
1876, 1, 27. Charles & Mary A. [Coates] recrq
1879, 9, 26. Chas. [Coat] relrq
1880, 3, 25. Charles & Martha Jane recrq

COBB
1811, 5, 25. Esther recrq
1811, 6, 29. Esther gct White Water MM, Ind.

COFFELT
1880, 3, 25. Charles W. [Coffett] recrq
1881, 4, 21. Julia Ann recrq
1881, 4, 21. Elizabeth A. recrq
1881, 4, 21. John Freeman recrq
1881, 4, 21. Frances L. recrq
1881, 4, 21. Cora May recrq
1881, 4, 21. John recrq
1889, 12, 26. John & Julia A. relrq
1891, 8, 27. Chas. W. relrq
1893, 3, 23. Addie relrq
1897, 7, 22. George & Frank dropped from mbrp
1897, 7, 22. Cora May dropped from mbrp
1915, 8, 26. Charles W. & s, Floy E., recrq

COFFMAN
1888, 4, 26. Mellie recrq
1889, 4, 25. Effie recrq
1901, 4, 25. Arch W. recrq
1913, 6, 26. Arch W. dropped from mbrp

COLE
----, --, --. ----- & Mary
Ch: Minnie b 1877, 5, 5
Louis J. " 1875, 7, 5

1885, 4, 23. Mary E. recrq
1885, 4, 23. James recrq
1885, 4, 23. Minna recrq
1907, 3, 28. Lewis gct Hopewell MM, O.

COLEMAN
1883, 5, 27. Frank b
1882, 6, 13. Minnie b

1906, 1, 25. Frank J. & Minnie M. recrq
1915, 2, 25. Frank & w, Minnie gct Miami MM, O.

COLLETT
1847, 2, 19. Rebecca d bur Caesars Creek
1849, 6, 18. Annie B. b

1823, 10, 30. Sarah (form McKay) dis mcd
1826, 8, 31. Virginia (form McKay) dis mcd

COLTER
1861, 6, 27. Lydia Job (form Colter) con mcd

COLVIN
1851, 2, 20. Phebe (form Farquhar) dis mcd
1857, 8, 27. Rebecca (form Mills) dis mcd
1906, 1, 25. M. Pearl recrq
1907, 9, 26. Hannah rocf Center MM, O.

COMER
1799, 3, 13. Mary, dt Robert & Martha, b
----, --, --. Stephen b 1773,12,14; m Mary ----- b 1775,11,15
Ch: John b 1800, 7, 1
Joseph " 1802, 4, 15
James " 1804, 2, 5
1802, 11, 28. Amos b
1804, 10, 5. Ann b
1823, 10, 2. Joseph, s Stephen & Mary, Wayne Co., Ind.; m in Caesars Creek MH, Hester COMPTON, dt Mathew & Rachel
1861, 5, 11. Martha b
1823, 11, 27. Hester Compton gct New Garden MM, Ind.

COMPTON
----, --, --. Amos b 1770,7,9 d 1824,9,14 bur Caesars Creek; m Rebecca ----- b 1767,8, 11 d 1844,10,5 bur Caesars Creek
Ch: Betty b 1794, 3, 30
Samuel " 1796, 8, 16
Mary " 1798, 12, 21
Rebecca " 1800, 11, 6
Lydia " 1803, 1, 20
Sally " 1805, 2, 13 d 1823, 8,31 bur Caesars Creek
John b 1807, 3, 1
Ann " 1812, 1, 13 " 1827, 3,23 bur Caesars Creek
----, --, --. Samuel Sr. b 1766,12,20 d 1850, 6,15 bur Caesars Creek; m Phebe ----- b 1774,--,-- d 1839,10,-- bur Caesars Creek
Ch: John b 1797, 8, 23
Elizabeth " 1800, 7, 25
Sarah " 1803, 8, 25
Joshua " 1807, 9, 20
Eli " 1809, 10, 20
Rebecca " 1812, 4, 18 d 1820, 3,21 bur Caesars Creek
Seth b 1814, 7, 17
----, --, --. Stephen b 1774,8,29 d 1862,7,14 bur Caesars Creek; m Dinah ----- b 1777, 8,29 d 1853,11,15 bur Caesars Creek
Ch: Henry b 1798, 1, 21
Sally " 1800, 9, 23
Amos
Samuel " 1805, 5, 4 d 1835, 1,13 bur Caesars Creek
William b 1808, 4, 11
Nancy " 1810, 10, 1
Hannah " 1813, 5, 13
John " 1816, 8, 10
Rebecca " 1822, 4, 28
----, --, --. Joshua & Rebekah
Ch: Nathan b 1800, 4, 12

COMPTON, Joshua & Rebekah, continued
Ch: Joshua b 1802, 4, 26
1802, 2, 15. Joshua d
1805, 2, 6. Samuel d
----, --, --. Joseph b 1782,6,18 d 1824,7,27; m Christiana ----- d 1820,2,10 bur Caesars Creek
Ch: Henry b 1806, 9, 2
Samuel " 1806, 9, 2
Matilda " 1808, 11, 21
Patty " 1811, 10, 16
Anna " 1815, 10, 23
Joseph m 2nd Catharine -----
Ch: Clarissa b 1822, 10, 8
----, --, --. John b 1772,12,29 d 1860,1,16; m Ann ----- d 1861,8,8
Ch: Lydia b 1808, 5, 13 d 1829, 7,16
Isaac Pedric " 1810, 12, 1 " 1840, 1,26
Hannah " 1814, 3, 10
Mary Ann " 1817, 1, 28 " 1850, 4, 3
Maria " 1819, 12, 17 " 1886,11,12
William Forsle " 1823, 3, 15
1817, 7, 31. Rachel m Samuel OWEN
1819, 10, 6. John, s Samuel & Phebe, Green Co., O.; m in Green Plain, Jane ENGLE, dt Joshua & Hannah, Clark Co., O.
1820, 3, 21. Rebecca, dt Ramuel & Phebe, b
1820, 6, 29. Betty m John MILLS
1821, 5, 17. Elizabeth d bur Joseph Compton's land
1823, 4, 3. Lydia m John JAY
1823, 4, 3. Sally m Wm. HORNER
1823, 10, 2. Rebecca m Elijah ELLIS
1823, 10, 2. Hester m Joseph COMER
1824, 4, 1. Rebeckah m John OWEN
----, --, --. Samuel b 1796,8,16 d 1861,3,12 bur Caesars Creek; m Ally ----- b 1804,3, 10 d 1885,8,14 bur Caesars Creek
Ch: Jesse b 1825, 1, 12
Rebecca " 1826, 10, 8
Nancy " 1828, 10, 12 d 1899, 5, 2 bur Caesars Creek
Amos b 1830, 12, 19
John M. " 1833, 5, 6 " 1833, 8, 9 bur Caesars Creek
Samuel T. " 1834, 8, 24 " 1834, 9,10 bur Caesars Creek
Martha b 1840, 4, 1 " 1841,12,22 bur Caesars Creek
Lydia b 1842, 12, 16
1825, 5, 5. Samuel, s Joseph & Christiana, Green Co., O.; m in Caesars Creek MH, Phebe WHITSON, dt David & Mary, Clinton Co., O.
Ch: Israel b 1826, 3, 15
Anna " 1829, 11, 16
Matilda " 1833, 1, 5
1826, 10, 12. Rebecca m John FURNAS
1826, 10, 12. Lydia m Clayton BROWN
1828, 11, 6. Samuel, s Stephen & Dinah, Green Co., O., d 1835,1,13; m in Caesars Creek MH, Tamar WILSON, dt Christopher & Mary, Warren Co., O.
1831, 1, 6. Sarah m Clayton BROWN
1831, 11, 30. Eli, s Samuel & Phebe, Green Co., O., b 1809,10,20 d 1883,8,16 bur Caesars Creek; m in Richland MH, Eunice WALTON, dt Edward & Deborah, Green Co.,O., b 1811,11,27 d 1879,9,30 bur Caesars Creek
Ch: Deborah b 1832, 12, 23
Phebe Ann " 1835, 4, 17
Elizabeth " 1837, 3, 3
Hannah " 1839, 7, 10
Sarah Jane " 1842, 9, 19 d 1862, 9,28
Rees A. " 1851, 3, 15 " 1851, 4, 9 bur Caesars Creek
Maria b 1855, 4, 20
1833, 10, 31. Matilda m Isaac FURNAS
1833, 11, 28. Hannah m Samuel COOK
----, --, --. Phares b 1813,11,2 d 1877,6,1; m Nancy ----- b 1810,1,20 d 1876,3,9 bur Caesars Creek
Ch: Joseph b 1834, 5, 11
Joel " 1837, 6, 7
Dinah " 1839, 9, 26
Henry " 1841, 7, 19
Martha Jane " 1844, 9, 16
James " 1844, 9, 16 d 1849, 6,18 bur Caesars Creek
Nancy Ann b 1847, 8, 13
----, --, --. John b 1807,3,1 d 1893,3,26 bur Caesars Creek; m Rebecca ----- b 1813,2,20
Ch: Eunice b 1834, 8, 9
Alice " 1836, 1, 7
Amos L. " 1837, 7, 30
----, --,---. John b 1816,8,10 d 1843,9,16 bur Caesars Creek; m Elizabeth ----- b 1813,7,14
Ch: Judith b 1836, 5, 30 d 1869,11, 9 bur Caesars Creek
James b 1840, 4, 21
1836, 9, 29. Patty m James HAWKINS
----, --, --. Seth b 1814,7,17 d 1887,1,24 bur Caesars Creek; m Mary ----- b 1813,3, 12 d 1863,7,19 bur Caesars Creek
Ch: Samuel b 1839, 8, 18
Eli " 1842, 12, 29 d 1884,12,18 bur Caesars Creek
Elijah b 1844, 1, 20
Jesse " 1846, 5, 7 " 1921, 9,20 bur Corwin
Benjamin b 1848, 7, 11
Charity " 1850, 8, 8 " 1850, 9, 4 bur Caesars Creek
Martha Ellen b 1851, 9, 19
1840, 4, 9. Rebecca m Job MILLS
1840, 4, 30. Mary Ann m John Furnas STEDDOM
----, --, --. William F. b 1823,3,15 d 1896,5, 1 bur Caesars Creek; m Catherine ----- b 1819,4,30
1841, 9, 24. Rebecca J. b
1845, 10, 9. William, s John & Ann, Warren Co., O.; m in Caesars Creek MH, Catherine

COMPTON, William, continued
MORGAN, dt Thomas & Ann, Clinton Co., O.
1848, 10, 12. Jesse, s Samuel & Ally, Green Co., O.; m in Caesars Creek MH, Esther SPRAY, dt Jesse & Mary, Clinton Co., O.
----, --, --. Jesse b 1825,1,12 d 1908,4,16 bur Caesars Creek; m Esther ----- b 1831,7,16 d 1919,3,10 bur Caesars Creek
Ch: Uriah b 1850, 9, 1 d 1896, 3,10 bur Caesars Creek
Martha b 1852, 4, 13 " 1914, 1, 1 bur Caesars Creek
John L. b 1854, 7, 12
Mary Ann " 1856, 8, 12
Lydia Jane " 1858, 11, 28
Elizabeth Alice " 1869, 8, 21 d 1904, 5, 9
Miriam " 1877, 1, 20
1851, 5, 1. Deborah m Amos JAY
1856, 3, 6. Eunice m John MENDENHALL
1853, 11, 2. Amos, s Samuel & Ally, Green Co., O.; m in Richland MH, Ann MENDENHALL, dt William & Betty, Green Co., O.
----, --, --. Amos b 1830,12,19 d 1880,6,28 bur Caesars Creek; m Ann ----- b 1830,11,26
Ch: Mary Elizabeth b 1854, 9, 17
Samuel T. " 1856, 5, 12
Emily Allice " 1858, 4, 12
William E. " 1860, 4, 1
Martha R. " 1862, 3, 26
Rhesa A. " 1864, 2, 7 d 1865,10,20 bur Caesars Creek
Walton b 1865, 12, 25
Lucy Ann " 1868, 7, 16
Ella C. " 1870, 12, 20
1854, 7, 12. John S. b
----, --, --. Amos S. b 1837,7,30; m Catherine M. ----- b 1842,4,24
1860, 10, 4. Phebe Ann m Micajah HAYWORTH
1861, 4, 20. Clara b
----, --, --. Joseph b 1834,5,11; m Ann R. ----- b 1834,5,4 d 1879,4,4
Ch: James Orville b 1862, 1, 19
Louisa Jane" 1864, 11, 12
Nancy D. " 1867, 11, 2 d 1897,11,25
1862, 4, 3. Lydia m Stephen MILLS
1863, 12, 3. Dinah m John C. COOK
----, --, --. Samuel B. b 1839,8,18; m Mary Ellen ----- b 1843,3,22
Ch: Horace Foster b 1867, 8, 25
Hettie Phebe " 1869, 5, 21
1867, 4, 4. Seth, s Samuel & Phebe, Green Co., O.; m in Caesars Creek MH, Ruth HAWKINS, dt Joseph & Sarah OREN, Randolph Co., Ind.
----, --, --. Joel T. b 1837,6,7 d 1885,9,15 bur Caesars Creek; m Susanna D. ----- b 1838,8,14 d 1889,2,11 bur Caesars Creek
Ch: Annie R. b 1869, 8, 31
Eva N. " 1876, 11, 17
----, --, --. Samuel T. b 1856,5,12; m Josephine ----- b 1852,10,14
----, --, --. Henry b 1841,7,19; m Mary E. ----- b 1851,6,19
Ch: Jennie b 1872, 2, 27
Westley G. " 1874, 9, 5
1876, 7, 31. Ella b
----, --, --. ----- m Rebecca J. ----- b 1841,9,24
Ch: Arrena b 1877, 7, 4
1887, 2, 28. Minnie May b
1888, 8, 8. Ralph J. b
----, --, --. Wm. E. b 1860,4,1; m Sarah J. ----- b 1867,11,29 d 1924,9,17 bur Spring Valley, O.
Ch: Adaline E. b 1889, 2, 26
Amos E. " 1891, 4, 10
Ethel F. " 1894, 2, 26
----, --, --. Walton b 1865,12,25; m Lillie M. ----- b 1889,12,12 (?)
Ch: Lester M. b 18-1, 3, 14
Lorena A. " 1894, 7, 27
----, --, --. Horace F. b 1867,8,25; m Lucy A. ----- b 1868,7,16
Ch: Marianna b 1892, 11, 27
Ina M. " 1898, 3, 27
1893, 6, 22. Miriam W. b
1895, 8, 6. Ruth Edna b
----, --, --. James O. b 1862,1,19; m Ella S. ----- b 1863,10,26
Ch: Joseph Edward b 1899, 9, 13
----, --, --. Forest D. b 1868,11,9; m Minnie F. ICENHOWER b 1877,9,28
----, --, --. Elmer J. b 1884,7,4; m Edith A. MENDENHALL b 1887,10,20
1914, 10, 7. Marianne m Raleigh Leon BOGAN

1815, 8, 25. Phebe & ch, John, Elizabeth, Sarah, Joshua, Eli, Rebeckah & Seth, recrq
1817, 11, 28. Elizabeth Haines (form Compton) dis mcd
1818, 10, 30. Henry dis mcd
1821, 7, 21. Joseph gct Mill Creek MM, to m Catherine Barnett
1821, 11, 23. Catherine rocf Mill Creek MM, dtd 1821,10,27
1822, 6, 28. Mary Saxton (form Compton) con mcd
1822, 12, 26. Amos con mcd
1823, 6, 26. Samuel con mcd
1824, 1, 29. Elizabeth Burnet (form Compton) con mcd
1824, 5, 27. Ally recrq
1824, 10, 28. Catherine & dt, Clarissa, gct Mill Creek MM
1825, 2, 24. Anna, minor, gct White Water MM, Ind.
1825, 7, 28. Amos gct Green Plain MM, O.
1826, 7, 27. Henry gct West Branch MM, O., to m Rachel Mendenhall

COMPTON, continued
1826, 8, 31. Joseph Furnas gct Center MM, O., to m Rebecca Compton
1827, 6, 28. Rachel Mendenhall rocf West Branch MM, O., dtd 1827,3,17
1827, 9, 27. John, s Mathew, gct Fairfield MM, Ind.
1828, 10, 30. Amos, s Mathew, gct White Lick MM, Ind.
1829, 9, 24. Wm. dis disunity
1829, 9, 24. John & w, Jane, & ch, Joshua, Phebe & Hannah Ann, gct Center MM, O.
1829, 10, 29. Hannah & Matilda dis jH
1829, 12, 31. Obadiah & Rachel gct Fairfield MM, Ind.
1830, 1, 28. Joshua gct Center MM, O., to m Edith BALLARD
1831, 3, 31. Joshua gct Center MM, O.
1831, 11, 30. Rachel & ch, Patty & Phares, gct West Branch MM, O.
1832, 4, 26. Ruth (form Hawkins) dis mcd
1834, 4, 26. Joshua & dt, Lucetta, rocf Center MM, O., dtd 1832,2,12
1832, 11, 22. Henry gct West Branch MM, O.
1832, 11, 22. Matilda rst
1833, 7, 25. Joshua dis mcd
1833, 9, 26. John gct Miami MM, O., to m Rebecca Steadham
1834, 1, 23. Isaac P. gct Miami MM, O.
1834, 3, 27. Rebecca rocf Miami MM, O., dtd 1834,2,19
1834, 4, 24. John, s Stephen, dis mcd
1835, 8, 27. Samuel, s Joseph, & w, Phebe, & ch, Israel, Anna & Matilda, gct Fairfield MM, Ind.
1835, 8, 27. Nancy rocf Center MM, O., dtd 1835,5,13
1835, 8, 27. Elizabeth Ann rocf Center MM, O., dtd 1835,5,13
1839, 10, 24. John rst
1839, 11, 21. Phares rst
1840, 1, 23. Judith, dt John & Elizabeth, recrq
1840, 2, 20. Seth con mcd
1840, 2, 20. Mary (form Hocket) con mcd
1840, 10, 22. Tamar & ch, Christopher & Benjamin, gct Fairfield MM, Ind.
1841, 9, 23. Joseph, Joel & Dinah, ch Phares, recrq
1845, 11, 27. Elizabeth (form Oren) dis mcd
1849, 4, 26. Elizabeth Ann & ch, Judith & James, gct Center MM, O.
1856, 9, 25. Elizabeth Linton (form Compton) dis mcd
1860, 3, 22. Joseph con mcd
1860, 7, 26. Ann R. rocf Fairfield MM, dtd 1860,6,16
1865, 5, 25. Hannah Haworth (form Compton) con mcd
1867, 3, 28. Judith Ann rocf Center MM, O., dtd 1867,2,13
1867, 7, 25. Benjamin gct Dover MM, to m Margaret Walthal
1867, 7, 25. Samuel B. con mcd
1868, 4, 23. Amos S. con mcd
1868, 4, 23. Elijah con mcd
1868, 5, 28. Catherine (form Mendenhall) con mcd
1868, 12, 24. Benjamin gct Dover MM
1869, 4, 22. Joel con mcd
1869, 4, 22. Susanna rocf Miami MM, O., dtd 1869,3,24
1870, 4, 21. Mary E. recrq
1871, 4, 27. Mary Eliza recrq
1875, 12, 23. Josephine rocf Wilmington MM, O.
1876, 5, 25. Samantha recrq
1877, 3, 22. Uriah & w, Samantha, gct North Branch MM, Ia.
1880, 12, 23. Miriam N., adopted dt Jesse & Esther, recrq
1881, 4, 21. Benjamin & w, Margaret, & ch, Augustus M., Thomas Walter, Seth & William F., rocf Dover MM, O., dtd 1881,5,19 (?)
1882, 1, 26. Samuel T. & w, Josephine, & ch, Alta B., gct Springfield MM, O.
1883, 6, 21. Fannie recrq
1884, 5, 22. Elijah & ch, Horace Forest D., Albert E. & Charles, gct Miami MM, O.
1887, 4, 21. Jesse M. gct Miami MM, O.
1894, 3, 22. Benjamin & w, Margaret, & ch, Augustus M., Thomas W., Seth Wm., Lizzie & Ethel, gct Platt Valley MM, Nebraska
1895, 8, 22. Ella Steddom recrq
1896, 3, 26. Phebe E. recrq
1898, 5, 26. Mary Elizabeth & ch, Nellie May & Charles Weldon, gct Marion MM, Ind.
1900, 3, 22. Ella recrq
1900, 3, 22. Ethel Sanders recrq
1900, 3, 22. Minnie May recrq
1900, 3, 22. Ralph G. recrq
1900, 3, 22. Miriam Minerva recrq
1900, 3, 22. Ruth Edna recrq
1905, 5, 25. Jesse C. & w, Priscilla, & dt, Mary Ann, rocf Miami MM, O.
1905, 7, 27. John recrq
1905, 12, 28. Walton & w, Lillie M., & ch, Lester M. & Lorena A., relrq
1913, 6, 26. Minnie May, Miriam Minerva & Ruth Edna, dropped from mbrp
1914, 1, 22. Neal recrq
1917, 7, 26. Neil dropped from mbrp
1919, 5, 22. Elizabeth Hurley rocf Center MM

CONFER
1880, 8, 26. Johanna recrq

CONLY
1825, 7, 28. Ruth (form Haynes) dis mcd

CONNER
----, --, --. John m Rachel ----- d 1814,12,11

Ch:			
William	b 1795, 10, 28	
John	" 1797, 4, 27	d 1797, 4,27
Catherine	" 1798, 4, 29	
Jesse	" 1800, 2, 12	
John	" 1801, 8, 10	

CONNER, John & Rachel, continued
Ch: Thomas b 1803, 1, 29
Mary " 1805, 5, 7
Rachel " 1807, 7, 29
Anna " 1809, 7, 27
Rebecca " 1811, 10, 4
Isaac " 1813, 9, 25

1831, 10, 13. Jesse, s John & Rachel, Warren Co., O.; m in Caesars Creek MH, Esther MILLS, dt Robert & Hannah FURNAS, Warren Co., O.

----, --, --. ----- m Martha H. ----- b 1861, 5,19
Ch: Sylvia M. b 1880, 9, 23

1815, 6, 23. John [Connor] & ch, Catharine, Rachel & Isaac, gct Miami MM, O.
1817, 3, 28. Wm. [Connor] gct New Garden MM; returned because he did not move
1818, 4, 24. William [Connor] gct New Garden MM, Ind.
1818, 10, 30. Thomas gct New Garden MM, Ind.
1820, 9, 29. John gct White Water MM, Ind.
1821, 2, 23. Jesse [Connor] gct West Branch MM, O.
1823, 12, 25. Jesse rocf West Branch MM, O., dtd 1823,10,18
1824, 10, 28. Mary gct Cherry Grove MM, Ind.
1825, 11, 24. Jesse gct West Branch MM, O.
1828, 11, 27. Anna [Connor] gct Cherry Grove MM, Ind.
1830, 1, 28. Anna [Conor] rocf Cherry Grove MM, Ind., dtd 1829,11,14
1830, 4, 29. Jesse [Connor] rocf West Branch MM, O., dtd 1830,5,15
1832, 3, 22. Rebecca [Connor] gct White River MM, Ind.
1834, 10, 23. Jesse [Connor] & w, Esther, & ch, Hannah & David Mills, & Mary Connor, gct Fairfield MM, Ind.
1834, 12, 25. Ann gct White Lick MM, Ind.
1859, 2, 24. Mary rocf Fairfield MM, Ind., dtd 1859,1,13
1861, 8, 22. Mary gct Fairfield MM, Ind.
1893, 4, 27. Martha H. & Sylvia M. recrq

CONWAY
1813, 9, 25. Elizabeth & ch, James, Lydia & Samuel recrq
1814, 1, 29. Elizabeth gct Miami MM, O.

COOK
----, --, --. Eli & Martha
Ch: James b 1785, 10, 3
Martha " 1787, 9, 22
Phebe " 1789, 12, 17
Nathan " 1792, 5, 28
Martha " 1791, 7, 24

----, --,---. Amos & Elizabeth
Ch: Levi b 1776, 11, 16
Mary " 1779, 5, 11
John " 1781, 1, 28
Dinah " 1783, 2, 6
Amos b 1785, 10, 13
Stephen " 1787, 11, 14
Abraham " 1792, 4, 19
Ruth " 1794, 11, 12

----, --,---. Isaac & Sarah
Ch: Seth b 1794, 7, 25
Rebecca " 1796, 4, 25
Robert " 1799, 5, 18
Mary " 1800, 10, 8

----, --, --. Joseph & Mary
Ch: John b 1796, 2, 20
Joseph " 1799, 7, 28
Uriah " 1801, 5, 7
Mary " 1803, 6, 3
Peter " 1805, 7, 1
Joseph m 2nd Elizabeth -----
Ch: Sarah b 1810, 2, 14
George " 1811, 1, 10
Rebecca " 1813, 12, 23
Ruth " 1815, 11, 13

----, --, --. Wright & Rebecca
Ch: Charity b 1800, 11, 9
Thomas " 1802, 5, 27
Isaac " 1804, 8, 13
Wright m 2nd Ann -----
Ch: Zachariah b 1809, 11, 14
John " 1811, 4, 10
Joseph " 1812, 12, 9

----, --,---. John b 1781,1,28 d 1861,9,22 bur Caesars Creek; m Dinah ----- d 1844, 7,12 bur Caesars Creek
Ch: Sally b 1806, 12, 25 d 1808, 7,26 bur Caesars Creek
Samuel b 1808, 2, 25
Elizabeth " 1810, 9, 15
Amos " 1814, 7, 10
Mary " 1815, 12, 26
Charity " 1820, 2, 26

1811, 5, 2. Olive m Moses HOCKETT
1812, 9, 10. Abraham, s Amos & Elizabeth, Warren Co., O.; m in Caesars Creek MH, Ruth HAWKINS, dt James & Sarah, Clinton Co., O.
1813, 9, 30. Isaac, s Thomas & Mary, Clinton Co., O., d 1820,11,13 ae 77 bur Caesars Creek; m in Caesars Creek MH, Charity LEWIS, dt Thomas & Rachel, Clinton Co., O., d 1822,11,13 ae 77 bur Caesars Creek
1813, 11, 4. Rebecca m David FRAZIER
1817, 9, 11. John, s Joseph & Mary, Clinton Co., O.; m in Caesars Creek MH, Mary FURNAS, dt Robert & Hannah, Warren Co., O.
1822, 11, 13. Charity d
1824, 11, 4. Thomas, s Wright & Rebecca, Union Co., Ind.; m in Caesars Creek MH, Mary DAVIS, Clinton Co., O.
1833, 11, 28. Samuel, s John & Dinah, Warren Co., O.; m in Caesars Creek MH, Hannah COMPTON, dt John & Ann, Warren Co., O.

----, --, --. Samuel b 1808,2,25 d 1855,2,19 bur Caesars Creek; m Hannah ----- b 1814,3 10
Ch: Mary

COOK, Samuel & Hannah, continued
Ch: Elizabeth b 1834, 10, 18
Ann P. " 1837, 7, 22
John C. " 1841, 9, 19
Maria " 1844, 2, 1 d 1921, 4, 9
bur Caesars Creek
Seth b 1846, 4, 13
Amos " 1849, 12, 3
William " 1852, 6, 15 d 1858, 3,20
bur Caesars Creek
Jonathan M. b 1854, 11, 8
1834, 10, 30. Mary m Moses WALTON
1836, 8, 31. Amos, s John & Dinah, Warren Co., O., b 1814,7,10; m in Richland MH, Hannah WALTON, Green Co., O., dt Edward & Deborah, Green Co., O., b 1818,10,2
Ch: John b 1837, 6, 17
Eunice " 1841, 7, 27
Samuel " 1843, 7, 6
Mary Annie " 1856, 5, 26 d 1859, 1,18
bur Caesars Creek
1837, 9 28. Charity m Jonathan MILLS
1844, 2, 1. Maria b
1845, 8, 29. Isaac, s Seth & Ruth, Wayne Co., Ind.; m in Caesars Creek MH, Mary S. REAGAN, dt Reason & Mary, Green Co., O.
1854, 11, 8. Jonathan b
1858, 2, 11. Mary Elizabeth m Amos MILLS
1859, 6, 2. Eunice m Joseph FURNAS
----, --, --. John b 1837,6,17; m Lydia Ann ----- b 1839,6,30
Ch: Lizzie S. b 1863,11, 5
1863, 1, 29. John, s Amos & Hannah, Warren Co., O.; m in Caesars Creek MH, Ann JAY, dt John & Lydia, Clinton Co., O.
1863, 12, 3. John C., s Samuel & Hannah, Warren Co., O., b 1841,9,19; m in Caesars Creek MH, Dinah T. COMPTON, dt Phares & Nancy, Clinton Co., O., b 1839,9,26
Ch: Louella D. b 1865, 7, 10
Mannah Maria " 1870, 8, 1
1864, 9, 11. Ann P. m George MILLS
1864, 12, 8. Samuel W., s Amos & Hannah, Warren Co., O.; m in Caesars Creek MH, Martha JAY, dt John & Lydia, Clinton Co., O.
1871, 5, 4. John, s Amos & Hannah, Hamilton Co., Ind.; m in Caesars Creek MH, Sarah T. JAY, dt John & Lydia
----, --, --. Seth b 1846,4,13; m Hannah J. ----- b 1846,11,28
Ch: Mary S. b 1869, 9, 25
Amelia E. " 1873, 6, 15

1811, 1, 26. Olive recrq
1811, 4, 27. John & w, Hannah, & ch, Lydia & Thomas, rocf Deep River MM, N. C., dtd 1810,9,3, endorsed by Center MM, O., 1811, 4,6
1811, 4, 27. Phebe Frost (form Cook) con mcd
1812, 4, 25. John & fam gct Mill Creek MM
1813, 7, 31. Ruth gct Miami MM, O.
1813, 12, 25. Isaac dis mcd
1814, 1, 29. Jacob & fam gct White Water MM, Ind.
1814, 5, 28. Isaac & w gct White Water MM, Ind.
1814, 10, 28. John gct Center MM, O.
1815, 9, 29. Rachel, Samuel, John, Nancy, Ruth & Mary, ch Isaac Jr., recrq
1816, 4, 26. Isaac Jr. & fam gct White Water MM, Ind.
1816, 5, 24. Robert gct Center MM, O., to m there
1816, 11, 29. Wright & fam gct White Water MM, Ind.
1817, 4, 25. John rocf Center MM, O., dtd 1817,3,15
1817, 8, 29. Robert gct New Garden MM, Ind.
1818, 1, 30. Seth gct Miami MM, O.
1818, 6, 26. Joseph Sr. & fam gct Silver Creek MM
1818, 6, 26. Joseph Jr. gct Silver Creek MM
1819, 2, 26. Mary gct New Hope MM, Ind.
1819, 7, 30. Isaac & w, Charity, gct Silver Creek MM, Ind.
1920, 6, 23. Charity rocf Silver Creek MM, Ind., dtd 1820,6,10
1822, 9, 26. John & w, Mary, & ch, Robert & Joshua, gct West Grove MM, Ind.
1823, 1, 30. Thomas Jr. rocf Short Creek MM, Ind., dtd 1822,12,16
1824, 5, 27. Thomas gct Short Creek MM, Ind.
1824, 12, 30. Mary gct Silver Creek MM, Ind.
1827, 5, 31. Thomas & w, Mary, & dt, Tamar, rocf Short Creek MM, Ind., dtd 1827,3,26

1832, 11, 22. Thomas dis disunity
1839, 5, 23. Mary & ch, Tamer, Rebecca, Josiah D., John & Wright, gct Newberry MM, O.
1841, 5, 27. Mary & Lydia rocf Chester MM, dtd 1840,12,24
1842, 9, 22. Sarah rocf Chester MM, Ind., dtd 1842,7,21
1844, 7, 25. Nancy rocf Fairfield MM, Ind., dtd 1844,5,16
1845, 1, 23. Mary gct Cherry Grove MM, Ind.
1845, 11, 27. Mary S. gct White Water MM, Ind.
1848, 3, 23. Nancy gct Fairfield MM, Ind.
1850, 8, 22. Lydia Hawkins (form Cook) dis mcd with first cousin
1851, 2, 20. Sarah Hawkins (form Cook) dis mcd
1859, 4, 21. John Jr. gct Fairfield MM, Ind., to m Mary Furnas
1860, 2, 23. John Jr. gct Bridgeport MM, Ind.
1862, 11, 27. John rocf Bridgeport MM, Ind., dtd 1862,10,30
1863, 6, 25. Hannah Josephine rocf White Water MM, Ind.
1865, 4, 27. John & w, Lydia Ann, & ch, Lizzie S., gct Greenwood MM, Ind.
1865, 9, 21. Amos & w, Hanah, gct Creenwood MM, Ind.

COOK, continued
1865, 10, 26. Samuel W. & w, Martha, gct Greenwood MM, Ind.
1867, 7, 25. Hannah Josephine Mathewman (form Cook) dis mcd
1870, 4, 21. Hannah J. recrq
1871, 8, 24. Sarah T. gct Greenwood MM, Ind.
1875, 8, 26. John C. & w, Dinah T., & ch, Luella D., Hannah Mariah & John Edgar, gct Wilmington MM, O.
1877, 9, 27. Amos gct Clear Creek MM, O., to m Elma C. Doster
1878, 2, 21. Elma C. rocf Clear Creek MM, O., dtd 1878,1,12
1880, 8, 26. Martha J. recrq
1880, 10, 28. Mary L. rocf Stillwater MM, Ind.
1881, 4, 21. Amos & w, Elma C., gct Miami MM, O.
1881, 5, 25. Seth C. & w, Hannah J., & ch, Bessie, Wm. & Mary, gct Miami MM, O.
1905, 3, 23. Martha J. gct Whittier MM, Calif.
1905, 4, 27. Amos rocf Miami MM, O.

COPELAND
1925, 7, 23. George B. & fam relrq

COPPOCK
1819, 12, 2. Aaron, s John & Anna, Clinton Co., O., b 1796,1,9; m in Caesars Creek MH, Mary FURNAS, dt John & Ruth, Clinton Co., O., b 1800,12,10
Ch: Ruth b 1820, 2, 16
Anna " 1822, 12, 8

1826, 2, 23. Aaron & w, Mary, & ch, Ruth, Anna & Lydia, gct White Lick MM, Ind.

COPSEY
----, --, --. Philip & Mary
Ch: Harry b 1867, 2, 10
William " 1869, 2, 14
Walter " 1870, 12, 21 d 1897, 5,26
Vernon " 1872, 5, 17
Archibald " 1875, 3, 2
Nellie M. " 1882, 8, 14
1875, 6, 25. Nina b
----, --, --. William b 1869,2,14; m Kate ---- b 1865,2,27
Ch: Carl b 1895, 12, 26
Bernice " 1897, 2, 1
----, --, --. Arch b 1875,3,2; m Bertina ----- b 1879,5,13
Ch: Laura M. b 1908, 1, 15

1873, 12, 25. Philip recrq
1876, 1, 27. Rosa recrq
1880, 3, 25. Eliza recrq
1896, 3, 26. Kate recrq
1896, 3, 26. Nina recrq
1906, 1, 25. Mertie recrq
1907, 5, 23. Bertina recrq
1911, 9, 21. Harry & w, Nina, gct Dayton MM, O.
1911, 9, 21. Philip & Laura, ch Arch & Bertina, recrq

CORNELL
1880, 3, 25. Lee recrq

COULTER
----, --, --. Asa m Lydia ----- b 1826,3,6
Ch: Mary J. E. b 1847, 4, 27
Martha A.R." 1850, 11, 16

1844, 12, 26. Lydia (form Ellis) con mcd
1853, 7, 28. Mary Jane Elizabeth & Martha Ann Rebecca, dt Lydia, recrq
1872, 7, 25. Mary E. Jobe (form Coulter) con mcd
1872, 7, 25. Martha A. Weekley (form Coulter) con mcd

COVOLT
1876, 1, 27. Clara recrq

COWAN
1910, 2, 24. Ida recrq

COX
1811, 7, 4. Hannah m Joel CLOUD
1815, 1, 5. John, s Richard & Jane, Green Co., O.; m in Caesars Creek MH, Ruth ALLEN, dt Jackson & Sarah, Green Co., O.
----, --, --. Isaac b 1791,4,14; m Mary ----- b 1795,3,1
Ch: Henry b 1819, 7, 2
Anna " 1823, 11, 5
Eli " 1825, 8, 28
1821, 5, 14. Thomas d ae 81
1829, 8, 25. Tamar, w Thomas, d

1812, 11, 20. David, John & Isaac rocf New Garden MM, dtd 1812,7,25
1815, 3, 24. Cert rec for Richard & w, Anna, & ch, Peter & William, from New Garden MM, N. C., dtd 1814,5,28, endorsed to Lick Creek MM, Ind.
1816, 9, 27. John & fam gct Lick Creek MM, Ind.
1817, 1, 24. David gct Miami MM, O., to m
1818, 3, 27. Isaac con mcd
1818, 4, 24. Mary (form Spray) con mcd
1820, 9, 29. David gct Miami MM, O.
1826, 3, 30. James dis disunity
1826, 6, 29. Hannah Spray (form Cox) con mcd
1830, 6, 24. Sarah, Celia & Susanna dis jH
1833, 11, 21. Isaac dis disunity
1836, 12, 22. John & ch, Ann & William, gct Massasinawa MM, Ind.
1843, 7, 27. Anna Martin (form Cox) con mcd
1845, 10, 23. Henry dis disunity
1846, 11, 26. Eli dis mcd
1858, 4, 22. Mary gct Bear Creek MM, Ia.

COY
1864, 6, 14. Simon Peter b

COY, continued
1903, 3, 26. Mattie recrq
1903, 3, 26. Simon P. recrq
1926, 11, 28. Simon Peter & Mattie dropped from mbrp

COYLE
1901, 4, 25. Wm. Lee & w, Florence, recrq
1917, 3, 22. Earle, Lee & Sarah Florence recrq

CRAIG
1850, 3, 31. James b

1875, 7, 22. James A. & w, Charity, gct Springfield MM, O.
1885, 4, 23. Sarah Frances & Amy Ether recrq
1887, 1, 27. Nancy recrq
1889, 12, 26. Francis relrq
1896, 3, 26. Chas. recrq
1900, 7, 24. Charles dropped from mbrp

CREIGHTON
----, --, --. Dr. Hamilton b 1829,8,4 d 1887, 11,18

1886, 3, 25. Hamilton & w, Nettie, & s, Charles, recrq
1891, 8, 27. S. Emma Guard relrq
1895, 11, 21. Jenette relrq
1901, 10, 24. Chas. dropped from mbrp

CREW
1911, 12, 28. Audra recrq
1914, 3, 26. Effie M. recrq
1914, 4, 23. Henry recrq

CRISPIN
1824, 12, 2. Mathias, s Francis & Elizabeth, Clark Co., O.; m in Caesars Creek MH, Sarah WHITE, dt Nathaniel & Phebe, Warren Co., O.

1815, 8, 25. Mathias & w, Mary, rocf Fairfield MM, O., dtd 1815,7,9
1825, 1, 27. Sarah [Crispen] gct Green Plain MM, O.

CRITES
----, --, --. ----- m Jane ----- b 1818,12,12
Ch: Phebe Malinda b 1854, 9, 10
John C. " 1856, 8, 21
Charles W. " 1858, 8, 21
James M. " 1859, 12, 18
Elmina J. " 1862, 12, 24

1874, 1, 22. John recrq
1879, 4, 24. Charles, James, Malinda & Elmina, recrq
1879, 4, 24. Jane recrq
1882, 5, 25. John gct Dover MM, O.
1883, 11, 22. John & fam rocf Dover MM, O.

1885, 9, 24. John & w, Ruthanna, & ch, Edith & Jesse W., gct Springfield MM, O.

CROWDER
1825, 8, 23. Abner W. b
1849, 5, 24. Abner recrq
1855, 7, 26. Abner W. dis mcd

CRUMLEY
1814, 7, 30. Jane (form Stanfield) dis mcd

CURLETT
1909, 3, 25. Lillian recrq

DAKIN
1842, 3, 24. Sarah (form Kelly) dis mcd
1884, 3, 27. Hamilton recrq
1884, 5, 22. Sarah A. & dt, Nellie R., recrq
1884, 4, 24. Sarah A. & Nellie R. recrq
1888, 7, 26 Annie Knee relrq
1891, 7, 23. Hamilton gct Miami MM, O.
1905, 7, 27. Cassie recrq

DALE
1917, 3, 22. Verna & Gertrude recrq
1923, 4, 29. Verna dropped from mbrp
1926, 11, 28. Gertrude dropped from mbrp

DALTON
1884, 3, 27. Adam recrq
1897, 7, 22. Adam dropped from mbrp

DANIELS
1873, 4, 24. John B. rocf Uxbridge MM, Mass.
1874, 8, 27. John B. gct Uxbridge MM, Mass.

DAVIS
1819, 10, 29. Mary rocf Center MM, O., dtd 1819,10,16
1905, 7, 27. Herbert recrq
1908, 3, 26. Cora G. recrq
1917, 3, 22. Walter & Anna Bella recrq
1919, 12, 25. Walter & w, Anna, gct Xenia MM, O.

DAWSON
1831, 3, 31. Isaac rocf Springborough MM, O., dtd 1831,3,29
1831, 11, 30. Isaac gct Marlborough MM

DAY
1877, 11, 22. Benjamin F. recrq
1884, 3, 27. Therman recrq
1885, 4, 23. Amanda, Viola, Josie, Minnie & Maggie recrq
1885, 7, 23. William H. recrq
1886, 2, 25. Joseph & w, Sarah, & ch, Leroy & Bessie, recrq
1893, 4, 27. Hannah recrq
1897, 7, 22. Sherman dropped from mbrp

DEDRICK
1889, 6, 27. Thomas [Dederick] recrq
1901, 10, 24. Thomas dropped from mbrp

DEDRICK, continued
1917, 3, 22. Ella & Eva recrq

DEHAVEN
----, --, --. Peter b 1827,12,15 d 1889,2,14 bur New Burlington; m Emeline ----- b 1835,4,18
Ch: Amos W. b 1870, 8, 23
Bertha E. " 1878, 4, 1

1870, 4, 21. Peter & Emeline recrq
1879, 4, 24. Albert & Emma recrq

DELIPLANE
1883, 6, 21. Wm. E. rocf Dover MM, O.
1884, 6, 26. William [Deleplane] gct Dover MM, O.

DEWITT
1818, 8, 28. Rebecca (form Thornborough) dis mcd

DIAMOND
1905, 6, 22. Robert C. rocf Center MM, O.
1905, 10, 26. Harriett [Dymond] recrq
1908, 11, 26. John [Dyamond] & w, Mary Belle, & ch, Edith, Helen & Emma, rocf Center MM, O.

DILL
1873, 12, 25. Charles recrq

DILLON
1833, 7, 4. Jesse, s Jonathan & Agness, Clinton Co., O.; m in Caesars Creek MH, Mary HAWKINS, dt William & Jemima, Warren Co., O.

1833, 10, 24. Mary gct Center MM, O.

DISHBROUGH
----, --, --. Joseph b 1876,5,21; m Ida May WILSON, dt Isaac & Euphemia, b 1870,7,3
Ch: Mary Dorothy b 1913, 10, 5
Charles
Edwin

1901, 12, 26. Joseph rocf Miami MM, O.
1905, 7, 27. Gertrude [Disbro] recrq
1905, 9, 21. Jennie [Disbro] recrq

DODD
1879, 4, 24. David & w, Sarah, recrq
1879, 4, 24. Thurman recrq
1884, 6, 26. Thermon gct Wilmington MM, O.
1884, 6, 26. David & w, Sarah, gct Wilmington MM, O.

DOLLIVER
1886, 10, 12. R. H., s James J. & Eliza J., Cherokee Co., Iowa; m Maryelle BARRETT, dt Isaac M. & Mary, Green Co., O.

1886, 11, 25. Marybelle Barrett relrq

DORMAN
1910, 4, 21. Elsie recrq

DOSTER
1877, 9, 27. Amos Cook gct Clear Creek MM, O., to m Elma C. Doster

DUDLEY
1925, 7, 23. Wm. F. & w relrq

DUNCAN
1813, 3, 27. Elizabeth gct New Garden MM,N.C.
1867, 12, 26. Tamer Ann con mcd

DUNIVANT
1878, 1, 24. Alice recrq
1880, 3, 25. Zadoc [Dunephant] recrq
1897, 7, 22. Zadock [Dunnevant] dropped from mbrp

DUREE
1843, 2, 20. Mary Speer b

DURNBAUGH
1925, 7, 23. Welber relrq
1925, 7, 23. Catherine relrq
1925, 7, 23. Elizabeth & Ida [Dunbaugh] relrq

EASTERLING
----, --, --. Caleb & Martha
Ch: Enoch b 1808, 10, 12
Mary " 1811, 9, 27
Thomas " 1816, 1, 1
Martha " 1818, 12, 19
Caleb " 1824, 5, 27
1820, 10, 5. Ann m Isaac WILSON
1829, 9, 10. Mary m Joseph FURNAS

1812, 4, 25. Caleb & w, Martha, & ch, Enoch & Mary, recrq
1812, 4, 25. Ann, an orphan in care of Caleb & Martha, recrq
1821, 11, 23. Ellanor Melton (form Easterling) con mcd
1830, 1, 28. Enoch con mcd
1832, 2, 23. Caleb & w, Martha, & ch, Thomas, Martha & Caleb, gct White Lick MM, Ind.
1833, 1, 24. Enoch gct Cherry Grove MM, Ind.

EDINGFIELD
1908, 10, 22. Erma recrq
1909, 12, 23. Franklin [Eddingfield] recrq

EDWARDS
1836, 1, 7. Allen, s William & Gemima, Clinton Co., O.; m in Caesars Creek MH, Mary SPRAY, dt James & Charity, Warren Co., O.
1825, 10, 6. Mary m Christopher HAWKINS
1826, 6, 1. Jane m Wm. HUSSEY
1829, 11, 5. Edith m John HAWKINS

EDWARDS, continued
1829, 2, 26. Hepsibah Hussey (form Edwards) con mcd
1838, 1, 25. William, Ruth & Jemima dis
1840, 4, 23. Jemima & Nancy, ch Jemima, gct Cincinnati MM, O.
1843, 1, 26. William gct Cincinnati MM, O.; returned for jas
1843, 1, 26. Sarah gct Cincinnati MM, O.
1843, 11, 23. Wm. dis jas
1848, 10, 26. Mary & ch, Elwood, Granderson, Charity, Ann, Henry, Emaline & Mandy Jane, gct Mississinewa MM, Ind.
1849, 8, 23. Allen dis
1851, 8, 28. Jemima rst at Cincinnati MM, O. on consent of this mtg
1861, 12, 26. Polly (form Moon) con mcd
1862, 4, 24. Polly gct White Lick MM, Ind.
1874, 4, 23. Mary & ch dropped from mbrp
1881, 2, 24. Emma H. & Bertha May recrq
1911, 3, 23. Ella recrq
1913, 6, 26. Ella dropped from mbrp
1925, 7, 23. Charles W. relrq

ELLIS
----, --, --. John b 1763,6,12 d 1836,4,3 bur on own farm; m Tamar ----- b 1763,3.21 d 1839,3,1
Ch: Elijah b 1801, 10, 20 d 1859, 6,20
Thomas " 1803, 12, 28 " 1836, 3,30
1823, 10, 2. Elijah, s John & Tamar, Green Co., O., b 1801,10,20 d 1859,6,20 bur on own farm; m in Caesars Creek MH, Rebecca COMPTON, dt Amos & Rebecca, Green Co., O., b 1800,11,6 d 1872,5,20
Ch: Lydia b 1826, 3, 6 d 1867, 2,--
John Compton " 1828, 5, 24 " 1832,11,18
Amos Coulson " 1831, 6, 22 " 1866, 5,2
Tamar Ann " 1833, 12, 13 " 1875, 5, 3
Rebecca Jane " 1837, 4, 14
Rachel Maria " 1840, 4, 30 " 1885, 1, 9
Samuel Henry " 1843, 3, 13 " 1819, 7,14
1856, 1, 29. India b
1860, 2, 29. Rachel M. m Thos. C. CARTER
----, --, --. Samuel H. b 1843,3,31 d 1919, 7,14 bur Massey Creek; m Guli Elma ----- b 1840,8,27 d 1879,3,27 bur Massey Creek
Ch: Elijah Harvey b 1872, 9, 29
Mary R. " 1878, 11, 21 d 1879, 5, 4 bur Massey Creek
1876, 8, 5. Lulu C. b
1907, 7, 27. Samuel C. b
1814, 1, 29. Nehemiah & w, Sarah, & ch, Mary & Robert, rocf Clear Creek MM, O., dtd 1814,11,25
1816, 5, 24. Thomas rocf Fairfield MM, O., dtd 1816,5,25
1816, 8, 30. Nehemiah & w, Sarah, & ch, Mary, gct Clear Creek MM, O.
1816, 8, 30. Robert gct Clear Creek MM, O.
1817, 6, 27. Lydia rocf Lost Creek MM, Tenn., dtd 1817,3,29
1817, 8, 29. Thomas con mcd
1819, 5, 28. Wm. & w, Hannah, & ch, Jacob, Elizabeth, Mary, Rebecca, Enos & Hannah, rocf Newberry MM, dtd 1819,3,25
1824, 9, 30. William & w, Hannah, & ch, Jacob, Elizabeth, Mary Rebecca, Ellis, Enos, Hannah & John, rocf Green Plain MM, O., dtd 1824,9,1
1831, 8, 25. Elizabeth dis mcd with first cousin
1833, 12, 28. Wm. & w, Hannah, & ch, Ellis, Enos, Hannah & Emily, gct Sugar River MM, Ind.
1844, 12, 26. Lydia Coulter (form Ellis) con mcd
1859, 9, 22. Tamer Ann Wheeler (form Ellis) con mcd
1859, 6, 23. Abner C. con mcd
1861, 2, 21. Rebecca Jane Fawcett (form Ellis) con mcd
1865, 5, 25. Emily A. rocf Plainfield MM. Ind., dtd 1865,5,3
1866, 1, 25. Emily A. & dt, Ella Everetta, gct Plainfield MM, Ind.
1868, 12, 24. Samuel H. con mcd
1869, 1, 28. Gulielma rocf Miami MM, O., dtd 1869,1,27
1881, 2, 24. Leonadis recrq
1883, 5, 24. A. J. & w, Polithia, recrq
1885, 6, 25. Elizabeth C. & ch gct Miami MM, O.
1886, 5, 27. J. W. recrq
1890, 11, 27. Indiana rocf Fairview MM, Ill.
1893, 2, 23. J. W. dis
1894, 6, 21. Martha rocf Dover MM
1896, 1, 23. Martha relrq
1903, 6, 25. Lula Pearson rocf Bridgeport MM. Ind.
1921, 3, 24. Indiana gct Xenia MM, O.
1922, 1, 26. Lulu & s, Clarkson, gct Xenia MM, O.

ELMORE
----, --, --. ----- m Lettie ----- b 1832,8.21 d 1896,8,21
Ch: Louisa A. b 1867, 3, 3

1817, 5, 30. Isaac & w, Mary, & ch, Reason,

ELMORE, continued
Stephen, Thomas, Rosanna, Abigail & Isaac, recrq
1821, 6, 27. Isaac & fam gct Blue River MM, Ind.
1879, 4, 24. Byron & w, Ellen, & ch, Jemima Laura, recrq
1879, 4, 24. Orma recrq
1879, 4, 24. Cora recrq
1883, 3, 22. Luelma recrq
1885, 4, 23. Luticia recrq
1901, 10, 24. Orma dropped from mbrp
1921, 5, 26. Lee Amy gct Xenia MM, O.

EMBREE
1811, 7, 27. Sarah Gilson (form Embree) con mcd
1815, 1, 27. Elijah dis disunity
1824, 5, 27. Thomas & w, Esther, gct Darby Creek MM, O.

ENGLE
----, --, --. Joshua b 1781,10,11; m Hannah ----- b 1781,5,15 d 1852,8,6 bur Xenia,O.
1819, 10, 6. Jane m John COMPTON
1817, 8, 29. Joshua & w, Hannah, & ch, Jane Elizabeth, Joshua, Hannah & Ann, rocf Miami MM, O., dtd 1817,7,30
1846, 11, 26. Joshua & w, Hannah, rocf Center MM, O., dtd 1846,10,14
1855, 1, 25. Joshua con mcd
1866, 3, 26. Joshua gct Wabash MM, Ind.

ENNIS
----, --, --. Thomas b 1820,12,10; m Harriet ----- b 1825,5,25

1876, 1, 27. William recrq
1876, 1, 27. Thomas recrq
1876, 2, 24. Harriet recrq
1876, 8, 24. Chas. & w, Mary, recrq
1876, 8, 24. Perry recrq
1878, 9, 26. Chas. & T. J. relrq
1878, 9, 26. W. M. relrq
1878, 10, 24. Perry relrq
1881, 4, 21. Perry recrq
1882, 6, 22. Perry dis disunity
1884, 3, 27. Thompson, William & Perry recrq
1884, 3, 27. Clara recrq
1885, 4, 23. Thomas J. recrq
1885, 4, 23. Della May recrq
1886, 1, 28. Della May relrq
1886, 3, 25. Thomas dis
1887, 1, 27. Hattie N. recrq
1888, 4, 26. Lemuel recrq
1896, 3, 26. Perry relrq
1896, 3, 26. Duff recrq
1897, 8, 26. Mary & ch, Clara & Queena, gct Van Wert MM, O.
1900, 7, 24. Hannah dropped from mbrp
1904, 4, 21. Driffy dropped from mbrp
1909, 8, 26. Myrtle recrq
1913, 6, 26. Myrtle gct Wilmington MM, O.

ERP
1880, 3, 25. George recrq

ESTEP
1895, 9, 26. Charles S. & w recrq
1895, 9, 26. Dr. C. E. & ch, Fern & Jessie, recrq
1896, 3, 26. Dr. Chas. S. dis

EVANS
1835, 12, 8. Isaac b
1857, 9, 28. Katie B. b

1829, 4, 30. Henry Fletcher gct Miami MM, O., to m Rachel Evans
1880, 3, 25. John S. & w, Mary E., & dt, Melissa, recrq
1895, 2, 21. John & Mary E. relrq
1895, 8, 22. Harriett Barret gct Indianapolis MM, Ind.
1899, 2, 23. Isaac recrq
1907, 3, 28. George W. recrq
1917, 3, 22. Elton & Erma recrq
1917, 3, 22. Elva A. recrq
1925, 7, 23. Elva, Elton & Erma relrq

EVERHART
1884, 3, 27. Willis recrq

EWING
1893, 1, 22. Claire, s Wm. A. & Julia, b

1902, 2, 20. Roy recrq
1905, 2, 3. Clara recrq
1906, 12, 27. Wm. relrq
1911, 12, 28. Clyde recrq
1925, 7, 23. Clyde relrq

FARQUHAR
----, --, --. Jonah b 1778,3,13; m Elizabeth ----- b 1790,1,4
Ch: Mahlon b 1810, 11, 18
Andrew " 1812, 11, 27
William " 1814, 8, 11 d 1814,10,22 bur Caesars Creek
William b 1815, 12, 15
Jacob " 1818, 4, 16
Allen " 1820, 2, 5 d 1820, 5,14 bur Caesars Creek
Benjamin b 1822, 2, 15
1850, 4, 4. Benjamin, s Jonah & Elizabeth, Clinton Co., O., b 1822,2,15; m in Caesars Creek MH, Ann JAY, dt David & Rebecca, Clinton Co., O., b 1829,7,9
Ch: Ruth Elma b 1851, 10, 27
William Henry " 1853, 9, 6 d 1854,12,14 bur Caesars Creek
Eunice Ellen b 1855, 7, 29 d 1877, 8,26 bur Jenkins Gr. Yd.
Lydia Maria b 1857, 11, 15 d 1875, 8,29

FARQUHAR, Benjamin & Ann, continued
Ch: bur Jenkins Gr. Yd.
Helena
Belle b 1861, 7, 31 d 1883, 2,19
bur Jenkins Gr. Yd.
David Jay b 1867, 9, 19
Wilbert
Morgan " 1872, 8, 24
----, --, --. Philip b 1828,2,16; m Sarah E.
----- b 1840,7,8
Ch: Iradel b 1861, 3, 7 d 1861, 8,17
James A. " 1862, 11, 1
Salathiel
D. " 1864, 1, 3
Linden W. " 1866, 4, 8 " 1867, 8,24
Viola M. " 1868, 4, 2
Mary I. " 1871, 1, 4

1818, 9, 25. Jonah rocf Center MM, O., dtd 1818,9,19
1819, 3, 26. Elizabeth & ch, Malon Andrew William & Jacob, recrq
1830, 9, 30. Jonah, Andrew & Mahlon dis jH
1837, 12, 28. Elizabeth dis jH
1843, 3, 23. Jacob dis mcd
1851, 1, 23. Amos dis mcd
1851, 2, 20. Phebe Colvin (form Farquhar) dis mcd
1861, 4, 25. Phillip con mcd
1869, 4, 22. Harriet Alice gct Cherry Grove MM, Ind.
1891, 8, 27. D. J. relrq

FAUCETT
----, --, --. Jonathan b 1828,8,2; m Huldah

Ch: Mary
Esther b 1856, 5, 22
Jonathan m 2nd Rebecca Jane ----- b 1837,4, 14
Ch: Tamar Ann b 1861, 5, 18
Elijah R. " 1863, 2, 3 d 1864, 2, 2
Charlotte
Lucinda " 1865, 9, 25 " 1869, 5,19
William Eli-
hu b 1871, 12, 8
Jesse H. " 1877, 3, 8
1880, 9, 23. Sylvia M. b

1861, 2, 21. Rebecca Jane (form Ellis) con mcd
1867, 7, 25. Mary Ester & Tamar Ann, step-dt & dt of Rebecca Jane, recrq
1893, 6, 22. Jonathan P. recrq
1917, 6, 21. Sylvia M. & dt, Myrtle, relrq
1917, 6, 21. Jesse H. & s, Homer, gct Xenia MM, O.

FAUS
1923, 4, 29. Cora Harner dropped from mbrp

FERGUSON
----, --, --. Clark [Furgeson] b 1786,6,24
d 1864,11,3 bur Massie Creek; m Mary
----- b 1785,9,20 d 1858,9,27 bur Massie Creek
Ch: Samuel b 1808, 10, 1
Elizabeth " 1810, 5, 2
Levi " 1812, 4, 21 d 1868, 2,12
bur Massie Creek
Charles b 1814, 5, 25
Isaac " 1816, 2, 10
Jacob " 1818, 3, 1
Clark " 1821, 9, 30
Ann " 1820, 2, 19 d 1835, 2,18
bur Massie Creek
Joseph b 1823, 7, 25 " 1824, 9, 9
bur Lees Creek
Mary b 1825, 1, 5
Aaron " 1827, 2, 2
Rachel " 1829, 1, 26 d 1829, 1,26
bur Massies Creek
Cyrus b 1830, 5, 11
1842, 12, 1. Clark, s Clark & Mary, Green Co., O.; m in Caesars Creek MH, Sarah FURNAS, dt Robert & Hannah, Warren Co.,O.
----, --, --. Aaron b 1827,2,2; m Mary -----
Ch: Evangeline b 1853, 5, 24
Sarah Emily
b 1858, 3, 28
Mary Eliza " 1860, 5, 11
Joseph Ri-
ley " 1864, 4, 11
Henrietta " 1867, 2, 1

1830, 2, 25. Clark & w, Mary, & ch, Elizabeth Levi, Charles, Isaac, Jacob, Ann, Clark, Mary & Aaron, rocf Lees Creek MM, O., dtd 1829,3,25
1834, 8, 28. Elizabeth [Furgeson] dis
1836, 10, 27. Chas. [Furgusson] con mcd
1840, 8, 22. Charles gct Dover MM
1841, 4, 22. Isaac [Furgason] gct Dover MM
1846, 9, 24. Clark & w, Sarah, & ch, Hannah W. & Mary E., gct Fairfield MM, Ind.
1849, 11, 22. Charles [Furgeson] rocf Dover MM, dtd 1849,9,13
1851, 1, 23. Jacob [Furgason] con mcd
1851, 8, 28. Jacob [Furgason] gct Mississinewa MM, Ind.
1851, 11, 27. Aaron [Furgason] con mcd
1852, 9, 23. Aaron gct Center MM, O.
1856, 2, 21. Mary [Furgason] dis mcd
1857, 10, 22. Sirus [Fergason] dis mcd
1859, 3, 24. Aaron [Furgason] rocf Spring Creek MM, Ia., dtd 1859,2,5
1860, 7, 26. Charles [Fergason] dis disunity
1865, 1, 26. Evangeline, Sarah Emily, Mary Eliza & Joseph Riley, ch Aaron, recrq
1872, 12, 26. Lucinda Catherine recrq
1894, 1, 25. Sarah E., Mary Eliza & Henrietta, relrq

FETZ
1912, 4, 25. Mary E. Carr relrq

FIELDS
1905, 10, 26. Wm. S. recrq

FLEMMING
1904, 5, 26. John recrq
1906, 3, 22. John D. gct Center MM, O.
1907, 9, 26. John [Fleming] & w, May, & dt, Mary Dena, rocf Center MM, O.

FLETCHER
1829, 3, 26. Henry rocf Fairfield MM, Ind., dtd 1829,3,7
1829, 4, 30. Henry gct Miami MM, O., to m Rachel Evans
1829, 11, 26. Rachel rocf Miami MM, O., dtd 1829,9,30
1836, 10, 27. Henry & w, Rachel, gct Vermillion MM, Ill.
1883, 3, 22. E. B. recrq
1892, 4, 21. John Wm. recrq
1914, 3, 26. George recrq
1915, 1, 28. Raymond Kennedy recrq
1923, 4, 29. Raymond dropped from mbrp
1923, 4, 29. John & May & ch dropped from mbrp
1925, 2, 22. Helen recrq
1925, 7, 23. George relrq
1926, 11, 28. Mary Chenoweth dropped from mbrp

FLOOI
1908, 12, 24. Ina recrq

FOLAND
----, --, --. Adolphus, s Azariah & Julia, b 1850,4,14; m Martha J. -----, dt Phares & Nancy COMPTON, b 1844,9,10

1892, 10, 27. Adolphus V. recrq

FOLKETH
1850, 7, 29. Jesse b
1878, 8, 17. Lucy b
1883, 10, 14. Clarissa b

1896, 11, 26. Clarence V. & Clarissa [Folkerth] ch Jesse, recrq
1911, 9, 21. Jesse, Lucy, Clarence & Clarissa [Folkerth] dropped from mbrp

FOSTER
1906, 5, 24. Samuel & w, Hannah, rocf Center MM, O.

FOWLER
1881, 2, 24. Wm. D. & Catharine recrq

FOX
1880, 7, 22. Rachel rocf West Branch MM, O., dtd 1880,6,17

FRAME
----, --, --. Nathan T. b 1835,12,19 d 1914, 12,27 bur Jamestown, O.; m Esther E. ----- b 1840,7,10 d 1920,6,11 bur Jamestown,O.
Ch: Tassie b 1862, 11, 13
Hettie " 1865, 8, 10
1885, 12, 29. Corrine m Wm. W. JOHNSON

1875, 2, 25. Nathan T. & w, Esther E., & ch, Itasca M. & Hettie C., rocf White Water MM, Ind., dtd 1875,1,27

FRAZIER
1813, 11, 4. David, s Francis & Elizabeth, Clinton Co., O.; m in Caesars Creek MH, Rebecca COOK, dt Isaac & Sarah. Warren Co., O.

1815, 6, 23. Rebecca gct Clear Creek MM, O.

FROST
1811, 4, 27. Phebe (form Cook) con mcd
1825, 12, 30. Phebe gct West Grove MM, Ind.

FULKERSON
1898, 12, 22. Susan recrq

FURNAS
----, --, --. John b 1765,8,5 d 1830,3,9 bur Caesars Creek (an elder); m Esther ----- b 1777,2,9 d 1795,9,13
Ch: Christopher
b 1791, 10, 18
John m 2nd Ruth ----- b 1776,8,29 d 1824, 9,21 bur Caesars Creek
Ch: Isaac b 1798, 12, 6
Mary " 1800, 12, 10
Joseph " 1802, 9, 24
Robert " 1803, 6, 3
1795, 9, 13. Esther d
----, --, --. Robert d 1863,2,16 bur Caesars Creek; m Hannah ----- d 1864,2,17 bur Caesars Creek
Ch: Mary b 1796, 11, 25
Esther " 1799, 1, 5
John " 1801, 3, 6
Seth " 1803, 3, 26
Joseph " 1805, 9, 9
Isaac " 1807, 11, 12 d 1839, 9,16 bur Caesars Creek
Dinah b 1810, 5. 5 " 1841, 9,10 bur Caesars Creek
Robert b 1812, 11, 22
Rebecca " 1815, 2, 9
Hannah " 1818, 1, 3
Sarah " 1822, 5, 29
1817, 9, 11. Mary m John COOK
1819, 12, 2. Mary m Aaron COPPOCK
1820, 7, 6. Esther m Daniel MILLS
----, --, --. Isaac b 1798,12,6; m Esly ----- b 1798,11,20
Ch: Allen b 1821, 3, 27
1824, 9, 21. Ruth d

FURNAS, continued
1826, 10, 12. John, s John & Mary, Clinton Co., O.; m in Caesars Creek MH, Rebecca COMPTON, dt Henry & Rebecca MILHOUSE, Green Co., O.
1827, 12, 6. Robert, s John & Ruth, Clinton Co., O., b 1803,6,3; m in Caesars Creek MH, Naomy WHITSON, dt Jordan & Mary, Warren Co., O.
Ch: John b 1829, 4, 5
Solomon " 1830, 11, 21 d 1833,11,11 bur Caesars Creek
Christopher b 1839, 3, 18
1829, 9, 10. Joseph, s Robert & Hannah, Warren Co., O.; m in Caesars Creek MH, Mary EASTERLING, dt Caleb & Martha, Clinton Co., O.
1830, 8, 5. Dinah m Robert MILHOUS
1832, 11, 1. Rebecca m Samuel STARBUCK
1833, 10, 31. Isaac, s Robert & Hannah, Warren Co., O., b 1807,11,12 d 1839,9,16; m in Caesars Creek MH, Matilda COMPTON, dt Joseph & Christianna, Green Co., O., b 1808 [4,21
Ch: Joseph b 1837, 4, 11
Isaac " 1839, 11, 6
1840, 2, 27. Hannah m Abner MILLS
1842, 12, 1. Sarah m Clark FERGUSON
----, --, --. Robert b 1812,11,22; m Phebe ----- d 1843,12,24 bur Caesars Creek
Ch: Samuel b 1843, 11, 7 d 1844, 7,13 bur Caesars Creek
Robert m 2nd Ann HOLLINGSWORTH b 1806,7,7 d 1850,7,29 bur Caesars Creek
Robert m 3rd Achsah ----- b 1831,8,25
Ch: John b 1861, 10, 31
Hannah Anna" 1863, 3, 31
1844, 1, 4. Matilda m Wm. MORGAN
1847, 9, 2. Joseph, s John & Ruth, Miami Co., Ind.; m in Caesars Creek MH, Patty HAWKINS dt Joseph & Christiana COMPTON
1859, 6, 2. Joseph, s Isaac & Matilda, Warren Co., O., b 1837,4,11; m in Caesars Creek MH, Eunice COOK, dt Amos & Hannah, Warren Co., O., b 1841,7,27
Ch: Walton C. b 1860, 4, 23
Anne Maria " 1863, 12, 21

1816, 9, 27. Christopher gct Mill Creek MM, to m
1817, 5, 30. Sarah rocf Mill Creek MM, dtd 1817,3,22
1817, 6, 27. Christopher & w, Sarah, gct Silver Creek MM
1818, 2, 27. Isaac gct Miami MM, O.
1821, 7, 21. Isaac & w, Esley, rocf Miami MM, O., dtd 1821,10,25
1823, 1, 23. John Jr. dis mcd
1826, 8, 31. Joseph gct Center MM, O., to m Rebecca Compton
1826, 9, 28. Isaac & w, Esley, & ch, Allen, Sarah & Mary, gct Fairfield MM, Ind.
1826, 9, 28. Seth gct Miami MM, O., to m Dinah Kindley
1827, 1, 25. Dinah Kindley rocf Miami MM, O., dtd 1826,12,27
1827, 4, 26. Elizabeth Ballard rocf Center MM, O., dtd 1827,1,20
1829, 10, 29. Seth & w, Dinah, dis jH
1829, 10, 29. Joseph & w, Mary, gct Fairfield MM, Ind.
1830, 8, 26. Joseph & w, Elizabeth, & ch, Isaac & Sarah, gct Center MM, O.
1838, 9, 27. Robert Jr. gct Fairfield MM, Ind., to m Phebe Whitson
1839, 12, 26. Phebe rocf Fairfield MM, Ind., dtd 1839,10,18
1847, 3, 25. Robert Jr. gct Miami MM, O., to m Anna Hollingsworth
1847, 8, 26. Anna rocf Miami MM, O., dtd 1847,7,21
1848, 4, 27. Joseph & ch, Samuel S., Orlando, Mary Jane & Ruth Ellen, rocf Fairfield MM, Ind., dtd 1848,1,13
1851, 11, 27. John dis mcd
1854, 4, 21. David dis jH
1856, 4, 24. Samuel dis jas
1857, 11, 26. Robert Jr. & w, Naomi, & s, Christopher, gct Fairfield MM, Ind.
1857, 11, 26. Mary Jane, Ruth Ellen, ch Jos. & Elizabeth, gct Fairfield MM, Ind.
1859, 4, 21. John Cook Jr. gct Fairfield MM, Ind., to m Mary Furnas
1859, 8, 25. Robert Jr. gct Fairfield MM, Ind., to m Axey Newby
1860, 2, 23. Achsah rocf Fairfield MM, Ind., dtd 1860,1,9
1860, 4, 26. Orlando dis mcd
1864, 8, 22. Robert & w, Achsah, & ch, John & Hannah, gct Beech Grove MM, Ind.
1864, 10, 22. Joseph & w, Patty, & dt, Anna M., gct Greenwood MM, Ind.
1865, 9, 21. Joseph & w, Eunice, & ch, Walter C. & Annie Maria, gct Greenwood MM, Ind.
1867, 12, 26. Isaac con mcd
1868, 5, 27. Isaac gct Miami MM, O.
1915, 1, 28. Fred recrq
1923, 4, 29. Lucile dropped from mbrp
1926, 11, 28. Fred dropped from mbrp

GADIS
1872, 2, 22. Sarah Jane [Gaddis] recrq
1879, 4, 24. Alaska recrq
1881, 11, 24. Jane relrq

GAINES
1880, 5, 27. Moses recrq
1899, 4, 27. Moses dropped from mbrp

GARD
1879, 4, 24. John & w, Margaret, & ch, William & Emma, recrq
1902, 2, 20. J. H. dropped from mbrp
1902, 4, 24. Margaret relrq
1913, 5, 22. Will & Harry dropped from mbrp

GARD, continued
1917, 9, 27. John recrq
1918, 1, 24. John gct Long Beach MM, Calif.

GARMAN
1884, 8, 28. Jacob & w, Ida, & ch, Orvil, Maude & Viola Bell, rocf Dover MM, O.

GARWOOD
1874, 1, 22. Sarah Thorn gct Oskaloosa MM,Ia.

GAUNT
1872, 10, 24. Martha A. recrq
1893, 5, 25. Hiram Cicero recrq

GEST
1836, 1, 23. Sarah b

1884, 5, 22. Sarah E. recrq
1892, 10, 27. Sarah E. relrq
1898, 12, 22. Sarah recrq

GIBERSON
1914, 1, 22. Roy Wilbur recrq
1914, 6, 25. Lillie & s, E. L. recrq
1917, 7, 26. Lillie G., Earl & Roy [Geiberson] dropped from mbrp

GIBSON
1828, 11, 5. Esther m Benjamin OWEN
1833, 9, 4. Maria L. m Benjamin WILDMAN

1819, 12, 27. Esther Coulson, Maria Louisa & Elijah Alfred, ch Sarah, recrq
1832, 8, 23. Thamar Ann, Rachel Jane, Deborah Frances, Hannah & Isaac Thorn, ch Sarah, recrq
1837, 1, 26. Sarah & ch, Elijah Alfred Thomas Ann Deborah Frances Hannah & Albert Thorn, gct White Lick MM, Ind.
1837, 9, 21. Rachel Jane gct White Lick MM, Ind.

GILPIN
1813, 6, 26. Sarah Mills (form Gilpin) con mcd
1823, 12, 25. John con mcd
1826, 9, 28. Thomas Jr. dis disunity
1832, 2, 23. Henry gct Dover MM, to m Esther Oran
1832, 6, 21. Esther rocf Dover MM, dtd 1832, 6,14
1835, 9, 24. Thomas gct Miami MM, O., to m Tacy Plummer
1836, 8, 25. Tracy rocf Miami MM, O., dtd 1836,5,25
1836, 9, 22. Rebecca Miller (form Gilpin) con mcd
1836, 11, 24. Joseph dis mcd
1840, 2, 20. Tacy gct Miami MM, O.
1840, 4, 23. Henry & w, Esther, & ch, Mary, Lydia & John Thomas, gct Center MM, O.
1841, 10, 28. James gct Cherry Grove MM, Ind.
1844, 8, 22. Tacy rocf Miami MM, O., dtd 1844,3,27
1844, 8, 22. Tacy rocf Miami MM, O., dtd 1844,3,27
1854, 8, 24. Tacy gct Three Rivers MM, Iowa
1860, 5, 24. Phebe [Gilpen] (form Oren) con mcd
1860, 9, 27. Phebe [Gilpen] gct Dover MM

GILSON
1811, 7, 27. Sarah (form Embree) con mcd

GITHENS
1880, 3, 25. Ida recrq
1881, 6, 23. Ida relrq

GOODE
1824, 9, 30. Margaret (form McKay) dis mcd

GOODBAR
1925, 7, 23. Harvey relrq

GORDEN
1887, 10, 27. William M. recrq

GRANT
----, --, --. Sarah b 1810,5,26 d 1896,1,15

1875, 11, 13. Sarah recrq

GREEN
1885, 4, 23. Willie recrq
1885, 4, 23. Minnie recrq
1908, 12, 24. Myrtle recrq
1910, 2, 24. Homer recrq

GRETSINGER
1879, 4, 24. Christopher & w, Annie, & ch, Nellie Mariah, recrq
1890, 4, 24. Mamie relrq
1911, 4, 27. Christopher & w, Anna, gct Xenia MM, O.

GRIFFITH
----, --, --. ----- b 1831,5,23; m Donna -----
Ch: Nannie b 1865, 7, 4

1887, 1, 27. Joseph W. & Dona Martha recrq
1890, 4, 24. Grace & Anna recrq
1911, 9, 21. Annie dropped from mbrp
1917, 7, 26. Dona Martha dropped from mbrp

GRIFFY
1846, 11, 15. William E. b

1873, 12, 25. Oliver recrq
1891, 7, 23. Oliver relrq
1896, 3, 26. Wm. E. recrq
1909, 1, 28. Wm. E. relrq

HACKNEY
1845, 5, 22. Susan D. (form Canby) dis mcd & jas
1896, 6, 25. N. Catherine [Hacney] relrq

HADLEY,
1883, 5, 24. Mahlon C. & w, Emily C., & ch, Arthur E. & Clara M., rocf Springfield MM, O.
1884, 4, 24. Mahlon C. & w, Esther C., & ch, Arthur E. & Clare M., gct Springfield MM, O.

HAINES
1815, 11, 30. Esther [Hains] m Pleasant TERREL
1817, 1, 9. Narcissa m Thos. P. ANTHONY

----, --, --. Eli b 1827,8,12 d 1897,6,18 bur Caesars Creek; m Emily S. ----- b 1837,2,7 d 1909,9,24
Ch: Stephen Allen b 1859, 9, 8 d 1866, 6,29 bur Caesars Creek
Mary Elizabeth b 1861, 9, 8 " 1866, 6,28 bur Caesars Creek
Jennie Maria b 1866, 3, 24
Zimri Forster " 1866, 3, 24
Ellanora A. " 1872, 7, 28 d 1917,12,28 bur Caesars Creek
Jesse Curtis b 1875, 4, 10 " 1919, 2,18 bur New Burlington
----, --, --. Zimri Foster, s Eli & Emily (McPherson), b 1868,2,9; m Ella ----- b 1870, 2,6 (Ella, dt Amos & Ann Compton)
Ch: Everett E. b 1893, 1, 24
Luther Grant " 1897, 1, 23
Homer " 1901, 5, 16
----, --, --. Luther G., s Zimri & Ella, b 1897,1,23; m Edith LAIRD, dt Charles & Carrie W., b 1899,7,2
Ch: Donald L. b 1918, 4, 17
Phyllis A. " 1923, 8, 23
----, --, --. Everett, s Zimri & Ella, b 1893, 1,24; m Ruth CAREY, dt Benjamin & Etta, b 1896,4,8
Ch: Willard E. b 1918, 7, 28
Marvin Zimri " 1921, 2, 6
Esther Jean " 1922, 4, 28
Carey Leigh" 1924, 8, 27
Errol Dean " 1927, 10, 2
1922, 10, 4. Homer H. m Lois A. TERRELL
----, --, --. Homer H., s Zimri & Ella, b 1901,5,16; m Lois TERRELL, dt Tasso & Millie, b 1903,9,6
Ch: Emily Lucile b 1923, 11, 1
Richard Allen " 1926, 3, 1

1814, 5, 28. John [Hains] & w, Betty, & ch, Stasia, Narcissa, Israel, Betty, Reuben, Ruth, John & Mary, rocf Miami MM, O., dtd 1814,3,30
1814, 5, 28. Esther [Hains] rocf Miami MM, O. dtd 1814,3,30
1816, 2, 23. Zimri [Hains] recrq
1817, 11, 28. Zimri [Hains] dis mcd
1817, 11, 28. Elizabeth [Hains] (form Compton) dis mcd
1817, 11, 28. Stacy [Hains] gct Fairfield MM, O., to m
1819, 5, 28. Judith rocf Fairfield MM, O., dtd 1818,5,30
1824, 8, 26. Betty Beamer (form Hains) dis mcd
1825, 5, 26. Reuben [Haynes] dis disunity
1825, 7, 28. Ruth Conly (form Haynes) dis mcd
1830, 9, 30. John [Hains] dis mcd
1838, 1, 25. Stacy [Haynes] & w, Judith, & ch, David, Amos, Sarah, Elizabeth, Samuel, Stacy, Allen, Martha N. & Judithann, gct Springfield MM
1840, 7, 23. Zimri & w, Elizabeth rst at Center MM, O., on consent of this mtg
1843, 5, 25. David rocf Springfield MM, dtd 1843,5,16
1847, 8, 26. David dis disunity
1859, 5, 26. Emily S. rocf Fairfield MM, O., dtd 1859,4,16
1859, 8, 25. Eli rocf Center MM, O., dtd 1859,7,13
1876, 8, 24. Louisa gct Wilmington MM, O.
1900, 3, 22. Daisy Lytle recrq
1914, 2, 26. Charles recrq
1914, 7, 30. Minnie B. & dt, Elizabeth Mildred, recrq
1918, 3, 28. Ruth Carey rocf Clear Creek MM, O.
1918, 3, 28. Edyth Laird recrq
1923, 1, 28. Lois T. rocf Fairview MM
1823, 8, 23. Phllis Ilene, dt Luther & Edith, recrq
1924, 8, 27. Carey Lee, ch Everett & Ruth, recrq
1926, 3, 1. Richard Allen, s Homer & Lois T., recrq
1927, 10, 2. Errol Dean, ch Everett & Ruth, recrq

HALSTEAD
1910, 4, 21. Thomas recrq

HAMMAR
1812, 1, 30. Margaret m Henry BENSON

1812, 7, 25. David dis disunity
1819, 12, 27. Charlotte & ch gct New Garden MM, Ind.
1833, 1, 24. David rst at Cherry Grove MM, Ind., on consent of this mtg

HAMPTON
1905, 7, 27. Anna recrq

HANSEL
1911, 12, 28. Bessie recrq

HARLAN
----, --, --. A. H. b 1848,5,19 d 1919,9,29 bur Corwin; m Diadema ----- b 1848,12,12
Ch: Thomas M. b 1870, 12, 16
Flora E. " 1879, 1, 26
Anna Maud " 1880, 3, 10
Wm. Haydock" 1892, 3, 3

1889, 2, 21. Thomas P. [Harland] recrq
1889, 2, 21. Diadem [Harland] & ch, Flora E. & Anna Maud, recrq
1894, 3, 22. Wm. Haydock, minor, recrq of mother, Diadema
1898, 8, 25. Mary T. Spray rocf Springfield MM, O.
1906, 3, 22. Thomas M. relrq
1909, 9, 23. Flora E. gct White Water MM, Ind.
1914, 7, 30. Alpheus H. recrq

HARMAN
----, --, --. ----- m Lizzie -----, dt David & Phoebe GAVIN, b 1858,8,22
Ch: Ida A. b 1878, 1, 21

1892, 4, 21. Ida, Elizabeth & David I. recrq
1901, 10, 24. David G. dropped from mbrp
1913, 5, 22. Lizzie D. dropped from mbrp

HARNER
----, --, --. Martin b 1841,6,28; m Martha J. ----- b 1846,3,3
Ch: Clement S. b 1866, 8, 15 d 1888, 5,16 bur Caesars Creek
Charles T. b 1868, 3, 4
Lillie M. " 1870, 2, 28
Clyde M. " 1872, 12, 15
Stella Jane" 1874, 9, 14
Jesse " 1876, 11, 7
Guy " 1878, 10, 7
Cracie Belle " 1880, 4, 12
Frank Wilson " 1882, 9, 21
Cleora " 1884, 3, 10
Ada L. " 1887, 9, 4 d 1888, 7,13 bur Caesars Creek
1869, 7, 29. Harry b
1874, 5, 22. Samuel b
1877, 7, 4. Arena B. b
----, --, --. ----- m Mary Eva ----- b 1860,12, 28
Ch: Lester A. b 1882, 8, 23
James R. " 1884, 9, 22
----, --, --. Charles T. b 1868,3,4; m Harriet P. ----- b 1869,5,21
Ch: Horace H. b 1893, 3, 25
Jennie Marie b 1895, 10, 2
Clement M. " 1899, 9, 6
Marybelle " 1902, 5, 22

1881, 2, 24. Martin & Martha recrq
1883, 3, 22. Clement recrq
1888, 9, 27. Martin relrq
1893, 4, 27. Wm. H. recrq
1893, 4, 27. Samuel recrq
1893, 4, 27. Ada recrq
1894, 2, 22. Clyde recrq
1894, 3, 22. Grace recrq
1901, 4, 25. Emily Alice recrq
1905, 7, 27. Elizabeth, Lella & Ruth recrq
1907, 4, 25. Samuel recrq
1908, 3, 26. Lester A. recrq
1909, 2, 25. Grace B. relrq
1911, 2, 23. Eva Moon relrq
1911, 3, 23. Harry & w, Emily Alice, relrq
1911, 3, 23. Ross relrq
1911, 7, 27. Guy & Frank dropped from mbrp
1913, 6, 26. Clyde relrq
1918, 2, 21. Arena C. gct Xenia MM, O.
1923, 4, 29. Clement dropped from mbrp
1925, 5, 31. Jennie Mills rocf Grassy Run MM, O.
1925, 7, 23. Edna relrq
1926, 11, 28. Clyde, Stella Jane & Guy dropped from mbrp

HARRIS
1811, 6, 29. Obadiah & w, Mary, & ch, Thomas, David, Rachel, Betsy, Susannah, Jonathan, John & Obadiah, rocf Piney Grove MM, S.C., dtd 1811,4,20
1811, 11, 30. Elizabeth rocf Pinny Grove MM, S. C., dtd 1811,4,20
1812, 8, 29. Obadiah & fam gct White Water MM, Ind.
1815, 8, 25. Elizabeth gct New Garden MM,Ind.

HARRISON
1885, 6, 2. Thomas H., s Timothy & Naomi, Wayne Co., Ind.; m in home of Isaac M. Barrett, Clarabel BARRETT, dt Isaac M. & Mary, Green Co., O.

1886, 9, 23. Claribel gct White Water MM, Ind.

HARSHBARGER
1908, 6, 25. Edgar & w, Julia, & ch, Iva, Glen D., Guy F. & Mary Opal, rocf West Branch MM, O.

HARTER
1861, 6, 20. William b
1863, 1, 14. Sarah b

HARTMAN
----, --, --. John b 1861,3,3; m Mary C. ----- b 1859,9,7
Ch: Ora L. b 1890, 7, 11

HARTMAN, continued
1886, 3, 25. Mary recrq
1893, 4,27. John L. recrq
1907, 3, 28. John C. & w, Mary, gct Hopewell MM, O.
1917, 4, 26. Bernice E. Hawkins gct Wilmington MM, O.
1921, 11, 24. Arthur & w, Bernice H., & ch, Margaret Ruth, Cecil Arthur & Rachel Nancy, rocf Wilmington MM, O.

HARVEY
1823, 11, 6. Caleb, s Joshua & Mary, Clinton Co., O.; m in Caesars Creek MH, Bathsheba NICHOLSON, dt Daniel & Elizabeth, Clinton Co., O.

1824, 2, 26. Bathsheba gct Springfield MM
1871, 2, 23. Simon D. rocf Miami MM, O., dtd 1871,2,22
1885, 2, 19. Ora (form Shafer) relrq
1925, 7, 23. Nora relrq

HASKET
1811, 10, 26. Ann & ch, Lydia, Mary, Isaac & Charity, rocf Miami MM, O., dtd 1811,8,28
1815, 5, 26. Ann & ch, Lydia, Mary, Isaac & Charity gct Miami MM, O.

HATHAWAY
1887, 1, 27. John, Ann, Garrett & Ivanetta recrq
1893, 8, 24. John & w relrq
1897, 7, 22. John dropped from mbrp

HAWES
1916, 2, 24. Nathan & Katie recrq

HAWKINS
----, --, --. Amos b 1769,1,7 d 1833,9,14 bur Caesars Creek; m Phebe ----- b 1769,2,18 d 1857,3,27 bur Caesars Creek
Ch: Jonathan b 1792, 9, 24
Mary " 1792, 9, 24
Margaret " 1795, 3, 15
Christopher" 1801, 3, 24 d 1830, 8, 5 bur Caesars Creek
Ruth b 1808, 11, 28
----, --, --. James b 1756,1,25 d 1840,11,24 bur Caesars Creek; m Sarah ----- b 1773,5,19 d 1871,3,26 bur Caesars Creek
Ch: Ruth b 1793, 3, 14
Dinah " 1795, 11, 22
Jehu " 1796, 10, 30
Benjamin " 1808, 4, 1
James " 1810, 6, 1
Amos " 1813, 5, 23
1796, 10, 12. Margaret, w Isaac Sr., d ae 49
----, --, --. John m Sarah ----- d 1820,3,28 bur Caesars Creek
Ch: Jesse b 1797, 7, 12
David " 1797, 5, 25 d 1802, 3,27 bur Caesars Creek
Ch: Dinah b 1802, 3, 9 d 1805,10, 7 bur Caesars Creek
Jonathan b 1805, 10, 7 " 1805,10, 7 bur Caesars Creek
Ann b 1809, 10, 31
Hannah " 1811, 11, 11
----, --, --. Amos d 1844,10,13 bur Caesars Creek; m Ann ----- d 1855,4,2 bur Caesars Creek
Ch: Henry b 1798, 7, 29
Mary " 1800, 2, 25
Rebecca " 1802, 7, 25
Martha " 1806, 4, 2
Ann " 1809, 10, 21
Amos " 1816, 4, 6
----, --, --. Isaac & Martha
Ch: Stephen b 1804, 10, 21 d 1804,11, 6
Mary " 1806, 7, 15
William " 1808, 9, 22
Rebecca " 1812, 4, 1
Ann " 1814, 7, 13
Sarah " 1817, 6, 29
1811, 11, 22. Edith b
1812, 9, 10. Ruth m Abraham COOK
1815, 12, 7. Dinah m William MILLS
1816, 12, 12. Margaret m James PARNELL
1818, 3, 5. Mary m Charles MILLS
----, --, --. Jehu b 1796,10,30; m Susanna ----- b 1799,6,10 d 1844,6,6 bur Caesars Creek
Ch: Ruth b 1819, 6, 30
Isaac " 1821, 10, 17
Sarah " 1823, 12, 29
Charity " 1825, 11, 20
Dinah " 1828, 8, 18
Eli " 1832, 6, 11
James " 1835, 5, 11
1821, 3, 1. Mary m Elijah MILLS
1821, 11, 29. Henry, s Amos & Ann, Warren Co., O., b 1798,7,29; m in Caesars Creek MH, Anna PEARSON, dt William & Anna, Clinton Co., O., d 1836,3,24 bur Caesars Creek
Ch: Mark b 1824, 1, 5
Noah " 1827, 4, 30
Charles " 1829, 12, 6
Jehu " 1832, 10, 10
Elijah " 1835, 5, 1
Henry m 2nd Lydia ----- b 1819,10,1
Ch: Linza E. b 1850, 12, 5
1825, 6, 19. Rebeckah m David JAY
1825, 10, 6. Christopher, s Amos & Phebe, Warren Co., O.; m in Caesars Creek MH, Mary EDWARDS, dt William & Jemima, Clinton Co., O.
1829, 11, 5. John, s Amos & Ann, Warren Co., O.; m in Caesars Creek MH, Edith EDWARDS, dt William & Jemmimah, Clinton Co., O.
1833, 7, 4. Mary m Jesse DILLON
1833, 9, 14. Amos d ae 64
1833, 10, 31. Hannah m James PARNELL

HAWKINS, continued
1834, 4, 3. Benjamin, s James & Sarah, Clinton Co., O., b 1808,4,1 d 1852,10,7 bur Caesars Creek; m Phamy MORGAN, dt Thomas & Ann, Green Co., O., b 1810,1,20
Ch: Sarah b 1836, 11, 18
Martha " 1840, 7, 28
1836, 9, 29. James, s James & Sarah, Clinton Co., O., b 1810,6,1 d 1839,11,23 bur Caesars Creek; m in Caesars Creek MH, Patty COMPTON, dt Joseph & Christian, Warren Co., O.
Ch: Joseph C.
1837, 3, 30. Ruth m John L. WALKER
1838, 12, 16. Elizabeth b
1840, 1, 30. Amos, s James & Sarah, Clinton Co., O., b 1813,5,23 d 1896,7,19 bur Caesars Creek; m in Caesars Creek MH, Massey SPRAY, dt John & Sarah, Clinton Co., O., b 1824,8,23 d 1891,9,27
Ch: James b 1841, 1, 7
Jehu " 1842, 2, 22 d 1921, 3,18
John " 1843, 12, 9 " 1924, 2,14
Jesse " 1846, 3, 21
Benjamin " 1848, 12, 23 " 1921, 2, 6
1840, 10, 1. Isaac, s Jehu & Susanna, Clinton Co., O.; m in Caesars Creek MH, Ann MILLS dt Elijah & Mary, Clinton Co., O.
Ch: Mary b 1841, 7, 12
Phamy " 1843, 3, 22 d 1843, 4,11
Susannah " 1846, 5, 30
1842, 11, 3. Amos, s Amos & Ann, b 1816,4,6 d 1852,9,30 bur Caesars Creek; m in Caesars Creek MH, Ruth OREN, dt Joseph & Sarah, form of Randolph Co., Ind., b 1815,11,4
Ch: Joseph b 1843, 8, 6
William " 1844, 9, 11 d 1857, 10, 1 bur Caesars Creek
Mary Ann b 1847, 9, 14
1843, 9, 28. Charity m John REAGAN
1846, 7, 13. Dinah m James STANTON
1847, 9, 2. Patty m Joseph FURNAS
1855, 8, 30. Sarah W. m Henry F. MILLS
1857, 7, 30. Joseph C., s James & Patty, Clinton Co., O.; m in Caesars Creek MH, Rebecca MOON, dt William & Hannah, Clinton Co., O.
1857, 10, 1. Martha m Samuel S. JAY
1857, 12, 31. Phamy m David JAY
1863, 9, 3. James, s Amos & Massey, Clinton Co., O., b 1841,1,7 d 1898,1,18 bur Caesars Creek; m in Caesars Creek MH, Mary MILLS Jr., dt Jonathan & Charity, Warren Co., O., b 1839,9,3 d 1877,3,13 bur Caesars Creek
Ch: William A.b 1864, 6, 24 d 1866, 7, 6 bur Caesars Creek
Carrie C. b 1866, 7, 18
Morris J. " 1868, 11, 21 " 1872, 7,20 bur Caesars Creek
Levi M. b 1874, 11, 17
1867, 4, 4. Ruth m Seth COMPTON
----, --, --. Joseph b 1843,8,6; m Martha Ann ----- b 1849,8,26
----, --, --. John b 1844,12,9; m Deborah T. ----- b 1849,1,3
Ch: Milton T. b 1871, 9, 7
----, --, --. Jesse b 1846,3,21; m Nancy C. ----- b 1853,8,23
Ch: Isabella M. b 1881, 5, 16
Bernice E. " 1890, 5, 5
----, --, --. Benjamin b 1848,12,23 d 1921,2,6 bur Corwin; m Viola K. ----- b 1857,7,30
Ch: Mary S. b 1881, 5, 2
Helen Esther " 1897, 11, 26
----, --, --. Harvey b 1860,8,1; m Naomi ----- b 1860,8,3
Ch: Paul b 1886, 10, 31
Mary

1812, 4, 25. James rst; dis by Cain Creek MM, S. C. which was laid down at this time
1817, 9, 26. Jehu con mcd
1817, 9, 26. Susanna (form Brock) con mcd
1818, 1, 30. Jonathan con mcd
1821, 8, 24. John gct Miami MM, O., to m Margery Horner
1821, 12, 28. Margery rocf Miami MM, O., dtd 1821,11,28
1822, 9, 26. Jesse gct White Water MM, Ind.
1822, 11, 28. Sarah & s, Isaac, recrq
1823, 7, 31. Jonathan & w, Sarah, & s, Isaac, gct West Union MM, Ind.; returned & sent to Milford MM, Ind.
1823, 9, 25. John & w, Margery, & ch, Ann & Hannah, gct White Lick MM, Ind.
1823, 11, 27. Jonathan & fam gct Milford MM, Ind.
1824, 9, 30. Isaac & w, Martha, & ch, Mary, William, Rebecca, Ann & Sarah, gct White Lick MM, Ind.
1826, 12, 28. Martha Mills (form Hawkins) dis mcd
1831, 12, 28. Thomas rocf New Garden MM, Ind., dtd 1831,12,17
1832, 4, 26. Ruth Compton (form Hawkins) dis mcd
1832, 9, 27. Ann rocf Fairfield MM, Ind., dtd 1832,9,13
1833, 1, 24. Thomas gct New Garden MM, Ind.
1833, 7, 25. Hannah roof Fairfield MM, Ind., dtd 1833,3,14
1834, 8, 28. Margery gct Fairfield MM, Ind.
1835, 8, 27. Ann gct Fairfield MM, Ind.
1838, 1, 25. John dis
1838, 1, 25. Edith dis
1838, 5, 24. Thomas & w, Mary, & ch, Jesse F. & Nathan, rocf Center MM, O., dtd 1838,3,14
1839, 2, 21. Thomas & w, Mary, & ch, Jesse, Nathan & Martha, gct Westfield MM, Ind.
1845, 5, 22. Edith rocf Springfield MM, dtd

HAWKINS, continued
1845,2,11
1845, 7, 24. Jehu gct Fairfield MM, Ind., to m Jane Mills
1846, 1, 22. Jane & dt, Mary Mills, rocf Fairfield MM, Ind., dtd 1845,11,1
1849, 9, 27. Jehu & w, Jane, & ch, Eli & James gct Fairfield MM, Ind.
1849, 12, 27. Isaac & w, Ann, & ch, Mary Susannah & Elijah, gct Fairfield MM, Ind.
1850, 6, 27. Mary Phamy (form Hawkins) con mcd
1850, 7, 25. Henry dis mcd to first cousin
1850, 8, 22. Lydia (form Cook) dis mcd to first cousin
1851, 1, 23. Noah dis mcd
1851, 2, 20. Sarah (form Cook) dis mcd
1853, 2, 24. Chas. dis mcd
1855, 7, 26. Mark dis mcd
1857, 10, 23. Elijah dis disunity
1857, 10, 23. Jehu dis disunity
1860, 8, 23. Joseph C. & w, Phebe, & ch, Mary Elizabeth & Amos James, gct Henkles Creek MM, Ind.
1866, 5, 26. Mary Ann Oren (form Hawkins) con mcd to her first cousin
1869, 3, 25. John con mcd
1869, 5, 27. Deborah T. rocf Center MM, O., dtd 1869,5,12
1870, 4, 21. Henry & Lydia, & F. Luisey, recrq
1871, 4, 27. Joseph con mcd
1872, 4, 25. John & w, Deborah T., & s, Milton T., gct Center MM, O.
1875, 5, 27. John rocf Center MM, O.
1880, 2, 26. Viola J. recrq
1881, 2, 24. Anna recrq
1881, 2, 24. Harvey recrq
1881, 3, 24. Nancy C. recrq
1881, 4, 21. John gct Center MM, O.
1897, 10, 28. Anna relrq
1899, 10, 26. Levi gct Wilmington MM, O.
1903, 3, 26. Anna recrq
1905, 4, 27. Benjamin & w, Viola K., & dt, Helen Esther, gct Miami MM, O.
1916, 6, 22. Harvey & w, Naomi, rocf Xenia MM, O.
1919, 9, 28. Harvey & w, Naomi, gct Xenia MM, O.

HAYDOCK
----, --, --. Trevor C. b 1874,9,27; m Isabella M. HAWKINS b 1881,5,6
Ch: Jesse
Eleanor b 1900, 5, 18

HAYWORTH
1860, 10, 4. Micajah H., s Elijah & Elizabeth, Clinton Co., O.; m in Caesars Creek MH, Phebe Ann COMPTON, dt Eli & Eunice, Clinton Co., O.
1867, 11, 4. Phebe Ann [Haworth] m Henry F. MILLS
1861, 4, 25. Phebe Ann [Haworth] gct Dover MM O.
1865, 5, 25. Hannah (form Compton) con mcd
1865, 8, 24. Hannah [Haworth] gct Dover MM,O.
1867, 5, 23. Phebe Ann rocf Dover MM
1900, 9, 27. Pearl McKibben [Haworth] gct Dover MM

HEATON
1908, 10, 22. Nellie S. recrq
1908, 10, 22. Ralph recrq
1908, 12, 24. Mary recrq

HEFNER
1868, 8, 27. Phebe (form Mills) con mcd

HELLER
1908, 1, 23. Dudley rocf Fairfield MM, O.
1908, 2, 20. Ina Frye recrq

HENDERSHOTT
1900, 3, 22. Lena recrq
1904, 4, 21. Lena dropped from mbrp

HENDERSON
----, --, --. ----- m Mourning ----- b 1814,6,24
Ch: James
Westley b 1864, 9, 13 (?)
Sarah
Frances " 1849, 2, 22

1854, 3, 23. Mourning & ch, James Wesley & Sarah Frances, rocf Center MM, O., dtd 1853,12,14
1856, 7, 24. Mourning & ch, James Wesley & Sarah Frances, gct Mill Creek MM, Ind.

HERMAN
1925, 7, 23. Lenna relrq

HESS
1913, 6, 26. Cert for Emma granted to Dayton MM, O., returned at her rq 1913,8,28
1922, 4, 27. Emma Moon relrq

HESTON
1813, 5, 29. Phineas & w, Sarah, & ch, Mary, Massey, Phebe, David, Mahlon, Margery, Elizabeth & Rebecca, recrq
1819, 7, 30. William rocf Miami MM, O., dtd 1819,5,26
1819, 11, 26. Ann rocf Miami MM, O., dtd 1819,9,26
1821, 6, 29. Phebe Melton (form Heston) con mcd
1821, 7, 27. Massa Clevenger (form Heston) con mcd
1822, 4, 26. Ann, w Amos, gct White Water MM, Ind.
1823, 5, 29. Mary Moody (form Heston) con mcd
1824, 8, 26. Phineas & fam gct Cherry Grove

HESTON, continued
MM, Ind.
1854, 10, 21. Elizabeth (form Canby) con mcd
1855, 10, 25. Elizabeth C. gct Elba MM, N. Y.

HIATT
1817, 9, 4. Rosannah [Hiett] m Jesse STOUT

1813, 9, 25. John [Hiett] & w, Mary, & ch, Gideon, Ruben, Rosemeal, Jesse, Anne, Rachel & Mary, rocf Clear Creek MM, O., dtd 1813,6,26
1818, 1, 30. Reuben [Hiatt] con mcd
1818, 4, 24. Reuben gct Center MM, O.
1818, 5, 29. John & fam gct Center MM, O.
1818, 5, 29. Gideon gct Center MM, O.
1819, 5, 28. Silas & w, Ann, & ch, Jordon, Armelia, Asenath, Irrena, Henry & Benajah, rocf Miami MM, O., dtd 1819,4,28
1819, 5, 28. Jesse rocf Derby Creek MM, O., dtd 1819,1,6 endorsed by Miami MM, O., 1819,3,31
1821, 3, 30. Silas & fam gct West Grove MM, Ind.
1822, 7, 26. Jesse gct West Grove MM, Ind.
1880, 3, 25. Flora [Hiett] recrq
1884, 3, 27. Frank [Hiet] recrq
1891, 7, 23. Frank relrq

HITCHCOCK
1884, 3, 27. Elietas [Hichcock] recrq
1897, 7, 22. Elistus dropped from mbrp

HICKMAN
----, --, --. ----- m Susan R. ----- b 1840,2, 14
Ch: Cora b 1877, 4, 20
Mary Ellen " 1879, 3, 16
Harry C. " 1884, 2, 5

1893, 4, 27. Susan R., Nina L., Cora M., Mary Ellen, Harry & David, recrq
1907, 4, 25. Ella, Cora, Mina recrq

HILL
----, --, --. John M. b 1852,9,11; m Mary A. ----- b 1855,8,12
1861, 11, 29. Martha E. b
----, --, --. Joseph H. b 1855,9,4 d 1896,4,20 m Lydia J. ----- b 1858,11,28
Ch: Jesse E. b 1887, 4, 8
----, --, --. Jesse E. b 1887,4,8; m Leola K. ----- b 1886,8,3
Ch: Marjorie Jane b 1919,1,26

1873, 5, 22. John M. & Joseph H., ch Elijah, rocf White Water MM, Ind., dtd 1873,4,23
1877, 4, 26. Enos W. & Martha E., ch Elijah & Rebecca, rocf Sugar River MM, Ind.
1883, 5, 24. John & w, Mary Ann, gct White Water MM, Ind.
1884, 5, 22. Martha E. gct White Water MM, Ind.
1884, 4, 24. Enos W. gct White Water MM, Ind.
1884, 4, 24. Martha E. gct White Water MM, Ind.
1887, 4, 21. Martha E. rocf White Water MM, Ind.
1887, 11, 24. Madora gct White Water MM, Ind.
1889, 6, 27. John M. & w, Mary A., rocf White Water MM, Ind.
1891, 2, 19. Enos & w, Dora, & ch, Ralph J., rocf White Water MM, Ind.
1900, 4, 26. Enos W. & w, Dora, & ch, Ralph J., gct Miami MM, O.
1918, 2, 21. Leona King rocf Fairmount MM, Ind.

HILLIARD
1925, 7, 23. Viola relrq

HIRE
1887, 3, 24. Flora A. rocf Van Wert MM, O.
1891, 7, 23. Hattie E. gct Van Wert MM, O.

HOCKETT
1811, 5, 2. Moses, s Anthony & Mary, Clinton Co., O.; m in Caesars Creek, Olive COOK, dt Isaac & Sarah

1812, 7, 25. Olive gct Center MM
1837, 5, 25. Mary [Hocket] rocf Fairfield MM, dtd 1837,3,23
1838, 11, 22. Ruth [Hocket] rocf Newberry MM, O., dtd 1838,10,22
1840, 2, 20. Mary Compton (form Hocket) con mcd

HODSON
1814, 3, 26. George rocf Center MM, N. C., dtd 1813,5,15, endorsed by Center MM, O., 1814,2,5
1814, 9, 23. John & w, Sarah, & ch, Delila, Rhoda & Nathan, rocf Clear Creek MM, O., dtd 1814,5,27
1814, 11, 25. Solomon & w, Elizabeth, & ch, Thomas, John, Jemima & Naomi, rocf Center MM, O., dtd 1814,7,2
1816, 2, 23. Solomon [Hodgson] & fam gct Fairfield MM, O.
1816, 2, 23. John [Hodgson] & fam gct Fairfield MM, O.

HOLLAND
----, --, --. John b 1847,3,20; m Mary E. ----- b 1854, 5, 16
Ch: Samuel b 1872, 8, 22
Willie " 1877, 11, 16
1882, 8, 14. Nellie b
----, --, --. Milton b 1861,3,12; m Lenora ----- b 1870,9,28
Ch: Raymond C. b 1888, 10, 19
Ethel R. " 1892, 6, 23
Ermel E. " 1895, 1, 6

HOLLAND, continued
1900, 6, 10. Mary C. b

1876, 3, 23. Joshua & w, Sarah Jane, recrq
1879, 4, 24. Joshua recrq
1880, 3, 25. John & w, Mattie, recrq
1880, 3, 25. Elgin recrq
1881, 4, 21. Charles recrq
1881, 9, 22. Joshua dis disunity
1884, 3, 27. Milton & Theodore, recrq
1885, 4, 23. Charity recrq
1886, 5, 27. Elgin dis disunity
1894, 2, 22. Charles relrq
1896, 4, 23. Rolena Compton relrq
1896, 8, 27. Theodore relrq
1898, 6, 23. Myrtle relrq
1900, 7, 24. Anna dropped from mbrp
1903, 4, 23. Hallie May recrq
1903, 9, 24. Myrtle recrq
1904, 4, 21. Raymond C. & Harry C. dropped from mbrp
1906, 1, 25. Lewis Smith recrq
1906, 1, 25. Rollena recrq
1906, 1, 25. Kent C. recrq
1906, 1, 25. Pharcs C. recrq
1906, 1, 25. Earl L. recrq
1911, 9, 21. Samuel dropped from mbrp
1913, 4, 24. Nora & dt, Ethel, relrq
1913, 6, 26. Mary Catherine gct Dayton MM, O.
1913, 6, 26. Wm. dropped from mbrp
1914, 1, 22. Clarence Leon recrq
1914, 6, 25. Mary Catherine dropped from mbrp

HOLLY
----, --, --. George W. b 1864,4,21; m Elizabeth A. ----- b 1869,3,12
Ch: Warren
Lester b 1888, 8, 20
Edith May " 1890, 3, 18
Mary Ellen " 1892, 11, 19

1887, 12, 22. George [Holley] recrq

HOLLINGSWORTH
1890, 1, 10. Lula, dt Simon & Emma (Beal), b

1847, 3, 25. Robert Furnas Jr. gct Miami MM, O., to m Anna Hollingsworth
1889, 11, 21. Eliza & dt, Roda, rocf Newberry MM, O.
1892, 7, 28. Rhoda Ann relrq
1894, 9, 27. Nathan relrq
1896, 10, 22. Nathan recrq
1898, 4, 21. Nathan & Eliza gct Fairmount MM, Ind.
1899, 9, 21. Susanna recrq
1904, 1, 28. Lula recrq
1926, 11, 28. Lulu dropped from mbrp

HOMER
1925, 7, 23. Walker & Elizabeth relrq

HONLACHER
1917, 4, 26. Florence Haycock relrq

HORNE
1818, 9, 25. William Sr. recrq

HORNER
1822, 9, 5. Jacob, s Thomas & Ann, Green Co., O.; m in Caesars Creek MH, Lydia McDONALD, dt William & Jemima, Clinton Co., O.
1823, 4, 3. William, s Jacob & Frances, Green Co., O.; m in Caesars Creek MH, Sally COMPTON, dt Stephen & Dinah, Green Co., O.

1821, 8, 24. John Hawkins gct Miami MM, O., to m Margery Horner
1822, 10, 31. Lydia gct Miami MM, O.
1823, 6, 26. Sally gct Miami MM, O.
1828, 1, 31. Lydia & ch, David & Fanny, rocf Springborough MM, dtd 1827,12,25
1829, 3, 26. Elizabeth rocf Springborough MM, dtd 1829,2,29
1834, 8, 24. Elizabeth gct Fairfield MM, Ind.
1835, 2, 19. Lydia dis disunity
1836, 11, 24. David, Frances & Jacob, ch Lydia, gct Fairfield MM, Ind.
1859, 7, 25. Lydia rst at Fairfield MM, Ind. on consent of this mtg
1886, 3, 25. Lillie, Charles & Stella recrq
1907, 1, 24. Walker recrq
1907, 3, 28. Jennie recrq
1907, 3, 28. Milo recrq

HORNIDAY
1871, 4, 27. Mary & s, Lemuel, rocf Elk MM, O., endorsed by Walnut Ridge MM, Ind., 1871,4,15
1873, 5, 22. Isaiah & w, Mary Jane, rocf Springfield MM, O., dtd 1873,4,19
1876, 6, 22. Isaiah & w, Mary Jane, & ch, Ezekiel, John W. & George Halita, gct Springfield MM, O.
1878, 9, 26. Mary & s, Lemuel, gct Fairfield MM, O.

HOSIER
1910, 2, 24. Emily recrq
1913, 5, 22. George dropped from mbrp
1914, 3, 26. George & w, Mary, & ch, Francis & Harry, recrq
1925, 7, 23. George, Mary, Francis & Harry relrq

HOUSEFELT
1844, 7, 3. Harman A. b

1870, 4, 21. Harmon recrq
1879, 1, 23. Harmon [Horisfelt] gct Center MM, O.

HOUSTON
1880, 3, 25. Mathew recrq

HOWE
1881, 2, 24. Elijah recrq
1915, 1, 28. Fannie recrq
1915, 1, 28. Ed recrq
1916, 10, 26. Jesse Bell, Reva & Lucy Leona recrq
1917, 7, 26. Alta Wright rocf Xenia MM, O.
1923, 4, 29. Edward & Alta dropped from mbrp
1926, 11, 28. Lucy Leone dropped from mbrp

HOWLAND
1873, 8, 28. Louisa rocf Dover MM
1892, 5, 26. George B. & w, Euphamia, & ch, Oren Clark, Laura & Benjamin, rocf Miami MM, O.
1894, 8, 23. Geo. & w, Fannie, & ch, Owen & Bennie relrq

HUBBARD
1907, 9, 26. James rocf Dover MM, O.

HUDGEL
1851, 10, 21. Almira b
1887, 3, 2. Cora Bell b

1897, 9, 23. Elmina recrq
1898, 4, 21. Cora A. recrq
1917, 7, 26. Almira [Hudgell] dropped from mbrp

HUFFMAN
1885, 4, 23. Emma R., Renna A. & Lucy M. recrq
1887, 12, 22. Clara B. recrq
1903, 12, 24. Levina gct Long Beech MM, Calif.
1906, 5, 24. Emma Hendershot rocf Center MM, O.
1907, 3, 28. Nancy rocf Center MM, O.
1909, 5, 27. Nancy gct Center MM, O.

HULTZ
----, --, --. Joseph b 1855,9,14; m Catherine ----- b 1860,2,28
Ch: Walter b 1884, 5, 9
Ethel S. " 1885, 8, 26
Wm. P. " 1889, 3, 3

1881, 2, 24. Sarah [Hults] recrq
1887, 1, 27. Joseph recrq
1887, 1, 27. Catherine L. recrq
1887, 2, 24. Walter, s Joseph, recrq

HUMSTON
1906, 12, 27. Mattie J. & ch, Hartzell W. & Ruth Gertrude, recrq

HUNT
1886, 12, 21. Maggie M. b

1818, 10, 30. Rebecca rocf Stroudsburgh MM, Pa., dtd 1818,5,21, endorsed by Marlborough MM, O., dtd 1818,6,17
1874, 1, 22. Mary A. recrq
1914, 12, 24. Mildred Marie & Helen Pauline, ch Maggie, recrq

HURLEY
----, --, --. Henry b 1819,10,28; m Sarah ----- b 1824,1,16
Ch: Francis W. b 1847, 9, 12
----, --, --. George S. b 1856,9,3; m Laura E. ----- b 1858,10,3
Ch: James C. b 1884, 8, 30
George " 1887, 11, 6
1886, 7, 1. Russell b
1889, 12, 24. Edgar b
1891, 5, 6. Glenna S. b

1871, 1, 26. Sarah recrq
1871, 4, 27. Francis recrq
1874, 1, 22. Benjamin recrq
1879, 4, 24. Charles & George recrq
1879, 4, 24. Henry M. & w, Lauretta, recrq
1879, 4, 24. Maggie D. recrq
1881, 2, 24. Wm. H. recrq
1881, 2, 24. Mamie recrq
1881, 9, 22. Francis dis disunity
1883, 3, 22. Arthur, Carrie & Mary recrq
1883, 3, 22. William recrq
1891, 10, 22. Chas. A. relrq
1897, 10, 28. Hortense relrq
1905, 2, 3. Edgar & Russell recrq
1908, 11, 26. Arthur W. & w, Hortense, & ch, Rosa A., Mary L. & Cory W., recrq
1911, 7, 27. Russell dropped from mbrp
1914, 3, 26. Raymond & w, Viola, & ch, Kenneth J., Pauline Florence, Cleo May, Donald Herbert, Ruth Elma & Evelyn Edith, recrq
1917, 4, 26. Raymond & w, Viola, & ch gct Ogden MM
1917, 7, 26. Edgar gct Wilmington MM, O.
1923, 4, 29. Russel dropped from mbrp

HUSSEY
1826, 6, 1. William, s Christopher & Jane, Highland Co., O.; m in Caesars Creek MH, Jane EDWARDS, dt Wm. & Jemima, Clinton Co. O.

1826, 9, 28. Jane Edwards gct Clear Creek MM, O.
1829, 2, 26. Hepsibath (form Edwards) con mcd
1829, 9, 24. Hepsabah gct Clear Creek MM,O.

ICENHOWER
----, --, --. Wm. M. b 1820,7,16 bur Jenkins Bur. Gr.; m Rachel ----- b 1820,6,11
Ch: Nancy J. b 1848, 3, 23
Marion " 1851, 7, 12
----, --, --. Marion b 1851,7,12 d 1921,9,28 bur Spring Valley; m Laura ----- b 1854,5,

ICENHOWER, Marion & Laura, continued
2
Ch: William H. b 1875, 11, 28
Minnie F. " 1877, 9, 28
Charles A. " 1885, 1, 15

1879, 4, 24. William & w, Rachel, recrq
1879, 4, 24. Marion & w, Laura, & ch, Wm. Henry & Minnie Florence, recrq
1879, 4, 24. Nancy J. recrq
1909, 3, 25. Lenna V. recrq
1913, 5, 22. Charles [Icehower] dropped from mbrp
1925, 7, 23. John Albert, Mary, Luella & Wm. Jr. relrq

INMAN
1812, 9, 26. Amelia gct West Branch MM, O.

IRONS
1906, 5, 24. Lena recrq
1908, 7, 23. Lena gct Miami MM, O.
1916, 6, 22. Lena & Ross rocf Miami MM, O.

JACKSON
----, --, --. Uriah S. b 1833,2,15 d 1899,6,20 bur Spring Valley; m Ann M. ----- b 1839,10,16
Ch: Amos B. b 1859, 8, 10
Martha R. " 1861, 4, 12
Annie E. " 1862, 12, 25
William F. " 1866, 2, 2
Massey L. " 1868, 11, 6

1870, 4, 21. Uriah S. recrq
1870, 10, 27. Ann & ch recrq
1891, 10, 22. Abbie Jane, Wm. & Amos relrq
1905, 7, 27. David & Mary, Hansford, Pearl & May recrq

JASPER
1874, 1, 22. Richard S. recrq
1881, 9, 22. Richard dis disunity

JAY
1821, 5, 21. Layton, s James & Jemima, Clinton Co., O., d 1860,8,3; m in Caesars Creek MH, Keturah BROCK, dt George & Charity, Clinton Co., O.
1821, 11, 1. Rhoda m Enoch NICHOLS
1823, 4, 3. John, s Layton & Elizabeth, Warren Co., O., b 1798,4,29 d 1881,1,27 bur Caesars Creek; m in Caesars Creek MH, Lydia COMPTON, dt Amos & Rebecca, Green Co., O., b 1803,1,20
Ch: Rebecca b 1824, 1, 2 d 1855,12, 3 bur Caesars Creek
Elizabeth b 1825, 10, 7
Amos " 1827, 9, 13
Layton " 1829, 4, 29 d 1860, 8, 3 bur Caesars Creek
Mary b 1830, 12, 31
Samuel
Ch: Spray b 1833, 3, 23
Elijah " 1835, 6, 29

Sarah " 1837, 4, 16
Lydia Ann " 1839, 6, 30
James " 1841, 10, 11
David " 1844, 3, 18
Martha " 1847, 3, 20

1825, 6, 9. David, s Layton & Elizabeth, Warren Co., O., b 1804,9,14; m in Caesars Creek MH, Rebeckah HAWKINS, dt Amos & Ann, Warren Co., O., d 1854,10,19
Ch: Amos b 1826, 4, 1 d 1854,10,19 bur Caesars Creek
Ruth b 1827, 10, 23
Ann " 1829, 7, 9
Elijah " 1831, 11, 11 d 1834, 2, 9
Henry " 1834, 3, 8 " 1855, 6,12 bur Caesars Creek
David m 2nd 1857,12,31, Phamy HAWKINS, dt Thomas & Ann MORGAN, Green Co., O., b 1810,1,20 d 1890,8,6 bur Martinsville
1834, 2, 9. Elizabeth d
1844, 10, 31. Elizabeth m Christopher SPRAY
1849, 9, 6. Mary m Jesse MILLS
1850, 4, 4. Ann m Benjamin FARQUHAR
1851, 5, 1. Amos, s John & Lydia, Clinton Co., O., b 1827,9,13; m in Caesars Creek MH, Deborah COMPTON, dt Eli & Eunice, Warren Co., O.
Ch: Eli b 1853, 12, 10
Mary Ann " 1856, 9, 21
1857, 10, 1. Samuel, s John & Lydia, b 1833, 3,23; m in Caesars Creek MH, Martha HAWKINS, dt Benjamin & Phamy, Green Co., O., b 1840,7,28
Ch: Benjamin D. b 1860, 4, 26
Arabel C. " 1865, 5, 27
Allen E. " 1869, 12, 24
Wilson T. " 1873, 6, 10
----, --, --. Elijah b 1835,6,29; m Adaline -----
Ch: Elma b 1863, 9, 8
Emma " 1864, 11, 21
1863, 1, 29. Lydia Ann m John COOK
1864, 12, 8. Martha m Samuel W. COOK
1868, 12, 31. Ruth m William MORGAN
----, --, --. James b 1841,10,11; m Eliza ---- b 1845,5,7
Ch: Eva C. b 1871, 2, 20
D. Russell " 1883, 3, 25
1871, 5, 4. Sarah T. m John COOK
----, --, --. David H. b 1844,8,18; m Hattie E. ----- b 1849,4,24
Ch: Josie E. b 1875, 3, 15
Adena S. " 1877, 5, 8
----, --, --. Samuel Gordon b 1851,5,22; m Martha S. ----- b 1853,7,29

1813, 9, 25. Elizabeth & ch, Patience, Char-

JAY, continued
lotte, William, John, James, Abigail, Mary, Elijah & Ann, rocf Union MM, dtd 1813,7,3
1816, 7, 25. Elizabeth & ch gct Union MM
1820, 2, 25. James & w, Jemima, & ch, Rhoda, Layton James Ed Dempsey Isaac Sarah & Anna, rocf Bush River MM, S. C., dtd 1819, 4,3 endorsed by West Branch MM, O., 1819, 12,18
1821, 2, 23. David gct New Garden MM, Ind.
1822, 7, 26. James & fam gct Cherry Grove MM, Ind.
1823, 1, 30. Lucinda (form Brock) con mcd
1823, 3, 27. Layton & w, Keturah, & s, Jehu, gct Cherry Grove MM, Ind.
1824, 1, 29. James rocf Union MM, dtd 1824, 1,3
1825, 4, 28. David rocf New Garden MM, Ind., dtd 1825,3,19
1835, 10, 22. James & w, Lucinda, & ch, Susanna, Mary, Keturah & Layton, gct Fairfield MM, Ind.
1862, 11, 27. Elijah con mcd
1863, 3, 26. Adaline recrq
1864, 11, 24. Amos & w, Deborah, & ch, Eli & Mary Ann, gct Greenwood MM, Ind.
1866, 5, 24. Elijah & w, Adaline, & ch, Elma & Emma, gct Greenwood MM, Ind.
1868, 10, 22. James C. con mcd
1869, 1, 28. Elisa rocf Back Creek MM, dtd 1868,12,17
1871, 12, 28. John & w, Lydia, gct Spicewood MM, Ind.
1872, 12, 26. Hattie E. rocf Newberry MM, O., dtd 1872,10,21
1873, 10, 23. Samuel Gordon recrq
1873, 10, 23. Martha Elizabeth recrq
1878, 2, 21. David H. & w, Hattie E., & dt, Josie E., gct Newberry MM, O.
1879, 4, 24. Madison recrq
1880, 5, 27. John & w, Lydia, rocf Spicewood MM, Ind.
1884, 9, 25. Madison dis
1885, 4, 23. Phama gct Newberry MM, O.
1886, 2, 25. Samuel S. & w, Martha, & ch, Allen E., Wilson T. & Arrena M., gct Newberry MM, O.
1887, 4, 21. James & w, Eliza, & ch, Eva C. & D. Russell, gct Newberry MM, O.
1887, 4, 21. Martha gct Miami MM, O.
1914, 12, 24. Gordon relrq
1922, 9, 2. Bevan m Frances E. WILSON

1843, 6, 22. Dinah (form Reagan) dis mcd
1847, 6, 24. Dinah rst rq
1870, 4, 21. Wm. A. & Ruth recrq
1879, 4, 24. Elen recrq
1889, 2, 21. Margaret recrq
1917, 4, 26. James recrq
1924, 2, 27. Frances E. gct Kokomo MM, Ind.
1925, 7, 23. James relrq

JEFFERS
1905, 4, 27. Ella recrq
1925, 7, 23. Ella R. relrq
1931, 4, 26. Velma Bennett [Jeffrey] relrq

JENKINS
1830, 3, 14. Ruth b
1850, 11, 27. Dinah m Isaac M. JOHNSON
1860, 12, 13. William A. b
1875, 8, 29. Lida b (dt Neri & Mary A. Moon)

JENNINGS
1909, 1, 28. Allie M. & Lucia recrq

JENSON
----, --, --. Loren b 1838,4,7; m Anna ----- b 1852,3,15
Ch: Jesse b 1870, 9, 23

1884, 3, 27. Jesse recrq
1888, 4, 26. Loren & Anna recrq
1898, 5, 26. Annie & s, Jesse, relrq
1911, 9, 21. Jesse dropped from mbrp

JESSOP
1821, 11, 8. Jonathan, s Thomas & Ann, Warren Co., O.; m in Caesars Creek MH, Patience MILLS, dt William & Lydia, Warren Co., O.
1837, 6, 23. Patience m Aaron LEWIS
1841, 9, 9. Charles, s Jonathan & Patience, Warren Co., O.; m in Caesars Creek MH, Hannah THORN, dt Thomas & Ann, Wabash Co., Ind.
1844, 10, 24. Thomas d bur Caesars Creek
1845, 4, 3. William, s Jonathan & Patience, Warren Co., O.; m in Caesars Creek MH, Dinah SPRAY, dt James & Charity, Warren Co., O.
Ch: Jonathan Y. b 1846, 7, 25
Samuel " 1849, 12, 15
Laura Jane " 1853, 11, 15
Horace " 1858, 9, 15 d 1860, 9, 6 bur Caesars Creek
1850, 10, 10. Daniel, s Jonathan & Patience, Warren Co., O., b 1825,12,12; m in Caesars Creek MH, Hannah Sophia YOUNG, dt James & Mary, Warren Co., O., b 1825,11,12
Ch: Amos b 1852, 7, 12
1823, 9, 25. Jonathan rocf Miami MM, O., dtd 1823,7,30
1846, 2, 19. Charles & w, Hannah, & dt, Charity, gct Fairfield MM, Ind.
1849, 7, 26. Wm. dis disunity
1853, 5, 26. Daniel & w, Hannah Sophia, & s, Amos C., gct Miami MM, O.
1860, 8, 23. Dinah dis disunity
1870, 4, 21. Jesse W. recrq
1872, 2, 22. Samuel S. gct Bridgeport MM, Ind.
1872, 5, 23. Jonathan J. gct Bridgeport MM, Ind.
1874, 3, 26. Martha E. gct Bridgeport MM, Ind.
1875, 2, 25. Jesse W. relrq

JESSUP, continued
1881, 6, 23. Samuel & w, Ellen, & ch, Jessie C. & Mary D., rocf Stillwater MM, Ind., dtd 1881,5,12
1891, 7, 23. Samuel & w, Ellen, & ch, Jesse C., Mary D. & Edith P., gct Bridgeport MM, Ind.

JOBE
1847, 4, 27. Mary J. E. b
1865, 11, 7. Hannah b

1861, 6, 27. Lydia [Job] (form Colter) con mcd
1872, 7, 25. Mary E. (form Coulter) con mcd

JOHNSON
1849, 2, 2. Almeda b
1850, 11, 27. Isaac M., s Anthony & Mary, Highland Co., O.; m in Richland MH, Dinah JENKINS, dt Reason & Mary REAGAN, Green Co., O.
----, --, --. Chillis T. b 1852,8,9; m Alice S. ----- b 1857,8,1
Ch: Rosa
Eunice b 1887, 6, 12
1885, 7, 20. Almeda m Marion WILDMAN
1885, 12, 29. William W., s Jesse S. & Amy, Green Co., O.; m in Jamestown, O., H. Corrinne FRAME, dt Nathan T. & Esther G., Green Co., O.

1810, 12, 29. Jesse & w, Elizabeth, & ch, Jonathan, Silas, Joshua, Sarah & Eli, rocf Cain Creek MM, N. C., dtd 1810,8,4, endorsed by Miami MM, O., 1810,11,28
1814, 4, 30. Richard Bloxom & gr s, Gideon Johnson, rocf Fairfield MM, O., 1814,1,29
1814, 12, 30. Ruth & dt, Elizabeth, rocf Fairfield MM, dtd 1814,3,26
1815, 8, 25. Jephtha rocf Fairfield MM, O., dtd 1814,12,31
1817, 11, 28. Jesse & fam gct New Garden MM, Ind.
1821, 6, 27. Gideon dis disunity
1849, 8, 23. Moses Walton gct Fairfield MM, O., to m Deborah Johnson
1851, 6, 26. Isaac M. rocf Fairfield MM, O., dtd 1851,5,17
1866, 6, 21. Isaac M. dis
1866, 9, 27. Dinah dis jas
1869, 10, 28. Joseph Anthony & w, Hannah Ellen, & ch, Henrietta A., Martha A., James A., Mary C. & Alice M., rocf Fairfield MM, O.
1872, 9, 26. Joseph Anthony & w, Hannah Ellen, & ch, Henrietta A., James A., Mary E., Alice M. & Hannah M., gct Fairfield MM, O.
1876, 3, 23. Almeda rocf Springfield MM, O.
1887, 2, 24. Chillis T. recrq
1893, 10, 26. Carrie L. gct Center MM, O.
1896, 11, 26. Clara recrq
1909, 5, 27. Lola recrq
1909, 5, 27. Lola recrq
1910, 2, 24. Albert recrq
1910, 3, 24. Ellen [Johnston] recrq

JONES
1881, 5, 14. Addie Minerva b
----, --, --. Richard, s Richard & Hannah, b 1839,9,13; m Mary E. CAREY, dt Elias & Jane, b 1838,9,1
----, --, --. Reuben b 1858,10,4; m Martha R. COMPTON, b 1862,3,26
Ch: Leroy A. b 1888, 12, 19
Herman F. " 1892, 9, 10
Carl G. " 1898, 2, 5

1847, 6, 24. Mary rocf Sugar River MM, Ind., dtd 1847,3,27
1848, 8, 24. Mary dis jas
1871, 3, 23. Samuel N. & w, Jane, & ch, Emaline H. & Martha A., rocf Walnut Ridge MM, Ind., dtd 1871,3,18
1878, 10, 24. Samuel N. & w, Jane, & ch, Mattie, gct Clear Creek MM, O.
1884, 1, 24. Reuben E. rocf Dover MM, O.
1887, 3, 24. George recrq
1887, 4, 21. Mary Potter recrq
1887, 4, 21. Rachel A. gct Miami MM, O.
1889, 6, 27. Samuel recrq
1890, 11, 27. Richard & w, Mary E., & ch rocf Fairview MM
1891, 5, 28. B. F. & w, Rachel, recrq
1898, 4, 21. E. Townsend & w, Rachel, rocf Wilmington MM, O.
1899, 4, 27. Addie Minerva recrq
1900, 7, 24. Addie Minerva dropped from mbrp
1905, 10, 26. Anna recrq
1908, 2, 20. Jennie recrq
1908, 3, 26. Honora & ch, Clinton A., Elmer R., Mary H., Gertrude E. & Cecil G. recrq
1908, 6, 25. Oscar gct Westfork MM, O.
1908, 12, 24. Cora, Albert R., Walter C. & Ethel recrq
1911, 1, 26. Dr. E. T. & w, Rachel K., gct Marlborough MM, N. Y.
1920, 10, 28. Ethel Curry rocf Center MM
1925, 7, 23. A. R. & Elsie relrq

KARNES
1905, 1, 26. Minnie Grace gct Hopewell MM,O.

KELLUM
1820, 1, 28. Samuel & w, Ann, & ch, Bulah & Lindley, rocf Springfield MM, N. C., dtd 1819,10,26, endorsed by Newberry MM, O., 1819,11,25
1820, 8, 25. Samuel & fam gct New Garden MM, Ind.

KELLY
1816, 8, 1. Mary m Thomas BENSON

1822, 9, 26. John dis disunity
1823, 12, 25. Chas. dis disunity

KELLY, continued
1825, 7, 28. Sarah & ch, Isaac, Eunice & Sarah, gct White Lick MM, Ind.
1830, 2, 25. Robert dis jH
1842, 2, 24. Isaac dis mcd
1842, 8, 25. Sarah gct Springfield MM
1842, 3, 24. Sarah Dakin (form Kelly) dis mcd
1842, 5, 26. Eunice Zell (form Kelly) dis mcd

KENWORTHY
----, --, --. John b 1774,3,10; m Rebecca ---- b 1777,2,27
Ch: Olive b 1802, 9, 13
William " 1803, 10, 23
Tamar " 1806, 1, 1 d 1812, 6,12 bur Caesars Creek
John b 1808, 3, 2
Isaac " 1810, 11, 6

1812, 4, 25. David [Kinworthy] & w, Dianah, & ch, Sarah, Mary, Betty, Dinah & David, rocf West Branch MM, dtd 1812,3,26
1813, 1, 30. Ann rocf West Branch MM, O.
1817, 10, 24. David & fam gct New Garden MM, Ind.
1818, 3, 27. Ann gct New Garden MM, Ind.
1819, 5, 28. John & fam gct New Garden MM,Ind.

KENNY
1879, 4, 24. Frank G. recrq

KEPHART
1883, 3, 22. Harry recrq

KERIC
1906, 1, 25. Ada M. Beach gct Miami MM, O.

KESTER
1828, 9, 25. Josiah Albertson & w, Hannah, & her s, Harmon Kester, rocf Springfield MM, dtd 1828,6,28
1837, 2, 23. Edith rocf Newberry MM, O., dtd 1836,10,17
1844, 10, 24. Edith & dt, Hannah, gct Newberry MM, O.

KINCAID
1875, 5, 30. Flora Pier b

1912, 5, 23. Flora Pier gct Dayton MM, O.

KINCK
1925, 7, 23. C. M., Mary E., Lloyd relrq
1925, 7, 23. Elbert & w relrq

KINDLEY
1826, 9, 28. Seth Furnas gct Miami MM, O., to m Dinah Kindley

KING
1889, 6, 27. Martha E. recrq
1889, 11, 21. Martha E. gct Miami MM, O.
1909, 9, 23. Bessie recrq
1911, 6, 22. Anna Anabe dropped from mbrp
1925, 7, 23. Bessie relrq

KIRK
1834, 2, 20. Emily recrq
1838, 3, 22. Emily gct Center MM, O.

KINSEY
1819, 12, 18. Fanney b
----, --, --. ----- m Isabella ----- b 1830, 9,9
Ch: Irene b 1858, 8, 21
Charles " 1870, 11, 16

1848, 5, 28. Fanny H. rocf Center MM, O., dtd 1848,4,12
1857, 11, 26. Fanny gct Pleasant Plain MM,Ia.
1875, 6, 24. Ella recrq
1875, 8, 26. Isabelle Anna recrq
1876, 1, 27. Addie recrq
1876, 1, 27. Christopher recrq
1878, 10, 24. C. B. relrq
1881, 4, 21. Christopher, Charles, Mary & Irene recrq
1882, 6, 22. Ella relrq
1883, 12, 27. Christopher dis disunity
1900, 7, 24. Charles dropped from mbrp

KISER
L874, 11, 6. Elizabeth C. b

1893, 12, 28. Elizabeth C. [Kizer] recrq

KITE
1925, 7, 23. John P. & Daisy relrq

KNEE
----, --, --. William b 1867,4,4; m Lola ----- b 1872,3,24

1881, 4, 21. Annie recrq
1896, 4, 23. Wm. & Lorena recrq
1911, 6, 22. Wm. dropped from mbrp

KNIGHT
1819, 9, 24. Samuel [Night] rocf New Garden MM, N. C., dtd 1817,8,30
1834, 3, 27. Samuel dis holding with the Universalist Doctrine

KUNTZ
1906, 9, 27. John recrq

LACKEY
1879, 4, 24. Lyle G. recrq

LACY
1816, 4, 26. Elizabeth (form Spray) dis mcd
1819, 1, 29. John recrq
1819, 3, 26. John gct New Garden MM, Ind.

LAMB
1780, 8, 20. Martha b

LAMB, continued
1791, 4, 15. Sarah, w Thomas, d
1791, 5, 4. Sarah b

LANCASTER
1821, 4, 27. Hannah (form Wright) con mcd
1825, 9, 25. Hannah gct Springfield MM, O.

LANE
1910, 3, 24. Lillie recrq

LASHLEY
1873, 1, 23. Isadora Belle recrq

LAURENS
1817, 3, 28. Milly [Lawrence] (form Vickers) dis mcd
1901, 7, 25. Josephine & James [Lawrens] rocf Selma MM, O.
1911, 9, 21. James & Josephine dropped from mbrp
1929, 1, 29. James relrq

LEACH
1881, 2, 24. Emma recrq

LEAMING
----, --, --. Ralph & Sarah
Ch: Edna b 1910, 3, 14
Helen " 1920, 3, 12
Margaret " 1921, 10, 25

1929, 3, 31. Edna recrq
1933, 3, 26. Helen recrq
1933, 4, 30. Margaret recrq

LEARNING
1904, 7, 28. Joseph S. & w, Mary, & ch, Ralph P., recrq
1905, 6, 22. Joseph S. & w, Mary, dropped from mbrp
1905, 12, 28. Ralph S. relrq

LEMAR
1872, 4, 26. Samuel Kenton b
1878, 11, 21. Raymond R. b

1879, 4, 24. John A. & w, Elizabeth, & ch, Ettie F., Mary E. & Alvie E., recrq
1883, 3, 22. Mary recrq
1887, 4, 21. John S. dis disunity
1892, 4, 21. Rolla recrq
1906, 9, 27. Samuel Kenton recrq
1913, 5, 22. Raymond R. dropped from mbrp
1923, 4, 29. Kenton dropped from mbrp

LEONARD
1894, 10, 25. Nancy A. C. gct Center MM, O.

LESH
1908, 3, 26. Dora recrq

LEVERTON
1906, 9, 27. James & w, Anna, recrq

LEWIS
1813, 9, 30. Charity m Isaac COOK
1822, 2, 23. Isaac, s Thomas & Rachel, Union Co., Ind.; m in Caesars Creek MH, Judith CADWALADER, dt Moses & Mary, Clinton Co., O.
1837, 6, 23. Aaron, s Evan & Sarah, Clinton Co., O.; m in Caesars Creek MH, Patience JESSOP, dt William & Lydia MILLS, Warren Co., O.

1814, 8, 27. Thomas & fam gct White Water MM, Ind.
1820, 8, 25. Hannah & ch, Thomas, Wm., Elizabeth, James, Preston, Appleberry & Cynthia rocf Silver Creek MM, Ind., dtd 1820,4,8
1822, 4, 26. Judith gct Silver Creek MM,Ind.
1822, 9, 26. Hannah & ch, William, Elizabeth, James, Preston Appleberry & Cynthia gct Short Creek MM, Ind.
1823, 4, 24. Thomas, s Wm., dis mcd
1823, 5, 29. Thomas, s Caleb, dis mcd
1824, 1, 29. Daniel rocf Miami MM, O., dtd 1824,1,26
1825, 4, 28. Thomas rst at Short Creek MM, Ind., on consent of this mtg
1825, 6, 30. Daniel gct Clear Creek MM, O.
1825, 7, 28. Caleb & w, Susanna, & ch, Isaac, Elizabeth, Charity, John, William, Eli, Zimri & Martha, gct Green Plain MM, O.
1833, 1, 24. Jesse & w, Hannah, & ch, Sarah & Caleb H., rocf Springfield MM, dtd 1832,10,13
1833, 5, 23. Abner & w, Rebecca, & ch, Ruth, Rhodema, Ruhamy & Alistus, rocf New Garden MM, Ind., dtd 1833,3,16
1835, 8, 27. Thomas rst at Sugar River MM, Ind., on consent of this mtg
1836, 5, 26. Jesse & w, Hannah, & ch, Sarah, Caleb H., Nancy & Elizabeth, gct Miami MM, O.
1839, 1, 24. Patience gct Clear Creek MM, O.
1840, 5, 28. Abner & w, Rebecca, & ch, Ruth, Rhodema, Ruthanna, Alistus & Alinza, gct White Lick MM, Ind.
1881, 2, 24. Adda recrq
1883, 11, 22. Wm. West & w, Mary Ann, & ch, Enos & Carrie, & ward, Addie Lewis, gct West Grove MM, Ind.
1925, 7, 23. Frank & Ruth relrq
1925, 7, 23. Daniel relrq

LICKLITER
1910, 2, 24. Leta recrq

LIGHTHISER
1880, 3, 25. James recrq
1884, 9, 25. James dis
1886, 4, 22. James recrq
1887, 1, 27. Edward [Lighthizer] recrq

LIGHTHIZER, continued
1896, 3, 26. James & Clara relrq
1897, 11, 25. Edward [Lighthizer] & w, Nellie, & ch, Howard & Edith, relrq
1900, 7, 24. George [Leighthizer] dropped from mbrp

LINCH
1879, 4, 24. Peter recrq
1881, 9, 22. Peter dis disunity

LINDENMUTH
1913, 5, 22. Bertha D. dropped from mbrp

LINDER
----, --, --. Caleb b 1849,10,5; m Florence ----- b 1864,11,10

1888, 4, 26. Caleb & Florence recrq
1911, 6, 22. Florence [Linden] dropped from mbrp

LINKHART
1881, 2, 24. Harry C. & Clara recrq
1881, 3, 24. Joseph recrq
1882, 1, 26. Joseph relrq
1897, 9, 23. Clara relrq

LINNIARD
1900, 7, 24. James dropped from mbrp

LINSCOTT
1898, 6, 23. Minerva recrq

LINTON
----, --, --. Amy b 1848,2,26 d 1897,11,26 bur Jenkins Bur. Gr.

1856, 9, 25. Elizabeth (form Compton) dis mcd
1879, 4, 24. Robert recrq
1880, 7, 22. Cary & w, Elizabeth, & dt, Eunice Ellen, rocf Stillwater MM, Ind.
1882, 5, 25. Robert & w, Almira, & ch, Ethel, gct Miami MM, O.
1893, 7, 27. Annie recrq

LIPINCOTT
1883, 3, 22. Charley recrq
1884, 6, 26. Charles gct Miami MM, O.

LITTLER
1821, 7, 21. Thomas rocf Hopewell MM, dtd 1820,12,7

LLOYD
1817, 1, 14. Phebe b d 1888,9,12 bur Caesars Creek

1837, 4, 27. Phebe (form Spray) con mcd
1869, 7, 22. Tilman [Loyd] & w, Deborah, rocf Greenwood MM, Ind., dtd 1869,5,26
1874, 1, 22. Samuel S. [Loyd] recrq
1914, 11, 26. Luella recrq

LUKINS
1874, 6, 25. Mary Emma & s, John, gct Miami MM, O.

LUMPKIN
----, --, --. Wm. H. b 1862,9,6; m Amy B. ----- b 1866,3,17
Ch: Albert J. b 1888, 2, 14
Edward R. " 1890, 6, 16
Elener T. " 1891, 11, 22 d 1893, 8,30 bur Caesars Creek
Mabel T. b 1894, 5, 13 " 1895, 9,25 bur Caesars Creek
Laurence L.b 1901, 11, 17
Russell M. " 1905, 8, 18
1888, 12, 24. Ida R. b

1884, 3, 27. W. H. recrq

LUNDY
1893, 10, 26. Lillian M. gct Center MM, O.

LYTLE
1901, 4, 25. Harry recrq
1912, 6, 27. Julia Maude recrq
1916, 3, 23. Harry & w, Maude, relrq
1918, 12, 26. Harry & w, Maude, recrq

McCARTHY
1911, 9, 21. Hettie Frame dropped from mbrp

McCOMAS
1888, 1, 26. Maggie recrq
1889, 3, 28. Maggie gct Miami MM, O.

McCONNELL
1875, 3, 25. James recrq

McCRAY
1896, 3, 26. William recrq
1897, 7, 22. Wm. Thomas dropped from mbrp
1910, 2, 24. Vernon recrq
1914, 12, 24. Dr. W. F. & w, Lettie, recrq

McDANIEL
1899, 4, 27. Wilmena Powell relrq
1909, 11, 25. Mary J. [McDaniels] recrq

McDONALD
1822, 9, 5. Lydia m Jacob HORNER

1873, 2, 20. Andrew & w, Asenath, & ch, Florence Amelia, Charles Albert, Mary Etta, Curtis, Eber & John Allen, recrq
1879, 4, 24. Alice & dt, Bertha Edna, recrq

McELROY
1907, 2, 21. Zetia relrq

McFADDEN
1891, 8, 27. Malinda gct Springfield MM

McGEE
1886, 3, 25. Joel & Martha recrq

McINTIRE
1882, 12, 20. Frank b

1870, 4, 21. John & Abigail recrq
1886, 3, 25. Henry & Edith recrq
1894, 4, 26. Edith [McIntyre] relrq
1901, 10, 24. Henry dropped from mbrp
1905, 2, 3. Frank recrq
1925, 7, 23. Henry relrq
1926, 11, 28. Frank dropped from mbrp
1931, 1, 25. May Catherine Wilson relrq

McKAY
1819, 9, 24. Abigail [McCoy] & ch, Sarah, George, Francis, Margaret, Virginia, Maria, Tilden & Levi, rocf Hopewell MM, Va., dtd 1819,5,6
1820, 4, 28. George dis disunity
1821, 8, 24. Abigail dis jas
1822, 7, 26. Francis dis disunity
1823, 10, 30. Sarah Collett (form McKay) dis mcd
1824, 9, 30. Margaret Goode (form McKay) di mcd
1826, 8, 31. Virginia Collett (form McKay) dis mcd
1829, 6, 25. Maria dis disunity
1832, 11, 22. Jonas Tilden dis disunity
1836, 5, 26. Levi D. dis mcd
1839, 10, 24. Mary Ann rocf Center MM, O., dtd 1839,8,14
1844, 4, 25. Jacob dis disunity

McKEE
1845, 9, 15. Evaline L. b
1848, 6, 4. Harriet Alice b
1850, 11, 5. Thos. Woodward b

1853, 3, 24. Thomas W., minor, recrq
1853, 3, 24. Emiline S. & Harriett Alice, minor ch, Thomas, recrq

McKIBBEN
1896, 1, 23. Cheniah & w, Amanda, & ch, Pearl, Maud, Maggie & Louella, rocf Center MM, O.
1900, 11, 22. Cheniah & w, Amanda, & ch, Maud Maggie & Louella, relrq

McKINNEY
----, --, --. Charles b 1854,6,4; m Elizabeth JOHNSON, b 1859,12,3
Ch: Carl b 1881, 12, 20
Allen " 1892, 7, 25
Sarah " 1898, 3, 1
Paul " 1900, 11, 6
----, --, --. Fred b 1883,8,15; m Nellie J. TURNER b 1884,11,14

1906, 5, 24. Charles [McKenney] & w, Levinna, & ch, Bessie, Allen, Sarah & Paul, rocf Fairfield MM, O.
1906, 5, 24. Carl A. rocf Fairfield MM, O.
1907, 6, 27. Fred rocf Fairfield MM, O.
1910, 12, 22. Fred D. & w, Nellie J., gct Xenia MM, O.
1918, 7, 25. Fred & w, Nellie, & dt, Freda, rocf Xenia MM, O.
1922, 4, 27. Susie & ch, Harold & Donald, recrq

McKINSEY
1813, 5, 29. Rebecca (form Spray) dis mcd

McMILLAN
1851, 10, 20. David J., s Josiah & Susanna, Clinton Co., O., b 1825,8,12; m in Caesars Creek MH, Eunice MILLS, dt William & Elizabeth, Warren Co., O., b 1836,2,13
Ch: John b 1852, 8, 23
Josiah " 1854, 6, 22
Mary Elizabeth " 1856, 8, 24
Susan P. " 1859, 12, 20
1849, 6, 21. David J. rocf Center MM, O., dtd 1849,5,16
1856, 1, 24. Clarkson rocf Center MM, O., dtd 1855,12,12
1860, 8, 23. David J. [McMilan] & w, Eunice, & ch, John Josiah, Mary Elizabeth Susan P. gct Bridgeport MM, Ind.
1863, 3, 26. Henry Spray gct Center MM, O., to m Mary Ann McMillan
1863, 9, 24. Levi Mills gct Center MM, O., to m Ruth McMillan
1866, 4, 26. Phebe (form Walker) con mcd
1866, 7, 26. Phebe H. gct Center MM, O.
1867, 4, 25. Clarkson gct Center MM, O.
1917, 12, 27. Robert & w, Pearl, rocf Smithfield MM
1922, 11, 26. Robert & w, Pearl, & ch, Rex, gct Springfield MM, O.

McNEAL
----, --, --. Leonidas Lee b 1854,1,11; m Hannah SPRAY b 1860,3,5

1898, 8, 25. Hannah Spray rocf Springfield MM, O.
1901, 4, 25. Leonidas Lee recrq
1906, 4, 26. Isaac Lionel, John G. & Mary Lee [McNeil] recrq
1913, 5, 22. Lee, Hannah & John G. dropped from mbrp
1925, 7, 23. Nello relrq

McPHERSON
1880, 1, 24. Hettie (Walton) b

1900, 6, 21. George W. rocf Fairfield MM, O.

MALONE
1896, 3, 26. John & Louella recrq
1900, 7, 24. John dropped from mbrp

MANN
----, --, --. John b 1810,3,22 d 1885,6,26; m Sarah Jane ----- b 1827,10,19
Ch: Emma L. b 1861, 10, 18
1855, 5, 26. Rachel E. b
1864, 1, 24. Ella May, dt Isaac & Keziah Bunnell, b

1872, 5, 23. Rachel E. recrq
1879, 4, 24. John & Jane recrq
1884, 6, 26. Nancy Catherine & Emma Luella recrq
1892, 4, 21. Horace, Ella B. & Harold S. recrq
1905, 3, 23. Horace & w, Nellie, & ch, Harold & Thurman, gct Whittier MM, Calif.

MANLEY
1887, 10, 27. Wm. F. & w, Lydia G., recrq
1889, 5, 23. Wm. T. & w, Lydia G., gct Westfield MM, Ind.

MANNINGTON
1884, 3, 27. Robert recrq
1894, 2, 22. Robert relrq

MARSHALL
1874, 4, 23. Elizabeth recrq
1881, 4, 21. Maggie recrq

MARTIN
1843, 7, 27. Anna (form Cox) con mcd
1855, 8, 23. Alfred & ch, Margaret, David, Isaac, Henry Macy, Mary Alice & James Albert, recrq
1856, 5, 22. Alfred & w, Anna, & ch, Margaret, David, Isaac, Henry Macy, Mary Alice & James Albert, gct Three Rivers MM, Ia.
1901, 4, 25. W. Jasper recrq
1903, 12, 24. Elma recrq
1913, 5, 22. W. Jasper & Flora dropped from mbrp

MASON
----, --, --. John B. b 1831,6,13; m Mary Jane ----- b 1838,4,11 d 1898,12,7
Ch: Joseph C. b 1860, 1, 25
David M. " 1866, 12, 23
Frank E. " 1871, 12, 3
----, --, --. Joseph C. b 1868,1,25; m Flora ----- b 1857,4,24
Ch: Irwin b 1893, 12, 2

1880, 3, 25. John B. & w, Mary J., & ch, David Montgomery & Frank Elvin, recrq
1881, 4, 21. Joseph C. recrq
1911, 9, 21. David W. dropped from mbrp
1913, 6, 26. Frank E. gct Dayton MM, O.
1922, 4, 27. Ervin P. relrq

MASTERS
1908, 11, 26. Mary recrq
1908, 12, 24. W. B. recrq
1914, 6, 25. Esther Thomas gct Xenia MM, O.

MATHEWMAN
1867, 7, 25. Hannah Josephine (form Cook) dis mcd

MATHEWS
1910, 2, 24. Milton recrq

MEFFORD
1900, 4, 26. Charles & w, Julia, & two ch rocf Smithfield MM, O., dtd 1900,1,20

MELTON
1821, 6, 29. Phebe (form Heston) con mcd
1821, 11, 23. Ellanor (form Easterling) con mcd
1830, 10, 28. Eleanor gct White Lick MM, Ind.
1830, 11, 25. Phebe gct White Lick MM, Ind.

MENDENHALL
----, --, --. John b 1759,3,6 d 1835,6,3 bur Caesars Creek; m Ruth ----- b 1767,4,4 d 1832,1,13 bur Caesars Creek
Ch: Richard b 1786, 3, 25
Joseph " 1787, 10, 2
Margaret " 1791, 6, 10
Aaron " 1793, 6, 4
Ruth " 1795, 4, 11
John " 1797, 7, 17
William " 1799, 10, 25
Catherine " 1801, 9, 19
Benjamin " 1804, 4, 26
Nathan " 1806, 4, 17
Ann " 1808, 10, 18
1813, 12, 29. Margaret m Athanasious BARRETT
1814, 11, 3. Obadiah, s Richard & Sarah, Green Co., O.; m in Caesars Creek MH, Sarah OWEN, dt Samuel & Margaret, Warren Co., O.
----, --, --. Benjamin b 1786,9,16; m Mary ----- b 1793,3,1
Ch: Zebulon b 1816, 9, 3
Ira " 1817, 12, 25
Lydia " 1819, 12, 8
Rebeckah " 1822, 6, 19
Sarah " 1824, 10, 29
1819, 11, 4. Ira, s Richard & Sarah, Green Co., O.; m in Caesars Creek MH, Sarah BALLARD, dt Joseph & Elizabeth, Clinton Co., O.
1825, 11, 2. William, s John & Ruth, Green Co., O., b 1789,12,25 d 1853,4,17 bur Caesars Creek; m Betty WALTON, dt Edward & Deborah, Green Co., O., b 1805,10,15 d 1869,3,1 bur Caesars Creek
Ch: Deborah b 1826, 10, 20
John " 1828, 12, 4
Ann " 1830, 11, 26
Hannah " 1833, 3, 25

MENDENHALL, William & Betty, continued
Ch: Edward b 1835, 3, 7
Samuel " 1837, 11, 30 d 1879, 4, 7 bur Caesars Creek
Ruth b 1840, 1, 31 d 1886, 5,26 bur Caesars Creek
Catherine b 1842, 4, 24
Margaret " 1844, 8, 16
William A. " 1848, 5, 30 d 1884, 3, 6 bur Caesars Creek
1826, 4, 12. Catherine m Samuel WALTON
1827, 10, 31. David, s Richard & Sarah, Green Co., O.; m in Richland MH, Maryann PERKINS, dt Thomas & Sarah, Green Co., O.
1832, 1, 13. Ruth, w John, d ae 64 bur Caesars Creek
1835, 6, 3. John d bur Caesars Creek
1852, 6, 9. Hannah m Elihu SPRAY
1853, 11, 2. Ann m Amos COMPTON
1855, 10, 31. Deborah m Abijah STEDDOM
1856, 3, 6. John, s William & Betty, Green Co., O., b 1828,12,4; m in Caesars Creek MH, Eunice COMPTON, dt John & Rebecca, Green Co., O., b 1834,8,9 d 1920,3,6 bur Spring Valley
Ch: Alice S. b 1857, 8, 1
William H. " 1859, 1, 21
Morrow W. " 1861, 3, 9
Anna R. " 1863, 7, 14 d 1876, 2, 2 bur Caesars Creek
Amy B. b 1866, 6, 17
Mary Catharine " 1868, 8, 29
Orval I. " 1871, 6, 1
Amos C. " 1873, 11, 18
Jennie E. " 1876, 4, 28
----, --, --. Samuel b 1837,11,30 d 1879,4,7 bur Caesars Creek; m ----- -----
Ch: Horace b 1868, 8, 8
Charles " 1871, 1, 23
----, --, --. William H. b 1859,1,21; m Mary E. ----- b 1858,12,27
Ch: Edith A. b 1886, 10, 20
Everett J. " 1898, 11, 3
----, --, --. Charles b 1871,1,23; m Nettie ----- b 1865,3,26
Ch: Hazel E. b 1894, 12, 14 d 1894,12,19

1815, 8, 25. Benjamin con mcd
1817, 4, 25. Aaron con mcd
1817, 8, 29. Mary & s, Zebulon, recrq
1819, 2, 26. Ruth Stanfield (form Mendenhall) dis mcd to first cousin
1819, 6, 25. Levina & ch, Cynthia & Margaret, recrq
1820, 4, 28. Joseph & fam gct Mill Creek MM
1823, 8, 28. Ira & w, Sarah, & ch, Joseph B. & Joel H., gct White Lick MM, Ind.
1823, 9, 25. Joseph & fam gct White Lick MM, Ind.
1823, 9, 25. Obadiah & fam gct White Lick MM, Ind.
1824, 8, 26. Richard Jr. & fam gct White Lick MM, Ind.
1825, 9, 29. Aaron & w, Levina, & ch, Cynthia, Joseph, Ann & John, gct White Lick MM, Ind.
1826, 7, 27. Henry Compton gct West Branch MM, O., to m Rachel Mendenhall
1827, 1, 25. James dis mcd
1827, 8, 30. Benjamin & w, Mary, & ch, Zebulon, Ira, Lydia, Rebecca, Sarah & Cary, gct Fairfield MM, Ind.
1828, 9, 25. Rebecca rocf Mill Creek MM, dtd 1828,6,28
1829, 9, 24. David & w, Maryann, & ch, Anna, gct White Lick MM, Ind.
1830, 3, 25. Nathan dis mcd
1833, 5, 23. Benjamin dis mcd
1836, 8, 25. Rebecca gct Westfield MM, Ind.
1836, 8, 25. Richard & w, Sarah, gct Westfield MM, Ind.
1859, 7, 25. James rst at Vermillion MM, Ill. on consent of this mtg
1867, 3, 28. Elizabeth Ann rocf Center MM, O., 1867,2,13
1868, 5, 28. Catherine Compton (form Mendenhall) con mcd
1868, 5, 28. Samuel con mcd
1871, 10, 26. Edward con mcd
1878, 9, 26. Edward & dt, Carrie, gct White Water MM, Ind.
1886, 11, 25. Alice Carey rocf White Water MM, Ind.
1893, 4, 27. Alice E. recrq (minor)
1896, 2, 20. Louella A. relrq
1896, 3, 26. Amos C. relrq
1902, 4, 24. Orval J. relrq
1909, 2, 25. Erma recrq
1917, 11, 22. Robert J. recrq
1917, 11, 22. Allen Kelly & w, Alma Jane, & ch Kelley & Maria, recrq
1919, 3, 27. Charles & w, Nettie, relrq
1919, 3, 27. Horace relrq
1919, 12, 25. Mary & ch relrq
1921, 4, 21. Anna recrq

MERRIMAN
1907, 9, 26. Maude rocf Ogden MM

MERSHOW
1874, 1, 22. Mary Asenath recrq

MESECHER
1873, 9, 25. Mary E. & ch, William, John H. & James F., recrq

MESKIMEN
1883, 4, 26. Mary E. Shumaker recrq
1884, 3, 27. Mary & Frank [Meskimer] recrq
1889, 12, 26. Jemima & May [Meskinner] relrq

MIDDLETON
1857, 8, 14. Mellie E. b
----, --, --. T. J. b 1850,8,25; m Mary R. ----- b 1856,12,27

MIDDLETON, continued
1878, 11, 13. Mary F. b

1880, 3, 25. Thomas & Mary recrq

MILHOUSE
----, --, --. Henry b 1736,5,1 d 1821,5,22 bur Caesars Creek; m Rebecca ----- b 1739, 8,11 d 1803,8,11 but Tyger River, S. C.
----, --, --. Robert & Sally
Ch: Henry b 1793, 5, 19
Samuel " 1796, 1, 23
John " 1797, 5, 22
Rebecca " 1799, 3, 22
Elizabeth " 1802, 11, 15
Ann " 1804, 1, 9
Robert " 1806, 4, 7
----, --, --. Henry b 1793,5,19; m Sarah ----- b 1793,2,25
Ch: Thomas b 1819, 1, 25
Margery " 1821, 10, 4
Elizabeth " 1825, 6, 19
Robert " 1828, 3, 22
1821, 5, 22. Henry [Milhous] d ae 85 bur Caesars Creek Gr. Yd.
1823, 10, 2. Anna [Milhous] m Samuel OWEN
1829, 5, 14. Samuel, s Robert & Sally, Clinton Co., O.; m in Caesars Creek MH, Sarah SCOTT, dt William & Amy SANDERS, Warren Co., O.
Ch: Henry b 1830, 2, 19
Mary " 1830, 2, 19
Charity " 1831, 9, 21
Amos " 1833, 8, 19
1829, 6, 4. Elizabeth [Milhous] m Wm. MILLS
1830, 6, 10. John, s Robert & Sally, Clinton Co., O.; m in Caesars Creek MH, Mary MILLS, dt John & Phebe, Clinton Co., O.
1830, 8, 5. Robert, s Robert & Sally, Clinton Co., O.; m in Caesars Creek MH, Dinah FURNAS, dt Robert & Hannah, Warren Co., O.
Ch: Isaac b 1832, 12, 28

1817, 7, 25. Henry [Milhous] Jr. gct Miami MM, O., to m
1818, 2, 27. Sarah [Milhous], w Henry, rocf Miami MM, O., dtd 1818,2,25
1834, 8, 28. Samuel [Milhous] & w, Sarah, & ch, John, Isam & Eli Scott, & Henry, Mary, Charity & Amos Milhous, gct Fairfield MM, Ind.
1834, 8, 28. Henry & w, Sarah, & ch, Thomas, Margery, Elizabeth & Robert, gct Fairfield MM, Ind.
1835, 4, 23. Robert [Milhous] Jr. & w, Dinah, & ch, Isaac, gct Fairfield MM, Ind.
1835, 8, 27. Robert [Milhous] & w, Sally, & dt, Ann, gct Fairfield MM, Ind.
1836, 8, 25. John & w, Mary, & ch, Phebe, gct Fairfield MM, Ind.
1836, 9, 22. Rebecca [Milhous] gct Fairfield MM, Ind.

MILLER
1861, 1, 6. Sarah d ae 80 bur Caesars Creek

1815, 7, 28. Sarah rocf Hopewell MM, dtd 1815,3,9
1815, 7, 28. John & w, Jane, & ch, Jonas & Elizabeth, rocf Hopewell MM, dtd 1815,3,9
1816, 11, 29. Jonas dis disunity
1818, 9, 25. Elizabeth gct Darby Creek MM,O.
1819, 1, 29. Cert rec for John & w, Margaret, & ch, Joshua, Elizabeth, Mary Rebecca, Thomas & Jane, from Fairfield MM, O., dtd 1816,5,25, endorsed to Darby Creek MM, O.
1836, 9, 22. Rebecca (form Gilpin) con mcd
1840, 2, 20. Rebecca gct Cherry Grove MM,Ind.
1881, 2, 24. Anna recrq
1881, 2, 24. Lydia L. & Wm. C., recrq
1887, 7, 28. Joseph & w, Louisa, recrq
1891, 10, 22. Jonathan L. rocf Center MM,O.
1892, 4, 21. Burrell & Clara recrq
1892, 11, 24. Zoe T. recrq
1893, 4, 27. Louis & Caroline recrq
1894, 9, 27. Joseph & dt, Clara, relrq
1897, 8, 26. Sarah gct Van Wert MM, O.
1899, 1, 27. Jonathan & w, Zoe, gct New Hope MM, Ind.
1899, 7, 27. Jonathan & w, Zoe, gct New Hope MM, Ind.
1901, 7, 25. Jonathan L. & w, Zoe I., rocf New Hope MM, Ind.
1902, 3, 27. Carolyn relrq
1906, 4, 26. Jonathan T. & w, Zoe L., relrq

MILLS
----, --, -- John b 1775,--,--; m Phebe ----- b 1783,5,9
Ch: William b 1803, 1, 1
Mark " 1804, 9, 25
Mary " 1807, 4, 25
Rachel " 1809, 9, 4
Ames " 1811, 7, 9
Lydia " 1813, 6, 24
1814, 8, 9. John d ae 84 bur Caesars Creek
1815, 5, 4. Enoch, s John & Mary, Clinton Co., O., b 1793,12,19; m in Caesars Creek MH, Patsy SCOTT, dt James & Lydia, Warren Co., O., b 1793,6,11 d 1823,9,3 bur Caesars Creek
Ch: Caleb b 1816, 2, 27
Abner " 1817, 9, 14
Seth " 1819, 10, 7 d 1825, 8, 2
Demsy " 1821, 7, 17
Enoch m 2nd 1824,11,4, Mary SANDERS, dt William & Amy, Warren Co., O.
Ch: Cyrus b 1826, 1, 15
Ada " 1827, 12, 4 d 1829, 8,27
Ruth " 1829, 4, 5
1815, 12, 7. William, s William & Lydia, Warren Co., O., b 1792,4,2; m in Caesars Creek MH, Dinah HAWKINS, dt James & Sarah, Warren Co., O.
Ch: Job b 1817, 9, 1
James " 1818, 11, 22

MILLS, William & Dinah, continued
Ch: Jehu b 1821, 4, 17
Charles " 1824, 6, 30
William m 2nd in Caesars Creek MH, 1829, 6,4, Elizabeth MILHOUSE, dt Robert & Sally, Clinton Co., O.
Ch: Rebecca b 1833, 6, 23
Amos " 1843, 10, 16
1818, 3, 5. Charles, s William & Lydia, Warren Co., O.; m in Caesars Creek MH, Mary HAWKINS, dt Amos & Phebe, Warren Co., O., d 1818,12,13
Ch: Jonathan b 1818, 12, 26
1819, 6, 15. Lydia b
1820, 6, 29. John, s Joseph & Sarah, Clinton Co., O.; m in Caesars Creek MH, Betty COMPTON, dt Amos & Rebecca, Green Co., O.
1820, 7, 6. Daniel, s William & Lydia, Warren Co., O.; m in Caesars Creek MH, Esther FURNAS, dt Robert & Hannah, Warren Co., O.
1821, 11, 8. Patience m Jonathan JESSUP
1821, 3, 1. Elijah, s John & Mary, Clinton Co., O., b 1796,2,27 d 1844,11,22 bur Caesars Creek; m Mary HAWKINS, dt Amos & Ann, Warren Co., O., b 1800,2,25
Ch: Ann b 1822, 5, 21
Rebecca " 1824, 11, 28
Martha " 1827, 12, 28 d 1829, 8,25 bur Caesars Creek
John b 1829, 8, 22
Amos " 1831, 5, 9
Phillip " 1833, 3, 13
Elihu " 1835, 3, 15
Dinah " 1836, 10, 17 d 18--,5,22 bur Caesars Creek
Phebe b 1844, 6, 25
1822, 4, 28. Rebecca b
1824, 9, 2. David, s William & Lydia, Warren Co., O.; m in Caesars Creek MH, Malona BROCK, dt George & Charity, Clinton Co.,O.
1826, 4, 6. Mark, s John & Phebe, Clinton Co., O.; m in Caesars Creek MH, Charity SANDERS, dt William & Amy, Warren Co., O.
Ch: Daniel b 1827, 2, 16
Amos " 1828, 8, 23
Amy " 1830, 9, 17
1827, 8, 2. William, s John & Phebe, Clinton Co., O., b 1803,1,1; m in Caesars Creek MH, Elizabeth COOK, dt John & Dinah, Warren Co., O.
Ch: Jesse b 1831, 2, 27
Eunice " 1836, 2, 18
Phebe " 1839, 11, 20
Charity " 1852, 8, 29
1829, 8, 25. Martha d
1830, 6, 10. Mary m John MILHOUS
1831, 2, 27. Jesse, s Wm. & Elizabeth, b
1831, 10, 13. Esther m Jesse CONNER
1833, 11, 7. Rachel m Daniel SANDERS
1836, 2, 18. Eunice b
1837, 9, 28. Jonathan, s Charles & Mary, Warren Co., O., b 1818,12,26 d 1864,2,24; m in Caesars Creek MH, Charity COOK, dt John & Dinah, Warren Co., O., b 1820,2,26 d 1860, 1860,8,27 bur Caesars Creek
Ch: Mary b 1839, 9, 3
Levi " 1844, 3, 14
1840, 2, 27. Abner, s Enoch & Patsy, Marion Co., Ind.; m in Caesars Creek MH, Hannah FURNAS, dt Robert & Hannah, Warren Co.,O.
1840, 9, 1. Job, s William & Dinah, b 1817, 9,1; m in Caesars Creek MH, Rebecca COMPTON, dt Stephen & Dinah, Green Co., O., b 1822,4,28
Ch: Stephen b 1843, 2, 24
William " 1849, 10, 15
1840, 10, 1. Ann m Isaac HAWKINS
1845, 10, 15. James, s William & Dinah, Warren Co., O., b 1818,11,22; m in Richland MH, Ruth WALTON, dt Samuel & Catherine, Green Co., O., b 1827,6,18
Ch: Samuel W. b 1846, 7, 13
1847, 8, 5. Mary m Uriah SPRAY
1849, 9, 6. Jesse, s William & Elizabeth, Warren Co., O., b 1831,2,27; m in Caesars Creek MH, Mary JAY, dt John & Lydia, Clinton Co., O., b 1830,12,31
Ch: Dinah b 1850, 6, 17 d 1855, 6,10 bur Caesars Creek
Lydia Ann b 1851, 8, 16
Elizabeth " 1856, 12, 23 d 1863, 4,28
Eunice Annie " 1864, 11, 15
1851, 10, 30. Eunice m David McMILLAN
1852, 3, 4. Rebecca m Jehu SPRAY
1855, 8, 30. Henry, s John & Elizabeth, Green Co., O., b 1829,12,5; m in Caesars Creek MH, Sarah W. HAWKINS, dt Benjamin & Phamy, Green Co., O., b 1836,11,18 d 1863, 4,18 bur Caesars Creek
Ch: Benjamin H. b 1857, 2, 1
Martha Elizabeth " 1859, 1, 30
John Lindley " 1861, 12, 2 d 1863, 9,10
Henry F. m 2nd Phebe A. ----- b 1835,4,17
Ch: George D. b 1871, 8, 8
----, --, --. George b 1834,5,24; m Ann P.----- b 1837,7,22
1858, 2, 11. Amos, s Mark & Charity, Marion Co.,Ind.;m in Caesars Creek MH, Mary Elizabeth COOK, dt Samuel & Hannah, Warren Co., O.
1862, 4, 3. Stephen, s Job & Rebecca, Green Co., O., b 1843,2,24 d 1919,3,29 bur Caesars Creek; m in Caesars Creek MH, Lydia COMPTON, dt Samuel & Ally, Green Co., O., b 1842,12,16 d 1879,12,23
Ch: Alice Rebecca b 1868, 8, 7 d 1879, 7,16 bur Caesars Creek
Amos Charles b 1874, 9, 17 " 1876, 9,29 bur Caesars Creek
Stephen m 2nd Mary E. ----- b 1854,4,3
Ch: Flora Etta b 1885, 8, 2

MILLS, Stephen & Mary E., continued
Ch: Harvey P. b 1887, 12, 4
1863, 9, 3. Mary Jr. m James HAWKINS
1864, 9, 1. George, s John & Betty, Green Co., O.; m in Caesars Creek MH, Ann P. COOK, dt Samuel & Hannah, Warren Co., O.
1866, 8, 18. Orville b d 1894,2,8
1867, 11, 4. Henry F., s John & Betty, Prebble Co., O.; m in Caesars Creek MH, Phebe Ann HAWORTH, dt Eli & Eunice COMPTON, Clinton Co., O.
----, --, --. Warren Elmer b 1864,6,23; m Nancy D. ----- b 1867,11,2 d 1897,11,25
Ch: Joseph O. b 1896, 11, 4
----, --, --. George D. b 1871,8,8; m Luella B. ----- b 1872,9,3 d 1922,3,13 bur Corwin
Ch: Linley E. b 1897, 5, 16

1813, 6, 26. Sarah (form Gilpin) con mcd
1818, 1, 30. Thomas dis mcd
1820, 3, 24. John & s, Joseph, recrq
1821, 3, 30. Betty gct White Water MM, Ind.
1821, 6, 27. John gct White Water MM, Ind.
1822, 4, 26. Sarah, w Alexander, gct Miami MM, O.
1822, 10, 31. Daniel & w, Esther, & dt, Hannah, gct West Grove MM, Ind.
1825, 1, 27. David dis
1825, 1, 27. Malona dis
1826, 7, 27. Esther & ch, Hannah & David, rocf White Lick MM, Ind., dtd 1826,5,13
1826, 12, 28. Martha (form Hawkins) dis mcd
1827, 6, 28. John & w, Betty gct White Water MM, Ind., to replace lost cert
1827, 9, 27. John & w, Betty, & ch, William, Amos, John & Elizabeth, gct White Water MM, Ind., to replace lost cert
1830, 10, 28. Enoch & w, Mary, & ch, Caleb, Abner, Dempsey, Cyrus & Ruth, gct Fairfield MM, Ind.
1833, 8, 22. Mark & w, Charity, & ch, Daniel, Amos & Amy, gct Fairfield MM, Ind.
1834, 10, 23. Jesse Connor & w, Esther, & ch, Hannah & David Mills, & Mary Connor, gct Fairfield MM, Ind.
1834, 11, 27. Charles gct Springfield MM, to m Ann Harvey
1835, 2, 19. Chas. gct Miami MM, O.
1836, 8, 25. John & w, Phebe, & ch, Amos & Lydia, gct Fairfield MM, Ind.
1837, 8, 24. Melona rst
1838, 2, 22. Layton, Elijah, Thomas & Isaac, ch David & Melona, recrq
1839, 7, 25. Lydia recrq
1839, 8, 22. David & w, Malona, & ch, Layton Elijah Isaac & Thomas, gct Fairfield MM, Ind.
1841, 10, 28. Hannah & s, Seth, gct Fairfield MM, Ind.
1844, 2, 22. Jehu con mcd
1845, 7, 24. Jehu Hawkins gct Fairfield MM, Ind., to m Jane Mills
1846, 1, 23. Jane Hawkins & dt, Mary Mills, rocf Fairfield MM, Ind., dtd 1845,11,1
1849, 5, 24. Chas. dis mcd
1850, 10, 24. James & w, Ruth, & ch, Samuel & Wm. Allen, gct Fairfield MM, Ind.
1851, 4, 24. John gct Fairfield MM, Ind.
1851, 11, 27. John dis mcd
1852, 1, 22. Amos dis disunity
1852, 1, 22. Amos dis disunity
1853, 10, 27. Wm. & w, Elizabeth, ch, Amos, gct Fairfield MM, Ind.
1853, 10, 27. Lydia gct Fairfield MM, Ind.
1854, 5, 25. George rocf White Water MM, Ind., dtd 1854,4,26
1854, 6, 22. Elihu dis disunity
1855, 7, 26. Henry F. rocf White Water MM, Ind., dtd 1855,6,27
1857, 8, 27. Rebecca Colvin (form Mills) dis mcd
1858, 6, 24. Mary Elizabeth gct Fairfield MM, Ind.
1863, 1, 22. Wm. & w, Elizabeth, & ch, Phebe G. & Charity, gct Bridgeport MM, Ind.
1863, 9, 24. Levi gct Center MM, O., to m Ruth McMillan
1865, 4, 27. Jesse & w, Mary, & ch, Lydia Ann & Eunice Anna, gct Greenwood MM, Ind.
1865, 10, 26. Levi gct Center MM, O.
1868, 8, 27. Phebe Hefner (form Mills) con mcd
1870, 4, 21. Philip recrq
1876, --, 23. Alice recrq
1881, 2, 24. Milton, Anna, Laura, Franklin, Chas. & Esther, recrq
1882, 10, 26. Mary recrq
1883, 12, 27. Lydia J. rocf Stillwater MM, Ind., dtd 1883,12,6
1884, 1, 24. Elmer recrq
1889, 2, 21. Orval P. recrq
1889, 7, 25. Arlie recrq
1895, 2, 21. Luella B. rocf Dover MM, O.
1898, 5, 26. Sarah A. recrq
1900, 9, 27. Benjamin N. & w, Lydia J., & ch, Ray P., gct Miami MM, O.
1901, 10, 24. Stephen dropped from mbrp
1906, 2, 22. George D., Louella B. & Lindley E., gct Miami MM, O.
1909, 9, 23. Dena recrq
1913, 5, 22. Wm. dropped from mbrp
1913, 5, 22. Frank dropped from mbrp
1913, 5, 22. Arthur dropped from mbrp
1913, 5, 22. Charles dropped from mbrp
1913, 5, 22. Jesse dropped from mbrp
1914, 3, 26. Hannah Isabel Painter gct Xenia MM, O.
1925, 7, 23. Harry relrq

MITCHENER
----, --, --. Lawrence, s Samuel & Margaret, b 1886,8,9; m Ethel COMPTON, dt Wm. & Sarah, b 1894,2,26

1885, 4, 23. Samuel C. [Mitchiner] recrq
1908, 6, 25. Lawrence [Michener] recrq

MITCHENER, continued
1910, 2, 24. Virgo recrq
1914, 3, 26. Thurman recrq
1917, 3, 22. Alice & Margaret recrq
1917, 3, 22. Walter & Horace recrq
1917, 3, 22. Margaret & dt, Florence, recrq
1926, 8, 29. Lawrence [Mitchner] & w, Ethel, rocf New Burlington MM

MITCHELL
1876, 1, 27. George & Dorcas recrq
1889, 12, 26. Geo. W. & Dorcas relrq

MOBLEY
1925, 7, 23. Grace & Jeannette relrq

MOCK
1925, 7, 23. C. S. & w relrq

MOFFETT
1813, 9, 26. Francis W. b

1870, 12, 22. Francis W. recrq
1891, 8, 27. F. W. relrq
1906, 4, 26. Amanda L. recrq

MONDY
1881, 2, 24. Amanda recrq
1907, 4, 25. Amanda recrq

MONTGOMERY
1881, 2, 24. Sidney & Owen recrq
1882, 12, 28. Owen dis disunity
1884, 11, 27. Sidney gct Miami MM, O.

MOODY
1815, 9, 29. Mary (form Allen) con mcd
1818, 8, 28. Abigail (form Cloud) con mcd
1819, 9, 24. Ruth recrq
1820, 7, 28. Samuel recrq
1822, 8, 30. Samuel & w, Ruth, gct Cherry Grove MM, Ind.
1823, 5, 29. Mary (form Heston) con mcd
1823, 9, 25. Mary gct Cherry Grove MM, Ind.

MOON
----, --, --. Aaron b 1832,3,16 d 1899,6,19; m Eunice ----- b 1826,4,2
Ch: Oliver b 1853, 6, 7
Arthur " 1854, 10, 28
Edgar " 1857, 8, 29 d 1858, 8, 3
Mary Eva " 1860, 12, 28
John Demrus " 1862, 11, 27 d 1887,11,23
1857, 7, 30. Phebe m Jos. C. HAWKINS
----, --, --. Neri b 1838,10,15; m Mary-ann Elizabeth ----- b ----,10,24 d 1922,3,8 bur Caesars Creek
Ch: William Bazzle b 1864, 1, 14
Eunice Ellen " 1867, 3, 16
Alfred
Alonzo b 1870, 10, 11 d 1871, 4, 9
Massy Jemima " 1860, 9, 6 " 1864, 2,27
Lucy Belle " 1872, 8, 30
Elida J. " 1875, 8, 29
----, --, --. Oliver b 1853,6,7; m Lucetta E. ----- b 1855,2,7 d 1887,12,7
Ch: Nora E. b 1878, 7, 26
Charles H. " 1880, 8, 15
Mary Emma " 1882, 10, 10
Russell W. " 1885, 3, 14
Albert D. " 1887, 3, 21
Oliver m 2nd Eva L. ----- b 1870,1,29

1856, 4, 24. Phebe rocf Newberry MM, O., dtd 1856,3,17
1858, 7, 22. Neri rocf Newberry MM, O., dtd 1858,6,21
1858, 7, 22. Polly rocf Newberry MM, O., dtd 1859,7,19
1860, 3, 22. Neri con mcd
1860, 7, 26. Neri gct Henkles Creek MM, Ind.
1862, 9, 25. Neri rocf Henkles Creek MM, Ind., dtd 1862,7,29, endorsed by Miami MM, O., 1862,9,24
1868, 9, 24. Wm. B., s Neri, recrq
1870, 4, 21. Mary A. recrq
1872, 12, 26. Aaron & w, Eunice E., & ch, Oliver, Arthur, Mary, Eva & John, rocf Smithfield MM, O., dtd 1872,10,21
1875, 7, 22. Aaron & w, Eunice E., & ch, Oliver, Arthur, Mary E. & John, gct West Branch MM, O.
1880, 3, 25. Clara recrq
1880, 7, 22. Aaron & w, Eunice, & ch, Arthur, Eva & John, rocf West Branch MM, O., dtd 1880,6,17
1881, 4, 21. Alpheus recrq
1883, 7, 26. Oliver rocf West Branch MM, O.
1884, 3, 27. Lucetta recrq
1886, 4, 22. Elizabeth recrq
1887, 5, 26. Mellie rocf Newberry MM, O.
1889, 1, 24. Neri & w, Mary, relrq
1891, 8, 27. Alpheus relrq
1892, 11, 24. Eva recrq
1896, 3, 26. Harriett recrq
1900, 7, 24. Harriett dropped from mbrp
1905, 7, 27. Samuel rocf Newberry MM, O.
1910, 2, 24. Charles, Ida, Mary & Milton recrq
1911, 6, 22. Russell dropped from mbrp
1911, 7, 27. Wm. B. dropped from mbrp
1912, 5, 23. Neri recrq
1913, 6, 26. Charles H. gct Dayton MM, O.
1913, 6, 26. Oliver & w, Eva L., gct Dayton MM, O.
1917, 8, 23. Clyde M. recrq

MOORE
1892, 2, 25. Junietta relrq
1925, 7, 23. Ruth, Eleanor & Eloise relrq

MOORMAN
1824, 2, 25. Henry T. b
1843, 3, 29. James, s Thomas Sr. & Aphracia, Green Co., O., b 1791,2,10; m in Richland MH, Mary SEXTON, dt Amos & Rebecca COMPTON, Green Co., O., b 1798,12,22 d 1877,3, 20 bur Caesars Creek

1844, 12, 26. Sarah & Hannah Sexton, ch Mary Moorman, recrq
1845, 10, 23. James rocf Dover MM, dtd 1845, 7,17
1855, 4, 26. Henry T. [Morman] rocf Dover MM, dtd 1855,1,18
1856, 2, 21. Henry T. gct White Water MM,Ind.
1910, 3, 24. Barrett G. recrq
1912, 12, 26. Frank & w rocf Jamestown MM

MORGAN
1819, 4, 30. Catharine b
1834, 4, 3. Phamy m Benjamin HAWKINS
1844, 1, 4. William, s Thomas & Ann, Warren Co., O., b 1816,11,26 d 1897,1,19 bur Caesars Creek; m in Caesars Creek MH, Matilda FURNAS, dt Joseph & Christiana COMPTON, b 1808,4,21 d 1864,10,7 bur Caesars Creek
Ch: James H. b 1844, 12, 24
Martha
Ann " 1846, 5, 30
William m 2nd 1868,12,31 in Caesars Creek MH, Ruth JAY, dt David & Rebecca, Clinton Co., O., b 1827,10,23
1845, 10, 9. Catherine m Wm. COMPTON
----, --, --. ----- m Annie L. ----- b 1867,1, 24
Ch: William H. b 1891, 4, 2
Carl S. " 1894, 1, 19
James W. " 1901, 1, 31
Winifred " 1902, 10, 11

1815, 3, 24. Elizabeth & ch, Jonathan, Isaac & Asa, rocf Fairfield MM, O., dtd 1814,8, 27
1816, 11, 29. Jonathan con mcd
1816, 11, 29. Ann (form Bloxom) con mcd
1818, 5, 29. Jonathan dis disunity
1833, 4, 25. Phamy recrq
1839, 9, 26. Catherine recrq
1843, 7, 27. Wm. recrq
1878, 9, 26. Thomas relrq
1881, 2, 24. John & Mary recrq
1881, 4, 21. James H. gct Miami MM, O.
1883, 5, 24. Martha A. gct Miami MM, O.
1889, 12, 26. Lizzie relrq
1890, 5, 22. Martha A. rocf Miami MM, O.
1900, 3, 22. James H. & w, Anna, & ch, Wm. H. & Carl S., rocf Miami MM, O., dtd 1900,2,21
1914, 6, 25. Ruth Edna Compton recrq

MORRIS
----, --, --. Warner, s John H. & Louisa, b 1857,5,5; m Maria COMPTON, dt Eli & Eunice, b 1855,4,28
Ch: LeeRoy b 1880, 7, 17
Lyle C. " 1882, 7, 9

1877, 5, 24. Catherine J. recrq
1886, 3, 25. Jeremiah & Eunice recrq
1886, 3, 25. Warner recrq
1886, 3, 25. Leroy recrq
1886, 3, 25. Lyle C. recrq
1892, 1, 28. Jerry & Eunice relrq
1913, 6, 26. LeRoy gct Dayton MM, O.
1919, 3, 27. Lyle C. & Martha E. relrq

MOSS
1831, 8, 22. Elizabeth b

1876, 1, 27. Andrew & Elizabeth recrq
1876, 1, 27. Julia recrq
1878, 10, 24. Andrew relrq
1880, 3, 25. Andrew recrq
1897, 7, 22. Lewis dropped from mbrp
1900, 7, 24. Harrison dropped from mbrp

MULL
1874, 5, 28. Noah & Margaret recrq
1897, 7, 22. ----- dropped from mbrp

MURPHY
1899, 9, 21. Rosa Holland relrq
1908, 12, 24. Albert recrq
1914, 1, 22. Willie recrq
1917, 7, 26. Willie dropped from mbrp

MURRELL
----, --, --. Ulysses Grant b 1868,6,19; m Ora H. ----- b 1868,7,17
Ch: Cordelia b 1898, 12, 19

1897, 8, 25. Ulysses Grant & w, Ora H., rocf Wilmington MM, O.
1905, 9, 21. U. G. & w, Ora, & ch, Cordelia & Mable, gct Wilmington MM, O.

MURRY
1883, 3, 22. Robert recrq

MUSSETTER
1872, 6, 27. Maria recrq

MYERS
1834, 1, 24. Mary m Thomas ROBERDS

1831, 10, 27. Mary [Miers] recrq
1906, 2, 22. Minnie [Miars] rocf Center MM,O.
1916, 5, 25. Clifford D. [Miars] rocf Wilmington MM, O.

NEWBY
1859, 8, 25. Robert Furnas Jr. gct Fairfield MM, Ind., to m Axey Newby

NEWCOMER
1925, 7, 23. Grace relrq

NICHOLS
----, --, --. James b 1770,9,1; m Ann ----- b 1778,5,5
Ch: Enoch b 1803, 4, 14
Elijah " 1805, 10, 9 d 1814,12, 4 bur Caesars Creek
William b 1807, 11, 17
Joseph " 1816, 11, 18
1821, 11, 1. Enoch, s James & Anna, Clinton Co., O.; m in Caesars Creek MH, Rhoda JAY, dt James & Jemima, Clinton Co., O.
----, --, --. Anson L. b 1818,12,15; m Elizabeth J. ----- b 1837,2,22
1823, 4, 24. Enoch & w, Rhoda, & ch, Elijah, gct Cherry Grove MM, Ind.
1828, 2, 28. Enoch & w, Rhoda, & ch, Elijah, Mark & Edith, rocf Cherry Grove MM, Ind., dtd 1827,11,10
1828, 9, 25. Enoch & w, Rhoda, & ch, Elijah, Mark, Edith & James, gct Cherry Grove MM, Ind.
1831, 12, 28. Wm. dis disunity
1855, 8, 23. Wm. rst at Salem MM, Ia., on consent of this mtg
1890, 10, 23. Anson S. & w, Lizzie, recrq
1903, 9, 24. Anson & w, Elizabeth, relrq

NICHOLSON
1823, 11, 6. Bathsheba m Caleb HARVEY

1811, 6, 29. Elizabeth recrq
1812, 6, 27. Daniel & ch, Bathsheba, Jesse & Valentine, recrq
1829, 10, 29. Valentine dis jH
1829, 11, 26. Daniel dis jH
1829, 12, 31. Jesse dis jH
1830, 7, 27. Elizabeth dis jH
1831, 8, 25. Lydia dis jH
1832, 3, 22. Elizabeth & George, minors, ch Daniel, gct Duck Creek MM, Ind.

NOAH
1880, 3, 25. John O. recrq
1894, 2, 22. J. I. & w relrq
1903, 7, 23. Eva recrq
1904, 6, 23. Eva relrq

NOGGLE
1883, 3, 22. David recrq
1885, 4, 23. Bell recrq
1885, 4, 23. Ella L. C., Pearl C., Wm. C., Henry O. & Jesse F. recrq
1899, 4, 27. David J. & w, Ella L., & ch, Pearl C., Wm. C., Henry S., Jesse F., Mary Jane, Myrtle C. & Nannie G. dropped from mbrp

NORRIGAN
1876, 1, 27. Elizabeth recrq

OGLESBEE
1899, 10, 26. Martha Morgan gct Miami MM, O.
1908, 5, 28. Martha A. M. & Alice Mae rocf Miami MM, O.
1910, 6, 23. Eva Foland gct Center MM, O.
1916, 9, 21. Alice Mae relrq

OREN
1842, 11, 3. Ruth m Amos HAWKINS

----, --, --. Ira & Mary Ann
Ch: Alva W. b 1866, 12, 29
William A. " 1869, 6, 29

1817, 3, 28. James & w, Margaret, rocf Center MM, O., dtd 1816,9,21
1824, 3, 25. Joseph, s James, recrq
1824, 4, 29. James & w, Margaret, & ch, Joseph, John, Susanna, Elijah & William, gct Green Plain MM, O.
1832, 2, 23. Henry Gilpin gct Dover MM, to m Esther Oran
1841, 11, 25. Ruth, Phebe, Hannah & Elizabeth rocf Sparrow Creek MM, Ia., dtd 1841,9,13
1841, 11, 25. Jane rocf Sparrow Creek MM, Ia., dtd 1841,9,13, endorsed to Center MM, O.
1842, 8, 25. Hannah dis disunity
1845, 11, 27. Elizabeth Compton (form Oren) dis mcd
1860, 5, 24. Phebe Gilpen (form Oren) con mcd
1866, 5, 26. Mary Ann (form Hawkins) con mcd to first cousin
1869, 9, 23. Mary Ann & ch, Alva W. & William A., gct Poplar Run MM, Ind.
1876, 12, 28. Asaneth rocf Center MM, O., dtd 1876,12,13

OSBORN
1883, 4, 26. Wilson J. & w, Sarah J., & ch, Josie Bell, recrq
1884, 6, 26. Alice relrq
1885, 3, 26. Cynthia recrq
1885, 4, 23. Edwin M. recrq
1885, 4, 23. Cynthia recrq
1888, 4, 26. Alice recrq
1897, 7, 22. Edward M. dropped from mbrp
1900, 7, 24. Sarah dropped from mbrp
1900, 7, 24. Wesley dropped from mbrp
1904, 4, 21. Bertha, Argus & Idena dropped from mbrp
1916, 2, 24. Idena recrq

OWENS
----, --, --. Samuel m Margery ----- d 1812,2, 8
Ch: Sarah b 1796, 8, 15
Ephraim " 1797, 12, 23 d 1805, 7,13
John " 1800, 9, 29
Mary " 1802, 6, 7
Benjamin " 1805, 2, 6
Samuel " 1806, 11, 19
Charity " 1809, 1, 9

OWENS, Samuel, continued
Samuel m 2nd Rachel ----- d 1822,2,19 bur Caesars Creek
Ch: Jonathan b 1818, 7, 15
Ann " 1820, 7, 5
James " 1822, 2, 18
1814, 11, 3. Sarah m Obadiah MENDENHALL
1817, 7, 31. Samuel, s Ephraim & Mary, Warren Co., O.; m in Caesars Creek MH, Rachel COMPTON, dt John & Esther CAMPBELL, Warren Co., O.
1823, 10, 2. Samuel, s Ephraim & Mary, Warren Co., O.; m in Caesars Creek MH, Anna MILHOUSE, dt George & Sarah STRAWN, Clinton Co., O.
1824, 4, 1. John, s Samuel & Margery, Warren Co., O.; m in Caesars Creek MH, Rebeckah COMPTON, dt Mathew & Rachel, Warren Co.,O.
1828, 11, 5. Benjamin, s Samuel & Margaret, Clinton Co., O.; m in Richland MH, Esther C. GIBSON, dt Montillion & Sarah, Green Co., O.
Ch: Samuel Griffin b 1829, 10, 30
Sarah " 1931, 9, 12
1846, 3, 5. Tamar d
1860, 5, 9. Samuel, s John & Rebecca, Hendricks Co., Ind.; m in Richland MH, Dinah WALTON, dt Moses & Mary, Green Co., O.

1825, 10, 27. John & w, Rebeckah, & s, Amos, gct White Lick MM, Ind.
1826, 9, 28. Samuel & w, Anna, & ch, Mary, Charity, Jonathan, Anne & James, gct White Lick MM, Ind.
1829, 5, 28. Benjamin & w, Esther C., gct Green Plain MM, O.
1830, 4, 29. Benjamin & w, Esther C., rocf Green Plain MM, O., dtd 1830,4,7
1837, 9, 21. Benjamin & w, Esther C., & ch, Samuel Griffin, Sarah Maria & Mary Annie, gct White Lick MM, Ind.
1860, 7, 26. Dinah gct Bridgeport MM, Ind.

PAINTER
----, --, --. Joseph C. b 1819,5,21; m Hannah S. ----- b 1822,3,21 d 1892,7,29 bur Caesars Creek
1860, 8, 3. Naomi b
1863, 2, 23. Hannah b
1865, 8, 1. John Henry b
1866, 3, 29. Harriet M. m Hampton W. TERRELL

1866, 1, 25. Joseph C. & w, Hannah S., & ch, Harriet M., Mary Emma, Naomi, Hannah & Joseph, rocf Dover MM
1894, 1, 25. Elva Hinshaw rocf Wilmington MM, O.
1897, 6, 24. J. Henry & w, Elva, & ch, Donald H., Herbert J. & Helen M., gct Wilmington MM, O.

PAIST
1818, 5, 29. Charles & w, Abigail, & s, James, rocf Center MM, O., dtd 1818,3,21

PARKER
1878, 8, 22. Hannah rocf Green Plain MM, O.

PARNELL
1816, 12, 12. James, s James & Esther, Warren Co., O.; m in Caesars Creek MH, Margaret HAWKINS, dt Amos & Phebe, Warren Co., O.
Ch: Amos b 1818, 8, 3
John " 1819, 10, 30
Phebe " 1822, 4, 4
Jonathan " 1825, 4, 21
Mary " 1827, 10, 30
Ruth " 1831, 1, 7
1833, 10, 31. James, s James & Esther, Warren Co., O.; m in Caesars Creek MH, Hannah HAWKINS, dt John & Sarah, Warren Co., O.

1816, 11, 29. James [Parnel] rocf Miami MM, O., dtd 1816,10,30
1835, 8, 27. James & w, Hannah, & ch, Amos, John, Phebe, Jonathan, Mary & George, gct Fairfield MM, Ind.

PATTY
1813, 3, 27. Charles [Paty] dis disunity
1820, 7, 28. Chas. & w gct New Garden MM,Ind.

PATTON
1883, 3, 22. Allie recrq

PAXTON
1908, 3, 26. Elias & fam rocf Center MM, O.

PEACEMAKER
1909, 7, 22. Foster & w, Myrtle, & dt, Thelma, rocf Center MM, O.

PEARSON
1821, 11, 29. Anna m Henry HAWKINS
1850, 9, 27. Levi, s Thomas & Mary, Miami Co., O., b 1823,12,13; m in Caesars Creek MH, Mary SPRAY, dt John & Sarah, b 1830, 7,11
Ch: Sarah Jane b 1851, 8, 8
Jehu S. " 1854, 2, 3
Marcus John " 1856, 7, 8
Thomas Elwood " 1858, 9, 12
Margery O. " 1862, 1, 23
Massey Emma " 1863, 8, 4 d 1866, 9,23 bur Caesars Creek
Eunice Anna b 1866, 2, 23
Jesse William " 1867, 9, 15

PEARSON, continued
1816, 3, 29. William rocf Miami MM, O., dtd 1815,12,27
1818, 3, 27. Wm. dis jas
1851, 2, 20. Mary S. gct Union MM
1860, 3, 22. Mary & ch, Sarah Jane, Jehu S., Marcus John & Thomas Elwood, rocf West Union MM, Ind., dtd 1860,3,12
1866, 2, 22. Mary S. dis disunity
1870, 6, 23. Levi rst
1881, 7, 28. Marcus J. gct Bangor MM, Ia.
1885, 12, 24. Jehu I. gct Des Moines MM, Ia.

PEDRICK
1846, 5, 13. Hannah d ae 88 bur Caesars Creek

PEELLE
1882, 10, 26. Mary Esther gct Dover MM, O.
1905, 6, 22. Mary Emma Vantress rocf Center MM, O.
1905, 6, 22. Alonzo rocf Dover MM, O.

PEER
----, --, --. George Francis b 1847,6,10 d 1892,3,1 bur Spring Valley; m Frankie ----- b 1854,3,8 d 1890,12,18

PEGG
1814, 4, 30. John & fam rocf Deep River MM, N. C., endorsed to White Water MM, Ind.

PENNEWITT
1900, 7, 24. Melissa E. dropped from mbrp

PENNINGTON
1906, 9, 27. Parker rocf Center MM, O.
1906, 10, 25. Reverence recrq
1925, 7, 23. Rowena B. relrq

PEPPER
1868, 8, 21. Irene Kinsey b

1911, 6, 22. Irene Kinsey dropped from mbrp

PERKINS
1827, 10, 31. Maryann m David MENDENHALL

1826, 1, 26. Thomas [Pirkins] & w, Sarah, & ch, Joseph, Mary Ann, Pheninah, Isaac, Abijah, Sarah & John K., rocf Center MM,O., dtd 1825,10,15
1829, 5, 28. Thomas dis jH
1829, 8, 27. Sarah & ch, Isaac, Abijah, Sarah & John Kelly, gct White Lick MM, Ind.
1829, 9, 24. Joseph gct White Lick MM, Ind.

PERRIN
1910, 2, 24. George T., Eliza, Pearl, Estella & Walter, recrq
1913, 5, 22. George T., Eliza, Pearl & Estella dropped from mbrp
1913, 11, 27. Leta Lickliter gct Xenia MM, O.

PETERSON
1886, 1, 26. Hattie E. b
----, --, --. Isaac O. b 1870,8,11; m Jennie E. ----- b 1876,4,28
Ch: William E. b 1905, 4, 30
----, --, --. Carl L. b 1888,6,22; m Bessie L. McKINNEY b 1888,4,4

1886, 1, 28. Cora relrq
1898, 6, 23. Isaac O. recrq
1898, 6, 23. Halliel Holland relrq
1908, 7, 23. Carl recrq
1909, 6, 24. Archie E. recrq
1915, 1, 28. Ruthanna recrq
1919, 4, 24. Archie relrq
1919, 12, 25. Olive Wilson relrq
1925, 7, 23. Garfield, Hattie E. & Ruthanna relrq

PHAMY
1850, 6, 27. Mary (form Hawkins) con mcd

PIER
1884, 4, 24. George F. & w, Frankie, rocf Springfield MM, O.
1884, 7, 27. Flora, dt Geo. Frank & Frankie, recrq

PIMM
1919, 7, 24. Lewis G. & w, Mary B., rocf Salem MM, O.
1920, 8, 26. Lewis G. [Pim] & w, Mary, gct Xenia MM, O.

PLANK
1877, 11, 23. Nancy recrq
1881, 4, 21. Mollie M. recrq
1883, 9, 27. Mary relrq

PLUMMER
1838, 3, 29. Emily N. m Thomas SANDERS

1835, 9, 24. Thomas Gilpin gct Miami MM, O., to m Tacy Plummer
1837, 12, 28. Emily N. rocf Fairfield MM, dtd 1837,7,20

POST
1910, 2, 24. Lizzie recrq

POWELL
1867, 4, 28. Amanda b

1883, 3, 22. Thomas E. & w, Ura, rocf Fairfield MM, O., dtd 1883,3,17
1884, 4, 24. Thomas [Powel] & w, Ura, gct Newberry MM, O.
1887, 12, 22. Jenetta & Amanda recrq
1892, 4, 21. Wilmena recrq

POWERS
1916, 4, 27. Hazel Stingley relrq

PRAMER
1879, 4, 24. John recrq
1884, 4, 24. John dis

PRATT
1897, 8, 25. Ivanette Hathaway relrq

PRICE
1906, 1, 25. Elijah, Emma S., Flora Elizabeth & Mamie Ann, recrq
1906, 2, 22. Bertha & Walter, ch Elijah, recrq
1917, 2, 22. Emma & ch, Bertha G., Paul & Evan recrq

PRITCHART
----, --, --. Benjamin b 1819,9,10 d 1877,3,31 bur Jenkins Bur. Gr.; m Abigail ----- b 1834,10,18
Ch: Lara A. b 1855, 1-,22

1870, 6, 23. Benjamin recrq
1871, 4, 27. Emma [Prichard] recrq
1871, 5, 25. Daniel R. recrq
1884, 6, 26. Daniel & w, Emma, & ch gct Miami MM, O.
1885, 7, 23. Daniel & w, Elizabeth, & ch, Alonzo, rocf Miami MM, O.
1890, 4, 24. Anna (Adda) relrq

PRUITT
1838, 9, 27. Charles Wilson gct Fairfield MM, Ind., to m Elizabeth Pruitt

PUGH
1903, 12, 24. Mary gct Miami MM, O.

QUINN
1908, 12, 24. Ralph & w & ch, Robert, Mildred, Mabel M., Elias, George W. & Mary M., recrq

RALSTON
1901, 2, 21. Elizabeth Marshall gct Walnut Ridge MM, Ind.

RAMSEY
1897, 5, 27. Catherine Ryan recrq

RAMY
1862, 4, 24. Mary gct Wabash MM, Ind.

RANDEL
----, --, --. Jonas & -----
Ch: Rebecca b 1785, 6, 4
John " 1787, 11, 16
Jehu " 1790, 7, 27
Jonathan " 1793, 2, 27
Walter " 1795, 6, 20
Elizabeth " 1797, 10, 11

1878, 10, 24. Emma [Randal] gct West Branch MM, O.

RAYLE
1888, 6, 21. Eunice Ella gct Union Grove MM, Ind.

REAGAN
1818, 4, 19. Reason, s Thomas & Rachel, Warren Co., O., b 1797,10,13 d 1864,1,5; m in Caesars Creek MH, Mary SPRAY, dt Samuel & Mary, Clinton Co., O., b 1798,6,30 d 1852,3,17 bur Caesars Creek
Cj: John b 1818, 12, 21
Dinah " 1821, 1, 22
Rachel " 1825, 2, 22 d 1848, 4,26 bur Caesars Creek
Mary b 1829, 1, 5 d 1847, 8, 7 bur Caesars Creek
Hannah b 1832, 2, 5
1843, 9, 28. John, s Reason & Mary, Green Co., O., b 1818,12,21; m in Caesars Creek MH, Charity HAWKINS, dt Jehu & Susanna, Clinton Co., O.
Ch: Reason b 1844, 7, 7
William " 1846, 2, 20
Sarah Ann " 1848, 2, 19
Eli H. " 1850, 6, 1
Jehu S. " 1853, 2, 4
1845, 8, 29. Mary S. m Isaac COOK
1845, 10, 1. Rachel m Moses WALTON

1812, 10, 31. Ruel [Ragan] gct Miami MM, O., to m
1813, 11, 27. Reason dis mcd
1814, 1, 29. Dinah (form Wilson) dis mcd
1817, 10, 24. Thomas & w, Rachel, & ch, Reason, John, Wiley & Wm., recrq
1818, 3, 27. Jesse dis mcd
1818, 3, 27. Susannah (form Sanders) dis mcd
1820, 9, 29. Reason & w & ch gct West Grove MM, Ind.
1800, 12, 29. Thos. [Ragan] & fam gct West Grove MM, Ind.
1824, 11, 25. Mary, w Ruel, rocf Miami MM, O., dtd 1824,9,29
1824, 12, 30. Ruel [Ragan] & w, Mary, & ch, Samuel Huston Elihu Mary Patience Lydia & Rachel, gct Cherry Grove MM, Ind.
1829, 12, 31. Reason & w, Mary, & ch, John, Dinah, Rachel & Mary, rocf Milford MM, Ind., dtd 1829,11,28
1830, 2, 25. Reason & w, Dinah rst at Fairfield MM, Ind., on consent of this mtg
1831, 4, 28. Reason & w, Mary, & ch, John, Dinah, Rachel & Mary, gct Miami MM, O.
1838, 3, 22. Reason & w, Mary, & ch, John, Dinah, Rachel, Mary & Hannah, rocf Miami MM, O., dtd 1838,1,24
1843, 6, 22. Dinah Jenkins (form Reagan) dis mcd
1850, 12, 26. Hanah Bonner (form Reagan) dis mcd
1855, 1, 25. John & w, Charity, & ch, Reason,

REAGAN, continued
Wm. J., Sarah Ann, Eli H. & Jehu S., gct Fairfield MM, Ind.
1855, 1, 25. Reason gct Fairfield MM, Ind.

REDDICK
1894, 2, 22. Frank recrq

REED
1816, 8, 30. Amasa & w, Sarah, rocf Uxbridge MM, dtd 1816,5,31
1828, 6, 26. Amesa & w, Sarah, dis jas
1835, 11, 26. Sarah Ann Robinson (form Reed) dis mcd
1835, 12, 24. Mary dis jas
1885, 4, 23. Margery recrq
1886, 3, 25. Wm. recrq
1900, 3, 22. Eva recrq

REEDER
1884, 3, 27. David recrq
1885, 2, 19. Jane relrq
1897, 7, 22. David dropped from mbrp
1897, 7, 22. Jane dropped from mbrp

REESE
1908, 6, 25. Rosa recrq
1925, 7, 23. Rosa & Charles & s relrq

REEVES
1870, 9, 12. Elmer D. b
----, --, --. John b 1850,12,12; m Katie ----- b 1852,5,20
Ch: Ora F. b 1878, 5, 13
William A. " 1880, 8, 25
John W. " 1882, 9, 4
Freddie G. " 1886, 5, 4
----, --, --. Robert b 1822,10,15 d 1897,2,28
----, --, --. ----- m Belle -----, dt Wm. H. & Charlotte BLAIR, b 1850,8,10 d 1918,8,11
Ch: Josephine J. b 1883, 1, 21
Raymond " 1886, 5, 28
Frank P. " 1889, 4, 7
----, --, --. Harry b 1872,4,20; m Eva N. ----- b 1875,11,17
Ch: Morris J. b 1896, 2, 27
----, --, --. George S. b 1880,7,31; m Etta MILLS b 1887,8,21

1877, 3, 22. Robert [Reaves] recrq
1881, 4, 21. Frances B. [Reaves] recrq
1885, 4, 23. John J. recrq
1885, 4, 23. Catherine recrq
1885, 6, 25. Ora Francis & Wm. Abraham [Reaves], ch John, recrq
1892, 4, 21. Harry & Wm. [Reaves] recrq
1894, 4, 26. Bell recrq
1896, 3, 26. Josephine, J. Raymond & Frankie R., ch Bell, recrq
1901, 4, 25. Elmer D. recrq
1901, 4, 25. George Sullivan recrq
1901, 4, 25. Ethel recrq
1906, 1, 25. Harry B. & w, Eva, & ch, Morris & Gilbert, gct White Water MM, Ind.
1909, 1, 28. Ora F. relrq
1909, 4, 22. Laura recrq
1913, 5, 22. George S., Etta Mills, Wm. H., Raymond, Elma & Frank dropped from mbrp
1913, 6, 26. John & Katie dropped from mbrp
1917, 7, 26. Laura & John W. dropped from mbrp
1920, 2, 12. Josephine relrq
1925, 2, 22. Claire Ewing relrq

RICHARDS
1828, 8, 27. Neomi rocf Center MM, O.
1839, 5, 23. Naomi gct Fairfield MM, Ind.

RIDDELL
1837, 4, 26. Robert [Ridell] b

1871, 4, 27. Robert recrq
1874, 3, 26. Lydia J. recrq
1913, 5, 22. Robert [Riddel] dropped from mbrp

RILEY
1875, 3, 28. Wm. b
1877, 2, 27. Rosella b
----, --, --. David F. b 1867,9,7; m Dora J. ----- b 1870,11,29
Ch: Clarence A. b 1887, 10, 11
Hazel R. " 1891, 12, 10
Flossie M. " 1894, 9, 19
Helen R. " 1903, 8, 16

1896, 3, 26. Rosella recrq
1898, 4, 21. Wm. recrq
1903, 4, 23. David T. recrq
1904, 3, 24. Clarence H. recrq
1908, 2, 20. Dora J. & ch, Hazel R., Flossie M. & Helen R., recrq
1911, 9, 21. Wm. dropped from mbrp
1916, 4, 27. Helen relrq

RHODE
1811, 4, 27. Thomas, Caleb & Semour [Roads], ch Mary, recrq
1817, 11, 28. Thomas [Rhode] gct Center MM, O., to m
1818, 7, 24. Mary [Rhoad] rocf Center MM, O., dtd 1818,5,16
1820, 5, 26. Caleb dis mcd
1820, 7, 27. Semour dis disunity
1829, 9, 24. Thomas & w, Mary, & ch, Sarah Esther Elizabeth Mary John & Joseph, gct White Lick MM, Ind.

ROBERDS
----, --, --. Thomas m Ann WHITSON
Ch: Rebeckah b 1787, 8, 8
Walter " 1789, 10, 2
David " 1792, 8, 18

ROBERDS, continued
1834, 1, 24. Thomas, s Thomas & Ann, Wayne Co., Ind.; m in Caesars Creek MH, Mary MYERS, dt Ralph & Prudence, Clinton Co.,O.

1826, 6, 29. Mary (form Allen) dis mcd
1834, 6, 26. Mary gct White Water MM, Ind.
1884, 4, 24. Asenath gct Dover MM, O.

ROBERTSON
1820, 10, 27. Mary (form Walters) dis mcd

ROBINETT
1907, 10, 24. Levisa recrq

ROBINSON
1872, 8, 30. Lucy Belle, dt Neri & Mary A. Moon, b

1835, 11, 26. Sarah Ann (form Reed) dis mcd
1872, 6, 27. Nelson recrq
1885, 7, 23. Lewis recrq
1901, 10, 24. Lewis dropped from mbrp
1923, 4, 29. Mary dropped from mbrp

ROHRBACK
1916, 2, 24. Susan recrq
1922, 2, 23. Goldie recrq

ROLAND
1913, 5, 22. Henry & sister, Jane, rocf Xenia MM, O.

ROMINE
1872, 4, 25. Emily recrq
1881, 2, 24. Dora recrq

----, --, --. Emily b 1813,9,20 d 1886,10,15 bur Caesars Creek

ROONEY
----, --, --. Michael [Roney] b 1829,4,1; m Virginia -----, dt John & Lydia Anderson, b 1841,11,11
Ch: Charley
Creighton b 1870, 4, 6
Harry Walter " 1872, 2, 24
Samuel T. " 1884, 2, 21

1874, 1, 22. Michael & w, Virginia, & ch, Charles C. & Harry Walter, recrq
1901, 10, 24. Harry dropped from mbrp
1901, 10, 24. Charles C. dropped from mbrp
1913, 5, 22. Samuel F. dropped from mbrp

RUDDICK
1824, 4, 29. John recrq
1824, 5, 27. Urxala recrq
1825, 1, 27. John & w, Ursala, gct Center MM, O.
1917, 3, 22. Agnes recrq
1917, 4, 26. Rosa recrq

RUST
1900, 3, 22. Marilla recrq

RYAN
1870, 6, 23. Ephraim E. recrq
1871, 10, 26. Ephraim relrq
1872, 6, 27. Ephraim recrq
1898, 5, 26. Catherine Ramsey relrq

SADDERS
1894, 9, 27. Abigail Pritchard relrq

SANDERS
----, --, --. Joel b 1751,8,9 d 1819,9,18 bur Caesars Creek; m Sarah ----- d 1828,10,26
----, --, --. William & Amy
Ch: Sarah b 1803, 1, 3
Mary " 1804, 9, 20
Charity " 1806, 6, 12
Barbara " 1808, 1, 4 d 1811, 3,28 bur Caesars Creek
Daniel b 1809, 3, 22
Ruth " 1810, 7, 25 " 1818,12,29 bur Caesars Creek
Rebecca b 1812, 11, 27
Joel " 1814, 3, 5
Eli " 1815, 12, 6
Libby " 1817, 12, 29
Elihu " 1819, 9, 6
Rhoda " 1821, 7, 8
William " 1823, 3, 1
1813, 9, 30. Sarah m John SPRAY
1824, 11, 4. Mary m Enoch MILLS
1826, 4, 6. Charity m Mark MILLS
1827, 5, 30. Miriam d (sister of Joel)
1833, 11, 7. Daniel, s William & Amy, Warren Co., O.; m in Caesars Creek MH, Rachel MILLS, dt John & Phebe, Clinton Co., O.
1838, 3, 29. Thomas, s Jonathan & Lydia, Warren Co., O.; m in Caesars Creek MH, Emily PLUMMER, dt Asa & Grace, Clinton Co., O.
1845, 6, 25. Rebecca A. b

1811, 8, 31. Massey con mcd
1811, 11, 30. Anny & ch, Sarah, Mary, Charity, Daniel & Ruth, recrq
1812, 10, 31. William rst; dis by Wrightsborough MM, S. C., since laid down
1815, 1, 27. Miriam con mcd
1818, 3, 27. Susannah Reagan (form Sanders) dis mcd
1820, 9, 29. Jesse dis disunity
1821, 6, 27. Sarah Scott (form Sanders) dis mcd
1822, 7, 26. Alice (form Allen) con mcd
1825, 3, 31. Miriam gct White Lick MM, Ind.
1827, 11, 29. Massey gct Fairfield MM, Ind.
1832, 10, 25. Wm. & w, Amy, & ch, Joel, Eli, Libby, Elihu, Rhoda, William & James Scott, gct Fairfield MM, Ind.
1832, 10, 25. Rebecca, dt Wm., gct Fairfield MM, Ind.
1832, 11, 22. Mary recrq

SANDERS, continued
1836, 8, 25. Daniel & w, Rachel, & ch, Lydia, gct Fairfield MM, Ind.
1838, 2, 22. Thomas Jr. rocf Clear Creek MM, O., dtd 1838,2,2
1839, 4, 25. Thomas & w, Emily N., gct Fairfield MM, Ind.
1875, 5, 27. Roster recrq
1878, 4, 25. Droster relrq
1884, 9, 25. Roster dis
1896, 3, 26. Rebecca recrq
1913, 6, 26. Ermel E. gct Dayton MM, O.; returned at her rq 1813,8,28
1914, 6, 25. Ermel E. dropped from mbrp

SANDERSON
1905, 7, 27. Frank rocf Sabina MM, O.
1905, 7, 27. Francis rocf Sabina MM, O.

SATTERTHWAIT
1873, 10, 27. Fannie Vance b
1900, 6, 21. Frances Vance gct Miami MM, O.
1907, 4, 25. Fanny Vance rocf Miami MM, O.

SEXTON
1837, 3, 7. Sarah, dt Mary, b
1840, 2, 7. Hannah, dt Mary, b
1843, 3, 29. Mary m James MOORMAN

1822, 6, 28. Mary [Saxton] (form Compton) con mcd
1844, 12, 26. Sarah & Hannah [Saxton] ch Mary Moorman, recrq

SAYERS
1872, 2, 22. John H. recrq
1872, 2, 22. Lottie recrq
1898, 1, 27. Wilbur recrq
1875, 9, 23. Wm. [Saires] recrq
1890, 4, 24. Wm. [Sears] gct Miami MM, O.

SCAMMAHORN
1889, 2, 21. Cora May [Scamahorn] recrq
1900, 3, 22. Eunice & Helen recrq
1911, 9, 21. Helen dropped from mbrp

SCHELL
1885, 4, 23. Ira recrq
1897, 7, 22. Ira dropped from mbrp

SCHWIBOLD
1925, 7, 23. Ethel relrq

SCOTT
1815, 5, 4. Patsy m Enoch MILLS
----, --, --. William & Sarah
Ch: John b 1822, 1, 25
Isum " 1823, 8, 12
Eli " 1824, 11, 8
James " 1826, 2, 25
1829, 5, 4. Sarah m Samuel MILHOUS

1815, 2, 24. Patsey recrq
1821, 6, 27. Sarah (form Sanders) dis mcd
1827, 12, 27. Sarah rst
1828, 5, 29. John Isum, Eli & James, ch Sarah, recrq
1834, 8, 28. Samuel Milhouse & w, Sarah, & ch, John, Isam & Eli Scott, & Henry, Mary, Charity & Amos Milhouse, gct Fairfield MM, Ind.

SCROGGY
----, --, --. Francis b 1847,11,30; m Sary J. ----- b 1848,3,22
Ch: Wilber b 1874, 7, 5
Alpha H.
----, --, --. Ira E. b 1850,7,28; m Mary E. ----- b ----, 2, 8
Ch: Walter A. b 1882, 10, 18 d 1884, 3, 4
Raymond C. " 1886, 4, 12
Jesse Edgar " 1889, 4, 24 " 1891, 8,10
Herman A. " 1894, 7, 18
----, --, --. Thomas m Anna ----- b 1863,3,8
Ch: Naomi C. b 1894, 4, 23
Jesse J. " 1896, 8, 9
Carric " 1897, 11, 23

1870, 4, 21. Ira recrq
1870, 4, 21. Francis B. recrq
1879, 4, 24. Elizabeth recrq
1883, 3, 22. Sallie recrq
1883, 4, 26. Thomas recrq
1898, 2, 24. Hattie recrq
1908, 3, 26. Annie & ch, Naomi C., Jessie J., Cory D., Robert E., Joseph N., Jennie R. & Lydia E., gct Wilmington MM, O.
1913, 5, 22. Francis W., Wilbert & Alpha dropped from mbrp
1914, 4, 23. Raymond relrq
1918, 1, 24. Raymond C. recrq

SEARS
1877, 7, 26. Edward & w, Anna, recrq

SEVERS
1870, 4, 21. Lydia recrq
----, --, --. Lydia Ann b 1846,10,10 d 1895,12 14 bur Jenkins Bur. Gr.

SEVORT
1925, 7, 23. Zella & ch relrq

SEWELL
1880, 3, 25. Amanda recrq

SHAFER
1871, 9, 21. Lucinda & Mary Jane recrq
1872, 12, 25. Christine Lauretta & Sarah Ella Ora, ch Lucinda, recrq
1885, 2, 19. Ora Harvey (form Shafer) relrq
1885, 5, 28. Lucinda & dt dropped from mbrp

SHAMBAUGH
1839, 10, 15. Sarah A. b

SHAMBAUGH, continued
1884, 6, 26. I. N. & w, Sarah Ann, recrq
1897, 1, 28. Mildred Esther, dt Elizabeth, recrq
1911, 5, 25. Hazel, Helen & Levi J. recrq
1921, 2, 24. Horace & w, Emma, recrq
1925, 7, 23. Horace relrq

SHANE
1913, 5, 22. Fred dropped from mbrp

SHAW
1881, 4, 21. Martha & Hanna recrq
1884, 3, 27. George, Minnie & James recrq
1897, 7, 22. George & James dropped from mbrp
1897, 7, 22. Martha dropped from mbrp
1897, 7, 22. Minnie dropped from mbrp
1922, 2, 23. John H., Effie Marie, Jesse Paul, Helen Augusta, Eva Josephine & Thelma Wilma, recrq

SHEETS
----, --, --. Franzy & Mary Helen
Ch: Ernest b 1915, 2, 23
June " 1916, 6, 9

1933, 4, 30. June & Ernest recrq

SHEPHERD
----, --, --. Charles Randolph, s Daniel & Hannah, b 1859,8,24; m Lydia Ellen WILSON, dt Amos & Mary B., b 1854,7,31
Ch: Frank b 1884, 11, 6
Mary Lena " 1887, 7, 10
Cora Louisa " 1891, 11, 11
Ernest " 1893, 6, 19
Amos Wilson " 1897, 7, 12

1881, 2, 24. Lizzie recrq
1882, 5, 25. Albert recrq
1905, 2, 3. Lena recrq
1905, 2, 3. Cora recrq
1905, 7, 27. Helen recrq

SHERWOOD
1872, 10, 28. Malinda b

1900, 6, 21. Malinda rocf Miami MM, O.

SHOCKLEY
1915, 3, 25. Nola recrq
1926, 11, 28. Viola dropped from mbrp

SHOEMAKER
1886, 4, 22. Abraham recrq
1897, 7, 22. Abraham dropped from mbrp
1897, 7, 22. Mary dropped from mbrp

SHORT
1908, 12, 24. Mary recrq

SIMMS
1867, 8, 31. Alice b
----, --, --. Joseph C. b 1839,12,8; m Frances M. ----- b 1835,6,8
Ch: William B. b 1871, 12, 18
Charles C. " 1875, 1, 22

1880, 3, 25. Joseph E. [Sims] recrq
1881, 4, 21. Francis M., Willie B. & Chas. Cliff [Sims] recrq
1884, 3, 27. George V. [Sims] recrq
1891, 2, 19. G. Val [Sims] relrq
1896, 3, 26. Minnie [Sims] recrq
1898, 5, 26. Alice [Syms] rocf Miami MM, O.
1909, 2, 25. Lawrence recrq
1911, 9, 21. Wm. B. dropped from mbrp
1917, 7, 26. Joseph C., Francis M. & Lawrence [Sims] dropped from mbrp

SIMMONS
1811, 12, 28. Abigail recrq

SIMPSON
1886, 3, 25. Eleazar recrq
1900, 3, 22. Elizabeth [Simson] recrq
1901, 5, 23. Edward [Simison] relrq
1910, 2, 24. Helen [Simison] recrq

SINCLAIR
----, --, --. Emerson m Pearl CREAGER b 1898, 7,16
Ch: Ladonna L. b 1917, 11, 19
Louise L. " 1921, 6, 10
Lowell L. " 1922, 11, 23
Louella " 1930, 3, 19

1933, 3, 26. Pearl & Ladonna & Louise recrq
1933, 4, 30. Lowell recrq
1933, 6, 25. Louise recrq

SINNARD
1884, 3, 27. James, Rebecca, Silas, Nancy E. & Sarah J. recrq
1884, 3, 27. Flora E. recrq
1884, 3, 27. William W. recrq
1913, 5, 22. Wm. W. dropped from mbrp

SLEEPER
1818, 11, 4. Charles, s Samuel & Patience, Clark Co.; m in Green Plain, Anne WILLIS, dt William & Henrietta, Clark Co., O.
1819, 12, 8. Keturah m Seth WILLIAMS

1818, 8, 28. Samuel & w, Patience, & ch, Keturah, Avis, Budder & Jacob, rocf Marlborough MM, dtd 1818,7,15
1818, 8, 28. Charles rocf Marlborough MM, dtd 1818,7,15
1827, 5, 31. Elizabeth rocf Miami MM, O., dtd 1827,4,25
1830, 6, 24. Elizabeth dis jH
1837, 3, 23. William Meridith, minor, gct

SLEEPER, continued
ND MM, Pa.

SMALLEY
1906, 11, 22. Daniel C. recrq
1907, 4, 25. Cora [Smaley] recrq

SMEDLEY
1886, 3, 25. Margaret recrq
1886, 6, 24. Margaret relrq

SMITH
1861, 10, 27. Frank B. b
1872, 5, 8. Nettie b
1884, 6, 12. James Bruce b
1893, 4, 18. Eunice b

1814, 2, 26. Elizabeth & s, Seth, rocf Fairfield MM, dtd 1812,7,25, endorsed by Center MM, O., 1813,11,6
1815, 7, 28. Seth roff Newhope MM, Tenn., dtd 1815,2,8
1819, 7, 30. James rocf Smithfield MM, R. I., dtd 1816,11,28
1819, 12, 27. Elizabeth dis
1821, 4, 27. Elizabeth rst
1821, 11, 28. James rocf Springfield MM, R. I., dtd 1816,11,28
1822, 3, 22. James gct Miami MM, O.
1874, 1, 22. Ann recrq
1881, 4, 2. Anna recrq
1884, 3, 27. Frank R. recrq
1884, 3, 27. Mary recrq
1885, 6, 25. Mary Ellen gct Portland MM, Ind.
1888, 4, 26. Nettie recrq
1897, 7, 22. Rose dropped from mbrp
1901, 4, 25. Clara May recrq
1901, 4, 25. James Bruce recrq
1907, 12, 26. Bruce & sister, Clara, relrq
1908, 12, 24. Lawrence & Pearl recrq
1909, 4, 22. Bruce & Clara recrq
1917, 3, 22. Urshel recrq
1917, 7, 26. Eunice dropped from mbrp
1921, 4, 21. Reva Marie recrq
1925, 7, 23. Mary E. & Donald relrq
1925, 7, 23. Marshall relrq

SMITTLE
1907, 3, 28. Thomas H. & Cathron recrq

SNELLEN
1879, 4, 24. George recrq
1881, 2, 24. Carrie [Snelley] recrq

SOHNS
----, --, --. Lewis & Elizabeth
Ch: Lula Belle b 1915, 5, 15
Anna

1927, 8, 28. Lulu B. [Sons] recrq

SOWARD
1874, 5, 28. Elisha recrq
1878, 12, 26. T. J. relrq

SPEER
----, --, --. Samuel [Spear] d 1857,2,2 bur Caesars Creek; m Lydia ----- d 1852,8,19 bur Caesars Creek
----, --, --. James b 1808,4,23 d 1853,12,19 bur Caesars Creek; m Mary ----- b 1810,9,19 d 1887,12,28 bur Caesars Creek
Ch: John F. b 1837, 12, 31
Henry
Lydia M. " 1842, 12, 8
Benjamin H." 1845, 5, 19
----, --, --. Samuel [Spear] b 1835,9,29; m Eliza ----- b 1836,11,25
Ch: James b 1858, 4, 16 d 1864, 8,21
Henry " 1861, 10, 18 " 1864, 8,21

1826, 8, 31. Samuel [Spear] & w, Lydia, rocf Springfield MM, N. C., dtd 1826,6,7
1834, 2, 20. Nancy (form Stanfield) con mcd
1850, 10, 24. Mary [Spear] recrq
1852, 12, 25. James [Spear] recrq
1853, 3, 24. John F., Lydia M. & Benjamin H. [Spear] ch James, recrq
1859, 1, 27. Samuel [Spear] & w, Eliza, & s, James, rocf Vermillion MM, Ill., dtd 1859,1,1
1861, 11, 21. John F. gct Bridgepoty MM, Ind., to m Mary Spray
1864, 3, 24. John gct Bridgeport MM, Ind.
1865, 4, 27. Samuel [Spear] & w, Eliza, gct Vermillion MM, Ill.
1866, 1, 25. Mary gct Ash Grove MM, Ill.
1867, 9, 26. Benjamin H. gct Ash Grove MM, Ill.
1875, 11, 13. Ann [Sphar] recrq
1876, 12, 28. Mary recrq
1902, 1, 23. John F. & Mary E., & ch, Grace Anna, S. Orricy rocf Dover MM, dtd 1902,1,16
1904, 5, 26. Leonidas & w, Martha J., & ch, Cleo F., Leon Spray, Ray Cyrus & Paul Stanley, rocf Dover MM, O.
1908, 7, 23. John F., Mary E., Grace A. & Orricy, gct White Water MM, Ind.
1908, 12, 24. John T. & w, Mary E., & ch, Grace A. & Orricy, gct White Water MM,Ind.
1911, 9, 21. Grace dropped from mbrp
1911, 9, 21. Anna dropped from mbrp
1913, 6, 26. Mattie & ch, Cleo F., Leon, Ray, Paul Stanley & Ralph, gct Dayton MM, O.; returned at her rq
1917, 7, 26. Leonidas E. & w, Mattie E., & ch, Cleo F., Leon, Ray, Paul Stanley & Ralph, dropped from mbrp

SPELLMAN
1910, 2, 24. Hattie, Ella, Bertha & Elsie recrq
1925, 7, 23. Ella relrq

SPENCER
1886, 3, 25. Elmer & Mary recrq
1908, 12, 24. Fay recrq
1910, 4, 21. George & Augusta E. recrq

SPRAY
----, --, --. Samuel b 1758,3,23 d 1836,3,20 bur Caesars Creek; m Mary ----- b 1760, 12,18 d 1843,6,18 bur Caesars Creek
Ch: John b 1790, 2, 15
James " 1793, 8, 17
Dinah " 1794, 10, 9
Samuel " 1796, 4, 30
Mary " 1798, 6, 30
Jesse " 1801, 2, 5
----, --, --. Mordecai b 1767,2,3; m Sarah ----- b 1770,3,25
Ch: Mary b 1795, 3, 1
Henry " 1797, 12, 22
William " 1801, 11, 6
Jesse " 1803, 11, 5
John " 1807, 5, 17
1813, 9, 30. John, s Samuel & Mary, Warren Co., O.; m in Caesars Creek MH, Sarah SANDERS, dt John & Massey, Warren Co., O.
----, --, --. John b 1790,2,15 d 1853,6,6 bur Caesars Creek; m Sarah ----- b 1796,6,24 d 1840,7,31 bur Caesars Creek
Ch: Jesse b 1815, 7, 9
Margery " 1817, 8, 16
Dinah " 1819, 2, 22
Martin " 1821, 9, 3 d 1845, 2, 5 bur Caesars Creek
Massie b 1824, 8, 23
Jehu " 1826, 7, 25
Elihu " 1828, 9, 22 " 1899, 9,13 bur in Kansas
Mary b 1830, 7, 11
Sarah " 1837, 9, 20
----, --, --. James b 1793,8, 7; m Charity ----- d 1866,10,30 bur Caesars Creek
Ch: Phebe b 1817, 1, 14
Mary " 1818, 9, 28
Susannah " 1823, 1, 23
Isaac " 1825, 7, 8
Samuel " 1830, 2, 15 d 1847, 2,19 bur Caesars Creek
----, --, --. Samuel & Esther
Ch: Elizabeth b 1818, 8, 19
James " 1821, 8, 21
John " 1824, 9, 29
1818, 4, 9. Mary m Reason REAGAN
----, --, --. Jesse b 1801,2,5 d 1881,1,1 bur Caesars Creek; m Mary ----- b 1803,6,3 d 1844,5,4 bur Caesars Creek
Ch: Joseph b 1820, 11, 27
Samuel " 1822, 10, 3
Christopher " 1824, 10, 1
John " 1826, 11, 13 d 1842, 9, 3 bur Caesars Creek
Uriah b 1828, 10, 29
Esther " 1831, 7, 16 d 1919, 3,10 bur Caesars Creek
Ch: James b 1833, 11, 28 d 1868, 9,21 bur Caesars Creek
Amos b 1838, 3, 10
Maryann " 1840, 6, 29 " 1860, 9,25 bur Caesars Creek
Dinah b 1843, 6, 19 " 1864, 5,18 bur Caesars Creek
Jesse m 2nd Rebecca ----- d 1871,9,8 bur Caesars Creek
1835, 4, 2. Elizabeth m James WILSON
1836, 1, 7. Mary m Allen EDWARDS
1836, 3, 3. Margery m Samuel T. STEDDOM
----, --, --. Jesse Jr. b 1815,7,9; m Eunice ----- b 1815,2,11
Ch: John b 1837, 7, 24 d 1842, 1,18 bur Caesars Creek
Henry b 1839, 11, 2
1839, 4, 4. Joseph, s Jesse & Mary, Clinton Co., O.; m in Caesars Creek MH, Dinah WILSON, dt Christopher & Mary, Warren Co., O.
1839, 4, 4. Dinah m Lewis WALKER
1840, 1, 30. Massey m Amos HAWKINS
1840, 7, 2. Elizabeth m George WHITE
1841, 9, 9. Samuel, s Jesse & Mary, Clinton Co., O.; m in Caesars Creek MH, Rachel WALKER, dt William & Martha, Clinton Co., O.
Ch: Mary b 1846, 4, 28
1844, 10, 31. Christopher, s Jesse & Mary, Clinton Co., O., b 1824,10,1; m in Caesars Creek MH, Elizabeth JAY, dt John & Lydia, Clinton Co., O., b 1825,10,7
Ch: John b 1845, 9, 15
Jesse " 1848, 10, 8
James " 1851, 9, 8
Lydia Jane " 1854, 12, 1
1845, 4, 3. Dinah m Wm. JESSOP
1847, 8, 5. Uriah, s Jesse & Mary, Clinton Co., O.; m in Caesars Creek MH, Mary MILLS dt Thomas & Jane
1848, 10, 12. Esther m Jesse COMPTON
1850, 9, 27. Mary m Levi PEARSON
1852, 3, 4. Jehu, s John & Sarah, Clinton Co., O.; m in Caesars Creek MH, Rebecca MILLS, dt William & Elizabeth, Warren Co., O.
1852, 5, 5. Harlan, ch Isaac & Rebecca, b
1852, 6, 9. Elihu, s John & Sarah, b 1828,9, 22; m in Richland MH, Hannah MENDENHALL, dt William & Betty, Green Co., O.
Ch: William Allen b 1854, 2, 15
----, --, --. Amos b 1838,3,16; m Elizabeth Ellen ----- b 1837,5,10 d 1863,3,14 bur Caesars Creek
Ch: Clara Emma b 1857, 6, 26
Eli N. " 1860, 8, 7
Charles Franklin " 1862, 9, 24
Amos m 2nd Sarah Ann ----- d 1919,3,20 bur St. Mary's, O.
Ch: Alva G. b 1865, 9, 18

SPRAY, continued
----, --, --. Henry b 1839,11,2; m Mary A. ----- b 1843,12,23

1811, 9, 28. James & ch, Benjamin, Rebecah, Elizabeth, William, Elias & James, recrq
1813, 5, 29. Rebecca McKinsey (form Spray) dis mcd
1814, 1, 29. Benjamin dis disunity
1816, 4, 26. Elizabeth Lacy (form Spray) dis mcd
1816, 5, 24. James Jr. dis mcd
1818, 1, 30. Samuel Jr. dis mcd
1818, 4, 24. Mary Cox (form Spray) con mcd
1819, 9, 24. William dis mcd
1819, 10, 29. Jesse gct Silver Creek MM, Ind., to m
1819, 12, 27. Wm., s Mordecai, dis
1820, 4, 28. Esther & dt, Elizabeth, recrq
1820, 5, 26. Mary, w Jesse, rocf Silver Creek MM, Ind., dtd 1820,5,13
1823, 4, 24. Jesse, s Mordecai, dis disunity
1823, 4, 24. Elias con mcd
1824, 4, 29. Charity & ch, Phebe, Mary & Susanna, recrq
1824, 10, 28. James, s James, dis disunity
1824, 11, 25. Elias dis disunity
1825, 4, 28. James dis mcd
1826, 6, 29. Hannah (form Cox) con mcd
1828, 7, 21. John, s Mordecai, dis disunity
1829, 11, 26. Henry dis disunity
1830, 6, 24. Hannah dis jH
1833, 1, 24. Jesse rst
1834, 5, 22. Jesse gct White River MM, Ind.
1836, 7, 28. Jesse Jr. gct Miami MM, O., to m Eunace Stedom
1837, 3, 23. Eunice Steddom rocf Miami MM, O., dtd 1837,1,25
1837, 8, 24. Samuel & w, Esther, & ch, James John Henry Wilson & Mary, gct Fairfield MM, Ind.
1837, 4, 27. Phebe Lloyd (form Spray) con mcd
1840, 4, 23. Elizabeth recrq
1841, 5, 27. Susanna Bradford (form Spray) dis mcd
1842, 8, 25. Joseph & w, Dinah, & ch, Mary W. & Jesse, gct Fairfield MM, Ind.
1846, 2, 19. Jesse gct Miami MM, O., to m Rebecca Burnett
1846, 9, 24. Rebecca rocf Miami MM, O., dtd 1846,5,27
1846, 11, 26. Isaac dis mcd
1847, 12, 25. Uriah & w, Mary, gct Fairfield MM, Ind.
1848, 8, 24. Samuel & w, Rachel, & ch, Mary & William W., gct Fairfield MM, Ind.
1853, 10, 27. Jehu & w, Rebecca, & ch, Sarah Elizabeth, gct Fairfield MM, Ind.
1855, 11, 22. Elihu & w, Hannah, & ch, Wm. Allen, gct Honey Creek MM, Ind.
1857, 11, 26, Sarah gct Fairfield MM, Ind.
1858, 10, 28. Sarah gct Bear Creek MM, Ia.
1858, 12, 23. Amos con mcd
1860, 4, 26. Elizabeth Ellen & dt, Clara Ema, recrq
1861, 11, 21. John F. Speer gct Bridgeport MM, Ind., to m Mary Spray
1863, 3, 26. Henry gct Center MM, O., to m Mary Ann McMillan
1863, 8, 27. Mary Ann rocf Center MM, O.
1864, 1, 28. Samuel & w, Rachel, & ch, Mary, Wm. W., Esther & Jesse Milton, rocf Fairfield MM, Ind.
1864, 2, 25. James & w, Charity, gct Springfield MM, O.
1865, 2, 23. Amos con mcd
1865, 3, 23. Sarah Ann recrq
1866, 4, 26. Mary gct Fairfield MM, Ind.
1866, 4, 26. Christopher & w, Elizabeth, & ch, John Jesse James & Lydia Jane, gct Greenwood MM, Ind.
1866, 8, 23. Samuel & w, Rachel, & ch, Wm. W., Esther & Jesse Milton, gct Fairfield MM, Ind.
1892, 3, 24. Henry & Mary relrq
1898, 8, 25. Isaac T. rocf Springfield MM, O.

SPROUT
1876, 1, 27. E. T. recrq
1884, 9, 25. Penn dis
1901, 4, 25. Clarence recrq

SQUIRES
1857, 3, 12. Belle b

1908, 12, 24. Isadore Bell gct White Water MM, Ind.
1919, 9, 28. Isadore rocf Dayton MM, O.

STANFIELD
----, --, --. William b 1767,8,15 d 1842,5,23 bur Caesars Creek; m Charity MENDENHALL b 1767,2,15 d 1853,8,10 bur Caesars Creek
Ch: Jane b 1792, 9, 19
Samuel " 1793, 11, 26
Jane " 1795, 2, 24
Mary " 1797, 7, 4
William " 1804, 8, 13 d 1805,10,18 bur Caesars Creek
Nancy b 1808, 1, 2 " 1845, 7,21 bur Caesars Creek
1801, 7, 5. Massy b
1840, 9, 29. Charity b

1814, 7, 30. Jane Crumley (form Stanfield) dis mcd
1815, 7, 28. Mary dis
1818, 5, 29. Samuel dis disunity
1819, 1, 29. John dis mcd to first cousin
1819, 2, 26. Ruth (form Mendenhall) dis mcd to first cousin
1834, 2, 20. Nancy Speer (form Standfield) con mcd
1870, 6, 23. Ruth recrq
1871, 4, 27. James Jr. & Charity recrq
1879, 4, 24. Evan J. recrq

STANFIELD, continued
1884, 7, 27. James gct Springfield MM, O.
1902, 2, 20. Lida recrq
1905, 2, 3. Hazel recrq
1911, 7, 27. Chanty dropped from mbrp

STANLEY
----, --, --. Olive T. b 1848,12,20 d 1877,1, 9 bur Sharon
1851, 1, 1. Isaiah b
1855, 4, 20. Franklin b
----, --, --. Robert, s Frank & Amelia, b 1888, 2,25; m Adeline COMPTON, dt Wm. & Sarah, b 1889,2,26
Ch: Charles Edward b 1910, 1, 18
Mary Edith " 1911, 9, 7
Wayne Compton " 1913, 9, 12
Sarah " 1918, 3, 31

1870, 4, 21. Oliver recrq
1870, 8, 25. Isaiah recrq
1871, 4, 26. Francis recrq
1877, 8, 23. Isaiah dis disunity
1877, 8, 23. Francis dis
1885, 4, 23. Eva recrq
1886, 3, 25. Cynthia & Edith recrq
1887, 1, 27. Florence A. recrq
1891, 5, 28. Franklin recrq
1892, 4, 21. Maggie recrq
1896, 4, 23. Eva relrq
1901, 10, 24. Isaiah recrq
1905, 2, 3. Robert & Howard recrq
1915, 1, 28. Jesse recrq
1917, 3, 22. Mabel C., Howard & Birdella recrq
1923, 4, 29. Jesse, Howard, Birdella & Mabel dropped from mbrp
1925, 11, 29. Robert & fam gct Beech Grove MM

STANTON
1846, 7, 13. James, s William & Margaret, Green Co., O.; m in Caesars Creek MH, Dinah HAWKINS, dt Jehu & Susanna, Clinton Co., O.

1847, 3, 25. James & w, Dinah, gct Dover MM

STAR
1880, 5, 27. Elizabeth recrq

STARBUCK
1832, 11, 1. Samuel, s Gayer & Susanna, Clinton Co., O.; m in Caesars Creek MH, Rebecca FURNAS, dt Robert & Hannah, Warren Co., O.

1833, 3, 31. Rebecca Furnas gct Dover MM, O.

STEDDOM
1836, 3, 3. Samuel T., s John & Alice, Warren Co., O.; m in Caesars Creek MH, Margery SPRAY, dt John & Sarah, Clinton Co., O.
1840, 4, 30. John Furnas, s Samuel & Susanna, Warren Co., O.; m in Caesars Creek MH, Mary Ann COMPTON, dt John & Ann, Warren Co., O.
1855, 10, 31. Abijah, s John & Alice, Warren Co., O.; m in Richland MH, Deborah MENDENHALL, dt William & Betty, Green Co., O.

1833, 9, 26. John Compton gct Miami MM, O., to m Rebecca STEADHAM
1836, 6, 23. Margery gct Miami MM, O.
1836, 7, 28. Jesse Spray Jr. gct Miami MM, O., to m Eunace Stedom
1846, 3, 26. Mary Ann gct Miami MM, O.
1856, 4, 24. Deborah gct Miami MM, O.
1865, 9, 21. Ann C. rocf Miami MM, O., dtd 1865,7,26
1865, 9, 21. Alice rocf Miami MM, O., dtd 1865,7,26
1910, 7, 28. Edward R. rocf White Water MM, Ind., dtd 1910,7,21

STEELE
1825, 2, 27. Earl b

1896, 3, 26. Earl recrq
1917, 7, 26. Earl dropped from mbrp

STEFFENSON
1904, 6, 23. Maggie & ch, Marshal & Helen, gct Dublin MM, Ind.

STEINMAN
1826, 10, 11. Edith b

1900, 3, 22. Edith recrq
1911, 6, 22. Edith dropped from mbrp

STEPHENS
1884, 3, 27. Alonzo recrq
1886, 4, 22. Ella [Stephen] recrq
1895, 8, 22. Alonzo & w, Ella, & ch, Alpha, gct Miami MM, O.

STILES
1882, 9, 1. Nancy b

1870, 4, 21. Nancy recrq
1871, 4, 27. Isaac recrq
1921, 4, 21. Alice May & Leora Isabelle recrq
1922, 2, 23. Hilbe D. & w, Mary Belle, & ch, Elva Lucile, recrq

STINGLEY
1891, 3, 26. Rose recrq
1891, 8, 27. Albert rocf Center MM, O.
1893, 10, 26. Mary J. gct Center MM, O.

STOCKMAN
1908, 2, 20. Mary recrq

STOCKMAN, continued
1911, 6, 22. Mary gct White Water MM, Ind.

STOOPS
1901, 4, 25. Lizzie recrq
1903, 11, 26. Lizzie dropped from mbrp

STOUT
1817, 9, 4. Jesse, s Isaac & Susannah, Clinton Co., O.; m in Caesars Creek MH, Rosannah HIETT, dt John & Mary, Green Co., O.

1818, 2, 27. Rosanna gct Center MM, O.

STRATTON
1820, 9, 29. John rocf Darby MM, dtd 1820,6,17
1821, 7, 21. John gct West Grove MM, Ind.
1831, 7, 28. Mary (form Haines) dis mcd
1905, 12, 28. Lydia recrq

STRICKLE
1896, 3, 26. George & Katie recrq
1900, 7, 24. George & Kate dropped from mbrp

STUBS
1883, 11, 22. Emma rocf Elk MM, O.

STUMP
1914, 7, 30. Melvina & ch, Leighfee & Luella, recrq
1917, 7, 26. Melvina & Leighfee dropped from mbrp

SURFACE
1883, 3, 22. Edward recrq

SWADNER
1893, 4, 27. Owen recrq
1905, 5, 25. Owen & Ada dropped from mbrp

SWAGART
1908, 12, 24. Edith & Margaret recrq
1925, 7, 23. Margaret [Swigart] relrq

SWAIN
1816, 1, 26. Paul & w, Unice, & ch, Hepsabah, Judah, Rebecca, Francis, Mary & Thomas, rocf West Branch MM, dtd 1816,12,28
1818, 6, 26. Paul & fam gct White Water MM, Ind.

SWEET
1842, 5, 26. Mary Ann rocf Sugar River MM, Ind., dtd 1842,2,26
1845, 11, 27. Mary Ann gct Mill Creek MM,O.

TACKLER
1893, 4, 27. Schuman G. recrq

TANNON
1910, 3, 24. Ola recrq

TENDER
1896, 3, 26. Maggie Holland relrq

TERREL
1815, 11, 30. Pleasant, s David & Mary, Highland Co., O.; m in home of Thos. Embree, Esther HAINS, dt John & Elizabeth, Green Co., O.
1866, 3, 29. Hampton W., s John H. & Elizabeth, Clinton Co., O.; m in Caesars Creek MH, Harriet M. PAINTER, dt Joseph C. & Hannah S., Warren Co., O.
1922, 10, 4. Lois A. m Homer H. HAINES

1816, 5, 22. Esther gct Fairfield MM, O.
1866, 8, 23. Harriett M. gct Fairfield MM,O.
1880, 3, 25. Amanda recrq
1902, 4, 24. Mary S. Hawkins gct Clear Creek MM, O.
1925, 7, 23. Robert W. & Nancy M. relrq

THOMAS
1874, 9, 14. Stella Janice b
1882, 11, 7. Esther b

1907, 3, 28. Orma & Grace recrq
1908, 2, 20. Esther recrq
1923, 4, 29. Jennie dropped from mbrp

THOMPSON
1874, 1, 22. Eli recrq
1874, 4, 23. Hannah [Thomson] rocf Dover MM, O., dtd 1874,3,19
1879, 4, 24. Almira recrq
1882, 5, 25. Eli & w, Hannah, gct Miami MM, O.
1903, 3, 26. Frank & w, Elizabeth, relrq
1908, 9, 24. Edith C. recrq

THORN
1841, 9, 9. Hannah m Charles JESSOP

1824, 11, 25. William & w, Rachel, & ch, Thomas, Hannah, Esther, Isaac, Elijah, Elihu, Sarah & Wm., gct Goshen MM
1841, 7, 22. Hannah rocf Short Creek MM, O., dtd 1841,5,18
1845, 7, 24. Sarah Jr. rocf Green Plain MM, O., dtd 1844,10,16
1845, 7, 24. Elizabeth, minor, rocf Green Plain MM, O., dtd 1844,10,16
1846, 1, 22. Elizabeth gct Fairfield MM, Ind.
1848, 8, 24. Elizabeth rocf Fairfield MM, Ind., dtd 1848,7,13

THORNBURGH
1813, 12, 25. Rebecca & ch, Rachel & Rebecca, rocf West Branch MM, dtd 1813,9,23
1816, 11, 29. Thomas & ch, Thomas & William, rocf West Branch MM, dtd 1816,11,24
1816, 11, 29. Thomas dis mcd
1818, 8, 28. Rebecca Dewit (form Thornborough) dis mcd

THORNBURGH, continued
1819, 1, 29. Wm. dis mcd
1823, 4, 24. Thomas & w, Rebecca, & dt, Rachel, gct Springfield MM, Ind.
1918, 11, 21. Ralph [Thornburg] rocf Fairfield MM, O.
1920, 11, 25. Ralph & w, Erma, gct Xenia MM,O.

TRACY
1910, 2, 24. Charles recrq
1910, 4, 21. Laura recrq

TRUBEE
1913, 6, 26. Bessie Boots gct Dayton MM, O.; returned at her rq 1913,8,28
1914, 6, 25. Bessie Boots dropped from mbrp

TRUE
1838, 5, 24. Ann (form Wilson) con mcd

TRUSS
1883, 4, 26. John recrq

TURNER
1901, 4, 25. Mary recrq
1904, 4, 21. Mary dropped from mbrp
1904, 9, 22. Nellie recrq

UNDERWOOD
1914, 12, 24. Toner & w, Jennie E., recrq

UPP
1881, 2, 24. Martha, May J. & Nannie recrq
1908, 10, 22. Martha recrq

VANCE
1873, 10, 27. Fanny M. b

1886, 3, 25. Fannie recrq

VANDERBURGH
1872, 8, 22. Ellen & Natella Harry recrq

VANDERWORT
1827, 4, 24. Minnie Wilson relrq

VANWINKLE
1871, 7, 20. Bessie b

1916, 3, 23. Bessie relrq

VETTERS
1880, 3, 25. Chas. Edward recrq
1881, 9, 22. Chas. [Vetter] recrq

VICKERS
1814, 8, 27. Celia & ch, John, Armelia, Joseph, Mary Ann & Ruth Jane, rocf Center MM, O., dtd 1814,8,6
1817, 3, 28. Milly Lawrence (form Vickers) dis mcd
1817, 11, 28. John dis disunity
1890, 4, 24. Calvin C. recrq
1891, 11, 26. C. C. relrq
1925, 7, 23. Ben relrq

WADE
1910, 2, 24. Dove recrq

WALES
1816, 7, 26. Elizabeth, w Geo., rocf Deep Creek MM, N. C., dtd 1815,7,1, endorsed by Fairfield MM, O., 1815,7,29

WALKER
----, --, --. William d 1846,2,19 bur Center; m Martha -----
Ch: Mordecai b 1801, 1, 13
Azel " 1802, 11, 21
David F. " 1804, 12, 20
Phebe F. " 1807, 4, 21
Eli " 1809, 10, 22
Asa " 1812, 7, 6
John S. " 1815, 8, 13
Lewis " 1819, 8, 11
Rachel " 1821, 11, 9
1837, 3, 30. John L., s William & Martha, Clinton Co., O.; m in Caesars Creek MH, Ruth HAWKINS, dt Jehu & Susannah, Clinton Co., O.
Ch: Elizabeth b 1839, 3, 25
Jehu " 1841, 8, 8
Benjamin Lewis " 1844, 8, 21
1839, 4, 4. Lewis, s William & Martha, Clinton Co., O., b 1819,8,11 d 1844,1,1; m in Caesars Creek MH, Dinah SPRAY, dt John & Sarah, Clinton Co., O., d 1843,5,18 bur Caesars Creek
Ch: Phebe H. b 1840, 5, 3
Sarah S. " 1842, 1, 29
1841, 9, 9. Rachel m Samuel SPRAY

1834, 11, 27. William & w, Martha, & ch, John Simpson Lewis & Rachel, rocf Center MM, O., dtd 1834,10,15
1835, 8, 27. Mordecai rocf New Garden MM, Ind., dtd 1835,4,18
1836, 6, 23. Mordecai gct Springfield MM
1843, 11, 23. Wm. & w, Martha, gct Springfield MM
1845, 4, 24. John S. & w, Ruth, & ch, Elizabeth, Jehu H. & Benjamin Lewis, gct Springfield MM
1866, 4, 26. Phebe McMillan (form Walker) con mcd
1869, 7, 22. Sarah J. gct Wilmington MM, O.

WALSH
1851, 8, 28. Edward recrq
1852, 10, 28. Edward dis disunity

WALTERS
1820, 10, 27. Mary Robertson (form Walter dis mcd

WALTHAL
1867, 7, 25. Benjamin Compton gct Dover MM, to m Margaret Walthal

WALTON
----, --, --. Edward b 1777,1,3 d 1867,4,10 bur Caesars Creek; m Deborah ----- b 1775, 4,10 d 1842,9,11 bur Caesars Creek
Ch: Samuel b 1804, 3, 26
Betty " 1805, 10, 15
Mary " 1807, 10, 12 d 1810, 7, 6 bur Caesars Creek
Moses b 1809, 6, 27
Eunice " 1811, 11, 27
Edward " 1814, 1, 30
John " 1816, 10, 1 d 1830, 6,27
Hannah " 1818, 10, 2
1825, 11, 2. Betty m Wm. MENDENHALL
1826, 4, 12. Samuel, s Edward & Deborah, Green Co., O., b 1804,3,26 d 1844,3,9; m in Richland, Catherine MENDENHALL, dt John & Ruth, Green Co., O., b 1801,9,19 d 1864, 4,16 both bur Caesars Creek
Ch: Ruth b 1827, 6, 18
Milo " 1829, 9, 22
Edward " 1832, 1, 5
John " 1835, 9, 8 d 1860,11, 5 bur Caesars Creek
Moses b 1840, 7, 22
William " 1843, 1, 27
1831, 11, 30. Eunice m Eli COMPTON
1834, 10, 30. Moses, s Edward & Deborah, Green Co., O., b 1809,6,27 d 1897,1,8 bur Caesars Creek; m in Caesars Creek MH, Mary COOK, dt John & Dinah, Warren Co., O., b 1815,12,26 d 1844,3,15 bur Caesars Creek
Ch: Dinah b 1835, 11, 6
Hannah " 1837, 1, 20
Samuel " 1838, 11, 25
Deborah " 1840, 10, 29 d 1922, 7,21 bur Spring Valley
Elizabeth b 1842, 11, 28
Moses m 2nd in Richland MH, 1845,10,1, Rachel REAGAN, dt Reason & Mary, Green Co., O., b 1825,2,22 d 1848,4,26 bur Caesars Creek
Ch: Moses b 1846, 12, 27
Moses m 3rd Deborah JOHNSON, b 1824,1,28
Ch: Mary b 1850, 6, 17 d 1855, 1,22 bur Caesars Creek
Rachel b 1852, 7, 23 " 1855, 1,20 bur Caesars Creek
Edward T. b 1855, 5, 6 " 1856, 9, 8 bur Caesars Creek
John b 1858, 11, 30
Homer " 1860, 4, 2
Isaac L. " 1863, 8, 20
Ethen A. " 1865, 8, 29
Attie " 1868, 6, 2 d 1869,12,20 bur Caesars Creek
----, --, --. Edward Jr. m Polly ----- b 1814, 1,30
Ch: Elizabeth Ann b 1836, 7, 15
Deborah Catherine " 1838, 2, 4
1836, 8, 31. Hannah m Amos COOK
1845, 10, 15. Ruth m James MILLS
1860, 5, 9. Dinah m Samuel OWEN
1866, 11, 26. Elizabeth m Marion WILDMAN
----, --, --. Moses b 1846,12,27; m Ellen ----- b 1848,7,30
Ch: John E. b 1869, 3, 11
Bessie R. " 1871, 7, 20
Judson Todd" 1875, 10, 7
Rosella " 1881, 12, 20
Samuel Moses b 1884, 2, 9
Joseph Hefford " 1888, 1, 9
Mary Lydia " 1890, 3, 11
----, --, --. Samuel b 1838,11,25; m ----- ---
Ch: Edith b 1869, 11, 27
----, --, --. Edward R. b 1832,1,5; m Alice ----- b 1836,1,7 d 1918,4,--
Ch: Ruth Etta b 1872, 4, 10
Rebecca Catherine " 1874, 5, 14
Anna E. " 1876, 9, 11
Hettie " 1880, 1, 24
1876, 4, 1. Wm. E. b
----, --, --. John b 1858,11,30; m Martha E. ----- b 1859,1,30
Ch: Henry T. b 1887, 5, 3
Herman " 1895, 3, 31
----, --, --. John Edward b 1869,3,11; m 2nd Sarah Alice ----- b 1877,9,14
Ch: Bessie Louella b 18-7, 4, 14
Edith Echo " 1898, 10, 9
Grace " 1900, 12, 19
Helen Marie" 1902, 10, 21
Dorothy Way" 1904, 5, 28
Sarah L. " 1906, 11, 21
Edward Reed" 1909, 1, 30

1812, 4,25. Edward & w, Deborah, & ch, Samuel, Betty & Moses, rocf Hopewell MM, dtd 1811,10,7, endorsed by Miami MM, O., 1811, 12,25
1814, 2, 26. Mary [Walten] rocf Fairfield MM, dtd 1812,7,25, endorsed by Center MM, O., 1813,11,6
1834, 12, 25. Edward Jr. con mcd
1836, 3, 24. Polly rocf Fairfield MM, Ind., dtd 1836,2,18
1849, 8, 23. Moses gct Fairfield MM, O., to m Deborah Johnson
1851, 1, 23. Deborah rocf Fairfield MM, Ind., dtd 1850,10,19
1851, 9, 25. Edward Jr. & w, Polly, & ch, Elizabeth Ann & Deborah Catherine, gct Fairfield MM, Ind.
1862, 2, 20. Hannah Alexander (form Walton) con mcd

WALTON, continued
1862, 12, 25. Moses A. con mcd
1864, 12, 22. Milow con mcd
1865, 2, 23. Deborah gct Bridgeport MM, Ind.
1865, 2, 23. Julietta rocf Dover MM
1866, 5, 24. Samuel con mcd
1867, 12, 26. Moses A. dis jas
1868, 5, 28. Moses Jr. con mcd
1871, 3, 23. Edward con mcd
1871, 3, 23. Alice con mcd
1871, 6, 22. Edward B. & w, Alice, gct Summit Grove MM, Iowa
1872, 5, 23. Edward R. & w, Alice, rocf Summit Grove MM, Ia.
1873, 12, 26. Mary & Ellen B. recrq
1886, 8, 26. Nilow & w, Julietta, relrq
1897, 2, 25. Sarah Alice recrq
1903, 2, 19. Robert S. relrq
1912, 4, 25. Wm. gct Dayton MM, O.
1914, 6, 25. Lucy & ch, Mildred, Velma & Genevive Loyd, recrq
1914, 6, 25. Almeda recrq
1916, 2, 24. Nellie Dar recrq
1916, 11, 23. Wm. & w, Mary, roc
1919, 6, 26. Helen Marie, Dorothy Mae, Deborah Sarah, Bee & Toddy Leon, recrq

WARD
1881, 2, 24. Mary E. recrq
1883, 3, 22. Alpha T. recrq
1883, 3, 22. John J. recrq
1883, 3, 22. William & Mary recrq
1883, 3, 22. Alpheus recrq
1884, 6, 26. Alpheus C. gct Miami MM, O.

WARNER
1816, 11, 29. Mary & ch, John, Elizabeth, Levi, William, Isaac & Abner, rocf Fairfield MM, O., dtd 1816,7,27
1816, 11, 29. Lydia rocf Fairfield MM, O., dtd 1816,7,27

WASHBURN
1909, 3, 25. Ethel recrq

WATSON
1869, 11, 3. William b
1868, 2, 27. Emily b

WAY
----, --, --. Sarah b 1784,4,20 d 1812,2,2 bur Caesars Creek

1811, 1, 26. Henry & w, Charlotty, & ch, Mary, Anna, Charlotty, Henry & William, rocf Center MM, N. C., dtd 1810,8,18, endorsed by Miami MM, O., 1810,12,1
1811, 1, 26. Joseph & w, Sarah, & ch, Rachel, Jonathan & Joel, rocf Center MM, N. C., dtd 1810,8,18
1811, 12, 28. Henry & w, Charlotte, & ch, Mary, Anna, Charlottee, Henry & William, gct White Water MM, Ind.
1812, 3, 28. Joseph & ch, Rachel, Jonathan & Joel, gct White Water MM, Ind.

WEAN
1908, 2, 20. Charles A. recrq
1908, 5, 28. Mrs. Chas. recrq
1911, 9, 21. Charles & Pearl Lucile dropped from mbrp
1916, 2, 24. Arthur & Gertrude recrq

WEEKLEY
1872, 7, 25. Martha A. (form Coulter) con mcd

WEISS
1925, 7, 23. Lillian relrq

WELLER
----, --, --. Samuel b 1826,11,30; m Catharine ----- b 1835,7,29

1873, 12, 25. Carrie E. recrq
1874, 12, 24. Samuel & w, Catherine, recrq
1911, 6, 22. Catherine dropped from mbrp

WEST
1866, 10, 11. William, s David & Ruth, Clinton Co., O., b 1841,5,6; m in Caesars Creek MH, Mary Ann WILSON, dt Enos & Rebecca B., Warren Co., O., b 1844,9,30
Ch: Enos b 1867, 12, 24
Carrie " 1873, 1, 26

1862, 8, 28. David & s, Charles, rocf Newberry MM, O., dtd 1832,5,23
1866, 7, 26. David & s, Chas., gct Miami MM, O.
1867, 1, 24. Mary Ann gct Newberry MM, O.
1868, 11, 26. William & w, Mary Ann, & s, Enos rocf Newberry MM, O.
1883, 11, 22. Wm. & w, Mary Ann, & ch, Enos & Carrie & ward, Addie Lewis, gct West Grove MM, Ind.

WHARTON
1874, 12, 24. James Dixon [Warton] & w, Sarah Jane, recrq
1875, 7, 22. Dixon [Warton] & w, Sarah Jane, gct Miami MM, O.; returned 1875,11,13 because they rem back
1889, 6, 27. Kansas recrq
1891, 8, 27. Kansas relrq
1897, 3, 25. Emma Leach relrq

WHEELER
1859, 9, 22. Tamer Ann (form Ellis) con mcd
1891, 8, 27. Sarah gct Wilmington MM, O.

WHITAKER
1884, 7, 24. Mary J. gct Miami MM, O.
1914, 5, 28. W. L. [Whitacre] & dt, Reva C., recrq
1917, 7, 26. Reva [Whitacer] dropped from mbrp

WHITE
1824, 12, 2. Sarah m Mathias CRESPIN
1840, 7, 2. George, s Nathaniel & Phebe, Warren Co., O., b 1798,10,14; m in Caesars Creek MH, Elizabeth SPRAY, dt William & Dinah, b 1820,9,18
Ch: Phebe S. b 1841, 8, 24
Lydia F. " 1843, 3, 23

1813, 11, 27. Mary rocf Hopewell MM, Va., dtd 1813,10,4
1813, 11, 27. Nathaniel & ch, John & Jesse, rocf Hopewell MM, Va., dtd 1813,10,4
1813, 12, 25. Sarah rocf Hopewell MM, Va., dtd 1813,10,4
1817, 2, 21. Jesse dis disunity
1817, 6, 27. John dis mcd
1824, 9, 30. George rocf Hopewell MM, dtd 1824,3,6
1834, 2, 20. John gct Fairfield MM, Ind.
1847, 8, 26. George & w, Elizabeth, & ch, Phebe, Lydia & Moses, gct Salem MM, O.
1878, 11, 21. Sarah J. gct Bangor MM, Ia.
1883, 5, 24. Wm. A. recrq
1910, 2, 24. John A. recrq
1910, 2, 24. Mary R. recrq

WHITEHEAD
1910, 2, 24. Mary recrq
1910, 3, 24. Elias G., Rebecca & Gertrude recrq
1910, 4, 21. Charlotte recrq

WHITINGDON
1900, 7, 24. Josie Osborn dropped from mbrp

WHITSON
----, --, --. Solomon b 1741,4,2; m Phebe ----- b 1745,5,25 d 1801,6,13

Ch:					
Ann	b 1766,	12,	27		
David	" 1769,	3,	8		
Silas Willis	" 1771,	2,	28	d 1771,	3,11
Mary	" 1772,	2,	11	" 1798,12,30	
Willis	" 1774,	5,	9		
Jordan	" 1777,	3,	3	" 1847,	1, 1
Samuel	" 1779,	10,	31		
Phebe	" 1781,	10,	30	" 1791,	5, 6
Solomon	" 1784,	5,	7	" 1798,	6, 1
John	" 1787,	6,	24		
Rowland	" 1789,	8,	13	" 1789,	9, 9

----, --, --. David b 1769,3,8; m Mary ----- b 1763,5,2
Ch: Phebe b 1801, 6, 25
----, --, --. Jordan b 1777,3,3 d 1847,4,1 bur Caesars Creek; m Mary ----- b 1789,4,20
Ch: Naomi b 1805, 12, 27
Solomon " 1807, 10, 12
Thomas " 1810, 2, 8
Mary Ann " 1812, 11, 2
----, --, --. Samuel d 1819,9,18 bur Caesars Creek; m Barbara -----
Ch: William b 1809, 7, 15
Joel b 1810, 9, 25
David " 1812, 7, 2
Sarah " 1814, 3, 3
Phebe " 1816, 1, 1
Ann " 1818, 3, 3
Charity " 1820, 2, 8
1821, 5, 24. Samuel d
1825, 5, 5. Phebe m Samuel COMPTON
1827, 12, 6. Naomy m Robert FURNAS

1813, 7, 31. John gct Elk MM, O.; returned for mcd
1814, 3, 26. John dis mcd
1830, 2, 25. Solomon dis disunity
1830, 2, 25. Thomas dis disunity
1831, 12, 29. Mary Ann dis disunity
1835, 8, 27. David & w, Mary, gct Fairfield MM, Ind.
1835, 9, 24. Barbara & ch, Sarah, Phebe, Ann & Charity, gct Fairfield MM, Ind.
1835, 9, 24. William, Joel & David Jr. gct Fairfield MM, Ind.
1838, 9, 27. Robert Furnas Jr. gct Fairfield MM, Ind., to m Phebe Whitson
1840, 8, 22. Ann dis jas
1925, 7, 23. Eva T. relrq

WICKERSHAM
1884, 3, 27. Enoch, Harriet & James recrq
1884, 3, 27. Horace Guy recrq
1886, 3, 25. James dis
1900, 7, 24. Horace dropped from mbrp

WILDMAN
1833, 9, 4. Benjamin, s John & Elizabeth, Clark Co., O.; m in Richland MH, Maria L. GIBSON, dt Montillion & Sarah, Green Co., O.
1885, 7, 30. Marion, s Edward & Hannah, Clark Co., O.; m in home of Moses WALTON, Almeda M. JOHNSON, dt Malen & Mahala, Leesburg, O.

1813, 10, 30. John [Wileman] & w, Elizabeth, & ch, Deborah, Hannah, William, Edward, Benjamin, Ann & Seneca, rocf Mt. Pleasant MM, Va., dtd 1812,11,20
1834, 1, 23. Maria L. gct Green Plain MM, O.
1869, 9, 23. Elizabeth gct Green Plain MM, O.
1886, 9, 23. Almedia gct Green Plain MM, O.

WILEY
1805, 2, 7. Ruth b

1836, 11, 24. Ruth rocf Center MM, O., dtd 1836,10,12
1857, 11, 26. Ruth gct Pleasant Plain MM, Ia.

WILLIAMS
1819, 12, 8. Seth, s Ennion & Martha, Highland Co., O.; m in Green Plain, Keturah SLEEPER, dt Samuel & Patience, Clark Co., O.

WILLIS
1818, 11, 4. Anne m Chas. SLEEPER

1814, 4, 30. William & w, Henrietta, & ch, Andrew, Elijah, Anna, William, Westley, Levi & Mildred, rocf Fairfield MM, dtd 1814,3,26

WILLIAMS
1814, 6, 25. Peter & w, Nancy, & ch, Mary, rocf Fairfield MM, O., dtd 1814,4,30
1820, 2, 25. Keturah gct Fairfield MM, O.
1821, 4, 27. Sarah rocf White Water MM, Ind., dtd 1820,10,28
1881, 2, 24. Louella recrq
1883, 3, 22. Edgar recrq
1883, 4, 26. Edgar recrq
1883, 11, 22. Enos Wilson & ward, Louella Williams, gct West Grove MM, Ind.
1908, 2, 20. Emma relrq
1908, 9, 24. Salinda recrq

WILSON
----, --, --. John d 1794,5,12 ae 50; m Dinah COON
Ch: Mary b 1760, 12, 18
Jehu " 1763, 1, 1
Seth " 1764, 12, 7
Phebe " 1769, 2, 18
Esther " 1771, 2, 9
Sarah " 1773, 5, 19
Christopher " 1775, 8, 15
Hannah " 1778, 7, 28
John " 1782, 2, 28 d 1784, 2,23
----, --, --. Jehu & Sarah
Ch: Betty b 1791, 10, 10
Dinah " 1794, 3, 14
John " 1796, 12, 17
Isaac " 1799, 7, 26
Seth " 1801, 7, 23
Amos " 1803, 1, 10
Ruth " 1806, 9, 17
Gideon " 1812, 3, 3
----, --, --. Seth b 1764,12,7 d 1846,7,13 bur Caesars Creek; m Martha ----- b 1773,11,21 d 1851,12,8 bur Caesars Creek
----, --, --. Christopher d 1859,4,3 ae 83; m Mary ----- d 1846,9,12 ae 62
Ch: John b 1801, 11, 26
Thomas " 1803, 8, 2
Hannah " 1805, 7, 8
Tamar " 1807, 7, 21
Eli " 1809, 10, 6
James " 1811, 3, 3
Charles " 1813, 2, 4
Dinah " 1815, 9, 20
Martha " 1819, 1, 27
Jehu " 1821, 6, 11
Seth " 1823, 5, 24 d 1833, 9,15 bur Caesars Creek
Huldah b 1825, 8, 10 " 1826, 7,18 bur Caesars Creek
1820, 10, 5. Isaac, s Jehu & Sarah, Warren Co., O.; m in Caesars Creek MH, Ann EASTERLING, dt Henry & Eleanor, Clinton Co., O.
Ch: Enos b 1821, 12, 2
Amos " 1826, 2, 17
Martha " 1828, 7, 29
----, --, --. John m Lydia ----- b 1799,11,16
Ch: Joshua b 1823, 2, 1
Samuel " 1825, 3, 9
----, --, --. John & Ann
Ch: Sarah b 1824, 8, 8
Gideon " 1825, 8, 8
Martha Ann " 1827, 2, 18
Jehu " 1829, 1, 16 d 1829, 7,20
1826, 7, 13. Huldah d
1828, 11, 6. Tamar m Samuel COMPTON
1829, 4, 2. Hannah m David BURNET
1833, 9, 15. Seth d
1835, 4, 2. James, s Christopher & Mary, Warren Co., O.; m in Caesars Creek MH, Elizabeth SPRAY, dt Samuel & Esther, Warren Co., O.
1839, 4, 4. Dinah m Joseph SPRAY
----, --, --. Enos b 1821,12,2; m Rebecca B. ----- b 1819,1,24 d 1879,5,20 bur Caesars Creek
Ch: Mary Ann b 1844, 9, 30
Phebe " 1846, 4, 5
Sarah " 1848, 5, 15 d 1853, 9,25 bur Caesars Creek
Isaac b 1850, 2, 18
Elizabeth Caroline " 1855, 5, 18
Amos " 1857, 5, 27
----, --, --. Amos b 1826,2,17 d 1907,11,29 bur Caesars Creek; m Mary B. ----- b 1822, 7,26 d 1897,2,17 bur Caesars Creek
Ch: Spencer B. b 1852, 7, 27
Lydia Ellen " 1854, 7, 31
Samuel " 1858, 5, 10
Enos B. " 1861, 2, 27
Walter T. " 1863, 5, 8
John " 1869, 11, 18
----, --, --. Amos & Mary B.
Ch: Enos b 1861, 2, 27
Samuel " 1858, 5, 10
1866, 10, 11. Mary Ann m William WEST
----, --, --. Isaac b 1850,2,18; m Euphemia ----- b 1848,1,3
Ch: Minerva R. b 1873, 7, 20
Ida May " 1876, 7, 3
----, --, --. Osborn b 1856,1,15; m Sarah J. ----- b 1860,11,19
Ch: Josie b 1881, 11, 1
Bertha " 1884, 12, 19
Argus " 1888, 12, 6
James " 1890, 6, 6
Idena " 1895, 11, 1
1888, 5, 19. Wilbur b
----, --, --. Walter, s Amos & Mary, b 1863, 5,8; m Jennie Maria HAINES, dt Eli & Emily, b 1866,3,24
Ch: Raymond H. b 1889, 3, 15

WILSON, Walter & Jennie Maria, continued
Ch: Edgar
Jesse b 1892, 6, 15
Olive
Emily " 1899, 5, 26
----, --, --. John, s Amos & Mary, b 1869,11, 18; m Ellanora HAINES b 1872,7,28
Ch: Albert b 1903, 7, 12
----, --, --. Raymond, s Walter & Jennie M., b 1887,3,15; m Jennie HURLEY, dt Ernest E. & Ella, b 1891,5,6
Ch: Mary-Kathryn b 1912, 6, 23
Jeanette " 1918, 6, 28
----, --, --. Weldon, s John & Ellanora, b 1897,6,7; m Lelah BOGAN, dt W. E. & Mary, b 1898,8,16
Ch: Gerald b 1921, 4, 13
1922, 9, 2. Frances E. m Bevan JENKINS

1814, 1, 29. Dinah Reagan (form Wilson) dis mcd
1817, 5, 30. Lydia con mcd
1819, 11, 26. Jehu & fam gc
1819, 11, 26. John gc
1822, 8, 30. John con mcd
1822, 8, 30. Lydia recrq
1825, 9, 29. John & w, Lydia, & ch, Joshua & Samuel, gct White Lick MM, Ind.
1829, 7, 30. Eli con mcd
1829, 10, 29. Thos. dis jH
1831, 12, 28. John & w, Anna, & ch, Sarah, Gideon & Martha Ann, rocf Milford MM, Ind., dtd 1831,11,26
1833, 7, 25. Mary Jr. recrq
1834, 8, 28. James & Huldah, ch Eli & Mary, recrq
1835, 8, 27. John & w, Anna, & ch, Sarah, Gideon & Marthann, gct Milford MM, Ind.
1837, 8, 24. James & w, Elizabeth, & ch, Esther C., gct Fairfield MM, Ind.
1838, 5, 24. Ann True (form Wilson) con mcd
1838, 9, 27. Charles gct Fairfield MM, Ind., to m Elizabeth Pruitt
1838, 12, 27. Charles gct Fairfield MM, Ind.
1839, 8, 22. Christopher & w, Mary, & s, Jehu, gct Fairfield MM, Ind.
1839, 8, 22. Eli & w, Mary, & ch, James C., Huldah, Jehu, Elizabeth C. & Thomas Jefferson, gct Fairfield MM, Ind.
1839, 8, 22. Charles gct Fairfield MM, Ind.
1839, 8, 22. Martha gct Fairfield MM, Ind.
1843, 9, 21. Enos gct Center MM, O., to m Rebecca Ballard
1844, 7, 25. Rebecca B. rocf Center MM, O., dtd 1844,6,12
1851, 11, 27. Sarah dis
1852, 3, 25. Amos con mcd
1853, 8, 25. Mary rocf Center MM, O.; dtd 1853,5,18
1871, 11, 23. Isaac con mcd
1878, 7, 25. Euphamy recrq
1880, 4, 22. Amos Jr. gct West Grove MM,Ind.
1883, 11, 22. Enos & ward, Louella Williams, gct West Grove MM, Ind.
1905, 2, 3. Wilbur recrq
1915, 1, 28. Mary Elsie recrq
1932, 6, 26. Gerald gct Spring Valley MM
1933, 4, 30. Harriett recrq

WINFIELD
1906, 12, 27. Vergil E. & w, Effie L., & ch, Thelma, recrq

WINTERS
1877, 7, 26. R. Alma relrq
1881, 2, 24. Ruth A., Mariah E. & Myrtle recrq

WOLFARD
1883, 3, 22. Lewis recrq
1884, 3, 27. Felix & Josephine recrq

WOLLENBURG
1908, 2, 20. M. Edith recrq

WOOD
1884, 3, 27. Ebeneezer & Geo. A. recrq
1900, 1, 25. Carrie C. gct Wilmington MM,O.

WOOLARD
1903, 1, 22. Clara recrq
1913, 4, 24. Clara relrq

WOOLFORD
1897, 7, 22. Phelix dropped from mbrp

WOOLMAN
1818, 4, 24. Ruth (form Bond) con mcd
1818, 6, 26. Eber rocf Evesham MM, N. J., dtd 1818,2,6

WOOTEN
1899, 6, 22. Elmer rocf Des Moines MM, Ia.
1911, 9, 21. Elmer O., Itasca F. & Esther dropped from mbrp

WORLEY
1877, 7, 26. Thomas recrq
1897, 7, 22. Thomas & Chas. W. dropped from mbrp
1897, 7, 22. Lucinda & Effie dropped from mbrp

WRIGHT
1881, 12, 20. Rosella b

1814, 6, 25. James & w, Catharine, & ch, John, Joab, Hannah, Lydia, George, Judith & James Allen, rocf Fairfield MM, O., dtd 1813,12,15
1816, 5, 24. Charlotty recrq
1818, 2, 27. Charlotte Coat (form Wright) dis mcd
1819, 5, 28. Richard & w, Rachel, & ch, Jane, Jonathan & Levi, rocf Hopewell MM, Va.,

WRIGHT, continued
dtd 1819,1,7
1821, 4, 27. Hannah Lancaster (form Wright) con mcd
1887, 1, 27. William recrq
1897, 7, 22. Wm. dropped from mbrp
1906, 3, 22. Minerva, Florence & Flora recrq
1906, 11, 22. Wm. & Alla J. recrq
1910, 2, 24. George W. recrq
1912, 4, 25. Moses Walton recrq
1913, 5, 22. George dropped from mbrp
1915, 1, 28. Sarah E. recrq

WYSONG
----, --, --. Alfred b 1850,1,5; m Eva ----- b 1854,11,17
Ch: Levi b 1-95, 7, 13

1885, 4, 23. Eva recrq
1896, 3, 26. Alphred recrq
1908, 7, 23. Eva & s, Levi, gct Miami MM, O.
1916, 6, 22. Eva rocf Miami MM, O.

* * * * * * *

ACTON
1925, 7, 23. John & Susie L. relrq

COOK
1827, 8, 2. Elizabeth m Wm. MILLS

DAVIS
1824, 11, 4. Mary m Thos. COOK

ELLIS
1829, 3, 26. Jacob dis mcd
1831, 5, 26. Rebecca gct Sugar River MM,Ind.

YATKINS
1842, 11, 3. Hiram b
1844, 3, 19. Sarah b

YEIGH
1879, 4, 24. H. B. recrq
1884, 9, 25. Lewis [Yei] dis

YEO
1852, 5, 27. Martha Ann rocf West Grove MM, Ind., dtd 1852,5,8
1855, 11, 22. Martha Ann gct White Water MM, Ind.
1881, 2, 24. Emma recrq
1883, 7, 26. Amanda dis
1888, 1, 26. Alice relrq
1911, 12, 28. Emma recrq

YOUNG
1850, 10, 10. Hannah Sophia m Daniel JESSOP

1847, 9, 23. Hannah Sulphia recrq
1901, 4, 25. James E. & w, Sarah C., rocf Miami MM, O.
1911, 6, 22. James E. & Sarah C. dropped from mbrp

ZELL
1842, 5, 26. Eunice (form Kelly) dis mcd

* * * * * * *

1831, 5, 26. Mary gct Sugar River MM, Ind.

MENDENHALL
1896, 6, 11. Erma M. b

SCAMMAHORN
1887, 7, 16. Helen M. b

WILDMAN
1866, 11, 28. Marion, s Edward & Hannah, Clark Co., O.; m in Richland MH, Elizabeth WALTON, dt Moses & Mary, Green Co., O.

WILSON
1821, 3, 11. Dinah d (an elder)

FAIRFIELD MONTHLY MEETING

Fairfield Monthly Meeting, located in Highland County, Ohio, near the town of Leesburg,was opened the 7 Mo. 18, 1807. It was set off from Miami Monthly Meeting by authority of Redstone Quarterly Meeting, Pa. A meeting for worship had been established at Fairfield about two years prior to the opening of the monthly meeting.

A list of names of Friends who were early members of Fairfield Monthly Meeting includes Jesse Baldwin, Hannah Baldwin, Elizabeth Ballard, overseer, Jonathan Barrett, Richard Barrett, Sarah Barrett, John Beals, Lois Beals, Sarah Beals, Walter Canaday, Patience Carr, Samuel Coffin, Mordicai Ellis, Milly Ellyson, clerk, Agatha Elsey, Evan Evans, Jesse George, elder, Mercy George, Martha Henley, George Hodgson, John Hodson, Daniel Huff, Aaron Hunt, John Hunt, Phinehas Hunt, Rachel Hunt, Sarah Hunt, Jacob Jackson, Ann Jackson, Ashley Johnson, overseer, James Johnson, Sarah Johnson, Elisha Kenworthy, Thamer Kenworthy, William Lupton, Bathsheba Lupton, Zebulon Overman, Mary Overman, Nathaniel Pope, Martha Pope, Thomas Sanders, John Seers, Joseph Small, overseer, Shedrick Stafford, Strangeman Stanley, Bowater Sumner, Rebecca Sumner, Isaac Todhunter, Josiah Tomlinson, elder, Ennion Williams, clerk and elder, William Williams, overseer, Martha Williams, overseer, Phebe Williams, overseer, William Willis, overseer, Jemima Wright.

ABBOTT
1886, 7, 17. Eva & Ellen recrq
1889, 3, 16. Ella H. relrq

ABERS
1872, 7, 20. James M. & w, Eliza A., recrq

ACHOR
----, --, --. Samuel & Martha
Ch: Mary Jane b 1851, 2, 20
Ellwood " 1853, 2, 27

1849, 1, 20. Joseph recrq
1849, 1, 20. Eunice recrq
1849, 7, 21. Elizabeth Minerva, Sarah Jane, Samuel D. & George Riley, ch Joseph & Eunice, recrq
1849, 12, 15. Samuel recrq
1849, 12, 15. Martha, w Samuel, recrq
1853, 1, 15. Joseph & w, Eunice, & ch gct Newberry MM
1865, 1, 21. Samuel dis engaging in military service
1866, 10, 20. Sarah Ann [Acre] recrq
1866, 12, 15. Martha dis jas
1869, 8, 21. Sarah Ann gct Clear Creek MM
1878, 8, 17. George & Mary Jane dropped from mbrp
1878, 10, 19. Mary J. dropped from mbrp
1925, 5, 7. Georgia recrq

ADAMS
1824, 8, 25. Joseph d bur Fairfield
1836, 5, 19. Isaac d ae 45 bur Fairfield
1836, 10, 13. Mary d ae 73 bur Fairfield
1839, 3, 4. Joseph d ae 79 bur Fairfield
1859, 5, 30. Phebe, dt Michael & Mahala Frye, b

1818, 8, 29. Joseph & w, Edith, rocf Hopewell MM, dtd 1817,6,11
1826, 7, 29. Cert rec for Isaac from Hopewell MM, Va., dtd 1825,11,10; endorsed to Lees Creek MM
1826, 7, 29. Cert rec for Joseph & w from Hopewell MM, Va., dtd 1825,11,10, endorsed to Lees Creek MM
1826, 12, 30. Jonathan rocf Hopewell MM, Va., dtd 1826,7,9
1829, 8, 29. Edith Starbuck (form Adams) dis mou
1832, 9, 20. Jonathan dis mou
1832, 10, 25. Mary Jane gct Center MM
1832, 10, 25. Rachel & Eliza Adams, ch Edith Starbuck, gct Goshen MM
1834, 8, 21. Hannah recrq
1842, 11, 24. Jeremiah recrq
1843, 7, 20. Asa L. dis mcd
1856, 6, 21. Zephaniah dis disunity
1859, 4, 16. John recrq
1859, 4, 16. Catherine, w John, recrq
1872, 1, 20. Charles recrq
1872, 4, 20. Francis Marion recrq
1872, 4, 20. Sarah Ann recrq
1873, 7, 19. Frank M. & w, Achsie P., con mcd
1875, 3, 20. Absalom, Jr. recrq
1875, 3, 20. Elias H. recrq
1877, 5, 19. Absalom & Ann recrq
1879, 4, 19. Flora rocf Newberry MM, O., dtd 1879,2,17
1880, 5, 15. Catherine recrq
1881, 9, 17. Franklyn M. & w, Achsia P., & ch, Sarah E. & Jesse W., gct Rose Hill MM, Kansas
1883, 11, 17. Absalom & Absalom Jr. dropped from mbrp
1883, 11, 17. Charles dropped from mbrp
1884, 1, 19. Henry S., s Valentine, recrq
1884, 1, 19. Valentine recrq
1884, 1, 19. Sarah gct Green Castle MM, Kans.
1884, 6, 21. Rosa recrq
1884, 7, 19. Katie relrq
1886, 2, 20. Wilson recrq
1886, 3, 20. Belle recrq
1886, 7, 17. Cora recrq
1886, 8, 21. Elias & Flora gct Argonia MM, Kans.
1887, 1, 15. Elias Jr. relrq
1889, 4, 20. Otho recrq
1893, 5, 20. Otho dropped from mbrp
1893, 5, 20. Rosa dropped from mbrp
1902, 2, 15. Bessie relrq

ADAMSON
1808, 3, 26. Susanna rocf Mt. Pleasant MM, Tenn., dtd 1807,10,31
1809, 8, 26. Susannah rqct Short Creek MM, Tenn.
1811, 2, 28. Susanna gct Lost Creek MM, Tenn. (first cert lost)

AITKEN
1896, 7, 18. Melvina W. dropped from mbrp

ALDERMAN
1842, 3, 24. Rebecca (form Ladd) con mcd

ALDERSON
1858, 4, 17. Sarah Jane (form Cowgill) con mcd
1858, 9, 18. Sarah Jane gct Plainfield MM

ALLBRIGHT
1835, 4, 23. Ruth rocf Westland MM, N. Y., dtd 1834,11,20
1836, 6, 23. Ruth gct Hartland MM, N. Y.

ALLEN
1857, 10, 22. Joseph, s Solomon & Amy, Parke Co., Ind.; m at Hardins Creek, Mahala B. STALKER, dt Eli & Gennett, Highland Co.,O.
1879, 1, 15. S. Catherine d bur Sabina

1811, 8, 31. Kesiah [Allin] (form Jackson) dis mcd
1858, 4, 17. Mahala B. gct Bloomfield MM,Ind.

ALLEN, continued
1873, 3, 15. Andrew recrq
1876, 9, 16. Andrew J. dis

ANDERSON
1826, 10, 4. Rachel d ae 84 bur Fairfield

1811, 3, 30. William rocf South River MM, Va., dtd 1811,1,12
1811, 3, 30. Rachel rocf South River MM, Va., dtd 1811,1,12
1814, 2, 26. William dis disunity
1818, 10, 31. Sarah (form Milner) dis mcd
1818, 12, 26. Sarah dis mcd
1870, 8, 20. Hannah A. recrq
1870, 8, 20. James recrq
1870, 8, 20. Mary recrq
1870, 8, 20. William Sylvester, s James, recrq
1873, 9, 20. Thomas J. & w, E. Jane, & s, Charles Earnest, recrq
1884, 2, 16. James C. & w, Hannah E., dis
1886, 7, 17. Allie recrq
1893, 5, 20. Allie dropped from mbrp
1898, 4, 16. Abner D., Wesley dropped from mbrp
1898, 4, 16. Dollie dropped from mbrp

ANDREWS
----, --, --. Calvin m Margery LADD
Ch: Rodney
Brice
1812, 5, 30. Cert rec for ch of Hannah Darby (form Andrews) from Cane Creek MM, N.C., dtd 1810,3,3, endorsed to Fall Creek MM
1872, 2, 17. Margery (form Ladd) dis mcd
1877, 2, 17. Margery recrq
1883, 4, 21. Calvin & ch, Price & Rodney, recrq
1912, 11, 16. Calvin's d rpd

ANSEVIN
1925, 2, 12. Imogene Thornburg relrq

ANTHONY
1814, 9, 24. Cert rec for Rhoda & ch, Samuel, Parsons, Thomas, Clark, Charles & Jane Wood, from Cedar Creek MM, Va., dtd 1812, 12,12, endorsed to Clear Creek MM

ANTRIM
1812, 6, 27. Thomas & w, Rachel, & ch, Benjamin, Aden, John & Rachel, recrq
1870, 7, 16. Joseph recrq
1871, 1, 21. Lucinda rocf Clear Creek MM, dtd 1870,12,10
1873, 4, 19. Eliza [Antram] recrq
1873, 4, 19. Louisa [Antram] recrq
1877, 7, 21. Lucinda [Antrum] gct Newberry MM

ARNOLD
1894, 3, 17. Isaac & Emma recrq

ARRASMITH
1882, 3, 18. Abner recrq
1882, 3, 18. Sarah E. recrq
1882, 3, 18. Elizabeth [Arasmith) recrq
1893, 2, 18. Lincoln recrq
1896, 7, 18. Abner, Josie E., John & Charles dropped from mbrp
1899, 2, 18. Reed & Hannah recrq
1910, 6, 18. Hannah [Arrowsmith] relrq

ARTHER
1810, 4, 28. Agness dis mcd

ATHE
1871, 9, 16. John recrq
1871, 9, 16. Mary recrq

ATKINSON
1846, 9, 19. Hannah Fisher (form Atkinson) dis mcd
1847, 6, 19. Alice Burnet (form Atkinson) dis mcd
1837, 11, 23. Hannah, Alice & Thomas L., ch John & Jane, rocf Dover MM, dtd 1837,6,15

AUSTIN
1873, 4, 19. Lydia A. con mcd

AYRES
1872, 6, 15. William Sr. recrq

BACON
1914, 4, 18. George & w recrq
1914, 4, 18. Ada recrq

BAGLEY
1871, 8, 19. William recrq
1871, 8, 19. Mary Ann recrq

BAILEY
1809, 4, 29. Thomas & s, John & Christopher, rocf South River MM, dtd 1808,11,12
1809, 4, 29. Elizabeth [Baley] & dt, Mary, rocf South River MM, dtd 1808,11,12
1851, 5, 17. Nathan gct Dover MM, to m Sarah Bailey
1856, 7, 19. Marmaduke Brackney & w, Susanna, & niece, Phebe Bailey, rocf Dover MM, dtd 1856,5,15
1867, 1, 19. Phebe Sayers (form Bailey) con mcd
1869, 4, 17. Sidney con mcd
1869, 5, 15. Sidney M. gct Dover MM, O.
1905, 10, 21. Clara Olive gct Clear Creek MM

BALDWIN
1809, 11, 23. William, s Uriah & Hannah, Highland Co., O.; m at Clear Creek, Elizabeth HUNT, dt Phinehas & Elizabeth, Highland Co., O.

1809, 11, 25. Margaret rocf Plainfield MM, dtd 1809,9,23

BALDWIN, continued
1809, 12, 30. William rocf New Garden MM, N.C. dtd 1809,9,30
1812, 8, 29. Enos dis disunity
1813, 5, 29. William & fam gct Darby Creek MM
1821, 6, 30. Cert rec for Jesse & w, Catherine, from Fall Creek MM, dtd 1821,6,23, endorsed to White Water MM, Ind.

BALLARD
1809, 1, 5. Elizabeth m Joseph HIATT

1808, 6, 25. Cert rec for William from Mt. Pleasant MM, Va., dtd 1808,2,27, endorsed to Center MM
1810, 7, 28. Rachel & dt, Nancy, rocf Westfield MM, dtd 1810,5,12
1810, 8, 25. Archer & s, Stephen, Aaron & Amos, rocf Westfield MM, dtd 1810,5,12
1811, 3, 30. Archer dis disunity
1811, 6, 29. Rachel dis disunity
1812, 1, 25. Cert rec for Jerman & fam from Mt. Pleasant MM, Va., dtd 1811,4,27, endorsed to Fall Creek MM
1830, 7, 31. Susanna (form Moorman) dis mcd
1844, 5, 23. Joseph Burgess gct Center MM, to m Phebe Ballard
1851, 12, 20. Eleanor con mcd
1852, 5, 15. Center MM was given permission to rst Elinor
1852, 6, 19. Eleanor gct Center MM
1861, 1, 19. Elizabeth (form Barrett) con mcd
1861, 5, 18. Elizabeth gct Center MM

BALLENTINE
1907, 3, 16. Esther recrq
1912, 1, 20. Lavon recrq
1914, 4, 19. Reba & Olive recrq
1920, 4, 21. Alice recrq
1922, 4, 13. Burch, Elizabeth, Oakley & Ruth Erma, recrq

BALON
1860, 5, 19. Hannah Elizabeth [Balen] (form Reader) dis mcd
1872, 4, 20. John recrq
1873, 3, 15. John relrq

BANKS
1853, 6, 15. Gulielma M. d bur Fairfield

1853, 1, 15. Julielma M. (form Cherry) con mcd

BANKSON
1874, 4, 23. Elizabeth d ae 77 bur Wilmington

1833, 2, 21. Elizabeth rocf Springfield MM
1834, 9, 25. Mary Ann, Isaac E., Esther E., Ruth C., Lydia C., Susannah & William, ch Elizabeth, recrq
1836, 9, 22. Elizabeth, dt Elizabeth, recrq
1837, 4, 20. Elizabeth & ch, Mary Ann, Esther, Isaac, Ruth, Lydia, Susanna, William & Elizabeth, gct Clear Creek MM
1865, 12, 16. Elizabeth rocf Springfield MM, dtd 1865,11,18
1865, 12, 16. Elizabeth E. rocf Springfield MM, dtd 1865,11,18
1870, 2, 19. Isaac recrq

1872, 1, 25. Lewis C., s Joel, Hamilton Co., Ind.; m Deborah A. GREEN, dt Levi, Highland Co., O.

BARKER
1872, 4, 20. Deborah Ann gct Greenwood MM, Ind.

BARNES
1914, 2, 21. Earl recrq
1919, 5, 19. Earl & fam relrq

BARR
1891, 3, 21. Lizzie relrq

BARRETT
1808, 11, 30. Rachel, dt Jonathan & Rachel, b
1809, 6, 29. Eleanor m John SANDERS
----, --, --. Jesse & Margaret
Ch: Ellenor b 1816, 6, 24
Eliza " 1818, 1, 17
Maria " 1820, 2, 4 d 1838, 6,30 bur Fairfield
David b 1821, 8, 20
Daniel " 1823, 9, 12
Levi " 1825, 9, 29
Sarah " 1827, 11, 2
John " 1829, 11, 27 d 1838, 7, 8 bur Fairfield
Jesse b 1831, 11, 18
Silas " 1834, 9, 6 d 1838, 7, 1 bur Fairfield
1822, 4, 11. Levi, s Jonathan & Rachel, Highland Co., O.; m at Walnut Creek, Susannah ELLIS, dt Mordecai & Sarah, Fayette Co.,O.
Ch: Milton b 1823, 3, 4
Lydia " 1825, 1, 22
Mordecai " 1828, 7, 20
Eli " 1832, 10, 12
Sally " 1834, 6, 26
Anna " 1836, 8, 16
Richard " 1838, 8, 29
Levi m 2nd Delilah -----
Ch: Joseph b 1847, 7, 9
Jesse "" 1853, 7, 24
1824, 9, 8. Lydia m Thomas DUTTON
1829, 4, 29. Ellis, s Jonathan & Rachel, Highland Co., O.; m at Fairfield, Anna LADD, dt Jacob & Elizabeth, Highland Co., O.
Ch: Denson b 1830, 7, 3
Jonathan " 1831, 9, 13
Jacob " 1832, 9, 18

BARRETT, Ellis & Anna, continued
Ch: Rebecca b 1833, 12, 25 d 1851, 7,11 bur Fairfield
Rachel b 1835, 1, 30
Ellis " 1836, 3, 28
Elizabeth " 1837, 11, 22
Anna " 1839, 8, 7
James " 1842, 10, 26
1829, 10, 7. Rachel m Jordan LADD
1837, 4, 23. Rachel d bur Fairfield
1840, 3, 29. Jonathan d ae 77 bur Fairfield
1841, 3, 17. Susanna d bur Fairfield
1844, 1, 20. Richard d ae 83 bur Fall Creek
1845, 11, 20. David, s Jesse & Margaret, Highland Co., O.; m at Walnut Creek, Melicent JURY, dt William & Elizabeth, Fayette Co., O.
Ch: Jesse William b 1846, 8, 25
Enos Jewry " 1848, 11, 18
Elizabeth " 1857, 9, 1
1847, 9, 22. Daniel, s Jesse & Margaret, Highland Co., O.; m at Fairfield, Hannah CHANDLER, dt Eli & Mary, Highland Co., O.
Ch: John Chandler b 1850, 6, 6
William Curry " 1848, 10, 23
----, --, --. Denson & Hannah
Ch: George Edgar b 1857, 3, 1
William Austin " 1859, 2, 28
Elias M. " 1861, 5, 1
Clara C. " 1864, 10, 18
1859, 10, 17. Rachel d ae 91 bur Fairfield
1860, 7, 31. Ellis d ae 67 bur Fairfield
1861, 5, 23. Anna m Asa HOCKETT
1861, 11, 21. Lydia m Eli NEWLIN
1863, 5, 8. Ellis d bur Fairfield
1868, 3, 26. Joseph M., s Levi & Delilah, Highland Co., O.; m at Fall Creek, Mary E. MAGOON, dt Alfred & Elizabeth, Highland Co., O.
----, --, --. Joseph & Mary E.
Ch: Levi b 1868, 9, 23
Alfred " 1870, 1, 12
Anna " 1872, 5, 4
1871, 3, 17. Levi d ae 71y (an elder)
----, --, --. C. Leslie m Sarah Eunice McVEY, dt Isaac & Martha Job, b 1871,2,12
Ch: Vivian Maurine b 1897, 6, 5
Clinton Delos " 1900, 6, 22
Lawrence Doan " 1903, 6, 24
----, --, --. Harry Milton, s Eli S. & Rebecca (Dicks), b 1878,2,9; m Bertha B. McKINLEY, dt Chas. & Levina (Johnson), b 1879,5,9
Ch: Chas. Vernon b 1901, 4, 11
Harry Wraymond b 1903, 5, 1
Carrie Bertha " 1905, 6, 3

1812, 4, 25. Benjamin dis mcd
1815, 7, 29. Jesse con mcd
1823, 2, 22. Margaret recrq
1823, 3, 29. Elenor, Eliza, Mariah & David, ch Jesse & Margaret, recrq
1845, 12, 20. Levi gct Newberry MM, to m Delila Moon
1846, 3, 21. Delila rocf Newbury MM, dtd 1846,3,16
1847, 2, 19. Mahala rocf Newberry MM, dtd 1847,2,15
1847, 9, 18. Milton & w, Mahala, gct Newberry MM
1851, 9, 20. Jesse & w, Margaret, & s, Jesse, gct Honey Creek MM, Ind.
1851, 9, 20. Daniel & w, Hannah, & ch, William Cary & John Chandler, gct Honey Creek MM, Ind.
1851, 9, 20. Eliza gct Honey Creek MM, Ind.
1851, 9, 20. Sarah gct Honey Creek MM, Ind.
1851, 9, 20. Levi rqct Honey Creek MM, Ind.
1851, 12, 20. Mordecai dis disunity
1853, 3, 19. Thomas recrq
1853, 4, 16. Eleanor, Benjamin & Catherine, ch Thomas, recrq
1853, 9, 17. David & w, Millicent, & ch, Jesse William & Enos, gct Honey Creek MM, Ind.
1854, 4, 15. Denson con mcd
1854, 12, 16. Eli dis disunity
1855, 11, 17. Jonathan dis mcd
1856, 3, 15. Hannah recrq
1856, 4, 19. Rachel Anna, ch Denson & Hannah, recrq
1859, 12, 17. Jacob con mcd
1860, 4, 21. David Barrett & w, Milicent, & ch, Jesse William, Enos Jewry & Elizabeth Barrett, also a niece, Margaret Ellen Ellis, rocf Salem MM, Ind., dtd 1860,3,8
1860, 11, 17. Minerva Jane rocf Center MM, dtd 1860,10,17
1861, 1, 19. Elizabeth Ballard (form Barrett) con mcd
1861, 2, 16. Ellis con mcd
1862, 5, 17. Jacob & w, Minerva, gct Center MM
1865, 8, 19. Anna M. Wright (form Barrett) con mcd
1865, 9, 16. Richard gct New Salem MM, Ind., to m Malinda Stanbrough
1865, 12, 16. Richard gct New Salem MM, Ind.
1868, 10, 17. Eleanor George (form Barrett) con mcd
1869, 2, 20. Benjamin, s Thomas, con mcd
1869, 5, 15. Mary E. rocf Dover MM
1870, 2, 19. Ann Maria recrq
1870, 2, 19. Hester & Thomas recrq of parents, Thomas & Mariah
1870, 3, 19. Robert W. recrq

BARRETT, continued
1871, 1, 21. Jesse W. con mcd
1871, 2, 18. Clarence, Amon Edward & Clara Bell, ch Martha Ellen, recrq
1871, 2, 18. Ellen recrq
1871, 6, 17. James G. con mcd
1871, 8, 19. Abi (form Johnson) con mcd
1871, 8, 19. Elizabeth recrq
1871, 8, 19. Gideon recrq
1871, 8, 19. James recrq
1871, 8, 19. John recrq
1871, 8, 19. Nancy recrq
1871, 8, 19. Ruth Anna recrq
1872, 2, 17. Richard C. recrq
1873, 3, 15. Richard L. recrq
1873, 3, 15. Jane recrq
1873, 5, 17. Mary & Eddie recrq
1873, 5, 17. Rhoda & Phoebe recrq
1873, 10, 18. Enos J. & w, Lavinia, con mcd
1873, 12, 20. Sallie gct New Hope MM, Ind.
1874, 7, 18. James, Ruth & James G. gct Londonderry MM
1874, 7, 18. Nancy Ellen, Gideon F. & Elizabeth, gct Londonderry MM
1877, 1, 20. Rebecca J. recrq
1877, 2, 17. Eli S. recrq
1880, 12, 18. Ellen relrq
1883, 4, 21. Jonas T., Mary E., M. Ella, Lora, Laura & Arthur recrq
1883, 6, 16. Mary E. recrq
1884, 12, 22. Emma A. relrq
1890, 4, 19. Rueben P., Phebe L., Maude, Augusta, Georgie & A. H., recrq
1893, 5, 20. Jonas & M. E. dropped from mbrp
1893, 5, 20. Clara L. dropped from mbrp
1893, 6, 17. Mary J. recrq
1894, 3, 17. Mary Guthrie dis disunity
1895, 4, 2. Maud & Josephine A. recrq
1896, 6, 20. Lida roc
1896, 10, 17. Leslie recrq
1898, 4, 16. Amon dropped from mbrp
1901, 3, 16. Adam, Rose Eugenia & ch, Roxie, Joseph C., Claude E., Benjamin, Austa E. & Bertha O. recrq
1904, 12, 17. Frank rocf Hopewell MM, dtd 1904,12,3
1905, 4, 15. Ione dropped from mbrp
1906, 10, 20. Frank [Barrette] gct Amo MM,Ind.
1909, 6, 19. Frank gct Amo MM, Ind. (a minister)
1912, 10, 19. R. P. & w, Phebe, & dt, Louise, gct Wilmington MM
1912, 10, 19. Hubert gct Wilmington MM
1913, 2, 15. Adam & w & ch, Roxa, Joseph, Claude, Glenn, Lula, Helen & Russell, relrq
1913, 6, 21. J. Arthur & w, Minnie, relrq
1914, 1, 17. B. H., Lida, Austie & Bertha relrq
1916, 6, 17. Roy relrq

BARRICK
1811, 2, 28. Nancy & Elizabeth Barrick, gr dt John Timberlake, recrq
1825, 5, 28. Aaron Chalfont gct Clear Creek MM, to m Elizabeth Barrix
1829, 12, 26. Jane [Barick] (form McPherson) dis mcd

BARTHOLF
1871, 9, 16. James recrq
1871, 9, 16. Rebecca recrq
1874, 7, 18. James [Bertholf] gct Londonderry MM

BASHAM
1871, 5, 20. Rebecca Ann recrq

BATEMAN
1824, 6, 26. Deborah gct Miami MM

BAY
1892, 2, 20. John recrq
1898, 4, 16. John dropped from mbrp

BEALS
----, --, --. John B. & Lois [Bales]

Ch:				
Eunice	b	1785,	1,	2
Isaac	"	1788,	4,	14
Mary	"	1790,	12,	5
Jonathan	"	1793,	7,	24
Jane	"	1796,	3,	10
Sarah	"	1799,	1,	3
Nathan	"	1801,	7,	9
Lois	"	1804,	7,	10
Bowater	"	1806,	2,	26
Ruth	"	1808,	8,	20

1801, 8, 29. Thomas d ae 82 bur Fairfield
----, --, --. John & Mary

Ch:				
Jesse	b	1804,	10,	1
Mary	"	1806,	4,	6
Esther	"	1807,	8,	10

----, --, --. Abraham & Mehitabel

Ch:				
Bethiah	b	1806,	4,	23
Prisila	"	1807,	11,	4
Mary	"	1809,	8,	28
Metilda	"	1811,	5,	3
Sarah	"	1813,	7,	14

1806, 8, 9. Lois d
1807, 12, 1. Isaac d
1808, 6, 29. Elizabeth m John THORNBROUGH
1811, 12, 12. Rachel [Beales] m Joseph THORNBROUGH
1813, 7, 6. Sarah d ae 89 bur Fairfield
1813, 9, 21. Abraham d bur Fairfield
1816, 12, 12. Jane m John HODGSON

1808, 1, 30. Daniel, the younger, dis mcd
1808, 1, 30. Katherine con mcd
1809, 1, 28. Daniel rocf Mt. Pleasant MM, Va., dtd 1808,8,27
1809, 1, 28. Priscilla rocf Lost Creek MM, dtd 1806,5,31, endorsed by Miami MM
1809, 10, 28. Rachel dis joining Methodists
1809, 11, 25. Priscilla Rion (form Beals) dis
1810, 5, 31. Jacob, s Daniel, dis

BEALS, continued
1810, 9, 29. Mary Conner (form Beals) dis mcd
1811, 4, 27. Jacob [Beales] & s, Solomon & John, rocf New Hope MM, Tenn., dtd 1810,11, 17; endorsed by Center MM
1811, 4, 27. Cert rec for Elizabeth [Beales] from New Hope MM, dtd 1810,8,17, endorsed by Center MM
1812, 11, 28. Daniel Jr. dis disunity
1813, 7, 30. Jonathan dis mcd
1814, 11, 26. Lydia dis
1815, 5, 27. Ruth [Bales] gct Clear Creek MM
1816, 12, 28. Nathan rocf Clear Creek MM, dtd 1816,11,9
1818, 8, 29. Nathan dis
1819, 5, 29. Hannah [Beal] rocf Hopewell MM, dtd 1819,2,4
1819, 5, 29. Rachel [Beal] rocf Hopewell MM, Va., dtd 1819,2,4
1819, 5, 29. William [Beal] rocf Hopewell MM, Va., dtd 1819,2,4
1822, 8, 31. Elizabeth Hiatt (form Beal) dis mcd
1823, 11, 29. Abijah dis disunity
1827, 7, 28. William [Beal] gct Hopewell MM, Va.
1827, 8, 25. Mary dis
1829, 4, 25. Mehetabel & ch, Bethiel Matilda & Sarah, gct Duck Creek MM, Ind.
1829, 7, 25. Hannah [Beal] gct Green Plain MM
1832, 10, 25. Rachel [Beal] gct Sugar River MM, Ind.
1833, 1, 24. John B. gct White River MM, Ind.
1833, 10, 24. Jacob dis jas
1833, 12, 26. White River MM was given permission to rst Jacob
1834, 9, 25. White River MM was given permission to rst Daniel

BEARD
1871, 8, 19. Mary Ann [Beird] recrq
1881, 5, 21. Lydia recrq
1886, 7, 17. Jettie recrq
1886, 7, 17. Elizabeth & N. B. recrq
1896, 7, 18. Jettie dropped from mbrp
1898, 4, 16. Lydia dropped from mbrp

BEAUCHAMP
1811, 7, 27. Cert rec for William & fam from Piney Grove MM, S. C., dtd 1811,4,20, endorsed to White Water MM

BECK
1884, 4, 19. Adam Mason & w, Mary Jane, recrq
1884, 5, 17. Mable recrq
1911, 9, 16. Mable gct Newberry MM, Oregon
1913, 11, 15. Mabel O. rocf Newburg MM, Oregon

BEERY
1873, 5, 17. Daniel & Edwin recrq

BEESON
1808, 10, 20. Rebeckah [Beason] (form Worley) dis mcd
1809, 5, 27. Benjamin [Beson] rocf Westfield MM, dtd 1807,10,10
1810, 4, 28. Richard [Beson] rocf Westfield MM, dtd 1809,12,9
1810, 4, 28. Amasa [Beson] & s, William, rocf Westfield MM, dtd 1809,12,9
1810, 4, 28. Mary rocf Westfield MM, N. C., dtd 1809,12,9
1810, 4, 28. Mary, 2nd & dt, Ann, rocf Westfield MM, N. C., dtd 1809,12,9
1836, 3, 24. Martha (form Wright) con mcd
1844, 9, 21. Martha & ch, Caroline, Daniel W., Jane & Joel Wright, gct Center MM
1846, 10, 17. Martha, w Ruel, & ch, Caroline, Daniel W., Jane & Joel Wright, rocf Center MM, dtd 1846,9,16
1866, 10, 20. Mary Ann (form Thornburg) con mcd
1870, 3, 19. Hannibal & Elizabeth T. recrq
1870, 3, 19. Anna, John & Charles, ch Hannibal & Elizabeth T., recrq of parents
1878, 3, 16. Hannibal & fam gct Cincinnati MM
1880, 6, 19. Hannibal & w, Elizabeth, & ch, Anna, John, Charles & Caroline, rocf Cincinnati MM

BELFORD
1857, 8, 15. Maria [Belfred] (form Hardy) dis mcd
1894, 3, 17. James & Sarah A. recrq

BELL
1818, 4, 25. Rebecca (form Chandler) con mcd
1825, 6, 25. Alexander recrq
1826, 6, 24. Mary, Jane, Hannah & Nancy, ch Alexander & Rebecca, recrq
1826, 11, 26. Alexander & w, Rebecca, & ch, Mary Jane, Hannah Nancy & John, gct Green Plain MM

BENBOW
1812, 6, 27. Cert rec for John & w, Charity, & ch, Miriam & Evan, from New Garden MM, N. C., dtd 1810,9,29; endorsed by White Water; endorsed by this mtg to Center MM

BENEGAR
----, --, --. George & Mary Jane
Ch: James Wesley b 1862, 5, 12
Ellis Ellsworth " 1864, 11, 8
Lee Clark " 1867, 8, 3
Cyrus Wister " 1867, 11, 7

BENNETT
1809, 2, 25. Mary rocf Hopewell MM, dtd 1808,8,1
1822, 8, 31. Mary gct Green Plain MM
1838, 4, 26. Mary (form Ellis) con mcd
1838, 6, 21. James Lee, Joseph & Mahala Ann,

BENNETT, continued
ch Jabez, rocf Phila. MM for Northern Dist., dtd 1838,1,23

BENTLEY
1818, 1, 31. Elizabeth rst by rq with consent of New Garden MM
1820, 12, 30. Cert rec for Lydia from Chesnut Creek MM, endorsed to Lees Creek MM

BERRY
1876, 6, 17. John recrq
1893, 2, 18. Belle recrq

BETTS
1835, 9, 30. Christopher, s Aaron & Ann, Clinton Co., O.; m at Fairfield, Lydia HUFF, dt Daniel & Sarah, Highland Co., O.

1810, 1, 27. William rocf Mt. Pleasant MM, Va., dtd 1809,8,26
1810, 1, 27. Mary rocf Mt. Pleasant MM, Va., dtd 1809,8,26
1814, 5, 28. Mary gct Center MM
1836, 2, 25. Lydia gct Newberry MM

BINEGAR
1862, 4, 19. Mary Jane (form Johnson) con mcd
1867, 3, 16. Ulysses N. Johnson, minor s Mary Jane [Benegar] recrq
1871, 4, 15. James W. & Ellis E., ch George & Jane, recrq

BINFORD
1826, 8, 26. Cert rec for James & ch endorsed to Springborough MM

BIRD
1902, 11, 15. Vista L. dropped from mbrp

BISHOP
1867, 12, 21. Margaretta H. gct South River (or Spring Creek) MM, Ia.

BLACKBURN
1871, 2, 18. Horace A., Jessie, William, Emma, Franklin & Lillie, ch George & Amelia, recrq

BLOXSOM
1808, 9, 24. Richard Bloxsom & s, Charles, & gr ch, Richard Obidiah & Gideon Johnson, rocf Concord MM, O., dtd 1808,6,23
1808, 9, 24. Ann [Blocksom] & dt, Ann & Mary, & gr dt, Unity & Jerusha Johnson, rocf Concord MM, dtd 1808,6,23
1812, 1, 25. William & w, Mary, & ch, James, Ann Elizabeth, Mariah Priscilla & Mary, rocf Still Water MM, dtd 1811,4,30
1812, 1, 25. Gregory rocf South River MM, Va. dtd 1811,10,12
1814, 1, 29. Richard Bloxsom & gr s, Gideon Johnson, gct Cesars Creek MM
1814, 1, 29. Gregory con mcd
1814, 3, 26. Charles gct Ceasars Creek MM
1814, 3, 26. William & fam gct Ceasars Creek MM
1814, 10, 29. Gregory gct Cesars Creek MM

BOATMAN
1881, 4, 16. Sarah M. recrq

BOCOCK
1809, 4, 29. Nancy (form Johnson) con mcd

BOND
1811, 9, 28. Cert rec for Samuel & fam from Westfield MM, dtd 1810,11,10, endorsed to Fall Creek MM
1813, 9, 25. Edward & w, Mary, rocf Mount Pleasant MM, Va., dtd 1812,11,28
1814, 10, 29. Edward & w, Mary, gct Ceasar's Creek MM
1861, 8, 17. Elgar Brown Jr. gct White Water MM, to m Sarah Bond

BONECUTTER
1820, 2, 28. Phebe rst with consent of Hopewell MM
1837, 2, 23. Phebe Johnson (form Bonecutter) dis mcd

BONHAM
1883, 4, 21. Nannie recrq
1896, 7, 18. Nannie dropped from mbrp

BOON
1871, 12, 16. Charles & Dorcas rocf Spiceland MM, Ind., dtd 1871,11,4

BOOTH
1871, 8, 19. Curtis recrq
1871, 8, 19. David recrq
1871, 8, 19. George recrq
1871, 8, 19. John Henry recrq
1871, 8, 19. Lizzie recrq
1871, 8, 19. Maggie recrq
1874, 7, 18. David gct Londonderry MM

BOOTS
1817, 8, 30. Rhoda (form Man) dis mcd

BORUM
1819, 11, 3. Katherine m George OAKLEY
1832, 7, 7. Sarah d
1836, 7, 22. Judith d ae 68 bur Fairfield
1839, 2, 27. Obed A. d bur Fairfield
1858, 11, 14. Catherine d ae 66 bur Fairfield

1809, 11, 25. Judith & ch, Obed A., Catherine & Sarah, rocf South River MM, dtd 1809,8,12
1822, 4, 27. Obed A. con mcd
1847, 2, 27. Alice recrq
1847, 6, 19. Mary E. [Boram] (form Terrell)

BORUM, continued
con mcd
1851, 1, 18. Jane (form Wright) dis mcd
1853, 5, 21. Ruth E. (form Terrell) con mcd
1854, 6, 17. Ruth E. gct Greenfield MM, Ind.
1870, 2, 19. Obed recrq
1880, 11, 20. Sarah J. Thornburg (form Borun) recrq
1881, 12, 17. Mary E. & ch gct Lawrence MM, Kans.
1882, 8, 19. Eva M. & Anna gct Lawrence MM, Kans.
1884, 3, 15. Obed gct Argonia MM, Kans.

BOSWELL
1867, 1, 19. Joseph & w, Lavina E., rocf Chesterfield MM, O., dtd 1866,12,26
1868, 7, 18. Joseph & w, Lavina, gct Wilmington MM, O.

BOWEN
1902, 2, 15. Spencer & George recrq
1924, 3, 6. George gct Greenfield MM

BOWERS
1871, 3, 18. Benjamin recrq
1871, 3, 18. George W., Sarah E., Benjamin F., David M. & Henry H., recrq
1871, 3, 18. Sarah recrq
1879, 5, 17. George M. gct Union MM, Minn.
1910, 6, 18. Henry H., Sarah Ellen, Benjamin F. & David M. relrq

BOWLES
1812, 3, 28. Ruth (form Hoggatt) con mcd

BRACKNEY
1856, 12, 7. Marmaduke d ae 62

1809, 2, 25. Elizabeth (form Branson) dis mcd
1856, 7, 19. Marmaduke & w, Susanna, & niece, Phebe Bailey, rocf Dover MM, dtd 1856,5,15
1856, 7, 19. Eli & w, Rachel, & s, Marmaduke, rocf Dover MM, dtd 1856,5,15
1856, 10, 18. Mahlon rocf Dover MM, dtd 1856,8,14
1862, 3, 15. Eli dis disunity
1863, 4, 18. Mahlon gct Center MM
1866, 10, 20. Rachel & ch, Marmaduke, Sally Mary, Pleasant, Joseph & Ida, gct Dover MM, O.
1866, 12, 15. Susanna gct Dover MM, O.

BRADFIELD
1826, 5, 19. Hannah (form Wilkins) dis mcd
1870, 2, 19. Sarah Catherine recrq

BRADLEY
1893, 5, 20. Annie (form Driscall) dropped from mbrp

BRANSON
1811, 6, 4. Jane d
1809, 2, 25. Elizabeth (form Branson) dis mcd (Elizabeth Brackney)
1809, 12, 30. Jacob dis mcd
1812, 10, 31. David & w recrq
1812, 10, 31. Hannah recrq
1813, 2, 27. Nathan & Thomas, ch David, recrq
1813, 2, 27. Jane, Abigail, Charity & Mary, ch David, recrq
1851, 11, 15. Sarah A. gct Flushing MM

BROWN
1820, 3, 1. Elgar, s Joel & Rachel, Highland Co., O.; m at Fairfield, Mary HUFF, dt Daniel & Sarah, Highland Co., O.
----, --, --. Samuel L. & Grace
Ch: Sarah A. b 1838, 11, 30
Jesse S. " 1840, 2, 16
Mary A. " 1841, 7, 25
Phebe J. " 1844, 12, 5
Rebecca " 1848, 1, 14
Elizabeth " 1851, 10, 10
Edna " 1856, 9, 5
1842, 8, 12. Rachel d ae 74 bur Fall Creek
1855, 2, 26. William d ae 76 bur Fall Creek
----, --, --. Elgar & Sarah
Ch: Emma Laura b 1862, 6, 10
Mary Lydia " 1865, 4, 4
1871, 2, 9. Sarah d bur Fall Creek

1809, 10, 28. Thomas rocf Deep Creek MM, N.C., dtd 1809,7,1
1809, 10, 28. Mary & dt, Gulielma & Ann, rocf Deep Creek MM, N. C., dtd 1809,7,1
1820, 5, 27. Mary gct Clear Creek MM
1851, 1, 18. Lydia Browning (form Brown) dis mcd
1852, 4, 17. James dis jas
1853, 10, 15. William dis jas
1857, 11, 17. Isaac dis mcd
1859, 6, 18. Sarah Ann dis
1860, 9, 15. Mary Jane dis jas
1861, 8, 17. Elgar Jr. gct White Water MM, to m Sarah Bond
1861, 12, 21. Clinton recrq
1862, 3, 15. Sarah rocf White Water MM, dtd 1862,1,22
1862, 8, 26. Phebe Jane Sloonaker (form Brown) dis mcd
1862, 12, 20. David dis jas
1863, 12, 19. Clinton relrq
1865, 2, 18. Mary Ann Buzzard (form Brown) dis mcd
1866, 8, 18. Samuel & w, Grace, & ch, Rebecca, Elizabeth & Edna, gct Clear Creek MM
1870, 3, 19. Henry recrq
1870, 6, 18. Sarah Jane recrq
1870, 6, 18. Shadrach S., Isaac R., Simon W., Thurman J. & Elma L., ch Henry & Sarah J., recrq of parents
1870, 6, 18. Charles E. recrq
1873, 5, 17. George recrq
1873, 5, 17. Isaac recrq

BROWN, continued
1909, 3, 20. Blanch recrq
1909, 3, 20. Helen recrq
1914, 4, 19. Thelma recrq
1922, 4, 13. Blanche & dt, Thelma, relrq

BROWNING
1851, 1, 18. Lydia (form Brown) dis mcd

BRYANT
1817, 6, 28. Cert rec for Allen from Mt. Pleasant MM, Va., dtd 1817,4,26, endorsed to Clear Creek MM
1817, 6, 28. Cert rec for Baley from Mt. Pleasant MM, Va., dtd 1817,4,26, endorsed to Lees Creek MM

BUFFINGTON
1835, 4, 23. Joseph [Buffinton] rocf Birmingham MM, Pa.
1835, 9, 24. Mifflin recrq
1837, 4, 20. Joseph dis disunity
1838, 2, 22. Mifflen M. gct Clear Creek MM
1871, 3, 18. Mifflin M. recrq
1873, 8, 16. Mifflin M. [Buffinton] con mcd

BUNDY
1857, 9, 23. Rebecca d ae 75 bur Fairfield
1858, 2, 2. Zadoc d ae 81 bur Fairfield

1855, 7, 21. Zadoc & w, Rebecca, rocf Newberry MM, dtd 1855,5,21

BURGESS
----, --, --. Daniel & Ruth
Ch: Anna b 1806, 10, 1
John " 1808, 1, 10
Sarah " 1810, 4, 28
Oliver " 1812, 2, 6
Joseph " 1814, 3, 31
Deborah " 1816, 4, 26
Tacy " 1818, 10, 31
Beverly " 1821, 7, 31
Mahala " 1823, 5, 7
1813, 10, 13. John Tompkins, s Thomas & Betty, b
1815, 11, 30. Martha, w Joseph C., d bur Fairfield
1817, 6, 11. Joseph, s Jonathan & Margaret, Highland Co., O.; m at Fairfield, Penelope JOHNSON, dt James & Penelope, Highland Co., O.
----, --, --. James m Penelope ----- (2nd w)
Ch: James b 1818, 3, 8
Samuel " 1819, 9, 13
Jonathan " 1821, 7, 13
Martha " 1823, 11, 21
1822, 6, 27. Deborah d near 80y bur Fairfield
1824, 9, 15. Elizabeth m Jesse HARVEY
1827, 10, 1. Mary H. m Simon D. HARVEY
1828, 3, 9. Deborah d bur Fairfield
----, --, --. Oliver & Rachel
Ch: Sarah b 1835, 6, 15
Daniel b 1836, 11, 28
John L. " 1841, 5, 13
William " 1844, 7, 26
Ann Eliza " 1846, 11, 25
Martha " 1848, 5, 27
Emily " 1851, 5, 1
1835, 8, 26. Tacy Jennett m Eli STALKER
1841, 1, 27. Ann m John STALKER
1842, 1, 27. Drusilla d ae 70 bur Fairfield
----, --, --. Joseph H. & Juliet
Ch: Aaron b 1844, 4, 26
Valena " 1846, 4, 9
1844, 2, 28. Mahala m Mahlon JOHNSON
----, --, --. Joseph & Phebe
Ch: Spencer b 1845, 4, 3
Deborah " 1846, 12, 12
Rebecca Ann " 1849, 1, 7
Jordan " 1850, 11, 21
Ruth " 1853, 1, 22
Mary " 1856, 1, 24
Joseph " 1858, 10, 23
Phebe " 1858, 10, 23
----, --, --. Beverly & Malinda
Ch: Lydia Ann b 1847, 7, 22
Eli " 1854, 1, 5
Harvey
Ellen " 1857, 7, 3
Emma Elva " 1866, 4, 23
1852, 6, 7. John d ae 83 bur Fairfield
1858, 3, 15. Ruth d ae 74 bur Fairfield
1859, 5, 30. Penelope d ae 76 bur Leesburgh
1872, 6, 20. Daniel d ae 101y 3m 12d bur Fairfield

1810, 11, 24. Daniel [Burges] rocf South River MM, dtd 1810,8,11
1810, 11, 24. Ruth [Burgis] & dt, Anne & Sarah, rocf South River MM, dtd 1810,8,11
1812, 1, 25. John & w, Drucilla, rocf South River MM, Va., dtd 1811,10,12
1812, 1, 25. Deborah rocf South River MM, Va., dtd 1811,10,21
1813, 10, 30. Thomas & w, Elizabeth, & ch, Elizabeth, Joseph, Jesse, Moses, Mary, Tacy & Martha, rocf South River MM, Va., dtd 1813,8,14
1813, 11, 27. Martha & ch, Elliza & Sarah, rocf South River MM, Va., dtd 1813,8,14
1814, 2, 26. Daniel gct Cesars Creek MM
1820, 8, 26. Leticia [Burges] rocf South River MM, Va., dtd 1820,4,8
1826, 9, 30. Joseph H. gct Newberry MM
1827, 5, 26. Jesse gct Springfield MM
1827, 6, 30. Fall Creek MM was given permission to rst Tabitha
1828, 10, 25. Joseph C. dis disunity
1829, 7, 25. Moses gct Newbury MM
1829, 11, 28. Penelope & ch, James, Samuel, Jonathan & Martha, also Eliza, gct White Lick MM, Ind.
1830, 1, 30. Sarah Roberts (form Burgess) con mcd
1832, 3, 22. Penelope & ch, James, Samuel,

BURGESS, continued
Jonathan & Martha, rocf Sugar River MM, Ind. dtd 1831,12,10
1835, 1, 22. Jesse & w, Elizabeth, & ch, Mary, Emily & Thomas, rocf Springfield MM
1835, 7, 23. Martha gct Miami MM
1835, 7, 23. Tacy gct Miami MM
1835, 7, 23. Thomas & w, Betty, gct Miami MM
1835, 9, 24. John Tompkins gct Miami MM
1835, 9, 24. Oliver con mcd
1835, 12, 24. Leticia gct Miami MM
1836, 1, 21. Jesse & w, Elizabeth, & ch, Mary Emily & Thomas H., gct Miami MM
1836, 10, 20. Rachel recrq
1837, 2, 23. Sarah, dt Oliver & Rachel, recrq
1838, 5, 24. James dis disunity
1842, 8, 25. Joseph rocf Miami MM, dtd 1842, 7,27
1843, 4, 20. Joseph H. gct Fall Creek, to m Juliet Johnson
1843, 7, 20. Juliet rocf Fall Creek MM, dtd 1843,7,19
1844, 5, 23. Joseph gct Center MM, to m Phebe Ballard
1845, 5, 17. Phebe rocf Center MM, dtd 1845,3, --
1845, 9, 20. Jonathan [Burges] dis mcd
1847, 2, 19. Beverly con mcd
1847, 11, 20. Joseph H. & w, Juliet, & ch, Aaron B. & Valena, gct Miami MM
1849, 3, 17. Martha Spencer (form Burgess) con mcd
1851, 6, 21. Samuel con mcd
1854, 8, 19. Sarah Worthington (form Burgess) con mcd
1854, 10, 21. Malinda recrq
1854, 11, 18. Lydia Ann & Eli, ch Beverly & Malinda, recrq
1855, 3, 17. Oliver & w, Rachel, & ch, Daniel, John, William, Ann Eliza, Martha & Emily, gct Henkles Creek MM
1858, 5, 15. John gct Westfield MM
1858, 12, 18. Samuel dis mcd
1862, 8, 26. Sarah Furgerson (form Burgess) con mcd
1869, 5, 15. Lydia Ann Parker (form Burgess) con mcd
1870, 2, 19. Olive D. Erskine (form Burgess) con mcd

BURKHARDT
1872, 7, 20. John recrq

BURNET
1847, 6, 19. Alice (form Atkinson) dis mcd

BURNS
1871, 8, 19. Gabriel recrq
1871, 8, 19. George [Burnes] recrq
1873, 3, 15. Leah & Sarah recrq
1874, 7, 18. Leah & dt gct Clear Creek MM
1874, 7, 18. George gct Londonderry MM
1874, 7, 18. Sarah & dt, Sarah, gct Clear Creek MM

BURNSIDE
1826, 5, 19. Cert rec for Mary from Deep Creek MM, N. C., dtd 1825,11,5; endorsed to New Garden MM, Ind.

BURRIS
----, --, --. John & Frances
Ch: Milley b 1794, 9, 19
Daniel " 1797, 2, 21
Betty " 1799, 4, 23
Rebecca " 1801, 1, 5

1808, 5, 28. Daniel [Burriss] rocf Westfield MM, N. C., dtd 1808,1,9
1810, 4, 28. Tabitha (form Sumner) dis mcd
1810, 7, 28. John C. [Burres] & w recrq
1810, 7, 28. Deborough [Buris] recrq
1811, 1, 26. Barclay [Burres], s John C., recrq
1811, 1, 26. Mahala & Susannah, ch John C., recrq
1884, 5, 17. Nancy recrq
1893, 5, 20. Nancy dropped from mbrp

BURTON
1871, 6, 17. Peyton recrq
1871, 6, 17. Martha recrq
1872, 5, 18. Davis S. & w, Mary A., & ch, Martha M., Mary A., Sarah M., Rosa B. & Payton, rocf Poplar Run MM, Ind., dtd 1872,4,13
1874, 9, 19. David L. & ch, Martha M., Mary A., Sarah M., Rosa B. & Peyton, gct Poplar Run MM, Ind.
1878, 8, 17. Pyyton dropped from mbrp
1914, 2, 21. Winfield Scott & Elva Rebecca recrq
1917, 2, 17. Maud dropped from mbrp

BUTLER
----, --, --. Samuel & Ursala
Ch: Mourning b 1791, 8, 9
Nathan " 1793, 8, 27
Lucy " 1795, 10, 26
Lydia " 1797, 10, 8
Tabitha " 1799, 8, 16
Simmons " 1802, 3, 17
Sarahan " 1804, 9, 19
Elizabeth P. b 1808, 11, 2
Susanna " 1811, 6, 18
Agatha " 1813, 9, 5
1812, 12, 2. William, s Joseph & Miriam, Clinton Co., O.; m at Fairfield, Esther LADD, dt Garrard & Sarah, Highland Co.,O.
1814, 2, 2. Lucy m William PIKE
1820, 10, 5. Samuel d ae 55 bur Fairfield

1809, 7, 29. Daniel, s James & Benjamin, rocf Upper MM, Va., dtd 1808,8,20
1809, 7, 29. Sarah & dt, Mary Susanna & Ann,

BUTLER, continued
rocf Prince George MM, Va., dtd 1808,8,20
1810, 8, 25. Daniel gct Miami MM
1813, 3, 27. Mourning Young (form Butler) dis mcd
1813, 3, 27. Esther gct Center MM
1820, 11, 25. Simmons dis disunity
1820, 12, 30. Nathan con mcd
1821, 8, 25. Ursala & dt, Elizabeth & Susannah, gct Clear Creek MM
1827, 1, 27. Sarah Ann dis jas
1827, 9, 29. Elizabeth rocf Clear Creek MM, dtd 1827,8,11
1829, 12, 26. Ursly rocf Clear Creek MM, dtd 1829,12,12
1831, 8, 22. Ursala Moorman (form Butler) con mcd
1832, 4, 26. Agatha gct Cherry Grove MM, Ind.
1832, 6, 21. Elizabeth dis disunity
1838, 5, 24. Nathan dis disunity

BUZZARD
1865, 2, 18. Mary Ann (form Brown) dis mcd
1882, 4, 15. Frank & Silemma recrq
1893, 5, 20. Frank dropped from mbrp

CADEMY
1870, 5, 21. James [Cadamy] recrq
1878, 5, 18. John [Cadamy] dis disunity
1882, 4, 15. Laura recrq
1884, 5, 17. John [Cadamy] recrq
1884, 6, 17. Joseph recrq
1885, 5, 16. Cora B., Anta May & Effie Pearl Walen, ch Laura Cademy, recrq
1887, 1, 15. John relrq
1887, 4, 16. Cora recrq

CALVER
1871, 6, 17. Jacob & Nancy recrq

CAMPBELL
1900, 3, 17. William & Ella recrq
1902, 4, 19. Benjamin recrq
1907, 3, 16. Fay recrq

CANTER
1875, 2, 20. David & Nancy recrq
1875, 2, 20. John W., s David & Nancy, recrq
1884, 3, 15. David H. & w, Nancy, relrq

CAPS
1841, 4, --. Sarah d ae 84

CAREY
----, --, --. Zenas & Lydia
Ch: Cyrus b 1829, 10, 13
Jonathan " 1831, 3, 10
Huldah " 1832, 8, 4
1831, 6, 2. Benjamin, s Jonathan & Ruth, Clinton Co., O.; m at Lees Creek, Elizabeth MARTIN, dt Abraham & Mary, Highland Co., O.
1833, 2, 28. Charlotte m Eli FELPS
1866, 3, 21. Isaac, s Jonathan & Ruth, Hamilton Co., Ind.; m at Fairfield, Rachel J. GREEN, dt Anthony & Mary Johnson, Highland Co., O.

1817, 6, 28. Cert rec for Jonathan [Cary] & w, Ruth, & ch, Zenas, Samuel, Benjamin, Mary Charlotte & Sylvanus, from Mt. Pleasant MM, Va., dtd 1817,4,26, endorsed to Lees Creek MM
1817, 6, 28. Cert rec for Samuel [Cary] Sr. & w, Rachel, & s, Elias, from Mt. Pleasant MM, Va., dtd 1817,4,26, endorsed to Clear Creek MM
1817, 6, 28. Cert rec for Samuel [Cary] Jr. & w, Anna, & ch, Daniel, Elizabeth, Thomas & Elias, from Mt. Pleasant MM, Va., dtd 1817,4,26, endorsed to Clear Creek MM
1818, 3, 28. Mary [Cary] dis mcd
1831, 7, 21. Benjamin & w, Elizabeth, gct Springfield MM, O.
1832, 4, 26. Benjamin & w rocf Springfield MM
1833, 3, 21. Samuel & w, Sarah, & ch, John F. & Ruth B., rocf Springfield MM
1833, 11, 21. Benjamin & fam gct Fairfield MM, Ind.
1833, 11, 21. Jonathan & fam gct Fairfield MM, Ind.
1834, 11, 20. Samuel & w, Sarah, & ch, John F., Ruth B. & Sylvester, gct Fairfield MM,Ind.
1835, 9, 24. Zenas & w, Lydia, & ch, Eli, Mary, Cyrus, Jonathan & Huldah, gct Fairfield MM, Ind.
1866, 6, 16. Rachel G. [Cary] & dt, Cordelia Bays Green, gct Richland MM, Ind.
1873, 3, 15. Maria Melissa recrq
1875, 6, 19. Marie Malissa & s, Walter, gct Newberry MM
1878, 5, 18. Annie E. gct Clear Creek MM

CARMEAN
1896, 6, 20. Elizabeth & Olive [Carmeans] recrq
1897, 4, 17. George recrq
1898, 4, 16. Thomas [Carmine] recrq
1901, 3, 16. Bert recrq
1907, 4, 20. Thomas gct Marshalltown, Ia.

CARR
1813, 4, 20. Benjamin d ae 70 bur Fairfield
1817, 9, 10. Thomas, s Benjamin & Patience, Highland Co., O.; m at Fairfield, Jemima STANLEY, Highland Co., O.
1820, 12, 16. Hezekiah, s Benjamin & Patience, Highland Co., O.; m at Fairfield; Esther CHALFONT, dt William & Ruth, Highland Co., O.
Ch: Bulah b 1821, 10, 11
Louisa " 1822, 10, 18
Benjamin " 1824, 8, 28
William " 1826, 9, 24
Bidell " 1828, 9, 8
Elizabeth " 1830, 11, 9 d 1839, 7,25

CARR, Benjamin & Esther, continued
Ch: bur Fairfield
Hezekiah b 1832, 12, 16 d 1839, 7,30
Elles " 1835, --, -- " 1839,12,17
bur Fairfield
Nathan b 1837, 7, 29
Mary Jane " 1840, 7, 21
----, --, --. Benjamin & Permely
Ch: Esther b 1821, 10, 7
Aaron " 1823, 12, 5
Hezekiah " 1826, 1, 5
Cyrus " 1828, 8, 20
Evan " 1830, 12, 10
Amos " 1833, 4, 27
Mary Jane " 1836, 10, 9
----, --, --. Iredel & Elizabeth
Ch: Mary Jane b 1856, 2, 4 d 1859,12,28
bur Fairfield
James Wesley b 1857, 9, 26
Hannah Cordelia " 1859, 8, 1
Elmer O. " 1861, 8, 5
Emma E. " 1863, 8, 13
Rachel Ann " 1865, 8, 10
1861, 5, 30. Benjamin W. d bur Fairfield
1863, 6, 8. Hezekiah d ae 72 bur Fairfield
1866, 10, 10. Hannah Cordelia d bur Fairfield

1820, 8, 26. Benjamin gct Lees Creek MM, to m
1821, 4, 28. Pamelia rocf Lees Creek MM, dtd 1821,--,--
1824, 2, 28. Thomas & w, Jemima, & ch, Rachel Huldah & Amos, gct Springfield MM, Ind.
1831, 12, 22. Patience gct Springfield MM,Ind.
1832, 8, 23. Benjamin & w, Permelia, & ch, Esther, Aaron, Hezekiah A., Cyrus & Evan, gct Cherry Grove MM, Ind.
1836, 2, 25. Benjamin & w, Permelia, & ch, Hester, Aaron, Hezekiah A., Cyrus, Evan & Amos, rocf White River MM, dtd 1835,12,21
1838, 10, 25. Benjamin & w, Permelia, & ch, Esther, Aaron, Hezekiah A., Cyrus, Evan, Amos & Mary Jane, gct Springfield MM,Ind.
1841, 4, 22. Eliza Steward (form Carr) dis mcd
1854, 6, 17. Iredell con mcd
1854, 8, 19. Elizabeth recrq
1855, 12, 16. William dis mcd
1860, 8, 18. Benjamin W. con mcd
1862, 12, 20. Nathan con mcd
1883, 4, 21. Andrew recrq

CARSON
1811, 11, 30. Cert rec for Bowater from Westfield MM, dtd 1810,11,10, endorsed to Fall Creek MM
1851, 8, 16. Sarah gct Honey Creek MM, Ind.
1857, 1, 17. Rachel (form Johnson) dis mcd
1857, 3, 21. Rachel recrq
1869, 7, 17. Lydia A., Madison M., Mary E. & Cyrus W., ch Rachel M., recrq

CARTER
1910, 6, 18. John W. relrq
1911, 3, 18. Marion, Jane, Blanch, William, Charles & Howard, roc
1921, 8, 3. William gct Bethel MM, Kans.
1922, 4, 13. Orpha & s, Beryl, recrq
1925, 5, 7. William & Ocie rocf Colorado Springs MM, Colo.

CARVER
1821, 2, 28. James, s Henry & Tabitha, Harrison Co., O.; m at Fairfield, Mary FERGUSON dt Nimrod & Anna, Highland Co., O.

1821, 4, 28. Mary gct Flushing MM
1822, 12, 28. James & w, Mary, rocf Flushing MM, 1822,11,22
1827, 8, 25. James & w, Mary, gct Flushing MM

CASHATT
1810, 6, 30. Thomas & s, John, Joseph, Thomas & David, rocf Cane Creek MM, N. C.
1810, 6, 30. Ann & dt, Margaret & Rachel, rocf Cane Creek MM, N. C., dtd 1809,9,2

CASS
1870, 12, 17. Jacob recrq
1871, 3, 18. Benjamin & Phebe recrq
1871, 3, 18. Cynthia A. recrq
1871, 3, 18. Lydia recrq

CECIL
1844, 4, 25. Mary (form Johnson) dis mcd

CHALFONT
1818, 11, 11. Abner, s Wm. & Ruth, Highland Co., O.; m at Fairfield; Ruth LUPTON, dt Asa & Hannah, Highland Co., O.
Ch: Margaret b 1819, 10, 2
Sarah " 1821, 8, 15
1820, 12, 16. Esther m Hezekiah CARR
1827, 1, 31. Bulah M. m Gerrard LADD
1830, 12, 29. Priscilla m Samuel MYRES

1808, 12, 31. Ruth rocf Mt. Pleasant MM, Va., dtd 1808,8,27
1814, 3, 26. William [Chalfinch] & w, Ruth, & ch, Esther, Abner, Mary, Aaron, William, Jacob, Beulah, Priscilla, Nathan & Jonathan, rocf Clear Creek MM, dtd 1814,2,24
1823, 3, 29. Abner & w & ch, Margaret & Sarah, gct Clear Creek MM
1825, 5, 28. Aaron gct Clear Creek MM, to m Elizabeth Barrix
1826, 2, 26. Aaron gct Clear Creek MM
1827, 1, 27. William Jr. con mcd
1827, 6,30. Aaron & w, Elizabeth, & dt, Mary, rocf Clear Creek MM, dtd 1827,5,12
1829, 1, 31. Aaron [Chalfond] & fam gct White Water MM; returned 1829,6,27, because of thir rem back
1829, 7, 25. William Jr. dis jH

CHALFONT, continued
1830, 4, 24. William dis jH
1830, 7, 31. Elizabeth dis jH
1830, 11, 27. Jonathan dis jH
1830, 11, 27. Nathan dis jH
1830, 11, 27. Ruth dis jH
1831, 1, 29. Jacob dis
1870, 3, 19. Hester Leuie recrq
1870, 3, 19. Nathan & Adaline recrq
1870, 3, 19. Ortla Glenford, s Nathan & Adaline, recrq of parents
1871, 2, 18. Ada recrq
1902, 11, 15. Glenn dropped from mbrp

CHALLENDER
1877, 5, 19. Andrew & Henry recrq
1882, 1, 21. Jaeson [Chalender] relrq

CHANCE
----, --, --. Isaac & Sarah
Ch: Atwell b 1814, 10, 29
William " 1816, 12, 22
Asa " 1819, 7, 14
1832, 11, 29. Tilghman, s Isaac & Sarah, Highland Co., O.; m at Lees Creek, Ann HAINES, dt Enos & Mary, Highland Co., O.
1833, 8, 26. Levi, s Tilman & Ann, b
1833, 12, 25. Isaac Jr. d bur at Fairfield
1835, 1, 3. William d bur Fairfield
1857, 3, 2. Sarah, w Isaac, d ae 76 bur Fairfield

1813, 4, 29. Isaac recrq
1816, 2, 24. Sarah recrq
1816, 5, 25. Iarrot, Nancy, Tilman, Isaac, David & Atwell, ch Isaac, recrq
1825, 6, 25. Nancy Hardy (form Chance) con mcd
1828, 2, 23. Parrot gct Green Plain MM; returned next mo
1829, 2, 28. Parrot con mcd
1830, 3, 27. Tilghman gct Green Plain MM
1831, 5, 28. Tilghman rocf Green Plain MM, dtd 1831,2,2
1832, 1, 26. David dis disunity
1836, 10, 20. Tilghman & w, Ann, & ch, Levi & Joshua, gct Westfield MM, Ind.
1837, 7, 20. Atwell dis mcd
1838, 4, 26. Asa dis disunity
1870, 3, 19. Atwell & Elizabeth J. recrq
1870, 3, 19. Mary E. & Adda Jane, ch Atwell & Elizabeth J., recrq of parents
1871, 2, 18. Isaac recrq
1878, 10, 19. Isaac dropped from mbrp
1905, 6, 17. Elizabeth J. relrq
1905, 6, 17. Emma, dt Elizabeth J., relrq

CHANDLER
1798, 11, 11. Rebecca, dt William & Hannah, b
1847, 9, 22. Hannah m Daniel BARRETT

1818, 4, 25. Rebecca Bell (form Chandler) con mcd
1844, 12, 21. Eli & w, Mary, & ch, John C., Mary, Elisha M., Marie P., Elizabeth Ann, Matilda B. & Bennett, rocf Flushing MM, dtd 1844,11,21
1844, 12, 21. Catherine rocf Flushing MM, dtd 1844,11,21
1844, 12, 21. Enoch rocf Flushing MM, dtd 1844,11,21
1844, 12, 21. Hannah rocf Flushing MM, dtd 1844,11,21
1847, 10, 16. Enoch dis mcd
1854, 11, 18. Eli & w, Mary, & ch, Maria P., Elizabeth Ann, Matilda B. & Bennett, gct Honey Creek MM, Ind.
1855, 10, 20. John dis mcd
1856, 10, 18. Elisha gct Clear Creek MM

CHANEY
1807, 9, 26. Sarah (form Jackson) dis mcd

CHENOWETH
1912, 2, 17. Mr. & Mrs. [Chinetwith] recrq
1916, 3, 18. Reece & Rosa relrq

CHERRY
1849, 11, 28. Milly M. m Hazael D. GREEN
1857, 9, 24. William, s Richard & Martha, Highland Co., O.; m at Hardins Creek, Elizabeth Ellen HADLEY, dt James & Sarah, Highland Co., O.
1857, 1, 13. Richard d ae 77 bur Fairfield
1869, 6, 14. William d bur Fairfield
1866, 11, 26. Richard d ae 77 bur Fairfield
----, --, --. J. A. m Eliza E. LADD, dt Franklin & N. R. (McVey), b 1859,12,27
Ch: Walter Ray b 1887, 6, 27
Ralph Elroy" 1889, 5, 1

1818, 12, 26. Martha rocf Clear Creek MM, dtd 1818,12,12
1840, 5, 21. Richard recrq
1840, 9, 24. Milly, Richard & William, ch Richard & Martha, recrq
1841, 12, 23. Gulielma recrq
1853, 1, 15. Julielma M. Banks (form Cherry) con mcd
1871, 6, 17. E. Ellen & ch, Corey Maud, Arthur Lee & James Pursey, gct Lawrence MM, Kans.
1900, 3, 17. Walter Ray & Ralph Elroy recrq

CHEW
1867, 1, 19. William & w, Julia Ann, recrq

1873, 8, 16. Rees recrq
1873, 8, 16. Minerva Adelaid recrq
1873, 9, 20. Eva, dt William & Julia Ann, recrq
1873, 9, 20. R. Matilda, N. Sarah & L. Louisa recrq

CLARK
1877, 5, 19. Hannah recrq
1883, 7, 21. Hannah relrq

CLARK, continued
1885, 12, 19. Henry recrq
1896, 9, 19. Henry J. gct Clear Creek MM
1902, 11, 15. Hannah dropped from mbrp

CLAYBORNE
1871, 8, 19. George recrq

CLAYPOLE
1870, 12, 17. Sarah & Mariah recrq

CLEARWATER
1811, 8, 31. Hannah rocf New Hope MM, dtd 1810,12,22
1825, 7, 30. Hannah [Clairwater] gct Dover MM
1827, 7, 27. Hannah gct Cherry Grove MM
1837, 10, 26. Hannah gct Westfield MM, Ind.

CLICKNER
1904, 2, 20. Ott recrq

CLIFTON
1913, 2, 15. Wilbur recrq
1922, 4, 13. Frances & s, Wilbur, relrq

CLINESS
1912, 10, 19. Augusta B. gct Wilmington MM

CLUFF
1901, 3, 16. Margery & Elizabeth recrq
1905, 4, 15. Elizabeth & Margery gct Hopewell MM
1907, 1, 19. Cert granted for Elizabeth & Marjorie, dtd 1905,4,15, not sent; retained mbrp here
1907, 4, 20. Elizabeth & Marjory dropped from mbrp

CLYDE
1870, 12, 17. Hiram recrq

COALE
1808, 7, 30. Eleanor & dt, Sarah, rocf Hopewell MM, dtd 1808,1,6
1861, 8, 17. Sarah [Cole] (form Hardy) dis mcd

COCKERELL
1855, 4, 20. Phebe [Cockrell] d ae 58 bur Cochran

1824, 5, 29. Phebe (form Mooney) con mcd
1863, 7, 18. Mary V. [Cockerill] (form Hadley) con mcd

COFFIN
1808, 9, 11. Samuel, s Samuel & Mary, Highland Co., O.; m at Clear Creek, Dinah KENWORTHY, dt David & Thamer, Highland Co., O.
1809, 12, 21. David, s Samuel & Mary, Highland Co., O.; m at Clear Creek, Mary KINWORTHY, dt David & Thamer, Highland Co., O.
1808, 2, 27. Olive con mcd
1808, 6, 25. David rocf Deep River MM, N. C., dtd 1807,11,2, endorsed by Miami MM
1837, 12, 21. Gerrard M. Johnson gct Clear Creek MM, to m Mary Coffin

COLLIER
1814, 5, 28. Cert rec for Samuel & s, William, from Contentne MM, N. C., dtd 1814, 2,12; endorsed to Clear Creek MM
1814, 5, 28. Cert rec for Margaret & dt, Miriam & Mary, from Contentne MM, N. C., dtd 1814,2,12, endorsed to Clear Creek MM
1870, 2, 19. Hannah E. recrq
1872, 4, 20. Mahala J. recrq

COLLINS
1870, 3, 19. John & Margaret recrq
1872, 4, 20. Mahala recrq
1873, 3, 15. Ellie B. & ch, Maggie & Almerin, recrq
1873, 7, 19. Eleanor & ch, Almarin & Maggie, gct Cincinnati MM, O.
1893, 5, 20. Eva dropped from mbrp

COMER
1812, 11, 28. Phebe recrq

COMPTON
1860, 1, 21. Anna [Cumpton] (form McPherson) con mcd
1860, 6, 16. Ann W. gct Cesars Creek MM

CONARD
1881, 5, 21. Enos & fam rocf Clear Creek MM, dtd 1881,4,9
1886, 8, 21. Phebe, Anna & Maria rocf Clear Creek MM
1895, 10, 19. Walter V. gct Wilmington MM, O.
1901, 4, 20. Anna relrq
1903, 2, 21. Phebe recrq

CONGER
1871, 8, 19. Eliza recrq
1874, 7, 18. Eliza gct Londonderry MM

CONNER
1810, 9, 29. Mary (form Beals) dis mcd

COOK
1809, 3, 28. Joseph, s Isaac & Charity, Warren Co., O.; m at Clear Creek, Elizabeth MILLS, dt Reuben & Cicila. Highland Co.,O.
1809, 3, 28. Wright, s Isaac & Charity, Warren Co., O.; m at Clear Creek, Ann HODGSON, dt John & Naomy, Highland Co., O.

1809, 5, 27. Elizabeth gct Center MM
1809, 5, 27. Ann gct Center MM
1824, 1, 24. Amy (form Winders) dis mcd
1873, 3, 15. Richard recrq
1904, 3, 19. Elmer recrq
1905, 4, 15. Ella recrq

COOK, continued
1907, 2, 16. Emma rocf Clear Creek MM
1908, 3, 21. Ellis rocf Clear Creek MM
1909, 3, 20. Roxollie D. relrq
1910, 9, 17. Elmer gct Hopewell MM
1911, 3, 18. Ella gct Hopewell MM

COOPER
1867, 7, 20. Sibil con mcd
1867, 11, 16. Sibil J. gct Pleasant Plain MM, Ia.
1871, 3, 18. Cedora recrq
1876, 2, 19. Amy recrq
1877, 3, 17. Eli & w, Sarah, rocf Hopewell MM, dtd 1877,3,3
1877, 5, 19. Morris & w, Alice, & ch, Cora & Alvin, recrq
1886, 4, 17. Amy Johnson (form Cooper) gct Newberry MM
1898, 4, 16. Alvin dropped from mbrp

CORWIN
1883, 4, 21. John recrq
1883, 12, 15. John [Corwan] relrq
1886, 7, 17. Samuel recrq
1889, 3, 16. Samuel Jr. recrq
1893, 5, 20. John dropped from mbrp
1907, 4, 20. Samuel dropped from mbrp

CORY
1818, 3, 28. Mary dis mcd

COURTNEY
1871, 8, 19. Calvin recrq

COVAN
1886, 7, 17. Mattie recrq
1893, 5, 20. Mattie dropped from mbrp

COWGILL
1815, 5, 3. Elisha, s John & Catherine, Clinton Co., O.; m at Fairfield, Rebecca PERDUE, dt Mentor P. & Jemima, Highland Co., O.
1821, 1, 10. Asa, John & Catherine, Clinton Co., O.; m at Fairfield, Margaret LUPTON, dt Asa & Hannah, Highland Co., O.
1851, 9, 2. Oscar d bur Fall Creek
1860, 11, 22. Lucinda m Jacob HADLEY
1865, 3, 30. Benjamin F., s Jonathan B. & Lucinda, Highland Co., O.; m at Fall Creek Jemima JOHNSON, dt Gerrard & Mary C., Highland Co., O.
1866, 9, 21. John B. d bur in Illinois
1867, 3, 11. Jesse d

1808, 7, 30. Benjamin & Henry, minors, rocf Hopewell MM, Va., dtd 1808,1,4
1815, 9, 30. Rebecca gct Clear Creek MM
1821, 6, 30. Margaret gct Clear Creek MM
1822, 3, 30. Asa rocf Clear Creek MM, dtd 1822,2,9
1822, 8, 31. Elisha & w, Rebecca, & ch, Gulielma & Hannah, rocf Springfield MM, dtd 1822,6,29
1824, 11, 27. Elisha & w, Rebeca, & ch, Gulielma Perdue, Hannah Coats & Bennett, gct Springfield MM
1827, 8, 25. Asa [Cowgil] & w, Margarett, & s, John, gct Fall Creek MM
1858, 4, 17. Sarah Jane Alderson (form Cowgill) con mcd
1860, 4, 21. John B. con mcd
1861, 2, 16. Lucinda Hadley & s, Jonathan B. Cowgill, gct Springfield MM, O.
1861, 6, 15. Ellen W. gct Springfield MM, O.
1863, 6, 20. Benjamin F. gct Clear Creek MM
1864, 8, 20. Milton dis mcd
1865, 8, 19. Samira gct Clear Creek MM
1866, 12, 15. Benjamin recrq
1866, 12, 15. Rachel, w Benjamin, recrq
1866, 12, 15. Charles G., Josephine & Jessie, ch Benjamin & Rachel, recrq
1868, 10, 18. Samuel C. gct Spiceland MM, Ind. to m Caroline Macy
1869, 4, 17. Caroline M. rocf Spiceland MM, Ind., dtd 1869,4,3
1870, 3, 19. Dinah K. Unthank (form Cowgill) con mcd
1871, 2, 18. Edwin con mcd
1871, 5, 20. Ellen C. rocf Spiceland MM, dtd 1871,4,1
1873, 5, 17. Jonathan & Ellen [Cowgil] recrq
1873, 5, 17. Katie recrq
1874, 1, 17. Katie & Mollie gct Springfield MM, O.

COWMEN
1864, 2, 20. Tacy Jonet (form Stalker) con mcd

COX
1809, 7, --. Thomas Sr. d ae 73 bur Clear Creek
1811, 7, 3. Gertrude m Elihu HIATT
1815, 8, 30. Mary m Josiah HUNT

1808, 2, 27. Jehu rocf New Garden MM, N. C., dtd 1807,9,26, endorsed by Center MM, O.
1808, 2, 27. Hester rocf New Garden MM, dtd 1807,8,26, endorsed by Center MM, O.
1808, 3, 26. Thomas Sr. rocf Cane Creek MM, N. C., dtd 1807,9,5
1808, 3, 26. Thomas Jr. & s, Stephen, Thomas & Joshua, rocf Cane Creek MM, N. C., dtd 1807,9,5
1808, 3, 26. Sarah & dt, Mary Martha & Katharine, rocf Cane Creek MM, N. C., dtd 1807, 9,5
1808, 3, 26. Sarah rocf Cane Creek MM, N. C., dtd 1807,9,5
1808, 5, 28. Enoch & s, Moorman & Enoch, rocf Cane Creek MM, N. C., dtd 1807,7,3, endorsed by Miami MM
1808, 5, 28. Gertrude & dt, Gertrude, Hannah, Phebe & Mary, rocf Deep Creek MM, N. C.,

COX, continued
dtd 1807,10,3
1808, 9, 24. Mary Harvey (form Cox) con mcd
1808, 10, 29. Samuel & s, Nathan, Jeremiah & Samuel, rocf Cane Creek MM, N. C., dtd 1808,3,5
1808, 10, 29. Lydia & dt, Jane & Lydia, rocf Cane Creek MM, N. C., dtd 1808,3,5
1812, 11, 28. Jehue & fam gc
1812, 11, 28. Esther gct White Water MM
1813, 9, 25. Phebe Hinton (form Cox) dis mcd
1814, 9, 24. Enoch & w, Gertrude, & ch, Mary & Enoch, gct Lick Creek MM, Ind.
1815, 4, 29. Enoch Jr. dis mcd
1815, 9, 30. Enoch & w, Gertrude, gct Blue River MM, Ind.
1817, 3, 29. Harmon gct Blue River MM, Ind.
1839, 6, 20. Charity (form Johnson) dis mcd
1842, 8, 25. Edna (form Johnson) dis mcd
1870, 3, 19. Edna recrq
1870, 3, 19. Harriet Pauline & Sabina Emerella, ch Edna, recrq
1870, 6, 18. Abraham & Sarah recrq
1870, 12, 17. Jacob recrq
1873, 3, 15. Andrew M. recrq
1875, 12, 18. Alfred J. recrq
1878, 10, 19. Alfred dropped from mbrp
1883, 11, 17. A. M. dropped from mbrp
1884, 5, 17. Joseph recrq
1886, 9, 18. Andrew recrq
1890, 12, 20. Joe gct Columbus MM, O.
1893, 5, 20. S. E. & P. dropped from mbrp
1897, 2, 20. Mary recrq
1901, 4, 20. Doris recrq
1901, 4, 20. Sallie P. recrq
1902, 1, 18. Mary relrq
1905, 10, 21. Hugh & w, Clara, recrq
1910, 1, 16. Chloe Gilbert gct West Fork MM
1917, 3, 17. Anna Mae recrq

CRANFORD
1910, 6, 18. Charles relrq

CRAVEN
1870, 2, 19. Thomas W. recrq
1877, 2, 17. Sanson [Cravin] recrq
1884, 7, 19. Charles gct Clear Creek MM
1884, 7, 19. Lansing F. & w, Nancy Jane, gct Clear Creek MM, O.

CRAWFORD
1873, 3, 15. Samuel H. recrq
1873, 8, 16. Atlantic con mcd
1879, 3, 15. Charles recrq
1893, 5, 20. Samuel & fam dropped from mbrp
1910, 6, 18. Charles relrq

CREELL
1871, 3, 18. William M. recrq

CREW
1812, 6, 27. Joshua [Cruise] con mcd
1819, 6, 26. Judith & dt, Elizabeth, gct Newberry MM
1819, 10, 30. John con mcd
1820, 5, 27. John gct Newberry MM
1823, 7, 26. Joshua gct Newberry MM
1827, 7, 28. John rocf Newbury MM, dtd 1827, 7,26
1827, 7, 28. Joshua rocf Newbury MM, dtd 1827 7,26
1833, 6, 20. Joshua gct Clear Creek MM
1833, 10, 24. John gct Sugar River MM, Ind.

CRISPIN
----, --, --. John & Rachel
Ch: Joshua b 1811, 5, 6
Ann " 1813, 8, 15

1809, 10, 28. Mathias & John recrq
1810, 1, 27. Mary recrq
1810, 1, 27. Rachel recrq
1811, 12, 28. Thomas, Charles & Isaac Postgait & Davis Crispin, s & step-s of John Crispin, recrq
1811, 12, 28. Mary Postgate, dt John & Rachel Crispin, recrq
1812, 6, 27. Elizabeth recrq
1815, 7, 29. Mathias & w, Mary, gct Cesars Creek MM
1818, 10, 31. Elizabeth Wing (form Crispin) dis mcd
1831, 7, 21. David dis
1832, 5, 24. Ann dis disunity
1832, 12, 20. Joshua dis mcd
1847, 8, 21. Pleasant Plain MM, Ia. was given permission to rst David
1847, 9, 18. John Jr. gct Pleasant Plain MM, Ia.
1847, 11, 20. Benjamin dis jas

CUNNINGHAM
1889, 3, 16. Ida recrq
1893, 5, 20. Ida dropped from mbrp

DAILY
1875, 4, 17. Eliza A. recrq

DARBY
1812, 5, 30. Cert rec for ch of Hannah (form Andrews) from Cane Creek MM, N. C., dtd 1810,3,3, endorsed to Fall Creek MM

DAVIS
1851, 8, 22. Jane d ae 87 bur Fall Creek
1870, 9, 22. Mary A. m William THORNBERRY
1876, 6, 12. Mary A. E. d bur Fairfield
1880, 2, 26. Sadie M. m Richard C. GREEN
----, --, --. A. J. & Hattie E.
Ch: Ralph
Waldo b 1892, 10, 9
Paul Estel " 1900, 7, 4
----, --, --. J. E. & Mary
Ch: Russell b 1903, 1, 7
Robert " 1906. 11, 30

DAVIS, continued
1811, 8, 31. Cert rec for John & fam from Lost Creek MM, dtd 1810,6,30, endorsed to Fall Creek MM
1816, 8, 31. Fanny dis mcd
1833, 6, 20. Peter dis disunity
1834, 3, 20. John dis disunity
1834, 11, 20. Mary (form Haines) con mcd
1835, 9, 24. Mary & dt, Elizabeth, gct Fairfield MM, Ind.
1837, 5, 25. Thomas dis mcd
1845, 3, 15. Jordan rocf Clear Creek MM, dtd 1845,3,8
1847, 7, 17. Sarah (form Terrill) con mcd
1847, 8, 21. Jacob dis mcd
1851, 5, 17. John & w, Mary, & dt, Emily, rocf Clear Creek MM, dtd 1851,4,12
1852, 9, 18. Sarah gct Clear Creek MM
1854, 9, 16. Josee, s Martin, dec, rocf Westfield MM, Ind., dtd 1854,6,29
1855, 3, 17. Jane (form Terrell) con mcd
1855, 7, 21. Jane gct Clear Creek MM
1857, 12, 19. John & w, Mary, & ch, Emily, Caroline & Rachel Almeda, gct Dover MM,O.
1861, 5, 18. Mary Ann, Martha Ester, Phebe Elizabeth, Lydia Ellen, Daniel,Jesse, Harmon & Sarah Maria, ch Jordan, recrq
1866, 6, 16. Tristram & w, Welmet, & ch, Levi, Elizabeth & Henry, gct Bear Creek MM, Ia.
1868, 3, 21. Jordan con mcd
1868, 9, 19. Mary Ann rocf Springfield MM, O., dtd 1868,8,15
1871, 4, 15. Jane con mcd
1871, 5, 20. Evangeline recrq
1872, 4, 20. Sarah Ann recrq
1873, 5, 17. Nancy & Ettie recrq
1873, 5, 17. Ermina, dt Nancy, recrq
1877, 5, 19. Lydia recrq
1880, 5, 15. Hattie E. recrq
1881, 9, 17. Lydia gct Rose Hill MM, Kans.
1882, 6, 17. Lindley Murray Green gct Sand Creek MM, Ind., to m Alice M. Davis
1884, 7, 19. Jay & w, Harriett E., & ch, Fred L., Samuel E., Joseph & Leta E., gct Clear Creek MM, O.
1885, 7, 17. Jordan relrq
1886, 2, 20. Dora recrq
1888, 12, 15. A. J. & w, H. E., & ch, Frederick L., Samuel E., Joseph H., Letta E. & Icy May, rocf Clear Creek MM
1889, 3, 16. Thomas L. & w, Edna, & ch, Birchie S., Jesse L., Mary L., Harry Wilber & David Allen, rocf Clear Creek MM,O.
1891, 4, 18. Martha recrq
1893, 5, 20. Dan dropped from mbrp
1893, 5, 20. Jesse dropped from mbrp
1893, 6, 17. Thomas Lorenzo & fam gct Kokomo MM
1895, 4, 2. Ida recrq
1897, 4, 17. Samuel & w, Mary, rocf Clear Creek MM
1899, 1, 21. Mattie L. recrq
1904, 2, 20. Thomas T. & Nancy rocf Hopewell MM
1909, 3, 20. Thomas J. rocf Clear Creek MM
1909, 4, 17. Mae recrq
1909, 4, 17. Roberta Jane, dt Mae, rec as an associate mbr
1910, 10, 15. A. J. dropped from mbrp
1914, 1, 17. Mary recrq
1914, 1, 17. Russel & Robert recrq
1918, 4, 20. Mary rocf Leesburg MM, O.
1920, 4, 21. Sarah Catharine recrq

DECKER
----, --, --. Albert & Lydia A.
Ch: Edith b 1871, 4, 12
Malissa " 1872, 11, 28
Mary " 1875, 1, 4

1870, 2, 19. Sylvester & Albert recrq
1870, 8, 20. Albert con mcd
1870, 8, 20. Lydia con mcd
1870, 11, 19. Webster con mcd
1871, 8, 19. Mary E. recrq
1872, 2, 17. Levina con mcd
1874, 7, 18. Ellen gct Londonderry MM
1879, 11, 15. Sylvester relrq
1886, 7, 17. Levina & ch, Alpharetta, Rachel, Louie & Maggie, gct Maryville MM, Tenn.
1910, 6, 18. Edith, Melissa & Mary relrq

DENNON
1870, 6, 18. Mary Ann recrq
1870, 12, 17. Jimmy J., Alda W. & Rachel E., ch Hiram & Mary Ann, recrq

DEURO
1818, 4, 25. James H. rocf Buckingham MM, Pa., dtd 1817,12,1

DEVO
1884, 5, 17. Mary J. & Charles Frederick recrq
1893, 5, 20. Charles dropped from mbrp
1893, 5, 20. Mary J. dropped from mbrp

DEVOSS
1871, 5, 20. Samuel recrq
1872, 8, 17. Samuel con mcd
1872, 9, 21. Margaret [DeVoss] con mcd

DICKS
1819, 2, 4. Nathan, s William & Agatha, Warren Co., O.; m at Dry Run, Sally JOHNSON, dt Elijah & Elizabeth, Ross Co., O.

1819, 6, 26. Sally gct Miami MM

DILLON
1814, 12, 31. Nathan & w, Mary, & dt, Ruth, rocf Center MM, dtd 1814,7,2
1831, 7, 21. Ruth (form Hoskins) con mcd
1832, 11, 22. Ruth gct Vermillion MM, Ill.
1855, 12, 15. Anna (form Wright) dis mcd

DILLON, continued
1867, 8, 17. Anna & ch, Mary Jane, Martha Ellen, Lydia Arabel, William Alvin & Ettie May, gct Three River MM, Ia.

DIRK
1825, 6, 25. Hannah [Derk] rst by rq with consent of Hopewell MM
1826, 5, 19. Hannah gct Lees Creek MM

DIRKEY
1871, 8, 19. Rachel recrq
1874, 7, 18. Rachel gct Londonderry MM

DIVINE
1873, 7, 19. Joseph recrq

DIXON
1869, 12, 18. Hiram recrq
1870, 1, 15. Julia Ann, w Hiram, recrq
1870, 3, 19. Finley, Rebecca E., Permelia & Catherine recrq
1870, 3, 19. Serentha J., Onedas & one ch not named, ch Finley, recrq
1870, 3, 19. Purley, Maria, Winnie, Hiram P., Ella & Simon E., ch Hiram, recrq
1870, 4, 16. George A. recrq
1870, 6, 18. Charles C., s Joseph & Jane, recrq of parents
1870, 6, 18. Silas recrq
1870, 6, 18. Tamer recrq
1870, 6, 18. Joseph, Jane & Simon recrq
1870, 7, 16. Ruth & Mary Ann recrq
1870, 7, 16. Hiram P., s George A. & Ruth, recrq
1870, 8, 20. Nathan & w, Elizabeth, recrq
1870, 12, 17. William recrq

DORAN
1871, 3, 18. William & James recrq

DOSTER
----m --, --. John & Mary
Ch: Elma H. b 1849, 5, 29
Mary M. " 1851, 6, 29
Clarissa N." 1854, 3, 22
1857, 11, 5. John d bur Walnut Creek

1829, 1, 31. Catherine (form Mooney) con mcd
1848, 6, 17. John recrq
1848, 7, 15. Mary (form Mooney) con mcd
1849, 7, 21. Harriett (form Ellis) con mcd
1869, 4, 17. Mary & ch, Ella, Matilda & Clara, gct Clear Creek MM
1871, 3, 18. John Q. recrq
1871, 3, 18. Martha recrq
1871, 3, 18. Savilla recrq

DOUGHERTY
1890, 4, 19. John & Eliza F. recrq
1896, 7, 18. John & Eliza dropped from mbrp

DOUGLAS
1881, 4, 16. Emma R. gct Union MM, Minn.

DOWELL
1871, 3, 18. Almarinda recrq

DOWNE
1870, 6, 18. Jane recrq

DOWNIE
1871, 6, 17. Jane recrq

DOWNING
1871, 8, 19. James & Catherine recrq

DOYLE
1887, 4, 16. Mary J. recrq

DRAPER
1815, 2, 1. Josiah, s Joseph & Lydia, Highland Co., O.; m at Fairfield, Jemima WRIGHT, dt John & Jemima

1811, 7, 27. Cert rec for Josiah & fam from Back Creek MM, N. C., dtd 1811,4,27, endorsed to Fall Creek MM
1815, 5, 27. Jemima gct Fall Creek MM

DRISCOLL
1889, 3, 16. Anna [Driscol] recrq
1893, 5, 20. Annie Bradley (form Driscoll) dropped from mbrp
1902, 2, 15. Harry [Driskill] recrq

DUER
----, --, --. John H. bur at Buckingham, Bucks Co., Pa.

DUFF
1839, 4, 25. Matilda (form Ladd) dis mcd

DUNCAN
1870, 3, 19. James F. recrq

DUNN
1883, 4, 21. Charles recrq
1886, 10, 16. Blanche & Whitfield dropped from mbrp
1898, 4, 16. Charles dropped from mbrp

DUPOY
1886, 7, 17. Lillie recrq
1887, 3, 19. Lillie relrq

DURBIN
1886, 10, 16. John dropped from mbrp

DURNELL
1873, 4, 19. Cornelia A. recrq
1873, 5, 17. John F., Nora E. & Mary E., ch Harmannis & Cornelia, recrq
1876, 1, 15. Ida Belle [Dernel] relrq

DUTTON
----, --, --. David & Phebe
Ch: Mary b 1809, 3, 16
Jonathan " 1812, 5, 25
Lydia " 1815, 5, 23
1816, 3, 22. David d bur Walnut Creek
1818, 2, 5. Phebe m Mordecai ELLIS
1821, 1, 4. Margaret m John ELLIS
1823, 7, 30. Hannah m Ashley M. JOHNSON
1824, 9, 8. Thomas, s David & Phebe, Highland Co., O.; m at Fairfield, Lydia BARRETT, dt Jonathan & Rachel, Highland Co.,O.
Ch: David b 1826, 3, 30
Jonathan " 1829, 6, 18
Silas " 1833, 8, 28
Lewis " 1835, 9, 5
1832, 9, 9. Silas d bur Fairfield
1848, 9, 6. Lydia d bur Fairfield

1829, 6, 27. Mary gct Green Plain MM
1830, 5, 29. Jonathan E. gct Green Plain MM, endorsed back 1831,2,26
1833, 11, 21. Jonathan dis mcd
1835, 7, 23. Lydia gct Green Plain MM
1851, 9, 20. Thomas & w, Elizabeth, & s, Lewis, gct Honey Creek MM, Ind.
1851, 10, 18. David dis mcd
1854, 12, 16. Jonathan dis disunity
1855, 12, 15. Sidney (form Ladd) dis mcd
1860, 5, 19. Lewis rocf Clear Creek MM, dtd 1860,5,12
1861, 10, 19. Jonathan recrq
1861, 10, 19. Sidney recrq
1861, 11, 16. Rachel Almeda, Lewis Clarkson & Jeremiah Thomas, ch Jonathan & Sydney, recrq
1864, 1, 16. Sidney E., w Jonathan B., & ch, Rachel A., Lewis C., Jeremiah T. & Clara E., gct New Salem MM, Ind.
1864, 4, 16. Jonathan gct New Salem MM, Ind.

EARLE
1900, 6, 16. Cassin [Earl] relrq
1911, 6, 17. Ray & Ida dropped from mbrp

EASTER
1882, 4, 15. Rosetta & Marion A. recrq
1883, 1, 20. John C. & w, Lydia A., & ch, John W. & Viola B., recrq
1890, 4, 19. Ida recrq
1893, 5, 20. John & fam dropped from mbrp
1894, 10, 20. Kittie recrq

EASTLACK
1846, 8, 15. Ruth (form Thornburg) dis mcd
1849, 9, 15. Marmaduke gct Clear Creek MM

EASTMAN
1848, 9, 4. Susanna d ae 84 bur Bloomingsburgh
1856, 3, 23. James d ae 88 bur Bloomingsburgh

1820, 12, 30. James & s, David, rocf Sandwich MM, New Hampshire, dtd 1819,11,18
1820, 12, 30. Susannah, w James, rocf Sandwich MM, New Hampshire, dtd 1819,11,18
1823, 11, 29. David gct Westfield MM; cert returned without being presented
1828, 12, 27. David dis mcd

EDWARDS
1877, 3, 17. Jesse, Asenath, Robert Jr. & Anna recrq
1877, 3, 17. Marion & Stanley, ch Jesse, recrq
1881, 5, 21. Robert & fam gct Union MM, Minn.
1897, 2, 20. Birtha recrq
1897, 12, 18. Marion relrq
1902, 1, 18. Jesse relrq
1902, 1, 18. Emily H. relrq
1904, 4, 16. Asenath relrq
1904, 9, 17. Bertha relrq
1907, 4, 20. Stanley dropped from mbrp
1922, 5, 4. James & w, Mary Elizabeth, & ch, Lawrence & Burch Carter, rocf Fairview MM, O.

ELLIOTT
1870, 3, 19. Ewen W. & Ruth recrq
1870, 3, 19. Leonidas & Elva, ch Ewen W., recrq
1886, 7, 17. Cynthia & Benjamin recrq
1898, 4, 16. Benjamin dropped from mbrp
1898, 4, 16. Cynthia dropped from mbrp

ELLIS
----, --, --. Mordecai, Fayette Co., O. & Sarah
Ch: Mordecai b 1805, 2, 2
Mordecai m 2nd 1818,2,5, Phebe DUTTON, Fayette Co., O.
Ch: David b 1820, 7, 18
----, --, --. Jehu & Phebe
Ch: Nehemiah b 1806, 3, 2
Mary " 1808, 3, 20
Sarah " 1810, 6, 8
----, --, --. Thomas m Lydia REES d 1863,2,1 ae 88 bur Walnut Creek
Ch: Margaret b 1806, 6, 1
Thomas " 1808, 3, 5
Solomon " 1809, 2, 28
Lydia " 1812, 6, 23
William " 1814, 9, 30
Rees " 1816, 4, 30
Delilah " 1819, 9, 20
Uriah " 1819, 9, 20
1813, 8, 15. David, s Thomas & Margaret, Fayette Co., O.; m at Walnut Creek, Hannah ELLIS, dt Thomas & Lydia, Fayette Co., O.
Ch: Mary b 1814, 5, 12
Elizabeth " 1815, 10, 12
Elijah " 1817, 10, 1
Sophia " 1819, 3, 4
Thomas " 1820, 12, 6
Morris Rees" 1823, 8, 4

ELLIS, David & Hannah, continued
Ch: Levi b 1825, 3, 27
David " 1828, 3, 23
James " 1830, 5, 12
Lydia " 1833, 1, 4
Hannah Ellin
b 1834, 12, 15
1816, 8, 18. Sarah, w Mordecai, d bur Walnut Creek
1816, 10, 16. Lydia d bur Walnut Creek
1819, 10, 5. Delilah d bur Walnut Creek
1819, 10, 13. Uriah d bur Walnut Creek
1821, 1, 4. John, s Thomas & Lydia, Fayette Co., O.; m Margaret DUTTON, dt David & Phebe, Fayette Co., O.
1821, 7, 23. Phebe d bur Walnut Creek
1821, 8, 1. David d bur Walnut Creek
----, --, --. John & Margaret
Ch: David b 1822, 1, 29
Jonathan " 1824, 4, 14
Eli " 1825, 12, 9
Francis " 1827, 4, 25
Harriett " 1829, 7, 5
Mary Jane " 1831, 8, 1
James W. " 1834, 3, 15
Wesley M. " 1836, 8, 1
Sarah A. " 1838, 7, 20
John Calvin" 1841, 4, 15
Margaret H." 1843, 6, 26
Cyrus " 1845, 6, 23
1822, 4, 4. Margaret m David WRIGHT
1822, 4, 11. Susannah m Levi BARRETT
1824, 4, 7. Mordecai, s Mordecai & Mary, Fayette Co., O.; m at Fairfield, Rachel STANBROUGH, dt Nehemiah & Mary, Clinton Co., O.
1826, 8, 4. Eli d bur Walnut Creek
1833, 10, 26. James d bur Walnut Creek
----, --, --. Levi & Mariah
Ch: Athaliah b 1839, 11, 21
Caroline " 1843, 3, 28
Rufus " 1845, 8, 22
1841, 3, 4. Elizabeth m William WASSON
----, --, --. Elijah & Jane
Ch: David
William b 1845, 5, 17
Joseph Rees" 1846, 6, 9
Cyrenius " 1847, 11, 10
Margaret
Ellen " 1850, 4, 25
Isaac Lar-
kin " 1852, 11, 17 d 1857, 6,11 bur Walnut Creek
1845, 4, 5. Wesley Merrion [Elles] d bur Walnut Creek
1845, 5, 12. Sophia, w James, d bur Walnut Creek
1845, 5, 12. James Elwood, s James & Sophia, b
----, --, --. Thomas m Mary Ellen BENNETT d 1863,1,15 bur Walnut Creek
Ch: Martha
Jane b 1851, 6, 9
Ch: Hannah
Amilda b 1853, 3, 28
Rebeccah
Ellen " 1855, 2, 12
Mary Ann " 1859, 10, 21
1852, 1, 15. Thomas d ae 79 bur Walnut Creek
1852, 12, 6. Jane, w Elijah, d bur Walnut Creek
1855, 9, 20. Rachel m Samuel EMBREE
1856, 1, 31. Hannah Ellen m Joseph JOHNSON
1856, 11, 20. James d bur Walnut Creek
1860, 2, 13. Margaret d bur Walnut Creek
1866, 1, 10. Emily E. d
1869, 4, 22. Rebecca E., dt Thomas, d bur Walnut Creek
1871, 4, 19. Hannah d bur Walnut Creek

1809, 11, 25. Mary rocf Plainfield MM, dtd 1809,9,23
1812, 9, 26. Nehemiah & w, Sarah, & ch, Mary & Robert, rocf Lost Creek MM, dtd 1812,7,25
1813, 2, 27. Mary Moon (form Ellis) dis mcd
1814, 12, 31. Cert rec for William & w, Hannah, & ch, Jacob, Elizabeth, Mary & Rebecca, from New Hope MM, Tenn., dtd 1814, 3,13, endorsed to Clear Creek MM
1815, 5, 27. Eleanor Smith (form Ellis) dis mcd
1815, 7, 29. Job con mcd

1815, 8, 26. Rees dis disunity
1816, 5, 25. Thomas gct Cesars Creek MM
1816, 6, 29. Job dis disunity
1818, 3, 28. David dis disunity
1819, 10, 30. Anna Moon (form Ellis) dis mcd
1820, 1, 29. Martha dis
1824, 1, 31. Samuel con mcd
1826, 2, 25. Isaac dis
1827, 1, 27. Levi dis mcd
1828, 1, 26. Samuel gct White Lick MM, Ind.
1828, 4, 26. Mordecai Jr. gct White Lick MM, Ind.
1830, 9, 25. Thomas Jr. dis mcd
1830, 12, 25. James dis disunity
1832, 4, 26. Solomon dis mcd
1833, 2, 21. John dis disunity
1835, 2, 26. Sarah rocf Flushing MM, endorsed by Fall Creek MM
1836, 1, 21. William dis mcd
1837, 6, 22. Sarah gct Cherry Grove MM, Ind.
1837, 8, 24. Rees dis disunity
1838, 4, 26. Mary Bennett (form Ellis) con mcd
1839, 3, 21. Levi rst by rq
1839, 4, 25. Maria recrq
1839, 5, 23. William rst by rq
1839, 6, 20. Elizabeth recrq
1839, 7, 25. John rst
1839, 10, 24. Ruth rst by rq with consent of Goshen MM
1840, 9, 24. Thomas Rees & Matilda, ch William, recrq

ELLIS, continued
1841, 2, 25. James gct Goshen MM
1842, 4, 21. Sophia dis
1843, 4, 20. Elizabeth & ch, Thomas Rees, Matilda & Mary Elizabeth, gct Goshen MM
1843, 8, 24. William dis
1844, 11, 16. Elijah con mcd
1844, 11, 16. Jane (form Jury) con mcd
1845, 1, 18. James rocf Goshen MM, dtd 1844, 12,21
1845, 3, 15. Sophia rocf West Grove MM, Ind., dtd 1844,12,14
1846, 10, 17. Elizabeth, Thomas R., Matilda M. & Mary E., rocf Goshen MM, dtd 1856,7,18
1847, 9, 18. Jonathan dis jas
1848, 1, 15. David dis disunity
1849, 4, 21. Morris Rees dis mcd
1849, 7, 21. Harriett Doster (form Ellis) con mcd
1851, 2, 15. Levi, Jr. con mcd
1851, 2, 15. Thomas con mcd
1851, 5, 17. Elizabeth, w William, & ch, Thomas Rees, Margaret Matilda, Mary Elizabeth, Albert & Almeda, gct Mississinewa MM, Ind.
1851, 7, 19. Mary Ellen recrq
1852, 4, 17. Sophia rst
1855, 6, 16. Mary Jane Johnson (form Ellis) dis mcd
1856, 1, 19. David Ellis dis mcd
1857, 6, 20. Athaliah Strangely (form Ellis) dis mcd
1859, 3, 19. Elijah con mcd
1859, 12, 17. Eliza B. rocf Springfield MM, dtd 1859,11,19
1860, 4, 21. David Barrett & w, Milicent, & ch, Jesse William, Enos Jewry & Elizabeth Barrett, also a niece, Margaret Ellen Ellis, rocf New Salem MM, Ind., dtd 1860, 3,8
1860, 4, 21. Francis dis mcd
1860, 4, 21. Lydia Margaret Fishback (form Ellis) con mcd
1862, 7, 19. Alice Matilda recrq
1864, 6, 18. Daniel Webster & Emily Elizabeth, ch Levi Jr., recrq
1864, 9, 17. Pleasant Plain MM, Ia. was given Permission to rst Isaac
1865, 8, 19. Calvin con mcd
1866, 4, 21. Calvin gct South River MM, Ia.
1866, 6, 16. Cyrus dis bearing arms
1866, 8, 18. Harmannus recrq
1866, 8, 18. Martha, w Harmannus, recrq
1869, 7, 17. Sylvester recrq
1869, 7, 17. Alice Adaline, dt Sylvester, recrq
1869, 7, 17. Lizzy recrq
1870, 5, 21. Theodore recrq
1870, 7, 16. James Ellwood con mcd
1870, 7, 16. Syreaneas con mcd
1870, 7, 16. Rebecca (form Terrill) con mcd
1871, 1, 21. Thomas con mcd
1871, 1, 21. Mary (form Levey) con mcd
1871, 3, 18. Leneas H. & Cordie S. recrq
1873, 3, 15. Joseph R. con mcd
1873, 3, 15. Lydia Jane recrq
1914, 6, 20. Lillie Ross relrq

ELLISON
1904, 10, 15. Mason & w, Flora, recrq

ELMORE
1817, 5, 31. Cert rec for John from Lost Creek MM, Tenn., dtd 1817,4,26, endorsed to Lees Creek MM

ELWOOD
1884, 5, 17. Cyrus Arthur recrq
1889, 2, 16. Cyrus dis disunity
1890, 4, 19. Kate recrq
1893, 5, 20. Kate dropped from mbrp
1893, 5, 20. Will dropped from mbrp

ELZEY
1821, 9, 11. Agatha d ae 61 bur Fairfield

1822, 11, 30. Priscilla gct West Grove MM, Ind.
1823, 2, 22. William & ch, Kezia, Gerrard & Esther, gct West Grove MM, Ind.

EMBREE
1855, 9, 20. Samuel, Fayette Co., O.; m at Walnut Creek, Rachel ELLIS

1868, 4, 18. Samuel & w, Rachel, gct Chesterfield MM, O.
1873, 7, 19. Samuel & w, Rachel, rocf Chesterfield MM, dtd 1873,5,10
1890, 12, 20. Philip D. & Virginia gct Pennsville MM, O.

ENOCHS
1899, 4, 15. Maggie recrq
1910, 6, 18. Maggie [Enoch] relrq

ERSKINE
1871, 1, 27. Ethel Eulania, dt Jacob H. & Olive D., b

1870, 2, 19. Olive D. (form Burgess) con mcd

ESTELL
1872, 12, 21. William recrq
1874, 6, 20. Meribah recrq

EVANS
1847, 9, 18. Evan d ae 94 bur Lees Creek
1873, 9, 10. Susan d bur Fairfield

1811, 8, 31. Lydia Gossett (form Evans) dis mcd
1813, 1, 30. John dis disunity
1814, 5, 28. Rachel Holeman (form Evans) dis mcd
1870, 2, 19. John & Susan recrq
1879, 10, 18. Mary Ann rocf Hopewell MM, dtd

EVANS, continued
1879,10,4
1882, 4, 15. Catherine & William recrq
1886, 7, 17. Amos recrq
1886, 7, 17. Emerson recrq
1886, 7, 17. Sarah R. recrq
1886, 10, 16. Leroy & Margaret dropped from mbrp
1889, 3, 16. Glenn & Harry recrq
1889, 6, 15. Emerson gct Hopewell MM
1893, 5, 20. Will dropped from mbrp
1896, 4, 18. Cary recrq
1896, 7, 18. Marianna dropped from mbrp
1898, 4, 16. Amos dropped from mbrp
1898, 4, 16. Sarah dropped from mbrp
1911, 6, 17. Harry dropped from mbrp
1920, 9, 28. Darnie McPherson relrq
1921, 9, 14. Carey & fam relrq
1926, 8, 5. Carey & Chloe recrq

EWING
1879, 11, 15. Samuel recrq
1883, 5, 19. Samuel & w, Mary, gct Hopewell MM, O.

FAIRLEY
1873, 5, 17. Mary [Fairly] recrq
1901, 4, 20. Jennie relrq
1903, 3, 21. Charles E. & Winnie O. recrq

FARRINGTON
1814, 4, 30. Elizabeth (form Newby) con mcd
1814, 9, 24. Elizabeth gct Fall Creek MM

FERGUSON
----, --, --. Clark & Mary
Ch: Levi b 1812, 4, 24
Charles " 1814, 5, 25
Isaac " 1816, 2, 10
1821, 2, 28. Mary m James CARVER

1812, 1, 25. Clark recrq
1812, 1, 25. Mary [Fergerson] recrq
1812, 9, 26. Samuel & Elizabeth, ch Clark, recrq
1815, 9, 30. Nimrod & w, Ann, & ch, Mary & Isaac, rocf South River MM
1829, 11, 28. Nimrod & w, Anna, & ch, Isaac, Elizabeth, William Edney, Richard, Rebecca & Nimrod, gct White Lick MM, Ind.
1830, 6, 26. Samuel rocf Lees Creek MM, dtd 1830,5,15
1832, 2, 23. Samuel gct Newberry MM
1862, 8, 26. Sarah [Furgerson] (form Burgess) con mcd
1862, 12, 20. Sarah gct Newberry MM

FERNEAN
1894, 3, 17. Harry & Bertha recrq

FERNOW
1911, 7, 13. Thelma Lucile, dt Jesse B. & Ida, b
1895, 7, 20. Jessie B. roc
1896, 4, 18. Jessie B. & w, glt Presbyterian Church, Frankfort, Ohio
1902, 4, 19. Jesse B. & w, Ida D., rolf Presbyterian Church

FETRO
1874, 2, 21. Jacob & w, Amy, & ch, Sarah, Isabel & Jacob, recrq
1886, 2, 20. Joseph [Fittro] recrq

FIGGINS
1871, 3, 18. Zadoc recrq
1871, 3, 18. Elizabeth & Nancy Ann recrq
1874, 2, 21. Elijah Jr. recrq
1878, 2, 16. Elizabeth & dt, Alice & Nancy, gct Hopewell MM
1878, 11, 16. Zadock & Elijah gct Hopewell MM

FISHBACK
1860, 4, 21. Lydia Margaret (form Ellis) con mcd
1902, 1, 18. Annie relrq

FISHER
1809, 6, 28. Alice m John FREZER
----, --, --. John & Mary
Ch: Rebecca b 1819, 4, 8
Jane " 1821, 7, 21
Nancy " 1823, 3, 29
Hiram " 1827, 1, 9
Rachel " 1829, 12, 19
Nathan " 1831, 10, 12
Sidney " 1834, 5, 30
1820, 5, 4. Elizabeth m William JUREY
----, --, --. Hiram & Rebecca
Ch: Jane b 1821, 9, 26
Mary " 1823, 5, 7
Amos " 1825, 1, 27
Elizabeth " 1827, 2, 25
Jemima " 1829, 4, 13
Isaac " 1831, 4, 22
1824, 9, 18. Jane d ae 71 bur Walnut Creek
1828, 8, 30. James d ae 84 bur Walnut Creek
1828, 9, 27. Hiram d bur Walnut Creek
1840, 5, 5. Rachel d ae 55 bur Lees Creek
1863, 1, 24. Nathan d
1863, 12, 31. Cephas d ae 84 bur Lees Creek

1808, 4, 30. Mary McAdams (form Fisher) dis mou with her first cousin
1808, 11, 26. James dis disunity
1811, 10, 26. Thomas dis mcd
1812, 7, 25. Margaret (form Hoggatt) con mcd
1813, 7, 30. Susannah rocf Center MM, dtd 1812,12,5
1818, 3, 28. Rachel recrq
1818, 9, 29. John con mcd
1821, 5, 26. Hiram con mcd
1822, 6, 29. Mary recrq
1822, 6, 29. Rebecca recrq
1823, 7, 26. Jane, dt Hiram & Rebecca, recrq
1823, 7, 26. Rebecca & Jane, ch John & Mary,

FISHER, continued
recrq
1824, 3, 27. Jane Woodard (form Fisher) con mcd
1827, 7, 28. John & w, Mary, & ch, Rebecca, Jane, Hiram & Nancy, gct Lees Creek MM
1830, 3, 27. Hiram & w, Rebecca, & ch, Jane, Mary, Amos, Elizabeth & Jemima, gct Lee's Creek MM
1834, 4, 24. Margaret gct Fairfield MM, Ind.
1835, 1, 22. Thomas, John & Samuel, ch Aphas & Rachel, recrq
1835, 1, 22. Hannah recrq
1838, 12, 20. Hiram & w, Rebecca, & ch, Jane, Mary, Amos, Elizabeth, Jemima, Isaac & Susanna, gct Dover MM, O.
1839, 11, 21. Susanna gct Salem MM, Ia.
1840, 11, 26. Cephas rst by rq with consent of New Hope MM, Tenn.
1841, 7, 22. Cephas con mcd
1841, 12, 23. Rebecca Smith (form Fisher) con mcd
1843, 3, 23. Hiram & part of his fam rocf Dover MM, dtd 1842,9,15, endorsed by Fall Creek MM, 1843,1,25
1844, 4, 25. Penelope (form Johnson) dis mcd
1845, 11, 15. Thomas dis mcd
1846, 6, 20. John Jr. con mcd
1846, 9, 19. Hannah (form Atkinson) dis mcd
1846, 9, 19. Jane dis
1847, 9, 18. Hiram & w, Rebecca, & ch, Amos, Jemima, Isáac & Susanna, gct Dover MM
1858, 11, 20. Samuel dis mcd
1861, 8, 17. Nancy T. Pyle (form Fisher) con mcd
1869, 4, 17. John Jr. gct Clear Creek MM,Ind.
1870, 2, 19. John Sr., Mary & Rachel transferred to Clear Creek MM

FLETCHER
1868, 7, 18. Mary Ann rocf Cincinnati MM, dtd 1868,5,21
1869, 12, 18. Sarah M. recrq

FORSHA
1886, 2, 20. Wilson & Amanda recrq
1899, 3, 18. Elizabeth recrq
1907, 4, 20. Wilson & Elizabeth dropped from mbrp

FOSTER
1810, 12, 29. Charity (form Jackson) dis mcd
1915, 5, 15. John Randolph & w, Nancy Isabelle, recrq

FOUST
1870, 6, 18. Abagail recrq
1870, 6, 18. Cynthia Ann, Ida May & Samuel, ch Abigail, recrq

FOWLER
1816, 5, 25. Phebe (form Hoggatt) con mcd

FOX
1822, 3, 30. Cert rec for Margaret from South River MM, Va., endorsed to Green Plain MM
1873, 3, 15. Mary recrq

FRAZIER
1809, 6, 28. John [Frezer], s Aaron & Jane, Highland Co., O.; m at Fairfield, Alice FISHER, dt James & Jane, Highland Co., O.
1810, 12, 5. Gideon, s Francis & Elizabeth, Clinton Co., O.; m at Lees Creek, Ann HOGGATT, dt Stephen & Margaret, Highland Co., O.
1812, 10, 7. Sarah m Isaac HOGGATT
1812, 11, 11. Thomas, s Francis & Elizabeth, Clinton Co., O.; m at Lees Creek, Hannah HOGGATT, dt Stephen & Margaret, Highland Co., O.
1843, 6, 23. Jonah, s Ezekiel & Rebecca, Clinton Co., O.; m at Fairfield, Sarah WRIGHT, dt David & Mary Terrell, Highland Co., O.
1856, 11, 12. Jonah [Frazer] d ae 62 bur Fairfield

1809, 5, 27. John rocf Warrinton MM, dtd 1809 4,19
1809, 11, 25. Alice [Frasure] gct Center MM
1810, 9, 29. Francis [Fraizer] & s, Davis, Thomas, Gidian & Frances, rocf Center MM, N. C., dtd 1810,4,28
1811, 1, 26. John & s, Nathan, rocf Center MM, N. C., dtd 1810,4,24
1811, 1, 26. Lydia [Frasure] rocf Center MM, N. C., dtd 1810,4,21
1812, 4, 25. James & w, Susannah, & ch, Levinah, Samuel, John, Frances, Elizabeth, Sarah, Susanna & James, rocf Center MM, N. C., dtd 1811,4,20
1812, 7, 25. Center MM was given permission to rst Mary
1812, 12, 26. John & fam gct Center MM
1812, 12, 26. Alse [Frazer] gct Center MM
1843, 7, 20. Jonah rocf Dover MM, dtd 1843, 7,13
1848, 9, 16. Jonah & fam gct Dover MM
1855, 1, 20. Jonah [Frazer] & w, Sarah, rocf Dover MM, dtd 1854,12,14
1878, 7, 20. Sarah gct Spring River MM, Kans.
1895, 4, 2. Gertie [Frazer] recrq
1895, 4, 2. Mary M. [Frazer] recrq
1907, 4, 20. Mary & Gertie [Frazer] dropped from mbrp

FRY
1840, 5, --. Margaret Elizabeth [Frye], dt James & Maria, b
----, --, --. Michael & Mahala
Ch: Glendora R.b 1870, 3, 19
Cora Etta " 1873, 3, 13
1874, 9, 7. Cora Etta d bur Oak Grove

1869, 6, 19. Michael & w, Mahala, & ch, Harriet Jane, Thomas Jefferson, Malinda Cathe-

FRY, continued
rine, Phebe Ellen, Andrew Jackson, Joseph William & Martha Esther, recrq
1870, 2, 19. James & Mary recrq
1870, 2, 19. John William, George W., Oscar D., Hannah J., Nicholas, Alice & Ellen, ch James & Mary, recrq
1881, 6, 18. John W. & w, Christena, & ch, Sophronia C., Sallie A. & John W., recrq
1883, 9, 15. Olga J. rocf Clear Creek MM
1893, 5, 20. Christina [Frye] dropped from mbrp
1893, 5, 20. Jefferson, Jack & Joseph [Frye] dropped from mbrp
1893, 5, 20. John W. [Frye] dropped from mbrp
1893, 5, 20. Nick [Frye] dropped from mbrp
1893, 5, 20. Sallie A. & J. W. [Frye] Jr. dropped from mbrp
1893, 5, 20. Sophronia C. [Frye] dropped from mbrp
1895, 3, 16. John & Olga [Frye] relrq
1900, 3, 17. Sherman recrq
1905, 4, 15. Sherman dropped from mbrp
1910, 6, 18. Glendora & Daniel [Frye] relrq

GALADAY
1808, 12, 31. Ruth rocf Center MM, O., dtd 1808,9,3

GALLIMORE
1812, 6, 27. William rocf Mt. Pleasant MM, dtd 1812,3,28
1818, 9, 26. William gct Centre MM

GAMBLE
1884, 5, 17. George & w, Elizabeth, recrq
1893, 5, 20. George dropped from mbrp
1893, 5, 20. Elizabeth dropped from mbrp

GARNER
1854, 4, 19. Jephthah, s William & Ann, Clinton Co., O.; m at Fairfield, Martha B. McPHERSON, dt John & Maria

1854, 6, 17. Martha B. gct Newbury MM

GARRETT
1825, 3, 26. Rebecca [Garret] (form Todhunter) dis mcd
1871, 8, 19. Catherine recrq
1871, 8, 19. Isham recrq

GELLAR
1871, 3, 18. Moses recrq

GEORGE
1809, 7, 21. Jesse d bur Fall Creek

1831, 5, 28. Tabitha gct Newberry MM
1849, 3, 17. Richard con mcd
1849, 10, 20. Richard gct Pleasant Plain MM,Ia.
1868, 10, 17. Eleanor (form Barrett) con mcd
1883, 4, 21. Elva & Melvina recrq

GILBERT
----, --, --. William m Mabel E. McVEY, dt Isaac & Martha (Job), b 1856,7,6
Ch: Walter b 1883, 7, 11
----, --, --. Walter & Rose
Ch: Howard
Leroy b 1910, 5, 2
Doris
Beryl " 1913, 3, 26

1878, 5, 18. William recrq
1910, 4, 16. Rose recrq

GILBREATH
1826, 10, 28. Martha (form Johnson) dis mcd

GILL
1828, 12, 27. Susanna & ch, John, Susana & Salkill, rocf Short Creek MM

GILPIN
1870, 4, 16. Lyman & Miles recrq

GLASCOCK
1871, 3, 18. Priscilla (form Morrison) con mcd

GOFF
1886, 7, 17. Ellen recrq

GOODSON
1831, 10, 20. Priscilla & ch, Rodah, Harriet, Polly, Solomon, Alexander & Uriah, roc
1832, 1, 26. Rhoda Wollard (form Goodson) dis mcd

GORDON
1877, 2, 17. Sarah J. recrq
1883, 6, 16. John W. recrq
1905, 4, 15. John dropped from mbrp
1905, 4, 15. Mary rel from mbrp

GORMAN
----, --, --. Orville & Annie
Ch: Harry b 1898, 5, 9
Mildred " 1903, 12, 23

1886, 7, 17. Maggie [Gormin] recrq
1887, 4, 16. Joseph & Mary recrq
1902, 11, 15. Maggie dropped from mbrp
1907, 11, 16. Orville & w, Anna, & ch, Harry & Mildred, roc

GOSSETT
1811, 8, 31. Lydia (form Evans) dis mcd
1873, 4, 19. Amariah & Lydia recrq
1874, 9, 19. Amariah & w, Lydia, gct Fairmount MM, Ind.
1886, 3, 20. John recrq
1887, 7, 16. John relrq
1895, 4, 2. John recrq

GRANDLE
1914, 7, 18. Hettie rocf Hopewell MM

GRAVES
1809, 8, 26. William & s, John, rocf Cane Creek MM, dtd 1806,8,5, endorsed by Miami MM
1809, 8, 26. Mary & Annie rocf Cane Creek MM, N. C., dtd 1806,7,5, endorsed by Miami MM
1871, 3, 18. Marina recrq
1895, 3, 16. Lella [Grave] relrq

GREEN
1835, 2, 15. Ruth m Thomas THORN
1839, 3, 6. Levi, s Isaac & Hannah, Clinton Co., O.; m at Fairfield, Elizabeth HUFF, dt Daniel & Sarah, Highland Co., O.
Ch: Sarah Huff b 1840, 1, 11
Levi m 2nd 1847,4,21, Grace JOHNSON, dt Anthony & Mary, Highland Co., O.
Ch: Deborah Ann b 1848, 2, 14
Isaac Anthony " 1849, 5, 15
William Dewsbury " 1851, 4, 18
Mary Hannah" 1853, 4, 21
Thomas T. " 1857, 9, 23
1840, 4, 2. Charlotte m Levi HAINES
1843, 3, 6. Elizabeth d
----, --, --. Jesse & Alice
Ch: Anna P. b 1844, 9, 11
John G.P. " 1846, 6, 26
William P. " 1848, 2, 9
----, --, --. Jonathan & Mary
Ch: Achsah P. b 1848, 11, 23
John Hamilton " 1855, 4, 12
Charlotte H. " 1858, 4, 22 d 1861, 1,13
Jesse Wilson " 1860, 7, 30
Ruth M. " 1852, 9, 2
1849, 5, 30. Ruth m Isaac McPHERSON
1849, 11, 28. Hazael D. m Milly M. CHERRY
1850, 5, 23. Isaac d ae 64 bur Fairfield
1851, 1, 28. Anna, dt Elias & Achsah, b
1851, 5, 31. Rhoda, w Joseph, d bur Fall Creek
----, --, --. Hazael D. & Milly M.
Ch: Linley Murray b 1853, 3, 29
Isaac William " 1855, 9, 23
Richard C. " 1857, 4, 18
Julia Ellen" 1858, 11, 27
Martha Hannah " 1860, 4, 17
Rodema Estel " 1863, 5, 8
Charlotte E. " 1864, 11, 12
Hazael D. m 2nd Naomi -----
Ch: Mary Anna b 1867, 2, 8 d 1869, 4,17 bur Fairfield
Elvira Ruth b 1869, 8, 2 " 1869, 8,14 bur Fairfield
Alise H. b 1873, 9, 23
1853, 9, 21. John, s John & Rachel, Highland Co., O.; m at Fairfield, Rachel JOHNSON, dt Anthony & Mary, Highland Co., O.
Ch: Isaac Linton b 1854, 5, 30
Cordelia Bays " 1856, 3, 14
1853, 11, 21. Margaret F. m Davis S. PAINTER
1854, 10, 15. Isaac d
1855, 10, 18. Hannah d ae 72 bur Fairfield
1856, 11, 23. John Jr. d
1857, 1, 11. Rachel, w John, d ae 69 bur Fairfield
1859, 6, 24. John d ae 72 bur Fairfield
1860, 11, 11. Milly d bur Fairfield
1860, 12, 7. Rachel Ann, dt Jonathan, d
1862, 5, 1. Hazael D. m Naomi C. SMITH
1866, 3, 21. Rachel J. m Isaac CAREY
1868, 6, 25. Daniel M., s Jonathan & Mary, Highland Co., O.; m at Oak Grove, Gulielma SMITH, dt Evan & Abigail, Fayette Co., O.
1869, 3, 25. William Edgerton, s Daniel M. & Gulielma, b
1872, 1, 25. Deborah A. m Lewis C. BARKER
1880, 2, 26. Richard C., s Hazael D. & Milly M., Highland Co., O.; m at home of Jordan Davis in Lexington, Highland Co., O., Sadie M. DAVIS, dt Jordan & Phebe, Highland Co., O.
----, --, --. Percy [Greene] m Anna JENKINS
Ch: Warren J. b 1913, --, --
Ruth Matilda " 1915, --, --
1913, 3, 26. Robert Meredith [Greene] b

1809, 11, 25. John rocf Deep River MM, N. C., dtd 1809,9,4
1810, 12, 29. Isaac rocf Mt. Pleasant MM, Va., dtd 1810,9,29
1810, 12, 29. Hannah & dt, Ruth & Mary, rocf Mt. Pleasant MM, Va., dtd 1810,9,29
1815, 1, 28. Cert rec for Jesse from Mt. Pleasant MM, Va., dtd 1814,9,24, endorsed to Center MM
1815, 11, 25. John & w, Rachel, & s, Elias, rocf Mt. Pleasant MM, Va., dtd 1815,6,26
1841, 8, 26. Elias gct Goshen MM, to m Achsah Paxson
1842, 5, 26. Jesse gct Newberry MM
1842, 12, 22. Jonathan con mcd
1843, 6, 22. Jesse rocf Newberry MM, dtd 1843,5,22
1843, 8, 24. Jesse gct Goshen MM, to m Alice Paxson
1844, 5, 23. Alice (form Paxon), w Jesse,

GREEN, continued
rocf Goshen MM, dtd 1844,3,16
1846, 6, 20. Sarah Paxson (form Green) con mcd
1847, 9, 18. Mary recrq
1851, 2, 15. Jesse & w, Alice, & ch, Anne P., John G. P., William P. & Angeline G., gct Goshen MM
1852, 4, 17. John Jr. gct Wabash MM, Ind., to m Mary Ann Votaw
1853, 3, 19. Daniel M., Rachel Anna & Hannah Elizabeth, ch Jonathan, recrq
1858, 10, 16. Elias & w, Achsah, & ch gct Goshen MM, O.
1866, 6, 16. Rachel G. Cary & dt, Cordelia Bays Green, gct Richland MM, Ind.
1869, 3, 20. Isaac A. gct Richland MM, Ind., to m Rebecca Harold
1870, 4, 16. Isaac A. gct Richland MM, Ind.
1870, 11, 19. Daniel M. & w, Gulielma, gct Newberry MM, O.
1874, 2, 21. Grace recrq
1877, 9, 15. Matilda J. rocf Clear Creek MM, dtd 1877,9,8
1877, 11, 17. Levi & w, Grace, & s, Thomas T., gct Richland MM, Ind.
1877, 11, 17. Mary H. gct Richland MM, Ind.
1879, 3, 15. Adaline recrq
1879, 5, 17. William D. & w gct Union MM, Minn.
1880, 2, 21. Oralonzo, s John & Adaline, recrq
1881, 9, 17. John H. & w, Adaline, & ch, Orie L. & Stella May, gct Rose Hill MM, Kans.
1881, 9, 17. Jonathan & w, Mary, & ch, Hanna E. & Jesse W., gct Rose Hill MM, Kans.
1881, 9, 17. Naomi C. gct Rose Hill MM, Kans.
1881, 9, 17. Richard C. gct Rose Hill MM, Kans.
1882, 6, 17. Lindley Murray gct Sand Creek MM, Ind., to m Alice M. Davis
1882, 6, 17. Elizabeth gct Rose Hill MM, Kans.
1883, 1, 20. Mary Alice rocf Sand Creek MM, dtd 1882,10,7
1883, 10, 20. Richard C. & w, Sadie, & ch, Grace L. & Mary, gct Poplar Ridge MM, Ind.
1885, 3, 21. Richard C. & fam rocf Poplar Ridge MM, dtd 1885,3,12
1889, 11, 16. Richard C. & w, Sadie, & ch gc
1890, 2, 15. Dr. Lindley M. [Greene] & fam gct Indianapolis MM, Ind.
1892, 6, 18. Mary Luella [Greene] recrq
1892, 12, 17. Richard H. & w, Sadie, & ch, Mary Ethel, Grace L. & Charles Herbert, rocf Wilmington MM, dtd 1892,11,12
1893, 10, 21. Richard C., Sadie D., Grace L., Mary E. & C. Herbert gct Springfield MM,O.
1893, 10, 21. Hazel D., Naomi C., Julia E., Alice H. & Mary gct Wilmington MM, O.
1893, 10, 21. William D. & w, Matilda, & ch gct Wilmington MM, O.
1900, 1, 20. William D. & w, Matilda G., & ch, Earnest L., Percy E. & Frances W., rocf Center MM
1902, 1, 18. Ernest L. gct Wilmington MM
1902, 11, 15. Isaac [Greene] dropped from mbrp
1912, 9, 21. Anna Jenkins [Greene] rocf Wilmington MM
1923, 3, 1. William D. & w, Matilda P., gct Xenia MM
1924, 7, 3. Percy & fam gct Dover MM

GRICE
1870, 3, 19. Mary recrq
1870, 3, 19. Jesse H. & Fredson E., ch Mary, recrq of mother
1876, 4, 15. Flora M. recrq

1883, 11, 17. Jesse dropped from mbrp
1893, 5, 20. Fred dropped from mbrp
1897, 4, 17. Jane & Hattie rocf Clear Creek MM
1898, 4, 16. Fredson dropped from mbrp

GRIFFIN
1808, 12, 31. James [Griffen] rocf Back Creek MM, N. C., dtd 1808,8,27
1810, 2, 24. Jacob [Griffen] & fam gct White Water MM
1810, 2, 24. Mary gct White Water MM

GRIFFITH
1830, 4, 19. John d ae 63 bur Circleville,O.
1832, 12, 8. Mary d ae 67 bur Circleville,O.
1837, 7, 25. Amos d bur at home near Circleville, Pickaway Co., O.
1849, 11, 30. John d bur near Circleville, O.
1861, 12, --. Mary d ae near 76y bur at home near Circleville, Pickaway Co., O.

1808, 7, 30. John rocf Hopewell MM, Va., dtd 1808,1,4
1808, 7, 30. Mary [Grifeth] rocf Hopewell MM, dtd 1808,1,6
1838, 6, 21. Amos & w, Mary, & ch, Susannah, Ruth, William & John, rocf Deer Creek MM, dtd 1837,3,9

GRIGG
1808, 2, 27. Joseph V. rocf Westfield MM, dtd 1807,12,12
1808, 2, 27. Moses H. rocf Westfield MM, dtd 1807,12,12
1808, 2, 27. Phebe rocf Westfield MM, dtd 1807,12,12
1810, 2, 24. Moses H. dis disunity
1810, 5, 26. Joseph V. gct Westfield MM

GRIM
1884, 6, 12. Pearl, dt John & Martha, b

1904, 3, 19. Ethel & Pearl recrq

GRIMES
1808, 11, 26. Rachel & ch, Jonathan, Josiah,

GRIMES, continued
Jesse, Mary & Rachel, rocf New Hope MM, Tenn., dtd 1808,9,17

GROVE
1854, 3, 24. Lydia Davis, dt Jordan & Phebe Davis, b 1854,3,24

GRUBB
1870, 2, 19. Leander [Grub] recrq
1870, 6, 18. Jane V. recrq
1870, 6, 18. George W., Mary V. & Thomas J., ch Jane V., recrq of parents
1878, 10, 19. Leander [Grubbs] dropped from mbrp

GRUMMAN
1870, 6, 18. Georgiana recrq
1870, 6, 18. Catherine, Eddy, Lovey, Luty, Monnie & Jesse, ch Georgianna, recrq of parent

GUTHRIE
1865, 10, 7. Minnie, dt Addary P. & Martha A. (Ladd) Pushee, b
----, --, --. S. B. m Sallie HOLMES
Ch: Hannibal
Eugene b 1897, 2, 18
Anna Lavonna " 1901, 9, 24

1876, 5, 20. Zachariah T. & John Henry recrq
1876, 5, 20. Margaret recrq
1883, 4, 21. Nettie & Mary A. [Gutherie] recrq
1886, 7, 17. S. B. recrq
1893, 12, 16. John Henry dis

HADLEY
1829, 2, 11. James, Jr., s James & Anne, Clinton Co., O.; m at Fairfield, Sarah HUFF, dt Daniel & Sarah, Highland Co., O.
----, --, --. James & Sarah
Ch: James Albert b 1848, 4, 11
Harriet " 1849, 11, 3
1853, 10, 17. Sarah Ann m Levi WOODARD
1857, 9, 24. Elizabeth Ellen m William CHERRY
1860, 11, 22. Jacob, s John & Lydia, Clinton Co., O.; m at Fall Creek, Lucinda COWGILL, dt Frederick & Elizabeth, Highland Co.,O.
1865, 3, 26. Sarah, w James, d bur Fairfield

1808, 6, 25. Ann & dt, Edith Mary Sarah & Thamar, recrq
1808, 7, 30. James rocf Cane Creek MM, N.C., dtd 1808,3,5
1808, 7, 30. James & Jeremiah, s James, recrq
1829, 10, 31. Sarah gct Newberry MM
1846, 1, 17. James & w, Sarah, & ch, Daniel H., Sarah Ann, Mary, Alfred, Elizabeth Ellen, Sinthy Jane & Juliet, rocf Newbury MM, dtd 1846,1,12
1852, 4, 17. Daniel H. con mcd
1861, 1, 19. Julia Polk (form Hadley) con mcd
1861, 2, 16. Lucinda Hadley & s, Jonathan B. Cowgill, gct Springfield MM, O.
1863, 7, 18. Mary V. Cockerill (form Hadley) con mcd
1866, 11, 17. C. Jane Thomas (form Hadley) con mcd
1867, 2, 16. C. Jane Thomas (form Hadley) gct New Garden MM, Ind.
1869, 1, 16. Alfred gct Plainfield MM, Ind., to m Kezia K. Overman
1869, 6, 19. Keziah K. rocf Plainfield MM, Ind., dtd 1869,6,--
1870, 3, 19. James Albert gct Springfield MM, Kans.
1870, 8, 20. James gct Duck Creek MM, to m Emily G. Saint
1870, 9, 17. Harriet M. gct Springfield MM, Kans.; returned 1870,12,17 because of mcd
1870, 12, 17. Harriet M. Stanton (form Hadley) con mcd
1871, 2, 18. James gct Milford MM, Ind.
1872, 5, 18. Alfred & w, Keziah, & ch gct Newberry MM, O.
1873, 9, 20. Ellen J. recrq

HAINES
1817, 12, 3. Stacy, s John & Betty, Green Co., O.; m at Fairfield, Judith TERRELL, dt David & Mary, Highland Co., O.
1832, 11, 29. Ann m Tilghman CHANCE
1835, 4, 30. Elizabeth [Hanes] m James MORRIS
1840, 4, 2. Levi, s Enos & Mary, Highland Co., O.; m at Lees Creek, Charlotte GREEN, dt John & Rachel, Clinton Co., O.
Ch: Rachel b 1840, 12, 26
Elias " 1842, 3, 25
Mary Elizabeth " 1844, 1, 22
Eli C. " 1846, 7, 15
1843. 1. 17. Elias d bur Lees Creek

1858, 11, 24. Eli, s Zimri & Elizabeth, Green Co., O.; m at Fairfield, Emily T. McPHERSON, dt Stephen & Mary

1815, 12, 30. Enos [Hains] & w, Mary, & ch, Hester, Joshua, Mahlon, Sarah, Lydia Ann Mary & Levi, rocf Miami MM, dtd 1815,2,22
1818, 5, 30. Judith gct Cesars Creek MM
1834, 11, 20. Mar6 Davis (form Haines) con mcd
1842, 6, 23. Joshua gct Westfield MM, Ind.
1844, 1, 25. Ruth Starns (form Hains) dis mcd
1844, 12, 21. Enos gct Westfield MM, Ind.
1848, 8, 19. Levi & w, Charlotte, & ch, Rachel, Mary Elizabeth & Eli, gct Mississinawa MM, Ind.
1859, 4, 16. Emily gct Cesars Creek MM
1870, 2, 19. Isaac W. Haines, adopted s Henry Runnels, recrq
1870, 7, 16. John G. rocf Wabash MM, Ind.,

HAINES, continued
dtd 1870,6,11
1872, 4, 20. Mahlon Jr. recrq
1872, 4, 20. Clara E. recrq
1872, 4, 20. Lizzie M., Frank E. & Anna E., ch Mahlon & Clara, recrq
1882, 4, 15. Frank recrq
1882, 4, 15. Elizabeth recrq
1882, 10, 21. John & w & fam gct Argonia MM, Kans.
1893, 11, 8. Jane relrq
1896, 6, 20. Ella Brown recrq
1905, 4, 15. Mary dropped from mbrp
1905, 10, 21. David & w, Samantha, recrq
1909, 3, 20. Clara E. relrq
1910, 6, 18. Wilson relrq
1910, 8, 13. David & w, Samantha, & ch gct Hopewell MM
1911, 9, 16. Claudies E. & Mark dropped from mbrp
1920, 4, 21. Eber H. & w, Edna Peelle, & ch, Helen Josephine, Donald Eber & Marjorie Jane, rocf Grassy Run MM, O.
1928, 6, 5. Joseph, Donald & Marjorie rec in active mbrp

HAMILTON
1892, 6, 18. Ida E. recrq

HARDY
----, --, --. William & Nancy
Ch: Darius E. b 1835, 3, 3
Mariah " 1839, 6, 4
Sarah " 1842, 1, 26
Ezra W. " 1847, 7, 25
1866, 8, 9. Nancy d bur Fairfield

1825, 6, 25. Nancy (form Chance) con mcd
1834, 4, 24. William recrq
1857, 8, 15. Maria Belfred (form Hardy) dis mcd
1858, 12, 18. Davis dis mcd
1861, 8, 17. Sarah Cole (form Hardy) dis mcd
1870, 3, 19. Aaron B. & Ellen C. recrq
1870, 3, 19. Nancy A. & John W., ch Aaron & Ellen C. recrq of parents
1882, 3, 18. E. D. recrq
1883, 4, 21. Nettie recrq
1883, 11, 17. Aaron B. & fam dropped from mbrp
1883, 11, 17. Edward dropped from mbrp
1886, 7, 17. Fred E. recrq
1889, 3, 16. William recrq
1892, 10, 15. Ollie rocf Clear Creek MM
1893, 5, 20. Ed dropped from mbrp
1896, 7, 18. William Jr. dropped from mbrp
1901, 6, 15. Olive, w William, gct Clear Creek MM
1905, 4, 15. Fred dropped from mbrp

HARPER
1917, 4, 21. Ruth recrq

HARRINGTON
1814, 9, 24. Elizabeth gct Fall Creek MM

HARRIS
1883, 2, 17. Jacob T. & Hannah E. recrq

HARROLD
1810, 4, 28. Richard & s, William & Thomas, rocf Westfield MM, dtd 1809,12,9
1810, 4, 28. Mary [Harrel] & dt, Rebecca & Arcada, rocf Westfield MM, N. C., dtd 1809,12,9
1820, 5, 27. Cert rec for Jacob & fam endorsed to Still Water MM
1869, 3, 20. Isaac A. Green gct Richland MM, Ind., to m Rebecca [Harold]

HARTMAN
1874, 2, 21. Isaac & w, Eliza, recrq

HARVEY
1824, 9, 15. Jesse, s Caleb & Sarah, Clinton Co., O.; m at Fairfield, Elizabeth BURGESS, dt Thomas & Elizabeth, Highland Co., O.
1827, 10, 1. Simon D., s Isaac & Lydia, Clinton Co., O.; m at Fairfield, Mary H. BURGESS, dt Thomas & Elizabeth, Highland Co., O.

1808, 9, 24. Mary (form Cox) con mcd
1809, 12, 30. Michel recrq
1810, 7, 28. Michael & s, Elias, gct White Water MM
1810, 8, 25. Mary rqct White Water MM
1824, 12, 25. Elizabeth gct Springfield MM
1828, 4, 26. Mary H. gct Miami MM

HASTING
1893, 8, 19. Melissa [Hastings] recrq
1895, 4, 2. Mary J. recrq
1898, 1, 15. Mary J. relrq

HAUCHER
1915, 10, 16. Leonard rocf Hopewell MM

HAWORTH
1812, 1, 1. Sarah m James HORTON
1816, 12, 5. Charity m Thomas POSTGAIT
1817, 1, 2. Jonathan m Sarah McPHERSON

1810, 5, 26. Phebe (form Thornbrough) dis mcd
1810, 11, 24. James [Hayworth] dis
1812, 11, 28. George dis mcd
1813, 3, 27. Jane (form Thornbrough) dis mcd
1821, 7, 28. Lees Creek MM was given permission to rst James [Hayworth] & w, Phebe
1830, 3, 27. Fairfield MM, Ind. was given permission to rst George & w, Jane
1851, 7, 19. Elisabeth [Hayworth] (form Terrell) con mcd
1909, 10, 16. Frances Willard [Hayworth] gct

HAWORTH, continued
S. Cleveland MM

HAY
1871, 8, 19. Lizzie recrq

HELLER
1898, 4, 16. Ida recrq
1902, 4, 19. Dudley recrq
1908, 1, 18. Dudley gct Caesars Creek MM

HENDERSON
-----,--, --. George m Selemma BUZZARD
Ch: Earl Brown
Damon Vernon
Mary Ester b 1902, 10, 7

1886, 7, 17. George recrq
1896, 5, 16. Charles & Estie recrq
1898, 4, 16. Chlce dropped from mbrp

HENDRICKS
1813, 11, 22. Ruth d near 80y bur at Fairfield

1811, 3, 30. Ruth [Hendrick] rocf South River MM, Va., dtd 1811,1,12

HENLEY
1812, 9, 28. Martha, Highland Co., O.; m at Clear Creek, Jonathan LINDLEY

1829, 9, 26. John [Henly] rocf Fall Creek MM, dtd 1829,9,19
1830, 11, 27. John dis jH
1870, 3, 19. John [Henly] recrq

HERSON
1871, 8, 19. Ann recrq

HIATT
----, --, --. Christopher & Jemima

Ch:				
Asher	b 1803,	7,	17
Samuel	" 1805,	8,	9
Mahala	" 1809,	3,	8
Elizabeth	" 1811,	7,	24

----, --, --. Joseph & Hannah

Ch:			
Olive	b 1808,	12,	22
Rebekah	" 1813,	2,	22
Hermon	" 1814,	6,	7

1809, 1, 5. Joseph, Highland Co., O.; m at Fall Creek, Elizabeth BALLARD, Highland Co., O.
1810, 10, --. Mahala d
1811, 7, 3. Elihu [Hiett], s John & Mary, Highland Co., O.; m at Fairfield, Gertrude COX, dt Enoch & Gertrude

Ch:			
Enoch	b 1812,	4,	25
Mary	" 1813,	9,	8
Rachel	" 1817,	5,	2
Oliver	" 1819,	5,	8
Harriet	" 1821,	2,	13
Elvinah	" 1823,	2,	6
Asenath Ellen	b 1823,	2,	6

1815, 2, 15. Asaph, s Asher & Mary, Clinton Co., O.; m at Fairfield, Rebecca HUNT, dt Abner & Mary, Highland Co., O.
1826, 7, 23. Gertrude d bur Fairfield
1833, 9, 11. Harriet d bur Fairfield
1859, 4, 13. Nathan, s Nathan, d ae 69 bur Fall Creek
1866, 2, 22. Louisa m William PEELLE

1808, 3, 26. Jacob [Hiett] rocf Mt. Pleasant MM, Va., dtd 1808,1,30
1808, 3, 26. Susanna [Hiett] rocf Mt. Pleasant MM, Va., dtd 1808,1,30
1808, 10, 29. Joseph [Highett] rocf Mt. Pleasant MM, Va., dtd 1808,8,27
1808, 10, 29. Joseph [Hiett] Jr. rocf Mt. Pleasant MM, Va., dtd 1808,8,27
1809, 12, 30. Benjamin [Hiett] & s, Nathan, Amaziah, Harmon, Ithamar, Joseph, Benjamin & Henry, rocf Mt. Pleasant MM, Va., dtd 1809,9,30
1809, 12, 30. Mary & dt, Levina, Rebecca, Sarah, Ruth Hannah Mourning & Mary, rocf Mt. Pleasant MM, Va., dtd 1809,11,11
1810, 1, 27. John [Hiett] & s, Elihue John Reuben & Jesse, rocf Mt. Pleasant MM, Va. dtd 1809,8,26 (also s, Gidian)
1810, 1, 27. Mary [Hight] & dt, Rosanah, Anna Rachel & Mary, rocf Mt. Pleasant MM, Va., dtd 1809,8,26
1810, 5, 26. Joseph [Hiett] con mcd
1810, 6, 30. Hannah con mou
1810, 12, 29. Christopher & s, Asher & Samuel, rocf Mt. Pleasant MM, Va., dtd 1810,8,25
1810, 12, 29. Jemima & dt, Anne, rocf Mt. Pleasant MM, Va., dtd 1810,8,25
1811, 4, 27. Absalom & s, David, Aaron, James, Hiram, Joseph, Absalom & Cornelius, rocf Mt. Pleasant MM, Va., dtd 1810,6,30
1811, 4, 27. Ann & dt, Phebe & Hannah, rocf Mt. Pleasant MM, Va., dtd 1810,6,30
1811, 5, 25. John & s, Hervey & Greenberry, rocf Mt. Pleasant MM, Va., dtd 1810,6,30
1811, 5, 25. Rachel & dt, Christine & Ruth, rocf Mt. Pleasant MM, Va., dtd 1810,6,30
1812, 3, 28. Cert rec for Richard & fam from Mt. Pleasant MM, Va., dtd 1812,7,28, endorsed to Fall Creek MM
1812, 5, 30. Cert rec for Isham & fam from New Garden MM, dtd 1811,11,2, endorsed to Darby Creek MM
1813, 10, 30. Cert rec for Jonathan & w, Rachel, & ch, Johh, Silas, Josiah, Lydia, Mary, Jonathan, George Richard, Rachel, Sarah & Nathan, from Mt. Pleasant MM, dtd 1813,3,28, endorsed to Clear Creek MM
1813, 10, 30. Cert rec for William & s, Charles, from Deep River MM, N. C., endorsed to Westfield MM, N. C.
1814, 5, 28. Christopher & w, Elizabeth, & ch, Solomon, Jonathan & Levina, rocf Mt. Pleasant MM, dtd 1813,9,25

HIATT, continued
1815, 5, 27. Joseph [Hiett] & w, Hannah, & ch, Olive, Rebecca & Hermin, gct Lick Creek MM, Ind.
1815, 6, 24. Rebekah gct Clear Creek MM
1816, 7, 27. Christopher & w, Elizabeth, & ch, Jonathan & Levina, rocf Clear Creek MM
1816, 12, 26. Jacob [Hiett] & w, Susannah, gct Blue River MM, Ind.
1822, 8, 31. Elizabeth (form Beal) dis mcd
1825, 5, 28. Milford MM was given permission to rst Elizabeth
1828, 5, 21. Elihu dis mcd
1830, 9, 25. Enoch dis disunity
1830, 9, 25. Mary & Eunice dis disunity
1830, 10, 30. Mary (form Terrell) con mcd
1831, 9, 22. Mary gct Newbury MM
1834, 7, 24. Rachel Tompkins (form Hiatt) dis mcd
1835, 10, 22. Enos & Delilah, minors, rocf White River MM
1839, 4, 25. Oliver dis mcd
1841, 6, 24. Elvira Ann McBride (form Hiatt) dis mcd
1842, 7, 21. Enos & Delilah, ch Solomon & Esther, gct Westfield MM, Ind.
1849, 6, 16. Louisa (form McPherson) con mcd
1850, 1, 19. Wilson rocf Chesterfield MM, dtd 1849,11,17
1850, 9, 21. Elisha rocf Clear Creek MM, dtd 1850,9,14
1851, 5, 17. Mary & ch, Martha, Deborah & Lydia Ann, rocf Clear Creek MM, dtd 1851, 4,12
1853, 12, 17. Mary & ch, Martha, Deborah & Lydia Ann, gct Clear Creek MM
1854, 7, 15. Elisha & w, Louisa, gct Spring Creek MM, Ia.
1855, 2, 17. Wilson dis mcd
1862, 1, 18. Elisha & w, Louisa, rocf Spring-Creek MM, Ia., dtd 1861,12,7
1865, 4, 15. Spring Creek MM, Ia. was given permission to rst Wilson
1911, 10, 21. Georgiana B. gct Wilmington MM

HICKS
1872, 6, 5. Henry H., s Clark D. & Anne, b

1901, 3, 16. Charles H. recrq
1907, 4, 20. Charles dropped from mbrp

HILL
1810, 1, 27. William rocf Back Creek MM, N.C.
1811, 4, 27. William & fam gct White Water MM
1811, 4, 27. Mary gct White Water MM
1903, 9, 19. Nina recrq
1904, 3, 19. Hattie recrq

HILTON
1818, 11, 27. Samuel rocf Darby Creek MM, dtd 1818,6,20

HINSHAW
1870, 6, 18. Mary recrq

HINTON
1813, 9, 25. Phebe (form Cox) dis mcd
1834, 8, 21. Sarah (form Sanders) dis mcd

HIXSON
1883, 9, 15. Ann & ch rocf Clear Creek MM
1898, 10, 15. Annie Rose & Walter recrq
1899, 5, 20. Sarah E. rocf Clear Creek MM
1901, 4, 20. Maud & Addie recrq
1902, 11, 15. Walter dropped from mbrp

HODGIN
1884, 6, 21. Sarah gct Bangor MM, Ia.

HODGSON
----, --, --. Solomon & Chloe
Ch: Rebecca b 1809, 6, 20
Lydia " 1813, 1, 21
1808, 6, 13. Zachariah [Hodson], s John & Naomi, Highland Co., O.; m at Clear Creek, Katherine HUNT, dt Phinehas & Elizabeth, Highland Co., O.
1809, 3, 1. George, s John & Mary, Highland Co., O.; m at Fairfield, Mary NIXON, dt Peirce & Peninah, Highland Co., O.
1809, 3, 28. Ann m Wright COOK
1811, 1, 30. John, s John & Naomi, Highland Co., O.; m at Fairfield, Sarah MILLS, dt Thomas & Jemimah, Highland Co., O.
1816, 12, 12. John Hodgson, s Solomon & Chloe, Highland Co., O.; m at Lees Creek, Jane BEALS, dt John B. & Lois, Highland Co.,O.
----, --, --. Hezekiah & Ann [Hodson]
Ch: Ann b 1831, 3, 29
Eliza H. " 1833, 3, 3
Malinda " 1834, 12, 13
Hannah " 1837, 1, 30
Rebecca " 1840, 3, 7
----, --, --. John & Rebecca
Ch: Lydia b 1831, 10, 1
Emily " 1837, 1, 22
Flavius " 1846, 6, 26
1840, 12, 22. Malinda d bur Lees Creek
1840, 12, 26. Ann d bur Lees Creek
1840, 12, 26. Hannah d bur Lees Creek
1857, 9, 23. Emily [Hodson] m Zadoc MILLER
1863, 11, 28. Rebecca d bur Fairfield
----, --, --. Flavious J. m Mary Ann TERRY, dt Wm. P. & Ophelia (Garrett), b 1847,2,11
Ch: John William b 1870, 9, 23

1808, 2, 27. George rocf New Garden MM, N.C., dtd 1807,8,29, endorsed by Center MM,O.
1808, 2, 27. Jane Ann rocf New Garden MM, dtd 1807,8,29, endorsed by Center MM
1808, 2, 27. John & s, John, Henry, Benjamin & Uriah, rocf Center MM, N. C., dtd 1807, 8,15, endorsed by Center MM, O.
1808, 2, 27. Sarah & dt, Charity, Naomy, Sa-

HODGSON, continued
rah & Abigail, rocf Center MM, N. C., dtd 1807,8,15, endorsed by Center MM, O.
1808, 2, 27. Ann rocf Center MM, N. C., dtd 1807,8,15, endorsed by Center MM, O.
1808, 2, 27. Zachariah rocf Center MM, N. C., dtd 1807,8,15, endorsed by Center MM, O.
1808, 12, 31. Solomon & s, John Hezekiah & Moses, rocf New Garden MM, dtd 1808,8,27, endorsed by Center MM
1808, 12, 31. Chloe & dt, Elizabeth, Mary & Rachel, rocf New Garden MM, N. C., dtd 1808, 8,2
1810, 6, 30. Zacheriah dis mcd
1811, 8, 31. Charity dis
1812, 4, 25. Jonathan & w, Mary, & ch, Enos, Mathew, Elizabeth, Sarah, Jonathan & John, rocf Center MM, N. C., dtd 1811,9,21, endorsed by Center MM
1815, 7, 29. Elizabeth dis
1816, 4, 27. John & w, Sarah, & ch, Delilah, Rhoda, Nathan & Ruth, rocf Cesars Creek MM, dtd 1816,2,23
1816, 4, 27. Jonathan & w, Mary, & ch, Mathew, Elizabeth, Sarah, Jonathan & John, rocf Clear Creek MM, dtd 1816,2,10
1816, 4, 27. Solomon & w, Elizabeth, & ch, Thomas, John, Jemima & Naomi, rocf Cesars Creek MM, dtd 1816,2,23
1816, 12, 24. John & w, Sarah, & ch, Delila, Rhoda, Nathan & Ruth, gct New Garden MM, Ind.
1817, 1, 25. Solomon & w, Elizabeth, & ch, Thomas, John, Jemima & Anna, gct New Garden MM, Ind.
1834, 5, 22. Mary [Hodson] & dt, Mary, gct Clear Creek MM
1834, 8, 21. John & w, Rebecca, & dt, Lydia, gct Clear Creek MM
1836, 5, 26. Jonathan [Hodson] dis disunity
1836, 5, 26. Solomon [Hodson] dis mcd
1837, 5, 25. Joseph [Hodson] dis mcd
1842, 11, 24. Hezekiah & w, Anna, & ch, Cyrus, Lewis, John, Martha, Ann, Eliza & Rebecca, gct Clear Creek MM
1849, 6, 16. John [Hodson] & w, Rebecca, & ch, Lydia, Emily & Flavius, rocf Clear Creek MM, dtd 1849,6,9
1858, 9, 18. Lydia Ladd (form Hodson) con mcd
1870, 9, 17. Flavious [Hodson] con mcd
1871, 4, 15. Jonathan [Hodson] & w, Sarah, rocf Cherry Grove MM, Ind., dtd 1871,4,8
1871, 5, 20. Mary A. [Hodson] recrq
1871, 11, 18. Jonathan & w, Sarah, gct Cherry Grove MM, Ind.
1887, 4, 16. Sarah M., Chloe & Alonzo [Hodson] recrq
1890, 4, 19. Mertie [Hodson] recrq
1895, 4, 2. Mary [Hodson] recrq
1918, 3, 16. Virginia Syferd [Hodson] gct Leesburg MM, O.
1921, 9, 14. Alonzo [Hodson] & fam relrq

HOGGATT
----, --, --. David & Sarah [Hockett]
Ch: Phebe b 1806, 1, 29
Alice " 1808, 2, 2
Mary " 1810, 2, 5
Sarah " 1812, 4, 22
Agness " 1815, 2, 7
1810, 12, 5. Ann m Gideon FRAZIER
1812, 10, 7. Isaac, s Stephen & Margaret, Highland Co., O.; m at Upper East Fork, Sarah FRAZIER, dt Francis & Elizabeth, Clinton Co., O.
1812, 11, 11. Hannah m Thomas FRAZIER
1857, 1, 22. Seth [Hockett], s Jonathan & Mary, Clinton Co., O.; m at Walnut Creek, Rebecca SIMMONS, dt Thomas & Eleanor
1861, 5, 23. Asa S. [Hockett], s William & Cina, Clinton Co., O.; m at Hardins Creek, Anna BARRETT, dt Levi & Susannah, Highland Co., O.

1810, 1, 27. Philip & s, John & Phillip, rocf New Garden MM, N. C., dtd 1804,9,24
1810, 1, 27. Alice & dt, Ruth, rocf New Garden MM, N. C., dtd 1808,9,24, endorsed by Back Creek MM, 1809,8,26
1810, 8, 25. Benjamin & s, Eli & Neri, rocf Westfield MM, dtd 1810,3,10
1810, 8, 25. Charity rocf Westfield MM, N.C. dtd 1810,3,10
1810, 11, 24. William gct Center MM, to m
1811, 1, 26. Moses & ch gct Center MM
1811, 3, 30. Rachel rocf Center MM, dtd 1811, 2,2
1811, 5, 25. Philip & fam gct White Water MM
1811, 5, 25. Alice gct White Water MM
1811, 5, 25. Joseph & s, John, rocf New Garden MM, N. C., dtd 1811,3,30
1811, 5, 25. Ann & dt, Margarett, Jane & Rachel, rocf New Garden MM, N. C., dtd 1811, 3,30
1811, 7, 27. Anthony rocf Westfield MM, N.C., dtd 1810,1,13
1812, 3, 28. Ruth Rowles (form Hoggatt) con mcd
1812, 6, 27. Nathan & w, Elizabeth, rocf New Garden MM, N. C., dtd 1812,2,29
1812, 7, 25. Margaret Fisher (form Hoggatt) con mcd
1813, 9, 25. Benjamin rocf Westfield MM, N.C. dtd 1813,7,9
1815, 9, 20. Cert rec for Jonathan & fam from Mt. Pleasant MM, Va., dtd 1815,7,29, endorsed to Clear Creek MM
1816, 1, 27. Hezekiah & w, Martha, & ch, Tabitha, Nathan, Mary, Edith, Zadock & Milly, rocf Center MM, N. C., dtd 1815,8, 19
1816, 2, 24. Isaac & w, Sarrah, & ch, Elizabeth & Margaret, gct New Garden MM, Ind.
1816, 5, 25. Phebe Fowler (form Hoggatt) con mcd
1816, 11, 30. Joseph con mcd

HOGGATT, continued
1817, 2, 22. Joseph gct New Garden MM, Ind.
1817, 2, 22. Stephen & w, Margaret, & ch, Stephen, Edward, Margaret, John & Betsy, gct New Garden MM, Ind.
1824, 9, 28. Cert rec for Elizabeth & ch from White Water MM, endorsed to Clear Creek MM
1835, 1, 22. Mary [Hocket] rocf Newbury MM
1837, 3, 23. Mary gct Cesars Creek MM
1851, 4, 19. Elizabeth [Hockett] (form Huff) dis mcd
1857, 1, 17. Matilda [Hockett] (form Simmons) dis mcd
1857, 6, 21. Rebecca R. [Hockett] & ch gct Newberry MM
1861, 8, 17. Anna B. [Hockett] gct Newberry MM

HOLE
1907, 12, 21. Harry R. & w, Leora E., & ch, Harrison H., roc
1908, 7, 18. Harry R. & w, Leora E., & ch, Harrison H. & Miriam L., gct Yorktown MM, N. Y.
1909, 9, 18. Harry R., minister, & w, Leora E., & ch, Harrison H. & Miriam L., rocf Yorktown MM, N. Y.
1911, 9, 16. Harry R. & w, Leora E., & ch, Harrison H., Miriam L. & Winston L., gct Smithfield MM, Woonsocket, R. I.

HOLEMAN
1814, 5, 28. Rachel (form Evans) dis mcd

HOLIDAY
1898, 2, 19. Lilly M., Naomi & James rocf Wilmington MM
1898, 5, 21. Mrs. James relrq
1898, 5, 21. Lillie Maud relrq
1915, 1, 16. Lillie Maud [Holaday] roc

HOLLINGSWORTH
1877, 6, 16. Esther recrq
1884, 9, 20. Esther gct Newbury MM
1891, 5, 16. Ida relrq
1914, 1, 17. Marion rmt Grace Elizabeth Huff

HOLLOWAY
1825, 7, 23. John W., s John & Lovicy, b

1809, 8, 26. Thomas rocf Hopewell MM, dtd 1809,3,6
1809, 2, 25. Elizabeth [Halloway] rocf Hopewell MM, dtd 1808,8,1
1810, 4, 28. George rocf Hopewell MM, dtd 1809,4,3
1811, 9, 28. George dis mcd
1812, 11, 28. William & w, Sally, & ch, John, Isaac, Betsy, Pleasant, Samuel, George, Sally & William, rocf South River MM, Va., dtd 1812,8,8
1813, 12, 25. Thomas dis disunity
1824, 4, 24. John & ch, Joab, Elizabeth & Sarah M., rocf Lees Creek MM, dtd 1824,2,21
1825, 1, 29. Cert rec for Abner & fam from Duck Creek MM, N. C., endorsed to Newbury MM
1826, 9, 30. John & ch, Joab, Elizabeth, Sarah M. & John W., gct Springfield MM,Ind.

HOLMES
----, --, --. Raleigh m Jennie B. BARRETT, dt John & Mary, b 1858,2,9
Ch: Maude b 1896, 3, 15

1886, 7, 17. Charles recrq
1886, 7, 17. Ralph E. & Sallie recrq
1895, 4, 2. Emma J. recrq
1896, 7, 18. Charles dropped from mbrp
1909, 1, 16. Raleigh, Jennie B. & Maud H. rocf Hopewell MM
1915, 5, 15. Ethel Pearl & Maria Oca recrq

HOPKINS
1830, 4, 24. Martha (form Pope) dis mcd
1907, 4, 20. Lillie Setty dropped from mbrp
1907, 4, 20. Martha Van Winkle dropped from mbrp

HORNADAY
1878, 11, 16. Mary & s rocf Cesars Creek MM, dtd 1878,9,26
1881, 7, 16. Mary gct Clear Creek MM

HORR
1879, 2, 20. Mamie, dt Wm. & Mabel (McVey) Gilbert, b

HORSEMAN
1816, 10, 26. Joseph [Horsman] rst by rq with consent of Hopewell MM
1825, 1, 29. Joseph [Horsman] dis jas
1848, 8, 19. Hannah (form Wright) con mcd
1850, 10, 19. Hannah gct Pleasant Plain MM,Ia.
1870, 2, 19. Fanny [Horsman] recrq
1877, 5, 19. Silas, Lydia, Jessie & Bessie recrq

HORTON
1812, 1, 1. James, s James & Margaret, Highland Co., O.; m at Lees Creek, Sarah HAWORTH, dt James & Mary, Highland Co., O.

Ch:		
	Jesse	b 1812, 9, 2
	Rachel	" 1813, 12, 4
	William	" 1815, 3, 17
	Mary	" 1816, 12, 16
	Howard	" 1818, 3, 30
	Margaret	" 1819, 12, 21

1866, 5, 15. Jacob d ae 85 bur Frankfort, Ia.

1809, 5, 27. James rocf Westfield MM, dtd 1809,2,11
1824, 10, 30. James & w, Sarah, & ch, Jesse, Rachel, William, Mary, Howard, Margaret Anna & David, gct White Lick MM
1835, 11, 26. Malinda (form Johnson) dis mcd

HORTON, continued
1845, 9, 20. Jacob recrq
1845, 9, 20. Phebe recrq
1851, 6, 21. Lewis, s Malinda Terrell, recrq
1851, 7, 19. Charity Ann recrq
1855, 10, 20. Samuel C. Terrell & w, Malinda, & ch, Charity Ann & Lewis Horton, ch Malinda by a form m & James J., Sarah V. & Samuel, gct Middle River MM, Ia.

HOSKINS
----, --, --. Moses & Elizabeth
Ch: Malinda b 1811, 9, 11
Joseph " 1813, 5, 15
Moses " 1814, 12, 18
Rachel " 1818, 4, 19
Ellis " 1821, 12, 3
1814, 3, 12. Joseph d bur Lees Creek
----, --, --. Isaac & Rachel
Ch: Mary b 1829, 10, 31
Joel & Josiah " 1831, 8, 14
Martha " 1834, 3, 23
Jane " 1837, 4, 8
Lydia " 1839, 2, 24
Josephus " 1841, 4, 26
1833, 9, 3. Malinda d bur Lees Creek

1811, 5, 25. Moses [Huskins] Jr. rocf New Garden MM, dtd 1811,3,30
1811, 5, 25. Elizabeth [Houskins] rocf New Garden MM, N. C., dtd 1811,3,30
1811, 7, 27. John [Huskins] & s, William & Isaac, rocf New Garden MM, N. C., dtd 1811,3,30
1811, 7, 27. Hannah [Houskins] & dt, Ann, rocf New Garden MM, N. C., dtd 1811,3,30
1812, 2, 29. George rocf New Garden MM, N.C., dtd 1811,3,30
1814, 12, 31. Moses [Huskins] & w, Ruth, & ch, Joseph, Hannah, Eli & Ruth, rocf Center MM, dtd 1814,7,2
1815, 9, 30. Moses Jr. & w, Elizabeth, & ch, Malinda & Moses, roc
1831, 5, 28. Malinda Thornburg (form Hoskins) con mcd
1831, 7, 21. Ruth Dillon (form Hoskins) con mcd
1834, 2, 20. Rachel Stanley (form Hoskins) dis mcd
1835, 10, 22. George gct Clear Creek MM
1842, 3, 24. Moses con mcd
1842, 5, 26. Ellis gct Salem MM, Ia.
1842, 11, 24. Isaac & w, Rachel, & ch, Mary, Joel, Josiah, Martha, Jane, Lydia & Josephus, gct Clear Creek MM
1842, 11, 24. Moses [Hoskens] gct Salem MM,Ia.
1884, 6, 17. Joseph, Rebecca, Estelle & Ardillia [Hoskens] recrq
1887, 4, 16. Minnie recrq
1889, 3, 16. Walter recrq
1892, 10, 15. Rachel Alma [Haskins] rocf Clear Creek MM
1903, 6, 20. Maud Milner [Hosking] gct Cleveland MM

HUDDLE
1870, 6, 18. Charles Sumner recrq

HUFF
1815, 2, 28. Lydia, dt Daniel & Sarah, b
1816, 1, 12. Daniel d ae 68 bur Fairfield
1816, 10, 13. Rebecah m Samuel SANDERS
1818, 4, 8. Jmmes, s Daniel & Sarah, Highland Co., O.; m at Fairfield, Sidney WRIGHT, dt Edward & Hannah, Highland Co., O.
Ch: Mary Ann b 1819, 1, 5 d 1826, 9, 4 bur Fairfield
Daniel b 1820, 11, 2 " 1826, 9,11 bur Fairfield
Hannah b 1823, 7, 25 " 1826, 9,14 bur Fairfield
Sarah b 1825, 11, 24 " 1826, 9,14 bur Fairfield
Sidney b 1827, 8, 14
James M. " 1829, 4, 17 " 1830, 9, 5 bur Fairfield
Elizabeth b 1831, 9, 2
Eunice " 1834, 10, 6
Ruth Ann " 1837, 2, 14
William W. H. " 1839, 12, 30
Lydia Eliza " 1842, 2, 24 d 1846, 5, 1 bur Fairfield
1820, 3, 1. Mary m Elgar BROWN
1823, 10, 2. John d bur Fairfield
1825, 9, 28. Rachel m Jacob HUNT
1826, 3, 9. Jesse d bur Fairfield
1829, 2, 11. Sarah m James HADLEY, Jr.
1833, 11, 18. Margaret d ae 76 bur Richland, Ind.
1835, 9, 30. Lydia m Christopher BETTS
1838, 11, 20. Sarah d ae 64y 21d bur Fairfield
1839, 3, 6. Elizabeth m Levi GREEN
1842, 3, 3. Daniel, s Daniel & Elizabeth, Highland Co., O.; m at Lees Creek, Ruth McPHERSON, dt Daniel & Mary, Highland Co., O.
1844, 10, 23. Sidney H. m Israel TERRELL
1850, 4, 19. Daniel d ae 75y 9m 7d bur Fairfield
1852, 9, 22. Ruth m Jonathan SANDERS
----, --, --. John & Mary Jane
Ch: Sarah Cordelia b 1853, 4, 6
Juliet " 1855, 5, 6
Francis Linley " 1857, 7, 17
Ella " 1859, 6, 5
----, --, --. William W. H., s James & Sidney (Wright), b 1839,12,31; m Phebe J. TERRELL
Ch: Maggie Morris b 1869, 6, 25
Daniel " 1872, 5, 17

HUFF, William W. H. & Phebe J., continued
Ch: Haines b 1875, 1, 4
Russell " 1877, 10, 21
J. Guy " 1879, 12, 28
Terrell Chalmers " 1882, 2, 4
Gracie Elizabeth " 1886, 10, 5
----, --, --. Haines m Anna Grace PEET
Ch: Geo. Wm. b 1904, 1, 25
Rufus " 1905, 11, 25
Hester
Gladys Marguerite" 1911, 8, 20
Ruth Mildred " 1914, 4, 22
May " 1916, 2, --
----, --, --. Terrell Chalmers, s William W. H. & Phebe J. (Terrell), b 1882,2,4; m Ella STEVENS, dt Henry & Alice, b 1886,11,12
Ch: Austin Terrell b 1909, 1, 20
Curtis Elton " 1911, 5, 30
Henry Harrison b 1913, 6, 21

1808, 4, 30. Daniel & gr s, William S. Hutchings, rocf Deep Creek MM, N. C., dtd 1808, 3,5
1808, 4, 30. Margaret rocf Deep Creek MM, N. C., dtd 1808,3,5
1811, 7, 27. Daniel, Jr. & s, James, Daniel, John & Jesse, rocf Deep Creek MM, N. C., dtd 1811,4,6
1811, 7, 27. Sarah & dt, Rebecca, Rachel, Mary & Sarah, rocf Deep Creek MM, dtd 1811, 4,6
1814, 5, 28. Daniel & w, Sarah, & ch, James, Rebecca, Daniel, Rachel, Mary, John, Sarah, Jesse & Elizabeth, rocf Clear Creek MM
1819, 9, 25. Cert rec for John & fam from Deep Creek MM, N. C., endorsed to New Garden MM, Ind.
1820, 7, 29. James & w, Sidney, & dt, Mary Ann, gct White Water MM, Ind.
1820, 9, 30. Daniel, Jr. gct Fall Creek MM, to m
1822, 8, 31. James & w, Sidney, & ch, Mary Ann & David, rocf White Water MM, dtd 1822,2,23
1823, 5, 31. Daniel, Jr. & w, Nancy, & dt, Juliet, gct Fall Creek MM
1829, 6, 27. Daniel Jr. & w, Nancy, & ch, Juliet, Mary, Sarah & John, roc
1832, 2, 23. Daniel Jr. & w, Nancy, & ch, Juliet, Mary, Sarah, John & Mahlon, gct Fall Creek MM
1851, 4, 19. Elizabeth Hockett (form Huff) dis mcd
1853, 5, 21. John con mcd
1854, 3, 18. Eunice Tiffin (form Hough) dis mcd
1854, 10, 21. Juliet Murdock (form Huff) con mcd
1854, 11, 18. Mary Jane rocf Dover MM, dtd 1854,7,13
1856, 7, 19. Mary B. (form Ladd) dis mcd
1856, 8, 16. Mahlon dis mcd
1856, 11, 15. Jesse dis mcd
1858, 7, 17. Daniel & w, Nancy, & s, Daniel Wheeler, gct Flushing MM, O.
1861, 7, 20. Aaron dis mcd
1862, 10, 18. John dis disunity
1868, 2, 15. William con mcd
1868, 2, 15. Phebe J. (form Terrell) con mcd
1883, 4, 21. Ruth E., Adda & Francis L. recrq
1883, 4, 21. Allie J. & Maggie recrq
1889, 5, 18. David [Hough] recrq
1894, 11, 17. Daniel gct Cleveland MM, O.
1897, 12, 18. Frank L. & Alice M. gct Hopewell MM
1903, 2, 21. Grace Peet recrq
1914, 1, 17. Ruth E. relrq
1914, 1, 17. Grace Elizabeth rmt Marion Hollingsworth
1916, 2, 19. Hester Phebe & Rebecca Mae recrq

HULETT
1845, 9, 26. Sarah Corlies d ae 78

HULL
1915, 5, 15. Dr. James R. & Lydia Ruth recrq

HUMPHREY
1870, 12, 17. Esther recrq

HUNT
1807, 12, 10. Aaron, s Phinehas & Elizabeth, Highland Co., O.; m at Fall Creek, Hannah MOFFITT, dt Hugh & Hannah, Ross Co., O.
1808, 6, 13. Katherine m Zachariah HODSON
1809, 11, 23. Elizabeth m William BALDWIN
1815, 2, 15. Rebecca m Asaph HIATT
1815, 8, 30. Josiah, s Abner & Mary, Highland Co., O.; m at Fairfield, Mary COX, dt Enoch & Gertrude, Highland Co., O.

1816, 9, 19. Lavina, dt Josiah & Mary, b
----, --, --. Nathan & Rachel
Ch: James b 1826, 7, 4
Jesse " 1827, 10, 13
Aaron B. " 1830, 2, 26
Daniel " 1832, 6, 1
Jacob G. " 1835, 1, 21
Lydia Ann " 1841, 2, 4
Nathan m 2nd Sarah -----
Ch: David Bailey b 1854, 7, 21
1825, 9, 28. Jacob, s Nathan & Lydia, Highland Co., O.; m at Fairfield, Rachel HUFF, dt Daniel & Sarah, Highland Co., O.

HUNT, continued
1834, 12, 31. Lavina m Jesse NORDYKE
1848, 9, 8. Rachel, w Nathan, d ae 48 bur Fairfield
1850, 2, 20. Josiah d ae 60 bur Fairfield
1855, 10, 17. Jesse d bur Newbury

1808, 3, 26. Jonathan & s, Barnabas & John, rocf Deep River MM, N. C., dtd 1805,9,2
1808, 3, 26. Phebe & dt, Margaret, rocf Deep River MM, N. C., dtd 1805,9,2
1808, 3, 26. Stephanes rocf Deep River MM, N. C., dtd 1805,1,7
1808, 3, 26. Elizabeth rocf Deep River MM, N. C., dtd 1805,1,7
1808, 3, 26. Sarah & dt, Hannah, rocf New Garden MM, N. C., dtd 1806,9,27
1808, 3, 26. Libni, Ezra & Hanuel, s Sarah, rocf New Garden MM, N. C., dtd 1806,9,27
1808, 3, 26. Miriam rocf New Garden MM, N.C., dtd 1806,8,30
1808, 3, 26. Asa rocf New Garden MM, N. C., dtd 1807,1,31
1809, 7, 29. Stephanes dis
1809, 7, 29. Uriah dis mcd
1811, 1, 26. Elizabeth rocf Mt. Pleasant MM, Va., dtd 1810,8,25
1811, 10, 26. Elizabeth & s, John & Silis, rocf Westfield MM, dtd 1810,10,13
1812, 11, 28. Nicholas & fam gct Darby Creek MM
1812, 11, 28. Elizabeth gct Darby Creek MM
1812, 12, 26. Aaron dis disunity
1813, 5, 29. Hannah & ch gct Darby Creek MM
1813, 9, 25. Eleazer gct Darby Creek MM
1813, 10, 30. Abner & w, Mary, & ch, Elizabeth, Rebeckah & Josiah, rocf Clear Creek MM, dtd 1813,10,28
1825, 1, 29. Nathan rocf Newberry MM, dtd 1824,12,25
1830, 12, 25. Abner & w, Mary, & dt, Elizabeth, gct Newbury MM
1845, 3, 15. David Wright gct Newberry MM, to m Ruth Hunt
1851, 5, 17. Nathan gct Dover MM, to m Sarah Bailey
1852, 1, 17. Sarah rocf Dover MM, dtd 1851,11,13
1854, 8, 17. Mary gct Richland MM, Ia.
1855, 4, 21. Nathan & w, Sarah, & ch, Jacob G., Lydia Ann & David Bailey, gct Newbury MM
1855, 6, 16. Aaron L. gct Newberry MM
1856, 10, 18. James gct Newberry MM
1876, 11, 18. Mary Ann gct Westfield MM, Ind.

HUSSEY
1812, 4, 9. Sarah m Isaac WILLIAMS

1808, 3, 26. Sarah [Huzza] & ch, Sarah, Stephen, Mary, Priscilla, William & John, recrq
1809, 4, 29. Christopher [Huzza] rocf Cane Creek MM, N. C., dtd 1808,9,3
1809, 6, 24. Joshua [Huzza] & s, Thomas & Stephen, rocf Cane Creek MM, dtd 1808,8,5
1809, 6, 24. Sarah rocf Cane Creek MM, dtd 1808,11,5
1809, 10, 28. Stephen rocf Cane Creek MM, dtd 1809,7,8
1809, 10, 28. Martha & dt, Martha, rocf Cane Creek MM, N. C., dtd 1809,7,1
1809, 12, 30. Martha Underwood (form Hussey) dis mcd
1896, 3, 21. Ray C., Earl & Ida recrq
1897, 4, 17. Eliza rocf Clear Creek MM
1913, 9, 20. Robert recrq

HUSTON
1886, 10, 16. Mary dropped from mbrp

HUTCHINS
1808, 4, 30. Daniel Huff & gr s, William S. [Hutchings] rocf Deep Creek MM, N. C., dtd 1808,3,5
1824, 4, 24. William dis mcd

HUTSON
1809, 4, 29. Margaret rocf Lost Creek MM, dtd 1808,9,24

HUTTON
1821, 12, 6. Sarah m John WINDER
1822, 9, 11. Levi, s John, Fayette Co., O.; m Rebecca LADD, dt Jacob, Highland Co.,O.
Ch: Elizabeth

R.	b 1823,	9, 11
John	" 1825,	7, 7
Jordan L.	" 1827,	4, 2

1812, 1, 25. Mercy recrq
1816, 12, 28. Levi, Sarah & Epimonondas, ch Mary, recrq
1817, 10, 25. John rst by rq with consent of Westland MM
1824, 4, 24. John & w, Mary, & s, Epimonandas, gct Green Plain MM
1830, 4, 24. Levi & w, Rebecca, & ch, Elizabeth, John & Jordan, gct Green Plain MM

INGHAM
1824, 4, 28. Deborah m John BATEMAN

1811, 7, 27. Hezekiah rocf Buckingham MM,Pa., dtd 1811,4,1
1811, 7, 27. Isiah rocf Gwynedd MM, Pa., dtd 1811,3,28
1815, 1, 28. Hezekiah con mcd
1815, 1, 28. Isiah dis mcd
1815, 11, 25. Deborah rocf Salsbury MM, Pa., dtd 1815,7,4
1824, 6, 26. Hezekiah dis
1826, 11, 25. Mary Ingham & niece, Anny Swain, gct Springborough MM

ISH
1871, 8, 19. Catherine recrq
1871, 8, 19. Mary recrq

JACKSON
1807, 9, 26. Sarah Chaney (form Jackson) dis mcd
1808, 2, 27. Elizabeth Roox (form Jackson) dis mcd
1810, 12, 29. Charity Foster (form Jackson) dis mcd
1811, 8, 31. Kesiah Allin (form Jackson) dis mcd
1812, 4, 25. Uriah dis disunity
1817, 1, 25. Amer dis disunity
1898, 2, 19. Nettie H. relrq
1909, 3, 20. Emma recrq

JAMES
1841, 6, 24. David & w, Mary, & ch, Mary, Levi C., Atticus S., Alfred P., Jonathan H., Lindley M., Sarah & Dillon H., rocf West Grove MM, Ind., dtd 1841,5,8
1841, 11, 25. David & w, Mary, & ch, Mary H., Levi C., Aticus S., Alfred R., Jonathan H., Linley M., Sarah & Dillen H., gct Clear Creek MM

JARVIS
1879, 3, 15. Lizzie M. recrq

JAYJOHN
1871, 8, 19. Eliza recrq

JENKINS
1850, 11, 16. Isaac M. Johnson gct Ceasars Creek MM, to m Dinah Jenkins
1894, 3, 17. John recrq
1898, 4, 16. John dropped from mbrp

JESSOP
1811, 9, 28. Thomas rocf Mt. Pleasant MM, Va., dtd 1811,5,25
1811, 11, 30. Mary rocf Mt. Pleasant MM, Va., dtd 1811,5,25
1812, 5, 30. Thomas & w, Ann, & ch, Jonathan, Prudence, Richard, Mary, Thomas & Anna, rocf Deep River MM, N. C., dtd 1811,11,4, endorsed by White Water MM
1812, 6, 27. Isaac rocf Mt. Pleasant MM, dtd 1812,3,28
1812, 6, 27. Nathan & w, Sarah, & ch, Isaac & Thomas, rocf Mt. Pleasant MM, dtd 1812,3, 28
1814, 11, 26. Isaac gct White Water MM
1814, 12, 31. Nathan & w, Sarah, & ch, Isaac, Thomas, Phebe & Mary, gct White Water MM
1815, 5, 27. Thomas [Jesup] & w, Ann, & ch, Jonathan, Prudence, Richard, Mary, Thomas, Anna Huldah & Rebecca, gct Clear Creek MM
1816, 11, 30. Thomas & w, Mary, gct Blue River MM, Ind.
1817, 11, 29. Cert rec for Ann from New Garden MM, N. C., dtd 1817,9,27, endorsed to Lees Creek MM

JOB
1869, 7, 17. Archibald recrq
1869, 7, 17. Ellen recrq
1869, 7, 17. Russell Orville, Caroline V., Ella Florence, Thomas P., Rufus E. & Sarah E., ch Archibald & Ellen, recrq
1872, 6, 15. Sally recrq

JOHN
1808, 3, 26. Ebeneezer rocf Westfield MM, dtd 1807,12,13, endorsed by Lost Creek MM, Tenn., & by Miami MM, O.

JOHNSON
----, --, --. Ashley & Milly
Ch: James E. b 1806, 9, 6
Clark " 1808, 7, 19
Ruth " 1812, 10, 1
1810, 1, 11. Jephthah, s Ashley & Mildred, Highland Co., O.; m at Walnut Creek, Ruth SMITH, dt Seth & Elizabeth, Highland Co., O.
1812, 1, 1. Simeon, s Joseph & Agatha, Highland Co., O.; m at Fairfield, Nancy JOHNSON, dt William & Agatha, Highland Co.,O.
1812, 2, 6. Lydia m Joseph THORNBROUGH
----, --, --. Moorman & Lydia
Ch: Pamelia b 1813, 5, 22
Silas Heston " 1816, 10, 23
Emily " 1818, 8, 1
Elias " 1820, 7, 30
Rachel Moorman " 1822, 7, 31
Caroline Agnes " 1826, 3, 1
Adaline " 1828, 1, 18
Cyrus Clarkson " 1830, 9, 10
Eliza Ellen " 1833, 3, 21
James M. " 1835, 3, 31
1813, 12, 29. Jerusha m Jury TODHUNTER
1815, 4, 15. Rachel m Allen LUPTON
1816, 3, 16. Caroline d bur Jamy Johnson's on Fall Creek
1816, 10, 2. Anthony, s James & Penelope, Highland Co., O.; m at Fairfield, Mary LUPTON, dt Wm. & Bathsheba, Highland Co., O.
Ch: Mahlon b 1817, 7, 15
Grace " 1819, 6, 28
Sarah " 1821, 9, 7
Deborah " 1824, 1, 28
Davis " 1826, 2, 12
James Allen " 1828, 2, 7
Isaac McPherson " 1830, 4, 22
Rachel " 1832, 6, 21

JOHNSON, Anthony & Mary, continued
Ch: Joseph
Anthony b 1835, 10, 10
----, --, --. Jesse & Mary
Ch: Jerdan b 1817, 6, 20
Elias " 1818, 11, 12
Edna " 1820, 6, 4
Michael " 1822, 4, 5
Penelope C." 1824, 11, 13
Mary " 1827, 1, 11
1817, 1, 29. Kitty Winstone Johnson m William MORMAN
1817, 6, 11. Penelope m Joseph BURGESS
1817, 10, 8. Elvy d bur Jamy Johnson's on Fall Creek
1819, 2, 4. Sally m Nathan DICKS
1819, 9, 10. Emily d bur James Johnson's
1820, 1, 26. Penelope d ae 75 bur Fairfield
1820, 4, 13. Mary d ae 38 bur Fairfield
1822, 10, 30. Watkins, s Joseph & Agatha, Highland Co., O.; m at Fairfield, Elizabeth MOORMAN, dt Charles & Elizabeth, Highland Co., O.
1823, 1, 29. Martha m Joel WRIGHT
1823, 5, 19. Agatha d ae 73 bur James Johnson's
1823, 7, 30. Ashley M., s Ashley & Milly, Highland Co., O.; m at Fairfield, Hannah DUTTON, dt David & Phebe, Highland Co., O.
1823, 8, 18. Elizabeth d bur James Johnson's on Fall Creek
1824, 8, 10. James d bur Fairfield
1824, 8, 14. William d ae 84 bur James Johnson's
1824, 12, 16. William d ae 90 bur Fairfield
1827, 9, --. Penelope d bur Fairfield
1829, 9, 6. Adaline d bur James Johnson's
1829, 10, 2. Mary d bur Fairfield
1830, 7, --. Susanna d ae 94 bur Fairfield
1834, --, --. Milly, w Ashley, d ae 68 bur Fairfield
1837, 2, 16. Elizabeth H. d bur Fairfield
1838, 2, 17. Joseph John d bur James Johnson's
----, --, --. Gerrard M. & Mary
Ch: Harvey b 1839, 6, 13
Warren " 1841, 1, 19
Semira " 1842, 6, 5
Abi " 1844, 2, 10
Cibil " 1846, 8, 19
1840, 10, 31. Sarah d ae 71 bur Fairfield
1841, 6, 25. Caroline Agness d bur James Johnson's
1841, 7, 27. Eliza Ellen d bur James Johnson's
1842, 4, 3. Pamela d bur in Johnson Bur. Gr.
1842, 12, 28. Addison, s Barclay & Sarah, Highland Co., O.; m at Fairfield, Emily MOORMAN, dt William & Kitty, Highland Co., O.
1843, 5, 3. Elizabeth d ae 75 bur Fairfield
1844, 2, 28. Mahlon, s Anthony & Mary, Highland Co., O.; m at Fairfield, Mahala BURGESS, dt Daniel & Ruth, Highland Co., O.
Ch: Beverly B. b 1844, 12, 12
Almeda " 1849, 2, 1
1845, 2, 18. Elias P. d bur James Johnson's
1845, 4, 20. James A. d ae 70 bur Fairfield
1846, 8, 20. James M. d bur James Johnson's
1847, 4, 21. Grace m Levi GREEN
1847, 7, 21. James d ae 88 bur fam gr yd
1848, 6, 26. Ashley, s William & Susanna, d ae 91 bur Fairfield
1849, 9, 19. Deborah m Moses WALTON
1850, 5, 13. Juliann d bur Fairfield
1853, 7, 1. Mahala d bur Fairfield
1853, 9, 21. Rachel m John GREEN
1856, 1, 31. Joseph A., s Anthony & Mary, Highland Co., O.; m at Walnut Creek, Hannah Ellen ELLIS, dt David & Hannah, Fayette Co., O.
1856, 4, 8. Moorman d ae 68
----, --, --. Anthony & Hannah Ellen
Ch: Henrietta A.
b 1857, 12, 7
Martha Ann " 1859, 7, 29
James Arthur " 1860, 2, 20
Mary Cordelia " 1863, 6, 19
1857, 1, 9. Susannah d ae 81
1860, 9, 19. Mildred d ae 76 bur Fairfield
1863, 3, 13. Agness d ae 76 bur Fairfield
1863, 12, 1. Judith d ae 85 bur Fairfield
1865, 3, 30. Jemima m Benjamin F. COWGILL
1866, 8, 5. Anthony d ae 79 bur Fairfield
1876, 11, 11. Mary d ae 84 bur Fairfield
1883, 12, 14. Leta Davis Johnson, dt A. J. & Hattie E., b
----, --, --. Eli J., s John & M. J., b 1856, 10,12; m Elizabeth L. KING, dt John & Emily, b 1860,12,26
Dt: Lillian
Maud b 1887, 11, 28
1908, 4, 25. Alvin b

1808, 2, 27. Rachel rocf Deep Creek MM, dtd 1807,4,11, endorsed by Miami MM
1808, 4, 30. Jonathan con mcd
1808, 9, 24. Richard Bloxsom & s, Charles, & gr ch, Richard Obidiah & Gideon Johnson, rocf Concord MM, O., dtd 1808,6,23
1808, 9, 24. Ann Blocksom & dt, Ann & Mary, & gr dt, Unity & Jerusha Johnson, rocf Concord MM, dtd 1808,6,23
1808, 11, 26. Micajah rocf South River MM, Va., dtd 1807,11,14
1808, 11, 26. Rachel & dt, Cumfort, rocf South River MM, Va., dtd 1807,11,4
1809, 1, 28. Edith rocf Deep Creek MM, N. C., dtd 1807,7,4, endorsed by Miami MM
1809, 1, 28. Mary rocf Deep Creek MM, N. C., dtd 1807,7,4, endorsed by Miami MM
1809, 1, 28. Ashle, minor, rocf Deep Creek MM, dtd 1807,4,4
1809, 4, 29. Nancy Bocock (form Johnson) con mcd

JOHNSON, continued
1809, 5, 27. Simeon rocf South River MM, Va., dtd 1809,2,11
1809, 11, 25. Jonathan dis disunity
1810, 2, 24. Nancy rocf Goos Creek MM, Va., dtd 1809,12,27
1810, 7, 28. Mary dis disunity
1810, 8, 25. Mildred & dt gct Ceasars Creek MM
1810, 9, 29. Elija, James, Gidion Nicholes, William & David, s Mary, rocf Deep Creek MM, N. C.
1810, 12, 29. Elijah & s, Garland & James, rocf Cedar Creek MM, Va., dtd 1810,7,14
1810, 12, 29. Elizabeth & dt, Sarah & Martha, rocf Ceder Creek MM, Va., dtd 1810,7,14
1811, 1, 26. James & s, Bartlett, rocf South River MM, Va., dtd 1810,9,8
1811, 1, 26. Rachel & dt, Lydia Susanna Nancy Polly & Melly, rocf South River MM, Va., dtd 1810,9,8
1811, 2, 23. Thomas M. dis disunity
1811, 4, 27. Susannah gct Center MM
1811, 9, 28. Cert rec for John W. from South River MM. dtd 1810,9,8, endorsed to Center MM
1811, 10, 26. Morman gct Fall Creek MM, to m
1812, 2, 29. Joseph rocf South River MM, Va., dtd 1811,10,22, endorsed by Center MM
1812, 4, 25. David dis disunity
1812, 6, 27. Mary & ch gct Mill Creek MM
1812, 7, 25. Ashley Jr. dis disunity
1812, 8, 29. Simeon dis disunity
1812, 11, 28. William & w, Susannah, rocf South River MM, Va., dtd 1812,8,8
1812, 11, 28. William Jr. rocf South River MM, Va., dtd 1812,10,10
1813, 4, 24. James & w, Penelope, & dt, Elizabeth, Sarah, Judith, Mary, Penelope, Agnes & Rachel, rocf Goose Creek MM, dtd 1813,2,24, endorsed by Miami MM
1813, 4, 24. Anthony rocf Goose Creek MM, dtd 1813,2,24, endorsed by Miami MM
1813, 4, 24. Jesse rocf Goose Creek MM, dtd 1813,2,24, endorsed by Miami MM
1813, 8, 28. Joseph dis mcd
1813, 11, 27. Susanna gct Center MM
1813, 12, 25. Abner dis disunity
1814, 1, 29. Richard Bloxsom & gr s, Gideon Johnson, gct Cedars Creek MM
1814, 3, 26. Joseph & ch, Polly, Kitty, Winston, Elvira, Watkins, Caroline, Alfred Carrell, rocf South River MM, Va., dtd 1813,10,9, endorsed by Fall Creek MM
1814, 3, 26. Micajah dis disunity
1814, 6, 25. Thomas G. dis disunity
1814, 12, 31. Jephthah gct Cesar's Creek MM
1815, 1, 28. Daniel dis mcd
1815, 1, 28. Unity dis mcd
1815, 6, 24. John W. & w, Milly, & ch, Gerrard Moorman, John Lynch & Benjamin Watkins, rocf Center MM, dtd 1815,5,20
1815, 6, 24. Lydia rocf Fall Creek MM
1815, 7, 29. David dis
1816, 1, 27. Christopher con mcd
1816, 1, 27. Jesse con mcd
1816, 2, 24. Agatha Upp (form Johnson) dis mcd
1816, 6, 29. Mary recrq
1817, 2, 12. Abner rst
1818, 8, 29. Pleasant & w, Nancy, & ch, Thomas M., Affrica, William C., Edwin E., Virgil H., Paulina P. & Gerves L., gct Centre MM
1818, 9, 29. Abner gct Fall Creek MM, to m
1819, 7, 31. Lydia rocf South River MM, Va., dtd 1819,5,11
1820, 4, 29. Mary con mcd
1820, 9, 30. James B. gct Miami MM, to m
1821, 1, 27. James A. recrq
1821, 7, 28. Milly recrq
1822, 1, 26. John, James Ellison, Mary, Jesse Clark, Payton, Bolin Anthony & Penelope, ch James A., recrq
1822, 10, 30. A testimony ordered against Obadiah for jas
1823, 2, 22. Abner gct Green Plain MM
1823, 10, 25. Thomas E. dis disunity
1824, 3, 27. Rhoda rocf Miami MM, dtd 1824,2,25
1824, 4, 24. Agatha (form Moorman) dis mcd
1824, 7, 31. Rachel, w Micaja, & ch gct Center MM; returned & accepted
1825, 4, 30. William Jr. dis
1825, 10, 29. Anna Watson (form Johnson) dis mcd
1825, 11, 26. Charles dis disunity
1825, 12, 21. Clark dis disunity
1826, 1, 28. Christopher dis disunity
1826, 1, 28. Mary dis disunity
1826, 6, 24. Anne Johnson (form Johnson) dis mcd
1826, 10, 28. Sarah, Mary & Susanna dis disunity
1826, 10, 28. Martha Gilbreath (form Johnson) dis mcd
1828, 1, 26. Elijah & w, Elizabeth, gct Springborough MM
1828, 1, 26. James B. & w & ch, Overton, Harriett W. & Martha, gct Springborough MM
1828, 12, 27. John Lynd dis disunity
1829, 6, 27. Ashley M. & w, Hannah, & ch, Harriett & Cyrus, gct Green Plain MM
1829, 6, 27. James E. dis disunity
1829, 7, 25. James P. dis disunity
1829, 7, 25. John W. dis jH
1829, 11, 28. James C. dis disunity
1830, 4, 24. Sally H. Overman (form Johnson) dis mcd
1830, 10, 30. John H. dis disunity
1831, 2, 26. Ruth dis disunity
1831, 5, 28. Elizabeth (form Wright) con mcd
1831, 9, 22. Comfort McCoy (form Johnson) dis mcd
1831, 10, 20. Nancy & ch, Delilah Albertine, Caroline Agnes, Arzilla, Martha Ann, Melvina, Julia Ann & Eliza Ann, gct Dover MM

JOHNSON, continued
1832, 7, 26. Joseph gct Dover MM
1833, 1, 24. Agness Vanpelt (form Johnson) dis mcd
1833, 2, 21. Hannah & ch, Louisa, Cyrus & John, gct Sugar River MM, Ind.
1833, 5, 23. Nancy Moorman (form Johnson) dis mcd
1834, 6, 26. Joseph rocf Dover MM, dtd 1834, 12,19
1835, 1, 22. William dis disunity
1835, 11, 26. Malinda Horton (form Johnson) dis mcd
1837, 1, 26. Jesse dis mcd
1837, 2, 23. Phebe (form Bonecutter) dis mcd
1837, 12, 21. Gerrard M. gct Clear Creek MM, to m Mary Coffin
1837, 12, 21. Peter dis
1838, 6, 21. Mary rocf Clear Creek MM, dtd 1838,5,22
1839, 6, 20. Charity Cox (form Johnson) dis mcd
1840, 8, 20. Lynch A. dis mcd
1841, 8, 26. Rachel Small (form Johnson) dis mcd
1842, 2, 24. Bolling A. dis disunity
1842, 6, 29. Christopher H., s John W. & Milly, Highland Co., O.; m Sisley A. TERRILL, at Fairfield
1842, 8, 25. Edna Cox (form Johnson) dis mcd
1842, 10, 20. Peyton dis disunity
1842, 10, 20. Silas H. dis
1843, 2, 23. Emily gct Fall Creek MM
1843, 2, 23. John, s Abner, rocf Sugar River MM, Ind., dtd 1842,9,17, endorsed by Fall Creek MM, 1843,2,22
1843, 4, 20. Joseph H. Burgess gct Fall Creek to m Juliet Johnson
1844, 1, 25. Uriah D. dis mcd
1844, 2, 22. Sarah Ladd (form Johnson) con mcd
1844, 4, 25. Mary Cecil (form Johnson) dis mcd
1844, 4, 25. Penelope Fisher (form Johnson) dis mcd
1844, 5, 23. Cyrus dis disunity
1844, 5, 23. Jesse C. dis disunity
1844, 8, 17. Matilda Marvin (form Johnson) dis mcd
1845, 1, 18. Allen H. dis mcd
1845, 7, 19. Eli P. rocf Dover MM, dtd 1845, 6,19
1846, 6, 20. Mary dis
1847, 4, 17. Jordan dis
1847, 5, 15. Elias dis mcd
1847, 7, 17. Milly W. Mendenhall (form Johnson) con mcd
1847, 8, 21. Levi M. dis disunity
1847, 10, 16. Julian (form McPherson) con mcd
1848, 7, 15. John Van Pelt gct Sugar River MM, Ind.
1849, 10, 20. Barclay & w, Sarah, & ch, Leah, Barclay & Ellwood, gct Pleasant Plain MM, Ia.
1849, 10, 20. Linton gct Pleasant Plain MM,Ia.
1849, 10, 20. Linton gct Pleasant Plain MM, Ia.
1849, 10, 20. Sidney & Melissa gct Pleasant Plain MM, Ia.
1850, 1, 19. Eli P. dis mcd
1850, 6, 15. Davis dis mcd
1850, 11, 16. Isaac M. gct Ceasars Creek MM, to m Dinah Jenkins
1850, 12, 31. Cyrus C. dis mcd
1851, 4, 19. Gerrard M. & w, Mary C., & ch, Hervey, Warren, Samira, Abi, Sibel & Orpha, gct Honey Creek MM, Ind.
1851, 5, 17. Isaac M. gct Ceasars Creek MM
1852, 6, 19. Christopher H. & w, Sicily, & ch, Elizabeth Olive, Mary Mildred & Pleasant Irving, gct Newbury MM
1853, 10, 15. Benjamin W. gct Spring Creek MM, Ia.
1853, 10, 15. Milly & dt, Elizabeth, gct Spring Creek MM, Ia.
1855, 2, 17. Jervis L. rocf Dover MM, dtd 1855,1,18
1855, 6, 16. Susannah gct Pleasant Plain MM, Ia.
1855, 6, 16. Mary Jane (form Ellis) dis mcd
1855, 11, 17. James dis mcd
1856, 1, 19. Mahlon dis mcd
1856, 6, 21. Mary Jane recrq
1857, 1, 17. Rachel Carson (form Johnson) dis mcd
1860, 2, 18. Jarvis L. gct Dover MM
1862, 4, 18. Mary Jane Binegar (form Johnson) con mcd
1862, 9, 20. Mary C. & ch, Samira, Abi, Cibil Orpa & Warren, rocf Clear Creek MM, dtd 1862,9,13
1865, 10, 21. Beverly gct Henkles Creek MM, Ind.
1866, 2, 17. Almedia gct Springfield MM, O.
1867, 3, 16. Ulysses N. Johnson, minor s Mary Jane Benegar, recrq
1869, 5, 15. Michal gct Kokomo MM, Ind.
1869, 10, 16. Joseph Anthony & w, Hannah Ellen, & ch, Henrietta A., Martha A., James A. Mary C. & Alice M., gct Ceasars Creek MM, O.
1870, 3, 19. Elias recrq
1870, 6, 18. Francis M. recrq
1870, 6, 18. Joseph Newton, s Francis M., recrq of parent
1871, 3, 18. Davis recrq
1871, 3, 18. Malinda recrq
1871, 3, 18. Charles M., Thomas E., Clara A., Emma E. & Lottie J., ch Davis & Malinda, recrq
1871, 8, 19. Abi Barrett (form Johnson) con mcd
1872, 11, 16. Elizabeth recrq
1873, 3, 15. David B. recrq
1873, 5, 17. Joseph A. & w, Hannah Ellen, & ch, Henrietta A., James A., Mary C., Alice M., Martha A. & Hannah M., rocf Cesar's Creek MM, dtd 1872,9,26
1882, 3, 18. Eli J. & John C. recrq

JOHNSON, continued
1882, 4, 15. Elizabeth L. recrq
1883, 4, 21. Cynthia recrq
1884, 7, 19. Warren gct Clear Creek MM, O.
1886, 4, 17. Amy (form Cooper) gct Newberry MM
1887, 4, 16. Raymond A. & Nancy A. recrq
1890, 12, 20. J. C. relrq
1892, 10, 15. Mary rocf Clear Creek MM
1893, 4, 15. Nancy relrq
1893, 5, 20. John J. dropped from mbrp
1893, 5, 20. Cynthia dropped from mbrp
1894, 3, 17. Arthur recrq
1895, 4, 2. Matilda & Lizzie M. recrq
1896, 1, 18. Edna recrq
1896, 2, 15. Matilda & dt, May, gct Marion MM, Ind.
1896, 7, 18. Raymond A. dropped from mbrp
1896, 7, 18. Emma, Nona E. & Minnie B. dropped from mbrp
1897, 4, 17. Lorena & Everett M. rocf Clear Creek MM
1900, 12, 15. Irena M. recrq
1902, 1, 18. Charles W. recrq
1907, 3, 16. Charles recrq
1921, 11, 2. Albert recrq
1922, 1, 5. Rena V. relrq

JONES
1808, 5, 28. Richard rocf Deep Creek MM, N. C., dtd 1808,3,5
1808, 5, 28. Jamima rocf Deep Creek MM, N.C., dtd 1808,3,5
1816, 10, 26. Richard & w, Jemima, gct Mill Creek MM
1839, 1, 24. Abigail con mcd
1869, 12, 18. Jacob & w, Elizabeth, recrq
1869, 12, 18. Mason recrq
1870, 6, 18. Catherine recrq
1870, 6, 18. Joshua & Elizabeth recrq
1870, 6, 18. Alice H., dt Joshua & Elizabeth, recrq
1870, 9, 17. Eliza recrq
1873, 5, 17. John & Sophia E. recrq
1874, 3, 21. John & w, Sophia, relrq
1877, 5, 19. Ada & Eva recrq

JURY
1820, 5, 4. William, s Lewis & Elizabeth, Fayette Co., O.; m at Walnut Creek, Elizabeth FISHER, dt James & Jane, Highland Co., O.

Ch:		
John M.	b	1821, 2, 13
Enos	"	1822, 9, 6
Milicent	"	1824, 2, 16
Jane	"	1826, 4, 20
Elizabeth	"	1828, 2, 20
Isaac	"	1829, 11, 26
Ezra	"	1832, 4, 6
Abner	"	1833, 12, 29
Milton	"	1837, 5, 20
Eleanor	"	1839, 5, 26

1821, 9, 23. John M. d bur Walnut Creek
1833, 2, 22. Elizabeth d bur Walnut Creek
1833, 2, 22. Ezra d bur Walnut Creek
1845, 11, 20. Milicent m David BARRETT
1856, 7, 29. Isaac d bur Walnut Creek
1859, 3, 24. Abner d bur Walnut Creek
1859, 10, 23. Margaret d ae 61 bur Walnut Creek
1861, 7, 24. William d ae 65 bur Walnut Creek

1838, 4, 26. Margaret recrq
1844, 11, 16. Jane Ellis (form Jury) con mcd
1850, 7, 20. Enos [Jewry] con mcd
1850, 7, 20. Sidney (form Wright) con mcd
1856, 10, 18. Enos & w, Sidney, & her s, Clarkson Wright, gct Middle River MM, Ia.

KEARNS
1902, 11, 15. Jessie H. dropped from mbrp
1903, 3, 21. James recrq

KEEN
1871, 2, 18. John M. & Mary recrq

KEITH
1910, 5, 25. Russell Delbert, s Arthur & Blanche, b

1870, 2, 19. Jeremiah A. & Martha recrq
1870, 2, 19. Sarah Alice & Cordelia B., ch Jeremiah & Martha, recrq
1873, 5, 17. Elizabeth Frances recrq
1874, 2, 21. Eli recrq
1878, 10, 19. Eli & Elizabeth dropped from mbrp
1887, 7, 16. Jerry, Martha & Sarah relrq
1908, 3, 21. Arthur & dt, Arline, recrq
1908, 3, 21. Blanche recrq

KELSEY
1870, 9, 17. Rebecca recrq

KENDALL
1809, 5, 27. William & s, Joseph, William, Enion & Isaac, rocf Springfield MM, N.C., dtd 1806,9,6, endorsed by Miami MM
1809, 5, 27. Elizabeth rocf Springfield MM, N. C., dtd 1806,9,6, endorsed by Miami MM
1815, 6, 24. Joseph dis mcd
1815, 7, 29. Elizabeth [Kendal] & s, Isaac, gct Center MM
1815, 8, 26. Ennion dis disunity
1815, 9, 30. William dis disunity

KENNET
1914, 4, 18. Ella recrq

KENWORTHY
1808, 9, 11. Dinah m Samuel COFFIN
1808, 9, 12. Thomas, s Elisha & Mary, b
1809, 12, 21. Mary [Kinworthy] m David COFFIN

1808, 3, 26. Elisha & s, Jehu & Silis, rocf

KENWORTHY, continued
Cane Creek MM, dtd 1807,3,7
1808, 3, 26. Mary [Kinworthy] & dt, Sarah, Rachel, Thamar & Mary, rocf Cane Creek MM, N. C., dtd 1807,3,7
1808, 7, 30. William dis mcd

KESTER
1887, 9, 17. Carey D. & w, Nancy J., & ch, Milton, Leroy & Ada, rocf Newbury MM
1893, 5, 20. Carey & fam dropped from mbrp

KEYS
1871, 3, 18. Ida M. recrq

KIER
1869, 12, 18. Mary E. con mcd
1870, 2, 19. Mary E. transferred to Clear Creek MM

KING
1813, 4, 24. Rachel (form More) dis mcd
1818, 5, 30. Chloe (form Slaughter) con mcd
1822, 1, 26. William receq
1831, 10, 20. Chooe gct White Lick MM, Ind.

KINZER
1880, 12, 18. Luella recrq
1883, 4, 21. Daniel & w, Mary, rocf Clear Creek MM
1884, 7, 19. Ella relrq

KIRBY
1904, 2, 20. James & Alice recrq
1904, 2, 20. Alice recrq
1819, 10, 30. Ruth [Kerby] rocf South River MM, Va., dtd 1819,4,1, endorsed by Clear Creek MM 1819,7,10

KIZER
1856, 3, 15. Mary (form Simmons) dis mcd
1873, 9, 20. Louisa recrq

KLINE
1910, 6, 18. Mary gct Clear Creek MM

LADD
----, --, --. Jacob & Elizabeth
Ch: Jacob b 1809, 4, 4
Denson " 1811, 2, 6
Elisabeth " 1813, 1, 30
Michal " 1817, 1, 16
1812, 7, 29. Lydia m John OREN
1812, 12, 2. Esther m William BUTLER
----, --, --. Asa & Mary
Ch: William C. b 1818, 10, 28
Elizabeth " 1821, 3, 11
Rebecca " 1823, 3, 10
Ruth " 1825, 3, 14
Isaac M. " 1827, 6, 9
Elwood " 1829, 6, 8
Jonathan B." 1831, 12, 20
Franklin " 1834, 8, 22
Ch: Martha Ann b 1837, 4, 27
----, --,---. Jeremiah & Rebecca
Ch: Matilda b 1822, 6, 24
Samuel " 1824, 10, 19
Jacob " 1826, 8, 14
Isaiah " 1828, 5, 27
Sidney H. " 1830, 2, 24
Alfred " 1832, 4, 5
Grace " 1834, 1, 26
Rachel " 1836, 1, 7
Rebecca " 1841, 4, 30
1822, 9, 11. Rebecca m Levi HUTTON
1827, 1, 31. Gerrard, s Jacob & Elizabeth, Highland Co., O.; m at Fairfield, Bulah M. CHALFONT, dt Wm. & Ruth, Highland Co., O.
Ch: John R. b 1828, 7, 17
Mary B. " 1830, 10, 28
William W. " 1832, 12, 16
Margaret " 1835, 3, 15
1828, 8, 3. Isaac M. d bur Fairfield
1829, 4, 29. Anna m Ellis BARRETT
1829, 10, 7. Jordan, s Jacob & Elizabeth, Highland Co., O.; m at Fairfield, Rachel BARRETT, dt Jonathan & Rachel, Highland Co., O.
Ch: Levi b 1830, 11, 23
Asa " 1833, 11, 9
1831, 11, 30. Sarah G. m John S. ROBERTS
1833, 11, 9. William C. d bur Fairfield
1835, 9, 14. Beulah M. d bur Fairfield
1836, 11, 7. Rachel, dt Jared & R., b
1837, 3, 16. Margaret d bur Fairfield
1840, 1, 25. Michael d bur Fairfield
----, --, --. Jeremiah & Rebecca
Ch: Mahala Jane b 1841, 4, 30
Jeremiah " 1845, 12, 10
Lewis " 1849, 9, 4
Margaret " 1850, 11, 23
1843, 9, 14. Elizabeth d ae 69 bur Fairfield
1845, 12, 8. Mahala J. d bur Fairfield
1846, 11, 6. Jeremiah d bur Fairfield
1849, 11, 21. Elizabeth P. m Thomas DUTTON
1850, 6, 24. Jacob d ae 82y 11m 11d (an elder)
1850, 8, 21. Jacob, s Jeremiah & Mary A. R., Highland Co., O.; m at Fairfield, Hannah B. McPHERSON, dt Daniel & Anna, Highland Co., O.
Ch: Anne M. b 1852, 10, 14
Eunice E. " 1855, 1, 7
Oscar Elwood " 1858, 10, 27
Jacob P. " 1860, 11, 4
1857, 4, 10. Victoria, dt Harmon & Jane Davis, b
1858, 8, 6. Margaret d bur Fairfield
----, --, --. Thomas Ellwood & Lydia
Ch: Harold b 1859, 4, 9
John A. " 1860, 3, 12
Franklin " 1864, 11, 20
----, --, --. Jonathan & Louisa
Ch: Emerson B. b 1860, 3, 13

LADD, Jonathan & Louisa, continued
Ch: John
Everet b 1863, 10, 14
Arthur
Langden " 1866, 10, 10
Mary Lu-
ella " 1869, 4, 23
----, --, --. Asa J. & Lydia B.
Ch: Mary Ellen b 1860, 10, 13
Arthur E. " 1862, 10, 4
Rebecca
Elmira " 1865, 1, 7
Ida " 1868, 9, 30
1860, 6, 15. Jacob d bur Fairfield
1860, 11, 18. Jacob P., s Jacob, d
1861, 3, 3. Ellwood Oscar, s Jacob P., d

1864, 3, 1. Asa d ae 69 bur Fairfield
----, --, --. Franklin & Nancy
Ch: Elwood G. b 1865, 1, 26
Jennie D. " 1867, 8, 25
Nettie M. " 1870, 2, 17
Arthur G. " 1874, 1, 3
1868, 12, 5. Arthur d bur Fairfield
1870, 2, 15. Mary Luella, dt Jonathan, d bur Fairfield
1870, 9, 22. Hannah G. m James MORRIS
1881, 11, 15. Elsie M., dt Geo. & Millie, b
----, --, --. John A. m Clara E. McVEY, dt Isaac & Martha, b 1859,4,10
Ch: Ora b 1887, 12, 9
----, --, --. J. Everett, s Jonathan & Louise, b 1863,10,14; m Maggie -----
Ch: J. Ollie b 1890, 10, 20
----, --, --. Frank, s Thos. E. & Lydia, b 1864,10,20; m Josephine -----
Ch: Mark b 1891, 12, 25
----, --, --. Louis, s Denson & Betsy, b 1854,5,13; m Ida EASTER
Ch: Maud
Amelia b 1896, 3, 15
Harriet
Viola " 1898, 8, 27
----, --, --. Arthur C. m Olive C. McPHERSON, dt Josiah & Esther, b 1881,1,19
Ch: Elbert
Clinton b 1906, 2, 2
Meredith " 1908, 7, 18
Rendell
McPherson " 1910, 8, 9

1808, 7, 30. Jacob & s, Asa, Jeremiah & G. Jordan, rocf Upper MM, Va., dtd 1808,3,19
1808, 7, 30. Elizabeth & dt, Anna, Sarah, Rebeckah & Margaret, rocf Gravelly Run MM, Va., dtd 1808,3,1
1808, 7, 30. Gerrard rocf Upper MM, Va., dtd 1808,3,19
1808, 7, 30. Priscilla, Lydia & Hester rocf Gravelly Run MM, Va., dtd 1808,3,1
1809, 4, 29. Lydia dis
1811, 5, 25. Lydia rst
1821, 9, 29. Jeremiah con mcd
1822, 10, 30. Mary Ann Rebecca rocf Darby Creek MM, dtd 1822,9,21
1830, 12, 25. Gerrard dis disunity
1836, 3, 24. Jacob Jr. dis mcd
1839, 4, 25. Jeremiah dis disunity
1839, 4, 25. Matilda Duff (form Ladd) dis mcd
1842, 3, 24. Rebecca Alderman (form Ladd) con mcd
1843, 3, 23. Denson con mcd
1844, 2, 22. Sarah (form Johnson) con mcd
1850, 12, 31. Isaiah con mcd
1855, 7, 21. Thomas E. con mcd
1855, 12, 15. Sidney Dutton (form Ladd) dis mcd
1856, 1, 19. Franklin dis mcd
1856, 2, 16. Rebecca Lewallen (form Ladd) dis mcd
1856, 7, 19. Mary B. Huff (form Ladd) dis mcd
1856, 9, 20. Rebecca dis jas
1858, 5, 15. Alfred dis mcd
1858, 9, 18. Thomas Elwood con mcd
1858, 9, 18. Lydia (form Hodson) con mcd
1859, 3, 19. Jonathan con mcd
1859, 7, 16. Eliza recrq
1859, 7, 16. Louiza recrq
1859, 12, 17. Asa Jr. con mcd
1860, 11, 17. Lydia rocf Center MM, dtd 1860, 10,17
1861, 12, 21. Martha Ann Pushey (form Ladd) con mcd
1866, 5, 19. Jacob recrq
1866, 5, 19. Nancy R., w Franklin, recrq
1866, 5, 19. Eliza Estelle, Charlie Ozborn, Henry Adna & Ellwood Grant, ch Franklin & Nancy, recrq
1868, 9, 19. Isaiah & dt, Emma Jane, gct Poplar Run MM, Ind.
1870, 3, 19. Franklin recrq
1870, 3, 19. Margery recrq
1870, 3, 19. Ruth Alma, Denson Jr., Ezekiel Lewis & Mary Elizabeth recrq
1871, 2, 18. Mary Ann recrq
1871, 2, 18. Betsy recrq
1872, 2, 17. Margery Andrews(form Ladd) dis mcd
1872, 2, 17. Ruth Small (form Ladd) con mcd
1873, 3, 15. Margaret & Cordelia recrq
1874, 2, 21. John recrq
1874, 2, 21. Louisa recrq
1878, 5, 18. John W. dis disunity
1878, 8, 17. Catherine rocf Hopewell MM, dtd 1878,7,6
1878, 10, 19. J. R. dropped from mbrp
1880, 5, 15. Pleasant recrq
1881, 3, 19. Mildred E. recrq
1883, 4, 21. William Glenn recrq
1884, 6, 17. William, Jonathan & Myrtie recrq
1886, 7, 17. Anna recrq
1887, 4, 16. Josephine recrq
1887, 4, 16. Maggie A. recrq
1887, 11, 19. Denson & w, Catherine, & ch

LADD, continued
gct Hopewell MM
1895, 4, 2. Ora recrq
1902, 11, 15. Adney dropped from mbrp
1907, 4, 20. Annie gct Wilmington MM
1907, 7, 20. Annie dropped from mbrp
1910, 6, 18. Jonathan relrq
1911, 6, 17. William dropped from mbrp
1912, 12, 21. Ida dropped from mbrp
1914, 4, 18. Henrietta recrq
1919, 5, 19. Arthur G. & w, Olive C., & ch, Elbert C., Meredith A. & Randall M., rocf Whittier MM, Calif.
1921, 9, 14. Arthur C. & fam gct Leesburg MM, O.

LANTZ
1871, 8, 19. Charlotte recrq
1871, 8, 19. Emily recrq
1871, 9, 16. Mary Magdeline recrq
1874, 7, 18. Emily & Mary gct Londonderry MM

LARKINS
1869, 10, 16. Alonzo & s, Joseph, rocf Clear Creek MM, dtd 1869,9,11
1870, 3, 19. Levina recrq
1870, 7, 16. Alonzo & w, Lavina, & ch, Joseph W. & Sarah Margaret, gct Clear Creek MM
1926, 3, 4. Alonzo E. & Elizabeth [Larkin] rocf Clear Creek MM
1932, 4, 14. Alonzo's d rpd

LARRICK
1873, 3, 15. William & Nancy recrq
1886, 3, 20. Etta recrq
1909, 3, 20. William & Ida M. recrq

LAWRENCE
1915, 2, 20. James recrq
1917, 3, 17. Lulu recrq

LAZENDY
1879, 5, 17. Sarah E. recrq
1898, 1, 15. Lizzie relrq

LEA
1817, 6, 28. Ann rocf South River, Va., dtd 1816,11,9
1817, 6, 28. Elizabeth rocf South River MM, Va., dtd 1816,11,9
1821, 6, 30. Ann gct Clear Creek MM

LEAKY
1834, 10, 23. Elizabeth gct Clear Creek MM

LEAVERTON
1869, 6, 5. Ella, w John, dt John & Mary Huff, b
----, --, --. Stanley m Mamie RIDGWAY
Ch: Hubert b 1910, 10, 8
Joseph " 1912, 2, 6
Helen Louise b 1914, 12, 9
1903, 3, 21. Stanley recrq
1914, 6, 20. Mrs. Jessie & dt, Eva, recrq
1914, 6, 20. Edgar E., s Jessie, recrq
1915, 7, 17. Jessie & ch, Eva & Edgar E., relrq

LEVEY
1869, 4, 17. Mary recrq
1871, 1, 21. Mary Ellis (form Levey) con mcd

LEWALLEN
1856, 2, 16. Rebecca (form Ladd) dis mcd

LEWIS
1862, 2, 23. Charles M., s Milton & Catherine b
1860, 8, 18. Milton & w, Catherine, recrq
1860, 8, 18. Martha Ann, Jane, Alice & Ellen, ch Milton & Catherine, recrq
1860, 8, 18. Clinton recrq
1866, 1, 20. Mary Jane, w Dewitt Clinton Lewis, & ch, Ellis, Caroline, Isaac N., Lewis & Julia E., recrq
1871, 8, 19. George recrq

LIMES
1854, 8, 8. Athaliah d ae 68 bur Walnut Creek
1863, 12, 17. William d ae 85 bur Walnut Creek

1840, 8, 20. Athaliah recrq
1853, 8, 20. William recrq

LINDLEY
1812, 9, 28. Jonathan, Harrison Co., Ind.; m at Clear Creek, Martha HENLEY, Highland Co., O.

1812, 11, 28. Martha & ch gct White Water MM

LINK
1889, 7, 20. Chas., s Lafayette & Mary Jane, b
1903, 3, 21. Charles recrq
1911, 4, 15. Maud Barrett relrq

LIVINGSTON
1871, 8, 19. Harriet recrq
1871, 8, 19. Holden recrq
1874, 5, 16. Holden relrq

LOGAN
----, --, --. Jasper & Eva
Ch: Luella b 1905, 11, 20
Paul Robert " 1908, 10, 22
Katherine Clodine " 1914, 10, 29
1910, 11, 20. Elizabeth Elaine b

LOGAN, continued
1895, 4, 2. Jasper E. recrq
1903, 3, 21. Eva recrq

LUCAS
1871, 8, 19. Jane recrq
1903, 2, 21. Ella & Maud recrq
1904, 3, 19. Barbara & Jacob recrq
1904, 3, 19. Maggie May recrq
1903, 9, 19. Minnie recrq
1910, 2, 19. Barbara & dt, Minnie, gct Wilmington MM
1912, 5, 18. Margaret relrq

LUKER
1870, 2, 19. David & Mary Ann recrq
1870, 2, 19. Enoch, George W., Amy E. & Thomas W., recrq of parents, David & Mary Ann
1890, 9, 20. Enoch & George dis
1893, 5, 20. William dropped from mbrp

LUNDY
1808, 11, 26. Nathan dis training with the militia
1811, 8, 31. Susannah (form Schooly) dis mcd
1811, 9, 28. Eli rocf Mt. Pleasant MM, Va., dtd 1810,12,29
1811, 11, 30. Ann rocf Mt. Pleasant MM, Va., dtd 1810,12,29
1812, 11, 28. James & w & ch, Enoch, William, Jesse, Anne & Levi, rocf Mt. Pleasant MM, Va., dtd 1812,6,26
1812, 11, 28. Amos rocf Still Water MM, dtd 1812,10,27
1813, 1, 30. Susanna rst
1814, 2, 26. Amos & fam gct Center MM
1814, 2, 26. Susannah [Lunda] gct Center MM
1815, 5, 27. James & w, Elizabeth, & ch, Enoch William, Jesse, Ann, Levi, James & John gct Center MM
1816, 2, 24. Center MM was given permission to rst Nathan

LUPTON
1811, 2, 8. William d ae 55 bur Fairfield
1815, 4, 15. Allen, s William & Bathsheba, Highland Co., O.; m at Fairfield, Rachel JOHNSON, dt James & Penelope, Highland Co., O.
1816, 10, 2. Mary m Anthony JOHNSON
1818, 11, 11. Ruth m Abner CHALFONT
1821, 1, 10. Margaret m Asa COWGILL
1847, 1, 22. Bathsheba d ae 86 bur Fairfield
1852, 7, 8. Chas. b
1876, 10, 6. Everett L. b

1814, 8, 27. Jonathan dis mcd
1818, 12, 26. Ruth rocf Hopewell MM, dtd 1818, 9,10
1820, 2, 26. Solomon & w, Rachel, & ch, Lydia, Joseph A., Grace, Margaret, Rebecca & Elizabeth, gct Darby Creek MM
1820, 11, 25. David dis
1823, 11, 29. William gct Clear Creek MM, to m Ann Nordyke
1826, 8, 26. William gct Clear Creek MM
1829, 11, 28. Rachel & ch, Julian, Penelope, Bathsheba, James, Elizabeth, William & Charlotte, gct White Lick MM, Ind.
1830, 5, 29. Isaac gct White Lick MM, Ind.
1830, 8, 28. Allen dis disunity
1832, 10, 25. Mahlon rpd mcd
1873, 2, 15. David E. & w, Ellen, recrq
1873, 2, 15. Charles E., s David E. & Ellen, recrq
1873, 3, 15. Reese recrq
1874, 2, 21. Elias & Elizabeth recrq
1881, 9, 17. Rice W. & w, Ruth, & ch, Cordelia E., William C. & Mary Jane, gct Rose Hill MM, Kans.
1889, 2, 16. Rebecca M. recrq
1893, 5, 20. Rebecca dropped from mbrp
1902, 11, 15. Ellen dropped from mbrp
1907, 3, 16. Elias & w gct Clear Creek MM,O.
1910, 6, 18. Lansen E. relrq

LUTTRELL
1866, 2, 17. Margaretta (form Smith) dis mcd

LYLE
1886, 3, 20. Thurman recrq
1890, 9, 20. Thurman dis

McADAMS
1808, 4, 30. Mary (form Fisher) dis mou
1817, 11, 29. Mary recrq
1838, 4, 26. Mary [McAdam] gct Miami MM

McBRIDE
1841, 6, 24. Elvira Ann (form Hiatt) dis mcd

McCLAIN
1826, 3, 25. Mary (form Robinson) dis mcd

McCLURE
1877, 5, 19. Taylor & Sarah recrq
1881, 6, 18. Joseph A. [McLure] & w, Malinda J., & ch, Gertrude W. & Marion C., recrq
1883, 7, 21. Robert T. dis disunity
1885, 4, 18. Joseph dis disunity
1885, 7, 17. Sadie relrq
1887, 4, 16. Gertie recrq
1889, 3, 16. Marion recrq
1893, 5, 20. Arthur J. droppped from mbrp
1893, 5, 20. Marion dropped from mbrp
1902, 11, 15. Harry & Allie dropped from mbrp
1903, 2, 21. Alice recrq

McCOY
1855, 4, 24. Polly d bur at James Johnson's
1857, 8, 26. Susan, dt John & Joanna Oren, b

1831, 9, 22. Comfort (form Johnson) dis mcd
1873, 5, 17. Lorrihanna recrq
1879, 3, 15. Rees recrq

McCOY, continued
1879, 3, 15. Hannah recrq
1884, 2, 16. Ella recrq
1886, 2, 20. Robert A. & Parthenia recrq
1896, 7, 18. Ada Chance dropped from mbrp
1898, 4, 16. Andrew dropped from mbrp
1899, 2, 18. Lenna recrq
1901, 3, 16. J. H. & w, Jessie, & ch, Gertrude & Rosa, recrq
1901, 4, 20. Ethel recrq
1904, 3, 19. John recrq
1907, 4, 20. Henry, Jesse, Gertrude & Rosa dropped from mbrp
1910, 6, 18. Reece relrq
1917, 2, 17. Archie dropped from mbrp

McDANIEL
1889, 2, 16. Randolph & Mary Ann recrq
1893, 5, 20. R. [McDaniels] & w dropped from mbrp

McDONALD
1869, 2, 20. Emma D. recrq of guardian, Joseph Peitsmeyer

McGEE
1870, 9, 17. Luella recrq

McKINLEY
1871, 4, 15. Elizabeth, Ezra & Avilla J. recrq

McKINNEY
1810, 7, 28. Obadiah rocf Westfield MM, N. C., dtd 1809,11,11
1810, 7, 28. William rocf Westfield MM, N. C. dtd 1809,10,14
1810, 12, 29. Obadiah & William dis disunity
1870, 3, 19. Alfred & w, Phebe, & ch, Charles A., Anderson & Sarah Louisa, recrq
1886, 7, 17. Levina recrq
1890, 4, 19. Charles recrq
1891, 9, 18. Bertha I., Carl A., Fred D. & Bessie L. [McKinsey], ch Charles & w recrq
1906, 4, 21. Charles & w, Levina, & ch, Carl A., Bessie L., Alfred Allen, Sarah Phebe & Charles Paul, gct Caesars Creek MM
1907, 4, 20. Fred gct New Burlington

McLAUGHLIN
1870, 3, 19. Joseph recrq
1870, 3, 19. Sarah recrq
1870, 3, 19. Fanny Floid, James & William, ch Joseph & Sarah, recrq of parents
1878, 5, 18. Joseph dis disunity
1878, 10, 19. Sarah dropped from mbrp
1883, 4, 21. Sarah recrq
1887, 4, 16. James W. recrq
1893, 5, 20. J. W. dropped from mbrp

McLINTOCK
1811, 8, 31. Charity (form Trimble) dis mcd

McMANNIS
1871, 8, 19. James recrq
1871, 8, 19. Maria recrq
1871, 9, 16. Jesse recrq
1871, 9, 16. Mary J. recrq

McMILLAN
1909, 11, 20. John & w, Esther, rocf Van Wert MM

McNEAL
1874, 7, 18. Mary H. recrq

McNICHOL
1893, 9, 7. Leslie, s Robert & Sarah E., b

1904, 3, 19. Robert & Leslie recrq
1904, 3, 19. Sarah E. rocf Hopewell MM

McPHERSON
----, --, --. Isaac & Betty
Ch: Ann b 1806, 3, 18
William " 1806, 1, 21
Jane " 1810, 1, 23
John " 1812, 7, 14
Lydia " 1814, 9, 22
Mary " 1817, 3, 4
Ruth " 1819, 6, 18
Grace " 1821, 11, 19
1817, 1, 2. Sarah m Jonathan HAWORTH
----, --, --. Stephen & Mary
Ch: Isaac b 1823, 2, 4
Atlantic " 1825, 5, 21
Daniel " 1827, 6, 9
Louisa " 1829, 6, 1
Josiah " 1831, 11, 10
Ann " 1834, 5, 4
Emily " 1837, 2, 7
Lydia " 1840, 2, 2
Margaret " 1842, 10, 25
Marion " 1845, 3, 7
1826, 7, 8. Atlantic d bur Lees Creek
1826, 10, 29. Isaac d bur Fairfield
1828, 1, 2. Ann M. m Joseph TERRELL
1829, 9, 14. Daniel d bur Lees Creek
1832, 3, 3. Daniel d ae 73 bur Lees Creek
1834, 4, 23. Betty, w Isaac, d ae 50 bur Fairfield
1842, 3, 3. Ruth m Daniel HUFF
1845, 3, 12. Daniel d bur Fairfield
----, --, --. John & Maria
Ch: Sidney b 1847, 1, 15
Jesse " 1849, 1, 21
Lydia Mariah " 1851, 6, 7
Malinda C. " 1853, 10, 16
1849, 5, 30. Isaac, s Stephen & Mary, Highland Co., O.; m at Fairfield, Ruth GREEN, dt John & Rachel, Clinton Co., O.
1850, 8, 21. Hannah G. m Jacob LADD
1853, 12, 8. Mary d ae 84 bur Fairfield
1854, 4, 19. Martha B. m Sephthah GARNER
1858, 11, 24. Emily T. m Eli HAINES

McPHERSON, continued
1860, 11, 19. Isebelle d bur Fairfield
----, --, --. Isaac B. m Rebecca Jane CRAWFORD dt Joseph & Margaret, b 1843,9,10
Ch: Elcie O. b 1864, 12, 5
Walter " 1867, 6, 27
Linley M. " 1869, 5, 24
William C. " 1873, 6, 27
1868, 2, 20. Phebe A. m Jesse PEELLE
----, --, --. Marion & Mary E.
Ch: Cora Ann b 1869, 1, 3
Edna J.
George W.
Almeda " 1878, 2, 20
Bertha " 1881, 7, 27
Ethel " 1884, 10, 4
1873, 10, 27. Stephen d ae 74 bur Fairfield
1875, 2, 22. Ruth d bur Fairfield
1876, 5, 8. Stella, dt Jesse & Angeline, b
1877, 9, 20. Walter R., s Joshiah & Martha Esther, b
----, --, --. Josiah, s Stephen & Mary, b 1831,11,10; m Esther DAVIS, dt Jordan & Phebe, b 1849,2,10
Dt: Edna b 1891, 2, 3

1814, 11, 26. Daniel & w, Mary, & ch, Sarah, Ruth, Daniel, Stephen, John, Charlotte, Joseph Merrab, Rachel & Benjamin, rocf Mt. Pleasant MM, Va., dtd 1814,8,27
1829, 12, 26. Jane Barick (form McPherson) dis mcd
1830, 4, 24. William dis disunity
1831, 1, 29. John dis disunity
1831, 8, 25. Merab dis
1831, 12, 22. Joseph gct Clear Creek MM, to m Ruth Carey
1832, 4, 26. Ruth rocf Clear Creek MM
1833, 3, 21. Joseph & w, Ruth, gct Clear Creek MM
1837, 1, 26. Benjamin dis mcd
1840, 3, 26. Ruth & Grace dis disunity
1846, 5, 16. John recrq
1846, 5, 16. Maria recrq
1846, 7, 18. Julian, William, Joseph, John, Mariam, Isaac Bourd & Phebe, ch John & Mariah, recrq
1847, 9, 18. Hannah G. recrq
1847, 10, 16. Julian Johnson (form McPherson) con mcd
1849, 6, 16. Louisa Hiatt (form McPherson) con mcd
1857, 2, 21. William P. (or C.) gct Spring Creek MM, Ia.
1858, 5, 15. Joseph gct Westfield MM, Ind.
1858, 9, 18. Joseph C. gct Spring Creek MM, Ia.
1859, 6, 18. Josiah con mcd
1859, 6, 18. Edna (form Terrell) con mcd
1860, 1, 21. Anna Cumpton (form McPherson) con mcd
1860, 6, 16. Josiah & w, Edna, gct Newberry MM
1865, 6, 17. Isaac B. con mcd
1867, 5, 18. Ruth G. con mcd
1868, 3, 21. Marion con mcd
1868, 4, 18. Mary Amney West (form McPherson) con mcd
1868, 9, 19. Josiah & s, Carey, rocf Newberry MM, dtd 1868,5,18
1869, 4, 17. John W. gct White Water MM, Ind.
1870, 2, 19. Benjamin & Rachel recrq
1870, 2, 19. Harrison & Joseph H. recrq of parents, Benjamin & Rachel
1870, 2, 19. Rebecca Jane & Nancy Jane recrq
1870, 3, 19. William & Mary recrq
1870, 3, 19. Lydia E. & Emaline recrq
1870, 6, 18. Mary E. rocf Wabash MM, dtd 1868,6,11
1878, 4, 20. Angie & ch relrq
1878, 4, 20. Jesse dis
1880, 1, 17. Mary M., Morris M., Ruth Anna & Jane, minors, rocf Newberry MM, dtd 1879,10,20
1881, 9, 17. Marion gct Rose Hill MM, Kans.
1884, 7, 19. Annie gct Clear Creek MM, O.
1884, 7, 19. Rachel gct Clear Creek MM, O.
1885, 2, 22. Elsie O. relrq
1887, 9, 17. Joseph H. gct Dover MM
1897, 2, 20. Emiline gct Wilmington MM
1900, 6, 16. George gct Caesar's Creek MM
1902, 11, 15. Walter dropped from mbrp
1902, 11, 15. Theresa dropped from mbrp
1904, 3, 19. Roscoe recrq
1908, 3, 21. Ella & ch, Harry Maxwell & Catherine M., recrq
1909, 3, 20. Darnie Mae recrq
1909, 9, 18. Walter recrq
1910, 6, 18. Harrison relrq
1911, 12, 16. Walter R. & w, Ella, & ch, Maxwell, Katharine & Carey Ellis, gct Whittier MM, Calif.
1923, 4, 5. Walter relrq

McVEY
----, --, --. Neuman Isaac, s Isaac & Martha, b 1867,5,17; m Josephine BARRETT
Ch: Harold b 1897, 4, 25
Herbert " 1899, 9, 28
Kenneth
Adrian " 1906, 12, 16
----, --, --. Noah Alva, s Isaac & Martha, b 1866,2,7; m Cora -----
Ch: Mildred b 1898, 1, 28
Helen
Anita " 1907, 9, 25

1870, 12, 17. Ruth recrq
1872, 6, 15. Irving M. recrq
1873, 3, 15. Alcina recrq
1873, 3, 15. Ina, Turner, William & Franklin, ch William I. & Alcina, recrq
1874, 1, 17. Isaac & w, Martha, & dt, Mabel, recrq
1874, 1, 17. Clara E., Frank S., Alfred J., Noah A., Isaac N., Minnie M. & Sarah U.,

McVEY, continued
ch Martha & Isaac, recrq
1890, 12, 20. Alfred I. gct Clear Creek MM
1895, 12, 21. N. Alva & Newman I. gct Clear Creek MM
1898, 10, 15. Newman & w, Josephine, & ch, Harold, rocf Clear Creek MM
1900, 1, 20. Alva & w, Cora, & ch, Mildred, rocf Clear Creek MM
1900, 2, 17. Ruth gct Springfield MM
1907, 2, 16. Burlie D. relrq
1908, 9, 19. F. L. relrq
1914, 7, 18. Warren recrq
1917, 2, 17. James P. recrq
1922, 4, 13. Vernon & Thelma recrq
1927, 2, 3. Mary B. rocf Wilmington MM

MACKLIN
1884, 5, 17. Newton & w, America, recrq
1893, 5, 20. Newton [Maclin] dropped from mbrp
1893, 5, 20. America [McLin] dropped from mbrp

MACY
1868, 10, 18. Samuel C. Cowgill gct Spiceland MM, Ind., to m Carolina Macy

MAGOON
1868, 3, 26. Mary E. m Joseph M. BARRETT

1863, 9, 19. Alfred rocf St. Albans MM, Maine, dtd 1863,7,21
1864, 1, 16. Mary E., Olive J., Josiah, William O., Parthena & Albert, ch Alfred, recrq
1864, 11, 19. Alfred & ch, Mary, Josiah, William, Parthena & Albert, gct Dover MM, O.
1865, 12, 16. Alfred & ch, Josiah, Parthenia & Albert, rocf Dover MM, dtd 1865,11,16
1868, 3, 21. William, s Alfred, rocf Dover MM, dtd 1868,2,13

MAN
1812, 2, 29. Joseph & w, Elizabeth, & ch, Aaron, Rhoda, John & Warner, rocf Farmington MM, N. Y., dtd 1811,6,27
1816, 8, 31. Elizabeth dis disunity
1817, 8, 30. Rhoda Boots (form Man) dis mcd
1821, 1, 27. Joseph dis disunity
1824, 1, 31. Warner [Mann] dis mcd
1830, 10, 30. Benjamin dis disunity
1835, 11, 26. Joseph gct White River MM, Ind.

MANIFOLD
1888, 10, 16. Samuel dropped from mbrp
1905, 4, 15. Samuel recrq

MARINE
1811, 5, 25. Cert rec for Jonathan from Piney Grove MM, S. C., dtd 1811,2,16, endorsed to White Water

MARSH
1871, 3, 18. James D. & Sarah recrq

MARTIN
1831, 6, 2. Elizabeth m Benjamin CAREY

1831, 3, 26. Elizabeth recrq
1871, 8, 19. Mary recrq
1871, 12, 16. John [Martins] recrq
1896, 1, 18. Minnie & Elizabeth recrq
1921, 10, 5. Frank P. & w, Pearl E., rocf Cleveland MM, O.
1922, 4, 13. Ruby recrq
1923, 10, 4. Frank P. & w, Pearl E., gct Dayton MM, O.

MARVIN
1844, 8, 17. Matilda (form Johnson) dis mcd

MATTHEWS
1886, 7, 17. Maggie [Mathews] recrq
1898, 4, 16. Maggie dropped from mbrp
1911, 6, 17. Myrtle dropped from mbrp

MEEKER
1871, 3, 18. Lydia recrq

MENDENHALL
1847, 7, 17. Milly W. (form Johnson) con mcd
1848, 11, 18. Moses & ch, William & Joseph, rocf White Lick MM, Ind., dtd 1848,9,13
1849, 12, 15. Moses & w, Milly W., & ch, William & Joseph, gct Pleasant Plain MM, Ia.

MERCER
1875, 4, 17. Sylvester recrq
1882, 7, 15. Jason & w rocf Center MM, dtd 1882,6,14
1883, 11, 17. Sylvester relrq
1886, 1, 16. Theodore recrq
1888, 7, 21. Eunice Emily gct Green Castle MM, Kans.
1889, 2, 16. Jason & w, Mary, gct Clear Creek MM
1893, 10, 21. Theodore gct Clear Creek MM
1913, 9, 20. Theodore, Jane & Anna rocf Clear Creek MM

MERCHANT
1851, 3, 15. Isaac recrq
1869, 7, 17. Isaac [Marchant] con mcd
1873, 4, 19. Louisa recrq
1883, 11, 17. Isaac dropped from mbrp

MERRILL
1873, 8, 16. William recrq
1874, 5, 16. Frances recrq

MICHAEL
1917, 2, 17. Phoebe [Michaels] dropped from mbrp
1928, 6, 5. Harold Jr. & Emily rec as associate mbr

MICHAEL, continued
1931, 2, 12. Nina relrq

MICHENER
1871, 3, 18. Joseph recrq

MILLER
1857, 9, 23. Zador, s Isaac & Martha, Clermont Co., O.; m at Fairfield, Emily HODSON dt John & Rebecca, Highland Co., O.

1808, 4, 30. Ann & Sarah rocf South River MM, Va., dtd 1808,1,9
1809, 3, 29. John & s, Joshua, rocf Plainfield MM, dtd 1808,10,22
1816, 5, 25. John & w, Margaret, & ch, Joshua, Elizabeth, Mary, Rebeckah, Thomas & Jane, gct Ceasars Creek MM
1817, 9, 27. Susannah rocf Fall Creek MM, dtd 1817,8,23
1833, 8, 22. Susanna dis disunity
1858, 12, 18. Emily H. gct Clear Creek MM
1869, 9, 18. Isabelle recrq
1872, 7, 20. Hiram recrq
1873, 5, 17. Dora recrq

MILLS
----, --, --. Daniel & Elizabeth
Ch: Keziah b 1809, 2, 26
Sarah " 1810, 11, 22
Thomas " 1813, 1, 24
Ames " 1814, 11, 26
1809, 3, 28. Elizabeth m Joseph COOK
1811, 1, 30. Sarah m John HODGSON
----, --, --. James m Orpha BERRY
Ch: J. Oscar b 1887, 4, 14; m Lelia HILL
Roscoe " 1888, 7, 16

1808, 2, 27. Elizabeth rocf New Garden MM, dtd 1807,8,29, endorsed by Center MM
1808, 3, 26. Richard rocf Deep Creek MM, N. C., dtd 1806,9,6
1810, 5, 26. Richard gct Center MM, to m
1812, 5, 30. Nancy rocf Center MM, dtd 1812, 1,4
1816, 3, 30. Richard & w, Nancy, & ch, Elizabeth, Jemima & Rachel, gct New Garden MM, Ind.
1817, 6, 28. Daniel & w, Elizabeth, & ch, Hezekiah, Sarah, Thomas, Maris & Lavena, gct New Garden MM, Ind.
1902, 2, 15. Oscar recrq
1905, 4, 15. Lewis V. recrq
1905, 4, 15. Roscoe recrq
1905, 4, 15. Mrs. Christina recrq
1913, 2, 15. Lewis G. & w, Christina, relrq

MILNER
1827, 6, 8. Luke d bur Fairfield
1828, 9, 22. Anna d ae 68 bur Fairfield
1836, 7, 8. Mary E., dt Robert & Rebecca Denny, b
1840, 6, 25. Sarah d ae 60 bur at family gr. yd.
1843, 1, 11. Beverly d ae 86 bur Fairfield
1853, 10, 8. Amos d ae 60 bur Fairfield
----, --, --. Fremont Beverly, s Alfred & Nancy E., b 1862,10,25; m Ella W. WALKER, dt Benj. & Margaret, b 1865,3,29
Ch: Alfred W. b 1893, 4, 7
Clyde Alonzo " 1899, 8, 2
Arthur Hackney " 1902, 6, 14
Howard Edwin " 1906, 11, 2
Chas. Fremont " 1909, 8, 18

1808, 4, 30. Beverly [Milliner] & s, Beverly, Amos, Joseph, John, Oliver & Luke, rocf South River MM, Va., dtd 1808,1,9
1809, 2, 25. R. Dudley [Milliner] rocf Plainfield MM, dtd 1808,9,24
1809, 2, 25. Mary & dt, Anne Katy & Ruth, rocf Plainfield MM, dtd 1808,9,24
1809, 3, 25. Margaret [Millner] & dt, Elizabeth, rocf Plainfield MM, dtd 1808,10,22
1814, 5, 28. Robert D. [Milliner] dis disunity
1815, 6, 24. Beverly [Milliner] Jr. dis mcd
1815, 6, 24. Hannah (form Wright) dis mcd
1818, 10, 31. Sarah Anderson (form Milner) dis mcd
1824, 1, 31. John con mcd
1824, 5, 29. Joseph dis mcd
1824, 10, 30. Oliver dis disunity
1829, 8, 29. John dis disunity
1829, 11, 28. Beverly con mcd
1829, 11, 28. Mary & ch, Anna Katherine Ruth Rachel & Josiah gct White Lick MM, Ind.
1832, 12, 20. Amos gct Sugar River MM, Ind.
1834, 7, 24. Sarah recrq
1843, 11, 23. Amos rocf Sugar River MM, Ind., dtd 1843,7,29
1870, 3, 19. Thomas recrq
1870, 3, 19. Nancy E. recrq
1870, 3, 19. Robert D., John A., Clary E., Rebecca S., Fremont B. & Louisa F., ch Nancy E., recrq of mother
1871, 7, 15. Michal J. rocf Kokomo MM, Ind., dtd 1871,5,10
1883, 4, 21. Sally & Ruth A. recrq
1887, 9, 17. Sallie relrq
1890, 4, 19. Sallie recrq
1892, 10, 19. Ella recrq
1893, 6, 17. Maud recrq
1894, 3, 17. Moses S. & Frank recrq
1896, 7, 18. Robert D. & John A. dropped from mbrp
1901, 3, 16. Henry recrq
1902, 1, 18. Mary Ann recrq
1902, 10, 18. Fremont B. & w, Ella, & ch, Alfred, Clyde & infant s rocf Hickory Valley MM, Tenn.

MILNER, continued
1912, 9, 21. Frank P. & w, Ann, & ch, Harry & Willis, gct Hopewell MM
1914, 1, 17. Rachel E. gct Hopewell MM

MITCHELL
1896, 5, 16. Jesse recrq

MOFFITT
1800, --, --. Hugh d early in 1800
1807, 12, 10. Hannah m Aaron HUNT

1809, 10, 28. Jeremiah [Moffit] rocf Cane Creek MM, dtd 1809,9,2
1810, 3, 24. Ruth [Moffit] rocf Cane Creek MM, N. C., dtd 1809,5,6
1812, 11, 28. Solomon [Moffett] recrq
1815, 1, 28. Solomon gct Lick Creek MM, Ind.

MONTJOY
1837, 11, 23. Bathsheba (form Pope) dis mcd

MOON
1808, 11, 26. Daniel & s, Joseph, William, Richard, Jeremiah, Samuel & John, rocf Lost Creek MM, dtd 1808,9,30
1808, 11, 26. Ruth rocf Lost Creek MM, Tenn., dtd 1808,7,30
1810, 6, 30. Joseph rocf Lost Creek MM, dtd 1809,5,27
1813, 2, 27. Mary (form Ellis) dis mcd
1819, 10, 30. Anna (form Ellis) dis mcd
1843, 10, 26. Lydia (form Wright) con mcd
1845, 12, 20. Levi Barrett gct Newberry MM, to m Delila Moon
1849, 4, 21. Jacob recrq
1849, 12, 15. Margaret Ellen & Aaron, ch Jacob & Lydia, recrq
1850, 10, 19. Jacob & w, Lydia, & ch, Margaret Ellin, Aaron & Edward, gct Pleasant Plain MM, Ia.
1871, 3, 18. Ella recrq
1874, 7, 18. Lydia E. gct Newberry MM

MOONEY
1844, 10, 22. James d ae 77 bur Walnut Creek
1857, 12, 23. Catherine, w James, d ae 93 bur Walnut Creek

1811, 5, 25. Catherine recrq
1817, 4, 26. Phebe recrq
1822, 7, 27. Catherine, Polly & James, ch Catherine, recrq
1824, 5, 29. Phebe Cockerell (form Mooney) con mcd
1829, 1, 31. Catherine Doster (form Mooney) con mcd
1832, 12, 20. James dis mcd & jas
1833, 4, 25. James Sr. recrq
1848, 7, 15. Mary Doster (form Mooney) con mcd

MOORE
1811, 4, 27. Joseph con mcd
1811, 11, 30. Ann [Moor] & ch, Sarah, Rachel & Phebe, recrq
1811, 12, 28. Samuel, Lindley & Joseph [Moor], s Anna, recrq
1812, 1, 25. Rachel [Moor] recrq
1813, 4, 24. Rachel King (form More) dis mcd
1818, 6, 27. Margaret (form Pike) con mcd
1828, 12, 27. Margaret gct New Garden MM, Ind.
1870, 12, 17. Taylor & Harriet [More] recrq
1870, 12, 17. Louiza & Susan recrq
1877, 3, 17. Emma recrq
1877, 5, 19. Nancy recrq
1907, 4, 20. Kittie dropped from mbrp

MOORMAN
1816, 1, 31. Nancy m John OVERMAN
1817, 1, 29. William, s Charles & Elizabeth, Highland Co., O.; m at Fairfield, Kitty Winstone JOHNSON, dt Joseph & Agatha, Highland Co., O.
Ch: Joseph
Watkins b 1818, 1, 19
Collins " 1819, 9, 16
Emmily " 1821, 12, 19
Nancy " 1824, 8, 31
Elizabeth " 1827, 4, 20
Edwin " 1832, 10, 25
William
Thomas " 1835, 3, 20
Mary Agness" 1837, 12, 15
Lydia Ann " 1837, 12, 16
John Winston " 1841, 7, 10
1821, 2, 19. Collins d bur Fairfield
1822, 10, 30. Elizabeth m Watkins JOHNSON
1823, 10, 3. Charles d bur James Johnson's on Fall Creek
1827, 4, 30. Elizabeth d bur James Johnson's
1832, 10, 25. Edwin d bur James Johnson's
1842, 12, 28. Emily m Addison JOHNSON

1808, 3, 26. Africai rocf South River MM, dtd 1808,5,9
1808, 3, 26. Chiles, Thomas, James & Charles [Morman], s Thomas & Africa, rocf South River MM, Va., dtd 1807,5,9
1808, 3, 26. Micajah [Morman] & s, Thomas, rocf South River MM, Va., dtd 1807,10,10
1808, 3, 26. Susanna & dt, Africai, rocf South River MM, dtd 1807,10,10
1808, 3, 26. Charles [Mormon] & s, William & Robert, rocf South River MM, dtd 1806, 9,13
1808, 3, 26. Betsy & dt, Nancy, Fanny, Betsy & Agathy, rocf South River MM, dtd 1806,9,13
1810, 5, 26. Affrica gct Center MM
1810, 5, 26. Childas [Morman] gct Center MM
1810, 8, 25. Micajah [Morman] gct Center MM
1810, 9, 29. Susanna gc
1811, 6, 29. Cert rec for Uriah [Morman] &

MOORMAN, continued
fam from Piney Grove MM, S. C., dtd 1811,4, 20, endorsed to White Water MM
1811, 6, 29. Cert rec for Hannah & dt, Maris, from Piney Grove MM, S. C., dtd 1811,4,20, endorsed to White Water MM
1811, 6, 29. Zachariah [Morman] & gr s, Eli, rocf Piney Grove MM, S. C., dtd 1811,4,20
1811, 6, 29. Mary & dt, Susannah, rocf Piney Grove MM, S. C., dtd 1811,4,20
1812, 1, 25. Zachariah [Morman] & fam gct White Water MM
1812, 1, 25. Mary & dt, Susannah, gct White Water MM
1821, 9, 29. Robert dis disunity
1824, 3, 27. Agatha Johnson (form Moorman) dis mcd
1827, 9, 29. Thomas gct Fall Creek MM
1830, 6, 26. Susannah Ballard (form Moorman) dis mcd
1831, 8, 25. Ursala (form Butler) con mcd
1832, 4, 26. Ursala gct Cherry Grove MM, Ind.
1833, 5, 23. Nancy (form Johnson) dis mcd
1842, 3, 24. Joseph dis mcd
1845, 11, 15. William & fam gct Pleasant Plain MM, Ia.
1845, 11, 15. Elizabeth gct Pleasant Plain MM
1845, 11, 15. Nancy gct Pleasant Plain MM, Ia.
1846, 5, 16. John T. & w, Mary, & ch, Childers E., Malinda, William H. & Chiles, rocf Fall Creek MM, dtd 1846,4,20
1846, 5, 16. Lydia rocf Fall Creek MM, dtd 1846,4,20
1849, 8, 18. John T. & w, Mary, & ch, Childress E., Malinda, William H., Chiles & Sarah, gct Pleasant Plain MM, Ia.
1850, 7, 20. Lydia gct Pleasant Plain MM, Ia.
1852, 10, 16. Jesse rocf Dover MM, dtd 1852,7, 15
1859, 2, 19. Jesse dis mcd
1870, 8, 20. Nancy recrq

MORGAN
1826, 5, 3. David B., s Hugh & Judith, Highland Co., O.; m at Fairfield, Grace WILLIAMS, dt Enion & Martha, Highland Co.,O.
1831, 10, 7. Judith d ae 63 bur Fairfield
1834, 1, 23. Hugh d ae 69 bur Fairfield

1809, 11, 25. David rocf Plainfield MM, dtd 1808,4,23
1809, 11, 25. Elizabeth [Morgin] & dt, Hannah, rocf Plainfield MM, O., dtd 1808,4,23
1809, 11, 25. Jonathan, Isaac & Asa, s Elizabeth, rocf Plainfield MM, dtd 1808,4,23
1813, 5, 29. David gct Miami MM
1814, 8, 27. Elizabeth & three s gct Cesars Creek MM
1824, 4, 24. Hugh & w, Judith, & s, David Bruce, Gerrard Johnson & John Watkins, rocf South River MM, Va., dtd 1823,9,13, endorsed by White Water MM, Ind.
1829, 3, 28. David B. dis jH
1829, 3, 28. Grace dis jH
1830, 4, 24. John W. dis disunity
1830, 8, 28. Gerrard J. dis jH
1832, 4, 26. Elizabeth (form Thornburg) dis mcd
1844, 8, 17. Plato, s David B., gct Cincinnati MM

MORRIS
1835, 4, 30. James, s Isaac & Millicent, Clinton Co., O.; m at Lees Creek, Elizabeth HANES, dt Enos & Mary, Highland Co., O.

Ch:		
John	b	1837, 8, 7
Mary	"	1839, 4, 26
Enos	"	1840, 10, 22
Isaac	"	1842, 12, 29
Isaiah	"	1844, 12, 1
Jeremiah	"	1846, 5, 1
Sarah Ann	"	1848, 3, 25
Mahlon	"	1849, 10, 20
Eleanor	"	1851, 9, 25
Lydia	"	1852, 4, 28(?)
Martha	"	1855, 2, 21
James	"	1856, 6, 28

James m 2nd Hannah -----

Ch:		
Charley	b	1863, 2, 25
Wilson	"	1865, 10, 26

James m 3rd 1870,9,22 at Oak Grove, Hannah G. LADD, dt Daniel & Anna McPHERSON, Highland Co., O.

Ch: Walter E. b 1872, 8, 26

1843, 3, 3. Isaac, s James, d bur Fairfield
1844, 8, 1. John, s James, d bur Fairfield
1849, 7, 13. Sarah Ann, dt James, d bur Fairfield
----, --, --. Jonathan & Serepta

Ch:		
Emmet	b	1863, 2, 25
Minta	"	1878, 6, 19

1864, 1, 13. Lydia d bur Fairfield
----, --, --. Enos, s James & Elizabeth, b 1840,10,27; m Elizabeth MORRISON, dt John & Jane, b 1840,12,30

Ch:		
Emma	b	1864, 12, 2
Alonzo	"	1868, 3, 11

1835, 1, 22. James acknowledged a mbr; Mt. Pleasant MM, Va. had been laid down & a cert was not available
1839, 2, 21. David con mcd
1857, 9, 19. Mary Pavy (form Morris) dis mcd
1862, 4, 19. James gct Center MM, to m Hannah Whinery
1862, 9, 20. Hannah & ch, Albert & Sarah Whinery, rocf Center MM, dtd 1862,8,13
1866, 1, 20. Enos con mcd
1866, 8, 18. Jonathan recrq
1866, 8, 18. Sarepta, w Jonathan, recrq
1866, 8, 18. Jane, Emmit & Mary, ch Jonathan, recrq
1867, 7, 20. Isaiah con mcd
1868, 11, 21. Ruth rocf Newberry MM, dtd 1868,9,21

MORRIS, continued
1870, 3, 19. Lucinda recrq
1870, 3, 19. William P. recrq
1870, 6, 18. Caroline recrq
1870, 6, 18. Emma R., Bennajah R., Willard, Ruth M. & Flora Jane, ch William R. & Catherine, recrq of parents
1870, 6, 18. Lavina recrq
1870, 7, 16. Zachariah recrq
1870, 10, 15. Elizabeth recrq
1870, 10, 15. Emma, dt Enos & Elizabeth, recrq
1871, 7, 15. Mahlon con mcd
1871, 7, 15. Sarah con mcd
1871, 12, 16. Zachariah gct Spring Creek MM,Ia.
1872, 7, 20. Mary recrq
1877, 9, 15. Isaiah relrq
1879, 6, 21. Benjamin F. & ch, Effa J., William E. & Henry J., rocf Mississinew MM, Ind., dtd 1879,6,11
1879, 12, 20. Benjamin & w, Lydia M., & ch, Effie J. & William E., gct Poplar Run MM, Ind.
1881, 1, 15. Zadoc recrq
1882, 10, 21. Hannah & s gct Argonia MM, Kans.
1883, 9, 15. Jennie B. rocf Clear Creek MM
1884, 3, 15. Jeremiah gct Center MM
1885, 7, 17. Ruth dropped from mbrp
1885, 7, 17. Sarah relrq
1888, 12, 15. Benjamin F. & w, Lydia, & dt, Alvaretta, rocf Farmland MM, Ind.
1892, 1, 16. Benjamin F. & w, Lydia Maria, & ch, Alvaretta & Albert, gct Wilmington MM, O.
1893, 5, 20. Wilson & Dennie dropped from mbrp
1895, 3, 16. Luretta & James & w, Jennie, relrq
1897, 4, 17. Ruth recrq
1898, 10, 15. Ruth gct Wilmington MM, O.
1908, 3, 21. Jonathan's d rpd
1908, 4, 18. Eldo relrq
1920, 7, 28. Alonzo gct Sabina MM
1927, 1, 6. Edith Thornburg relrq

MORRISON
----, --, --. Thomas W. & Mary Atlantic
Ch: Alson W.
John Q. b 1875, 11, 3

1845, 10, 18. Priscilla recrq
1861, 2, 16. Mary Atlantic (form Smith) con mcd
1869, 6, 19. Thomas W. & ch, Jennie & Gilbert Gurey, recrq
1870, 2, 19. John W. recrq
1871, 3, 18. Priscilla Glascock (form Morrison) con mcd

MORSE
1825, 7, 30. Gershom Perdue gct Goshen MM, to m Abigail Morse

MOSS
1871, 5, 20. Mary J. recrq

MURDOCK
1855, 1, 9. Juliet d bur Fall Creek

1854, 10, 21. Juliet (form Huff) con mcd

MYERS
1830, 12, 29. Samuel [Myres], s Samuel & Ollah, Clinton Co., O.; m at Fairfield, Priscilla CHALFONT, dt William & Ruth, Highland Co., O.
1837, 2, 22. William H., s Samuel & Priscilla, b
1869, 6, 13. Biola Gertrude, dt William H., b
1870, 3, 19. John [Meyers] recrq
1870, 3, 19. Ellen recrq
1870, 3, 19. Charles William Henry [Meyers], s John & Elen, recrq of parents
1870, 11, 19. Nancy rocf Newberry MM, dtd 1870,9,19
1878, 10, 19. John & Ellen dropped from mbrp
1886, 7, 17. John & Mary J. recrq
1889, 3, 16. Zebedee & George [Meyers] recrq
1898, 4, 16. William dropped from mbrp
1898, 4, 16. Zeb dropped from mbrp
1901, 3, 16. George C. & Sarah J. [Myres] recrq
1901, 11, 15. George Jr. relrq
1904, 2, 20. George & w, Sarah J., gct Hopewell MM

MURRY
1902, 11, 15. Lindley dropped from mbrp

NANCE
1850, 7, 20. Sarah recrq
1861, 8, 17. Lydia & dt, Laura, recrq

NAYLOR
1919, 3, 15. Gladys Cox relrq

NELSON
1879, 1, 18. Elizabeth rocf Wilmington MM, dtd 1878,12,20
1902, 11, 15. Elizabeth dropped from mbrp

NEWBRY
1915, --, --. Kenneth Lloyd, s Lee & Stella, b
1913, 7, 19. Lee & w, Stella, & s, Harrold, recrq

NEWBY
1811, 8, 31. Esther & dt, Rachel, rocf Mt. Pleasant MM, dtd 1810,11,24
1811, 9, 28. Nathan & s, Joseph, Thomas, Robert, Isaac & William, rocf Mt. Pleasant MM, Va., dtd 1810,11,24
1812, 11, 28. Josiah rocf Back Creek MM, N.C.,

NEWBY, continued
dtd 1811,11,26
1812, 11, 28. Elizabeth rocf Back Creek MM, N. C., dtd 1812,10,26
1814, 4, 30. Elizabeth Farrington (form Newby) con mcd
1815, 9, 30. Josiah dis
1816, 11, 30. Nathan & w, Esther, & ch, Joseph, Thomas, Robert, Isaac, Rachel & Nathan, gct Blue River MM, Ind.
1818, 6, 27. Cert rec for William & fam from Back Creek MM, N. C., dtd 1817,8,30, endorsed to Fall Creek MM
1870, 2, 19. Lucinda recrq

NEWELL
1871, 3, 18. Lewis [Newel] recrq
1871, 3, 18. Emma B., Ulysses & Cary Jane recrq
1871, 3, 18. Carrie J. recrq
1880, 6, 19. Lewis & fam gct Wilmington MM,O.

NEWLIN
1861, 11, 21. Eli, s John & Esther, Clinton Co., O.; m at Hardins Creek, Lydia BARRETT dt Levi & Susannah, Highland Co., O.

1862, 1, 18. Lydia B. gct Newberry MM

NIXON
1809, 3, 1. Mary m George HODGSON

1808, 5, 28. Mary & dt, Rachel, rocf Deep Creek MM, N. C., dtd 1808,3,5
1808, 7, 30. William rocf Deep Creek MM, N. C., dtd 1808,4,2
1808, 7, 30. Elizabeth rocf Deep Creek MM, N. C., dtd 1808,4,2

NORDYKE
1834, 12, 31. Jesse, s Micajah & Charity, Highland Co., O.; m Lavina HUNT, dt Josiah & Mary, Highland Co., O.
Ch: Albert H. b 1835, 10, 20
Mary E. " 1837, 4, 21
Calvin J. " 1840, 1, 18
Sary Emly " 1841, 12, 21
Linley M. " 1844, 6, 5
Hannah Ellen " 1847, 1, 26
Harvey D. " 1848, 12, 29
Ellwood " 1851, 4, 15
1852, 4, 4. Elwood, s Jesse, d bur Fairfield

1808, 12, 31. Hiram [Noridyke] con mcd
1830, 7, 31. Jesse rocf Clear Creek MM, dtd 1830,5,8
1834, 4, 24. Jesse gct Clear Creek MM
1836, 2, 25. Jesse rocf Clear Creek MM, dtd 1836,2,23
1843, 7, 20. Clear Creek MM was given permission to rst Eunice
1854, 8, 19. Jesse & w, Levina, & ch, Albert H., Mary Elizabeth, Calvin J., Sarah Emily, Linley M., Hannah Ellen, Harvey D. & Aaron B., gct Richland MM, Ia.

OAKLEY
1819, 11, 3. George, s William & Frances, Warren Co., O.; m at Fairfield, Katherine BORUM, dt John & Judith, Highland Co.,O.

OGBORN
1849, 11, 17. Henry M., minor, rocf Springfield MM, dtd 1849,9,15
1859, 1, 15. Henry [Ogburn] dis mcd
1868, 11, 21. Henry recrq
1868, 11, 21. Eliza recrq
1868, 11, 21. Dicy Ella, Matilda A., Florence C. & Pamelia F., ch Eliza & Henry M., recrq

OLDHAM
1829, 6, 27. Anne (form Warner) dis mcd

OREN
1812, 7, 29. John, s Joseph & Abigail, Clinton Co., O.; m at Fairfield, Lydia LADD, dt Gerrard & Sarah, Highland Co., O.

1812, 11, 28. Lydia gct Center MM
1870, 2, 19. Laura E. con mcd
1878, 9, 21. Mary, Sarah Ann & Susan rocf Center MM, dtd 1878,6,12

OSBURN
1811, 7, 27. John [Ozbun] & s, John, rocf Center MM, N. C., dtd 1811,4,20
1811, 7, 27. Mary rocf Center MM, N. C., dtd 1811,4,20
1811, 7, 27. Sarah & dt, Susanna & Elizabeth, rocf Center MM, N. C., dtd 1811,4,20
1813, 4, 24. Cert rec for Daniel [Ozbun] & w, Mourning, & s, Exum, from Center MM, N. C., dtd 1812,4,18, endorsed to Clear Creek MM

OVERMAN
----, --, --. Zebulon & Mary
Ch: Dempsey b 1783, 9, 24
Mary " 1789, 1, 22
Enoch " 1792, 10, 29
Elias " 1794, 12, 11
John " 1797, 5, 18
Nathan " 1799, 11, 21
Anna " 1803, 3, 25
1816, 1, 31. John, s Zebulon & Mary, Highland Co., O.; m at Fairfield, Nancy MOORMAN, dt Charles & Elizabeth, Highland Co., O.
1841, 10, 20. Obadiah d ae 93 bur Fall Creek

1810, 7, 28. Nancy recrq
1816, 7, 27. Nancy gct Fall Creek MM
1830, 4, 24. Sally H. (form Johnson) dis mcd
1869, 1, 16. Alfred Hadley gct Plainfield MM, Ind., to m Kezia K. Overman

OVERMAN, continued
1873, 5, 17. Vernon & Alva recrq
1873, 5, 17. William recrq

OWENS
1910, 12, 17. Maud relrq

PAINE
1907, 3, 16. Frank [Pain] recrq
1907, 4, 20. Lettie rocf Hopewell MM
1907, 11, 16. Frank & w, Letitia, gct Sabina MM

PAINTER
1853, 11, 21. David S., s Jacob & Naomi, Wabash Co., Ind.; m at Fairfield, Margaret F. GREEN, dt Isaac & Hannah, Clinton Co.,O.

1854, 2, 18. Margaret F. gct Wabash MM, Ind.
1866, 3, 17. Hampton W. Terrell gct Cesars Creek MM, to m Harriet M. Painter
1867, 7, 20. Mary recrq
1874, 3, 21. Sarah A. recrq

PARKER
1869, 5, 15. Lydia Ann (form Burgess) con mcd
1870, 2, 19. William & w recrq
1874, 2, 21. Adam recrq
1887, 11, 19. Isaac & w, Francis, gct Short Creek MM

PARR
1882, 3, 18. Andrew F. recrq
1883, 4, 21. Andrew recrq
1883, 4, 21. Lucinda A. recrq
1884, 5, 17. Mary recrq
1893, 5, 20. Andrew F. & Lucinda dropped from mbrp
1893, 5, 20. Mary dropped from mbrp
1896, 7, 18. Spencer & Alferd dropped from mbrp

PARRETT
1870, 6, 18. Silas & Huldah recrq
1870, 6, 18. Cora Bell, George & Elmer, ch Silas & Huldah, recrq

PARISHO
1815, 3, 25. Cert rec for James [Parrishro] & fam from Mt. Pleasant MM, Va., dtd 1814, 1,29, endorsed to Lick Creek MM, Ind.

PARSON
1811, 7, 27. Joshua rocf Westland MM, dtd 1810,10,27
1817, 10, 25. Ann rst by rq with consent of Westland MM
1817, 11, 29. Mary, Jacob, Samuel Jairus William & Margaret, ch Joshua, recrq
1820, 1, 29. Joshua & w, Ann, & ch, Mary, Jacob, Samuel James (Jarius?), William & Margaret, gct New Garden MM, Ind.
1833, 6, 20. Margaret Sidney & Elisha rocf White River MM

PATTERSON
1817, 6, 28. Cert rec for William from Deep Creek MM, N. C., dtd 1815,11,4, endorsed to Center MM
1887, 11, 19. Lucinda gct Short Creek MM

PATTON
1884, 9, 28. Esta Henderson, dt Chas. & Ella, b
----, --, --. J. E. & Lena [PATTEN]
Ch: Gladys b 1901, 9, 12
Wilbur " 1905, 5, 15

1872, 10, 19. James & w, Ruth, & ch, Mary Elizabeth, Sarah Arbelle, Euphema Alice, William T. Sherman, James M. & Seymore, recrq
1874, 2, 21. Susan recrq
1875, 2, 20. Warren J. recrq
1876, 5, 20. Hardenia Ellen recrq
1877, 5, 19. William recrq
1882, 4, 15. Sarah A. recrq
1882, 5, 20. William relrq
1884, 12, 20. Warren J. dis
1884, 12, 20. Sarah A. relrq
1901, 3, 16. Geo. Wm. & w, Drusilla, recrq
1906, 6, 16. Geo. Wm. & w, Drusilla, gct West Fork MM
1914, 4, 18. John & w, Lena, & ch, Gladys & Wilbur, recrq
1915, 2, 20. William H. [Patten] recrq

PAVEY
1857, 9, 19. Mary [Pavy] (form Morris) dis mcd
1907, 4, 20. Margaret E. recrq

PAXSON
1849, 10, 24. John, s John & Anna, Fayette Co., O.; m at Fairfield, Amy Eleanor SMITH, dt Louisa Reeder, Fayette Co., O.
----, --, --. Elias G. & Mary E.
Ch: Irena b 1872, 12, 13
Olie J. " 1874, 11, 8

1841, 8, 26. Elias Green gct Goshen MM, to m Achsah Paxson
1843, 7, 20. Reuben rocf Goshen MM, dtd 1843,5,20
1843, 8, 24. Jesse Green gct Goshen MM, to m Alice Paxson
1844, 5, 23. Alice Green (form Paxon), w Jesse, rocf Goshen MM, dtd 1844,3,16
1846, 6, 20. Reuben con mcd
1846, 6, 20. Sarah (form Green) con mcd
1847, 2, 19. Reuben gct Goshen MM
1847, 9, 18. Sarah [Paxon] gct Goshen MM
1849, 9, 15. John Jr. rocf Goshen MM, dtd 1849,8,18
1849, 12, 15. John [Paxon] & w, Anna, & ch, William & Asaph, rocf Goshen MM, dtd

PAXSON, continued
dtd 1849,10,20
1851, 7, 19. John & w, Anna, & s, Aseph H., gct Goshen MM
1852, 2, 21. William gct Goshen MM
1852, 4, 17. John Jr. & w, Amy Ellen, & ch, Eliza Ann, gct Goshen MM
1864, 7, 16. Reuben & w, Sarah, & ch, Rachel G., Elias G., James, John, Margaret Ann, Mary Jane, Jonathan G. & Ruth Alice, rocf Goshen MM, O., dtd 1864,5,21
1864, 10, 16. William rocf Goshen MM, dtd 1864,8,20
1864, 11, 19. Ruth G. [Paxton] & ch, Mary Ellen, Anna Elizabeth, Florence N. & Thomas F., rocf Green Plain MM, dtd 1864,9,14
1865, 4, 15. Reuben & w, Sarah, & ch, Rachel J., Elias G., James, John, Margaret Ann, Mary Jane, Jonathan P. & Ruth Alice, gct Newbury MM
1866, 1, 20. William & w, Ruth, & ch, Mary Ellen, Anna Elizabeth, Florence N. & Thomas F., gct Goshen MM, O.
1871, 3, 18. Elias G. rocf Newberry MM, dtd 1871,2,20
1872, 7, 20. Elias G. con mcd
1872, 7, 20. Mary E. con mcd
1873, 5, 17. Reuben [Paxton] & w, Sarah, & ch, Rachel G., John, Margaret A., Mary J., Jonathan G. & Ruth A.,rocf Newberry MM, dtd 1873,4,--
1881, 9, 17. Elias G. & w, Mary E., & ch, Irena B., Olie J., Sarah L. & Maud G., gct Rose Hill MM, Kans.
1881, 9, 17. Sarah, Rachel G., Margaret A. & Jonathan G., gct Rose Hill MM, Kans.
1881, 9, 17. Ruth A. gct Rose Hill MM, Kans.
1883, 11, 17. John [Paxton] dropped from mbrp

PEARCE
1851, 6, 21. Charles dis disunity

PEARSON
1813, 10, 30. John & w, Hannah, & ch, Joseph & Rebecca, rocf Mt. Pleasant MM, Va., dtd 1810,11,24
1814, 5, 28. Cert rec for Jonathan & William from Contentne MM, N. C., dtd 1814,2,12, endorsed to Clear Creek MM
1815, 7, 29. Cert rec for Mark & w from Fall Creek MM, endorsed to Centre MM
1818, 10, 31. John & w Hannah, & ch, Joseph, Rebecca, Asenath, Jesse & Hezekiah, gct Centre MM

PEELLE
1866, 2, 22. William, s John & Lydia, Clinton Co., O.; m at Oak Grove, Louisa HIATT, dt Stephen & Mary McPherson, Highland Co., O.
1868, 2, 20. Jesse, s William & Clarissa, Clinton Co., O.; m at Oak Grove, Phebe A. McPHERSON, dt John & Maria, Highland Co.,O.
1808, 9, 24. John [Peal] rocf Concord MM, O., dtd 1808,3,24
1808, 9, 24. Lydia [Peel] rocf Concord MM, dtd 1808,5,24
1866, 5, 19. Louisa gct Dover MM, O.
1868, 6, 20. Phebe A. gct Dover MM, O.
1895, 2, 16. Louisa [Peele] roc

PEITSMEYER
1856, 5, 22. Joseph, s Christian & Luiza, Ross Co., O.; m at Walnut Creek, Eliza L. PERDUE, dt Gershom & Abigail, Fayette Co., O.
Ch: Isaac Christian b 1858, 10, 25
Louisa Abigail " 1861, 7, 23
Mary Esther " 1863, 1, 18
Charles Gershom " 1864, 10, 20
Eliza Olivia " 1866, 6, 23
Joseph Morse " 1867, 9, 9
Grace Amy " 1870, 3, 21
Elizabeth Hannah " 1872, 1, 17
Anna Jane " 1873, 5, 7
1872, 10, 27. Anna d bur Walnut Creek

1850, 6, 15. Joseph [Peitsmeyre] rocf Baltimore MM, for Eastern & Western Districts, dtd 1850,2,7
1855, 2, 17. Charles rocf Baltimore MM for Eastern & Western Districts, dtd 1854,11,9
1858, 2, 21. Charles gct Clear Creek MM, to m Gulielma M. Sanders
1859, 1, 15. Gulielma rocf Clear Creek MM, dtd 1858,12,11
1861, 3, 16. Gulielma gct Miami MM
1866, 2, 17. Charles gct Miami MM
1868, 3, 21. Edward [Peitsmeyers] rocf 2 months mtg of friends held at Minden, in Prussia, dtd 1868,1,5
1868, 5, 16. Edward gct Clear Creek MM, O.
1869, 2, 20. Anna, Otto & Martha recrq of guardian, Joseph Peitsmeyer
1869, 2, 20. Emma D. McDonald recrq of guardian, Joseph Peitsmeyer

PENROSE
1888, 2, 18. Mary R. relrq

PERDUE
1815, 5, 3. Rebecca m Elisha COWGILL
----, --, --. Gershom & Elizabeth
Ch: Hannah b 1821, 12, 20
Gershom m 2nd Abigail -----
Ch: Elizabeth b 1827, 4, 4
Esther " 1829, 2, 11
Isaac " 1831, 3, 12
Jacob " 1831, 3, 12
Menton Pimm" 1833, 4, 28

PERDUE, Gershom & Abigail, continued
Ch: Eliza b 1835, 11, 22
Thomas
Kite " 1838, 7, 30
1822, 2, 22. Elizabeth, w Gershom, d bur Fairfield
1828, 7, 8. Elizabeth d bur Fairfield
1833, 8, 3. Jemima d ae 81 bur Fairfield
1856, 5, 22. Eliza L. m Joseph PEITSMYER
1857, 10, 11. Isaac, s Gershom, d bur Walnut Creek
1863, 1, 2. Gulielma d ae 85 bur Walnut Creek
1865, 3, 19. Stephen d ae 82 bur Walnut Creek
----, --, --. Thomas Kite & Jane
Ch: Whittier b 1869, 3, 19
Miriam " 1871, 1, 12
Edith " 1872, 12, 12

1813, 10, 30. Gershom rocf Goose Creek MM, Va., dtd 1813,9,2
1813, 10, 30. Jacob rocf Goose Creek MM, Va., dtd 1813,9,2
1813, 10, 30. Stephen rocf Goose Creek MM, Va., dtd 1813,9,2
1813, 11, 27. Jemimah & dt, Rebeckah, rocf Goose Creek MM, Va., dtd 1813,9,2
1815, 7, 29. Jacob gct Chester MM, Pa., to m
1815, 12, 30. Sarah rocf Chester MM, Pa., dtd 1815,11,27
1817, 12, 27. Jemima gct Center MM
1818, 8, 29. Jacob & w, Sarah, gct Chester MM, Pa.
1818, 10, 31. Gershom gct Miami MM, to m
1819, 5, 29. Elizabeth rocf Miami MM, dtd 1819,2,24
1822, 8, 31. Jemimah rocf Springfield MM, dtd 1822,4,27
1824, 4, 24. Gulielma rocf South River MM, Va., dtd 1823,12,13
1825, 7, 30. Gershom gct Goshen MM, to m Abigail Morse
1826, 1, 28. Abigail rocf Goshen MM, dtd 1825, 12,19
1840, 1, 23. Hannah gct Miami MM
1868, 7, 18. Thomas K. con mcd
1870, 11, 19. Jane M. recrq

PERRIN
1884, 1, 19. Elias recrq
1884, 1, 19. Riece E., s Elias, recrq
1890, 9, 20. Elias & Luchama dis
1910, 6, 18. Reece relrq

PERRY
1893, 5, 20. Fredona F. dropped from mbrp

PHELPS
1833, 2, 28. Eli [Felps], s John & Mariam, Highland Co., O.; m at Lees Creek, Charlotte CAREY, dt Jonathan & Ruth, Clinton Co., O.

1833, 11, 21. Eli & w gct Fairfield MM, Ind.
1836, 9, 22. Meriam & ch, Joel, Martin, Martha, John & Mary, gct Westfield MM, Ind.

PICKERING
----, --, --. William & Ruth
Ch: Sidney b 1824, 9, 7
John " 1827, 4, 6
Hannah " 1829, 6, 18
Rachel " 1831, 10, 30
1826, 2, 1. Elenor m James REES
1826, 3, 27. Jonathan d ae 65 bur Lees Creek

1817, 10, 25. Cert rec for Isaac from Hopewell MM, Va., dtd 1816,11,7, endorsed to Plainfield MM
1824, 4, 24. William & w, Ruth, & ch, David, Sary & Eleanor, rocf Hopewell MM, Va., dtd 1824,2,5, endorsed by Fall Creek MM
1824, 4, 24. David rocf Hopewell MM, Va., dtd 1824,2,5, endorsed by Fall Creek MM
1824, 4, 24. Jonathan Sr. rocf Hopewell MM, dtd 1824,2,5, endorsed by Fall Creek MM
1824, 4, 24. Jonathan Jr. rocf Hopewell MM, Va., dtd 1824,2,5, endorsed by Fall Creek MM
1824, 4, 24. Eleanor rocf Hopewell MM, Va., dtd 1824,1,8, endorsed by Fall Creek MM
1824, 4, 24. Lydia rocf Hopewell MM, Va., dtd 1824,1,8, endorsed by Fall Creek MM
1825, 11, 26. David dis
1826, 7, 29. William & w, Ruth, & ch, David, Sarah, Eleanor & Sidney, gct Lees Creek MM
1828, 7, 26. Jonathan gct Lees Creek MM
1828, 7, 26. Lydia gct Lees Creek MM
1840, 11, 26. William & w, Ruth, & ch, David, Sarah, Elenor, Sidney, John, Hannah, Rachel & Phebe, gct Salem MM, Ia.
1865, 9, 16. Sarah recrq

PICKETT
1800, --, --. William d early in 1800 bur at Dry Run or Salt Creek

1813, 12, 25. Cert rec for Rebecca from Mt. Pleasant MM, Va., dtd 1813,8,28, endorsed to Fall Creek MM

PIKE
1812, 12, 8. John, s William & Phebe, b
1812, 12, 15. Phebe d bur Clear Creek
1814, 2, 2. William, s Nathan & Elizabeth, Highland Co., O.; m at Fairfield, Lucy BUTLER, dt Samuel & Usala, Highland Co., O.
1822, 5, 8. Rachel m William STANBROUGH
1825, 6, 29. Abigail m John WRIGHT
1826, 8, 30. Samuel, s John & Leah, Highland Co., O.; m at Fairfield, Elizabeth C. POPE, dt Wm. & Grace, Highland Co., O.
Ch: Martha H. b 1827, 8, 5
William W. " 1829, 6, 6
1830, 3, 3. Ruth m Judah ROBERTS
1830, 12, 1. Elizabeth, w Samuel, d bur

PIKE, continued
Fairfield

1811, 11, 30. William & s, Nathan & Tristram, rocf Deep River MM, N. C., dtd 1811,8,5
1811, 10, 26. Phebe & dt, Abigail, rocf Deep River MM, N. C., dtd 1811,5,5
1814, 4, 30. Lucy gct Clear Creek MM
1817, 8, 30. Margaret rocf Fall Creek MM, dtd 1816,12,21
1818, 2, 28. Hannah (form Reams) con mcd
1818, 6, 27. Margaret Moore (form Pike) con mcd
1818, 8, 29. Hannah gct Lees Creek MM
1820, 5, 27. Rachel, Samuel, Abigail, Ruth & John, ch John, roc dtd 1820,4,22
1827, 3, 31. Cert rec for Hannah from Lees Creek MM, endorsed to Clear Creek MM
1828, 4, 26. Samuel dis disunity
1828, 4, 26. Hannah rocf Clear Creek MM, dtd 1828,4,12
1828, 5, 21. John recrq
1832, 10, 25. John [Pyke] & w, Hannah, & s, John, gct New Garden MM, Ind.

PITZER
1886, 3, 20. Albert, Clara, Lizzie, Anna & Ella recrq
1890, 9, 20. Albert, Clara, Lizzie, Annie & Ella dis

PLUMMER
1813, 10, 30. Asa & w, Grace, & ch, Eli, Jesse, Ezra, Tacy & Lot, rocf South River MM, Va., dtd 1813,8,14
1820, 8, 26. Asa dis disunity
1825, 4, 30. Eva, minor, gct Miami MM
1825, 10, 29. Tacy [Plumer] dis
1826, 12, 30. Eli dis disunity
1828, 6, 28. Jesse dis mcd
1831, 2, 26. Lot dis mcd
1831, 7, 21. Tacy rst by rq
1833, 7, 25. Mahala gct Springfield MM
1835, 7, 23. Tacy gct Miami MM
1837, 7, 20. Emily gct Cesars Creek MM
1840, 7, 23. Grace gct Miami MM

POFF
1873, 3, 15. James W. recrq
1874, 4, 18. Joseph D. & w, Sarah W., & ch, Rachel F. & Stephen W., recrq
1883, 11, 17. Luke, Rachel, James & Stephen dropped from mbrp

POLK
1861, 1, 19. Julia (form Hadley) con mcd
1862, 7, 19. Julia gct Clear Creek MM
1909, 9, 18. Addie recrq

POPE
----, --, --. William & Grace
Ch: Elizabeth b 1806, 3, 2
Bathsheba " 1814, 8, 12
Lewis J. b 1819, 10, 9
Alfred " 1822, 2, 10
Aquila " 1824, 8, 31
1826, 8, 30. Elizabeth L. m Samuel PIKE
1843, 7, 25. Lewis John d bur Fairfield
1844, 9, 2. William d ae 62 bur Fairfield

1809, 9, 30. Nathaniel & s, John, recrq
1812, 11, 28. Samuel rocf New Garden MM, N.C., dtd 1813,9,26
1830, 4, 24. Martha Hopkins (form Pope) dis mcd
1830, 4, 24. William Jr. dis disunity
1837, 11, 23. Bathsheba Montjoy (form Pope) dis mcd
1849, 9, 15. Grace gct Salem MM, Ia.
1850, 1, 19. Alfred gct Salem MM, Ia.
1850, 1, 19. Aquilla gct Salem MM, Ia.

POSTGAIT
1816, 12, 5. Thomas, s Charles & Rachel, Highland Co., O.; m at Lees Creek, Charity HAWORTH, dt James & Mary, Highland Co.,O.

1811, 12, 28. Mary [Postgate], dt John & Rachel Crispin, recrq
1811, 12, 28. Thomas, Charles & Isaac Postgait & Davis Crispin, s & step s of John Crispin, recrq

POWELL
1870, 6, 18. Susan E. recrq
1872, 4, 20. Thomas E. & w, Ura, rocf Newberry MM, dtd 1872,3,18
1883, 3, 17. Thomas E. [Powel] & w gct Cesars Creek MM
1896, 3, 21. Robert R. [Powel] recrq
1917, 10, 20. Gerald recrq

POWERS
1852, 4, 17. Mary (form Rains) dis mcd & jas

PRICE
1886, 7, 17. William recrq
1893, 5, 20. Wm. dropped from mbrp

PRIEST
----, --, --. Andrew & Cordelia
Ch: Mary Edith b 1888, 9, 30
Jacob Leslie " 1892, 11, 9
Raymond E. " 1894, 2, 11
Noble L. " 1898, 10, 10

1877, 2, 17. John D. & Amanda Jane recrq
1882, 3, 18. Andrew recrq
1883, 3, 18. Anna A. & Emma A. recrq
1883, 4, 21. Thomas & Laura recrq
1884, 10, 18. Alice dis
1884, 12, 22. Amanda J. relrq
1893, 5, 20. Thos. dropped from mbrp
1893, 5, 20. Anna & Emma dropped from mbrp
1898, 4, 16. John dropped from mbrp

PRIEST, continued
1898, 4, 16. Sadie dropped from mbrp
1901, 3, 16. Wm. M. recrq
1902, 11, 15. Amanda dropped from mbrp
1909, 9, 18. Cordelia dropped from mbrp
1911, 4, 15. Flora P., Andrew, William, George, John & Elias, relrq
1914, 4, 18. George & w, Margarite, & ch, Dean & Mildred, recrq
1914, 4, 18. William & w, Mamie, & ch, Herbert, recrq

PUCKETT
1809, 5, 27. Benjamin & s, James, Moses & Daniel, rocf Westfield MM, dtd 1809,4,8
1809, 5, 27. Catherine & dt, Elizabeth, Keziah, Mary & Phebe, rocf Westfield MM, dtd 1809,4,8
1877, 3, 17. Nathan [Pucket] recrq
1877, 3, 17. Nancy M. [Pucket] recrq
1878, 9, 21. Taylor & w, Jane, & ch, rocf Clear Creek MM, dtd 1878,7,10
1878, 9, 21. Nathan & w gct Hopewell MM
1878, 10, 19. Taylor & w, Jane, & ch gct Cherry Grove MM, Ind.

PUMMEL
1875, 2, 20. Alexander H. recrq
1875, 2, 20. Mary E. recrq
1890, 9, 20. Hamilton & Mary [Powel] dis

PUSHIE
----, --, --. ----- & Martha
Ch: Minnie M. b 1865, 10, 2
Mellie F. " 1866, 12, 3
1868, 12, 16. Nellie d bur Fairfield
1877, 7, 15. Walter H. [Pushee], s Adney P. & Martha, b

1861, 12, 21. Martha Ann [Pushey] (form Ladd) con mcd
1883, 4, 21. Minnie & Addie recrq
1893, 5, 20. Addie dropped from mbrp
1914, 6, 20. Margaret & ch, Harley & Arthur, recrq

PYLE
1861, 8, 17. Nancy T. (form Fisher) con mcd
1862, 1, 18. Nancy J. gct Springfield MM
1872, 5, 18. Cert rec for David S. & w & ch endorsed to Clear Creek MM

RADLEY
1884, 6, 17. Cornelius recrq

RAINS
1852, 4, 17. Mary Powers (form Rains) dis mcd & jas
1886, 10, 16. David & Catherine dropped from mbrp

RATCLIFF
1808, 5, 28. Amos [Ratliff] & s, Jehu, Amos & Moses, rocf Cane Creek MM, N. C., dtd 1807.10,7, endorsed by Miami MM
1808, 5, 28. Eleanor [Ratliff] & dt, Margaret Ann, Sarah Eleanor & Elizabeth, rocf Cane Creek MM, N. C., dtd 1807,3,7
1809, 6, 24. Mildred rocf South River MM, Va., dtd 1809,1,14
1810, 6, 30. Abner & s, John, Abner & Isaac, rocf Cane Creek MM, N. C.
1810, 6, 30. Sarah & dt, Ann Margaret & Dorcas, rocf Cane Creek MM, N. C., dtd 1809, 9,2
1810, 8, 25. Harrison rst by rq with consent of Waynook MM, Va.
1810, 10, 27. Edom & s, Edom Jacob John Joel Thomas & Jesse, rocf Cane Creek MM, N.C., dtd 1809,10,7
1810, 10, 27. Rachel & dt, Sarah Elizabeth Rachel & Margaret, rocf Cain Creek MM, N. C., dtd 1809,10,7
1815, 2, 25. Cert rec for Joseph [Ratliff] from Deep Creek MM, N. C., dtd 1815,10,1, endorsed to White Water MM
1815, 2, 25. Cert rec for Rebecca [Ratliff] & dt, Jane, Huldah & Anne, from Deep Creek MM, N. C., dtd 1814,11,5, endorsed to White Water MM
1815, 2, 25. Cert rec for Jonathan [Ratliff] & s, Elias, from Deep Creek MM, N. C., dtd 1815,10,1, endorsed to White Water MM
1815, 2, 25. Cert rec for Sarah [Ratliff] from Deep Creek MM, N. C., dtd 1814,11,5, endorsed to White Water MM
1817, 3, 29. Harrison [Ratclif] & w, Mildred, gct Short Creek MM
1870, 3, 19. Ezekiel recrq

RAWLINSON
1877, 5, 19. Thomas recrq
1878, 10, 19. Thomas [Rollinson] dropped from mbrp
1882, 4, 15. Ann recrq
1907, 3, 16. Maymie recrq

RAY
1870, 7, 16. Rachel J. recrq
1870, 9, 17. Mary A. recrq

REAMS
----, --, --. Elijah & Sarah
Ch: Jose b 1813, 1, 28
Rebecca " 1814, 12, 15
Hannah " 1816, 11, 28
Mary " 1818, 8, 12
Jeremiah " 1820, 6, 23
William W. " 1823, 1, 17
Jonathan " 1824, 12, 2
1854, 4, 10. John [Reems] d ae 84 bur Fairfield

1811, 11, 30. Elijah rocf Jack Swamp MM, N. C., dtd 1811,9,7
1811, 11, 30. Hannah rocf Jack Swamp MM,N.C.,

REAMS, continued
dtd 1811,9,7
1812, 7, 25. Sarah recrq
1812, 8, 29. Cert rec for William & fam from Jack Swamp MM, N. C., dtd 1811,9,7, endorsed to Darby Creek MM
1812, 8, 29. David & Peter recrq of father, Elijah
1818, 2, 28. Hannah Pike (form Reams) con mcd
1822, 12, 28. Letia rocf Darby Creek MM, dtd 1822,9,21
1826, 1, 28. Elijah [Reames] & w, Sarah, & ch, David, Peter R., Joseph, Rebecca, Hannah, Mary, Jeremiah, William W. & Jonathan, gct Goshen MM
1849, 1, 29. John con mcd
1850, 6, 15. John [Ream] con mcd
1852, 6, 19. Lettis gct Clear Creek MM

REEDER
1836, 6, 30. Enos, s Joseph & Hannah, Carroll Co., O.; m at Lees Creek, Louiza SMITH, dt James & Atlantic, Fayette Co., O.
Ch: Hannah E. b 1837, 9, 14
Joseph " 1839, 4, 29
Enos m 2nd Zilpah -----
Eh: Thomas Elwood b 1866, 3, 28
John Sherman " 1868, 1, 18
1839, 5, 19. Louisa, w Enos, d bur Lees Creek
1839, 9, 26. Joseph, s Enos & Louisa, d bur Lees Creek

1836, 11, 24. Amy Eleanor Smith, dt Louisa Reeder, recrq
1847, 6, 19. Enos con mcd
1860, 5, 19. Hannah Elizabeth Balen (form Reader) dis mcd
1870, 2, 19. Zilpah recrq
1871, 3, 18. Deborah, Webster, Emma & Eunice recrq
1886, 8, 21. Amanda gct Maryville MM, Tenn.
1893, 5, 20. Levi & Sherman [Reader] dropped from mbrp
1893, 6, 17. Zilphia [Reader] & dt, Emma, gct Mill Creek MM, Ind.
1908, 4, 18. Ethel Grim [Reader] gct Springfield MM

REES
1826, 2, 1. James, s William & Charity, Highland Co., O.; m at Fairfield, Elenor PICKERING, dt Jonathan & Phebe, Highland Co., O.

1808, 11, 26. James & s, Thomas & William, rocf Lost Creek MM, Tenn., dtd 1808,7,30
1808, 11, 26. Jane [Reace] rocf Lost Creek MM, Tenn., dtd 1808,7,30
1809, 1, 28. Ann [Reace] rocf Hopewell MM, dtd 1808,1,4
1810, 1, 27. Caleb [Reece] & s, William & France, rocf Mt. Pleasant MM, Va., dtd 1809,8,26
1810, 1, 27. Sarah [Reace] & dt, Elizabeth Ann Sarah & Jane, rocf Mt. Pleasant MM, Va., dtd 1809,8,26
1813, 9, 25. Cert rec for Caleb & s, Michael, from Springfield MM, N. C., dtd 1811,9,7, endorsed to Fall Creek MM
1826, 3, 25. Eleanor gct Lees Creek MM
1831, 9, 22. William gct Fairfield MM, Ind.
1832, 2, 23. Thomas gct Clear Creek MM
1832, 10, 25. James & w, Elenor, & ch, Nancy, Charity & Phebe Elmore, Lydia, James & John, gct Fall Creek MM
1834, 9, 25. Joel gct Fall Creek MM
1848, 3, 18. Lucinda (form Wilcox) dis mcd & jas
1870, 6, 18. William [Reese] recrq
1905, 10, 21. Abraham [Reese] recrq

REMLEY
1871, 3, 18. William & Martha recrq

REYNOLDS
1856, 8, 16. Levi Smith gct Bloomfield MM, to m Rachel Reynolds
1870, 2, 19. Henry & Clarissa [Runnels] recrq
1870, 2, 19. Isaac W. Haines, adopted s Henry [Runnels], recrq

RHOADS
1871, 8, 19. Sarah [Rhodes] recrq
1873, 5, 17. Enos recrq
1904, 2, 20. Alva [Roads] recrq
1907, 4, 20. Alvah dropped from mbrp

RHONIMUS
1902, 1, 18. Martha relrq

RICE
1873, 5, 17. Margaretta recrq

RION
1809, 11, 25. Priscilla (form Beals) dis mou

ROBERTS
1830, 3, 3. Judah, s Thomas & Hannah, Highland Co., O.; m at Fairfield, Ruth PIKE, dt John & Leah, Highland Co., O.
Ch: Charles b 1830, 12, 12
Samuel " 1832, 9, 4
1831, 11, 30. John S., s Joseph & Jane, Highland Co., O.; m at Fairfield, Sarah G. LADD, dt Jacob & Elizabeth, Highland Co., O.
Ch: William b 1832, 9, 21
Gerrard " 1834, 1, 7
Michael L. " 1835, 4, 6
Lydia Ann " 1837, 3, 7
Elias " 1841, 8, 29
1834, 3, 15. Gerrard d bur Fairfield

ROBERTS, continued
1835, 12, 24. Michael L. d bur Fairfield
1841, 9, 9. Elias d bur Fairfield
1860, 1, 7. Thomas d bur at his home
----, --, --. William & Nancy
Ch: Charley D. b 1866, 1, 3
Wilson P. " 1868, 12, 7

1829, 2, 28. Joseph rocf Fall Creek MM, dtd 1829,2,21
1829, 7, 25. John & Moses [Robarts] rocf Fall Creek MM, dtd 1829,7,18
1829, 9, 26. Judah rocf Fall Creek MM, dtd 1829,9,19
1829, 12, 26. Ann [Robarts] rocf Fall Creek MM, dtd 1829,12,19
1830, 1, 30. Sarah (form Burgess) con mcd
1830, 3, 27. Joseph con mcd
1830, 8, 28. Joseph & w, Sarah, gct White Lick MM, Ind.
1832, 2, 23. Moses rocf Uwhlan MM, endorsed by Fall Creek MM
1834, 8, 21. Judah & w, Ruth, & ch, Charles & Samuel, gct Fairfield MM, Ind.
1834, 12, 25. Ann & minor brother, Moses, gct Sugar River MM, Ind.
1837, 3, 23. Moses dis disunity
1850, 1, 19. Abraham gct Westfield MM, Ind.
1851, 8, 16. Joseph gct Westfield MM, Ind.
1855, 5, 19. Joseph rocf Westfield MM, dtd 1855,2,1
1863, 3, 21. William con mcd
1870, 3, 19. Nancy recrq
1870, 3, 19. Emma Elva, dt William & Nancy, recrq of parents
1870, 10, 15. Elizabeth recrq
1874, 2, 21. Lydia A. [Robberts] recrq
1878, 3, 16. Thomas recrq
1889, 5, 18. Thomas & s, Irving, gct Newberg MM, Ore.

ROBINSON
1825, 3, 28. Elizabeth P. m Azel WALKER

1812, 4, 25. Cert rec for John & fam from Mt. Pleasant MM, Va., dtd 1811,11,30, endorsed to Derby Creek MM
1814, 9, 24. Joshua & w, Anna, & ch, Banner, John, Elizabeth, Mary, Hannah & Mahala, rocf Mt. Pleasant MM, dtd 1814,8,27
1819, 8, 28. Eliza (form Terry) dis mcd
1821, 6, 30. Banner dis mcd
1823, 7, 26. Joshua rqct Darby Creek; not granted
1823, 7, 26. Ann & ch, John, Elizabeth, Mary Ann, Mahala, Martha, Sally, Eli, George & Caleb, gct Darby Creek MM
1825, 2, 26. Cert granted to Darby Creek MM, 1823,7,26 for Ann & ch returned & accepted
1825, 4, 30. Joshua rpd mcd
1825, 10, 29. Joshua & ch, Mahala, Martha, Sarah Meriah & George, gct Goshen MM
1826, 3, 25. Mary McClain (form Robinson) dis mcd
1828, 12, 27. Hannah [Robeson] dis
1830, 11, 27. John dis mcd

ROGERS
1868, 2, 15. Michael recrq
1873, 11, 15. Michael gct Vermillion MM, Ill.
1893, 2, 18. Lucy [Rodgers] recrq

ROOX
1808, 2, 27. Elizabeth (form Jackson) dis mcd

ROSE
1893, 2, 18. Joseph, Maud & Netta recrq
1902, 2, 15. Melissa recrq
1903, 3, 21. Jessie recrq
1912, 7, 20. Annie & Nettie dropped from mbrp
1914, 2, 21. Carrie recrq
1917, 4, 21. Carrie relrq
1924, 4, 3. Joseph E. & w, Melissa J., relrq

ROSHER
1895, 4, 2. John recrq

ROSS
1846, 5, 16. Enos acknowledged a mbr
1851, 8, 16. Elizabeth recrq
1851, 9, 20. Eilliam Erskine, Martha Ann, Alfred Simmons, Almira Jane & Ellis Rees, ch Enos & Elizabeth, recrq
1854, 11, 18. Enos & w, Elizabeth, & ch, William E., Martha Ann, Alfred S., Elmira J Jane, Ellis R. & Samuel E., gct Dover MM
1870, 6, 18. Margaret recrq
1870, 9, 17. Amanda Jane recrq
1897, 1, 16. David T. & w, Lillian, rocf Clear Creek MM

ROWE
1864, 6, 18. Rebecca S. [Roe] rocf Dover MM, dtd 1864,5,19
1868, 1, 18. Rebecca gct Dover MM, O.
1901, 3, 16. Earl recrq
1904, 3, 19. Martin recrq
1910, 6, 18. Martin gct Clear Creek MM

RUTHERFORD
1870, 6, 18. John & Mary Ann recrq
1870, 6, 18. Maggie E., dt Benjamin & Mary Ann, recrq of parents

SAGER
1927, 8, 4. Edna McPherson relrq

SAINT
1870, 8, 20. James Hadley gct Duck Creek MM, to m Emily G. Saint

ST. CLAIR
1818, 10, 31. Martha recrq
1819, 5, 25. George & w gct Clear Creek MM

SAMMONS
1871, 3, 18. Benjamin F., Leonard G. & Charles W. recrq

SANDERS
----, --, --. Thomas & Betsy
Ch: John b 1808, 3, 19
Nathaniel " 1810, 6, 12
----, --, --. Jonathan & Lydia
Ch: Elizabeth b 1809, 10, 18
Mary " 1811, 6, 13
1809, 6, 29. John, s John & Milly, Highland Co., O.; m at Fall Creek, Eleanor BARRETT, dt Richard & Sarah, Highland Co., O.
1809, 8, 19. John d bur Clear Creek
1810, 4, 14. Jesse, s John & Eleanor, b
1816, 10, 13. Samuel, s John & Milly, Highland Co., O.; m at Fairfield, Rebecca HUFF, dt Daniel & Sarah, Highland Co., O.
1837, 11, 14. Addison d bur Fairfield
----, --, --. Thomas & Emmily
Ch: Deborah Ann b 1839, 4, 4 d 1851,10,15 bur Walnut Creek
Daniel Webster b 1840, 8, 17 " 1842, 8, 7 bur Walnut Creek
Levi H. b 1842, 8, 10
David Lewis" 1844, 11, 2 " 1846, 8,15 bur Walnut Creek
Maria L. b 1846, 8, 24
Lydia Elma " 1849, 11, 3
Grace A. " 1851, 5, 15
Eliza A.
1845, 10, 22. Rachel m Manson TERRELL
1852, 9, 22. Jonathan, s John & Milly, Highland Co., O.; m at Fairfield, Ruth HUFF, dt Daniel & Mary McPherson, Highalnd Co., O.
1873, 9, 21. Ruth d ae 79 bur Fairfield

1816, 2, 24. Jonathan & w, Lydia, & ch, Sally, Elizabeth, Mary, Gulielma & Thomas, rocf Clear Creek MM, dtd 1815,12,9
1816, 9, 29. Samuel rocf Clear Creek MM, dtd 1816,8,10
1817, 2, 22. Jonathan & w, Lydia, & ch, Sarah, Betsy, Mary, Gulielma & Thomas, gct Clear Creek MM
1829, 5, 30. Rebecca dis jH
1834, 8, 21. Sarah Hinton (form Sanders) dis mcd
1839, 6, 20. Thomas & w, Emily, rocf Ceasars Creek MM, dtd 1839,4,25
1841, 12, 23. John H. gct Fall Creek MM; cert not accepted, returned 1842,3,24
1841, 12, 23. Thomas & w, Emmily, & ch, Deborah Ann & Daniel Webster, gct Miami MM
1842, 8, 25. John H. dis disunity
1846, 11, 21. Thomas & w, Emily, & ch, Deborah Ann, Levi & David Lewis, rocf Center MM, dtd 1845,10,15, endorsed by Clear Creek MM 1846,11,14
1848, 12, 16. David gct Newberry MM
1853, 1, 15. Ruth gct Clear Creek MM
1855, 4, 21. Thomas & w, Emily N., & ch, Levi H., Maria L., Lydia E., Grace A. & Eliza Arbelle, gct Three River MM, Ia.
1858, 2, 21. Charles Peitsmeyer gct Clear Creek MM, to m Gulielma M. Sanders
1870, 3, 19. Nathaniel & Mariah recrq
1881, 12, 17. Mary & Ellen rocf Clear Creek MM, dtd 1881,11,12
1883, 9, 15. Sarah Emily rocf Clear Creek MM
1890, 4, 19. Thos. recrq
1911, 9, 16. Charles R. recrq

SANDERSON
1916, 9, 16. Frank & Frances rocf Xenia MM

SARVER
1890, 4, 19. Frank & Elizabeth recrq
1914, 6, 20. Ruth recrq

SAUL
1857, 9, 19. Louisa recrq

SCHOOLEY
1810, 1, 27. William rocf Mt. Pleasant MM, Va., dtd 1809,8,26
1810, 1, 27. Susanah rocf Mt. Pleasant MM, Va., dtd 1809,8,26
1811, 8, 31. Susannah Lundy (form Schooly) dis mcd
1821, 9, 29. Christopher Terrell gct Green Plain MM, to m Elizabeth Schooley

SCOTT
1895, 12, 21. Thomas L. & w, Lydia A., rocf Hopewell MM
1896, 1, 18. Ella rocf Hopewell MM
1901, 3, 16. Oral recrq
1902, 2, 15. Estel recrq
1905, 9, 16. T. L. & w, Lydia, & ch, Lois, Margaret & Thelma Elizabeth, gct Sabina MM, O.
1909, 4, 17. Oral relrq
1911, 10, 21. Estel & w, Edna, & dt, Margaret, gct Hopewell MM

SEARCH
1884, 2, 16. Eva relrq

SEARS
----, --, --. John & Penelope
Ch: Polly b 1809, 12, 22
Pleasant " 1812, 1, 29
Christopher" 1814, 8, 3
John " 1817, 2, 12
1817, 7, 12. John d bur Fairfield

1817, 11, 29. Penelope & ch, Dolly Pleasant Christopher & John, gct Center MM
1867, 1, 19. Phebe [Sayers] (form Bailey)

SEARS, continued
con mcd
1867, 7, 20. Phebe G. [Sayers] & ch, Lillian Clinton, gct Center MM, O.

SEITZ
1901, 3, 16. Rhoda A., Bishop, Melissa, William, Charles E. & Sydney R. recrq
1903, 1, 17. Rhoda [Sites] dropped from mbrp
1912, 6, 15. Bishop dropped from mbrp

SELLARS
1886, 10, 16. E. dropped from mbrp

SETTY
1895, 4, 2. George, Olive J. & Lillie G. recrq
1907, 4, 20. George & Olive dropped from mbrp

SEXTON
----, --, --. Chas. & Cora
Ch: Nora
Geneva b 1902, 1, 23
Chas. Edwin " 1904, 4, 2
Marion G. " 1906, 4, 12

1915, 2, 20. Cora & ch, Nora Geneva, Charles Edwin & Marion A., recrq

SHACKLEFORD
----, --, --. John, s Wilson & Mary E., b 1862,4,23; m Edna McPHERSON, dt Marion & Mary, b 1870,9,17
Dt: Mary b 1902, 4, 23

1886, 1, 16. John recrq

SHAFER
1870, 6, 18. Elizabeth C. & Mary E. recrq

SHARP
1874, 2, 21. Joseph B. & w, Mary A., recrq
1874, 2, 21. Cyrus B., Louis M., John W. & Aldis A., ch Joseph B. & Mary A., recrq
1882, 4, 15. Cyrus, Lewis, John & Aldis recrq
1884, 6, 21. Bowman dis
1885, 8, 15. Cyrus relrq
1893, 5, 20. Aldis dropped from mbrp
1893, 5, 20. Louis dropped from mbrp
1901, 4, 20. Jesse recrq
1911, 6, 17. Frank dropped from mbrp

SHELEY
1884, 5, 17. Amos R. & w, Carrie Earl, recrq
1893, 5, 20. Amos R. [Shealy] & w dropped from mbrp

SHERIFF
1871, 8, 19. Hannah recrq

SHIN
1809, 4, 29. George & s, Frances, rocf Hopewell MM, dtd 1808,8,3
1809, 4, 29. Elizabeth [Shinn] rocf Hopewell MM, dtd 1808,10,3
1811, 9, 28. George dis disunity
1811, 10, 26. Elizabeth dis disunity

SHOCKEY
1884, 4, 19. William & Jane recrq
1893, 5, 20. William dropped from mbrp
1893, 5, 20. Jane dropped from mbrp

SIDWELL
1811, 11, 30. Lemuel & Levi, s Levi, rocf Notingham MM, dtd 1811,7,5

SIMERS
1871, 8, 19. Alfred recrq

SIMMONS
----, --, --. Samuel & Rebecca
Ch: Gulielma b 1840, 12, 5
John " 1843, 7, 21
Jacob " 1845, 8, 26
1841, 10, 19. Jane Ellen d bur Walnut Creek
1842, 4, 3. Samuel Powel d bur Walnut Creek
1848, 10, 30. Lydia d bur Walnut Creek
1848, 11, 24. Sylvester d bur Walnut Creek
1852, 5, 12. Samuel d bur Walnut Creek
1857, 1, 22. Rebecca m Seth HOCKETT

1825, 2, 26. Rebecca rocf Hopewell MM, dtd 1824,9,9
1838, 8, 23. Samuel recrq
1838, 10, 25. Thomas W., Jane E., Josiah W., Rebecca Ann, Samuel P., Alfred R., Sylvester, Mary E. & Matilda, ch Samuel & Rebecca, recrq
1845, 6, 21. Rebecca Ann dis
1849, 4, 21. Thomas William con mcd
1850, 4, 20. Josiah Westly dis disunity
1851, 7, 19. Thomas William con mcd
1852, 4, 17. Thomas William gct Dover MM
1853, 5, 21. Alfred Rees dis
1856, 3, 15. Mary Kizer (form Simmons) dis mcd
1857, 1, 17. Matilda Hockett (form Simmons) dis mcd
1883, 2, 17. Jane recrq
1890, 11, 15. Mary T. gct Denver MM, Colo.
1816, 2, 17. Sarah Mildred & Wilmuth E., ch Pearl, recrq

SIMPSON
1821, 9, 21. Anna, w John, d ae 66 bur Dry Run

1815, 11, 25. Anna rocf Abington MM, Pa., dtd 1815,5,29

SINCLEAR
1817, 10, 25. George rocf New Garden MM, dtd ----,6,19
1819, 5, 29. George & w, Martha, gct Clear Creek MM

SITTRO
1874, 8, 6. Jacob d bur Fall Creek

SLAUGHTER
1905, 9, 26. Stanley Earl, s Chas. & Bertha, b
----, --, --. Marcus & Clara
Ch: John Jackson b 1911, 7, 31
Chas. Edward " 1914, 4, 15

1813, 10, 30. Chloe recrq
1818, 5, 30. Chloe King (form Slaughter) con mcd
1820, 9, 30. Anna (form Wright) con mcd
1834, 3, 20. Anna gct Green Plain MM
1902, 2, 15. Charles & Bertha recrq
1914, 4, 18. Bertha relrq
1914, 7, 18. Marcus A. & ch, John Jackson & Charles Edward, recrq
1914, 7, 18. Clara rocf Newberry MM

SLOONAKER
1862, 8, 26. Phebe Jane (form Brown) dis mcd

SMALL
1811, 3, 4. Gideon d bur Fall Creek

1813, 5, 29. Cert rec for Jacob from Westfield MM, dtd 1810,11,10, endorsed to Center MM
1841, 8, 26. Rachel (form Johnson) dis mcd
1872, 2, 17. Ruth (form Ladd) con mcd
1890, 4, 19. Abner & Anna recrq
1893, 5, 20. Ruth A. dropped from mbrp

SMITH
1810, 1, 11. Ruth m Jephthah JOHNSON
1812, 4, 15. Hannah d bur Fairfield
----, --, --. Evan & Abigail
Ch: Abner b 1831, 2, 2
Barclay " 1833, 3, 15
Amos " 1836, 1, 30
Hannah " 1838, 4, 27
Margaretta " 1841, 2, 9
Atalantic " 1841, 2, 9
John " 1843, 11, 16
Gulielma " 1846, 4, 27
Mary Elizabeth " 1848, 11, 19
Havilah " 1853, 7, 28
1836, 6, 30. Louisa m Enos REEDER
1847, 12, 15. Lydia Ann, dt Job & Charlotte, b
1848, 6, 1. James, d ae 73y 8m 16d bur Fairfield (an elder)
1849, 10, 24. Amy Eleanor m John PAXSON
----, --, --. James & Catherine
Ch: Josiah b 1851, 1, 9
Lindley M. " 1852, 7, 17
Eldra E. " 1854, 7, 25
Almira R. " 1856, 12, 14
Laura Bell " 1859, 2, 8
Ch: Phebe L. b 1861, 9, 16
Henry A. " 1864, 3, 13
David W. " 1865, 10, 9
Charlie " 1869, 5, 11
Vannje C. " 1872, 4, 18
Minnie " 1875, 11, 4
1853, 4, 28. Lydia Morris, dt James & Elizabeth Morris, b
1854, 2, 27. Amos d
----, --, --. Zimry & Sarah
Ch: Orlando b 1860, 10, 31
Fanny C. " 1862, 8, 5
Luella J. " 1864, 5, 12
Rachel " 1866, 8, 1
Otho E. " 1868, 8, 10
1860, 9, 29. Atlantic d ae 82 bur Fairfield
1861, 9, 20. Walter Lincoln, s John P. & Mariah, b
1862, 5, 1. Naomi C. m Hazael D. GREEN
1862, 10, 22. Walter Lincoln d
1863, 9, 27. Orlando d
1865, 8, 24. Rachel m Alonzo E. THORNBURG
1868, 6, 25. Gulielma m Daniel GREEN
1874, 3, 19. Nancy C. d
1877, 3, 17. Minnie d bur Fairfield
1884, 8, 28. Elma L., dt John & Clara Ladd, b
----, --, --. Thos. T. & Paulina
Ch: Clifford b 1885, 1, 28
Wraymond " 1891, 12, 6
----, --, --. Franklin D., s Tristrim & A., b 1856,4,21; m Lizzie -----
Ch: Elmer b 1889, 8, 16
Iva " 1893, 10, 3
Laura " 1895, 9, 16
Stanley " 1899, 12, 1
Vernon " 1901, 9, 19
Russell Franklin " 1905, 8, 3
1910, 8, 18. Nettie Virginia, dt Lycurgas & Emma, b

1811, 7, 27. Ephraim rocf Westland MM, dtd 1810,11,24
1811, 7, 27. Jacob rocf Westland MM, dtd 1810 11,24
1811, 7, 27. Hannah rocf Westland MM, dtd 1810,11,24
1812, 7, 25. Elizabeth gct Center MM
1815, 5, 27. Eleanor (form Ellis) dis mcd
1816, 3, 30. James & w, Atlantick, & ch, Amos, Job, Mary, Lydia, Evan, Louiza & George, recrq
1817, 6, 28. Ephraim dis mcd
1821, 2, 24. Jacob gct New Garden MM, Ind.
1832, 9, 20. George con mcd
1834, 11, 20. Louisa recrq
1835, 9, 24. Abigail & ch, Abner & Barclay, recrq
1836, 11, 24. Amy Eleanor Smith, dt Louisa Reeder, recrq
1841, 12, 23. Rebecca (form Fisher) con mcd
1844, 6, 15. Rebecca gct Mississinewa MM,

SMITH, continued
Ind.
1847, 9, 18. George gct Pleasant Plain MM
1847, 10, 16. Job recrq
1847, 11, 20. Charlotte recrq
1848, 2, 19. Levi, John, Zimri, Naomi, Ruth, Mary, Atlantic & Rachel, ch Job & Charlotte, recrq
1849, 10, 20. Lydia gct Salem MM, Ia.
1850, 3, 16. James con mcd
1850, 12, 21. Catherine recrq
1855, 4, 21. Barclay con mcd
1856, 3, 15. Sophia recrq
1856, 8, 16. Levi gct Bloomfield MM, to m Rachel Reynolds
1856, 11, 15. Oliver, s Barclay & Sophia, recrq
1857, 6, 20. Rachel rocf Bloomfield MM, Ind., dtd 1857,5,6
1858, 10, 16. Levi & w, Rachel, gct Bloomfield MM, Ind.
1859, 2, 19. John con mcd
1859, 2, 19. Abner dis mcd
1859, 7, 16. Maria E. rocf Spring Creek MM, Ia., dtd 1859,7,5
1860, 2, 18. Zimri con mcd
1860, 5, 19. Ruth M. Stout (form Smith) con mcd
1861, 2, 16. Mary Atlantic Morrison (form Smith) con mcd
1862, 7, 19. Sarah F., w Zimri, & s, Orlando, recrq
1863, 3, 21. Abner D. recrq
1866, 2, 17. Margaretta Luttrell (form Smith) dis mcd
1866, 11, 17. John & w, Maria E., & ch, Mary Alice, Julia Ella, Emma Malissa & Charlotte, gct Spring Creek MM, Ia.
1867, 8, 17. Lydia & ch, Estel & Rufus, recrq
1868, 9, 19. Barclay & w, Sophia, & ch, Oliver G., Everett W., Edgar O. & Ida May, gct Poplar Run MM, Ind.
1869, 6, 19. Zimri & w, Sary, & ch, Fanny C., Luella M., Rachel A. & Otto E., gct Newbury MM, O.
1870, 2, 19. Ordwa recrq
1870, 3, 19. Anor recrq
1870, 3, 19. Isaac M., Franklin D. & Joseph W., ch Anor, recrq
1870, 5, 21. Jacob recrq
1870, 5, 21. William H. recrq
1870, 7, 16. Tristram recrq
1871, 3, 18. Isaac recrq
1871, 3, 18. Jeremiah W. recrq
1871, 3, 18. Jonathan & Julia recrq
1871, 7, 15. William con mcd
1871, 7, 15. Lydia con mcd
1871, 8, 19. Peter recrq
1871, 8, 19. Mary recrq
1872, 4, 20. Abner con mcd
1872, 4, 20. Elizabeth recrq
1873, 3, 15. James recrq
1873, 3, 15. Maria Ann & Ella E. recrq
1873, 3, 15. Mary & Anna recrq
1874, 1, 17. Nathan recrq
1874, 7, 18. Peter & Mary E. gct Londonderry MM
1874, 7, 18. Rebecca Jane recrq
1878, 10, 19. Ordway dropped from mbrp
1881, 9, 17. Havilah & w, Susan, relrq
1884, 7, 19. Isaiah & Lindley gct Clear Creek MM, O.
1885, 4, 18. James & fam gct Clear Creek MM
1886, 7, 17. Vada recrq
1886, 10, 16. Thomas & Elgar dropped from mbrp
1889, 3, 16. Lizzie recrq
1891, 5, 16. Mary Ellen relrq
1891, 5, 16. Vada relrq
1893, 2, 18. Alice E. relrq
1893, 5, 20. Abner D. & fam dropped from mbrp
1893, 5, 20. Abner A. dropped from mbrp
1893, 5, 20. Joseph W. dropped from mbrp
1902, 11, 15. Rebecca dropped from mbrp
1903, 3, 21. Clifford, Harrison & Raymond recrq
1905, 4, 15. Roy Vernon recrq
1907, 4, 20. Lena Chalfont relrq
1907, 4, 20. Roy Vernon dropped from mbrp
1908, 3, 21. Emma recrq
1915, 5, 15. Sarah recrq
1916, 9, 16. Harrison dropped from mbrp
1923, 4, 5. Emma & Nettie Virginia relrq

SMITHIN
1817, 2, 22. Elizabeth (form Thornbury) con mcd

SMITHSON
1846, 9, 19. Mary (form Terrill) dis mcd
1873, 3, 15. Lucinda E. recrq
1889, 3, 16. Alta H. rocf Woolson MM, Ia.
1896, 10, 17. Alta gct Clear Creek MM, O.

SMOOT
1888, 2, 18. Mary J. relrq
1910, 6, 18. Verdie E. relrq

SNIDER
1906, 1, 20. Charles & Homer recrq

SPARGER
1812, 7, 25. Cert rec for Rachel from Westfield MM, N. C., dtd 1810,12,8, endorsed to Fall Creek MM

SPEARS
1877, 5, 19. Margery recrq

SPENCE
----, --, --. J. F. & M. Etta
Ch: Edna b 1887, 6, 21
Minnie " 1888, 9, 22

1904, 2, 20. M. Etta rocf Hopewell MM

SPENCER
1849, 3, 17. Martha (form Burgess) con mcd
1903, 3, 21. Winnie & Edna recrq

STAFFORD
1809, 4, 29. Stacy dis

STALKER
1835, 8, 26. Eli, s Nathan & Mary, Clinton Co., O.; m at Fairfield, Tacy Jennett BURGESS, dt Daniel & Ruth, Highland Co., O.
Ch: Mahala B. b 1837, 7, 30
Nathan " 1839, 6, 18
Mary Ann " 1843, 2, 18
Daniel B. " 1844, 11, 6
Sarah Emily" 1847, 5, 29

1841, 1, 27. John, s John & Mary, Highland Co., O.; m at Fairfield, Anna BURGESS, dt Daniel & Ruth, Highland Co., O.
1853, 8, 19. Eli d bur Fairfield
1857, 10, 22. Mahala B. m Joseph ALLEN

1836, 3, 24. Tacy Jennette gct Springfield MM
1837, 9, 21. Eli & w, Tacy Genette, rocf Springfield MM, dtd 1837,5,16
1841, 1, 21. John rocf Cherry Grove MM, Ind., dtd 1841,1,13
1842, 6, 23. John & w, Anna, & dt, Ruth, gct Westfield MM, Ind.
1864, 2, 20. Tacy Jenet Cowmen (form Stalker) con mcd
1866, 11, 17. Daniel con mcd
1867, 9, 21. Mary Ellen recrq
1869, 9, 18. Emily Wright (form Stalker) con mcd

STANBROUGH
1822, 5, 8. William, s Solomon & Tabitha, Clinton Co., O.; m at Fairfield, Rachel PIKE, dt John & Leah, Highland Co., O.
1824, 4, 7. Rachel m Mordecai ELLIS

1822, 7, 27. Rachel gct Center MM
1823, 10, 25. Rachel recrq
1865, 9, 16. Richard Barrett gct New Salem MM, Ind., to m Malinda Stanbrough

STANLEY
1817, 9, 10. Jemima m Thomas CARR
1829, 6, 20. Strangeman d ae 84 bur Fairfield

1810, 4, 28. Anthony [Standley] & s, William & John, rocf New Garden MM, N. C., dtd 1809,11,25
1810, 4, 28. Hannah & dt, Ruth & Sarah, rocf New Garden MM, N. C., dtd 1809,11,25
1811, 11, 30. Hannah [Standley] rocf Mt. Pleasant MM, Va., dtd 1811,2,23
1812, 12, 26. Elizabeth recrq
1813, 11, 27. John rst by rq with consent of New Garden MM
1814, 6, 25. Anthony & fam gct Center MM
1818, 10, 31. Hannah gct Center MM
1830, 7, 31. Jemima & s, Strangeman, gct Springfield MM, Ind.
1834, 2, 20. Rachel (form Hoskins) dis mcd

STANTON
1810, 10, 27. Latham & s, Daniel, William & Stephen Butler Stanton, rocf South River MM, dtd 1810,9,8
1810, 10, 27. Hulday & dt, Hephsabeth, Elizabeth, Gulielma & Hunnicutt, rocf South River MM, dtd 1810,9,8
1811, 10, 26. Cert rec for Latham 1810,10,27 endorsed to Miami MM
1825, 12, 21. Cert rec for James & fam & ch of John, dec, from Western Branch MM, Va., endorsed to Springborough MM
1870, 12, 17. Harriet M. (form Hadley) con mcd
1871, 1, 21. Harriet M. gct Springfield MM, Kans.

STARBUCK
1829, 8, 29. Edith (form Adams) dis mcd
1832, 10, 25. Rachel & Eliza Adams, ch Edith Starbuck, gct Goshen MM

STARNS
1844, 1, 25. Ruth (form Hains) dis mcd
1901, 10, 19. William [Stearns] recrq
1910, 4, 16. Mrs. Mary recrq

STEPHENS
1808, 3, 26. Gideon & s, Samuel, rocf New Garden MM, N. C., dtd 1806,10,25
1808, 3, 26. Mary & dt, Lydia, rocf New Garden MM, N. C., dtd 1807,10,25
1873, 5, 17. Cassius & Cornelius [Stevens] recrq
1874, 6, 20. Julia [Stevens] recrq
1904, 3, 19. Ella [Stevens] recrq

STEPHENSON
1871, 8, 19. James & John recrq

STEWART
1911, 6, --. Mary Verita b

1841, 4, 22. Eliza [Steward] (form Carr) dis mcd
1876, 5, 20. David C. & Elizabeth J. recrq
1889, 2, 16. Sarah E. recrq
1889, 3, 16. Esther recrq
1890, 1, 18. David C. & w, Elizabeth, relrq
1893, 5, 20. Esther dropped from mbrp
1893, 5, 20. Sarah dropped from mbrp
1904, 2, 20. Minor, Annie, John, Ora & Elsie recrq
1907, 3, 16. Minor & w, Annie, & ch gct Clear Creek MM
1909, 3, 20. Eldon Frank recrq
1920, 6, 16. Frank dropped from mbrp
1922, 6, 1. Vereta dropped from mbrp

STOUT
----, --, --. Simon & Ruth
Ch: Orpah Jane b 1862, 10, 9
Alida May " 1866, 5, 7
Allen I. " 1869, 1, 19
Alvin H. " 1869, 1, 19

1860, 5, 19. Ruth M. (form Smith) con mcd
1860, 10, 20. Ruth gct Bloomfield MM, Ind.
1863, 2, 21. Simon & w, Ruth, & dt, Orpha Jane, rocf Bloomfield MM, Ind., dtd 1863, 1,14
1871, 6, 17. Simon & w, Ruth, & ch, Orpa Jane, Alida May & Alvin H., gct Spring Creek MM, Ia.

STRANGELY
1857, 6, 20. Athaliah (form Ellis) dis mcd

STRATTON
1855, 12, 15. Judith (form Terrell) con mcd
1856, 4, 19. Judith gct Springfield MM

STRETCH
1869, 6, 26. Martha, w Aaron, d bur Clear Creek

1869, 5, 15. Aaron & w, Martha, & ch, David Wilson, Thomas Wesley & Etta May, recrq
1871, 6, 17. Aaron con mcd

STOWE
1901, 2, 16. Rodema relrq
1912, 4, 20. Stanley B. & w, Nellie Kearns, recrq
1912, 4, 20. Carrie Genevieve, dt Stanley & Nellie, rec as associate mbr
1916, 1, 15. Ruth Todhunter rocf Wilmington MM
1916, 1, 15. Willard H. recrq
1921, 5, 4. Genevieve recrq
1925, 12, 3. Stanley B., Nellie & Genevieve relrq

STUBBS
1883, 2, 17. Lizzie & Albert recrq
1891, 6, 20. Albert M. & w, Lizzie, relrq

SUMNER
1809, 7, 13. Rebeckah m Joshua WRIGHT
1829, 7, 1. Thomas, Highland Co., O.; m at Fairfield, Martha WILLIAMS

1808, 12, 31. Joseph & s, Samuel & Thomas, rocf Westfield MM, dtd 1808,10,8
1808, 12, 31. Abigail & dt, Phebe, Ann & Elizabeth, rocf Westfield MM, N. C., dtd 1808, 10,8
1809, 3, 25. Caleb & s, Caleb, rocf Westfield MM, N. C., dtd 1808,1,12
1809, 3, 25. Mary & dt, Mary & Tabitha, rocf Westfield MM, N. C., dtd 1808,11,12
1809, 10, 28. Thomas rocf Westfield MM, dtd 1809,9,9
1809, 10, 28. Hannah & dt, Hannah Lydia Rebecca & Abigail, rocf Westfield MM, N. C., dtd 1809,9,9
1810, 4, 28. Tabitha Burris (form Sumner) dis mcd
1829, 10, 31. Martha gct Fall Creek MM
1869, 4, 19. Robert & w, Tabitha, recrq

SUMPTION
1870, 6, 18. Benjamin & Susan recrq
1870, 6, 18. Amos R., James T., Hannah M., John L., Joseph A. & Mary Ann, ch Benjamin & Susan, recrq of parents

SWAIN
1821, 5, --. Anna d ae 39 bur Dry Run

1815, 11, 25. David [Swayn] & w, Anna, & ch, Jonathan I., Anna & Isaiah, rocf Abington MM, Pa., dtd 1815,5,29
1824, 10, 30. David con mcd
1826, 11, 26. Mary Ingham & niece, Anny Swain, gct Springborough MM
1831, 7, 21. Jonathan gct White Water MM; returned because he joined Hicksites
1832, 5, 24. David & s, Isaiah, gct Bloomfield MM, Ind.
1833, 11, 21. Jonathan dis jH

SWEENEY
1882, 4, 15. James & Anna [Sweney] recrq
1887, 3, 19. James & w, Anna, gct Clear Creek MM
1892, 12, 17. James [Sweeny] & w, Anna, rocf Clear Creek MM, O., dtd 1892,11,12

SWISSHELM
1892, 5, 21. George W. [Swishelm] & w, Rosa L., recrq
1894, 3, 17. George relrq
1914, 3, 21. Jennie recrq

SWONGER
1886, 2, 20. Robert recrq
1887, 4, 16. Anna recrq
1896, 3, 21. Henry E. recrq
1897, 2, 20. Maud recrq
1901, 4, 20. Louie recrq
1902, 11, 15. Henry dropped from mbrp

SYFERD
1862, 2, 17. Cordelia Keith, dt Jer. & Martha Keith, b

1886, 2, 20. William W., Jane & Cordelia N., recrq
1886, 3, 20. Thomas [Syford] recrq
1896, 11, 21. Phillip J. & w, Araminta, recrq
1904, 3, 19. Adaline recrq
1907, 12, 21. Araminta J. gct Sabina MM
1908, 3, 21. Virginia & Martha recrq

SYFERD, continued
1915, 7, 17. Martha dropped from mbrp
1918, 3, 16. Amy & Corda gct Leesburg MM, O.
1918, 3, 16. Belle's d rpd

TAYLOR
1895, 3, 16. Malinda C. relrq

TEMPLIN
1873, 5, 17. Caroline, Lettie & Oscar recrq
1903, 3, 21. William W. recrq
1915, 2, 20. Letitia recrq

TERRELL
----, --, --. Pleasant & Esther
Ch: John H. b 1815, 10, 3
Israel A. " 1818, 2, 17
David " 1820, 2, 5
Mary E. " 1829, 9, 24
Narcissa " 1831, 2, 20
Ruth " 1834, 4, 21
1817, 12, 3. Judith m Stacy HAINES
----, --, --. Christopher & Elizabeth
Ch: Manson b 1822, 9, 21
Sicily " 1824, 7, 28
Mary " 1826, 10, 19
Sarah " 1828, 7, 15
Israel " 1830, 2, 4
Elizabeth " 1831, 9, 14
Judith " 1833, 6, 11
Pleasant " 1839, 2, 2
Edna " 1839, 1, 2
1827, 5, 2. Sarah [Terrill] m Jonah WRIGHT
1828, 1, 2. Joseph, s David & Mary, Highland Co., O.; m at Fairfield, Ann McPHERSON, dt Isaac & Elizabeth, Highland Co., O.
Ch: Jane b 1832, 4, 30
William M. " 1834, 11, 27
David F. " 1836, 5, 16
1835, 12, 10. David d bur Fairfield
1839, 1, 3. Ann d bur Fairfield
----, --, --. John H. & Elizabeth [Terrill]
Ch: Hampton W. b 1840, 10, 18
Pleasant " 1843, 3, 16
Ruth Ann " 1844, 11, 8
Phebe Jane " 1846, 8, 6
David Edgar " 1847, 10, 8
Mary Edna " 1849, 10, 8
Flora Annis " 1853, 1, 20
1840, 8, 8. Pleasant d ae 49 bur Fairfield
1841, 9, 15. Christopher d bur Fairfield
1842, 6, 29. Sisley A. m Christopher JOHNSON
1844, 10, 23. Israel, s Pleasant & Esther, Highland Co., O.; m at Fairfield, Sidney H. HUFF, dt James & Sidney, Highland Co., O.
1845, 10, 22. Manson, s Christopher & Elizabeth, Highland Co., O.; m Rachel SANDERS, dt Samuel & Rebecca, Highland Co., O.
----, --, --. Israel A. & Sarah
Ch: James H. b 1846, 3, 22
Israel Allen b 1848, 2, 24
Sarah H. " 1852, 1, 6
William G. " 1854, 9, 29
George " 1857, 2, 6
Clarai " 1859, 3, 11
Charles Earnice " 1866, 1, 4
Anna " 1869, 6, 4
----, --, --. Manson & Rachel
Ch: Christopher C. b 1846, 12, 1
Samuel S. " 1848, 1, 8
Martha Elma " 1849, 8, 13
Edwin " 1850, 10, 30
1846, 2, 21. Esther d bur Fairfield
1850, 12, 30. Adalyne, dt Samuel & Mary Davis, b
1853, 8, 1. Mary d ae 86 bur Fairfield
1859, 3, 10. Christopher d bur Fairfield
1862, 3, 27. Eliza A., dt Thomas & Clarinda, b
1864, 4, 28. David E., s M. & R., d bur Springfield, Kans.
----, --, --. Rutherford m Harriet M. THORNBURG, dt Edward & Rachel, b 1868,1,9
Dt: Helen Avelyne b 1899, 1, 3

1811, 3, 30. Mary (form Wright) dis mcd
1815, 10, 28. Pleasant gct Ceasars Creek MM, to m
1816, 6, 29. Esther rocf Cesars Creek MM, dtd 1816,5,24
1821, 9, 29. Christopher gct Green Plain MM, to m Elizabeth Schooley
1822, 6, 29. Elizabeth rocf Green Plain MM, dtd 1822,--,--
1826, 3, 25. David [Terrel] Jr. con mcd
1827, 5, 26. David Jr. gct Lees Creek MM
1830, 10, 30. Mary Hiatt (form Terrell) con mcd
1839, 5, 23. Samuel C. recrq
1839, 11, 21. John H. gct Clear Creek MM, to m Elizabeth Williams
1840, 7, 23. Elizabeth rocf Clear Creek MM, dtd 1840,7,21
1840, 8, 20. Clarinda (form Woodard) con mcd
1843, 8, 24. Joseph con mcd
1846, 9, 19. Mary Smithson (form Terrill) dis mcd
1847, 6, 19. Mary E. Boram (form Terrell) con mcd
1847, 6, 19. Narcissa Wright (form Terrill) con mcd
1847, 7, 17. Sarah Davis (form Terrill) con mcd
1847, 9, 18. Samuel C. con mcd
1848, 6, 17. David dis mcd
1851, 4, 19. James L. & Sarah V., ch Samuel C., recrq
1851, 5, 17. Malinda rst by rq
1851, 6, 21. Lewis Horton, s Malinda Terrell,

TERRELL, continued
recrq
1851, 7, 19. Elisabeth Hayworth (form Terrell) con mcd
1853, 5, 21. Ruth E. Borum (form Terrell) con mcd
1853, 6, 18. Joseph dis disunity
1855, 3, 17. Jane Davis (form Terrell) con mcd
1855, 6, 16. Israel, Jr. con mcd
1855, 10, 20. Samuel C. & w, Malinda, & ch, Charity Ann & Lewis Horton, ch Malinda by a form m, & James J., Sarah V. & Samuel Terrell, gct Middle River MM, Ia.
1855, 12, 15. Judith Stratton (form Terrell) con mcd
1856, 5, 17. Mary E. rocf Dover MM, dtd 1856, 4,17
1856, 10, 18. Clarinda gct Middle River MM,Ia.
1859, 6, 18. Edna McPherson (form Terrell) con mcd
1860, 5, 19. William Manson dis mcd
1861, 7, 20. Thomas & w, Clarinda, & ch, Nancy E., Rebecca J., Christopher M. & Lewis P., rocf South River MM, Ia., dtd 1861,5,25
1861, 7, 20. Martha A. rocf South River MM, Ia., dtd 1861,5,25
1865, 4, 15. David con mcd
1866, 3, 17. Hampton W. gct Cesars Creek MM, to m Harriet M. Painter
1866, 8, 18. Manson & w, Rachel, & ch, Christopher Cornelius, Samuel S., Martha E., Edwin, Pleasant A., Lycurgus, Frank, Emma Ann & Willie A., gct Springfield MM, Kans.
1866, 9, 15. Harriet M. rocf Caesers Creek MM, dtd 1866,8,23
1866, 11, 17. Hampton W. & w, Harriet M., gct Clear Creek MM, O.
1868, 2, 15. Phebe J. Huff (form Terrell) con mcd
1869, 5, 15. Pleasant M. gct Raysville MM, Ind.
1870, 2, 19. Israel A. & w, Sydney H., & ch, James H., Allen P., Sarah H., William G., Charles E. & Anna E., transferred to Clear Creek MM
1870, 2, 19. John H. & w, Elizabeth, & ch, Ruth A., David E. & Flora A., transferred to Clear Creek MM
1870, 7, 16. Rebecca Ellis (form Terrill) con mcd
1872, 7, 20. David F. con mcd
1872, 7, 20. Adaline E. [Terrill] recrq
1877, 5, 19. Harry recrq
1882, 4, 15. Rutherford recrq
1883, 11, 17. Harry E. relrq
1884, 5, 17. Harry recrq
1885, 2, 21. Harry relrq
1885, 10, 17. Rutherford relrq
1899, 3, 18. Helen E., dt Rutherford & Hattie M., recrq
1900, 5, 19. James H.'s d rpd
1906, 1, 20. Clayton & fam relrq
1907, 4, 20. David W., Samuel H. & Roy dropped from mbrp

TERRY
1851, 10, 25. Mary A. E., dt John & Elizabeth Slaughter, b
1857, 2, 25. Laura, dt Wm. & Ophelia, b
----, --, --. Fred & Addie

Ch:		
Thos. Carlton	b	1891, 9, 28
Edward Eugene	"	1893, 6, 6
Harold	"	1897, 11, 25

1808, 5, 28. Thomas & s, David Jeremiah, Jeduthan & John, rocf South River MM, Va., dtd 1808,1,9
1808, 5, 28. Sarah [Terrey] & dt, Elizabeth, rocf South River MM, Va., dtd 1808,1,9
1819, 8, 28. Eliza Robinson (form Terry) dis mcd
1823, 5, 31. Thomas & w, Sarah, & ch, David, Jeremiah, Jeduthen & John P., gct Allum Creek MM
1847, 4, 17. Caroline (form Wright) con mcd
1855, 8, 18. Caroline dis jas
1870, 3, 19. Thomas recrq
1870, 3, 19. Thomas F., Eugene F. & Frant F., ch Thomas J., recrq
1870, 3, 19. William P. & Ophelia recrq
1870, 3, 19. Laura, dt William & Ophelia, recrq of parents
1871, 5, 20. Edward F. recrq
1879, 7, 19. Mary A. recrq
1879, 7, 19. Vista F. recrq
1883, 4, 21. Caroline E., Freddie & Vista F. recrq
1907, 3, 16. Annie recrq
1909, 10, 16. Florence Cordelia relrq
1909, 10, 16. Grant Frederic & w, Addie A., relrq
1920, 6, 16. Mary gct Leesburg MM, O.

TETER
1891, 11, 17. Howard, s Edward & Allie, b

1903, 3, 21. Howard recrq

THOMAS
1810, 6, 30. Rachel recrq
1811, 5, 25. Cert rec for Benjamin from Piney Grove MM, S. C., dtd 1811,2,16, endorsed to White Water MM
1811, 5, 25. Cert rec for John & s, Jesse & Hendley, from Piney Grove MM, S. C., dtd 1811,2,16, endorsed to White Water MM
1811, 12, 28. Francis & s, Luke, rocf Contentney MM, N. C., dtd 1811,8,10
1866, 11, 17. C. Jane (form Hadley) con mcd
1867, 2, 16. C. Jane (form Hadley) gct New Garden MM, Ind.
1872, 4, 20. Mary (form Tompkins) con mcd

THOMPSON
1821, 8, 25. Amy rocf Newbury MM, dtd 1821,4, 26
1824, 9, 28. Margaret (form Winder) dis mcd
1871, 8, 19. William recrq

THORN
1835, 2, 15. Thomas, s William & Rachel, Green Co., O.; m at Lees Creek, Ruth GREEN dt Isaac & Hannah, Clinton Co., O.

1835, 3, 26. Ruth gct Green Plain MM

THORNBURGH
----, --, --. Edward & Phebe
Ch: Sarah b 1780, 8, 3
Ann " 1782, 1, 27
Mary " 1785, 6, 27
Nathan " 1787, 7, 18
Joseph " 1789, 6, 21
Phebe " 1791, 10, 2
Jane " 1795, 5, 16
Edward " 1798, 1, 16
Jacob " 1801, 3, 7
Edward m 2nd Keziah -----
Ch: Hannah b 1804, 7, 27
Keziah " 1806, 1, 13
Rebecca " 1807, 6, 30
Rachel " 1810, 5, 8
----, --, --. John & Elizabeth
Ch: Rachel B. b 1807, 2, 27
Louisa J. " 1812, 1, 14
Isaac Norton " 1817, 3, 24
1808, 6, 29. John [Thornbrough], s Joseph & Rachel, Highland Co., O.; m at Fairfield, Elizabeth BEALS, dt Daniel & Susannah, Highland Co., O.
1811, 12, 12. Joseph [Thornbrough], s Edward & Phebe, Highland Co., O.; m at Lower East Fork, Rachel BEALES, dt Daniel & Susannah, Highland Co., O.
1812, 2, 6. Joseph [Thornbrough], s Joseph & Rachel, Highland Co., O.; m at Lower East Fork, Lydia JACKSON, dt Jacob & Ann, Clinton Co., O.
----, --, --. Edward & Rachel Ann
Ch: Mary Ann b 1844, 5, 30
Hannah W. " 1846, 9, 4
Lydia Ann " 1848, 11, 1
William W. " 1850, 10, 6
Silas H. " 1852, 12, 24
Matilda Jane " 1855, 4, 8
John Milton " 1857, 7, 30
Rachel Emma " 1859, 8, 6
Samuel Charles " 1861, 12, 17
Frances Elizabeth " 1866, 2, 12
Harriet Ellen " 1868, 1, 9
1845, 3, 9. Elizabeth d ae 59 bur Fairfield
1849, 1, 30. William d ae 66 bur Lees Creek
1865, 11, 9. Lydia d ae 77 bur Fairfield
1865, 8, 24. Alonzo E., s Thomas & Nancy, Mahaska Co., Ia.; m at Oak Grove, Rachel SMITH, dt Job & Charlotte, Fayette Co.,O.
1868, 10, 13. Joel d
1870, 9, 22. William J. [Thornberry], s Abel & Rhoda, Fayette Co., O.; m at Oak Grove, Mary A. DAVIS, dt Jordan & Phebe, Highland Co., O.
1874, 9, 12. John d ae 91
1878, 5, 5. L. A. d bur Newvenna
----, --, --. Chas., s Edward & Rachel, b 1861,12,17; m America -----
Dt: Bessie Mae b 1887, 11, 13
----, --, --. Milton, s Edward & Rachel, b 1857,7,30; m Charlotte E. GREENE, dt Hazel & Naomi, b 1864,11,12
Dt: Edith M. b 1888, 3, 15
1911, 9, 29. Marvin b

1808, 3, 26. John [Thornbrough] rocf New Garden MM, N. C., dtd 1808,2,27
1808, 3, 26. Joseph [Thornbrough] rocf New Garden MM, N. C., dtd 1808,2,27
1810, 5, 26. Phebe Haworth (form Thornbrough) dis mcd
1810, 10, 27. Ann [Thornbrough] dis
1812, 2, 29. Isaac [Thornburgh] & w, Rebecca, & ch, John, Joab, Elizabeth, Joseph, Job, Margaret, Isaac Edward & Alexander, rocf New Garden MM, N. C., dtd 1811,11,2
1813, 3, 27. Jane Haworth (form Thornbrough) dis mcd
1813, 12, 25. Abel [Thornbrough] dis disunity
1816, 5, 25. Susannah [Thornbrough] rocf Clear Creek MM, dtd 1816,5,--
1816, 10, 26. Joseph & w, Rachel, rocf New Garden MM, N. C., dtd 1816,8,31
1816, 11, 30. Joel & w, Anna Jessop, rocf New Garden MM, N. C., dtd 1816,8,31
1816, 11, 30. William & w, Lydia, & ch, Samuel & Jessop, rocf New Garden MM, N. C., dtd 1816,10,26
1817, 2, 22. Elizabeth Smithin (form Thornbury] con mcd
1817, 9, 27. Lees Creek MM was given permission to rst Ann
1819, 4, 24. Springfield MM was given permission to rst Abel [Thornbrough]
1831, 3, 26. Isaac [Thornburgh] & fam gct White River MM, Ind.
1831, 5, 28. Alexander con mcd
1831, 5, 28. Malinda (form Hoskins) con mcd
1831, 8, 25. Joel & w, Ann, & ch, Cyrus, William W., Mary Ann & Lydia Jane, gct Duck Creek MM, Ind.
1832, 1, 26. Louisa Woodmansie (form Thornburgh] dis mcd
1832, 5, 24. Elizabeth Morgan (form Thornburg) dis mcd
1832, 7, 26. Hannah dis disunity
1832, 8, 23. Isaac gct Clear Creek MM

THORNBURG, continued
1832, 9, 20. Edward Jr. gct White River MM, Ind.
1835, 4, 23. Joseph dis jH
1835, 4, 23. Lydia dis jH
1835, 10, 22. Alexander dis mcd
1836, 8, 25. Joseph & Isaac, ch Isaac, gct White River MM, Ind.
1836, 8, 25. Ch of Alexander gct White Water MM, Ind.
1836, 12, 22. Joseph dis mcd
1840, 6, 25. Samuel con mcd
1841, 5, 20. Ann Wright (form Thornburg) con mcd
1841, 7, 22. Isaac N. dis disunity
1842, 3, 24. Edward dis mcd
1846, 3, 21. Rachel Ann recrq
1846, 8, 15. Ruth Eastlock (form Thornburg) dis mcd & joining Separatists
1848, 7, 15. Edward rst by rq
1848, 12, 16. Mary Ann & Hannah W., ch Edward & Rachel Ann, recrq
1852, 2, 21. Jesse dis mcd
1856, 7, 19. Samuel W. [Thornburgh] gct Clear Creek MM
1865, 8, 19. Jacob dis mcd
1866, 3, 17. Rachel M. gct Spring Creek MM, Ia.
1866, 10, 20. Mary Ann Beeson (form Thornburg) con mcd
1870, 1, 15. Abel [Thornberry] rocf Springfield MM, dtd 1869,12,18
1870, 1, 15. William J. [Thornberry] rocf Springfield MM, dtd 1869,12,18
1870, 2, 19. Edward & w, Rachel, & ch, Hannah W., Lydia A., William W., Silas H., Matilda Jane, Rachel Emma, Samuel Charles, Frances E., Hariet E. & John Milton, transferred to Clear Creek MM
1871, 12, 10. Nancy con mcd
1872, 1, 20. Nancy gct Poplar Run MM, Ind.
1874, 4, 18. William J. & w, Mary A., gct Mill Creek MM, Ind.
1877, 9, 15. Edward & w, Rachel Ann, & ch, John Milton, Rachel Emma, Samuel C., Frances E. & Harriet E., rocf Clear Creek MM, dtd 1877,9,8
1877, 9, 15. William W. & w, Victoria, & ch, Clarence & Mary S., rocf Clear Creek MM, dtd 1877,9,8
1878, 1, 19. Hannah W. rocf Clear Creek MM, dtd 1877,12,8
1878, 1, 19. Lydia A. rocf Clear Creek MM, dtd 1877,12,8
1878, 1, 19. Silas rocf Clear Creek MM, dtd 1877,12,8
1880, 11, 20. Sarah J. (form Borum) recrq
1881, 9, 17. Silas H. gct Rose Hill MM, Kans.
1881, 9, 17. Sarah gct Rose Hill MM, Kans.
1886, 1, 16. America recrq
1892, 1, 16. Silas H. & w, Sarah, & ch, Carrie M., Raymond B. & Nellie, gct Wilmington MM, O.
1901, 12, 21. Silas H. & w, Sarah B., & ch, Carrie M., Raymond, Nellie E., Ralph W. & Imogene, rocf Wilmington MM
1903, 11, 21. Clarence E. gct Jonesboro MM
1904, 6, 18. Edward's d rpd
1907, 11, 16. Herbert gct Back Creek MM, Ind.
1911, 3, 18. Minnie relrq
1911, 9, 16. Clinton gct Alliance, O.
1912, 7, 20. W. W. & w, Victoria A., & ch, Charles H., Howard Paul, Russel W., Mary Stella, Annie Ethel & Rachel May, gct Urbana MM, O.
1914, 4, 18. Jesse & w, Addie, & ch, Marvin, roc
1917, 2, 17. Raymond gct Center MM
1918, 9, 21. Ralph gct Caesars Creek MM, O.
1923, 5, 3. S. H. & w, Sarah, & dt, Nellie, gct Leesburg MM, O.
1932, 4, 14. Milton's d rpd

THORP
1895, 4, 2. Delia recrq
1897, 4, 17. Delia relrq

TIFFIN
1854, 3, 18. Eunice (form Hough) dis mcd

TIMBERLAKE
1811, 2, 11. Jonathan, s Richard & Mary, b

1809, 4, 29. Richard rocf South River MM, dtd 1808,11,12
1809, 12, 30. John & s, John, rocf South River MM, Va., dtd 1809,11,11
1809, 12, 30. Mary & dt, Agness Mourning Sallie & Judith, rocf South River MM, Va., dtd 1809,11,11
1810, 4, 28. Richard gct Center MM, to m
1811, 2, 28. Nancy & Elizabeth Barrick, gr dt John Timberlake, recrq

TIMMONS
1870, 6, 18. Shadrock R. & Rachel recrq
1870, 6, 18. Mary Ann recrq
1870, 7, 16. Charity recrq
1870, 12, 17. Azariah recrq
1871, 3, 18. Mary recrq

TODHUNTER
1813, 12, 29. Jury, s Isaac & Eleanor, Fayette Co., O.; m at Fairfield, Jerusha JOHNSON, dt William & Sarah, Highland Co., O.
1821, 8, 3. Isaac d ae 65 bur Walnut Creek
1839, 12, 21. Elenor, w Isaac, d ae 84 bur Walnut Creek
1846, 2, 21. Jephthah d bur Fairfield
----, --, --. Abner Jr. & Emiline

Ch:		
Ida M.	b	1857, 6, 30
Henry M.	"	1862, 6, 27
Anna M.	"	1864, 7, 17
Martha A.	"	1866, 7, 20
Minnie		

TODHUNTER, Abner & Emiline, continued
Ch: Lauretta b
----, --, --. Amos & Emily E.
Ch: Laura C. b 1860, 10, 23
Horace Scott " 1863, 2, 4
Layton Wilson " 1866, 3, 30
Clayton Vincent " 1866, 3, 30
1865, 11, 29. Horace Scott, s Amos & Emily, d bur Walnut Creek
1866, 3, 28. Elizabeth, w Abner Sr. d ae 72 bur Walnut Creek

1808, 7, 30. Isaac Jr. dis
1811, 2, 23. John recrq
1812, 4, 25. Rebecca recrq
1814, 2, 26. Abner con mcd
1815, 4, 29. John & w, Rebecca, gct Cincinnati MM
1818, 1, 31. Margaret Woodard (form Todhunter) con mcd
1818, 4, 25. Jury dis disunity
1818, 9, 29. Jacob con mcd
1822, 5, 25. Rebecca rocf Cincinnati MM, dtd 1822,3,28
1825, 3, 26. Rebecca Garret (form Todhunter) dis mcd
1827, 8, 25. Jerusha & ch, William, Lewis, Charles, Caroline, Isaac Newton & John, gct Green Plain MM
1838, 3, 22. Jephthat recrq
1838, 8, 23. Rebecca recrq
1839, 8, 22. Amos recrq
1841, 3, 25. Milton recrq
1846, 3, 21. Elizabeth recrq
1848, 4, 15. Amos con mcd
1852, 4, 17. Milton gct Dover MM
1852, 12, 18. John recrq
1858, 1, 16. Emily E. recrq
1862, 2, 15. Oscar B., Mary L., Lucetta E., Allise M. & Clara E., ch Amos & Emily E., recrq
1866, 4, 21. Abner recrq
1866, 4, 21. Emeline recrq
1867, 3, 16. Ida M., Henry M. & Anna M., ch Abner & Emeline, recrq
1871, 3, 18. Aaron recrq
1873, 3, 15. Sarah recrq
1873, 8, 16. George F. recrq
1873, 10, 18. Milton recrq

TOLL
1880, 10, 17. Lida Grogg, dt Andrew J. & Sarah, b

1886, 7, 17. Eliza recrq
1915, 6, 19. Paul recrq (later discovered to be birthright mbr)
1920, 6, 16. Harry & w, Louise, & ch, Paul, gct Leesburg MM, O.

TOMLINSON
1807, 11, 12. Josiah, Highland Co., O.; m at Clear Creek, Milley ELLYSON, Highland Co., O.

TOMPKINS
1834, 7, 24. Rachel (form Hiatt) dis mcd
1867, 7, 20. John recrq
1867, 7, 20. Elizabeth, w John, & ch, Addie Elvira, William Edgar & Charles Ellsworth, recrq
1870, 3, 19. Jacob, Rachel, Mary & Nancy recrq
1872, 4, 20. Mary Thomas (form Tompkins) con mcd

TOWNSEND
1878, 2, 16. Eldora rocf Clear Creek MM, dtd 1878,1,12
1893, 5, 20. Eldora dropped from mbrp

TOY
1871, 8, 19. Sarah recrq

TRENT
1895, 4, 2. Florence V. recrq

TRESHAM
1853, 11, 16. Mary Jane (form Wright) con mcd
1856, 10, 18. Jane gct Middle River MM, Ia.

TRIMBLE
1810, 9, --. John d ae 67 bur on Kinikonick
1810, 9, --. Rachel, w John, d bur on Kinikonick

1810, 9, 29. Catherine dis jas
1811, 7, 27. Rachel (form Woodrow) dis mcd
1811, 8, 31. Charity McLintock (form Trimble) dis mcd
1870, 2, 19. James W. rocf Elmwood MM, Ill., dtd 1869,12,25

TYO
1871, 8, 19. S. M. recrq

UNDERWOOD
1809, 12, 30. Martha (form Hussey) dis mcd

UNTHANK
1870, 3, 19. Dinah K. (form Cowgill) con mcd
1870, 4, 16. Dinah K. gct Spiceland MM, Ind.

UPP
1816, 2, 24. Agatha (form Johnson) dis mcd

VAN GRUNDY
1871, 5, 20. Etna [Vangrundy] recrq
1871, 6, 17. Edwin recrq

VAN PELT
1852, 10, 31. John d ae 76 bur Fall Creek
1856, 4, 2. Mary, w John, d ae 78 bur Fall

VAN PELT, continued
Creek

1831, 4, 30. Aaron Winder gct Fall Creek MM, to m Phebe Van Pelt
1833, 1, 24. Agness (form Johnson) dis mcd
1842, 9, 22. Katherine gct Dover MM
1856, 2, 16. Ann gct Red Cedar MM, Ia.
1870, 3, 19. Lucy recrq
1877, 9, 15. Lucinda dis disunity

VAN WINKLE
1886, 7, 17. Martha (Vanwinkle) recrq
1890, 4, 19. Henry recrq

VARLEY
1887, 4, 16. Grace recrq
1893, 5, 20. Grace dropped from mbrp
1915, 5, 15. Perry & w, Mary Elizabeth, & ch, Grace, Percell & Stella Blanche, recrq

VEDER
1838, 3, 22. Enos rocf Sandy Spring MM, dtd 1837,12,22

VICKERS
1825, 6, 25. Isaac & w, Abigail, & ch, Edwin, Samuel N., William M. & Thomas, rocf Clear Creek MM, dtd 1825,6,11
1827, 6, 30. Isaac M. & w, Abigail, & ch, Edwin, Samuel N., William & Thomas, gct Elk MM

VORE
1846, 9, 19. John & w, Susanna, & ch, Hazael, Eli, Sarah & John, rocf Chester MM, Ind., dtd 1846,7,23
1847, 11, 20. John & w, Susanna, & ch, Eli, John & Sarah, gct Clear Creek MM
1849, 5, 19. Asael gct Clear Creek MM

VOTAW
1852, 4, 17. John Green Jr. gct Wabash MM, Ind., to m Mary Ann Votaw

WADE
1826, 8, 5. Mary Ann, dt Thos. & Edith, b

1870, 3, 19. Mary Ann recrq
1871, 8, 19. George L. recrq
1873, 5, 17. Richard recrq

WALEN
1885, 5, 16. Cora B., Anta May & Effie Pearl Walen, ch Laura Cademy, recrq

WALES
1815, 3, 25. Isaac & w, Ruth, & ch, Mary Jane, Nancy & Thomas Montgomery, rocf Deep Creek MM, N. C., dtd 1815,1,7
1815, 7, 29. Cert rec for George [Wails] & w, Elizabeth, from Deep Creek MM, N. C., dtd 1815,1,7, endorsed to Cesars Creek MM
1815, 9, 20. Isaac & w, Ruth, & ch, Mary Jane, Nancy & Thomas Montgomery, gct Miami MM

WALKER
1825, 3, 28. Azel, s William & Martha, Clinton Co., O.; m at Fairfield, Elizabeth P. ROBINSON, dt Joshua & Ann, Champaign Co., O.
1826, 4, 29. Elizabeth gct Center MM
1870, 1, 15. Joshua R. rocf Springfield MM, dtd 1869,12,18
1870, 2, 19. Eliza Jane recrq
1870, 6, 18. Benjamin & Margaret recrq
1870, 12, 17. Benjamin R., Leonidas, Emza & Margaret L., ch Benjamin & Margaret, recrq
1884, 7, 19. Joshua & w, Eliza Jane, gct Wilmington MM, O.
1893, 5, 20. J. R. dropped from mbrp
1900, 6, 16. Eliza J. rocf Wilmington MM
1902, 2, 15. Anna recrq

WALLACE
1886, 7, 17. William recrq
1887, 4, 16. Elizabeth recrq
1889, 3, 16. Carey recrq
1893, 5, 20. Carey dropped from mbrp
1893, 5, 20. Elizabeth dropped from mbrp
1902, 11, 15. William dropped from mbrp
1904, 3, 19. Lesta recrq
1907, 3, 16. Fay recrq
1909, 3, 20. Carey M. & Elizabeth recrq

WALTON
1849, 9, 19. Moses, s Edward & Deborah, Green Co., O.; m at Fairfield, Deborah JOHNSON, dt Anthony & Mary, Highland Co., O.

1850, 10, 19. Deborah gct Cesars Creek MM

WALTERS
1812, 7, 25. Mary gct Center MM

WARNER
----, --, --. Isaac & Mary
Ch: Lydia b 1796, 7, 28
John " 1798, 7, 12
Elizabeth " 1802, 9, 22
Levi " 1804, 10, 22
William " 1807, 2, 28
Isaac " 1809, 2, 26
Abner " 1811, 4, 11
----, --, --. Levi & Massey
Ch: Ann b 1806, 7, 28
Joseph " 1807, 10, 2
Mary " 1809, 8, 24
Rachel " 1811, 9, 29
Massey " 1813, 10, 5
Levi " 1815, 6, 2
Simeon " 1817, 10, 22
Lyda " 1819, 9, 10

WARNER, Levi & Massey, continued
Ch: Abner b 1821, 8, 2
1811, 4, 21. Mary [Worner] d bur Dry Run
1814, 8, 23. Mary, dt Levi & Massey, d bur Dry Run
1817, 7, 24. Levi, s Levi & Massey, d bur Dry Run
1819, 9, 17. Rachel, dt Levi & Massy, d bur Dry Run

1809, 11, 25. Mercy con mcd
1811, 3, 30. Levi rocf Wilmington MM, dtd 1810,8,10
1814, 3, 26. Mary con mcd
1816, 7, 27. Mary & ch, Nancy, John, Elizabeth, Levi, William, Isaac & Abner, gct Ceasars Creek MM
1816, 7, 27. Lydia gct Cesars Creek MM
1823, 3, 29. Levi con mcd
1829, 6, 27. Anne Oldham (form Warner) dis mcd
1829, 9, 26. Levi dis jH
1829, 11, 28. Elizabeth dis jH
1831, 11, 24. Joseph dis mcd
1872, 7, 20. Mary recrq

WARNING
1906, 2, 8. Clarence Ladd, s Benj. & Retta, b

1905, 4, 15. Benjamin & Retta recrq

WASHBURN
1871, 2, 18. George & Amelia Ann recrq
1876, 5, 20. George & w dis disunity
1876, 6, 17. Amelia Ann dis
1886, 7, 17. Frank recrq
1893, 5, 20. Frank dropped from mbrp
1894, 3, 17. Amelia recrq

WASSON
1841, 3, 4. William, s Calvin & Mary, Fayette Co., O.; m at Walnut Creek, Elizabeth ELLIS, dt David & Hannah, Fayette Co., O.
Ch: Emily b 1842, 4, 10
Hannah Ann " 1843, 8, 24
Thomas Elwood " 1845, 2, 14
Mary Jane " 1848, 4, 10
P. Alwilda

1840, 9, 24. William rocf Alum Creek MM, dtd 1840,9,22
1855, 12, 15. Calvin & w, Mary, & ch, Eliza Ann & Asa, rocf Pipe Creek MM, dtd 1855, 11,3
1856, 11, 15. Calvin & w, Mary, & ch, Eliza Ann & Asa, gct West Union MM, Ind.
1858, 11, 20. William & w, Elizabeth, & ch, Emily, Hannah Ann, Thomas Elwood, Mary Jane & Priscilla Alwilda, gct Plainfield MM, Ind.

WATKINS
1815, 2, 25. Sally [Wadkins] rocf Cedar Creek MM, Va., dtd 1814,12,10

WATSON
1821, 11, 24. Jonathan J. rocf Buckington MM, Pa., dtd 1821,10,1
1825, 8, 27. Jonathan I. gct Cincinnati MM
1825, 10, 29. Anna (form Johnson) dis mcd

WATTS
1917, 2, 17. Raymond & Elizabeth, ch Maud, recrq

WAY
1823, 1, 1. Robert, s Samuel & Hannah, Warren Co., O.; m at Fairfield, Abigail WILLIAMS, dt Enion & Martha, Highland Co., O.

1823, 3, 29. Abigail gct Miami MM
1828, 2, 23. Robert & w, Abigail, & ch, Mary Anne & Phatran, rocf Clear Creek MM, dtd 1828,2,9
1828, 11, 29. Robert dis jH
1829, 7, 25. Abigail dis jH

WEAVER
1882, 4, 15. Charles A. recrq
1888, 6, 16. Jane recrq
1910, 6, 18. Charles relrq

WEBSTER
----, --, --. Taylor d early in 1800 bur at Dry Run or Salt Creek

1811, 8, 31. Elizabeth con mou
1819, 7, 31. Elizabeth gct West Branch MM,O.
1826, 1, 28. Taylor gct White Water MM,Ind.
1837, 1, 26. William dis mcd

WEECE
1870, 6, 18. William recrq

WELLS
1871, 3, 18. John F. & Anna recrq
1871, 3, 18. Matilda E., James F. & Sarah E., ch John F. & Annie, recrq

WERTSEL
1872, 11, 20. Lydia d bur Walnut Creek

WEST
1868, 4, 18. Mary Amney (form McPherson) con mcd
1868, 7, 18. Mary Ann gct Newberry MM
1877, 2, 17. Harrison & w recrq
1877, 2, 17. Jane recrq
1878, 8, 17. Harrison & fam dropped from mbrp
1880, 1, 17. Mary Margaret & ch, Morris, Ruth Ann & Sarah Jane, rocf Newberry MM, dtd 1879,10,20
1885, 10, 17. Mary M. & ch, Sarah J., relrq

WEST, continued
1886, 3, 20. Morris recrq
1886, 7, 17. Jennie recrq
1887, 3, 19. Jennie relrq
1892, 3, 19. Ettie M. recrq
1894, 3, 17. Leslie recrq
1896, 7, 18. Leslie dropped from mbrp
1896, 7, 18. Morris dropped from mbrp
1904, 2, 20. Thomas recrq
1908, 7, 18. Sadie Shepert rocf Wilmington MM
1914, 1, 17. Thomas relrq

WHINERY
1862, 4, 19. James Morris gct Center MM, to m Hannah Whinery
1862, 9, 20. Hannah Morris & ch, Albert & Sarah Whinery, rocf Center MM, dtd 1862,8,13

WHITBY
1870, 7, 16. Nancy recrq
1902, 11, 15. William & w dropped from mbrp

WHITE
1849, 7, 31. Elgar Toms, s Francis, d bur Fall Creek

1812, 7, 25. Elizabeth & s gct Center MM
1850, 11, 16. Francis & w, Sarah, & ch, Lydia Jane, gct Salem MM, Ia.

WHITLACK
1872, 8, 17. Sarah S. recrq

WHITSEL
1870, 1, 15. Susan J. & ch, Lida F., & Adda Rachel, rocf Springfield MM, dtd 1869,12, 18
1873, 3, 15. Inis recrq

WILCOX
1839, 8, 22. Martha rst by rq
1841, 5, 20. Lucinda & Martha Jane, ch Martha, recrq
1846, 6, 20. Martha dis jas
1848, 3, 18. Lucinda Rees (form Wilcox) dis mcd & jas

WILDMAN
1827, 5, 26. Thomas Winder gct Green Plain MM, to m Hannah Wildman

WILEY
1878, 9, 21. Ella recrq

WILKINS
1817, 9, 27. Joseph & w, Sarah, & ch, Tamzon, William, John, Thomas, Hannah & Francisco, rocf Fall Creek MM, dtd 1817,9,20
1822, 6, 29. Joseph Jr. rst with consent of New Garden MM
1822, 7, 27. Thomas dis disunity
1822, 9, 28. William dis mcd
1825, 11, 26. John gct Lee's Creek MM
1825, 11, 26. Joseph & w, Sarah, & s, Francis, gct Lees Creek MM
1826, 5, 19. Hannah Bradfield (form Wilkins) dis mcd
1827, 5, 26. Joseph Jr. gct Goshen MM
1833, 11, 21. Joseph & w gct Cherry Grove MM, Ind.
1870, 6, 18. Rebecca recrq
1871, 5, 20. William recrq

WILLETS
1809, 10, 28. Nancy & Anna, ch William, recrq
1817, 5, 31. Joseph rocf Plainfield MM, dtd 1817,4,24
1820, 9, 30. Joseph [Willits] gct Still Water MM

WILLIAMS
----, --, --. Enion & Martha
Ch: Clark b 1796, 1, 29
Seth " 1798, 6, 24
Abigail " 1802, 1, 24
Enion " 1804, 1, 24
Isaac " 1806, 10, 14
Jacob " 1806, 10, 14
Grace " 1809, 8, 14
1808, 2, 23. Isaac, s Jonathan & Phebe, b
----, --, --. William & Phebe
Ch: Joseph b 1810, 5, 23
John " 1812, 8, 14
1812, 4, 9. Isaac, s Owen & Catherine, Highland Co., O.; m at Clear Creek, Sarah HUSSEY, dt Christopher & Sarah, Highland Co., O.
1812, 7, 29. Peter, s Enion & Martha, Highland Co., O.; m at Fairfield, Nancy Willis, dt William & Henrietta, Highland Co., O.
1823, 1, 1. Abigail m Robert WAY
1826, 5, 3. Grace m David B. MORGAN
1827, 2, 4. Ennion d ae 68 bur Fairfield
1829, 7, 1. Martha m Thomas SUMNER
----, --, --. William & Martha
Ch: Guy b 1889, 7, 12
Henry Glenn" 1898, 1, 2

1810, 9, 29. Isaac recrq
1814, 4, 30. Peter & fam gct Cesars Creek MM
1816, 6, 29. Clark gct Clear Creek MM
1819, 10, 30. Seth gct Cesars Creek MM, to m
1820, 3, 25. Keturah rocf Cesars Creek MM, dtd 1820,2,25
1825, 12, 31. Seth & w, Kitturah, & ch, Samuel & Avis, gct Green Plain MM
1829, 11, 28. Isaac dis jH
1830, 8, 28. Jacob dis disunity
1831, 1, 29. Ennion dis disunity
1839, 11, 21. John H. Terrell gct Clear Creek MM, to m Elizabeth Williams
1871, 6, 17. William recrq
1873, 3, 15. Esther Perdue con mcd
1873, 5, 17. Allen recrq
1883, 2, 17. Ettie recrq
1886, 11, 20. Etta relrq

WILLIAMS, continued
1895, 4, 2. Don H. recrq
1895, 4, 2. William & w, Martha, recrq
1901, 3, 16. Guy recrq
1902, 11, 15. Etta dropped from mbrp
1904, 3, 19. Don L. relrq
1905, 12, 16. Inez recrq

WILLIAMSON
1871, 3, 18. Harrison recrq
1871, 3, 18. Charity recrq
1871, 3, 18. Cora J. recrq
1873, 3, 15. Adam Jackson recrq
1873, 3, 15. Rhoda A. recrq
1873, 7, 19. George A., William T., Samuel A., John McC., Harriet M. & Sarah Estella, ch A. Jackson & w recrq
1876, 12, 16. Adam J. & fam gct Greenwood MM, Ind.
1878, 8, 17. Harrison & fam dropped from mbrp

WILLIS
1812, 7, 29. Nancy m Peter WILLIAMS
1842, 10, 24. Joel d ae 78 bur Fairfield
1847, 9, 13. Hannah d ae 79 bur Lees Creek

1811, 8, 31. Henrietta recrq
1814, 3, 26. William & fam gct Cesars Creek MM
1831, 9, 22. Hannah, w Joel, gct Cherry Grove MM
1831, 10, 20. Joel gct Cherry Grove MM, Ind.
1842, 8, 25. Joel & w, Hannah, rocf Westfield MM, Ind., dtd 1842,7,7
1843, 6, 22. Lydia, minor, rocf Cherry Grove MM, Ind., dtd 1842,12,10

WILSON
1834, 12, 25. Cert rec for Henry from Deep Creek MM, N. C., endorsed to Duck Creek MM, Ind.
1839, 8, 22. Martha recrq
1846, 6, 20. Martha dis jas

WILSTACH
1874, 7, 18. Cornelius & Sarah gct Londonderry MM

WINDER
----, --, --. Abner & Hope [Winders]

Ch:		
	John	b 1803, 6, 22
	Thomas	" 1804, 12, 24
	Sarah	" 1806, 11, 23
	Aaron	" 1808, 11, 9
	Joshua	" 1810, 7, 8
	James	" 1812, 3, 19
	Abner	" 1814, 7, 20
	Henry	" 1816, 10, 19
	Elizabeth	" 1819, 6, 19
	Levi	
	Moses	
	Caleb	

1812, 6, 24. Margaret d ae 71 bur Dry Run
1819, 4, 5. John d ae 82 bur Dry Run
1821, 12, 6. John, s Abner & Hope, Ross Co., O.; m at Walnut Creek, Sarah HUTTON, dt John & Mary, Fayette Co., O.

1809, 12, 30. John, Thomas & Allen [Winders], ch Abner, recrq
1809, 12, 30. Sarah [Winders], dt Abner & Hope, recrq
1821, 12, 24. John, s James, dis mcd
1824, 1, 24. Amy Cook (form Winders) dis mcd
1824, 9, 28. Margaret Thompson (form Winder) dis mcd
1825, 12, 31. John & w, Sarah, & ch, David, Davidson & Sewell, gct Green Plane MM
1827, 5, 26. Thomas gct Green Plain MM, to m Hannah Wildman
1827, 10, 27. Hannah rocf Green Plain MM, dtd 1827,9,5
1831, 4, 30. Aaron gct Fall Creek MM, to m Phebe Van Pelt
1831, 11, 24. Thomas & w, Hannah, & ch, John, Edward & Aaron, gct Green Plain MM
1832, 11, 22. James A., minor s Abner, gct Springborough MM
1833, 5, 23. Phebe rocf Fall Creek MM
1834, 3, 20. John con mcd
1835, 11, 26. James rocf Springborough MM
1836, 5, 26. James con mcd
1837, 8, 24. Abner, Jr. gct Goshen MM
1837, 8, 24. Joshua gct Goshen MM
1837, 9, 21. Abner & w, Hope, & ch, Sarah, Elizabeth, Levi, Moses & Caleb, gct Goshen MM (s: Henry, not included)
1838, 7, 26. Henry dis mcd & jas
1838, 8, 23. James gct Goshen MM
1838, 10, 25. Aaron & w, Phebe, & ch, Mary V., Margaret & Sarah Elizabeth, gct Goshen MM

WING
1818, 10, 31. Elizabeth (form Crispin) dis mcd
1820, 8, 26. Cincinnati MM was given permission to rst Elizabeth

WINKLE
----, --, --. Samuel m Almira B. SMITH, dt James & Catharine, b 1856,12,14

Ch:		
	Cecil Ross	b 1881, 7, 8
	Oral Guy	" 1885, 11, 17
	Loren Fay	" 1890, 9, 13

1878, 2, 16. James P. rocf Clear Creek MM, dtd 1878,1,12
1878, 7, 20. Samuel recrq
1886, 2, 20. Elizabeth recrq
1889, 5, 18. James dis
1898, 9, 17. James recrq

WINN
1871, 8, 19. Mathilda recrq

WISE
1890, 4, 19. Josie R. recrq
1890, 4, 19. H. F. & Edward S. recrq
1891, 4, 18. W. F. relrq
1893, 6, 17. Josie relrq
1896, 7, 18. Edward dropped from mbrp

WITTER
1815, 6, 24. Jonathan dis mcd

WITTY
1825, 4, 30. James con mcd
1825, 5, 28. James gct Dover MM

WOLF
1887, 4, 16. Joel & Lida J. recrq
1898, 1, 15. Joel relrq

WOOD
1871, 5, 20. George R. & dt, Ellen, rocf Chesterfield MM, dtd 1870,9,10
1884, 5, 17. Bell recrq

WOODARD
1822, 2, 15. Margaret d bur Walnut Creek
1853, 10, 17. Levi, s Luke & Avis, Wayne Co., Ind.; m at Hardins Creek, Sarah Ann HADLEY dt James & Sarah, Highland Co., O.

1818, 1, 31. Margaret (form Todhunter) con mcd
1822, 6, 29. Clarenda recrq
1824, 3, 27. Jane (form Fisher) con mcd
1832, 11, 22. Abishai, Clarissa, Minerva, William & Adaline, ch Jane, recrq
1834, 6, 26. Isaac M. rocf Birmingham MM, dtd 1834,5,28
1838, 4, 26. Isaac M. & w, Jane, & ch, Abisha, Minerva, William & Mary, gct Miami MM
1840, 8, 20. Clarinda Terrell (form Woodard) con mcd
1854, 1, 21. Sarah Ann gct New Garden MM, Ind.

WOODMANSEE
1832, 1, 26. Louisa [Woodmansie] (form Thornburgh) dis mcd
1884, 4, 19. Charles & ch, Edna M., Wilbur E. & Eland L., recrq
1891, 7, 18. Charles [Woodmancy] relrq
1902, 11, 15. Edna [Woodmanse] dropped from mbrp
1917, 6, 17. Geneva & s, Herman, recrq

WOODROW
1809, 4, 29. Joseph rocf Hopewell MM, dtd 1808,10,3
1809, 4, 29. Elizabeth rocf Hopewell MM, dtd 1808,10,3
1809, 4, 29. Rachel rocf Hopewell MM, dtd 1808,10,3
1809, 6, 24. Joshua & s, Watson & Joshua, rocf Hopewell MM, dtd 1808,10,3
1809, 6, 24. Ann & dt, Elizabeth & Rachel, rocf Hopewell MM, dtd 1808,10,3
1811, 6, 29. Joseph dis disunity
1811, 7, 27. Rachel Trimble (form Woodrow) dis mcd
1886, 12, 18. Clara recrq

WOOLARD
1874, 1, 5. John b
----, --, --. Frank m Frances Olive MILBURN, dt Wesley & Jemima, b 1873,1,11
Ch: Lewis Glenn b 1900, 10, 20
Horace Clinton " 1904, 10, 16
Harry Delbert " 1908, 1, 4
Sarah Elizabeth " 1910, 3, 19
Edgar V. " 1902, 10, 1

1832, 1, 26. Rhoda [Wollard] (form Goodson) dis mcd
1870, 2, 19. James & Merab recrq
1872, 6, 15. Mary J. recrq
1872, 11, 16. Elizabeth M. recrq
1881, 9, 17. Mary J. & William F. gct Rose Hill MM, Kans.
1885, 5, 16. Daniel & Mary recrq
1886, 3, 20. Joseph, Elizabeth, William & Frank recrq
1889, 3, 16. Daniel, Jennie, Wilson P., Milton S. & Myrta M. recrq
1893, 5, 20. Daniel, Wilson & Mertie dropped from mbrp
1893, 5, 20. Jennie & Milton dropped from mbrp
1915, 5, 15. Frances & ch, Edgar Vernon, Horace Clinton, Harry Delbert & Sarah Elizabeth, recrq
1915, 5, 15. Lewis Glenn recrq

WOOLSEY
1872, 3, 16. Marianne recrq

WORLEY
1808, 10, 20. Rebeckah Beason (form Worley) dis mcd
1809, 2, 25. Jacob dis disunity
1811, 5, 25. Ruth rocf Westfield MM, N. C., dtd 1810,8,11
1871, 3, 18. Ella recrq

WORMALDORF
1872, 4, 20. David recrq
1874, 6, 20. David [Wormaldurf] relrq

WORRELL
1883, 2, 17. Mary E. & William B. recrq
1883, 2, 17. Ruth recrq

WORTH
1873, 3, 15. Andrew G. recrq

WORTHINGTON
1854, 8, 19. Sarah (form Burgess) con mcd
1869, 4, 17. Rachel, Nancy, Armilla & Arthur, ch Sarah, recrq
1869, 5, 15. Sarah & ch, Rachel, Nancy, Armelda & Arthur, gct Henkles Creek MM, Ind.

WRIGHT
1809, 7, 13. Joshua, s John & Jemimah, Highland Co., O.; m at Fall Creek, Rebeckah SUMNER, dt Bowater & Rebeckah, Highland Co., O.
1815, 2, 1. Jemima m Josiah DRAPER
1818, 4, 8. Sidney m James HUFF
1822, 4, 4. David, s Edward & Hannah, Highland Co., O.; m at Walnut Creek, Margaret ELLIS, dt Thomas & Lydia, Fayette Co., O.
Ch: Jonathan b 1823, 8, 12
Lydia " 1824, 10, 7
Edward " 1826, 11, 17
Sidney " 1828, 1, 3
Hannah " 1829, 12, 25
John " 1831, 6, 24
Jane " 1834, 3, 21
Anna " 1836, 4, 6
David " 1838, 9, 3
Eleanor " 1841, 9, 18
David m 2nd Ruth -----
Ch: William Dillen b 1848, 10, 3
Jacob H. " 1846, 4, 24
Rachel " 1849, 10, 3
1823, 1, 29. Joel, s John & Jemima, Highland Co., O.; m at Fairfield, Martha JOHNSON, dt Ashley & Milly, Highland Co., O.
Ch: Thomas Clarkson b 1823, 8, 16
Edwin Wadkins " 1825, 8, 26
Ashley Johnson " 1827, 5, 9
Caroline " 1828, 10, 30
Daniel Webster " 1830, 9, 7
Jane " 1832, 4, 18
Joel " 1834, 1, 11
1825, 6, 29. John, s James & Catherine, Clinton Co., O.; m at Fairfield, Abigail PIKE, dt John & Leah, Highland Co., O.
1827, 5, 2. Jonah, s John & Jemimah, Highland Co., O.; m at Fairfield, Sarah TERRELL, dt David & Mary, Highland Co., O.
Ch: Pleasant b 1828, 2, 19
Lindley Murray " 1830, 3, 12
Mary " 1832, 7, 8
Rachel " 1834, 8, 6
David " 1837, 3, 7
John " 1840, 4, 5
1828, 8, 14. Jemima d ae 80 bur Fairfield
1831, 10, 23. Jacob d bur Fairfield
1832, 1, 18. Doctor J., s Joseph & Susannah, b
1833, 8, 24. Joseph d ae 59 bur Fairfield
1833, 10, 14. Joel d ae 44 bur Fairfield
1835, 1, 29. Jane d bur Fairfield
1837, 8, 8. Susanna d bur Fairfield
----, --, --. John & Ann
Ch: Joel T. b 1841, 11, 20
William E. " 1844, 9, 16
Levi " 1847, 9, 11
Rachel " 1847, 10, 3
Joseph " 1854, 2, 7
Edward W. " 1856, 12, 20
1841, 9, 13. Jonah d ae 60 bur Fairfield
1841, 12, 29. Margaret d bur Fairfield
1842, 4, 12. John d bur Fairfield
1843, 6, 23. Sarah m Jonah FRAIZER
1848, 8, 27. Jacob H., s David, d bur Fairfield
1848, 9, 16. Lindley Murray d bur Fall Creek
1851, 3, 12. William, s John, d bur Fairfield
1855, 10, 17. Hannah d ae 95 bur Fairfield
1864, 7, 14. Rachel d ae 77 bur Fairfield
----, --, --. Joel F. & Ann
Ch: Lydia Ann b 1866, 6, 20
Rachel Elva" 1869, 3, 1
1868, 9, 22. Rachel Ann d bur Fairfield

1808, 7, 30. John rocf Hopewell MM, Va., dtd 1808,2,1
1809, 8, 26. John recrq
1809, 8, 26. Catherine recrq
1810, 8, 25. Elizabeth & Mary Timberlake rocf Center MM, dtd 1810,8,7
1810, 11, 24. James rst by rq with consent of New Hope MM
1810, 12, 29. John, Joab & George, ch James, recrq
1810, 12, 29. Hannah Lydia & Judith, ch James, recrq
1811, 3, 30. Mary Terrell (form Wright) dis mcd
1811, 11, 30. Joseph dis mcd
1812, 7, 25. Betty, James, Phebe, Sampson & Hannah, ch John, recrq
1812, 10, 31. Sarah recrq
1812, 10, 31. Elizabeth gct Center MM
1813, 5, 29. Joseph rst by rq
1813, 12, 25. James & fam gct Cesars Creek MM
1814, 7, 30. Joshua & fam gct Fall Creek MM
1814, 10, 29. Joseph gct Clear Creek MM
1815, 6, 24. Hannah Milner (form Wright) dis mcd
1817, 1, 25. John gct New Garden MM, Ind.
1817, 2, 22. Rebecca gct New Garden MM, Ind.
1820, 9, 30. Anna Slaughter (form Wright) con mcd
1823, 10, 25. John rocf Green Plain MM, dtd 1823,9,20
1824, 5, 29. Joab Jr. rocf Green Plain MM, dtd 1824,5,22
1824, 10, 30. Ruth recrq
1825, 12, 31. Joab & w, Ruth, & dt, Amy, gct Newberry MM

WRIGHT, continued
1826, 11, 25. Joseph & ch, Elizabeth, John, Milton & Owen, rocf Newbury MM, dtd 1826, 10,26
1830, 1, 30. Susanna recrq
1830, 4, 24. Lot, s Joseph, recrq
1831, 5, 28. Elizabeth Johnson (form Wright) con mcd
1832, 11, 22. John & w, Abigail, & ch, Mary Jane, Nathan & Catherine, gct Duck Creek MM, Ind.
1836, 3, 24. Martha Beeson (form Wright) con mcd
1838, 5, 24. John dis disunity
1840, 3, 26. Owen W. dis disunity
1840, 3, 26. Thomas C. dis disunity
1840, 9, 24. Lot & Doctor J., minor ch Joseph, gct Newbury MM
1841, 5, 20. Ann (form Thornburg) con mcd
1843, 10, 26. Lydia Moon (form Wright) con mcd
1844, 2, 22. John recrq
1844, 4, 25. Joel T., s John & Ann, recrq
1844, 12, 21. Ashley, minor, gct Center MM
1845, 3, 15. David gct Newberry MM, to m Ruth Hunt
1845, 12, 20. Ruth rocf Newbury MM, dtd 1845, 9,15
1847, 4, 17. Caroline Terry (form Wright) con mcd
1847, 5, 15. Edwin con mcd
1847, 6, 19. Narcissa (form Terrill) con mcd
1847, 7, 17. Rachel recrq
1848, 8, 19. Hannah Horseman (form Wright) con mcd
1848, 12, 16. Ashley rocf Center MM, dtd 1848, 10,18
1849, 2, 17. Pleasant gct Dover MM
1849, 4, 21. Joseph & w, Lydia, & ch, Henry C., Eleanor C. & David Sands, gct Clear Creek MM
1850, 3, 16. Ashley J. dis disunity
1850, 7, 20. Sidney Jury (form Wright) con mcd
1851, 1, 18. Jane Borum (form Wright) dis mcd
1851, 2, 15. Edward gct Pleasant Plain MM,Ia.
1852, 10, 16. Jonathan gct Three River MM, Ia.
1853, 11, 16. Mary Jane Tresham (form Wright) con mcd
1855, 12, 15. Anna Dillon (form Wright) dis mcd
1856, 1, 19. John Jr. gct Three River MM, Ia.
1856, 2, 16. Narcissa A. dis jas
1856, 10, 18. Daniel dis mcd
1858, 7, 17. Edwin dis jas
1858, 7, 17. Hannah recrq
1861, 11, 16. Eleanor gct South River MM, Ia.
1861, 12, 21. David Jr. con mcd
1865, 8, 19. Joel T. con mcd
1865, 8, 19. Anna M. (form Barrett) con mcd
1868, 5, 16. David & s, Edward S., gct South River MM, Ia.
1869, 9, 18. Emily (form Stalker) con mcd
1870, 3, 19. Amon recrq
1870, 3, 19. Lindley M. & Hannah E. recrq
1870, 3, 19. Albert, Anna & Clifford, ch Lindley M. & Hannah E., recrq of parents
1873, 1, 18. Levi dis mcd
1874, 2, 21. Mary recrq
1874, 12, 19. Sarah Amanda recrq
1878, 1, 19. Joel H. relrq
1878, 7, 20. Lindley M. & fam gct Spring River MM, Kans.
1878, 10, 19. Amon & fam gc
1882, 4, 15. Joel H. recrq
1886, 7, 17. Martha & Mary recrq
1887, 11, 19. J. D. & w, Martha, gct Newbury MM
1893, 5, 20. Sarah dropped from mbrp
1895, 12, 21. Joel T. & w, Anna M., rocf Hopewell MM
1896, 9, 19. Joshua & w, Mary, & ch, Mary, rocf Newberry MM
1898, 3, 19. Frank O. rocf Clear Creek MM
1898, 3, 19. Kate recrq
1899, 2, 18. Henry H. & Esther C. recrq
1899, 4, 15. Dr. Frank O. & w, Katherine, relrq
1907, 3, 16. Eunice recrq
1909, 9, 18. Joel F. & w, Elizabeth E., gct Wilmington MM
1910, 7, 16. Ellen relrq
1912, 7, 20. Eunice B. dropped from mbrp
1914, 1, 17. William A., Edward, Madge & Bessie recrq
1914, 1, 17. Mary Crute rocf Clear Creek MM, dtd 1914,1,10
1918, 2, 16. W. A. & w, Mary Crulet, & ch, Edward, Madge & Bessie, gct Leesburg MM,O.

WYATT
1915, 5, 15. William recrq

YOKUM
1886, 2, 20. Anna recrq
1893, 5, 20. Anna dropped from mbrp

YOUNG
1813, 3, 27. Mourning (form Butler) dis mcd
1873, 5, 17. Lizzie recrq

ZIMMERMAN
1873, 9, 20. S. Anna recrq
1904, 3, 19. Zatharine recrq

* * * * * * *

CONARD
1890, 5, 19. Mary Jane, dt A. J. & Hattie E., b

DILLON
1861, 2, 16. Anna [Dillen] recrq
1861, 6, 15. Mary Jane, Martha Ellen & Lydia

DILLON, continued
Arabelle, ch Anna, recrq
1867, 7, 20. William, s Anna, recrq

DUTTON
1849, 11, 21. Thomas, s David & Phebe, Highland Co., O.; m at Fairfield, Elizabeth P. LADD, dt Jacob & Elizabeth, Highland Co., O.

HAINES
1871, 2, 18. Annie M. con mcd

STALKER
1840, 7, 17. Nathan d bur Fairfield

WRIGHT
1851, 10, 16. Sarah Ann, dt John & Joanna, b

FALL CREEK MONTHLY MEETING

Fall Creek Monthly Meeting in Highland County was set off from Fairfield Monthly Meeting at a meeting of Miami Quarterly Meeting held 5 Mo. 11, 1811. One of the first acts of the new meeting was to appoint a committee to confer with a similar committee of the Fairfield Monthly Meeting to establish the boundaries. The men selected were Richard Barrett, Josiah Thomasson, Walter Canady, Caleb Sumner, Obediah Small and Joseph Small.

The boundary established was as follows: "The new road leading from New Lancaster to Chillicothe; thence up the state road to the Indian Ford on Paint Creek; thence up Paint Creek to the mouth of Rattlesnake (fork of Paint); thence up Rattlesnake to the mouth of Fall Creek; thence the road leading to Hillsborough; thence the new state road to West Union."

The meeting ran very smoothly until mid year of 1829 when quite a serious upheaval was experienced due to so many members following the teaching of Elias Hicks. Due to disownments and removals, the Fall Creek Monthly Meeting came to a close in 1848 when they began meeting with the Fairfield Monthly Meeting near Leesburg, Highland County.

RECORDS

AIKERS
1849, 11, 17. Rachel (form Jackson) dis mou & jas (H)

ALDERSON
1823, 2, 15. Phebe (form Ballard) dis mcd

AMOS
1842, 3, 23. Matilda (form Rees) dis mcd (H)

ANDREWS
1812, 8, 22. Thomas, Mary, Sarah, Hannah & David, ch Hannah, rocf Cane Creek MM, dtd 1810,3,3 end by Fairfield MM 1812,5,30
1812, 11, 21. Mary Barney (form Andrews) dis mcd
1814, 5, 21. Thomas dis disunity
1817, 7, 19. Sarah Parson (form Andrews)dis mcd
1821, 12, 22. Hannah dis

ANTHONY
----, --, --. Thomas & Judith (H)
Ch: Clark b 1823, 10, 11
Almerid " 1825, 3, 22
Ovilla " 1826, 11, 29

1832, 4, 21. Judith & ch gct White Water MM, Ind. (H)
1834, 7, 19. Rachel Baker (form Anthony) con mcd (H)
1835, 11, 21. Rhoda Townsend (form Anthony) dis mcd (H)
1838, 3, 17. Ruth con mcd (H)

ANTRIM
1828, 8, 23. Sarah gct White Water MM, Ind.
1828, 3, 22. Daniel rmt Sarah Hiatt

ARNOTT
1832, 9, 7. Homer recrq

ARTHUR
1843, 10, 21. Ann (form Larkin) dis mou (H)

BAILEY
----, --, --. Thomas & Elizabeth (H)
Ch: Judith b 1816, 3, 22
Ansalem
Jr. " 1820, 8, 16
Elizabeth " 1823, 4, 17
Moses " 1825, 1, 13
Ann " 1814, 5, 21 (sic)
Hannah " 1827, 11, 12
1828, 8, 31. Hannah d bur Clear Creek
1829, 9, 20. Ann d bur Clear Creek

1833, 12, 21. Joseph dis mcd (H)
1834, 3, 22. Judith [Daley] dis disunity (H)
1841, 6, 19. Elizabeth McMillen (form Bailey) dis mcd (H)
1853, 8, 20. Moses dis mcd (H)

BAKER
----, --, --. Amasa & Sarah (H)
Ch: George H. b 1811, 3, 14
John " 1812, 10, 10
Mary " 1814, 10, 23
Joseph " 1817, 1, 26
Nathan " 1819, 5, 7
Elizabeth " 1820, 12, 11
Lydia Ann " 1822, 4, 22
Susannah " 1824, 9, 15
William " 1828, 8, 17
Enos " 1830, 11, 28
1828, 8, 19. Nathan d bur Clear Creek
1833, 9, 15. Elizabeth d bur Clear Creek
1836, 7, 28. Geo. H., s Amasa & Sarah, Highland Co., O.; m in Fall Creek MH, Margaret BOND, dt John & Rachel, Frederick Co., Va. (H)
Ch: Amba b 1841, 10, 27
Mary " 1847, 2, 12
1843, 4, 28. Mary m Jesse M. FOULKE (H)
1845, 4, 23. Susannah m Benj. JOHNSON (H)

1823, 11, 22. Amasa & fam rocf Chester MM, Pa., dtd 1823,8,28, end by Plainfield MM, O., 1823,10,23
1831, 10, 22. George con mcd (H)
1831, 10, 22. Hannah (form Wright) con mcd (H)
1834, 7, 19. John con mcd (H)
1834, 7, 19. Rachel (form Anthony) con mcd (H)
1845, 10, 18. Joseph dis mcd (H)
1851, 12, 20. George & w, Margaret, & two ch gct Fall Creek MM, Ind. (H)
1854, 3, 18. Amasa & w, Sarah, gct Fall Creek MM, Ind. (H)
1853, 8, 20. Lydia Peale (form Baker) dis mcd (H)

BALDWIN
1834, 11, 5. Charity d bur in Michigan (H)

1812, 8, 22. Walter dis disunity
1813, 4, 17. Uriah dis disunity
1814, 2, 19. Daniel dis disunity
1814, 9, 17. Olive (form Hiatt) dis mcd
1815, 10, 21. Jesse & w, Hannah, & ch, Sarah & Sophah, gct Clear Creek MM
1816, 6, 22. Richard dis disunity
1819, 2, 20. Jesse & fam gct New Garden MM, Ind.
1820, 10, 21. Jesse rocf Clear Creek MM, dtd 1820,10,14, to m Catharine Sexton
1820, 11, 18. Jesse rmt Catharine Sexton
1821, 6, 23. Jesse & w, Catharine, gct Fairfield MM
1827, 11, 17. Jesse & w, Miriam, rocf Springfield MM, Ind., dtd 1827,9,15
1829, 2, 21. Jesse & w, Miriam, gct Goshen MM
1832, 7, 21. Charity (form Tomlinson) con

BALDWIN, continued
mcd (H)

BALLARD
1812, 3, 21. Jerman & w, Rachel, & ch, Wm., Phebe Anslum, Elizabeth Edith & Rebecca, rocf Mt. Pleasant MM, dtd 1811,4,27 end by Fairfield MM 1812,1,25
1813, 9, 18. Stephen dis mcd
1813, 10, 29. Byron & w, Sarah, & ch, Levina, Aden, Uriah, Jesse, Mary, Betsy & Wm., rocf Westfield MM, dtd 1812,12,12
1814, 1, 22. Levina rmt Amaziah Hiatt
1817, 1, 18. Nancy Claypool (form Ballard) dis mcd
1817, 11, 22. Ansalom dis mcd
1820, 7, 22. Aden rmt Phebe Sumner
1820, 10, 21. Aaron dis disunity
1822, 2, 15. Phebe Alderson (form Ballard) dis mcd
1823, 4, 19. Elizabeth (form Overman) dis mcd
1823, 10, 18. Adin & fam gct White Lick MM, Ind.
1825, 4, 23. Edith Eperson (form Ballard) con mcd
1826, 1, 21. Jesse dis
1826, 11, 18. Abigail rocf Westfield MM, N. C. dtd 1826,5,13
1827, 2, 17. Uriah dis mcd
1830, 3, 20. Abigail dis joining Separatists
1830, 4, 17. Wm. dis disunity
1833, 12, 25. Mary dis
1836, 11, 23. Elizabeth gct Fairfield MM, Ind.
1839, 11, 20. Elizabeth rocf Fairfield MM, Ind., dtd 1839,8,15
1843, 11, 22. Jesse rst at White Lick MM on consent of this mtg

BANTZ
1930, 11, 5. O. Perry & w recrq

BAREFIELD
1815, 12, 23. Millicent, Damaris & Jonathan, gr ch of Zadock Bundy, rocf Mt. Pleasant MM, Va., dtd 1815,1,28
1817, 8, 23. Milley [Barfield] dis disunity
1817, 8, 23. Demaris dis disunity
1824, 8, 21. Jonathan dis mcd

BERNARD
1814, 1, 22. Uriah [Barnard] & w, Elizabeth, & ch, Love, Hannah, Anna, Elizabeth, Mary, George, Wm. & John, rocf White Water MM, Ind., dtd 1813,11,27
1814, 7, 23. Elizabeth Swain (form Bernard) con mcd
1818, 7, 18. Uriah & fam gct New Garden MM, Ind.
1820, 4, 22. Lydia, Frederic & Jemima, ch Frederic, rocf New Garden MM, N. C., dtd 1819,3,28
1823, 3, 22. Subal rocf New Garden MM, N. C., dtd 1822,9,28 end by New Garden MM, Ind., 1823,2,14
1824, 2, 21. Frederick gct Honey Creek MM, Ind.
1825, 12, 24. Mary [Barnard] rocf Honey Creek MM, Ind.
1827, 1, 20. Elizabeth recrq
1828, 4, 19. Lydia Morris (form Bernard) con mcd
1828, 11, 23. Jamima Combs (form Bernard) dis mcd

BARNETT
1817, 1, 18. Sarah rmt Barclay Johnson
1825, 9, 17. Mary [Barnet] (form Canaday) con mcd

BARNEY
1812, 11, 21. Mary (form Andrews) dis mcd

BARRETT
1821, 5, 19. Amy dis
1822, 2, 16. Sidney rmt Moses Roberts
1825, 4, 23. Richard Jr. dis mcd

BEALS
1829, 8, 22. Jacob Carson Jr. gct Newberry MM, to m Esther Beals

BEESON
1812, 4, 18. William rmt Mary Sumner
1812, 4, 18. Richard rmt Milley Burris
1813, 11, 20. Benjamin dis disunity
1813, 12, 18. Bethiah rocf Center MM, N. C., dtd 1813,10,16
1817, 1, 18. Mary gct Newberry MM
1817, 6, 21. Ann rmt Josiah Carson
1818, 9, 19. Mary rocf Newberry MM, dtd 1818,8,27
1822, 9, 21. Amasa & w, Mary, gct New Garden MM, Ind.
1825, 11, 19. Wm. & fam gct White Lick MM, Ind.
1826, 4, 22. Milley & fam gct White Lick MM, Ind.
1841, 10, 23. Lydia (form Pickering) con mcd (H)
1845, 5, 19. Ann (form Overman) dis mcd
1847, 10, 23. Anne [Beesan] (form Overman) dis mou

BENNETT
1837, 11, 18. Joseph rocf Deer Creek MM, dtd 1837,9.14 (H)

BEVAN
1825, 2, 19. Cert rec for Stacy & w, Lydia, & ch, John, Owen, Samuel, Abel & Elizabeth, from Flushing MM, dtd 1824,6,25, end to Center MM

BLIZZARD
1822, 12, 21. Elizabeth rocf New Garden MM, N. C., dtd 1822,8,31

BLIZZARD, continued
1825, 11, 19. Elizabeth gct White Water MM, Ind.

BOGAN
1930, 10, 1. Mr. & Mrs. Bogan gct Spring Valley MM, O.

BOND
1836, 7, 28. Margaret m Geo. H. BAKER (H)

1811, 10, 19. Samuel & s, Amasa, rocf Westfield MM, N. C., dtd 1810,11,10, end by Fairfield MM 1811,7,28
1811, 10, 19. Charity rocf Westfield MM, N. C., dtd 1810,11,10, end by Fairfield MM
1814, 6, 18. Abigail Moor, w Asa L., & ch, Sarah Bond & Jane & Miriam Moor & step dt, Leah Moor, rocf Piney Woods MM, N. C., dtd 1814,4,2
1815, 9, 23. Samuel & w, Charity, gct New Garden MM, Ind.
1836, 6, 18. Margaret rocf Hopewell MM, dtd 1836,5,5 (H)

BRANSON
1837, 3, 18. Ruth rocf Short Creek MM, dtd 1836,8,25 (H)
1840, 3, 21. Priscilla recrq (H)
1842, 2, 19. Priscilla Fletcher (form Branson) con mcd (H)
1848, 4, 18. Samuel rmt Sarah A. Huff

BROWN
1829, 3, 21. Elgar & w, Mary, & ch, Sarah H. & Wm., rocf Clear Creek MM, dtd 1829, 3,14
1838, 8, 22. Wm. & w, Grace, & s, Isaac, rocf Short Creek MM, dtd 1838,8,21
1838, 8, 22. Samuel rocf Short Creek MM, dtd 1837,11,21, end by Clear Creek 1838,8,21
1838, 8, 18. Grace (form Pickering) con mou (H)
1838, 11, 21. Samuel con mcd
1843, 12, 20. Sarah H. rmt Francis White
1844, 4, 24. Sarah Ann, Jesse L. & Mary Ann, ch Samuel & Grace, recrq
1845, 11, 22. Grace dis jas (H)

BUNDY
1815, 12, 23. Zadock & w, Rebeckah, & ch, Wm., Mary, Anna, Caleb, John & Caroline, rocf Mt. Pleasant MM, Va., dtd 1815,1,28
1815, 12, 23. Millicent, Damaris & Jonathan Barefield, gr ch Zadock Bundy, rocf Mt. Pleasant MM, Va., dtd 1815,1,28
1825, 5, 21. Zadock dis disunity
1825, 5, 21. Wm. dis disunity
1825, 7, 23. Mary Scott (form Bundy) dis mcd
1825, 8, 20. Rebecca dis disunity
1828, 12, 20. Ann Easter (form Bundy) dis mcd
1835, 5, 20. Caleb dis mcd
1835, 9, 23. John dis disunity
1841, 9, 22. Zadock rst at Newberry MM on consent of this mtg
1842, 6, 22. James & Hannah gct Newberry MM
1842, 8, 24. Rebecca rst at Newberry MM

BURGESS
1843, 6, 21. Joseph H. rmt Juliett Johnson
1843, 7, 19. Juliett gct Fairfield MM

BURRIS
1812, 4, 18. Milley rmt Richard Beeson
1818, 5, 23. John C. dis mcd
1818, 12, 19. Daniel Jr. dis mcd
1830, 7, 22. Daniel rocf Caesars Creek MM, dtd 1820,3,24
1820, 9, 19. Mary recrq
1822, 5, 18. Christine (form Hiatt) dis mcd
1823, 10, 18. Bartley & Mahala gct White Lick MM, Ind.
1826, 4, 22. John & fam gct White Lick MM, Ind.
1826, 10, 21. Joseph dis mcd
1827, 2, 17. Frances, w John, & ch, Luke & John, gct White Lick MM, Ind.
1827, 7, 21. Tabitha recrq
1827, 11, 17. Tabitha gct White Lick MM, Ind.
1828, 9, 20. John gct White Lick MM, Ind.
1828, 12, 20. Stephen gct Duck Creek MM, Ind.

BURSON
1816, 1, 20. Ann (form Small) dis mcd

BUSSEY
1857, 10, --. Emma b
1934, 3, 21. Sarah d

CADWALADER
1815, 7, 22. Byram rocf Miami MM, dtd 1815,4, 26
1819, 11, 20. Byram dis mcd

CAIN
1840, 1, 20. William, s Wm. & Mary, b (H)

1838, 6, 16. Wm. & Mary B., & ch, Thornton & Mary Jane, rocf Chesterfield MM, dtd 1838,5,8 (H)
1842, 4, 16. Wm. & ch gct Green Plain MM (H)

CANADAY
1821, 6, 23. John rocf West Grove MM, Ind., dtd 1820,7,8
1821, 8, 18. John dis mcd
1825, 6, 18. Nathan dis mcd
1825, 9, 17. Mary Barnet (form Canaday) con mcd
1828, 9, 20. Henry gct Clear Creek MM, to m Drusilla Hussey
1829, 8, 22. John gct Cherry Grove MM, Ind.
1831, 1, 22. Christopher dis disunity
1831, 3, 19. Henry dis
1833, 9, 25. Margaret Moorman (form Canaday) dis mcd

CANADAY, continued
1834, 10, 22. Anna Jr. dis disunity
1835, 4, 22. Bowater dis mcd
1835, 5, 20. Drucilla & ch, Wm. Riley Madison & Nathan, rocf Clear Creek MM, dtd 1835,3, 24
1838, 5, 23. Drucilla & ch, Wm. Riley, Matison & Nathan, gct Vermillion MM, Ill.
1844, 5, 22. Walter & w gct Salem MM, Ia.

CARROLL
1840, 6, 25. Enos, s Joseph & Elizabeth, Highland Co., O.; m in Fall Creek MH, Mary Ann SMITH, dt Eli & Mary, Warren Co., O. (H)

1839, 9, 21. Joseph [Carrol] & w, Elizabeth, & ch, Enos, Edward, Mary, John, Emmet, Elizanna, Rebecca H., Joseph, Sarah & Rolon, rocf New Garden MM, dtd 1838,10,25 (H)
1840, 8, 22. Mary Sheppard (form Carroll) con mcd (H)
1842, 12, 17. Edward gct Centre MM, to m Levina Birdsel (H)
1843, 7, 22. Enos & w, Mary Ann, & two ch gct Miami MM (H)
1843, 9, 10. Elizabeth & seven ch gct Camden MM, Ind. (H)

CARSON
1812, 4, 18. Bowater rocf Westfield MM, dtd 1818,11,10, end by Fairfield MM, 1811,11, 30
1816, 3, 23. Josiah, Silas, Uriah & Jacob rocf Westfield MM, dtd 1814,11,12
1817, 6, 21. Josiah rmt Ann Beeson
1819, 1, 23. Josiah & w, Ann, rocf New Garden MM, Ind.
1819, 6, 19. Clementine (form Pierce) con mcd
1822, 5, 18. Sarah dis mcd
1823, 11, 22. Sally rmt Enos George
1824, 8, 21. Salley rocf Westfield MM, N. C., dtd 1824,7,10
1825, 2, 19. Jacob Jr. gct New Garden MM, Ind.
1825, 4, 23. Uriah rmt Phebe George
1827, 6, 23. Jacob Jr. rocf New Garden MM, Ind., dtd 1827,1,2, end by Newberry MM, 1827,5,24
1828, 10, 18. Uriah & w, Phebe, & dt, Mary Ann, gct Fairfield MM, Ind.
1829, 8, 22. Jacob Jr. gct Newberry MM, to m Esther Beals
1830, 2, 20. Esther rocf Newberry MM, dtd 1829,11,26
1832, 5, 23. Jacob Jr. & fam gct Newberry MM
1837, 8, 23. Clemma gct Westfield MM, Ind.
1843, 8, 23. Jacob & w gct Fairfield MM, Ind.

CHADWICK
1823, 4, 19. Anna rocf New Garden MM, N. C., dtd 1823,2,14
1823, 10, 18. Anna gct Silver Creek MM, Ind.

CHALFONT
----, --, --. Abner & Ruth [Chalfant] (H)

Ch:				
Margaret	b	1819,	10,	2
Sarah	"	1821,	8,	15
William P.	"	1823,	11,	21
Asa L.	"	1826,	1,	30
Edwin	"	1828,	4,	5

1836, 8, 20. Wm. Jr. dis disunity (H)
1836, 10, 22. Martha (form Ridgeway) dis mcd (H)
1837, 6, 17. Martha dis mcd (H)

CHAPLUN
1923, 12, 12. Harry recrq

CHARLES
1841, 9, 23. Thomas rmt Charlotte Johnson
1841, 11, 24. Charlotte gct Richland MM, Ind.

CHRISMAN
1930, 9, 14. Wm. d

1921, 12, 3. Clarence & Dena recrq
1829, 12, 4. Dena relrq
1931, 2, 4. Wilma Jean, minor, recrq

CLARK
1847, 11, 20. Martha rocf White Water MM, Ind. (H)

CLAYPOOL
1817, 1, 18. Nancy (form Ballard) dis mcd

COFFIN
1812, 3, 21. Olive dis joining Baptist Society
1839, 11, 20. John Cowgill gct Clear Creek MM, to m Lydia Coffin

COMBS
1828, 11, 23. Jamima (form Bernard) dis mcd

CONARD
1847, 5, 21. Martha, dt Joseph & Rebecca, b (H)

1846, 10, 17. Joseph & w, Rebecca, & ch, Lewis, Charles, Franklin, Susanna & Sarah, rocf Little Brittain MM, Pa., dtd 1846,8, 15 (H)
1850, 5, 18. Benjamin & w, Eliza, & ch, Almira, Cornelius, Alice R., George R., Wm. & Elwood H., gct Little Brittain MM, Lancaster Co., Pa. (H)
1852, 7, 17. Lewis dis mcd (H)

COOK
----, --, --. Elmer, s Wm. & Eliza J., b 1886,11,12; m Bessie Ione TROTH, dt Nathan & Mary J., b 1887,10,23

COOPER
1837, 6, 21. Jesse, s John & Jane, Highland Co., O.; m in Clear Creek MH, Eleanor REES, dt Thos. & Eleanor, Highland Co., O.
1840, 6, 25. Phebe Jane m John M. OVERMAN (H)
1841, 2, 25. Leah m Dempsy OVERMAN (H)

1836, 9, 17. Amos & fam rocf Sadsbury MM, dtd 1836,6,8 (H)
1837, 3, 18. Jesse rocf Sadsbury MM, dtd 1837,2,8 (H)
1837, 9, 20. John, Phebe Jane, Leah, Amos & Yarnel, ch Amos & Jane, rocf Sadsbury MM, Pa., dtd 1837,5,2
1841, 10, 23. Ann recrq (H)
1841, 12, 22. Phebe Jane Overman (form Cooper) dis mcd
1841, 12, 22. Leah Overman (form Cooper) dis mcd
1844, 3, 23. John gct Short Creek MM, to m Elma Griffith (H)
1844, 9, 23. John dis mcd
1844, 11, 16. Elma rocf Short Creek MM, dtd 1844,6,20 (H)

COWGILL
----, --, --. J. B., s Benj. & Rachel, b 1846,9,19 d 1931,7,28; m Ellen PARKER, dt Samuel & Mary, b 1851,5,7 d 1926,7,10

1816, 4, 20. Sarah rmt Elias Overman
1826, 4, 22. Benj. dis
1828, 5, 24. Asa & w, Margaret, & s, John, rocf Fairfield MM, dtd 1827,8,25
1830, 3, 20. Asa & fam gct Center MM, O.
1832, 3, 21. Jonathan dis disunity
1839, 11, 20. John gct Clear Creek MM, to m Lydia Coffin
1840, 5, 20. Lydia rocf Clear Creek MM, dtd 1840,4,21
1841, 7, 21. Lydia rmt Joseph Wright
1844, 1, 24. Henry recrq
1845, 10, 20. Lucinda recrq
1845, 11, 17. John Bernard, Sarah Jane, Milton, Eleanor, Benjamin Franklin & Oscar, ch Lydia, recrq
1922, 7, 1. Carrie, Harry, Frank Roderick & Sarah Ellen, gct Wilmington MM, O.
1932, 7, 6. Mary Jean, John Parker & Paul Raymond recrq

COX
1812, 4, 18. Nathan dis mcd & joining Methodist Society
1812, 5, 23. Lydia dis
1812, 5, 23. Jeremiah dis joining Methodist Society
1812, 6, 26. Jane Redford (form Cox) dis mcd & joining Methodist Society
1812, 7, 13. Margery dis
1812, 11, 21. Patience Mooney (form Cox) dis mcd
1813, 11, 18. Joshua dis mcd
1814, 10, 22. Wm., John, Ruth, Ann, Patience, Lydia & Mary, ch Benjamin, recrq
1814, 10, 22. Ann & ch, Ruth Ann, Patience, Lydia & Mary, recrq
1816, 4, 20. Lydia Redfern (form Cox) dis mcd
1817, 11, 22. Benjamin & fam gct New Garden MM, Ind.
1818, 7, 18. Isaiah gct New Garden MM, Ind.
1818, 11, 21. John & fam gct New Garden MM, Ind.
1828, 11, 28. Joshua rst at White River MM, Ind. on consent of this mtg

CRAIGHEAD
1844, 8, 19. Sarah (form Overman) dis mcd

CROZER
1842, 8, 24. Joshua W. rocf Flushing MM, dtd 1842,6,--
1844, 1, 24. Joshua W. dis mcd

DARLINGTON
1830, 3, 20. Anna rocf Clear Creek MM, dtd 1830,2,13

DAVIDSON
1821, 12, 3. Ora Lee & Ella recrq

DAVIS
1811, 9, 21. John & s, Thomas, Elihu John William & Tristrum, rocf Lost Creek MM, dtd 1810,6,30, end by Fairfield MM, 1811, 8,31
1811, 9, 21. Jane & dt, Sarah, rocf Lost Creek MM, dtd 1810,6,30
1812, 5, 23. Thomas dis disunity
1812, 11, 21. Elihu dis mcd
1814, 6, 18. Love con mcd
1817, 3, 22. Love gct New Garden MM, Ind.
1821, 1, 20. John Jr. dis
1921, 6, 23. Rebecca (form Sumner) con mcd
1821, 11, 17. Rebecah gct Springfield MM, Ind.
1822, 4, 25. Hester (form Willson) con mcd
1823, 4, 19. Tristram con mcd
1823, 10, 18. Welmet recrq
1824, 6, 19. Wm. dis mcd
1824, 7, 24. Hester gct Lick Creek MM, Ind.

DINGEE
1842, 7, 23. Hannah (form Jackson) con mou (H)
1843, 6, 17. Charles [Dingy] rocf Center MM, dtd 1843,6,15 (H)

DIXON
1816, 4, 20. Lydia recrq
1821, 12, 22. Lydia dis jas

DODD
1846, 1, 19. Joseph & w, Ann, rocf Sommerset MM, dtd 1845,12,29

DOWNING
1836, 7, 23. Wm. & w, Phebe, rocf Sadsbury MM, dtd 1836,6,8 (H)

DRAPER
1811, 8, 24. Josiah & w, Miriam, & ch, Jesse, Joseph, Josiah, John, Joshua, Elizabeth, Miriam & Maryann, rocf Back Creek MM, N. C., dtd 1811,4,27, end by Fairfield MM, 1811,7,27
1813, 10, 20. Elizabeth rmt Jesse Small
1815, 1, 21. Josiah gct Fairfield MM, to m Jemima Wright
1815, 6, 17. Jemima rocf Fairfield MM, dtd 1815,5,27
1816, 9, 21. Miriam gct New Garden MM, Ind.
1816, 11, 23. Jesse dis mcd
1818, 2, 21. Josiah & fam gct White Water MM, Ind.
1819, 3, 20. Joseph dis mcd

DUFF
1820, 11, 18. Daniel rmt Nancy Vanpelt

EASLACK
1845, 4, 19. Ruth (form Thornbury) con mcd (H)

EASTER
1828, 12, 20. Ann (form Bundy) dis mcd

EDWARDS
1837, 10, 21. Elizabeth rocf Westland MM, Pa., dtd 1837,9,4 (H)

ELLIS
1834, 5, 17. Jonathan & w, Martha, & ch, Theodore, Peter Marsh, Martha, Solomon, Jehu & Catharine, rocf Flushing MM, Mich., dtd 1834,3,22 (H)
1834, 5, 17. Jonathan Jr. rocf Flushing MM, dtd 1834,3,22 (H)
1834, 10, 20. Martha & ch, Peter, Martha, Solomon & Catharine, rocf Flushing MM, dtd 1834,7,24
1834, 12, 24. Sarah rocf Flushing MM, dtd 1834,3,20
1836, 6, 18. Jonathan Jr. con mcd (H)
1836, 6, 22. Peter dis jH
1836, 9, 17. Jonathan M. & fam gct White Water MM, Ind. (H)
1836, 10, 22. Jonathan Jr. gct White Water MM, Ind. (H)
1837, 11, 22. Martha & ch, Martha, Solomon & Catharine, gct Chester MM, Ind.
1838, 7, 21. Theodore dis mcd (H)
1839, 11, 16. Jonathan rocf White Water MM, Ind., dtd 1839,7,24 (H)
1840, 2, 19. Mary rocf Sandy Spring MM, dtd 1839,11,22
1841, 12, 18. Jonathan Jr. gct White Water MM, Ind. (H)
1843, 8, 23. Mary gct Lick Creek MM

EPERSON
1825, 4, 23. Edith (form Ballard) con mcd
1827, 1, 20. Edith [Epison] gct Fairfield MM, Ind.

FAIRLY
1844, 4, 20. Sophia [Fairby] (form Overman) dis mou (H)
1844, 5, 22. Sophia (form Overman) dis mcd

FISHER
1843, 1, 25. Cert rec for Hiram & w, Rebecca, & ch, Amos, Elizabeth, Jemima, Isaac & Susannah, from Dover MM, end to Fairfield MM

FLETCHER
1827, 11, 17. Nancy (form Newby) con mcd
1836, 12, 21. Nancy gct Clear Creek MM
1842, 1, 22. Rebecca (form Pickering) con mcd (H)
1842, 2, 19. Priscilla (form Branson) con mou (H)

FOULKE
1843, 4, 28. Jesse M., s Judah & Sarah, Highland Co., O.; m in Clear Creek MH, Mary BAKER, dt Amasa & Sarah, Highland Co., O. (H)

1843, 7, 22. Mary gct Short Creek MM (H)

FRASINGTON
1814, 11, 19. Elizabeth rocf Fairfield MM, dtd 1814,9,24

GEORGE
----, --, --. John & Leah (H)

Ch:		
Sarah L.	b	1830, 7, 21
Isaac	"	1832, 5, 4
Abner	"	1833, 6, 11
Amy	"	1834, 12, 3
David	"	1837, 6, 7
Lydia	"	1839, 10, 4
Cyrus	"	1841, 3, 9
Mary R.	"	1843, 3, 14

1822, 8, 24. Isaac rmt Anna Sumner
1823, 11, 22. Enos rmt Sally Carson
1824, 11, 20. Isaac & fam gct White Lick MM, Ind.
1825, 4, 23. Phebe rmt Uriah Carson
1825, 10, 22. Amy recrq
1826, 11, 18. Enos & fam gct White Lick MM, Ind.
1826, 11, 18. Jesse gct Fairfield MM, Ind.
1828, 5, 24. Amy rocf Clear Creek MM, dtd 1828,4,12

GEORGE, continued
1830, 10, 23. John & w, Leah, rocf Hopewell MM, Va., dtd 1830,7,8 (H)
1830, 12, 18. Evan & w, Hannah, & ch, Richard Lewis & John Band, rocf Hopewell MM, Va., dtd 1830,7,8 (H)
1831, 1, 22. James & w, Mary, & s, David, rocf Hopewell MM, Va., dtd 1830,9,9 (H)
1831, 1, 22. Jesse rocf Hopewell MM, Va., dtd 1830,9,9 (H)
1831, 3, 17. James rmt Lydia Pearce
1831, 4, 23. Richard rocf Hopewell MM, Va., dtd 1830,12,9 (H)
1831, 4, 23. Mary rocf Hopewell MM, Va., dtd 1830,12,9 (H)
1831, 4, 23. Ruth, Rachel, Sarah & Mary Jr. rocf Hopewell MM, Va., dtd 1830,12,9 (H)
1831, 9, 21. James & w, Lydia, gct Fairfield MM, Ind.
1833, 8, 17. James Jr. rocf Hopewell MM, Va., dtd 1833,5,9 (H)
1836, 1, 23. Jesse dis mcd (H)
1839, 10, 23. Mercy & Elizabeth gct Fairfield MM, Ind.
1840, 4, 22. Isaiah gct Fairfield MM, Ind.
1841, 2, 24. Richard rocf Back Creek MM, Ind., dtd 1840,9,19
1841, 11, 24. Ellis recrq
1842, 1, 19. Jesse B., James L. & HenryC., ch Ellis, recrq
1843, 4, 19. Ellis & fam gct Richland MM, Ind.
1843, 11, 22. Mary rocf Back Creek MM, Ind.
1845, 5, 19. Mary gct Richland MM, Ind.
1851, 8, 23. John & w, Leah, & ch gct Fall Creek MM, Ind. (H)
1851, 8, 23. Ruth, Sarah & Mary gct Fall Creek MM, Ind. (H)
1852, 2, 21. Evan & w, Hannah, & ch gct Fall Creek MM, Ind. (H)
1852, 2, 21. John B. Jr. gct Fall Creek MM, Ind.

GIBSON
1825, 2, 19. Arcada (form Harrold) dis mcd

GILL
1831, 4, 23. Susannah & ch gct Green Plain MM

GORLEY
1923, 1, 6. Mary relrq

GRAVES
1812, 6, 26. Mary Hunter (form Graves) dis mcd & joining Methodist Society
1812, 7, 13. Amy dis joining Methodist Society

GREEN
1842, 11, 23. Rhoda rocf Clear Creek MM, dtd 1842,10,18

GREGG
1826, 8, 29. Phebe dis disunity

GRIFFITH
1844, 3, 23. John Cooper gct Short Creek MM, to m Elma Griffith (H)

GUIRE
1815, 9, 23. Rachel (form Small) con mcd
1816, 1, 20. Sarah [Guyer] gct Blue River MM, Ind.

HAMMOND
1928, 2, 24. Grace d

1929, 7, 3. Leroy & Louise, minors, recrq
1929, 12, 4. Sylvia recrq

HARLAN
1849, 4, 21. Martha (form Sanders) con mou (H)

HART
1812, 11, 21. Elizabeth & ch, John, Elizabeth, Rebecca & Silas, rocf Westfield MM, dtd 1810, 10,15, end by Fairfield MM, 1811, 10,26; cert returned

HARTMAN
1926, 8, 4. Ora relrq

HARVEY
1847, 9, 20. James rmt Minerva Johnson
1847, 12, 20. Minerva gct Miami MM, O.

HAYWOOD
1925, 8, 4. Elizabeth d
1926, 6, 14. Joseph d

HELLER
1841, 8, 21. Martha R. (form Timberlake) con mou (H)

HENDERSON
1839, 7, 20. Sally (form Lewis) dis mou (H)

HENLEY
1827, 8, 18. John rocf Clear Creek MM, O., dtd 1827,5,22
1829, 9, 19. John gct Fairfield MM

HERRELD
1815, 12, 23. Rebeckah Sumner (form Herreld) con mcd
1824, 11, 20. Jacob [Harrold] & fam gct White Lick MM, Ind.
1825, 2, 19. Arcada Gibson (form Harrold) dis mcd
1825, 2, 19. Wm. [Harreld] dis mcd

HIATT
----, --, --. Christopher & Jemima (H)
Ch: Amos b 1817, 3, 18

HIATT, Christopher & Jemima, continued
Ch: Mary b 1819, 3, 17
Abner " 1821, 2, 16
Clarkson " 1823, 6, 25
Elwood " 1825, 10, 30
1834, 4, 20. Mary d bur Fall Creek
1845, 3, 27. Hannah m Josiah JACKSON (H)

1812, 4, 18. Richard [Hiett] & w, Sarah, & ch, Anna, William, David & Susannah, rocf Mt. Pleasant MM, dtd 1828,7,28 end by Fairfield MM, 1812,3,23
1813, 11, 20. Olive Catharine, Wm. & Howard, ch Azariah, roc dtd 1812,11,14
1814, 1, 22. Amaziah rmt Levina Ballard
1814, 9, 17. Olive Baldwin (form Hiatt) dis mcd
1816, 4, 20. Katharine Walter (form Hiatt) dis mcd
1816, 5, 18. David dis disunity
1818, 2, 21. Rebeckah Reece (form Hiatt) dis mcd
1818, 5, 23. Benjamin gct Clear Creek MM
1818, 9, 19. Mary rocf Clear Creek MM, dtd 1818,8,8
1819, 1, 23. John, Enoch & Catharine rocf Deep Creek MM, N. C., dtd 1818,10,3
1819, 1, 23. Absalom rocf Deep Creek MM, N.C.
1820, 12, 23. Phebe Reese (form Hiatt) dis mcd
1820, 10, 21. Harmon con mcd
1821, 8, 18. Ann dis mcd to first cousin
1822, 5, 18. Christine Burris (form Hiatt) dis mcd
1822, 6, 22. Aaron dis mcd
1823, 7, 19. Absalom & fam gct Milford MM, Ind.
1823, 10, 18. Ruth rmt Josiah Jackson
1823, 10, 18. James gct Milford MM, Ind.
1823, 10, 18. Harmon & fam gct White Lick MM, Ind.
1824, 3, 20. Amaziah dis mcd
1824, 9, 18. Richard & fam gct Milford MM, Ind.
1825, 1, 22. Catharine dis
1825, 6, 18. Aaron & John rst at Milford MM, Ind. on consent of this mtg
1825, 6, 18. Wm. dis disunity
1826, 2, 18. Benjamin Jr. dis disunity
1827, 3, 24. Benjamin Jr. gct White Lick MM, Ind.
1827, 5, 19. John & fam gct Duck Creek MM, Ind.
1827, 5, 19. Joseph dis disunity
1827, 9, 22. Enoch dis disunity
1828, 2, 16. Rachel (form Overman) dis mcd
1828, 3, 22. Howard dis mcd
1828, 3, 22. Sarah rmt Daniel Antrim
1828, 5, 24. Rachel dis mcd
1829, 7, 18. Benjamin & Mary dis jH
1830, 4, 17. Hannah dis jH
1830, 9, 18. Henry dis jH
1831, 2, 19. Absalom dis disunity
1832, 2, 22. Mourning dis jas
1832, 5, 19. Henry dis mcd (H)
1833, 5, 22. Lavina dis disunity
1834, 3, 22. Mourning dis joining Methodist Society (H)
1834, 12, 20. Rachel Tompkins (form Hiatt) con mcd (H)
1839, 2, 16. Amos con mou (H)
1839, 8, 21. Sarah dis jH
1839, 2, 16. Mary Lausenby (form Hiatt) con mou (H)
1840, 2, 15. Mary Ann rocf Centre MM, O., dtd 1839,9,19
1844, 8, 17. Abner dis mcd (H)
1847, 2, 20. Clarkson gct Miami MM, to m Jane Hollingsworth (H)
1849, 6, 16. Elwood con mcd (H)

HIBBERD
1829, 11, 21. Hannah & three ch gct Springborough MM (H)
1834, 11, 22. Sarah (form Sanders) dis mcd (H)
1824, 9, 18. Rebeckah gct White Lick MM, Ind.

HOCKET
1836, 10, 22. Lucinda (form Jackson) con mcd (H)
1849, 10, 20. Jacob con mou (H)
1850, 10, 19. Rhoda recrq (H)

HODGSON
1811, 11, 23. Jonathan rmt Phebe Sumner

HOGE
1839, 10, 24. Elisha rmt Lydia Vanpelt
1840, 2, 19. Lydia gct Flushing MM, O.

HOGGATT
1834, 10, 18. Josiah con mcd (H)

HOLLINGSWORTH
1847, 2, 20. Clarkson Hiatt gct Miami MM, O., to m Jane Hollingsworth (H)
1850, 10, 19. Mahlon & w, Mary, & ch, Edward H., James M., Rebecca C., Charles M. & Rachel Ann, rocf Miami MM, dtd 1850,7,24 (H)

HUFF
1821, 1, 20. Nancy gct Fairfield MM
1823, 8, 23. Daniel Jr. & w, Nancy, & dt, Juliet, rocf Fairfield MM, dtd 1823,5,13
1829, 5, 25. Daniel & w, Nancy, & ch, Juliet, Mary, Sarah & John, gct Fairfield MM
1832, 3, 21. Daniel Jr. & w, Nancy, & ch, Juliet, Mary, Sarah, John & Mahlon, gct Fairfield MM
1836, 6, 18. Margaret (form Reece) dis mcd (H)
1846, 6, 22. Mary Wood (form Huff) dis mcd
1848, 4, 18. Sarah A. rmt Samuel Branson

HULIT
1812, 2, 22. Sarah rocf Shrewsbury MM, dtd

HULIT, continued
1810,10,15, end by Miami MM

HUMPHREY
1884, 9, 18. Netty, dt Westley & Laura, b

HUNT
1824, 6, 19. Eleanor gct Clear Creek MM
1829, 4, 18. Hanuel & w, Eleanor, & ch, Sarah, Asenith & Ezra, rocf Clear Creek MM, dtd 1829,4,11
1831, 6, 22. Hanuel & fam gct Clear Creek MM

HUNTER
1812, 6, 26. Mary (form Graves) dis mcd & joining Methodist Society

HUSSEY
1828, 9, 20. Henry Canaday gct Clear Creek MM, to m Drucilla Hussey

HUTSON
1831, 5, 21. Phebe (form Worley) dis mcd

JACKSON
----, --, --. Jesse & Ann (H)
Ch: Malinda b 1815, 7, 20
Nathan " 1816, 12, 7
Joseph " 1817, 9, 16
Elizabeth " 1820, 10, 6
Jacob " 1820, 5, 6 (sic)
Asenath " 1825, 1, 5
Lydia " 1826, 5, 20
Thomas " 1831, 9, 18
----, --, --. Curtis & Lydia (H)
Ch: Lucinda b 1816, 7, 22
Hannah " 1817, 10, 28
Phebe " 1819, 8, 21
John W. " 1821, 12, 25
Jury T. " 1824, 3, 18
Amra " 1827, 1, 23
Thomas L. " 1830, 9, 17
----, --, --. Josiah & Ruth (H)
Ch: Helena b 1824, 10, 4
William " 1826, 10, 6
Jacob Jr. " 1828, 8, 31
Sarah " 1833, 1, 19
1835, 8, 27. Ann d bur Fairfield
1843, 7, 9. Ruth d bur Newberry, O.
1845, 3, 27. Josiah, s Jacob & Ann, Clinton Co., O.; m in Fall Creek MH, Hannah HIATT, dt Benjamin & Mary, Highland Co., O. (H)
1848, 7, 16. Josiah d bur Newberry, O.

1815, 11, 18. Curtis rmt Lydia Sumner
1816, 3, 23. Lydia gct Clear Creek MM
1822, 11, 23. Betsy rocf Westfield MM, N. C., dtd 1822,9,14
1823, 10, 18. Josiah rmt Ruth Hiatt
1824, 3, 20. Ruth gct Newberry MM
1833, 9, 14. Jesse & w, Ann, "left Orthodox Church to join Hicksites (H)
1836, 10, 22. Lucinda Hocket (form Jackson) con mcd (H)
1842, 7, 23. Hannah Dingee (form Jackson) con mou (H)
1845, 1, 18. Jacob, dec, testimonial prepared for him (H)
1849, 11, 17. Rachel Aikers (form Jackson) dis mou & jas (H)
1849, 12, 22. Asenath & Lydia dis jas (H)
1849, 4, 21. Helena West (form Jackson) con mou (H)

JAMES
1842, 1, 19. John & w, Esther, rocf Clear Creek MM, dtd 1841,12,21
1844, 4, 24. John & w gct Salem MM, Iowa

JESSOP
1811, 11, 23. Sarah rocf Westfield MM, N. C., dtd 1811,11,10, end by Fairfield MM
1815, 4, 22. Sarah dis
1817, 11, 22. Timothy & w, Susannah, & ch, Rachel, Martin, Lewis & John rocf Westfield MM, N. C., dtd 1817,11,8
1821, 8, 18. Ann rocf Lees Creek MM, dtd 1821,7,21
1821, 11, 17. Timothy & w, Mary, rocf New Garden MM, N. C., dtd 1821,9,29
1822, 11, 23. Timothy [Jessup] & w, Mary. gct New Garden MM, Ind.
1826, 4, 22. Rachel Ritter (form Jessop) con mcd
1826, 4, 22. Timothy H. & fam gct White Lick MM, Ind.

JOHN
1815, 10, 21. Ebanezer gct Clear Creek MM

JOHNSON
1845, 4, 23. Benjamin, s Joseph & Betsey, Washington Co., O.; m in Clear Creek MH, Susannah BAKER, dt Amasa & Sarah, Highland Co., O. (H)

1811, 11, 23. Moorman rmt Lydia Johnson
1811, 11, 23. Lydia rmt Moorman Johnson
1815, 6, 17. Lydia gct Fairfield MM
1817, 1, 18. Barclay rmt Sarah Barnett
1818, 1, 21. Abner rmt Hannah Vanpelt
1823, 2, 15. Hannah & dt, Louisa, gct Green Plain MM
1825, 3, 19. Polly McCoy (form Johnson) con mcd
1836, 7, 20. Hannah (form Overman) dis jH
1837, 5, 20. Hannah (form Overman) dis mcd (H)
1841, 9, 23. Charlotte rmt Thomas Charles
1842, 12, 21. Addison gct Fairfield MM, to m Emily Moorman
1843, 2, 22. John & Rhoda, ch Abner, rocf Sugar River MM, dtd 1842,9,17; cert for John endorsed to Fairfield MM
1843, 3, 22. Emily rocf Fairfield MM, dtd

JOHNSON, continued
1843,2,23
1843, 6, 21. Juliett rmt Joseph H. Burgess
1845, 6, 21. Susannah gct Miami MM (H)
1845, 10, 20. Addison & fam gct Salem MM
1847, 9, 20. Minerva rmt James Harvey
1848, 12, 23. Tacy B. (form Jones) con mou (H)
1850, 11, 16. Miller gct Fall Creek MM, Ind. (H)

JONES
1824, 3, 20. Ann (form Pierce) dis mcd
1834, 1, 18. John & w, Deborah, & ch, Wm., Joseph Tompkins, Tacy Burgess & John Amos, rocf Deercreek MM, Md., dtd 1833,11,17 (H)
1848, 12, 23. Tacy B. Johnson (form Jones) con mou (H)
1849, 6, 16. Wm. con mos (H)

KARNES
----, --, --. Joseph m Gertrude MILLER, dt Dickerson & Juliana, b 1847,3,9
Ch: Harry O. b 1873, 10, 23
George " 1880, 5, 22
Clyde " 1882, 11, 4
Clarence " 1887, 10, 17
1892, 12, 24. Blanch, w Clarence, dt Harry & Myrtle Dewitt, b
1932, 7, 6. Loren Elwood recrq

KENWORTHY
1927, 3, 2. Helen Rowe gct Whittier MM, Calif.

KINLEY
1814, 1, 22. Ann gct Miami MM

KISLING
1932, 7, 6. John F. & w, Mary J., & ch, Eunice Juanita, John G., Gladys E. & Mary Ellen, recrq

LARKIN
----, --, --. Joseph W. & Margaret (H)
Ch: Alonzo M. b 1841, 8, 13
Jesse F. " 1842, 11, 6
1841, 9, 12. Joseph d bur Clear Creek (H)

1837, 5, 20. Joseph [Larkens] & w & dt, Ann, rocf Short Creek MM, dtd 1837,3,23 (H)
1837, 6, 17. Joseph W. [Larkens] rocf Short Creek MM, dtd 1837,3,23 (H)
1837, 6, 17. Reece [Larkens] & w, Agnes, & ch, Charles, Rachel, Ann, Joseph & John, rocf Short Creek MM, dtd 1837,3,23 (H)
1838, 8, 18. John S. [Larken] & w, Sarah, & ch, Isaac & Mary Ann, rocf Short Creek MM, dtd 1837,5,25 (H)
1840, 9, 19 Joseph W. [Larkens] gct Short Creek MM, to m Margaret Yost (H)
1842, 2, 19. Margaret rocf Short Creek MM, dtd 1841,9,23 (H)
1843, 10, 21. Ann Arthur (form Larkin) dis mou (H)
1852, 6, 19. Chas. dis mcd (H)

LAUSENBY
1839, 2, 16. Mary (form Hiatt) con mou (H)

LEWIS
----, --, --. Jehu & Eleanor (H)
Ch: Betsy b 1812, 9, 17
Joel " 1814, 3, 18
Moses " 1816, 4, 24
Aaron " 1818, 2, 12
Amos " 1821, 3, 6
Daniel " 1823, 3, 17
Esther " 1825, 7, 20
Uriah " 1828, 11, 19
----, --, --. Enoch & Mourning (H)
Ch: Jonah b 1814, 3, 13
Elizabeth " 1817, 2, 4
Sally " 1818, 10, 10
John " 1820, 8, 4
Mary " 1823, 5, 3
Clark " 1825, 6, 19
Ann " 1827, 7, 22
----, --, --. Daniel & Priscilla (H)
Ch: Charles b 1829, 5, 30
Christopher" 1831, 9, 16
Sarah Ann " 1835, 2, 4
Albert " 1836, 10, 12 d 1841, 8,15 bur Clear Creek
Alvah b 1839, 3, 8 d 1841, 8, 9 bur Clear Creek
Mary b 1841, 7, 15
George " 1843, 5, 1
Rachel " 1845, 9, 28 d 1846, 9,23 bur Clear Creek
1847, 11, 28. Daniel d bur Clear Creek
1850, 1, 23. Priscilla (form Hussey) m Amos UNDERWOOD (H)
1893, 2, 17. George H. d bur 3 miles south of Richmond, Ind.
1907, 12, 6. Sarah Ann d bur 3 miles south of Richmond, Ind.

1833, 2, 16. Betsy Woodmansee (form Lewis) dis mcd (H)
1837, 11, 18. Jehu & fam gct White Water MM, Ind.
1838, 7, 21. Joel dis mcd (H)
1839, 7, 20. Sally Henderson (form Lewis) dis mou (H)

LOVETT
1926, 5, 17. J. S. d

LUNDY
1839, 5, 22. Mary (form Overman) dis mcd
1839, 8, 17. Mary (form Overman) con mou (H)
1844, 7, 20. Aaron rocf Centre MM, dtd 1844, 6,13

LUPTON
1846, 1, 17. Wm. & w, Mary, rocf Hopewell MM, Va., dtd 1845,10,9 (H)

McCOY
1825, 3, 19. Polly (form Johnson) con mcd

McMILLEN
1841, 6, 19. Elizabeth (form Bailey) dis mcd (H)

MENDENHALL
1820, 2, 19. Richard & w, Polly, & ch, Alexander, Peter, Charity, Temple, Ezekiel, Lydia, Irene, Moses, James Clemmons & John Milton, rocf Springfield MM, N. C., dtd 1819,9,8, end by Clear Creek MM 1820, 2,12.
1823, 10, 18. Richard & fam gct White Lick MM, Ind.

MEREDITH
1840, 8, 22. Ellen (form Overman) con mcd (H)
1841, 12, 22. Eleanor (form Overman) dis mcd
1931, 2, 4. Paul Robert recrq

MILLER
1815, 9, 23. Susanna rocf New Garden MM, O., dtd 1814,12,15
1817, 8, 23. Susanna gct Fairfield MM

MILLIKAN
1811, 7, 13. Lydia (form Barrett) dis mcd

MITCHELL
1921, 12, 3. Mercides recrq

MOFFITT
1812, 12, 13. Joseph recrq
1818, 9, 19. Jeremiah gct White Water MM, Ind.
1818, 9, 19. Hannah & dt gct White Water MM, Ind.
1820, 10, 21. Joseph gct New Garden MM, Ind.

MONTGOMERY
1877, 1, 1. J. L. b

1822, 6, 22. Mary dis mcd
1927, 4, 6. Theodore Leslie relrq

MOONEY
1812, 11, 21. Patience (form Cox) dis mcd

MOORE
1812, 5, 23. Josiah & w, Elizabeth, & ch, Jonathan, Lydia & Isabel, rocf Pinewood MM, dtd 1812,3,7
1812, 5, 23. Isabel rocf Piney Woods MM, N. C., dtd 1812,3,7
1814, 6, 18. Thos. & s, Wm. & Thos. rocf Piney Woods MM, N. C., dtd 1814,4,2
1814, 6, 18. Abigail, w Asa L., & ch, Sarah Bond, Jane & Miriam Moor & step dt, Leah Moor, rocf Piney Woods MM, N. C., dtd 1814,4,2
1815, 4, 22. Thos. & w, Abigail, & ch, Wm., Leah, Jane, Abigail & Thos., gct White Water MM, Ind.
1843, 11, 22. Betsey gct White Lick MM, Ind.

MOORMAN
1816, 1, 20. John Overman gct Fairfield MM, to m Nancy Moorman
1828, 2, 16. Thomas rocf Fairfield MM, dtd 1827,9,29
1830, 4, 17. Thomas dis disunity
1833, 9, 25. Margaret (form Canaday) dis mcd
1836, 11, 23. Lydia rocf Dover MM, dtd 1836, 8,18
1840, 12, 23. John T. recrq
1842, 12, 21. Addison Johnson gct Fairfield MM to m Emily Moorman
1846, 4, 20. John T. & fam gct Fairfield MM
1846, 4, 20. Lydia gct Fairfield MM

MORRIS
1824, 10, 23. David rocf Chestnut Creek MM, Va., dtd 1824,8,28, endorsed to Lees Creek MM
1828, 4, 19. Lydia (form Bernard) con mcd
1829, 5, 25. Lydia gct Lees Creek MM
1844, 10, 21. Milly dis jas

MORROW
1921, 12, 3. Letta Lee recrq
1923, 12, 12. Clarence O. recrq
1932, 7, 6. J. D. & Alice recrq

NEWBY
1818, 8, 22. Wm. & w, Sarah, & ch, Eleanor, Isaac, Nancy, Elizabeth, Nathan & Josiah, rocf Back Creek MM, N. C., dtd 1817,8,30, end by Fairfield MM, 1818,6,27
1827, 11, 17. Nancy Fletcher (form Newby) con mcd
1831, 12, 21. Isaac dis mcd
1833, 5, 22. Wm. & w, Sarah, & ch, Elizabeth, Nathan, Josiah, Demcy & Sarah, gct Clear Creek MM

NIXON
1825, 1, 22. Wm. & w, Martha, & ch, Mary, Susannah, Peninah, Martha Ann, Wm. & Ann, rocf Uwchlan MM, Pa., dtd 1824,6,5
1825, 1, 22. Cert rec for Sarah from Uwchlan MM, Pa., dtd 1824,6,5, endorsed to Springboro MM
1825, 1, 22. Cert rec for Hannah from Uwchlan MM, Pa., dtd 1824,6,5, endorsed to Springboro MM
1826, 8, 29. Samuel rocf Uwchlan MM, Pa., dtd 1825,10,6
1827, 10, 20. Samuel dis mcd

OVERMAN
----, --, --. Elias & Sarah (H)
Ch: John M. b 1817, 11, 10
Demsey C. " 1819, 3, 13
Eleanor " 1822, 1, 19
Lydia " 1825, 1, 21
William P. " 1828, 7, 8
Martha
Nathan
Elizabeth
Mary Ann
Elias
1840, 6, 25. John Milton, s Elias & Sarah, Highland Co., O.; m in Fall Creek MH, Phebe Jane COOPER, dt Amos & Jane, Highland Co., O. (H)
1841, 2, 25. Dempsey, s Elias & Sarah, Highland Co., O.; m in Fall Creek MH, Leah COOPER, dt Amos & Jane, Highland Co., O. (H)
----, --, --. W. O. b 1857,10,29 d 1921,3,11

1812, 7, 13. Mary Jr. dis
1814, 2, 19. Elisha dis mcd
1816, 1, 20. John gct Fairfield MM, to m Nancy Moorman
1816, 3, 23. Enoch con mcd
1816, 4, 20. Elias rmt Sarah Cowgill
1816, 8, 24. Nancy rocf Fairfield MM, dtd 1816,7,27
1817, 8, 23. Enos & Eli, ch Isaac, recrq
1821, 7, 21. Nathan dis mcd
1821, 11, 17. John dis disunity
1823, 4, 19. Elizabeth Ballard (form Overman) dis mcd
1824, 11, 20. Nancy & ch, Enos, Eli, Rachel, Elijah, Rhoda, Isaac, Nancy & Sarah, rocf White Lick MM, dtd 1824,10,13
1826, 7, 22. Anne rmt Charles Postgate
1826, 8, 19. Nancy rmt George Raines
1827, 4, 21. Zebulon gct White Water MM, Ind., to m Elizabeth Small
1828, 2, 16. Elizabeth rocf White Water MM, Ind., dtd 1827,11,28
1828, 2, 16. Rachel Hiatt (form Overman) dis mcd
1828, 3, 22. Eli dis disunity
1828, 4, 19. Enos dis disunity
1828, 11, 22. Enoch dis disunity
1829, 3, 21. Rebecca/Raines (form Overman) dis mcd
1829, 7, 18. Zebulon & Elizabeth & Mary dis jH
1830, 2, 20. Wm. dis mcd
1830, 5, 22. Nancy, w John, dis jH
1830, 5, 22. Sarah, w Enoch, dis jH
1830, 12, 18. Mary dis disunity
1832, 10, 24. Rhoda dis jas
1833, 3, 20. Nancy dis jas
1834, 4, 19. Elijah dis mcd & joining militia (H)
1834, 7, 19. Rhoda & Nancy dis jas (H)
1834, 7, 23. Elijah dis jH
1836, 7, 20. Hannah Johnson (form Overman) dis jas
1837, 5, 20. Hannah Johnson (form Overman) dis mcd (H) [mcd
1839, 5, 22. Mary Lundy (form Overman) dis
1839, 8, 17. Mary Lundy (form Overman) con mou (H)
1840, 2, 19. Isaac dis mcd
1840, 8, 19. John M. dis jH
1840, 8, 22. Ellen Meredith (form Overman) con mcd (H)
1841, 8, 25. Demcey dis mcd
1841, 12, 22. Eleanor Meredith (form Overman) dis mcd
1841, 12, 22. Phebe Jane (form Cooper) dis mcd
1841, 12, 22. Leah (form Cooper) dis mcd
1842, 4, 20. Achilles dis mcd
1842, 11, 23. Lydia & William, ch Elias & Sarah, gct Salem MM, Ia.
1844, 3, 20. Levi dis disunity
1844, 4, 20. Sophia Fairby (form Overman) dis mou (H)
1844, 5, 22. Sophia Fairly (form Overman) dis mcd
1844, 8, 19. Sarah Craighead (form Overman) dis mcd
1845, 5, 19. Ann Beeson (form Overman) dis mcd
1846, 9, 21. Elias dis
1847, 7, 19. Jesse B. dis disunity
1847, 10, 23. Anne Beesan (form Overman) dis mcd (H)
1921, 12, 3. Norman M. recrq

PARSON
1817, 7, 19. Sarah (form Andrews) dis mcd

PATTON
1927, 10, 15. Sarah E. d

1925, 1, 7. Sarah E. recrq

PEARSON
1812, 6, 26. Mark & w, Elizabeth, rocf Mt. Pleasant MM, dtd 1812,3,28
1814, 3, 18. Mark & w gct Fairfield MM
1815, 3, 18. Mark [Pierson] & w gct Fairfield MM

PEEL
1815, 3, 18. John gct Center MM
1853, 8, 20. Lydia [Peale] (form Baker) dis mcd (H)

PERRY
1878, 8, --. Walter [Perie] b

1921, 12, 3. Homer & Cecil recrq
1922, 1, 7. Blanch rocf Hopewell MM

PICKET
1814, 2, 19. Rebeckah rocf Mt. Pleasant MM, Va., dtd 1813,8,28, end by Fairfield MM,

PICKET, continued
1813,12,25

PICKERING
1838, 11, 27. Jonathan d bur Fall Creek (H)

1824, 4, 17. Cert rec for Jonathan Sr., Jonathan Jr. & David, from Hopewell MM, Va., dtd 1824,2,5, endorsed to Fairfield MM
1824, 4, 17. Cert rec for Wm. & w, Ruth, & ch, David, Sarah & Eleanor, from Hopewell MM, Va., dtd 1824,2,5, endorsed to Fairfield MM
1824, 4, 17. Cert rec for Eleanor & Lydia from Hopewell MM, Va., dtd 1824,1,8, endorsed to Fairfield MM
1833, 8, 17. Benjamin & w, Mercy, & ch, Grace, Jonathan, Phebe, Lydia, Rebecca, Rachel, Hannah & Sarah, rocf Hopewell MM, Va., dtd 1833,5,9 (H)
1838, 8, 18. Grace Brown (form Pickering) con mou (H)
1841, 10, 23. Lydia Beeson (form Pickering) con mcd (H)
1842, 1, 22. Rebecca Fletcher (form Pickering) con mcd (H)

PIERCE
----, --, --. Benjamin & Catharine [Pearce] (H)

Ch:		
	Jacob	b ----, --, --
	Nathan	" 1825, 2, 6
	Ruth	" 1827, 7, 6
	Charles	" 1829, 3, 4

1814, 11, 19. Wm. & s, David, rocf Mt. Pleasant MM, dtd 1814,7,30
1818, 10, 24. Manuel & w, Elizabeth, & ch, Meribah, Clemma, Anne, Lydia & John, rocf Shrewsberry MM, dtd 1818,3,2
1819, 6, 19. Clementine Carson (form Pierce) con mcd
1824, 3, 20. Ann Jones (form Pierce) dis mcd
1824, 10, 23. Benjamin [Peirce] recrq
1825, 1, 22. Catharine [Peirce] recrq
1826, 2, 18. John [Peirce] dis disunity
1829, 7, 18. Benjamin [Pearce] dis jH
1830, 1, 4. Catharine [Peirce] dis jH
1831, 3, 17. Lydia [Pearce] rmt James George
1832, 5, 19. Benjamin dis disunity (H)
1832, 5, 19. Jacob recrq (H)
1839, 1, 23. Meriba [Pearce] gct Dover MM, Ind.
1841, 9, 18. Jacob dis mcd (H)
1847, 3, 22. Nathan [Pearce] dis disunity

PIKE
1815, 5, 20. Leah & ch, Margaret, Rachel, Samuel, Abigail & Ruth, rocf Mt. Pleasant MM, Va., dtd 1813,12,25
1816, 12, 21. Margaret gct Fairfield MM
1820, 4, 22. Ch of John gct Fairfield MM

POOL
1827, 1, 20. Joshua rocf White Water MM, Ind., dtd 1826,11,22

POSTGATE
1826, 7, 22. Charles rmt Anne Overman
1829, 5, 25. Anne [Posegate] & ch, Mary Ann & Isaac, gct Clear Creek MM

PUCKET
1812, 2, 22. Mary rocf Westfield MM, dtd 1810,10,15, end by Fairfield MM
1814, 7, 23. Mary gct Clear Creek MM

RAINES
1820, 4, 22. George [Reins] recrq

1826, 8, 19. George rmt Nancy Overman
1829, 3, 21. Rebecca (form Overman) dis mcd
1829, 8, 22. George dis jH
1830, 1, 4. Nancy dis jH
1848, 7, 22. Nancy Wire (form Rains) dis mou

REDFORD
1812, 6, 26. Jane (form Cox) dis mcd & joining Methodist Society
1816, 4, 20. Lydia (form Cox) dis mcd

RIDGEWAY
1835, 4, 18. Martha & Martha Jr. rocf White Water MM, Ind., dtd 1835,1,28 (H)
1836, 10, 22. Martha Chalfont (form Ridgeway) dis mcd (H)

REES
1837, 6, 21. Eleanor m Jesse COOPER

1813, 10, 29. Caleb [Riece] & s, Michael, rocf Fairfield MM, dtd 1813,9,21
1815, 12, 23. Sarah [Riece] dis joining Methodist Society
1817, 4, 19. Wm. gct New Garden MM, Ind.
1818, 2, 21. Wm. dis mcd
1818, 2, 21. Rebeckah [Reece] (form Hiatt) dis mcd
1818, 7, 18. Caleb dis disunity
1818, 10, 24. Caleb [Reece] & fam gct New Garden MM, Ind.
1819, 7, 24. Michael dis mcd
1820, 12, 23. Phebe [Reese] (form Hiatt) dis mcd
1820, 12, 23. Phebe [Reece] (form Sumner) dis mcd
1833, 1, 23. James & w, Eleanor, & ch, Ann, Charity, Lydia, James & John, rocf Fairfield MM, dtd 1832,10,25
1834, 8, 23. Thos. [Riece] & w, Eleanor, & ch, Wm., Margaret, Mary Eleanor, Evan, John, Josiah, Matilda Jane & Elisha, rocf Hopewell MM, Va., dtd 1834,6,5 (H)
1834, 8, 23. Thomas [Riece] Jr. rocf Hopewell MM, Va., dtd 1834,6,5 (H)
1834, 8, 23. Alfred [Riece] rocf Hopewell

REES, continued
MM, Va., dtd 1834,6,5 (H)
1834, 8, 23. Joel [Riece] rocf Hopewell MM, Va., dtd 1834,6,5 (H)
1835, 11, 25. James & fam gct Fairfield MM, Ind.
1835, 11, 25. Joel gct Fairfield MM, Ind.
1836, 4, 16. Jesse [Reece] dis mcd (H)
1836, 6, 18. Margaret Huff (form Reece) dis mcd (H)
1840, 7, 22. Ann [Reece] gct Westfield MM, Ind.
1842, 3, 23. Matilda Amos (or Ames) (form Rees) dis mcd (H)

RITTER
1826, 4, 22. Rachel (form Jessup) con mcd
1827, 3, 24. Rachel gct Fairfield MM, Ind.

ROADS
1928, 5, 4. Edwin C. d
1934, 1, 1. Effie d

1820, 9, 23. Ann gct New Garden MM, Ind.

ROBERTS
1821, 12, 22. Abel & w, Eleanor, & s, Moses, rocf Clear Creek MM, dtd 1821,12,8
1822, 2, 16. Moses rmt Sidney Barrett
1823, 8, 23. Thomas & w, Hannah, & ch, Abraham, John, Judah, Joseph, Lewis, Margaret, Ann, Abel & Ephraim, rocf Short Creek MM, O., dtd 1823,4,22
1825, 2, 19. John dis mcd
1825, 6, 18. John rocf Gwynnedd MM, Pa., dtd 1825,3,3
1825, 6, 18. Ann rocf Uwchlan MM, Pa., dtd 1825,4,7
1825, 6, 18. Stephen & Moses, ch Moses, rocf Uwchlan MM, Pa., dtd 1825,4,7
1826, 5, 18. Joseph, minor, rocf Uwchlan MM, Pa., dtd 1825,9,8
1829, 2, 21. Joseph gct Fairfield MM
1829, 9, 19. Judah gct Fairfield MM
1832, 1, 25. Moses rocf Uwchlan MM, dtd 1831,11,10
1836, 5, 25. Joseph con mcd
1836, 6, 22. Lewis gct Westfield MM, Ind.
1837, 2, 22. Abel & fam gct Newberry MM
1838, 5, 23. Abel Jr. gct Westfield MM, Ind.
1840, 3, 25. Ann Vanpelt (form Roberts) con mcd
1840, 8, 22. Ezekiel rocf Plainfield MM, dtd 1840,6,18 (H)
1844, 12, 23. Ephraim con mcd
1854, 3, 18. Ezekiel gct Plainfield MM (H)

ROGERS
1834, 4, 19. Massy (form Warner), dt Levi & Eliza, dis mcd (H)
1839, 9, 25. Lydia dis mcd
1921, 12, 3. Ruby Faye & Dorothy Lee recrq

RUDDUCK
1830, 3, 22. Sarah d bur Fall Creek

SAMS
1923, 12, 12. Floyd recrq

SANDERS
----, --, --. John & Eleanor (H)
Ch: Jesse b 1810, 4, 14 d 1829, 7, 5 bur Clear Creek
Hezekiah b 1812, 8, 8 " 1835, 9,18 bur Clear Creek
Addison b 1814, 4, 25 " 1814,12,21 bur Clear Creek
Cyrus b 1817, 9, 28
Richard B. " 1820, 8, 11

----, --, --. Samuel & Rebecca (H)
Ch: Sarah b 1817, 8, 5
John H. " 1819, 2, 20
Addison " 1822, 4, 12
Rachel " 1826, 4, 1
David " 1828, 2, 27
Samuel " 1831, 9, 16
Martha " 1831, 9, 16
1831, 2, 20. Samuel d bur Fairfield
----, --, --. Richard & Jane (H)
Ch: Eleanor b 1847, 4, 10
Elma Ann " 1849, 7, 7

1831, 11, 19. John gct Miami MM, to m (H)
1832, 5, 19. Rachel M. rocf Miami MM, dtd 1832,2,29 (H)
1834, 11, 22. Sarah Hinton (form Sanders) dis mcd (H)
1842, 3, 23. John H. rocf Fairfield MM, dtd 1841,12,23
1843, 10, 21. John H. dis mou (H)
1846, 9, 19. Richard B. gct Miami MM, to m Jane Whitacre (H)
1847, 4, 17. Jane rocf Miami MM, O., dtd 1846,12,23 (H)
1849, 4, 21. Martha Harlan (form Sanders) con mou (H)
1852, 2, 21. Caroline Amelia H., adopted dt John & Rachel, recrq (H)

SCOTT
1825, 7, 23. Mary (form Bundy) dis mcd

SEXTON
1819, 12, 18. Catharine rocf Center MM, O., dtd 1819,11,20
1820, 11, 18. Catharine rmt Jesse Baldwin

SHARP
1836, 10, 22. Phebe rocf Sadsbury MM, dtd 1836,5,4 (H)

SHEPPARD
1840, 8, 22. Mary (form Carroll) con mcd (H)

SHOEMAKER
1932, 7, 5. Joan b
1840, 3, 2. Thomas d bur Clear Creek (H)
1840, 3, 2. Abi d bur Clear Creek (H)

1839, 4, 20. Thomas & w, Abi, & ch, Edwin, Isaac B., Ann & Elizabeth T., rocf Short Creek MM, dtd 1839,2,21 (H)
1843, 7, 22. Edwin, Isaac B., Anna & Elizabeth T., ch Thos. & Abi, dec, gct Little Brittain MM, Pa. (H)

SMALL
1813, 10, 30. Jesse rmt Elizabeth Draper
1813, 11, 20. Jesse rocf White Water MM, Ind., dtd 1813,10,30
1815, 4, 22. Obadiah & w, Isabel, gct White Water MM
1815, 9, 23. Sarah & ch, Jonathan Amos, Ann, Ruth, Nathan & Sarah, gct White Water MM, Ind.
1815, 9, 23. Samuel, s Sarah, gct Clear Creek MM
1815, 9, 23. Rachel Guire (form Small) con mcd
1815, 10, 21. Joshua, Joseph, Jesse & Elizabeth, ch Joseph, gct New Garden MM, Ind.
1816, 1, 20. Ann Burson (form Small) dis mcd
1826, 1, 21. Jesse & fam gct New Garden MM, Ind.
1827, 4, 21. Zebulon Overman gct White Water MM, Ind., to m Elizabeth Small
1829, 7, 18. Ephraim rocf White Water MM, Ind., dtd 1828,12,24
1837, 7, 19. Clarkey gct Mississinewa MM, Ind.
1841, 7, 21. Ephraim dis mcd

SMITH
1840, 6, 25. Mary Ann m Enos CARROLL (H)

1832, 12, 22. Moses Tomlinson gct Miami MM, to m Ruth Smith (H)
1839, 4, 20. Nathan rocf Short Creek MM, dtd 1839,2,21 (H)
1840, 2, 15. Mary Ann recrq (H)
1849, 6, 16. Nathan con mou
1928, 6, 7. Jacob & Margaret relrq

SOALE
1922, 2, 4. Phoebe, Bessie & Nancy relrq

SPARGER
1812, 9, 19. Rachel rocf Westfield MM, dtd 1810,12,8, endorsed by Fairfield MM, 1812, 7,25

STULTZ
1929, 12, 4. Mary Margaret recrq

SUMMERS
1831, 7, 23. Isaac & fam gct White Water MM, Ind.(H)

SUMNER
1838, 5, 30. Thomas d ae 81y 5m 10d (an elder)

1811, 11, 23. Phebe rmt Jonathan Hodgson
1812, 4, 18. Mary rmt Wm. Beeson
1812, 9, 19. Hannah Walter (form Sumner) dis mcd
1813, 9, 18. Bowater Jr. dis mcd
1814, 1, 22. Isaac dis disunity
1815, 12, 23. Caleb con mcd
1815, 12, 23. Rebeckah (form Herreld) con mcd
1819, 1, 23. Isaac rst
1820, 7, 22. Phebe rmt Aden Ballard
1820, 12, 23. Phebe Reece (form Sumner) dis mcd
1821, 6, 23. Rebecka Davis (form Sumner) con mcd
1821, 12, 22. Allen dis
1822, 7, 20. Rachel recrq
1822, 8, 24. Anna rmt Isaac George
1822, 12, 21. Matilda, Amy & Elizabeth, ch Isaac, recrq
1826, 12, 23. Samuel con mcd
1827, 2, 17. Caleb gct Fairfield MM, Ind.
1829, 4, 18. Isaac dis jH
1829, 4, 18. Absalom dis jH
1829, 6, 20. Thomas gct Fairfield MM, to m Martha Williams
1829, 10, 24. Caleb & fam gct Fairfield MM, Ind.
1830, 2, 20. Rachel dis jH
1830, 2, 20. Thomas dis mcd
1830, 2, 20. Martha rocf Fairfield MM, dtd 1829,10,31
1831, 4, 23. Abigail [Sumners] dis disunity
1834, 1, 22. Samuel gct Milford MM, Ind.
1834, 8, 20. Martin con mcd
1838, 5, 19. Olive con mcd (H)
1838, 7, 25. Martha gct Cincinnati MM
1834, 10, 20. Joseph & fam gct Fairfield MM, Ind.
1834, 10, 20. Marton & fam gct Fairfield MM, Ind.
1834, 10, 20. Esther gct Duck Creek MM, Ind.

SWAIN
1814, 7, 23. Elizabeth (form Bernard) con mcd

SWISSHELM
1921, 12, 3. Mabel recrq

THOMPSON
1930, 4, 14. Martha d

THORNBURGH
----, --, --. Joseph & Lydia [Thornburg] (H)

Ch:		
	Joel	b 1816, 7, 27
	Jacob	" 1818, 6, 2
	Ruth	" 1825, 8, 4

1837, 6, 17. Joseph & fam recrq (H)
1845, 4, 19. Ruth Easlack (form Thornbury)

THORNBURGH, continued
con mcd (H)

TIMBERLAKE
----, --, --. John & Amy (H)
Ch: Joseph
Rhoads b 1819, 9, 23
Martha R. " 1821, 3, 2
Lydia " 1826, 3, 25
Mary Ann " 1823, 1, 27 (sic)
John P. " 1828, 1, 17
Pleasant " 1831, 5, 5
Harmon " 1833, 6, 28
Asenath " 1836, 11, 11

1841, 8, 21. Martha R. Heller (form Timberlake) con mcd (H)

TOMLINSON
1833, 9, 26. Milly d bur Fall Creek
----, --, --. Moses & Ruth (H)
Ch: Paul b 1834, 7, 26
Rachel " 1837, 4, 25
1835, 4, 9. Josiah d bur Fall Creek

1815, 6, 17. Mark dis
1823, 9, 20. Sarah dis
1826, 9, 23. Jacob dis mcd
1829, 4, 18. Moses dis jH
1829, 7, 18. Josiah & Milley dis jH
1829, 12, 19. Wm. dis jH
1830, 2, 20. Josiah Jr. dis jH
1830, 4, 17. Dinah, Olive & Charity dis jH
1832, 7, 21. Charity Baldwin (form Tomlinson) con mcd (H)
1832, 12, 22. Moses gct Miami MM, to m Ruth Smith (H)
1833, 5, 15. Ruth rocf Miami MM, dtd 1833,2, 20 (H)
1845, 4, 19. John con mcd (H)

TOMPKINS
1834, 1, 18. Sarah rocf Deercreek MM, Md., dtd 1833,10,17 (H)
1834, 1, 18. Jacob rocf Deercreek MM, Md., dtd 1833,9,12 (H)
1834, 8, 23. Jacob con mcd (H)
1834, 12, 20. Rachel (form Hiatt) con mcd (H)

TOWNSEND
1835, 11, 21. Rhoda (form Anthony) dis mcd (H)

TRUEBLOOD
1825, 12, 24. Miriam rocf White Water MM, Ind., dtd 1825,11,19
1827, 1, 20. Meriam gct White Water MM, Ind.

TROTH
----, --, --. Nathan m Mary J. DIVEN, dt James & Catherine, b 1853,6,28
Ch: Florence
Belle b 1885, 10, 23 d 1930, 2,21
Jessie C. b 1890, 2, 25

TURNER
1923, 12, 12. Clarence recrq

UNDERWOOD
1850, 1, 23. Amos, s Zephaniah & Rebecca, Clinton Co., O.; m in Clear Creek MH, Priscilla LEWIS, dt Christopher & Sarah HUSSEY, Highland Co., O. (H)

1850, 4, 20. Amos rocf Center MM, dtd 1850, 4,18 (H)
1853, 6, 18. Amos & w gct Center MM (H)

VANPELT
1815, 2, 13. John & w, Mary, & ch, Hannah, Jonathan, Ann, Mary Katy, Elisha, Mahlon & Phebe, rocf Plainfield MM, dtd 1814,11, 26
1818, 1, 21. Hannah rmt Abner Johnson
1820, 11, 18. Nancy rmt Daniel Duff
1821, 6, 23. Jonathan dis
1822, 5, 18. Mary Jr. dis mcd
1825, 4, 23. Catharine con.mcd
1826, 2, 18. Catharine gct Lees Creek MM
1828, 4, 19. Elisha dis mcd
1831, 6, 22. Phebe rmt Aaron Winder
1832, 1, 25. Sarah rocf Flushing MM, dtd 1831,5,26
1836, 6, 22. Mahlon dis mou
1839, 10, 24. Lydia rmt Elisha Hoge
1840, 3, 25. Ann (form Roberts) con mcd

WALKER
1930, 10, 30. Wm. d

WALTER
1812, 9, 19. Hannah (form Sumner) dis mcd
1816, 4, 20. Katharine (form Hiatt) dis mcd

WARD
1812, 9, 19. Thomas recrq
1822, 10, 19. Thomas gct Cherry Grove MM, Ind.

WARNER
----, --, --. Levi m Elizabeth WEBSTER, a wd (H)
Ch: Massey b 1813, 10, 5
Simion " 1817, 10, 22
Lydia " 1819, 9, 10
Abner " 1821, 8, 2
Joshua
Woodrow " 1825, 10, 6
Levi Woodrow " 1825, 10, 6
Pennington " 1830, 1, 25

1833, 7, 20. Levi & w, Eliza, & ch gct Green Plain MM (H)
1834, 4, 19. Massy Rogers, dt Levi & Eliza, WARNER, dis mcd (H)

WAY
----, --, --. Robert & Abigail (H)
Ch: Mariannie b 1823, 11, 1 d 1828,12,29 bur Clear Creek
Phocion b 1826, 3, 14
Elias " 1828, 7, 18

1838, 5, 19. Robert & fam gct Springborough MM (H)
1844, 8, 17. Robert & w, Abigail, & ch, Phocian R., Elias H., Samuel C., Jacob W. & David, rocf Springborough MM, dtd 1844, 5,23 (H)
1846, 8, 22. Robert & fam gct Miami MM (H)

WEBSTER
----, --, --. ----- & Elizabeth (H)
Ch: William b 1814, 10, 4
Hugh " 1818, 10, 13

WEST
1849, 4, 21. Helena (form Jackson) con mou (H)
1821, 12, 3. Willie & Helen recrq
1922, 2, 4. Millie recrq

WHITACRE
1846, 9, 19. Richard B. Sanders gct Miami MM, to m Jane Whitacre (H)

WHITE
1843, 4, 19. Francis rocf Blue River MM, Ind., dtd 1843,2,4
1843, 12, 20. Francis rmt Sarah H. Brown

WILKINS
1815, 9, 23. Joseph & w, Sarah, & ch, Tamzon, Wm., John, Thos., Hannah & Frances, rocf New Garden MM, O., dtd 1814,12,15
1817, 9, 20. Joseph & fam gct Fairfield MM

WILLIAMS
1829, 6, 20. Thomas Sumner gct Fairfield MM, to m Martha Williams

WILLIS
1821, 9, 22. Joel & w, Hannah, & s, Jesse, rocf Lees Creek MM, dtd 1821,7,21
1822, 5, 18. Betsey dis mcd
1822, 5, 18. Jesse dis mcd
1828, 5, 24. Joel & w, Hannah, gct Lees Creek MM

WILSON
1813, 9, 18. John & w, Milicent, & ch, Isaac, Elizabeth, rocf Rich Square MM, N. C., dtd 1812,11,21
1816, 5, 18. Esther & dt, Esther, & s, Joseph, rocf Center MM, N. C., dtd 1815,8,13
1816, 6, 22. Michael rocf Center MM, N. C., dtd 1816,8,19
1817, 5, 24. Michael dis mcd
1817, 6, 21. Wm. rocf Centre MM, N. C., dtd 1815,8,19, end by Lick Creek MM, Ind.
1818, 5, 23. Joseph dis mcd
1822, 4, 25. Hester Davis (form Willson) con mcd
1822, 6, 22. Michael rst rq
1827, 3, 24. Joseph rst
1827, 8, 18. Rebecca recrq
1827, 11, 17. Michael & w, Rebecca, gct Duck Creek MM, Ind.
1828, 7, 19. Phebe recrq
1828, 10, 18. Wm. gct Duck Creek MM, Ind.
1828, 10, 18. Joseph & w gct Duck Creek MM, Ind.
1829, 10, 24. John & fam gct Fairfield MM, Ind.
1834, 5, 21. Esther gct Duck Creek MM, Ind.

WINDER
1831, 6, 22. Aaron rmt Phebe Vanpelt

WIRE
1848, 7, 22. Nancy (form Rains) dis mou

WOLF
1929, 10, 2. W. W. & w & dt, Elsie & Eveline, relrq
1932, 7, 6. Pearl E., Jean E. & Mildred E. recrq

WOOD
1911, 8, 9. Helen Louise, dt Lewis & Rosa, b

1839, 3, 20. Susannah dis mcd
1846, 6, 22. Mary (form Huff) dis mcd
1921, 12, 3. Helen Louise recrq

WOODMANSEE
1833, 2, 16. Betsy (form Lewis) dis mcd (H)

WORLEY
1811, 10, 19. Hiram dis disunity
1813, 9, 18. Milly dis
1815, 3, 18. Katy dis
1815, 9, 23. Polly dis mcd
1822, 8, 24. John dis disunity
1824, 9, 18. Jacob Jr. dis disunity
1826, 3, 18. Stephen dis disunity
1831, 5, 21. Phebe Hutson (form Worley) dis mcd

WRIGHT
1814, 7, 23. Joshua & w, Rebecca, & ch, Sarah, Isaac, Jonathan & Betsey, rocf Fairfield MM, dtd 1814,6,25
1815, 1, 21. Josiah Draper gct Fairfield MM, to m Jemima Wright
1821, 9, 22. Joshua & fam gct Honey Creek MM, Ind.
1831, 10, 22. Hannah Baker (form Wright) con mcd (H)
1841, 7, 21. Joseph rmt Lydia Cowgill
1841, 9, 22. Joseph rocf Clear Creek MM, dtd

WRIGHT, continued
1841,8,24
1823, 12, 12. Frank recrq

YOST
1840, 9, 19. Joseph W. Larkens gct Short Creek MM, to m Margaret Yost (H)

CLEAR CREEK MONTHLY MEETING

Clear Creek Monthly Meeting, located three-fourths of a mile east of Samantha, Clinton County, Ohio, was set off from Fairfield Monthly Meeting 12 Mo. 24, 1812.

Among the charter members were James Hadley and Rachel Hunt, clerks; Daniel Huff, John Beals, Jonathan Sanders, Joseph Hockett, James Griffin, Christopher Heath, Charity Nordike, Sarah Hodgson, Ruth Chaffant and Mary Kenworthy, overseers. Other families represented in the charter membership were Ellis, Timberlake, Stafford, Baldwin, Moon, Prechett, Brown, Jackson, Mills, Williams, Hoggatt, Presey, Coffin, Ratcliff, Cox.

RECORDS

ABBOTT
1881, 4, 9. John B. [Abbot] recrq
1882, 1, 14. J. B. relrq
1903, 5, 9. W. Elworth, Minnie & Fay [Abbot] rocf Sabina MM, O.
1903, 11, 14. Lorena relrq
1904, 12, 10. Elsworth & dt, Faye, gct Wilmington MM

ACHOR
1858, 12, 7. Elizabeth D., dt John & Ann, b

1850, 10, 12. Rachel [Acre] (form Jackson) dis mcd & jas
1855, 11, 10. John & w, Ann, & ch, Thomas Dillon, Martha Jane, Survetus Taylor & Sarah Ann, recrq
1869, 9, 11. Sarah Ann rocf Fairfield MM, dtd 1869,8,21
1871, 2, 11. Thomas rpd mcd; dropped from mbrp
1871, 4, 8. Thomas D. rpd mcd; dropped from mbrp
1873, 1, 10. Sarah gct Richland MM, Ia.
1883, 8, 11. Survetus T. dropped from mbrp
1883, 8, 11. Cora V. dropped from mbrp
1897, 2, 13. Euphemia A. rocf Center MM
1900, 12, 8. John & w, Euphemia, gct Wilmington MM

ACKERMAN
1877, 10, 13. Laura O. relrq

ADAMS
1855, 9, 8. Ann (form Hodson) dis mcd
1869, 4, 10. Louisa recrq
1869, 4, 10. Eliza J. recrq
1878, 1, 12. Louisa dropped from mbrp
1886, 2, 12. Loami A. recrq
1886, 2, 12. Belle recrq
1892, 6, 11. J. M. & w dropped from mbrp
1895, 5, 11. Laomi recrq
1895, 5, 11. Bell recrq
1895, 5, 11. Opha recrq

ALBERTSON
1821, 6, 15. Rebecca m Ezra HUNT

1820, 7, 8. Rebecca recrq

ALLEN
1873, 5, 10. Owega recrq

ANDREW
1873, 3, 8. Nancy Ellen recrq
1878, 1, 12. Ellen [Andrews] dropped from mbrp
1894, 1, 13. Milton rocf Westfork MM, O.
1895, 9, 14. Lillian rocf Westfork MM
1904, 6, 7. Ida rocf Newberry MM
1906, 3, 10. Milton & w, Ida May, gct Westfork MM

ANTHONY
----, --, --. Joseph & Rhoda
Ch: Samuel Parsons b 1792, 12, 2
Thomas Clark " 1796, 6, 1
Charles " 1798, 3, 30
Jane Wood " 1804, 2, 21
Joseph " 1805, 10, 31
Rhoda Moorman " 1807, 9, 20
Sarah " 1811, 9, 25
Rachel " 1813, 5, 3
Penelope " 1814, 8, 30
Christopher " 1816, 9, 9
1822, 10, 24. Thomas C., s Joseph & Rhoda, Clinton Co., O.; m in Clear Creek MH, Judith TIMBERLAKE, dt John & Mary, Highland Co., O.
1823, 1, 22. Jane W. m Thos. HUSSEY

1814, 12, 30. Rhoda, w Joseph, & ch, Samuel Parson, Thomas Clark, Charles & Jane Wood, rocf a monthly mtg held at Cedar Creek, Hanover Co., dtd 1812,12,12
1817, 3, 8. Samuel gct Cincinnati MM
1817, 4, 12. Charles & w, Elizabeth, & ch, Eliza, Judith, Henrietta, Sally & Joseph, gct Miami MM, O.
1818, 3, 14. Rhoda & ch, Charles, Jane Wood, Joseph, Rhoda Moorman, Sarah Rachel Penelope & Christopher, gct Cincinnati MM
1821, 6, 9. Rhoda & ch, Jane Wood, Joseph, Rhoda Moorman, Sarah, Rachel, Penelope, Christopher & Elizabeth, rocf Cincinnati MM, dtd 1820,9,21
1821, 8, 12. Cert rec for Charles & w, Elizabeth, & ch, Susan Evans, from Cincinnati MM, dtd 1821,6,28, endorsed to Miami MM
1823, 4, 12. Charles dis disunity
1825, 4, 19. Abraham Nordyke Jr. gct Miami MM, to m Henrietta P. Anthony
1826, 4, 8. Thomas C. dis disunity
1828, 6, 13. Rhoda dis jH
1829, 4, 11. Joseph dis mcd
1829, 8, 8. Rhoda M. & Judith dis jH
1833, 2, 19. Sarah Fletcher (form Anthony) dis mcd
1834, 9, 23. Penelope dis disunity
1835, 3, 24. Rachel Baker (form Anthony) dis mcd & jH
1838, 4, 24. Christopher Jr. dis mcd

ANTRIM
1870, 11, 12. Lucinda (form Michael) con mcd
1871, 1, 14. Lucinda gct Fairfield MM

ARTHUR
1868, 5, 9. Laura E. & Mary E. recrq
1869, 7, 10. Laura E. Jones (form Arthur) con mcd

ARTHUR, continued
1870, 5, 14. Martha A. recrq
1873, 5, 10. Edwin & Ann recrq

BABB
1875, 4, 10. Elizabeth recrq

BAILEY
----, --, --. Thomas & Elizabeth
Ch: Mary b 1804, 4, 9
John " 1806, 1, 21
Christopher" 1807, 9, 12
Joseph " 1809, 12, 7
Sarah " 1811, 7, 26
Ann " 1814, 5, 21
Judith " 1816, 3, 22
Thomas " 1818, 1, 6
Ansalum " 1820, 8, 16
Elizabeth " 1822, 4, 17
1818, 7, 18. Thomas d bur Clear Creek
1820, 11, 16. Mary m Aaron COX
1923, 2-, --. Martha Leone m Robert JOHNSON

1828, 8, 9. John dis mcd
1829, 4, 11. Thomas dis jH
1829, 9, 12. Elizabeth dis jH
1830, 3, 13. Christopher dis mcd
1830, 8, 14. Joseph dis jH
1830, 10, 14. Sarah dis disunity
1841, 8, 24. Elizabeth McMullen (form Bailey) dis mcd
1846, 6, 13. Ansalem dis jH
1850, 9, 14. Asa Nordyke gct Dover MM, to m Almedia Bailey
1857, 10, 10. Thamer (form Hiatt) dis mcd
1868, 5, 9. Joseph recrq
1871, 1, 14. Joseph rpd mcd; retained mbrp
1871, 2, 11. Martha rpd mcd; retained mbrp
1905, 11, 11. Clara Olive rocf Fairfield MM
1909, 11, 13. John H. & Jane rocf Friends Chapel, Ind.
1920, 6, 12. Alvin Arthur & dt, Anna Jean, recrq
1920, 6, 12. Leone recrq
1931, 5, 4. Alvin & w, Elma, gct Leesburg MM, O.

BAKER
1824, 9, 15. Susannah, dt Amasa & Sarah, b

1823, 12, 13. Amasa & w, Sarah, & ch, George H., John Y., Mary, Joseph & Lydia, rocf Chester MM, Pa., dtd 1823,8,25, endorsed by Plainfield MM & Fall Creek MM
1826, 7, 8. Nathan & s, Amos, rocf Chester MM, Pa., dtd 1826,4,24
1828, 9, 14. Sarah dis jH
1829, 3, 14. Amasa dis jH
1830, 8, 14. George dis jH
1830, 10, 14. John dis jH
1834, 10, 21. Mary dis jH
1835, 3, 24. Rachel (form Anthony) dis mcd & jH
1842, 6, 21. Susannah dis disunity
1842, 6, 21. Lydia dis disunity
1842, 11, 22. Joseph dis disunity
1845, 1, 11. Susannah (form Bankson) dis mcd

BALDWIN
1813, 4, 22. Sarah & ch, Jesse, Elizabeth, Phinehas & Hannah, gct Darby Creek MM
1815, 11, 11. Jesse & w, Hannah, & ch, Sarah & Sophia, rocf Fall Creek MM, dtd 1815,10, 21
1818, 3, 14. Sophia gct Darby Creek MM
1820, 10, 14. Jesse gct Fall Creek MM

BALLARD
1814, 3, 2. David, s Moorman & Minerva, Clinton Co., O.; m in East Fork MH, Mary OZBUN, dt John & Sarah, Clinton Co., O.
1841, 9, 22. David F., s William & Phebe, Green Co., O.; m in East Fork MH, Priscilla LEWIS, dt Amos & Phebe, Clinton Co., O.

1814, 8, 26. Mary gct Centre MM
1815, 1, 27. Thomas & w, Sarah, rocf South River MM, Va., dtd 1814,9,10, endorsed by Center MM
1819, 3, 13. Thomas & w, Sarah, & ch, Elizabeth & Barkley, gct Miami MM
1824, 3, 13. Thomas & w, Sarah, & ch, Elizabeth, Barclay, Achilles, Rachel & Adison, rocf Miami MM, dtd 1824,3,25
1825, 8, 13. Thomas & w, Sarah, & ch, Elizabeth, Barclay, Achilles, Rachel & Addison, gct Miami MM
1842, 9, 20. Priscilla gct Centre MM
1845, 11, 8. David F. & w, Priscilla, & s, Asa N., rocf Centre MM, dtd 1843,5,17 (1845?)
1852, 9, 11. Priscilla & ch, Asa N., Louisa, Mary, Evaline & Asenath B., rocf Salem MM, Ia., dtd 1851,10,15
1865, 12, 9. Louisa Cline (form Ballard) dis mcd & jas
1866, 8, 11. Asa N. gct Dover MM, O.
1866, 8, 11. Mary & Evaline gct Dover MM
1866, 8, 11. Priscilla & ch, Asenath & Wm., gct Dover MM

BANKSON
1837, 5, 23. Elizabeth & ch, Marian, Esther, Isaac, Ruth, Lydia, Susannah, William & Elizabeth, rocf Fairfield MM, dtd 1837,4, 20
1839, 10, 22. Esther Savage (form Bankson) dis mcd
1844, 6, 8. Lydia Hoskins (form Bankson) dis mcd
1844, 11, 9. Mary Ann gct Springfield MM
1844, 11, 9. Ruth gct Springfield MM
1844, 11, 9. Elizabeth & ch, William & Elizabeth, gct Springfield MM
1845, 1, 11. Susannah Baker (form Bankson)

BANKSON, continued
dis mcd
1846, 6, 13. Isaac dis disunity

BARRETT
1863, 7, 11. Ezekiel recrq
1878, 1, 12. Ezekiel dropped from mbrp

BARRICK
1825, 6, 23. Elizabeth m Aaron CHALFANT

1829, 11, 14. John dis mcd
1834, 9, 23. Nancy Becner (form Barrick) rpd mcd; dec

BATEMAN
1836, 11, 22. John W. Timberlake gct Springborough MM, to m Rachel J. Bateman

BASHER
1914, 2, 14. Delilah recrq

BEAN
1869, 4, 10. Margaret recrq

BEALS
1815, 9, 21. Susannah m John THORNBROUGH

1815, 7, 28. Ruth rocf Fairfield MM, dtd 1815,5,27
1816, 1, 13. Jacob & w, Ann, & ch, Jesse & Lydia, recrq
1816, 3, 19. Elizabeth (form Pucket) con mcd
1816, 3, 19. John Jr. con mcd
1816, 11, 9. Nathan gct Fairfield MM

BEARD
1878, 4, 13. Hannah relrq

BEARY
1857, 7, 11. Sarah Ann (form Michael) dis mcd
1857, 10, 10. Sarah Ann recrq
1858, 12, 11. Sarah Ann gct Dover MM
1862, 12, 13. Sarah Ann [Bera] rocf Dover MM, dtd 1862,9,18
1874, 1, 19. Cyrus A. [Beery] gct Richland MM, Ind.
1875, 6, 12. Sarah Ann gct Newberry MM
1881, 12, 10. Cynthia [Berry] recrq

BEAWR (?)
1883, 8, 11. Margaret A. dropped from mbrp
1883, 8, 11. Frank dropped from mbrp
1883, 8, 11. Elizabeth dropped from mbrp
1883, 8, 11. Elma dropped from mbrp

BECNER
1834, 9, 23. Nancy (form Barrick) rpd mcd; dec

BEESON
1873, 3, 8. William C. recrq
1873, 3, 8. Samantha E. recrq
1873, 3, 8. Edwin, s Wm. C. & Samantha E., recrq
1888, 11, 12. William dropped from mbrp
1888, 11, 12. Mattie dropped from mbrp
1888, 11, 12. Edwin dropped from mbrp

BELFORD
1887, 2, 12. John W. recrq
1892, 6, 11. John dropped from mbrp

BERNARD
1867, 3, 9. Jane Emily (form Hoskins) con mcd
1869, 4, 10. Thomas J. recrq
1869, 4, 10. James K. recrq
1869, 4, 10. Keziah recrq
1869, 4, 10. Harriet recrq
1869, 4, 10. Chas. B. recrq
1869, 4, 10. Elijah recrq
1869, 4, 10. Harriet J. recrq
1869, 4, 10. John R., minor ch, recrq of parents
1869, 4, 10. Geo. W. recrq
1869, 4, 10. Harriet C. recrq
1869, 4, 10. Chas. O. recrq
1869, 4, 10. Martha A. recrq
1869, 4, 10. James E. recrq
1874, 4, 11. Joanna & Laura May recrq
1877, 3, 11. George W. recrq
1877, 3, 11. George W. Jr. & w, Jane, & dt, Abba, recrq
1878, 8, 10. Columbia recrq
1887, 2, 12. Thomas Judson recrq
1888, 7, 14. Judson dropped from mbrp
1888, 7, 14. George dropped from mbrp
1888, 7, 14. Edwin dropped from mbrp
1888, 7, 14. Keziah dropped from mbrp
1888, 7, 14. Mattie dropped from mbrp
1888, 7, 14. Abbie dropped from mbrp
1888, 7, 14. James K. dropped from mbrp
1892, 6, 11. Cora dropped from mbrp
1892, 6, 11. John dropped from mbrp
1892, 6, 11. Charles dropped from mbrp
1892, 6, 11. Thomas J. & fam dropped from mbrp
1895, 5, 11. Charles O. & Ella & ch, James Everett, Myrtle & Charles Rodney recrq
1895, 5, 11. Thomas recrq
1896, 4, 11. John B. recrq
1898, 11, 12. G. W. dropped from mbrp
1898, 11, 12. Judson dropped from mbrp
1899, 12, 9. George W. dropped from mbrp
1900, 4, 14. Oscar E. recrq
1900, 4, 14. George W. & Cora B. & ch, Aleta & Georgia, recrq
1902, 1, 11. Sarah J. & dt, Beth, relrq
1902, 6, 14. Jud recrq
1912, 5, 11. Jud dropped from mbrp

BERRY
1899, 1, 14. Cynthia dropped from mbrp

BINGER
1899, 6, 10. Mary Jane rocf Hopewell MM
1900, 10, 13. Mary J. [Binegar] gct Hopewell MM

BLAIR
1873, 5, 10. Sarah (form Richman) rpd mcd; dropped from mbrp
1892, 2, 13. Emma gct Wilmington MM

BOATMAN
1914, 11, 14. Anna Ridgeway dropped from mbrp

BOND
1819, 12, 16. Daniel, s Edward & Anna, Wayne Co., Ind.; m in Clear Creek MH, Mary HUSSEY, dt Christopher & Sarah, Highland Co., O.

1820, 2, 12. Mary gct New Garden MM, Ind.
1848, 10, 14. Eunice rocf Dover MM, Ia., dtd 1848,7,19
1865, 12, 9. Eunice Nugent (form Bond) con mcd

BONWELL
1842, 5, 24. Nathaniel recrq

BORDEN
1893, 2, 11. Dudley dropped from mbrp
1894, 7, 14. Milburn dropped from mbrp
1895, 10, 12. Milburn dropped from mbrp
1898, 7, 9. Wilburn dropped from mbrp

BOWERS
1905, 8, 12. James G. recrq

BOWLS
1818, 7, 11. Ruth & ch, Jonah & William, gct White Water MM, Ind.

BOWMAN
1917, 9, 8. Alfred C. recrq
1917, 9, 8. Oneta B. recrq
1917, 9, 8. Paul recrq
1917, 9, 8. Pauline recrq

BOYD
1850, 5, 11. Elizabeth dis joining M. E. Church

BRACKNEY
1846, 10, 10. Lewis Nordyke gct Dover MM, to m Rachel Brackney

BRADEN
1831, 3, 12. Juliet rocf Cherry Grove MM, Ind., dtd 1830,5,8
1838, 4, 24. Juliet gct New Garden MM, Ind.

BRADFIELD
1819, 10, 9. Cynthia & ch, Mary, Samuel, Elias, Rachel, Jonas & Cary, rocf Carmel MM, held at Elkrun, dtd 1819,3,20
1824, 11, 13. Elias dis
1825, 10, 8. Samuel dis mcd
1826, 3, 11. Tamer (form Davis) dis mcd
1826, 9, 9. Rachel Burton (form Bradfield) dis mcd
1834, 12. 23. Jonas dis mcd
1835, 11, 24. Carey gct Cherry Grove MM, Ind.

BRANNON
1912, 2, 10. Charles Wm. recrq

BREAKNALL
1894, 7, 14. Lee dropped from mbrp
1898, 7, 9. Lee dropped from mbrp

BREWER
1871, 1, 14. Elizabeth recrq
1871, 1, 14. Etta recrq
1873, 3, 8. John W. recrq
1873, 3, 8. David F. recrq
1873, 3, 8. Martha recrq
1875, 3, 13. Mattie relrq
1880, 1, 10. John Wm. & David Franklin recrq
1880, 1, 10. Etta relrq
1883, 5, 12. Joel recrq
1883, 5, 12. Martha recrq
1889, 2, 9. John recrq

BROWDER
1909, 2, 13. Mildred & Harmon recrq
1909, 2, 13. Henrietta, minor, recrq
1910, 1, 8. Edward recrq
1920, 4, 10. E. H. & w, Amy, gct Leesburg MM, O.
1920, 4, 10. Harmon & Henrietta gct Leesburg MM, O.

BROWN
----, --, --. Edgar & Mary
Ch: Sarah H. b 1824, 4, 24
Joel " 1825, 5, 15 d 1828, 8,28 bur Fairfield
Daniel H. b 1826, 6, 28 " 1828, 8, 9 bur Fairfield
Rachel Ann b 1827, 10, 10 " 1828, 8,14 bur Fairfield
William b 1828, 12, 14

1820, 2, 12. Elgar gct Fairfield MM, to m
1820, 7, 8. Mary rocf Fairfield MM, dtd 1820,5,27
1821, 3, 10. Joel dis
1828, 3, 14. Elgar & w, Mary, & ch, Sarah H. & Wm., gct Fall Creek MM
1830, 7, 10. William dis mcd
1830, 9, 10. Joshua dis disunity
1838, 8, 21. Cert rec for Wm. & w, Grace, & ch, Isaac, from Short Creek MM, O., dtd 1837,11,21, endorsed to Fall Creek MM
1838, 8, 21. Cert rec for Samuel from Short Creek MM, dtd 1837,11,21, endorsed to

BROWN, continued
Fall Creek MM
1839, 11, 19. Rachel gct Fall Creek MM
1866, 10, 13. Samuel & w, Grace, & ch, Rebecca, Elizabeth & Edna, rocf Fairfield MM
1874, 7, 11. Lydia N. recrq
1877, 3, 11. William H. recrq
1878, 3, 9. William dis
1882, 4, 8. Dr. Edward W. recrq
1885, 3, 14. George N. recrq
1885, 6, 13. Dr. E. W. dropped from mbrp
1892, 12, 10. Lydia W. (form Conard) relrq
1894, 7, 14. George W. dropped from mbrp
1899, 3, 11. Wm. & w, Margrate, & s, Walter, recrq
1899, 3, 11. Sarah & ch, Mary, Mabel, Harry & Homer, recrq
1900, 6, 9. William & Maggie relrq
1918, 9, 14. Mary dropped from mbrp
1918, 9, 14. Mabel dropped from mbrp
1918, 9, 14. Harry dropped from mbrp
1918, 9, 14. Homer dropped from mbrp
1931, 4, 8. Sarah dropped from mbrp

BRYANT
1817, 7, 12. Allen rocf Mt. Pleasant MM, Va., dtd 1817,4,26, endorsed by Fairfield MM
1817, 10, 11. Allen dis disunity

BUFFINGTON
1838, 5, 22. Mifflin M. rocf Fairfield MM, dtd 1838,2,22
1840, 6, 23. Mifflin M. gct Springfield MM
1842, 10, 18. Mifflin M. gct Springfield MM, O., Clinton Co.
1856, 2, 7. Mifflin M. dis disunity

BURNETT
1869, 4, 10. George recrq
1869, 4, 10. Martha J. recrq
1874, 4, 11. George relrq

BURNS
1874, 8, 8. Leah & dt, Sarah, rocf Fairfield MM, dtd 1874,7,18
1882, 1, 14. Leah gct Newberry MM

BURTON
1826, 9, 9. Rachel (form Bradfield) dis mcd
1909, 3, 13. Ballard recrq

BUTLER
1821, 9, 8. Ursula & dt, Elizabeth & Susannah, rocf Fairfield MM, dtd 1821,8,25
1827, 8, 11. Elizabeth gct Fairfield MM
1829, 12, 12. Ursula gct Fairfield MM
1830, 8, 14. Susannah dis jH
1871, 3, 11. Elisha M. & w, Keziah D., rocf Spiceland MM, dtd 1871,2,4
1876, 5, 13. Elisha & w, Keziah, gct Wilmington MM

BUTTERWORTH
1886, 6, 12. Etta gct Wilmington MM

CADE
1887, 4, 9. Thomas E. recrq
1891, 5, 9. Etta recrq
1893, 2, 11. Addie dropped from mbrp
1893, 2, 11. Thomas dropped from mbrp
1893, 2, 11. Henry dropped from mbrp
1894, 7, 14. Etta dropped from mbrp
1898, 5, 14. Sarah recrq
1898, 7, 9. Elta dropped from mbrp
1903, 2, 14. Arthur recrq
1904, 4, 9. Adeline recrq
1906, 2, 10. Henry recrq
1907, 7, 13. Harry recrq
1910, 7, 9. Sarah recrq
1910, 7, 9. Frances White recrq
1912, 5, 11. Henry & Adaline dropped from mbrp
1916, 9, 9. Harry dropped from mbrp
1916, 9, 9. Francis dropped from mbrp

CADEMY
1877, 6, 7. Carrie recrq

CADWALADER
1823, 3, 19. Joseph [Cadwallader], s Moses & Mary, Highland Co., O.; m in East Fork MH, Catharine COX, dt Thomas & Sarah, Clinton Co., O.

1819, 8, 14. Jesse & w, Amy, & ch, John, Isaac, Moses, Mahlon, Silas, Betsy & Jonah, rocf South River MM, Va., dtd 1819,5,1
1820, 12, 9. John dis jas
1821, 3, 10. Jesse dis jas
1821, 2, 10. Amy dis jas
1822, 3, 9. Moses dis jas
1824, 7, 10. Joseph rocf Miami MM, dtd 1824, 4,26
1825, 5, 14. Tamer con mcd
1825, 6, 11. Isaac & w, Tamer, gct White Lick MM, Ind.
1828, 10, 11. Joseph dis disunity
1829, 9, 12. Catharine dis jH
1830, 2, 13. Betsy dis jH
1830, 11, 13. Mahlon dis joining "Dunkers Society"
1830, 12, 11. Silas dis joining Dunkards Society
1834, 5, 20. Jonah dis disunity

CAMMACK
1865, 2, 11. George W. recrq
1865, 3, 11. Mary [Camack] (form Pidgon) con mcd
1866, 3, 10. George W. & w, Mary, & ch, Willie, gct White Water MM, Ind.
1886, 11, 13. Irvin H. rocf Amboy MM, Ind.
1888, 5, 12. Ervin & w, Michael, gct Whittier MM, Calif.

CANADAY
1828, 10, 22. Henry, s Walter & Ann, Highland Co., O.; m in East Fork MH, Drucilla HUSSEY, dt Joshua & Sarah, Highland Co., O.

1835, 3, 24. Drucilla & ch, Wm. Riley, Madison & Nathan, gct Fall Creek MM

CANTLEY
1870, 11, 12. Alice (form Carey) con mcd
1874, 4, 11. George M. recrq
1888, 1, 14. George & fam gct Wichita MM, Kans.

CANTRELL
1884, 3, 8. James & w, Alcinda, & ch, Clayton, recrq
1885, 4, 11. James M. & fam gc
1899, 4, 8. Charles [Cantrill] recrq
1908, 1, 11. Chas. relrq

CAREY
----, --, --. John & Margaret
Ch: Isaac b 1812, 8, 25
Elias " 1814, 4, 23
John " 1816, 3, 17
Mary " 1818, 10, 15
Abigail " 1820, 4, 27
Peninah " 1822, 10, 23
----, --, --. Samuel & Ann
Ch: Sarah
Lemert b 1819, 2, 15 d 1820, 3,13 bur Clear Creek
Jonathan b 1820, 9, 20
David M. " 1822, 5, 6
Rhoda " 1824, 5, 9
John " 1826, 8, 16
Rachel " 1828, 11, 22
1820, 10, 28. Thomas d bur Clear Creek
1823, 9, 6. Samuel d bur Salt Creek Graveyard
1831, 5, 19. Daniel, s Samuel & Anne, Highland Co., O.; m in Clear Creek MH, Anne COFFIN, dt David & Mary, Highland Co., O.
1832, 2, 2. Ruth m Joseph McPHERSON
1834, 10, 2. Elizabeth m David KESTER
----, --, --. John & Eliza [Cary]
Ch: Elias b 1836, 11, 19
Penninah " 1838, 9, 11
Margaret G." 1839, 12, 20
Daniel " 1841, 6, 14 d 1841, 8, 8 bur Clear Creek
1838, 11, 1. Mary m Owen WEST
1843, 11, 2. Abigail m Martin WEST
1843, 11, 30. Rhoda m John GREEN
1844, 12, 14. Ruth Anna, dt Isaac & Elizabeth, b
----, --, --. Jonathan & Abigail J.
----, --, Gurney B. b 1856, 8, 4
Charles E. " 1863, 8, 26
1924, 6, 3. Arthur L. m Anna M. FARR
1932, 6, 18. Arthur L. d (an elder)

1815, 7, 28. John & w, Margaret, & ch, Ruth, Robert, Isaac & Elias, rocf Mt. Pleasant MM, Va., dtd 1815,5,27
1817, 7, 12. Samuel [Cary] & w, Rachel, & s, Elias, rocf Mt. Pleasant MM, Va., dtd 1817,4,26 endorsed by Fairfield MM
1817, 7, 12. Samuel [Cary] Jr. & w, Anna, & ch, Daniel, Elizabeth, Thomas & Elias, rocf Mt. Pleasant MM, Va., dtd 1817,4,26 endorsed by Fairfield MM
1819, 5, 8. Elias [Cary] con mcd
1830, 5, 8. Robert gct Newberry MM, to m Susannah Moon
1830, 11, 13. Susannah rocf Newberry MM, dtd 1830,10,28
1832, 5, 22. Robert & w, Susannah, gct Newberry MM
1833, 10, 22. Isaac gct Newberry MM, to m Elizabeth Moon
1834, 4, 22. Elias Jr. gct Newberry MM
1835, 10, 20. John Jr. gct Newberry MM, to m Eliza Moon
1836, 9, 20. Eliza rocf Newberry MM, dtd 1836,5,23
1838, 2, 20. Elias Jr. con mcd
1840, 10, 20. Daniel & w, Anne, & ch, David, Thomas Elwood, Priscilla & Sarah Anne, gct Newberry MM
1842, 2, 22. John Jr. & w, Eliza, & ch, Elias, Penina & Margaret, gct Newberry MM
1843, 4, 18. Isaac & w, Elizabeth, & ch, William, John, Jesse, Margaretjane & Daniel, rocf Newberry MM, dtd 1843,4,17
1844, 12, 14. David M. gct Newberry MM, to m Rebecca Hiatt
1845, 11, 8. Elias dis disunity
1846, 11, 14. Rebecca rocf Newberry MM, dtd 1846,5,11
1846, 11, 14. Jonathan con mcd
1850, 2, 9. Samuel & w, Anna, gct Newberry MM
1850, 5, 11. Elias gct Newberry MM
1850, 5, 11. Isaac & w, Elizabeth, & ch, Wm. M., John H., Jesse G., Margaret Jane, Daniel M., Ruth Anna, Sarah Ellen & Mary E., gct Back Creek MM, Iowa [Note by Mrs. J.E. McMullan I think this must be Ia. the old abbreviation for Ind.]

1850, 8, 10. John gct Newberry MM
1855, 9, 8. Abigail Jane recrq
1855, 11, 10. Katharine A., Arthur L. & Emily, ch Jonathan & Abigail, recrq
1867, 5, 11. William & w, Almira, & ch, Alonzo, Eliza R., Mary Ann, Margaret H., Lenna Alice & Benjamin C. recrq
1870, 11, 12. Alice Cantley (form Carey) con mcd
1871, 2, 11. Thomas L. rpd mcd; retained mbrp
1871, 2, 11. Amos H. rpd mcd; retained mbrp
1871, 3, 11. Anna J. rpd mcd; retained mbrp
1874, 4, 11. Elizabeth recrq
1877, 8, 11. Thomas L. & s, Walter, gct New-

CAREY, continued
1877, 8, 11. Thos. L. & s, Walter, gct Newberry MM
1877, 10, 13. Mary Ann & Maggie relrq
1878, 6, 8. Anna E. rocf Fairfield MM, O., dtd 1878,5,18
1880, 7, 9. Amos H. & w, Anna, & ch, Frank, Ida & Pearl, gct Springfield MM, O.
1884, 9, 13. Thomas L. & w, Melissa, & s, Walter Homer, rocf Newberry MM, O.
1885, 3, 14. Florence B. recrq
1886, 3, 13. Adda recrq
1886, 6, 12. Ruth A. recrq
1887, 3, 12. Clifton O., Elizabeth M. & David E., ch Samuel A. & Ruth, recrq
1889, 2, 9. Charles E. gct Oak Ridge MM, Ind.
1894, 7, 14. Luena A. dropped from mbrp
1894, 7, 14. Alonzo M. dropped from mbrp
1900, 4, 14. Hattie C. recrq
1900, 4, 14. Olga Kezia, dt James, recrq
1902, 1, 11. Albert & w, Ruth A., & ch, Bertha L., Clifton O., Elizabeth M., David E. & Mary Ellen, gct Wilmington MM, O.
1902, 6, 14. Harley gct Wilmington MM
1907, 4, 13. Frank & fam gct Westfork MM, O.
1908, 3, 14. Wm.'s d rpd (an elder)
1910, 5, 10. Velma recrq
1914, 7, 11. Elwood dropped from mbrp
1916, 5, 13. Sarah Ann recrq
1917, 5, 12. Thadeus gct Ogden MM
1918, 10, 11. Cora McPherson rocf Leesburg MM, dtd 1919,9,18
1921, 2, 12. Herbert recrq
1922, 2, 11. Cora's d rpd (an elder)
1924, 7, 12. Jesse H. & w, Velma, & ch, Helen, Robert, Alice, Orba, Neal, John & Eleanor, gct Wilmington MM, O.
1824, 7, 12. Anna M. Farr rocf Oskaloosa MM, Ia.
1926, 1, 9. Virginia & Raymond dropped from mbrp
1931, 4, 8. Irvin dropped from mbrp
1931, 4, 8. Ruth Woodard dropped from mbrp

CARTER
1871, 3, 11. Leonard recrq
1871, 3, 11. Margaret J. recrq
1871, 3, 11. Julia A. recrq

1878, 1, 12. Leonard & w, Margaret J., gct Wilmington MM, O.
1889, 3, 9. Samuel & ch, Mary E. & Eva, rocf Oak Ridge MM, Ind., dtd 1889,1,15
1891, 11, 14. Mary Emily rocf Oak Ridge MM, Ind.
1893, 5, 13. Samuel & dt, Rachel Eva, rocf Oak Ridge MM, Ind.
1894, 7, 14. Mary Emily dropped from mbrp
1895, 7, 13. Samuel & dt, Eva, gct Newberry MM
1898, 7, 9. Mary E. dropped from mbrp
1921, 2, 12. Mae recrq
1926, 1, 9. May dropped from mbrp

CARTWRIGHT
1877, 3, 11. Marshall recrq
1878, 3, 9. Marshall dis

CASHATT
1815, 6, 23. John dis mcd
1816, 9, 14. Thomas dis disunity
1819, 5, 8. Margaret Ruse (form Cashatt) con mcd
1819, 6, 12. Joseph dis mcd
1821, 11, 10. Rachel Reese (form Cashett) dis mcd
1822, 3, 9. Ann & ch, Thomas, David, Mariah, Sarah, Eleanor, gct Newberry MM

CECIL
1889, 5, 11. Ella recrq
1898, 11, 12. Ella dropped from mbrp

CHALFANT
----, --, --. Abner & Ruth [Chalfont]
Ch: Margaret b 1819, 10, 2
Sarah " 1821, 8, 15
William " 1823, 11, 21
Asa L. " 1826, 1, 30
Edwin " 1828, 4, 5
1825, 6, 23. Aaron, s William & Ruth, Highland Co., O.; m in Clear Creek MH, Elizabeth BARRICK, dt Russel & Mary, Ky.

1813, 4, 22. William [Chaffant] & ch, Esther, Abner, Mary, Aaron, William, Jacob, Bulah, Priscilla, Nathan H. & Jonathan B. recrq
1814, 2, 24. Wm. & w, Ruth, & ch, Esther, Abner, Mary, Aaron, Wm., Jacob, Beulah, Priscilla, Nathan & Jonathan, gct Fairfield MM
1823, 4, 12. Abner [Chaffant] & w, Ruth, & ch Margaret & Sarah, rocf Fairfield MM, dtd 1823,3,29
1826, 4, 8. Aaron rocf Fairfield MM, dtd 1826,2,25
1827, 5, 12. Aaron & w, Elizabeth, & dt, Mary, gct Fairfield MM
1829, 8, 8. Ruth [Chaffant] dis jH

CHALLENDER
1871, 3, 11. Charles A. recrq
1871, 3, 11. Mary Jane recrq
1872, 7, 13. Charles A. dis disunity
1872, 12, 14. Mary Jane dis
1873, 1, 11. Martha J. dis disunity
1881, 4, 9. Chas. [Chalender] recrq
1882, 4, 8. Chas. [Chalander] dis disunity

CHANCE
1871, 3, 11. Reuben recrq
1871, 3, 11. Isaac recrq
1874, 3, 14. Isaac dis
1876, 12, 9. Reuben dis disunity
1878, 5, 11. Rosanna dis disunity
1887, 2, 12. Isaac recrq

CHANCE, continued
1893, 2, 11. Isaac dropped from mbrp
1904, 9, 10. Isaac recrq
1912, 5, 11. Isaac dropped from mbrp
1917, 3, 10. Isaac recrq

CHANDLER
1856, 12, 13. Elisha rocf Fairfield MM, dtd 1856,11,18
1858, 2, 13. Elisha dis disunity

CHANEY
1873, 7, 12. Harriett P. (form Conard) rpd mcd; dropped from mbrp
1881, 4, 9. Jacob recrq
1883, 8, 11. Jacob dropped from mbrp
1885, 3, 14. Homer & w, Belle, & ch, Cora, recrq
1909, 11, 13. James Wesley & Hattie, rocf Wilmington MM
1910, 3, 12. James Wesley & Hattie relrq
1926, 1, 9. Wm. dropped from mbrp
1928, 3, 8. Belle dropped from mbrp
1929, 3, 14. Bell recrq

CHAPLIN
1877, 3, 11. Adda recrq
1878, 1, 12. Ada relrq
1878, 1, 12. Ada dropped from mbrp

CHARLES
1865, 3, 11. William R. & w, Hannah C., & ch, Rufus O., Lee P. & Eva C., recrq
1866, 4, 14. Wm. R. & w, Hannah E., & ch, Rufus O., Lee P. & Eva C., gct Dover MM

CHERRY
1818, 9, 12. Martha con mcd
1818, 12, 12. Martha gct Fairfield MM

CHRISTENBERRY
1914, 6, 13. Harry recrq

CHRISTIAN
1913, 5, 10. Edith recrq
1914, 7, 11. Edith dropped from mbrp

CHRISTY
1843, 11, 21. Mary Ann (form Nordyke) dis mcd

CLARK
1887, 4, 9. John H. recrq
1887, 4, 9. Nellie recrq
1888, 6, 9. John dis jas
1896, 10, 10. Henry rocf Fairfield MM

CLEAVER
1871, 3, 11. Hiram recrq
1871, 3, 11. Unice recrq

CLEMENS
1885, 8, 8. Leroy S. & fam rocf Middle Point MM, O.
1894, 7, 14. Sarah L. [Clemons] dropped from mbrp
1898, 7, 9. Sarah L. dropped from mbrp
1899, 5, 13. Sarah relrq

CLINE
1865, 12, 9. Louisa (form Ballard) dis mcd & jas
1866, 6, 9. Susannah rpd mcd; dropped from mbrp
1910, 8, 13. Mary Ladd rocf Fairfield MM

COATS
1816, 6, 8. Hannah (form Cowgill) con mcd
1822, 11, 9. Aquilla recrq
1869, 4, 10. Martha E. recrq
1869, 4, 10. Benjamin F. recrq
1869, 4, 10. James A. recrq
1869, 4, 10. Isaac recrq
1878, 1, 12. Isaac dropped from mbrp
1892, 6, 11. Martha [Coates] & ch dropped from mbrp

COFFIN
----, --, --. Samuel m Dinah ----- d 1832,3, 25 bur Clear Creek
Ch: Mary b 1809, 6, 10
Lydia " 1812, 1, 20
Levina " 1815, 11, 24
----, --, --. David & Mary
Ch: Anna b 1811, 1, 1
Priscilla " 1812, 8, 13
Jesse " 1815, 8, 22
Daniel " 1822, 11, 11
1831, 5, 19. Anne m Daniel CAREY
1832, 11, 29. Priscilla m Joseph H. MOON
1837, 1, 25. Levina m Benjamin WHITE
1838, 2, 1. Mary m Gerard M. JOHNSON
1838, 11, 1. Samuel, s Samuel & Mary, dec, Highland Co., O.; m in Clear Creek MH, Hannah WRIGHT, dt Joseph & Ann GILBERT, Highland Co., O.
1840, 1, 2. Lydia m John COWGILL
1861, 4, 6. Samuel d bur Clear Creek

1819, 8, 14. Mary rocf Lick Creek MM, dtd 1818,10,31, endorsed to Lees Creek MM
1822, 8, 10. Mary rocf Lees Creek MM, dtd 1822,6,15
1840, 6, 23. Jesse gct Newberry MM
1841, 1, 19. Wm. Pike gct Walnut Ridge MM, Ind., to m Phebe Coffin
1844, 7, 13. Daniel gct Newberry MM, to m Patience Janney
1845, 8, 9. Patience rocf Newberry MM, dtd 1845,5,16
1846, 5, 9. Daniel & w, Patience, & ch, Eliza, gct Newberry MM

COLLIER
1814, 6, 24. Samuel & w, Margaret, & ch, Jonathan, Miriam & Mary, rocf Contentney MM, N. C., dtd 1814,2,12, endorsed by

COLLIER, continued
Fairfield MM
1814, 11, 25. Samuel & w, Margaret, & ch, Miriam, Jonathan & Mary, gct Darby Creek MM, O.

COLLIGNOW
1871, 5, 13. John B. recrq
1870, 7, 9. Joseph [Collingnow] recrq
1874, 3, 14. John B. dis

COLLINS
1869 4, 10. Elizabeth recrq
1869 4, 10. George recrq
1869, 4, 10. F. M. recrq
1869, 4, 10. Rebecca E. recrq
1869, 4, 10. Ellen J. recrq
1873, 3, 8. John Eli recrq
1873, 3, 8. Lucinda G. recrq
1875, 4, 10. Thomas recrq
1883, 11, 10. John E. relrq
1888, 7, 14. William dropped from mbrp
1892, 6, 11. Rebecca, Marian, Thomas & Ellen dropped from mbrp

CONARD
1871, 12, 13. Sarah [Connard] m Aaron B. NORDYKE

1864, 3, 12. Sarah recrq
1866, 6, 9. Lewis & w, Edith M., & ch, Harriet P., Chas. W., Joseph W., Sarah E. & Susannah L., recrq
1868, 3, 14. Martha recrq
1868, 8, 8. Rebecca [Connard] recrq
1868, 8, 8. Lydia Ann [Connard] recrq
1869, 4, 10. Phebe [Connard] recrq
1869, 4, 10. Lewis [Connard] recrq
1869, 4, 10. Maria [Connard] recrq
1871, 1, 14. Matilda recrq
1871, 3, 11. Lydia [Connard] recrq
1872, 5, 11. Emily recrq
1872, 6, 8. Walter, s Emily, recrq
1873, 3, 8. Alfred recrq
1873, 7, 12. Harriett P. Chaney (form Conard) con mcd
1875, 3, 13. Enos recrq
1877, 5, 12. Mary recrq
1878, 9, 14. Dora relrq
1878, 11, 19. Joseph relrq
1880, 3, 18. Charles relrq
1880, 4, 9. Enos & w, Emily, & ch, Walter & Homer, gct Fairfield MM
1880, 4, 9. Amea recrq
1883, 8, 11. Lewis gct Newberry MM, O.
1883, 10, 13. Edith, Sarah & Susannah relrq
1886, 8, 14. Phoebe, Maria & Anna gct Fairfield MM
1887, 2, 12. Emma J. recrq
1893, 5, 13. Lenna May recrq
1894, 2, 10. Lydia relrq
1894, 2, 10. Lewis rocf Newberry MM
1902, 6, 14. Frank recrq
1902, 6, 14. James recrq
1902, 6, 14. Bertha recrq
1902, 6, 14. Stella recrq

CONNELL
1929, 10, 30. Alice m Chas. M. LUCK
1931, 9, 29. Catharine m Martin LUCK
1909, 2, 13. Mae recrq
1909, 2, 13. Alice recrq
1915, 10, 9. Olive Bogan [Connal] rocf Wilmington MM
1921, 2, 12. Alice & Glenn recrq

CONWAY
1869, 4, 10. John recrq
1883, 8, 11. John dropped from mbrp

COOK
1877, 10, 17. Amos, s Samuel & Hannah, Warren Co., O.; m in house of John DOSTER, Elma DOSTER, dt John & Mary, Fayette Co., O.
1924, 6, 11. Nellie m Stanley R. LAYMON

1813, 12, 23. Thomas rocf Deep River MM, N.C., dtd 1813,11,1
1876, 3, 11. Dennis M. recrq
1878, 1, 12. Elma C. gct Caesars Creek MM, O.
1889, 5, 11. Ada recrq
1893, 4, 8. Mattie dropped from mbrp
1894, 7, 14. Addie dropped from mbrp
1907, 2, 9. Emma gct Fairfield MM
1908, 3, 14. Ellis gct Fairfield MM
1909, 2, 13. Flora recrq
1909, 2, 13. Nellie recrq
1912, 5, 11. Almira Carey dropped from mbrp

CORMELL
1887, 4, 9. Kate recrq
1887, 4, 9. Lewis & ch, Frank, Oscar B. & Moletus Elbert, recrq

COWGILL
1822, 4, 18. John d bur Newberry
1822, 4, 29. Catharine d bur Newberry
1840, 1, 2. John, s Henry & Elenor, Highland Co., O.; m in Clear Creek MH, Lydia COFFIN dt Samuel & Dinah, Highland Co., O.

1813, 8, 26. John Jr. & w, Susannah, & s, James, rocf Hopewell MM, dtd 1812,5,14, endorsed by Centre MM
1814, 6, 24. William rocf Hopewell MM, Va., dtd 1813,11,4
1815, 2, 24. John & w, Catherine, & ch, Asa & Amos, rocf Hopewell MM, dtd 1814,9,8
1815, 2, 24. Elisha rocf Hopewell MM, dtd 1814,9,8
1815, 2, 24. Ann rocf Hopewell MM, dtd 1814, 9,8
1815, 4, 28. Elisha gct Fairfield MM, to m
1815, 9, 9. Anne Hays (form Cowgill) dis mcd
1815, 12, 9. Elisha & w, Rebecca, gct Centre MM

COWGILL, continued
1815, 10, 14. Rebecca rocf Fairfield MM, dtd 1815,9,30
1816, 6, 8. Hannah Coats (form Cowgill) con mcd
1818, 1, 10. Amos gct Center MM, to m
1818, 7, 11. Amos gct Newberry MM
1818, 7, 11. William gct Hopewell MM, Va.
1822, 2, 9. Asa gct Fairfield MM
1840, 4, 21. Lydia gct Fall Creek MM
1841, 6, 22. Joseph Wright gct Fall Creek MM, to m Lydia Cowgill
1863, 8, 8. Benjamin F. rocf Fairfield MM, dtd 1863,6,20
1866, 5, 12. Samira rocf Fairfield MM, dtd 1865,8,19
1876, 5, 13. Benjamin F. & w, Samira, & s, Leslie W., gct Smyrna MM, Ia.

COX
1813, 2, 2. Sarah d bur Clear Creek
1814, 1, 5. Martha m John Hockett
1819, 12, 15. Thomas Jr., s Thomas & Sarah, Clinton Co., O.; m in East Fork MH, Rachel HOCKETT, dt Joseph & Ann, Clinton Co., O.
1820, 11, 16. Aaron, s Thomas & Sarah, Clinton Co., O.; m in Clear Creek MH, Mary BAILY, dt Thomas & Elizabeth, Highland Co., O.
Ch: Elizabeth b 1821, 8, 15
Milton " 1824, 6, 20
Vincent " 1826, 8, 5
1823, 3, 19. Catharine m Joseph CADWALADER
1853, 4, 1. Esther d bur East Fork

1819, 1, 9. Stephen gct White Water MM, Ind.
1819, 8, 14. Sarah rocf South River MM, Va., dtd 1819,5,1
1828, 9, 13. Joseph dis mcd
1830, 5, 8. Thomas dis jH
1830, 5, 8. Aaron dis disunity
1830, 5, 8. Sarah dis jH
1830, 9, 11. Mary dis jH
1831, 10, 18. Esther rocf Blue River MM, Ind., dtd 1831,8,6
1841, 2, 23. Nathan Wasson gct Milford MM, Ind., to m Maria Cox
1844, 9, 14. Aaron dis mcd
1845, 11, 8. Joseph dis disunity
1846, 5, 9. Mary Jane dis disunity
1846, 5, 9. Betsy Ann dis disunity
1848, 4, 8. Vincent dis mcd
1851, 11, 8. Rachel & ch, Wm. & Rachel, gct Hincles Creek MM, Ind.
1851, 12, 13. Sarah gct Hinkles Creek MM, Ind.
1873, 3, 8. Hannah E. recrq
1877, 3, 11. Albert recrq
1877, 3, 11. Joseph recrq
1878, 1, 12. Adaline gct White River MM, Ind.
1883, 8, 11. Joseph W. dropped from mbrp
1884, 1, 12. Sallie recrq
1885, 3, 14. Sarah recrq
1890, 11, 8. Sallie relrq
1891, 4, 11. Albert dropped from mbrp
1896, 2, 8. William rocf Westfork MM, O.
1903, 5, 9. Louise R. recrq

CRAIG
1868, 10, 10. Rebecca M. recrq
1871, 3, 11. James M. recrq
1880, 4, 10. James gct Wilmington MM

CRAVEN
1884, 8, 9. Lansing F. & w, Nancy Jane, & s, Charley, rocf Fairfield MM
1897, 9, 11. Lansing & w, Nancy, & ch, Charles & Ernest, gct Marion MM, Ind.

CREW
1844, 2, 23. Elizabeth (form Anthony) dis mcd

CROUCHER
1866, 6, 9. Rebecca & ch, Margaret Ann Prather, Jesse Elma Croucher & Mary Caroline Croucher, recrq
1869, 4, 10. Rebecca & ch, Margaret Ann, Prather, Jessie Elma & Mary Caroline, gct Union MM, Mo.

CRUTE
1885, 3, 14. Clara, Mary & Mintie recrq

CURL
1821, 3, 10. Cert rec for Samuel from Middleton MM, dtd 1817,12,15, endorsed to Darby Creek MM

CURTIS
1869, 4, 10. James C. recrq
1869, 4, 10. Mary E. recrq
1869, 4, 10. Stephen C., minor ch recrq of parents
1869, 4, 10. David T. recrq
1869, 4, 10. Nancy M. recrq
1869, 4, 10. Chas. E. recrq

1884, 3, 8. Frank recrq
1887, 2, 12. Edward A. recrq
1887, 2, 12. Lucinda recrq
1887, 2, 12. Thomas recrq
1887, 2, 12. Ella Bernard recrq
1887, 2, 12. William recrq
1887, 2, 12. Fronia recrq
1889, 5, 11. Catharine recrq
1889, 5, 11. Dovie recrq
1892, 6, 11. Stephen, Maria, Charles & Fronia dropped from mbrp
1893, 5, 13. Estella T. recrq
1898, 11, 12. Edward A. dropped from mbrp
1898, 11, 12. Lucinda dropped from mbrp
1902, 5, 10. Jennie recrq
1902, 5, 10. Abbie H. recrq
1903, 3, 14. Thomas recrq
1908, 6, 13. Lucy dropped from mbrp
1909, 3, 13. Carrie recrq
1909, 3, 13. Jessie recrq

CURTIS, continued
1909, 3, 13. Ethel recrq
1912, 5, 11. Thomas dropped from mbrp

DALTON
1907, 8, 10. Estella Curtis gct Wilmington MM

DARBYSHIRE
1890, 4, 12. Jennie S. recrq
1894, 7, 14. Jennie dropped from mbrp

DARICK
1889, 5, 11. John & w, Rachel, recrq

DARLINGTON
1817, 11, 8. Anna rocf Hopewell MM, dtd 1817,9,4
1830, 2, 13. Anna gct Fall Creek MM

DARROW
1818, 1, 10. Mary (form Nordyke) dis mcd

DAVIS
----, --, --. Harmon d 1862,2,26 bur Clear Creek; m Martha -----
Ch: Daniel b 1813, 10, 19
Mary " 1815, 9, 7
Jordon " 1818, 4, 1
Ruth " 1820, 4, 4
Thomas " 1822, 8, 9
John " 1824, 9, 11
Lydia " 1827, 8, 7
Harmon " 1830, 10, 8 d 1849, 3,15 bur Clear Creek
Martha b 1832, 10, 30
Esther Osborn " 1835, 12, 13 d 1837, 6, 1 bur Clear Creek
1835, 4, 30. Mary m Jonathan HIATT
1836, 12, 1. Daniel, s Harmon & Martha, Highland Co., O.; m in Clear Creek MH, Ann HIATT, dt Jehu & Tamer, Highland Co., O.
Ch: Jehu b 1837, 9, 7
----, --, --. Thomas & Sarah
Ch: Lorena Hinman b 1847, 12, 24
Christopher Harmon " 1849, 5, 17 d 1849, 9,16 bur Clear Creek
Wesley Taylor b 1851, 1, 26
Israel Arthur " 1852, 11, 30 d 1854, 3,13 bur Clear Creek
Sarah Elizabeth b 1855, 3, 9
1853, 2, 21. Thomas A. d bur Clear Creek
----, --, --. Harmon & Jane
Ch: Martha Ann b 1855, 6, 4 d 1863, 8,30 bur Clear Creek
Victoria Titala b 1857, 4, 10
Ch: Joseph T. b 1859, 7, 7 d 1863,11,27 bur Clear Creek
Mary Jane b 1861, 4, 11
1859, 4, 12. Lieuella, dt Joshua & Elizabeth, b
1825, 1, 8. Betsey recrq
1825, 11, 12. John & ch, Martin & Tamer, rocf Chestnut Creek MM, Va., dtd 1825,2,26
1826, 3, 11. Tamer Bradfield (form Davis) dis mcd
1828, 5, 10. Betsy gct Springborough MM
1828, 4, 11. Lydia recrq
1829, 11, 14. Betsy dis jH
1834, 4, 22. Martin con mcd
1836, 4, 19. Martin gct Westfield MM, Ind.
1838, 2, 20. Daniel & w, Ann, & s, Jehu, gct Chesterfield MM
1838, 10, 13. John & w, Lydia, rocf Westfield MM, Ind.
1840, 1, 21. Ruth Engle (form Davis) con mcd
1842, 4, 19. Jorden con mcd
1845, 3, 8. Jordon gct Fairfield MM
1845, 6, 14. Lydia rocf Westfield MM, Ind., dtd 1845,5,8
1846, 9, 12. Lydia gct Westfield MM
1847, 3, 13. Elizabeth recrq
1847, 9, 11. Thos. M. con mcd
1848, 1, 8. Lydia Margaret rocf Westfield MM, Ind., dtd 1847,11,11
1848, 9, 9. Lydia rocf Westfield MM, dtd 1848,6,8
1849, 4, 14. John con mcd
1849, 9, 8. Lydia Strech (form Davis) dis mcd
1851, 4, 12. John & w, Mary, & ch, Emily, Minerva, gct Fairfield MM
1852, 11, 13. Sarah rocf Fairfield MM, dtd 1852,9,18
1854, 8, 12. Mahlon rocf Westfield MM, Ind., dtd 1854,6,29
1854, 12, 9. Harmon con mcd
1855, 5, 12. Martha Stretch (form Davis) dis mcd
1855, 9, 8. Thos. E. dis disunity
1855, 10, 13. Jane rocf Fairfield MM, dtd 1855,7,21
1855, 11, 10. Thomas M. dis disunity
1856, 12, 13. Mahlon dis disunity
1858, 1, 9. Thos. M. recrq
1858, 4, 10. Joshua F. recrq
1858, 4, 10. Elizabeth recrq
1858, 6, 12. Mary rocf Newberry MM, dtd 1858,5,17
1859, 3, 12. Valentine, s Joshua & Elizabeth, recrq
1860, 11, 10. Joshua F. & w, Elizabeth, & ch, Valentine & Luella, gct Newberry MM
1863, 8, 8. Joshua F. & w, Elizabeth, & ch, Valentine, Luella & Sarah Lydia, rocf Newberry MM, dtd 1863,3,23
1865, 1, 14. Joshua F. dis mcd
1866, 3, 10. Valentine, Luella & Sarah Lydia, ch Joshua F., gct Richland MM, Ind.

DAVIS, continued
1867, 5, 11. Delila Mills (form Davis) con mcd
1867, 12, 14. Lorena H. Johnson (form Davis) con mcd
1872, 3, 9. Handy T. recrq
1872, 4, 13. Margaret recrq
1872, 7, 13. Samuel recrq
1874, 6, 13. Hattie E. & Laura B. recrq
1877, 3, 11. Lorenzo recrq
1877, 3, 11. James E. recrq
1877, 3, 11. Edna recrq
1879, 10, 11. Amos J. recrq
1883, 8, 11. Handy T. & w, Margaret, & ch gct Wilmington MM
1884, 1, 12. Lewis E. recrq
1884, 8, 9. Harriet E., w Jay, & ch, Frederick L., Samuel E., Joseph & Letta, rocf Fairfield MM
1888, 10, 13. A. J. & fam gct Fairfield MM
1889, 2, 9. Thomas L. & w, Edna, & ch, Birchie S., Jesse L., Mary L., Harry W. & David Allen, gct Fairfield MM
1895, 4, 13. Wesley T. relrq
1897, 4, 10. Samuel & w, Mary, gct Fairfield MM, O.
1899, 5, 13. Thos. J. recrq
1900, 4, 14. Sarah M. rocf Newberry MM, O.
1901, 6, 8. James Orland recrq
1901, 6, 8. Chas. Merlin recrq
1909, 3, 13. Thomas J. gct Fairfield MM
1915, 1, 9. J. Orland & w, Sadie, & ch, Merlin, Mary H. & Kathleen, gct Ogden MM

DAWSON
1881, 4, 9. John recrq
1881, 4, 9. Mary recrq
1881, 4, 9. Henry recrq
1885, 5, 9. Henry relrq
1887, 11, 12. John dropped from mbrp
1887, 11, 12. Mary dropped from mbrp

DENNY
1896, 5, 9. Julia & Robert recrq

DICKEY
1830, 4, 10. Phebe Jane & Elizabeth rocf Newberry MM, dtd 1830,3,25
1830, 5, 8. Nimrod & w, Ann, & ch, Charity, Matilda, Lucinda, Mary Ann, James & Aseneth, rocf Newberry MM, dtd 1830,4,23
1833, 1, 22. Elizabeth dis
1833, 6, 18. Nimrod & w, Ann, & ch, Charity, Matilda, Lucinda, Mary Ann, James & Asenith, gct Newberry MM
1833, 6, 18. Jane gct Newberry MM
1833, 8, 20. Phebe gct Newberry MM

DOAN
1839, 4, 23. Alfred Timberlake gct Centre MM, to m Phebe Doan

DODD
1897, 1, 9. Emma recrq
1898, 3, 12. Dessie recrq
1907, 7, 13. Bertha recrq
1912, 5, 11. Dessie & Emma dropped from mbrp
1921, 6, 1. Elizabeth recrq
1928, 6, 14. Leslie & w, Mary, rocf Hopewell MM

DOGGETT
1837, 7, 18. Milly (form Sanders) dis mcd

DOSTER
1877, 10, 17. Elma m Amos COOK

1869, 5, 8. Mary & ch, Elma C., Mary Matilda & Clara W., rocf Fairfield MM, dtd 1869,4,17
1873, 5, 10. Miller C. recrq

DOUGLAS
1862, 7, 12. Robert W. [Duglas] & w, Margaret A., & ch, David Franklin & George Gifford, rocf Dover MM, dtd 1862,5,15
1868, 3, 14. Chloe rocf Dover MM, dtd 1868,2,13
1868, 3, 14. John Henry & w, Miriam, & ch, Chloe Anna, Jesse C., Miriam C. & John Henry, rocf Dover MM, dtd 1868,2,13
1868, 6, 13. Robert W. & w, Margaret A., & ch David F., Geo. W. & Anna B., gct Wilmington MM
1874, 5, 9. John Henry & w, Miriam C., & ch, Chloe, Anna, Jesse Carter, Miriam, John Henry Jr., Christine & Mary Leckey, gct Wilmington MM, O.
1878, 1, 12. Chloe gct Wilmington MM

DOVE
1871, 3, 11. Jacob recrq
1873, 3, 8. Stephen C. recrq
1873, 3, 8. Riley G. recrq
1873, 3, 8. Mary Jane recrq
1873, 3, 8 Mary C. recrq
1873, 3, 8. Netta recrq
1873, 3, 8. Milla recrq
1873, 12, 13. Beltesshazzar & w, Nancy Emeline, & ch, Alice May & Wilber, rocf Newberry MM, dtd 1873,7,21
1878, 1, 12. Bellashazzer & w, Nancy Emeline, & ch, Alice May, Wilbur A., Myrtle & Martha, gct Newberry MM, O.
1883, 8, 11. Stephen C. dropped from mbrp
1883, 8, 11. Mary Jane dropped from mbrp
1883, 8, 11. Riley G. dropped from mbrp
1883, 8, 11. Nettie dropped from mbrp
1883, 8, 11. Lizzie M. dropped from mbrp
1883, 8, 11. William dropped from mbrp

DRAKE
1896, 4, 11. Virginia recrq
1900, 4, 14. Eliza J. recrq
1912, 5, 11. Eliza dropped from mbrp

DRISKILL
1869, 4, 10. John H. [Driscal] recrq
1869, 4, 10. Anna [Driscal] recrq
1869, 4, 10. Simon [Driscal] recrq
1869, 4, 10. Hannah [Driscal] recrq
1871, 4, 8. Hannah relrq
1871, 9, 9. Simon dis disunity
1873, 3, 8. David [Driskall] recrq
1873, 3, 8. Cynthia A. [Driskall] recrq
1873, 3, 8. Martha A. [Driskall] recrq
1873, 3, 8. Mary E. [Driskall] recrq
1873, 3, 8. Lizzie [Driskall] recrq
1873, 3, 8. Martha E. [Driskall] recrq
1878, 3, 9. John dis
1881, 4, 9. David [Driscoll] recrq
1883, 5, 12. Emma [Driscoll] recrq
1883, 8, 11. David [Driscoll] relrq
1883, 8, 11. Phebe Ann [Driscoll] dropped from mbrp
1883, 8, 11. Isom dropped from mbrp
1883, 8, 11. Emma [Driscoll] dropped from mbrp
1883, 8, 11. Sina [Driscoll] dropped from mbrp
1883, 8, 11. George H. [Driscall] dropped from mbrp
1885, 6, 13. Emma [Driscall] dropped from mbrp
1886, 5, 8. Isom recrq
1886, 5, 8. Louie recrq
1886, 5, 8. Emma recrq
1886, 5, 8. Lina recrq
1886, 5, 8. Lorenza recrq
1887, 4, 9. George & Noah recrq
1891, 10, 10. Horatio [Driscol] recrq
1893, 2, 11. George dropped from mbrp
1893, 2, 11. Lorenzo dropped from mbrp
1893, 2, 11. Isam dropped from mbrp
1893, 2, 11. Noah dropped from mbrp
1894, 7, 14. Lewis [Driskall] dropped from mbrp
1895, 5, 11. William recrq
1898, 3, 12. Noah [Driscol] & w, Rosa, & s, Harry, recrq
1898, 7, 9. Lewis [Driskall] dropped from mbrp
1898, 11, 12. Cynthia A. [Driscol] dropped from mbrp
1898, 11, 12. J. W. [Driscol] dropped from mbrp
1898, 11, 12. Martha Ann [Driscol] dropped from mbrp
1898, 11, 12. William [Driscol] dropped from mbrp
1901, 5, 11. Mary Wilson [Driscoll] dropped from mbrp
1901, 6, 8. Pheba A. recrq
1902, 4, 12. Frank [Driscoll] recrq
1904, 4, 9. Bessie [Driscoll] recrq
1912, 5, 11. Frank & Bessie [Driscoll] dropped from mbrp
1913, 4, 12. Sina [Driscoll] dropped from mbrp
1914, 3, 14. Bessie [Driscoll] dropped from mbrp
1916, 8, 12. Sina [Driscall] dropped from mbrp

DUNCAN
1881, 4, 9. Thos. Sr. recrq
1882, 6, 10. Thomas relrq
1928, 4, 12. Bessie Mercer rocf Fairview MM

DUTTON
1854, 5, 13. Lewis rocf Honey Creek MM, dtd 1854,4,8
1860, 5, 12. Lewis gct Fairfield MM; returned for mcd

EARL
1883, 8, 11. Carrie A. dropped from mbrp

EASTLACK
1863, 2, 4. Marmaduke d bur Clear Creek

1849, 11, 10. Marmaduke [Easlack] rocf Fairfield MM, dtd 1849,9,15

EATON
1889, 2, 9. James recrq
1898, 4, 9. James relrq
1910, 7, 9. James recrq

EDWARDS
1826, 5, 17. William Hussey gct Caesars Creek MM, to m Jane Edwards
1865, 8, 12. Hannah (form Hockett) dis mcd
1866, 6, 9. Hannah rocf Miami MM, dtd 1866, 5,23
1873, 1, 11. Asenath (form Magoon) dis mcd
1875, 4, 10. Sarah S. recrq
1876, 2, 12. Hannah gct Cincinnati MM
1886, 3, 13. Charles recrq
1887, 4, 9. Frank recrq
1893, 10, 14. Frank relrq
1894, 7, 14. Charles dropped from mbrp
1900, 6, 8. Charles dropped from mbrp
1902, 6, 14. James recrq
1904, 12, 10. Sarah dropped from mbrp
1910, 7, 9. Mary E. C. rocf Wilmington MM

ELISON
1828, 9, 14. Eunice (form Hunt) dis mcd

ELLIOTT
1869, 4, 10. William recrq
1869, 4, 10. David recrq
1869, 4, 10. Alexander recrq
1869, 4, 10. Jesse recrq
1869, 4, 10. Eliza J. recrq
1869, 4, 10. Catharine recrq
1869, 4, 10. Susan recrq
1869, 4, 10. Malinda recrq
1870, 11, 12. Elizabeth recrq
1878, 1, 12. Alexander, Jesse, Eliza J., Catharine & Susan, gct Newberry MM, O.

ELLIOTT, continued
1878, 1, 12. David & w & ch dropped from mbrp
1878, 1, 12. Malinda dropped from mbrp

ELLIS
1817, 11, 20. Robert, s Nehemiah & Sarah, Clinton Co., O.; m in Clear Creek MH, Susannah LEWIS, dt Enoch & Sarah, Highland Co., O.
1818, 6, 15. Mary m Benjamin HIETT
1818, 7, 27. Susannah d bur East Fork (w of Robert)
1818, 8, 20. Sarah d bur East Fork
1822, 7, 31. Nehemiah d bur Newberry
1833, 8, 24. Jonathan, s Jonathan & Lydia, Belmont Co., O.; m in Clear Creek MH, Susannah TIMBERLAKE, dt Richard & Mary, Highland Co., O.
Ch: Lydia
Mary b 1837, 5, 11
Jonathan W." 1840, 2, 25
Richard T. " 1840, 2, 25
Joshua " 1842, 10, 17 d 1843, 1,14 bur Clear Creek
Aquilla b 1845, 11, 6

1813, 11, 25. Nehemiah & w, Sarah, & ch, Mary & Robert, gct Caesars Creek MM
1815, 2, 24. William & w, Hannah, & ch, Jacob, Elizabeth, Mary & Rebecca, rocf New Hope MM, Tenn., dtd 1814,3,12, endorsed by Fairfield MM
1816, 11, 9. Nehemiah & w, Sarah, rocf Caesars Creek MM, dtd 1816,8,30
1816, 11, 9. Robert rocf Caesars Creek MM, dtd 1816,8,30
1816, 11, 9. Mary rocf Caesars Creek MM, dtd 1816,8,30
1819, 10, 9. Robert gct Newberry MM
1822, 1, 12. Mordecai rocf Newberry MM, dtd 1821,12,27
1824, 11, 13. Mordecai dis
1830, 11, 13. Mordecai rst at White Lick MM, Ind., on consent of this mtg
1833, 6, 18. Jonathan Sr. rocf Flushing MM, O., dtd 1833,4,25
1848, 2, 12. Jonathan & w, Susannah, & ch, Lydia Mary, Jonathan N., Richard T. & Aquilla, gct Springfield MM

EMMONS
1841, 11, 24. Joseph, s Thomas & Mary, m in Clear Creek MH, Mary W. TIMBERLAKE, dt Richard & Mary, Highland Co., O.

1842, 1, 18. Mary M. gct Goshen MM

ENGLE
----, --, --. Jesse & Ruth
Ch: Elizabeth b 1839, 11, 11
Harmon " 1841, 4, 21
Samuel " 1843, 8, 23
Martha " 1845, 7, 20
John b 1849, 10, 30 d 1865, 2,15 bur Clear Creek
Jesse b 1852, 11, 1 " 1854, 4,27 bur Clear Creek
Martha b 1855, 7, 13
Lindley " 1858, 7, 21
1843, 12, 31. Elizabeth d bur Clear Creek (dt Samuel)

1830, 7, 10. Elizabeth recrq
1840, 1, 21. Ruth (form Davis) con mcd
1841, 6, 22. Stacy recrq
1843, 10, 24. Stacy con mcd
1850, 7, 13. Stacy gct Newberry MM
1867, 11, 9. Elizabeth Johnson (form Engle) con mcd
1871, 2, 11. Samuel rpd mcd; retained mbrp
1871, 2, 11. Mary E. rpd mcd; retained mbrp
1881, 4, 9. Lindley relrq
1894, 4, 14. Walter relrq
1900, 10, 13. Cora rocf Hopewell MM
1926, 1, 9. Dudley dropped from mbrp

EVANS
1827, 1, 13. Jonathan Haworth gct Lees Creek MM, to m Hester Evans
1852, 1, 10. Priscilla rocf Newberry MM, dtd 1851,12,15
1861, 2, 9. Priscilla gct Elk MM
1883, 5, 12. Jennie recrq
1890, 7, 12. Jennie dropped from mbrp

FANNING
1923, 5, 12. John recrq
1931, 4, 8. John dropped from mbrp

FARQUHAR
1822, 4, 13. Allen rocf Centre MM, dtd 1822, 2,16
1822, 10, 12. Allen dis disunity

FARR
1924, 6, 3. Anna M. m Arthur L. CAREY

FENNER
1868, 3, 14. Lydia Elizabeth recrq
1868, 9, 12. Lydia E. Hussey (form Fenner) con mcd
1887, 4, 9. Effie recrq
1928, 4, 12. Charles & Dwight recrq
1931, 4, 8. Chas. & Wright dropped from mbrp

FETTERLING
1890, 4, 12. Walter J. & Maud E. recrq
1893, 2, 11. Walter & Maude [Fettering] dropped from mbrp

FISHBACK
1906, 12, 8. Mrs. Ada & s, Harry, recrq
1911, 3, 11. Ada & s, Harry relrq

FISHER
1874, 1, 15. Amos, s John & Hannah, Clinton

FISHER, Amos, continued
Co., O.; m in Fairview, O., Ruth A. TERRELL dt John H. & Elizabeth, Clinton Co., O.

1850, 11, 9. Amos rocf Dover MM, dtd 1850,8, 19
1853, 6, 11. Amos dis mcd & joining Anti-Slavery Friends
1863, 2, 14. Cert rec for Hiram & w, Rebecca, & ch, Susannah, from Dover MM, endorsed to Cherry Grove MM, Ind.
1869, 4, 10. Jane recrq
1869, 4, 10. Rachel recrq
1869, 4, 10. Hannah recrq
1869, 4, 10. Rebecca recrq
1869, 4, 10. Harriet recrq
1869, 4, 10. Phebe J. recrq
1869, 4, 10. Thomas recrq
1869, 4, 10. Joseph recrq
1869, 4, 10. Amos recrq
1869, 5, 8. John Jr. rocf Fairfield MM, dtd 1869,4,17
1870, 2, 12. John Sr. set off from Fairfield MM
1870, 2, 12. Mary set off from Fairfield MM
1870, 2, 12. Rachel set off from Fairfield MM
1871, 3, 11. Thomas recrq
1873, 3, 8. Wm. H. recrq
1873, 3, 8. Azariah recrq
1873, 3, 8. Rachel A. recrq
1875, 2, 13. Thos. dis disunity
1875, 4, 10. James recrq
1878, 1, 12. James dropped from mbrp
1878, 1, 12. Rachel dropped from mbrp
1883, 2, 10. Eliza J. recrq
1883, 8, 11. Rachel dropped from mbrp
1883, 8, 11. Joseph relrq
1883, 12, 18. Jennie recrq
1883, 12, 18. Joseph rst
1886, 4, 10. Henry gct Wilmington MM
1888, 5, 12. Lydia E. recrq
1890, 2, 8. Joseph & w, Jennie, relrq
1893, 5, 13. Mary E. recrq
1895, 5, 11. Austin recrq
1895, 5, 11. Estel recrq
1900, 7, 14. Emma L. recrq
1907, 4, 13. Elver J. & w, Emma, gct Wilmington MM, O.
1913, 5, 10. Clesee Jean gct Fairview MM

FITTRO
1885, 3, 14. Minerva recrq
1894, 7, 14. Minerva dropped from mbrp

FLETCHER
1833, 2, 19. Sarah (form Anthony) dis mcd
1837, 2, 21. Nancy rocf Fall Creek MM, dtd 1836,12,21
1843, 8, 22. Nancy dis joining Baptists

FLYNN
1869, 4, 10. Sarah A. recrq

FOLK
1823, 8, 9. Samuel rocf Bradford MM, Pa., dtd 1823,6,4
1826, 6, 10. Samuel gct Richland MM, Pa.

FORD
1924, 11, 26. James E. m Margaret SANDERS

FORDICE
1901, 6, 8. Olive recrq

FOSTER
1889, 5, 11. John & Jemima recrq
1894, 7, 14. John dropped from mbrp

FRAUN
1869, 4, 10. Jesse M. recrq

FRAZIER
1813, 4, 1. Moses, s Ezekiel & Rebecca, Clinton Co., O.; m in Clear Creek MH, Lydia PUSEY, dt Nathan & Mary
1816, 9, 19. Jonah, s Ezekiel & Rebecca, Clinton Co., O.; m in Clear Creek MH, Mary HADLEY, dt James & Ann, Highland Co., O.

1813, 8, 26. Lydia gct Center MM
1813, 10, 28. David gct Caesars Creek MM, to m
1815, 1, 27. John & w, Lydia, & ch, Nathan, Charlotte & Francis Henry, gct White Water MM, Ind.
1815, 11, 11. Rebecca rocf Caesars Creek MM, dtd 1815,6,23
1816, 3, 9. Guidean [Frazure] & w, Ann, & ch, Stephen, Thomas & Margarette, gct New Garden MM, Ind.
1816, 12, 14. Mary gct Centre MM
1816, 12, 14. Francis & w, Elizabeth, & ch, Elizabeth Ann Susannah & Francis, gct New Garden MM, Ind.
1817, 3, 8. Thomas & w, Hannah, & ch, Lydia & Joseph, gct New Garden MM, Ind.
1818, 2, 14. James dis disunity
1818, 11, 14. Susanah & ch, Samuel, John, Elizabeth, Frances, Sarah, Susanna, Maryann, James & Isaiah, gct New Garden MM, Ind.
1819, 3, 13. David & w, Rebecca, & ch, Seth & Saran, gct New Garden MM, Ind.
1845, 11, 8. Rebecca [Frazer] (form Oren) dis mcd
1852, 11, 13. Joel Hoskins gct Dover MM, to m Lydia P. Frazier
1864, 7, 9. Lydia Ann gct Dover MM
1889, 2, 9. Abraham & Kate J. recrq
1894, 7, 14. Abram [Frazer] dropped from mbrp
1902, 5, 10. Effie Oma recrq

FRY
1883, 8, 11. Olga gct Fairfield MM
1895, 5, 11. Jackson recrq
1895, 5, 11. Virginia recrq

FRY, continued
1895, 5, 11. Charles recrq
1895, 5, 11. William recrq
1895, 5, 11. Howard recrq
1895, 5, 11. Nettie recrq

GAFFNEY
1887, 4, 9. Rachel [Gofney] recrq
1897, 1, 9. Bessie [Goffney] recrq
1900, 4, 14. Bessie dropped from mbrp
1904, 4, 9. Bessie recrq

GALLIDAY
1840, 1, 21. Ruth gct Vermillion MM, Ill.

GARDNER
1813, 10, 28. Elizabeth (form Ratcliff) con mcd
1822, 1, 12. Rachel (form Ratcliff) dis mcd
1822, 3, 9. Eleanor [Garner] gct Newberry MM
1869, 4, 10. Catharine recrq
1869, 4, 10. Roselle recrq
1869, 4, 10. Chas. M., minor ch, recrq of parents
1869, 4, 10. James R., minor ch, recrq of parents
1869, 4, 10. Anna S., minor ch, recrq of parents
1869, 12, 11. Charles M., James & Anna S., ch Russel & Catharine, recrq
1880, 3, 13. Chas. M. dis disunity
1882, 4, 8. James R. dis
1887, 11, 12. Anna L. dropped from mbrp
1893, 2, 11. Harry M. dropped from mbrp
1894, 7, 14. Jesse B. dropped from mbrp
1894, 7, 14. Kate dropped from mbrp
1898, 7, 9. Jessie B. dropped from mbrp
1898, 7, 9. Kate dropped from mbrp

GARNETT
1882, 2, 11. Augustus P. recrq
1889, 4, 13. Augusta dropped from mbrp

GEORGE
1827, 6, 9. Amy rocf Fall Creek MM, dtd 1827,5,19
1828, 4, 12. Amy gct Fall Creek MM

GIBSON
1903, 11, 14. Albion & w, Martha, roc
1905, 11, 11. Albian M. & w, Martha, gct Hopewell MM

GIFFHORN
1884, 2, 9. Bell gct Cleveland MM, O.

GIFFORD
1861, 10, 12. Thos. R. Nordyke gct White Water MM, Ind., to m Elizabeth A. Gifford

GILBERT
1886, 6, 12. Nathan & w, Amy, recrq
1889, 2, 9. Charles S. recrq
1889, 3, 9. Charles L. recrq
1905, 3, 11. Annie recrq

GILLAND
1889, 2, 9. David J. & Laura recrq
1893, 10, 14. Laura relrq

GILPIN
1883, 5, 12. Elizabeth (form Hill) relrq

GLADDELL
1877, 3, 11. Sarah recrq

GLENN
1889, 2, 9. Elizabeth recrq
1901, 6, 8. Elizabeth dropped from mbrp

GORMAN
1899, 7, 8. Orville recrq
1901, 5, 11. Anna gct Center MM
1905, 6, 10. Orville & w, Anna, & ch, Harry & Mildred, rocf Center MM
1907, 11, 9. Orville & fam gct Fairfield MM

GRAVATT
1881, 4, 9. Joseph recrq
1886, 10, 9. Joseph A. relrq

GRAVES
1883, 2, 10. Andrew & w, Martha, recrq
1888, 7, 14. A. J. dropped from mbrp

GRAHAM
1815, 6, 29. Rachel m Christopher HUSSEY

1815, 2, 24. Mary Hunt (form Grayham) con mcd
1828, 11, 8. Rachel dis disunity

GREEN
1828, 1, 8. Asa B., s David & Mary, b
1843, 11, 30. John, s Robert & Mary, Highland Co., O.; m in Clear Creek MH, Rhoda CAREY dt Samuel & Anne, Highland Co., O.
----, --, --. Sewel & -----
Ch: Thomas
Edgar b 1857, 3, 23
Mariah Alma " 1858, 9, 8
1857, 9, 4. Thomas E., s S. & T., d bur Clear Creek
1858, 7, 12. John Wm., s S. & T., d bur Clear Creek
1865, 1, 31. Lillian M., dt Eli & Samantha, b

1814, 6, 24. John gct Lick Creek MM, Ind.
1827, 7, 14. David & w, Mary, rocf Springfield MM, dtd 1827,6,30
1829, 4, 11. David & w, Mary, & ch, Asa B., gct Springfield MM
1837, 6, 20. Joseph rocf Lisburn MM, Ireland dtd 1836,12,15

GREEN, continued
1842, 1, 18. Rhoda (form Wright) con mcd
1842, 1, 18. Joseph dis mcd
1842, 10, 18. Rhoda gct Fall Creek MM
1843, 8, 22. John rocf Newberry MM
1846, 11, 14. John & w, Rhoda C., & s, Robert, gct Centre MM
1853, 6, 11. Sewell rocf Centre MM, dtd 1853, 4,13
1855, 8, 11. Tamar recrq
1855, 9, 8. Francis Marion & John Wm., ch Sewell & Tamar, recrq
1860, 10, 13. Sewell & w, Tamer, & ch, Francis Marion & Maria Elma, gct Cincinnati MM
1862, 1, 11. Rachel M. & ch, Thomas Homer, Susan Mary, Ruth Emma, Robert Oscar, Martha Elizabeth & Theodocia Eva, rocf Newberry MM, dtd 1862,11,18
1864, 8, 13. Sewell & ch, Francis Marion, Maria Alma & David Alonzo, rocf Cincinnati MM
1864, 11, 12. Eli rocf Miami MM, dtd 1864,9,21
1865, 3, 11. Israel C. recrq
1865, 8, 12. Eli H. & w, Samantha N., & dt, Lillian N., gct Plainfield MM, Ind.
1866, 5, 12. Sewell con mcd
1867, 11, 9. John Sewel rocf Newberry MM, dtd 1867,9,23
1868, 5, 9. Israel C. & w, Rachel M., & ch, Thomas Hamer, Susan Mary, Ruth Emma, Robert Oscar, Martha Elizabeth & William Walter, gct Spring Creek MM
1868, 5, 14. Robert L. rocf Newberry MM, dtd 1868,3,23
1868, 8, 8. Saline recrq
1871, 1, 14. Robert gct Centre MM
1871, 2, 11. John S. rpd mcd; retained mbrp
1871, 2, 11. Rebecca rpd mcd; retained mbrp
1871, 3, 11. Cynthia Ann recrq
1871, 3, 11. Jesse recrq
1873, 8, 9. Cynthia Ann relrq
1877, 9, 8. Matilda J. gct Fairfield MM
1878, 1, 12. Sewell & ch, David A., Harlen P. & Jesse, gct Richland MM, Ind.
1878, 1, 12. Francis M. & Mariah Alma gct Richland MM, Ind.
1878, 3, 9. Jesse dis disunity
1879, 3, 18. John S. & w, Rebecca, & ch, Mary Luela & Clarence, relrq
1879, 4, 12. Alma Hammer (form Green) gct Westfield MM, Ind.
1881, 4, 9. David recrq
1883, 5, 12. Bessie recrq
1886, 5, 8. Jesse recrq
1887, 11, 12. David dropped from mbrp
1891, 5, 9. Cynthia recrq
1891, 6, 13. Belle recrq
1893, 2, 11. Bessie dropped from mbrp
1901, 6, 8. Cynthia & Belle relrq
1904, 4, 9. Cynthia A. recrq
1916, 9, 9. Cynthia & Bell dropped from mbrp

GREGORY
1884, 1, 12. Servetus & Martha A. recrq
1885, 8, 8. Survetus & w gct Wilmington MM
1887, 2, 12. Nathan recrq
1898, 11, 12. Nathan dropped from mbrp
1899, 4, 8. Nathan & w, Mary, & ch, Sherman, recrq

GRICE
1869, 4, 10. Jemima Jane recrq
1869, 4, 10. Rachel A. recrq
1869, 4, 10. Harriet E. recrq
1869, 4, 10. Sarah E. recrq
1869, 4, 10. James E., minor ch, recrq of parents
1869, 4, 10. Thomas E., minor ch, recrq of parents
1869, 4, 10. William E., minor ch, recrq of parents
1869, 4, 10. Pleasant A., minor ch, recrq of parents
1869, 4, 10. John D., minor ch, recrq of parents
1897, 4, 10. Jane & Harriet gct Fairfield MM, O.
1898, 11, 12. Wm. E. dropped from mbrp
1898, 11, 12. Pleasant A. dropped from mbrp
1898, 11, 12. John D. dropped from mbrp
1908, 1, 11. James relrq

GRIFFIN
1822, 10, 12. James & w, Priscilla, & s, Benjamin, gct West Grove MM, Ind.

GRIFFITH
1893, 4, 8. Josiah & w, Mary A., & ch, Leslie, Emma & John W., recrq
1914, 7, 11. Elma & Earl dropped from mbrp
1926, 1, 9. Leslie dropped from mbrp
1926, 1, 9. Carey dropped from mbrp
1926, 1, 9. Laurence dropped from mbrp
1933, 1, 12. Mary A. relrq

GRIM
1909, 3, 13. Ostie Ridgway relrq

GULLIAND
1893, 2, 11. David dropped from mbrp

HADLEY
1816, 9, 19. Mary m Jonah FRAZIER

1817, 7, 12. Edith gct Newberry MM
1818, 2, 14. James & w, Ann, & ch, Tamer, Sarah, James, Jeremiah, Margaret, Ann, John & Jane, gct Newberry MM
1875, 6, 12. Emma C. gct Wilmington MM
1876, 1, 8. Frank & w, Emma, rocf Wilmington MM, dtd 1875,12,17
1892, 6, 11. Stella dropped from mbrp
1894, 6, 9. Stella relrq
1927, 7, 14. Gladys recrq

HAGERMAN
1883, 5, 12. George E. recrq
1887, 4, 9. Everett gct Cincinnati MM

HAGGARDY
1912, 5, 11. Homer dropped from mbrp

HAGUE
1868, 3, 14. William & w, Margaret, recrq
1894, 8, 11. Wm. & w relrq

HAINES
1870, 2, 12. William & w, Elizabeth J., & dt, Mantie, recrq
1871, 7, 8. Wm. dis
1878, 1, 12. Elizabeth dropped from mbrp
1883, 8, 11. Manite dropped from mbrp
1909, 12, 11. Harry [Haynes] & w, Lida, & dt, Ica, rocf Ogden MM
1910, 7, 9. Harvey [Haynes] & w, Lida, & dt, Ica, rocf Beech Grove MM
1917, 11, 10. Ruth Carey gct Ceasars Creek MM, O.

HAM
1833, 11, 19. Thomas M. Sanders gct White Water MM, Ind., to m Sarah Ham Jr.

HAMILTON
1907, 4, 13. Samuel & w, Anna, recrq
1907, 11, 9. S. H. & w gct Fairfield MM
1912, 4, 13. Mary E. recrq
1929, 2, 14. Samuel & w, Myrtle, dropped from mbrp

HAMMER
1879, 4, 12. Alma (form Green) gct Westfield MM, Ind.

HAMPTON
1896, 2, 8. Jessie Sanders gct White Water MM, Ind.
1896, 8, 8. Bessie Sanders gct White Water MM, Ind., changed to Chester MM

HANIFUR
1889, 2, 9. Michael recrq
1893, 2, 11. Michael [Hanifer] dropped from mbrp

HARDESTY
1869, 4, 10. James recrq
1883, 8, 11. James dropped from mbrp
1889, 2, 9. Della recrq
1889, 2, 9. James T. recrq
1889, 2, 9. Flora recrq
1893, 2, 11. James J. dropped from mbrp
1896, 12, 12. Della dropped from mbrp

HARDY
1892, 8, 13. Celia rocf Fairfield MM
1901, 7, 13. William recrq
1901, 7, 13. Olive & s rocf Fairfield MM
1906, 2, 10. William W. & w, Olive, & s, Aldo dropped from mbrp

HARE
1901, 1, 12. Emma T. & s, Joseph E., gct Anderson MM

HARKNESS
1874, 3, 14. Jesse S. & w, Cynthia T., rocf Allum Creek MM, dtd 1874,2,19
1875, 1, 9. Jesse & w, Cynthia T., gct Allum Creek MM

HARLAN
1882, 1, 14. Nathaniel F. & w, Sarah, & s, Warren E., rocf Springfield MM
1886, 4, 10. Nathaniel & w, Sarah, & s, Warren E., gct Miami MM, O.

HARRIS
1866, 7, 14. Mary recrq
1866, 7, 14. Charles H. recrq
1868, 2, 8. Mary E. relrq
1869, 2, 13. Chas. H. dis disunity
1869, 4, 10. James L. recrq
1878, 1, 12. James dropped from mbrp
1887, 4, 9. Robert & w, Lucy, recrq
1894, 7, 14. Robert dropped from mbrp
1899, 1, 14. Lucy dropped from mbrp

HARRISON
1871, 3, 11. Clara recrq
1881, 4, 9. John recrq
1882, 9, 9. John relrq
1885, 6, 13. Clara E. dropped from mbrp

HARTLEY
1912, 7, 13. Harold recrq
1914, 7, 11. Harold dropped from mbrp

HARVEY
1827, 7, 16. Caleb, s William & Elizabeth, Clinton Co., O.; m in Clear Creek MH, Ann LEWIS, dt Evan & Sarah, Highland Co., O.

1827, 9, 8. Ann [Harvy] gct Springfield MM

HASTINGS
1869, 4, 10. Martha J. recrq
1891, 10, 10. Cassius & Susan recrq
1894, 7, 14. Cassius dropped from mbrp
1902, 4, 12. Wilber recrq
1912, 5, 11. Wilbur dropped from mbrp

HAUGHTON
1826, 12, 9. Maria rocf Silver Creek MM, Ind., dtd 1826,3,25, endorsed to Cincinnati MM
1834, 4, 22. Wm. & w, Salley, & ch, Richard Elwood & Lucy, rocf Salem MM, Ind., dtd 1834,4,22
1838, 5, 22. Wm. [Houghton] & w, Sally, & ch, Richard, Elwood & Lucy, gct Miami MM

HAYDOCK
1865, 6, 16. Wm. rocf Miami MM, dtd 1865,5,24
1872, 12, 14. Wm. T. & w, Emily L., & ch, Millie, gct Cincinnati MM

HAYS
1815, 9, 9. Anne (form Cowgill) dis mcd

HAWORTH
1855, 1, 21. Mary A. d bur East Fork

1826, 8, 12. Jonathan & ch, Daniel, Mary, George & Mahlon, rocf White River MM, Ind., dtd 1826,4,1
1827, 1, 13. Jonathan gct Lees Creek MM, to m Hester Evans
1830, 4, 10. Esther rocf Lees Creek MM, dtd 1830,2,20
1835, 11, 24. Jonathan & w, Esther, & ch, David, Mary, George, William & Joel, gct Fairfield MM
1842, 1, 18. David rocf Westfield MM, Ind., dtd 1841,12,9
1842, 9, 20. Daniel dis mcd
1855, 6, 9. Ezekiel Jr. rocf Newberry MM, dtd 1855,5,21
1856, 12, 13. Ezekiel & w, Martha, & s, Sylvester, gct Dover MM
1869, 5, 8. Thomas C. recrq
1869, 11, 13. Nancy rocf Honey Creek MM, dtd 1869,9,11
1870, 2, 12. Rebecca Jane recrq
1871, 1, 14. Sarah & Flora recrq
1872, 12, 14. Sarah E. & ch, Flora A., Samuel C. & Clayton M., gct Newberry MM
1873, 6, 14. Nancy & dt, Rebecca Jane, gct Wilmington MM, O.
1878, 1, 12. Thomas C., Nancy & Rebecca J. [Hayworth] gct Wilmington MM, O.
1917, 3, 10. Glenna recrq

HEDRICK
1873, 5, 10. Lydia recrq
1878, 6, 8. Oliver R. recrq
1879, 12, 13. Oliver R. dis
1881, 3, 12. Oliver recrq
1881, 4, 9. Oliver Elmer recrq
1881, 4, 9. Mary E. recrq
1881, 4, 9. Martha J. recrq
1887, 11, 12. Martha & Mary dropped from mbrp
1893, 2, 11. Oliver Elmer dropped from mbrp
1901, 5, 11. Angie May dropped from mbrp
1912, 5, 11. Flora dropped from mbrp

HELLER
1841, 4, 20. Martha (form Timberlake) dis mcd
1885, 3, 14. Elizabeth B. recrq

HELMIT
1887, 2, 12. J. T. recrq
1898, 11, 12. J. T. [Helmet] dropped from mbrp

HENLEY
1814, 8, 26. John rocf Lick Creek MM, Ind., dtd 1814,7,30
1827, 5, 12. John gct Fairfield MM

HENRY
1894, 1, 13. William & w, Julia, & s, Wm., rocf Wilmington MM
1895, 9, 14. Wm. & w & s, Wm., gct Wilmington MM

HIATT
1816, 10, 17. John, s Jonathan & Rachel, Champaign Co.; m in Clear Creek MH, Sarah KENWORTHY, dt Elisha & Mary, Highland Co., O.
Ch: Isaac b 1817, 9, 10
Mary " 1819, 3, 7
Rachel " 1821, 11, 7
1818, 6, 15. Benjamin, s Joseph & Hannah, Highland Co., O.; m in East Fork MH, Mary ELLIS, dt Nehemiah & Sarah, Clinton Co., O.
1822, 1, 14. Eleazar, s Solomon & Susannah, Wayne Co., Ind.; m in Clear Creek MH, Gulielma SANDERS, dt John & Milly
----, --, --. Jonathan m Jemimah ----- d 1834,3,6 bur Clear Creek
Ch: Elisha b 1826, 4, 4
Lewis " 1827, 11, 13
Wilson " 1829, 12, 20
----, --, --. Jesse & Ruthanna
Ch: Mary b 1832, 3, 12
Rachel " 1834, 1, 25
Elijah " 1835, 7, 18
1835, 4, 30. Jonathan, s John & Tamer, Highland Co., O.; m in Clear Creek MH, Mary DAVIS, dt Harmon & Martha, Highland Co., O.
Ch: Martha b 1836, 2, 3
1836, 12, 1. Ann m Daniel DAVIS
----, --, --. Amos & Lydia
Ch: Harmon b 1846, 8, 16
Daniel " 1849, 12, 16 d 1851, 9,21 bur Clear Creek
Lydia D. b 1853, 2, 12
Jonathan " 1855, 12, 19

1816, 12, 14. Sarah gct Darby MM
1818, 6, 13. John & w, Sarah, & s, Isaac, rocf Darby Creek MM, dtd 1818,2,21
1818, 8, 8. Mary gct Fall Creek MM
1818, 12, 12. Solomon gct Lees Creek MM
1822, 3, 9. Gulielma gct White Water MM, Ind.
1825, 6, 11. John & w, Sarah, & ch, Isaac, Mary, Rachel & Silas, gct White Lick MM, Ind.
1832, 2, 21. Jehu & w, Tamer, rocf Somerset MM, dtd 1831,12,26
1832, 2, 21. Jonathan & w, Jemima, & ch, Elisha, Lewis & Wilson, rocf Summerset MM, dtd 1831,12,26

HIATT, continued
1832, 2, 21. Susannah rocf Summerset MM, dtd 1831,12,26
1832, 2, 21. Jesse rocf Summerset MM, dtd 1831,12,26
1832, 2, 21. Ann rocf Summerset MM, dtd 1831, 12,26
1832, 2, 21. Amos rocf Summerset MM, dtd 1831,12,26
1832, 2, 21. Ruth Anna rocf Short Creek MM, O., dtd 1831,12,20
1833, 6, 18. Amos con mcd
1837, 2, 21. Susannah gct Pennsville MM, O. (Morgan Co.)
1837, 2, 21. Jesse & w, Ruthanna, & ch, Mary, Rachel & Elijah, gct Pennsville MM, O.
1837, 2, 21. Jehu & w, Tamer, gct Pennsville MM, O.
1837, 9, 19. Jonathan & w, Mary, & ch, Elisha, Lewis, Wilson & Martha, gct Pennsville MM, O.
1844, 12, 14. David M. Carey gct Newberry MM, to m Rebecca Hiatt
1846, 3, 14. Thomas, Jehu, Jesse & Amos, ch Amos, recrq
1846, 3, 14. Lydia & ch, Tamer, Elizabeth & Ann, recrq
1847, 6, 12. Elisha rocf Chesterfield MM, dtd 1847,3,20
1849, 4, 14. Elisha con mcd
1850, 1, 12. Mary & ch, Martha, Deborah & Lydia Ann, rocf Chesterfield MM, dtd 1849, 12,15
1850, 9, 14. Elisha gct Fairfield MM
1851, 4, 12. Mary & ch, Martha, Deborah & Lydia Ann, gct Fairfield MM
1854, 1, 14. Mary & ch, Martha, Deborah & Lydia Ann, rocf Fairfield MM, dtd 1853,12, 17
1855, 11, 10. Martha dis disunity
1856, 7, 12. Thomas dis mcd
1856, 12, 13. Jehu dis disunity
1857, 9, 12. Martha recrq
1857, 10, 10. Amos & w, Lydia, & ch, Elizabeth, Ann, Jesse, Amos, Harmon, Lydia & Jonathan, gct Spring Creek MM, Ia.
1857, 10, 10. Amos J. rocf Newberry MM, dtd 1857,8,16
1857, 10, 10. Harriett rocf Newberry MM, dtd 1857,9,21
1857, 10, 10. Thamer Bailey (form Hiatt) dis mcd
1863, 4, 11. Thomas recrq
1863, 4, 11. Caroline recrq
1866, 4, 15. Florence E. & Victory A., ch Amos J. & Martha, recrq
1871, 5, 13. Mary Kinzee (form Hiatt) rpd mcd; membership retained
1873, 8, 9. Florence E. Thompson (form Hiatt) rpd mcd; mbrp retained
1874, 7, 11. Caroline H. relrq
1878, 12, 14. Amos J. & w, Martha, & ch, Thomas Lincoln, Emily Alice, Anna Jane, Wm. Grant, Minnie Isabel & Bertha May, and Odsar Thompson, a gr s, gct Wilmington MM,O.
1881, 11, 12. Caroline H. recrq
1881, 11, 12. Caroline [Hyatt] recrq

HIBBERD
1826, 9, 21. Dalton, s Jacob & Hannah, b

1824, 7, 10. Isaac & w, Hannah, & ch, Phebe, Lydia, Mary Ann, Jesse & Sarah D., rocf Chester MM, Pa., dtd 1824,4,26
1826, 3, 11. Jacob dis disunity
1828, 4, 11. Hannah dis jH
1829, 4, 11. Hannah dis jH
1831, 4, 9. Lydia, Maryann & Jesse, ch Micajah, gct Springborough MM

HILL
1843, 4, 10. Thomas, s Nathan & Elizabeth, Hancock Co., Ind.; m in East Fork MH, Melissa HODSON, dt Matthew & Hannah, Clinton Co., O.
Ch: Hannah
Elizabeth b 1844, 3, 23
Sarah Ann " 1846, 7, 24
William
Wilson " 1847, 11, 30
1865, 2, 15. Daniel, s Henry & Achsah, Randolph Co., Ind.; m in East Fork MH, Martha Ann HUSSEY, dt Stephen & Rachel B., Clinton Co., O.

1845, 12, 13. Thomas Jr. rocf Walnut Ridge MM, Ind., dtd 1845,11,15
1850, 6, 8. Thomas & w, Milissa, & ch, Hannah, Elizabeth, Sarah Ann & Wm. Wilson, gct Walnut Ridge MM, Ind.
1865, 4, 8. Martha Ann gct Cincinnati MM
1867, 6, 8. Daniel & w, Martha Ann, & s, Chas. R., rocf Cincinnati MM, dtd 1867, 5,16
1868, 8, 8. Adaline rocf Sugar River MM, Ind., dtd 1868,7,11
1873, 9, 13. Daniel gct Green Plain MM, to m Tamar Thorn
1874, 2, 14. Tamar T. rocf Green Plain MM, dtd 1874,1,14
1877, 10, 13. Eliza relrq
1883, 5, 12. Elizabeth Gilpin (form Hill) relrq
1887, 8, 13. Daniel & w, Tamar, & ch, Murray & Emma, gct White Water MM, Ind.

HIMILLER
1871, 3, 11. William recrq
1929, 3, 14. Wm.'s d rpd

HINES
1866, 9, 8. Rebecca recrq
1868, 3, 14. John recrq

HINSHAW
1813, 10, 28. Margaret con mcd

HINSHAW, continued
1824, 9, 11. Margaret gct Newberry MM

HIXON
1871, 2, 11. Annie rpd mcd; retained mbrp
1883, 8, 11. Anna, Minnie M., Orlie C., Arthur, Mirtie M. [Hixzon] gct Fairfield MM
1887, 4, 9. May recrq
1898, 11, 12. Sarah E. dropped from mbrp
1899, 4, 8. Sarah E. gct Fairfield MM

HOCKETT
1814, 1, 5. John, s Joseph & Ann, Clinton Co., O.; m in East Fork MH, Martha COX, dt Thomas & Sarah, Clinton Co., O.
Ch: Lewis b 1815, 1, 16
Thomas " 1818, 4, 12
Mary " 1821, 7, 24
Elizabeth " 1824, 5, 11
Sarah Ann " 1828, 2, 26
Hannah " 1833, 11, 10
1814, 4, 6. Ann m Jesse JACKSON
1816, 10, 23. Jane m Libney HUNT
1819, 12, 15. Rachel m Thomas COX Jr.
1829, 12, 23. Jonathan, s Jonathan & Mary, Clinton Co., O.; m in East Fork MH, Mary NORDYKE, dt Micajah & Charity, Clinton Co., O.
1832, 10, 12. Ann d bur East Fork
1840, 7, 2. Levi, s Jesse & Mary, Clinton Co., O.; m in Clear Creek MH, Lydia PIKE, dt Wm. & Lucy, Highland Co., O.

1813, 11, 25. Phillip rocf White Water MM, Ind., dtd 1813,6,26
1814, 1, 27. Alice & ch, John & Philip, rocf White Water MM, Ind., dtd 1812,12,26, endorsed by Miami MM
1819, 9, 11. Nathan & w, Elizabeth, & ch, Eleazer, Jabez, Lydia & Nancy, gct White Water MM, Ind.
1831, 12, 20. Mary gct Newberry MM
1833, 8, 20. Eleazor gct White Lick MM, Ind.
1833, 8, 20. Elizabeth & ch, Lydia, Nancy, Elizann, Emely, Joseph & Cyrus, gct White Lick MM, Ind.
1834, 10, 21. Lois rocf Newberry MM, dtd 1834,9,22
1836, 2, 23. Jonathan & w, Mary, & ch, Esther, Sarah & Henry, rocf Newberry MM, dtd 1835, 10,19
1837, 4, 18. Lewis dis mcd
1837, 7, 18. Joseph gct Walnut Ridge MM, Ind.
1838, 3, 20. Lois gct Newberry MM
1840, 3, 24. Jonathan & w, Mary, & ch, Esther, Sarah, Henry & Barclay, gct Goshen MM
1840, 9, 22. Lydia gct Newberry MM
1841, 1, 19. Thomas con mcd
1841, 1, 19. Sarah (form Newby) con mcd
1845, 8, 9. Elizabeth rocf Newberry MM, dtd 1845,5,12
1846, 11, 14. Mary Leeka (form Hockett) rpd mcd
1855, 1, 13. Thomas & w, Sarah, & ch, Nancy Ellen, Wm., Martha Jane & John, gct Newberry MM
1865, 8, 12. Hannah Edwards (form Hockett) dis mcd
1869, 6, 12. Josiah & w, Mary, & ch, Jacob, also Naomi Hockett, a minor in his care, rocf Oak Ridge MM, Ind.
1871, 2, 11. Phebe Ann & ch, Hannah Ann & Oliver J., rocf Oak Ridge MM, dtd 1870, 10,11
1871, 3, 11. Joseph recrq
1873, 7, 22. Joseph & w, Phebe Ann, & ch, Hannah Ann, Oliver J. & John, gct Oak Ridge MM, Ind.
1874, 1, 10. Samantha rocf Newberry MM, dtd 1873,12,13
1875, 12, 11. Josiah & w, Mary, & ch, Jacob Powell & Naomi, gct Oak Ridge MM, Ind.
1894, 4, 14. Jacob & w & ch, Oscar B., Lewis & Earl J., gct Fairmount MM, Ind.

HODSON
----, --, --. John & Sarah [Hodgson]
Ch: Mary b 1808, 9, 7
Allen " 1809, 12, 30
George " 1812, 2, 29
Rachel " 1814, 8, 31
----, --, --. John Jr. & Sarah [Hodgson]
Ch: Delilah b 1811, 11, 7
Rhoda " 1812, 11, 19
1815, 2, 14. Benjamin [Hodgson] d bur Clear Creek
1821, 10, 18. Matthew [Hodgson], s Jonathan & Mary, Clinton Co., O.; m in Clear Creek MH, Hannah HUNT, dt Asa & Sarah, Highland Co., O.
1823, 2, 20. John [Hodgson] d bur Clear Creek
1843, 4, 10. Melissa m Thos. HILL
1849, 1, 12. Anna d bur East Fork
----, --, --. John & Sarah Ann
Ch: Anna Jane b 1850, 7, 24
William " 1852, 8, 1
Martha Elina " 1856, 1, 30

1814, 5, 27. John [Hodgson] & w, Sarah, & ch, Delilah, Rhoda & Nathan, gct Caesars Creek MM
1816, 2, 10. Jonathan [Hodgson] & w, Mary, & ch, Matthew, Elizabeth, Sarah, Jonathan & John, gct Fairfield MM
1816, 10, 12. Jane Manlove (form Hodgson) con mcd
1817, 9, 13. Henry [Hodgson] gct White Water MM, Ind.
1817, 12, 13. Enos [Hodgson] dis disunity
1819, 4, 10. Levina [Hodgson] & ch, Rachel, James, Mary & Enos, gct New Garden MM, Ind.
1821, 10, 13. Matthew [Hodgson] rocf Lees

HODSON, continued
Creek MM, to m Hannah Hunt
1821, 11, 10. Naomi Shockley (form Hodgson) dis mcd
1822, 6, 8. Hannah [Hodgson] gct Lees Creek MM
1823, 6, 14. Uriah [Hodgson] dis jas
1824, 3, 13. Abigail [Hodgson] dis jas
1825, 1, 8. Sarah [Hodgson] dis jas
1825, 1, 8. Anna (form Hoskins) con mcd
1825, 8, 13. Anna [Hodgson] gct Lees Creek MM
1825, 8, 13. Matthew [Hodgson] & w, Hannah, & ch, Sarah Ann & Melissa, rocf Lees Creek MM, dtd 1825,7,16
1829, 9, 12. Allen [Hodgson] dis disunity
1830, 3, 13. George [Hodgson] Jr. dis mcd
1831, 8, 23. Enos [Hodgson] rst at Cherry Grove MM, Ind. on consent of this mtg
1832, 12, 18. Sarah [Hodgson] & dt, Mary & Rachel, gct Newberry MM
1834, 12, 23. Mary [Hodgson] & dt, Mary, rocf Fairfield MM, dtd 1834,5,22
1834, 12, 23. John [Hodgson] & w, Rebecca, & dt, Lydia, rocf Fairfield MM, dtd 1834,8,21
1837, 1, 24. Geo. [Hodgson] & w, Mary, gct Newberry MM
1842, 9, 20. Sarah Ann Hoskins (form Hodgson) con mcd
1843, 1, 24. Hezekiah & w, Anne, & ch, Cyrus, Lewis, John, Martha, Ann, Eliza & Rebecca, rocf Fairfield MM, dtd 1842,11,24
1849, 1, 13. Cyrus [Hodgson] con mcd
1849, 6, 9. John & w, Rebecca, & ch, Lydia Emily & Flavius, gct Fairfield MM
1850, 11, 9. John con mcd
1851, 11, 8. Matthew [Hodgson] & w, Hannah, & ch, John Milton, gct Walnut Ridge MM, Ind.
1851, 12, 13. Asa gct Walnut Ridge MM, Ind.
1853, 9, 10. Lewis dis mcd
1853, 10, 8. Martha dis disunity
1853, 10, 8. Eliza dis disunity
1855, 9, 8. Ann Adams (form Hodson) dis mcd
1855, 11, 10. Hezekiah dis disunity
1858, 7, 10. Rebecca dis joining M. E. Church
1869, 4, 10. Lewis recrq
1869, 4, 10. Phebe recrq
1869, 4, 10. Thos. recrq
1869, 4, 10. Lydia recrq
1869, 4, 10. Lewis A. recrq
1869, 4, 10. Rebecca recrq
1869, 4, 10. Rebecca, minor, recrq of parents
1869, 4, 10. Caroline, minor, recrq of parents
1869, 4, 10. Cyrus, minor, recrq of parents
1869, 4, 10. Eva, minor, recrq of parents
1872, 2, 10. Joseph Jr. recrq
1873, 3, 8. Jonathan recrq
1873, 3, 8. Milton recrq
1873, 3, 8. Emily J. recrq
1873, 3, 8. Ella N. recrq
1873, 3, 8. Evelena, dt Jonathan & Emily J., recrq
1877, 3, 11. Lillie recrq
1884, 3, 8. Ida recrq
1886, 10, 9. John relrq
1886, 10, 9. Clarissa relrq
1886, 10, 9. Cyrus relrq
1887, 2, 12. Thomas & Hannah recrq
1887, 11, 12. William dropped from mbrp
1888, 6, 9. Iva dropped from mbrp
1888, 6, 9. Ettie dropped from mbrp
1888, 6, 9. Chloe dropped from mbrp
1898, 11, 12. Ira dropped from mbrp
1898, 11, 12. Nellie M. dropped from mbrp
1899, 12, 9. Rosetta & Chloe dropped from mbrp
1902, 6, 14. Carry recrq
1912, 2, 10. Stella & ch, Virgil, Russell & Virginia recrq

HOGGATT
1814, 6, 1. Alice d bur East Fork

1813, 9, 23. David & w, Dorcas, & ch, Nathan, Ruth, Agnes & David, rocf Mt. Pleasant MM, dtd 1812,9,26, endorsed by White Water MM, Ind.
1815, 4, 28. Phillip con mcd
1815, 10, 14. Jonathan & ch, Seth, Anna, Jesse, Mahlon & Jonathan, rocf Mt. Pleasant MM, dtd 1815,7,29, endorsed by Fairfield MM
1815, 11, 11. Phillip & s, John, gct Darby Creek MM
1817, 3, 8. Phillip gct White Water MM, Ind.
1824, 10, 9. Elizabeth & ch, Eleazor, Lydia, Ann & Eliza, rocf White Water MM, Ind., dtd 1824,6,19, endorsed by Fairfield
1846, 11, 14. Elizabeth Vanwinkle (form Hoggatt) dis mcd

HOLE
1880, 3, 12. Anna E. rocf West Union MM, Ind.

HOLADAY
1867, 9, 14. Sarah Jane [Holiday] (form West) con mcd
1867, 10, 12. Sarah Jane [Holiday] gct Newberry MM
1877, 12, 8. Lorenzo D. [Holliday] & w, Nancy J., & ch, Lorie O. & Charles, rocf Newberry MM, O., dtd 1877,7,23
1883, 10, 13. Charles rocf Newberry MM, O., dtd 1883,9,17
1884, 6, 14. Raleigh & Angeline [Holladay] rocf Newberry MM, O.
1885, 6, 13. Angie [Holliday] dropped from mbrp
1893, 2, 11. Raleigh [Holladay] dropped from mbrp
1894, 7, 14. Charles [Holliday] Sr. dropped from mbrp
1896, 4, 11. Loren [Holladay] relrq
1897, 1, 9. Charles [Holladay] recrq
1897, 1, 9. Nora [Holladay] recrq

HOLADAY, continued
1897, 1, 9. Viola recrq
1910, 7, 9. Charles & w, Nora, & ch, Nellie & Wm., gct Wilmington MM
1911, 11, 11. Nancy & dt, Ruth, gct Wilmington MM, O.
1912, 5, 11. Charles E. dropped from mbrp
1912, 5, 11. Bertie dropped from mbrp
1912, 5, 11. Earnest dropped from mbrp
1916, 9, 9. Viola dropped from mbrp

HOLLAWAY
1817, 8, 9. William & w, Sarah, & ch, Isaac, Elizabeth, Pleasant, Samuel, George, Sarah & William, gct Lees Creek MM
1817, 12, 13. John con mcd
1819, 3, 13. John gct Newberry MM

HOLLINGSWORTH
1886, 5, 8. James recrq
1890, 7, 12. James dropped from mbrp

HOLLOWELL
1904, 1, 9. Mary Anna gct High Point MM, N.C.

HOLMS
1885, 3, 14. William [Holme] recrq
1887, 4, 9. May recrq
1887, 4, 9. Rosa recrq
1889, 4, 13. May & Rosa dropped from mbrp
1893, 4, 8. Branson recrq
1894, 7, 14. William [Holmes] dropped from mbrp

HORNADAY
1881, 8, 13. Mary rocf Fairfield MM
1883, 1, 13. Mary relrq

HOSKINS
1840, 10, 28. Mary Jane m Isaac LEWIS
1841, 9, 1. Hannah m Lemuel LEWIS
----, --, --. Isaac m Rachel ----- d 1854,3,6 bur East Fork
Ch: Hannah b 1843, 3,17 d 1844,11,11 bur East Fork
1846. 12, 13. John d bur East Fork
----, --, --. Joel & Lydia B.
Ch: Isaac Albert b 1856, 5, 30

1815, 7, 28. Moses Jr. & w, Elizabeth, & ch, Malinda & Moses, gct Fairfield MM
1818, 1, 10. George con mcd
1821, 3, 10. Geo. gct Lees Creek MM
1825, 1, 8. Anna Hodson (form Hoskins) con mcd
1829, 10, 15. Isaac gct Lees Creek MM
1833, 4, 23. William dis mcd
1836, 2, 23. George rocf Fairfield MM, dtd 1835,10,22
1841, 1, 19. Elizabeth Newby (form Hoskins) con mcd
1842, 9, 20. Sarah Ann (form Hodgson) con mcd
1843, 1, 24. Isaac & w, Rachel, & ch, Mary, Joel, Josiah, Martha, Jane, Lydia & Josephus, rocf Fairfield MM, dtd 1842,11,24
1844, 6, 8. Lydia (form Bankson) dis mcd
1849, 6, 9. Asenith (form Hunt) dis mcd
1849, 9, 8. John dis mcd
1852, 11, 13. Joel gct Dover MM, to m Lydia P. Frazier
1854, 2, 11. Joel gct Newberry MM
1856, 6, 14. Joel & w, Lydia P., & s, Moses F., rocf Newberry MM, dtd 1856,5,19
1857, 6, 13. Joel & w, Lydia P., & ch, Moses F. & Isaac A., gct Dover MM
1857, 11, 14. Josiah dis mcd
1858, 3, 13. Lydia & Jane gct Dover MM
1858, 3, 13. Isaac & s, Joseph, gct Dover MM
1866, 5, 12. Jane Emily recrq
1866, 6, 9. Sarah Ann gct Walnut Ridge MM, Ind.
1867, 3, 9. Jane Emily Bernard (form Hoskins) con mcd
1868, 3, 14. Mary recrq
1868, 3, 14. George & w, Asenath, & dt, Mary Jane, recrq
1869, 4, 10. John recrq
1869, 4, 10. John recrq
1869, 4, 10. William recrq
1869, 4, 10. Mary Ann recrq
1869, 4, 10. Emily S. recrq
1869, 4, 10. Ida M. recrq
1869, 4, 10. Mary C. recrq
1869, 4, 10. David M. recrq
1870, 4, 9. George & w, Acenath, & ch, Mary Jane, gct Walnut Ridge MM, Ind.
1871, 8, 12. Alma rpd mcd; retained mbrp
1878, 1, 12. Mary C. gct Walnut Ridge MM, Ind.; cert returned with information she did not reside in limits
1884, 3, 8. Maria J. recrq
1887, 2, 12. Minnie recrq
1887, 2, 12. David recrq
1887, 2, 12. Raymond Reed, s J. W. & Jennie, recrq
1892, 8, 13. Rachel gct Fairfield MM
1898, 11, 12. Minnie Blanche dropped from mbrp
1902, 6, 14. Harley Roy recrq
1906, 12, 8. Joseph & Maud Milner rocf Cleveland MM
1908, 10, 10. Joseph & w, Maud, gct Maryville MM, Tenn.

HOUGH
1814, 5, 27. Daniel [Huff] & w, Sarah, & ch, Joseph, Rebecca, Rachel, Daniel, Mary, John, Sarah, Jesse & Elizabeth, gct Fairfield MM
1852, 9, 11. Jonathan Sanders gct Fairfield MM, to m Ruth [Huff]
1876, 5, 13. Zeri & w, Miriam, & adopted dt, Susan C. Teas, rocf New Garden MM, Ind., dtd 1876,4,15
1879, 3, 8. Zeri & w, Mariam, gct New Gar-

HOUGH, cohtinued
den MM, Ind.

HOUSTED
1877, 3, 11. Wm. A. recrq
1878, 6, 8. William relrq

HOWARD
1908, 11, 14. Mattie C. rocf Wilmington MM

HUBBARD
1846, 11, 14. Bathsheba (form Sanders) dis mcd
1869, 3, 13. Wm. G. rocf White Water MM, Ind.
1870, 11, 12. Wm. G. gct Short Creek MM, O., to m Lydia Hussey
1873, 7, 12. Lydia H. & ch rocf Short Creek MM, O., dtd 1873,6,25
1880, 1, 10. Wm. G. & w, Lydia, & ch, Penrose, Walter & Wm., gct Columbus MM, O.

HULL
1881, 4, 9. Elizabeth recrq
1887, 11, 12. Eliza dropped from mbrp

HUNNICUTT
1895, 3, 9. Callie Nordyke gct Whittier MM, Calif.

HUNT
----, --, --. Asa & Priscilla
Ch: Miriam b 1785, 9, 30
Libni " 1791, 8, 4
Asa m 2nd Sarah -----
Ch: Ezra b 1797, 7, 17
Hannah " 1799, 1, 31
Eber " 1801, 10, 28 d 1821, 3,20 bur Clear Creek
Harriet b 1804, 1, 18
Asa " 1807, 5, 25
Jesse " 1809, 11, 26
Eunice " 1811, 10, 4
1815, 5, 4. Miriam m Isaac KENWORTHY
1816, 10, 23. Libney, s Asa & Rachel, Highland Co., O.; m in East Fork MH, Jane HOCKETT, dt Joseph & Ann, Clinton Co., O.
Ch: Alfred b 1817, 7, 25
Eber " 1818, 12, 21
Ann " 1820, 7, 10
Miriam " 1821, 9, 18
John " 1823, 3, 13
Margaret " 1824, 12, 22
Priscilla " 1828, 11, 19
Isaac " 1830, 3, 16
1821, 10, 18. Hannah m Matthew HODGSON
1825, 9, 20. Margaret d bur East Fork
1818, 12, 3. Barnabas, s Jonathan & Phebe, Highland Co., O.; m in Clear Creek MH, Hannah LEWIS, dt Evan & Sarah, Highland Co., O.
1821, 6, 15. Ezra, s Asa & Sarah, Highland Co., O.; m in Clear Creek MH, Rebecca ALBERTSON, dt Feraby GRIFFIN, Highland Co., O.
1841, 2, 24. Pleasant, s Barnabas & Hannah, Wayne Co., Ind.; m in Clear Creek MH, Ann WILLIAMS, dt Wm. & Phebe, Highland Co.,O.

1813, 1, 28. Abner & w, Mary, & ch, Josiah & Rebecca, rocf Mt. Pleasant MM, dtd 1812, 9,26, endorsed by Fairfield MM
1813, 10, 28. Abner & w, Mary, & ch, Elizabeth, Rebecca & Joseph, gct Fairfield MM
1815, 5, 26. John Jr. gct White Water MM, Ind.
1815, 2, 24. Ira con mcd
1815, 2, 24. Mary (form Greyham) con mcd
1816, 5, 11. Ira & w, Mary, gct New Garden MM, Ind.
1816, 12, 14. Cert rec for Jacob & w, Lydia, & ch, Rachel, Nathan, Robert, Thomas, Ruth, Jesse, Rebecca & Reuben, from Mt. Pleasant MM, Va., dtd 1816,9,28, endorsed to Newberry MM, O.
1818, 9, 12. Jonathan & w, Phebe, & ch, Margaret, John, Hulda, Jesse, Phebe, Elizabeth, Rachel, Mary & Bula, gct Newgarden MM, Ind.
1819, 5, 8. Barnabas & w, Hanah, gct New Garden MM, Ind.
1821, 10, 13. Ezra & w, Rebecca, gct Cherry Grove MM, Ind.
1823, 10, 11. Hanuel gct Fall Creek MM, to m Eleanor Newby
1824, 8, 14. Eleanor rocf Fall Creek MM, dtd 1824,6,19
1828, 9, 14. Eunice Elison (form Hunt) dis mcd
1829, 2, 14. Jesse dis mcd
1829, 4, 11. Hanuel & w, Eliona, & ch, Sarah, Asenith & Ezra, gct Fall Creek MM
1830, 3, 13. Asa con mcd
1830, 8, 14. Lydia (form Stevens) con mcd
1831, 8, 23. Hanuel & w, Eleanor, & ch, Sarah Asenath & Ezra, rocf Fall Creek MM, dtd 1831,6,22
1834, 12, 23. Jesse Nordyke gct Fairfield MM, to m Levina Hunt
1836, 8, 23. Hanuel con mcd
1836, 12, 20. Hanuel & ch, Sarah, Asenith, Ezra, Nancy, Jane & James, gct Milford MM, Ind.
1837, 7, 18. Libni & w, Jane, & ch, Alfred, Ann, Miriam, John, Priscilla, Isaac, Rebecca, Joseph & Jane, gct Walnut Ridge MM, Ind.
1839, 1, 22. Asa & w, Lydia, & ch, Mary Ann, Levi Stevens & Cyrus Adison, gct Walnut Ridge MM, Ind.
1839, 9, 24. Sarah gct Walnut Ridge MM, Ind.
1841, 5, 18. Ann gct New Garden MM, Ind.
1848, 6, 10. Nancy Jane rocf Duck Creek MM, Ind., dtd 1848,4,20
1848, 10, 14. Asenith rocf Walnut Ridge MM, Ind., dtd 1848,9,16
1849, 6, 9. Asenith Hoskins (form Hunt) dis mcd

HUNT, continued
1849, 8, 11. Nancy Jane dis joining M. E. Ch.
1900, 7, 14. Clyde rocf Newberry MM
1900, 7, 14. James & w, Sarah Rebecca, rocf Newberry MM
1912, 5, 11. Clyde dropped from mbrp

HUNTER
1910, 4, 9. Frank recrq

HUSSEY
----, --, --. Christopher & Sarah
Ch: Stephen b 1793, 8, 16 d 1850, 7,28 bur Clear Creek
Sarah b 1795, 2, 17
Mary " 1797, 3, 13
Priscilla " 1800, 9, 3
William " 1802, 2, 28
Betsy " 1805, 3, 1
John " 1806, 11, 15
Kerenhappoch b 1809, 7, 28
Eunice " 1812, 11, 6
----, --, --. Joshua & Sarah
Ch: Thomas b 1800, 11, 4
Stephen " 1804, 10, 23
Drusilla " 1806, 9, 17
William " 1808, 3, 16
Nathan " 1810, 8, 16
Sarah " 1815, 10, 15
1812, 3, 9. Stephen d bur East Fork
1814, 4, 14. Sarah d bur Clear Creek
1815, 6, 29. Christopher, s Stephen & Martha, Highland Co., O.; m in Newberry MH, Rachel GRAHAM, dt Jacob & Ann JACKSON, Clinton Co. O.
Ch: Christopher b 1816, 7, 26
Lydia " 1816, 7, 26
1816, 10, 24. Stephen, s Christopher & Sarah, Highland Co., O.; m in Clear Creek MH, Katharine WILLIAMS, dt Wm. & Phebe, Highland Co., O., d 1847,7,31 bur Clear Creek
Ch: Joshua b 1818, 5, 20
Sarah " 1820, 6, 26
William " 1822, 11, 10
Christopher" 1824, 12, 21
Robert W. " 1827, 2, 13
Joseph " 1829, 8, 8
John " 1831, 10, 13
Hiram " 1833, 10, 26 d 1836, 3,19 bur Clear Creek
Elizabeth Ann b 1836, 3, 23
Cyrus " 1838, 11, 4
Phebe W. " 1841, 1, 7
1819, 12, 16. Mary m Daniel BOND
1823, 1, 22. Thomas, s Joshua & Sarah, Highland Co., O.; m in East Fork MH, Jane W. ANTHONY, dt Joseph & Rhoda, Clinton Co.,O.
1825, 9, 15. Priscilla m Daniel LEWIS
1828, 10, 22. Drucilla m Henry CANADAY
----, --, --. Sephen & Rachel B.
Ch: Edwin b 1830, 10, 31 d 1832, 2, 6
Ch: Isaac T. b 1832, 5, 2 d 1848,12,29
Martha Ann " 1834, 1, 15
Silas " 1836, 4, 11 " 1838, 4,13
John M. " 1838, 2, 6
Ch bur East Fork
1830, 12, 9. Martha d bur East Fork
1832, 10, 20. John d bur Clear Creek
1841, 5, 5. Joseph d bur Clear Creek
1844, 4, 14. Robert d bur Clear Creek
1846, 9, 23. Rachel d bur Clear Creek
1849, 3, 26. Joshua d bur East Fork
1865, 2, 15. Martha Ann m Daniel HILL

1825, 8, 13. Kerenhapock Kelvey (form Hussey) dis mcd
1826, 5, 17. William gct Caesars Creek MM, to m Jane Edwards
1827, 1, 13. Jane rocf Caesars Creek MM, dtd 1826,9,26
1828, 1, 12. Jane D. rocf Springfield MM, dtd 1827,11,24
1829, 10, 15. John & w, Jane, & s, Isaac, gct Miami MM
1829, 10, 15. Stephen gct Lees Creek MM, to m Rachel Thornburgh
1829, 11, 14. Hepseba rocf Caesars Creek MM, dtd 1829,9,24
1830, 6, 12. Rachel rocf Lees Creek MM, dtd 1830,4,17
1831, 3, 12. Jane dis disunity
1831, 7, 19. Nathan dis mcd
1832, 7, 24. Eunice Underwood (form Hussey) dis mcd
1833, 4, 23. William dis mcd
1835, 6, 23. Thomas dis disunity
1835, 7, 21. William dis disunity
1836, 11, 22. Christopher Jr. dis mcd
1837, 7, 18. Lydia Moberly (form Hussey) dis mcd
1837, 11, 21. Stephen dis disunity
1841, 7, 20. Sarah Smith (form Hussey) dis mcd
1844, 2, 20. Stephen recrq
1846, 1, 10. Joshua Jr. dis jas
1846, 12, 12. Christopher gct Miami MM
1847, 11, 13. Christopher rocf Miami MM, dtd 1847,9,22
1847, 12, 11. William dis disunity & taking part in War with Mexico
1848, 2, 12. Jane, w Wm., & ch, John Milton, Martha A., Lydia, Alfred, Rachel, William Henry, Esther N. & Jane, gct Union MM
1848, 2, 12. Cyrus, Charles, Alonzo & Adison, ch Thos. & Jane, gct Union MM
1848, 7, 8. Christopher Jr. dis disunity
1848, 9, 9. Sarah Jr. dis jas
1857, 6, 13. Phebe Tyson (form Hussey) dis mcd
1858, 5, 8. Martha Ann recrq
1860, 8, 11. Cyrus dis mcd & joining M. E. Church
1863, 8, 8. Nathan & w, Julia A., recrq
1865, 6, 16. John M. con mcd

HUSSEY, continued
1866, 2, 10. Julia gct Dover MM
1866, 6, 9. Adaline (form Newby) con mcd
1866, 4, 14. Anna R. recrq
1866, 4, 14. Joshua recrq
1866, 6, 9. William recrq
1866, 7, 14. James recrq
1868, 9, 12. Lydia E. (form Fenner) con mcd
1869, 4, 10. Eliza recrq
1869, 4, 10. Frank, minor ch, recrq of parents
1869, 4, 10. Ella, minor ch, recrq of parents
1869, 4, 10. Jennie, minor ch, recrq of parents
1869, 4, 10. Isaac, minor ch, recrq of parents
1870, 11, 12. Wm. G. Hubbard gct Short Creek MM, O., to m Lydia Hussey
1872, 4, 13. Martha Ann gct Union MM, Mo.
1878, 1, 12. William dropped from mbrp
1887, 2, 12. Frank E. relrq
1891, 11, 14. Rachel B. gct White Water MM, Ind.
1891, 11, 14. Homer gct White Water MM, Ind.
1891, 11, 14. Mary, dt John M. & Annie, gct White Water MM, Ind.
1892, 1, 9. John M. & Annie dropped from mbrp
1893, 2, 11. Ottie dropped from mbrp
1897, 3, 13. Melvin recrq
1897, 4, 10. Eliza gct Fairfield MM, O.
1898, 11, 12. Isaac F. dropped from mbrp
1902, 5, 10. Melvin dropped from mbrp

HUTSON
1815, 3, 24. Margaret gct White Water MM, Ind.

JACKSON
1814, 4, 6. Jesse, s Jacob & Ann, Clinton Co., O.; m in East Fork MH, Ann HOCKETT, dt Joseph & Ann, Clinton Co., O.

1815, 10, 14. Curtis gct Fall Creek MM, to m
1816, 5, 11. Lydia rocf Fall Creek MM, dtd 1816,3,23
1826, 6, 10. Jesse & w, Ann, & ch, Milinda, Joseph, Jacob & Asenath, rocf Newberry MM, dtd 1826,3,23
1826, 9, 9. Phebe rocf Cherry Grove MM, Ind. dtd 1826,4,8, endorsed by Dover MM
1834, 5, 20. Ann dis jas
1834, 6, 24. Jesse dis jas
1838, 7, 24. Joseph dis disunity
1846, 3, 14. Asenith dis disunity
1846, 3, 14. Lydia dis disunity
1845, 7, 12. Jacob dis mcd & jas
1846, 3, 14. Asenath dis jas
1846, 3, 14. Lydia dis jas
1850, 10, 12. Rachel Acre (form Jackson) dis mcd & jas
1859, 9, 10. Malinda dis jas

JAMES
1842, 10, 26. Mary H. m Asa NORDYKE
1855, 10, 17. David, s Isaac & Sarah, Clinton Co., O.; m in East Fork MH, Deborah STEPHENS, dt Gideon & Mary, Highland Co., O.

184-, 12, 22. John & w, Esther, rocf White Water MM, Ind., dtd 1840,11,25
1841, 6, 22. Cert rec for David & w, Mary, & ch, Mary, Levi C., Atticus S., Alfred P., Jonathan H., Lindley M., Sarah & Dillin H., from West Grove MM, Ind., dtd 1841,5,8, endorsed to Fairfield MM
1841, 12, 21. John & w, Hester, gct Fairfield MM
1843, 1, 24. Allen rocf Carmel MM, dtd 1842, 10,15
1844, 10, 12. David & w, Mary, & ch, Levi C., Atticus L., Alfred P., Jonathan H., Sarah, Lindley H. & Anna B., gct Newberry MM
1855, 12, 8. Deborah gct Newberry MM
1876, 3, 11. David & w, Deborah S., rocf Wilmington MM, dtd 1876,2,18
1889, 4, 13. Ann (form McFadden) rocf Springfield MM, dtd 1889,2,16
1898, 8, 13. Anna gct Wilmington MM

JANNEY
1844, 7, 13. Daniel Coffin gct Newberry MM, to m Patience Janney

JEFFRIES
1886, 5, 8. Eliza & Sarah recrq
1887, 4, 9. Anderson recrq
1890, 7, 12. Sadie & Eliza dropped from mbrp

JESSOP
1815, 6, 23. Thomas & w, Ann, & ch, Jonathan, Prudence, Richard, Mary Thomas, Anna Huldah & Rebecca, rocf Fairfield MM, dtd 1815,5,27
1817, 1, 11. Thomas & w, Ann, & ch, Jonathan, Prudence, Richard, Mary, Thomas, Anna, Huldah & Rebecca, gct Miami MM, O.
1837, 6, 20. Amos Lewis gct Caesar Creek MM, to m Patience Jessup

JOHN
1815, 11, 11. Ebenazar rocf Fall Creek MM, dtd 1815,10,21

JOHNSON
1825, 4, 19. Sarah d bur Clear Creek
1838, 1, 21. Gerard M., s John W. & Milley, Highland Co., O.; m in Clear Creek MH, Mary COFFIN, dt Samuel & Dinah, Highland Co., O.
1841, 7, 11. Rachel d bur Clear Creek (w Elisha)
1854, 5, 2. Sarah d bur Clear Creek
1923, 2, --. Robert m Martha Leone BAILEY
1925, --, --. Clyde m Della McCALL

JOHNSON, continued
1813, 12, 23. Wm. dis disunity
1814, 6, 24. Richard dis disunity
1817, 3, 8. Polly recrq on consent of Cedar Creek MM, Va.
1817, 9, 13. William & w, Polly, recrq
1819, 4, 10. Sally (form Timberlake) dis mcd
1820, 9, 9. Sarah M. recrq
1819, 1, 9. Jesse, Thomas, John, Robert & George, ch William, recrq
1821, 4, 14. James dis
1823, 10, 11. Sarah recrq
1826, 12, 9. Jesse dis mcd
1827, 2, 16. Thomas dis disunity
1831, 10, 18. John dis disunity
1832, 2, 21. Robert dis disunity
1833, 8, 20. Wm. & w, Polly, & s, George, gct Newberry MM
1838, 5, 22. Mary gct Fairfield MM
1857, 5, 9. Mary C. & ch, Hervy, Warren, Semira, Abi Sibil & Orpah, rocf Honey Creek MM, dtd 1857,4,11
1862, 9, 13. Mary C. & ch, Sibil & Orpah, minors, & Warren, Samira & Abi, not minors, gct Fairfield MM
1867, 11, 9. Elizabeth (form Engle) con mcd
1867, 12, 14. Lorena (form Davis) con mcd
1869, 7, 10. Jesse K. recrq
1873, 3, 8. Maria E. recrq
1873, 5, 10. Emma S. recrq
1873, 5, 10. Rachel recrq
1878, 1, 12. Elizabeth dropped from mbrp
1879, 9, 13. Alfred recrq
1879, 9, 13. Emma gct Louisville, Ky.
1880, 9, 10. Anna M. & ch, James E., John W., Anna Mary & Chas. F., rocf Wilmington MM
1880, 10, 9. Isaac T. rocf Wilmington MM
1882, 2, 11. Isaac T. gct Wilmington MM, Del. cert returned 1882,5,13
1883, 3, 10. James B. gct New York MM, N. Y.
1884, 8, 9. Warren rocf Fairfield MM
1885, 3, 14. William & Mary Amanda recrq
1885, 6, 13. Alfred & Annie M. & Anna Mary & Charles F. gct Rose Hill MM, Kans.
1887, 4, 9. Martha A. recrq
1889, 4, 13. Albert E. dropped from mbrp
1889, 11, 9. Henry & w, Elizabeth, & ch, Edgar R., Azalia M. & Albertia A., gct Wichita MM, Kans.
1892, 8, 13. Mary E. gct Fairfield MM
1893, 8, 12. Cert for Warren endorsed to Hopewell MM
1896, 5, 9. Leonard recrq
1896, 5, 9. Annie Smith rocf Fairfield MM
1897, 4, 10. Everett & Lorena gct Fairfield MM, O.
1898, 8, 13. Junius rocf Wilmington MM
1900, 4, 14. Charles & Cora E. recrq
1901, 12, 14. Isaac F. gct Germantown MM, Pa.
1902, 7, 12. William & Mary dropped from mbrp
1906, 2, 10. Effie & ch, David & Glenn recrq
1908, 2, 8. J. Will gct Wilmington MM
1912, 5, 11. John W. dropped from mbrp
1916, 9, 9. Effie dropped from mbrp
1916, 9, 9. David dropped from mbrp
1916, 9, 9. Glenn dropped from mbrp

JONES
1869, 4, 10. Samuel A. recrq
1869, 6, 12. Daniel recrq
1869, 7, 10. Laura E. (form Arthur) con mcd
1879, 5, 10. Samuel & w, Jane, & ch, Martha, gct Chester MM, Ind.
1885, 3, 14. Tacy B. recrq
1885, 3,14. Annie recrq
1887, 4, 9. R. Frank recrq
1887, 4, 9. William & Hannah recrq
1894, 7, 14. Frank dropped from mbrp
1894, 7, 14. Daniel dropped from mbrp
1894, 7, 14. William dropped from mbrp
1899, 1, 14. Anna dropped from mbrp

KEARNS
1887, 4, 9. Charles recrq
1899, 1, 8. Chas. [Kernes] relrq

KELLEY
1881, 4, 9. William recrq
1883, 6, 9. Emily recrq
1885, 3, 14. Laura recrq
1886, 3, 13. Mary [Kelly] recrq
1890, 4, 12. Emily relrq
1893, 9, 19. Mary gct Harveyville MM, Kans.
1893, 9, 19. Laura & ch, Bertha, Walter, Leroy & Jessie, gct Harveyville MM, Kans.
1894, 7, 14. Martha A. dropped from mbrp

KELVEY
1825, 8, 13. Kerenhapock (form Hussey) dis mcd

KENT
1891, 6, 13. Flora recrq
1894, 7, 14. Flora dropped from mbrp
1898, 7, 9. Flora dropped from mbrp

KENWORTHY
----, --, --. Elisha & Mary
Ch: Ira b 1811, 4, 27
Jesse " 1813, 12, 5
Lydia " 1816, 5, 27
1811, 6, 16. Mary d bur Clear Creek
1815, 5, 4. Isaac, s David & Tamer, Highland Co., O.; m in Clear Creek MH, Miriam HUNT, dt Asa & Priscilla, Highland Co.,O. (Isaac d 1853,9,18 bur East Fork)
Ch: Asa b 1817, 6, 22 d 1839,10,20 bur Walnut Ridge
Mary b 1820, 4, 30
1816, 10, 17. Sarah m John HIATT
1822, 1, 17. Rachel m Hudson MIDDLETON
1835, 3, 7. Tamer d bur Clear Creek
1835, 5, 6. David d bur Clear Creek
1841, 10, 21. Mary m Josiah NEWBY

KENWORTHY, continued
1826, 1, 14. Elisha & w, Mary, & ch, Silas, Thomas, Ira, Jesse & Lydia, gct White Lick MM, Ind.
1826, 1, 14. John gct White Lick MM, Ind.
1830, 11, 13. Joshua gct White Lick MM, Ind.

KERNS
1885, 3, 14. Minnie & Martha Gertrude recrq

KESTER
1834, 10, 2. David, s Peter & Hannah, Clinton Co., O.; m in Clear Creek MH, Elizabeth CAREY, dt Samuel & Ann, Highland Co., O.

1835, 1, 20. Elizabeth gct Newberry MM
1884, 6, 14. Miles rocf Newberry MM, O.
1887, 11, 12. Miles gct Newberry MM, O.
1893, 4, 8. Pearl recrq
1894, 7, 14. Miles rocf Newberry MM, O.
1894, 7, 14. Pearl dropped from mbrp
1901, 10, 12. Mary F. gct Newberry MM
1915, 10, 9. Milton L. & w, Cora Clarke, recrq

KINSEY
1867, 11, 9. Samuel B. & w, Rachel G., & ch, Hannah Ann, Jane, Mary Ann, Samuel B., Harrison M. & Rachel Ella, rocf Short Creek MM, dtd 1867,8,22
1871, 5, 13. Mary (form Hiatt) rpd mcd; retained mbrp
1872, 12, 14. Hannah Ann Spencer (form Kinzy) rpd mcd; retained mbrp
1880, 7, 10. Samuel dis disunity
1880, 8, 14. Samuel B. Jr. dis disunity
1881, 4, 9. Samuel Jr. recrq
1893, 11, 11. Mary A. relrq
1894, 7, 14. Harry M. dropped from mbrp
1898, 7, 9. Harry M. dropped from mbrp

KINZER
1929, 2, 23. Jane d ae 79

1872, 1, 13. Daniel recrq
1883, 4, 14. Daniel & w, Mary, gct Fairfield MM
1887, 6, 19. Sarah Jane & ch, Myrtie & Robert, recrq

KIER
1869, 4, 10. Francis M. [Kiser] recrq
1870, 2, 12. Mary E. set off from Fairfield MM
1871, 1, 14. Francis M. con mcd

KIRBY
1819, 7, 10. Ruth rocf South River MM, Va., dtd 1819,5,1, endorsed to Fairfield MM
1869, 4, 10. Nancy recrq
1869, 4, 10. James recrq
1869, 10, 9. Eliza & Eliza Jane recrq
1872, 1, 13. James rpd mcd; retained mbrp
1872, 4, 13. Caroline M. recrq
1898, 11, 12. James dropped from mbrp
1898, 11, 12. Bessie dropped from mbrp

KNEADLER
1884, 6, 8. Belle (form Pulse) relrq

KNEISLEY
1926, 1, 9. Rena Vansant dropped from mbrp

KNOTTS
1882, 6, 10. Milton & s, James W., recrq
1885, 11, 14. Milton dis
1891, 2, 14. Robert [Knott] dropped from mbrp

KOCHLER
1856, 4, 12. Asenath (form Lewis) dis mcd
1866, 4, 14. Asenath recrq

KRAMER
1889, 10, 12. Mary J. gct White Water MM, Ind.

LADD
1869, 8, 14. Ellen (form Lowman) con mcd
1883, 8, 11. Ellen dropped from mbrp
1883, 8, 11. Cyrus R. dropped from mbrp
1883, 8, 11. William dropped from mbrp
1898, 11, 12. Abbey dropped from mbrp

LANE
1863, 10, 31. Joseph S. & s, Henry D., recrq
1865, 9, 9. Joseph S. & s, Henry D., gct Dover MM, O.

LANGSTAFF
1880, 2, 14. Ida M. rocf Cincinnati MM, O., dtd 1880,3,18
1883, 11, 10. Ida relrq

LARICK
1893, 5, 13. Ocie recrq
1893, 5, 13. Chas. Clinton recrq
1893, 5, 13. Bertha recrq
1893, 5, 13. Ida recrq
1893, 5, 13. Lora recrq

LARKIN
1862, 9, 21. Hepsibah d bur Clear Creek
1924, 7, 19. Margaret m J. B. MAST

1867, 2, 9. Alonzo M. recrq
1868, 5, 9. Mary F. recrq
1869, 6, 12. Alonzo M. [Larkins] con mcd
1869, 9, 11. Alonzo M. & s, Joseph, gct Fairfield MM
1870, 7, 18. Alonzo & w, Lavina, & ch, Joseph & Sarah Margarette, rocf Fairfield MM, dtd 1870,7,16
1891, 2, 14. Mary dropped from mbrp
1914, 4, 11. Alice & Margaret recrq
1926, 1, 9. Joseph relrq

LARKIN, continued
1926, 2, 13. Alonzo M. & Elizabeth gct Fairfield MM

LAYMON
1924, 6, 11. Stanley R. m Nellie COOK

LEA
1817, 6, 14. Cert rec for Ann from South River MM, Va., dtd 1816,11,9, endorsed to Fair field MM
1817, 6, 14. Cert rec for Elizabeth from South River MM, Va., dtd 1816,11,9, endorsed to Fairfield MM [6,30
1821, 7, 14. Ann rocf Fairfield MM, dtd 1821,
1900, 7, 13. I. Gurney [Lee] rocf Neuse MM,N.C
1903, 3, 14. I. Gurney [Lee] gct E. Goshen MM
LEAKA
1834, 12, 23. Elizabeth [Leaky] rocf Fairfield MM, dtd 1834,10,23
1846, 11, 14. Mary (form Hockett) rpd mcd
1854, 8, 12. Jonathan & ch, Sarah, Elizabeth, Harvey, Milton & Alpheus, recrq
1868, 12, 12. Lucinda B. rocf Spiceland MM, dtd 1868,11,19
1871, 7, 8. Lucinda relrq to join M. E. Ch.
1873, 1, 11. Sarah [Leera] recrq
1891, 2, 14. Sylvanus relrq
1894, 7, 14. Jonathan dropped from mbrp
1894, 7, 14. Harvey relrq
1898, 1, 8. Alpheus relrq
1898, 7, 9. Jonathan dropped from mbrp
1901, 6, 8. Martha E. Mulane (form Leeka) relrq

LEGGETT
1881, 4, 9. Jacob recrq
1885, 12, 12. Jacob [Legett] dis
1904, 4, 9. Jacob Henry [Liggett] recrq
1907, 7, 13. Jesse recrq
1912, 5, 11. Jacob, Caroline & Jesse dropped from mbrp
1914, 2, 14. Elva & Charles recrq

LEVERTON
1874, 4, 11. John recrq
1877, 3, 11. Milton recrq
1877, 6, 9. Eliza recrq
1883, 8, 11. George W. [Leaverton] dropped from mbrp
1887, 4, 9. John T. & w, Mary A., & ch, Joseph V., Frank, Minnie J., Etta Cora, Lelia A. & Emma E., recrq
1891, 11, 14. John T. & fam relrq
1894, 7, 14. John [Leaverton] dropped from mbrp
1894, 7, 14. Hattie [Leaverton] dropped from mbrp
1914, 3, 14. Mamie Ridgeway [Leaverton] gct Fairfield MM, O.

LEWIS
1814, 3, 13. Jonah, s Enoch & Eliza, b
1816, 3, 14. Enoch, s Evan & Sarah, Highland Co., O.; m in Clear Creek MH, Mourning TIMBERLAKE, dt John & Mollie, Highland Co., O.
Ch: Elizabeth b 1817, 2, 4
Sally " 1818, 10, 10
John " 1820, 8, 4
Mary " 1823, 5, 3
Clark " 1825, 6, 19
Ann " 1827, 7, 22
1817, 1, 1. Amos, s Evan & Sarah, Highland Co., O.; m in East Fork MH, Phebe NORDYKE dt Micajah & Charity, Clinton Co., O., d 1835,6,10 bur East Fork
Ch: Isaac
Aquilla b 1822, 11, 12
Priscilla " 1824, 4, 4
Syrina " 1825, 7, 20
Assenath " 1827, 8, 25
Caleb " 1828, 12, 28 d 1837, 9,13 bur East Fork, Clinton Co., O.
Jesse b 1833, 2, 23 d 1836,12,26 bur East Fork, Clinton Co., O.
Lydia Ann b 1838, 7, 23 d 1849,10, 9 bur East Fork
Evan b 1840, 12, 13 " 1854, 5, 1 bur East Fork
1817, 11, 20. Susannah m Robert ELLIS
1818, 2, 17. Sarah d bur Clear Creek
1818, 9, 17. Nathan, s Evan & Sarah, Hamilton Co.; m in Clear Creek MH, Rachel THOMAS, dt Josiah & Rachel, Hamilton Co.
Ch: Josiah b 1819, 7, 10
Sarah " 1820, 12, 10
Martha " 1822, 3, 2
Ann " ----, 7, 22
1818, 12, 3. Hannah m Barnabas HUNT
----, --, --. Jehu & Eleanor
Ch: Amos b 1821, 3, 6
Daniel " 1823, 3, 17
1823, 10, 3. Even d bur Clear Creek
1825, 9, 15. Daniel, s Joel & Sarah, Highland Co., O.; m in Clear Creek MH, Priscilla HUSSEY, dt Christopher & Sarah, Highland Co., O.
1827, 7, 16. Ann m Caleb HARVEY
1840, 2, 23. Sarah d bur Clear Creek
1840, 10, 28. Isaac, s Amos & Phebe, Clinton Co., O.; m in East Fork MH, Mary Jane HAWKINS, dt John & Hannah, Clinton Co., O.
Ch: Ellis A. b 1842, 4, 6
Emily " 1844, 1, 14
Hannah Ann " 1849, 7, 2
1841, 9, 1. Lemuel, s Amos & Phebe, Clinton Co., O.; m in East Fork MH, Hannah HOSKINS dt John & Hannah, Clinton Co., O.
1841, 9, 22. Priscilla m David BALLARD.
----, --, --. Aquilla & Harriett
Ch: Caroline E.b 1847, 11, 27 d 1851, 7,27

LEWIS, Aquilla & Harriett, continued
Ch: Isaac N. b 1849, 5, 28 d 1854, 4,12 bur East Fork
Elijah Fletcher b 1851, 3, 16 " 1854, 4,30 bur East Fork
Charles Evan b 1852, 3, 9 " 1854, 4,30 bur East Fork
Amos T. b 1859, 10, 16

1814, 10, 28. Evan & w, Sarah, & ch, Ann, Amos, Susannah, Abner, Hannah & Jesse, rocf George Creek MM, Va., dtd 1814,8,4
1815, 4, 28. Enoch & s, Jonah, rocf Center MM, dtd 1815,3,4
1819, 6, 12. Jehu & w, Eleanor, & ch, Betsy, Joel, Moses & Aaron, rocf Miami MM, dtd 1819, 5, 26
1821, 12, 5. Nathan rocf Cincinnati MM, dtd 1821,3,29
1822, 6, 8. Nathan & w, Rachel, & ch, Isaiah, Sarah & Martha, gct Cherry Grove MM, Ind.
1823, 1, 11. Abner gct Cherry Grove MM, Ind.
1824, 3, 13. Joel & w, Sarah, rocf Miami MM, dtd 1824,3,25
1825, 7, 9. Daniel rocf Caesars Creek MM, dtd 1825,6,30
1828, 5, 10. Jesse gct Springfield MM
1828, 9, 14. Eleanor dis jH
1828, 9, 14. Mourning dis jH
1829, 2, 14. Jehu dis joining Separatists
1829, 4, 11. Enoch dis jH
1829, 4, 11. Betsey dis disunity
1831, 1, 8. Sarah dis jH
1831, 4, 9. Joel dis jH
1834, 6, 24. Moses dis disunity
1834, 7, 22. Elizabeth dis disunity
1834, 7, 22. Sally dis disunity
1837, 6, 20. Amos gct Caesars Creek MM, to m Patience Jessup
1837, 8, 22. Jonah con mcd
1838, 3, 20. Jonah gct Miami MM
1839, 3, 19. Patience rocf Caesars Creek MM, dtd 1839,1,24
1846, 1, 10. Amos dis mcd
1848, 4, 8. Aquilla con mcd
1848, 7, 8. Lemuel & w, Hannah, & s, John, gct Newberry MM
1848, 8, 12. Harriet & ch, Caroline E., recrq
1852, 10, 9. Amos & Nancy recrq
1853, 11, 12. Isaac dis
1856, 4, 12. Asenath Kochler (form Lewis) dis mcd
1865, 4, 8. Isaac recrq
1877, 11, 10. Hannah gct Green Plain MM
1877, 11, 10. Ellis A. gct Wilmington MM
1883, 5, 12. Emma C. recrq
1883, 5, 12. William R. recrq
1886, 11, 13. Isaac & Mary Jane gct Wilmington MM, O.
1891, 5, 9. Catharine rocf Wilmington MM
1893, 2, 11. Kate dropped from mbrp
1894, 8, 11. William R. gct Center MM

LIDDELL
1917, 9, 8. Kathren M. recrq

LIEURANCE
1909, 5, 10. Alva recrq

LINDLEY
1868, 9, 12. Miriam (form Newby) con mcd
1869, 4, 10. Mariam gct Honey Creek MM
1885, 7, 11. A. H. & w, Nannie, & ch, Lilian rocf Honey Creek MM, Ia. (old abbreviation for Ind.?)
1890, 7, 12. A. H. dropped from mbrp
1912, 5, 11. Lillian dropped from mbrp

LINKHART
1895, 4, 13. Elizabeth rocf Center MM
1895, 8, 10. John & dt, Cleo C., recrq
1906, 4, 14. John & w, Elizabeth, & dt, Cleo, gct Ogden Mtg

LINTON
1893, 4, 8. William recrq
1894, 7, 14. Willie dropped from mbrp

LIVEZEY
1868, 6, 13. Wm. B. [Livzey] rocf Chesterfield MM, dtd 1868,4,29
1869, 6, 12. William [Livezy] con mcd
1873, 5, 10. Mary H. S. recrq
1885, 6, 13. Anna dropped from mbrp
1890, 7, 12. Nellie dropped from mbrp
1912, 5, 11. Bertha & Mary dropped from mbrp

LOVINGFOSS
1874, 6, 13. Louis [Lovingpass] recrq
1874, 6, 13. William [Lovingpass] recrq
1874, 6, 13. Alice [Lovingpass] recrq
1878, 1, 12. William dropped from mbrp
1878, 1, 12. Lewis dropped from mbrp
1878, 1, 12. Jennie dropped from mbrp
1878, 1, 12. Alice dropped from mbrp

LOWMAN
1866, 9, 8. Ellen recrq
1869, 8, 14. Ellen Ladd (form Lowman) con mcd

LUCA
----, --, --. Elizabeth d

LUCK
1929, 10, 30. Charles M. m Alice CONNELL
1931, 9, 29. Martin m Catharine CONNELL
1831, 4, 8. Charles recrq
1933, 2, 9. Martin recrq

LUPTON
1824, 1, 28. William, s William, Highland Co., O.; m in East Fork MH, Anna NORDYKE, dt Israel & Mary, Clinton Co., O.

LUPTON, William & Anna, continued
Ch: Mary
Emeline b 1825, 5, 4
Hezekiah " 1827, 9, 9 d 1828, 7,16 bur East Fork
Elizabeth b 1829, 5, 22
Israel " 1831, 11, 6
Rebecca " 1834, 1, 9
William
Lewis " 1836, 2, 20

1823, 8, 14. Anna gct Fairfield MM; returned 1824,12,11
1827, 6, 9. William rocf Fairfield MM, dtd 1826,8,26
1842, 9, 20. Wm. & w, Anna, & ch, Mary Emeline, Elizabeth, Israel Nordyke, Rebecca, Maria, William Lewis, Morgan, Elmore & Lydia Ann, gct Salem MM, Ia.
1849, 8, 11. Elizabeth dis jas
1853, 12, 10. Israel dis mcd
1907, 5, 11. Elias & w, Elizabeth, rocf Westfork MM, O.
1926, 1, 9. Elizabeth relrq
1931, 4, 8. Elizabeth dropped from mbrp

LUTTRELL
1912, 12, 14. Clayton & w, Margaret, rocf New Martinsburgh MM, dtd 1912,10,5
1913, 10, 11. O. C. & w, Margaret, relrq

LYNN
1872, 6, 8. Hannah recrq

LYTLE
1885, 3, 14. John recrq
1889, 4, 13. John dropped from mbrp
1889, 6, 8. Albert recrq

McCALL
1925, --, --. Della m Clyde JOHNSON

1909, 2, 13. Anna recrq
1923, 5, 12. Della recrq
1928, 4, 12. Anna gct New Vienna MM
1931, 4, 8. Della dropped from mbrp

McCLAREN
1887, 4, 9. Josie recrq
1887, 4, 9. Roy recrq
1902, 1, 11. Roy [McLaren] relrq

McCLINTON
1873, 5, 10. James D. & Rachel & ch, James M., Kate E. & Edwin M., recrq
1878, 9, 14. James D. [McClintock] relrq
1883, 8, 11. Rachel [McClintock] dropped from mbrp
1883, 8, 11. James N. [McClintock] dropped from mbrp
1883, 8, 11. Edwin M. [McClintock] dropped from mbrp
1883, 8, 11. Nellie T. [McClintock] dropped from mbrp

McCOLGIN
1883, 5, 12. Anna recrq
1883, 5, 12. John recrq
1883, 5, 12. Bell recrq
1885, 6, 13. John dropped from mbrp
1885, 6, 13. Anna dropped from mbrp
1885, 6, 13. Bell dropped from mbrp

McCOY
1867, 2, 9. Harvey W. & ch, Frank Wm. & Mary Idamay, recrq
1867, 2, 9. Jesse E. recrq
1867, 2, 9. Mary W. recrq
1868, 6, 13. Robert C. recrq
1868, 6, 13. Harvey W. relrq
1869, 6, 12. Harvey W. recrq
1872, 9, 14. Harvey W. & w, Mary, & ch, Frank Wm. & Ida May, gct Pipe Creek MM
1872, 12, 14. Robert C. & w, Elizabeth, & ch, gct Pipe Creek MM
1873, 6, 14. Jesse E. gct Pipe Creek MM, Ind.
1885, 3, 14. Philander & w, Rachel, & ch, Samuel, recrq
1894, 7, 14. Filander dropped from mbrp
1894, 7, 14. Rachel dropped from mbrp
1894, 7, 14. Samuel dropped from mbrp
1896, 2, 8. Ruth relrq
1902, 6, 14. Harry P. recrq

McCUNE
1881, 4, 9. Thomas & Margaret recrq
1882, 9, 9. Thomas relrq
1885, 6, 13. Margcrct droppcd from mbrp
1886, 3, 13. Edger recrq
1887, 4, 9. Thomas & Arthur recrq
1889, 2, 9. Maggie recrq
1889, 2, 9. Valeria B. recrq
1889, 2, 9. Clara D. recrq
1889, 4, 9. Edward dropped from mbrp
1893, 2, 11. Thomas dropped from mbrp
1901, 5, 11. Arthur relrq
1903, 2, 14. Thomas recrq

McDANIEL
1843, 5, 23. Elizabeth (form Wright) dis mcd
1846, 7, 11. Lucy (form Wright) dis mcd
1878, 1, 12. Elvira dis jas
1885, 3, 14. Nannie recrq
1896, 12, 12. J. F. recrq
1902, 7, 12. Frank dropped from mbrp
1906, 12, 8. Mary & dt, Reba May, gct Wilmington MM

McDONALD
1886, 10, 9. Martha E. relrq

McFADDEN
1883, 8, 11. Lydia A. dropped from mbrp
1883, 8, 11. Eva dropped from mbrp

McKINNEY
1897, 5, 8. J. H. recrq
1898, 3, 12. Anna & Lucy [McKinsey] recrq
1912, 5, 11. Henry J. [McKenney] dropped from mbrp

McLAREN
1885, 3, 14. Thomas recrq
1885, 3, 14. Margaret recrq
1885, 3, 14. Susan recrq
1885, 3, 14. Sarah recrq
1885, 3, 14. Margaret Bell recrq
1887, 4, 9. Roy recrq

McMULLEN
1841, 8, 24. Elizabeth (form Bailey) dis mcd

McNICKOL
1887, 4, 9. John recrq
1899, 1, 14. John [McNicol] dropped from mbrp

McPHERSON
1832, 2, 2. Joseph, s Daniel & Mary, Highland Co., O.; m in Clear Creek MH, Ruth CAREY, dt John & Margaret, Highland Co.,O.
Ch: Mary
Margaret b 1848, 12, 14

1832, 3, 20. Ruth gct Fairfield MM
1833, 4, 23. Joseph & w, Ruth, roc
1834, 4, 22. Joseph & w, Ruth, gct Newberry MM
1842, 8, 23. Joseph & w, Ruth, & s, Daniel, rocf Newberry MM, dtd 1842,7,18
1854, 3, 11. Joseph & w, Ruth, & ch, Daniel & Mary Margarett, gct Back Creek MM, Ind.
1884, 8, 9. Annie M. rocf Fairfield MM
1884, 8, 9. Rachel rocf Fairfield MM
1897, 9, 11. Anna gct Marion MM, Ind.

McVEY
1869, 4, 10. Edmond recrq
1869, 4, 10. Martha E. recrq
1891, 1, 10. Alfred rocf Fairfield MM, O., dtd 1890,12,20
1895, 12, 14. Josephine Barrett rocf Hopewell MM
1895, 12, 14. Cora Barrett rocf Hopewell MM
1896, 1, 11. Isaac Newman rocf Fairfield MM
1896, 1, 11. Alva rocf Fairfield MM
1898, 7, 9. Newman I. & w & s, Harold, gct Fairfield MM
1898, 11, 12. Ed dropped from mbrp
1900, 1, 13. Alva & w, Cora, & dt, Mildred, gct Fairfield MM
1902, 6, 14. Elijah recrq
1909, 5, 10. Alfred relrq
1916, 6, 10. Leroy & w, Adelia, & ch, Ada Alice, James Carl, Bessie M., Wm. H., Thelma & Harold, rocf Center MM, dtd 1916,5,17

McWILLIAMS
1869, 4, 10. John recrq
1874, 3, 14. John dis

MAGOON
1864, 1, 9. Asenath, dt Alfred, recrq
1873, 1, 11. Asenath Edwards (form Magoon dis mcd

MALONE
1871, 2, 15. Alice E. m Pleasant M. TERRELL

1865, 4, 8. John & w, Mary A., & ch, P. Harrison, Edwin T. James T., John W., Wm. L. & Henry G., rocf Newberry MM, dtd 1865,4,17
1865, 4, 8. Alice E. rocf Newberry MM, dtd 1865,4,17
1868, 3, 14. Hezekiah rocf Newberry MM, dtd 1868,3,23
1868, 3, 14. Chas. B. rocf Newberry MM, dtd 1868,3,23
1877, 12, 8. Levi H. relrq
1882, 7, 8. Chas. O. & s, Harrison, gct Salem MM, O.
1882, 7, 8. James S. gct Salem MM
1886, 3, 13. Mary A. gct Cleveland MM, O.
1886, 3, 13. Edwin T. relrq
1886, 9, 11. Wm. L. relrq
1890, 11, 8. Emma & ch, May & Bessie, recrq
1892, 6, 11. H. P. & w, Emma, & ch, May & Bessie, gct Wilmington MM
1914, 11, 14. Mildred Bowder dropped from mbrp

MALOTT
1826, 1, 9. Elsa Stewart dropped from mbrp

MANLOVE
1816, 10, 12. Jane (form Hodgson) con mcd
1830, 12, 11. Rachel & Ann, dt Ann, recrq
1834, 11, 18. Jane & ch, Rachel & Ann, gct Sugar River MM, Ind.

MANSFIELD
1869, 6, 12. Henry recrq

MASON
1896, 6, 13. Wm. P. recrq
1901, 8, 10. Samuel P. dropped from mbrp
1901, 9, 14. Sarah gc

MASSEY
1867, 2, 9. William recrq
1867, 10, 12. Mary recrq
1867, 12, 14. Wm. A., James E. & Chas. A., ch Wm., recrq
1877, 11, 8. William [Massa] dis
1878, 3, 9. Wm. dis disunity
1878, 3, 9. Charles dis
1879, 3, 18. Edwin dis

MAST
1924, 7, 19. J. B. m Margaret LARKIN

1928, 4, 12. Margaret Larkin relrq

MATTHEWS
1841, 7, 20. Eliza (form Nordyke) dis mcd
1887, 2, 12. Clara recrq
1887, 2, 12. Ollie recrq
1902, 6, 14. Oscar recrq
1902, 6, 14. Lucy & s, Fred C., recrq

MAYLOR
1883, 2, 10. Wm. recrq
1883, 2, 10. Mattie recrq

MENDENHALL
1820, 2, 12. Cert rec for Richard & w, Polly, & ch, Alexander, Peter, Charity, Temple, Ezekiel, Lydia, Irena, Moses, James Clemmons & John Milton, from Springfield MM, N. C., dtd 1819,9,8, endorsed to Fall Creek MM

MENTE
1898, 8, 13. William dropped from mbrp

MERCER
1929, 1, 12. Opal m Walter MURRAY

1889, 3, 9. Jason & w, Mary, rocf Fairfield MM, O., dtd 1889,2,16 (w dec)
1890, 3, 8. Jane recrq
1890, 7, 12. Jason dropped from mbrp
1893, 11, 11. Theodore rocf Fairfield MM
1913, 6, 14. Theodore & w & dt, Anna, gct Fairfield MM
1928, 4, 12. Opal rocf Fairview MM
1928, 4, 12. Jeanette & Janie recrq
1929, 4, 11. Hilda & Catharine, minors, recrq

MICHAEL
1856, 7, 12. Sarah Ann recrq
1857, 6, 13. Sarah Ann Beary (form Michael) dis mcd
1866, 8, 11. Lucinda recrq
1870, 11, 12. Lucinda Antrim (form Michael) con mcd
1907, 7, 13. Alva & Alma [Michaels] recrq

MIDDLETON
1822, 1, 17. Hudson, s Hudson & Deborah, Highland Co., O.; m in Clear Creek MH, Rachel KENWORTHY, dt Elisha & Mary, Highland Co., O.

1825, 10, 8. Rachel & s, Ira, gct White Lick MM, Ind.

MIERS
1877, 3, 11. Henry recrq
1878, 1, 12. Henry [Miars] dropped from mbrp

MILLARD
1875, 3, 13. Elizabeth relrq

MILLER
1859, 1, 8. Zadock & s, John E., rocf Newberry MM, dtd 1858,12,20
1859, 1, 8. Emily H. rocf Fairfield MM, dtd 1858,12,18
1865, 5, 13. Samuel & w, Charity, & ch, Martha Jane, rocf Newberry MM, dtd 1865,4,17
1868, 1, 11. Levi & w, Mariah, & ch, James Madison, Francis, Austin, Mariah B. & Henry Clay, rocf Newberry MM, dtd 1867,10, 21
1869, 5, 8. Frances Turpin (form Miller) con mcd
1869, 6, 12. James con mcd
1871, 4, 8. Lizzie recrq
1871, 7, 8. Martha rocf Newberry MM, dtd 1871,5,22
1877, 11, 10. James M. & w, Elizabeth, & s, Claud, gct Springfield MM
1884, 6, 14. Ruth A. rocf Newberry MM, O.
1887, 4, 9. Henry gct Cincinnati MM
1889, 9, 14. J. Everett relrq
1892, 5, 14. Zadok & w, Emily, & ch, Flora J., Newton, Ralph & Alice, gct Whittier MM, Calif.
1892, 5, 14. Isaac N. gct Whittier MM, Calif.
1892, 5, 14. Alice gct Whittier MM, Calif.
1893, 2, 11. Austin dropped from mbrp
1903, 4, 11. Claud rocf Wilmington MM
1905, 4, 8. Claud gct Wilmington MM
1906, 11, 8. Memorial for Ruth, dec

MILLS
1813, 2, 25. Joseph & w, Hannah, & ch, Sarah, John & Joseph, rocf Deep River MM, N. C., dtd 1812,9,7, endorsed by White Water MM, Ind.
1813, 2, 25. Jonathan & w, Sarah, & ch, John & Samuel, rocf Deep River MM, N. C., dtd 1812,9,7, endorsed by White Water MM, Ind.
1813, 2, 25. Hezekiah rocf Deep River MM, N. C., dtd 1812,9,7, endorsed by White Water MM, Ind.
1814, 2, 24. Hezekiah gct White Water MM, Ind.
1814, 8, 26. Jonathan & w, Sarah, & ch, John, Samuel & Anna, gct White Water MM, Ind.
1815, 2, 24. Sarah Moon (form Mills) con mcd
1867, 5, 11. Delila (form Davis) con mcd
1866, 8, 10. Delila gct Newberry MM
1898, 5, 14. Myrtle Rayburn gct Dover MM

MILNER
1850, 8, 10. Susannah recrq
1850, 10, 12. Ruth, Wm. & Jesse, ch Susannah, recrq
1851, 4, 12. Joseph recrq
1854, 8, 12. Priscilla Ann, dt Susanna, recrq
1854, 11, 11. Susannah & ch, Ruth, Wm. Jesse & Priscilla Ann, gct Back Creek MM, Ind.

MILNER, continued
1858, 4, 14. Joseph [Millner] gct Oak Ridge MM, Ind.
1862, 11, 8. Susanna & ch, Wm. T., Jesse J. & Priscilla Ann, rocf Back Creek MM, Ind.
1866, 7, 14. Susannah & ch, Priscilla A., gct Cottonwood MM
1867, 10, 12. Jesse J. con mcd
1868, 3, 14. Jesse J. gct Oak Ridge MM, Ind.
1868, 12, 12. Wm. G. gct Cottonwood MM

MINNICK
1931, 4, 8. Louise Cox dropped from mbrp

MOBERLY
1923, 10, 25. Roy m Rebecca WILLIAMS
1837, 7, 18. Lydia (form Hussey) dis mcd

MOCKLENPAGE
1882, 1, 14. August W. recrq
1883, 5, 12. Anna [Mochlenpage] recrq

MOON
----, --, --. Daniel & Ruth
Ch: Jean b 1810, 2, 10
Zimri " 1812, 11, 12
1813, 8, 4. William, s Daniel & Ruth, Clinton Co., O.; m in East Fork MH, Ann RATCLIFF, dt Amos & Eleanor, Clinton Co., O.
Ch: Amos b 1814, 5, 13
Daniel " 1815, 7, 7
1819, 4, 15. Jeremiah, s Daniel & Ruth, Clinton Co., O.; m in Clear Creek MH, Rachel NIXON, dt George & Mary HODGSON, Highland Co., O.
Ch: Mary b 1820, 3, 26
Geo. Hodgson " 1823, 4, 18
1832, 11, 29. Joseph H., s William & Jane, Clinton Co., O.; m in Clear Creek MH, Priscilla COFFIN, dt David & Mary, Highland Co., O.
1837, 2, 2. John, s William & Ann, Clinton Co., O.; m in Clear Creek MH, Ursula PIKE, dt Wm. & Lucy, Highland Co., O.

1815, 2, 24. Sarah (form Mills) con mcd
1816, 4, 13. Henry recrq
1819, 8, 14. Jeremiah rocf Newberry MM, dtd 1819,7,29
1826, 3, 11. Jeremiah & w, Rachel, & ch, Mary & Geo. H., gct Newberry MM
1830, 5, 8. Robert Carey gct Newberry MM, to m Susannah Moon
1833, 5, 21. Priscilla gct Newberry MM
1833, 10, 22. Isaac Carey gct Newberry MM, to m Elizabeth Moon
1835, 10, 20. John Carey Jr. gct Newberry MM, to m Eliza Moon
1837, 5, 23. Ursula gct Newberry MM
1839, 10, 22. Huldah (form Pike) con mcd
1840, 2, 18. Huldah gct Newberry MM

MOORE
1845, 6, 14. Sarah Emily rocf Springfield MM, dtd 1845,5,13
1847, 2, 17. Sarah Emily gct Springfield MM
1869, 4, 10. John B. recrq
1869, 4, 10. Nancy recrq
1869, 4, 10. Mary recrq
1869, 4, 10. Geo. recrq
1869, 4, 10. Grafton recrq
1869, 4, 10. Caroline recrq
1869, 4, 10. John W. recrq
1869, 4, 10. Douglas recrq
1869, 4, 10. Flavus J. recrq
1872, 9, 14. George W. rpd mcd; retained mbrp
1873, 3, 8. Anna recrq
1874, 1, 10. Lydia recrq
1876, 3, 11. John W. dis disunity
1877, 3, 11. Samuel J. & Salina recrq
1883, 5, 12. Jessie recrq
1884, 3, 8. Ellen recrq
1885, 6, 13. Jesse dropped from mbrp
1887, 4, 9. Austin recrq
1887, 4, 9. Charles recrq
1888, 7, 14. Flavius J. dropped from mbrp
1888, 7, 14. John B. dropped from mbrp
1889, 5, 11. Anna recrq
1891, 4, 11. Austin dropped from mbrp
1893, 5, 13. Emma recrq
1893, 5, 13. Jane recrq
1896, 4, 11. Stanley recrq
1898, 11, 12. Graftian A. dropped from mbrp
1898, 11, 12. Samuel J. dropped from mbrp
1898, 11, 12. Salina dropped from mbrp
1898, 11, 12. Meret Elmore dropped from mbrp
1902, 4, 12. Isaac & Eliza A. recrq
1902, 6, 14. Oceanus C. recrq
1902, 6, 14. Earl F. recrq
1904, 4, 9. Blanch Ida recrq
1906, 7, 14. John Benjamin, Samuel Ayers, Robert Wain & Clara Marcilla, ch Samuel & Emma, recrq
1909, 4, 10. John recrq
1910, 7, 9. Gladys recrq
1912, 5, 11. John dropped from mbrp
1916, 9, 9. Isaac dropped from mbrp

MOORMAN
1817, 9, 13. Cert rec for Archilus from Back Creek MM, N. C., dtd 1816,9,28, endorsed to New Garden MM, Ind.
1869, 4, 10. Alfred J. recrq
1869, 4, 10. Gilbert recrq
1869, 4, 10. Richard F. recrq
1869, 4, 10. Jane recrq
1869, 4, 10. Mary R. recrq
1869, 4, 10. Nancy J. recrq
1869, 4, 10. Hannah E., minor, recrq
1869, 4, 10. Ariann, minor, recrq
1873, 3, 8. Arianna recrq
1878, 1, 12. Mary Alice gct Center MM, O.
1883, 8, 11. Alfred dropped from mbrp
1883, 8, 11. Mary Rebecca dropped from mbrp

MOORMAN, continued
1883, 8, 11. Nancy J. dropped from mbrp
1883, 8, 11. Hannah dropped from mbrp
1883, 8, 11. Rachel Fisher dropped from mbrp
1888, 6, 9. Nancy [Morman] dropped from mbrp
1888, 6, 9. Rebecca [Morman] dropped from mbrp

MOREY
1855, 8, 11. Margaret (form Nordyke) dis mcd & joining M. E. Ch.
1869, 4, 10. Benjamin F. [Moory] recrq
1869, 4, 10. George A. [Moory] recrq
1871, 8, 12. Daniel B. [Mory] recrq
1871, 9, 9. Sarah J. recrq
1874, 8, 8. Benjamin dis
1878, 1, 12. Daniel B. recrq
1878, 3, 9. Sarah Jane gct Wilmington MM, O.

MORRIS
1883, 8, 11. Jennie B. gct Fairfield MM

MORRISON
1881, 8, 13. Thomas W. & w, Mary A., & ch, Jennie L., Gilbert G., Alson W., Lindley M. & John, rocf Fairfield MM
1885, 6, 13. William, Mary A., Jennie L., Alson W., Lindley M. & John I., gct Fairfield MM
1887, 11, 12. Gilbert dropped from mbrp

MULANE
1901, 6, 8. Martha E. (form Leeka) relrq

MULLENIX
1923, 9, 8. Edna Sanders relrq

MURPHEY
1924, 10, 11. Elva m Glenn STORER

1824, 8, 14. Cynthia (form Wildman) dis mcd
1921, 2, 12. Zola & ch, Truman, Elma & Elva, recrq
1924, 3, 8. Elma rmt Wilbur Woodyard
1931, 4, 8. Truman [Murphy] dropped from mbrp

MURRAY
1929, 1, 12. Walter m Opal MERCER

NELSON
1887, 11, 12. Elizabeth recrq

NEWBY
----, --, --. Demsey & Elizabeth
Ch: Sarah Jane b 1840, 10, 27
John Westly " 1843, 4, 18
William Milton " 1845, 9, 29
Caroline Elizabeth " 1852, 1, 30
1841, 10, 21. Josiah, s William & Sarah, Clinton Co., O.; m in East Fork MH, Mary KENWORTHY, dt Isaac & Mariam, Clinton Co., O.
Ch: Semantha Ellen b 184-, 9, 19
Miriam Elizabeth " 184-, 1, 20
Isaac K. " 1850, 7, 9 d 1852, 9, 3 bur East Fork
Emma Caroline b 1853, 6, 30
William Albert " 1855, 11, 17
1860, 9, 1. Sarah d bur East Fork

1823, 10, 11. Hanuel Hunt gct Fall Creek MM, to m Eleanor Newby
1833, 6, 18. William & w, Sarah, & ch, Elizabeth, Nathan, Josiah, Demcy & Sarah, rocf Fall Creek MM, dtd 1833,5,22
1837, 7, 18. Nathan dis mcd
1840, 11, 24. Dempsy con mcd
1841, 1, 19. Sarah Hockett (form Newby) con mcd
1841, 1, 19. Elizabeth (form Hoskins) con mcd
1865, 12, 9. Jane Nordyke (form Newby) con mcd
1866, 6, 9. Adaline Hussey (form Newby) con mcd
1868, 6, 13. John con mcd
1868, 9, 12. Miriam Lindley (form Newby) con mcd
1869, 4, 10. Dempsy & w, Elizabeth, & dt, Caroline, gct Cottonwood MM, Kans.
1869, 4, 10. Wm. Milton gct Cottonwood MM, Kans.
1869, 4, 10. John W. gct Cottonwood MM
1869, 6, 12. Josiah con mcd
1873, 5, 10. Julia A. recrq
1897, 11, 13. Julia relrq
1912, 5, 11. William dropped from mbrp

NEWELL
1871, 2, 11. Margaret Emily rpd mcd; retained mbrp
1888, 3, 10. Margaret Emeline relrq

NEWLIN
1855, 12, 8. Eli & w, Lydia, & ch, Charles, Wm. & Temple, rocf White Lick MM, Ind., dtd 1855,11,14
1856, 6, 14. Charles gct White Lick MM, Ind.
1857, 1, 10. Ely & w, Lydia, & ch, William & Temple, gct Newberry MM

NEWMAN
1894, 7, 14. Hattie dropped from mbrp

NEWTON
1909, 6, 12. John C. recrq
1912, 5, 11. John dropped from mbrp

NIXON
1802, 11, 5. Rachel, dt Mary, b
1819, 4, 15. Rachel m Jeremiah MOON

1826, 10, 14. Henrietta & Ann P., ch Samuel, rocf Uwchlan MM, Pa., dtd 1825,10,2

NORDYKE
----, --, --. Micajah m Charity ----- d 1854, 6,5 bur East Fork
Ch: Phebe b 1798, 3, 9
Sarah " 1800, 12, 2
Isaac " 1802, 7, 18
Mary " 1804, 11, 27
Ellis " 1807, 7, 7
Henry " 1809, 5, 16
Samuel " 1811, 3, 16
Jesse " 1813, 6, 21
David " 1815, 7, 27
Asa " 1817, 10, 25
Lewis " 1820, 12, 18
Hannah " 1823, 11, 2
1814, 5, 13. Mary d bur East Fork
1817, 1, 1. Phebe m Amos LEWIS
1819, 11, 17. Sarah m Elisha THOMAS
1824, 1, 28. Anna m Wm. LUPTON
1825, 9, 23. Abraham d bur East Fork
----, --, --. Abraham & Henrietta
Ch: Mary Angelina b 1826, 6, 7
Eliza " 1827, 7, 25
Hezekiah " 1829, 2, 1
Morgan Elmore " 1830, 11, 8
Martha Helen " 1832, 10, 21 d 1834,10,19 bur East Fork
Charles A. b 1834, 5, 19
Israel " 1836, 7, 1
1829, 12, 23. Mary m Jonathan HOCKETT
----, --, --. David & Lydia J
Ch: Rhoda Ann b 1838, 9, 20
Joseph Thornburg " 1840, 10, 4
Edward L. " 1843, 10, 7
----, --, --. Henry & Phebe
Ch: Thomas R. b 1839, 11, 20
Aaron B. " 1842, 3, 5
Edith H. " 1846, 1, 8
Isabella A." 1852, 6, 10 d 1862,12,30 bur East Fork
Caroline E.b 1858, 5, 22
1840, 6, 24. Hannah m Stephen PEEBLES
1842, 10, 26. Asa, s Micajah & Charity, Clinton Co., O.; m in East Fork MH, Mary H. JAMES, dt David & Mary, Clinton Co., O.
Ch: Ellen C. b 1843, 10, 4
----, --, --. Lewis & Rachel
Ch: Eli M. b 1848, 10, 28
Susannah B." 1851, 3, 16
Isaac E. " 1853, 7, 14
Alpheus " 1856, 8, 2
Edmund " 1859, 9, 5
Ch: Mary Bell b 1862, --, --
184-, 7, 29. Mary, w Asa, d bur East Fork
1848, 10, 16. Ellen C., dt Asa & Mary, d bur East Fork
----, --, --. Asa & Almedia
Ch: Mary Frances b 1851, 8, 11
Michael " 1855, 1, 25
Edgar M. " 1860, 10, 28
1871, 12, 13. Aaron B., s Henry & Phebe, Clinton Co., O.; m in New Vienna, O., Sarah CONARD, dt Joseph & Rebecca, Clinton Co., O.
1871, 12, 13. Edith H. m James H. TERRELL

1816, 9, 14. Benajah gct Centre MM, to m
1818, 1, 10. Mary Darrow (form Nordyke) dis mcd
1818, 9, 12. Ann rocf Center MM, dtd 1818, 5,16
1820, 4, 8. Hezekiah dis
1825, 4, 19. Abraham Jr. gct Miami MM, to m Henrietta P. Anthony
1826, 3, 11. Hiram dis disunity
1826, 10, 14. Henrietta P. rocf Miami MM, dtd 1825,12,28
1827, 7, 14. Isaac dis mcd
1830, 5, 8. Jesse, s Micajah, rocf Fairfield MM
1830, 5, 8. Jesse, s Micajah, gct Fairfield MM
1831, 3, 12. Elmore dis disunity
1833, 3, 19. Ann rocf Fairfield MM, Ind., dtd 1833,1,17
1834, 6, 24. Jesse rocf Fairfield MM, dtd 1834,4,24
1834, 12, 23. Jesse gct Fairfield MM, to m Levina Hunt
1835, 2, 23. Jesse gct Fairfield MM
1836, 4, 19. Henry gct Springfield MM, to m Phebe Rich
1836, 7, 19. Samuel dis mcd
1837, 5, 23. Phebe rocf Springfield MM, dtd 1837,3,4
1837, 9, 19. David gct White Water MM, Ind., to m Lydia J. Thornburgh
1839, 1, 22. Lydia J. rocf White Water MM, Ind., dtd 1838,11,28
1839, 10, 22. Ellis dis mcd
1839, 10, 22. James con mcd
1841, 7, 20. Eliza Matthews (form Nordyke) dis mcd
1842, 8, 23. Abraham & w, Henrietta P., & ch, Mary, Angeline, Eliza, Hezekiah, Morgan E., Charles A., Henrietta P. Jr. & Abram Andrews, gct Salem MM, Ia.
1842, 10, 18. James dis disunity
1843, 9, 19. Eunice rst on consent of Fairfield MM
1843, 11, 21. Mary Ann Christy (form Nordyke) dis mcd
1846, 2, 14. Cyrus dis disunity
1846, 4, 11. David & w, Lydia, & ch, Rhoda,

NORDYKE, continued
Ann, Joseph T., Edward S. & Sylvanus, gct White Water MM, Ind.
1846, 10, 10. Lewis gct Dover MM, to m Rachel Brackney
1847, 3, 13. Rachel A. rocf Dover MM, dtd 1847,2,18
1849, 5, 12. Eunice gct Centre MM
1850, 2, 9. Ann dis jas
1850, 4, 13. Rebecca dis disunity
1850, 6, 8. Benjamin dis disunity
1850, 9, 14. Asa gct Dover MM, to m Almedia Bailey
1851, 2, 8. Almedia rocf Dover MM, dtd 1851, 1,16
1852, 9, 11. Unice rocf Center MM, dtd 1852, 6,16
1854, 6, 10. Elijah dis disunity
1855, 8, 11. Margaret Morey (form Nordyke) dis mcd & joining M. E. Ch.
1855, 10, 13. Eunice gct Richland MM, Iowa
1861, 10, 12. Thos. R. gct White Water MM, Ind., to m Elizabeth A. Gifford
1863, 6, 13. Benajah recrq
1864, 4, 9. Elizabeth A. & ch, Mary Isabel & Clayton B., rocf White Water MM, Ind., dtd 1864,2,24
1865, 2, 11. Lewis & w, Rachel Ann, & ch, Eli M., Susanna B., Isaac E., Alpheus, Edmund & Mary B., gct Spring Creek MM, Ia.
1865, 12, 9. Jane (form Newby) con mcd
1866, 5, 12. Caroline recrq
1868, 1, 11. Elijah recrq
1869, 4, 10. Sarah J. & s, Frank, gct Cottonwood MM, Kans.
1869, 6, 12. Thomas K. con mcd
1870, 6, 11. Mary A. recrq
1875, 11, 10. Almedia (form Peebles) gct Spring Creek MM, Ia.
1878, 1, 12. Elijah & w, Caroline, gct Wilmington MM, O.
1880, 6, 12. Mary A. relrq
1883, 11, 10. Harriet A. rocf Wilmington MM
1885, 6, 13. Wm. M. dropped from mbrp
1886, 11, 13. Edgar M. & w, Hattie A., & ch, Milton, gct Wilmington MM, O.
1888, 5, 12. Clayton B. gct Whittier MM, Calif
1888, 12, 8. Asa & w, Almedia, gct Wilmington MM
1888, 12, 8. Mary Frances gct Wilmington MM
1890, 3, 8. Thomas R. relrq
1892, 12, 10. Aaron B. & dt, Irene, gct Whittier MM, Calif.
1894, 7, 14. Herbert dropped from mbrp
1894, 7, 14. Inez dropped from mbrp
1897, 1, 9. Loren recrq
1897, 6, 12. Ella S. rocf Newberry MM, O.
1898, 7, 9. Herbert & Inez dropped from mbrp
1902, 7, 12. Loran dropped from mbrp
1916, 12, 9. Ella gct Newberry MM

NUGENT

NUME
1885, 3, 14. John W. & w, Ora, recrq
1889, 4, 13. John dropped from mbrp
1894, 7, 14. Ora dropped from mbrp

OAKLEY
1818, 4, 11. George recrq
1819, 4, 10. George gct Miami MM

O'CONNER
1869, 4, 10. John recrq
1878, 1, 12. John dropped from mbrp

OGBORN
1840, 1, 9. Samuel F. d bur Fairfield

OREN
1843, 10, 13. Lydia Ann, dt Alex & Lydia, b
1844, 1, 24. Ruth m John THOMAS, Jr.

1843, 1, 24. Lydia Jr. & ch, James, Ezekiel, Hannah, John F., Phebe, Alexander & Moses F., rocf Dover MM, dtd 1842,12,15
1843, 1, 24. Rebecca rocf Dover MM, dtd 1842,12,15
1843, 1, 24. Ruth rocf Dover MM, dtd 1842, 12,15
1844, 5, 21. Lydia [Oron] & ch, James, Ezekiel, Hannah, John F., Phebe, Alexander, Moses F. & Lydia Ann, gct Center MM
1845, 11, 8. Rebecca Frazer (form Oren) dis mcd
1872, 3, 9. Rebecca F. dis mcd
1872, 4, 13. Henry G. recrq
1873, 3, 8. Esther B. recrq
1878, 1, 12. Esther gct Dover MM, O.
1878, 1, 12. Henry G. gct Center MM, O.
1878, 8, 10. John & ch, Daniel & John, rocf Centre MM, O.
1878, 8, 10. Chalkley rocf Center MM
1883, 5, 12. Henry G. relrq
1883, 8, 11. John A. dropped from mbrp
1887, 4, 9. John recrq

OSBORNE
1891, 2, 14. Eliza rocf Cincinnati MM

OVERMAN
1816, 7, 13. Sarah (form Baldwin) con mcd
1816, 12, 14. Sarah gct Fall Creek MM
1902, 2, 8. Frank W. rocf Cincinnati MM, dtd 1901,11,10

OVERTAKE
1872, 4, 13. Henry C. & w, Margaret J., & ch, John F. & Lucinda, recrq
1872, 11, 9. Henry C. [Overtakes] & w, Margaret, & ch, John F. & Lucinda E., gct Saline MM

OWENS
1869, 4, 10. Richard recrq
1869, 4, 10. Robert C. recrq

OWENS, continued
1869, 4, 10. Martha recrq
1869, 12, 11. Chasteen, Isaac A. & Cashius E., ch Rob. & Martha, recrq
1871, 3, 11. William recrq
1878, 1, 12. William & Richard dropped from mbrp
1883, 8, 11. Charleen [Owen] dropped from mbrp
1883, 8, 11. Isaac E. [Owen] dropped from mbrp
1883, 8, 11. Cassius E. [Owen] dropped from mbrp
1883, 8, 11. Henry M. [Owen] dropped from mbrp
1883, 8, 11. Sarah S. [Owen] dropped from mbrp
1883, 8, 11. William C. [Owen] dropped from mbrp
1883, 10, 13. Robert C. [Owen] dropped from mbrp

OZBURN
1814, 3, 2. Mary [Ozbun] m David BALLARD

1813, 6, 24. Daniel & w, Mourning, & ch, Exum, rocf Centre MM, N. C., dtd 1812,4,28 endorsed by Fairfield MM
1814, 9, 23. John rocf Center MM, N. C., dtd 1812,9,19, endorsed by Miami MM
1814, 9, 23. Isabel rocf Springfield MM, N. C., dtd 1812,9,5, endorsed by Miami MM
1816, 1, 13. Jonathan [Ozburn] & w, Isabella, & s, Elwood, gct New Garden MM, Ind.
1816, 12, 12. John & w, Sarah, & ch, Susanna, John & Elizabeth, gct New Garden MM, Ind.
1818, 5, 9. Daniel & w, Mourning, & ch, John & Asenath, gct New Garden MM, Ind.
1840, 1, 21. Samuel & w, Eliza B., & s, Henry M., rocf White Water MM, Ind., dtd 1839,11, 22
1841, 6, 22. Eliza B. & ch, Henry, Marshall & Isaac Samuel, gct Springfield MM

PAGE
1912, 5, 11. Anna Mochlen dropped from mbrp

PAINTER
1820, 8, 17. Thomas, s David & Martha, Green Co., O.; m in Clear Creek MH, Mary WILLIAMS, dt William & Phebe, Highland Co.,O.

1820, 10, 14. Mary gct Centre MM

PARIS
1869, 6, 12. Sarah recrq
1876, 4, 8. Lida recrq

PEARL
1871, 3, 11. Edward recrq
1887, 11, 12. Edwin dropped from mbrp

PEARSON
1814, 6, 24. Jonathan & William [Pierson] rocf Contentney MM, N. C., dtd 1814,2,12 endorsed by Fairfield MM
1814, 11, 25. Jonathan gct Darby Creek MM, O.
1814, 11, 25. William gct Darby MM, O.
1871, 11, 11. George & w, Sarah T. H., recrq
1872, 6, 8. George & w, Sarah T. C., relrq

PEEBLES
1840, 6, 24. Stephen, s Stephen & Sarah, Warren Co., O.; m in East Fork MH, Hannah NORDYKE, dt Micajah & Charity, Clinton Co. O.

1840, 12, 22. Hannah gct Springborough MM
1874, 1, 10. Almedia rocf Chesterfield MM, dtd 1873,12,22

PEELLE
1887, 1, 8. Jesse & w, Margaretta, & ch, Bertha, Clara S. & William Ruskin, rocf Marysville MM
1893, 9, 19. Jesse & w, Margeretta, & ch, Clara S. & Wm. Ruskin, gct Blue Island MM, Ill.
1893, 9, 19. Bertha gct Blue Island MM, Ill.

PEITSMYER
1858, 9, 16. Charles, s Christian & Louisa, Highland Co., O.; m in Clear Creek MH, Gulielma M. SANDERS, dt Thomas & Sarah, Highland Co., O.

PEMBERTON
1894, 3, 10. Clara rocf Newberry MM
1895, 8, 10. Walter recrq

PENCE
1925, 8, 29. Glenn m Mildred WRIGHT

1927, 7, 21. Mildred Wright dropped from mbrp

PENN
1890, 2, 8. Louie R. relrq

PERKINS
1814, 9, 23. Elizabeth rocf New Garden MM, dtd 1813,12,25

PERRIN
1896, 12, 12. Mary recrq
1902, 4, 12. Frank recrq
1905, 7, 8. Verna recrq
1914, 3, 14. Elmer rocf Fairview MM
1926, 1, 9. Frank & Verna relrq

PIDGEON
1864, 6, 11. Charles [Pigeon] & w, Catharine, & ch, Louise M., Chas. A., Henry H. & Cornelia C., rocf Dover MM, dtd 1864,5,19
1864, 6, 11. Julia A. [Pigeon] rocf Dover MM dtd 1864,5,19

PIDGEON, continued
1864, 7, 9. Mary [Pigeon] rocf Dover MM, dtd 1864,6,16
1865, 3, 11. Mary Camack (form Pidgon] con mcd
1866, 3, 10. Louisa Starbuck (form Pidgeon) con mcd
1869, 4, 10. Charles & w, Catharine, & ch, Cornelia & Henry, gct Dover MM, O.
1869, 4, 10. Julia gct Dover MM, O.
1869, 4, 10. Chas. B. recrq
1869, 5, 8. Addison [Pigeon], s Chas., gct Dover MM
1885, 4, 11. Chas. & Elizabeth relrq

PIERCE
1818, 11, 14. William rocf Deep River MM, N.C. dtd 1814,10,3, endorsed by White Water MM, Ind.
1826, 10, 14. Charity recrq
1835, 11, 24. Moses [Pearce] recrq
1837, 11, 21. William & w, Charity, gct Cherry Grove MM, Ind.
1837, 11, 21. Moses M. gct Cherry Grove MM, Ind.
1883, 12, 18. Matilda gct Oak Run MM, Ind.

PIKE
1812, 12, 8. John, s Wm. & Phebe, b
1812, 12, 15. Phebe d bur Clear Creek
----, --, --. William m Lucy ----- d 1839,6,16 bur Clear Creek
Ch: James b 1814, 11, 5
Huldy " 1817, 6, 16
Ursula " 1819, 4, 4
Levi " 1820, 5, 27
Lydia " 1822, 8, 31
Mary " 1824, 10, 1
Ann " 1826, 5, 9
Hannah " 1828, 7, 22
Samuel " 1830, 7, 29
William " 1834, 3, 16
Eli " 1836, 9, 3
1818, 8, 31. Abigail d bur Clear Creek
1837, 2, 2. Ursula m John MOON
1840, 7, 2. Lydia m Levi HOCKETT
----, --, --. Samuel & Lydia
Ch: Harriet Ellen b 1856, 2, 26
Martha Isodre " 1857, 12, 1
Marietta " 1860, 1, 6
Ida May " 1863, 6, 12 d 1864, 3,30 bur Clear Creek
Carrie b 1865, 3, 18

1814, 1, 27. William gct Fairfield MM, to m
1814, 5, 27. Lucy rocf Fairfield MM, dtd 1814,4,30
1819, 8, 14. Tristram, s Wm., gct White Water MM, Ind.
1821, 4, 14. Tristram rocf White Water MM, Ind., dtd 1820,12,30
1824, 4, 10. Tristram dis disunity
1827, 4, 14. Hannah rocf Lees Creek MM, dtd 1826,11,8, endorsed by Fairfield MM
1828, 4, 12. Hannah gct Fairfield MM
1830, 3, 13. John dis mcd
1839, 6, 18. Levi dis disunity
1839, 10, 22. Huldah Moon (form Pike) con mcd
1841, 1, 19. William gct Walnut Ridge MM, Ind., to m Phebe Coffin
1841, 6, 22. Phebe rocf Walnut Ridge MM, Ind.
1841, 10, 19. Wm. & w, Phebe, & ch, Mary Ann, Hannah, Samuel, William & Eli, gct Walnut Ridge MM, Ind.
1843, 4, 18. James gct Newberry MM
1843, 4, 18. James gct Newberry MM
1858, 5, 8. Samuel & w, Lydia, & ch, Harriett Ellen & Martha Isadore, rocf Newberry MM, dtd 1858,4,19
1894, 7, 14. Samuel & fam dropped from mbrp

PINKERTON
1890, 3, 8. Richard P., Ruth A. & Charlotte recrq
1893, 2, 11. Albert dropped from mbrp

PITSER
1881, 4, 9. William recrq
1884, 6, 14. Wm. [Pitzer] relrq

PITSMYER
1858, 12, 11. Gulielma gct Fairfield MM
1868, 6, 13. Edward [Pietmier] rocf Fairfield MM, dtd 1868,5,16
1869, 9, 11. Edward [Pietsmire] gct WD MM; this cert was returned at Edward's rq & a sojourn cert granted

POLK
1862, 9, 13. Julia rocf Fairfield MM, dtd 1862,7,19
1896, 4, 11. Eva recrq

POND
1887, 2, 12. Sylvester recrq

POPE
1818, 2, 10. Samuel d bur Clear Creek
1824, 1, 23. Nathaniel d bur Clear Creek

1815, 4, 28. John dis disunity
1818, 12, 12. Nathaniel dis disunity

POSTGATE
1829, 9, 12. Charles rocf Lees Creek MM, dtd 1829,4,18
1830, 10, 14. Charles dis disunity
1831, 5, 14. Anna dis disunity
1846, 1, 10. Mary Ann Woodmansee (form Postgate) dis mcd
1850, 8, 10. Martha [Posegate] dis joining M. E. Ch.
1858, 9, 11. Isaac N. dis joining Baptist Ch.

POWELL
1869, 6, 12. Jacob, minor in care of Josiah Hockett, rocf Oak Ridge MM, Ind.
1875, 12, 11. Jacob gct Oak Ridge MM, Ind. with Josiah Hockett & w

POWERS
1877, 3, 10. Katie, minor in care of Isaac & Mary J. Lewis, recrq

PRATHER
1853, 11, 12. Rebecca (form Sanders) dis mcd

PRESTON
1904, 4, 9. Jennie recrq
1916, 9, 9. Jennie dropped from mbrp

PRICE
1871, 3, 11. Julia recrq
1873, 5, 10. John recrq
1876, 7, 8. Clara Jane, dt Gideon & Julia, recrq
1877, 4, 14. Melissa & Elijah recrq
1877, 11, 10. John dis disunity
1887, 11, 12. Elijah & Melissa gct Springfield MM

PRIEST
1909, 2, 13. Edith recrq

PUCKETT
1814, 7, 29. Mary rocf Fall Creek MM, dtd 1814,7,23
1816, 3, 19. Elizabeth Beals (form Pucket) con mcd
1816, 4, 13. James recrq
1817, 5, 10. Joseph & ch, Tirey, Welcome, Benjamin & Micajah, gct Newberry MM
1877, 6, 9. Taylor & w, Jane, & dt, Mary, rocf Cherry Grove MM, Ind., dtd 1877,5,12
1878, 8, 10. Taylor & w, Jane, & dt, Mary, gct Fairfield MM

PULSE
1881, 4, 9. Bell recrq
1884, 6, 8. Belle Kneadler (form Pulse) relrq

PURDY
1897, 6, 12. Hugh [Purdie] recrq
1920, 4, 10. Anna, Grace & Helen gct Leesburg MM, O.

PUSEY
1813, 4, 1. Lydia m Moses FRAZIER
1814, 11, 3. Margaret m Wm. STANTON
1832, 7, 9. Mary d bur Clear Creek

1813, 9, 23. Nathan gct Westland MM, Pa.
1814, 5, 24. Mary Jr. dis
1815, 1, 27. Joel gct Centre MM
1816, 10, 12. Mary & s, Wm., gct Westland MM, Pa.
1816, 10, 12. George, s Mary, gct Hopewell MM, Va.

PYLE
1872, 6, 8. David S. & w, Nancy F., & ch, Tamar Anna, Sarah Malinda, Esther & Rachel, rocf Toledo MM, Kans., dtd 1872,4,27
1873, 4, 12. David S. & w, Nancy F., & ch, Sarah, Malinda, Esther & Rachel, gct Springfield MM, O.
1873, 4, 12. Tamar Anna gct Springfield MM,O.

QUIGLEY
1889, 2, 9. Michael recrq
1894, 1, 13. Michael relrq

RAMBO
1871, 3, 11. Benjamin [Rumbo] recrq
1871, 3, 11. Jane [Rumbo] recrq
1871, 3, 11. Robert [Rumbo] recrq
1871, 4, 8. Isaac [Rumbo] & w, Deborah Rachel, & ch, Jane M., recrq
1873, 9, 13. Jane Rhonimus (form Rambo) con mcd
1878, 3, 9. Isaac dis disunity
1883, 2, 10. William recrq
1887, 4, 9. Isaac recrq
1893, 2, 11. Herman dropped from mbrp
1893, 2, 11. Louis dropped from mbrp
1895, 5, 11. Tillie recrq
1897, 1, 9. Monte & Ruth recrq
1898, 4, 9. Monte & Ruth dropped from mbrp
1898, 11, 12. Tillie dropped from mbrp
1902, 6, 14. William recrq
1903, 2, 14. Ada recrq
1908, 1, 11. Wm. & w gct Newberry MM, O.
1912, 5, 11. Isaac dropped from mbrp

RATCHFORD
1914, 8, 8. Joseph recrq
1926, 1, 9. Joseph [Rachford] dropped from mbrp

1914, 8, 8. Joseph recrq

RATCLIFF
1808, 3, 30. Thomas, s Amos & Elenor, b
1813, 8, 4. Ann m Wm. MOON

1813, 10, 28. Sarah Smith (form Ratcliff) con mcd
1813, 10, 28. Elizabeth Gardner (form Ratcliff) con mcd
1815, 6, 23. Edom Jr. con mcd
1817, 5, 10. Amos & w, Eleanor, & ch, John, Abner, Elizabeth, Amos, Moses & Thomas, gct Newberry MM
1817, 11, 8. Abner & w, Sarah, & ch, Ann, John, Margaret, Dorcas, Abner, Isaac, Sarah, Thomas & Jesse, gct Newberry MM
1820, 9, 9. John dis mcd
1820, 9, 9. Jacob con mcd
1822, 1, 12. Rachel Gardner (form Ratcliff)

RATCLIFF, continued
dis mcd
1823, 4, 12. Jacob or Isaiah (both given on separate records) gct Newberry MM
1823, 4, 12. Edom & w, Rachel, & ch, Joel, Margaret, Thomas, Jesse & Ann, gct Newberry MM
1823, 4, 12. Sarah gct Newberry MM
1832, 4, 24. Edom gct Newberry MM

RAYBURN
1883, 5, 12. Lydia recrq
1883, 5, 12. Marley recrq
1883, 5, 12. Wm. C. recrq
1889, 2, 9. Thomas W. recrq
1889, 2, 9. Emeline recrq
1889, 2, 9. Myrtie recrq
1890, 4, 12. May recrq
1901, 6, 8. Nellie recrq
1901, 7, 13. William dropped from mbrp
1917, 4, 14. Wm. C. recrq

REAMS
1852, 9, 11. Lettice rocf Fairfield MM, dtd 1852,6,19
1878, 1, 12. Lettice gct Hopewell MM., O.

REED
1889, 7, 13. Myrtle B. recrq
1894, 7, 14. Belle dropped from mbrp

REES
1832, 5, 2. Thomas, s James & Jane, Clinton Co., O.; m in East Fork MH, Esther STEPHENS dt Gideon & Mary, Highland Co., O.
Ch: Zeno b 1833, 2, 14
Caroline " 1834, 9, 2
Elmore " 1844, 1, 11

1819, 5, 8. Margaret [Ruse] (form Cashatt) con mcd
1821, 11, 10. Rachel [Reese] (form Cashatt) dis mcd
1822, 3, 9. Margaret [Ruse] gct Newberry MM
1832, 3, 20. Thomas rocf Fairfield MM, dtd 1832,2,23
1846, 11, 14. Thomas & w, Hester, & ch, Zeno, Caroline & Elmore, gct Westfield MM

RENN
1873, 5, 10. Charles A. recrq
1878, 1, 12. Charles dropped from mbrp

RHODES
1823, 1, 11. Lydia rocf Short Creek MM, O., dtd 1822,11,19
1826, 11, 11. Lydia gct Short Creek MM, O.
1928, 4, 12. Clarence [Roads] & w, Faye, & ch, Rendell & Dorothy, recrq

RHONIMUS
1873, 9, 13. Jane (form Rambo) con mcd
1878, 1, 12. Jane dropped from mbrp

RHOTEN
1904, 12, 10. Maud Edwards dropped from mbrp

RICH
1871, 7, 8. Thomas rocf Springfield MM, dtd 1871,6,17

RICHARDSON
1876, 6, 10. John W. & ch, Ollie & Mary C., rocf Center MM, O., dtd 1876,5,17
1878, 1, 12. John C. dropped from mbrp
1885, 3, 14. E. M. recrq
1886, 3, 13. Charity B. recrq
1889, 12, 14. Emmit dis disunity
1894, 7, 14. Minnie dropped from mbrp
1894, 7, 14. Libbie dropped from mbrp

RICHMOND
1871, 3, 11. Sarah A. recrq
1873, 5, 10. Sarah Blair (form Richmond) rpd mcd; dropped from mbrp

RIDDLE
1903, 7, 11. James recrq

RIDGEWAY
1845, 1, 11. Elizabeth (form Sanders) con mcd
1885, 3, 14. Richard & w, Mary McCoy, recrq
1915, 2, 13. Martha [Ridgway] dropped from mbrp
1915, 2, 13. Richard [Ridgway] & w, Mary, & ch, Grace, Elizabeth, Robert, Wilbur, Joseph & David H., gct Hopewell MM

ROBBINS
1898, 11, 12. Martha J. dropped from mbrp

ROBERTS
1819, 6, 12. Abel & w, Eleanor, & s, Moses, rocf Flushing MM, dtd 1818,12,25
1821, 12, 8. Abel & w, Eleanor, & s, Moses, gct Fall Creek MM

ROGERS
1885, 3, 14. Wm. A. recrq
1885, 3, 14. Wallace recrq
1885, 3, 14. Walter B. recrq
1885, 3, 14. J. Wesley recrq
1894, 7, 14. Willie dropped from mbrp
1894, 7, 14. Wesley dropped from mbrp
1902, 7, 12. Walace & w dropped from mbrp

ROSS
1894, 3, 10. Frank recrq
1897, 1, 9. David F. & w, Lillie, gct Fairfield MM

ROUTH
1870, 8, 13. Alice (form Underwood) con mcd
1873, 5, 10. Alice relrq

ROWE
1887, 4, 9. Lizzie recrq

ROWE, continued
1893, 2, 11. Lizzie dropped from mbrp
1910, 7, 9. Bessie recrq
1910, 7, 9. Martha rocf Fairfield MM
1914, 3, 14. Mark & w, Bessie, relrq

ROWEN
1874, 4, 11. Mary R. recrq
1878, 1, 12. Mary K. dropped from mbrp

RUDE
1904, 4, 9. Amanda recrq
1905, 1, 14. Joseph & w recrq
1920, 4, 10. Elizabeth Chaney [Rudy] relrq

RUNK
1871, 3, 11. John D. H. recrq
1883, 8, 11. Dorsey F. dropped from mbrp
1885, 3, 14. Clara recrq
1897, 1, 9. Charles relrq

RUSSELL
1874, 6, 13. Mary Jane recrq
1878, 1, 12. Mary dropped from mbrp

SANDERS
----, --, --. Jonathan m Lydia ----- d 1848,10, 2 bur Clear Creek
Ch: Sally b 1808, 2, 23 d 1836, 6, 7 bur Clear Creek
Elizabeth b 1809, 10, 18
Mary " 1811, 6, 13
----, --, --. John m Eleanor ----- d 1822,9,12
Ch: Jesse b 1810, 4, 14 d 1829, 7, 5 bur Clear Creek
Hezekiah b 1812, 8, 8
Addison " 1814, 4, 23 " 1814,12,21 bur Clear Creek
Cyrus b 1817, 9, 28
Richard " 1820, 8, 11
----, --, --. Thomas d 1856,9,9 bur Clear Creek; m Elizabeth -----
Ch: Nathaniel Pope b 1810, 6, 12
Martha " 1812, 9, 15
Milley " 1815, 6, 8
Samuel " 1817, 6, 1
Elizabeth Pope " 1819, 8, 14
John M. " 1823, 11, 1
Rebecca " 1825, 11, 5
Frances C. " 1828, 2, 24
William " 1829, 12, 27 d 1836, 3,20 bur Clear Creek
Thos. Chalkley b 1831, 9, 22 " 1831,12, 6 bur Clear Creek
----, --, --. Jonathan & Lydia
Ch: Gulielma Maria b 1813, 8, 23
Thomas " 1815, 9, 9
Rebecca " 1817, 11, 20
David " 1820, 1, 16
Ch: Bathsheba b 1822, 7, 6
Barclay " 1824, 10, 11
William P. " 1827, 3, 8
Jonathan " 1830, 1, 29
1819, 9, 5. Elizabeth d bur Clear Creek (w Thos. M.)
1822, 1, 14. Gulielma m Eleazar HIATT
1827, 8, 27. Rebecca d bur Lynn Mtg, Randolph Co., Ind.
1831, 8, 9. Elizabeth d bur Clear Creek
1831, 9, 23. Judith d bur Clear Creek (dt Thomas M.)
----, --, --. Thomas & Sarah
Ch: Gulielma Maria b 1834, 11, 16
Mary Caroline " 1836, 4, 20
Sarah Emily " 1838, 2, 9
Hezekiah H." 1840, 5, 23
Ellen " 1842, 11, 17
Lindley M. " 1846, 10, 8 d 1854, 4, 5 bur Clear Creek
1858, 9, 16. Gulielma m Chas. PEITSMYER
1924, 11, 26. Margaret m James E. FORD

1815, 12, 9. Jonathan & w, Lydia, & ch, Sarah, Elizabeth, Mary, Gulyelmy & Thomas, gct Fairfield MM
1816, 8, 10. Samuel gct Fairfield MM
1817, 3, 8. Jonathan & w, Lydia, & ch, Sally Elizabeth Mary Gulielma & Thomas, rocf Fairfield MM, dtd 1817,2,22
1822, 6, 8. Thomas con mcd
1823, 6, 14. Judith rocf Cherry Grove MM, Ind., dtd 1823,2,13
1830, 10, 14. Hezekiah dis jH
1832, 5, 22. Nathaniel dis disunity
1832, 12, 18. Martha Wood (form Sanders) dis mcd
1833, 11, 19. Thomas M. gct White Water MM, Ind., to m Sarah Ham Jr.
1833, 11, 19. Mary Timberlake (form Sanders) con mcd
1834, 6, 24. Sarah rocf White Water MM, Ind., dtd 1834,1,22
1837, 7, 18. Gulielma Woodmansee (form Sanders) dis mcd
1837, 7, 17. Milly Doggett (form Sanders) dis mcd
1838, 2, 20. Thos. gct Caesars Creek MM
1839, 8, 20. Samuel dis disunity
1841, 5, 18. Cyrus gct Salem MM, Ia.
1845, 1, 11. Elizabeth Ridgeway (form Sanders) con mcd
1845, 8, 9. Richard dis disunity
1846, 9, 12. John M. dis disunity
1846, 11, 14. Cert rec for Thomas & w, Emily, & ch, Deborah Ann, Levi & David, from Center MM, dtd 1845,10,15, endorsed to Fairfield MM
1846, 11, 14. Bathsheba Hubbard (form Sanders) dis mcd

SANDERS, continued
1848, 9, 9. Barclay gct White Lick MM, Ind.
1848, 11, 11. David gct White Lick MM, Ind.

1850, 12, 14. Jonathan Jr. dis joining M. E. Ch.
1852, 9, 11. Jonathan gct Fairfield MM, to m Ruth Huff
1853, 2, 12. Ruth rocf Fairfield MM, dtd 1853,1,15
1853, 11, 12. Rebecca Prather (form Sanders) dis mcd
1868, 5, 9. Jonathan L. recrq
1869, 4, 10. Wm. P. gct Union MM, Mo.
1869, 5, 8. Martha E. recrq
1869, 9, 11. Sarah, Mary, Caroline & Ellen gct White Water MM, Ind.
1869, 10, 9. Elvira recrq
1872, 10, 12. Sarah Sr., Mary C. & Ellen rocf White Water MM, Ind., dtd 1872,8,28
1881, 11, 12. Mary C. & Ellen gct Fairfield MM
1883, 8, 11. Sarah E. gct Fairfield MM
1887, 4, 9. Tennyson recrq
1894, 7, 14. Tennyson dropped from mbrp
1904, 4, 9. Hezekiah H., Martha E., Wilbur & Elma Pearl, gct S. 8th St. Mtg, Richmond, Ind.
1910, 5, 14. Euclid recrq
1914, 4, 11. Edna, Margaret & Ethel recrq

SAUM
1894, 3, 10. Lida Reyburn relrq

SAVAGE
1839, 10, 22. Esther (form Bankson) dis mcd

SCOTT
1926, 1, 9. Martha Griffith dropped from mbrp

SETTLES
1873, 5, 10. Mary recrq
1878, 1, 12. Mary [Settle] dropped from mbrp

SEWELL
1870, 9, 10. Sarah A. rocf Mississinewa MM, dtd 1870,8,17
1873, 11, 8. Sarah Ann relrq

SHAFER
1872, 1, 13. Mary, Ellen & Margaret recrq
1872, 3, 9. Matilda Jane & Rosina, ch Mary, recrq

SHARP
1822, 3, 9. Susanna rocf Providence MM, Pa., dtd 1820,11,21
1877, 3, 11. Eli N. recrq
1885, 3, 14. Samuel & w, Sarah, recrq
1898, 11, 12. Martha J. dropped from mbrp

SHEPHERD
1869, 4, 10. John F. recrq
1869, 12, 11. Wm. L. [Shephard] & w, Sidney E., & dt, Mary Alice, recrq
1883, 2, 10. Martha E. recrq
1888, 7, 14. John [Sheppard] dropped from mbrp
1896, 4, 11. Frank, Sarah L. & Ora [Shephard] recrq
1898, 5, 14. Lucy relrq
1902, 4, 12. Lena & M. Emily [Sheperd] recrq
1903, 2, 14. Eugene recrq
1912, 5, 11. Verne dropped from mbrp

SHERIDAN
1912, 12, 14. Mary Edith rocf Westfork MM, O.

SHOCKLEY
1821, 11, 10. Naomi (form Hodgson) dis mcd
1883, 10, 13. Cora D. relrq

SHOEMAKER
1871, 2, 11. Martha J. rpd mcd; retained mbrp
1873, 5, 10. Flora recrq
1886, 5, 8. Jennie relrq
1899, 1, 14. Fanny & Cora E. dropped from mbrp

SHOOK
1877, 3, 11. Allen recrq
1899, 1, 14. Allen dropped from mbrp

SIMMONS
1868, 3, 14. John C. recrq
1878, 1, 12. Charles [Simons] dropped from mbrp

SINCLAIR
1819, 6, 12. Geo. & w, Martha, rocf Fairfield MM, dtd 1819,5,29
1893, 5, 13. Melvina relrq

SLETHUM
1884, 1, 12. Levi recrq

SLOANAKER
1868, 9, 12. Phebe J. & dt, Cora Ellen, recrq

SMALL
1815, 11, 11. Samuel rocf Fall Creek MM, dtd 1815,9,23
1817, 12, 13. Samuel gct White Water MM, Ind.

SMALLEY
1869, 4, 10. Rachel recrq
1878, 1, 12. Rachel & Eliza Jane dropped from mbrp

SMITH
1813, 10, 28. Sarah (form Ratcliff) con mou
1841, 7, 20. Sarah (form Hussey) dis mcd
1844, 9, 14. Richard Timberlake gct Cincinnati MM, to m Mahala Smith

SMITH, continued
1873, 3, 8. Elmer E. recrq
1873, 3, 8. Marcella W. recrq
1873, 3, 8. Rebecca S. recrq
1877, 11, 8. Hannah L. gct Green Plain MM
1878, 1, 12. Lydia dropped from mbrp
1878, 1, 12. Rebecca S. & ch, Elmer E. & Marcella W., dropped from mbrp
1884, 1, 12. George W. recrq
1884, 3, 8. Clarence & Elizabeth recrq
1884, 7, 12. Levi & Rachel rocf Bloomingdale MM, Ind.
1884, 8, 9. Isaiah & Lindley rocf Fairfield MM
1885, 4, 11. Isaiah relrq
1885, 5, 9. James & w, Catharine F., & ch, David M., Charlie, Laura B., Phebe L. & Henry A., rocf Fairfield MM
1885, 7, 11. Rachel relrq
1885, 12, 12. Clarence dis disunity
1890, 7, 12. Lizzie dropped from mbrp
1901, 8, 10. Levi & w, Lizzie, dropped from mbrp
1902, 6, 14. Leda Diana recrq
1909, 7, 10. Wm. relrq

SMITHSON
1869, 4, 10. Celie recrq
1871, 1, 14. Martha J. recrq
1871, 9, 9. Celia recrq
1875, 3, 13. Martha J. relrq
1896, 11, 14. Alta rocf Fairfield MM
1918, 9, 14. Josephine dropped from mbrp
1918, 9, 14. Maud Wright dropped from mbrp

SNEAD
1814, 1, 27. Sarah rocf South River MM, Va., dtd 1813,9,11, endorsed by Miami MM
1814, 7, 29. Sarah gct South River MM, Va.

SOUTHARD
1875, 4, 10. Ann Eliza recrq
1898, 2, 12. Lillian recrq

SPANGLER
1871, 1, 14. Jane recrq

SPENCER
1872, 12, 14. Hannah Ann (form Kinzy) rpd mcd; mbrp retained
1878, 1, 12. Hannah A. & ch, Ada & Eva, gct Oskaloosa MM, Ia.

STACKHOUSE
1897, 1, 9. Mary recrq
1897, 2, 13. Frank recrq
1897, 2, 13. Orville C., minor, recrq
1904, 4, 9. Josie recrq
1907, 7, 13. Orville recrq
1912, 5, 11. Alice dropped from mbrp
1916, 9, 9. Frank dropped from mbrp
1916, 9, 9. Wilbur dropped from mbrp

STAFFORD
1813, 4, 22. James dis disunity
1820, 10, 14. John dis mcd
1850, 1, 12. Shaderack con mcd

STANLEY
1817, 5, 10. Cert rec for Samuel & w, Susanna, & ch, Elizabeth, Martha & Susanna, from Deep Creek MM, N. C., dtd 1817,3,1, endorsed to Newberry MM, O.
1817, 5, 10. Cert rec for George from Deep Creek MM, N. C., dtd 1817,3,1, endorsed to Newberry MM, O.
1817, 5, 10. Cert rec for Nancy from Deep Creek MM, N. C., dtd 1817,3,1, endorsed to Newberry MM, O.

STANTON
1814, 11, 3. William, s James & Ann, Clinton Co., O.; m in Clear Creek MH, Margaret PUSEY, dt Nathan & Mary, Highland Co., O.

1815, 1, 27. Margaret gct Centre MM, O.

STARBUCK
1866, 3, 10. Louisa (form Pidgeon) con mcd
1866, 8, 10. Louisa gct Springfield MM, O.
1909, 2, 13. Jesse C. & w, Osie, & ch, Raymond, Leo & Willie A., rocf Dover MM
1911, 7, 8. Jesse & fam gct Grassy Run MM, O.

STEEL
1892, 6, 11. Harriett J. dropped from mbrp

STEPHENS
1832, 5, 2. Esther m Thos. REES
1854, 2, 10. Gideon d bur East Fork
1855, 9, 21. Mary d bur East Fork
1855, 10, 17. Deborah m David JAMES

1829, 11, 14. Samuel dis mcd
1830, 8, 14. Lydia Hunt (form Stevens) con mcd
1837, 8, 22. Evan [Stevens] gct Newberry MM
1839, 2, 19. Thomas [Stevens] dis disunity
1871, 3, 11. Vincent T. recrq
1871, 3, 11. Mary recrq
1874, 8, 8. Vincent & Mary [Stevens] relrq
1884, 3, 8. William A. [Stevens] recrq
1890, 7, 12. Wm. A. [Stevens] dropped from mbrp

STETHEN
1887, 2, 12. Levi recrq

STEWART
1907, 4, 13. Minor & w, Anna, & ch, John, Ora & Elsie, rocf Fairfield MM
1926, 1, 9. Minor & w, Elizabeth A., & ch, John & Ora, dropped from mbrp

STILLWELL
1887, 5, 11. Mary recrq
1891, 5, 9. Lemuel recrq
1912, 5, 11. Lemuel & Mary dropped from mbrp

STORER
1924, 10, 11. Glenn m Elva MURPHEY

STOTLER
1891, 10, 10. Martha recrq
1898, 6, 11. Leota recrq

STRATTON
1874, 11, 14. Flora & Francis, ch of John H., rocf Newberry MM, dtd 1874,9,21
1878, 1, 12. Francis gct Springfield MM, O.
1883, 8, 11. Flora E. gct Springfield MM
1883, 11, 10. Cert for Flora E. returned & she was dropped from mbrp
1926, 2, 13. Adda recrq

STRETCH
1849, 9, 8. Lydia [Strech] (form Davis) dis mcd
1855, 5, 12. Martha (form Davis) dis mcd

STROUP
1893, 4, 8. William recrq
1894, 7, 14. William dropped from mbrp

SUMMERS
1901, 6, 8. Wm. Morris recrq
1902, 6, 14. Blanch recrq
1906, 2, 10. Wm. & w, Adeline, gct Wilmington MM

SWEENEY
1887, 5, 14. James & w, Anna, rocf Fairfield MM
1892, 11, 12. James & w gct Fairfield MM

SWIFT
1910, 1, 8. Rachel Alice relrq

SWISSHELM
1924, 1, 12. Cora relrq

TABOR
1874, 3, 14. Isaac & w, Sarah, rocf Allum Creek MM, dtd 1874,2,19
1875, 1, 9. Isaac & w, Sarah, gct Allum Creek MM

TAYLOR
1885, 3, 14. Mary J. recrq
1893, 2, 11. Mary J. relrq
1895, 5, 11. Almeda recrq
1897, 5, 8. Luella recrq
1901, 5, 11. Louella dropped from mbrp

TEAS
1876, 5, 13. Susan C., adopted dt Zeri & Miriam Hough, rocf New Garden MM, Ind., dtd 1876,4,15
1879, 3, 8. Sarah gct New Garden MM, Ind.

TERRELL
1823, 9, 13. Martha d bur Clear Creek
1840, 1, 2. John, s Pleasant & Esther, Highland Co., O.; m in Clear Creek MH, Elizabeth WILLIAMS, dt William & Phebe, Highland Co., O.
1871, 2, 15. Pleasant M., s John H. & Elizabeth W., Clinton Co., O.; m in New Vienna O., Alice E. MALONE, dt John C. & Mary Ann, Clinton Co., O.
1871, 12, 13. James H., s Israel A. & Sidney H., Clinton Co., O.; m in New Vienna, Edith H. NORDYKE, dt Henry & Phebe, Clinton Co., O.
1872, 7, 17. Sarah H. m Benjamin TRUEBLOOD
1874, 1, 15. Ruth A. m Amos FISHER

1815, 4, 28. Jane recrq
1816, 6, 8. Patty rocf South River MM, Va., dte 1815,10,20
1840, 7, 21. Elizabeth gct Fairfield MM
1867, 1, 12. Hampton & w, Harriett M., rocf Fairfield MM, dtd 1866,11,17
1870, 2, 12. Israel A. & w, Sidney H., & ch, James H., Allen J., Sarah H., Wm. G., Chas. E. & Anna E., set off from Fairfield MM
1870, 2, 12. John H. & w, Elizabeth, & ch, Ruth A., David E. & Flora A., set off from Fairfield MM
1871, 7, 8. Pleasant M. rocf Raysville MM, dtd 1871,6,24
1872, 4, 13. David E. rpd mcd; retained mbrp
1872, 5, 11. Sarah recrq
1875, 7, 10. Pleasant M. & w, Alice E., & ch, Hezekiah, gct Cincinnati MM
1877, 3, 11. Pleasant M. & w, Alice, & ch, Hezekiah, rocf Cincinnati MM, dtd 1877,1,18
1882, 3, 11. David E. & w, Sarah, gct Union MM, Minn.
1886, 3, 13. Alice & ch gct Cleveland MM, O.
1887, 4, 9. Clayton recrq
1890, 1, 11. Elva R. rocf Hopewell MM
1891, 8, 8. Anna M. (form Harris) rocf Miami MM
1893, 4, 8. Charles recrq
1897, 1, 9. Clayton & w, Nannie, & ch, Glen & Ada, gct Fairfield MM
1902, 5, 10. Mary H. rocf Caesars Creek MM
1902, 11, 8. Millie roc
1903, 10, 10. Matilda C. & fam gct Wilmington MM, O.

THARP
1877, 3, 11. Eli N. recrq
1878, 3, 9. Eli N. dis
1885, 3, 14. Eli Wm. recrq
1885, 3, 14. Cora recrq
1887, 4, 9. Maud recrq

THARP, continued
1894, 7, 14. Samuel dropped from mbrp
1894, 7, 14. Arthur dropped from mbrp
1894, 7, 14. Maud dropped from mbrp
1894, 7, 14. Cora dropped from mbrp
1894, 7, 14. Annie dropped from mbrp
1926, 1, 9. Arthur & Anna dropped from mbrp

THOMAS
1818, 9, 17. Rachel m Nathan LEWIS
1819, 11, 17. Elisha, s Edward & Mary, Warren Co., O.; m in East Fork MH, Sarah NORDYKE, dt Micajah & Charity, Clinton Co., O.
----, --, --. Isaac & Sarah
Ch: Micajah W. b 1820, 10, 8
Joseph E. " 1822, 3, 19
1844, 1, 24. John Jr., s John & Esther, Clinton Co., O.; m in East Fork MM, Ruth OREN, dt Alexander & Lydia, Clinton Co., O.

1820, 10, 14. Elisha rocf Miami MM
1825, 12, 10. Elisha dis disunity
1831, 11, 22. Sarah & ch, Micajah W., Joseph E., Eliza A., Silvester L., Erastus & Elizabeth, gct Arba MM, Ind.
1836, 6, 21. Micajah W., Joseph E., Eliza Ann, Silvester S., Erastus N. & Elizabeth, ch Elisha, rocf New Garden MM, Ind., dtd 1836,5,21
1843, 7, 18. Sarah rst on consent of Arby MM, Ind.
1844, 11, 9. Ruth gct Dover MM
1883, 8, 11. Sarah dropped from mbrp
1883, 8, 11. Sylvester dropped from mbrp
1883, 8, 11. Erastus dropped from mbrp
1883, 8, 11. Elizabeth dropped from mbrp

THOMPSON
1826, 12, 9. Lucy, w Joseph D., & ch, Alfred, Edwin & Maria, rocf Silver Creek MM, dtd 1826,3,25
1872, 1, 13. Wm. D. recrq
1873, 8, 9. Wm. D. & w, Florence E. (form Hiatt) rpd mcd; retained mbrp
1878, 12, 14. Oscar, gr s Amos J. Hiatt, gct Wilmington MM, O.
1883, 3, 10. Wm. D. & w, Mary E., & ch, Freddie T. & J. Leslie, gct Union MM, Minn.

THORN
1873, 9, 13. Daniel Hill gct Green Plain MM, to m Tamar Thorn

THORNBURG
1815, 9, 21. John [Thornbrough], s Isaac & Rebecca, Clinton Co., O.; m in Newberry MH Susannah BEALES, dt Daniel & Susannah, Clinton Co., O.
1816, 5, 11. Susannah [Thornbrough] gct Fairfield MM
1829, 10, 15. Stephen Hussey gct Lees Creek MM, to m Rachel [Thornburgh]
1832, 9, 18. Isaac rocf Fairfield MM, dtd 1832,8,23
1837, 9, 19. David Nordyke, gct White Water MM, Ind., to m Lydia J. Thornburgh
1841, 4, 20. Rhoda & ch, Mary Ann, Rachel, Susannah & William G., rocf White Water MM, Ind., dtd 1841,2,24
1854, 12, 9. Isaac [Thornburgh] con mcd
1856, 10, 11. Samuel [Thornburgh] rocf Fairfield MM, dtd 1856,7,19
1858, 9, 11. Isaac [Thornburgh] dis disunity; reversed by QM 1859,6,11
1864, 8, 13. Elizabeth [Thornburgh] & ch recrq
1866, 5, 12. Cyrus [Thornburgh] recrq
1866, 5, 12. Jane W. [Thornburgh] & ch, Lydia William & Lewis recrq
1866, 5, 12. Hannah & Phebe Jane [Thornburgh] recrq
1868, 2, 8. Cyrus [Thornburgh] con mcd
1869, 4, 10. Matilda Ann [Thornburgh] recrq
1870, 2, 12. Edward & w, Rachel A., & ch, Hannah W., Lydia A., Wm. W., Silas H., Matilda Jane, John Milton, Rachel Emma, Samuel Chas., Frances E. & Harriet E., set off from Fairfield MM
1877, 9, 8. William W. & w, Victoria, & ch, Clarence, gct Fairfield MM
1877, 9, 8. Edward & w, Rachel Anna, & ch, John W., Rachel E., Samuel C., Frances E. & Harriet E., gct Fairfield MM
1877, 12, 8. Silas & w, Hannah W., & ch, Lydia A., gct Fairfield MM
1881, 12, 10. Christopher relrq
1884, 7, 12. Sarah relrq
1887, 4, 9. Sarah recrq again
1902, 6, 14. Lamar recrq
1903, 2, 14. Allie relrq
1914, 3, 14. Jesse & w, Adda, & s, Marvin, gct Fairfield MM, O.
1920, 4, 10. Cyrus gct Leesburg MM, O.

THROCKMORTON
1914, 6, 13. Foster Sheridan recrq
1914, 8, 8. Iva & s, Jefferson, recrq

TILTON
1896, 4, 11. William recrq
1923, 1, 13. Minnie H. relrq

TIMBERLAKE
----, --, --. Richard m Mary ----- d 1840,9, 28 bur Clear Creek
Ch: Jonathan b 1811, 2, 11
Susannah " 1812, 8, 29
John W. " 1814, 4, 23
Mary " 1815, 9, 29
Alfred " 1817, 4, 12
Elizabeth " 1819, 3, 4
Rebecca " 1820, 11, 1 d 1842, 9,18 bur Clear Creek

TIMBERLAKE, Richard & Mary, continued
Ch: Acquilla b 1825, 1, 6
1816, 3, 14. Mourning m Enoch LEWIS
----, --, --. John & Amy
Ch: Joseph R. b 1819, 9, 23
Martha " 1821, 3, 2
Maryann " 1823, 1, 27
Lydia " 1826, 3, 25
John Phillip
b 1828, 1, 17
1822, 10, 24. Judith m Thos. C. ANTHONY
1827, 3, 14. John d bur Clear Creek
1833, 8, 24. Susannah m Jonathan ELLIS
1835, 12, 25. Molley d bur Clear Creek
1836, 9, 13. Mary d bur near Peru, Ind.
----, --, --. John W. & Rachel
Ch: Hannah b 1837, 12, 22 d 1841,10, 1 bur Clear Creek
Mary E. b 1840, 7, 28
Milton " 1842, 5, 3
John B. " 1844, 8, 3
Richard " 1847, 1, 24
Mahlon " 1849, 5, 2
William " 1851, 12, 19
----, --, --. Alfred & Phebe
Ch: Mary B. b 1841, 4, 11
Eliza D. " 1843, 5, 9
Caroline " 1845, 1, 15
Edward " 1846, 12, 9
Susannah E." 1849, 4, 17
1841, 11, 24. Mary W. m Joseph EMMONS

1818, 9, 12. John gct Salem MM, to m
1819, 2, 13. Amy rocf Salem MM, dtd 1818,12,23
1819, 4, 10. Sally Johnson (form Timberlake) dis mcd
1828, 6, 13. Amy dis jH
1829, 3, 14. John dis jH
1829, 10, 15. Jonathan gct Miami MM
1832, 3, 20. Jonathan rocf Miami MM, dtd 1832,1,25
1833, 11, 19. Mary (form Sanders) con mcd
1834, 12, 23. Jonathan gct Springfield MM
1836, 11, 22. John W. gct Springborough MM, to m Rachel J. Bateman
1837, 4, 18. Rachel rocf Springborough MM, dtd 1837,3,21
1839, 4, 23. Alfred gct Centre MM, to m Phebe Doan
1839, 7, 23. Alfred gct Centre MM
1841, 4, 20. Martha Heller (form Timberlake) dis mcd
1841, 6, 22. Mary Ann dis disunity
1844, 9, 14. Richard gct Cincinnati MM, to m Mahala Smith
1845, 8, 9. Alfred & w, Phebe, & ch, Mary B., Eliza D. & Caroline, rocf Dover MM, dtd 1845,6,19
1845, 10, 11. Mahala rocf Cincinnati MM, dtd 1845,7,17
1847, 5, 8. Aquilla gct White Lick MM, Ind
1848, 2, 12. Elizabeth gct Springfield MM
1849, 11, 10. Alfred & w, Phebe, & ch, Mary B., Eliza D., Caroline, Edward & Susannah E., gct Centre MM
1850, 9, 14. John W. dis
1852, 4, 10. Joseph R. gct Salem MM, Ia.
1853, 8, 13. Richard gct Springfield MM
1854, 12, 9. Rachel B. & ch, Mary Elizabeth, Milton, John Bateman, Richard, Mahlon, William & Deborah Ann, gct Goshen MM

TODD
1869, 4, 10. James recrq
1869, 4, 10. Nancy recrq
1869, 4, 10. John W., minor ch, recrq of parents
1869, 4, 10. Elizabeth, minor ch, recrq of parents
1878, 1, 12. James & ch, John W. & Elizabeth, dropped from mbrp

TOWNSEND
1847, 3, 18. Isaac, s Josiah & Abigail, Highland Co., O.; m in East Fork MH, Penninah CAREY, dt John & Margaret

1846, 8, 8. Isaac recrq
1848, 12, 9. Isaac & w, Peninah, & dt, Abigail Emily, gct Newberry MM
1874, 4, 11. Eldora recrq
1878, 1, 12. Eldora gct Fairfield MM
1895, 5, 11. Emma Spencer rocf White Water MM, Ind.
1897, 2, 13. Emma S. gct Newberry MM, O.

TREFTZ
1895, 3, 9. Etta relrq

TROUT
1832, 7, 24. Zillah (form Wildman) dis mcd

TRUEBLOOD
1872, 7, 17. Benjamin, s Joshua & Esther, Wayne Co., Ind.; m in home of Israel A. Terrell, Sarah H. TERRELL, dt Israel A. & Sidney H., Clinton Co., O.

1873, 8, 9. Sarah H. gct Spring Creek MM,Ia.

TULLIS
1895, 5, 11. Walter recrq

TURPIN
1869, 5, 8. Frances (form Miller) con mcd
1887, 11, 12. Ida Belle gct Wilmington MM
1887, 11, 12. Fannie dropped from mbrp

TYSON
1857, 6, 13. Phebe (form Hussey) dis mcd

UNDERWOOD
1832, 7, 24. Eunice (form Hussey) dis mcd
1866, 6, 9. James & w, Eunice, & dt, Alice, recrq
1870, 8, 13. Alice Routh (form Underwood)

UNDERWOOD, continued
con mcd

VANCE
1887, 4, 9. Hugh S. recrq
1894, 7, 14. Hugh dropped from mbrp

VANSANT
1909, 2, 13. John & Rena recrq

VANWINKLE
1846, 11, 14. Elizabeth (form Hoggatt) dis mcd
1870, 3, 12. Clarinda recrq
1872, 5, 11. Clarinda gct Newberry MM

VAUGHN
1887, 4, 9. Abe recrq
1889, 4, 13. Abe dropped from mbrp
1894, 7, 14. Elsie dropped from mbrp
1895, 4, 13. Ida recrq
1901, 7, 13. Ida dropped from mbrp
1904, 12, 10. Amy Bailey rocf Friends Chapel MM, Ind.
1909, 2, 13. Marguerite & Errol, minors, recrq
1920, 4, 10. Errol & Marguerite gct Leesburg MM, O.
1928, 1, 18. Nellie relrq

VERNON
1833, 1, 22. Jesse rocf Stillwater MM, O., dtd 1832,11,24
1836, 3, 22. Jesse gct Stillwater MM, O.

VICKERS
1823, 9, 13. Isaac M. & w, Abigail, & ch, Edwin, Samuel N., William M. & Thomas, rocf Bradford MM, Pa., dtd 1823,5,7
1825, 6, 11. Isaac M. & w, Abigail, & ch, Edwin, Samuel N., William M. & Thomas, gct Fairfield MM

VONESSEN
1869, 4, 10. Matilda recrq
1878, 1, 12. Matilda dropped from mbrp

VORE
1848, 1, 8. John & w, Susannah, & ch, Eli, John & Sarah, rocf Fairfield MM, dtd 1847, 11,20
1849, 6, 9. Azel rocf Fairfield MM, dtd 1849,5,19
1850, 12, 14. Eli [Vorr] dis joining M. E. Ch.
1853, 1, 8. John & w, Elizabeth, & s, John, gct Dover MM, Ind.
1853, 1, 8. Azel con mcd
1853, 9, 10. Azel gct White Water MM, Ind.

WADDLE
1882, 8, 12. Phebe Jane gct Wilmington MM,O.

WARD
1819, 11, 13. Grace rocf Centre MM, N. C., dtd 1819,9,18
1820, 1, 8. Obed & w, Mary, & ch, Susanna, Timothy, George & Rachel, rocf Centre MM, N. C., dtd 1819,9,18
1822, 8, 10. Obed & w, Mary, & ch, Susanna, Timothy, George & Rachel, gct West Grove MM, Ind.
1822, 11, 9. Grace gct West Grove MM, Ind.
1875, 4, 10. Marshall & w, Gala Ann, recrq
1878, 1, 12. Marshall & fam dropped from mbrp
1881, 4, 9. Charles & Agnes recrq

WARDEN
1873, 3, 8. Rosanna recrq
1885, 3, 14. Isaac recrq

WASSON
----, --, --. Calvin & Mary
Ch: William b 1819, 6, 20
Nathan " 1821, 3, 14
Elizabeth " 1824, 1, 30
Sarah " 1826, 5, 18
Mary Jane " 1830, 3, 25
Calvin " 1832, 2, 24
Eliza Ann " 1838, 3, 25

1840, 8, 18. Calvin [Warson] & w, Mary, & ch, William, Nathan, Elizabeth, Sarah, Mary Jane, Calvin & Eliza Ann, rocf West Grove MM, Ind.
1840, 9, 22. Wm. [Warson] gct Fairfield MM
1841, 2, 23. Nathan gct Milford MM, Ind., to m Maria Cox
1841, 9, 21. Nathan gct Milford MM, Ind.
1842, 1, 18. Calvin & w, Mary, & ch, Elizabeth, Sarah, Mary Jane, Calvin, Eliza Ann & Asa, gct Newberry MM

WATTS
1926, 1, 9. Flora Cook dropped from mbrp

WAY
1825, 11, 12. Robert & w, Abigail, & dt, Miriame, rocf Springborough MM, dtd 1825,9, 27
1828, 2, 9. Robert & w, Abigail, & ch, Maryanne & Photian, gct Fairfield MM

WELCH
1814, 12, 30. Samuel & w, Chloe, & ch, Martha, Amos, Judith, Betsy, Sally, Webster & Sally, rocf Deep Creek MM, dtd 1814,10,1
1816, 6, 8. Samuel & w, Chloe, & ch, Martha, Amos, Judith, Betsy, Sally, Webster & Samuel (Sally above) gct Miami MM, O.

WEST
1838, 11, 1. Owen, s William & Mary, Clinton Co., O.; m in Clear Creek MH, Mary CAREY, dt John & Margaret, Highland Co., O.
Ch: Rhoda
Ellen b 1852, 4, 28
Charles

WEST, Owen & Mary, continued
Ch: Wilson b 1854, 12, 7
Owen Lindley " 1857, 7, 30
Mary Elizabeth " 1859, 11, 23
1843, 11, 2. Martin, s William & Sarah, Clinton Co., O.; m in Clear Creek MH, Abigail CAREY, dt John & Margaret, Highland Co., O.
1846, 10, 15. Charles O., s Wm. & Sarah, Clinton Co., O.; m in Clear Creek MH, Rachel D. CAREY, dt Samuel & Anna, Highland Co., O.

1814, 9, 23. Owen & w, Elizabeth, & ch, James, Payton, Elizabeth, Amelia, Rebecca & John, recrq
1814, 9, 23. Owen & Thomas, s Owen & Elizabeth, recrq
1839, 1, 22. Mary gct Newberry MM
1844, 4, 23. Abigail C. gct Newberry MM
1845, 9, 13. Benjamin recrq
1847, 7, 10. Rachel gct Newberry MM
1850, 3, 9. Owen & w, Mary, & ch, Sarah Jane, Abigail C., Margaret Emely, Jehiel G. & Joseph Milton, rocf Newberry MM, dtd 1850,2,11
1870, 6, 11. William & w, Nancy, recrq
1873, 3, 8. Jehiel rpd mcd; retained mbrp
1873, 4, 15. Jehiel gct Newberry MM
1881, 4, 9. Walter recrq
1882, 4, 8. Walter dis disunity
1885, 1, 10. J. M. gct Newberry MM
1885, 3, 14. Edwin Quinn recrq
1885, 3, 14. Wilson W. recrq
1885, 3, 14. Frank M. recrq
1885, 6, 13. Lindley A. gct Newberry MM, O.
1885, 6, 13. James M. gct Newberry MM, O.
1895, 5, 11. Roy recrq
1898, 3, 12. Lafayette & Effie recrq
1898, 4, 9. Owen & w, Lizzie, rocf Newberry MM, O.
1898, 5, 14. Rachel recrq
1918, 9, 14. Wilson W. dis disunity

WHETLEY
1869, 4, 10. Alexander recrq

WHITE
1837, 1, 25. Benjamin, s Josiah & Elizabeth, Washington Co., Ind.; m in Clear Creek MH, Levina COFFIN, dt Samuel & Dinah, Highland Co., O.

1837, 5, 23. Lavina gct Blue River MM, Ind.
1842, 7, 19. Levina & ch, Josephine & Lydia, rocf Blue River MM, Ind., dtd 1842,7,18
1852, 12, 11. Levina & ch, Josephine, Lydia, Mary, Henry, Wilson & Elizabeth, gct Newberry MM
1887, 4, 9. Arthur recrq

WILDMAN
1817, 11, 8. Rebeckah & dt, Lilla, rocf Redstone MM, dtd 1816,11,20
1817, 11, 8. Cinthy rocf Redstone MM, dtd 1816,11,20
1817, 11, 8. Townsend rocf Redstone MM, dtd 1816,12,25
1822, 1, 12. Townsend dis mcd
1824, 8, 14. Cynthia Murphey (form Wildman) dis mcd
1832, 7, 24. Zillah Trout (form Wildman) dis mcd

WILLETTS
1818, 4, 11. Henry gct Lees Creek MM
1830, 5, 8. Sarah rocf Union MM, N. C., dtd 1829,10,28
1832, 3, 20. Sarah [Willets] gct New Garden MM, Ind.

WILLIAMS
----, --, --. Isaac & Sarah
Ch: Betsy b 1813, 2, 23
Christopher " 1814, 10, 13
Owen " 1817, 4, 22
----, --, --. William d 1860,11,13 bur Clear Creek; m Phebe ----- d 1857,6,1 bur Clear Creek
Ch: Elizabeth b 1814, 6, 5
Ann " 1816, 10, 10
Jonathan " 1820, 4, 17
Phebe " 1823, 5, 16
1816, 10, 24. Katharine m Stephen HUSSEY
1820, 8, 17. Mary m Thomas PAINTER
1840, 1, 2. Elizabeth m John TERRELL
1841, 2, 24. Ann m Pleasant HUNT
1923, 10, 25. Rebecca m Roy MOBBERLY

1816, 7, 13. Clark rocf Fairfield MM, dtd 1816,6,29
1817, 7, 12. Isaac & w, Sarah, & ch, Betsy, Christopher & Owen, gct White Water MM, Ind.
1820, 4, 8. Clark gct Miami MM
1824, 8, 14. Robert dis
1824, 8, 14. Isaac dis
1825, 5, 14. Josiah gct Centre MM
1830, 12, 11. John dis
1834, 9, 23. Joseph dis disunity
1842, 4, 19. Jonathan dis mcd
1844, 3, 19. William dis disunity
1865, 5, 13. Phebe gct Chester MM
1868, 3, 14. Eliza J. recrq
1869, 4, 10. Wm. C. recrq
1869, 4, 10. James K. recrq
1871, 3, 11. Cora recrq
1871, 4, 8. Francis recrq
1873, 1, 11. Jonathan & w, Sarah, & s, Chas. O., recrq
1873, 1, 11. Laura Emma & Caroline Matilda recrq
1873, 3, 8. Worth R. recrq
1878, 1, 12. Wm. C. dropped from mbrp
1883, 8, 11. Sarah S. dropped from mbrp
1884, 1, 12. Jennie recrq

WILLIAMS, continued
1885, 3, 14. Charles Gustavus recrq
1885, 5, 9. James K. relrq
1889, 2, 9. James K. & Emma recrq
1893, 2, 11. James dropped from mbrp
1893, 2, 11. Emma dropped from mbrp
1899, 1, 14. Laura E. dropped from mbrp
1899, 1, 14. Charley O. dropped from mbrp
1926, 1, 9. Charles G. & Lyman dropped from mbrp

WILSON
1883, 5, 12. James H. recrq
1884, 12, 13. J. H. dis
1897, 1, 9. Mary recrq
1901, 9, 14. Emma C. relrq
1912, 2, 10. Susan McLoren relrq
1912, 4, 13. Mary E. recrq
1912, 4, 13. Claybon recrq
1912, 4, 13. Henry recrq
1912, 4, 13. Perrin recrq
1912, 4, 13. Ora E. recrq

WINKLE
1869, 4, 10. James P. recrq
1878, 1, 12. James P. gct Fairfield MM, O.

WINTERS
1929, 2, 24. Nancy d ae 37

1927, 7, 14. Nancy recrq
1927, 7, 14. Ruby, minor, recrq

WISE
1881, 4, 9. Harvey recrq
1883, 8, 11. Harvey dropped from mbrp
1893, 2, 11. Hugh dropped from mbrp
1897, 1, 9. James recrq
1897, 5, 8. Melissa, w James, & ch, Eliza, Nora, Rodna, Mary, Arwilda & Caroline, recrq
1902, 4, 12. James Jr. recrq
1906, 2, 10. James Sr. & w, Melissa, & ch, Rodney, Nora, Caroline, Armilda, Mary, James Jr., Olive & Joseph F., dropped from mbrp

WOOD
1832, 12, 18. Martha (form Sanders) dis mcd
1867, 3, 9. Martha recrq
1884, 1, 12. Henry recrq
1884, 3, 8. Frank recrq
1898, 11, 12. Henry dropped from mbrp

WOODYARD
1924, 3, 8. Wilbur m Elma MURPHEY

1913, 5, 10. Ruth recrq
1914, 4, 11. Joseph recrq
1930, 3, 12. Elma Murphey dropped from mbrp
1931, 4, 8. Joseph dropped from mbrp

WOODELL
1877, 6, 9. Angie recrq

WOODMANSEE
1837, 7, 18. Gulielma (form Sanders) dis mcd
1846, 1, 10. Mary Ann (form Postgate) dis mcd
1885, 6, 13. Ella dropped from mbrp
1919, 12, 13. Edith dropped from mbrp

WOODROW
1824, 2, 14. Rachel & Elizabeth dis disunity
1828, 11, 8. John dis disunity
1829, 2, 14. Joshua Jr. dis disunity
1829, 3, 14. Joshua dis jH
1830, 5, 8. Ann dis disunity
1835, 8, 18. Hellena dis disunity
1839, 10, 22. David gct Cincinnati MM

WOODY
1911, 1, 14. Eva Terrell gct Knoxville MM, Tenn.

WOOSLEY
1889, 11, 9. Lillie recrq

WRIGHT
----, --, --. John & Hannah
Ch: Jonathan b 1817, 10, 25
Rebecca " 1820, 6, 14
1822, 1, 21. John d bur Clear Creek
1838, 11, 1. Hannah m Samuel COFFIN
1839, 9, 15. Thomas d bur Clear Creek
1840, 10, 13. Rebecca d bur Clear Creek
1844, 7, 28. Letticia d bur Clear Creek
----, --, --. Joseph & Lydia
Ch: Jonathan B. b 1850, 4, 14
Elwood " 1852, 8, 29
Emma " 1856, 4, 19
1851, 11, 22. Benjamin d bur Clear Creek
1925, 8, 29. Mildred m Glenn PENCE

1815, 1, 27. Joseph rocf Fairfield MM, dtd 1814,10,29
1815, 4, 28. Joseph gct Centre MM
1815, 3, 24. Joseph gct Centre MM
1816, 7, 13. John & w, Hannah, & ch, Ann, Joseph & David, rocf New Garden MM, dtd 1816,3,14
1817, 11, 8. Letitia rocf Middleton MM, dtd 1817,4,14
1820, 2, 12. Benjamin recrq
1821, 7, 14. Thomas & Mary recrq
1828, 8, 9. Benjamin dis
1829, 2, 4. Susanna rocf Silver Creek MM, Ind., dtd 1828,11,22
1836, 12, 20. Susannah gct White Water MM, Ind.
1836, 5, 24. Jonathan dis disunity
1837, 11, 21. David dis disunity
1837, 12, 19. Mary dis disunity
1840, 3, 24. Rhoda recrq
1841, 6, 22. Joseph gct Fall Creek MM, to m

WRIGHT, continued
Lydia Cowgill
1841, 8, 24. Joseph gct Fall Creek MM
1842, 1, 18. Rhoda Green (form Wright) con mcd
1843, 5, 23. Elizabeth McDaniel (form Wright) dis mcd
1846, 7, 11. Lucy McDaniel (form Wright) dis mcd
1849, 5, 12. Joseph & w, Lydia, & ch, Henry C., Eleanor C. & Davis S., rocf Fairfield MM, dtd 1849,4,21
1850, 11, 9. Mahala recrq
1866, 4, 14. Jonathan recrq
1866, 5, 12. Henry C. con mcd
1866, 5, 12. Sarah M. recrq
1869, 4, 10. Keziah recrq
1869, 4, 10. Robert recrq
1869, 4, 10. Elizabeth recrq
1869, 4, 10. Emma L., minor, recrq of parents
1869, 4, 10. Melissa F. recrq
1869, 4, 10. John H. recrq
1869, 4, 10. Henry P. recrq
1870, 11, 12. Jonathan relrq
1871, 1, 14. David H. recrq
1871, 2, 11. George recrq
1871, 3, 11. David H. & w, Phebe J. rpd mcd; mbrp retained
1872, 2, 10. Levi recrq
1872, 2, 10. Louisa recrq
1872, 12, 9. David S. gct Salem MM, Ia.
1873, 3, 8. Levi Jr. recrq
1873, 3, 8. Hannah recrq
1873, 3, 8. Maud H. recrq
1873, 3, 8. Claud S. recrq
1873, 4, 12. George dis disunity
1873, 10, 11. David H. relrq
1874, 4, 11. Lucurgus B. recrq
1875, 9, 11. Jonathan B. gct Salem MM, Ia.
1877, 10, 13. Henry C. relrq
1878, 1, 12. Levi & w, Louisa, & ch, Phebe J., gct Wilmington MM, O.
1878, 1, 12. Levi Jr. dropped from mbrp
1881, 4, 9. Anthony & Elizabeth recrq
1883, 5, 12. Frank C. recrq
1885, 3, 14. James E. & Sarah C. recrq
1885, 3, 14. Thadeus W. recrq
1885, 3, 14. Benjamin F. recrq
1885, 4, 11. Katie recrq
1885, 7, 11. Ellen C. gct Wilmington MM
1886, 3, 13. Charles W. recrq
1886, 3, 13. Melvina recrq
1887, 4, 9. Hattie recrq
1888, 6, 9. Emma & Frankie dropped from mbrp
1889, 2, 9. Elsie A. & Eldora recrq
1892, 3, 12. James E. relrq
1892, 9, 10. Eldora relrq
1893, 4, 8. Gurney recrq
1893, 4, 8. Joseph recrq
1894, 7, 14. Thadeus dropped from mbrp
1894, 7, 14. Benjamin dropped from mbrp
1894, 7, 14. Fred dropped from mbrp
1894, 7, 14. Martha dropped from mbrp
1894, 7, 14. Nellie dropped from mbrp
1896, 3, 14. Lizzie Gustin recrq
1897, 12, 11. Charles W. relrq
1898, 3, 12. Frank O. gct Fairfield MM
1899, 1, 14. Lycurgus B. dropped from mbrp
1899, 4, 8. Emma gct Wilmington MM
1899, 8, 12. Chas. W. gct Chicago MM, Ill.
1900, 3, 10. Elsie relrq
1904, 4, 9. Lizzie relrq
1907, 4, 13. Bertha E. recrq
1907, 9, 14. Julia gct Newberry MM
1908, 4, 11. Alonzo relrq
1910, 1, 8. Bert E. relrq
1914, 1, 10. Mary Crute gct Fairfield MM, O.
1914, 4, 11. Mildred recrq
1914, 7, 11. Bell dropped from mbrp
1931, 4, 8. Bertha dropped from mbrp

YORK
1903, 5, 9. Lewis H. & w, Charlotta, & ch, Harley Edward, Lola Fern, Walter Lewis, Dewey Raymond & John Theodore, recrq
1906, 4, 14. Lewis H. & w, Charlotte, & ch, Harley E., Leota F., Walter L., Dewey R. & John T., relrq

YOUNG
1885, 3, 14. Reuben & w, Ellen, recrq

* * * * * * *

CARY
----, --, --. David & Rebecca
Ch: Thomas
Lindley b 1845, 11, 9
Amos H. " 1847, 7, 1
Samuel Albert " 1849, 5, 29
Anne " 1850, 11, 1
David F. " 1852, 5, 6 d 1857, 6,21 bur Clear Creek
Harriet E. b 1854, 1, 2
Elwood O. " 1855, 11, 22
James Edgar " 1857, 12, 1
Charles Newton " 1859, 3, 27
Matthew " 1861, 4, 27
Minervia " 1863, 3, 24
Thadeus L. " 1865, 2, 18
1846, 10, 15. Rachel D. m Charles O. WEST
1847, 3, 18. Penninah m Isaac TOWNSEND

JONES
1849, 1, 11. Samuel & w, Jane, & ch, Mattie, rocf Caesars Creek MM, dtd 1878,11,21

HIATT

1813, 8, 26. John & w, Mary, & ch, Gideon, Rueben, Rozannah, Jesse, Anne, Rachel & Mary, gct Caesars Creek MM, O.

1813, 8, 26. John Jr. dis mou

1813, 11, 25. Jonathan & w, Rachel, & ch, John, Silas, Josiah, Lydia, Mary, Jonathan, George, Richard, Rachel, Sarah & Nathan, rocf Mt. Pleasant MM, dtd 1813,3, 27, endorsed by Fairfield MM

1814, 6, 24. John gct Darby Creek MM, O.

1814, 6, 24. Christopher & w, Elizabeth, & ch, Solomon, Jonathan & Levinah, rocf Mt. Pleasant MM, dtd 1813,9,25, endorsed by Fairfield MM

1814, 10, 28. Jonathan & w, Rachel, & ch, Silas, Josiah, Lydia, Mary, Jonathan, George, Richard, Sarah, Rachel & Nathan, gct Darby Creek MM

1815, 1, 27. Asaph gct Fairfield MM, to m

1815, 10, 14. Rebecca rocf Fairfield MM, dtd 1815,6,24

1816, 6, 8. Christopher & w, Elizabeth, & ch, Jonathan & Levina, gct Fairfield MM

NEWBERRY MONTHLY MEETING

The early settlement of Martinsville, Ohio, is practically co-incident with Newberry Monthly Meeting since almost all the early settlers were Friends. The first of whom we have any authentic account was John Wright who settled within the present limits of the town in 1806. He assisted in establishing the first meeting which was held in his home in 1810 under the direction of Clear Creek Monthly Meeting.

Soon after John Wright, came many other settlers. The Moons and Garners settled just east of Martinsville in 1808 and John Beals, northeast, Christopher Hiatt, west, and Jacob Jackson, south, in 1810. Among the other earliest Friends to settle here were Owen West, who came in 1808, Daniel Puckett in 1810, William West in 1811, Joseph Mills in 1814, Jacob Hunt in 1816, Thomas Hunt in 1817, and Aaron Betts in 1819. To these may be added the name of James Hadley, who was not only prominent in church, but also in township affairs.

The monthly meeting records show that the first monthly meeting was held on twelfth month, second, 1816. It took its name from Newberry County, or District, in South Carolina. It was set off from Clear Creek Monthly Meeting by Fairfield Quarterly Meeting, 11 Mo. 2, 1816. The first business transaction was the appointment of John Beals, Owen West, Benjamin Puckett and David Moon as a committee to select a clerk for the new meeting and Christopher Hiatt was chosen. A similar committee of women friends consisting of Mary Beales, Phoebe Ellis, Ann Jackson, Hannah Mills and Rachel Hunt reported the name of Hannah Mills for the first clerk of women friends.

The first members received into the new meeting were by a certificate of removal from Mt. Pleasant Monthly Meeting in Grayson County, Virginia, dated 9 Mo. 26, 1816, and directed to Clear Creek Monthly Meeting for Jacob Hunt and wife, Lydia, together with their children, Rachel, Nathan, Robert, Thomas, Ruth, Jesse, Rebecca and Ruben. The first minister was Jacob Jackson who, together with his sons, Curtis and Josiah, settled just south of Martinsville.

An indulged meeting under the direction of Newberry Monthly Meeting was granted to Turtle Creek Friends, 11 Mo. 28, 1822, and was made a meeting for worship 11 Mo. 25, 1824, under the name of Greenburry Meeting. An indulged meeting was held for a number of years at Sugartree Branch, about two and a half miles northeast of Martinsville. An indulged meeting was granted to Westfork, near Westboro, First Month 25, 1827, which was made a meeting for worship in 1833, a preparative meeting in 1840 and a monthly meeting in 1891. An indulged meeting was also granted to Sycamore and one to Clermont Friends in Clermont County in 1853.

RECORDS

ACHOR
----, --, --. Joseph b 1822,5,16; m Eunice ----- b 1822,6,3
Ch: Elizabeth Minerva b 1844, 7, 7
Sarah Jane " 1846, 3, 4
Samuel Davis " 1847, 10, 12
George Riley " 1849, 6, 30
Thomas Claton " 1851, 11, 16
Lydia Ann " 1854, 4, 25
Mary Margaret " 1856, 5, 7
1859, 8, 9. Mary M. d
1933, 1, 19. Mildred d

1853, 2, 5. Joseph & w, Emma, & ch, Elizabeth M., Sarah J., Samuel D., George R. & Thomas C., rocf Fairfield MM, dtd 1853,1,5
1865, 5, 22. Elizabeth Corder (form Achor) dis mou
1865, 12, 18. Joseph & w, Eunice, & ch, Samuel, George R., Thomas & Lydia Ann, gct Back Creek MM, Ind.
1866, 2, 19. Sarah J. gct Oak Ridge MM, Ind.
1895, 4, 20. Clement recrq
1887, 8, 22. Clement dropped from mbrp
1902, 2, 13. Maud Miller relrq
1911, 7, 13. Bruce recrq
1911, 7, 13. Wayne recrq
1926, 5, 23. Mildred Brewer recrq

ADAMS
1879, 2, 17. Flora gct Westfield MM, Ind.

ADDINGTON
1870, 9, 19. Ayner J. gct New Garden MM, Ind.

ALBERTSON
----, --, --. Josiah b 1784,1,12 d 1866,10,15 bur Newberry; m Hannah ----- b 1783,11,28 d 1866,8,8 bur Newberry
----, --, --. Isaiah & Alice
Ch: Chalkley b 1811, 3, 20
Benjamin " 1813, 6, 15

1832, 5, 21. Joseph & w, Hannah, rocf Caesars Creek MM, dtd 1832,3,22
1872, 12, 23. Chockley recrq
1877, 9, 17. Benjamin rocf Springfield MM, O., dtd 1877,7,21
1879, 11, 17. Benjamin relrq

ALLEN
1874, 2, 23. John & w, Matilda Ann, & ch, Joseph Warren & Wm. Franklin, recrq

ANDERSON
----, --, --. Robert W. b 1842,7,31; m Lydia Jane ----- b 1839,10,6
Ch: Charles b 1868, 9, 19

1867, 5, 20. Elizabeth recrq
1867, 5, 20. Lydia Jane recrq
1870, 1, 17. Robert W. recrq
1887, 5, 23. Robert W. dropped from mbrp

ANDREW
1840, 3, 27. Sarah, dt Henry & Jane d bur Westfork
1840, 10, 28. Jonathan, s Henry & Jane, Clinton Co., O.; m in Westfork MH, Elizabeth GARNER, dt Wm. & Ann, Clinton Co., O., b 1819,9,6 (Jonathan b 1821,1,26)
Ch: Henry b 1846, 12, 14
William G. " 1852, 8, 5
----, --, --. Joseph b 1816,1,19; m Sarah ----- b 1821,12,10
Ch: Martha Jane b 1842, 10, 17
William Henry " 1843, 4, 21
Elizabeth " 1845, 12, 13
Anna " 1847, 12, 18
Elias " 1849, 10, 24
Jonathan
Susannah
Hannah Isabella
1844, 11, 20. William, s Henry & Jane, Clinton Co., O., b 1818,11,21 d 1856,12,15 bur Westfork; m in Westfork MH, Ruth GARNER, dt William & Ann, Clinton Co., O., b 1822, 4,13
Ch: Jacob b 1845, 8, 16
Mary " 1847, 4, 7
Lydia Ann " 1848, 5, 13
Sarah " 1850, 5, 7 d 1850, 5,10 bur Westfork
Robert b 1851, 7, 18
James Rileigh " 1854, 8, 15
Nancy Jane " 1856, 9, 29
1846, 9, 21. Henry d bur Westfork

----, --, --. Jacob H., s Wm. & Ruth, b 1845, 8,16; m Frances A. McCRARY, dt John & Anna, b 1843,3,2
Ch: John Milton
Lizzie M. b 1869, 11, 27
William P. " 1872, 2, 23
Lillian C. " 1873, 12, 21
Samuel C. " 1876, 2, 26
James Gilbert " 1878, 2, 25
1870, 1, 28. Arrie Jane d
----, --, --. Robert E., s Wm. & Ruth, b 1852, 7,18; m Clarinda VAN WINKLE, dt Wm. & Elizabeth, b 1833,8,18
Ch: Fred
Mable b 1891, 1, 1

ANDREW, continued
1826, 5, 16. Mahlon Hockett gct Springfield MM, to m Anna Andrew
1839, 4, 22. Henry & w, Jane, & ch, William, Jonathan & Sarah, rocf Springfield MM, dtd 1839,4,16
1848, 8, 14. Joseph & w, Sarah, & ch, Martha Jane, William Henry, Elizabeth & Ann, rocf White Lick MM, Ind., dtd 1848,7,12
1858, 6, 21. Joseph & w, Sarah, & ch, Martha Jane, William Henry, Anna, Elias, Jonathan, Susanna & Hannah Isabel, gct White Lick MM, Ind.
1863, 3, 23. Henry con mou
1866, 4, 23. Lydia Ann Carter (form Andrew) con mou
1866, 4, 23. Grace (form Puckett) con mou
1867, 4, 22. Joseph M. recrq
1867, 4, 22. John E. recrq
1867, 7, 22. Margaret E. & s, Charles Emmet, recrq
1867, 12, 23. Joseph & w, Grace, & s, Otis L., gct Plainfield MM, Ind.
1868, 6, 22. Jacob con mou
1873, 8, 18. Elizabeth & s, Wm. G., gct Eagle Creek MM, Ind.
1873, 8, 18. Margaret Ellen & ch, Charles Emmett, Erminnie & Thomas Ellwood, gct Eagle Creek MM, Ind.
1874, 1, 19. William G. gct Greenwood MM, Ind.
1874, 2, 23. Frances A. recrq
1874, 3, 23. Henry gct Greenwood MM, Ind.
1877, 6, 18. Jonathan dis disunity
1879, 8, 21. William G. rocf Greenwood MM, Ind., dtd 1879,7,2
1881, 3, 21. Rachel Ann & ch, Clifton G. & Earl J., recrq
1888, 9, 17. Elizabeth rocf Greenwood MM, Ind., dtd 1888,8,29
1919, 12, 18. Milton & w, Ida, rocf Westfork MM, O.

ANTHONY
1827, 10, 26. Charles & w, Elizabeth, & ch, Sarah & Joseph, rocf Miami MM, dtd 1827,7,25
1827, 10, 26. Judith rocf Miami MM, dtd 1827,7,25
1830, 7, 29. Judith Nordyke (form Anthony) con mou
1830, 8, 26. Joseph dis mou
1833, 1, 23. Sarah Nordyke (form Anthony) con mou
1835, 9, 21. Charles gct Mississinewa MM, Ind.

ANTRAM
1815, 8, 15. Lucinda, w Joseph, dt Joshua & Lydia Davis, b

1877, 8, 20. Lucinda rocf Fairfield MM, O., dtd 1877,7,21

ARMSTRONG
1893, 2, 20. Lenora (form Hunt) gct Whittier MM, Calif.

ARNOLD
----, --, --. John m Nancy McKIBBEN, dt Joseph & Hester, b 1823,6,29 d 1896,3,1
Ch: Emma b 1863, 4, 23

1876, 5, 22. Nancy rocf Caesars Creek MM, O., dtd 1876,4,27

AUSTIN
1870, 1, 17. Ruth gct Vermillion MM, Ill.

AXALINE
1872, 9, 23. Rachel con mou
1879, 1, 20. Homer & Clyde, ch Rachel A., recrq
1879, 2, 17. Rachel A. & ch, Homer & Clyde, gct Cincinnati MM, O.

BAILEY
1845, 4, 24. David, s Daniel & Mary, Clinton Co., O.; m in Newberry MH, Mary JANNEY, dt Joseph & Elizabeth, Clinton Co., O.

1845, 10, 13. Mary gct Dover MM
1848, 6, 12. Mary J. & s, Joseph, rocf Dover MM, dtd 1848,5,18
1852, 12, 6. Mary & s, Joseph, gct Dover MM
1873, 2, 17. Samantha recrq
1874, 5, 18. Jonathan & w, Rebecca, rocf Dover MM, dtd 1874,5,16
1877, 2, 19. Jonathan & w gct Dover MM, O.

BAKER
----, --, --. Addison m Anna Delilah HOLLADAY, dt Wm. & Ann, b 1852,2,8
Ch: Francis
Augustus b 1872, 9, 10
Meta Almeda" 1877, 11, 1

1871, 11, 20. Anna D. (form Holoday) con mou
1885, 12, 21. Annie D. relrq

BALLARD
----, --, --. Amos b 1837,11,22; m Elizabeth ----- b 1835,3,25
Ch: Rebecca b 1861, 8, 2
Anna " 1863, 1, 13
Olive " 1864, 4, 8
Phebe Alice" 1867, 2, 22
Elva " 1869, 2, 27

1862, 6, 23. Amos & w, Elizabeth, & dt, Rebecca, rocf Centre MM, dtd 1862,5,14
1871, 3, 20. Amos & w, Elizabeth, & ch, Rebecca, Anna, Olive, Phebe Alice & Elva, gct Springfield MM, O.

BARDSLEY
1881, 3, 21. Mary recrq

BARNHILL
1889, 4, 22. Celeste Terrill relrq

BARRETT
1846, 1, 23. Levi, s Jonathan & Rachel, Highland Co., O.; m in Newberry MH, Delilah MOON, dt Joseph & Sarah, Clinton Co., O.
1846, 10, 22. Milton, s Levi & Susannah, Highland Co., O.; m in Newberry MH, Mahala MOON, dt Jesse & Phebe, Clinton Co., O.
Ch: Susannah b 1847, 12, 28
Phebe " 1850, 9, 12
Sarah Lydia" 1851, 12, 11

1846, 3, 16. Delilah gct Fairfield MM
1847, 2, 15. Mahala gct Fairfield MM
1847, 10, 11. Milton & w, Mahala, rocf Fairfield MM, dtd 1847,9,18
1853, 12, 19. Milton & w, Mahala, & ch, Susanna, Phebe & Sarah Lydia, gct Honey Creek MM, Ind.
1861, 4, 22. Asa S. Hockett gct Fairfield MM, O., to m Anna Barrett
1861, 10, 21. Eli Newlin gct Fairfield MM, to m Lydia Barrett

BATES
1885, 12, 21. Eliza recrq
1892, 10, 17. Eliza gct Wilmington MM, O.

BEALS
----, --, --. Jacob b 1788,6,8; m Ann ----- b 1787,12,1
Ch: Joel b 1817, 1, 2
Curtis " 1820, 9, 1
1822, 2, 28. Thomas, s John & Mary, Clinton Co., O.; m in Newberry MH, Nancy STANLEY, dt Samuel & Susannah, Clinton Co., O.
1822, 12, 29. Lemuel, s Thomas & Ann, b
1827, 2, 1. Jacob, s Daniel & Katherine, Clinton Co., O.; m in Newberry MH, Charity HOCKETT, dt Benjamin & Charity, Clinton Co., O.
----, --, --. Jesse & Dinah
Ch: Richard b 1829, 7, 25
Jacob C. " 1831, 11, 29
1828, 4, 4. Jacob d
1829, 9, 10. Esther m Jacob CARSON

1817, 3, 3. Sollomon [Beales] dis mou
1819, 3, 25. Mary [Beales] gct Lees Creek MM, O.
1820, 9, 28. Amy Thompson (form Beals) con mou
1822, 9, 26. Matilda recrq
1823, 2, 20. Daniel [Bealls] dis
1825, 5, 26. Daniel gct White Lick MM, Ind.
1825, 5, 26. John Jr. gct New Garden MM, Ind.
1826, 10, 12. Susannah gct Cherry Grove MM, Ind.
1826, 10, 12. Matilda gct Cherry Grove MM, Ind.
1827, 10, 26. Jesse gct Miami MM, to m Dinah Moon
1828, 7, 24. Catharine & ch, Susannah, Elizabeth, Hannah, Samuel, Amos, Mahala, Rachel & Daniel, gct White River MM, Ind.
1829, 11, 26. Jacob Jr. & w, Charity, & ch, Lucinda & Eli, gct White River MM, Ind.
1830, 5, 27. Lydia Moon (form Beals) dis mou
1830, 4, 22. Jesse Jr. dis disunity
1830, 12, 23. Thomas & w, Nancy, & ch, Lemuel & Mary, gct Milford MM, Ind.
1832, 10, 22. Jacob dis
1833, 5, 20. David rst at White River MM on consent of this mtg
1833, 9, 23. Jesse & w, Dinah, & ch, Richard & Jacob, gct Fairfield MM, Ind.
1835, 1, 19. Elizabeth gct Sugar River MM, Ind.
1835, 3, 23. John dis
1835, 8, 17. Mary, w John, & dt, Mary, gct Fairfield MM, Ind.
1838, 6, 18. John gct Westfield MM, Ind.
1841, 9, 20. Curtis dis mou
1842, 4, 18. Joel dis mou
1850, 9, 16. Mary Jane (form Moon) dis mou

BEARY
1877, 4, 14. Sarah Ann d

1875, 6, 21. Sarah Ann rocf Clear Creek MM, O., dtd 1875,6,12

BEASON
1818, 8, 27. Mary gct Fall Creek MM

BERGER
1886, 4, 19. Fanny recrq
1889, 2, 18. Enoch & Floren recrq
1922, 4, 13. Ora West gct Westfork MM, O.

BETTS
----, --, --. Aaron b 1782,9,11 d 1866,9,20 bur Newbury; m Anna ----- d 1866,7,31 ae 80y bur Newbury
Ch: Mary b 1807, 3, 8 d 1823, 8,18 bur Fairfield
William b 1809, 9, 9
Christopher" 1813, 5, 30
Susannah " 1816, 8, 17 d 1818,10,-- bur Newberry
Priscilla b 1818, 9, 28
1831, 9, 22. William, s Aaron & Ann, Clinton Co., O.; b 1809,9,9; m in Newberry MH, Anna HADLEY, dt James & Ann, Clinton Co., O., b 1812,2,3
Ch: Mary Jane b 1832,10, 9 d 1846,10,29 bur Newbury
Christopher W. b 1834, 1, 30 d 1851,12,12 bur Newbury
Aaron S. b 1835, 10, 13
Priscilla E. "1837,10, 10 " 1838,10,10 bur Newbury
James P. b 1837, 10, 12

BETTS, William & Anna, continued
Ch: Anna C. b 1841, 9, 19
William C. " 1843, 10, 7
Sarah Emaline " 1845, 8, 11 d 1846, 6,27
John H. " 1847, 7, 17 " 1847, 7,25
George E. " 1849, 6, 16
Charles Arthur " 1850, 10, 23 " 1851, 9,13 bur Newbury
Eva Beth b 1852, 11, 17
Albert Lawrence " 1855, 3, 11
Walter G. " 1858, 5, 22
----, --, --. Christopher b 1813,5,30 d 1870, 10,14; m Lydia HUFF, dt Daniel & Sarah, b 1815,2,28
Ch: William A. M. b 1837, 2, 13
Rebecca Ann" 1838, 8, 24
Sarah Ellin" 1840, 3, 26 d 1840, 7,27 bur Newbury
James Edwinb 1842, 3, 14
Aaron Homerb 1845, 2, 6
Martha Emily b 1847, 1, 25
Rachel Alice " 1849, 6, 13
Mary Olevia" 1851, 11, 16
Daniel Webster " 1854, 1, 7
Lydia Luella " 1856, 3, 20
Susan " 1858, 4, 7

1837, 9, 28. Priscilla m Evan STEPHENS
1857, 8, 27. Rebecca A. m George JANNEY
1859, 6, 30. Madison, s C. C. & Lydia, Clinton Co., O.; m in Newberry MH, Caroline JANNEY, dt Joseph & Elizabeth
----, --, --. Wm. A. M. b 1837,2,13; m Caroline ----- b 1839,7,30
Ch: Lizzie b 1862, 6, 25
Thomas Wade" 1864, 6, 17
----, --, --. James E. m Missouri GADDIS
Ch: Anna H. b 1870, 5, 10
Wm. C. " 1871, 12, 15
1927, 3, 18. Anna d
1927, 10, 11. James E. d
1932, 3, 16. Homer d

1819, 11, 25. Aaron & w, Anna, & ch, Mary, William, Christopher & Priscilla, rocf Chestnut Creek MM, Va., dtd 1819,8,28
1835, 9, 21. Christopher gct Fairfield MM, to m Lydia Huff
1836, 4, 18. Lydia rocf Fairfield MM, dtd 1836,2,25
1864, 6, 20. Caroline Jackson (form Betts) con mou
1869, 2, 22. William S. & w, Anna, & ch, George E., Evaline & Albert, gct Union MM
1872, 10, 21. James Edwin con mou
1876, 4, 17. Madison & w, Caroline, & ch, Lizzie & Wade, gct Wilmington MM, O.
1883, 10, 22. Madison & w, Caroline, & ch, Lillie, Russel & Thomas Wade, gct Wilmington MM, O.
1894, 1, 22. James E. gct Wilmington MM, O.
1901, 3, 14. James E. rocf Westfork MM, O., dtd 1901,2,16
1903, 5, 14. James E. relrq
1909, 1, 14. Horner gct White Water MM, Ind.
1913, 3, 20. Sadie recrq
1919, 7, 17. James Edwin recrq
1931, 2, 15. Elizabeth rocf Dayton MM, O.

BILDERBACK
1881, 3, 21. Edwin recrq
1887, 8, 22. E. A. dropped from mbrp

BISHOP
1813, 5, 4. Amy Ann, w John, dt Shepherd & Lydia Randall, b

1870, 1, 17. Amy Ann recrq

BLACK
1849, 8, 22. Margaret A. b
1869, 8, 14. Robert W. b

1870, 3, 21. Margaret Ann recrq
1870, 3, 21. Robert W. recrq
1873, 2, 17. Joseph R. & w, Clarissa, & ch, Sarah A., Matilda C., William H., Mary E., Oma L. & Allen, recrq
1887, 5, 23. Clarissa & ch, Allen E., Ruth Matilda & John A., gct Springfield MM, O.
1887, 5, 23. Margaret Ann & Robert W. dropped from mbrp
1887, 5, 23. Joseph R., Wm. H. & Malinda C. dropped from mbrp

BOGAN
1873, 5, 19. Hannah O. con mou
1873, 6, 23. Hannah O. gct Springfield MM, O.
1873, 9, 22. William E., Elnora & Annie Mary, ch Hannah, gct Springfield MM, O.

BOND
1873, 12, 22. John A. J. & w, Sarah, & dt, Rosanna, recrq
1887, 5, 23. John A. J., Sarah J. & Rosanna dropped from mbrp

BOTTS
----, --, --. George W. b 1836,5,24; m Lydia ----- b 1834,11,23
Ch: Mary E. b 1857, 1, 20
Francis M. " 1860, 8, 11
Joseph " 1862, 4, 3
Isaac N. " 1864, 4, 14 d 1875, 6,12 bur Sabina
Noah M. b 1866, 1, 26
James H. " 1868, 7, 1
1870, 2, 21. George recrq

BOTTS, continued
1870, 3, 21. Letitia recrq
1870, 3, 21. Mary E. recrq
1870, 3, 21. Francis M. recrq
1870, 3, 21. Henry recrq
1870, 3, 21. Isaac N. recrq
1870, 3, 21. Noah M. recrq
1870, 3, 21. James H. recrq
1885, 12, 21. William recrq
1886, 11, 22. Lutitia & Frank relrq
1886, 11, 22. Noah relrq
1886, 11, 22. Henry relrq

BOYD
1869, 4, 19. Susannah Moon (form Boyd) con mou
1883, 11, 19. John T. rocf Springfield MM, O., dtd 1883,9,15
1894, 2, 19. John T. dropped from mbrp

BRANDENBURG
----, --, --. Moses D. [Brandenburgh] b 1834, 2,1; m Rebecca A. ----- b 1836,7,10
Ch: Lawrence b 1856, 2, 11
Laura Z. " 1857, 8, 31
Templin " 1858, 8, 28
Rodney " 1860, 3, 5
Kitty Ann " 1861, 9, 24
Mary A. " 1862, 11, 25
Frank " 1865, 12, 2

1870, 2, 21. Moses & w, Rebecca, & ch, Lawrence, Laura, Templin, Rodney, Kitty, Mary & Frank, recrq
1871, 10, 23. Moses & w, Rebecca, & ch, Laurence, Laura, Templin, Rodney, Kitty, Mary & Frank, gct Springfield MM, O.
1886, 1, 18. Frank & w, Mary A., & ch, George E., Susan Myrtle, Raymond W. & Flora E., recrq

BRANSON
1853, 9, 20. Thomas, s David & Mary, Clinton Co., O., b 1834,5,19; m in Newberry MH, Mary Jane WASSON, dt Calvin & Mary, b 1830,7,10
Ch: Mary Emma b 1854, 7, 7
Jesse K. " 1856, 7, 12
Willis " 1858, 1, 17 d 1858, 3, 5

1845, 4, 14. Daniel H. Moon gct Elk MM, to m Mary Branson
1846, 11, 16. Thomas, s Mary Moon rocf Elk MM dtd 1846,9,19
1859, 7, 18. Thomas & w, Jane, & ch, Mary Emma & Jesse R., gct Mill Creek MM, Ind.

BRIGHT
1888, 10, 22. Ernest recrq

BRITTON
1866, 12, 17. Lydia Jane (form Moon) con mou

BROWN
----- m Jane ----- b 1835,9,20
Ch: Charles b 1856, 9, 25
Esther J. " 1859, 10, 23

1861, 7, 22. Jane & ch, Charles & Esther rocf Walnut Ridge MM, Ind.
1863, 11, 23. Jane & ch, Charles & Esther J., gct Plainfield MM, Ind.
1866, 12, 17. Mary Ellen (form Moon) dis mou
1885, 6, 22. Mattie relrq
1886, 6, 21. Mary relrq
1913, 4, 24. Kathleen recrq

BRUNSON
1838, 4, 23. Elizabeth (form Moon) dis mou
1842, 6, 20. Elizabeth rstrq
1851, 5, 12. Elizabeth gct Honey Creek MM, Ind.
1853, 6, 20. Elizabeth rocf Honey Creek MM, Ind., dtd 1853,4,9
1855, 2, 19. Elizabeth gct New Salem MM, Ind.
1859, 1, 17. Elizabeth [Bronson] rocf New Salem MM, Ind., dtd 1858,12,9
1868, 2, 17. Elizabeth [Bronson] gct Richland MM, Ind.

BUNDY
----, --, --. William S. m Martha A. ROWAN, dt Jeremiah & Hannah, b 1823,5,4
----, --, --. Edom Talbot & -----
Ch: John M. b 18--, 1, 25
Nancy J. " 1842, 4, 15
Edom Talbot m 2nd Jane ----- b 1816,5,12
Ch: Lindley M. b 1848, 11, 1
Orange L. " 1852, 12, 30
Joseph E. " 1855, 1, 1
James " 1857, 4, 5
1859, 2, 4. John d
1863, 7, 28. Lydia d

1837, 8, 21. Lydia recrq
1841, 9, 20. Zadock rst at Fall Creek MM on consent of this mtg
1842, 7, 18. James & Hannah, ch Zadock, rocf Fall Creek MM, dtd 1842,6,22
1842, 9, 19. Rebecca rst on consent of Fall Creek MM
1842, 10, 17. Sarah recrq
1842, 10, 17. Mary recrq
1843, 5, 22. James dis jas
1844, 3, 18. John, Marion & Nancy Jane, ch Mary, recrq
1846, 12, 14. Jane (form Moon) con mou
1849, 2, 12. John recrq; dis by Mt. Pleasant MM, Va., which has been laid down; their consent not given
1855, 5, 21. Zadoc & w, Rebecca, gct Fairfield MM
1856, 8, 18. Edom T. & ch, Lindley, Orange & Joseph Edwin, recrq
1859, 3, 21. Edom T. & w, Jane, & ch, John Marion, Nancy Jane, Lindley Murry, Orange

BUNDY, continued
Lisbon, Joseph Edwin & James Alexander, gct Oak Ridge MM, Ind.
1859, 5, 23. John M. con mou
1859, 9, 19. Edom T. & w, Jane, & ch, Lindley Murry, Orange Lisbon, Joseph Edwin & James Alexander, rocf Oak Ridge MM, Ind., dtd 1859,9,13
1859, 10, 17. John M. gct Oak Ridge MM, Ind.
1864, 11, 21. Edom T. & w, Jane, & ch, Lindley M., Orange Lisbon, Joseph Edmond & James Alexander, gct
1873, 12, 22. Martha A. recrq

BURGE
1873, 5, 19. Martha Jane con mou
1873, 6, 23. Martha Jane gct Springfield MM, O.
1873, 9, 22. Charles & Jesse Clyde, ch Martha Jane, gct Springfield MM, O.

BURGESS
1826, 11, 23. Joseph H. rocf Fairfield MM, dtd 1826,9,30
1829, 9, 24. Joseph rocf Fairfield MM, dtd 1829,7,25
1831, 5, 26. Joseph H. con mou
1831, 12, 19. Joseph gct Miami MM
1835, 2, 23. Joseph gct Springfield MM

BURGETT
1927, 4, 17. Eva Carter relrq

BURGHER
1885, 1, 19. Elemor recrq
1885, 5, 18. Andrew [Burger] recrq

BURNS
1882, 1, 23. Leah rocf Clear Creek MM, O., dtd 1882,1,14
1887, 5, 23. Leah relrq

BEARD
1881, 3, 21. Nancy [Byard] recrq

1886, 6, 21. Jacob & w, Pamelia, & dt, Laura Ann, rocf Springfield MM, O., dtd 1886,5, 15
1888, 2, 20. Lizzie recrq
1888, 9, 17. Elwood rocf Wilmington MM, O., dtd 1888,8,11
1892, 2, 22. Luther A., s Elwood & Lizzie, recrq
1892, 3, 21. Elwood & w, Lizzie, & s, Luther A., gct Cincinnati MM, O.
1899, 7, 13. Nancy [Byard] gct Wilmington MM, O.

CADWALADER
1835, 3, 29. Eliza b
----, --, --. Abner b
1842, 7, 30. Ezra b
1848, 10, 16. Eliza, Abner & Ezra, minors, recrq (ch Joseph)

CALDWELL
1893, 7, 17. Chancellor P. recrq

CAREY
----, --, --. Samuel, s Samuel & Rachel, b 1785,12,2 d 1879,2,13; m Anna ----- b 1786,6,27
1830, 6, 3. Robert [Cary], s John & Margaret, Highland Co., O.; m in Newberry MH, Susanna MOON, dt Joseph & Eliza, Clinton Co., O., b 1813,2,20

Ch: Joseph M. b 1832, 8, 16
Margaret " 1834, 3, 10
Eliza " 1836, 1, 29
Samuel " 1839, 7, 28
John " 1841, 6, 5
Ruth " 1843, 8, 20
Rachel " 1846, 8, 31
Jane " 1849, 7, 28
Isaac " 1851, 2, 24
Anna Elizabeth " 1853, 5, 14

----, --, --. Daniel b 1810,5,2; m Anna ----- b 1811,1,1

Ch: David b 1832, 3, 8
Thomas Elwood " 1833, 7, 15
Joseph " 1834, 11, 29 d 1835,1,26 bur Clear Creek
Priscilla b 1837, 9, 12
Sarah Ann " 1839, 11, 7
Mary Elizabeth " 1842, 12, 21
Lemuel " 1846, 8, 28 d 1847, 9,19
Samuel Lewis " 1848, 7, 13
Jesse Franklin b 1851, 3, 23

Daniel m 2nd Hannah ----- b 1825,11,4

Ch: Elva Jane b 1858, 5, 28
Lydia N. " 1860, 7, 18

1833, 11, 28. Isaac, s John & Margaret, Highland Co., O.; m in Newberry MH, Elizabeth MOON, dt Wm. & Jane, Clinton Co., O., b 1814,3,16

Ch: William M. b 1834, 11, 2
John " 1836, 1, 10
Jesse G. " 1838, 3, 8
Margaret Jane " 1840, 5, 31

1835, 12, 3. John, s John & MArgaret, Highland Co., O., b 1816,3,17; m in Newberry MH, Eliza MOON, dt Joseph & Eliza, Clinton Co., O., b 1817,9,12 d 1847,9,26 bur Newbury

Ch: Elias b 1836, 11, 9
Peninah " 1838, 9, 11
Margaret G." 1839, 12, 20
Daniel " 1841, 6, 14 d 1841, 8,8 bur Clear Creek

CAREY, John & Eliza, continued
Ch: Pleasant b 1842, 8, 18
Susanna " 1844, 3, 14
Charles A.2 1845, 12, 12
Naomi " 1847, 8, 14 d 1848, 1,11 bur Newbury
1837, 11, 2. Elias, s John & Margaret, Clinton Co., O., b 1814,4,23; m in Newberry MH, Jane MOON, dt Henry & Sarah, Clinton Co., O., b 1819,10,26
Ch: Mary Elizabeth b 1838, 9, 1
Sarah M. " 1840, 10, 30
Hannah M. " 1843, 2, 3
Martha Emily b 1845, 5, 29
John Henry " 1848, 11, 14
Rachel " 1850, 4, 1
Anna " 1852, 7, 29
Isaac " 1856, 2, 18
Irena " 1858, 9, 7
James Walter " 1862, 2, 15
1843, 8, 28. Mary Elizabeth, dt C. D. & Arena, d bur Newbury
1844, 12, 26. David M., s Samuel & Ann, Highland Co., O.; m in Newberry MH, Rebecca HIATT, dt Thomas & Harriett, Clinton Co., O.
----, --, --. David b 1832,3,8; m Rebecca Jane ----- b 1837,11,20
Ch: Anna E. b 1854, 6, 30
Madira " 1857, 7, 13
Edgar " 1863, 3, 27
----, --, --. Thomas E. b 1833,7,15; m Lydia ----- b 1833,6,1
Ch: Ida b 1854, 9, 3
Alonzo " 1857, 6, 6 d 1857,12,21 bur Newbury
Lewella b 1858, 12, 2
Alpheus " 1860, 12, 28 d 1861, 3, 3 bur Newbury
Eva b 1862, 4, 15
1854, 3, 5. Lydia Margaret d
----, --, --. John b 1826,8,16; m Elizabeth ----- b 1827,11,23
Ch: Enoch L. b 1859, 4, 12
Samuel F. " 1861, 8, 25
Nathan H. " 1863, 10, 1
1866, 12, 19. Anna d ae 80y bur Newbury
----, --, --. Thomas L., s David M. & Rebecca, b 1845,11,9; m Melissa HENRY, dt Wm. & Nancy, b 1846,11,15
Ch: Walter D. b 1871, 6, 16
Homer " 1873, 4, 20
William H. " 1874, 8, 5
Harley " 1876, 2, 6
Elwood " 1877, 11, 29

1830, 10, 28. Susanna gct Clear Creek MM
1832, 6, 18. Robert & w, Susannah, rocf Clear Creek MM, dtd 1832,5,22
1834, 5, 19. Isaac rocf Clear Creek MM, dtd 1834,4,22
1834, 5, 19. Elias rocf Clear Creek MM, dtd 1834,4,22
1834, 9, 22. Daniel Kester gct Clear Creek MM, to m Elizabeth Carey
1836, 5, 23. Eliza gct Clear Creek MM
1838, 10, 22. Owen West gct Clear Creek MM, to m Mary Carey
1840, 11, 23. Daniel & w, Ann, & ch, David, Thomas Ellwood, Priscilla & Sarah Ann, rocf Clear Creek MM, dtd 1840,10,20
1842, 3, 21. John & w, Eliza, & ch, Elias, Penninah & Margaret G., rocf Clear Creek MM, dtd 1842,2,22
1843, 4, 17. Isaac & fam gct Clear Creek MM
1843, 10, 23. Martin West gct Clear Creek MM, to m Abigail Carey
1846, 5, 11. Elias & w, Jane, & ch, Mary Elizabeth, Sarah Margaret, Hannah & Martha Emily, gct Centre MM
1846, 5, 11. Rebecca gct Clear Creek MM
1846, 9, 14. Charles O. West gct Clear Creek MM, to m Rachel D. Carey
1847, 8, 16. Elias & w, Jane, & ch, Mary Elizabeth, Sarah Margaret, Hannah M. & Martha Emaly, rocf Center MM, dtd 1847,6,16
1848, 3, 13. Daniel dis disunity
1849, 3, 12. John gct Mississinewa MM, Ind., to m Lydia Hollingsworth
1849, 6, 11. John & ch, Elias, Peninah, Margaret G., Pleasant & Susannah, gct Back Creek MM, Ind.
1850, 3, 11. Samuel & w, Anna, rocf Clear Creek MM, dtd 1850,2,9
1850, 6, 10. Elias rocf Clear Creek MM, dtd 1850,5,11
1850, 8, 12. John rocf Clear Creek MM, O., dtd 1850,8,10
1850, 11, 11. Margaret Moon (form Carey) con mou
1850, 11, 11. Charles A. gct Back Creek MM, Ind.
1851, 7, 11. Joseph dis mou
1851, 8, 11. Elias & w, Jane, & ch, Mary Elizabeth, Sarah Margaret, Hannah M., Martha Emaly, John Henry & Rachel, gct Back Creek MM, Ind.
1853, 9, 19. Robert & w, Susanna, & ch, Eliza, Samuel, John, Ruth, Rachel, Jane, Isaac & Anna Elizabeth, gct Back Creek MM, Ind.
1854, 8, 21. David con mou
1854, 9, 18. Thomas E. con mou
1854, 10, 23. Lydia (form Moon) con mou
1855, 6, 18. Hannah (form Green) dis mou
1855, 9, 17. Rebecca Jane & dt, Ann Elizabeth, recrq
1855, 9, 17. Hannah dis mou
1855, 11, 19. Samuel, Daniel, Mary Ann, Jonathan, Rachel, Jane, Silas & Cynthia, ch Elias & Mary, recrq
1855, 11, 19. Priscilla Moon (form Carey) dis

CAREY, continued
mou
1855, 11, 19. Mary recrq
1856, 8, 18. John gct Centre MM, to m Elizabeth Lundy Jr.
1856, 11, 17. Margaret rocf Back Creek MM, Ind. dtd 1856,10,16
1857, 2, 23. Elizabeth rocf Centre MM, dtd 1856,11,12
1858, 11, 22. Elias & w, Jane, & ch, Hannah M., Martha Emily, John Henry, Rachel, Anna, Isaac Milton & Irena, rocf Oak Ridge MM, Ind., dtd 1858,10,12
1861, 10, 21. Hannah recrq
1862, 6, 23. Margaret gct Back Creek MM, Ind.
1864, 4, 18. Altha & Alpheus, ch Daniel & Hannah, recrq
1864, 4, 18. Hannah, w David, & ch by his first m, Samuel Lewis, Jesse Franklin, Elva Jane, Lydia N., Altha & Alpheus, gct Richland MM, Ind.
1864, 5, 23. Nancy Jane gct Richland MM,Ind.
1865, 3, 20. David & w, Rebecca Jane, & ch, Ann E., Dora & Edgar, gct Richland MM, Ind.
1865, 4, 17. Thomas E. & w, Lydia, & ch, Ida M., Luella & Eva, gct Richland MM, Ind.
1865, 7, 17. Anna Nordyke (form Carey) con mou
1866, 1, 22. Elias & w, Jane, & ch, Martha Emily, John H., Rachel, Ann, Isaac Milton, Irena & James Walter, gct Cincinnati MM
1866, 11, 19. Martha E. rocf Cincinnati MM, dtd 1866,10,18
1866, 12, 17. Elias & w, Mary, & ch, Rachel J., Jonathan, Silas, Cynthia & John, gct Gilead MM, Mo.
1867, 8, 19. Samuel con mou & military service
1867, 8, 19. Daniel con mou & military service
1867, 10, 21. John & w, Elizabeth, & ch, Enoch L., Samuel F. & Nathan H., and an adopted dt, Sarah Alcinda Green, gct Center MM, O.
1868, 1, 20. Mary Emily Simpson (form Carey) con mou
1868, 3, 23. Elias & w, Jane, & ch, John Henry, Rachel, Anna, Isaac Milton, Irena & James Walter, gct Plainfield MM, Ind.
1868, 3, 23. Samuel & Daniel gct Gilead MM, Mo.
1875, 7, 19. Marie Malissa & s, Walter, rocf Fairfield MM, dtd 1875,6,19
1877, 9, 17. Thomas L. & s, Walter, rocf Clear Creek MM, O., dtd 1877,8,11
1884, 7, 21. Thomas L. & w, Melissa, & ch gct Clear Creek MM, O.

CARNAHAN
1832, 4, 17. Imogene Dolph relrq

CARR
1889, 3, 18. Nory A. recrq

CARROLL
----, --, --. George b 1865,3,9 d 1906,3,5; m Cammie M. TOWNSEND, dt J. M. & Esther, b 1863,2,20
Ch: Inez M. b 1888, 12, 16
Esther " 1890, 1, 31
Willard Townsend " 1893, 2, 4
Lucile " 1904, 11, 4

1883, 10, 22. Mary & ch, William Jesse Anna, gct Wilmington MM, O.
1887, 7, 18. Cammie gct Miami MM, O.
1894, 2, 19. George E. & w, Cammie M., & ch, Inez & Esther, rocf Miami MM, O., dtd 1894,1,24

CARSON
1829, 9, 10. Jacob, s Jacob & Martha, Highland Co., O.; m in Newberry MH, Esther BEALS, dt John & Mary, Clinton Co., O.
Ch: Achsah b 1834, 3, 25

1827, 5, 24. Jacob rocf New Garden MM, Ind., dtd 1827,5,20
1829, 11, 26. Esther gct Fall Creek MM
1832, 6, 18. Jacob & w, Esther, & dt, Dinah, rocf Fall Creek MM, dtd 1832,5,23
1834, 7, 21. Jacob & w, Esther, & ch, Dinah & Achsa, gct Fairfield MM, Ind.

CARTER
1826, 11, 10. Delilah, dt Nathaniel & Nancy, b
----, --, --. Samuel, s Enoch & Elizabeth, b 1873,5,1; m Lydia Ann ANDREW, dt Wm. & Ruth, b 1848,5,13
Ch: Alice D. b 1867, 7, 31
Mary Emily " 1870, 4, 16
Clarence Elton " 1878, 1, 20 d 1879, 4,23 bur Westboro

1866, 2, 19. Cyrus E. & w, Lydia B., & s, George M., & gr dt, Susannah L. Carter, rocf Dover MM, dtd 1866,1,18
1866, 2, 19. Susannah L. rocf Dover MM, dtd 1866,1,18 (gr dt Cyrus E. & Lydia B.)
1866, 4, 23. Lydia Ann (form Andrew) con mou
1866, 10, 22. Lydia Ann gct Springfield MM,O.
1866, 10, 22. Elias & w, Jane, & ch, John Henry, Rachel, Anna, Isaac, Milton, Irena & James Walter, rocf Cincinnati MM, dtd 1866,10,18
1867, 7, 22. Enoch & dt, Susannah L., rocf Springfield MM, O., dtd 1867,7,20
1867, 7, 22. Samuel & w, Lydia Ann, rocf Springfield MM, O., dtd 1867,7,20
1867, 7, 22. Elizabeth J. rocf Springfield MM, O., dtd 1867,7,20
1867, 12, 23. Delilah rocf Springfield MM,O.,

CARTER, continued
dtd 1867,11,16
1870, 4, 18. Cyrus E. dis mou
1870, 11, 21. Elizabeth rocf Chesterfield MM, dtd 1870,10,8
1873, 2, 17. Enoch & dt gct Cottonwood MM, Kans.
1873, 2, 17. Samuel & w, Ludia, & ch, Alice & Emma, gct Cottonwood MM, Kans.
1873, 12, 22. Elizabeth Linkhart (form Carter) con mou
1874, 1, 19. Samuel & w, Lydia, & ch, Alice D., Mary E. & Wm. C., gct Center MM, O.
1876, 6, 19. Samuel & w, Lydia, & ch, Alice D. & Mary Emily, rocf Center MM, O., dtd 1876,6,14
1885, 5, 18. Samuel & w, Lydia A., & ch, Alice D., Mary E. & Rachel E., gct Oak Ridge MM
1895, 9, 19. Samuel & dt, Eva, rocf Clear Creek MM, O., dtd 1895,7,13

CASHATT
----, --, --. Thomas [Cashat] m Ann ----- b 1771,9,30
Ch: David b 1807, 6, 1
Eleanor " 1815, 7, 23
1858, 6, 4. Ann d ae 86

1822, 3, 28. Ann & ch, Thomas, David, Maria Sarah & Elanor, rocf Clear Creek MM, dtd 1822,3,9
1827, 6, 28. Thomas dis mou
1828, 6, 26. Maria Gilliland (form Curshal) dis mou
1830, 6, 24. Sarah Ruse (form Cashatt) dis mou
1836, 5, 23. Eleanor Hart (form Cashatt) dis mou

CHALFONT
1830, 12, 23. Samuel Miers gct Fairfield MM, to m Priscilla Chalfont

CHAMBERLAIN
1889, 2, 18. Etta Belle recrq
1889, 3, 18. Jacob recrq

CHAPMAN
1933, 10, 2. Gertrude d

1883, 2, 19. Silas & w, Lucy, recrq
1888, 10, 22. Silas dis

CHEW
----, --, --. Ephraim & Rachel
Ch: William b 1815, 2, 14
Mary " 1815, 2, 14
Isaac " 1816, 6, 30
Hannah " 1817, 12, 31
Abigail " 1819, 10, 23
Lydia " 1819, 10, 23
Nathan " 1821, 10, 17
John M. b 1827, 6, 23
Joseph M. " 1830, 3, 6

1818, 10, 29. Ephraim & w, Rachel, & ch, William, Mary & Isaac, rocf Centre MM, dtd 1818,10,17
1820, 2, 24. John rocf Center MM, dtd 1819, 10,16
1830, 11, 25. John dis disunity
1836, 5, 23. William dis mou
1838, 6, 19. Mary Knight (form Chew) con mou
1838, 7, 23. Ephraim & w, Rachel, & ch, Isaac, Hannah, Lydia, Abigail, Nathan, Milton & Joseph, gct Spiceland MM, Ind.

CHICKSTON
1873, 7, 21. Eviline (form Hiatt) con mou

CHRISTOPHER
1896, 6, 18. Blanch relrq

CLARK
----, --, --. Elmore b 1839,1,31; m Sarah A. ----- b 1826,5,17
Ch: Elwworth b 1864, 6, 13
Phebe L. " 1866, 6, 19
Rebecca E. " 1868, 10, 7

1853, 7, 18. Tamar (form Moon) con mou
1861, 8, 19. Sarah Ann (form Moon) con mou
1865, 3, 20. Elmore recrq
1865, 3, 20. Ellsworth recrq (s Elmore)
1874, 4, 20. Elmore & fam gct Center MM, Ia.
1875, 3, 22. Elmore relrq
1883, 2, 19. Verona recrq
1883, 3, 19. Verona gct Cincinnati MM, O.
1885, 9, 21. Lindley rocf Springfield MM,O., dtd 1885,8,14
1886, 4, 19. At. T., Nancy, Wm. Guy & Joseph Boyd, recrq
1893, 11, 20. A. T., Nancy, Wm. Guy & Joseph B. dropped from mbrp
1894, 3, 22. Lindley gct Wilmington MM, O.

CLAY
1870, 2, 21. John Henry recrq

CLELAND
----, --, --. Larkin, s James & Phebe, b 1832,12,2 d 1904,3,5; m Melcena MITCHELL, dt Samuel K. & Charlotte, b 1833,12,13 d 1891,8,16 bur Martinsville
Ch: Henry B. b 1855, 4, 6
Phebe " 1858, 3, 8
Nancy Jane " 1862, 6, 17

1870, 1, 21. Larkin recrq
1870, 1, 21. Melcina recrq
1870, 1, 21. Henry B. recrq
1870, 1, 21. Phebe recrq
1870, 1, 21. Nancy Jane recrq
1881, 2, 21. James recrq
1927, 8, 4. Caroline [Clelland] d

CLEMENS
1892, 11, 21. Ella (form Murphy) gct Van Wert MM, O.

CLINE
----, --, --. Charles, s Geo. W. & Mattie J., b 1869,2,14; m Martha J. HUNT, dt John & Phebe, d 1875,2,15 bur Newbury

1881, 3, 21. Fredy recrq
1887, 8, 22. Fred dropped from mbrp
1894, 1, 22. Charles gct Kokomo MM, Ind.

CLUXTON
----, --, --. Carey m Evelyn HIATT, dt Clarkson & Jane, b 1852,10,28
Ch: Chloe b 1874, 1, 14
1914, 1, 26. Evelyn Hiatt d
1915, 6, 8. Richard, s Clayton & Halcy, b
1931, 8, 12. Halcy d

1894, 8, 23. Clara recrq

COAT
1883, 10, 22. Sarah L. gct Wilmington MM, O.

COFFIN
1843, 2, 10. Elizabeth d bur Newbury
1844, 7, 25. Jesse, s David & Mary, Clinton Co., O., b 1815,8,22; m in Newberry MH, Emily JANNEY, dt Joseph & Elizabeth, Clinton Co., O., b 1818,8,26
Ch: Edwin b 1845, 4, 22
Alpheus " 1846, 11, 5
Adaline " 1848, 1, 30
Wilson " 1850. 2, 22

1844, 7, 25. Daniel, s David & Mary, Highland Co., O., b 1822,11,11; m in Newberry MH, Patience JANNEY, dt Joseph & Elizabeth, Clinton Co., O., b 1825,1,1 d 1857,7,16 bur Newbury
Ch: Eliza b 1845, 7, 5
Caroline " 1847, 10, 23
Rufus " 1850, 11, 1 d 1851,12,22 bur Newbury
Eva b 1852, 10, 31
Lora " 1855, 11, 14
Oscar " 1857, 7, 5

1832, 11, 19. Joseph H. Moon gct Clear Creek MM, to m Priscilla Coffin
1840, 7, 20. Jesse rocf Clear Creek MM, dtd 1840,5,23
1841, 4, 19. Jesse gct Centre MM, to m Elizabeth Whinery
1841, 9, 20. Elizabeth rocf Centre MM, dtd 1841,8,18
1845, 6, 16. Patience gct Clear Creek MM
1846, 6, 11. Daniel & w, Patience, & dt, Eliza, rocf Clear Creek MM
1853, 8, 22. Jesse & w, Emily, & ch, Edwin, Alpheus, Adaline & William, gct White Water MM, Ind.
1855, 11, 19. Daniel & w, Patience, & ch, Eliza, Caroline & Eva, gct Greenfield MM
1857, 2, 23. Daniel & w, Patience, & ch, Eliza, Caroline & Eva, rocf Greenfield MM, Ind., dtd 1857,1,17
1859, 4, 18. Daniel con mou
1859, 12, 19. Susan rocf White Water MM, Ind., dtd 1859,11,23
1860, 3, 19. Daniel & w, Susan, & ch, Eliza Caroline, Eva & Charles C., gct Back Creek MM, Ind.

COLE
1835, 10, 4. Philip C., s John & Hannah, b

1881, 3, 21. Philip C. recrq
1885, 2, 23. Phillip G. relrq

COLLINS
1933, 10, 19. Nancy d

1920, 6, 17. Laura Beard rocf Westfork MM, O.
1921, 3, 17. Lewis recrq

COLVIN
1876, 3, 20. Pricilla & s, Amaziah, recrq
1897, 2, 18. Priscilla & Amaziah, gct Rose Hill MM, Kans.

CONARD
1883, 9, 17. Lewis rocf Clear Creek MM, O., dtd 1883,8,11
1894, 2, 19. Lewis gct Clear Creek MM, O.

CONNEL
1819, 12, 23. Lucinda b (dt Wm. & H. Sheals)

1841, 1, 18. Lucinda rocf Dover MM, dtd 1840, 11,19

CONOVER
1876, 4, 17. Corinthe recrq

COOK
1865, 6, 26. Narcissa d

1839, 6, 17. Mary & ch, Tamar, Rebecca, Josiah D., John & Wright, rocf Caesars Creek MM, dtd 1839,5,23
1840, 10, 19. Mary & ch, Tamar, Rebecca, Josiah D., John K. & Wright, gct Back Creek MM, Ind.
1870, 2, 21. Ambrose recrq

COONS
----, --, --. Abraham G. W. b 1833,7,4; m Mary -----
Ch: Sarah
Ellen b 1857, 12, 8
John Henry " 1860, 3, 22

COONS, Abraham G. W. & Mary, continued
Ch: Thomas
Sherman b 1864, 12, 7
Abraham G. W. m 2nd Mariah D. MEEDS, dt John & Mary, b 1846,3,17
Ch: Joseph Davis b 1869, 4, 6
Charles Martin " 1872, 5, 23

1870, 1, 17. A. G. W., Maria D., Sarah, John H. & Thomas S. recrq
1887, 5, 23. Maria dropped from mbrp

COPPOCK
1860, 9, 26. Lyndley, s Layton & Elnor, Howard Co., Ind., b 1837,8,18; m in Westfork MH, Martha GARNER, dt William & Ann, Clinton Co., O., b 1838,10,13
Ch: William F. b 1861, 8, 9
Emma " 1862, 9, 9
Jesse L. " 1863, 11, 30
Anna " 1865, 3, 13
Riley G. " 1866, 9, 29
Elizabeth " 1868, 3, 18
Della P. " 1872, 3, 16
Lewis " 1874, 9, 23

1865, 6, 19. Lindley rocf Honey Creek MM, Ind., dtd 1865,5,13
1867, 3, 18. Mary E. recrq
1867, 8, 19. Wesley rocf Union MM, dtd 1867, 5,15
1868, 12, 21. Lindley & w, Martha, & ch, William Layton, Emma, Jesse Lucell, Anna, Rileigh G. & Elizabeth, gct Richland MM, Ind.
1874, 6, 22. Wesley & w, Mary E., & ch, Almeda & Clarence A., gct Union MM, O.
1879, 1, 20. Lindley & w, Martha, & ch, William L., Emma, Jesse L., Anna, Riley G., Elizabeth, Della P. & Lewis, rocf Oak Ridge MM, Ind.
1881, 1, 17. Lindley & w, Martha, & ch, William L., Emma, Jesse L., Anna, Riley G., Elizabeth, Della P. & Lewis, gct Union MM, O.

CORDER
1865, 5, 22. Elizabeth (form Achor) dis mou

CORNELL
----, --, --. John m Lizzie CAREY, dt Chas. & Rachel, b 1851,3,29
Ch: Blanche b 1870, 4, 12

1870, 5, 25. Mary Elizabeth con mou
1881, 2, 21. Elizabeth relrq

COUTS
1842, 10, 2. Frances M. [Courto] b
1859, 7, 1. Victoria [Courto] b
1861, 9, 21. Mary [Courto] b
1864, 2, 13. Lizzie [Courto] b

1870, 1, 17. Francis M., Victory, Mary & Elizabeth [Courts] recrq
1878, 10, 21. Frances & dt, Victoria, dis disunity
1887, 5, 23. Victoria, Mary Lizzie dropped from mbrp

COVERDALE
1914, 4, 16. Hattie dropped from mbrp

COWGILL
----, --, --. Elisha & Rebecca
Ch: Gulielma b 1818, 3, 25
Hannah " 1820, 9, 30
Bennet " 1823, 5, 14
Cyrus " 1825, 2, 25
Ann " 1827, 8, 5
Jemima I. " 1830, 4, 25
----, --, --. Amos b 1794,10,13; m Edith ----- b 1799,7,25
Ch: Calvin b 1819, 1, 7
Hiram " 1820, 5, 19
Lydia " 1822, 2, 6
Olive Ann " 1824, 1, 3
Abi " 1825, 6, 28
Nathan " 1827, 8, 8
Catherine " 1830, 9, 22
Maris M. " 1832, 2, 20
----, --, --. ----- m Mary Jane ----- b 1843, 11,5 d 1876,8,5 bur Vienna M. E. Gr.
Ch: Bertha Frances b 1867, 11, 19
Vira Emely " 1875, 1, 22 d 1875, 8, 4 bur Vienna M. E. Gr.
John Frederic b 1867, 6, 30 " 1876, 8,31 bur Vienna M. E. Gr.

1818, 10, 29. Amos rocf Clear Creek MM, dtd 1818,7,11
1818, 10, 29. Edith rocf Centre MM, O., dtd 1818,9,19
1829, 10, 29. Elisha & w, Rebecca, & ch, Gulielma, Hannah, Bennett, Cyrus & Ann, rocf Centre MM, dtd 1829,5,13
1836, 5, 23. Amos & w, Edith, & ch, Calvin, Hiram, Lydia, Olive Ann, Abi, Nathan, Catherine, Maris & Margaret, gct White River MM, Ind.
1837, 8, 21. Elisha & fam gct White River MM, Ind.
1848, 1, 10. Hannah rocf Sparrow Creek MM, Ind., dtd 1845,8,14
1866, 12, 17. Mary Alma (form Stevens) con mou
1868, 2, 17. Mary Jane (form Mills) con mou
1869, 8, 23. Alma & dt, Lilly D., gct Union MM, Mo.
1881, 11, 21. Sarah, w Geo., rocf Wilmington MM, O., dtd 1881,10,14
1920, 8, 26. Sarah recrq

COX
----, --, --. Jesse W., s Wm. & Miriam, b 1843,4,22; m Sarah M. GARNER, dt James & Grace, b 1845,6,26
Ch: Alonzo J. b 1866, 7, 25
Bertha " 1869, 9, 4
James " 1871, 11, 30
William " 1874, 12, 15

1877, 2, 19. Jesse & w, Sarah, & ch, Alonzo, Bertha, James & William, rocf Fairview MM, Ill., dtd 1876,12,16
1881, 3, 21. Milton & w, Eliza, recrq
1886, 11, 22. Milton & Elisha relrq
1891, 6, 22. Jesse relrq
1891, 12, 21. Bertha J. gct Westfork MM, O.
1891, 12, 21. Sarah M. & ch, James & William, gct Westfork MM, O.

COY
1877, 7, 23. Mary A. recrq
1882, 6, 19. Mary relrq

CRAWFORD
----, --, --. Jonas, s John & Elizabeth, b 1834,8,6; m Elizabeth HOCKETT, dt Seth & Nancy, b 1832,10,17 d 1917,12,21
Ch: Florence b 1859, 12, 10
Alice " 1856, 9, 25
----, --, --. George Webster b 1842,4,20; m Sarah E. ----- b 1845,1,20
Ch: George C. b 1868, 6, 12

1855, 5, 21. Elizabeth (form Hockett) con mou
1860, 12, 17. Elizabeth dis jas
1870, 2, 21. Jonas & Elizabeth recrq
1870, 2, 21. George & Sarah E. recrq
1870, 3, 21. Florence Emma recrq
1875, 12, 20. George W. & w, Sarah E., relrq
1876, 8, 21. Alice M. recrq
1886, 3, 22. George S. & w recrq
1891, 1, 19. Anna relrq

CRAMPTON
1927, 3, 13. Cleo Fife rocf Wilmington MM, O.
1927, 4, 17. Earl Hudley recrq
1927, 4, 17. Ruthanna [Cramton], infant dt Earl & Cleo, recrq

CREW
1820, 1, 27. Judith & dt, Elizabeth, rocf Fairfield MM, dtd 1819,6,26
1820, 8, 24. John rocf Fairfield MM, dtd 1820,5,27
1820, 6, 22. Elizabeth Ratliff (form Crew) con mou
1823, 9, 25. Joshua rocf Fairfield MM, dtd 1823,7,26
1827, 7, 26. John gct Fairfield MM
1827, 7, 26. Joshua gct Fairfield MM
1832, 7, 23. Matilda recrq

CRITE
----, --, --. George m Elizabeth A. OWEN, dt Wm. G. & Martha A., b 1847,1,31
Ch: Gracie C. b 1875, 7, 10

CROCKETT
1881, 3, 21. James recrq

CRUIT
1876, 5, 22. Lizzie rocf Wilmington MM, O., dtd 1876,4,14
1881, 3, 21. George A. recrq
1881, 3, 21. Gracy recrq
1881, 3, 21. George E. recrq
1885, 2, 23. George dis disunity
1889, 4, 22. Elizabeth & ch, Gracie C. & George E., gct Dover MM, O.

CRUMLEY
1881, 5, 23. Henry rocf Wilmington MM, O., dtd 1881,4,15
1883, 2, 19. Mollie recrq
1887, 8, 22. Henry dropped from mbrp
1898, 3, 17. Mary E. rocf Wilmington MM, O., dtd 1898,2,12
1898, 3, 17. Blanch rocf Wilmington MM, O., dtd 1898,2,12
1932, 7, 17. Charles & w, Esther, & dt, Rose, recrq
1932, 8, 14. Charles Sr. & w recrq

CRUSE
1835, 5, 18. Matilda McCoy (form Cruse) dis mou

CUNNINGHAM
----, --, --. Charles J. b 1832,4,30; m Lizzie ----- b 1836,1,23
Ch: Dalton b 1863, 1, 19
Frank " 1867, 3, 19 d 1883, 9, 6

1867, 5, 20. Charles recrq
1870, 1, 17. Elizabeth recrq
1870, 1, 17. Dalton H. recrq
1870, 1, 17. Frank recrq
1878, 6, 17. Charles dis disunity
1885, 7, 20. Elizabeth A. gct Kokomo MM, Ind.

DALE
1853, 5, 23. Perry recrq

DANIELS
1827, 3, 29. Sarah O. (form Holloway) con mou

DAUGHERTY
----, --, --. Alfred, s James & Mary Ann, b 1827,7,12; m Mary Jane WILSON, dt George & Ellen, b 1829,9,15

DAVIS
----, --, --. Joshua F. b 1833,9,11; m Elizabeth ----- b 1830,4,26

DAVIS, Joshua F. & Elizabeth, continued
Ch: Valentine b 1856, 12, 7
Lewella " 1859, 4, 11
Sarah Lydia " 1861, 1, 29
----, --, --. Morris b 1837,8,25; m Hannah ----- b 1843,4,6
Ch: Luvenia b 1861, 6, 21
Ada " 1862, 12, 16
Ora E. " 1867, 5, 26
Effie Z. " 1869, 3, 27
----, --, --. Ebeneezer, s Timothy & Barbara, b 1830,4,26; m Susannah SIMCOX, dt Job & Hannah, b 1837,12,24
Ch: Clara Ellen b 1877, 3, 6

1849, 6, 10. Mary (form Hiatt) con mou
1855, 11, 19. Elizabeth (form Green) dis mou
1860, 11, 19. Joshua & w, Elizabeth, & ch, Valentine & Luella, rocf Clear Creek MM, dtd 1860,11,10
1861, 6, 17. Hannah (form Kester) dis mou
1863, 3, 23. Joshua F. & w, Elizabeth, & ch, Valentine, Luella & Sarah Lydia, gct Clear Creek MM
1870, 2, 21. Morris, Hannah, Luvena, Ada, Orra E. & Effa Z., recrq
1876, 5, 22. Ebeneezer recrq
1876, 5, 22. Morris & w, Hannah, & ch, Luvenia, Ada, Ora E., Effie V., Sarah D. & Stella, gct Mississinewa MM, Ind.
1900, 3, 15. Sarah W. gct Clear Creek MM, O.

DEMPSEY
1870, 2, 21. John recrq

DICKERSON
----, --, --. William m Eliza ----- b 1848,8,22
Ch: Rebecca E. b 1868, 3, 4
Ida Belle " 1870, 2, 28

1867, 10, 21. Eliza (form Wilson) con mou
1886, 1, 18. Ida recrq
1886, 1, 18. Rebecca E. recrq
1890, 1, 20. Rebecca dis

DICKEY
1822, 11, 26. Asenath, dt Nimrod & Ann, b
1828, 5, 1. Sarah m John RATCLIFF

1821, 12, 27. Nimrod & w, Anna, & ch, Sarah Phebe, Jane, Elizabeth Charity, Matilda, Lucinda, Mary Ann & James, recrq
1823, 5, 29. Sarah rocf Lees Creek MM, dtd 1823,4,19
1830, 3, 25. Phebe gct Clear Creek MM
1830, 3, 25. Jane gct Clear Creek MM
1830, 3, 25. Elizabeth gct Clear Creek MM
1830, 4, 22. Nimrod & w, Ann, & ch, Charity, Matilda, Lucinda, Mary Ann, James & Asenith, gct Clear Creek MM
1833, 7, 22. Nimrod & w, Anna, & ch, Charity, Malinda, Lucinda, Mary Ann, James & Asenith, rocf Clear Creek MM, dtd 1833,6,18
1833, 7, 22. Jane rocf Clear Creek MM, dtd 1833,6,18
1834, 3, 17. Phebe rocf Clear Creek MM, dtd 1833,8,20
1834, 6, 23. Sarah Ann gct White River MM, Ind.
1835, 8, 17. Matilda Puckett (form Dickey) con mou

1836, 8, 22. Lucinda Hunt (form Dickey) con mou
1836, 9, 19. Nimrod & w, Ann, & ch, Phebe, Jane, Charity, Mary Ann, James & Asenath, gct Duck Creek MM, Ind.

DILKS
1860, 1, 23. Anna (form Moon) dis mou
1870, 2, 21. John I. & Anna recrq

DINGY
1843, 8, 21. Hannah (form Jackson) dis mou
1872, 4, 22. Ann recrq
1872, 6, 17. Lydia recrq

DOAN
1884, 2, 18. Sylvia (form Hunt) relrq
1901, 7, 18. Sant & w, Sylvia, & ch, Wm. Earl Chas. Henry & Mabel, recrq
1917, 5, 17. Agnes & s, Nelson, recrq
1924, 8, 24. Charles & family relrq

DODD
1855, 9, 17. Sarah (form West) dis mou

DOLPH
1821, 4, 14. Catherine & Jessie recrq
1926, 4, 18. Imogene recrq
1930, 5, 18. Ernest recrq
1932, 1, 17. Ora recrq

DONLEY
1885, 1, 19. George W. recrq
1886, 1, 18. John W. & w, Nancy, & ch, J. Walter, Wilsher L., Mary M. & Riie Ann, recrq
1887, 5, 23. George W. dropped from mbrp
1887, 5, 23. John W. & ch dropped from mbrp

DONOHOE
----, --, --. Quincy Clay, s John & Abigail, b 1825,11,11; m Mary HAMMER, dt Wm. & Jane, b 1829,9,20

1871, 3, 20. Mary con mou
1871, 3, 20. Quinn C. recrq
1883, 2, 19. Q. C. [Donoho] relrq

DOUGHERTY
1870, 1, 17. Alfred & Mary Jane recrq
1870, 2, 21. Turisse [Dority] recrq

DOUGLAS
1873, 1, 20. David & w, Lydia M., rocf Litchfield MM, Me.
1874, 5, 18. David [Douglass] & w, Lydia M., gct West Branch MM, O.

DOVE
----, --, --. Beltshazzer, s Elizabeth, b 1845,5,16; m Emeline HAMMER, dt Isaac & Esther, b 1849,9,19
Ch: Alice b 1871, 2, 24
Wilbur A. " 1873, 2, 16
Mirtilla " 1875, 3, 6
Mattie " 1877, 9, 16

1867, 6, 17. Belteshazzer G. recrq
1869, 6, 21. Belteshazzer G. con mou
1869, 7, 19. Emiline recrq
1873, 7, 21. B. F. & w, Nancy Emiline, & ch, Alice May & Wilbur, gct Clear Creek MM,O.
1878, 2, 18. Belteshazzer & w, Nancy Emeline, & ch, Alice May, Wilbur A., Myrtle & Martha, rocf Clear Creek MM, O., dtd 1878,1, 12

DRAKE
1890, 1, 27. Sylvia M., dt John, b

1877, 11, 19. Mary Jane (form Garner) relrq
1886, 4, 19. John recrq

DUMFORD
----, --, --. Elias, s Elias & Sabilta, b 1853, 9,6; m Olive E. ----- b 1854,8,26
Ch: Harry W. b 1874, 7, 6
Emily Annetta " 1876, 3, 22
1875, 7, 23. Harvey W., s Elias & Olive, d
1878, 4, 1. Sarah Sevilla, dt Elias S. & Olive E., b

1876, 4, 17. Elias recrq
1889, 5, 20. Elias & w, Olive E., recrq

DUNGAN
1881, 3, 21. John H. & w, Louisa, & ch, Clyde W. & Mary, recrq
1887, 5, 23. Louisa, Clyde W. & Mary A. dropped from mbrp

DURBAN
----, --, --. Wm. Joseph, s Wm. & Nancy, b 1828,3,16; m Ellen CRAFT, dt John & Rachel, b 1836,7,30
Ch: Adda Mary b 1863, 1, 1
George B. " 1864, 9, 29
Charles C. " 1866, 11, 14
Artie E. " 1868, 8, 29
Josephine " 1870, 4, 13

1876, 3, 20. William J., Ellen & Carrie B. [Durbin] recrq

EDWARDS
1883, 10, 22. Jonathan Conroy recrq; he d before rq was granted but his name was recorded
1883, 11, 19. Emma recrq
1906, 2, 15. Emma relrq

ELDER
1887, 8, 22. Joseph dropped from mbrp

ELLIOTT
1819, 7, 21. Alexander, s Wm. & Elizabeth, b
----, --, --. William & Ann
Ch: Susannah b 1843, 10, 26 d 1878, 6,25
Catharine " 1846, 4, 26
Jesse " 1850, 12, 13

1878, 2, 18. Alexander & ch, Jesse, Eliza J., Catharine & Susan, rocf Clear Creek MM, O., dtd 1878,1,12

ELLIS
----, --, --. John & Phebe
Ch: Charity b 1812, 6, 24 d 1824, 1,26
Elizabeth " 1814, 6, 20
Abraham " 1817, 5, 21
Anna " 1820, 4, 19
Mary " 1824, 2, 3
1819, 12, 2. Robert, s Nehemiah & Sarah, Clinton Co., O., b 1794,9,25; m in Newbury MH, Anna MOON, dt Jonathan & Mary HOCKETT, Clinton Co., O., b 1796,6,18
Ch: Susannah b 1820, 7, 6
Sarah " 1821, 12, 26
James M. " 1823, 11, 26
Dorcas " 1825, 9, 1
Jonathan " 1827, 7, 3
Seth " 1830, 1, 3
Jehu " 1833, 3, 22
Lydia Ann " 1835, 10, 7
Nancy Jane " 1839, 8, 14
----, --, --. Carey b 1816,10,5; m Mary b 1814,9,14
Ch: Elizabeth b 1837, 12, 26
Samuel " 1839, 12, 10
Daniel " 1842, 4, 19
Mary Ann " 1844, 6, 18
Jonathan " 1846, 8, 23
Rachel Jane " 1848, 11, 23
Silas " 1851, 7, 12
Lydia Margaret " 1854, 1, 22
Cynthia " 1855, 7, 11
John " 1858, 10, 31
1845, 7, 23. James, s Robert & Anna, Clinton Co., O., b 1823,11,26; m in Westfork MH, Louisa MOON, dt Daniel & Rachel, Clinton Co., O.
Ch: Edwin b 1846, 9, 30
Rachel Ann " 1852, 9, 18
Elwood " 1857, 4, 19
Daniel H. " 1850, 7, 28 d 1852,11,27

ELLIS, James & Louisa, continued
bur Back Creek, Ind.
Ch: Daniel H. b 1850, 7, 28 d 1852,11,27
bur Back Creek, Ind.
Sarah L. b 1859, 4, 3
Robert " 1863, 2, 2

1819, 3, 25. William & fam gct Cesars Creek MM
1819, 3, 25. Hannah & dt gct Cesars Creek MM
1819, 10, 28. Robert rocf Clear Creek MM, dtd 1819,10,8
1821, 12, 27. Mordecai gct Clear Creek MM
1825, 7, 27. Jehu & w, Phebe, & ch, Bulah, Nehemiah, Sarah, Elizabeth, Abraham & Anna, gct White Lick MM, Ind.
1825, 7, 27. Hiram gct White Lick MM, Ind.
1827, 6, 28. Ann (form Moon) con mou
1828, 7, 24. Ann gct White Lick MM, Ind.
1837, 10, 23. Robert dis disunity
1838, 4, 23. Sarah Green (form Ellis) dis mou
1842, 8, 22. Robert rst rq
1843, 11, 20. Robert & fam gct Springfield MM
1846, 5, 11. Susannah rocf Centre MM, dtd 1846,4,14
1847, 2, 15. Robert & w, Anna, & ch, Susannah, Seth, Jehu, Lydia Ann & Nancy Jane, gct Springborough MM
1850, 1, 14. Jonathan dis disunity
1851, 11, 10. James & w, Louiza, & ch, Edwin & Daniel H., gct Back Creek MM, Ind.
1856, 4, 21. James M. & w, Louiza, & ch, Edwin & Rachel Ann, rocf Back Creek MM, Ind., dtd 1856,3,13
1865, 4, 17. Daniel McPherson gct Center MM, O., to m Lydia Mary Ellis
1868, 6, 22. Edwin C. con mou
1869, 3, 22. Mary A. recrq
1871, 3, 20. James M. & w, Louisa, & ch, Rachel A., Elwood O., Sarah L., Robert, Walter & Myrtie E., gct Richland MM, Ind.
1871, 3, 20. Edwin C. & w, Mary, & s, Leon Orland, gct Elk MM, O.
1876, 10, 23. Mary A. & dt, Leona May, rocf Back Creek MM, Ind., dtd 1876,9,14
1888, 1, 23. Leona May relrq

EVANS
----, --, --. ----- m Mary ----- b 1808,12,28
Ch: Moses b 1834, 7, 25
Priscilla " 1836, 4, 28
Matilda " 1837, 12, 3
Margaret " 1839, 3, 24
Isom " 1840, 12, 7
Mary " 1842, 4, 5

1833, 4, 22. Mary (form Puckett) dis mou
1840, 3, 23. Mary rst
1842, 10, 17. Moses, Priscilla, Matilda Ann, Margaret, Isam & Mary, ch Mary, recrq
1846, 4, 13. Mary Parker (form Evans) dis mou
1851, 5, 12. Moses gct Highland Co. MM, Ind.
1851, 12, 15. Priscilla gct Clear Creek MM
1852, 9, 4. Moses dis mou & jas
1857, 8, 17. Matilda Ann Moore (form Evans) dis mou

FALLIS
1847, 5, 11. Susan m Milton HOLLINGSWORTH

1847, 4, 12. Susan N. rocf Springfield MM, dtd 1847,3,20

FARQUHAR
1887, 5, 22. Laurenna (form Hunt) gct Wilmington MM, O.

FAWCETT
1929, 8, 25. Harry M. & w, Bertha, & ch, Mary & Wm. L., recrq

FENTON
1883, 2, 19. Cora Alice recrq
1883, 3, 19. Cora A. gct Cincinnati MM, O.

FERGUSON
1832, 6, 18. Samuel rocf Fairfield MM, dtd 1832,2,23
1835, 9, 21. Samuel gct Dover MM
1862, 12, 22. Sarah rocf Fairfield MM, dtd 1862,12,20
1864, 10, 17. Sarah gct Springfield MM

FESSANT
----, --, --. William b 1800,12,20 d 1858,11, 23 bur Newbury

1855, 12, 17. William [Fessent] rocf Nottingham MM, England, dtd 1855,8,30

FISHER
----, --, --. Joshua m Eleanor Jane HAMMER b 1840,1,21 (dt Elisha & Elizabeth)
Ch: Mary Emma b 1871, 1, 7
Adia Ruth " 1875, 8, 13
Laura A. " 1873, 12, 5
1880, 8, 22. Elias M. d bur Westboro, O.
1832, 1, 23. Phebe (form Moon) con mou
1832, 8, 20. Phebe gct Sugar River MM, Ind.
1870, 1, 17. E. Jane recrq
1878, 1, 21. Elias M. recrq
1885, 7, 20. Elenor relrq
1921, 1, 13. Rebecca recrq

FOSTER
1885, 11, 23. Isaac & w, Abigail A., recrq
1889, 11, 18. Isaac gct Newhope MM, Ind.

FOX
1836, 1, 28. Jacob S. b

1871, 12, 18. Jacob dis disunity
1879, 9, 22. Almira & ch, Clara D., Alice M., Elizabeth, Margaret E. & George I., recrq
1887, 5, 22. Clara P., Alice M., Margaret,

FOX, continued
Elizabeth & George J. dropped from mbrp

FREEBORN
----, --, --. David B., s David & Mary, b 1829,6,25 d 1905,4,18; m Anna Eliza HENDEE dt Wm. & Ann, b 1828,5,12 d 1917,11,4
Ch: Orcelia G. b 1852, 3, 20
Etta S. " 1859, 8, 2

1870, 2, 21. David, Ann Eliza, Orcelia & Ella recrq

FREEDLEY
1887, 5, 22. Angenetta relrq

FRESH
1877, 2, 19. Caroline (form Moon) gct Peace MM, Kans.

FRISK
1887, 5, 23. Thomas dropped from mbrp

GADDIS
1883, 2, 19. Thomas B. & w, Carey B., recrq
1887, 1, 17. Thomas B. & w, Carrie B., relrq
1900, 5, 17. Thomas D. & w, Carrie B., & s, Tilden H., recrq
1920, 10, 14. Ethel Gibson relrq
1922, 5, 18. Carrie relrq

GALLIHER
1870, 2, 21. Mary recrq
1870, 9, 19. Mary gct Springfield MM, O.

GARLAND
1930, 7, 30. Clarence, s Daniel & Joanna, b

1894, 10, 18. Clara recrq
1897, 9, 16. Joanna recrq

GARNER
1809, 3, 26. Rileigh, s James & Mary, b
----, --, --. John b 1795,6,1 d 1831,6,8 bur West Fork; m Elenor ----- b 1799,6,11
Ch: Mary b 1818, 2, 12 d 1847, 9,15 bur Westfork
Amos b 1820, 6, 8
Elizabeth " 1822, 3, 25
James " 1825, 9, 7 d 1831, 7, 2 bur West Fork
Irena b 1828, 3, 27
William " 1830, 6, 9 " 1831, 6, 2 bur West Fork
----, --, --. William b 1794,4,20; m Ann ----- dt Joseph & Ruth HOCKETT, b 1797,8, 1
Ch: John b 1818, 3, 1
Elizabeth " 1819, 9, 6
James " 1820, 10, 16
Ruth " 1822, 4, 13
Jesse " 1823, 12, 13
Mary " 1825, 7, 28
Ch: Rebecca b 1827, 10, 1
Susannah " 1829, 7, 12
Jephthat " 1831, 12, 11
Nancy " 1833, 4, 18
Rileigh " 1835, 6, 10
Rachel " 1836, 8, 16
Martha " 1838, 10, 13
----, --, --. Ira b 1816,1,13; m Margaret ----- b 1821,5,28
Ch: Martha Ann b 1841, 3, 8
Joseph " 1842, 9, 12
Milton " 1844, 3, 26
Rebecca Jane b 1846, 1, 29
Richard G. " 1850, 3, 23
Pleasant " 1852, 1, 28
Mary Matilda " 1854, 5, 19
Asa " 1856, 11, 1
Asenath Isabel " 1858, 11, 19
Charlie Augustus " 1862, 10, 25
1840, 10, 28. Elizabeth m Jonathan ANDREW
1840, 12, 30. John, s William & Ann, Clinton Co., O., b 1818,3,1; m in Westfork MH, Ann HOLADAY, dt John & Susannah, Clinton Co., O., b 1818,3,7
Ch: William b 1841, 11, 17 d 1842, 9,28
Job S. " 1843, 6, 21 " 1864, 9,21
Amaziah " 1845, 9, 4
Henry M. " 1850, 8, 6 " 1864, 9,18
Rebecca Jane " 1853, 2, 22
John Irwin " 1855, 1, 31
James Allen " 1858, 9, 15
Thomas E. " 1860, 3, 21 d 1863, 9, 8
1842, 9, 28. William d bur Westfork
1843, 5, 19. Jesse d bur Westfork
1843, 10, 3. Mary d bur Westfork
1844, 9, 26. James, s William & Ann, Clinton Co., O., b 1820,10,16; m Grace MOON, dt Joseph & Sarah, Clinton Co., O., b 1823,3, 2
Ch: Sarah M. b 1845, 6, 26
Ann " 1847, 2, 21
Joseph " 1848, 12, 11 d 1870,11, 7 bur Westfork
William b 1850, 11, 12
Jesse " 1853, 2, 2
Mary Jane " 1855, 2, 5
Elizabeth A" 1857, 6, 7
Martha Ellen " 1859, 12, 25
Lindley " 1862, 1, 24 d 1868, 9,11 bur Westfork
Levina b 1864, 6, 20 " 1869, 9,17
Ollive " 1866, 12, 2
1844, 11, 20. Ruth m Wm. ANDREW
1845, 7, 23. Rebecca m Wm. PYLE
1849, 9, 20. Irena m John SIMCOX
1850, 4, 24. Susannah m Asa B. GREEN

GARNER, continued
1851, 6, 16. William d bur Westfork
----, --, --. Jeptha b 1831,12,11; m Martha ----- b 1833,5,26
Ch: Juliann b 1855, 2, 21
Maria M. " 1856, 7, 18
William Orlando " 1858, 3, 31
Emma
----, --, --. William, s James & Grace (Moon) b 1850,11,12; m Louisa HAMMER, dt John & Drusilla, b 1854,7,19
Ch: Hattie b 1874, 10, 10
Frank " 1876, 4, 29
----, --, --. Amos R., s John & Eleanor, b 1820, 6,8 d 1905,2,11; m 2nd Martha S. SEWELL, dt David & Martha, b 1835,9,2 d 1913,9,26
Ch: Eldon C. b 1875, 10, 13
1882, 2, 14. Nancy d bur Westfork
1883, 9, 14. Mont, s Jesse & Maranda, b
1890, 2, 7. Mont J. d
1914, 3, 20. Nancy d

1818, 2, 2. Ann rocf Lees Creek MM, dtd 1818,1,17
1820, 9, 28. Elizabeth gct West Grove MM, Ind.
1820, 9, 28. Elizabeth gct West Grove MM, Ind.
1821, 4, 26. William & ch, John, Elizabeth & James, recrq
1822, 3, 28. Eleanor rocf Clear Creek MM, dtd 1822,3,9
1823, 1, 23. John recrq
1827, 11, 22. Rebecca (form West) con mou
1835, 4, 20. Mary Hammer (form Garner) dis mou
1843, 12, 18. Amos con mou
1854, 3, 20. Jeptha gct Fairfield MM, to m Martha B. McPherson
1854, 8, 21. Martha B. rocf Fairfield MM
1855, 12, 17. Margaret & ch, Martha Ann, Joseph, Milton, Rebecca Jane, Richard, Pleasant B. & Mary Matilda, recrq
1856, 8, 18. Ira recrq
1858, 4, 19. James & w, Grace, & ch, Sarah M., Ann, Joseph, Wm., Jesse, Mary Jane & Elizabeth, gct Oak Ridge MM, Ind.
1860, 5, 21. Riley con mou
1861, 9, 23. Riley gct West Union MM, Ind.
1863, 6, 22. James & w, Grace, & ch, Ann, Joseph Wm., Jesse, Mary Jane, Elizabeth A., Martha Ellen & Lindley, rocf Oak Ridge MM, Ind.
1863, 12, 21. Martha Ann dis jas
1863, 12, 21. Rebecca Jane dis jas
1868, 2, 17. Milton dis disunity & military service
1869, 1, 18. Ann gct Richland MM, Ind.
1870, 2, 21. Rileigh recrq
1870, 3, 21. Jeptha & ch, Julia A., Maria M., William O. & Martha Emma, gct Westfield MM, Ind.
1872, 9, 23. Ameziah con mou
1873, 2, 17. Amos R. con mou
1873, 3, 17. Martha S. rocf Springfield MM, O., dtd 1873,2,15
1876, 6, 19. Louiza & s, Frank, recrq
1877, 3, 19. Ann rocf Oak Ridge MM, Ind., dtd 1877,2,13
1877, 11, 19. Mary Jane Drake (form Garner) relrq
1885, 12, 21. Mattie & dt, Hyacinth, recrq
1886, 1, 18. Rebecca recrq
1886, 5, 17. Albert recrq
1888, 1, 23. Mollie A. relrq
1889, 3, 18. William H. recrq
1891, 6, 22. Mary B. & Sarah E. recrq
1894, 2, 19. Albert dropped from mbrp
1895, 1, 17. William & w, Louisa, & ch, Hattie, Frank, Ethel, Cecil & Velma, rocf Westfork MM, O., dtd 1894,12,15
1897, 8, 26. John rocf Minneapolis MM, Minn., dtd 1897,7,8
1898, 6, 16. William & w, Louisa, & ch, Ethel, Cecil & Velma, gct Westfork MM, O.
1912, 10, 17. Nancy recrq

GARRETT
----, --, --. William m Mary E. ANDREW, dt Wm. & Ruth, b 1847,4,7
Ch: Effie Viola b 1869, 3, 4
Charles Leroy " 1870, 11, 26
Andrew Orvil " 1872, 4, 8

1868, 6, 22. Mary E. con mou
1889, 3, 18. Joseph G. recrq
1893, 11, 20. Joseph dropped from mbrp

GASKELL
----, --, --. Milton S., s Thomas & Mary, b 1811,10,5; m Louisa TRIBBY, dt Joseph & Ruth, b 1806,6,29

1874, 10, 19. Milton S. [Gaskill] & w, Louise, rocf Wilmington MM, O., dtd 1874,8,14

GAUSE
1863, 9, 8. Thomas E. d bur West Fork
1864, 9, 10. Henry M. d bur West Fork

1884, 4, 21. Samuel & w, Mary Jane, & ch, Elkana B., Esther F. & Morris, rocf Springfield MM, O., dtd 1884,3,15

GEHRON
1928, 11, 23. Edith d 1928,11,23

1928, 4, 15. Chris & w, Edith, & dt, Mondalee, recrq

GEORGE
1931, 7, 18. Tabitha rocf Fairfield MM, dtd 1831,5,28

GIBSON
----, --, --. ----- m Rachel HUNT, dt Jacob & Lydia, b 1798, 10, 1 d 1878,12,31
Ch: Sarah b 1831, 7, 18
Caleb L. " 1836, 2, 11
Jesse A. " 1838, 1, 26
Louiza Jane" 1841, 10, 12
1856, 3, 27. Sarah A. m Stover SIMCOX
----, --, --. Caleb, s Absalom & Rachel, b 1836,2,11 d 1906,1,11; m Nancy BROWN
Ch: Orlando M. b 1860, 9, 9
William T. " 1862, 2, 21
Jessie E. " 1863, 6, 4
Ida M. " 1864, 11, 28
Francis M. " 1866, 5, 1
Charles A. " 1872, 5, 10
Adie G. " 1873, 8, 30
Oliver O. " 1876, 8, 3
1876, 9, 30. Absalom d
1928, 3, 8. Alta, w Chas., dt S. & Emma Wallace, d

1829, 11, 26. Rachel (form Hunt) con mou
1830, 8, 26. Rachel gct Springfield MM
1833, 3, 18. Rachel rocf Springfield MM, dtd 1833,2,12
1851, 1, 13. Caleb S., Jesse A. & Louiza Jane, ch Rachel, recrq
1851, 1, 13. Sarah recrq
1859, 4, 18. Sarah Elizabeth (form Moon) con mou
1860, 5, 21. Caleb S. con mou
1867, 2, 18. Louiza Holaday (form Gibson) con mou
1867, 12, 23. Jesse con mou
1868, 1, 20. Mary Emily (form Carey) con mou
1868, 3, 23. Jesse & w, Martha E., gct Plainfield MM, Ind.
1869, 12, 30. Oscar, Frank, William Thomas & Mary, ch Sarah E., recrq
1870, 1, 17. Sarah E. & ch gct Vermillion MM, Ill.
1871, 5, 22. Absalom recrq
1893, 11, 20. W. T. & A. G. dropped from mbrp
1911, 7, 13. Eva M. & Ethel recrq
1916, 1, 13. Harsha & Helen recrq

GILLILAND
1828, 7, 24. Maria (form Curshal) dis mou

GLASGO
1877, 6, 18. Josephine (form Jackson) relrq

GOLDSBERRY
1873, 5, 19. Robert [Goolsberry] & w, Jennie, & ch, William, Janette, Leander & Lula, recrq
1887, 5, 23. Robert, Jennie, William & Leander, dropped from mbrp

GRAHAM
1928, 2, 28. Jewse, s Enoch & Rachel, Clinton Co., O.; m in Newberry MH, Phebe WRIGHT, dt John & Sary, Clinton Co., O.
----, --, --. Josiah b 1803,3,1 d 1856,4,2; m Mary ----- b 1804,7,13
Ch: Josiah b 1836, 3, 27 d 1858,1,23 (an adopted nephew)
Hannah I. Pennington b 1845, 12, 7

1825, 7, 27. Josiah con mou
1826, 2, 23. Jonathan dis mou
1829, 9, 24. Jesse dis disunity
1831, 1, 27. Phebe dis jH
1842, 7, 18. Mary recrq
1852, 10, 11. Josiah & w, Mary, & Hannah Isabel Pennington, an adopted ch, gct Duck Creek MM, Ind.
1856, 4, 21. Josiah & w, Mary, & adopted ch, Josiah Graham, & Hannah Isabel Pennington, -----
1868, 10, 19. Mary gct Springfield MM, O.
1886, 1, 18. Lovina recrq

GRAYBILL
1881, 3, 21. Nancy recrq
1886, 5, 17. Ed recrq

GREEN
----, --, --. Robert b 1792,11,14 d 1843,4,5 bur Newbury; m Mary ----- b 1799,11,2 d 1840,2,14 bur Newbury
Ch: Joseph b 1818, 1, 9
Jehiel " 1819, 7, 20
John " 1821, 6, 13
Joel " 1824, 3, 21
Israel " 1826, 6, 10
Mahlon " 1828, 12, 6
Ruth " 1831, 11, 18
Robert B. " 1835, 9, 1
Rebecca I. " 1838, 3, 31 d 1838,10,12 bur Newbury
1842, 9, 1. Joseph, s Robert & Mary, Clinton Co., O., b 1818,1,9; m in Newbury MH, Roda WEST, dt William & Sarah, Clinton Co., O., b 1819,4,15
Ch: Mary Emily b 1843, 11, 23
William W. " 1845, 5, 7
Robert A. " 1847, 3, 26
Sarah Ellen " 1849, 4, 14
Owen W. " 1856, 2, 10 d 1862, 3, 7
Joseph Lindley " 1858, 8, 19
----, --, --. John, s Robert & Mary, b 1821, 6,13 d 1906,12,11 bur Martinsville; m Rhoda CAREY, dt Samuel & Anne, b 1824,5,9
Ch: Robert L. b 1844, 8, 6
Samuel " 1844, 8, 6 d 1844, 11,6
David C. " 1846, 11, 19
Eli (Eliel)" 1849, 2, 3
Thomas Elwood " 1851, 3, 16
Joseph P. " 1853, 11, 27 d 1854, 8,30

GREEN, John & Rhoda, continued
Ch: Enos b 1855, 9, 23
Mary " 1858, 11, 8
Anne " 1861, 3, 23
Alie E. " 1866, 5, 22
----, --, --. Aaron b 1818,10,20; m Rachel ---- b 1826,2,21
Ch: Nancy Jane b 1844, 12, 25
John Sewell" 1847, 12, 22
----, --, --. Isaac C. b 1826,6,13; m Rachel M. ----- b 1829,5,23
Ch: Thomas Homer b 1849, 10, 27
Susan Mary " 1851, 8, 28
1850, 4, 24. Asa B., s David & Mary, Clinton Co., O.; m in Westfork MH, Susanna GARNER, dt William & Ann, Clinton Co., O., b 1829, 7,12
Ch: William G. b 1851, 2, 15
John Riley " 1853, 3, 21
David Warren " 1855, 1, 2
----, --, --. Robert B., s Robert & Mary, b 1835,9,1; m Sarah A. WEST, dt Peyton & Sarah, b 1835,7,25
Ch: Charles E. b 1856, 8, 11
Peyton W. " 1858, 7, 19
Carrie E. " 1862, 10, 14
Josiah E. " 1865, 5, 23 d 1895, 2, 8 bur Martinsville
Mary E. b 1868, 4, 22
Cora A. " 1872, 5, 20
----, --, --. Daniel M., s Jonathan & Mary M., b 1844,2,21; m Gulielma SMITH, dt Evan & Abigail, b 1846,4,27
Ch: William Edgerton b 1869, 3, 25
Walter Douglas " 1871, 7, 6
Laura Elma " 1873, 5, 10
Jonathan Evan " 1875, 10, 17
Mary Hannah" 1879, 2, 26
----, --, --. Harry J., s Eliah & Carrie, b 1879,12,29; m Mary L. LEONARD, dt C. B. & Mary, b 1883,11,18
1903, 9, 22. Edith M. b

1823, 12, 25. Robert & w, Mary, & ch, Joseph, Jahiel & John, recrq
1838, 4, 23. Sarah (form Ellis) dis mou
1842, 7, 18. Johiel gct Centre MM, to m Rachel Lundy
1842, 9, 19. Jesse rocf Fairfield MM, dtd 1842,5,26
1843, 5, 22. Jesse gct Fairfield MM
1843, 7, 17. John gct Clear Creek MM
1843, 10, 23. Rachel rocf Centre MM, dtd 1843, 3,15
1846, 1, 12. Aaron & w, Rachel, & dt, Nancy Jane, rocf Centre MM, dtd 1845,7,16
1846, 5, 11. Ruth gct Center MM
1846, 12, 14. Jehiel & w, Rachel, & s, Joel, gct Centre MM, O.
1847, 9, 13. Miles H. Moon gct Centre MM, to m Charlotte D. Green
1848, 3, 13. Joel gct Centre MM, to m Elizabeth Schooley
1848, 4, 10. Israel C. gct Dover MM, to m Rachel Morman
1848, 9, 11. John C. & w, Rhoda, & ch, Robert & David C., rocf Centre MM, dtd 1848, 6,14
1850, 4, 15. Joel gct Mississinewa MM, Ind.
1850, 8, 12. Susannah gct Springfield MM, O.
1850, 11, 11. John rocf Centre MM, dtd 1850, 9,18
1851, 3, 10. Jesse & w, Sarah, & ch, Ruth, Jesse & Sarah Jane, rocf Centre MM, dtd 1850,10,13
1851, 5, 12. Hannah & Elizabeth rocf Centre MM, dtd 1851,3,12
1851, 9, 15. John Hockett gct Springfield MM, to m Mary Ann Green
1852, 7, 3. John Jr. con mou
1852, 8, 7. Asa B. & w, Susannah, & s, William G., roc dtd 1852,6,19
1852, 8, 7. Miriam (form Schooley) con mou
1852, 9, 4. Rachel rocf Dover MM, dtd 1852, 7,15
1853, 6, 20. Israel C. dis disunity
1854, 5, 20. Mahlon con mou
1854, 7, 17. Cert for Asa B. & w, Susannah, & ch, William G. & John Riley, granted to Miami MM, O., endorsed back to this mtg 1854,12,--
1854, 10, 23. Mahlon gct Mississinewa MM, Ind.
1855, 6, 18. Hannah Carey (form Green) dis mou
1855, 11, 19. Robert Barclay dis mou
1855, 11, 19. Elizabeth Davis (form Green) dis mou
1856, 12, 26. Cyrus Moon gct Springfield MM, to m Jane Green
1858, 1, 18. Asa B. & w, Susannah, & ch, William G., John Rileigh, David Warren & Martha Emily, gct West Union MM, Ind.
1861, 11, 18. Rachel & ch, Thomas, Homer, Susan Mary Ruth Emma, Robert Oscar, Martha Elizabeth & Theodocia Eva, gct Clear Creek MM
1864, 3, 21. Jehiel & w, Rachel, & ch, Joel Wm., James Robert, Aseph Leander, Amanda Jane & Lieu Emma Catherine, rocf Springfield MM, O., dtd 1864,2,20
1865, 10, 23. Parker rmt Mary E. Moon
1867, 5, 20. John & s, Arthur M., gct Bangor MM, Ia.
1867, 9, 23. John Sewell gct Clear Creek MM, O.
1867, 10, 21. Sarah, Alcinda, adopted dt of John & Elizabeth Carey, gct Center MM, O.
1867, 10, 21. Sarah Ann & ch, Charles Edwin Payton W., Carrie Estella & Josiah, recrq
1868, 3, 23. Robert L. gct Clear Creek MM, O.
1868, 3, 23. Robert L. gct Clear Creek MM, O.

GREEN, continued
1868, 6, 22. William gct Spring River MM, Kans. or Mo.
1868, 11, 23. Hannah Isabel con mou
1868, 12, 21. Hannah Isabel gct Springfield MM
1870, 2, 21. Joseph & w, Rhoda, & ch, Robert Amos, Sarah Ellen, Joseph Lindley & niece, Anna West, gct Spring River MM, Mo.
1870, 2, 21. Robert B. recrq
1870, 5, 25. David C. dis mou
1870, 12, 19. Daniel M. & w, Gulielma, & s, William Edgerton, rocf Fairfield MM, O., dtd 1870,12,17
1873, 2, 17. Thomas E. gct Center MM
1879, 10, 20. Annie recrq
1881, 9, 19. Daniel & w, Gulielma, & ch, Gurney, William E., Walter, Laura E. & Jonathan E. & Mary, gct Rose Hill MM, Kans.
1893, 11, 20. Charles & Peyton dropped from mbrp
1900, 6, 14. Sarah Ann gct Cincinnati MM, O.
1903, 3, 19. Mary L. rocf Center MM, O., dtd 1903,2,18
1914, 4, 16. Cora dropped from mbrp

GRICE
1818, 2, 16. William b

1854, 6, 19. Jemima (form Hiatt) dis mou
1870, 1, 17. William recrq

GRUBB
1864, 11, 21. Charles W. recrq
1867, 3, 18. Charles W. dis disunity

HADLEY
1795, 11, 2. Susannah b
----, --, --. James b 1774,1,31 d 1845,8,19; m Anna ----- b 1778,2,16
Ch: Edith b 1796, 7, 17
Mary " 1798, 1, 1
Tamer " 1799, 11, 4
Sarah " 1801, 10, 1
James " 1803, 8, 20
Jeremiah " 1805, 11, 10
Margaret " 1808, 8, 15
Anna " 1812, 2, 3
John " 1814, 3, 28
Jane " 1816, 11, 23
Joshua " 1820, 3, 23
----, --, --. James b 1803,8,20; m Sarah ----- b 1807,3,30
Ch: Daniel H. b 1830, 1, 5
Sarah Ann " 1831, 3, 31
Mary " 1832, 8, 26
Alfred " 1834, 1, 5
Elizabeth Ellen " 1835, 12, 20
Cynthia Jane " 1837, 10, 19
Juliet " 1839, 8, 11
1839, 10, 31. Joshua D., s James & Ann, Clinton Co., O., b 1820,3,23; m in Newberry MH, Rachel LUNDY, dt Amos & Susannah
Ch: William B. b 1841, 9, 13
Amos L. " 1842, 10, 12
James E. " 1844, 11, 6
Mary Ann " 1846, 4, 7
1841, 7, 4. Jane d bur Newbury
1845, 3, 19. Ann d bur Newbury
----, --, --. William, s Wm. & Susannah, b 1832,3,14 d 1900,10,8; m Rebecca Jane HUNT, dt Jonathan & Margaret, b 1838,2,4
Ch: Ida Belle b 1858, 3, 16 d 1876,10,24 bur Martinsville, O.
Emma S. b 1861, 11, 29
Frank W. " 1865, 5, 9
Annie J. " 1867, 8, 23
1868, 4, 22. Annie d
----, --, --. Alfred, s James & Sarah, b 1834,1,5; m Keziah K. OVERMAN, dt Eli & Piety, b 1836,2,2
Ch: Elmer T. b 1871, 11, 24
Royal " 1874, 11, 27
Clifton " 1877, 2, 10
1899, 7, 4. Miriam G., dt F. W. & Winnie, b

1817, 8, 4. Edith rocf Clear Creek MM, dtd 1817,7,12
1818, 3, 2. James & w, Anne, & ch, Thamer, Sarah, James, Jeremiah, Margaret Ann, John. Jane, rocf Clear Creek MM, dtd 1818,2,14
1829, 1, 29. James gct Fairfield MM, to m Sarah Huff
1830, 2, 25. Sarah rocf Fairfield MM, dtd 1829,10,31
1831, 9, 19. Jeremiah gct Centre MM
1839, 11, 18. John con mou
1846, 1, 12. James & w, Sarah, & ch, Daniel H., Sarah Ann, Mary, Alfred, Elizabeth Elen, Cyntha Jane & Juliet, gct Fairfield MM, O.
1846, 6, 11. Joshua D. & fam gct Cincinnati MM
1848, 10, 16. Joshua D. & w, Rachel, & ch, Amos L. & James, rocf Cincinnati MM, dtd 1848,8,17
1848, 12, 11. William West gct Springfield MM, to m Sophia Hadley
1851, 1, 13. John gct Springfield MM, O.
1851, 12, 15. Joshua D. dis jas
1853, 2, 5. Rachel dis jas
1857, 3, 23. Rebecca Jane (form Hunt) dis mou
1865, 11, 20. Susanna rocf Springfield MM, O., dtd 1865,11,18
1865, 11, 20. William & w, Rebecca, & ch, Oda, Bell, Emma & Frank W., rocf Springfield MM O., dtd 1865,11,18
1872, 6, 17. Alfred & w, Keziah, & s, Elmer F., rocf Fairfield MM, dtd 1872,5,18
1879, 2, 17. Susannah gct Springfield MM, O.
1882, 2, 20. Alfred & w, Keziah R., & ch, Elmer F., Royal, Clifton & Leila, gct Springfield MM, Kans.
1894, 1, 22. Mary F. gct Springfield MM, O.
1894, 1, 22. Sarah A. gct Springfield MM, O.

HADLEY, continued
1895, 8, 22. Winnie recrq
1907, 8, 18. Atwell M. & w, Sarah A., & ch, Hershel, Ethel, Reba, Edith Vivian & Herbert, rocf Springfield MM, O.
1908, 2, 13. Frank W. & w, Winnie, & dt, Miriam, relrq
1910, 8, 25. Abigail J. gct Ypsilanta MM, Mich.

HAGERMAN
1861, 6, 17. Lydia (form Miller) dis mou & jas

HAINES
1853, 2, 22. Rebecca Jane, w Robert, dt John & Mary Ann Garner, b
----, --, --. M. M. b 1832,2,2; m Naomi CURL, b 1831,6,10
Ch: Maria L. b 1854, 10, 21
Andrew J. " 1855, 12, 23
Joel E. " 1857, 10, 12
Mary Maranda b 1857, 12, 23
Emma F. " 1862, 2, 13
Cora Ellen" 1864, 12, 6
James A. Brisben " 1867, 3, 2
Arthur " 1870, 4, 27
Hattie " 1873, 3, 23
1858, 11, 19. Belle, w Andrew, dt Ira & Margaret Garner, b

1863, 8, 17. Elwood & w, Aphracia, & ch, Lydia Emily, Israel Thomas, Ann Isabel & Zimri Samuel, rocf Dover MM
1867, 10, 21. Ellwood & w, Aphracia, & ch, Lydia Emily, Israel Thomas, Ann Isabel, Zimri Samuel, gct Spring Creek MM, Ia.
1870, 1, 17. Mordecai recrq
1870, 1, 17. Naomi recrq
1870, 1, 17. Maria recrq
1870, 1, 17. Andrew J. recrq
1870, 1, 17. Joel recrq
1870, 1, 17. Mary M. recrq
1870, 1, 17. Emma F. recrq
1870, 1, 17. Cora E. recrq
1870, 1, 17. James B. recrq
1872, 6, 17. Mary con mou
1875, 2, 22. Mary relrq
1878, 7, 22. Mordecai M. & Andrew relrq
1882, 8, 21. Rebecca Jane relrq
1889, 2, 18. Eva & ch, Rowena M. & Norma L. recrq
1891, 7, 20. Charley C. & ch, Freddy Melville, Lulu May & Ona Oberta, rocf Lick Creek MM, Ind.

HAISLEY
1859, 8, 22. James M. Hunt rqct Oak Ridge MM, Ind., to m Emma Haisley

HAISTINGS
1885, 8, 17. Charlotte recrq

HALL
----, --, --. Moses & Sarah
Ch: Ruth b 1838, 3, 3
Amos " 1839, 9, 4
Margaret " 1840, 12, 10
Ellwood " 1843, 1, 16
Alfred " 1845, 1, 19
Phebe " 1847, 1, 8
Marion " 1849, 12, 5

1844, 4, 22. Sarah recrq
1844, 4, 22. Moses recrq
1844, 5, 20. Ruth, Amos, Margaret & Elwood, ch Moses & Sarah, recrq
1855, 2, 19. Moses & w, Sarah, & ch, Ruth, Amos, Margaret, Ellwood, Alfred, Phebe, Marion & Mary Emiline, gct Cherry Grove MM, Ind.
1886, 1, 18. Emma C. recrq
1881, 3, 21. Daniel recrq
1887, 8, 22. Daniel dropped from mbrp
1889, 3, 18. Almeda recrq

HAMMER
----, --, --. James, s Wm. & Jane, b 1812,1, 5; m Mary GARNER, dt John & Eleanor, b 1818,1,12
Ch: Jane b 1832, 9, 6
Martha " 1839, 9, 23
John G. " 1842, 1, 25 d 1842, 6,14 bur Westfork
Amos G. b 1843, 6, 7
William R. " 1846, 1, 13
James G. " 1850, 5, 27
Irena " 1853, 3, 23
Noah " 1859, 9, 24
Mary Ellen " 1863, 9, 14

----, --, --. ----- m Elizabeth ----- b 1801, 10,5
Ch: William b 1837, 10, 19
Esther Ann " 1841, 9, 2
Margaret E." 1848, 1, 25
----, --, --. Elisha, s William & Jane, b 1813 2,6; m Elizabeth ----- b 1801,10,10
Ch: Francis M. b 1859, 4, 8
----, --, --. Wilfred, s Isaac & Esther, b 1844,8,20; m Sarah MOON, dt James & Levina, b 1842,12,29
Ch: Melvina b 1865, 12, 15
Emma " 1868, 12, 14
Levi " 1871, 1, 4
James Riley" 1877, 3, 6
Isaac Rauley b 1877, 3, 6
Emerson " 1868, 12, 14 (twin to [Emma)
----, --, --. Amos G., s James & Mary, b 1843,6,7; m Martha CONSTABLE, dt John & Dorothy, b 1848,8,17
Ch: Florella b 1872, 9, 15

HAMMER, continued
Ch: Maretta b 1874, 7, 10
Leroy " 1876, 7, 20
1877, 7, 11. Leroy d bur Westfork
1877, 7, 27. Florella d bur Westfork

1835, 4, 20. Mary (form Garner) dis mou
1842, 11, 21. Thomas recrq
1844, 6, 10. Mary rstrq
1844, 6, 10. Elizabeth rstrq
1844, 7, 15. Jane, Martha & Amos G., ch James, recrq
1853, 9, 19. Elizabeth gct Back Creek MM, Ind.
1856, 10, 20. Elizabeth & ch, Elleanor Jane, Esther Ann & Margaret Emily, rocf Back Creek MM, Ind., dtd 1856,9,18
1857, 5, 18. Elisha rocf Back Creek MM, Ind., dtd 1857,4,16
1857, 12, 21. Elisha dis disunity
1859, 6, 20. Eleanor Jane dis
1863, 7, 20. Esther Ann Watson (form Hammer) dis mou
1864, 9, 19. Martha Moon (form Hammer) dis mou
1865, 4, 17. Sarah E. (form Moon) con mou
1865, 8, 21. Mary Emily Stogden (form Hammer) dis mou
1867, 2, 18. Wilford recrq
1868, 2, 17. Elisha recrq
1869, 7, 19. Francis, minor, recrq
1872, 7, 22. Amos con mou
1872, 8, 19. Riley rpd mou & jas
1873, 5, 19. Martha recrq
1878, 7, 22. James G. relrq
1878, 10, 21. Margaret Jane & ch, Audsley D. & Manford, recrq
1885, 12, 21. Charles recrq
1886, 1, 18. Peter & w, Amanda, & ch, Jesse, Daisy & Curtis, recrq
1886, 1, 18. Mattie recrq
1889, 4, 22. Emma rocf Wilmington MM, O., dtd 1889,4,13

HAMMERSLEY
1889, 2, 18. David F. & Fannie A. recrq
1889, 2, 18. Elizabeth E. recrq

HANKS
1857, 3, 23. Sarah Jane (form Puckett) dis mou

HANLIN
1880, 6, 21. Annie gct Smyrna MM, Ia.

HANNAH
1918, 4, 17. Arena relrq

HARDEN
1877, 2, 19. Sarah Ann (form Moon) gct Peace MM, Kans.

HARRIS
----, --, --. Samuel m Ruth Ann Taylor, dt Geo. & Sarah, b 1814,1,19
Ch: Marion b 1844, 9, 8
Lewis " 1854, 2, 11
----, --, --. Malinda J., w Marion, dt Wm. & Nancy PURCELL, -----

1874, 2, 23. Francis M. & w, Malinda, & s, William, recrq
1874, 2, 23. Lewis & Ruth Ann & Lena recrq
1877, 4, 23. William relrq
1879, 7, 21. Marion dis disunity
1887, 8, 22. Louis dropped from mbrp
1920, 4, 15. Clara Cluxton relrq

HARROLD
1858, 10, 28. Nathan, s Andrew & Mary, Clinton Co., O.; m in Newberry MH, Anna KESTER, dt Daniel & Elizabeth, Clinton Co., O., b 1837,6,26
Ch: Mary
Alice b 1860, 1, 4
Anna
Elizabeth " 1862, 3, 4
Anna Kester Harrold m 2nd John LLEWELLYN
1878, 8, 7. Mary Elizabeth, dt Nathan & Anna, d bur Martinsville

1846, 11, 16. Leah S. rocf Richland MM, dtd 1846,10,7
1856, 7, 21. James J. gct Richland MM, Ind.
1859, 8, 22. Anne gct Center MM
1863, 3, 23. Anna & ch, Mary Alice & Anna Elizabeth, rocf Center MM, dtd 1863,3,18
1868, 3, 23. Anna [Harold] rmt John Llewellyn

HART
1836, 5, 23. Eleanor (form Cashatt) dis mou
1924, 3, 13. Mabel Mancher relrq

HARTMAN
----, --, --. George b 1849,5,21 d 1932,7,16; m Anna -----
Ch: Nellie b 1906, 1, 16

1894, 8, 23. George & ch recrq

HARVEY
----, --, --. Nathaniel, s Isaac & Sarah, b 1843,6,30; m Irena MOON, dt Moses & Elizabeth, b 1845,1,19
Ch: Della b 1872, 8, 10
Junetta " 1870, 10, 16

1849, 11, 12. Caleb E. rocf Mississinewa MM, Ind., dtd 1849,8,15
1869, 3, 22. Irena (form Moon) con mou
1875, 4, 19. Nathaniel & w, Irena, & ch, Genetta & Della, rocf Springfield MM, O., dtd 1875,3,20

HAWK
1887, 1, 7. Albert, s Eli & Araminta, b

HAWORTH
1817, 9, 4. George D., s Malon & Phebe, Clinton Co., O.; m in Newberry MH, Edith HADLEY, dt James & Ann
1818, 11, 12. Ezekiel, s Mahlon & Phebe, Clinton Co., O., b 1799,10,30; m in Newberry MH, Elizabeth WEST, dt Owen & Elizabeth, Clinton Co., O., b 1799,11,15
Ch: Malissa b 1819, 9, 22 d 1820, 9,21 bur Newbury
Rebecca b 1821, 5, 31
Mahlon " 1823, 3, 23
Owen " 1825, 4, 15
Flemmon " 1826, 12, 3 d 1836, 3, 5 bur Newbury
Phebe b 1828, 1, 8
Ezekiel " 1829, 5, 7
Elizabeth " 1831, 1, 14
Uriah " 1832, 10, 25
Elijah " 1834, 4, 15
James W. " 1835, 11, 17
Isaiah " 1837, 10, 27
Mary " 1839, 5, 23 d 1844, 2,23 bur Newbury
Susannah b 1842, 8, 28
1846, 12, 14. Phebe m Wm. S. HUNT

1818, 4, 6. Edith gct Center MM, O.
1819, 3, 25. Elizabeth gct Center MM, O.
1820, 5, 25. Emilia (form West) con mou
1820, 6, 22. Ezekiel & w, Elizabeth, & dt, Lilissa, rocf Center MM, dtd 1820,6,17
1840, 9, 21. Rebecca Ruse (form Haworth) dis mou
1846, 4, 13. Owen con mou
1849, 7, 16. Mahlon dis mou
1850, 3, 11. Nancy (form Hiatt) con mou
1852, 3, 16. Elizabeth rocf Fairfield MM, dtd 1852,2,21
1852, 6, 5. Elizabeth Thornburg (form Hayworth) dis mou
1853, 7, 18. Nancy gct Honey Creek MM, Ind.
1853, 7, 18. Elizabeth gct Honey Creek MM, Ind.
1853, 8, 22. Owen dis disunity
1853, 9, 19. Ezekiel con mou
1855, 5, 21. Ezekiel Jr. gct Clear Creek MM, O.
1858, 5, 17. Uriah dis mou
1860, 7, 23. Elijah dis mou
1861, 5, 20. Susannah Patchel (form Hayworth) con mou
1862, 8, 18. Isaiah dis mou
1864, 5, 23. Jane (form Janney) con mou
1865, 3, 20. Jane gct Dover MM
1870, 9, 19. Ezekiel dis disunity
1872, 12, 23. Sarah E. & ch, Flora A., Samuel C. & Clayton M., rocf Clear Creek MM, O.
1887, 7, 18. Mary J. gct Dover MM
1917, 11, 15. Mabel Doan gct Dover MM

HAYES
1896, 3, 6. Mariah d bur Wilmington
1899, 2, 25. Joel d bur Bethel

1886, 1, 18. Joel [Hays] & w, Mary Ann, rocf Springfield MM, O., dtd 1886,1,16
1889, 7, 22. Maria rocf Wilmington MM, O., dtd 1889,5,--
1894, 5, 17. E. Marie relrq

HAYNES
1861, 1, 21. Sophronia Ann (form Snider) con mou
1861, 4, 22. Sophronia Ann [Haines] gct Springfield MM, O.

HAZARD
1910, 12, 15. Ernest & w, Pearl, & dt, Ellen, rocf Wilmington MM, O.
1925, 3, 15. Ernest & fam gct Wilmington MM, O.

HEARTSOCK
1893, 9, 18. Arabelle J., dt Byron, recrq

HENLEY
1836, 8, 22. Reuben Hunt gct White Water MM, Ind., to m Rebecca Henley
1868, 4, 10. Aaron B. Hunt gct Carthage MM, Ind., to m Ann Henley

HERALD
1848, 11, 22. James J., s Andrew & Mary L., Clinton Co., O.; m in Westfork MH, Sarah MOON, dt Joseph & Rachel, Clinton Co.,O.

1848, 5, 15. Leah Moon (form Herald) con mou

HERRON
----, --, --. John m Rhoda ----- dt Chas. O. & Rachel D. CAREY (or WEST) b 1853,8,21 d 1877,8,28
1877, 4, 9. Clyde [Herrin], s John W. & Rhoda, b

1886, 4, 19. Clara recrq
1889, 4, 22. Clyde, s Rhoda, recrq

HESTER
1850, 5, 23. Amos, s Robert & Mary, Clinton Co., O.; m in Newberry MH, Esther HOCKETT dt Jonathan & Mary, Clinton Co., O.

1848, 11, 13. Amos rocf Dover MM, dtd 1848,9,14
1853, 10, 17. Esther & ch gct Back Creek MM, Ind.

HIATT
----, --, --. Asaph & Rebecca
Ch: Asher b 1816, 6, 15
Zimri " 1819, 6, 13 d 1820,--,-- bur Newbury
Mahala b 1821, 1, 13
Caleb " 1824, 12, 8

HIATT, continued
1824, 4, 1. Christopher, s Amos & Priscilla, Clinton Co., O.; m in Newberry MH, Martha STANLEY, dt Samuel & Susannah, Clinton Co., O.
Ch: Amos b 1825, 1, 8
----, --, --. Thomas & Harriett
Ch: Rebecca b 1827, 2, 11
Amos " 1828, 1, 14
Nancy " 1829, 4, 11
Priscilla " 1830, 8, 6
Mary " 1832, 2, 2
Lydia " 1834, 1, 31
Jamima " 1835, 7, 16
Harriet Ellen " 1837, 5, 11
1827, 1, 4. Lydia m David HOCKETT
1828, 5, 1. Elizabeth m James WRIGHT
1829, 6, 28. Rebecca d bur Newbury
1831, 8, 21. Priscilla d bur Newbury
1837, 3, 7. Thomas d bur Newbury
1844, 12, 26. Rebecca m David M. CAREY
----, --, --. Collumbus m Martha H. ----- b 1835,9,24
Ch: Emlen b 1854, 7, 31
Ellen " 1855, 9, 23
Allis " 1856, 12, 20
Ann " 1858, 5, 4
William H. " 1860, 4, 29
1896, 10, 13. Clarkson d
1905, 8, 26. Sarah d
1908, 10, 5. Jane, w Clarkson, d
1919, 10, 18. Catherine d

1818, 11, 26. Priscilla & ch, Thomas, Christopher, Lydia, Jemimah & Aaron Lindley, rocf Clermont MM, Va., dtd 1818,9,26
1819, 1, 28. Eli recrq
1819, 10, 28. Jesse & w, Viry, recrq
1819, 11, 25. Sarah, Jonathan, Curtis & Nathan, ch Jesse, recrq
1822, 3, 28. Asher con mou
1823, 8, 28. Josiah Jackson gct Fall Creek MM, to m Ruth Hiatt
1826, 3, 23. Jesse & fam gct Dover MM
1826, 8, 24. Thomas con mou
1827, 1, 25. Eli gct Cherry Grove MM, Ind.
1827, 2, 22. Harriet recrq
1827, 8, 23. Lucy recrq
1829, 9, 24. Christopher dis jH
1829, 10, 29. Asher dis jH
1830, 4, 22. Christopher & w, Martha, & ch, Amos & Susannah, gct Milford MM, Ind.
1830, 11, 25. Jemimah dis jH
1831, 1, 27. Lucy dis jH
1831, 2, 24. Samuel dis mou
1831, 11, 21. Mary rocf Fairfield MM, dtd 1831,9,22
1832, 5, 21. Asaph gct White Water MM, Ind., to m Sarah Smith
1832, 1, 23. Anna Wright (form Hiatt) dis mou
1832, 10, 22. Sarah rocf White Water MM, Ind., dtd 1832,7,25
1833, 10, 21. Asaph & w, Sarah, & ch, Asher, Mehala & Caleb, gct Milford MM, Ind.
1839, 2, 18. Mary Ann (form Lundy) dis mou
1839, 2, 18. Amos dis mou
1839, 4, 22. Mary Lazenby (form Hiatt) dis mou
1843, 6, 19. Abner dis mou
1848, 2, 14. Clarkson dis mou
1848, 9, 11. Elwood dis mou
1849, 6, 10. Mary Davis (form Hiatt) con mou
1849, 8, 13. Mary B. rocf Dover MM, dtd 1849, 7,19
1850, 3, 11. Nancy Haworth (form Hiatt) con mou
1853, 6, 20. Amos J. con mou
1854, 6, 19. Jemima Grice (form Hiatt) dis mou
1855, 5, 21. Martha H. rocf Springfield MM, O., dtd 1855,5,19
1855, 5, 21. Lydia Pike (form Hiatt) con mou
1856, 12, 26. Mary gct Springfield MM
1857, 8, 17. Emlen, Ellen & Alice H., ch Martha, recrq
1857, 8, 17. Amos G. gct Clear Creek MM, O.
1857, 9, 21. Harriet gct Clear Creek MM, O.
1858, 7, 19. Ann, infant dt Martha, recrq
1861, 10, 21. William H., s Columbus, recrq
1864, 6, 20. Elwood recrq
1864, 7, 18. Rosabell, Frank, Thomas C., Clinton & Newton, ch Elwood & Mary, recrq
1864, 11, 21. Mary rocf Dover MM, dtd 1864,9, 15
1865, 5, 22. Sarah M. gct Minneapolis MM, Minn.
1865, 8, 21. Ellwood & w, Mary, & ch, Rosabel, Frank, Thomas, Clinton & Newton, gct Spring Creek MM, Iowa
1866, 5, 21. Christopher C. & ch, John G. & Mary T., recrq
1868, 4, 10. Columbus & w, Martha, & ch, Emma, Ella, Alice, Ann, Wm., John, Mary T. & Rettie Sophia, gct Summit Grove MM, Ia.
1871, 11, 20. Evelyn recrq
1873, 7, 21. Eviline Chickston (form Hiatt) con mou
1881, 3, 21. Clarkson recrq
1881, 3, 21. Jane recrq
1881, 3, 21. Lora recrq
1881, 3, 21. Francis M. recrq
1881, 3, 21. Eddie recrq
1881, 3, 21. Francisco recrq
1881, 3, 21. Catherine recrq
1881, 3, 21. Macie M. recrq
1886, 10, 18. Edwin J. gct Wilmington MM, O.
1894, 1, 22. Duella gct Wilmington MM, O.
1894, 10, 18. Sarah M. recrq
1899, 1, 19. Albert P. rocf Union MM, Minn., dtd 1898,4,16
1907, 9, 19. Francisco relrq
1917, 1, 18. Howard recrq
1921, 4, 14. Clarkson & Esther recrq

HIGGINS
1887, 8, 22. John dropped from mbrp

HILDRETH
1885, 8, 17. Sarah E. roc

HINSHAW
----, --, --. Absolem [Henshaw], s John & Margaret, b 1828,8,24; m Eadeth WEST, dt Peyton & Sarah, b 1833,2,14
Ch: Viola b 1855, 5, 29
Caroline E." 1856, 9, 17
Frank W. " 1858, 5, 31
Sarah Addie" 1860, 7, 18
Florence M." 1862, 4, 8
Minnie Dora" 1864, 2, 15
Margaret G." 1866, 8, 6
William T. " 1868, 10, 26
Henrietta J" 1873, 2, 1
----, --, --. Garner b 1836,6,13; m Maria ---- b 1836,11,11
Ch: Anna b 1864, 1, 2
Orie " 1866, 7, 17
Elva " 1869, 1, 22

1824, 10, 28. Margaret rocf Clear Creek MM, dtd 1824,9,11
1831, 11, 21. Nancy recrq
1832, 1, 23. Abel rocf Holly Spring MM, N.C., dtd 1830,10,16
1836, 3, 21. Abel [Henshaw] & w, Nancy, gct Cherry Grove MM, Ind.
1843, 3, 20. Margaret [Henshaw] recrq
1852, 2, 16. Margaret Norton (form Hinshaw) dis mou
1855, 6, 18. Edith (form West) con mou
1865, 2, 20. Absalom & ch, Viola A., Caroline E., Frank W., Sarah A., Florence N. & Minnie D., recrq
1866, 3, 19. John Garner & w, Maria, & dt, Anna, recrq
1874, 3, 23. Garner & w, Maria, & ch, Anna, Orrie & Elva, gct Wilmington MM, O.
1893, 11, 20. Henrietta dropped from mbrp

HIXON
1910, 6, 24. Marianna [Hixson], dt C. L. & Melcena, b
1928, 3, 7. Joseph [Hixson] d

1870, 2, 21. Joseph recrq
1880, 1, 19. Emily recrq
1881, 3, 21. Christian & Mary E. recrq
1883, 6, 18. Christian E. dis disunity
1886, 11, 22. Mary E. relrq
1895, 9, 19. Thomas recrq
1897, 1, 14. Carl recrq
1914, 4, 16. Lelia [Hixson] & dt, Emily, recrq
1926, 4, 18. Emily recrq

HOCKETT
----, --, --. Benjamin b 1772,12,9; m Charity ----- b 1778,3,16
Ch: Hannah b 1796, 11, 28
Rachel " 1798, 10, 8
Leah " 1800, 6, 20
Sarah " 1801, 11, 10
Eli " 1803, 4, 7
Neri " 1806, 6, 2 d 1836,11,17
Charity " 1807, 12, 10
Phebe " 1810, 5, 2
Loes " 1811, 12, 12
Mary " 1813, 3, 12
Jonathan " 1815, 5, 13
Edith " 1816, 11, 20
Ruth " 1820, 8, 8
1818, 1, 8. Sarah m Richard MOON
1818, 2, 2. Dorcas d bur Newbury
1819, 11, 11. John, s Jonathan & Mary, Clinton Co., O.; m in Newbury MH, Mary MOON, dt Daniel & Ruth
----, --, --. Jesse b 1799,4,18; m Mary -----
Ch: Levi b 1820, 9, 16
Daniel " 1821, 12, 26
Ruth " 1823, 9, 6
Eliza " 1825, 12, 25
Charles " 1828, 1, 23
Zimri " 1830, 1, 17
Anna " 1831, 11, 21
Sarah " 1833, 12, 26
Jane " 1835, 12, 19
Mahlon " 1838, 5, 18 d 1863, 4,26 bur Memphis, Tenn.
Jonathan b 1840, 3, 16
Uriah " 1844, 9, 9
----, --, --. Seth b 1794,4,21; m Nancy ---- b 1797,5,15
Ch: Mary b 1821, 8, 21
Asa " 1823, 8, 1
Anna " 1825, 2, 1
James " 1827, 10, 7
John " 1830, 5, 11 d 1860,12,28 bur Newbury
Elizabeth b 1832, 10, 17
Pleasant " 1834, 8, 30
Seth m 2nd Rebecca SEMANS b 1804,1,9
Ch: Gulielma Semans b 1844, 5, 12
John Semans" 1843, 7, 21
Jacob Semans b 1845, 8, 26
1824, 9, 2. Rachel m Daniel MOON
1825, 8, 4. Phebe m Jesse MOON
----, --, --. Mahlon b 1801,10,8; m Anna ----- b 1806,8,7
Ch: Mary Jane b 1827, 7, 4
Alvah " 1828, 11, 13
Susannah " 1831, 8, 15
Ruth " 1833, 8, 30
Henry A. " 1835, 10, 16
Hannah " 1838, 9, 16
Sarah Elizabeth b 1843, 3, 2
William Edwin " 1845, 8, 25

HOCKETT, continued
----, --, --. David, s David & Dorcas, b 1805, 5,23; m Lydia ----- b 1807,2,26
Ch: Albert b 1827, 11, 12
Amos " 1829, 7, 31
William " 1831, 6, 20
----, --, --. David m 2nd Rebecca -----, dt Jacob & Lydia Hunt, b 1813,4,16
Ch: Lydia Jane b 1841, 5, 24
Francis Lindley " 1847, 10, 1
Lewis Edgar " 1849, 11, 26 d 1850, 8, 1 bur Newbury
1827, 1, 4. David, s David & Dorcas, Clinton Co., O.; m in Newbury MH, Lydia HIATT, dt Amos & Priscilla, Clinton Co., O.
1827, 2, 1. Charity m Jacob BEALS
1828, 9, 4. Agnes m John MILLS
----, --, --. Jonathan b 1803,10,29; m Mary ----- b 1804,11,27
Ch: Esther b 1830, 10, 16
Sarah " 1832, 1, 24
Henry " 1833, 12, 31
Barclay " 1837, 7, 19
1829, 9, 9. Charity d bur Newbury
1834, 8, 3. Jonathan d bur Newbury
1834, 11, 27. Lydia d bur Newbury
1834, 1, 2. Neri, s Benjamin & Charity, Clinton Co., O., b 1806,6,2; m in Newbury MH, Rachel SMITH, dt John & Sarah, Highland Co., O., b 1815,5,19 (Neri d 1836, 11,17)
Ch: William b 1835, 1, 31
1836, 10, 27. David, s David & Dorcas, Clinton Co., O.; m in Newberry MH, Rebecca HUNT, dt Jacob & Lydia, Clinton Co., O.
----, --, --. William b 1817,3,29; m Sena ----- b 1818,9,29
Ch: Asa b 1839, 12, 7
1838, 12, 27. Lois m Joseph MILLS
----, --, --. Pleasant b 1834,8,30; m Matilda ----- b 1838,4,18 d 1857,11,14 bur Newbury
Pleasant m 2nd Guli Elma ----- b 1840,5,12
----, --, --. Zimri b 1820,1,12; m Lucinda ----- b 1820,7,—
Ch: Allen b 1840, 9, 13
Lydia " 1842, 7, 22
Milton " 1844, 4, 22
Lewis " 1847, 8, 13
Nancy " 1849, 2, 8
Silas " 1851, 6, 2
Alonzo " 1851, 8, 24 (sic)
John " 1857, 10, 9
Nuton " 1860, 4, 1
----, --, --. Thomas, s John & Martha, b 1818,4,12; m Sarah NEWBY, dt Wm. & Sarah, b 1820,9,16
Ch: Nancy Elen b 1840, 12, 13
William " 1842, 11, 7
Martha Jane " 1845, 12, 29
John Edwin " 1853, 7, 11
Ch: Lorenzo b 1858, 12, 7
----, --, --. Levi m 2nd Lydia -----
Ch: Asa b 1841, 3, 21
Mary " 1843, 3, 2
Jesse P. " 1844, 10, 24
Ann " 1847, 5, 27
William P. " 1848, 6, 23
Levi m 3rd Mary E. ----- b 1834,9,11 d 1856,7,8 bur Westfork
Ch: Jonas b 1854, 7, 19
Elizabeth " 1856, 7, 7
Levi m 4th Sarah A. ----- dt Thos. & Charlotte CURD, b 1820,7,4
Ch: Jesse b 1844, 6, 23
Jonas " 1854, 7, 19
Emma " 1862, 8, 27
1840, 12, 2. Daniel, s Jesse & Mary, Clinton Co., O.; m in Westfork MH, Betsy HOLADAY, dt Susannah, Clinton Co., O.
1841, 6, 14. Lydia Jane d
1841, 9, 14. William d bur Newbury
1841, 10, 27. Ruth m Jesse F. HOLODAY
1842, 7, 13. David d ae 77 bur Newbury
1843, 9, 20. Asa, s Seth & Nancy, b 1823,8,7, m in Newberry MH, Elizabeth WASSON, dt Calvin & Mary, Clinton Co., O., b 1824,1, 30
Ch: Albert b 1844, 6, 29
Ellwood " 1847, 10, 5
1847, 5, 30. Ann d
1848, 9, 20. Alvah, s Mahlon & Ann, Clinton Co., O., b 1828,11,13; m in Newberry MM, O., Lydia HUNT, dt Thomas & Jane, Clinton Co., O., b 1828,3,22 d 1851,7,16 bur Westfork
Ch: Thomas Lisbon b 1849, 10, 8
Anna Jane " 1851, 3, 8
Susan Alice " 1852, 10, 19
Jabez " 1856, 7, 18 d 1857, 8,19 bur Westfork
Adaline b 1858, 5, 18 " 1858, 9, 3 bur Westfork
1848, 9, 21. Susanna m Jonathan HOLE
1850, 5, 23. Esther m Amos HESTER
----, --, --. James b 1827,10,7; m Mary Jane ----- b 1832,9,20
Ch: Julian Edgar b 1851, 10, 12
Francis Alvin " 1853, 10, 26
Louiza " 1855, 12, 2
Seth " 1858, 2, 23
Alwilda " 1860, 3, 22
Sylvia " 1862, 7, 31
----, --, --. John b 1830,5,11; m Lydia ----- b 1834,1,22
Ch: Clarinda b 1853, 5, 26
Alpheus " 1856, 5, 27
1854, 11, 1. Mary Jane m Wm. HUNT
----, --, --. Wm. R., s Neri & Rachel, b 1835,1,31; m Ellen B. BYE, dt Reading &

HOCKETT, Wm. R. & Ellen B., continued
Sarah, b 1836,4,26
Ch: Alonzo b 1858, 8, 7
Frank E. " 1861, 5, 20
Annie E. " 1863, 9, 24
----, --, --. Lewis b 1815,1,16; m Lucinda ----- b 1816,2,27
Ch: Clara b 1859, 11, 18
1861, 1, 7. Seth, s Jonathan, d
1862, 9, 13. Jesse d bur Westfork
1859, 11, 30. Sarah Elizabeth m Thos. SIMCOX
----, --, --. Allen, s Zimri & Lucinda, b 1840,9,13; m Martha E. -----, dt Isaac & Edna MOON, b 1846,6,22
Ch: Della b 1864, 5, 17 d 1872, 8, 3 bur Martinsville, O.
Charles S. b 1867, 4, 1
William A. " 1876, 9, 22
----, --, --. William, s Thos. & Sarah, b 1842,11,7; m Ellen -----, dt Saml. & Elizabeth EWING, b 1838,2,2
Ch: Irene b 1864, 12, 6
Eugene " 1867, 7, 5
Thomas A. " 1869, 10, 14
Mattie " 1872, 4, 24
----, --, --. Elbridge b 1845,12,30; m Ruth ----- b 1844,5,5
Ch: Hattie M. b 1869, 10, 27
----, --, --. Francis L., s David & Rebecca, b 1847,10,1; m Rachel CAREY, dt Elias & Jane, b 1850,4,1
Ch: Hattie A. b 1870, 4, 5
Homer C. " 1875, 12, 11

1817, 2, 3. Anna Moon (form Hockett) con mcd
1817, 6, 2. Benjamin & w, Charity, & ch, Rachel, Leah, Sarah, Eli, Neri, Charity, Phebe, Loes, Mary, Jonathan & Edith, rocf Lees Creek MM, dtd 1817,5,17
1817, 12, 1. Joseph & w, Ruth, & ch, Elizabeth, Jesse, Jacob, Rachel, Susanna & Josiah, rocf Lees Creek MM, dtd 1817,10,18
1818, 4, 6. Seth dis mou
1818, 10, 29. Elizabeth Moon (form Hockett) con mou
1818, 11, 26. Rachel Moon (form Hockett) con mou
1821, 2, 22. Leah gct West Grove MM, Ind.
1821, 8, 23. Wm., stepson of Wm. Moon, recrq
1823, 1, 23. Ruth Mills (form Hockett) con mcd
1823, 3, 27. Jesse dis mou
1823, 4, 24. Nathan dis mou
1825, 6, 23. Eli dis mou
1826, 5, 16. Mahlon gct Springfield MM, to m Anna Andrew
1826, 7, 27. Leah Jenkins (form Hockett) dis mou
1826, 11, 23. Anna rocf Springfield MM, dtd 1826,10,28
1829, 10, 29. Jonathan rqct Clear Creek MM, to m Mary Nordyke
1830, 2, 25. Joseph dis disunity
1830, 6, 24. Ruth dis jH
1830, 6, 24. Jacob con mou
1832, 3, 19. Mary rocf Clear Creek MM, dtd 1831,12,20
1832, 7, 23. Jesse dis
1832, 12, 17. Jonathan dis disunity
1833, 11, 18. Benjamin rstrq
1834, 4, 21. Susannah Milner (form Hockett) con mou
1834, 9, 22. Mary gct Fairfield MM
1834, 9, 22. Lois gct Clear Creek MM
1835, 3, 23. Josiah dis mou & joining Separatists
1835, 10, 19. Jonathan & fam gct Clear Creek MM
1836, 2, 22. Benjamin dis disunity
1836, 4, 18. Edith Kester (form Hockett) con mou
1836, 10, 17. Lucinda (form Jackson) dis mou
1837, 1, 23. Jacob dis jH
1838, 6, 18. Lois rocf Clear Creek MM, dtd 1838,3,20
1838, 10, 22. Ruth gct Cesars Creek MM
1839, 4, 22. Levi con mou
1839, 9, 23. William con mou
1839, 9, 23. Sinia (form Smith) con mou
1840, 5, 18. Jesse rstrq
1840, 6, 22. Levi gct Clear Creek MM, to m Lydia Pike
1841, 1, 18. Rachel Moon (form Hockett) con mou
1842, 9, 19. Nancy & ch, Asa, Anne, James, John, Elizabeth & Pleasant, recrq
1842, 10, 17. Lucinda recrq
1842, 12, 19. Benjamin rstrq
1844, 9, 16. Eliza Osborn (form Hockett) con mou
1844, 10, 19. Jonathan & w, Mary, & ch, Esther, Sarah, Henry & Barclay, rocf Goshen MM, dtd 1844,10,19
1845, 1, 13. Elizabeth recrq
1845, 5, 12. Elizabeth gct Clear Creek MM
1846, 1, 12. Seth con mou
1848, 8, 14. Anne Pennington (form Hockett) con mou
1850, 10, 14. Jonathan dis disunity
1851, 2, 10. John dis mou
1851, 4, 14. Anna Watkins (form Hockett) dis disunity
1851, 4, 14. Amos dis mou
1851, 5, 12. Zimri dis disunity
1851, 9, 15. John gct Springfield MM, to m Mary Ann Green
1852, 4, 3. James con mou
1853, 2, 5. Levi con mou
1853, 3, 21. Mary Elizabeth recrq
1853, 4, 18. John gct Springfield MM
1853, 10, 17. Mary & ch, Henry N. & Barclay, gct Back Creek MM, Ind.
1853, 10, 17. Sarah gct Back Creek MM, Ind.
1854, 1, 23. Ruth Holoday (form Hockett) con mou
1854, 1, 23. Wm. R., s Rachel Moon, gct

HOCKETT, continued
White River MM, Ind.
1854, 12, 18. Zimri rstrq
1855, 2, 19. Thomas & w, Sarah, & ch, Nancy Ellen, William, Martha Jane & John Edwin, rocf Clear Creek MM, dtd 1855,1,13
1855, 4, 23. Albert dis mou
1855, 5, 21. Elizabeth Crawford (form Hockett) con mou
1855, 5, 21. John & w, Mary Ann, & dt, Clarinda, rocf Springfield MM, O., dtd 1855, 5,19
1855, 6, 18. Mary Jane recrq
1855, 7, 23. Julian Edgar & Francis Alvin, ch James A., recrq
1855, 11, 19. Allen, Lydia, Lewis, Milton, Nancy, Silas & Alonzo, ch Lucinda, recrq
1856, 8, 18. Daniel dis mou
1856, 12, 26. Seth gct Fairfield MM, O., to m Rebecca Simmons
1857, 2, 23. Nathan & Jemima rst at Goshen MM on consent of this mtg
1857, 5, 18. Pleasant dis mou
1857, 6, 22. Rebecca & ch, Gulielma, John & Jacob Simmons, rocf Fairfield MM, O., dtd 1857,6,20
1857, 8, 17. Pleasant recrq
1857, 8, 17. Matilda recrq
1857, 8, 17. Josiah rst at Oak Ridge MM, Ind. on consent of this mtg
1857, 10, 19. Levi dis disunity
1858, 3, 3. Hannah m Reuben G. HUNT
1858, 4, 19. Amos recrq
1858, 7, 19. Asa & w, Elizabeth W., & ch, Albert Elwood & Elizabeth W., gct Mill Creek MM, Ind.
1859, 4, 18. Pleasant con mou
1859, 8, 22. Elma (form Simmons) con mou
1859, 10, 17. Mary Jr. dis
1859, 10, 17. Mahlon Jr. con mou
1860, 2, 20. Mahlon & w, Anna, & s, William Edwin, gct West Union MM, Ind.
1860, 2, 20. Alva & w, Lydia, & ch, Thomas Lisbon, Anna Jane, Susan Alice & Almedia, gct West Union MM, Ind.
1860, 1, 23. Nancy Ellen Hodson (form Hockett) dis mou
1860, 5, 21. Zimri dis disunity
1860, 10, 22. Jonathan dis mou
1860, 11, 19. James & w, Mary Jane, & ch, Julian Edgar, Francis A., Louiza, Seth & Alwilda, gct Plainfield MM, Ind.
1861, 2, 18. Asa dis disunity
1861, 2, 18. Pleasant & w, Julielma, & dt, Martha Jane, gct Dover MM
1861, 2, 18. Rebecca S. & ch, John & Jacob Semans, gct Dover MM
1861, 2, 18. Henry A. gct West Union MM, Ind.
1861, 4, 22. Asa S. gct Fairfield MM, O., to m Anna Barrett
1861, 4, 22. Jesse & w, Mary, & s, Uriah, gct Dover MM
1861, 7, 22. Sarah gct Dover MM
1861, 6, 17. Mary Ann & ch gct Springfield MM
1861, 8, 19. Anna B. rocf Fairfield MM, dtd 1861,8,17
1861, 9, 23. James G. & w, Mary Jane, & ch, Julian Edgar, Francis Alvin, Louiza, Seth W. & Alwilda, rocf Plainfield MM, Ind., dtd 1861,7,31
1862, 6, 23. Jesse & w, Mary, & s, Uriah, rocf Dover MM, dtd 1862,6,19
1864, 7, 18. William dis mou
1865, 2, 20. Lydia Turner (form Hockett) con mou
1865, 5, 22. Allen con mou
1865, 7, 17. Martha J. Hodson (form Hockett) dis mou
1865, 11, 20. John & Newton, ch Lucinda, recrq
1866, 4, 23. Allen & ch, Della, gct Dover MM
1866, 4, 23. Allen & dt, Della, gct Dover MM, Ohio
1866, 5, 21. Zimri recrq
1867, 2, 18. Lewis & w, Lucinda, & dt, Clara, recrq
1867, 5, 20. William & w, Eleanor C., & ch, Alonzo, Franklin C. & Annie Elizabeth, recrq
1867, 7, 22. Nancy (or Mary) relrq
1867, 12, 23. Lewis dis jas
1868, 5, 18. Milton dis mou & jas
1868, 6, 22. Mary Ann & ch, Clarinda, John Alpheus & Nancy Jane, rocf Springfield MM, O., dtd 1868,5,16
1868, 8, 17. David W. & w, Rebecca, gct Fairview MM, Ill.
1868, 8, 17. Francis L. con mou
1868, 9, 21. Francis L. gct Fairview MM, Ill.
1868, 12, 21. Allen & ch, Della & Charley, rocf Dover MM, dtd 1868,11,19
1869, 5, 17. James G. & w, Mary Jane, & ch, Julian, Francis, Seth, Louisa, Alwilda & Murray, gct Ash Grove MM, Ill.
1869, 9, 20. Mary Ann & ch, Clarinda, Alpheus & Nancy, gct Springfield MM, O.
1869, 12, 30. Seth & w, Rebecca J., & ch, Louiza & Margaret Ellen, recrq
1870, 1, 17. Seth & fam gct Vermillion MM, Ill.
1870, 1, 17. William recrq
1870, 1, 17. Ellen recrq
1870, 1, 17. Irene recrq
1870, 1, 17. Eugene recrq
1870, 1, 17. Thomas S. recrq
1870, 1, 17. William P. recrq
1870, 1, 17. Sarah recrq
1870, 1, 17. Emma recrq
1870, 1, 17. Jonas recrq
1870, 1, 17. Jonathan recrq
1870, 1, 17. Elldridge recrq
1870, 1, 17. Ruth A. recrq
1870, 1, 17. Hattie M. recrq
1870, 1, 17. Fanny recrq
1870, 2, 21. Martha E. recrq
1871, 1, 23. Caroline recrq

HOCKETT, continued
1871, 2, 20. Zimri & w, Lucinda, & ch, Silas, Alonzo, John & Newton, gct Ash Grove MM, Ill.
1871, 7, 17. Uriah J. con mou
1871, 8, 21. Wm. P. con mou
1873, 4, 21. William & w, Sina, gct Mill Creek MM, Ind.
1873, 4, 21. Asa C. & w, Anne, & ch, Emma, Orthey, Alvin, Alma, Sina & Levi, gct Mill Creek MM, Ind.
1873, 4, 21. Amos gct Wilmington MM, O.
1873, 5, 19. Amos gct Wilmington MM, O.
1873, 11, 17. Jesse J. & w, Sarah Ann, rocf Springfield MM, dtd 1873,10,18
1873, 11, 17. Samantha con mou
1873, 12, 22. Samantha gct Clear Creek MM, O.
1874, 3, 23. Lewis & w, Lucinda J., & dt, Clara, gct Wilmington MM, O.
1874, 3, 23. Jesse & w, Sarah Ann, rocf Springfield MM, O., dtd 1873,10,19
1875, 2, 22. David W. & w, Rebecca, rocf Fairview MM, Ill., dtd 1875,1,23
1875, 2, 22. Francis L. & w, Rachel, & dt, Hattie A., rocf Fairview MM, Ill., dtd 1875,1,23
1875, 9, 20. Sarah rocf Dover MM, O., dtd 1875,8,19
1881, 6, 20. Sarah E. gct Cincinnati MM, O.; returned 1882,1,23
1883, 7, 23. Francis L. & w, Rachel, & ch, Hattie & Homer, gct Wilmington MM, O.
1883, 7, 23. David gct Wilmington MM, O.
1883, 9, 17. Sarah E. gct Wilmington MM, O.
1884, 7, 21. Uriah gct Cincinnati MM, O.
1886, 1, 18. Sarah relrq
1887, 5, 23. Jonas, Jonathan M. & Fannie dropped from mbrp
1887, 8, 22. Henry rocf Mill Creek MM, Ind., dtd 1887,7,30
1887, --, 10. Mary Ann & Clarkson M. rocf Greenfield MM, Ind.
1888, 1, 23. William P. relrq
1909, 7, 15. Charles S. relrq

HOCKMAN
1870, 3, 21. Michael recrq
1870, 3, 21. Minerva recrq
1870, 3, 21. Anna T. recrq
1870, 3, 21. Tilford E. recrq
1870, 3, 21. Granville P. recrq
1870, 3, 21. Ada B. recrq
1870, 3, 21. Rosa Belle recrq
1887, 5, 23. Michael, Minerva, Anna T., Tilford E., Granville, Ada D. & Rosa Bell dropped from mbrp

HODSON
1834, 9, 13. Edwin W. b
----, --, --. Simeon, s George G. & Mary, b 1830,9,1; m Mary L. ----- dt James M. & Sarah CUNNINGHAM, b 1830,8,10
Ch: Florence b 1853, 6, 5
Charles b 1856, 8, 26
Etta " 1859, 6, 12
Anna " 1862, 4, 23
1855, 8, 14. Eliza E. b
1851, 2, 28. Sarah d bur Westfork
----, --, --. John Dalton, s George & Mary Ann, b 1839,1,9; m Martha Jane HOCKETT, dt Thomas & Sarah, b 1845,12,29

1833, 1, 21. Sarah & dt, Mary & Rachel, rocf Clear Creek MM, dtd 1832,12,18
1837, 2, 20. George & w, Mary, rocf Clear Creek MM, dtd 1837,1,24
1837, 7, 17. Mary Jr. dis
1839, 2, 18. George & w, Mary, gct Walnut Ridge MM, Ind.
1857, 8, 17. Zadoc Miller gct Fairfield MM, to m Emily Hodson
1860, 1, 23. Nancy Ellen (form Hockett) dis mou
1865, 7, 17. Martha J. (form Hockett) dis mou
1867, 2, 18. John D. & w, Martha Jane, recrq
1867, 2, 18. Mary L. & ch, Florence, Charles I., Marietta & Annie, recrq
1870, 1, 17. Simeon recrq
1870, 2, 21. Ira recrq
1870, 3, 21. Ira gct Center MM, O.
1870, 3, 21. Edwin W. & Eliza Emma recrq
1872, 8, 19. Edwin relrq
1887, 5, 23. Eliza Emma dropped from mbrp
1889, 1, 21. Charles H. relrq
1889, 11, 18. Simeon & w, Mary L., relrq

HOGGERTY
1888, 12, 17. Anna F., William F. & Leslie T. recrq
1893, 11, 20. Anna F., William & Leslie G. dropped from mbrp

HOLADAY
----, --, --. John [Holladay] b 1784,2,10 d 1852,9,1 bur Westfork; m Susanna ----- b 1785,6,16 d 1866,1,15
Ch: Hannah b 1808, 11, 13
Robert " 1811, 12, 12
William " 1813, 6, 19
Betsy " 1816, 1, 15
Mary Ann " 1818, 3, 7
Jesse F. " 1820, 10, 31
Susannah " 1824, 9, 25
John " 1828, 1, 30
----, --, --. Robert [Holladay] b 1811,12,12; m Hannah -----, dt Henry & Jane ANDREW, b 1813,4,13
Ch: Thomas F. b 1835, 1, 27
Jonathan " 1836, 7, 1
Betsy " 1837, 12, 13
Louiza " 1839, 11, 19
John H. " 1842, 3, 19
Milton M. " 1843, 6, 16 d 1849,11,27 bur Westfork
Samuel b 1845, 3, 22

HOLADAY, Robert & Hannah, continued
Ch: Joseph M. b 1847, 10, 24
Job " 1850, 2, 12
Malon " 1852, 6, 17
Pleasant " 1855, 1, 5 d 1855, 1,16 bur Westfork
William W. b 1857, 7, 5
----, --, --. William [Holladay] b 1813,6,19 d 1862,7,20 bur Westfork; m Ann ----- dt Nathaniel & Nancy CARTER, b 1813,9,13
Ch: Enoch b 1836, 7, 17
Asa " 1838, 10, 17
Hannah " 1840, 10, 25
John C. " 1845, 6, 16
Susanna " 1847, 9, 28
Emily Jane " 1850, 9, 28 d 1851, 2, 8 bur Westfork
Anna Delilah b 1852, 2, 8
1840, 12, 2. Betsey [Holoday] m Daniel HOCKETT
1840, 12, 30. Ann [Holoday] m John GARNER
1841, 10, 27. Jesse F., s John & Susannah, Clinton Co., O., b 1820,10,31; m in Westfork MH, Ruth HOCKETT, dt Jesse & Mary, b 1823,9,6
Ch: Daniel b 1843, 1, 4
David " 1844, 3, 16
Betsy " 1846, 5, 9
Charles " 1848, 4, 5
Angeline " 1850, 5, 20
James W. " 1852, 5, 24
Lorenzo D. " 1854, 5, 29
Lafayette " 1856, 6, 12 d 1857, 1,20 bur Westfork
Hiram E. b 1857, 11, 12
Sarah A. " 1860, 5, 8
Jess H. " 1862, 12, 15
Alvah " 1867, 9, 16
1843, 9, --. Daniel [Hollowday] d bur Westfork
----, --, --. John, s John & Susanna, b 1828, 1,30; m Ruth M. -----, dt Mahlon & Anna HOCKETT, b 1833,8,30 d 1889,10,12 bur Westboro
Ch: Elwood b 1853, 10, 1
Francis M. " 1856, 5, 26
Milton " 1858, 6, 14
1864, 2, 13. Robert d bur West Fork
----, --, --. Jonathan, s Robert & Hannah, b 1836,7,1 d 1918,4,13; m Louisa J. ----- dt Absalom & Rachel GIBSON, b 1842,10,12 d 1926,3,12
Ch: Elbridge b 1866, 7, 13
Ellworth " 1866, 7, 13 d 1867, 8,19
Robert Clayton " 1868, 5, 11
Walter " 1870, 5, 22 d 1870, 6, 2
Harley C. " 1873, 8, 11
----, --, --. Enoch, s Wm. & Ann, b 1836,7,17; m Sarah J. -----, dt Owen & Mary WEST, b 1840,5,12
Ch: Lindley O. b 1867, 8, 2
Evaline A. b 1868, 12, 23
Mary E. " 1871, 9, 3
Maggie E. " ----, 8, 17
Lizzie A. " 1877, 8, 26
----, --, --. Samuel, s Robert & Hannah, b 1847,3,27; m Patience ----- dt Frederick D. & Mary Ann POBST, b 1844,9,6
Ch: Rosse E. b 1869, 7, 14
Mary Alice " 1872, 6, 21
Lilly Adaline " 1875, 8, 17
Lida Evaline " 1875, 8, 17
----, --, --. Charles [Holladay], s Jesse & Ruth, b 1848,4,5; m Susannah FRITTS
Ch: Rolla b 1869, 10, 3
Angeline " 1872, 3, 3

1839, 11, 18. William [Holiday] & w, Ann, & ch, Enoch & Asa, rocf Springfield MM, dtd 1839,11,12
1840, 1, 20. Robert [Holiday] & w, Hannah, & ch, Thomas, Jonathan, Betsy Jane & Louisa, rocf Springfield MM, dtd 1840,1, 14
1840, 3, 23. John [Holiday] & w, Susannah, & ch, Jesse F., Susanna & John, rocf Springfield MM, dtd 1840,3,17
1840, 3, 23. Betsy [Holiday] rocf Springfield MM, dtd 1840,3,17
1840, 3, 23. Mary Ann [Holiday] rocf Springfield MM, dtd 1840,3,17
1854, 1, 23. Ruth (form Hockett) con mou
1854, 1, 23. John con mou
1865, 5, 22. Betty H. Moon (form Holaday) con mou
1866, 6, 18. Jonathan con mou
1867, 2, 18. Louiza [Holoday] (form Gibson) con mou
1867, 10, 21. Sarah J. rocf Clear Creek MM, O., dtd 1867,10,12
1867, 11, 18. Angeline Wolf (form Holaday) dis mou
1867, 12, 23. Enoch [Holoday] con mou
1868, 1, 20. Susannah Simpson (form Holaday) con mou
1868, 2, 17. John Henry [Holoday] dis mou
1869, 3, 22. Samuel A. con mou
1869, 5, 17. David [Holladay] con mou
1869, 6, 21. Nancy B. Williams (form Holaday) con mou
1869, 6, 21. David [Holoday] gct Fairview MM, Ill.
1870, 1, 17. Patience [Holliday] recrq
1870, 4, 18. Betty J. Roberts (form Holaday) con mou
1870, 8, 22. Charles con mou
1870, 12, 19. Jesse F. & w, Ruth, & ch, James W., Lorenzo D., Hiram E., Amanda, Jesse H. & Alva, gct Wilmington MM, O.
1871, 11, 20. Anna D. Baker (form Holoday) con mou
1872, 6, 17. Thomas F. gct West Union MM,

HOLADAY, continued
Ind.
1872, 12, 23. Jesse F. & w, Ruth, & ch, James W., Lorenzo D., Hiram E., Amanda, Jesse H. & Alvah, rocf Wilmington MM, O.
1877, 7, 23. Lorenzo D. & w, Nancy J., & ch, Charles Emmett & Lora, gct Clear Creek MM, O.
1881, 3, 21. Jesse F. & w, Ruth, & ch, Jesse & Alva, gct Wilmington MM, O.
1881, 3, 21. Laura recrq
1883, 9, 17. Charles [Holoday] gct Clear Creek MM, O.
1883, 10, 22. Asa [Holoday] gct Wilmington MM, O.
1884, 5, 19. Raleigh & Angeline [Holoday] gct Clear Creek MM, O.
1884, 5, 19. Thomas F. & w, Sarah Ann, & ch, Edna, Ethel & Laura, rocf West Union MM, Ind., dtd 1884,5,5
1885, 2, 23. Thomas F. & w, Sarah A., & ch, Ethel B., Edna, Laura & Chester, gct West Union MM, Ind.
1888, 2, 20. Nancy recrq
1888, 7, 23. Mary & dt, Elva, recrq
1909, 11, 18. Elsworth rocf Westfork MM, O., dtd 1909,7,17

HOLE
1848, 9, 21. Jonathan, s Jonah & Elizabeth, Clinton Co., O., b 1825,12,13; m in Newberry MH, Susannah HOCKETT, dt Mahlon & Ann, Clinton Co., O., b 1831,8,15
Ch: Francis Orlando b 1853, 5, 23
Florence Eva " 1854, 9, 23
Anna Elizabeth " 1857, 1, 21
----, --, --. Frank m Maria BAILEY, dt Wilson & Sarah, b 1856,4,24
Ch: Laura Elliott b 1875, 10, 4
Francis Rolland " 1876, 10, 9

1848, 4, 10. Jonathan rocf Goshen MM, dtd 1847,12,18
1848, 5, 15. Elizabeth & Jonah Jr. rocf Goshen MM, dtd 1847,12,18
1851, 8, 11. Elizabeth gct Goshen MM
1853, 5, 23. Jonah gct Vermillion MM, Ill.
1860, 12, 17. Jonathan & w, Susannah, & ch, Francis Orlando, Florena-Eva, Ann Elizabeth & Charles Emerson, gct West Union MM, Ind.
1873, 5, 19. Francis Orlando & Eva rocf West Union MM, Ind., dtd 1873,5,5
1875, 12, 20. Maria & dt, Laura Elliott recrq

HOLLINGSWORTH
1800, 1, 25. Esther, w James, dt Thomas & Jane Cadwalader, b
1847, 5, 11. Milton, s Thomas & Susannah, Clinton Co., O.; m in Newbury MH, Susan FALLIS, dt Amos & Lydia, Clinton Co., O.
1853, 10, 15. Franklin b
1893, 1, 22. Irvin T. b

1846, 7, 13. Milton rocf Salem MM, Ind., dtd 1826,5,23
1849, 3, 12. John Carey gct Mississinewa MM, Ind., to m Lydia Hollingsworth
1849, 9, 10. Milton & w, Susan M., & dt, Joanna Inez, gct Salem MM, Ia. (Ind.?)
1870, 2, 21. Frank recrq
1871, 3, 20. James recrq
1875, 9, 20. James H. gct Greenplain MM, O.
1883, 3, 19. Abner recrq
1884, 10, 20. Esther rocf Fairfield MM, O., dtd 1884,9,20
1888, 4, 23. Nathan & w, Eliza, & dt, Rhoda Ann, rocf Springfield MM, O., dtd 1888,3,17
1889, 11, 18. Nathan & fam gct Cesars Creek MM, O.
1892, 5, 23. Frank relrq
1894, 3, 22. Abner relrq
1897, 5, 13. Elva T. relrq

HOLLOWAY
----, --, --. Abner d 1846,5,31 ae 80 bur Newbury; m Elizabeth -----
Ch: Sarah b 1804, 1, 20
Mary " 1811, 9, 21
Isaac " 1814, 1, 25
----, --, --. Jesse [Holaway] b 1800,7,26; m Ellenor ----- b 1810,2,25
Ch: Margaret b 1828, 8, 6
Abner " 1830, 12, 6
John " 1833, 4, 15
Amos " 1834, 8, 29
1830, 8, 5. Mary [Holoway] m Joseph PUCKETT
1833, 10, 28. John d ae 8- bur Newbury

1819, 4, 22. John rocf Clear Creek MM, dtd 1819,3,13
1819, 4, 22. Joab recrq of parent, John
1820, 2, 24. John & s, Joab, gct Lees Creek MM
1825, 2, 24. Abner & w, Elizabeth, & ch, Jesse, Sarah, Mary & Isaac, rocf Deep Creek MM, N. C., dtd 1824,3,6, endorsed by Fairfield MM
1826, 8, 24. Jesse con mou
1827, 3, 29. Ellenor recrq
1827, 3, 29. Sarah Daniels (form Holloway) con mou
1836, 10, 17. Isaac con mou
1837, 5, 20. Isaac gct White River MM, Ind.
1838, 11, 19. Jesse dis jas
1839, 3, 18. Eleanor dis jas
1848, 8, 14. Isaac [Holaway] & w, Matilda, & ch, Betsy, Cyntha & Asenath, rocf Sparrow Creek MM, dtd 1846,3,19; Matilda d before the cert was rec

HOLLOWAY, continued
1850, 1, 14. Isaac [Holiway] dis mou
1850, 12, 16. Elizabeth [Holoway] gct Poplar Run MM, Ind.
1850, 1, 13. Elizabeth, Cynthia Ann, Asenith & Mary Jane [Holoway] gct Poplar Run MM, Ind.
1851, 12, 15. Abner, John & Amos [Holoway] gct Back Creek MM, Ind.
1852, 6, 5. Margaret Mills (form Holaway) con mou
1852, 9, 4. Timothy [Holoway] gct Back Creek MM, Ind.
1862, 4, 21. Rachel [Holaway] (form Moon) con mou
1862, 10, 20. Rachel gct Back Creek MM, Ind.

HOLMES
1873, 7, 21. Annie (form Mills) con mou

HOMAN
1885, 12, 21. William Jacob recrq

HONEYCUT
1848, 1, 10. Jacob Ratliff gct Dover MM, to m Mary Honeycut

HOOK
1840, 1, 2. Israel C. b

1870, 1, 17. I. C. recrq
1878, 5, 20. Israel C. dis disunity

HOPKINS
1833, 8, 19. Hannah (form Smith) con mou
1851, 5, 12. Hannah gct Honey Creek MM, Ind.

HOSKINS
----, --, --. Joel b 1831,8,14; m Lydia ----- b 1838,2,28
Ch: Moses Frazier b 1853, 9, 2
1859, 1, 27. Isaac, s John & Hannah, Clinton Co., O.; m in Newbury MH, Anna HUNT, dt Henry & Sarah MOON

1854, 7, 17. Lydia P., w Joel, rocf Dover MM, dtd 1854,5,18
1854, 7, 17. Moses F., s Joel & Lydia, recrq
1856, 5, 19. Joel & w, Lydia P., & s, Moses F., gct Clear Creek MM
1859, 11, 21. Lydia rocf Dover MM, dtd 1859,9,15
1859, 11, 21. Jane rocf Dover MM, dtd 1859,9,15
1860, 1, 23. Isaac & s, Joseph, rocf Dover MM, dtd 1859,10,13
1860, 10, 22. Jane & Lydia gct Dover MM
1860, 11, 19. Josephus gct Dover MM
1861, 6, 17. Isaac & w, Anna, gct Dover MM

HUCHINS
1873, 12, 22. William & w, Mary Ann, & ch, Annie Gertrude & Elizabeth Margaret, recrq

HUDGEL
----, --, --. John, s Joseph & Louisa M.; m Marcelina -----, dt Robert & Fannie, b 1840,7,15 (John b 1849,3,21)
Ch: Ethel May b 1876, 9, 24

1872, 12, 23. John & w, Elizabeth, recrq
1878, 4, 22. John relrq
1881, 3, 21. John recrq

HUFF
1829, 1, 29. James Hadley gct Fairfield MM, to m Sarah Huff
1835, 9, 21. Christopher Betts gct Fairfield MM, to m Lydia Huff
1888, 2, 20. Daniel relrq

HUMPHREY
1916, 7, 13. Ora [Humphry] & w, Cora B., & ch, Goldie Ronia, Raymond, Bertha, Mildred, Leala, Dennis J. & Leonard Donald, rocf Miami MM, O.
1917, 11, 15. Ora & w & ch gct Dover MM

HUNNICUTT
1896, 11, 19. Martha rocf Whittier MM, Calif., dtd 1896,10,10
1897, 7, 15. Martha gct Walnut Ridge MM, Ind.

HUNT
----, --, --. Jacob b 1774,10,10; m Lydia ----- b 1774,2,8 d 1858,4,22 bur Newbury
Ch: Rachel b 1798, 10, 1
Nathan " 1800, 2, 28
Robert " 1802, 1, 25
Mary " 1803, 12, 10
Thomas " 1806, 2, 11
Ruth " 1808, 2, 13
Jesse " 1810, 6, 27 d 1851, 9, 2 bur Newbury
Rebecca b 1813, 4, 16
Reuben " 1815, 6, 17
----, --, --. Thomas & Susanna
Ch: Jonathan b 1804, 12, 29
John " 1807, 5, 1
Jacob " 1810, 6, 27
Amos " 1813, 5, 19
William S. " 1816, 8, 27
Mary Ann " 1822, 8, 7
----, --,--- Susan Elizabeth d ae 75
1807, 9, 30. Mary d
----, --, --. Nathan, s Jacob & Lydia, b 1800, 2,28; m Rachel ----- b 1800,9,8 d 1848,9,8 bur Newbury
Ch: James b 1826, 7, 4
Jesse " 1827, 10, 13 d 1855,10,11 bur Newbury
Aaron Betts b 1830, 2, 26
Daniel " 1832, 6, 1
Jacob Green" 1835, 1, 21

HUNT, Nathan & Rachel, continued
Ch: Lydia Ann b 1841, 2, 4 d 1918,11, 1
Nathan m 2nd Sarah -----, dt Daniel & Mary BAILEY, b 1814,6,9 d 1901,9,6
Ch: David Bailey b 1854, 7, 21 d 1926, 5,25
----, --, --. Thomas b 1806,2,11; m Jane ----- b 1805,10,17
Ch: Lydia b 1828, 3, 22
William " 1829, 8, 23
Asa " 1830, 11, 17
Reuben " 1833, 5, 25
Mary J. " 1836, 6, 17
Jabez " 1840, 8, 26
James R. " 1842, 8, 29
Martha " 1855, 12, 30 (adopted)
1828, 11, 6. Jonathan, s Thomas & Susannah, Clinton Co., O., b 1804,12,29; m in Newbury MH, Margaret HADLEY, dt James & Ann, Clinton Co., O., b 1808,8,15
Ch: Aaron B. b 1829, 8, 30 d 1843, 8,24 bur Newbury
Elmira b 1832, 12, 11
Mary Ann " 1835, 6, 27 d 1853,12,26 bur Westfork
Rebecca J.b 1838, 2, 4
James E. " 1841, 1, 5
S. Emma " 1843, 10, 15
Martha " 1846, 9, 2
Albert " 1848, 7, 20
1833, 9, 29. Jesse, s Jacob & Lydia, b 1810, 6,27; m in Newberry MH, Anna MOON, dt Henry & Sarah, Clinton Co., O., b 1815,5,25
Ch: Joseph M. b 1834, 5, 19
Milton L. " 1836, 2, 2
Thomas E. " 1838, 2, 11
Mary " 1842, 2, 21
Sarah Lydia" 1847, 2, 17
----, --, --. John, s Thomas & Susannah, b 1807,5,1 d 1891,7,9; m Phebe -----, dt Wm. & Martha WALKER, b 1807,4,21 d 1892, 3,20 both bur Newberry
Ch: Martha Jane b 1834, 10, 6
Eliza Ann " 1836, 9, 1
Maria Elizabeth " 1839, 1, 9 d 1839,12,20 bur Newbury
William Lindley b 1840, 12, 11
John Milton" 1844, 1, 28
Susan Amelia " 1845, 10, 14
Harriett Ellen " 1849, 4, 24
----, --, --. Jacob, s Thomas & Susannah, b 1810,6,27; m Eliza -----
Ch: Mary Elizabeth b 1834, 11, 6
Susannah G." 1837, 2, 29 d 1858, 8,19 bur Newbury
Thomas J. b 1840, 10, 10
Jonathan L." 1843, 1, 29
Ch: Sidney E. b 1848, 11, 7 d 1923,12,24
Matilda C. " 1854, 12, 20 " 1933,12,27
1834, 9, 28. Abner d ae 83
1836, 8, 26. Amos, s Thomas & Susannah, Clinton Co., O., b 1813,5,19; m in Newberry MH, Hannah MOON, dt Henry & Sarah, Clinton Co., O., b 1817,4,1
Ch: Sarah Elen b 1837, 9, 9
Leuiza Jane " 1839, 11, 14
William Henry " 1843, 5, 31
Anna " 1846, 6, 28
Mary Almeda" 1848, 10, 30
Jesse Milton " 1851, 6, 26
Francis Orvine " 1853, 12, 18
Alice G. " 1857, 9, 28
Susannah " 1861, 1, 15
1839, 11, 27. Mary d ae 86 bur Newbury
----, --, --. Reuben, s Jacob & Lydia, b 1815,6,17; m Rebecca -----, dt Micajah & Gulielma HENLEY, b 1817,8,30
Ch: Gulielma Mariah b 1840, 5, 8
Thomas Clarkson " 1842, 3, 17
1844, 4, 9. Jacob d bur Newbury
1845, 4, 24. Ruth m David WRIGHT
1846, 11, 6. William S., s Thomas & Susannah Clinton Co., O., b 1816,8,27 d 1892,1,15; m in Newberry MH, Phebe HAWORTH, dt Ezekiel & Elizabeth, Clinton Co., O., b 1828,1,8
Ch: Charles Edwin b 1848, 7, 31
Aaron " 1851, 2, 13 d 1921, 1,20
Isaiah " 1853, 1, 20
Susan " 1856, 4, 20
Sylvia " 1859, 3, 28
Olaver " 1861, 7, 14
William S. " 1870, 3, 8
Charles E. " 1848, 7, 31
----, --, --. William S. m Phebe HAWORTH, dt Ezekiel & Elizabeth, b 1828,1,8
Ch: Charles E. b 1848, 7, 31 d 1925, 4,10
Isaiah " 1854, 1, 20 " 1924, 3,27
William S. " 1870, 3, 8 " 1919, 3, 1
1848, 2, 24. Mary m John R. SMITH
1848, 9, 20. Lydia m Alvah HOCKETT
1853, 4, 19. Almira m Hiram E. MOON
1854, 11, 1. William, s Thomas & Jane, Clinton Co., O., b 1829,8,23; m in Westfork MH, Mary Jane HOCKETT, dt Mahlon & Anna, Clinton Co., O., b 1827,7,4
Ch: Ruth Emly b 1855, 12, 12
Joanna " 1857, 8, 4
1856, 2, 28. Asa, s Thomas & Jane, b 1830,11, 17; m in Westfork MH, Martha SIMCOX, dt Job & Catherine, Clinton Co., O., b 1833, 8,28
Ch: Martha b 1855, 12, 30

HUNT, continued
1856, 1, 6. Martha d
1856, 4, 8. Milton d
1858, 3, 3. Reuben G., s Thomas & Jane, Clinton Co., O., b 1833,5,25; m in Westfork MH, Hannah HOCKETT, dt Mahlon & Anna, Clinton Co., O., b 1838,9,16
1859, 1, 31. Thomas d ae 81 bur Newbury
1859, 1, 27. Anna (nee Moon) m Isaac HOSKINS
1859, 11, 10. Daniel d bur Newbury
1860, 2, 22. Gulielma d bur Newbury
1860, 10, 23. Elwood d bur Newbury
----, --, --. Joseph b 1834,5,19; m Emily ----- b 1841,1,25
Ch: Elwood b 1861, 4, 3
Elva " 1863, 3, 15
Wilson H. " 1865, 3, 8
1861, 10, 31. Jacob G., s Nathan & Rachel, Clinton Co., O.; m in Newberry MH, Sarah F. JAMES, dt David & Mary
----, --, --. Jacob G., s Nathan & Rachel, b 1835,1,21; m Sarah F. JAMES, dt David & Mary, b 1838,12,1
Ch: Daniel Huff b 1863, 3, 6
Walter D. " 1865, 4, 5
Clarkson N." 1867, 12, 10
Luther N. " 1874, 1, 19
----, --, --. James E., s Jonathan & Margaret, b 1841,1,5; m Sarah R. CLUXTON, dt Wm. & Margaret, b 1843,1,15
Ch: Clinton b 1863, 5, 28
Gertrude " 1866, 7, 4
Mary " 1868, 9, 7
Clara " 1870, 8, 8
Emma " 1876, 9, 26
----, --, --. Thomas P. b 1840,10,10; m Mary E. ----- b 1848,8,10
Ch: Cliffton H.b 1865, 8, 30
Harry H. " 1868, 4, 29
----, --, --. Thomas Clarkson, s Reuben & Rebecca, b 1842,3,17; m Marianna BAILEY, dt Jonathan & Rebecca T., b 1843,9,1
Ch: Laurena b 1866, 10, 20
Hattie Emma " 1868, 11, 25
Lenora R. " 1870, 11, 12
Elma Ethaleen " 1875, 7, 1
Eva I. " 1877, 9, 18
Iva E. " 1877, 9, 18
Gladis May " 1881, 6, 4
Herbert Bailey " 1886, 7, 15
----, --, --. Milton, s Jesse & Anna, b 1836,2,2 d 1907,5,4; m Sarah E. ----- dt James & Mary J. WRIGHT, b 1845,9,29 d 1915,4,20
Ch: Wright b 1868, 1, 15
Reid " 1870, 4, 20
----, --, --. Aaron Betts, s Nathan & Rachel, b 1830,2,26; m Ann H. -----, dt Thos. & Abigail HENLEY, b 1835,5,24
Ch: Florence E.b 1870, 6, 7
Gurney L. b 1874, 5, 4
----, --, --. Ella M., w C. E., dt Timothy & Mary DOAN, b 1850,1,6 d 1913,9,7
1874, 9, 1. Eliza d
1924, 4, 2. Alverett, w Will, dt Henry & Rachel LONG, d
1934, 1, 28. Anna B., w David B., d

1817, 1, 6. Jacob & w, Lydia, & ch, Rachel, Nathan, Robert, Thomas, Ruth, Jesse, Rebecca & Reuben, rocf Mt. Pleasant MM, Va., dtd 1816,9,26
1817, 3, 3. John & fam gct White Water MM, Ind.
1818, 11, 26. Thomas & w, Susannah, & ch, Jonathan, John, Jacob, Amos & William Sewel, rocf Clermont MM, Va., dtd 1818,9,26
1824, 12, 23. Nathan gct Fairfield MM
1827, 4, 26. Robert gct Springfield MM, to m Ruth Madden
1827, 9, 27. Thomas Jr. con mou
1827, 9, 27. Robert S. rocf Springfield MM, dtd 1827,8,25
1829, 6, 25. Robert & w, Ruth, & s, Cyrus, gct Springfield MM
1829, 11, 26. Rachel Gibson (form Hunt) con mou
1831, 1, 27. Abner & w, Mary, & dt, Elizabeth, rocf Fairfield MM, dtd 1830,12,25
1832, 10, 22. John gct Center MM, to m Phebe Walker
1833, 6, 17. Phebe F. rocf Center MM, dtd 1833,5,15
1834, 9, 22. Jacob Jr. con mou
1836, 8, 22. Reuben gct White Water MM, Ind., to m Rebecca Henley
1836, 8, 22. Lucinda (form Dickey) con mou
1836, 11, 21. Lucinda gct Milford MM, Ind.
1837, 2, 20. Rebecca rocf White Water MM, Ind., dtd 1836,11,23
1843, 7, 17. Eliza & ch, Mary, Elizabeth, Susan & Thomas Ensley, recrq
1844, 7, 15. Jane & ch, Lydia, William, Asa, Reuben, Mary, Jane, Jabez & James R., recrq
1851, 5, 12. Strafford rocf Salem MM, Iowa, dtd 1850,12,18
1852, 9, 4. Stafford gct Hinkles Creek MM, Ind.
1853, 2, 5. Thomas T. & w, Nancy D., & ch, Hannah B., Eliza K., Laura, Mary J. & Margaret, rocf New Garden MM, N. C., dtd 1852,12,29
1853, 6, 20. Thomas & fam gct Milford MM, Ind.
1854, 8, 21. Cyrus L. & w, Margaret Ann, & s, Oliver W., rocf Springfield MM, O., dtd 1854,8,19
1855, 5, 21. Nathan & w, Sarah, & ch, Jacob B., Lydia Ann & David Bailey, rocf Fairfield MM, dtd 1855,4,21
1855, 5, 21. William S. & w, Phebe, & ch, Charles Edwin, Aaron & Josiah, gct Dover

HUNT, continued
MM
1855, 8, 20. Aaron B. rocf Fairfield MM, dtd 1855,6,16
1856, 11, 17. James rocf Fairfield MM, dtd 1856,10,18
1857, 3, 23. Rebecca Jane Hadley (form Hunt) dis mou
1858, 4, 19. Martha Jane Cline (form Hunt) con mou
1858, 5, 17. William T. & w, Phebe, & ch, Charles Edwin, Aaron, Isaiah & Susannah Elizabeth, rocf Dover MM, dtd 1858,4,15
1859, 5, 25. Mary Elizabeth Whinery (form Hunt) con mou
1859, 8, 22. James M. rqct Oak Ridge MM, Ind., to m Emily Haisley
1860, 2, 20. Reuben G. & w, Hannah, gct West Union MM, Ind.
1860, 5, 21. Eliza West (form Hunt) con mou
1860, 10, 22. Emily rocf Oak Ridge MM, Ind., dtd 1860,9,11
1861, 3, 18. William & w, Mary Jane, & ch, Ruth Emaly, Joana & Linton D., gct West Union MM, Ind.
1861, 11, 18. Thomas & w, Jane, & s, James, gct West Union MM, Ind.
1861, 11, 18. Mary, Jane, Jabez, Asa B. & Martha gct West Union MM, Ind.
1863, 5, 18. James E. con mou
1865, 8, 21. Amos & w, Hannah, & ch, Sarah Ellen, Louiza J., Wm. Henry, Annie E., Mary Almedia, Jesse M., Francis Orvine, Alice G. & Susan A., gct West Union MM, Ind.
1865, 9, 18. Clarkson con mou
1865, 11, 20. Margaret C. rocf Goshen MM, dtd 1865,9,23
1866, 1, 22. Marianna rocf Dover MM, dtd 1865,12,14
1866, 11, 19. Thomas J. con mou
1867, 3, 18. Milton L. con mou
1867, 3, 18. James con mou
1867, 4, 25. Emma rmt Mahlon Thomas
1867, 12, 23. William H. dis mou & jas
1868, 1, 20. William dis disunity
1868, 4, 10. Aaron B. gct Carthage MM, Ind., to m Ann Henley
1868, 8, 17. Ann H. rocf Carthage MM, Ind., dtd 1868,7,18
1868, 10, 19. James & w, Margaret C., & dt, Abigail May, gct Goshen MM
1870, 2, 21. Mary E. recrq
1870, 3, 21. Jonathan & w, Margaret, & s, Alfred, gct New Garden MM, Ind.
1870, 4, 18. Susan McIllhenry (form Hunt) con mou
1871, 9, 18. Sarah E. recrq
1872, 1, 22. Thomas Elwood & Wilson A., ch Joseph M., gct Dover MM, O.
1872, 1, 22. Elva, dt Joseph, gct Oak Ridge MM, Ind.
1873, 11, 17. Sarah R. recrq
1875, 1, 18. Maria E. recrq
1875, 2, 22. Cyrus L. & w, Margaret, & ch, Oliver, Robert Edgar, Palmer Nathan & Gladdis May, gct Peace MM, Kans.
1878, 4, 22. Thomas I. & w, Mella, & ch, Clifton & Harrie, relrq
1884, 2, 18. Sylvia Doan (form Hunt) relrq
1887, 5, 23. Laurenna Farquhar (form Hunt) gct Wilmington MM, O.
1888, 9, 17. Hattie E. gct Whittier MM, Calif
1891, 12, 21. Clark N. gct Cincinnati MM, O.
1893, 3, 20. T. Clarkson & w, Marianna, & ch, Ethaleen, Eva J., Iva E., Gladdis May & Herbert Bailey, gct Chicago MM, Ill.
1893, 10, 23. Jacob G. & w, Sarah F., & s, Luther C., gct Wilmington MM, O.
1894, 2, 19. Clinton dropped from mbrp
1894, 6, 14. Rebecca gct Whittier MM, Calif.
1896, 7, 16. Ann rocf Hopewell MM, O., dtd 1896,6,6
1896, 9, 17. Alvaretta rocf Westland MM, Ind.
1897, 5, 13. Ann H. gct Carthage MM, Ind.
1898, 9, 15. Arthur recrq
1900, 6, 14. James & w, Sarah Rebecca, gct Clear Creek MM, O.
1900, 6, 14. Maud gct Clear Creek MM, O.
1900, 6, 14. Clyde gct Clear Creek MM, O.
1903, 10, 15. Luther M. rocf Wilmington MM, O., dtd 1903,10,10
1905, 2, 23. Lenna recrq
1906, 8, 23. Luther M. & w, Lenna, relrq

HUNTER
1926, 4, 18. Harriett recrq

HUTSON
1826, 6, 22. Margaret (form Ratcliff) con mou
1828, 10, 23. Margaret & dt gct Duck Creek MM, Ind.

INGLE
1850, 7, 15. Stacy rocf Clear Creek MM, O., dtd 1850,7,13
1851, 10, 13. Stacy gct Westfield MM, Ind.

IRVIN
1915, 6, 17. Eldora gct Wilmington MM, O.

IZZARD
1836, 6, 20. Mary (form Moon) dis mou
1842, 7, 18. Mary rstrq
1849, 2, 12. Mary gct Springfield MM, O.

JACKSON
----, --, --. Jesse & Ann
Ch: Malinda b 1815, 7, 20
Nathan " 1816, 12, 7 d 1818, 2,27 bur Newberry
Joseph b 1818, 9, 16
Betsy " 1820, 10, 6 d 1821, 2,16 bur Newberry
Jacob b 1822, 5, 6
Asenath " 1825, 1, 5

JACKSON, continued
----, --, --. Jury T., s Curtis & Lydia, b 1824,3,18; m Dorotha -----, dt Wm. & Jane HAMMER, b 1827,9,5
1847, 1, 25. Lydia J. b
1848, 5, 22. Lydia M., dt Josiah & Hannah, b
----, --, --. Erastus & Josephine
Ch: Blanche b 1887, 3, 23
Clara " ----, 11, 15

1823, 8, 28. Josiah gct Fall Creek MM, to m Ruth Hiatt
1824, 4, 22. Ruth rocf Fall Creek MM, dtd 1824,3,30
1826, 3, 23. Jesse & fam gct Clear Creek MM
1829, 11, 26. Jacob dis disunity
1830, 6, 24. Curtis dis jH
1830, 7, 29. Lydia & Ruth dis jH
1830, 8, 26. Ann dis jH
1830, 10, 28. Josiah dis jH
1836, 10, 17. Lucinda Hockett (form Jackson) dis mou
1843, 8, 21. Hannah Dingy (form Jackson) dis mcd
1846, 5, 11. Jury dis mou
1848, 5, 15. John dis mou
1848, 11, 13. Helena West (form Jackson) dis mou
1849, 5, 14. Hellena West (form Jackson) dis mou
1849, 5, 14. Ann Williams (form Jackson) dis mou
1864, 6, 20. Caroline (form Betts) con mou
1867, 4, 22. Lydia Jane recrq
1867, 5, 20. Jury T. & w, Dorothy, recrq
1869, 8, 23. Jacob & w, Caroline, & ch, William W. & Annetta H., gct Union MM, Mo.
1870, 1, 17. Martha M. recrq
1870, 1, 17. Helena W. recrq
1870, 1, 17. Josiah recrq
1870, 1, 17. Josephine recrq
1870, 1, 17. Margaret C. recrq
1870, 1, 17. Curtis recrq
1870, 2, 21. Lydia M. recrq
1877, 6, 18. Josephine Glasgo (form Jackson) relrq
1878, 7, 22. Lydia J., Margaret C., Helena W., Curtis & Joshua, gct Oskaloosa MM, Ia.
1880, 1, 19. Lydia J., Margaret C., Curtis, Helena W. & Josiah, rocf Oskaloosa MM, Ia., dtd 1879,11,1
1885, 8, 17. Frank & w, Josephine, & ch, Oscar & Floren B., recrq
1889, 11, 18. Lydia J. gct Whittier MM, Calif.
1915, 10, 14. Lydia gct Whittier MM, Calif.

JAMES
----, --, --. David b 1803,5,11; m Mary ----- b 1803,3,30 d 1853,4,15 bur Westfork
Ch: Levi C. b 1828, 10, 20
Atticus S. " 1830, 10, 16
Alfred P. " 1832, 12, 19
Jonathan H." 1835, 4, 4
Lindley M. b 1837, 1, 1 d 1859, 4,16
Sarah " 1838, 12, 1
Dillon H. " 1841, 3, 3
Anna B. " 1843, 1, 16
Lydia " 1845, 4, 18
David m 2nd Deborah ----- b 1812,10,26
1861, 10, 31. Sarah F. m Jacob G. HUNT

1844, 10, 14. David & w, Mary, & ch, Levi C., Atticus S., Alfred P., Jonathan H., Sarah, Lindley M., Dillon H. & Anna B., rocf Clear Creek MM, dtd 1844,10,12
1855, 1, 22. John rocf Salem MM, Iowa, dtd 1854,8,16, endorsed by Goshen MM 1854,11, 18
1855, 9, 17. David gct Clear Creek MM, to m Deborah Stevens
1855, 12, 17. Deborah T. rocf Clear Creek MM, dtd 1855,12,8
1856, 2, 18. Jonathan H. gct Centre MM, to m Mary Jane Shepherd
1858, 10, 18. John gct South River MM, Iowa
1860, 7, 23. Alfred P. dis mou
1860, 9, 17. Anna B. dis jas
1865, 1, 23. Mary, Jane & dt, Ella N., rocf Center MM, dtd 1864,12,14
1868, 11, 23. Jonathan H. & w, Mary J., & ch, Elva H. & Lydia Frances, gct Wilmington MM, O.
1869, 1, 18. David & fam gct Wilmington MM, O.
1876, 4, 17. Atticus S. & dt, Ethel M., gct New York MM, N. Y.

JANNEY
----, --, --. Joseph b 1791,3,8 d 1852,3,13 bur Newberry; m Elizabeth ----- b 1795,7, 13 d 1851,12,15 bur Newberry
Ch: Mary b 1817, 1, 1
Emily " 1818, 8, 26
Rebecca " 1822, 2, 24
Patience " 1824, 1, 1
Lot " 1826, 1, 24
Jane " 1828, 3, 7
George " 1830, 2, 6
Stephen " 1832, 7, 1
William " 1835, 1, 8
Caroline " 1839, 7, 30
1835, 1, 8. William b
1840, 7, 1. Paulina Ann b
1844, 7, 25. Patience m Daniel COFFIN
1845, 4, 24. Mary m David BAILEY
1845, 4, 24. Rebecca m John MILTON
1846, 6, 25. Joseph, s Mary (form Janney) b (Joseph Bailey)
1857, 8, 27. George, s Joseph & Elizabeth, Clinton Co., O., b 1830,2,6 d 1867,1,19; m in Newberry MH, Rebecca A. BETTS, dt Christopher & Lydia, Clinton Co., O., b 1838,8,24
Ch: Reynold b 1858, 7, 4
Madison " 1861, 1, 14
1859, 6, 30. Caroline m Madison BETTS

JANNEY, continued
1842, 9, 19. Elizabeth & ch, Lot, Jane, George, Stephen, William & Caroline, recrq
1842, 9, 19. Emila, Rebecca & Patience recrq
1843, 2, 20. Joseph recrq
1843, 3, 20. Mary recrq
1844, 7, 25. Emily m Jesse Coffin
1853, 8, 22. Caroline gct White Water MM, Ind.
1859, 5, 23. Caroline rocf White Water MM, Ind., dtd 1859,4,27
1859, 11, 21. William con mou
1859, 11, 21. Pelena (form Stephens) con mou
1864, 5, 23. Jane Haworth (form Janney) con mou
1866, 4, 23. Lydia (form White) con mou
1866, 8, 20. Lydia gct Ash Grove MM, Ill.
1867, 12, 23. Stephen con mou
1868, 3, 23. Stephen gct Ash Grove MM, Ill.
1869, 8, 23. William & w, Paulina, & dt, Alma F., gct Union MM, Mo.
1883, 10, 22. Rebecca Ann gct Wilmington MM, O.
1883, 10, 22. Reynold gct Wilmington MM, O.

JAY
----, --, --. James, s John & Lydia, b 1841, 10,11 d 1928,5,9; m Eliza COFFIN, dt Daniel & Patierce, b 1845,7,5
Ch: Eva C. b 1870, 2, 20
Russell "
----, --, --. David, s John & Lydia, b 1844,8, 18 d 1923,6,5; m Hattie E. HUNT, dt John & Phebe, b 1849,4,24 d 1930,1,17
Ch: Josie E. b 1875, 3, 15 d 1892,12, 9 bur Wilmington
1899, 8, 18. Harold M., s W. T. & Hattie, d
1903, 4, 3. Walton G. b or d
1909, 9, 26. Miriam Madeline, dt Russell & Mary Ethel, b
1926, 11, 9. Martha H. d

1872, 9, 23. Hattie E. con mou
1872, 10, 21. Hattie E. gct Cesars Creek MM, O.
1878, 3, 18. David H. & w, Hattie E., & dt, Josie E., rocf Ceasers Creek MM, O., dtd 1878,2,21
1885, 5, 18. Phama rocf Ceasars Creek MM, O., dtd 1885,4,23
1886, 1, 18. Samuel S. & w, Martha, & ch, Allen E., Wilson T. & Arrena, rocf Caesars Creek MM, O., dtd 1886,2,25
1887, 5, 23. James & w, Eliza, & ch, Eva C. & D. Russell, rocf Ceasars Creek MM, O., dtd 1887,4,21
1898, 1, 13. Dora M. & s, Cassius M., gct Whittier MM, Calif.
1907, 2, 14. Mary Ethel Green rocf Wilmington MM, O.
1920, 3, 18. Russell D. & w, Mary Ethel, & ch, Miriam Madeline & James Wilbur, relrq
1924, 6, 15. Ella recrq

JENKINS
1826, 7, 27. Leah (form Hockett) dis mou

JESSUP
1856, 8, 18. Daniel & w, Hannah L., & s, Amos, rocf Fairfield MM, Ind., dtd 1856,7, 17
1863, 5, 18. Daniel & w, Hannah Sophia, & ch, Amos C., Mary Emma & Charles W., gct Back Creek MM, Ind.

JOHN
1828, 3, 22. Ebenezar d ae 70 bur Newberry

1825, 11, 24. Samuel & ch, Priscilla, Jesse, Jonathan & Samuel, recrq
1826, 6, 22. Elizabeth rst on consent of Newhope MM, Tenn.
1830, 4, 22. Samuel & w, Elizabeth, & ch, Priscilla, Jesse, Jonathan, Samuel & Ebeneezer, gct White Lick MM, Ind.

JOHNSON
1807, 5, 9. Thomas B., s Wm. & Mary, b
----, --, --. John W., s Wm. & Mary, b 1809,4, 4; m Jane BOTTS, dt Williamson & Sarah, b 1820,4,1
1835, 3, 12. William d ae 78 bur Newberry
1836, 11, 26. Mary d ae 64 bur Newberry
----, --, --. George b 1813,6,13; m Ruth ----- b 1818,12,10 d 1849,6,19
Ch: Mary b 1842, 5, 11
Thomas H. " 1845, 8, 3
Robert Barclay " 1849, 6, 19
----, --, --. Christopher H., s John W. & Milly, b 1819,2,8; m Sisley -----, dt Chris. & Elizabeth TERRELL, b 1824,7,28 d 1901,8,3
Ch: Elizabeth Olive b 1843, 7, 22
Mary Mildred " 1846, 1, 8
Pleasant Irvin " 1850, 4, 14
John Christopher " 1854, 3, 4 d 1859, 9, 4 bur Westfork
Sisley Ann b 1859, 8, 23 " 1927, 3,18
Duelah " 1864, 11, 13
1842, 4, 22. Elizabeth Olive b
1846, 5, 30. John H., s Thomas & Elizabeth, b
----, --, --. Benjamin F., s Thomas & Elizabeth, b 1836,9,5; m Louisa JACKSON, dt Curtis & Lydia, b 1837,8,9
1863, 10, 29. Mary M. m John KESTER

1834, 3, 17. William & w, Polly, & s, George, rocf Clear Creek MM, dtd 1833,8,20
1841, 6, 21. Ruth (form Moon) con mou
1841, 5, 17. George con mou
1852, 8, 7. Christopher & w, Sicily, & ch, Elizabeth Olive, Mary Mildred & Pleasant Irving, rocf Fairfield MM, dtd 1852,6,17
1862, 2, 17. George & s, Henry, gct Pipe Creek MM, Ind.

JOHNSON, continued
1862, 2, 17. Mary gct Pipe Creek MM, Ind.
1870, 2, 21. Thomas B. recrq
1870, 2, 21. John H. recrq
1870, 2, 21. Benjamin F. recrq
1870, 2, 21. Louisa recrq
1870, 2, 21. John W. recrq
1870, 2, 21. Jane recrq
1870, 2, 21. Oliver H. recrq
1870, 2, 21. Sarah Ellen recrq
1881, 3, 21. Rosellie recrq
1881, 3, 21. Harley recrq
1881, 3, 21. Minnie recrq
1881, 3, 21. Francis M. recrq
1881, 3, 21. Emme recrq
1886, 1, 18. Sarah E. recrq
1886, 1, 18. Edward S. recrq
1893, 11, 20. Frances M. & Emma dropped from mbrp

JONES
----, --, --. Charles, s James & Sarah H., b 1854,10,16; m Sarah E. KESTER, dt Miles & Jane, b 1858,12,21
Ch: Orval S. b 1878, 2, 7

1822, 7, 25. Abigail rocf Chestnut MM, Va., dtd 1821,12,2
1824, 11, 23. Abigail gct Lees Creek MM, O.
1847, 2, 15. Samuel N. & w, Jane, & s, Wiley B., rocf Elk MM, dtd 1846,12,19
1850, 8, 12. Samuel N. & w, Jane, & ch, Wiley B. & Lemuel, gct Back Creek MM, Ind.
1864, 8, 22. Richard & w, Mary Elizabeth, & ch, Wm. Arthur, John Albert, Jemima Jane, Martha Estella & Daniel Henry, rocf Wabash MM, dtd 1864,5,14
1867, 12, 23. Richard & w, Mary E., & ch, William Arthur, John Albert, Jane, Martha Estella & Daniel, gct Plainfield MM, Ind.
1870, 6, 20. Joseph T. & w, Elizabeth, & ch, Henrietta, Margaret Louisa, Anna, Frank, recrq
1873, 8, 18. Olive E. recrq
1876, 4, 17. Charles E. recrq
1878, 3, 18. Sarah E. (form Kester) relrq
1881, 3, 21. William Henry recrq
1887, 8, 22. Wm. H. dropped from mbrp
1911, 2, 16. Viola gct Oskaloosa MM, Ia.
1911, 4, 13. Minnie recrq
1920, 12, 16. Maud M. & ch, Mary Ellen, Lucile May & John Marshall, recrq
1933, 4, 16. Mary & Lucile relrq

JOSEPH
1906, 10, 18. Thomas & w, Gertrude, & ch, Hazel, Elma & Ray, rocf Westfork MM, O.
1907, 7, 18. Thomas & w, Gertrude, & ch, Hazel, Elma & Raymond, relrq

JUDKINS
----, --, --. Stanton B. b 1833,7,18; m -----
Ch: Madora b 1870, 6, 29

1869, 4, 19. Stanton B. recrq

KEITH
1883, 4, 23. Louisa & ch, Minnie B. & Walter, recrq
1885, 1, 19. Elisha & ch, Jesse & Bessie, recrq

KELLIS
1886, 1, 18. Frank V. & w, Catharine E., & ch, Laura L., Emma Z., Frank E. & Howard, recrq
1886, 4, 19. John W. recrq
1887, 8, 22. John dropped from mbrp
1893, 11, 20. John W. dropped from mbrp

KELLUM
1819, 11, 25. Noah & w, Esther, & ch, Jesse, Noah, Asenith, Amos, Esther & Asher, rocf Springfield MM, N. C., dtd 1819,10,6
1819, 11, 25. Christopher rocf Springfield MM, N. C., dtd 1819,10,6
1819, 11, 25. Cert rec for Samuel & w, Ann, & ch, Buly & Lindley, from Springfield MM, N. C., dtd 1819,10,6, endorsed to Cesars Creek MM, O.
1819, 12, 23. Christopher gct Springfield MM, to m
1820, 5, 25. Elizabeth rocf Springfield MM, dtd 1820,3,25
1822, 2, 21. Jesse gct West Grove MM, Ind.
1822, 3, 28. Christopher & fam gct West Grove MM, Ind.

KELSO
1848, 3, 13. Diantha (form Moon) con mou
1855, 4, 23. Diantha gct Sugar Plain MM, Ind.
1860, 2, 20. Diantha rocf Sugar Plain MM, Ind., dtd 1860,1,7
1867, 7, 22. William G. & ch, John Riley, Joseph Marion, James Andrew, Hiram Edwin, Mary Ann & Ayner Jane, recrq
1869, 3, 22. William J. & w, Diantha, & ch, John Riley, Joseph Marion, Hiram Edwin, Mary Ann, Abner Jane & Daniel Orland, gct Center MM, O.

KENWORTHY
1827, 12, 27. Margaret (form Ratcliff) dis mou
1830, 7, 29. Ann (form Ratcliff) dis mou

KESTER
----, --, --. Daniel, s Peter & Hannah, b 1809,5,31; m Elizabeth -----, dt Samuel & Anna CAREY, b 1812,6,14
Ch: Miles b 1835, 8, 30
Anna " 1837, 6, 26
John " 1839, 9, 24
Carey D. " 1841, 12, 20
Hannah " 1843, 4, 6
Rachel " 1845, 5, 27 d 1845,12,28 bur Newberry

KESTER, Daniel & Elizabeth, continued
Ch: Mary b 1846, 12, 19
Sarah " 1849, 2, 11
Tamer E. " 1851, 6, 5 d 1851, 9,17 bur Newberry
Jesse b 1852, 11, 24
Daniel
Samuel " 1855, 3, 7 d 1874, 1, 6 bur Newberry
1858, 10, 28. Anna m Nathan HARROLD
1863, 10, 29. John, s Daniel & Elizabeth, Clinton Co., O., b 1839,9,26 d 1912,3,22; m in Newberry MH, Mary M. JOHNSON, dt Christopher H. & Sisely, Clinton Co., O., b 1846,1,8 d 1927,8,26
Ch: Orland W. b 1864, 7, 19
Olive E. " 1867, 7, 2 d 1868, 9,14
Daniel O. " 1870, 10, 19 d 1932,10,21
Clemmie E. " 1877, 4, 29
Stanley " " 1913, 7,17
----, --, --. Miles b 1835,8,30; m Jane -----
Ch: Sylvia b 1865, 6, 28
Emma A. " 1867, 8, 10
Elwood " 1872, 5, 1 d 1873, 7,30 bur Newberry
----, --, --. Carey D., s Daniel & Elizabeth, b 1841,12,20; m Nancy Jane -----, dt Wm. & Delilah BETTERTON, b 1846,8,16
Ch: Delilah
Ettie b 1868, 3, 4
Eva Elizabeth " 1873, 1, 23 d 1873, 8,24
Milton Leroy " 1875, 9, 15
----, --, --. Jesse, s Daniel & Elizabeth, b 1852,11,24; m Lenna -----, dt Samuel & Ruth HARRIS, b 1850,6,2 d 1878,4,30 bur Martinsville, O.
Ch: Ida A. b 1876, 11, 29
1876, 9, 26. Emma Hunt, w Geo., dt James E. & Rebecca HUNT, b
1879, 12, 9. Minnie L., w Stanley, dt A. L. & Mary HENDEE, b
1898, 12, 1. Warren W., s D. M. & Mary, b
1932, 10, 21. Daniel d

1831, 7, 18. Daniel rocf Centre MM, dtd 1831,6,15
1833, 4, 22. Harmon rocf Caesars Creek MM, dtd 1833,1,24
1834, 9, 22. Daniel gct Clear Creek MM, to m Elizabeth Carey
1835, 2, 23. Elizabeth rocf Clear Creek MM, dtd 1835,1,20
1836, 4, 18. Harmon dis mou
1836, 4, 18. Edith (form Hockett) con mou
1836, 10, 17. Edith gct Caesars Creek MM
1844, 2, 16. Edith & dt, Hannah, rocf Caesars Creek MM, dtd 1844,1,27
1846, 9, 14. Edith & ch, Hannah, gct Westfield MM, Ind.
1850, 4, 15. Harmon rst at Westfield MM, Ind. on consent of this mtg
1857, 8, 17. Miles dis mou
1861, 6, 17. Hannah Davis (form Kester) dis mou
1865, 2, 20. Miles recrq
1867, 6, 17. Mary Lutteral (form Kester) con mou
1870, 6, 20. Carey D. dis mou
1871, 4, 17. Sarah Llewellyn (form Kester) dis mou
1874, 2, 23. Carey D. & w, Nancy Jane, & ch, Delilah E., recrq
1874, 2, 23. Sarah E. recrq
1878, 3, 18. Sarah E. Jones (form Kester) relrq
1884, 5, 19. Miles gct Clear Creek MM, O.
1887, 7, 18. Carey D. & w, Nancy J., & ch, Milton Leroy & Ada, gct Fairfield MM, O.
1887, 8, 22. Jesse & Delilah dropped from mbrp
1887, 11, 21. Miles rocf Clear Creek MM, O., dtd 1887,11,12
1894, 6, 14. Miles gct Clear Creek MM, O.
1901, 10, 17. Mary F. rocf Clear Creek MM, O., dtd 1901,10,12
1913, 3, 20. Donald recrq
1913, 3, 20. George recrq
1913, 3, 20. Emma recrq

KIBLY
1870, 2, 21. Thomas E. recrq
1876, 2, 21. Thomas E. [Kibby] relrq

KIGER
1881, 3, 21. Vina recrq
1894, 2, 19. Vina dropped from mbrp

KING
----, --, --. Elijah & Mary Ann
Ch: Franklin F. b 1856, 3, 4
Nancy Ellen " 1858, 10, 12

1870, 1, 17. Nancy E. & Franklin F. recrq

KIRBY
1899, 3, 2. Richard d bur Martinsville
1912, 11, 15. Sarah Ann d

1886, 4, 19. Ricaard & Sarah Ann recrq

KNIGHT
1838, 6, 19. Mary (form Chew) con mou
1839, 3, 18. Mary gct Mississinewa MM, Ind.

KNOTT
1838, 7, 2. Helen M., dt Oliver V. & Mary P., b

1876, 1, 17. Helen recrq
1881, 3, 21. Annie recrq
1891, 7, 20. Helen M. relrq

KNOTT, continued
1893, 11, 20. Anna dropped from mbrp

KNOWLAND
1879, 2, 2. Esto [Knowlan], ch Joseph H. & Mary A., b

1879, 2, 17. Joseph H. & s, Joseph H., recrq
1887, 7, 18. Joseph & w, Mary Alice, & ch, Esto, gct Mississinewa MM, Ind.

LADD
1870, 3, 21. Mary & Jesse P. recrq
1870, 3, 21. Henry C. & Minerva Ann recrq
1871, 4, 17. Isaiah & ch, Emma Jane & Mary Ellen, rocf Poplar Run MM, Ind., dtd 1871, 3,16

LANGSTAFF
----, --, --. Benjamin P. b 1806,6,5; m Catharine ----- b 1807,7,5
Ch: Laban b 1835, 9, 5

1851, 9, 15. Benjamin P. & w, Catherine, & s, Laban, rocf Cincinnati MM, O., dtd 1851,8, 21
1865, 8, 21. Benjamin & Catherine gct West Union MM, Ind.
1865, 8, 21. Laban gct West Union MM, Ind.

LARICK
1881, 9, 19. Olive recrq
1894, 2, 19. Olive dropped from mbrp

LARROWE
1859, 1, 17. Mary (form Moon) con mou

LAZENBY
1839, 4, 22. Mary (form Hiatt) dis mou
1865, 5, 22. Mary recrq
1869, 4, 19. Mary gct Union MM, Mo.

LEAGUE
1840, 10, 19. Ann (form Ruse) dis mou

LEAR
1889, 2, 18. Low & Zimri recrq
1890, 10, 20. Winnie recrq

LEWIS
----, --, --. Lemuel b 1818,11,28; m Hannah ----- b 1815,1,2
Ch: John b 1848, 2, 6

1848, 8, 14. Lemuel & w, Hannah, & s, John, rocf Clear Creek MM, dtd 1848,7,8
1855, 7, 23. Lemuel dis disunity
1860, 1, 23. Lemuel rst rq
1930, 12, 14. Geneva Moon relrq

LIEURANCE
----, --, --. Pierson b 1848,1,25; m Cordelia ----- d 1933,12,27
Ch: Rhue D. b 1875, 6, 26
Ettie Leota " 1880, 1, 16
----, --, --. David b 1852,3,17 d 1928,7,14; m Sidney HUNT
Ch: Laurenna Maud b 1883, 9, 18
1928, 7, 14. David d

1891, 2, 23. Piercon, David, Etta Leota & Lourenna Maud, recrq

LIGHT
1894, 5, 17. Mary (form Green) gct Westfork MM, O.

LIGHTFOOT
----, --, --. Thomas b 1819,5,28; m Malinda ----- b 1823,10,21
Ch: Jeptha b 1840, 7, 20

1840, 10, 19. Melinda (form Moon) con mou
1841, 11, 22. Thomas recrq
1842, 4, 18. Jephtha, s Thos., recrq
1842, 8, 22. Thomas & fam gct Richland MM, Ind.

LINKHART
1873, 12, 22. Elizabeth (form Carter) con mou
1874, 1, 19. Elizabeth & dt, Nellie Revelle, gct Center MM, O.

LITTLE
----, --, --. Hezekiah, s Hezekiah & Delilah, b 1832,12,25; m Mary Ann ----- dt James & Leah HOOVER, b 1834,3,15
Ch: Martha V. b 1858, 4, 3
Annetty B. " 1860, 5, 14
Luadia " 1864, 7, 25

1873, 5, 19. Annetta B. recrq
1876, 2, 21. Hezikiah & w, Mary, & ch, Mary Ann, Martha & Luanda, recrq
1878, 10, 21. Hezekiah dis disunity
1879, 3, 17. Mary Ann relrq

LLEWELLYN
----, --, --. John, s Wm. & Sarah, b 1829,2, 18; m Anna HERROLD, dt Daniel & Elizabeth KESTER, b 1837,6,26
Ch: Sarah Lydia b 1868, 12, 1 d 1869, 8,29
Martha Hanna " 1870, 7, 8
Edgar " 1874, 11, 21
Samuel Joseph " 1876, 6, 29

1868, 3, 23. John rmt Anna Harold
1868, 6, 22. John rocf Chesterfield MM, dtd 1868,--,--
1869, 8, 23. John & w, Anna, & ch, Mary Alice, Harold, Anna Elizabeth, Harold &

LLEWELLYN, continued
Sarah Lydia, gct Chesterfield MM
1871, 1, 23. John [Lewellyn] & w, Anna, & ch, Mary Alice, Anna Elizabeth, Harold & Martha Hannah, rocf Chesterfield MM, dtd 1870, 12,10
1871, 4, 17. Sarah (form Kester) dis mou
1871, 5, 22. Sarah relrq
1882, 8, 21. John & ch, Martha J., Edgar & Samuel J., gct Mississinewa MM, Ind.

LONG
-----, --, --. Rachel, w Henry, dt Pleasant & Huldah MOON, b 1844,11,15 d 1929,9,1

1893, 4, 17. Rachel gct Westland MM, Ind.
1821, 2, 17. Rachel rocf Greenfield MM, Ind.

LOVE
----, --, --. Belta G. b 1845,5,16; m Emaline ----- b 1849,9,19
Ch: Mary R. b 1869, 3, 9

LUKENS
1929, 5, 19. Edith Greene gct Miami MM, O.

LUNDY
1839, 10, 31. Rachel m Joshua D. HADLEY

1836, 12, 19. Mary Ann, Rachel, Dempsey & Aaron, orphans, rocf Center MM, dtd 1836,4, 9
1839, 2, 18. Mary Ann Hiatt (form Lundy) dis mou
1842, 7, 18. Johiel Green gct Centre MM, to m Rachel Lundy
1842, 8, 22. Dempsey dis mou
1855, 7, 23. Aaron dis disunity
1856, 8, 18. John Carey gct Centre MM, to m Elizabeth Lundy Jr.

LUTTRELL
----, --, --. Robert H. [Lutrell], s Robert & Fannie, b 1844,9,2; m Mary -----, dt Daniel & Elizabeth KESTER, b 1846,12,9
Ch: Fanny E. b 1867, 8, 28 d 1867, 9,18 bur Newbury
Chloe E. b 1868, 10, 12
Ulissius D." 1870, 8, 11

1867, 6, 17. Mary [Lutteral] (form Kester) con mou
1867, 9, 23. Robert H. [Lutterell] recrq
1880, 10, 18. R. H. relrq
1881, 3, 21. Chloa E. & Ulyssis, ch Robert Holland, gct Springfield MM, O.; redirected to Wilmington MM, O. 1881,6,20

LYONS
1864, 4, 18. Mary (form West) con mou

McCALL
1821, 10, 25. John & w, Margaret, & ch, Mary Susanna, Dorcas, William & John, recrq
1830, 12, 23. John & w, Margaret, & ch gct White Water MM, Ind.
1831, 4, 28. John dis disunity

McCOY
1835, 5, 18. Matilda (form Cruse) dis mou
1847, 6, 14. Anna (form Moon) con mou
1861, 12, 23. Ann gct Oak Ridge MM, Ind.

McCRARY
1805, 10, 8. Anna, w John, dt Geo. & Mary GREEN, b

McCRAY
1870, 2, 21. Anna recrq

McDURMOTT
1876, 3, 20. Patrick B. recrq

McILHENNY
1871, 7, 12. John J., s A. C. & Sue A. (Hunt) b
1870, 4, 18. Susan [McIllhenry] (form Hunt) con mou

McKIBBEN
1858, 3, 8. Phebe, w Joseph, dt Larkin & Melcena CLELAND, b

1929, 8, 25. Etta May recrq

McKINNEY
1870, 1, 17. Jesse recrq
1870, 4, 18. Jesse gct Springfield MM, O.
1872, 9, 23. Jesse rocf Springfield MM, dtd 1872,8,17
1887, 5, 23. Jesse dropped from mbrp

McKINSEY
1886, 4, 19. Jacob & ch, Gracie Pearl, Charley J., Samuel R., Lesley Howard recrq
1886, 4, 19. Cora recrq

McLINN
1830, 7, 29. Mary dis disunity

McMILLAN
----, --, --. Joshua F., s Jonathan & Rebecca, b 1853,10,18; m Mary E. LEWIS, dt John W. & Hannah, b 1860,11,10
Ch: Viola H. b 1882, 12, 23
L. Dora " 1885, 12, 13
Evaline " 1888, 12, 11
Carl L. " 1901, 9, 3

1907, 7, 18. Joshua & w, Mary E., & ch, Lena & Carl, rocf Dover MM
1907, 7, 18. L. Dora rocf Dover MM
1907, 7, 18. Viola H. rocf Dover MM
1918, 8, 29. Esther Carroll gct Center MM,O.

MCPHERSON
1834, 8, 26. Daniel, s Joseph & Ruth, b
1842, 4, 10. Hannah, w Hiram, dt Joseph M. & Lois MILLS, b
----, --, --. Josiah b 1831,11,10; m Edna ----- b 1838,2,2
Ch: Francis M. b 1860, 7, 8
Carey Lee " 1862, 9, 5
----, --, --. Joseph C., s John & Maria, b 1835 12,15 d 1889,7,8; m Caroline E. -----, dt Peyton & Sarah WEST, b 1845,7,13 d 1927,8, 4
Ch: Florence b 1865, 4, 14 d 1908, 2,29
Clara " 1867, 9, 17
Sarah " 1869, 11, 27
Edward Everett " 1871, 10, 12
Mary " 1874, 12, 15 d 1901,10,13
Minnie " 1878, 2 , 5 " 1894, 5,19
Raymond

1834, 5, 19. Joseph & w, Ruth, rocf Clear Creek MM, dtd 1834,4,22
1842, 7, 18. Joseph & w, Ruth, & s, Daniel, gct Clear Creek MM
1854, 3, 20. Jeptha Garner gct Fairfield MM, to m Martha B. McPherson
1860, 7, 23. Josiah & w, Edney, rocf Fairfield MM, dtd 1860,6,16
1864, 6, 20. Ruth & dt, Mary Margaret, rocf OR MM, Ind., dtd 1864,4,14, endorsed by Cincinnati MM, 1864,5,19 (Oak Ridge MM)
1864, 7, 18. Daniel rocf ORMM, Ind., dtd 1864,6,14 (Oak Ridge MM)
1865, 1, 23. Joseph C. rocf Spring Creek MM, Ia., dtd 1865,1,7
1865, 4, 17. Daniel gct Center MM, O., to m Lydia Mary Ellis
1865, 7, 17. Caroline con mou
1867, 2, 18. Daniel gct Gilead MM, Mo.
1868, 3, 23. Josiah con mou
1868, 5, 18. Josiah & s, Carey, gct Fairfield MM, O.
1868, 8, 17. Ruth Morris (form McPherson) con mou
1879, 10, 20. Mary Margaret & ch gct Fairfield MM
1894, 5, 17. Minette relrq

MADDEN
1827, 4, 26. Robert Hunt gct Springfield MM, to m Ruth Madden

MAGEE
1881, 3, 21. Joseph recrq
1881, 3, 21. Missouri recrq
1881, 3, 21. Wm. Webster recrq
1881, 3, 21. Edith Maria recrq
1881, 3, 21. Archer James recrq
1881, 3, 21. Alice Gertrude recrq
1886, 4, 19. Joseph & w, Missouri, & ch, Wm. Webster, Edith Mariah, Archer, James & Alice Gertrude, relrq

MALONE
----, --, --. John & Mary Ann
Ch: Hezekiah P.b 1841, 9, 13
Alice Elvira " 1843, 8, 21
Charles Oskar " 1844, 11, 28
Levi Harison " 1847, 3, 16
Frances Emaly " 1849, 8, 31 d 1853, 2,14
Edwin Meadow " 1851, 10, 1
James Scott" 1853, 6, 6
John Walter" 1857, 8, 10
1853, 5, 23. John & w, Mary Ann, & ch, Hezekiah P., Charles E., Levi H. & Edwin T., rocf Marlborough MM, O., dtd 1853,3,9
1865, 4, 17. John & w, Mary A., & ch, Edwin T., James S., John W., William L. & Henry G., gct Clear Creek MM, O.
1865, 4, 17. Alice E. gct Clear Creek MM, O.
1868, 2, 17. H. P. con mou
1868, 3, 23. Harry P. & Charles O. gct Clear Creek MM, O.

MANKER
1886 4, 19. Sanford & Maryetta recrq
1887, 1, 17. Ida A. recrq
1887, 1, 17. Albert N. recrq
1887, 1, 17. Alpheus O. recrq
1887, 1, 17. Harley A. recrq
1910, 2, 24. Albert [Mancher] & w & ch gct Westfork MM, O.
1914, 4, 16. Albert & w, Beryha, & ch, Lesta, Harley, Mabel, Estel, Stanley, Maud Louise & Mildred Lucile, rocf Westfork MM, O., dtd 1914,3,21
1924, 10, 19. Grace [Mancher] recrq
1929, 2, 17. Estel relrq

MARIS
1838, 6, 1. Hannah, w Temple, dt John & Agnes MILLS, b

MARSHALL
1870, 2, 21. John J., Mary E., Norah H. & Eva, recrq
1876, 10, 23. Mary C. & ch, Nora H., Eva L., Annie E., Minnie B. & Allie M., gct Springfield MM, O.

MEEKER
1856, 8, 12. John Q., s Jefferson & Martha, b

1876, 4, 17. John Q. recrq
1894, 10, 18. Charlie recrq

MENDENHALL
1859, 9, 29. Jesse N., s John & Eunice, Grant Co., Ind.; m in Newberry MH, Hannah M. CAREY, dt Elias & Jane, Clinton Co.,O.

MENDENHALL, continued
1820, 11, 23. Stephen [Mendinghall] rocf New Garden MM, N. C., dtd 1820,2,26, endorsed by New Garden MM, Ind., 1820,10,21
1821, 6, 28. Stephen [Mendinghall] gct Springfield MM
1860, 6 18. Hannah gct Oak Ridge MM, Ind.

MICHAEL
1843, 6, 4. Wm. W., s John & Lucinda, b

1870, 2, 21. William W. [Michaels] recrq
1881, 3, 21. Mattie [Michels] recrq

MILLER
----, --, --. Isaac b 1802,3,24; m Martha ----- b 1810,10,15
Ch: Zadock b 1834, 1, 20
Deborah Ann" 1836, 9, 13
Wilmer " 1841, 6, 28
Isaac Newton " 1846, 9, 25
----, --, --. ----- & Charity
Ch: James Harrison b 1837, 10, 19
Lydia Elizabeth " 1840, 12, 16
Sarah Charity " 1844, 5, 12
Martha Jane" 1848, 1, 4
----, --, --. Levi & Maria
Ch: James Madison b 1838, 1, 17
Mordecai " 1846, 5, 22
Francis " 1842, 10, 20
Austin " 1850, 5, 15
Mariah " 1852, 8, 17
Henry Clay " 1854, 9, 17
1858, 4, 29. Deborah Ann m Benajah PARKER
----, --, --. Wilmer, s Isaac & Martha, b 1840,6,28; m Mary E. -----, dt Robert & Mary FULTON, b 1845,7,3 d 1925,7,21
Ch: Jesse A. b 1862, 11, 1
Charles F. " 1865, 1, 1 d 1865,10,11 bur Newberry
Edward b 1866, 8, 6
Leonard Survetus " 1869, 3, 5
Willie
Virgil
1869, 4, 11. Isaac d

1839, 4, 22. Lucinda (form Moon) dis mou
1841, 12, 20. Lucinda rst
1842, 4, 18. Mary (form Moon) con mou
1851, 5, 12. Lucinda gct Honey Creek MM, Ind.; returned for jas
1852, 5, 1. Lucinda dis jas
1854, 6, 19. Isaac & w, Martha, & ch, Zadoc, Deborah Ann, Wilmer & Isaac Newton, rocf Sandy Spring MM, dtd 1854,5,26
1854, 8, 21. Charity P. & ch, James Harrison, Lydia Elizabeth, Sarah Charity & Martha Jane, rocf Upper Springfield MM, dtd 1854,6,24
1855, 9, 17. Levi recrq
1855, 11, 19. Levi rst at Sandy Spring MM on consent of this mtg
1856, 2, 18. Mary, w Levi, & ch, James Madison, Mordecai, Francis, Austin, Maria & Henry Clay, rocf Cincinnati MM, dtd 1856,2,14
1857, 8, 17. Zadoc gct Fairfield MM, to m Emily Hodson
1858, 12, 20. Zadoc & s, John E., gct Clear Creek MM
1860, 6, 18. Samuel rst on consent of Sandy Spring MM, O.
1861, 6, 17. Lydia Hagerman (form Miller) dis mou & jas
1862, 6, 23. Wilmer con mou
1863, 10, 19. Sarah Charity dis jas
1865, 4, 17. Samuel & w, Charity, & dt, Mary Jane, gct Clear Creek MM, O.
1870, 2, 21. Mary E. recrq
1871, 6, 19. Martha gct Clear Creek MM, O.
1876, 2, 21. I. Newton relrq
1884, 5, 19. Ruth A. gct Clear Creek MM, O.
1887, 2, 21. Jessie Troth (form Miller) relrq
1901, 7, 18. Lola H. & dt, Marjory Jay, recrq
1913, 12, 18. Marjorie J. relrq

MILLS
1828, 9, 4. John, s Joseph & Hannah, Clinton Co., O., b 1793,3,1 d 1880,4,11 bur Martinsville, O.; m in Newberry MH, Agnes HOCKETT, dt David & Dorcas, b 1802,11,1
Ch: Clarkson W.b 1829, 8, 20
Lewis " 1831, 9, 21
Joseph H. " 1833, 8, 26
Dorcas " 1836, 2, 19
Hannah " 1838, 7, 1
Sarah Jane " 1840, 3, 16 d 1841, 9,12 bur Newbury
David b 1842, 3, 23
1834, 2, 26. Joseph d ae 81 bur Newberry
1836, 5, 26. Hannah d ae 94 bur Newberry
1836, 8, 7. Ruth, w Joseph M., d bur Newberry
1836, 12, 1. Clarkson d bur Newberry
1838, 12, 27. Joseph, s Joseph & Hannah, Clinton Co., O., b 1799,12,12; m in Newberry MH, Lois HOCKETT, dt Benjamin & Charity, b 1811,12,12 (B & D record says 2nd w)
Ch: Joseph Maris b 1839, 7, 18
John M. " 1841, 1, 22
Clarkson " 1842, 4, 10
Hannah " 1842, 4, 10
Mary Jane " 1843, 11, 5
Jabez " 1846, 4, 30
Ann " 1848, 7, 5
Albert " 1851, 10, 15
Sarah " 1853, 4, 20
1845, 2, 20. Rebecca m Ezra MOON

MILLS, continued
1857, 10, 29. Lewis, s John & Agnes, b 1831,9, 21; m in Newberry MH, Catherine B. TOWNSEND, dt Josiah & Abigail, b 1826,9,23
Ch: Mary Anna b 1858, 12, 22
Walter T. " 1860, 7, 5
Clara J. " 1863, 5, 2 d 1863, 7,16
Corah B. " 1864, 1, 3 " 1865,12,18
1859, 12, 29. Dorcas A. m John PEELLE Jr.
1863, 6, 6. Emma Bell d
----, --, --. Jabas b 1846,4,30; m Delila ----- b 1844,10,11
Ch: Regina b 1866, 4, 29
Edgar " 1868, 2, 22
----, --, --. Joseph H., s John & Agnes, b 1833,8,26 d 1927,5,4; m Nancy -----
Ch: Minnie
Elva b 1867, 8, 31
Flora B. " 1870, 8, 24
----, --, --. David, s John & Agnes, b 1843, 3,23; m Lydia M. -----, dt James & Eliza MOON, b 1854,12,20 d 1930,8,18
Ch: Murry D. b 1877, 3, 2
1877, 3, 5. Lois d
1927, 5, 3. Joseph d

1820, 4, 27. Joseph Jr. dis training with militia
1823, 1, 23. Ruth (form Hockett) con mcd
1840, 3, 23. Joseph dis
1840, 4, 20. Lois dis
1842, 8, 22. Rebecca recrq
1844, 3, 18. Reuben rocf Chesterfield MM, dtd 1843,12,16
1851, 2, 10. Reuben dis
1852, 6, 5. Margaret (form Holaway) con mou
1852, 12, 6. Margaret gct Back Creek MM, Ind.
1859, 7, 18. Joseph M. & w, Lois, & ch, John Milton, Hannah, Mary Jane, Jabez H., Anne & Albert, recrq
1865, 9, 18. Jabez con mou
1867, 8, 19. Joseph H. con mou
1867, 8, 19. Della rocf Clear Creek MM, O., dtd 1867,8,10
1867, 10, 21. Levi & w, Maria, & ch, James, Frances, Austin, Maria & Henry, gct Clear Creek MM, O.
1868, 2, 17. Mary Jane Cowgill (form Mills) con mou
1873, 7, 21. Annie Holmes (form Mills) con mou
1876, 5, 22. Lewis M. & w, Catharine B., & ch, Mary Alma & Walter, gct Cincinnati MM, O.
1879, 5, 19. Delila & ch, Rigena, Edgar & Lucille Ella, gct Poplar Ridge MM, Ind.
1887, 8, 22. David C. & w, Lydia, & ch, Murray D. & Anna O., relrq
1888, 4, 23. Lewis M. & w, Catherine B., rocf Cincinnati MM, O., dtd 1888,3,--
1893, 11, 20. Flora B. dropped from mbrp
1894, 1, 22. Lewis & Catherine gct Cincinnati MM, O.
1899, 6, 15. Lewis M. & w, Catherine, rocf Cincinnati MM, O., dtd 1899,6,9

MILNER
1834, 4, 21. Susannah (form Hockett) con mou
1837, 4, 17. Susannah dis disunity
1850, 7, 15. Susannah rst at Clear Creek MM, on consent of this mtg

MINEHART
1889, 3, 18. Josie recrq
1894, 2, 19. Jose dropped from mbrp

MITCHEL
1886, 1, 18. Oliver A. recrq
1886, 1, 18. Oliver recrq

MONCE
1889, 2, 18. Edwin S. recrq
1889, 3, 18. Ulysses L. recrq
1890, 7, 21. Ulysses & w, Clara, & ch, Howard & Vivian, gct Miami MM, O.
1890, 10, 20. Edwin S. relrq

MONROE
1840, 7, 5. Mary A., dt John B. & Dorcas S., b

MONTGOMERY
1914, 4, 16. Lena dropped from mbrp

MOON
1796, 6, 18. Anna b
1801, 9, 19. James b
1802, 12, 23. Sarah b
----, --, --. Joseph b 1783,7,19; m Sarah ----- b 1781,12,12 d 1846,2,14
Ch: Ann b 1803, 11, 15
Thomas " 1805, 5, 22
Jesse " 1807, 7, 1
Phebe " 1809, 9, 19
Delilah " 1811, 11, 14
Mary " 1814, 2, 27
Jane " 1816, 5, 12
James " 1818, 7, 2
Seth " 1820, 11, 17 d 1833, 3,24 bur Newberry
Grace b 1823, 5, 2
Tamar " 1825, 9, 4
----, --, --. William b 1777,1,25; m Jane ----
Ch: Daniel b 1804, 4, 11
Joseph H. " 1806, 6, 9
Henry " 1808, 7, 13
Ann " 1811, 8, 31 d 1828, 8, 5 bur Newberry
Elizabeth b 1814, 3, 16
----, --, --. Jesse b 1788,1,30; m Rebecca -----
Ch: Benjamin b 1808, 8, 21 d 1828, 1,27 bur Newberry
James b 1810, 9, 1
Ann " 1812, 7, 19
William " 1814, 9, 29
Mary " 1817, 3, 7

MOON, Jesse & Rebecca, continued
Ch: Elizabeth b 1819, 2, 4
Solomon " 1820, 12, 28
----, --, --. Joseph b 1791,8,18; m Eliza -----
Ch: Susannah b 1813, 2, 20
Ruth " 1815, 6, 4
Eliza " 1817, 9, 12
Jeseph m 2nd Rachel ----- HOCKETT, dt Benj. & Charity, b 1798,10,18 d 1879,7,26
Ch: Pleasant b 1819, 5, 20
Eli " 1820, 12, 17
Daniel " 1822, 9, 20 d 1842, 6,11 bur Newberry
Leah b 1824, 10, 12
Richard " 1826, 8, 21
Sarah " 1828, 6, 5
William " 1831, 3, 9
Stephen " 1835, 2, 6
Robert " 1836, 12, 17
Phebe " 1839, 2, 21
Anna " 1841, 6, 7
Mary " 1833, 2, 25
----, --, --. William b 1795,4,11; m Anna ----- b 1792,10,16
Ch: Amos b 1814, 5, 13 d 1814, 8,13 bur Newberry
Daniel R. b 1815, 7, 7
John R. " 1818, 2, 1
Eleanor " 1820, 4, 13
Moses " 1822, 3, 15
Ezra " 1824, 3, 8
Miles " 1827, 10, 21
Hiram " 1830, 3, 7
Ruth " 1832, 8, 19
Huldah " 1837, 12, 24
Lewis " 1834, 9, 21
----, --, --. Henry b 1790,11,29; m Sarah ---- b 1792,1,1
Ch: Ann b 1815, 5, 25
Hannah " 1817, 1, 4
Jane " 1819, 10, 26
Mary " 1821, 11, 2
John Milton" 1824, 11, 8
1817, 7, 10. Mary, dt Anna, b
1818, 1, 8. Richard, s Daniel & Ruth, Clinton Co., O.; m in Newberry MH, Sarah HOCKETT, dt Benjamin & Charity, Clinton Co., O.
----, --, --. Thomas b 1798,3,14; m Elizabeth ----- b 1800,5,7 d 1842,2,19 bur Newberry
Ch: Ruth b 1818, 12, 10
Isaiah " 1820, 1, 2
Joseph H. " 1821, 11, 22
Jacob " 1823, 5, 31
Nathan " 1825, 7, 8
Joel " 1827, 5, 5
Jehu " 1828, 9, 14
Ann " 1830, 9, 13
Jane " 1832, 7, 17
Rachel " 1833, 12, 7
Thomas " 1836, 5, 19
Jason " 1837, 12, 18
Ch: John b 1839, 4, 8
Thomas m 2nd Sarah ----- d 1858,8,7 bur Westfork
Ch: Elkanah b 1847, 7, 14
Jabez " 1849, 6, 20
Margaret " 1852, 3, 21
Sarah Elizabeth " 1854, 8, 23
----, --, --. Richard b 1798,2,12; m Sarah ----- b 1801,11,10
Ch: Lucinda b 1818, 12, 22
Malinda " 1820, 10, 21
Mary " 1823, 8, 21
Silas " 1826, 10, 5
Charity " 1829, 12, 22
Mathew " 1832, 4, 6
Elias " 1837, 4, 22
William Riley " 1839, 10, 1
----, --, --. William m Hannah ----- b 1796, 11,28 d 1842,11,30 bur Newberry
Ch: Nathan b 1819, 12, 7
Jane " 1821, 3, 29
Charity " 1823, 1, 12
Asenath " 1825, 9, 23
Benjamin " 1827, 6, 25
Samuel " 1829, 10, 24
Esther " 1831, 10, 2
Hannah " 1834, 6, 16
Phebe " 1837, 3, 9
Neri " 1838, 10, 15
Polly " 1840, 5, 23
Seth " 1842, 2, 17
----, --, --. Jeremiah b 1800,1,15; m Rachel ----- b 1803,11,5
Ch: Mary b 1820, 11, 5
George " 1823, 4, 18
Ann " 1826, 4, 28
Jane " 1829, 3, 20
Elizabeth " 1831, 2, 27
Nixon " 1833, 10, 14
Havilah " 1837, 8, 28
1819, 11, 11. Mary m John HOCKETT
1819, 12, 2. Anna (nee Hockett) m Robert ELLIS
----, --, --. Solomon b 1803,1,21; m Hannah ----- b 1803,3,3
Ch: Mary b 1823, 11, 26
Lydia " 1824, 11, 19
Cyrus " 1826, 1, 1
Allen " 1827, 5, 12
Lewis " 1828, 12, 20
John C. " 1830, 5, 1
Aaron " 1832, 3, 16
Arksy Ann " 1833, 12, 17
Jane " 1835, 11, 23
Malinda " 1837, 11, 12
Sarah E. " 1839, 11, 12
William T. " 1841, 8, 2 d 1851, 8,15 bur Newberry
Ruth b 1843, 8, 24
Solomon " 1846, 1, 5
Infant s " 1849, 3, 9

MOON, continued
Ch: Samantha
Louella b 1853, 7, 21 (an adopted gr dt)
1824, 5, 31. Elizabeth, w George, b
1824, 8, 31. Ann, w Joseph Sr., d bur Newberry
1824, 9, 2. Daniel, s Wm. & Jane, b 1804,4, 11; m in Newberry MH, Rachel HOCKETT, dt Joseph & Ruth, Clinton Co., O., b 1806,10, 10 d 1843,7,31 bur Westfork
Ch: Louisa b 1825, 7, 20
Susannah " 1827, 5, 2
Joab " 1829, 12, 9
Christopher" 1831, 8, 21
Lydia " 1833, 6, 1
Asaph " 1836, 1, 26
Jacob " 1839, 6, 28
Daniel m 2nd Mary -----
Ch: William K. b 1846, 1, 29
Rachel Jane " 1847, 7, 13
Lindley M. " 1849, 11, 17 d 1850, 8,21 bur Newberry
Silas b 1852, 5, 6 " 1853, 1,18
1825, 8, 4. Jesse, s Joseph & Sarah, Clinton Co., O., b 1807,7,1; m in Newberry MH, Phebe HOCKETT, dt Benjamin & Charity, Clinton Co., O., b 1810,5,2
Ch: Melissa b 1826, 5, 7
Mahala " 1828, 8, 20
Barclay " 1832, 4, 10
Caleb " 1834, 10, 10
Sarah " 1836, 12, 23
Benjamin H." 1839, 12, 3
Joseph B. " 1842, 9, 11
David I. " 1845, 4, 13
Seth " 1848, 7, 25
----, --, --. Thomas, s Joseph & Sarah, b 1805,5,27 d 1902,9,9; m Mary ----- b 1807, 9,7 d 1859,3,9
Ch: Sarah Ann b 1826, 5, 17
Diantha " 1827, 8, 9
Thomas W. " 1829, 1, 23
Mqry Jane " 1831, 4, 17 d 1852, 7,27
Phebe " 1833, 7, 19
James C. " 1835, 11, 11
Joseph B. " 1838, 6, 4 d 1840, 2,22
Daniel " 1842, 8, 3
Simon Peter " 1845, 5, 1
Andrew " 1847, 9, 20
Jesse " 1849, 11, 4
Lydia Margaret " 1852, 9, 1 d 1853, 7,28
Thomas m 2nd Hannah S. SHEPHERD, dt Jesse & Elizabeth, b 1821,12,10
----, --, --. Samuel b 1805,9,10; m Mary ----- b 1809,8,19
Ch: Ann b 1826, 9, 4
Enos " 1828, 11, 4
Henry P. " 1830, 6, 21
Jeremiah " 1832, 8, 21
Hannah " 1834, 11, 27
Ch: Ruth b 1837, 1, 17
John P. " 1839, 3, 21
Calvin " 1841, 5, 22
Daniel " 1843, 6, 22
Allen " 1845, 3, 24
Zimri " 1847, 2, 18
Edom " 1849, 4, 22
----, --, --. John b 1807,2,25; m Judith ----- b 1806,9,24
Ch: Vashti b 1826, 12, 25
Abigail " 1828, 11, 27
Esther " 1830, 2, 12
Elwood " 1831, 11, 22
Levi " 1831, 11, 22
1827, 3, 1. Jane m Benoni PRESNAL
1828, 1, 5. Benjamin, s Wm. & Jane, d bur Newberry
1830, 6, 3. Susanna m Robert CARY
----, --, --. Joseph b 1806,6,9 d 1865,5,15; m Priscilla ----- b 1812,8,13
Ch: Dinah b 1833, 11, 11
Mary Ellen " 1836, 4 , 14
Anna Isabelle " 1838, 12, 20
Reuben C. " 1841, 9, 28 d 1842,10, 19 bur Newberry
Lydia Jane b 1843, 10, 14
Sylvanus " 1849, 4, 29
1833, 4, 14. Joseph d ae 83 bur Newberry
1833, 8, 29. Anna m Jesse HUNT
1833, 11, 28. Elizabeth m Isaac CARY
1834, 3, 28. Ruth d bur Newberry
1834, 5, 9. Elizabeth H. b
1834, 9, 8. Dinah d bur Newberry
1835, 1, 12. Sarah, dt Daniel & Ruth, d bur Newberry
1835, 12, 3. Eliza m John CAREY
1835, 12, 10. Jane d bur Newberry
1836, 3, 20. Ruth m David WEST
1836, 8, 26. Hannah m Amos HUNT
1837, 11, 2. Jane m Elias CAREY
----, --, --. John R., s Wm. & Ann, b 1818,2, 1; m Ursala ----- d 1838,6,12 bur Clear Creek, O.
Ch: Levi b 1838, 3, 6
John R. m 2nd Rachel -----, dt John & Sarah SMITH, b 1815,5,19
Ch: Narcissa b 1840, 10, 26
Leander " 1842, 10, 9
Alfred " 1844, 8, 26
Alvin " 1846, 3, 27 d 1864, 7,13 bur Newberry
Sarah Ann b 1848, 8, 10
1837, 3, 2. James, s Joseph & Sarah, Clinton Co., O., b 1818,7,2; m in Newberry MH, Lavinah SMITH, dt John & Sarah, Highland Co., O., b 1816,10,16
Ch: Amos b 1838, 4, 9
Sarah Elizabeth " 1842, 12, 29
Levi " 1846, 11, 10
William T. " 1850, 11, 29
1838, 8, 18. Levi d bur Westfork

MOON, continued
----, --, --. Daniel R. b 1815,7,15; m Esther -----
Ch: Levina b 1839, 1, 28
Lindley " 1841, 1, 1
Loena " 1842, 10, 12
Ezra " 1844, 3, 9
Amos R. " 1846, 1, 21
Hiram H. " 1847, 9, 19
Ira " 1849, 5, 16
Ann " 1852, 5, 21
----, --, --. Pleasant b 1819,5,20; m Huldah ----- b 1817,6,16 d 1863,5,25
Ch: Lucy b 1840, 2, 12
Daniel " 1841, 3, 3 d 1841, 4,25
Parker " 1842, 3, 30
Carey " 1842, 3, 30 d 1853, 6, 3
Rachel " 1844, 11, 15
Joseph " 1845, 11, 15
Sarah Elizabeth " 1846, 4, 14
Mary Ann " 1848, 1, 26
William J. " 1849, 5, 12 d 1849, 8,21
Samuel " 1850, 9, 26
Harvey " 1852, 7, 27
James Arthur " 1854, 3, 3
Stephen O. " 1855, 9, 19 d 1855,12,19
Lindley Murry " 1857, 3, 21
Elwood " 1858, 7, 4 d 1858, 8,28
Manary B. " 1859, 6, 19 " 1859, 7,31
----, --, --. Pleasant b 1819,5,20 (s Joseph D. & Rachel); m Susannah TERRELL, dt John & Jane, b 1818,6,2
1840, 12, 29. Daniel d bur Clear Spring, Ind.
1841, 4, 18. Daniel d bur Westfork
1841, 7, 28. Moses, s William & Ann, b 1822, 3,15; m in Westfork MH, Elizabeth WILSON, dt Joseph & Abigail, Clinton Co., O., b 1823,2,20
Ch: Job b 1842, 11, 15
Irena " 1845, 1, 19
Eleanor " 1847, 5, 6 d 1923, 7,14
Harvey " 1851, 7, 11
Albert " 1854, 8, 4
William D. " 1857, 11, 1
Talbert " 1859, 2, 16 d 1863, 5,22
Amanda " 1861, 8, 25
1842, 7, 11. Calvin d bur Westfork
1842, 8, 3. Daniel C. b
1843, 12, 31. Daniel d bur Westfork
1844, 3, 28. Mary m James WHINERY
1844, 9, 26. Grace m James GARNER
1845, 2, 20. Ezra, s William & Ann, b 1824, 3,8; m in Newberry MM, Rebecca MILLS, dt Hezekiah & Dorcas, b 1822,9,12
Ch: Jonathan b 1846, 4, 28
Dorcas Ann " 1848, 11, 30
1845, 4, 24. John Milton, s Henry & Sarah, Clinton Co., O., b 1824,11,8; m in Newberry MH, Rebecca JANNEY, dt Joseph & Elizabeth, Clinton Co., O., b 1822,2,25
Ch: Clarkson b 1846, 4, 22
Linton " 1848, 6, 3
Lisbon " 1853, 1, 12 d 1854, 9,27
Ella " 1857, 8, 2
Dora " 1863, 9, 23
1845, 7, 23. Louisa m James ELLIS
1845, 10, 6. Joseph D. d bur Newberry
1846, 1, 10. Solomon d bur Newberry
1846, 1, 23. Delilah m Levi BARRETT
1846, 2, 14. Sarah d bur Newberry
1846, 8, 20. Richard, s Joseph & Rachel, Clinton Co., O., b 1826,8,21; m in Newberry MH, Mary SCHOOLEY, dt Nathan & Sarah, Clinton Co., O., b 1830,2,16
Ch: Eunice Jane b 1849, 1, 17
1846, 10, 22. Mahala m Milton BARRETT
1848, 11, 22. Sarah m James J. HERALD
----, --, --. Cyrus b 1826,1,1; m ----- -----
Ch: Elwood b 1849, 2, 19
Cyrus m 2nd Jane G. ----- b 1829,8,30
Ch: Nelson b 1857, 12, 5
Lydia " 1860, 6, 1
Annie " 1862, 9, 25
----, --, --. Nathan B. b 1825,7,8; m Leah ----- b 1827,10,27
Ch: Andrew H. b 1849, 6, 18
Mary Elizabeth " 1851, 2, 23
----, --, --. Miles & Charlotte
Ch: Isaac G. b 1849, 11, 7
1849, 9, 4. Seth, s Jesse & Phebe, d bur Newberry
1849, 12, 3. Jabez d bur Newberry
----, --, --. Thomas b 1829,1,23; m Margaret ----- b 1834,3,10
Ch: John C. b 1850, 9, 6
Robert " 1851, 9, 8
Caroline " 1852, 10, 25
Eliza Jane " 1854, 7, 26
Mary Lydia " 1856, 3, 25
Nathan W. " 1858, 6, 19
Sarah Ann " 1860, 9, 25
Louella " 1863, 5, 16
Susannah " 1865, 7, 19
Martha Emily " 1867, 2, 25
Henry " 1869, 1, 15
1850, 6, 10. William d ae 77 bur Newby
1851, 1, 23. Obadiah, s Enos & Rachel, b
1851, 2, 17. Mary, w Richard, d bur Westfork
1852, 1, 19. Ruth, w Daniel, d ae 82 bur Westfork
----, --, --. Aaron b 1832,3,16; m Eunice ----- b 1826,4,2
Ch: Oliver b 1853, 6, 7
Arthur " 1854, 10, 28
Edgar " 1857, 8, 29
Mary Ann " 1860, 12, 27
----, --, --. Wilkerson T., s James & Sarah, b 1833,5,5; m Lydia -----, dt Jacob & Anna HOCKETT, b 1834,8,9
Ch: Sanford A. b 1853, 6, 14

MOON, continued
Ch: Erlistus
J. b 1856, 7, 31
Walter E. " 1858, 2, 23
Eva " 1862, 2, 20
Elbridge " 1865, 3, 2
Annie " 1866, 9, 6
1853, 4, 19. Hiram E., s William & Ann, Clinton Co., O., b 1874,12,10; m in Newberry MH, Almira HUNT, dt Jonathan & Margaret, Clinton Co., O.
1853, 7, 28. Margaret Lydia, dt Thomas & Mary, d bur Newberry
----, --, --. William Ellis b 1830,3,7; m Almira ----- b 1832,12,11
Ch: Mary
Louesa b 1854, 2, 2
Ossian " 1856, 8, 31
Emma Bell " 1863, 5, 26 d 1863, 6, 6
----, --, --. James C. b 1835,11,11; m Eliza M. -----, dt Robert & Susannah CAREY, b 1836,1,29
Ch: Lydia M. b 1854, 12, 20
John T. " 1856, 7, 2
Mary J. " 1858, 2, 11
Robert E. " 1860, 2, 20
Susanna A. " 1862, 1, 4
Dallis N. " 1864, 5, 2
Ange Netta " 1866, 3, 2
Minnie
Olive " 1868, 3, 17
William H. " 1870, 5, 13
Frances
Marion " 1872, 9, 24
Hiram Edwin" 1874, 12, 10
1854, 3, 21. Joseph H. b
1854, 9, 23. Florence Eva, w Emerson, dt Jonathan & Susan HOLE, b
----, --, --. Richard E. b 1825,8,20; m Mary E. ----- b 1836,1,7
Ch: Amanda E. b 1855, 11, 9
Margaret E." 1858, 5, 9
John H. " 1859, 10, 9
Susannah " 1862, 6, 9
Charles W. " 1866, 2, 16
Cora " 1868, 6, 16 d 1868, 6,18
----, --, --. Thomas J., s Thomas & Elizabeth, b 1836,3,19; m Lida E. McPHERSON, dt Wm. & Mary, b 1846,11,15
1857, 2, 9. Solomon d bur Newberry
----, --, --. Robert, s Joseph & Rachel, b 1836,12,17; m Mary Edith DEILKS, dt John & Jerusha, b 1838,1,1
Ch: Daniel C. b 1858, 3, 4 d 1878,11,10 bur Westboro
Mary b 1859, 5, 29
Jenetie " 1860, 7, 12
Martha " 1862, 5, 6
Alice " 1865, 5, 28
Ella May " 1867, 8, 22
Joseph Harley " 1869, 12, 3
Amos G. " 1872, 4, 23
Ch: Emma
Jerusha b 1874, 6, 1
John Dalton" 1876, 5, 19
George " 1879, 4, 17 d 1879, 4,17 bur Westboro
----, --, --. Joseph H., s Thomas & Elizabeth, b 1821,11,22; m Lucinda B. HOCKETT, dt Nathan & Polly
Ch: Charles
Allen b 1858, 10, 27
Maria " 1861, 2, 14
Joseph E. " 1862, 12, 6
Rachel " 1868, 8, 18
1858, 8, 3. Edgar d bur Newby
1859, 6, 25. Henry d bur Newbury
1860, 5, 6. Mary d
1860, 7, 24. Walter, s John W. & Samira, b
----, --, --. Amos S., s James & Levina, b 1838,4,9; m Lydia Jane -----, dt Isaac & Esther HAMMER, b 1842,2,2
Ch: Arthur H. b 1861, 8, 6 d 1862,12,13 bur Westfork
Arminda b 1864, 1, 25
Armandus " 1866, 10, 19
Clarence " 1869, 10, 24
Annie " 1875, 3, 16
1861, 7, 1. Ella d bur Newbury
1863, 5, 15. Joseph H. d bur Newberry
1863, 11, 4. Joseph d ae 80 bur Newberry
1863, 12, 9. Lewis d
----, --, --. Alfred, s John R. & Rachel, b 1844,8,26; m Abbie -----, dt Chas. & Mary RUSSELL, b 1838,5,23
Ch: William b 1866, 3, 22
Edwin J. " 1871, 12, 3
Ann B. " 1875, 10, 18
----, --, --. Jesse H. b 1842,4,17; m Annie L. ----- b 1846,3,18
Ch: Dorothy B. b 1866, 4, 11
Alice L. " 1868, 8, 2
----, --, --. Levi b 1846,11,10; m Mary E. -----, dt Isaac & Esther HAMMER, b 1846, 10,22
Ch: Arthur b 1866, 10, 26
William H. " 1867, 11, 21
Lilley " 1872, 3, 3
1866, 6, 8. Cora A. b
----, --, --. Andrew b 1847,9,20; m Elizabeth ----- b 1850,6,12
Ch: Minnie Dolphenia b 1867, 8, 7
Charles H. " 1869, 4, 25
Mary Etta " 1871, 9, 17 d 1872, 8,11 bur Newberry
Ida May " 1873, 6, 16
Thomas W. " 1875, 8, 1
1867, 3, 17. Arthur d
----, --, --. Simon P. b 1845,5,1; m Rebecca ----- b 1846,6,19
Ch: Hattie Delilah b 1868, 5, 9
1867, 12, 17. Otto J. b
1868, 4, 28. Rebecca d ae 46

MOON, continued
----, --, --. William F., s James C. & Levina, b 1850,10,29; m Arminda -----, dt Mathias & Sarah POBST, b 1852,11,23
Ch: Clara L. b 1871, 10, 20
Willis D. " 1876, 6, 6
----, --, --. Daniel C. m Ella MOON, dt Moses & Elizabeth, b 1847,5,6 d 1923,7,14
Ch: Enos Finley b 1872, 1, 11
----, --, --. Harvey, s Moses & Elizabeth, b 1851,7,11; m Australia J. -----, dt Wm. & Nancy HITCH, b 1854,6,19
Ch: Calvin P. b 1875, 5, 16 d 1876, 1, 5 bur Westfork
Birtsel b 1877, 5, 10
----, --, --. Erlistus J., s W. T. & Lydia, b 1856,7,3; m Maria L. -----, dt Mordecai & Naomi HAINES, b 1854,10,21
Ch: Etta b 1875, 12, 31
1877, 4, 7. Daniel C. d
1889, 2, 28. Nina, dt Othello & Gertrude, b
1913, 9, 19. Eva May d
----, --, --. Harry, s Carey E. & Allie, b 1884,1,18; m Ethel CONNOR, dt Taylor & Cora, b 1887,4,7
Ch: Mary Louise b 1917, 3, 24
1931, 8, 12. Haley d

1817, 2, 3. Anne (form Hockett) con mcd
1817, 4, 17. Anna recrq of parents, Henry & Sarah
1818, 4, 6. Mary recrq of parent, Anna
1818, 10, 29. Elizabeth (form Hockett) con mou
1818, 11, 26. Rachel (form Hockett) con mou
1818, 11, 26. Joseph Jr. dis mou
1819, 3, 25. Jeremiah gct Clear Creek MM, to m
1819, 7, 29. Joseph & w, Sarah, & ch, Ann, Thomas, Jesse, Phebe, Delilah, Mary, Jane & James, recrq
1819, 7, 29. Jeremiah gct Clear Creek MM
1821, 2, 22. Rachel gct West Grove MM, Ind.
1821, 8, 23. William & ch, Daniel, Joseph, Henry, Ann, Elizabeth, Nathan, Jane & step-s, Wm. Hockett, recrq
1821, 8, 23. Jesse recrq
1821, 9, 27. Hannah rst on consent of Lees Creek MM, O.
1822, 1, 24. Ann recrq
1822, 3, 28. Benjamin, James, Nancy, Wm., Mary, Elizabeth & Solomon, ch Jesse, recrq
1822, 5, 23. Thomas recrq
1823, 7, 24. Rachel rocf West Grove MM, Ind., dtd 1823,1,14
1825, 2, 24. Samuel gct Milford MM, Ind., to m Mary Presnall
1825, 7, 27. Thomas Jr. dis mou
1826, 1, 26. John gct Miami MM, to m Judith Moon
1826, 2, 23. Benjamin dis mou
1826, 4, 27. Jeremiah & w, Rachel, & ch, Mary & George H., rocf Clear Creek MM, dtd 1826,3,11
1826, 12, 28. Judith rocf Miami MM, dtd 1826, 9,27
1827, 1, 25. Mary rocf Duck Creek MM, Ind., dtd 1826,11,30
1827, 6, 28. Ann Ellis (form Moon) con mou
1827, 10, 26. Jesse Beals gct Miami MM, to m Dinah Moon
1829, 4, 23. John rstrq
1829, 11, 26. Ann Nordyke (form Moon) con mou
1829, 12, 24. Judith dis jH
1830, 3, 25. Susannah, Ruth, Eliza, Pleasant, Eli, Daniel, Leah, Richard & Sarah, ch Joseph D., recrq
1830, 5, 27. Lydia (form Beals) dis mou
1830, 7, 29. Henry con mou
1831, 6, 20. John dis
1831, 6, 20. James con mou
1832, 1, 23. Phebe Fisher (form Moon) con mou
1832, 11, 19. Joseph H. gct Clear Creek MM, to m Priscilla Coffin
1832, 12, 17. William dis disunity
1832, 12, 17. Zimri dis mou
1833, 6, 17. Priscilla rocf Clear Creek MM, dtd 1833,5,21
1833, 9, 23. Richard dis
1834, 2, 17. Judith & ch, Vashti, Abigail, Esther, Ellwood & Levi, gct Fairfield MM, Ind.
1834, 10, 20. Solomon & w, Hannah, & ch, Mary, Lydia, Cyrus, Allen, Lewis, John Carter, Aaron & Acsha Ann, recrq
1836, 6, 20. Mary Izzard (form Moon) dis mou
1837, 1, 23. Mary Wright (form Moon) con mou
1837, 1, 23. John gct Clear Creek MM, to m Ursola Pike
1837, 6, 19. Ursola rocf Clear Creek MM, dtd 1837,5,23
1837, 7, 17. Daniel R. con mou
1838, 1, 22. Mary Puckett (form Moon) con mou
1838, 4, 23. Esther rocf Pennsville MM, dtd 1838,2,15
1838, 4, 23. Elizabeth Brunson (form Moon) dis mou
1839, 1, 21. Jane dis
1839, 1, 21. Jeremiah & w, Rachel, & ch, Mary, George, Ann, Elizabeth, Jane, Nixon & Havilah, gct Walnut Ridge MM, Ind.
1839, 4, 22. Lucinda Miller (form Moon) dis mou
1839, 7, 22. Solomon Jr. dis mou
1839, 8, 19. Pleasant con mou
1839, 9, 23. Nathan dis disunity
1840, 10, 19. Melinda Lightfoot (form Moon) con mou
1840, 10, 19. Isaiah con mou
1840, 11, 23. John R. con mou
1841, 1, 18. Rachel (form Hockett) con mou
1841, 4, 19. Mary recrq
1841, 4, 19. Thomas Jr. rst rq
1841, 4, 19. Eleanor Porter (form Moon) con

MOON, continued
mou
1841, 5, 17. Richard rst rq
1841, 6, 21. Ruth Johnson (form Moon) con mou
1841, 9, 20. Richard & w, Sarah, & ch, Silas, Charity, Mathew, Elias & William, gct Richland MM, Ind.
1841, 11, 22. Sarah Ann, Diantha, Thomas, Mary Jane, Phebe & James, ch Thomas Jr., recrq
1841, 12, 20. Huldah rst
1842, 4, 18. Mary Miller (form Moon) con mou
1842, 4, 18. Margaret (form Smith) dis mou
1842, 4, 18. Henry H. dis jas
1842, 4, 18. James S. con mou
1842, 5, 23. Charity dis disunity
1842, 6, 20. James recrq
1842, 12, 19. Eli con mou
1844, 3, 18. Thomas gct Duck Creek MM, Ind., to m Sarah Pressnell
1844, 7, 15. Sarah rocf Duck Creek MM, Ind., dtd 1844,5,23
1844, 9, 16. Elizabeth (form Smith) con mou
1845, 4, 14. Daniel H. gct Elks MM, to m Mary Branson
1845, 6, 16. Lydia Pennington (form Moon) con mou
1845, 12, 15. Joseph H. dis mou
1846, 6, 15. Mary Smithson (form Moon) con mou
1846, 7, 13. Jacob con mou
1846, 9, 14. Nancy Ousley (form Moon) con mou
1846, 11, 16. Mary & s, Thomas Branson, rocf Elk MM, dtd 1846,9,19
1846, 12, 14. Jane Bundy (form Moon) con mou
1846, 12, 14. Susanna Walkup (form Moon) con mou
1847, 6, 14. Anna McCoy (form Moon) con mou
1847, 9, 13. Miles H. gct Centre MM, to m Charlotte D. Green
1848, 3, 18. Diantha Kelso (form Moon) con mou
1848, 3, 13. Nathan con mou
1848, 5, 15. Leah (form Herald) con mou
1848, 5, 15. Elias, William Riley & Sarah Jane, rocf Westfield MM, Ind., dtd 1847, 12,9
1848, 5, 15. Charlotte D. rocf Centre MM, dtd 1848,3,15
1848, 9, 11. Cyrus con mou
1849, 2, 12. Miles H. & Charlotte D. gct Centre MM
1849, 7, 16. Esther dis jas
1849, 8, 13. Eli dis jas & m after his w had divorced him
1849, 9, 10. Enos con mou
1849, 9, 10. William con mou
1850, 9, 16. Mary Jane Beals (form Moon) dis mou
1850, 10, 14. Leah dis jas
1850, 10, 14. Thomas W. con mou
1850, 11, 11. Margaret (form Carey) con mou
1850, 11, 11. Miles H. & w, Charlotte D., & ch, Isaac, rocf Centre MM, dtd 1850,10,16
1850, 11, 11. Mary rocf Duck Creek MM, Ind., dte 1850,9,22
1851, 4, 14. Jehu dis disunity
1851, 5, 12. Jesse gct Honey Creek MM, Ind.
1851, 5, 12. James S. gct Honey Creek MM,Ind.
1851, 5, 12. Sarah Jane gct Honey Creek MM, Ind.
1851, 6, 16. Allen dis disunity
1851, 8, 11. John Carter dis joining a secret society
1851, 12, 15. Jacob gct Back Creek MM, Ind.
1851, 12, 15. Ezra & w, Rebecca, & ch, Jonathan & Dorcas Ann, gct Back Creek MM, Ind.
1852, 3, 16. Asenith dis disunity
1852, 3, 16. Joel dis mou
1852, 4, 3. Hannah dis jas
1852, 5, 1. Christopher dis disunity
1852, 9, 4. Samuel & w, Mary, & ch, Jeremiah, Hannah, Ruth, John P., Allen, Zimri, Edom & Mary Jane, gct Mississinewa MM, Ind.
1852, 9, 4. Enos & w, Rachel, & s, Obadiah, gct Mississinewa MM, Ind.
1852, 9, 4. Henry Jr. gct Mississinewa MM, Ind.
1853, 2, 5. Joab con mou
1853, 2, 5. Samuel dis mou
1853, 3, 21. Aaron con mou
1853, 5, 23. Ellwood, s Cyrus, recrq
1853, 7, 18. Tamar Clark (form Moon) con mou
1853, 9, 19. Malissa gct Honey Creek MM, Ind.
1853, 10, 17. Jesse & w, Phebe, & ch, Caleb T., Benjamin, Sarah H., Joseph B. & David I., gct Honey Creek MM, Ind.
1853, 12, 19. Richard dis mou
1854, 1, 23. John R. & w, Rachel, & ch, William R. Hockett (form m), Narcess, Leander, Alfred, Alvin, Sarah Ann, David & John Eldridge, gct White River MM, Ind.
1854, 2, 20. Eunice E. & s, Oliver, recrq
1854, 5, 20. Daniel R. & w, Esther, & ch, Levina, Lindley, Loena, Ezra, Amos R., Hiram, Ira & Ann, gct White River MM, Ind.
1854, 7, 17. James C. Jr. dis mou
1854, 10, 23. Lydia Carey (form Moon) con mou
1854, 12, 18. Thomas W. & w, Margaret, & ch, John C., Caroline & Eliza Jane, gc
1855, 5, 21. Barclay gct New Salem MM
1855, 11, 19. Priscilla (form Carey) dis mou
1856, 3, 19. Phebe gct Caesars Creek MM
1856, 88, 18. Stephen dis mou
1856, 8, 18. Samantha Luella recrq
1856, 9, 22. Joab dis jas
1856, 12, 26. Cyrus gct Springfield MM, to m Jane Green
1856, 12, 26. Nathan & w, Leah, & ch, Andrew H. & Mary Elizabeth, gct Back Creek MM, Ind.
1857, 4, 20. Eliza rocf Back Creek MM, Ind., dtd 1857,3,19
1857, 6, 22. Jane G. rocf Springfield MM, O., dtd 1857,6,20
1857, 6, 22. Robert dis mou
1857, 10, 19. Huldah Young (form Moon) dis

MOON, continued
1857, 10, 19. Huldah Young (form Moon) dis mou
1858, 1, 18. Asaph dis mou
1858, 3, 22. Isaiah gct Oak Ridge MM, Ind.
1858, 4, 19. Lewis dis disunity
1858, 6, 21. Neri gct Caesars Creek MM
1858, 7, 19. Seth gct Cesars Creek MM
1858, 7, 19. Polly gct Ceasors Creek MM
1859, 1, 17. Mary Larrowe (form Moon) con mou
1859, 3, 21. Solomon L. rst rq
1859, 4, 18. Solomon L. gct Winnesheik MM, Iowa
1859, 4, 18. Anna Isabel Snyder (form Moon) con mou
1859, 4, 18. Sarah Elizabeth Gibson (form Moon) con mou
1859, 6, 20. Daniel H. & w, Mary, & ch, William & Rachel Jane, gct Elk MM
1859, 7, 18. Thomas J. con mou
1859, 12, 19. Thomas Sr. con mou
1860, 1, 23. Phebe dis jas
1860, 1, 23. Anna Dilks (form Moon) dis mou
1860, 5, 21. Thomas & ch, Elkanah, Margaret & Sarah E., gct Back Creek MM, Ind.
1860, 7, 23. Jane dis jas
1860, 8, 20. Phebe Smith (form Moon) con mou
1860, 9, 17. Rachel gct New Salem MM
1860, 10, 22. John D. dis mou
1860, 10, 22. Amos con mou
1861, 6, 17. Lucy dis jas
1861, 7, 22. Jason dis mou
1861, 8, 19. Sarah Ann Clark (form Moon) con mou
1861, 11, 18. Eleanor (Holoway) rst at Back Creek MM, Ind., on consent of this mtg
1862, 4, 21. Rachel Holaway (form Moon) con mou
1862, 5, 19. Priscilla & ch, Orpha, Myrta & Olive, recrq
1863, 4, 20. Eliza gct Oak Ridge MM, Ind.
1863, 6, 22. Lydia J. recrq
1863, 9, 21. Thomas J. dis disunity
1863, 9, 21. Elizabeth dis jas
1863, 11, 23. Phebe recrq
1864, 5, 23. Cyrus & w, Jane, & ch, Elwood, Nelson, Lydia & Anna, gct Springfield MM,O.
1864, 7, 18. Rachel rocf New Salem MM, Ind., dtd 1864,9,30
1864, 9, 19. Martha (form Hammer) dis mou
1865, 4, 17. Sarah E. Hammer (form Moon) con mou
1865, 5, 22. Betty H. (form Holaday) con mou
1865, 5, 22. Thomas W. & w, Margaret, & ch, John, Caroline, Eliza Jane, Nathan & Sarah Ann, rocf Back Creek MM, dtd 1865,2,16
1865, 6, 19. Miles & w, Charlotte D., & ch, Isaac G., Enoch L., Daniel W., William C. & Quintillius V., gct Bangar MM, Ia.
1865, 10, 23. Mary E. rmt Parker Green
1866, 1, 22. Simon P. con mou
1866, 6, 18. Levi con mou
1866, 9, 17. Jacob K. gct Richland MM, Ind.
1866, 12, 17. Mary Ellen Brown (form Moon) dis mou
1867, 1, 21. Richard & w, Mary, & ch, Amanda, Ellen, Margaret Emily, John, Susannah & Charles William, recrq
1866, 12, 17. Lydia Jane Britton (form Moon) con mou
1867, 2, 18. Leander & w, Martha, & ch, Francis Orville, recrq
1867, 2, 18. Joseph H. recrq
1867, 3, 18. Lucinda & ch, Charles A., Maria & Joseph, recrq
1867, 3, 18. Robert & w, Mary E., & ch, Daniel Edward, Mary, Genette, Martha & Alice, recrq
1867, 5, 20. Wilkerson T. & w, Lydia, & ch, Erlestus, Walter E., Eva, Elbridge & Annie, recrq
1867, 5, 20. Mary E. recrq
1867, 7, 22. Samantha B. rocf Springfield MM, O., dtd 1867,7,20
1867, 10, 21. Elizabeth recrq
1867, 12, 23. Leander & w, Martha, & ch, Francis Orville & James H., gct Plainfield MM, Ind.
1868, 2, 17. Priscilla & ch, Orpha, Myrta, Olive & Morton, gct Richland MM, Ind.
1868, 6, 22. Parker & w, Mary Emily, & s, Leonidas, gct Spring River MM, Kans. or Mo.
1868, 9, 21. Sarah M. gct Bangor MM, Ia.
1868, 9, 21. Ellen con mou
1868, 9, 21. Sarah M. gct Bangor MM, Ia.
1868, 11, 23. Thomas gct Wilmington MM, O., to m Hannah Shepherd
1869, 2, 22. Aaron & w, Eunice Ellen & ch, Oliver, Arthur, Mary Eva & John Dewrus, gct Springfield MM, O.
1869, 3, 22. Priscilla S. gct Bangor MM, Ia.
1869, 3, 22. Irena Harvey (form Moon) con mou
1869, 4, 19. Susannah (form Boyd) con mou
1869, 4, 19. Pleasant con mou
1869, 8, 23. Hiram E. & w, Almira, & ch, Louisa, Ossian & Margaret, gct White Water MM, Ind.
1869, 11, 22. Hannah S. rocf Wilmington MM, O., dtd 1869,11,16
1870, 1, 17. Hannah & dt, Arksy Ann, Malinda & Martha, gct Vermillion MM, Ill.
1870, 1, 17. Alfred H., Abby S. & William R. recrq
1870, 1, 17. Arminda, Joseph H., Sarah & Sanford recrq
1870, 2, 21. Rachel & James recrq
1870, 2, 21. Rebecca recrq
1870, 2, 21. Jesse F. recrq
1870, 2, 21. Daniel H. recrq
1870, 2, 21. Dorothy B. recrq
1870, 2, 21. Alice L. recrq
1870, 3, 21. William T. con mou
1870, 5, 25. Mary A. Waltz (form Moon) con mou
1871, 4, 17. Daniel C. recrq

MOON, continued
1871, 5, 22. Daniel & w, Betsy, & ch, Cora & Otto, gct Wilmington MM, O.
1871, 7, 17. James H. & w, Sarah, gct Elk River MM, Kans.
1871, 7, 17. Joseph H. & w, Samantha B., gct Elk River MM, Kans.
1872, 4, 22. Julia Ann recrq
1872, 8, 19. John C. con mou
1872, 9, 23. Jesse relrq
1873, 4, 21. Andrew & w, Elizabeth, & ch, Minnie D. & Charles H., gct Center MM,Ia.
1873, 12, 22. Rachel recrq
1874, 1, 19. Thomas W. recrq
1874, 2, 23. Jesse H. & w & ch, Dorothy B., Alice L. & Lucy, gct Ironton MM, Wis.
1874, 7, 20. James C. & w, Eliza, & ch, Lydia Margaret, John Thos., Mary Jane, Robert Ellwood & Susan, rocf Winneshiek MM, dtd 1874,5,23
1874, 8, 17. Lydia C. rocf Fairfield MM, dtd 1874,7,18
1874, 11, 23. Thomas J. recrq
1876, 4, 17. Walter recrq
1876, 6, 19. Ansie recrq
1877, 2, 19. Thomas W. & w, Margaret, & ch, Nathan, Sarah Ann Hardin (form Moon), Luella, Susannah, Martha, Emily, Henry, Amaziah, Alma & Thomas, gct Peace MM, Kans.
1877, 2, 19. Caroline Fresh (form Moon) gct Peace MM, Kans.
1877, 2, 19. Jane Weaver (form Moon) gct Peace MM, Kans.
1872, 2, 19. John gct Peace MM, Kans.
1877, 3, 19. James C. Jr. relrq
1878, 7, 22. John Jr. relrq
1879, 3, 17. Eliza E. & ch, Harley & Walter West, gct Union MM, O.
1879, 7, 21. Adalask W. recrq
1879, 7, 21. Arthur relrq
1880, 9, 20. Minnie relrq
1881, 2, 21. Phebe gct Newhope MM, O.
1881, 3, 21. Charles H. recrq
1881, 3, 21. Andrew recrq
1881, 3, 21. Elizabeth recrq
1881, 3, 21. Clarence recrq
1881, 3, 21. Elmira M. recrq
1881, 3, 21. Lee recrq
1881, 8, 22. Eliza & ch, Robert E., Dallas N., Angenetta, Minnie O., William H., Francis M., Hiram E. & Bertha, gct Springfield MM, O.
1883, 10, 22. Thomas J. & w, Lydia, & dt, Cora, gct Wilmington MM, O.
1884, 3, 18. Adalask & w, Abie, & dt, Ora, gct Minneapolis MM, Minn.
1885, 2, 23. Wilson T. & w, Lydia, & s, Jacob, rocf Pleasant Hill MM, Kans.
1885, 5, 18. Jamima & ch, Raymond, Lilly & Carl recrq
1886, 1, 18. Lottie & ch, Francis & Andrew, recrq
1886, 4, 19. John Wesley, Loreena & Myra, recrq
1886, 4, 19. Minnie Ollie recrq
1886, 4, 19. Maggie G. recrq
1886, 10, 18. William T. & fam gct Red Wood MM, Minn.
1886, 10, 18. Maggie G. relrq
1887, 2, 21. Rebecca relrq
1887, 4, 18. Thomas relrq
1887, 5, 23. Sanford dropped from mbrp
1887, 8, 22. Andrew, Elizabeth, Charles & Ida May dropped from mbrp
1887, 8, 22. Walter Clarence dropped from mbrp
1889, 3, 18. Carl recrq
1889, 11, 18. Alfred H., Abby S. & Edwin J. relrq
1891, 3, 23. Emma dis
1891, 4, 20. John T. gct Cincinnati MM, O.
1891, 4, 20. Joseph Harley relrq
1893, 11, 20. Lindley dropped from mbrp
1893, 11, 20. Loranna dropped from mbrp
1893, 12, 18. Thomas rst rq
1894, 1, 22. Gertrude gct Cincinnati MM, O.
1894, 2, 19. Elmina dropped from mbrp
1894, 2, 19. Minnie O. dropped from mbrp
1896, 8, 20. Carl A. relrq
1898, 9, 15. Galen recrq
1899, 3, 16. Gertrude relrq
1902, 6, 19. Mary Halcie & Eva Mae recrq
1903, 11, 19. Hannah S. gct Indianapolis MM, Ind.
1905, 6, 22. Bertha Cox rocf Westfork MM, O., dtd 1905,5,20
1905, 7, 13. Samuel gct Caesars Creek MM,O.
1915, 10, 14. Harry & w, Ethel, recrq
1917, 6, 21. Leighton recrq
1921, 4, 14. Elmer, Naomi & Ruby recrq
1924, 1, 17. Naomi relrq
1926 4, 18. Madge Brown recrq

MOONY
1881, 3, 21. Sidney C. recrq
1893, 11, 20. Sidney dropped from mbrp

MOORE
1862, 4, 30. Joseph, s Mordecai & Rachel, Hamilton Co., Ind.; m in Westfork MH, Rachel GARNER, dt William & Ann, Clinton Co., O.

1857, 8, 17. Matilda Ann (form Evans) dis mou
1862, 10, 20. Rachel G. gct Westfield MM, Ind.

MOORMAN
1848, 4, 10. Israel C. Green gct Dover MM, to m Rachel [Morman]

MORGAN
1866, 4, 23. Josephine E. (form White) con mou
1866, 8, 20. Josephine gct Ash Grove MM, Ill.

MORRIS

MORRIS
1868, 8, 17. Ruth (form McPherson) con mou
1881, 12, 19. Benjamin F. & w, Maria, & dt, Effa J., rocf Poplar Run MM, Ind., dtd 1881,11,19
1882, 6, 19. Hannah gct Spicewood MM, Ind.
1885, 12, 21. John S. recrq

MORROW
----, --, --. Warren d 1934,5,11; m Lettie S. THORNBURGH, dt Jesse & Elizabeth, b 1854, 9,4
Ch: Charles W. b 1877, 11, 8
Mary E. " 1879, 8, 21
Florence " 1882, 7, 27
Helen " 1884, 3, 18
Inez " 1886, 6, 11

1880, 1, 19. Warren recrq
1880, 2, 23. Charlie W. & Mary Elizabeth, ch Warren & Letta, recrq
1888, 4, 23. Susan B. relrq

MURPHY
1888, 5, 21. Mary E. recrq

MYERS
1852, 7, 5. Amelia d
1868, 3, 13. John d
1892, 5, 15. Ralph J., s Henry & Eva, b

1821, 9, 27. Samuel [Mires] recrq
1830, 12, 23. Samuel gct Fairfield MM, to m Priscilla Chalfont
1841, 8, 23. Samuel dis
1842, 10, 17. Permelia [Mires] recrq
1866, 5, 21. John F. & w, Nancy, recrq
1870, 9, 19. Nancy [Mire] gct Fairfield MM
1892, 8, 18. Eva C. [Miars] & s, Ralph J., gct Wilmington MM, O.

NEALL
1845, 11, 26. Eliza Elen b
1855, 6, 18. Eliza Ellen recrq
1865, 12, 18. Eliza E. [Neeld] rmt Eliel W. West

NEFFNER
1843, 3, 23. Annie, w Henry, dt Edward & Annie COLE, b
----, --, --. R. T., s Henry & Anna, b 1878, 7,11 d 1916,1,11
1919, 10, 16. Henry d

1877, 3, 19. Annie [Nefner] recrq
1894, 10, 18. Artie recrq
1898, 9, 15. Margaret recrq
1916, 2, 17. Henry recrq

NEWLIN
----, --, --. Eli b 1808,12,4; m Lydia ----- b 1805,6,10
Ch: Esther b 1835, 1, 20
Charles b 1840, 7, 22
William " 1843, 7, 26
Temple " 1850, 3, 17

1857, 1, 19. Eli & w, Lydia, & ch, William & Temple, rocf Clear Creek MM, dtd 1857,1, 10
1859, 4, 18. Charles rocf White Lick MM, Ind., dtd 1859,3,16
1860, 7, 23. Charles, minor, gct Plainfield MM
1860, 10, 22. Esther rocf Centre MM, dtd 1860,8,14
1861, 10, 21. Eli gct Fairfield MM, to m Lydia Barrett
1862, 3, 17. Lydia B. rocf Fairfield MM, dtd 1862,1,18
1863, 11, 23. Eli & w, Lydia B., & ch, William & Temple, gct Plainfield MM, Ind.
1863, 11, 23. Esther gct Plainfield MM, Ind.

NEWMAN
1841, 4, 24. Nancy A. b
1872, 3, 23. Hattie b
1883, 9, 1. George b
1884, 2, 19. Lillie C., dt Geo. & Anna, b
1892, 12, 21. Lillie C., dt Geo. & Anna, d

1886, 4, 19. Ella recrq
1886, 4, 19. Nancy A. recrq
1887, 8, 22. Nancy dropped from mbrp
1889, 3, 18. George & w, Nancie A., & ch, Hattie E. & Lillie C., recrq
1889, 3, 18. Annie recrq
1893, 11, 20. George & Nancy A. dropped from mbrp

NEWTON
1889, 2, 18. William recrq
1889, 2, 18. Charles recrq
1889, 2, 18. Ida May recrq

NIXON
1817, 9, 1. William & w, Elizabeth, gct Newgarden MM, Ind.

NOLDER
1870, 2, 21. Samuel M. recrq
1872, 4, 22. Samuel A. con mou
1872, 5, 20. Samuel N. gct Back Creek MM, Ind.

NORDYKE
----, --, --. John b 1809,8,1; m Ann ----- b 1812,7,19
Ch: Sylvester b 1842, 6, 24
Solomon " 1845, 3, 31
Albert H. " 1850, 6, 27
John M. " 1853, 12, 7
1923, 5, 29. Luther d

1829, 10, 29. Jonathan Hockett rqct Clear Creek MM, to m Mary Nordyke
1829, 11, 26. Ann (form Moon) con mou

NORDYKE, continued
1830, 7, 29. Judith (form Anthony) con mou
1833, 1, 23. Sarah (form Anthony) con mou
1833, 2, 28. Judith gct Springfield MM, Ind.
1843, 10, 20. Sarah gct Springfield MM, Ind.
1851, 5, 12. Ann gct Honey Creek MM, Ind.
1856, 8, 18. John & s, Sylvester, Solomon, Albert & John Milton, recrq
1865, 7, 17. Anna (form Carey) con mou
1866, 8, 20. Sylvester B. con mou
1866, 10, 22. John & w, Nancy, & ch, Albert & John Milton, gct Gilead MM, Mo.
1866, 10, 22. Sylvester B. & w, Mary Anna, & s, Charley, gct Gilead MM, Mo.
1897, 3, 18. Ella S. gct Clear Creek MM, O.
1917, 1, 18. Ella roc
1923, 3, 15. Luther recrq

NORTON
1852, 2, 16. Margaret (form Hinshaw) dis mou

NOYES
----, --, --. William m Mary ----- b 1863,2,--
Ch: Estella b 1882, 7, 3
Georgia " 1884, 9, 22 d 1891, 6,24 bur Martinsville
Bessie b 1889, 11, 21

1891, 2, 23. Mary & ch, George & Bessie, recrq
1891, 2, 23. Estella recrq

O'CONNELL
1889, 3, 18. William recrq

O'DONALS
1854, 12, 18. Sarah gct Poplar Run MM, Ind.

OSBORN
----, --, --. William b 1818,12,18; m Eliza ----- b 1825,12,25
Ch: Mary Ann b 1845, 1, 9
Margaret " 1846, 5, 22
Samantha " 1847, 10, 17
Hannah " 1849, 5, 6
Elenora " 1851, 4, 17
Martha Jane" 1854, 5, 8

1844, 9, 16. Elizabeth (form Hockett) con mou
1845, 6, 16. Eliza gct Springfield MM, O.
1846, 5, 11. Wm. & w, Eliza, & dt, Mary Ann, rocf Springfield MM, O., dtd 1846,4,14
1860, 1, 23. Eliza dis disunity
1861, 6, 17. William & ch, Mary Ann, Margaret Samantha, Hannah, Elnora & Martha Jane, gct Springfield MM, O.
1861, 8, 19. Eliza rst at Springfield MM on consent of this mtg
1867, 8, 19. William & w, Eliza, & ch, Hannah, Elnora, Martha J. & Anna C., rocf Springfield MM, O., dtd 1867,8,17
1873, 6, 23. William & w, Eliza, & ch, Elnora, Anna C. & Jesse Wm., gct Springfield MM, O.
1875, 4, 19. Courtis recrq
1885, 12, 21. Omer recrq
1886, 1, 18. Syrena recrq
1890, 2, 17. Alfred & w, Martha, & s, Frank T., rocf Springfield MM
1916, 7, 13. Anna Mancher rocf Westfork MM,O.

OUSLEY
----, --, --. John, s Richard & Elizabeth, b 1833,11,7 d 1920,5,31; m Ollie M. WALKER, dt Lewis & Mary, b 1842,6,12 d 1924,9,13
Ch: Cassius
Carl b 1874, 4, 27
----, --, --. Wm. Henry [Owsley], s Moses & Nancy, b 1852,9,14; m Catharine D. MURPHY, dt Greenberry & Jerusha
Ch: Anna
Louisa b 1874, 9, 18

1846, 9, 14. Nancy (form Moon) con mou
1861, 10, 21. Wm. Henry, s Moses, recrq
1870, 2, 21. John D. & Ollie recrq
1873, 12, 22. Catherine recrq
1879, 12, 22. Cert for William H. & w, Catherine, & ch, Annie L. & Ethel H., granted to Winneshiek MM, Ia., returned 1881,11, 21 when they moved back here
1881, 3, 21. Harvey & w, Mary, & ch, Lille & Clarence, recrq
1886, 4, 19. Carrie receq
1887, 8, 22. Harvey, Mary, Lillie & Clarence dropped from mbrp
1888, 3, 19. William Henry & w, Catherine D., & ch, Anna L., Ethel H. & Nellie, relrq
1890, 4, 21. Wm. Henry & w, Catherine D., & ch, Anna L., Ethel, Nettie & Maud E. relrq

PAGE
1911, 4, 13. Alice recrq
1914, 4, 16. Charles recrq
1920, 5, 13. Alta recrq
1927, 4, 17. Grant recrq

PARKER
1858, 4, 29. Benajah, s Benajah & Grace, Wayne Co., Ind.; m in Clermont, Deborah Ann MILLER, dt Isaac & Martha, Clearmont Co., O.

1822, 2, 21. George Stanley gct White Water MM, Ind., to m Jamima Parker
1846, 4, 13. Mary (form Evans) dis mou
1858, 7, 19. Eleanor Stephens (form Parker) con mou
1858, 9, 20. Deborah A. gct Raysville MM,Ind.
1889, 2, 18. Phebe recrq

PARREN
1881, 3, 21. George recrq
1887, 8, 22. George dropped from mbrp

PARREN, continued
1889, 3, 18. George, Sarah [Perrin] & ch, Elias, Bertha & John H., recrq
1889, 3, 18. Melvin [Perrin] recrq

PATCHEL
1861, 5, 20. Susannah (form Hayworth) con mou

PAXTON
1865, 6, 19. Reuben & w, Sarah, & ch, Rachel G., Elias G., James, John, Margaret Ann, Mary Jane, Jonathan G. & Ruth Alice, rocf Fairfield MM, Ind., dtd 1865,4,15
1871, 2, 20. Elias G. gct Fairfield MM
1873, 4, 21. Reuben & w, Sarah, & ch, Rachel J., John, Margaret A., Mary J., Jonathan G. & Ruth A., gct Fairfield MM, O.
1873, 11, 17. Mary J. recrq
1885, 2, 23. James & Mary Jane & Francis Marion, gct Argona MM, Kans.

PEARSON
1817, 3, 3. Mary rocf Fall Creek MM, dtd 1817,1,13

PEEBLES
1844, 7, 15. Elijah rocf Centre MM, dtd 1844,8,14
1845, 8, 11. Elijah gct Milford MM, Ind.

PEELLE
1859, 12, 29. John Jr., s William & Clarissa, Clinton Co., O.; m in Newberry MH, Dorcas A. MILLS, dt John & Agness, Clinton Co., O.

1930, 9, 22. Walter d bur Sabina
1930, 10, 20. Walter d

1860, 3, 19. Dorcas gct Dover MM, O.
1886, 11, 22. Emma relrq
1922, 7, 13. Walter & s, Hubert Wayne, rocf Grassy Run MM, O.
1922, 7, 13. Mae, w Walter, rocf Wilmington MM, O.

PEMBERTON
1894, 2, 19. Clara gct Clear Creek MM, O.

PENNINGTON
----, --, --. Levi b 1784,6,20 d 1868,5,26 bur Newbury; m 2nd Jane ----- b 1801,10,31
----, --, --. Wm. R. b 1824,11,25; m Anna ----- b 1825,2,1
Ch: John b 1849, 2, 14
Edwin " 1850, 12, 5
Mary E. " 1852, 9, 14
Lydia Jane " 1854, 9, 26
Nancy Emma " 1856, 4, 30
Martha Elma " 1857, 10, 13
Josiah " 1860, 5, 5 d 1860, 8, 5 bur Newberry
Caroline b 1861, 4, 5
1848, 8, 19. Lydia d
1845, 6, 16. Lydia (form Moon) con mou
1848, 8, 14. Anne (form Hockett) con mou
1852, 9, 4. Hannah Isabel, minor, recrq
1852, 10, 11. Hannah Isabel, adopted ch Josiah & Mary Graham, gct Back Creek MM, Ind.
1855, 4, 23. Levi & w, Jane, rocf Sandy Spring MM, O., dtd 1855,3,23
1855, 7, 23. William R. & ch, John, Edwin, Mary Elizabeth & Lydia Jane, recrq
1867, 8, 19. William & w, Ann, & ch, John, Edward, Mary, Lydia, Nancy, Ella, Caroline & Frank, gct Dover MM

PERCELL
1849, 8, 20. Francis A. b

PERKINS
1822, 7, 11. Martha m Abner RATCLIFF

1822, 2, 21. Martha recrq

PFISTER
----, --, --. Lewis b 1844,12,1; m Sarah Jane -----, dt John & Rachel MOON, b 1848,10,9
Ch: Melcena b 1868, 4, 1 d 1868, 8,18
Lenna Margaret " 1869, 5, 24
Orlando " 1873, 3, 4

1870, 2, 21. Lewis & Sarah & Lena M. recrq
1885, 9, 21. Lewis relrq
1895, 4, 18. Sarah A. relrq
1913, 2, 13. Lewis, Sarah A. & Gertrude recrq

PICKERING
1911, 10, 19. Rose rocf University MM, Kans.

PICKETT
1899, 12, 24. James d

1881, 3, 21. James Barclay recrq
1881, 3, 21. Eliza recrq
1881, 3, 21. Mary E. recrq

PIKE
----, --, --. James b 1814,11,5; m Juliann ----- b 1821,3,11 d 1854,1,17 bur Newberry
Ch: William J. b 1844, 10, 30
John " 1846, 6, 8 d 1849, 9, 4 bur Newberry
Daniel K. b 1848, 5, 22
Aner Jane " 1850, 11, 3
Thomas Elwood " 1852, 11, 4

1837, 1, 23. John Moon gct Clear Creek MM, to m Ursola Pike
1840, 6, 22. Levi Hockett gct Clear Creek MM, to m Lydia Pike
1843, 5, 22. James rocf Clear Creek MM, dtd 1843,4,18
1843, 12, 18. Sarah (form Smith) con mou

PIKE, continued
1845, 2, 10. James con mou
1846, 6, 11. Julia Ann recrq
1847, 10, 11. Samuel, William & Eli, orphans, rocf Walnut Ridge MM, Ind., dtd 1847,8,21
1849, 6, 11. William J. & John, ch James, recrq
1855, 5, 21. Lydia (form Hiatt) con mou
1855, 7, 23. Samuel con mou
1858, 4, 19. Samuel & w, Lydia, & ch, Harriet Elen & Martha Isadore, gct Clear Creek MM
1859, 7, 18. James con mou
1860, 4, 23. James gct New Garden MM, Ind.
1862, 7, 21. Daniel Kester & Thomas Ellwood gct Cherry Grove MM, Ind.
1862, 7, 21. William gct New Garden MM, Ind.

POBST
1887, 1, 17. Laura recrq
1889, 2, 18. James recrq

POND
1870, 2, 21. David, Eleanor, Levi W. & Sylvester recrq
1876, 5, 22. David & w gct Springfield MM,O
1878, 4, 22. Levi gct Springfield MM

PORTER
1841, 4, 19. Eleanor (form Moon) con mou
1866, 4, 23. Hannah (form Puckett) con mou

POTTER
1867, 12, 23. Hannah & dt, Cordovia May, gct Plainfield MM, Ind.
1881, 3, 21. Jesse F. recrq
1893, 11, 20. Jesse T. dropped from mbrp

POWELL
1871, 4, 17. Thomas E. & fam recrq
1871, 3, 18. Thomas E. & w, Urie, gct Fairfield MM
1884, 7, 21. Thomas & w, Ura, rocf Cesars Creek MM, O., dtd 1884,5,22

PRESNAL
1827, 3, 1. Benoni, s Daniel & Pleasant, Henry Co., Ind.; m in Newberry MH, Jane MOON, dt Daniel & Ruth, Clinton Co., O., b 1810,2,10
Ch: Jeremiah b 1828, 3, 11
William " 1829, 9, 31
James " 1831, 2, 4
Henry " 1832, 5, 17

1825, 2, 24. Samuel Moon gct Milford MM, Ind. to m Mary [Presnall]
1830, 4, 22. Jane gct Duck Creek MM, Ind.
1831, 10, 17. Jane & ch, Jeremiah & Wm., rocf Duck Creek MM, Ind., dtd 1831,9,29
1834, 9, 22. Jane & ch, Jeremiah, William, James, Henry & Mary, gct Duck Creek MM, Ind.
1844, 3, 18. Thomas Moon gct Duck Creek MM, Ind., to m Sarah [Pressnell]

PRESTON
1930, 5, 18. Walter recrq
1932, 4, 17. Litten O. & w, Blanche B., recrq

PUCKETT
----, --, --. James b 1788,10,24; m Margaret -----
Ch: Mary b 1808, 12, 28
Moses " 1811, 9, 11
Joseph " 1814, 3, 5
Thomas " 1816, 2, 2
Henry " 1820, 12, 14
Gulielma " 1823, 5, 2
Lydia " 1825, 4, 1
Margaret " 1827, 3, 15
Barclay " 1829, 11, 29
Arzilla " 1832, 6, 29
1812, 3, 14. Benjamin, s Benjamin & Catherine, b
----, --, --. Richard & Susannah
Ch: Thomas b 1830, 6, 20
Daniel " 1832, 7, 7
Enos " 1834, 1, 13
Tamer " 1835, 12, 2
1830, 8, 5. Joseph, s James & Margaret, Clinton Co., O., b 1814,5,3; m in Newberry MH, Mary HOLAWAY, dt Abner & Elizabeth, Clinton Co., O., b 1811,9,21
Ch: Isaac b 1831, 5, 7 d 1832, 8,15 bur Newberry
Aaron b 1832, 12, 3
Elizabeth " 1834, 11, 4 d 1835, 1, 9 bur Newberry
John b 1836, 1, 7
Jeremiah "" 1838, 1, 18
James R. " 1839, 12, 30
1830, 8, 5. Moses, s James & Margaret, Clinton Co., O., b 1811,9,11; m in Newberry MH, Nancy WEST, dt George & Mary, Clinton Co., O., b 1814,10,4
Ch: Nathan b 1832, 8, 28
Mary Jane " 1835, 2, 28
Martha Ann " 1837, 12, 17
Levina " 1840, 4, 30
----, --, --. Daniel b 1818,5,18; m Mary ----- b 1814,2,27
Ch: Sarah Jane b 1838, 2, 17
Hannah " 1839, 10, 20
Delilah Ann" 1842, 10, 8 d 1843, 5,20 bur Newberry
Grace b 1844, 6, 16
Thomas Elwood " 1847, 11, 3 " 1849, 6,19 bur Newberry
Tamer b 1849, 11, 26
Joseph M. " 1852, 5, 4
Talbot B. " 1855, 5, 31
Daniel Roberts " 1858, 4, 10

1817, 7, 7. Joseph & ch, Tira, Welcome,

PUCKETT, continued
Benjamin & Micajah, rocf Clear Creek MM, dtd 1817,5,10
1818, 5, 4. Mary, Moses, Joseph & Thomas, ch James, recrq
1818, 7, 6. Isom, John, Alice, Sally & Pheriby, ch Zachariah, rocf Westfield MM, N. C., dtd 1817,9,13
1818, 8, 3. Jincy rocf Westfield MM, N. C., dtd 1818,6,23
1818, 8, 27. Eli [Pucket] dis disunity
1818, 9, 24. James [Pucket] Jr. dis mou
1819, 3, 25. Moses dis mou
1919, 10, 28. Mary gct New Garden MM, Ind.
1819, 4, 22. Joseph & ch gct New Garden MM, Ind.
1819, 10, 28. Isom, John, Alice, Sally & Pheraby, ch Zachariah, gct New Garden MM, Ind.
1819, 10, 28. Mary [Pucket] gct New Garden MM, Ind.
1820, 2, 24. Jincy gct New Garden MM, Ind.
1820, 3, 23. Catharine & dt gct New Garden MM, Ind.
1820, 3, 23. Benjamin & fam gct New Garden MM, Ind.
1820, 6, 22. Keziah [Pucket] dis
1822, 3, 28. Benjamin & w, Catherine, & ch, Mary, Pheby & Benjamin, rocf New Garden MM, Ind., dtd 1822,2,16
1824, 5, 27. Benjamin & fam gct New Garden MM, Ind.
1824, 5, 27. Leah rocf West Grove MM, Ind., dtd 1824,4,13
1824, 8, 26. Rebecca rocf New Garden MM, dtd 1824,6,19
1824, 10, 28. Mary gct New Garden MM, Ind.
1825, 2, 24. Keziah rst
1825, 3, 24. Malinda, dt Keziah, recrq
1825, 9, 22. Keziah & dt gct New Garden MM, Ind.
1825, 9, 22. Rebecca & s gct New Garden MM, Ind.
1829, 12, 24. Moses dis disunity
1833, 4, 22. Mary Evans (form Puckett) dis mou
1833, 10, 21. Richard & w, Susannah, & ch, Thomas & Daniel, rocf White River MM, dtd 1833,6,17, endorsed by Elk MM
1834, 5, 19. Ch of James recrq
1835, 8, 17. Thomas con mou
1835, 8, 17. Matilda (form Dickey) con mou
1836, 5, 23. Moses & w, Nancy, & ch, Nathan & Mary, gct Westfield MM, Ind.
1836, 11, 21. Thomas & w, Matilda, & dt, Mary Ann, gct Duck Creek MM, Ind.
1837, 3, 20. Daniel Jr. rocf Elk MM, dtd 1837,2,18
1837, 4, 17. Richard & w, Susannah, & ch, Thomas, Daniel, Enos & Tamar, gct Elk MM
1838, 1, 22. Mary (form Moon) con mou
1838, 1, 22. Daniel dis mou
1838, 2, 19. Moses & w, Nancy, & ch, Nathan & Mary Jane, rocf Westfield MM, Ind., dtd 1837,12,7
1838, 7, 23. Mary, w Daniel, gct White River MM, Ind.
1839, 10, 21. Joseph dis disunity
1840, 4, 20. Henry dis disunity
1840, 9, 21. Margaret recrq
1841, 5, 17. Mary & ch, Sarah Jane & Hannah, rocf Sparroe Creek MM, Ind., dtd 1841,4, 12
1842, 9, 19. Moses & fam gct Richland MM, Ind.
1843, 3, 20. Lydia dis jas
1843, 3, 20. Margaret Ann dis jas
1843, 11, 20. Daniel rst
1843, 11, 20. Gulielma dis jas
1849, 6, 11. James B. dis mou
1851, 1, 13. Mary & ch, Aaron, John, Amelia, Olive Ann, Eliza, Joseph & Benjamin, gct Honey Creek MM, Ind.
1851, 5, 12. Margaret gct Honey Creek MM, Ind.
1857, 3, 23. Sarah Jane Hanks (form Puckett) dis mou
1866, 4, 23. Grace Andrew (form Puckett) con mou
1866, 4, 23. Hannah Porter (form Puckett) con mou
1867, 12, 23. Daniel & w, Mary, & ch, Tamar, Joseph M., Talbot B. & Daniel Roberts, gct Plainfield MM, Ind.
1881, 3, 21. Eliza recrq
1881, 3, 21. Charles recrq
1881, 3, 21. Frank recrq
1881, 3, 21. Albert recrq
1881, 3, 21. Bell recrq
1881, 3, 21. Gertie recrq
1887, 8, 22. Albert, Belle & Gertie dropped from mbrp
1887, 8, 22. Frank & Charles dropped from mbrp
1894, 2, 19. Mary dropped from mbrp

PURCELL
1877, 4, 23. Francis A. recrq

PURKEY
1913, 3, 20. Gay recrq
1913, 3, 20. Neale recrq

PUTMAN
1924, 1, 17. Eva Gibson relrq

PYLE
1845, 7, 23. William, s John & Esther, Clinton Co., O.; m in Westfork MH, Rebecca GARNER, dt Wm. & Ann, Clinton Co., O., b 1827,10,1
Ch: Esther Ann b 1847, 2, 21

1846, 4, 13. Rebecca gct Springfield MM, O.
1847, 6, 11. William & w, Rebecca, & dt, Esther Ann, rocf Springfield MM, O., dtd

PYLE, continued
1847,5,15
1851, 9, 15. William & w, Rebecca, & s, Jehu Evan, gct Springfield MM, O.

RALSTON
1895, 5, 16. Mary d bur West Elkton, O.

1893, 12, 18. John W. & w, Mary H., rocf Elk MM, dtd 1893,10,23
1896, 3, 19. John W. gct Van Wert MM, O.

RAMBO
1908, 1, 16. William & w, Effie, rocf Clear Creek MM, O.
1914, 4, 16. William & Effie dropped from mbrp

RANDALL
1894, 3, 22. John & w, Mary, rocf Springfield MM, O., dtd 1894,2,17
1908, 3, 19. John & w, Mary, gct Wilmington MM, O.

RATCLIFF
----, --, --. Amos b 1765,2,1; m Elenor ----- b 1768,3,25
Ch: John b 1788, 9, 13
Margaret " 1790, 9, 12
Ann " 1792, 10, 10
Abner " 1794, 12, 5
Sarah " 1797, 2, 19
Elenor " 1799, 6, 11
Elizabeth " 1805, 10, 5
Amos " 1803, 11, 12 (sic)
Moses " 1806, 7, 20
Thomas " 1808, 3, 30
----, --, --. Edom & Rachel
Ch: Jacob b 1793, 3, 26
Joel " 1800, 2, 13
Jesse " 1807, 12, 4
1799, 1, 16. Elizabeth b
1810, --, --. Jacob b 1793,3,26 d 1863,1,28; m 2nd Mary -----
----, --, --. John m Elizabeth ----- d 1869,9, 24 ae 70 bur Newberry
Ch: Judith b 1820, 11, 29
Eleanor " 1822, 4, 1
Anna " 1824, 1, 21
Abner " 1825, 12, 25
John " 1828, 4, 18
Elizabeth " 1830, 4, 25
Rachel " 1832, 6, 6
1822, 7, 11. Abner, s Amos & Elenor, Highland Co., O., b 1794,12,5; m in Newberry MH, Martha PERKINS, dt Robert & Martha
Ch: John b 1823, 9, 1
Amos " 1824, 7, 2
Eleanor " 1826, 8, 13
Ann " 1829, 9, 10
Thomas " 1830, 4, 13
1823, 9, 9. Edom d
1828, 5, 1. John, s Abner & Sarah, Clinton Co., O.; m in Newberry MH, Sarah DICKEY, dt Nimrod & Ann, Clinton Co., O.
Ch: Ann b 1829, 4, 11
Abner " 1831, 5, 29
1828, 10, 22. Amos d bur Greenberry
1831, 8, 23. Ann m Dempsey REECE
----, --, --. Thomas & Rebecca
Ch: Sarah Jane b 1839, 3, 2
Elizabeth
Ann " 1840, 12, 14
John T. " 1843, 1, 17
1841, 1, 28. Jesse, s Abner & Sarah, Clinton Co., O.; m in Newberry MH, Elizabeth TERRILL, dt John & Jane, Clinton Co.,O.
Ch: Susan b 1842, 3, 1
Amos " 1843, 7, 3
1845, 12, 25. Dorcas m John SMITH
1850, 8, 7. Rachel d

1817, 7, 7. Amos [Ratliff] & w, Ellenor, & ch, John, Abner, Elizabeth, Amos, Moses, Thomas, roc
1817, 12, 1. Abner [Ratliff] & w, Sarah, & ch, Ann, John, Margaret, Dorcas, Abner, Isaac, Sarah, Thomas & Jesse, rocf Clear Creek MM, dtd 1817,11,8
1820, 6, 22. John [Ratliff] con mou
1820, 6, 22. Elizabeth [Ratliff] (form Crew) con mou
1823, 5, 29. Jacob [Ratliff] rocf Clear Creek MM, dtd 1823,4,12
1823, 6, 23. Edom [Ratliff] & w, Rachel, & ch, Joel, Thomas, Margaret, Jesse & Ann, rocf Clear Creek MM, dtd 1823,4,12
1823, 6, 23. Sarah [Ratliff] rocf Clear Creek MM, dtd 1823,4,12
1825, 8, 25. Thomas dis mou
1826, 6, 22. Margaret Hutson (form Ratcliff) con mou
1826, 7, 27. Joel con mou
1827, 12, 27. Amos Jr. con mou
1827, 12, 27. Margaret Kenworthy (form Ratcliff) dis mou
1830, 7, 29. John dis disunity
1830, 7, 29. Ann Kenworthy (form Ratcliff) dis mou
1830, 9, 23. Abner Jr. dis disunity
1830, 9, 23. Jesse con mou
1830, 11, 25. Abner Sr. dis disunity
1832, 2, 20. Joel gct Springfield MM, Ind.
1832, 5, 21. Edom rocf Clear Creek MM, dtd 1832,4,24
1833, 11, 18. Thomas dis mou
1834, 7, 21. Edom dis disunity
1834, 12, 22. Elizabeth dis disunity
1835, 10, 19. Isaac gct Deep Creek MM, Ind.
1835, 12, 21. John & w, Sarah, & ch, Ann & Abner, gct Deep Creek MM, Ind.
1836, 9, 19. Amos [Ratliff] & w, Eleanor, gct Deep Creek MM, Ind.
1836, 9, 19. Abner [Ratliff] & w, Martha, & ch, John, Amos, Eleanor, Ann, Thomas, Martha & Elizabeth, gct Deep Creek MM, Ind.

RATCLIFF, continued
1836, 9, 19. Moses gct Deep Creek MM, Ind.
1839, 6, 17. Rebecca (form Terrill) con mou
1839, 6, 17. Thomas [Ratliff] con mou
1842, 12, 19. Elizabeth recrq
1843, 12, 18. Nathan con mou
1848, 1, 10. Jacob gct Dover MM, to m Mary Honeycut
1848, 6, 12. Thomas & w, Rebecca, & ch, Sarah Jane, Elizabeth Ann, John T. & Margaret H., gct Duck Creek MM, Ind.
1852, 10, 11. Jesse & w, Elizabeth, & ch, Susan, Amos, Abner, John Milton & Cyrus, gct Honey Creek MM, Ind.
1853, 2, 5. Sarah gct Honey Creek MM, Ind.
1853, 3, 21. Nathan gct Honey Creek MM, Ind.
1853, 3, 21. Silas gct Honey Creek MM, Ind.
1856, 12, 26. Sarah Terrell (form Ratcliff) dis mou

REECE
1831, 8, 23. Dempsey, s Hannah PRESNAL, Henry Co., Ind.; m in Newberry MH, Ann RATLIFF, dt Abner & Sarah, Clinton Co., O.

1832, 4, 23. Ann [Rees] gct Duck Creek MM, Ind.
1850, 4, 15. Sarah [Reese] (form Terrell) con mou
1850, 11, 11. Sarah [Rece] gct Duck Creek MM, Ind.
1870, 2, 21. Thomas recrq
1884, 9, 22. Jane [Reese] recrq

REYNOLDS
1889, 2, 18. Frank recrq
1889, 2, 18. Charlie recrq
1894, 2, 19. Frank dropped from mbrp

RICHARDSON
1926, 4, 6. Helen, dt Harley & Rhue, d

1923, 4, 19. Helen recrq

RILEIGH
1851, 5, 12. Elias William gct Honey Creek MM, Ind.

RISH
1873, 5, 19. Thomas recrq

ROBERTS
1837, 4, 17. Abel & w, Eleanor, & gr s, Moses B., rocf Fall Creek MM, dtd 1837,2,22
1837, 11, 20. Abel & w, Eleanor, & gr s, Moses B., gct Dover MM
1870, 4, 18. Betty J. (form Holaday) con mou
1870, 5, 23. Betsey J. gct Elk MM, O.
1886, 7, 19. Lora M. gct Fairview MM, Mo.

ROBUCK
1889, 2, 18. Pearl S. & Gracie E. recrq

ROTHER
1867, 2, 18. Jane recrq

ROUTSAW
1877, 4, 23. Mary A. recrq

RUBLE
1843, 11, 20. Ruth (form Ruse) dis mou

RUDY
1886, 4, 19. Lizzie recrq
1887, 8, 22. Lizzie dropped from mbrp
1889, 2, 18. Nichodemus & w, Elizabeth, & ch, Mary May, Alice & Leroy, recrq
1889, 2, 18. Frank & John recrq

RUNK
1925, 8, 23. Leota Mancher relrq

RUSE
----, --, --. Thomas, s Michael & Rachel, b 1811,7,3; m Margaret -----
Ch: Ann b 1818, 1, 30
Ruth " 1823, 2, 13
1911, 3, 5. Jennie d

1822, 1, 24. Thomas recrq
1822, 2, 21. Ann & Aaron, ch Thos., recrq
1822, 3, 28. Margaret [Roose] rocf Clear Creek MM, dtd 1822,3,9
1830, 6, 24. Sarah (form Cashatt) dis mou
1840, 9, 21. Rebecca (form Haworth) dis mou
1840, 10, 19. Ann League (form Ruse) dis mou
1843, 11, 20. Ruth Ruble (form Ruse) dis mou

SAMS
1889, 2, 18. Nettie recrq

SANDERS
1828, 2, 27. David b

1849, 4, 16. David rocf Fairfield MM, dtd 1848,12,16
1855, 9, 17. David con mou
1868, 9, 21. David con mou
1868, 10, 19. David & s, Addison, gct Wilmington MM, O.

SCHOOLEY
1846, 8, 20. Mary m Richard MOON

1846, 1, 12. Mary & Hannah, minors, rocf Centre MM, dtd 1845,11,12
1848, 3, 13. Joel Green gct Centre MM, to m Elizabeth Schooley
1850, 3, 11. Miriam, minor, rocf Center MM, dtd 1850,2,13
1851, 3, 10. Hannah Smith (form Schooley) con mou
1851, 5, 12. Aaron rocf Centre MM, dtd 1861, 4,16
1852, 8, 7. Miriam Green (form Schooley) con mou

SCOTT
1889, 2, 18. William B. recrq

SELLARS
1934, 2, 18. Esther Hiatt relrq

SEWELL
1862, 1, 20. Sarah Ann recrq
1866, 12, 17. Sarah Ann gct Chester MM
1868, 2, 17. Sarah Ann rocf Chesterfield MM, dtd 1868,1,29
1869, 9, 20. Sarah Ann gct Mississinewa MM, Ind.

SHANK
----, --, --. Jacob D., s Henry & Mary, b 1839, 7,23; m Sarah E. HIGGINS, dt Joseph & Katharine, b 1850,6,5
Ch: C. Leroy b 1881, 3, 8
Harry Waldo" 1889, 3, 5

1897, 11, 18. Jzcob & w, Sarah, & ch, Leroy & Harry W., rocf Westfork MM, O., dtd 1897, 10,16

SHAPER
1930, 6, Abraham

1915, 9, 16. Abraham & w recrq

SHAW
1864, 4, 18. Thomas E. rocf Birch Lake MM, dtd 1864,4,2
1868, 5, 18. Thomas E. con mou
1879, 9, 22. Martha J. & dt, Melvina, recrq
1881, 9, 19. Thomas E. gct Arch St. MM, Phila., Pa.
1882, 6, 19. Thomas E. gct Phila.; presented to Vandalia MM, Mich.
1887, 5, 23. Martha J. & Melvina dropped from mbrp
1901, 11, 14. Ida Manker rocf Westfork MM, O., dtd 1901,10,19

SHELDON
1840, 9, 15. Lucinda b
1869, 6, 11. Melissa b
1871, 1, 28. Benjamin b
1873, 3, 1. Lucy b
1875, 1, 29. Charles b
1877, 2, 3. Joan b
1879, 9, 3. George b
1882, 12, 11. Oman b
1885, 7, 20. Leroy b
1889, 7, 28. Frank b

1874, 9, 21. Ruth relrq
1889, 2, 18. Melissa & ch, Benjamin, Lucy, Charles, Joanna, George L., Omar & Leroy recrq
1889, 2, 18. Frank recrq

SHEPHERD
1856, 2, 18. Jonathan James gct Centre MM, to m Mary Jane Shepherd
1868, 11, 23. Thomas Moon gct Wilmington MM, O., to m Hannah Shepherd

SHIELDS
----, --, --. Joseph A. b 1815,10,25; m Gulia E. ----- b 1823,5,2
Ch: Sarah E. b 1852, 10, 25
Elma M. " 1856, 11, 16
Priscilla " 1858, 6, 4
Josephine " 1860, 11, 6
Moses B. " 1866, 9, 17

1870, 2, 21. Joseph, Gulielma, Sarah & Emma recrq
1870, 3, 21. Priscilla recrq
1870, 3, 21. Josephine recrq
1870, 3, 21. Moses B. recrq
1876, 7, 17. Joseph A. gct Union MM, Ind.
1887, 5, 23. Sarah, Emma, Priscilla, Josephine & Moses P. dropped from mbrp

SHERIFF
1801, 1, 23. John b
1827, 11, 27. Lusinda [Shurraf] b

1871, 3, 20. Lucinda recrq
1871, 3, 20. Lucinda [Shariff] recrq
1878, 2, 18. John recrq

SIMCOX
----, --, --. Job, s John & Mary, b 1803,4, 12; m Hannah -----, dt John & Susannah HOLLADAY, b 1808,11,13
Ch: Lydia b 1826, 5, 3
John " 1827, 11, 8
Stover " 1831, 9, 2
Martha " 1833, 8, 28
Thomas " 1836, 2, 8
Susanna " 1837, 12, 24
Betsy " 1840, 7, 12
William Owsley (adopted s)
1849, 9, 20. John, s Job & Catherine, Clinton Co., O., b 1827,11,8; m in Newberry MH, Irena GARNER, dt John & Elenor, b 1828,3,27
Ch: Mary b 1850, 9, 15
Job " 1852, 10, 15
Lisbon " 1856, 9, 27
Martha " 1858, 9, 11
Lindley " 1860, 9, 29
Elma " 1863, 8, 22 d 1864,10, 1
1856, 2, 28. Martha m Asa HUNT
1856, 3, 27. Stover, s Job & Catherine, Clinton Co., O., b 1831,9,25; m Sarah A. GIBSON, dt Absolom & Rachel, b 1831,7,18
Ch: Milton H. b 1857, 6, 23
Clara Emma " 1859, 12, 2
Francis T. " 1861, 1, 6
1859, 11, 30. Thomas, s Job & Catherine, Clinton Co., O., b 1836,2,8; m in Westfork MH

SIMCOX, Thomas, continued
Sarah Elizabeth HOCKETT, dt Mahlon & Anna, Clinton Co., O., b 1843,3,2
Ch: Alvah H. b 1860, 12, 24
John Henry " 1862, 5, 19
1889, 12, 18. Harley b

1840, 1, 20. Job & w, Hannah, & ch, Lydia, John, Stover, Martha, Thomas & Susannah, rocf Springfield MM, dtd 1840,1,14
1845, 5, 12. Lydia gct Spiceland MM, Ind.
1867, 12, 23. Thomas & w, Sarah Elizabeth, & ch, Alvah H., John Henry, Lydia Jane & Alma Lora, gct Plainfield MM, Ind.
1872, 6, 17. Stover & w, Sarah, & ch, Milton N., Clara Emma, Francis Thomas, Eva, Catherine Elma, Louisa & Martha, gct Fairview MM, Ill.
1885, 2, 23. Jobe relrq
1889, 5, 20. Annie M. recrq

SIMMS
1928, 5, 25. Hannah Jane [Simmes] d 1928,5,25

1901, 7, 18. Hannah J. recrq

SIMMONS
----, --, --. Joseph & Eva
Ch: Josephine b 1887, 9, 26
Seraphina " 1885, 2, 5
1924, 9, 14. Pearl d

1856, 12, 26. Seth Hockett gct Fairfield MM,O. to m Rebecca Simmons
1857, 6, 22. Gulielma, John & Jacob, ch Rebecca Hockett, rocf Fairfield MM, O., dtd 1857,6,20
1859, 8, 22. Elma Hockett (form Simmons) con mou
1881, 3, 21. Joseph C. recrq
1881, 3, 21. Eva M. recrq
1881, 3, 21. Turner W. recrq
1881, 3, 21. Pearl recrq
1881, 3, 21. Alice recrq
1885, 8, 17. Joseph C. dis disunity
1911, 4, 13. Bell recrq
1913, 3, 20. Gladys recrq

SIMONTON
1881, 3, 21. William recrq
1886, 11, 22. William relrq

SIMPSON
----, --, --. David Butler, s Simeon & Martha, b 1844,2,24; m Susanna G. -----, dt Wm. & Ann HOLLADAY, b 1847,9,28
Ch: William E. b 1867, 9, 25
Martha A. " 1869, 12, 31
Mary Alice " 1872, 7, 25
Lenna S. " 1875, 6, 28
Simeon " 1878, 3, 14

1868, 1, 20. Susannah (form Holaday) con mou

1870, 1, 17. David B. recrq

SLAUGHTER
1914, 6, 18. Mrs. M. A. gct Fairfield MM

SMITH
----, --, --. John b 1792,11,9 d 1860,3,28 bur Newberry; m Sarah ----- b 1786,12,15 d 1836,10,27
Ch: Hannah b 1814, 2, 24
Rachel " 1815, 5, 19
Levina " 1816, 10, 16
Cina " 1818, 9, 29
Sarah " 1820, 4, 9
Margaret " 1821, 12, 7
Elizabeth " 1824, 5, 31
John R. " 1826, 6, 13
William R. " 1829, 3, 28
John m 2nd Dorcas ----- b 1804,5,12
Ch: Ephraim b 1850, 4, 20
1834, 1, 2. Rachel m Neri HOCKETT
1837, 3, 2. Lavinah m James MOON
1845, 12, 25. John, s William & Margaret, Clinton Co., O.; m in Newberry MH, Dorcas RATCLIFF, dt Abner & Sarah, Clinton Co.,O.
Ch: Ephraim b 1850, 4, 20 [b 1804,5,12
1848, 2, 24. John R., s John & Sarah, Clinton Co., O., b 1826,6,13; m in Newberry MH, Mary HUNT, dt Thomas & Susannah, Clinton Co., O., b 1822,8,7 d 1848,2,24 bur Westfield
Ch: Sarah E. b 1849, 6, 6 d 1849,11,28 bur Newberry
Thomas Arthur b 1851, 1, 1 " 1920,10,17
Susan Caroline " 1854, 8, 17
Eliza E. " 1860, 3, 18
----, --, --. William b 1839,3,28; m Hannah ----- b 1832,10,1
Ch: Sarah E. b 1851, 2, 12
Rachel M. " 1854, 3, 22 d 1856, 1,12 bur Newberry
Mary E. b 1856, 3, 28
Ema Jane " 1859, 8, 28
----, --, --. Eliza Emma b 1860,3,18 d 1922, 10,31
----, --, --. Ambrose, s John W. & Sarah, b 1835,9,30; m Phebe -----, dt Thomas & Mary MOON, b 1833,7,19
Ch: John T. b 1861, 3, 24
James Andrew " 1862, 10, 16
Mary Abbarilla " 1864, 12, 18
Daniel William " 1866, 8, 30
Simon Alonzo " 1870, 3, 31
Jesse H. " 1872, 6, 9
Nancy E. " 1875, 6, 19
Effie M. " 1879, 6, 14
1927, 11, 12. Phebe M. d

SMITH, continued
----, --, --. Zimri, s Job & Charlotte, b 1833,3,8; m Sarah F. LUTTRELL, dt Robert & Fannie, b 1838,3,28
Ch: Fannie C. b 1862, 8, 5
Luella J. " 1864, 5, 12
Rachel A. " 1866, 8, 1
Cordelia B." 1870, 9, 9
Halla Z. " 1872, 10, 26
Olive
Blanch " 1874, 10, 13
1879, 6, 14. Effie, dt Arthur T. & Phebe, b
1927, 11, 12. Phebe d
1820, 4, 27. John & ch, Hannah, Rachel, Lavina, Sinah & Sarah, recrq
1832, 5, 21. Asaph Hiatt gct White Water MM, Ind., to m Sarah Smith
1833, 8, 19. Hannah Hopkins (form Smith) dis mou
1839, 9, 23. Sinia Hockett (form Smith) con mou
1839, 8, 19. Mary rocf Springfield MM
1843, 12, 18. Sarah Pike (form Smith) con mou
1844, 9, 16. Elizabeth Moon (form Smith) con mou
1851, 3, 10. Wm. con mou
1851, 3, 10. Hannah (form Schooley) con mou
1855, 5, 21. William R. & w, Hannah, & ch, Sarah Ellen & Rachel Amanda, gct White River MM, Ind.
1860, 2, 20. William R. & w, Hannah, & ch, Sarah Elen, Mary Elizabeth & Emma Jane, rocf White River MM, Ind., dtd 1860,2,4
1860, 8, 20. Ambrose recrq
1860, 8, 20. Phebe (form Moon) con mou
1861, 9, 23. Dorcas Thornburgh (form Smith) con mou
1862, 8, 18. Ephraim, s Dorcas Thornburgh, gct Poplar Run MM, Ind.
1868, 11, 23. William R. & w, Hannah, & ch, Elizabeth Emma & Emerson, gct Wilmington MM, O.
1869, 9, 20. Zimri & w, Sarah, & ch, Fanny C., Louella J., Rachel A. & Alta E., rocf Fairfield MM, dtd 1869,6,19
1884, 8, 18. William recrq
1886, 1, 18. Cyrus & Samuel recrq
1886, 4, 19. Ellen recrq
1887, 8, 22. Ambrose, James, John & Ellen dropped from mbrp
1888, 1, 23. Phebe & ch, Daniel Wm., Sarah Amanda & Nancy Elizabeth, relrq
1888, 4, 23. Zimri & w, Sarah, relrq
1893, 11, 20. Zimri, Sarah T., Fannie, Louella, Rachel A., Cordelia, Hallie J. & Olive B. dropped from mbrp
1898, 9, 15. Effie M. & Lena M. recrq
1901, 4, 18. Phebe M. recrq
1901, 7, 18. Anna G., Clara E. & Charles J. recrq
1907, 7, 18. Goldie A. recrq
1914, 4, 16. Goldie Ann dropped from mbrp
1924, 12, 21. Alfred V. recrq

SMITHSON
1846, 6, 15. Mary (form Moon) con mou
1857, 1, 19. Jane (form Terrell) dis mou
1869, 12, 30. Frank, Solomon, Lewis, Carter, ch Mary, recrq
1870, 1, 17. Mary & ch gct Vermillion MM, Ill.
1886, 4, 19. Louie, Sarah & Frank recrq

SNEAD
1886, 1, 18. Christine & ch, Lee, Eva, Frank, Lizzie & Mark recrq
1889, 3, 18. Martimer & s, James Oran, recrq

SNYDER
----, --, --. Phillip b 1794,6,16; m Eliza -----, dt Chas. & Elizabeth ANTHONY, b 1800,3,18
Saphfronia b 1838, 1, 29 (Eliza's dt)

1834, 8, 18. Eliza rocf Cincinnati MM, dtd 1834,7,17
1855, 4, 23. Sophronia Ann recrq
1859, 1, 17. Philip [Snider] recrq
1859, 4, 18. Anna Isabel (form Moon) con mou
1861, 1, 21. Sophronia Ann Haynes (form Snider) con mou
1886, 4, 19. Sand [Snider] recrq
1886, 4, 19. James [Snider] recrq
1887, 8, 22. Samuel dropped from mbrp
1888, 4, 23. Estella relrq
1892, 12, 19. Anne J. gct Marshalltown MM, Ia.
1893, 2, 20. Jennie gct Marshalltown MM, Ia.
1893, 11, 20. Samuel dropped from mbrp

SOUTHARD
----, --, --. Forester E. [Southerd], s James & Mary J., b 1852,1,24 d 1931,11,26; m Lillian A. ANDREW, dt Jacob & Frances, b 1873,12,21

1906, 4, 19. Foster E. recrq
1906, 4, 19. Lillian recrq

SPENCER
1894, 10, 18. Isaac & Leota M. recrq

SPIELMAN
1887, 8, 22. Seymore dropped from mbrp

STAMATS
1929, 8, 18. Artemiss d

1885, 8, 17. Artemesa & s, Frank, rocf Wilmington MM, dtd 1885,7,11
1898, 3, 17. Arthur rocf Wilmington MM, O., dtd 1898,2,12
1914, 4, 16. Arthur dropped from mbrp

STANBROUGH
1851, 2, 10. Elizabeth rocf Westfield MM, Ind., dtd 1851,1,2
1853, 8, 22. Elizabeth dis

STANLEY
----, --, --. George & Jemima
Ch: Samuel b 1822, 12, 12
Jeremiah " 1824, 7, 13
Isaac " 1825, 12, 15
1822, 2, 28. Nancy m Thomas BEALS
1824, 4, 1. Martha m Christopher HIATT

1817, 6, 2. Samuel & w, Susannah, & ch, Elizabeth, Martha, Susanna, rocf Deep Creek MM, N. C., dtd 1817,3,1
1817, 6, 2. George & Nancy rocf Deep Creek MM, N. C., dtd 1817,3,1
1822, 2, 21. George gct Whitewater MM, Ind., to m Jamima Parker
1822, 10, 24. Jemimah rocf White Water MM, Ind., dtd 1822,7,20
1829, 2, 26. George & w, Jemimah, & ch, Samuel, Jeremiah Parker, Isaac & Keren Newby, gct Milford MM, Ind.
1830, 3, 25. Samuel & w, Susannah, & ch, Elizabeth & Susannah, gct Milford MM, Ind.

STEPHENS
1837, 9, 28. Evan, s Gideon & Mary, Clinton Co., O., b 1808,11,10; m in Newberry MH, Priscilla BETTS, dt Aaron & Nancy, Clinton Co., O., b 1818,9,28
Ch: Paulina Ann b 1840, 7, 1
Mary Alma " 1845, 10, 9
Lydia Elva " 1852, 3, 29
William L. " 1855, 9, 7
----, --, --. John m Eleanor -----, dt Wm. & Ann MOON, b 1828,4,13
Ch: Permelia Jane b 1858, 12, 12
Huldah Ann " 1860, 9, 4

1855, 9, 17. David James gct Clear Creek MM, to m Deborah Stevens
1858, 7, 19. Eleanor (form Parker) con mou
1859, 11, 21. Pelena Janney (form Stephens) con mou
1866, 12, 18. Mary Alma Cowgill (form Stevens) con mou
1869, 8, 23. Evan & w, Priscilla, & ch, Lydia Elva, William & adopted dt, Paulina Stephens, gct Union MM, Mo.
1869, 8, 23. Paulina gct Union MM, Mo. (adopted dt Evan & Priscilla Stephens)
1870, 1, 17. Permelia J. & Hulda A. [Stevens] recrq
1873, 12, 22. Alpheus [Stevens] recrq

STEPHENSON
1899, 7, 13. Emma rocf Wilmington MM, O., dtd 1899,6,11
1914, 4, 16. Emma [Stevenson] dropped from mbrp

STEWART
1886, 1, 18. Hester A. recrq
1886, 1, 18. Henry J. [Steward] & s, Robert & George Wm., recrq

STOGDEN
----, --, --. John W., s Thomas & Jeanetta, b 1837,6,24; m Margaret E. HAMMER, dt Elisha & Elizabeth, b 1848,1,25
Ch: Anna J. b 1865, 8, 9
Ada Belle " 1877, 12, 18

1865, 8, 21. Mary Emily (form Hammer) dis mou
1870, 1, 17. Margaret [Stogdon] recrq
1877, 2, 19. William [Stogdon] recrq
1891, 1, 19. Wm. & Margaret Emily relrq

STRAIN
1874, 7, 20. David recrq

STRATE
----, --, --. Francis W., s Seth & Sarah, b 1846,7,16; m Anna HOLLINGSWORTH, dt Elias & Lydia, b 1847,11,8
Ch: Mary R. b 1873, 3, 22
James C. " 1875, 7, 25

1875, 6, 21. Francis M. [Strait] & w, Annie, & dt, Mary R., rocf Middleport MM, Ill., dtd 1875,5,15
1893, 11, 20. Francis, Anna, James C. & Mary R. [Straight] dropped from mbrp

STRATTON
1867, 8, 19. John Haines & ch, Francis Irvin & Flora Ellen, rocf Springfield MM,O., dtd 1867,8,17
1873, 12, 22. John H. & w, Lydia, & ch, John, Joseph, David, Lorena, Arrena & Clara, gct Springfield MM
1874, 9, 21. Flora & Frances, ch John H., gct Clear Creek MM, O

STRAW
1836, 8, 26. Elizabeth, dt John & Patience STEWARD, b

1873, 5, 19. Elizabeth recrq
1885, 5, 18. Charles &, s, Sylvester, Lindley & Melvin, recrq

SWAIN
1927, 6, 19. Lola Katherine recrq

TAYLOR
1883, 9, 14. Osa, s Abert & Leila, b

1864, 11, 21. Rebecca Ann recrq
1864, 12, 19. Rebecca Ann gct Oak Ridge MM, Ind.
1886, 1, 18. Elisha recrq
1886, 6, 21. M. Evalyn recrq
1906, 4, 19. Osa recrq

TERRELL

----, --, --. John [Terrill] m Jane -----
b 1785,7,29
Ch: William b 1812, 11, 29
Rebecca " 1814, 4, 7
Elizabeth " 1816, 5, 26
Susanna " 1818, 6, 2
James " 1820, 2, 14
Catherine " 1822, 9, 5
Benjamin " 1823, 8, 7
Sarah " 1825, 8, 30
Jane " 1830, 12, 25

1841, 1, 28. Elizabeth [Terrill] m Jesse RATCLIFF

----, --, --. Benjamin, s John & Jane, b 1823, 8,7 d 1905,1,1; m Asenath JOHNSON, dt Robert & Milly, b 1840,8,9
Ch: Celesta
Jane b 1864, 12, 2
Elizabeth " 1866, 1, 6 d 1923, 7, 2
Edward
Everett " 1867, 9, 1
Beecher " 1869, 4, 22
Francis
Robert " 1870, 12, 13
Milly " 1873, 3, 4

1823, 2, 20. William, Rebecca, Elizabeth, Susannah, James & Catharine [Terrel], ch John, recrq
1824, 8, 26. Benjamin [Terrel] recrq cf parents, John & Jane
1825, 10, 27. Sarah [Terrel] & dt, Jane, recrq of parent
1831, 4, 28. Jane [Terrel] recrq of mother, Jane
1839, 6, 17. Rebecca Ratcliff (form Terrill) con mou
1846, 4, 13. William con mou
1846, 11, 16. Wm. gct Vermillion MM, Ill.
1850, 5, 15. Sarah Reese (form Terrell) con mou
1856, 12, 26. Sarah (form Ratcliff) dis mou
1857, 1, 19. Jane Smithson (form Terrell) dis mou
1859, 8, 22. James con mou
1864, 12, 19. Asenith rocf Honey Creek MM, Ind., dtd 1864,12,10
1865, 2, 20. Benjamin con mou
1868, 11, 23. James gct Honey Creek MM, Ind.
1900, 6, 14. Beecher gct Indianapolis MM,Ind.
1902, 10, 16. Millie gct Clear Creek MM, O.
1909, 11, 18. B. J. relrq
1914, 3, 19. Florence Morrow recrq
1914, 3, 19. Charles Warren, Florence Asenath & Esther Inez, recrq
1916, 2, 17. Estella recrq

THOMAS

1867, 4, 25. Mahlon rmt Emma Hunt
1867, 11, 18. Emma H. gct New Garden MM, Ind.

THOMPSON

----, --, --. Eli b 1829,9,10; m Jane -----
b 1835,12,19
Ch: Laura b 1858, 8, 6
Ella " 1860, 6, 15
Jaspar " 1862, 4, 12
Mahlon " 1863, 3, 22
Effie " 1866, 10, 20

1820, 9, 28. Amy (form Beals) con mou
1821, 4, 26. Amy gct Fairfield MM
1857, 9, 21. Jane (Hockett) dis jas
1863, 6, 22. Jane recrq
1881, 3, 21. Sarah E. & Charles recrq
1885, 5, 18. Jane recrq
1886, 1, 18. Anna L. recrq
1886, 1, 18. Lawrence recrq
1886, 5, 17. Carrie recrq
1889, 3, 18. Joanna [Thomson] & ch, Elmer H., Carrie & Ada, recrq
1890, 1, 20. John C. recrq
1890, 1, 20. Andrew recrq
1915, 9, 16. Grace recrq
1916, 1, 13. Thomas & w, Marie, recrq

THORNBURGH

1852, 6, 5. Elizabeth [Thornburg] (form Hayworth) dis mou
1861, 9, 23. Dorcas (form Smith) con mou
1862, 8, 18. Dorcas & s, Ephraim Smith, gct Poplar Run MM, Ind.
1873, 3, 17. Lettie recrq

THORNHILL

1829, 9, 20. Mary b
----, --, --. ----- & Ann
Ch: Homer b 1871, 2, 19 d 1872, 2,18
bur Westfork
Wilber b 1872, 10, 26
Jennie " 1875, 2, 2

1870, 2, 21. Mary recrq
1870, 8, 22. Ann con mou
1881, 3, 21. Emma Zerilda recrq
1883, 10, 22. Emma Zerilda relrq

THRUSHER

1894, 8, 23. Maggie C. rocf Westfork MM, O., dtd 1894,7,21
1898, 3, 17. Maggie relrq

TOMLIN

1890, 9, 22. Harriett rocf Wilmington MM, O., dtd 1890,9,13

TOMLINSON

1820, 6, 28. Robert & w, Lydia, & s, Milton, rocf Springfield MM, N. C., dtd 1821,3,7
1822, 2, 21. Robert & fam gct West Grove MM, Ind.

TOWNSEND

----, --, --. Abigail, w Josiah, dt Thomas &

TOWNSEND, Abigail, continued
Lavina HOLLOWAY, b 1796,9,9 d 1878,5,21
----, --, --. Isaac b 1827,9,27; m Peninah
----- b 1822,10,23
Ch: Abigail
Emily b 1847, 12, 17
Josiah Dayton " 1849, 5, 24
John Thomas " 1851, 8, 9
Lydia Margaret " 1855, 3, 3
Mary Catherine " 1857, 10, 29
Warren B. " 1860, 11, 25
----, --, --. Dayton H., s Josiah & Abigail, b 1829,12,31; m Rachel -----, dt James & Esther HOLLINGSWORTH, b 1828,9,26 d 1905, 1,4
Ch: Emma R. b 1858, 12, 1 d 1896,11,14
Oliver J. " 1861, 2, 6
Mildred " 1863, 4, 10 " 1878, 2, 5 bur Newberry
Austin D. b 1866, 1, 7 " 1867, 4,24 bur Newbury
Elva b 1869, 12, 31
Virgil " 1872, 8, 1 " 1910, 3,20
----, --, --. Josiah M., s Josiah & Abigail, b 1832,2,16 d 1870,1,23; m Esther J. WEST, dt Peyton & Sarah, b 1839,3,25
Ch: Orland b 1860, 1, 18
Clinton H. " 1861, 6, 23 d 1862, 7, 5
Cammie M. " 1863, 2, 20
Sarah A. " 1865, 3, 11
Josiah Jr. " 1867, 11, 18
Herbert H. " 1869, 11, 2
George A. " 1873, 7, 15
Melville May " 1876, 3, 25
----, --, --. Orlando & Mary
Ch: Loyd M. b 1885, 6, 15
Horace " ----, 9, 15
1922, --, --. Mary d
1927, 3, 2. Harriet Marie, dt Lloyd & Ada, b
1933, 2, 10. Emma Spencer, w Oliver J., d bur Corwin

1849, 1, 15. Isaac & Peninah & dt, Abigail Emaly, rocf Clear Creek MM, dtd 1848,12,9
1850, 6, 10. Abigail & ch, Dayton H. & Josiah M., rocf Centre MM, O., dtd 1850,4,17
1854, 9, 18. Isaac & w, Penina, & ch, Abigail, Josiah Dayton & John Thomas returned
1859, 6, 20. Dayton H. con mou
1859, 11, 21. Josiah M. con mou
1859, 11, 21. Esther Jane (form West) con mou
1861, 9, 23. Isaac & w, Peninah, & ch, Abigail Emily, Josiah Dayton, John Thomas, Lydia Margaret, Mary Catherine & Warren B. gct Cincinnati MM
1867, 10, 21. Rachel recrq
1888, 2, 20. Mary recrq
1897, 3, 18. Emma Spencer rocf Clear Creek MM, O., dtd 1897,2,13
1906, 2, 15. Horace recrq
1906, 2, 15. Lloyd recrq
1915, 3, 18. Ada & s, Wm. Eugene, recrq
1921, 4, 14. Floyd, Dana & Harold recrq
1921, 6, 23. Hattie Rand recrq

TRENARY
----, --, --. John L., s Frank & Nancy, b 1895,2,26 d 1930,9,27; m Susan SPENCER, dt Friend & Hannah, b 1881,11,29
Ch: Martha Louise b 1905, 5, 16

1918, 3, 14. Susan & dt, Martha, relrq

TROTH
1887, 2, 21. Jessie (form Miller) relrq

TURNER
1815, 12, 10. Susan d
1931, 6, 29. C. W. d

1865, 2, 20. Lydia (form Hockett) con mou
1870, 2, 21. Eva recrq
1886, 4, 19. Susan recrq
1889, 3, 18. Charles W. recrq
1893, 11, 20. Cora A. dropped from mbrp
1895, 2, 14. Bell recrq
1895, 8, 22. Sallie recrq
1901, 4, 18. Bell relrq

UTMAN
1886, 4, 19. Stella recrq

VANCE
1846, 11, 5. Amanda S. b

1870, 2, 21. Amanda recrq
1874, 8, 17. Elma rocf Saline MM, dtd 1874, 7,11
1874, 9, 21. Elma relrq
1874, 10, 19. Emery rocf Saline MM, Ill., dtd 1874,9,12
1880, 4, 19. Emery H. gct Saline MM, Ill.

VANWINKLE
1872, 5, 20. Clarinda rocf Clear Creek MM, dtd 1872,5,11

WALKER
1809, 10, 12. Eli, s Wm. & Martha, b
----, --, --. H. F. m Samantha M. DEAKIN, dt James & Susan, b 1842,9,26
Ch: Willie D. b 1871, 11, 16

1832, 10, 22. John Hunt gct Center MM, to m Phebe Walker
1870, 2, 21. Samantha M. recrq
1872, 9, 23. Eli rocf Centre MM, dtd 1872, 7,17
1881, 3, 21. Samantha relrq
1886, 1, 18. Ann E. recrq

WALKER, continued
1886, 1, 18. Mary L. & dt, Minnie, recrq
1889, 5, 20. Margaret recrq
1893, 11, 20. Margaret dropped from mbrp
1895, 1, 17. Elizabeth relrq
1898, 1, 13. Willie D. relrq
1898, 9, 15. Rebecca recrq

WALKUP
----, --, --. Anderson m Susannah MOON, dt Daniel & Rachel, b 1827,5,2
Ch: Rachel
Emma b 1865, 12, 29
Martha " 1868, 7, 25

1846, 12, 14. Susanna (form Moon) con mou
1888, 2, 20. Daniel recrq

WALTZ
1870, 5, 25. Mary A. (form Moon) con mou
1871, 6, 19. Mary A. gct Union MM, Mo.

WARREN
1881, 3, 21. George & John recrq
1887, 8, 22. George & Wilshire dropped from mbrp
1889, 11, 18. Eva N. gct Wilmington MM, O.
1893, 11, 20. John dropped from mbrp

WASSON
----, --, --. Calvin & Mary
Ch: William b 1819, 6, 20
Nathan " 1821, 3, 14
Elizabeth " 1824, 1, 30
Sarah " 1826, 5, 18
Mary Jane " 1830, 1, 10
Calvin H. " 1832, 2, 24
Eliza Ann " 1838, 3, 25
Asa B. " 1841, 8, 2
1842, 9, 20. Elizabeth m Asa HOCKETT
1853, 9, 20. Mary Jane m Thos. BRANSON

1842, 2, 24. Calvin & w, Mary, & ch, Elizabeth, Sarah, Mary Jane, Calvin, Eliza Ann & Asa, rocf Clear Creek MM, dtd 1842,1,18
1853, 9, 19. Calvin & w, Mary, & ch, Eliza Ann & Asa, gct Pipe Creek MM, Ind.

WATKINS
1851, 4, 14. Anna (form Hockett) dis disunity

WATSON
1863, 7, 20. Esther Ann (form Hammer) dis mou

WEAVER
1877, 2, 19. Jane (form Moon) gct Peace MM, Kans.

WEBB
1881, 3, 21. John recrq
1894, 2, 19. John dropped from mbrp

WELLS
1834, 2, 17. Thomas & w, Hannah, rocf Miami MM, dtd 1833,12,25
1836, 4, 18. Thomas & w, Hannah, gct Miami MM
1887, 8, 22. Ella dropped from mbrp

WESEMAN
1922, 9, 14. Amelia & dt, Betty Ethel, recrq

WEST
----, --, --. George b 1788,3,27; m Mary ----- b 1790,11,22
Ch: Thomas b 1813, 7, 9
Nancy " 1814, 10, 4
Elizabeth " 1816, 5, 1
John " 1817, 9, 16
Samuel " 1820, 5, 6
Christopher" 1821, 7, 10
Benjamin " 1823, 2, 1
George " 1824, 5, 22
Jesse " 1825, 8, 8
Mary " 1827, 8, 10
Hannah " 1833, 2, 25
1818, 5, 14. Thomas, s Owen & Elizabeth, Clinton Co., O., b 1794,6,18; m in Newberry MH, Tamar HADLEY, dt James & Ann, Clinton Co., O., b 1799,11,4
Ch: Sarah b 1819, 8, 2
Elizabeth " 1822, 7, 10
Jeremiah H." 1824, 12, 17
Anna " 1827, 1, 27
Mary " 1830, 10, 25
Josiah M. " 1833, 7, 11
1818, 11, 12. Elizabeth m Ezekiel HAWORTH
1820, 5, 4. Peyton, s Owen & Elizabeth, Clinton Co., O., b 1798,4,20; m in Newberry MH, Sarah HADLEY, dt James & Ann, Clinton Co., O., b 1801,10,1 d 1876,6,--
Ch: James H. b 1821, 3, 2
Joseph " 1822, 11, 21
William " 1824, 12, 18
Peyton M. " 1827, 8, 22
Elisha B. " 1830, 7, 30
Edith H. " 1833, 2, 14
Sarah Ann " 1835, 7, 25 d 1862, 8,27 bur Newberry
Esther Janeb 1839, 3, 25
Jeremiah H." 1842, 1, 27
Caroline E." 1845, 7, 13
Hannah M. " 1848, 2, 18
1822, 3, 4. Elizabeth d
1829, 4, 27. Elial b
1830, 9, 29. Nancy m Moses PUCKETT
1830, 10, 5. Sarah, w David, d
1836, 3, 30. David, s William & Sarah, Clinton Co., O., b 1813,11,22; m in Westfork MH, Ruth MOON, dt Joseph D. & Eliza, Clinton Co., O., b 1815,6,4
Ch: Sarah b 1836, 12, 31
Daniel " 1838, 2, 15
Eliza " 1839, 8, 9
William " 1841, 5, 6

WEST, David & Ruth, continued
Ch: Mary b 1843, 11, 28
Robert " 1848, 11, 18
Rhoda " 1851, 10, 22
Charles " 1853, 10, 20
Anna " 1860, 2, 4
----, --, --. Owen b 1816,6,11 d 1900,6,10 ae 83y 11m 29d
----, --, --. Oliver & Mary
Ch: Sarah Jane b 1840, 5, 12
Abigail C. " 1842, 2, 19
Margaret Emily 2 1844, 4, 4
Jehiel " 1846, 9, 24
1842, 9, 1. Roda m Joseph GREEN
----, --, --. Martin b 1821,9,13 d 1863,10,7; m Abigail -----, dt John & Margaret CAREY, b 1820,4,27 d 1902,11,30
Ch: John William b 1845, 6, 29
Eliel W. " 1846, 10, 5
James Asa " 1849, 4 , 23 d 1867,12,7
Daniel H. " 1852, 5, 8
Isaac C. " 1854, 5, 4 " 1877, 3,--
Sarah Margaret " 1856, 6, 10
Elias C. " 1860, 5, 2
Samuel L. " 1863, 2, 6 " 1864, 3, 2
----, --, --. Charles O., s Wm. & Sarah, b 1824,3,9 d 1904,5,28; m Rachel D. ----- dt Samuel & Ann CAREY, b 1828,11,22
Ch: Sarah Ann b 1847, 8, 6 d 1862, 8,27
Daniel C. " 1849, 8, 9 " 1914, 1,19
Mary E. " 1851, 3, 29
Rhoda Emley " 1853, 8, 21
Linley H. " 1856, 10, 12 d 1858, 7,14
Thomas Elwood " 1861, 10, 22 " 1898, 7,31
Milton E. " 1864, 10, 24
Willard W. " 1874, 4, 2
Elizabeth " 1851, 3, 29
Rhoda " 1853, 8, 21
----, --, --. Elisha B., s Peyton & Sarah H., b 1830,7,30; m Rebecca -----, dt John & Elizabeth CRAWFORD, b 1835,10,4
Ch: Webster B. b 1853, 2, 20
Oliver H. " 1854, 7, 11
Florella " 1856, 8, 17
Peyton " 1860, 8, 21
Lizzie B. " 1863, 3, 21
Esther J. " 1865, 10, 29
George " 1872, 12, 19
----, --, --. James H. & Helena
Ch: Edwin P. b 1851, 2, 18 d 1926,12,13
Arthur W. " 1855, 12, 9
Otis T. " 1860, 10, 30
----, --, --. James H., s Peyton & Sarah, b 1821,3,2 d 1903,6,28; m Marianna McPHERSON dt John & Maria, b 1831,12,15 d 1907,7,23
Ch: Helena b 1868, 12, --
John M. " 1871, 1, 22 d 1929, 8, 3
James " 1872, 5, 2
Ch: Melcena b 1874, 10, 27 d 1913,10,17
----, --, --. Peyton M., s Peyton & Sarah, b 1827,8,22 d 1897,4,8; m Sarah JACKSON, b 1834,1,20
Ch: Marietta b 1855, 8, 14
Clara Myrta" 1862, 4, 15
Francis Marion " 1865, 8, 17
Josiah E. " 1868, 10, 14
Peyton M. m 2nd Dianna DEAN
Ch: Hattie D. b 1870, 4, 25
Harry " 1871, 4, 25
C. Roy " 1873, 6, 23
Musa " 1876, 12, 3
----, --, --. Eliel, s Wm. & Sarah, b 1828,4, 27 d 1910,3,3; m Eliza A. -----, dt John & Phebe HUNT, b 1836,9,1 d 1928,1,24
1860, 2, 13. Ruth d
1860, 3, 24. Rhoda d
1860, 5, 14. Rhoda d
----, --, --. Eliel W. b 1846,10,5; m Eliza Ellen -----, dt Joseph & Ellen NEELE, b 1845,11,26
Ch: Clara b 1866, 9, 15 d 1866,11,18
Hattie E. " 1867, 9, 26
Harley " 1870, 8, 23
Walter " 1873, 4, 2
Jesse B. " 1875, 11, 19 d 1876, 9,30
----, --, --. John W., s Martin & Abigail, b 1845,6,29; m Rosalie BARBER, dt Henry & Lucinda, b 1853,10,29
Ch: Sylvia A. b 1870, 4, 21
Orpha L. " 1872, 2, 2
Adelbert C." 1878, 2, 1
----, --, --. Jeremiah, s Peyton & Sarah, b 1842,1,27 d 1880,12,30; m Louisa UNDERWOOD, dt Ezekiel & Anna, b 1846,10,30
Ch: Emma b 1872, 9, 21
Stella " 1876, 11, 23
----, --, --. Jehiel G., s Owen & Mary, b 1846,9,24; m Betsy Jane SIMCOX, dt Job & Hannah, b 1840,7,12
Ch: Larena A. b 1874, 1, 3
Mary Anne " 1875, 6, 10
Frances W. " 1878, 3, 6
----, --, --. Daniel H., s Martin & Abigail, b 1852,5,8 d 1932,10,2; m Margaret ----- dt Geo. & Elizabeth MOON, d 1932,9,2
Ch: Arthur b 1877, 9, 28
Amy " 1882, 2, 3
William W. " 1885, 8, 1
Fred " 1889, 3, 26 d 1902, 1,24
----, --, --. James m Anna M. MOON, dt C. C. & Melissa, b 1861,12,15
Ch: Winnie b 1879, 9, 8
Genevra " 1881, 6, 4
Merle " 1883, 2, 2
----, --, --. Lindley O., s Owen & Mary, b 1859,7,30; m Emma -----
Ch: Raymond J. b 1890, 6, 11
Edgar C. " 1892, 8, 13
Mary Iona " 1888, 6, 15 d 189-, 3, 8
1898, 8, 13. Wendall P., s M. E. & Lenna, b

WEST, continued
1900, 6, 10. Owen d
----, --, --. John M. m Clarence(?) -----
Ch: Joanna b 1905, 5, 6
William " 1907, 4, 25
----, --, --. James H., s John M. & C., b 1902,10,4 d 1923,7,11; m Louie ----- d 1930,6,30
Ch: Maxine b 1923, 8, 4
1928, 1, 21. Eliza A. d
1929, 8, 25. John M. d
1930, 6, 30. Louie d
1930, 7, 30. Clarance d
1932, 9, 2. Margaret Moon d

1817, 11, 3. William & w recrq
1820, 5, 25. Emilia Hayworth (form West) con mou
1821, 2, 22. George recrq
1821, 2, 22. James dis mou
1822, 8, 29. Mary recrq
1822, 9, 26. Thomas, Nancy, Elizabeth, John, Samuel & Christopher, ch George, recrq
1824, 6, 24. Owen dis
1827, 11, 22. Rebecca Garner (form West) con mou
1831, 8, 22. John dis mou
1831, 9, 19. William dis
1834, 10, 20. George & w, Mary, & ch, Elizabeth, Samuel, Christopher, Benjamin, George, Jesse, Mary & Hannah, gct Fairfield MM, Ind.
1835, 4, 20. Peyton dis
1836, 2, 22. John dis disunity
1837, 6, 19. Thomas, s Geo., dis disunity
1837, 11, 20. Thomas dis
1838, 1, 22. Tamer & ch, Sarah, Elizabeth, Jeremiah, Anna, Mary & Isaiah, gct Dover MM
1838, 10, 22. Owen gct Clear Creek MM, to m Mary Carey
1839, 4, 22. Mary rocf Clear Creek MM, dtd 1839,1,22
1841, 5, 17. David & w, Ruth, & ch, Sarah, Daniel, Eliza & William, gct Dover MM
1842, 8, 22. Peyton rst rq
1843, 8, 21. William rst
1843, 10, 23. Martin gct Clear Creek MM, to m Abigail Carey
1844, 5, 20. Abigail C. rocf Clear Creek MM, dtd 1844,4,23
1845, 4, 14. David & w, Ruth, & ch, Sarah, Daniel, Eliza, William & Mary, rocf Dover MM, dtd 1845,3,13
1846, 9, 14. Charles O. gct Clear Creek MM, to m Rachel D. Carey
1847, 7, 12. Rachel D. rocf Clear Creek MM, dtd 1847,7,10
1848, 11, 13. James H. con mou
1848, 11, 13. Helena (form Jackson) dis mou
1848, 12, 11. William gct Springfield MM, to m Sophia Hadley
1849, 1, 15. William H. con mou
1849, 5, 14. William gct Springfield MM, O.
1849, 5, 14. Hellena (form Jackson) dis mou
1849, 8, 13. Peyton M. dis disunity
1850, 2, 11. Owen & w, Mary, & ch, Sarah Jane, Abigail C., Margaret Emaly, Jehiel G. & Joseph Milton, gct Clear Creek MM
1850, 10, 14. William H. dis disunity
1852, 7, 3. Joseph dis mou
1853, 6, 20. Elisha B. con mou
1855, 6, 18. Edith Hinshaw (form West) con mou
1855, 9, 17. Sarah Dodd (form West) dis mou
1859, 11, 21. Esther Jane Townsend (form West) con mou
1860, 5, 21. Eliza (form Hunt) con mou
1861, 7, 22. Eliza Ann dis
1862, 2, 17. David con mou
1862, 3, 17. Elisha B. dis disunity
1862, 6, 23. David & s, Charles, gct Cesars Creek MM
1864, 4, 18. Mary Lyons (form West) con mou
1865, 2, 20. Peyton M. & w, Sarah, & ch, Marietta & Clara Myrta, recrq
1865, 4, 17. Elisha B. & w, Rebecca, & ch, Webster B., Oliver H., Peyton & Lizzie Bell, recrq
1865, 12, 18. Eliel W. rmt Eliza E. Neeld
1866, 9, 17. William gct Cesars Creek MM, O., to m Mary Ann Wilson
1867, 2, 18. Mary Ann rocf Caesars Creek MM, O., dtd 1867,1,24
1867, 6, 17. Catharine gct Honey Creek MM, Ind.
1868, 6, 22. James H. con mou
1868, 8, 17. Mary Anne rocf Fairfield MM, dtd 1868,7,18
1868, 9, 21. Mary Margaret con mou
1868, 11, 23. William & w, Mary, & s, Enos, gct Cesars Creek MM, O.
1868, 11, 23. Robert con mou
1870, 2, 21. Anna, niece of Jos. & Mary GREEN, gct Spring River MM, Mo.
1870, 2, 21. John William con mou
1870, 2, 21. Edwin P. recrq
1870, 3, 21. John W. gct Cincinnati MM, O.
1870, 3, 21. Cassius J., Arthur W. & Otis T. recrq
1873, 4, 21. Jehiel rocf Clear Creek MM, O., dtd 1873,4,21
1873, 4, 21. Jeremiah H. con mou
1873, 4, 21. Bettie J. con mou
1873, 4, 21. Rosilla recrq
1873, 11, 17. Louisa recrq
1875, 2, 22. John W. & ch, Sylvia C. & Orva L., rocf Cincinnati MM, O., dtd 1874,12, 17
1881, 3, 21. Eva recrq
1881, 3, 21. Margaret recrq
1881, 3, 21. Annie recrq
1881, 3, 21. Clarence recrq
1881, 3, 21. Muretta P. recrq
1881, 3, 21. Carol C. recrq
1882, 2, 20. John William & w, Rosa, relrq

WEST, continued
1883, 8, 20. Charlotte F. recrq
1883, 10, 22. Louisa & ch, Emma & Stella, gct Wilmington MM, O.
1885, 7, 20. Lindley O. & James Milton rocf Clear Creek MM, O., dtd 1885,6,13
1888, 2, 20. Clary recrq
1889, 3, 18. Annie M. & ch, Winnie, Genevia & Merl, recrq
1893, 11, 20. Clara dropped from mbrp
1893, 11, 20. Webster dropped from mbrp
1893, 11, 20. Oliver H. dropped from mbrp
1893, 11, 20. Flora B. dropped from mbrp
1893, 11, 20. Peyton dropped from mbrp
1893, 11, 20. Lizzie dropped from mbrp
1893, 11, 20. Esther J. dropped from mbrp
1893, 11, 20. George dropped from mbrp
1893, 11, 20. Elisha B. dropped from mbrp
1894, 1, 22. Annie M. & ch, Minnie, Ginevra & Merle, gct Kokomo MM, Ind.
1894, 2, 19. Anna dropped from mbrp
1898, 6, 16. Owen rocf Clear Creek MM, O., dtd 1898,4,9
1898, 6, 16. Mary E. rocf Clear Creek MM, O., dtd 1898,4,9
1898, 9, 15. James Harvey recrq
1899, 8, 24. Abigail rocf Westfork MM, O., dtd 1899,7,15
1908, 3, 19. Andrew S. recrq
1909, 10, 14. Carey & w & ch, Leslie Mellie Earl & Fred, rocf Westfork MM, O., dtd 1909,9,18
1909, 12, 16. Joanna & Wm. H., ch John M., recrq
1913, 11, 13. Cora Garner rocf Westfork MM, O., dtd 1913,10,18
1913, 12, 18. Williard & dt, Rachel & Mildred, relrq
1915, 3, 18. Mary Elizabeth relrq
1918, 4, 17. Lovie & ch, William, Fred, Russell & John, recrq
1921, 2, 17. Paxton gct Wilmington MM, O.
1921, 2, 17. Carl gct Wilmington MM, O.
1929, 7, 14. Ethel recrq
1930, 5, 18. John recrq

WHARTON
1873, 5, 19. Isaac recrq
1873, 5, 19. Huldah & s, Walter, rocf Center MM, O., dtd 1872,10,16
1873, 6, 23. Harley, s Isaac, recrq
1887, 5, 23. Isaac dropped from mbrp

WHINERY
1834, 11, 6. Mary E. b
1844, 3, 28. James, s Zimri & Judith, Clinton Co., O.; m in Newberry MH, Mary MOON, dt Henry & Sarah, Clinton Co., O.
1863, 11, 4. Lenna L., dt Warren & Mary E., b

1841, 4, 19. Jesse Coffin gct Centre MM, to m Elizabeth Whinery
1843, 9, 18. James rocf Centre MM, dtd 1843, 8,16
1845, 9, 15. James & w, Mary, & s, Arthur, gct Centre MM
1859, 5, 25. Mary Elizabeth (form Hunt) con mou
1894, 1, 22. Lenna gct Sabina MM, O.
1900, 6, 14. Mary E. gct Sabina MM, O.

WHITACRE
1926, 11, 12. Emmerson d

1923, 12, 13. Emmerson & w, Nannie, recrq

WHITE
----, --, --. Benjamin m Lavena ----- b 1815, 11,24

Ch:				
Josephine	b 1838,	5,	17
Lydia	" 1840,	8,	29
Mary	" 1843,	2,	10
Henry W.	" 1846,	2,	6
Elizabeth	" 1850,	1,	28

1853, 2, 5. Levina & ch, Josephine, Lydia, Mary, Henry Wilson & Elizabeth, rocf Clear Creek MM, dtd 1852,12,11
1866, 1, 22. Lavina & ch, Henry & Elizabeth, gct Ash Grove MM, Ill.
1866, 4, 23. Josephine E. Morgan (form White) con mou
1866, 4, 23. Lydia Janney (form White) con mou

WILLET
1881, 3, 21. John recrq
1887, 8, 22. John dropped from mbrp

WILLIAMS
1---, --, --. William A., s James H. & Ann, b 1848,8,3; m Nancy B. -----, dt ----- HOLLOWAY, b 1843,6,3
----, --, --. James Harvey, s Isaac & Sarah, b 1827,12,11; m Ann JACKSON, dt Curtis & Lydia, b 1827,1,28

Ch:			
Isaac	b 1853,	2,	18
Lisbon	" 1856,	6,	4
Francis Edward	" 1858,	10,	5
Sarah Ellen	" 1861,	6,	15
Thomas	" 1865,	8,	17
Wm. Anderson	" 1848,	8,	3

1849, 5, 14. Ann (form Jackson) dis mou
1869, 6, 21. Nancy B. (form Holaday) con mou
1869, 3, 22. James H. & ch, Isaac, Lisbon, Francis Edwin, Sarah & Thomas, recrq
1870, 1, 17. William A. recrq
1886, 1, 18. Frederick recrq
1887, 11, 21. Anderson & w, Nancy, & s, Frederick, gct Haveland MM, Kans.
1891, 7, 20. Mary F. recrq

WILLIAMSON
1927, 12, 16. Blanche d

1884, 8, 18. Florence & s, Raymond, gct Minneapolis, Minn.
1932, 4, 17. Marjorie recrq

WILSON
----, --, --. William b 1803,5,26 d 1874,5,10; m Rebecca -----, dt George & Mary CARLILE, dt 1813,5,24
Ch: Elizabeth b 1834, 9, 11
Eliza " 1848, 8, 22
John C. 2 1851, 10, 5
Daniel D. " 1861, 11, 26
1841, 7, 28. Elizabeth m Moses MOON
----, --, --. Thomas, s Wm. & Nancy, b 1847,10, 14; m Louisa HARPER, dt Benjamin & Frances J., b 1844,3,7
Ch: Robert M. b 1878, 2, 17

1840, 3, 23. Elizabeth recrq
1856, 6, 23. Rebecca recrq
1863, 5, 18. Eliza A., John C. & Daniel, ch Rebecca, recrq
1866, 9, 17. William West gct Cesars Creek MM, O., to m Mary Ann Wilson
1867, 10, 21. Eliza Dickerson (form Wilson) con mou
1871, 7, 17. William S. recrq
1877, 2, 19. Thomas & w, Louisa, recrq
1881, 3, 21. Lizzie recrq
1881, 3, 21. Emme recrq
1881, 3, 21. Hattie recrq
1881, 3, 21. John recrq
1881, 3, 21. Eliza recrq

1883, 4, 23. Louisa relrq
1884, 6, 18. John dis disunity
1886, 1, 18. Mariah & ch, Minna, Lizzie & Nettie, recrq
1887, 8, 22. Emma dropped from mbrp
1888, 6, 18. Eli recrq
1891, 3, 23. Mina relrq
1893, 11, 20. Eliza [Willison] dropped from mbrp
1893, 11, 20. Lizzie [Willison] dropped from mbrp
1897, 11, 18. Florence recrq
1905, 11, 16. Elsie gct Spiceland WM, Ind.

WINEGAR
1886, 1, 18. Isaac recrq
1891, 1, 19. Ed relrq

WINFIELD
1889, 2, 18. John D. & w, Alice A., & ch, Mary Y., Charles A. & Frank Y., recrq

WINTERS
1906, 2, 20. Lucy Elizabeth, dt John C. & Gertrude (Chapman), b

WOLF
1867, 7, 22. Margaret F. rocf Springfield MM, O., dtd 1867,7,20
1867, 11, 18. Angeline (form Holaday) dis mou

WOOD
1886, 1, 18. William A. & Ann L. recrq
1886, 4, 19. Francis M. recrq
1893, 11, 20. Francis M. dropped from mbrp

WRIGHT
----, --, --. Joshua m Rebecca ----- d 1831, 5,5 bur Newbury
Ch: Isaac S. b 1811, 4, 4
Jonathan H." 1812, 5, 28
Betsy " 1813, 9, 30
Matilda " 1816, 5, 1 d 1831,11,18 bur Newbury
Polly b 1819, 6, 23
Amos " 1823, 11, 30
William P. " 1825, 11, 10
Addison " 1827, 11, 16
Lydia " 1829, 6, 19
----, --, --. John & Sarah
Ch: Hannah b 1811, 5, 29
Rachel " 1814, 2, 10
Jemima " 1814, 2, 10
Jonathan " 1816, 9, 26
Jesse " 1820, 3, 2 d 1832, 4,-- bur Newbury
Mahala b 1822, 7, 26
1828, 2, 28. Phebe m Jesse GRAHAM
1828, 5, 1. James, s John & Sarah, Clinton Co., O.; m in Newberry MH, Elizabeth HIATT, dt Christopher & Jamima, Clinton Co., O.
Ch: Louisa b 1829, 1, 24
1845, 4, 24. David, s Edward & Hannah, Highland Co., O.; m in Newberry MH, Ruth HUNT dt Jacob & Lydia, Clinton Co., O.
----, --, --. Theodore, s Abel & Rebecca, b 1850,1,13; m Lizzie MOON, dt Pleasant & Huldah, b 1849,4,14
Ch: Frank b 1875, 3, 10
Walter " 1877, 12, 3

1821, 4, 26. Joseph rocf Center MM, dtd 1821,3,17
1823, 9, 25. Betsy, John, Rice & Owen, ch Joseph, recrq
1823, 10, 23. Joshua & w, Rebecca, & ch, Sarah, Isaac, Jonathan, Betsy, Matilda & Polly, rocf Honey Creek MM, Ind., dtd 1823 6,14
1825, 11, 24. Joshua dis disunity
1826, 4, 27. Joab & w, Ruth, & dt, Amey, rocf Fairfield MM, dtd 1825,12,31
1826, 10, 26. Joseph & ch, Elizabeth, John Milton & Owen, gct Fairfield MM
1829, 2, 23. Joab & fam gct Centre MM, O.
1829, 4, 23. John dis jH
1830, 6, 24. Sarah Jr. dis disunity
1830, 11, 25. James dis jH

WRIGHT, continued
1830, 11, 25. Sarah dis jH
1830, 11, 25. Elizabeth dis jH
1830, 11, 25. Sampson dis disunity
1832, 3, 19. Jemima dis disunity
1832, 3, 19. Rachel dis disunity
1832, 5, 21. Elizabeth dis disunity
1832, 5, 21. Anna (form Hiatt) dis mou
1834, 5, 19. Isaac dis mou
1835, 11, 23. Jonathan dis disunity
1837, 1, 23. Mary (form Moon) con mou
1837, 4, 17. Jonathan dis disunity
1845, 9, 15. Ruth gct Fairfield MM

* * * * * * *

CAREY
1859, 9, 29. Hannah m Jesse H. MENDENHALL

GARNER
1860, 9, 26. Martha m Lindley COPPOCK
1862, 4, 30. Rachel m Joseph MOORE

HADLEY
1831, 9, 22. Ann m Wm. BETTS

HUNT
1836, 10, 27. Rebecca m David HOCKETT
1847, 4, 29. Martha d bur Newbury

KESTER
1927, 8, 25. Mary M. d

MOON
----, --, --. Pleasant & Susannah

1864, 1, 18. Sarah M. rocf Minneapolis MM, Minn., dtd 1863,11,12
1873, 12, 22. Theodore recrq
1881, 7, 18. James recrq
1881, 10, 17. Sampson & w, Annie, recrq
1887, 12, 19. J. D. & w, Martha, & dt, Mary, rocf Fairfield MM, dtd 1887,11,19
1894, 3, 22. Theodore & ch, Frank M., Walter A., Elva N., Artlees, Leslie, Jessie L. & Minnie A., gct Wilmington MM, O.
1896, 6, 18. J. D. & w, Martha, & dt, Mary, gct Fairfield MM, O.
1913, 3, 20. Hugh & Robert recrq

* * * * * * *

Ch: Samuel b 1850, 9, 26
James
Arthur " 1854, 3, 3
Linley " 1857, 3, 21

PERRIN
1893, 11, 20. George, Sarah, Elias, Bertha, John H. & Melvin, recrq

SIMS
----, --, --. Hannah J., w Anslam, dt Wm. & Mary Fitzgerald, b 1840,12,3 d 1928,6,2

TOWNSEND
1857, 10, 29. Catherine B. m Lewis MILLS

WEST
1868, 10, 29. Sarah J. d

LEES CREEK MONTHLY MEETING

Lees Creek Monthly Meeting, located one and a half miles northwest of New Lexington, Highland County, was set off from Fairland Monthly Meeting by Fairfield Quarterly Meeting, 3 Mo. 15, 1817. This monthly meeting was laid down 2 Mo. 19, 1831.

Solomon Hodgson was the clerk, and Jonathan Hodgson and John Thornbrough were overseers. Other family names recorded are McPherson, Hockett, Evans, Branson, Beals, Green, Jackson, Crispin, Stanley, Hayworth and Antrim.

RECORDS

ADAMS
1926, 8, 19. Joseph rocf Hopewell MM, dtd 1825,11,10, endorsed by Fairfield MM, 1826,7,29
1826, 8, 19. Isaac rocf Hopewell MM, dtd 1825,10,6, endorsed by Fairfield MM, 1826, 7,29

ANTRIM
1821, 3, 17. Thomas & fam gct Springfield MM, Ind.

BANKSON
1824, 9, 18. Elizabeth recrq

BEALS
1818, 7, 18. Sarah dis
1819, 4, 17. Mary & s, Isaac, rocf Newberry MM, dtd 1819,3,25
1820, 11, 16. Mary gct New Garden MM, Ind.
1822, 7, 20. Nathan con mcd
1823, 3, 15. Nathan gct Springfield MM, Ind.
1824, 11, 20. John con mcd
1825, 12, 17. Ruth rmt Solomon Falkner
1826, 6, 17. Curtis & fam gct Cherry Grove MM, Ind.
1827, 4, 21. John gct Cherry Grove MM, Ind.
1827, 5, 25. Boheter dis mcd

BENTLEY
1821, 2, 17. Lydia rocf Chestnut Creek MM, Va., dtd 1819,11,27, endorsed from Fairfield MM, O., 1820,12,30

BOND
1819, 10, 16. Edward & w, Mary, rocf Cesars Creek MM, O., dtd 1819,9,24
1821, 7, 21. Edward & w gct Cesars Creek MM,O.

BRANSON
1821, 10, 20. Thomas con mcd
1822, 4, 20. Nathan dis disunity
1823, 1, 18. Isaac recrq
1823, 3, 15. Isaac gct Springfield MM, Ind.
1825, 6, 18. Thomas gct White River MM, Ind.
1826, 1, 21. David dis disunity
1826, 3, 18. Hannah dis

BRYANT
1817, 7, 19. Beulah rocf Mt. Pleasant MM, Va., dtd 1817,4,24, endorsed by Fairfield MM, 1817,6,28

CAREY
1817, 8, 16. Jonathan & w, Ruth, & ch, Zenas, Samuel, Benjamin, Mary Charlotte & Sylvanus, rocf Mt. Pleasant MM, Va., dtd 1817,4,26, endorsed by Fairfield MM, 1817, 6,28
1824, 1, 17. Zenas rmt Lydia Haines
1827, 11, 17. Samuel rmt Sarah Felps
1831, 1, 15. Samuel & fam gct Springfield MM

CARR
1820, 10, 21. Benjamin rmt Parmelia Evans

CLAIRWATER
1830, 8, 21. Hannah rocf Cherry Grove MM, Ind., dtd 1828,12,13, endorsed by Dover MM, 1830,2,18

COFFIN
1819, 9, 18. Mary rocf Lick Creek MM, dtd 1818,10,31, endorsed by Clear Creek MM, O., dtd 1819,8,14

CRISPEN
1824, 5, 15. John con mcd
1828, 2, 28. Phebe rst on consent of Hopewell MM, Va.
1829, 6, 20. John dis jH
1829, 7, 18. Phebe dis
1829, 11, 21. David rmt Rachel McPherson

DAVIS
1824, 11, 20. Peter rst on consent of New Garden MM, N. C.
1825, 12, 17. Mary recrq
1825, 12, 17. Thomas John & Jacob, ch Peter, recrq
1829, 3, 25. Harmon & fam gct Clear Creek MM
1829, 4, 18. Mary dis disunity
1830, 12, 18. Peter dis disunity

DERK
1826, 8, 19. Hannah rocf Fairfield MM, dtd 1826,5,19

DILLON
1818, 10, 17. Hannah dis

EASTLACK
1822, 5, 18. Marmaduke recrq

ELMORE
1817, 6, 21. John rocf Lost Creek MM, Tenn., dtd 1817,4,26, endorsed by Fairfield MM, 1817,5,31
1818, 1, 17. John rmt Ann Thornborough
1818, 3, 21. Nathan Thornbrough, s Ann Elmore recrq

EVANS
1820, 10, 21. Parmelia rmt Benjamin Carr
1827, 2, 17. Esther rmt Jonathan Hayworth
1830, 2, 1. Frances dis

FALKNER
1825, 12, 17. Solomon rmt Ruth Beals

FERGUSON
1830, 5, 15. Samuel gct Fairfield MM

FISHER
1828, 2, 28. John & w, Mary, & ch, Rebeccah Jane Nancy & Hiram, rocf Fairfield MM, dtd 1827,7,28
1830, 4, 17. Hiram & w, Rebecca, & ch, Jane Mary Amos Elizabeth & Jemima, rocf Fairfield MM

FOWLER
1817, 8, 16. Phebe gct New Garden MM, Ind.

HAINES
1819, 9, 18. Esther rmt Solomon Hiatt
1824, 1, 17. Lydia rmt Zenas Carey
1826, 3, 18. Mahlon con mcd

HARRIS
1825, 7, 16. Jane dis

HAYWORTH
1817, 8, 16. William con mcd
1819, 3, 20. Wm. & fam gct New Garden MM,Ind.
1820, 11, 16. David gct New Garden MM, Ind.
1821, 8, 18. James rst on consent of Fairfield MM
1822, 1, 19. Edward, Mary Ann & Joel, ch James, recrq
1824, 10, 16. James & fam gct White River MM, Ind.
1824, 10, 16. Jonathan & fam gct White River MM, Ind.
1825, 1, 15. James Jr. & fam gct White Lick MM, Ind.
1827, 2, 17. Jonathan rmt Esther Evans

HIATT
1819, 1, 16. Solomon rocf Clear Creek MM
1819, 5, 15. Christopher & fam gct New Garden MM, Ind.
1819, 9, 18. Solomon rmt Esther Haines
1820, 1, 15. Solomon gct New Garden MM, Ind.
1821, 4, 21. Jonathan rpd mcd

HOCKETT
1817, 5, 17. Benjamin & fam gct Newberry MM
1817, 6, 21. David & fam gct White Water MM, Ind.
1817, 8, 16. Hannah dis
1817, 10, 18. Wm. & fam gct New Garden MM,Ind.
1817, 10, 18. Joseph & fam gct New Garden MM, Ind.
1818, 10, 17. Hezekiah & fam gct New Garden MM, Ind.
1819, 1, 16. Sarah & ch, Phebe Alice Mary Agness & Joseph rocf White Water MM, Ind., dtd 1818,12,26
1822, 7, 20. Sarah & ch gct Cherry Grove MM, Ind.

HODGSON
1821, 9, 15. Mathew gct Clear Creek MM, to m Hannah Hunt
1822, 7, 20. Hannah rocf Clear Creek MM, dtd 1822,6,8
1823, 8, 16. John dis disunity
1824, 8, 21. Hezekiah con mcd
1825, 6, 18. Moses dis mou
1825, 7, 16. Mathew & fam gct Clear Creek MM, O.
1826, 1, 21. Anna rocf Clear Creek MM, dtd 1825,8,13
1826, 10, 21. Jane gct Springfield MM, Ind.
1830, 11, 20. John rmt Rebecca Hodgson
1830, 11, 20. Rebecca rmt John Hodson

HOLAWAY
1817, 9, 20. William & w, Sarah, & ch, Isaac, Elizabeth, Pleasant, Samuel, George, Sarah & Wm., rocf Clear Creek MM, O., dtd 1817,8,9
1818, 1, 17. Elizabeth [Hollaway] rmt Joab Thornborough
1819, 10, 16. Isaac [Holoway] con mcd
1820, 3, 18. John [Hollaway] & s, Joab, rocf Newberry MM, dtd 1820,2,24
1820, 4, 15. Betsy [Hollaway], dt John, recrq
1821, 12, 15. Pleasant [Holoway] dis mou
1822, 5, 18. Isaac [Holoway] dis disunity
1822, 5, 18. Louvicy [Holoway] dis
1823, 11, 15. Samuel dis mcd
1823, 11, 15. George dis mcd
1824, 2, 21. John & ch gct Fairfield MM
1826, 10, 21. Wm. & fam gct Springfield MM, Ind.

HOSKINS
1820, 12, 16. Joseph dis mcd
1821, 4, 21. George rocf Clear Creek MM, O., dtd 1821,3,10
1825, 5, 21. Eli dis mcd
1825, 5, 21. Moses Jr. con mcd
1828, 7, 19. Moses dis disunity
1829, 11, 21. Isaac rocf Clear Creek MM, dtd 1829,10,15

HUNT
1821, 9, 15. Mathew Hodgson gct Clear Creek MM, to m Hannah Hunt

HUSSEY
1829, 11, 21. Stephen rmt Rachel Thornburgh

JACKSON
1818, 3, 21. Wm. dis disunity
1818, 3, 21. Mary dis
1821, 7, 21. Jesse dis mcd

JESSOP
1817, 12, 17. Ann rocf New Garden MM, N. C., dtd 1817,11,29, endorsed by Fairfield MM, 1817,11,29

JOHNSON
1827, 5, 25. Abner rocf Fairfield MM, dtd 1823,2,22, endorsed by Green Plain MM, O., dtd 1827,5,2

JOHNSON, continued
1827, 5, 25. Hannah & dt, Louisa, rocf Fall Creek MM, dtd 1823,5,24, endorsed by Green Plain MM, O., 1827,5,2
1829, 10, 17. Abner dis disunity

JONES
1825, 1, 15. Abigail rocf Newberry MM

KINWORTHY
1821, 12, 15. Hudson Middleton gct Clear Creek MM, to m Rachel Kinworthy

McPHERSON
1821, 12, 15. Stephen rmt Mary Smith
1827, 1, 20. Charlotte rmt Job Smith
1829, 6, 20. John dis mcd
1829, 11, 21. Rachel rmt David Crispin

MIDDLETON
1821, 7, 21. Hudson rocf Salem MM, dtd 1821, 4,23
1821, 7, 21. Levi rocf Middleton MM, dtd 1821,4,23
1821, 9, 15. Levi con mcd
1821, 12, 15. Hudson gct Clear Creek MM, to m Rachel Kinworthy
1825, 6, 18. Hudson gct White Lick MM, Ind.
1826, 6, 17. Levi & fam gct White Lick MM, Ind.

MORRIS
1825, 1, 15. David rocf Chestnut Creek MM, Va., dtd 1824,8,28, endorsed by Fall Creek MM, O., 1824,10,23
1829, 7, 18. Lydia rocf Fall Creek MM, dtd 1829,5,25

OVERMAN
1826, 4, 15. Charles Postgate gct Fall Creek MM, to m Anna Overman

PHELPS
1827, 4, 21. Meriam & ch, Sarah, Eli, Joel, Martin, Martha, John & Mary recrq
1827, 11, 17. Sarah [Felps] rmt Samuel Carcy

PICKERING
1826, 1, 21. James Rees gct Fairfield MM, to m Elenor [Pickron]
1826, 8, 19. Wm. & fam rocf Fairfield MM, dtd 1826,7,29
1828, 10, 18. Jonathan rocf Fairfield MM, dtd 1828,7,26
1828, 10, 18. Lydia rocf Fairfield MM, dtd 1828,7,26

PIKE
1818, 9, 19. Hannah rocf Fairfield MM, dtd 1818,8,29

POSTGATE
1825, 11, 19. Thomas & fam gct Honey Creek MM, Ind.
1826, 4, 15. Charles gct Fall Creek MM, to m Anna Overman
1829, 4, 18. Charles [Posegate] gct Clear Creek MM

REES
1826, 1, 21. James gct Fairfield MM, to m Elenor Pickron
1826, 5, 20. Eleanor rocf Fairfield MM, dtd 1826,3,25
1830, 9, 18. Jonathan rocf Newhope MM, Tenn., dtd 1830,4,17

SMITH
1821, 12, 15. Mary rmt Stephen McPherson
1822, 11, 16. Amos rmt Margaret Thornbrough
1827, 1, 20. Job rmt Charlotte McPherson
1827, 7, 21. Louisa dis
1828, 6, 21. Job dis
1828, 6, 21. Charlotte dis
1829, 7, 18. Amos & fam gct White River MM, Ind.
1830, 10, 16. Evan con mcd

STANLEY
1817, 7, 19. John gct New Garden MM, Ind.

TERREL
1827, 8, 18. David Jr. rocf Fairfield MM, dtd 1827,5,26

THORNBURGH
1817, 10, 18. Ann [Thornbrough] rst on consent of Fairfield MM
1818, 1, 17. Ann [Thornborough] rmt John Elmore
1818, 1, 17. Joab [Thornborough] rmt Elizabeth Hollaway
1818, 3, 21. Nathan [Thornborough], s Ann Elmore, recrq
1818, 4, 18. Nathan [Thornborough] rmt Ann Wright
1818, 6, 20. Isaac [Thornborough] Jr. rocf New Garden MM, N. C., dtd 1818,3,28
1818, 9, 19. Nathan [Thornborough] & w gct New Garden MM, Ind.
1819, 9, 18. Edward [Thornborough] & fam gct New Garden MM, Ind.
1819, 9, 18. Joseph [Thornborough] & fam gct New Garden MM, Ind.
1820, 6, 17. Joseph [Thornbrough] Jr. con mcd
1821, 12, 15. Joseph Jr. dis disunity
1822, 4, 20. Nathan, minor, gct Cherry Grove MM, Ind.
1822, 11, 16. Margaret [Thornbrough] rmt Amos Smith
1825, 7, 16. John Jr. & fam gct Smithfield MM, Ind.
1825, 9, 17. Job con mcd
1826, 8, 19. Joab & fam gct Smithfield MM, Ind.
1826, 8, 19. Job & fam gct Smithfield MM,

THORNBURGH, continued
Ind.
1828, 10, 18. Isaac Jr. dis
1829, 10, 17. Joseph & w gct Cherry Grove MM, Ind.
1829, 11, 21. Rachel rmt Stephen Hussey

VANPELT
1826, 3, 18. Catherine rocf Fall Creek MM, dtd 1826,2,16

WILKINS
1828, 5, 17. John dis mcd

WILKINSON
1825, 12, 17. Joseph & w, Sarah, & s, Francis, rocf Fairfield MM, dtd 1825,11,26
1825, 12, 17. John rocf Fairfield MM, dtd 1825,11,26

WILLETS
1817, 12, 17. Charity rocf Deep River MM, N. C., dtd 1817,9,1
1817, 12, 17. Charity Jr. rocf Deep River MM, N. C., dtd 1817,9,1
1818, 5, 16. Henry rocf Clear Creek MM, O., dtd 1818,4,11
1820, 7, 16. Henry gct Stillwater MM
1820, 7, 16. Charity gct Stillwater MM
1820, 7, 16. Charity Jr. gct Stillwater MM

WILLIS
1818, 6, 20. Joel & w, Hannah, & s, Jesse, rocf New Garden MM, N. C., dtd 1818,3,28
1818, 6, 20. Jonathan & w, Hannah, & ch, Joel & Isaac, rocf New Garden MM, N. C., dtd 1818,3,28
1821, 7, 21. Joel & fam gct Fall Creek MM
1821, 8, 18. Jonathan & fam gct Cherry Grove MM, Ind.
1828, 6, 21. Joel & w, Hannah, rocf Fall Creek MM, dtd 1828,5,24

WRIGHT
1817, 9, 20. Ann recrq
1818, 4, 18. Ann rmt Nathan Thornborough

HOPEWELL MONTHLY MEETING

Hopewell Monthly Meeting, Highland County, Ohio, was established 12 Mo. 3, 1874, by Fairfield Quarterly Meeting. It was made up of Walnut Creek, Hardin's Creek and Fall Creek Preparative Meetings. It is now (1946) made up of Centerfield and Hardins Creek Meetings and is held alternately at the two places.

RECORDS

ABBOTT
1900, 6, 2. W. E. & w, Minnie, & ch, Fay, rocf Sabina MM & relrq

ABERS
1878, 3, 2. Eliza relrq

ADAMS
1889, 6, 1. John H. recrq
1892, 4, 2. John H., Bell, Gerta B. & Johnny H. relrq

ALEXANDER
1911, 3, 4. Rufus recrq

ANDERSON
1914, 6, 13. Elmer E., Sarah Isabelle & Ruth recrq

AULT
1892, 2, 6. Elizabeth recrq
1904, 9, 1. Elizabeth & dt, Anna, relrq

AUSTIN
1884, 10, 4. Lydia A. & dt, Olive E., gct Plainfield MM, Ind.

BACKENSTOE
1917, 4, 14. Nannie recrq

BADGLEY
1914, 6, 13. Cassius & Olive recrq
1925, 7, 10. Cash & Olive relrq

BALDWIN
1912, 2, 10. Ernest recrq
1914, 2, 14. Bessie, Fred & Lena recrq
1916, 7, 7. Oren A., minor s Ernest & Bessie, recrq
1916, 7, 8. Helen Cordelia, minor dt Fred & Lena, recrq

BANKS
1914, 10, 18. Sarah J. d

1889, 5, 4. James, Sarah Jane & Myrta recrq
1901, 11, 2. Sidney recrq
1912, 7, 13. Sidney relrq

BARNES
1898, 6, 4. Earnest recrq

BARRETT
1820, 10, 24. Rhoda, w Geo. W., dt Wm. & Mary, -----, b
1839, 2, 6. Mary, w John, dt Joseph & Nancy Davis, b
1842, 10, 26. James J., s Ellis & Anna, b
----, --, --. David, s Jesse & Margaret, b 1821,8,20; m Millicent JURY, dt Wm. & Elizabeth, b 1824,2,16
----, --, --. Denson, s Ellis & Anna, b 1830, 7,3; m Hannah WRIGHT, dt Wm. & Rachel, b 1825,7,13

Ch:				
Rachel A.	b 1855,	1,	3	
George E.	" 1857,	3,	30	
William W.	" 1859,	2,	28	d 1932,11,14
Clara C.	" 1864,	10,	18	

----, --, --. Richard L. b 1805,3,-- d 1877, 10,--; m 2nd Mary Jane WILEY, dt Joseph & Ann, b 1822,3,22

Ch:			
Mary	b 1855,	4,	16
Edgar	" 1857,	8,	21

----, --, --. Joseph, s Levi & Delilah, b 1847,7,9; m Mary MAGOON

Ch:			
Levi	b 1868,	9,	23
Alfred	" 1870,	1,	12
Anna	" 1872,	5,	4

Joseph m 2nd Virginia Frances McDANIEL, dt Randolph & Mary, b 1857,3,31

Ch:			
Leslie	b 1876,	12,	13
David	" 1878,	5,	17
Mary	" 1880,	3,	10

----, --, --. Richard Cyrus, s Richard L. & Sarah, b 1839,7,23; m Abi JOHNSON, dt Jarad M. & Mary C., b 1844,2,19

Ch:			
Richard Warren	b 1872,	7,	11
Walter C.	" 1875,	10,	3
Sarah E.	" 1881,	10,	11
Mary C.	" 1887,	5,	21

1871, 2, 24. Malinda, dt Jesse & Mary, b
----, --, --. Enos J., s David & Millicent (Jury), b 1848,11,18; m Lavena TODHUNTER, dt Amos & Emily, b 1850,10,6

Ch:			
Horace Leslie	b 1874,	1,	3
Ralph E.	" 1883,	12,	2
Mabel E.	" 1888,	8,	29

----, --, --. Ralph E. m Edith JOHNSON

Ch:			
C. Maynard	b 1908,	10,	24
E. Iona	" 1910,	3,	11
Frederick Enos	" 1915,	6,	15

1930, 11, 5. Maggie d

1876, 5, 6. John recrq
1877, 4, 7. Mary recrq
1877, 4, 7. Virginia F. recrq
1878, 7, 6. Phebe dropped from mbrp
1882, 4, 5. Mary Jane recrq
1882, 11, 4. Emma recrq
1884, 2, 2. Frances recrq
1884, 6, 9. Benjamin relrq
1884, 10, 4. James G. gct Kansas City MM, Mo.
1885, 1, 3. Thomas & w & dt dis
1889, 5, 4. Cora recrq
1889, 8, 3. Maggie recrq
1890, 12, 6. Etta relrq
1893, 3, 4. Stanley recrq
1893, 5, 6. Homer dropped from mbrp
1895, 2, 2. Elsie recrq
1895, 10, 5. Mary A. gct Columbus MM, O.
1896, 6, 6. Lida gct Fairfield MM, O.

BARRETT, continued
1897, 4, 3. W. O. Vernon relrq
1897, 5, 1. James G. relrq
1897, 10, 2. Frank rocf Wilmington MM, dtd 1897,7,10
1901, 4, 6. Fannie recrq
1901, 9, 7. Nellie recrq
1901, 10, 5. Cyrus & w, Abbie, & ch, Sarah Elizabeth & Mary Coffin, gct Wilmington MM, O.
1902, 3, 1. Walter relrq
1903, 9, 5. Denson gct Wilmington MM, O.
1904, 12, 3. Frank gct Fairfield MM, O.
1905, 2, 4. Warren relrq
1907, 3, 2. Elsa relrq
1911, 1, 7. Edith recrq
1912, 2, 10. Jessie recrq
1912, 3, 9. Nora recrq
1913, 4, 12. Pearl recrq
1914, 2, 14. Bertha, Lydia & Benjamin recrq
1915, 12, 1. Byrdia recrq
1917, 4, 14. Ethel recrq
1927, 8, 12. Mary & Lydia Ann gct Leesburg MM, O.

BAYHAM
1901, 4, 6. George & w & ch roc

BEARD
1895, 2, 2. Edgar recrq

BEATS
1893, 5, 6. Emma L. dropped from mbrp

BENNETT
1911, 3, 4. Frederick recrq

BEYRIE
1879, 5, 3. Edwin gct Poplar Ridge MM, Ind.

BINEGAR
1910, 11, 3. Lois Todhunter d

1899, 5, 6. Mary J. gct Clear Creek MM, O.
1900, 12, 1. Mary J. rocf Walnut Creek MM

BOGGESS
1892, 6, 4. Sarah recrq
1897, 3, 5. David [Boggus] recrq
1904, 9, 1. Sarah [Bogess] relrq
1904, 11, 5. Mattie relrq

BOILS
1858, 2, 6. Bell, dt Neal & Elizabeth, b

BOON
1876, 7, 1. Charles gct Spiceland MM, Ind.

BORDEN
1893, 8, 5. C. A. recrq
1900, 12, 1. Myrtle recrq

BOWERS
1879, 6, 7. Henrietta Arabella gct Union MM, Minn.
1885, 3, 7. Flora relrq

BOYLES
1876, 3, 4. Bell recrq

BROWN
1820, 7, 10. Isaac b
----, --, --. Elgar Jr., s Elgar & Mary, b 1835,11,16; m Sarah BOND, dt Benj. & Lydia, b 1836,12,16
Ch: Emma L. b 1862, 6, 11
Mary L. " 1865, 4, 4
Mattie E. " 1867, 9, 17
Sadie " 1870, 8, 23 d 1871,2 9
Joseph A. " 1872, 2, 13
Bessie I. " 1876, 8, 21

1880, 9, 4. Elgar & w, Sarah, & ch, Emma, Mary, Martie, Joseph & Bessie, gct Spiceland MM, Ind.
1880, 9, 4. Emma gct Spiceland MM, Ind.
1884, 4, 5. Sarah recrq
1885, 2, 7. Elijah, Eliza & Vinta recrq
1891, 6, 6. Ellie & Louie recrq •
1892, 6, 4. Saida recrq
1892, 10, 1. E. A. dis disunity
1893, 3, 4. Bertie G. recrq
1894, 4, 7. Vinta relrq
1895, 2, 2. Frank recrq
1895, 2, 2. Arch & Bert recrq
1897, 5, 1. Caroline recrq
1899, 4, 1. Arch dropped from mbrp
1900, 11, 3. Elijah gct West Fork MM, O.
1901, 7, 6. Caroline dropped from mbrp
1923, 12, 8. Geneva recrq

BUDD
1891, 8, 1. Leroy W., Anne Eliza, Melvin W., Mary & Berry recrq
1891, 8, 1. Otice, Jennie & Orlan recrq
1892, 9, 5. Ann E. relrq
1893, 3, 4. Otis & fam relrq

BUNTON
1906, 7, 7. Letta dropped from mbrp

BURGESS
----, --, --. Joseph, s Daniel & Ruth, b 1814, 3,31; m Phebe BALLARD, dt Spencer & Rebecca, b 1816,4,15 d 1907,9,2
Ch: Spencer W. b 1845, 4, 3
Rebecca " 1849, 1, 7
Jordan " 1850, 11, 21
Ruth " 1853, 1, 22
Mary B. " 1856, 1, 24
Joseph " 1858, 10, 23
Phebe " 1858, 10, 23
----, --, --. Joseph & Ruth
Ch: Jordan b 1850, 11, 21
Joseph " 1858, 10, 23

BURGESS, continued
----, --, --. Beverly, s Daniel & Ruth, b 1821,7,31; m Malinda LEONARD, dt John & Lydia, b 1825,9,22
Ch: Harvey A. b 1857, 7, 3
Emma E. " 1866, 4, 23
Eli " 1854, 1, 5 d 1934, 1,12
----, --, --. Eli M., s Beverly & Malinda, b 1854,1,5; m Ida M. TODHUNTER, dt Abner & Emiline, b 1857,5,30
Ch: Maud b 1877, 4, 23
1907, 3, 30. Robert d

1883, 8, 4. Beverly & w, Malinda, dis
1883, 8, 4. Joseph & w, Phebe, dis
1892, 5, 7. Maud recrq
1899, 4, 1. Joseph & w, Phebe, rst rq
1899, 4, 1. Beverly & w, Malinda, rst rq
1904, 4, 2. Eunice M. & Judith E. recrq
1910, 4, 2. Robert dropped from mbrp
1912, 2, 10. John H. recrq
1927, 9, 9. Harvey dropped from mbrp

BURNETT
1901, 12, 7. Alice T. relrq

BUSSEY
----, --, --. Wm. H. b 1854,10,--; m Emma BROWN b 1857,10,--
1862, 3, --. George b
1864, 3, --. James b

1884, 4, 5. Wm. & Emma L. [Bussy] recrq
1891, 12, 5. James H. recrq
1892, 2, 6. George A. recrq
1911, 4, 4. Lorella recrq
1913, 1, 11. Elizabeth recrq

BUZZARD
1860, 6, 19. Luella, dt Wm. & Sarah, b

1876, 5, 6. Louella recrq

CALDWELL
1895, 2, 2. David & Emma recrq
1904, 5, 7. David & w, Emma, dropped from mbrp
1912, 4, 13. J. M. & Mary recrq
1922, 1, 4. Ione recrq

CALVIN
1900, 7, 7. Edith dropped from mbrp

CAMPBELL
1889, 6, 1. Eva recrq
1893, 5, 6. Eva dropped from mbrp

CANDY
1824, 5, 25. Samuel, s David & Mary, b

1876, 3, 4. Newton recrq
1876, 5, 6. Samuel & Mary recrq
1878, 7, 6. Milton dis
1878, 7, 6. Mary dropped from mbrp

CARMINE
1897, 4, 3. Ashford & Clara E. recrq

CARMEAN
1882, 4, 5. John & Wm. J. [Carnean] recrq
1898, 3, 5. Harry, Sadie & Willie recrq
1915, 2, 12. George recrq
1922, 1, 4. John recrq
1923, 12, 8. George dropped from mbrp
1924, 12, 13. Blanche, Wayne & Floyd recrq
1927, 9, 9. Johnny dropped from mbrp

CARSON
1877, 1, 6. Nancy recrq
1884, 5, 3. Ellen recrq
1898, 3, 5. McClan, Rosetta & Ellba recrq

CARTER
1908, 4, 4. Thomas C. & fam roc
1919, 2, 8. Almina relrq

CARY
1913, 1, 11. Elmer & Elizabeth recrq

CASS
1924, 12, 13. Burch recrq

CHAPLIN
1919, 10, 11. Effie Elliott relrq

CHAPMAN
1876, 3, 4. Frank recrq

CHEW
----, --, --. William b 1816,3,12; m Julianna TODHUNTER, dt Abner & Elizabeth, b 1816,3, 20
Ch: Matilda b 1844, 12, 3
Sarah
Louisa " 1847, 9, 13
Rees E.
Minerva A.
Eva " 1870, 2, 22

1885, 7, 4. Wm. & w, Julia Ann, gct Wilmington MM

CHRISMAN
1901, 9, 7. Wm., Amanda & John recrq
1911, 4, 4. Josephine & Grace recrq
1913, 1, 11. Mary recrq
1915, 12, 1. Estella, Margery & Carrie recrq
1916, 11, 11. Wilber L., Carl O. & Wendell L., minors, recrq
1917, 3, 10. Carrie & Emma recrq
1920, 3, 13. Wilbur & Carl recrq

CLAY
1915, 2, 12. Madge recrq

CLEMENTS
1891, 6, 6. Emma & Hattie recrq
1913, 1, 11. Raymond, Margaret & Dorothy recrq

CLEMSON
1892, 6, 4. Anna recrq

CLINE
1907, 3, 2. Jennie recrq

COAL
1891, 8, 1. Lucinda recrq

COCKERILL
1832, 8, 26. Mary, w James, dt James & Sarah Hadley, b

1881, 12, 3. Ina B. recrq
1884, 5, 3. Nellie & Walter [Cockrill], ch James, recrq
1885, 4, 11. James [Cockerell] recrq
1890, 3, 1. Ina relrq
1898, 12, 3. Nellie [Cockerell] gct Wilmington MM
1901, 10, 5. James [Cockerall] gct Wilmington MM, O.

COLE
1917, 4, 14. J. L. recrq
1923, 12, 8. J. L. dropped from mbrp

COOK
1906, 4, 7. Wm. & Eliza recrq
1910, 10, 1. Elmer roc
1911, 4, 4. Ella recrq
1914, 2, 14. Almira recrq

COOPER
1875, 4, 3. Sallie recrq
1877, 3, 3. Eli & w gct Fairfield MM
1877, 5, 5. Amy recrq
1895, 2, 2. Charles recrq
1898, 3, 5. Lettie recrq
1898, 7, 2. Samuel J. Ewing & w, Mary Ellen, & adopted ch, Chas. Cooper, gct Fairmount MM, Ind.
1914, 2, 14. Earnest recrq

COPELAND
1912, 2, 10. Samuel, Adelia, Cordie & Roy recrq
1923, 12, 8. Samuel, Delia, Lee & Stella dropped from mbrp

COURTNEY
1877, 3, 3. William [Cortney] recrq
1878, 7, 6. Wm. gct Cedar Creek MM, Ia.

COWGILL
1802, 6, 10. Benjamin, s Henry & Eleanor, b
----, --, --. John, s Henry & Eleanor, b 1810,10,2; m Lydia COFFIN, dt Samuel & Dinah, b 1812,12,20
Ch: Mary E. b 1841, 10, 25
David " 1853, 2, 27
1855, 3, 19. Charles G., s Benjamin & Rachel, b
----, --, --. Jonathan B., s Benjamin & Rachel, b 1846,9,19; m Ellen PARKER, dt Samuel & Mary, b 1851,5,7
Ch: William B. b 1869, 12, 25
Berch M. " 1872, 10, 28
Albert G. " 1875, 9, 28
Clarence O." 1878, 4, 11

1875, 3, 6. Samuel S. & w, Sarah E., & ch, S. Macy, Luzena T. & Lydia M., gct Duck Creek MM, Ind.
1876, 3, 4. Charles G. recrq
1884, 4, 5. Lydia S. recrq
1895, 2, 2. Ethel, Imo & Chloe recrq
1897, 3, 5. Burch M. recrq
1898, 7, 2. Earnest gct Indianapolis MM, Ind.
1899, 1, 7. Birch gct Fairmount MM, Ind.
1899, 1, 7. Earnest gct Indianapolis MM, Ind.
1901, 9, 7. T. Roy & Martha B. recrq
1905, 6, 3. David & fam gct Paomi MM, Colo.
1911, 4, 4. Carrie recrq
1916, 11, 11. Harry, Frank, Roderick & Sarah Ellen, minors, recrq
1920, 3, 13. Frank, Roderick & Sarah Ellen recrq

COWMAN
1818, 10, 30. Jennette, w John, dt Daniel & Ruth Burgess, b

1895, 2, 2. Laura recrq
1904, 2, 6. Inez [Cowmans] relrq

COWNE
1914, 2, 14. Reuben recrq
1923, 12, 8. Reuben dropped from mbrp

COX
1896, 11, 7. Myrta relrq
1901, 4, 6. Robert & Sarah recrq
1906, 7, 7. Robert dropped from mbrp

CREAMER
1913, 4, 12. Ollie recrq

CROCK
1913, 5, 10. Austie Stephens relrq

CROPPER
1895, 2, 2. Mary J., Etta & Lowell recrq
1915, 2, 12. Albert recrq
1923, 12, 8. Albert dropped from mbrp

CURTAIN
1910, 4, 2. Margaret recrq

DAVIDSON
1917, 3, 10. Clara recrq
1920, 3, 13. Beryl recrq

DAVIS
----, --, --. Thomas T., s Joseph & Nancy, b 1837,5,26; m Nancy COLLINS, dt John & Susan, b 1837,8,4
Ch: Mary E. b 1860, 3, 24
Emma " 1866, 4, 21
1932, 8, 3. Jennie d

1876, 3, 4. Thomas F. recrq
1878, 7, 6. Jennie dropped from mbrp
1884, 4, 5. Joseph C., Wm. J. & Anna recrq
1891, 4, 4. J. Harvey recrq
1904, 2, 6. Thomas & Nancy gct Fairfield MM, O.
1910, 4, 2. Henry, Mary, Charles dropped from mbrp
1917, 11, 10. Harley & Jennie recrq

DAWS
1908, 8, 29. Plympton d

1907, 3, 2. Henry, Mary & Charlie recrq
1908, 7, 4. Plympton recrq
1908, 7, 4. Margaret recrq

DEVON
1876, 3, 4. Frank M. recrq

DEVOS
1850, 2, 17. Nancy, w Samuel, dt Thos. P. & Clarinda Terrell, b

1884, 5, 3. Samuel [Devoss] & w, Nancy, & ch, Clara G., Bertha E. & David J., recrq

DICKENSON
1891, 8, 1. Charles, Ola & Roy C. recrq
1904, 10, 1. Chas., Ola & Ray C. dropped from mbrp

DILL
1884, 5, 3. James & w, Eliza, & ch, Anna A. & Elizabeth J., recrq

DIVEN
----, --, --. Frank, s James & Catharine, b 1852,9,11; m Sarah FETTRO, dt Jacob & Amy, b 1851,6,11
Ch: Charles b 1877, 5, 1
James " 1879, 1, 30
Mary

1906, 8, 4. Inez Elsie [Divens] recrq
1909, 7, 3. Elsie Barrett [Divens] relrq

DODDS
1932, 8, 31. Mary E. d

1892, 5, 7. Carrie & Ollie recrq
1895, 3, 2. Wilbur & Ray recrq
1897, 5, 1. Leslie recrq
1897, 6, 5. Isaac & Mary recrq
1901, 6, 1. Zilla recrq
1905, 1, 7. Ray & Wilbur dropped from mbrp
1912, 2, 10. Margaery L. recrq
1912, 2, 10. Otto recrq
1914, 2, 14. Joseph recrq
1928, 6, 8. Leslie & Mary gct Samantha Mtg

DORAN
1878, 7, 6. James & Wm. dropped from mbrp

DOSTER
1905, 3, 4. Lewis dropped from mbrp

DOUGHERTY
1897, 5, 1. Henrietta recrq
1899, 10, 7. Henrietta relrq

DOWELL
1832, 9, 6. Almarinda, w Geo., dt Levi & Mariah Ellis, b

1905, 3, 4. Almarinda [Dowel] dropped from mbrp

DRACE
1915, 4, 10. Margaret recrq

DUDLEY
1914, 6, 13. Clara recrq

DUKE
1897, 3, 5. Martha recrq

DUNCAN
1891, 6, 6. Lee recrq

DUTTON
1918, 7, 13. Dorothy Dean recrq

DWYER
1889, 5, 4. Joseph J. & Sarah Jane recrq
1922, 2, 11. Sarah gct Leesburg MM, O.

EARL
1917, 4, 14. Nettie recrq

EASTER
1884, 6, 9. Amy relrq
1891, 6, 6. Rachel recrq
1893, 5, 6. Wm. & Edward dropped from mbrp
1923, 12, 9. Blanch dropped from mbrp

EDMOND
1891, 8, 1. Annie recrq

ELLIOTT
1881, 3, 5. James & fam recrq
1901, 7, 6. James, Jane, Ida, Vernon, Earnest & Jody dropped from mbrp
1912, 2, 10. Mary E. recrq

ELLIS
1817, 10, 1. Elijah, s David & Hannah, b
1820, 3, 4. Sophia, dt David & Hannah, b
1820, 10, 10. Eliza, dt Abel & Rhoda Thornburg, b
----, --, --. Levi m Maria DOSTER, dt John, b 1800,6,22
Ch: Caroline b 18--, 3, 28
1820, 12, 6. Thomas, s David & Hannah, b
1826, 11, 30. Mary, dt John & Mourning Arthur, b
1845, 5, 17. David W., s Elijah & Jane, b
1846, 6, 9. Joseph R., s Elijah & Jane, b
----, --, --. Harmanus, s Levi & Maria, b 1827,8,2; m Martha FISHBACK, dt Thomas & Martha, b 1832,9,15
Ch: Conda S. b 1853, 6, 4
Malven Ursula " 1875, 1, 16
Harmanus m 2nd Elizabeth J. ----- b 1839,4,28
----, --, --. Cyrenus, s Elijah & Jane, b 1848,11,10; m Rebecca TERRELL, dt T. P. & Clarinda, b 1852,7,28
Ch: Lavelle b 1871, 3, 17
Lester " 1879, 11, 5
1875, 4, 23. Etta, dt Joseph R. & Lydia (Zimmerman), b
----, --, --. Joseph R. & Mary E. (Mary E. b 1862,8,17)
Ch: Harley b 1881, 12, 19
Elijah Leroy " 1888, 8, 29
Ruth May " 1891, 4, 3
Ada " 1895, 4, 25

1878, 7, 6. Lizzie dropped from mbrp
1878, 7, 6. Linius relrq
1882, 11, 4. Martha dis
1884, 5, 3. Mary E. & ch, Harley G., recrq
1892, 4, 2. Eliza gct Amboy MM, Ind.
1898, 3, 5. Harley & Leroy recrq
1898, 3, 5. Rebecca recrq
1900, 3, 3. Harley relrq
1901, 12, 7. D. Webster relrq
1905, 3, 4. Harmanus & Lizzie dropped from mbrp
1905, 6, 3. Harley recrq
1907, 3, 2. Zella recrq
1907, 3, 2. Wm. A. recrq

ELTON
1884, 4, 5. Frank recrq

ENGLE
1900, 9, 1. Cora gct Clear Creek MM, O.

ERSKINE
1846, 12, 12. Olive D., dt Joseph & Phebe Burgess, b

1884, 6, 9. Olive D. & dt, Ethel, relrq
1894, 5, 5. Maud recrq
1895, 2, 2. Wm. recrq
1895, 2, 2. Sarah & Addie recrq
1915, 4, 10. Clarence & Viola recrq
1915, 6, 12. Heressi relrq
1929, 4, 12. Irene, Lucile & Robert recrq

ERVING
1876, 9, 2. Mary E. recrq

ESTLE
----, --, --. James & Rebecca
Ch: William b 1820, 5, 19
Meriba " 1823, 11, 5

EVANS
1879, 10, 4. Mary Ann gct Fairfield MM, O.
1883, 7, 7. Samuel & w, Mary Ann, rocf Fairfield MM, O.
1884, 4, 5. Charles, Emma & Alva recrq
1889, 5, 4. John Emmerson & Leone Catherine recrq
1904, 3, 5. Charles [Evens] relrq
1904, 5, 7. Sarah [Evens] recrq
1911, 4, 4. Emerson relrq
1924, 11, 9. Clara R. relrq

EWING
1891, 6, 6. Cooper M. & William recrq
1898, 7, 2. Samuel & Mary & adopted ch, Chas. Cooper, gct Fairfield MM, O.

FAIRLEY
----, --, --. Cyrus W. b 1849,--,--; m Hannah ----- b 1857,--,--
1861, 10, --. Christina, dt James & Mary, b
1877, --, --. Charley b
1879, --, --. Rosa b
1883, --, --. Herman b

1876, 5, 6. Christina recrq
1889, 6, 1. John recrq
1891, 6, 6. Rosa recrq
1893, 5, 6. John dropped from mbrp
1903, 8, 1. Ruth relrq
1903, 9, 5. Grant & w, Callie, gct Wilmington MM, O.
1905, 11, 4. Wilmer relrq
1914, 2, 14. Walter recrq
1928, 7, 13. Walter relrq

FANNING
1891, 6, 6. John recrq

FENNER
1893, 5, 6. Lucy & Frank dropped from mbrp

FETTRO
----, --, --. Jacob m Amy WHITE, dt Wm. & Dorcas, b 1816,--,--
Ch: Isabel b 1855, --, --
Jacob " 1859, --, --

1884, 6, 9. Jacob & w, Luella, & dt, Grace

FETTRO, continued
& Ethel relrq

FIGGINS
1878, 3, 2. Elizabeth [Figgans] & dt, Alice E. & Nancy M., roc
1897, 6, 5. Thomas E., Elizabeth & Minnie (Figgons] recrq
1906, 7, 7. Cora dropped from mbrp
1927, 9, 9. Cora dropped from mbrp
1932, 2, 12. Elizabeth gct Leesburg MM, O.

FINIGAN
1893, 5, 6. Ella dropped from mbrp

FISHBACK
1878, 7, 6. Lydia Margaret dropped from mbrp

FORAKER
1931, 1, 8. Emma C. d

1914, 5, 9. John H., Emma C., George J. & Mayme M. recrq

FOREMAN
1910, 3, 5. Sarah Jane Evans relrq

FORTE
1922, 3, 11. Fay recrq
1927, 9, 9. Fay dropped from mbrp

FORTIER
1907, 3, 2. Henry, Elbert & Waunita N. recrq

FULKERSON
1929, 10, 5. Sarah E. d

1914, 6, 13. Sarah recrq

GARMAN
1895, 4, 6. Ellie G. recrq

GEBHART
1901, 4, 6. Margaret recrq

GEORGE
1878, 7, 6. Ellen dropped from mbrp

GIBSON
1905, 12, 2. Abion M. & w recrq
1911, 4, 4. Olive recrq

GLEADELL
----, --, --. Thomas [Gleadall], s Ambrose & Hannah, b 1845,3,30; m Euphemia TEMPLIN, dt Milton & Margaret, b 1850,4,21
Ch: Mirtie b 1875, 6, 20
Elmer " 1877, 8, 28
Maggie " 1880, 1, 16

1875, 1, 2. Euphemia [Gladle] recrq
1876, 3, 4. Thomas [Gladle] recrq
1889, 5, 4. Henry, Frant T. & Mary [Gladle] recrq
1889, 5, 4. Myrta [Gladle] recrq
1889, 6, 1. Harvey [Gladle] recrq
1895, 2, 2. Wm. recrq
1896, 5, 2. Harry gct Marion MM, Ind.
1901, 7, 6. Henry [Gladall] dropped from mbrp
1916, 7, 8. Pearl Leota, dt Elmer & Minnie, recrq
1920, 3, 13. Frank gct Leesburg MM, O.
1923, 7, 14. Euphemia & Myrtle gct Leesburg MM, O.

GRANDELL
1892, 5, 7. Berta recrq
1914, 6, 13. Hattie [Grandle] gct Fairfield MM, O.

GRAY
1884, 5, 3. Lilly [Grey], dt Milly, recrq
1898, 7, 2. Lizzie recrq
1911, 9, 9. Lizzie dropped from mbrp

GRIFFITH
1877, 3, 3. Edward recrq
1895, 2, 2. Edward M. & Dora A. recrq
1899, 4, 1. Edward & Dora G. dropped from mbrp

GRIM
1892, 12, 3. John, Martha & Elsa recrq
1906, 10, 6. John & Martha relrq

GRIMSLEY
1882, 4, 5. George L. & Lucinda recrq
1895, 3, 2. Isaiah recrq
1901, 7, 6. Isaiah [Grisley] dropped from mbrp

GROVE
1898, 6, 4. Walter, Ida & Mark recrq
1899, 4, 1. M. C. dropped from mbrp
1914, 6, 13. George & Elizabeth recrq
1916, 9, 9. Lizzie [Groves] relrq

HADLEY
1895, 2, 2. Ambrose M. gct Hazeldell MM, Ind.

HAINES
1893, 3, 4. Lucy Maybel, Alma Clarinda, Louis Paul, Phyllis Irena recrq
1894, 6, 2. Frank & w, Alveretta, relrq
1896, 5, 2. Ella Brown gct Fairfield MM, O.
1910, 9, 3. David, Samantha & Mary roc

HAINSWORTH
1891, 2, 7. Eliza recrq
1897, 4, 3. Eliza gct Sabina MM, O.

HALE
1917, 11, 10. Kittie recrq

HALE, continued
1921, 7, 9. Kittie gct Marysville MM, Tenn.

HAMILTON
1904, 9, 1. R. F. & Minnie relrq
1906, 4, 7. Huston recrq
1915, 6, 12. M. O. & w recrq
1916, 7, 8. Hubert Floyd, s Huston & Maggie, recrq
1916, 7, 8. Helen Euphemia, dt Huston & Maggie, recrq
1916, 7, 8. Truman Leslie, Lloyd Wesley & Rexie Ione, ch Rosco & Minnie, recrq
1927, 9, 9. Houston & Maggie dropped from mbrp

HAMMER
1922, 1, 4. Lacy recrq

HAMMOND
1911, 4, 4. Vernon recrq
1920, 3, 13. Grace L. recrq

HANCHER
1912, 3, 9. Leonard recrq
1915, 10, 9. Leonard gct Fairfield MM, O.

HARRISON
1905, 2, 4. Wm. recrq

HART
1907, 6, 1./ Louie relrq

HARTMAN
1907, 6, 1. John C. & w, Mary, rocf Caesars Creek MM, O.
1907, 6, 1. Mary & s, Lewis Cole, rocf Caesars Creek MM, O.

HAYWOOD
1895, 2, 2. Joseph recrq
1905, 2, 4. Bessie recrq

HESS
1923, 12, 8. Nina Milner dropped from mbrp

HIGHMILLER
1876, 3, 4. John recrq
1878, 7, 6. John dis
1878, 7, 6. Ellie relrq

HILL
1875, 12, 4. Nancy Tompkins gct North Branch MM, Iowa
1895, 2, 2. Wm. H. recrq
1895, 2, 2. Bertha recrq
1895, 2, 2. Emma recrq
1898, 6, 4. Jesse recrq
1899, 4, 1. Jesse dropped from mbrp
1905, 6, 3. Maud relrq
1911, 9, 9. Wm., Emma & Bertha dropped from mbrp
1914, 2, 14. May Tompkins gct Whittier MM, Calif.

GIRE
1903, 3, 7. Ida relrq

HOLIDAY
1905, 2, 4. Carrie E. recrq

HOLMES
1890, 6, 7. Rollie H. recrq
1896, 11, 7. Melvin & w, Cora, recrq
1897, 3, 5. Harley S. recrq
1909, 1, 2. Raleigh, Jennie B. & Maud H. gct Fairfield MM, O.
1911, 3, 4. Frank recrq

HORNES
1901, 10, 5. M. C. & w, Cora, & ch relrq

HOSKINS
1916, 8, 11. Maude d
----, --, --. Maud M., w Joseph, dt Moses & Rachel E. Milner, b 187-,3,19 d 1916,8,11
1930, 2, 4. Ada Mills d

1914, 6, 13. Joseph & w, Maud, recrq
1923, 12, 8. Lela Rebecca recrq

HOTCHER
1876, 3, 4. Birch recrq

HUDSON
1932, 7, 7. Sarah J. d

1914, 6, 13. Burton, Zetta, Melvine, Clifford & Robert Lee recrq
1914, 6, 13. Sarah J. recrq
1918, 7, 13. Wm. recrq
1923, 12, 8. Harold & Helen Ruth recrq

HUEY
1889, 6, 1. Russell recrq
1901, 7, 6. Russel [Hughey] dropped from mbrp

HUFF
1934, 1, 7. Frank d
1930, 11, 23. Alice d

1898, 1, 1. Frank L. & Alice M. rocf Fairfield MM, O., dtd 1897,12,18
1914, 6, 13. Ralph recrq

HULL
1915, 12, 1. Clarence recrq

HUNGERFORD
1902, 6, 7. Oliver relrq

HUNT
1896, 6, 6. Anna gct Newberry MM, O.

HYERS
1891, 6, 6. Letha recrq

JACKSON
1895, 2, 2. John recrq

JAMES
1901, 4, 6. Edgar, Sarah E., Elsa Margaret recrq
1906, 12, 1. Edward & w relrq

JOB
1905, 3, 4. Archabald dropped from mbrp

JOHNSON
1841, 1, 19. Warren b
----, --, --. Jarad M. m Mary COFFIN, dt Samuel & Dinah, b 1809,6,10
Ch: Orpha b 1849, 4, 18
1859, 3, 18. Charles, s Davis & Malinda, b
1879, 7, 5. Ulysses N. gct Acksworth MM, Ia.
1881, 5, 7. Joseph A. gct Howard Lake MM, Minn.
1882, 4, 1. Warren gct Fairfield MM
1884, 5, 3. Allen recrq
1884, 5, 3. Wm. & Christopher recrq
1884, 5, 3. Mahala recrq
1884, 11, 1. Allen T. & w, Mahala, gct Dover MM, O.
1890, 3, 1. Mahala J. rocf Dover MM, O.
1892, 3, 5. Clinton & Wm. relrq
1893, 10, 7. Warren gct Wichita MM, Kans.
1895, 3, 2. Shepherd & Harry recrq
1896, 9, 5. Davis dropped from mbrp
1896, 10, 3. Warren gct Wichita MM, Kans.

JONES
1904, 1, 30. May d

1901, 7, 6. Susanna & ch, Mary Turner & John & Edward Jones, recrq

JURY
----, --, --. Wm. m Elizabeth ----- b 1794,2,2 d 1890,1,20 bur Walnut Creek
Ch: Milton b 1838, 5, 26
Ellen " 1840, 5, 20

KEARNS
1847, 3, 9. Gertrude, w Joseph, dt Dickinson & Juliana Miller, b

1875, 1, 2. Gertrude recrq
1882, 4, 5. Eliza recrq
1884, 4, 5. Joseph recrq
1894, 4, 7. Anna [Keerns] relrq
1916, 11, 11. Louella [Karns], minor, recrq
1916, 11, 11. Marie [Karns], minor, recrq
1916, 11, 11. Carey M. [Karns], minor, recrq
1916, 11, 11. Joseph [Karns], minor, recrq
1916, 11, 11. Jennie [Karns], minor, recrq
1916, 11, 11. George [Karns], minor, recrq
1916, 11, 11. Isaac [Karns], minor, recrq
1920, 3, 13. Clarence, Blanche, Edna Marie, Luella May, Carey M. & Jennie, recrq

KEATTS
1900, 10, 6. Louisa Coal gct Springfield MM, O.

KELLY
1885, 4, 11. Effie recrq
1907, 3, 2. Florence E. Tompkins relrq

KERSEY
1914, 6, 13. Virgil, Arthur C., Robert M. & Mary recrq
1925, 7, 10. Robert, Mary, Arthur & Virgil dropped from mbrp

KEYS
1878, 7, 6. Ida dropped from mbrp

KNEALER
1922, 1, 4. Edith recrq
1927, 9, 9. Edith dropped from mbrp

KRAMER
1894, 2, 3. Charles & w, Alva, gct Wilmington MM, O.

LADD
1808, 11, 30. Rachel, dt Jonathan & Rachel Barrett, b (Rachel, w Jordan)
----, --, --. Asa J. m Lydia BALLARD, dt Benajah & Rebecca, b 1836,8,16 d 1907,3,14
Ch: Arthur E. b 1862, 10, 4
Rebecca E. " 1865, 1, 7
Rachel E. " 1868, 9, 30
1917, 8, 26. Lewis, s Denson & Betsey B., d

1878, 7, 6. Catharine gct Fairfield MM, O.
1901, 7, 6. Arthur dropped from mbrp
1911, 4, 4. Lucile recrq
1911, 9, 9. Denson, Kathryn, Thomas, Louie & Vernon dropped from mbrp
1917, 7, 14. Lewis rocf Leesburg MM, O.
1927, 9, 9. Jordon & Carrie dropped from mbrp

LARKIN
1914, 6, 13. Pearl Anderson, Willard E. & Richard recrq
1922, 1, 4. Pearl A. relrq

LEASURE
1910, 4, 2. Alonzo recrq

LEAVERTON
1931, 7, 7. Lavina d

1889, 6, 1. Alice [Leverton] recrq
1912, 2, 10. Grace recrq
1914, 6, 13. Lavinia M. recrq

LEMLIE
1911, 9, 9. Jessie dropped from mbrp

LENIES
1901, 4, 6. Charles, Sallie & Harry recrq

LEWIS
1891, 6, 6. Caleb & w, Rhoda, rocf Wilmington MM, O., dtd 1891,4,11
1892, 7, 2. Caleb & w, Rhoda, gct Greenville MM, Ia.

LIMES
1907, 3, 2. Clara & Lenore recrq
1910, 6, 4. Hazel recrq

LITTLE
1889, 5, 4. Alcina recrq

LOOMIS
1891, 8, 1. Oscar & Jennie & Everett, Raymond, Jessie, Bessie & Benjamin, recrq
1894, 3, 3. Oscar & fam relrq

LOVETT
1911, 4, 4. Sampson & Reola recrq

LUCAS
1918, 7, 13. Floy Hudson recrq
1918, 7, 13. Sarah Catharine recrq
1918, 7, 13. Paul Hudson recrq
1923, 12, 8. James Lamar recrq
1925, 11, 23. Floy Hudson & ch, Sarah Catharine, Paul Hudson & James Lamar, dropped from mbrp

LUTTRELL
1908, 12, 5. Robert H. & w roc

McCONNAUGHEY
1922, 1, 4. Roy, Hattie & Velma recrq

McCORMICK
1891, 8, 1. Albert & Annabelle recrq
1904, 10, 1. Albert & Anna [McCormack] dropped from mbrp

McCOY
1884, 4, 5. Charley recrq

McCRAY
1891, 8, 1. Amelia & Joseph recrq
1904, 10, 1. Joseph & Amelia dropped from mbrp

McKINNEY
----, --, --. Alfred, s Obadiah & Sarah, b 1824,10,10; m Phebe DAVIS, dt Caleb & Minerva, b 1830,3,31
Ch: Charles A. b 1845, 6, 4
Anderson " 1855, 12, 2
1924, 11, 28. Anderson d
1890, 4, 5. Charles A. gct Fairfield MM, O.
1892, 12, 3. Anna B. recrq
1912, 4, 13. Rose Towne recrq
1915, 2, 12. Ruby recrq

McNEAL
1811, 10, --. Mary, w Daniel W., dt Robert E. & Bathsheba Lanum, b

1884, 9, 16. Mary gct Wilmington MM, O.

McNICKEL
1904, 3, 5. Sarah E. gct Fairfield MM

McPHERSON
----, --, --. Harrison m Dora ----- b 1857,2, 18
Ch: Ethel
Blanch b 1880, 6, 6
Mary

1901, 12, 7. Dora & dt, Mary, gct Wilmington MM, O.
1901, 12, 7. Blanch gct Wilmington MM, O.

McVEY
1895, 11, 2. Cora Barrett gct Clear Creek MM, O.
1895, 12, 7. Josephine Barrell gct Clear Creek MM, O.

MAGOON
----, --, --. Alfred b 1821,1,21; m Elizabeth -----
Ch: Josiah
Albert
Frank b 1866, 4, 29
Hiram " 1869, 1, 27

1881, 5, 7. Josiah gct Howard Lake MM, Minn.
1882, 4, 1. Josiah gct Union MM, Minn.
1885, 1, 3. Alfred gct Union MM, Minn.

MAHAN
1905, 2, 4. Bertelle recrq

MANNING
1893, 3, 4. Louisa recrq

MAXWELL
1895, 2, 2. Thomas recrq
1911, 9, 9. Thomas dropped from mbrp

MERCER
1898, 5, 7. Leona recrq
1905, 2, 4. John & Jane relrq
1920, 3, 13. Charlie, Fay, Wilbur, Virginia & Kennith recrq

MERCHANT
1906, 12, 1. Isaac recrq

MERIDETH
1889, 6, 1. Benjamin & Leslie recrq
1893, 5, 6. Benjamin & Leslie dropped from mbrp
1913, 6, 14. Edward recrq
1915, 6, 12. Anna recrq
1916, 11, 11. Mabel, minor, recrq
1920, 3, 13. Mabel M. recrq

MERRILL
1878, 7, 6. Wm. gct White River MM, Ind.

MILLER
1890, 12, 6. Wm. & w, Emily S., gct Wilmington MM, O.

MILLIGAN
1884, 4, 5. Emma & Elnora recrq
1892, 6, 4. George recrq

MILLS
1905, 1, 7. Henry dropped from mbrp
1917, 11, 10. Lelia recrq

MILNER
1934, 4, 28. Stanley d

1914, 2, 14. Rachel E. rocf Fairfield MM, O., dtd 1914,1,17
1914, 2, 14. Stanley recrq
1915, 2, 12. Nina recrq
1923, 12, 8. Nettie C. dropped from mbrp
1923, 12, 8. Grace dropped from mbrp
1929, 4, 12. Winnifred recrq

MONTGOMERY
----, --, --. Robert, s Thomas & Hannah, b 1836,2,9; m Rachel FETTRO, dt Jacob & Amy, b 1845,11,30
Ch: John L. b 1877, 1, 1
Lulua " 1879, 5, 1
William
Mary

1876, 3, 4. A. Newton recrq
1876, 3, 4. A. Harvey recrq
1876, 3, 4. R. Marshall recrq
1876, 3, 4. Rachel recrq
1883, 6, 2. Huldah recrq
1884, 6, 9. Newton & w, Dora, & ch, Bertha, Elva, Nina & Wilbur, relrq
1891, 6, 6. W. H. recrq
1897, 3, 5. Milton recrq
1911, 4, 4. Bessie recrq
1914, 2, 14. Cora recrq
1915, 6, 12. Leslie & Homer recrq
1916, 11, 11. Carrie, minor, recrq

MOON
1878, 7, 6. Mary dropped from mbrp
1901, 4, 6. Mary E. recrq

MOORE
1891, 4, 4. Smith, Nancy & Lizzie relrq

MOOREHEAD
1923, 12, 8. Geo., Adelaide, Bernice & Jessie May dropped from mbrp

MORGAN
----, --, --. Orpha gct New Sharon MM, Ia.

MORRIS
1898, 6, 4. Martha recrq

MORRISON
1889, 6, 1. Mary, Robert & Mamie recrq

MORROW
1884, 6, 9. Delia relrq
1898, 2, 5. Inas recrq
1910, 9, 3. Lois Marie recrq
1911, 4, 4. Adelia relrq
1915, 2, 12. Vernon recrq
1915, 4, 10. Albert recrq
1915, 12, 1. Lee recrq

MULL
1920, 3, 13. Blanch May recrq

MURRY
1895, 2, 2. Wm. recrq
1903, 9, 5. Ruth Barrett [Murrey] gct Springfield MM, O.

MYERS
1898, 6, 4. Iota [Meyers] recrq
1904, 3, 5. George C. & Sarah J. rocf Fairfield MM, dtd 1904,2,20
1906, 7, 7. George & Sarah dropped from mbrp

NALER
1895, 3, 2. Wm. recrq

NANCE
1811, 10, 29. Sarah, dt Campbel & Elizabeth, b

NEDLER
1907, 3, 2. Alonzo recrq
1907, 3, 2. Belle recrq

NEFF
1920, 3, 13. Marion, Mabel, Henry & Lillie May recrq

NEWBY
1822, 10, 12. Lucinda, w Isaac, dt Richard & Mary Lucas, b

1889, 6, 1. Ewing recrq
1901, 5, 4. Wm. A. & father & mother & brother gc
1907, 3, 2. John M. gct Wilmington MM, O.

OGBORN
----, --, --. Henry M., s Samuel & Eliza, b 1837,7,28; m Eliza DOWELL, dt David P. & Dicey, b 1839,9,4
Ch: Matilda b 1861, 7, 18
Flora C. " 1865, 9, 5
Amelia F. " 1867, 8, 18
Grace " 1869, 3, 5
William " 1873, 1, 20
Earnest " 1874, 12, 29

1885, 3, 7. Amelia & Grace relrq
1886, 3, 6. Henry M. & w, Eliza Jane, & ch, Wm. Layton & Earnest Francis, gct Ambor MM, Ind.

OLINGER
1877, 5, 5. Jane recrq

OREN
----, --, --. Alfred, s John & Elizabeth, b 1845,4,9; m Laura E. NANCE b 1854,5,8
Ch: Charles B. b 1871, 4, 19
Elizabeth L. " 1872, 10, 26
Levi B. " 1874, 11, 19
John A. " 1877, 3, 7
Joanna A. " 188-, 11, 24

1899, 10, 7. Levi relrq
1904, 3, 5. Ruth gct Dover MM
1904, 3, 5. Lizzie relrq
1905, 1, 7. Charles dropped from mbrp
1911, 4, 4. J. A. relrq

OSBORN
1876, 9, 2. Wm. & w, Eliza, & ch, Anna H. & Jesse Wm., rocf Springfield MM, O., dtd 1876,8,19
1879, 9, 6. Wm. & fam gct Wilmington MM, O.

OVERMAN
----, --, --. Elias & Ruth
Ch: Wm. O. b 1857, 10, 29
Vernon " 1860, 1, --
Alva " 1862, 3, 24
1863, 7, 14. Adelia, dt Dempsey & Amanda, b

1877, 3, 3. Adelia recrq
1884, 4, 5. Norman recrq
1892, 10, 1. Norman dis disunity
1897, 5, 1. Wm. recrq
1903, 8, 1. William & w, Libbie Tompkins, dropped from mbrp
1911, 4, 4. Helen recrq
1915, 12, 1. Cornelia recrq
1916, 11, 11. Robert, minor, recrq
1920, 3, 13. Robert recrq

PAIN
1907, 3, 2. Libbie gct Fairfield MM, O.

PAINTER
1882, 2, 4. Sarah Alice gct Dover MM, O.
1882, 5, 6. Mary gct Dover MM, O.
1892, 8, 6. Lydia A. relrq

PARKER
----, --, --. Adam, s Samuel & Mary, b 1846, 4,22; m Lydia BURGESS, dt Beverly & Malinda, b 1847,7,22
Ch: Walter F. b 1869, 6, 25
Beverly B. " 1870, 12, 25
Charles " 1872, 11, 21
Samuel O. " 1878, 3, 9

1878, 6, 1. Wm. & w, Harriett, & dt, Carrie Ellen, gct Syrna MM, Iowa
1884, 10, 4. Adam & w, Lydia Ann, gct Greenplain MM, O.

PARSHAL
1930, 9, 7. Tina d

1914, 6, 13. Tina recrq
1914, 6, 13. Austie recrq
1924, 3, 8. Allie relrq

PATTRAGE
1904, 3, 5. Bell & Cora recrq

PATTON
1876, 5, 6. Anna recrq

PAULEY
----, --, --. Rufus T., s Chas. & Angeline, b 1847,7,16; m Mary BOILES, dt Neal & Elizabeth, b 1848,9,1

1875, 1, 2. Rufus F. & Mary G. recrq
1898, 6, 4. James, Samantha, Louella & Chance recrq

PAYTON
1914, 6, 13. Archie recrq
1922, 1, 4. Clyde & Anna recrq
1923, 12, 8. Joseph E. & Richard Allen recrq

PERRY
----, --, --. John [Peery] b 1847,2,7; m Mary MONTGOMERY, dt James & Mary, b 1846,3,25
Ch: Walter b 1878, 8, --
Ernest
1933, 2, 15. Charles d

1877, 9, 1. John [Peery] & w recrq
1895, 3, 2. Verley recrq
1911, 9, 9. Mary [Perie] dropped from mbrp
1914, 6, 13. Blanche recrq
1915, 10, 9. Charles W. recrq
1916, 6, 10. Edward recrq
1917, 8, 11. Walter [Perie] recrq
1918, 7, 13. Howard Dewitt recrq
1919, 5, 10. John [Perie] relrq
1921, 12, 10. Blanche gct Fall Creek MM

PEITSMEYER
1853, 2, 17. Emma b
----, --, --. Ernest & Albertine
Ch: Otto b 1857, 4, 9
Mattie " 1861, 4, 10
----, --, --. Joseph, s Christian & Louisa, b 1824,4,7; m Eliza PERDUE, dt Gershom & Abigail, b 1835,11,22
Ch: Isaac C. b 1858, 10, 25
Louisa A. " 1861, 7, 23
Mary E. " 1863, 1, 18
Charles G. " 1864, 10, 20
Eliza O. " 1866, 6, 23
Joseph M. " 1867, 9, 9
Grace A. d 1879, 1,14
Elizabeth H. b 1872, 1, 17
Anna J. " 1873, 5, 7
Gilbert C. " 1876, 10, 10
Hattie E. " 1878, 8, 29

1901, 12, 7. Nancy Dunhue recrq
1902, 4, 5. Chas. Eugene, minor s Chas. & Anne, recrq
1910, 3, 5. Mary relrq

PERDUE
----, --, --. Gershom, s Mentor P. & Jemima, b 1790,12,28 d 1885,2,18; m Abigail MOISE, dt Ephraim & Elizabeth, b 1797,3,25 d 1878, 5,27
Ch: Jacob b 1831, 3, 12
Mentor P. " 1833, 4, 28
----, --, --. Thomas K., s Gershom & Abigail, b 1838,7,30; m Jane M. SMITH, dt Isaac & Mary, b 1847,2,24
Ch: Whittier b 1867, 3, 19
Myra " 1871, 1, 12
Edith " 1872, 12, 12
Alice " 1875, 4, 26
Morton " 1877, 11, 12
Homer " 1880, 4, 22
Lizzie " 1882, 4, 19
Helen " 1885, 2, 17
Gladis " 1887, 12, 26

1903, 12, 5. Alice gct Searsboro MM, Ia.

PIERCE
1923, 1, 13. Elizabeth Ridgeway relrq

PIGGOT
1923, 12, 8. Albert dropped from mbrp

PINDLE
1914, 6, 13. Nancy J. recrq
1923, 4, 14. Nancy J. relrq

POLLY
1884, 4, 5. Eva recrq

POST
1901, 9, 7. Cora recrq
1911, 9, 9. Cora dropped from mbrp
1913, 1, 11. Charles & Bessie recrq

PUCKETT
1915, 2, 12. Ocie recrq
1916, 6, 10. Clinton, Emma, Mary, Bertha & Nora recrq
1916, 6, 10. Nan recrq
1923, 12, 8. Nan relrq

PUMPHREY
1915, 12, 1. Mettie recrq

PURDY
1904, 12, 3. Rose relrq

RAY
1915, 4, 10. John & Mae recrq

REAMES
----, --, --. Joel m Lettice MARMAN, dt Samuel & Peggy, b 1811,11,14
Ch: Matilda b 1841, 6, --

1875, 1, 2. Matilda recrq
1878, 3, 2. Lettice [Reams] roc

RECTOR
1892, 12, 3. Eliza recrq
1895, 2, 2. Addie recrq
1895, 3, 2. Henry recrq
1897, 5, 1. John recrq
1897, 6, 5. Myrtle, Rosa & Cora recrq
1898, 10, 1. Addie dropped from mbrp
1901, 7, 6. Henry dropped from mbrp
1909, 3, 6. Fam of Rector dropped from mbrp

REED
1905, 8, 5. Iota gct Center MM, O.

REES
1859, 3, 5. Ella, w W. O., dt H. M. & Eliza Ogborn, b

1914, 6, 13. Jennie [Reese] recrq

REYNOLDS
1929, 7, 7. John M. d

1892, 6, 4. Anna recrq
1914, 6, 13. John M. & Charlette recrq
1917, 11, 10. Anna recrq

ROADS -
----, --, --. Lewis & Martha [Rhoades]
Ch: Enos b 1852, --, 2
Dora " 1856, 1, 21
William " 1858, 2, 9
Frances " 1861, 2, 5

1876, 3, 4. Dora E. recrq
1876, 3, 4. Frank recrq
1876, 3, 4. Wm. L. recrq

ROADS, continued
1877, 3, 3. Enos H. [Roades] recrq
1913, 1, 11. Nellie recrq
1915, 8, 14. Madge recrq
1921, 4, 9. Lindley [Rhodes] recrq

RICE
1878, 3, 2. Margaret dis

RIDGWAY
1930, 6, 9. Richard H. d

1915, 3, 13. Richard & w, Mary, & ch, Elizabeth, Robert, Wilbur, Joseph & David H., rocf Clear Creek MM, O.

RILEY
1892, 7, 2. John rocf Friends Chapel MM
1895, 3, 2. Isadora C., w John, rocf Des Moines MM, Ia.
1901, 1, 5. John gct Cleveland MM, O.

ROBERTS
1832, 3, 21. Wm., s John & Sarah, b
1838, 8, 5. Nancy A., dt James & Elizabeth Wolf, b

1892, 8, 6. Wm. & Nancy relrq
1893, 3, 4. Jennie relrq
1905, 1, 7. Wilson, James, Wm. & Warren dropped from mbrp

ROSENBOWER
1909, 11, 2. J. R., Lydia, Herbert & Nellie recrq

ROSS
1911, 4, 4. S. J., Ollie, James, Frank, Willie & Mary recrq
1912, 12, 14. S. J. & fam relrq

ROWE
1899, 6, 3. J. W. recrq

SANDERS
1884, 2, 2. Bell recrq
1889, 6, 1. Stanley recrq
1893, 5, 6. Stanley dropped from mbrp

SCOTT
1928, 3, 31. Janie d

1889, 5, 4. Thomas L. recrq
1891, 4, 4. Walter relrq
1892, 5, 7. Rosa & Ellie recrq
1893, 3, 4. Walter recrq
1895, 12, 7. Thomas S. & w, Lydia A., gct Fairfield MM, O.
1895, 12, 7. Ellie relrq
1911, 11, 11. Estell & w, Edna, & dt, Margaret, rocf Fairfield MM, dtd 1911,10,21
1914, 2, 14. Charles recrq
1914, 2, 14. Lizzie recrq
1916, 7, 8. John, s Chas. & Lizzie, recrq
1918, 3, 9. Elizabeth relrq
1923, 12, 8. Estel, Edna & Margaret dropped from mbrp
1923, 12, 8. John & Charles dropped from mbrp
1925, 12, 11. Alfred, Janie, Minnie & Robert Elwood recrq

SEAMAN
1924, 12, 13. Edgar recrq

SEMLE
1898, 3, 5. Jesse recrq

SETTY
1897, 5, 1. Albert & Hattie Ann [Setts] recrq
1901, 7, 6. Albert & Hattie A. [Setty] dropped from mbrp
1904, 10, 1. Albert D. & Nancy [Setta] recrq
1912, 9, 14. Icy Ruth recrq
1914, 2, 12. Byron recrq
1916, 7, 8. Mary Alice Leota, Violet May Hattie, Gertrude Anna Victoria, ch Albert & Nancy, recrq
1923, 12, 8. Byron dropped from mbrp
1927, 10, 7. Albert & Nancy relrq

SHAKLEFORD
1878, 7, 6. Simon dropped from mbrp

SHOCKLEY
1911, 3, 4. Wm. & Alice recrq

SIMBRO
1892, 6, 4. Zelphia Ann, Lettie & Zerelda recrq
1911, 9, 9. Lettie, Zerilda & Zillpha Ann dropped from mbrp

SIMES
1904, 3, 5. Jane recrq

SIMMONS
1884, 4, 5. John recrq

SKEEN
1895, 2, 2. Thomas recrq
1901, 9, 7. Maud recrq

SLUSHER
1891, 2, 7. George recrq
1902, 8, 2. Geo. relrq

SMACK
1823, 12, 8. Charles & Ida recrq
1823, 12, 8. Chauncey Malcom recrq
1823, 12, 8. Marlene recrq

SMALL
1918, 4, 30. Mary d

SMALL, continued
1902, 3, 1. Florence recrq
1911, 2, 10. Ephraim recrq
1912, 4, 13. Jane recrq
1913, 1, 11. Mary recrq
1914, 2, 14. Austie recrq
1919, 4, 12. E. O. relrq

SMITH
1829, 4, 2. Lydia, w Jacob, dt Levi & Maria Ellis, b
1860, 10, 5. Ella E., dt Jeremiah & Martha, b
1861, 10, 16. Estel b
1863, 7, 11. Rufus b
----, --, --. Isaac, s Anthony & Leah, d 1906, 10,--; m Mary SMITH, dt S----- & Ann, b 1827,12,9
Ch: Orpha b 1868, 9, 12

1875, 4, 3. Mary recrq
1875, 4, 3. Orpha, minor dt Isaac & Mary, recrq
1878, 7, 6. Lydia dis disunity
1878, 7, 6. Jonathan & Julia dropped from mbrp
1884, 5, 3. Conrad & w, Mary, & ch, Genesis, Arley & Nolia, recrq
1884, 5, 3. Wm. & w, Sarah, & ch, Dussey, Stella, Charley recrq
1884, 5, 3. Julia recrq
1893, 5, 6. Sarah dropped from mbrp
1895, 1, 20. Orpha relrq
1901, 4, 6. Andrew J. recrq
1905, 3, 4. Estil dropped from mbrp
1912, 3, 9. Jacob L. & Margaret L. recrq

SNIDER
1876, 3, 4. Mahlon recrq
1878, 7, 6. Mahlon dropped from mbrp
1891, 8, 1. Charles & Ella recrq

SOALE
1913, 1, 11. Phebe recrq
1917, 3, 10. Bessie recrq
1920, 3, 13. Chas. E. & Nancy P. recrq

SOUTHARD
1890, 4, 5. S. C. & w, Alice, recrq
1892, 9, 5. S. C. & w, Alice C. relrq
1900, 9, 1. Dr. S. C. & w, Alice, rocf Sabina MM, dtd 1900,8,8
1907, 4, 6. Dr. S. C. & w, Alice, gct Center MM, O.

SPELLMAN
1891, 8, 1. Margaret, Gay & Hugh recrq
1904, 10, 1. Albert, Guy & Hugh dropped from mbrp

SPENCE
1838, 4, 25. Mary E., w Wm., dt Stephen & Lydia Worley, b
1904, 2, 6. M. Etta gct Fairfield MM, O.

SPRINGER
1897, 3, 5. Fred G. recrq

STEPHENS
----, --, --. John & Elizabeth
Ch: Cassius b 1853, 3, 6
Cornelius " 1857, 6, 10
1912, 7, 2. Myrtla Stout d

1884, 4, 5. Ann B. recrq
1891, 6, 6. Elwood recrq
1892, 2, 5. John W., Alice & Bertha B. recrq.
1901, 9, 7. Charley, Agusta & Myrtle recrq
1911, 4, 4. Madge recrq
1913, 1, 11. Mary recrq
1914, 2, 14. Chlo & Vernon recrq
1916, 7, 8. Norma Pearl, dt Vernon & Chloe, recrq

STONE
1877, 7, 7. Eliza recrq
1879, 1, 3. Eliza gct Wilmington MM, O.

STONEKING
1895, 7, 6. Eliza H. recrq
1904, 10, 1. Eliza dropped from mbrp
1917, 3, 10. May [Stonaker] recrq

STOOPS
1889, 6, 1. Samuel recrq
1893, 5, 6. Samuel dropped from mbrp
1895, 3, 2. Zot recrq
1915, 4, 10. Myrtle recrq
1916, 6, 10. Alta recrq

STOUT
1875, 8, 7. John rmt Lucetta Todhunter
1876, 9, 2. Lucetta T. gct Sandy Creek MM, Ind.

STOWE
1912, 4, 13. Nellie Karnes gct Fairfield MM, O.

STRAIN
1911, 9, 9. Emma dropped from mbrp

SUMNER
----, --, --. Robert, s Absalom & Priscilla, b 1827,7,4; m Tobitha Fettro, dt Jacob & Amy, b 1837,11,6
Ch: Sarah E. b 1872, 8, 6

SWAIN
1884, 4, 5. Rachel & Joseph recrq

SWEARINGER
1914, 2, 14. Thomas recrq
1924, 3, 8. Thos. W. relrq

SWISSHELM
1895, 2, 2. Susie recrq

TAYLOR
1892, 6, 4. Frank recrq
1895, 2, 2. Rosa recrq
1901, 7, 6. Frank dropped from mbrp
1921, 4, 9. N. H. recrq

TEMPLIN
1825, 12, 18. Margaret, w J. M., dt Joel & Lettice Reames, b

1876, 3, 4. Margaret H. [Templen] recrq
1878, 7, 6. Letitia & Caroline dropped from mbrp
1878, 7, 6. Oscar dropped from mbrp
1882, 4, 5. Sylvanus & Ellen M. recrq
1882, 4, 5. Sylvanus & Ellen M. recrq
1884, 4, 5. Wm. recrq
1889, 5, 4. Wm. & Ella recrq
1901, 7, 6. Wm. dropped from mbrp
1910, 3, 5. Sylvanus & Ella dropped from mbrp

TERRELL
----, --, --. Thomas P. b 1816,12,10; m Clarinda WOODARD, dt Isaac & Eleanor, b 1820,4,9
Ch: Martha M. b 1842, 9, 13
Lewis P. " 1857, 1, 24
E. Annetta " 1862, 3, 27
Christopher M. " 1855, 5, 20
----, --, --. Lewis P. m Clara SMITH, dt Isaac & Mary, b 1854,9,17
Ch: ----- b 1883, 7, 8
----- " 1885, 2, 25
----- " 1888, 12, 2
----, --, --. Christopher M., s Thos. P. & Clarinda, b 1855,5,20; m Elizabeth BARRETT dt David & Millicent, b 1857,9,1
Ch: Clara A. b 1878, 10, 17
Clyde
Leona
Minnie " 1885, 12, 29
Orlando " 1888, 8, 29

1889, 10, 5. Elva R. gct Clear Creek MM, O.
1898, 3, 5. Leona & Minnie recrq
1906, 1, 6. Clara recrq
1910, 4, 2. Clyde dropped from mbrp

THIRMAN
1876, 3, 4. Hick recrq

THOMSON
1892, 6, 4. James M. recrq

THORNBERRY
1789, 11, 16. Abel b d 1880,8,29

TODHUNTER
----, --, --. Jacob, s Isaac & Eleanor, b 1795, 12, 14; m Rebecca DOSTER, dt John & Lydia, b 1798,2,10
1818, 12, 14. Milton, s Isaac, b
1830, 12, 8. Aaron, s Abner & Elizabeth, b
----, --, --. Amos, s Abner & Elizabeth, b 1818,2,18; m Emily E. McNEAL, dt Samuel W. & Mary, b 1828,1,28
Ch: Oscar B. b 1848, 7, 4
Alice M. " 1855, 4, 16
Clara E. " 1857, 10, 17
Laura C. " 1860, 10, 23
Layton W. " 1866, 3, 30
Bessie C.E." 1868, 11, 17
Lucy E. " 1871, 6, 5

1875, 8, 7. Lucetta rmt John Stout
1880, 12, 4. Oscar B. gct Cincinnati MM, O.
1884, 5, 3. Melissa recrq
1884, 9, 16. Amos & w, Emily E., & ch, Clara E., Laura C., Layton W., Bessie C. E. & Lucy E., gct Wilmington MM, O.
1884, 11, 1. Milton gct Dover MM, O.
1890, 1, 4. Bell recrq

TOMPKINS
----, --, --. Jacob, s John & Sarah, b 1800, 9,22; m Rachel HIATT, dt Elihu, b 1817,2,5
----, --, --. John, s Jacob & Rachel (Hiatt), b 1835,10,20; m Elizabeth NEWBY, dt Isaac & Lucinda, b 1845,8,26
ChP Addie E. b 1864, 6, 16
William E. " 1865, 7, 17
Charles E. " 1867, 2, 14
Sarah E. " 1872, 1, 1
Mary E. " 1874, 9, 22
1911, 11, --. John, s Jacob & Rachel, d
1916, 1, --. Elizabeth, w John, d
1914, 4, --. William d

1884, 4, 5. Wm. & Pluma recrq
1889, 6, 1. Lillie I. & Nannie C. recrq
1891, 6, 6. Marley recrq
1893, 5, 6. Charles dropped from mbrp
1912, 2, 10. Lindley recrq
1912, 3, 9. Gertrude recrq
1915, 2, 12. Ruth recrq

TOWNSEND
1878, 7, 6. Ines relrq

TROTH
1891, 8, 1. Nathan recrq
1905, 5, 6. Jennie recrq
1909, 7, 3. Florence Bell, Bessie Ione & Jessie recrq

TURNER
1901, 7, 6. Susanna Jones & ch, Mary Turner & John & Edward Jones recrq

UHLEN
1878, 2, 2. Ellie S. relrq

UHLEN, continued
1919, 7, 12. Bessie E. Stephens [Uhlan] relrq

UNTHANK
1881, 7, 2. Dinah & ch, Joseph C. & Martha C., rocf Spiceland MM, Ind.
1889, 9, 7. Dinah K. gct Wilmington MM, O.
1889, 9, 7. John gct Wilmington MM, O.

VALENTINE
1920, 3, 13. Ethel recrq

VARLEY
1897, 5, 1. Emma recrq
1901, 7, 6. Parry dropped from mbrp

VERNON
1893, 3, 4. W. O. recrq

WALKER
1876, 3, 4. Alexander recrq
1892, 6, 4. Wm. recrq
1895, 2, 2. Alex recrq
1897, 3, 5. Sarah Jane, Clara & Lloyd recrq
1898, 6, 4. Mary recrq
1910, 1, 1. Grace recrq
1911, 9, 9. Sarah, Alexander, Mary & Johnson dropped from mbrp
1914, 2, 14. Wm. & Alva recrq

WALLACE
1895, 2, 2. Leslie recrq
1911, 9, 9. Leslie dropped from mbrp

WALN
1877, 4, 7. Ann & Millie recrq
1884, 5, 3. Thomas recrq
1890, 7, 5. Martha recrq
1906, 4, 7. Joseph Wm. recrq

WARDEN
----, --, --. Dallis, s Isaac & Belinda, b 1844,6,18; m Anna R. BARRETT, dt Geo. W. & Rhoda, b 1856,2,3

1879, 4, 5. Dallas & Rebecca recrq
1892, 10, 1. Dallis dis disunity
1895, 2, 2. Dallas recrq

WASHBURN
1884, 4, 5. Samson B. & Jessie Florence recrq

WEAVER
1901, 4, 6. Bessie recrq

WEBB
1898, 6, 4. John W. & Sallie recrq
1901, 9, 7. Bessie recrq
1911, 9, 9. J. W. & Sallie dropped from mbrp

WELLER
1877, 3, 3. Peter S. & Sarah Louiza recrq
1904, 12, 3. Louiza relrq

WEST
1893, 5, 6. Isaac C. dropped from mbrp
1896, 4, 4. Robert & w, Lizzie, dropped from mbrp
1914, 6, 13. Thomas C. recrq

WHEATON
1898, 3; 5. Rachel recrq
1911, 9, 9. Rachel dropped from mbrp

WHETZEL
1884, 5, 3. Addie recrq

WHITEHEAD
1898, 6, 4. Wm. recrq
1911, 9, 9. Wm. dropped from mbrp

WEYER
1876, 3, 4. Daniel [Wier] recrq
1876, 5, 6. Ella recrq
1884, 4, 5. Wm., Lydia A. & Lizzie recrq

WILLEMAN
1897, 3, 5. Adam A., Huldah & M. Belle recrq

WILLIAMS
1829, 2, 11. Esther P., dt Gershom & Abigail Perdue, b

1878, 7, 6. Allen dropped from mbrp

WILLIAMSON
1933, 5, 10. Jennie d

1891, 8, 1. Louisa recrq
1914, 2, 14. Minor & Jennie recrq

WILSON
1884, 5, 3. Samantha recrq
1893, 3, 4. John & w, Sarah, recrq
1901, 4, 6. John & Mary B. recrq
1910, 4, 2. John dropped from mbrp

WINEGAR
1897, 3, 5. Isabel, Taylor & Richard recrq
1898, 6, 4. A. J. recrq
1911, 9, 9. Taylor & Richard dropped from mbrp

WIRE
1853, 11, 21. Daniel, s Harrison & Huldah, b

WISE
1895, 3, 2. Edward, Louie & May recrq
1901, 7, 6. Edward, Louey & May dropped from mbrp

WOLF
1901, 9, 7. Wm. & Anna recrq
1906, 4, 7. Fred relrq

WOLF, continued
1914, 6, 13. Clyde recrq
1915, 6, 12. Elsie & Evelyn recrq
1918, 7, 13. Lucile recrq

WOOD
1914, 1, 10. Lou F. recrq
1914, 2, 14. Rosa recrq
1916, 11, 11. Helen, minor, recrq

WORLEY
1877, 3, 3. Susannah recrq
1879, 4, 5. Wm. Mack recrq

WORNICKS
1876, 5, 6. Lettie A. recrq

WORNSTAFF
1898, 3, 5. Guy recrq
1902, 4, 5. Guy relrq

WRIGHT
----, --, --. David D., s Edward & Hannah, b 1800,8,6; m Ruth HUNT, dt Jacob & Lydia, b 1808,2,13
Ch: William b 1847, 10, 3
Rachel H. " 1849, 10, 3 d 1907,5,31
----, --, --. John, s Wm. & Rachel, b 1818,3,17; m Ann THORNBURG, dt Wm. & Lydia, b 1822,2,11
----, --, --. Joel T., s John & Ann, b 1841,11,20; m Anna M. BARRETT, dt Ellis & Anna, b 1839,8,7
Ch: Lydia A. b 1866, 6, 20
Rachel E. " 1869, 3, 1
Elizabeth E. b 1871, 9, 9
----, --, --. Joseph H., s John & Ann, b 1854,2,7; m Sarah L. McKINNEY, dt Alfred & Phebe, b 1857,3,23
Ch: Jessie b 1877, 4, 2

1895, 12, 7. Joel T. & w, Anna M., gct Fairfield MM, O.
1895, 12, 7. Elizabeth E. gct Fairfield MM,O.
1905, 10, 7. Jane relrq
1910, 3, 5. Charles & J. H. dropped from mbrp

YARGER
1927, 9, 9. America dropped from mbrp

ZELLAR
1898, 3, 5. Etta recrq

ZIMMERMAN
1850, 4, 23. Annie, w Jacob, dt Wm. P. & Rebecca Todhunter, b

1901, 4, 6. Maggie recrq
1905, 12, 2. Olive recrq

CENTER MONTHLY MEETING

Center Monthly Meeting, located in Clinton County, Ohio, three miles northwest of Wilmington was set up on the 2 Mo. 7, 1807. A meeting for worship appears to have been held since about 1805. The new monthly meeting was set off from Miami Monthly Meeting by authority of Redstone Quarterly Meeting, Pa.

A list of names of those persons who were early members of Center Monthly Meeting includes Robert Andrews, Daniel Bailey, Morman Ballard, Elizabeth Barnard, Mary Barrett, William Butler, Joseph Cloud, Stephen Compton, Rebecca Compton, overseer, Charity Cook, Isaac Cook, elder, Thomas Cox, Rachel Embree, Thomas Emery, Benjamin Farquhar, David Faulkner, Ellen Faulkner, Judith Faulkner, Martha Faulkner, Susanna Faulkner, John Furnace, Ruth (Doan) Haines, William Harvey, Sarah Hawkins, overseer, George Hayworth, Joanna Hayworth, Mary Hayworth, Phebe Hayworth, Rachel Henderson, overseer, Richard Henderson, overseer, Center Preparative, John Henley, Francis Hester, Mary Hester, overseer, Patience Hines, Achsah Hodgson, Amos Hodgson, Jacob Jackson, Robert Kilby, Abigail Leonard, Rachel Lewis, Nathan Linton, David McMillan, Hannah McMillan, Richard Mendenhall, Anne Milhouse, Henry Millhouse, Robert Millhouse, overseer, Caesars Creek Preparative, Sarah Milhouse, assistant clerk, Jane Moon, Salina Moon, Samuel Owens, overseer, Caesars Creek Preparative, David Painter, Isaac Perkens, Phenia Perkins, clerk and elder, Sarah (Hayworth) Rice, Esther (Lewis) Roads, John Sanders, Mary Sanders, Lydia Smith, Mary Spray, Samuel Spray, William Stanton, Rebecca (Clark) Steward, Ann Stout, John Stout, clerk, Margaret Stout, John Stubs, Mary Thatcher, Joanna Vanhorn, Martha Walker, Mordecai Walker, William Walker, Robert Whitacre, David Whitson, Mary Whitson, Enoch Wickersham, Betty Wilson, Jehu Wilson, Sarah Wilson, elder, Elizabeth Wright, clerk, Joel Wright, Jonathan Wright, elder, Susannah Wright.

In 1828 the Hicksite separation divided the monthly meeting into two branches. The Orthodox branch appears to have had the larger membership and to have retained the record books of the original meeting. The Hicksite branch was laid down in 1864. The Orthodox branch was laid down in 1921.

RECORDS

ACHOR
1896, 12, 16. Euphemia Ann gct Clear Creek MM, O.

ADAIR
1843, 11, 30. Sabilla Ann (form Scott) dis mou & jas (H)

ADAMS
1843, 1, 4. Eunice b
1869, 12, 11. Harley, s Joseph & Eunice, b

1829, 2, 18. William dis disunity
1829, 4, 15. Milly dis jH
1833, 1, 16. Mary Jane & dt, Edith S., rocf Fairfield MM, dtd 1832,10,25
1906, 3, 14. Wilson & w, Effie J., & ch, Bertha N., Rosa B., Lirenna D., Mary J. & Susanna, rocf Dover MM
1910, 2, 16. Bertha recrq

ADSIT
1825, 9, 17. Isabella & ch, Elizabeth & Mary Ann, recrq
1841, 2, 17. Elizabeth N. rpd married to Thomas W. McMullan
1841, 4, 14. Thomas Rich prcf Springfield MM, to m Isabella Adsit
1841, 5, 12. Isabella rmt Thomas Rich
1841, 6, 16. Isabella Rich & dt, Mary Ann Adsit, gct Springfield MM

ALBERSON
1817, 5, 17. Josiah recrq

ALEXANDER
1886, 8, 18. Zora dis disunity

ALLEN
----, --, --. Abraham b 1796,5,3; m Cata ----- b 1800,6,26 (H)

Ch:					
David B.	b 1819,	9,	2		
Fanny H.	" 1822,	5,	23		
Elizabeth	" 1824,	9,	20		
Mary S.	" 1827,	7,	21	d 1844, 8, 4 bur Center	
Martha	" 1830,	1,	18		
Isaac	" 1832,	11,	10		
Sarah	" 1836,	3,	2		
Jacob	" 1839,	1,	17		
Lydia Maria					

1820, 8, 19. Abraham & w, Cata, & s, David, rocf Oswego MM, N. Y.
1828, 9, 17. Abraham dis jH
1829, 1, 14. Cata dis jH
1831, 6, 18. Elcy [Alen], w Jacob, rocf New York MM, dtd 1830,8,4 (H)
1836, 6, 16. Elcy H. gct Cincinnati MM (H)
1843, 4, 13. Abraham dis disunity (H)
1843, 4, 13. Daniel B. dis disunity (H)
1844, 9, 18. David dis joining Separatists
1846, 1, 15. Cata dis disunity (HP

ALMOND
1812, 7, 4. Cert rec for Matthew from Piney Grove MM, S. C., dtd 1812,2,15, endorsed to White Water MM

ALVIS
1897, 4, 14. Frank rocf Springfield MM

ANDERSON
1807, 10, 3. Eli rocf Northwest Fork MM, Md., dtd 1807,7,2
1808, 1, 2. Eli rmt Mary Thatcher
1830, 10, 13. Eli dis jH
1831, 2, 16. Mary dis jH
1832, 6, 13. Julianna Moore (form Anderson) dis mou
1836, 9, 14. Thomas T. gct White Lick MM, Ind.
1836, 9, 14. Elijah, Joel P., Eli, Jr. and Martha Ruth, ch Eli & Mary, gct White Lick MM, Ind.
1842, 9, 14. White Lick MM granted permission to rst Mary
1842, 12, 14. White Lick MM, Ind. granted permisiion to rst Eli
1906, 2, 14. Russell recrq
1906, 4, 18. John recrq
1914, 2, 18. John & w, Elizabeth, & s, Russel, gct Xenia MM

ANDREW
----, --, --. Robert b 1782,2,11; m Ellen ----- b 1789,6,21

Ch:				
William	b 1808,	12,	14	
Ruth D.	" 1810,	5,	14	
Jesse	" 1812,	8,	10	
Aaron	" 1814,	8,	28	
Henry	" 1816,	4,	28	
Hannah	" 1818,	1,	3	
Jane	" 1819,	11,	28	
John	" 1821,	10,	25	
Eli	" 1823,	9,	23	
Jehu	" 1825,	5,	24	
Andy Tate	" 1827,	7,	17	d 1828, 5,20 bur at New Hope

1831, 9, 29. Ruth d bur New Hope
1832, 2. 15. Ellen d bur New Hope

1807, 10, 3. Robert [Andrews] rpd married to Ellen Faulkner
1811, 2, 2. Samuel [Andrews] rocf Spring MM, N. C., dtd 1810,8,25
1815, 10, 21. Henry & w, Jane, & ch, Robert, John, Anna & Hannah, rocf Sadsbury MM, dtd 1815,7,4
1818, 6, 20. Delilah [Andrews] & ch, William John & Hannah, recrq
1831, 3, 16. William dis disunity
1833, 5, 15. Jesse F. dis mou
1834, 5, 14. Aaron dis disunity

ANDREW, continued
1836, 3, 16. Henry com for mou & training in militia
1836, 6, 15. Henry [Andrews] dis disunity
1842, 8, 17. John dis disunity
1843, 9, 13. Eli dis jas
1843, 9, 13. Jane dis jas
1845, 2, 12. Jehu dis joining Separatists
1853, 3, 16. Stanton dis mou & jas
1853, 3, 16. Mary (form Faulkner) dis mou & jas
1853, 10, 12. Robert gct Mississiniwa MM, Ind.
1869, 6, 16. Caroline gct Springfield MM
1910, 2, 16. Nettie [Andrews] recrq

ANTRIM
1817, 6, 21. Ann & ch, Joseph Hiram John Joshua Elizabeth Aaron Edmond & Charity Ann, rocf Hopewell MM, Va., dtd 1817,1,8
1823, 7, 19. Deborah (form Whitson) dis mou
1823, 10, 18. Sarah [Antram] dis mou
1829, 2, 18. Joseph dis jH

ARNETT
----, --, --. Thomas b 1791,6,30; m Rachel FAULKNER b 1809,6,20
Ch: David b 1827, 1, 8 d 1828, 7,23
Martha W. " 1830, 12, 7 " 1834, 1,17

1825, 6, 18. Thomas rocf Union MM, N. C., dtd 1825,4,27
1826, 1, 21. Thomas rpd married to Rachel Faulkner
1847, 5, 12. Thomas & w, Rachel, gct Miami MM

ARNOLD
1807, 10, 3. Jesse recrq
1814, 1, 1. Jesse rmt Jane Linton
1814, 4, 2. Jane gct Cesars Creek MM

ARY
1820, 1, 15. Sally (form Bailiff) dis mou
1830, 10, 13. Sally [Airey] dis jH
1900, 3, 14. Corwin recrq
1900, 6, 13. Guy recrq
1919, 2, 12. Goldie relrq

ATCHISON
1913, 2, 12. Harry, Roxie, Emma, Charles, Mildred, Maud & Elmer recrq
1913, 6, 18. Benjamin & Louisa Ethel, ch Harry & Roxie, recrq
1919, 3, 12. Mrs. Harry & ch gc

ATKINSON
----, --, --. Joseph & Susannah
Ch: Cephas b 1790, 11, 5
Robert " 1795, 5, 27
Margaret " 1797, 9, 14
John " 1800, 4, 12
William " 1803, 2, 22
Thomas " 1806, 8, 17
Isaac " 1809, 4, 16

----, --, --. Charles b 1796,6,21; m Lydia ----- b 1800,12,20
Ch: Jane b 1821, 4, 12
David " 1822, 10, 14
Susannah " 1824, 9, 26
Jesse " 1826, 6, 27
Levi " 1828, 2, 2

1811, 8, 3. Susannah & ch, Robert, Margaret, John, William, Thomas & Isaac, rocf Warrington MM, dtd 1811,5,23
1811, 8, 3. Cephas rocf Warrington MM, dtd 1811,5,23
1815, 7, 15. Margaret Oren (form Atkinson) rpd mou
1815, 10, 21. Cephus rmt Abigail Oren
1816, 4, 20. Cephas & w, Abigail, gct Caesars Creek MM
1819, 2, 20. Robert dis mou
1819, 10, 16. Charles recrq
1820, 7, 15. Charles rmt Lydia Oren
1822, 12, 21. John gct Green Plain MM
1826, 4, 15. Thomas [Atkeson] con mou
1826, 9, 16. Thomas gct Green Plain MM
1829, 5, 16. Charles & fam recrq (H)
1829, 5, 16. Lydia recrq (H)
1832, 7, 18. Isaac dis mou
1833, 6, 12. Susannah gct Green Plain MM
1839, 12, 19. Charles & w, Lydia, & ch, Jane, David, Susanna, Jesse, Levi, Alice, James, Moses & Lydia, gct White Water MM, Ind.(H)

BABB
1887, 5, 19. Mata, dt Isaiah & Lydia Ann, d
1911, 1, 16. Sarah A. d ae 71y
1831, 11, 16. Jane (form Wall) dis mou
1879, 1, 15. Clara Louisa recrq
1879, 1, 15. Alice Ann recrq
1879, 1, 15. Mary Emma recrq
1879, 1, 15. Hattie Harley recrq
1879, 1, 15. Sarah Ann recrq
1879, 1, 15. Marietta recrq
1879, 1, 15. Orville Clinton recrq
1879, 2, 12. Henry & ch, Burtha E. & Burly M., recrq
1883, 7, 18. Elizabeth & Eliza, ch Sarah Ann, recrq
1886, 3, 17. Lydia Ann recrq
1886, 4, 14. Israel recrq
1888, 2, 15. Alpheus W. recrq
1888, 2, 15. Charley recrq
1888, 2, 15. Eli recrq
1891, 4, 15. Clayton recrq
1895, 6, 12. Clinton & w, Anne, & ch gct Wilmington MM
1895, 6, 12. Eli gct Sabina MM
1895, 7, 19. Alpheus gct West Fork MM
1895, 7, 19. Charlie W. gct West Fork MM
1895, 12, 18. Oriana gct Sabina MM
1901, 4, 17. Clyde recrq
1901, 12, 18. Eli & w, Orianna, rocf Springfield MM, O., dtd 1901,11,16
1903, 2, 18. Bertha recrq

BARB, continued
1918, 7, 17. E. L. & w, Orianna, & ch, Anna B., gct Wilmington MM

BAILEY
----, --, --. Daniel & Mary
Ch: Martha b 1808, 7, 26
Susannah " 1810, 2, 9
George " 1811, 6, 24
Sarah " 1814, 6, 9
David " 1815, 11, 1
1816, 6, 9. Judith b
1831, 10, 26. Thomas b

1807, 10, 3. Daniel rmt Mary Hayworth
1815, 5, 20. Rebecca & ch, Hiram, Sally, Abidan, Joseph, Mary, John & Rebecca, rocf Stillwater MM, dtd 1815,2,28
1816, 4, 20. Hiram gct Stillwater MM, O.
1816, 10, 19. Susannah & ch, Almeda, Robert Barclay, Judith, Daniel, James Edwin & Mary Byrum, roc
1817, 6, 21. Hiram rocf Stillwater MM, O., dtd 1817,2,22
1820, 11, 18. Hiram [Baily] gct Miami MM
1822, 2, 16. Susannah rmt Caleb Kirk
1822, 2, 16. Elizabeth rocf Stillwater MM, dtd 1821,12,22
1823, 12, 20. Elizabeth rmt Jesse Barnett
1825, 11, 19. Judith Stanley (form Bailey) con mou
1826, 7, 15. Abidon con mou
1826, 10, 21. Abiden [Baley] gct White Lick MM, Ind.
1827, 8, 18. Robert B. gct Dover MM, to m Lucy Banghum
1828, 4, 19. Robert B. gct Dover MM
1828, 5, 17. Robert Thomas prcf Dover MM, to m Almedia Bailey
1828, 6, 21. Almeda rmt Robert Thomas
1829, 8, 12. Sarah Cadwalader (form Bailey) con mou
1830, 4, 14. Caleb Kirk & w, Susannah, & her ch, Daniel, James, Edwin & Mary Byram Baily, gct Dover MM
1830, 5, 12. Hiram & w, Rachel, & ch, Elijah T., Joseph B., David D. & Rebecca, gct Arba MM, Ind.
1831, 2, 16. Abidon rocf Fairfield MM, Ind., dtd 1830,8,7
1831, 3, 16. John Stout, Jr. gct Dover MM, to m Mary B. Baily
1831, 8, 17. John rpd mou
1831, 8, 20. Nathan rocf Center MM, Pa., dtd 1831,2,10 (H)
1832, 3, 14. John con mou
1832, 5, 16. John gct Fairfield MM, Ind.
1833, 4, 17. Eliza Ann rocf Goshen MM, dtd 1832,9,15
1834, 4, 16. Rebecca Ballard (form Baily) con mou
1834, 4, 17. Nathan [Baily] gct Elk MM (H)
1836, 7, 13. Abidon dis disunity
1852, 9, 16. Asenath [Baily] (form Underwood) dis mcd (H)
1865, 9, 13. David rpd mou
1901, 3, 13. Josiah H. & w, Sydnie M., rocf Dover MM, dtd 1901,1,14
1908, 11, 18. Amos [Baily] gct Wilmington MM
1916, 10, 18. Sidney M. gct Dover MM
1917, 4, 18. Veda recrq
1921, 2, 16. Stella & Veda gct Wilmington MM, O.

BAILIFF
1808, 12, 3. Sarah [Bayliff] & ch, Daniel, Leah, Sarah, Mary & Martha, recrq
1809, 4, 1. Joshua & w, Margaret, & ch, Sally Elizabeth & Susanna, recrq
1810, 3, 3. Thomas recrq
1817, 3, 15. Joshua dis mou
1820, 1, 15. Sally Ary (form Bailiff) dis mou
1823, 11, 15. Joshua [Bayliff] recrq
1824, 9, 18. Elizabeth Thomas (form Bayliff) dis mou
1825, 6, 18. Sarah rmt Josiah Williams
1827, 2, 17. Mary Curl (form Bailiff) dis mou
1828, 12, 17. Susanna Thomas (form Bailiff) dis mou
1829, 1, 14. Daniel [Bayliff] dis disunity
1829, 4, 15. Able [Bayliff] dis disunity
1830, 11, 17. Polly dis disunity
1832, 4, 18. Leah [Bayliff] rmt David Faulkner
1832, 5, 16. Joel dis jas
1833, 4, 17. Eliza Ann rocf Goshen MM, dtd 1832,9,15
1834, 11, 12. Daniel dis disunity
1837, 6, 14. Judith Curl (form Bailiff) dis mou
1838, 6, 13. Lydia Murphey (form Bailiff) dis mou
1839, 5, 15. Eliza Ann gct Springfield MM
1840, 1, 15. Springfield MM was granted permission to rst Daniel
1843, 6, 14. Ann Bone (form Bailiff) dis mou
1906, 12, 12. Amos recrq

BALES
1854, 4, 24. Rebecca Ann, dt Zimri & Elizabeth Haines, d ae 19y 8m 24d

BALLARD
----, --, --. Jesse F. & Fereby
Ch: Thomas Chalkley b 1836, 11, 30
William " 1838, 6, 12
Phebeann " 1840, 3, 18
1838, 11, 29. William F., s William & Nancy, Clermont, O.; m at Center, Hannah TAYLOR, dt Israel & Mary, Warren Co., O. (H)
1839, 9, 11. Rebecca d ae 61 bur at Center
----, --, --. John & Lydia
Ch: Jordan b 1840, 8, 21
Rebecca

BALLARD, John & Lydia, continued
Ch: Jane b 1841, 9, 24
Thomas Elwood " 1846, 12, 24 d 1863,11,10 bur Center
Alpheus b 1830, 11, 27
1842, 10, 17. Asa N., s David & Priscilla, b
----, --, --. Jordan b 1813,8,13; m Eleanor ----- b 1816,6,24
Ch: Spencer b 1852, 6, 9
Jesse " 1855, 1, 3
1852, 9, 5. Spencer d ae 8ly 7d bur Center
1861, 8, 2. Rebecca, dt Amos & Elizabeth, b
1876, 7, 5. Olive d

1808, 8, 8. William rocf Mt. Pleasant MM, Va., dtd 1808,2,27
1808, 11, 5. Enoch recrq
1808, 12, 3. David & w, Mary, & ch, Anne & Asa, rocf Mt. Pleasant MM, Va., dtd 1808,8,27
1809, 7, 1. William rmt Phebe Faulkner
1809, 8, 5. Simon rmt Barbara Rhinehart
1810, 1, 6. Cert rec for Nathan & w, Martha, & ch, Ahira, Sarah, Rhoda, David & Samuel, from Mt. Pleasant MM, Va., dtd 1809,9,30, endorsed to Miami MM
1810, 2, 3. John & w, Dinah, & ch, Lydia, Eunice, Jesse, Jonathan & William, rocf Mt. Pleasant MM, Va., dtd 1809,9,30
1810, 3, 3. Jacob, s Enoch, recrq
1811, 12, 7. Ann Rich (form Ballard) con mou
1813, 12, 4. Joseph & w, Elizabeth, & ch, Rhoda, John, Sarah, Mary Alice, David, Susannah, Joel & Juliann, rocf Mt. Pleasant MM, Va., dtd 1813,7,25
1814, 2, 5. David, Jr. gct Clear Creek MM, to m
1815, 3, 4. Mary rocf Clear Creek MM, dtd 1814,8,28
1815, 8, 19. David gct Darby Creek MM, to m
1815, 11, 18. Martha rocf Darby Creek MM
1816, 1, 20. Rebecca rmt Thomas Cary
1816, 12, 21. John rqct Caesars Creek MM
1817, 12, 20. Thomas Rhodes prcf Caesars Creek MM, to m Mary Ballard
1818, 1, 17. Mary rmt Thomas Rhodes
1818, 9, 19. Mary & ch gct New Garden MM, Ind.
1818, 9, 19. Nathan & ch, David, Samuel & Elizabeth, rocf Miami MM, dtd 1818,6,24
1819, 1, 16. Sarah gct Caesars Creek MM
1819, 1, 16. Joseph & fam gct Caesars Creek MM
1820, 4, 15. John dis mou
1823, 11, 15. David & Samuel, ch Nathan, gct Chester MM, Ind.
1824, 1, 17. Lydia rmt Jesse Doan
1825, 7, 16. John Whitson gct Springfield MM, to m Dinah Ballard
1825, 12, 17. James Whitson gct Springfield MM to m Unice Ballard
1826, 2, --. Edith Vestal (form Ballard) con mou
1826, 10, 21. Elizabeth rmt Joseph Furnace
1827, 10, 20. Caleb Davis prcf Miami MM, dtd 1827,9,26, to m Minerva Ballard
1827, 11, 31. Minerva rmt Caleb Davis
1828, 5, 17. Simon & w, Barbarah, & ch, Ruth, Rachel, Mourman, Catharine, Isaac, Daniel, Adam & Joel, gct Vermilion MM, Ill.
1830, 2, 17. Joshua Compton prcf Caesars Creek MM, dtd 1830,1,28, to m Edith Ballard
1830, 3, 17. Benajah dis disunity
1830, 3, 17. Edith rmt Joshua Compton
1830, 10, 13. Nathan Jr. dis jH
1832, 11, 14. Matilda Kinsie (form Ballard) con mou
1834, 4, 16. Rebecca (form Baily) con mou
1834, 9, 17. Wilson Carter prcf Springfield MM, dtd 1834,9,16, to m Judith F. Ballard
1834, 10, 15. Judith F. rmt Wilson Carter
1835, 8, 12. Jesse F. gct Springfield MM, to m Pharaba G. Wilson
1836, 4, 13. Phariba J. rocf Springfield MM, dtd 1836,3,15
1836, 6, 15. Joseph con mou
1836, 11, 17. Joseph con mou (H)
1839, 10, 16. John P. Honeycutt prcf Springfield MM, to m Susannah Ballard
1839, 11, 13. Susannah H. rmt John P. Honeycutt
1840, 10, 15. Hannah gct Miami MM (H)
1840, 11, 18. John con mou
1840, 11, 18. Hannah (form Taylor) dis mou & joining separatists
1841, 9, 15. David gct Clear Creek MM, to m Priscilla Lewis
1842, 9, 14. Jesse F. & w, Pheraba, & ch, Thomas Chalkley, William & Phebe Ann, gct Springfield MM
1842, 10, 12. Priscilla rocf Clear Creek MM, dtd 1842,9,20
1843, 5, 17. David F. & w, Priscilla, & ch, Asa N., gct Clear Creek MM
1843, 10, 18. Enos Wilson prcf Caesars Creek MM, to m Rebecca Ballard
1843, 11, 15. Rebecca rmt Enos Wilson
1844, 6, 12. Joseph Burgess prcf Fairfield MM to m Phebe Ballard
1844, 7, 17. Phebe rmt Joseph Burgess
1844, 11, 13. Joseph gct Dover MM
1845, 3, 12. Phebe Burgess (form Ballard) gct Fairfield MM
1849, 1, 17. Jesse gct West Branch MM, to m Mary Mote
1849, 6, 13. Mary M. rocf West Branch MM, dtd 1849,4,26
1849, 7, 18. Asa dis mou
1852, 3, 17. Jordon con mou
1852, 11, 17. Eleanor rocf Fairfield MM
1852, 11, 17. Mary Wilson (form Ballard) con mou
1852, 12, 15. Jehu & w, Mary, gct Honey Creek MM, Ind.
1853, 5, 18. Mary dis disunity
1853, 6, 15. Lydia & ch recrq

BALLARD, continued
1853, 7, 13. Mourning Henderson (form Ballard) con mou
1853, 9, 14. Benajah rst
1853, 10, 12. Amos, Lydia, Sally Mary, John Harvey & Allen, ch Benajah, recrq
1854, 4, 12. Phebe rocf Elk MM
1854, 5, 17. Phebe gct Honey Creek MM, Ind.
1861, 5, 18. Amos rpd mou
1861, 6, 12. Elisabeth rocf Fairfield MM
1862, 5, 14. Amos & w, Elizabeth, & dt, Rebecca, gct Newberry MM
1865, 9, 13. John & w, Lydia, & s, Alpheus, gct Caesars Creek MM
1865, 9, 13. Jordan gct Caesars Creek MM
1865, 9, 13. Rebecca Jane gct Caesars Creek MM
1878, 11, 13. John & w, Lydia, rocf Caesars Creek MM
1894, 3, 14. Joseph recrq
1913, 2, 12. Donald & Nadine transferred from associate to active mbrp
1920, 6, 17. Reva recrq

BANES
1848, 10, 19. Wilson rpd mou (H)
1852, 4, 15. Thomas con mcd (H)
1853, 10, 13. Watson dis mcd (H)
1854, 2, 16. Isaac & w, Hannah, gct Miami MM (H)
1854, 6, 15. Cert granted Isaac & w returned by Miami MM, because they did not live within limits of that mtg (H)
1855, 1, 18. Isaac & w, Hannah, gct Honey Creek MM, Ind. (H)
1855, 1, 18. Thomas gct Honey Creek MM, Ind. (H)

BANGHAM
1812, 9, 5. Benjamin [Bangam] & w & ch, Zachariah M., Elizabeth, Mary, Lucy Humphrey, Martha & Agnes, recrq
1820, 10, 21. Mary [Banghum] rmt Lewis Johnson
1827, 8, 18. Robert B. Bailey gct Dover MM, to m Lucy Bangham
1841, 8, 18. Jonathan prcf Dover MM, to m Jane Fawcett
1841, 9, 15. Jonathan rmt Jane Fawcett
1842, 9, 14. Jane gct Dover MM

BARNARD
1808, 2, 6. Elizabeth rmt Richard Mendinghall
1809, 2, 4. Ann rmt Joseph Mendenhall

BARNETT
----, --, --. Thomas & Theodate
Ch: Jesse b 1800, 9, 6
James " 1802, 5, 14
William " 1804, 3, 10
John " 1805, 10, 28
Jane " 1808, 1, 31
Nancy " 1810, 4, 30
Melesent " 1812, 4, 3
William b 1814, 7, 30
Thomas " 1817, 11, 20
Amos " 1820, 3, 8

1808, 1, 2. Mary rmt Amos Hodson
1812, 12, 5. Athanations gct Caesars Creek MM
1823, 12, 20. Jesse rmt Elizabeth Bailey
1826, 9, 16. Mary [Barnet] dis disunity

BARRETT
1829, 12, 11. Minerva b
1832, 9, 18. Jacob b
1888, 1, 26. Elizabeth d bur at Hastings, Neb.
1893, 10, 4. Minerva, w Jacob, d bur at Springfield

1826, 7, 16. Elizabeth rocf Carmell MM
1829, 3, 18. Elizabeth gct Carmel MM, O.
1832, 10, 17. Elizabeth [Barret] rocf Carmel MM, dtd 1832,7,21
1860, 5, 16. Minerva Jane (form Vestal) rpd mou
1860, 10, 17. Minerva Jane gct Fairfield MM
1862, 7, 16. Jacob [Barret] & w, Minerva Jane, rocf Fairfield MM
1883, 4, 18. Elizabeth recrq

BATH
1889, 6, 6. Bessie G. b
1889, 11, 28. Robert K. b

1881, 6, 15. Frederic recrq
1883, 4, 18. Harry F. recrq
1883, 4, 18. Edwin J. recrq
1884, 6, 18. Harry F. gct Wilmington MM
1895, 7, 17. Lydia relrq
1902, 1, 15. Fred C. & w, Rata K., & ch, Robert K., J. Harold & Elizabeth, gct Wilmington MM, O.

BAXTER
1830, 11, 24. Mary, w J., d bur Center

BAYLESS
1917, 3, 14. Marie, Helen & Roy recrq

BAYLIFF
----, --, --. Thomas & Sarah
Ch: Daniel b 1799, 3, 31
Leah " 1802, 3, 21
Sarah " 1803, 9, 6
Mary " 1806, 5, 28
Martha " 1808, 8, 4 d 1831,10,26 bur at New Hope
Abel b 1810, 9, 11
Anna " 1813, 2, 5
Judith " 1816, 6, 9
----, --, --. Joshua & Margaret
Ch: Amos b 1809, 8, 29 d 1814, 1,14 bur at New Hope
Polly b 1811, 1, 30

BAYLIFF, Joshua & Margaret, continued
Ch: Joel b 1812, 8, 29
Lydia " 1812, 8, 29
Daniel " 1816, 5, 22
1816, 6, 15. Margaret d ae 23d bur New Hope
1831, 11, 9. Thomas d ae 64y 1m 24d bur New Hope
1845, 3, 8. Sarah d ae 71 bur New Hope
1846, 7, 29. Joshua d ae 72y 7m 23d

BEALS
1811, 3, 2. Cert rec for Joab [Beal] from New Hope MM, endorsed to Fairfield MM
1825, 10, 15. Solomon Faulkner gct Lees Creek MM, to m Ruth [Bayles]
1837, 2, 16. Isaac B. rocf Goose Creek MM, dtd 1836,3,17, endorsed by Miami MM, 1836, 12,21 (H)

BEANS
1843, 9, 14. Isaac & w, Hannah, & s, Watson T., rocf Wrightstown MM, Pa., dtd 1843,5,3 (H)
1843, 9, 14. Thomas rocf Wrightstown MM, Pa., dtd 1843,5,3 (H)
1843, 10, 19. Wilson J. rocf Wrightstown MM, Pa., dtd 1843,5,3 (H)

BEESON
1844, 12, 18. Martha & ch, Caroline, Daniel H., Jane & Joel Wright, rocf Fairfield MM, dtd 1844,9,21
1846, 9, 16. Martha [Beason] & ch, Caroline, Daniel W., Jane & Joel, gct Fairfield MM

BELL
1842, 9, 15. Isaac gct Camden MM, Ind. (H)

BENBOW
1812, 8, 1. John & w, Charity, & ch, Miriam & Evan, rocf New Garden MM, N. C., dtd 1810,9,29
1814, 10, 1. John & fam gct White Water MM
1815, 3, 4. John & w, Charity, & ch, Miriam, Evan, Benjamin, Aaron & Moses, gct White Water MM

BENNETT
1810, 3, 3. Ann (form Dillen) dis mou
1862, 7, 16. Jacob & w, Minerva, rocf Fairfield MM
1871, 3, 15. Sarah Jane [Bennet] recrq
1871, 4, 12. Sarah Jane [Bennet] gct Elk MM

BENSON
1809, 9, 2. William dis mou & attending musters

BETTS
1814, 8, 6. Mary rocf Fairfield MM, dtd 1814,5,28

BEVAN
----, --, --. Owen [Biven] m Mary HIATT
Ch: Lewis b 1829, 9, 6
Abel " 1831, 10, 27
Elizabeth " 1835, 3, 30
1836, 5, 23. Stacy d ae 69y 1m 15d bur Center
----, --, --. Abel b 1810,2,18; m Charlotte F. ----- b 1814,10,18
Ch: Phineas R. b 1837, 11, 15 d 1860, 7,23 bur New Hope
Robert b 1839, 4, 20 " 1859, 3, 7 bur New Hope
Mary Jane b 1841, 8, 23
Phanny Ann " 1843, 1, 22
Sarah Elizabeth " 1849, 7, 2
Hansel Malinda " 1851, 11, 7
Emma " 1853, 4, 10
1844, 11, 22. Euphenia A. b
1845, 9, 22. Lydia E. b
1847, 3, 12. Hannah L. b
1865, 2, 22. Lydia, w Stacy, d ae 91y 8m 24d bur New Hope

1825, 4, 16. Stacy & w, Lydia, & ch, John, Owen, Samuel & Elizabeth, rocf Flushing MM, dtd 1824,6,25, endorsed by Fall Creek MM, 1825,2,19
1827, 11, 27. John [Biven] dis mou
1828, 12, 17. Owen [Biven] rpd married to Mary Hiatt
1834, 11, 12. Elizabeth Griffith (form Biven) dis mou
1835, 8, 12. Owen [Biven] dis disunity
1835, 8, 12. Samuel [Biven] dis disunity
1836, 9, 14. Abel [Biven] rmt Charlotte Fawcett
1837, 9, 13. Abel & w, Charlotte, gct Springfield MM
1837, 12, 13. Mary, wd Owen, & ch, Lewis, Abel & Elizabeth, gct Dunkirk MM, Ind.
1839, 11, 13. Abel & w, Charlotte, & ch, Phineas R. & Robert, rocf Springfield MM, dtd 1839,10,15
1846, 9, 12. Abel & w, Charlotte, & ch, Phineas R., Robert, Mary Jane, Phamy Ann, Stacy & Lydia Ellen, gct Springfield MM
1849, 8, 15. Abel & w, Charlotte, & ch, Phenias R., Robert, Mary Jane, Phamy Ann, Stacy, Lydia Ellen & Hannah Louisa, rocf Springfield MM, dtd 1849,5,19
1868, 8, 18. Mary J. rmt William Gallimore
1878, 12, 18. Stacy gct Cherry Grove MM, Ind.
1892, 10, 13. Abel & w, Charlotte T., gct Dover MM
1914, 5, 13. Horace L. rocf Springfield MM

BICKHART
1889, 4, 13. Jacob & Elizabeth recrq
1889, 12, 18. Jacob [Bichart] & w, Elizabeth, gct Wilmington MM

BIRDSALL
1825, 2, 25. Wm. H. b
1827, 11, 15. Rachel b
1840, 2, 20. Samuel, s William & Ruth, Clinton Co., O.; m at Center, Ann HIATT, dt Hezekiah & Ann, Clinton Co., O. (H)
1841, 11, 5. Joseph d bur at Center
1843, 1, 26. Levinia m Edward G. CARROLL (H)
----, --, --. Charles M. & Annie
Ch: Mary E. b 1876, 4, 5
Tracy " 1877, 8, 3
Mabel d 1877, 9, 5
Mabel " 1882, 12, 7
William " 1882,12,13
1890, 12, 22. Rachel L., w William H., d bur Springfield Cemetery
1882, 12, 7. Wm. & Vera (twins) b
1900, 6, 4. Wm. d

1813, 10, 2. Daniel rocf Oblong MM, N. Y., dtd 1811,11,18
1814, 3, 5. Zada & ch, Patty M., James A., Hannah A. & Sarah, recrq
1827, 1, 20. Daniel & w, Zada, & ch, James, Albert, Hannah Almirah, Sarah, Lydia, Phebe & Priscilla, gct Cincinnati MM
1827, 1, 20. Martha Melissa gc
1836, 6, 16. Rachel P. & Martha rocf Goose Creek MM, Va. (H)
1836, 7, 14. Andrew [Birdsel] & ch, Thomas W., Rachel P., Joseph, Martha, George & Edward, rocf Goose Creek MM, Va. (H)
1838, 5, 17. William & ch, Samuel, Hannah, Levenia, William H. & Thomas, rocf Indian Spring MM, Md., dtd 1838,3,7, endorsed by Miami MM, 1838,4,25 (H)
1838, 5, 17. Elizabeth rocf Indian Spring MM, Md., dtd 1838,3,7, endorsed by Miami MM, 1838,4,25 (H)
1838, 5, 17. Rachel rocf Indian Spring MM, Md., dtd 1838,3,7, endorsed by Miami MM, 1838,4,25 (H)
1838, 11, 20. William gct Miami MM, to m Ruth Wales (H)
1841, 9, 15. Mary Ann (form Hiatt) dis mou & jH
1842, 12, 15. Elizabeth Hoyle (form Birdsall) con mou (H)
1843, 11, 30. William dis (H)
1845, 2, 19. Thomas W. C. dis disunity (H)
1846, 6, 18. Ruth gct Miami MM (H)
1847, 10, 14. Hannah dis jas (H)
1848, 3, 14. Rachel Sabin (form Birdsall) con mou (H)
1848, 10, 19. Thomas gct White Water MM, to m Mary B. Thistlethwaite (H)
1849, 7, 19. Rachel Longstreth (form Birdsall) con mou (H)
1850, 1, 17. Mary T. [Birdsal] rocf White Water MM (H)
1852, 5, 13. Thomas B. [Birdsal] & w, Mary B., & ch, Albert A., gct White Water MM (H)
1854, 6, 15. Edward con mcd (H)
1855, 1, 18. William H. con mcd (H)
1857, 5, 14. George F. con mcd (H)
1863, 9, 17. Rachel L. rocf Wrightstown MM, Pa., dtd 1863,4,8 (H)
1868, 4, 15. William H. & w, Rachel L., recrq
1869, 1, 13. Charles M. recrq
1899, 6, --. Charles M. & w, Anna, & ch, Grace & Vera, gct White Water MM, Ind.

BOGAN
1910, 2, 16. Zoe recrq

BOND
1891, 4, 15. Rosa recrq

BONE
1843, 6, 14. Ann (form Bailiff) dis mou
1877, 3, 14. James C. recrq
1885, 2, 19. Lincoln dropped from mbrp
1885, 12, 16. Lucian relrq
1888, 5, 16. Susan recrq
1889, 6, 12. Ella Mary recrq
1889, 6, 12. Eliza recrq
1910, 3, 16. Callie recrq
1920, 10, 13. Kelly relrq

BORING
1921, 2, 16. Damarris M. gct Wilmington MM, O.

BRACKNEY
1863, 11, 18. Mahlon rocf Fairfield MM
1911, 4, 12. John & w, Lillian, & ch, Charlotte, Loren, Charles, Ruth & John William, rocf Wilmington MM, O.
1913, 2, 12. Charlotte, Loren & Charles transferred from associate to active mbrp

BRADSHAW
1907, 4, 17. Harley [Brodshaw] recrq
1914, 3, 18. Harley relrq

BRANN
----, --, --. James b 1848,12,26; m Mercy Ann ----- b 1850,6,6
Ch: Maria b 1871, 3, 27
Roscoe " 1880, 7, 9
1853, 9, 29. Emma J. (form McKee) b

1871, 3, 15. Samuel L. recrq
1871, 4, 12. Mercie A. rocf Springfield MM
1873, 12, 17. James W. recrq
1883, 9, 12. Catharine rocf Dover MM
1889, 12, 18. James W. & fam gct Wilmington MM
1906, 3, 14. Catharine gct Wilmington MM
1906, 3, 14. Clifford gct Wilmington MM

BRAY
1834, 10, 15. Lucy (form Taylor) dis mou

BREEDLOVE
1877, 3, 14. Lizzie recrq
1885, 12, 16. Mary relrq

BRINDLE
1904, 1, 13. Addie & Alma gct Wilmington MM

BROCK
1808, 5, 7. Charity & ch, Elijah, Ruth, Susannah, Kiturah & Lucinda, rocf Bush River MM, S. C., dtd 1806,9,27

BROOK
----, --, --. William [Brooks] b 1802,2,25; m Lydia L. ----- b 1805,4,16
Ch: Samuel b 1833, 5, 30
Gilpin " 1834, 10, 18
Sarah " 1839, 1, 9
Lydia Maria" 1842, 2, 1
----, --, --. Abraham & Elizabeth [Brooke]
Ch: Henry
Howard b 1833, 10, 31
Caroline
Elizabeth " 1835, 7, 26
1844, 2, 6. Samuel [Brooke] d bur in home lot at Oakland

1838, 2, 15. Abraham & w, Elizabeth, & ch, Henry & Caroline, rocf Marlborough MM, dtd 1837,10,28 (H)
1838, 6, 14. William & w, Lydia, & ch, Samuel & Gilpin, rocf Marlborough MM, dtd 1838,2,21 (H)
1838, 11, 14. Henry Howard & Caroline Elizabeth, beth, ch Abraham & Elizabeth, rocf Marlborough MM, dtd 1838,9,25
1839, 5, 16. Samuel [Brooke] & w, Sarah, rocf Marlborough MM, dtd 1839,3,23 (H)
1839, 7, 17. James B. rocf Springborough MM, dtd 1839,6,25
1841, 3, 17. Samuel & Gilpin [Brooks] ch William & Lydia, rocf Marlborough MM
1843, 11, 30. Abraham [Brooke]dis disunity (H)
1844, 4, 18. William [Brooke] dis disunity (H)
1845, 7, 17. Margaret [Brooke] dis disunity (H)
1848, 10, 17. Lydia & ch, Samuel, Gilpin, Sarah & Lydia, gct Marlboro MM, O. (H)
1850, 4, 18. Samuel & Gilpin, ch William, gct Marlboro MM
1854, 8, 17. Henry [Brooke] gct Marlborough MM (H)

BROOMHALL
1832, 12, 12. Elizabeth [Bromhaul] dis mou
1833, 1, 16. Rachel (form Kinsey) dis mou
1867, 7, 17. Rachel recrq

BROWN
1843, 6, 3. Anne d bur at Center

1827, 11, 27. John [Brow] prcf Miami MM, dtd 1827,10,31, to m Mary W. Carpenter
1827, 12, 15. John rmt Mary W. Carpenter
1828, 1, 19. Mary W. gct Miami MM
1835, 7, 16. Azariah rocf Little Britton MM, dtd 1835,5,16 (H)
1835, 7, 16. Rachel rocf Little Britain MM, dtd 1835,4,18 (H)
1835, 7, 16. Arin rocf Little Britain MM, dtd 1835,4,18 (H)
1837, 4, 12. John & w, Mary, & ch, Aaron W. & Eliza Ann, rocf Miami MM, dtd 1836,12,21
1838, 10, 18. Rachel McMillan (form Brown) dis mou (H)
1841, 5, 12. Elizabeth Jefferes (form Brown) rocf Nottingham & Little Brittan MM
1842, 8, 17. John gct Miami MM, to m Elizabeth R. Jones
1843, 4, 12. John & ch, Aaron W. & Ann Eliza, gct Miami MM
1865, 4, 26. Mary Maria (form Haines) rpd mou
1865, 11, 15. Mary Maria gct Springfield MM, Ind.
1888, 2, 15. J. Frank recrq
1888, 2, 15. Ella N. recrq
1888, 3, 14. Frank & w, Ella N., gct Dover MM
1901, 7, 17. John F. & w, Ella, & s, Earl, rocf Dover MM
1901, 11, 13. Clement gct Wilmington MM, O.
1913, 11, 12. Frank & w, Ella, gc

BRUCE
1849, 2, 17. Charles M. b

1876, 3, 15. Charles M. recrq
1885, 12, 16. Charles relrq

BRYAN
1813, 9, 4. Polly dis mou
1823, 11, 15. James recrq

BUCKLEY
1921, 2, 16. Bessie Miars relrq

BUCKNER
1826, 11, 18. Ann gct Vermillion MM

BULLEN
1910, 2, 16. Elvert L. recrq
1910, 2, 16. Claybourne, Estella, Herbert L., James Ansther & Ada Ruth recrq
1919, 3, 12. Elvert [Bullin] dropped from mbrp

BURCH
1905, 4, 12. George A. & w, Florence, recrq
1906, 5, 16. George & Florence gct Cesars Creek MM

BURDEN
1827, 10, 20. Peter [Bourden] rocf Miami MM, dtd 1827,7,25
1828, 5, 17. Peter [Borden] dis mou
1887, 5, 18. ----- dis disunity
1889, 6, 12. Franklin recrq
1889, 6, 12. Laura recrq

BURDEN, continued
1889, 6, 12. Edward recrq
1894, 3, 14. Frank recrq
1894, 3, 14. Sam recrq
1919, 3, 12. Frank dropped from mbrp

BURGESS
1844, 6, 12. Joseph prcf Fairfield MM, to m Phebe Ballard
1844, 7, 17. Joseph rmt Phebe Ballard
1845, 3, 12. Phebe (form Ballard) gct Fairfield MM

BURSON
1838, 7, 18. Edward & w, Jemima, & ch, John W. & Lydia, rocf Springborough MM, dtd 1838,5,22
1842, 9, 14. Brooks Johnson prcf Miami MM, to m Lydia Burson
1842, 10, 12. Lydia rmt Brooks Johnson
1849, 11, 14. John dis disunity
1852, 5, 12. Edward & w, Jemima, gct Miami MM

BURTON
1907, 2, 13. Samuel & w, Rebecca, & ch, Willard Ray & Glenn Addison, recrq
1907, 2, 13. William & w, Mary E., & ch, Clarence & Lena, recrq

BUSKLER
1813, 4, 3. Joanna Buskler, gr dt Joanna Hayworth, recrq

BUTLER
----, --, --. William m Mary ----- d 1811,5,7 ae 36
Ch: David b 1798, 7, 27
Jonathan " 1800, 5, 28
Michal " 1802, 4, 10
Elizabeth " 1805, 5, 6
William " 1807, 9, 17
William m 2nd Esther TODD (m 1812,12,2)
Ch: Joseph b 1813, 9, 22
James " 1815, 3, 5 d 1822, 4,13
Jesse " 1816, 9, 29 " 1816,12, 6
Lydia " 1817, 10, 16
Priscilla " 1820, 9, 4
Edward " 1822, 5, 28

1812, 11, 7. William gct Fairfield MM, to m
1813, 5, 1. Esther rocf Fairfield MM, dtd 1813,3,27
1822, 10, 19. Michal gct West Grove MM, Ind.
1822, 11, 16. David & w, Mary, gct West Grove MM, Ind.
1822, 12, 21. William & w, Esther, & ch, Jonathan, Elizabeth, William, Joseph, Lydia, Priscilla & Edwin, gct West Grove MM, Ind.
1822, 12, 21. Cert rec for Lemuel & fam from Uper MM, Va., endorsed to White Water MM, Indiana.
1893, 5, 17. George B. White & w, Sarah Rufina, & niece, Edna Butler, rocf Springfield MM, dtd 1893,4,15
1896, 1, 15. George B. White & w, Sarah Rufina & niece, Edna Butler, gct Springfield MM

BUTTERWORTH
1822, 5, 18. Samuel rpd married to Hannah L. Taylor
1822, 7, 20. Hannah gct Miami MM
1826, 7, 15. William rmt Elizabeth Linton
1826, 10, 21. Elizabeth gct Miami MM

BYARD
1910, 2, 16. Elizabeth recrq

BYRD
1910, 2, 16. Thomas McArthur recrq

CADWALADER
1829, 8, 12. Sarah (form Bailey) con mou
1840, 3, 18. Sarah gct New Garden MM, Ind.
1845, 6, 18. John prcf Miami MM, to m Rachel Farquhar
1845, 7, 16. John rmt Rachel Farquhar
1845, 12, 17. Jane (form Fallis) con mou
1846, 7, 15. Jane N. gct Miami MM
1848, 9, 13. Rachel gct Miami MM
1854, 12,13. John T.. & w, Rachel, & ch, Albert D., Isaac H. & John F., rocf Miami MM
1854, 12, 14. Hester gct Miami MM (H)
1855, 3, 15. Isaiah Welch gct Miami MM, to m Leah Cadwalader (H)

CANNIDY
1808, 1, 2. Mary, gr ch Mary Sanders, recrq

CAREN
1846, 7, 15. Elias & w, Jane, & ch, Mary Elizabeth, Sarah Margaret, Hannah & Martha Emily, rocf Newberry MM

CARMAN
1845, 2, 13. Ruth rocf Hopewell MM, Va., dtd 1844,10,10 (H)
1854, 6, 15. Ruth gct Miami MM (H)
1877, 3, 14. Millard H. recrq
1881, 6, 15. Millard dis disunity

CARPENTER
----, --, --. Jacob & Elizabeth
Ch: Edward b 1815, 2, 2
Thomas " 1817, 11, 12
1819, 7, 23. Edward d
1825, 10, 26. Thomas C. d
1836, 2, 15. Isaac d ae 56y 3m 5d bur Center, O.
1838, 11, 12. Abraham d ae 63
1852, 3, 25. Jacob d bur Center
----, --, --. Abraham bur at Center

1815, 10, 21. Isaac & w, Mercy, & ch, Ezra Lydia Calvin Esther Walter & Sarah, rocf

CARPENTER, continued
Duanesburgh, N. Y., dtd 1815,9,29
1815, 10, 21. Jacob & w, Elizabeth, & ch, Eliza Mary & Edward, rocf Hudson MM, N.Y., dtd 1815,8,22
1820, 8, 19. Eliza D. rmt Joseph Doan Jr.
1823, 4, 19. Lydia rmt Amos Fallis
1826, 3, 18. Ezra gct Pearl Street MM, N.Y.
1827, 11, 27. John Brow prcf Miami MM, dtd 1827,10,31, to m Mary W. Carpenter
1827, 12, 15. Mary W. rmt John Brown
1828, 10, 15. Esther rmt Dean King
1828, 12, 17. Jacob & w, Elizabeth, & ch, William & Matthew, gct Cincinnati MM
1829, 3, 18. Esther King (form Carpenter) gct White Water MM, Ind.
1830, 1, 13. Jacob & w, Elizabeth, & William Comstock, minor, rocf Cincinnati MM,dtd 1829,12,31
1830, 10, 13. Calvin gct Cincinnati MM
1834, 6, 17. Abraham & w, Anna, rocf Amawalk MM, N. Y., dtd 1834,4,11
1834, 6, 17. Nathaniel & w, Zermiah, & ch, Catharine, Mary & Edwin, rocf Amawalk MM, N. Y., dtd 1834,4,11
1834, 10, 15. Walter T. rmt Susan Mabee
1834, 11, 12. Walter T. & w, Susan M., gct Cincinnati MM
1835, 3, 18. Sarah rmt David McMillan Jr.
1836, 7, 13. Walter & w, Susan, & s, Charles, rocf Cincinnati MM, dtd 1836,6,16
1841, 5, 12. Walter T. & w, Susan M., & s, Charles Grey, gct Springfield MM
1843, 2, 15. Nathaniel & w, Zeriah, & ch, Catharine,Mary T. & Edwin, gct Cincinnati MM
1843, 2, 15. Anna gct Cincinnati MM

CARR
1889, 11, 13. Jane relrq

CARROLL
1843, 1, 26. Edward G., s Joseph & Elizabeth, Blackford Co., Ind.; m at Center, Levinia BIRDSALL, dt William & Ruth, Clinton Co., O. (H)

1833, 7, 17. David [Carrol] gct Springfield MM
1843, 9, 14. Levinia gct Camden MM, Ind. (H)
1846, 1, 15. Rebecca H., Joseph, Sarah, Solon, John & Eliza Ann, minors, rocf White Water MM, dtd 1845,11,28

CARTER
----, --, --. George, s John & Ann, b 1782,3, 8; m Miriam WILSON, dt Jesse & Elizabeth, b 1787,2,2
Ch: Jesse b 1806, 3, 2
John " 1808, 3, 28
Samuel " 1810, 3, 19
Wilson " 1812, 9, 25
Cyrus " 1815, 3, 5

1875, 12, 28. William d (s Samuel & Lydia)

1811, 12, 7. George & w, Meriam, & ch, Jesse, John & Samuel, rocf Spring MM, N. C., dtd 1811,8,31
1812, 5, 2. Nathaniel rocf Spring MM, N.C., dtd 1811,8,31
1814, 7, 2. Nancy, w Nathaniel, & ch, Jane, John B., Susannah, Enoch & Ann, recrq
1833, 8, 14. Enoch prcf Springfield MM, dtd 1833,8,13, to m Elizabeth Faulkner
1833, 9, 18. Enoch rmt Elizabeth Faulkner
1834, 3, 12. Elizabeth gct Springfield MM
1834, 9, 17. Wilson prcf Springfield MM, dtd 1834,9,16, to m Judith F. Ballard
1834, 10, 15. Wilson rmt Judith F. Ballard
1835, 2, 18. Judith F. gct Dover MM
1856, 2, 16. George D. prcf Dover MM, dtd 1856,1,17, to m Elizabeth Haines
1856, 3, 12. George rmt Elizabeth Haines
1856, 9, 17. Elizabeth gct Dover MM
1874, 3, 18. Samuel & w, Lydia A., & ch, Alice D., Mary E. & William C., rocf Newberry MM, dtd 1874,1,19
1876, 6, 15. Samuel & w, Lydia Ann, & ch, Alice D. & Mary Emily, gct Newberry MM,O.

CARVER
1839, 9, 19. George & w, Ann, & ch, Maryhannah & Martha Jane, rocf Byberry MM, Pa., dtd 1839,4,30 (H)
1842, 4, 14. Eli rocf Byberry MM, Pa., dtd 1841,9,28 (H)
1843, 11, 30. George & w, Ann, & ch, Mary Hannah, Martha Jane, Jacob M. & Charles Ann, gct Miami MM (H)
1843, 12, 14. Eli gct Miami MM (H)
1845, 4, 17. Rachel Read (form Carver) con mou (H)
1845, 4, 17. Mary H. Croasdale (form Carver) con mou (H)

CARY
----, --, --. John [Carey] b 1826,8,16; m Elizabeth ----- b 1827,11,23
Ch: Enoch L. b 1859, 4, 12
Samuel F. " 1861, 8, 25
Nathan H. " 1863, 10, 1
1887, 3, 14. Dallas J. b
1888, 5, 18. Mary E. b

1815, 11, 16. Thomas rocf Mt. Pleasant MM, dtd 1815,9,30
1816, 1, 20. Thomas rmt Rebecca Ballard
1817, 4, 19. Thomas & w, Rhoda, & dt, Elizabeth, gct Caesars Creek MM
1817, 4, 19. Mary [Cory] (form Osborne) dis mou
1846, 7, 15. Elias & w, Jane, & ch, Mary Elizabeth, Sarah Margaret, Hannah & Martha Eunty, rocf Newberry MM, dtd 1846,3,11
1847, 6, 16. Elias & w, Jane, & ch,Mary

CARY, continued
Elizabeth, Sarah Margaret, Hannah M. & Martha Emily, gct Newberry MM
1856, 9, 17. John [Carey] prcf New Burry MM, to m Elizabeth Lundy
1856, 10, 15. John [Carey] rmt Elizabeth Lundy
1856, 11, 12. Elizabeth gct Newberry MM
1867, 12, 18. John [Carey] & fam rocf Newberry MM, dtd 1867,10,21
1887, 6, 15. John & w dis disunity
1908, 3, 18. Bula McElwee [Corey] rocf Dover MM
1912, 1, 7. Nathan [Carey] gct Whittier MM, Calif.
1913, 2, 12. Esther [Carey] transferred from associate to active mbrp
1914, 10, 14. Louise B. [Carey] rocf Springfield MM
1917, 3, 14. Dallas J. [Carey] & w, Beula, & s, Harold, gct Wilmington MM

CHANDLER
1885, 10, 14. Calvin d

1885, 5, 15. Calvin B. rec in mbrp

CHARLES
1863, 9, 16. Matthew prcf White Water MM, Ind., to m Eliza D. Timberlake
1863, 10, 14. Matthew rmt Eliza D. Timberlake
1864, 10, 12. Eliza D. gct White Water MM

CHEW
1816, 12, 21. John rocf Mt. Pleasant MM, Va., dtd 1816,9,28
1817, 1, 18. Martha con mou
1817, 4, 19. Ephraim & w, Rachel, & ch, William & Mary, rocf Mt. Pleasant MM, Va., dtd 1816,9,28
1818, 10, 17. Ephraim & w, Rachel, & ch, William, Mary & Isaac, gct Newberry MM
1818, 12, 19. Samuel & w, Abigail, & ch, Alice Mary Rueben & Ruth, rocf Chestnut Creek MM, Va., dtd 1818,7,26
1819, 10, 16. John gct Newberry MM

CLARK
1808, 3, 5. Rebecca Stuart (form Clark) dis mou
1809, 11, 4. Jonathan dis disunity
1858, 12, 15. George D. Haworth gct White Water MM, to m Sarah Clark

CLEAVER
1820, 2, 19. Sarah recrq (con misconduct)
1821, 9, 15. Sarah gct Springfield MM

CLELLAND
----, --, --. John Wm. [Clealand] b 1836,11,2; m Sarah Ann ----- b 1849,12,17
Ch: Marietta b 1868, 1, 12
Martin Luther " 1869, 7, 11
Isaac Thomas b 1871, 1, 21
Martha Ellen " 1873, 4, 12 d at ae of 15d
John Wm. " 1874, 7, 14 " " " " 1y 6m 20d
Rebecca Jane " 1876, 7, 8

1875, 8, 18. William & w, Sarah Ann, & ch, Marietta, Martin Luther, Thomas & John William, rocf Springfield MM, dtd 1875,6,19
1881, 3, 16. William & w, Sarah Ann, & ch, Marietta, Luther, Thomas & Rebecca Jane, gct Springfield MM, O.

CLEMMER
1909, 4, 14. Daisy Howell rocf Wilmington MM, O.

CLINE
1834, 6, 17. Rachel (form Leonard) dis mou
1836, 12, 14. Eleanor (form Leonard) dis mou
1889, 6, 12. Israel recrq
1889, 6, 12. Mary recrq

CLOUD
1810, 7, 7. Joseph rmt Mary Hunt

COATE
----, --, --. John b 1785,7,19; m ----- -----
Ch: Joseph b 1810, 11, 1
Elijah " 1812, 7, 20
Hiram " 1815, 9, 8
Rebecca " 1817, 6, 26
Martha " 1819, 3, 26
Lindley M. " 1821, 9, 9
John m 2nd Mary BAUGHAM b 1802,8,30
Ch: Esther b 1829, 7, 8
Humphrey " 1830, 12, 5 d 1833, 8,30
Lucy " 1832, 4, 9
Cyrus " 1835, 3, 20
Benjamin " 1836, 7, 11
----, --, --. Elijah b 1812,7,20; m Rebecca ----- b 1813,8,17
Ch: Hiram b 1833, 11, 20
----, --, --. Hiram & Rachel
Ch: Elizabeth Painter b 1839, 9, 9
Elijah Smith " 1841, 12, 25
Ophelia Adelaide D. b 1844, 7, 10
Alvin P. " 1848, 3, 18 d 1849, 5,21 bur New Hope
Alice S. b 1848, 3, 18
Mercy Ann " 1850, 6, 6
Rebecca Mary " 1853, 11, 29

COATE, Joseph & Agnes, continued
Ch: Elizabeth
B. b 1833, 3, 14
Nancy " 1834, 12, 22
John " 1836, 10, 21
Martha " 1838, 11, 28
Mary " 1841, 2, 15 d 1844, 1, 2
1866, 9, 24. Lucian Clare, s Elijah & Mary E., b
1824, 8, 21. Aquilla [Coats] & w, Rachel, & s, Isaac Lewis, rocf Hopewell MM, dtd 1824,5,6
1829, 7, 15. Aquila [Coats] dis jH
1829, 12, 16. Rachel [Coats] dis jH
1834, 12, 17. John [Cote] & w, Mary, & ch, Hiram, Rebecca, Martha, Lindley M., Esther & Lucy Cote, & Lewis Johnson, s Mary by form m, rocf Union MM, dtd 1834,11,12
1835, 4, 15. Joseph T. [Cote] & w, Agnes, & dt, Elizabeth, rocf Union MM, dtd 1835,2,18
1835, 11, 18. Elijah & w, Rebecca, & s, Hiram, rocf Union MM, dtd 1835,9,16
1836, 5, 18. Elijah & w, Rebecca, & s, Hiram, gct Caesars Creek MM
1837, 4, 12. Rebecca [Coat] rmt David Curl
1838, 12, 12. Hiram [Coats] rmt Rachel W. Painter
1841, 8, 18. William Longstreth prcf Miami MM, to m Martha Coate
1841, 9, 15. Martha rmt William Longstreth
1843, 12, 13. Joseph T. dis joining Separatists
1844, 4, 17. Agnes dis joining Separatists
1844, 6, 12. Lindley M. dis joining Separatists
1845, 1, 15. John [Coat] dis joining Separatists
1845, 9, 17. Martha (form Painter) dis mou
1848, 9, 13. Edwin Hadley prcf Springfield MM, to m Esther Coate
1848, 10, 18. Esther rmt Edwin Hadley
1854, 6, 14. Mary B. & s, Cyrus, gct Springfield MM
1855, 4, 14. Springfield MM granted permission to rst John
1857, 4, 15. John Jr. gct Springfield MM
1857, 4, 15. Elizabeth B., Nancy & Martha gct Springfield MM
1858, 11, 17. Springfield MM was granted permission to rst Joseph T. [Coat] & w, Agnes
1866, 5, 16. Elijah S. con mou & taking part in military service
1866, 7, 18. Ezekiel N. Kirk & w, Elizabeth P. (form Coate) con mou
1869, 5, 14. Hiram & w, Rachel, & ch, Rebecca Mary & Hiram Alvin, gct Springfield MM
1869, 5, 14. Alice S. gct Springfield MM
1869, 5, 14. Mercie A. gct Springfield MM
1869, 5, 14. Elijah S. gct Springfield MM

COFFIN
1808, 7, 2. Deborah rocf Little River MM, N. C., dtd 1808,3,26
1808, 12, 3. Deborah Johnson (form Coffin) dis mou & jas
1841, 5, 12. Jesse prcf Newberry MM, to m Elizabeth Whinery
1841, 6, 16. Jesse rmt Elizabeth Whinery
1841, 8, 18. Elizabeth (form Whinery) gct Newberry MM

COLE
1829, 12, 16. Rachel dis jH

COLLETT
1809, 7, 1. Rebecca rocf Hopewell MM, dtd 1809,7,6(?)
1897, 9, 15. Alice (form Dedrick) relrq

COLVIN
1907, 9, 18. Hannah gct Ceasars Creek MM

COMELY
1868, 4, 11. Mary recrq

COMPTON
----, --, --. John & Jane
Ch: Joshua b 1823, 2, 4
Phebe " 1825, 8, 19
Samuel " 1827, 1, 22
Hannah Ann " 1828, 7, 29
Sarah " 1831, 2, 10
Martha " 1833, 12, 30 d 1839, 4,18
Mary M. " 1838, 4, 11
1831, 7, 31. Edith d ae 19y 4d bur New Hope

1808, 7, 2. Rachel, w Matthew, & ch, Esther, Betty & Rebeckah, recrq
1809, 4, 1. Matthew recrq
1809, 7, 1. John & w, Ann, & dt, Lydia, rocf Miami MM, dtd 1809,5,6
1829, 10, 14. John & w, Jane, & ch, Joshua, Phebe & Hannah Ann, rocf Caesars Creek MM, dtd 1829,9,24
1830, 2, 17. Joshua prcf Caesars Creek MM, dtd 1830,1,28, to m Edith Ballard
1830, 3, 17. Joshua rmt Edith Ballard
1831, 6, 15. Joshua rocf Caesars Creek MM, dtd 1831,3,31
1832, 2, 15. Joshua & dt, Lucetta, gct Caesars Creek MM
1833, 6, 12. Nancy (form Thornburgh) con mou
1834, 11, 12. Elizabeth Ann (form Thornburgh) con mou
1835, 5, 13. Nancy & Elizabeth Ann gct Caesars Creek MM
1846, 1, 14. Isaac Votaw prcf White River MM, Ind., to m Phebe Compton
1846, 2, 18. Phebe rmt Isaac Votaw
1849, 6, 13. Elizabeth Ann & ch, Judith & James, rocf Cesars Creek MM, dtd 1849,4,26
1851, 9, 17. John & w, Jane, & ch, Mary C., Nathan & Rebecca Jane, gct Mississiniwa MM, Ind.
1851, 9, 17. Joshua E. gct Mississiniwa MM, Ind.

COMPTON, continued
1851, 9, 17. Hannah Ann & Sarah gct Mississiniwa MM, Ind.
1860, 2, 15. James rpd mou; dropped from mbrp
1866, 12, 12. Elizabeth Ann Mendenhall (form Compton) rpd mou
1867, 2, 13. Elizabeth Ann Mendenhall & dt, Judith Ann Compton, gct Caesars Creek MM
1919, 3, 12. Elizabeth Hurley gct Caesars Creek MM

COMSTOCK
1828, 7, 16. Elizabeth, William & Matthew, ch Ebenezar, dec, & Anna, rocf Hudson MM, N. Y., dtd 1828,2,20
1828, 12, 17. Elizabeth, William & Matthew gct Cincinnati MM
1830, 1, 13. Jacob Carpenter & w, Elizabeth, & William Comstock, minor, rocf Cincinnati MM, dtd 1829,12,31
1830, 8, 18. Cert rec for Anna & ch, Mary, Susan, Sarah & Emeline, from Hudson MM, N. Y., dtd 1828,5,20, endorsed to Cincinnati MM
1836, 7, 13. William gct Cincinnati MM

CONGER
1908, 3, 1. Ira d ae 60y 7m 3d

1874, 4, 15. Eri recrq
1879, 1, 15. Ira recrq
1881, 4, 13. Sarah Ann recrq
1883, 6, 13. Sarah dis disunity
1888, 2, 15. George recrq
1888, 2, 15. Charley recrq
1888, 2, 15. Oliver recrq
1889, 6, 12. Irena recrq
1896, 2, 12. Lena recrq
1897, 4, 14. Missouri Etta recrq
1897, 4, 14. Vena Viola recrq
1901, 4, 17. Joseph recrq
1901, 4, 17. Orange recrq
1903, 2, 18. Nora M. recrq
1906, 2, 14. George recrq

CONNER
----, --, --. John & Rachel
Ch: Wm. b 1795, 10, 28
Catherine " 1798, 4, 29
Jesse " 1800, 2, 12
John " 1801, 8, 10
Thomas " 1802, 1, 29
Nancy " 1805, 5, 7
Rachel " 1807, 7, 29

COOK
1848, 10, 5. Amos, s Amos & Elizabeth, Warren Co., O.; m at Center, Mary WHITSON, dt Ezekiel & Mary Thomas, Clinton Co., O. (H)

1807, 10, 3. Joseph & ch, John, Joseph, Uriah, Mary & Peter, rocf Bush River MM, S. C., dtd 1807,5,30
1808, 5, 7. Phebe recrq
1809, 3, 4. Joseph gct Fairfield MM, to m
1809, 3, 4. Wright gct Fairfield MM, to m
1809, 7, 1. Ann rocf Fairfield MM, dtd 1809, 5,27
1809, 7, 1. Elisabeth rocf Fairfield MM, dtd 1809,5,27
1811, 4, 6. Cert rec for John from Deep River MM, dtd 1810,9,3; endorsed to Caesars Creek MM
1813, 12, 4. Amos rmt Susannah Perkins
1814, 3, 5. Susannah gct Miami MM
1814, 12, 3. John rocf Caesars Creek MM, dtd 1814,10,28
1816, 9, 21. Robert rmt Mary Hoggatt
1817, 1, 18. Mary gct New Garden MM, Ind.
1817, 3, 15. John gct Caesars Creek MM
1848, 12, 17. Mary gct Miami MM (H)

CORDON
1875, 10, 13. Rachel (form Jefferis) gct Dragoon MM, Kans.

COSS
1874, 3, 18. Cert rec for Benjamin & w, Phebe, from Londonderry MM, endorsed to Wilmington MM

COTTON
1807, 10, 3. Richard & w, Ann, rocf Bush River MM, S. C., dtd 1807,5,30

COWGILL
1812, 8, 1. John [Cougal] & w, Susannah, & s, James, rocf Hopewell MM, dtd 1812,5,14
1813, 8, 7. Cert rec 1812,8,1 for John & fam endorsed to Clear Creek MM
1815, 12, 16. Elisha & w, Rebecca, rocf Clear Creek MM, dtd 1815,12,9
1818, 2, 21. Amos rmt Edith Mendinghall
1818, 9, 19. Edith gct Newberry MM
1829, 5, 13. Elisha & w, Rebecca, & ch, Gulielma, Hannah, Bennet, Cyrus & Ann, gct Newbury MM
1830, 6, 16. Asa & w, Margaret, & ch, John & Hannah, rocf Fall Creek MM, dtd 1830,3, 20
1846, 8, 12. John P. dis jas
1846, 12, 16. Hannah gct Springfield MM
1847, 3, 17. Edwin gct Springfield MM
1854, 8, 16. Edwin rocf Springfield MM

COX
----, --, --. Samuel b 1797,3,19; m Edith W. ----- b 1795,3,14
Ch: Thomas M. b 1823, 4, 15
Susannah " 1826, 2, 11
Deborah " 1830, 10, 24
----, --, --. Thomas d 1856,2,7 ae 63 bur Chester; m Mary ----- d 1840,8,18 ae 37y 1m 9d bur at Chester

1820, 5, 20. Samuel rocf Monallen MM, Pa.,

COX, continued
dtd 1820,3,22
1821, 10, 20. Thomas rocf Monallen MM, dtd 1821,5,23, endorsed by New Garden MM, Ind., dtd 1821,9,15
1821, 12, 15. Samuel rmt Edith McMillan
1822, 4, 20. Thomas rmt Mary McMillan
1824, 3, 20. Susan rocf White Water MM
1824, 10, 16. Susannah rmt Josiah McMillan
1830, 12, 15. Thomas dis disunity
1831, 2, 16. Amy gct White River MM, Ind.
1831, 6, 15. Samuel & w, Edith, & ch, Thomas M., Susannah & Deborah, gct White River MM, Ind.
1836, 11, 16. Thomas rst
1839, 2, 13. Amy rocf New Garden MM, dtd 1838,12,15
1841, 12, 15. Elizabeth rocf White River MM, Ind., dtd 1841,11,6
1842, 9, 14. Elizabeth rmt Omri Schooley
1843, 4, 12. John rocf White River MM
1844, 8, 14. John gct Cherry Grove MM, Ind., to m Ann Reese
1844, 8, 14. Amy gct White River MM, Ind.
1848, 10, 18. John gct White River MM, Ind.

CRAWFORD
1885, 7, 15. Dr. George B. & w, Jennie, recrq
1909, 3, 17. Dr. George B. & w, Jennie, relrq

CRESWELL
1907, 10, 19. Cynthia A. d ae 62y 4m 20d bur in Millers Cemetery

1877, 3, 14. John [Criswell] & w, Cynthia A., & ch, Keziah, Sarah A. & Louetta A., recrq
1899, 6, --. John relrq
1903, 4, 15. Keziah relrq

CREWS
1816, 3, 16. Hannah rocf New Garden MM, N. C.
1816, 12, 21. Sarah roc
1818, 1, 17. Sarah recrq
1818, 11, 21. Hannah gct Miami MM
1819, 3, 20. Sarah [Cruse] gct Miami MM
1819, 10, 16. John [Crew] gct Newberry MM
1841, 11, 17. Susannah (form Taylor) dis mou & jH
1851, 8, 13. Mary [Crew] rocf Upper Springfield MM, O., dtd 1851,7,26
1851, 10, 15. Mary [Crew] rmt Josiah McMillan
1857, 7, 15. John A. [Crew] & w, Joanna, & ch, Alfeus, Mary, James, Thomas C., Sarah Ann & Margaret E., rocf Dover MM

CROASDALE
1845, 4, 17. Mary H. (form Carver) con mou (H)
1845, 7, 17. Amos rocf Byberry MM, Pa., dtd 1842,3,29 (H)
1845, 12, 18. Amos con mou (H)
1851, 8, 14. Amos [Crowsdale] & ch, Lydia & Emily, gct Fall Creek MM
1851, 11, 13. Cert for Amos [Crowsdale] & ch, returned with information he did not reside within limits of Fall Creek Mtg (H)
1855, 10, 18. Lydia & Emma [Croesdale] gct Byberry MM, Pa. (H)

CROCKETT
1894, 2, 14. James rocf Newberry MM

CRUMLY
1848, 7, 12. Mary (form Doan) dis mou
1849, 7, 19. Mary (form Doan) con mou (H)

CURL
1836, 8, 29. Joseph d bur New Hope
1862, 7, 29. Sarah d bur New Hope
1867, 11, 7. Joel d bur New Hope
1870, 2, 1. Mary d bur New Hope

1818, 10, 17. Elias rocf Darby Creek MM, dtd 1818,9,19
1819, 6, 19. Elias con mou
1819, 12, 18. Elias gct Darby Creek MM
1820, 8, 19. Martha rocf Darby Creek MM, dtd 1820,4,5 (held at Goshen)
1822, 1, 19. James rocf Darby Creek MM, dtd 1821,9,5
1823, 9, 20. Elias & w, Martha, & ch, Catharine & Sarah, gct Darby Creek MM
1825, 3, 19. James dis mou
1825, 11, 19. Joel [Curle] rocf Goshen MM, dtd 1825,8,20
1827, 2, 17. Joel dis mou
1827, 2, 17. Mary (form Bailiff] dis mou
1827, 5, 19. Joseph & w, Sarah, & gr ch, David & Eliza, rocf Goshen MM, dtd 1827,4,21
1827, 7, 21. John rocf Goshen MM, dtd 1827,4, 21
1827, 10, 20. Benjamin rocf Goshen MM, dtd 1827,7,21
1829, 5, 13. Benjamin dis disunity
1833, 7, 17. David gct Springfield MM
1834, 2, 12. Catharine, Elizabeth & Sarah, ch Elias, rocf Goshen MM, dtd 1833,1,18
1834, 4, 16. Thomas Miller prcf Springborough MM, dtd 1834,3,25, to m Eliza Curl
1834, 5, 14. Eliza rmt Thomas Miller
1837, 4, 12. David rmt Rebecca Coat
1837, 5, 17. Rebecca gct Springfield MM
1837, 6, 14. Judith (form Bailiff) dis mou
1838, 12, 12. Catherine gct Springborough MM
1839, 6, 12. Sarah & Elizabeth gct Springfield MM
1842, 7, 13. Elias & ch, Amy, Jemima, Joseph F., Jacob P., Naomi, Gulielma Maria & David, recrq
1842, 8, 17. Rachel rocf Springfield MM, dtd 1842,7,12
1843, 2, 15. Eliza rocf Springfield MM
1843, 9, 13. Elizabeth gct White Lick MM,Ind.
1844, 4, 17. Rachel & ch, Amy, Jemima, Joseph, Jacob, Nancy, Gulielma Mariah, David & Rachel, gct White Lick MM, Ind.

CURL, continued
1846, 5, 13. Elias dis disunity
1862, 6, 18. Joel & w, Mary, rst

CURRY
1910, 3, 16. Elmer, Abbie, Viola, William H. & Anna M., recrq
1913, 2, 12. Chester recrq

CURTIS
1916, 3, 15. Carl recrq
1916, 4, 12. Virgil & Earl Wilson, ch Carl & Rose, recrq

DAKIN
1818, 7, 18. Thankful recrq
1821, 5, 19. Rockyfeller recrq
1822, 12, 21. Rockyfeller gct Green Plain MM
1824, 4, 17. James & Elias [Daken] rocf Oblong MM, N. Y.
1824, 6, 19. Rockyfellar rocf Green Plain MM, dtd 1824,5,22
1825, 9, 17. Rockyfeller gct Philadelphia MM, Pa.
1829, 5, 13. James dis jH
1829, 5, 13. Elias dis jH
1838, 2, 15. Philip & w, Sarah L., & ch, James V., Zebulon B. & Rachel L., rocf Upper Springfield MM, N. J., dtd 1837,6,12 (H)
1841, 3, 18. Sarah L. & ch, James V., Zebulon B., Rachel L. & William Henry, gct Plainfield & Rahway MM, N. J.

DANIEL
1839, 7, 17. William, Robert Bond, Martha Jane, Lydia & Rebecca, ch Robert & Martha, rocf Hopewell MM, Va., dtd 1839,5,2, endorsed by Springfield MM, 1839,7,16
1839, 8, 15. Robert & w, Martha, & ch, William F., Martha Jane, Robert B., Lydia E. & Rebeccah Ann, rocf Hopewell MM, dtd 1839,5,9 (H)
1848, 1, 13. Martha Jane Howard (form Daniel) con mou (H)
1851, 11, 13. Robert B. con mcd (H)
1861, 4, 18. Rachel [Daniels] (form Tomlinson) con mcd (H)

DAVIS
----, --, --. Caleb, s Elisha & Alice, Clinton Co., O.; m Mannerva BALLARD b 1805,11, 11 d 1836,9,11 bur Center
Ch: Rebecca b 1828, 8, 18
Phebe " 1830, 3, 31
Elisha " 1832, 2, 8
Spenser " 1834, 2, 1
Mannerva " 1835, 11, 20
Caleb m 2nd 1844,12,26 at Center, Martha STOUT, dt Isaac & Susanna, Clinton Co.,O.
Ch: Isaac S. b 1845, 12, 11
Elizabeth A. " 1848, 1, 14
Ch: Charles B. b 1850, 4, 16
1846, 12, 24. Isaac L. d
----, --, --. Calvin & Lydia M.
Ch: Adella M. b 1869, 2, 27
Luella H. " 1871, 5, 13
Eslie A. " 1874, 7, 11

1818, 12, 19. Mary Davis & John, Daniel & Harmon Kester; ch Hannah Kester, recrq
1819, 10, 16. Mary gct Caesars Creek MM
1827, 10, 20. Caleb prcf Miami MM, dtd 1827,9, 26, to m Minerva Ballard
1827, 11, 31. Caleb rmt Minerva Ballard
1829, 2, 21. Mary recrq (H)
1829, 5, 13. Rachel dis jH
1829, 12, 16. Caleb dis jH
1830, 8, 21. Caleb & w, Ann, & ch, Amos, Mary, Penington, Elizabeth, Sarah Ann & Jane Eliza, rocf Center MM, Pa., dtd 1830,8,7 (H)
1830, 8, 21. Charles rocf Center MM, dtd 1830,7,8 (H)
1830, 8, 21. Margaret roc (H)
1831, 6, 18. Elisha rocf Center MM, Pa., dtd 1831,5,5 (H)
1831, 6, 18. Alice rocf Center MM, Pa., dtd 1831,5,5 (H)
1832, 11, 14. Minerva dis jH
1833, 3, 16. Rachel, w Thomas, gct Milford MM, Ind. (H)
1833, 6, 15. Charles dis mou (H)
1833, 11, 14. Elisha gct Milford MM, Ind. (H)
1834, 4, 17. Amos con mou (H)
1835, 5, 14. Mary Nickleson (form Davis) con mou (H)
1837, 11, 16. Eliza Jane gct Milford MM (H)
1839, 12, 19. Pennington gct Fall Creek MM, Ind. (H)
1840, 1, 16. Sarah gct Fall Creek MM, Ind. (H)
1840, 1, 16. Margaret gct Fall Creek MM, Ind. (H)
1849, 7, 18. Rebecca Maze (form Davis) dis mou
1850, 4, 18. Rebecca Maise (form Davis) dis mcd (H)
1854, 3, 15. Allen & w, Hannah, rocf West Grove MM, Ind.
1854, 12, 13. Joseph E. prcf Wabash MM, Ind., to m Phebe Haines
1855, 1, 17. Allen & w, Hannah, gct Sugar River MM, Ind.
1855, 2, 14. Joseph L. rmt Phebe Haines
1855, 4, 18. Phebe H. gct Wabash MM, Ind.
1857, 11, 9. Elisha dis mcd (H)
1866, 4, 18. Burthenia O. (form Painter) rpd mou
1866, 6, 13. Burthenia O. gct Dover MM
1867, 6, 12. William S. & w, Berthenia, & s, Joseph, rocf Dover MM
1869, 4, 14. Lidia (form McMillan) rpd mou
1870, 4, 13. William S. & fam gct Dover MM
1874, 4, 15. John Calvin recrq

DAVIS, continued
1875, 3, 17. Hannah A. rocf Cherry Grove MM, Ind., dtd 1875,1,13
1875, 8, 18. Charles B. recrq
1876, 3, 15. Charles & w, Hannah, gct Cherry Grove MM, Ind.
1883, 9, 12. Louella H., dt Calvin W., gct Wilmington MM, O.
1886, 3, 17. Russel recrq
1886, 3, 17. Lydia recrq
1889, 6, 12. John recrq
1889, 11, 13. John recrq
1903, 2, 18. Williard L. recrq

DEAN
1895, 6, 12. Deborah L. (form Spencer) dropped from mbrp

DEARDUFF
1823, 6, 21. Apharacia (form Johnson) con mou

DEDRIC
1843, 8, 24. Mary b

1874, 4, 15. Mary [Dedric] recrq
1887, 3, 16. Alece V. recrq
1897, 9, 15. Alice Collett (form Dedrick) relrq

DENNIS
1838, 5, 16. Nathan prcf Springfield MM, Ind., to m Mary Lamar
1838, 6, 13. Nathan rmt Mary Lemar
1838, 8, 15. Mary gct Springfield MM, Ind.

DEVOE
1910, 3, 16. Robert recrq

DeWITTE
1911, 9, 13. William recrq

DICKINSON
1908, 10, 14. Jonathan & ch, Oren & Marianna, rocf Poughkeepsie MM
1914, 4, 15. Jonathan & w, Clara, & ch, Oren & Marianna, gct Wilmington MM

DICKS
1810, 3, 3. Peter rmt Elizabeth Vestal
1812, 10, 3. Zachariah [Dix] gct White Water MM, Ind.
1813, 10, 2. Elizabeth [Dix] & ch gct White Water MM
1818, 1, 17. Nathan [Dix] rocf Cincinnati MM, dtd 1817,11,20
1818, 7, 18. Achilles rocf Cincinnati MM, dtd 1818,3,19
1819, 1, 16. Nathan gct Fairfield MM, to m

DILLINGHAM
1908, 2, 12. Clifton recrq

DILLON
----, --, --. Jonathan b 1785,1,8; m Agnes ----- b 1785,4,11
Ch: Jesse b 1806, 11, 20
Richard Henry " 1809, 10, 29
Samuel " 1811, 12, 13
Joseph " 1813, 11, 9
Elizabeth L. " 1816, 1, 24
Jonathan " 1818, 2, 21
Sarah " 1820, 1, 29
1823, 10, 3. Jesse d
----, --, --. Jesse b 1806,11,20; m Mary ----- b 1806,11,28
Ch: Isaac b 1827, 1, 22
Albert " 1827, 10, 1
Sarah Ann " 1830, 9, 23
Calvin " 1832, 3, 29
Mary Jane " 1834, 7, 17
William " 1835, 9, 23

1807, 11, 28. Jesse [Dillen] & w, Hannah, & ch, Luke, Hannah & Abigale, rocf New Garden MM, N. C., dtd 1807,9,25
1809, 2, 4. Jonathan & w, Agnes, & s, Jesse, rec in mbrp; cert granted them by New Garden MM, N. C., had been "consumed by fire"
1809, 8, 5. Thomas dis disunity
1810, 3, 3. Ann Bennett (form Dillen) dis mou
1810, 10, 5. Betty (form Wright) con mou
1811, 9, 7. Hannah [Dillen] rmt William Wright
1813, 4, 3. Luke rmt Charity Wright
1813, 4, 3. Nathan rmt Mary Hoskins
1814, 5, 7. Walter dis disunity
1814, 7, 2. Abigail rmt Isaac Wright
1814, 7, 2. Nathan & w, Mary, & dt, Ruth, gct Fairfield MM
1818, 9, 19. William dis mou
1819, 3, 20. Joseph gct New Garden MM, Ind.
1820, 3, 18. Absalom gct Springfield MM, to m
1820, 7, 15. Absalom gct Springfield MM
1821, 2, 17. Jane Fife (form Dillon) con mou
1824, 9, 18. Cert rec for Joseph from New Garden MM, Ind., dtd 1825,11,15, endorsed to Dover MM
1833, 12, 18. Mary rocf Caesars Creek MM, dtd 1833,10,24
1834, 3, 12. Richard H. gct New Garden MM, Ind., to m Elizabeth Unthank
1834, 8, 13. Elizabeth rocf New Garden MM, Ind., dtd 1834,5,17
1836, 4, 13. Jonathan & w, Agnes, & ch, Elizabeth, Jonathan & Sarah, gct Duck Creek MM, Ind.
1836, 4, 13. Richard H. & w, Elizabeth, & ch, Allen, gct Duck Creek MM, Ind.
1836, 9, 14. Jesse & w, Mary, & ch, Isaac, Albert, Sarah Ann, Mary Jane & William, gct Duck Creek MM, Ind.

DILLON, continued
1837, 4, 12. Joseph gct Duck Creek MM, Ind.
1838, 1, 17. Calvin gct New Garden MM, Ind.
1838, 2, 14. Samuel gct Spiceland MM, Ind.

DINGEE
1840, 12, 30. Bathsheba d

1832, 7, 21. Bathsheba rocf Middleton MM, dtd 1831,12,8 (H)
1832, 7, 21. Ruth rocf Middleton MM, dtd 1831,12,8 (H)
1832, 7, 21. Martha rocf Middleton MM, dtd 1831,12,8 (H)
1832, 8, 18. John [Dingey] & w, Bethshebe, & ch, Charles & John, rocf Middle Town MM (H)
1833, 9, 18. Charles & John [Dingy], ch John & Bethsheba, rocf Middleton MM, dtd 1833, 6,6
1843, 1, 19. Charles con mou (H)
1843, 6, 15. Charles gct Fall Creek MM (H)
1844, 5, 16. John dis mou (H)
1849, 5, 16. Charles [Dingy] dis mou
1849, 5, 16. John Milton [Dingy] dis mou

DIXON
1889, 6, 12. Wilson [Dexson] recrq
1889, 6, 12. Thomas [Dexson] recrq
1889, 6, 12. Emma [Dexson] recrq
1889, 6, 12. Lennie [Dexson] recrq
1894, 3, 14. Cora recrq
1894, 3, 14. Cynthia recrq
1919, 3, 12. Cynthia Middleton dropped from mbrp

DOAN
----, --, --. Joseph Jr. b 1794,5,25; m Eliza CARPENTER b 1802,2,18
Ch: Phebe b 1821, 5, 6
Edward " 1823, 4, 20
Nathan " 1824, 12, 17
Thomas " 1826, 12, 28
Jacob " 1828, 9, 15
Jemima " 1830, 9, 29
Mary " 1833, 2, 26
Joseph " 1835, 5, 17
Isaac " 1837, 11, 26
Elizabeth " 1843, 1, 1
----, --, --. Jonathan & Phebe
Ch: John b 1823, 2, 5
Azariah " 1824, 12, 17
Absolam " 1827, 7, 7 d 1839, 7, 4
Calvin " 1830, 5, 7
Joseph " 1832, 7, 23 " 1834, 7,25
Jonathan " 1836, 5, 20
David " 1839, 8, 7
----, --, --. William & Betsey
Ch: Maria E. b 1825, 7, 9
Robert E. " 1831, 7, 23
Joseph W. " 1836, 3, 7
1831, 1, 15. Edward d bur Center
1836, 8, 12. Lydia d bur Wilmington
1838, 5, 28. Joseph Sr. d bur at Wilmington
1838, 11, 15. Spencer d bur Wilmington
1839, 3, 1. Rebecca Jane d bur Wilmington
----, --, --. John & Sarah Jane
Ch: Mary
Ellen b 1850, 1, 31
Calvin " 1851, 8, 10
William " 1853, 2, 25
Francis " 1855, 2, 10
Lucinda " 1856, 5, 13
Albert " 1858, 3, 4
Ulissas " 1864, 11, 7
----, --, --. Robert E. & Maria
Ch: Clinton M. b 1858, 11, 19
Charles A. " 1865, 10, 10 d 1866, 9, 6
----, --, --. Joseph & Deborah
Ch: Wendell P. b 1859, 8, 23 d 1861, 1, 8 bur at Center
Harrison J. b 1861, 11, 10
1861, 3, 1. Joseph d bur Center
1864, 5, --. Eva Arometta, dt Jonathan & Naomi, b
1869, 4, 24. William d
1873, 3, 11. Eliza d bur Center

1808, 2, 6. Ruth Haines (form Doan) con mou
1810, 3, 3. John con mou
1813, 3, 6. Elizabeth Haines (form Doan) con mou
1817, 4, 19. John gct New Garden MM, Ind.
1818, 12, 19. William rmt Betsy Eashus
1820, 8, 19. Joseph Jr. rmt Eliza D. Carpenter
1822, 5, 18. Jonathan rmt Phebe Wall
1822, 6, 15. Jacob gct Miami MM, to m Hannah Stubbs
1824, 1, 17. Jesse rmt Lydia Ballard
1826, 2, --. Rachel Hines (form Doan) dis mou
1826, 8, 19. Jacob gct Miami MM
1829, 7, 15. Joseph Sr. dis jH
1831, 10, 12. Elisha dis disunity
1832, 7, 18. Jesse dis jH
1833, 2, 13. Lydia dis jH
1839, 5, 15. Alfred Timberlake prcf Clear Creek MM, to m Phebe Doan
1839, 6, 12. Phebe rmt Alfred Timberlake
1840, 1, 16. Jesse con mou (H)
1840, 2, 13. Rebecca F. con mou (H)
1848, 7, 12. Mary Crumly (form Doan) dis mou
1848, 8, 16. John gct Dover MM, to m Mary Jane Shield
1848, 8, 16. Asariah dis mou
1848, 8, 16. Israel dis mou
1849, 7, 19. Mary Crumly (form Doan) con mou (H)
1849, 8, 16. Amanda (form Stratton) dis mou (H)
1850, 6, 12. Nathan dis mou
1850, 7, 17. Sarah Jane rocf Dover MM, dtd 1850,3,16
1855, 3, 14 Thomas gct Mississiniwa MM, Ind.

DOAN, continued
1855, 6, 13. Edwin Hadley prcf Springfield MM, to m Jemima Doan
1855, 7, 18. Jemima rmt Edwin Hadley
1857, 12, 16. Thomas Walthall prcf Dover MM, to m Maria E. Doan
1858, 1, 13. Marion E. rmt Thomas Walthall
1858, 10, 13. Joseph Jr. rmt Deborah E. Taylor
1859, 1, 12. Robert E. rpd mou
1859, 3, 16. Maria M. (form McMillan) rpd mou
1866, 12, 12. Isaac dis mou
1868, 5, 13. Joseph & fam gct White Water MM, Ind.
1870, 11, 16. Eliza, Mary & Elizabeth gct White Water MM
1872, 12, 16. Joseph William gct Dover MM

DODD
1900, 3, 14. William [Dodds] & w & two ch recrq
1904, 10, 12. William & w, Josie, & ch, Carl & Goldie, relrq
1915, 9, 15. Charles & w, Ollie, & ch, Vergil, recrq
1921, 3, 16. Clarence & w, Ollie, relrq

DOUGHERTY
1860, 6, 13. Elizabeth (form Vestal) rpd mou

DUDLEY
1917, 3, 14. Blanch gct Xenia MM

DUNCAN
1808, 12, 3. Elizabeth rocf Bush River MM, S. C., dtd 1807,8,29

DUNN
1877, 3, 14. William M. recrq
1885, 12, 16. William relrq

DWIGGIN
1812, 8, 1. Cert rec for Mary from New Garden MM, dtd 1812,4,28, endorsed to White Water MM
1819, 9, 18. Sarah [Dwiggins] recrq

DYMOND
1897, 8, 27. Robert Lestlie d bur Center
1899, 2, 7. Helen b
1901, 2, 4. Emma b

1881, 6, 15. Robert [Diamond] recrq
1883, 4, 18. John recrq
1905, 6, 14. Robert gct Cesars Creek MM
1908, 11, 18. John & w, Mary Bell, & ch, Edith, Helen & Emma, gct Cesars Creek MM

EACHUS
1829, 3, 24. Robert [Eaches] d ae 67y 4m 1d bur Center, O.
1842, 9, 21. Phebe [Eaches] d ae 74y 8m 26d bur Center
1808, 5, 7. Betsy, John Julian & David F., ch Phebe, recrq
1818, 12, 19. Betsy [Eashus] rmt William Doan
1820, 9, 16. Robert recrq
1822, 1, 19. Juliana [Eaches] rmt John Perkins
1828, 1, 19. David dis disunity

EDGINGTON
1916, 3, 15. Oakley recrq

EDMUNDSON
1833, 11, 14. Esther [Edmonson] rocf Pipe Creek MM, dtd 1833,8,17 (H)
1833, 11, 14. Thomas [Edmonson] & w, Elizabeth, & ch, William, Thomas, Maria, Ann & John, rocf Pipe Creek MM, dtd 1833,8,17(H)
1834, 4, 17. Thomas & w, Elizabeth, & ch, Thomas, Mariah, Ann & John, gct Green Plain MM (H)
1834, 4, 17. William gct Green Plain MM (H)
1834, 5, 15. Ester [Edmonson] gct Green Plain MM (H)

ELLENBERGER
1917, 3, 14. Joseph & Myrtle recrq

ELLIS
1809, 6, 3. Sarah rocf New Hope MM, Tenn., dtd 1808,9,17
1821, 3, 17. Sarah (form Williams) dis mou
1822, 9, 21. Sarah gct Honey Creek MM, Ind.
1853, 4, 13. Jonathan & w, Susannah, & ch, Lydia Mary, Jonathan W., Richard S. & Aquila, rocf Springfield MM
1865, 5, 17. Daniel McPherson prcf Newberry MM, to m Lydia Mary Ellis
1865, 6, 14. Lydia Mary rmt Daniel McPherson
1871, 5, 17. Mary Rebecca & ch, Alice, recrq
1895, 1, 16. Christopher & w recrq
1895, 3, 13. Charles recrq
1896, 10, 14. Christopher relrq
1897, 4, 14. Mary relrq
1899, 5, 17. Charles relrq

ELLISON
1917, 5, 23. Anna & Laura recrq

ELMORE
1840, 6, 17. Bloomfield MM rq permission to rst Elizabeth (form Harvey) in mbrp (rq not granted)
1847, 9, 15. Vermillion MM, Ill was granted permission to rst Elizabeth (form Harvey)

EMBREE
1808, 3, 5. Rachel rmt William Thorn

EMENS
1905, 11, 15. Edith recrq

ENGLE
1843, 6, 14. Hannah Ann rocf Green Plain MM,

ENGLE, continued
dtd 1842,7,13
1844, 6, 12. Joshua & w, Hannah, rocf Green Plain MM, dtd 1844,4,17
1846, 6, 17. Hannah Ann Vanmeter (form Engle) dis mou
1846, 10, 14. Joshua & w gct Caesars Creek MM

EVANS
1842, 5, 18. Mary Ann (form Fawcett) dis mou
1851, 11, 12. Jacob Taylor gct Spiceland MM, Ind., to m Sarah Evans

FALLIS
1814, 7, 2. Richard & w, Phebe, & ch, Mary Lydia Rachel Eliza John & Thomas, rocf Redstone MM, dtd 1814,3,16
1814, 10, 1. John & w, Mary, & ch, Esther, Amos & Sarah, rocf Redstone MM, dtd 1814, 7,1
1817, 2, 15. Isah [Fallas] recrq
1823, 4, 19. Amos rmt Lydia Carpenter
1823, 5, 17. Cyrus Farquhar gct Springfield MM, to m Lydia Fallis
1823, 6, 21. Lydia gct Springfield MM
1826, 12, 16. Richard & fam roc
1826, 12, 16. Phebe & ch, Nancy Harriet Jane & Phebe, rocf Springfield MM
1826, 12, 16. Eliza rocf Springfield MM
1830, 8, 18. Eliza Tong (form Fallis) dis mou
1833, 9, 18. Nancy Lapham (form Fallis) con mou
1837, 12, 13. Harriet gct Miami MM
1838, 11, 14. Eli McMillan gct Springfield MM, to m Lydia Fallis
1839, 3, 13. Lydia McMillan, w Eli, & ch, Turner W., John, Isaac & Susan M. Fallis, rocf Springfield MM, dtd 1839,3,12
1844, 2, 14. Thomas gct Miami MM
1844, 6, 12. Isaac C. gct Cincinnati MM
1844, 7, 17. Elizabeth M. gct Springfield MM
1844, 7, 17. Susan M. gct Springfield MM
1845, 12, 17. Jane Cadwalader (form Fallis) con mou
1845, 12, 17. Phebe gct Miami MM
1846, 11, 18. Turner W. [Follis] dis mou
1846, 11, 18. John [Follis] dis mou
1848, 8, 16. John rpd mou
1849, 1, 17. John gct Miami MM
1850, 7, 18. John con mcd (H)
1850, 12, 19. Isaiah dis jas (H)
1851, 5, 15. John gct Miami MM (H)
1851, 8, 14. Elizabeth gct Miami MM (H)

FANGHNDER
1887, 3, 16. Eva recrq
1887, 5, 18. Viola M. & Paul I., ch Eva, recrq

FARQUHAR
----, --, --. Benjamin [Farquar] b 1766,5,8 d 1827,8,8; m Rachel ----- b 1773,3,31 d 1841,9,1 ae 68y 5m 1d

Ch:	Uriah	b 1795, 5, 5
	Cyrus	" 1796, 7, 4
	Allen	" 1798, 7, 18
	Jonathan	" 1800, 4, 21 d 1825, 7, 2
	Josiah	" 1802, 2, 19
	Susannah	" 1804, 10, 16
	Edwin	" 1807, 7, 3 d 1808, 4,20
	Rebecca	" 1810, 9, 9
	Rachel	" 1815, 9, 6

----, --, --. Francis & Hannah Ann [Farquar]

Ch:	Milton J.	b 1860, 3, 17
	Harriet A.	" 1862, 3, 4
	Henry B.	" 1864, 9, 10

1808, 8, 8. Jonah rocf Pike MM, dtd 1808,4, 16
1808, 8, 8. Mahlon rocf Baltimore MM for West Dist., dtd 1807,12,9
1809, 4, 1. Jonah con mou
1813, 4, 3. Jonah gct Pipe Creek MM, Md.
1815, 3, 4. Jonah rocf Pipe Creek MM, dtd 1814,10,15
1815, 7, 14. Uriah gct Miami MM
1818, 9, 19. Jonah gct Caesars Creek MM
1822, 2, 16. Allen gct Clear Creek MM
1823, 5, 17. Cyrus gct Springfield MM, to m Lydia Fallis
1829, 12, 16. Josiah rmt Abi Linton
1831, 9, 14. Rebecca Strickel (form Farquhar) con mou
1833, 11, 13. Cyrus & w, Lydia, & ch, Richard, Henry & Louisa, gct Cincinnati MM
1844, 4, 17. Abi Sparks (form Farquhar) con mou
1845, 6, 18. John Cadwalader prcf Miami MM, to m Rachel Farquhar
1845, 7, 16. Rachel rmt John Cadwalader
1846, 4, 13. Louisa rocf Cincinnati MM, dtd 1846,3,15
1846, 7, 15. Abi Sparks & ch, Benjamin & Francis Farquhar, gct Salem MM, Ind.
1852, 3, 17. Aby Sparks & s, Benjamin & Frances Farquhar, rocf Salem MM, dtd 1852,3,27
1853, 1, 12. Louisa Hill (form Farquhar) con mou
1854, 5, 17. Susannah Lytles (form rquhar) con mou
1856, 4, 16. Benjamin gct Springfiel MM
1858, 10, 13. Francis rmt Hannah Ann ..cMillan

FAULKNER
1749, 6, 26. David b d 1821,1,30
1760, 10, 3. Judith b d 1843,4,23 bur New Hope
----, --, --. Jesse b 1785,4,24; m Hannah ----- b 1781,10,6

Ch:	Susannah	b 1806, 12, 20
	Judith	" 1808, 3, 29 d 1812,11,16
	Lydia	" 1810, 7, 9
	David	" 1811, 9, 25
	Joel	" 1813, 3, 1 d 1814, 9,23
	Phebe	" 1814, 12, 26
	Mary	" 1816, 8, 26

FAULKNER, continued

----, --, --. David b 1790,9,10 d 1853,6,26; m Mary ----- b 1790,10,23 d 1830,7,13 bur New Hope

Ch: John b 1812, 8, 27
Elizabeth " 1814, 1, 1
Joel " 1816, 4, 13
Thomas " 1818, 4, 25
Judith " 1821, 12, 27
Rachel " 1824, 9, 12
Phebe " 1826, 12, 11
Mary " 1830, 6, 14

David m 2nd Leah ----- b 1802,3,23

Ch: Sarah b 1833, 11, 6
Elias " 1835, 9, 24
Anna " 1838, 1, 30
Lucinda " 1840, 4, 5
Angelina " 1843, 3, 31

1867, 9, 29. Lucien b

----, --, --. Harvey C. b 1843,5,25; m Sarah E. ----- b 1847,4,14

Ch: Amos E. b 1869, 7, 14
David Walter " 1870, 12, 4
Cora Mary " 1873, 2, 21
Samuel " 1878, 8, 24

1876, 8, 16. Leah d bur New Hope
1885, 4, 25. Adna A. b

1807, 10, 3. Ruth rmt William Stanton
1807, 10, 3. Ellen rmt Robert Andrews
1808, 1, 2. Susannah rmt John Holladay
1808, 8, 6. David rocf Hopewell MM, dtd 1808,6,6
1808, 8, 6. Elizabeth roc
1809, 1, 7. Jesse Jr. recrq
1809, 7, 1. Phebe rmt William Ballard
1811, 8, 3. Thomas, s Robert, dis mou
1812, 2, 1. David Jr. con mou
1812, 2, 1. Mary rmt Thomas Johnson
1812, 3, 7. Mary recrq
1812, 8, 1. Thomas, s David, dis mou
1814, 9, 3. Jesse & w, Hannah, & ch, Susannah Lydia David & Joel Wright, rocf Miami MM, dtd 1814,2,23
1815, 7, 14. Hannah rmt Joel Pusey
1815, 9, 16. Elizabeth rmt Jesse Shepherd
1816, 5, 18. Judith rmt John Johnson
1819, 1, 16. Caleb Stratton prcf Darby Creek MM, dtd 1819,12,19, to m Jane Faulkner
1819, 2, 20. Jane rmt Caleb Stratton
1825, 7, 16. Susannah Griffith (form Faulkner) con mou
1825, 10, 15. Solomon gct Lees Creek MM, to m Ruth Bayles
1826, 1, 21. Rachel rmt Thomas Arnett
1826, 5, 23. Ruth rocf Lees Creek MM, dtd 1826,2,18
1827, 3, 17. Jesse recrq
1827, 11, 27. Jesse Jr. dis disunity
1828, 1, 19. Solomon dis jas
1829, 2, 18. David Jr. dis disunity
1829, 5, 13. Elizabeth & ch, Isaiah M. & Nathan, gct White River MM, Ind.
1829, 5, 13. Ruth & ch gct Dunkirk MM, Ind.
1831, 3, 16. Lydia S. Johnson (form Faulkner) con mou
1832, 1, 18. Eliza rocf Green Plain MM, dtd 1831,12,7
1832, 4, 18. David rmt Leah Bayliff
1833, 5, 15. John dis disunity
1833, 7, 17. Phebe Murphy (form Faulkner) dis mou
1833, 8, 14. Enoch Carter prcf Springfield MM dtd 1833,8,13, to m Elizabeth Faulkner
1833, 9, 18. Elizabeth rmt Enoch Carter
1833, 12, 18. Thomas Hawkins rocf New Garden MM, Ind., to m Mary Faulkner
1834, 1, 15. Mary rmt Thomas Hawkins
1836, 6, 15. Anna Witherbee (form Faulkner) dis mou
1836, 7, 13. Jesse gct White Lick MM, Ind.
1838, 11, 14. Jesse & w, Hannah, & ch, Abijah & Juliann, gct White Lick MM, Ind.
1839, 2, 13. Hannah Stephans (form Faulkner) dis mou
1839, 3, 13. Eliza gct White Lick MM, Ind.
1839, 8, 14. Hannah Stephens (form Faulkner) dis mou
1841, 6, 16. Judith Garmen (form Faulkner) con mou
1843, 9, 13. Joel dis jas
1849, 9, 12. Rachel McCay (form Faulkner) dis mou
1850, 1, 16. Phebe rmt Thomas Williams
1853, 3, 16. Mary Andrew (form Faulkner) dis mou & jas
1856, 7, 16. Sarah dis jas
1863, 7, 15. Lucina Lewis (form Faulkner) rpd mou;dropped from mbrp
1863, 8, 12. Angeline dis jas
1868, 3, 18. Sarah rpd mou
1872, 3, 13. Harvey C. recrq
1888, 2, 15. James recrq
1889, 4, 17. Viola [Falkner] recrq
1894, 6, 13. Thomas H. & w, Minnie Bell, & s, Howard P., recrq
1897, 4, 14. Cora May & ch, Leroy H., Russell J. & Harry T., recrq
1900, 1, 17. James W. [Foulkner] & w relrq
1902, 12, 17. Amos E. relrq
1914, 3, 18. Bessie Cleora & Etta Leona recrq

FAWCETT

----, --, --. Robert b 1792,11,1; m Mary ----- b 1793,5,30 d 1860,12,7 bur New Hope

Ch: Charlotte T. b 1814, 10, 18
Jane " 1816, 11, 24
Mary Ann " 1819, 3, 2
Milton " 1821, 9, 24
John " 1824, 2, 17
Sarah P. " 1826, 5, 12 d 1854,2,27 bur New Hope
Jonathan P. b 1828, 8, 3
Elizabeth " 1831, 2, 4

FAWCETT, Robert & Mary, continued
Ch: Levi E. b 1833, 4, 3
Rebecca P. " 1840, 6, 16
1842, 2, 11. Mary d ae 73 bur New Hope
----, --, --. John & Phebe
Ch: Caroline b 1848, 6, 26
Isaac P. " 1849, 11, 22
Lorenzo D. " 1851, 3, 24

1825, 6, 18. Alban rocf Hopewell MM, dtd 1825,4,7
1825, 8, 20. Phebe rec with permission of Hopewell MM
1829, 9, 16. Alban dis disunity
1831, 11, 16. Phebe [Fasset] dis jH
1832, 11, 14. Mary rocf Flushing MM, held at Gurnsey, dtd 1832,4,26
1833, 1, 16. Lucinda rocf Flushing MM, dtd 1832,4,26
1833, 4, 17. Robert & w, Mary, & ch, Charlotte, Jane, Mary Ann, Milton, Sarah B., Jonathan P. & Elizabeth, rocf Flushing MM, dtd 1833,1,24
1833, 9, 18. Lucinda Oglesbee (form Fawcett) dis mou
1833, 9, 19. Elijah [Fosset] recrq (H)
1833, 11, 13. Lucinda Oglesby (form Fawcett) dis mou
1834, 8, 14. Elijah [Faucet] & w, Phebe, gct Goshen MM (H)
1836, 9, 14. Charlotte rpd married to Abel Biven
1841, 8, 18. Jonathan Bangham prcf Dover MM, to m Jane Fawcett
1841, 9, 15. Jane rmt Jonathan Bangham
1842, 5, 18. Mary Ann Evans (form Fawcett) dis mou
1845, 11, 12. Milton rmt Sarah Haines
1846, 10, 14. John rmt Phebe Painter
1852, 4, 14. D aniel B. Walthall prcf Dover MM, to m Elizabeth Fawcett
1852, 5, 12. Elizabeth H. rmt Daniel B. Walthall
1852, 9, 15. Milton & w, Sarah, & s, Mordecai H., gct Mississiniwa MM, Ind.
1853, 2, 16. John P. & w, Phebe W., & ch, Caroline W. & Isaac P., gct Honey Creek MM, Ind.
1854, 1, 18. Elizabeth Ann (form Painter) dis mou
1856, 3, 12. Jonathan dis mou
1857, 2, 18. Levi rpd mou
1862, 2, 12. Rebecca Wile (form Fawcett) rpd mou

FIFE
1821, 2, 17. Jane (form Dillon) con mou

FISHER
1811, 10, 5. Susannah (form Hodgson) con mou
1812, 3, 7. Susannah dis mou
1812, 12, 5. Susannah gct Fairfield MM
1820, 10, 21. Martha recrq
1824, 7, 17. Achsah (form Starbuck) con mou
1882, 2, 15. Frank recrq
1886, 3, 17. James W. & w, Frances A., & s, Russel Davis, recrq
1888, 2, 15. Frank recrq
1904, 12, 14. Frank dropped from mbrp

FLEMING
1905, 4, 12. Nellie [Flemming] recrq
1906, 5, 16. May B. [Flemings] recrq
1906, 6, 13. John D. recrq
1907, 9, 18. John & w, Mary, & dt, Mary Dena, gct Caesars Creek MM

FOLAND
1907, 6, 13. George & w, Jennie, rocf Wilmington MM, O.

FONDLER
1887, 3, 16. Eva recrq
1887, 5, 18. Viola M. & Joel L. Shepherd, ch Eva Fondler, recrq

FORD
1838, 9, 12. Ruth (form Jones) dis mou

FOSTER
1901, 4, 17. Samuel & Hannah recrq
1906, 5, 16. Samuel & Hannah gct Cesars Creek MM

FOULKE
1891, 4, 15. William A. recrq

FOX
1882, 11, 14. Emma Leonard relrq

FRAZIER
1808, 3, 5. Alexander [Frazer] rocf New Hope MM, dtd 1806,10,18, endorsed by Miami MM
1808, 12, 3. Elizabeth [Frazure] & ch, Ezekiel, Moses, Jonah & Lydia, rocf New Hope MM, dtd 1807,11,21
1809, 12, 2. John [Frazer] & w, Alice, rocf Fairfield MM, dtd 1809,11,25
1812, 2, 1. Alexander [Fraizer] con mou & paying muster fine
1812, 9, 5. Mary recrq
1813, 2, 6. John & w, Alice, rocf Fairfield MM, dtd 1812,12,26
1813, 3, 6. Moses gct Clear Creek MM, to m
1813, 9, 2. Lydia rocf Clear Creek MM, dtd 1813,8,26
1816, 8, 17. Jonah gct Clear Creek MM, to m
1817, 2, 15. Mary rocf Clear Creek MM
1820, 3, 18. Lydia rmt Alexander Oren
1843, 9, 13. David Painter gct Dover MM, to m Mary Frazier
1848, 10, 18. Jonathan McMillan gct Dover MM, to m Rebecca Frazier
1849, 1, 18. William rocf Dunning Creek MM, dtd 1848,11,15 (H)

FRAZIER, continued
1849, 9, 13. William gct Dennings Creek MM, Pa. (H)
1866, 3, 14. Martha W. (form Walker) rpd mou
1866, 5, 16. Martha W. gct Dover MM

FREELAND
1916, 3, 15. John Wesley & w recrq
1916, 3, 15. Walter recrq

FREEMAN
1879, 9, 27. Sylvester, s Granville & Nicie, b

1879, 1, 15. Granville & w, Miza, & ch, Samantha, Viola & Eliza Ellen, recrq

FRONTE
1888, 5, 16. William Alfred recrq

FRYE
1906, 4, 18. Nicholas, Lovina, Everett, Edith, Leroy & Leona recrq
1906, 5, 16. Oscar, James J., Mary A. & Carl recrq
1921, 2, 16. Nick, Lavinna & Roy [Fry] gct Wilmington MM, O.

FURGASON
----, --, --. Samuel m Melissa MOORMAN, dt Thomas & Dosha, d 1855,3,22 ae 30y 10m 20d
Ch: Webster
Monroe b 1846, 3, 7
Arthur Hale " 1850, 4, 27
Thomas
Clark " 1854, 9, 9

1847, 7, 17. Melissa & ch, Maria Eliza, Ellen Jane & Esther Amanda [Ferguson] rocf Dover MM, dtd 1847,6,17
1854, 5, 18. Aaron [Ferguson] rocf Caesars Creek MM
1856, 1, 16. Aaron [Ferguson] gct Spring Creek MM, Ia.
1856, 6, 18. Samuel & w, Melissa, & ch, Maria Eliza, Ellen Jane, Esther Amanda, Webster Monroe, Arthur Hale & Thomas Clark, gct Spring Creek MM, Ia.

FURNANCE
----, --, --. Joseph b 1802,9,24; m Elizabeth BALLARD b 1810,6,2
Ch: Isaac b 1827, 7, 20
Sarah " 1829, 1, 17
Ahira B. " 1831, 1, 13
Samuel " 1833, 1, 14
Orlando " 1835, 10, 8
Robert Barclay " 1838, 3, 3 d 1838, 9, 9

1830, 1, 15. Isaac [Furnace] rmt Esley Wright
1820, 2, 19. Esly (form Wright) gct Miami MM
1826, 10, 21. Joseph [Furnace] rmt Elizabeth Ballard
1827, 1, 20. Elizabeth [Furnis] gct Caesars Creek MM
1830, 11, 17. Joseph [Furnace] & w, Elizabeth, & ch, Isaac & Sarah, rocf Caesars Creek MM, dtd 1830,8,27
1839, 1, 16. Joseph & w, Elizabeth, & ch, Isaac, Sarah S., Ahiza B., Samuel S. & Orlando, gct Fairfield MM, Ind.

GAGE
1830, 12, 15. Mary Ann (form Stanbrough) dis mou

GALLADY
1808, 9, 3. Ruth gct Fairfield MM

GALLIMORE
1819, 8, 21. William rocf Fairfield MM, dtd 1819,9,18
1823, 9, 20. Mary [Gallemore] recrq
1823, 11, 15. William, Elisha, Levicey, Catharine, John & Polly, ch William & Mary, recrq
1868, 8, 18. William rmt Mary J. Bevan
1868, 9, 16. Mary Jane gct Dover MM
1878, 7, 17. Isaiah M. & w, Mary J., & ch, Ertie M., recrq

GARMAN
1841, 6, 16. Judith [Garmen] (form Faulkner) con mou
1843, 9, 13. Judith [Garmon] dis jas
1897, 4, 14. Orval recrq
1901, 5, 15. Orville & w, Anna M., & ch, [ll Harry J., rocf Clear Creek MM, dtd 1901,5,
1905, 5, 17. Orval [Garmond] & fam gc

GARRETSON
1821, 5, 19. Aaron & w, Hannah, rocf Dunnings Creek MM, dtd 1820,12,13
1823, 6, 21. Aaron & w, Hannah, & ch, Thomas, gct Dunnings Creek MM, Pa.

GASKILL
1830, 10, 13. Hannah dis disunity

GAUNT
1828, 8, 13. Mary [Gant] (form Hiatt) dis mou
1835, 8, 12. White River MM, Ind. was granted permission to rst Mary

GAUSE
1895, 11, 13. Esther rocf West Fork MM, dtd 1895,10,19
1911, 5, 17. Esther gct West Fork MM

GILLAM
1918, 9, 18. Ernest Allen & John Calvin, ch Daniel & Lily May, recrq

GILPIN
----, --, --. Henry & Esther
Ch: Mary b 1833, 5, 29

GILPIN, Henry & Esther, continued
Ch: Ruth b 1835, 2, 7 d 1839,10, 6
Lydia " 1836, 12, 7
Levi " 1839, 1, 27 " 1839, 2,22
John Thos. " 1839, 12, 28
Rebecca " 1842, 5, 6

1809, 9, 2. Thomas & w, Mary, & ch, Sarah, John, Rebeckah, Thomas & Henry, rocf Center MM, Va., dtd 1809,3,10
1840, 5, 13. Henry & w, Esther, & ch, Mary, Lydia & John Thomas, rocf Caesars Creek MM, dtd 1840,4,23
1844, 8, 14. Henry dis joining Separatists
1844, 8, 14. Esther dis joining Separatists
1860, 5, 16. Mary Hester (form Gilpin) rpd mou; dropped from mbrp
1860, 5, 16. Lydia Mowen (form Gilpin) rpd mou; dropped from mbrp

GLASS
1845, 7, 16. Mary (form Haworth) dis mou

GOOD
1855, 6, 14. Charles & w, Betsy, & ch, Mary Ann, Elizabeth F., Martha E., Ellis, Lydia C., Evan & Rachel L., rocf Little Britain MM, Pa., dtd 1855,3,17

GORDON
1861, 5, 18. Milton M. Taylor gct Spiceland MM, Ind., to m Emily Gordon

GRANT
1829, 1, 14. Mary dis mou

GRAY
1832, 3, 14. Ann (form Shipley) con mou
1873, 3, 12. Rebecca & Ann gct Ash Grove MM, Ill.

GREEN
----, --, --. Rueben, s Isaac & Mary, b 1770, 7,28; m Rhoda BALLARD, dt David & Mary, b 1775,3,1
Ch: Isaac b 1797, 10, 4 d 1808, 6,22
Mary " 1799, 4, 7
David " 1800, 6, 2
Lydia " 1801, 12, 9 d 1803, 8,13
Robert " 1803, 6, 26
Asa " 1805, 1, 5
Anna " 1807, 1, 2 d 1812, 9,25
Abigail " 1808, 10, 19
John " 1810, 7, 27
Susannah " 1812, 9, 29
Rowland " 1814, 11, 10
Rhoda " 1817, 7, 7
----, --, --. Jesse m Sarah DAVIS
Ch: Isaac b 1816, 3, 14
Aaron " 1818, 10, 20
Charlotte " 1820, 12, 20
Sewel " 1823, 3, 22
Hannah " 1825, 11, 4
Ch: John Jr. b 1828, 1, 28
Elizabeth " 1830, 4, 26
Ruth " 1833, 6, 16
Jesse " 1836, 4, 15
Sarah " 1839, 12, 27
1825, 4, 11. John Sr. d ae 68y 29d
----, --, --. Isaac & Anna
Ch: Allen b 1836, 10, 29
Sarah " 1838, 12, 24
Wilson " 1842, 2, 11
1843, 12, 24. Ruth, w John, d ae 84y 2m 14d bur at Center
----, --, --. Jehiel & Rachel
Ch: Joel William b 1844, 11, 21
Mary Elizabeth " 1848, 5, 5 d 1849,11,11 bur at Chester
James Robert b 1849, 9, 16
Asaph Leander d 1853, 3,26
1844, 8, 6. Robert L. b
1874, 6, 25. Bertha b

1811, 12, 7. Ruben & w, Rhoda, & ch, Mary, David, Robert, Asa, Anne, Abigail & John, rocf Mt. Pleasant MM, Va., dtd 1811,9,28
1815, 2, 4. Jesse rocf Mt. Pleasant MM, Va., dtd 1814,9,24
1816, 2, 17. Jesse con mou
1816, 11, 16. Alice rocf Mt Pleasant MM, Va.
1816, 11, 16. John & w, Ruth, & ch, Mary, Abigail & Charlotte, rocf Mt. Pleasant MM, Va., dtd 1816,9,28
1823, 8, 16. Mordecai Walker, Jr. gct Springfield MM, to m Mary Green
1824, 4, 17. Sarah & ch, Isaac, Aaron, Charlotte & Sewel, recrq
1825, 1, 15. Charlotte rmt Enoch Lundy
1828, 12, 17. Abigail rmt Jesse Lundy
1833, 6, 15. Ann recrq (H)
1836, 2, 17. Isaac rmt Anna Schooley
1842, 8, 17. Jehiel prcf Newberry MM, to m Rachel Lundy
1842, 9, 14. Jehiel rmt Rachel Lundy
1843, 3, 15. Rachel gct Newberry MM
1843, 12, 13. Aaron rmt Rachel Schooley
1845, 7, 16. Aaron & w, Rachel, & ch, Nancy Jane, gct Newberry MM
1846, 7, 15. Ruth rocf Newberry MM, dtd 1846, 3,11
1847, 2, 17. John & w, Rhoda C., & s, Robert, rocf Clear Creek MM, dtd 1846,11,14
1847, 3, 17. Jehiel & w, Rachel, & ch, Joel William, rocf Newberry MM, dtd 1846,12,14
1847, 9, 15. Miles H. Moon prcf Newberry MM, to m Charlotte D. Green
1847, 10, 13. Charlotte D. rmt Miles H. Moon
1847, 11, 17. Sewel con mou
1848, 4, 12. Joel prcf Newberry MM, to m Elizabeth Schooley
1848, 5, 17. Joel rmt Elizabeth Schooley

GREEN, continued
1848, 6, 14. John & w, Rhoda C., & ch, Robert & David, gct Newberry MM
1850, 3, 13. Elizabeth, w Joel, gct Mississiniwa MM, Ind.
1850, 9, 18. John gct Newbury MM
1850, 11, 13. Jesse & ch, Ruth Jesse & Sarah Jane, gct Newberry MM
1851, 3, 12. Hannah & Elizabeth gct Newberry MM
1853, 4, 13. Sewell gct Clear Creek MM
1853, 4, 13. William Paxson prcf Goshen MM, to m Ruth Green
1853, 5, 18. Ruth rmt William Paxson
1853, 7, 13. Ruth Paxton (form Green) gct Goshen MM
1854, 3, 15. Polly rocf West Grove MM, Ind.
1854, 10, 18. Isaac & w, Anna, & ch, Allen, Sarah, Wilson, Rachel Ann, Susannah & Enos, gct Mississiniwa MM, Ind.
1855, 1, 17. Polly gct Sugar River MM, Ind.
1856, 7, 16. Jehiel & w, Rachel, & ch, Joel William, James Robert & Aseph Leander, gct Springfield MM
1871, 2, 15. Robert L. rocf Clear Creek MM
1873, 4, 16. Thomas E. rocf Newberry MM, dtd 1873,2,17
1879, 5, 14. Robert L. & dt, Bertha, relrq
1887, 6, 15. Allice dis disunity
1897, 12, 15. William D. & w, Matilda, & ch, Ernest L., Percy E. & Francis W., roc
1899, 12, 13. William D. & w, Matilda, & ch gct Fairfield MM, O.
1900, 5, 16. Richard C. & w, Sadie D., & ch, Grace L., Mary & Herbert, rocf Ogden MM,O.
1902, 1, 15. Richard C. & w, Sadie D., & ch, Grace L., Mary E. & C. Herbert, gct Wilmington MM, O.
1903, 2, 18. Mary L. gct Newberry MM, O.

GRIFFITH
1810, 5, 5. Hannah recrq
1819, 6, 19. Elizabeth recrq
1821, 6, 16. Elizabeth rmt James Johnson
1822, 11, 16. Nancy (form Moreman) con mou
1825, 7, 16. Susannah (form Faulkner) con mou
1831, 1, 18. Susannah dis jH
1832, 8, 15. Nancy Osborn gct Miami MM
1834, 11, 12. Elizabeth (form Biven) dis mou
1836, 8, 17. Nancy Osborn rocf Miami MM, dtd 1836,7,27
1844, 7, 17. John Sr. recrq
1845, 12, 17. John Sr. gct White Lick MM, Ind.
1846, 12, 16. Nancy gct White Lick MM, Ind.
1895, 3, 13. Henry recrq
1900, 1, 17. Henry dropped from mbrp

GRIMES
----, --, --. George & Susannah
Ch: Asa G. b 1841, 12, 22
Elizabeth " 1848, 4, 28

1842, 1, 12. George & w, Susannah, & dt, Martha Jane, rocf Springfield MM, dtd 1841,7,13
1844, 2, 14. George & w, Susannah S., & ch, Martha Jane & Asa J., gct Springfield MM
1847, 5, 12. George M. & w, Susannah, & ch, Martha Jane, Jacob L. & Amos D., rocf Springfield MM, dtd 1847,2,20
1851, 12, 17. Martha Jane, Jacob, Amos D. & Elizabeth, ch George & Sarah, gct Mill Creek MM (cert returned)
1852, 12, 15. Martha Jane, Jacob, Elizabeth, Amos & Alfred,gct Honey Creek MM, Ind.
1853, 3, 16. George con mou
1854, 1, 18. George gct Honey Creek MM, Ind.

GRIST
1824, 6, 19. Ann rocf Miami MM
1824, 6, 19. Joseph & w, Mary, & ch, Isaac, John, Amy, Mary & Micajah, rocf Miami MM, dtd 1824,5,26
1825, 2, 19. Ann [Griste] gct Springborough MM
1825, 3, 19. Joseph [Griest] & w, Mary, & ch, Isaac, John, Amy, Mary & Micajah, gct Springboro MM

HACKNEY
1803, 7, 4. Deborah L. b

1843, 2, 15. John Lewis recrq
1843, 6, 14. Deborah L. recrq
1906, 2, 14. Wilbur recrq
1906, 2, 14. Edward & w, Rose, & ch, Sherman Raymond & Wilford Haines, recrq
1914, 9, 6. Howard & Robert recrq
1917, 7, 18. Volcah recrq

HADLEY
----, --, --. John b 1770,12,23; m Lydia ----- b 1774,1,17
Ch: William b 1795, 7, 18
Simon " 1796, 11, 1
Elizabeth " 1798, 6, 14
Joshua " 1799, 9, 15 d 1808, 4,15
Jacob " 1801, 3, 3
Isaac " 1802, 12, 9
Eli " 1804, 9, 27
John " 1806, 10, 3
Thomas " 1808, 8, 21
Jonathan " 1810, 8, 10
Ruth " 1812, 11, 15
Jane " 1815, 7, 20
----, --, --. Jeremiah & Esther
Ch: John Smith b 1840, 1, 14
James William " 1840, 1, 14
1891, 4, 20. Ruth E., w Joshua, d bur Springfield
1893, 6, 24. Joshua d bur Springfield

1807, 11, 28. John & w, Lydia, & ch, William Simon, Joshua, Jacob, Eli, Isaac, John & Elizabeth, rocf Cane Creek MM, N. C., dtd

HADLEY, continued
1807,9,5
1814, 5, 7. William gct Lick Creek MM, Ind., to m
1815, 5, 2. Sarah rocf Lick Creek MM, Ind., dtd 1814,10,9
1815, 10, 21. William & w, Sarah, & ch, John, Ruth, Jonathan, Anne, Joshua, Sarah, William & Jane, rocf Spring MM, dtd 1815,8,26
1815, 11, 16. Jonathan [Haley] rocf Spring MM, dtd 1815,9,30
1815, 12, 16. Jonathan rmt Rebecca Harvey
1816, 8, 17. William & fam gct Lick Creek MM, Ind.
1816, 11, 16. Ruth rmt William Harvey
1817, 1, 18. Simon rmt Ann Kersey
1817, 1, 18. William & w, Sarah, & ch, Jonathan, rocf Lick Creek MM, Ind., dtd 1816, 12,28
1817, 11, 15. John rmt Ruth Hale
1818, 3, 21. Joshua rocf Silver Creek MM, Ind., dtd 1818,3,14
1818, 5, 16. Joshua rmt Rebecca Towel
1818, 12, 19. Elizabeth rmt Ezekiel Hornada
1831, 11, 16. Jeremiah rocf Newberry MM, dtd 1831,9,19
1835, 9, 16. Jeremiah con mou
1838, 7, 16. Jeremiah gct White Water MM, Indiana, to m Esther Smith
1838, 8, 15. Jonathan prcf Springfield MM, to m Mary Linton
1838, 9, 12. Jonathan rmt Mary Linton
1840, 7, 15. Esther & ch, John S. & James W., rocf White Water MM, Ind., dtd 1840,4.22
1840, 8, 12. Mary (form Linton) gct Springfield MM
1842, 12, 14. Jonathan prcf Springfield MM, to m Eliza B. Mabie
1843, 1, 18. Jonathan rmt Eliza B. Mabie
1843, 2, 15. Eliza B. gct Springfield MM
1843, 8, 16. James Linton gct Springfield MM, to m Ann M. Hadley
1846, 1, 15. Ann rocf White Water MM, dtd 1845,12,24 (H)
1847, 3, 17. Jeremiah & w, Esther, & ch, John Smith, James William, Jane Ann & Samuel S., gct Cincinnati MM
1848, 9, 13. Edwin prcf Springfield MM, to m Esther Coate
1848, 10, 18. Edwin rmt Esther Coate
1849, 5, 16. Esther C. gct Springfield MM
1852, 9, 15. Emiline & ch, William Lawrence & Clark Hinman, recrq
1853, 4, 13. John C. rocf Springfield MM
1853, 8, 17. Cyrus Linton gct Springfield MM, to m Eliza Hadley
1854, 3, 15. John C. & w, Emiline, & ch, William Lawrence & Clark Henman, gct White Water MM, Ind.
1855, 6, 13. Edwin prcf Springfield MM, to m Jemima Doan
1855, 7, 18. Edwin rmt Jemima Doan
1856, 1, 16. Jemima D. gct Springfield MM
1859, 11, 16. Jonathan & w, Mary L., & ch, Rachel Ann, Mary Jane, Caroline Elizabeth, Lydia, Seth Silver, Nathan & William, rocf Springfield MM
1866, 3, 14. Rachel Ann Hale (form Hadley) rpd mou
1866, 5, 16. Rachel Ann gct Springfield MM
1867, 7, 17. Mary L. & ch, Lydia, Seth Silver, Nathan L., William & Martha Annillie, gct Lynn Grove MM, Ia.
1867, 7, 17. Elizabeth gct Lynn Grove MM,Ia.
1885, 4, 15. Joshua & w, Ruth E., rocf Springfield MM, dtd 1885,2,21

HAINES
1800, 7, 25. Elizabeth b
1809, 6, 30. Jane b
1811, 12, 5. Samuel [Hains] b
1818, 10, 24. Samuel [Hanes] b
1824, 9, 14. Mary b
1827, 12, 25. Hannah [Haine] b
1832, 1, 10. Clayton b
----, --, --. Zimri & Elizabeth
Ch: Asaph b 1841, 8, 3
Mary Mariah" 1844, 7, 27
----, --, --. Elwood & Apharacio
Ch: Lydia Emily
b 1846, 12, 13
Israel " 1848, 11, 28
Ann Isabel " 1850, 9, 3
Zimri L. " 1853, 2, 20
1850, 10, 15. Juliann [Hains] b
1854, 11, 15. Elisha b
----, --, --. Eber b 1825,1,20; m Mary ----- b 1830,3,9 d 1905,12,27 ae 75y
Ch: Zimri
Dennison b 1855, 6, 4
Thaddeus A." 1858, 1, 10
Webster " 1863, 4, 22
Willimene " 1863, 4, 22 d 1863, 5,29 bur New Hope
Mary Mariah
b 1866, 1, 13
Watts " 1872, 2, 28
1857, 8, 9. Eli b
----k --, --. Samuel & Mary
Ch: Aaron b 1859, 10, 17 d 1862, 2, 9 bur New Hope
Priscilla b 1860, 7, 13
1861, 12, 6. Hannah [Hains] b
----, --, --. Samuel & Mary
Ch: Alfred b 1865, 12, 31
Mary Emma " 1867, 5, 2
1868, 7, 16. Phebe d bur New Hope
1868, 8, 26. Zimri d bur New Hope
1871, 7, 11. Mary Elizabeth b
1873, 8, 14. Alvin Z. b
----, --, --. Zimri b 1848,9,24; m Elizabeth C. ----- b 1854,8,15
Ch: Harlin b 1873, --, 15
1875, 5, 14. Amos d bur New Hope
1875, 9, 10. Joshua, s Jacob & Mary, d bur Center

HAINES, continued
1876, 5, 5. Samuel, s Zimri & Elizabeth, b
1885, 8, 24. Corwin E. b
1888, 2, 17. Thomas H. b
1889, 6, 9. Samuel d
1889, 6, 11. Roy M. b
1893, --, --. Elden b
1904, 11, 6. Samuel d ae 86y 13d
1907, 1, 3. Mary d ae 82y 5m 17d

1808, 2, 6. Ruth (form Doan) con mou
1813, 3, 6. Elizabeth (form Doan) con mou
1831, 2, 19. William rocf Flushing MM, dtd 1830,12,25 (H)
1836, 8, 17. Susannah (form Lundy) dis mou
1840, 6, 17. Elizabeth gct Dover MM
1840, 8, 12. Zimri & w, Elizabeth, & ch, Samuel, Sarah, Elwood, Eber, Eli, Phebe, Clayton, Rebecca, Elizabeth & Zimri, Jr., recrq
1842, 7, 13. Samuel con mou
1845, 11, 12. Elwood gct Dover MM, to m Apharacia Moormon
1845, 11, 12. Sarah rmt Milton Fawcett
1847, 9, 15. Apharacia rocf Dover MM, dtd 1847,8,19
1848, 6, 14. Eber con mou
1854, 5, 17. Margaret M. & dt, Margaret Elizabeth, recrq
1854, 12, 13. Joseph E. Davis prcf Wabash MM, Ind., to m Phebe Haines
1855, 2, 14. Phebe rmt Joseph L. Davis
1855, 2, 14. Elwood & w, Apharacio, & ch, Lydia Emily, Israel Thomas, Ann Isabella & Zimri S., gct Dover MM
1856, 2, 16. George D. Carter prcf Dover MM, dtd 1856,1,17, to m Elizabeth Haines
1856, 3, 12. Elizabeth rmt George Carter
1856, 9, 17. Clayton dis mou
1858, 11, 17. Eli gct Fairfield MM, to m Emily McPherson
1858, 11, 17. Mary & ch, Eunice, Amos, Sarah Elizabeth, Zimri, Julie Ann, Phebe, Elisha & Eli, recrq
1859, 7, 13. Eli gct Caesars Creek MM
1865, 4, 26. Mary Maria Brown (form Haines) rpd mou
1867, 7, 17. Samuel recrq
1868, 5, 13. Clayton & w, Lydia, & ch, Maria Alice & Sarah Emily, recrq
1870, 3, 16. Asaph con mou
1871, 5, 17. Joshua & w, Jane, recrq
1873, 11, 12. Zimri rpd mou
1874, 2, 18. Elizabeth C. recrq
1877, 2, 14. Sarah Catharine [Haynes] & dt, Laura, recrq
1883, 6, 13. Zimri D. relrq
1883, 7, 18. Mary recrq
1885, 6, 17. William & w, Emma,recrq
1887, 3, 16. Louisa E. & dt, Lizzie, recrq
1888, 4, 16. Silvenia recrq
1896, 2, 12. Estella & s, Eldon Ray, recrq
1900, 2, 14. William [Haynes] & w, Emma, gct Wilmington MM, O.
1907, 2, 14. Corwin, Lydia & Edith recrq
1907, 4, 17. Ebor K. recrq
1909, 3, 17. Emma Hunt recrq
1909, 5, 12. Eli & w, Louise E., & ch, Bernice E. & Sylvester T., gct Wilmington MM
1912, 10, 16. D. W. & w, Estella, gct Wilmington MM
1912, 10, 16. Eldon gct Wilmington MM
1913, 2, 12. Bernard recrq
1913, 6, 18. Eber gct Grassy Run MM
1914, 2, 18. Samuel & dt, Pearl, gct Xenia MM
1919, 3, 12. Venice, Pearl, William, Mary E. & Earl [Haynes] dropped from mbrp
1920, 6, 17. Ralph & Addie recrq

HALE
1851, 9, 6. Jacob d

1810, 9, 1. Jacob & w, Martha, & ch, Samuel, Elizabeth, William, Eli, Ruth, Lydia, Martha, Jacob, Joseph & Armoni, rocf Cane Creek MM, N. C., dtd 1809,10,7
1813, 1, 2. Samuel H. dis mou
1814, 11, 5. Elizabeth rmt James Massey
1816, 9, 21. Lydia rmt John Harlan
1817, 7, 19. William dis mou
1817, 11, 15. Ruth rmt John Hadley
1829, 3, 21. Martha recrq (H)
1862, 8, 14. Mary Roseberry (form Hale) con mcd (H)
1866, 3, 14. Rachel Ann (form Hadley) rpd mou
1866, 5, 16. Rachel Ann gct Springfield MM

HALEY
1886, 5, 12. Thomas S. recrq
1919, 3, 12. Thomas dropped from mbrp

HALL
1829, 5, 16. Jacob recrq (H)

HALTON
1840, 12, 16. Abraham & w, Ann, & ch, Amos & Robert, gct White River MM, Ind.

HAMILTON
1911, 5, 17. H. H. recrq
1913, 2, 12. Ray recrq

HAMMAR
1809, 9, 2. David recrq

HAMPTON
1884, 6, 1. Isaac b
1884, 7, 29. Isaac d
1884, 9, 17. Rebecca d
1888, 6, 23. Ethel May b

1838, 3, 14. Margaret (form Smith) dis mou
1861, 11, 13. Zimri Whinery gct Chester MM, Ind., to m Rachel M. Hampton
1886, 3, 17. Orange recrq

HAMPTON, continued
1894, 11, 14. Orange & w, Clara, relrq

HANSEL
1846, 7, 16. Oliver W. b
1871, 3, 15. Oliver recrq
1907, 6, 13. Frances [Hansell] recrq

HANSON
1921, 4, 13. Florence gct Wilmington MM

HARLAN
1866, 8, 3. George [Harlin], s Barclay & Caroline, b d 1866,8,29 bur at Wilmington

1808, 2, 6. Edith [Harlon] & ch, Hannah, Enoch, John & Rebecca, rocf Springfield MM, N. C., dtd 1806,11,1
1809, 12, 2. Nathan [Harlin] & w, Sarah, & ch, Martha, Edith, Lydia, Nathan & Enoch, rocf Springfield MM, dtd 1809,2,4
1809, 12, 2. William [Harlin] & w, Charity, & ch, Margaret, Enoch, Ruth, David & Susannah, rocf Springfield MM, dtd 1809,2,4
1810, 12, 1. Hannah (form Morrison) rocf Miami MM, dtd 1810,10,31
1811, 4, 6. Hannah [Harlin] (form Morrison) con mou
1812, 10, 3. Solomon [Harlon] rocf Spring MM, N. C., dtd 1811,11,2
1814, 10, 1. Enoch rmt Elizabeth Harvey
1815, 11, 16. Solomon [Harlen] con mou
1816, 9, 21. John rmt Lydia Hale
1818, 10, 17. Margaret Ryan (form Harlan) con mou
1836, 6, 15. Edith recrq (form dis by Springfield MM)
1839, 2, 13. Edith [Harlin] gct Miami MM
1839, 9, 19. Lucy, w Enoch, & ch, Margaretann, Martha, Elizabeth, David R., Nathaniel E., Isaac F. & Emery B., recrq (H)
1840, 2, 17. Jabez dis jas
1840, 4, 15. Jabez [Halan] rocf Springfield MM
1845, 2, 13. Mary (form Massy) dis mou
1848, 8, 16. Caroline Elizabeth (form Haworth) con mou

HARLOW
1829, 10, 17. Enoch recrq (H)

HARMON
1897, 9, 15. Eunice dropped from mbrp

HAROLD
----, --, --. Andrew & Mary [Herald]
Ch: James J. b 1824, 11, 4
Leah T. " 1827, 10, 27
Margarett " 1830, 6, 10
Eli & Samuel " 1833, 7, 20
Sally & Elizabeth " 1835, 3, 25
Nathan " 1837, 10, 11

1835, 4, 12. Sally [Heareld] d
1837, 10, 22. Mary [Herald] d
----, --, --. Nathan d 1862,12,30 ae 25y 2m 18d; m Anna -----
Ch: Mary Allice b 1860, 1, 4
Anna Elizabeth " 1862, 3, 4

1829, 11, 18. Andrew [Harrold] & w, Mary, & ch, James Johnson & Leah Schooley, rocf Union MM, dtd 1829,9,23
1830, 11, 17. Jonathan [Harrold] Jr. rocf Union MM, N. C., dtd 1830,7,28
1831, 7, 13. Jonathan gct New Garden MM, Ind.
1831, 9, 14. Andrew & w, Mary L., & ch, James J., Leah S. & Margaret, gct New Garden MM, Ind.
1833, 11, 13. Andrew [Harrold] & w, Mary, & ch, James Johnson, Leah Schooley, Margaret, Eli & Samuel, rocf New Garden MM, dtd 1833,10,19
1844, 2, 14. Andrew & ch, James, Leah S., Margaret, Samuel, Eli & Elizabeth, gct Richland MM, Ind.
1846, 11, 18. James T. rocf Richland MM, Ind., dtd 1846,10,7
1848, 9, 13. James gct Newberry MM
1858, 10, 13. Nathan gct Newberry MM, to m Ann Kester
1859, 10, 12. Anna [Harrold] rocf Newberry MM, dtd 1859,8,22
1863, 3, 18. Anna & ch, Mary Alice & Anna Elizabeth, gct Newberry MM

HARRIS
1888, 5, 16. Marion & w, Malinda, recrq
1890, 5, 14. Marion dropped from mbrp
1892, 4, 13. Ernest recrq
1895, 6, 12. Malinda dropped from mbrp
1897, 10, 13. Ernest gct Miami MM

HARRISON
1827, 5, 19. William H. rmt Anne Stout
1827, 5, 19. Anne gct Green Plain MM
1829, 7, 15. William H. [Harison] & w, Anna, rocf Green Plain MM, dtd 1829,6,3
1830, 12, 15. William H. [Harison] & w, Ann, & ch, John A., gct Green Plain MM
1835, 10, 15. William & w, Anna, & ch, John, Stephen & Martha Ann, gct Miami MM (H)

HARTMAN
1883, 4, 18. Lida recrq

HARVEY
----, --, --. William & Mary
Ch: John b 1800, 7, 16
Eli " 1803, 3, 9
David " 1805, 4, 3
Sarah " 1807, 11, 23
Elizabeth " 1811, 2, 11
----, --, --. Joshua b 1779,7,15; m Mary -----

HARVEY, Joshua & Mary, continued
----- b 1782,8,24 d 1813,4,26
Ch: Hannah b 1801, 8, 16
Caleb " 1803, 5, 5
Simon " 1805, 11, 27
Levi " 1808, 12, 20
Robert " 1811, 7, 14
Joshua m 2nd Mary ----- d 1816,2,14
Ch: Ann & Jehu b 1816, 2, 14
1809, 5, 24. Deborah & Martha, twins, dt Isaac & Lydia, b
1813, 1, 2. Lydia d
----, --, --. Caleb J. & Rebecca J.
Ch: Jeremiah b 1863, 2, 18
Joseph " 1864, 10, 18 d 1864,11, 3

1807, 1, 8. Caleb & w, Sarah, & ch, Jesse, Joshua & Hannah, rocf Cane Creek MM, N. C., dtd 1806,9,6
1807, 1, 8. Joshua & w, Mary, & ch, Hannah, Caleb & Simon, rocf Cane Creek MM, N. C., dtd 1806,8,30
1807, 1, 8. William rocf Cane Creek MM, N.C. dtd 1806,8,30
1807, 1, 8. Eli & w, Mary, & ch, William, Lydia, Martha, Elizabeth, Ann & Mary, rocf Spring MM, N. C., dtd 1806,8,30
1807, 1, 8. Isaac & w, Lydia, & ch, Ruth, Elizabeth, Rebeckah, William, Harlan & Simon, rocf Spring MM, N. C., dtd 1806,8, 30
1807, 8, 1. Elizabeth [Hervey] rocf Spring MM, N. C., dtd 1806,9,27
1807, 10, 3. William gct Miami MM
1808, 6, 4. William & w, Mary, & ch, John Elis David & Sarah, rocf Spring MM, dtd 1806,3,26
1810, 1, 6. Cert rec for Caleb from Spring MM, N. C., endorsed to White Water MM
1810, 1, 6. Cert rec for Mary from Spring MM, N. C., endorsed to White Water MM
1810, 2, 3. William, Jr. gct White Water MM
1810, 7, 7. Samuel gct Miami MM, to m
1810, 10, 5. Rebecca rocf Miami MM, dtd 1810, 8,26
1810, 11, 3. Ezekiel Horneday, minor, under care of Isaac Harvey, recrq
1813, 2, 6. Ann [Hervey] rocf Springfield MM, N. C., dtd 1811,8,3
1814, 10, 1. Elizabeth rmt Enoch Harlan
1815, 3, 4. Joshua rmt Mary Moon
1815, 5, 20. Isaac gct Cincinnati MM, to m
1815, 10, 21. Lydia rmt Simon Moon
1815, 11, 18. Agatha rocf Cincinnati MM
1815, 11, 18. Ruth Towel (form Harvey) con mou
1815, 12, 16. Rebecca rmt Jonathan Hadley
1816, 11, 16. William rmt Ruth Hadley
1817, 5, 17. Samuel & w, Rebecca, & fam gct White Water MM, Ind.
1817, 8, 21. Henry declared intention of m with Ann Madden
1817, 9, 20. Henry prcf White Water MM, to m Ann Madden
1818, 4, 18. Ann gct West Grove MM, Ind.
1819, 1, 16. Elizabeth dis disunity
1840, 6, 17. Bloomfield MM rq permission to rst Elizabeth Elmore (form Harvey) (rq not granted)
1847, 9, 15. Vermillion MM, Ill. was granted permission to rst Elizabeth Elmore (form Harvey)
1848, 4, 12. Isaac Schooley gct Springfield MM, to m Deborah L. Harvey
1855, 9, 12. Caleb prcf Springfield MM, to m Rebecca Jeffries
1855, 10, 17. Caleb J. rmt Rebecca Jeffries
1856, 3, 12. Rebecca J. gct Springfield MM
1862, 12, 17. Caleb J. & w, Rebecca, & s, Charles, rocf Springfield MM
1867, 8, 14. Caleb J. & w, Rebecca J., & ch, gct Cottonwood MM, Kans.

HASKET
1871, 3, 15. Jesse & w, Betsy, recrq
1875, 5, 12. Betsy, w Jesse, dec, gct Waynesville MM
1875, 11, 17. Cert granted 1875,5m for Betsy returned by Miami MM

HATTON
1814, 3, 5. George roc dtd 1814,1,15
1815, 1, 7. Edward rocf Stillwater MM, dtd 1814,10,25
1815, 1, 7. George gct Miami MM
1815, 5, 20. George gct Cincinnati MM
1815, 12, 16. Edward gct Cincinnati MM

HAUSEFELT
1879, 3, 12. Harmon rocf Caesars Creek MM
1883, 12, 12. Harmon relrq
1886, 3, 17. Harmon A. recrq

HAWKINS
----, --, --. Thomas & Mary
Ch: Jesse F. b 1834, 9, 21
Nathan " 1836, 9, 30
----, --, --. Elizabeth M., dt John & Deborah T., b 1872,12,5 d 1883,3,28
1884, 5, 23. Ethel Mary b
1918, 6, 11. Ethel May m Thomas Leaton WALL

1807, 9, 5. Amos & w, Phebe, & ch, Jonathan, Mary Margaret & Christopher, rocf Cane Creek MM, S. C., dtd 1807,3,20
1807, 9, 5. Amos & w, Ann, & ch, Henry, Mary, Rebecca & Martha, rocf Cane Creek MM, S. C., dtd 1807,3,20
1833, 12, 18. Thomas prcf New Garden MM, Ind., to m Mary Faulkner
1834, 1, 15. Thomas rmt Mary Faulkner
1835, 6, 17. Thomas rocf New Garden MM, Ind., dtd 1835,2,21
1838, 3, 14. Thomas & w, Mary, & ch, Jesse F. & Nathan, gct Caesars Creek MM
1869, 4, 14. Deborah T. (form McMillan) rpd

HAWKINS, continued
mou
1869, 5, 12. Deborah T. gct Caesars Creek MM
1872, 6, 12. John & w, Deborah T., & s, Milton T., rocf Caesars Creek MM, dtd 1872,4, 25
1875, 4, 14. John gct Caesars Creek MM
1881, 6, 15. John rocf Caesars Creek MM, dtd 1881,5,26
1913, 2, 12. Violet Rose transferred from associate to active mbrp
1921, 2, 16. Milton J. gct Wilmington MM, O.

HAWORTH
----, --, --. James [Hayworth] b 1781,2,16; m Rachel ----- b 1782,1,1
Ch: George b 1801, 9, 14
Ruth " 1804, 3, 23
Sarah " 1806, 1, 28
Jonathan " 1808, 11, 27
James Wright " 1811, 3, 13
Eli " 1814, 3, 10
----, --, --. George D. b 1797,5,29; m Edith HADLEY b 1796,7,11
Ch: Anne b 1818, 5, 28 d 1821, 6,23 bur Dover
Elkanah " 1820, 2, 11 " 1820,10,26 bur Dover
Jonah F. b 1821, 10, 6 " 1828, 5,31
Mary " 1824, 2, 4
Caroline " 1826, 11, 3
George D. " 1829, 4, 18
James Malon " 1831, 11, 19
Edith Emeline " 1838, 9, 27
----, --, --. George D. & Rebecca
Ch: Laura Bell b 1854, 12, 29
James R. " 1858, 6, 28
Frank White" 1864, 5, 6

1807, 10, 3. George [Hayworth] rmt Joanna Vanhorn
1807, 10, 3. Mary [Hayworth] rmt Daniel Bailey
1807, 10, 3. Sarah Reece (form Hayworth) con mou
1809, 4, 1. William [Hayworth] dis mou
1809, 7, 1. Ruth [Hayworth] (form Wright) dis mou
1813, 4, 3. Joanna Buskler, gr dt Joanna [Hayworth] recrq
1814, 10, 1. George & Ruth, ch James, recrq
1814, 11, 5. Phebe Haworth, gr ch Sarah Wright, recrq
1817, 8, 16. George D. [Hayworth] Jr. gct Newberry MM, to m
1818, 4, 18. Edith [Hayworth] rocf Newberry MM, dtd 1818,3,5
1818, 12, 19. Richard [Hayworth] & w, Susannah, & ch, Rachel & Sarah, gct Silver Creek MM, Ind.
1819, 1, 16. George dis disunity
1819, 5, 15. Elizabeth rocf Newberry MM, dtd 1819,3,25
1819, 11, 20. Phebe rmt Charles M. Johnson
1820, 1, 15. Dillon dis mou & disunity
1820, 6, 17. Ezekiel & w, Elizabeth, & dt, Melissa, gct Newbury MM
1821, 7, 21. Samuel dis disunity
1821, 8, 18. John [Hayworth] & w, Elizabeth, & ch, Moorman, Susann, George, Mahlon, Minerva, Allen, John & Herman, gct Honey Creek MM, Ind.
1822, 10, 19. James [Hayworth] & w, Racher, & ch, George, Ruth, Sarah, Jonathan, James, Eli, Mahlon, Susannah & William, gct Honey Creek MM, Ind.
1823, 9, 20. George rst
1825, 2, 19. George H. & w, Joanna, gct Honey Creek MM, Ind.
1825, 2, 19. Joanna gct Honey Creek MM, Ind.
1872, 5, 19. George D. & w, Edith, & ch, Jonah, Mary & Caroline E., rocf Dover MM, dtd 1827,5,5
1836, 9, 14. Vermilion MM, Ill. was granted permission to rst William
1845, 7, 16. Mary Glass (form Hsworth) dis mou
1848, 8, 16. Caroline Elizabeth Harlan (form Haworth) con mou
1853, 11, 13. James con mou
1855, 4, 18. George Jr. con mou
1855, 4, 18. Rebecca [Hayworth] (form Hoage) con mou
1858, 12, 15. George D. gct White Water MM, to m Sarah Clark
1859, 6, 15. Sarah rocf White Water MM, dtd 1859,5,25
1860, 2, 15. Edith Emily Moody (form Haworth) rpd mou
1871, 10, 18. Isaiah rmt Mary Johnson
1872, 6, 12. Mary [Hayworth] gct Dover MM

HAYCOCK
1834, 3, 13. Jane rocf Uwchlon MM, Pa., dtd 1833,11,4 (H)

HAYES
1910, 2, 16. Venice, Pearl, William H., Mary E. & Earl B., recrq

HAZARD
1877, 8, 17. Lorain, dt Frank & Louella, b
----, --, --. Herbertm Hannah ----- d 1879,12, 10
Ch: Anna R. b 1879, 11, 2
Clara S. " 1879, 11, 2

1829, 9, 16. John dis disunity
1874, 5, 13. Herbert recrq
1879, 1, 15. Francis D. recrq
1890, 9, 17. Frank & w & s, Lorain & Ethelbert, gct Wilmington MM, O.
1906, 5, 16. Clara [Hazzard] gct Wilmington MM

HAZARD, continued
1912, 12, 18. Herbert & w, Flora, & ch, Clifton, & Mary, gct Wilmington MM, O.

HEMELRIGHT
1831, 6, 15. Elizabeth [Hemelwright] rocf Hopewell MM, Va., dtd 1831,3,2
1842, 6, 15. Elizabeth gct Springfield MM

HENDERSHOT
1894, 3, 14. Lola recrq
1896, 2, 12. Emma recrq

HENDERSON
1815, 3, 4. Richard & w, Rachel, & ch, Isaac, Sarah, Keziah & William, gct White Water MM
1853, 7, 13. Mourning (form Ballard) con mou
1853, 10, 12. James Westley & Sarah Frances, ch Mourning, recrq
1853, 12, 14. Mourning & ch, James Westley & Sarah Frances, gct Caesars Creek MM

HESTER
----, --, --. Francis & Mary

Ch:		
	Rachel	b 1807, 1, 4
	Henry	" 1809, 1, 15
	William	" 1811, 2, 9
	Isaac	" 1812, 12, 9

1811, 10, 5. Elizabeth rmt Evan Stanbrough
1815, 6, 11. Ruth rmt Nehemiah Stanbrough
1819, 10, 30. Thomas rmt Mary Leonard
1819, 11, 20. Thomas & w, Mary, gct New Garden MM, Ind.
1860, 5, 16. Mary (form Gilpin) rpd mou; dropped from mbrp

HESTON
1831, 5, 21. Samuel & w, Susan R., & ch, Edward T., Arthur L., Rebecca Ann, George G. & Joseph L., rocf Baltimore MM for Western District dtd 1831,4,8 (H)
1831, 5, 21. Jane rocf Baltimore MM for Western District, dtd 1831,4,8 (H)
1836, 3, 17. Samuel & w, Susannah, & seven ch gct White Water MM, Ind. (H)
1842, 9, 15. Letitia gct Springborough MM, O. (H)

HIATT
----, --, --. Hezekiah b 1786,3,22; m Ann PERKINS b 1785,4,21 (H)

Ch:		
	Sarah	b 1811, 4, 7
	Isaac	" 1813, 1, 4
	Allen	" 1814, 12, 15
	Maryann	" 1816, 12, 3
	Susannah	" 1819, 1, 4
	Lydia	" 1821, 3, 5
	Narcissa	" 1823, 5, 16
	Pheniah	" 1825, 4, 13
	Amos	" 1827, 6, 28

1833, 5, 23. Sarah m Joseph WHINERY (H)
1840, 2, 20. Mary Ann m Samuel BIRDSALL
1853, 4, 25. Narcissa d bur Center
1892, 12, 29. Mamie M., dt Eber & Mary Haines, d bur Sugar Grove Cemetery, near Wilmington

1810, 5, 5. Hezekiah rocf New Garden MM, N. C., dtd 1809,9,30
1810, 9, 1. Hezekiah rmt Ann Perkins
1815, 5, 20. Lydia & ch, Hester & Jehu, rocf Mt. Pleasant MM, dtd 1815,1,28
1815, 12, 16. Jesse [Hyatt] & fam recrq
1816, 1, 20. Sarah [Hyatt] rocf New Garden MM, N. C.
1816, 6, 15. Lydia rmt Jacob Jessop
1816, 9, 25. Jesse [Hyatt] & fam recrq
1816, 12, 21. Joel & w, Mary, & ch, Allen, Guli Elma, Isom & Joel, rocf New Garden MM, N. C., dtd 1816,8,31
1817, 4, 19. Eleazar & w, Anna, & ch, Eliza & Jesse, rocf New Garden MM, N. C., dtd 1816,11,30
1818, 5, 16. Eleazar & w, Anna, & ch, Eliza, Jesse & Daniel, gct Miami MM
1818, 6, 20. Mary recrq
1818, 7, 18. Reubin rocf Caesars Creek MM, dtd 1818,4,24
1818, 8, 15. Gideon rocf Caesars Creek MM, dtd 1818,5,29
1818, 8, 15. John & w, Mary, & ch, Jesse, Anna Rachel & Mary, rocf Caesars Creek MM, dtd 1818,5,29
1818, 11, 21. Sarah gct Miami MM, O.
1820, 3, 18. Gideon con mou
1820, 6, 17. John & w, Mary, & ch, Jesse, Anna, Rachel & Mary, gct Springfield MM, Ind.
1820, 11, 18. Gideon gct Springfield MM, Ind.
1821, 3, 17. Hezekiah dis disunity
1821, 5, 19. Jesse [Hyatt] & ch, Joseph, Lewis, Elizabeth & Mary, gct Springfield MM
1824, 6, 19. Mary & ch, Margaret & Samuel, rocf Cherry Grove MM, Ind., dtd 1824,4,10, endorsed by Springfield MM, 1824,5,29
1826, 1, 21. Hezekiah rst
1826, 2, 18. John & w, Mary, rocf White River MM, Ind., dtd 1825,12,10
1826, 6, 17. Jesse & ch, Lewis & Mary, rocf Springfield MM, dtd 1826,5,15
1828, 2, 16. Lewis gct Springfield MM, to m Charity Kimbrough
1828, 8, 13. Mary Gant (form Hiatt) dis mou
1828, 11, 12. Hezekiah dis jH
1828, 12, 17. Mary rmt Owen Biven
1829, 1, 14. Ann dis jH
1829, 4, 15. Jesse rmt Sarah Masson
1829, 11, 18. John & w, Mary, gct Fairfield MM, Ind.
1830, 11, 17. Jesse Hiatt & w, Sarah, & ch, Ira, Ruth, Jonathan, Stephen & Mary Hannah Mason & Rachel Hiatt, gct Vermillion MM, Ill.

HIATT, continued
1833, 2, 13. Rueben dis disunity
1834, 12, 17. Sarah Whinery (form Hiatt) dis mou & jH
1837, 3, 15. Lewis gct Springfield MM
1838, 7, 18. Margaret [Hiat] dis disunity
1839, 7, 18. Mary Ann con mou (H)
1839, 11, 13. Mary [Hyatt], w Rueben, & ch, Elihu, Stephen, Martha, Charles, Rueben & Samuel M., gct Salem MM, Ia.
1841, 9, 15. Mary Ann Birdsall (form Hiatt) dis mou
1844, 11, 13. Lydia Stump (form Hiatt) dis mou
1845, 12, 18. Lydia Stump (form Hiatt) dis mou (H)
1846, 4, 16. Isaac con mou (H)
1846, 5, 14. Phaniah Oglesby (form Hiatt) con mou (H)
1846, 11, 18. Pheniah Oglesbee (form Hiatt) dis mou & joining Separatists
1847, 3, 17. Stephen dis mou
1847, 3, 17. Elihu dis mou
1847, 8, 18. Isaac dis mou
1852, 6, 17. Amos C. con mcd (H)
1852, 10, 13. Martha D. (form Hutton) con mcd (H)
1853, 1, 13. Martha D. gct White Water MM (H)
1899, 3, 15. Angie gct Wilmington MM, O.

HILL
1853, 1, 12. Louisa (form Farquhar) con mou
1853, 9, 14. Louisa gct Greenwich MM

HINES
1828, 9, 24. Jesse d bur Center, O.
1830, 12, 6. Patience d

1821, 8, 18. Isaac dis mou
1826, 2, --. Rachel (form Doan) dis mou
1826, 5, 23. Rachel dis disunity
1826, 11, 18. Jesse [Hinds] rmt Sarah Stanley
1829, 2, 18. Nathan dis jH
1830, 6, 16. Sarah dis jH
1830, 12, 15. Sarah [Hinds] rmt Mahlon Kirk
1842, 11, 5. Hannah rmt Edwin Whinery

HOBS
1809, 4, 1. George dis mou

HOBSON
1807, 11, 28. William & w, Sarah, & ch, Bailey and Peggy, & gr ch, George & Hannah, rocf Cane Creek MM, N. C., dtd 1807,9,5
1810, 5, 5. Joseph & fam rocf Cane Creek MM, dtd 1810,3,3
1810, 5, 5. Hannah Polk (form Hobson) dis mou
1812, 12, 5. Joseph dis disunity

HODGENS
1815, 2, 5. Mary Stanborough (form Hodgens) con mou

HODGSON
----, --, --. Hur b 1767,5,16 d 1851,2,6; m Elizabeth ----- b 1769,--,-- d 1794,7,10
Ch: Mary b 1790, 7, 2 d 1807,11, 2
Isaac " 1792, 3, 19
Hur m 2nd Achsah ----- b 1779,1,25 d 1841, 10,6 bur Center
Ch: Jesse b 1798, 10, 15
Jonathan " 1800, 2, 6 d 1811,11,16
Jehu " 1802, 1, 19
John " 1804, 4, 30
Elizabeth " 1806, 11, 4
Hannah " 1809, 2, 20
Uri " 1811, 9, 9
Ira " 1811, 9, 9 d 1841, 7,28
Nathan " 1815, 3, 24
1816, 10, 23. Mary, dt Nathan Hines, d ae 38 bur Center
1819, 4, 10. Joel b
1824, 11, 2. Jehu d
1868, 11, 5. Elizabeth d bur Center

1808, 1, 2. Amos [Hodson] rmt Mary Barnett
1808, 2, 6. Mary [Hodson] rocf New Garden MM, N. C., dtd 1807,9,26 (d before arrival of cert)
1810, 10, 6. Jonathan rocf New Garden MM, N. C., dtd 1810,3,31
1811, 1, 5. Rachel rmt William Hoggatt
1811, 10, 5. Jonathan gct Fall Creek MM, to m
1811, 10, 5. Susannah Fisher (form Hodgson) con mou
1812, 4, 8. Jonathan rocf Center MM, N. C., dtd 1811,8,21
1812, 11, 7. Amos dis disunity
1813, 9, 4. Joel [Hodson] con mou
1814, 2, 5. Lydia Hoskins (form Hodgson) dis mou
1814, 7, 2. Solomon & w, Elizabeth, & ch, Thomas, John, Jemima & Naomi, gct Caesars Creek MM
1814, 7, 2. Moses gct Cesars Creek MM
1820, 10, 21. Isaac rmt Hannah Leonard
1820, 12, 16. Isaac & w, Hannah, gct New Garden MM, Ind.
1821, 3, 17. Jesse dis disunity
1827, 9, 15. Anna con mou
1828, 7, 16. John dis mou
1835, 5, 13. Anna dis jas
1839, 1, 16. Uri con mou
1839, 2, 13. Mary (form Thornburgh) con mou
1840, 1, 15. Uri gct Westfield MM, Ind.
1840, 4, 15. Mary [Hodson] gct Westfield MM, Ind.
1840, 11, 18. Nathan dis mou
1844, 1, 17. Joel con mou
1869, 9, 15. Lidia [Hodson] recrq
1870, 4, 13. Ira [Hodson] rocf Newberry MM, dtd 1870,3,21
1883, 8, 15. Hannah [Hodson] gct Peace MM, Kans.

HOGE

----, --, --. Asa H. b 1804,2,2 d 1849,1,22 bur Center; m Rebecca McPherson LUPTON, b 1811,5,17 d 1833,12,22 bur Center
Ch: John M. b 1831, 2, 24 d 1839, 5, 4 bur Center
Mary Thamosin " 1832, 9, 20
Rebecca Lupton " 1833, 3, 10

1834, 1, 15. Asa & w, Rebecca, & ch, John McPherson, Mary Thomazin & Rebecca, rocf Hopewell MM, dtd 1834,12,4
1845, 12, 17. Asa H. gct Cincinnati MM
1855, 4, 18. Rebecca Hayworth (form Hoage) con mou

HOGGATT

----, --, --. Moses & Olive [Hockett]
Ch: Isaac b 1812, 2, 14
Ann " 1813, 8, 12
Rebecca " 1814, 12, 23
Agnes " 1816, 7, 17

1811, 1, 5. William rmt Rachel Hodgson
1811, 2, 2. Rachel gct Fairfield MM
1811, 2, 2. Moses [Hocket] & ch, Margaret, Mary, Sarah & Prudence, rocf Fairfield MM, dtd 1811,1,26
1811, 4, 6. Moses gct Caesars Creek MM, to m
1812, 8, 1. Olive rocf Caesars Creek MM, dtd 1812,7,25
1816, 9, 21. Mary rmt Robert Cook
1817, 1, 18. Moses & w, Olive, & ch, Sarah, Prudence, Isaac, Ann, Rebecca & Agnes, gct New Garden MM, Ind.
1817, 2, 15. Margaret [Hocket] gct New Garden MM, Ind.

HOLLAND

1832, 7, 21. Salina con mou (H)

HOLLADAY

1807, 10, 3. John rocf Spring MM, N. C., dtd 1807,7,25
1807, 10, 3. William rocf North West Fork MM, Md., dtd 1807,7,2
1808, 1, 2. John rmt Susannah Faulkner

HOLLINGSWORTH

1822, 1, 8. Lydia, dt Israel, d bur Center
----, --, --. Samuel m Jane A. ----- d 1837,8, 29 ae 36y 7m bur Center
Ch: Israel b 1824, 9, 16
Jonathan " 1827, 1, 8
Hannah " 1828, 8, 31
Sarah Ann " 1831, 2, 2
Elizabeth " 1832, 9, 29
Phebe " 1834, 9, 17
Samuel " 1837, 8, 22 d 1837,10, 9 bur Center
Samuel m 2nd Emily -----
Ch: Mary W. b 1842, 1, 11
David " 1843, 4, 12
1826, 1, 6. Sarah d
----, --, --. Asaph m Anna WICKERSHAM
Ch: Valentine b 1828, 10, 11 d 1849,10, 9
Lydia " 1830, 11, 11
Pierce " 1833, 7, 10
Enoch " 1837, 5, 3
Israel H. " 1843, 1, 1
1835, 10, 14. Anna d bur Center
1842, 2, 13. Israel d bur Center
1846, 7, 17. Asaph d bur Chester
----, --, --. Pierce & Sarah Jane
Ch: Isadore b 1856, 8, 5 d 1857,10,15 bur Chester
Emma " 1859, 12, 20
Calvin R. " 1860, 12, 23 d 1861, 6, 1
Asaph E. " 1862, 6, 2
1861, 1, 20. Ella, dt Enoch & Hester Ann, b
1865, 7, 19. James W., s Pierce & Mary (Sarah) Jane, b

1813, 12, 4. Sarah rocf Center MM, Pa., dtd 1813,10,16
1816, 2, 17. Israel & ch, Samuel Aseph Lydia James & Ann, rocf Center MM, Pa., dtd 1815,10,14
1820, 1, 15. Mary rocf White Water MM, Ind., dtd 1818,12,26
1820, 2, 19. John & w, Mary, & dt, Elizabeth, rocf Miami MM, dtd 1819,11,24
1820, 12, 16. Samuel rmt Jane Ann McMillan
1825, 8, 15. John & fam gc
1827, 8, 18. John & w, Mary, & ch, Elizabeth, Mirza, Hannah & Samuel, gct White Lick MM, Ind.
1827, 9, 15. Asaph rmt Anna Wickersham
1827, 12, 15. Jarrus dis mou
1827, 12, 15. Susannah rocf Silver Creek MM, dtd 1827,9,22
1828, 4, 19. Sophia rocf Union MM, dtd 1828, 1,18

1834, 1, 15. Sophia rmt James Lundy
1838, 12, 12. Samuel rmt Emily Kirk
1844, 7, 17. Samuel dis joining separatists
1847, 6, 16. Iwrael dis mou
1850, 10, 16. Sarah Ann dis disunity
1854, 4, 12. Lydia H. Rockhill (form Hollingsworth) dis mou
1855, 5, 16. Pierce rmt Sarah Jane Whinery
1856, 1, 16. Phebe Jackson (form Hollingsworth) rpd mou; dropped from mbrp
1857, 4, 15. Jonathan gct Wabash MM, Ind.
1858, 10, 13. Charles H. Kirk prcf White Water MM, to m Rachel Hollingsworth
1858, 11, 17. Rachel rmt Charles H. Kirk
1859, 7, 13. Enoch rpd mou
1859, 7, 13. Hester Ann (form Snider) rpd mou
1860, 6, 13. Seth Smith prcf Green Plain MM, to m Anna Hollingsworth

HOLLINGSWORTH
1860, 7, 18. Hannah rmt Seth Smith
1860, 9, 12. Hannah Smith (form Hollingsworth) & Harriet Hollingsworth, a minor under her care, gct Green Plain MM
1860, 10, 18. Mahlon & w, Mary P., & ch, Edward W., James M., Charles M., Rachel Ann, Aquilla W., Esther Jane & Harriet, gct Prairie Grove MM, Ia.
1864, 4, 13. David (or Daniel) gct Wabash MM
1866, 2, 14. Josiah, s Samuel, dec, gct Bangor MM, Ia.
1866, 3, 14. Pierce & w, Sarah Jane, & ch, Emmer Asaph & James N., gct Bangor MM, Ia.
1868, 7, 15. Isaac gct Green Plain MM
1870, 1, 12. Eli & w, Hester Ann, & ch, Ella & Inez, gct Wilmington MM
1897, 4, 14. Marion recrq

HONEYCUTT
1839, 10, 16. John P. prcf Springfield MM, to m Susannah Ballard
1839, 11, 13. John P. rmt Susannah H. Ballard
1840, 7, 15. Susannah H. [Hunnicutt] gct Springfield MM

HOPKINS
1855, 10, 18. Priscilla rocf Baltimore MM, dtd 1855,8,9, endorsed by Miami MM

HORNEDAY
1810, 11, 3. Ezekiel, minor, under care of Isaac Harvey, recrq
1818, 12, 19. Ezekial [Hornada] rmt Elizabeth Hadley

HORNER
1911, 4, 12. Ethel Henley gct Xenia MM

HORTON
1875, 10, 13. Rachel gct Dragoon MM, Kans.

HOSKINS
1812, 1, 4. Moses & w, Ruth, & ch, William, Jonathan, Mary, Joseph, Hannah, Eli & Ruth, rocf New Garden MM, N. C., dtd 1811, 7,27
1813, 4, 3. Mary rmt Nathan Dillon
1814, 2, 5. Jonathan dis mou
1814, 2, 5. Lydia (form Hodgson) dis mou
1814, 7, 2. Moses [Haskins] & w, Ruth, & ch, Joseph, Hannah, Eli & Ruth, gct Fairfield MM

HOUGHEY
1823, 5, 17. Barnett recrq
1824, 1, 17. Margaret & ch, Elizabeth Ann & John, recrq

HOUSTON
1906, 2, 14. Rebecca & Ardella recrq

HOWARD
1848, 1, 13. Martha Jane (form Daniel) con mou (H)

HOWELL
1913, 2, 12. Blanch recrq

HOWLAND
1827, 6, 16. Mary recrq
1827, 8, 18. Barnabas recrq
1841, 8, 18. Barnabas & w, Mary, & dt, Lydia, gct Springfield MM
1872, 9, 18. Barnabas rocf Springfield MM

HOYLE
1842, 12, 15. Elizabeth (form Birdsall) con mou

HUDGE
1874, 6, 17. Ellis recrq

HUDGEL
1874, 4, 15. Newton recrq
1878, 9, 18. Newton gct Newberry MM
1879, 2, 12. Newton's cert returned by Newberry MM; relrq

HUFFMAN
1829, 8, 27. Christopher b
1832, 10, 29. Harriett b
1885, 7, 13. Emma Jane b

1874, 4, 15. Christopher C. & w, Hariet A., recrq
1874, 4, 15. Angie Amanda recrq
1883, 4, 18. George W. & w, Margaret, & ch, Dellis Elmer Francis Marion & Oliver Alvie, recrq
1894, 3, 14. Ella recrq
1896, 2, 12. Amanda recrq
1899, 3, 15. Christopher & w gct Wilmington MM, O.
1906, 5, 16. Emma Hendershot gct Cesars Creek MM
1907, 2, 12. Nancy recrq
1907, 3, 13. Nancy gct Caesars Creek MM
1909, 7, 14. Nancy rocf Cesars Creek MM
1913, 5, 14. Clement & w, Emma, rocf Xenia MM
1919, 3, 12. Maude dropped from mbrp

HULL
1886, 5, 12. Charles recrq
1886, 5, 12. Julia recrq
1888, 2, 15. Archy recrq
1891, 4, 15. Ida recrq
1892, 1, 13. Charles & fam relrq

HUMPSTON
1902, 3, 12. John E. & w, Harriett, & ch, Asa B. & Anna D., recrq
1914, 4, 15. John A., Harriett, Asa & Anna gct Xenia MM

HUNT
1810, 7, 7. Mary rmt Joseph Cloud
1832, 12, 12. John rmt Phebe F. Walker
1833, 5, 15. Phebe F. gct Newberry MM
1841, 10, 13. Phareby rocf Springfield MM, dtd 1841,9,18
1842, 9, 14. Pharaba gct Springfield MM
1908, 2, 12. Bernard T. recrq
1914, 9, 6. Alice recrq
1915, 5, 12. Dorris recrq

HURLEY
1887, 3, 16. Vella relrq
1894, 3, 14. Jerema D. recrq
1896, 11, 18. Ida recrq
1907, 2, 12. Edith & Ethel recrq
1910, 2, 16. Howard Noah recrq
1910, 2, 16. Elizabeth [Harley] recrq
1913, 2, 12. Ralph transferred from associate to active mbrp

HUTCHINS
1884, 1, 16. Maria Alice gct West Branch MM

HUTTON
1839, 8, 15. Martha con mou (H)
1852, 10, 13. Martha D. Hiatt (form Hutton) con mcd (H)

INSMINGER
1826, 9, 16. Jane recrq
1826, 12, 16. Jane gct Vermillion MM, Ill.

JACKS
1913, 2, 12. Claud, Leona & Mani recrq

JACKSON
1884, 2, 16. Dora Ann b

1856, 1, 16. Phebe (form Hollingsworth) rpd mou; dropped from mbrp
1881, 12, 14. Harvey F. & w, Anna J., & ch, Nellie E., recrq
1887, 11, 16. H. F. relrq
1887, 11, 16. Anna J. relrq
1887, 11, 16. Nellie E. relrq
1887, 11, 16. Dora A. relrq
1887, 11, 16. Ruth L. relrq

JAMES
----, --, --. Jonathan & Mary Jane
Ch: Elvie H. b 1857, 9, 6
William
Linton " 1861, 12, 6

1848, 10, 18. Evan dis mou
1856, 3, 12. Jonathan prcf Newberry MM, to m Mary Jane Shepherd
1856, 4, 16. Jonathan rmt Mary Jane Shepherd
1864, 12, 14. Mary Jane gct Newberry MM

JAY
1809, 7, 1. Layton & fam gct West Branch MM

JEFFERIS
----, --, --. Job E. [Jeffries] b 1811,1,29; m Elizabeth ----- b 1804,6,27
Ch: Rebecca B. b 1835, 12, 30
Jeremiah " 1837, 8, 21
Rachel " 1839, 3, 5
Hannah " 1842, 5, 4
1846, 1, 2. Job [Jeffers] d bur Center
1878, 8, 9. Harriett d
1879, 7, 21. T. J., s Joshua, b
1887, 1, 2. Hannah d bur Center
1902, 9, 21. Rebecca H. d bur Springfield

1810, 9, 1. Job [Jeffreys] & s, Darlington, rocf Miami MM, dtd 1810,7,25
1822, 4, 20. Elizabeth (or Hannah) & ch, Hannah, Joab & Job, recrq
1823, 8, 16. Abraham rocf Bradford MM, Pa.
1823, 8, 16. Hannah rocf Bradford MM, Pa., dtd 1823,7,5
1824, 4, 17. Abraham [Jefferas] con mou
1824, 7, 17. Hannah gct Miami MM
1824, 8, 21. Darlington [Jefferas] dis mou
1825, 5, 21. Abraham gct White Water MM, Ind.
1825, 8, 20. Hannah gct Miami MM
1836, 8, 17. Job [Jefferies] Jr. con mou
1837, 8, 16. Joab [Jeffaries] con mou
1841, 5, 12. Elizabeth [Jefferes] (form Brown) rocf Nottingham & Little Brittan MM, dtd 1841,4,9
1853, 3, 16. Job E. [Jeffries] dis mou
1853, 5, 18. Harriet M. recrq
1855, 6, 13. Joab [Jeffries] dis disunity
1855, 9, 12. Caleb Harvey prcf Springfield MM to m Rebecca Jeffries
1855, 10, 17. Rebecca [Jeffries] rmt Caleb J. Harvey
1860, 1, 18. Hannah [Jeffries] gct Springfield MM
1861, 10, 16. Joshua M., Nancy Ann, William Preston & Mary Belle, ch Harriet, recrq
1862, 9, 17. Hannah S. rocf Springfield MM, dtd 1862,8,16
1875, 10, 16. Rachel Cordon (form Jefferis) gct Dragoon MM, Kans.
1879, 1, 15. Lydia C. [Jefferies] recrq
1881, 9, 14. Rebecca [Jeffries] rocf Springfield MM
1892, 9, 14. Joshua & w, Lydia, & ch, Isaac J., Eulalia, Wayne, Ann Mary & Luther, gct Wilmington MM

1914, 4, 15. Preston [Jeffries] gct Wilmington MM
1917, 4, 18. Russell [Jeffris] recrq

JENKINS
1825, 7, 28. John b
1843, 1, 19. Jane b
1846, 11, 24. Mary Elizabeth, dt Evan & Martha, b
1864, 11, 3. Phebe b

JENKINS, continued
1841, 5, 12. Evan H. prcf Mill Creek MM, to m Martha Shepherd
1841, 6, 16. Evan H. rmt Martha Shepherd
1841, 11, 17. Martha S. gct Mill Creek MM
1848, 11, 15. Evan H. & w, Martha L., & ch, Siles Newton, David Harvey & Mary Elizabeth, rocf Mill Creek MM, dtd 1848,8,15
1851, 1, 15. Evan H. & ch, Silas Newton, David Harvey & Mary Elizabeth, gct Mill Creek MM
1856, 2, 13. Deborah T. (form Painter) dis mou
1876, 3, 15. John & w, Sarah Jane, & dt, Phebe, recrq
1904, 12, 14. John & Fanny dropped from mbrp
1906, 5, 16. John rocf Wilmington MM

JESSOP
1863, 9, 24. Joseph P., s Richard & Rebecca, Warren Co., O.; m at Center, Mary B. LEWIS, dt Daniel & Priscilla, Clinton Co., O. (H)

1816, 6, 15. Jacob rmt Lydia Hiatt
1816, 12, 21. Lydia & ch gct White Water MM

JOHNSON
----, --, --. Martha b 1815,6,23 d 1830,12,13 bur New Hope
----, --, --. John & Judith
Ch: Brooks b 1817, 8, 3
Joel W. " 1819, 7, 29
David " 1821, 8, 14
Phebe " 1823, 8, 28
Rhoda " 1826, 2, 1
1819, 8, 14. Amos b
1821, 11, 13. Lewis, s Mary (later w John Coate), b
----, --, --. James m Elizabeth GRIFFITH
Ch: Rhoda Ann b 1822, 6, 27
John Griffith " 1824, 1, 22
Alfred " 1825, 10, 28
Evan " 1827, 10, 21
Thatcher L." 1829, 11, 4
Hannah Mariah " 1832, 1, 4
Mary B. " 1834, 3, 10
1822, 5, 20. Lydia b
1824, 12, 31. Solomon F. b
----, --, --. Lewis m Rachel ----- b 1818,1, 14
Ch: Ahirah b 1843, 9, 20
Sarah Ann " 1847, 2, 8
Mary " 1849, 6, 8
Joseph R. " 1852, 5, 4
Elizabeth L. b 1856, 5, 26
----, --, --. Ahira b 1843,9,20; m Margaret Ann ----- b 1845,6,21
Ch: Arthur b 1867, 1, 24
Hannah P. " 1868, 11, 8
Irena " 1872, 2, 22
Ora Anna b 1874, 12, 17
1875, 12, 11. Rachel b

1808, 12, 3. Deborah (form Coffin) dis mou & jas
1810, 10, 6. Micajah rocf Fairfield MM, dtd 1810,8,25
1811, 3, 2. Mildred & dt, Elizabeth, rocf Fairfield MM, dtd 1810,8,25
1811, 6, 1. Samuel & w, Susanna, & ch, Thomas, Samuel, Moreman, James, John, George, Susannah, Lydia & Joseph, rocf South River MM, dtd 1810,9,3
1811, 6, 1. Moreman & w, Elizabeth, & ch, Christopher, Thomas, Charles, Achiles & John Milton, rocf South River MM, dtd 1810,11,10
1811, 11, 2. John W. & w, Milly, & s, Garrard Moreman, rocf South River MM, dtd 1810, 9,8
1811, 12, 7. Micajah dis mou
1811, 12, 7. Rhoda dis mou
1812, 1, 4. Cert rec for Joseph Jr. from South River MM, endorsed to Fairfield MM
1812, 2, 1. Thomas rmt Mary Faulkner
1813, 5, 1. Micajah gct Miami MM
1813, 6, 5. Joseph dis disunity
1814, 2, 5. Susannah rocf Fairfield MM, dtd 1813,11,27
1814, 11, 5. John & w, Lydia, & ch, Rhoda Elizabeth Mary Susannah Thomas Lydia & Anna, rocf Mt. Pleasant MM, Va., dtd 1813,11,27
1815, 3, 4. Christopher E. dis disunity
1815, 5, 20. John W. & w, Milley, & ch, Gerrard Moorman, John Linch & Benjamin Wadkins, gct Fairfield MM
1815, 7, 15. Elizabeth Moreman (form Johnson) dis mou
1815, 8, 19. Thomas & w, Ann, & ch, Isaac & Ann, rocf Mt. Pleasant MM, dtd 1815,2,26
1816, 5, 18. John rmt Judith Faulkner
1816, 10, 19. Ann rmt Benajah Nordyke
1818, 4, 18. Rhoda Thornborough (form Johnson) con mou
1818, 8, 15. Charles gct Fairfield MM
1819, 1, 16. Pleasant & w, Nancy, & ch, Thomas M., Alfrica, William C., Edwin E., Paulina P. & Jervis L., rocf Fairfield MM, O., dtd 1818,8,29
1819, 6, 19. Isaac dis disunity
1819, 11, 20. Charles M. rmt Phebe Haworth
1820, 7, 15. Thomas dis mou
1820, 8, 19. James dis mou
1820, 10, 21. Lewis rmt Mary Banghum
1821, 4, 21. Elizabeth recrq
1821, 6, 16. James rmt Elizabeth Griffith
1821, 6, 16. Charles M. dis disunity
1821, 10, 20. Achilles dis disunity
1823, 2, 15. John con mou
1823, 3, 15. James & fam gct Miami MM
1823, 6, 21. Apharacia Dearduff (form Johnson) con mou

JOHNSON, continued
1824, 4, 17. Thomas rmt Susannah Johnson
1824, 4, 17. Susannah rmt Thomas Johnson
1824, 5, 15. Martha recrq
1824, 9, 18. George W. rmt Apharacia Moorman
1827, 6, 16. Thomas dis disunity
1827, 10, 20. Mary dis
1828, 9, 17. Ann Turner (form Johnson) dis mou
1830, 5, 12. James & fam rocf Miami MM, dtd 1830,2,24
1831, 3, 16. Lydia S. (form Faulkner) con mou
1832, 5, 16. Lydia S. & dt, Juliann, gct White Lick MM, Ind.
1832, 7, 18. James & w, Elizabeth, & ch, Rhoda Ann, John Griffith, Alfred, Evan Lewis, Thatcher-Stratton & Hannah Maria, rocf Dover MM,dtd 1832,3,19
1834, 11, 12. John & w, Judith, & ch, Brooks, Joel W., David F., Phebe, Rhoda M., Eli & Rachel A., gct Miami MM
1834, 12, 17. John Cote & w, Mary, & ch, Hiram, Rebecca, Martha, Lindley M., Esther & Lucy Cote & Lewis Johnson, s Mary by form m, rocf Union MM, dtd 1834,11,12
1837, 1, 18. James & w, Elizabeth, & ch, Rhody Ann, John J., Alfred, Evan L., Thatcher L., Hannahmariah, Mary B. & Rebecca, gct Miami MM
1837, 3, 15. Amos, Lydia & Solomon, ch Thomas & Mary, gct Dover MM
1842, 9, 14. Lewis rmt Rachel Stanton
1842, 9, 14. Brooks prcf Miami MM, to m Lydia Burson
1842, 10, 12. Brooks rmt Lydia Burson
1842, 11, 16. Lydia B. gct Springborough MM
1852, 2, 18. Isaac Painter gct West Union MM, Ind., to m Joanna T. Johnson
1853, 8, 18. James A. & w, Rebecca, rocf Miami MM, dtd 1853,6,22 (H)
1853, 9, 15. Hannah E., Sarah E. & Clarke, ch James A., recrq (H)
1856, 12, 18. James A. & w, Rebecca, & ch, Hannah E., Sarah E. & Clarke, gct Fall Creek MM, Ind.
1865, 9, 13. Ahairah gct Dover MM, to m Margaret Ann Painter
1866, 2, 14. Margaret Ann rocf Dover MM
1866, 2, 14. Ruth (form Lundy) rpd mou
1866, 6, 13. Ruth L. gct Spring Creek MM, Ia.
1871, 10, 18. Mary rmt Isaiah Haworth
1874, 1, 14. Rebecca M. recrq
1876, 12, 13. Joseph gct Dover MM
1885, 2, 18. Emma R. gct Spiceland MM, Ind.
1887, 6, 15. Lewis & w, Rachel, dis disunity
1887, 6, 15. Sarah Ann dis disunity
1893, 11, 15. Carrie L. rocf Cesars Creek MM
1899, 6, --. Mary B. & s, Harold, gct White Water MM, Ind.
1900, 4, 18. Margaret A. gct Wilmington MM,O.
1902, 6, 18. William H. & Mary recrq
1903, 3, 18. Arthur relrq
1906, 2, 14. William McKinley, Wilbur, Charles Walter F. recrq
1911, 9, 13. Margaret H. rocf Wilmington MM
1915, 3, 17. Charles & w, Edith, & s, Carshall, gct Wilmington MM

JONES
----, --, --. Isaac b 1784,8,6 d 1856,9,2; m Phebee OREN b 1792,9,22
Ch: Ruth b 1811, 10, 18
Miriam " 1813, 8, 15 d 1823, 1,12 bur Center
Abigail " 1814, 10, 23
Mary Ann " 1816, 2, 15 d 1825,10, 6 bur Center
Huldah " 1817, 8, 7
Lydia " 1819, 2, 13 d 1825,10,16 bur Center
Sarah " 1820, 10, 20 " 1835, 4, 7 bur Center
Rebecca " 1822, 9, 28 " 1825,10,20 bur Center
Phebe " 1824, 5, 5
Evan " 1826, 3, 15
John " 1827, 2, 22
James " 1828, 12, 24
Margaret " 1831, 1, 10
Isaac " 1832, 8, 12 d 1832, 9,20 bur Center
----, --, --. Benjamin d 1858,4,9 ae 52y 11m 15d bur near Center; m Cynthia A. JOHNSON
Ch: Sarah C. b 1842, 9, 24
Micajah I. " 1844, 8, 21
Eliza S. " 1846, 11, 29 d 1865, 8, 3 bur Center
Rebecca Emily " 1849, 3, 28
Martha Ann " 1851, 4, 19 d 1867, 5,15 bur Center
Joseph Edwin " 1853, 5, 12
George Catlit " 1855, 7, 4
John Howard" 1857, 8, 14

1825, 9, 17. Samuel, minor under care of Samuel Stanton, recrq
1826, 1, 21. Elenor (form Whitson) dis mou
1826, 7, 15. Jesse Kersey recrq
1828, 10, 15. Isaac & w, Phebe, & ch, Ruth, Abigail, Huldah, Sarah & Phebe, recrq
1829, 5, 13. James recrq
1837, 8, 16. Jesse dis mou
1838, 9, 12. Ruth Ford (form Jones) dis mou
1839, 1, 16. Edward Thomas prcf Dover MM, to m Huldah Jones
1839, 2, 13. Huldah rmt Edward Thomas
1839, 6, 12. Huldah Thomas (form Jones) gct Dover MM
1839, 6, 12. Daniel prcf Miami MM, to m Hannah Mabie
1839, 7, 17. Daniel rmt Hannah Mabie
1839, 10, 16. Hannah M. gct Miami MM
1840, 2, 12. Abigail Richards (form Jones)

JONES, continued
dis mou
1841, 11, 17. Phebe rmt John Schooley
1842, 8, 17. John Brown gct Miami MM, to m Elizabeth R. Jones
1850, 6, 12. Benjamin & w, Cynthia A., & ch, Sarah C., Micajah J., Eliza S. & Rebecca E., rocf Upper Springfield MM, O., dtd 1850,5,25
1852, 5, 12. John dis mou
1854, 1, 18. Margaret Luzena (form Jones) dis mou
1871, 2, 15. Cynthia A. & ch, Joseph E., George C. & John Howard, gct Wilmington MM
1872, 3, 13. Micajah rpd mou
1898, 3, 17. Cert rec for E. Townsend & w, Rachel, from Wilmington MM, O., endorsed to Cesars Creek MM
1920, 9, 15. Ethel C. gct Caesars Creek MM

KENDALL
1815, 9, 16. Elizabeth & s, Isaac, rocf Fairfield MM, dtd 1815,7,20

KENNEY
1903, 2, 18. Robert S. recrq
1903, 3, 18. Anna Huff (Kinney] recrq
1903, 7, 15. Nannie Huff [Kinney] rocf Dover MM
1903, 11, 18. Effie & Etha, ch Robert & Nannie, recrq
1905, 4, 12. Louetta & Alta, ch Robert & Anna, recrq
1919, 3, 12. Effie, Louella, Alta & Edward dropped from mbrp

KERSEY
1812, 11, 7. Thomas & w, Rebecca, & ch, Thomas, Rebecca & Carter, rocf Springfield MM, N. C., dtd 1811,8,3
1813, 2, 6. John [Kirsey] rocf Springfield MM, dtd 1811,8,3
1813, 7, 3. John con mou
1815, 2, 4. John & dt, Elizabeth, gct Miami MM
1817, 1, 18. Ann rmt Simon Hadley
1820, 4, 15. Springfield MM was granted permission to rec Rebecca, Jr.

KESTER
1818, 11, 21. Hannah recrq
1818, 12, 19. Mary Davis & John, Daniel & Harmon Kester, ch Hannah, recrq
1819, 11, 20. Thomas & w gct New Garden MM, Ind.
1823, 1, 18. Hannah & ch, John & Harmon, gct Springfield MM
1831, 6, 15. Daniel gct Newberry MM
1858, 10, 13. Nathan Harold gct Newberry MM, to m Ann Kester

KIBBY
1909, 10, 13. Ambrose & w, Louisa, & dt, Laura, rocf Wilmington MM
1910, 2, 16. Oscar recrq
1910, 2, 16. Effie recrq

KILDOW
----, --, --. Michael b 1831,6,24; m Margaret Ann ----- b 1836,4,17
Ch: Eliza Jane b 1860, 3, 2
Joseph A. " 1862, 3, 1
Eunice Louvenia " 1865, 4, 23
Viola " 1868, 7, 25
Eber Azel " 1872, 7, 23
Harvey Allen " 1874, 4, 13
1876, 9, 19. Eliza Jane, dt Michael L. & Margaret Ann, d

1870, 7, 13. Margaret Ann, w Michael, & ch, Eliza Jane, Joseph Abraham, Eunice Lewvenia & Viola, recrq
1871, 4, 12. Michael recrq
1889, 12, 19. Joseph gct Wilmington MM
1897, 9, 15. Azel & Allen [Kildon] dropped from mbrp

KIMBROUGH
1850, 8, 15. Jeremiah d

1828, 2, 16. Lewis Hiatt gct Springfield MM, to m Charity Kimbrough
1829, 4, 18. Jeremiah recrq (H)

KING
----, --, --. Dean & Esther
Ch: Almyra b 1836, 3, 5
Louisa " 1837, 9, 22
Levinus " 1840, 2, 31
Edward " 1842, 10, 27
Henry " 1845, 4, 15
Sarah Clarissa " 1849, 5, 11

1828, 9, 17. Dean rocf White Water MM, dtd 1828,8,27
1828, 10, 15. Dean rmt Esther Carpenter
1829, 3, 18. Esther (form Carpenter) gct White Water MM, Ind.
1831, 4, 13. Thomas & w, Sarah, & ch, Israel, Hannah, Elizabeth, Mary Ann, Rachel, Thomas Clarkson, Naomi & Allen, gct Duck Creek MM, Ind.
1834, 8, 13. Dean & w, Esther, & ch, Mercy Ann, Mary & Calvin, rocf White Water MM, dtd 1834,5,28
1838, 5, 16. Mary rocf White Water MM, Ind., dtd 1838,4,15
1838, 11, 14. Mary gct White Water MM, Ind.
1847, 1, 12. Mary rocf White Water MM, Ind., dtd 1847,11,25
1849, 2, 14. Mercy Ann Painter (form King) dis mou
1854, 9, 13. Dean & w, Esther, & ch, Mary,

KING, continued
Calvin C., Almira, Louisa, Livinus, Edward, Henry F., Sarah Clarissa & Anna Maria, gct Wabash MM, Ind.

KINLEY
1807, 11, 28. John rmt Betty Wilson
1809, 10, 7. Betty gct Miami MM

KINNINGS
1913, 2, 12. Robert recrq

KINSEY
----, --, --. John & Elenor
Ch: Lewis b 1826, 6, 22
Milton " 1828, 7, 30
John " 1830, 7, 26 d 1839, 4,12 bur Center
Louisa " 1832, 7, 1
Ruth " 1834, 7, 28
Macy " 1837, 3, 25
Nathan L. " 1840, 8, 2

1827, 7, 21. John & w, Elenor, & ch, Jonathan B. & Samuel B., rocf Flushing MM, dtd 1827,4,21
1827, 10, 20. Ruth rocf Flushing MM, dtd 1827, 4,27
1827, 12, 15. Christopher & fam rocf Flushing MM, dtd 1827,6,22
1828, 12, 17. Susannah rmt John Stout Jr.
1830, 9, 15. Edmund dis disunity
1832, 11, 14. Matilda [Kinsie] (form Ballard) con mou
1833, 1, 16. Rachel Broomhall (form Kinsey) dis mou
1835, 10, 14. Mary Ann McCoy (form Kinsey) con mou
1836, 5, 18. Ruth Wiley (form Kinsey) con mou
1836, 6, 15. Christopher dis disunity
1841, 11, 17. John dis disunity
1848, 4, 12. Fanney H. gct Caesars Creek MM
1857, 7, 15. Matilda gct Western Plain MM,Ia.

KIRK
----, --, Thomas & Sarah
Ch: Israel b 1810, 12, 26
Hannah " 1813, 2, 7
Elizabeth " 1815, 4, 1
Mary Ann " 1817, 8, 26
Rachel " 1820, 1, 20
Jacob " 1822, 2, 10
Thomas Clarkson " 1825, 4, 14
Naomi " 1827, 6, 19
----, --, --. Timothy b 1800,4,23; m Rebecca -----
Ch: Elizabeth C. b 1826, 7, 17
Rachel W. " 1827, 10, 21 d 1828,10,21
Timothy m 2nd Hannah T. ----- b 1814,12,12
Ch: Wilson T. b 1834, 9, 8
1828, 11, 27. Ezekiel d

----, --, --. Malon b 1802,10,22; m Sarah ---- b 1807,5,3
Ch: Nathan b 1832, 11, 17
John " 1834, 9, 15
Jesse " 1836, 7, 11
Ezekiel " 1838, 7, 16
Isaac " 1840, 10, 28 d 1841, 5,12 bur Chester
Isaiah b 1845, 11, 3
----, --, --. Nathan & Abigail
Ch: Willis b 1854, 8, 7
Joseph P. " 1858, 3, 11
Edwin " 1862, 9, 7
----, --, --. Ezekial b 1838,7,16; m Elizabeth P. ----- b 1839,9,9
Ch: A. Lincoln b 1867, 1, 16
Rachel A. " 1870, 11, 15
1874, 5, 21. Gilbert Mahlon b
1874, 12, 16. Elbert J. b
1881, 4, 16. Mahlon d

1812, 12, 5. Ezekiel & w, Hannah, & ch, William, Sarah, Timothy & Mahlon, rocf Center MM, dtd 1812,9,24
1812, 12, 5. Hannah rocf Center MM, Pa., dtd 1812,9,19
1816, 11, 16. Thomas & w, Sarah, & ch, Israel, Hannah & Elizabeth, rocf Center MM, Pa., dtd 1816,9,14
1822, 2, 16. Caleb rmt Susannah Bailey
1823, 5, 17. Hannah rmt Abraham Moore
1824, 2, 21. Sarah W. gct White Water MM,Ind.
1824, 9, 18. William gct West Grove MM, Ind., to m Rachel Wickersham
1824, 11, 20. Timothy con mou
1825, 11, 19. Rebecca rocf White Water MM
1825, 12, 17. William gct West Grove MM, Ind.
1830, 4, 14. Caleb Kirk & w, Susannah, & her ch, Daniel, James Edwin & Mary Byram Bailey, gct Dover MM
1830, 12, 15. Mahlon rmt Sarah Hinds
1831, 4, 13. Thomas & w, Sarah, & ch, Israel, Hannah, Elizabeth, Mary Ann, Rachel, Thomas Clarkson, Naomi & Allen, gct Duck Creek MM, Ind.
1831, 9, 14. Rebecca dis jH
1832, 9, 12. Milton McMillan gct Duck Creek MM, Ind., to m Elizabeth Kirke
1833, 5, 15. Timothy gct Allum Creek MM, to m Hannah Townsend
1833, 8, 14. Ann recrq
1834, 7, 16. Hannah rocf Allum Creek MM, dtd 1834,2,20
1836, 4, 13. Timothy & w, Hannah, & ch, Elizabeth E. & Wilson F., gct White Water MM, Ind.
1836, 11, 16. Hannah Sr. gct White River MM, Ind.
1838, 4, 18. Emily rocf Caesars Creek MM, dtd 1838,3,22
1838, 12, 12. Emily rmt Samuel Hollingsworth
1853, 10, 12. Nathan rmt Abigail Whinery
1858, 10, 13. Charles H. prcf White Water MM,

KIRK, continued
to m Rachel Hollingsworth
1858, 11, 17. Charles H. rmt Rachel Hollingsworth
1859, 11, 16. Rachel gct Plainfield MM, Ind.
1861, 3, 13. John rpd mou
1866, 7, 18. Ezekiel N. & w, Elizabeth P. (form Coate) con mou
1867, 2, 13. Nathan & w, Abigail, & ch, Willis, Joseph P. & Edwin Whinery, gct Bangor MM, Ia.
1871, 6, 14. Elizabeth Ann recrq
1873, 7, 16. Elizabeth Ann gct Wilmington MM
1892, 7, 13. Ida recrq
1893, 2, 15. Cleo E. & Rollo S., minors, rec-in mbrp
1895, 4, 17. Jesse H. gct Wilmington MM
1898, 5, 18. Angeline rocf Ogden MM
1913, 2, 12. Cecil, Jesse & Wilbur transferred from associate to active mbrp
1913, 4, 16. Edwin, s Elbert J. & Margaret, recrq
1919, 3, 12. Ralph dropped from mbrp
1921, 2, 16. Angelina gct Wilmington MM, O.

LADD
1860, 10, 17. Lydia gct Fairfield MM

LAMAR
1830, 5, 12. Hannah [Lemar] & ch, Mary, Osborn, Samuel & Ruth, rocf White Lick MM
1837, 7, 12. Osborn dis disunity
1838, 5, 16. Nathan Dennis prcf Springfield MM, Ind., to m Mary Lamar
1838, 6, 13. Mary [Lemar] rmt Nathan Dennis
1839, 12, 18. Hannah & dt, Ruth, gct Springfield MM, Ind.
1842, 7, 13. Samuel [Lemar] gct Springfield MM, Ind.

LAMBURN
1832, 5, 19. Isaac rocf Cherry St. MM, Phila., dtd 1831,5,18 (H)

LANCASTER
1828, 12, 17. Rachel dis jH

LAPHAM
1833, 9, 18. Nancy (form Fallis) con mou
1834, 4, 16. Nancy L. gct Cincinnati MM

LARRICK
1896, 5, 13. William & w, Nancy, rocf Fairfield MM
1903, 3, 18. William & Nancy [Larrieck] relrq

LEACH
1839, 6, 13. Joseph & w, Ann, & ch, John, Sarah Jane & Hannah, rocf Warrington MM, dtd 1839,3,21 (H)
1867, 2, 13. Cush recrq
1889, 7, 17. Eva relrq

LEHMAN
1830, 5, 12. Hannah & ch, Mary, Osborn, Samuel & Ruth, rocf White Lick MM, Ind., dtd 1829,11,14
1833, 7, 17. Levina [Leamon] (form Smith) dis mou

LEONARD
1837, 11, 30. Abigal d ae 96y 7m bur Center
----, --, --. Bezillar b 1823,6,15; m Susan H. ----- b 1820,--,--
Dt: Emma A. b 1852, 3, 2
1854, 11, 11. Emma b
1854, 11, 11. Lucinda b
----, --, --. Calvin B. b 1845,6,18; m Rebecca M. ----- b 1846,4,2
Ch: Alta Dell b 1868, 11, 13
Cora P. " 1870, 4, 8
Della M. " 1875, 9, 2
----, --, --. Calvin B. & Mary
Ch: Arthur C. b 1879, 1, 5
Walter E. " 1881, 8, 1
Mary E. " 1883, 11, 18
1881, 10, 18. Walter E. d
1890, 2, 26. Rebecca M., w C. B., d
1897, 10, 22. Joseph d bur Center
1899, 11, 13. Abbie d bur Center
1901, 3, 12. Brazille d bur near Xenia

1807, 5, 2. John & w, Abigail, rocf Center MM, N. C., dtd 1807,2,28
1808, 12, 3. Abigail & Sarah rocf Center MM, N. C., dtd 1808,9,17
1810, 5, 5. Sarah Rees (form Leonard) con mou
1819, 10, 30. Mary rmt Thomas Hester
1820, 10, 21. Hannah rmt Isaac Hodgson
1821, 3, 17. Thomas dis mou & disunity
1825, 11, 19. Ezekiel dis disunity
1829, 5, 13. Rebecca dis jH
1830, 5, 12. Ruth dis jH
1835, 4, 15. Rachel Cline (form Leonard) dis mou
1836, 12, 14. Eleanor Cline (form Leonard) dis
1844, 8, 15. Rebecca gct Clear Creek MM, Ill. (H)
1844, 8, 15. Ruth gct Clear Creek MM, Ill. (H)
1853, 10, 13. Susan H. con mcd (H)
1871, 3, 15. Barzillai & w, Susannah, & dt, Emma A., recrq
1874, 4, 15. Joseph & w, Abigail, & ch, Albert G. & Edgar S., recrq
1876, 3, 15. Colvin B. & w, Rebecca, & ch, Alta Dell, Cora P. & Della M., recrq
1876, 3, 15. Emma E. & Lucinda recrq
1894, 11, 14. Nancy A. C. rocf Caesars Creek MM, dtd 1894,10,25
1894, 12, 12. Parmelia recrq
1907, 2, 12. De Ella gct Bloomingdale MM, Ind.

LESTER
1871, 3, 15. William & w, Eunice, & ch, Martha Ellen, Angeline & Walter H., recrq

LEWIS
----, --, --. Enoch m Elizabeth ----- d 1814, 4,21
Ch: Jonah b 1814, 3, 13
1835, 11, 7. John d ae 74y 6m 27d bur Center, O.
1863, 9, 24. Mary B. m Joseph P. JESSOP (H)
----, --, --. Jacob & Amanda
Ch: Elsie b 1868, 12, 13
Seth " d 1894, 3,16 bur Sugar Grove

1807, 11, 7. Esther Roads (form Lewis) con mou
1813, 11, 6. Enoch & w, Elizabeth, rocf Goose Creek MM, Va., dtd 1813,9,2
1815, 3, 4. Enoch & s, Jonah, gct Clear Creek MM
1826, 9, 16. John & Elizabeth recrq
1841, 9, 15. David Ballard gct Clear Creek MM, to m Priscilla Lewis
1850, 1, 17. Amos Underwood gct Fall Creek MM, O., to m Priscilla Lewis (H)
1860, 1, 18. Hannah (form Painter) rpd mou; dropped from mbrp
1863, 7, 15. Lucina (form Faulkner) rpd mou; dropped from mbrp
1869, 1, 13. Amanda rpd mou
1871, 3, 15. Jacob recrq
1886, 5, 12. Lydia J. recrq
1886, 5, 12. Alice E. recrq
1888, 2, 15. Roy recrq
1894, 9, 12. William R. rocf Clear Creek MM
1897, 2, 17. William R. relrq
1897, 4, 14. Jacob relrq
1898, 9, 14. Eva rocf Springfield MM
1921, 2, 16. Eva gct Wilmington MM, O.

LINKHART
1871, 3, 23. Mellia b
1871, 3, 27. Elizabeth L. b
1897, 8, 29. Thomas d ae 59y

1874, 3, 18. Elizabeth [Linkheart] & dt, Nellie Revelle, rocf Newberry MM, dtd 1874, 1,19
1885, 5, 12. Thomas & w, Mary, & ch, Milton S., George L., Herbert B. & Dallas E., recrq
1895, 1, 16. Elizabeth J. gct New Vienna MM
1895, 2, 13. Nellie relrq
1895, 6, 12. Dallas relrq
1898, 1, 12. George relrq
1904, 12, 14. Milton & Herbert dropped from mbrp

LINTON
----, --, --. Nathan b 1778,1,18 d 1858,1,11 bur Center; m Rachel ----- b 1790,1,17 d 1859,4,30
Ch: Elizabeth b 1807, 7, 29
Abi " 1808, 11, 25
Samuel
Smith b 1810, 11, 17
Seth " 1812, 10, 5
David " 1815, 1, 30
James " 1817, 1, 17
Mary " 1819, 4, 21
Nathan " 1821, 3, 21 d 1824,11,14 bur Center
Benjamin " 1823, 5, 7
Cyrus " 1825, 4, 17
Ruth " 1827, 4, 23
----, --, --. Seth b 1812,12,5; m Sarah Ann ----- b 1819,12,7
Ch: Nathan M. b 1838, 3, 18
Nancy " 1840, 3, 1
Rachel " 1841, 10, 8
Joshua " 1843, 4, 2
Oliver " 1845, 8, 5
Amanda " 1848, 11, 11
----, --, --. Cyrus & Lidia
Ch: Samuel S. b 1848, 7, 8
Olive " 1855, 6, 18
Lydia " 1859, 12, 9
Edwin C. " 1862, 10, 14
----, --, --. James William & Edith
Ch: Abigail Ann b 1850, 3, 19
Charles J. " 1853, 8, 7
Elizabeth " 1855, 7, 4
Maria E. " 1857, 5, 6
----, --, --. Joshua & Olive
Ch: Walter b 1865, 7, 19
Seth " 1871, 11, 18 d 1875, 3,23 bur Center
Alida C. " 1873, 7, 6 " 1875, 3,14 bur Center
Myra " 1878, 5, 1
1870, 7, 5. Ada, dt Oliver & Sally, b
1875, 3, 11. Sally, dt N. M., d
1893, 5, 29. Sarah Ann, w Seth, d bur Springfield
1895, 11, 5. Seth d bur Springfield

1807, 1, 8. Daniel rocf Westland MM, dtd 1807,4,25
1810, 10, 6. Elizabeth rmt John Satterthwaite
1814, 1, 1. Jane rmt Jesse Arnold
1819, 6, 19. William & w, Hannah, & ch, William, Samuel, David, Albert, Thomas, Harriet, John, Sarah, Isaiah & Hannah, rocf Smithfield MM, dtd 1819,3,22
1819, 6, 19. Elizabeth rocf Smithfield MM, dtd 1819,3,22
1820, 12, 16. Elizabeth rmt Joseph Thatcher
1823, 1, 18. William Jr, dis mou
1826, 1, 21. Albert dis jas
1826, 7, 15. Elizabeth rmt William Butterworth
1826, 9, 16. Samuel B. dis disunity
1826, 12, 16. Harriet dis jas
1827, 5, 19. Thomas dis disunity
1829, 12, 16. Abi rmt Josiah Farquhar
1831, 5, 18. Samuel dis mou
1832, 6, 13. William & w, Hannah, & ch,

LINTON, continued
John, Sarah, Isaiah, Hannah, Rachel & Anna R., gct Cincinnati MM
1835, 3, 18. Elizabeth & ch, Jonathan B. & James William, recrq

1836, 8, 17. Seth gct Springfield MM, to m Sarah Ann Moore
1837, 8, 16. Sarah Ann rocf Springfield MM, dtd 1837,7,11
1838, 8, 15. Jonathan Hadley prcf Springfield MM, to m Mary Linton
1838, 9, 12. Mary rmt Jonathan Hadley
1840, 8, 12. Mary Hadley (form Linton) gct Springfield MM
1842, 1, 12. David dis mou
1843, 8, 16. James gct Springfield MM, to m Ann M. Hadley
1845, 9, 17. Benjamin dis mou
1845, 9, 17. Ruth rmt Benjamin Whinery
1845, 12, 17. Jonathan B. gct Miami MM
1845, 12, 17. Elizabeth F. & s, James William, gct Miami MM
1846, 8, 12. Jonathan rocf Miami MM, dtd 1846, 5,27
1846, 8, 12. Elizabeth F. & s, James William, rocf Miami MM, dtd 1846,5,27
1848, 10, 18. Lydia rocf Springfield MM, dtd 1848,7,15
1849, 4, 18. James W. rmt Edith Shepherd
1851, 8, 13. James gct Springfield MM
1853, 8, 17. Cyrus gct Springfield MM, to m Eliza Hadley
1854, 7, 12. Eliza rocf Springfield MM, dtd 1854,6,17
1857, 6, 17. Jonathan rpd mou; dropped from mbrp
1860, 3, 14. Nathan rpd mou; dropped from mbrp
1860, 6, 13. Nancy rmt Isaac McMillan
1863, 9, 16. Rachel Snowden (form Linton) rpd mou
1866, 1, 17. Joshua rpd mou
1866, 10, 17. Elizabeth gct Indianapolis MM, Ind.
1868, 7, 15. Joshua & s, Walter, gct Springfield MM, O.
1868, 7, 15. Edith & ch, Abigail Ann, Charles J., Elizabeth,Maria D., Alma H. & Sarah Frances, gct Indianapolis MM, Ind.
1869, 7, 14. Oliver rpd mou
1871, 3, 15. Sarah A. Jr. recrq
1872, 3, 13. Loftus Walter & w, Sarah R., & gr ch, Seth & Sarah Ann, recrq
1872, 9, 18. Joshua & w, Olive, & ch, Walter, Elsa & Seth H., rocf Springfield MM
1878, 7, 17. James W. gct Indianapolis MM, Ind.
1892, 9, 14. Walter gct Springfield MM, O.
1893, 6, 14. Joshua & w, Olive, & dt, Myra, gct Wilmington MM
1893, 6, 14. Elsie gct Wilmington MM
1898, 3, 17. Loftus W. relrq

LISTER
1898, 12, 29. Walter d bur Gallipolis, O.
1899, 1, 18. Wm. d bur Nat'l Soldiers Home, Dayton, O.

LONG
1830, 8, 18. Eliza (form Fallis) dis mou

LONGSTRETH
1818, 1, 17. Jacob rocf Phila. MM, Pa., dtd 1817,5,29, endorsed by Miami MM
1818, 6, 20. Jacob dis mou
1841, 8,18. William prcf Miami MM, to m Martha Coate
1841, 9, 15. William rmt Martha Coate
1842, 2, 16. Martha gct Miami MM
1849, 7, 19. Rachel (form Birdsall) con mou (H)
1852, 2, 19. Rachel B. gct Miami MM (H)
1907, 2, 12. Benjamin recrq

LOUDER
1817, 8,16. Celia rocf Center MM, N. C.
1821, 10, 20. Celia dis mou & disunity

LUCAS
1849, 7, 18. Mary (form William) dis mou

LUKENS
1826, 3, 18. Miriam [Lukins] rocf Smithfield MM, dtd 1825,12,19
1840, 3, 19. Elizabeth & dt, Susan J., rocf Marlborough MM, dtd 1840,2,22 (H)
1842, 12, 15. Joseph dis mou (H)
1901, 12, 18. Sarah Snowden gct Wilmington MM

LUNDY
----, --, --. James m Elizabeth ----- d 1832, 4,30 bur Centre

Ch:		
	Enoch	b 1802, 11, 20
	William	" 1804, 3, 27
	Jesse	" 1805, 9, 19
	Anna	" 1807, 7, 18
	Levi	" 1809, 7, 29
	James	" 1811, 4, 10
	John	" 1813, 6, 18
	Susannah	" 1815, 10, 8
	Cyrus	" 1817, 12, 22
	Elizabeth	" 1820, 7, 5
	Asenith	" 1822, 10, 13
	Rachel	" 1825, 5, 1

James m 2nd Sophia ----- d 1835,1,22 bur Centre
James m 3rd Sarah ----- d 1844,10,26 bur Centre
Ch: Elizabeth b 1844, 1, 22
1802, 11, 27. Charlotte b
----, --, --. Amos & Susannah (H)

Ch:		
	Maryann	b 1818, 8, 22
	Rachel	" 1820, 2, 5
	Dempsey	" 1822, 1, 7
	Aaron	" 1826, 2, 24

1821, 1, 7. Cyrus d ae 3y 1m 7d bur Centre

LUNDY, continued
----, --, --. Enoch & Charlotte
Ch: Alice b 1825, 12, 15
Elizabeth " 1827, 11, 23
1725, 9, --. Elizabeth d bur Centre
1828, 8, 21. Enoch d ae 24y 9m 1d bur Centre, O.
----, --, --. Jesse & Abagail [Londy]
Ch: Enoch b 1830, 7, 18
Ruth " 1831, 10, 9
Elizabeth " 1833, 3, 30
Margarett " 1835, 9, 17
John " 1837, 1, 10
James " 1837, 1, 10
----, --, --. Levi b 1809,7,29; m Sarah ----- b 1813,9,7
Ch: Lydia W. b 1833, 2, 27
Calvin " 1835, 6, 14
Margaret S." 1837, 7, 19
1837, 8, 29. John d
1839, 6, 21. Phebe b
1844, 12, 23. Elizabeth, dt James & Sarah, d
1853, 10, 22. Abigail d ae 58y 10m 3d bur Chester
1854, 11, 29. James d ae 77y 1m 10d bur Chester
1864, 1, 10. Calvin b
1865, 10, 6. Henry Irwin, s James & Sarah N., b
1870, 12, 1. Sarah M. d bur Chester
1871, 3, 22. Huldah d bur Chester
1876, 5, 8. Franklin b
1876, 7, 7. Franklin d bur Center

1814, 4, 2. Amos & w, Susannah, & s, William Schooly, rocf Fairfield MM, dtd 1814,2,26
1815, 6, 11. James & w, Elizabeth, & ch, Enoch, William, Jesse, Ann, Levi, James & John, rocf Fairfield MM, dtd 1815,5,27
1816, 2, 17. Nathan & w, Amy, & ch, Susannah, John, Amos, Nickolas, Enoch, Samuel & Nathan, recrq
1817, 2, 15. Nathan & fam gct Derby Creek MM
1823, 11, 15. James & w, Elizabeth, & ch, Enoch, William, Jesse, Anna, Levi, James, John, Susannah, Elizabeth & Asenith, rocf Springfield MM, O., dtd 1823,8,13
1825, 1, 15. Enoch rmt Charlotte Green
1826, 10, 21. William rmt Maria Ann Smith
1828, 12, 17. Jesse rmt Abigail Green
1828, 12, 17. Amos dis jH
1828, 12, 17. Susannah dis jH
1831, 5, 18. William dis jH
1831, 6, 15. Levi rmt Sarah Wickersham
1834, 1, 15. James rmt Sophia Hollingsworth
1835, 3, 18. James dis mou
1836, 8, 17. Susannah Haines (form Lundy) dis mou
1836, 9, 14. Mary Ann, Rachel, Dempsey & Aaron, ch Amos, gct Newberry MM
1837, 4, 12. Mariah Ann & ch, Israel, Enoch, Eliza Ann & Ruth, gct Springfield MM
1840, 1, 15. Elizabeth & ch, Aaron B., Josaphine E., Thomas N., Marion E., Ezrah & Mercy Ann, gct Springfield MM
1840, 8, 12. Joseph Oren prcf Dover MM, to m Asenith Lundy
1840, 9, 16. Asenath rmt Joseph Oren
1840, 12, 16. John dis mou
1841, 9, 15. Levi & w, Sarah, & ch, Lydia W., Calvin & Margaret S., gct Mississiniwa MM, Ind.
1841, 10, 13. James rmt Sarah Schooley
1842, 8, 17. Jehiel Green prcf Newberry MM, to m Rachel Lundy
1842, 9, 14. Rachel rmt Jehiel Green
1844, 5, 16. Demcy dis mou (H)
1844, 6, 13. Aaron, minor, gct Fall Creek MM (H)
1853, 5, 17. Asaph H. Paxson prcf Goshen MM, to m Margaret Lundy
1854, 6, 14. Margaret rmt Asaph Paxson
1856, 9, 17. John Carey prcf New Burry MM, to m Elizabeth Lundy
1856, 10, 15. Elizabeth rmt John Carey
1859, 1, 12. Enoch rpd mou
1860, 5, 16. Elizabeth Osborn (form Lundy) rpd mou
1860, 8, 15. Honey Creek MM, Ia. granted permission to rst James
1865, 8, 16. Jesse gct Dover MM, Ind., to m Hulda Smith
1865, 12, 13. James rpd mou
1865, 12, 13. Hulda rocf Dover MM, Ind., dtd 1865,10,25
1866, 2, 14. Ruth Johnson (form Lundy) rpd mou
1867, 5, 15. Sarah Mary & s, Calvin J., recrq
1875, 11, 17. James & ch, Henry Irving, Horace E. & Walter J., gct Spring Creek MM, Ia.
1893, 11, 15. Lillian M. rocf Cesars Creek MM
1908, 3, 18. Ruth M. rocf Dover MM
1913, 2, 12. Frank, Lindley & James transferred from associate to active mbrp

LUPTON
1834, 2, 13. Richard R. & w, Anna, & ch, Joseph A. & Elizabeth Ann, rocf Hopewell MM, dtd 1833,11,7 (H)
1835, 7, 16. Richard R. & w, Anna, & ch, Joseph Abijah & Elizabeth Ann, rocf Springborough MM, dtd 1834,12,25 (H)
1842, 9, 15. Richard R. & w, Ann, & ch, Joseph Abijah, Elizabeth Ann & Esther Jane, gct White Water MM, Ind.

LUSTER
1889, 6, 12. Hannah recrq

LUZENA
1854, 1, 18. Margaret (form Jones) dis mou

LYTLES
1854, 5, 17. Susannah (form Farquhar) con mou

McCOWAN
1840, 2, 13. Maria con mou (H)
1840, 5, 13. Mariah [McCowen] (form Taylor) dis mou & joining Separatists
1840, 10, 15. Maria gct Miami MM (H)

McCOY
1835, 10, 14. Mary Ann (form Kinsey) con mou
1839, 8, 14. Mary Ann gct Caesars Creek MM

McDONALD
1884, 10, 15. James & w, Sarah, & ch, Nettie, Frank & Russel, rocf Springfield MM, dtd 1884,9,20
1886, 3, 17. James & fam gct Wilmington MM
1906, 2, 14. George & w recrq
1906, 3, 14. Russell & Ruth, ch George & Lecy, recrq

McGLADDERY
1866, 8, 5. Ann, w James, d

1860, 8, 15. James recrq
1860, 10, 17. Ann [McGladary] recrq

McKAY
1849, 9, 12. Rachel [McCay] (form Faulkner) dis mou
1892, 3, 16. Lida relrq
1904, 7, 13. Ella May, dt Priscilla, recrq
1907, 2, 12. Howard & Harold recrq
1910, 11, 16. Maynard F. recrq
1914, 2, 18. Ada Turner rocf Wilmington MM
1914, 4, 15. Ila Haworth rocf Dover MM
1915, 3, 17. Harold & w, Ila Haworth, gct Dover MM
1916, 4, 12. Robert Franklin recrq
1916, 4, 12. Edith Starbuck rocf Dover MM
1917, 4, 18. Howard & w, Edith S., & ch, Robert, gct Dover MM
1917, 10, 24. Priscilla & ch, Mary Elba & Maynard J., gct Wilmington MM

McKEE
----, --, --. Eli A. b 1827,1,31; m Elizabeth ----- b 1833,11,9
Ch: Charles O. b 1856, 5, 10
Adda " 1868, 5, 20
Alma " 1868, 5, 20

1870, 7, 13. Eli A. & w, Elizabeth, & ch, Emily Jane, Charles O., Alma C. & Ada C., recrq
1914, 9, 6. Charles O. gct Wilmington MM

McKENZIE
1913, 2, 12. Lucile recrq

McKIBBEN
1894, 10, --. Cheniah & w, Amanda, & ch, Minnie Pearl, Maud, Maggie & Lou Ella, rocf Dover MM
1895, 12, 18. Cheniah & w, Amanda, & ch, Minnie Pearl, Maud, Maggie & Lou Ella, gct Cesars Creek MM

McMILLAN
----, --, --. David d 1844,12,20 ae 72y 9m 18d bur Center; m Hannah -----
Ch: Josiah b 1798, 5, 10
Eli " 1799, 9, 23
Deborah " 1801, 12, 4
Mary " 1803, 9, 7
David " 1805, 2, 3
Ann " 1807, 1, 6 d 1863, 3, 5 bur Chester
Milton b 1809, 9, 8
Jonathan " 1812, 6, 27
Hannah J. " 1814, 12, 1 d 1823,12, 6 bur Center
Thomas W. " 1817, 9, 2
1818, 3, 26. Rebecca Ann d bur Chester
1820, 2, 29. Martha b
1821, 11, 1. Thomas d ae 58y 6m 9d bur Center
1822, 10, 13. Rebecca b
----, --, --. Josiah m Susannah ----- d 1843, 12,15 bur Chester
Ch: David J. b 1825, 8, 12
Hannah " 1827, 6, 12
Mary M. " 1830, 6, 28
Clarkson M." 1832, 10, 27
Thomas M. " 1832, 4, 6
Susannah M." 1837, 6, 21 d 1853,11, 7 bur Chester
Ann C. b 1840, 3, 17
Josiah m 2nd Mary ----- d 1854,4,12 bur Chester
----, --, --. Milton b 1809,9,8; m Elizabeth M. ----- b 1816,4,1 d 1841,5,18 bur Chester
Ch: Sarah K. b 1834, 11, 6 d 1843, 8, 6 bur Chester
Mariah b 1836, 8, 8
Calvin M. " 1838, 1, 28 d 1838, 1,29 bur Chester
Hannah Ann b 1838, 12, 15
Ezra " 1841, 4, 3 d 1841, 4, 4 bur Chester
----, --, --. David d 1861,1,22 bur Centerp m Sarah -----
Ch: Isaac C. b 1836, 5, 23
Alfred " 1838, 5, 15 d 1838, 8,30
Jediah " 1844, 7, 6
----, --, --. Jonathan b 1812,6,27; m Susannah ----- b 1821,1,7
Ch: Emma b 1838, 10, 21
Lydia Emily" 1840, 12, 16
Calvin " 1843, 2, 13 d 1831, 4, 3 bur Chester
Enoch W. b 1844, 4, 8
Jonathan m 2nd Rebecca -----
Ch: Sarah Ann b 1849, 8, 7
Joshua F. " 1854, 10, 18
Oliver Milton b 1855, 10, 1
Moses

McMILLAN, continued
Ch: Clinton b 1861, 1, 13
Mary
Elizabeth " 1864, 7, 3
Susannah H. d 1852, 12,29
Sarah H. " 1851, 8, 14
----, --, --. Eli m Lydia ----- d 1842,7,22
bur Chester
Ch: Elizabeth b 1840, 2, 25 d 1840, 3, 2
Eli " 1841, 1, 1
Eli m 2nd Martha -----
Ch: Lydia b 1845, 3, 10
Neomi " 1847, 2, 13
Hannah M. " 1850, 4, 3
----, --, --. Thomas W. b 1817,9,20 d 1889,5,1
bur Chester; m Elizabeth ----- b 1820,9,11
d 1877,4,23
Ch: Isabella R.b 1842, 6, 3 d 1842, 8,29
bur Chester
Mariam b 1843, 12, 23
Deborah " 1849, 3, 1
Eliza Jane " 1851, 5, 7
Horace G. " 1853, 12, 25
Parmer A. " 1857, 3, 1 d 1874, 3, 3
1846, 8, 19. Susannah d
1846, 9, 18. Hannah d ae 71y 5m 11d
1852, 12, 29. Sarah H. [McMillen], w Eli, d
bur Chester
----, --, --. Newton b 1802,4,9; m Sarah -----
b 1831,11,10
Ch: Thomas
Dick b 1860, 5, 20
Sarah L. " 1862, 8, 11
Chase Grant" 1864, 8, 28
----, --, --. Isaac C. & Nancy L.
Ch: David R. b 1861, 3, 29 d 1864,4,1
Seth L. " 1863, 2, 15
Walter " 1865, 11, 22
----, --, --. Josiah & Rebecca Ann
Ch: Joseph b 1861, 8, 24
Jane " 1863, 10, 23
1864, 3, 14. Sanford, s Emmer & Susan, b
1866, 4, 4. Elvira, dt Eli Jr. & Rachel, b
1867, 1, 16. Eva, dt Enoch, b
1870, 7, 9. Eli d bur Chester
----, --, --. Shipley & Sarah A.
Ch: Edna R. b 1875, 7, 3
Ada B. " 1877, 12, 10
1876, 7, 19. Martha d
1877, 6, 20. Josiah d
----, --, --. Oliver M. & Eliza
Ch: Glenard b 1879, 9, 14
Hondora " 1881, 4, 26
Leroy J.V. " 1879, 12, 22
1879, 6, 18. Orville J., s Joshua F. & Mary,
b
1879, 11, 27. Ella, dt Newton, d
1882, 12, 23. Viola b
1884, 1, 5. Thomas Henry b
1885, 6, 19. Esther Jacob b
1885, 7, 11. Sarah d
1888, 1, 11. Evalend b
1894, 8, 14. Newton d bur Center

1811, 2, 2. Thomas [McMillen] & w, Jane, &
ch, Edith & Deborah, rocf Center MM, Pa.,
dtd 1810,10,13
1811, 4, 6. Jonathan [McMillen] gct Short
Creek MM, to m
1811, 12, 7. David [McMillen] dis mou
1812, 1, 4. Hannah rocf Plainfield MM, dtd
1811,8,24
1820, 12, 16. Jane Ann rmt Samuel Hollingsworth
1821, 12, 15. Edith rmt Samuel Cox
1822, 4, 20. Mary rmt Thomas Cox
1824, 5, 15. Deborah rmt Jesse Taylor
1824, 10, 16. Josiah rmt Susannah Cox
1828, 11, 12. William dis jH
1830, 12, 15. David dis disunity
1832, 9, 12. Milton gct Duck Creek MM, Ind.,
to m Elizabeth Kirke
1832, 12, 12. Mary Emily rmt Thomas C. Shipley
1833, 5, 15. Elizabeth rocf Duck Creek MM,
Ind., dtd 1833,4,25
1833, 7, 17. Jonathan dis disunity
1834, 5, 14. Hannah L. [McMillin] & dt,
Eliza, gct Cincinnati MM
1835, 3, 18. David Jr. rmt Sarah Carpenter
1836, 5, 18. Jonathan Wright prcf Salem MM,
dtd 1836,4,23, to m Deborah McMillan
1836, 7, 13. Deborah J. rmt Jonathan Wright
1836, 10, 12. Jane [McMillon] gct Salem MM,
Ind.
1837, 5, 17. Newton dis mou
1837, 12, 13. Jonathan rmt Susannah Wickersham
1838, 2, 14. Cincinnati MM rq permission to
rst Jonathan (not granted)
1838, 10, 18. William dis mou (H)
1838, 10, 18. Rachel (form Brown) dis mou (H)
1838, 11, 14. Eli gct Springfield MM, to m
Lydia Fallis
1839, 3, 13. Lydia, w Eli, & ch, Turner W.,
John, Isaac C. & Susan M. Fallis, rocf
Springfield MM, dtd 1839,3,12
1841, 2, 17. Thomas W. [McMullan] rmt Elizabeth N. Adsit
1842, 11, 5. Cincinnati MM rst Jonathan
1843, 12, 13. David rst
1844, 1, 17. Milton dis mou
1844, 4, 17. Harriet (form Whinery) dis mou
1844, 6, 12. Eli con mou
1844, 10, 16. Martha McMillan & dt, Hester Ann
Snider, recrq
1844, 11, 19. Harriet (form Whinery) dis mou
(H)
1848, 10, 18. Jonathan gct Dover MM, to m
Rebecca Frazier
1849, 4, 18. Rebecca rocf Dover MM, dtd 1849,
2,15
1849, 5, 16. David gct Caesars Creek MM
1849, 6, 13. Hannah rmt Ezra Whinery
1851, 10, 15. Josiah rmt Mary Crew
1855, 12, 12. Clarkson gct Caesars Creek MM
1857, 12, 16. Lydia Emily rmt Samuel Whinery
1858, 10, 13. Hannah Ann rmt Francis Farquhar
1859, 3, 16. Maria M. Doan (form McMillan)

McMILLAN, continued
rpd mou
1860, 6, 13. Emer H. [McMillen] gct Springfield MM, to m Susan Thatcher
1860, 6, 13. Isaac rmt Nancy Linton
1860, 9, 12. Josiah [McMillen] gct New Garden MM, to m Rebecca Ann Whinery
1861, 1, 16. Rebecca Ann rocf New Garden MM, O.
1863, 4, 15. Henry Spray prcf Caesar Creek MM, to m Mary Ann McMillen
1863, 5, 13. Mary Ann rmt Henry Spray
1863, 8, 15. Mary Ann Spray (form McMillan) gct Caesars Creek MM
1863, 10, 14. Levi Mills prcf Caesars Creek MM, to m Ruth W. McMillen
1863, 11, 18. Ruth [McMillen] rmt Levi Mills
1864, 9, 14. Susan [McMillen] & ch, Sanford, rocf Springfield MM
1866, 2, 14. Eli Jr. rpd mou
1866, 2, 14. Enoch [McMillen] rpd mou
1866, 9, 12. Phebe H. rocf Caesars Creek MM
1867, 6, 12. Clarkson rocf Caesars Creek MM
1867, 9, 18. Ann Maria recrq
1868, 4, 11. Ann C. Wall (form McMillen) rpd mou
1868, 5, 16. Enoch & w & ch, Eva A., gct Bangor MM, Ia.
1869, 4, 14. Deborah T. Hawkins (form McMillan) rpd mou
1869, 4, 14. Lidia Davis (form McMillan) rpd mou
1871, 3, 15. Emma H. & s, Sanford, gct Springfield MM
1871, 3, 15. Newton & w, Sarah, & ch, Thomas Dick, Sarah L. & Chase Grant, recrq
1873, 12, 17. Shipley rocf Wilmington MM
1879, 6, 18. Nancy L. & ch, Seth L. & Walter T., rocf Wilmington MM
1879, 6, 18. Sarah rocf Wilmington MM
1883, 4, 18. Maria Louisa & ch, Glenora M., Leroy J. & Hondora K., recrq
1885, 9, 17. Shipley & w, Sarah, & ch, Edna & Ada, gct Wilmington MM
1886, 5, 12. Mary E. recrq
1889, 5, 15. Thomas Dick gct Wilmington MM
1890, 7, 16. Joseph gct Dover MM
1893, 4, 12. Joseph & w, Emma, & ch, Rebecca Mary, Vera Ann & Robert J., rocf Dover MM
1894, 3, 14. Rebecca [McMillen] & s, Moses C., & dt, Mary Elizabeth, gct Wilmington MM
1895, 6, 12. Martha Blanch recrq
1897, 4, 14. Alice M. recrq
1897, 12, 15. Joshua F. & w, Mary E., & ch, Charles, Viola, Eldora & Evalena, gct Dover MM, O.
1905, 3, 5. Mary E. recrq
1909, 5, 12. Elizabeth H. rocf Harveyville MM, Kans.
1910, 2, 16. Esper recrq
1910, 3, 16. Joseph & w, Emma, & ch, Rebecca M., Vera A., Robert, Willis, Mark, Dillen, Ruth, Ever, Adelbert & Mabel, gct Springfield MM
1910, 12, 14. Joseph & w, Emma, & ch, Rebecca Mary, Vera Ann, Robert D., Willis, Mark, Dillon, Ruth, Eva, Adelebert, Mabel & Herbert, rocf Springfield MM
1913, 2, 12. Carl transferred from associate to active mbrp
1913, 2, 12. Mark, Dillon & Ruth transferred from associate to active mbrp
1913, 3, 12. Mary Probasco rocf Wilmington MM
1914, 12, 16. Joseph & w, Emma, & ch, Rebecca Mary, Vera Ann, Robert J., Willis, Mark, Ruth, Dillon, Eva, Adelbert, Mable & Herbert, gct Miami MM
1918, 11, 20. Esther Carroll rocf Newberry MM
1920, 3, 17. John & w, Esther, rocf Miami MM
1920, 7, 14. Walter T. & w, Blanch Martha, & ch, Isaac, Kirk & Harriett, gct Wilmington MM

McNEAL
1886, 3, 17. Lee relrq

McPHERSON
1858, 11, 17. Eli Haines gct Fairfield MM, to m Emily McPherson
1865, 5, 17. Daniel prcf Newberry MM, to m Lydia Mary Ellis
1865, 6, 14. Daniel rmt Lydia Mary Ellis
1904, 7, 13. Nina V. gct Wilmington MM

McVEY
1909, 1, 13. Leroy & w, Ardella, & ch, Bessie M., William H., Ada, Olive & James Carl, rocf Dover MM
1916, 5, 17. Leroy & w, Adelia, & ch, Bessie M., William H., Ada Ollie & James Carl, gct Clear Creek MM

MABIE
1846, 4, 11. Deborah [Maibie] d ae 42

1833, 11, 13. John [Mabee] & dt, Eliza B., Deborah, Catharine F., Susan & Hannah H., rocf Amawalk MM, N. Y., dtd 1833,9,13
1834, 10, 15. Susan [Mabee] rmt Walter T. Carpenter
1837, 5, 17. Catharine F. [Mabee] rmt Jonathan Timberlake
1839, 6, 12. Daniel Jones prcf Miami MM, to m Hannah Mabie
1839, 7, 17. Hannah rmt Daniel Jones
1842, 12, 14. Jonathan Hadley prcf Springfield MM, to m Eliza B. Mabie
1843, 1, 18. Eliza B. rmt Jonathan Hadley
1846, 11, 18. John gct Springfield MM

MADDEN
1811, 3, 2. Hannah [Maden] con mou
1811, 12, 7. George & w, Elizabeth, & ch, Hiram, Solomon, John, Ann, Rebecca, Mary

MADDEN, continued
Ruth & Deborah, rocf Spring MM, N. C., dtd 1811,8,31
1817, 8, 21. Ann declared intention of m with Henry Harvey
1817, 9, 20. Henry Harvey prcf White Water MM, to m Ann Madden

MADSON
1913, 6, 18. Ella recrq

MAISE
1849, 7, 18. Rebecca [Maze] (form Davis) dis mou
1850, 4, 18. Rebecca (form Davis) dis mcd (H)

MARBLY
1879, 1, 15. Jacob recrq

MARSHALL
1911, 1, 18. James recrq
1919, 3, 12. James dropped from mbrp

MARTINDALE
1877, 3, 14. William recrq
1877, 5, 16. John & w, Mary Ann, recrq
1889, 2, 13. Vincent dis disunity
1900, 6, 13. John [Martyndale] relrq

MASON
1821, 5, 2. Nancy E. b

1828, 11, 12. Sarah & ch, Nathan, Iry, Ruth, Jonathan, Stephen & Mary, rocf Flushing MM, dtd 1828,1,25
1829, 4, 15. Sarah [Masson] rmt Jesse Hiatt
1830, 11, 17. Jesse Hiatt & w, Sarah, & ch, Ira, Ruth, Jonathan, Stephen & Mary Hannah Mason & Rachel Hiatt, gct Vermillion MM, Ill.
1871, 7, 12. Stacy & w, Elizabeth, recrq
1875, 10, 13. Stacy relrq

MASSEY
1807, 1, 8. James rocf Center MM, N. C., dtd 1806,9,20
1809, 11, 4. Jane gct White Water MM
1814, 11, 5. James rmt Elizabeth Hale
1828, 11, 12. James D. [Massie] dis jH
1829, 4, 15. Elizabeth dis jH
1845, 2, 13. Mary Harlan (form Massy) dis mou

MASTER
1912, 7, 17. Edith Marie recrq

MATTHEWS
1810, 9, 1. Oliver & fam gc
1811, 10, 5. Oliver & w, Phebe, & ch, Joel, William, Ann, Jonathan & Susannah, rocf Miami MM, dtd 1811,8,28
1815, 12, 16. Oliver & w, Phebe, & ch, Joel, William, Ann, Jonathan, Susannah & Elizabeth, gct Miami MM

MEANDER
1874, 4, 15. Joseph recrq

MEGREGAR
1823, 2, 15. Maria con mou

MELLEN
1892, 3, 16. James & w, Ella, & ch, Halleck Joseph & Teymiah, dropped from mbrp

MENDENHALL
1769, 10, 28. Stephen b
1776, 11, 11. Ann b
----, --, --. Absolom & Alice D.
Ch: Elizabeth
A. b 1834, 7, 5
Sarah J. " 1837, 8, 15
1843, 4, 8. Stephen d bur Center
1848, 12, 2. Ann d at her home

1808, 2, 6. Nathan [Mendingham] & w, Ann, & ch, Edith, Hiram, Olive, Moris & Elizabeth, rocf Springfield MM, N. C., dtd 1807,8,1
1808, 2, 6. Richard [Mendinghall] rmt Elizabeth Barnard
1809, 2, 4. Joseph rmt Ann Barnard
1818, 2, 21. Edith [Mendinghall] rmt Amos Cowgill
1823, 2, 15. Ann recrq
1829, 5, 13. Ann dis jH
1831, 9, 17. Stephen recrq (H)
1833, 3, 16. Alice gct Milford MM, Ind. (H)
1836, 2, 18. Alice rocf Milford MM, dtd 1835,12,17 (H)
1840, 5, 14. Absalum & ch, Elizabethann & Sarah Jane, recrq (H)
1853, 11, 17. Absalom & w, Alice, & ch, Elizabeth Ann & Sarah Jane, gct White Water MM, Ind. (H)
1866, 12, 12. Elizabeth Ann (form Compton) rpd mou
1867, 2, 13. Elizabeth Ann & dt, Judith Ann Compton, gct Caesars Creek MM

MERCER
1870, 8, 17. Jason & w, Mary, recrq
1882, 6, 14. Jason & w, Mary, gct Fairfield MM, O.

MERSON
1888, 2, 15. Clara P. recrq

MIARS
1833, 8, 23. Isaiah F. b
1837, 4, 23. Matilda b
1843, 4, 20. Margaret b
1845, 2, 6. Sarah b
1845, 2, 6. Abigail b
1848, 9, 2. James W. b
1850, 10, 5. Rebecca b
1856, 12, 6. Louella b
1858, 9, 20. Sophronia A. b

MIARS, continued
1861, 5, 26. Emma B. b
1862, 2, 26. Mary Eliza b
1865, 10, 20. Corwin b
1868, 3, 11. Henry b
1875, 2, 15. Sally, w David, d
----, --, --. James M. m Nancy A. ----- d 1884, 8,25 bur Center
Ch: Earl b 1879, 12, 21
Lindley " 1882, 1, 23
Oliver B. " 1884, 3, 30

1820, 1, 15. Sarah (form Stout) con mou
1866, 11, 14. Samuel [Myers] recrq
1866, 11, 14. Catharine [Myars] recrq
1874, 4, 15. Sarah [Myers] recrq
1876, 3, 15. Isaiah F. & w, Matilda, recrq
1876, 3, 15. Mary Eliza, Corwin & Henry, ch Isaiah, recrq
1876, 3, 15. James W. recrq
1876, 3, 15. Sophronia, Emma B., Abigail, Mary Ellen, Rebecca M., Margaret J. & Louella J., recrq
1879, 1, 15. Annie, Elva, Mary Eliza, Isaiah & Nicholas recrq
1879, 1, 15. Joseph & ch, Haines & Mary Eliza, recrq
1888, 2, 15. Martin recrq
1888, 2, 15. Sarah S. recrq
1889, 12, 18. Joseph relrq
1892, 9, 14. Henry gct Wilmington MM, O.
1896, 2, 12. Mary E. gct Carmel MM, Ind.
1901, 4, 17. Lindley recrq
1901, 4, 17. Ollie recrq
1903, 2, 18. Anna & Bessie [Mires] recrq
1906, 1, 17. Nicholas D. & w, Alice B., & dt, Minnie M., gct Ceasers Creek MM
1910, 2, 16. Edith [Myers] recrq
1910, 2, 16. Linley John recrq
1910, 2, 16. Lula recrq
1910k 2, 16. Maud recrq
1913, 11, 12. Willie B. recrq
1913, 12, 17. Hannah Foster rocf Xenia MM
1917, 1, 17. Cora B. recrq
1920, 10, 13. Sarah gct Wilmington MM
1921, 2, 16. Willie & Hannah gct Wilmington MM, O.

MIDDLETON
1910, 2, 16. Belle recrq
1910, 12, 14. Mary E. recrq
1912, 3, 13. Lizzie M. relrq
1916, 3, 15. Bell dropped from mbrp
1917, 6, 13. J. Raymond recrq
1919, 3, 12. Mary E. dropped from mbrp
1920, 1, 14. Elizabeth recrq

MILLER
1848, 2, 20. Margaret d ae 84y 10m 20d bur Chester

1809, 6, 3. Margaret rocf Warrington MM, held at Newberry, dtd 1809,4,19
1834, 4, 16. Thomas prcf Springborough MM, dtd 1834,3,25, to m Eliza Curl
1834, 5, 14. Thomas rmt Eliza Curl
1834, 11, 12. Eliza gct Springborough MM
1883, 9, 12. Jonathan rocf Farmland MM, dtd 1883,8,11
1891, 9, 16. Jonathan L. gct Cesars Creek MM
1898, 6, 15. Henry Oldine recrq
1910, 2, 16. Henry E. relrq

MILLICAN
1813, 2, 6. Eli [Milikin] & w, Mary, & ch, William Thomas & John, rocf Springfield MM, dtd 1811,8,3
1815, 3, 4. Eli [Miliken] dis disunity
1827, 1, 20. Springfield MM was granted permission to rst Eli

MILLS
1867, 1, 6. Harriet C., dt Levi & Ruth, b

1810, 7, 7. Richard rmt Mary Ozborn
1812, 1, 4. Nancy gct Fairfield MM
1863, 10, 14. Levi prcf Caesars Creek MM, to m Ruth W. McMillen
1863, 11, 18. Levi rmt Ruth McMillen
1865, 11, 15. Levi rocf Caesars Creek MM, dtd 1865,10,26
1875, 8, 18. Emma gct Dover MM

MITCHEL
1849, 3, 15. Sarah (form Whinery) dis mou (H)
1859, 9, 14. Hannah D. & Robert R. rocf ND MM, Pa.
1859, 9, 14. Jehu More prcf Springfield MM, to m Hannah D. Mitchel
1859, 10, 12. Hannah D. rmt Jehu More
1879, 1, 15. Marietta B. recrq
1897, 12, 15. Estella S. [Mitchell] recrq

MITCHENER
1897, 9, 15. Alice dropped from mbrp

MOODY
1860, 2, 15. Edith Emily (form Haworth) rpd mou

MOON
----, --, --. James b 1768,12,31; m Saline LEONARD b 1771,--,--

1808, 12, 3. John & w, Dinah, & ch, Aaron, Jonathan, James, Enoch & Sarah, rocf New Garden MM, N. C., dtd 1808,8,27
1813, 9, 4. Richard & w, Vashti, & ch, Dinah, Judith, Miriam, Vashti & Asenath, rocf New Garden MM, N. C., dtd 1813,2,27
1813, 9, 4. Simon & w, Judith, & dt, Jane, rocf New Garden MM, N. C., dtd 1813,2,27
1813, 9, 4. Mary rocf New Garden MM, N. C. dtd 1813,3,27
1813, 10, 2. Simon Jr. rocf New Garden MM,

MOON, continued
N. C., dtd 1813,2,27
1815, 3, 4. Mary rmt Joshua Harvey
1815, 10, 21. Simon rmt Lydia Harvey
1816, 6, 15. Simon Jr. & w, Lydia, gct Miami MM
1816, 9, 21. Richard & w, Vashti, & ch, Dinah, Judith, Maryann, Vashti & Asenath, gct Miami MM
1816, 9, 21. Simon & fam gct Miami MM
1816, 11, 16. Jane gct Miami MM
1819, 8, 21. John dis mou

1828, 10, 15. Selina dis jH
1828, 11, 12. James dis jH
1830, 9, 15. Enoch gct Green Plain MM
1847, 9, 15. Miles H. prcf Newberry MM, to m Charlotte D. Green
1847, 10, 13. Miles H. rmt Charlotte D. Green
1848, 3, 15. Charlotta D. gct Newberry MM
1849, 4, 18. Miles H. & w, Charlotte D., rocf Newberry MM, dtd 1849,2,12
1850, 10, 16. Miles C. & w, Charlotte D., & s, Isaac G. gct Newbury MM

MORGAN
1834, 4, 16. Martha rocf Hopewell MM, Va., dtd 1834,1,1
1849, 11, 15. Martha (form Peirce) con mou (H)
1850, 7, 18. Martha gct Miami MM (H)

MOORE
----, --, --. Abraham b 1786,6,2; m Susannah ----- b 1790,6,7 d 1822,2,13 bur Center
1851, 5, 22. James, s Andrew & Elizabeth, Clinton Co., O.; m at Center, Priscilla Jane UNDERWOOD, dt Amos & Mary, Highland Co., O. (H)
1854, 7, 16. Pricilla Jane (Underwood) d
----, --, --. Jehu & Hannah
Ch: Mary H. b 1860, 7, 11
Franklin J." 1861, 12, 11
Albert K. " 1862, 4, 29
Frederick " 1865, 12, 22
1866, 12, 23. Mary B., w Franklin, dt Alfred & Phebe Timberlake, d bur Center, Ind. (resided at Thorntown, Ind.)
1813, 12, 4. Joshua rocf Center MM, Pa., dtd [1813,10,16
1814, 9, 3. Joshua rmt Nancy Stratton
1816, 2, 17. John rocf Center MM, Pa., dtd 1815,10,14
1823, 5, 17. Abraham rmt Hannah Kirk
1827, 10, 20. Abraham & w, Hannah, & ch, Hannah, Jacob & Abraham, gct Duck Creek MM
1832, 6, 13. Juilianna (form Anderson) dis mou
1832, 7, 18. Joseph dis disunity & jH
1832, 9, 12. Abigail dis disunity & jH
1836, 8, 17. Seth Linton gct Springfield MM, to m Sarah Ann Moore
1846, 3, 19. Sarah [Moor] & ch, Lydia Ann, David R., Milton Y., Samuel S., Edward T., Sarah Elizabeth & Elmira, rocf Center MM, Pa., dtd 1845,7,9, endorsed by Marlborough MM 1845,10,25 (H)
1850, 11, 14. James [More] rocf West Branch MM, Pa., dtd 1850,10,31 (H)
1855, 5, 17. James gct Fall Creek MM, Ind. (H)
1859, 9, 14. Jehu [More] prcf Springfield MM, to m Hannah D. Mitchel
1859, 10, 12. Jehu [More] rmt Hannah D. Mitchel
1865, 4, 12. Franklin prcf Sugar River MM, Ind., to m Mary B. Timberlake
1865, 5, 17. Franklin rmt Mary B. Timberlake
1865, 5, 17. Joshua M. rocf Hopewell MM,Ind.
1865, 7, 12. Mary B. gct Sugar River MM,Ind.
1868, 3, 18. Rachel W. rpd mou
1868, 3, 18. Ophelia rpd mou
1868, 4, 15. Rachel W. gct Springfield MM,O.
1868, 7, 15. Ophelia A. gct Springfield MM
1885, 6, 17. Andrew dis disunity
1886, 8, 18. Hannah D. gct Springfield MM,O.
1887, 1, 12. Wilson recrq
1910, 2, 16. Isaac, Mary U., Edna, Ema, Paulina & Ruthanna recrq
1910, 2, 16. Thomas, Nusetta, Mattie & Bell recrq
1913, 2, 12. Pearl recrq

MOORMAN
1854, 4, 23. Micajah Clark d bur New Hope

1809, 9, 2. Susanna & gr dt, Dosha Paxton, rocf South River MM, Va., dtd 1809,9,9(?)
1810, 5, 5. Alrica [Moreman] & ch, Thomas James & Charles, rocf Fairfield MM, dtd 1810,5,26
1810, 5, 5. Childs [Moreman] rocf Fairfield MM, dtd 1810,5,26
1811, 3, 2. Elizabeth rocf Cedar Creek MM, Va., dtd 1810,9,3
1811, 6, 1. Childs [Moreman] con mou & attending musters
1811, 6, 1. Micajah [Moreman] & w, Susannah, & ch, Aphraca, Thomas, Mildred & Christopher, rocf Fairfield MM, dtd 1810,9,29
1811, 6, 1. Molly rocf South River MM, dtd 1809,9,9
1811, 12, 7. Dosha [Moreman] (form Paxton) dis mou
1812, 8, 1. Thomas [Morman] & w, Dosha, recrq
1813, 1, 2. Thomas [Morman] recrq
1815, 7, 14. James dis mou
1815, 7, 14. Elizabeth [Moreman] (form Johnson) dis mou
1817, 4, 19. Charles [Morman] con mou
1818, 9, 19. Lydia & ch, Charlotte E., Nancy John Thomas & Ruebin, rocf South River MM, Va. dtd 1817,12,13
1820, 8, 19. Charlotte E. Reaves (form Moorman) dis mou
1822, 11, 16. Polly [Moreman] dis disunity
1822, 11, 16. Nancy Griffith (form Moreman) con mou

MOORMAN, continued
1823, 7, 19. James [Morman] & w, Elizabeth, & ch, Emily, Manson H. & Mary, recrq
1823, 10, 18. Nancy (Morman], dt Thomas (or James P.) & Dosha, recrq
1824, 6, 19. Matilda & ch, Betsy Ann, Mariah & Micajah, recrq
1824, 9, 18. Apharacia rmt George W. Johnson
1834, 1, 15. Thomas Thornburgh gct Dover MM, to m Nancy Moorman
1841, 11, 17. Jesse Painter gct Dover MM, to m Susannah Moorman
1845, 11, 12. Elwood Haines gct Dover MM, to m Apharacia Moormon
1849, 6, 13. Thomas C. [Morman] & ch, Lucy Ann, Micajah C., Benjamin B. & John H., rocf Dover MM, dtd 1849,5,17
1850, 6, 12. Lucy Ann rmt David A. Painter
1853, 12, 14. Thomas C. con mou
1855, 4, 18. Thomas C. & ch, Benjamin B. & John Hampton, gct Dover MM
1865, 6, 14. Henry T. rocf Dover MM
1872, 10, 16. Henry T. gct Dover MM
1878, 3, 13. Mary Alice [Morman] rocf Clear Creek MM, dtd 1878,1,12

MORRIS
1838, 6, 22. Ruth d ae 33y 4m 3d bur Center

1823, 9, 20. Ruth (form Stanley) con mou
1862, 5, 14. James prcf Fairfield MM, to m Hannah Whinery
1862, 6, 18. James rmt Hannah Whinery
1862, 8, 13. Hannah (form Whinnery) & ch, Albert & Sarah Whinery, gct Fairfield MM
1868, 9, 16. John & w, Mary, recrq
1871, 6, 14. John & w, Mary, gct Miami MM
1884, 5, 19. Jerry rocf Fairfield MM, dtd 1884,3,15
1895, 6, 12. Jerry relrq

MORRISON
1810, 12, 1. Hannah Harlan (form Morrison) rocf Miami MM, dtd 1810,10,31
1811, 4, 6. Hannah Harlin (form Morrison) con mou

MORROW
1917, 6, 13. Harry Franklin & w, Lavina K., & dt, Lucile, recrq

MOTE
1849, 1, 17. Jesse Ballard gct West Branch MM, to m Mary Mote
1850, 11, 13. Joseph prcf West Branch MM, to m Martha Painter
1850, 12, 18. Joseph rmt Martha Painter
1851, 1, 15. Martha P. gct West Branch MM

MOWEN
1860, 5, 16. Lydia (form Gilpen) rpd mou; dropped from mbrp

MULLEN
----, --, --. Isaiah M. b 1843,3,1; m Eunice D. ----- b 1842,1,9
Ch: Flora b 1862, 5, 14
Charlie " 1871, 3, 9
Harley " 1871, 3, 9
Alpheus " 1875, 1, 14
1883, 9, 3. Clyde D. [Mullin] d

1830, 6, 16. Jacob Taylor gct Springborough MM, to m Ann Mullen
1875, 3, 17. Isaiah & w, Eunice Medora, & ch, Flora, Charley, Harley & Alpha, recrq
1877, 3, 14. Henry L. recrq
1877, 6, 13. James & w, Ellenor, & ch, Hallie O., Joseph H. & Levina P., recrq
1880, 5, 12. Henry relrq
1881, 6, 15. Isaiah dis disunity
1885, 12, 16. Dora relrq

MURPHY
1856, 4, 20. Martha [Murphey] d

1822, 10, 19. Martha recrq
1833, 7, 17. Phebe (form Faulkner) dis mou
1838, 6, 13. Lydia [Murphey] (form Bailiff) dis mou
1898, 3, 17. James & dt, Estella, recrq

MUSSETTER
1907, 4, 17. Clarence W. recrq
1908, 12, 16. Alvin & w, Sarah, recrq
1911, 4, 12. Minnie Carl recrq

NAGGLE
1913, 2, 12. Lena [Nagle] recrq
1913, 4, 16. Lena L. relrq

NANZER
1863, 6, 17. John & w, Melinda, & ch, George Henry & William Harland, rocf Cincinnati MM, dtd 1863,5,21
1866, 7, 18. John gct Morris MM, N. Y.

NEWLIN
1809, 4, 1. John & w, Esther, & ch, Eli, rocf Miami MM, dtd 1809,5,6
1858, 7, 14. Esther rocf White Lick MM
1860, 8, 15. Esther gct Newberry MM

NICKLESON
1829, 4, 18. Joshua [Nickerson] recrq (H)
1835, 5, 14. Mary (form Davis) con mou (H)
1836, 6, 16. Mary gct Milford MM, Ind. (H)

NIXON
1841, 7, 14. Sarah rocf White Water MM, dtd 1841,6,23
1846, 10, 14. Mordicai W. Painter gct Chester MM, Ind., to m Mary Nixon
1848, 11, 15. Sarah Ann gct Hopewell MM, Ind.

NORDYKE
1816, 10, 19. Benajah rmt Ann Johnson
1818, 5, 16. Ann gct Clear Creek MM
1849, 6, 13. Eunice rocf Clear Creek MM, dtd 1849,5,12
1852, 6, 16. Eunice gct Clear Creek MM
1912, 11, 13. Frank rocf Ogden MM
1912, 11, 13. Nellie Leonard, w Frank, recrq

O'BRIAN
1822, 1, 19. Thomas rocf Cincinnati MM, dtd 1821,10,25
1824, 3, 30. Thomas gct Miami MM

OGLESBEE
1844, 7, 11. Rebecca A. b
1845, 6, 18. Christopher R. b
1854, 10, 5. Rebecca b
----, --, --. Reece & Rebecca
Ch: Eric b 1877, 2, 16
Roy
Edward
Floid

1819, 5, 15. Phebe [Oglesby] rocf Hopewell MM, dtd 1818,12,10
1833, 11, 13. Lucinda [Oglesby] (form Fawcett) dis mou
1846, 5, 14. Phaniah [Oglesby] (form Hiatt) con mou (H)
1846, 11, 18. Pheniah (form Hiatt) dis mou & joining Separatists
1876, 3, 15. Christopher R. & w, Rebecca A., recrq
1876, 8, 16. Ruth [Oglesby] & dt, Anna, rocf Springfield MM, dtd 1875,6,18
1880, 12, 15. Reece relrq
1892, 3, 16. Rebecca relrq
1898, 3, 17. Ruth & dt, Anna, relrq
1901, 4, 17. Edward D. recrq
1901, 4, 17. Floyd H. recrq
1901, 4, 17. Oscar Leroy recrq
1906, 3, 14. Errick J. & w, Lenna, & dt, Winnifred, recrq
1910, 7, 13. Eva Foland rocf Caesars Creek MM
1912, 4, 17. Mary Emily rocf Wilmington MM
1912, 5, 15. Sarah Margaret & Mary Esther recrq
1912, 6, 12. Alonzo & ch, Priscilla Gladys, Leontine, Francis & Robert, recrq
1912, 7, 17. Mary Bell recrq
1921, 2, 16. Eva & Reece gct Wilmington MM,O.
1921, 2, 16. Floyd gct Wilmington MM, O.

OREN
----, --, --. John A. b 1817,10,2; m Joanna ----- b 1823,5,12
Ch: Alfred b 1845, 2, 9
Mary " 1---, 8, 5
James " 1846, 3, 4
Sarah A. " 1849, 11, 16
Chalkley " ----, --, --
Margaret b 1851, 10, 10
Susan " 1857, 8, 26
Daniel B. " 1863, 1, 27
----, --, --. Joseph m Rachel ----- b 1817,2,7
Ch: Thomas H. b 1850, 5, 13
James E. " 1852, 10, 24
Alvin " 1854, 9, 3
Mary " 1856, 3, 14
Sarah H. " 1858, 10, 25
1876, 1, 11. Joanna d bur Fairfield
1884, 7, 9. Sarah d ae 26y (a minister)

1812, 4, 8. John rocf New Hope MM, Tenn., dtd 1811,8,21
1812, 7, 4. John gct Fairfield MM, to m
1812, 12, 5. Lydia rocf Fairfield MM, dtd 1812,11,28
1814, 10, 1. John Jesse Elihu Jane Lydia & Ruth, ch John, recrq
1815, 5, 20. Abigail recrq
1815, 7, 15. Margaret (form Atkinson) rpd mou
1815, 10, 21. Abigail rmt Cephus Atkinson
1816, 5, 18. James recrq
1816, 9, 21. James & w, Margaret, gct Caesar's Creek MM
1819, 9, 18. Alexander recrq
1820, 3, 18. Alexander rmt Lydia Frazier
1820, 7, 15. Lydia rmt Charles Atkinson
1830, 3, 20. Jane recrq (H)
1840, 8, 12. Joseph prcf Dover MM, to m Asenith Lundy
1840, 9, 16. Joseph rmt Asenath Lundy
1841, 11, 17. Asenath gct Dover MM
1841, 12, 15. Abigail rocf Sparrow Creek MM, dtd 1841,11,25
1841, 12, 15. Jane rocf Sparrow Creek MM, dtd 1841,9,13, endorsed by Caesars Creek MM, 1841,11,25
1842, 12, 14. Jane Underwood (form Oren) dis mou
1844, 6, 12. Lydia, & ch, James, Ezekiel, Hannah, John F., Phebe, Alexander, Moses F. & Lydia Ann, rocf Clear Creek MM, dtd 1844,5,21
1848, 6, 14. Hannah rmt Enoch Wickersham
1849, 3, 14. Lydia & ch, John F., Phebe, Alexandria, Moses & Lydia, gct Birch Lake MM, Mich.
1856, 12, 17. James dis mou
1857, 7, 15. John A. & w, Joanna, & ch, Alfeus, Mary, James, Thomas C., Sarah Ann & Margaret E. rocf Dover MM
1866, 9, 12. Rachel & ch, Mary B. & Sarah H., recrq
1868, 4, 15. Joseph & ch, Thomas, David, James Elihu & Alvin, recrq
1869, 11, 17. Joseph & w, Rachel L., & ch, Thomas, David, James E., Alvin, Mary & Sarah, rocf Wilmington MM
1870, 9, 14. Alfred con mou
1871, 2, 15. Asenith rocf Dover MM
1875, 5, 12. Joseph dis disunity

OREN, continued
1876, 12, 13. Asenath gct Carsars Creek MM
1877, 9, 12. Jesse N. & w, Mary B., & ch, Charles H., Arthur E. & Clara J., recrq
1878, 6, 12. Mary, Sarah Ann & Susan gct Fairfield MM, O.
1878, 7, 17. John A. & s, Chalkley, gct Clear Creek MM
1878, 7, 17. Alfred & James gct Hopewell MM, O. (or Center MM)
1880, 2, 18. Alvin gct Dover MM
1881, 10, 12. Alvin rocf Dover MM, dtd 1881, 9,15
1885, 5, 15. James E. dis disunity
1887, 6, 15. Mary relrq
1917, 3, 14. Philip M. & Leslie recrq

OSBORN
1866, 4, 3. Margaret J., dt Peter & Elizabeth, b

1810, 7, 7. Mary [Ozborn] rmt Richard Mills
1816, 2, 17. William [Osburn] rocf Back Creek MM, N. C., dtd 1815,8,26
1816, 5, 18. David [Osbourn] & w, Elizabeth, & ch, Jonathan, Hessy, Elizabeth, Rebecca, Lydia & Miriam, gct New Garden MM, Ind.
1817, 4, 19. Mary Cory (form Osborne) dis mou
1818, 4, 18. Margaret (form Rhinehart) con mou
1850, 5, 18. Caroline & ch, Mary, Emily, Edward Francis Hannah & Daniel Henman, recrq
1860, 5, 16. Elizabeth (form Lundy) rpd mou
1860, 12, 12. Elizabeth gct Springfield MM
1864, 5, 18. Peter Jr. & w, Elizabeth, & ch, Angeline & Ruth Ellen, rocf Springfield MM, dtd 1864,4,16
1875, 12, 15. Peter & w, Elizabeth, & ch, Elizabeth Angeline, Ruth Ellen, Margaret Jane & Clark, gct Springfield MM
1883, 12, 12. William H. [Osbern] & w, Martha, & ch, Joseph B. & George Edwin, rocf Springfield MM, dtd 1883,11,17
1886, 5, 12. Scott & w, Mary A., & ch, Charles J., recrq
1889, 4, 17. William & w, Martha, & s, George E., gct Wilmington MM
1889, 4, 17. Edward gct Wilmington MM
1909, 11, 17. Joseph & w, Elizabeth, & s, Harry, gct Miami MM

OWNES
1827, 1, 20. Mary recrq

PADGETT
1904, 1, 13. Alice gct Dover MM

PAINTER
----, --, --. David b 1771,11,1 d 1844,5,23
1764, 3, 12. Martha b d 1839,7,30
----, --, --. Jesse b 1789,1,1; m Elizabeth ----- b 1795,5,2 d 1860,3,12 bur New Hope
Ch: Rachel W. b 1817, 6, 8
David b 1818, 9, 2
Samuel S. " 1820, 5, 31
Martha " 1822, 3, 27
Mordecai W." 1824, 1, 16
Lidia " 1825, 11, 28
----, --, --. Jacob & Naomi
Ch: Sarah b 1817, 7, 3
Joseph " 1819, 5, 21
David " 1822, 8, 24
Hannah " 1825, 2, 2
Julian " 1828, 1, 19
Martha L. " 1830, 4, 8
Thomas " 1833, 10, 27
1820, 1, 16. Mary, dt Moses & Lydia Fraizer, b
----, --, --. Thomas b 1797,5,23; m Mary ----- b 1800,12,28
Ch: William b 1821, 4, 28
Jesse " 1823, 1, 26
Phebe W. " 1826, 5, 26
David Anderson " 1828, 5, 25
Isaac " 1830, 4, 22
Martha " 1832, 11, 6
Elizabeth Ann " 1834, 8, 14
Mary " 1837, 1, 30
Rebecca " 1839, 1, 13
Eliza " 1840, 1, 12
Louisa " 1841, 1, 19
Asenith " 1842, 5, 10
----, --, --. Jesse & Susannah
Ch: Rhoda b 1843, 4, 21
John " 1844, 11, 16
Docia " 1847, 1, 19
Helena " 1849, 1, 8
Virginia " 1851, 4, 15
Dayton " 1853, 9, 4
1843, 8, 3. Harriet M., dt Joseph C. & Hannah L., b
----, --, --. David d 1863,12,6 bur New Hope; m Mary -----
Ch: Deborah b 1845, 1, 3
Berthina " 1847, 2, 16
Lydia E. " 1849, 1, 2
Jesse " 1850, 12, 11
Mary " 1852, 10, 24
Moses " 1855, 7, 23
Martha C. " 1857, 8, 13
David A. " 1859, 8, 30
1847, 9, 16. Edmund Franklin, s Mordecai & Mary, b
1852, 8, 25. Lorenzo D. d ae 1y 3m bur New Hope
1867, 6, 21. Jesse d bur New Hope
1888, 6, 5. Roy D. b
1888, 5, 23. Ethel L. b
1897, 1, 28. Mary d ae 77y

1815, 3, 4. Jacob gct Darby Creek MM, to m
1815, 9, 11. Naomi rocf Darby Creek MM, dtd 1815,8,19
1816, 9, 21. Jesse rmt Elizabeth Smith

PAINTER, continued
1820, 11, 19. Mary rocf Clear Creek MM, dtd 1820,10,14
1830, 10, 13. Elizabeth dis jH
1830, 12, 15. Jesse dis disunity
1838, 5, 16. Sarah rmt Eli Thornburgh
1838, 12, 12. Rachel W. rmt Hiram Coats
1841, 6, 16. William gct Short Creek MM
1841, 11, 17. Jesse gct Dover MM, to m Susannah Moorman
1842, 6, 15. Susannah rocf Dover MM, dtd 1842,4,14
1842, 8, 17. Joseph C. gct Dover MM, to m Hannah Shields
1842, 10, 12. William rocf Short Creek MM
1842, 11, 5. Samuel dis mou
1843, 3, 15. Hannah S. rocf Dover MM, dtd 1842,12,15
1843, 9, 13. David S. gct White Lick MM
1843, 9, 13. David gct Dover MM, to m Mary Frazier
1844, 1, 17. William con mou
1844, 2, 14. Mary rocf Dover MM, dtd 1844,1, 18
1844, 4, 17. Jesse & w, Elizabeth, & ch, Joseph G. & Hannah A., rst
1844, 4, 17. Joseph C. & w, Hannah L., & dt, Harriett M., gct White Lick MM
1845, 6, 18. William dis mou
1845, 8, 13. Jacob & w, Naomi, & ch, Hannah, Julian, Martha S. & Thomas, gct White Lick MM, Ind.
1845, 9, 17. Martha Coate (form Painter) dis mou
1846, 10, 14. Phebe rmt John Fawcett
1846, 10, 14. Mordicai W. gct Chester MM, Ind., to m Mary Nixon
1847, 2, 17. Mary rocf Chester MM, Ind., dtd 1846,12,24
1849, 2, 14. Mercy Ann (form King) dis mou
1850, 3, 13. Mordecai W. & w, Mary H., & ch, Edmund Franklin & Amanda Jane, gct Mississiniwa MM, Ind.
1850, 6, 12. David A. rmt Lucy Ann Moorman
1850, 11, 13. Joseph Mote prcf West Branch MM, to m Martha Painter
1850, 12, 18. Martha rmt Joseph Mote
1851, 4, 16. Lydia S. rmt Josiah Thornburgh
1851, 6, 18. Joseph S. dis jas
1852, 2, 18. Isaac gct West Union MM, Ind., to m Joanna T. Johnson
1852, 8, 18. Joanna T. rocf West Union MM, Ind.
1852, 11, 17. Thomas & w, Mary, & ch, Mary, Rebecca, Louisa & Asenath, gct Honey Creek MM, Ind.
1852, 12, 15. Rebecca F. Semans (form Painter) dis mou
1853, 3, 16. Isaac & w, Joanna, & s, Thomas Ashley, gct Honey Creek MM, Ind.
1854, 1, 18. Elizabeth Ann Fawcett (form Painter) dis mou
1854, 1, 18. David A. dis mou
1855, 4, 18. Jesse & w, Susannah, & ch, Rhoda, John, Theodocia, Helena, Virginia & Dayton, gct Three River MM, Ia.
1860, 1, 18. Hannah Lewis (form Painter) rpd mou; dropped from mbrp
1865, 9, 13. Ahairah Johnson gct Dover MM, to m Margaret Ann Painter
1863, 4, 18. Burthenia O. Davis (form Painter) rpd mou
1866, 12, 12. Mordecai J. Walker & w, Deborah L. (form Painter) con mou
1875, 8, 18. Jesse Moses, Mary Frances & Martha relrq
1888, 2, 15. Jesse S. & w, Irene J., & s, Morris E., recrq
1888, 4, 18. Demo & ch recrq
1888, 4, 18. Aletha L., w David, & ch, Orville E. & Dora F., recrq
1896, 12, 16. Jesse relrq
1898, 7, 13. David & fam relrq
1897, 9, 15. Irene & ch, Maurice, Roy & Bertha, relrq

PAIST
1815, 12, 16. Charles rocf Chester MM, Pa., dtd 1815,10,30
1816, 2, 17. Charles rmt Abigail Perkins
1818, 3, 21. Charles & w, Abigail & s, James, gct Caesars Creek MM

PARKER
1895, 4, 17. William recrq
1897, 12, 15. William relrq
1916, 3, 15. Pearl recrq

PARLOTT
1877, 5, 16. William C. [Parlot] & w, Sarah E., & ch, Frances C., recrq
1879, 7, 16. William C. & w, Elizabeth, relrq
1887, 3, 16. David E. [Parlette] recrq
1889, 4, 13. David E. gct Mississiniwa MM

PATTERSON
1817, 7, 19. William rocf Deep Creek MM, N. C., dtd 1815,11,4, endorsed by Fairfield MM, 1817,6,28
1818, 8, 15. Sarah rocf Deep Creek MM, N. C., dtd 1818,6,6
1818, 9, 19. Mary recrq
1886, 5, 12. John recrq
1888, 2, 15. Clara S. recrq
1897, 4, 14. Bessie recrq

PATTY
1808, 5, 7. Charles recrq

PAXSON
1836, 5, 2. Asaph b
1858, 3, 16. James H. b
1862, 8, 8. Elias G. b
1865, 5, 22. Newton W. b
1873, 5, 19. Eldora A. b
1901, 11, 11. Aseph d ae 68y 6m 9d

PAXSON, continued
1901, 11, 11. Aseph d ae 68y 6m 9d
1936, 9, 19. Margaret b

1809, 9, 2. Susanna Moorman & gr dt, Dosha Paxton, rocf South River MM, Va., dtd 1809,9,9(?)
1811, 12, 7. Dosha Moreman (form Paxton) dis mou
1843, 12, 13. Mary Ann [Paxton] recrq
1853, 4, 13. William prcf Goshen MM, to m Ruth Green
1853, 5, 18. William rmt Ruth Green
1853, 7, 13. Ruth [Paxton] (form Green) gct Goshen MM
1854, 5, 17. Asaph H. prcf Goshen MM, to m Margaret Lundy
1854, 6, 14. Asaph rmt Margaret Lundy
1854, 7, 12. Margaret L. [Paxton] gct Goshen MM
1856, 2, 13. Mary Ann Tibbles (form Paxon) dis mou
1870, 4, 13. Asaph [Paxon] & fam rocf Goshen MM
1895, 7, 17. Aseph [Paxton] & w, Margaret, gct Sabina MM
1896, 5, 13. Nora T. [Paxton] & ch, Charles Robert & Eldora Elizabeth, recrq
1905, 5, 17. Margaret [Paxton] rocf Sabina MM
1908, 3, 18. Elias G. & w, Nora I., & ch, Charles Robert, Eldora Elizabeth, Leona Margaret & Glen Dawson, gct Cesars Creek MM

PEACEMAKER
1907, 2, 12. Foster & w, Myrtle, & ch, Thelma, recrq
1909, 6, 16. Foster & fam gct Cesars Creek MM

PEARSON
1819, 5, 15. John & w, Hannah, & ch, Joseph, Rebecca, Asenath, Jesse & Kesiah, rocf Fairfield MM, dtd 1818,10,31

PEEBLES
1832, 10, 17. Cert rec for James S. from Springborough MM, dtd 1832,7,24; returned to Springborough MM since he had returned there
1833, 7, 17. Cert rec for John & w, Mary Ann, from Springborough MM, dtd 1832,9,25, endorsed to Dover MM
1842, 9, 14. Elijah recrq
1844, 8, 14. Elijah gct Newberry MM

PEELLE
1870, 8, 17. Sarah E. gct Dover MM
1875, 8, 18. Esther [Peele] gct Dover MM
1875, 8, 18. Harriet M. [Peele] gct Dover MM
1905, 6, 14. Mary Vantress gct Cesars Creek MM
1906, 3, 14. Lydia Deborah gct Wilmington MM

1829, 10, 17. Paul rocf Green Plain MM, dtd 1829,2,9 (H)
1839, 3, 14. Paul gct Milford MM, Ind. (H)
1889, 6, 12. Lina M. recrq
1889, 6, 12. Wilson C. recrq
1889, 6, 12. Charles recrq
1891, 10, 14. Nora rocf Springfield MM, dtd 1891,8,15
1893, 2, 15. Carrie, minor, rec
1894, 3, 14. S. Parker recrq
1906, 9, 12. Parker gct Ceasars Creek MM

PERDUE
1818, 3, 21. Jemima rocf Fairfield MM

PERKINS
----, --, --. Isaac b 1762,6,30 d 1828,10,3, bur Center; m Pheniah LEONARD b 1763,3,14 d 1840,3,26 bur Center
1825, 11, 20. Priscilla, dt John & Julia Ann, b
1810, 9, 1. Ann rmt Hezekiah Hiatt
1813, 3, 6. Susannah rocf Deep Creek MM, N. C., dtd 1812,9,5
1813, 12, 4. Susannah rmt Amos Cook
1816, 2, 17. Abigail rmt Charles Paist
1816, 4, 20. Lydia Whinery (form Perkins) con mou
1821, 7, 21. Thomas & w, Sarah, & ch, Joseph, Mary Ann, Phineas, Isaac, Abijah & Sarah, rocf Miami MM, dtd 1821,5,30
1822, 1, 19. John rmt Juliana Eaches
1825, 10, 15. Thomas & w, Sarah, & ch, Joseph, Mary Ann, Pheniah, Isaac, Abijah, Sarah & John K., gct Caesars Creek MM
1829, 2, 18. Phenia dis jH
1829, 5, 13. John dis jH
1830, 11, 17. Selina dis jH
1838, 3, 15. John L. con mou (H)
1845, 8, 19. Priscilla H. dis disunity
1866, 7, 18. Priscilla recrq
1869, 12, 15. Priscilla gct Wilmington MM

PETERSON
1820, 11, 19. Clarence recrq

PEW
1829, 9, 19. Martha recrq (H)

PHILIPS
1812, 12, 5. James rocf Warrington MM, dtd 1812,9,24
1816, 2, 17. James [Phillips] rpd mou
1825, 10, 15. James dis

PICKET
1813, 7, 3. Joseph & w, Priscilla, & ch, Tamer, Anna, Lydia, Mary & Sarah, rocf Elk MM, dtd 1813,6,5
1817, 12, 20. Joseph & w, Priscilla, & ch, Thamar, Anne, Lydia, Mary, Sarah & Joseph, gct White Water MM, Ind.

PIERCE
----, --, --. Richard [Peirce] b 1783,--,--; m Mary ----- b 1787,--,-- (H)
Ch: Miriam b 1821, 5, 18
John F. " 1823, 7, 18
James " 1826, 3, 30
Martha " 1827, 7, 29
Esther W. " 1829, 6, 24
1852, 9, 23. Esther m Andrew CADWALADER (H)

1814, 12, 3. Richard rocf Wilmington MM, dtd 1814,4,1
1828, 9, 17. Richard dis jH
1828, 11, 12. Mary dis jH
1841, 8, 18. Miriam Williamson (form Pierce) dis mou
1846, 12, 16. John dis joining separatists
1849, 11, 15. Martha Morgan (form Peirce) con mou (H)
1850, 1, 17. Miriam Williamson (form Pierce) con mcd (H)

PIKE
1822, 4, 20. William Stanbrough gct Fairfield MM, to m Rachel Pike

PITCHER
1840, 8, 12. Abigail (form Thornburgh) dis mou

PLACE
1830, 6, 19. Maurice gct Green Plains MM (H)

POLK
1810, 5, 5. Hannah (form Hobson) dis mou

POORMAN
1910, 2, 16. George & Ella recrq

PRICE
1874, 4, 15. Parker recrq
1879, 1, 15. Calvin & w, Eliza Jane, & ch, Flora Bell, recrq
1880, 3, 17. Parker dis disunity
1885, 5, 15. Calvin dis disunity
1887, 5, 18. Eliza & dt, Flora Burden, relrq

PUSEY
----, --, --. Joel b 1794,2,13; m Hannah ----- b 1793,9,11
Ch: Martha b 1816, 7, 7
Jesse F. " 1820, 10, 18

1815, 4, 15. Joel rocf Caesars Creek MM, dtd 1815,1,27
1815, 7, 14. Joel rmt Hannah Faulkner
1820, 5, 20. Joel & w, Hannah, & ch, Martha, gct Miami MM
1821, 7, 21. Joel & w, Hannah, & ch, Martha & Jesse F., rocf Miami MM, dtd 1821,5,30
1834, 12, 17. Joel & w, Hannah, & ch, Martha, Jesse F. & Rachel, gct Spiceland MM, Ind.

PYLE
1886, 5, 12. Elizabeth recrq
1886, 6, 16. Allen rocf Toledo MM, Kans.
1888, 7, 18. Allen & w relrq

QUINBY
1832, 12, 12. Elizabeth recrq
1837, 3, 15. Aaron B., Josephine E., Thomas M., Miriam E., Ezra A. & Mercy Ann, ch Elizabeth, recrq
1840, 1, 15. Elizabeth & ch, Aaron B., Josaphine E., Thomas M., Miriam E. & Mary Ann, rqct Springfield MM (not granted)

RAWLS
1844, 5, 7. Elizabeth, dt Burwell & Sarah, d ae 15y 8m 9d bur Center

1835, 12, 16. Cert rec for Burwell & w, Sarah, & ch from Sandy Spring MM, dtd 1835,10,6, endorsed to Dover MM
1844, 2, 14. Michael rocf Springfield MM, dtd 1844,2,13
1844, 2, 14. Burwell & w, Sarah, & ch, Jonathan, Elizabeth, William, Esther, Jesse, John & Sarah Jane, rocf Springfield MM, dtd 1843,12,12
1845, 7, 16. Burwell dis disunity
1845, 12, 17. Sarah & ch, William, Esther, Jesse John & Sarah Jane, gct Walnut Ridge MM, Ind.
1846, 6, 17. Jonathan gct Walnut Ridge MM, Ind.
1846, 12, 16. Jonathan dis mou

REAGAN
1810, 2, 3. Reasin & s, Reasin Reuel & Jesse recrq

REAVES
1820, 8, 19. Charlotte E. (form Moorman) dis mou

REES
1807, 10, 3. Sarah [Reece] (form Hayworth) con mou
1810, 5, 5. Sarah (form Leonard) con mou
1824, 11, 20. Sarah gct Honey Creek MM
1844, 8, 14. John Cox gct Cherry Grove MM, Ind., to m Ann Reese

REED
1845, 4, 17. Rachel [Read] (form Carver) con mou (H)
1905, 9, 13. John rocf Hopewell MM
1905, 10, 18. James Edward recrq
1914, 2, 18. Bernice Virginia, adopted dt Edward & Iota, recrq

RENNELS
1907, 4, 17. Clyde recrq
1907, 4, 17. Sarah Goldie & Stephen Hire recrq

RENNELS, continued
1908, 12, 16. Clara recrq

RHINEHART
----, --, --. Adam & Catharine [Rinehart]
Ch: Jeremiah b 1789, 5, 13
Rachel " 1790, 12, 22
Barbara " 1792, 9, 1
George " 1794, 5, 15
Margaret " 1796, 3, 10
Solomon " 1798, 1, 27
Ann " 1799, 12, 16
Jacob " 1802, 1, 8
Lydia " 1804, 2, 7
Isaac " 1806, 3, 2
Catharine " 1807, 12, 20
Adam " 1811, 4, 7
Joel " 1814, 4, 21
Martha " 1817, 2, 23
Asa " 1817, 2, 23

1808, 2, 6. Adam & w, Catharine, & ch, Jeremiah, Barbara, George, Margaret, Solomon, Ann, Jacob, Lydia & Isaac, rocf Cane Creek MM, N. C., dtd 1807,9,5
1809, 8, 5. Barbara rmt Simon Ballard
1813, 8, 7. George [Rinard] dis disunity
1814, 5, 7. Jeremiah [Rinard] dis disunity
1818, 4, 18. Margaret Osborn (form Rhinehart) con mou
1818, 4, 18. Ann Smith (form Rhinehart) con mou
1818, 9, 19. Solomon [Rinard] dis mou
1823, 4, 19. Cherry Grove MM, Ind. was granted permission to rst Solomon
1826, 2, 18. White Water MM, Ind. was granted permission to rst Jeremiah [Rhineheart]

RHODES
1807, 11, 7. Esther [Roads] (form Lewis) con mou
1817, 12, 20. Thomas prcf Caesars Creek MM, to m Mary Ballard
1818, 1, 17. Thomas rmt Mary Ballard
1818, 5, 16. Mary [Rhode] gct Caesars Creek MM

RICH
1811, 12, 7. Ann (form Ballard) con mou
1817, 8, 16. Cert rec for Samuel & fam from New Garden MM, dtd 1817,8,28, endorsed to Miami MM
1821, 2, 17. Samuel rocf Miami MM
1821, 3, 17. Samuel rmt Lydia Thomas
1821, 5, 19. Lydia gct Miami MM
1841, 4, 14. Thomas prcf Springfield MM, to m Isabella Adsit
1841, 5, 12. Thomas rmt Isabella Adsit
1841, 6, 16. Isabella Rich & dt, Mary Ann Adsit, gct Springfield MM

RICHARDS
1820, 1, 15. Nancy rocf Center MM, Pa., dtd 1819,6,19
1828, 6, 21. Naomi gct Caesars Creek MM
1840, 2, 12. Abigail (form Jones) dis mou

RICHARDSON
1869, 8, 18. John W. & ch, Henry T., Henrietta M., Sarah Esther, Ollie P. & Mary Clarinda, rocf Springfield MM
1872, 1, 17. John W. rpd mou
1876, 4, 12. Henrietta M. & Sarah Esther gct Springfield MM
1876, 5, 17. John W. & ch, Olive & Mary C., gct Clear Creek MM

RILEY
1917, 5, 23. Florence recrq

RISON
1834, 4, 16. Mary (form Stanton) dis mou & jas

ROBINSON
1825, 3, 19. Azel Walker gct Fairfield MM, to m Elizabeth Robinson

ROCKHILL
1817, 5, 18. Ruth b
1830, 11, 11. Lydia H. b
1877, 2, 10. Serena Bell, dt Jonathan & Mary, b
1897, 3, 13. Calvin d bur Chester

1810, 8, 4. Elizabeth rocf Falls MM, Pa., dtd 1810,4,4, endorsed by Fairfield MM
1827, 6, 16. Elizabeth rocf Springfield MM, dtd 1827,5,--
1834, 2, 12. Sarah rocf Phila. MM, Pa., dtd 1832,7,26, endorsed by Cincinnati MM, 1833,10,17
1834, 8, 13. Elizabeth dis jH
1854, 4, 12. Lydia H. (form Hollingsworth) dis mou
1858, 7, 14. Lydia H. recrq
1860, 11, 14. Calvin recrq
1862, 2, 12. Calvin & w, Lydia H., gct Greenwood MM, Ind.
1867, 6, 12. Calvin & w, Lydia, rocf West Grove MM, Ind.
1874, 4, 15. Jonathan E. recrq
1874, 4, 15. Mary recrq
1874, 4, 15. Ruth recrq
1889, 6, 12. Charles recrq
1898, 5, 18. Lydia H. gct Green Plain MM, O.
1899, 4, 12. J. H. & w, Mary, relrq

ROGERS
1880, 5, 10. Lydia R. [Rodgers] b
1882, 9, 17. John Edward [Rodgers], s John & Clara, b

1879, 1, 15. John F. & s, Allen D., recrq
1879, 1, 15. Clara A. [Rodgers] recrq
1888, 11, 14. John [Rodgers] relrq

ROGERS, continued
1905, 11, 15. Leona recrq
1906, 2, 14. Ray recrq
1906, 2, 14. Roy recrq
1913, 1, 15. Roy & Ray gct Wilmington MM

ROLLINSON
1905, 3, 5. Catherine Parlette gct Wilmington MM

ROSE
1895, 3, 13. Andrew recrq
1904, 12, 14. Andrew dropped from mbrp

ROSEBERRY
1862, 8, 14. Mary (form Hale) con mcd (H)

ROSS
1840, 8, 16. Emma b
1868, 12, 17. Loulu b
1870, 3, 4. Oatas b
1871, 11, 17. Eldon b
1873, 10, 28. Jennie b
1875, 5, 14. Albert b

1876, 8, 16. Emeline rocf New Garden MM, dtd 1875,8,21
1886, 4, 14. Oris gct Wilmington MM, O.
1895, 3, 13. Emaline & ch, Jennie, Elden & Alberta, gct Wilmington MM
1899, 2, 15. Cora Leonard relrq

RUBLE
1812, 6, 16. Walter dis mou
1813, 4, 3. Owen dis disunity
1815, 2, 4. Samuel Jr. dis mou & bearing arms

RUDDUCK
1815, 10, 21. Cert rec for Sarah from Springfield MM, endorsed to Fall Creek MM
1825, 3, 19. John [Redick] & w, Ursula, rocf Caesars Creek MM, dtd 1825,1,27

RUTHERFORD
----, --, --. John & Sylvia
Ch: Susannah G. b 1861, 6, 14
Mary Jane " 1864, 1, 27

RUTLEGE
1913, 2, 12. Katie recrq

RYAN
1818, 10, 17. Margaret (form Harlan) con mou

SABIN
----, --, --. Warren m Margaret ----- d 1843, 1?,24
Ch: Martha M. b 1827, 7, 31
Lydia Smith " 1829, 10, 24
John M. " 1832, 1, 19
Stuart " 1834, 4, 26

1823, 2, 15. Warren recrq
1826, 3, 18. Margaret recrq
1828, 11, 12. Warren dis jH
1829, 7, 15. Margaret dis jH
1835, 11, 19. William recrq (H)
1839, 2, 14. Lydia, w William, & ch, Matilda, Sarah, Mary, Paul & Elizabeth, recrq (H)
1839, 2, 14. William & w, & ch, Matilda, Sarah, Mary, Paul & Elizabeth, gct Miami MM (H)
1841, 4, 15. Warren dis disunity (H)
1848, 3, 14. Rachel (form Birdsall) con mou (H)
1885, 6, 17. George [Sabine] rocf Wilmington MM
1901, 4, 17. Mary Ann & Ora Louisa recrq
1903, 2, 18. Bessie M. recrq
1909, 7, 14. George & w, Mary, & dt, Ora, gct Springfield MM

SANDERS
1808, 1, 2. Mary Cannidy, gr ch Mary Sanders, recrq
1808, 3, 5. Joel & fam recrq
1808, 6, 4. Barbara rmt Samuel Whitson
1809, 1, 7. John dis disunity
1844, 5, 15. Thomas & w, Emily, & ch, Deborah Ann & Levi H., rocf Miami MM, dtd 1844,4,24
1845, 10, 15. Thomas & w, Emily, & ch, Deborah Ann, Levi & David Lewis, gct Clear Creek MM
1860, 10, 18. Richard B. & w, Jane, & dt, Elma Ann, gct Prairie Grove MM, Ia. (H)

SATTERTHWAITE
1810, 8, 4. John [Satterthwait] rocf Falls MM, Pa., dtd 1810,3,7
1810, 10, 6. John rmt Elizabeth Linton
1811, 1, 5. Elizabeth gct Miami MM

SAVILLE
1868, 7, 14. Caldonia b

1866, 6, 13. John Franklin recrq
1868, 8, 12. Margaret R. [Savill] recrq
1878, 12, 18. Frank & fam relrq
1885, 12, 16. Franklin [Savill] & w relrq

SAYRES
1866, 8, 13. Lillian C., dt Phebe, b

SCHOOLEY
----, --, --. Samuel b 1784,8,25 d 1844,1,27 bur Center; m Rachel JOHNSON b 1792,2,27 d 1863,4,11
Ch: Margarett b 1809, 10, 20 d 1809,12,23
Ann " 1810, 10, 30
Benjamin " 1813, 2, 23
John " 1815, 8, 6
Leah " 1818, 1, 28
Isaac " 1820, 9, 22
Thomas " 1823, 8, 6

SCHOOLEY, Samuel & Rachel, continued
Ch: Elizabeth b 1827, 11, 12
Samuel " 1834, 8, 27
----, --, --. Nathan & Sarah
Ch: Aaron b 1818, 6, 4
Nancy " 1820, 2, 3 d 1827,10,15
Omri " 1822, 12, 16
Ezra " 1824, 2, 16 d 1827,11,14
Rachel " 1826, 2, 21
Benjamin " 1828, 2, 16
Mary " 1830, 2, 16
Hannah " 1832, 10, 1
Miriam " 1835, 3, 8
Unice " 1837, 3, 12 d 1839, 8,14
1842, 12, 5. John, s Ira, b

1812, 9, 5. John [Schooly] & w, Susannah, & ch, Isaac & Asenath, rocf Elk MM, dtd 1812,7,4
1813, 7, 3. Benjamin & w, Rebecca, rocf Mt. Pleasant MM, dtd 1813,9,26
1817, 2, 15. Nathan rocf Mt. Pleasant MM, Va. dtd 1816,10,26
1817, 4, 19. Nathan rmt Mary Stanbrough
1821, 1, 20. Nathan & w, Sarah, & ch, Aaron & Nancy, rocf Springfield MM, dtd 1820,11, 25
1827, 8, 18. William con mou
1830, 11, 17. William dis disunity
1834, 12, 17. Samuel & w, Rachel, & ch, Anna, Benjamin, John, Leah, Isaac, Thomas & Elizabeth, rocf Deep Creek MM, N. C., dtd 1833,11,2, endorsed by White Lick MM, Ind., 1834,9,17
1836, 2, 17. Anna rmt Isaac Green
1840, 3, 18. Aaron con mou
1841, 3, 17. Leah Wickersham (form Schooley) dis mou
1841, 3, 17. Benjamin gct Mississiniwa MM, Ind., to m Lucinda Stout
1841, 10, 13. Sarah rmt James Lundy
1841, 11, 17. John rmt Phebe Jones
1842, 9, 14. Omri rmt Elizabeth Cox
1843, 12, 13. Rachel rmt Aaron Green
1844, 9, 18. Omry & w, Elizabeth, & s, William H., gct White Lick MM, Ind.
1845, 7, 16. Omri & s, William H., rocf White Water MM, Ind.
1845, 11, 12. Mary & Hannah gct Newberry MM
1845, 11, 12. John & w, Phebe, & ch, Ira & Lydia Ann, gct Mississiniwa MM, Ind.
1846, 9, 16. Omri dis mou
1847, 7, 14. Benjamin gct Mississiniwa MM, Ind.
1848, 4, 12. Isaac gct Springfield MM, to m Deborah L. Harvey
1848, 4, 12. Joel Green prcf Newberry MM, to m Elizabeth Schooley
1848, 5, 17. Elizabeth rmt Joel Green
1850, 2, 13. Miriam gct Newberry MM
1851, 4, 16. Aaron gct Newberry MM
1852, 3, 18. Isaac gct Springfield MM
1852, 6, 16. William gct Mississiniwa MM, Ind.
1852, 8, 18. Thomas gct Poplar Run MM, Ind.
1853, 2, 16. Benjamin dis mou
1855, 3, 14. Thomas & w, Elizabeth, & ch, Rebecca Jane, gct Mississiniwa MM, Ind.
1859, 7, 13. Isaac gct Springfield MM
1860, 3,14. Samuel rpd mou
1874, 4, 15. Samuel gct Sugar Creek MM, Ind.

SCOTT
1830, 4, 17. Charles recrq (H)
1830, 7, 17. Charles gct Green Plain MM (H)
1832, 9, 15. Timothy & w, Hannah, & ch, Sabilla Ann & Isaiah, recrq (H)
1839, 8, 14. Ann, w William, rocf Springborough MM, dtd 1839,5,21
1843, 11, 30. Sabilla Ann Adair (form Scott) dis mou & jas (H)
1845, 7, 16. Ann Eliza, William E. & John L., rocf Springborough MM, dtd 1845,2,1
1845, 9, 17. Ann & ch, Ann Eliza, John L. & Louisa, gct White Water MM, Ind.
1857, 11, 9. Isaiah dis mcd (H)

SEARS
1818, 2, 21. Penelope & ch, Polly Pleasant Christopher & John, rocf Fairfield MM, dtd 1817,11,29
1836, 9, 14. Pleasant dis mou
1867, 8, 14. Phebe G. & ch, Lillian Clinton, rocf Fairfield MM, dtd 1867,7,20

SEMANS
1852, 12, 15. Rebecca F. (form Painter) dis mou

SEWELL
1844, 9, 19. Elizabeth (form West) dis mou (H)

SEXTON
1813, 11, 6. Mary rocf Plainfield MM, dtd 1813,9,25
1813, 11, 6. Cert rec for Catherine from Plainfield MM, dtd 1813,9,25, endorsed to Miami MM
1814, 4, 2. Maria recrq
1814, 11, 5. Catharine rocf Miami MM, dtd 1814,8,31
1815, 5, 20. Mary rmt Israel Taylor
1819, 11, 20. Catherine gct Fall Creek MM

SHARP
1888, 2, 15. George recrq
1888, 2, 15. Roy recrq
1892, 9, 14. Delilah gct Springfield MM
1915, 11, 17. Thomas J. rocf Wilmington MM

SHEPHERD
----, --, --. Jesse [Shepperd] b 1793,9,21; m Elizabeth ----- b 1792,6,14
Ch: Susannah b 1817, 12, 19
Martha " 1820, 1, 29

SHEPHERD, Jesse & Elizabeth, continued
Ch: Hannah b 1821, 12, 11
Jacob " 1824, 5, 18
Amaziah " 1826, 5, 24
1866, 10, 26. Francis J., s Allen & Angelina, b

1814, 7, 2. Jesse rocf Hopewell MM, dtd 1813,11,4
1814, 12, 3. Susannah & dt, Susanna, rocf Miami MM, dtd 1814,4,27
1815, 9, 16. Jesse rmt Elizabeth Faulkner
1817, 2, 15. Susannah dis disunity
1834, 8, 13. Jesse & w, Elizabeth, & ch, Susannah, Martha, Hannah, Jacob, Amaziah, Edith, Thomas & Allen, gct Springfield MM
1841, 4, 14. Martha rocf Mill Creek MM, dtd 1841,4,13
1841, 5, 12. Hannah [Sheppherd] rocf Mill Creek MM, dtd 1841,4,13
1841, 5, 12. Evan H. Jenkins prcf Mill Creek MM, to m Martha Shepherd
1841, 6, 16. Martha rmt Evan H. Jenkins
1841, 8, 18. Jesse & w, Elizabeth, & ch, Jacob, Amaziah, Thomas, Allen, Edith & Mary Jane, rocf Mill Creek MM, dtd 1841,6,15
1849, 4, 18. Edith rmt James W. Linton
1849, 9, 12. Jacob dis mou & jas
1850, 11, 13. Jesse & fam gct Mill Creek MM
1850, 11, 13. Elizabeth & ch, Thomas & Mary Jane,gct Mill Creek MM
1850, 12, 18. Hannah gct Mill Creek MM
1851, 5, 14. Amaziah & Allen gct Mill Creek MM, O.
1851, 7, 16. Amaziah's cert returned; dis mou
1854, 12, 13. Elizabeth & dt, Mary Jane, rocf Mill Creek MM, dtd 1854,11,14
1854, 12, 13. Hannah rocf Mill Creek MM
1855, 7, 18. Thomas rocf Mill Creek MM
1856, 3, 12. Jonathan James prcf Newberry MM, to m Mary Jane Shepherd
1856, 4, 16. Mary Jane rmt Jonathan James
1857, 7, 15. Allen rocf Mill Creek MM
1887, 5, 18. Viola M. & Joel L. Shepherd, ch Eva Fondler, recrq
1895, 2, 13. Joel L. & Viola M. relrq

SHERIDAN
1814, 12, 3. John & ch, Hannah, Elizabeth, William, Rachel, George & John, recrq

SHIELDS
1808, 2, 6. Hannah rocf New Hope MM, Tenn., dtd 1807,3,2
1819, 10, 16. John, Rebecca, Elizabeth, Maryann & Lydia, ch Hannah, recrq
1819, 12, 18. William recrq
1842, 8, 17. Joseph C. Painter gct Dover MM, to m Hannah Shields
1848, 8, 16. John Doan gct Dover MM, to m Mary Jane Shield

SHIPLEY
1831, 7, 13. Ann rocf New York MM, N. Y., dtd 1831,6,1
1831, 7, 13. William & w, Phebe, & ch, Ann, Elizabeth C., Mary P., Caroline, Henry & William, rocf New York MM, N. Y., dtd 1831,6,1
1831, 7, 13. Thomas C. rocf New York MM, N. Y., dtd 1831,6,1
1832, 3, 14. Ann Gray (form Shipley) con mou
1832, 12, 12. Thomas C. rmt Mary Emily McMillan
1834, 5, 14. Ann gct Cincinnati MM
1834, 5, 14. William & w, Phebe, & ch, Elizabeth C., Mary P., Caroline, Henry & William, gct Cincinnati MM
1834, 5, 14. Thomas C. & w, Mary Emily, gct Cincinnati MM
1835, 5, 13. John W. rocf New York MM, N.Y., dtd 1833,7,3

SHORT
1874, 2, 18. William H. recrq
1885, 12, 16. William relrq
1893, 8, 15. Catherine E. recrq
1894, 9, 12. William H. rst
1895, 3, 13. John recrq
1899, 9, 13. John relrq
1900, 3, 14. Phebe dropped from mbrp

SHUPERT
1915, 6, 16. George & w, Ida, rocf Wilmington MM

SIMS
----, --, --. Wm. b 1826,8,29; m Nancy Ellen ----- b 1834,4,4
Ch: Rebecca
Jane b 1856, 7, 28
Ruth Ellen " 1861, 7, 7
Wm. D. " 1863, 1, 7
Delilah " 1867, 3, 1
1878, 5, 9. Martha E., w Joseph, d
1895, 3, 13. William d bur Springfield Territory
1899, 2, 2. Nancy Ellen [Simms] d bur Springfield

1869, 12, 15. William & w, Nancy Ellen, & ch, Rebecca Jane, Ruth Ellen, William D. & Delilah, recrq
1874, 4, 15. Joseph E. recrq
1895, 7, 19. Joseph gct West Fork MM
1913, 10, 15. Sarah L. & Helen U. [Simms], ch Rose, relrq
1920, 11, 19. William J. [Simms] & w, Rose B., relrq

SKIMMINGS
1913, 2, 12. Helen recrq

SMALL
1813, 10, 2. Jacob rocf Westfield MM, S. C., dtd 1812,11,10
1818, 3, 21. Jacob gct New Garden MM, Ind.

SMITH
1812, 10, 8. Elijah b
1837, 10, 5. Henry, s Joseph & Lydia, Clinton Co., O.; m at Wilmington, Sarah WHINERY, dt Thomas & Lydia, Clinton Co., O. (H)
Ch: Isaiah b 1839, 12, 3
Lydia W. " 1842, 3, 24
1866, 8, 18. Sarah, w Samuel S., d bur at Wilmington
1878, 9, 4. Newton Edward, s Duane & Elizabeth, b
1890, 8, 24. Rachel E., dt William & Irene, b
1892, 12, 26. Ann, mother Lydia H. Rockhill, d bur Chester
1901, 11, --. Elijah d

1812, 2, 1. Mordecai gct Miami MM
1813, 1, 2. Elizabeth & s, Seth, rocf Fairfield MM, dtd 1812,7,25
1813, 11, 6. Cert rec 1813,1,2 for Elizabeth & s endorsed to Caesars Creek MM
1816, 9, 21. Elizabeth rmt Jesse Painter
1818, 4, 18. Ann (form Rhinehart) con mou
1822, 2, 16. Jane (form Thornburgh) dis mou
1824, 4, 17. Samuel dis disunity
1825, 11, 19. Thomas & Eve & ch, Maria Ann, Thomas, Rachel & Deborah, rocf Lick Creek MM, Ind.
1826, 10, 21. Maria Ann rmt William Lundy
1827, 2, 17. Prudence & Lavina rocf Westland MM, Pa., dtd 1826,12,28
1828, 9, 17. Joseph dis
1829, 2, 18. Lydia dis jH
1829, 5, 13. Joseph Jr. dis disunity
1829, 8, 12. Thomas dis disunity & jH
1829, 9, 16. Eve dis disunity
1830, 6, 16. Rebedca dis jH
1830, 6, 16. Lydia Jr. dis jH
1830, 7, 14. Henry dis disunity & jH
1831, 9, 14. William dis disunity
1833, 7, 17. Levina Leamon (form Smith) dis mou
1837, 4, 12. John, Rachel, Deborah & Thomas Jr., ch Thomas, gct Springfield MM
1837, 6, 14. William dis mou
1838, 3, 14. Margaret Hampton (form Smith) dis mou
1838, 4, 18. Henry dis mou & joining Separatists
1838, 7, 16. Sarah (form Whinery) dis mou
1838, 7, 16. Jeremiah Hadley gct White Water MM, Ind., to m Esther Smith
1839, 1, 16. Elijah dis mou
1847, 4, 17. Sarah rocf Miami MM, dtd 1847,2,27
1860, 6, 13. Seth prcf Green Plain MM, to m Anna Hollingsworth
1860, 7, 18. Seth rmt Hannah Hollingsworth
1860, 9, 12. Hannah Smith (form Hollingsworth) & Harriet Hollingsworth, a minor under her care, gct Green Plain MM
1865, 8, 16. Jesse Lundy gct Dover MM, Ind., to m Hulda Smith
1871, 4, 12. Susan (or Lucina) recrq
1871, 4, 12. Mary M. recrq
1874, 4, 15. Margaret recrq
1874, 9, 16. Duane & w, Elizabeth, & ch, Mary Estella, recrq
1874, 11, 7. Elijah recrq
1877, 3, 14. Charlex M. & w, Martha L., & ch, Jacob A. & Dean, recrq
1880, 5, 12. Martha L. & ch, Jacob A. & Dean, relrq
1880, 6, 16. Charles W. dis disunity
1883, 4, 18. Ellen recrq
1884, 1, 16. Anne rocf Green Plain MM, dtd 1884,12,12(?)
1885, 12, 16. Lucian & w, Mary, relrq
1885, 12, 16. Duane & w, Elizabeth, & ch, Mary Estella, Ida & Newton, relrq
1888, 5, 16. Ellen gct Springfield MM, O.
1889, 6, 12. John recrq
1889, 6, 12. Angie recrq
1891, 2, 18. William & dt, Rachel Elizabeth, recrq
1894, 3, 14. Charley recrq
1894, 3, 14. Jennie recrq
1894, 3, 14. Elsmer, minor, recrq
1894, 9, 12. Dr. Lucian & w, Mary, rst
1895, 3, 13. Clara gct Wilmington MM
1905, 1, 18. William & w recrq
1906, 2, 14. Rachel recrq
1913, 2, 12. Lucian, Homer, Oren & Mildred transferred from associate to active mbrp
1913, 10, 15. Phebe & dt, Marie, recrq
1913, 10, 15. John, s Phebe, recrq
1915, 3, 17. William H. & w, Irene, & ch gct Springfield MM

SNIDER
1844, 10, 16. Martha McMillan & dt, Hester Ann Snider, recrq
1859, 7, 13. Hester Ann Hollingsworth (form Snider) rpd mou

SNOWDEN
----, --, --. Richard b 1800,3,19; m Mary ----- b 1808,5,14 (H)
Ch: Lewis
Philip b 1840, 4, 25
William F. " 1842, 8, 7
----, --, --. Edward b 1836,10,17; m Rachel ----- b 1841,10,8
Ch: Mary W. b 1864, 11, 5
Sarah A. " 1867, 3, 23 d 1867, 4,14 bur Center
Alton L. " 1868, 8, 11
Seth " 1877, 1, 3
Sarah A. " 1879, 10, 17
1892, 11, 27. Charles Edwin, h Rachel L., d bur Sugar Grove Cemetery near Wilmington

SNOWDEN, continued
1838, 9, 13. Richard & w, Mary, & ch, Sarah A., Ellen Jane, Henry Allen & Charles Edward, rocf Indian Spring MM, dtd 1838,8,8
1861, 8, 14. Amanda, form mbr Sandy Springs MM, Md., since laid down, recorded a mbr
1863, 9, 16. Rachel (form Linton) rpd mou
1867, 5, 15. Charles Edward recrq
1867, 11, 13. Sarah Amanda gct Miami MM
1890, 7, 16. Celia Kite recrq
1901, 12, 18. Rachel L. gct Wilmington MM
1904, 1, 13. Seth gct Wilmington MM
1914, 5, 13. Alta & w, Celia, & ch, Sarah, Edward, Myrtle, Arthur, Mary & Roy Tomkins, gct Wilmington MM

SQUIRE
1892, 7, 13. Eva H. recrq

SOUTHARD
1907, 4, 17. S. C. & w, Alice C., recrq
1912, 5, 15. Alice C. relrq

SPARKS
1844, 4, 17. Abi (form Farquhar) con mou
1846, 7, 15. Abi Sparks & ch, Benjamin & Francis Farquhar, gct Salem MM, Ind.
1852, 3, 17. Aby Sparks & s, Benjamin & Frances Farquhar, rocf Salem MM, dtd 1852,3,27
1869, 8, 18. Abi gct Wilmington MM

SPENCER
1879, 1, 15. John B. & w, Hannah, & ch, Deborah L., George E. & Harry E., recrq
1885, 12, 16. John B. relrq
1895, 6, 12. Deborah L. Dean (form Spencer) dropped from mbrp
1897, 9, 15. Hannah, George & Harry dropped from mbrp

SPOND
1881, 3, 16. Oscar [Spohn] recrq
1886, 5, 12. Clara recrq
1889, 11, 13. Oscar & w dropped from mbrp

SPRAY
1863, 4, 15. Henry prcf Caesar Creek MM, to m Mary Ann McMillen
1863, 5, 13. Henry rmt Mary Ann McMillan
1863, 8, 12. Mary Ann (form McMillan) gct Caesars Creek MM
1921, 2, 16. Bertha gct Wilmington MM, O.

SPROUSE
1894, 3, 14. David recrq
1907, 2, 12. Goldie & ch, James Ransom, Lucile Way, Russle Leonard & Harold Edwin, recrq
1910, 12, 14. David & w, Goldie, & ch, James Holson, Lucile May, Russell Leonard & Harold Edwin, relrq
1913, 4, 16. David & w, Goldie, & ch, James B., Russell, Lucille & Harold, recrq

SPURGEON
1901, 11, 13. Daniel B. & w, Lida, recrq
1907, 4, 17. Daniel & Goldie recrq
1907, 7, 17. Daniel & w, Lida, & gr ch, Daniel & Goldie, gct Wilmington MM, O.

STACKHOUSE
1895, 7, 19. James W. & w, Eliza E., & ch, Alice D., Selva, Hermon & Lottie, rocf Springfield MM

STAFFORD
1839, 9, 18. Sarah (form Williams) con mou
1853, 9, 11. Sarah gct Mississiniwa MM, Ind.

STALKER
1810, 2, 3. Nathan & w, Mary, & ch, Elenor & Lydia, rocf Mt. Pleasant MM, Va., dtd 1809,9,30

STANBROUGH
----, --, --. Evan b 1790,5,17; m Elizabeth ----- b 1795,2,5

Ch:		
	Mary	b 1814, 1, 14
	Solomon	" 1815, 6, 15
	Tobitha	" 1817, 1, 11
	Rachel	" 1818, 12, 7
	John	" 1820, 11, 18
	Francis Hester	" 1822, 12, 19
	William	" 1824, 12, 13
	Elizabeth	" 1827, 1, 1

----, --, --. Nehemiah b 1792,3,23; m Ruth ----- b 1798,9,25
Ch: Ann b 1816, 3, 3

----, --, --. William b 1803,5,30; m Rachel ----- b 1802,3,2

Ch:		
	Samuel	b 1823, 5, 14
	Isaac	" 1825, 1, 7
	Leah	" 1826, 10, 8
	Mary	" 1828, 10, 14
	Rachel	" 1830, 8, 18

1832, 4, 24. Solomon d bur Center MM

1810, 9, 1. Evan recrq
1811, 10, 5. Evan rmt Elizabeth Hester
1812, 10, 20. James [Stambrough] & fam gct West Grove MM, Ind.
1814, 8, 5. Nehemiah recrq
1815, 2, 5. Mary [Stanborough] (form Hodgens) con mou
1815, 5, 20. Solomon & w, Tabitha, & ch, Elizabeth Sarah Rachel William Mary Ann & Isaac, recrq
1815, 6, 11. Nehemiah rmt Ruth Hester
1817, 4, 19. Mary rmt Nathan Schooley
1821, 10, 20. James & w, Mary, & ch, Isaac, Jonathan & Phebe, gct West Grove MM, Ind.
1822, 4, 20. William gct Fairfield MM, to m Rachel Pike
1822, 8, 17. Rachel rocf Fairfield MM, dtd 1822,7,21
1823, 10, 18. Nehemiah & w, Ruth, & ch, Ann,

STANBROUGH, continued
Thomas, Francis & James, gct Milford MM, Ind.
1830, 12, 15. Mary Ann Gage (form Stanbrough) dis mou
1831, 1, 12. Evan & w, Elizabeth, & ch, Mary, Solomon, Tabitha, Rachel, John, Francis Hester, William, Elizabeth & Jane, gct Milford MM, Ind.
1834, 3, 12. Isaac con mou
1834, 8, 13. William & w, Rachel, & ch, Samuel, Leah, Mary, Rachel & Elizabeth, gct Fairfield MM, Ind.
1834, 8, 13. Elizabeth gct Fairfield MM, Ind.
1834, 8, 13. Isaac gct Fairfield MM, Ind.
1834, 8, 13. Tabitha gct Fairfield MM, Ind.

STANLEY
----, --, --. Anthony & Hannah
Ch: William b 1801, 8, 30
John " 1803, 3, 29
Ruth " 1805, 2, 19
Sarah " 1807, 5, 3
Micajah " 1810, 2, 3
Isaac " 1812, 3, 15
Samuel " 1814, 11, 24 d 1816, 8,17 bur Center, O.
Rebecca b 1817, 11, 11
Elizabeth " 1821, 7, 26
----, --, --. William b 1801,3,30; m Judith ----- b 1808,2,25
Ch: Josiah Elwood b 1826, 9, 22

1814, 7, 2. Anthony & w, Hannah, & ch, William, John, Ruth, Sarah, Micajah & Isaac, rocf Fairfield MM, dtd 1814,6,25
1817, 2, 15. Cert rec for James & fam endorsed to Miami MM
1819, 5, 15. Hannah rocf Fairfield MM
1823, 9, 20. Ruth Morris (form Stanley) con mou
1825, 11, 19. Judith (form Bailey) con mou
1826, 1, 21. John con mou
1826, 11, 18. Sarah rmt Jesse Hinds
1830, 8, 18. Anthony & w, Hannah, & ch, Micajah, Isaac, Rebecca & Elizabeth, gct White Lick MM, Ind.
1832, 11, 14. John gct Vermillion MM, Ill.
1837, 4, 12. William & w, Judith, & ch, Josiah Elwood, James Edwin, Susannah & Hannah, gct Vermillion MM, Ill.

STANTON
----, --, --. William & Martha
Ch: Jesse b 1808, 6, 24
Hiram " 1810, 10, 25
Ann " 1812, 10, 23
William m 2nd Margaret -----
Ch: Mary P. b 1815, 8, 27
Rachel " 1818, 1, 15
James " 1820, 8, 22
1852, 12, 7. Samuel d ae 76
1807, 10, 3. William rmt Ruth Faulkner
1808, 7, 2. Frederick rocf Upper MM, Va.
1810, 10, 6. Frederick gct Miami MM, to m
1811, 8, 3. Hannah rocf Miami MM, dtd 1811, 7,24
1812, 7, 4. Frederick & w gct Miami MM
1814, 10, 1. William gct Clear Creek MM, to m
1815, 4, 15. Margaret rocf Clear Creek MM, dtd 1815,1,27
1817, 8, 16. Latham rocf Dover MM, N. C., dtd 1817,1,18
1823, 8, 16. William dis mou
1825, 9, 17. Samuel Jones, minor under care of Samuel Stanton, recrq
1826, 1, 21. William rst
1826, 2, 18. Ann gct Springborough MM
1828, 11, 12. William dis jH
1830, 2, 20. William con mou (H)
1831, 1, 18. Jesse F. dis mou
1832, 5, 16. Ann rocf Springborough MM, dtd 1832,3,20
1833, 4, 17. Sarah rocf Dover MM, dtd 1832, 10,18
1833, 6, 12. Hiram & w, Sarah, & s, John, gct New Garden MM, Ind.
1834, 4, 16. Mary Rison (form Stanton) dis mou & jas
1834, 5, 14. Ann gct New Garden MM, Ind.
1836, 8, 17. James gct Spiceland MM, Ind.
1838, 12, 12. James rocf Spiceland MM, Ind., dtd 1838,11,21
1839, 1, 16. Cert rec for Jesse & fam from Center MM, N. C. (returned)
1839, 9, 18. James gct Caesars Creek MM
1842, 9, 14. Rachel rmt Lewis Johnson
1848, 4, 12. James & w, Dinah, & ch, Susannah, rocf Dover MM, dtd 1848,2,16
1849, 4, 18. White Lick MM was granted permission to rst Jesse F.
1849, 5, 16. James & w, Dinah, & dt, Susannah, gct Fairfield MM, Ind.

STARBUCK
----, --, --. Gayer b 1777,8,10; m Susannah ----- b 1780,9,2
Ch: Mary b 1808, 2, 12
Hezekiah " 1810, 3, 9 d 1811, 2, 5
Samuel " 1812, 9, 27
Clarissa " 1815, 5, 6
Joel " 1817, 7, 13
Jesse G. " 1819, 10, 8

1808, 1, 2. Gayer & w, Susannah, & ch, Abigail, Hannah, Moses & Achsah, rocf New Garden MM, N. C., dtd 1807,8,29
1817, 8, 21. Abigail rmt James Wright
1824, 7, 17. Achsah Fisher (form Starbuck) con mou
1913, 1, 15. Charles & w, Estella, & ch, Hubert & Pauline, rocf Springfield MM
1913, 2, 12. Hazel & Frankie recrq
1913, 3, 12. Earnest rocf Dover MM

STARBUCK, continued
1913, 3, 12. Gladys, w Earnest, recrq
1916, 4, 12. Charles & w, Stella, & ch, Herbert & Pauline, gct Dover MM

STARR
1902, 2, 12. Mary Etta Timberlake gct Wilmington MM, O.

STEPHENS
1839, 8, 14. Hannah (form Faulkner) dis mou

STEWART
1808, 3, 5. Rebecca [Stuart] (form Clark) dis mou
1895, 2, 13. Joseph & s, Arthur, recrq
1901, 4, 17. Arthur recrq

STINGLEY
1880, 10, 13. William Allison [Stingly] & w, Alice, recrq
1885, 6, 17. Calvin & Albert recrq
1886, 4, 14. Alice dropped from mbrp
1891, 6, 17. Albert [Stingly] gct Cesars Creek MM
1893, 11, 15. Mary J. rocf Cesars Creek MM
1896, 2, 12. Gilead & Nancy recrq
1910, 2, 16. William & Elizabeth recrq
1913, 2, 12. Alie, Luther & Clarence recrq
1920, 6, 17. Charles recrq

STOOPS
1878, 9, 18. Sarah Alcinda gct Richland MM, Ind.
1905, 2, 5. Sina Pennington (form Stoopes) gct Wilmington MM, O.

STOUT
----, -- --. John d 1836,2,26 ae 68y 2m 21d bur Center; m Ann ----- d 1834,9,3 ae 65y 1m 21d bur Center
Ch: Margaret b 1789, 7, 22
Geo. " 1791, 9, 11
Dinah " 1794, 3, 3
Mary " 1797, 3, 16
Sarah " 1799, 6, 23
Stephen " 1802, 9, 21
Anne " 1806, 2, 26
John " 1809, 2, 24
Elihu " 1814, 8, 19 d 1818, 1,26

1808, 6, 4. Isaac & w, Susannah, & ch, Sarah, Jesse, Phebe, Rebeckah, Lydia & Matilda, rocf Lost Creek MM, Tenn., dtd 1807,10,31
1808, 2, 6. Margaret rmt Enoch Wickersham
1812, 1, 4. Dinah Wilds (form Stout) con mou
1813, 4, 3. Mary dis disunity
1817, 8, 16. Jesse gct Caesars Creek MM, to m
1817, 12, 20. George con mou
1818, 4, 18. Rosanna rocf Caesars Creek MM, dtd 1818,2,27
1818, 6, 20. Phebe recrq
1819, 12, 18. David gct New Garden MM, Ind.
1820, 1, 15. Sarah Miars (form Stout) con mou
1823, 1, 18. Stephen con mou
1823, 10, 18. Anna rocf Springfield MM, Ind.
1826, 1, 21. George & w, Phebe, & ch, Hannah, Lucinda, Naomi & John, gct Dover MM
1827, 5, 19. Anne rmt William H. Harrison
1828, 5, 17. Stephen & w, Anna, & ch, Eliza, Micajah & Jesse, gct Dover MM
1828, 12, 17. John Jr. rmt Susannah Kinsey
1829, 4, 18. Isaac & w, Susannah, & ch, Isaac & Isaiah, recrq (H)
1829, 7, 18. Mary & Martha recrq (H)
1831, 3, 16. John Jr. gct Dover MM, to m Mary B. Baily
1832, 9, 12. Mary B. rocf Dover MM, dtd 1832,6,14
1834, 11, 13. Mary Stubbs (form Stout) con mou (H)
1838, 2, 14. John dis jas
1838, 4, 18. Mary B. dis jas
1840, 6, 18. Isaac H. con mou (H)
1840, 7, 16. Isaac H. gct Miami MM (H)
1841, 3, 17. Benjamin Schooley gct Mississiniwa MM, Ind., to m Lucinda Stout
1844, 4, 18. Isaiah con mou (H)
1852, 3, 18. Isaac, Jr. gct Miami MM (H)
1852, 8, 19. Isaac's cert returned by Miami MM because his mbrp was already there (H)

STRATTON
----, --, --. Joseph b 1770,2,6; m Dosha ---- b 1773,2,5
Ch: David b 1793, 11, 23
Susannah " 1795, 11, 2
Nancy " 1797, 11, 10
Joseph " 1800, 1, 9
Micajah " 1802, 1, 22
Esther " 1804, 2, 4
Benjamin " 1812, 4, 26
----, --, --. David b 1793,11,23; m Ruth -----
Ch: Stephen T. b 1818, 10, 1
Amanda " 1827, 3, 1
Edward Linch " 1829, 9, 17
David m 2nd Harriett HINMAN b 1807,7,1
Ch: Letitia Emaline b 1834, 7, 29
Marthy Emily " 1837, 3, 31
Joseph Daniel " 1839, 4, 9
Benjamin Clark " 1841, 4, 2
David William " 1843, 4, 10
1839, 1, 13. Martha Emily d
----, --, --. Ruth bur Lytles Creek

1811, 3, 2. Joseph & w, Dosha, & ch, David, Dusannah, Nancy, Joseph, Micajah & Esther, rocf South River MM, Va., dtd 1810,

STRATTON, continued
11,10
1811, 4, 6. Mahlon & w, Sarah, & ch, Levy, David, Susannah, Mary & Mahlon, rocf South River MM, Va., dtd 1807,10,14
1813, 1, 2. Susanna rmt Thomas Thatcher
1814, 9, 3. Nancy rmt Joshua Moore
1815, 5, 20. David gct Cincinnati MM
1816, 11, 16. David rmt Ruth Thatcher
1817, 10, 18. David rocf Cincinnati MM, O., dtd 1817,8,21
1819, 1, 16. Caleb prcf Darby Creek MM, dtd 1819,12,19, to m Jane Faulkner
1819, 2, 20. Caleb rmt Jane Faulkner
1829, 2, 18. David dis jH
1829, 4, 18. Harriet & dt, Amanda, recrq (H)
1833, 4, 17. Sarah rocf Dover MM, dtd 1832,10, 18
1833, 10, 16. Caleb & w, Jane, & ch, Ruth, Eliza, Jesse F. & Thomas A., gct White Lick MM, Ind.
1840, 11, 18. Stephen [Stratten] dis mou
1844, 4, 18. Stephen dis mou (H)
1849, 8, 16. Amanda Doan (form Stratton) dis mou (H)
1851, 8, 14. Lewis Underwood gct Westfield MM, to m Sarah B. Stratton (H)
1855, 5, 17. Edward [Stratten] dis mcd (H)

STRICKEL
1831, 9, 14. Rebecca (form Farquhar) con mou
1838, 8, 15. Rebecca [Strickle] dis disunity

STROUD
1839, 5, 15. Jacob & w, Ann M., & ch, Sarah B., Mary D. & Emily H., rocf Marlborough MM, dtd 1839,3,26
1839, 5, 15. Eleanor rocf Marlborough MM, dtd 1839,1,29
1839, 11, 13. Parvin Wright prcf Short Creek MM, dtd 1839,10,22, to m Ellen Stroud
1839, 11, 13. Ellen rmt Parvin Wright
1841, 11, 17. Sally B. gct Short Creek MM
1843, 5, 17. Jacob & w, Ann M., & ch, Mary B., Emily H. & William, gct Short Creek MM

STUBBS
1822, 6, 15. Jacob Doan gct Miami MM, to m Hannah Stubbs
1834, 11, 13. Mary (form Stout) con mou (H)
1835, 12, 17. Mary gct Elk MM (H)

STUDWAN
1815, 10, 21. Sarah recrq

STUMP
1844, 11, 13. Lydia (form Hiatt) dis mou
1845, 12, 18. Lydia (form Hiatt) dis mou (H)
1915, 6, 16. Rachel & dt, Mary Charlotte, relrq

SWOPE
1904, 12, 14. Sarah dropped from mbrp

SYMCOCK
1817, 2, 15. John rocf Mt. Pleasant MM, Va., dtd 1816,10,26

TAYLOR
----, --, --. Isral d about 1824; m Mary ----- b 1787,9,29

Ch: Hannah	b 1816, 1, 30
Maria	" 1817, 2, 8
Sarah	" 1818, 12, 9
Susanna	" 1822, 6, 17

1822, 11, 27. Israel d bur Center
----, --, --. Jesse b 1798,2,20; m Deborah McMILLAN b 1801,12,4

Ch: Israel	b 1825, 5, 5
David	" 1826, 6, 22
Jacob	" 1828, 5, 5
Jonathan	" 1830, 5, 18 d 1830, 6,13
Jesse Jr.	" 1831, 9, 20 " 1833,11,30
Hannah N.	" 1834, 3, 13
Milton	" 1836, 5, 13
Deborah E.	" 1839, 3, 20
Mary L.	" 1841, 1, 28
Ann Eliza	" 1812, 12, 6 d 1844, 8,16 bur Chester

1828, 8, 12. Hannah, w Jacob, d bur Center
1838, 11, 29. Hannah m William F. BALLARD (H)
1853, 3, 31. Jesse Frank, s Isaac, b

1813, 12, 4. Jacob & w, Hannah, & ch, Elizabeth, Jesse, Naomi & Hannah, rocf Center MM, Pa., dtd 1813,10,16
1813, 12, 4. Israel rocf Center MM, Pa., dtd 1813,10,16
1815, 5, 20. Israel rmt Mary Sexton
1815, 7, 14. Elizabeth rmt Joel Wright
1818, 7, 18. Kinchin recrq
1822, 5, 18. Hannah L. rmt Samuel Buttweworth
1823, 2, 15. Jacob dis disunity
1824, 5, 15. Jesse rmt Deborah McMillan
1828, 2, 16. Richard & w, Lucy, & ch, Hannah & Emily, rocf Dover MM, dtd 1827,10,6
1829, 2, 18. Mary dis jH
1830, 6, 16. Jacob gct Springborough MM, to m Ann Mullen
1830, 11, 17. Ann rocf Springborough MM
1831, 6, 15. Jacob & w, Ann, gct Springborough MM
1833, 4, 17. Naomi gct Silver Creek MM, Ind.
1834, 10, 15. Lucy Bray (form Taylor) dis mou
1839, 12, 19. Mary & dt, Sarah & Susan, gct Miami MM (H)
1840, 10, 14. Mariah McCowen (form Taylor) dis mou & joining Separatists
1840, 11, 18. Hannah Ballard (form Taylor) dis mou & joining Separatists
1841, 11, 17. Susannah Crews (form Taylor) dis mou & jH
1846, 1, 14. Sarah dis joining Separatists
1849, 12, 12. Israel con mou

TAYLOR, continued
1851, 11, 12. Jacob gct Spiceland MM, Ind., to m Sarah Evans
1852, 4, 14. Sarah E. rocf Spiceland MM, Ind., dtd 1852,3,25
1852, 6, 16. David M. gct Cincinnati MM
1852, 6, 16. Israel gct Miami MM
1854, 4, 12. Jacob & w, Sarah E., & s, Jesse Frank, gct Spiceland MM, Ind.
1858, 10, 13. Deborah E. rmt Joseph Doan Jr.
1860, 5, 16. Mary C. Wickersham (form Taylor) rpd mou
1860, 6, 13. Jesse & w, Deborah, gct Bridgeport MM, Ind.
1860, 11, 14. Hannah L. gct Bridgeport MM,Ind.
1861, 5, 18. Milton M. gct Spiceland MM, Ind., to m Emily Gordon
1861, 12, 18. Milton M. gct Spiceland MM, Ind.
1866, 6, 13. John recrq
1907, 2, 12. Joseph & w, Minnie, & ch, Roy & Carl, recrq
1910, 2, 16. Rosco recrq
1913, 2, 12. Carl & Roy transferred from associate to active mbrp
1919, 3, 12. Roscoe dropped from mbrp

TERRELL
1880, 9, 15. Elias recrq

THATCHER
1808, 1, 2. Mary rmt Eli Anderson
1808, 2, 6. Ruth rocf Hopewell MM, dtd 1807,3,2, endorsed by Miami MM, 1808,1,14
1811, 1, 5. Thomas gct White Water MM, Ind., to m
1812, 10, 3. Thomas dis disunity
1813, 1, 2. Thomas rmt Susanna Stratton
1813, 6, 1. David recrq
1814, 6, 4. David con mou
1815, 5, 20. David gct Cincinnati MM
1816, 11, 16. Ruth rmt David Stratton
1820, 12, 16. Joseph rmt Elizabeth Linton
1835, 8, 12. Joseph Sr. con mou
1836, 1, 13. Joseph Jr. gct Springfield MM
1837, 7, 12. Joseph [Thacher] & w, Elizabeth, & ch, Jesse, Ruth, William, David, Hannah, Thomas, Stephen & John,gct Springfield MM
1860, 6, 13. Emer H. McMillen gct Springfield MM, to m Susan Thatcher

THISTLETHWAITE
1848, 10, 19. Thomas Birdsall gct White Water MM to m Mary B. Thistlethwaite

THOMAS
----, --, --. Isaac B. & Jane M.
Ch: Thamsin b 1834, 12, 13
Isaac L. " 1839, 2, 12
1836, 10, 19. Mary m John WHITSON (H)
----, --, --. Lewis b 1838,3,30; m Terressa ----- b 1830,10,30
Ch: Wm. A. b 1865, 9, 11
Elmore A. " 1867, 5, 3
1817, 9, 20. John rocf Dunings Creek MM, dtd 1817,4,16
1817, 9, 20. Jane & s, Robert, rocf Dunnings Creek MM, dtd 1817,4,16
1817, 9, 20. Ann & Jane rocf Dunnings Creek MM
1817, 12, 20. Lydia rocf Dunnings Creek MM
1818, 9, 19. Ann rpd mou
1819, 7, 17. Ann gct Miami MM
1821, 1, 20. Esther & ch, Jane, Edward R. & Ellis, recrq
1821, 3, 17. Lydia rmt Samuel Rich
1824, 6, 19. Ann & ch, Chalkley & Mary, rocf Miami MM, dtd 1824,5,26
1824, 9, 18. Elizabeth (form Bayliff) dis mou
1828, 5, 17. Robert prcf Dover MM, to m Almedia Bailey
1828, 6, 21. Robert rmt Almeda Bailey
1828, 12, 17. Susanna (form Bailiff) dis mou & jH
1832, 8, 15. Almedia & ch, Mary Ann & Uriah, gct Dover MM
1832, 12, 15. Isaac B. & w, Jane, rocf Hopewell MM, Va., dtd 1832,10,4(H)
1836, 3, 17. Mary rocf Hopewell MM, dtd 1835,5,7 (H)
1839, 1, 16. Edward prcf Dover MM, to m Huldah Jones
1839, 2, 13. Edward rmt Huldah Jones
1839, 6, 12. Huldah (form Jones) gct Dover MM
1852, 5, 13. Isaac B. & w, Jane, & ch, Tamson M. & Isaac L., gct White Water MM,Ind.
1875, 3, 17. Lewis & w, Terressa, & ch, William A. & Ellmer A., recrq
1884, 11, 12. Lewis relrq
1888, 2, 15. Lewis recrq
1891, 11, 18. E. A. relrq
1902, 4, 16. Lewis & w, Teressa, relrq
1904, 12, 14. Alpha dropped from mbrp

THOMPSON
1839, 5, 15. Martha (form Thornburg) con mou
1841, 2, 17. Martha gct Cherry Grove MM, Ind.
1903, 2, 18. Lulu recrq
1906, 2, 14. Harry recrq

THORN
1808, 1, 2. William rocf Short Creek MM, dtd 1809,12,19
1808, 3, 5. William rmt Rachel Embree

THORNBURGH
----, --, --. Richard & Judith
Ch: Shadrach b 1801, 10, 24
Abigail " 1804, 5, 11
Thomas " 1806, 8, 10
Martha " 1808, 12, 5
Mary " 1810, 10, 5
Jonathan " 1812, 1, 10
----, --, --. Joel & Dinah
Ch: Eli P. b 1819, 8, 19
James A. " 1822, 10, 8

THORNBURGH, Joel & Dinah, continued
Ch: William b 1824, 11, 19
Josiah " 1828, 7, 28
1830, 11, 27. Richard d
----, --, --. Eli & Sarah
Ch: Naomi P. b 1833, 1, 2
Jemimah
Ann " 1841, 5, 6
Dinah " 1843, 8, 1
----, --, --. Thomas & Sarah
Ch: Sarah Emely
b 1835, 4, 18
Malissa
Jane " 1837, 5, 12
1837, 10, 5. Judith d ae 29y 8m 12d bur New Hope
1850, 5, 17. Dinah, w Joel, d ae 68y 4m bur New Hope
1861, 5, 3. Joel d ae 84y 1m 21d bur New Hope
1865, 11, 16. William N. b
1867, 5, 19. Joel [Thornburg] b
1867, 6, 10. Emmazetta [Thornburg] b
1899, 12, 30. Joel d bur Xenia

1808, 8, 8. Richard [Thornberry] & w, Judith, & ch, Shadrick, Abigail & Thomas, rocf New Garden MM, N. C., dtd 1807,10,31
1817, 12, 20. Joel & ch, Jane Thomas Judith Jemimah Nancy Betsy & Joel, recrq
1818, 2, 21. Dinah rocf Miami MM
1818, 4, 18. Rhoda [Thornborough] (form Johnson) con mou
1822, 2, 16. Jane Smith (form Thornburgh) dis mou
1829, 6, 17. Shadrack dis disunity
1833, 6, 12. Nancy Compton (form Thornburgh) con mou
1834, 1, 15. Thomas gct Dover MM, to m Nancy Moorman
1834, 11, 12. Elizabeth Ann Compton (form Thornburgh) con mou
1835, 7, 15. Nancy Ann rocf Dover MM, dtd 1835,3,19
1837, 5, 17. Jonathan dis disunity
1838, 5, 16. Eli rmt Sarah Painter
1839, 2, 13. Thomas [Thornburg] & w, Nancy, & ch, Sarah Emily & Melissa Jane, gct Dover MM
1839, 2, 13. Mary Hodgson (form Thornburgh) con mou
1839, 5, 15. Martha Thompson (form Thornburg) con mou
1840, 8, 12. Abigail Pitcher (form Thornburgh) dis mou
1841, 2, 17. Judith gct Westfield MM, Ind.
1841, 5, 12. Thomas dis disunity
1844, 5, 15. Eli [Thornburg] & w Sarah, & ch, Naomi, Jemima Ann & Dinah, gct Springborough MM
1850, 9, 18. Mordecai Walker prcf Springfield MM, to m Jemima Thornburg
1850, 10, 16. Jemima rmt Mordecai Walker
1851, 2, 12. Jemima Walker (form Thornburgh) gct Springfield MM
1851, 4, 16. Josiah rmt Lydia S. Painter
1864, 9, 14. Josiah & w, Lydia S., gct Wabash MM Ind.
1868, 12, 16. Joel [Thornburg] con mou
1870, 9, 14. William [Thornburg] rpd mou
1917, 3, 14. Raymond B. [Thornburg] rocf Fairfield MM

TIBBLES
1856, 2, 13. Mary Ann (form Paxon) dis mou

TIMBERLAKE
----, --, --. Alfred b 1817,4,12; m Phebe ---- b 1821,5,6
Ch: Mary B. b 1841, 4, 11 d 1866,12,23 bur Center
Eliza D. " 1843, 5, 9
Caroline " 1845, 1, 15 " 1896, 2,16 bur Center
Edward " 1846, 12, 9
Susannah E." 1849, 4, 17
Annie
Elizabeth " 1852, 11, 9
Charles " 1854, 9, 25
Evaline " 1857, 10, 2
Rebecca
Emily " 1859, 7, 7
Marietta " 1867, 6, 8
1860, 1, 1. Richard d bur Center
1900, --, --. Alfred d bur near Richmond
1901, 4, 4. Phebe d bur near Richmond

1810, 5, 5. Richard prcf Fairfield MM, to m Mary Wright
1810, 5, 5. Richard rmt Mary Wright
1810, 8, 4. Elizabeth & Mary gct Fairfield MM
1837, 5, 17. Jonathan rmt Catharine F. Mabee
1837, 8, 16. Catharine F. gct Springfield MM
1839, 5, 15. Alfred prcf Clear Creek MM, to m Phebe Doan
1839, 6, 12. Alfred rmt Phebe Doan
1839, 8, 14. Alfred rocf Clear Creek MM, dtd 1839,7,23
1844, 4, 17. Alfred & w, Phebe, & ch, Mary B. & Eliza D., gct Dover MM
1849, 12, 12. Alfred & w, Phebe, & ch, Mary B., Eliza D. Caroline, Edward & Susannah E., rocf Clear Creek MM
1856, 4, 16. Richard rocf Springfield MM
1863, 9, 16. Matthew Charles prcf White Water MM, Ind., to m Eliza D. Timberlake
1863, 10, 14. Eliza D. rmt Matthew Charles
1865, 4, 12. Franklin Moore prcf Sugar River MM, Ind., to m Mary B. Timberlake
1865, 5, 17. Mary B. rmt Franklin Moore
1868, 7, 15. Edward gct White Water MM, Ind.
1873, 12, 17. Susannah E. gct White Water MM

TOLBAT
1812, 2, 1. John & w, Mary, rocf Mt. Pleasant MM, Va., dtd 1811,8,31

TOMLINSON
1861, 4, 18. Paul con mcd (H)
1861, 4, 18. Rachel Daniels (form Tomlinson) con mcd (H)
1876, 5, 17. Mary Jane & ch, Nellie E., Eber J. & Lizzie Irene, gct Smyrna MM, Ia.

TONG
1830, 8, 18. Eliza (form Fallis) dis mou

TOWEL
1815, 11, 18. Ruth (form Harvey) con mou
1816, 5, 18. Ruth gct Lick Creek MM
1818, 3, 21. Rebecca rocf Lick Creek MM
1818, 5, 16. Rebecca rmt Joshua Hadley

TOWNSEND
1833, 5, 15. Timothy Kirk gct Allum Creek MM, to m Hannah Townsend
1839, 2, 13. Abigail recrq
1842, 12, 14. Catharine B., Daton H. & Josiah M., ch Abigail, recrq
1850, 4, 17. Abigail & ch, Dayton H. & Jonah H., gct Newbury MM
1850, 4, 17. Catharine B. gct Newbury MM

TROUT
1890, 10, 15. W. Alfred gct Wilmington MM

TUCKER
1913, 11, 12. Margaret, Nellie I. & Anna B. recrq
1917, 4, 18. Margaret, Nellie J. & Anne B. gct Ogden MM

TURNER
1815, 11, 17. Elijah b
----, --, --. John b 1849,9,16; m Margaret E. ----- b 1848,12,23
Ch: Elijah H. b 1870, 10, 26
Mary Emily " 1872, 10, 16
Frances L. " 1875, 6, 17
Eber W. " 1878, 7, 15
1899, 5, --. Elijah d

1807, 6, 6. Mary rocf Lost Creek MM, dtd 1807,2,28
1828, 9, 17. Ann (form Johnson) dis mou
1828, 11, 12. Anna dis jH
1862, 7, 16. Elijah recrq
1871, 4, 12. Margaret E. rpd mou
1871, 5, 17. John recrq
1884, 4, 16. John & w, Margaret, & ch, Elijah H., Mary Emmily, Fannie Leura, Eber Walter, Priscilla & Amy, gct Wilmington MM

UNDERWOOD
----, --, --. Amos b 1786, 8, 18; m Mary SHERK b 1791,9,16 (H)
Ch: Reuben b 1814, 10, 17
Isaac " 1816, 9, 30
John " 1818, 10, 26
Zephariah " 1820, 11, 10
Amos b 1823, 3, 5
Lewis " 1825, 3, 16
Asenath " 1827, 4, 24
Thomas Elwood " 1829, 8, 22
Priscilla Jane " 1831, 12, 10
William " 1834, 6, 5
Elihu " 1839, 2, 17
1843, 7, 27. Reuben d bur Center
1847, 12, 13. Mary d bur Center
1850, 3, 11. Thomas E. d bur Center
1850, 5, 18. Amos d bur Center
1851, 5, 22. Priscilla Jane m James MOORE
1867, 4, 11. Amos d bur Center
1878, 11, 13. Isaac d
1887, 2, 27. Lewis d
1893, 3, 4. William d
1899, 2, 6. Anna d bur Center
1900, 4, 17. Zephaniah d bur Miami
1818, 7, 18. Ezekiel, Rebecca, Hannah & Deborah, rocf Center MM, Pa., dtd 1817,11, 15 (ch William)
1824, 10, 16. Hannah rmt Joseph Wilson
1826, 4, 15. Rebecca dis disunity
1826, 4, 15. Ezekiel dis mou
1826, 7, 15. Mary, w Amos, & ch, Rueben, Isaac, John, Zephaniah, Amos & Lewis, rocf Carmel MM on Elk Run, dtd 1826,5,20
1826, 7, 15. Rebecca & Mary rocf Carmell MM
1829, 3, 18. Rebecca gct Carmel MM, O.
1829, 3, 18. Mary gct Carmel MM, O.
1831, 6, 15. Deborah Vore (form Underwood) dis mou
1832, 9, 15. Amos & ch, Asenath H., Thomas Elwood & Priscilla Jane, recrq (H)
1832, 9, 15. Rebecca rocf Carmal MM, dtd 1832,6,16 (H)
1832, 10, 17. Rebecca rocf Carmel MM, dtd 1832,7,21
1832, 10, 17. Mary rocf Carmel MM, dtd 1832,7, 21
1842, 12, 14. Jane (form Oren) dis mou
1847, 2, 18. John con mou (H)
1847, 8, 19. Isaac rocf Carmel MM, dtd 1847, 4,17 (H)
1848, 9, 14. Amos con mou (H)
1850, 1, 17. Amos gct Fall Creek MM, O., to m Priscilla Lewis (H)
1850, 4, 18. Amos gct Fall Creek MM (H)
1851, 8, 14. Lewis gct Westfield MM, to m Sarah B. Stratton (H)
1852, 9, 16. Asenath Baily (form Underwood) dis mcd (H)
1853, 7, 14. Amos & w, Priscilla, rocf Clear Creek MM, dtd 1853,6,18 (H)
1854, 3, 16. Lewis & John gct Fall Creek MM, Ind. (H)
1854, 4, 13. Amos & w, Priscilla, & ch, William & Elihu, gct Miami MM (H)
1854, 6, 15. Cert rec for Mary Ann & Rebecca Jane from Carmel MM, dtd 1853,12,17, endorsed to Miami MM (H)

UNDERWOOD, continued
1856, 8, 14. Isaac con mcd (H)
1861, 9, 19. Isaac gct Miami MM (H)
1874, 4, 15. Anne recrq
1874, 4, 15. Phebe A. recrq

UNTHANK
1834, 3, 12. Richard H. Dillon gct New Garden MM, Ind., to m Elizabeth Unthank

VANHORN
1807, 8, 1. Joanna & dt, Rebecca, rocf Bush MM, S. C., dtd 1807,4,25, endorsed by Miami MM, 1807,8,13
1807, 10, 3. Joanna rmt George Haworth
1828, 7, 16. Rebecca gct Vermillion MM, Ill.

VANMETER
1846, 6, 17. Hannah Ann(form Engle) dis mou

VANTRESS
----, --, --. Calvin R. & Nancy
Ch: Nancy H. b 1879, 11, 14
Willie R. d 1892, 8,18

1853, 11, 16. Deborah [Vantres] recrq
1879, 2, 12. Calvin & w, Lydia, & ch rocf Ackworth MM, Ia.
1906, 3, 14. Calvin gct Wilmington MM

VERMILLION
1887, 3, 16. Ella recrq
1894, 1, 17. Ella [Vermilian] relrq

VESTAL
1803, 6, 29. Edith b
1827, 9, 9. Elizabeth b
1835, 12, 17. Rachel b
1839, 12, 11. Spencer b
1841, 12, 9. Olive E. b

1810, 3, 3. Elizabeth rmt Peter Dicks
1824, 2, 21. Cert rec for Sarah from Cane Creek MM, N. C., endorsed to Cherry Grove MM, Ind.
1826, 2, --. Edith (form Ballard) con mou
1842, 11, 16. John, Elizabeth C., Minerva Jane, Clark, Rachel, Spencer W. & Olive Emily, ch Samuel & Edith, recrq
1860, 5, 16. Minerva Jane Barrett (form Vestal) rpd mou
1860, 6, 13. Elizabeth Dougherty (form Vestal) rpd mou
1869, 7, 14. Spencer H. rpd mou

VICKERS
1814, 8, 6. Celia & ch, John, Amelia, Joseph, Mary Ann & Ruth Jane, gct Caesars Creek MM
1816, 11, 16. William dis disunity
1823, 1, 18. Green Plain MM was given permission to rst William

VORE
1827, 7, 21. Jane (form Witson) dis mou
1831, 6, 15. Deborah (form Underwood) dis mou

VOTAW
1837, 7, 12. Hannah D. & Mary Ann, ch Benjamin, rocf Salem MM, O., dtd 1835,11,12, endorsed by Chester MM, Ind., 1837,3,22
1838, 2, 14. Phebe & dt, Hannah & Phebe, rocf Salem MM, dtd 1837,8,23
1840, 10, 14. Phebe & dt, Hannah & Phebe, gct Chester MM, Ind.
1846, 1, 14. Isaac prcf White River MM, Ind., to m Phebe Compton
1846, 2, 18. Isaac rmt Phebe Compton
1846, 5, 13. Phebe C. gct White River MM, Ind.
1846, 9, 16. Hannah gct Mississiniwa MM,Ind.
1848, 5, 17. Mary Ann gct Mississiniwa MM, Ind.

WADE
1873, 7, 16. James A. [Weade] recrq
1885, 12, 16. James relrq

WALES
1838, 11, 20. William Birdsall gct Miami MM, to m Ruth Wales (H)

WALKER
----, --, --. William & Martha
Ch: Mordecai b 1801, 1, 13
Azael " 1802, 11, 21
David F. " 1804, 12, 20
Phebe F. " 1807, 4, 21
Eli " 1809, 10, 22
Asa " 1812, 7, 6
Simpson " 1815, 8, 13
----, --, --. Azel b 1774,4,21; m Hannah ----- b 1782,2,1
Ch: William b 1803, 3, 17
Josiah Jackson " 1805, 3, 16
Lewis M. " 1807, 10, 10
Joseph S. " 1809, 7, 18
Rachel " 1811, 7, 7
Ruth " 1813, 8, 7
Elijah " 1815, 3, 31
Betsy Ann " 1818, 5, 1
Abel " 1819, 7, 28
Samuel " 1821, 10, 6
1808, 5, 26. Jemima b
1822, 3, --. Eleanor b
1824, 10, 21. Azel b
1830, 4, 1. Mordecai d bur Center
1835, 5, 7. Azel d bur Clinton Co., O.
1843, 10, 15. Elijah d
1845, 11, 3. Mary A. b
1855, 7, 15. Hannah d
----, --, --. Mordecai D. b 1846,12,17; m Deborah S. ----- b 1845,3,1 d 1907,10,3 ae 62y 9m bur Wilmington

WALKER, Mordecai D. & Deborah S., continued
Ch: Elizabeth d 1860,10,22
bur Lylles Creek
Frank W. b 1867, 8, 21
Alpheus D. " 1872, 6, 10
1872, 8, 25. Louis M. d bur Sugar Grove
1873, 8, 16. Josiah Jackson d
1875, 8, 12. Rachel d bur Sugar Grove
1875, 8, 22. Ruth d bur Sugar Grove
1885, 3, 5. Azel d
1886, 1, 28. Betsy d bur Sugar Grove
1886, 8, 31. William d bur Sugar Grove
1887, 8, 10. Joseph S. d bur Sugar Grove
1888, 6, 12. Mordecai d
1897, 2, 20. Abel d bur Sugar Grove

1813, 6, 1. Mordecai & w, Rachel, rocf Miami MM, dtd 1813,4,28
1819, 3, 20. Mordecai Jr. gct Miami MM
1820, 11, 18. Mordecai Jr. rocf Miami MM, dtd 1820,9,27
1823, 8, 16. Mordecai Jr. gct Springfield MM, to m Mary Green
1824, 1, 17. Mary rocf Springfield MM
1825, 3, 19. Azel gct Fairfield MM, to m Elizabeth Robinson
1825, 11, 19. Azel & w, Eve, & ch, Maria-Ann Henry Margaret John William Rachel & Deborah, rocf Lick Creek MM, dtd 1824,11,20, endorsed by Miami MM 1825,10,26
1826, 5, 23. Elizabeth P. rocf Fairfield MM, dtd 1826,4,29
1828, 10, 15. Hannah dis jH
1828, 11, 12. Azel dis jH
1829, 12, 16. David dis disunity
1830, 11, 17. Rebecca (form Wall) dis mou
1831, 3, 16. Mordecai & w, Mary, & ch, Azel & Rhoda G., gct Springfield MM
1832, 12, 12. Phebe F. rmt John Hunt
1833, 2, 13. Eli dis mou
1833, 7, 17. Josiah J. dis joining Separatists
1834, 6, 18. Rachel & Ruth dis jH
1834, 10, 15. William & w, Martha, & ch, John Simpson, Lewis & Rachel, gct Caesars Creek MM
1835, 5, 13. Azel Jr. & w, Elizabeth P., & ch, Edward B., Isaac, Cyrus, John R. & Eliza Ann, gct Springfield MM
1835, 8, 12. Asa con mou
1836, 2, 17. Asa gct Springfield MM
1838, 5, 16. William dis disunity
1838, 7, 16. Lewis M. dis mou
1838, 9, 12. Joseph S. dis joining Separatists
1842, 9, 14. Rebecca rst
1843, 1, 19. Lewis con mou (H)
1850, 9, 18. Mordecai prcf Springfield MM, to m Jemima Thornburg
1850, 10, 16. Mordecai rmt Jemima Thornburgh
1851, 2, 12. Jemima (form Thornburgh) gct Springfield MM
1853, 4, 13. Mordecai & w, Jemima, & ch, Rachel, Elizabeth M., Mary Ann & Martha, rocf Springfield MM
1853, 5, 18. Isaac rocf Springfield MM
1853, 8, 17. Rebecca gct Fairfield MM, Ind.
1853, 11, 16. Azel & w, Eleanor, & ch, Mordecai J., rocf Springfield MM, dtd 1853,10,15
1854, 9, 14. Lewis M. con mcd (H)
1855, 4, 14. Isaac C. dis mou
1860, 12, 12. Springfield MM, Kans. was granted permission to rst David
1866, 3, 14. Martha W. Frazier (form Walker) rpd mou
1866, 12, 12. Mordecai J. & w, Deborah S. (form Painter) con mou
1871, 4, 12. Eli & Hannah recrq
1885, 9, 17. Elva gct Wilmington MM
1888, 6, 13. Mordecai & dt, Mary Ann, gct Springfield MM, O.
1890, 2, 12. Ella Dell recrq
1896, 12, 16. Frank W. & w, Ella D., & ch, Reva E. & Lora M., relrq
1904, 12, 14. Alpha dropped from mbrp

WALL
----, --, --. Azariah b 1772,9,1 d 1853,8,29 bur Center; m Rebecca ----- b 1778,3,24 d 1837,10,13
Ch: Phebe b 1797, 11, 17
John " 1798, 11, 22
William " 1802, 4, 29
Thomas " 1803, 11, 23
Absolam " 1805, 2, 10
Rebeccah " 1807, 1, 26
Jane " 1811, 5, 6
Azariah
Leech " 1816, 8, 2
1845, 5, 28. B. Frank b
1851, 10, 28. Christina b
----, --, --. Robert D. b 1839,2,29; m Ann C. ----- b 1840,3,17
Ch: Bayard T. b 1868, 1, 23 d 1870,1,12
bur Chester
Mahlon
Henry b 1871, 3, 2
Thomas
Leighton " 1872, 11, 5
1871, 3, 2. Henry M., s Isaac & Ruth, b
1872, 5, 3. Eunice O. b
1873, 1, 4. Eunice d bur Center
1873, 7, 1. Alphronso O. b
1875, 3, 8. Zelta V. b
1893, 1, 22. Azariah d bur Center

1809, 12, 2. Azariah & w, Rebeckah, & ch, Phebe, John, Thomas, Absalom & Rebeckah, rocf Center MM, Pa., dtd 1809,3,18
1822, 5, 18. Phebe rmt Jonathan Doan
1829, 7, 15. Absalom dis mou & disunity
1830, 11, 17. Rebecca Walker (form Wall) dis mou
1831, 8, 17. Thomas dis mou
1831, 11, 16. Jane Babb (form Wall) dis mou
1838, 7, 16. Azariah Jr. dis mou
1839, 3, 13. John gct Dover MM

WALL, continued
1868, 4, 11. Ann C. (form McMillen) rpd mou
1870, 5, 18. Robert D. recrq
1871, 3, 15. Azariah & w, Eunice, recrq
1871, 3, 15. Phebe recrq
1871, 5, 17. Mahlon & w, Mary, recrq
1872, 7, 11. Lucy Alice recrq
1874, 4, 15. Franklin & ch, Vinnie Corene & Alphonso, recrq
1874, 4, 15. Amy Christina recrq
1893, 5, 17. Alice gct Muncie MM, Ind.
1894, 3, 14. Rebecca & ch, Nellie E., recrq
1895, 3, 13. Viola K. relrq
1897, 12, 15. M. Henry & w, Hannah B., gct Wilmington MM, O.
1910, 3, 16. Granville recrq
1917, 5, 23. M. Henry & w, Hannah, & ch, Margaret & George R., roc

1919, 3, 12. Eunice dropped from mbrp

WALTERS
1813, 1, 2. Mary [Walter] rocf Fairfield MM, dtd 1812,7,25
1813, 11, 6. Cert rec 1813,1,2 for Mary endorsed to Caesars Creek MM

WALTHALL
1852, 4, 14. Daniel B. prcf Dover MM, to m Elizabeth Fawcett
1852, 5, 12. Daniel B. rmt Elizabeth H.Fawcett
1852, 6, 16. Elizabeth H. gct Dover MM
1857, 12, 16. Thomas prcf Dover MM, to m Maria E. Doan
1858, 1, 13. Thomas rmt Marion E. Doan
1858, 2, 17. Maria E. gct Dover MM
1859, 4, 13. Thomas [Walthal] & w, Maria E., & ch, Margaret & Sarah, rocf Dover MM
1864, 10, 12. Thomas [Walthal] & w, Maria E., & ch gct Dover MM

WALTON
1836, 12, 3. Charles s A. & Anna, b

1836, 10, 12. Abraham & w, Ann, & s, Amos, rocf Chester MM, dtd 1836,6,22
1840, 12, 16. Abram & w, Ann, & ch, Amos & Robert, gct White River MM, Ind.

WANZER
1865, 1, 3. Malinda d bur Cincinnati

1863, 6, 17. John & w, Malinda, & ch, George Henry & William Haviland, roc
1866, 8, 15. John & s, George H. & William H., gct Ypsilanti MM, Mich.

WARNER
1850, 7, 18. Joshua W. rocf Green Plain MM(H)
1850, 9, 19. Mahala H. recrq (H)

WATSON
1913, 2, 12. Charles & Lelia recrq

WAY
1810, 7, 7. Paul & dt, Hannah, rocf Center MM, N. C., dtd 1809,10,21
1810, 7, 7. Levinah rocf New Garden MM, N. C., dtd 1809,9,30
1810, 12, 1. Cert rec for Henry & fam from Center MM, N. C., dtd 1810,8,18, endorsed to Caesars Creek MM
1810, 12, 1. Cert rec for Joseph from Center MM, N. C., dtd 1810,8,18, endorsed to Caesars Creek MM
1811, 2, 2. Seth & w, Sarah, & ch, Thomas, Lydia & Hannah, rocf Center MM, N. C., dtd 1810,8,18
1812, 3, 7. Seth & w, Sarah, & ch, Thomas, Lydia & Hannah, gct White Water MM, Ind.
1814, 11, 5. Robert rocf Dunnings Creek MM, dtd 1814,7,13
1816, 10, 19. Paul & fam gct New Garden MM, Ind.
1818, 12, 19. Robert gct Miami MM
1824, 6, 19. Hannah rocf Dunings Creek MM

WEAD
1848, 8, 31. James A. b

WEBSTER
1841, 9, 4. Lydia R. d bur Monmouth, Ill.

1837, 6, 15. Lydia rocf Little Britton MM, Pa., dtd 1837,2,18 (H)
1846, 8, 13. William R. con mou (H)
1846, 9, 17. William R. gct Miami MM

WELCH
1829, 7, 15. Esther dis jH
1838, 3, 14. Turner & ch, Mary, Martha Ann, John, Isaiah, James & Robert Barclay, gct Sugar River MM, Ind.
1850, 1, 17. John gct Miami MM, to m Ann Whitacre (H)
1850, 2, 14. Martha A. gct Miami MM (H)
1855, 3, 15. Isaiah gct Miami MM to m Leah Cadwalader (H)

WEST
1844, 9, 4. Isaac A. d bur Center

1837, 8, 17. Isaac & w, Letitia, & ch, Hannah Ann, Louisa K. & Robert K., rocf Indian Spring MM, Md., dtd 1837,7,5 (H)
1837, 8, 17. Elizabeth rocf Indian Spring MM, Md., dtd 1837,7,5 (H)
1840, 7, 16. Charles rocf Indian Spring MM, Md., dtd 1840,3,4 (H)
1842, 12, 15. Charles con mou (H)
1844, 9, 19. Elizabeth Sewell (form West) dis mou (H)
1855, 8, 16. Letitia gct Miami MM (H)
1859, 5, 19. John L. & ch, Henry, Mary,

WEST, continued
Charles, Edward, Sarah & Richard, rocf White Water MM, Ind., dtd 1859,4,27 (H)
1860, 4, 19. John L. & ch, Mary E., Edward, Charles, Sarah & Richard, gct White Water MM, Ind.
1866, 9, 12. Rebecca recrq

WHARTON
1811, 3, 2. Cert rec for Silas from Falls MM, Pa., endorsed to Miami MM
1868, 1, 15. Huldah recrq
1872, 10, 16. Hulda & s, Walter, gct Newberry MM
1889, 6, 12. Fannie recrq

WHINERY
----, --, --. Thomas b 1779,10,5; m Ruth ----- b 1787,8,15
Ch: Phebe b 1808, 7, 18
Joseph " 1810, 4, 20
Edwin " 1812, 5, 20
Mark " 1813, 5, 7
Harriet " 1816, 1, 13
Sarah M. " 1818, 6, 15
Josiah " 1820, 10, 5
Enos " 1824, 8, 26
Allen " 1826, 4, 16 d 1855, 4, 2 bur Center
1833, 5, 23. Joseph, s Thomas & Ruth, Clinton Co., O.; m at Center, Sarah HIATT, dt Hezekiah & Ann, Clinton Co., O. (H)
----, --, --. Vincent b 1807,7,18; m Phebe ----- b 1810,12,12 (H)
Ch: Edward B. b 1834, 6, 5
Jemima R. " 1835, 12, 19
Holland G. " 1837, 8, 8
Lydia Ellen " 1841, 4, 1
Albin " 1843, 4, 16
1837, 10, 5. Sarah m Henry SMITH (H)
----, --, --. Zimri m Judith ----- d 1859,3,20 bur Chester
Ch: Isabella A. b 1839, 8, 2
Wright " 1845, 10, 9
1839, 1, 19. Ruth d bur Center
1844, 1, 15. Ann b
1844, 9, 3. Lydia Emily d bur Wilmington
1844, --, --. Jane Ann d bur Wilmington
1842, 10, 10. Halland d bur Wilmington
1842, 10, 11. Judith d bur Wilmington
1842, 10, 24. David d bur Wilmington
----, --, --. Edwin & Hannah
Ch: Zimri b 1845, 1, 10
Eliza " 1847, 12, 22
Albert " 1850, 2, 4
Sarah " 1853, 9, 8
----, --, --. Benjamin & Ruth
Ch: Calvin b 1846, 11, 3
Rachel Jane " 1849, 2, 24
Edwin " 1855, 12, 22 d 1857, 9,11
Ch: bur Center
Frank b 1858, 2, 27
James L. " 1860, 6, 7
Samuel G. " 1865, 6, 8
----, --, --. Ezra & Hannah M.
Ch: Judith E. b 1853, 3, 5
Mary Bell " 1858, 2, 28
Walter P. " 1861, 5, 19
Elsworth " 1864, 1, 31
1855, 8, 15. Edwin d bur Chester
1856, 8, 12. Thomas d
----, --, --. James & Mary
Ch: Eva b 1857, 5, 11
Alpheus " 1859, 4, 13
Oliver M. " 1863, 12, 19
----, --, --. Samuel & Lydia Emely
Ch: Charles Rollin b 1858, 11, 24
Jonathan M." 1860, 11, 17
Annie Jane " 1863, 9, 10
1864, 5, 26. Lorenzo V. b
1870, 10, 6. Alvaretta, dt Zimri & Ann, b
1870, 10, 10. Alvaretta d bur Chester
1871, 10, 30. Hannah L. b
1874, 7, 5. Edwin & Eva, ch Zimri & Ann, b

1809, 4, 1. Thomas & w, Ruth, & dt, Phebe, rocf Warrington MM, dtd 1809,4,19
1813, 10, 2. Thomas [Whinnery] rocf Warrington MM, dtd 1813,7,22
1816, 4, 20. Lydia (form Perkins) con mou
1826, 5, 21. John recrq
1825, 6, 18. Lydia dis disunity
1829, 2, 18. Thomas dis jH
1829, 2, 18. Ruth dis jH
1831, 3, 16. Joseph dis joining Separatists
1832, 10, 20. Thomas & w, Lydia, & ch, Sarah, William H., Esther, David, Lydia Emily, Judith, Thomas Milton & Nathan H., rocf New Garden MM, dtd 1832,7,26 (H)
1832, 10, 20. Vincent rocf New Garden MM, dtd 1832,7,26 (H)
1832, 10, 20. Jane Ann rocf New Garden MM, O., dtd 1832,7,26 (H)
1834, 3, 13. Vincent con mou (H)
1834, 4, 17. Holland rocf New Garden MM, dtd 1834,2,20 (H)
1834, 5, 14. William, Esther, David, Lydia Emilia, Judith & Thomas Milton, ch Thomas & Lydia, rocf New Garden MM, O., dtd 1834, 3,20
1834, 5, 14. Jane Ann & Sarah rocf New Garden MM, O., dtd 1834,3,20
1834, 6, 19. Phebe R. rocf New Garden MM, dtd 1834,1,23 (H)
1834, 12, 17. Sarah (form Hiatt) dis mou & jH
1835, 10, 14. Judith & ch, Edwin, Elizabeth, James, Benjamin, Ezra, Abigail & Samuel, rocf New Garden MM, dtd 1835,8,20
1836, 3, 17. Achilles rocf New Garden MM, dtd 1836,1,21 (H)
1838, 7, 16. Sarah Smith (form Whinery) dis mou

WHINERY, continued
1841, 5, 12. Jesse Coffin prcf Newberry MM, to m Elizabeth Whinery
1841, 6, 16. Elizabeth rmt Jesse Coffin
1841, 8, 18. Elizabeth Coffin (form Whinery) gct Newberry MM
1842, 11, 5. Edwin rmt Hannah Hines
1843, 4, 13. Achilles dis mou (H)
1843, 7, 13. Thomas Jr. dis disunity (H)
1843, 8, 16. James gct Newberry MM
1844, 4, 17. Harriet McMillan (form Whinery) dis mou (H)
1844, 11, 19. Harriet McMillan (form Whinery) dis mou (H)
1845, 6, 18. William dis disunity
1845, 7, 16. Sarah dis joining Separatists
1845, 9, 17. Benjamin rmt Ruth Linton
1846, 1, 14. James & w, Mary, & s, Arthur, rocf Newbury MM, dtd 1845,9,15
1846, 2, 19. Esther dis disunity (H)
1846, 3, 18. Esther dis joining Separatists
1846, 8, 13. Josiah dis mou (H)
1846, 9, 16. Josiah dis mou
1849, 3, 15. Sarah Mitchel (form Whinery) dis mou (H)
1849, 3, 15. Thomas Jr.dis mou (H)
1849, 6, 13. James & w, Mary, & ch, Arthur & Enos, gct Springfield MM
1849, 6, 13. Ezra rmt Hannah McMillan
1851, 4, 17. Enos dis mcd (H)
1851, 12, 17. Enos dis mou
1853, 10, 12. Abigail rmt Nathan Kirk
1853, 10, 12. Ezra & w, Hannah, & dt, Judith E.. gct Springfield MM
1854, 7, 12. James & w, Mary, & ch, Arthur, Enos & Henry, rocf Springfield MM, dtd 1854,6,17
1854, 10, 19. Mark con mcd (H)
1855, 5, 16. Sarah Jane rmt Pierce Hollingsworth
1857, 4, 15. Ezra & w, Hannah M., & ch, Judith E. & Susannah M., rocf Springfield MM
1857, 12, 16. Samuel rmt Lydia Emily McMillan
1858, 11, 17. Isabella Wilson (form Whinery) rpd mou
1860, 5, 16. James & w, Mary, & ch, Arthur, Enos, Henry, Eva & Alpheus, gct White Water MM, Ind.
1860, 8, 15. Zimri recrq
1860, 9, 12. Josiah McMillen gct New Garden MM, to m Rebecca Ann Whinery
1861, 11, 13. Zimri gct Chester MM, Ind., to m Rachel M. Hampton
1862, 4, 16. James & w, Mary, & ch, Arthur, Enos, Henry, Adelaide & Alpheus, rocf White Water MM, Ind.
1862, 5, 14. Rachel M. rocf Chester MM, Ind., dtd 1862,4,24
1862, 5, 14. James Morris prcf Fairfield MM, to m Hannah Whinery
1862, 6, 18. Hannah rmt James Morris
1862, 8, 13. Hannah Morris (form Whinnery) & ch, Albert & Sarah Whinery, gct Fairfield MM
1864, 4, 13. Ann recrq
1865, 9, 13. Samuel & w, Lydia, & ch gct Bangor MM
1865, 12, 13. Arthur rpd mou
1865, 12, 13. Zimri W. rpd mou
1866, 1, 17. Benjamin & w, Ruth L., & ch, Calvin, Rachel Jane, Frank, James & Samuel, gct Bangor MM
1866, 2, 14. James & fam gct White Water MM, Ind.
1866, 2, 14. Ezra & w, Hannah, & ch, Judith E., Susannah M., Mary Bell, Walter T. & Ellsworth, gct Bangor MM, Ia.
1866, 7, 18. Zimri & w, Rachel, gct Bangor MM, Ia.
1868, 4, 15. Isaiah & w, Hannah, & ch, William Henry & Frank Garwood, recrq
1869, 10, 13. Arthur gct Bangor MM, Ia.
1874, 11, 18. Zimri W. & fam gct Bangor MM,Ia.
1876, 4, 12. Zimri W. & w, Ann, & ch, Lorenza, Hannah Loretta, Eva M. & Edwin T., rocf Bangor MM, Ia., dtd 1876,3,18
1880, 3, 17. Zimri W. & w, Ann, & ch, Lorenza V. & Eva M., gct Peace MM, Kansas

WHITACRE
1850, 1, 17. John Welch gct Miami MM, to m Ann Whitacre (H)

WHITE
----, --, --. Thomas d 1846,6,28 ae 81y 6m 28d bur Center; m Sabillah ----- d 1844,7,1 ae 78y 8m 21d bur Center

1822, 1, 19. Thomas & w, Sabilla, rocf Upper Evesham MM, N. J., dtd 1821,9,8
1823, 8, 16. Sarah recrq
1848, 10, 18. Ashley gct Fairfield MM
1872, 4, 17. Sarah F. gct Indianapolis MM,Ind.
1893, 5, 17. George B. & w, Sarah Rufina, & niece, Edna Butler, rocf Springfield MM, d dtd 1893,4,15
1896, 1, 15. George B. & w, Sarah Rufina, & niece, Edna Butler, gct Springfield MM

WHITSON
1836, 10, 19. John, s Thomas & Elizabeth, Clinton Co., O.; m at Wilmington, Mary THOMAS, dt Ezekiel & Rebecca (H)
1848, 10, 5. Mary m Amos COOK (H)

1808, 6, 4. Samuel rmt Barbara Sanders
1809, 9, 2. Mary, w Jordon, & ch, Naomi & Solomon, recrq
1820, 12, 16. John & w, Margaret, & ch, Sarah James Lindley Ellen Jane & John, rocf Center MM, Pa., dtd 1820,7,15
1820, 12, 16. Deborah rocf Center MM, Pa., dtd 1820,7,15
1823, 7, 19. Deborah Antrim (form Whitson) dis mou
1825, 7, 16. John gct Springfield MM, to m

WHITSON, continued
Dinah Ballard
1825, 12, 17. James gct Springfield MM, to m Unice Ballard
1826, 1, 21. Elenor Jones (form Whitson) dis mou
1827, 7, 21. Jane Vore (form Witson) dis mou
1829, 7, 15. James dis disunity
1829, 7, 15. John dis disunity
1830, 10, 13. Dinah dis jH
1830, 10, 13. Eunice dis jH
1831, 6, 15. George Jr. com mou & disunity
1831, 9, 14. John dis disunity

WICKERSHAM
----, --, --. William b 1775,12,21 d 1839,6,17 bur Center; m Rachel ----- b 1783,9,20 d 1867,5,23 (H)
Ch: David b 1806, 7, 14
Robert " 1808, 8, 31
James " 1810, 10, 13
William Jr." 1813, 9, 15
Levi " 1816, 10, 3
Eliza " 1819, 3, 18 d 1888,10,11
Thomas " 1822, 8, 6
----, --, --. Enoch b 1778,8,13 d 1862,11,8 bur Chester; m Margarett ----- b 1789,7,22
Ch: Anna b 1809, 10, 23
James " 1811, 8, 31
Sarah " 1813, 9, 7
John " 1816, 1, 30
Abner " 1818, 7, 31
Susannah " 1821, 1, 7
Lydia " 1823, 8, 30 d 1833, 2, 5 bur Chester
Noah b 1827, 1, 27
Enoch " 1829, 9, 14
1838, 5, 14. Joseph C. b
----, --, --. Enoch & Hannah
Ch: Asaph H. b 1849, 5, 18 d 1853, 1,14 bur Chester
James b 1851, 2, 2
----, --, --. Joseph & Mary
Ch: Florence L. b 1863, 2, 22
Nantilla " 1865, 7, 9
Elizabeth " 1866, 8, 28
Mary A. " 1868, 12, 3
1869, 12, 21. Mary C. d bur Chester

1808, 2, 6. Enoch rmt Margaret Stout
1808 3, 5. Margaret gct Miami MM
1809, 4, 1. William & w, Rachel, & ch, David & Robert, rocf Warrington MM, dtd 1808,12,21
1810, 12, 1. Enoch & w, Margaret, & dt, Anne, rocf Miami MM, dtd 1810,10,31
1824, 9, 18. William Kirk gct West Grove MM, Ind., to m Rachel Wickersham
1827, 9, 15. Anna rmt Asaph Hollingsworth
1829, 2, 18. William dis jH
1829, 6, 17. Rachel dis jH
1831, 2, 16. James dis jH
1831, 4, 13. David dis jH
1831, 6, 15. Sarah rmt Levi Lundy
1831, 11, 19. Edward J. & w, Susanna, & ch, Rebecca C., Jesse & Jane M., rocf Warrington MM, Pa., dtd 1830,12,22 (H)
1832, 1, 18. Robert dis jH & disunity
1834, 5, 14. James dis disunity
1837, 6, 14. John con mou
1837, 11, 16. Edward & fam gct Milford MM (H)
1837, 12, 13. Susannah rmt Jonathan McMillan
1840, 8, 12. John gct Mississiniwa MM, Ind.
1840, 9, 16. Abner dis mou
1841, 3, 17. Leah (form Schooley) dis mou
1844, 7, 18. Robert dis mou (H)
1845, 7, 16. Eliza dis joining Separatists
1846, 2, 18. Thomas dis disunity
1847, 3, 17. John rocf Mississiniwa MM, Ind., dtd 1846,7,15
1847, 12, 16. David con mou (H)
1848, 6, 14. Enoch rmt Hannah Oren
1851, 7, 16. Noah gct Mississiniwa MM, Ind.
1852, 6, 16. John gct Mississiniwa MM, Ind.
1852, 7, 15. Thomas rpd mcd (H)
1852, 12, 16. Levi dis jas (H)
1855, 9, 12. Enoch & w, Hannah, & s, James, gct Winesheak MM, Ia.
1860, 5, 16. Mary C. (form Taylor) rpd mou
1873, 12, 17. Joseph C. rocf Wilmington MM
1874, 4, 15. James recrq
1889, 6, 12. Sarah J. recrq

WIKALL
1879, 12, 17. Rebecca & ch, Arabella, Lemella & Rosa Ella, gct Middle Point MM, O.

WILES
1812, 1, 4. Dina [Wilds] (form Stout) con mou
1825, 10, 16. Dinah [Wilds] rocf Springfield MM, Ind.
1827, 7, 21. Dinah gct Dover MM
1833, 5, 15. Dinah rocf Dover MM, dtd 1832, 7,19
1833, 5, 15. Sarah rocf Dover MM, dtd 1832, 7,19
1862, 2, 12. Rebecca [Wile] (form Fawcett) rpd mou

WILEY
1836, 5, 18. Ruth (form Kinsey) con mou
1836, 10, 12. Ruth gct Caesars Creek MM

WILLIAMS
----, --, --. Josiah m Sarah ----- b 1803,9,6
Ch: James L. b 1826,11,23
Thomas B." 1828, 9, 29
Mary " 1830, 2, 8
Orpha " 1831, 9, 14

1825, 5, 21. Josiah rocf Clear Creek MM, dtd 1825,5,14
1825, 6, 18. Josiah rmt Sarah Bailiff
1829, 5, 13. Josiah dis disunity

WILLIAMS, continued
1836, 3, 16. Margaret rocf White Lick MM, Ind., dtd 1835,12,16
1836, 3, 16. Malinda rocf White Lick MM, Ind., dtd 1835,12,16
1837, 3, 15. Margaret & Malinda gct Duck Creek MM, Ind.
1839, 9, 18. Sarah Stafford (form Williams) con mou
1849, 7, 18. Mary Lucus (form Williams) dis mou
1850, 1, 16. Thomas rmt Phebe Faulkner
1851, 11, 12. Thomas & w, Phebe, & dt, Mehiah Ann, gct Mississiniwa MM, Ind.
1852, 4, 14. James L. dis mou 1851,12,17
1865, 11, 15. Cassandra rocf Birch Lake MM, dtd 1865,9,2
1891, 3, 18. Alta T. relrq
1902, 4, 16. Benjamin F. recrq
1906, 4, 18. Edgar recrq
1906, 4, 18. Clara recrq
1906, 5, 16. Charles A. recrq
1906, 6, 13. William Minor & w, Theodosha, & ch, Oscar Elmer & Anna Marie, recrq
1913, 12, 17. Grace Laurence & s, Maynard E., recrq

WILLIAMSON
1841, 8, 18. Miriam (form Pierce) dis mou
1850, 1, 17. Miriam (form Pierce) con mcd (H)
1850, 7, 18. Mariam gct Miami MM (H)
1910, 3, 16. Ollie recrq

WILSON
1807, 11, 28. Betty rmt John Kinley
1808, 7, 2. Seth & w, Martha, recrq
1824, 10, 16. Joseph rmt Hannah Underwood
1824, 12, 18. Hannah gct Allum Creek MM
1835, 8, 12. Jesse F. Ballard gct Springfield MM, to m Pharaba G. Wilson
1843, 10, 18. Enos prcf Caesars Creek MM, to m Rebecca Ballard
1843, 11, 15. Enos rmt Rebecca Ballard
1844, 6, 12. Rebecca B. gct Caesars Creek MM
1852, 11, 17. Mary (form Ballard) con mou
1853, 5, 18. Mary gct Caesars Creek MM
1858, 11, 17. Isabella (form Whinery) rpd mou
1865, 8, 16. Isabella gct Bangor MM, Ia.
1888, 11, 14. Katherine & ch, Minnie, Elsie & Emmerson, recrq
1889, 6, 12. Joseph recrq
1899, 5, 17. Joseph relrq
1901, 7, 17. Viola Foland rocf Wilmington MM
1910, 2, 16. Marion & Marie recrq
1910, 4, 10. Sarah & ch, Chlorine & Madge, recrq
1913, 2, 12. Alta recrq
1914, 9, 6. Marion & w, Mary, gct Springfield MM
1919, 3, 12. Alta dropped from mbrp

WITHERBEE
1836, 6, 15. Anna (form Faulkner) dis mou

WOOD
1834, 1, 15. Isaac & w, Lydia, rocf Hopewell MM, dtd 1833,12,4
1834, 1, 15. Robert roc
1836, 6, 15. Robert dis mou

WOOLERY
1847, 7, 26. John A. [Wolary] b
1850, 4, 3. Hanna M. [Wolary] b
----, --, --. J. Asbury m Naomi B. ----- d 1873,12,15
Dt: Martha E. b 1872, 12, 15
J. Asbury m 2nd Hannah -----
Ch: Loren C. b 1874, 12, 8 d 1876, 4, 5
Lindley J. " 1877, 7, 16
1879, 6, 12. Hannah M. d

1871, 3, 15. Louisa [Woolary] recrq
1873, 12, 17. J. A. rocf Wilmington MM
1875, 5, 12. J. Asberry con mou
1894, 3, 14. Lindley recrq
1912, 4, 17. Lindley & w, Flora, & ch, Ethel, Carl, Loren, Edward & Hannah, granted cert to Sabin MM

WOOLMAN
1825, 12, 17. Eber rocf Green Plain MM, dtd 1825,8,3
1829, 9, 16. Eber dis
1830, 7, 14. Ruth rocf Green Plain MM, dtd 1830,5,5
1845, 7, 16. Ruth gct Mississiniwa MM, Ind.
1846, 3, 18. Ruth's cert to Mississiniwa MM, Ind. returned, because she had jas
1846, 9, 16. Ruth dis jas

WRIGHT
----, --, --. Joale b 1800,6,4; m Ruth ----- b 1802,12,9
Ch: Amey b 1824, 5, 4
Hannah " 1825, 12, 25
Juliann " 1827, 10, 29
Catharine " 1830, 2, 1
Griffith " 1833, 2, 23
Joel " 1835, 6, 14
Phebe " 1837, 6, 28
Mary Emily " 1840, 5, 1 d 1841, 7,13 bur New Hope

1809, 7, 1. Ruth Hayworth (form Wright) dis mou
1810, 1, 6. Jonathan Jr. gct Miami MM
1810, 3, 3. John & w, Margaret, & ch, James, Abraham, Isaac, Jacob, Ann, Solomon & Sarah, rocf New Hope MM, dtd 1810,--,7
1810, 5, 5. Richard Timberlake prcf Fairfield MM, to m Mary Wright
1810, 5, 5. Mary rmt Richard Timberlake
1810, 10, 5. Betty Dillon (form Wright) con mou

WRIGHT, continued
1811, 9, 7. William rmt Hannah Dillen
1812, 12, 5. Cert rec for Elizabeth from Center MM, Pa., dtd 1812,9,19, endorsed to Miami MM
1813, 3, 6. Joel gct Miami MM
1813, 4, 3. Charity rmt Luke Dillon
1813, 11, 6. Jonathan & w, Susannah, gct Miami MM
1813, 11, 6. Susanna Jr. & Rebecca gct Miami MM
1814, 7, 2. Isaac rmt Abigail Dillon
1814, 11, 5. Phebe Haworth, gr ch Sarah Wright, recrq
1815, 5, 20. Joseph rocf Clear Creek MM, dtd 1815,4,28
1815, 7, 14. Joel rmt Elizabeth Taylor
1815, 11, 18. Elizabeth gct Cincinnati MM
1817, 4, 19. William & w, Hannah, & ch, Luke, James & Jesse, gct New Garden MM, Ind.
1817, 8, 21. James rmt Abigail Starbuck
1818, 4, 18. James & w, Abigail, gct New Garden MM, Ind.
1818, 5, 16. Abraham rpd mou
1818, 8, 15. Esley recrq
1819, 2, 20. John & w, Margaret, & ch, Isaac, Jacob, Ann, Solomon, John, Margaret, Phebe, Rees, Hannah, William & Lydia, gct New Garden MM, Ind.
1819, 3, 20. Abraham dis disunity
1819, 10, 16. Jacob con mou
1820, 1, 15. Esley rmt Isaac Furnace
1820, 2, 19. Esly Furnace (form Wright) gct Miami MM
1820, 11, 18. Jacob gct New Garden MM, Ind.
1821, 3, 17. Joseph gct Newberry MM
1824, 9, 18. White Water MM was granted permission to rst Abraham
1826, 11, 18. Jacob gct White River MM, Ind.
1829, 2, 18. Joab & w, Ruth, & ch, Amy, Hannah & Julian, rocf Newberry MM, dtd 1829, 2,3
1836, 5, 18. Jonathan prcf Salem MM, dtd 1836,4,23, to m Deborah McMillan
1836, 7, 13. Jonathan rmt Deborah J. McMillan
1836, 8, 13. Deborah J. gct Salem MM, Ind.
1839, 11, 13. Parvin prcf Short Creek MM, dtd 1839,10,22, to m Ellen Stroud
1839, 11, 13. Parvin rmt Ellen Stroud
1840, 1, 15. Ellen S. gct Short Creek MM
1841, 9, 15. Joab & w, Ruth, & ch, Amy, Hannah, Julian, Catharine, Griffith, Joel & Phebe, gct White Lick MM, Ind.
1845, 2, 12. Ashley rocf Fairfield MM

WRIGHTSMAN
1809, 7, 1. Abigail con mou

YARGER
1909, 4, 14. Rachel S. relrq

* * * * * * *

AVERY
1913, 2, 12. Ethel recrq

BALLARD
----, --, --. William & Phebe
Ch: Jesse Faulkner b 1810, 10, 10
Edith " 1812, 7, 27
Susannah H." 1815, 1, 21
Judith " 1817, 1, 14
1853, 7, 13. William d ae 68y 6m 23d

COMPTON
1841, 12, 15. Nathan Linton, s John & Jane, b

GREEN
1797, 5, 30. Alice b
1818, 5, 4. Alice, dt Isaac & Mary, d ae 56

HADLEY
1843, 2, 19. Jane Ann, dt Jeremiah & Esther, b

HOLLINGSWORTH
1830, 7, 31. Susannah d ae 75y 3m 15d (a minister)

HUDGEL
1859, 6, 10. James N. b

KILGOUR
1894, 2, 14. Elizabeth recrq

PAINTER
1856, 2, 13. Deborah T. Jenkins (form Painter) dis mou

RUDDICK
1829, 7, 15. John [Reddock] dis jH

STOUT
----, --, --. Isaac b 1768,4,14; m Susanna ----- b 1769,5,1
Ch: Phebe b 1798, 3, 27
Mary " 1808, 5, 28
Martha " 1808, 5, 28
Isaac " 1810, 8, 9
Isaiah " 1815, 3, 2
1844, 12, 26. Martha m Caleb DAVIS

WALL
----, --, --. Mahlon b 1810,5,31 d 1890,4,22
----, --, --. Mary b 1813,3,20 d 1890,1,25 bur Center
1918, 6, 11. Thomas Leaton m at Chester, Ethel May HAWKINS

WILLIAMS
1808, 10, 1. Betty [William] & dt, Sarah, rocf New Hope MM, dtd 1808,4,23
1821, 3, 17. Sarah Ellis (form Williams) dis [mou

EXTRACTS FROM EARLY MARRIAGE CERTIFICATES FOUND IN BOOK A.

This book was lost for years, but it has recently been found and copied. Deeming the book irretrievably lost, we prepared all other material for publication and paged it. This made it necessary to insert the following extracts from early marriage certificates with special paging.

ADSIT
1840, 1, 21. Elizabeth m Thos. W. McMILLAN
1841, 4, 22. Isabella, wd, m Thos. RICH

ANDERSON
1807, 3, 12. Eli, Green Co., O., s James & Ann, both dec, Kent Co., Del.; m at Centre Mary THATCHER, dt Stephen, dec, & Ruth

ANDREW
1807, 8, 10. Robert, Green Co., O., s Wm. & Hannah, Orange Co., N. C.; m at Centre, Ellen FAULKNER, dt Jesse & Ruth, dec

ARNOLD
1813, 12, 13. Jesse, s Geo. & Rachel, Clinton Co., O.; m at Centre Mtg, Jane LINTON, dt Samuel & Elizabeth

ATKINSON
1815, 9, 20. Cephas, s Joseph & Susannah, Clinton Co., O.; m at Centre Mtg, Abigail OREN, dt John & Ruth, dec
1820, 6, 22. Charles, s Thomas & Alice, both dec, Clinton Co., O.; m in Dover Mtg, Lydia OREN, dt John & Ruth, dec

BAILEY
1815, 9, 20. Rebeccah m Enoch BALLARD
1822, 1, 24. Susanna, m Caleb KIRK
1823, 11, 18. Elizabeth m Jesse BARNET
1828, 5, 21. Almedia m Robert THOMAS

BAILIFF
1825, 5, 26. Sarah m Josiah WILLIAMS
1832, 3, 22. Leah [Bayliff] m David FAULKNER

BALLARD
1809, 6, 8. Wm., s David & Mary, Warren Co., O.; m in "mtg held on waters of Anderson's Fork of Caesers Creek", Phebe FAULKNER, dt David & Judith, Green Co., O.
1809, 7, 5. Simeon, s Moorman & Minerva, Warren Co., O.; m in Centre Mtg, Barbary RINEHART, dt Adam & Catherine
1815, 9, 20. Enoch, s Moorman & Minerva, dec, Clinton Co., O.; m in Centre Mtg, Rebecah BAILEY, dt Abiden & Sarah, both dec
1815, 12, 20. Rhoda m Thomas CAREY
1817, 12, 25. Mary m Thomas RHODE
1823, 12, 31. Lydia m Jesse DOAN
1826, 9, 20. Elizabeth m Joseph FURNAS
1827, 10, 24. Minerva m Caleb DAVIS
1830, 3, 4. Edith m Joshua COMPTON
1834, 9, 25. Judith F. m Wilson CARTER
1843, 10, 25. Rebecca m Enos WILSON
1844, 6, 19. Phebe m Joseph BURGESS

BANGHAM
1820, 9, 21. Mary m Lewis JOHNSON
1841, 8, 26. Jonathan, s Benjamin & Lucy, Clinton Co., O.; m in Newhope MH, Jane FAWCETT, dt Robert & Mary, Clinton Co., O.

BARNETT
1807, 12, 16. Mary m Amos HODGSON
1808, 1, 6. Elizabeth m Richard MENDENHALL
1809, 5, 11. Ann m Joseph MENDENHALL
1823, 11, 18. Jesse [Barnet], s Thomas & Theodate, Clinton Co., O.; m at Dover MH, O., Elizabeth BAILEY, dt Abidan & Mourning

BEVANS
1828, 11, 19. Owen, s Stacy & Lydia, Clinton Co., O.; m in Centre MH, Mary HIATT, dt Jesse & Martha, dec
1836, 8, 25. Abel, s Stacy, dec, & Lydia, Clinton Co., O.; m in Newhope MH, Charlotte T. FAUCETT, dt Robert & Mary, Green Co., O.
1868, 2, 20. Mary m Wm. GALLEMORE (Mary Jane)

BROWN
1827, 11, 21. John, Waynesville, s Asher & Mary, Warren Co., O.; m in Centre Mtg, Mary W. CARPENTER, dt Jacob & Phebe, dec, Clinton Co., O.

BURGESS
1844, 6, 19. Joseph, s Daniel & Ruth, Highland Co., O.; m in Centre MH, Phebe BALLARD, dt Spencer & Rebecca, Clinton Co., O.

BURSON
1842, 9, 22. Lydia m Brooks JOHNSON

BUTLER
1822, 3, 27. David, s William & Mary, dec, Clinton Co., O.; m in Centre Mtg, Mary SMITH, dt Joseph & Lydia, Clinton Co., O.

BUTTERWORTH
1822, 4, 4. Samuel, s Benjamin & Rachel, Warren Co., O.; m in Centre Mtg, Hannah TAYLOR, dt Jacob & Hannah, Clinton Co.,O.
1826, 6, 21. William, s Benjamin & Rachel, Warren Co., O.; m in Centre Mtg, Elizabeth LINTON, dt Nathan & Rachel, Clinton Co.,O.

CADWALLADER
1845, 6, 26. John T., s Mahlon & Elizabeth, dec, Warren Co., O.; m in Wilmington MH, Rachel FARQUHAR, dt Benj. & Rachel, both dec, Clinton Co., O.

CAREY
1815, 12, 20. Thomas, s Samuel & Rachel, Grayson Co., Va.; m in Springfield Mtg, Rhoda BALLARD, dt Joseph & Elizabeth, Clinton Co., O.
1856, 9, 25. John [Cary], s Samuel & Anne, Clinton Co., O.; m in Chester MH, Elizabeth LUNDY, dt Enoch, dec, & Charlotte, Clinton Co., O.

CARPENTER
1820, 7, 19. Eliza D. m Joseph DOAN,Jr.
1823, 3, 19. Lydia m Amos FALLIS
1827, 11, 21. Mary W. m John BROWN
1828, 9, 24. Esther m Dean KING
1834, 9, 24. Walter T., s Isaac & Mercy, dec, Clinton Co., O.; m in Centre MH, Susan MABEE, dt John & Elizabeth, dec, Clinton Co., O.
1845, 2, 25. Sarah m David McMILLAN, Jr.

CARTER
1833, 8, 22. Enoch, s Nathaniel & Nancy, Clinton Co., O.; m in Newhope MH, Elizabeth FAULKNER, dt David & Mary, dec, Green Co., O.
1834, 9, 25. Wilson, s George & Miriam, Clinton Co., O.; m in Newhope MH, Judith F. BALLARD, dt Wm. & Phebe, Green Co., O.
1852, 2, 21. George, s John & Hannah, Clinton Co., O.; m in Newhope MH, Elizabeth HAINES, dt Zimri & Elizabeth, Green Co.,O.

CHARLES
1863, 9, 23. Mathew, s Nathan & Mary, Wayne Co., Ind.; m in Centre MH, Eliza D. TIMBERLAKE, dt Alfred & Phebe, Clinton Co.,O.

CLOUD
1810, 6, 7. Joseph, Warren Co., O.; m in Caesar's Creek MH, O., Mary HUNT

COATE
1837, 2, 23. Rebecca m David CURL
1838, 11, 22. Hiram, s John & Esther, dec, Green Co., O.; m in Newhope MH, Rachel W. PAINTER, dt Jesse & Elizabeth, Green Co.,O.
1841, 8, 26. Martha m Wm. LONGSTRETCH
1848, 9, 21. Esther m Edwin HADLEY

COFFIN
1841, 5, 19. Jesse, s David & Mary, Clinton Co., O.; m in Centre MH, Elizabeth WHINNERY dt Zimri & Judith, Clinton Co., O.

COMPTON
1830, 3, 4. Joshua, s Samuel & Phebe, Green Co., O.; m in Newhope MH, Edith BALLARD, dt Wm. & Phebe, Green Co., O.
1846, 1, 15. Phebe m Isaac VOTAW

COOK
1813, 11, 10. Amos, s Amos & Elizabeth, Warren Co., O.; m in Centre Mtg, Susannah PERKINS dt Isaac & Ann, dec, Clinton Co., O.
1816, 8, 21. Robert, s Isaac & Sarah, dec, Warren Co., O.; m in Centre Mtg, Mary HOCKET, dt Moses & Rebecka, dec, Clinton Co., O.

COWGILL
1818, 1, 21. Amos, s John & Cathrine, Clinton Co., O.; m in Sites Creek MH, Edith MENdinghall, dt Nathan & Ann, Clinton Co., O.

COX
1821, 12, 5. Samuel, s Joshua, dec, & Amy, Wayne Co., Ind.; m in Centre Mtg, Edith McMILLAN, dt Thomas, dec, & Jane, Clinton Co., O.
1822, 3, 20. Thomas, s Joshua, dec, & Amy, Wayne Co., Ind.; m in Centre Mtg, Mary McMILLAN, dt David & Hannah, Clinton Co.,O.
1824, 9, 22. Susanna m Josiah McMILLAN
1842, 9, 1. Elizabeth m Omri SCHOOLEY

CREW
1851, 9, 24. Mary m Josiah McMILLAN

CURL
1834, 4, 24. Eliza m Thos. MILLER
1837, 2, 23. David, s Samuel & Susanna, dec, Logan Co., O.; m in Newhope MH, Rebecca COATE, dt John & Esther, dec, Green Co.,O.

DAVIS
1827, 10, 24. Caleb, Clinton Co., O., s Elisha & Alice, dec, Huntingdon Co., Pa.; m in Centre Mtg, Minerva BALLARD, dt Spencer & Rebecca, Clinton Co., O.
1854, 12, 14. Joseph L., s John & Lydia, Wabash Co., Ind.; m in Newhope MH, Phebe HAINES, dt Zimri & Elizabeth, Green Co.,O.

DENNIS
1838, 5, 17. Nathan, s William & Delilah, Wayne Co., Ind.; m in Centre MH, Mary LAMAR, dt Isaac & Hannah, Clinton Co., O.

DICKS
1810, 3, 7. Peter, s Zacharias, dec, & Ruth, Warren Co., O.; m in Centre Mtg, Elizabeth VESTAL, dt Samuel, dec & Mary CARTER, Chatham Co., N. C.

DILLON
1811, 8, 8. Hannah m Wm. WRIGHT
1813, 3, 11. Luke, s Jesse & Hannah, Clinton Co., O.; m in Centre Mtg, Charity WRIGHT, dt James, dec, & Sarah, Clinton Co., O.
1813, 3, 17. Nathan, s Daniel Jr. & Ann, Clinton Co., O.; m in Centre Mtg, Mary HOSKINS, dt Moses & Ruth
1814, 6, 9. Abigail, m Jesse WRIGHT

DOAN
1818, 11, 23. William, s Joseph & Jemima, Clinton Co., O.; m in Centre Mtg, Betsy EACHUS, dt Robert & Pheby, Clinton Co., O.
1820, 7, 19. Joseph Jr., s Joseph & Jemima, Clinton Co., O.; m in Centre Mtg, Eliza D. CARPENTER, dt Jacob & Phebe, dec, Clinton Co., O.
1822, 4, 4. Jonathan, s Joseph & Jemima, Clinton Co., O.; m in Centre Mtg, Phebe WALL, dt Azariah & Rebecca, Clinton Co.,O.
1823, 12, 31. Jesse, s Joseph & Jemima, Clinton Co., O.; m in Centre Mtg, Lydia BALLARD, dt Spencer & Rebecca, Clinton Co.,O.
1839, 5, 2. Phebe, m Alfred TIMBERLAKE
1855, 6, 20. Jemmima m Edwin HADLEY
1857, 12, 23. Maria E. m Thomas WALTHALL
1858, 9, 23. Joseph Jr., s Joseph & Eliza, Clinton Co., O.; m in Chester MH, Deborah E. TAYLOR, dt Jesse & Deborah, Clinton Co., O.

EACHUS
1818, 11, 23. Betsy m Wm. DOAN
1821, 12, 26. Julianna m John PERKINS

ELLIS
1865, 5, 24. Lydia/Mary m Daniel McPHERSON

EMBREE
1808, 2, 8. Rachel m Wm. THORNE

FALLIS
1823, 3, 19. Amos, s John & Mary, Clinton Co., O.; m in Centre Mtg, Lydia CARPENTER, dt Isaac & Mercy, dec, Clinton Co., O.

FARQUHAR
1829, 12, 2. Josiah, s Benjamin, dec, & Rachel, Clinton Co., O.; m in Centre MH, Abi LINTON, dt Nathan & Rachel, Clinton Co.,O.
1858, 9, 23. Francis, s Josiah, dec, & Abi, Clinton Co., O.; m in Chester MH, Hannah Ann McMILLAN, dt Milton & Elizabeth, both dec, Clinton Co., O.
1845, 6, 26. Rachel m John L. CADWALLADER

FAULKNER
1807, 10, 8. Ellen m Robert ANDREW
1807, 10, 8. Martha m Wm. STANTON
1807, 12, 2. Susanna m John HOLADAY
1809, 6, 8. Phebe m Wm. BALLARD
1812, 1, 9. Mary m Thomas JOHNSON
1815, 6, 21. Hannah m Joel PUSEY
1815, 8, 23. Elizabeth m Jesse SHEPPARD
1816, 5, 22. Judith m John JOHNSON
1819, 1, 21. Jane m Caleb STRATTON
1825, 12, 22. Rachel m Thomas ARNETT

1833, 8, 22. Elizabeth m Enoch CARTER
1833, 12, 19. Mary m Thos. HAWKINS
1849, 12, 20. Phebe m Thos. B. WILLIAMS

FAWCETT
1836, 8, 25. Charlotte T. m Abel BEVANS
1841, 8, 26. Jane m Jonathan BANGHAM
1845, 10, 23. Milton, s Robert & Mary, Green Co., O.; m in Newhope MH, Sarah HAINES, dt Zimri & Elizabeth, Green Co., O.
1846, 9, 24. John, s Robert & Mary, Green Co., O.; m in Newhope MH, Phebe W. PAINTER dt Thomas & Mary, Green Co., O.
1852, 4, 22. Elizabeth H. m Daniel B. WALTHAIL

FRAZIER
1820, 2, 24. Lydia m Alexander OREN

FURNAS
1819, 12, 29. Isaac, Warren Co., O., s John & Ruth, Clinton Co., O.; m in Centre Mtg, Esly WRIGHT, dt Thos. & Elizabeth, dec, Miami Co., O.
1826, 9, 20. Joseph, s John & Ruth, dec, Clinton Co., O.; m in Centre Mtg, Elizabeth BALLARD, dt Nathan & Martha, dec, Wayne Co., Ind.

GALLEMORE
1868, 2, 20. William, s Elisha, dec, Clinton Co., O.; m in Newhope MH, Mary Jane BEVANS dt Abel & Charlotte, Green Co., O.

GREEN
1824, 12, 23. Charlotte m Enoch LUNDY
1828, 11, 20. Abigail m Jesse LUNDY
1836, 1, 21. Isaac, s Jesse & Sarah, Clinton Co., O.; m in Chester MH, Anne SCHOOLEY, dt Samuel & Rachel, Clinton Co., O.
1842, 9, 1. Jehiel, s Robert & Mary, dec, Clinton Co., O.; m in Chester MH, Rachel LUNDY, dt James & Elizabeth, dec, Clinton Co., O.
1843, 11, 23. Aaron, s Jesse & Sarah, Clinton Co., O.; m in Chester MH, Rachel SCHOOLEY, dt Nathan, dec, & Sarah, Clinton Co., O.
1847, 9, 23. Charlotte D. m Miles H. MOON
1848, 4, 20. Joel, s Robert & Mary, both dec, Clinton Co., O.; m in Chester MH, Elizabeth SCHOOLEY, dt Samuel, dec, & Rachel
1853, 4, 14. Ruth m Wm. PAXON

GRIFFITH
1821, 5, 23. Elizabeth m James JOHNSON

HADLEY
1815, 11, 13. Jonathan, s Simon & Elizabeth, Chatham Co., N. C.; m in Springfield Mtg, Rebecca HARVEY, dt Isaac & Lydia, dec, Chatham Co., N. C.
1816, 11, 7. Ruth m Wm. HARVEY
1816, 12, 26. Simon, s John & Lydia, Clinton Co., O.; m in Springfield Mtg, O., Ann KERSEY, dt Thomas & Rebecca, Clinton Co., O.
1817, 10, 30. John, s Wm. & Sarah, Clinton Co., O.; m in Springfield Mtg, Ruth HALE,

HADLEY, John & Ruth, continued
dt Jacob & Martha, Clinton Co., O.
1818, 4, 30. Joshua, s Simon & Elizabeth, Chatham Co., N. C.; m in Springfield Mtg, Rebecca TOWEL, dt Jesse & Hannah, dec, Clinton Co., O.
1818, 11, 26. Elizabeth m Ezekiel HORNADY
1838, 8, 22. Jonathan, s William & Sarah, dec, Clinton Co., O.; m in Centre MH, Mary LINTON, dt Nathan & Rachel, Clinton Co., O.
1848, 9, 21. Edwin, s Jonathan & Olive, dec, Clinton Co., O.; m in Newhope MH, Esther COATE, dt John & Mary, Green Co., O.

HAINES
1845, 10, 23. Sarah m Milton FAWCETT
1852, 2, 21. Elizabeth m George CARTER
1854, 12, 14. Phebe m Joseph L. DAVIS

HALE
1814, 11, 17. Elizabeth m James MASSEY
1816, 8, 22. Lydia m John HARLAN
1817, 10, 30. Ruth m John HADLEY

HARLAND
1814, 10, 6. Enoch, s Enoch & Edith, Clinton Co., O.; m in Springfield Mtg, Elizabeth HARVEY, dt Isaac & Lydia, Clinton Co., O.
1816, 8, 22. John, s Enoch, dec, & Edith, Clinton Co., O.; m in Springfield Mtg, Lydia HALE, dt Jacob & Martha, Clinton Co., O.

HARRISON
1827, 3, 21. William H., s Wm., dec, & Martha, Clark Co., O.; m in Centre Mtg, Ann STOUT, dt John & Anne, Clinton Co.,O.

HARVEY
1814, 10, 6. Elizabeth m Enoch HARLAND
1815, 2, 15. Joshua, s Wm., dec, & Elizabeth, Clinton Co., O.; m in Centre Mtg, Mary MOON, dt Simon & Judith, Clinton Co., O.
1815, 9, 28. Lydia m Simon MOON
1815, 11, 13. Rebecca m Jonathan HADLEY
1816, 11, 7. Wm., s Eli & Mary, Clinton Co., O.; m in Springfield Mtg, Ruth HADLEY, dt William & Sarah, Clinton Co., O.
1817, 9, 25. Henry, s Caleb & Mary, dec, Wayne Co., Ind.; m in Springfield Mtg, Ann MADEN, dt Geo. & Elizabeth, Clinton Co., O.
1855, 10, 19. Caleb I.(or J.), s Isaac & Sarah, Clinton Co., O.; m at Center MH, O., Rebecca JEFFRIES, dt Job & Elizabeth, both dec, Clinton Co., O.

HAWKINS
1833, 12, 19. Thomas, s Nathan & Rebecca, Wayne Co., Ind.; m in Newhope MH, Mary FAULKNER, dt Jesse Jr. & Hannah, Green Co., O.

HAWORTH
1807, 10, 7. George Sr., Warren Co., O.; m in Centre Mtg, Joanna VANHORN, wd, Warren Co., O.
1813, 12, 8. Richard, s George & Susan, dec, Clinton Co., O.; m in Centre Mtg, Susanna HENDERSON, dt Richard & Rachel, Clinton Co., O.
1819, 10, 18. Phebe m Charles M. JOHNSON
1871, 9, 20. Isaiah M., s Richard M. & Elizabeth, dec, Clinton Co., O.; m in Centre MH, Mary JOHNSON, dt Lewis & Rachel, Clinton Co., O.

HENDERSON
1813, 12, 8. Susanna, m Richard HAWORTH

HESTER
1811, 9, 18. Elizabeth m Evan STANBROUGH
1815, 5, 24. Ruth m Nehemiah STANBROUGH
1819, 9, 22. Thomas, s Francis & Mary, Clinton Co., O.; m in Centre Mtg, Mary LEONARD dt Ezekiel & Rebecca, Clinton Co., O.

HIATT
1810, 8, 8. Hezekiah, Clinton Co., O., s Solomon & Sarah, Guilford Co., N. C.; m Ann PERKINS, dt Isaac & Ann, dec, Clinton Co., O.
1816, 5, 23. Lydia, m Jacob JESSOP
1828, 11, 19. Mary m Owen BEVAN
1829, 3, 25. Jesse, s Wm. & Susannah, dec, Clinton Co., O.; m in Centre MH, Sarah MAXSON, dt Christopher & Mary KINSEY, Clinton Co., O.

HINES
1826, 10, 26. Jesse, s Nathan & Patience, Clinton Co., O.; m in Chester Mtg, Sarah STANLEY, dt Anthony & Hannah, Clinton Co., O.
1830, 12, 1. Sarah m Mahlon KIRK
1842, 10, 20. Hannah m Edwin WHINERY

HOCKET
1816, 8, 21. Mary m Robert COOK

HODGSON
1810, 12, 11. Rachel m Wm. HOGGATT
1807, 12, 16. Amos, s Thomas, dec, & Patience, Warren Co., O.; m in Centre Mtg, Mary BARNETT, dt Athanasius & Jane, Warren Co., O.
1820, 9, 27. Isaac, s Hur & Elizabeth, dec, Clinton Co., O.; m in Centre Mtg, Hannah LEONARD, dt Ezekiel & Rebecca, Clinton Co., O.

HOGGATT
1810, 12, 11. Wm., s Stephen & Margaret, Highland Co., O.; m in Centre Mtg, Rachel HODGSON, dt Thoc., dec, & Patience, Clinton Co., O.

HOLADAY
1807, 12, 2. John, Green Co., O., s Robert & Hannah, Orange Co., N. C.; m in Centre Mtg, Susanna FAULKNER, dt Robert & Elizabeth, dec, Green Co., O.

HOLLINGSWORTH
1820, 11, 22. Samuel, s Israel & Ann, dec, Clinton Co., O.; m in Centre Mtg, Jane Ann McMILLAN, dt Jonathan & Ann, dec, Clinton Co., O.
1827, 8, 23. Asaph, s Israel & Ann, dec, Clinton Co., O.; m in Chester MH, Anne WICKERSHAM, dt Enoch & Margaret, Clinton Co., O.
1833, 12, 25. Sophia m James LUNDY
1838, 11, 22. Samuel, s Israel & Ann, dec, Clinton Co., O.; m in Chester MH, Emily KIRK, dt Josiah & Elizabeth, Clinton Co.,O.
1855, 4, 26. Pierce, s Asaph, dec, & Anne, Clinton Co., O.; m in Chester MH, Jane WHINERY, dt Zimri & Judith, Clinton Co.,O.
1858, 10, 21. Rachel m Charles W. KIRK
1860, 6, 21. Anne m Seth SMITH

HORNADY
1818, 11, 26. Ezekiel, s Ezekiel, dec, & Mary, Clinton Co., O.; m in Springfield Mtg, Elizabeth HADLEY, dt John & Lydia, Clinton Co., O.

HOSKINS
1813, 3, 17. Mary m Nathan DILLON

HUNNICUTT
1839, 10, 24. John P., s Thomas, dec, & Elizabeth, Clinton Co., O.; m in Hopewell MH, Susannah H. BALLARD, dt Wm. & Phebe, Green Co., O.

HUNT
1810, 6, 7. Mary m Joseph CLOUD
1832, 11, 21. John, s Thos. & Susannah, Clinton Co., O.; m in Centre MH, Phebe F. WALKER, dt Wm. & Martha, Clinton Co., O.

JAMES
1856, 3, 19. Jonathan H., s David & Mary, dec, Clinton Co., O.; m Mary Jane SHEPPERD, dt Jesse & Elizabeth, Clinton Co., O.

JEFFRIES
1855, 10, 19. Rebecca m Caleb I. HARVEY

JENKINS
1841, 5, 13. Evan H., s Robert & Jemima, Miami Co., O.; m in Centre MH, Martha SHEPHERD, dt Jesse & Elizabeth, Clinton Co.,O.

JESSOP
1816, 5, 23. Jacob, s Thomas & Sarah, dec, Wayne Co., Ind.; m in Springfield Mtg, Lydia HIATT, wd Jehu, dt Wm. & Deborah, dec, STANFIELD, Clinton Co., O.

JOHNSON
1812, 1, 9. Thos., s Samuel & Susannah, Green Co., O.; m in "mtg held at Anderson's Fork", Mary FAULKNER, dt David & Judith, Green Co., O.
1816, 5, 22. John, s John, dec, & Rhoda, Green Co., O.; m in Centre Mtg, Judith FAULKNER, dt David & Judith, Green Co.,O.
1816, 9, 26. Ann m Benajah NORDYKE
1819, 10, 18. Chas. M., s Moreman & Elizabeth, dec, Clinton Co., O.; m in Dover Mtg, Phebe HAWORTH, dt Absalom & Phebe, dec, Clinton Co., O.
1820, 9, 21. Lewis, s John & Rhoda, Clinton Co., O.; m at Dover Mtg, Mary BANGHAM, dt Benjamin & Lucy, Clinton Co., O.
1821, 5, 23. James, s John, dec, & Rhoda, Clinton Co., O.; m in Centre Mtg, Elizabeth GRIFFITH, dt John & Hannah, Clinton Co., O.
1824, 3, 24. Susannah m Thomas JOHNSON
1824, 3, 24. Thomas m Susannah JOHNSON (Thomas, s Pleasant & Nancy, Green Co.,O.; m in Seneca MH, Susannah JOHNSON, dt Samuel & Susannah, Green Co., O.)
1824, 8, 25. George W., s Samuel & Susanna, Green Co., O.; m in Seneca Mtg, Apharicia MOORMAN, dt Micajah C. & Susanna, Green Co., O.
1842, 8, 24. Lewis, s Lewis, dec, & Mary, Clinton Co., O.; m in Centre MH, Rachel STANTON, dt Wm. & Margaret, Clinton Co.,O.
1842, 9, 22. Brooks, s John & Judith, Warren Co., O.; m in Wilmington MH, Lydia BURSON, dt Edward & Jemima, Clinton Co., O.
1871, 9, 20. Mary m Isaiah M. HAWORTH

JONES
1839, 1, 24. Huldah m Edward THOMAS
1839, 6, 20. Daniel, s Daniel, dec, & Elizabeth, Warren Co., O.; m in Wilmington MH, Hannah H. MABIE, dt John & Elizabeth, Clinton Co., O.
1841, 10, 21. Phebe m John SCHOOLEY

KERSEY
1816, 12, 26. Ann m Simon HADLEY

KINDLEY
1807, 11, 19. John, s Edward & Margaret, Warren Co., O.; m Betty WILSON, dt Jehu & Sarah

KING
1828, 9, 24. Dean, s John & Mary, Wayne Co., Ind.; m in Centre MH, Esther CARPENTER, dt Isaac & Mercy, dec, Clinton Co., O.

KINSEY
1828, 11, 19. Susannah m John STOUT, Jr.

KIRK
1822, 1, 24. Caleb, s Ezekiel & Hannah, Clinton Co., O.; m in Dover Mtg, Susanna BAILEY, dt Barclay, dec, & Judith BALLARD, of Va.
1823, 4, 23. Hannah m Abraham MOORE
1823, 12, 24. Isaiah, s Benjamin & Elizabeth, Wayne Co., Ind.; m in Centre Mtg, Sarah W. KIRK, dt Ezekiel & Hannah, Clinton Co., O.
1823, 12, 24. Sarah W. m Isaiah KIRK
1830, 12, 1. Mahlon, s Ezekiel, dec, & Hannah, Clinton Co., O.; m in Centre MH, Sarah HINES, dt Anthony & Hannah STANLEY, Vermillion Co., Ill.
1838, 11, 22. Emily m Samuel HOLLINGSWORTH
1853, 9, 21. Nathan, s Mahlon & Sarah, Clinton Co., O.; m in Centre MH, Abigail WHINERY, dt Zimri & Judith, Clinton Co.,O.
1858, 10, 21. Charles W., Wayne Co., Ind., s Israel, dec, & Sarah, Union Co., O.; m in Chester MH, Rachel HOLLINGSWORTH, dt Aseph, dec, & Anna, Clinton Co., O.

LAMAR
1838, 5, 17. Mary m Nathan DENNIS

LEONARD
1819, 9, 22. Mary m Thomas HESTER
1820, 9, 27. Hannah m Isaac HODGSON

LINTON
1810, 9, 5. Elizabeth m John SATTERTHWAIT
1813, 12, 13. Jane m Jesse ARNOLD
1820, 11, 22. Elizabeth m Joseph THATCHER
1826, 6, 21. Elizabeth m Wm. BUTTERWORTH
1829, 12, 2. Abi m Josiah FARQUHAR
1838, 8, 22. Mary m Jonathan HADLEY
1845, 8, 11. Ruth m Benj. WHINERY
1849, 3, 21. James W., s William, dec, & Elizabeth, Clinton Co., O.; m in Centre MH, Edith SHEPHERD, dt Jesse & Elizabeth, Clinton Co., O.
1860, 5, 23. Nancy m Isaac McMILLAN

LONGSTRETCH
1841, 8, 26. William, Warren Co., O., s Benjamin & Isabella, dec, Monmouth Co., Va.; m in Newhope, Martha COATE, dt John & Esther, dec, Green Co., O.

LUNDY
1824, 12, 23. Enoch, s James & Elizabeth, Clinton Co., O.; m in Chester Mtg, Charlotte GREEN, dt John & Ruth, Clinton Co., O.
1826, 8, 24. William, s James & Elizabeth, Clinton Co., O.; m in Chester Mtg, Mariah Ann SMITH, dt Thomas & Eve, Clinton Co.,O.
1828, 11, 20. Jesse, s James & Elizabeth, Clinton Co., O.; m in Chester MH, Abigail GREEN, dt John, dec, & Ruth, Clinton Co., O.
1831, 7, 1. Levi, s James & Elizabeth, Clinton Co., O.; m at Centre MH, Sarah WICKERSHAM, dt Enoch & Margaret, Clinton Co., O.
1833, 12, 25. James, s Amos & Ann, both dec, Clinton Co., O.; m at Center MH, O., Sophia HOLLINGSWORTH, dt Joel & Anna, Clinton Co., O.
1841, 3, 9. James, s Amos & Ann, both dec, Clinton Co., O.; m at Chester MH, O., Sarah SCHOOLEY, wd Nathan, dt Solomon & Tabitha STANBROUGH, Hamilton Co., O.
1840, 8, 20. Asenath m Joseph OREN
1842, 9, 1. Rachel m Jehiel GREEN
1854, 5, 18. Margaret m Asaph PAXSON
1856, 9, 25. Elizabeth m John CARY

McMILLAN
1820, 11, 22. Jane Ann m Samuel HOLLINGSWORTH
1821, 12, 5. Edith m Samuel COX
1822, 3, 20. Mary m Thomas COX
1824, 4, 21. Deborah m Jesse TAYLOR
1824, 9, 22. Josiah, s David & Hannah, Clinton Co., O.; m in Centre Mtg, Susanna COX, dt Joshua, dec, & Amy, Randolph Co., Ind. Josiah m 2nd 1851,9,24 at Center MH, O., Mary CREWS, dt Obediah & Mary, both dec, Mahoning Co., O.
1832, 11, 21. Mary/Emily m Thos. C. SHIPLEY
1835, 2, 25. David Jr., s David & Hannah, Clinton Co., O.; m in Centre MH, Sarah CARPENTER, dt Isaac & Mercy, dec, Clinton Co., O.
1836, 5, 26. Deborah J. m Jonathan WRIGHT
1837, 11, 23. Jonathan, s David & Hannah, Clinton Co., O.; m in Chester MH, Susannah H. WICKERSHAM, dt Enoch & Margaret, Clinton Co., O.
1840, 1, 21. Thomas W., s David & Hannah, Clinton Co., O.; m in Wilmington MH, Elizabeth ADSIT, dt Parmer, dec, & Isabella, Clinton Co., O.
1849, 5, 24. Hannah m Ezra WHINERY
1857, 11, 26. Lydia Emily m Samuel WHINERY
1858, 9, 23. Hannah Ann m Francis FARQUHAR
1860, 5, 23. Isaac, s David & Sarah, Clinton Co., O.; m in Centre MH, Nancy LINTON, dt Seth & Ann, Clinton Co., O.
1863, 4, 23. Mary Ann m Henry SPRAY
1863, 10, 21. Ruth W. m Levi MILLS

McPHERSON
1865, 5, 24. Daniel, s Joseph & Ruth, Clinton Co., O.; m in Centre MH, Lydia May ELLIS, Clinton Co., O.

MABEE
1834, 9, 24. Susan m Walter T. CARPENTER
1837, 4, 19. Catherine F. m Jonathan TIMBERLAKE
1839, 6, 20. Hannah H. m Daniel JONES
1842, 12, 22. Eliza B. m Jonathan HADLEY

MADEN
1817, 9, 25. Ann m Henry HARVEY

MALLARD
1839, 10, 24. Susannah H. m John P. HUNNICUTT

MASSEY
1814, 11, 17. James, Clinton Co., O., s -enu, dec, & Ruth, Orange Co., O.; m in Springfield Mtg, Elizabeth HALL, dt Jacob & Martha, Clinton Co., O.

MAXSON
1829, 3, 25. Sarah m Jesse HIATT

MENDENHALL
1808, 1, 6. Richard, s John & Ruth, Green Co., O.; m in Centre Mtg, Elizabeth BARNETT, dt Athanasius & Jane, Green Co., O.
1809, 5, 11. Joseph, s John & Ruth, Green Co., O.; m in Centre Mtg, Ann BARNETT
1818, 1, 21. Edith [Mendinghall] m Amos COWGILL

MILLER
1834, 4, 24. Thomas, s Solomon & Ruth, Warren Co., O.; m in Newhope MH, Eliza CURL, dt Samuel & Susannah, dec

MILLS
1810, 6, 7. Richard, s Thomas, dec, & Jamima, Clinton Co., O.; m Nancy OZBUN, dt David & Elizabeth
1863, 10, 21. Levi, s Jonathan & Charity, dec, Warren Co., O.; m in Centre MH, Ruth W. McMILLAN, dt Milton, dec, & Harriet S., Clinton Co., O.

MITCHEL
1859, 9, 21. Hannah D. m Jehu MOORE

MOON
1815, 2, 15. Mary m Joshua HARVEY
1815, 9, 28. Simon, s Simon & Judith, Clinton Co., O.; m in Springfield Mtg, Lydia HARVEY, dt Eli & Mary, Clinton Co., O.
1847, 9, 23. Miles H., Newberry MM, s Wm. & Ann, Clinton Co., O.; m in Chester MH, Charlotte D. GREEN, dt Jesse & Sarah, Clinton Co., O.

MOORE
1814, 8, 11. Joshua, Clinton Co., O., s Thos., dec, & Sarah, Center MM, Pa.; m in Springfield MH, Nancy STRATTON, dt Joseph & Dosha, Clinton Co., O.
1823, 4, 23. Abraham, s John & Mary, both dec, of Pa.; m in Centre Mtg, Hannah KIRK, dt Ezekiel & Hannah, Clinton Co., O.
1859, 9, 21. Jehu, s Joshua & Nancy, Clinton Co., O.; m in Centre MH, Hannah D. MITCHEL dt Franklin & Sarah, dec, Clinton Co., O.
1865, 4, 19. Franklin, Sugar River MM, Montgomery Co., Ind., s Jacob & Tacy B.; m in Centre MH, Mary B. TIMBERLAKE

MOORMAN
1824, 8, 25. Apharicia, m Geo. W. JOHNSON
1850, 5, 23. Lucy Ann, m David A. PAINTER

MORRIS
1862, 5, 22. James, s Isaac, dec, & Millicent, Clinton Co., O.; m in Chester MH, Hannah WHINERY, dt Jesse, dec, & Sarah, Clinton Co., O.

MOTE
1850, 11, 14. Joseph, s David Jr. & Barbara, Miami MM, O.; m in Newhope MH, Martha PAINTER, dt Thos. & Mary, Green Co., O.

NORDYKE
1816, 9, 26. Benajah, s Israel & Mary, Clinton Co., O.; m in Springfield, Ann JOHNSON dt Thomas dec & Ann, Clinton Co., O.

OREN
1815, 9, 20. Abigail m Cephas ATKINSON
1820, 2, 24. Alexander, s John & Ruth, dec, Clinton Co., O.; m in Dover Mtg, Lydia FRAZIER, dt Ezekiel & Rebecca, Clinton Co., O.
1820, 6, 22. Lydia m Chas. ATKINSON
1840, 8, 20. Joseph, s James & Margaret, Clinton Co., O.; m in Chester MH, Asenath LUNDY, dt James & Elizabeth, dec, Clinton Co., O.
1848, 5, 25. Hannah m Enoch WICKERSHAM

OZBUN
1810, 6, 7. Nancy m Richard MILLS

PAINTER
1816, 8, 28. Jesse, s David & Martha, Green Co., O.; m in Centre Mtg, Elizabeth SMITH, dt Joseph & Lydia, Clinton Co., O.
1838, 4, 26. Sarah m Eli THORNBURGH
1838, 11, 22. Rachel W. m Hiram COATE
1846, 9, 24. Phebe W. m John FAWCETT
1850, 5, 23. David A., s Thomas & Mary, Green Co., O.; m in Newhope MH, Lucy Ann MOREMAN dt Thos. & Martha, dec, Green Co., O.
1850, 11, 14. Martha m Joseph MOTE
1851, 3, 20. Lydia S. m Josiah THORNBURGH

PAIST
1816, 1, 24. Charles, s James & Elizabeth, Providence, Pa.; m Abigale PERKINS, dt Isaac & Phenina, Clinton Co., O.

PAXON
1853, 4, 14. William, s John & Anna, Logan Co., O.; m in Chester MH at a mtg appoined for that purpose, Ruth GREEN, dt Robert

PAXON, William & Ruth, continued
& Mary, both dec, Clinton Co., O.
1854, 5, 18. Asaph [Paxson], s John & Anna, Logan Co., O.; m in Chester MH, Margaret LUNDY, dt Jesse & Abigail, dec, Clinton Co., O.

PERKINS
1810, 8, 8. Ann m Hezekiah HIATT
1813, 11, 10. Susannah m Amos COOK
1816, 1, 24. Abigaile m Charles PAIST
1821, 12, 26. John, s Isaac & Pheniah, Clinton Co., O.; m in Centre, Julianna EACHUS, dt Robert & Phebe, Clinton Co., O.

PUSEY
1815, 6, 21. Joel, s Nathan, dec, & Mary, Clinton Co., O.; m in Centre Mtg, Hannah FAULKNER, dt Jesse & Ruth, dec, Green Co., O.

RHODE
1817, 12, 25. Thomas, s John & Mary, Warren Co., O.; m in Springfield Mtg, Mary BALLARD dt Joseph & Elizabeth, Clinton Co., O.

RICH
1821, 2, 22. Samuel, Warren Co., O., s Samuel & Dinah, both dec, Guilford Co., N. C.; m in Dover Mtg, Lydia THOMAS, dt John, dec in Pa., & Jane, Clinton Co., O.
1841, 4, 22. Thomas, Clinton Co., O., s Samuel & Dinah, both dec, Stokes Co., N. C.; m in Wilmington MH, Isabella ADSIT, wd Palmer, Clinton Co., O.

RINEHART
1809, 7, 5. Barbary m Simeon BALLARD

SANDERS
1808, 5, 12. Barbara m Samuel WHITSON

SATTERTHWAIT
1810, 9, 5. John, Warren Co., O., s Wm. & Mary, Bucks Co., Pa.; m in Centre Mtg, Elizabeth LINTON, dt Samuel & Elizabeth, dec, Bucks Co., Pa.

SCHOOLEY
1817, 3, 19. Nathan, s Samuel & Elizabeth, Grayson Co., Va.; m in Centre Mtg, Sarah STANBROUGH, dt Solomon & Tabitha, Clinton Co., O.
1836, 1, 21. Anne m Isaac GREEN
1841, 9, 3. Sarah m James LUNDY
1841, 10, 21. John, s Samuel & Rachel, Clinton Co., O.; m in Chester MH, Phebe JONES, dt Isaac & Phebe, Clinton Co., O.
1842, 9, 1. Omri, s Nathan, dec, & Sarah, Clinton Co., O.; m in Chester MH, Elizabeth COX, dt Joshua & Mariah, Randolph Co., Ind.
1843, 11, 23. Rachel m Aaron GREEN
1848, 4, 20. Elizabeth m Joel GREEN

SEXTON
1815, 4, 19. Mary m Israel TAYLOR

SHEPHERD
1815, 8, 23. Jesse [Sheppard], s Moses & Susannah, Green Co., O.; m in Centre Mtg, Elizabeth FAULKNER, dt Robert & Elizabeth, dec, Green Co., O.
1841, 5, 13. Martha m Evan H. JENKINS
1849, 3, 21. Edith m James W. LINTON
1856, 3, 19. Mary Jane [Shepperd] m Jonathan H. JAMES

SHIPLEY
1832, 11, 21. Thomas C., s Wm. & Phebe, Clinton Co., O.; m in Centre MH, Mary Emily McMILLAN, dt Jonathan & Hannah

SMITH
1816, 8, 28. Elizabeth m Jesse PAINTER
1822, 3, 27. Mary m David BUTLER
1826, 8, 24. Mariah Ann m Wm. LUNDY
1860, 6, 21. Seth, s Seth & Elizabeth, both dec, Clark Co., O.; m in Chester MH, Anne HOLLINGSWORTH, dt Enoch & Margaret WICKERSHAM, Clinton Co., O.

SPRAY
1863, 4, 23. Henry, s Jesse & Eunice, Clinton Co., O.; m in Centre MH, Mary Ann McMILLAN dt Thos. W. & Elizabeth, Clinton Co., O.

STANBROUGH
1811, 9, 18. Evan, s Solomon & Tabitha, Clinton Co., O.; m in Centre Mtg, Elizabeth HESTER, dt Francis & Mary, Clinton Co., O.
1815, 5, 24. Nehemiah, s Sollomon & Tabitha, Clinton Co., O.; m in Centre Mtg, Ruth HESTER, dt Francis & Mary, Clinton Co.,O.
1817, 3, 19. Sarah m Nathan SCHOOLY

STANLEY
1826, 10, 26. Sarah m Jesse HINES

STANTON
1807, 10, 8. Wm. Xenia, Green Co., O., s James, dec, & Ann, Green Co., O.; m in Centre Mtg, Martha FAULKNER, dt Jesse & Ruth, dec
1842, 8, 24. Rachel m Lewis JOHNSON

STARBUCK
1817, 10, 2. Abigail m James WRIGHT

STOUT
1808, 1, 6. Margaret m Enoch WICKERSHAM
1827, 3, 21. Ann m Wm. H. HARRISON

STRATTON
1812, 12, 9. Susanna m Thomas THATCHER
1814, 8, 11. Nancy m Joshua MOORE
1816, 10, 23. Davis, s Joseph & Dosha, Clinton

STRATTON, David, continued
Co., O.; m in Centre Mtg, Ruthy THATCHER, dt Stephen, dec, & Ruth, Clinton Co., O.
1819, 1, 21. Caleb, Green Co., O., step-s of Joseph CURL & own s of his w, Sarah, Logan Co., O.; m in Newhope Mtg, Jane FAULKNER, dt Jesse & Ruth, Green Co., O.
1828, 11, 19. John Jr., s John & Ann, Clinton Co., O.; m in Centre MH, Susannah KINSEY, dt Christopher & Mary, Clinton Co., O.

STROUD
1839, 11, 20. Ellen m Parvin WRIGHT

TAYLOR
1815, 4, 19. Israel, s Jacob & Hannah, Clinton Co., O.; m in Centre Mtg, Mary SEXTON, dt Mashach & Hannah, dec, Fayette Co., Pa.
1815, 6, 21. Elizabeth m Joel WRIGHT
1822, 4, 4. Hannah m Samuel BUTTERWORTH
1824, 4, 21. Jesse, s Jacob & Hannah, Clinton Co., O.; m in Centre Mtg, Deborah McMILLAN dt David & Hannah, Clinton Co., O.
1858, 9, 23. Deborah E. m Joseph DOAN, Jr.

THATCHER
1807, 12, 3. Mary m Eli ANDERSON
1812, 12, 9. Thomas, Clinton Co., O., s Stephen, dec, & Ruth, Green Co., O.; m in Centre Mtg, Susanna STRATTON, dt Joseph & Dosha, Clinton Co., O.
1816, 10, 23. Ruthy m David STRATTON
1820, 11, 22. Joseph, s Stephen, dec, Berkley Co., Va.; m in Centre Mtg, Elizabeth LINTON, dt William & Hannah, Clinton Co., O.

THOMAS
1821, 2, 22. Lydia m Samuel RICH
1828, 5, 21. Robert, s John, dec, & Jane, Clinton Co., O.; m in Centre MH, Almedia BAILEY, dt Josiah, dec, & Susannah "now KIRK", Clinton Co., O.
1839, 1, 24. Edward, s John & Esther, Clinton Co., O.; m in Chester MH, Huldah JONES, dt Isaac & Phebe, Clinton Co., O.

THORNE
1808, 2, 8. Wm., Green Co., O., s Isaac, dec, & Hannah, Jefferson Co., O.; m in Cesars Creek MH, Rachel EMBREE, dt Thomas & Ester, Green Co., O.

THORNBURGH
1838, 4, 26. Eli, s Joel & Dinah, Clinton Co., O.; m in Newhope MH, Sarah PAINTER, dt Jacob & Naomi, Clinton Co., O.
1850, 9, 26. Jemima m Mordecai WALKER
1851, 3, 20. Josiah, s Joel & Dinah, dec, Green Co., O.; m in Newhope MH, Lydia S. PAINTER, dt Jesse & Elizabeth, Green Co., O.

TIMBERLAKE
1810, 5, 7. Richard, s John & Mollie, Highland Co., O.; m in Centre Mtg, Mary WRIGHT, dt Jonathan & Susanna, Highland Co., O.
1837, 4, 19. Jonathan, s Richard & Mary, Clinton Co., O.; m in Centre MH, Catherine F. MABIE, dt John & Elizabeth, dec, Clinton Co., O.
1839, 5, 2. Alfred, s Richard & Mary, Highland Co., O.; m in Centre MH, Phebe DOAN, dt Joseph & Eliza, Clinton Co., O.
1863, 9, 23. Eliza D. m Mathew CHARLES
1865, 4, 19. Mary B. m Franklin MOORE

TOWEL
1818, 4, 30. Rebecca m Joshua HADLEY

UNDERWOOD
1829, 9, 21. Hannah m Joseph WILSON

VANHORN
1807, 10, 7. Joanna, wd, m Geo. HAYWORTH, Sr.

VESTAL
1810, 3, 7. Elizabeth m Peter DICKS

VOTAW
1846, 1, 15. Isaac, Jay Co., Ind., s John & Rebecca, both dec; m in Newhope MH, Phebe COMPTON, dt John & Jane, Green Co., O.

WALKER
1832, 11, 21. Phebe F. m John HUNT
1850, 9, 26. Mordecai, s Wm., dec, & Martha, Clinton Co., O.; m in Newhope MH, Jemima THORNBURG, dt Joel & Dinah, Green Co., O.

WALL
1822, 4, 4. Phebe m Jonathan DOAN

WALTHALL
1852, 4, 22. Daniel B., Dover MM, s William B. & Martha, Clinton Co., O.; m in Newhope MH, Elizabeth H. FAUCETT, dt Robert & Mary, Green Co., O.
1857, 12, 23. Thomas, s William B. & Martha, Clinton Co., O.; m in Centre MH, Maria E. DOAN, dt Wm. & Betsey, Clinton Co., O.

WHINERY
1841, 5, 19. Elizabeth m Jesse COFFIN
1842, 10, 20. Edwin, s Zimri & Judith, Clinton Co., O.; m in Chester MH, Hannah HINES, dt Jesse, dec, & Sarah, Clinton Co., O.
1845, 8, 11. Benjamin, s Zimri & Judith, Clinton Co., O.; m in Centre MH, Ruth LINTON, dt Nathan & Rachel, Clinton Co.,O.
1849, 5, 24. Ezra, s Zimri & Judith, Clinton Co., O.; m in Chester MH, Hannah McMILLAN, dt Joshua & Susannah, dec, Clinton Co.,O.
1853, 9, 21. Abigail m Nathan KIRK
1855, 4, 26. Jane m Pierce HOLLINGSWORTH

WHINERY, continued
1857, 11, 26. Samuel, s Zimri & Judith, Clinton Co., O.; m in Chester MH, Lydia Emily McMILLAN, dt Jonathan & Susannah, dec, Clinton Co., O.
1862, 5, 22. Hannah m James MORRIS

WHITSON
1808, 5, 12. Samuel, Warren Co., O., s Solomon & Phebe; m in Ceasors Creek, Barbara SANDERS, dt Joel & Sarah, Warren Co., O.

WICKERSHAM
1808, 1, 6. Enoch, Warren Co., O., s James & Sarah, dec, York Co., Pa.; m in Centre Mtg, Margaret STOUT, dt John & Anne, York Co., Pa.
1827, 8, 23. Anne m Asaph HOLLINGSWORTH
1831, 7, 1. Sarah m Levi LUNDY
1837, 11, 23. Susannah H. m Jonathan McMILLAN
1848, 5, 25. Enoch, s Enoch & Margaret, Clinton Co., O.; m in Chester MH, Hannah OREN, dt Alexandria & Lydia, Clinton Co., O.

WILLIAMS
1825, 5, 26. Josiah, Green Co., O., s Wm. & Phebe, Highland Co., O.; m in Newhope Mtg, Sarah BAILIFF, dt Thomas & Sarah, Green Co., O.
1849, 12, 20. Thomas B., s Josiah, dec, & Sarah (now STAFFORD), Green Co., O.; m in Newhope MH, Phebe FAULKNER, dt David & Mary, dec, Green Co., O.

WILSON
1807, 11, 19. Betty m John KINDLEY
1829, 9, 21. Joseph, s Samuel, dec, & Hannah, Clinton Co., O.; m in Chester Mtg, Hannah UNDERWOOD, dt Wm. & Deborah, dec, Clinton Co., O.
1843, 10, 25. Enos, s Isaac, dec, & Ann (now TRUE), Warren Co., O.; m in Centre MH, Rebecca BALLARD, dt Spencer & Rebecca, dec, Clinton Co., O.

WRIGHT
1810, 5, 7. Mary m Richard TIMBERLAKE
1811, 8, 8. Wm., s James & Sarah, Clinton Co., O.; m in "Upper MH on Todds Forks", Hannah DILLON, dt Jesse & Hannah, Clinton Co., O.
1813, 3, 11. Charity m Luke DILLEN
1814, 6, 9. Jesse, s James, dec, & Sarah, Clinton Co., O.; m in "Upper MH on Todds Fork" Abigail DILLON, dt Jesse & Hannah, Clinton Co., O.
1815, 6, 21. Joel, Cincinnati, O., s Jonathan & Susanna, Hamilton Co., O.; m auspices Center MM, O., Elizabeth TAYLOR, dt Jacob & Hannah, Clinton Co., O.
1817, 10, 2. James, s John & Margaret, Clinton Co., O.; m in Dover MH, Abigail STARBUCK, dt Gayer & Susannah
1819, 12, 29. Esly m Isaac FURNAS
1836, 5, 26. Jonathan, s Jonathan & Susannah, both dec, Fayette Co., Ind.; m in Chester MH, Deborah J. McMILLAN, dt Thomas, dec, & Jane, Clinton Co., O.
1839, 11, 20. Parvin, s Benjamin, dec, & Hannah, Belmont Co., O.; m in Centre MH, Ellen STROUD, dt Jacob & Ann, Clinton Co., O.

* * * * * * *

ARNETT
1825, 12, 22. Thomas, s Valentine & Sarah, dec, Green Co., O.; m in Newhope MH, Rachel FAULKNER, dt David, dec, & Judith, Center MM, O.

FAULKNER
1832, 3, 22. David, s Robert & Elizabeth, dec, Green Co., O.; m in Newhope MH, Leah BAYLIFF, dt Thomas, dec, & Sarah, Green Co., O.

SPRINGFIELD MONTHLY MEETING

Springfield Monthly Meeting, located on Tods Fork, five and a half miles west of Wilmington, was set off from Center Monthly Meeting 11 Mo. 26, 1818.

Among the members were Jacob Beard and family, Jacob Hadley and family, Azel Walker and family, Henry T. Davis, John Harvey, Benjamin Farquhar and family, Eugene Hadley, Jane Gaskill and Susannah Gallop.

RECORDS

ADAMS
1821, 1, 27. Achsa (form Hobson) con mou
1825, 8, 27. Arksah Macklin (form Adams) dis mou
1827, 7, 28. Wm. & w, Mellescent, attached to Center MM, O.

ADSET
1841, 4, 13. Thomas Rich gct Centre MM, to m Isabella Adset
1841, 7, 13. Mary Ann rocf Centre MM, O., dtd 1841,6,16

ALBERTSON
1819, 12, 25. Alice & ch, Chalkley & Benjamin, recrq
1824, 2, 28. Josiah rmt Hannah Kester
1828, 6, 28. Josiah & w, Hannah, & her s, Harmon Kester, gct Cesars Creek MM, O.
1837, 6, 11. Chalkley dis disunity
1838, 4, 17. Benjamin dis disunity
1874, 7, 18. Benjamin recrq
1877, 7, 21. Benjamin gct Newberry MM, O.
1899, 3, 18. John recrq

ALBRIGHT
1898, 11, 19. Amanda relrq

ALLEN
1854, 5, 20. Daniel C. rmt Elizabeth Hadley
1854, 7, 15. Daniel C. & ch, John & Charles, rocf Spiceland MM, Ind., dtd 1854,6,7
1859, 2, 19. Job D., minor, s Daniel C., rocf Spiceland MM, Ind.
1874, 2, 21. Daniel C. gct Shawnee MM, Kans.
1874, 5, 16. Samuel recrq
1874, 10, 17. Charles & Job D. gct Shawnee MM, Kans.
1877, 3, 17. Rebecca L. & Sarah M. recrq
1878, 7, 20. Marion S. & ch, Orrilla B., Olive M., Mary L. & Annetta, recrq

ANDERSON
1930, 3, 5. Noah E. & Hattie recrq (G)
1930, 4, 3. Martha recrq (G)

ANDREW
----, --, --. Samuel b 1783,12,14 d 1871,7,18; m Delilah BAKER b 1787,8,19 d 1856,2,13
Ch: William b 1806, 7, 21
John " 1808, 9, 22
Hannah " 1812, 1, 27
Susannah " 1819, 4, 24
----, --, --. Henry b 1777,2,12; m Jane MILLS b 1783,11,5
Ch: Anne b 1806, 8, 7
Robert " 1809, 2, 14 d 1823, 5,21
John " 1811, 3, 11
Hannah " 1813, 4, 13
Joseph " 1816, 1, 14
William " 1818, 11, 21
Ch: Jonathan b 1821, 1, 26
Sarah " 1825, 1, 8
----, --, --. William m Ruth ----- d 1852,10, 19 bur Springfield
Ch: Eliza Jane b 1832, 7, 3
Hannah " 1833, 12, 5
Samuel " 1835, 7, 28
Delilah " 1837, 2, 13
Isaac H. " 1838, 11, 28
John Thomas " 1841, 1, 3
William Henry " 1842, 9, 14
Jacob " 1844, 6, 20
Lydia " 1846, 7, 1
Wilson Hobbs " 1850, 9, 11
----, --, --. Ira b 1818,1,20; m Mary E. ----- b 1826,2,2
Ch: Elwood G. b 1856, 12, 17
----, --, --. Eden b 1820,3,1; m Nancy ----- b 1821,11,15
Ch: Amanda J.T.b 1860, 4, 10 (adopted)
----, --, --. Samuel & Louisa
Ch: Hannah Elma b 1860, 11, 18
Nancy Elizabeth " 1862, 3, 8
John B. " 1863, 10, 1
Ruth Ellen " 1866, 8, 4
Anna D. " 1872, 5, 18
1866, 2, 25. Americus J. b
1866, 8, 4. Ruth E. b
----, --, --. Wm. Henry b 1842,9,14; m Caroline ----- b 1845,7,11
Ch: Mary Ruth b 1870, 11, 4
1898, 2, 15. Susannah McFadden d ae 78 bur Wilmington
1910, 6, 21. Susannah, dt Robert & Frances (Green), b

1826, 7, 29. Anna rmt Mahlon Hockett
1830, 3, 16. Hannah rmt Jacob Hale
1831, 1, 11. William rmt Ruth Hadley
1834, 5, 13. Hannah rmt Robert Holaday
1836, 6, 14. John, s Samuel, con mou
1837, 1, 17. John Jr. dis mou
1837, 1, 17. Mary (form Smith) dis mou
1839, 4, 16. Henry & w, Jane, & ch, William Jonathan & Sarah, gct Newberry MM, O.
1842, 5, 17. Joseph con mou
1843, 12, 12. Joseph & w, Sarah, & dt, Martha Jane, gct White Lick MM, Ind.
1847, 4, 17. Susannah rmt John McFadden
1858, 10, 17. Hannah Hiatt (form Andrew) con mou
1859, 8, 20. Samuel Jr. dis disunity
1859, 8, 20. Samuel Jr. dis disunity
1859, 11, 19. John B. dis mou
1860, 3, 21. Louisa (form Hornaday) con mou
1862, 7, 19. Isaac con mou
1862, 9, 20. Mary Jane (form Osborn) con mou
1866, 6, 16. Lydia Anson (form Andrew) con mou

ANDREW, continued
1866, 8, 18. John T. con mou
1867, 7, 20. Elizabeth recrq
1868, 7, 18. Mary Ellen recrq
1868, 8, 15. Nancy Jane & adopted dt, Amanda Jane T., recrq
1868, 12, 19. William H. con mou
1871, 1, 21. Caroline rocf Center MM, O.
1871, 2, 18. Sarah Emily recrq
1871, 2, 18. Ira & w, Mary E., & ch, Elwood, recrq
1871, 2, 18. Samuel & w, Hannah E., & ch, Nancy & John B., recrq
1871, 2, 18. Eden recrq
1871, 2, 18. Sarah Emily recrq
1872, 10, 19. Cyrus & w, Clarissa, recrq
1876, 7, 15. John Thomas & w, Mary Ellen, & ch, Americus J., Clinton R., Mary B. & Ruth Ella, gct Smyrna MM, Ia.
1876, 7, 15. William H. & w, Caroline, & ch, Mary R. & Walter T., gct Smyrna MM, Ia.
1876, 7, 15. John B. recrq
1877, 8, 18. Samuel & w, Louisa, & ch, Hannah Elma, Nancy Elizabeth, John B., Ruth Ellen & Anna D., gct Smyrna MM, Ia.
1879, 3, 15. Jacob H. dis disunity
1881, 5, 21. Miles recrq
1891, 6, 20. Sarah Emily Pyle (form Andrews) relrq
1911, 1, 21. Frances Green rocf Lansdown MM, Pa.
1911, 6, 17. Susanna, dt Robert & Frances, recrq
1926, 1, 30. Susanna gct Westtown MM, Pa.

ANSON
1827, 4, 28. Hannah recrq
1866, 6, 16. Lydia (form Andrews) con mou
1871, 11, 18. George H. & w, Susan L., & ch, Semer E., Minnie B. & Willis A., recrq
1876, 7, 15. Lydia H. & ch, Alice J., & Mary A., gct Smyrna MM, Ia.

ANTRAM
1820, 2, 28. Joseph rmt Mary Fallis
1822, 12, 28. Elizabeth More (form Antrim) dis mou
1823, 3, 29. Hiram dis mou
1823, 8, 30. Joseph con mou
1823, 11, 29. John Jr. dis mou
1825, 6, 25. Ann & ch, Aaron Edmund Charity Ann, gct Miami MM, O.
1827, 7, 28. Joseph attached to Center MM, O.
1828, 3, 29. Joshua dis disunity

ARCHDEACON
----, --, --. George H., s N. & Ann M., b 1869,6,10; m Bertha H. CUSHMAN, dt W. H. & Sarah E., b 1876,1,12
Ch: Bruce
Burdette b 1907, 10, 4

1922, 2, 18. Hurley & w, Bertha, & s, Bruce Burdette, recrq
1925, 5, 17. Hurley & w, Bertha & s, Bruce, relrq

ARMSTRONG
1901, 1, 19. Amora recrq

ARTHUR
1894, 4, 21. C. W. & fam recrq
1895, 7, 20. C. A. & w relrq

AUGBURN
1841, 9, 14. Eliza B. & ch, Henry Marshal & Isaac Samuel, rocf Clear Creek MM, O., dtd 1841,6,22

AUSTIN
1836, 11, 15. Mary (form Pyle) con mou
1843, 10, 17. Mary dis jas
1886, 8, 21. Samantha L. rocf Maple Grove MM, Ill., dtd 1886,5,22

BABB
1900, 11, 17. Eli & w, Orianna, rocf Sabina MM, O., dtd 1900,10,10

BAILEY
----, --, --. Frank C. b 1877,2,25; m Katie C. SMITH, dt Joseph & Ann (Osborn), b 1880,2,14.
Ch: Russell W. b 1901, 5, 12 d 1926, 8,16
Bernice
May " 1903, 2, 4 " 1919, 6,21
Carl J. " 1906, 7, 12
1927, 5, 1. Samuel d bur Clarksville

1893, 3, 18. Samuel Oscar & w recrq
1907, 12, 21. Wm. V. & ch, Walter E., Lillian & Herman T., recrq
1909, 3, 20. Mrs. W. H. recrq
1910, 1, 15. Katie rocf Ogden MM, O.
1910, 1, 15. Frank R. & ch, Russell W., Bernice May & Carl J., recrq
1910, 11, 19. Wm. B. & fam gct Dayton MM, O.
1915, 3, 20. Sarah E. relrq

BAILIFF
1839, 6, 11. Eliza Ann rocf Center MM, O., dtd 1839,5,15
1840, 3, 17. Daniel rst on consent of Centre MM, O.
1840, 3, 17. Thomas, Joshua M., Elijah & David, ch Daniel, recrq
1841, 8, 17. Daniel & w, Eliza, & ch, Thomas, Joshua M., Elijah, David & Anna Mariah, gct White Lick MM, Ind.

BAKER
1874, 1, 17. Samuel & w, Jennie, & ch, Frank M. & Leonidas, recrq
1881, 4, 16. Jennie recrq
1881, 5, 21. Clara recrq
1882, 4, 15. George recrq

BAKER, continued
1889, 6, 15. Samuel & ch, Frank Leonidas & Harley, gct Wilmington MM, O.

BALLARD
1826, 2, 26. Martha d (an elder)
1826, 7, 26. Martha, w David, d ae 57
1826, 7, 28. Asa d
1853, 3, 31. Jane d
----, --, --. Amos b 1835,2,25; m Elizabeth ----- b 1837,11,22

Ch:				
Rebecca	b 1861,	8,	2
Annie	" 1863,	1,	11
Olive	" 1864,	4,	8
Phebe A.	" 1867,	2,	22
Elva	" 1869,	2,	27
Mary J.	" 1873,	4,	9

1821, 10, 27. Lydia rmt John Harvey
1825, 8, 27. Dinah rmt John Whitson
1826, 1, 28. Dinah rmt James L. Whitson
1827, 1, 27. Jonathan gct Fairfield MM, Ind.
1827, 7, 28. William, Joseph & Mourning attached to Center MM, O.
1831, 8, 16. Jonathan rocf Fairfield MM, Ind., dtd 1831,8,16
1832, 3, 13. Jonathan gct Miami MM, O.
1834, 9, 16. Wilson Carter gct Centre MM, O., to m Judith F. Ballard
1835, 10, 13. Jesse F. rmt Phariba J. Wilson
1836, 3, 15. Pheriba J. gct Center MM, O.
1838, 9, 11. Eli Hadley gct New Garden MM, Ind., to m Mary Balard
1839, 2, 12. Jane [Balard], dt Mary Hadley, rocf New Garden MM, Ind., dtd 1838,12,15
1839, 10, 15. John P. Hunnicutt gct Center MM, O., to m Susannah H. Balard
1842, 10, 11. Jesse F. & w, Pheriba, & ch, Thomas Chalkley, William & Phebe Ann, rocf Centre MM, O., dtd 1842,9,14
1843, 10, 17. Jesse F. & w, Phariby, & ch, Thomas C., William, Phebe Ann & Jesse, gct Smithfield MM, Ind.
1862, 4, 19. Henry Harvey gct West Union MM, Ind., to m Sarah Ballard
1871, 4, 15. Amos & w, Elizabeth, & ch, Rebecca, Ormie, Olive, Phebe, Alice & Elva, rocf Newberry MM, O.
1896, 12, 19. Amos & fam gct Wilmington MM, O.

BANGHAM
1866, 9, 15. Esther rocf New Garden MM, Ind., dtd 1866,8,18
1868, 4, 18. John C. & ch recrq
1868, 12, 19. John C. gct Salem MM, Ia.; returned unused 1874,10,17
1874, 10, 17. John C. & ch, Ella M., Cyrus, Lavina & Anna Lucy, gct Wilmington MM, O.
1882, 1, 21. Benjamin relrq

BANKSON
1829, 6, 16. Elizabeth rocf Lees Creek MM, O., dtd 1829,2,21
1833, 1, 15. Elizabeth gct Fairfield MM, O.
1845, 2, 11. Elizabeth & ch, William & Elizabeth, rocf Clear Creek MM, O., dtd 1844, 11,9
1845, 2, 11. Ruth rocf Clear Creek MM, O., dtd 1844,11,9
1845, 4, 15. Mary Ann rocf Clear Creek MM, O., dtd 1844,11,9
1851, 6, 21. Ruth C. Lacey (form Bankson) dis mou
1856, 6, 21. William dis mou
1865, 11, 18. Elizabeth E. gct Fairfield MM,O.
1865, 11, 18. Elizabeth gct Fairfield MM, O.
1868, 8, 18. Mary Ann Davis (form Bankson) gct Fairfield MM

BARBER
1874, 5, 16. George & w, Sarah E., & s, George W., recrq

BARRETT
1885, 6, 20. Ella M. (form Harvey) gct Cesars Creek MM, O.

BATES
1877, 3, 17. Anice recrq

BAUGHAM
1849, 8, 19. Simon Hadley gct Dover MM, O., to m Rachel M. Baugham

BEAN
1868, 8, 15. Mary Ann (form Rich) con mou

BEARD
----, --, --. Jacob & Pamelia

Ch:				
Rosanna Jane	b 1848,	2,	23 d 1850, 4, 6
Amos Elwood	" 1851,	8,	3
Susannah Elma	" 1854,	5,	10
Sarah Delilah	" 1857,	11,	30
Laura Ann	" 1860,	8,	29

1852, 1, 17. Jacob & w, Permelia, & s, Amos Elwood, recrq
1857, 8, 15. Jacob & w, Pamelia, & ch, Amos Elwood & Susannah Elma, gct Honey Creek MM, Iowa
1860, 5, 19. Jacob & w, Pamelia, & ch, Amos Elwood, Susannah Elma & Sarah, rocf Rocksylvania MM, Ia., dtd 1860,2,23
1881, 11, 19. Jacob & w, Permelia, & dt, Laura, rocf Wilmington MM, O.
1886, 5, 15. Laura Ann gct Newberry MM, O.
1886, 5, 15. Jacob & w, Pamelia, gct Newberry MM, O.

BEATTY
1929, 12, 5. Dora May recrq (G)

BEAVER
1857, 6, 20. Miriam (form Quinby) dis mou

BELL
1870, 4, 10. Martha (form Kersey) con mou
1873, 11, 15. Martha & ch, Lutitia & Charles K., gct Wilmington MM, O.

BETTS
1880, 3, 20. Hattie P. [Bettz] recrq
1883, 11, 17. John recrq

BEVAN
----, --, --. Lewis H., s Owen & Mary, b 1830,9 6; d 1914,5,12; m Jane HADLEY b 1834,10,23 d 1883,8,7
Ch: Orlando b 1857, 9, 21
Frank " 1859, 11, 3
Emmett " 1861, 9, 21
----,--, --. Orlando, s Lewis & Jane (Hadley) b 1857,9,21 d 1933,4,23 bur Springfield; m Ella H. HADLEY, dt Harlan H. & Susannah, b 1859,8,30
Ch: Horace L. b 1884, 12, 22
Hugh Isaac " 1887, 5, 1
Orville " 1888, 10, 19
Mary Louise " 1890, 10, 30
Geneva W. " 1892, 11, 9
Ralph A. " 1896, 11, 4
Nina E. " 1898, 6, 22
----, --, --. Emmet, s Lewis & Jane, b 1861,1, 21; m Eva VanDERVOORTE, dt John & Lida (Turner), b 1865,1,29
Ch: Anna b 1891, 6, 18
Lula " 1894, 8, 11
Lewis " 1894, 8, 11
----, --, --. Hugh Isaac, s Orlando & Ella (Hadley), b 1887,5,1; m Bessie REDFERN
Ch: Harlan J. b 1911, 3, --
Anora " 1912, 7, 12
Donald Herbert " 1914, --, -- d 1915, 5, 5
Mary Genevieve " 1917, 7, 24
----, --, --. Lewis Jr., s Emmett & Eva (Vanderwoort), b 1894,8,11; m Naomi HADLEY, dt Wm. & Lizzie (Harvey), b 1897,2,10
Ch: Emmet Eugene b 1928, 9, 24
----, --, --. Ralph, s Orlando & Ella H., b 1896,11,4; m Jane MADDEN, dt Douglas & Cora G., b 1900,7,6

1837, 12, 12. Abel & w, Charlotte, rocf Centre MM, O., dtd 1837,9,13
1839, 10, 15. Abel & w, Charlotte, & ch, Phinehas R. & Robert, gct Centre MM, O.
1846, 12, 19. Abel & Charlotte T., & ch, Phinehas R., Robert, Mary Jane, Phamy Ann, Stacy & Lydia Ellen, rocf Centre MM, O., dtd 1846,12,8
1849, 5, 17. Abel & w, Charlotte, & ch, Phineas R., Robert, Mary Jane, Phany Ann, Stacy, Lydia Ellen & Hannah Louisa, gct Centre MM, O.
1857, 1, 17. Jane [Biven] (form Hadley) dis mou
1866, 5, 19. Lewis H. rocf Poplar Run MM, Ind., dtd 1866,3,15
1866, 10, 20. Jane & ch, Orlando, Franklin & Edward E., recrq
1870, 8, 20. Lewis H. & w, Jane, & ch, Orland Franklin & Elwood Emet, gct Cincinnati MM, O.
1874, 4, 18. Lewis H. & w, Jane, & ch, Orlando, Franklin & Edward Emmitt, rocf Cincinnati MM, O.
1908, 1, 18. Bessie E. recrq
1909, 11, 20. Eva & ch, Anna, Lula & Lewis recrq
1914, 3, 21. Orville gct Ogdon MM, O.
1914, 4, 18. Horace gct Center MM, O.
1918, 4, 20. Florence Emma recrq
1918, 4, 20. Lucille R., Myra F., Nida E. & Carlton A., ch Frank & Anna, recrq
1920, 12, 18. Anna A. recrq
1921, 6, 18. Naomi H. rocf Wilmington MM, O.
1924, 6, 22. Geneva W. relrq
1931, 3, 23. Amora gct Wilmington MM, O.

BIDDLECUM
1823, 2, 10. William [Biddlecomb] b
1925, 3, 26. Martha d bur Springfield

1867, 10, 17. William [Biddlecome] recrq
1876, 3, 18. Wm. relrq
1910, 4, 10. Jason & w, Martha, rocf Back Creek MM, Ind., dtd 1910,3,17
1910, 9, 19. Homer rocf Back Creek MM, Ind., dtd 1910,7,14
1914, 9, 12. Homer G. gct Xenia MM, O.
1914, 10, 17. Anna M. V. gct Xenia MM, O.

BINKLEY
1881, 4, 16. Henry recrq
1883, 11, 17. Eva recrq
1913, 2, 15. John Howard recrq
1913, 5, 17. Charles H., Mary C. & Irene recrq
1918, 1, 19. Charles & w, Mary, & ch, Irene & John Howard, relrq

BLACK
1887, 6, 18. Clarissa & ch rocf Newberry MM, O., dtd 1887,5,23
1895, 1, 19. Clarissa & ch gct White Water MM, Ind.
1895, 1, 19. Allen gct White Water MM, Ind.
1895, 1, 19. Matilda(Black)Dailey gct White Water MM, Ind.

BOBBITT
1929, 7, 22. Lucile Probasco relrq

BOGAN
----, --, --. J. Waller, s John & Martha J., b 1860,3,18; m Anna Elizabeth GRAY, dt Andrew & Martha, b 1860,2,23
Ch: Vernon
Leroy b 1884, 2, 4
Martha
Olive " 1885, 11, 26
John A. " 1888, 1, 15
Bessie Bell" 1889, 11, 18
----, --, --. Vernon LeRoy, s Walter & Lizzie, b 1911,11,9; m Nina PROBASCO, dt Wm. & Anna
Ch: Robert W. b 1913, 2, 23
Ruth Anna " 1920, 4, 10
----, --, --. John A. [Brogan], s J. Walter & Anna Elizabeth, b 1888,1,15; m Rosa CLARKE dt Elwood & Ella
Ch: J. Rendell b 1912, 10, 22
Meredith " 1914, 10, 25
Virginia " 1915, 11, 14
Priscilla " 1921, 7, 18
Walter Elwood " 1927, 3, 16

1871, 9, 16. Lina [Bogen] recrq
1873, 7, 19. Hannah rocf Newberry MM, O., dtd 1873,6,23
----, --, --. William E., Elnora & Annie Mary, ch Hannah, rocf Newberry MM, O., dtd 1873,9,22
1873, 8, 16. Lina Gray (form Bogan) con mou
1873, 9, 20. George W. [Bogen] recrq
1885, 4, 18. J. Walter & w, Lizzie, & ch, Vernon Leroy & Martha Olive, recrq
1896, 3, 21. Martha recrq
1897, 3, 20. Ida recrq
1897, 3, 20. Inez recrq
1897, 3, 20. Nellie recrq
1897, 3, 20. Clara recrq
1910, 7, 16. Rosa Clark rocf Ogden MM, O.
1913, 1, 18. J. Walter & w, Anna Elizabeth, & ch, Olive & Bessie B., gct Wilmington MM, O.
1914, 12, 19. Anna recrq
1922, 3, 18. George & Hannah gct Miami MM, O.

BOND
1859, 2, 19. Zimri rmt Julia Ann Mendenhall
1859, 5, 21. Julia Ann gct Poplar Run MM, Ind.

BOWMAN
1874, 5, 16. Valeria & s, Frank, recrq
1874, 5, 16. Mary recrq
1874, 5, 16. Carrie recrq
1874, 5, 16. Joseph & w, Sarah, & ch, Rebecca E., Annie M., Floretta, Irea, Maggie, Myrlie & May, recrq
1875, 4, 17. Samuel S. recrq
1883, 11, 17. Eliza recrq
1897, 9, 18. Joseph & fam gct Topeka MM, Kans.
1901, 4, 20. Samuel & Valira transferred to Ogden MM, O.

BOWSER
1898, 11, 19. Elijah recrq
1921, 6, 18. Della dropped from mbrp
1925, 7, 19. DeWitt relrq

BOYD
1881, 5, 21. John T. recrq
1883, 9, 15. John T. gct Newberry MM, O.

BRACKNEY
1853, 12, 17. George rmt Judith Haines
1854, 7, 15. Judith Ann gct Dover MM

BRANDENBURG
----, --, --. Moses D. b 1834,2,1; m Rebecca A. ----- b 1836,7,10
Ch: Lawrence b 1856, 2, 11
Laura B. " 1857, 8, 31
Templin " 1858, 8, 28
Rodney " 1860, 3, 5
Hittie A. " 1861, 9, 24
Mary " 1862, 11, 25
Frank " 1865, 12, 2

1871, 12, 16. Moses & w, Rebecca, & ch, Lawrence, Laura, Templin, Rodney, Kittie, Mary & Frank, rocf Newberry MM, O., dtd 1871,10,23

BRANN
1871, 1, 21. Mercie A. (form Coate) con mou
1871, 3, 18. Mercie A. gct Center MM, O.

BRIGGS
1925, 11, 22. J. Emery, Willard & Nellie recrq
1925, 11, 22. Wendell recrq

BROWN
----, --, --. Charles m Louie M. HADLEY, dt James & Isabella (Moore) d 1930,6,6 bur Springfield
Ch: Norman
Hadley b 1915, 3, 19

1858, 5, 15. Samuel rmt Elizabeth W. Hadley
1868, 12, 18. Elizabeth H. gct Miami MM, O.
1862, 9, 20. Joseph Mather gct Miami MM, O., to m Mary Ann Brown
1874, 5, 16. William & w, Eliza, & ch, Annie E., recrq
1876, 5, 20. Daniel recrq
1877, 1, 20. Thomas & w, Mary E., & ch, William E., Cora B., Alva C., Mertie M. & Leona P., recrq
1891, 2, 21. Daniel relrq
1901, 4, 20. Eliza transferred to Ogden MM, O.
1901, 4, 20. Annie E. transferred to Ogden MM, O.
1911, 6, 17. Charles & ch, Ruth Isabelle &

BROWN, continued
Edith Adelaide, recrq
1925, 7, 19. Blanch Davis relrq

BRYAN
1930, 2, 6. John Woodward & Letha Marie & Achilles G. recrq (G)
1932, 1, 7. William Eugene, s Rev. A. G. & Letha M., b 1931,9,12 (G)
1932, 2, 4. Marguerite Francella recrq (G)
1932, 10, 6. Rev. A. G. & w, & s, Wm. Eugene, gct Stone Quarry MM (G)

BUCK
1822, 6, 29. Lucy recrq
1822, 9, 28. Lucy rmt Enoch Harlan, Jr.

BUFFINGTON
1841, 1, 12. Mifflin F. rocf Clear Creek MM, O., dtd 1840,6,23
1842, 2, 15. Mifflin M. con mou
1842, 7, 12. Mifflin M. gct Clear Creek MM, O.

BULLEN
----, --, --. Isaac Clayhorn b 1884,5,16; m Mary Estella ----- b 1883,11,11
Ch: Hubert Lee b 1905, 4, 7
James Arthur " 1907, 1, 13
Ruth Ida " 1909, 12, 27
Harold William " 1911, 2, 28
Virgil Byron " 1913, 4, 13
John Spencer " 1915, 5, 20

1923, 9, 16. Isaac Claybourne & w, Mary Estella, & ch, Hubert Lee, James Arthur, Ruth Ida, Harold Wm., Virgil Byron & John Spencer, rocf Chester MM
1933, 4, 23. I. C. & fam gct Wilmington MM,O.

BURGE
1873, 7, 19. Jane rocf Newberry MM, O., dtd 1873,6,23
1873, 7, 19. Jonathan D. recrq
1873, 10, 18. Charles & Jesse, ch Martha, rocf Newberry MM, O., dtd 1873,9,22
1886, 6, 19. Jonathan D. & w, Martha J., & ch, Chas. C. & Jesse C., gct Wilmington MM, O.
1891, 3, 21. J. D. & w, Martha J., & ch, Chas. C. & Jesse C., gct Cincinnati MM, O.

BURGESS
----, --, --. Jesse b 1805,11,8; m Elizabeth HARVEY b 1811,2,11
Ch: Mary Emily b 1830, 1, 10

1824, 7, 31. Jesse Harvey gct Fairfield MM, O., to m Elizabeth Burgess
1827, 8, 25. Simon D. Harvey gct Fairfield MM, O., to m Mary Burgess
1827, 10, 27. Jesse rocf Fairfield MM, O., dtd 1827,5,26
1829, 3, 17. Jesse rmt Elizabeth Harvey
1831, 11, 15. Jesse & w, Elizabeth, & dt, Mary Emily, gct Cincinnati MM, O.
1832, 7, 17. Jesse & w, Elizabeth, & dt, Mary Emily, rocf Cincinnati MM, O., dtd 1832,6,14
1834, 12, 16. Jesse & w, Elizabeth, & ch, Mary Emily & Thos. H., gct Fairfield MM
1835, 3, 17. Moses rocf Newberry MM, O., dtd 1835,2,23
1835, 8, 11. Eli Stalker gct Fairfield MM, O. to m Tacy Jennette Burgess
1837, 6, 13. John T. rmt Elizabeth Harvey
1837, 10, 17. Elizabeth gct Miami MM, O.
1838, 7, 17. Moses gct Miami MM, O.

BURNET
1845, 4, 15. John Pyle gct Miami MM, O., to m Mary Ann Burnet

BURRIS
1901, 4, 20. Carrie transferred to Ogden MM, O.

BUTLER
1823, 5, 31. Jacob Hadley gct White Water MM, Ind., to m Mary Butler
1893, 4, 15. Edna, niece of Geo. D. & Sarah Rufina White, gct Center MM, O.

BYRN
----, --, --. Mary b 1846,8,20; m ----- -----
Ch: Cary T. b 1871, 1, 1
Ella May " 1872, 10, 2

1874, 2, 21. Mary Elizabeth [Burns] & ch, Carrie T. & Ella Mary, recrq

CADWALADER
----, --, --. Joseph b 1832,12,23; m Jane ----- b 1838,11,12
Ch: William C. b 1858, 12, 9
Frank " 1865, 5, 4

1874, 4, 18. Joseph & w, Eliza, & ch, Clinton & Frank, recrq
1901, 1, 19. Belle recrq

CALLACE
1901, 4, 20. Tillia A. transferred to Ogden MM, O.
1901, 4, 20. Cynthia transferred to Ogden MM, O.
1901, 4, 20. Benjamin H. transferred to Ogden MM, O.
1901, 4, 20. Elmer M. & Jane transferred to Ogden MM, O.

CAMMACK
1850, 1, 19. James rmt Elizabeth Hadley

CAMP
1874, 5, 16. Clark & w, Ruth Ann, & ch, Mary Jane, Isabele & Effie May, recrq
1878, 4, 20. Clark dis
1920, 4, 17. Bell gct Wilmington MM, O.

CAMPBELL
1856, 9, 20. Malinda gct Miami MM, O.

CANADAY
1830, 4, 13. William Millikan gct West Grove MM, Ind., to m Charity Canaday

CANE
1874, 3, 21. Simon recrq

CARDER
1874, 5, 16. Frederick recrq
1876, 5, 20. Ambrose & w, Hannah, & ch, Mirwama, Emerson C., recrq
1880, 5, 15. Iva, Itha & Ebler recrq
1893, 1, 21. Ambrose, Hannah, Emmerson, Itha, Iva & Eberle, recrq

CAREY
1831, 2, 15. Samuel & w, Sarah, & s, John, rocf Lees Creek MM, O., dtd 1831,1,15
1831, 9, 13. Benjamin & w, Elizabeth, rocf Fairfield MM, dtd 1831,7,21
1832, 2, 14. Benjamin & w, Elizabeth, gct Fairfield MM, O.
1833, 2, 12. Samuel & w, Sarah, & ch, John F. & Ruth B., gct Fairfield MM, O.
1881, 8, 20. Amos & w, Anna, & ch, Frank, Ida & Pearl, rocf Clear Creek MM, O., dtd 1881,7,9
1914, 9, 12. Louis B. gct Center MM, O.
1931, 11, 5. Charles J. & w, Jennie P., & ch, Edna Marie, rocf Mt. Pleasant MM, O. (G)
1933, 1, 5. May recrq (G)

CARPENTER
----, --, --. Walter T. b 1811,1,1; m Susan M. ----- b 1811,12,27
Ch: Charles G. b 1836, 8, 6
Albert F. " 1842, 8, 6 d 1843, 3, 5
Elizabeth " 1829, 4, 25

1823, 2, 23. Amos Fallis gct Centre MM, to m Lydia Carpenter
1841, 6, 15. Walter T. & w, Susan M., & s, Charles Gray, rocf Center MM, O., dtd 1841,5,18
1844, 10, 15. Walter T. & w, Susan M., & s, Charles G., gct Cincinnati MM, O.
1847, 11, 20. Walter T. & w, Susan M., & ch, Charles G. & Caroline, rocf Cincinnati MM, O., dtd 1847,10,21
1849, 1, 20. Nathaniel & w, Zeruiah, rocf Cincinnati MM, O., dtd 1848,11,16
1849, 2, 17. Edwin rocf Cincinnati MM, O., dtd 1848,11,16
1849, 2, 17. Anna rocf Cincinnati MM, O., dtd 1848,11,16
1849, 2, 17. Mary rocf Cincinnati MM, O., dtd 1848,12,21
1851, 7, 19. Edwin rmt Louisa Hale
1852, 6, 19. Mary T. rmt Wm. T. Pyle
1857, 1, 17. Walter T. & w, Susan M., & ch, Charles G., Caroline & Elizabeth, gct White Water MM, Ind.
1858, 3, 20. Nathaniel & w, Zeruiah, gct White Water MM, Ind.
1858, 3, 20. Anna gct White Water MM, Ind.
1858, 11, 20. Edwin & w, Louisa, & ch, Laura A. & Caroline E., gct White Water MM, Ind.

CARTER
----, --, --. Nathaniel b 1779,6,21; m Nancy BAKER, b 1781,10,17
Ch: Jane b 1802, 2, 17
John Baker " 1804, 2, 1
Susanna " 1806, 3, 10
Enoch " 1808, 12, 10
Ann " 1813, 9, 14
Delilah " 1826, 11, 10
----, --, --. George b 1782,3,8; m Miriam WILSON, b 1787,2,2 d 1878,1,19 bur Grassy Run
Ch: Jesse b 1806, 2, 2
John " 1808, 2, 28
Samuel " 1810, 3, 19 d 1832, 2, 5 bur Lytles Creek
Wilson b 1812, 9, 25
Cyrus " 1815, 3, 5
Louiza " 1817, 12, 5
George " 1822, 4, 30 d 1845, 1, 8 bur Lytles Creek
----, --,---. Enoch m Elizabeth ----- d 1864, 8,23 bur Lytles Creek
Ch: Mary b 1835, 6, 15 d 1856, 8,27
David " 1837, 4, 20
Nathaniel " 1838, 11, 11 d 1856, 8,27
John " 1840. 8, 6 " 1877, 5,12
Rachel " 1841, 10, 15 " 1842, 10,13
Samuel " 1843, 5, 1
Hiram " 1845, 4, 14 d 1850,10,29
Phebe Ann " 1847, 1, 14 " 1848, 9,10
Elizabeth Jane " 1849, 3, 27
Susannah Delilah " 1853, 2, 14
----, --, --. John & Sarah
Ch: Mary b 1836, 5, 5
Nancy " 1837, 11, 17
Jane " 1840, 7, 9
William " 1842, 3, 31
----, --, -- Leonard b 1835,4,30; m Eliza Ann ----- b 1833,4,27
Ch: Adolphus A. b 1854, 9, 20
Perry J. " 1856, 1, 11
Ida Bell " 1866, 7, 22
Laura M. " 1870, 3, 3

CARTER, continued
David b 1837,4,20; m Sarah Emily -----
Ch: Laura b 1861, 2, 2 d 1861, 3,23
Lauretta " 1863, 4, 30
Elmer J. " 1865, 7, 5
1842, 12, 15. Nathaniel d ae 63y 8m 15d (a minister)
----, --, --. John & Mary
Ch: Eva D. b 1866, 12, 26
Almon E. " 1869, 4, 2

1822, 7, 27. Jane Gaskill (form Carter) con mou
1828, 10, 14. Susannah rmt Asa Green
1828, 12, 16. Jesse con mou
1829, 4, 14. Jesse gct Dover MM, O.
1829, 4, 14. Jesse gct Dover MM, O.
1829, 8, 21. John rmt Hannah Milikan
1830, 4, 13. John & w, Hannah, gct Dover MM, O.
1833, 10, 15. John B. rmt Sarah Smith
1833, 8, 13. Enoch gct Center MM, O., to m Elizabeth Faulkner
1834, 4, 15. Elizabeth rocf Centre MM, O., dtd 1834,3,12
1834, 9, 16. Wilson gct Centre MM, O., to m Judith F. Ballard
1835, 3, 17. Wilson gct Dover MM
1835, 10, 13. Ann rmt Wm. Holliday
1836, 11, 15. Louisa rmt Jehu Pyle
1838, 9, 11. Cyrus con mou
1838, 12, 11. Cyrus gct Dover MM
1845, 4, 15. Wilson & w, Judith T., & ch, William B. & Elizabeth, rocf Dover MM, dtd 1845,3,13
1847, 11, 20. Wilson & w, Judith, & ch, William B. & Elizabeth, gct Dover MM, O.
1854, 7, 15. Cyrus E. rst on consent of Dover MM, O.
1855, 12, 15. Cyrus E. gct Dover MM, O.
1857, 11, 21. George gct Dover MM, O.
1860, 1, 21. David F. rmt Sarah Emily Moore
1864, 7, 16. Mary Ann (form Wire) con mou
1864, 11, 19. Mary Ann gct Dover MM
1866, 8, 18. Mary Ann recrq
1866, 8, 18. William dis mou
1866, 8, 18. John con mou
1866, 8, 18. Samuel con mou
1866, 11, 17. Lydia Ann rocf Newberry MM, O., dtd 1866,10,22
1867, 7, 20. Enoch & dt, Susanna E., gct Newberry MM, O.
1867, 7, 20. Samuel & w, Lydia Ann, gct Newberry MM, O.
1867, 7, 20. Elizabeth Jane gct Newberry MM, O.
1867, 7, 20. Enoch & dt, Susanna D., gct Newberry MM, O.
1867, 7, 20. Samuel & w, Lydia Ann, gct Newberry MM, O.
1867, 7, 20. Elizabeth gct Newberry MM, O.
1867, 11, 16. Delilah gct Newberry MM, O.
1869, 4, 17. John B. gct Cottonwood MM, Kans.
1871, 2, 18. Leonard J. & w, Eliza Ann, & ch, Perry, Jackson, Adolphus, Alonzo, Ida Belle & Laura May, recrq
1871, 10, 20. Nathaniel gct Cottonwood MM, Kan.
1871, 10, 20. Asa gct Cottonwood MM, Kans.
1871, 10, 20. Jane gct Cottonwood MM, Kans.
1878, 9, 21. Leonard J. & dt, Ida Bell & Laura May, relrq
1881, 5, 21. Leonard J. recrq
1881, 11, 19. Eva gct Wilmington MM, O.
1883, 3, 17. Eva rocf Wilmington MM, O.
1883, 7, 21. Leonard & w, Margaret, rocf Wilmington MM, O., dtd 1884,7,20
1891, 12, 19. Phebe Ann recrq
1891, 4, 18. Washington, Amelia & Peter, recrq
1895, 10, 19. Delila rocf West Fork MM, O.

CAST
1912, 2, 9. Ellen d

CATTELL
1930, 11, 6. Everett L. & w, Catharine (De Vol) rocf Sullivant Avenue MM, Columbus, O. (G)
1931, 4, 2. David DeVol, s Everett & Catharine, b 1931,2,8 (G)

CELLS
1885, 4, 18. Charles & w, Lucie (or Susie) recrq

CHEW
1819, 11, 21. Alice rmt Joshua Harvey
1822, 7, 27. Ruth rmt Harlan Harvey
1824, 11, 27. Reuben rmt Rebecca Madden
1825, 1, 29. Mary Maden (form Chew) con mou
1829, 9, 15. Martha dis jH
1838, 5, 15. Reuben & w, Rebecca, & ch, Miles, Malinda, Emily, Angeline, Mary & Ruth, gct Bloomfield MM, Ind.
1851, 1, 18. Reuben & ch, Mary & Ruth, rocf Rush Creek MM, Ind., dtd 1850,10,17, end by Miami MM, O., 1850,11,20
1851, 1, 18. Angeline rocf Rush Creek MM, Ind., dtd 1850,10,17
1851, 1, 18. Emily rocf Rush Creek MM, Ind., dtd 1850,10,17
1851, 5, 17. Emily gct Miami MM, O.
1851, 5, 17. Angeline gct Miami MM, O.
1851, 6, 12. Reuben & ch, Mary & Ruth, gct Miami MM, O.

CLARE
1882, 12, 16. George W. & Mary Josephine recrq
1885, 3, 21. George W. dis disunity
1885, 10, 17. Josephine relrq

CLARK
----, --, --. Elwood b 1850,7,23; m Ellen HADLEY b 1851,11,25
Ch: Eva D. b 1873, 5, 1 d 1873, 9, 4

CLARK, Elwood & Ellen, continued
Ch: Marris b 1874, 6, 25
----, --, --. Camp b 18-4,9,17; m Ruth A. ----- b 1849,6,20
Ch: Mary J. b 1869, 9, 4
Isabel " 1871, 7, 20
Effie May " 1873, 3, 15
Flora " 1875, 3, 31
1852, 6, 4. Alvin, s Jemima Clark Osborn, b
1855, 3, 26. Lindley b
1856, 11, 1. Cassius b

1853, 9, 17. David L. Hadley gct Walnut Ridge MM, Ind., to m Abigail G. Clark
1865, 12, 16. Chas. Osborn gct New Garden MM, Ind., to m Jemima Clark
1866, 2, 17. Jemima Osborn & ch, Elwood, Alvin, Lindley & Cassius Clark, rocf New Garden MM, Ind., dtd 1860,3,17
1873, 7, 19. Elwood con mou
1873, 7, 19. Ellen (form Hadley) con mou
1885, 8, 14. Lindley gct Newberry MM, O.
1885, 8, 15. Clestea B. & ch, Estella M. & Tacy V., recrq
1893, 12, 16. Cassius & w, Bell, & ch gct Wilmington MM, O.
1897, 3, 20. Alvin gct Newburg MM, Ore.

CLAYTON
1880, 5, 15. Belle recrq

CLAWSON
1831, 12, 13. Jonathan D. Hadley gct White Water MM, Ind., to m Susanna W. Clawson
1851, 1, 18. Wm. T. Harvey gct White Water MM, Ind., to m Ann Clawson

CLEAVER
1821, 10, 27. Sarah [Cleever] rocf Center MM, O., dtd 1821,9,15
1824, 1, 21. Daniel recrq
1825, 5, 11. Sarah [Clever], dt David & Sarah, recrq
1829, 1, 13. David dis jH
1829, 1, 13. Sarah dis jH
1829, 12, 15. Matilda (form Stout) dis mou
1839, 9, 17. Caroline [Clever] dis jH

CLELAND
----, --, --. William b 1836,11,2; m Sarah A. ----- b 1849,12,17 d 1916,2,26
Ch: Mary E. b 1868, 1, 12
Luther " 1869, 7, 11
Thomas " 1871, 1, 21
John W. " 1874, 7, 14
----, --, --. ----- m Delila J. ----- b 1850, 7,15
Ch: Cora A. b 1872, 11, 16
1850, 12, 24. James b
1896, 4, 21. Ruth Etta [Clelland] b d 1932, 12,3
1913, 9, 18. Clarence Raymond [Clelland] d
1924, 5, 12. Irena Isabell [Clelland] d
1872, 5, 18. Rebecca recrq
1874, 5, 16. William & w, Sarah Ann, & ch, Mary Ella, Luther & Thomas, recrq
1874, 5, 16. Delilah Jane & dt, Cora A., recrq
1874, 5, 16. James recrq
1875, 6, 19. Wm. & w, Sarah, & ch, Marietta, Marten Luther, Thomas & John, gct Center MM, O.
1881, 3, 19. Wm. & w, Sarah Ann, & ch, Mary Etta, Luther Thos., & Rebecca Jane, rocf Center MM, O., dtd 1881,3,16
1910, 2, 16. Elva recrq
1912, 3, 16. Ida & ch, Ruth Etta, Irena Belle, Clarence Raymond, Earl Wm. & Carl Emmett, recrq
1918, 4, 20. Thomas dropped from mbrp
1926, 6, 20. Charles dropped from mbrp

CLEVENGER
1899, 11, 18. Lissie dis

CLINE
----, --, --. Madison F., s John & Mary A., b 1862,2,28 d 1930,12,1 bur Springfield; m Eliza J. TROUT, dt John & Julia A., b 1862,6,8
Ch: Belva Mabel b 1886, 9, 1
Ambert Albert " 1887, 8, 29

1926, 6, 20. Albert dropped from mbrp

CLIPARD
1845, 9, 16. Deborah (form Smith) dis mou

CLIVER
1911, 11, 18. Etta S. relrq

COATS
----, --, --. John B. b 1836,10,21; m Delilah B. ----- b 1837,3,13
Ch: Ruth Eva b 1860, 7, 7
Mary Agness" 1863, 11, 8
Lincoln " 1865, 7, 3
Joseph William " 1869, 7, 21 d 1869, 7,24
----, --, --. Hiram Alvin, s Hiram & Rachel (Painter), b 1862,7,11; m Flora HALE, dt Wm. & Mary (Ent)
Ch: Donald Wm. b 1896, 11, 6
Lester Hershel " 1898, 8, 3
Kenneth " 1901, 5, 9
Mary Elizabeth " 1906, 7, 19
Lovesa May " 1908, 11, 20
1869, 8, 23. Wm. Kirk, s Elijah & Mary E., b
1871, 1, 21. Merrick, s Orlistus & Anna D., b

1837, 2, 14. David Curl gct Centre MM, O., to m Rebecca Coate

COATS
1848, 8, 19. Edwin Hadley gct Center MM, O., to m Esther[Coate]
1854, 8, 19. Mary B. [Coate] & s, Cyrus, rocf Center MM, O., dtd 1854,6,14
1854, 8, 19. Mary B. rocf Center MM, O., dtd 1854,6,14
1855, 4, 21. John rst on consent of Center MM, O.
1857, 5, 16. John Jr. rocf Center MM, O., dtd 1857,4,15
1857, 5, 16. Elizabeth B., Nancy & Martha rocf Center MM, O., dtd 1857,4,15
1858, 10, 17. Elizabeth Haney (form Coate) con mou
1858, 11, 20. Josiah T. & w, Agnes, rst on consent of Center MM, O. (also ch, Loran Alphonso & Orlistes)
1859, 5, 21. John [Coate] rmt Delilah Andrew
1863, 12, 19. Martha rmt Wm. N. Osborn
1869, 6, 19. Hiram & w, Rachel W., & ch, Rebecca Mary & Hiram Alvin, rocf Center MM, O., dtd 1869,5,12
1869, 6, 19. Elijah S., Alice S. & Merie [Coate] rocf Center MM, O., dtd 1869,5,12
1869, 8, 21. Mary E. recrq
1870, 8, 20. Annie D. recrq
1871, 1, 21. Mercie A. Brann (form Coate) con mou
1871, 2, 18. Rachel W. recrq
1871, 5, 20. Joseph T. & w, Agness & s, Lorin Alphonso, gct Wilmington MM, O.
1871, 5, 20. Nancy gct Wilmington MM, O.
1873, 6, 21. Joseph T. & w, Agnes, & dt, Nancy & Loran, rocf Wilmington MM, O.
1874, 1, 17. Hiram recrq
1880, 2, 21. Orlestus & w, Annie D., & ch, Merrick D., Leo Guy & Annie Maud, gct Wilmington MM, O.
1882, 9, 16. Agnes gct Wilmington MM, O.
1882, 9, 16. Nancy gct Wilmington MM, O.
1893, 10, 4. H. A. rmt Flora Hale
1901, 1, 19. Flora recrq
1901, 1, 19. H. A. recrq
1925, 11, 22. Lester relrq

COLLICE
1874, 5, 16. Jane E. recrq
1874, 5, 16. Cynthia & ch, Benna H., Lillie & Elmer M., recrq

COLLINS
----, --, --. James, s Levi & Martha (Branon), b 1858,11,28; m Laura May ----- b 1869,5,6
Ch: Joseph L. b 1888, 4, 2
Nathan K. " 1891, 6, 27
Harry E. " 1893, 11, 11
May Amelia " 1897, 7, 18
Charles Ward " 1900, 11, 14
Melva D. " 1908, 1, 14
Elva E. " 1908, 1, 14

1851, 8, 16. Lewis G. & w, Sarah D., & dt, Susan E., rocf Nine Partners MM, dtd 1851,5,15
1854, 4, 15. Lewis G. & w, Sarah D., & dt, Jane, gct Milford MM, Ind.
1889, 4, 20. William & Mary recrq
1894, 11, 17. Laura May recrq
1897, 3, 20. Laura relrq
1907, 1, 19. Wm. A. relrq
1920, 4, 17. James dropped from mbrp

COMPTON
1882, 2, 18. Samuel T. & w, Josephine, & dt, Alta B., rocf Caesars Creek MM, O.
1888, 12, 15. Samuel T. & w, Josephine, & ch, Alta B., Ally C. & John W., gct Wilmington MM, O.

CONKLIN
1889, 4, 20. John recrq
1890, 1, 19. John W. relrq
1897, 8, 14. John relrq

CONNAR
1874, 10, 17. Susan recrq

COOK
1891, 11, 21. John & w, Sarah, rocf Vandalia MM
1904, 7, 16. Winifred Harvey gct Miami MM, O.

COOPER
1857, 9, 19. William recrq
1914, 1, 17. Everett recrq
1915, 9, 18. Louise H. recrq
1920, 4, 17. Everett dropped from mbrp
1920, 4, 17. Louise H. dropped from mbrp
1921, 7, 16. Carl & w, Elizabeth, & ch, Eva Lucile, Thelma Louise, Irene Rebecca, George Willard & Helen Juanita, recrq

CORT
1895, 1, 19. Margaret Hooten & dt, Cressie Mildred Hooten, rocf Wilmington MM, O.

COWDEN
1908, 7, 18. Blanch L. gct Wilmington MM, O.

COWGILL
1822, 6, 29. Elisha & w, Rebecca, & ch, Gulielma & Hannah, gct Fairfield MM
1824, 12, 25. Elisha & Rebecca, & ch, Guli Elma Hannah & Bennette, rocf Fairfield MM, O., dtd 1824,11,27
1827, 7, 28. Elisha & w, Rebecca, & ch, Guli-elma, Hannah, Bennett & Cyrus, attached to Center MM, O.
1847, 3, 20. Hannah rocf Center MM, O., dtd 1846,12,16
1847, 5, 15. Edwin rocf Centre MM, O., dtd 1847,3,17
1849, 7, 21. Hannah L. rmt Wm. Longstreth
1854, 7, 15. Edwin gct Center MM, O.

COWGILL, continued
1860, 10, 20. Jacob C. Hadley gct Fairfield MM, O., to m Lucinda Cowgill
1861, 3, 16. Jonathan B., s Lucinda Hadley, rocf Fairfield MM, dtd 1861,2,16
1861, 8, 17. Ellen M. rocf Fairfield MM, O., dtd 1861,6,15
1861, 8, 17. Ellen W. rocf Fairfield MM, dtd 1861,6,15
1864, 3, 19. Ellen W. rmt Micajah C. Hadley
1871, 10, 21. Jonathan B. rmt Louisa Kimbrough
1874, 2, 21. Katie & Mollie rocf Fairfield MM, O., dtd 1874,1,17
1884, 2, 16. Mary E. gct Wilmington MM, O.

COZADD
1894, 10, 20. James & Kittie recrq

CRAIG
----, --, --. James A., s Addison & Dortha, b 1850,3,31; m Charity S. STANFIELD, dt John & Mary b 1848,7,27 d 1907,12,17 bur Dayton
Ch: Mary E. b 1877, 12, 7

1823, 10, 25. Thomas Kersey gct Miami MM, O., to m Lititia Craig
1875, 8, 21. James A. & w, Charity, rocf Caesars Creek MM, O., dtd 1875,7,22
1896, 8, 18. James A. & fam relrq
1912, 9, 21. James gct Dayton MM, O.
1915, 3, 20. Mary E. relrq

CRAMER
1880, 5, 15. Lucius recrq
1883, 4, 21. Lucy M. recrq

CREWS
1819, 1, 30. Ruth recrq
1819, 3, 27. Mary rmt William Harvey
1822, 8, 31. Ruth Stratton (form Crews) con mou
1828, 9, 24. Hannah rocf Miami MM, O., dtd 1825,5,25
1827, 6, 27. Rebecca recrq
1828, 4, 26. Rebecca gct Miami MM, O.
1830, 1, 12. Hannah gct Miami MM, O.

CRISINBERY
----, --, --. Peter V., s Wm. & Nancy, b 1881,2,23; m Grace GROVE, dt Oscar & Elizabeth, b 1886,7,20
Ch: Floyd
Vernon b 1913, 8, 17
Mildred
Elizabeth " 1918, 5, 9

1925, 10, 25. P. V. & w, Grace, & ch, Floyd & Mildred, recrq
1934, 3, 4. Floyd relrq

CRITES
1885, 11, 21. John C. & w, Anna, & ch, Edith M. & Jesse, rocf Cesars Creek MM, O., dtd 1885,9,24
1929, 12, 22. Wendell S. rocf Ogden MM, O.

CURL
----, --, --. Elias b 1813,2,14 d 1861,3,14 bur Springfield; m Sarah ----- b 1825,10,12 d 1878,1,20
Ch: Eliza Ann
Elwood d 1870, 10, 23
Oliver " 1867, 2, 25
Martha H. b 1853, 11, 24
David " 1856, 10, 3
Henry H. " 1859, 8, 25
----, --, --. David b 1814,7,21; m Rebecca COATE b 1817,6,21
Ch: Esther b 1838, 5, 23 d 1915, 5,18 bur Springfield
Eliza b 1842, 10, 27 d 1853,10, 6
Samuel " 1845, 4, 13
Hiram " 1847, 2, 3 d 1922, 3,19 bur Springfield
Rhoda M. b 1849, 9, 8
----, --, --. Samuel, s David & Rebecca, b 1844,5,30 d 1906,10,31 bur Springfield; m Lydia MORRIS, dt John, b 1842,5,8 d 1910,1,9 bur Springfield
Ch: Frank b 1871, 8, 30
Flora " 1875, 9, 23
Viola " 1883, 9, 3
----, --, --. Hiram m Katie KELLY
Ch: Daniel
Stacy b 1890, 9, 15
Channing
David " 1892, 1, 19

1821, 9, 29. Elias Fisher & Rebecca, minors, rocf Derby Creek MM, dtd 1821,9,15
1826, 10, 12. Anna rocf Goshen MM, dtd 1826, 10,15
1833, 11, 12. David rocf Center MM, O., dtd 1833,7,17
1834, 10, 14. Anna rmt Levi Harvey
1836, 5, 17. Rebecca rmt Lewis N. Miller
1837, 2, 14. David gct Centre MM, O., to m Rebecca Coate
1837, 7, 11. Rebecca rocf Centre MM, O., dtd 1837,5,17
1839, 8, 13. Sarah & Elizabeth rocf Centre MM, O., dtd 1839,7,17
1842, 5, 17. Rachel recrq
1842, 7, 12. Rachel gct Centre MM, O.
1843, 1, 17. Elizabeth gct Centre MM, O.
1843, 11, 14. Elias F. rmt Sarah Elizabeth Haines
1871, 1, 21. Sarah E. & ch, Martha H., Henry H. & David, gct Wilmington MM, O.
1871, 1, 21. Eliza Ann gct Wilmington MM, O.
1871, 2, 18. Samuel con mou
1877, 2, 17. Lydia recrq
1891, 3, 21. Naomi P. rocf Westland MM, dtd 1891,3,7
1901, 1, 19. Flora recrq

CURL, continued
1907, 1, 19. Daniel Stacy & David Channing, ch Hiram, recrq
1911, 6, 17. Frank gct Wilmington MM, O.
1916, 9, 16. Olive M. rocf Wilmington MM, O.
1916, 9, 16. Alonzo recrq
1925, 7, 19. Channing relrq
1931, 4, 19. Alonzo & w, Olive, gct Miami MM, O.

CURTIS
1921, 1, 15. Lucinda d bur New Antioch

1920, 9, 18. Frank & w, Lucinda, & ch, Alice, Lucy, Opal, Martha & Bertsell, recrq
1922, 11, 18. Belle recrq
1925, 7, 19. Frank & w dropped from mbrp
1926, 6, 20. Opal, Martha & Bertsell dropped from mbrp

DAILY
1895, 1, 19. Matilda Black gct White Water MM, Ind.

DAKIN
1821, 5, 21. Preserved rst on consent of Oblonge MM, N. Y.
1826, 7, 29. Nary (form Harvey) con mou
1829, 9, 15. Preserved dis jH
1831, 8, 16. Mary gct White Lick MM, Ind.
1930, 1, 19. Aus recrq

DAMEL
1839, 7, 16. William, Robert Bond, Martha Jane, Lydie & Rebecca, ch Robert & Martha, rqcf Hopewell MM, Va.

DARBEY
1893, 1, 21. Samuel recrq

DAUGHERTY
1874, 5, 16. Frances recrq
1874, 5, 16. Benjamin recrq
1874, 5, 16. William recrq
1877, 11, 17. Frank relrq

DAVIS
----, --, --. Robert b 1809,1,14; m Mary ----- b 1812,12,22
Ch: Mariah b 1837, 7, 6
1890, 7, 19. Carrie, dt Silas & Ruth (Thatcher), b
1922, 1, 4. Silas, s Hiram, d

1853, 2, 19. Henry rocf Nine Partners MM, N. Y., dtd 1852,9,15
1854, 10, 21. Henry T. con mou
1867, 6, 15. Allen rocf Miami MM, O., dtd 1867,5,22
1868, 8, 15. Mary Ann (form Bankson) gct Fairfield MM
1870, 4, 10. Ruth recrq
1870, 4, 16. Ruth recrq
1871, 2, 18. Silas rocf Dover MM
1874, 1, 17. Robert & w, Mary, recrq
1874, 1, 17. Mariah recrq
1888, 6, 16. Silas & fam rocf Miami MM, O., dtd 1888,4,25
1902, 2, 15. Ola Chamberlain rocf West Fork MM, O.
1902, 2, 15. Silas & w, Ruth, & dt, Carrie B., rocf Ogden MM, O.
1902, 8, 25. Silas & w, Ruth, gct Ogden MM, O.
1913, 12, 20. Blanch E., dt Chas. & Alice, recrq
1920, 3, 20. Leroy S. & w, Ola, relrq
1922, 3, 18. Edith Bogan gct Miami MM, O.

DAVISON
1831, 3, 15. Mary dis mou

DEAM
----, --, --. Chas. E. m Bertha Ruth SIRCLE, dt Minnie R., b 1895,9,9 (G)
Ch: Roger
Francis b 1925, 6, 16

1930, 2, 6. Mrs. Ruth recrq (G)
1932, 10, 6. Ruth & s, Roger, recrq (G)

DEBOARD
1894, 1, 20. William recrq
1894, 10, 20. Isaac [Debord] & w, Anna, recrq
1895, 5, 18. Leroy [Debord] recrq
1898, 4, 16. Ivy [Debord] dis
1899, 3, 18. James & w, Maggie, & ch, James Marion, Myrtle, Ottie & Clifford, recrq
1899, 11, 18. Will & Roy dis

DECK
1912, 12, 21. Joe V. recrq
1926, 2, 26. J. V. & w, Martha, recrq

DEDRICK
1887, 4, 16. Anna L. recrq

DELEANY
1874, 7, 18. Callie May recrq

DENNY
----, --, --. Martin V. b 1843,10,17; m Permela MILLIKAN b 1848,3,10
Ch: Henry H. b 1867, 8, 26
John W. " 1872, 5, 25
----, --, --. Emery Loring, s Levi Milton & Susan Frances (Ford), b 1881,1,9; m Josie Beryl MEANS, dt Joseph Francis & Ida May (Wright), b 1862,7,30 (G)
1874, 3, 21. Martin V. & w, Permelia, & ch, Henry H. & John W., recrq

DICKS
1819, 3, 27. Nathan gct Miami MM, O.
1820, 1, 29. Achilles D. rmt Hannah Harvy
1824, 7, 31. Achilles & w, Hannah, & ch,

DICKS, continued
Wm. Calvin & Levi, gct Miami MM, O.

DILLON
1820, 4, 20. Absalom rmt Gulielma Hiatt
1820, 8, 26. Absalom rocf Center MM, dtd 1820,7,15
1821, 5, 21. Absalom dis
1825, 9, 24. Gulielma gct Milford MM, Ind.

DIONNE
1881, 4, 16. Lewis recrq

DISBROW
1847, 1, 16. Alice Jane (form Maden) dis mou

DOAN
1831, 10, 26. Ephraim, s John & Eunice, b
----, --, --. Ann H., dt Eli & Sarah, b 1833,2, 8 d 1867,8,7 bur Springfield
----, --, --. E. & A. N.
Ch: William H. b 1861, 6, 14
John " 1863, 3, 8
James " 1865, 7, 15 d 1868, 1,27 bur Springfield
----, --, --. Calvin B., s John & Sarah (Shields), b 1852,8,10 d 1924,1,21 bur San Diego, Calif.; m Martha Emma THATCHER b 1853,3,16
Ch: Edith
Jessie b 1889, 2, 8 d 1922,3,23 bur San Diego

1855, 5, 19. Edwin Hadley gct Center MM, O., to m Jemima Doan
1860, 9, 15. Ephraim rmt Ann Harvey
1861, 2, 16. Ann H. gct Westfield MM, Ind.
1861, 11, 16. Ephraim & w, Ann, & s, William H., rocf Westfield MM, Ind., dtd 1861,10,1
1868, 11, 21. Ephraim gct Plainfield MM, Ind., to m Jane Hadley
1869, 3, 20. Jane rocf Plainfield MM, Ind., dtd 1869,3,3
1870, 5, 21. Ephraim & w, Jane, & ch, Wm. H. & John, gct Plainfield MM, Ind.
1870, 11, 19. Clarinda (form Hockett) con mou
1871, 8, 19. Clarinda gct Ash Grove MM, Ill.
1876, 3, 18. Isaac recrq
1906, 4, 21. Calvin & w, Martha E., & dt, Edith Jessie, rocf Chicago MM, Ill.
1925, 1, 18. Emma gct San Diego MM, Calif.

DONALDS
1865, 11, 18. Sarah M. (form Thatcher) con mou

DOUGHERTY
1921, 4, 11. Ida Maxine, dt Wm. & Florence B., b

1920, 9, 18. Wm. Joseph recrq

DOUGLAS
1846, 11, 21. Cornelius & w, Phebe N., & dt, Mary, rocf Vassalborough MM, Me., dtd 1846,10,14
1847, 5, 15. Cornelius & w, Phebe N., & dt, Mary, gct White Water MM, Ind.
1848, 1, 15. Cornelius & w, Phebe N., & dt, Mary, rocf White Water MM, Ind., dtd 1847,12,22
1849, 10, 20. John N. & w, Sarah, & dt, Maria, rocf St. Albans MM, Me., dtd 1849, 7,24
1854, 10, 21. Cornelius & w, Phebe N., gct Dover MM
1855, 2, 17. Mary gct Dover MM
1892, 7, 16. Elizabeth (Smith) & ch, Harriet E., Thomas J., Chas. A. & Edward S. Smith relrq

DOWN
1881, 4, 16. William & w, Sarah, recrq

DOWNARD
----, --, --. William b 1839,11,5; m Clara ----- b 1846,2,1
Ch: Lizzie b 1871, 3, 17

1871, 2, 18. William & w, Clara, recrq

DOWNING
1913, 2, 15. Luther Ruble recrq
1913, 3, 15. Wilbur Sherman recrq
1915, 2, 20. L. Ruble relrq
1921, 6, 18. Wilbur Sherman dropped from mbrp

DRAKE
1899, 4, 15. Andrew & w, Ida, & ch, Mary, Leonard C., John W. & Louie Belle, recrq
1903, 6, 20. A. J. & fam relrq

DUDLEY
1874, 1, 17. Martha recrq
1876, 3, 18. Garland recrq

DUNLAP
1883, 11, 17. Ruth recrq

DUNN
1886, 2, 18. Mary Frances, dt Wash. & Anne Stover, b (G)

1920, 4, 17. Clara relrq

EARLY
1912, 12, 21. Albert & w, Louie, & dt, Mildred Marie, recrq

EBON
1925, 7, --. Sarah d bur Lebanon

EDWARDS
1826, 5, 15. Joshua rmt Sarah Harvey

EDWARDS, continued
1826, 8, 28. Sarah gct Miami MM, O.
1827, 1, 27. Ruth rmt Joshua Hadley
1827, 10, 27. Jane rmt John Hussey
1829, 1, 13. Joshua & w, Sarah, & dt, Eliza, rocf Miami MM, O., dtd 1828,8,27
1829, 4, 14. Archibald & w, Ann, & ch, Mary, John Isaac Rebecca Harlan H. & Eleanor C., gct Miami MM, O.
1829, 4, 14. Elizabeth gct Miami MM, O.
1829, 1, 13. Lydia gct Miami MM, O.
1830, 6, 15. Joshua & w, Sarah, & dt, Mary Jane, gct Miami MM, O.
1831, 12, 13. Wm. Newlin gct Miami MM, O., to m Mary Edwards
1835, 10, 13. Isaac rmt Nancy Harvey
1835, 12, 15. Nancy gct Miami MM, O.
1854, 6, 17. Edith & ch, Mary Avilla & William H., recrq
1858, 8, 21. Joshua & w, Sarah, & ch, Nathaniel & John, rocf Miami MM, O., dtd 1858, 7,21
1861, 2, 16. Nathaniel Jr. dis disunity
1866, 11, 17. John dis disunity
1873, 1, 18. Joshua con mou
1897, 1, 16. Bert dis

ELLIS
----, --, --. Howard, s Marion, b 1891,7,22; m Mary DAVIS, dt J. O., b 1893,12,14
Ch: Maynard b 1917, 6, 29
Elwood " 1919, 11, 15
Francis " 1921, 9, 27
Richard " 1922, 11, 13
Mamie " 1826, 8, 3

1843, 12, 12. Robert & w, Anna, & ch, Susanna, James M., Dorcas, Jonathan, Seth, Jehu, Lydia Ann & Nancy Jane, rocf Newberry MM, dtd 1843,11,20
1844, 10, 15. Dorcas rmt John Miller
1844, 11, 12. James M. gct Newberry MM, O.
1846, 4, 14. Susanna gct Newberry MM, O.
1846, 5, 12. Robert & w, Ann, & ch, Jonathan, Seth, Jehu, Lydia Ann & Nancy Jane, gct Newberry MM, O.
1848, 2, 19. Jonathan & w, Susanna, & ch, Lydia, Mary, Jonathan W., Richard T. & Aquilla, rocf Clear Creek MM, O., dtd 1848,2,12
1853, 3, 19. Jonathan & w, Susanna, & ch, Lydia Mary, Jonathan, Richard & Aquilla, gct Center MM, O.
1859, 6, 18. Eliza (form Ogborn) con mou
1859, 11, 19. Eliza B. gct Fairfield MM
1927, 6, 19. Howard & w, Mary, & ch, Charles Maynard, James Elwood Francis & Richard, roc

ELLISON
1896, 1, 18. Nellie recrq
1896, 2, 15. Frank recrq

ELSTON
1880, 5, 16. Lilbie & Mary Jane recrq
1880, 5, 16. Horrace, Kemper & Chas. recrq
1883, 11, 17. Sallie E. recrq

EMERY
1883, 11, 17. Ella recrq

ENGLE
1915, 7, 23. Marie Madeline, dt J. H., b (G)

1930, 1, 2. Margaret recrq (G)
1931, 4, 2. Marie Madaline recrq (G)

EVANS
1859, 10, 15. William R. rmt Margaret A. Hadley
1860, 2, 18. Margaret Ann gct Miami MM, O.

1929, 12, 5. Bessie recrq (G)

FALLIS
1819, 2, 27. Mary rmt Richard Peirce
1819, 4, 24. Elizabeth & ch, Miriam, Rachel & Ann recrq
1820, 2, 28. Mary rmt Joseph Antram
1821, 2, 24. Jonathan rst on consent of Redstone MM, Pa.
1823, 2, 23. Amos gct Center MM, to m Lydia Carpenter
1823, 6, 28. Lydia Carpenter rocf Center MM, dtd 1823,6,21
1823, 6, 28. Lydia rmt Cyrus Farquhar
1824, 3, 27. Sarah rmt Eli Harvey
1824, 11, 27. Rachel rmt Amos Welch
1825, 5, 28. Amos dis disunity
1826, 10, 28. Eliza gct Centre MM
1826, 10, 28. Richard & w, Phebe, & ch, John, Thomas, Nancy, Harriett, Jane & Phebe, gct Center MM, O.
1828, 9, 16. John dis disunity
1828, 12, 16. Jonathan dis disunity
1829, 5, 12. Isaiah dis jH
1829, 7, 14. Mary dis jH
1829, 7, 14. Elizabeth dis disunity
1836, 7, 12. Rachel McGuire (form Fallis) dis mou
1836, 8, 16. Miriam gct Dover MM
1836, 9, 13. Esther & John, ch Isaiah & Elizabeth, gct Green Plain MM, O.
1839, 1, 15. Lydia rmt Eli McMillan
1839, 3, 12. Turner W., John, Isaac C. & Susan A., ch Lydia McMillan, gct Center MM, O.
1839, 12, 17. Miriam Tharp (form Fallis) dis mou
1844, 9, 17. Susan M. rocf Centre MM, O., dtd 1844,7,17

FARQUHAR
----, --, --. Benjamin b 1830,12,5; m Mary B. HADLEY b 1836,2,24
Ch: Ruth b 1862, 10, 4

FARQUHAR, continued
Ch: Charles b 1864, 9, 9
Naomi Jane " 1864, 11, 14 (?)

1823, 6, 28. Cyrus rmt Lydia Fallis
1823, 9, 27. Lydia gct Center MM, O.
1856, 4, 19. Benjamin rocf Center MM, O., dtd 1856,4,16
1856, 6, 21. Benjamin rmt Ruth Hawkins
1861, 12, 21. Benjamin rmt Mary B. Hadley
1893, 11, 18. Minnie B. relrq

FAULKNER
1833, 8, 13. Enoch Carter gct Center MM, O., to m Elizabeth Faulkner

FERGUSON
1854, 9, 9. H. b

1865, 1, 21. Sarah rocf Newberry MM, O., dtd 1864,10,17
1866, 5, 19. Webster M. rocf Spring Creek MM, Ia.
1874, 1, 17. Thomas recrq
1880, 4, 17. Cynthia recrq
1881, 5, 21. Minnie & Clement recrq
1886, 4, 17. Samuel recrq

FERRIS
1894, 1, 20. Gilbert recrq
1921, 6, 18. Gilbert & Luther dropped from mbrp

FIERS
1921, 9, 17. Wm. & fam gct Ogden MM, O.

FISHER
----, --, --. Elias b 1768,5,10 d 1845,12,22; m Hannah ----- b 1776,3,19 d 1852,7,26
Ch: Anna Cloud b 1812, 2, 17 (adopted)
Rebecca Cloud " 1817, 1, 23 (adopted)
Elias Fisher Cloud " 1819, 12, 14 d 1861, 3,14 (adopted)
1845, 12, 23. Elias d ae 77 y 7m 12d (a minister)
1852, 7, 26. Hannah d ae 76y 4m 6d (an elder)

1821, 3, 21. Elias & w, Hannah, rocf Cincinnati MM, O., dtd 1821,3,1
1832, 7, 17. Anna K. rocf Carmel MM, dtd 1832,1,21
1833, 6, 11. Ruth rocf Carmel MM, dtd 1833, 3,16
1835, 5, 12. Ann K. & Ruth gct Miami MM, O.
1836, 8, 16. Eli Harvey gct Miami MM, O., to m Ruth Fisher
1837, 8, 15. Anna K. rocf Miami MM, O., dtd 1837,7,26
1838, 3, 13. Anna K. rmt Wm. Lindley
1847, 9, 21. Asahel E. rocf Salem MM, O., dtd 1849,4,25
1854, 8, 19. Asahel gct Miami MM, O.
1877, 5, 19. Frank recrq

FLACK
--33, --, --. Nancy b
1867, 8, 15. Mary b

1867, 11, 16. Nancy recrq
1897, 8, 14. James relrq

FLANDERS
1898, 3, 19. John rocf Wilmington MM, O.

FORDYCE
1874, 2, 21. Ida E. recrq
1874, 2, 21. Ada [Foredyce] recrq
1874, 5, 16. William F. & w, Henrietta, & ch, Wm. & Alberta C., recrq
1874, 5, 16. Oscar recrq
1874, 5, 16. Alice recrq
1893, 1, 20. Ray recrq
1901, 4, 20. Albert C. & Permelia transferred to Ogden MM, O.

FRANKS
1855, 3, 13. John b

1871, 2, 18. John A. [Frank] recrq

FRAZIER
1850, 12, 21. Rebecca (form Millikin) dis mou
1913, 3, 15. Glenn recrq
1921, 6, 18. Glen dropped from mbrp

FREESTONE
1827, 1, 27. Daniel gct Chester MM, Ind.

FREEZE
1895, 3, 16. Thomas & w & ch recrq

FRY
1880, 5, 16. Hershel recrq
1881, 4, 16. Willard & w, Lue Ellen, & ch, Perlie & Blanch, recrq

FRYER
1933, 3, --. James M. d

1826, 6, 20. Anna dropped from mbrp
1826, 6, 20. Mathew dropped from mbrp
1826, 6, 20. Wilbur dropped from mbrp
1826, 6, 20. Orville dropped from mbrp
1892, 3, 19. James M. [Friar] recrq
1894, 1, 20. James Madison recrq
1907, 9, 20. Anna rocf Ogden MM, O.
1920, 5, 15. Thelma relrq
1922, 4, 15. Leona relrq
1931, 12, 13. James M. & w, Annie, recrq

FUGATE
1878, 7, 20. Merretta recrq
1878, 7, 20. Martha recrq

FUGATE, continued
1878, 7, 20. Annie E. recrq

FULGHUM
1837, 11, 14. Charles Osborn gct New Garden MM, Ind., to m Catherine Fulghum
1856, 4, 19. Hiram Hadley gct White Water MM, Ind., to m Hannah Fulghum
1890, 6, 21. Woodard & w, Amy, rocf Raysville MM, Ind., dtd 1890,5,24

GALEMAN
1872, 2, 17. Eunice W. & dt, Alcinda, recrq

GALLOP
1868, 2, 15. Susanna [Gallops] (form Hale) con mou
1869, 9, 18. Martha Jane con mou
1870, 5, 21. Susannah gct Wilmington MM, O.
1875, 7, 17. Martha J. [Gallup] & ch, Cora & Etta, gct Wilmington MM, O.

GARDNER
1848, 10, 21. Joseph & w, Eliza, & ch, Mary & Theodore, gct Salem MM, Ia.

GARNER
1845, 6, 17. William Pyle gct Newberry MM, O., to m Rebecca Garner
1850, 3, 16. Asa B. Green gct Newberry MM, O., to m Susanna Garner
1873, 1, 18. Martha L. (form Sewell) con mou
1873, 2, 15. Martha S. gct Newberry MM, O.
1900, 2, 17. Clara recrq

GASKILL
1822, 7, 27. Jane (form Carter) con mou
1847, 3, 20. William, s Jane, recrq
1857, 8, 15. Jane gct Honey Creek MM, Iowa
1860, 4, 21. Jane rocf Rocksylvania MM, Ia., dtd 1860,2,23
1882, 7, 15. Maria Louisa recrq

GAUSE
1866, 5, 19. Samuel rmt Mary J. Harvey
1866, 6, 16. Mary Jane gct Duck Creek MM, Ind.
1872, 5, 18. Samuel & w, Mary Jane, & ch, Elcana B. & Esther F., rocf Miami MM, O.
1876, 3, 18. Samuel & w, Mary Jane, & ch, Elkana B. & Esther F., gct Wilmington MM, O.
1877, 11, 17. Samuel & w, Mary Jane, & ch, Elcana B., Ester F. & Enos, rocf Wilmington MM, O.
1884, 3, 15. Samuel & w, Mary Jane, & ch, Elkanah B., Esther F. & Maurice, gct Newberry MM, O.

GERHARD
1915, 2, 20. Louis, s Christian & Mary, recrq

GIBSON
1830, 9, 14. Rachel rocf Newberry MM, O., dtd 1830,8,26
1833, 2, 12. Rachel gct Newburg MM

GOLLAHER
1870, 11, 19. Mary rocf Newberry MM, O., dtd 1870,9,19

GOODWIN
1852, 11, 20. Eliza A. (form Lundy) dis mou

GOOLMAN
1873, 11, 15. Eunice W. & dt, Alcinda F., gct Indianapolis MM, Ind.
1875, 7, 17. Eunice W. [Goulman] & ch, Alcinda F., gct Mill Creek MM, Ind.

GRAHAM
1868, 11, 21. Mary rocf Newberry MM, O., dtd 1868,10,19
1872, 6, 15. Mary gct Ackworth MM, Ia.

GRAY
----, --, --. Thomas & Mabel Annette (G)
Ch: Russell
William b 1912, 7, 17
Howard
Leonard " 1909, 10, 19

1873, 8, 16. Lina (form Bogan) con mou
1879, 4, 19. John W. recrq
1885, 4, 18. Walter [Grey] recrq
1889, 4, 20. John T. recrq
1894, 4, 21. Sarah B. recrq
1897, 9, 18. Angeline gct Wilmington MM, O.
1918, 4, 20. John T. dropped from mbrp
1932, 2, 4. Howard Leonard recrq (G)
1933, 4, 6. Russell Wm. recrq (G)

GREATHOUSE
1901, 1, 19. Charles Henry recrq
1901, 1, 19. Linton Smart recrq
1901, 1, 19. Dora Amanda recrq
1901, 1, 19. Mary Millie recrq
1901, 1, 19. Sarah Martin recrq
1924, 4, 20. Sarah (Greathouse) Law relrq
1924, 6, 22. Dora relrq
1925, 7, 19. Charles dropped from mbrp

GREEN
----, --, --. Reuben b 1770,7,28; m Rhoda BALLARD b 1775,3,1 d 1843,2,10
Ch: Isaac b 1797, 10, 4 d 1808, 6,22
Mary " 1799, 4, 7
David " 1800, 6, 2
Lydia " 1801, 12, 9 d 1803, 8,13
Robert " 1803, 6, 26
Asa " 1805, 1, 5
Anna " 1807, 1, 2 d 1812, 9,25
Abigail " 1808, 10, 19
John " 1810, 7, 27
Susann " 1812, 9, 29
Rowland " 1814, 11, 10
Rhoda " 1818, 7, 7

GREEN, continued
----, --, --. David b 1800,6,2; m Mary JESSOP b 1805, 4, 9
Ch: Asa B. b 1828, 1, 8
Jonathan " 1829, 7, 18
Elijah " 1831, 4, 24
Thomas " 1832, 11, 3
Rhoda Ann " 1834, 5, 16
Eli " 1836, 12, 5
Rebecca " 1839, 10, 4
Albert " 1845, 2, 20
Levi " 1847, 5, 17
William " 1849, 8, 20
----, --, --. Asa b 1805,1,5 d 1893,3,15 bur Springfield; m Susanna -----
Ch: Jane b 1829, 8, 30
Reuben " 1831, 11, 24
Mary Ann " 1834, 1, 22
Cyrus " 1836, 10, 12
Gulielma " 1839, 10, 16
John C. " 1842, 7, 9
Samuel G. " 1845, 9, 21
Nancy Emily" 1849, 9, 28
William G. " 1851, 2, 15
----, --, --. Rowland b 1819,11,10; m Absillet THOMAS b 1815,5,17 d 1871,8,31
Ch: William T. b 1838, 7, 8 d 1841,11,13
Mary Jane " 1841, 11, 20 " 1863,12,18
Clarkson T." 1845, 6, 7 " 1871,10,11
1844, 2, 3. Ellen b (w Samuel G.)
----, --, --. Isaiah & Ella
Ch: Bert Franklin
Myrtle Evelyn
Bernice Ellen b 1909, 11, 1
Arthur Edward " 1911, 12, 30
Laura Elizabeth

1823, 9, 27. Mary rmt Mordecai Walker
1823, 9, 27. Robert gct White Water MM, Ind.
1826, 10, 12. Robert & w, Mahala, rocf White Water MM, Ind., dtd 1826,8,23
1826, 11, 25. David gct Miami MM, O., to m Mary Jessop
1827, 2, 24. Mary rocf Miami MM, O., dtd 1827, 1,31
1827, 6, 27. David & w, Mary, gct Clear Creek MM, O.
1828, 10, 14. Asa rmt Susannah Carter
1829, 3, 17. Abigail rmt Eli Hadley
1829, 5, 12. David & w, Mary, & ch, Asa B., rocf Clear Creek MM, O., dtd 1829,4,11
1831, 5, 17. Robert gct New Garden MM, Ind.
1832, 9, 11. John gct Goshen MM, O., to m Mary Ann Watkins
1832, 11, 13. John gct Goshen MM, O.
1835, 9, 15. Rowland gct New Garden MM, Ind., to m Absillet Thomas
1835, 12, 15. Absillet rocf New Garden MM, Ind., dtd 1835,11,21
1838, 1, 16. Susannah Moore (form Green) con mou
1850, 3, 16. Asa B. gct Newberry MM, O., to m Susanna Garner
1850, 8, 17. Susanna rocf Newberry MM, O., dtd 1850,8,12
1851, 10, 18. Jonathan gct Goshen MM, O.
1852, 6, 17. Asa B. & w, Susannah, & s, William G., gct Newberry MM, O.
1851, 10, 18. Mary Ann rmt John Hockett
1852, 6, 19. Asa B. & w, Susanna, & s, Wm. G., gct Newberry MM, O.
1853, 4, 16. David & w, Mary, & ch, Thomas, Eli, Rebecca, Albert, Levi & William, gct Miami MM, O.
1853, 4, 16. Rhoda Ann gct Miami MM, O.
1854, 3, 18. Rhoda rmt Daniel Young
1854, 7, 15. Elijah C. gct Miami MM, O.
1856, 8, 16. Jehiel & w, Rachel, & ch, Joel Wm., James Robert & Aseph Leander, rocf Center MM, O., dtd 1856,7,16
1857, 2, 21. Jane rmt Cyrus Moon
1859, 3, 19. Gulielma More (form Green) con mou
1860, 5, 19. Jonathan & w, Rachel, & ch, Asa Oscar, Mary Emely & Anna Louisa, rocf Miami MM, O., dtd 1860,4,25
1863, 4, 18. Jonathan & w, Rachel B., & ch, Asa Oscar, Mary Emily & Anna Louise, gct Plainfield MM, Ind.
1864, 2, 20. Jehiel & w, Rachel, & ch, Joel Wm., James Robert, Aseph Leander & Lieuenna Catharine, gct Newberry MM, O.
1865, 2, 18. Cyrus gct Plainfield MM, Ind.
1867, 2, 16. Ellen H. recrq
1867, 6, 15. Polly rocf Miami MM, O., dtd 1867,5,22
1867, 6, 15. Samuel G. con mou
1868, 8, 15. John C. con mou
1868, 10, 17. Nancy E. rmt Timothy C. Kimbrough
1869, 8, 21. Hannah Isabelle rocf Newberry MM, O., dtd 1868,12,21
1872, 6, 15. John C. & w, Hannah Isabel & ch, Orlando & Claudia, gct Ackworth MM, Ia.
1874, 1, 17. Asa recrq
1874, 5, 16. Rowland gct Richland MM, Ind., to m Elizabeth Harold
1874, 10, 17. Rowland gct Richland MM, Ind.
1878, 7, 20. Hannah Isabel & ch, Orlando W. & Flora M., rocf Acworth MM, Ia., dtd 1878,6,22
1881, 11, 19. Samuel T. & w, Ella, gct Wilmington MM, O.
1883, 3, 17. Samuel & w, Ellen, rocf Wilmington MM, O.
1888, 6, 16. Jacob & fam rocf Westland MM, dtd 1888,4,7
1888, 9, 15. Lydia Annetta, dt Jacob H. & Anna M., gct Birmingham MM, Pa.
1893, 11, 18. Richard C. & fam rocf Fairfield

GREEN, continued
MM
1894, 12, 15. Lizzie & dt gct Wilmington MM, O.
1913, 1, 18. Isaiah & w, Ellen M., & ch, Bert Franklin, Myrtle Evelyn, Bernice Ellen & Arthur Edward, recrq
1926, 3, 26. Sophia recrq

GRIEST
1854, 7, 15. Edwin dis mou

GRIFFIN
1823, 3, 29. Samuel rmt Lydia Reynard
1823, 10, 25. Lydia gct West Grove MM, Ind.

GRIFFITH
1827, 12, 29. Ruth (form Harlan) dis mou

GRIMES
1838, 12, 11. George recrq
1839, 10, 15. George gct Miami MM, O., to m Susanna Shepherd
1840, 4, 14. Susannah rocf Miami MM, O., dtd 1840,2,19
1841, 7, 13. George & w, Susanna, & dt, Martha Jane, gct Centre MM, O.
1841, 7, 13. George & w, Susanna, & dt, Martha Jane, gct Centre MM, O.
1844, 4, 16. George & w, Susannah, & ch, Martha Jane & Asa G., rocf Centre MM, O., dtd 1844,2,14

GRIST
1850, 8, 17. Edwin rocf Sugar River MM, Ind., dtd 1850,6,3

GROVE
----, --, --. Homer, dt Oscar, b 1890,5,20; m Chloe DECK, dt George, b 1891,8,30
Ch: Howard b 1913, 8, 2
Heber " 1918, 4, 22

1929, 12, 22. Hamer & w, Chloe, & ch, Howard & Heber, recrq

GUDGEON
1881, 2, 19. Mina recrq
1888, 7, 21. Silas recrq

HADLEY
----, --, --. William b 1768,12,2; m Sarah CLARK b 1769,1,13 d 1837,10,2
Ch: Mary b 1792, 7, 27
David " 1794, 4, 27
John " 1796, 7, 17 d 1868, 1, 8 bur Clarksville
Ruth b 1798, 8, 25
Jonathan " 1800, 8, 20
Ann " 1802, 8, 31
Joshua " 1804, 12, 2
Sarah " 1805, 10, 24
William " 1808, 12, 17 d 1844, 3,21 bur Clarksville
Ch: Jane b 1808, 3, 3
son " 1815, 11, 19 d 1815,11,22
----, --, --. John b 1770,12,23 d 1832,4,13; m Lydia HARVEY b 1774,10,17 d 1852,9,16
Ch: William b 1795, 7, 18
Simon " 1796, 11, 1
Elizabeth " 1798, 6, 14
Joshua " 1799, 9, 15 d 1808,4,15
Jacob " 1801, 3, 3
Isaac " 1802, 12, 9 d 1839, 7,22
Eli " 1804, 9, 27
John " 1806, 10, 3
Thomas " 1808, 8, 21 " 1828, 6, 5
Jonathan " 1810, 8, 10
Ruth " 1812, 11, 15 d 1852,10,19
Jane " 1815, 7, 20
----, --, --. David b 1794,4,27; m Sarah LINDLEY b 1796,9,7
Ch: Hannah b 1816, 1, 1
William " 1818, 2, 12
Samuel " 1820, 6, 24 d 1820, 7,16
Mary " 1821, 6, 3
Isaiah " 1824, 1, 23
David " 1827, 2, 8
Sarah " 1830, 2, 29
Lindley " 1833, 2, 9
Chambers " 1836, 4, 19
Abraham " 1841, 2, 16
----, --, --. Jonathan b 1793,3,14; m Rebecca HARVEY b 1795,1,17 d 1876,6,19 bur Springfield
Ch: Elizabeth b 1816, 12, 3 d 1868, 4,15 bur Springfield
Lydia b 1818, 12, 6
Samuel " 1821, 1, 30
Ruth " 1825, 9, 1 d 1877, 2,15 bur Springfield
Isaac b 1828, 4, 26 " 1843, 8,19 bur Springfield
Simon b 1822, 12, 11
Deborah " 1830, 11, 26
Milton " 1833, 2, 19
Harlan H. " 1835, 10, 21
----, --, --. Simon d 1870,5,13 bur Springfield; m Ann ----- d 1843,9,28 bur Springfield
Ch: Jabez H. b 1817, 9, 29
Rebecca " 1819, 12, 18
Lydia " 1822, 1, 15 d 1847, 5,19 bur Springfield
John b 1824 4, 20 " 1835, 7,28 bur Springfield
Julia Ann b 1827, 3, 4
Ann K. " 1830, 2, 3 " 1843, 9,28 bur Springfield
Mary M. b 1832, 12, 13
----, --, --. Jacob b 1801,3,3 d 1879,2,11 bur SPringfield; m Mary BUTLAR b 1801,3,6 d 1858,7,20 bur Springfield
Ch: Samuel b 1824, 5, 18
Eliza Ann " 1826, 1, 12
William Beale " 1830, 5, 21

HADLEY, continued
Ch: Ellwood b 1832, 11, 9
Mary B. " 1836, 12, 24
Susanna Jane " 1838, 10, 15
Naomi C. " 1845, 4, 5
----, --, --. Jonathan b 1800,8,20; m Olive MENDENHALL b 1803,7,11 d 1840,11,19
Ch: Edwin b 1826, 5, 16
William Clark " 1828, 1, 21
Eliza " 1830, 2, 15
Rebecca Jane " 1833, 10, 5
Ann " 1836, 3, 27
John " 1838, 11, 15
Olive " 1840, 11, 19 d 1842, 7,11
Jonathan m 2nd Eliza ----- b 1846,4,26
Ch: Sarah Elizabeth b 1844, 5, 25 d 1844,12,16
Jonathan m 3rd Elizabeth -----
Ch: Albert b 1849, 8, 5 d 1875, 7,26
Charles " 1850, 11, 5
Francis " 1852, 10, 2
----, --, --. Isaac & Lydia
Ch: Calvin C. b 1826, 7, 8
Elizabeth " 1828, 5, 21
Phebe " 1830, 6, 19
Almira " 1832, 10, 23
Henry " 1835, 2, 21 d 1836, 1,30 bur Springfield
Rebecca Helen b 1836, 12, 16
Harriet " 1839, 12, 12 d 1841, 9,27 bur Springfield
----, --, --. Joshua b 1804,12,2; m Ruth E. EDWARDS b 1806,4,17
Ch: Anna b 1827, 10, 26 d 1839, 7, 2
Miles " 1829, 11, 27
Archibald " 1832, 3, 18
Jane " 1834, 10, 23
Abraham " 1837, 2, 1 d 1839, 7,14
William P. " 1840, 12, 1
Olive " 1844, 1, 16
Seth " 1848, 1, 14
----, --, --. Eli b 1804,9,27 d 1854,11,29; m Abigail GREEN b 1808,10,19 d 1837,4,30
Ch: Mahalah G. b 1829, 11, 13
Gulielma " 1830, 11, 17
Thomas " 1832, 9, 21
Micajah C. " 1834, 9, 20
Rhoda E. " 1836, 7, 14
Eli m 2nd Mary -----
----, --, --. John b 1806,10,3; m Ann WILDMAN b 1810,4,15 d 1848,4,21 bur Springfield
Ch: Hiram b 1833, 3, 17
Elizabeth " 1834, 5, 3
Margaret Ann " 1836, 10, 13
Henry " 1838, 3, 5
Deborah " 1839, 10, 16 d 1840,10, 3 bur Springfield
Ruth b 1841, 2, 28 " 1842, 7,13

Ch: Seth S. b 1846, 6, 20
----, --, --. William b 1808,12,17; m Sophia ----- b 1812,11,10
Ch: Sarah Jane b 1833, 12, 13
Martha " 1835, 9, 24
Ann " 1837, 4, 1
Clark " 1838, 11, 9
Allen " 1840, 9, 23
Mary T. " 1844, 4, 25
----, --, --. Jonathan D. b 1810,8,10 d 1872, 9,23 bur Springfield; m Susannah ----- b 1812,5,14 d 1874,10,27 bur Springfield
Ch: Louisa b 1836, 11, 8 d 1859,11, 7 bur Springfield
Mahlon b 1835, 2, 13
John William " 1839, 12, 22
Evan " 1842, 9, 20
1829, 11, 27. Miles b
1832, 3, 18. Archabald b (s J. & R.)
----, --, --. Wm. L. b 1818,2,12; m Mary N. NICHOLSON b 1819,11,2
Ch: John N. b 1840, 7, 16
Artemus N. " 1842, 2, 6 d 1868, 6, 3 bur Springfield
Sarah Elizabeth " 1844, 11, 10
1842, 12, 15. William d ae 74 (an elder)
----, --, --. Samuel m Mary Jane HARVEY
Ch: Martha Ann b 1845, 2, 13 d 1875, 2,15
James " 1846, 7, 27
Ansalem " 1848, 8, 4
Calvin " 1850, 8, 15
Emma " 1853, 12, 15 d 1830,10,28 bur Springfield
Anna b 1855, 11, 2 d 1931, 1,30 bur Springfield
Edwin b 1857, 10, 24
Esther " 1860, 10, 9 d 1863,10, 7
Marietta " 1865, 4, 20
William P. " 1872, 8, 24
----, --, --. Eli S. d 1868,9,7; m Theodocia -----
Ch: Chester b 1849, 3, 14
John William " 1846, 8, 12 d 1848,12,20
Ellen b 1851, 11, 25
Ruth " 1854, 3, 25
Warren " 1856, 9, 19
Alonzo " 1858, 12, 18
----, --, --. Simon & Rachel
Ch: Joseph Edgar b 1849, 7, 26 d 1850, 7,26 bur Springfield
Lucy Caroline b 1851, 6, 22
Martha Emeline " 1852, 10, 27
Joseph C. " 1855, 1, 16
Benjamin B." 1857, 8, 1
Albert J. " 1859, 12, 22
Cyrus M. " 1863, 4, 9
----, --, --. Samuel & Ruth S.

HADLEY, Samuel & Ruth S., continued
Ch: Orlando b 1851, 12, 25
Emily " 1853, 11, 2
Alice " 1856, 2, 27
Mary D. " 1860, 4, 8
Anna " 1862, 7, 31
Eva Jane " 1864, 3, 10
1852, 2, 24. David d ae 57y 8m 27d (an elder)
1852, 9, 16. Lydia d ae 78y 8m (an elder)
----, --, --. David & Abigail
Ch: Byrom C. b 1854, 10, 14 d 1855, 4,14 bur Clarksville
George C. b 1856, 5, 31
Woodro Warner " 1860, 4, 10
----, --, --. Milton & Lucy
Ch: Isaac H. b 1855, 8, 21
Otis " 1868, 5, 27
1854, 11, 29. Eli d ae 50y (an elder)
----, --, --. William & Rebecca Jane
Ch: Ida Belle b 1858, 3, 16
Emma S. " 1861, 11, 29
----, --, --. W. B. & R. J.
Ch: Flora M. b 1858, 4, 5
Ada E. " 1859, 8, 19
1857, 12, 5. William d ae 88y 7m 26d (an elder)
----, --, --, Harlan H. b 1835,10,21; m Susanna KIMBRO, dt Thomas & Elizabeth KIMBROUGH, b 1836,11,15
Ch: Ella b 1859, 8, 30
Atwell " 1861, 7, 28
Isaac P. " 1863, 4, 2
Horace A. " 1865, 9, 21
Ruth Edna " 1873, 3, 28
----, --, --. John W. b 1839,12,22; m Sarah E. WORTHINGTON b 1842,4,9
Ch: William Edgar b 1861, 1, 31
Mary Anna " 1862, 9, 15
----, --, --. Thomas m Amanda Maria PYLE
Ch: Anna Winn b 1862, 9, 27
Harriett Isabel " 1863, 12, 5
Morris W. " 1871, 10, 14
Bertha M. " 1873, 6, 24
----, --, --. Columbus b 1836,4,19; m Ann Elizabeth HIGGINS b 1846,9,29
Ch: Mary Catharine b 1863, 9, 22 d 1864, 9, bur Clarksville
Joseph W. b 1865, 2, 27
Elnora " 1867, 4, 7
1864, 8, 1. Milly b
----, --, --. Micajah C. b 1834,9,20; m Ellen COWGILL
Ch: Weldon S. b 1866, 2, 1
Gertrude " 1869, 12, 12
1866, 12, 12. Anna b
1868, 1, 8. John d
----, --, --. James, s Samuel L. & Mary (Harvey), b 1846,7,27 d 1917,4,25; m Isabella A. MOORE, dt John H. & Ruth, b 1850,9,23
Ch: Edgar L. b 1870, 10, 7
Alonta " 1875, 2, 26
Louie May " 1879, 9, 9
Everett Murray " 1882, 5, 27
Bertha A. " 1894, 2, 1
Ruthanna " 1887, 6, 27
Mary Edith " 1892, 9, 25
----, --, --. Orlando, s S. H. & Ruth (Smith), b 1851,12,25; m Harriet E. HAWORTH, dt Richard & Elizabeth (West) b 1856,9,7
Ch: Florence E. b 1880, 3, 25
Ruthanna " 1883, 7, 14
1875, 5, 31. Zenas, s Evan & Susannah N., b
1875, 8, 15. Minnie Johns, dt Rodney G. & Anna, b
----, --, --. Atwell M., s Harlan H. & Susan, b 1861,7,28; m Sarah A. TOWNSEND, dt Josiah M. & Ester J., b 1865,3,11
Ch: Hershel T. b 1891, 2, 15
Ethel K. " 1893, 11, 25
Reba M. " 1895, 9, 7
Edith W. " 1897, 11, 10
Vivian M. " 1900, 7, 30
Herbert H. " 1902, 1, 26
----, --, --. Maurice, s Archibald & Mary (Andrews), b 1873,7,16; m Carrie Bell McKENNY, dt Robert & Susan (Wolfe), b 1874,9,8 d 1933,4,16 bur Springfield
Ch: Veda b 1895, 9, 19
Mary " 1898, 9, 8
William " 1902, 3, 23
Olive " 1903, 11, 13
Donald Leroy " 1908, 9, 21
Raymond Morris
Doris " 1912, 8, 21
----, --, --. Everett Murry, s James & Isabella (Moore), b 1882,5,27; m Anna Ethel CRITES, dt John & Ann (Peelle)
Ch: Howard J. b 1910, 7, 9
Herbert " 1912, 8, 24
Anna Edith " 1914, 8, 5
James Murry " 1916, 3, 7
Jesse William " 1918, 11, 8
Franklin Everett " 1920, 10, 23
Theodore " 1929, 1, 4
Calvin Charles " 1925, 2, 10
1920, 1, 16. Farinda d
----, --, --. Calvin m Emma MULLEN
Ch: Samuel
M. Etta
Albert
Gilpin d 1923, 9,18
1926, 5, 17. William d

1823, 5, 31. Jacob gct White Water MM, Ind.,

HADLEY, continued
to m Mary Butler
1824, 1, 21. Mary rocf White Water MM, Ind., dtd 1823,10,18
1824, 2, 28. William rmt Ann Harvey
1824, 2, 28. Ann rmt Eli Hale
1824, 11, 27. Ann gct White Lick MM, Ind.
1825, 5, 11. Jonathan rmt Olive Mendenhall
1826, 3, 25. Isaac con mou
1826, 10, 28. Joshua & w, Rebecca, & ch, Jesse, Anna, James & Isaac, gct White Lick MM, Ind.
1827, 1, 27. Joshua rmt Ruth Edwards
1828, 3, 29. Lydia Jr. & s, Caleb, recrq
1829, 3, 17. Eli rmt Abigail Green
1830, 5, 11. Susannah (form Thatcher) dis mou
1830, 4, 13. Wm. Jr. dis mou
1830, 7, 13. Sarah dis jH
1830, 11, 16. Jane rmt Abraham Hawkins
1831, 1, 11. Ruth rmt Wm. Andrew
1831, 2, 15. Ruth dis jH
1831, 7, 12. John Jr. gct Green Plain MM, O., to m Ann Wildman
1831, 12, 13. Jonathan D. gct White Water MM, Ind., to m Susanna W. Clawson
1832, 1, 17. Ann rocf Green Plain MM, O., dtd 1832,1,4
1832, 4, 17. Sarah rmt Peter Osborn
1832, 8, 14. Susannah W. rocf White Water MM, Ind., dtd 1832,4,25
1833, 7, 16. William Jr. con mou
1833, 7, 16. Sophia (form Thompson) con mou
1834, 1, 14. Jane rmt Seneca Wildman
1835, 1, 13. Hannah rmt Wm. Osborn Jr.
1835, 7, 14. Deborah Thatcher (form Hadley) con mou
1838, 8, 14. Jonathan, s Wm., gct Center MM, O., to m Mary Linton
1838, 9, 11. Eli gct New Garden MM, Ind., to m Mary Balard
1839, 2, 12. Mary & dt, Jane Balard, rocf New Garden MM, Ind., dtd 1838,12,15
1840, 6, 16. William, s David, con mou
1840, 12, 15. Mary rocf Centre MM, O., dtd 1840,8,12
1842, 12, 13. Jonathan gct Centre MM, O., to m Eliza B. Mabie
1843, 3, 14. Eliza B. rocf Center MM, O., dtd 1843,2,15
1843, 10, 17. Ann M. rmt James Linton
1844, 1, 16. Samuel L. rmt Mary Jane Harvey
1845, 12, 16. Lydia rmt James Smith
1846, 4, 14. Alfred Jr. dis mou
1846, 9, 19. Isaiah gct White Lick MM, Ind., to m Emily Hadley
1846, 9, 19. Isaiah Hadley gct White Lick MM, Ind., to m Emily Hadley
1846, 11, 21. Eli dis mou
1846, 12, 19. Theodosia (form Stanton) dis mou
1847, 1, 16. Isaiah gct White Lick MM, Ind.
1847, 4, 17. Milton con mou
1847, 5, 15. Samuel M. gct Miami MM, O., to m Emily Johnson
1848, 6, 17. Jonathan rmt Elizabeth Timberlake
1848, 2, 19. Emily J. rocf Miami MM, O., dtd 1848,1,26
1848, 3, 18. Simon gct Springborough MM, O., to m Mary J. O'Neal
1848, 6, 17. Susanna recrq
1848, 8, 19. Edwin gct Center MM, O., to m Esther Coate
1848, 9, 16. Simon gct Dover MM, O., to m Rachel M. Baugham
1848, 11, 18. Carter con mou
1849, 1, 20. Mary J. rocf Springborough MM, O., dtd 1848,12,26
1849, 1, 20. Sophia rmt Wm. West
1849, 4, 21. Rachel M. rocf Dover MM, O., dtd 1849,3,15
1849, 5, 19. Mahala J. rmt Isaac Thomas
1849, 8, 18. Esther C. rocf Center MM, O., dtd 1849,5,16
1849, 11, 18. Milton gct Honey Creek MM, Ia.
1850, 1, 19. Elizabeth rmt Jane Cammack
1850, 2, 16. Mahala H. Warner (form Hadley) dis mou
1850, 5, 18. Eliza A. rmt Samuel Henley
1850, 12, 21. Samuel H. gct Green Plain MM, O. to m Ruth Smith
1851, 4, 19. John C. rocf Newberry MM, O., dtd 1851,1,13
1851, 9, 20. Ann Hazard (form Hadley) con mou
1851, 9, 20. Ruth S. rocf Green Plain MM, O., dtd 1851,7,19
1851, 9, 20. Rachel L. rocf Green Plain MM, dtd 1851,8,12
1851, 10, 16. Phebe D. More (form Hadley) con mou
1851, 10, 18. Almira rmt Alfred Wilson
1852, 2, 21. Louisa rmt Joseph Mather
1852, 2, 21. Eli L. & Theodosia rst & ch, Chester & Ellen recrq
1852, 12, 18. John, Artemus & Sarah Elizabeth, ch Wm. L., recrq
1853, 1, 15. John C. gct Center MM, O.
1853, 8, 20. Mary N. recrq
1853, 9, 17. David L. gct Walnut Ridge MM, Ind., to m Abigail G. Clark
1853, 9, 17. Wm. C. con mou
1853, 9, 17. Eliza rmt Cyrus Linton
1853, 11, 19. Sarah Jane More (form Hadley) con mou
1854, 5, 20. Elizabeth rmt Daniel C. Allen
1854, 10, 21. Martha H. Hiatt (form Hadley) con mou
1854, 10, 21. Abigail J. rocf Walnut Ridge MM, Ind., dtd 1854,7,15
1855, 1, 20. Milton con mou
1855, 5, 19. Lucy M. recrq
1855, 5, 19. Edwin gct Center MM, O., to m Jemima Doan
1856, 2, 16. Jemima D. rocf Center MM, O., dtd 1856,1,16
1856, 3, 15. John gct Springborough MM, O.,

HADLEY, continued
to m Rhoda Stanton
1856, 4, 19. Hiram gct White Water MM, Ind., to m Hannah Fulghum
1856, 4, 19. William B. dis mou
1856, 5, 17. Rebecca Jane dis mou
1856, 5, 17. Eli dis mou
1856, 5, 17. Lindley dis mou
1856, 6, 21. Rhoda G. & dt, Lydia G. Stanton, rocf Springborough MM, O., dtd 1856,5,20
1857, 1, 17. Jane Biven (form Hadley) dis mou
1857, 3, 21. Hiram gct White Water MM, Ind.
1857, 5, 16. Wm. B. & w, Rebecca Jane, recrq
1857, 8, 15. Mahlon C. dis mou
1858, 5, 15. Elizabeth W. rmt Samuel Brown
1858, 6, 19. Anna M. Welsh (form Hadley) con mou
1858, 6, 19. Miles con mou
1858, 10, 16. Elwood gct White Water MM, Ind., to m Ann Pedrick
1859, 2, 19. Harlan H. con mou
1859, 2, 19. Susannah (form Kimbrough) con mou
1859, 4, 16. Archibald con mou
1859, 5, 21. Ann P. rocf White Water MM, Ind. dtd 1859,4,27
1859, 9, 17. Jonathan & w, Mary, & ch, Rachel Anna, Mary Jane, Caroline, Elizabeth, Lydia, Seth Silvers, Nathan & William, gct Center MM, O.
1859, 10, 15. Margaret A. rmt Wm. R. Evans
1860, 4, 21. John Wm. rmt Sarah Ellin Worthington
1860, 7, 21. Clark W. con mou
1860, 10, 20. Mahlon C. & w, Emily Caroline, & s, Walter, recrq
1860, 10, 20. Jacob C. gct Fairfield MM, O., to m Lucinda Cowgill
1861, 2, 16. Jabes H. con mou
1861, 3, 16. Lucinda & s, Jonathan B. Bowgill, rocf Fairfield MM, dtd 1861,2,16
1861, 4, 20. Jonathan D. & w, Susannah W., & s, Evan H., gct Miami MM, O.
1861, 5, 18. Edwin & w, Jemima, & ch, Eliza, Olive & Eleen, gct Miami MM, O.
1861, 5, 18. 'Rebecca Helen Wildman (form Hadley) con mou
1861, 8, 17. Thomas con mou
1861, 12, 21. Mary B. rmt Benjamin Farquhar
1862, 3, 15. Amanda Meriah recrq
1862, 6, 21. Elwood & w, Anna P., & dt, Corrilla M., gct White Water MM, Ind.
1862, 7, 19. Julia KcKencie (form Hadley) con mou
1862, 10, 18. Jonathan & w, Elizabeth T., & ch, Albert, Charles, Francis, Eveline, Calvin, Caroline, Jonathan, gct Rocksylvania MM, Ia.
1862, 12, 20. Allen dis disunity
1863, 5, 16. Sarah Caroline recrq
1863, 7, 18. John rmt Mary Newlin
1863, 7, 18. Artemus N. gct Miami MM, O., to m Elizabeth M. Jones
1863, 7, 18. Chambers con mou
1863, 7, 18. Ann Elizabeth recrq
1864, 3, 19. Micajah C. rmt Ellen W. Cowgill
1864, 6, 18. John Jr. & w, Rhoda G., & s, Seth S., gct Springborough MM, O.
1864, 7, 16. Jeremiah rmt Rebecca Hadley
1864, 7, 16. Rebecca rmt Jeremiah Hadley
1864, 12, 17. Rebecca C. gct White Water MM, Ind.
1865, 2, 18. Olive Linton (form Hadley) con mou
1865, 7, 15. Henry gct Springborough MM, O.
1865, 9, 16. Elizabeth M. rocf Miami MM, O., dtd 1865,7,26
1865, 11, 18. William & w, Rebecca Jane, & ch, Idabell, Emma & Frank W., gct Newberry MM, O.
1865, 11, 18. Susannah Sr. gct Newberry MM, O.
1866, 5, 19. Deborah J. recrq
1867, 1, 19. Abraham H. con mou
1867, 7, 20. Ann gct Summit Grove MM, Ia.
1867, 7, 20. Mary T. gct Summit Grove MM, Ia.
1867, 8, 17. Mahlon C. & w, Emily C., & ch, Walter & Arthur, gct Springborough MM, O.
1868, 3, 21. Rhoda Ann rmt Jeremiah Kimbrough
1868, 4, 18. Artemus & w, Elizabeth, & ch, Elsie, Mary & Samuel W., gct White Water MM, Ind.
1868, 4, 18. Wm. Beal & w, Rebecca Jane, & ch Flora & Ada, gct White Water MM, Ind.
1868, 11, 21. Ephraim Doan gct Plainfield MM, Ind., to m Jane Hadley
1869, 5, 15. Thomas & w, Amanda, & ch, Annie & Harriett J., gct Rocksylvanie MM, Ia.
1870, 2, 19. Adaline & Laura, ch Miles, recrq
1870, 3, 19. James con mou
1870, 3, 19. Isabel A. con mou
1870, 7, 16. Mahlon C. & w, Emily G., & ch, Walter & Arthur E., rocf Springfield MM, O., dtd 1870,6,21
1870, 7, 16. Thomas & w, Amanda M., & ch, Anna W. & Hattie J., rocf Rocksylvania MM, Ia., dtd 1870,6,18
1870, 8, 20. Miles H. & fam gct Cincinnati MM, O.
1870, 12, 17. Lucy C. rmt Jesse H. Harvey
1871, 2, 18. Sarah Caroline recrq
1871, 5, 20. Jonathan D. & w, Susannah, rocf Springborough MM, O.
1871, 5, 20. Evan H. & w, Susan W., rocf Springborough MM, O., dtd 1871,4,25
1871, 6, 17. Chester G. con mou
1872, 3, 16. Calvin & w, Emma B., con mou
1872, 8, 17. Mary gct Plainfield MM, Ind.
1872, 12, 21. Susan N. recrq
1873, 7, 19. Ellen Clark (form Hadley) con mou
1874, 1, 17. Milton & w, Lucy M., & ch, Isaac H. & Otis, gct Miami MM, O.
1874, 1, 17. Thomas recrq
1874, 2, 21. Simon & w, Rachel, & ch, Joseph C., Benjamin B., Albert J. & Cyrus M., gct Wilmington MM, O.

HADLEY, continued
1874, 2, 21. Martha E. gct Wilmington MM, O.
1875, 6, 19. Farinda recrq
1876, 3, 18. Chester G. & w, Eunice M., & ch, James F. & Martha T., gct Deer Creek MM, Ind.
1877, 1, 20. Deborah relrq
1878, 2, 16. Harriet rocf Dover MM, O., dtd 1878,1,17
1879, 3, 15. Laura relrq
1879, 3, 15. Thomas & w, Amanda, & ch, Anna W., Hattie I., Morris W. & Bertha M., gct Rocksylvania MM, Ia.
1879, 3, 15. Susanna rocf Newberry MM, O., dtd 1879,2,17
1880, 4, 17. Lucinda rocf Wilmington MM, O., dtd 1880,3,19
1880, 9, 18. W. C. & dt relrq
1883, 4, 21. Mahlon C. & w, Emily C., & ch, Arthur E. & Clara M., gct Cesars Creek MM, O.
1884, 4, 19. George C. gct Rochester MM, N.Y.
1884, 5, 17. Ruth S. gct Wilmington MM, O.
1884, 5, 17. Alice gct Wilmington MM, O.
1884, 5, 17. Eva J. gct Wilmington MM, O.
1884, 5, 17. Ann gct Wilmington MM, O.
1884, 7, 19. Mahlon C. & w, Emily C., & ch, Arthur E. & Clara M., rocf Cesars Creek MM, O., dtd 1884,5,22
1884, 10, 18. Seth gct Toledo MM, Kans.
1884, 10, 18. Mary A. & J. Carlton, minors, gct Toledo MM, O.
1885, 2, 21. Joshua & w, Ruth E., gct Center MM, O.
1887, 5, 21. Isaac P. relrq
1888, 2, 18. Atwood relrq
1888, 3, 17. Edwin relrq
1888, 4, 21. Mahlon C. & fam relrq
1889, 8, 17. Archibald relrq
1890, 1, 18. Evan H. & w, Susan, & s, Zenas G., gct Wilmington MM, O.
1890, 1, 18. Cora L. gct Wilmington MM, O.
1890, 3, 15. Orlando & w, Hattie E., & ch, Florence E. & Ruthanna, gct Wilmington MM, O.
1890, 7, 19. Atwell recrq
1890, 8, 16. Horace H. relrq
1891, 4, 18. Woodrow W. gct Blue Jacket MM
1891, 7, 18. Nora Outland (form Hadley) gct Goshen MM, O.
1891, 11, 21. Edwin & s, Arthur, recrq
1892, 7, 16. Ida & Anna relrq
1892, 11, 19. Clifford V. relrq
1894, 2, 17. Mary T. rocf Newberry MM, O.
1894, 2, 17. Sarah A. rocf Newberry MM, O.
----, --, --. Louetta gct Wilmington MM, O.
1895, 9, 21. Sarah Ellen & dt, Luella, gct Wilmington MM, O.
1896, 3, 21. Orlando & w & ch, Florence E. & Ruth Annie, rocf Wilmington MM, O., dtd 1896,3,14
1898, 8, 13. Ellen C. & Adilla, gct Wilmington MM, O.
1898, 10, 15. Alonzo gct Goshen MM, O.
1898, 10, 15. Elizabeth(Hadley)Watkins gct Goshen MM, O.
1899, 2, 18. Mary F. gct Wilmington MM, O.
1900, 5, 19. Abigail J. gct Newberry MM, O.
1901, 1, 19. Park, Flora & Marie recrq
1902, 4, 19. Miles & w, Sarah C., gct Wilmington MM, O.
1906, 3, 17. Edwin & fam relrq
1906, 9, 15. Wm. P. & fam relrq
1906, 11, 19. Carrie recrq
1907, 7, 20. Atwill & w, Sarah, & ch, Hershel T., Ethel K., Reba M., Edith W., Vivian M. & Hubert H., gct Newberry MM, O.
1907, 11, 16. Alanta gct Wilmington MM, O.
1909, 11, 20. Anna Ethel C. rocf Ogden MM, O.
1910, 6, 18. Orlando & fam gct Wilmington MM, O.
1914, 9, 12. Parker & Flora relrq
1916, 4, 15. Edgar L. relrq
1917, 9, 15. Cora C. rocf Grassy Run MM, O.
1917, 10, 20. Adelaide G. recrq
1921, 12, 17. Adalaide G. gct Huntington Park MM, Calif.
1923, 1, 20. Mary Howard recrq
1923, 2, 17. Dorothy Jean recrq
1926, 3, 26. Zene G. rocf Ogden MM, O.
1926, 6, 20. Joseph & w dropped from mbrp
1926, 6, 20. Nathan dropped from mbrp
1926, 12, 27. Edwin rocf Detroit MM, Mich.
1929, 12, 22. Minnie Johns recrq
1934, 3, 25. Wm. & fam relrq

HAINES
----, --, --. Caleb b 1776,12,21 d 1830,12,12 bur Springfield; m Sarah TOWEL b 1777,10, 18 d 1825,6,27

Ch:			
Jesse	b 1801, 11, 26	
Joshua	" 1803, 11, 24	d 1831, 1,15
Hannah	" 1806, 6, 26	
Eli	" 1808, 12, 12	d 1809, 1, 7
Isaac	" 1809, 11, 27	
Rebecca	" 1813, 9, 15	
Elizabeth	" 1816, 11, 4	

----, --, --. Stacy & Judith

Ch:		
David	b 1818, 10, 1	
Noah	" 1820, 3, 16	d 1823,--,--
Mary	" 1822, 2, 12	" 1824,--,--
Amos	" 1823, 4, 20	
Sarah E.	" 1825, 10, 12	
Samuel T.	" 1827, 12, 31	
John	" 1829, 7, 28	d 1829, --,--
Stacy A.	" 1831, 9, 10	
Martha	" 1834, 7, 28	
Judith A.	" 1836, 12, 31	
Edwin	" 1839, 2, 19	
Calvin	" 1841, 9, 5	

1824, 12, 25. Martha [Haynes] (form Harlan) con mou
1832, 8, 14. Martha gct Miami MM, O.
1838, 4, 17. Stacy & w, Judith, & ch, David, Amos, Sarah, Elizabeth, Samuel, Stacy

HAINES, continued
Allen, Martha N. & Judith Ann, rocf Cesars Creek MM, O., dtd 1838,1,25
1841, 8, 17. David con mou
1843, 5, 16. David gct Caesars Creek MM, O.
1843, 11, 14. Sarah Elizabeth rmt Elias F. Curl
1847, 1, 16. Amos rmt Elizabeth Ann Hunt
1853, 12, 17. Judith rmt Geo. Brackney
1855, 4, 21. Samuel dis mou
1855, 5, 19. Amos & w, Elizabeth, & ch, Lydia Ann & Stacy Edwin, gct Back Creek MM, Ind.
1856, 1, 19. Martha Moore (form Haines) con mou
1861, 4, 20. Edwin A. con mou
1861, 5, 18. Sophronia rocf Newberry MM, O., dtd 1861,4,22
1868, 11, 21. Calvin con mou
1872, 5, 18. Edwin A. & w, Sophronia, & ch, Carrie E., Elmer E. & Flora M., gct Spring River MM, Kans.
1876, 4, 15. Calvin & ch, Albert W. & Harvey, gct White River MM, Ind.

HALE
----, --, --. Jacob b 1802,7,12; m Hannah ANDREW b 1812,1,7
Ch: ----- b 1835, 11, 10
----- " 1838, 10, 10
----- " 1843, 12, 23
----, --, --. Alfred b 1841,12,23; m Rachel HADLEY b 1842,7,26
Ch: Mary Alice b 1865, 12, 5
Clark J. " 1868, 10, 17
Emma " 1873, 3, 30

1821, 12, 29. Martha rmt Hiram Mendenhall
1824, 2, 28. Eli rmt Ann Hadley
1828, 4, 26. Joseph dis
1828, 9, 16. Jacob dis jH
1829, 2, 17. Martha dis jH
1830, 3, 16. Jacob rmt Hannah Andrew
1830, 6, 15. Armonia dis jH
1830, 9, 14. Polly dis jH
1832k 11, 13. Elizabeth rocf Miami MM, O., dtd 1832,10,24
1850, 12, 21. Ann rmt Micajah Johnson
1851, 3, 15. Mary, Sarah Ann & Alfred C., ch Ann Johnson, gct Miami MM, O.
1851, 7, 19. Louisa rmt Edwin Carpenter
1854, 7, 15. William T. gct Miami MM, O.
1856, 5, 19. Miles M. gct Miami MM, O.
1858, 5, 15. William dis mou
1866, 6, 16. Rachel Ann rocf Center MM, O., dtd 1866,5,16
1866, 7, 21. Alfred con mou
1868, 2, 15. Susanna Gallops (form Hale) con mou
1883, 12, 15. Sarah C. rocf Wilmington MM, O., dtd 1883,12,14
1884, 1, 19. Elwood & ch, Minnie Bell, Albert V. & Naomi R. recrq
1892, 3, 19. Flora & Esther recrq
1893, 10, 4. Flora rmt H. A. Coate
1895, 1, 19. Alice recrq
1898, 8, 13. Esther gct Wilmington MM, O.
1906, 11, 17. Sarah Tomlinson rocf Wilmington MM, O.
1910, 2, 16. Inez recrq
1920, 4, 17. Inez relrq

HALL
1895, 3, 16. Thomas & Edith recrq
1896, 7, 18. Thomas dis
1897, 1, 16. Clark J. & w, Alice, & ch, R. Edith & Herman R., gct Wilmington MM, O.
1913, 2, 15. Jesse Ione recrq
1920, 6, 19. Etta Cleland recrq
1921, 6, 18. Jesse Stone dropped from mbrp
1922, 4, 15. Etta relrq

HALSTEAD
1911, 9, 16. DeElla Harvey relrq

HAM
1879, 2, 15. Finley F. & w, Martha Jane, & s, Fred, recrq
1897, 3, 20. F. F. & w, Martha, & dt, Lucy Elizabeth, gct Wilmington MM, O.

HAMMER
1925, 6, 21. Eugene, Victor & Robert Thomas, ch Clara, recrq

HAMPTON
1819, 6, 26. Julia & ch, Emily, Oliver & Henry Dennis, rocf Short Creek MM, O., dtd 1819,1,19, end by Cincinnati MM
1819, 7, 31. Rebecca con mou
1824, 6, 26. Julia dis disunity
1825, 9, 24. Rebecca gct Milford MM, Ind.
1828, 9, 24. Rebecca gct Chester MM, Ind.
1834, 7, 15. Henry Dennis gct Buckingham MM, Pa.
1836, 9, 13. Emily gct Springborough MM
1836, 9, 13. Oliver & Eliza C., ch Chas. & Julia, gct Springborough MM
1837, 10, 17. Emily dis disunity
1874, 5, 16. Robert W. recrq
1889, 4, 20. Milton recrq
1896, 3, 21. John W. recrq

HANEY
----, --, --. Charles, s Abram & Elizabeth, b 1863,7,23; m Eva D. CARTER, dt John & Mary Ann, b 1866,12,25
Ch: Elizabeth b 1906,12, 4

1866, 5, 19. Abraham M. & ch, Ella Mary, Joseph W. & John C., recrq
1858, 10, 17. Elizabeth (form Coate) con mou
1871, 3, 18. Abram M. & w, Elizabeth B., & ch gct Wilmington MM, O.
1875, 7, 17. Elizabeth B. & ch, Ella, Joseph J., Charles & Lila, rocf Wilmington

HANEY, continued
MM, O., dtd 1875,6,18
1925, 11, 22. Charles & w, Eva, & dt, Elizabeth, rocf Wilmington MM, O.

HARLAN
1788, 9, 14. Hannah b d 1863,2,-- bur Springfield
----, --, --. Enoch d 1866,7,26 bur Springfield; m Elizabeth -----
Ch: Lydia b 1815, 10, 23
Mahlon " 1817, 10, 31
Carter " 1819, 9, 13
Mary Ann " 1821, 3, 15 d 1839, 9,27 bur Springfield
John b 1823, 2, 14 " 1906,12,25 bur Springfield
Nathaniel b 1825, 4, 20
Isaac " 1827, 3, 1
Samuel " 1829, 10, 16
Aaron " 1832, 3, 23 d 1839, 8,20 bur Springfield
Wilson b 1834, 5, 10 " 1916, 2,12
Sarah Caroline " 1836, 3, 20
----, --, --. John C. & Lydia (Hale)
Ch: Jacob b 1824, 1, 1 d 1911, 4,--
James " 1829, 9, 30 " 1913, 3, 1
----, --, --. Wm. H., s Nathaniel & Lydia, b 1838,12,31 d 1918,5,6; m Anna HALE, dt Armonia & Elizabeth (Edwards) b 1847,4,9
1866, 5, 1. Mary, dt Samuel, b
1866, 4, 1. May, dt Samuel & Hannah, b

1822, 9, 28. Enoch Jr. rmt Lucy Buck
1823, 5, 31. Jane recrq
1823, 6, 28. Rebecca Ann, John Milton, David F. & Wm. Foster, ch Solomon & Jane, recrq
1824, 11, 27. Ann Varner (form Harlan) con mou
1824, 12, 25. Martha Haynes (form Harlan) con mou
1827, 7, 28. William dis disunity
1827, 12, 29. Ruth Griffith (form Harlan) dis mou
1828, 2, 23. Nathan Jr. dis disunity
1828, 6, 24. Lydia Sabin (form Harlan) dis mou
1828, 12, 16. David dis mou
1829, 9, 15. John dis jH
1829, 11, 17. Enoch dis jH
1830, 3, 16. Charity & Nathan dis jH
1830, 4, 13. Enoch, s Nathan, dis jH
1830, 5, 11. Solomon dis jH
1830, 9, 14. Edith, dt Wm., dis jH
1830, 9, 14. Lucy dis jH
1830, 10, 12. Edith, dt Nathan, dis jH
1830, 11, 16. Prudence dis jH
1832, 6, 12. Jane dis disunity
1833, 4, 16. William dis mou
1835, 9, 15. Nathaniel dis jH
1836, 1, 12. Jabez con mou
1836, 6, 14. Edith rst at Centre MM, O. on consent of this mtg
1836, 7, 12. Sarah rst
1838, 11, 13. Rebecca Ann dis disunity
1839, 5, 14. Sarah gct Miami MM, O.
1839, 8, 13. Hannah dis disunity
1839, 9, 17. John M. dis disunity
1840, 2, 11. Jabez gct Centre MM, O.
1840, 7, 14. David Ferris, Wm. Foster, Rachel Fallis, Jonathan & Solomon, ch Solomon, gct Dover MM
1840, 7, 14. John, s Nathan, gct Miami MM, O.
1842, 8, 16. Margaret Ann Oiler (form Harlan) dis mou
1842, 10, 11. Hannahmariah Elizabeth dis disunity
1842, 12, 13. Rebecca dis disunity
1844, 12, 17. Mahlon con mou
1845, 6, 17. Jacob dis mou
1846, 3, 17. Mahlon dis
1846, 11, 21. John dis mou
1849, 7, 21. Maria rocf Bloomfield MM, Ind., dtd 1849,3,7
1852, 1, 17. Nathaniel dis mou
1853, 12, 17. Enoch & Lucy B. rst
1854, 2, 18. Martin R. [Harlin] con mou
1854, 9, 16. Barclay W. & w, Susannah M., ch Enoch & Lucy, recrq
1859, 10, 15. Carter B. & w, Maria, & dt, Mary Elizabeth, gct Miami MM, O.
1859, 12, 17. Wilson con mou
1867, 9, 21. David K. recrq
1868, 12, 19. Samuel con mou
1872, 3, 16. John Jr. & w, Elizabeth, & ch, Emma & Oliver, recrq
1881, 3, 19. Nathaniel F. & w, Sarah A., & s, Warren, recrq
1881, 11, 19. Nathaniel & w, Sarah, & s, Warren, gct Wilmington MM, O.
1882, 6, 17. Carter & w, Mariah, rocf Miami MM, O., dtd 1882,4,26
1883, 3, 17. Jacob & w, Sarah, recrq
1892, 5, 21. Wm. H. recrq

HAROLD
1874, 5, 16. Rowland Green gct Richland MM, Ind., to m Elizabeth Harold

HARRELL
1874, 5, 16. Benjamin & w, Louisa, & ch, Ella E., Lura M. & Dolly M., recrq
1901, 4, 20. Benj. & w, Louisa, transferred to Ogden MM, O.

HARRIER
----, --, --. Albert & Laura (G)
Ch: Helen Jane b -----, 10, 14
Florence Elizabeth " 1897, 2, 26

1930, 1, 2. Florence [Herrier] recrq (G)
1931, 4, 2. Helen Jane recrq (G)
1931, 4, 2. Mrs. Eleanor (Felger) [Herrier] rocf Cleveland MM, O. (G)

HARRIS
1881, 4, 16. Isaac recrq
1896, 3, 21. Alfred & w recrq
1908, 1, 18. Ruth Ellen recrq
1911, 6, 17. Henry R. & w, Alma E., recrq
1920, 12, 18. Ruth Ellen gct Miami MM, O.
1924, 3, 16. Henry & fam relrq

HARTMAN
1834, 6, 17. Maris con mou
1838, 7, 17. Maris gct Dover MM
1874, 2, 21. James recrq
1874, 3, 21. Anna recrq
1874, 5, 16. Susan & ch, Nora May & James William, recrq
1877, 3, 17. Jane W. recrq

HARTSOCK
1922, 3, 18. Allen Z. & ch, Kenneth J. & Sarah Katharine, recrq
1925, 11, 22. Viola recrq
1925, 11, 22. Anna Louise recrq
1925, 11, 22. Joseph Walter recrq

HARVEY
----, --, --. Elizabeth, dt Nathaniel & Ann Carter b 1737,6,16 d 1832,2,18
----, --, --. Eli b 1762,1,13 d 1822,4,14; m Mary STANFIELD b 1764,4,21 d 1823,4,15
Ch: William b 1791, 6, 15
Ann " 1801, 3, 7
Mary " 1805, 3, 11
Son " 1806, 3, 14 d 1806, 3,23
Cynthia " 1808, 3, 18
----, --, --. William b 1769,4,10 d 1858,12,5 bur Springfield; m Mary VESTAL b 1768,4,7 d 1863,11,13 bur Springfield
Ch: John (or Jehu) b 1800, 7, 16
Eli " 1803, 3, 9
David " 1805, 4, 3
Sarah " 1807, 11, 23
Elizabeth " 1811, 2, 11
1816, 2, 14. Nancy, dt Joshua & Mary, b (raised in fam of Caleb Haines)
----, --, --. Henry b 1797,4,6; m Ann MADEN, b 1797,11,14
Ch: George Maden b 1818, 8, 21
Caleb Elwood " 1821, 3, 10
Mary " 1823, 9, 21
Elizabeth " 1825, 9, 15 d 1826, 7, 5
Deborah " 1825, 9, 15
Nathan " 1828, 3, 31 " 1828, 4, 3
Rebecca " 1828, 3, 31 " 1828, 4,26
Samuel B. " 1830, 7, 22
Henry C. " 1833, 12, 19
Ann B. " 1836, 8, 31
----, --, --. William b 1791,6,15; m Ruth HADLEY b 1798,8,25
Ch: David b 1819, 9, 7 (?)
Eli " 1819, 6, 2
Ch: Jonathan b 1821, 9, 20
Sarah " 1823, 8, 13
Mahlon " 1826, 2, 26
Rebecca " 1828, 4, 16
----, --, --. John b 1800,7,16; m Lydia BALLARD b 1800,11,9
Ch: James b 1822, 7, 1
Mary Ann " 1823, 10, 18
Elias " 1825, 6, 10
Martha " 1827, 10, 27
Eunice " 1829, 2, 22
----, --, --. Caleb b 1803,5,5; m Bathshebe NICHOLSON b 1802,2,24
Ch: Asenath b 1824, 8, 20
Amos " 1826, 6, 6
Silas " 1830, 2, 7
----, --, --. Eli b 1803,3,9 d 1872,4,15 bur Springfield; m Sarah FALLIS b 1804,2,16 d 1835,7,12 bur Springfield
Ch: Mary Jane b 1825, 1, 17
Lydia " 1826, 12, 16 d 1852, 3, 4 bur Center
William Penn " 1828, 11, 16 " 1917, 9, 7 bur Springfield
Esther b 1830, 10, 13 " 1859,10,18
Ann " 1833, 2, 8 " 1867, 8, 7
Sarah " 1835, 4, 10 " 1855, 4,24 bur Springfield
Eli m 2nd Ruth FISHER b 1811,6,29
Ch: Joseph F. b 1837, 7, 14 d 1837, 8,12 bur Springfield
Isaac b 1838, 7, 30 " 1846, 4,13 bur Springfield
Hannah b 1840, 2, 4 " 1865, 9, 1 bur Springfield
John b 1842, 10, 8
James W. " 1846, 2, 11
Sina Ann " 1852, 10, 28
1825, 6, 27. Sarah d (an elder)
----, --, --. Isaac b 1809,11,27 d 1883,8,11 bur Springfield; m Sarah EDWARDS b 1812, 11,7
Ch: Caleb b 1832, 11, 7
Elizabeth " 1835, 3, 6
Mary Jane " 1836, 8, 22
William " 1839, 7, 24
Rebecca " 1841, 5, 22
Nathaniel " 1843, 6, 30
Abigail C. " 1846, 6, 11 d 1864, 6,18 bur Springfield
Jesse H. b 1849, 4, 10
Enos F. " 1853, 2, 2 d 1871,10,10 bur Springfield
----, --, --. Levi & Anna
Ch: Susannah b 1835, 7, 31
Mary " 1837, 1, 31
Hannah F. " 1838, 11, 17
----, --, --. William Penn & Nancy
Ch: Willis M. b 1858, 8, 21
Eli " 1860, 9, 23
Joshua " 1862, 9, 18
John H. " 1863, 12, 14 d 1866, 2, 7

HARVEY, William Penn & Nancy, continued
Ch: Seth
1917, 9, 7. Wm. P., s Eli & Sarah, d bur Springfield
----, --, --. Nathaniel, s Isaac & Sarah (Edwards), b 1843,6,30; m Irena MOON, dt Moses & Elizabeth, d 1919,12,3
1863, 11, 13. Mary d ae 96 (an elder)
----, --, --. Nathaniel & Irena
Ch: Jenetta b 1870, 10, 16
De Ella " 1873, 8, 10
1872, 4, 15. Eli d ae 70 (an elder)
----, --, --. Jesse & Caroline
Ch: Lizzie
Viola b 1873, 8, 29
Elsie R. " 1875, 11, 22
----, --, --. Jesse H., s Isaac & Sarah (Edwards) b 1849,4,10 d 1933,5,23; m Lucy H. HADLEY, dt Simon & Rachel (Bangham), b 1851,6,23
Ch: Elsie R. b 1875, 11, 23
Rachel Myra" 1877, 2, 7
1884, 3, 24. Martha, dt Willis & Kate (Cowgill), b
----, --, --. Willis m Jennie PETERS, dt James & Amanda (Smith), b 1860,12,18
Ch: Inda b 1891, 3, 26
Ernest " 1893, 3, 16

1819, 3, 27. William rmt Mary Crews
1819, 9, 25. Henry & w, Ann, & s, George Maden, rocf West Grove MM, Ind., dtd 1819, 6,12
1819, 11, 21. Joshua rmt Alice Chew
1820, 1, 29. Hannah [Harvy] rmt Achilles D. Dicks
1821, 7, 28. William Jr. & fam gct Miami MM, O.
1821, 10, 27. John rmt Lydia Ballard
1822, 7, 27. Harlan rmt Ruth Chew
1823, 9, 27. Caleb Jr. gct Ceasars Creek MM, O., to m Bathsheba Nicholson
1824, 1, 21. William & fam rocf Miami MM, O., dtd 1823,9,24
1824, 3, 27. Eli rmt Sarah Fallis
1824, 3, 27. Bathsheba rocf Cesars Creek MM, O., dtd 1824,2,26
1824, 7, 31. Jesse gct Fairfield MM, O., to m Elizabeth Burgess
1824, 2, 28. Ann rmt William Harvey
1825, 1, 29. Elizabeth rocf Fairfield MM, O., dtd 1825,12,25 (1824?)
1825, 2, 26. Henry & w, Ann, & ch, Geo. M., Caleb & Mary, gct White Water MM, Ind.
1825, 5, 28. David con mou
1825, 11, 26. Isaac & w, Agatha, gct Mill Creek MM, O.
1826, 5, 15. Sarah rmt Joshua Edwards
1826, 5, 15. Isaac & w, Agątha, rocf Mill Creek MM, dtd 1826,4,22
1826, 7, 29. Mary Dakin (form Harvey) con mou
1826, 10, 12. Henry & w, Ann, & ch, George, Caleb, Mary & Deborah, rocf White Water MM, Ind., dtd 1826,9,27
1827, 6, 27. Caleb gct Clear Creek MM, O., to m Ann Lewis
1827, 8, 25. Simon D. gct Fairfield MM, O., to m Mary Burgess
1827, 9, 29. Ann rocf Clear Creek MM, O., dtd 1827,9,8
1828, 3, 29. Martha & Deborah gct Miami MM,O.
1828, 3, 29. Isaac & w, Agatha, gct Miami MM, O.
1828, 3, 29. William & w, Mary, & ch, Joseph D., Jane, Isaac & Mariah, gct Miami MM, O.
1828, 4, 26. Simon D. gct Miami MM, O.
1828, 3, 29. Joseph Stratton gct West Grove MM, Ind., to m Rebecca Harvey
1828, 6, 24. Hannah rmt Jesse Lewis
1828, 12, 16. Mary, Sarah, Isaac & Davis, ch Rebecca Stratton, rocf West Grove MM, Ind., dtd 1828,6,14
1829, 1, 13. Harlan & w, Ruth, & ch, Lydia, Milton, Nancy & Ellwood, gct Miami MM, O.
1829, 3, 17. Elizabeth rmt Jesse Burgess
1829, 11, 17. Mary (form Maden) con mou
1830, 5, 11. Jesse & w, Elizabeth, & ch, Wm. Forster, Sarah T. & Thomas B., gct Miami MM, O.
1830, 6, 15. David gct Miami MM, O.
1830, 7, 13. Mary gct Bloomfield MM, Ind.
1830, 8, 17. Wm. Jr. & w, Ruth, & ch, David Eli Jonathan Sarah, Mahlon, Rebecca & William, gct White Lick MM, Ind.
1831, 8, 16. William & w, Mary, gct Miami MM, O.
1831, 10, 11. Isaac gct Miami MM, O., to m Sarah Edwards
1831, 10, 11. Mary gct White Lick MM, Ind.
1831, 10, 11. Cynthia gct White Lick MM, Ind.
1831, 12, 13. Sarah, Isaac & Davis, minor ch Rebecca Stratton, gct Miami MM, O.
1831, 12, 13. Mary, dt Samuel, gct Miami MM,O.
1832, 1, 17. Rebecca gct Miami MM, O.
1832, 3, 13. John & w, Lydia, & ch, James, Mary Ann, Elias, Martha, Eunice & John Meader, gct Miami MM, O.
1832, 3, 13. Sarah rocf Miami MM, O., dtd 1832,2,29
1832, 5, 15. Simon Jr. con mou
1834, 2, 11. Robert gct White Lick MM, Ind.
1834, 11, 11. Abraham & w, Jane, & s, Wm., rocf Miami MM, O., dtd 1834,9,24
1834, 10, 14. Levi rmt Anna Curl
1834, 10, 14. John rmt Mahala Plummer
1834, 12, 16. Mahala gct Miami MM, O.
1835, 1, 13. Ann rmt Chas. Mills
1835, 10, 13. Nancy rmt Isaac Edwards
1836, 8, 16. Eli gct Miami MM, O., to m Ruth Fisher
1836, 11, 15. Caleb & w, Bathsheba, & ch, Asenith, Amos P., Silas, Mary & George, gct Miami MM, O.
1837, 4, 11. Ruth rocf Miami MM, O., dtd 1837,2,22

HARVEY, continued
1837, 6, 13. Elizabeth rmt John T. Burgess
1838, 4, 17. Jehu gct Bloomfield MM, Ind.
1838, 8, 14. Joshua & w, Alice, & ch, Abigail & Samuel, gct Bloomfield MM, Ind.
1840, 4, 14. Levi & w, Anna, & ch, Susannah, Mary M. & Hannah, gct Bloomfield MM, Ind.
1840, 4, 14. Levi & w, Anna, & ch, Susanna, Mary M. & Hannah F., gct Bloomfield MM, Ind.
1841, 1, 12. George M. dis mou
1843, 7, 11. Caleb E. con mou
1844, 1, 16. Mary Jane rmt Samuel L. Hadley
1845, 8, 12. Caleb E. gct Mississinewa MM, Ind.
1847, 9, 18. Lydia rmt Cyrus Linton
1848, 5, 20. Deborah L. rmt Isaac Schooley
1849, 5, 19. Hiram Maden Jr. gct Bloomfield MM, Ind., to m Hannah C. Harvey
1850, 3, 16. Esther rmt Jeremiah J. Kimbrough
1851, 1, 18. William T. gct White Water MM, Ind., to m Ann Clawson
1851, 11, 15. Ann C. rocf White Water MM, Ind., dtd 1851,9,24
1855, 4, 21. William P. rmt Nancy Moore
1855, 8, 18. Caleb J. gct Center MM, O., to m Rebecca Jefferis
1856, 5, 17. Rebecca J. rocf Center MM, O., dtd 1856,3,12
1858, 12, 18. Elizabeth rmt Wm. Thorn
1860, 9, 15. Ann rmt Ephraim Doan
1862, 4, 19. Henry gct West Union MM, Ind., to m Sarah Ballard
1862, 7, 19. Henry gct White Lick MM, Ind.
1862, 10, 18. Caleb J. & w, Rebecca J., & s, Charles, gct Center MM, O.
1864, 10, 15. William gct Richland MM, O., to m Sarah Elma Hockett
1865, 10, 21. Sarah E. Hockett (now Harvey) rocf Center MM, N. C., dtd 1864,6,18, end by Richland MM, Ind., 1865,6,18
1866, 5, 19. Mary J. rmt Samuel Gause
1867, 8, 17. William & w, Sarah Ellen, & ch, Lina C. & Luther T., gct Cottonwood MM, Kans.
1868, 12, 19. John con mou
1869, 2, 20. John gct Wilmington MM, O.
1869, 5, 15. Nathaniel con mou
1869, 6, 19. Irena rocf Newberry MM, O., dtd 1869,4,19
1870, 12, 17. Jesse H. rmt Lucy C. Hadley
1871, 2, 18. Sarah & Nancy recrq
1871, 8, 19. James W. & w, Alice W., con mou
1873, 10, 18. Ruth gct Spiceland MM, Ind.
1873, 11, 15. Lina gct Spiceland MM, Ind.
1873, 12, 20. James & w, Alice S., gct Spiceland MM, Ind.
1874, 1, 17. Isaac recrq
1874, 2, 21. Ann & Martha recrq
1875, 3, 20. Nathaniel & w, Irena, & ch, Jennette & DeElla, gct Newberry MM, O.
1881, 5, 21. Anna M. recrq
1882, 3, 18. Fred H. recrq
1882, 5, 22. George S. recrq
1882, 12, 16. Bernard recrq
1883, 4, 21. Aaron & fam rocf Wilmington MM, O., dtd 1883,4,20
1883, 11, 17. Aaron & w, Maria E., & ch, S. Bernard, Charlie E., Nellie E. & George W., gct Minneapolis MM, Minn.
1884, 11, 15. Fred H. gct Minneapolis MM, Minn.
1885, 4, 18. Jennie recrq
1885, 6, 20. Ella M. Barrett (form Harvey) gct Cesars Creek MM, O.
1887, 11, 19. Eli gct Cincinnati MM, O.
1896, 4, 18. Nathaniel & fam rocf West Fork MM, O., dtd 1896,3,20
1897, 2, 20. Joshua relrq
1897, 7, 17. James dis
1900, 5, 19. Seth relrq
1901, 1, 19. Jessie H. recrq
1901, 6, 15. Wm. P. dropped from mbrp
1915, 1, 16. Wm. P. recrq
1916, 3, 18. Jennie & dt, Inda, & s, Ernest, relrq
1920, 5, 15. Nathaniel relrq

HAWKINS
----, --, --. Abraham b 1808,5,20; m Jane HADLEY b 1811,3,3
Ch: Son b 1831, 3, 21 d 1831, 3,21
William " 1833, 4, 16
Ruth " 1836, 6, 17
Isaac " 1838, 8, 10
Sarah H. " 1840, 7, 14
Mary Ann " 1843, 1, 18
Eli " 1846, 2, 16
Walter C. " 1848, 1, 13
Annette " 1850, 12, 30
----, --, --. Isaac & Ruth
Ch: Mary Elizabeth b 1840, 10, 4
Sarah Emlin" 1843, 7, 17
----, --, --. William m Mary Ellen HUTCHISON b 1840,10,8
Ch: John H. b 1866, 8, 30

1830, 11, 16. Abraham rmt Jane Hadley
1831, 3, 15. Jane gct Miami MM, O.
1839, 6, 11. Israel rmt Ruth Pyle
1840, 8, 11. Isaac rocf Miami MM, O., dtd 1840,6,24
1843, 5, 16. Seth rocf Miami MM, O., dtd 1842,11,23
1845, 2, 11. Edith gct Ceasars Creek MM, O.
1856, 5, 19. Isaac & w, Ruth, & ch, Mary Elizabeth, Sarah Emlin, Seth, Louiza Jane, Caroline Margaret & William P., gct East Grove MM, Iowa
1856, 6, 21. Ruth rmt Benjamin Farquhar
1858, 6, 19. William H. con mou
1861, 4, 20. Sarah N. rmt John Howard Johnson
1862, 10, 18. Mary Ellen, w Wm. H., & s, John

HAWKINS, continued
H. recrq (w Wm. H.)
1863, 10, 17. Abraham & w, Jane, & ch, Eli N., Walter C. & Annetta, gct Spring Creek MM, Ia.
1864, 5, 21. Isaac C. gct Miami MM, O., to m Susan Mather
1872, 8, 17. Wm. H. & w, Mary Ellen, & s, John, gct Spring Creek MM, Ia.

HAWTHORN
1891, 2, 21. George W. & w, Samantha, & ch, Ethel & Catherine E., recrq
1891, 2, 21. Geo. & w, Samantha, & ch, Ethel & Catherine E., recrq
1901, 4, 20. Catharine E. & Ethel transferred to Ogden MM, O.

HAYS
1876, 5, 20. Joel recrq
1876, 5, 20. Alice recrq
1876, 11, 18. Mary Ann recrq
1886, 1, 16. Joel & w, Mary Ann, gct Newberry MM, O.
1894, 1, 20. John & w, Anna, & ch, Bell, Warren & Laura, recrq
1900, 1, 20. John & w, Annie, & ch, Marie Pearl, & infant s, gct Miami MM, O.

HAZARD
----, --, --. Allen d 1864,3,24 bur Springfield; m Ann K. HADLEY b 1830,2,3
Ch: Henrietta b 1852, 4, 23
Julia Rebecca " 1854, 6, 6
Lydia Jane " 1857, 1, 19 d 1878, 2,20 bur Springfield
Harriet H. b 1859, 7, 27

1851, 9, 20. Ann (form Hadley) con mou
1862, 3, 15. Allen & ch, Julia R., Lydia J. & Harriett H., recrq
1874, 1, 17. Sarah L. [Hazzard] recrq

HEMILRIGHT
1842, 7, 12. Elizabeth rocf Centre MM, O., dtd 1842,6,15

HENLEY
1850, 5, 18. Samuel rmt Eliza A. Hadley
1850, 12, 21. Eliza Ann gct White Water MM, Ind.

HENRY
1874, 5, 16. James M. & w, Hannah, & ch, Rettie, Cynthia, Lula & Ida recrq
1893, 1, 21. Ina recrq
1901, 4, 20. James & w, Hannah, & ch, Retta, Cynthia, Lulu & Stella, transferred to Ogden MM, O.
1901, 4, 20. Charles & Zenas dropped from mbrp

HIATT
1819, 6, 26. Allen con mou
1820, 4, 20. Gulielma rmt Absalom Dillon
1820, 11, 25. Rhoda rocf New Garden MM, N. C., dtd 1820,6,21
1821, 6, 30. Jesse & ch, Joseph, Lewis, Elizabeth & Mary, rocf Center MM, dtd 1821,5,17
1822, 7, 27. Elizabeth Kimber (form Hiatt) con mou
1824, 5, 29. Cert rec for Mary & ch, Margaret & Samuel, from West Grove MM, Ind., dtd 1824,4,16, end to Center MM, O.
1824, 8, 28. Isom dis mou
1825, 2, 26. Allen & w, Rhoda, & ch, Susannah, Gulielma & Milton, gct Milford MM, Ind.
1825, 7, 30. Joel & w, Mary, & ch, Joel & Joshua, gct Milford MM, Ind.
1826, 5, 15. Jesse & ch, Lewis & Mary, gct Centre MM
1828, 4, 26. Lewis rmt Charity Kimbrough
1837, 7, 11. Lewis rocf Centre MM, O., dtd 1837,3,15
1837, 8, 15. Lewis & w, Charity, & ch, John K.W., Martha Ann, Jesse Thomas & Joseph, gct White River MM, Ind.
1854, 10, 21. Martha H. (form Hadley) con mou
1855, 5, 19. Martha H. gct Newberry MM, O.
1857, 2, 21. Mary rocf Newberry MM, O., dtd 1856,12,22
1858, 10, 17. Hannah (form Andrew) con mou
1859, 6, 18. Hannah gct Cherry Grove MM, Ind.
1859, 6, 18. Mary gct Cherry Grove MM, Ind.
1863, 6, 20. Hannah rocf Cherry Grove MM, Ind., dtd 1863,5,9
1868, 12, 19. Hannah & ch, Ida Bell, Alonzo & Sarah J., recrq
1876, 7, 15. Hannah & ch, Ida Bell, Alonzo A. & Sarah Jane, gct Smyrna MM, Ia.
1914, 2, 21. R. Ida [Hyatt] relrq

HILL
1881, 12, 17. Caroline recrq
1881, 9, 17. Ella & Nancy recrq
1883, 11, 17. James A. recrq
1909, 10, 16. Helen Irene recrq

HOBBS
1845, 10, 14. Wilson rocf White Water MM, Ind., dtd 1845,7,23, end by Miami MM, O., 1845,8,27
1846, 9, 19. Wilson gct West Grove MM, Ind., to m Zalinda Williams
1849, 1, 20. Zalinda & s, Orville A. W., rocf West Grove MM, Ind., dtd 1848,7,8
1853, 11, 19. Wilson & w, Zelinda, & ch, Orville A. W., Mary Zelinda & Walton, gct Bloomfield MM, Ind.

HOBSON
1820, 10, 28. Aaron gct West Grove MM, Ind.
1821, 1, 27. Jane & ch, Evan, Elizabeth, Mary

HOBSON, continued
John, David & Allen, gct West Grove MM, Ind.
1821, 1, 27. Achsah Adams (form Hobson) con mou

HOCKETT
----, --, --. ----- m Mary A. GREEN b 1834,1, 22
Ch: Clarinda b 1853, 5, 26
Alpheus " 1856, 5, 27
Nancy Jane " 1861, 3, 31

1826, 7, 27. Mahlon rmt Anna Andrew
1826, 10, 28. Anna gct Newberry MM, O.
1851, 10, 18. John rmt Mary Ann Green
1853, 6, 18. John rocf Newberry MM, O., dtd 1853,4,18
1855, 5, 19. John & w, Mary Ann, & dt, Clarinda, gct Newberry MM, O.
1861, 7, 17. Mary Ann & ch, Clarinda, John, Alpheus & Nancy Jane, rocf Newberry MM, O., dtd 1861,6,17
1864, 10, 15. Wm. Harvey gct Richland MM, O., to m Sarah Elma Hockett
1868, 5, 16. Mary Ann & ch, John Alpheus, Nancy Jane & Clorinda, gct Newberry MM,O.
1869, 10, 16. Mary Ann & ch, Clarinda, John Alpheus & Nancy Jane, rocf Newberry MM,O.
1870, 11, 19. Clarinda Doan (form Hockett) con mou
1871, 9, 16. Jesse J. & w, Sarah Ann, recrq
1873, 10, 18. Jesse J. & w, Sarah, gct Newberry MM, O.
1874, 3, 21. Isaac & w, Rhoda A., & ch, David A., Woodrow W. & Edward, recrq
1880, 5, 15. Cora, Eva & Retta recrq
1882, 4, 15. Mary Ann gct Watseka MM, Ill.
1882, 4, 15. Nancy Jane gct Watseka MM, Ill.
1888, 3, 17. Isaac & w relrq
1888, 5, 19. Rhoda A. & ch, Edward & Hensie, relrq
1893, 1, 21. J. A. & w, Mary E., & ch, Elden E. & Myrtle B., relrq
1910, 1, 15. Mary Etta & Gertrude recrq
1920, 4, 17. Marietta & Gertrude dropped from mbrp

HOIT
1854, 5, 20. Eliza Jane con mou
1860, 5, 19. Eliza Jane gct Salem MM, Ia.

HOLADAY
1834, 5, 13. Robert rmt Hannah Andrew
1836, 10, 13. William [Holliday] rmt Ann Carter
1837, 5, 16. Hannah [Holliday] rmt Job Simcock
1839, 11, 12. William [Holoday] & w, Ann, & ch, Enoch & Asa, gct Newberry MM, O.
1840, 1, 14. Robert & w, Hannah, & ch, Thomas, Jonathan, Betsy Jane & Louisa, gct Newberry MM, O.
1840, 3, 17. John & w, Susanna, & ch, Jesse F., Susanna & John, gct Newberry MM, O.
1840, 3, 17. Betsy gct Newberry MM, O.
1840, 3, 17. Mary Ann gct Newberry MM, O.
1840, 3, 17. John & w, Susanna, & ch, Jesse F., Susannah & John, gct Newberry MM, O.
1840, 3, 17. Betsy gct Newberry MM, O.
1840, 3, 17. Mary Ann gct Newberry MM, O.

HOLE
----, --, --. Eli b 1794,12,29; m Ann HADLEY b 1802,8,30
Ch: Malinda b 1825, 2, 27
William Hadley " 1826, 4, 12
Louisa " 1828, 6, 20
Martha Jane " 1830, 8, 4 d 1835,2,18
Miles Miller " 1833, 2, 1
Mary " 1835, 2, 20
Alfred Clark " 1839, 2, 18
Sarah Ann " 1839, 4, 27
Caroline " 1842, 6, 18

HOLLINGSWORTH
1886, 12, 18. Nathan & w, Eliza, & dt, Rhoda, rocf Westland MM, dtd 1886,11,27
1888, 3, 17. Nathan & w, Eliza, & dt, Rhoda, gct Newberry MM, O.

HOLMES
1926, 3, 26. Bertha recrq

HOOK
----, --, --. Harold, s Frank & Nellie L., b 1896,10,24; m Esther CAREY, dt Enoch & Jane M., b 1899,11,11
Ch: John Melville b 1926, 10, 30
Caroline Revelle " 1929, 6, 17
Dorothy Evonne " 1933, 12, --

1925, 10, 25. Harold recrq
1925, 11, 22. Esther Carey rocf Chester MM
1926, 4, 18. Frank & w, Nellie Revelle, & ch, Earl, Mary Elizabeth, Lucile & Frank Jr. recrq

HOOTEN
1895, 1, 19. Margaret (Hooten) Cort & dt, Cressie Mildred Hooten, rocf Wilmington MM, O.

HORNADAY
----, --, --. Ezekiel & Elizabeth
Ch: John b 1820, 2, 29 d 1887, 8, 4
Jehu " 1821, 9, 22 " 1837, 7,5
Isaiah " 1823, 7, 19
Jane " 1825, 3, 2 " 1826, 9, 6
Mary " 1826, 10, 16 " 1862, 9,22

HORNADAY, Ezekiel & Elizabeth, continued
Ch: William b 1828, 8, 24
Eleanor " 1830, 10, 10
Simon " 1833, 5, 11 d 1835,10, 1
Lydia " 1835, 12, 26
Eli " 1838, 6, 5 " 1839, 9,18
Isaac " 1840, 3, 24 " 1840, 3,25
----, --, --. John m Martha ----- d 1852,1,15 bur Springfield
Ch: Josiah Forster b 1846, 1, 10 d 1851, 6,21 bur Springfield
Ann Elizabeth b 1850, 7, 26

1843, 3, 14. John gct Miami MM, O., to m Martha Kersey
1843, 12, 12. Martha rocf Miami MM, O., dtd 1843,10,25
1852, 11, 20. Ezekiel gct Chester MM, Ind., to m Hannah Mendenhall
1853, 4, 16. Hannah & ch, Julia Ann, Delitha E., Elam K. & Wm. E. Mendenhall, rocf Chester MM, Ind., dtd 1853,2,24
1854, 2, 18. John & dt, Anna Elizabeth, gct Vermillion MM, Ill.
1854, 2, 18. William gct Vermillion MM, Ill.
1854, 2, 18. Mary gct Vermillion MM, Ill.
1855, 4, 21. Ellen & Lydia gct Vermillion MM, Ill.
1860, 3, 21. Louisa Andrew (form Hornaday) con mou
1860, 6, 16. Mary rocf Dover MM, dtd 1860,5, 17
1860, 8, 18. John & dt, Anna Elizabeth, rocf Vermillion MM, Ill., dtd 1860,6,2
1864, 1, 16. John & w, Mary, & dt, Anna E., gct Dover MM
1872, 1, 20. Isaiah [Horniday] con mou
1872, 9, 21. Mary J. [Horniday] recrq
1873, 4, 19. Isaiah F. [Horniday] & w, Mary Jane, gct Caesars Creek MM, O.
1876, 7, 15. Isaiah & w, Mary Jane, & ch, Ezekiel, John W. & George Kalita, rocf Cesars Creek MM, O., dtd 1876,6,22
1877, 4, 21. John [Horneday] & w, Mary, & ch, Daniel Allen & Ezekiel Albert, rocf Dover MM, O., dtd 1877,4,19
1877, 4, 21. Anna E. rocf Dover MM, O., dtd 1877,4,19
1884, 1, 19. Ezekiel & w, Hannah, gct White River MM, Ind.
1885, 2, 21. John & w, Mary, & ch, Allen & Albert, gct Wilmington MM, O.
1885, 3, 21. Ezekiel rocf White River MM, Ind., dtd 1885,3,7

HORNEY
1860, 3, 21. Susan L. rocf WD MM, dtd 1860,2, 15
1873, 5, 17. Susan L. gct Hinkles Creek MM, Ind.

HOSKINS
1905, 5, 20. Nellie Curl gct Dover MM, O.

HOUP
1883, 1, 20. Daniel M. & w, Kate C., & dt, Gracie L., recrq
1886, 1, 16. Katie C. relrq

HOWARD
1859, 5, 15. Amanda Mary, dt Adam & Martha J. Osborn, d
----, --, --. Raymond B. m Nina BEVAN, dt Orlando & Ella, b 1898,6,22
Ch: Harold John b 1923, 12, 26

1881, 4, 16. Frank recrq
1891, 9, 19. James rocf Van Wert MM, O.
1893, 5, 20. Susan M. & s, Charles, recrq
1899, 3, 18. Ada recrq
1899, 4, 15. Wm. & w, Amanda, & ch, Eva, May, Clem, Grover, Alfred, Frank, Wm. & Ida, recrq
1909, 3, 20. William, Amanda, Ada, Alfred, Della, Eva, Frank, George, Ida & Mary, dropped from mbrp
1909, 4, 17. Frank & w gct Marion MM, Ind.
1914, 1, 17. Raymond B., s Eli & Julia F., recrq
1927, 4, 17. Raymond & w, Nina B., & s, Harold John, relrq

HOWE
1877, 3, 17. William & w, Mariah, recrq

HOWELL
1802, 1, 3. Elizabeth b
----, --, --. Aaron b 1827,5,5; m Louisa ----- b 1829,7,23
Ch: Isabelle b 1856, 2, 14
----, --, --. John K. b 1840,5,31; m Sallie ----- b 1839,5,14
Ch: Flora E. b 1861, 12, 16
Benjamin S." 1863, 11, 2
Mary A. " 1865, 11, 11
Francis B. " 1868, 3, 2
Emeline M. " 1870, 2, 22
Lutie A. " 1871, 7, 4
Charles W. " 1872, 2, 20
1865, 9, 18. Charles E. b
1866, 11, 22. Arthur W. b

1860, 1, 21. Elizabeth [Howel] recrq
1862, 8, 15. Sarah Ellen (form Osborn) con mou
1866, 12, 15. John K. & w, Sarah, & ch, Flora, Benjamin & Adaline, recrq
1871, 2, 18. Aaron [Howel] & w, Louisa, & dt, Isabella, recrq
1875, 5, 15. Elizabeth & ch, Etta May & Daisy Dean, gct Millcreek MM, Ind.
1877, 4, 21. Wm. C. recrq (living in Calif.)
1879, 3, 15. John K. & w, Sallie A., & ch,

HOWELL, continued
Flora E., Benjamin S., Mary A., Francis B., Emaline M., Lutie A., Charles H. & Everette C., gct Dover MM, O.

HOWLAND
1842, 2, 15. Barnabas & w, Mary, & dt, Lydia rocf Center MM, O., dtd 1841,8,18
1872, 8, 17. Barnabas gct Center MM, O.
1877, 3, 17. Ruth E. Williams recrq

HUBBARD
1844, 3, 12. Jehiel L. rocf New Garden MM, Ind., dtd 1844,2,17
1850, 11, 16. Jehiel L. gct White Water MM, Ind.

HUFF
1891, 9, 19. Gracie B. gct Wilmington MM, O.

HUFFMAN
1881, 5, 21. Amos recrq
1882, 12, 16. Kate & ch, Gracie, Willie & Mary, recrq
1891, 9, 19. Amos & w, Kate W., & ch, Willie & Millie, gct Wilmington MM, O.

HUGHS
1899, 3, 18. Frank & Sarah recrq
1899, 5, 20. Ethel recrq

HULSE
1891, 3, 21. Ann recrq

HUMPHREYS
1876, 5, 20. James & ch, Emma F., Jane E., Lizzie A., Jennie M., William H., Minnie & Mentie recrq
1876, 6, 17. Emma relrq
1877, 3, 17. David L. recrq

HUMSTON
1931, 8, 9. Glenn, s Halleck, b (G)

1931, 6, 4. Glenn recrq (G)

HUNNICUTT
1839, 5, 14. John P. rocf Dover MM, dtd 1839,2,14
1839, 10, 15. John P. gct Center MM, O., to m Susannah H. Balard
1840, 8, 11. Susannah H. rocf Centre MM, O., dtd 1840,7,15
1842, 11, 15. John P. & w, Susanna H., & dt, Phebe Ann, gct Dover MM

HUNT
----, --, --. Robert b 1802,1,25; m Ruth MADEN b 1803,11,12
Ch: Cyrus L. b 1828, 6, 2
Elizabeth M. " 1829, 9, 17
Lydia " 1831, 2, 26
Ann b 1833, 1, 25
Nathan " 1835, 4, 28
Mary " 1836, 10, 19
Edith " 1839, 1, 7
Henry " 1841, 1, 27
George M. " 1843, 2, 19
Rachel " 1845, 4, 10

1827, 5, 26. Robert rmt Ruth Maden
1827, 8, 25. Ruth S. gct Newberry MM, O.
1829, 8, 11. Robert & w, Ruth, & s, Cyrus, rocf Newberry MM, O., dtd 1829,6,25
1841, 10, 12. Elizabeth rocf Smithfield MM, Ind., dtd 1841,9,18
1842, 10, 11. Pheriba rocf Centre MM, O., dtd 1842,9,14
1844, 12, 17. Pheriba Shields (form Hunt) dis mou
1847, 1, 16. Elizabeth Ann rmt Amos Haines
1853, 9, 17. Margaret Ann recrq
1854, 4, 15. Cyrus L. con mou
1854, 8, 19. Cyrus L. & w, Margaret Ann, & s, Oliver W., gct Newberry MM, O.
1856, 1, 19. Elizabeth M. Stubbs (form Hunt) con mou
1856, 1, 19. Mary rmt Enos P. Stubbs
1860, 7, 21. Nathan gct Elk MM, O., to m Esther T. Stubbs
1861, 7, 21. Nathan gct Elk MM, O., to m Esther T. Stubbs
1861, 1, 19. Ruth S. & ch, Henry H., George M. & Rachel G., gct Elk MM, O.
1861, 1, 19. Lydia C. gct Elk MM, O.
1861, 1, 19. Ann gct Elk MM, O.
1861, 1, 19. Edith S. gct Elk MM, O.
1861, 2, 16. Nathan gct Elk MM, O.
1871, 2, 18. Thomas recrq
1874, 9, 19. John T. gct Camden MM

HUSSEY
1827, 10, 27. John rmt Jane Edwards
1827, 11, 24. Jane gct Clear Creek MM, O.

HUTCHINSON
1874, 3, 21. William recrq
1874, 5, 16. Oscar recrq

HYDE
1898, 11, 19. George recrq

IZZARDS
1849, 6, 16. Mary rocf Newberry MM, dtd 1849,2,12

JAMES
1889, 2, 16. Anna McFadden gct Clear Creek MM, O.
1932, 7, 7. Ella rocf Urbana MM, O. (G)

JAY
1893, 4, 15. Leona S. gct Oak Ridge MM, Ind.

JEFFRIES
----, --, --. George m Mary Ellen HARLAN, dt Jacob & Sarah (Smith) b 1845,10,20
Ch: Bland b 1873, 5, 29

1853, 4, 16. Harriett M. (form More) rst at Center MM on consent of this mtg
1855, 8, 18. Caleb J. Harvey gct Center MM, O., to m Rebecca [Jefferis]
1860, 2, 18. Hannah S. [Jefferes] rocf Center MM, O., dtd 1860,1,18
1862, 8, 15. Hannah S. gct Center MM, O.
1881, 5, 21. Rebecca H. gct Center MM
1883, 3, 17. Mary Ellen recrq
1891, 3, 21. Blanch L. recrq

JENKS
----, --, --. David b 1847,9,20; m Emily THATCHER b 1852,8,11
Ch: Rodney b 1871, 4, 5
Joseph O. " 1873, 5, 30

1871, 7, 15. Emily [Jinks] (form Thatcher) con mou
1874, 1, 17. David recrq
1878, 12, 21. David dis disunity
1879, 6, 21. Maria rocf Back Creek MM, Ind.
1882, 12, 16. George & w, Hannah E., & ch, Loren & Anna, recrq
1889, 4, 20. Elizabeth & ch, Loran A., Claudie & Geo. relrq

JESSOP
1826, 11, 25. David Green gct Miami MM, O., to m Mary Jessop

JOBE
1881, 4, 16. John recrq
1898, 8, 14. Frank dis

JOHNSON
1866, 8, 20. Alfretta J. b
1889, 9, 28. Leslie Earl b
1933, 3, 19. John H. d

1820, 1, 29. Elizabeth rmt Christopher Kellum
1823, 9, 27. John & w, Lydia, & ch, Mary Susanna Thomas Lydia & Anna, gct White Lick MM, Ind.
1847, 5, 15. Samuel M. Hadley gct Miami MM, O., to m Emily Johnson
1849, 7, 21. David F. & w, Catherine, & ch, Charles Albert, Calvin C. & John, rocf Cincinnati MM, O., dtd 1849,6,14
1850, 12, 21. Micajah rmt Ann Hale
1851, 3, 15. Ann & ch, Mary, Sarah Ann & Alfred C. Hale, gct Miami MM, O.
1856, 3, 15. David F. & w, Catharine C., & ch, Chas. Albert, Calvin C., John, Joel W., Caroline & Eli M., gct Miami MM, O.
1861, 4, 20. John Howard rmt Sarah N. Hawkins
1862, 8, 16. John Howard rocf Miami MM, O., dtd 1862,7,23
1863, 11, 21. John Howard & w, Sarah H., & ch, Allen Clifford, gct Spring Creek MM, Ia.
1866, 3, 17. Almeda rocf Fairfield MM, dtd 1866,2,17
1876, 2, 19. Almeda gct Caesars Creek MM, O.
1884, 12, 20. Joseph R. & Minerva I., & ch, Irvin H. & Mary Anna, rocf Dover MM, O., dtd 1884,12,18
1900, 10, 20. Joseph R. & w, Isabelle, gct Wilmington MM, O.
1900, 10, 20. Mary A. gct Wilmington MM, O.
1902, 2, 15. Irvin & fam gct New Garden MM, Ind.
1906, 11, 17. Leslie recrq
1909, 9, 18. John & w, Sarah, rocf Wilmington MM, O., dtd 1909,8,14
1924, 3, 16. Leslie dropped from mbrp
1926, 6, 20. Bertha M. dropped from mbrp

JONES
----, --, --. Thomas & Mary
Ch: John W. b 1842, 2, 10
Ella " 1853, 3, 31
----, --, --. Ethelbert b 1826,9,28; m Sarah A. ----- b 1837,6,26
Ch: Louella
Kate b 1857, 1, 5
Anna May " 1860, 5, 20
Charles W. " 1864, 2, 22
Hattie C. " 1873, 2, 28

1825, 7, 30. Narcissa recrq
1826, 2, 25. Mary rst on consent of Cane Creek MM, N. C.
1826, 8, 28. Mary gct Honey Creek MM, Ind.
1827, 3, 21. Narcissa gct Miami MM, O.
1851, 9, 20. Alfred H. & w, Mary R., & ch, Stephen Alfred & Mary Adalade, rocf China MM, Me., dtd 1851,8,19
1854, 4, 15. Alfred H. & w, Mary R., & ch, Stephen Alphred, Mary Adalade & Lindley Sebohm, gct China MM, Me.
1863, 7, 18. Artemus N. Hadley gct Miami MM, O., to m Elizabeth M. Jones
1865, 9, 16. Sarah M. rocf Miami MM, O., dtd 1865,7,26
1873, 10, 18. Ethelbert & w, Sarah, & ch, Franklin, Luellen, Kate, Anna May, Chas. Wm. & Hattie Clifford, rocf Wilmington MM, O., dtd 1873,8,15
1874, 3, 21. Ella recrq
1874, 3, 21. John W. recrq

KEATTS
1900, 11, 17. Lucinda Cole rocf Hopewell MM, O., dtd 1900,10,6

KELLUM
----, --, --. Elizabeth, dt Geo. & Mary (Myres) b 1832,1,11 d 1918,3,25

1820, 1, 29. Christopher rmt Elizabeth Johnson

KELLUM, continued
1820, 3, 25. Elizabeth gct Newberry MM, O.
1891, 5, 16. Elizabeth recrq

KELLY
1843, 2, 14. Sarah rocf Cesars Creek MM, O., dtd 1842,8,25
1845, 8, 12. Sarah gct Miami MM, O.
1847, 6, 19. Sarah dis

KERSEY
----, --, --. Thomas Sr. b 1759,9,15 d 1835, 8,10 bur Lytles Creek; m Rebecca CARTER, b 1759,7,11
----, --, --. Thomas Jr. b 1793,1,27 d 1870,9, 7 bur Lytles Creek; m Letitia CRAIG b 1801,1,23 d 1872,5,11 bur Lytles Creek
Ch: Ann b 1824, 10, 23 d 1842, 1,10 bur Litles Creek
William b 1826, 12, 24 " 1869, 9,22
John " 1829, 4, 3
Hannah " 1832, 1, 11 " 1841, 12,31 bur Litles Creek
Martha b 1834, 10, 22
Rebecca " 1838, 3, 12

1820, 4, 20. Rebecca rst on consent of Center MM, O.
1821, 3, 21. Daniel rocf Springfield MM, N. C., dtd 1821,2,7
1823, 3, 29. Daniel gct Cherry Grove MM, Ind.
1823, 10, 25. Thomas gct Miami MM, O., to m Letitia Craig
1824, 5, 29. Letitia rocf Miami MM, O., dtd 1824,4,28
1837, 7, 11. Carter dis mou
1843, 3, 14. John Hornaday gct Miami MM, O., to m Martha Kersey
1870, 4, 10. Martha Bell (form Kersey) con mou

KESTER
1823, 2, 23. Hannah & ch, John & Harmon, rocf Centre MM, O., dtd 1823,1,18
1824, 2, 28. Hannah rmt Josiah Albertson
1827, 12, 29. John dis disunity

KIMBROUGH
----, --, --. D. & Ester
Ch: Ora b 1868, 9, 24
Anna " 1870, 2, 4
----, --, --. Jeremiah b 1827,10,14; m Esther HARVEY b 1830,10,13 d 1859,10,18
Ch: Louisa b 1851, 5, 17
Jeremiah m 2nd Rhoda -----
Ch: Willard T. b 1870, 9, 21
Lulu S. " 1872, 6, 12
Clifford E." 1873, 12, 20
----, --, --. Timothy b 1846,6,30; m Nancy Emily ----- b 1849,9,28
Ch: Elva b 1870, 5, 10

1822, 7, 27. Elizabeth [Kimber] (form Hiatt) con mou
1822, 9, 28. Elizabeth con mou
1827, 6, 27. Sarah Jr. recrq
1827, 9, 29. Jeremiah & Charity recrq
1828, 4, 26. Charity rmt Lewis Hiatt
1829, 1, 13. Jeremiah dis jH
1830, 4, 13. Sarah Jr. dis jH
1836, 5, 17. Elizabeth gct White River MM, Ind.
1841, 3, 16. Elizabeth rocf White River MM, Ind., dtd 1841,1,9
1848, 8, 19. Jeremiah recrq
1850, 3, 16. Jeremiah J. rmt Esther Harvey
1854, 6, 17. Susanna recrq
1855, 10, 20. Permelia (form Wire) con mou
1859, 2, 19. Susanna Hadley (form Kimbrough) con mou
1866, 12, 15. Timothy recrq
1868, 3, 21. Jeremiah rmt Rhoda Ann Hadley
1868, 4, 18. Esther (form Bangham) con mou
1868, 10, 17. Timothy C. rmt Nancy E. Green
1870, 3, 19. Jeremiah & w, Rhoda Ann, gct Cincinnati MM, O.
1871, 2, 18. Dennice recrq
1871, 10, 21. Louisa rmt Jonathan B. Cowgill
1872, 6, 15. Lawson recrq
1872, 8, 17. Pamela & s, Ellsworth gct Miami MM, O.
1872, 11, 16. Jeremiah & w, Rhoda E., & ch, Willard T. & Lulu, rocf Cincinnati MM, O., dtd 1872,9,19
1874, 3, 21. Demetrius recrq
1874, 5, 16. Eddie recrq
1885, 4, 18. Demetrius & w, Esther C., & ch, Orah M., Anna B. & Estella E., gct Elk River MM, Kans.
1897, 4, 17. Willard [Kimbro] relrq
1902, 3, 15. Rhoda E., Lula & Ethel relrq
1902, 5, 17. Clifford relrq
1905, 12, 16. Raymond J. relrq
1926, 6, 20. Elva dropped from mbrp

KIMMER
1874, 1, 17. Samuel & w, Jane, & ch, Homer V. & Mary Alice, recrq

KING
----, --, --. James M., s Amos & Catherine (Murphy), b 1852,2,6; m Emma MOORE, dt Allen & Sarah (Murphy), b 1862,11,21
Ch: Wilbur b 1882, 6, 14
Arthur " 1884, 6, 30
Russell " 1886, 11, 13

1896, 2, 15. James recrq
1921, 6, 18. David & Maggie dropped from mbrp

KIRK
----, --, --. Elisha & Almira
Ch: Timothy b 1822, 8, 25 d 1859, 5,30
Harriet " 1826, 3, 5

KIRK, Elisha & Almira, continued
Ch: Eli b 1829, 1, 27 d 1853, 3, 8
Eleanor " 1832, 1, 31
Malissa " 1835, 2, 15 " 1842, 1,18
Lydia " 1837, 2, 23
Hester " 1838, 11, 23
Josiah " 1841, 3, 21 " 1841, 3,24
Levi " 1841, 3, 21 " 1841, 3,24
Emily " 1842, 10, 12 " 1858, 2,28

1839, 6, 11. Elisha & w, Almira, & ch, Timothy, Harriet, Eli, Eleanor, Melissa, Lydia & Hester, recrq
1850, 7, 20. Timothy gct Salem MM, Iowa
1853, 2, 19. Timothy rocf Richland MM, Ind., dtd 1853,1,6
1856, 5, 17. Timothy gct Mississinewa MM, Ind.
1860, 1, 21. Lydia Smith (form Kirk) con mou
1862, 7, 19. Esther Underwood (form Kirk) con mou
1884, 10, 18. Robert gct Cincinnati MM, O.

KIRKHAM
1932, 2, 4. Cora M. d (G)

1929, 12, 5. Cora Celesta May recrq (G)

KISER
1885, 4, 18. Jacob & w, Armilda, recrq

KLIPPARD
1878, 7, 20. William recrq

KNOWLTON
1846, 12, 19. Julia Ann gct Cincinnati MM, O.
1854, 2, 18. Julia Ann rocf Dover MM, dtd 1853,12,15
1865, 7, 15. Julia A. gct Spring Creek MM,Ia.

LACEY
1851, 6, 21. Ruth C. (form Bankson) dis mou
1884, 5, 17. Mary D. [Lacy] gct Wilmington MM, O.

LANCASTER
----, --, --. Edward, s John & Deborah (Richards), b 1848,11,8 d 1913,2,28 bur Springfield; m Phoebe LANCASTER, dt James & Allie (Townsend), b 1856,2,13
Ch: Marie Shank b 1894, 7, 21
Addie " d 1919, 8,--

1825, 3, 26. Rachel rocf Miami MM, O., dtd 1825,2,23
1825, 12, 31. Hannah, w Jesse, rocf Cesars Creek MM, O., dtd 1825,9,29
1827, 7, 28. Rachel & Hannah attached to Center MM, O.
1882, 12, 16. John & David recrq
1901, 1, 19. Adaline recrq
1901, 5, 18. Phebe & s, Edgar Berkhart, rocf Miami MM, O., dtd 1901,4,24
1901, 7, 20. Edward & dt, Maggie Marie, recrq
1924, 3, 16. Phebe relrq

LASHLEY
1902, 7, 19. Alfred rocf Miami MM, O.
1903, 9, 17. Robert Boone rocf Miami MM, O., dtd 1902,11,26
1905, 9, 16. Alfred & Robert gct Miami MM, O.

LAW
1924, 4, 20. Sarah Greathouse relrq

LAWRENCE
1871, 3, 18. James & w, Mary Ellen, recrq

LEACH
1893, 1, 21. Thomas & Grant recrq
1901, 4, 20. Thomas transferred to Ogden MM, O.
1901, 4, 20. Grant transferred to Ogden MM, O.

LENTZ
1876, 2, 19. John J. recrq
1884, 10, 18. John relrq

LEVER
1880, 5, 15. Eliza recrq
1880, 6, 19. Abiel & ch, Frank, Iva, Hannah & McClane, recrq

LEWIS
----, --, --. Clyde, s James & Eva O., b 1889, 6,14; m Coral MILLS, dt Warren & Margaret, b 1892,10,15
Ch: Russell b 1914, 12, 13
Ronald " 1921, 1, 18
Velma " 1923, 2, 2

1827, 6, 27. Caleb Harvey gct Clear Creek MM, O., to m Ann Lewis
1828, 6, 24. Jesse rmt Hannah Harvey
1832, 11, 13. Jesse & w, Hannah, & ch, Sarah & Caleb, gct Ceasars Creek MM, O.
1877, 11, 17. Emily H. gct Wilmington MM, O.
1895, 5, 18. Vennie dropped from mbrp
1897, 3, 20. Vernie recrq
1898, 5, 21. Eva gct Center MM, O.
1929, 12, 22. Clyde & w, Carol, & ch, Russell, Ronald & Velma, recrq

LIGGETT
1894, 6, 16. Anna Laura gct West Fork MM, O.

LINDLEY
----, --, --. William b 1787,1,18 d 1850,12, 28 bur Lick Creek, Ind.; m Ama K. ----- b 1806,4,8
Ch: Hannah E. b 1845, 3, 4 d 1855,12,4 bur Springfield

1838, 3, 13. William rmt Anna K. Fisher

LINDLEY, continued
1838, 4, 17. Anna K. gct Lost Creek MM, Ind.
1839, 9, 17. Ruth & Sarah B. rocf Blue River MM, Ind., dtd 1839,7,6
1851, 9, 20. Anna K. rocf Lost Creek MM, Ind., dtd 1851,7,19

LINTON
----, --, --. Joseph & Mariah
Ch: Mary E. b 1845, 7, 7
Alfred Alonzo " 1848, 5, 15
John Hadley " 1852, 4, 22
William C. " 1854, 11, 30
Ruth Ida " 1861, 6, 23
Joseph Eli " 1863, 4, 13
Charles Linton " 1866, 7, 18

1836, 10, 11. Seth rmt Mary Ann Moore
1837, 7, 11. Sarah Ann gct Centre MM, O.
1838, 8, 14. Jonathan Hadley, s Wm., gct Center MM, O., to m Mary Linton
1843, 10, 17. James rmt Ann M. Hadley
1847, 9, 18. Cyrus rmt Lydia Harvey
1848, 7, 15. Lydia gct Centre MM, O.
1851, 9, 20. James rocf Center MM, O., dtd 1851,8,13
1853, 9, 17. Cyrus rmt Eliza Hadley
1854, 6, 17. Eliza gct Center MM, O.
1865, 2, 18. Olive (form Hadley) con mou
1868, 8, 15. Joshua rocf Center MM, O., dtd 1868,7,15
1872, 8, 17. Joshua & w, Olive, & ch, Walter Elsa & Seth H., gct Center MM, O.
1892, 10, 15. Walter rocf Center MM, O.
1900, 7, 21. Walter & w, Gertrude, & ch, Fred W. & Eleanor, gct Wilmington MM, O.
1903, 9, 17. Alfred Alonzo & w, Wm. C., gct Wilmington MM, O.
1912, 3, 16. Stella recrq
1914, 9, 12. Carrie Margaret recrq

LIPPINCOTT
1907, 9, 21. Bessie rocf Ogden MM, O.
1910, 5, 21. Bessie gct Center MM, O.

LITTLETON
1885, 5, 16. Chancey recrq
1895, 7, 20. Chauncey T. & ch, Ernest N., Orpha A. & Wayne C., gct Chambersburg MM

LONGSHORE
1850, 10, 19. Eleanor Simons (form Longshore) con mou

LONGSTRETH
1849, 7, 21. William rmt Hannah L. Cowgil
1849, 10, 20. Hannah C. gct Miami MM, O.

LOSY
1880, 5, 15. A. K. recrq
1880, 6, 19. Lennie recrq

LOWES
1916, 10, 21. Martha H. gct Cincinnati MM, O.

LUDINGTON
1823, 5, 31. Sarah recrq
1823, 6, 28. Thomas recrq
1829, 1, 13. Thomas dis jH
1838, 6, 12. David recrq
1852, 9, 18. Mary recrq
1853, 5, 21. Lewis & Harrison, ch David, roc
1855, 4, 21. David con mou
1873, 7, 19. Lewis relrq

LUNDY
1823, 8, 30. James & w, Elizabeth, & ch, Enoch William Jesse Anna Levi James John Susanna Elizabeth & Asenith, gct Centre MM, O.
1837, 10, 17. Maria Ann & ch, Israel, Enoch, Eliza Ann & Ruth, rocf Center MM, O., dtd 1837,4,12
1846, 9, 19. Sarah B. Smith (form Lundy) dis mou
1852, 11, 20. Eliza A. Goodwin (form Lundy) dis mou
1852, 11, 20. Ruth Shaver (form Lundy) dis mou
1852, 9, 18. Israel dis mou

LUNSFORD
1922, 4, 15. James recrq
1926, 6, 20. James dropped from mbrp
1926, 6, 20. Alice dropped from mbrp

LUTTRELL
1890, 1, 18. Mary gct Cincinnati MM, O.

McBRIDE
----, --, --. John b 1838,9,8; m Mattie ----- b 1845,11,12
Ch: Willie b 1869, 3, 8
Mary " 1871, 9, 10
Albert " 1874, 12, 1

1874, 1, 17. John & w, Martha, & ch, Wm. & Mary, recrq
1897, 4, 17. John & w, Martha A., gct Columbus MM, O.

McCARTNEY
1930, 2, 6. Josephine E. recrq (G)

McCRAY
1860, 10, 18. Maude Jane d
1860, 11, 10. Mary Emily d
----, --, --. Thomas & Susannah
Ch: Mary b 1867, 5, 13
Arthur " 1869, 8, 12

1860, 1, 21. Mary Emily (form Osborn) con mou
1867, 4, 20. Susannah [McCrey] (form Maden) con mou

McCRAY, continued
1891, 1, 17. Wm. F. & w, Lettie, recrq
1898, 1, 15. Wm. & w, Letitia, gct Dublin MM, Ind.
1907, 12, 21. Minnie & Amelia recrq

McCULLUM
1881, 2, 19. Susan recrq

McDONALD
----, --, --. James b 1844,10,1; m Sarah ----- b 1843,9,4
Ch: Alvin W. b 1866, 7, 26
Mary Annetta " 1867, 9, 24

1867, 2, 16. James W. recrq
1884, 9, 20. James & w, Sarah, & ch, Nettie, Frank & Russell, gct Center MM, O.

McELIVER
----, --, --. Isaac b 1825,4,5; m Rhoda G. ----- b 1826,3,5
Ch: Charles E. b 1852, 11, 24

McELWEE
----, --, --. Wm. R., s Chas. & Kate (Jones); m Flora CURL, dt Samuel & Lydia (Morris) b 1875,9,23
Ch: Winifred b 1908, 7, 7
Helen " 1912, 2, 23

1874, 10, 17. Isaac R. recrq
1874, 10, 17. Charles recrq
1897, 5, 15. Chas. & fam gct Dover MM, O.
1914, 4, 18. Will rocf Dover MM

McFADDEN
----, --, --. John d 1871,7,6; m Susannah ANDREW
Ch: Samuel b 1847, 11, 24
Martha Jane" 1849, 8, 26
Esper Ann " 1851, 8, 27
Mary Elizabeth " 1853, 11, 25
James Lucien " 1857, 2, 22
Laura Delila " 1859, 12, 19
John William " 1862, 3, 28

1846, 4, 14. John recrq
1857, 4, 17. John rmt Susannah Andrew
1889, 2, 16. Anna(McFadden)James gct Clear Creek MM, O.

McGUIRE
1836, 7, 12. Rachel (form Fallis) dis mou

McKENCIE
1862, 7, 19. Julia (form Hadley) con mou
1871, 5, 20. Julia [McKecney] gct Wilmington MM, O.

McKINNEY
----, --, --. Alexander [McKenny] b 1847,12,4; m Rebecca Ann ----- b 1853,6,13
Ch: Sina Almeda b 1872, 4, 3
Charles S. " 1874, 6, 11

1870, 6, 18. Jesse [McKiney] rocf Newberry MM, O., dtd 1870,4,18
1872, 8, 17. Jesse gct Newberry MM, O.
1874, 5, 16. Alexander & w, Rebecca A., & dt, Sina A., recrq
1874, 5, 16. May recrq
1874, 5, 16. Rachel Ann recrq
1889, 4, 20. Ruth Emma recrq
1890, 9, 20. Emma [McKiney] relrq
1894, 11, 17. Obadiah & w rocf Wilmington MM, O.
1895, 5, 18. Eli & w & ch recrq
1895, 5, 18. Pearl gct Wilmington MM, O.
1897, 3, 20. John & Henry recrq
1897, 8, 14. Obadiah & w, Rachel, relrq
1898, 4, 16. H. M. dis
1898, 4, 16. Jesse recrq
1921, 9, 17. Earnest relrq

McMILLAN
----, --, --. Joseph b 1861,8,24; m Emma D. ----- b 1866,4,18
Ch: Rebecca Mary b 1889, 11, 16
Vera Ann " 1891, 2, 19
Robert J. " 1892, 4, 12
Willis O. " 1893, 10, 13
Mark E. C. " 1896, 2, 2
Dillon R. " 1900, 9, 20
Ruth Emma " 1902, 7, 13
Eva W. " 1904, 9, 5
Joseph Adelbert " 1906, 7, 25
Mable E. " 1908, 10, 16
Thomas Herbert " 1910, 4, 5
1893, 5, 2. Pearl, dt Wm. & Eva (Holliday) Warren, b
1928, 3, 5. Joseph L. [McMullen] d bur Springfield
----, --, --. Albert Earl [McMullen], s Joseph L. & Alice D., b 1893,3,28; m Mary HADLEY, dt James & Isabelle, b 1892,9,25
Ch: Isabelle Ann b 1931, 7, 7
James Lincoln " 1933, 11, 21

1839, 1, 15. Eli rmt Lydia Fallis
1839, 3, 12. Lydia & ch, Turner W., John, Isaac C. & Susan A. Fallis, gct Center MM, O.
1860, 7, 21. Emmor H. rmt Susan Thatcher
1864, 8, 20. Susan & s, Sanford, gct Center

McMILLAN, continued
MM, O.
1871, 4, 15. Emmor & w, Susan, & s, Sanford, rocf Center MM, O., dtd 1871,2,6
1910, 2, 16. Joseph & w, Emma D., & ch, Rebecca W., Vera Ann, Robert D., Willis O., Mark E. C., Dillon K., Ruth Emma, Eva W., J. Albert & Mable E., rocf Center MM
1910, 11, 19. Joseph & fam gct Center MM
1914, 4, 18. Alice J. rocf Ogden MM, O.
1914, 4, 18. Joseph Lincoln [McMullan] & dt, Oletha, recrq
1914, 4, 18. Albert Earl [McMullan] recrq
1916, 6, 17. Robert rocf Miami MM, O.
1917, 11, 17. Robert & w, Pearl, gct Ceasars Creek MM, O.
1922, 12, 16. Robert & w, Pearl, & s, Rex, rocf Ceasars Creek MM, O.

McNAMA
1897, 2, 20. Sarah M. gct Wilmington MM, O.

McRAY
1860, 11, 10. Mary E. (Osborn) d

1853, 11, 19. Mary Ann (form Maden) con mou

McVEY
1878, 7, 20. Deborah recrq
1900, 4, 21. Ruth rocf Fairfield MM

MABIE
1851, 8, 27. John d ae 76y 8m 2d (an elder)

1837, 4, 11. Jonathan Timberlake gct Centre MM, O., to m Catharine Mabie
1842, 12, 13. Jonathan Hadley gct Center MM, O., to m Eliza B. Mabie
1846, 12, 19. John rocf Centre MM, O., dtd 1846,11,18

MACKLIN
1825, 8, 27. Arksah (form Adams) dis mou

MADEN
----, --, --. Hiram b 1792,1,28; m Susanna STUART b 1800,11,10
Ch: George b 1829, 7, 10
Jehu " 1831, 1, 13
Hiram m 2nd Elizabeth OSBORN b 1803,2,27
Ch: William b 1835, 2, 27
John " 1837, 8, 11
Eli " 1839, 1, 14
Elizabeth Ann " 1841, 1, 23
Hiram " 1842, 7, 7
Susannah " 1844, 7, 3
Thomas Elwood " 1849, 7, 10
----, --, --. Harlan [Madden] b 1811,10,26; m Margaret ----- b 1814,7,25
Ch: Hannah b 1837, 2, 14 d 1842, 1,10
Rebecca Ann" 1846, 8, 17
Ch: Sally M. b 1853, 4, 9
----, --, --. George [Madden] b 1829,7,10; m Mary HORNADAY b 1826,10,16 d 1862,9,22
Ch: William H. b 1858, 1, 26
Alpheus E. " 1860, 8, 3
Lindon F. " 1862, 9, 19 d 1862,10,14
1871, 12, 22. Eli [Madden] d ae 92
1914, 6, 2. Cora [Madden] d

1819, 9, 25. Solomon con mou
1820, 1, 29. Solomon gct White Water MM, Ind.
1820, 3, 25. Edith recrq
1821, 6, 30. Solomon rocf White Water MM, Ind., dtd 1821,5,19
1824, 11, 27. Rebecca [Madden] rmt Reuben Chew
1825, 1, 29. Mary (form Chew) con mou
1825, 3, 26. Edith [Madden] rmt Joseph Stubbs
1826, 5, 15. Eli & ch, Harlan, John, George, Rhoena, Rebecca & Hiram, recrq
1826, 11, 25. Hiram gct White Water MM, Ind., to m Susannah Stewart
1827, 3, 31. Susannah rocf White Water MM, Ind., dtd 1827,2,28
1827, 4, 28. Ruth & ch, Elizabeth, Cyrus, Alice & John recrq
1827, 5, 26. Ruth rmt Robert Hunt
1829, 11, 17. Mary Harvey (form Maden) con mou
1824, 2, 11. Hiram rmt Elizabeth Osborn
1835, 7, 14. George & ch, Samuel & Edith, recrq
1836, 3, 15. Harlan rmt Margaret Osborn
1837, 4, 11. Solomon & w, Ruth, & ch, Elizabeth R., Cyrus W., Alice Jane, Mary Ann & Solomon, gct Dover MM
1837, 8, 15. George & w, Mary, & ch, Samuel C. & Edith, gct Bloomfield MM, Ind.
1845, 11, 11. Solomon & w, Ruth, & ch, Alice Jane, Mary Ann, Solomon, Moses, George, Wm. Henry & Rachel, rocf Dover MM, dtd 1845,9,18
1845, 11, 11. Cyrus W. rocf Dover MM, dtd 1845,9,18
1847, 1, 16. Alice Jane Disbrow (form Maden) dis mou
1847, 9, 18. Cyrus W. con mou
1849, 5, 19. Hiram Jr. gct Bloomfield MM, Ind., to m Hannah C. Harvey
1851, 6, 21. Hannah C. rocf Bloomfield MM, Ind., dtd 1851,3,5
1853, 11, 19. Mary Ann McRay (form Maden) con mou
1856, 4, 19. Cyrus W. [Madden] dis mou
1856, 8, 16. George [Madden] Jr. gct Vermillion MM, to m Mary Hornaday
1856, 12, 20. George [Madden] Jr. gct Vermillion MM, Ill.
1858, 10, 16. Jehu S. rmt Ruth Wildman
1859, 4, 16. Jehu S. [Madden] & w, Ruth W., gct Rocksylvania MM, Ia.
1859, 10, 15. Hiram [Madden] Jr. & w, Hannah C., & ch, Arthur & Anna Maria, gct Miami MM, O.

MADEN, continued
1860, 8, 18. Ruth & ch, William H, & Rachel, gct Dover MM
1863, 5, 16. George [Madden] & ch, Wm. & Alpheus E., rocf Vermillion MM, Ill., dtd 1863,4,4
1865, 12, 16. George [Madden] Jr. gct New Garden MM, Ind., to m Ruth Pyle
1866, 7, 21. George [Madden] Jr. & ch gct Spring Creek MM, Ia.
1867, 4, 20. Susanna McCrey (form Maden) con mou
1870, 8, 20. Solomon & Moses G. gct Dover MM
1871, 2, 18. Cyrus W. recrq
1872, 3, 15. Sarah [Madden] gct Spring Creek MM, Ia.
1872, 3, 15. Thomas Elwood [Madden] gct Wilmington MM, O.
1916, 9, 16. Clinton C. & Nellie C. [Madden] rocf Wilmington MM, O.

MADDOX
1889, 4, 20. Joseph, Harriett, Charles, Genevere & Hattie J. recrq

MARLATT
1923, 12, 17. Theodore d bur Springfield
1914, 8, 14. Rebecca d bur Springfield

1901, 1, 19. Mollie Anna Bell & Bertha recrq

MARSH
1846, 7, 14. Elias rmt Margaret Osborn
1846, 12, 19. Margaret & ch, Mary, Margaret & Thomas Osborn, rocf Walnut Ridge MM, Ind.

MARSHALL
1876, 11, 18. Mary C. & ch, Nora H., Eva L., Annie E., Minnie B. & Alice M., rocf Newberry MM, O., dtd 1876,10,23

MART
1871, 2, 18. Hannah recrq
1893, 5, 20. Stella Netta & Laura recrq

MARTIN
----, --, --. Viola May, dt John & Elizabeth Kellum, b 1853,5,16 d 1932,1,16 bur Springfield

1874, 5, 16. Andrew [Marten] recrq
1874, 5, 16. John recrq
1874, 5, 16. Charles recrq
1880, 9, 18. Chas. [Marten] & ch relrq
1892, 1, 16. Viola Mary recrq
1909, 7, 17. Theodore recrq

MASSEY
1827, 7, 28. James D. & w, Elizabeth, & ch, Mary, Anson L., Samuel Emsley & Eli attached to Center MM, O.

1930, 2, 6. Helen C. recrq (G)

MATHER
----, --, --. Joseph m Louisa ----- d 1859,11, 7 bur Springfield
Ch: Albert H. b 1852, 11, 30
Charles W. " 1858, 11, 19 d 1859, 2,14 bur Springfield
Joseph m 2nd Mary Ann -----
Ch: Carrie b 1865, 7, 1
Eva " 1873, 5, 12

1852, 2, 21. Joseph rmt Louisa Hadley
1854, 6, 17. Joseph rocf Miami MM, O., dtd 1854,5,24
1862, 8, 16. Joseph gct Miami MM, O., to m Mary Ann Brown
1863, 4, 18. Mary Ann rocf Miami MM, O., dtd 1863,3,25
1864, 5, 21. Isaac C. Hawkins gct Miami MM, O., to m Susan Mather
1879, 3, 15. Phebe E. rocf Dover MM, O., dtd 1879,4,17
1883, 10, 20. Albert H. & w, Phebe E., & ch, Omar B. & Ethel E., gct Dover MM, O.
1899, 11, 18. Esther L. & Mary A., gct Wilmington MM, O.

MAVERTY
1868, 9, 19. Lydia Ann (form Smith) gct Kokomo MM, Ind.

MENDENHALL
1821, 10, 27. Stephen & w, Elizabeth, rocf West Grove MM, Ind., dtd 1821,8,11
1821, 12, 29. Hiram rmt Martha Hale
1824, 12, 25. Stephen rocf Newberry MM, O., dtd 1821,6,28
1825, 5, 11. Olive rmt Jonathan Hadley
1828, 9, 16. Hiram dis jH
1829, 11, 17. Martha dis jH
1831, 2, 15. Nathan dis mou
1837, 8, 15. Nathan & w, Ann, gct White River MM, Ind.
1837, 8, 15. Hannah gct White River MM, Ind.
1837, 8, 15. Elizabeth gct White River MM, Ind.
1837, 8, 15. Rebecca gct White River MM, Ind.
1838, 1, 16. Rowena, Joseph, Martha Ann, Amos & Nathan, ch Hiram & Martha, gct White River MM, Ind.
1839, 9, 17. Stephen gct Sugar River MM, Ind.
1852, 11, 20. Ezekiel Hornaday gct Chester MM, Ind., to m Hannah Mendenhall
1853, 4, 16. Julia Ann, Delirga E., Elam K. & Wm. E., ch Hannah, rocf Chester MM, O., dtd 1853,2,24
1859, 2, 19. Julia Ann rmt Zimri Bond
1861, 12, 21. Delitha Vandervort (form Mendenhall) dis mou

MERDEN
1876, 4, 15. Susan & s, Ethelbert H., gct Kokomo MM, Ind.

MIARS
1882, 12, 16. Sallie, Mintie & Isaac recrq
1885, 1, 17. Isaac [Mires] & w, Anna, gct Minneapolis MM, Minn.
1891, 5, 16. Elizabeth recrq
1927, 9, 25. Olitha McMullen [Myers] relrq

MILES
1880, 5, 15. Emma recrq

MILLIKAN
----, --, --. Eli b 1782,9,17; m Mary KERSEY, b 1783,1,15
Ch: William b 1805, 9, 12
Thomas " 1808, 3, 1
John " 1810, 1, 15
Nathan " 1812, 2, 2
Zachariah " 1814, 6, 19 d 1819, 4,29
Almedie " 1816, 12, 9
Pamelia " 1819, 1, 24
Rebecca " 1821, 4, 10
Eli " 1824, 1, 11
----, --, --. John b 1820, 1, 15; m Margaret ----- b 1827,8,8
Ch: Sarah J. b 1847, 6, 12
John H. " 1850, 9, 9
Margaret E." 1851, 11, 20
Rachel C. " 1853, 5, 17
Eli W. " 1855, 7, 22
Almeda R. " 1857, 7, 26
Martha J. " 1860, 1, 1
Jesse D. " 1862, 1, 27
Priscilla E. " 1864, 11, 30
Thomas N. " 1867, 1, 16
Hannah C. " 1868, 3, 3

1827, 1, 27. Eli rst on consent of Center MM, O.
1829, 1, 13. Hannah recrq
1829, 8, 11. Hannah [Milikan] rmt John Carter
1830, 4, 13. Wm. gct West Grove MM, Ind., to m Charity Canaday
1830, 11, 16. Charity rocf West Grove MM, Ind.
1836, 12, 13. Thomas con mou
1837, 1, 17. Wm. & w, Charity, & ch, John, Charley, Mary, Emily & Sarah Ellen, gct Smithfield MM, Ind.
1842, 4, 12. Nathan dis disunity
1846, 8, 11. John dis mou
1850, 12, 21. Rebecca Frazier (form Millikin) dis mou
1856, 5, 17. Eli dis mou
1870, 8, 20. Margaret Eleanor [Milican] recrq
1871, 9, 16. John [Milican] rst
1871, 9, 16. Margaret [Milican], w John, & ch, Almedia R., Martha J., Jesse D. F., Priscilla E., Thomas N. & Hannah C., recrq
1871, 9, 16. Mary E. [Milican] recrq
1874, 3, 21. Sarah J. & Rachel C. [Milikan] recrq
1874, 3, 21. Eli [Milikan] recrq
1876, 5, 20. John H. relrq

MILLER
----, --, --. Lewis & Rebecca
Ch: Elias F. b 1837, 4, 20
Ruth N. " 1840, 3, 12
Hannah F. " 1842, 10, 12
1932, 2, 15. Kathleen Osborn d

1836, 5, 17. Lewis N. rmt Rebecca Curl
1836, 8, 16. Rebecca gct Springborough MM,O.
1840, 5, 12. Lewis N. & w, Rebecca, & s, Elias F., rocf Sugar River MM, Ind., dtd 1840,3,28
1844, 10, 15. John rmt Dorcas Ellis
1844, 11, 12. Dorcas gct Springborough MM
1853, 7, 16. Lewis N. & w, Rebecca, & ch, Elias F., Ruth N., Hannah F., Mary K., Joseph & Thomas, gct Springborough MM, O.
1877, 12, 15. James M. & w, Elizabeth, & s, Claud, rocf Clear Creek MM, O., dtd 1877,10,11
1881, 4, 16. Martha recrq
1892, 12, 19. James & w, Lizzie, gct Wilmington MM, O.
1921, 3, 19. Kathleen Osborn recrq

MILLS
1835, 1, 13. Charles rmt Ann Harvey
1835, 2, 17. Ann gct Miami MM, O.

MINOR
1828, 3, 29. Sarah (form Patterson) dis mou

MITCHELL
1859, 8, 20. Jehu Moore gct Center MM, O., to m Hannah D. Mitchel

MOHRMYER
1874, 5, 16. John recrq

MOOMA
1930, 5, 11. Lewis d
1918, 9, 21. Susan, w Lewis, d

1816, 9, 16. Lewis, Susan & Latha S. [Moomaw] recrq

MOON
1842, 5, 18. George m Susanna Osborn
----, --, --. Cyrus b 1826,1,1; m Jane GREEN b 1829,8,30
Ch: Elwood b 1849, 2, 19
Nelson " 1857, 12, 5
Lydia " 1860, 6, 1
Anna " 1862, 9, 25
Clarkson " 1868, 10, 10

1842, 11, 15. Susanna gct Walnut Ridge MM, Ind.
1857, 2, 21. Cyrus rmt Jane Green
1864, 6, 18. Cyrus & w, Jane, & ch, Elwood, Nelson, Lydia & Anna, rocf Newberry MM, O., dtd 1864,5,23
1867, 5, 18. Samantha B. (form Osborn) con mou

MOON, continued
1867, 7, 20. Samantha B. gct Newberry MM, O.
1869, 4, 17. Aaron & w, Eunice, & ch, Oliver Arthur, Mary Eva & John Demrus, rocf Newberry MM, O., dtd 1869,2,22
1869, 10, 18. Cyrus & w, Jane, & ch, Elwood Nelson Lydia, Anna, William A. & Clarkson, gct Vermillion MM, Ill.
1872, 11, 16. Aaron & w, Eunice, & ch, Oliver Arthur, Mary Eva & John D., gct Ceasars Creek MM, O.
1881, 8, 20. Eliza & ch, Robert E., Dallos N., Angenetta, Minnie D., William H., Francis M., Hiram E. & Bertha, rocf Newberry MM, O., dtd 1881,8,22

MOORE
----, --, --. Joshua b 1791,10,17 d 1874,2,7; m Nancy STRATTON b 1798,11,16
Ch: David S. b 1815, 8, 4 d 1816,11,26
John Haines" 1817, 9, 8
Sarah Ann " 1819, 12, 7
Micajah " 1821, 12, 23
William " 1824, 1, 7 d 1877,11,14
Joseph " 1826, 2, 10
Harriett " 1827, 11, 23
Nancy " 1829, 12, 19
Joshua " 1832, 2, 15
Benjamin " 1834, 2, 25 d 1836, 8, 4
Jehu C. " 1836, 12, 24
Seth " 1839, 1, 18 d 1865, 9, 8
----, --, --. ----- m Elizabeth ----- b 1788, 10,30 d 1874,8,13
Ch: Evaline b 1825, 11, 17 d 1912, 1,--
Sarah A. " 1820, 5, 20
----, , --. John b 1798, 8, 31; m Ann MOORE b 1805,7,6
Ch: Haines b 1825, 12, 9 d 1827,10, 7
Sarah " 1829, 11, 3
----, --, --. Isaac & Susanna [More]
Ch: Rhoda G. b 1837, 12, 7
Sarah Emily" 1839, 6, 25
----, --,--. John H. b 1817,9,8; m Ruth LINDLEY b 1817,8,28 d 1869,3,31 bur Springfield
Ch: Lindley M. b 1843, 2, 3
Oliver " 1845, 9, 20
Francis " 1847, 9, 10 d 1849, 2,19
Isabel " 1850, 9, 23
----, --, --. Harris b 1835,4,5; m Gulielma GREEN b 1839,10,17 d 1865,--,-- bur Lytles Creek
Ch: Francis b 1859, 7, 26
Eva " 1861, 11, 27
Harris m 2nd Rachel -----
Ch: Mary Ellen b 1868, 8, 11
Mordecai C." 1870, 6, 3
----, --, --. Micajah b 1821,12,25; m Margaret Ellen ----- b 1838,7,15
Ch: Robert H. b 1861, 6, 2
Benjamin " 1863, 4, 15
Thomas Seth" 1866, 6, 9
Emma J. " 1869, 3, 30

----, --, --. Thomas b 1844,1,29; m Sarah ----- b 1854,8,15
Ch: Clara M. b 1869, 4, 27
Clifton " 1870, 9, 26 d 1870,11,2
Jennetta " 1872, 10, 26
1912, 12, 27. Florence d
1914, 4, 4. Samuel d bur Springfield
1920, 1, 27. Carrie Elma, dt Taylor & Veda (Hadley), b
1924, 11, --. Sarah Jane d bur Springfield

1822, 11, 30. John dis disunity
1822, 12, 28. Elizabeth [More] (form Antrim) dis mou
1823, 6, 28. Elizabeth dis
1826, 11, 25. Anne rocf Centre MM, Pa., dtd 1826,9,7
1827, 9, 29. John rst
1831, 11, 15. Joshua dis
1832, 10, 16. John & w, Ann, & ch, Sarah, & Martha Ann, gct Duck Creek MM, Ind.
1836, 10, 11. Mary Ann rmt Seth Linton
1838, 1, 16. Susannah (form Green) con mou
1838, 8, 14. Susannah gct Spiceland MM, Ind.
1839, 4, 16. Susannah rocf Spiceland MM, Ind., dtd 1839,2,20
1840, 7, 14. John Haines
1840, 8, 11. Susannah dis
1842, 9, 13. Sarah Emily recrq
1844, 6, 11. Harriett dis
1845, 5, 13. Sarah Emily gct Clear Creek MM, O.
1846, 12, 19. Rhoda G. recrq of gr father Reuben Green
1847, 3, 20. Sarah Emily rocf Clear Creek MM, O., dtd 1847,2,13
1851, 10, 16. Phebe D. (form Hadley) con mou
1852, 4, 17. Phebe gct Honey Creek MM, Ind.
1853, 4, 16. Harriet M. (form More) Jeffries rst at Centre MM, O., on consent of this mtg
1843, 11, 19. Sarah Jane (form Hadley) con mou
1855, 5, 21. Nancy rmt Wm. P. Harvey
1856, 1, 19. Martha (form Haines) con mou
1858, 4, 17. Joshua Jr. gct Milford MM, Ind.
1859, 2, 19. Joseph con mou
1859, 3, 19. Gulielma [More] (form Green) con mou
1859, 7, 16. Harris C. recrq
1859, 8, 20. Joseph gct Hopewell MM, Ind.
1859, 8, 20. Jehu gct Center MM, O., to m Hannah D. Mitchel
1860, 1, 21. Sarah Emily rmt David F. Carter
1860, 2, 18. Adaline E. recrq
1861, 4, 20. Micajah con mou
1862, 4, 19. Joseph rocf Hopewell MM, Ind., dtd 1861,10,19
1862, 8, 15. Margaret E. rocf Dover MM, dtd 1862,6,19
1863, 5, 16. Adaline E. gct Oak Ridge MM, Ind.
1865, 8, 19. Isabel Ann (form Rich) con mou

MOORE, continued
1866, 2, 17. Lindley M. con mou
1868, 2, 15. Oliver con mou
1868, 2, 15. Harris C. con mou
1868, 4, 18. Rachel W. rocf Center MM, O., dtd 1868,4,15
1868, 8, 15. Ophelia rocf Center MM, O., dtd 1868,7,15
1870, 2, 18. Samuel & ch, Alfred B. & Hattie E., recrq
1871, 2, 18. Thomas & w, Sarah, & dt, Clara, recrq
1871, 2, 18. Caleb recrq
1871, 2, 18. Martha recrq
1871, 2, 18. Elizabeth recrq
1871, 2, 18. Evaline recrq
1874, 1, 17. Clark recrq
1877, 4, 21. John W. recrq
1878, 12, 21. Micajah C. dis disunity
1879, 1, 18. John W. relrq
1881, 4, 16. Edward recrq
1885, 2, 21. John H. gct Wilmington MM, O.
1885, 11, 21. Clark & w, Mary Alice, relrq
1886, 8, 21. Hannah D. rocf Center MM, O., dtd 1886,8,18
1887, 3, 19. Jehu C. & w, Hannah D., gct New York MM, N. Y.
1887, 3, 19. Albert R. gct New York MM, N.Y.
1887, 3, 19. Frederick L. gct N. Y. MM, N.Y.
1888, 3, 17. Oliver & fam relrq by letter to M. E. Church, Grenola, Kans.
1896, 2, 15. Allie & dt recrq
1906, 9, 15. Samuel & Sarah Jane rocf Ogden MM, O.
1909, 6, 19. Eveline rocf Ogden MM, O.
1918, 4, 20. Charlie & Allie dropped from mbrp
1920, 4, 17. Roy dropped from mbrp
1920, 5, 15. Veda Hadley gct Ogden MM, O.

MOORMAN
1842, 5, 18. Manson m Rachel Ann STRATTON

1843, 11, 14. Rachel Ann [Mormon] gct Dover MM
1867, 5, 18. Mary Ann (form Osborn) dis mou

MORRIS
1881, 5, 21. Isaac recrq

MORROW
1868, 9, 19. Susan L. rocf Miami MM, O., dtd 1868,8,26
1878, 5, 18. Susan L. relrq
1892, 8, 13. Samuel C. & Martha L. relrq

MOSIER
1895, 5, 18. James recrq
1896, 4, 18. James relrq

MOSGROVE
1874, 5, 16. Margaretta recrq
1892, 4, 16. Watson R. recrq
1901, 4, 20. Watson R. transferred to Ogden MM, O.

MOTE
1826, 6, 20. Dora dropped from mbrp

MOUNTS
1925, 7, 19. Belle dropped from mbrp

MULFORD
1894, 1, 20. Charles & w, Julia, & dt, Mable Ruth, recrq

MULLEN
1871, 3, 18. Emily B. recrq

MURDIN
1876, 4, 15. Susan D. & s, Ethelbert H., gct Kokomo MM, Ind.

MURDOCK
1866, 4, 21. James E. & w, Susan, & ch, James E., Wm. B. & Thomas F., recrq
1879, 8, 16. Susan B. & ch, James E., Wm. B. & Thomas F. relrq
1884, 10, 18. James gct Phila. MM, Pa.

MURPHY
1883, 11, 17. Laura recrq

MURRAY
1903, 9, 19. Ruth rocf Hopewell MM, O., dtd 1903,9,5
1922, 3, 18. Russel J. & Ruth Barrett gct Miami MM, O.

NEAL
1889, 4, 20. Samuel recrq

NEFF
1900, 12, 28. Isabel Frances, w Paul Adam, dt Benjamin & Louise J. White, b

1931, 6, 4. Isabelle Frances recrq (G)
1933, 4, 6. Frances relrq (G)

NEWBY
1860, 7, 21. Emily (form Pyle) con mou
1860, 12, 15. Nathan rocf Blue River MM, Ind., dtd 1860,12,8
1863, 10, 17. Nathan & w, Emily P., & s, Albert Edward, gct Blue River MM, Ind.

NEWBERRY
1844, 4, 16. Mary Ann (form Thornberry) dis mou
1856, 8, 16. Mary Ann recrq

NEWLAND
1911, 10, 21. Ira Earl recrq
1920, 4, 17. Ira dropped from mbrp

NEWLIN
----, --, --. Jno. b 1783,9,1 d 1821,6,21; m Esther STUBBS b 1786,8,28
Ch: Eli b 1808, 12, 4
William " 1810, 2, 22
Jane " 1811, 10, 29
Joshua " 1813, 9, 26
Sarah " 1815, 4, 10
Ruth " 1817, 1, 12
Jno. " 1818, 9, 15
David " 1820, 9, 17
Phinehas " 1822, 7, 4
Elias " 1822, 7, 4
Joel " 1824, 8, 26
Esther " 1826, 9, 12

1829, 1, 13. Eli rmt Lydia Osborn
1830, 11, 16. Eli & w, Lydia, gct Smithfield MM, Ind.
1831, 12, 13. William gct Miami MM, O., to m Mary Edwards
1832, 7, 17. Eli & w, Lydia, & dt, Esther, rocf Smithfield MM, Ind., dtd 1832,5,19
1832, 7, 17. Mary rocf Miami MM, O., dtd 1832, 5,23
1834, 3, 11. Jane gct White Lick MM, Ind.
1834, 3, 11. Sarah gct White Lick MM, Ind.
1834, 3, 11. Eli & w, Lydia, & ch, Esther & John, gct White Lick MM, Ind.
1834, 3, 11. Esther & ch, Joshua, Ruth, David, Elias, Phinehas, Joel & Esther, gct White Lick MM, Ind.
1836, 12, 13. William & w, Mary, & ch, Eleanor & John D., gct Miami MM, O.
1863, 6, 20. Mary rocf White Lick MM, Ind., dtd 1863,6,10
1863, 7, 18. Mary rmt John Hadley

NEWMAN
1829, 8, 30. Mary M. b
1859, 3, 30. Asenath b
1863, 3, 17. William b
1865, 6, 15. Franklin B. b

1874, 6, 20. Mary & ch, Asenath, Benjamin F. & Wm. recrq
1893, 1, 21. William recrq

NEWPORT
1899, 2, 18. James recrq

NICHOLSON
1823, 5, 31. Abigail recrq
1823, 9, 27. Caleb Harvey Jr. gct Cesars Creek MM, O., to m Bathsheba Nicholson

NIXON
1899, 3, 18. Everette & Anna recrq

NORDYKE
----, --, --. Micajah b 1833,5,3; m Anna E. ----- b 1836,3,15
Ch: Frank H. b 1854, 1, 3
Charles M. b 1856, 1, 21
Ida M. " 1858, 8, 5
Nora E. " 1861, 3, 30

1836, 6, 14. Henry rmt Phebe Rich
1837, 3, 14. Phebe gct Clear Creek MM, O.
1869, 9, 18. Micajah & w, Ann, & ch recrq
1872, 7, 20. Micajah T. relrq
1882, 12, 16. Florence Rosetta & Anna J. recrq

ODOMS
1881, 2, 19. Charles recrq

OGBORN
1849, 9, 15. Henry M. gct Fairfield MM
1859, 6, 18. Eliza Ellis (form Ogborn) con mou
1859, 8, 20. Isaac F. gct White Water MM, Ind.
1871, 2, 18. David H. [Ogburn] & w, Sarah E., & ch, Harriett M., recrq

OGLESBEE
----, --, --. ----- m Ruth HADLEY, dt Eli & Theodocia
Ch: Anna T. b 1873, 12, 1
1876, 6, 17. Ruth & dt, Anna T., gct Center MM, O.

O'HARA
1920, 1, 2. Emma Linton d

OILER
1842, 8, 16. Margaret Ann (form Harlan) dis mou
1854, 6, 17. Margaret A. rst
1859, 6, 18. Hannah rst
1865, 4, 15. Hannah Maria [Oyler] gct Cincinnati MM, O.

OLVIS
1881, 4, 16. Clay & w, Rebecca, recrq
1882, 12, 16. Frank recrq
1884, 4, 19. Wm. & w, Edna, & ch, Willie & Laverne, rocf Miami MM, O., dtd 1884,3,26
1885, 7, 18. Eva recrq
1891, 7, 18. Wm. P. & w, Edna, & ch, Wm. H., Lovina C., Sherman & Charles M., gct Miami MM, O.
1897, 3, 20. Frank gct Center MM, O.

O'NEAL
1868, 5, 15. Mathias d ae 71 bur Lytles Creek

1848, 3, 18. Simon Hadley gct Springborough MM, O., to m Mary J. O'Neal

ORR
----, --, --. George, s S. B. & Elizabeth, b 1874,2,26; m Gertrude HARVEY, dt Nathaniel & Irena (Moon), b 1880,6,1
Ch: Harry b 1896, 8, 27
Howard " 1899, 1, 11

ORR, George & Gertrude, continued
Ch: Asa b 1901, 2, 6
Odis " 1903, 9, 27
Lalia Lucile " 1910, 7, 7
Harold N.
Hershel B.

1898, 10, 15. Gertrude gct West Fork MM, O.
1906, 3, 17. Gertrude rocf West Fork MM, O.
1907, 1, 19. George & ch, Harry, Howard W., Osee & Otis recrq
1919, 4, 19. Jesse Kirk rocf Center MM, O.
1928, 4, --. Osee relrq
1930, 9, 21. Howard W. relrq
1933, 4, 23. George & w & ch, Harold & Hershel, relrq

ORVILLE
1889, 9, 21. Emma M. gct Cincinnati MM, O.

OSBORN
----, --, --. William b 1778,8,1; m Susanna SUOTHERLY(?) b 1771,4,20
Ch: Thomas b 1800, 2, 23
John " 1801, 5, 14
Elizabeth " 1803, 2, 27
Mary " 1805, 1, 2
Peter " 1807, 3, 4
William " 1808, 12, 5
Charles " 1811, 6, 10
Margaret " 1814, 7, 25
----, --, --. ----- & -----
Ch: Thomas b 1818, 12, 18
Margaret " 1821, 4, 2
Adam " 1823, 2, 1
Peter " 1825, 7, 31
Catherine " 1827, 7, 1
Mary " 1829, 6, 26
Elisha B. " 1831, 2, 16
Margaret " 1833, 3, 20
Thomas " 1835, 3, 24
Solomon " 1838, 12, 19 d 1843, 2,20
----, --, --. Peter b 1807,3,4 d 1874,11,17 bur Lytles Creek; m Sarah HADLEY b 1806, 10,22 d 1853,8,22 bur Lytles Creek
Ch: Alfred b 1833, 1, 5
Charles " 1834, 10, 8
William H. " 1837, 12, 2
Sarah Jane " 1840, 4, 20
John Thomas " 1843, 2, 5
Ruth Ann " 1845, 3, 26
Ellwood " 1847, 9, 12
Eli " 1850, 6, 22 d 1853, 3, 6
Peter m 2nd Eliza Ann ----- b 1817,8,8
Ch: Mary E. b 1856, 7, 23
Adeline " 1858, 11, 30
----, --, --. Charles b 1811,6,10 d 1876,1,1; m Elizabeth ----- d 1864,10,28
Ch: Sarah b 1838, 10, 27
Isaiah " 1840, 3, 10 d 1851, 3,21
Mary Jane " 1842, 1, 4
Mikle W. " 1843, 9, 26
Peter b 1845, 11, 9
Carolin " 1847, 9, 28
Elizabeth " 1849, 10, 5
Charles W. " 1851, 4, 14
Calvin " 1853, 1, 15 d 1865,12,12
Lydia " 1854, 10, 13
Frank " 1856, 11, 13
Clark " 1859, 3, 26
Delphina " 1861, 10, 9
Charles m 2nd Jemima ----- b 1821,9,24
----, --, --. William Jr. b 1814,5,12; m Hannah HADLEY b 1816,1,1 d 1863,9,26
Ch: Mary E. b 1838, 10, 29 d 1860,11,10
David " 1835, 12, 17 " 1867, 9,10
William C. " 1842, 12, 12 " 1843, 4,14
Isaiah H. " 1844, 4, 15
Seth " 1848, 1, 31
1842, 5, 18. Susanna m George MOON
----, --, --. Peter b 1825,7,31; m Margaret ----- b 1833,3,30
Ch: Angeline b 1861, 3, 1
Ruth E. " 1863, 2, 7
Margaret J." 1866, 4, 3
Clark " 1869, 9, 7
1861, 10, 3. William d (an elder)
1863, 9, 26. Hannah, w William, d
----, --, --. Alfred b 1833,1,5; m Martha E. ----- b 1841,10,1
Ch: Alletta b 1864, 2, 1
Walter S. " 1866, 7, 11
Sally T. " 1868, 9, 6
Olive A. " 1870, 8, 4
Ruth J. " 1872, 2, 21 d 1874,11,21
Frank L. " 1873, 11, 14
----, --, --. William H. & Martha C.
Ch: Joseph P. b 1864, 11, 23
George Eddy" 1866, 10, 25
----, --, --. Charles Jr. b 1834,12,11; m Mary OSBORN b 1847,3,18
Ch: Leona L. b 1867, 12, 1
Eli M. " 1868, 11, 2 d 1873,5,22
Paulina J. " 1870, 1, 5
Alice C. " 1871, 8, 14
Lucy E. " 1873, 3, 17
Frederick D. b 1874, 8, 17
----, --, --. David & Eleanor
Ch: Mary Emily b 1860, 10, 4
Hettie " 1862, 9, 2 d 1864, 1, 2
1867, 4, 6. Alice A. d
1867, 8, 25. Nancy Ellen d
1867, 9, 10. David S. d
----, --, --. Peter Jr. b 1845,11,9; m Anna THATCHER b 1849,5,28
Ch: ----- b 1867, 9, 17 d 1867, 9,17
Calvin " 1869, 2, 15
Clinton L. " 1870, 11, 29
Elizabeth D. b 1875, 6, 7
----, --, --. Seth W. b 1848,1,31; m Ann E. RAYBORN b 1846,7,10
Ch: Walter D. b 1868, 2, 14

OSBORN, Seth W. & Ann E., continued
Ch: Albert W. b 1870, 12, 17
Gilbert S. " 1872, 1, 18
----, --, --. Isaiah b 1845,4,15; m ----- -----
Ch: Nettie J. b 1869, 8, 13
dt " 1870, 12, 17
----, --, --. John T. b 1843,2,5; m Maranda ----- b 1848,7,9
Ch: Eva Rosa b 1870, 8, 19

1822, 5, 26. Peter, William, Charles, Mary & Margaret, ch Wm., recrq
1822, 5, 26. Elizabeth recrq
1822, 7, 27. Elizabeth Sr. gct West Grove MM, Ind.
1827, 4, 28. Charles & w, Hannah, & ch, Narcissa, Cynthia, Gideon S., Charles N., Parker Jordan & Benjamin, rocf Smithfield MM, Ind., dtd 1827,3,27
1828, 9, 16. Lydia rocf Smithfield MM, Ind.
1829, 1, 13. Lydia rmt Eli Newlin
1829, 1, 13. Charles & w, Hannah, & ch, Narcissa, Cynthia, Gideon S., Charles N., Parker, Jordan, Benjamin & Sarah, gct Miami MM, O.
1832, 4, 17. Peter rmt Sarah Hadley
1834, 2, 11. Elizabeth rmt Hiram Maden
1835, 1, 13. Wm. Jr. rmt Hannah Hadley
1836, 3, 15. Margaret rmt Harlan Maden
1836, 10, 11. Mary rmt Mordecai Walker
1837, 11, 14. Charles gct New Garden MM, Ind., to m Catherine Fulghum
1838, 4, 17. Elizabeth rocf New Garden MM, Ind., dtd 1838,1,20
1838, 12, 11. William, Susannah, Adam, Peter, Katherine, Mary, Elisha B., Margaret & Thomas, ch Margaret, recrq
1839, 2, 12. Solomon, s Margaret, recrq
1844, 12, 17. William Jr. con mou
1845, 8, 12. Eliza rocf Newberry MM, O., dtd 1845,6,18
1846, 4, 14. William & w, Eliza, & dt, Mary Ann, gct Newberry MM, O.
1846, 7, 14. Margaret rmt Elias Marsh
1846, 12, 19. Mary, Margaret & Thomas, ch Margaret Marsh, rocf Walnut Ridge MM, Ind.
1846, 12, 19. Catherine gct Walnut Ridge MM, Ind.
1847, 1, 16. Adam dis mou
1852, 5, 15. Elisha dis disunity
1854, 2, 18. Margaret rocf Walnut Ridge MM, Ind.
1854, 8, 19. Adam rst
1855, 8, 18. Peter gct Blue River MM, Ind., to m Eliza Ann Trueblood
1855, 9, 15. Peter Jr. dis mou
1856, 1, 19. Eliza Ann & s, Charles Trueblood, rocf Blue River MM, Ind., dtd 1856,1,5
1856, 6, 21. Abigail recrq
1860, 1, 21. Mary Emily McCray (form Osborn) con mou
1860, 1, 21. David S. con mou
1860, 4, 21. Nancy Ellen recrq
1860, 12, 15. Peter Jr. recrq
1861, 5, 18. Martha P. & ch, Mary R., Unice M., Martha J., Peter A., Elisha B., Eliza D. & Amanda M., recrq
1861, 5, 18. Elizabeth rocf Center MM, O., dtd 1860,12,12
1861, 8, 17. William rocf Newberry MM, O., dtd 1861,6,17
1861, 8, 17. Mary Ann, Margaret, Samantha, Hannah, Elnora & Martha Jane, ch Wm., rocf Newberry MM, O., dtd 1861,6,17
1861, 9, 21. Eliza rst on consent of Newberry MM, O.
1862, 8, 15. Sarah Ellen Howel (form Osborn) con mou
1862, 9, 20. Mary Jane Andrew (form Osborn) con mou
1862, 11, 16. Alfred rmt Martha Emily Stanton
1862, 11, 15. Sarah Jane rmt Wm. H. Walker
1863, 10, 17. William N. rmt Martha Coate
1864, 4, 16. Peter Jr. & w, Elizabeth, & ch, Angelkne & Ruth Ellen, gct Center MM, O.
1865, 1, 21. Margaret gct New Garden MM, Ind.
1865, 12, 16. Charles gct New Garden MM, Ind., to m Jemima Clark
1866, 2, 17. Ann rocf Dover MM, dtd 1866,1, 18
1866, 2, 17. Ann rocf Dover MM, O., dtd 1866, 1,18
1866, 4, 21. Jemimah & ch, Elwood, Alvin, Lindley & Cassius Clark, rocf New Garden MM, Ind., dtd 1860,3,17
1867, 4, 20. Annie J. (form Thatcher) con mou
1867, 5, 18. Mary Ann Moorman (form Osborn) dis mou
1867, 5, 18. Peter Jr. con mou
1867, 5, 18. Margaret Wolf (form Osborn) con mou
1867, 5, 18. Charles Jr. con mou
1867, 5, 18. Samantha B. Moon (form Osborn) con mou
1867, 6, 15. Adam con mou
1867, 8, 17. William & w, Eliza, & ch, Hannah, Elnora, Martha & Anna C., gct Newberry MM, O.
1868, 1, 18. Mary R. con mou
1868, 1, 18. Isaiah con mou & military service
1868, 1, 18. Seth con mou & military service
1868, 10, 17. Ruth Ann Smith (form Osborn) con mou
1869, 12, 18. John T. con mou
1871, 2, 18. Ann Eliza recrq
1871, 2, 18. Maranda recrq
1873, 7, 19. Wm. & w, Eliza, & ch, Elnor, Anna C. & Jesse Wm., rocf Newberry MM, O., dtd 1873,6,23
1874, 5, 16. Stephen & w, Lydia A., recrq
1875, 12, 18. Peter & w, Elizabeth, & ch, Angeline, Ruth Ellen, Margaret Jane & Clark, rocf Center MM, O., dtd 1875,12,15
1876, 8, 19. William & w, Eliza, & ch, Anna

OSBORN, continued
C. & Jesse Wm., gct Hopewell MM, O.
1880, 3, 20. Peter A. gct Deer Creek MM, Ind.
1880, 9, 18. Martha J. gct Oak Ridge MM, Ind.
1882, 11, 18. Lida T. & ch, Vannette J., Fay H. & Floyd I., recrq
1883, 1, 20. Eva M. & dt, Maud H., recrq
1883, 11, 17. Isaiah H. & w, Lida T., & ch, Fay H., Vannetta J. & Floyd I., gct Union MM, Mo.
1883, 11, 18. Wm. H. & w, Martha E., & ch, Joseph & Edwin, gct Center MM, O.
1886, 3, 20. Effa A. recrq
1889, 12, 21. Alfred & w, Martha E., & s, Frank gct Newberry MM, O.
1890, 10, 18. Isaiah H. & w, Lida T., & ch, Fay, Floyd & Randall, gct Des Moines MM, Ia.
1890, 10, 18. Vanette gct Des Moins MM, Ia.
1891, 9, 19. Elwood & w, Effie E., gct Wilmington MM, O.
1893, 1, 21. I. H. & fam rocf Des Moines MM, Ia.
1894, 6, 16. J. T. gct West Fork MM, O.
1894, 6, 16. Maranda gct West Fork MM, O.
1895, 7, 20. Alletta gct West Fork MM, O.
1895, 7, 20. Ollie gct West Fork MM, O.
1895, 7, 20. Sallie gct West Fork MM, O.
1896, 4, 18. Seth W. & w, Ann, Eliza & ch, Walter Albert & Gilbert, gct Columbus MM, O.
1897, 8, 14. Pauline gct Indianapolis MM, Ind.
1920, 4, 17. Frank dropped from mbrp

OUTLAND
1891, 7, 18. Nora (form Hadley) gct Goshen MM, O.

PAINTER
1851, 6, 21. Cert rec for Thomas from West Union MM, Ind., dtd 1851,3,10, end to Dover MM, O.

PATTERSON
1828, 3, 29. Sarah Minor (form Patterson) dis mou

PATTON
1871, 2, 18. John recrq

PEDRICK
1858, 10, 16. Elwood Hadley gct White Water MM, Ind., to m Ann Pedrick

PEEBLES
1840, 11, 17. Elihu rmt Mary Ann Rawls
1843, 4, 11. Elihu & w, Mary Ann, & dt, Sarah Ann, gct Springborough MM, O.

PENNINGTON
1882, 12, 16. Stephen P. recrq
1882, 12, 16. Nora recrq
1891, 8, 15. Nora gct Center MM, O.

PERDUE
1822, 4, 27. Jemima gct Fairfield MM

PEYTON
1831, 6, 14. Mary rocf Hopewell MM, Va., dtd 1831,4,6
1842, 10, 11. Mary gct Vermillion MM, Ill.

PHILIPS
1906, 7, 21. Kate Bailey relrq

PIER
1883, 5, 19. George F. & w, Frances, rocf Van Wert MM, O., dtd 1883,4,28
1884, 5, 17. Geo. & w, Frankie, gct Cesars Creek MM, O.

PIERCE
1819, 2, 27. Richard rmt Mary Fallis
1827, 7, 28. Richard [Peirce] & w, Mary, & ch, Mariam, John & James, attached to Center MM, O.

PIKE
1848, 5, 20. Deborah gct Mississinewa MM, Ind.

PLUMMER
1833, 8, 13. Mahala rocf Fairfield MM, O., dtd 1833,7,25
1834, 10, 14. Mahala rmt John Harvey

POND
1876, 7, 15. David & w, Ellenor, rocf Newberry MM, O., dtd 1876,5,22
1877, 3, 17. Jennie recrq
1877, 3, 17. Rosa Ellen recrq
1877, 3, 17. Nancy J. recrq
1878, 7, 20. Phebe A. & ch, Zenas I. & Annie E., recrq
1878, 10, 19. Levi rocf Newberry MM, O., dtd 1878,4,22

PRAY
1852, 4, 17. Enos & w, Elvira, & ch, William S., Elizabeth M., Martha H., Rachel, Sybil J., Ruth J., Joseph & Anna Maria, rocf West Branch MM, O., dtd 1852,4,15
1857, 3, 21. Enos G. & w, Elvira, & ch, Martha, Rachel, Sybil J., Rhoda J., Joseph J., Anna Mariah, Samuel Dilwin & Enos Edwin, gct Milford MM, Ind.
1847, 3, 21. Wm. S. gct Milford MM, Ind.
1857, 3, 21. Elizabeth M. gct Milford MM, Ind.
1880, 5, 15. Nida & Mark recrq
1880, 5, 15. Mattie recrq

PRICE
1823, 4, 26. Samuel rocf Miami MM, O., dtd 1822,12,25
1887, 12, 17. Elijah & w rocf Clear Creek MM, O., dtd 1887,12,12

PRICE, continued
1921, 1, 30. Mildred Early relrq

PRINGLE
1883, 11, 17. Susan J. recrq

PRITCHARD
----, --, --. Calvin W. & Anna M. b 1837,4,14
Ch: William H. b 1866, 11, 14

1863, 12, 19. Calvin W. rmt Anna M. Pyle
1864, 2, 20. Anna gct Blue River MM, Ind.
1866, 6, 16. Calvin W. & w, Anna M., rocf Blue River MM, Ind., dtd 1866,6,9
1868, 9, 19. Calvin W. & w, Anna M., & s, Wm., gct Wilmington MM, O.

PROBASCO
----, --, --. William m Anna REED
Ch: Charles D. b 1893, 8, 20
Robert M. " 1895, 9, 20
William A. " 1900, 2, 2
Mary Lucile" 1904, 8, 21
----, --, --. Robert M. m Myra HARVEY, dt Jesse & Carrie H., b 1897,2,7
Ch: Harold R. b 1921, 6, 22
Raymond H. " 1924, 7, 31
Mary Catherine " 1929, 3, 31

1891, 9, 19. Mary Anna gct Wilmington MM, O.
1909, 10, 16. Charles Donald, Robert M., Wm. Arthur & Mary Lucile, ch W. H., recrq
1910, 7, 16. Nina recrq
1928, 4, --. Don & fam gct Dover MM, O.
1929, 7, 21. Wm. Arthur relrq

PRYOL
1877, 4, 21. Jeremiah recrq
1881, 3, 19. Jeremiah dis

PURSLER
1897, 3, 20. Rebecca Mary gct South Wabash MM, Ind.

PYLE
----, --, --. William b 1788,3,11 d 1875,7,20 bur Clarksville; m Mary HADLEY b 1792,7,27 d 1848,2,7
Ch: Samuel b 1812, 9, 22
Jehu " 1814, 9, 8
Mary " 1816, 11, 22
Ruth " 1819, 5, 16
John " 1822, 11, 21
David " 1825, 1, 16
Sarah " 1827, 11, 9
William " 1830, 2, 3
Ann Maria " 1837, 4, 14
----, --, --. Jehu b 1795,12,25 d 1859,1,29; m Esther STRATTON b 1804,2,4 d 1897,10,26
Ch: Joseph b 1822, 7, 16 d 1824, 6, 8
William " 1822, 7, 16
David S. " 1824, 8, 27
Abigail b 1826, 5, 24 d 1835,10,10
Caleb " 1828, 12, 17 " 1837, 3, 1
Nancy " 1831, 1, 27 " 1837, 3,16
Lindley " 1832, 12, 7 " 1837, 3, 8
Emily " 1835, 8, 28
Mary " 1837, 10, 10 " 1842,11, 1
John " 1840, 7, 29 " 1856, 4,17
Malinda " 1843, 11, 22
----, --, --. Rebecca, dt Wm. & Anna Garner, b 1823,10,1 d 1916,3,23 bur Springfield
----, --, --. Jehu b 1814,9,8; m Louise CARTER b 1817,12,5
Ch: Ruth b 1837, 8, 15
Samuel " 1840, 3, 22
Meriam " 1843, 4, 17
----, --, --. David & Sarah
Ch: Joseph S. b 1848, 2, 23
Abijah H. " 1854, 5, 7
Mary E. " 1862, 11, 15
----, --, --. David S. m Sarah T. ----- d 1856,11,3 bur Clarksville
Ch: Allen H. b 1849, 8, 27
Thomas Henry " 1851, 3, 21 d 1869,12, 5 bur St. George, Kans.
Esther Jane b 1852, 12, 20 d 1853, 9,30 bur Clarksville
Tamer Anna b 1854, 11, 13 " 1878, 3,24 bur Springfield
Mary Emily b 1856, 9, 28
David S. m 2nd Nancy T. -----
Ch: Sarah Malinda b 1862, 6, 20
Esther " 1864, 1, 8
Rachel " 1865, 9, 18
----, --, --. Thomas, s Samuel & Isabella, b 1848,9,5 d 1907,5,4 bur Springfield; m Olive HARLAN, dt John & Elizabeth, b 1850, 10,4 d 1925,2,18 bur Springfield
Ch: Albert b 1877, 3, 6 d 1931,10, 2
Woodrow " 1879, 10, 28
Charley " 1870, 6, 26
----, --, --. Charley, s Thos. & Olive (Harlan), b 1870,6,26; m Minnie M. GRAHAM, dt Davis & Mary, b 1870,3,2
Ch: Ada Laura b 1890, 10, 13
Howard O. " 1893, 11, 13
Graham " 1896, 3, 25
Irena " 1898, 5, 27
Martha " 1901, 8, 22

1820, 4, 29. Esther (form Stratton) con mou
1822, 2, 25. Jehu Jr. recrq
1836, 11, 15. Jehu rmt Louisa Carter
1836, 11, 15. Mary Austin (form Pyle) con mou
1838, 4, 17. Samuel dis mou
1839, 6, 11. Ruth rmt Israel Hawkins
1845, 2, 11. Jehu & w, Abigail, recrq
1845, 4, 15. John gct Miami MM, O., to m Mary Ann Burnet
1845, 6, 17. Wm. gct Newberry MM, O., to m Rebecca Garner

PYLE, continued
1846, 1, 13. Mary Ann rocf Miami MM, O., dtd 1845,11,26
1846, 6, 16. Rebecca rocf Newberry MM, O., dtd 1846,4,13
1847, 2, 20. David gct Miami MM, O., to m Esther Stedom
1847, 5, 15. Wm. Jr. & w, Rebecca, & dt, Esther Ann, gct Newberry MM, O.
1847, 10, 16. Esther S. rocf Miami MM, O., dtd 1847,7,21.
1848, 8, 19. David S. gct Dover MM, O., to m Sarah T. West
1849, 10, 20. Sarah T. rocf Dover MM, dtd 1849,8,16
1851, 5, 17. William rmt Lydia Smith
1851, 10, 18. William & w, Rebecca, & s, Jehu Evan, rocf Newberry MM, O., dtd 1851,9,15
1852, 6, 19. Wm. T. rmt Mary T. Carpenter
1852, 9, 18. Sarah rmt Moses Steddom
1854, 7, 15. David S. & w, Sarah T., & ch, Allen H. & Thomas Henry, gct Dover MM
1856, 6, 21. John & w, Mary Ann, gct West Grove MM, Ia.
1856, 12, 20. David & w, Esther, & ch, Joseph & Abijah, gct Miami MM, O.
1858, 3, 20. Wm. L. & w, Mary T., & ch, Charles C. & Marietta, gct White Water MM, Ind.
1858, 5, 15. David & w, Esther S., & ch, Joseph S. & Abijah, rocf Miami MM, O., dtd 1858,3,23
1860, 1, 21. Wm. Jr. & w, Rebecca, & ch, Jehu Evan, David Lindley & John Wm., gct West Union MM, Ind.
1860, 5, 19. David S. & ch, Allen H., Thomas Henry & Thamer Ann, rocf Dover MM, dtd 1860,4,13
1860, 7, 21. Emily Newby (form Pyle) con mou
1861, 1, 19. William L. & w, Mary, & ch, Charles C. & Marietta, rocf White Water MM, Ind., dtd 1860,12,26
1861, 2, 16. Jehu H. & w, Louisa, & ch, Samuel W., Miriam C., Mary Ann, Abraham, George C. & Louiza, gct New Garden MM, Ind.
1861, 2, 16. David S. con mou
1861, 2, 16. Ruth gct New Garden MM
1862, 2, 15. Nancy J. rocf Fairfield MM, dtd 1862,1,18
1863, 4, 18. William L. & w, Mary T., & ch, Chas. C., Marietta & Anna C., gct Bridgport MM, Ind.
1865, 4, 15. David S. & w, Nancy F., & ch, Allen H., Thomas Henry, Tamar Ann, Sarah Malinda & Esther, gct Oak Ridge MM, Ind.
1865, 12, 16. Geo. Madden Jr. gct New Garden MM, Ind., to m Ruth Pyle
1866, 6, 16. Melinda Snowden (form Pyle) con mou
1868, 4, 18. David & w, Esther, & ch, Joseph, Abijah H. & Mary C., gct White Water MM, Ind.
1871, 3, 18. Wm. & w, Rebecca, & ch, John Evan, David Lindley, John Wm., Joseph Luther & Mary Abigail, rocf West Union MM, Ind., dtd 1871,2,6
1872, 4, 20. Mary recrq
1872, 8, 17. Wm. & w, Lydia, gct Indianapolis MM, Ind.
1873, 5, 17. David S. & w, Nancy T., & ch rocf Clear Creek MM, O., dtd 1873,4,12
1873, 5, 17. Tamar Ann rocf Clear Creek MM, O., dtd 1873,4,12
1881, 5, 21. Thomas & w, Olive, & ch, Chas. W., Albert C., Woodrow B. & Alfred C., recrq
1883, 12, 15. David S. dis disunity
1884, 12, 20. Wm. relrq
1885, 2, 21. Wm. recrq
1888, 1, 21. A. C. & w, Emma, & s, Walter, gct Wilmington MM, O.
1891, 11, 21. J. E. & w, Mary P., relrq
1893, 8, 12. Rachel J. relrq
1891, 6, 20. Sarah Emily (form Andrews) relrq
1891, 11, 21. Evan & w, Mary, relrq
1925, 7, 19. Charles & w dropped from mbrp
1926, 6, 20. Omar dropped from mbrp
1926, 6, 20. Graham dropped from mbrp
1926, 6, 20. Martha dropped from mbrp
1926, 6, 20. Irene dropped from mbrp

QUINBY
1840, 4, 14. Elizabeth & ch, Aaron B., Jesaphine E., Thos. M., Miriam E., Ezra A. & Mercy Ann, rocf Center MM, O., dtd 1840, 1,15
1847, 1, 16. Aaron dis mou
1853, 1, 15. Thomas M. con mou
1857, 6, 20. Miriam Beaver (form Quinby) dis mou
1858, 6, 19. Josephine E. Washburn (form Quinby) con mou

RAYBURN
----, --, --. Samuel [Rayborn] b 1814,3,2; m Susannah ----- b 1821,3,2
Ch: Laura B. b 1853, 11, 19
James " 1842, 2, 5

1842, 10, 11. Susannah [Raburn] dis mou
1868, 9, 19. Susanna [Raburn] recrq
1871, 2, 18. Samuel & ch, Laura B. & James W., recrq
1897, 4, 17. Samuel & w, Susanna, gct Columbus MM, O.
1897, 4, 17. James W. gct Columbus MM, O.

RANDALL
1880, 3, 20. Wm. S. B. & w, Mary, recrq
1880, 5, 16. Charles & Sarah recrq
1880, 5, 15. Alverdie recrq
1883, 11, 17. John D. & Mary recrq
1894, 2, 17. John & w gct Newberry MM, O.

RAWLES
1840, 5, 12. Burwell & w, Sarah, & ch, Micajah, Michael, Jonathan, Elizabeth, William, Esther, Jesse, John & Sarah Jane, rocf Dover MM, O., dtd 1840,4,16
1840, 5, 12. Mary Ann rocf Dover MM, O., dtd 1840,4,16
1840, 11, 17. Mary Ann rmt Elihu Peebles
1843, 12, 12. Burwell [Rawls] & w, Sarah, & ch, Jonathan, Elizabeth, Esther, John, Jesse & Sarah Jane, gct Center MM, O.
1844, 2, 13. Michel [Rawls] gct Center MM, O.

REAMS
1908, 12, 4. Mary Louise, w Gleen Maurise, dt Earl & Gertrude Sise, b (G)

1930, 3, 5. Glenn M. rocf Goshen MM (G)

REDDICK
1869, 3, 20. Phebe (form Spray) con mou

REDFERN
1918, 4, 20. Emma H. dropped from mbrp

REED
1861, 2, 2. Emma, dt Mary A. Stillings, b

1881, 5, 21. Maggie B. recrq

REEDER
1919, 10, 21. Martha d

1894, 3, 14. Martha J. & s, Harvey W., recrq
1908, 6, 20. Ethel Grim rocf Fairfield MM

RENDLES
1876, 5, 20. Jane recrq

RENNER
----, --, --. E. Marshall, s Gilman & Mahala G., b 1860,11,2; m Alice H. HALE, dt Alfred & Rachel (Hadley), b 1865,12,5
Ch: Clarence b 1893, 6, 10
Robert " 1897, 7, 17

1896, 2, 15. Marshall recrq
1901, 1, 19. Marshall & Allie recrq
1915, 4, 17. Marshall & w, Alice, & s, Robert, gct Wilmington MM, O.
1915, 4, 17. Clarence H. gct Wilmington MM,O.

REYNARD
1822, 3, 30. Jacob rmt Elizabeth Sheridan
1822, 4, 27. Jacob & w gct West Grove MM, Ind.
1823, 3, 29. Lydia rmt Samuel Griffin
1825, 5, 28. Catherine rmt Job Simcock
1830, 6, 15. Adam dis mou
1834, 11, 11. Adam Jr. rst at White River MM on consent of this mtg
1835, 9, 15. Joel dis mou
1837, 7, 11. Asa dis disunity

RICH
----, --, --. Thomas b 1785,7,4 d 1872,3,14; m Ann BALLARD b 1783,4,4 d 1839,1,9
Ch: Edith b 1811, 11, 22
Phebe " 1813, 11, 26
Bartley " 1815, 3, 15
1860, 7, 14. Isabella d ae 65y 9m 5d (an elder)

1830, 1, 12. Edith & Phebe, ch Thos. & Ann, recrq
1836, 6, 14. Phebe rmt Henry Nordyke
1841, 4, 13. Thomas gct Center MM, to m Isabella Adset
1841, 7, 13. Isabela rocf Centre MM, O., dtd 1841,6,16
1846, 1, 13. Robert B. dis mou
1862, 5, 17. Isabella Ann, Thomas, Elizabeth C., Robert B., Jemima R. & Mary Emily, ch Mary Ann, recrq
1865, 8, 19. Isabel Ann Moore (form Rich) con mou
1868, 8, 15. Mary Ann Bean (form Rich) con mou
1871, 6, 17. Thomas gct Clear Creek MM, O.
1879, 1, 18. Thomas P. gct Pipe Creek MM, Ind.

RICHARDSON
1866, 9, 15. John W. & ch, Henry T., Henrietta M., Sarah E., Alvin T. M. & Mary C., recrq
1869, 7, 17. John W. & ch, Henry, Henriette, Sarah, Esther, Oliver & Mary Clarinda, gct Center MM, O.
1876, 11, 18. Henrietta M. & Sarah Esther, gct Clear Creek MM, O.
1896, 2, 15. Anthony recrq
1904, 3, 19. R. Edna relrq
1904, 12, 17. Anthony & w, Amanda, & dt, Lizzie, gct Wilmington MM, O.

RILEY
1874, 1, 17. William S. & w, Sarah Jane, & s, Charles, recrq

ROADS
1894, 10, 20. Edith recrq

ROCKHILL
1827, 5, 26. Elizabeth gct Centre MM, O.
1896, 2, 15. Millie gct Wilmington MM, O.

ROSENBERGER
1923, 9, 16. Alonzo A. recrq

ROUSH
1933, 5, 4. Ruth Elizabeth relrq (G)

RUBLE
1819, 9, 25. Henry dis mou
1820, 4, 20. William dis mou
1820, 8, 26. Rachel Wright (form Ruble) dis

RUBLE, continued
mou
1826, 1, 28. Samuel & w, Rachel, & s, Levitt, gct White River MM, Ind.

RUSSELL
----, --, --. Samuel E., s Samuel B. & Emily, b 1890,9,26; m Mildred Grace HORMELL, dt Clarence & Lelia, b 1895,7,9
Ch: Frieda
Emily b 1915, 9, 8
Mary Ellen " 1918, 3, 24

1925, 11, 22. Samuel E. & Mildred recrq
1925, 11, 22. Freda Emly recrq
1927, 1, 23. Samuel E. & fam relrq

RYAN
1829, 9, 11. Margaret dis jH

SABIN
1828, 6, 24. Lydia (form Harlan) dis mou
1909, 9, 18. George & w, Mary, & dt, Ola, rocf Center MM, O., dtd 1909,7,14
1915, 11, 20. George W. gct Dayton MM, O.

SARVER
1926, 12, 27. Ruby rocf Wilmington MM, O.
1926, 12, 27. Hazel & Viola recrq

SCALES
1880, 5, 16. Joseph recrq
1880, 5, 16. Naomi recrq
1881, 2, 19. Georgenie & Martha, ch Ruth, recrq

SCHOOLEY
1840, 5, 8. Nelson b

1819, 3, 27. John & fam gct Newgarden MM, Ind.
1820, 11, 26. Nathan & fam gct Centre MM
1820, 12, 30. Benjamin & w, Rebecca, & ch, gct New Garden MM, Ind.
1848, 5, 20. Isaac rmt Deborah L. Harvey
1852, 5, 15. Isaac [Schooly] rocf Center MM, O., dtd 1852,2,18
1872, 10, 19. Marshall dis mou
1872, 10, 19. Isaac & w, Deborah, & ch, Anna M., Elizabeth C., Charles S., Elmer E. & Frank Wilber, gct Milford MM, Ind.
1874, 4, 18. Nelson [Schooly] recrq

SCOTT
1881, 2, 19. Quincy & Walter, ch Hannah A., recrq
1881, 11, 19. Susan rocf Wilmington MM, O.
1889, 4, 20. Frank recrq

SEARS
1924, 12, 28. Arthur & w, Anne, & ch, Mildred, Florence, Frances Lucile & Harry, rocf Flat Fork MM

SEIGLER
1909, 3, 20. Harry dropped from mbrp

SETTLES
1898, 1, 15. Cert rec for Minnie from Miami MM, O., end to Ogden MM, O.
1899, 3, 18. Amizer & w, Eliza, & ch, Archie, Kelsie & Cora recrq
1899, 4, 15. Mary recrq

SETTY
1930, 1, 2. Ann recrq (G)

SEVERS
1912, 5, 3. Margaret d

1877, 3, 17. George W. [Sever] & w, Massie, recrq
1897, 1, 16. George L. [Sever] & w, Minnie, relrq
1911, 9, 16. George L. [Seavers] & w, Margaret, recrq
1912, 12, 21. George gct Wilmington MM, O.

SEWELL
1871, 9, 16. Martha recrq
1873, 1, 18. Martha L. Garner (form Sewell) con mou

SEWARD
1881, 4, 16. Joseph recrq

SHANER
1914, 12, 19. Mary Elizabeth & Stella May, ch Lewis & Myrtle, recrq
1920, 4, 17. Mary E. & Stella May dropped from mbrp

SHANK
1923, 7, 16. Samuel, s James & Martha C., d bur Clarksville

1874, 5, 16. Jacob D. & w, Sarah E., & ch, Mary Alfretta, Joseph H. & Leonard, recrq
1874, 5, 16. George H. recrq
1874, 5, 16. Mary M. recrq
1876, 5, 20. Lucian, step s John Stump, recrq
1876, 6, 17. Florence M. recrq
1877, 7, 21. George H. gct Miami MM, O.
1882, 4, 15. George Henry rocf Miami MM, O., dtd 1882,3,22
1886, 4, 17. George H. relrq
1891, 2, 21. Lucius relrq
1894, 6, 16. Jacob & w, Sarah, & ch gct West Fork MM, O.
1894, 6, 16. Joseph E. relrq
1901, 4, 20. Samuel, Mary A., Earl, Murrell, Raymond & Arthur transferred to Ogden MM, O.
1915, 1, 16. E. Ray rocf Ogden MM, O.
1918, 5, 18. Samuel & w, Mary, & ch, Earl, Muriel & Leo, rocf Ogden MM, O.
1924, 3, 16. Marie relrq

SHANK, continued
1925, 3, 22. Leo relrq
1926, 6, 20. Ray dropped from mbrp

SHANNON
1891, 1, 17. Ada relrq

SHARP
1874, 5, 16. Elizabeth recrq
1892, 10, 15. Dellie rocf Center MM, O.
1894, 3, 14. Laura & fam recrq

SHAVER
1852, 11, 20. Ruth (form Lundy) dis mou

SHAW
1881, 8, 11. Mary Belle, w Rufus, dt James & Annie Elizabeth Fergusson, b (G)

SHAWHORN
1891, 1, 17. Adie relrq

SHEPHERD
----, --, --. William W. b 1821,3,20; m Elizabeth ----- b 1829,9,10

1834, 11, 11. Jesse & w, Elizabeth, & ch, Susannah, Martha, Hannah, Jacob, Amaziah, Edith, Thomas & Allen, rocf Centre MM, O., dtd 1834,8,13
1836, 8, 16. Jessy & w, Elizabeth, & ch, Martha, Hannah, Jacob, Amaziah, Edith, Thomas & Allen, gct Miami MM, O.
1836, 11, 15. Susanna gct Miami MM, O.
1839, 10, 15. George Grimes gct Miami MM, O., to m Susanna Shepherd
1871, 2, 18. William W. & w, Elizabeth A., recrq
1874, 1, 17. William W. recrq
1883, 1, 20. Wm. W. [Sheppard] & w, Elizabeth gct Wilmington MM, O.

SHERIDAN
1822, 3, 30. Elizabeth rmt Jacob Reynard
1822, 4, 27. John & fam gct West Grove MM, Ind.

SHIDAKER
----, --, --. Mary E., dt J. W. & Eliza (Moon) Slack, b 1850,7,16 d 1927,3,21 bur Miami

1907, 5, 18. Mary E. recrq

SHIELDS
1844, 12, 17. Pheriba (form Hunt) dis mou

SHOEMAKER
----, --, --. George b 1825,2,21; m Elizabeth ----- b 1833,6,10
Ch: Amos D. b 1857, 3, 3
Raymond W. " 1859, 3, 27
Emerson W. " 1860, 11, 22
John E. " 1864, 1, 18
Henry M. b 1865, 4, 16
Edward E. " 1866, 4, 17

1871, 11, 18. George & w,, Elizabeth, & ch, Amos D., Raymon W., Emmerson W., John Elmer, Henry M. & Edward, recrq
1882, 3, 18. Elizabeth relrq
1887, 2, 19. Amos D. gct West Grove MM, Ind.

SIMCOCK
1823, 10, 25. Job recrq
1825, 5, 28. Job rmt Catherine Reynard
1837, 5, 16. Job rmt Hannah Holliday
1840, 1, 14. Job & w, Hannah, & ch, Lydia, John Stover, Martha Jane, Thomas & Susanna, gct Newberry MM, O

SIMONS
1850, 10, 19. Eleanor (form Longshore) con mou
1851, 2, 15. Eleanor gct White Water MM, Ind.
1893, 1, 21. Henley recrq

SKINNER
1901, 4, 20. Lura M. transferred to Ogden MM, O.

SLY
1881, 4, 16. Benjamin F. & w, Mollie, & ch, Minnie May, Edie R., Jacob S., Willie H., Ulysses S. & Carle C. recrq

SMITH
----, --, --. Henry b 1829,4,15; m Emma ----- b 1837,10,7
Ch: Minnie b 1860, 4, 26
John H. " 1874, 8, 15
----, --, --. Joseph H. b 1842,4,27; m Ruth A. OSBORN b 1845,3,26
Ch: Lizzie M. b 1869, 5, 7
----, --, --. Alfred, s Edward & Jane (Collins), b 1849,3,25 d 1920,5,9; m Calista Emiline BOGAN, dt John & Harriet (Gray), b 1853,2,24 d 1929,11,10
Ch: Lizzie May b 1895, 12, 14 d 1909, 1,23 bur Clarksville
1915, 11, 8. Irena d

1822, 2, 23. Ann gct West Grove MM, Ind.
1828, 11, 11. Mary & ch, Sarah, Mary & Eri rocf Smithfield MM, N. C., dtd 1827,11,14 endorsed by Duck Creek MM, Ind.
1833, 10, 15. Sarah rmt John B. Carter
1835, 5, 12. Eri dis disunity
1837, 1, 17. Mary Andrew (form Smith) dis mou
1837, 10, 17. John, Rachel, Deborah & Thomas, ch Thomas, rocf Centre MM, O., dtd 1837,4, 12
1838, 12, 11. Rachel Whitaker (form Smith) dis mou
1839, 6, 11. Mary gct Newberry MM, O.
1839, 12, 17. John dis disunity
1845, 9, 16. Deborah Clipard (form Smith)

SMITH, continued
dis mou
1845, 12, 16. James rmt Lydia Hadley
1846, 2, 17. Lydia gct Miami MM, O.
1846, 9, 19. Sarah B. (form Lundy) dis mou
1850, 7, 20. Lydia & dt, Lydia Ann, rocf Miami MM, O., dtd 1850,6,26
1850, 12, 21. Samuel H. Hadley gct Green Plain MM, O., to m Ruth Smith
1851, 5, 17. Lydia rmt Wm. Pyle
1857, 11, 21. Mary M. dis mou
1860, 1, 21. Lydia (form Kirk) con mou
1867, 7, 20. Elizabeth recrq
1868, 9, 19. Lydia Ann Maverty (form Smith) gct Kokomo MM, Ind.
1868, 10, 17. Ruth Ann (form Osborn) con mou
1871, 2, 18. Joseph H. recrq
1872, 4, 20. Henry recrq
1874, 1, 17. Emily & dt, Minnie, recrq
1876, 4, 15. Daniel & w, Ann, recrq
1876, 4, 15. James recrq
1888, 3, 17. Henry & w, Emily, relrq
1888, 6, 16. Ellen rocf Center MM, O., dtd 1888,5,16
1889, 4, 20. Alfred & Calista recrq
1891, 6, 20. Alfred E. recrq
1891, 11, 21. Lizzie & ch, Theodore & Mable, rocf Vandalia MM, Mich., dtd 1891,11,14
1892, 7, 16. Elizabeth Douglas (form Smith) & ch, Harriet E., Thomas J., Chas. A. & Edward S. Smith, relrq
1893, 3, 18. Catharine Emeline recrq
1896, 2, 15. Charles W. & w recrq
1896, 3, 21. Clyde recrq
1896, 10, 17. James E. & fam gct Wilmington MM, O.
1898, 6, 23. Charles dis
1915, 4, 17. Wm. H. & w, Irene, & s, Clarence, rocf Center MM, O.
1919, 2, 15. Anora Fitzpatrick relrq

SNODGRASS
1881, 2, 19. Jacob recrq

SNOOK
1889, 4, 20. Nathan K. & Edward recrq

SNOWDEN
1815, 5, 20. William H. b
1819, 11, 13. Lydia b
----, --, --. Robert, s Wm. & Lydia M. (Carter), b 1841,6,21; m Malinda PYLE, dt Jehu & Esther, b 1843,11,22
Ch: William J. b 1868, 2, 28
Ester Anna " 1876, 10, 21

1866, 6, 16. Melinda (form Pyle) con mou
1874, 1, 17. Robert P. recrq
1874, 1, 17. Wm. H. & w, Lydia, recrq
1881, 5, 21. M. P. recrq
1901, 1, 19. Malinda P. recrq
1921, 2, 19. Robert P. & w, Malinda P., gct Wilmington MM, O.
1921, 2, 19. William J. gct Wilmington MM,O.
1921, 2, 19. Esther Anna gct Wilmington MM,O.

SPENCER
----, --, --. Franklin m Jane C. ----- b 1819,5,13
Ch: Mary R. b 1853, 11, 23
Strickland " 1855, 1, 6
Leigh Thomas " 1858, 1, 7
----, --, --. John K. b 1831,6,26; m Priscilla ----- b 1831,1,25
Ch: Mary E. b 1855, 9, 29
Thomas R. " 1857, 4, 6
John K. " 1859, 4, 26
Sarah E. " 1861, 7, 7 d 1862, 8,13
Francis " 1863, 6, 29
Russell S. " 1865, 3, 4

1856, 9, 20. Franklin recrq
1866, 3, 17. John K. & w, Priscilla, & ch, Mary E., Thomas R., John K., Frances & Russel T. recrq
1869, 7, 17. John K. & w, Priscilla, & ch, Mary E., Thomas R. J. K., Francis, Russell T. & Caroline, gct Miami MM, O.
1871, 2, 18. Jane Caroline & ch, Mary R., Strickland & Leigh Thomas, recrq
1877, 1, 20. Strickland gct Hardshaw East MM, Eng.
1888, 2, 18. Leigh Thomas gct Preston MM, Eng. Lancashire; this cert returned for mou
1890, 3, 15. Mary R. gct Hardshaw MM, Eng.
1892, 2, 20. Leigh Thomas gct Hardshaw MM, Eng.
1892, 2, 20. Caroline J. gct Hardshaw MM, Eng.
1892, 2, 20. Mary R. gct Hardshaw MM, Eng.

SPRAY
1823, 12, 24. Rebecca b
----, --, --. Isaac & -----
Ch: Phebe J. b 1847, 10, 9
Sammie L. " 1854, 5, 5
Mary F. " 1854, 5, 5
Ada May " 1856, 7, 14
John C. " 1858, 4, 26
Hannah A. " 1860, 3, 5
Catharine C. b 1862, 9, 8

1864, 5, 21. James & w, Charity, rocf Cesars Creek MM, O., dtd 1864,2,25
1865, 5, 19. Rebecca & ch, Phebe, Samuel Lawrence, Mary Florence, Ida May, John C., Hannah Ann & Catherine C., recrq
1869, 3, 20. Phebe Reddick (form Spray) con mou
1870, 6, 18. Isaac recrq

SROUFE
1862, 8, 8. George Delbert, s Andrew &

SROUFE, continued
Edith, b (G)

STACKHOUSE
1893, 4, 15. James & w recrq
1894, 1, 20. Eliza & ch, Delcena, Thurman, Lottie & Sullivan, recrq
1895, 5, 18. James & w, Eliza, & ch, Alice D., Selva, Herman & Lottie, gct Center MM, O.

STALKER
----, --, --. Nathan & Mary
Ch: Eleanor b 1807, 10, 11
Lydia " 1809, 1, 29
John " 1810, 9, 19
Eli " 1812, 1, 9
David " 1813, 5, 27
Mary " 1816, 5, 23
Sarah " 1817, 10, 9
Rhoda " 1822, 7, 19

1835, 8, 11. Eli gct Fairfield MM, O., to m Tacy Jennette Burgess
1835, 9, 15. John gct White Water MM, Ind.
1836, 8, 16. Tacy Jennette rocf Fairfield MM, dtd 1836,3,24
1837, 3, 14. John rocf White Water MM, Ind., dtd 1836,8,24
1837, 4, 11. Nathan & w, Mary, gct Cherry Grove MM, Ind.
1837, 4, 11. John gct Cherry Grove MM, Ind.
1837, 4, 11. David gct Cherry Grove MM, Ind.
1837, 4, 11. Mary Jr. gct Cherry Grove MM, Ind.
1837, 5, 16. Eli & w, Tacy Gennette, gct Fairfield MM

STANFIELD
1884, 10, 18. James rocf Cesars Creek MM, O.
1898, 12, 17. James relrq

STANTON
1836, 9, 13. William R. rmt Ruth Thatcher
1837, 1, 17. Ruth gct Springborough MM, O.
1837, 12, 12. William rmt Theodosia Thatcher
1838, 6, 12. Theodocia gct Springborough MM,O.
1839, 5, 14. William & w, Theodosia, rocf Springborough MM, O., dtd 1839,2,26
1846, 12, 19. Theodosia Hadley (form Stanton) dis mou
1856, 3, 15. John Hadley gct Springborough MM, O., to m Rhoda Stanton
1856, 6, 21. Lydia G., dt Rhoda G. Hadley, rocf Springborough MM, O., dtd 1856,5,20
1856, 6, 21. Rebecca M. rocf Springborough MM, O., dtd 1856,5,20
1862, 12, 15. Martha Emily rmt Alfred Osborn
1864, 6, 18. Rebecca M. gct Springborough MM, O.
1864, 6, 18. Lydia G. gct Springborough MM,O.
1866, 8, 18. James E. con mou
1867, 3; 16. James E. & ch gct Bangor MM, Ia.
1867, 3, 16. James E. gct Bangor MM, Ia.

STARBUCK
1866, 7, 21. Adin L. rocf Dover MM, O., dtd 1866,7,19
1866, 9, 15. Louisa rocf Clear Creek MM, O., dtd 1866,8,11
1907, 10, 19. Charles & w, Stella, & ch, Herbert & Pauline, rocf Dover MM, O.
1912, 12, 21. Charles & fam gct Center MM, O.

STARKEY
----, --, --. Frank Pierce, s Eli & Alice S., b 1879,9,26; m Gertrude Belle SNYDER, dt Perry & Julia W., b 1882,3,14
Ch: Frances
Belle b 1913, 3, 29

1927, 4, 17. Frank & fam recrq
1931, 4, 19. Frank P., Gertrude B. & Frances B., relrq

STATLER
1868, 10, 17. Lydia (form Thatcher) con mou
1892, 1, 16. Mary, Emma G. & Della, dt Samuel & Lydia, gct Wilmington MM, O.
1892, 1, 16. Lydia gct Wilmington MM, O.

ST. CLAIR
1891, 3, 21. Ada gct Cincinnati MM, O.

STEDDOM
1847, 2, 20. David Pyle gct Miami MM, O., to m Esther Stedom
1852, 9, 18. Moses rmt Sarah Pyle
1853, 1, 15. Sarah gct Miami MM, O.

STEVENSON
1869, 12, 18. Mary & s, John R., rocf Dover MM, O., dtd 1869,11,18
1873, 5, 17. Mary [Stephenson] & s, Robert, gct Springfield MM, Kans.
1874, 5, 16. James M. recrq
1875, 4, 17. Amanda & ch, Carrie, Edgar Miner & Annie L. recrq

STEWART
1826, 11, 25. Hiram Maden gct White Water MM, Ind., to m Susannah Stewart

STILES
1851, 1, 18. Robert & w, Rachel, & dt, Amy Ann, rocf Allum Creek MM, O., dtd 1850,12, 26
1854, 1, 24. Robert & w, Rachel, & ch, Amyann & Caroline, gct Allum Creek MM, O.

STILLINGS
----, --, --. James b 1805,9,16; m Mary A. ----- b 1825,4,2

1874, 1, 17. James & w, Mary A., & dt, Emma Reed, recrq

STOLL
1900, 3, 5. Jennie Reams rocf Goshen MM (G)

STOUT
----, --, --. Jesse b 1794,2,23; m Rosanna HIATT b 1798,7,21
Ch: Charlotte b 1818, 7, 21
Isaac " 1822, 9, 7
Elijah " 1824, 7, 1
Susannah " 1826, 8, 17
1871, 4, 6. William B. d ae 83y 5m 25d

1819, 11, 27. Jesse & w, Rosanna, & dt, Charlotte, gct Newgarden MM, Ind.
1822, 7, 27. Phebe & Lydia gct Cherry Grove MM, Ind.
1822, 12, 28. Sarah dis mou
1823, 5, 31. Sarah dis mou
1823, 12, 27. Rebecca rmt Nathan Thornburgh
1826, 2, 25. Jesse & w, Rosanna, & ch, Charlotte, Isaac & Elijah, rocf White River MM, Ind., dtd 1825,10,12
1828, 12, 16. Isaac dis setting up mtg contrary to discipline
1829, 1, 13. Jesse & w, Rosanna, & ch, Charlotte, Isaac, Elijah, Susanna & Stephen, gct Vermillion MM, Ill.
1829, 1, 13. Susannah dis disunity
1829, 4, 14. Phebe rocf Cherry Grove MM, Ind., dtd 1829,1,10
1829, 12, 15. Matilda Cleaver (form Stout) dis mou
1830, 4, 13. Martha & Mary dis jH
1832, 8, 14. Isaac Jr. dis jH
1835, 4, 11. Phebe rpd mou; Vermillion MM, Ill. asked to treat with her
1835, 7, 14. Jesse & ch, Charlotte, Isaac, Elijah, Susanna & Stephen, rocf Vermillion MM, Ill., dtd 1835,5,2
1835, 11, 17. Jesse dis mou
1837, 12, 12. Jane D. rocf Springborough MM, O., dtd 1837,10,24
1839, 9, 17. Jane gct Miami MM, O.
1840, 6, 16. Isaac, Elijah, Susannah & Stephen, ch Jesse & Rosanna, gct Elk MM, O.
1840, 6, 16. Isaac, Elijah, Susanna & Stephen ch Jesse, gct Elk MM, O.; cert returned, they were not there
1841, 6, 15. Isaiah dis mou
1847, 4, 17. Jane rocf Miami MM, O., dtd 1846,11,25
1854, 2, 18. Jane gct Miami MM, O.
1866, 10, 20. William B. recrq
1881, 4, 16. Isaiah & w, Sarah, & s, Clyde, recrq
1888, 6, 16. Isaiah gct Winchester MM, Ind.

STRATTON
----, --, --. Micajah b 1802,1,22 d 1857,5,12
----, --, --. Micajah & Mary
Ch: John Haines b 1831, 5, 12
Joseph " 1834, 8, 27 d 1859, 5,19
Ruth Ann b 1837, 3, 29
Mary Elizabeth " 1840, 5, 24 d 1841, 9,17
1842, 5, 18. Rachel Ann m Manson MOORMAN
----, --, --. John W. b 1831,3,12; m Judith ----- b 1833,6,11 d 1861,9,23
Ch: Mary E. b 1855, 6, 22
Frances J. " 1857, 9, 22
Flora E. " 1866, 2, 15
John W. m 2nd Lydia L. ----- b 1843,3,21
Ch: Joseph b 1864, 2, 27
John " 1864, 2, 27
David " 1866, 6, 4
Lorena " 1868, 10, 23
Arrena " 1868, 10, 23
Clara " 1872, 4, 28
Mary E. " 1874, 7, 19
Clarence Victor " 1877, 12, 13
----, --, --. Theodocia & -----
Ch: James E. b 1839, 8, 10
Martha Emily " 1841, 10, 1
Theodocia now m to ----- Hadley
1845, 7, 1. Micajah b d 1856,8,23
1850, 7, 27. Narcissa b d 1874,8,14

1820, 4, 29. Esther Pyle (form Stratton) con mou
1822, 8, 31. Ruth (form Crews) con mou
1823, 1, 25. Ruth gct White Water MM, Ind.
1826, 1, 28. David Jr. dis
1826, 8, 26. Joseph Jr. gct White Water MM, Ind.
1826, 8, 26. David con mou
1827, 7, 28. David & s, Stephen, attached to Center MM, O.
1828, 3, 29. Joseph gct West Grove MM, Ind., to m Rebecca Harvey
1828, 12, 16. Rebecca & ch, Mary Sarah, Isaac & David Harvey, rocf West Grove MM, Ind., dtd 1828,6,14
1830, 4, 13. Sarah Jr. dis disunity
1830, 12, 14. Micajah dis mou & jH
1831, 10, 11. Benjamin gct White Water MM, Ind.
1831, 12, 13. Rebecca & Edward, ch Rebecca, wd Joseph,& Sarah, Isaac & Davis Harvey, ch by a form m to Samuel H. Harvey, gct Miami MM, O.
1832, 4, 17. Rebecca dis jH
1832, 8, 14. Mahlon Jr. dis mou
1838, 4, 17. Micajah & w, Mary, & ch, John Haines, Joseph & Ruth Ann, recrq
1854, 10, 21. John Haines con mou
1856, 9, 20. Judith rocf Fairfield MM, dtd 1856,4,19
1863, 6, 20. John Haines con mou
1867, 8, 17. John Haynes & ch, Francis Irvin & Flora Ellen, gct Newberry MM, O.
1871, 2, 18. Mahlon & w, Harriett, & ch, Clarrie E., Mary E., Amanda F. & Almina A., recrq
1874, 2, 21. Albert & w, Anna E., & ch, Al-

STRATTON, continued
fred C. & Albert E., recrq
1874, 2, 21. John H. & w, Lydia, & ch, John, Joseph, David, Sorena, Arrena & Clara, rocf Newberry MM, O., dtd 1873,12,22
1878, 2, 16. Francis rocf Clear Creek MM, O., dtd 1878,1,12
1883, 9, 15. Flora E. rocf Clear Creek MM, O., dtd 1883,8,11

STROUD
1925, 7, 19. Hazel dropped from mbrp

STUBBS
1825, 3, 26. Joseph rmt Edith Madden
1825, 6, 25. Edith gct Elk MM, O.
1841, 1, 12. Charlotte gct Elk MM, O.
1856, 1, 19. Elizabeth M. (form Hunt) con mou
1856, 1, 19. Enos P. rmt Mary Hunt
1856, 5, 19. Elizabeth gct Elk MM, O.
1856, 6, 21. Mary H. gct Elk MM, O.

STUMP
1876, 5, 20. Lucian Shank, step s John Stump, recrq
1876, 6, 17. John & w, Margaret, recrq
1876, 6, 17. Mary recrq
1894, 6, 16. John & w, Margaret, gct West Fork MM, O.
1901, 4, 20. John & w rocf West Fork MM, O.

STURGEON
1893, 3, 18. Lewis recrq

SUMMER
1876, 3, 18. William recrq
1876, 5, 20. Adaline & ch, Harriet Emma & Stephen, recrq
1913, 3, 15. Eugene Foust recrq
1921, 6, 18. Eugene F. dropped from mbrp

SUTTON
1913, 3, 15. Roxie Lucile recrq
1913, 4, 19. Harley & w & ch, Winnie Ardena, Izita,Fabel & Edgar Ardel, recrq
1926, 6, 20. Harley & fam dropped from mbrp

TALBOT
1813, 12, 31. Mary d
1823, 4, 15. John d

TAYLOR
1825, 1, 26. Hannah, dt Richard & Lucy, b

1823, 1, 25. Richard recrq
1823, 11, 29. Lucy recrq
1826, 4, 29. Richard & w, Lucy, & dt, Hannah, gct Dover MM
1897, 3, 20. Iva recrq
1930, 1, 2. Mary Jane rocf Oak Grove MM, Tenn. (G)

TERRELL
1896, 8, 18. Lorana M. gc

THARP
1839, 12, 17. Miriam (form Fallis) dis mou

THATCHER
----, --, --. Joseph d 1857,5,3; m Deborah ----- d 1862,8,--
Ch: Mary Ellen b 1834, 9, 24 d 1854,12,25
William H. " 1837, 10, 30 " 1857, 9,18
Susan " 1840, 7, 29
Sarah " 1843, 9, 4
Lydia Mariah " 1846, 7, 20
Anna J. " 1849, 5, 2
Emily " 1852, 8, 11
Oliver J. " 1857, 11, 10

1827, 7, 28. Joseph J. attached to Center MM
1830, 5, 11. Susanna Hadley (form Thacher) dis mou
1835, 7, 14. Deborah (form Hadley) con mou
1835, 12, 15. Jesse dis mou
1835, 11, 17. Martha con mou
1836, 4, 12. Joseph Jr. rocf Center MM, O., dtd 1836,2,17
1836, 9, 13. Ruth rmt Wm. R. Stanton
1837, 9, 12. Joseph & w, Elizabeth, & ch, Jesse, Ruth, William, David, Hannah, Thomas, Stephen & John, rocf Centre MM, O., dtd 1837,7,12
1837, 12, 12. Theodosia rmt Wm. Stanton
1844, 12, 17. Thomas con mou
1845, 6, 17. Elizabeth rocf White Water MM, Ind., dtd 1845,2,26
1846, 3, 17. Joseph & w, Elizabeth, & ch, Wm. David, Hannah, Thomas Stephen John & Ann, gct Salem MM, Ia.
1848, 2, 19. David con mou
1848, 12, 16. Thomas & w, Elizabeth, & ch, Lucinda & Jesse, gct Mississinewa MM, Ind.
1849, 7, 21. Joseph & w, Deborah, & ch, Mary Ellen, William, Susanna, Sarah, Lydia Maria & Anna F., gct Milford MM, Ind.
1852, 8, 21. Deborah & ch, Wm., Insam, Sarah, Lydia Maria & Anna J., rocf Milford MM, Ind., dtd 1852,4,24
1854, 2, 18. Joseph rocf Milford MM, Ind., dtd 1854,1,28
1860, 7, 21. Susan rmt Emmor H. McMillan
1865, 11, 18. Sarah M. Donalds (form Thatcher) con mou
1867, 4, 20. Annie J. Osborn (form Thatcher) con mou
1867, 9, 21. David gct Spring Creek MM, Ia.
1868, 10, 17. Lydia Statler (form Thatcher) con mou
1870, 4, 16. Jesse recrq
1871, 7, 15. Emily Jinks (form Thatcher) con mou
1878, 7, 20. Jesse dis disunity
1880, 3, 20. Oliver J. gct Wilmington MM, O.

THATCHER, continued
1880, 4, 17. Jesse recrq
1881, 5, 21. Jesse Jr. recrq

THOMAS
1835, 9, 15. Rowland Green gct New Garden MM, Ind., to m Absillet Thomas
1849, 5, 19. Isaac rmt Mahama J. Hadley
1849, 8, 18. Mahala G. gct New Garden MM, Ind.
1902, 5, 17. George & w gct Miami MM, O.

THOMPSON
1831, 5, 17. Sophia recrq
1833, 7, 16. Sophia Hadley (form Thompson) con mou
1875, 4, 17. John & w, Ellen, recrq
1887, 3, 19. James recrq
1887, 5, 21. Elizabeth recrq
1893, 9, 16. Hannah recrq
1897, 3, 20. Ellsworth recrq

THORN
1858, 12, 18. William rmt Elizabeth Harvey
1859, 2, 19. Elizabeth H. gct Green Plain MM, O.

THORNBERRY
----, --, --. Abel & Rhoda [Thornburg]
Ch: John
Thomas b 1843, 4, 10 d 1858, 1,10

1819, 5, 29. Abel [Thornburgh] rst on consent of Fairfield MM, O.
1819, 7, 31. Lydia [Thornborough] recrq of parents, Abel & Rhoda
1819, 9, 25. Abel [Thornborough] & w, Rhoda, & dt, Lydia, gct White Water MM, Ind.
1823, 12, 27. Nathan [Thornburgh] rmt Rebecca Stout
1824, 1, 21. Rebecca [Thornburgh] gct Cherry Grove MM, Ind.
1841, 5, 11. Rhoda & ch, Mary Ann, Rachel, Susanna & William J., rocf White Water MM, Ind., dtd 1841,4,20
1844, 4, 16. Mary Ann Newberry (form Thornberry) dis mou
1850, 8, 17. Mordecai Walker gct Centre MM, O., to m Jemimah [Thornburgh]
1856, 2, 16. Susannah J. Whitsel (form Thornbury) dis mou
1860, 6, 16. Wm. J. gct West Union MM, Ind.
1865, 5, 20. William rocf West Union MM, Ind., dtd 1865,4,3
1866, 8, 18. Abel recrq
1869, 12, 18. Wm. G. gct Fairfield MM, O.

THRASHER
1877, 6, 16. Gilbert & w, Hannah, & ch, John, Sarah E., Martha & Lydia, rocf Dover MM, O., dtd 1877,6,14
1897, 11, 20. Gilbert [Thresher] & ch, Sarah E., Lydia, John & Martha, dropped from mbrp

TICE
1894, 1, 20. Albert recrq
1898, 4, 16. Nathan & w, Amy, & ch, Wallace, Maggie Edith & Amy Loretta, gct Raysville MM, Ind.

TIMBERLAKE
----, --, --. Jonathan & Catherine
Ch: Sarah b 1838, 4, 14
Amelia " 1840, 8, 15

1835, 1, 13. Jonathan rocf Clear Creek MM, O., dtd 1834,12,23
1837, 4, 11. Jonathan gct Centre MM, O., to m Catherine Mabie
1837, 10, 17. Catherine rocf Centre MM, O., dtd 1837,8,16
1848, 6, 17. Elizabeth rmt Jonathan Hadley
1853, 9, 17. Richard rocf Clear Creek MM, O., dtd 1853,8,13
1856, 2, 16. Richard gct Center MM, O.
1859, 2, 19. Jonathan & w, Catharine, & ch, Amelia, Rebecca Mary, Anna Eliza & Arthur, gct White Water MM, Ind.
1859, 2, 19. Sarah Matilda gct White Water MM, Ind.

TOMLIN
1889, 8, 17. Isabel recrq

TOMPSON
1926, 3, 26. B. O. & w, Effie, & ch, Mynard, Lewis & Mary-Martha, rocf Wilmington MM,O.

TRIMMER
----, --, --. Samuel b 1829,4,27; m Jane ----- b 1831,10,21
Ch: H. V. b 1857, 7, 17
Mary Alice " 1859, 11, 7

TRUEBLOOD
1855, 8, 18. Peter Osborn gct Blue River MM, Ind., to m Eliza Ann Trueblood
1856, 1, 19. Charles, s Eliza Ann Osborn, rocf Blue River MM, Ind., dtd 1856,1,5
1867, 10, 17. Charles con mou
1868, 3, 21. Charles E. gct South River MM, Ia.

TUCKER
----, --, --. Ida M., dt Isaac & Rebecca S. Spray, b 1856,7,14 d 1911,--,--

TURNER
1882, 12, 16. Henry & w, Susan, & ch, Flo & Luther, recrq

UNDERWOOD
1862, 7, 19. Esther (form Kirk) con mou
1888, 6, 16. Ellen recrq

UPTON
1894, 1, 20. John W. recrq

UPTON, continued
1895, 5, 18. Newton & w, Malinda, & ch, Bessie, recrq
1895, 12, 21. Mary recrq
1897, 12, 18. Newton & w, Malinda, dis

URTON
----, --, --. Ezra b 1832,11,14; m Mary Ann ----- b 1832,3,6
Ch: Charles A. b 1856, 3, 19
John W. " 1859, 8, 7
Malissa " 1861, 2, 28
George W. " 1863, 5, 5

1872, 7, 20. Ezra & w, Mary A., & ch, Charles A., Malissa J., John W. & George, recrq
1885, 4, 18. Serepta recrq
1885, 6, 20. Ezra & w, Mary A., gct Wilmington MM, O.
1885, 6, 20. Melissa gct Wilmington MM, O.
1891, 9, 19. George & w, Serepta, & ch, Cleo, gct Dover MM, O.
1899, 3, 18. Oliver recrq

VANCE
1927, 5, 15. Belva gct Beech Grove MM, Ind.

VAN CLEVE
1880, 4, 17. Luther & w, Retta, recrq
1891, 5, 16. Luther rocf Van Wert MM, O., dtd 1891,3,28

VANDERVORT
1861, 12, 21. Delitha (form Mendenhall) dis mou

VANDOREN
1911, 7, 15. Anna M. recrq

VARNER
1824, 11, 27. Ann (form Harlan) con mou
1837, 10, 17. Ann gct Miami MM, O.

VILLARS
1914, 9, 12. Wm. & w, Laura, recrq
1928, 7, 22. Wm. & w, Laura, relrq

WAITES
----, --, --. Samuel m Ida Bell LONG, dt Harper & Mary Ellen, b 1875,3,31
Ch: Edith
Marie b 1910, 5, 20

1913, 3, 15. Vernie Edward recrq
1913, 3, 15. Hazel Mary recrq
1913, 3, 15. Ida Bell & ch, Clara Bell & Edith Marie, recrq
1913, 4, 19. Goldie recrq
1921, 6, 18. Verne Edward dropped from mbrp

WALKER
----, --, --. Mordecai b 1801,1,13; m Mary GREEN b 1799,4,7 d ----,9,18
Ch: Azel b 1824, 10, 21
Rhoda G. " 1826, 3, 5
William " 1827, 10, 2 d 1829, 7,24
Mordecai m 2nd Mary OSBORN b 1805,1,2
Ch: Rachel b 1839, 7, 6
Elizabeth " 1842, 7, 6
----, --, --. John R., s Azel & Elizabeth, b 1827,11,26; m ----- -----
Ch: Russell b 1864, 10, 17
----, --, --. Cyrus, s Azel & Elizabeth, b 1829,1,4; m ----- -----
Ch: Nellie B. b 1865, 2, 6
----, --, --. Azel & Elizabeth
Ch: Edward B. b 1826, 3, 12
Isaac " 1827, 7, 30
Cyrus " 1829, 1, 4
John R. " 1830, 11, 26
William " 1832, 11, 14 d 1833, 1,19
Eliza Ann " 1833, 12, 17
Martha Jane" 1835, 11, 8
Lewis " 1837, 12, 4
Calvin " 1843, 9, 6
Amos J. " 1845, 12, 1
----, --, --. Asa & Maria
Ch: Joshua R. b 1835, 7, 26
William H. " 1839, 12, 31
Bruce Mc. " 1855, 8, 22
1864, 7, 3. Hattie S., dt Wm. H. & Sarah J., b
1823, 9, 27. Mordecai rmt Mary Green
1823, 11, 29. Mary gct Center MM, O.
1831, 5, 17. Mordicai & w, Mary, & ch, Azel & Rhoda G., rocf Centre MM, O., dtd 1831, 3,16
1835, 1, 13. Mordecai gct New Garden MM, Ind.
1835, 9, 15. Azel Jr. & w, Elizabeth P., & ch, Edward B., Isaac, Cyrus, John R. & Eliza Ann, rocf Centre MM, O., dtd 1835,5, 13
1836, 7, 12. Mordicai rocf Ceasars Creek MM, O., dtd 1836,5,24
1836, 10, 11. Mordecai rmt Mary Osburn
1842, 9, 13. Sally Maria recrq
1842, 10, 11. Joshua R. & Wm. H., ch Asa, recrq
1843, 12, 12. William & w, Martha, rocf Caesars Creek MM, O., dtd 1843,11,23
1845, 5, 13. John S. & w, Ruth, & ch, Elizabeth, Jehu H. & Louis, rocf Cesars Creek MM, O., dtd 1845,4,24
1846, 3, 19. Azel rmt Eleanor Walter
1848, 2, 19. Edward W. dis joining military company
1848, 10, 21. John L. & w, Ruth, & ch, Elizabeth, Jehu & Benjamin L., gct Fairfield MM, Ind.
1850, 8, 17. Mordecai gct Center MM, O., to m Jemima Thornburgh
1851, 4, 19. Jemima rocf Center MM, O., dtd 1851,2,12
1853, 2, 19. Mordecai & w, Jemima, & ch, Rachel, Elizabeth M., Mary Ann & Martha, gct Center MM, O.

WALKER, continued
1853, 4, 16. Isaac gct Centre MM, O.
1853, 10, 15. Azel Jr. & w, Eleanor, & s, Mordecai J., gct Center MM, O.
1860, 1, 21. John B. con mou
1862, 8, 16. Cyrus M. con mou
1862, 11, 15. William H. rmt Sarah Jane Osborn
1862, 12, 20. Cyrus M. gct Wabash MM, Ind.
1866, 6, 16. Joshua R. con mou
1869, 12, 18. Joshua R. gct Fairfield MM, O.
1874, 1, 17. Asa recrq
1882, 9, 16. Maria gct Wilmington MM, O.
1886, 1, 16. Bruce Mack dis disunity
1888, 7, 21. Mordecai & Mary Ann rocf Center MM, O.
1891, 9, 19. Charles A. gct Wilmington MM, O.
1891, 9, 19. Wm. H. & w & ch, Roy, gct Wilmington MM, O.

WALLACE
1879, 6, 21. Mary A. rocf Back Creek MM, Ind.
1887, 3, 19. Winfield recrq

WALTER
1842, 4, 12. Eleanor recrq
1846, 3, 17. Eleanor rmt Azel Walker

WARD
1874, 5, 16. Isaac recrq
1877, 6, 16. Isaiah dropped from mbrp
1889, 4, 20. Dr. Chas. recrq
1889, 4, 20. Mary, w Dr. Chas., recrq
1918, 4, 20. May dropped from mbrp

WARRMAN
----, --, --. George W. b 1842,7,16; m Mary A. OSBORN b 1845,1,9
Ch: Ethel b 1867, 9, 13
Adah " 1869, 11, 2

1874, 1, 17. George W. & w, Mary A., & ch, Ethel & Adah, recrq
1877, 6, 16. George W. dis disunity

WARNER
1850, 2, 16. Mahala H. (form Hadley) dis mou
1890, 5, 19. Ethel gct Cincinnati MM, O.

WARREN
----, --, --. William, s James & Sarah (Wiltsher), b 1867,2,24; m Eva HOLADAY, dt Enoch & Sarah (West), b 1867,12,25
Ch: Luther E. b 1891, 3, 9
Pearl E. " 1893, 5, 2
Ralph T. " 1902, 7, 4
Clifton J. " 1904, 10, 8

1909, 1, 16. Wm. & fam recrq
1921, 10, 15. Luther gct East Vasselboro MM, Me.
1923, 3, 18. Lucile Starkey recrq
1934, 3, 4. Luther & w & two ch rocf Friendsville MM, Tenn.

WASHBURN
1858, 6, 19. Josephine E. (form Quinby) con mou

WATKINS
1832, 9, 11. John Green gct Goshen MM, O., to m Mary Ann Watkins
1898, 10, 15. Elizabeth Hadley gct Goshen MM, O.

WATSON
1881, 4, 16. Hattie recrq

WEBB
----, --, --. Ralph, s Oliver & Sylvia, b 1896,5,8; m Mary HADLEY, dt Maurice & Carrie, b 1898,9,8
Ch: Virgene
May b 1924, 5, 25
Ralph Dale " 1928, 8, 17

1929, 12, 22. Ralph & ch, Virgene May & Ralph Dale, recrq
1930, 1, 2. Roy recrq (G)

WELFORD
1900, 1, 20. Charles & w, Julia, gct Cesars Creek MM, O.

WELCH
1819, 12, 25. Esther con mcd
1821, 10, 27. Turner rst on consent of Deep Creek MM, N. C.
1824, 11, 27. Amos rmt Rachel Fallis
1825, 2, 26. Rachel gct Miami MM, O.
1827, 7, 28. Turner & w, Esther, & ch, Mary, Martha & John, attached to Center MM, O.
1858, 6, 19. Anna M. (form Hadley) con mou
1859, 2, 19. Ann M. gct Miami MM, O.

WELLER
1914, 1, 17. Oscar rocf Wilmington MM, O.
1921, 9, 17. Oscar & Anna relrq
1926, 6, 20. Ada Pyle dropped from mbrp

WELLS
1889, 4, 20. George recrq

WEST
----, --, --. William m Sophia HADLEY
Ch: Alpheus b 1849, 10, 28
William E. " 1851, 7, 13
Elwood H. " 1855, 9, 7

1848, 8, 19. David S. Pyle gct Dover MM, O., to m Sarah T. West
1849, 1, 20. Wm. rmt Sophia Hadley
1849, 6, 16. William rocf Newberry MM, O., dtd 1849,5,14
1867, 7, 20. Sophia & ch, Alpheus T., Wm. E. & Elwood H., gct Summit Grove MM, Ia.
1906, 2, 17. Eva Mather gct Wilmington MM,O.

WHARTON
1897, 3, 20. Albert & Minnie recrq
1902, 5, 17. Albert gct Miami MM, O.

WHITAKER
1838, 12, 11. Rachel (form Smith) dis mou

WHINERY
1849, 8, 18. James & w, Mary, & ch, Arthur & Enos, rocf Center MM, O., dtd 1849,6,13
1853, 10, 15. Ezra & w, Hannah, & dt, Judith E., rocf Center MM, O.
1854, 6, 17. James & w, Mary, & s, Arthur Enos & Henry, gct Center MM, O.
1857, 2, 21. Ezra & w, Hannah, & ch, Judith & Susanna, gct Center MM, O.

WHITE
1891, 2, 21. George B. & w, Sarah Rufing, rocf Walnut Ridge MM, Ind.
1893, 4, 15. George B. & w, Sarah Rufina, & niece, Edna Butler, gct Center MM, O.
1897, 12, 18. Annie E. recrq
1898, 1, 15. Wm. recrq
1912, 1, 20. Wm. relrq

WHITSEL
1856, 2, 16. Susannah J. (form Thornbury) dis mou
1856, 10, 18. Susannah J. recrq
1859, 6, 18. Susanna J. gct Miami MM, O.
1861, 4, 20. Susannah rocf Miami MM, O., dtd 1861,3,29
1869, 12, 18. Susan J. & ch, Lida F. & Adda Rachel, gct Fairfield MM, O.

WHITSON
1825, 8, 27. John rmt Dinah Ballard
1826, 1, 28. James L. rmt Dinah Ballard
1827, 7, 28. Dinah, & Eunice attached to Center MM, O.

WHIPP
1932, 5, 5. Thelma Elizabeth & Alice Louise recrq (G)

WILDMAN
----, --, --. Seneca & Jane
Ch: Ruth b 1834, 12, 11
John " 1836, 8, 25 d 1840, 9,17 bur Springfield
Jonathan H. b 1838, 5, 6
Elizabeth " 1840, 6, 23
William " 1843, 3, 31
Hiram " 1845, 2, 26
Lydia Ann " 1847, 3, 8
Thomas " 1849, 1, 27 d 1850,11, 9 bur Springfield

1831, 7, 12. John Hadley Jr. gct Green Plain MM, O., to m Ann Wildman
1833, 9, 17. Seneca rocf Green Plain MM, O., dtd 1833,8,24
1834, 1, 14. Seneca rmt Jane Hadley
1857, 8, 15. Jonathan H. dis mou
1858,10, 16. Ruth rmt Jehu S. Maden
1859, 7, 11. Seneca & w, Jane, & ch, Elizabeth, Wm. H., Hiram, Lydia Anne & Oliver, gct Rocksylvania MM, Ia.
1861, 5, 18. Rebecca Helen (form Hadley) con mou
1861, 12, 21. Rebecca gct Honey Creek MM, Ind.

WILKERSON
1897, 9, 18. Frank & w recrq
1897, 11, 20. Perry dis
1909, 3, 20. Myrtle dropped from mbrp
1913, 3, 15. Edwin Legrand recrq
1921, 6, 18. Edwin LeGrand dropped from mbrp

WILLIAMS
1822, 8, 31. Mary rocf Buckingham MM, Pa., dtd 1822,3,4, end by Fairfield MM, O., dtd 1822,4,27
1846, 9, 19. Wilson Hobbs gct West Grove MM, Ind., to m Zalinda Williams
1877, 3, 17. Mary W. recrq
1889, 4, 20. Webster recrq
1897, 3, 20. Webster, Clyde, Edward recrq
1909, 3, 20. Simeon & Emma dropped from mbrp
1925, 7, 19. Webster dropped from mbrp

WILSON
1832, 1, 17. Asa gct Sugar River MM, Ind.
1835, 4, 14. Pheriba rocf Smithfield MM, Ind. dtd 1835,1,17
1835, 10, 13. Phariba J. rmt Jesse F. Ballard
1851, 10, 18. Alfred rmt Almira Hadley
1851, 12, 20. Almira gct Honey Creek MM, Ind.
1887, 10, 15. Sarah J. (Milican) gct Pleasant Plain MM, Kans.
1892, 3, 19. Sarah recrq
1897, 3, 20. Ella recrq
1899, 5, 20. Essie recrq
1899, 11, 18. Ella relrq
1914, 10, 17. Marion & w, Mary, & ch, Clyde, Chlorine & Madge, rocf Center MM, O.
1924, 4, 20. Marion & w, Mary P., & ch, Chlorine, Clyde & Madge, relrq

WINFIELD
----, --, --. John, s Joseph & Elanor J., b 1852,2,24; m Alice A. HARLAN, dt James & Sarah, b 1855,2,14
Ch: Frank b 1882, 1, 14
----, --, --. Frank, s John & Alice A. (Harlan); m Marie HADLEY, dt Isaac Parker & Florence (Weeks), b 1885,7,22 (John b 1882 1,14)
Ch: Mary C. b 1906, 7, 4

1892, 11, 19. Thomas J. recrq
1893, 3, 18. John recrq
1898, 4, 16. T. J. & Pearl May recrq
1899, 9, 16. John & w, Addie, & ch, Charles & Frank, rocf West Fork MM, O.

WINFIELD, continued
1904, 5, 21. Charles & w & s, Robert L., gct Miami MM, O.
1924, 4, 20. Frank & fam relrq

WIRE
1855, 10, 20. Permelia Kimbrough (form Wire) con mou
1863, 8, 15. Mary Ann recrq
1864, 7, 16. Mary Ann Carter (form Wire) con mou

WOLF
----, --, --. Benjamin b 1847,2,16; m Maggie F. ----- b 1846,5,22
Ch: Atlanta G. b 1867, 8, 10
William A. " 1868, 10, 7
Velara E. " 1870, 3, 27
Myrtie B. " 1872, 4, 11
Charley N. " 1873, 8, 20

1867, 5, 18. Margaret (form Osborn) con mou
1867, 7, 20. Margaret F. gct Newberry MM, O.
1874, 4, 18. Margaret F. & ch, Atlanta Georga, William Alonzo, Velora Eliza, Myrtie Belle & Charlie Henry, rocf Newberry MM, O., dtd 1874,3,23
1874, 6, 20. Benjamin F. recrq
1876, 4, 15. John recrq
1888, 3, 17. John S. relrq
1894, 1, 20. Atlanta relrq
1930, 2, 6. Eva May recrq (G)

WOOTON
1893, 10, 21. Ellen gct Wilmington MM, O.

WORLEY
----, --, --. Charles Bland, s James B. & Rebecca (Owen), b 1884,2,28; m Freda OSBORN, dt Peter & Emma (Winfield), b 1889,1,13
Ch: Charles B. Jr. b 1920, 12, 31

1930, 12, 28. C. Bland, Freda O. & Charles B. rocf Wilmington MM, O.

WORTHINGTON
1852, 7, 11. Sarah Ellen & Wm. Clark, ch Mary, recrq
1860, 4, 21. Sarah Ellin rmt John Wm. Hadley
1866, 8, 18. Wm. C. con mou
1867, 2, 16. Rhoda C. rocf Carthage MM, Ind., dtd 1867,1,5
1867, 4, 20. Isaac recrq
1868, 10, 17. Isaac & w, Rhoda C., gct Wilmington MM, O.
1882, 3, 18. Malissa J. recrq

WRIGHT
1820, 8, 26. Rachel (form Ruble) dis mou
1821, 8, 25. Isaac rocf New Garden MM, Ind., dtd 1821,6,8
1825, 8, 27. Isaac gct White River MM, Ind.

WYSONG
----, --, --. Eugene m Emma PIERSON, dt Robert & Emma, b 1878,7,14
Ch: Carl E. b 1901, 11, 8
Raymond " 1903, 11, 14
Mary " 1905, 5, 7
Loren Adelbert " 1908, 11, 18

1891, 3, 21. Elnora gct Cincinnati MM, O.
1909, 7, 17. Emma & ch, Carl, Raymond & Mary recrq
1920, 4, 17. Emma dropped from mbrp
1920, 4, 17. Loren Adelbert dropped from mbrp
1920, 4, 17. Carl dropped from mbrp
1920, 4, 17. Raymond dropped from mbrp
1920, 4, 17. Mary dropped from mbrp

YEO
1874, 5, 16. William H. & w, Elizabeth, recrq
1891, 5, 16. Wm. [Yoe] gct White Water MM, Ind.

YOUNG
1854, 3, 18. Daniel rmt Rhoda Green
1884, 3, 15. Laura B. relrq
1896, 2, 15. George recrq

ZEIGLER
1895, 4, 20. Martin recrq

* * * * * * *

McKINNEY
1921, 9, 17. Jane relrq

MILLIKAN
1874, 10, 17. John H. recrq

STRATTON
1859, 3, 20. Mary b

DOVER MONTHLY MEETING

Dover Monthly Meeting, four miles northeast of Wilmington, was set off from Center Monthly Meeting 9 Mo. 4, 1824.

Charter members were Isaac and Anna Haskins, John T. Starbuck and family, Isaiah M. and Tamer West, Josiah Haskins and family, Amos Jenkins, Mary Emily Pyle, Susannah Brackner, Anna Arnold and Hannah Thomson.

RECORDS

ABERNATHY
1838, 2, 15. Nancy W. (form Moorman) dis mou

ADAMS
1902, 3, 13. Wilson S. recrq
1902, 3, 13. Effie recrq
1902, 3, 13. Bertha M. recrq
1902, 3, 13. Rosa E. recrq
1902, 3, 13. Lorena D. recrq
1902, 3, 13. Mary J. recrq

1906, 2, 15. Wilson & w, Effie, & ch, Bertha W., Rosa B., Lorenna D., Mary J. & Susanna, gct Center MM

ALDRIDGE
1874, 2, 19. Joseph recrq
1880, 5, 10. Lena & Jane recrq
1880, 5, 10. Wm. recrq
1888, 5, 17. Jane & ch, Eva, recrq
1900, 2, 15. David & w, Jane, recrq
1905, 2, 16. Charles & w, Mary, & s, Fred, relrq
1906, 3, 15. Alton relrq
1908, 6, 18. David dropped from mbrp
1909, 9, 16. Gladys gct Wilmington MM

ALEXANDER
1851, 5, 15. Elizabeth (form Moorman) con mou
1865, 5, 18. Aubine, ch Elizabeth, recrq
1878, 1, 16. Elizabeth & s, Aubine, gct Spring Creek MM, Ia.

ALLEN
1873, 2, 13. Joel A. & w, Mary C., & dt, Josephine, recrq
1873, 3, 13. Lucinda recrq
1883, 5, 17. Orville M. recrq
1899, 6, 15. Isaphine & Ralph relrq
1915, 11, 18. Ida M. rocf Urbana MM, O.
1916, 10, 19. Ida M. gct Upland MM, Ind.

ANDERSON
1876, 4, 13. George, Mary & Josephine recrq
1878, 2, 14. Josephine relrq
1887, 7, 14. B. H. & w, Margaret, recrq
1909, 5, 13. Junette recrq

ANDREWS
1905, 2, 16. Ollie recrq

ANSON
1933, 4, 23. Grace recrq

ANTRAM
1925, 1, 6. John M. d ae 99y 6m 18d

1855, 6, 14. Rebecca Ann (form Wall) dis mou
1867, 4, 18. Hiram [Antrim] recrq
1872, 1, 18. John M. & w, Catharine, & ch, Arthur D. & Frank W., recrq

1899, 1, 19. Carrie recrq
1902, 1, 16. Carrie E. gct Wilmington MM, O.
1918, 2, 14. Orville Paris recrq
1923, 11, 25. Mary gct Caesars Creek MM, O.

ARNOLD
1846, 12, 17. Anna M. (form West) con mou
1868, 5, 14. Anna set off with Wilmington MM, O.

ARY
1902, 5, 2. Wm. recrq
1902, 11, 13. Carrie gct Green Plain MM
1905, 3, 16. Elsie Vannersdoll (form Ary) relrq

ATKINSON
----, --, --. Charles, s Thomas, b 1796,6,21; m Lydia OREN, dt John & Ruth, b 1800,12, 20

Ch: Jane b 1821, 4, 12
David " 1822, 10, 14
Susannah " 1824, 9, 26
Jesse " 1826, 6, 26
Levi " 1828, 2, 2

----, --, --. John & Jane

Ch: Hannah b 1827, 6, 2
Alice " 1828, 10, 12
Thomas L. " 1829, 11, 28

----, --, --. Temple & Esther

Ch: Sarah Jane b 1854, 8, 20
Isaac W. " 1857, 10, 13
David H. " 1860, 3, 19
Clara E. " 1863, 3, 26
Mary M. " 1868, 7, 16

1827, 2, 3. Jane rocf Warrington MM, Pa., dtd 1826,12,20
1829, 1, 15. Lydia dis jH
1830, 10, 14. Jane dis jH
1837, 6, 15. Hannah Alice & Thomas L., ch John & Jane, gct Fairfield MM
1840, 8, 13. David, Susannah, Jesse & Levi, ch Chas. & Lydia, gct Mississinewa MM, Ind.
1840, 8, 13. Jane gct Mississinewa MM, Ind.
1849, 11, 15. Cephas gct Mississinewa MM
1852, 3, 18. Esther (form Rawls) con mou
1853, 10, 13. Esther F. gct Cherry Grove MM, Ind.
1859, 7, 14. Esther rocf Cherry Grove MM, Ind., dtd 1859,11,16
1867, 2, 14. Temple & ch, Sarah Jane, Isaac Wm., David & Clara Emma, recrq
1885, 4, 16. David A. & William dropped from mbrp
1885, 7, 16. David & Jane & ch relrq

BAILEY
----, --, --. Daniel d 1844,7,12 ae 66y 6m 12d bur Dover; m Mary ----- d 1868,7,24 bur Dover

Ch: Martha b 1808, 7, 26

BAILEY, Daniel & Mary, continued
Ch: Susannah b 1810, 2, 9
George " 1811, 6, 24
Sarah " 1814, 6, 9
William " 1817, 4, 6
Josiah " 1818, 6, 30
Joanna " 1820, 5, 12
Elizabeth " 1822, 1, 12
Rebecca " 1823, 12, 31 d 1846, 3,18 bur Dover
Daniel " 1826, 4, 8
Mary " 1828, 4, 11

1827, 9, 20. Robert B., s Josiah & Susannah, Clinton Co., O.; m in Dover MH, Lucy BANGHAM, dt Benjamin & Lucy, Clinton Co., O.
Ch: Benjamin H. b 1828, 8, 6
Josiah " 1830, 2, 19
Lindley M. " 1831, 12, 23
Mary C. " 1834, 3, 2
Gulielma " 1837, 10, 4

1829, 5, 28. Micajah, s David & Silviah, Clinton Co., O.; m in Dover MH, Phebe HAWORTH, dt Mahlon & Phebe, Clinton Co., O., d 1843,9,14 ae 36y 4m 4d bur Dover
Ch: David H. b 1830, 9, 27
Silviah Caroline " 1832, 11, 17
Susannah " 1835, 3, 7
Rebecca Mary " 1837, 9, 8
Mahlon G. " 1840, 5, 11
Phebe " 1843, 9, 3

1831, 3, 24. Mary B. m John STOUT

1831, 4, 20. Daniel Jr., s Josiah & Susannah, Clinton Co., O.; m in Seneca MH, Elizabeth MOORMAN, dt Micajah C. & Susannah, Green Co., O.
Ch: Susannah b 1832, 4, 25
Almedia " 1834, 11, 22
Granderson Edwin " 1837, 3, 3
Elizabeth Ann " 1839, 2, 21
Adderson Mills " 1841, 9, 6 d 1845, 4,21
Barclay Thomas " 1843, 12, 29
Micajah " 1846, 9, 18

1831, 12, 1. Martha m John OREN, Jr.

1832, 6, 21. George, s Daniel & Mary, Clinton Co., O.; m in Dover MH, Lydia SHIELDS dt Wm. & Hannah, Clinton Co., O.
Ch: Delitha Ann b 1833, 4, 23
William " 1835, 7, 16
Sylvia " 1837, 10, 30
Josiah H. " 1842, 2, 14
Hannah Mary " 1839, 11, 22
Allen " 1846, 8, 10 d 1847, 8,28
Enos " 1849, 7, 30

1835, 10, 15. Susannah m Thos. HUNNICUTT

1836, 9, 22. Elizabeth m Abijah JOHNSON

1840, 11, 25. David, s Daniel & Mary, Clinton Co., O.; m in Seneca MH, Elizabeth MOORMAN, dt Charles T. & Matilda, Green Co., O., d 1841,11,9 ae 24y 3m 19d

1841, 7, 25. Silviah, w David, d ae 61y

1846, 6, 25. Joseph, s David & Mary, b

1842, 3, 24. Jonathan, s David & Silviah, Clinton Co., O.; m in Wilmington MH, Rebecca T. FRAZIER, dt Jonah & Mary D., Clinton Co., O.
Ch: Mary Anna b 1843, 9, 1
Sarah Emily " 1845, 5, 25 d 1848,12,17
Edwin Frazier " 1848, 2, 12
James W. " 1852, 8, 25

1842, 11, 24. Josiah, s Daniel & Mary, Clinton Co., O.; m in Dover MH, Mary JENKINS, dt Jacob & Hannah, Clinton Co., O.
Ch: Hannah b 1844, 7, 15
Albert " 1846, 6, 15
Mariana " 1862, 6, 20

1844, 4, 25. Joannah m John A. ORAN

1847, 12, 10. David d

1850, 9, 26. Almedia m Asa NORDYKE

1851, 6, 26. Sarah m Nathan HUNT

1852, 11, 19. Delithia m Pharos COMPTON

1854, 6, 26. David d ae 78y 4m 14d

----, --, --. William d 1866,11,6 ae 31y 3m 21d; m Maria -----
Ch: Corwin Allen b 1857, 9, 14
Clifton Dennis " 1859, 12, 28

1827, 12, 1. David & w, Sylvia, & ch, Micajah, Elizabeth, Jonathan & Almeda, rocf Springborough MM, dtd 1827,10,30

1830, 4, 14. Mary B. roc

1831, 6, 16. Thos. E. gct Union MM

1838, 6, 14. Robert B. & w, Lucy, & ch, Benjamin Hamilton, Isaiah, Lindley M., Mary C., Gulielma & Martha, gct New Garden MM, Ind.

1845, 11, 13. Mary J. rocf Newberry MM, dtd 1845,--,13

1846, 4, 16. Micajah & ch, David H., Silviah C. & Susannah, gct Cincinnati MM, O.

1848, 5, 18. Mary J. & s, Joseph, gct Newberry MM

1848, 9, 14. Elizabeth Sr. dis jas

1853, 1, 13. Mary Jane & ch, Joseph, rocf Newberry MM, dtd 1852,12,9

1855, 12, 13. Asenath recrq

1856, 6, 19. Phebe, niece of Marmaduke & Susannah Brackney, gct Fairfield MM

1858, 2, 18. Maria T. recrq

1858, 6, 17. Elizabeth Ann Fogle (form Bailey) con mou

1860, 9, 19. Daniel & w, Asenath, & ch, Amos H., Nathan H., Edith E. & David M.,

BAILEY, continued
gct Hopewell MM
1860, 12, 13. Mary J. Fisher (form Bailey) con mou
1861, 1, 17. Hannah Mary Carle (form Bailey) con mou
1861, 1, 17. Susannah Becket (form Bailey) con mou
1881, 3, 14. Granderson dis disunity
1865, 7, 13. Mary Anna Hunt (form Bailey) con mou
1865, 12, 14. Elizabeth (form Carter) con mou
1866, 9, 20. Josiah H. con mou
1869, 6, 17. Sidney M. rocf Fairfield MM, O.
1870, 2, 17. Enos P. con mou
1871, 3, 16. Sarah E. recrq
1871, 4, 13. Elizabeth recrq
1872, 3, 14. Emma recrq
1872, 3, 14. Albert con mou
1872, 3, 14. Barclay con mou
1873, 1, 16. Grandison & Ellen recrq
1874, 2, 19. Jonathan recrq
1874, 5, 14. Jonathan & w gct Newberry MM
1876, 3, 16. Clinton & Fanney recrq
1877, 3, 15. Jonathan & w, Rebecca T., rocf Newberry MM
1877, 3, 15. Micajah relrq
1882, 6, 15. Josiah H. & w, Sidney, & ch, Eva, Luther G. & Louella, gct Deer Creek MM, Ind.
1885, 10, 15. Albert J. gct Wilmington MM, O.
1886, 3, 18. Josiah H. & w, Sidnie, & ch, Eva, Luther & Luella, rocf Deer Creek MM, Ind.
1887, 7, 14. Jonathan & w, Rebecca T., gct Pasadena MM, Calif.
1901, 2, 18. J. H. & w gct Center MM
1901, 6, 13. Lizzie dropped from mbrp
1901, 11, 14. Emma relrq
1902, 11, 13. Belle gct Wilmington MM, O.
1903, 10, 15. Gwenn E. dropped from mbrp
1909, 5, 13. Elmer gct Wilmington MM, O.
1916, 11, 16. Sidney M. rocf Center MM

BAKER
1901, 6, 13. Raymond dropped from mbrp

BALLARD
----, --, --. Israel m Elizabeth SHIELDS, dt Wm. & Hannah, b 1806,6,4
Ch: Lydia b 1834, 2, 7
Mary Jane " 1836, 2, 18
Hannah " 1839, 1, 8

1833, 8, 15. Elizabeth (form Shields) con mcd
1835, 9, 17. Elizabeth gct Elk MM
1837, 6, 15. Elizabeth rocf Elk MM, dtd 1837,2,18
1835, 9, 17. Elizabeth gct Miami MM, O.
1842, 8, 18. Elizabeth & ch, Lydia, Mary Jane & Hannah, recrq
1850, 6, 13. Lydia Starbuck (form Ballard) dis mou
1861, 3, 14. Hannah Thomson (form Ballard) con mou
1863, 7, 16. Mary Jane Malanger (form Ballard) con mou
1866, 8, 16. Priscilla & ch, Asenath & Wm., rocf Clear Creek MM, O., dtd 1866,8,11
1866, 8, 16. Mary & Eveline rocf Clear Creek MM, O., dtd 1866,8,11
1866, 8, 16. Asa N. rocf Clear Creek MM, dtd 1866,8,11
1867, 1, 17. David F. rocf Salem MM, Ia.
1868, 5, 14. Mary Douglas (form Ross) con mou
1868, 6, 18. Mary gct Pipe Creek MM, Ind.
1868, 8, 13. Susan recrq
1871, 4, 13. David F. & w, Priscilla, gct Saline MM, Ill.
1871, 4, 13. Asenath gct Saline MM, Ill.
1871, 11, 16. Asa N. gct Saline MM, Ill.

BANGHAM
----, --, --. Benjamin d 1856,10,4 ae 80y 4m 25d; m Lucy -----
Ch: Benjamin b 1814, 3, 14
Nancy " 1816, 2, 26
John C. " 1818, 3, 11
Jonathan " 1820, 4, 14
Rachel " 1822, 9, 19
Thomas E. " 1825, 4, 24
1820, 2, 24. Elizabeth d bur Dover
1824, 12, 9. Zachariah M., s Benjamin & Lucy, Clinton Co., O.; m in Dover MH, Elizabeth JOHNSON, dt John & Susannah, Clinton Co., O.
Ch: Lucy Ann b 1825, 9, 15
Zachariah M. " 1827, 12, 22
1827, 9, 20. Lucy m Robert B. BAILEY
1828, 2, 7. Martha m Thomas C. MOORMAN
1832, 4, 20. Agnes m Joseph T. COATE
----, --, --. Humphrey & Mary
Ch: Agnes b 1834, 2, 27
Martha Ann " 1834, 2, 4
Caroline Elizabeth " 1836, 4, 1
Jonathan P." 1838, 7, 24
Isabella " 1840, 5, 10 d 1841, 1,18
1839, 2, 21. Nancy m John COGGESHALL
----, --, --. Jonathan d 1855,5,16; m Jane ----- d 1847,5,4
Ch: Robert F. b 1843, 5, 26 d 1855,11, 7
Martha " 1844, 8, 27
Jane W. " 1850, 7, 20
William Francis " 1852, 2, 26
Rachel H. " 1854, 2, 23
1848, 10, 26. Rachel M. m Simon HADLEY
1849, 8, 23. Jonathan, s Benjamin & Lucy, Clinton Co., O.; m in Dover MH, Martha A. WALTHALL, dt Wm. & Martha, Clinton Co.,O.
1869, 10, 21. Jane W. m Isaac J. THOMAS

1832, 6, 14. Agnes Bangham Coat gct Union MM
1834, 7, 17. Mary & ch, Agnes & Martha, rocf

BANGHAM, continued
Union MM, dtd 1834,4,6
1839, 10, 17. Ann rocf New Garden MM, dtd 1839, 8,17
1840, 12, 17. John & fam gct New Garden MM, Ind.
1842, 9, 15. Jane rocf Center MM, dtd 1842,9, 14
1842, 10, 13. Lucy Ann dis jas
1843, 5, 18. Humphrey & w, Mary, & ch, Agnes, Martha Ann, Caroline Elizabeth, Jonathan & Phebe, gct New Garden MM, Ind.
1846, 8, 13. Elizabeth dis disunity
1906, 9, 13. Wm. F. & w, Maggie, & ch, Ramona & Wm. Laribee, gct Pasadena MM, Calif.
1908, 3, 19. Ida & Gertrude gct Pasadena MM, Calif.

BARBER
1907, 4, 18. Della dropped from mbrp

BARLETT
1880, 5, 10. Marrell recrq

BARLOW
1879, 6, 19. James M. & w, Margaret, & ch, Alvaretta Josephine, Lewis Stanley, Susan Mary, Harry & George F., recrq
1879, 6, 19. Charles & w, Martha A., recrq
1882, 1, 19. Chas. H. & w, Martha A., & ch relrq
1887, 6, 16. Chas. H. & w, Mattie A., recrq
1905, 3, 16. Angeline relrq

BARNETT
1825, 8, 6. James V. gct White Lick MM, Ind.
1825, 8, 6. Jesse & w, Elizabeth, & ch, Melissa Ann, gct White Lick MM, Ind.
1826, 5, 22. Jonathan & w, Margaret, & ch, John, Ruth, Jesse, Catharine, Joseph & William, rocf Caesars Creek MM, O., dtd 1826,2,23
1827, 10, 6. Thomas & w, Theodate, & ch, Ann Mildred Wilson Thos. Amos Curtis & Isaac, gct Fairfield MM, Ind.
1827, 10, 6. Jane gct Fairfield MM, Ind.
1827, 12, 1. Arthenations & w, Margaret, & ch, John, Ruth, Jesse, Catharine, William Joseph & Jane, gct Fairfield MM, Ind.
1827, 12, 1. Jane Sr. gct Fairfield MM, Ind.
1907, 4, 18. Walter [Barnet] recrq

BARRETT
1869, 4, 15. Mary (form Magoon) gct Fairfield MM

BAUGHAM
1875, 7, 15. Gertrude H. rocf Springdale MM, Ia., dtd 1855,4,17

BAXLA
1909, 5, 13. Abe & w, Rose, recrq

BAUGHN
1910, 10, 3. Kate relrq

BAYHAM
1899, 1, 19. George C. & w, Mary Alice, & ch, Lena M., James O., Olen J., Edwin F., recrq
1901, 2, 18. George & fam gct Hopewell MM

BEAL
1854, 10, 19. Henrietta (form Peebles) con mou
1855, 8, 16. Henrietta P. [Beall] gct Middle River MM, Warren Co., Iowa
1874, 2, 19. Viola V. [Bales] recrq

BEARY
1859, 1, 13. Sarah Ann rocf Clear Creek MM, O., dtd 1858,12,11
1862, 9, 18. Sarah Ann gct Clear Creek MM, O.

BECKET
1861, 1, 17. Susannah (form Bailey) con mou
1869, 3, 18. Susannah [Beckett] gct Elwood MM

BECKFORD
1864, 9, 15. Elizabeth (form Gallemore) con mou

BEIGHLE
1879, 6, 19. Samuel recrq

BENTLEY
1854, 8, 3. Sarah d
----, --, --. Benjamin d 1869,6,13; m Emma -----
Ch: John E. b 1839, 1, 9
Isaiah " 1841, 7, 12
Jeremiah " 1843, 4, 5
Jesse " 1847, 2, 22
Sarah E. " 1851, 11, 17
Cyrus C. " 1855, 10, 20
----, --, --. Isaiah, s Benj. & Emma, b 1841, 7,12; m Geretty ----- b 1843,3,22
Ch: Elias
Russell b 1866, 10, 28
Charles C. " 1869, 2, 29

1833, 8, 15. Sally (form Hiel) con mcd
1841, 11, 18. Emma (form Peelle) con mou
1858, 4, 15. Benjamin & w, Emma, & ch, Isaiah Jeremiah Jesse, Elizabeth & Cyrus, recrq
1867, 3, 14. Isaiah con mou
1871, 10, 19. Jeretta recrq
1873, 9, 18. Jesse con mou
1874, 2, 19. Mary E. recrq
1885, 1, 15. Isaiah & w, Jeretta, & ch, Russell, Chas., Viola, Clarence, Mable & Walter, relrq
1901, 1, 17. Katie F. relrq
1905, 3, 16. Ottie recrq

BENTLEY, continued
1907, 3, 14. Archie relrq
1908, 12, 17. Inez H. relrq

BERRY
1899, 12, 14. Thomas R. & ch, Otto C. & Walter S., recrq

BEUHLER
1912, 3, 14. Myrtle (form McElwee) relrq

BEVAN
1868, 1, 16. Wm. P. Gallemore gct Center MM, to m Mary Jane Bevan

BISHOP
1906, 4, 19. Ralph Elding recrq

BLOOM
1873, 10, 16. Wm. recrq of John N. & Sarah T. Douglas with whom he made his home

BOCOCK
1826, 5, 22. Penelope (form Sears) con mcd
1827, 8, 24. Penelope & dt, Mary Lewis, gct Green Plain MM, O.

BOND
1863, 9, 17. Mary D. (form West) con mou
1864, 4, 14. Mary D. gct Spring Creek MM, Ia.

BORTON
1900, 2, 15. Edward & w, Leah Ellen, & ch, Alda O., Orville J. & Jesse R., relrq

BOWYER
1874, 3, 19. Margaret gct Elk MM

BRACKNEY
----, --, --. Marmaduke & Susanna
Ch: Marmaduke b 1794, 1, 8 (father's d)
Mahlon H. " 1825, 9, 4
Rachel " 1827, 7, 27
Phebe " 1829, 11, 26 d 1839, 8,26
George " 1831, 1, 6
Eli " 1834, 2, 21
Mary " 1838, 9, 2
1846, 10, 22. Rachel A. m Lewis NORDYKE
1854, 6, 25. Marmaduke, s, Eli & Rachel, b
----, --, --. George & Judith A.
Ch: Stacy Allen b 1855, 3, 5
Mahlon " 1857, 7, 4
Edwin " 1859, 8, 21
George Howard " 1861, 11, 15
Lewis Calvin " 1864, 7, 9
Sarah Mable " 1868, 6, 19

1825, 2, 5. Susannah (form Haworth) con mcd
1836, 5, 19. Mahlon H., Rachel, Phebe, George & Eli, ch Marmaduke & Susannah, recrq
1854, 8, 17. Judith Ann gct Springfield MM, dtd 1854,7,15
1854, 8, 17. Rachel (form Wright) con mou
1855, 7, 19. Mary Terrell (form Brackney) con mou
1856, 5, 15. Marmaduke & w, Susannah, & niece, Phebe Bailey, gct Fairfield MM
1856, 6, 19. Eli & w, Rachel, & s, Marmaduke, gct Fairfield MM
1856, 8, 14. Mahlon H. gct Fairfield MM
1866, 10, 18. Eli recrq
1866, 11, 15. Rachel & ch, Marmaduke, Sally, Mary, Pleasant, Joseph & Ida, rocf Fairfield MM, O., dtd 1866,10,20
1867, 1, 17. Susannah rocf Fairfield MM, O., dtd 1866,12,15
1868, 5, 14. Susannah set off with Wilmington MM, O.
1870, 8, 18. Eli gct Wilmington MM, O.
1870, 8, 18. Eli & w, Rachel, & ch, Marmaduke, Callie Mary, Pleasant, Joseph, Ida, Eli & Susan, gct Wilmington MM, O.
1884, 5, 15. Geo. & w, Judith Ann, & ch, Louis C., Sarah Mabel, John & Anna C., gct Wilmington MM, O.

BRADDS
1885, 6, 18. Rebecca & Estie recrq
1886, 9, 16. John W. & Alva recrq
1901, 6, 13. John dropped from mbrp

BRAGG
1840, 2, 13. Clarissa [Brag] (form Hunt) con mou
1884, 7, 17. Ann rocf Caesars Creek MM, O.

BRANN
1883, 5, 19. Catharine gct Center MM, O.

BREWER
1884, 3, 13. Dennis & w, Lovetta, & ch, Irvin, Eliza E., Thos. Roy & Ida May recrq
1884, 12, 18. Miller recrq
1900, 3, 15. Dennis & w & ch relrq
1908, 12, 17. Marie dropped from mbrp
1913, 1, 16. Clara dropped from mbrp
1914, 11, 19. Miller T. & dt, Eva M., gct Wilmington MM

BRIGGS
----, --, --. William L. m Rebecca ----- b 1840,6,2
Ch: Thomas Franklin b 1859, 12, 21
William J. " 1861, 9, 15
Oresia Caroline b 1867, 2, 1
Uriah Pearson " 1869, 1, 20
Lewis Yan-

BRIGGS, William L. & Rebecca, continued
Ch: cy b 1871, 9, 5
----, --, --. John b 1828,9,7; m Emily M.
----- b 1830,6,17 d 1869,10,27
Ch: Charles M. b 1860, 2, 23
Sarah O. " 1862, 7, 20
Mary E. " 1864, 4, 11

1863, 5, 14. Emily recorded a mbr
1864, 12, 15. John & ch, Mary Etta, recrq
1865, 12, 14. Emily rocf Dover MM, N. C.
1866, 8, 16. Wm. & ch, Thos., Franklin & Wm. J., recrq
1866, 10, 18. Rebecca rocf Dover MM, N. C., dtd 1866,8,30
1871, 12, 14. John N. con mou
1871, 12, 14. Margaret con mou
1906, 4, 19. Ralph recrq
1907, 7, 18. Lee dropped from mbrp

BROCK
1909, 5, 13. Mary E. recrq

BRONSON
1862, 9, 17. Seler N. d ae 39y 6d

BROWN
----, --, --. William b 1834,9,23; m Jane
----- b 1838,1,20
Ch: William
Lawson b 1857, 10, 9
John Franklin b 1859, 8, 1
Albert Russel " 1865, 8, 8

1850, 11, 14. Virgin Shaner (form Brown) rpd mou; d before completed
1866, 9, 13. Wm. Jr. & w, Jane, & ch recrq
1878, 2, 14. Wm. L. & John F. relrq
1886, 10, 14. Wm. T. & w, Jane, & dt, Clara, gct Wilmington MM, O.
1888, 1, 19. Jasper & w, Isadora, & dt, Jennie E., recrq
1888, 5, 17. Frank & w, Ella, rocf Center MM, O.
1901, 6, 13. John Frank & w gct Center MM

BRUNSON
1853, 11, 17. Mariah W. (form Moorman) con mou

BRYON
1852, 1, 15. Mary E. (form Thomas) dis mou

BUNDY
----, --, --. Isaac C. b 1842,7,21 d 1870,7,2; m Eliza A. ----- b 1845,10,24
Ch: Frank E. b 1870, 2, 4 d 1870,11,29

1870, 4, 14. Isaac & w, Eliza Ann, & ch, Frank E., recrq

BUNTING
1882, 4, 13. Theodore M. recrq
1886, 6, 17. Theodore M. relrq

BUSH
1876, 4, 13. Owen recrq
1876, 4, 13. Amanda recrq
1876, 4, 13. Hannah recrq
1876, 4, 13. Lucy recrq
1878, 2, 14. Owen F. relrq

BURRIS
1876, 4, 13. Wm. recrq
1876, 4, 13. James recrq
1876, 4, 13. John Jr. recrq
1876, 4, 13. Elizabeth E. recrq
1876, 4, 13. Amanda recrq
1876, 4, 13. Elizabeth recrq
1876, 4, 13. Ann recrq
1876, 4, 13. Emma recrq
1889, 3, 14. John L. gct Wilmington MM, O.

BURTON
1883, 1, 18. Lavina V. Washington relrq

CALHOUN
1867, 2, 14. Newton J. recrq
1868, 8, 13. Newton J. dis

CAMMACK
1885, 4, 16. Willie recrq
1885, 4, 16. Nellie recrq
1885, 4, 16. Cornelia C. recrq
1885, 4, 16. Charlie H. recrq
1885, 4, 16. John W. recrq
1901, 6, 13. Cornelia dropped from mbrp
1913, 7, 17. Charles gct Wilmington MM

CAREY
1908, 2, 13. Beulah McElwee gct Center MM

CARROLL
1861, 1, 17. Hannah Mary (form Bailey) con mou
1862, 5, 15. Jane (form Huskins) con mou
1866, 8, 16. Deborah con mou
1870, 4, 14. Solon recrq
1870, 12, 15. Hannah M. & ch, George E. & John, gct Miami MM, O.
1872, 2, 15. Jane & ch, Olive B., gct Wilmington MM
1874, 8, 13. Jane & dt, Olive B., rocf Wilmington MM, O., dtd 1874,7,17
1879, 12, 18. Solon & fam gct Caesars Creek MM, O.
1887, 4, 14. Susan M. recrq

CARSON
1907, 12, 19. John M. & w, Ruth, rocf Wilmington MM

CARTER
----, --, --. Jesse, s Geo. & Miriam, b 1806,

CARTER, continued
b 2-2-; m Malinda BENTLEY, dt Benjamin & Rebecca, b 1813,3,5
Ch: John b 1829, 8, 21
Miriam " 1831, 8, 31
William " 1833, 6, 11 d 1839,10,13
Rebecca " 1836, 2, 3
George Lewis " 1838, 2, 6
Thomas " 1840, 10, 12
Ann " 1843, 8, 20
Elizabeth " 1845, 12, 27
Jesse W. " 1849, 4, 10
Cyrus " 1852, 1, 6
----, --, --. John & Hannah
Ch: George b 1830, 4, 10
Louisa " 1832, 6, 12
Elihu " 1833, 3, 9
Isaac " 1835, 2, 7
James " 1838, 4, 6 d 1839, 7,20 bur Grassy Run
John M. b 1841, 11, 13
Joseph G. " 1844, 3, 8
Elizabeth E. " 1847, 2, 28 d 1855,10, 5
----, --, --. Wilson d 1854,5,9; m Judith ----
Ch: William b 1835, 12, 11
Elizabeth " 1840, 11, 19
1840, 10, 23. Samuel (note says b or d)
1843, 11, 12. Wilson (note says b or d)
1850, 10, 16. George (note says b or d)
1851, 11, 19. Elihu, s John & Hannah, Clinton Co., O.; m in Grassy Run MH, Susannah PEELLE, dt Wm. & Clarissa, Clinton Co., O., d 1854,5,4
Ch: James Allen b 1853, 4, 8 d 1853, 7,12
Elihu m 2nd Esther B. ----- d 1863,4,17
Ch: John W. b 1857, 3, 17
Susannah " 1858, 8, 17
Rufus M. " 1862, 11, 22
1853, 10, 19. Louisa m David WALTHALL
1855, 6, 30. Susan Alice, dt Isaac & Phebe, b
1856, 3, 19. Elizabeth m John JESSUP
1856, 3, 19. Cyrus E., s George & Miriam, Clinton Co., O.; m in Grassy Run MH, Lydia B. PEELLE, dt John & Lydia B., Clinton Co., O.
1856, 4, 23. Miriam m John H. DOUGLASS
----, --, --. William & Abigail
Ch: Emily b 1857, 3, 13
Malinda " 1859, 4, 4
William P. " 1862, 1, 13
----, --, --. William B. & Martitia
Ch: Ann Mariah b 1858, 1, 26
Millicent " 1859, 7, 15
----, --, --. George & Elizabeth
Ch: Hannah Louisa b 1858, 4, 6
Elizabeth E. " 1859, 9, 29
Ch: Sybil J. b 1861, 5, 11
Anna M. " 1863, 7, 19
Zimri H. " 1865, 6, 29
John Henry " 1867, 3, 11
George Hamilton " 1869, 2, 6
1858, 12, 22. Artemas N., s Cyrus & Susannah, Green Co., O., b 1838,9,21; m in Grassy Run MH, Fidelia HUNT, dt Lewis & Rebecca, Clinton Co., O., b 1843,3,19 d 1864,7,22
Ch: Susannah b 1860, 2, 2
Cyrus F. " 1862, 4, 30 d 1863, 5,24
1860, 1, 25. Judith F. m Wm. John LOCKE
----, --, --. John M. b 1841,11,13; m Susannah F. ----- b 1844,11,21
Ch: David Elmore b 1862, 12, 16 d 1865,12,10
Alonzo Clinton " 1864, 5, 19
Hannah Pemelia " 1865, 11, 29
1865, 12, 7. Harry Edgar, s Joseph & Sarah M., b
1868, 5, 14. George d ae 87

1830, 6, 17. John & w, Hannah, rocf Springfield MM, dtd 1830,4,13
1835, 3, 19. Judith F. rocf Center MM, dtd 1835,2,18
1835, 9, 17. Malinda recrq
1835, 9, 17. John, Miriam & Wm., ch Jesse & Malinda, recrq
1845, 3, 13. Wilson & w, Judith, & ch, Wm. B. & Elizabeth, gct Springfield MM
1848, 1, 13. Wilson & w, Judith F., & ch, Wm. B. & Elizabeth, rocf Springfield MM, dtd 1847,11,20
1852, 11, 18. John gct Mississinewa MM, Ind.
1855, 10, 18. Esther B. recrq
1855, 11, 15. Isaac gct Back Creek MM, Ind.
1856, 9, 18. Elizabeth rocf Center MM, dtd 1856,9,17
1857, 8, 13. Marticia recrq
1857, 11, 19. George & w, Mariam, rocf Springfield MM, dtd 1857,10,17
1860, 1, 19. Cyrus E. & w, Lydia B., gct Springfield MM, N. C.
1860, 2, 16. Thos. C. gct Caesars Creek MM, O., to m Rachel M. Ellis
1860, 4, 19. Judith F. gct Springfield MM
1860, 4, 19. Wm. B. & w, Marticia, & ch, Ann Maria & Milicent B., gct Springfield MM, Ia.
1860, 5, 17. Thos. C. gct Caesars Creek MM, O.
1860, 11, 15. John Jr. rocf Back Creek MM, dtd 1860,10,18
1861, 1, 17. Cyrus E. & w, Lydia B., rocf Springfield MM, N. C., dtd 1860,12,5
1861, 2, 14. Wilson's d rpd; memorial comm appointed
1862, 3, 13. John M. con mou
1863, 8, 13. Susan F. & s, Elmore, recrq

CARTER, continued
1863, 7, 16. John gct Cottonwood MM, Kans.
1864, 2, 18. Elihu con mou
1865, 1, 19. Mary Ann rocf Springfield MM, O., dtd 1864,11,19
1865, 2, 16. Elihu & w, Mary Ann, & ch, John Wm., Susannah P., Hannah B. & Rufus, gct Wabash MM, Ind.
1865, 3, 16. Samuel C. & Wilson E. gct Plainfield MM, Ind.
1865, 5, 18. Joseph G. con mou
1865, 6, 15. Jesse & w, Malinda, & s, Cyrus, gct Cottonwood MM, Kans.
1865, 12, 14. Elizabeth Bailey (form Carter) con mou
1866, 1, 18. Cyrus B. & w, Lydia B., & gr ch Geo. M. & Susannah F., gct Newberry MM,O.
1866, 7, 19. Artemas N. rpd mou; dropped from mbrp
1867, 9, 19. Wm. & w, Abigail, & ch, Emily Malinda & Wm. P., gct Cottonwood MM, Kans.
1874, 2, 19. Sarah M. recrq
1882, 3, 16. Malinda rocf Cottonwood MM, Kans.
1885, 7, 16. George L. relrq
1904, 11, 17. G. Hamilton & w, Laura E., & ch, L. Sibyl, Walter Everett, Almira E. & Ruth May, gct Goshen MM, O.
1908, 2, 13. Winnifred recrq
1908, 12, 17. Clinton gct White Water MM, Ind.
1909, 5, 13. G. H. & w, Laura, & ch, Sibyl, Walter, Elizabeth, Ruth & John, rocf Westland MM, O.
1910, 3, 17. Elihu & w, Callie, & dt, Opal, relrq

CAVENDER
1901, 6, 13. Mrs. & Ida dropped from mbrp

CHAMBERS
1926, 9, 26. Ruthanna Hare gct Wilmington MM

CHARLES
1866, 5, 17. Wm. R. & w, Hannah E., & ch, Rufus O., Lee P. & Eva C., rocf Clear Creek MM, O.

CLABAUGH
1876, 4, 13. Ruth recrq
1876, 12, 14. Jane [Clabough] recrq
1878, 2, 14. Jane & Ruth relrq

CLARK
1876, 12, 14. Phebe recrq
1878, 2,14. Elizabeth dropped from mbrp
1880, 12, 16. Elizabeth gct Blue River MM, Ind.
1885, 4, 16. Angeline recrq
1887, 7, 14. Alonzo A. & w, Mary E., & ch, John, Jeremiah, Jennie, Gilbert & Edgar, recrq
1889, 8, 15. Lillie May recrq

CLAWSON
1889, 12, 19. Elizabeth Sears relrq

CLEARWATER
----, --, --. Jachab & Sarah Jane
Ch: Charlie b 1855, 2, 13
Esther B. " 1857, 9, 17
Joseph W. " 1860, 10, 1
John T. " 1863, 11, 3

1830, 2, 18. Cert rec for Hannah from Cherry Grove MM, Ind., dtd 1828,12,13, endorsed to Lea's Creek MM
1852, 12, 16. Sarah Jane (form Rawls) con mou
1866, 9, 13. Jacob & ch recrq
1870, 8, 18. Jacob & ch, Chas., Esther, Joseph & John, gct Mississinewa MM, Ind.

CLEMMENS
1905, 2, 16. Fred & Katie relrq

CLEVENGER
1871, 4, 13. Francis E. recrq
1872, 3, 14. Sarah recrq
1877, 4, 19. Francis & Sarah dis disunity

CLIFTON
1876, 4, 13. Thos. recrq
1877, 5, 17. Thos. dropped from mbrp

COATE
1828, 8, 15. John, s Marmaduke & Mary, Miami Co., O.; m in Dover MH, Mary JOHNSON, dt Benjamin & Lucy, Clinton Co., O.
1832, 4, 20. Joseph T., s John & Esther, Miami Co., O.; m in Dover MH, Agnes BANGHAM, dt Benjamin & Lucy, Clinton Co., O.
1828, 10, 16. Mary & s, Lewis Johnson, gct Union MM
1832, 6, 14. Agnes (form Bangham) gct Union MM

COGGESHALL
1839, 2, 21. John, s Tristram & Elizabeth, Wayne Co., Ind.; m in Dover MH, Nancy BANGHAM, dt Benjamin & Lucy, Clinton Co., O.

1839, 5, 16. Nancy gct New Garden MM, Ind.

COMPTON
1852, 11, 19. Pharos, s Henry & Rachel, Miami Co.; O.; m in Dover MH, Delitha BAILEY, dt George & Lydia, Clinton Co., O.
1867, 8, 22. Benjamin, s Seth & Mary, Green Co., O.; m in Dover MH, Margaret WALTHALL dt Thomas & Elizabeth Ann, Clinton Co., O.

1853, 3, 17. Delitha Ann [Comton] gct West Branch MM
1860, 9, 13. Hicajah H. Haworth gct Caesars Creek MM, O., to m Phebe A. Compton

COMPTON, continued
1869, 1, 17. Benjamin rocf Caesars Creek MM, O., dtd 1868,12,27
1873, 3, 13. Jehu, Anna & Chas. recrq
1873, 3, 13. Elwood recrq
1873, 3, 13. Katy recrq
1881, 5, 19. Benjamin & fam gct Caesars Creek MM, O.

CONGER
1911, 12, 14. Gertrude recrq

CONKLIN
1908, 2, 13. Elmer J. & Iona E. recrq
1909, 7, 15. Dora E. relrq

CONNEL
1840, 6, 18. Lucinda (form Shields) con mou
1840, 11, 19. Lucinda gct Newberry MM

CONNER
1907, 4, 18. Lile & Emma recrq

CONSTANT
1902, 3, 13. Bert recrq
1911, 12, 14. Ione recrq
1913, 7, 17. Gertrude Conger dropped from mbrp
1914, 2, 19. Edna recrq

COOK
1902, 3, 13. Wm. H. & Malinda J. recrq
1918, 7, 18. Esther rocf New Castle MM, Ind.
1919, 10, 17. Esther gct New Garden MM

COOPER
1907, 4, 18. Mrs. J. W. recrq

COX
1872, 3, 14. William recrq
1872, 6, 13. Henry recrq
1873, 3, 13. Robert & w, Tamsen R., & ch, Emma J., John W. H. & Franklin N., recrq
1878, 4, 18. Wm. P. relrq
1882, 4, 13. Henry, Robert & Rebecca relrq

CREAMER
1847, 1, 14. Lydia [Cramer] (form Johnson) dis mou
1873, 3, 13. Beach recrq
1906, 4, 19. Frank & Olive recrq

CREEDEN
1887, 7, 14. John & w, Manerva, & s, Hiram, recrq
1887, 7, 14. William recrq
1887, 8, 19. John recrq
1889, 6, 13. John & w, Minerva, & ch, Hiram & Wm., dis disunity

CRISSENBERRY
1879, 4, 17. Annie relrq

CRITES
1882, 5, 18. Ruth Anna rocf Wilmington MM
1882, 6, 15. John rocf Caesars Creek MM
1883, 11, 15. John & w, Ruth Anna, & dt, Edith, gct Caesars Creek MM, O.

CROSS
1874, 4, 16. Thomas L. recrq
1877, 5, 17. Thos. L. dis
1904, 1, 14. Geo. T. & w, Emma, dropped from mbrp

CRUDER
1909, 4, 15. Hallie recrq

CRUIT
1889, 5, 16. Elizabeth & ch, Grace C. & George E., rocf Newberry MM, O.

CULBERTSON
1876, 4, 13. Robert & Nancy recrq

CUMMINS
1873, 1, 16. Robert G. & Flora M. recrq
1873, 2, 13. Emma recrq
1873, 2, 13. Francis J. recrq
1873, 2, 13. Walkup Nimrod recrq
1873, 3, 13. Townsend M. recrq
1873, 3, 13. Martha recrq
1882, 4, 13. Robert & w, Flora M., & ch, Worthie L., Blanchie & Horace D., relrq

CURL
1877, 8, 16. Anthony & w, Mary E., & ch, Alonzo S., Salathiel P., Sarah E. & Emma, recrq
1887, 4, 14. Susan M. recrq (Carroll on women's minutes)
1903, 4, 16. Lena gct Wilmington MM
1913, 9, 18. Orville dropped from mbrp

DALTON
1902, 3, 13. Charles recrq
1909, 12, 16. Earl dropped from mbrp

DASKIN
1904, 2, 18. Laura B. relrq

DAUGHERTY
1876, 4, 13. James C. & Susan recrq
1884, 9, 18. James C. & w, Susan, & ch, Lawrence, rocf Mississinewa MM, Ind.

DAVIS
1832, 6, 21. Hiram, s Joshua & Elizabeth, Clinton Co., O.; m in Dover MH, Mary Ann SHIELDS, dt Wm. & Hannah, Clinton Co.,O.
Ch: Elizabeth b 1833, 3, 9
Rebecca Jane " 1834, 8, 15
Ellis " 1836, 7, 22
John Thos. " 1837, 12, 5
William " 1839, 3, 12

DAVIS, Hiram & Mary Ann, continued
Ch: George B. b 1841, 9, 11
Joseph " 1843, 12, 22 d 1863, 8,22
Silas " 1845, 11, 21
Lewis W. " 1847, 12, 8
Calvin
Hiram " 1850, 5, 5 d 1852, 6, 3
----, --, --. John & Mary
Ch: Joseph
Wesley b 1859, 1, 2
John Albert " 1861, 4, 26

1855, 12, 13. Elizabeth Shields (form Davis) dis mou
1858, 2, 18. John & w, Mary, & ch, Emily, Caroline & Rachel Almedia, rocf Fairfield MM, dtd 1857,12,19
1862, 9, 18. John dis mou
1866, 7, 19. Berthenia O. rocf Center MM
1867, 5, 16. Wm. L. & fam gct Centre MM
1868, 2, 13. Geo. B. dis disunity
1868, 12, 17. Lewis dis jas
1870, 4, 14. Lewis recrq
1870, 7, 17. Wm. L. & fam rocf Center MM
1870, 12, 15. Silas con mou
1871, 1, 19. Silas gct Springfield MM
1871, 4, 13. States & Martha recrq
1872, 3, 14. John recrq
1873, 1, 16. Victoria V. recrq
1875, 1, 14. James P. recrq
1875, 9, 16. James dis
1881, 3, 17. Mary Ann gct Miami MM, O.
1882, 1, 19. Wm. L. & fam gct Mississinewa MM, Ind.
1882, 10, 19. Lewis & w & ch, Rebecca, Lavena, Eveline, Wm. S., Eldena & Clifford, gct Deer Creek MM, Ind.
1886, 12, 16. Louie Palmer relrq
1887, 1, 13. Silas & w, Ruth, & ch, Ann, Alice Jane & Leroy, gct Miami MM, O.
1888, 1, 19. Hiram recrq
1888, 6, 14. Rollah recrq
1911, 12, 14. Eunice gct Wilmington MM

DEARDORFF
1832, 10, 18. Apharacia gct Sugar River MM, Ind.

DEFEBAUGH
1860, 1, 19. Ann (form Gallemore) con mou
1861, 11, 14. Ann [Deffebaugh] dis disunity

DEGROAT
1837, 7, 13. Emily (form Moorman) dis mou

DELEPLANE
1883, 2, 15. Wm. [Dellaplane] recrq
1883, 5, 17. Wm. E. [Delaplane] gct Caesars Creek MM, O.
1884, 3, 13. Lewis [Delaplane] recrq
1884, 4, 17. Carrie recrq
1884, 8, 14. Wm. rocf Caesars Creek MM, O.
1887, 1, 13. Lewis R. relrq
1888, 4, 19. Wm. E. & w, Carrie, & ch, Guy E., gct Wilmington MM, O.

DENNIS
1860, 3, 22. Thomas, s Thomas & Elizabeth, Wayne Co., Ind.; m in Dover MH, Lucy Ann PEEBLES, dt John & Michael, Clinton Co., O.

1860, 9, 13. Lucy Ann gct Springfield MM
1863, 9, 17. Emily (form Peebles) con mou
1864, 2, 18. Emily gct Springfield MM, Ind.

DEREMUS
1885, 7, 16. Emma recrq

DILLON
----, --, --. Luke & Charity
Ch: Naomi b 1813, 12, 14
James " 1815, 11, 12
Hannah " 1817, 11, 12 d 1832, 2,6 bur Dover
Jonathan " 1820, 2, 12
William " 1822, 5, 30
Sarah " 1825, 7, 29
Ruth " 1827, 8, 16
1823, 10, 3. Jess d

1825, 8, 6. Betty gct Honey Creek MM, Ind.
1826, 5, 22. Ann (form Unthank) con mcd
1826, 12, 2. Joseph gct Vermillion MM, Ill.
1826, 12, 2. John gct Vermillion MM, Ill.
1826, 12, 2. Daniel gct Vermillion MM, Ill.
1828, 1, 5. Ann, w Daniel, gct Vermillion MM, Ill.
1829, 3, 19. Daniel Sr. gct Vermillion MM, Ill.
1830, 7, 15. Luke & w, Charity, & ch, Naomi, James W., Hannah, Jonathan, Wm., Sarah & Ruth, gct Vermillion MM, Ill.

DOAN
1848, 8, 24. John, s Jonathan & Phebe, Clinton Co., O.; m in Dover MH, Sarah Jane SHIELDS, dt William & Hannah, Clinton Co., O.

1850, 5, 16. Sarah Jane gct Center MM
1868, 6, 18. Adaline (form Patten) con mou
1873, 1, 16. Joseph W. rocf Dover MM, O. (?)

DODD
1907, 4, 18. Lenna recrq
1907, 4, 18. Mary recrq
1911, 12, 14. Virgil recrq

DONALDSON
1885, 11, 19. Glendora B. recrq
1886, 9, 16. Wenona recrq

DOSTER
1908, 3, 19. Bell recrq

DOUGLAS
----, --, --. David F. b 1796,7,16 d 1863,12,3; m Chloe ----- b 1800,12,27
----, --, --. John & Sarah
Ch: Mariah b 1847, 11, 24
Lydia E. " 1854, 6, 26 d 1857, 1, 4
Phebe Ann " 1857, 10, 17
Mary Narcissa " 1860, 8, 30
1856, 4, 23. John H. [Douglass], s David, Clinton Co., O.; m in Grassy Run MH, Miriam CARTER, dt Jesse & Malinda, Clinton Co., O.
Ch: Chloe Anna b 1857, 2, 13
Jesse Carter b 1859, 4, 21
Mirium " 1861, 1, 31
John Henry Jr. " 1863, 7, 8
----, --, --. Robert W. b 1834,11,11; m Margaret A. ----- b 1833,10,20
Ch: David Franklin b 1857, 6, 15
George Gifford " 1859, 7, 29

1842, 1, 13. Elizabeth (form Madden) dis mou
1854, 6, 15. John N. & w, Sarah T., & dt, Mariah, rocf Springfield MM
1854, 11, 16. Cornelius & w, Phebe N., rocf Springfield MM, dtd 1854,10,21
1855, 3, 15. John Henry [Douglass] gct St. Albans MM, Me.
1856, 11, 13. Mary Everest (form Douglas) dis mou
1858, 8, 18. John Henry [Douglass] & w, Marium, & ch, Chloe, gct St. Albans MM, Me.
1859, 8, 18. John Henry [Douglass] & w, Merium, & ch, Chloe Ann & Jesse Carter, rocf St. Albans MM, Me., dtd 1859,7,26
1860, 4, 19. Margaret A. & ch, David Franklin & Geo. Gifford, recrq
1860, 5, 17. David & w, Chloe, rocf St. Albans MM, Me., dtd 1860,1,24
1862, 5, 14. Robert Walter & w, Margaret A., & ch, David Franklin & Geo. Gifford, gct Clear Creek MM, O.
1865, 12, 14. Maria Jackson (form Douglas) con mou
1868, 2, 13. Chloe gct Clear Creek MM, O.
1868, 2, 13. John Henry & w, Miriam C., & ch, Chloe Ann, Jesse C., Miriam & John Henry, gct Clear Creek MM, O.
1868, 6, 18. Mary gct Pipe Creek MM
1875, 1, 14. Cornelius & w, Phebe N., gct Wilmington MM, O.

DUGAN
1869, 2, 18. Susan & ch, Chas. M. & Harriet L. & Sarah Jane, recrq
1882, 2, 16. Susan & ch, Chas. M., Harriet L. & Sarah J., relrq

DUNN
1911, 12, 14. Edward H. & Clara A. recrq
1911, 12, 14. Geva K. recrq
1911, 12, 14. Ottis Edward recrq
1911, 12, 14. Robert Leslie recrq
1911, 12, 14. Davis Wesley recrq
1911, 12, 14. Lestie Helen recrq
1911, 12, 14. Lester Harris recrq
1917, 11, 15. Ed. & Clara relrq

DWIGGINS
----, --, --. Zimri b 1827,7,20; m Phebe ----- b 1828,8,20
Ch: Charles B. b 1850, 4, 3
Moses F. " 1852, 4, 25
James Farr " 1855, 8, 9
Lizzie " 1858, 9, 21
----, --, --. Robert J. b 1832,2,1; m Rebecca B. ----- b 1834,3,31
Ch: Charles Edwin b 1856, 12, 13
Sarah May " 1862, 10, 15
Emma Elena " 1866, 4, 18
Clara Anna " 1868, 11, 1 d 1870, 9,10
Eva Matilda " 1870, 10, 9
1861, 4, 30. Sarah d ae 75y 9m 11d

1849, 10, 18. Phebe (form Fraizer) con mou
1860, 6, 14. Zimri & ch, Chas. B., Moses F., James F. & Lizzie, recrq (h & ch of Phebe)
1866, 6, 14. Robert J. & w, Rebecca B., & ch, Chas. E., Sally, Mary & Emma, recrq
1881, 3, 17. Moses F. gct White Water MM, Ind.
1888, 1, 19. Clara E. & ch, Arthur R., recrq
1913, 3, 13. Anna recrq
1913, 4, 17. Howard C. & Edith Lucile, minor ch of Anna, recrq

EARLY
1878, 4, 18. Lafayette & w, Susan J., recrq
1878, 4, 18. Marietta recrq
1879, 6, 19. Moses P. & w, Elizabeth, & ch, Sarah V., Orlando M. & Mary M., recrq
1879, 6, 19. Alfred & w, Susan O., & dt, Rosa F., recrq
1879, 6, 19. Irena & ch, Mary A. & John F. recrq
1881, 12, 15. Alfred & w, Susan, & ch, Rosa, relrq
1885, 4, 16. Lafayette & w released
1885, 4, 16. Melccinia released
1885, 4, 16. Marietta released
1885, 4, 16. Irena released
1886, 2, 18. Anne recrq

EDWARDS
1875, 10, 14. David & w, Martha J., & ch, Nettie & Eliza E., rocf Cincinnati MM, dtd 1875,9,16

EDWARDS, continued
1877, 3, 15. David & fam gct Wilmington MM,O.

ELDRED
1889, 8, 15. Flora E. rocf Wilmington MM, O.

ELLIS
1850, 6, 13. Jemima (form Fisher) dis mou
1855, 12, 13. Martha C. (form Moorman) dis mou
1860, 2, 16. Thos. C. Carter gct Caesars Creek MM, O., to m Rachel M. Ellis
1901, 6, 13. Stella dropped from mbrp
1906, 1, 18. H. B. & w, Katie A. & Orville, recrq
1907, 7, 18. Bonnir dropped from mbrp
1931, 4, 26. Ethel Martin & s, Richard Dale, recrq

ELLISON
1873, 3, 13. Samuel Wm. recrq

ENGLISH
1887, 8, 19. W. A. recrq

ENT
1885, 4, 16. Emma J. recrq

EVEREST
1856, 11, 13. Mary (form Douglas) dis mou
1866, 5, 17. Cornelius J., gr s Cornelius Douglas, recrq
1908, 6, 18. Elmer & Sherman dropped from mbrp

FENKER
1908, 3, 19. Henry & Hattie recrq

FERGUSON
1836, 11, 23. Smmuel, s Clark & Mary, Clear Creek, O.; m in Seneca MH, Melissa MOORMAN, dt Thomas P. & Dosha, Green Co., O.
Ch: Maria
Eliza b 1838, 12, 25
Ellen Jane " 1841, 4, 17
Esther
Amanda " 1843, 10, 3
----, --, --. Wm. J. b 1833,5,31; m Rosanna ----- b 1834,9,21
Ch: Virgil F. b 1856, 1, 17
Sidney L. " 1857, 3, 29
Mary Ann " 1858, 7, 8
Almira " 1860, 1, 21
Mellissa " 1861, 7, 3

1847, 6, 17. Mellissa & ch, Maria Eliza, Ellen Jane & Esther Amanda, gct Center MM
1849, 9, 13. Chas. gct Cesars Creek MM, O.
1863, 8, 13. Wm. & w, Rosanna, & ch, Virgil F., Almira & Malissa, recrq
1906, 4, 19. Adam & Florence recrq

FEW
1876, 11, 16. Joseph recrq
1878, 2, 14. Joseph dropped from mbrp

FISHER
1829, 8, 13. Martha gct Vermillion MM, Ill.
1830, 9, 16. Achsah gct Vermillion MM, Ill.
1839, 8, 15. Hiram & w, Rebecca, & ch, Jane, Mary, Amos, Elizabeth, Jemimah, Isaac & Susannah, rocf Fairfield MM, dtd 1839,12, 20
1842, 9, 15. Hiram & w, Rebecca, & ch, Amos, Elizabeth, Jemima, Isaac & Susannah, gct Fall Creek MM
1848, 3, 16. Jane Mason (form Fisher) dis disunity
1848, 3, 16. Mary dis disunity
1848, 3, 16. Hiram & w, Rebecca, & ch, Amos, Jemimah, Isaac & Susannah, rocf Fairfield MM, dtd 1847,9,18
1850, 6, 13. Jemima Ellis (form Fisher) dis mou
1850, 8, 19. Amos gct Clear Creek MM, O.
1860, 12, 13. Mary J. (form Bailey) con mou
1862, 7, 17. Hiram & w, Rebecca, & ch, Susannah, gct Clear Creek MM, O.
1866, 1, 18. Mary J. gct Sugar Plain MM, Ind.

FIX
1878, 2, 14. Martha relrq

FLOTA
1873, 10, 16. Katy recrq of Wm. & Louisa Peebles

FLOWERS
1876, 8, 17. Jane recrq
1878, 3, 14. Jane relrq

FLOYD
1883, 5, 17. Joseph recrq

FOGLE
1856, 6, 17. Elizabeth Ann (form Bailey) con mou
1874, 2, 19. Wm. B. recrq
1878, 4, 18. Wm. B. relrq

FOLLEY
1885, 7, 16. Samuel relrq

FORD
1879, 3, 13. Tailor recrq
1879, 3, 13. William recrq
1879, 3, 13. Mary Elizabeth recrq
1879, 3, 13. John J. & Sarah recrq
1879, 6, 19. John recrq
1880, 5, 10. Eliza recrq
1885, 4, 16. John released
1885, 7, 16. William & Lydia relrq
1901, 6, 13. Charlie dropped from mbrp
1901, 6, 13. Sarah dropped from mbrp
1901, 6, 13. Elizabeth dropped from mbrp

FRANKS
1873, 5, 15. Lucy recrq
1876, 3, 16. Katie recrq
1880, 1, 15. Lucy dis disunity

FRAZIER
----, --, --. John m Alice FISHER dt James & Jane, b 1777,8,14
Ch: Alexander b 1810, 3, 25
Jane " 1811, 2, 28
Mary " 1813, 5, 10
Elizabeth " 1816, 8, 13
Aaron " 1819, 9, 17
Hannah " 1823, 3, 18
----, --, --. Moses, s Ezekiel & Rebecca, b 1791,8,4; m Lydia PUSEY, dt Nathan & Mary, b 1787,12,15 d 1823,10,5 bur Dover
Ch: Joshua b 1814, 1, 7
Ezekiel " 1815, 12, 20
Nathan " 1817, 12, 28 d 1826, 8,16 bur Dover
Mary " 1820, 1, 16
Rebecca " 1822, 10, 13
Moses m 2nd Elizabeth ----- b 1799,6,3
Ch: Hannah b 1826, 2, 23
Phebe " 1828, 8, 30
Jonah " 1830, 8, 30
Lydia Pusey" 1833, 2, 27
James F. " 1835, 3, 29
John " 1837, 6, 25
Caroline Elizabeth " 1845, 12, 5 d 1865, 2,21 bur Dover
----, --, --. Jonah, s Ezekiel & Rebecca, b 1795,3,12; m Mary HADLEY, dt James & Anne, b 1798,1,1
Ch: Son b 1817, 5, 14 d 1817, 5,15 bur Dover
Maria " 1818, 9, 26 " 1818,10, 9 bur Dover
James " 1819, 8, 19 " 1819,10,19 bur Dover
Rebecca " 1820, 9, 9 " 1820,11,20 bur Dover
Rebecca T. " 1821, 11, 2
Son " 1825, 5, 9 " 1825, 5,11 bur Dover
Dt " 1826, 8, 31 " 1826, 8,31
Son " 1827, 9, 16 " 1827, 9,16
" " 1829, 8, 15 " 1829, 8,15
" " 1830, 10, 1 " 1830,10, 1
" " 1832, 11, 11 " 1832,11,11
Dt " 1833, 8, 25 " 1833, 8,25
" " 1834, 6, 3 " 1834, 6, 3
----, --, --. Alexander, s Ezekiel & Rebecca, b 1825,9,30; m Mary JOHNSON, dt Elisha & Jane, b 1787,7,25
Ch: Ashley b 1813, 6, 21 d 1820, 8,21 bur Dover
Moses " 1815, 3, 30 " 1820, 8, 5 bur Dover
Jane " 1817, 2, 26
James " 1819, 4, 11
William b 1823, 1, 15 d 1826, 9,23 bur Dover
Elisha " 1825, 3, 26
Edith " 1821, 4, 2 " 1826, 9,30 bur Dover
1821, 8, 16. Rebecca d bur Dover
1833, 5, 20. Ezekiel d ae 80y 5m 18d
1831, 12, 1. Jane [Frazer] m Joseph PEARSON
1836, 11, 24. Mary m Jacob L. OREN
1838, 3, 6. Ezekiel Jr. d ae 50y 15d
1841, 5, 20. Elizabeth m Ephrim OREN
1842, 3, 24. Rebecca T. [Fraizer] m Jonathan BAILEY
1843, 9, 21. Mary [Fraizer] m David PAINTER
1847, 5, 14. Hannah m Isaac THORNBURY
1848, 10, 26. Rebecca [Frasure] m Jonathan McMILLAN
1852, 11, 25. Lydia P. [Frazer] m Joel HOSKINS
1877, 10, 25. Hannah [Fraizer] m James STANTON

1825, 10, 1. Elizabeth [Fraizer] rocf Green Plain MM, O., dtd 1825,9,7
1837, 1, 19. Jane [Fraizer] con mou
1837, 11, 16. Alexander [Fraizer] & w, Jane, gct Mississinewa MM, Ind.
1838, 4, 19. Joshua [Fraizer] gct Arch St. MM, Phila., Pa.
1843, 7, 13. Jonah [Fraizer] gct Fairfield MM
1848, 10, 19. Jonah [Fraizer] & w, Sarah, & ch, Lindley Murray, Mary Jane & Rachel Wright, rocf Fairfield MM, dtd 1848,9,16
1852, 4, 15. Mary [Fraizer] gct Mississinewa MM, Ind.
1852, 10, 14. Elisha [Fraizer] gct Mississinewa MM, Ind.
1854, 4, 18. John [Fraizer] & w, Alice, gct Cherry Grove MM, Ind.
1854, 12, 14. Jonah [Fraiser] & w, Sarah, gct Fairfield MM
1864, 8, 18. Lydia Ann [Fraizer] gct Clear Creek MM, O.
1866, 5, 17. Martha W. [Fraizer] rocf Centre MM, dtd 1866,5,16
1875, 11, 18. John & fam gct Carthage MM, Ind.

GALLEMORE
----, --, --. William & Mary
Ch: Elisha b 1811, 4, 9
Levisa " 1813, 8, 17
Catharine " 1815, 8, 13
John " 1819, 12, 19
Mary " 1822, 1, 8
----, --, --. William [Gallimore] d 1867,4,12; m Sarah ----- d 1860,3,4
Ch: Susannah b 1832, 8, 6 d 1836, 4,11 bur in Ind.
Catherine b 1833, 10, 14
Mary Jane " 1835, 3, 26
Phebe " 1837, 4, 14 d 1837,12,21
Nathan " 1838, 10, 26 " 1849, 4,30
Ann " 1840, 11, 10
Lewis " 1842, 6, 17 " 1846, 7, 8

GALLEMORE, William & Sarah, continued
Ch: Moses b 1844, 7, 1 d 1845, 6,24
Latham " 1845, 10, 13
Isaiah " 1848, 7, 22
Elisha " 1853, 3, 6
----, --, --. Elisha [Gallimore] m Eliza ----- b 1811,5,21 d 1865,10,18
Ch: Joseph b 1837, 2, 24
Cyrus " 1839, 5, 8 d 1844, 7,20
James " 1842, 2, 26 " 1860,11,10
William P. " 1844, 4, 7
Emily J. " 1846, 5, 15
Mary " 1848, 11, 8
Ann Eliza " 1856, 6, 22
----, --, --. John [Gallamore] b 1819,12,19 d 1864,7,6; m Martha ----- b 1820,7,28
Ch: Elijah b 1840, 7, 27
James M. " 1845, 2, 11
Elizabeth " 1847, 4, 27
1840, 10, 28. Mary [Gallimore] d ae 60
----, --, --. Joseph [Gallimore] m Rebecca Jane ----- b 1839,4,24
Ch: Ann Eliza b 1858, 5, 11
Elizabeth Ellen " 1860, 5, 22
Martha Jane" 1862, 9, 22
James William " 1865, 2, 25
Syrus E. " 1868, 10, 24

1831, 3, 17. Sally [Galemore] (form Hunt) con mcd
1833, 7, 10. Levicy Miers (form Gallemore) dis mcd
1836, 7, 14. William Jr. & fam gct Westfield MM, Ind.
1837, 2, 16. Catharine Ogan (form Gallemore) con mou
1837, 10, 19. Mary Hunt (form Gallemore) con mou
1840, 4, 16. Eliza recrq
1851, 5, 15. Mary Jane Thornbury (form Gallemore) dis mou
1859, 12, 15. John & Martha recrq
1860, 1, 19. Elijah, Elizabeth & James, ch John & Martha, recrq
1860, 1, 19. Ann Defebaugh (form Gallemore) con mou
1862, 5, 14. Joseph recrq
1864, 9, 15. Emily Hoskins (form Gallemore) con mou
1864, 9, 15. Elizabeth Beckford (form Gallemore) con mou
1865, 5, 18. Elijah con mou
1865, 12, 14. Meria recrq
1866, 4, 19. Rebecca Jane & ch, Ann Eliza, Elizabeth Elen, Martha Jane & James Wm., recrq
1867, 6, 13. James dis disunity
1867, 10, 17. Martha rpd mou; droped from mbrp
1868, 1, 16. Wm. P. gct Center MM, to m Mary Jane Bevan
1868, 1, 16. Elisha gct Miami MM, O., to m Sarah Amanda Snowden
1868, 10, 15. Mary J. rocf Center MM, dtd 1868,9,16
1871, 12, 14. Latham con mou
1874, 1, 15. Elisha Jr. relrq
1877, 11, 15. Isaiah & Latham relrq
1879, 5, 15. Rosanna [Gallimore] recrq
1883, 12, 13. Elijah & w, Maria, dis disunity
1885, 7, 16. John W. relrq
1885, 7, 16. Louisa L. relrq
1885, 7, 16. Marietta L. relrq
1885, 7, 16. Jennie G. relrq
1885, 7, 16. Edgar R. relrq
1886, 6, 17. Mary J. & ch, Oscar, Flora & Wm., gct Wilmington MM, O.
1887, 7, 14. Ettie recrq
1889, 8, 15. Mary Jane & ch, Oscar & Wm. B., rocf Wilmington MM, O.
1902, 4, 17. James Wm. & w, Florence, & ch, Adna R. & Letha L., gct Wilmington MM, O.
1906, 2, 15. Oscar [Gallimore] gct Sabina MM

GARRETSON
1879, 3, 13. Thos. recrq
1881, 3, 17. Thos. [Garreson] & w gct Miami MM, O.

GILBERT
1871, 11, 16. Sarah Ann (form Peelle) con mou
1872, 1, 18. Sarah Ann gct Hopewell MM, Ind.

GILLAM
1921, 9, 15. Dan gct Chester MM
1928, 7, 29. Jennie recrq
1928, 7, 29. Roger Miriam, minor, recrq

GILPIN
1832, 3, 22. Henry, s Thomas & Mary, Clinton Co., O.; m in Dover MH, Esther ORAN, dt John & Lydia, Clinton Co., O.

1832, 6, 14. Esther gct Caesars Creek MM, O.
1860, 11, 15. Phebe rocf Caesars Creek MM, O., dtd 1860,9,27
1864, 6, 16. Henry [Gilpen] & ch, Rachel, Rebecca Jane, Levisa & Martha, recrq
1866, 2, 15. Rachel Woolery (form Gilpin) con mou
1871, 1, 19. Louisa Haworth (form Gilpin) con mou

GINN
1885, 6, 18. Blanche B. recrq
1885, 7, 16. Sarah recrq
1886, 6, 17. Fannie recrq
1881, 3, 15. John M. recrq
1889, 5, 16. Anna recrq
1889, 8, 15. Sally recrq

GIRARD
1904, 7, 14. Nettie gct Caesars Creek MM

GLASS
1841, 4, 15. Mary (form Moorman) dis mou
1879, 3, 13. Laban & Julia recrq
1885, 7, 16. Sabin & Julia relrq

GLASSCOCK
1885, 7, 16. Rhoda C. recrq

GLOVER
1876, 4, 13. Edmund recrq
1907, 4, 18. Sarah & John dropped from mbrp

GOINS
1907, 7, 18. Chester & Inez dropped from mbrp

GORMAN
1881, 6, 16. Jacob & w, Ida, & ch, Willie, Orville & Modie, recrq
1884, 8, 14. Jacob [Garman] & w, Ida, & ch, Orville, Maude & Violet Belle, gct Caesars Creek MM, O.

GOTHERMAN
1889, 1, 17. James recrq

GRAVES
1898, 12, 15. Evalyn T. gct Goshen MM, O.

GRAY
1902, 3, 13. Gibbens & Emma recrq
1911, 12, 14. Mabel recrq
1919, 7, 17. Mabel dropped from mbrp

GREEN
1848, 4, 19. Israel C., s Robert & Mary, Clinton Co., O.; m in Seneca MH, Rachel MOORMAN, dt Thomas P. & Dosha, Green Co., O.

1852, 7, 15. Rachel M. gct Newberry MM
1924, 9, 29. Percy E. & w, Anna J., & ch, Ruth M., Robert M., Faith D. & Philip E., roc

GRIFFITH
1834, 9, 18. Paulina P. (form Johnson) dis mcd

GURLEY
1875, 4, 15. Alpheus Newton & w, Frances M., & s, John W., recrq
1885, 7, 16. Alpheus N. & Frances M. relrq

HADLEY
1848, 10, 26. Simon, s Jonathan & Rebecca, Clinton Co., O.; m in Dover MH, Rachel M. BANGHAM, dt Benjamin & Lucy, Clinton Co., O.

1849, 3, 15. Rachel M. gct Springfield MM
1878, 1, 17. Harriet E. (form Haworth) gct Springfield MM, O.
1879, 5, 15. Simon & fam rocf Wilmington MM
1883, 6, 14. Simon & w, Rachel, & s, Cyrus, gct Honey Creek MM, Ia.
1898, 12, 15. J. C. & w gc
1901, 9, 19. Simon rocf Wilmington MM, O.
1902, 5, 2. Simon gct Miami MM, O.

HAINES
1845, 11, 19. Elwood, s Zimri & Elizabeth, Green Co., O., b 1822,8,24; m in Seneca MH, Apharacia MOORMAN, dt Thomas P. & Dosha, Green Co., O., b 1822,11,20
Ch: Lydia
Emily b 1846, 12, 13
Israel
Thos. " 1848, 11, 28
Ann Isabel " 1850, 9, 3
Zimri L. " 1853, 2, 20
Martha
Alice " 1859, 9, 12 d 1862,10, 8
1862, 7, 22. Elizabeth d

1840, 7, 16. Elizabeth rocf Center MM, dtd 1840,6,17
1847, 8, 19. Apharacia gct Center MM
1855, 3, 15. Elwood & w, Apharacia, & ch, Lydia Emily, Israel Thos., Ann Isabella & Zimri L., rocf Center MM, dtd 1855,2,14
1863, 7, 16. Elwood & w, Apharacia, & ch, Lydia E., Israel T., Anna J., Zimri L., gct Newberry MM
1867, 7, 18. Francis E. [Haynes] recrq
1873, 3, 13. Allen & Lucy recrq
1878, 4, 18. Wm. D. & w, Hannah, & ch, Olive May, Mary E., Ida Bell & Nathan O., recrq

HAMILTON
1871, 4, 13. John W. & w, Mildred, & ch, Eli Elizabeth J., Martha A. & Chas. L., recrq
1877, 4, 19. John & Mildred dis disunity

HAMMACK
1869, 5, 13. Lydia (form Peelle) con mou
1872, 4, 18. John H. recrq
1902, 6, 19. John Henry [Hammock] & w, Lydia, gct Sabina MM, O.

HAMPTON
1872, 4, 18. Ezekiel & w, Martha E., & ch, Naomi, Flora B., Augusta Artemesa, Andrew & Lizzie, recrq
1884, 9, 18. Flora relrq

HANKISON
1872, 3, 14. Holmes recrq
1885, 7, 16. Joseph H. & w, Sarah J., & s, James, relrq

HARE
1900, 3, 15. Eliza & ch, Henry D., Walter T. & Edith M., rocf Wilmington MM
1914, 2, 19. Ruthanna recrq
1926, 9, 26. Henry gct Wilmington MM

HARLAN
1840, 8, 13. David Ferris, William Forster, Rachel Fallis, Jonathan & Solomon, ch Solomon, rocf Springfield MM, dtd 1840, 7,14
1846, 8, 13. Rachel Fallis dis disunity

HARNESS
1887, 8, 19. Samuel Augustus & w, Cynthia L., recrq
1889, 4, 18. Samuel & w, Cynthia, dropped from mbrp

HAROLD
1872, 3, 14. Harvey & w, Matilda, & ch, Henrietta, Mary & Caroline, recrq
1885, 7, 16. Henrietta, Mary R. & Caroline relrq

HARRIS
1885, 4, 16. George W. & w released

HARRISON
1835, 2, 19. Wm. H. & w, Ann, & ch, John Stephen & Martha Ann, rocf Green Plain MM, dtd 1834,11,29
1837, 7, 13. Anna dis disunity
1836, 11, 17. Ann & ch, John, Stephen, Martha Ann & Ruth Anna, gct Miami MM, O.
1837, 7, 13. John Stephen, Martha Ann & Ruth Anna, gct Mississinewa MM, Ind.

HART
1876, 4, 13. Joab recrq
1876, 4, 13. Caroline recrq
1907, 4, 18. John & Susan recrq

HARTLEY
1908, 9, 17. Alma Carter rstrq

HARTMAN
1838, 8, 16. Maris rocf Springfield MM, dtd 1838,7,17
1881, 5, 19. Prudence recrq

HATCH
1901, 5, 16. Ora B. relrq

HAUGHE
----, --, --. Barnet & Margaret
Ch: Elizabeth b 1818, 9, 12
Nancy " 1821, 6, 19 d 1837, 2, 8
John A. " 1822, 2, 28
Polly Ann " 1825, 7, 22
Stephen S. " 1827, 3, 31
Allen B. " 1829, 8, 12

1832, 4, 18. Margaret [Hawhay] dis disunity
1838, 1, 18. Elizabeth Turner (form Hawhay) dis mou
1844, 8, 15. Polly Ann Starbuck (form Haughey) dis mou

HAWORTH
----, --, --. Mahlon, s Geo. & Susannah, b 1775,10,23 d 1850,3,23; m Phebe FRAZIER dt Ezekiel & Rebecca, b 1775,7,27 d 1853, 5,20
Ch: Rebecca b 1794, 12, 3 d 1815 5,-- bur Dover
George " 1798, 5, 29
Ezekiel " 1800, 10, 30
Susannah " 1803, 7, 17
Phebe " 1807, 5, 10
Mary " 1804, 12, 5 d 1820, 9,-- bur Dover
Mahlon " 1809, 8, 20
Elijah " 1815, 3, --
James " 1817, 10, -- " 1826, 8,-- bur Dover
Richard " 1823, 7, 1
John F. " 1812, 4, 1 " 1814, 4,-- bur Dover
1834, 10, 23. Elijah, s Mahlon & Phebe, Clinton Co., O.; m in Dover MH, Elizabeth WALTHALL, dt William & Martha, Clinton Co., O.
Ch: Micjah Henry b 1835, 10, 7 d 1861,10, 1
William " 1837, 5, 12
Martha " 1839, 9, 14
Elijah " 1849, 9, 9
Phebe E. " 1854, 7, 20
1843, 3, 23. Richard [Hayworth], s Mahlon & Phebe, Clinton Co., O.; m in Wilmington MH, Elizabeth WEST, dt Thomas & Tamer, Clinton Co., O.
Ch: Thomas Mahlon b 1844, 6, 17
James M. " 1846, 4, 11 d 1865,10, 3
Isaiah M. " 1848, 8, 16
Frances Emily B. " 1852, 5, 23
Caroline " 1854, 9, 9
Harriet Ellen " 1856, 9, 7
Anna Elizabeth " 1862, 10, 12 d 1862,11, 9
Clinton " 1869, 3, 23
----, --, --. Ezekiel & Martha
Ch: Sylvester b 1855, 10, 14
Caroline " 1857, 11, 26
Lawrence " 1861, 2, 4
Alla Jane " 1863, 1, 31
----, --, --. Henriann b 1861,12,17 d 1862,5, 27 (dt Micajah H. & Phebe Ann)
----, --, --. William b 1837,5,12; m Hannah -----
Ch: Eunice Emma b 1866, 6, 1
Alvida Elizabeth " 1868, 11, 14

1825, 2, 5. Susannah Brackney (form Haworth) con mcd
1827, 5, 5. Geo. D. & w, Edith, & ch, Jonah,

HAWORTH, continued
1857, 1, 15. Ezekiel & w, Martha, & ch, Sylvester, rocf Clear Creek MM, O., dtd 1856,12,13
1857, 9, 17. Martha Hoskins (form Haworth) dis mou
1860, 9, 13. Micajah H. gct Caesars Creek MM, O., to m Phebe A. Compton
1861, 5, 16. Phebe Ann rocf Caesars Creek MM, O., dtd 1861,4,25
1864, 4, 14. Richard con mou also taking part in military service
1865, 5, 18. Wm. con mou
1865, 5, 18. Jane rocf Newberry MM, O., dtd 1865,3,20
1865, 9, 14. Hannah C. rocf Caesars Creek MM, dtd 1865,8,24
1867, 5, 16. Phebe Ann gct Caesars Creek MM,O.
1871, 1, 19. Elijah M. con mou
1871, 1, 19. Louisa (form Guilpin) con mou
1871, 8, 17. Isaiah M. [Hayworth] gct Center MM, to m Mary Johnson
1872, 7, 18. Mary [Hayworth] rocf Center MM, O., dtd 1872,6,12
1872, 8, 15. Thos. M. [Hayworth] con mou
1878, 1, 17. Harriet E. Hadley (form Haworth) gct Springfield MM, O.
1885, 7, 16. Richard & w, Jane, & ch, Lenora P. & Clinton, relrq
1887, 9, 15. Mary Jane rocf Newberry MM, O., dtd 1887,7,18
1889, 5, 16. Ora gct Wilmington MM, O.
1900, 11, 15. Pearl rocf Caesars Creek MM, O., dtd 1900,9,27
1902, 3, 13. Ida recrq
1902, 3, 13. Chas. C. recrq
1909, 3, 18. Ida M. relrq
1911, 12, 14. Alvida gct Wilmington MM
1913, 9, 18. Edward gct Wilmington MM
1914, 7, 16. Charles relrq
1915, 1, 14. Orion gct Wilmington MM
1917, 12, 13. Mabel Doan rocf Newberry MM
1921, 3, 17. Jennie & Elizabeth gct Wilmington MM
1931, 4, 26. E. C. relrq

HAWS
1878, 4, 18. Thos. & w, Sarah L., & ch, Harriet A., recrq
1878, 4, 18. George W. & w, Martha, & ch, James L., recrq
1887, 3, 17. Thos. & w, Sarah, & dt, Hattie, relrq

HAYES
1908, 9, 17. Alpha recrq

HEATH
1879, 3, 13. James recrq
1901, 6, 13. James dropped from mbrp

HEFNER
1879, 3, 13. Samuel & Mary recrq

HENRY
1861, 3, 14. Lydia (form Hoskins) dis mou
1884, 5, 15. Julia gct Wilmington MM, O.

HESTER
1826, 9, 7. Robert, s Francis & Mary, Wayne Co., Ind.; m in Dover MH, Mary STARBUCK, dt Gaynor & Susannah, Clinton Co., O.
Ch: Amos b 1827, 5, 9
Zimri " 1828, 10, 9
Joel " 1843, 10, 19
1852, 9, 23. Mary m Isaac LAMB

1827, 10, 6. Mary gct Milford MM, Ind.
1848, 9, 14. Amos gct Newberry MM
1858, 9, 16. Joel dis mou

HIATT
----, --, --. Jesse & Levisa
Ch: Isom b 1826, 12, 17
Jonathan " 1812, 9, 9 (?)
Mahala " 1822, 12, 22
Elizabeth Ann " 1832, 6, 11

1826, 6, 3. Jesse & w, Lavisa, & ch, Sarah, Jonathan, Curtis, Nathan, Susannah & Mahala, rocf Newberry MM, O., dtd 1826,3,23
1835, 10, 15. Jesse & w, Levisha, & ch, Curtis, Nathan, Susannah, Isham & Betsy Ann, gct White Lick MM, Ind.
1843, 1, 19. Susannah (form Pearson) dis mou
1848, 1, 13. Mary (form Moorman) con mou
1849, 7, 19. Mary B. gct Newberry MM
1864, 9, 15. Mary gct Newberry MM, O.
1866, 2, 15. Wm. Peelle gct Fairfield MM, O., to m Louisa Hiatt

HIEL
1833, 8, 15. Sally Bentley (form Hiel) con mcd

HIGHT
1874, 2, 19. Martha E. recrq

HILL
1876, 4, 13. Amelia C. recrq
1878, 2, 14. Amelia C. dropped from mbrp

HINSHAW
----, --, --. Barclay gct Springborough MM

HIRT
1904, 1, 14. Valentine rocf Wilmington MM
1904, 1, 14. Lida & ch recrq
1915, 1, 14. Valentine gct Wilmington MM

HOCKET
----, --, --. Pleasant b 1834,8,30; m Julia Elma ----- b 1840,12,5
Ch: Matilda
Jane b 1861, 10, 14
Jesse

HOCKET, Pleasant & Julia Elma, continued
Ch: William
b 1864, 10, 1
1866, 2, 2. Ida May d

1861, 4, 18. Pleasant & w, Julia Elma, & ch, Malinda Jane, rocf Newberry MM, O., dtd 1861,2,18
1861, 4, 18. Rebecca S. & ch, John & Jacob Simmons, rocf Newberry MM, dtd 1861,2,18
1861, 5, 16. Jesse & w, Mary, & s, Uriah, rocf Newberry MM, dtd 1861,4,22
1861, 8, 15. Sarah rocf Newberry MM, dtd 1861,2,27
1864, 1, 14. Rebecca Roe (form Hockett) con mou
1866, 6, 14. Allen & ch, Della, rocf Newberry MM, dtd 1866,4,23
1868, 10, 15. Pleasant & fam gct Ash Grove MM, Ill.
1868, 11, 19. Allen & ch, Della & Charlie, gct Newberry MM
1869, 1, 14. Julia Elma & ch, Malinda Ann, Wm. & John Henry, gct Ash Grove MM, Ill.
1870, 9, 15. Pleasant gct Ash Grove MM, Ill.
1875, 8, 19. Sarah gct Newberry MM, O.
1886, 6, 17. David rocf Wilmington MM
1886, 6, 17. Frank & w, Rachel, & ch, Hattie & Homer, rocf Wilmington MM, O.

HODGE
1907, 7, 18. Ella dropped from mbrp

HODGSON
----, --, --. Amos & Mary

Ch:		
Nancy	b 1809, 2, 12	
Rebecca	" 1810, 11, 20	
Thomas	" 1812, 7, 18	
Daniel	" 1814, 5, 26	
William	" 1816, 8, 15	
Nathan	" 1818, --, 20	
Allen	" 1821, 2, 20	
Levi	" 1826, 6, 22	
Jesse	" 1829, 4, 25	

1827, 9, 6. Jonathan, s Hur & Achsah, Clinton Co., O., d 1842,1,6 ae 41y 11m; m in Dover MH, Rebecca HODGSON, dt Amos & Mary, Clinton Co., O., d 1840,8,28

Ch:		
Jehu	b 1828, 6, 24	
Zimri	" 1829, 10, 12	
Jane	" 1831, 9, 9	
Mary	" 1834, 1, 23	
Lewis	" 1836, 3, 16	d 1845, 4, 2
Sarah	" 1838, 3, 4	" 1840,12,20

1828, 12, 18. Rebecca (form Starbuck) con mcd
1830, 10, 14. Mary dis jH
1833, 3, 14. Nancy, dt Amos & Mary, gct Vermillion MM, Ill.
1833, 3, 14. Thos., Daniel, Nathan, William, Allen, Levi & Jesse, ch Amos & Mary, gct Vermillion MM, Ill.
1844, 11, 14. Rebecca dis joining Separatists

1872, 9, 19. Cyrus L. [Hodson] recrq
1872, 9, 19. Isaiah [Hodson] recrq
1872, 9, 19. Edith [Hodson] recrq
1872, 9, 19. Willie [Hodson] recrq
1876, 4, 13. Mary & Drucilla [Hodson] recrq
1878, 2, 14. Mary & Drucilla [Hodson] dropped from mbrp
1885, 4, 16. Isaiah [Hodson] dropped from mbrp
1904, 1, 14. Ellsworth [Hodson] recrq

HOLE
1905, 6, 22. Harry R. & w, Leora, rocf Salem MM, O.
1907, 12, 19. Harry R. & w, Leora E., & s, Harrison, gct Fairfield MM

HOMAN
1873, 5, 15. Lucinda recrq

HOOVER
1874, 2, 19. Mary & ch, Lewis S. & Clara C., recrq
1874, 2, 19. Chas. recrq
1874, 3, 19. Leander & Amanda recrq
1879, 5, 15. Milton & w, Mary E., & s, Frank, recrq
1880, 5, 10. Emma recrq
1882, 4, 13. Emma relrq
1882, 4, 13. Clara relrq
1884, 3, 13. Martha E. recrq
1885, 7, 16. Lewis S. relrq
1888, 5, 17. Jessie recrq
1903, 2, 19. Milton & w gct Wilmington MM
1903, 5, 14. Grover E., s Milton & Ella, gct Wilmington MM
1906, 4, 19. Alice M. recrq

HORNADA
1859, 8, 25. John, s Ezekiel & Elizabeth, Clinton Co., O.; m in Dover MH, Mary BAILEY, dt Daniel & Mary, Clinton Co.,O.
Ch: D. Allen b 1869, 8, 21

1860, 5, 11. Mary [Horneday] gct Springfield MM, O.
1864, 2, 18. John & w, Mary, & dt, Anna, rocf Springfield MM, dtd 1864,1,16
1865, 3, 16. John W. [Horneday] & w, Mary, & ch, Annie Elizabeth, gct Rocksylvania MM, Ia.
1866, 1, 18. John W. [Horneday] & fam rocf Rocksylvania MM, Ia.
1877, 4, 19. John & w, Mary, & ch gct Springfield MM, O.
1877, 4, 19. Annie E. gct Springfield MM, O.

HOSKINS
1852, 11, 25. Joel, s Isaac & Rachel, Clinton Co., O.; m in Dover MH, Lydia P. FRAZER, dt Moses & Elizabeth, Clinton Co., O.
Ch: Moses

HOSKINS, continued
Ch: Fraizer b 1853, 9, 20
Isaac Albert " 1856, 5, 30
Wm. Arthur " 1859, 7, 18
Hannah Mary " 1862, 6, 24 d 1863, 8, 1
----, --, --. Josiah b 1831,8,14; m Martha A. ----- b 1839,9,14
Ch: Horace Everett b 1859, 12, 21
Elijah " 1864, 7, 19
----, --, --. Josephas & Emily
Ch: William E. b 1865, 7, 3 d 1866, 7,30
Eliza A. " 1867, 8, 19
Louella " 1869, 5, 15

1854, 5, 18. Lydia P. gct Newberry MM
1857, 7, 16. Joel rocf Clear Creek MM, O., dtd 1857,6,13 (Joel & fam)
1857, 9, 17. Martha (form Haworth) dis mou
1858, 3, 18. Martha recrq
1858, 4, 15. Jane & Lydia rocf Clear Creek MM, O., dtd 1858,3,13
1859, 1, 13. Isaac gct Newberry MM, O., to m Anna Hunt
1859, 9, 15. Jane & Lydia gct Newberry MM, O.
1859, 10, 13. Isaac & s, Josephus, gct Newberry MM, O.
1860, 11, 15. Jane & Lydia rocf Fairfield MM, dtd 1860,10,22
1861, 3, 14. Lydia Henry (form Hoskins) dis mou
1861, 8, 15. Isaac & w, Anna, rocf Newberry MM, dtd 1861,6,17
1862, 5, 15. Anna M. Mercer (form Huskins) con mou
1864, 9, 15. Emily (form Gallemore) con mou
1864, 10, 15. Josephus rpd mou
1868, 5, 14. Jsaac & Anna set off with Wilmington MM
1868, 5, 14. Josiah set off with Wilmington MM, O.
1868, 5, 14. Martha set off with Wilmington MM, O.
1868, 5, 14. Horace Everest set off with Wilmington MM, O.
1868, 5, 14. Gertrude set off with Wilmington MM, O.
1868, 5, 14. Elijah set off with Wilmington MM, O.
1879, 8, 14. Isaac rocf Wilmington MM, O.
1903, 1, 15. Nettie recrq
1905, 6, 22. Nellie Curl rocf Springfield MM
1906, 2, 15. Clarence & w, Nettie K., gct Wilmington MM
1918, 7, 18. Josephine gct Whittier MM, Calif.

HOSTETTER
1871, 4, 13. Samuel & Elenor recrq
1878, 4, 18. Samuel relrq
1879, 3, 13. Samuel recrq
1904, 11, 17. Samuel recrq

HOWARD
1900, 3, 15. Frank & w, Lillie, recrq
1910, 10, 3. Frank & w, Lillie, & s, Waldo, gct Sabina MM, O.

HOWELL
1879, 5, 15. John K. & fam rocf Springfield MM
1881, 7, 14. John K. & fam relrq

HOWLAND
1872, 11, 14. Louisa recrq
1873, 7, 17. Louisa gct Caesars Creek MM, O.

HOXIE
1867, 4, 18. Chas. [Hoxey] & w, Louisa, & ch, Rhoda E., Chas. E., Susannah A. & Howard A., rocf Sidnel MM, Me., dtd 1867, 2,28
1870, 8, 18. Chas. & w, Louisa J., & ch, Rhoda E., Edward, Susannah A. & Howard A., gct Lynn Grove MM, Ia.
1872, 4, 18. Chas. & fam rocf Lynn Grove MM, Ia.
1878, 2, 14. Louisa G. relrq
1885, 7, 16. Edward E. & Susan A. relrq

HUBBARD
1907, 5, 16. James gct Caesars Creek MM, O.

HUFF
1853, 8, 18. Mary Jane (form Wright) con mou
1854, 7, 13. Mary Jane gct Fairfield MM
1888, 1, 19. Nannie E. recrq
1888, 1, 19. Rachel J. recrq
1888, 1, 19. Rebecca E. recrq

HUFFMAN
1907, 4, 18. Lee Otis dropped from mbrp
1909, 3, 18. Ethel & Cora Esther dropped from mbrp

HUGHES
1904, 5, 19. Ethel Pidgeon gct Wilmington MM
1905, 2, 16. Theodore & Mary recrq
1907, 4, 18. John, Mattie & Belle recrq

HUMPHREY
1914, 2, 19. Will [Humphry] & w, Sarah, recrq
1914, 2, 19. Frank [Humphry] & w, Ada, recrq
1917, 12, 13. Ora & w, Dora B., & ch, Goldie, Roma, Raymond, Bertha, Mildred Leala, Dennis J. & Leonard Donald, rocf Newberry MM
1919, 3, 13. Wm. & w, Sarah, & ch, Henry, Walter, Charlie, Zelma & Freda, gct Ogden MM
1920, 9, 16. Ora & w, Dora B., & ch, Goldie, Mabel, Roma, Raymond, Bertha, Mildred Leola, Dennis J. & Leonard Donald, dropped from mbrp

HUNNICUTT
----, --, --. William P. & Edna

HUNNICUTT, William P. & Edna, continued
Ch: Mordecai b 1827, 9, 8
Burwell " 1829, 7, 26
Margaret " 1833, 8, 28
1830, 5, 27. Ann m John PEEBLES
1832, 10, 25. John T., s Margaret, Clinton Co., O., d 1854,2,12; m in Dover MH, Sarah HUNNICUTT, dt Samuel & Phebe, Clinton Co., O.
Ch: Elizabeth Ann b 1834, 7, 13 d 1844, 4, 6
Mary Emily " 1836, 2, 16
William H. " 1839, 7, 20
1835, 10, 15. Thomas, s Thomas & Elizabeth, Clinton Co., O.; m in Dover MH, Susannah BAILEY, dt Daniel & Mary, Clinton Co., O
Ch: Catharine b 1837, 6, 13
David " 1838, 8, 15
John Oliver" 1840, 4, 12
Daniel B. " 1842, 3, 19
Mahlon " 1843, 6, 14 d 1844,11,11
Mary Elizabeth " 1844, 10, 25
Wilson " 1846, 8, 18
Thomas " 1848, 5, 28
Ann Eliza " 1851, 4, 1
1843, 1, 18. Elizabeth d ae 64y 9m 23d bur Dover
----, --, --. John P. & Susannah
Ch: Phebe Ann b 1840, 9, 28
Elizabeth Jane " 1843, 7, 11
David B. " 1851, 12, 23
Mary B. " 1851, 12, 23 d 1852, 1,12
1844, 5, 6. Samuel d ae 30y 10m
1844, 11, 21. Micajah, s Thomas & Elizabeth; m in Dover MH, Sarah WALTHALL, dt Wm. & Martha, Clinton Co., O.
1848, 1, 20. Mary E. m Jacob RATCLIFF
1852, 9, 30. Martha J. m John OREN
----, --, --. David & Martha
Ch: Irina b 1866, 4, 27
Charley " 1867, 8, 16
Edward T. " 1868, 10, 3
1878, 9, 12. Mary E. m John F. SPEER

1827, 12, 1. Elizabeth & ch, Mary Ann, John P., Micajah, Thos. & Martha Jane, rocf Upper MM, Va., dtd 1828,3,17
1829, 12, 17. Wm. P. & w, Edna, & ch, Mordecai P. & Burwell, rocf Stillwater MM, dtd 1828,9,26, endorsed by Springborough MM
1832, 8, 16. Samuel & ch, Sarah Priscilla Chappel & Samuel, rocf Western Branch MM, Va., dtd 1832,7,28
1835, 11, 19. Geo. E. gct Duck Creek MM, Ind.
1835, 5, 14. Ephraim, Robert B., Able & Susannah, rocf Western Branch MM, Va., dtd 1835,3,28
1839, 2, 14. John P. gct Springfield MM
1839, 9, 19. Priscilla dis
1843, 3, 16. John & w, Susannah H., & ch, Phebe Ann, rocf Springfield MM, Ind., dtd 1842,11,15
1846, 3, 19. Wm. P. & w, Edney, & ch, Burwell & Margaret, gct Pennsville MM, O.
1848, 8, 17. Sarah Sr. dis jas
1855, 1, 18. John P. gct Honey Creek MM, Ind.
1855, 1, 18. John T. & ch, Phebe Ann, Elizabeth Jane & David B., gct Honey Creek MM
1857, 2, 19. Mary Emily dis disunity
1858, 4, 15. Catharine Underwood (form Hunnicutt) con mou
1865, 1, 19. Wm. H. dis disunity
1865, 7, 13. David con mou
1865, 12, 14. Martha Ann (form Ross) con mou
1871, 12, 14. Wilson & Mary con mou
1878, 8, 15. John F. Speer rocf Bridgeport MM, Ind., to m Mary E. Hunnicutt
1884, 8, 14. Daniel B. gct Lawrence MM, Kans.
1902, 9, 18. Irene gct Hopewell MM
1910, 3, 17. Frank & w, Laura, & ch, Mary Pauline, Leslie & Priscilla, gct Sabina MM
1914, 9, 17. Charles & w, Delena, & ch, Walter & Robert, gct Wilmington MM, O.
1921, 9, 15. Frank, Lura, Priscilla & Susannah, rocf Wilmington MM
1923, 1, 18. Frank & w, Lura, & ch, Priscilla & Susannah, gct Wilmington MM

HUNT
----, --, --. Joel m Mary ----- d 1849,11,28
Ch: Sally b 1813, 3, 21
Lewis Clark " 1814, 10, 1
Joel " 1816, 10, 8
Clarissa " 1822, 12, 24
Mary Ann " 1825, 1, 20
Moses Starbuck " 1827, 4, 20
Elizabeth " 1830, 5, 9
Hezekiah " 1822, 12, 24
----, --, --. Lewis b 1814,10,1; m Rebecca ----- b 1815,3,17
Ch: Almeda b 1838, 1, 17 d 1858, 1,24
Milton " 1840, 4, 16
Fidelia " 1843, 3, 19
Barton " 1845, 9, 20
Granville " 1849, 12, 20 d 1849,12,27
Hiram H. " 1851, 6, 2
Henry " 1856, 8, 17
----, --, --. Joel Jr. b 1816,10,8; m Mary ----- d 1858,3,17
Ch: Mariah b 1838, 6, 17
Jesse " 1840, 12, 30
Rebecca Jane b 1842, 5, 6
Joel Jr. m 2nd Elizabeth -----
Ch: Elizabeth b 1846, 11, 13
Mary A. " 1849, 9, 2
Allen " 1852, 8, 6
----, --, --. Hezekiah b 1822,12,24 d 1865,9,23; m Rachel L. ----- b 1821,12,21
Ch: Stephen F. b 18-7, 1, 15 d 1870, 8,12
Delitha Ann" 1853, 1, 26
Eliza Jane " 1854, 4, 29

HUNT, Hezekiah & Rachel L., continued
Ch: Jefferson T.
b 1857, 1, 5
Almeda " 1859, 11, 20 d 1861, 3,17
Claton " 1861, 4, 20
1851, 6, 26. Nathan, s Jacob & Lydia, Highland Co., O.; m in Dover MH, Sarah BAILEY, dt Daniel & Mary, Clinton Co., O.
1858, 12, 22. Fidelia m Artemas N. CARTER
----, --, --. Milton & Margaret
Ch: Artemesa b 1863, 12, 1 d 1864,10, 6
Martha Elma" 1864, 9, 5 " 1865,12, 3
1863, 12, 16. Reuben b

1826, 3, 7. Joel & w, Mary, & ch, Sally, Lewis, Joel, Clarissa, Hezekiah & Mary Ann, rocf Dover MM, N. C., dtd 1825,10,22
1831, 3, 17. Sally Gallcmore (form Hunt) con mcd
1837, 10, 19. Mary (form Gallemore) con mou
1840, 2, 13. Clarissa Brag (form Hunt) con mou
1843, 1, 19. Mary Ann Pearson (form Hunt) dis mou
1847, 10, 19. Rebecca & ch, Almeida, Milton, Phidelia & Burton, recrq
1851, 11, 13. Sarah gct Fairfield MM
1852, 6, 17. Elizabeth Williams (form Hunt) con mou
1855, 2, 15. Deborah Ann recrq
1855, 6, 14. Wm. L. & w, Phebe, & ch, Chas. Edwin, Aaron & Isaiah, rocf Newberry MM, dtd 1855,5,21
1857, 11, 19. Maria Shela (form Hunt) con mou
1858, 4, 15. Wm. & w, Phebe, & ch, Chas. E., Aaron, Isaiah & Susannah E., gct Newberry MM, O.
1859, 1, 13. Isaac Hoskins gct Newberry MM, O., to m Anna Hunt
1859, 2, 17. Milton con mou
1859, 7, 14. Jesse dis mou
1859, 9, 15. Joel Jr. con mou
1860, 2, 16. Elizabeth recrq
1860, 4, 19. Rachel & ch, Stephen, Delitha Ann, Elisa Jane, Jefferson T. & Almeda, recrq
1860, 11, 15. Rebecca Jane dis disunity
1860, 11, 15. Margaret Jane & s, John L., recrq
1864, 6, 16. Joel & w, Elizabeth, & ch, Elizabeth, Mary Ann & Allen, gct Cottonwood MM, Kans.
1865, 7, 13. Mary Abba (form Bailey) con mou
1865, 12, 14. Marianna Bailey gct Newberry MM, O.
1866, 4, 19. Milton gct Cottonwood MM, Kans.
1866, 4, 19. Mary Anna Bailey gct Newberry MM, O.
1866, 11, 15. Milton & w, Margaret, & s, John L., gct Cottonwood MM, Kans.
1869, 8, 19. Barton con mou
1869, 10, 14. Barton gct Cottonwood MM, Kans.
1872, 2, 15. Thos. Elwood & Wilson rocf Newberry MM, O., dtd 1872,1,22
1883, 5, 17. Briton recrq
1885, 12, 17. Clayton dis disunity
1887, 7, 14. Hattie & ch, Ottie C. & Mandy E., recrq
1887, 7, 14. Della recrq
1889, 3, 14. Thomas Elwood gct Wilmington MM, O.
1907, 7, 18. Wilson A. dropped from mbrp

HUSSEY
1866, 9, 19. Julia A. (nee Thompson) m Micajah F. MOORMAN

1848, 12, 14. Louisa rocf Salem MM, Iowa, dtd 1848,9,13
1866, 5, 17. Julia [Husy] rocf Clear Creek MM, O.

INLOW
1915, 7, 15. Rena Hurley dropped from mbrp

IRELAND
1907, 4, 18. Alice recrq

JACKS
1876, 4, 13. William recrq
1876, 4, 13. Daniel recrq
1876, 4, 13. Celia recrq
1877, 5, 17. Daniel dropped from mbrp
1884, 10, 16. Wm. gct Wilmington MM, O.

JACKSON
1865, 12, 14. Maria (form Douglas) con mou
1872, 3, 14. Lucretia recrq
1874, 2, 19. Irvin H. recrq
1875, 7, 15. Lucretia gct Van Wert MM, O.
1876, 12, 14. Evan H. relrq
1877, 1, 18. Evan H. recrq again
1907, 3, 14. Osie recrq

JANUARY
1878, 5, 16. Robert P. recrq
1902, 4, 17. Clara Pagett gct Wilmington MM, O.
1906, 2, 15. Garnett P. rocf Wilmington MM
1906, 4, 19. Maw recrq

JASPER
1904, 1, 14. Clyde dropped from mbrp

JEFFRIES
1888, 5, 17. Alice relrq
1901, 6, 13. Roper dropped from mbrp

JENKINS
1842, 11, 24. Mary m Josiah BAILEY
1847, 5, 23. Hannah d ae 58y 5m 11d

1839, 3, 14. Hannah & ch, Israel, Mary & Ann, rocf Hopewell MM, dtd 1838,12,6
1868, 5, 14. Ann set off with Wilmington MM, O.

JENKINS, continued
1874, 2, 19. Martha recrq
1885, 6, 18. Clary recrq

JESSOP
1856, 3, 19. John, s Elijah, dec, & Emily (now Peelle), Clinton Co., O.; m in Grassy Run MH, Elizabeth CARTER, dt Wilson & Judith, Clinton Co., O.
Ch: Wilson C. b 1857, 6, 14
Samuel L. " 1863, 3, 2

1870, 1, 13. John [Jessup] & w, Elizabeth Ann, & ch, Wilson C., Samuel S. & Josephine gct Poplar Run MM

JOHNSON
----, --, --. Samuel & Susannah
Ch: Dosha G. b 1811, 11, 22
David B. " 1824, 1, 9
1820, 11, 11. James, s Chas. M. & Phebe, b
----, --, --. Pleasant & Nancy
Ch: Eli P. b 1821, 9, 29
Nancy G. " 1823, 2, 23
----, --, --. Lewis Jr., s Lewis & Mary, b 1821,11,14 d 1821,12,28 bur Dover
----, --, --. James & Elizabeth
Ch: Rhoda Ann b 1822, 6, 27
John G. " 1824, 1, 22
Alfred " 1825, 10, 28
Evan L. " 1827, 10, 21
Thatcher S." 1829, 11, 4
Hannah Maria " 1832, 1, 4
1823, 10, 4. Susannah d bur Seneca
1824, 12, 9. Elizabeth m Zachariah M. BAUGHMAN
----, --, --. John m Martha ----- d 1830,10, 24 ae 27y 1m 12d bur Seneca
Ch: Jesse Faulkner b 1827, 6, 6
Juleann " 1829, 4, 17 d 1840, 9,22 bur Seneca
Joel " 1830, 10, 12
----, --, --. George W. & Apharacia
Ch: Jehu b 1827, 6, 22
Joel " 1829, 4, 20
1828, 8, 15. Mary m John COATE
1832, 3, 11. Ann b
1836, 9, 22. Abijah, s Micajah & Elizabeth, Warren Co., O.; m in Dover MH, Elizabeth BAILEY, dt David & Sylvia, Clinton Co.,O.
1837, 8, 8. Chalkley Thos. b
1840, 1, 5. Mary Evans b
1844, 2, 11. Joseph d ae 80y 4m 10d bur Seneca
1844, 8, 9. Susannah d ae 62y 11m 17d bur Concord
----, --, --. Mildred d 1852,1,18 ae 86y 10m 3d bur Seneca (w of Christopher, dt Micajah & Susannah Moorman)
1856, 1, 13. Nancy d bur Seneca, Green Co.,O.
----, --, --. Jarvis L. b 1818,1,29; m Jane ----- b 1829,10,28
Ch: Edith V. b 1855, 8, 14 d 1862, 9,26
William " 1858, 4, 25
Mary E. " 1860, 3, 16
Edwin C. " 1863, 2, 27
Harry " 1865, 2, 5
Frank " 1867, 1, 5
Oliver " 1869, 3, 10 d 1869,12,25
1865, 9, 21. Ahira, s Lewis & Rachel, Clinton Co., O.; m in Dover MH, Margaret Ann PAINTER, dt Joseph C. & Hannah, Clinton Co., O.

1827, 4, 7. Lydia con mou
1837, 11, 3. Samuel gct White Lick MM, Ind.
1829, 8, 13. Susannah gct Vermillion MM, Ill.
1830, 5, 13. James W. & w, Elizabeth, & ch, Rhoda Ann, John G., Evan L., Alfred & Thatcher S., rocf Miami MM, O., dtd 1830, 2,24, endorsed by Center MM, 1830,5,12
1830, 11, 18. Joseph gct White Lick MM, Ind.
1831, 11, 17. Nancy & ch, Delilah Albertine, Caroline Agnes, Arzilla, Martha Ann, Melvina, Julia Ann & Eliza Ann, rocf Fairfield MM, dtd 1831,10,20
1832, 4, 19. James & w, Elizabeth, & ch, Rhoda Ann, John Griffith, Alfred Evan, Lewis Thatcher Stratton & Mannah Maria, gct Center MM
1832, 10, 18. Wm. C. gct Sugar River MM, Ind.
1833, 12, 19. Joseph gct Fairfield MM, O.
1832, 11, 15. Nancy, w Simon, dis jH
1832, 11, 15. Delilah Albertine dis jH
1834, 9, 18. Paulina P. Griffith (form Johnson) dis mou
1835, 8, 13. Susannah dis disunity
1836, 9, 15. Arzilli Wilson (form Johnson) dis mou
1836, 12, 15. Elizabeth gct Miami MM, O.
1837, 3, 16. Dosha dis disunity
1837, 7, 13. Amos, Lydia & Solomon, ch Thos. & Mary, rocf Center MM, dtd 1837,6,15
1842, 1, 13. Abigail & w, Elizabeth, & ch, Silvia & John Kelley, rocf Springborough MM, dtd 1841,10,23
1844, 9, 19. Larkin Fauster, Mary Ann, Thos. Elwood, Wm. Lewis, Samuel Pleasant & Juliann, ch Thos. M. & Susannah, gct Springboro MM
1845, 6, 19. Eli P. gct Fairfield MM
1845, 11, 13. Martha Ann Wadkins (form Johnson) dis mou & jas
1846, 4, 16. Abijah & w, Elizabeth B., & ch, Silviah B., John & Micajah D., gct Miami MM, O.
1847, 1, 14. Lydia Cramer (form Johnson) dis mou
1849, 10, 18. Samuel gct Springborough MM
1854, 9, 14. Elizabeth (form Moorman) con mou
1855, 1, 18. Jervis gct Fairfield MM
1855, 4, 19. Nancy G. Smith (form Johnson) dis mou

JOHNSON, continued
1860, 6, 14. Jarvis L. rocf Fairfield MM, dtd 1860,3,17
1863, 3, 19. Elizabeth (form Wall) dis mou
1866, 1, 18. Margaret gct Center MM
1871, 4, 13. Theodore recrq
1871, 4, 13. Pascal recrq
1871, 4, 13. James recrq
1871, 4, 13. Daniel C. recrq
1871, 4, 13. John recrq
1871, 4, 13. Rufus recrq
1871, 4, 13. Mary E. recrq
1871, 8, 17. Isaiah M. Hayworth gct Center MM, to m Mary Johnson
1873, 1, 16. Lunettie J. recrq
1875, 3, 18. Peter & w, Comfort, recrq
1876, 3, 16. Mary recrq
1876, 4, 13. Tolbert recrq
1876, 4, 13. Temperance & Laura recrq
1876, 5, 18. Belle rocf Elk MM, O., dtd 1876,3,23
1876, 6, 15. James S., Emily Jane & Alice May, ch Talbolt & Temperance, recrq
1877, 1, 18. Joseph rocf Center MM, O.
1879, 3, 13. Nancie & Rose recrq
1879, 3, 13. Annie recrq
1880, 5, 10. Jennie recrq
1882, 1, 19. Jennie relrq
1883, 4, 19. James H., Rufus, John, Daniel & Mary, gct Honey Creek MM, Iowa
1884, 11, 13. Allen T. & w, Mahala, rocf Hopewell MM, O.
1884, 12, 18. Joseph & w, M. Belle, & ch, Irven H. & Mary Ann, gct Springfield MM,O.
1887, 6, 16. A. L. & w gct Hopewell MM, O.
1888, 1, 19. Curtis Marion recrq
1903, 3, 19. Charles & w, Mary, recrq
1903, 9, 17. Grace & Nellie recrq
1909, 5, 13. Charles, Mary, Grace & Nellie relrq

JONES
1866, 3, 15. Elizabeth con mou
1867, 11, 14. Elizabeth dis disunity
1874, 2, 19. Sarah recrq
1881, 5, 19. Reuben recrq
1884, 1, 17. Reuben gct Caesars Creek MM, O.
1908, 1, 16. Lindley & w, Lida, & dt, Elma, rocf Friendsville MM, Tenn.
1908, 1, 16. Marvin H., minor s Lindley & Lida, recrq
1910, 9, 15. J. Lindley & fam gct Sabina MM

JORDAN
1907, 4, 18. Eroscoe recrq
1907, 4, 18. Pearl recrq
1908, 3, 19. Roscoe H. & w, Pearl, relrq

KEARNS
1872, 2, 15. John & Emily recrq
1874, 2, 19. Alfred T. [Kernes] recrq
1878, 5, 16. John E., Emily & Alfred [Kerns] relrq

KIRK
1830, 4, 14. Caleb [Kerk] & w, Susanna, & ch, Daniel & James E., roc
1838, 9, 13. Susannah dis disunity
1853, 6, 16. Caleb gct New Garden MM

KERSEY
1871, 5, 13. Amos W. & Sarah recrq
1888, 4, 19. Amos gct Springfield MM, N. C.

KERTICE
1878, 4, 18. Jane Shirk relrq

KESLER
1872, 3, 14. Martin recrq

KIGER
1901, 6, 13. Minnie dropped from mbrp

KINGERY
1888, 4, 19. Ada gct Mississinewa MM, Ind.

KINNEY
1903, 2, 19. Naomi Huff gct Center MM

KINSEY
1848, 3, 23. Elizabeth Ann m Thos. WALTHALL

KNICK
1907, 4, 18. Charles [Nick] recrq
1907, 6, 20. Mary recrq
1907, 6, 20. Myrtle recrq
1907, 6, 20. Blanch recrq
1907, 6, 20. Elbert recrq

KNOWLTON
1852, 10, 19. Julia Ann rocf Cincinnati MM, dtd 1852,9,16
1853, 12, 15. Julia Ann gct Springfield MM

LACKEY
1928, 1, 22. Leota Stevens gct Mt. Airy MM, N. C.

LAMB
----, --, --. Isaac & Catharine
Ch: John W. b 1844, 4, 9
Jehu B. " 1846, 2, 27
Emariah B. " 1848, 6, 27
1852, 9, 23. Isaac, s John & Sarah, Clinton Co., O.; m in Dover MH, Mary HESTER, dt Gaynor & Susannah STARBUCK, Clinton Co.,O.

1827, 9, 1. Rebecca [Lam] (form Pierson) con mcd
1841, 7, 15. Isaac & w, Catharine, rocf Piney Woods MM, N. C., dtd 1841,4,3
1854, 2, 16. Rebecca dis jas
1872, 3, 14. Geo. & w, Henrietta, & ch, Rebecca, Hannah & Willis, recrq
1872, 3, 14. Eri recrq
1885, 7, 16. John W. relrq
1908, 6, 18. Willis dropped from mbrp

LAMBERT
1866, 6, 14. Catharine recrq

LANCASTER
1882, 3, 16. John C. recrq
1885, 9, 17. Sallie recrq
1908, 9, 17. Alice Sears recrq

LANE
1865, 8, 17. Hannah D. rocf St. Albans MM, Me.
1865, 9, 14. Joseph S. & s rocf Clear Creek MM, O., dtd 1865,9,9
1867, 8, 15. Joseph S. & w, Hannah D., & s, Henry D., gct Lynn Grove MM
1885, 6, 18. Louella recrq
1901, 6, 13. James & Luella dropped from mbrp

LARKINS
1870, 5, 19. John W. & w, Nancy M., & ch, Isaac James, John Wm., Asa & Thos. Eli, recrq
1881, 2, 17. John & fam gct Hopewell MM, O.
1901, 6, 13. Mannie & Paul [Larkin] dropped from mbrp

LEEKY
1855, 4, 19. Ruth (form Thomas) dis mou

LEMONS
1874, 2, 19. Jasper recrq
1878, 2, 14. Jasper dropped from mbrp
1907, 4, 18. Carrie & Lillie [Lemmon] recrq

LEWIS
1871, 4, 13. Eva con mou
1871, 4, 13. Eva gct Saline MM, Ill.

LIGHT
1884, 5, 15. Wm. A. recrq

LINKHART
1913, 7, 17. Mary C. recrq

LITTLE
1885, 7, 16. Margaret relrq

LOCKE
1860, 1, 25. William, s John & Lucretia, Wayne Co., Ind.; m in Grassy Run MH, Judith F. CARTER, dt Wm. & Phebe BALLARD

1860, 4, 19. Judith F. [Loch] gct Springfield MM, Ind.

LONT
1901, 6, 13. John dropped from mbrp
1901, 6, 13. Hallie dropped from mbrp

LORD
1866, 1, 18. Cyrus W. recrq

LOVELL
1867, 1, 17. Anna recrq

LUELLEN
1889, 1, 17. Thos. Albert recrq

LUNDY
1908, 2, 13. Ruth M. gct Center MM

LYNCH
1876, 4, 13. Malissa recrq
1885, 7, 16. Melissa relrq
1908, 6, 18. Eva dropped from mbrp
1908, 6, 18. Joseph gct Sabina MM, O.

McCARTNEY
1876, 12, 14. Mary recrq

McCLURE
1878, 2, 14. Jane dropped from mbrp

McCONNELL
1904, 1, 14. Jennie dropped from mbrp

McDANIEL
1906, 4, 19. Raymond recrq

McDONALD
1900, 3, 15. Aaron & w & ch, Grace, relrq

McELWEE
1904, 1, 14. Ethelbert J. gct Ogden MM
1908, 1, 16. Ethelbert & w, Myrtle, rocf Ogden MM
1912, 3, 14. Myrtle Beuhler (form McElwee) relrq
1914, 2, 19. Will gct Springfield MM
1920, 9, 16. Kate gct Wilmington MM

McFARLAND
1901, 6, 13. Archie dropped from mbrp

McGINNIS
1871, 4, 13. Samuel M. recrq

McKAY
1915, 4, 15. Harold & w, Ida Haworth, rocf Center MM
1916, 3, 16. Edith Starbuck gct Center MM
1917, 4, 19. Howard F. & w, Edith S., & s, Robert, rocf Center MM
1921, 2, 17. Howard F. & w, Edith S., & ch, Robert F. & Donald S., gct Miami MM, O.
1921, 2, 17. E. Harold & w, Ila H., & s, Allen H., gct Miami MM, O.

McKIBBEN
1888, 1, 19. Chemiah & w, Amanda E. & Minnie T., Maud & Maggie, recrq

McMILLAN
1848, 10, 26. Jonathan, s David & Hannah, Clinton Co.,O., m in Dover MH, Rebecca

McMILLAN, continued
FRASURE, dt Moses & Lydia, Clinton Co., O.

1849, 2, 15. Rebecca gct Center MM
1907, 6, 20. Joshua F. & w, Mary E., & ch, Viola H., L. Dora, Lena & Carl, gct Newberry MM
1909, 1, 14. Charles gct Miami MM, O.

McNEAL
1907, 7, 18. John & w, Mary, dropped from mbrp
1907, 7, 18. Ada dropped from mbrp
1907, 7, 18. Hazel dropped from mbrp
1907, 9, 19. Allie Carter [McNeil] relrq
1909, 9, 16. Thomas & w, Sallie, & ch, Carlos, Mary M., Ella, Herburt, Walter, Imogene & Carrie Mabel, relrq

MCPHERSON
1868, 2, 13. Jesse Peelle gct Fairfield MM, O., to m Phebe A. McPherson
1873, 1, 16. Henry C. recrq
1874, 2, 19. Elmore recrq
1878, 2, 14. Elmore dropped from mbrp
1887, 11, 17. Joseph rocf Fairfield MM, O.

McVEY
1902, 3, 13. Leroy M. & w, Ardiela, & ch, Bessie M. & Wm. H., recrq
1908, 12, 17. Roy & w, Della, & ch, Bessie, Willie, Ada, Olive & James Carl, gct Center MM

MADDEN
----, --, --. Solomon, s Geo. & Elizabeth, b 1793,9,28; m Ruth ROBINS, dt Moses & Alice, b 1802,8,8
Ch: Cyrus b 1822, 9, 22
Alice Jane " 1824, 3, 5
Mary Ann " 1830, 1, 4
Solomon " 1832, 11, 3
Moses
George " 1837, 10, 10
William " 1840, 5, 14
Rachel " 1843, 7, 26
1820, 7, 6. Elizabeth, dt Moses & Alice Robins, b

1837, 4, 13. Solomon & w, Ruth, & ch, Elizabeth R., Cyrus W., Alice Jane, Maryann & Solomon, rocf Springfield MM, O., dtd 1837,4,11
1842, 1, 13. Elizabeth Douglas (form Madden) dis mou
1845, 9, 18. Solomon & w, Ruth, & ch, Alice Jane, Mary Ann, Solomon, Moses, George, William, Henry & Rachel, gct Springfield MM
1845, 9, 18. Cyrus W. gct Springfield MM
1860, 9, 13. Ruth & ch, Wm. H. & Rachel, rocf Lytles Creek MM, dtd 1860,8,18
1870, 10, 13. Solomon & Joseph G. rocf Springfield MM, O.

MAGOON
1864, 12, 15. Alfred & ch, Mary E., Josiah, Wm. O., Parthena & Albert, rocf Fairfield MM, O., dtd 1864,11,19
1865, 11, 16. Alfred & ch, Josiah, Parthena & Albert, gct Fairfield MM, O.
1868, 2, 13. Wm., s Alfred, gct Fairfield MM, O.
1869, 4, 15. Mary Barrett (form Magoon) gct Fairfield MM

MAHAFFY
1901, 6, 13. Nathan A. [Mahaffey] & w, Sarah, & ch, Goldie M. & Clarence W., rocf Wilmington MM
1904, 2, 18. Nathan & w, Sara Alice, & ch, Clarence, Goldie dropped from mbrp
1906, 4, 19. George & Irena recrq

MALLANGER
1863, 7, 16. Mary Jane [Malanger] (form Ballard) con mou
1886, 9, 16. Mary J. gct Mt. Air MM, Osbern Co., Kans.

MARTIN
1866, 9, 13. Mary (form Pearson) dis mou
1873, 2, 13. Chas. L. & w, Mary, & ch, Clara A., Wm. H. & Ann E., recrq
1902, 5, 2. Anna recrq
1906, 2, 15. Annie gct Sabina MM
1909, 5, 13. Anna S. A. recrq

MASON
1848, 3, 16. Jane (form Fisher) dis disunity
1878, 2, 14. Wm. F. relrq

MATHER
1883, 11, 15. Albert H. & w, Phebe E., & ch, Omar B. & Ethel E., rocf Springfield MM,O.

MATTHEWS
1879, 4, 17. Phebe E. gct Springfield MM

MELINGER
1886, 9, 16. Mary J. gct Mt. Air MM, Osborn Co., Kans.

MELVIN
1906, 4, 19. Will recrq
1908, 6, 18. Will dropped from mbrp

MERCER
1862, 5, 15. Anna M. (form Thomas) dis mou

MERRITT
1906, 4, 19. Milton recrq
1908, 6, 18. Milton [Merrit] dropped from mbrp

MIARS
1833, 7, 10. Levicy [Miers] (form Gallemore) dis mou
1872, 9, 19. Orlando & Marcia recrq
1888, 9, 13. Orlando dis disunity
1889, 1, 17. Marcia dis disunity
1902, 11, 13. Chas. E. & Esther L. recrq
1903, 11, 19. Chas. E. & w, Esther L., gct Bridgeport MM, Ind.
1907, 4, 18. Dora [Myers] recrq

MILLER
1861, 3, 14. Isaiah Peelle gct Springboro MM, to m Susan Miller
1886, 9, 16. Rosa recrq

MILLS
----, --, --. Jonathan C. & Rhoda
Ch: Calvin W. b 1845, 2, 25
Lewis B. " 1850, 1, 14
Albert H. " 1852, 10, 25
Elias P. " 1855, 8, 20
Elizabeth Ann " 1858, 1, 1

1845, 2, 13. Rhoda (form Peelle) con mou
1872, 8, 15. Calvin W. & w, Fannie E., con mou
1874, 2, 19. Joseph recrq
1876, 1, 13. Emma rocf Center MM, O.
1876, 4, 13. William & Nancy recrq
1880, 5, 10. James recrq
1882, 2, 16. Albert H. & fam gct Wilmington MM
1882, 7, 13. Jemimah J. rocf Fairview MM, Ill.
1883, 3, 15. Alfred recrq
1883, 3, 15. Emma recrq
1883, 3, 15. Claude J., s E. P. & Emma J., recrq
1885, 7, 16. Wm. & Nancy relrq

MINSHALL
1886, 9, 16. Bertha recrq

MITCHELL
1914, 9, 17. Grace recrq

MOCK
1873, 3, 13. Cassius & Almeda recrq
1878, 4, 18. Cassius & w, Almedia, relrq

MOON
1875, 3, 18. Thomas E. rocf Fairview MM, Ill.
1889, 3, 14. T. Elwood & w, Louisa P., & ch, Elsie, Orlando, Wm. P. & Oland J., gct Wilmington MM, O.

MOORE
1861, 1, 17. Margaret (form West) con mou
1862, 6, 19. Margaret E. gct Springfield MM

MOORMAN
----, --, --. Micajah d 1860,4,28 bur Seneca, Green Co., O.; m Susannah -----
Ch: Apharacia b 1802, 11, 30
Thomas C. " 1805, 4, 17
Mildred " 1807, 9, 22
Christopher" 1810, 1, 25
Elizabeth " 1812, 8, 14
Nancy W. " 1815, 5, 7
Reuben " 1818, 1, 20
Polley " 1820, 12, 17
John " 1822, 9, 23
----, --, --. Thomas P. & Dosha
Ch: Nancy b 1812, 7, 30
John " 1814, 5, 5
Malissa " 1816, 5, 2
Thos. Clark" 1818, 5, 9
Susannah " 1820, 10, 14
Apharacia " 1822, 11, 20
Mary " 1824, 12, 24
Elizabeth " 1827, 3, 3
Rachel " 1829, 5, 23
Martha " 1831, 4, 14
James Ellis" 1833, 7, 26
Paxon Hope " 1835, 9, 17 d 1859, 5,17 bur Seneca Green Co., O.
Wm. Newton b 1838, 8, 8
1813, 11, 3. Reuben, s Reuben & Lydia, b
----, --, --. James m Elizabeth ----- d 1840, 11,23 ae 45y 6m 5d bur Seneca
Ch: Emily b 1816, 1, 9
Manson " 1818, 2, 18
Mary " 1821, 1, 10
Henry T. " 1824, 2, 25
John C. " 1826, 10, 13
Mildred " 1829, 9, 10
Elizabeth " 1832, 8, 31
James Christopher " 1835, 9, 5
Reuben Chiles " 1838, 10, 6 d 1853, 2,20 bur Seneca
1816, 2, 6. John d bur Seneca, Green Co.,O.
----, --, --. Charles & Matilda
Ch: Betsy Ann b 1817, 7, 20
Maria " 1819, 11, 1
Micajah F. " 1824, 2, 8
Marshall " 1826, 2, 26
Jesse " 1828, 4, 10
Matthew " 1830, 6, 15
Malinda " 1832, 12, 11
Chas. Thos." 1835, 3, 30
Paschal Lewis " 1837, 8, 30
Eli Watson " 1840, 7, 4
Matilda Ann " 1842, 12, 3 d 1844,10,20 bur Seneca
Margaret Matilda " 1845, 1, 3
1820, 10, 14. Susannah d bur Seneca, Green Co., O.

MOORMAN, continued
1820, 12, 17. Polley d bur Seneca, Green Co., O.
1822, 10, 16. John d bur Seneca, Green Co., O.
1822, 12, 28. Susannah d bur Seneca, Green Co., O.
1817, 1, 3. Elizabeth d bur Dover
1825, 10, 6. Micajah Sr., s Thomas & Apharacia, Green Co., O.; m in Dover MH, Ann THOMAS, dt John & Jane, Clinton Co., O.
1828, 2, 7. Thomas C., s Micajah C. & Susannah, Green Co., O.; m in Dover MH, Martha BANGHAM, dt Benjamin & Lucy, d 1848,10,15 ae 38y 9m 10d bur Seneca
Ch: Lucy Ann b 1831, 5, 3
Micajah " 1834, 7, 8
Benjamin B." 1837, 2, 26
John Hampton " 1844, 7, 24
Thomas C. m 2nd Martha Ann -----
Ch: Rueben Albert b 1857, 1, 12
Alva Augburn " 1853, 4, 23
Nancy Elizabeth " 1859, 5, 6
Christopher Elsworth " 1862, 8, 3
Mary Alzina" 1864, 10, 15 d 1867, 4, 6
Thomas E. " 1867, 1, 11 " 1867,10,25
Barckley " 1872, 9, 22
1834, 1, 22. Nancy m Thos. THORNBURGH
1836, 11, 23. Melissa m Samuel FERGUSON
1840, 11, 25. Elizabeth m David BAILEY
1841, 11, 24. Susannah m Jesse PAINTER
----, --, --. Manson H. d 1869,9,30; m Rachel -----
Ch: James Leander b 1844, 7, 10 d 1846, 6,28 bur Seneca
Sally Mary b 1847, 11, 11
Levi Stratton " 1849, 3, 26
Frank Hope " 1857, 3, 28
1845, 11, 19. Apharacia m Elwood HAINES
1848, 4, 19. Rachel m Israel C. GREEN
----, --, --. Marshall & Martha
Ch: Alpheus b 1850, 4, 27
Algerney " 1852, 2, 22
Sarah Eveline " 1854, 3, 25
Americus " 1856, 2, 26
Charles Clinton " 1858, 3, 27
Rufus " 1861, 2, 17
Martha Ann " 1863, 7, 27
1851, 8, 18. Apharacia, wd Thos. Sr., dt John & Mary Hope, d bur Seneca, Green Co., O. ae 99y lacking 6d
----, --, --. Matthew & Martha M.
Ch: Rozetta Harriet b 1857, 2, 1
Charles William b 1859, 2, 26
Ch: Alice Matilda b 1862, 9, 18
Harry Leroy " 1864, 11, 15
----, --, --. Charles Thos. b 1835,3,30; m Sarah Jane -----
Ch: Fenton Thomas b 1857, 11, 10
Marcella Jane " 1859, 9, 4
John Allen " 1861, 8, 6
Margaret Matilda " 1864, 8, 9 d 1865,11,--
----, --, --. James Christopher b 1835,9,5; m Susannah H. ----- b 1839,10,30 d 1868, 4,15
Ch: William F. b 1860, 11, 20 d 1861,10,28
Laura Elizabeth " 1862, 9, 18 " 1863,12,24
Chloe Alice" 1864, 11, 11
James Sheridan " 1869, 6, 24 " 1868, 5,22
1866, 3, 4. Ann d bur Seneca, Green Co., O.
1866, 9, 19. Micajah F., s Charles & Matilda, Green Co., O.; m in Grassy Run MH, Julia A. HUSSEY, dt Thomas & Nancy THOMPSON, Guilford Co., N. C.

1834, 9, 18. Mildred dis
1836, 8, 18. Lydia gct Fall Creek MM, O.
1837, 7, 13. Emily Degroat (form Moorman) dis mou
1838, 2, 15. Nancy W. Abernathy (form Moorman) dis mou
1841, 4, 15. Mary Glass (form Moorman) dis mou
1844, 1, 18. Rachel Ann rocf Springfield MM, dtd 1843,11,14
1845, 7, 17. James gct Caesars Creek MM, O.
1848, 1, 13. Mary Hiatt (form Moorman) con mou
1849, 5, 17. Thomas C. & ch, Lucy Ann, Micajah C., Benjamin B. & John H., gct Center MM
1849, 9, 13. Thomas C. gct Miami MM, O.
1851, 5, 15. Elizabeth Alexander (form Moorman) con mou
1852, 7, 15. Jesse gct Fairfield MM
1853, 11, 17. Mariah W. Brunson (form Moorman) con mou
1854, 9, 14. Elizabeth Johnson (form Moorman) con mou
1855, 1, 18. Henry T. gct Caesars Creek MM,O.
1855, 12, 13. Martha E. Ellis (form Moorman) dis mou
1856, 5, 15. Martha Ann recrq
1856, 10, 16. Thomas P. & w, Dosha, & ch, Paxton Hope & Wm. Newton, gct Spring Creek MM, Ia.
1857, 5, 14. Matthew & w, Martha, & ch, Rosetta Harriet, recrq
1857, 6, 14. Martha Ann & ch, Alpheus Al-

MOORMAN, continued
journey, Sarah Eveline & Americus, recrq
1858, 8, 19. Benjamin B. con mou
1859, 10, 13. Thos. C. gct South River MM, Iowa
1859, 12, 15. Henry T. rocf White Water MM, Ind., dtd 1859,11,23
1860, 4, 19. James Jr. con mou
1860, 5, 17. Chas. T. & w, Sarah Jane, & ch, Trenton Thos. & Marcella Jane, recrq
1860, 6, 14. Susannah Ruth recrq
1865, 3, 16. Henry T. gct Center MM
1869, 10, 17. Malinda Paulin (form Moorman) con mou
1870, 11, 17. John H. con mou
1871, 4, 13. Watson & Sarah recrq
1871, 4, 13. David & Catharine recrq
1871, 4, 13. Genevra recrq
1871, 4, 13. Elizabeth recrq
1871, 4, 13. Susannah recrq
1871, 4, 13. Caroline recrq
1872, 3, 14. Elnora, Mary & Manerva recrq
1872, 7, 18. Hannah recrq
1872, 8, 15. James C. con mou
1872, 10, 17. Henry T. rocf Center MM, dtd 1872,10,16
1874, 2, 19. Wm. C. recrq
1876, 3, 16. Allice recrq
1876, 9, 14. Manerva dis
1878, 2, 14. Harry T. & Anna M., ch David & Catherine, recrq
1878, 9, 19. John Hampton relrq
1879, 3, 13. Louisa & Mary recrq
1885, 7, 16. Eli relrq
1885, 7, 16. Chas. Jr. relrq
1885, 7, 16. Jesse relrq
1885, 7, 16. John H. relrq
1885, 7, 16. Benjamin relrq
1885, 8, 13. Wm. D. & ch, Chas. R., recrq
1885, 8, 13. Nettie E. recrq
1888, 7, 19. Alvah & w, Mary, relrq
1889, 8, 15. Lillie recrq
1901, 6, 13. James S. dropped from mbrp
1901, 6, 13. Stella dropped from mbrp
1907, 4, 18. Mary, Frank & Howard recrq

MORGAN
1901, 6, 13. Ola dropped from mbrp

MORRIS
1879, 3, 13. John C. & Jennie recrq
1906, 4, 19. Homer & Fannie recrq
1906, 4, 19. Clara recrq
1906, 4, 19. Pryor recrq

MORROW
1888, 12, 13. Celia gct Wilmington MM, O.
1899, 3, 16. Fannie recrq

MUNGO
1880, 5, 10. Scott recrq

MURRELL
1880, 5, 10. Eveline & Jennie recrq
1882, 6, 15. Jane & Evaline relrq
1887, 2, 17. Grant recrq
1887, 7, 14. Mary recrq
1906, 4, 19. Stella recrq
1909, 5, 13. S. J. recrq

NEWSUM
1875, 4, 15. John L. recrq
1878, 2, 14. John L. [Newsom] dropped from mbrp

NICELY
1902, 5, 2. Minnie recrq

NIDY
1880, 5, 10. Margaret E. recrq

NORDYKE
1846, 10, 22. Lewis, s Micajah & Charity, Clinton Co., O.; m in Dover MH, Rachel A. BRACKNEY, dt Marmaduke & Susannah, Clinton Co., O.
1850, 9, 26. Asa, s Micajah & Charity, Clinton Co., O.; m in Dover MH, Almedia BAILEY, dt David & Silviah, Clinton Co., O.

1847, 2, 18. Rachel M. gct Clear Creek MM, O.
1851, 1, 16. Almedia gct Clear Creek MM, O.

NUNN
1906, 4, 19. Catharine recrq
1906, 4, 19. Milton O. recrq
1906, 4, 19. Marion recrq
1906, 4, 19. Mary recrq
1906, 4, 19. Martha recrq

OGAN
1837, 2, 16. Catharine (form Gallemore) con mou
1850, 9, 19. Catharine gct Miami MM, O.

OLIVER
1880, 5, 10. Sarah M. recrq
1907, 7, 18. Amos dropped from mbrp
1908, 6, 18. Emma Ellison dropped from mbrp

O'NEAL
1904, 5, 19. Lizzie dropped from mbrp

OREN
----, --, --. John & Lydia
Ch: Jacob b 1813, 4, 3
Esther " 1814, 3, 25
Ephraim " 1815, 3, 27
David " 1819, 12, 24 d 1821, 8,21 bur Dover
----, --, --. Joseph & Sarah
Ch: Absalom b 1814, 4, 26
Ruth " 1815, 11, 4
Phebe " 1817, 7, 8
Hannah " 1819, 3, 8

OREN, Joseph & Sarah, continued
Ch: Jane b 1820, 10, 20
John " 1822, 8, 13
Elizabeth " 1825, 12, 30
Lydia " 1829, 10, 16
Sarah " 1826, 12, 20 d 1827,10, 6 bur Dover
Abigail " 1831, 12, 24
Mary Ann " 1836, 3, 28

----, --, --. Alexander, s John & Ruth, b 1794,4,24; m Lydia FRAZIER, dt Ezekiel & Rebecca, b 1797,12,26
Ch: Rebecca b 1821, 1, 3
Ruth " 1823, 1, 9
James " 1825, 1, 29
Ezekiel " 1827, 7, 21
Hannah " 1829, 11, 21
John F. " 1832, 10, 20
Phebe " 1835, 2, 10
Alexander " 1837, 7, 1

1831, 12, 1. John Jr., s John & Ruth, Clinton Co., O.; m in Dover MH, Martha BAILEY dt Daniel & Mary, Clinton Co., O.
Ch: Elie b 1832, 9, 14
Daniel B. " 1835, 4, 18 d 1863, 5,25
Eliza " 1836, 11, 25
Mary " 1840, 1, 16 " 1840, 2,26
Asa " 1840, 1, 16
Henry " 1842, 12, 28 " 1863, 3, 4
Lewis " 1845, 3, 29 " 1848,12,14
Martha " 1847, 11, 4
Isabella " 1853, 10, 31

1848, 3, 21. Martha d ae 39y 7m 25d
1832, 3, 22. Esther [Oran] m Henry GILPIN
1836, 11, 24. Jacob L., s John & Lydia, Clinton Co., O., b 1813,4,3; m in Dover MH, Mary FRAZIER, dt John & Alice
Ch: Angeline b 1838, 4, 21

1840, 4, 17. Ruth m Joseph PEARSON
1841, 5, 20. Ephraim, s John & Lydia, Clinton Co., O.; m in Dover MH, Elizabeth FRAZIER, dt John & Alice, Clinton Co., O.
Ch: Levi b 1842, 2, 22

1842, 12, 17. Elizabeth, dt Joseph & Asenath, b
1844, 4, 25. John A. [Oran], s James & Margaret, Clinton Co., O.; m in Dover MH, Joannah BAILEY, dt Daniel & Mary, Clinton Co., O.
Ch: Alfred b 1845, 4, 9
Mary " 1846, 8, 4
James " 1848, 3, 4
Thomas Chalkley " 1849, 11, 16
Sarah Ann " 1851, 10, 16
Margaret Ellen " 1855, 9, 10

1852, 9, 30. John, s John & Ruth, Clinton Co., O.; m in Dover MH, Martha J. HUNNICUTT, dt Thomas & Elizabeth, Clinton Co.,O.

1825, 12, 3. Joseph & w, Sarah, & ch, Absalom, Ruth, Phebe Hannah Jane & Elizabeth, recrq
1829, 7, 16. Jane dis jH
1836, 8, 18. Absalom gct White River MM, Ind.
1837, 4, 13. Phebe gct White River MM, Ind.
1837, 4, 13. Ruth, dt Joseph, gct White River MM, Ind.
1837, 4, 13. Sarah & ch, Hannah Jane, John, Elizabeth Lydia Abigail & Mary Ann, gct White River MM, Ind.
1839, 4, 18. James & w, Margaret, & ch, Elijah & Wm., rocf Green Plain MM, dtd 1839,2,23
1839, 4, 18. Susannah rocf Greenplain MM, dtd 1839,2,23
1841, 12, 16. Lydia & Mary Ann rocf Sparroe Creek MM, Ind., dtd 1841,9,13
1841, 10, 14. Jacob L. & w, Mary, & ch, Angeline, Isaiah & Allis, gct Cherry Grove MM, Ind.
1842, 2, 17. Asenath rocf Center MM, dtd 1841,11,17
1842, 9, 15. Susannah Starbuck (form Oren) con mou
1842, 12, 15. Lydia & ch, James Ezekiel, Hannah, John F., Phebe, Alexander & Moses, gct Clear Creek MM, O.
1842, 12, 15. Ruth gct Clear Creek MM, O.
1842, 12, 15. Rebecca gct Clear Creek MM, O.
1844, 7, 18. Elizabeth & s, Levi, gct Cherry Grove MM, Ind.
1844, 8, 15. Lydia Sr. dis jH
1844, 8, 15. Asenath dis joining Separatists
1856, 12, 18. Eliza Spear (form Oren) dis mou
1857, 5, 14. John A. & w, Joanna, & ch, Alfred, Mary, James, Thomas C., Sarah Ann & Margaret E., gct Center MM
1861, 4, 18. Margaret & Asenath recrq of Uncle & Aunt, Joel Starbeck & w
1861, 7, 18. Elizabeth Williams (form Oren) dis mou
1867, 10, 17. Martha South (form Oren) con mou
1870, 2, 17. Lydia gct Poplar Run MM
1870, 12, 15. Asenath gct Center MM
1873, 3, 13. James & Anna recrq
1877, 7, 18. Asa dis disunity
1878, 2, 14. Henry rocf Clear Creek MM, O., dtd 1878,1,12
1878, 2, 14. Henry G. rocf Clear Creek MM,O.
1879, 1, 16. Lydia rocf Poplar Run MM, Ind.
1880, 2, 19. Alvin rocf Center MM, O., dtd 1880,2,--
1881, 9, 15. Alvin gct Center MM, O.
1882, 1, 19. Lydia gct Poplar Run MM, Ind.
1904, 3, 17. Ruth rocf Hopewell MM, dtd 1904,3,5

OSBORN
1865, 11, 16. Ann con mou
1866, 1, 18. Ann gct Fairfield MM

PAGETT
1904, 1, 14. Alice rocf Center MM

PAGETT, continued
1904, 1, 14. Edward & ch, Harry L. & Myra E., recrq

PAINTER
1841, 11, 24. Jesse, s Thomas & Mary, Green Co., O.; m in Senecca MH, Susannah MOORMAN, dt Thomas P. & Dosha, Green Co., O.
1842, 8, 25. Joseph C., s Jacob & Naomi, Green Co., O.; m in Dover MH, Hannah SHIELDS, dt Wm. & Hannah, Clinton Co., O.
Ch: Mary Emy b 1850, 11, 2
Jacob " 1856, 3, 4 d 1862, 2, 6
Naomi " 1860, 8, 3
Hannah " 1863, 2, 25
Joseph H. " 1865, 3, 1
1843, 9, 21. David, s Jesse & Elizabeth, Green Co., O.; m in Dover MH, Mary FRAZIER dt Moses & Lydia, Clinton Co., O.
1865, 9, 21. Margaret Ann m Ahira JOHNSON

1842, 4, 19. Susannah gct Center MM
1842, 12, 15. Hannah L. gct Center MM
1844, 1, 18. Mary gct Center MM
1847, 2, 18. Joseph C. & w, Hannah S., & ch, Harriet M. & Margaret Ann, rocf White Lick MM
1851, 12, 18. David S. gct Wabash MM, Ind.
1856, 3, 13. Thos. gct West Union MM
1866, 1, 18. Joseph C. & w, Hannah, & ch, Harriet M., Mary Emma, Naomi Hannah & Joseph Henry, gct Caesars Creek MM, O.
1882, 2, 16. Sarah Alice gct Hopewell MM, O.
1882, 5, 18. Mary rocf Hopewell MM, O.
1883, 3, 15. Mary gct Van Wert MM, O.
1912, 11, 14. Lillian P. gct Wilmington MM,O.

PALMER
1872, 3, 14. Wj. H. & w, Carrie B., & ch, Lucy M., Lizzie E., Blanchie & John, recrq
1881, 5, 19. Carrie recrq
1882, 1, 19. Carrie gct Honey Creek MM, Ia.
1884, 2, 14. Wm. H. & w, Carrie, & ch, Lizzie, John, Blanche & Clarence, gct Rose Hill MM, Kans.

PANKETT
1873k 6, 19. Lucretia Bell recrq

PARISH
1873, 1, 16. Thos. H. recrq
1879, 3, 13. Margaret recrq

PARKINSON
1905, 7, 13. Joseph & w relrq

PARLOTT
1871, 1, 19. Margaret Jane, minor in care of Nathaniel Woolary, recrq
1871, 1, 19. Jemima, adopted ch Nathaniel Woolary, recrq

PATTEN
1866, 8, 16. Evaline recrq
1868, 6, 18. Adaline Doan (form Patten) con mou
1884, 3, 13. Cyrus recrq

PATTERSON
----, --, --. John & Rebecca
Ch: Polly b 1824, 11, 11
Elizabeth " 1826, 2, 8
William " 1828, 5, 2 d 1847,10,25
Mary " 1830, 9, 30 " 1850, 9,21
Elisha " 1833, 2, 19 " 1851, 2,26
Isom " 1835, 3, 5
Lydia " 1837, 5, 20
Daniel " 1840, 4, 17
Rebecca Jane " 1844, 5, 6

1827, 1, 6. John & w, Rebecca, & ch, Sarah & Elizabeth, recrq
1842, 8, 18. Elizabeth Rhinehart (form Patterson) dis mou
1843, 6, 15. Sally dis jas
1859, 9, 15. Isom dis disunity
1861, 9, 19. Lydia dis disunity
1870, 8, 18. Rebecca gct Miami MM, O.; returned 1871,1,19

PATTON
1901, 6, 13. Scott dropped from mbrp

PAULIN
1869, 7, 20. Charles A., s Enos & Malinda, b

1869, 10, 17. Malinda (form Moorman) con mou
1905, 2, 16. David & Lelia [Paullin] recrq

PEARSON
1785, 6, 31. Martha b
----, --, --. John d 1859,11,23; m Hannah ----- d 1840,7,18 ae 55y 2m 5d
Ch: Joseph b 1807, 7, 12
Rebecca " 1809, 11, 8
Asenath " 1812, 6, 4
Jesse " 1815, 3, 24
Keziah " 1815, 3, 24
Rachel " 1818, 3, 4 d 1827, 3,14
Lydia " 1820, 10, 30
Susannah " 1823, 12, 14
1831, 12, 1. Joseph, s John & Hannah, Green Co., O.; m in Dover MH, Jane FRAZIER, dt John & Alice, Clinton Co., O.
Ch: Alice b 1832, 9, 23
Abner " 1833, 11, 25
John F. " 1835, 8, 10
----, --, --. Jesse & Achsah
Ch: Rachel b 1840, 4, 6
Anne " 1844, 7, 9
George " 1846, 3, 19
Thomas " 1847, 8, 27
Mary " 1849, 10, 14
John " 1852, 10, 17

PEARSON, Jesse & Achsah, continued
Ch: James b 1854, 1, 19
Henry " 1858, 3, 14
1840, 4, 17. Joseph, s John & Hannah, Grant Co., Ind.; m in Dover MH, Ruth OREN, dt John & Ruth, Clinton Co., O.

1827, 9, 1. Rebecca Lam (form Pierson) con mcd
1832, 7, 19. Aseneth Studavin (form Pearson) dis mcd
1834, 8, 14. Keziah dis
1836, 11, 17. Joseph & w, Jane, & ch, Alice, Abner & John F., gct Mississinewa MM, Ind.
1840, 6, 18. Ruth gct Mississinewa MM, Ind.
1843, 1, 19. Lydia dis disunity
1843, 1, 19. Susannah Hiatt (form Pearson) dis mou
1843, 1, 19. Mary Ann (form Hunt) dis mou
1848, 1, 13. Mary (form Peelle) con mou
1848, 9, 14. Alice rocf Mississinewa MM, Ind., dtd 1848,7,12
1855, 6, 14. Mary E. rocf Milford MM, dtd 1855,5,26
1856, 2, 14. Thos. B. & w, Mary E., gct Hopewell MM
1856, 6, 19. Achsa, w Jesse, & ch recrq
1860, 4, 19. Martha recrq
1860, 5, 17. Thos. B. & w, Mary E., & ch, Axum & Margaret Susan, rocf Milford MM, Ind., dtd 1860,4,28
1861, 3, 14. Rachel dis disunity
1866, 9, 13. Mary Martin (form Pearson) dis mou
1872, 6, 13. Isaac recrq
1873, 2, 13. Eli & Esther & s, Harry W., recrq
1873, 9, 18. Thos. con mou
1873, 9, 18. George con mou
1876, 4, 13. Chas. G. & w, Rachel, & ch, Joseph F., Walter & Franklin, recrq
1878, 2, 14. George relrq
1878, 6, 13. Albert & Jane recrq
1880, 5, 10. Buma & ch, John H., Wm. T. & Eva May, recrq
1884, 4, 17. Lon A. recrq
1885, 7, 16. Thomas C. relrq
1885, 7, 16. Albert & Jane relrq
1889, 3, 14. Eli & ch, Harry W. & Laura M., gct Wilmington MM
1889, 6, 13. Chas. dis disunity
1907, 3, 14. Susan Carter gct Sabina MM, O.

PEEBLES
----, --, --. John d 1873,5,1; m Michal ----- d 1873,6,5
Ch: Caroline b 1824, 3, 25 d 1846, 6,19
Lucy Ann " 1825, 10, 18
Henrietta " 1827, 8, 18
Samuel " 1830, 3, 22
Elizabeth " 1832, 3, 19
Julietta " 1834, 9, 4
Joshua " 1837, 4, 15
Ch: Emily b 1839, 9, 8
Almedia " 1841, 10, 13
Deborah " 1844, 4, 10
David " 1845, 12, 4
1835, 8, 30. Sarah, wd James, d bur Dover
1830, 5, 27. John, s Stephen & Sarah, Warren Co., O.; m in Dover MH, Mary Ann HUNNICUTT, dt Thomas & Elizabeth, Clinton Co., O.
Ch: Elizabeth Hollowell b 1834, 3, 26
Stephen Thomas " 1834, 9, 22
Benjamin Franklin " 1836, 12, 26
Micajah " 1839, 6, 2
William Henry " 1841, 7, 8
Mary Jane " 1842, 9, 19
1860, 3, 23. Lucy Ann m Thos. DENNIS

1828, 7, 17. John & w, Michal, & ch, Caroline, Lucy Ann & Henrietta, rocf Springborough MM, dtd 1828,4,29
1829, 4, 16. Elijah & w, Christian, & ch, Pleasant Dilworth, Catharina Oliver Emlen & Deborah, rocf Upper MM, Va., dtd 1829,2,21
1829, 7, 16. Elijah & w, Christianna, & ch, Pleasant Dilworth Catharine, Oliver Emlin & Deborah, gct Miami MM, O.
1831, 11, 17. Mary Ann gct Springboro MM
1833, 8, 15. John & w, Mary Ann, rocf Springborough MM, dtd 1832,9,25, endorsed by Center MM 1833,7,17
1833, 12, 19. Reuben & w, Rhoda, rocf New Garden MM, Ind., dtd 1833,10,19
1835, 11, 19. Deborah gct Springboro MM, O.
1835, 3, 19. Sarah rocf Springborough MM, dtd 1835,2,17
1835, 3, 19. Deborah rocf Springborough MM, dtd 1835,2,17
1835, 5, 14. Pleasant Dilworth, Oliver Emlin, Catharine & Deborah, rocf Miami MM, dtd 1835,4,22
1838, 8, 16. Catharine Rawls (form Peebles) dis mou
1844, 12, 19. Deborah dis jas
1851, 3, 13. John E. & w, Mary Ann, & ch, Elizabeth Hollowell, Stephen Thos., Benjamin Franklin, Micajah Hunnicutt, Wm. H. & Mary Jane, gct Wabash MM, Ind.
1852, 9, 16. Samuel gct Cincinnati MM
1854, 10, 19. Henrietta Beal (form Peebles) con mou
1863, 9, 17. Emily Dennis (form Peebles) con mou
1864, 12, 15. July Etta Walton (form Peebles) con mou
1866, 4, 19. Joshua dis disunity
1869, 6, 17. David con mou
1872, 11, 14. Almeda relrq
1874, 2, 19. William recrq

PEELLE

----, --, --. John d 1869,12,1; m Lydia ----- d 1856,12,2
Ch: Mary b 1813, 7, 27
Rhoda " 1815, 8, 20
Emma " 1818, 5, 11
Mark " 1821, 1, 11
Lydia " 1828, 2, 8

1832, 11, 22. William, s John & Lydia, Clinton Co., O.; m in Dover MH, Clarissa STARBUCK, dt Gaynor & Susannah, Clinton Co., O., d 1864,10,4 ae 50y (an elder)
Ch: Moses b 1834, 1, 17 d 1835, 3, 1
Aaron " 1834, 1, 17 " 1834, 1,17
Susannah " 1835, 11, 3
Josiah " 1837, 0, 18 " 1838, 6,21
John " 1839, 3, 23
Isaiah " 1840, 11, 17
Jesse " 1842, 11, 5
Reuben " 1845, 8, 1
Wilson " 1848, 1, 12
Lydia C. " 1850, 4, 13 d 1851, 3, 1
Asa " 1852, 3, 4 " 1854, 5,18
Louisa " 1854, 12, 3
Elihu C. " 1857, 10, 21 " 1861, 1,22

1833, 11, 24. Rhoda, w Reuben, d ae 81y 9m
1834, 8, 18. Reuben d ae 73

----, --, --. Reuben m Emily ----- b 1809,11, 14
Ch: Abigail b 1837, 12, 9
Lydia " 1839, 8, 17
Elizabeth " 1841, 7, 27
Elias " 1843, 4, 10
William " 1845, 7, 1
Enos " 1847, 6, 27
Sarah Ann " 1849, 10, 22
Jonathan R." 1853, 5, 29

----, --, --. Mark, s John & Lydia, b 1821,1, 11; m Mary Eleanor ----- b 1830,4,18
Ch: Margaret Emily b 1849, 2, 8
Elijah J. " 1851, 5, 10
Seth " 1854, 4, 15
Lydia " 1857, 1, 5
John P. " 1859, 3, 4

1851, 11, 19. Susannah m Elihu CARTER
1856, 1, 23. Abigail m Wm. CARTER
1856, 3, 19. Lydia B. m Cyrus E. CARTER

----, --, --. John b 1837,5,23; m Dorcas A. ----- b 1836,3,19
Ch: Clarkson b 1862, 9, 5 d 1864, 2,11
Leroy " 1864, 4, 24
Alice Jane " 1866, 1, 21
John W. " 1867, 11, 4
Henry E. " 1870, 1, 5

----, --, --. Josiah b 1840,11,17; m Susan M. ----- b 1838,3,30
Ch: Ruth Anna b 1862, 12, 12
Chas. Edward " 1865, 11, 26
Luther Allen " 1873, 4, 16 d 1873, 8, 9
Minnie R. " 1869, 11, 19 (adopted)

----, --, --. Elias H. b 1843,4,10; m Aromethea ----- b 1846,5,18
1868, 7, 29. Frank A. b
1870, 8, 20. Cary b d 1870,9,27
1870, 8, 22. Annetta, dt Jesse & Phebe, b

1841, 11, 18. Emma Bentley (form Peelle) con mou
1845, 2, 13. Rhoda Mills (form Peelle) con mou
1848, 1, 13. Mary Pearson (form Peelle) con mou
1850, 10, 17. Mary E. & ch, Margaret E., recrq
1850, 10, 17. Emily & ch, Abigail, Lydia, Elizabeth, Elias, Wm. C., Enos & Sarah Ann, recrq
1860, 5, 17. Dorcas A. rocf Newberry MM, O., dtd 1860,3,19
1861, 3, 14. Isaiah gct Springboro MM, to m Susan Miller
1861, 8, 15. Susan M. rocf Springboro MM, dtd 1861,6,25
1866, 2, 15. Wm. gct Fairfield MM, O., to m Louisa Hiatt
1866, 6, 14. Louisa rocf Fairfield MM, O., dtd 1866,5,19
1868, 2, 13. Jesse gct Fairfield MM, O., to m Phebe A. McPherson
1868, 7, 16. Phebe N. rocf Fairfield MM, O.
1868, 11, 19. Elias H. con mou
1869, 5, 13. Lydia Hammack (form Peelle) con mou
1870, 8, 18. Sarah E. rocf Center MM
1870, 8, 18. Wm. C. con mou
1872, 11, 16. Sarah Ann Gilbert (form Peelle) con mou
1872, 6, 13. Lydia Arametha recrq
1873, 4, 17. Jesse & w, Phebe A., & ch, Annetta & Bertha, gct Marysville MM, Tenn.
1873, 10, 16. Minna R. recrq (adopted ch of Isaiah & Susan Peelle)
1876, 1, 13. Esther & Harriet M. rocf Center MM, O.
1878, 9, 19. Isaiah & fam gct Wilmington MM,O.
1879, 8, 14. Emma E. rocf Milford MM, Ind.
1879, 12, 18. Ella recrq
1882, 11, 16. Mary rocf Caesars Creek MM, O.
1887, 1, 15. Harriett Florence rocf Westland MM, O., dtd 1887,8,6
1900, 9, 13. Josie recrq
1901, 7, 18. Seth & fam gct Wilmington MM
1902, 4, 17. Orrin G. gct Wilmington MM, O.
1903, 3, 19. Leroy & w, Annabelle, & ch, Emory, Lawrence, Alfred Earl & Virgil LeRoy, rocf Wilmington MM
1903, 10, 15. Frank A. & w, Virginia B. R., gct Wilmington MM, O.
1904, 10, 13. Bertha recrq
1905, 5, 16. Alonzo gct Caesars Creek MM, O.
1905, 9, 14. Edna recrq
1906, 4, 19. Walter D. recrq
1908, 2, 13. Weldon recrq
1908, 12, 17. Henry gct White Water MM, Ind

PEELLE, continued
1909, 9, 16. J. Will gct White Water MM, Ind.
1910, 3, 17. Weldon gct Dayton MM

PENLAND
1905, 1, 19. Stella Bailey relrq

PENNINGTON
1867, 11, 14. Wm. & w, Ann, & ch rocf Newberry MM, O.
1871, 2, 16. Wm. R. & w, Anna, & ch, John Edwin, Mary C., Nancy E., Martha E., Caroline & Benjamin F., gct South River MM,Ia.
1887, 7, 14. Chas. & Ann rocf Green Plain MM, O.
1906, 9, 13. Lee relrq

PIDGEON
----, --, --. John M. b 1834,2,2; m Caroline P. ----- b 1839,3,12
Ch: Ida May C. b 1860, 1, 11
Carl J. " 1861, 7, 11
Charles " 1863, 2, 12
1866, 9, 20. David A., s Charles & Catharine, Clinton Co., O.; m in Dover MH, Hannah BAILEY, dt Josiah & Mary T., Clinton Co., O.
Ch: Laura Bell b 1867, 7, 7 d 1869, 7, 5
Minnie Cornelia " 1869, 9, 22

1863, 3, 19. Chas. & w, Catherine, & ch, John, Mary J., Julia A., Samuel T., Daniel A., Louisa M., Chas. A., Henry H. & Caroline C., rec in mbrp
1863, 5, 14. Caroline & ch, Ida May, Carol J. & Charlie T., recrq
1864, 5, 19. Chas. & w, Catharine, & ch, Louise M., Chas. A., Henry H. & Caroline, gct Clear Creek MM, O.
1864, 5, 19. Julia A. gct Clear Creek MM, O.
1864, 6, 16. Mary gct Clear Creek MM, O.
1865, 11, 16. Elizabeth con mou
1865, 11, 16. Chas. & fam gct Clear Creek MM, O.
1866, 4, 19. Elizabeth Peelle gct Springfield MM, Ind.
1869, 5, 13. Chas. & w, Catharine, & ch, Cornelia & Henry, rocf Clear Creek MM, O.
1869, 5, 13. Julia rocf Clear Creek MM, O.
1869, 6, 17. Addison rocf Clear Creek MM,O.
1877, 6, 14. Samuel T. relrq
1882, 1, 19. David A. & fam gct Honey Creek MM, Iowa
1906, 1, 18. Oscar Leonard [Pidgion] recrq
1906, 9, 13. Ella recrq
1907, 7, 18. Charles [Pigeon] dropped from mbr.
1911, 3, 16. Willard T. recrq
1917, 2, 15. Homer relrq
1919, 3, 13. Oscar L. gct Knoxville MM, Tenn.
1923, 9, 23. Henry & w, Ella, & s, Willard, gct Wilmington MM, O.

PIKE
1873, 1, 16. Rebecca recrq

PILCHER
1886, 6, 17. Orlando & Sattie recrq
1902, 6, 19. Orland & fam dropped from mbrp

PLANKETT
1886, 4, 15. B. Franklin gct Wilmington MM,O.

PLUMMER
1883, 3, 15. Park S. & w, Mary, recrq
1888, 1, 19. Park & w, Mary L., & ch, Chas. & David, recrq

POCKETT
1872, 9, 19. Benjamin F. recrq

POPE
1877, 1, 18. James L. & w, Elizabeth, & ch, Louisa Jane, Mary Ann, Martha R., Henrietta, Sarah M. & Ira Clinton, rocf Vanwert MM, O.
1884, 1, 17. James L. & w, Martha E., & ch, Louisa J., Martha R., Mary A., Henrietta E., Sarah M., Ira C., Emma B. & Lorenzo D., relrq
1902, 5, 2. Cora recrq
1909, 5, 13. Frank & w, Minnie, recrq

POWELL
1900, 3, 15. Frank & w relrq

PROBASCO
1928, 5, 27. Charles Donald, Lulu B., Eva Lucile, Lewis Donald, Wm. Emmitt & Carol Lee, rocf Springfield MM

PURCELL
1902, 3, 13. Lena recrq
1909, 12, 16. Ella & Leana relrq

PYLE
1848, 9, 21. Davis S., s John & Esther, Clinton Co., O.; m Sarah WEST, dt Thomas & Tamor, Clinton Co., O.
Ch: Tamar Ann b 1854, 11, 13
Mary Emily " 1856, 10, 28
1856, 11, 3. Sarah T. d

1849, 8, 16. Sarah T. gct Springfield MM
1854, 8, 17. David S. & w, Sarah T., & ch, Allen H. & Thos. Henry, rocf Springfield MM, dtd 1854,7,15
1860, 4, 19. David S. & ch, Allen T., David Henry & Tamar Anna, gct Springfield MM
1868, 5 14. Mary Emily set off with Wilmington MM, O.

RAILEY
1870, 8, 18. Elizabeth & ch gct Cottonwood MM, Kans.
1872, 4, 18. Edwin & Martha recrq

RATCLIFF
1848, 1, 20. Jacob, s Edom & Rachel, Highland Co., O.; m in Dover MH, Mary E. HUNNICUTT, dt Ephraim & Margaret, Prince George Co., Va.

1848, 4, 13. Mary E. gct Newberry MM
1885, 6, 18. Ettie recrq

RAWLS
1836, 2, 18. Sarah Jane, dt Burnwell & Sarah, b

1835, 12, 17. Burwell & w, Sarah, & ch, Mary Ann, Micajah, Michal, Jonathan, William, Elizabeth, Esther, John & Jesse, rocf Sandy Springs MM, dtd 1835,11,6, endorsed by Center MM, 1835,12,16
1838, 8, 16. Catharine (form Peebles) dis mou
1840, 4, 16. Burwell & w, Sarah, & ch, Micajah, Michal, Jonathan, Elizabeth, William, Esther, Jesse, John & Sarah Jane, gct Springfield MM
1840, 4, 16. Mary Ann gct Springfield MM, O.
1850, 6, 13. Esther F. rocf Springborough MM, dtd 1850,5,21
1850, 6, 13. Jesse, John & Sarah Jane, ch Sarah, dec, rocf Springborough MM, dtd 1850,5,21
1852, 3, 18. Esther Atkinson (form Rawls) con mou
1852, 12, 16. Sarah Jane Clearwater (form Rawls) con mou

REYNOLDS
1876, 4, 13. Lewis recrq
1876, 4, 13. George recrq
1879, 6, 19. Lewis C. recrq
1880, 3, 18. Lewis relrq

RHINEHART
1842, 8, 18. Elizabeth (form Patterson) dis mou

RICE
1876, 4, 13. Devolzo E. recrq
1876, 4, 13. Sarah L. relrq
1876, 6, 15. Jesse D. & Lilly Jessie Bell, ch Devalzo E. & Sarah L., recrq

RICHARDSON
1876, 4, 13. Jesse recrq
1878, 2, 14. Jesse dropped from mbrp

RILEY
1879, 6, 19. Silas M. recrq
1885, 4, 16. Silas W. released

ROBERTS
1838, 1, 18. Abel & w, Elenor, & gr s, Moses B. Roberts, rocf Newberry MM, dtd 1837,11,20
1839, 8, 15. Abel & w, Elenor, & gr s, Moses B. Roberts, gct Westfield MM, Ind.
1884, 7, 17. Asenath rocf Caesars Creek MM,O.
1905, 2, 16. John recrq

ROBINETT
1872, 11, 14. Anna recrq
1881, 4, 14. Emma [Robinet] recrq
1881, 5, 19. Zenas & w, Levica, & ch, Eliza, Sarah, Carl & Mary, recrq
1881, 5, 19. Emma recrq
1885, 8, 13. Thos. [Robbinett] rocf Wilmington MM, O.
1888, 1, 19. Leah Ellen & Elma recrq

ROBINSON
1873, 3, 13. James F. [Robison] recrq
1873, 3, 13. Elisha [Robison] recrq
1873, 3, 13. Sarah [Robison] recrq
1878, 2, 14. Frank Orlando, Idelia May, Chas. Alvin & Reuben Warren, ch James F. & Ann E., recrq
1885, 6, 18. Dellie M. recrq

ROSS
----, --, --. Enos b 1810,2,1; m Elizabeth ----- b 1811,6,29 d 1864,10,21

Ch: William Erskine b 1836, 7, 2 d 1861, 3,20
Martha Ann " 1838, 9, 1
Alfred Simmons " 1840, 7, 24
Almira Jane " 1842, 6, 25
Ellis Rees " 1844, 10, 20
Samuel Enos " 1852, 10, 8

----, --, --. Alfred S. b 1840,7,24; m Martha G. -----

Ch: James Albert b 1868, 2, 24
Carrie Ellen " 1870, 8, 20

1855, 1, 18. Enos & w, Elizabeth, & ch, Wm. E., Martha Ann, Alfred L., Elmira Jane, Ellis R. & Samuel E., rocf Fairfield MM, dtd 1854,11,18
1865, 12, 14. Martha Ann Hunnicutt (form Ross) con mou
1867, 7, 18. Alfred L. con mou
1867, 11, 14. Martha G. recrq
1868, 5, 14. Mary Douglas (form Ross) con mou
1874, 2, 19. Enos recrq
1884, 12, 18. Eva O. H. rocf Wilmington MM,O.
1899, 3, 16. James A. relrq
1905, 12, 14. Ellis & w, Eva O. H., & ch, Alberta L. & Rebecca J., gct Wilmington MM
1905, 12, 14. Almira Jane gct Wilmington MM,O.
1905, 12, 14. Nellie gct Wilmington MM, O.

ROTHERFORD
1857, 7, 16. John [Rutherford] & fam rocf Cincinnati MM, dtd 1857,5,21
1868, 5, 14. Sylvia set off with Wilmington MM, O.
1868, 5, 14. Adia set off with Wilmington MM, O.
1868, 5, 14. Susannah set off with Wilmington MM, O.
1868, 5, 14. Jannie set off with Wilmington MM, O.

ROWE
1864, 1, 14. Rebecca [Roe] (form Hockett) con mou
1864, 5, 19. Rebecca S. gct Fairfield MM
1868, 3, 19. Rebecca rocf Fairfield MM, O., dtd 1868,1,18
1868, 10, 15. Rebecca gct Ash Grove MM, Ill.
1872, 7, 18. Rebecca [Rue] rocf Ash Grove MM, Ill., dtd 1872,5,29

RUNNELLS
1878, 6, 13. George relrq
1878, 7, 18. Lewis relrq
1887, 7, 14. Cora recrq

RUSSELL
1911, 12, 14. Lon dropped from mbrp

SANDERSON
1879, 6, 19. Foster recrq
1880, 5, 10. Geo. recrq
1884, 9, 18. George relrq
1885, 4, 16. Foster released
1888, 4, 19. Foster recrq

SAPP
1885, 4, 16. Dora recrq
1902, 5, 2. Emery recrq

SAUNDERS
1855, 5, 17. Malissa Jane [Sanders] (form Thornburg) dis mou
1879, 3, 14. Mary recrq
1889, 1, 17. Mamie dis disunity

SCOTT
1908, 2, 13. Orville recrq

SEARS
1826, 5, 22. Penelope Bocock (form Sears) con mcd
1831, 7, 14. Christopher & John, ch Penelope, gct Miami MM, O.
1878, 3, 14. Nancy recrq
1878, 2, 14. Nancy recrq
1880, 4, 15. John & w, Mary Ann, & dt, Elizabeth & Jane, recrq
1885, 7, 16. Nancy relrq
1885, 8, 13. Nancy recrq

SESLER
1877, 4, 19. Martin dis disunity
1880, 5, 10. Joseph M. recrq

SEWELL
1889, 3, 14. Elizabeth Ann gct Wilmington MM, O.

SHANER
1850, 11, 14. Virgin (form Brown) rpd mou; d before completed
1878, 4, 18. Mary M. & ch, Melcenia, recrq
1879, 6, 19. Frederick & ch, Stephen J., Allen B., Minnie M. & Annie M., recrq
1885, 4, 16. Fredrick & w released
1901, 6, 13. Hattie dropped from mbrp

SHANNON
1900, 3, 15. J. C. & Elzina B., recrq
1900, 10, 18. Lucy rocf Green Plain MM, O., dtd 1900,9,12

SHAW
1867, 8, 15. John M. recrq
1869, 9, 16. John M. gct Mississinewa MM, Ind.
1876, 4, 13. James recrq
1876, 4, 13. Temperance recrq
1876, 4, 13. Louisa recrq
1876, 6, 15. Wm. S., Wyatt P. & Elmira, ch James, recrq

SHEELY
----, --, --. George [Sheley] b 1836,9,11; m Mariah ----- b 1837,10,1
Ch: Joseph
Allen b 1858, 10, 21
Elizabeth " 1861, 5, 7

1857, 11, 19. Maria [Shela] (form Hunt) con mou
1860, 1, 19. George recrq
1860, 2, 16. Joseph Allen, s Geo. & Meriah, recrq
1864, 6, 16. Geo. [Shealey] & w, Mariah, & ch, Joseph, Allen & Mary Elizabeth, gct Cottonwood MM, Kans.
1871, 4, 13. Elizabeth recrq

SHIELDS
----, --, --. William d 1865,5,1 ae 81; m Hannah ----- d 1869,7,4 ae 84
Ch: Elizabeth b 1806, 6, 4
Rebecca " 1808, 5, 8
Mary Ann " 1810, 7, 2
Lydia " 1812, 2, 12
John " 1814, 6, 11
Lucinda " 1819, 12, 13
Hannah " 1822, 3, 21
Margaret " 1824, 7, 24
Maria " 1829, 10, 19 d 1838, 1,25
Sarah Jane " 1831, 6, 26
1832, 6, 21. Lydia m George BAILEY

SHIELDS, continued
1832, 6, 21. Mary Ann m Hiram DAVIS
1842, 8, 25. Hannah m Joseph C. PAINTER
1848, 8, 24. Sarah Jane m John DOAN

1833, 8, 15. Elizabeth Ballard (form Shields) con mou
1840, 6, 18. Lucinda Connell (form Shields) con mou
1841, 9, 16. Rebecca Walker (form Shields) con mou
1852, 12, 16. Margaret Starbuck (form Shields) con mou
1855, 12, 13. Elizabeth (form Davis) dis mou

SHIRK
1871, 4, 13. Sarah F. recrq
1904, 3, 17. Anna recrq

SHOOP
1871, 4, 13. Elizabeth recrq
1871, 4, 13. Martha G. recrq
1871, 4, 13. Charles recrq

SHORT
1885, 4, 16. Fielding recrq

SIMMONS
1864, 7, 14. John con mou
1864, 9, 15. John gct Spring Creek MM, Ia.
1869, 1, 14. Jacob gct Three Rivers MM, Ia.
1903, 10, 15. Emma Aldridge dropped from mbrp

SLUSHER
1905, 12, 14. George rocf Hopewell MM
1910, 5, 19. George relrq

SMALL
1876, 4, 13. Eli recrq
1876, 4, 13. Mary recrq
1876, 6, 15. Clara Jane & James H., ch Eli & Mary, recrq
1878, 2, 14. Eli dropped from mbrp
1878, 2, 14. Mary dropped from mbrp

SMITH
1855, 4, 19. Nancy G. (form Johnson) dis mou
1871, 4, 13. Frederick recrq
1873, 3, 14. Martha recrq
1873, 3, 13. Luther recrq
1874, 2, 19. Elizabeth recrq
1878, 4, 18. John F. & Elizabeth relrq
1879, 4, 17. John F. recrq
1883, 5, 17. Esther recrq
1888, 1, 19. Tacie, Wm. J. & Angie recrq
1904, 1, 14. Cora dropped from mbrp

SNOWDEN
1878, 1, 16. Elisha Gallemore gct Miami MM, O., to m Sarah Amanda Snowden

SNYDER
1900, 9, 13. A. T. recrq
1900, 9, 13. Ida E. recrq
1901, 6, 13. A. T. & w, Ida E., relrq

SOUTH
1867, 10, 17. Martha (form Oren) con mou
1867, 11, 14. Martha gct Ash Grove MM, Ill.

SOWLES
1914, 2, 19. Lucile recrq
1917, 2, 15. Florence Lucile [Soles] gct Sabina MM

SPEAR
1878, 9, 12. John F. [Speer], s James & Mary, Bridgeport, Ind.; m in home of bride's mother, Mary E. HUNNICUTT, dt Thomas & Susannah, Clinton Co., O.

1856, 12, 18. Eliza (form Oren) dis mou
1871, 4, 13. Samuel & w, Eliza, & ch, Eli & John, rocf Ash Grove MM, Ill., dtd 1871, 3,1
1874, 2, 19. Samuel recrq
1878, 8, 15. John F. [Speer] rocf Bridgeport MM, Ind., to m Mary E. Hunnicutt
1879, 8, 14. Mary rocf Ash Grove MM, Ill.
1881, 12, 15. John F. [Speer] & ch, Leonedas E. & Esther A., rocf Bridgeport MM, Ind.
1889, 1, 17. Solomon Carey, Effie Jane & Thos. L., recrq
1902, 1, 16. John F. [Spur] & w, Mary E., & ch, Grace Anna & S. Orricy, gct Caesars Creek MM, O.
1904, 4, 14. Leonidas E. [Spur] & w, Martha J. & ch, Cleo F., Leon Spray, Ray Cyrus & Paul Stanley, gct Caesars Creek MM, O.
1906, 4, 19. Almeda recrq
1906, 4, 19. Zeph [Speer] recrq
1912, 3, 14. Louise Turner rocf Wilmington MM
1921, 3, 17. Carey [Spears] & w, Minnie, & dt, Ada, gct Wilmington MM, O.
1921, 3, 17. Wm. [Spears] gct Wilmington MM, O.
1921, 5, 19. Elizabeth Linkhart [Spears] recrq
1922, 12, 14. Frank [Speer] gct Grassy Run MM, O.

SPURGEON
1888, 3, 15. Andrew J. & w, Amanda J., recrq

STANLEY
1824, 3, 4. Hannah d ae 86y 3m bur Grassy Run

STANTON
1877, 10, 25. James, s William & Margaret, Marion Co., Ind.; m in Dover MH, Hannah FRAZIER, dt Moses & Elizabeth, Clinton Co., O.

1832, 4, 18. Sarah (form Unthank) con mcd
1832, 10, 18. Sarah gct Center MM

STANTON, continued
1847, 5, 13. James & w, Dinah, rocf Caesars Creek MM, dtd 1847,3,25
1848, 3, 16. James & w, Dinah, & dt, Susannah, gct Center MM
1878, 2, 14. James rocf Beech Grove MM, Ind.
1881, 5, 19. Jehu L. rocf Beech Grove MM, Ind.
1882, 6, 15. Jehu gct Honey Creek MM, Iowa
1883, 11, 15. Louis rocf Honey Creek MM, Ia.
1884, 4, 17. Lucinda recrq
1886, 2, 18. Louis J. & fam relrq
1912, 10, 17. Lewis Jehu recrq
1916, 12, 14. Lewis J. relrq

STARBUCK
----, --, --. Gayer d 1866,12,30 ae 89y 4m 20d; m Susannah ----- d 1861,12,3 ae 87y 3m 1d

Ch:	Samuel	b 1812, 9, 27
	Clarissa	" 1815, 5, 6
	Joel	" 1817, 7, 15
	Jesse	" 1819, 10, 8
	Asa	" 1821, 11, 18 d 1844,12,28 bur Dover

1826, 9, 7. Mary m Robert HESTER
1830, 6, 10. Hezekiah d ae 81
1832, 11, 22. Clarissa m Wm. PEELLE
----, --, --. Jesse & Anna

Ch:	Adin	b 1844, 5, 10
	Asa	" 1846, 3, 3
	Martha	" 1848, 1, 29
	Mary D.	" 1851, 1, 29 d 1855,10,12
	Susannah	" 1853, 4, 26
	Ezra	" 1855, 6, 20 d 1856, 9, 5
	Joseph	" 1857, 5, 28 " 1857, 6,12
	William	" 1858, 5, 12
	Sarah	" 1860, 10, 17
	Jesse H.	" 1864, 11, 26

1929, 1, 27. Asa d ae 82y 10m

1825, 5, 7. Hezekiah & w, Judith, rocf Dover MM, N. C., dtd 1825,3,17
1825, 9, 3. Rebecca rocf Dover MM, N. C., dtd 1825,3,19
1828, 12, 18. Rebecca Hodson (form Starbuck) con mcd
1830, 9, 16. Judith gct Mill Creek MM
1833, 5, 16. Rebecca rocf Cesars Creek MM, O., dtd 1833,2,21
1834, 8, 14. Samuel & w, Rebecca, gct Fairfield MM, Ind.
1842, 9, 15. Susannah (form Oren) con mou
1843, 4, 13. Amy rocf Fairfield MM, Ind., dtd 1843,2,16
1844, 8, 15. Polly Ann (form Haughey) dis mou
1849, 3, 15. Susannah Jr. dis joining Separatists
1850, 6, 13. Lydia (form Ballard) dis mou
1852, 12, 16. Margaret (form Shields) con mou
1856, 5, 15. Susannah rst
1866, 4, 19. Aiden con mou
1865, 7, 19. Aden L. gct Springfield MM
1867, 2, 14. Moses rst
1867, 2, 14. Moses gct South River MM, Ia.
1868, 3, 19. John T. & ch, Josephine, Wm. A., Nathan T. & Clary Ann, recrq
1868, 5, 14. John T. set off with Wilmington MM, O.
1868, 5, 14. Margaret set off with Wilmington MM, O.
1868, 5, 14. Josephine set off with Wilmington MM, O.
1868, 5, 14. William A. set off with Wilmington MM, O.
1868, 5, 14. Nathan T. set off with Wilmington MM, O.
1868, 5, 14. Clary Ann set off with Wilmington MM, O.
1868, 11, 19. Asa con mou
1870, 8, 18. Susannah recrq
1870, 8, 18. Susannah dis
1871, 10, 19. Adin L. & w, Louisa, & ch, Nellie, rocf Wilmington MM, O., dtd 1871,8,18
1879, 6, 19. John F. & w, Margaret, & ch, Nathan I., Clara A. & Albert, rocf Wilmington MM
1879, 6, 19. Wm. A. rocf Wilmington MM
1883, 6, 14. John relrq
1887, 7, 14. Mary relrq
1898, 12, 15. Wm. R. relrq
1901, 10, 17. Osie & ch, Raymond & Leo, rocf Plainfield MM, Ind.
1904, 2, 18. Aden Jr. dropped from mbrp
1906, 2, 15. Albert & w, Lizzie, & s, Arthur, gct Wilmington MM
1907, 9, 19. Aden Charles & w, Stella, & ch, Hobert & Pauline, gct Springfield MM
1907, 10, 17. Maurice B. gct Wilmington MM
1909, 1, 14. Jesse C. & w, Osee, & ch, Ray Leo & Willie A., gct Fairview MM
1913, 2, 13. Ernest gct Center MM
1914, 9, 17. Goldie recrq
1914, 9, 17. Marion recrq
1914, 9, 17. Jesse & w, Osee, & ch, Raymond Leo & Willie, rocf Grassy Run MM, O.
1915, 1, 14. Bertha Shugart recrq
1916, 5, 18. Charles & w, Stella, & ch, Herbert & Pauline, rocf Center MM
1919, 11, 13. Wm. & w & s, Franklin, gct Wilmington MM, O.

STEPHENS
1885, 4, 16. Lewis recrq
1902, 3, 13. Webster E. recrq
1902, 7, 17. Dennis & s, Donald L., recrq
1915, 1, 14. Howard Wilson, s Dennis & w recrq
1915, 7, 15. Webster dropped from mbrp

STEPHENSON
1868, 4, 16. Mary & s, John R., rocf Dover MM, N. C., dtd 1868,3,5
1869, 11, 18. Mary & s, John, gct Springfield MM

STEWART
1872, 4, 18. George recrq
1872, 9, 19. William recrq
1873, 6, 19. Joseph E. & w, Rose, & ch, Flora E., recrq
1877, 5, 17. Wm. [Steward] dis disunity
1887, 7, 14. Irena & ch, Therman B., recrq
1899, 9, 14. Mary Lancaster gct Sabina MM,O.
1903, 3, 19. Jennie Crumley rocf Wilmington MM
1908, 6, 18. Jennie C. gct Sabina MM, O.

STINSON
1871, 4, 13. Jefferson & Rebecca recrq
1874, 2, 19. Effie recrq
1877, 8, 16. Thos. J. & w, Rebecca, & ch, Effie, gct Hopewell MM
1878, 6, 13. Thos. & w, Rebecca, & dt, Effie, gct Hopewell MM
1886, 2, 18. Edgar recrq
1901, 7, 18. Edgar S. C. gct Miami MM, O.

STITCHWORTH
1869, 12, 16. Ann con mou
1881, 1, 14. Ann [Stitsworth] relrq

STONE
1883, 5, 17. Abraham J. & w, Caroline, recrq

STOUT
----, --, --. George & Phebe
Ch: Hannah b 1819, 7, 20
Lucinda " 1821, 3, 1
Naoma " 1823, 3, 9
John " 1825, 1, 21
Anna " 1826, 10, 15
Phebe " 1829, 2, 15
Elizabeth " 1831, 4, 7
Eliza Jane " 1833, 5, 6
1831, 3, 24. John, s John & Ann, Clinton Co., O.; m in Dover MH, Mary B. BAILEY, dt Josiah & Susannah, Clinton Co., O.

1826, 2, 7. George & w, Phebe, & ch, Hannah, Lucinda, Naomi & John, rocf Center MM, dtd 1826,1,21
1828, 8, 11. Stephen & fam rocf Center MM, dtd 1828,5,17, endorsed to Vermillion MM, Ill.
1832, 6, 14. Mary B. gct Center MM
1836, 9, 15. George & w, Phebe, & ch, Hannah Lucinda Naomi John Anna Phebe L. Elizabeth Eliza Jane & Sarah, gct Mississinewa MM, Ind.
1873, 4, 17. Matthew gct New Garden MM, Ind.

STRONG
1879, 3, 13. Esther Ann recrq
1885, 7, 16. Esther A. relrq

STROUP
1908, 6, 18. Ella dropped from mbrp

STUDAVIN
1832, 7, 19. Aseneth (form Pearson) dis mcd

STURGEON
1872, 4, 18. John recrq
1872, 6, 13. Margaret recrq
1874, 2, 19. Jeremiah recrq
1877, 11, 15. Jeremiah relrq
1880, 5, 10. Jeremiah recrq
1883, 4, 19. Jeremiah relrq
1906, 4, 19. Lou M. recrq
1906, 4, 19. Ella recrq
1906, 4, 19. Jesse recrq
1906, 4, 19. Cora recrq

SUMMERS
1872, 6, 13. Melvina recrq

TADHUNTER
1859, 10, 13. Milton dis disunity

TAYLOR
1826, 1, 7. Lavica (form Unthank) con mcd
1826, 6, 3. Richard & w, Lucy, & dt, Hannah, rocf Springfield MM, dtd 1826,4,29
1827, 6, 10. Richard & w, Lucy, & ch, Hannah & Emily, gct Center MM

TELFAIR
1910, 3, 17. Alice Green rocf Ogden MM
1910, 3, 17. Wm. B. & dt, Alice G., recrq

TERRELL
1855, 7, 19. Mary (form Brackney) con mou
1856, 4, 17. Mary Brackney gct Fairfield MM

THATCHER
1908, 7, 16. George rocf Wilmington MM

THES
1876, 4, 13. David recrq
1876, 4, 13. Hannah recrq
1878, 2, 14. David & Hannah dis disunity

THOMAS
----, --, --. John b 1778,--,13; m Esther ----- b 1781,8,1 d 1846,7,9
Ch: Jane b 1813, 10, 28
Edward " 1816, 7, 28
Ellis R. " 1819, 6, 17 d 1821, 7,26 bur Dover
John " 1821, 10, 1 " 1855, 1, 9 bur Dover
----, --, --. Jesse & Nanna
Ch: Chalkley b 1819, 1, 23
Mary Evans " 1820, 6, 29
1825, 10, 6. Ann m Micajah MOORMAN
----, --, --. Robert & Almedia
Ch: Uriah b 1829, 7, 8
Mary Ann " 1831, 10, 25
Clarkson " 1833, 5, 21
Caroline Elizabeth " 1835, 6, 19

THOMAS, Robert & Almedia, continued
Ch: Louiza
Jane b 1837, 3, 27
Alva Curtis " 1839, 8, 1
Frances " 1841, 7, 4
Mariah Emily " 1842, 12, 2
Chalkley " 1844, 6, 1
1835, 8, 11. Jane d bur Dover
----, --, --. Edward d 1858,1,3; m Huldah -----
Ch: Ann Maria b 1840, 1, 21
Sarah " 1841, 6, 25
Isaac J. " 1845, 3, 22
John " 1849, 2, 28
James Arthur " 1856, 3, 28
----, --, --. John d 1848,9,17 ae 26y 11m 17d; m Ruth -----
Ch: Calvin b 1844, 12, 5
John A. " 1846, 11, 28 d 1853,10, 4
1851, 2, 27. John Jr. d
1869, 10, 21. Isaac J., s Edward & Huldah, Clinton Co., O.; m in Dover MH, Jane W. BANGHAM, dt Jonathan & Martha A., Clinton Co., O.
Ch: Clara Elma b 1870, 7, 31

1833, 1, 17. Almeda & ch, Uriah & Mary Ann, rocf Center MM, dtd 1832,8,15
1844, 11, 14. Almedia dis joining Separatists
1845, 4, 17. Ruth rocf Clear Creek MM, O., dtd 1844,11,9
1845, 5, 15. Jane dis joining Separatists
1848, 10, 19. Uriah, Mary Ann, Clarkson, Caroline Elizabeth, Louisa Jane, Alva Curtis, Frances J., Mariah Emily & Chalkley, ch Robert & Almedia, gct New Garden MM, Ind.
1849, 5, 17. Ruth & ch, Calvin & John A., gct Birch Lake MM, Mich.
1852, 1, 15. Mary E. Bryon (form Thomas) dis mou
1853, 5, 19. Ruth & ch, Calvin & Alexander, rocf Birch Lake MM, Mich., dtd 1853,2,5
1855, 4, 19. Ruth Leeky (form Thomas) dis mou
1860, 7, 19. Sarah Wall (form Thomas) dis mou
1862, 5, 15. Anna M. Mercer (form Thomas) dis mou
1872, 4, 17. Uriah gct New Garden MM, Ind.
1874, 3, 19. Hannah gct Caesars Creek MM,O.
1903, 3, 19. Lewis & w, Terresa, rocf Center MM
1903, 11, 19. Isaac gct Miami MM
1908, 12, 17. Alice Haworth dropped from mbrp
1911, 3, 16. Joseph gct Ogden MM

THOMPSON
1861, 3, 14. Hannah [Thomson] (form Ballard) con mou
1868, 5, 14. Hannah set off with Wilmington MM, O.
1874, 3, 19. Hannah gct Caesars Creek MM, O.
1884, 9, 18. Rebecca relrq
1911, 12, 14. Vesper recrq
1915, 7, 15. Vesper dropped from mbrp

THORNBURG
1834, 1, 22. Thomas [Thornburgh], s Joel & Dinah, Green Co., O.; m in Seneca MH, Nancy MOORMAN, dt Thomas P. & Dosha, Green Co., O.
Ch: Sarah Emily b 1835, 4, 18
Melissa Jane " 1837, 5, 12
Alonzo " 1839, 4, 24
Dosha Dinah " 1841, 9, 28
Nancy Elizabeth " 1844, 12, 13
Judith Mary" 1847, 9, 23
Joel Thomas " 1850, 2, 25

1835, 3, 17. Nancy Ann gct Centre MM
1839, 4, 18. Thomas [Thornburgh] & w, Nancy, & ch, Sarah Emily & Melissa Jane, rocf Center MM, dtd 1839,2,15
1855, 5, 17. Malissa Jane Sanders (form Thornburg) dis mou
1864, 5, 19. Thomas & w, Nancy, & ch, Nancy E., Judith M. & Joel Thos., gct Spring Creek MM, Ia.
1864, 5, 19. Alonzo E. gct Spring Creek MM, Ia.
1864, 5, 19. Sarah E.& Dosha D. gct Spring Creek MM, Ia.

THORNBURY
1847, 5, 14. Isaac, s Nathan & Rebecca, Randolph Co., Ind.; m in Dover MH, Hannah FRAZIER, dt John & Alice, Clinton Co., O.

1850, 11, 14. Hannah gct Cherry Grove MM, Ind.
1850, 11, 14. Elizabeth Manerva (form Woodard) dis mou
1851, 5, 15. Mary Jane (form Gallemore) dis mou
1888, 4, 19. Mary recrq

THORP
1874, 2, 19. Joseph recrq
1876, 7, 13. Joseph E. dis disunity
1885, 7, 16. Viola V. relrq
1887, 7, 14. Huldah recrq

THRUSHER
1871, 1, 19. Gilbert T. & w, Hannah, & ch, Hannah Ella, John Emery, Sarah Edna & Mary Martha Anna, recrq
1877, 6, 14. Gilbert & fam gct Springfield MM, O.

TIDD
1904, 3, 17. Oscar & Versie recrq

TIMBERLAKE
1844, 4, 18. Alfred & w, Phebe, & ch, Mary B. & Eliza D., rocf Center MM, dtd 1844, 4,17
1845, 6, 19. Alfred & w, Phebe, & ch, Mary B., Eliza D. & Caroline, gct Clear Creek MM, O.

TOBIN
1901, 6, 13. Emma dropped from mbrp

TODHUNTER
1884, 11, 13. Milton rocf Hopewell MM, O.

TOLLY
1880, 6, 17. Samuel & w, Rebecca, & ch, Lottie Naomi, Church, Catharine, Eliza & Bertha Anne, recrq

TURNER
1838, 1, 18. Elizabeth (form Hawhay) dis mou
1874, 2, 19. Jesse recrq
1878, 2, 14. Jesse relrq
1906, 9, 13. Mary P. relrq
1908, 12, 17. Mamie gct Wilmington MM, O.

UNTHANK
----, --, --. John, s John & Sarah, b 1780, 6,29; m Mary MASON, dt Thos. & Elizabeth, b 1782,12,15

Ch:			
Leveicy	b 1804, 10, 4	d 1850,10,15
Ann	" 1806, 3, 18	" 1832, 4,26
Jonathan	" 1807, 12, 27	
Sarah	" 1809, 12, 12	
Elizabeth	" 1811, 11, 4	
Mary	" 1813, 8, 17	
Joseph	" 1815, 11, 10	
Rebecca	" 1817, 10, 6	
John Allen	" 1819, 12, 18	
Beulah	" 1821, 12, 28	d 1823, 7,22
William M.	" 1824, 9, 6	

1825, 6, 4. John & w, Mary, & ch, Jonathan, Sarah Elizabeth, Mary Rebecca, Joseph John Allen & William, rocf Chester MM, Ind., dtd 1825,4,20
1825, 11, 5. Ann rocf Chester MM, Ind., dtd 1825,9,21
1825, 11, 5. Lavica rocf Chester MM, Ind., dtd 1825,5,18
1826, 1, 7. Lavicia Taylor (form Unthank) con mcd
1826, 5, 22. Ann Dillon (form Unthank) con mcd
1831, 4, 14. Rachel rocf White Water MM, Ind., dtd 1830,11,24
1832, 4, 18. Sarah Stanton (form Unthank) con mcd
1832, 10, 18. John & w, Mary, & ch, Elizabeth Mary, Joseph, Rebecca, John Allen & Wm. M. gct New Garden MM, Ind.
1839, 7, 18. Rachel gct New Garden MM, Ind.

UNDERWOOD
1858, 4, 15. Catharine (form Hunnicutt) con mou
1879, 3, 13. Henry & Arthama recrq
1905, 1, 19. Kelly & ch relrq
1905, 1, 19. Clarkson relrq
1911, 12, 14. Evan dropped from mbrp

VANAKEN
1885, 4, 16. Marcellus recrq

VANDERWORT
1912, 1, 8. Lucius & w recrq
1923, 3, 25. Myra Pagett relrq
1925, 1, 26. Lucius & w & two ch, Pauline & Margaret, gct Wilmington MM

VANNOY
1876, 4, 13. Daniel & Amanda [Vannay] recrq
1880, 5, 10. Wm. J. recrq
1881, 7, 14. W. J. [Vanney] dis disunity
1883, 12, 13. Daniel relrq

VANNERSDOLL
1905, 3, 16. Elsie (form Ary) relrq

VANPELT
1842, 10, 13. Catharine rocf Fairfield MM, dtd 1842,9,22
1902, 7, 17. Lena M. Spear relrq

VARVEL
1928, 7, 29. Ellen Miley recrq
1929, 4, 28. Ellen Miley relrq

WADKINS
1845, 11, 13. Martha Ann (form Johnson) dis mou & jas

WALKER
1841, 9, 16. Rebecca (form Shields) con mou
1881, 5, 19. Rebecca gct Wilmington MM

WALL
1857, 1, 4. Mary d

1842, 6, 16. Mary & ch, Rebecca Ann & Elizabeth, recrq
1855, 6, 14. Rebecca Ann Antram (form Wall) dis mou
1860, 7, 19. Sarah (form Thomas) dis mou
1863, 3, 19. Elizabeth Johnson (form Wall) dis mou
1888, 1, 19. Minnie recrq

WALTHALL
----, --, --. William & Martha

Ch:		
Elizabeth	b 1811, 11, 26
Sarah	" 1813, 9, 28
Martha	" 1816, 6, 6

WALTHALL, William & Martha, continued
Ch: William b 1818, 1, 25
Thomas " 1820, 8, 25
Daniel Bailey " 1823, 3, 26
David " 1825, 1, 23
1824, 2, 15. Wm. B. d ae 83
1834, 10, 23. Elizabeth m Elijah HAWORTH
1844, 11, 21. Sarah m Micajah HUNNICUTT
1848, 3, 23. Thomas, s William & Martha, Clinton Co., O.; m in Dover MH, Elizabeth Ann KINSEY, dt Absalom & Margaret, Clinton Co., O., d 1856,6,8 ae 30y 8m 6d
Ch: Margaret b 1849, 1, 7 d 1865, 3,13
Sarah " 1851, 3, 24
Thomas m 2nd Marie E. -----
Ch: Eliza P. b 1869, 4, 20
1849, 8, 23. Martha A. m Jonathan BANGHAM
1853, 10, 19. David, s William B. & Martha, Clinton Co., O.; m in Grassy Run MH, Louisa CARTER, dt John & Hannah, Clinton Co., O.
Ch: John Gurney b 1854, 8, 11
Edith Ellen " 1858, 5, 8
Hannah Alta " 1862, 5, 8 d 1863, 5, 3
Josiah T. " 1864, 6, 9
Ezra Allen " 1868, 3, 13
----, --, --. Daniel & Elizabeth
Ch: Robert M. b 1861, 1, 7
Elijah D. " 1863, 1, 16
John F. " 1864, 11, 26
1867, 8, 22. Margaret m Benjamin COMPTON
1870, 6, 10. Martha d ae 85y 10m 8d

1830, 11, 18. Wm. B. & w, Martha, & ch, Elizabeth, Sarah Martha Ann Wm. B., Thos. Daniel B. & David, rocf Upper MM, Va., dtd 1830,8,18
1842, 1, 13. Wm. B. gct Vermillion MM, Ill.
1852, 7, 15. Elizabeth H. rocf Center MM
1852, 11, 18. Daniel B. & w, Elizabeth H., gct Honey Creek MM, Ind.
1858, 2, 18. Maria E. rocf Center MM, dtd 1858,2,17
1859, 3, 17. Thomas & w, Mariah E., & ch, Margaret & Sarah, gct Center MM
1860, 11, 15. Daniel B. & w, Elizabeth, & ch, Wm., Levi F., Sarah Emily & Mary Martha, rocf Honey Creek MM, Ind., dtd 1860,10,13
1864, 10, 15. Thos. & w, Maria, & ch, Margaret & Sarah, rocf Center MM, dtd 1864,10, 12
1865, 3, 16. Daniel B. & w, Elizabeth H., & ch, Wm. A., Levi F., Sarah E., Mary M., Robert M., Elijah D. & John F., gct Rocksylvania MM, Iowa
1866, 1, 18. Daniel B. & fam rocf Rocksylvania MM, Iowa
1869, 11, 18. Daniel B. & w, Elizabeth, & ch, Wm., Levi F., Sarah E., Mary M., Robert M., Elijah D., John F. & Samuel, gct Rocksylvania MM, Ia.
1870, 4, 14. David & w, Louisa C., & ch, John G., Edith E., Josiah F. & Ezra A., gct Back Creek MM
1886, 12, 16. Thos. & w, Marie E., & dt, Eliza P., gct Wilmington MM, O.
1901, 6, 13. Fletcher dropped from mbrp

WALTON
1864, 12, 15. July Etta (form Peebles) con mou
1865, 2, 16. Juliette gct Caesars Creek MM,O.
1865, 4, 18. Julietta rocf Caesars Creek MM, O., dtd 1865,2.23

WASHINGTON
1876, 12, 14. Levina V. recrq
1880, 5, 10. Benjamin recrq
1889, 4, 18. Benjamin dropped from mbrp

WATSON
1871, 4, 13. Sarah recrq
1871, 4, 13. Charles recrq
1871, 4, 13. Isabell recrq
1874, 2, 19. Rose A. recrq
1878, 4, 13. John & ch, Chas. L., Calvin & Charlotte recrq
1878, 7, 18. Chas. & w, Isabella, dis disunity
1885, 6, 18. Sarah recrq

WEAVER
1906, 4, 19. Alfretta recrq

WEIMER
1881, 5, 19. Cora & Rosa recrq
1911, 11, 16. J. W. & Gladys S. [Weiner] recrq
1911, 12, 14. Leo recrq
1916, 10,19. J. H. & w, Gladys, relrq
1921, 1, 13. Leo [Wymer] gct Wilmington MM

WELCH
1870, 2, 17. Margaret recrq

WELLER
1902, 3, 13. Earl recrq
1909, 12, 17. Earl dropped from mbrp
1911, 12, 14. Ernest recrq
1912, 3, 14. Wm. J., Ella J. & Homer recrq

WEST
1838, 7, 13. Margaret Ellen, dt Thos. & Tamar, b
----, --, --. David & Ruth
Ch: William b 1841, 5, 6
Mary " 1844, 2, 28
1841, 8, 31. Jeremiah A. d ae 16y 8m 14d

1838, 3, 15. Tamer & ch, Sarah, Elizabeth, Jeremiah, Anna, Mary & Isaiah, rocf Newberry MM, O., dtd 1838,1,22
1841, 8, 19. David & w, Ruth, & ch, Sarah, Daniel, Ezra & William, rocf Newberry MM,

WEST, continued
dtd 1841,7,19
1845, 3, 13. David & w, Ruth, & ch, Sarah, Daniel, Elizabeth, Wm. & Mary, gct Newberry MM
1846, 12, 17. Anna M. Arnold (form West) con mou
1861, 1, 17. Margaret Moore (form West) con mou
1863, 9, 17. Mary D. Bond (form West) con mou
1868, 5, 14. Tamer & s, Isaiah M., set off with Wilmington MM, O.

WHEELER
1902, 9, 18. Dora Sapp rocf New Garden MM, N. C.

WHINERY
1907, 9, 17. Joseph H. & w, Edna H., & ch, Fileta & Raymond, rocf Winona MM, O.

WHITE
1872, 6, 13. Nancy Jane recrq
1887, 2, 17. Thos. & Sally recrq
1887, 6, 16. Joseph & w, Mary J., recrq
1899, 12, 14. Thomas A. & ch, Frank J., Winona G. & Pauline E., gct Sabina MM

WHITTINGTON
1879, 3, 13. Eliza & Luettie recrq
1885, 1, 15. Eliza relrq

WIGGINS
1872, 3, 14. Nancy recrq
1878, 2, 14. Jane dis jas
1878, 2, 14. Florence dis jas
1878, 2, 14. Nancy dis jas

WILES
1827, 9, 1. Diana rocf Center MM, dtd 1827, 7,21
1832, 8, 19. Diana gct Center MM

WILKINSON
1901, 3, 14. Minna relrq
1902, 5, 2. Gertrude recrq

WILLIAMS
1830, 11, 18. Rachel rocf White Water MM, Ind., dtd 1830,7,28
1831, 9, 15. Rachel gct West Grove MM, Ind.
1852, 6, 17. Elizabeth (form Hunt) con mou
1856, 3, 13. Elizabeth dis jas
1861, 7, 18. Elizabeth (form Oren) dis mou
1874, 2, 19. Riley & w, Alice, & ch, Israel P. & Chas. Wm., recrq
1874, 2, 19. Huldah J. recrq
1874, 5, 14. Carie Alice, dt Huldah Ellen, recrq
1878, 2, 14. Huldah E. & dt, Cora A., relrq

WILLIS
1879, 7, 17. Isaac recrq
1882, 4, 13. Richard & Eliza recrq
1883, 12, 13. Richard & w gct Cincinnati MM
1885, 4, 16. Isaac released
1888, 12, 13. Alice gct Muncie MM, Ind.
1923, 3, 25. Wm. [Wellis] relrq

WILSON
1836, 9, 15. Arzilli (form Johnson) dis mou
1876, 4, 13. Wm. H. recrq
1878, 2, 14. James recrq
1887, 8, 18. W. W. gct Pleasant Plain MM, Kans.

WINSLOW
1863, 5, 14. Joseph & w, Eunice, rocf St. Albans MM, Me., dtd 1863,2,24
1856, 12, 14. Joseph & w, Eunice, gct Sidney MM, Me.

WOODARD
1851, 4, 14. William d

1843, 6, 15. Jane & ch, Alisha, Elizabeth Minerva, William & Mary Adaline, rocf Miami MM, dtd 1863,9,21
1850, 11, 14. Elizabeth Manerva Thornbury (form Woodard) dis mou
1851, 7, 17. Jane & dt, Mary Adaline, gct Cherry Grove MM, Ind.

WOODMANSEE
1905, 2, 16. Mary S. dropped from mbrp

WOOLERY
1866, 2, 15. Rachel (form Gilpin) con mou
1871, 1, 19. Nathanial [Woolary] & adopted ch, Jemima Parlott, recrq

WRIGHT
----, --, --. Isaac & Abigail

Ch:		
	James	b 1815, 2, 12
	Jesse	" 1817, 4, 28
	George	" 1820, 1, 1
	Martha	" 1823, 1, 14
	Jonathan	" 1825, 4, 22
	Hanah	" 1827, 10, 28
	Sarah	" 1830, 8, 26
	Dillon	" 1833, 11, 1

1830, 9, 16. Sarah gct Vermillion MM, Ill.
1836, 9, 15. Jesse & w, Abigail, & ch, Jesse George Martha Jonathan Hannah Sarah & Dillon, gct Mississinewa MM, Ind.
1853, 8, 18. Mary Jane Huff (form Wright) con mou
1854, 8, 17. Rachel Brackney (form Wright) con mou

WRIGHTSMAN
1829, 9, 17. Abigail dis jH

YARNELL
1901, 3, 14. Winnie [Yarnall] recrq

YARNELL, continued
1903, 10, 15. Eugene dropped from mbrp
1907, 4, 18. Beulah recrq

YOWELL
1901, 3, 14. Mary Willa relrq

* * * * * * *

BAILEY
1859, 8, 25. Mary m John HORNADA
1866, 9, 20. Hannah m David PIDGEON

MOORMAN
1831, 4, 20. Elizabeth m Daniel BAILEY, Jr.

1904, 2, 18. Mary dropped from mbrp

ZURFACE
1931, 12, 27. Ruth Elizabeth Young & ch, Harold Eugene, Virginia Eilene & Melba May, rocf Wilmington MM

* * * * * * *

FRAZIER
----, --, --. John & Lydia [Fraizure]
Ch: Mary
Elizabeth b 1864, 9, 28
Hannah P. " 1869, 10, 12

WILMINGTON MONTHLY MEETING

Wilmington Monthly Meeting began as an indulged meeting from Center Monthly Meeting in 1825. A monthly meeting was granted by Center Quarterly Meeting in 1868 with a membership of 178, mostly from Center, Dover and Springfield meetings.

RECORDS

ABBOTT
1908, 1, 1. Fay m Charles BASHORE
1911, 2, 26. Margaret m Wm. PUMMELLE

1905, 1, 11. Elsworth & Fay [Abbot] rocf Clear Creek MM, O.
1905, 1, 11. Minnie [Abbot] recrq
1921, 6, 15. Ellsworth & Minnie dropped from mbrp

ACHOR
1901, 1, 17. John G. d ae 80
1909, 10, 6. George d ae 75
1917, 3, 17. Maria S. d
1926, 7, 23. Euphemia B. d

1901, 2, 9. John C. & w, Euphemia, rocf Fairview MM, O., dtd 1900,12,8

ADAMS
1897, 9, 9. Sarah d ae 82
1923, 10, 7. Susanna m Allen MARTIN

1870, 3, 18. Edward recrq
1870, 4, 15. Sarah recrq
1876, 8, 18. Edward dis
1877, 2, 16. David M. recrq
1882, 3, 17. Elizabeth & dt, Fannie, recrq
1885, 5, 9. J. Clinton & w, Jennie, & ch, Lowell, recrq
1885, 6, 13. Edward dropped from mbrp
1889, 1, 12. Fannie & Maggie relrq
1919, 10, 8. Mary L. rocf Kansas City MM, Mo.
1921, 3, 9. Wilson, Effie J., Susanna & Mildred, roc
1921, 4, 13. Glenna M. recrq
1922, 7, 12. Mary L. C. gct Waynesville MM,O.
1926, 4, 14. Mary L. C. rocf Miami MM, O.

ALAXANDER
1872, 4, 19. Sarah Ella Lecta recrq

ALBAN
1873, 4, 18. James S. & Ann E. recrq
1885, 6, 13. James, Emily & Ann dropped from mbrp

ALBRO
1929, 12, 10. Minnie Huffman dropped from mbrp

ALDRIDGE
1927, 12, 31. Gladys m Wm. VAN NESSLEY

1909, 10, 9. Gladys [Aldreige] rocf Dover MM, O.
1913, 12, 17. George Tellfair recrq

ALLEN
----, --, --. Marion L. b 1835,3,25; m Rebecca L. THOMASON b 1838,12,26
Ch: Sarah M. b 1860, 9, 3
Olive M. b 1863, 11, 1
Mary L. " 1865, 11, 22
Orilla B. " 1867, 8, 4
Annetta " 1872, 7, 6

1877, 2, 16. George & James recrq
1886, 4, 10. Chas. J. & w, Emma A., recrq
1888, 4, 14. Anna relrq

ALLISON
1899, 9, 9. James & w, Cora, recrq
1900, 2, 10. James & w, Cora, relrq

AMES
1919, 6, --. Clarence m Virginia GLASS

1914, 2, 11. Jessie recrq
1921, 6, 15. Jessie dropped from mbrp
1929, 4, 10. Virginia Glass relrq

AMOS
1877, 2, 16. George recrq

ANDERS
1909, 3, 10. Foster m Viola SMITH

1913, 6, 11. Viola relrq

ANDERSON
1910, 9, 18. Dorothy E. m David Edward ALDER

1870, 3, 18. Wm. H. & w, Jane, & ch, Charles, Ella & John W., recrq
1886, 1, 9. Wm. H. & fam relrq
1920, 11, 10. Melissa Urton relrq

ANDREW
1794, 12, 3. Elizabeth b
1853, 4, 26. Mary Emily b
----, --, --. Ira b 1818,1,30; m Mary SMITH b 1826,2,2
Ch: Elwood G. b 1856, 12, 17
1925, 8, 3. Paul m Ruth OREN

1900, 1, 13. Wm. H. & w, Caroline, rocf Smyrna MM, Ia., dtd 1899,11,4
1931, 6, 10. Paul J. recrq

ANTRAM
1898, 7, 26. John d ae 97
1911, 11, 28. Ada m Chas. Herbert GREEN

1897, 12, 11. John recrq
1902, 2, 8. Bell recrq
1902, 3, 8. Carrie E. rocf Dover MM, O.
1902, 5, 10. Ada recrq

ARMSTRONG
1922, 3, 7. Vesta m Russell PROBASCO

1921, 7, 13. Vesta & s, Ellis K., recrq

ARNOLD
1921, 2, 9. Truman Dewitt recrq
1929, 10, 9. Ruth recrq
1929, 10, 9. Versa recrq

ARROWSMITH
1909, 11, 16. Grace m Daniel CLARK
1918, 8, 10. Goldam Jesse HOLADAY

1914, 4, 8. Goldie recrq

ARTHUR
1903, 9, 12. Edwin P., s Bertha, recrq

ASKEW
1874, 7, 17. Sarah (form McBeth) dis mcd

AUSTIN
1905, 6, 10. Elizabeth, dt Dr. G. M. & Elma, b
1910, 2, 19. Lulu m Laurence MACE
1916, 12, 14. Lena m Huston TALMADGE
1919, 9, 12. Faith m Gurney TERRELL
1927, 2, 1. Samantha d
1930, 10, 25. Dr. J. M. d
1932, 10, 11. Elizabeth m Svend M. PETERSON

1898, 4, 9. Samantha rocf Ogden MM, O., dtd 1898,3,26
1903, 10, 10. G. M. & w, Elma & Faith, recrq
1905, 1, 11. Mary recrq
1906, 2, 10. Lulu & Lena recrq
1911, 7, 8. John B. recrq

AYERS
1907, 12, 24. Wm. M. m Florence S. LYLE
1929, 11, 30. Arthur G. m Mary Louise BISHER

1916, 6, 14. Margaret & Pauline recrq
1921, 6, 15. Florence S. dropped from mbrp

BABB
----, --, --. Frank m Hannah OSBORN b 1848,2, 17
Ch: Caroline b 1870, 8, 16
Elizabeth " 1872, 9, 21
Charles O. " 1875, 8, 3 d 1875,10,18
1905, 5, 23. Rebecca d ae 60
1905, 6, 30. Wm. R. d ae 70
1908, 8, 9. David d ae 66
1921, 5, 25. Ruth C. m Scott MOLYNEAUX
1927, 4, 20. Hannah O. d
1931, 2, 24. Harriett d
1932, 3, 17. Hannah d

1870, 11, 18. Hannah (form Osborne) con mcd
1873, 3, 14. David & w, Hannah, recrq
1873, 4, 18. Sarah recrq
1874, 3, 20. Jasper recrq
1874, 3, 20. Mary recrq
1874, 3, 20. Sarah recrq
1876, 5, 19. Rebecca recrq
1885, 6, 13. Jasper dropped from mbrp
1889, 4, 13. Wm. R. & w, Eliza W., & ch, Wm. R. Jr., Wilbur T., Marion E., Charles F. & Calvin M., recrq
1895, 8, 10. Clinton & w, Annie, & ch, Vedith, Eva, Albert & Esther, rocf Center MM, O., dtd 1895,4,17
1905, 6, 10. Clinton & w, Anna, & ch, Vedith, Eva, Albert & Esther, gct Caesars Creek MM, O.
1906, 6, 9. Eliza W. relrq
1907, 5, 11. Wm. R. Jr., Marion S. & Calvin M. dropped from mbrp
1907, 5, 11. Wilbur T. & Chas. F. dropped from mbrp
1912, 2, 10. Viola recrq
1912, 11, 13. Harriett M., Ruth C. & Daniel J., recrq
1918, 8, 21. Eli & w, Orianna, & dt, Anna Barbara, rocf Center MM, O.
1919, 5, 14. Carey Henry recrq

BACON
1915, 6, 30. Francis Rogers m Edith FARQUHAR in Wilmington MH

1915, 10, 13. Edith Farquhar gct Lansdowne MM, Pa.

BAHAN
1885, 6, 13. William & Mary Flora dropped from mbrp

BAILEY
----, --, --. David H. m Maria S. ----- b 1837,6,1
Ch: Corwin A. b 1858, 9, 14
Clifton D. " 1859, 12, 29
Susan
Antoinette d 1877,12,10
1909, 11, 17. Elsie m Dr. KINZEL
1916, 11, 23. Albert I. d
1917, 8, 16. H. K. m Jeanette TAYLOR
1923, 3, 14. Lucretia Bell m W. H. JONES
1925, 8, 27. Mary E. d

1868, 12, 15. David H. rocf Cincinnati MM, O., dtd 1868,11,19
1881, 8, 19. Maria dis
1885, 11, 13. Albert I. rocf Dover MM
1886, 2, 13. Mary E. recrq
1899, 8, 12. Corwin relrq
1900, 8, 11. Luella recrq
1901, 5, 11. Harlan relrq
1902, 12, 13. Bell rocf Dover MM, O.
1904, 3, 12. Elsie recrq
1904, 4, 9. Wm. A. recrq
1904, 7, 9. Belle relrq
1908, 8, 8. Belle recrq
1908, 12, 12. Amos rocf Center MM, O.
1908, 12, 12. Addie S. recrq
1909, 6, 12. Elmer rocf Dover MM, O.
1916, 12, 13. Minnie Howell recrq
1917, 5, 9. Nell, Juanita & Alma Elizabeth

BAILEY, continued
ch Elmer & Minnie, recrq
1921, 3, 9. Stella & Veda rocf Center MM, O., dtd 1921,2,16
1921, 3, 9. W. A. recrq
1921, 12, 14. Wm. relrq
1929, 6, 12. Neil dropped from mbrp

BAILIFF
1921, 6, 15. Amos dropped from mbrp
1921, 6, 15. Addie dropped from mbrp

BAKER
----, --, --. Samuel W. d 1905,3,25 ae 60; m Jennie JONES
Ch: Frank M. b 1869, 9, 8
Leonidas " 1873, 1, 26
Harley " 1874, 8, 11
1911, 4, 22. Homer Richard, s Earle & Minnie, b
1911, 10, 25. Lee d
1913, 9, 27. Frances Susie, dt Earl & Minnie, b
1921, 1, 20. Frank d

1889, 4, 13. Ella recrq
1889, 8, 10. Samuel & ch, Leonidas Frank & Harley, rocf Springfield MM, O.
1909, 4, 10. Jennie recrq
1909, 8, 14. Earle rocf West Fork MM, O., dtd 1909,7,17
1909, 9, 11. Minnie & s, Chas. Gilbert, recrq
1913, 1, 8. Susanna Bessie recrq
1913, 1, 8. Wm. Anderson recrq
1913, 6, 11. John R. recrq
1914, 2, 11. Wm. Anderson relrq
1921, 6, 15. Harley dropped from mbrp
1926, 11, 10. Earl R. & fam gct Westfork MM,O.

BALES
1909, 6, 23. Thomas m Ada PROBASCO
1910, 3, 23. Emery m Elizabeth E. MAGEE
1910, 3, 24. Jane d ae 49
1914, 5, 29. Mary Elizabeth, dt Thos. & Ada, b
1915, 6, 13. Wm. Chas., s Thos. & Ada, b
1916, 6, 17. Lorena m Frank R. ELLIOTT
1929, 1, 9. Ilo d

1904, 4, 9. Emery R. recrq
1904, 4, 9. Thomas U. recrq
1906, 6, 9. Jane recrq
1906, 8, 11. Ilo H., dt Jane, recrq
1911, 2, 11. Emory relrq
1927, 6, 8. Mary Elizabeth recrq

BALLARD
----, --, --. Benajah b 1797,10,19; m Phebe ----- b 1806,11,19
Ch: Sallie M. b 1838, 8, 4
Allen " 1847, 4, 25
John " 1841, 10, 15
----, --, --. Amos b 1835,2,25 d 1911,2,23 ae 76; m Elizabeth BARRETT b 1837,11,22 d 1880,3,23 bur Springfield
Ch: Rebecca b 1861, 8, 2
Anna " 1863, 1, 13
Olive " 1864, 4, 8
Phebe Alice " 1867, 2, 22
Elva " 1869, 2, 27
Mary Jane " 1873, 4, 9
Almeda Hester " 1876, 9, 7
Bertha E. " 1876, 10, 11
----, --, --. John b 1841,10,15; m Louisa ----
Ch: Eleanor b 1868, 12, 10
Emma
1870, 1, 5. Phebe d
1921, 6, --. Martha d
1922, 12, 22. Allen d

1870, 3, 18. Lucinda recrq
1892, 2, 13. Martha & ch, Ellroy & Edna Marie, rocf Cesars Creek MM, O.
1894, 9, 8. Willa recrq
1897, 1, 9. Amos, Rebecca, Olive E., Alice, Elva, Mary J., Almeda H. & Bertha E., rocf Springfield MM, O., dtd 1896,12,19
1897, 2, 13. Fred W. recrq
1898, 5, 14. Lucinda dropped from mbrp
1902, 5, 10. Fred W. & w, Bessie T., gct Cleveland MM, O.
1903, 2, 14. Lucinda dropped from mbrp
1907, 4, 13. John, Louisa & Eleanor dropped from mbrp
1909, 5, 8. Alice relrq
1912, 12, 11. Willa gct Moorstown MM, N. J.
1914, 4, 8. Elva & Mary gct Lindsey MM, Calif.
1914, 10, 14. Jesse D. recrq
1920, 12, 8. Rebecca gct Long Beach MM, Calif.
1921, 6, 15. Elroy dropped from mbrp

BANGHAM
1912, 11, 13. Loren E. d

1874, 11, 20. John C. & ch, Ella M., Cyrus, Lovina & Anna Lucy, rocf Springfield MM, O., dtd 1874,10,17
1874, 12, 18. Lydia recrq
1886, 4, 10. Mary E. recrq
1889, 4, 13. John & w, Lydia, & s, Wm., gct Cesars Creek MM, O.
1889, 4, 13. Levina gct Cesars Creek MM, O.
1889, 4, 13. Anna gct Cesars Creek MM, O.
1898, 2, 12. Cyrus gct Cesars Creek MM, O.
1908, 5, 19. Wm. J. & w, Elizabeth C., & ch, Mabel E., rocf Caesars Creek MM, O.
1909, 2, 13. John C. rocf Long Beach MM, Calif.
1911, 5, 13. Loren E. recrq
1924, 9, 10. Alberta recrq
1925, 9, 9. Alberta relrq
1926, 8, 11. Wm. J. & w, Elizabeth C., & dt, Mable E., gct Cincinnati MM, O.

BARLOW
1900, 6, 22. Alzina W. d ae 54

1873, 4, 18. Annie & Miriam recrq
1874, 3, 20. Henry C. & w, Elgina, recrq
1897, 2, 13. Fred J. relrq
1897, 3, 12. Bessie recrq

BARRERE
1921, 6, 2. Helen m Isaac McMULLAN

BARRETT
1907, 5, 25. Denson d ae 76
1907, 7, 27. Richard Cyrus d ae 68
1911, 6, 14. Georgianna m Harold C. HIATT
1918, 4, 22. Hurbert A. m Sarah Lucile BRIGGS
1920, 2, 7. Hubert, s Hubert A. & Lucile Briggs, b
1924, 10, 11. Abi d
1925, 6, 26. Ethel Kathleen, dt Hubert & Lucile (Briggs), b
1925, 11, 4. Mary m James McVEY

1885, 4, 11. Frank recrq
1886, 4, 10. Wm. Elmer recrq
1889, 11, 9. Rosa B. P. recrq
1897, 7, 10. Frank gct Hopewell MM, O.
1901, 10, 12. Richard Cyrus & w, Abi, & dt, Sarah Elizabeth & Mary Coffin, rocf Hopewell MM, O., dtd 1901,10,5
1903, 9, 12. Denson rocf Hopewell MM, O., dtd 1903,9,5
1905, 3, 8. Richard Warren rocf Hopewell MM, O., dtd 1905,2,4
1905, 3, 8. Wm. Elmer & w, Rose, & ch, Hellen, gct 12th St. MM, Phila., Pa.
1912, 11, 13. Reuben Putman & w, Phebe L., & ch, Hubert A. & Mary Louise, rocf Fairfield MM, O., dtd 1912,10,19

BASHORE
1908, 1, 1. Charles m Fay ABBOTT

1925, 5, 13. Mary Louise recrq

BASSETT
1921, 6, 14. Leo J. m Louise PROBASCO

BATES
1892, 11, 12. Eliza rocf Newberry MM, O., dtd 1892,10,13

BATH
1905, 11, 16. Dorothy, dt Fred C. & Rata, b
1922, 2, 23. Bertha m Mark Clinton PEELLE

1902, 2, 8. Fred C. & w, Rachel K., & ch, Robert K., J. Harroll & Elizabeth, rocf Center MM, O., dtd 1902,1,15
1921, 12, 14. Robert gct Chester MM

BAUGHAM
1909, 3, 22. John C. d ae 91

BAYARD
1909, 6, 30. Charles m Lenna CLARK

BAYHAM
1873, 4, 18. William A. recrq

BAYLESS
1911, 12, --. Anna m Richard FAHEY
1926, 11, 30. Helen Myrtle m Henry DALTON

1908, 5, 19. Anna Brewer recrq

BEARD
1881, 10, 14. Jacob & w, Permelia, & dt, Laura, gct Springfield MM, O.
1888, 8, 11. Elwood gct Newberry MM, O.

BECK
1921, 11, 10. Tessie C. m Frank OREN

BELL
1909, 4, 17. Richard m Lorna HOOVER
1917, 3, 21. Martha d
1916, 5, --. John d

1874, 1, 16. Martha & ch, Lucretia & Chas. H., rocf Springfield MM, dtd 1873,11,1
1883, 4, 20. John recrq
1895, 6, 8. Olive recrq
1898, 12, 12. Charles dis
1926, 1, 13. Martha Ellen recrq
1929, 10, 9. Virginia recrq of parents

BELLOWS
1909, 10, 9. Meda Ballard relrq

BENDEN
1921, 2, 9. Pierce E., Anna K., Bertha L., Marie E. & Robert W., recrq

BENHAM
1891, 7, 11. Mary rocf Miami MM, O., dtd 1891,4,22
1895, 5, 11. Mary dropped from mbrp

BENNETT
1907, 5, 11. Anna May Jefferis relrq

BENTLEY
1909, 10, 14. Delbert Morris, s Ervin & Daisy, b

1908, 1, 11. Ervin I. rocf Dover MM, O.
1908, 1, 11. Daisey recrq
1917, 5, 9. Ervin I. & w, Daisy F., & s, Morris, gct Sabina MM, O.

BENTZ
1897, 4, 2. Sarah d

BERLIN
1876, 6, 16. Mary E. recrq
1902, 3, 8. Dessie recrq

BERLIN, continued
1914, 11, 11. Wm. & w, Cora, & ch, Mary, Nola & Espy, rocf Ogden MM, O., dtd 1914, 10,24
1921, 3, 9. Wm. & Cora & dt, Nolia, gct Ogden MM, O.
1927, 10, 12. Ancil & w, Vinta, & his dt, Harriett, recrq
1929, 12, 10. Espy dropped from mbrp

BESCH
1920, 12, 8. M. Zora & Helen L. recrq
1929, 11, 13. Zora & dt, Helen, gct First Friends Church, Los Angeles, Calif.

BETTS
1907, 9, 19. Madison d ae 70

1876, 6, 16. Madison & w, Caroline J., & ch, Lizzie & Thomas Wade, rocf Newberry MM, O., dtd 1876,4,17
1877, 2, 16. Mary recrq
1883, 11, 16. Madison & w, Caroline, & ch, Lizzie Russel & Thomas Wade, rocf Newberry MM, O., dtd 1883,10,22
1894, 2, 10. James E. rocf New Berry MM, O., dtd 1894,1,22
1898, 2, 12. James E. gct West Fork MM, O.
1908, 12, 12. Caroline & Elizabeth gct White Water MM, Ind.

BEVAN
----, --, --. Lewis H. b 1830,9,6; m Jane HADLEY, b 18--,3,18
Ch: Orlando b 1857, 9, 21
Frank " 1858, 11, 3
Emmet " 1861, 1, 21
1921, 3, 16. Lewis m Naomi HADLEY

1921, 5, 11. Naomi Hadley gct Springfield MM
1924, 8, 20. Orville & w, Mina J., & ch, Wm. O., Reba Jane & Betty Jean, rocf Ogden MM, O., dtd 1924,7,27
1931, 4, 1. Anora rocf Springfield MM, O.

BIAS
1926, 6, 9. Clarence recrq
1927, 6, 8. Jennings recrq

BICKETT
1926, 12, 10. Donald m Kathryn PEELLE

BICKHART
1890, 1, 11. Jacob & w, Elizabeth, rocf Centre MM, O., dtd 1889,12,18
1890, 2, 8. Anna L. recrq
1898, 4, 9. Jacob & fam dropped from mbrp

BIGGS
1894, 12, 8. Mary recrq
1895, 4, 13. Grace recrq

BISHER
1929, 11, 30. Mary Louise m Arthur G. AYERS

BLAIR
1892, 3, 12. Emma Lewis rocf Clear Creek MM, O., dtd 1892,2,13
1904, 2, 12. Ruth recrq
1915, 9, 18. Emma L. & Ruth gct Whittier MM, Calif.

BLAKELEY
1877, 2, 16. John A. recrq
1877, 2, 16. Daniel recrq
1889, 3, 9. Imogene recrq

BLANCHARD
1926, 7, 14. Pauline Ayers relrq

BLESSING
1918, 3, 30. Earl S. m Mary TODHUNTER

1926, 3, 31. Mary Todhunter dropped from mbrp

BLISS
1918, 5, 18. Marion m Mildred JONES

BLOOM
1877, 11, 25. Eunice d bur New Antioch
1912, 6, 27. Ella d
1919, 11, 30. Melissa d

1873, 4, 18. Ella recrq
1873, 6, 20. Eunice & Melissa recrq

BLOSSOM
1928, 7, 23. Paul m Harriet FARQUHAR

1931, 2, 11. Harriett Farquhar gct W. Richmond MM, Ind.

BOARD
1877, 2, 16. Lucy Ann & ch, Emila, Wm. & Clarinda recrq
1884, 10, 17. Emily, Clarinda & L. A. dropped from mbrp

BODKIN
1907, 5, 11. Rebecca Jane Haworth dropped from mbrp

BOGAN
----, --, --. Geo. W. b 1847,5,11; m Hannah OSBORN b 1849,5,5
Ch: William E. b 1868, 12, 3
Elnora " 1870, 6, 20
Bertie F. 2"1876, 3, 13
Clara Bell " 1879, 5, 9
Nellie May " 1882, 8, 29
Edith Grace" 1890, 3, 17
----, --, --. Walter b 1860,3,18; m Anna Elizabeth ----- b 1860,2,23
Ch: Vernon Leroy " 1884, 2, 14

BOGAN, Walter & Anna Elizabeth, continued
Ch: Martha
Olive b 1885, 11, 26
Jonny A. " 1888, 1, 15
Bessie Bell
b 1889, 11, 18
1913, 11, 12. Olive m Frank Leslie CONNELL

1889, 10, 12. Nancy J. recrq
1913, 2, 12. J. Walter & w, Anna Elizabeth, & dt, Olive & Bessie B., rocf Springfield MM, O., dtd 1913,1,18

BOLES
1906, 2, 10. Rorena recrq

BOND
1889, 10, 12. Lucy Jane recrq

BONFIELD
1913, 4, 14. Wilma Evylin recrq

BORING
1921, 6, 24. Evelyn Jane, dt Carl & Damarris, b

1911, 5, 13. Corda recrq
1921, 3, 9. Demaris M. rocf Center MM, O., dtd 1921,2,16
1921, 4, 13. Carl M. recrq
1921, 5, 11. Corda relrq

BOSWELL
----, --, --. Joseph b 1828,9,13; m Lavina E. ----- b 1830,2,26
----, --, --. Levi M. & Isabelle F.
Ch: Martha E. b 1872, 10, 24
Alice C.

1868, 8, 11. Joseph H. & Levina E. rocf Fairfield MM, O., dtd 1868,7,18
1871, 7, 14. Rachel rocf Chesterfield MM, dtd 1871,6,10
1872, 3, 15. Isabella F. recrq
1873, 4, 18. Levi recrq
1873, 4, 18. Alice recrq
1873, 6, 20. Alice, minor dt Levi & Isabelle, rocf Chesterfield MM, dtd 1873,6,14
1874, 10, 16. Joseph & w, Levina, & ch, Mary M., gct Union MM, Howard Lake, Minn.
1874, 10, 16. Rachel gct Union MM, Minn.
1877, 4, 20. Levi & w, Isabelle, & ch, Alice Cora & Martha Ellen, gct Minneapolis MM, Minn.

BOSWORTH
1913, 6, 11. Clifford Eugene recrq of parents

BOTTS
1903, 10, 10. Wm. & Etta rocf West Fork MM, O., dtd 1903,9,19
1921, 6, 15. Wm. dropped from mbrp

BOWYER
1914, 3, 27. Margaret d

1900, 10, 13. Maggie rocf Elk MM, O., dtd 1900,7,26
1908, 2, 8. Margaret rst; name dropped by mistake

BOYD
1919, 3, 12. Oscar recrq
1928, 2, 8. Opal W. & ch, Paul Fisher & Mary Ruth, recrq

BOYERS
1919, 3, 12. Minnie recrq

BRACKNEY
1802, 7, 17. Susannah b
----, --, --. Eli b 1834,2,24; m Rachel ----- b 1834,8,6
Ch: Marmaduke b 1854, 6, 25
Sarah M. " 1856, 9, 6 d 1870,12, 8 bur Dover
Pleasant " 1858, 12, 22
Joseph " 1861, 4, 5
Ida Ann " 1864, 8, 8
Eli " 1866, 9, 7
Susannah " 1869, 1, 6 d 1869, 1,27
Mahlon " ----, --, -- " 1872, 8, 8
----, --, --. Mahlon H. b 1825,9,3, s Marmaduke & Susanna; m Martha ----- d 1907,9, 26 ae 77
Ch: May L. b 1866, 8, 8
Fanny
U. C.
Albert M.
1910, 3, 2. Uriah Clifford d ae 49
1919, 1, 3. Lewis d
1920, 11, 21. George d
1921, 5, 5. Lauren m Clarice TURNER
1922, 3, 22. Judith Ann d
1923, 2, 20. Tella d
1928, 11, 12. Kate d
1931, 6, 2. S. Allen d

1870, 3, 18. Martha & ch, Clara, Fanny, Albert M. & Uriah Clifford, recrq
1870, 9, 16. Eli & w, Rachel, & ch, Marmaduke, Sally, Mary, Pleasant, Joseph, Ida, Eli & Susanna, rocf Dover MM, O.
1875, 4, 16. Eli & w, Rachel, & ch, Marmaduke, Pleasant, Joseph, Eli, Ida, Susanna & Louis, gct Union MM
1884, 5, 15. Geo. & w, Judith Ann, & ch, Lewis C., Sarah M., Anna H. & John, rocf Dover MM, O., dtd 1884,5,15
1894, 7, 14. S. A. rocf Dover MM, O., dtd 1894,5,17
1907, 3, 9. Albert N. dropped from mbrp
1911, 4, 8. John & w, Lillian, & ch, Charlotte B., Loren, Chas. E., Ruth & Geo. Wm., gct Center MM, O.
1921, 2, 9. Tella F. recrq

BRACKNEY, continued
1921, 11, 9. Katie B. recrq
1932, 4, 13. Hazel Smith recrq
1932, 5, 11. Loren rocf Chester MM

BRADSHAW
1913, 7, --. ----- m Hallie HAMILTON

BRANDENBURG
----, --, --. Moses D. b 1834,2,1; m Rebecca GALLAHER b 1836,7,10
Ch: Lawrence b 1856, 2, 11
Laura " 1857, 8, 31
Templin " 1858, 9, 28
Rodney " 1860, 3, 5
Katie " 1861, 9, 24
Mary " 1862, 11, 25
Frank " 1865, 12, 2

1921, 2, 9. Calvin E. recrq

BRANN
1926, 1, 1. Ruth Esther m Leroy THOMPSON
1927, 6, 15. Harriett m John NOVROLD

1890, 1, 11. James & w, Marcy Ann, & ch, Maria E. & Roscoe C., rocf Center MM, O., dtd 1889,12,19
1901, 12, 14. Clement L. rocf Center MM, O.
1902, 10, 11. Clement & w, Irene, gct Whittier MM, Calif.
1906, 4, 14. Catharine & Clifford rocf Center MM, O., dtd 1906,3,14
1912, 5, 8. Clement & w, Irene M., & ch, Ruth Ester & Harriett M., rocf Whittier MM, Calif.
1929, 8, 21. Roscoe dropped from mbrp
1929, 10, 9. Joe Edwin recrq of parents

BRANNON
1889, 5, 11. Frank, adopted s Joseph H. Camp, recrq
1907, 3, 9. Frank dropped from mbrp
1907, 3, 9. Alexander dropped from mbrp
1914, 10, 14. Hazel recrq

BRAZIL
1873, 3, 14. Sarah recrq
1874, 3, 20. John M. recrq
1876, 4, 14. Charles E. recrq
1881, 5, 20. Jesse recrq
1881, 5, 20. Jennie recrq
1899, 1, 14. Sarah gct Wichita MM, Kans.; returned 1900,3,10
1899, 1, 14. Chas. D. gct Wichita MM, Kans.
1900, 3, 10. Sarah gct Lowell MM, Kans.

BREWER
----, --, --. Irvin & Dora
Ch: Franklin
Lundy b 1908, 3, 25
Mary Nell " 1909, 4, 13
1916, 7, 3. Vedith m Frank SUTHERLAND
1906, 2, 10. Irvin & w, Dora, & ch, Edna May, Vedith L. & Hazel recrq
1914, 12, 9. Millte T. & dt, Eva M., rocf Dover MM
1914, 12, 9. Clara, w Miller, recrq
1919, 5, 14. Eva May relrq
1926, 3, 31. Mary Nell dropped from mbrp

BRIGGS
1918, 4, 22. Sarah Lucile m Hubert A. BARRETT
1921, 6, 28. Ronald C. m Nellie Marie YARGER
1933, 2, 7. Ronald d

1908, 6, 12. Mary Estella recrq
1908, 11, 14. Abel & w, Ethel, & ch, Sarah Lucile & Ronald Cast, recrq
1921, 4, 13. Myrtle roc
1921, 4, 13. Rebecca recrq

BRINDLE
1904, 2, 13. Addie rocf Center MM, O., dtd 1904,1,13
1904, 2, 13. Alma rocf Center MM, O., dtd 1904,1,13

BRONSON
1898, 4, 9. Eliza dropped from mbrp
1907, 4, 13. Mary Belle dropped from mbrp

BROWN
1902, 10, 24. Jane d ae 64
1906, 9, 22. Robert Maxwell, s Albert J. & Ada, b
1907, 12, 24. Dana m May McELWEE
1918, 2, 5. William T. d
1918, 5, 24. Martha d

1883, 9, 14. Alfred rocf Walnut Ridge MM, Ind.
1886, 3, 13. Emma recrq
1886, 12, 11. Wm. & Jane & ch, Clara, rocf Dover MM, O.
1888, 8, 11. Effie Afton rocf Amboy MM, Ind., dtd 1888,8,4
1890, 5, 10. Alfred & w, Effie A., & s, Paul Howard, gct Walnut Ridge MM, Ind.
1897, 4, 10. Martha recrq
1898, 4, 9. Cora recrq
1898, 7, 9. Elva Wright relrq
1899, 9, 9. Dana T. recrq
1903, 9, 12. Robert J. & w, Ada C., & ch, Sidney F., Althea & Helen M., rocf Indianapolis MM, Ind.
1908, 4, 11. May M. recrq
1913, 1, 8. Lenora recrq
1916, 7, 12. Alfert J. & w, Ada C., & ch, Sydney, Althea, Helen & Robert M., gct Mndianapolis MM, Ind.

BRUNSON
1873, 4, 18. Eliza recrq
1873, 4, 18. Courtland & Mary Belle recrq
1878, 5, 17. Cortland dis

BRYAN
1913, 7, --. Jessie m Eldon HAINES
1926, 7, 12. Anna E. d
1931, 3, 24. S. K. m Blanch McMILLAN

1900, 5, 12. Laura Tyra recrq
1906, 3, 10. Ida recrq
1909, 3, 13. Louisa recrq
1910, 2, 10. Josie & Clara Belle recrq

BUCKLEY
1911, 2, 28. Harry m Lucretia THATCHER

1925, 1, 14. Lucretia recrq

BULLEN
1933, 5, 10. Isaac Clayton & w, Mary Estelle, & ch, Hubert Lee, Harold William, Virgil Byron & John Spencer, rocf Springfield MM

BUNTAIN
1873, 4, 18. Annie recrq
1874, 3, 20. Mary recrq
1876, 4, 14. Clinton recrq
1878, 2, 15. Clinton dis
1892, 6, 11. Susanna relrq

BURDEN
1894, 5, 12. Flora [Burdin] recrq
1907, 5, 11. Flora dropped from mbrp
1926, 3, 31. Pierce H., Anna K., Bertha L., Marie E. & Robert W. dropped from mbrp

BURGE
----, --, --. Jonathan D. b 1850,7,25; m Martha J. OSBORN b 1856,5,8
Ch: Charles C. b 1870, 10, 8
Jesse C. " 1872, 10, 13

1886, 7, 10. Jonathan D. & w, Martha, & ch, Charles C. & Jesse C., rocf Springfield MM, O., dtd 1886,6,19
1899, 4, 8. Charles C. rocf Cincinnati MM,O., dtd 1899,3,10

BURK
1890, 9, 13. Wilbur recrq
1895, 3, 9. Wilbur relrq

BURKHART
1886, 2, 13. Phebe Hartman relrq

BURNETT
1885, 4, 11. Thomas & w, Cora, & ch, Nettie Louise, recrq
1885, 4, 11. Charles recrq
1892, 5, 14. Thomas relrq
1907, 5, 11. Cora relrq

BURNS
1876, 5, 19. Rachel recrq

BURTON
----, --, --. ----- m Annes PATTON

1902, 3, 8. Richard, Anna, Emmet & Maggie recrq
1906, 3, 10. Hazel recrq
1907, 5, 11. Anna, Maggie & Emmett relrq
1907, 5, 11. Hazel gct West Fork MM, O.

BUSSEY
1907, 11, 9. George & w, Nannie, & s, Homer, recrq
1931, 4, 1. Homer relrq

BUTLER
1876, 5, 19. Elisha & w, Keziah D., rocf Clear Creek MM, O., dtd 1876,5,13
1885, 4, 11. Elisha M. gct Columbus MM, O.

BUTTERWORTH
1886, 7, 10. Charles & s, Arthur, recrq
1886, 7, 10. Ettie rocf Clear Creek MM, O.
1898, 10, 8. Chas. C. & w, Etta, & ch, Arthur & Esther, relrq

BYARD
1895, 4, 13. Clyde recrq
1899, 8, 12. Nancy rocf Newberry MM, O., dtd 1899,7,13
1905, 2, 8. Clyde & Nancy dropped from mbrp

BYRNE
----, --, --. R. J. m Mary ANDREW b 1846,8,20
Ch: Carrie T. b 1871, 1, 1
Ella M. " 1872, 10, 22

CADDEN
1911, 1, 12. James J. m Edna CARROLL

CADWALADER
----, --, --. Joseph b 1832,12,23; m Eliza Jane JONES b 1840,11,12
Ch: William C. b 1858, 12, 9
Frank " 1865, 5, 4
1926, 9, 4. Mildred Jean, dt Rayburn & Ruth (Winson), b

1907, 5, 11. Mary dropped from mbrp

CAMMACK
1915, 10, 19. Ivan Oglesbee, s Chas. & Anna, b

1913, 5, 14. Charles rocf Dover MM

CAMP
----, --, --. Clark m Mary J. ----- b 1868,9,22
Ch: Isabella b 1870, 7, 19
Effa May " 1873, 5, 15
Florra " 1875, 3, 13

1889, 5, 11. Joseph Henry & w, Elizabeth, &

CAMP, continued
adopted s Frank Brannon, recrq
1889,. 5, 11. Anna Belle & Ulysses Grant recrq
1889, 9, 14. Alice recrq
1907, 3, 9. Elizabeth & ch, Anna Belle, Ulysses Grant & Alice, dropped from mbrp
1921, 6, 15. Hazel Brannon dropped from mbrp

CAMPBELL
1920, 9, 8. Frances d
1929, 3, 30. Gertrude m James MONROE

1904, 3, 12. Eva recrq
1914, 7, 8. Catherine recrq
1920, 8, 11. Orville O. & w, Lula E., & ch, Gertrude, Evelyn & Francis, recrq
1927, 5, 11. Eva dropped from mbrp

CANADAY
1877, 5, 18. Sarah recrq

CANDLE
1909, 12, 12. Mary Glass relrq

CANTRILL
1932, 2, 26. Blanch d

1913, 4, 14. Blanche, Guy E. & Robert Elmo [Cantrell] recrq

CAREY
1906, 4, 5. Samuel Albert d ae 56
1914, 12, 20. Joseph d
1920, 5, 20. Mary m Clarence MERKER
1922, 3, 8. Marjorie, dt Dallis & Bulah, b
1924, 12, 5. Charles Enoch, s Dallas & Beulah, b
1927, --, --. Dean, s Jesse & Velma, b
1929, 12, 14. Harley d
1933, 1, 24. Ruth d

1878, 12, 20. Elizabeth Nelson gct Fairfield MM, O.
1895, 8, 10. Mary J. Thomas relrq
1902, 2, 8. Albert & w, Ruth, & ch, Bertha L., Clifton O., Elizabeth M., David E. & Mary Ellen, rocf Clear Creek MM, O., dtd 1902,1,11
1902, 7, 12. Harley rocf Clear Creek MM, O.
1907, 3, 9. Anna Barlow dropped from mbrp
1908, 1, 11. Harold Nevin recrq of father, Clifton D.
1911, 4, 8. Joseph M. rocf Kedron MM, Minn.
1911, 4, 8. Albert, Miriam & Elizabeth recrq
1917, 4, 11. Dallas & w, Beula, & s, Harold, rocf Center MM, O., dtd 1917,3,14
1921, 4, 13. Mary M. recrq
1921, 4, 13. Thadeus roc
1922, 9, 13. David E. relrq
1924, 4, 9. Miriam relrq
1924, 9, 10. Jesse & w, Velma, & ch, Helen, Robert, Alice, Orba, Neal, John & Eleanor, rocf Clear Creek MM, O.

CARPENTER
1907, 5, 11. May relrq

CARR
1909, 12, 29. LaRue m Mary Baker LINTON

1930, 11, 12. Mary Linton relrq
1931, 3, 11. Mary Linton recrq

CARROLL
1911, 1, 12. Edna m James J. CADDEN
1914, 8, 1. Ilo m Edward SNOWDEN
1918, 5, 29. Edith m Neil MOUNTS

1872, 3, 15. Jane & ch, Olive B., rocf Dover MM, O.
1874, 7, 17. Jane & dt, Olive B., gct Dover MM, O.
1883, 11, 16. Mary & ch, Wm. & Jessie Anna, rocf Newberry MM, O., dtd 1883,10,22
1890, 4, 12. Soleon rocf Caesars Creek MM, O., dtd 1890,3,27
1896, 8, 8. Solon relrq
1906, 6, 9. Eva Snead rocf West Fork MM, O., dtd 1906,7,21
1907, 8, 10. Mary gct Whittier MM, Calif.
1909, 12, 12. Edith recrq

CARSON
1891, 4, 11. John M. & Ruth recrq
1907, 12, 14. John M. & w, Ruth, gct Dover MM, O.

CARTER
----, --, --. John m Mary KIMBROUGH b 1841, 11,26 d 1928,4,26
Ch: Eva b 1866, 12, 26
Almond " 1869, 4, 2
1907, 8, 15. Elizabeth m James EDWARDS
1916, 11, 26. Almon m Masie KELLY

1878, 4, 19. Leonard & w, Margaret, rocf Clear Creek MM, O.
1882, 1, 20. Eva rocf Springfield MM, O., dtd 1881,11,19
1883, 3, 16. Eva gct Springfield MM, O.
1883, 7, 20. Leonard & w, Margaret, gct Springfield MM, O.
1892, 4, 9. Joseph G. & w, Margaret, & s, John L., recrq
1907, 3, 9. Marion, Jennie, Blanch, Lizzie, Willie, Charlie & Howard, recrq
1911, 3, 11. Marion, Jane, Blanche, Elizabeth, Wm., Chas. & Howard, gct Fairfield MM, O.
1912, 11, 13. Mary A. & Almon rocf Ogden MM,O.

CARTWRIGHT
1907, 5, 11. Louisa Burnett relrq

CARVER
1907, 3, 9. Maud E. Clark relrq

CAST
1894, 12, 8. Ollie recrq
1895, 1, 12. Ellen Hooten & dt, Cressie Mildred Hootin, gct Springfield MM, O.
1907, 5, 11. Ollie relrq
1932, 3, 23. Irene recrq

CERTAIN
1873, 4, 18. Duncan, Matilda J. & Sarah A. recrq
1873, 4, 18. Sarah A. & Duncan M. recrq
1885, 2, 14. Duncan relrq
1885, 6, 13. Sarah A. & Matilda J. dropped from mbrp

CHAMBERS
1926, 10, 13. Ruth Anna Hare rocf Dover MM
1926, 10, 13. Robert recrq
1929, 8, 21. C. Robert & w, Ruth Anna H., relrq

CHANCE
1880, 4, 16. Cyrus & w, Margaret, & ch, Chas. Wm., Bertha May & Zella Jane, recrq
1885, 5, 9. Charles recrq
1885, 7, 11. Margaret dropped from mbrp
1885, 9, 12. Cyrus & ch, Chas. H., Bertha & Zella, relrq

CHANEY
1901, 3, 9. Charles recrq
1901, 11, 9. J. W. & w, Hattie, recrq

CHANNEL
1930, 9, 10. Walter F. & w, Edith T., & s, Billy, recrq

CHEW
1885, 9, 12. William & w, Julia Ann, rocf Hopewell MM, dtd 1885,7,4

CHISM
1815, 6, 25. Sarah d
1915, 10, 20. Matilda d
1929, 8, 12. Elizabeth d

1909, 11, 13. Matilda, Sarah & Elizabeth recrq

CLARK
----, --, --. Jesse & Jemima
Ch: Lindley b 1855, 3, 26
Cassius " 1856, 11, 1
Elwood " 1850, 7, 2
----, --, --. Elwood b 1850,7,2; m Ella HADLEY, b 1851,11,25
Ch: Morris W. b 1874, 6, 25
Gulielma " 1875, 12, 18
Alvin DeWitt " 1877, 6, 28
Pearly May " 1879, 5, 28
1909, 6, 30. Lenna m Charles BYARD
1909, 11, 16. Daniel m Grace ARROSMITH
1888, 3, 10. Margaret recrq
1894, 2, 10. Cassius & w, Belle, & ch, Maggie A., Lena M., Daniel J. & Jesse C., rocf Springfield MM, O., dtd 1893,12,16
1894, 2, 10. Maud & Tacy, ch Cassios, recrq
1894, 5, 12. Lindley rocf Newberry MM, O., dtd 1894,3,22
1894, 8, 11. Samantha & ch, Jemima B., Atwood, Alta, Arthur, Edith & Charles, recrq
1897, 9, 11. Naomi Farquhar relrq
1906, 3, 10. Edith, Lena & Dannie recrq
1907, 5, 11. Samantha relrq

CLELAND
1903, --, --. Rebecca Daugherty, w John, b
----, --, --. Alexander m Delilah SIMPSON, b 1851,7,4
Ch: Cora Ann b 1872, 11, 6
Twilight " 1876, 7, 12

CLEMENS
1897, 12, 11. Leroy F. & w, Ella, & s, Claude, rocf Van Vert MM, O., dtd 1897,11,27
1903, 2, 14. Leroy [Clemmens] & w, Ella, & ch, Claude, gct Ogden MM, O.
1920, 5, 12. Ella rocf Ogden MM, O.

CLEVELAND
1912, 4, 20. Elizabeth d

1878, 1, 18. Wm. recrq
1878, 3, 15. Elizabeth Ann & dt, Estella, recrq

CLIFFORD
----, --, --. P. J. m Anna SIMMONS

CLINE
----, --, --. Madison J. b 1862,2,28; m Eliza TROUTE b 1862,6,8
Ch: Belva Mable b 1886, 9, 1
Ambert Albert " 1887, 8, 29
1907, 7, 12. Sarah d ae 90

1873, 3, 14. Sarah recrq
1876, 5, 19. Mary V. recrq
1877, 2, 16. Jennie recrq
1877, 2, 16. John A. recrq
1885, 5, 9. Louella recrq
1921, 6, 15. Cora Brown & Thelma dropped from mbrp

CLINNESS
1921, 12, 25. Augusta Barrett m Dr. W. J. TRAINOR

1912, 11, 13. Augusta J. rocf Fairfield MM, O., dtd 1912,11,19

COATE
----, --, --. Joseph T. b 1810,1,11 d 1880,7, 29 bur Springfield; m Agnes BANHAM b 1812, 2,24 d 1899,7,16 ae 87
Ch: Nancy b 1834, 12, 22
John B. " 1836, 10, 21
----, --, --. Hiram b 1815,9,8 d 1884,12,7 bur Springfield; m Rachel W. PAINTER b 1817,6,8
Ch: Rebecca
Mary b 1853, 11, 29
Hiram Alvin" 1862, 7, 11
----, --, --. John B. b 1836,10,21; m Delilah ANDREW b 1837,3,7
Ch: Mary Agnes b 1862, 11, 8
Lincoln " 1865, 7, 3
----, --, --. Elijah b 1841,12,25; m Mary E. LAFFERTY b 1845,1,30
Ch: William K. b 1869, 8, 23
Hiram W. " 1872, 6, 23
Vernon L. " 1876, 11, 24
Zenas A. " 1880, 9, 8
----, --, --. Orlistus L. b 1848,1,24; m Annie D. HARLAN b 1848,5,30
Ch: Merrick D. b 1871, 1, 21
Leo Guy " 1872, 5, 16
Annie Maud " 1874, 6, 14
----, --, --. Hiram Alvin b 1862,7,11; m Flora HALE
Ch: Hershel H. b 1895, 11, 25
Donald William " 1896, 11, 6
Lester Hershel " 1898, 8, 3
1904, 6, 23. Nancy d ae 69
1912, 5, 7. Sarah Lydia d

1871, 6, 16. Joseph T. & w, Agnes, & s, Loran, rocf Springfield MM, O., dtd 1871,5,20
1871, 6, 16. Nancy rocf Springfield MM, O., dtd 1871,5,20
1873, 6, 20. Joseph T. & w, Agnes, & ch, Nancy & Loren A., gct Springfield MM, O.
1880, 3, 19. Orlistus S. & w, Anna D., & ch, Merrick D., Leo Guy & Anna Maud, rocf Springfield MM, O., dtd 1880,2,21
1882, 10, 20. Agnes rocf Springfield MM, O., dtd 1882,9,16
1882, 10, 20. Nancy rocf Springfield MM, O., dtd 1882,9,16
1883, 11, 16. Sarah L. Hunt rocf Newberry MM, O., dtd 1883,10,22
1921, 6, 15. Orlistis & dt, Anna Maude, gct Detroit MM, Mich.

COCKERELL
1908, 6, 7. James d ae 80
1908, 12, 10. Nellie S. m Clinton MADDEN

1898, 11, 12. Ina H. recrq
1898, 12, 12. Nellie rocf Hopewell MM, O., dtd 1898,12,3
1901, 10, 12. James rocf Hopewell MM, O., dtd 1901,10,5
1918, 7, 10. Ina Hadley gct First Friends Church, Indianapolis, Ind.
1933, 1, 11. Ina H. [Cockerill] rocf Indianapolis MM, Ind.

COIL
1929, 2, 9. Urban d

1923, 1, 10. Urban & w, Emma, recrq

COLE
1877, 2, 16. Robert T. & w, Nancy J., & s, Ira Lee, recrq
1877, 2, 16. Nancy J. recrq
1887, 12, 10. Jeremiah relrq

COLLINS
1874, 3, 20. Sarah C. recrq
1914, 10, 14. Hazel recrq
1927, 6, 8. Mason recrq
1927, 11, 19. Manson gct Beech Grove MM
1933, 4, 12. Walter & w, Mable, & ch, Paul, Walter Jr. & Mary Louise, recrq

COMER
1895, 4, 13. Eliza Jane recrq

COMPTON
1897, 9, 18. Alta B. d ae 20
1908, 4, 28. John L. m Leta M. SHARP
1914, 1, 25. Mabel m Robert R. DOAN

1875, 12, 17. Josephine Starbuck gct Cesars Creek MM, O.
1889, 1, 12. Samuel T. & w, Josephine, & ch, Alta B., Ally C. & John W., rocf Springfield MM, O., dtd 1888,12,15
1890, 1, 11. Blanch recrq
1926, 3, 10. R. L. relrq
1927, 2, 16. Cleo Fife gct Newberry MM
1929, 11, 13. John relrq

CONDEN
1931, 9, 1. Wm. T. d

CONLEY
1898, 11, 11. Miriam Barlow d

CONARD
1895, 6, 8. Carrie [Connard] recrq
1895, 12, 14. Walter V. rocf Fairfield MM,O., dtd 1895,10,19
1912, 6, 12. Stella rocf Fairview MM
1919, 5, 21. Robert recrq

CONNELL
1913, 11, 12. Frank Leslie m Olive BOGAN

1914, 6, 10. Olive Bogan gct Clear Creek MM, O.

CONNOR
1929, 6, 12. Helen Stratton dropped from mbrp

CONOVER
1906, 3, 10. Rena recrq
1924, 5, 14. Hester recrq

COOK
1899, 3, 31. Hannah d ae 28
1909, 12, 12. Dinah d ae 70

1875, 9, 17. John & w, Dinah, & ch, Louella D., Hannah Maria & John Edgar, rocf Cesars Creek MM, O., dtd 1875,8,26
1922, 4, 12. Lovetta relrq
1927, 4, 13. Maynard relrq

COOLE
1890, 6, 14. Henry Crew gct Baltimore MM, Md., to m Helen C. Coole

COOPER
1924, 5, 14. Augusta recrq

COPPERAS
1905, 11, 11. Alice P. Jennings relrq

CORBEAN
1890, 9, 13. William recrq
1893, 4, 8. Samuel recrq
1907, 4, 13. Wm. & Samuel [Corbin] dropped from mbrp

COREY
1911, 2, 3. Joseph M. m Dorcas PEELLE

CORNELL
1926, 1, 23. Elizabeth d

1908, 2, 8. Elizabeth recrq
1914, 10, 14. Adine recrq

COSS
1874, 4, 17. Benjamin & w, Phebe, & ch, Virgil, Eunice, Jacob & Minnie, rocf Londonderry MM, O., dtd 1874,1,3, endorsed by Center MM, O., 1874,3,18
1877, 4, 20. Benjamin & w, Phebe, & ch, Virgil, Eunice, Jacob & Minnie, gct Londonderry MM, O.

COVERDALE
1907, 11, 28. Grace m Harley PLYMIRE

1902, 3, 8. Sally & Grace recrq

COWDER
1908, 8, 8. Blanch L. rocf Springfield MM, O.
1908, 8, 8. Wm. T & ch, Donald H., recrq

COWGILL
----, --, --. Kate b 1862,3,3 d 1894,3,14 (orphaned ch whom Ellen (Cowgill) Hadley took to raise)
1863, 5, 10. Millie E. b (an orphan ch whom Ellen (Cowgill) Hadley took to raise)
1873, 3, 13. Harry H. b
1919, 6, 12. Ruthanna m Lewis C. MOON
1920, 2, 26. Alice m Raymond STARBUCK

1881, 10, 14. Sarah gct Newberry MM, O.
1884, 4, 18. Mary E. rocf Springfield MM, dtd 1884,2,15
1898, 2, 12. John B. & w, Ida S., & s, Carl, recrq
1906, 10, 13. John, Ida & Carl gct Cincinati MM, O.
1919, 6, 11. Ruthanna rocf Alum Creek MM,O.
1920, 1, 14. Alice recrq
1921, 6, 15. John, Ida & Carl dropped from mbrp
1922, 8, 9. Clarence & w, Carrie, & ch, Harry, Frank, Roderick, Sarah Ellen, Don & Thomas, rocf Fall Creek MM, O.

COYLE
1917, 9, 12. Urban & Emma recrq

CRAIG
----, --, --. James A. b 1850,3,31; m Charity STANFIELD b 1848,7,27
Ch: Mary E. b 1877, 12, 7
1910, 8, 12. Alonzo m Dollie GRAY

1880, 5, 14. James rocf Clear Creek MM, O.
1898, 10, 8. James recrq

CRAMPTON
1924, 11, 25. Ira Hundley m Cleo M. FIFE

CRANE
1933, 8, 9. Fred & w, Emma, & s, Robert, gct Xenia MM, O.

CRAWFORD
1880, 4, 16. George recrq
1882, 6, 16. John recrq
1883, 5, 18. Leona recrq
1888, 8, 11. John relrq
1890, 4, 12. Leona relrq
1898, 4, 9. George dropped from mbrp

CREW
1873, 6, 20. Deborah A. & ch, Henry, Caroline L. & Winona B., rocf Chesterfield MM
1885, 6, 13. Pleasant dropped from mbrp
1890, 6, 14. Henry gct Baltimore MM, Md., to m Helen C. Coole
1903, 12, 12. Caroline Ladd relrq
1905, 3, 8. Winona gct Phila. MM, Pa.
1908, 11, 14. Wm. Henry, s Henry, recrq

CRISWELL
1904, 12, 10. Ursula recrq
1907, 12, 14. Lou Esther recrq
1910, 7, 9. Ursula, Ursul & Lou Esther gct Marion MM, Ind.

CRITES
1909, 6, 15. Willis m Pauline JONES
1911, 7, 21. Marjean, dt Willis & Pauline, b

1882, 4, 14. Anna Peelle gct Dover MM, O.
1910, 9, 10. Willis rocf Ogden MM, O.
1921, 1, 12. Willis & w, Pauline, & ch, Marjean & Judith, relrq

CROUSE
1930, 6, 5. Adeline d

1876, 5, 19. Minervia recrq
1880, 4, 16. Susan F. & ch, Wm. H. & Ida May, recrq
1880, 4, 16. Fransena recrq
1880, 4, 16. Emma T. recrq
1883, 1, 19. Wm. recrq
1883, 2, 16. Wm. & fam gct Union MM, Minn.
1895, 4, 13. Melvina recrq
1899, 5, 13. Cora & Ivolen recrq
1907, 10, 12. Minerva dropped from mbrp
1913, 1, 8. Iva Lou relrq
1921, 3, 9. Geo. E. & Adeline rocf Ogden MM, O., dtd 1921,2,26

CRUMLEY
1825, 11, 3. Henry B. b

1870, 3, 18. Henry B. [Crumly] recrq
1873, 4, 18. Clark, Mollie & Rosanna recrq
1873, 4, 16. Rosalta recrq
1877, 9, 14. Mollie dis
1881, 4, 15. Henry B. gct Newberry MM, O.
1894, 7, 14. Blanch recrq
1895, 6, 8. Jennie & Laura recrq
1898, 2, 12. Mary E. & Blanch gct Newberry MM, O.
1907, 4, 13. Laura dropped from mbrp

CRUSE
1870, 3, 18. Pleasant recrq

CRUTE
1872, 1, 19. Lizzie (form Owens) con mcd
1876, 4, 14. Elizabeth gct Newberry MM, O.

CUMMINGS
1894, 7, 14. Flora recrq

CURL
----, --, --. David b 1814,7,20 d 1882,9,12 bur Springfield; m Rebecca COATE b 1817, 6,21 d 1884,8,25 bur Springfield
Ch: Esther b 1839, 5, 23
Hiram " 1848, 2, 3
Rhoda M. " 1850, 9, 8
----, --, --. Samuel b 1844,5,30; m Lydia MORRIS b 1842,5,8
Ch: Frank M. b 1871, 8, 30
Flora E. " 1875, 9, 23
1875, 12, 5. Eliza A. d bur Springfield
1878, 1, 20. Sarah E. d bur Springfield
1932, 7, 20. Frank d

1871, 2, 17. Sarah & ch, Martha H., David & Henry, rocf Springfield MM
1871, 2, 17. Eliza Ann rocf Springfield MM
1873, 4, 18. Chas. recrq
1898, 2, 12. Hannah P. Doan gct Chicago MM, Ill.
1903, 5, 9. Lena rocf Dover MM, O.
1911, 7, 8. Frank M. rocf Springfield MM,O., dtd 1911,6,7
1911, 7, 8. Sarah Melissa recrq
1916, 9, 13. Olive recrq
1921, 6, 15. David dropped from mbrp

CURTIS
1925, 12, 2. Ercil m Hester FISHER
1926, 12, 15. Richard Bruce, s Ercil & Helen (Fisher), b

1876, 12, 15. Elizabeth A. [Custis] recrq
1877, 2, 16. Azariah [Custis] & w, Elizabeth, & ch, Frank & Effie, recrq
1877, 2, 16. Charles [Custis] recrq
1877, 2, 16. Harrison [Custis] recrq
1877, 2, 16. Anna [Custis] recrq
1877, 2, 16. Wm. H. [Custis] recrq
1877, 2, 16. Jennie [Custis] recrq
1883, 2, 16. Jennie dropped from mbrp
1884, 6, 26. Harrison dis
1886, 4, 10. Kate & Caroline [Custis] recrq
1889, 3, 9. Grace [Custis] recrq
1889, 4, 13. Sanford [Curts] recrq
1890, 5, 10. Charles & Ivy recrq
1914, 10, 14. Harvey & Lillian recrq
1926, 3, 31. Wm. Ercil recrq
1929, 12, 10. Harvey dropped from mbrp

DABE
1912, 1, 1. Frank m Louise GLASS
1918, 4, 2. Verna m Leslie D. JEFFERIS
1918, 12, 24. Freda Louise m Wilbur SPEARS
1923, 1, 25. Josephine d

1908, 5, 19. Freda Louise recrq
1908, 5, 19. Verna Marie recrq

DAILEY
1925, 8, 12. Morris m Eva WOOD

1895, 7, 13. Zarilda Jesse recrq
1914, 10, 14. Milo [Daily] recrq

DALTON
1905, 4, 29. Lee Anna H., dt Pomp A. & Nellie F., b
1907, 5, 14. Elon Custis, s Dennis & Estella C., b
1907, 6, 22. Lee Anna d ae 2
1908, 10, 25. Edith Louise, dt Pomp A. & Nellie, b
1910, 4, 15. Nellie Farquhar d ae 34
1926, 11, 30. Henry m Helen Myrtle BAYLESS

DALTON, continued
1901, 3, 9. Dennis recrq
1904, 3, 12. Pomp A. recrq
1924, 6, 11. Naomi & Elon recrq
1930, 1, 8. Pomp & dt, Edith Louise, relrq

DARBEYSHIRE
1846, 2, 8. John N. b

1870, 3, 18. Sarah Ann [Darbyshare] recrq
1870, 3, 18. John [Darbyshare] recrq
1873, 4, 18. Lucy & Maggie [Darbeyshare] recrq
1885, 5, 9. Oliver N. recrq
1885, 6, 13. Lucy dropped from mbrp
1885, 6, 13. John A. dropped from mbrp
1886, 5, 8. James recrq
1888, 7, 14. Rhoda C. W. [Derbyshire] gct Ypsilanti MM, Mich.
1898, 4, 9. Sarah [Darbeshire] dropped from mbrp
1906, 10, 13. Emma [Darbyshire] gct Xenia MM, O.

DAUGHERTY
1922, 6, 21. Frank m Marie FAWCETT

DAVIS
1901, 4, 15. Bell d ae 54
1902, 10, 26. Elizabeth d ae 75
1926, 7, 14. Margaret Stoop Watson d

1870, 4, 15. Jenette E. recrq
1873, 3, 14. Geo. B. recrq
1875, 6, 18. Elizabeth J. recrq
1880, 6, 18. Mary Elizabeth Glenn relrq
1883, 10, 19. Louella H. rocf Centre MM, O., dtd 1883,9,12
1883, 11, 16. Handy T. & w, Margaret, & ch rocf Clear Creek MM, O., dtd 1883,8,11
1885, 6, 13. G. B. dropped from mbrp
1892, 6, 11. Bell recrq
1912, 1, 13. Eunice rocf Dover MM
1914, 10, 14. Omal recrq
1919, 5, 14. Harold Bennett recrq
1921, 2, 9. John I. & Bertha D. recrq
1921, 12, 14. Louella relrq
1924, 5, 14. Mildred E. recrq
1924, 12, 10. Orland & w, Sadie, rocf Beach Grove MM, Ind.
1925, 3, 11. Dale recrq
1928, 3, 14. Onal relrq
1930, 5, 14. John I. & Bertha relrq

DEACLY
1908, 1, 11. Jemimah Clark relrq

DEAKIN
1914, 3, 11. Maria Brann relrq

DeCAMP
1870, 7, 29. Mary Elizabeth d
1871, 1, 7. William E., s Chas. & Matilda,

1870, 3, 18. Charles & w, Matilda Louisa, & dt, Mary Edith, recrq
1898, 4, 9. Charles, Matilda L. & ch, Mary E., Wm. E. & Lambert, dropped from mbrp

DELAPHANE
1898, 1, 8. Wm. dropped from mbrp
1907, 4, 13. Gibson dropped from mbrp
1907, 5, 11. Martha [Deleplane] relrq
1921, 6, 15. Carrie dropped from mbrp

DENNIS
1879, 11, 14. David W. rocf White Water MM, Ind., dtd 1879,9,24
1881, 7, 15. David Worth gct White Water MM, Ind.

DEWEESE
1889, 4, 13. Lulu & Nellie recrq

DIBOL
1914, 10, 14. Conklin recrq

DICKENSON
1920, 2, 8. Jonathan d
1920, 4, 11. Clara O. d
1921, 3, 4. Marianne [Dickinson] m George PACK

1914, 5, 13. Jonathan & w, Clara, & ch, Oren & Marianna, rocf Center MM, O., dtd 1914,4,15

DILLON
1895, 6, 8. Martha recrq

DIXON
----, --, --. William b 1817,7,12; m Eliza A. ----- b 1818,1,25
Ch: Homer b 1856, 3, 18

1869, 5, 11. Wm. & w, Eliza Ann, & s, Homer, recrq
1898, 4, 9. Homer dropped from mbrp
1907, 12, 14. Lydia Sayers relrq
1919, 5, 14. Nellie Marie recrq
1921, 6, 15. Nellie Marie dropped from mbrp
1927, 6, 8. Lester recrq
1927, 11, 19. Lester gct Beech Grove MM

DOAK
1913, 5, 9. Marianna, dt Clara H., b

1911, 7, 8. James Herbert, s Joseph & Clara, recrq
1913, 5, 14. Marianna, dt Clara H., recrq

DOAN
----, --, --. Azariah W. b 1824,12,17 d 1911, 8,22 ae 88; m Martha G. ----- b 1828,9,7 d 1908,12,22

DOAN, Azariah & Martha G., continued
Ch: Corwin F. b 1849, 8, 9
Phebe E. " 1851, 4, 24 d 1869,11,19 bur Sugar Grove
William A. b 1857, 4, 4
Joseph L. " 1862, 4, 10
Alice Rebecca b 1866, 3, 15
Walker " 1867, 12, 29
Maria Fannie " 1872, 3, 13
----, --, --. John b 1823,2,5; m Sarah J. ---- b 1831,6,25
Ch: Mary E. b 1850, 1, 31
Calvin " 1851, 8, 10
William " 1853, 2, 25
Francis M. " 1855, 2, 16
Lucinda C. " 1856, 5, 13
Albert " 1858, 3, 4
Hannah P. " 1860, 2, 17
Lewis " 1862, 5, 13
Ulyses G. " 1864, 10, 7
George B. " 1867, 4, 4
Eddie " 1871, 6, 30
----, --, --. Robert E. d 1919,2,24; m Maria ----- b 1836,8,8 d 1920,6,9
Ch: Clinton M. b 1858, 11, 19
Albert W. " 1860, 8, 25 d 1915, 8, 7
Burritt T. " 1862, 9, 16
Frank L. " 1867, 7, 21
----- R. " 1873, 7, 2
----, --, --. Jonathan b 1836,5,20; m Louisa -----
Ch: Eva b 1864, 5, 22
Emma " 1865, 7, 30
Lizzie " 1866, 9, 1
Calvin
1872, 3, 12. Burrett L. d bur Sugar Grove
1873, 9, 25. Lizzie M. d
1874, 3, 13. Louisa N. d
1902, 12, 5. Frank L. d ae 37
1911, 4, 8. Hazel m Ralph McPHERSON
1913, 8, --. Calvin d
1914, 1, 25. Robert R. m Mabel COMPTON
1914, 9, 20. Wm. d
1915, 6, 30. Charles m Hazel MOORE
1915, 11, --. David d
1918, 9, 17. Joe T., s Chas. & Hazel (Moore) b
1918, 11, 9. Esther m Charles STARBUCK
1919, 8, 7. Evaline d
1920, 3, 10. Eunice d
1925, 10, 28. Joseph T. d
1927, 10, 31. Walker d
1928, 9, 25. Norman d

1870, 3, 18. Martha & ch, Phebe E., William A. & Joseph T., recrq
1870, 3, 18. Louisa & dt, Eva, recrq
1871, 1, 20. Jonathan Sr. con mcd
1873, 4, 18. Eliza E. recrq
1873, 4, 18. Jesse E. recrq
1876, 4, 14. John recrq
1876, 5, 19. Martha M. & Henrietta recrq
1881, 8, 19. Lina relrq
1885, 6, 13. David dropped from mbrp
1886, 4, 10. Anna & dt, Florence, recrq
1888, 1, 14. Annie & Florence relrq
1898, 2, 12. Sarah J. gct Chicago MM, Ill.
1888, 2, 12. George B. gct Chicago MM, Ill.; returned at his rq 1899,5,13
1898, 4, 9. Jesse dropped from mbrp
1903, 2, 14. Corwin, Eliza, Bertha, Mabel & Henrietta dropped from mbrp
1903, 9, 12. Wm., Francis N., Lewis & Ulyses G. relrq
1905, 6, 10. Everett recrq
1906, 2, 10. David W. recrq
1906, 3, 10. Elma McIntyre recrq
1906, 3, 10. David & Annie L. recrq
1907, 3, 9. Mary rocf Westfield MM, Ind.
1907, 10, 12. George C. dropped from mbrp
1908, 5, 19. Frances Louella & Norman H., ch Alma, recrq
1908, 6, 13. Mary gct Westfield MM, Ind.
1929, 3, 13. Alma recrq

DODD
1884, 8, 15. David & w & s, Thurman, rocf Cesars Creek MM, O., dtd 1884,6,26
1898, 4, 9. David & Thurman dropped from mbrp

DOE
1909, 11, 2. Henrietta M. d ae 49

DODSON
1898, 2, 12. Clara gct Cincinnati MM, O., returned at her rq 1898,8,12
1921, 6, 15. Clara Hocket dropped from mbrp

DONALDSON
1897, 3, 13. Nora recrq
1903, 2, 14. Nora dropped from mbrp

DONOHUE
1911, 4, 18. Rachel McDonald m Benj. H. GLASS

DOUGLAS
----, --, --. Robert W. b 1834,11,11; m Margaret ----- b 1833,10,20
Ch: Franklin b 1857, 6, 15
George G. " 1859, 7, 29 d 1870, 1,13
Annie B. " 1864, 9, 27
Chas. Baily" 1872, 5, 10
1881, 5, 22. Chloe d

1868, 7, 14. Robert W. & w, Margaret Ann, & ch, David Franklin, George Gifford & Anna Bell, rocf Clear Creek MM, O., dtd 1868,6, 13
1874, 5, 15. John Henry & w, Miriam C., & ch, Chloe Anna, Jesse Carter, Miriam, John Henry, Christine & Mary Lecky, rocf Clear Creek MM, O., dtd 1874,5,9
1875, 1, 15. Cornelius & w, Phebe, rocf Dover

DOUGLAS, continued
MM, O., dtd 1875,1,14
1878, 3, 15. Chloe rocf Clear Creek MM, O., dtd 1878,1,12
1878, 7, 18. Jesse C. gct St. Albans MM, Me.
1881, 2, 18. David Franklin gct Union MM, Minn.
1884, 2, 15. Robert W. & ch, Anna & Charlie, gct West Branch MM, O.
1885, 10, 10. John Henry & w, Miriam C., & ch, Mellie, John Henry & Christine A., gct Des Moines MM, Ia.

DOWNING
1909, 12, 25. Carl m Olivia McKIBBEN

1913, 4, 14. Oliva McKibben relrq

DRAKE
1919, 10, 16. Lawrence m Opal LANE

1873, 4, 18. Annie recrq
1898, 4, 9. Ann dropped from mbrp

DRISCOL
1902, 3, 8. Fronia recrq

DUDLEY
----, --, --. Peter & Nancy
Ch: Martha b 1837, 4, 17
Garland " 1858, 5, 24
1913, 5, 17. Martha d

1886, 4, 10. Frank recrq
1898, 2, 12. Martha rocf Ogden MM, O., dtd 1898,1,22
1898, 8, 13. John recrq
1919, 5, 14. Eva May recrq

DUNHAM
1870, 3, 18. George P. recrq
1880, 7, 16. Geo. W. relrq

DUNN
1883, 5, 18. James Oregon, s George D., recrq
1898, 2, 12. James Oregon gct Chicago MM, Ill. returned for jas
1898, 5, 14. James O. relrq

DUNNEGAN
1879, 4, 18. James recrq
1898, 4, 9. James [Dunnigan] dropped from mbrp

DUNSMITH
1932, 8, 10. Theodore m Elsie FIFE

DURBIN
1880, 4, 16. Louella & Addie recrq
1883, 5, 18. Josie recrq
1898, 4, 9. Luella & Ida dropped from mbrp

DWIGGINS
1873, 4, 18. Mary recrq
1921, 6, 15. Mary dropped from mbrp

EARLY
1890, 6, 14. Cora A. Moon relrq

EDWARDS
1838, 3, 12. Rebecca, dt Thomas & Letitia Kersey, b
----, --, --. Wm. H. & Edith
Ch: William H. b 1854, 2, 6
Mary A. " 1852, 4, 9
1907, 8, 15. James m Elizabeth CARTER
1911, 10, 7. Lewis m Elsie HAINES
1927, 8, 17. Bonnie m Luther LUKINS

1877, 3, 16. David & w, Martha J., & ch, Nettie & Eliza E., rocf Dover MM, O., dtd 1877,3,15
1885, 10, 10. Levi F. rocf Spiceland MM, Ind. dtd 1885,9,5
1886, 4, 10. Elvie recrq
1891, 11, 14. Levi T. & ch, Edward Aiken & Earl Nelson, gct 12th St. MM, Phila., Pa.
1895, 6, 8. Arthur recrq
1899, 3, 11. Arthur relrq
1910, 6, 11. Mary E. Carter gct Clear Creek MM, O.
1913, 4, 14. Mary J. recrq
1928, 2, 8. Lewis T. recrq

ELDER
1910, 9, 18. David Edward m Dorothy E. ANDERSON

1909, 7, 10. David Edward recrq

ELDRED
1886, 4, 10. Harry S. recrq
1889, 7, 13. Flora gct Dover MM, O.

ELLIOTT
1909, 5, 1. Robert Clark, s Jesse & Virginia, b
1913, 9, 17. Curtis m Louise URTON
1916, 6, 17. Frank R. m Lorena BALES
1917, 7, 21. Frank Roy, s Frank & Lorena, b
1919, 8, 31. Saretta m Luther WARREN

1880, 4, 16. Kate recrq
1908, 12, 12. Jesse J. & Virginia C. recrq
1913, 2, 12. Frank recrq
1913, 11, 12. Louise Urton gct Damascus MM, O.
1916, 11, 8. Seretta recrq
1919, 5, 14. Jesse & w, Virginia, & ch, Robert Clark, relrq
1920, 12, 8. Frank & w, Lorena, & ch, Frank Jr., gct West Richmond MM, Ind.

ELLIS
1915, 10, 8. Ivan d

ELLIS, continued
1924, 7, 24. Linnaeus d
1932, 4, 3. Uriah d

1886, 3, 13. Linneus & w, Laura, & s, Ovan, recrq
1894, 7, 14. Uriah recrq
1894, 7, 14. Clarence Homer recrq
1894, 10, 13. Alice rocf Dover MM, O., dtd 1894,9,13
1895, 6, 8. Elizabeth relrq
1932, 3, 23. Clarence dropped from mbrp

ENNIS
1913, 7, 30. Myrtle rocf Caesars Creek MM,O.
1913, 12, 17. Mary recrq
1914, 2, 11. Dessie recrq

ENT
1925, 5, 18. Margaret d

1873, 3, 14. Margaret recrq
1873, 4, 18. Milton L. & w, Clara, recrq
1879, 2, 10. Clara & ch, Maria Estella & Emma, gct Tongonoxie MM, Kans.

ERNEST
1921, 6, 15. Kate Elliott dropped from mbrp

ERTEL
1927, 6, 8. Jack recrq

ESTES
1871, 5, 19. Lewis A. & w, Huldah C., & ch, Thomas Rowland, rocf Westland MM, Ind., dtd 1871,4,27
1871, 5, 19. Ludovic rocf Westfield MM,Ind., dtd 1871,4,24
1874, 10, 16. Lewis H. & w, Huldah C., & s, Thomas Rowland & Niece, Anna J. Hoag, gct Westfield MM, Ind.
1879, 8, 15. Ludovica gct Spiceland MM, Ind.

EVANS
1906, 9, 8. Fronia gct Sabina MM, O.
1924, 5, 14. Anna recrq
1926, 6, 9. Arthur recrq
1927, 6, 8. Arthur recrq
1928, 4, 11. George Fullerton recrq

EWBANK
1927, 6, 29. Charles m Olive HADLEY

1931, 4, 1. Chas. T. [Eubank] recrq

FAHEY
1912, 11, --. Richard m Anna BAYLESS

1921, 6, 15. Anna Bayliss dropped from mbrp

FAIRLEY
1931, 2, 8. Callie B. d
1933, 8, 4. C. Grant m Sarah Ethel McCOY

1903, 9, 12. Grant & w, Callie, rocf Hopewell MM, O., dtd 1903,9,5

FARBER
1911, 12, 18. Chas. K. m Etha WYSONG

FARLING
----, --, --. ----- m Lavina ----- b 1825,10, 19
Ch: Christopher b 1853, 3, 28
Samuel " 1857, 12, 14
Fietta " 1860, 11, 1
Abraham " 1861, 12, 12
Barbara E. " 1863, 10, 2
Sarah L. " 1865, 11, 13
Amos " 1867, 8, 6
1853, 3, 17. Rhoda b

1873, 5, 16. Rhoda gct Union MM, O.
1873, 5, 16. Levina & ch, Christopher, Fietta Abraham, Barbara E., Sarah L., Amos & Samuel, gct Union MM, O.

FARR
1923, 11, 14. Wendell G. & w, Faye F., & ch, Florence Marion & Elizabeth, rocf Chicago MM, Ill.
1927, 6, 8. Marion recrq

FARQUHAR
----, --, --. Benjamin b 1830,12,5 d 1905,2,5 ae 74; m Mary B. ----- b 1836,2,24 d 1899, 1,22
Ch: Ruth b 1862, 10, 3
Charles " 1864, 9, 9
Naomi J. " 1866, 11, 14
Caroline " 1868, 7, 5
Mary G. " 1872, 4, 11
Oscar J. " 1875, 12, 7
1913, 4, 14. Hannah d ae 74
1913, 9, 16. Benjamin m Mary VANDERVOORT
1914, 6, 24. Francis H. m Mary Evelyn KELLY
1915, 1, 30. Rebecca m Carlton McQUISTON
1915, 6, 30. Edith m Francis Rogers BACON in Wilmington MH
1916, 6, 14. Mary Elizabeth, dt Benj. & Mary, b
----, --, --. Francis H. m Mary KELLY
Ch: Evelyn b 1918, 4, 2
Harold Francis " 1919, 12, 8
Thomas Carlton " 1922, 4, 15
Milton Kelly " 1926, 6, 15
1920, 5, 11. Chas. Benj., s Benj. & Mary, b
1924, 3, 7. Francis d
1927, 8, 20. Robert m Hildegarde JACOB
1928, 7, 23. Harriett m Paul BLOSSOM
1929, 4, 9. Milton J. d

1869, 5, 11. Francis & w, Hannah Ann, & ch, Milton P., Harriett A. & Henry B., gct

FARQUHAR, continued
White Water MM, Ind.
1873, 1, 17. Francis & w, Hannah Ann, & ch, Milton J., Harriet A. & Henry B., rocf White Water MM, Ind., dtd 1872,11,27
1887, 6, 11. Laurena Hunt rocf Newberry MM, O., dtd 1887,5,23
1888, 6, 9. Mary Ada rocf Westland MM, O., dtd 1888,4,7
1889, 2, 7. Nellie recrq
1892, 5, 14. Francis & w, Hannah, & adopted dt, Nellie, gct Chicago MM, Ill.
1892, 5, 14. Milton J. & w, Laurenna, & ch, Rebecca Avi & Francis Hunt, gct Chicago MM, Ill.
1892, 5, 14. Henry & w, Mary Ada, gct Chicago MM, Ill.
1896, 1, 11. Francis & w, Hannah A., & dt, Nellie, rocf Chicago MM, Ill., dtd 1895,12,18
1896, 1, 11. Henry B. & w, Mary Ada, & ch, Edith Melrose & Esther Lois, rocf Chicago MM, Ill., dtd 1895,12,18
1897, 8, 14. Milton J. & w, Laurenna, & ch, Rebecca Abi & Francis J., rocf Chicago MM, Ill.
1903, 10, 10. Camilla McMillan recrq
1903, 10, 10. Robert Roy, s Oscar, recrq
1914, 12, 9. Mary Vandervoort recrq
1927, 6, 29. Robert Hamilton gct 12th St. MM, Phila., to m R. Hildegarde Jacob

FAWCETT
1922, 6, 21. Marie m Frank DAUGHERTY

1914, 10, 14. Marie recrq
1919, 2, 11. Lora & ch, Marion & Ruth, recrq

FELLOW
1886, 10, 9. Henry & w, Melissa, rocf Mississinewa MM, Ind., dtd 1886,7,--, endorsed by Westfield MM, Ind., 1886,9,2
1887, 10, 8. Henry C. & w, Melissa, gct Tonganoxie MM, Kans.

FENDER
1873, 4, 18. Fred recrq

FERREE
1921, 4, 13. Ray & w recrq

FIFE
1922, 9, 1. Clinton m Audna GALLIMORE
1924, 9, 20. Wm. Clinton, s Clinton & Audra, b
1924, 11, 25. Cleo M. m Ira Hundley CRAMPTON
1932, 8, 10. Elsie m Theodore DUNSMITH

1914, 10, 14. Cleo recrq
1919, 5, 14. Elsie Jane recrq
1926, 3, 31. Audna Gallimore relrq

FINEGAN
1880, 4, 16. Peter recrq

FINOUT
1873, 4, 18. Matilda recrq
1874, 7, 17. Matilda [Fineout] dis

FIRMAN
1921, 4, 13. Andrew & w, Louisa, recrq

FISHER
1911, 2, 19. Emma H. d ae 36
1914, 4, 3. Cyrus d
1914, 7, 22. Ruth Esther, dt Clyde & Anna, b
1915, 2, 13. James d
1917, 4, 29. Earl, s Clyde & Anna, b
1923, 12, 26. Lydia d
1925, 12, 2. Hester m Ercil CURTIS
1926, 1, 1. Azariah m Luranna HODSON
1926, 9, 18. Mary Ruth m Kenneth WINTERS
1926, 10, 7. Albert m Bertha HUMPHREY
1932, 5, --. Azariah d

1873, 3, 14. Mary recrq
1886, 5, 8. Wm. Henry rocf Clear Creek MM,O.
1889, 4, 13. James & w, Charlotte, recrq
1891, 8, 8. Homer recrq
1907, 6, 8. Albert rocf Clear Creek MM, O.
1907, 6, 8. Elver J. & w, Emma H., rocf Clear Creek MM, O.
1913, 11, 12. O. Clyde, Anna & Hester rocf Fairview MM
1917, 5, 9. Oliver recrq
1921, 4, 13. Azariah & Lydia E.roc
1921, 6, 15. Homer dropped from mbrp
1926, 3, 10. Luranna A. recrq
1927, 6, 8. Ruth Esther recrq

FITZPATRICK
1876, 5, 19. Ellen recrq
1881, 8, 19. Ellen gct Miami MM, O.

FLANDERS
1825, 12, 25. John A. b

1870, 3, 18. John A. recrq
1898, 2, 12. John A. gct Springfield MM, O.

FLEMING
1906, 5, 12. John D. rocf Cesars Creek MM,O.
1906, 6, 9. John D. gct Center MM, O.

FLORA
1873, 4, 18. Mary E. recrq

FLOYD
1932, 3, 23. Helen recrq

FOLAND
1895, 6, 8. George & Jennie recrq
1897, 4, 10. Ota recrq
1907, 4, 13. George & Jennie gct Center MM,O.
1925, 9, 9. Ella McCray recrq

FOLAND, continued
1926, 7, 14. Ella McCon gct Dayton MM, O.
1930, 4, 9. Ella M. recrq

FOLGER
1929, 1, 1. Joan Marie, dt Hershel & Beatrice, b

1925, 10, 14. O. Hershel & w, Beatrice, rocf Salem MM, Mass.

FORD
1873, 4, 18. Jane A. recrq

FOREMAN
1910, 2, 10. Horace E. recrq
1910, 3, 12. Anna recrq

FOSTER
1932, 8, 10. Anna Mills rocf Grassy Run MM,O.
1932, 10, 12. Lester recrq

FRANKLIN
1914, 7, 30. Lucy m Glenn HARVEY
1915, 6, --. Mary m Hayden KERSHNER

1904, 1, 8. Benj. S., Samuel Glass, Lucy Maria Alice, Lawrence Haworth, Stacy Byron & Richard, ch Byron & Emma, recrq
1906, 4, 14. Byron dropped from mbrp

FRAZIER
----, --, --. James Farr b 1835,3,21; m Rachel S. ----- b 1836,1,17
Ch: Joseph
Burr b 1869, 4, 5
Carsen " 1870, 12, 22 d 1871, 7,10 bur Dover
Cora
Clifford
Homer

1870, 10, 14. Rachel & s, Joseph Burr, rocf Milford MM, Ind.
1871, 4, 14. James Farr rocf Gilead MM, Mo., dtd 1871,3,25
1873, 4, 18. James C. recrq
1884, 4, 18. J. Farr & w, Rachel, & ch, Cora, Clifford & Homer, gct Chester MM, Ind.
1889, 5, 11. James & w, Hannah, & ch, John Henry & Zephaniah, recrq
1889, 5, 11. Martha Ann & dt, Margaret Jane Morris, recrq
1889, 5, 11. Andrew J. & w, Mary Jane, recrq
1907, 3, 9. John Henry dropped from mbrp
1907, 3, 9. Zephamah dropped from mbrp
1907, 3, 9. Andy dropped from mbrp
1907, 3, 9. Mary Jane dropped from mbrp
1932, 3, 23. Virginia recrq

FREELAND
1906, 3, 10. Amos recrq
1907, 3, 9. Eliza Jane recrq
1921, 6, 15. Amos [Freland] dropped from mbrp
1921, 6, 15. Eliza [Freland] dropped from mbrp

FREEMAN
1901, 6, 8. Granville recrq

FREEZE
1913, 12, 17. Garland D. recrq

FREEZAN
1921, 6, 15. Garland dropped from mbrp

FRITTS
1886, 5, 8. Jasper recrq

FRYE
1925, 12, 2. Levinna
1927, 5, 31. Nicholas d

1921, 3, 9. Nicholas, Levinna & Roy rocf Center MM, O., dtd 1921,2,16

FULTON
1928, 7, 11. Sarah d

1905, 11, 11. Sarah J. recrq

FULTZ
1873, 4, 18. Mary R. recrq
1873, 4, 18. Annie recrq
1874, 3, 20. Jennie recrq

FURGUSON
1810, 4, 28. Sarah (Burgess), w Samuel, b

GADDIS
1894, 7, 14. Ella recrq

GALLAHER
1844, 12, 1. Mary J., dt Harvey & Ann, b

1874, 3, 20. James recrq

GALLIETT
1926, 10, 13. Henry B. & Effa relrq

GALLIMORE
1922, 9, 1. Audna m Clinton FIFE
1923, 10, 18. Letha m Clarence ROBINSON

1886, 7, 10. Mary J. & ch, Oscar M., Flora E. & Wm. B., rocf Dover MM, O.
1889, 7, 13. Mary & ch, Oscar & Wm. Gallimore, gct Dover MM, O.
1902, 4, 10. James W. & w, Florence, & ch, Audna R. & Letha C., rocf Dover MM, O.

GALLUP
1902, 2, 28. George d ae 27
1907, 6, 1. Susannah d ae 68

1870, 6, 17. Susanna N. rocf Springfield MM, O., dtd 1870,5,21

GALLUP, continued
MM, O., dtd 1870,5,21
1875, 9, 17. Martha Jane [Gallop] & ch, Cora & Estella, rocf Springfield MM, O., dtd 1875,7,17
1881, 5, 20. Emma [Gallop] recrq
1897, 11, 13. Estella relrq
1902, 4, 12. Cora & Martha relrq
1923, 1, 10. H. B. & w recrq

GARNER
1927, 10, 12. James recrq
1928, 2, 8. Birdie recrq
1931, 8, 5. Marion & w, Alice, recrq

GARRISON
1889, 5, 11. Lillie recrq
1907, 3, 9. Lillie dropped from mbrp

GASKILL
1916, 2, --. Mahlon d
1925, 3, 13. Laura d

1873, 4, 18. Milton S. recrq
1873, 6, 20. Louisa rocf Miami MM, O., dtd 1873,5,21
1874, 8, 14. Milton S. & w, Louisa, gct Newberry MM, O.
1876, 5, 19. Laura recrq
1889, 4, 13. Mahlon R. [Gaskil] recrq

GASKINS
1877, 2, 16. Dr. Aaron J. & w, Celia Ann, recrq
1881, 5, 20. James recrq
1889, 3, 9. Essie Alton recrq

GAUSE
----, --, --. Samuel b 1820,5,18; m Mary Jane HARVEY, b 1836,8,22
Ch: Elkanah B. b 1868, 8, 30
Esther F. " 1871, 1, 9
Enos " 1876, 7, 28

1876, 4, 14. Samuel & w, Mary Jane, & ch, Elkanah B. & Ester F., rocf Springfield MM, O., dtd 1876,3,18
1877, 10, 19. Samuel & w, Mary Jane, & ch, Elkanah Beard, Esther F. & Enos, gct Springfield MM, O.

GLASS
----, --, --. Geo. D. H. m Brazella ----- d 1875,8,18
Ch: Mary B. b 1870, 9, 22
Geo. D. H. m 2nd Mattie H. CURL d 1878,2, 15 bur Sugar Grove
Ch: George b 1879, 2, --
1912, 9, 23. Alice d
1919, 6, --. Virginia m Clarence AMES
1924, 2, 9. George d
1925, 5, 10. Ella A. d
----, --, --. Samuel R. & Mary H.
Ch: Samuel W.
Emma E.

1870, 3, 18. Samuel R. & w, Mary H., & ch, Samuel W. & Emma E., recrq
1870, 3, 18. George D. H. & w, Bruzilla, recrq
1883, 5, 18. Alice recrq
1897, 4, 10. Edith recrq
1908, 5, 19. Alice Nell, dt Robert, recrq
1927, 2, 16. Robert G. & Alice Nell relrq

GLENN
1874, 2, 28. Emma d
----, --, --. John & Sarah [Glenna]
Ch: John A.
Mary
Emma
Amanda J.
Susie E.
Samuel E.

1870, 3, 18. John & w, Sarah, & ch, John A., Mary, Emma, Amanda J., Susan E. & Samuel E., recrq
1876, 4, 14. Samuel recrq
1880, 3, 19. Elizabeth relrq
1897, 4, 10. Effie recrq
1897, 5, 8. Leo S. recrq
1904, 4, 9. Samuel E., Effie, Leo & John A. dropped from mbrp

GEIGER
1907, 12, 14. Laura Todhunter relrq

GEORGE
1893, 7, 8. Mattie Wood gct Kansas City MM, Mo.

GERARD
1878, 12, 20. Fanny Grand relrq

GIBSON
1922, 5, 20. Ruth m Donald TUTTLE

1872, 11, 15. Jesse A. & w, Martha Emily & ch, Sarah M., rocf Newberry MM
1879, 5, 16. Jess A. & w, Martha E., & ch, Sarah M. & Georgie Annie, gct Back Creek MM, Ind.
1908, 3, 4. Albion M. & w, Martha E., rocf Hopewell MM, O.
1911, 12, 9. Albion M. & w, Martha E., gct Rose Valley MM, Kans.
1919, 3, 12. Ruth Eleanor recrq

GIFFIN
1874, 3, 20. George W. [Giffen] recrq
1877, 2, 16. Anna recrq
1879, 4, 18. David recrq

GILBERT
1895, 6, 8. Oscar recrq

GLASGOW
1877, 2, 16. Louis N. recrq

GOSSIN
1907, 2, 9. Emma Stewart relrq

GRANDSTAFF
1897, 4, 10. William recrq
1903, 1, 10. Wm. dropped from mbrp

GRAY
1901, 1, 7. Adam d ae 75
1910, 8, 12. Dollie m Alonzo CRAIG
1914, 1, 9. George d

1897, 10, 9. Angeline rocf Springfield MM,O., dtd 1897,9,18
1897, 10, 9. George W. & ch, Sanford P., Mary D., Joseph R., James W. & Dollie C., recrq
1899, 6, 15. Adam recrq
1907, 4, 13. Park & Mary dropped from mbrp
1919, 5, 14. Walter relrq
1924, 5, 14. Florence recrq
1930, 11, 12. Oscar recrq

GREEN
----, --, --. Asa b 1805,1,5; m Susannah CARTER b 1806,3,16 d 1898,3,27
Ch: Reuben b 1831, 11, 24
Mary Ann " 1834, 1, 22
----, --, --. Samuel G. b 1845,9,21; m Ellen KIMBROUGH b 1844,2,3
1899, 4, 18. Hazael D. d ae 77
1909, 6, 11. Naomi C. d ae 73
1911, 11, 28. Charles Herbert m Ada ANTRAM
1912, 6, 12. Percy m Anna JENKINS
1917, 1, 2. Alice Doan m Ralph JOHNSON
1930, 5, 30. Lois d

1876, 6, 16. Mary recrq
1882, 1, 20. Samuel G. & w, Ella, rocf Springfield MM, O., dtd 1881,11,19
1883, 3, 16. Samuel G. & w gct Springfield MM, O.
1889, 12, 14. Richard E. & w, Sadie, & ch, Grace L., Mary Ethel & Charles Herbert, rocf Fairfield MM, O., dtd 1889,11,16
1890, 4, 12. Lindley M. & w, Alice D., & ch, Inez & Pliny F., rocf Fairfield MM, O., dtd 1890,2,15
1891, 7, 11. Amanda recrq
1892, 11, 12. Richard C. & fam gct Fairfield MM, O.
1893, 11, 11. Wm. D. & w, Matilda, & ch, Ernest L., Percy E. & Francis W., rocf Fairfield MM, O., dtd 1893,10,21
1893, 11, 11. Hazael D. & w, Naomi, & ch, Julia & Alice H., rocf Fairfield MM, O., dtd 1893,10,21
1893, 11, 11. Mary rocf Fairfield MM, O., dtd 1893,10,21
1895, 1, 12. Lizzie Smith & dt, Mabel Smith, rocf Springfield MM, O., dtd 1894,12,15
1897, 11, 13. William D. & w, Matilda, & ch, Ernest L., Frances W. & Percy E., gct Center MM, O.
1899, 5, 13. Elizabeth Wilson relrq
1901, 10, 12. Alice Doan relrq
1902, 2, 8. Richard C. & w, Sadie D., & ch, Grace L., Mary E. & Hubert C., rocf Center MM, O., dtd 1902,1,15
1902, 3, 8. Ernest L. rocf Fairfield MM, O., dtd 1902,1,18
1903, 2, 14. Ernest L. relrq
1903, 9, 12. L. M. & w, Lizzie E., & ch, Pliny T., gct Pasadena MM, Calif.
1903, 9, 12. Inez A. gct Pasadena MM, Calif.
1904, 1, 9. Albert L. recrq
1912, 6, 12. Ernest gct Dayton MM, O.
1912, 8, 7. Anna Jenkins gct Fairfield MM,O.
1914, 10, 14. Alice D. recrq
1917, 3, 14. Charles Herbert & w, Ada A., relrq
1918, 2, 13. Julia E. gct Long Beach MM, Calif.
1921, 3, 9. Lois & Hannah rocf Ogden MM,O., dtd 1921,2,26
1927, 7, 20. Alice recrq
1927, 8, 26. Alice m ----- -----
1928, 11, 14. C. Herbert & w, Ada, recrq

GREGORY
1923, 5, 4. Sirvetus d

1885, 9, 12. Sylvester & w, Martha, rocf Clear Creek MM, O., dtd 1885,8,8
1886, 5, 8. Nancy recrq
1904, 6, 11. Raymond B. recrq
1905, 1, 11. Blanche recrq
1911, 2, 11. Raymond B. relrq
1921, 3, 9. Raymond B. recrq
1921, 3, 9. Kennett H. recrq
1921, 3, 9. Christine E. recrq
1921, 3, 9. Blanche recrq
1933, 4, 12. Martha recrq

GREGG
1918, 2, 13. Hazel West relrq

GRICE
1918, 2, 21. Jane m Charles W. STOLTZ
1920, 2, 7. Mildred m Walter SPELLMAN
1922, 7, 3. Ruth m Donald E. HARE

1904, 2, 13. Nora Marie recrq
1908, 12, 12. Ruthanna & Alma J. recrq
1908, 12, 12. Lella E. & Mildred recrq

GRIFFITH
----, --, --. William Brooks b 1810,5,16; m Elizabeth ----- b 1812,4,25
Ch: Francis
Marion b 1841, 8, 1 d 1903, 8, 2
Samuel B.
1912, 11, 13. Samuel d

GRIFFITH, continued
1870, 3, 18. Francis Marion recrq
1870, 3, 18. W. B. recrq
1871, 3, 17. Elizabeth recrq
1873, 4, 18. Samuel B. recrq

GRISSEN
1897, 4, 10. Elizabeth recrq

GUINN
1870, 3, 18. Allen T. recrq

GUSTIN
1926, 10, 7. Milburn m Phoebe SMITH

1870, 3, 18. Norah & Alice, ch Jonathan, recrq
1880, 4, 16. Wm. C. recrq
1883, 4, 20. Alice relrq
1898, 2, 12. Wm. E. gct Cincinnati MM, O.

GUTHRIE
1899, 9, 9. James recrq
1900, 2, 10. Robert recrq
1900, 6, 9. James & Robert gct Ogden MM, O.
1906, 2, 10. James D. & w, Bessie N., & ch, Austin T., Forest G. & Carl L., recrq
1921, 6, 15. James & w, Bessie, & ch, Austin T., Forrest G. & Carl, dropped from mbrp

HACKNEY
1886, 11, --. James L. d bur Sugar Grove

1873, 4, 18. Mary recrq
1921, 11, 9. Edward & w, Rose, & ch, Raymond, Wilfred & Maynard, rocf Center MM, O.

HADLEY
----, --, --. Mary T. b 1792,1,10 d 1880,8,31 bur Springfield
1795, 11, 2. Susanna, dt Joseph & Dosha Stratton, b
----, --, --. Mary (Thomas) Jr. b 1808,3,28 d 1878,9,9 bur Springfield
----, --, --. Jonathan T. b 1793,3,14 d 1879,10,28 bur Springfield; m Rebecca HARVEY b 1795,1,17 d 1876,6,20 bur Springfield
Ch: Lydia D. b 1818, 12, 6
Deborah L. " 1830, 11, 26
Harlan H. " 1835, 10, 21
----, --, --. Jacob b 1801,3,3; m Lucinda ----- b 1811,12,26
Ch: Susanna Jane b 1838, 10, 25
Naomi C. " 1845, 4, 5
----, --, --. William L. & Mary N.
Ch: John
Sarah E. b 1844, 11, 10
----, --, --. Samuel L. b 1821,1,30; m Mary G. HARVEY b 1825,1,17 d 1885,7,22 bur Springfield
Ch: James b 1846, 7, 27
Ansalem " 1848, 8, 4 d 1884,11,20
Ch: Emma b 1853, 12, 15
Anna " 1855, 11, 2
Edwin " 1857, 10, 24
William " 1872, 8, 24
----, --, --. Samuel H. b 1824,5,18; m Ruth L. SMITH b 1829,10,25
Ch: Orlando b 1851, 12, 25
Emily G. " 1853, 11, 2
Alice " 1856, 2, 27
Mary D. " 1860, 4, 8
Anna " 1862, 7, 31
Eva Jane " 1864, 3, 10 d 1888, 3,16
----, --, --. William C. b 1828,1,21; m ----------
Ch: Eugnne b 1853, 8, 6 d 1918, 3,15
Mary V. " 1860, 2, 14
William Clark " 1869, 7, 20
----, --, --. David L. b 1827,8,2 d 1898,1,22 bur Springfield; m Abigail J. CLARK b 1830,10,10
Ch: George C. b 1856, 5, 3
Woodrow Warner " 1860, 4, 11
----, --, --. Eli & Theodocia
Ch: Warren b 1856, 9, 19
Alonzo " 1858, 12, 18
1857, 10, 24. Edwin b
----, --, --. Harlan H. b 1835,10,21; m Susannah KIMBROUGH b 1836,11,15
Ch: Ella b 1859, 8, 30
Atwell M. " 1861, 7, 28
Isaac P. " 1863, 4, 2
Horace A. " 1865, 9, 21
Ruth Edna " 1873, 3, 28
----, --, --. John Wm. b 1839,12,22 d 1892,11,24 bur Springfield; m Sarah Ellen WORTHINGTON b 1842,9,4
Ch: William Edgar b 1861, 1, 31
Mary Anna " 1862, 9, 15
Lucetta W. " 1875, 4, 3
----, --, --. Thomas b 1832,9,21; m Amanda Maria PYLE b 1842,7,29
Ch: Anna Wim b 1862, 9, 27
Harriett Isabella " 1869, 12, 5
Morris W. " 1871, 10, 14
Bertha M. " 1873, 6, 24
----, --, --. Evan H. b 1842,9,20; m Susie NICKERSON b 1846,7,21
Ch: James Clark b 1864, 6, 19 d 1889, 5,10
Cora Louisa b 1869, 1, 17
Zenis Garland " 1875, 5, 13
----, --, --. Chambers b 1836,4,1 d 1874,7,13 m Ann HIGGINS b 1846,9,29
Ch: Joseph W. b 1865, 2, 22
Norah C. " 1867, 4, 7
Alonzo L. " 1869, 5, 30
Clifford V." 1871, 3, 10

HADLEY, continued
1865, 7, 3. Carrie B. b
----, --, --. Micajah C. b 1834,9,20 d 1889,5, 16 bur Springfield; m Ellen COWGILL b 1840,8,15
Ch: Milden T. b 1866, 2, 1
Gertrude W." 1869, 12, 13
Adilla M. " 1874, 11, 4
----, --, --. William b 1840,12,1; m Tarinda VANDOREN b 1844,10,9
Ch: Alvin b 1868, 11, 13
Alfred " 1870, 4, 14 d 1870, 5, 2
Arthalina " 1873, 3, 14
Nathan " 1875, 4, 14
Lucinda " 1878, 4, 5
1868, 6, 3. Sarah E. d
----, --, --. James b 1846,7,27; m Isabel MOORE b 1850,9,23
Ch: Edgar L. b 1870, 10, 7
Aloutie " 1875, 2, 26
Louie May " 1879, 9, 9
----, --, --. Calvin b 1850,8,15; m Emeline MULLEN b 1852,4,14
Ch: Elton P. b 1874, 1, 16
Marietta " 1876, 1, 23
1875, 7, 26. Albert d bur Sugar Grove
----, --, --. Alonzo b 1858,12,18; m Frances PRITCHARD
Ch: Ann
Jeanette b 1878, 3, 5
----, --, --. Orlando b 1851,12,25; m Harriett E. HAWORTH b 1856,9,7
Ch: Florence E.b 1880, 3, 25
Ruthanna
----, --, --. Wm. P. b 1872,8,24; m Lizzie V. HARVEY b 1873,8,29
Ch: Mary Naomi b 1897, 2, 10
Willard
Jesse " 1898, 6, 2
1897, 12, 26. Elizabeth d ae 78
1904, 12, 10. Clorinna d ae 19
----, --, --. Alonta & Belle
Ch: Robert
Allen b 1909, 10, 28
Clarence " 1911, 9, 15
1910, 7, 15. Oma C. d ae 65
1914, 12, 29. Edgar d
1916, 5, 24. Mabel Alice m U. S. IRELAND
1916, 6, 23. Miles d
1918, 11, 16. Sarah Ellen d
1921, 3, 16. Naomi m Lewis BEVAN
1921, 4, 3. Mary Katharine m Homer STULTZ
1923, 8, 8. Loren m Jeanette JANEY
1923, 11, 29. Mable m Roy M. SMART
----, --, --. Willard m Opal SCOTT
1926, 8, 14. Robert m Ethel SLACK
1926, 12, 23. Chas. d
1927, 2, 1. James Seth m Bessie SHADLEY
1927, 6, 29. Olive m Chas. EWBANK
1927, 7, 6. Louise m James TEMPLIN
1927, 7, 23. William d
1932, 1, 14. Sarah Caroline d
1932, 10, 17. Ellen d

1871, 5, 19. Elizabeth & ch, Charles, Francis, Evaline O., Calvin, Caroline & Jonathan, rocf Miami MM, O., dtd 1871,4,26
1871, 6, 16. Albert H. rocf Miami MM, O., dtd 1871,5,24
1874, 4, 17. Simon & w, Rachel, & ch, Joseph, Benjamin B. & Cyrus, rocf Springfield MM, O., dtd 1874,2,21
1874, 4, 17. Martha E. rocf Springfield MM, O., dtd 1874,2,21
1875, 6, 18. Emma C. rocf Clear Creek MM, O., dtd 1875,6,12
1875, 12, 17. Frank & w, Emma C., gct Clear Creek MM, O.
1879, 4, 18. Simon & w, Rachel M., & ch, Albert J. & Cyrus M., gct Dover MM, O.
1880, 3, 19. Lucinda gct Springfield MM, O.
1883, 4, 20. Mary recrq
1883, 8, 17. Joseph C. gct Honey Creek MM,Ia.
1884, 2, 15. Benjamin gct Honey Creek MM,Ia.
1884, 2, 15. Martha E. gct Honey Creek MM,Ia.
1884, 6, 26. Ruth S. & dt, Alice, rocf Springfield MM, O., dtd 1884,5,17
1884, 6, 26. Anna & dt, Eva J., rocf Springfield MM, O., dtd 1884,5,17
1885, 9, 12. Mary Virginia relrq
1886, 6, 12. Calvin gct Kokomo MM, Ind.
1886, 6, 12. Jonathan gct Kokomo MM, Ind.
1887, 9, 10. Carrie gct Kokomo MM, Ind.
1888, 9, 8. Elizabeth gct Kokomo MM, Ind.
1889, 12, 14. Simon & w, Rachel, rocf Honey Creek MM, Ia.
1890, 2, 8. Evan H. & w, Susan W., & s, Zenas, rocf Springfield MM, O., dtd 1890, 1,18
1890, 2, 8. Cora rocf Springfield MM
1890, 4, 12. Orlando & w, Hattie E., & ch, Florence E. & Ruth Anna, rocf Springfield MM
1892, 3, 12. Elizabeth T. & dt, Carrie, rocf Kokomo MM, Ind., dtd 1892,3,9
1892, 10, 8. Martha E. rocf Honey Creek MM, Ia., dtd 1892,9,24
1894, 3, 10. Anna relrq
1895, 12, 14. Sarah Ellen & Luetta, rocf Springfield MM, O.
1896, 4, 14. Orlando & fam gct Springfield MM, O.
1898, 9, 10. Wm. Edgar, Ellen C. & Adella rocf Springfield MM, O., dtd 1898,8,13
1899, 2, 11. Carrie E. gct Marion MM, Ind.
1899, 4, 8. Evan H. & w, Susan N., gct Ogden MM, O.
1900, 2, 10. Cora relrq
1901, 8, 10. Simon gct Dover MM, O.
1902, 5, 10. Miles & w, Sarah Caroline, rocf Springfield MM, O., dtd 1902,4,19
1903, 2, 14. Zenas gct Ogden MM, O.
1907, 12, 14. Alontie rocf Springfield MM,O., dtd 1907,11,16
1907, 12, 14. Mary Katherine, Mabel Elizabeth, Margaret Louise & James Seth, ch Alontie, recrq

HADLEY, continued
1908, 12, 12. Elsa & Bessie recrq
1910, 6, 11. Elsa & Rebecca relrq
1910, 7, 9. Orlando & w, Hattie E., rocf Springfield MM, O., dtd 1910,6,18
1910, 7, 9. Florence & Ruthanna rocf Springfield MM, O., dtd 1910,6,18
1914, 10, 14. Wm. P. & w, Lizzie, & ch, Naomi M., Willard I., Loren S., Robert E., Olivia & Wendell recrq

HAGUE
1907, 2, 25. Robert d ae 86
1919, 8, 4. Mary d
1923, 6, 5. Harry d
1925, 8, 1. Edith d

1892, 4, 9. Robert S. & w, Martha T., rocf Columbus MM, O., dtd 1892,4,3
1892, 4, 9. Harry W. & w, Mary T., & ch, Hazel E., Edith M., Claire C., William M. & Harry W. rocf Columbus MM, O., dtd 1892,4,3

HAINES
----, --, --. J. Monroe & Clara
Ch: Elsie C. b 1872, 3, 30
Charles M. " 1875, 6, 21 d 1876, 1,25 bur Sugar Grove
Edna b 1877, 1, 13
Sarah S. " 1842, 1, 29
1873, 10, 24. Sallie Mary d
1897, 7, 27. Mary Miars d ae 76
1902, 2, 17. Emma d ae 61
1905, 4, 24. Howard d ae 62
1909, 3, 14. Zimri d ae 94
1909, 6, 24. Harry m Edith McLAUGHLIN
1911, 10, 7. Elsie m Lewis EDWARDS
1913, 7, --. Eldon m Jessie BRYAN
1915, 1, 10. Fred d
1916, 9, 4. Bernice d
1918, 6, 21. Mary Haladay d
1926, --, --. Carl m Frances Marie TURNER
1928, 6, 27. Eldon m Portia ROBINSON
1932, 6, 7. Arthur Webster, s Eldon & Portia, b
1933, 1, 13. Louisa d

1870, 3, 18. J. Monroe recrq
1873, 3, 14. Howard & w, Sally Mary & ch, Lizzie Bell, recrq
1873, 4, 18. Susan recrq
1874, 3, 20. Lydia recrq
1874, 7, 17. Mary recrq
1875, 3, 19. Zimri recrq
1876, 5, 19. Ada [Haynes] recrq
1900, 3, 10. Wm. [Haynes] & w, Emma, rocf Center MM, O., dtd 1900,2,14
1902, 5, 10. Mary J. recrq
1902, 10, 11. Sarah Louisa recrq
1903, 7, 12. Fred H. recrq
1903, 10, 10. Mary F. rocf West Fork MM, O., dtd 1903,9,19
1905, 10, 14. Sarah Louisa gct Lowell MM, Kans.
1909, 6, 12. Eli, Louisa E., Bernard E. & Sylvester T., rocf Center MM, O.
1912, 11, 13. D. Webster & w, Estella, & s, Eldon, rocf Center MM, O., dtd 1912,10,16
1921, 2, 9. Opal E. recrq
1928, 11, 14. Portia Robinson recrq
1929, 8, 21. Frances Marie Turner relrq

HALE
1810, 4, 11. Elizabeth (Edwards), w Armonia, b
----, --, --. Jacob d 1925,11,29; m Hannah ANDREW b 1812,1,27 d 1895,6,4 bur Springfield
Ch: Alfred b 1841, 12, 23
----, --, --. Alfred b 1841,12,23 d 1914,11, 11; m Rachel A. HADLEY b 1842,7,26
Ch: Mary
Alice b 1865, 12, 5
Clark J. " 1868, 10, 17
Emma " 1873, 3, 30 d 1887, 4,22
Hannah G. " 1883, 2, 8
----, --, --. Clark J. b 1868,10,17; m Alice JACKSON b 1865,9,25
Ch: Rachel
Edith b 1892, 5, 14
Herman T. " 1895, 8, 28
1911, 4, 2. Layton m Jessie LUKINS
1932, 3, 25. Esther d

1876, 5, 19. Mary recrq
1883, 12, 14. Sarah Collins gct Springfield MM, O.
1886, 4, 10. Henry M. & ch, Harrie, Rosa Belle & Hattie, recrq
1897, 3, 13. Clark J. & w, Alice, & ch, R. Edith & Herman T., rocf Springfield MM,O., dtd 1897,1,16
1898, 9, 10. Esther M. rocf Springfield MM, O., dtd 1898,8,13
1901, 6, 8. Alfred & Hannah rocf Ogden MM, O., dtd 1901,5,25
1903, 1, 10. Jacob recrq
1906, 9, 8. Alice J. & ch, R. Edith & Herman T., relrq
1906, 10, 13. Sarah Tomlinson gct Springfield MM, O.
1910, 8, 13. Clark dropped from mbrp
1914, 4, 8. Alice Pate recrq

HAM
1908, 8, 28. Martha d ae 66

1897, 4, 10. Lucy Elizabeth rocf Springfield MM, O., dtd 1897,3,20
1903, 4, 11. Martha J. rocf Ogden MM, O., dtd 1903,3,28

HAMILTON
1912, 2, 17. Minnie m Chas. A. MOOTS
1913, 7, --. Hallie m ----- BRADSHAW
1917, 11, 24. Mary m Dwight STEPHENSON

HAMILTON, continued
1918, 4, 26. Belle d
1920, 6, 19. Grace m George RHOADES
1922, 6, 3. Wm. m Zella NEITERT
1925, 4, 2. Marion d

1909, 3, 13. Frances E. recrq
1910, 2, 10. Minnie & Hallie recrq
1913, 2, 12. Wm. V., Elmer U., Grace J. & Mary E., recrq
1913, 4, 14. Marion & Belle recrq
1924, 5, 14. Wm. Vance relrq
1931, 6, 10. Roy rocf Chester MM

HAMMER
1889, 4, 13. Emma Hastings gct Newberry MM,O.

HAMPTON
1898, 11, 17. Alice d

1898, 11, 12. Alice recrq

HANDMAN
1932, 6, 8. Ally Compton relrq

HANEY
----, --, --. Abraham M. b 1832,9,4; m Elizabeth B. COATE b 1833,3,14 d 1902,1,20 ae 69
Ch: Ella Mary b 1860, 2, 27
Joseph W. " 1861, 3, 15
John Charles " 1863, 7, 23
Delila C. " 1870, 9, 9
Abram " 1873, 6, 13
1906, 12, 4. Elizabeth, dt Chas. & Emma, b
1907, 9, 26. Lila m J. L. TRUMAN

1871, 4, 14. A. M. & w, Elizabeth, & ch, Ella Mary, Joseph W., John Charles & Delilah C., rocf Springfield MM, dtd 1871,3,18
1901, 6, 8. Elizabeth B. rocf Ogden MM, O., dtd 1901,5,25
1904, 4, 9. Chas. & Eva D. rocf Ogden MM,O., dtd 1904,3,26
1904, 4, 9. Lila C. rocf Ogden MM, O., dtd 1904,3,26
1925, 10, 14. Charles & w, Eva D., & ch, Elizabeth, gct Springfield MM

HANNAH
1912, 3, 11. Florence m Ernest HIRT

1902, 3, 8. James, Eva & Florence recrq
1906, 3, 10. Florence recrq

HANKS
1889, 4, 13. Austin J. & w, Sarah C., & ch, Clara & Laura, recrq
1892, 3, 12. Sarah C.& fam relrq

HANSON
1928, 7, 18. Florence recrq

1933, 6, 14. Florence N. gct Oskaloosa MM,Ia.

HARDMAN
1920, 6, 30. Charles m Ally Compton QUINN

HARE
1922, 7, 3. Donald E. m Ruth GRICE
1928, 8, 18. Henry m Katherine PEMBERTON

1900, 3, 10. Eliza W. & ch, Walter T., Henry I. & Edith M., gct Dover MM, O.
1926, 10, 13. Henry rocf Dover MM

HARLAN
----, --, --. Lydia b 1815,10,23 d 1884,12,1 bur Springfield
----, --, --. Enoch m Elizabeth KIMBROUGH b 1802,1,3
Ch: Samuel b 1829, 10, 16
Wilson " 1834, 5, 10
1827, 11, 3. Caroline E. b
1838, 12, 31. Wm. H., s Nathaniel & Lydia, b
----, --, --. John b 1823,2,14; m Elizabeth WILSON b 1828,10,18
Ch: Emma b 1854, 9, 28
Oliver T. " 1859, 11, 25 d 1888,12,23 bur Springfield
1866, 5, 1. May, dt Samuel & Hannah, b
1899, 4, 25. Lucy W. d ae 57

1873, 4, 18. Isaac H. recrq
1873, 4, 18. Newton recrq
1874, 3, 20. Lucy M. recrq
1885, 2, 14. Lucy W. recrq
1885, 6, 13. I. A. dropped from mbrp
1918, 7, 10. F. Margaret & dt, Maxine, recrq

HARNER
1929, 12, 10. Hattie Lukens dropped from mbrp

HAROLD
1907, 12, 23. Jones E. m Alice NORDYKE

1919, 10, 8. Earl J. & w, Clara O., & ch, Mary Elizabeth & Margaret C., rocf Salem MM, Mass.
1922, 9, 13. Earl J. & w, Clara, & ch, Mary Elizabeth & Margaret C., gct Marion MM, Ind.

HARRIS
1889, 4, 13. Adolphus & w, Kate, & ch, Roy & Estus, recrq
1892, 5, 14. Adolphus & w, Kate, relrq

HARSHA
1907, 5, 11. Rose Althea relrq

HART
1889, 4, 13. Mary recrq
1891, 6, 13. Charles H. recrq
1902, 4, 12. Charles H. relrq

HARTLEY
1883, 9, 14. Reuben H. rocf Oskaloosa MM,Ia.
1883, 9, 14. M. Libbie rocf Legrand MM, Ia.
1885, 8, 8. Reuben H. & w, M. Libbie, & s, Walter Earl, gct Des Moines MM, Ia.

HARTMAN
----, --, --. James b 1821,11,22; m Susan SHAFER
Ch: Nora May b 1871, 5, 7
James William " 1873, 8, 5
Hiram Ellsworth " 1876, 9, 1
1900, 9, 27. Elizabeth d ae 54
1916, 11, 30. J. Arthur m Bernice HAWKINS
Ch: Margaret Ruth b 1917, 9, 27
Cecil Arthur " 1918, 10, 5
Rachel Nancy " 1920, 11, 24

1876, 5, 19. Phebe recrq
1882, 6, 16. Elizabeth recrq
1885, 7, 11. Phebe gct White Water MM, Ind.; returned because she was not at that mtg
1896, 11, 14. Blanch recrq
1906, 2, 10. Arthur recrq
1921, 10, 12. Arthur & w, Bernice, & ch, Margaret Ruth, Cecil Arthur & Rachel, gct Caesars Creek MM, O.

HARVEY
1809, 3, 22. Samuel Clayton b
----, --, --. Isaac b 1809,11,27 d 1883,8,11 bur Springfield; m Sarah EDWARDS b 1812, 11,10
Ch: Rebecca b 1839, 7, 24
Jesse H. " 1849, 4, 10
----, --, --. Simon m Ann ----- b 1813,2,6
Ch: Martha b 1843, 11, 26
1842, 10, 8. John b
1843, 6, 30. Nathaniel b
----, --, --. Wm. P. b 1828,11,16; m Nancy MOORE b 1830,2,19 d 1898,1,28
Ch: Sarah Ann b 1856, 11, 28 d 1892,11,30
Willis M. " 1858, 8, 21
Eli " 1860, 9, 23
Joshua " 1862, 9, 1
Seth " 1865, 11, 1
James " 1867, 10, 1
----, --, --. Willis M. b 1858,8,21 d 1893,12, 20 bur Springfield; m Jennie PETERS
Ch: Inda
Earnest
----, --, --. Jesse H. b 1849,4,10; m Lucy Caroline HADLEY, b 1851,6,23
Ch: Lizzie Viola b 1873, 8, 29
Elsie R. " 1875, 11, 23
Olive Etta " 1880, 12, 1 d 1903,10,17
Rachel Myra" 1897, 2, 7

1873, 8, 4. Abraham d bur Sugar Grove
1907, 6, 30. Micajah d ae 73
1914, 7, 30. Glenn m Lucy FRANKLIN
1930, 2, 18. Anna B. d

1869, 3, 16. John rocf Springfield MM, O., dtd 1869,2,20
1873, 3, 14. Aaron recrq
1873, 4, 18. Freddy H. recrq
1873, 12, 19. Maria A. recrq
1877, 2, 16. James & w, Alice, & ch, Blancha, rocf Spiceland MM, Ind., dtd 1877,1,6
1883, 4, 20. Aaron & w, Maria E., & ch, Frederic, S. Bernard, Charles E., Nelliford E. & Geo. W., gct Springfield MM,O.
1885, 7, 11. James & fam gct Indianapolis MM, Ind.
1886, 7, 10. Miles W. & w, Elizabeth, & dt, Lucile, rocf Miami MM, O., dtd 1886,6,23
1891, 1, 10. Miles & dt, Lucile, gct Miami MM, O.
1894, 3, 10. Alice C. & s, Homer A., rocf Indianapolis MM, Ind., dtd 1894,2,22
1898, 2, 12. Alice C. & s, Homer, gct Ogden MM, O.
1904, 3, 12. Micajah & dt, Anna, rocf Miami MM, O., dtd 1904,2,24
1907, 10, 12. Samuel C. dropped from mbrp
1917, 8, 8. Lucy Franklin gct Fowler MM, Kans.

HARWOOD
1896, 1, 11. Jessie S. relrq

HASTINGS
1886, 4, 10. Emma recrq

HATHAWAY
1886, 11, 13. Alfred C. rocf Rollin MM, Mich.,
1888, 12, 8. Minnie recrq
1891, 4, 11. Alfred C. & w, Minnie R., & s, Francis W., gct White Water MM, Ind.

HAWKINS
1906, 1, 31. Mary E., dt Levi & Lena, b
1916, 11, 30. Bernice m J. Arthur HARTMAN
1919, 8, 11. Viola d
1921, 2, 6. Benjamin d
1926, 3, 30. Mary Walker d

1886, 5, 8. Nancy Clarinda recrq
1899, 11, 11. Levi M. rocf Caesars Creek MM, O., dtd 1899,10,26
1917, 5, 9. Bernice E. H. rocf Caesars Creek MM, O.
1918, 6, 12. Benjamin & w, Viola K., & dt, Helen E., rocf Grassy Run MM, O.
1921, 3, 9. Milton J. rocf Center MM, O., dtd 1921,2,16
1921, 3, 9. Mary I. recrq
1931, 7, 13. Helen gct Fairview MM
1921, 10, 12. Lee & Lena & dt, Mary Elizabeth,

HAWKINS, continued
relrq
1930, 2, 12. Milton gct Chester MM

HAWORTH
----, --, --. Geo. D. b 1797,5,29 d 1881,6,27; m Sarah ----- b 1802,7,7 d 1881,6,24
----, --, --. Frank & Emma
Ch: Ethel
Louisa b 1898, 10, 30
Ruth Olive " 1900, 2, 18
Helen Curl " 1903, 3, 8
1903, 5, 14. Rebecca d ae 69
1905, 4, 24. Carrie Antram d ae 24
1909, 12, 25. George D. m Edith MAGEE
1910, 2, 26. Harriett, dt Ralph & Hanna, b
1910, 3, 24. Edith m Orville WALL
1912, 4, 25. Emma d
1921, 6, 29. Mary d
1925, 11, 5. Ruth m Frank MARTIN
1930, 10, 2. Hannah d

1873, 3, 14. Elizabeth P., w James M., & s, James E., recrq
1873, 3, 14. James M. & w, Elizabeth P., & s, James E., gct Shawnee MM, Kans.
1873, 4, 18. James & Clinton recrq
1873, 4, 18. Charles recrq
1873, 7, 18. Nancy & dt, Rebecca Jane, rocf Clear Creek MM, O., dtd 1873,6,14
1878, 3, 15. Nancy, Rebecca Jane & Thomas C. rocf Clear Creek MM, O., dtd 1878,1,12
1889, 4, 13. Mary R. recrq
1889, 6, 8. Otis L. rocf Dover MM, O.
1898, 5, 14. Emma C. rocf Dover MM, O., dtd 1898,3,17
1898, 7, 9. James S. gct White Water MM,Ind.
1903, 2, 14. Clinton dropped from mbrp
1907, 4, 13. James Ridgley relrq
1907, 5, 11. Otis dropped from mbrp
1907, 5, 11. Ralph & Edith recrq
1912, 1, 13. Alvida rocf Dover MM
1913, 11, 12. Edward rocf Dover MM
1915, 1, 13. Orian rocf Dover MM
1921, 2, 9. Charles relrq
1921, 4, 13. Jennie & Elizabeth roc

HAYS
1889, 6, 8. Maria Walker gct Newberry MM,O.
1921, 4, 13. Erskine R., Ethel & Mildred [Hayes] recrq

HAZARD
----, --, --. Allen m Ann K. HADLEY b 1830,3,2
Ch: Gulia R. b 1854, 6, 6 d 1878, 2,20
Lydia Jane " 1857, 1, 19
Harriet H. " 1859, 7, 27 " 1885, 9,20
1905, 8, 3. Frank O., s Ethelbert & Nellie, b
1910, 5, 10. Mary Ellen, dt Earnest & Pearle, b
1911, 8, 6. Allen E., s Ethelbert & Nellie, b
1914, 8, 12. Mary m Horace TOWNSEND
1919, 8, 2. Ruth d
1920, 4, 6. Louella d
1921, 10, 24. Amy Ellen d
1926, 4, 10. Frank T. d
1926, 10, 19. Seth d
1931, 9, 20. Barbara Lee, dt Allen & Elizabeth (Irvin), b

1876, 4, 14. Seth recrq
1890, 9, 13. Frank & w, Louella J., & ch, Loren & Ethelbert, rocf Center MM
1895, 7, 13. Rtth A. & Emma rocf Springfield MM, O., dtd 1895,6,15
1901, 8, 10. Loren W. relrq
1902, 11, 8. Amy Ellen recrq
1906, 6, 9. Clara rocf Center MM, O., dtd 1906,5,16
1907, 11, 9. Pearle Certain recrq
1910, 11, 2. Ernest & w, Pearl, & ch, Mary Ellen, gct Newberry MM, O.
1913, 1, 8. Herbert & w, Flora, & ch, Clifton & Mary, rocf Center MM, O., dtd 1912, 12,18
1925, 4, 8. Ernest R. & w, Pearl, & ch, Mary Ellen & Roberta, rocf Newberry MM,O., dtd 1925,3,15
1931, 1, 14. Elizabeth Irwin recrq

HECKLEY
1928, 12, 3. Fred Jr. m Helen Leroy LINTON

HELMS
1880, 5, 14. Geo. W. recrq

HEMPSTEAD
1913, 4, 14. David Kinkead recrq

HENLEY
1923, 2, 14. Marvin rocf Deep River MM, N.C.
1926, 1, 13. Marvin J. relrq

HENRY
1906, 9, 10. Wm. Sr. d ae 68
1909, 9, 20. Wm. d ae 33
1930, 8, 4. Julia d

1884, 5, 15. William & s, Chas. A., Junius & Wm., recrq
1884, 5, 15. Julia A. rocf Dover MM, O., dtd 1884,5,15
1893, 12, 9. Wm. A. & w, Julia, & s, Wm., gct Clear Creek MM, O.
1895, 10, 12. Wm. & w, Julia, & ch, Wm., rocf Clear Creek MM, O., dtd 1895,9,14
1900, 3, 10. Wm. A. relrq
1905, 11, 11. Wm. Jr. recrq
1907, 4, 13. Charles dropped from mbrp

HEWES
1873, 4, 18. Susan recrq

HIATT
1910, 12, 29. Burritt m Pearl PEELLE
1911, 1, 11. Oliver m Alice LUKINS
1911, 6, 14. Harold C. m Georgianna BARRETT
----, --, --. Dorothy, dt Harold & Georgiana, b 1912,4,1 d 1912,4,6
----, --, --. Robert Barrett, s Harold C. & Georgianna (Barrett), b 1913,9,7 d 1913,9, 20
1914, 1, 1. Richard Mills, s Burrett & Pearl, b
1915, 3, 21. Charles Everett, s Oliver & Alice L., b
1915, 7, --. Harold d
1919,10, 22. Donald L., s Oliver & Alice L., b
1917, 4, 30. Robert Burritt, s Burritt & Pearl, b
1918, 2, 27. Anna Jean, dt Geo. A. & Bessie (Statler), b
1920, 7, 10. Howard Allen, s Geo. A. & Bessie (Statler), b
1921, 10, 15. Harold, s Burritt & Pearl, b
1921, 2, 20. Georgiana m Howard HUDSON
1921, 10, 29. Emily Jean, dt Russell & Della (Hadley) b
1922, 12, 16. Chas. d

1879, 1, 17. Amos J. & w, Martha, & ch, Thomas Lincoln, Emily Alace, Anna Jane, Willie Grant, Minnie Isabel & Bertha May, rocf Clear Creek MM, O.
1880, 10, 15. Amos J. & w, Martha, & ch, Thomas L., Emily A., Annie J., Wm. G., Minnie B. & Bertha M., gct Union MM, Minn.
1886, 12, 11. Edwin J. rocf Newberry MM, O., dtd 1886,10,18
1894, 2, 10. Duella rocf Newberry MM, O., dtd 1894,12,2
1899, 4, 8. Angeline rocf Center MM, O., dtd 1899,3,15
1903, 12, 12. Oliver recrq
1911, 11, 11. Georgianna B. rocf Fairfield MM, O., dtd 1911,10,21
1912, 2, 10. Pearl Peelle rocf Grassy Run MM, O.
1912, 12, 14. Howard Allen recrq of parents
1912, 12, 11. Charles C. recrq
1916, 7, 12. George A. recrq
1927, 4, 13. George & Bessie Statler, & ch, Anna Jean & Howard Allen, gct Xenia MM,O.
1929, 3, 13. George & w, Bessie S., & ch, Anne Jean & Howard Allen, rocf Xenia MM,O.

HIBBEN
1873, 4, 18. Patience M. recrq
1874, 10, 16. Patience M. gct Cincinnati MM,O.; returned because she wished to join M. E. Ch.
1875, 2, 19. Patience M. relrq

HILDEBRANT
1912, 3, 29. Henry m Elizabeth W. MILLER
1873, 4, 18. Thomas Q. [Hildebrandt] recrq
1874, 10, 16. T. Q. [Hildebrandt] gct Cincinnati MM, O.
1918, 6, 12. Elizabeth W. gct Leesburg MM

HILDRETH
1885, 7, 11. Sarah E. gct Newberry MM, O.
1898, 2, 12. Sarah gct West Fork MM, O.

HILL
1908, 9, 30. Katharyn m Lynn F. VANCE

1871, 11, 17. Louisa rocf Greenwich MM, dtd 1871,10,12
1873, 4, 18. Emma recrq
1881, 6, 17. John recrq
1886, 4, 10. Bertha recrq
1886, 5, 8. Wm. A. recrq
1890, 3, 8. Mariah recrq
1890, 5, 10. Alice recrq
1902, 4, 12. George R. recrq
1907, 5, 11. George R. relrq
1914, 10, 14. Walter recrq

HINES
1871, 7, 8. Charles McKenny, s Jesse & Rachel, b

1870, 4, 15. Jesse & w, Rachel, & ch, Edgar, recrq

HINKSON
1894, 7, 14. Frank & Anna recrq
1895, 2, 9. Maud recrq
1899, 6, 15. Grace recrq
1903, 10, 10. Maud dropped from mbrp
1921, 6, 15. Frank & Anna dropped from mbrp

HINSHAW
----, --, --. Ethel b 1877,8,15 d 1879,7,26 bur West Burough, O.
1903, 1, 22. Maria H. d ae 66

1874, 4, 17. Garner & w, Maria H., & ch, Annie, Orris & Elva, rocf Newberry MM, O., dtd 1874,3,23

HIRT
1912, 3, 11. Ernest m Florence HANNAH
1913, 4, 30. James Edwin, s Florence, b
1917, 12, 17. Grace m Carey HOLADAY

1904, 1, 9. Valentine gct Dover MM, O.
1913, 5, 14. James Edwin, s Florence, recrq
1915, 4, 14. Valentine & w, Alida, & s, Ernest, rocf Dover MM

HITCH
1894, 7, 14. John C. & Laura recrq
1894, 7, 14. Thomas B. & W. Vernon recrq
1906, 10, 13. John, Laura & Thomas B. dropped from mbrp
1921, 6, 15. Vernon dropped from mbrp

HOAG
1873, 3, 14. Anna recrq
1874, 10, 16. Lewis A. Estes & w, Huldah C., & s, Thos. Rowland, & niece, Anna J. Hoag, gct Westfield MM, Ind.

HOCKETT
----, --, --. John m Mary Ann GREEN b 1834,1, 22
Ch: John
Alpheus b 1856, 5, 27
Nancy Jane " 1861, 3, 31
1875, 8, 3. Loucinda d bur Westboro
1876, 10, 20. Louisė d bur Westboro
1877, 3, 24. Elizabeth d bur Sugar Grove
1916, --, --. Edith m Carey V. HODGSON

1870, 3, 18. Elizabeth recrq
1873, 4, 18. Lou recrq
1873, 6, 20. Amos rocf Newberry MM, O., dtd 1873,4,21
1874, 4, 17. Lewis & w, Lucinda, & dt, Clara, rocf Newberry MM, O., dtd 1874,3,23
1883, 8, 17. Francis L. & w, Rachel, & ch, Hattie E. & Homer C., rocf Newberry MM,O., dtd 1883,7,23
1883, 8, 17. David rocf Newberry MM, O., dtd 1883,7,23
1883, 10, 19. Sarah rocf Newberry MM, O., dtd 1883,9,17
1886, 5, 8. Frank & fam gct Dover MM, O.
1886, 5, 8. David gct Dover MM, O.

HODGE
1914, 10, 14. Howard recrq
1921, 6, 15. Howard dropped from mbrp

HODGIN
1913, 3, 18. Samuel Horace Jr., s Samuel H. & Olive J., b

1912, 10, 9. Samuel H. & w, Olive J., & dt, Olive M., rocf Newgarden MM, N. C.
1915, 9, 18. Samuel H. & w, Olive J., & ch, Olive Marion & Samuel H., Jr., gct Greensboro MM, N. C.

HODGSON
1916, --, --. Carey V. m Edith HOCKETT

1904, 11, 12. Carrie V. rocf Washington, D. C.
1920, 4, 14. Carey relrq

HODSON
1926, 1, 1. Luranna m Azariah FISHER

1902, 3, 8. J. recrq
1921, 3, 9. Helen recrq
1921, 3, 9. Harry recrq
1921, 3, 9. Jennie recrq

HOLADAY
1897, 12, 3. Wm. [Holiday] d ae 30
1909, 5, 1. Frederick Samuel [Holoday], s Robert & Bessie, b
1913, 10, 7. Ruth [Holoday] m Ashley INWOOD
1917, 1, 19. Samuel d
1917, 3, 21. Nellie m L. O. PAGE
1917, 12, 17. Carey m Grace HIRT
1918, 8, 10. Jesse m Golda ARROWSMITH
1922, 6, 29. Patience d
1929, 11, 29. Ross [Holliday] d

1871, 1, 20. Jesse F. [Halliday] & w, Ruth, & ch, James W., Lorenzo D., Hiram E., Amanda, Jesse H. & Alvah, rocf Newberry MM, O., dtd 1870,12,19
1872, 12, 20. Jesse F. [Holliday] & w, Ruth, & ch, James W., Lorenzo D., Hiram E., Amanda, Jesse H. & Alva, gct Newberry MM,O.
1881, 5, 20. Jesse F. [Holiday] & w, Ruth, & ch, Jesse Jr. & Alvah, rocf Newberry MM, O., dtd 1881,3,21
1883, 11, 16. Asa [Holiday] rocf Newberry MM, O., dtd 1883,11,22
1889, 3, 9. Mahalah & ch, Naomi Belle & Lillie Maud, recrq
1889, 3, 9. Wm. [Holiday] recrq
1898, 2, 12. Asa [Holiday] gct Fairfield MM, O.
1898, 2, 12. Lilly [Holiday] gct Fairfield MM, O.
1902, 4, 12. Susie [Holoday] relrq
1903, 2, 14. Asa & Lilly Maud gct Fairfield MM, O.
1903, 6, 13. Samuel [Holiday] & w, Patience, rocf West Fork MM, O., dtd 1903,5,16
1903, 9, 12. Alva relrq
1903, 10, 10. Ross & Lillian [Holiday] rocf West Fork MM, O., dtd 1903,9,19
1903, 12, 12. Robert [Holliday] rocf West Fork MM, O., dtd 1903,11,21
1904, 4, 9. Leona, DeWitt, Jesse & Camella [Holliday] dropped from mbrp
1907, 6, 8. Anna Osborn [Holoday] relrq
1910, 8, 13. Charles [Holladay] & w, Nora, & ch, Nellie & Wm., rocf Clear Creek MM, O.
1911, 12, 9. Nancy [Holoday] & dt, Ruth, rocf Clear Creek MM, O.
1915, 7, 14. Hattie [Holladay] recrq
1917, 3, 14. Elizabeth rocf West Fork MM,O., dtd 1917,2,17
1920, 12, 8. Nancy J. [Holoday] gct San Diego MM, Calif.
1921, 6, 15. Gold Arrosmith [Holoday] dropped from mbrp
1922, 6, --. Charles, Nora, William & Nellie gct Beech Grove MM, Ind.
1925, 2, 11. Robert E. [Holliday] & w, Bessie, & ch, Robert & Fredrick, gct Kokomo MM, Ind.

HOLE
1903, 10, 10. Frank rocf West Fork MM, O., dtd 1903,9,19

HOLE, continued
1921, 6, 15. Frank dropped from mbrp

HOLLINGSWORTH
----, --, --. Enoch b 1837,5,3; m Hestar A. ----- b 1839,12,22
Ch: Ella b 1861, 1, 20
Inez " 1869, 9, 9

1870, 2, 18. Enoch & w, Hester Ann, & ch, Ella & Inez, rocf Center MM, O., dtd 1870, 1,12.
1875, 5, 14. Enoch & w, Hester, & ch, Ella & Inez, gct Green Plain MM, O.
1881, 5, 20. J. Furnas & w, Susannah, & ch, Idella, Clifford, Mary L. W. & Eber rocf Miami MM, O., dtd 1881,3,23
1882, 2, 17. J. Furnas & w, Susannah P., & ch, Adella, Clifford, Mary L. W. & Eber, gct Miami MM, O.

HOLMES
1915, 6, 21. Raymond Waldo b
1931, 7, 13. David Ira, s Frank & Faye, b

1914, 4, 8. Margaret recrq
1914, 4, 8. Elizabeth recrq
1921, 3, 9. Frank & Otho Eugene recrq
1921, 3, 9. Faye recrq
1921, 4, 13. Eldon recrq

HOLTON
1907, 10, 12. Estella Custis rocf Clear Creek MM, O.

HONSTETT
1854, 1, 11. Adam b

HOOP
1914, 5, --. Shirley Maude m Harry D. Vance
1909, 3, 13. Bell, Zora, Shirley Maude & Marie J. recrq

HOOTEN
1893, 11, 11. Ellen rocf Springfield MM, O., dtd 1893,10,21
1893, 12, 9. Cressa Mildred, dt Ellen, recrq
1895, 1, 12. Ellen (Hooten) Cast & dt, Cressie Mildred Hooten, gct Springfield MM,O.

HOOVER
1909, 4, 17. Lorna m Richard BELL
1911, 12, 8. Grove m Alvada MORTON
1916, 9, 25. Ella d
1923, 1, 19. Milton d

1903, 4, 11. Milton & w, Ella, rocf Dover MM, O., dtd 1903,2,19
1903, 6, 13. Grover E., s Milton & Ella, recrq
1917, 5, 9. Arvada recrq

HOPERT
1902, 3, 8. Sadie L. recrq
1903, 10, 10. Sadie S. dropped from mbrp

HORNADAY
----, --, --. Ezekiel b 1796,2,26 d 1885,8,29; m Elizabeth HADLEY
Ch: John b 1820, 2, 29
Ezekiel m 2nd Hannah Clark MENDENHALL, b 1804,4,22
----, --, --. John b 1820,2,29 d 1887,8,4; m Martha KERSEY
Ch: Anna E. b 1850, 7, 26
John m 2nd Mary BAILEY d 1886,8,24
Ch: Daniel
Allen b 1869, 8, 24
E. Albert " 1872, 5, 9
----, --, --. Isaiah b 1823,7,19; m Mary Jane WATSON b 1837,11,17
Ch: John W. b 1874, 6, 8
George " 1875, 10, 18

1885, 4, 11. John & w, Mary, & ch, Allen & Albert, rocf Springfield MM, O., dtd 1885,2,21
1907, 4, 13. Albert dropped from mbrp

HORMELL
1921, 4, 13. Robert & Roy [Hornell] recrq
1926, 3, 31. Roy dropped from mbrp
1927, 2, 16. Robert relrq

HORSEMAN
1897, 10, 9. Lewis [Horsman] d ae 57
1902, 6, 18. Everett d
1914, 4, 14. Susanna d
1932, 7, 14. Alice d

1874, 3, 20. Lewis & w, Susanna, & ch, John E. & George E., recrq
1893, 2, 11. Alice recrq
1903, 2, 14. George E. dropped from mbrp
1907, 5, 11. Russel dropped from mbrp

HORTON
1920, 5, 12. George recrq

HOSKINS
----, --, --. Isaac b 1809,11,7 d 1873,11,17; m Anna ----- b 1815,5,25 d 1879,4,12 bur Mathiesville, O.
----, --, --. Josiah b 1831,8,14; m Martha A. ----- b 1839,7,14
Ch: Horace E. b 1859, 12, 21
Elijah " 1864, 7, 19
Gertrude " 1868, 3, 6
Isaac Russell
1874, 4, 13. Russell d
1915, 3, 13. Martha d

1879, 7, 18. Isaac gct Dover MM, O.
1906, 3, 10. Clarence & w, Nettie, rocf Dover MM, O., dtd 1906,2,15

HOSKINS, continued
1908, 10, 10. Clarence & Nettie K. relrq
1930, 11, 12. Mary B. & Mildred rocf Fairview MM
1930, 12, 10. Mary Elizabeth recrq

HOUP
1909, 3, 6. Kate d ae 58
1921, 3, 26. Daniel d

1909, 2, 13. Daniel rocf Sabina MM, O.
1909, 2, 13. Kate & Mabel rocf Sabina MM, O.

HOUSTET
1873, 5, 16. Adam gct Union MM, O.

HOWELL
----, --, --. Aaron b 1827,5,5; m Louisa MILLER b 1829,7,24
Ch: Isabella b 1856, 2, 14

----, --, --. John K. b 1840,5,31; m Sallie ANSON b 1839,5,14
Ch: Flora E. b 1861, 12, 16
Benjamin L." 1863, 11, 2
Mary A. " 1865, 11, 11
Francis B. " 1868, 3, 2
Emeline M. " 1870, 2, 22
Lutie A. " 1872, 4, 7
Charles H. " 1874, 2, 20
Everett C. " 1876, 4, 17

1892, 3, 12. John K. [Howel] & w, Sallie, recrq
1903, 10, 10. Rosa recrq
1909, 4, 10. Daisy [Howel] gct Center MM,O.

HUCKNEY
1870, 3, 18. James L. recrq

HUDSON
1921, 2, 20. Howard m Georgiana HIATT
1922, 2, 7. Phebe, dt Howard & Georgiana, b

1921, 3, 9. Carrie Ellen & Helen Louise, recrq
1921, 3, 9. Helen recrq
1927, 6, 8. Carrie Ellen recrq

HUFFMAN
1902, 5, 21. Kate d ae 52
1917, 3, 19. Christopher d
1920, 2, 1. Amos d

1891, 11, 14. Amos & w, Kate W., & ch, Willie & Minnie, rocf Springfield MM, O., dtd 1891,9,19
1891, 11, 14. Grace B. rocf Springfield MM,O., dtd 1891,9,19
1899, 4, 8. Christopher & w, Harriett, rocf Center MM, O., dtd 1899,3,15
1921, 6, 15. William dropped from mbrp

HUGHES
1883, 4, 20. Wm. Clifford [Hughie] recrq
1889, 4, 13. Edward W. recrq
1892, 9, 10. Edward W. gct West Fork MM, O.
1898, 4, 9. Wm. C. dropped from mbrp
1904, 6, 11. Ethel Pidgeon rocf Dover MM,O.
1917, 9, 12. Katherine recrq
1928, 2, 8. J. Elza recrq
1929, 6, 12. Mary Bracney dropped from mbrp

HULS
1919, 2, 8. Ella d

1885, 5, 9. Jane G. [Hulse] recrq
1898, 5, 14. James G. dropped from mbrp
1898, 10, 8. Samuel W. & w, Blanch, recrq
1903, 12, 12. Samuel W. [Hulls] & w, Blanch, & Vesta Mildred & Gertrude Elizabeth, relrq
1911, 7, 8. E. Ella recrq

HUMPHREY
1926, 10, 7. Bertha m Albert FISHER

1920, 4, 14. W. H. & w, Sarah, & ch, Chas. L., Jehua M., Walter J. & Freda N., rocf Ogden MM, O.

HUNNICUTT
1897, 9, 8. Anna E. d ae 41
1898, 6, 12. Harley E. d ae 19
1916, 11, 14. Susanna, dt Franklin & Lura, b
1919, 9, 5. Thomas Dick, s Walter & Margery, b
1922, 5, 29. Mary d
1926, 12, 24. Wilson d

1872, 4, 19. William P. recrq
1882, 12, 15. Wm. P. relrq
1895, 9, 14. Thomas E. & w, Anna E., & ch, Orville B. & Harley D., rocf Dover MM, O., dtd 1895,8,10
1896, 9, 12. Lura T. gct Dover MM, O.
1900, 8, 11. Thomas E. gct Marion MM, Ind.
1902, 2, 8. Wm. P. recrq
1903, 2, 14. W. P. dropped from mbrp
1906, 2, 10. Orville B. & Myra L. relrq
1906, 4, 14. Anna P. dropped from mbrp
1912, 1, 13. Franklin & w, Lura, & ch, Mary Pauline, Leslie Thomas & Priscilla M., rocf Sabina MM, O., dtd 1911,11,15
1914, 4, 8. Wilson & Mary rocf Dover MM
1919, 6, 11. Margaret & dt, Margory Jean, recrq
1914, 10, 14. Charles E. & w, Delena, & ch, Walter & Robert, rocf Dover MM
1921, 3, 9. Linton relrq
1921, 5, 11. Frank, Lura, Priscilla & Sussanna, gct Dover MM
1923, 1, 10. Frank & w, Lura, & ch, Priscilla & Susanna, rocf Dover MM
1929, 3, 13. Linton & w, Catherine, & ch, Eleanor Kathryn & Ann Linton, recrq

HUNT
1904, 8, 28. Mary E. d ae 61
1914, 1, 18. Thomas I. d
1918, 10, 14. Jacob G. d

1892, 5, 14. T. E. gct Chicago MM, Ill.
1893, 11, 11. Jacob G. & w, Sarah T., & s, Luther M., rocf Newberry MM, O., dtd 1893, 10,23
1894, 9, 8. Thomas I. & w, Mary E., recrq
1903, 10, 10. Luther M. gct Newberry MM, O.
1912, 11, 13. Arthur rocf West Fork MM, O., dtd 1912,11,16
1919, 5, 21. Helen C. & Dorothy recrq

HURLEY
1917, 9, 12. Edgar rocf Caesars Creek MM, O.

HUTCH
1889, 3, 9. Neva recrq

HUTCHINSON
1840, 2, 26. William, s Benjamin & Fanny, b
----, --, --. George & Sarah
Ch: Oscar b 1860, 3, 18
Elizabeth " 1858, 9, 10

HUXTABLE
1904, 8, 13. Mary F. relrq

INKS
1921, 7, 20. George m Vesta Eleanor MILLER

1929, 12, 10. Vesta Miller dropped from mbrp

INWOOD
1913, 10, 7. Ashley m Ruth HOLODAY

1920, 12, 8. Ruth H. gct San Diago MM, Calif.

IRELAND
1916, 5, 24. U. S. m Mabel Alice HADLEY

1895, 4, 13. Estella recrq
1929, 10, 9. Jane recrq of parents

IRONS
1874, 3, 20. Ella recrq

IRVIN
1919, 12, 22. Eldora McMillan d
1924, 9, 26. George B. d

1873, 4, 18. Loyal recrq
1878, 3, 15. Loyal dis
1915, 9, 18. Eldora rocf Newberry MM, O., dtd 1915,6,17
1916, 3, 8. George rocf Ogden MM, O.

JACKS
1883, 5, 18. Lizzie recrq
1884, 5, 15. Lizzie relrq
1884, 10, 17. Wm. rocf Dover MM
1907, 3, 9. Wm. dropped from mbrp

JACKSON
1874, 11, 20. Mary recrq

JACOB
1927, 8, 20. Hildegarde m Robert FARQUHAR

1927, 6, 29. Robert Hamilton Farquhar gct 12th St. MM, Phila., to m R. Hildegarde Jacob

JAMES
----, --, --. David b 1803,5,11; m Deborah S. ----- b 1812,10,26

----, --, --. Jonathan H. b 1835,4,4; m Mary J. ----- b 1836,10,15
Ch: Elvin H. b 1857, 9, 6
William L. " 1861, 2, 6 d 1862,12, 17
Lydia Frances b 1864, 10, 22
----- " 1873, 7, 28
1931, 7, 6. Ester Ann d

1868, 12, 15. Jonathan & w, Mary Jane, & ch, Elva H. & Lydia Frances, rocf Newberry MM, O., dtd 1868,11,23
1869, 2, 16. David & w, Deborah, rocf Newberry MM, O., dtd 1869,1,18
1875, 4, 16. Jonathan H. & w, Mary Jane, & ch, Elvin H. & Lydia Frances, gct Union MM, Minn.
1876, 2, 18. David & w, Deborah, gct Clear Creek MM, O.
1876, 5, 19. Mary recrq
1898, 2, 12. Naomi gct Fairfield MM, O.
1898, 6, 11. Ann C. rocf Ogden MM, O., dtd 1898,5,27
1898, 9, 10. Ann C. rocf Clear Creek MM,O., dtd 1898,8,13
1914, 10, 14. Raymond recrq
1924, 5, 14. Marie recrq

JANNEY
1923, 8, 8. Jeanette m Loren HADLEY

1883, 11, 16. Rebecca Ann & s, Reynolds, rocf Newberry MM, O., dtd 1883,10,22
1888, 7, 14. Rebecca A. & s, Reynolds, relrq

JANUARY
1902, 5, 10. Garnet recrq
1902, 5, 10. Clara Padget rocf Dover MM, O.
1906, 2, 10. Garnett P. gct Dover MM, O.
1908, 7, 11. Anna Linton relrq

JARVIS
1909, 4, 10. Olive Ballard relrq

JAY
1907, 1, 12. Mary Ethel Green gct Newberry

JAY, continued
MM, O.
1916, 1, 12. J. Edwin & w, Alice W., & s, Howard rocf Newgarden MM, N. C.

JEFFRIES
1918, 4, 2. Leslie D. m Verna DABE
1923, 1, 21. Julian, dt Leslie & Verna (Doak) b
1926, 1, 21. Peytan d
1928, 10, 17. Joshua d
1928, 12, 25. Wayne d

1892, 11, 12. Joshua & w, Lydia, & ch, I. J., Eulalia P., Wayne W., Anna M. & Luther, rocf Center MM, O., dtd 1892,10,12
1914, 3, 11. Leslie Darlington [Jefferis] recrq
1914, 5, 13. Preston rocf Center MM, O., dtd 1914,4,15
1919, 5, 21. Norma & Maynard [Jefferis] recrq
1929, 4, 10. Leslie & w, Verna D., & ch, Julianna, gct Whittier MM, Calif.

JENKINS
1903, 3, 3. Chas. M. d ae 48
1912, 6, 12. Anna m Percy GREEN
1917, 1, 15. Annie d
1922, 9, 2. Bevan m Frances WILSON

1873, 3, 14. Daniel recrq
1880, 4 16. Martha J. recrq
1885, 7, 11. Daniel & w gct Minneapolis MM, Minn.
1888, 4, 14. George recrq
1889, 4, 13. Josephine & ch, Salathiel, Augustine S., Omer E., Mildred V. & Street, recrq
1895, 6, 8. John recrq
1900, 4, 14. Chas. M. recrq
1906, 2, 10. John L. & Anna recrq
1906, 5, 12. John gct Center MM, O.
1906, 10, 13. George & w, Josephine, & ch, Salathiel, Augustine S., Omer E., Mildred V. & Street, gct Xenia MM, O.
1907, 4, 13. Martha dropped from mbrp
1913, 10, 18. Beven recrq
1914, 5, 13. David & Hallie recrq
1924, 3, 12. Bevan gct Kokomo MM, Ind.
1925, 12, 9. John L. relrq

JENKS
1849, 2, 2. Mariah, dt Lorenzo & Jedida Ann, b

1913, 3, 12. Dorothy Lucile recrq

JENNINGS
1898, 6, 11. Alice Peelle rocf Dover MM, O., dtd 1898,4,14

JOB
1834, 7, 9. Andrew, s Elbert & Rebecca, b
1877, 5, 18. Martha [Jobe] recrq
1886, 4, 10. Clara recrq
1903, 1, 10. Martha [Jobe] dropped from mbrp

JOHNSON
----, --, --. Alfred b 1825,10,28; m Anna M. ----- b 1827,2,19
Ch: Isaac T. b 1858, 2, 6
James B. " 1860, 4, 9
John W. " 1861, 12, 23
Anna Mary " 1868, 5, 25
Charlie F. " 1870, 8, 20
----, --, --. Joseph R. b 1852,5,26; m Minerva Isabel BENNETT b 1852,8,12
Ch: Irvin H. b 1875, 11, 18
Mary G. " 1877, 7, 2
1917, 1, 2. Ralph m Alice Doan GREENE
1923, 8, 18. Elmer F. m Myra PROBASCO
1929, 6, 8. Eleanor m Miles L. PEELLE
1932, 1, 31. Stanley L. m Helen Wright SNYDER
1932, 9, 27. J. Will d

1870, 7, 15. Alfred & w, Anna, & ch, Isaac Thorn, James Brooks, John William & Anna Mary, rocf Kokomo MM, Ind., dtd 1870,7,6
1877, 2, 16. Jared L. recrq
1878, 4, 19. Alfred rocf Columbus MM, O., dtd 1878,4,3
1879, 7, 18. Alfred relrq
1880, 8, 20. Isaac T. gct Clear Creek MM, O.
1880, 9, 17. Anna M. & ch, James B., John W., Anna Mary & Charles, gct Clear Creek MM,O.
1883, 4, 20. Sarah Ellen recrq
1883, 4, 20. Mary Elizabeth recrq
1884, 2, 15. J. L. dis
1885, 4, 11. Charles recrq
1888, 4, 14. Junius recrq
1888, 4, 14. Mrs. E. [Johnston] & dt, Icy Ellis, recrq
1899, 6, 15. Minnie Smith gct Newberry MM,O.
1900, 6, 9. Margaret A. rocf Center MM, O., dtd 1900,4,18
1900, 11, 10. Joseph R. & w, Isabel, rocf Springfield MM, O., dtd 1900,10,20
1900, 11, 10. Mary A. rocf Springfield MM,O., dtd 1900,10,20
1901, 3, 9. Fletcher recrq
1902, 10, 11. Joseph & fam gct Dover MM, O.
1903, 1, 10. Junius E. dropped from mbrp
1903, 12, 12. John H. & w, Sarah M., recrq
1904, 4, 9. John recrq
1906, 12, 8. Isaac T. rocf Frankford MM, Pa.
1907, 10, 12. Charles F. rocf Sterling MM, Kans.
1908, 3, 4. J. Will rocf Clear Creek MM, O.
1909, 8, 14. John H. & w, Sarah, gct Springfield MM
1911, 8, 12. Margaret A. gct Center MM, O.
1913, 2, 12. Dora recrq
1915, 4, 14. Charles & Ethel & s, Carshall, rocf Center MM, O., dtd 1915,3,17
1921, 6, 15. John dropped from mbrp
1926, 9, 8. Mary Catharine Price recrq of

JOHNSON, continued
foster parents, Wm. & Clara Johnson
1928, 3, 14. Ralph recrq
1929, 12, 10. Dora dropped from mbrp

JONES
----, --, --. Ethelbert b 1826,9,28 d 1907,8,29; m Sarah A. SEVAN b 1836,6,20 (Ethelbert d ae 80)
Ch: Frank b 1852, 5, 8
Louella C. " 1858, 1, 5
Anna May " 1861, 6, 22
Charles W. " 1864, 2, 22
Hattie C. " ----, 2, 28
1874, 2, 27. Eleanor d
1878, 4, 4. Rebecca E. d bur Sugar Grove
1899, 9, 23. Henry H. d ae 70
1900, 6, 5. Mary d ae 71
1908, 8, 25. Louis T. m Viola McMILLAN
1909, 6, 15. Pauline m Willis CRITES
1917, 3, 12. Helena Elizabeth d
1917, 5, 16. Lula m A. L. SENMAN
1927, 3, 4. Austin d
1931, 10, 3. Sarah d

1871, 2, 17. Cynthia & ch, Joseph E., George C. & John Howard, rocf Center MM, O., dtd 1871,2,15
1873, 3, 14. Henry recrq
1873, 3, 14. Emma recrq
1873, 3, 14. Sarah A. recrq
1873, 3, 14. Mary recrq
1873, 4, 18. Eleanor recrq
1873, 4, 18. Frank recrq
1873, 4, 18. Henry P. recrq
1873, 4, 18. Ethelbert recrq
1873, 4, 18. Sarah A. recrq
1873, 8, 15. Ethelbert & w, Sarah A., & ch, Franklin, Luella, Kate, Annie Mary, Chas. Wm. & Hattie Clifford, gct Springfield MM, O.
1874, 3, 20. Richard & w, Mary Elizabeth, & ch, Wm. Arthur, John Albert, Jemima Jane, Martha Estella, Daniel Henry, Flora & Leonard, rocf Fairview MM, dtd 1874,2,21
1874, 6, 19. Clinton recrq
1877, 11, 16. Henry P. dis
1879, 5, 16. Richard & w, Mary E., & ch, Martha Estella, Daniel H., Florie Leonard, Oscar & Milton, gct Fairview MM, Ill.
1879, 5, 16. Jemima Jane gct Fairview MM,Ill.
1885, 7, 11. Eleanor gct Kokomo MM, Ind.
1891, 7, 11. Micajah Jr. & Cynthia recrq
1893, 9, 9. Sarah A. recrq
1894, 7, 14. Bert L. recrq
1894, 7, 14. Eugene H. recrq
1894, 7, 14. Louis recrq
1894, 7, 14. Leon recrq
1897, 1, 9. E. Townsend & w, Rachel, recrq
1898, 2, 12. E. Townsend & w, Rachel, gct Center MM, O.
1898, 4, 9. Frank dropped from mbrp
1904, 3, 12. Bertrand L. relrq
1904, 5, 14. Austin & w, Edith, recrq
1904, 5, 14. Pauline & Mildred recrq
1905, 11, 11. Ethelbert & w, Sarah, rocf Ogden MM, O., dtd 1905,11,25
1907, 4, 13. Geo. C. dropped from mbrp
1907, 5, 11. Clinton dropped from mbrp
1907, 5, 11. Cynthia relrq
1910, 2, 10. E. Harold gct Indianapolis MM, Ind.
1910, 8, 13. Harold Joshua, s Louis & Viola, recrq
1910, 8, 13. Louis T. & s, Harold J., gct Oskaloosa MM, Ia.
1913, 4, 14. Wilbur recrq
1914, 1, 14. Lulu & ch, Helena Elizabeth & Mabel Catherine, recrq
1914, 10, 14. Bertha recrq
1921, 5, 11. Mabel Paine relrq
1923, 4, 11. Lucretia Bailey relrq
1929, 12, 10. Edith dropped from mbrp
1932, 3, 23. Dorothy recrq

KANE
1855, 1, 1. Simon, s Francis & Mary, b

KELLER
1908, 4, 5. Katharine Pauline, dt Karl & Charlotte, b

1921, 12, 14. Katharine [Kellar] relrq

KELSEY
1920, 8, 26. Ruth m Pearl ROBUCK
----, --, --. Hadley & Stella
Ch: Alma
Louise b 1926, 12, 15
David Culver " 1929, 2, 9

1920, 5, 12. Hadley & w, Estella, & ch, Lewis & Edwin, roc
1922, 7, 12. Robert rocf W. Richland MM,Ind.
1927, 10, 12. Robert M. relrq
1932, 8, 10. Anna L. rocf Plainfield MM,Ind.

KELSO
1898, 5, 5. Peter d ae 79
1915, 11, 17. Rachel d

1877, 2, 16. Peter & w, Rachel, recrq

KELLIS
1884, 3, 14. Eliza recrq

KELLY
1914, 6, 24. Mary Evelyn m Francis H. FARQUHAR
1915, 1, 2. Madora m Walter LINTON
1916, 9, 20. Russell m Myrtle STACKHOUSE
1916, 11, 26. Masie m Almon CARTER
1919, 5, 29. Thomas R. m Lael LACY

1891, 10. 10. Mariam recrq

KELLY, continued
1898, 4, 9. Mariam dropped from mbrp
1904, 2, 13. Dora E. rocf Londonderry MM, O.
1904, 2, 13. Mary E. rocf Londonderry MM, O.
1904, 2, 13. Thomas R. rocf Londonderry MM,O.
1921, 6, 15. Myrtle Stackhouse dropped from mbrp
1925, 11, 11. Thomas R. gct W. Richmond MM, Ind.

KENNETT
1913, 8, 22. Margaret d
1922, 6, 22. Samantha d

1891, 7, 11. Margaret Ann recrq
1893, 3, 11. Wesley & w, Samantha, recrq
1897, 4, 10. Blanch recrq
1910, 2, 10. Mary recrq
1924, 5, 14. Wesley [Kennet] gct Cuba MM

KENWORTHY
1922, 5, 23. Lenora d

1919, 6, 11. Murray & w, Lenora, & ch, Carroll B., Wilmer & Leonard, rocf Glenn Falls MM, N. Y.
1923, 9, 12. Carroll H. gct New London MM,Ind.
1923, 9, 12. Murray S. & s, Leonard, gct Washington MM, D. C.
1923, 9, 12. Wilmer gct New London MM, Ind.

KERSEY
1829, 4, 3. John, s Thomas & Letitia, b

KERSHNER
1915, 6, --. Hayden m Mary FRANKLIN

1916, 3, 8. Mary Franklin gct University MM, Kans.

KETZEL
1912, 5, 8. Ida Schoonover relrq

KIBBY
1901, 3, 5. Lily d ae 13

1876, 6, 16. Mary E. & ch, Norah B. & Oren, recrq
1900, 1, 13. Ambrose & w, Louisa C., & dt, Laura & Lillie, recrq
1903, 10, 10. Orin dropped from mbrp
1904, 1, 9. Ambrose, Louisa & Laura relrq
1909, 1, 9. Ambrose, Louisa & Laura recrq
1909, 10, 9. Ambrose & w, Louisa, & dt, Laura, gct Center MM, O.

KILDOW
1890, 1, 11. Joseph rocf Centre MM, O., dtd 1889,12,19
1907, 3, 9. James dropped from mbrp

KIMBER
1878, 2, 17. Marmaduke C. d

1875, 7, 16. Marmaduke C. rocf WD MM, Pa.

KIMBROUGH
----, --, --. Thomas m Elizabeth HIATT b 1803,1,15 d 1885,10,4 bur Springfield
Ch: Demetrius b 1839, 2, 23
1851, 5, 17. Louise, dt Jeremiah & Esther, b
----, --, --. John m Demas BEACH b 1817,11,22 d 1895,1,—
Ch: Lawson b 1853, 2, 9
J. Eddie " 1861, 12, 1
----, --, --. Demetrius b 1839,2,23; m Esther C. BANGHAM b 1844,11,21
Ch: Orah M. b 1868, 9, 24
Anna B. " 1870, 2, 4
Esther E. " 1872, 2, 3
----, --, --. Timothy C. m Nancy GREEN b 1849,9,28
Ch: Elva M. b 1870, 10, 5
Clark " 1875, 8, 7
J. Omer " 1876, 9, 5
----, --, --. Jeremiah b 1827,10,14 d 1898,1,16 bur Springfield; m Rhoda E. HADLEY b 1836,7,14 d 1868,3,26
Ch: Willard T. b 1870, 9, 21
Lulu L. " 1872, 6, 12
Clifford E." 1873, 12, 21
Raymond J. " 1875, 6, 9
Ethel M. " 1877, 12, 6
These cannot be ch of the above Rhoda E. if her d date is correct, J.E.McM.

KING
1909, 6, 10. William m May OSBORN
1912, 6, 5. Elizabeth Rogers m Leo J. McCOY

1921, 6, 15. Mae Osborn dropped from mbrp

KINZEL
1909, 11, 17. Dr. m Elsie BAILEY

1919, 5, 14. Elsie Bailey relrq

KIRK
----, --, --. John M. b 1834,9,15; m Mary Emily ----- b 1846,12,18 d 1916,2,--
Ch: Clorena b 1862, 3, 21
Maria " 1863, 10, 8
Sarah " 1865, 9, 28
Wilmer B. " 1872, 5, 23
1901, 3, 8. Mary d ae 82
1902, 12, 16. Jesse d ae 66
1908, 1, 15. John W. d ae 73
1922, 2, 18. Elizabeth d
1931, 12, 31. Angeline d

1868, 6, 16. Mary Emma & ch, Clarinda & Maria, recrq
1873, 7, 18. Elizabeth Ann rocf Centre MM,O., dtd 1873,7,16
1877, 7, 20. Mary recrq
1895, 5, 11. Jesse rocf Center MM, O., dtd 1895,4,17

KIRK, continued
1897, 4, 10. Emory recrq
1897, 4, 10. Warren recrq
1897, 4, 10. Rachel recrq
1900, 5, 12. Emory, Rachel, Warren, Sarah & Stanley, relrq
1913, 3, 12. Elizabeth rocf Center MM, O.
1921, 3, 9. Angeline rocf Center MM, O., dtd 1921,2,16

KIRTLEY
1910, 12, 7. Lottie H. m John McKECKNIE

KITTRELL
1900, 5, 12. John rocf Friendsville MM, Tenn., dtd 1900,5,5

KLINE
1921, 6, --. Mary d

1914, 10, 14. Thelma recrq

KLISE
1929, 12, 6. Mollie m Robert RENNIE

KNIGHT
1925, 1, 14. Hazel Starbuck recrq

KRAMER
1894, 2, 10. Charles & w, Alva, rocf Hopewell MM, O., dtd 1894,2,3
1902, 10, 11. Chas. S. relrq

LACY
1925, 4, 24. Helen d
1927, 10, 21. Richard m Wanda MOON

1873, 4, 18. Sarah A. recrq
1873, 4, 18. Arthur recrq
1874, 3, 20. Thomas recrq
1884, 6, 26. Mary D. rocf Springfield MM,O., dtd 1884,5,17
1898, 8, 13. Thomas dropped from mbrp
1903, 1, 10. Thomas dropped from mbrp
1903, 2, 14. Arthur dropped from mbrp
1903, 9, 12. Helen P. recrq
1921, 6, 15. Charles recrq
1924, 5, 14. Charles relrq

LAMER
1899, 11, 11. Frank S. & w, Zitella, rocf White Water MM, Ind., dtd 1899,10,25
1909, 3, 13. Franklin S. & w, Zitella, & ch, Miriam, gct S. 8th St. MM, Richmond, Ind.

LANCASTER
1885, 5, 9. Mary J. recrq

LANE
1919, 10, 16. Opal m Lawrence DRAKE
1823, 8, 26. Willard Eugene, s Elmer E. & Mary J., b
1912, 11, 13. Elmer recrq
1921, 3, 9. Mary J. rocf Center MM

LANGDON
1918, 5, 31. Mary Mills d

LAPPE
1877, 2, 16. John & Mary recrq
1883, 3, 16. Mary [Lappy] relrq

LARICK
1909, 1, 13. Floyd Charles, s Chas. & Maud, b

1899, 5, 13. Wm. & Ida recrq
1899, 8, 12. Ella relrq
1902, 4, 12. Maude recrq
1902, 7, 12. Charles rocf Clear Creek MM,O.

LAWES
1905, 6, 10. Herbert recrq

LAWSON
1883, 4, 20. Kate recrq
1883, 4, 20. Catharine recrq

LEAMING
1870, 3, 18. Samuel & w, Lydia, & s, Geo. H., recrq
1873, 4, 18. James recrq
1876, 8, 18. James dis
1879, 4, 18. Lydia H. gct Cincinnati MM, O.
1885, 6, 13. Samuel dropped from mbrp

LEE
1906, 3, 10. Ada Elliott rocf Greensboro MM, N. C.
1908, 1, 11. Ada Elliott gct South 8th St. MM, Richmond, Ind.

LEEKA
1922, 6, 28. Ernest m Ada M. ZELLAR

1914, 6, 10. Earnest recrq

LEIGH
1905, 2, 8. Catharine dropped from mbrp

LEMON
1931, 12, 24. Forest m Bertha MATHER

LENNINGER
1921, 6, 15. Rhena C. dropped from mbrp

LEONARD
1922, 11, 25. Calvin B. d
1924, 9, 28. Nancy A. C. d
1928, 12, 25. Emma d

1921, 8, 10. Calvin B. & Nancy A. C. rocf Center MM
1921, 12, 14. Emma rocf Center MM

LEWELLEN
1889, 3, 9. Henry recrq
1889, 3, 9. Edgar recrq
1889, 5, 11. George recrq

LEWIS
1898, 9, 22. Cora M. d ae 36
1917, 2, 8. Walter d
1922, 4, 4. Janetta Davis d

1870, 4, 15. Eva recrq
1873, 4, 18. A. F. & Ida recrq
1877, 12, 14. Emily H. rocf Springfield MM,O., dtd 1877,11,17
1877, 12, 14. Ellis A. rocf Clear Creek MM,O., dtd 1877,11,10
1881, 4, 15. Caleb H. & w, Rhoda A., rocf Saline MM, Ill.
1883, 5, 18. Chas. recrq
1883, 5, 18. Catharine recrq
1886, 12, 11. Isaac & w, Mary Jane, rocf Clear Creek MM, O.
1891, 4, 11. Catherine gct Clear Creek MM,O.
1891, 5, 9. Caleb H. & Rhoda A. gct Hopewell MM, O.
1892, 5, 14. Anna recrq
1898, 4, 9. Anna recrq
1898, 10, 8. Charles R. relrq
1903, 2, 14. Anna, Eva, Ida & Charles dropped from mbrp
1912, 2, 10. Walter C. recrq
1929, 12, 10. Caroline Babb dropped from mbrp

LIGHTNER
1877, 2, 16. S. B. & w, Ada, & ch, Frank & Mertie, recrq

LIMING
1899, 5, 13. Andrew & Daisy recrq
1903, 10, 10. Andrew & Daisy dropped from mbrp

LINKHART
1933, 4, 12. Edith C. & ch, Robert C., Richard N., Luther J. & Edward G., rocf Ogden MM, O., dtd 1933,2,26

LINTON
----, --, --. Cyrus b 1825,4,17 d 1914,3,26; m Eliza ----- b 1830,2,15
Ch: Samuel S. b 1848, 7, 8
Olive " 1855, 6, 18
Lydia " 1859, 9, 12
Edwin C. " 1862, 10, 14
1849, 5, 3. Kate Eldred, w Samuel S., b
1872, 5, 9. Guy, s S. S. & C., b d 1929,10, 31
1902, 8, 3. Eliza H. d ae 73
1909, 12, 23. Madge Osborn m Chas. D. SMITH
1909, 12, 29. Mary Baker m LaRue CARR
1912, 5, 29. Kate D. d
1912, 11, 30. Gertrude d
1915, 1, 2. Walter m Madora KELLY
1918, 1, 28. Joshua d
1920, 9, 4. Arnold m Rose SLIKER
1923, 1, 31. John d
1926, 4, 15. Olive b or d
1928, 12, 3. Helen Leroy m Fred HECKLEY, Jr.
1931, 6, 19. Ada d
1931, 8, 15. Samuel d
1931, 11, 30. Mary B. d
1932, 3, 18. Mary Etta d
1933, 1, 5. Alonzo A. d

1870, 4, 15. Katie recrq
1893, 7, 8. Joshua & w, Olive, & dt, Elsie, rocf Center MM, O., dtd 1893,6,14
1897, 4, 10. Anna M. recrq
1900, 8, 11. Walter & w, Gertrude, & ch, Fred W. & Elanor, rocf Springfield MM, O., dtd 1900,7,21
1902, 7, 12. James M. recrq
1903, 2, 14. Alfred Alonzo & w, Wm., rocf Springfield MM, O.
1903, 2, 14. Mary Butterworth & ch, Arnold Edward & Ethel, recrq
1903, 2, 14. Mary Etta & ch, Henry Jehu & Mary Baker, recrq
1913, 11, 12. Fred relrq
1920, 5, 12. John & Carrie M. recrq
1921, 2, 9. Helen Leroy recrq
1921, 11, 9. Ada rocf Center MM
1932, 3, 23. Wm. & fam gct First Friends Church, Richmond, Ind.

LIPPINCOTT
1910, 6, 11. Hazel m Stanley PENNINGTON

1884, 4, 18. Oswel rocf Miami MM, O., dtd 1884,3,26
1895, 6, 8. Emma, Howard & Hazel recrq
1915, 3, 10. Oswell & Emma relrq
1921, 6, 15. Howard & Joseph dropped from mbrp

LLOYD
1883, 4, 20. James & Julie A., & ch, Alice B., Minnie M., Carrie E. & Lizzie S., recrq
1896, 6, 13. James & fam relrq

LONG
1912, 1, --. Guy m Mary RHUDE

LONGSTRETH
1906, 12, 29. Horace d ae 27

1895, 6, 8. Horace & Gertrude recrq

LOTZ
1914, 4, 8. Earnest recrq
1916, 3, 8. Ernest gct Miami MM, O.

LOVE
----, --, --. Edmund m Hattie POND
1922, 6, 28. Hattie Pond d

LOVE
1914, 10, 14. Mabel & Opal recrq

LOVELL
1926, 6, 14. ----- m Ethel RAYBURN

1933, 6, 14. Ethel [Loveall] relrq

LOWES
1907, 6, 28. Mary, dt Herbert & Adilla, b
1913, 11, 12. Adilla d

1877, 2, 16. Cornelius [Lowe] & w, Jennetta, recrq
1916, 8, 9. Herbert gct Cincinnati MM, O.

LUCAS
1910, 2, 10. Dora recrq
1910, 3, 12. Minnie & Barbara rocf Fairfield MM, O.

LUDDINGTON
1858, 4, 8. Lydia b

1874, 3, 20. Lydia [Ludington] recrq
1886, 4, 10. Lewis [Ludington] recrq
1898, 4, 9. Lewis dropped from mbrp
1907, 4, 13. Daniel, George & Franklin dropped from mbrp
1907, 4, 13. Harvey dropped from mbrp
1907, 4, 13. Henry L. dropped from mbrp

LUDLUM
1874, 3, 20. Wm. T. recrq
1885, 2, 14. Wm. F. relrq

LUKINS
1909, 2, 2. Sarah Virginia, dt Carl & Sarah (Snowden), b
1911, 1, 11. Alice m Oliver HIATT
1911, 4, 2. Jessie m Layton HALE
1918, 7, 12. Elizabeth, dt Carl & Sarah (Snowden), b
1920, 6, 26. Robert Carl, s Harold & Violet (Rowe), b
1920, 9, 2. Harold m Violet ROWE
1925, 6, 6. Helen m Homer WRIGHT
1927, 8, 17. Luther m Bonnie EDWARDS
1932, 10, 9. Mary E. d

1895, 6, 8. Carl recrq
1895, 8, 10. Mary Emma & Hattie rocf Miami MM, O., dtd 1895,7,24
1897, 3, 13. Rachel & Nellie recrq
1897, 4, 10. Jessie [Lukens] recrq
1902, 1, 11. Sara Snowden [Lukens] rocf Center MM, O., dtd 1901,12,18
1903, 12, 12. Alice recrq
1906, 2, 10. Mabel recrq
1906, 3, 10. Luther recrq
1921, 12, 14. Robert Carl recrq of parents
1928, 3, 14. Bonnie Edward [Lukens] recrq

LUNDY
1921, 8, 3. Lindley L. m Pauline McPHERSON
1925, 2, 16. Richard McPherson, s Lindley & Pauline, b

1921, 12, 14. Lindley rocf Chester MM

LUSE
1925, 12, 9. Roena Berlin & ch, Wendell & Ronald Wright, gct Beach Grove MM

LUTTRELL
1881, 7, 15. Chloa & Ulyssis [Lettrell], ch R. H., rocf Newberry MM, O., dtd 1881,6, 21
1886, 4, 10. Robert H. [Lutterel] recrq
1890, 1, 11. R. H. [Lutteral] & ch gct Cincinnati MM, O.
1896, 7, 11. Robert H. & w, Mary, & s, Otto, rocf Cincinnati MM, O., dtd 1896,6,18
1908, 11, 14. Robert H. & w, Mary, gct Hopewell MM, O.
1910, 10, 8. Otto Clayton relrq

LYLE
1907, 12, 24. Florence S. m Wm. M. AYERS

1898, 4, 9. Florence recrq
1902, 1, 11. Ella Gaddis relrq

McBETH
1870, 3, 18. Sarah recrq
1874, 7, 17. Sarah Askew (form McBeth) dis mcd

McBRIDE
----, --, --. John b 1837,9,8; m Martha McGURTHY b 1845,11,12
Ch: William T. b 1869, 3, 8
Mary C. " 1871, 9, 10
Albert B. " 1875, 12, 1

McCALL
1858, 2, 20. Mary b

1870, 3, 18. Mary recrq

McCAMMISH
1923, 9, 15. Carl m Cordelia MURRELL

1926, 2, 10. Cordelia Murrell gct Winchester MM, Ind.

McCOLLISTER
1911, 3, 11. Tacy relrq

McCONNAUGHEY
1922, 11, 8. Elizabeth m Clarence PENNER

McCOY
1908, 11, 26. Richard Hugh, s Oliver & Elizabeth, b
1912, 6, 5. Leo J. m Elizabeth Rogers KING

McCOY, continued
1913, 10, 12. Margaret Barrett, dt Oliver & Elizabeth, b
1920, 3, 6. Robert Thorp, s Arthur H. & Eva (Thorpe), b
1933, 8, 4. Sarah Ethel m C. Grant FAIRLEY

1898, 12, 12. Hugh & ch, Mary Elsie, Sarah Ethel & Geo. J. recrq
1901, 3, 9. Blanch Hartman relrq
1903, 10, 10. Oliver R. recrq
1906, 2, 10. Arthur recrq
1913, 3, 12. Leo J. relrq
1914, 10, 14. Helen recrq
1919, 2, 11. Eva Thorpe recrq
1927, 6, 8. Margaret recrq
1928, 1, 11. Arthur & w, Eva, & s, Robert, gct Fairview MM

McCRAY
----, --, --. Thomas m Susanna MADEN b 1840, 10,9
Ch: Anna Mary b 1867, 7, 4
Arthur William " 1869, 5, 13
Clayton Harlan b 1878, 1, 21
----, --, --. Arthur L. m Rebecca Ann MADEN b 1846,8,17
Ch: Olive E. b 1875, 8, 21

McCREIGHT
1894, 7, 14. Ed [McCright] recrq
1903, 2, 14. Edward dropped from mbrp
1914, 10, 14. Edith [McCraight] recrq
1928, 1, 11. Ethel relrq

McDANIEL
1907, 1, 12. Mary & dt, Reba May, rocf Clear Creek MM, O.
1910, 12, 10. Mary & Reba May relrq

McDONALD
----, --, --. James W. b 1844,10,1; m Sarah THATCHER b 1843,9,4 d 1930,4,13
Ch: Annetta M. b 1867, 9, 24
Frank L. " 1871, 11, 17
Thomas Russell " ----, 6, 30
1900, 3, 10. Sarah B. d ae 75
1905, 6, 5. Gerald Doan, s Frank & Fannie (Doan), b
1913, 11, 20. Russell d
1923, 6, 24. Frank d

1886, 4, 10. James W. & w, Sarah, & ch, Annetta M., Frank L., Russell T. & Wm. Estes, rocf Center MM, O., dtd 1886,3,17
1894, 1, 13. Samuel & w, Anna, & ch, George, Rose, Mabel, Samuel & Charles, recrq
1899, 6, 15. Sarah B. recrq
1900, 3, 10. Samuel & fam relrq

1929, 6, 12. Ester dropped from mbrp

McELWEE
----, --, --. Isaac R. b 1825,4,5; m Rhoda G. WALKER b 1826,3,5
Ch: Charles E. b 1852, 11, 24
----, --, --. Chas. E. b 1852,11,24; m Louella K. JONES b 1857,1,5
Ch: Ethbert J. b 1877, 3, 14
Stella A. " 1878, 9, 28
1907, 12, 24. May m Dana BROWN
1923, 3, 2. Kate d
1933, 5, 24. Minnie d

1904, 1, 9. Myrtle Sprague gct Ogdon MM,O.
1915, 2, 10. Minnie & Elizabeth recrq
1920, 10, 13. Kate rocf Dover MM

McFADDEN
----, --, --. John m Susannah ANDREW b 1819, 4,24
Ch: Samuel b 1847, 11, 24
Esper Ann " 1851, 8, 27
Mary Elizabeth " 1853, 11, 25
Laura D. " 1859, 12, 19
John W. " 1862, 3, 28

1898, 6, 11. Mary rocf Ogden MM, O., dtd 1898,5,27
1902, 4, 12. Mary relrq

McGLADDERY
1799, 12, --. James b d 1871,7,20

1871, 12, 15. Margaret E. recrq
1882, 10, 20. Margaret relrq

McGREGOR
1797, 5, 25. Maria b d 1878,9,21 bur Sugar Grove

McKAY
1914, 2, 11. Ada Turner gct Center MM, O.
1917, 12, 12. Priscilla & ch, Mary Elba & Maynard, rocf Center MM, O.

McKECHNIE
1910, 12, 7. John m Lottie H. KIRTLEY
1914, 8, 25. Joseph d
1922, 5, 21. Julia d

1871, 4, 14. Josiah B. recrq
1871, 6, 16. Julia rocf Springfield MM, O., dtd 1871,5,20
1871, 7, 14. John Wm., s Julia, recrq

McKEE
1931, 3, 26. Chas. O. d

1873, 4, 18. Martha recrq
1873, 4, 18. George recrq
1914, 5, 13. Minerva Ault recrq

McKEE, continued
1914, 10, 14. Charles O. rocf Center MM, O., dtd 1914,9,6

McKIBBEN
1908, 5, 13. Wm. d ae 64
1909, 12, 25. Olivia m Carl DOWNING

1895, 4, 13. Lula & Hannah recrq
1898, 5, 14. Wm. recrq
1907, 3, 9. Oliva [McKibbon] recrq
1923, 11, 14. Hannah relrq

McKINNEY
----, --, --. Alexander b 1848,4,19; m Rebecca CLELAND b 1853,6,12
Ch: Charles L. b 1874, 6, 11
1829, 1, 8. Rebecca, dt Samuel & Mary A., b
1913, 9, 8. Ruth Elizabeth b
1916, 8, 5. Ora m Wallace WULFECK
1918, 1, 5. Sarah, w Obadiah, d
1926, 3, 6. Charles Wm. m Verna WELLER
1927, 4, 12. Obediah d
1932, 9, 24. Wm. d

1886, 7, 10. Obediah & w, Rachel, recrq
1889, 8, 10. Lewis recrq
1893, 2, 11. Wm. recrq
1894, 9, 8. Obediah & w, Rachel, gct Springfield MM, O.
1895, 5, 11. Wm. D. relrq
1895, 7, 13. Pearl rocf Springfield MM, O., dtd 1895,5,18
1895, 9, 14. Wm. recrq
1896, 4, 11. Wm. relrq
1908, 10, 10. Wm. recrq
1909, 3, 13. Obadiah & w, Sarah, recrq
1914, 10, 14. James W., Howard & Clyde, recrq

McKENZIE
1893, 4, 8. Ella [McKinzie] & ch, Zella A., recrq
1897, 4, 10. Zella recrq
1911, 2, 11. Zella relrq

McLAUGHLIN
1909, 6, 24. Edith m Harry HAYNES

McMILLAN
----, --, --. David m Sarah ----- b 1813,8,10
Ch: Jediah H. b 1844, 6, 7 d 1877, 4,29 bur Calif.
1849, 7, 4. Burritt b
----, --, --. Isaac C. b 1836,5,24; m Nancy L. ----- b 1840,3,1
Ch: Seth L. b 1863, 2, 15
Walter T. " 1865, 11, 22 d 1928, 1,23
Clifton J. " 1867, 12, 21 " 1868,10,29 bur Sugar Grove Cemetery
Carrie E. b 1869, 11, 3 d 1872, 7,23 bur Sugar Grove Cemetery
----, --, --. Emmor b 1838,10,21 d 1884,3,6 bur Wilmington; m Susan THATCHER b 1840, 7,29
Ch: Sanford b 1864, 3, 14
Louetta " 1875, 9, 17
----, --, --. Eli Jr. b 1842,1,2 d 1870,11,16 bur Sugar Grove; m Phebe H. ----- b 1840, 5,2
Ch: Elven L. b 1866, 4, 4
Jessie " 1868, 6, 13
Fallis " 1870, 4, 23
1873, 12, 12. Burritt d
1874, 12, 13. Isaac d bur Sugar Grove
1875, 1, 19. Maria C. d bur Sugar Grove
1908, 8, 25. Viola m Louis T. JONES
1910, 4, 22. Rebecca d ae 72
1914, 1, 11. Shipley d
1921, 6, 2. Isaac m Helen BARRERE
1925, 10, 12. Dorothea Mae, dt Isaac & Helen B., b
1926, 10, 20. Moses d
1931, 3, 24. Blanch m S. K. BRYAN

1870, 3, 18. Burritt recrq
1870, 3, 18. Elizabeth recrq
1873, 4, 18. Mary E. recrq
1873, 4, 18. Shipley recrq
1873, 4, 18. William recrq
1874, 9, 18. Phebe & ch, Elveron Lewis, Jesse & Eli W. F., gct Union MM, Howard Lake, Minn.
1874, 11, 14. Shipley gct Centre MM, O.
1879, 5, 16. Nancy & ch, Seth L. & Walter T., gct Center MM, O.
1879, 5, 16. Sarah gct Center MM, O.
1880, 4, 16. Mary A. recrq
1885, 10, 10. Shipley & w, Sarah, & ch, Edna R. & Ada B., rocf Center MM, O., dtd 1885,9,16
1889, 4, 13. Sarah Ellen recrq
1889, 9, 14. Thomas Dick rocf Centre MM, O., dtd 1889,5,15
1894, 4, 14. Rebecca & ch, Moses & Mary E., rocf Center MM, O., dtd 1894,3,14
1903, 2, 14. William dropped from mbrp
1903, 2, 14. Thomas Dick dropped from mbrp
1910, 8, 13. Mary Probasco gct Center MM, O.
1920, 8, 11. Walter T. & w, Blanch Martha & ch, Kirk, Isaac & Harriett, rocf Center MM, O., dtd 1920,7,14
1922, 3, 8. Helen B. recrq
1928, 3, 14. Henry & Mary rocf Dover MM

McNEMA
1910, 6, 20. William [McNama] m Florence RILEY
1914, 8, 12. Mary Ann [McNama] d
1930, 1, --. Margaret d

1873, 3, 14. Mary A. recrq
1873, 3, 14. Abraham recrq
1873, 3, 14. William recrq
1873, 3, 14. Lawther recrq
1897, 3, 13. Sarah M. [McNama] rocf Fairfield MM, O., dtd 1897,2,20

McNEMA, continued
1906, 4, 14. Reba [McNama] dropped from mbrp

McNEAL
1884, 11, 14. Mary rocf Hopewell MM, dtd 1884, 9,6

McNEMAR
1927, 7, 20. Donald recrq

McPHAIL
1903, 5, 9. Caroline rocf Miami MM, O., dtd 1903,4,22
1903, 9, 12. Donald E. recrq

McPHERSON
1905, 5, 9. Anna d ae 54
1905, 9, 7. Neil, s Geo. B. & Nina, b
1910, 11, 1. George Myron, s Geo. & Neva, b
1911, 6, 10. Ralph m Hazel DOAN
1913, 4, 30. Fred d
1916, --, --. Hattie m Clifford MIARS
1921, 8, 3. Pauline m Lindley L. LUNDY
1928, 12, 1. Emma d
1933, 4, 14. Nancy Ellen, dt Neil & Cleo (Ames), b

1897, 3, 13. Emaline rocf Fairfield MM, O., dtd 1897,2,20
1897, 4, 10. Maud recrq
1898, 6, 11. Henry C. & w, Anna E., & ch, Elmer T., Ollie S., Frederick B., George B., Mauda R., Vada M., Lulu B. & Ralph W., rocf Dover MM, O., dtd 1898,4,14
1902, 1, 11. Dora & dt, Mary, rocf Hopewell MM, O., dtd 1901,12,7
1902, 1, 11. Blanch rocf Hopewell MM, O., dtd 1901,12,7
1904, 8, 13. Nina V. rocf Center MM, O., dtd 1904,7,13
1904, 8, 13. Pauline L., dt Geo. B. & Nina V., recrq
1929, 6, 12. George dropped from mbrp
1933, 4, 12. Oio recrq

McQUISTON
1915, 1, 30. Carlton m Rebecca FARQUHAR
----, --, --. Carl m Rebecca FARQUHAR
Ch: Mary Elma b 1918, 9, 12
Joan Worth " 1921, 10, 14
Robert Farquhar " 1928, 9, 11

1915, 6, 19. Rebecca Farquhar relrq
1916, 9, 13. Rebecca Farquhar rst
1916, 9, 13. Carl recrq
1916, 9, 13. Thomas Milton recrq of parents, Carl & Rebecca

McVEY
1925, 11, 4. James m Mary BARRETT
1841, 2, 26. Deborah, dt James & Mary, b
1919, 5, 21. Alfred I. & Mintha recrq
1926, 12, 8. Mary Barrett gct Fairfield MM

MACE
1910, 2, 19. Laurence m Lulu AUSTIN

1927, 2, 16. Lulu Austin relrq

MACY
1919, 5, 29. Lael m Thomas R. KELLY

MADEN
----, --, --. Eli & Hannah
Ch: Harlan b 1811, 10, 26 d 1901, 8,27 bur Springfield
John b 1813, 3, 13 " 1887,10,21 bur Springfield
George b 1814, 9, 3 " 1895, 3,30 bur Springfield
Roena b 1817, 2, 12 " 1895, 4, 5 bur Springfield
Rebecca b 1819, 1, 5
----, --, --. Harlan b 1811,10,26 d 1901,8,27 bur Springfield; m Margaret OSBORN b 1814,7,25 d 1893,10,2
Ch: Sally M. b 1853, 4, 9
----, --, --. Thomas E. m Phebe E. ----- b 1851,4,24 d 1874,9,22 bur Sugar Grove
Ch: Leon Doan b 1873, 10, 12 d 1874,10,4 bur Sugar Grove
1908, 12, 10. Clinton m Nellie S. COCKERILE

1872, 4, 19. Thomas Elwood rocf Springfield MM, dtd 1872,3,16
1897, 7, 10. Eleanor recrq
1898, 4, 9. Elwood dropped from mbrp
1902, 1, 11. Cyrus Clinton recrq
1916, 9, 13. C. Clinton & w, Nellie C., gct Springfield MM, O.

MAGEE
1909, 12, 25. Edith m Geo. D. HAWORTH
1910, 3, 23. Elizabeth E. m Emery BALES

MAHAFFEY
1901, 1, 12. Nathan A. & w, Sarah A., & ch, Goldie M. & Clarence W., recrq
1901, 5, 11. Nathan A. & fam gct Dover MM,O.

MALONE
1892, 7, 9. Hezekiah P. & w, Emma, & ch, May & Bessie, rocf Clear Creek MM, O., dtd 1892,6,11
1892, 7, 9. Wm. H. rocf Clear Creek MM, O., dtd 1892,6,11
1892, 7, 9. Carl rocf Clear Creek MM, O., dtd 1892,6,11
1897, 3, 13. Wm. H. relrq
1906, 4, 14. Hezekiah & w, Emma, & ch, May & Bessie, dropped from mbrp
1906, 4, 14. Carl dropped from mbrp

MANKER
1931, 4, 1. Alpheus O. & Tillie recrq

MANLOVE
1883, 4, 20. Sarah recrq
1885, 5, 9. Belle recrq

MANN
1914, 10, 14. Victor recrq
1919, 5, 14. Charlotte Marie & Wanda Caroline, recrq

MARBLE
1928, 12, 16. Frank d

1873, 4, 18. Frank & w, Emma L., recrq

MARLOW
1920, 10, --. Martha d

1915, 9, 18. James F. & w, Martha A., recrq
1921, 12, 14. James [Marlowe] relrq

MARSHALL
1891, 7, 11. Eva recrq

MART
1848, 7, 3. Moses b
1850, 12, 17. Sylvester b

1870, 3, 18. Sylvester recrq
1870, 3, 18. Moses recrq
1871, 11, 17. Jennie (form Patten) dis mcd
1873, 3, 14. Susie C. recrq
1873, 3, 14. Moses con mcd
1898, 2, 12. Sylvester gct Miami MM, O.
1898, 7, 9. Moses gct Ogden MM, O.

MARTIN
1877, 8, 16. Lizzie b
1915, 2, 3. Lucile m Roy WELLER
1920, 9, 21. Wm. Robert, s Robert & Anne, b
1923, 10, 7. Allen m Susanna ADAMS
1925, 11, 5. Frank m Ruth HAWORTH

1877, 2, 16. John & w, Anna, & ch, Minnie & Elijah, recrq
1877, 2, 16. Alfred & w, Elizabeth, recrq
1877, 4, 20. Jehu & w, Martha J., & ch, Samantha & Margaret E., recrq
1892, 2, 13. Francis Linton, s Francis & Lydia L., recrq
1895, 8, 10. Cyrus Griffin, s Francis & Lydia, recrq
1906, 9, 8. Sarah Elizabeth recrq
1912, 11, 13. Lucile, Robert M. & Waller E. recrq
1914, 10, 14. Ernestine recrq
1914, 10, 14. John recrq
1914, 10, 14. Ernestine recrq
1914, 10, 14. Russell recrq
1915, 1, 13. May recrq
1921, 12, 14. Wm. Robert recrq of parents
1926, 3, 31. Anna M. recrq
1929, 12, 10. Ernestine, John, Russell & Walter, dropped from mbrp

MASON
1832, 2, 22. Edith (Kimbrough), b

1905, 5, 13. Mary A. recrq

MATHER
----, --, --. Joseph b 1827,11,29 d 1888,4,1 bur Springfield; m Mary A. BROWN b 1834, 11,16 d 1924,4,29
Ch: Caroline B. b 1865, 7, 3
Esther L. " 1868, 5, 13
Eva " 1873, 5, 12
----, --, --. Albert H. b 1852,11,30; m Phebe HAWORTH
Ch: Omar B. b 1878, 1, 5
1931, 12, 24. Bertha m Forest LEMON

1900, 1, 13. Mary A. & dt, Esther, rocf Springfield MM, O., dtd 1899,11,18
1931, 3, 11. Bertha recrq

MAXFIELD
1900, 12, 6. James & Jennie recrq
1907, 5, 11. James & Jennie relrq

MEEKS
1915, 9, 9. Horace Wm. m Alice Caroline ROCKHILL

MENDENHALL
1902, 11, 8. Wm. Orville rocf Pleasant Plain MM, Ia.
1909, 11, 13. Wm. O. gct West Richmond MM, Ind.

MERKER
1920, 5, 20. Clarence m Mary CAREY
Ch: Charles Edward b 1921, 3, 4
Ruth Anna " 1922, 9, 19
Barbara Jean b 1924, 4, 22
Wendell Carey " 1926, 12, 17

1921, 11, 9. Clarence G. & s, Clarence, recrq
1927, 5, 11. Clarence & w, Mary Carey, & ch, Clarence Edward, Ruthanna, Barbara Jean & Wendal Carey, relrq

MERRILL
1874, 7, 17. Henry A. recrq
1875, 5, 14. Henry A. gct White River MM, Ind.

MESSENGER
1889, 4, 13. J. Ira recrq
1893, 6, 10. J. Ira gct Blue Island MM, Ill.

MIARS
1814, 12, 30. Catherine [Meyers] b
1870, 8, 4. Samuel [Meyers] d
1916, --, --. Clifford Miars m Hattie McPHERSON
----, --, --. Ralph & Sylvia
Ch: Martha
Louise b 1917, 6, 13
Harry S. " 1921, 1, 10
David " 1933, 1, 1
1926, 4, 25. Mary C. d
1930, 2, 15. Cora d
1932, 1, 17. Wm. B. d
1932, 4, 24. Henry B. d

1873, 4, 18. Eliza recrq
1892, 10, 8. Henry rocf Center MM, O., dtd 1892,9,14
1892, 10, 8. Eva G. & ch, Ralph J., rocf Newberry MM, O., dtd 1892,8,12
1898, 2, 12. Mary C. & ch, Clifford & Pearly E., recrq
1898, 2, 12. Eliza gct Ogden MM, O.
1906, 5, 12. Eliza gct Ogden MM, O.
1906, 9, 8. Fred recrq
1916, 5, 10. Clifford gct Cesars Creek MM,O.
1916, 9, 13. Sylvia Sanders recrq
1920, 11, 10. Sarah rocf Center MM, O., dtd 1920,10,13
1921, 3, 9. Willie & Hannah rocf Center MM, O., dtd 1921,2,16

MICHAEL
1906, 3, 23. Martha J. d ae 81

1889, 4, 13. Martha J. recrq

MILLIKAN
----, --, --. John [Milican] b 1810,1,15; m Margaret C. HIMELWRIGHT b 1827,8,2
Ch: Mary E. b 1845, 12, 3
Pamelia A. " 1848, 3, 11
Sarah J. " 1849, 6, 12
Margaret E." 1851, 11, 20
Rachel C. " 1853, 5, 17
Eli W. " 1855, 7, 22
Almedia R. " 1857, 7, 26
Martha J. " 1860, 1, 1
Jessie D.F." 1862, 1, 27
Priscilla E. " 1864, 11, 30
Thomas N. " 1867, 1, 16
Hannah C. " 1868, 3, 3
1917, 3, 18. Elizabeth d

1874, 11, 20. Sarah [Milican] recrq
1880, 4, 16. Priscilla [Millekin] recrq
1900, 7, 14. Isabel rocf Sabina MM, O., dtd 1897,1,5
1901, 7, 13. Bell relrq
1907, 4, 13. Thomas dropped from mbrp

MILLER
1906, 9, 11. James d ae 69
1912, 3, 29. Elizabeth W. m Henry HILDEBRANT
1921, 7, 20. Vesta Eleanor m George INKS

1889, 10, 12. Ernest Clyde recrq
1890, 12, 13. William & w, L. Emma, rocf Hopewell MM, O., dtd 1890,12,6
1891, 7, 11. Rhoda recrq
1892, 4, 9. James & w, Lizzie, & s, Claud, rocf Springfield MM, O., dtd 1891,12,19
1895, 4, 13. George & w, Katie, & ch, Bessie Viola, Stella May & Elizabeth, recrq
1903, 2, 14. Claude gct Clear Creek MM, O.
1903, 10, 10. Earnest C. dropped from mbrp
1905, 6, 10. Claude rocf Clear Creek MM, O.
1906, 9, 8. Mildred Marie recrq of parents
1907, 5, 11. Elvin Elizabeth relrq
1911, 5, 13. Grace Robuck rocf West Fork MM, O., dtd 1911,4,15
1913, 4, 14. Mollie & Vesla Eleanor recrq
1914, 1, 14. Oscar gct Springfield MM
1919, 5, 21. Thurman, Eugene James & Harold Thurman, recrq
1921, 6, 15. Claude & Mildred dropped from mbrp
1923, 12, 12. Wm. H. & w, L. Emma, gct Leesburg MM, O.

MILLS
----, --, --. Levi b 1844,3,14; m Ruth W. ----- b 1844,1,21 d 1919,4,22
Ch: Harriet C. b 1867, 1, 6
Robert J. " 1869, 10, 25
Mary H. " 1873, 1, 21
1875, 10, 23. Robert d
1917, 2, 8. Levi d
1931, 1, 13. Elias d

1882, 4, 14. Albert H. & w, Ann, & ch, Pearly, rocf Dover MM, O., dtd 1882,2,16
1886, 4, 10. Frank B. & w, Frankie S., & ch, Mary & Maynard, recrq
1890, 7, 12. Frankie relrq
1901, 9, 14. Levi & w, Ruth W., gct Oskaloosa MM, Ia.
1903, 9, 12. Frank B. relrq
1905, 10, 14. Levi & w, Ruth W., rocf Whittier MM, Calif.
1917, 4, 11. Maynard relrq
1926, 3, 31. Nora Grice relrq
1927, 11, 19. Elias P. & w, Myrtle R., & ch, Nellie M. & Alice M., rocf Grassy Run MM, O.

MIRZA
1904, 3, 12. Youel recrq
1921, 9, 14. Youel relrq

MISNER
1877, 2, 16. Wm. & w, Mary, recrq

MITCHELL
1873, 4, 18. Lizzie recrq

MOBERLY
1923, 3, 10. J. F. d
1926, 7, 29. Catharine d

1916, 5, 10. John F. & Catherine recrq

MODLEN
1909, 10, 9. Bertha Ballard relrq

MOHLER
1872, 2, 16. Joseph B. recrq

MOLYNEAUX
1821, 5, 25. Scott m Ruth C. BABB

MONROE
1929, 3, 30. James m Gertrude CAMPBELL

MOODY
1838, 9, 27. Edith Emma b d 1912,5,12

1872, 4, 19. L. R. recrq
1876, 5, 19. Clara recrq

MOON
1868, 12, 16. Thomas m Hannah SHEPERD in Wilmington MH
1872, 7, 22. Golden B. b
1907, 9, 1. Thomas J. d ae 71
1918, 10, 12. Bert G. d
1919, 6, 12. Lewis C. m in Wilmington MH, Ruthanna COWGILL
1921, 5, 20. Allen Lewis, s Lewis & Ruthanna C., b
1926, 12, 9. Lida E. d
1927, 10, 21. Wanda m Richard LACY
1929, 8, 12. Elizabeth Hadley d

1869, 11, 16. Hannah S. gct Newberry MM, O.
1870, 3, 18. Mary recrq
1870, 3, 18. Jephtha D. recrq
1871, 6, 16. Daniel C. & w, Betsy H., & ch, Cora A. & Otto, rocf Newberry MM, O., dtd 1871,5,22
1876, 4, 14. Milton W. recrq
1880, 3, 19. Ella Glenn relrq
1883, 11, 16. Thomas J. & w, Lydia, & ch, Cora, rocf Newberry MM,O., dtd 1883,10,22
1889, 4, 13. James & L. R. recrq
1889, 4, 13. T. E. & w, Louisa P., & ch, Elsie, Orland, Wm. P. & Oland J., rocf Dover MM, O.
1894, 6, 19. Mary C. recrq
1896, 5, 9. Della & dt, Beatrice B., gct Chicago MM, Ill.
1897, 4, 10. Ada Bell recrq
1897, 5, 8. Harry C. recrq
1897, 12, 11. Oscar rocf Marion MM, Ind., dtd 1897,11,10
1898, 5, 14. James O. relrq
1898, 7, 9. Milton M. dropped from mbrp
1898, 10, 8. Oscar gct Marion MM, Ind.
1899, 7, 8. Harvey & w, Australia, rocf West Fork MM, O., dtd 1899,6,17
1903, 1, 10. Minnie A. recrq
1903, 2, 14. Milton M. dropped from mbrp
1906, 10, 13. James O. dropped from mbrp
1907, 5, 11. Lois R. dropped from mbrp
1912, 1, 13. Lewis rocf Graham MM, N. C.
1915, 3, 10. Lulu recrq
1921, 3, 9. Olive R. rocf Sabina MM, O., dtd 1921,2,9
1921, 3, 9. Ralph L. recrq
1921, 3, 9. John E. recrq
1921, 3, 9. May E. recrq
1921, 6, 15. Harvey & Australia dropped from mbrp
1921, 12, 14. Lewis C. & w, Ruth Anna, & ch, Allen Lewis, gct Baltimore MM, Md.
1923, 6, 13. Olin & w, Mae, & ch, Ralph & John, relrq
1924, 1, 9. Lulu relrq
1925, 5, 13. Wanda recrq

MOORE
---- --, --. Nancy, w Joshua, dt Joseph & Dosha STRATTON, b 1797,11,16 d 1881,12,29 bur Springfield
----, --, --. Samuel & Elizabeth
Ch: Sarah A. b 1820, 5, 1
Evaline " 1825, 11, 17
----, --, --. Caleb b 1800,9,27 d 1892,3,16; m 2nd Martha BEER b 1809,4,9
Ch: Harris C. b 1835, 4, 5
----, --, --. John Haines b 1817,9,8 d 1877, 11,28; m Ruth LINDLEY
Ch: Lindley b 1843, 2, 3
----, --, --. John W., s Haines & Eliza, b 1826,10,10; m Martha HAINES, dt Stacy & Judith, b 1834,7,28 d 1919,3,11
----, --, --. Samuel b 1827,10,1; m Sarah Jane HADLEY b 1833,12,13
Ch: Clark b 1856, 2, 28
Alfred B. " 1861, 12, 30
Hettie " 1865, 4, 1
Charlie R. " 1869, 7, 7
----, --, --. Harris C. b 1835,4,5; m Gulielma GREEN
Ch: Francis I. b 1859, 7, 26
Eva " 1861, 11, 27
Harris C. m 2d Rachel WALKER, b 1839,7,6
Ch: Mary E. b 1868, 11, 8
----, --, --. Micajah b 1821,12,23; m Margaret Ellen WEST b 1838,7,15
Ch: Robert C. b 1861, 6, 20
Benjamin " 1863, 4, 15
Thomas Seth " 1866, 6, 9
Emma J. " 1869, 3, 30
Walter Hadley " 1875, 6, 10
1866, 8, 18. Louisa Nye b
----, --, --. Oliver C. b 1845,9,20; m Ophelia COATE b 1844,7,10

MOORE, Oliver C. & Ophelia, continued
Ch: Luther H. b 1868, 6, 8
Ruth A. " 1876, 3, 8
1868, 9, 8. Arthur K. b
----, --, --. Thomas E. b 1844,1,29; m Sarah REESE b 1854,8,15 d 1896,7,6 bur Wilmington
Ch: Clara May b 1870, 4, 27
Clifton " 1871, 10, 2 d 1871,11,10 bur Center
Jennetta Belle " 1872, 10, 26
Adelbert " 1876, 2, 10
Ottie " 1877, 7, 22
Viola " 1879, 4, 16
----, --, --. Clark b 1856,2,28; m Alice TRIMMER, dt Samuel & Jane, b 1859,11,7
1908, 9, 3. John Haines d ae 92
1915, 6, 30. Hazel m Charles DOAN
1916, 7, 18. Arthur d
1918, 3, 30. Verba d
1918, 8, 6. Joshua M. d
1918, 10, 9. Oscar m Estella YARGER
1921, 6, 16. Charles Oscar, s Oscar & Estella, b
1928, 11, 28. Mary A. d
1929, 8, 10. Estella Yarger d

1874, 3, 20. Isabel recrq
1885, 3, 14. Mary A. & s, Joseph, recrq
1885, 4, 11. John H. rocf Springfield MM, O., dtd 1885,2,21
1894, 5, 12. Emma rocf Cincinnati MM, O., dtd 1894,4,19
1898, 7, 9. Isabelle dropped from mbrp
1900, 6, 9. Martha H. rocf Ogden MM, O., dtd 1900,5,26
1903, 2, 14. Isabella dropped from mbrp
1904, 8, 13. Hazel Everett recrq
1912, 12, 11. Oscar A. & w, Veva, recrq
1919, 5, 14. Estella Yarger rocf Sabina MM,O.
1926, 7, 14. America & ch, Reba, Elizabeth & Mary Catharine, recrq

MOORMAN
1874, 3, 20. Thomas recrq
1885, 6, 13. Thomas dropped from mbrp

MOOTS
1912, 2, 17. Charles A. m Minnie HAMILTON

MORGAN
1903, --, --. Henry B. d ae 87
1919, 10, 24. Edwin Tasso m Mary Genevieve OLIVER
1926, 2, 28. Orpha d

1870, 3, 18. Henry B. & dt, Henrietta, recrq
1873, 4, 18. William H. recrq
1876, 5, 19. Jennie recrq
1907, 4, 13. Clarence & Mertie dropped from mbrp
1908, 6, 13. Orpha & s, Edwin Tasco rocf Paomia MM, Col.
1923, 4, 11. Edwin Tasso relrq

MORMAN
1874, 3, 29. Arthur d

MORRIS
1843, 4, 12. Thomas C., s Isaiah & Rhoda C., b
1929, 9, 23. Fannie d

1870, 3, 18. Thomas C. recrq
1876, 5, 19. Sarah recrq
1879, 11, 14. Earnestine P. rocf White Water MM, Ind., dtd 1879,10,23
1880, 12, 17. Thomas C. dis
1889, 3, 9. Elizabeth Maud recrq
1889, 5, 11. Margaret Jane, dt Martha A. Frazier, recrq
1889, 8, 10. Charles recrq
1892, 2, 13. Benjamin F. & w, Lydia Maria, & ch, Alvaretta & Albert, rocf Fairfield MM, O., dtd 1892,1,16
1898, 11, 12. Ruth rocf Fairfield MM, O., dtd 1898,10,15
1901, 6, 8. Joshua C. recrq
1903, 2, 14. Esther Pugh dropped from mbrp
1906, 10, 13. Sarah dropped from mbrp
1907, 3, 9. Charles & Elizabeth dropped from mbrp
1907, 3, 9. Margaret Jane dropped from mbrp
1907, 5, 11. Josiah C. relrq
1925, 4, 8. Fannie C. recrq

MORROW
1889, 1, 12. Celia rocf Dover MM, O.
1890, 5, 10. Rose recrq

MORTON
1911, 12, 8. Alvada m Grover HOOVER

1881, 5, 20. James M. & w, Maria, & ch, Calvin Wister, Clorinda Bell, Everett Perry & Ishmael Earl, recrq
1903, 11, 14. Ella M. relrq

MORY
1902, 8, 1. Daniel B. [Morey] d ae 80
1878, 3, 15. Daniel B. rocf Clear Creek MM, O., dtd 1878,1,12
1878, 3, 15. Sarah Jane rocf Clear Creek MM, O., dtd 1878,3,9
1912, 11, 13. Mary [Mowry] rocf Ogden MM,O.
1914, 10, 14. Verna [Mowry] recrq

MOSIER
1873, 3, 14. Harriet recrq
1906, 3, 10. Granville & Daisy T. recrq
1929, 6, 12. Granville & Daisy dropped from mbrp

MOSSBARGER
1923, 2, 27. Thomas M. m Nettie STRATTON

1925, 2, 11. Nellie Stratton [Mossberger] relrq

MOSMAN
1929, 12, 10. Frances Doan dropped from mbrp

MOUNTS
1918, 5, 29. Neil m Edith CARROLL

MOYERS
----, --, --. Samuel b 1809,--,--; m Catherine ----- b 1814,12,30

MULLEN
1932, 10, 12. Marie Ballard d

MUNGER
1902, 5, 10. Avis B. recrq
1926, 11, 10. Avis B. dropped from mbrp

MURRELL
1923, 9, 15. Cordelia m Carl McCAMMISH
1924, 9, 27. Mabel m Burch WILLIAMS

1890, 5, 10. Grant rocf Dover MM
1897, 8, 14. U. Grant & w, Ora, gct Cesars Creek MM, O.
1905, 11, 11. U. Grant & w, Ora, & ch, Cordelia M. & Mabel A., rocf Ceasars Creek MM, O.

NEITERT
1922, 6, 3. Zella m Wm. HAMILTON

NELSON
1849, 10, 6. Christopher C. b
1927, 1, 29. Arbella d

1870, 3, 18. Christopher C. recrq
1874, 3, 20. Lizzie recrq
1900, 5, 11. Arbelle & dt, Edna, recrq
1905, 10, 14. Edna E. relrq

NEWBY
1891, 9, 12. Jennie Brazil gct Kansas City MM, Mo.
1907, 3, 9. John M. rocf Hopewell MM, dtd 1907,3,2
1907, 3, 9. Anna May recrq
1907, 8, 10. Richard R. & w, Emma, & s, James M., rocf Providence MM, Ia.
1910, 10, 8. Richard R. & w, Emma, & ch, James M., gct Scipio MM, N. Y.
1912, 12, 13. John M. & w, Anna May, relrq

NEWEL
1880, 7, 16. Lewis & w, Jayne, & ch, Emma, Grant, Carrie, John P. & Adam H., rocf Fairfield MM, O., dtd 1880,6,19
1884, 10, 17. Jane, Emma & Carrie dropped from mbrp

NEWLIN
1900, 8, 11. Thomas & w, Olive W., & dt, Edna B., rocf Newburg MM, Oregon, dtd 1900,7,10
1902, 6, 14. Thomas & w, Olive W., & ch, Edna, gct Newgarden MM, N. C.

NEWMAN
1879, 6, 26. H. N. recrq
1884, 2, 15. Henry dis

NICHOLS
1881, 5, 20. Calvin recrq
1889, 4, 13. Agnes [Nicolot] recrq
1907, 3, 9. Calvin dropped from mbrp

NOLYE
1895, 6, 8. David C. & w, Elizabeth, & ch, Charles H., Lewis D. & Dlorence V., recrq
1903, 1, 10. David C. [Noltz] & w, Elizabeth, & ch, Charles, Dennis D. & Florence dropped from mbrp

NORDYKE
----, --, --. Micajah m Ann Elizabeth HENRY b 1836,3,15
Ch: Frank b 1854, 2, 3
Ida " 1858, 8, 5
Ella M. " 1861, 3, 30
1907, 12, 23. Alice m Jones E. HAROLD

1878, 2, 15. Elijah & w, Caroline, rocf Clear Creek MM, O., dtd 1878,1,12
1883, 4, 20. Callie recrq
1883, 10, 19. Harriet A. Farquhar gct Clear Creek MM, O.
1886, 12, 11. Edgar M. & w, Hattie, & s, Milton H., rocf Clear Creek MM, O.
1889, 1, 12. Asa & w, Almedia, & dt, Mary F., rocf Clear Creek MM, O.
1892, 5, 14. Edgar M. & w, Harriett & ch, Milton Henry & Almeda H., gct Chicago MM, Ill.
1892, 9, 10. Asa & w, Mary F., gct Whittier MM, Calif.

NORTON
1874, 3, 20. John H. recrq
1885, 6, 13. John dropped from mbrp

NORVALD
1927, 6, 15. John m Harriett BRANN
----, --, --. John & Harriet B.
Ch: John Jr. b 1929, 12, 6
Gretchen " 1933, 2, 22

1919, 3, 12. Grace Kersey recrq
1926, 2, 10. John R. recrq

O'CONNER
1910, 8, 13. Gertrude L. dropped from mbrp

OGBURN
----, --, --. David H. b 1843,7,3; m Sarah E. STRATTON b 1846,2,28
Ch: Harriet B. b 1871, 9, 24
Mahlon F. " 1875, 5, 19

OGLESBEE
1914, 4, 16. Franklin d
1916, 9, 10. Ruth d
1924, 7, 23. Rebecca d

1904, 4, 9. Franklin, Ruth & Anna recrq
1912, 4, 10. Mary Emily gct Center MM
1921, 3, 9. Floyd, Eva & Reece rocf Center MM, O., dtd 1921,2,16
1921, 8, 10. Rebecca rocf Center MM
1921, 11, 9. Edward rocf Center MM
1925, 3, 11. Robert rocf Newhope MM

OLIVER
1919, 2, 19. Asa m Hazel WOODS
1919, 10, 24. Mary Genevive m Edwin Tasso MORGAN
1921, 8, 6. Asa Lee, s Asa & Hazel (Woods), b
1925, 7, 5. George m Marguerite TODHUNTER

1921, 12, 14. Asa Lee recrq of parents

OLVIS
1905, 2, 8. Wm. & w, Edna R., & ch, Ella & Elmira, rocf Ogden MM, O., dtd 1905,1,28
1921, 6, 15. Edna & Elmira dropped from mbrp

ORBIN
1925, 9, 1. Sleve William m Anna Lou SAPP

OREN
----, --, --. Joseph, s James & Margaret, b 1816,4,6; m Rachel L. ----- b 1817,2,7
Ch: Thomas H. b 1850, 5, 13
David " 1851, 8, 4
James E. " 1852, 12, 24
Alvan " 1854, 9, 3
Mary B. " 1856, 12, 3
Sarah H. " 1858, 10, 25
1921, 11, 10. Frank m Tessie C. BECK
1925, 8, 3. Ruth m Paul ANDREWS

1869, 10, 12. Joseph & w, Rachel, & ch, Thomas, David, James E., Mary & Sarah, gct Centre MM, O.
1917, 9, 12. Anna & s, Frank, recrq
1920, 5, 12. Ruth recrq

ORSEN
1904, 12, 10. Mary Moon gct Douglas MM, Alaska

ORTON
1917, 4, 11. Helen C. recrq
1917, 4, 11. Luella Cook & Helen C. relrq

OSBORN
1844, 4, 15. Isaiah b
----, --, --. C. N. m Caroline ----- b 1819, 6,19
Ch: Edward b 1846, 4, 24
Hannah " 1848, 2, 17
Daniel " 1850, 4, 2
1847, 9, 12. Ellwood, s Peter & Sarah, b
----, --, --. Adam b 1823,2,1; m Martha P. CLARK
Ch: Martha J. b 1851, 10, 24
Peter Alfred " 1853, 12, 31
Elisha B. " 1856, 9, 2
Eliza D. " 1856, 9, 2
Amanda May " 1859, 5, 15
Adam m 2nd Ann Elizabeth (Henry) NORDYKE, b 1836,3,15
----, --, --. Peter m Eliza Ann MOORE, dt Joseph & Penina, b 1817,8,8
Ch: Adaline b 1858, 11, 30
----, --, --. Peter b 1826,7,31; m Elizabeth LUNDY b 1833,3,30
Ch: Angeline b 1861, 3, 1
Ruth Ellen " 1863, 2, 7
Margaret Jane " 1866, 4, 3
Clark " 1869, 9, 7
----, --, --. Alfred b 1833,1,5; m Martha Emly STANTON, b 1841,10,1
Ch: Allettia b 1864, 2, 1
Walter Stanton " 1866, 7, 12
Sarah Theodocia " 1868, 9, 6
Olive Ann " 1870, 8, 4
Ruth Irena " 1872, 2, 21 d 1874,11,21
Frank T. " 1873, 11, 14
----, --, --. Wm. H. b 1837,12,2 d 1905,3,17; m Martha COATE b 1838,11,28
Ch: Joseph Peter b 1864, 11, 23
George Eddie " 1866, 10, 25
----, --, --. Charles b 1834,12,11; m Mary R. OSBORN b 1847,2,18
Ch: Leona S. b 1867, 12, 1
Paulina J. " 1870, 1, 5
Alice C. " 1871, 8, 14
Lucy E. " 1873, 3, 17
Frederick " 1874, 8, 17
Catherine M. b 1876, 9, 17
Laura M. " 1878, 4, 20
Nellie A. " 1879, 6, 4
----, --, --. Seth b 1848,1,31; m Ann Eliza RAYBURN b 1846,7,10
Ch: Walter D. b 1868, 2, 14
Albert W. " 1869, 11, 12
Gilbert S. " 1872, 1, 8
1868, 8, 18. Vionette J. b
----, --, --. John Thomas b 1848,7,9; m Miranda OGLESBEE b 1848,7,9

OSBORN, John Thomas & Miranda, continued
Ch: Eva R. b 1870, 8, 19
----, --, --. Peter b 1846,11,9; m Anna THATCHER, b 1849,5,28
Ch: Calvin J. b 1869, 2, 15
Clinton " 1870, 11, 29
Elizabeth D. " 1873, 6, 7
Melissa " 1875, 6, 8
Melville S." 1877, 4, 9
----, --, --. Blanche L. b 1870,12,17 d 1876,1,3
1878, 12, 5. Fay b
1909, 6, 10. May m William KING
1911, 11, 23. Glenn m Minnie SIMMONS
1915, 9, 14. Martha d
1925, 10, 30. Elwood d
1926, 7, 5. Emma N. d

1870, 11, 18. Hannah Babb (form Osborne) con mcd
1873, 4, 18. Annie recrq
1879, 9, 19. Wm. & w, Eliza, & ch, Annie & Wm., rocf Hopewell MM, O.
1889, 5, 11. Eliza & s, Jesse Wm., gct Cincinnati MM, O.
1889, 9, 14. William & a, Martha, & s, George Eddie, rocf Centre MM, O., dtd 1889,4,17
1891, 11, 14. Elwood & w, Effie, rocf Springfield MM, O., dtd 1891,9,19
1898, 5, 14. Edward dropped from mbrp
1902, 6, 14. Jesse W. rocf Cincinnati MM,O.
1905, 11, 11. Emma U. & Mae rocf Ogden MM,O., dtd 1905,11,25(?)
1921, 6, 15. Minnie Loyd & Helen dropped from mbrp

OWENS
1870, 12, 16. Lizzie recrq
1872, 1, 19. Lizzie Cruit (form Owens) con mcd
1873, 4, 18. Ella recrq
1911, 11, 11. Edgar T. recrq
1929, 6, 12. Edgar dropped from mbrp

PACK
1921, 3, 4. George m Marianne DICKINSON

PADGET
1889, 6, 8. Charles recrq
1889, 10, 12. Alexander & w, Sarah Elizabeth Ann, & ch, Alice Ann, Farrell Benjamin & Lillie May, recrq
1898, 4, 9. Alexander, Phaso, Lilly May & Alice, dropped from mbrp
1898, 7, 9. Charles dropped from mbrp
1903, 1, 10. Charles dropped from mbrp

PAGE
1917, 3, 21. L. O. m Nellie HOLADAY

PAINE
1909, 10, 9. Mabel Jane recrq

PAINTER
1910, 9, --. Roy m Hazel THATCHER
1926, 1, 25. Lillian m Earl C. STARBUCK

1894, 1, 13. Elva Hinshaw gct Cesars Creek MM, O.
1897, 7, 10. J. Henry & w, Elva, & ch, Donald Hinshaw, Herbert Joseph & Helen Maria, rocf Cesars Creek MM, O., dtd 1897, 6,24
1909, 1, 9. Elva H. gct White Water MM,Ind.
1912, 2, 10. J. Henry gct Dayton MM, O.
1912, 11, 13. Maurice recrq
1912, 12, 11. Lillian Pidgeon rocf Dover MM
1912, 12, 11. George Edward & David Pidgeon recrq of parents, Maurice & w
1920, 4, 14. Herbert J. gct Haverford MM,Pa.
1920, 12, 8. Hazel T. relrq
1929, 2, 13. Maurice & David dropped from mbrp
1930, 7, 9. Elva & Henry rocf Dayton MM,O.

PALMER
1873, 3, 14. Mary Adaline recrq
1907, 3, 9. Mary Adeline dropped from mbrp

PARKER
1919, 6, 12. Douglas L. m in Wilmington MH, Rebecca ROSS
Ch: Anna Isabelle b 1922, 1, 19
Douglas Ross " 1923, 12, 28
Elizabeth Louise " 1928, 8, --

1914, 8, 26. Douglas L. rocf University MM, Kans.
1929, 8, 21. Douglas & w, Rebecca Ross, & ch, Anna Isabel, Douglas Ross & Elizabeth Louise, gct Matamoros MM, Mexico
1931, 7, 8. Douglas & w, Rebecca J., & ch, Anna Isabella, Douglass Ross & Elizabeth Louise, rocf Matamoros MM, Mexico
1931, 11, 11. Douglas & w, Rebecca Jane, & ch, Rebecca Jane, Anna Isabella, Douglas Ross & Elizabeth Louise, gct Glenn Falls MM, N. Y.

PATCH
1877, 2, 16. Francis recrq

PATTON
1870, 3, 18. Helen & ch, Alice & Isaac, recrq
1870, 4, 15. Jennie recrq
1871, 3, 17. Helen Pennington (form Patten) con mcd
1871, 11, 17. Jennie Mart (form Patten) dis mcd
1894, 7, 14. Anna recrq
1913, 12, 17. Annis recrq
1914, 10, 14. Blanch recrq

PATTON, continued
1924, 12, 10. D. Hubert & w, Gladys, & ch, Violet Lenore, recrq

PAUKETT
1886, 4, 10. Dora recrq
1886, 5, 8. R. Franklin rocf Dover MM, O.
1894, 3, 10. Frank [Pauckett] & w, Dora, relrq
1906, 10, 13. Clarence [Pauckett] gct Xenia MM, O.
1914, 6, 10. Clarence recrq

PAVEY
1877, 2, 16. Wm. & w, Mary, & ch, Wm., Frederic, Louis & Minnie, recrq

PAXON
1916, 11, 8. Nora & ch, Leona & Glenn, rocf Xenia MM, O.
1919, 5, 21. Glenn & Leona relrq
1920, 5, 12. Charles rocf Xenia MM, O.
1921, 3, 9. Nora relrq
1925, 1, 14. Charles rocf Sabina MM, O.

PEACOCK
1919, 5, 21. Thomas & Naomi recrq

PEARSON
1873, 4, 18. George, Angeline & Benjamin recrq
1885, 6, 13. George, Benjamin & Angeline dropped from mbrp
1886, 4, 10. Susie [Pierson] recrq
1889, 4, 13. Eli & ch, Harry W. & Laura M., rocf Dover MM
1890, 5, 10. Irene Louella recrq

PEEBLES
1920, 6, 1. Mary d

1893, 4, 8. Mary L. [Pebles] recrq
1896, 10, 10. Isabel recrq
1896, 11, 14. Edwin Auber recrq

PEDDICORD
1917, 5, 9. Oscar Jr. recrq

PEELLE
1898, 9, 15. John d ae 59
1904, 10, 3. Kathryn Marie, dt Waldo & Maude M., b
1904, 11, 28. Hazel Ellen, dt Roscoe & Bertha, b
1905, 7, 9. Isaiah d ae 64
1905, 10, 7. Orrin d ae 24
1910, 7, 12. Lydia D. d ae 35
1910, 7, 18. Oscar D., s Oscar & Lydia, b
1910, 12, 29. Pearl m Burritt M. HIATT
1911, 2, 3. Dorcas m Joseph M. COREY
1912, 6, 22. Seth d
1916, 9, 22. Susan d
1920, 7, 30. Wm. C. d
1922, 2, 23. Mark Clinton m Bertha BATH
1923, 1, 3. Margaretta d
1926, 5, 25. Elijah J. d
1926, 12, 10. Kathryn m Donald BICKETT
1928, 6, 28. Ellen m Clarence ROBINSON, in Wilmington MH
1929, 6, 8. Miles L. m Eleanor JOHNSON
1930, 3, 3. Esther B. d
1931, 11, 21. Sarah d

1878, 9, 20. Isaiah & w, Susan M., & ch, Ruth Annie, Chas. Edward & Isaiah Morris, rocf Dover MM, dtd 1878,9,19
1891, 8, 8. Enos P. & w, Hattie M., & ch, Gertrude & Elton, rocf Dover MM, O., dtd 1891,7,16
1894, 12, 8. Charles Edward gct Dover MM,O.
1894, 12, 8. John & w, Dorcas A., & ch, Harley H., Clarissa A. & Oscar V., rocf Dover MM, O., dtd 1894,11,15
1896, 5, 9. Wm. C. & w, Sarah, & ch, Elmer & Lillian, rocf Dover MM, O., dtd 1896,4,16
1896, 12, 12. Elijah J. & w, Esther B., & ch, Alvan A. & Roscoe E., rocf Dover MM, O., dtd 1896,11,19
1898, 6, 11. Leroy & w, Anna Belle, & ch, Emery S. & Alfred, rocf Dover MM, O., dtd 1898,4,14
1899, 2, 11. Jesse & w, Margaretta C., & ch, Wm. R., rocf Chicago MM, Ill.
1899, 2, 11. Clara S. rocf Chicago MM, Ill.
1899, 2, 11. Bertha rocf Chicago MM, Ill.
1901, 3, 9. Isaiah Morris & w, Alice H., & s, Russell G., gct Ogden MM, O.
1901, 8, 10. Seth & w, Mary Esther, & s, Mark Clinton, rocf Dover MM, O., dtd 1901,7,18
1902, 5, 10. Orrin G. rocf Dover MM, O.
1903, 2, 14. Leroy & w, Anna, & ch, Emory, Alfred Earl, Virgil Leroy & Lawrence D., gct Dover MM, O.
1903, 11, 14. Frank Alton & Virginia Rhonemus Bosworth, rocf Dover MM, O.
1904, 2, 13. Elmer & Elizabeth gct Sabina MM, O.
1905, 11, 11. J. Irving recrq
1906, 4, 14. Lydia Deborah rocf Center MM,O., dtd 1906,3,14
1906, 4, 14. Emma Lucile & Selma V., ch Oscar & Lydia B., rocf Center MM, O., dtd 1906,3,14
1908, 3, 4. Bertha Barbara & ch, Gladys Marie & Alice Arline, recrq

1909, 12, 12. Harley & w, Bertha, & ch, May Arlene & Gladys, gct White Water MM,Ind.
1910, 12, 10. Wm. R. & w, Edna Street gct Dayton MM, O.
1915, 12, 8. J. Irving & w, Edna C., & s, Miles L., recrq
1920, 4, 14. Oliver relrq
1921, 1, 12. Calvin W. gct Xenia MM, O.

PEELLE, continued
1922, 6, --. May Thompson gct Newberry MM,O.
1923, 5, 9. Thelma V. gct Xenia MM, O.
1925, 5, 13. Dorothy recrq

PEMBERTON
1928, 8, 18. Katherine m Henry HARE

1924, 1, 9. H. Elmer & w, Kate, & ch, Kathryn & Max, rocf Salem MM, Oregon
1928, 5, 9. Kate gct Whittier MM, Calif.
1928, 9, 12. H. Elmer & s, Max, gct Friendsville MM, Tenn.

PENNINGTON
1910, 6, 11. Stanley m Hazel LIPPINCOTT

1871, 3, 17. Helen (form Patten) con mcd
1880, 10, 15. John Henry recrq
1882, 6, 16. Isaac V. recrq
1882, 6, 16. Margaret Ann recrq
1883, 12, 14. Sarah M. & Ruth Ann recrq
1889, 10, 12. Laura Ann recrq
1894, 7, 14. Mary recrq
1903, 1, 10. Sarah M. dropped from mbrp
1903, 2, 14. Mary dropped from mbrp
1905, 3, 8. Sina Stoops rocf Center MM,O., dtd 1905,2,5
1906, 3, 10. Roscor recrq
1906, 4, 14. John Henry & Ruth Anna dropped from mbrp
1920, 2, 11. Hazel L. relrq

PERDUE
1899, 7, 8. Thomas & w, Jennie, & ch, Jesse Mable & Pearl Marie, recrq
1903, 2, 14. Thomas, Jennie, Jessie M. & Pearl M., dropped from mbrp

PERKINS
1904, 10, 9. Priscilla d ae 79

1869, 12, 17. Priscilla rocf Centre MM, O., dtd 1869,12,15

PERRIN
1899, 5, 13. Bertha recrq

PERSINGER
1886, 3, 13. Minnie recrq
1894, 7, 14. Rilla recrq
1902, 12, 13. Minnie relrq

PETERMAN
1925, 3, 13. Joseph McKinney d

PETERS
1919, 8, 27. Edward K. d

1874, 3, 20. Ed K. recrq
1893, 1, 14. Maria Evaline & dt, Edith Mary, recrq

PETERSON
1932, 10, 11. Svend M. m Elizabeth AUSTIN

1909, 5, 8. Lula gct Oakland MM, Calif.

PHILLIPS
1910, 4, 22. Caroline d ae 75

1895, 6, 8. Caroline [Philips] recrq
1904, 4, 9. Dorothy Simons dropped from mbrp

PICKENS
1895, 6, 8. Keziah recrq
1898, 5, 14. Keziah dropped from mbrp
1903, 1, 10. Keziah dropped from mbrp

PIDGEON
1843, 8, 22. Isaac H. b
1926, 12, 12. Henry H. d

1870, 3, 18. Isaac recrq
1898, 7, 9. Isaac H. dropped from mbrp
1923, 10, 14. Henry & w, Ella, & s, Willard, rocf Dover MM

PIERCE
----, --, --. John F. b 1824,7,18; m Eliza -----
Ch: Richard b 1870, 8, 23

1870, 3, 18. John F. recrq
1907, 4, 13. Willie & Dick dropped from mbrp

PLYMIRE
1907, 11, 28. Harley m Grace COVERDALE

1914, 2, 11. Grace C. relrq

POIGNIER
1888, 5, 12. Hattie Hosier relrq

POND
----, --, --. Hattie m Edmund LOVE

1912, 12, 11. Hattie rocf Fairview MM

PORTER
1927, 6, 25. Paul m Veda VANDERVOORT

POTTS
1879, 5, 16. Joseph recrq
1879, 9, 19. Joseph gct Marysville MM, Tenn.

PRATHER
1932, 3, 23. Mary Jean recrq

PRATT
1921, 4, 13. Doris & Roy recrq
1921, 4, 13. T. C. & w recrq
1921, 4, 13. Lillian recrq

PRETLOW
1901, 11, 9. Robert E. & Emma F., & ch,

PRETLOW, continued
Robert F. & Abigail, rocf Mill Creek MM, Ind.
1906, 8, 11. Robert E. & w, Emma T., & ch, Robert T. & Abbie, gct New York MM, N. Y.

PRICE
1875, 3, 25. Moody b
1909, 5, 7. Charles d
1910, 7, 10. Henry d ae 70
1925, 2, 20. Martha d

1873, 4, 18. Henry C., Martha J. & Charles F. recrq
1883, 3, 16. James recrq
1917, 2, 14. Moody relrq
1926, 9, 8. Mary Catharine recrq of foster parents, Wm. & Clara Johnson

PRITCHARD
----, --, --. Calvin W. b 1834,1,24; m Anna M. ----- b 1837,4,14 d 1871,4,4 bur Sugar Grove
Ch: William H. b 1866, 11, 14
Calvin D. " 1869, 2, 27
Clifford M." 1870, 10, 17
Carlton C. " 1870, 10, 17

1868, 10, 13. Calvin W. & w, Anna, & ch, Wm. H., rocf Springfield MM, O., dtd 1868,9,19
1873, 8, 15. Calvin & ch, Wm. H., Edwin D., Clifford M. & Carlton C., gct Indianapolis MM, Ind.

PROBASCO
1900, 3, 20. Wm. d ae 84
1901, 3, 3. Emily d ae 62
1909, 6, 23. Ada m Thomas BALES
1914, 10, 10. Mary Ann d
1921, 6, 14. Louise m Leo J. BASSETT
1922, 3, 7. Russell m Vesta ARMSTRONG
1923, 4, 13. Hannah d
1923, 8, 18. Myra m Elmer F. JOHNSON
1924, 10, --. Ruth m Robert SKIMMINGS
1929, 1, 6. James C. d

1873, 4, 18. James recrq
1873, 4, 18. Hannah J. recrq
1873, 4, 18. Lydia recrq
1873, 4, 18. William & w, Lydia, & ch, Emily & Hannah, recrq
1891, 11, 14. Mary Anna rocf Springfield MM, O., dtd 1891,9,19
1891, 12, 12. Mary H., Ada & Wm. Russel, ch Mary Anna, recrq
1901, 4, 13. Malidsa & dt, Bertha & Edith, rocf Sabina MM, O., dtd 1901,4,10
1901, 6, 8. Ethel recrq
1903, 9, 12. Louise recrq
1904, 2, 13. Ruth Anna, dt Chas. & Anna, recrq
1906, 3, 10. George W., Myra & Inez recrq
1914, 10, 14. John recrq

PUCKETT
1898, 7, 9. Flo & Clarence relrq

PUGH
1889, 4, 13. John R. & w, Elizabeth, & ch, Albert Eston, George David, Emma Mary & Clara Ethel, recrq
1907, 4, 13. Albert Eston, George, Mary & Clara Esther dropped from mbrp
1907, 4, 13. Elizabeth dropped from mbrp

PUGSLEY
1932, 4, 13. Perci & w, Sybil, & ch, Phyllis Jeanne, Charlotte Marie & Laura Bell Ruth, recrq

PUMMELLE
1911, 2, 26. William m Margaret ABBOTT

PURDY
1910, 10, 8. Ellison R. & w, Harriett W., & ch, Alexander C., rocf Oskaloosa MM, Ia.
1914, 6, 10. Jeanette H. rocf Oskaloosa MM, Ia.
1916, 12, 13. Alexander C. & w, Jeanette, gct West Richmond MM, Ind.
1919, 7, 30. Ellison R. & w, Harriett W., gct Minneapolis MM, Minn.

PURTEE
1927, 6, 8. Hazel recrq

PYLE
----- m Esther STRATTON, dt Joseph & Dosha, b 1804,2,4
Ch: William b 1822, 7, 16
----, --, --. William b 1822,7,16; m Rebecca GARNER b 1827,10,1
Ch: Jehu Evans b 1850, 5, 17
David Lindley " 1854, 10, 13
John W. " 1857, 9, 19
Joseph L. " 1863, 9, 8
Mary A. " 1868, 11, 22
----, --, --. David S. b 1824,8,27; m Nancy FISHER b 1823,5,29
Ch: Sarah Malinda b 1862, 6, 20
Esther " 1864, 1, 8
Rachel " 1865, 9, 18
----, --, --. Henry m Lydia OSBORN b 1854,10,13
Ch: Samuel C. b 1878, 9, 7
----, --, --. Jehu Evan b 1850,5,17; m Mary P. SNOWDEN b 1851,10,6
Ch: Louella Marie b 187-, 6, 10
William Howard " 1876, 9, 3
Carrie " 1880, 4, 30
1928, 1, 28. Mildred m Chas. SAPP

1888, 3, 10. Alfred Clark & w, Emma, rocf

PYLE, continued
Springfield MM, dtd 1888,1,21
1921, 6, 15. Emma dropped from mbrp
1921, 6, 15. Frank W., Mary & Margaret dropped from mbrp

QUINN
1920, 6, 30. Ally Compton m Chas. HARDMAN

1874, 6, 19. Dr. A. T. relrq
1909, 4, 10. Ally Compton relrq
1918, 1, 9. Ally Compton recrq

RAYBURN
----, --, --. Samuel b 1814,3,2; m Susannah STRATTON b 1821,3,2
Ch: James b 1858, 2, 8
Laura
1926, 6, 14. Ethel m ----- LOVELL

1906, 2, 10. Ethel [Raeburn] recrq

RALEIGH
1911, 4, 8. Cora m Robert D. SCHMIDT

1895, 6, 8. Cora recrq

RANDALL
1903, 4, 11. Grace H. relrq
1908, 11, 14. John D. [Randal] & w, Mary, rocf Newberry MM, O., dtd 1908,9,19
1921, 6, 15. John dropped from mbrp

RANNELLS
1892, 2, 13. Clara Kirk relrq
1921, 8, 10. Daisy Wright relrq

RAPP
1877, 6, 15. John recrq
1884, 6, 26. John dis

REASON
1893, 7, 8. Edward & w, Sadie, & ch, Paul & Percy, rocf Miami MM, O., dtd 1893,6,21
1893, 8, 12. Elsie M., dt Edward & Sadie, recrq
1903, 2, 14. Edward & w, Sadie, & ch, Elsie, Paul & Percy, gct Miami MM, O.

RECTOR
1874, 3, 20. Jennie recrq

REED
----, --, --. Wm. H. b 1829,4,7; m Priscilla ----- b 1823,6,15 d 1911,9,2 ae 88
Ch: Elizabeth b 1854, 10, 4
Louella " 1857, 8, 27
Lucinda " 1861, 5, 6
1861, 2, 2. Martha Emily, dt William & Mary A., b
1877, --, --. Ella d

1870, 3, 18. Wm. H. & w, Priscilla, & ch, Elizabeth Ann, Ella & Lucinda, recrq
1873, 3, 14. Martha A. recrq
1877, 2, 16. Samuel J. & w, Delilah Jane, & ch, John W., Samuel P., Ruth A., Catherine, Ella M. & Elmer E., recrq
1877, 10, 19. Elizabeth A. relrq
1879, 12, 19. Lucinda dis
1889, 7, 13. Henderson H. dis

REESEVILLE
1921, 3, 9. M. R. recrq

RENNER
----, --, --. Marshall b 1860,11,2; m Alice HALE b 1865,12,5
Ch: Clarence b 1893, 6, 10
Robert " 1897, 7, 17
1922, 11, 8. Clarence m Elizabeth McCONNAUGHEY
1925, 8, 23. Charles Marshall, s Clarence & Elizabeth, b
1929, 12, 6. Robert [Rennie] m Mollie KLISE

1915, 5, 12. Marshall & w, Alice, & ch, Clarence & Robert, rocf Springfield MM, O., dtd 1915,4,17
1926, 2, 10. Elizabeth McConnaughey recrq
1928, 11, 14. Clarence & Elizabeth M., & s, Chas. Marshall, relrq

REYNOLDS
1903, 10, 10. Oliver P. & w, Minnie R., & ch, Isaac P., Helen & Roy, rocf Marion MM, Ind., dtd 1903,10,7

RHOADES
1920, 6, 19. George m Grace HAMILTON
1927, 3, 23. Marilyn, dt George & Grace, b

1899, 2, 11. Frank B. & w, Myra A., recrq
1899, 4, 8. Edna Brown, dt Frank & Myra, recrq
1921, 2, 9. George recrq
1921, 6, 15. Frank B. & w, Myra, & dt, Edna, dropped from mbrp

RHUDE
1912, 1, --. Mary m Guy LONG

1906, 3, 10. Nancy & May recrq
1907, 3, 9. Mattie & Cora recrq
1918, 5, 8. Howard Leonidas recrq

RICHARDS
1873, 4, 18. Samuel, Helen, Miriam & Mary recrq
1885, 12, 10. Ellen relrq

RICHARDSON
1873, 12, 1. Olive d

1872, 10, 18. Benjamin Franklin recrq
1873, 3, 14. Emma & ch, Edith, Clara B. &

RICHARDSON, continued
Olive, recrq
1875, 12, 17. Emma C. relrq
1878, 6, 14. B. F. dis
1895, 6, 8. Martha L. recrq
1898, 4, 9. Martha dropped from mbrp
1905, 1, 11. Anthony & w, Lizzie, & ch, Amanda, rocf Springfield MM, O., dtd 1904,12, 17
1906, 10, 13. Martha L. dropped from mbrp
1909, 10, 9. Esther Sayers relrq

RIDGEWAY
----, --, --. Inez m Connell WILSON

1895, 4, 13. Frank recrq
1907, 10, 12. Edna recrq
1909, 12, 12. Mary relrq
1911, 10, 14. Inez recrq

RIGGLE
1853, 6, 6. Sarah E. [Rigle] b

1872, 4, 19. Sarah recrq
1873, 3, 14. Lucy recrq
1878, 12, 20. Lucy A. & dt, Sarah Leggit, gct Springfield MM, Ind.

RILEY
----, --, --. William S. b 1818,4,29; m Sarah J. BATEY b 1827,3,27
Ch: Charley L. b 1860, 12, 24
1910, 6, 20. Florence m Wm. McNAMA

1914, 10, 14. Ivy recrq
1914, 10, 14. Charlene F. recrq

ROBERTS
1877, 2, 16. Isaac & w, Margaret E., & ch, Clauda, Elonette & Homer C., recrq
1921, 4, 13. Velma & Raymond recrq
1921, 4, 13. John & w recrq

ROBINETT
1873, 4, 18. Thomas & Moses recrq
1885, 7, 11. Thomas [Robinet] gct Dover MM,O

ROBINSON
1923, 10, 18. Clarence m Letha GALLIMORE
1924, 9, 1. Letha Gallimore d
1924, 9, 1. Martha Ann b
1928, 6, 27. Portia m Eldon HAINES
1928, 6, 28. Clarence m in Wilmington MH, Ellen PEELLE
Ch: Roger Peelle b 1930, 12, 21
Norma Charlotte " 1933, 7, 24

1894, 7, 14. Wm. recrq
1921, 6, 15. Catherine dropped from mbrp
1923, 12, 12. Clarence recrq
1932, 3, 23. Catherine recrq

ROCKHILL
1915, 9, 9. Alice Caroline m Horace Wm. MEEKS
1928, 9, 12. Amelia d

1896, 4, 11. Amelia rocf Springfield MM, O., dtd 1896,2,18
1898, 7, 9. Susan Mart dropped from mbrp
1903, 2, 14. Susie M. dropped from mbrp
1906, 5, 12. Edward & Alice recrq
1927, 9, 14. Alice E. relrq

ROE
1909, 12, 12. Hellen recrq
1921, 6, 15. Helen dropped from mbrp

ROEBUCK
1920, 8, 26. Pearl m Ruth KELSEY
1921, 11, 6. Albert Warren, s Pearl & Ruth (Kesay), b

1917, 7, 11. Pearl rocf Westfork MM, O., dtd 1917,6,16

ROGERS
1894, 5, 12. Zettie [Roger] recrq
1894, 7, 14. Mary F. recrq
1894, 7, 14. Allen D. recrq
1913, 2, 12. Roy & Ray rocf Center MM
1913, 2, 12. Frank, Martha J. & Grant recrq
1921, 4, 13. Roy relrq

ROLLISON
1905, 5, 13. Catherine Parlette rocf Center MM, O., dtd 1905,3,5

ROSE
1920, 5, 12. Margaret recrq
1920, 5, 12. Nol L. recrq
1920, 5, 12. James E. recrq
1931, 4, 1. Edward J. recrq

ROSS
1906, 2, 5. Louella d ae 20
1919, 6, 12. Rebecca m in Wilmington MH, Douglas L. PARKER
1920, 3, 23. Almira Jane d
1921, 3, 15. Ellis d
1926, 12, 7. Emma d

1884, 11, 14. Eva O. H. gct Dover MM
1886, 5, 8. Orris rocf Center MM, O., dtd 1886,4,14
1889, 4, 13. Ordie L. recrq
1889, 4, 13. Blanch & Louella, ch Emma, recrq
1895, 4, 13. Emmaline & ch, Jennie, Elden & Albert, rocf Center MM, O., dtd 1895,3. 15
1895, 4, 13. Clara rocf Center MM, O., dtd 1895,3,15
1895, 5, 11. Lena B. & Louella G., dt Emaline, recrq

ROSS, continued
1904, 6, 11. Albert relrq
1905, 11, 11. Ellis & w, Eva O. H., & ch, Alberta L. & Rebecca J., rocf Dover MM, O., dtd 1905,12,14 (?)
1905, 11, 11. Ross, Nellie E. & Almira Jane rocf Dover MM, O., dtd 1905,12,14(?)
1908, 7, 11. Albert recrq
1910, 8, 13. Albert J. dropped from mbrp
1927, 1, 12. Eldon relrq

ROWE
1920, 9, 2. Violet m Harold LUKINS

RUBLE
1933, 4, 12. Stella recrq

RUDDICK
1870, 3, 18. William recrq
1871, 6, 16. Eliza J. recrq
1872, 4, 19. Anna recrq
1876, 5, 19. Ida [Rudduck] recrq

RUDE
1904, 1, 9. Elvira recrq

RUTHERFORD
----, --, --. John b 1827,5,5 d 1865,4,5; m Sylvia ----- b 1832,11,17 d 1918,10,3
Ch: Ada B. b 1855, 2, 13
Davidella b 1858, 3, 28 d 1862,10,29
Susanna G. " 1861, 6, 14
Mary Jane " 1864, 1, 27

SABIN
1884, 5, 15. Geo. W. rocf Miami MM, O., dtd 1884,4,23
1885, 5, 9. Geo. W. gct Centre MM, O.

SAMMONS
1889, 3, 9. Lexie recrq

SANDERS
1828, 2, 27. David b
1866, 1, 27. Addison b
1920, 2, 8. Grace Green d

1868, 11, 17. David & s, Adison, rocf Newberry MM, O., dtd 1868,10,19
1917, 5, 9. Richard John & Edwin Allen, ch Grace, recrq
1925, 6, 10. Richard John relrq
1926, 3, 31. Edwin Allen dropped from mbrp
1928, 11, 14. Edwin recrq

SAPP
1925, 9. 1. Anna Lou m Sleva Wm. ORBIN
1928, 1, 28. Charles m Mildred PYLE

1914, 2, 11. Emery J. rocf Jamestown MM
1914, 2, 11. Emma recrq
1914, 10, 14. Anna Lou, Charley & Helen recrq

SARVER
1925, 5, 13. Ruby recrq
1926, 12, 8. Ruby gct Springfield MM, O.

SAYRES
----, --, --. L. D. [Sayers] m Phebe G. ----- b 1843,9,3
Ch: Lillian b 1866, 8, 13
St. Clair " 1869, 3, 29
Esther Grace
b 1869, 3, 28(?)
1914, 1, 3. David d

1873, 4, 18. Davis L. recrq

SCHAIBER
1904, 3, 12. Ivan Victor recrq
1929, 12,10. Ivan Victor [Schiath] dropped from mbrp

SCHOONOVER
1908, 11, 21. Earl m Cazy TRENARY

1894, 7, 14. Anna, Ida & Effie recrq
1894, 7, 14. Earle recrq
1894, 9, 8. Nicholas recrq
1921, 6, 15. Earl dropped from mbrp

SCHUBERG
1910, 11, 14. Benjamin F. m Alice Emma GLASS

1912, 6, 12. Benjamin Franklin recrq

SCHULTZ
1921, 6, 15. Grace, William & Lindley dropped from mbrp

SCOTT
----, --, --. Opal m Willard HADLEY

1870, 4, 15. Irena recrq
1871, 5, 19. Irena dis
1881, 10, 14. Susan gct Springfield MM, O.

SCROGGY
1910, 3, 2. Naomi d ae 15

1908, 4, 11. Annie L. & ch, Naomi C., Jesse J., Carey D., Robert E., Joseph N., Jennie R. & Lydia E., rocf Caesars Creek MM, O.
1914, 12, 9. Jesse J. [Scoggy] relrq
1920, 4, 14. Jennie relrq
1921, 3, 9. Hazel relrq
1921, 4, 13. Anna, Carey D., Robert E. & Joseph M. relrq

SEEKINGS
1873, 5, 16. Mary gct Union MM, O.

SEIFORT
1903, 11, 14. Alta rocf Kokomo MM, Ind.
1921, 6, 15. Alta [Seigert] dropped from

SEIFORT, continued
mbrp

SENMAN
1917, 5, 16. A. L. m Lula JONES

SEVER
1913, 1, 8. George rocf Springfield MM, O., dtd 1912,12,21
1925, 4, 8. George [Severs] relrq

SEWELL
1883, 4, 20. Wm. J. recrq

SHADLEY
1827, 2, 1. Bessie m James Seth HADLEY

SHANKS
1933, 4, 12. Carl H. & Edith & Carl Herman Jr. recrq

SHARP
1907, 10, 7. Robert d ae 42
1908, 4, 28. Leta M. m John L. COMPTON

1889, 4, 13. Robert, John & Thomas recrq
1915, 10, 13. Thomas J. gct Center MM, O.
1921, 8, 10. Thomas rocf Center MM
1927, 6, 29. Thomas relrq

SHEPPARD
1833, 3, 1. Allen b
----, --, --. Wm. H. b 1820,3,20; m Elizabeth RIDDLE b 1828,9,10
1866, 10, 26. Francis J. b
1868, 12, 16. Hannah m in Wilmington MH, Thos. MOON
1899, 2, 8. Dr. W. W. d ae 77

1870, 3, 18. Angeline D. recrq
1883, 2, 16. Wm. W. & w, Elizabeth, rocf Springfield MM, dtd 1883,1,20
1885, 7, 11. Angeline & s, Frank, gct Minneapolis MM, Minn.
1886, 4, 10. Louise recrq

SHERENGER
1881, 5, 20. F. C. & w, M. F., & ch, Wm. Arthur, recrq

SHERMAN
1929, 12, 10. Lucile Peelle dropped from mbrp

SHEWALTER
1873, 4, 18. Elizabeth recrq
1873, 4, 18. Clarence W. recrq
1890, 5, 10. Mary E. [Showalter] relrq

SHOCKNEY
1893, 2, 13. Agnes E. Nicklow relrq

SHOWMAKER
----, --, --. George b 1825,2,21; m Elizabeth VAN DOREN b 1833.6.10
Ch: Amos D. b 1857, 3, 3
Raymon W. " 1859, 3, 27
Emerson W. " 1860, 11, 22
John E. " 1864, 12, 18
Edward E. " 1866, 8,17 d 1876,10,10
Henry M. " 186-, 4, 16

SHOOP
1888, 4, 14. Richard H. recrq
1890, 5, 10. May recrq

SHRIEVES
1908, 10, 10. Reba A. gct Dover MM, O.

SHUBERT
1914, 3, 19. Bertha m Everett STARBUCK

1899, 5, 13. Sadie & Bertha recrq
1899, 5, 13. George recrq
1899, 5, 13. Ida recrq
1915, 5, 12. George & w, Ida, gct Center MM, O.

SHULTZ
1908, 2, 8. Wm. & Grace rocf Ogdon MM, O., dtd 1907,11,23
1908, 4, 11. Lindley [Schultz] recrq

SILLICK
1877, 2, 16. Jennie recrq

SIMMONS
1911, 11, 23. Minnie m Glenn OSBORN
----, --, --. Anna m P. J. CLIFFORD

1925, 12, --. Don Jr., s Don & Ether (Ruble),b

1874, 3, 20. James K. recrq
1894, 7, 14. J. W., Annie L., Stella A., Lottie M., Nellie D., Minnie L., Marlie C. & Don W., recrq
1903, 2, 14. Marlie dropped from mbrp
1906, 4, 14. Estella dropped from mbrp
1906, 4, 14. J. W. dropped from mbrp
1917, 5, 9. Ethel Ruble recrq

SIMPSON
1898, 7, 8. Henry d ae 69

1874, 3, 20. Henry recrq
1895, 5, 11. Andrew & Zurellie recrq
1896, 2, 8. Etta recrq
1903, 1, 10. Andrew & Zurilla dropped from mbrp
1904, 4, 9. Etta dropped from mbrp
1914, 10, 14. Thelma recrq

SKIMMINGS
1924, 10, --. Robert m Ruth PROBASCO

1928, 3, 14. Robert [Skimming] rocf Dover MM

SLACK
1926, 8, 14. Ethel m Robert HADLEY

SLAGEL
1894, 7, 14. Dick recrq
1895, 8, 10. Dick [Slagle] relrq

SLIKER
1920, 9, 4. Rose m Arnold LINTON

SMART
1923, 11, 29. Roy M. m Mable HADLEY

1921, 2, 9. Carroll & Madaline L. recrq
1824, 3, 12. Mable E. Hadley relrq

SMITH
----, --, --. Daniel b 1809,4,15 d 1880,4,1 bur Wilmington; m Anna M. HARTMAN b 1816,6,1 d 1889,10,19 bur Wilmington
Ch: James E. b 1847, 3, 27
----, --, --. William R. b 1829,3,28; m Hannah ----- b 1832,10,10
Ch: Mary Elizabeth b 1856, 3, 28
Emma Jane " 1859, 8, 28
John Emerson " 1865, 3, 23
William Orla b 1869, 9, 10
----, --, --. Henry b 1849,4,15; m Emily ANDREW b 1838,10,15
Ch: Minnie b 1860, 4, 26
John Henry " 1874, 8, 15
----, --, --. Joseph H. b 1842,4,27; m Ruth Ann OSBORN b 1845,3,26 d 1928,11,19
Ch: Lizzie May b 1869, 5, 7
Fanny G. " 1878, 4, 21
----, --, --. James E. b 1847,3,27; m Mary E. OSBORN b 1856,7,23
Ch: Ella b 1879, 1, 22
1897, 8, 22. Hattie d ae 2
1909, 3, 10. Viola m Foster ANDERS
1909, 12, 23. Charles D. m Madge Osborn LINTON
1911, 4, 8. Robert D. m Cora RALEIGH
1912, 2, 4. Donald & Dorothy, ch Gilbert & Mary, b
1922, 12, 19. Caroline McPhail d
1926, 10, 7. Phoebe m Milburn GUSTIN
1929, 2, 2. James d
1930, 12, 12. Clara d

1868, 12, 15. Wm. P. & w, Hannah, & ch, Mary Elizabeth, Emma Jane & John Emmerson, rocf Newberry MM, O., dtd 1868,11,23
1873, 4, 18. Austin T. recrq
1876, 5, 19. Mary & Maggie recrq
1878, 5, 17. Wm. R. & w, Hannah, & ch, Mary Elizabeth Emma Jane, John Emerson & Wm. Orla, gct Plainfield MM, Ind.
1884, 4, 18. Wm. P. recrq
1884, 5, 15. Abi A. & Mintie recrq
1884, 6, 26. Mary & Maggie relrq
1890, 5, 10. Edward & Sarah recrq
1895, 1, 12. Lizzie (Smith) Green & dt, Mabel Smith, rocf Springfield MM, O., dtd 1894,12,15
1895, 2, 9. Gilbert & w, Mary Maranda & ch, Arthur T. & Mary T., recrq
1895, 4, 13. Minnie recrq
1896, 11, 14. James E. & w, Mary E., & ch, Ella J. & Lena M., rocf Springfield MM, O., dtd 1896,10,17
1897, 6, 17. Wm. recrq
1898, 4, 9. Austin dropped from mbrp
1900, 4, 14. Joseph H. & w, Ruth A., & s, Chas. D., rocf Ogden MM, O., dtd 1900,3,24
1903, 9, 12. Mabel J. gct Pasadena MM, Calif.
1903, 10, 10. Viola H., Ada L. & Alice E., recrq
1905, 11, 11. Lillian Holliday gct Newberry MM, O.
1906, 2, 10. Frank A. & Walker B. recrq
1906, 10, 13. Wm. McCoy dropped from mbrp
1907, 3, 9. William dropped from mbrp
1907, 8, 10. Jessie Carrol gct Whittier MM, Calif.
1907, 9, 14. Manda rocf Westland MM, O.
1907, 9, 14. Dora rocf Goshen MM, O.
1910, 2, 10. Anna recrq
1913, 4, 14. Charles relrq
1913, 12, 17. Fred S. recrq
1914, 2, 11. Maude recrq
1914, 10, 14. Bessie recrq
1919, 5, 21. Chester & Dorothy recrq
1921, 2, 9. Grover T. recrq
1921, 4, 13. Eleanor relrq
1921, 6, 15. Fred & Bessie dropped from mbrp
1925, 10, 14. Clarence & w, Goldie, recrq
1927, 6, 8. Helen recrq
1928, 6, 8. Frank A. gct Xenia MM, O.
1929, 6, 12. Walker dropped from mbrp
1929, 12, 10. Cora dropped from mbrp

SMITHSON
1902, 3, 8. Charles & Della & ch, Fred & Madge, recrq
1907, 10, 12. Dorothy recrq
1910, 2, 10. Bessie recrq

SNODGRASS
1930, 5, 14. Orville & w, May Marie, recrq

SNOWDEN
----, --, --. William b 1815,5,20 d 1885,2,25 bur Center; m Lydia M. CARTER b 1820,11,13
Ch: Robert P. b 1841, 6, 21
----, --, --. Robert P. b 1841,6,21; m Malinda PYLE b 1843,11,22
Ch: William J. b 1868, 2, 28
Esther Anna" 1876, 10, 21
1914, 8, 1. Edward m Ilo CARROLL
1922, 9, 18. William m Nettie WHITLOW
1925, 9, 13. Alta d
1925, 10, 18. Robert d
1931, 2, 14. William d

SNOWDEN, continued
1902, 1, 11. Rachel rocf Centre MM, O., dtd 1901,12,18
1904, 2, 13. Seth rocf Center MM, O., dtd 1904,1,13
1904, 2, 13. Flora P. recrq
1914, 6, 10. Alta & w, Celia, & ch, Myrtle, Sarah, Edward, Arthur, Mary & Roy Townsend, rocf Center MM, O., dtd 1914,5,13
1914, 7, 8. Myrtle relrq
1921, 3, 9. Robert & w, Malinda P., rocf Springfield MM, O., dtd 1921,2,19
1921, 3, 9. Wm. J. rocf Springfield MM, O., dtd 1921,2,19
1921, 3, 9. Esther Anna rocf Springfield MM, O., dtd 1921,2,19
1929, 3, 13. Celia & ch, Sarah, Edward Arthur & Mary, relrq

SNYDER
1932, 1, 31. Helen Wright m Stanley L. JOHNSON

1917, 2, 14. Helen recrq
1930, 6, 11. J. Earle & w, Harriett & ch, Douglas & J. Thad, recrq

SOCKMAN
1876, 4, 14. John recrq

SOUTH
1871, 6, 15. Enis, s Wm., b
1871, 7, 29. Lizzie G. d
1873, 5, 15. Enis d

SOUTHWORTH
1874, 3, 20. Wilbur S. recrq
1876, 8, 18. Wilbur D. dis

SPAID
1898, 12, 12. Mary Farquhar relrq

SPARKS
1899, 2, 10. Ethel Rebecca d ae 19
1917, 6, 30. Josiah W. d
1931, 2, 11. Laura B. d

1869, 10, 12. Abi rocf Center MM, O., dtd 1869,8,18
1874, 3, 20. Josiah W. recrq

SPEAR
1911, 3, 9. Fred m Louisa TURNER
1918, 12, 25. Wilbur [Spears] m FredaLouise DABE
1930, 12, 18. Edna Emily m Herman WOODMANSEE
1927, 2, 15. John Dana, s Wilbur & Freda (Dabe), b

1912, 4, 10. Louise Turner gct Dover MM, O.
1921, 4, 13. Carey, Minnie, Ada Emily & Wilbur [Spears] roc
1929, 4, 10. Wilbur [Spears] & w, Freda, & ch, Hugh, Mildred Jeanne & John Dana, gct Whittier MM, Calif.

SPELLMAN
1920, 2, 7. Walter m Mildred GRICE

SPENCER
1876, 4, 14. Frank recrq
1876, 5, 19. Emily recrq
1898, 5, 14. Frank & Emma dropped from mbrp
1903, 1, 10. Emma dropped from mbrp
1903, 2, 14. Frank dropped from mbrp
1925, 3, 11. Maurice & Leonard recrq

SPINKS
1896, 11, 14. Martin recrq

SPRAGUE
1925, 4, 22. Cornelia d
1931, 1, 15. George B. d

1901, 3, 9. Myrtle recrq
1903, 2, 14. George & w, Cornelia, & s, Karl L., recrq
1903, 2, 14. Maude M. recrq
1909, 4, 10. Frankie recrq
1914, 10, 14. Esther recrq
1920, 1, 14. Esther relrq
1921, 6, 15. Howard R. recrq
1928, 3, 14. Louise recrq

SPRAY
1793, 8, 17. James, s Samuel & Mary, b
----, --, --. Isaac b 1822,7,8; m Rebecca L. HARLAN b 1823,12,24
Ch: Phebe b 1849, 10, 19
Samuel L. " 1854, 5, 5
Mary F. " 1854, 5, 5
Ida M. b 1856, 7, 14
John C. " 1858, 4, 26
Hannah A. " 1860, 3, 5
Catharine C. b 1862, 9, 8
1907, 12, 9. Mary Ann d ae 63

1895, 6, 8. Henry & Mary Ann recrq
1921, 3, 9. Eva roc
1921, 3, 9. Bertha rocf Center MM, O., dtd 1921,2,16

SPROUSE
1914, 4, 8. Pearl Carey rocf Ogden MM, O., dtd 1914,3,28
1914, 4, 8. Floyd Carey recrq
1921, 2, 9. Charles recrq

SPURGEON
1908, 6, 8. Daniel d ae 69
1912, 4, 10. Lida d ae 66

1879, 4, 18. Ella recrq
1881, 5, 20. Minnie recrq
1886, 5, 8. Jesse A. & w, Lida J., & ch,

SPURGEON, continued
Frank & Mary B., recrq
1907, 8, 10. Daniel & w, Lida, & gr ch, Daniel & Goldie, rocf Center MM, O., dtd 1907,7,17
1915, 1, 13. Alvin C. & Goldie F. relrq

STACKHOUSE
1916, 9, 20. Myrtle m Russell KELLY

1914, 10, 14. C. W. & Myrtle recrq
1921, 6, 15. C. W. dropped from mbrp

STAMATS
1872, 5, 20. Frank [Stamates] b
1875, --, --. Peter A. [Stamater] d

1870, 3, 18. Peter A. [Stamates] & w, Artemissa, & s, Arthur, recrq
1885, 7, 11. Artemecia & s, Arthur, gct Newberry MM, O.
1898, 2, 12. Arthur gct Newberry MM, O.
1906, 10, 13. Arthur dropped from mbrp

STANLEY
1898, 7, 9. Mary A. dropped from mbrp

STANTON
1919, 12, 18. James Franklin d

1899, 10, 14. John T. & w, Emily, & ch, Louisa, Wm. E. & Mariella, rocf Bridgeport MM, Ind., dtd 1899,10,5
1899, 12, 9. Louisa [Staunton] relrq
1904, 6, 11. John F. & w, Emily, & ch, Marietta & Wm. G., gct White Water MM, Ind.
1911, 3, 11. Bessie Smith recrq
1914, 5, 13. Wm. & w, Bessie Smith, & ch, Wm.,Smith, Emily Maude & Elizabeth Ann, rocf White Water MM, Ind., dtd 1914,4,16
1915, 2, 10. Carlton W. rocf Plainfield MM, Ind.
1921, 6, 15. Carlton dropped from mbrp

STARBUCK
----, --, --. John L. b 1822,10,6; m Margaret ----- b 1824,7,24
Ch: Josephine b 1852, 10, 14
William A. " 1856, 3, 4
Nathan L. " 1859, 7, 8
Clara A. " 1864, 7, 19
Albert " 1869, 6, 15
----, --, --. Adin L. b 1844,5,10; m Louisa M. ----- b 1847,11,21
Ch: Nellie M. b 1867, 9, 23
1909, 9, 14. Clara Evelyn, dt Morris & Clara, b
1914, 3. 19. Everett m Bertha SHUPERT
1918, 11, 9. Charles m Esther DOAN
1920, 2, 26. Raymond m Alice COWGILL
1926, 1, 25. Earl C. m Lillian PAINTER
1930, 4, 10. Thomas Arthur, s Charles & Esther (Doan), b

1871, 8, 18. Aden & w, Louisa M., & dt, Nellie M., gct Dover MM, O.
1879, 5, 16. John T. & w, Margaret, & ch, Nathan T., Clara A. & Albert, gct Dover MM, O.
1879, 5, 16. William gct Dover MM. O.
1901, 7, 13. Cert rec for Asie & ch, Raymond, Leo from Plainfield MM, O., endorsed to Dover MM, O., 1901,8,10
1906, 3, 10. Albert & w, Lizzie, & s, Arthur, rocf Dover MM, O., dtd 1906,2,15
1907, 11, 9. Maurice B. rocf Dover MM, O.
1907, 11, 9. Granville A. recrq
1915, 1, 13. Bertha Shupert gct Dover MM
1919, 4, 9. Maurice & w, Clara, & ch, Granville A. & Clara Evylin, relrq
1919, 12, 10. Wm., Marianna & Franklin rocf Dover MM
1923, 10, 14. Wm. A. & w, Marianna, & s, Franklin, gct Whittier MM, Calif.
1926, 1, 13. Virginia recrq
1926, 6, 9. Chas. Richard & Martha Jr. recrq
1927, 10, 12. Chas. R. relrq
1928, 4, 11. Lillian Pidgeon relrq

STARR
1902, 3, 8. Mary Etta Timberlake rocf Centre MM, O., dtd 1902,2,12
1902, 5, 10. Clarence Raymond recrq
1917, 8, 8. Metta relrq
1926, 3, 31. Ruth Emma dropped from mbrp
1929, 12, 10. Raymond dropped from mbrp

STATLER
1930, 8, 31. Lydia d

1892, 4, 9. Lydia & dt, Mary, Emma T. & Della, rocf Springfield MM, O., dtd 1892, 1,16
1905, 1, 11. Bessie M. recrq

STEPHENS
1880, 4, 16. Lucinda recrq
1923, 3, 14. Leo M. [Stevens] & w, Stella, recrq

STEPHENSON
1917, 11, 24. Dwight m Mary HAMILTON

1895, 4, 13. Emma recrq
1899, 6, 15. Emma gct Newberry MM, O.

STEWART
1922, 2, 2. Emma d
1926, 3, 28. Pearl d
1929, 4, 15. Grace Kirk d
1931, 12, 22. Joseph d

1886, 8, 14. George recrq
1889, 4, 13. Wm. I. & w, Emma, & s, Pearl, recrq
1903, 1, 10. George dropped from mbrp

STEWART, continued
1903, 2, 14. Jennie Crumley gct Dover MM, O.
1919, 3, 12. Grace Kirk & ch, Wendell E., Carl L. & Robert J., rocf Center MM, O.
1921, 8, 10. Ella, Joseph, Arthur, Fred, Cora Mears & Donald, rocf Center MM
1926, 3, 10. Mable recrq
1929, 12, 10. Arthur dropped from mbrp
1931, 1, 14. Donald relrq

STIFF
1919, 8, 24. Priscilla d

STILLINGS
----, --, --. James, s John & Sarah, b 1805,9, 16 d 1882,7,4 bur Xenia, O.; m Mary A. CHOPSON b 1825,4,2

STODDARD
1876, 1, 21. Clarissa d bur Sugar Grove

1870, 3, 18. Henry P. recrq
1870, 12, 16. Clarissa D. recrq
1873, 3, 14. James E., Virginia B. & Harry A., ch Henry P. & Clarissa D., recrq
1885, 1, 16. Virginia B. relrq
1907, 10, 12. James Edwin & Harry C. dropped from mbrp

STOFFREGEN
1907, 3, 12. Francis Turpin b

1906, 9, 8. Harry Frederick Jr. recrq of parents
1909, 11, 13. Ida Belle Turpin relrq
1915, 10, 13. Ida B. Turpin recrq
1916, 4, 12. David Miller recrq of mother, Ida
1930, 7, 9. Ida B. & ch, H. Frederick Jr., Frances T. & David Miller, gct Cincinnati MM, O.

STOLTZ
1918, 2, 21. Charles W. m Jane GRICE

1929, 1, 9. Charles W. recrq

STONE
1879, 4, 18. Eliza rocf Hopewell MM, O., dtd 1879,3,1
1898, 6, 11. Laura rocf Ogden MM, O., dtd 1898,5,27
1898, 10, 8. Laura M. relrq

STOOPS
1895, 6, 8. Margaret, Walter & Frederick recrq
1906, 4, 14. Fred dropped from mbrp
1921, 6, 15. Walter & Sina dropped from mbrp

STOUT
1903, 10, 10. Florence recrq
1921, 11, 9. Drucella Leonard rocf Center MM
1921, 11, 2. Florence relrq

STOWE
----, --, --. Willard m Ruthanna TODHUNTER

1916, 1, 12. Ruth Todhunter gct Fairfield MM, O.

STRANAHAN
1904, 6, 11. Edgar & w, Irene, & dt, Esther, rocf Sabina MM, O., dtd 1904,6,8
1907, 9, 14. Edgar H. & w, Irene D., & dt, Esther, gct University MM, Kans.

STRATTON
----, --, --. Mahlon b 1809,9,25; m Harriet JENKS b 1825,6,24
Ch: Clara E. b 1856, 10, 28
Mary E. " 1858, 9, 4
Amanda F. " 1862, 6, 5
Almira A. " 1865, 8, 27
----, --, --. John H. b 1831,3,12; m Judith -----
Ch: Francis J. b 1857, 9, 22
Flora E. " 1860, 2, 15
John H, m 2nd Lydia McGAHEE b 1843,3,21
Ch: Joseph b 1864, 2, 27
John " 1864, 2, 27
David " 1866, 6, 4
Lorena " 1868, 10, 23
Arrena " 1868, 10, 23
Clara " 1872, 4, 28
May E. " 1874, 7, 19
Clarence Victor " 1877, 12, 13
Salina Ann " 1880, 11, 6
1923, 2, 27. Nettie m Thos. M. MOSSBARGER

1898, 6, 11. David J. rocf Ogden MM, O., dtd 1898,5,27
1911, 3, 11. David relrq
1921, 3, 9. Nettie recrq
1921, 4, 13. Helen Frances recrq
1925, 5, 13. Helen recrq
1926, 6, 9. Charles recrq

STREET
1874, 3, 20. Rose recrq
1886, 4, 10. Lola Montez recrq
1892, 3, 12. Jessie recrq
1897, 3, 13. Edna & Ardell recrq
1912, 6, 12. Mildred Ardella gct University MM, Kans.

STULTS
1921, 4, 3. Homer m Mary Katharine HADLEY
Ch: Elizabeth Gene b 1921, 12, 31

1921, 12, 14. Elizabeth Gene [Stultz] recrq of parents

STURGEON
1932, 11, 13. Letitia B. Weller d

SUMNER
----, --, --. Wm. M. b 1849,4,10 d 1927,2,25; m Adaline OGBURN b 1850,7,8 d 1912,12,4
Ch: Harriet E. b 1872, 2, 25
Stephen J. " 1874, 3, 22
Sarah E. " 1876, 5, 30

1906, 3, 10. William [Sumners] & w, Adeline, rocf Clear Creek MM, O.

SURFACE
1921, 3, 9. Bertha M. rocf Center MM

SUTHERLAND
1916, 7, 3. Frank m Vedith BREWER

SUTTON
1889, 4, 13. Sadie recrq

SWAIN
1929, 1, 9. Henrietta B. rocf Leesburg MM

SWINK
1880, 5, 14. Sarah recrq

SWISSHELM
1933, 4, 12. Ellen recrq

TAGGART
1887, 8, 13. Alice Hadley relrq

TALMADGE
1916, 12, 14. Huston m Lena AUSTIN

TAYLOR
1917, 8, 16. Jeanette m H. K. BAILEY
1919, 1, 9. Clifford d

1873, 4, 18. Wm. H. recrq
1874, 3, 20. Jeanette recrq
1877, 11, 16. Chloe Douglas gct Spiceland MM, Ind.
1885, 6, 13. Wm. H. dropped from mbrp
1886, 4, 10. Clifford D. recrq
1895, 6, 8. George recrq
1906, 2, 10. Jeanette recrq
1907, 5, 11. George dropped from mbrp
1924, 10, 11. Charles E. & w, Mayme, & dt, Maurine, recrq

TELFAIR
1927, 9, 14. John Peyton rocf Grassy Run MM, O.
1929, 6, 12. Peyton dropped from mbrp

TEMPLIN
1927, 7, 6. James m Louise HADLEY

1912, 4, 10. Lorena recrq
1914, 10, 14. Russell recrq
1929, 11, 13. Louise Hadley relrq

TENER
1916, 8, 9. Herman recrq
1922, 5, 10. Herman [Tever] gct Friendsville MM, Tenn.

TERRELL
----, --, --. Israel b 1830,2,4; m Mary E. ----- b 1838,9,2
Ch: George M. b 1857, 2, 6
Clara B. " 1859, 3, 11
Clinton S. " 1861, 1, 27
William H. " 1863, 6, 10
Susannah C." 1866, 2, 10
Albert
----, --, --. Everett m Susanna McKAY
Ch: Mary Matilda b 1912, 7, 19
Edward
Everett Jr. b 1923, 10, 6
1925, 7, 6. Mary d

1903, 11, 14. Matilda & ch, Randal H., Everett, Howard Vincent & Clara A., rocf Clear Creek MM, O., dtd 1903,10,10
1907, 5, 11. Wm. dropped from mbrp
1908, 10, 10. Mattie C. gct Clear Creek MM,O.
1908, 10, 10. Randall gct Clear Creek MM, O.
1908, 10, 10. Howard V. gct Clear Creek MM,O.
1912, 2, 10. Susanna recrq
1912, 2, 10. Allen McKay recrq of parents, E. Everett & Susanna
1919, 11, 12. Faith Austin gct Fairview MM
1929, 6, 12. Mary Louise dropped from mbrp

THATCHER
----, --, --. Jesse b 1815,1,8; m Martha REYNARD b 1817,2,23

1877, 4, 20. Mary Hannah con mcd
1880, 4, 16. Oliver J. rocf Springfield MM, O., dtd 1880,3,20
1881, 9, 16. Oliver J. relrq
1885, 6, 13. Mary dropped from mbrp
1891, 7, 11. Nancy recrq
1898, 2, 12. Mary E. gct Ogden MM, O.
1904, 6, 11. Harry & George recrq
1906, 2, 10. Lucretia & Hazel recrq
1908, 7, 11. George gct Dover MM, O.
1909, 7, 10. Nannie relrq

THOMAS
1874, 7, 17. Isaac & w, Mary Jane, & dt, Augusta, recrq
1897, 12, 11. Roberta recrq
1912, 12, 11. Louisa Doan relrq
1929, 10, 9. Roberta relrq

THOMPSON
1909, 9, 12. Lewis Elwood, s Birtzel & Effie,

THOMPSON, continued
b
1920, 8, 4. Mary Martha b
1926, 1, 1. Leroy & Ruth Esther
Ch: Mary
Harriett b 1928, 9, 11
J. Leroy " 1932, 5, 26

1876, 5, 19. Clara recrq
1877, 2, 16. McClelland recrq
1879, 1, 17. Oscar A. rocf Clear Creek MM, O.
1880, 10, 15. Oscar A., gr s Amos Hiatt, gct Union MM, Minn.
1881, 5, 20. Ella recrq
1899, 8, 12. Lawrence rocf West Fork MM, O., dtd 1899,7,15
1903, 2, 14. Hannah dropped from mbrp
1906, 2, 10. Leslie recrq
1907, 3, 9. Lawrence dropped from mbrp
1907, 4, 13. Clara dropped from mbrp
1909, 3, 13. Birtsel & w, Effie, & s, Maynard, recrq
1912, 12, 11. Franklin recrq
1914, 10, 14. Mary recrq
1917, 5, 9. Lutie A. recrq
1918, 8, 21. May & Ralph recrq
1926k 3, 10. B. O. & w, Effie, & ch, Maynard, Lewis & Mary Martha, gct Springfield MM,O.
1927, 7, 20. J. Leroy recrq
1928, 4, 11. Lida Lucile relrq
1929, 12, 10. Leslie dropped from mbrp

THORNBURG
1892, 2, 13. Silas H. & w, Sarah, & ch, Carrie M., Raymond & Nellie E., rocf Fairfield MM, O., dtd 1892,1,16
1901, 12, 14. Silas & fam gct Fairfield MM,O.

THORNE
----, --, --. John & Elizabeth
Ch: John
Alfred M.
Mary M. d 1899,4,25 ae 58
----, --, --. John & Susannah
Ch: Margrett
Elizabeth b 1877, 9, 18
1923, 8, 6. Alfred d

1870, 7, 15. Elizabeth [Thorn] & ch, Stephen, John, Alfred M. & Mary, rocf Miami MM,O., dtd 1870,6,20
1874, 3, 20. John W. [Thorn] recrq
1875, 1, 15. Eliza [Thorn] recrq
1875, 4, 16. Susannah recrq
1877, 2, 16. Lucy M. relrq
1885, 6, 13. John W. dropped from mbrp
1889, 4, 13. Lucy M. [Thorn] recrq
1902, 4, 12. Cornelia relrq

THORNTON
1832, 8, 16. Evan C. b
1835, 12, 14. Martha B. b
1870, 2, 18. Evan C. & w, Martha B., rocf Miami MM, O., dtd 1870,1,26
1874, 5, 15. Evan C. & w, Martha B., gct New Garden MM

TILLINGHAST
1924, 5, 14. Mary recrq

TODHUNTER
1897, 10, 24. Clara d ae 40
1901, 6, 3. Amos d ae 83
1909, 6, 17. Walter m Ora TRUITT
1918, 3, 30. Mary m Earl S. BLESSING
1925, 7, 5. Marguerite m George OLIVER
----, --, --. Ruthanna m Willard STOWE

1884, 11, 14. Amos & w, Emily, & ch, Clara E., Laura C., Layton W., Bessie C. & Lucy E., rocf Hopewell MM, dtd 1884,9,6
1897, 5, 8. Alice & Virgie recrq
1897, 7, 10. Walter, Mary, Ruth & Marguerite recrq
1913, 11, 12. Walter relrq

TOMLIN
1890, 7, 12. Harriett recrq
1890, 9, 13. Harriett gct Newberry MM, O.
1891, 7, 11. Peter recrq

TOMLINSON
1902, 1, 11. Sara recrq

TOWNSEND
1914, 8, 12. Horace m Mary HAZARD

TRAINOR
1921, 12, 25. Dr. W. J. m Augusta Barrett CLINNESS

1922, 12, 13. Augusta B. relrq

TREFZ
1921, 6, 29. Alice m George WRIGHT

1921, 4, 13. Alice recrq
1921, 4, 13. Oren recrq

TRENARY
1908, 11, 21. Cazy m Earl SCHOONOVER

TRICKY
1926, 1, 13. Hazel recrq

TRIMMER
----, --, --. Samuel b 1829,4,27; m Jane LUDLOW b 1831,11,21
Ch: Homer V. b 1857, 7, 17
Mary Alice " 1859, 11, 7

TROUT
1890, 12, 13. Alfred rocf Center MM, O.
1906, 10, 13. Alfred dropped from mbrp

TRUEBLOOD
----, --, --. Benjamin & Sarah
Ch: Irvin K. b 1875, 9, 26 d 1877, 7,14 bur Sugar Grove
Lyra D. b 1877, 9, 23
1914, 12, 15. Martha H. d

1874, 8, 14. Benjamin & w, Sarah, rocf Spring Creek MM, Ia., dtd 1874,8,1
1879, 8, 15. Benjamin & w & dt gct Oskaloosa MM, Ia.
1889, 4, 13. Alpheus & w, Almeda, & ch, Effie, Mary E. & Edna Winifred, rocf Amboy MM,Ind.
1896, 2, 8. Alpheus & w, Almeda, & dt, Edna Winifred, gct Winthrop MM, Me.
1896, 2, 8. Mary gct Winthrop MM, Me.
1896, 2, 8. Effie gct Winthrop MM, Me.

TRUITT
1909, 6, 17. Ora m Walter TODHUNTER

TRUMAN
1907, 9, 26. J. L. m Lila HANEY
1925, 12, 5. Lila Haney d

1922, 5, 10. Lita Lucile recrq of mother, Lita H.

TUCKER
1882, 11, 17. Newton recrq

TURNER
1911, 3, 9. Louisa m Fred SPEAR
1918, 8, 31. Margaret d
1921, 5, 5. Clarice m Lauren BRACKNEY
----, --, --. Frances Marie m Carl HAINES

1884, 5, 15. John & w, Margaret, & ch, Elijah N., Mary Emily, Fannie Laura, Eber, Walter, Priscilla & Amy, rocf Centre MM, O., dtd 1884,4,16
1909, 1, 9. Marie rocf Dover MM
1909, 1, 9. Aaron Waller & Francis Marie, ch Eber & Marie, recrq
1909, 3, 13. Elijah gct White Water MM, Ind.
1919, 5, 14. Ronald recrq
1921, 1, 12. Clarice recrq
1921, 3, 9. Charles recrq
1922, 10, 11. Eleanor recrq

TURPIN
1887, 12, 10. Ida Belle rocf Clear Creek MM,O.

TUTTLE
1922, 5, 20. Donald m Ruth GIBSON

TYSON
1885, 4, 11. Lena recrq

UNTHANK
1897, 10, 24. James Russell d ae 6

1876, 12, 15. James B. rocf Dover MM, Ind., dtd 1876,9,20
1889, 10, 12. Dinah K. rocf Hopewell MM
1889, 10, 12. John C. rocf Hopewell MM
1895, 7, 13. Dinah K. & John C. gct Hopewell MM, O.
1896, 4, 11. Emma & s, James R., recrq
1898, 6, 11. Dinah K. & w, John, gct Sharon MM, Ia. (form cert lost)
1903, 11, 14. James B. & w, Emma H., gct Dover MM, Ind.

UPP
1882, 12, 15. Jennie relrq
1907, 11, 9. James B. & Jennie S. recrq
1907, 11, 9. Charley B. recrq
1909, 4, 10. James E., Jennie S. & Chas. B. relrq

URTON
----, --, --. Ezra b 1832,11,14 d 1900,12,6; m Mary Ann WILSON b 1832,3,6 d 1930,12,26
Ch: Charles b 1854, 3, 19
John W. " 1857, 8, 7
Malissa J. " 1861, 2, 28
George W. " 1863, 5, 5
1913, 9, 17. Louise m Curtis ELLET

1882, 6, 16. Bennett recrq
1885, 7, 11. Ezra & w, Mary Ann, & dt, Melissa, rocf Springfield MM
1900, 6, 9. Mary A. Walker rocf Ogden MM,O., dtd 1900,5,26
1906, 10, 13. Bennett dropped from mbrp
1909, 8, 14. Louisa rocf Ogden MM, O., dtd 1909,7,24

VALEART
1882, 6, 16. Anna recrq

VANCE
1908, 9, 30. Lynn F. m Kathryn HILL
1913, 8, 7. Ethel Anna d
1914, 5, --. Harry D. m Shirley Maude HOOP

1885, 5, 9. Susan J. & ch, Cecil, Anna & Jane, recrq
1885, 5, 9. John, Linnie & Lucy, ch Susan, recrq
1907, 12, 14. Anna E. dropped from mbrp
1907, 12, 14. Lucy dropped from mbrp
1907, 12, 14. John dropped from mbrp; rst 1908,5,9
1907, 12, 14. Linnie dropped from mbrp; rst 1908,5,9
1909, 9, 11. Ethel Anna rst
1929, 6, 12. John dropped from mbrp

VANDEVORT
1912, 6, 13. Edith Clark d
1913, 9, 16. Mary [Vandervoort] m Benj. FARQUHAR
1927, 6, 25. Veda [Vandervoort] m Paul PORTER

VANDERVORT, continued
1897, 6, 17. Maud [Vandervoort] recrq
1897, 10, 9. Maud gct Cincinnati MM, O.
1903, 1, 10. Mora dropped from mbrp
1925, 2, 11. Lucius [Vanderwort] & w, Fannie, & ch, Pauline & Margaret, rocf Dover MM
1925, 2, 11. Veda, Virginia & Mary [Vanderwort] ch Lucius, recrq
1927, 6, 8. John recrq

VAN NESSLEY
1927, 12, 31. Wm. m Gladys ALDRIDGE

VANPELT
1911, 7, 18. Rebecca d ae 74

1904, 12, 10. Abner J. & w, Rebecca, recrq

VANTRESS
1930, 4, 22. Calvin d

1906, 4, 14. Calvin R. rocf Center MM, O., dtd 1906,3,14

VESTAL
1874, 3, 20. Jennie recrq
1903, 10, 10. Jennie dropped from mbrp

VOLKART
1906, 4, 14. Anna dropped from mbrp

WADDLE
1882, 11, 17. Phebe rocf Clear Creek MM, O., dtd 1882,8,12
1884, 4, 18. Wm. F. [Waddell] recrq

WAHU
1912, 12, 11. Yoo recrq
1916, 4, 12. Yoo gct Scipio MM, N. Y.

WAKEFIELD
----, --, --. Joseph J. b 1835,9,3; m Mary ----- b 1826,9,3
Ch: Mary
Louisa b 1855, 8, 22 d 1870,10,29 bur Sugar Grove
Eben H. b 1858, 12, 4
Benjamin
Frank " 1860, 2, 6
Lydia A. " 1862, 9, 4
Jane C.S.W.K.
b 1868, 9, 13

1870, 3, 18. Joseph J. & w, Mary, & ch, E. H., B. F., Mary L., Lydia & Jennie, recrq
1874, 7, 17. Joseph J. & fam gct Union MM,O.
1876, 12, 15. Joseph & w, Mary Ann, & ch, Frank, Eber, Lydia & Jane, rocf West Branch MM, O., dtd 1876,11,16
1879, 7, 18. Joseph J. & w, Mary A., & ch, Eber H., Lydia & Jane C., gct Gilead MM,O.
1899, 12, 9. Joseph rocf Rush Creek MM, O., dtd 1899,11,25
1906, 9, 8. Joseph J. relrq

WALKER
----, --, --. Azel b 1802,11,21 d 1869,5,8 bur Sugar Grove Cemetery; m Elizabeth ----
Ch: Eliza Ann
Martha Jane
Lewis C.
Calvin B.
Amos J.
----, --, --. Asa b 1812,7,6; m Maria ROBINSON b 1814,2,10
Ch: Joshua R. b 1835, 7, 26
William H. " 1839, 12, 31
1855, 8, 22. Bruce, s Asa & Maria, b
----, --, --. Cyrus M. b 1829,1,4; m Irene ----- b 1865,2,6
Ch: Irene
Lizzie Bue
----, --, --. John b 1830,11,30; m Amelia Jane -----
Ch: Addison J.
George H.S.
1877, 4, 28. John R. d
1917, 5, 18. Roy d

1869, 3, 16. Azel gct White Water MM, Ind. (canceled because of his d)
1869, 3, 16. Lewis C. gct White Water MM,Ind.
1869, 3, 16. Calvin B. gct White Water MM, Ind.
1869, 4, 13. Elizabeth, Eliza Ann & Martha Jane, gct White Water MM, Ind.
1869, 9, 14. Sarah rocf Caesars Creek MM,O., dtd 1869,7,22
1872, 4, 19. Irene recrq
1873, 4, 18. Amelia Jane & ch, Geo. H. S. & Lewis J., recrq
1873, 4, 18. Lizzie Bell recrq
1874, 10, 16. Sarah J. gct Union MM, Howard Lake, Minn.
1875, 5, 14. Jedidah recrq
1877, 11, 16. Cyrus W. dis
1881, 6, 17. Rebecca rocf Dover MM, O., dtd 1881,5,19
1882, 10, 20. Maria rocf Springfield MM, O., dtd 1882,9,16
1884, 8, 15. Eliza rocf Fairfield MM, O., dtd 1884,7,19
1884, 8, 15. Joshua R.'s cert from Fairfield refused
1885, 6, 13. Amelia J., George & Russel dropped from mbrp
1885, 10, 10. Elva rocf Center MM, O., dtd 1885,9,16
1891, 11, 14. Wm. H. & w, Sarah Jane, & s, Roy, rocf Springfield MM, O., dtd 1891,9,19
1891, 11, 14. Charles rocf Springfield MM,O., dtd 1891,9,19
1894, 7, 14. Jessie & Martha recrq
1900, 1, 13. Chas. A. relrq
1900, 6, 9. Eliza J. gct Fairfield MM, O.

WALKER, continued
1908, 10, 10. Joseph M. & w, Eugenia, & ch, Mary Frances, recrq
1919, 5, 14. Sarah recrq
1927, 6, 8. Goldie recrq
1929, 4, 10. Mary Frances relrq
1929, 11, 13. Jennie gct West Fork MM
1929, 12, 10. Joseph & Eugenia Cast dropped from mbrp

WALL
1904, 7, 7. George Robert, s Henry & Hannah, b
1910, 3, 24. Orville m Edith HAWORTH
1929, 4, 12. Alice d

1895, 9, 14. Viola recrq
1898, 1, 8. M. Henry & w, Hannah P., rocf Center MM, O.,dtd 1897,12,15
1907, 11, 9. M. Henry & w, Hannah, relrq
1911, 7, 8. Henry & w, Hannah, & ch, Margaret & George R., recrq
1917, 5, 9. Henry & w, Hannah, & ch, Margaret & George R., gct Center MM, O.
1921, 6, 15. Viola dropped from mbrp
1933, 4, ,2. Bessie recrq

WALLACE
1909, 5, 8. Everett & w, Edna, & ch, Catherine & May L., rocf Ogden MM, O.
1909, 12, 12. Grace recrq
1920, 3, 10. Everett, Edna, Catherine & Mary L., relrq
1921, 6, 15. Grace dropped from mbrp

WALTHAL
1887, 1, 8. Thomas & w, Maria E., & dt, Eliza P., rocf Dover MM, O.

WALTON
1906, 4, 3. Milo d ae 76
1910, 3, 18. Julia d ae 74

1893, 9, 9. Milo & w, Julia, recrq

WARD
1919, 10, 23. Harry m Elva WOOLARY
1921, 5, 8. Wilbert W., s Harry & Eva (Woolary), b

1921, 12, 24. Wilbert W. recrq of parents
1928, 2, 8. Alice M. recrq

WARREN
1919, 8, 31. Luther m Saretta ELLIOTT

1877, 5, 18. Rachel & dt, Jemima Pike, recrq
1877, 6, 15. Wm. recrq
1883, 3, 16. Wm. & w, Rachel, relrq
1890, 1, 11. Eva A. rocf Newberry MM, dtd 1889,12,23
1891, 10, 10. Eva H. gct West Fork MM, O.
1921, 11, 9. Saretta Elliott gct Vasselboro MM, Me.

WATSON
1918, 8, 4. John d ae 88
1918, 10, 10. Edith Stoops d

1873, 3, 14. Elizabeth & ch, Mary, Thurman & Margaret, recrq
1898, 4, 9. Elizabeth, Mary, Thomas & Margaret dropped from mbrp
1907, 1, 12. John M. rocf Vera MM, Indian Territory
1920, 10, 13. Shepherd Arthur & w, Florence, rocf Hesper MM, Kans.
1926, 10, 13. Clyde O. & w, Lena B., rocf Westfield MM, Ind.
1927, 10, 12. Shepherd Arthur & w, Florence, gct Beech Grove MM, Ind.
1929, 4, 10. Clyde O. & w, Lenna R., gct Carthage MM, Ind.

WAY
----, --, --. Daniel L. b 1838,9,8; m Mary Emily ----- b 1843,8,4
Ch: Mary Grace b 1866, 6, 7
Charle E. " 1868, 6, 9
William " 1870, 1, 26
Susie S. " 1872, 7, 23 d 1874, 3,12 bur Sugar Grove
David Leroy b 1875, 6, 20
1869, 3, 19. Charles Eugene d bur Sugar Grove Cemetery

1870, 3, 18. David L. recrq
1893, 1, 14. D. L. & fam relrq

WEBB
1921, 2, 9. Veda U. recrq
1929, 11, 13. Veda Mae gct Beech Grove MM

WEED
1905, 5, 13. Emma West gct Whittier MM, Calif.

WEEKS
1907, 10, 12. Minnie Wright dropped from mbrp

WEIMER
1926, 12, 14. Leo d

1921, 4, 13. J. W. & w recrq
1921, 9, 14. Leo rocf Dover MM

WELCH
1845, 1, 12. Oliver M. b

1870, 2, 18. Olive rocf Miami MM, O., dtd 1870,1,26

WELLER
1915, 2, 3. Roy m Lucile MARTIN
1926, 3, 6. Verna m Chas. Wm. McKINNEY

WELLER, continued
1894, 7, 14. Alonzo recrq
1894, 7, 14. Oscar recrq
1912, 3, 9. Roy recrq
1927, 5, 11. Roy D. & Lucile Martin dropped from mbrp
1932, 3, 23. Ethel recrq

WELTZ
1929, 3, 10. Anna R. b or d

WEST
1869, 12, 7. Tamar d
1924, 2, 24. Peyton Gale, ch Carl & Grace, b

1883, 11, 16. Louisa & ch, Emma & Stella, rocf Newberry MM, O., dtd 1883,10,22
1906, 3, 10. Eva Mather rocf Springfield MM,O.
1906, 3, 10. Margaretta & Lillian recrq of mother, Eva
1906, 3, 10. Daniel Win recrq
1908, 5, 19. Sadie Shubert gct Fairfield MM, O.
1908, 10, 10. Eva Mather & dt, Margaretta & Lillian, relrq
1917, 5, 9. Hazel recrq
1921, 3, 9. Carl & Peyton rocf Newberry MM, O., dtd 1921,2,17
1921, 3, 9. Grace, Mildred, Virgil, Stella J. & Robert Paul, recrq
1921, 6, 15. Daniel Wynne dropped from mbrp

WHEELER
1891, 10, 10. Sarah rocf Caesars Creek MM,O., dtd 1891,8,21
1901, 3, 9. Sarah relrq
1925, 11, 11. Blanch Ross relrq

WHINERY
----, --, --. Isaiah b 1832,7,8; m Hannah M. ----- b 1839,11,12
Ch: William H. b 1864, 7, 14
Frank G. " 1865, 9, 27
Robert C. " 1868, 8, 29
Celesta " 1870, 4, 4

1907, 5, 11. Wm. H., Frank G., Robert & Celesta dropped from mbrp

WHIPPS
1916, 12, 13. Nina Cook relrq

WHITACRE
1904, 3, 12. Joseph H. recrq
1921, 6, 15. Joseph H. dropped from mbrp

WHITE
1905, 2, 8. Ella J. Smith dropped from mbrp

WHITESIDE
1906, 3, 10. Margaretta recrq
1923, 6, 13. Jennie Ross gct Dayton MM, O.

WHITLOW
1922, 9, 18. Nettie m Wm. SNOWDEN

1919, 5, 21. ----- recrq

WHITMAN
1877, 2, 16. Charles & w, Ella, & dt, Charity, recrq

WHYLAND
1922, 5, 10. Fred S. recrq
1925, 10, 14. Fred S. relrq

WICAL
1925, 3, 11. Noel recrq
1925, 4, 8. Clara B. recrq
1927, 6, 8. Elizabeth recrq

WICKERSHAM
1873, 4, 18. Joseph C. recrq
1874, 5, 15. George recrq
1874, 11, 14. Joseph C. gct Centre MM, O.
1891, 3, 14. George [Wickham] relrq

WILKINS
1873, 3, 14. Louisa recrq

WILLHITE
1929, 6, 12. Mary McPherson dropped from mbrp

WILLIAMS
1924, 9, 24. Burch m Mable MURRELL

1873, 4, 18. Elleda L. recrq
1900, 8, 11. A. J. & w, Elizabeth E., recrq
1904, 4, 9. H. A. recrq
1906, 2, 10. Dr. A. J. & Eliza E., relrq
1921, 4, 13. Paul recrq
1929, 12, 10. H. A. dropped from mbrp

WILSON
1852, 10, 18. John b
----, --, --. Joshua [Willson] b 1825,9,13; m Elizabeth J. ----- b 1824,1,10
Ch: Ann Eliza b 1858, 2, 16
James H. " 1860, 3, 12
Laura E. " 1862, 7, 31
Edward F. " 1866, 9, 30
1897, 6, 28. John C. d ae 45
1922, 9, 2. Frances m Bevan JENKINS
----, --, --. Connell m Inez RIDGEWAY

1872, 6, 14. Joshua & w, Elizabeth, & ch, Ann Eliza, Laura, Jane & Edward, recrq
1873, 5, 16. John gct Union MM, O.

WILSON, continued
1875, 4, 16. Joshua & w, Elizabeth, & ch, Ann Eliza, Laura, Jane Elwood, gct Union MM
1893, 12, 9. Elizabeth recrq
1894, 7, 14. Wm. & Lizzie [Willison] recrq
1894, 7, 14. Ercy Earl [Willison] recrq
1895, 4, 13. John & w, Susan, & ch, Emory Kirk, Warren Kirk, Rachel Kirk & Stanley Kirk, recrq
1897, 4, 10. Nettie recrq
1898, 4, 9. Wm. & Lizzie [Willison] dropped from mbrp
1900, 5, 12. Susan relrq
1901, 5, 11. Otie Foland gct Center MM, O.
1902, 4, 12. Ercy Earl relrq
1903, 12, 12. Eunice recrq
1913, 2, 12. Eunice relrq
1921, 6, 15. Willard dropped from mbrp
1924, 10, 11. Inez Ridgeway gct South Cleveland MM, O.
1926, 1, 13. Anna Mae [Willison] recrq
1929, 6, 12. Anna Mae [Willison] dropped from mbrp

WINFIELD
----, --, --. John b 1852,2,24; m Alice A. HARLAN b 1855,2,14
Ch: Charles A. b 1877, 1, 15
Frank J. " 1883, 1, 14

WINKLE
----, --, --. Dwight & Georgiana
Ch: Barbara Alta b 1927, 10, 28
Betty Jo-anne " 1930, 9, 26

1914, 5, 13. Emma recrq
1914, 5, 13. Lillian recrq
1926, 3, 31. Dwight & Georgiana recrq
1926, 6, 9. Robert Eugene recrq

WINTERS
1926, 9, 18. Kennet m Mary Ruth FISHER

WOOD
1917, 8, 8. J. Densmore rocf Sandwich MM, N. H.
1920, 5, 12. Eva recrq
1932, 5, 11. J. Densmore relrq

1873, 4, 18. Isaac recrq
1889, 9, 14. Martha recrq
1889, 12, 14. Belle recrq
1893, 5, 13. Bell relrq
1900, 2, 10. Carrie C. rocf Caesars Creek MM, O., dtd 1900,1,25
1900, 2, 10. Pearly Miars relrq
1901, 1, 12. Callie recrq
1901, 5, 11. Daniel C. recrq
1903, 9, 12. Mary T., Ruth M. & Rhea, ch Daniel C. & Carrie C., recrq
1904, 1, 9. Isaac relrq
1909, 11, 13. Mary recrq
1912, 2, 10. Hazel recrq
1916, 3, 8. Daniel C. & w, Carrie C., & ch, Mary T., Ruth M. & Rhea E., relrq
1919, 2, 19. Hazel m Asa OLIVER
1925, 8, 12. Eva m Morris DAILEY

WOODMANSEE
1930, 12, 18. Herman m Edna Emily SPEAR
1932, 11, 30. Ada Spears d

WOODY
----, --, --. Waldo m Eva TERRELL
Ch: Mary Edith b 1913, 7, 29
Herman
Clayton " 1915, 1, 10 d 1916,2,13

1912, 9, 11. J. Waldo & w, Eva Terrell, rocf Knoxville MM, Tenn.
1919, 6, 11. J. Waldo & w, Eva T., & ch, Mary Edith, gct Newgarden MM, N. C.

WOLLARY
1915, 3, 11. Calvin d
1919, 10, 23. Elva m Harry WARD

1926, 5, 10. Malinda [Woolery] d

1873, 4, 18. J. A. [Woolery] recrq
1874, 11, 14. John A. gct Centre MM, O.
1913, 5, 14. Calvin, Melinda J. & Elva, recrq

WOOTEN
1915, 11, 10. Nellie rocf Miami MM, O., dtd 1915,9,22
1917, 9, 12. Nellie gct Stella MM, Kans.

WORKMAN
1927, 6, 8. Vergie recrq

WORLEY
1914, 2, 11. Freda Osborn rocf Ogden MM, O., dtd 1914,1,24
1914, 2, 11. Bland recrq
1930, 11, 12. C. Bland & w, Freda O., & s, Chas. Bland, gct Springfield MM

WORTHINGTON
----, --, --. Isaac b 1819,10,4; m Rhoda C. ----- b 1835,11,23

1868, 11, 17. Isaac & w, Rhoda C., rocf Springfield MM, O., dtd 1868,10,17

WRIGHT
1908, 12, 4. Victor Leon, s Dr. F. O. & Kate, b
1914, 12, 8. Joel T. d
1921, 6, 29. George m Alice TREFZ
1925, 6, 6. Homer m Helen LUKINS
1926, 9, 16. Patricia Ellen, dt Homer &

WRIGHT, continued
Helen, b
1929, 3, 30. David Harold b

1873, 3, 14. Sarah recrq
1878, 3, 15. Levi & w, Louisa & Phebe Jane, rocf Clear Creek MM, O., dtd 1878,1,12
1878, 12, 20. David H. recrq
1880, 4, 16. Jonathan B. & w, Louisa S., & dt, Grace L., rocf Miami MM, O., dtd 1880,3,24
1880, 6, 18. Ella A. Werntz recrq
1881, 5, 20. Callie recrq
1885, 9, 12. Ellen rocf Clear Creek MM, O., dtd 1885,7,11
1894, 5, 12. Theodore & ch, Frank M., Walter A., Elva N., Arthur, Leslie, Jessie L. & Minnie O., rocf Newberry MM, O., dtd 1894, 3,22
1895, 6, 8. Lizzie recrq
1898, 8, 18. Jonathan B. & w, Louisa, & ch, Grace L. & Paul H., gct Maryville MM,Tenn.
1899, 5, 13. Emma E. rocf Clear Creek MM, O., dtd 1899,4,8
1902, 2, 8. Minnie & ch, Mattie & Ralph, recrq
1902, 4, 12. Richard recrq
1903, 10, 10. Frank O. & w, Kate, recrq
1903, 10, 10. Elva N. dropped from mbrp
1903, 10, 10. Frank M. dropped from mbrp
1904, 10, 8. Gurney C. & w, Carrie Edith, & ch, Homer Elroy, recrq
1905, 11, 11. Gilbert, Minnie, Ralph B., Matilda A. & Florence C., relrq
1906, 6, 9. Daisy D. recrq
1907, 3, 9. Lizzie dropped from mbrp
1907, 5, 11. Leslie relrq
1908, 12, 12. Virgil A., s F. O. & Kate, recrq
1909, 2, 13. Leanna recrq
1909, 10, 9. Joel T. & Elizabeth rocf Fairfield MM, O.
1914, 2, 11. Rowena Berlin rocf Ogden MM,O., dtd 1914,1,24
1914, 10, 14. Wendall, Ronald & Rowena recrq
1926, 11, 10. Gurney & Carrie relrq
1932, 3, 23. Inez Ellen recrq

WULFECK
1916, 8, 5. Wallace m Ora McKINNEY

WYSONG
1911, 12, 18. Etha m Chas. K. McKINNEY

1897, 4, 10. Etha May recrq
1897, 7, 10. Lauren recrq

* * * * * * *

ALBAN
1873, 4, 18. Emily recrq

YARGER
1918, 10, 9. Estella m Oscar MOORE
1921, 5, 5. Edward d
1921, 6, 28. Nellie Marie m Ronald C. BRIGGS
1922, 4, 6. Nellie d

1914, 10, 14. Nellie recrq
1921, 4, 13. John L., Mary Alice & Edward E. recrq

YEO
----, --, --. William H. b 1842,3,4; m Elizabeth KIMBROUGH b 1840,1,16 d 1897,11,28

YOUNG
1922, 6, 14. Ruth m Carl ZURFACE

1887, 2, 12. M. C. & w, Phebe, & ch, Rhoda, Ernest & Lewis, rocf Saline MM, Ill.
1888, 1, 14. M. C. & fam gct Saline MM, Ill.
1911, 5, 13. Ruth recrq

ZEIGLER
1873, 3, 14. Geo. M. recrq
1907, 3, 9. George dropped from mbrp

ZELLAR
1922, 6, 28. Ada M. m Ernest LEEKA

ZURFACE
1922, 6, 14. Carl m Ruth YOUNG

1926, 1, 28. Bertha Adams d

1929, 10, 9. Harold Eugene, Virginia Ellene & Malva recrq of parents
1931, 12, 9. Ruth & ch, Harold, Virginia & Melba gct Dover MM

ZURMEHLY
1898, 3, 12. Mattie Walker relrq

* * * * * * *

COMPTON
1923, 9, 13. Samuel d
1929, 3, 19. Josephine d

DABE
1912, 11, 13. Donald Carl, s Frank & Louise, recrq

GLASS
1910, 11, 14. Alice Emma m Benj. F. SCHUBERG
1911, 4, 18. Benjamin H. m Rachel McDonald DONOHUE
1912, 1, 1. Louise m Frank DABE

JONES
1918, 5, 18. Mildred m Marion BLISS
1923, 3, 14. W. H. m Lucretia Bell BAILEY

PATTON
----, --, --. Annes m ----- BURTON

1903, 1, 10. Anna dropped from mbrp

THATCHER
1910, 9, --. Hazel m Ray PAINTER
1911 2, 28. Lucretia m Harry BUCKLEY

WEST BRANCH MONTHLY MEETING

West Branch Monthly Meeting, located in Miami County, Ohio, two miles southwest of West Milton, was opened on the 1 Mo. 7, 1807. It was set off from Miami Monthly Meeting by authority of Redstone Quarterly Meeting, Pa., and was the second monthly meeting to be established in southwestern Ohio. A meeting for worship had been established at West Branch about two years earlier.

A list of names of Friends who were early members of West Branch Monthly Meeting includes Henry Coate, Jane Coppock, John Coppock, Abiather Davis, Rachel Davis, an elder, William Elliman, Isaac Embree, Isaac Hollingsworth, James Hollingsworth, Nathan Hollingsworth, Sarah Hollingsworth, Susannah Hollingsworth, John Hoover, Benjamin Iddings, an elder, Phebe Iddings, David Jones, Mary Jones, Samuel Jones, an elder, Moses Kelly, Betty McCool, Gabriel McCool, Elizabeth McDonald, Joseph McDonald, Sarah McDonald, Caleb Mendenhall, Susannah Mendenhall, Jeremiah Mote, Jonathan Mote, Mary Mote, Timothy Mote, Henry Neal, Rebecca Neal, William Neal, Ephraim Owen, James Patty, Enoch Pearson, Mary Pearson, Sarah Pike, Ann Russell, Luranah Teague, Rebecca Teague, Samuel Teague, Grace Vernon, Nathaniel Vernon, George Zink, Mary Zink.

RECORDS

ABBOTT
----, -- --. John m (2) Sarah JONES
Ch: Samuel
Mary b 1816, 8, 14
John m 3rd Mary HANKS, dt T. & K., b 1792, 1,28
1819, 6, 22. Sarah, w John, d bur West Branch
----, --, --. Samuel m Rebecca MILES
Ch: Calvin b 1840, 1, 21
Wm. " 1841, 5, 19
Abijah " 1842, 8, 14
John Meader" 1844, 9, 20
1841, 5, 31. Wm., s Samuel d bur West Branch

1816, 11, 28. Sarah con mcd
1817, 6, 26. Sarah gct Union MM
1821, 7, 21. Mary rocf Union MM, dtd 1821,4,7
1822, 7, 20. John [Abot] recrq
1822, 7, 20. Mary, dt John, recrq
1838, 10, 18. Samuel M. gct Union MM, to m Rebecca Miles
1852, 10, 14. Samuel & fam gc
1855, 5, 17. John & w, Mary, & four gr ch gct Western Plain MM, Ia.

ADDINGTON
1807, 8, 22. John [Adington] & s, James, rocf Cain Creek MM, S. C., dtd 1806,9,20; endorsed by Miami MM, 1807,6,11
1807, --, --. Sarah & Elizabeth rocf Cane Creek MM, S. C., dtd 1806,9,20; endorsed by Miami MM, 1807,6,11
1808, 8, 28. Sarah Roberts (form Adington) dis mcd

AIRY
1822, 5, 18. John rocf White Water MM
1824, 11, 20. John gct White Water MM, Ind.

ALDRICH
1858, 8, 10. Caroline M. Aldrich, w Wm., d bur West Branch

ALLEN
1886, 1, 9. John recrq

ALLISON
----, --, --. Jonathan, s James, b 1800,10,12; m Hannah ----- b 1805,3,30
Ch: James b 1827, 6, 28
John " 1829, 10, 5
Wm. " 1832, 3, 31
David W. " 1834, 5, 17
Jonathan " 1837, 11, 23
Abraham " 1840, 8, 23
1840, 1, 31. Sarah Sr. d bur West Branch
1848, 2, 24. Sarah m John E. PEMBERTON

1839, 10, 17. Sarah & ch, Rebecca, Caleb & Priscilla, rocf Dunens Creek MM, Pa., dtd 1839,9,26
1842, 3, 17. Andrew, James, Thomas & Benjamin rocf Dunnings Creek MM, Pa., dtd 1840,7,30
1845, 6, 19. Jonathan & fam gct Mill Creek MM
1845, 11, 13. Benjamin dis disunity
1846, 5, 14. Thomas dis disunity
1848, 12, 14. Andrew con mcd
1852, 11, 18. James & Caleb gct Vermillion MM, Ill.
1855, 1, 18. Andrew dis mcd

ANDERSON
----, --, --. George & Marie
Ch: Robert
Duane b 1919, 12, 1
Francis
Russel " 1923, 9, 23
1928, 12, 31. George d

1903, 6, 13. Ellen M. & ch, Vinnie Edna, Joseph Irvin & George Edwin, rocf New Garden MM, dtd 1903,5,16
1913, 5, 10. Joseph dropped from mbrp

ANDREWS
1809, 5, 20. Robert & s, John & William, rocf Miami MM, dtd 1809,2,11

ANTHONY
1838, 3, 21. Harriet m Samuel T. COATE

1821, 7, 21. Susan (form Mendenhall) con mcd
1835, 11, 19. Susannah Wisener (form Anthony) dis mcd
1838, 3, 15. Samuel T. Coate prcf Union MM, dtd 1838,3,14, to m Harriet Anthony

APPLEGATE
----, --, --. John, s Robert & Elizabeth; m Hannah ADAMS, dt Thos. & Betty (Bridget)
Ch: Mary Caroline b 1829, 3, 15
Henry " 1832, 7, 10
Emma " 1834, 5, 7
Thos. Adams" 1836, 4, 29
The above ch not mbrs; b in England
Chas. Robert b 1838, 12, 30
Frances Elizabeth " 1841, 7, 8
Catharine Diana " 1846, 7, 3
----, --, --. Robert Chas. Applegate, s John & Hannah (Adams); m Lucinda LILLY, dt Wm. & Harriett
Ch: Matilda Emma b 1864, 6, --
Cornelia Edith " 1865, 10, 4
Myra Anna " 1867, 5, 9
Wm. Herschel " 1868, 5, 9
Henry Dorsey 1869, 7, 23

APPLEGATE, Robert Chas. & Lucinda, continued
Ch: Samuel
Pearson b 1871, 3, 29
Anna Leona " 1872, 6, 4
Stephen
Herbert " 1873, 10, 12
Lilly
Florence " 1875, 1, 22
Clarkson
Andrew " 1876, 10, 20
1884, 3, 10. Hannah, w John, dt Thos. & Bridget Adams, d bur West Branch
1918, 6, 14. Emma Alice d

1873, 3, 13. Robert Charles, s Hannah, & w, Lucinda, & ch, Matilda M., Caroline E., William H., Henry D., Samuel P. & Anna L., recrq
1873, 3, 13. Hannah & dt, Frances, recrq
1918, 3, 9. Emma Alice recrq

ARNETT
1902, 1, 11. Jeremiah recrq

ATTIC
1913, 5, 10. Lillie dropped from mbrp

BADGLEY
1914, 2, 14. George recrq

BAER
1883, 3, 15. Susan & s, Henry Clinton, recrq

BAILEY
----, --, --. Albert A., s James E. & Rebecca, b 1832,5,14; m Ann Elizabeth MACY, dt Aaron & M. Matilda, b 1832,10,1
Ch: Leslie W. b 1856, 7, 23
Lambert R. " 1859, 5, 1
Mary Nanville " 1864, 7, 13

1809, 5, 20. David rocf Back Creek MM, N. C., dtd 1807,3,28, endorsed by Miami MM, 1809, 4,8
1852, 10, 14. Phares Compton gct Dover MM, O., to m Delitha Ann Bailey
1863, 6, 17. Albert A. & w, Elizabeth, recrq
1867, 5, 16. Albert A. & w, Elizabeth, & ch, gct Salem MM, Ia.
1885, 9, 12. Alpha recrq
1891, 2, 14. May recrq

BAKER
1883, 1, 18. Emma recrq
1904, 3, 12. Mrs. Della Welbaum relrq

BALLARD
1849, 2, 22. Jehu, s William & Phebe, Greene Co., O.; m at West Branch, Mary MOTE, dt David & Barbara, Miami Co., O.

1809, --, --. Catharine [Balyard] & dt, Caroline, rocf Back Creek MM, N. C., dtd 1807, 3,18

BALLENGER
1811, 12, 11. Jesse, s James & Lydia, Miami Co., O.; m at Rocky Spring, Rebeckah WRIGHT, dt Joshua & Elizabeth, Montgomery Co., O.

1810, --, --. Lydia rocf New Hope MM, Tenn., dtd 1809,9,23
1813, 4, 22. Jesse rocf Mill Creek MM, dtd 1813,2,27
1819, 1, 16. Jesse & fam gct New Garden MM
1819, 1, 16. Rebecca gct New Garden MM

BALWIN
1872, 9, 19. Rachel rocf Chester MM, Ind.

BANGUM
1832, 7, 19. Mary rocf Green Plain MM, dtd 1832,5,26

BANISTER
1869, 1, 14. David recrq

BARBEE
1885, 9, 12. John recrq

BARKER
1808, 12, 17. Isaac & s, Thomas, Jacob & Abel, rocf Cane Creek MM, N. C., dtd 1808,5,7

BARNARD
1809, 8, 19. Samuel rocf Deep Creek MM, N.C., dtd 1808,3,5
1809, --, --. Catharine & dt, Catharine, rocf Deep Creek MM, N. C., dtd 1808,3,5

BARNHARDT
1886, 1, 9. Henry & w, Sarah, & ch, Icy, Ida May & J. W. Dorsey, recrq
1886, 1, 9. Noah & Nettie recrq
1889, 1, 12. Henry & fam relrq

BARRAT
1812, 3, 26. Mary con mcd

BEALL
1863, 5, 14. Henrietta [Beal] rocf White Water MM, Ind., dtd 1863,4,22
1867, 12, 19. Henrietta relrq
1885, 3, 19. William H. recrq
1895, 2, 9. William H. dropped from mbrp

BEARD
1811, 11, 28. Certificate rec for Hugh & w & ch, William, Thomas, Israel & Hiram, from Deep River MM, N. C.; endorsed to White Water MM
1811, 11, 28. Cert rec for John Jr. from Springfield MM, N. C., dtd 1808,3,6; endorsed to White Water MM

BEARD, continued
1883, 4, 17. Martha recrq
1908, 4, 11. Eva recrq

BEAUCHAMPS
1812, 7, 23. Cert rec for Matthew from Piney Grove MM, S. C., dtd 1811,2,16, endorsed to White Water MM

BEERY
1924, 8, 9. Hazel relrq

BEESON
1879, 1, 16. John Henry, Cordelia Jane, Maggie Belle, Cara E., Callie P., Nellie V., John Howard & Emma F., recrq
1909, 1, 9. John, Cordelia, Frank & Elmer, form mbr of Chambersburg MM, recrq
1909, 8, 14. John [Beesom] relrq
1913, 1, 13. Elmer G. [Beesom] relrq
1913, 5, 10. Cordelia & Frank [Besom] dropped from mbrp

BENBOW
1886, 6, 12. Clara gct Cherry Grove MM, Ind.
1917, 2, 10. Walter & fam gct Dayton MM, O.

BENDER
1927, 7, 13. Rhea dropped from mbrp

BENEDICT
1849, 3, 15. Robert Styles gct Alum Creek MM, to m Rachel Benedict

BENNETT
1885, 2, 19. Hattie recrq
1887, 4, 9. Anna recrq
1895, 2, 9. Laura dropped from mbrp
1907, 5, 11. Laura dropped from mbrp for lack of interest

BENTON
1820, 12, 16. Ann rocf Cincinnati MM, dtd 1820,10,19
1830, 12, 9. Ann dis disunity

BERGNER
1916, 12, 9. Mabel recrq
1919, 7, 12. Eliza [Burgner] recrq

BIRD
1924, 9, 13. George W. & w, Christie B., rocf Van Wert MM, O., dtd 1924,8,28
1926, 4, 10. George & w gct Raysville MM, Ind.

BLACKBURN
1923, 4, 14. Charles rec as associate mbr
1924, 5, 10. Mrs. recrq

BLACK
1885, 9, 12. Hattie recrq
1903, 4, 11. Clarence, h Ethel J., recrq
1903, 4, 11. Ethel J. rocf Cherry Grove MM
1904, 10, 8. Clarence & w, Ethel, gct New Garden MM, Ind.

BODINE
1909, 1, 9. Roy & Vesta, form mbr of Chambersburg MM, recrq
1913, 5, 10. Roy & Vesta dropped from mbrp

BOHSE
1909, 1, 9. Willie [Bohre], form mbr of Chambersburg MM, recrq
1913, 4, 10. Willie dropped from mbrp

BOLL
----, --, --. Wilbur m Sarah THOMAS, b 1873,4, 3 (Sarah, dt Joseph & Elizabeth)
Ch: Ruby
Edna
Estella
Lois
Esther

1925, 6, 13. Esther dropped from mbrp for jas
1909, 1, 9. Wilber, Sadie, Rubey, Edna, Estella & Lois, form mbr of Chambersburg MM, recrq
1909, 1, 9. Charlie & Nettie, form mbr of Chambersburg MM, recrq
1909, 1, 9. Nettie gct First Friends Church, Cedar Avenue, Cleveland, O.
1913, 5, 10. Charles dropped from mbrp
1922, 5, 13. Stella & Lois dropped from mbrp for jas
1930, 5, 14. Sadie relrq

BOND
1808, 10, 22. Jesse & s, Nathan Robert & John, rocf Mt. Pleasant MM, Va., dtd 1808, 1,30
1808, --, --. Phebe rocf Mt. Pleasant MM, dtd 1808,1,30
1809, 5, 20. William & s, Jesse, rocf Miami MM, dtd 1809,2,11
1886, 2, 13. Charles recrq
1887, 1, 8. Charles H. gct Union MM

BOOKER
1909, 1, 9. George, form mbr Chambersburg MM recrq
1909, 1, 9. Nellie, form mbr Chambersburg MM, recrq
1913, 5, 10. George & Nellie dropped from mbrp

BOWERS
----, --, --. Hezekiah D., s Jacob & Emeline F., b 1861,8,28; m Martha Ellen STULTZ, dt John & Abigail, b 1863,8,8

1885, 1, 15. Hezekiah D. & w, Martha Ellen, recrq

BOWLS
1807, 10, 17. David & s, George Fox, rocf Simons Creek MM, N. C., dtd 1807,4,18
1807, 10, 17. David Jr. rocf Simon's Creek MM, N. C., dtd 1807,4,18
1807, 10, 17. Ephraim Overman [Bowles] rocf Simons Creek MM, N. C., dtd 1807,4,18
1882, 1, 19. John & w, Sophia, & ch, Joseph, Ada E. & Wilber J., recrq
1884, 8, 14. Ellie, Charlie & Nettie [Bawls] ch John, recrq

BOWMAN
1911, 2, 11. W. O. recrq

BOYD
1818, 4, 23. Ann con mcd
1823, 10, 18. Ann [Boyde] gct Union MM
1833, 6, 13. Ann rocf Union MM, dtd 1833,6,12
1844, 1, 18. Ann dis jas

BOYER
1897, 2, 14. Harvey C. & w, Dora O., recrq
1901, 4, 13. Harvey C. & w relrq

BRAGG
1850, 8, 15. Ann & Jane rocf Cincinnati MM, dtd 1850,7,18
1852, 5, 13. Isaac William rocf Cincinnati MM, dtd 1852,3,18
1852, 9, 16. James dis jas
1856, 8, 14. Isaac W. dis mcd
1883, 12, 13. Ann gct Dorking Horsham and Guilford MM, England

BRANDENBURG
1885, 11, 14. Fowler recrq
1891, 7, 11. A. F. relrq

BREWER
1917, 6, 8. George d

1824, 11, 20. Susanna (form Wright) dis mcd
1914, 2, 14. Daniel B., Eva Mary, George O. & William A., ch George & Erma, recrq

BRICKER
1872, 3, 14. Mary, wd, recrq

BRIDENBAUGH
----, --, --. Paul m Christiana COMPTON
Ch: Flora b 1873, 3, 28
Elmer " 1875, 8, 3
Lydia " 1877, 1, 13
1877, 7, 1. Christiana C., w Paul, dt Henry & Rachel COMPTON, d bur West Branch
1926, 6, 17. Paul d
1927, 1, 4. Jane d

1877, 7, 19. Paul & ch, Flora, Elmor & Lydia, recrq
1883, 3, 15. Sarah recrq

BRODRICK
1856, 2, 26. Phebe m Reuben FARMER

1826, 5, 20. Sarah (form Wisener) dis mcd
1883, 2, 15. Walter & w, Carrie, recrq
1886, 2, 13. Samuel J. [Broderick] & w, Nannie M., recrq
1887, 7, 9. Isaac [Broderick] rocf Westland MM, O., dtd 1887,6,4
1887, 11, 12. Isaac gct Westland MM, O.
1890, 5, 9. Samuel & w gct Westland MM, O.

BROOKS
----, --, --. Nimrod b 1782,8,9 d 1855,10,5; m Elizabeth -----
Ch: Mary b 1806, 12, 15
Susan " 1809, 1, 24
Daniel " 1811, 4, 13
Ann " 1814, 8, 23
John " 1817, 7, 6
Larkin " 1820, 1, 12
Jesse " 1822, 10, 22
Henry " 1825, 10, 20
1863, 3, 5. Elizabeth (Thomas), w Nimrod, d bur South Fork

1817, 1, 23. Nimrod & w, Elizabeth, & ch, Mary, Susannah, Daniel & Ann, rocf Miami MM, dtd 1816,12,25
1819, 2, 20. Hanah rocf Silver Creek MM, dtd 1819,1,9
1824, 12, 18. Mary Hollingsworth (form Brooks) con mcd
1833, 7, 16. Daniel con mcd
1833, 7, 18. Priscilla (form Thomas) con mcd
1833, 8, 15. Susannah Cox (form Brooks) con mcd
1835, 8, 13. Anne Hollingsworth (form Brooks) con mcd
1836, 7, 14. Nimrod & fam gct Mississiniwa MM Ind.
1840, 7, 16. Daniel dis disunity
1843, 7, 13. Priscilla dis jas
1859, 4, 14. Benjamin dis mcd
1859, 12, 15. Elizabeth rocf Back Creek MM, Ind., dtd 1859,11,17

BROWN
1807, 12, 27. Ann, w Samuel, d bur Union
1824, 4, --. Thos., s Thos., d bur West Branch
1829, 7, 2. Samuel d bur West Branch
1841, 10, 3. Rebecca, w Benj., d bur West Branch
1865, 5, 30. Mary, 2nd w Samuel Sr., d bur West Branch

1807, 8, 22. Samuel Jr. rocf Bush River MM, S. C., dtd 1807,3,22
1810, 1, 20. Cert rec for Samuel from New Garden MM, N. C., dtd 1809,11,4, endorsed to Elk MM
1814, 2, 24. Samuel gct Union MM, to m
1814, 6, 23. Mary Brown & ch, Nicolas, Jacob

BROWN, continued
Naomi, Sarah, Michoes, Jonathan, Abraham & Joseph Tucker, rocf Union MM, dtd 1814,4,6
1816, 1, 25. Samuel, Jr. & fam gc
1816, 7, 25. Mary con mcd
1817, 7, 24. Mary gct Elk MM
1820, 5, 20. Thomas rocf Miami MM, dtd 1820,1, 26
1820, 5, 20. Cert rec for Samuel Jr. & fam from Union MM, dtd 1818,3,7, endorsed to Union MM
1825, 7, 16. Joshua & ch rocf Union MM, dtd 1825,7,2
1825, 7, 16. Nancy rocf Union MM, dtd 1825,7,2
1830, 3, 20. Nancy Tucker (form Brown) con mcd
1832, 1, 21. Joshua, s Samuel, gct Union MM
1836, 10, 13. Rebecca rocf Mill Creek MM, dtd 1836,9,13
1836, 11, 17. Sarah rocf Mill Creek MM, dtd 1836,9,13
1896, 5, 9. A. H. & James recrq
1913, 3, 8. D. H. recrq
1924, 11, 8. Sarah & Mabel recrq

BRUBAKER
1913, 4, 12. James & w, Lula, recrq
1919, 1, 11. Clara Jane, dt James & Lula, b rpd

BRUMBAUGH
1919, 12, 13. Eva [Brunbaugh] recrq
1924, 4, 12. Pearl recrq
1933, 3, 8. Mrsl Pearl relrq

BRYAN
1850, 8, 15. Elizabeth & ch, Ann, Mary Ann & Elizabeth, rocf Cincinnati MM, dtd 1850,7, 18
1852, 12, 16. Elizabeth & three dt gct Lisburn MM, Ireland

BUCKLEY
1907, 5, 11. Pauline Macy dropped from mbrp for lack of interest

BUNDY
1863, 4, 23. Joseph J., s Samuel & Priscilla, Howard Co., Ind.; m at West Branch, Elizabeth C. MOTE, dt John & Rhoda, Miami Co. O.

BUNKER
1808, 12, 17. John rocf New Garden MM, N. C., dtd 1805,10,30, endorsed by New Hope MM, N. C., dtd 1808,10,22

BURGESS
1879, 12, 18. David & w, Anna, & ch, Irene, Gaynor, Emmar Lewis & Edith Lina, recrq

BUTLER
1810, 1, 20. Cert rec for Bales & fam from New Garden MM, N. C., dtd 1809,7,29, endorsed to White Water MM

BUTTS
1893, 5, 26. James S., s Geo. L. & Mary R., d
1893, 6, 7. Geo. L., s Henry & Nellie R., d
1918, 12, 17. Paul d
1923, 2, 1. Geo., minister, d

1886, 2, 13. Joseph M. recrq
1886, 2, 13. George E. recrq
1886, 2, 13. Mary & William A. recrq
1886, 2, 13. James S. & Alice E. recrq
1892, 11, 12. Flora M. recrq
1893, 12, 9. George & w, Dora, gct another mtg or glt another Church
1897, 8, 13. William A. & w, Mary M., relrq
1911, 1, 14. George & w, Dora, & ch, Gertrude, Gladys, Mabel, Grant & Paul, recrq
1917, 10, 13. Mark, s Mr. & Mrs. George Butts, b rpd
1926, 5, 8. Dora & ch, Grant, Carl, Dorothy, Una, Mark & Neddie, relrq

BYRIES
1925, 6, 13. Ruby dropped from mbrp for jas

CADWALLADER
1906, 8, 8. Addalena recrq
1920, 5, 8. Almeda gct Laura MM

CAMPBELL
1836, 3, 17. John & fam gct Westfield MM, Ind.
1896, 11, 14. Jessee A. recrq
1897, 2, 14. Margaret recrq
1901, 2, 9. Victor & Mattie recrq
1902, 12, 13. Gladys recrq
1907, 5, 11. Margaret dropped from mbr;; jas

CAPRON
1878, 5, 16. Oliver & w, Sarah, rocf Mississiniwa MM, Ind.
1880, 7, 15. Oliver & w gct Deer Creek MM, Ind.
1880, 11, 18. Metcalf dis
1881, 1, 13. Cert for Oliver not accepted by Deer Creek MM, Ind.
1881, 5, 19. Oliver dis

CAREY
1807, 12, 19. Levina recrq
1881, 3, 17. Lindley & w, Rosella, & ch, Clyde N., rocf Back Creek MM, Ind.
1882, 8, 17. Lindley & w gct Deer Creek MM, Ind.

CARROL
1891, 3, 10. Harley recrq
1895, 12, 14. Amy & ch relrq
1915, 11, 13. Mrs. Amy recrq
1917, 6, 19. Ray J. recrq

CARROL, continued
1920, 9, 11. Celia relrq

CARTER
1883, 2, 15. Ella rocf Springfield MM, Kans.
1883, 3, 15. Isaac & dt, Ethel F., recrq
1885, 3, 19. John recrq
1902, 1, 11. John relrq
1925, 2, 14. J. W. & w, Ella, relrq

CASHNER
1909, 8, 14. Lizzie recrq
1911, 1, 14. Frank recrq
1911, 2, 11. David recrq
1913, 3, 8. Harry recrq
1920, 8, 14. Eva recrq
1924, 8, 9. Harry dropped from mbrp for joining another society

CASSELL
1918, 4, 13. Margaret recrq
1919, 12, 13. Margaret relrq

CASEY
1807, 12, 19. Levina recrq
1813, 2, 25. Lavina gct Caesars Creek MM
1819, 5, 15. Levina [Cacy] rocf Caesars, Creek MM, dtd 1818,11,27
1827, 4, 21. Lavina gct Honey Creek MM, Ind.

CHARLES
1809, 8, 19. John & s, Abram & Samuel, rocf Back Creek MM, N. C., dtd 1809,2,25

CHASE
1883, 4, 17. Daniel M. recrq
1895, 2, 9. Daniel N. dropped from mbrp

CHELLIS
1888, 9, 8. Rachel & Charles recrq

CHILDRESS
1825, 2, 19. Mary (form Waggoner) con mcd
1830, 10, 16. Mary [Childres] dis disunity
1887, 4, 9. Esther [Childers] recrq
1889, 5, 11. Esty [Childres] relrq

CHILDS
1887, 3, 12. J. W. & V. S. A. recrq
1895, 2, 9. J. M. & w, Alselea, dropped from mbrp

CLARK
1809, 11, 16. Cert rec for John & fam from Cane Creek MM, dtd 1808,9,3; endorsed to White Water MM

CLEGG
1890, 4, 12. Thomas rocf Union MM
1896, 4, 11. Thomas relrq

CLINGENFIELD
1862, 2, 13. Rebecca gct Honey Creek MM

COATE
1807, 10, 28. James, s Marmaduke & Mary, Miami Co., O.; m at Ludlow Creek, Luranah TEAGUE, dt Samuel & Rebecca, Miami Co., O.
1809, 8, 30. John, s Marmaduke & Mary, Miami Co., O.; m at Ludlow Creek, Esther TEAGUE, dt Samuel & Rebeckah, Miami Co., O.
1810, 11, 1. Joseph Teague Coate, s John & Esther, b
1810, 11, 7. Lydia m John DAVIS
1812, 7, 2. Elijah b [(Wilson), b
1818, 9, 16. Clarkson, s Henry & Rebecca
1821, 9, 20. Thomas Coate, s Moses & Elizabeth, Miami Co., O.; m at West Branch, Sarah PATTY, dt Anne, Montgomery Co., O.
1822, 11, 21. Joseph Coate, s Moses & Elizabeth, Miami Co., O.; m at West Branch, Lydia DAVICE, dt Abiather & Lydia, Miami Co., O.
1825, 6, 1. Hannah C., dt Samuel & Milly Pearson, 3rd w Henry W., b
1825, 6, 20. Mary T., w David M., dt Moses & Jane (Coppock) Teague, b d in 70th yr
----, --, --. Thomas, s Samuel & Margaret, b 1812,12,16; m Eliza RAGAN, b 1819,7,24

Ch:		
	Sarah	b 1837, 11, 29
	Mary	" 1839, 11, 27
	Emeline	" 1843, 3, 2
	Nancy	" 1846, 3, 13
	Alvah	" 1849, 5, 31
	Orrin	" 1857, 5, 25
	Eliza	" 1860, 7, 18

1838, 3, 21. Samuel T., s James & Lurana, Miami Co., O.; m at South Fork, Harriet ANTHONY, dt Daniel & Susannah, Miami Co., O.
1838, 12, 20. William, s Samuel & Margaret, Miami Co., O.; m at West Branch, Mary TUCKER, dt Jacob & Elizabeth, Miami Co.,O.
1842, 3, 24. John Coate, s Samuel & Margaret, Miami Co., O.; m at West Branch, Nancy CREW, dt Robert & Hannah FINNEY, Miami Co., O.
----, --, --. David M. Coate, s Henry & Rebecca (Wilson), b 1823,7,9; m Mary TEAGUE, dt Moses & Jane, b 1825,6,20

Ch:		
	John	b 1844, 9, 5
	Unnamed	" 1844, 9, 5
	Orrin	" 1854, 6, 15

1860, 6, 21. Jonathan C., s James & Lurana, Miami Co., O.; m at West Branch, Martha COMPTON, dt Henry & Rachel, Miami Co., O.
1866, 7, 14. Lydia, w Caleb, d bur Union
----, --, --. Ezra, s Moses; m Melissa THOMAS, dt D. & E.

Ch:		
	Idella	b 1868, 2, 4
	Anna Elizabeth	" 1869, 7, 11

----, --, --. Abijah J., s Joshua & Adila; m Mary M. COATE, dt Josias & Sarah

Ch:		
	Alvine	b 1870, 11, 16

1871, 1, 20. Mary M., dt Josias & Sarah, d bur Union

COATE, continued

----, --, --. John, s D. M. & Mary C.; m Lucinda S. EVERETT, dt S. & Ann (Branderburgh)
Ch: Edgar b 1873, 1, 28
Kittie E. " 1876, 10, 28 d 1877, 9, 6 bur Milton Cemetery

----, --, --. Orrin S., s D. M. & Mary (Teague) b 1854,6,10; m Belle dt A. C. & Lucinda (Hartzell), b 1857,10,25

1887, 3, 24. Martha, 3rd w John, dt Henry & Rachel COMPTON, d

1890, --, --. Nancy (Finney) (Crew) d bur Union (m John Coate after d of first h, Benjamin Crew)

1895, --, --. Casper, brother of John, d bur Dayton, O.

1917, 9, 3. Lucinda d

1920, 9, 1. Ned Cecil, s Cecil & Lydia, b

1922, 6, 26. John d

1923, 5, --. John J. d

1923, 6, 27. Leonard B., s Cecil & Lydia, b

1932, 8, 17. Belle d

1810, 8, 18. Jesse con mcd

1812, 7, 23. Henry & ch gct Miami MM

1823, 12, 20. Lydia gct Union MM

1828, 7, 19. Sarah gct Union MM

1833, 7, 16. Mark, Isaac & Hugh rocf Union MM, dtd 1833,7,17

1833, 7, 18. Sarah & dt, Anna & Elizabeth, rocf Union MM, dtd 1833,7,17

1838, 3, 15. Samuel T. prcf Union MM, dtd 1838,3,14, to m Harriet Anthony

1842, 10, 13. Nancy & s, Menalcas Crew, gct Union MM

1852, 6, 17. David M. & w, Mary, & s, John, rocf Union MM, dtd 1852,6,16

1859, 6, 16. Thomas & w, Eliza, & s, Alvah & Orrin, rocf Union MM

1869, 1, 14. Abijah & w, Mary M., & ch, Clara Almeida & David Orland, rocf Union MM, dtd 1869,1,13

1869, 2, 18. Robert H. & w, Vashti, rocf Union MM, dtd 1869,2,17

1869, 12, 16. Caleb rmd mcd

1870, 3, 16. Eliza & fam gct Cottonwood MM, Kans.

1870, 3, 16. Sarah, dt Eliza, gct Cottonwood MM, Kans.

1870, 3, 16. David J. Coppock gct Union MM, to m Margaret Coate

1870, 9, 15. Caleb gct Union MM

1873, 3, 13. John rpd mcd

1873, 8, 14. Thomas gc

1874, 5, 14. Anna, w Abijah, recrq

1874, 9, 17. Henry W. & w, Hannah, & s, Clarkson, rocf Union MM

1874, 10, 15. Martha C. & ch, Emma Anna E. & Lydia A., rocf Union MM

1875, 7, 15. Abijah & fam gct Union MM

1875, 8, 19. Melissa & ch rocf MM in Kansas

1875, 9, 16. Harris & fam gct Union MM

1875, 11, 18. John H. & w, Jane, & ch, Warren & Loretta, rocf Union MM

1876, 2, 17. Harry R. & w, Mary, recrq

1878, 10, 17. Caleb & dt, Jane & Florence, recrq

1879, 5, 15. Ida, w Warren C., recrq

1880, 2, 19. John J. & w, Eliza, & ch rocf Union MM, dtd 1880,2,18

1882, 3, 16. Belle, w Orrin S., & ch, Nellie & David M., Jr., recrq

1883, 3, 15. Lucinda & ch, Eddie & Mabel, recrq

1884, 2, 14. Mina recrq

1885, 9, 12. Thomas Elleman rocf Union MM, O., dtd 1885,8,12

1885, 11, 14. Ellwood roc

1885, 11, 14. Rosa J. relrq

1886, 2, 13. Marcus & Naomi recrq

1886, 2, 13. Carl E. recrq

1887, 4, 9. Robert & w, Jemima, & dt rocf Van Wert MM, O.

1887, 5, 14. John H. & w, Jane, gct Union MM

1889, 2, 9. N. C. gct Union MM, O.

1890, 10, 11. Thomas Elwood gct Union MM

1895, 2, 9. Gracie [Coates] recrq

1897, 2, 14. John recrq

1903, 2, 14. Alice, birthright mbr, recorded mbr by choice

1907, 5, 11. Warren, Idella, Ida, Albert, John & Annice dropped from mbrp for lack of interest

1907, 5, 11. Marcus, Omar & Charles dropped from mbrp for lack of interest

1907, 5, 11. Marguerite dropped from mbrp; jas

1909, 1, 9. Jemima & Wreford, form mbr of Chambersburg MM, recrq

1909, 2, 13. Jemima & s, Benjamin Wreford, gct Columbus MM

1909, 4, 10. Benjamin C. & w, Esther, rocf Union MM

1913, 3, 8. Cecil recrq

1916, 3, 11. Esther's d rpd

1916, 9, 9. Benjamin C. gct Union MM

1923, 11, 10. Loretta recrq

1923, 12, 8. Bessie & dt, Virginia, recrq

COFFIN

1807, 2, 21. Adam & s, Benjamin, Francis & Moses, rocf Deep Creek MM, N. C., dtd 1806,9,6

1807, --, --. Ann & dt, Catharine, Elizabeth, Jemima, Rebecca & Ann, rocf Deep Creek MM, N. C., dtd 1806,9,6

1897, 12, 11. Sarah E. & s, Howard E., relrq

COLBY

1889, 5, 11. Ella H. relrq

COMER

1809, 8, 19. Joseph rocf Miami MM, dtd 1809, 8,5

COMMONS
1816, 10, 31. John, s Robert & Ruth, Wayne Co., Ind.; m at West Branch, Elizabeth MOTE, dt John & Rachel, Miami Co., O.
1824, 2, 26. David, s Robert & Ruth, Wayne Co., Ind.; m at West Branch, Rachel MOTE, dt John & Rachel, Miami Co., O.
1840, 9, 24. Rachel m Job P. JAY

1809, 6, 17. Isaac rocf Mt. Pleasant MM, dtd 1808,1,30
1816, 10, 24. John prcf White Water MM, dtd 1816,9,28, to m Elizabeth Mote
1817, 1, 23. Elisabeth gct White Water MM, Ind.
1819, 3, 20. John rocf West Grove MM, dtd 1819,2,13
1819, 3, 20. Elizabeth & dt, Rachel, rocf West Grove MM, dtd 1819,2,13
1824, 6, 19. Rachel gct West Grove MM, Ind.
1826, 8, 19. John & fam gct Honey Creek MM, Ind.
1840, 9, 17. Job P. Jay prcf Mill Creek MM, to m Rachel Commons

COMPTON
1826, 8, 24. Henry, s Joseph & Christianna (Steddom), b 1806,9,6 d 1886,4,10 bur West Branch; m Rachel MENDENHALL, dt Joseph & Rachel, Miami Co., O., d 1884,1,23 bur West Branch
Ch: Patty b 1828, 12, 22
Phares " 1830, 10, 28
William " 1832, 10, 8
Nancy Ann " 1835, 4, 13 d 1839, 5,29
Isaac " 1837, 2, 24
Samuel " 1841, 3, 6 d 1849, 3, 1 bur West Branch
Christiana b 1843, 2, 22
Samantha " 1846, 1, 31
Mary " 1848, 2, 25 d 1860, 2,16 bur West Branch
Lydia b 1850, 4, 27
----, --, --. Phares m Delitha Ann BAILEY
Ch: Lydia Ellen b 1854, 3, 14
Rachel Emma " 1855, 7, 2
Sylvia Jane " 1857, 7, 5
Henry Allen " 1859, 6, 19
Anna Mary " 1863, 12, 29
Lindley Murray " 1868, 8, 27
1855, 12, 7. Rachel Emma, dt Phares, d bur West Branch
1860, 6, 21. Martha m Jonathan COATE
1861, 5, 23. William, s Henry & Rachel C., Miami Co., O., b 1832,10,10; m Sarah J. HUTCHINS, dt Daniel & Dorcas, Montgomery Co., O., b 1836,11,29 d 1872,4,1 bur Randolph Gr Yd
Ch: Oritla b 1863, 9, 15
William Compton d 1893,10,1
----, --, --. Isaac, s Henry & Rachel; m Rachel C. COATE, dt Henry & Phebe, b 1845,4,14
Ch: William H. b 1866, 8, 29
Omar C. " 1872, 12, 16
Alice H. " 1875, 5, 7
Gurney LeRoy " 1881, 1, 20
1878, 11, 8. Alice H., dt Isaac & Rachel, d bur West Branch

1827, 3, 17. Rachel gct Caesars Creek MM
1831, 12, 17. Rachel & dt, Paty, rocf Seacers Creek MM, dtd 1831,11,24
1852, 10, 14. Phares gct Dover MM, O., to m Delitha Ann Bailey
1853, 4, 14. Delitha Ann rocf Dover MM, dtd 1853,3,17
1866, 3, 15. Isaac rpd mcd
1866, 7, 19. Rachel C. rocf Union MM, dtd 1866,7,18
1876, 9, 14. Phares & fam gct Spiceland MM, Ind.
1903, 7, 11. William H. & Gurney relrq
1903, 7, 11. Isaac & Rachel relrq
1907, 5, 11. Mrs. W. H. recrq
1907, 5, 11. William & Gurney rst
1908, 2, 8. G. L. relrq
1911, 12, 9. William H. & w, H. Leota, gct Whittier MM, Calif.
1916, 10, 14. Rachel rocf Whittier MM, Calif., dtd 1916,9,6
1919, 4, 12. Rachel gct Whittier MM, Calif.

CONLEY
1892, 3, 12. Thomas & w, Mary, recrq

CONNELL
1894, 1, 13. Maggie M. recrq

CONNER
1821, 4, 21. Jesse rocf Caesars Creek MM, dtd 1821,2,23
1821, 10, 20. John rocf Caesars Creek MM, dtd 1820,9,29, endorsed by White Water MM, 1821,7,28
1823, 10, 18. Jesse gct Caesars Creek MM
1825, 12, 17. Jesse rocf Caesars Creek MM, dtd 1825,11,28
1830, 5, 15. Jesse gct Caesars Creek MM

COOPER
1808, 8, 28. Benjamin & ch, Benjamin, Joel, Absolom, John, Joseph, William & Mordecai, rocf Lost Creek MM, Tenn., dtd 1807,7,25
1808, --, --. Ferraba & dt, Pherraba & Sarah, rocf Lost Creek MM, Tenn., dtd 1807,7,25
1809, 10, 21. Isaac & ch, Prudence & Joseph, recrq
1809, 10, 21. Elizabeth recrq
1811, 3, 28. Isaac & w, Abigail, & dt, Welmet, rocf Miami MM, dtd 1811,2,27
1813, 6, 24. Joel con mcd
1814, 2, 24. Benjamin Jr. dis mcd
1821, 1, 20. Isaac & fam gct Mill Creek MM
1831, 4, 16. Maryann dis jH

COPPOCK
1809, 8, 2. Eunice m Robert PEMBERTON
1809, 11, 22. Moses, s James & Hannah, Miami Co., O.; m at Mill Creek, Lydia JAY, dt John & Betty
----, --, --. James, s Mose & Lydia, b 1814,11, 11; m Eleanor H. EVANS, dt Robert & Esther, b 1817,2,4
Ch: Esther b 1837, 8, 17
Samuel " 1839, 10, 7
Lydia " 1841, 9, 30
1839, 12, 31. David, s Dayton, b
----, --, --. James, s Wm. & Charity, b 1823, 9,6; m Maria McCONNEL, dt John & Elizabeth, b 1828,8,26
Ch: John Mc b 1852, 4, 25
Mary E. " 1854, 9, 6
Wm. P. " 1856, 8, 21
Corilla Ann" 1860, 5, 6
Ulipsus " 1869, 5, 6
1853, 5, 26. James, s Moses & Lydia, Miami Co., O.; m at West Branch, Susannah JAY, dt Elisha & Rebecca JONES, Miami Co., O.
1863, 4, 19. Charles H., s David, b
1867, 12, 25. Albert N., s David, d bur Union
1875, 3, 29. Jane, w James, dt Geo. & Mary Huntsman, d bur Union Graveyard
1918, 2, 18. Oscar d

1808, 3, 19. Benjamin & s, Joseph & William, rocf Bush River MM, S. C., dtd 1807,8,29
1808, --, --. Susannah & dt, Jane & Elizabeth, rocf Bush River MM, S. C., dtd 1807,8,29
1809, 11, 18. Moses rocf Miami MM, dtd 1809, --,--
1810, 6, 23. William con mcd
1810, 6, 23. Eunice recrq
1812, 7, 23. Jane, dt John, recrq
1833, 7, 16. Isaac Elleman gct Union MM, to m Elizabeth Coppock
1837, 3, 16. Mary (form Mote) con mcd
1837, 6, 15. Elijah rocf Union MM, dtd 1837, 5,17
1838, 5, 17. Elijah & fam gct Union MM
1867, 7, 18. David & w, Ann, & ch, Charles M. & Albert Newton, rocf Honey Creek MM, Ind., dtd 1867,6,8
1867, 12, 19. Isaac C. rocf Union MM, dtd 1867,12,18
1868, 7, 16. Jane Sr. rocf Union MM, dtd 1868,7,15
1870, 3, 16. David J. gct Union MM, to m Margaret Coate
1870, 7, 14. Margaret rocf Union MM, dtd 1870,7,13
1871, 4, 13. James & w, Maria, & ch, John W., Mary E., William P., Corilla A. & Ulysses G., rocf Union MM, dtd 1870,11,16
1873, 8, 14. Sampson & fam rocf Union MM
1874, 6, 18. Isaac C. & w gct Milford MM,Ind.
1875, 2, 18. Isaac C. & w, Martha Ellen, rocf Milford MM, Ind.
1886, 1, 9. Frank & w, Fannie, & ch, Samuel C., recrq
1886, 2, 13. William recrq
1890, 11, 8. Martha E. relrq
1893, 6, 10. Barbara (form Wagoner) rst (form dis mcd)
1894, 8, 11. Fannie relrq
1905, 10, 14. Oscar & Walter rocf Union MM
1907, 5, 11. Ulysses relrq
1911, 2, 11. Walter & Maud recrq
1918, 1, 12. Oscar recrq
1919, 12, 13. Isabel recrq

COTHRON
1809, 10, 21. Esther & ch, Ann, Jane Esther, Mark & David, recrq
1811, 8, 22. Hannah con mcd

COTTERAL
1905, 2, 11. Lucinda Varilla recrq
1908, 8, 8. Ephraim & s, Martin, recrq

COUSINS
1903, 2, 14. Bessie, Wendall & Harrison (Cussins) recrq
1907, 5, 11. Wendall & Harrison dropped from mbrp for lack of interest
1913, 5, 10. Bessie dropped from mbrp

COX
1808, 12, 21. Sarah m Evan THOMAS
1809, 9, 27. David, s John & Jemima, Montgomery Co., O.; m at West Branch, Phebe THOMAS, dt Jesse & Mary, Montgomery Co.,O.
Ch: David
Priscilla
John b 1817, 9, 25
Nehemiah " 1820, 11, 5
Simpson " 1822, 4, 5
1813, 9, 29. Elizabeth m Isaiah THOMAS
1819, 1, 21. Mary m William THOMAS
1833, 5, 21. Nancy, dt David & Susannah (Brooks), b
1848, 4, 23. Jemima, dt Elizabeth Tucker, b

1807, --, --. Hannah rocf Lost Creek MM, Tenn., dtd 1806,8,30
1807, --, --. Rebecca rocf Cane Creek MM, N. C., dtd 1807,11,7
1809, 6, 17. Benjamin rocf Cain Creek MM, N. C., dtd 1809,2,4
1809, 11, 16. John, Sr. & s, James, recrq
1809, 11, 18. Sarah recrq
1813, 4, 27. Catharine Swallow (form Cox) dis mcd
1813, 9, 23. Isaiah Thomas prcf Miami MM, dtd 1813,8,28, to m Elizabeth Cox
1814, 4, 28. John gc
1815, 2, 23. Jonathan Jr. gct Mill Creek MM
1819, 10, 16. John con mcd
1820, 10, 21. Joseph dis mcd
1822, 7, 20. Margaret dis
1823, 11, 15. William & fam gct Springfield MM, Ind.

COX, continued
1826, 5, 20. Jonathan dis disunity
1833, 1, 17. David dis disunity
1833, 1, 17. Isaac dis disunity
1833, 8, 15. Susannah (form Brooks) con mcd
1839, 7, 18. John & Nehemiah dis disunity
1839, 7, 18. Simpson dis disunity
1840, 4, 18. David dis disunity
1873, 4, 17. Jemima Cox, dt Esther Ann Thomas, gct New Garden MM, Ind.
1904, 11, 12. Phoebe rocf New Garden MM

CRAIG
1886, 2, 13. Mildred & Alfred B. recrq

CRAIGHEAD
1883, 3, 15. Robert recrq

CRAMPTON
1909, 1, 9. Earl, Grace, L. N., George & Osella L., form mbr of Chambersburg MM, recrq
1913, 5, 10. Earl, Grace, L. N., George & Osella dropped from mbrp

CRATTY
1893, 12, 5. Eliza H., w James H., dt James M. & Margaret (Parsons) Peirce d bur West Milton

1882, 3, 16. Eliza H. & grandson, Bertie, recrq

CRESS
1903, 2, 14. Dessie recrq
1913, 5, 10. Lenna dropped from mbrp
1923, 5, 12. Janie & Treva recrq
1932, 4, 13. Glenn & Cora (Criss) recrq

CREW
----, --, --. Benjamin m Nancy FINNEY, dt Robert, b 1808,9,23
Ch: Caspar W. b 1828, 7, 6
Menalcas Stanley " 1831, 9, 25 d 1898, 8,28
1833, 10, 4. Dr. Benj., s Littleberry d bur West Branch
1842, 3, 24. Nancy m John COATE

1828, 4, 19. Benjamin con mcd
1838, 5, 17. Nancy & ch, Casper W. & Menalcas S., recrq
1842, 10, 13. Nancy Coate & s, Menalcas Crew, gct Union MM
1849, 3, 15. Casper W. dis mcd
1853, 3, 17. Manalcus S. dis mcd
1883, 3, 15. Menalcas S. recrq

CRITTEN
1885, 2, 19. James F. & ch, Albert E., Eva J. & Louise, recrq

CROMAIN
1831, 5, 21. Ruth con mcd
1838, 6, 14. Ruth [Crumine] gct Union MM

CRUEA
1887, 3, 12. Austin & Allie recrq
1891, 2, 14. John recrq
1907, 5, 11. Mayme dropped from mbrp for lack of interest

CULLERS
1887, 2, 12. Andrew [Cullars] & w, Maggie, recrq
1909, 1, 9. Margaret, form mbr Chambersburg MM, recrq

CURTIS
1840, 5, 21. Andrew, s John & Catharine, Montgomery Co., O.; m at West Branch, Mary DAVIS, dt Samuel & Dorcas, Miami Co., O.

1810, 3, 17. Catharine & dt, Mary, recrq
1909, 1, 9. Lucy, form mbr Chambersburg MM, recrq
1913, 2, 7. Lucy gct Dayton MM, O.

DAVIDSON
1879, 1, 16. John Wesley recrq

DAVIS
----, --, --. Abiather b 1754,2,11; m Lydia -----
Ch: Amos b 1779, --, --
Rachel " 1781, --, --; m Henry CARTER
Rhoda " 1783, --, --; m Nathan GALBUTH
Samuel " 1785, 2, 20; m Dorcas JONES
John " 1787, --, --; m Lydia COATE
Mary " 1789, --, --; m Jos. IDDINGS
Seha " 1791, --, --
Benj. " 1793, --, --; 1st w Margaret (Fettig) WAREHAM
Sarah b 1795, --, --
Lydia " 1797, --, --; m Jos. COATE
----, --, --. Samuel, s Abiathar D., b 1785, 2,20; m Dorcas JONES dt Samuel, b 1784,9, 18 d 1841,5,29 bur West Branch
Ch: Keziah b 1807, 9, 8
Riley " 1809, 5, 16
Lindley " 1811, 1, 8
Nancy " 1813, 3, 3
Allen " 1815, 9, 16
Mary " 1817, 8, 28
1808, 12, 22. Mary m Joseph IDDINGS
1810, 11, 7. John, s Abiather & Lydia, Miami Co., O.; m at Union, Lydia COATE, dt Henry & Mary, Miami Co., O., d 1826,8,12 bur

DAVIS, John & Lydia, continued
bur West Branch
Ch: Henry b 1811, 8, 18
Samuel " 1813, 8, 2
Isaac " 1815, 3, 22
Jonathan " 1817, 3, 18
Mary " 1820, 10, 26
John m 2nd Elizabeth HAWORTH
Dt: Lydia b 1835, 12, 14
1821, 11, 25. Anna M., w David, dt John & Rhoda T. Motte, d bur Russiaville, Ind.
1822, 11, 21. Lydia [Davice] m Joseph COATE
1826, 8, 12. Sarah, dt Abiather, d bur West Branch
1840, 2, 20. Mary m Eli HOOVER
1840, 5, 21. Mary m Andrew CURTIS
1840, 9, 5. Abiathar Sr. d bur West Branch
----, --, --. Riley, s Samuel & Dorcas, b 1809, 5,17 d 1885,1,1; m Rachel MADDOCK, dt Nath., b 1814,12,30 d 1854,6,1 bur West Branch
Ch: John M. b 1841, 2, 27
Rollin " 1842, 11, 4
Henry M. " 1844, 2, 16
Joseph M. " 1846, 6, 4 d 1866,8,15 bur West Branch
Sarah E. b 1850, 8, 2
Phebe " 1853, 1, 6 d 1866,11,11 bur West Branch
Riley m 2nd Charlotte T. TOWNSEND, dt James & Rosanna, b 1813,7,27
1854, 4, 20. Betsy m Jesse JONES
1893, 11, 29. Samantha, w Hiram, dt John & Margaret Campbell, d bur Milton Cemetery, O.

1810, --, --. Cert rec for Sarah from Stillwater MM, O., dtd 1810,2,27, endorsed to Elk MM
1813, 10, 28. Rachel dis disunity
1814, 11, 24. Sarah & Lydia [Davice] dt Abiather, gct Elk MM
1815, 2, 23. Benjamin [Davies] gc
1815, 8, 24. Abiather & ch gct Elk MM
1817, 2, 27. Abiather & fam rocf Elk MM, dtd 1817,2,1
1817, 2, 27. Sarah & Lydia rocf Elk MM, dtd 1817,2,1
1817, 8, 28. Benjamin rocf Elk MM, dtd 1817, 8,8
1828, 7, 19. Benjamin dis mcd
1829, 9, 19. Isaac, s John, gct Union MM
1829, 12, 10. Mary, dt John, gct Union MM
1830, 8, 12. John gct Union MM, to m
1830, 12, 18. John & s, Jonathan, gct Union MM
1831, 11, 19. Samuel Jr. dis disunity
1831, 12, 17. Henry dis disunity
1832, 8, 18. Lindley dis disunity
1833, 7, 16. Simon & s, Ezra Wilson & Simon, rocf Mill Creek MM, dtd 1833,7,16
1833, 7, 18. Abigail & dt, Nancy & Ann, rocf Mill Creek MM, dtd 1833,7,16
1835, 2, 19. Jonathan rocf Union MM, dtd 1835,2,18
1835, 5, 14. Simon & fam gct Mill Creek MM
1835, 8, 13. Ezra dis mcd
1836, 4, 14. Allen dis disunity
1839, 4, 18. Jonathan dis mcd
1839, 5, 16. Eleanor C. (form Jones) dis mcd
1840, 4, 18. Riley gct Elk MM, to m Rachel Maddock
1845, 3, 13. Samuel dis mcd
1845, 6, 19. Ann dis mcd
1849, 5, 17. Eleanor C. rst
1855, 8, 16. Riley gct Elk MM, to m Charlotte T. Hunt
1855, 10, 18. Lydia gct Union MM
1856, 3, 13. Charlotte T. rocf Elk MM, dtd 1856,1,24
1887, 3, 12. Samantha recrq
1897, 2, 14. Mary A. (K.) recrq
1900, 8, 11. Catharine & ch, Iva I., Rayborn H. & John R., gct West Branch MM, held at West Milton
1907, 5, 11. John dropped from mbrp for lack of interest
1913, 5, 10. Iva dropped from mbrp
1918, 5, 11. Mrs. Mary, w John, recrq
1920, 1, 10. Luella Toms rocf White Water MM, Ind., dtd 1919,12,18
1923, 4, 14. Willa recrq

DEARTH
1888, 9, 8. Barbara, Alexander & Orion F. recrq

DEETRICK
1901, 9, 14. Olive E. (form Elleman) relrq

DeLOTTEE
1913, 5, 10. Minnie dropped from mbrp

DENNIS
----, --, --. Albert m Clara THOMAS, dt Joseph & Elizabeth, b 186-,7,8
Ch: Howard
Forrest
Glenn

1892, 3, 12. Albert H. & ch rocf Cherry Grove MM, Ind.
1903, 2, 14. Forrest, birthright mbr, recorded mbr by choice
1903, 11, 14. Albert & w, Clara, & ch, Howard, Forrest & Glenn, gct White Water MM, Ind.

DETVICK
1891, 2, 14. Emma recrq

DEXTER
1922, 4, 8. Lova Pearson relrq

DICKS
1809, 9, 23. Cert rec for Zacharias & w, Ruth, from Spring MM, N. C., dtd 1808,3,

DICKS, continued
24, endorsed to Center MM

DOHNER
1923, 4, 14. Emma Coate relrq
1925, 11, 14. Ella rocf Ludlow Falls MM, O.

DOUGHTY
1903, 2, 14. W. C. recrq
1903, 2, 14. Nellie, birthright mbr, recorded mbr by choice
1913, 5, 10. W. C. dropped from mbrp
1923, 11, 10. Paulin recrq

DOUGLAS
----, --, --. R. W. b 1834,11,11; m Margaret -----' b 1832,--,--
1919, 2, 18. Robert W. d

1874, 6, 18. David & w, Lydia, rocf Newberry MM, O.
1875, 3, 18. David & w gct Raysville MM, Ind.
1883, 6, 14. David F. [Douglass] & w, Emma L., rocf Union MM, Minn., dtd 1883,5,12
1884, 3, 13. Robert W. & fam rocf Wilmington MM, O.
1896, 11, 14. Effie J. [Douglass] rocf Cherry Grove MM, Ind.
1897, 2, 14. Emma T. [Douglass] recrq
1898, 11, 12. Charles B. & Effie gct White River MM, Ind.
1903, 2, 14. Edward, birthright mbr, recorded mbr by choice
1907, 4, 13. Mary Elsie rocf Amboy MM, Ind.
1907, 7, 13. Robert Jr. gct Indianapolis MM, Ind.
1912, 4, 13. Gifford T. & w, Elsie, & ch, Elaine & Esther, gct Berkley MM, Calif.
1921, 12, 10. David Franklin, Emma R. & Winnifred E., gct Berkley MM

DUDLEY
1916, 12, 9. Charles S. & w, Nellie, & ch, Fredda & Beulah, rocf Back Creek MM
1919, 11, 8. Charles & w, Nellie, & dt, Freeda & Beulah, gct Louisville MM, Ind.

DULIN
1830, 12, 9. Rhoda (form Mendenhall) con mcd
1844, 1, 18. Rhoda dis disunity

DUNKIN
1811, 5, 15. Jesse [Duncan], s Samuel & Mary, Miami Co., O.; m at Union MH, Elizabeth PEMBERTON, dt Richard & Lydia, Miami Co., O.
1807, 4, 18. Samuel & s, Amos & Isaac, rocf New Hope MM, Tenn., dtd 1806,7,19, endorsed by Miami MM, 1807,3,12
1807, --, --. Cert rec for Mary & dt, Sarah, Mary & Rachel, from New Hope MM, Tenn., dtd 1806,7,19, endorsed by Miami MM
1809, 9, 23. Amos [Dunken] con mcd
1809, 10, 21. Sarah Littlejohn (form Dunkin) dis mcd
1882, 1, 19. Sarah [Duncan] recrq

DYE
1883, 4, 17. Mandus recrq
1895, 2, 9. Mandus dropped from mbrp

EAKINS
1913, 3, 8. Catharine recrq

EARHART
1927, 3, 16. Catharine Elizabeth d

1911, 2, 11. Eph. recrq
1919, 12, 13. Roy, Bessie & Lester recrq

EDWARDS
1808, 11, 19. Mary & ch, David, Daniel, Charles, Spencer & Margaret, recrq
1821, 6, 16. Margaret dis jas
1822, 2, 16. Daniel dis mcd
1822, 5, 18. Charles dis disunity
1823, 8, 16. Mary gct New Garden MM, Ind.
1823, 10, 18. Spencer dis disunity
1842, 4, 14. David rpd mcd (could not be located)

ELAFRITZ
1907, 5, 11. Delphina relrq

ELLEMAN
1810, 11, 7. Drusilla m John PEMBERTON
1822, 2, 21. Isaac E., s William & Jane, Miami Co., O., b 1798,9,3; m at West Branch, Mary JONES, dt Wallace & Rachel, Miami Co., O., b 1802,3,22 d 1832,2,6 bur West Branch
Ch: Owen b 1823, 5, 3
Dorcas " 1824, 12, 29
Jordan " 1827, 5, 6
William " 1829, 9, 8
Isaac m 2nd Elizabeth E. COPPOCK, dt Benjamin & Susannah (Jay), b 1807,2,3
Ch: Mary b 1834, 7, 28
Benjamin " 1836, 4, 30
Jane " 1839, 4, 21 d 1877, 6,13 bur Union Graveyard
Isaac J. b 1840, 10, 29
Rachel C. " 1846, 11, 8
----, --, --. David W., s Enos & Margaret (Ward), b 1833,7,29; m Esther T. COATE, dt Elijah & Rebecca C., b 1838,1,18
Ch: John b 1855, 9, 29
Samantha Viola " 1858, 3, 22
Horatio P. " 1860, 3, 18
Wm. " 1862, 1, 18
Mary Rosella " 1864, 1, 11
Zehora Edgar " 1868, 1, 4
Lindley

ELLEMAN, David W. & Esther T., continued
Ch: Merrick b 1870, 9, 26
----, --, --. Isaac J. & Sarah Ann
Ch: Anna b 1865, 6, 25
Clara " 1868, 4, 27
Benj. Franklin " 1871, 2, 3
1918, 8, 22. John Sr. d
1919, 11, 17. Anna d
1925, 1, 13. Rachel, dt Ward & Vesta, b

1824, 4, 17. Isaac & infant s, Owen, rocf Union MM, dtd 1824,4,3
1833, 7, 16. Isaac gct Union MM, to m Elizabeth Coppock
1834, 1, 16. Elizabeth rocf Union MM, dtd 1833,12,18
1835, 2, 19. James & William rocf Union MM, dtd 1835,2mo
1837, 1, 19. Susannah Oaks (form Elleman) dis mcd
1837, 2, 16. Isaac & fam gct Union MM
1841, 6, 17. Jane Ghent (form Elleman) dis mcd
1846, 6, 18. William dis mcd
1846, 8, 13. James dis disunity
1867, 4, 18. David W. & w, Esther T., & ch, John, Samantha Viola, Horatio P., William & Mary Rosella, recrq
1867, 8, 15. Sarah Ann & s, William, recrq
1875, 1, 14. Isaac J. relrq
1875, 8, 19. Benjamin & fam rocf Caesars Creek MM
1876, 6, 15. Benjamin & fam gct Barclay MM, Kans.
1886, 1, 9. Mattie recrq
1886, 2, 13. Anna & ch, Elden L., Aubra E. & William A., recrq
1889, 7, 13. Isaac J. & w, Sarah A., & ch, Harvey, Peasley, Olive, Lula, Asa & Eber, rst
1892, 2, 13. David W. & fam gct Union MM, O.
1893, 6, 10. Jane Ghent (form Elleman) rst (form dis mcd)
1900, 11, 10. Zebora rocf Union MM, dtd 1900, 11,3
1900, 11, 10. Lindley M. & w, Flora A., & ch, rocf Union MM, dtd 1900,11,3
1901, 1, 12. David Jr. relrq
1901, 9, 14. Osa relrq
1901, 9, 14. Anna E. McGlother (form Elleman) relrq
1901, 9, 14. Olive E. Deetrick (form Elleman) relrq
1901, 9, 14. Pearl E. Furlong (form Elleman) relrq
1902, 3, 8. Lizzie Kessler recrq
1902, 3, 8. Isaac J. relrq
1902, 12, 13. Robert recrq
1903, 1, 10. William & w, Mattie M., rocf Union MM, O.
1906, 3, 10. Faye, birthright mbr, recorded mbr by choice
1906, 8, 8. Harold David, s Lizzie, recorded a birthright mbr
1908, 2, 8. Charles recrq
1911, 2, 11. Artie recrq
1911, 2, 11. Mrs. Bertha recrq
1913, 5, 10. Aubrey dropped from mbrp
1915, 1, 9. Juanita recrq
1915, 6, 12. Maxine, dt Artie & Bertha, b rpd
1916, 5, 13. Melvin & Mary rocf Union MM
1919, 11, 8. William & w, Mattie, rocf West Richmond MM, Ind.
1919, 12, 13. Mirriam & Ruth rec in active mbrp by rq
1919, 12, 13. Martha & Irlena recrq
1922, 5, 13. Vesta recrq
1923, 4, 14. Maxine rec in active mbrp by rq
1923, 4, 14. Dorothy, Esther & Kenneth rec as associate mbr

ELLER
1848, 7, 13. Rachel (form Mote) dis mcd

ELLIOT
1808, 6, 18. Israel rocf Lost Creek MM, Tenn., dtd 1807,9,26
1808, --, --. Wilmet & dt, Edith & Esther, rocf Lost Creek MM, Tenn., dtd 1807,9,26
1808, 6, 18. Jacob rocf Lost Creek MM, Tenn., dtd 1807,9,26
1808, --, --. Ann & dt, Olive, rocf Lost Creek MM, Tenn., dtd 1807,9,26
1926, 10, 13. Charles, Louella & Mary [Elliott] rocf Jonesboro MM, Ind., dtd 1826, 9,7

ELLIS
1887, 5, 14. Sarah Lydia Jones (form Ellis) rocf Back Creek MM, Ind.

EMBREE
1807, --, --. Margaret rocf New Hope MM, Tenn. dtd 1807,8,29
1810, 4, 21. James con mcd
1811, 6, 27. Mary recrq

EMMERSON
1878, 9, 19. Charles J. recrq

EMRICK
1885, 4, 16. George P. recrq
1887, 3, 12. Lucetta [Emerick] recrq
1906, 3, 10. Lucetta relrq

ENGLE
1883, 3, 15. John Calvin & w recrq
1883, 9, 13. John Calvin & w relrq

ENNIS
1882, 1, 19. Frances M. recrq
1888, 10, 13. Frank & w, Josephine, & ch, Forest, Clifford & Leota, gct Cleveland

ENNIS, continued
MM, O.

ENSLY
1823, 2, 15. Susannah dis mcd

ERVEN
1899, 12, 9. Willie S. recrq

EVANS
1807, 7, 18. Joseph & s, Robert, rocf Bush River MM, S. C., dtd 1806,8,30
1807, --, --. Rachel & dt, Nancy, Elizabeth & Rebecca, rocf Bush River MM, S. C., dtd 1806,8,30 (cert was directed to Miami MM, but was rec here)
1807, --, --. Rebecca rocf Bush River MM, S.C. dtd 1807,8,30
1810, 6, 23. Joseph & w, Esther, & ch, Robert, Aaron & Sarah, rocf Elk MM, dtd 1810,6,2
1813, 10, 28. Joseph & fam gct Miami MM
1813, 10, 28. Rachel gc
1832, 4, 21. Rebecca rocf Cincinnati MM, dtd 1832,1,26
1832, 4, 21. Susan rocf Cincinnati MM, dtd 1832,1,26
1832, 8, 16. Rebecca dis jH
1832, 8, 16. Susan dis jH

FAIR
1879, 1, 16. Mary B. recrq
1882, 11, 16. Samuel recrq

FARMER
----, --, --. William & Ruth
Ch: Rebecca b 1817, 12, 24
Mary " 1819, 5, 23
Sarah " 1821, 3, 20
Daniel
1822, 11, 21. Hannah m John THOMAS
1823, 8, 28. Mary d bur Rocky Spring
1823, 8, 14. Sarah, dt William, d bur Rocky Spring
1826, 10, 26. John, s Moses & Sarah, Randolph Co., Ind., b 1799,3,21 d 1885,6,13; m at West Branch, Elizabeth THOMAS, dt Isaac & Sarah, Montgomery Co., O., b 1801,5,5 d 1891,4,25
Ch: Isaac T. b 1827, 7, 29
Sarah P. " 1829, 9, 25
Wm. " 1831, 12, 6
Moses " 1834, 7, 9
Rachel " 1836, 4, 20
Serepta " 1837, 5, 27
Benj. " 1839, 8, 23
Abijah " 1841, 12, 4
Mary Ann " 1845, 7, 24
John Albert" 1848, 1, 2
1831, 4, 20. Philip, s Moses & Sarah, Montgomery Co., O., d 1886,6,20; m at South Fork, Susannah THOMAS, dt Abel & Ruth, Montgomery Co., O., d 1835,3,7 bur South Fork
Ch: Saryann b 1832, 6, 3
1834, 7, 13. Moses, s John, d bur South Fork
1836, 5, 20. Rachel, dt John, d bur South Fork
1850, 8, 27. Mary Ann, dt John, d bur West Branch
1856, 2, 26. Reuben, s Moses & Sarah, Randolph Co., Ind.; m at South Fork, Phebe BRODRICK, dt Thomas & Sarah Gilbert, Montgomery Co., O.

1808, 4, 23. William Jr. & s, John, rocf Bush River MM, S. C., dtd 1806,5,31, endorsed by Miami MM, 1808,3,10
1808, --, --. Prudence & dt, Matilda, rocf Bush River MM, S. C., dtd 1806,6,28, endorsed by Miami MM, 1808,3,10
1814, 1, 27. William & w, Rebecca, & s, Jesse, rocf New Garden MM, N. C., dtd 1813,10,30
1816, 9, 26. William gct Stillwater MM, to m
1817, 5, 22. Ruth rocf Stillwater MM, dtd 1817,2,22
1818, 5, 28. Jessy dis disunity
1820, 10, 21. William Jr. dis joining Methodist society
1820, 10, 21. John dis joining Methodist society
1820, 11, 18. Matilda dis joining Methodist society
1823, 4, 19. Hannah rocf Cherry Grove MM, Indiana, dtd 1823,2,13
1823, 9, 20. William Thomas gct Cherry Grove MM, to m Mary Farmer
1826, 9, 16. Philip rocf Cherry Grove MM, dtd 1826,8,12
1827, 6, 16. John rocf Cherry Grove MM, Ind., dtd 1827,1,13
1829, 12, 19. Philip gct Cherry Grove MM, Ind., to m Anna Mills
1830, 6, 19. Orry & Rebecca dis joining Methodist society
1831, 8, 20. William & w, Ruth, & ch gct White Lick MM, Ind.
1831, 9, 17. Prudence & dt gct Sugar River MM, Ind.
1835, 5, 14. Philip & dt gct Cherry Grove MM, Ind.
1851, 6, 19. Isaac con mcd
1851, 10, 16. Isaac gct Cherry Grove MM, Ind.
1852, 4, 15. William dis disunity
1866, 2, 15. John Albert dis disunity
1866, 10, 18. Abijah rmd mcd
1867, 1, 17. Benjamin dis mcd
1868, 4, 16. John & w, Elizabeth, gct Cherry Grove MM, Ind.

FAULKNER
1902, 3, 8. Mabel recrq
1903, 2, 14. Loren, Laura, Merle & Ethel recrq
1907, 5, 11. Merle dropped from mbrp for lack of interest

FAWCETT
1886, 2, 13. Rosa recrq

FEESE
1893, 1, 14. Ezra & Sophia recrq

FENHER
1909, 1, 9. Will, form mbr Chambersburg MM, recrq
1913, 5, 10. William [Fenhrer] dropped from mbrp

FETTERS
----, --, --. Flora, w George, dt P. & Christina C. Bridenbough, bur West Branch

1913, 3, 8. Marie recrq

FINNEY
1833, 3, 14. Elizabeth (Pemberton) d bur West Branch
1866, 7, 10. Robert d bur West Branch

1859, 10, 13. Robert recrq
1871, 4, 13. Elizabeth gct White Water MM

FISHER
1843, 3, 7. Isaac, Sr. d bur West Branch
1850, 1, 18. Caleb, s Isaac, d bur West Branch

1839, 10, 17. Isaac & w, Elizabeth, & ch, James, John, David & Caleb, rocf Providence MM, Pa. dtd 1839,8,1
1847, 8, 19. John dis mcd
1852, 6, 17. David dis mcd
1853, 8, 18. James dis mcd
1864, 6, 16. Anna recrq

FITZGERALD
1887, 4, 9. William & w, Donna M., recrq
1887, 4, 9. Donna M. & Anna J., dt William & w recrq
1888, 1, 14. Donna relrq
1892, 2, 13. William & fam relrq

FLATTERY
1909, 1, 9. Maggie [Flatter], form mbr of Chambersburg MM, recrq
1913, 5, 10. Maggie dropped from mbrp

FOLKER
1887, 3, 12. William [Falcker] recrq
1907, 5, 11. William dropped from mbrp for lack of interest

FOUTS
1811, 5, 8. Peter [Phouts] recrq
1824, 11, 20. Elizabeth (form Yount) con mcd
1832, 6, 14. Elizabeth dis disunity

FOWLER
1884, 8, 14. Jacob recrq
1886, 2, 13. Jacob relrq

FOX
1876, 3, 16. Rachel M. recrq
1913, 3, 8. Herbert recrq
1913, 3, 8. Susie recrq
1913, 3, 8. Clara & Ethel recrq
1920, 4, 10. Herbert relrq
1928, 6, 13. Clara & Ethel relrq

FUHR
1883, 3, 15. John D. recrq

FUNCKE
1888, 9, 8. Hallcarnia & William recrq

FURLONG
1891, 2, 14. Samuel & Christina recrq
1901, 9, 14. Pearl E. (form Elleman) relrq
1905, 4, 8. Christina dropped from mbrp; jas

FURNAS
1811, 7, 3. Mary m William JAY
1836, 3, 24. Lydia Hasket m John MOTTE Jr.
1874, 6, 6. Sally Furnas, w John, dt Joseph & Esther (Buffington) Evans, d bur Sugar Grove
1874, 7, 13. John, s James & Sarah, d bur Sugar Grove

1811, 5, 23. Joseph [Furnace] & w, Sarah, & ch, Mary, John, Samuel, Joseph, Benjamin, William & Sarah, rocf Miami MM, dtd 1809, 8,5
1861, 3, 14. Sarah Johnson (form Furnas) dis
1868, 3, 19. David dis mcd
1868, 4, 16. Elizabeth M. dis mcd
1871, 6, 15. Adam gct Miami MM

GADDIS
1818, 10, 22. William recrq
1825, 3, 19. William [Gaddes] dis joining Methodist society

GARBER
1924, 8, 9. Ethel dropped from mbrp for jas

GARDNER
1839, 2, --. Jemima, dt William G., d bur West Branch

1825, 7, 16. Jemima rocf Deep River MM, dtd 1825,3,3

GASSETT
1868, 2, 13. Nancy rpd mcd; dropped from mbrp

GILBERT
----, --, --. Thos m Sarah THOMAS
Ch: Elmira b 1850, 9, 15
Albert " 1853, 11, 7

1831, 2, 19. Nehemiah Thomas, Jr. gct Mil-

GILBERT, continued
ford MM, Ind., to m Phebe Gilbert
1850, 11, 14. Thomas rocf Hopewell MM, dtd 1850,10,19
1855, 1, 18. Thomas dis disunity
1862, 2, 13. Sarah gct Westfield MM, Ind.

GHENT
1841, 6, 17. Jane (form Elleman) dis mcd
1893, 6, 10. Jane (form Elleman) rst (form dis mcd)

GINGRICH
1918, 12, 11. Russell d

1913, 3, 8. Russel recrq

GORDON
1909, 7, 10. Myra recrq

GRAVE
1831, 5, 21. Mary [Graves] (form Thomas) dis mcd
1848, 6, 15. Linas Mote gct White Water MM, Ind., to m Hannah L. Grave
1855, 9, 13. Enoch Jones gct West Union MM, to m Lydia Ann Grave

GREEN
1885, 3, 19. Amanda recrq

GREGG
----, --, --. Smith, s Smith & Sarah (Ramsey), b 1820,12,21 d 1890,1,24 bur West Branch; m Rachel HUTCHINS, dt Isaac & Phebe, b 1825,2,22 d 1862,5,1 bur Randolph Gr Yd
Ch: Wm. Elwood b 1841, 11, 6
Martha Ann " 1846, 6, 5 d 1849, 1, 2 bur Randolph Gr Yd
Mary Ann b 1848, 12, 8
Annie E. " 1853, 3, 6 " 1869, 3,19 bur West Branch
Joseph b 1855, 5, 31
Willis " 1856, 11, 10
Wilbur " 1858, 12, 21 d 1881, 7,19
Rachel Persis " 1861, 9, 8 " 1879, 2,25 bur West Branch
Smith m 2nd 1863,--,-- Margaret S. HOLLINGSWORTH, wd Wright, dt Isaac & Eliza STANLEY, b 1835,3,8 d 1879,4,2 bur West Branch
Ch: Charles H. b 1866, 1, 18 d 1884, 7,13 bur West Branch
Martha S. b 1868, 3, 25
Smith m 3rd 1880,--,--, Mary (Furnas) MILES, dt Joseph & Patience (Mills) FURNAS d 1893,7,27 bur Union (m 1st Moses Mills)

1863, 9, 17. Smith gct Pipe Creek MM, Ind., to m Margaret Hollingsworth
1880, 7, 15. Mary, w Smith, rocf Union MM, dtd 1880,6,16

GREBHART
1888, 9, 8. Edward recrq

GRINDELL
1882, 4, 13. Lucinda recrq
1883, 1, 18. Sarah E. & Mary A. [Grindle] recrq
1883, 3, 15. Amanda M., Daniel F., William H., Francis A. & Ella Hall, ch Lucinda, recrq
1895, 2, 9. Lucinda & ch, Amanda, Sarah, Alice, William, Daniel & Frank, dropped from mbrp

GRISOM
1855, 11, 15. Eleanor C. Snyder (form Grisom) dis mcd

HAINES
1913, 3, 8. Ellis recrq

HALL
1926, 6, 18. Wesley d

1885, 7, 11. Lydia, wd, recrq
1887, 2, 12. William recrq
1888, 9, 8. Estella recrq
1913, 3, 8. Wesley recrq

HAMMEL
1883, 4, 17. Alice & A. J. recrq
1883, 4, 17. Elizabeth & dt, Minnie & Dora, recrq
1887, 3, 12. Laura recrq
1887, 4, 9. J. W. recrq
1888, 9, 8. John [Hamel] recrq
1888, 9, 8. A. F. [Hamel] recrq
1888, 9, 8. Mary [Hamel] recrq
1888, 9, 8. W. H. [Hamel] recrq
1907, 5, 11. Mrs. A. J. [Hamiel] dropped from mbrp for lack of interest

HANKS
1807, 12, 19. Keziah & ch, Thomas, Noah, Mary, John, James & Rachel, rocf Bush River MM, S. C., dtd 1807,3,28
1812, 4, 23. Thomas con mcd
1812, 4, 23. Martha (form McCoole) con mcd

HARMON
1930, 2, 13. Billie & Wanda rec as associate mbr

HARRINGTON
1847, 9, 16. Naomi (form Tucker) dis mcd

HARRIS
1812, 5, 28. Hannah con mcd
1910, 7, 9. Chester F. & w, Martha, rocf Oskaloosa MM, Ia., dtd 1910,6,2
1915, 1, 9. Martha recrq

HARSHBARGER
1917, 11, 12. Lloyd d
1930, 8, 29. Electa d
1930, 12, 8. Lowell Edwin, s Jim, b

1872, 2, 15. Samuel recrq
1886, 1, 9. Frederick recrq
1886, 2, 13. Martha recrq
1886, 2, 13. George & w, Lydia, & ch, Rose, Clara & Pearle, recrq
1886, 2, 13. Lloyd & w, Electa, recrq
1887, 3, 12. David recrq
1891, 2, 14. William & Anna recrq
1891, 3, 10. Olive recrq
1894, 1, 13. Howard recrq
1894, 1, 13. Rosa recrq
1895, 2, 9. Myrtle recrq
1907, 5, 11. George & Lydia dropped from mbrp for lack of interest
1907, 5, 11. Pearl, Clara & Rose dropped from mbrp; jas
1907, 5, 11. Edgar dropped from mbrp for lack of interest
1908, 6, 13. Edgar rst
1908, 6, 13. Edgar gct Cedars Creek MM
1913, 3, 8. Floyd recrq
1913, 3, 8. Callie recrq
1913, 5, 10. Fred & Martha dropped from mbrp
1915, 1, 9. Ruth recrq
1916, 12, 9. Loren recrq
1916, 12, 9. Mamie recrq
1918, 1, 12. Ruth relrq
1918, 8, 10. Dorothy, dt Loren & Mamie, b rpd
1919, 12, 13. Margaret recrq
1923, 4, 14. Lydia recrq
1923, 4, 14. Elizabeth recrq
1930, 1, 8. Jim & w, Marlin, recrq
1930, 1, 8. Norma Jean & Ruby Lavern, ch Jim & Marlin, rec as associate mbr

HART
1849, 8, 25. Mary, dt N. Hoover, d bur West Branch
----, --, --. Thos. Corwin, s John & Sarah; m Arrie L. MOTE, dt L. S. & C.
S: Willie b 1871, 8, 22 d 1872, 6,10

1875, 12, 16. Emma, w George, recrq
1876, 1, 13. Alice & James E. recrq

HARVEY
1891, 5, 16. Clara Frances, w Edwin, dt Thos. & Sarah Jay, d bur Elm Grove Cemetery

1877, 2, 15. Ruth rocf Spiceland MM, Ind.
1885, 7, 11. Rebecca H. Mote & ch, William R. Harvey & Alice Harvey, rocf Fairmount MM, Ind., dtd 1885,5,13
1888, 5, 12. Rebecca H. Mote, & ch, William R. Harvey & Alice Harvey, gct Fairmount MM, Ind.

HASKET
----, --, --. Isaac, s Isaac, b 1777,11,15; m Rebecca EVANS, dt Robert, b 1780,6,2
Ch: Lydia b 1804, 9, 16
Moses " 1807, 3, 9
Thomas " 1809, 11, 23
Robert " 1812, 2, 12
John " 1814, 9, 5
Joseph " 1817, 11, 11
Rebecca " 1820, 11, 24
Rhoda " 1825, 1, 27
1838, 10, 2. Robert, s Isaac, d bur West Branch
----, --, --. Thos. m Luvenia JONES, dt Thos. & Sarah, b 1815,12,22
Ch: Robert Evans b 1840, 2, 3
Chas. Lewis" 1841, 4, 26
Isaac Reece" 1843, 2, 19
Byron " 1845, 1, 5
Alvin " 1847, 6, 2
Thos. Ellwood " 1849, 1, 14
Melinda " 1851, 4, 17
Joseph Forster " 1853, 7, 1
Wm. Lindley" 1855, 6, 6
Ledru C. " 1856, 6, 5
Lydia Alice" 1859, 3, 28
----, --, --. John b 1814,9,5; m Mary MADDOCK, dt Frank & Phebe, b 1821,9,9
Ch: Rebecca b 1841, 10, 27
Phebe Ellen" 1846, 4, 14
1842, 2, 28. Rebecca Jr. dt Isaac, d bur West Branch
1849, 7, 16. Isaac, s Isaac, d bur West Branch
1862, 3, 20. Rhoda m Henry STEDDOM
----, --, --. Moses, s I. & R., b 1807,3,9; m Lucy A. MARCUM, dt Daniel & Eliza, b 1833,9,16
Ch: Chas. A. b 1864, 7, 25
Geo. Lester" 1867, 9, 27
Edna May " 1869, 10, 4
Joseph Henry " 1873, 10, 5
1864, 5, 9. Chas. L., s Thomas & Luvinia, d bur West Branch
1866, 3, 25. Rebecca, w I., d bur West Branch
1867, 3, 16. Thos. Elwood, s Thos. & Luvenia, d bur West Branch
1867, 6, 8. Wm. Lindley, s Thos. & Luvenia, d bur West Branch
1870, 12, 3. Lydia Alice, dt Thos. & Luvenia, d bur West Branch
1878, 2, 1. Moses, s Isaac & Rebecca, d bur West Branch
1880, 9, 12. John, s Isaac & Rebecca, d bur West Branch
1887, 11, 19. Thos., s Isaac & Rebecca (Evans) d bur West Milton
1889, 9, 20. Joseph, s Isaac & Rebecca (Evans), d

HASKET, continued
1890, 5, 25. Alvine, s Thos. & Luvenia d bur West Milton

1814, 4, 28. Isaac & w, Rebecca, & ch, Lydia, Moses, Thomas & Robert, rocf Union MM, dtd 1814,4,2
1840, 9, 17. John gct Elk MM, to m Mary MADDOCK
1840, 12, 17. Thomas con mcd
1841, 4, 15. John gct Elk MM
1843, 7, 13. John rocf Elk MM, dtd 1843,5,20
1864, 6, 16. Moses rpd mcd
1865, 6, 15. Lucy A. & s, Charles A., recrq
1868, 9, 13. Robert E. rpd mcd
1866, 12, 13. Robert & w, Elizabeth, gct Honey Creek MM, Ind.
1868, 12, 17. Joseph con mcd
1869, 2, 18. Joseph gct Kokomo MM, Ind.
1875, 12, 16. Maime, dt Lucy, recrq

HASTINGS
1808, 8, 28. William [Hasting] rocf Back Creek MM, N. C., dtd 1807,3,28, endorsed by Miami MM, 1808,8,11
1808, --, --. Sarah & dt, Ann, Catharine, Eunice & Wellmet, rocf Back Creek MM, N. C., dtd 1807,3,28, endorsed by Miami MM, 1808,8,11

HATCH
1870, 4, 14. Margaret Jane recrq

HATFIELD
1923, 11, 10. W. R. recrq

HAVENS
1832, 9, 13. Samuel rocf Miami MM, dtd 1832, 7,25

HAWORTH
1854, 4, 20. Betsy Davis m Jesse JONES

1872, 3, 14. Sampson recrq
1872, 5, 16. Esther & s, Walter T., rocf Union MM, dtd 1872,4,17
1913, 3, 8. Mabel recrq

HECKMAN
1818, 3, 26. Mary con mcd
1885, 1, 15. William H. (Hickman] & w, Sarah Elizabeth, & ch, Abbie L., Ora M. & Anson H., recrq
1887, 4, 9. Jesse [Hickman] recrq
1895, 2, 9. Jesse dropped from mbrp
1917, 8, 11. George E. recrq

HEISEY
1923, 4, 14. Ralph & w, Clara, recrq
1925, 12, 12. Dorothy & Bertha recrq
1931, 1, 14. Wilbur David, Willard Julius & Ruth Esther recrq
1932, 4, 13. Naomi recrq
1932, 4, 13. Herman recrq

HENLEY
1883, 11, 15. Jason rocf Carthage MM, Ind., dtd 1883,11,3
1885, 5, 9. Clarence Jay H. & Anna B., ch Jason & Rebecca E., rocf Carthage MM, Ind., dtd 1885,5,2
1885, 11, 14. Harvey G. roc
1892, 2, 13. Jason & fam gct Portland MM,Ind.
1895, 12, 14. Harvey G. & w, Emma, relrq

HERR
1887, 3, 12. George & Grace recrq
1907, 5, 11. George dropped from mbrp for lack of interest
1911, 2, 11. Walter recrq
1913, 3, 8. Harry recrq

HERRON
1923, 4, 14. May & Nellie recrq
1925, 6, 13. May & Nellie dropped from mbrp for jas

HESSON
1887, 4, 9. Eliza recrq
1891, 2, 14. Eliza [Heson] relrq
1893, 2, 11. Samuel recrq

HESS
1892, 9, 10. Flora recrq
1905, 10, 14. Nettie rocf Union MM
1913, 3, 8. Charles & Nettie recrq
1918, 1, 12. Treva recrq

HICKMAN
1837, 2, --. Mary, w Joseph, d bur West Branch
----, --, --. Wm., s Jeremiah & Abbey H., b 1854,1,22; m Sarah Elizabeth SHELLEY, b 1853,10,2
Ch: Abbey L. b 1875, 12, 11
Orey May " 1877, 6, 11
Anson H. " 1882, 5, 11

HILL
1808, 11, 24. Elizabeth m Jonathan JESSOP

1808, 3, 19. Jesse rocf Back Creek MM, N.C., dtd 1807,8,29
1808, 3, 19. Thomas & s, Thomas, Jonathan & Matthew, rocf Back Creek MM, N. C., dtd 1807,8,29
1808, 8, 28. Benjamin & s, John, Jacob, William & Joseph, rocf Mt. Pleasant MM, Va., dtd 1806,8,3, endorsed by Miami MM, 1808, 8,11
1808, --, --. Mary & ch, Sarah, rocf Mt. Pleasant MM, Va., dtd 1806,8,30; endorsed by Miami MM 1808,8,11
1809, 6, 17. Benjamin dis mcd
1815, 3, 23. White Water MM was given permission to rst Benjamin

HILL, continued
1829, 8, 15. John Thomas, s Isaac, gct Arby MM, Ind., to m Miriam Hill

HINES
1915, 1, 9. Mrs. Edna recrq

HISSONG
1923, 6, 13. La Von Arlene, dt Frank & Merle, b
1926, 7, 10. -----, s Frank & Merlie, b

1913, 5, 10. Clyde dropped from mbrp
1923, 2, 10. Frank recrq
1923, 4, 14. Glenna rec as associate mbr
1927, 7, 13. Elbert & Delbert dropped from mbrp
1933, 7, 12. Raymond Lee & w recrq
1933, 8, 9. Patricia Marie rec as associate mbr

HODGEN
1810, 1, 20. Robert & w, Ann, & ch rocf New Garden MM, dtd 1809,11,4

HOLLINGSWORTH
1806, 5, 15. Susannah m Elisha JONES
1809, 11, 24. Isaac d bur West Branch
----, --, --. Richard & Sarah
Ch: Parker b 1821, 5, 21
Moses " 1824, 11, 14
Ira " 1827, 4, 26
----, --, --. James m Mary BROOKS
Ch: Enos b 1825, 4, 25
Isaiah " 1829, 3, 7
Daniel " 1831, 6, 13
Henry " 1834, 8, 13
1830, 7, 31. Susannah d
1830, 12, 30. Susannah m John PEMBERTON
----, --, --. Isaiah, s Richard; m Sarah THOMAS, dt John, Sr.
Ch: Josiah b 1832, 5, 15
1859, 4, 8. Albert, s Wright & Margaret S., b

1807, 10, 17. George Jr. rocf Bush River MM, S. C. dtd 1805,8,31
1808, 10, 22. George con mcd
1808, 11, 19. George Sr. recrq
1810, 4, 21. Anna & ch, Rachel Suffiah Susannah & Joseph, recrq
1811, 11, 28. Carter con mcd
1812, 4, 23. James & fam gct Miami MM
1812, 9, 24. John dis mcd
1813, 9, 23. Joseph dis
1814, 4, 28. Carter gc
1816, 5, 23. Susannah gct White Water MM,Ind.
1823, 10, 18. George dis disunity
1824, 12, 18. Mary (form Brooks) con mcd
1825, 7, 16. Mary gct Silver Creek MM, Ind.
1829, 6, 11. Susannah rocf Union MM, dtd 1829,5,2
1829, 6, 20. Mary rocf Silver Creek MM, dtd 1829,2,28
1830, 8, 21. Sarah rocf Silver Creek MM, Ind., dtd 1830,6,26
1831, 7, 16. Parker, Moses & Irie, ch Sally, recrq
1831, 12, 17. Sarah (form Thomas) con mcd
1832, 1, 21. Isaiah recrq
1833, 3, 14. James & s, Enos, Isaiah &.Daniel recrq
1833, 6, 13. Richard recrq
1833, 7, 18. Ann (form Thomas) con mcd
1835, 8, 13. Anne (form Brooks) con mcd
1836, 7, 14. James & fam gct Mississiniwa MM, Ind.
1839, 4, 18. Richard & fam gct Mississiniwa MM, Ind.
1839, 11, 14. Richard & fam gct Mississiniwa MM, Ind.(cert granted 1839,4,18 not rec)
1840, 6, 18. Isaiah dis mcd
1852, 8, 19. Ann & s, Isaiah & Joseph, rocf Mississiniwa MM, Ind., dtd 1852,7,14
1853, 4, 14. Michael rocf Mississiniwa MM, Ind., dtd 1853,3,16
1855, 1, 18. Michael & fam gct Back Creek MM, Ind.
1856, 9, 18. Josiah dropped from mbrp
1863, 9, 17. Smith Gregg gct Pipe Creek MM, Ind., to m Margaret Hollingsworth
1867, 3, 14. Smith Gregg & w, Margaret, & ch, Mary Ann, Anna Elizabeth, Wilbur S. & Rachel Persis Gregg; Albert W. Hollingsworth & Charles H. Gregg, rocf Wabash MM, Ind., dtd 1867,2,19
1896, 1, 17. Joseph Furnas & w, Susannah, roc
1896, 1, 17. Eber rocf Miami MM, O.
1907, 1, 12. Joseph Earl gct Union MM
1908, 8, 8. Rev. Furnas & w, Susanna, gct Union MM
1908, 8, 8. Eber gct Union MM

HOLTON
1887, 2, 12. George E. rocf Union MM, O.

HOMAN
1888, 9, 8. Betsy & Aaron recrq
1888, 9, 8. Jane recrq

HONEYMAN
1913, 3, 8. Ralph recrq
1913, 4, 12. Callie recrq
1916, 12, 9. Margaret recrq
1924, 4, 12. Iris & s, Richard, recrq

HOOD
1930, 2, 12. Mrs. Louella recrq

HOOVER
----, --, --. John Sr. b 1760,--,--; m Sarah BYRKETT
Ch: Henry b 1785, --, --
Catharine " 1787, 9, 25
Susannah
Elizabeth " 1793, 9, 4

HOOVER, John & Sarah, continued
Ch: Solomon b 1795, 1, --
Noah " 1796, 6, 23
Abraham " 1798, 5, --
Jesse " 1800, --, --
John " 1804, --, --
Joseph " 1808, 2, 12
----, --, --. Jesse, s John & Sarah, d 1856, 12,--; m Rebecca YOUNT, dt John & Mary, d 1895,8,--
Ch: Eli b 1820, 7, 16
Delilah " 1822, 9, 18
Solomon " 1825, 9, 19
Elizabeth " 1827, 12, 20
Mary " 1830, 4, 2
Sarah " 1832, 2, 4
John G. " 1834, 6, 7
Benajah " 1837, 3, 27
Frederic G." 1843, 5, 14
1831, 11, 18. John Sr. d bur West Branch
1837, 10, 7. Andrew, s Noah, d bur West Branch
1838, 11, 22. Mahala m John JAY
1840, 2, 20. Eli, s Jesse & Rebecca, Miami Co., O.; m at West Branch, Mary DAVIS, dt John & Lydia, Miami Co., O.
Ch: Eunice b 1841, 7, 15
Allen " 1844, 2, 5
Jesse Clark" 1846, 9, 2
Rebecca J. " 1849, 7, 9
Henry Davis" 1852, 2, 2
1843, 12, 29. Sarah, w John Sr., d bur West Branch
1849, 8, 20. Frederick, s Jesse, d bur West Branch
1850, 11, 24. Elizabeth m Wm. MILES
1853, 3, 3. Mary, w Eli, dt J. Davis, d bur West Branch
1853, 3, 23. Sarah m Samuel JAY
1853. 4, 12. Eunice, dt Eli & Mary, d bur West Branch
1853, 8, 23. Mary m Enoch P. MILES
1853, 11, 24. Solomon, s Jesse & Rebecca, Miami Co., O.; m at West Branch, Margaret S. MOTE, dt Asa & Kezia, Miami Co., O.
1854, 8, 25. Olive Emeline, dt Solomon G. & Margaret S. (Mote), b
1855, 10, 17. Olive E., dt Solomon & Margaret, d bur West Branch
----, --, --. John C. m Esther JAY
Ch: Wm. Arthur b 1857, 9, 21
Sarah Ellen" 1859, 9, 24
Emma Elizabeth " 1865, 9, 14
1863, 6, 15. Michal, w Noah, dt Fred & Mary Yount, d bur West Branch
1866, 8, 8. Noah, s John & Sarah H., d bur West Branch

1807, 6, 20. Sarah & ch, Solomon, Elizabeth, Noah, Abraham, Jesse, John & Joseph, recrq
1807, 10, 17. Andrew & s, Henry & Andrew, rocf Miami MM, dtd 1807,10,8
1807, --, --. Elizabeth & dt, Rebecca Catharine & Sarah, rocf Miami MM, dtd 1807,10,8
1809, 6, 17. David dis mcd
1809, 7, 22. Sarah con mcd
1814, 5, 26. Solomon dis mcd
1814, 6, 28. Mary (form Jones) con mcd
1816, 12, 26. Noah con mcd
1816, 12, 26. Michal con mcd
1819, 12, 18. Abraham dis disunity
1820, 1, 15. Jesse con mcd
1822, 4, 19. Rebecca rocf Mill Creek MM, dtd 1822,2,23
1824, 3, 20. John Jr. dis mcd
1826, 9, 16. Joseph dis disunity
1842, 7, 14. Absalom dis disunity
1851, 9, 18. Frederic con mcd
1852, 6, 17. Enos dis mcd
1852, 6, 17. Deborah rocf Honey Creek MM, Ind., dtd 1852,5,8
1852, 12, 16. Frederic & w, Deborah, & dt gct Union MM
1854, 5, 18. Eli & fam gct Red Cedar MM, Ia.
1854, 7, 13. Jesse & w, Rebecca, & ch, gct Cedar MM, Ia.
1857, 8, 13. Solomon Y. & w, Margaret S., & dt gct Westland MM, Ia.
1860, 3, 15. Jason dis mcd
1863, 11, 19. John C. & w, & ch, William Arthur, Anna & Sarah Ellen, rocf LeGrand MM, Iowa
1870, 3, 16. Esther & ch gct Wabash MM, Ind.

HOPKINS
1919, 11, 8. Henry W. & w, Jennie, recrq

HORINE
1886, 2, 13. Mattie [Hoorine] recrq
1891, 12, 12. Mattie gct New Hope MM, Ind.

HORNER
1881, 12, 15. Lydia rocf Raysville MM, Ind.
1886, 10, 9. Lydia gct Spiceland MM, Ind.

HOWE
1888, 9, 8. Elnora recrq
1888, 9, 8. Estella recrq
1888, 9, 8. Molly recrq
1888, 9, 8. Amanda recrq

HOZER
1809, 5, 20. William & s, Nathan, rocf Back Creek MM, N. C., dtd 1807,3,28, endorsed by Miami MM, 1809,4,8

HUFFMAN
1910, 12, 10. Warren G. recrq
1913, 4, 12. Warren & Eva relrq

HUNT
1855, 8, 16. Riley Davis gct Elk MM, to m Charlotte T. Hunt
1862, 4, 17. Stephen W. recrq
1862, 5, 15. Stephen W. gct Red Cedar MM,Ia.
1930, 2, 13. Mrs. Anna recrq

HUNTER
1876, 1, 13. Harry recrq

HUTCHINS
1834, 4, 24. Daniel, s Isaac & Rebecca, Montgomery Co., O.; m at West Branch, Dorcas JONES, dt John & Sarah, Miami Co., O.
1854, 5, 10. Darius, s James & Sarah, b 1798, 12,3 d 1878,8,22 bur Randolph; m Mary Elizabeth ENNIS, dt Geo. & Sarah E.
1861, 5, 23. Sarah J. m William COMPTON
1863, 5, 21. Harris, s Isaac & Rebecca, Montgomery Co., O.; m at Randolph, Jemima JENKINS, dt Robert & Ann, Montgomery Co., O.
1866, 12, 10. Daniel H. d bur Randolph
1870, 9, 24. Rebecca, dt Abijah & Rachel H. Jones, d bur Randolph
1874, 1, 15. Dorcas m John MILES
1886, 3, 19. Myrtle L., infant dt Owen E. & M. Alice, d

1807, 12, 19. Benjamin & s, Isaac, & gr s, Jesse, rocf Deep Creek MM, N. C., dtd 1807, 8,1
1807, --, --. Judith [Hutchens] & dt, Dorothy & Lydia, & gr dt, Elizabeth Hutchens, rocf Deep Creek MM, N. C., dtd 1807,8,1 (cert was directed to Miami MM but was rec here)
1809, 6, 17. Rebecca [Huchins] con mcd
1809, 7, 22. Isaac con mcd
1834, 4, 17. Daniel prcf Mill Creek MM, dtd 1834,4,15, to m Dorcas Jones
1836, 2, 18. Dorcas gct Mill Creek MM
1845, 4, 17. Josiah [Huchens] rocf Mill Creek MM, dtd 1845,4,15
1845, 8, 14. Josiah [Huchens] dis mcd
1867, 4, 18. Isaac J. relrq
1868, 5, 14. Abigail gct West Union MM, Ind.
1874, 1, 15. John Miles rocf Milford MM, Ind., to m Dorcas [Hutchens]
1874, 5, 14. Elizabeth, w Darius, recrq
1879, 1, 16. Owen Edgar recrq
1882, 11, 16. Charles E. & w, Mary Virginia, & ch, Lillia May & Myrtle C., recrq
1884, 2, 14. Mary Alice & ch rocf Centre MM, O., dtd 1884,1,16
1890, 3, 8. Sarah F. relrq

HYRE
1903, 2, 14. Gertrude recrq

IDDINGS
1808, 12, 22. Joseph, s Benjamin & Phebe, Miami Co., O.; m at West Branch, Mary DAVIS, dt Abiather & Lydia, Miami Co., O.
1810, 1, 3. Milly m Samuel PEIRCE
1811, 1, 24. Benjamin, s Benjamin & Phebe, Miami Co., O.; m at West Branch, Sarah YOUNT, dt Henry & Mary, Montgomery Co.,O.
1919, 6, 10. Lawson J. d
1924, 5, 28. Priscilla d

1814, 4, 28. Benjamin gc
1814, 4, 28. Sarah & dt gct Mill Creek MM
1889, 4, 13. James L. & w, Priscilla, & ch, Jennette, rocf Miami MM, dtd 1889,3,27
1913, 3, 8. Mary gct Union MM

INGHAM
1810, 8, 18. Deborah rocf Bucks Co., Pa., dtd 1810,6,6
1810, 8, 18. Mary rocf Bucks Co., Pa., dtd 1810,7,4

INGLE
1887, 3, 12. John Calvin & Ruth recrq
1895, 2, 9. Manda & Nellie recrq
1907, 8, 10. J. C. & w relrq
1923, 1, 13. Mr. & Mrs. J. C. recrq

INMAN
1832, 6, 14. Elizabeth con mcd
1842, 5, 19. Elizabeth dis

INSCO
1807, 4, 18. James & w, Lydia, & dt, Beuley, Isabel, Joanna & Ann, rocf Bush River MM, S. C., dtd 1806,6,28 (cert was directed to Miami MM but was rec here)

JACKSON
1813, 3, 25. Lucy dis mcd
1815, 7, 27. Jemima con mcd
1820, 9, 15. Jemima gct Springfield MM

JACOBS
----, --, --. Earl & Vinnie
Ch: Marvin
Earl b 1916, 11, 28
Ruth E. " 1918, 9, 21
Rena L. " 1918, 9, 21
Mearl Lester " 1920, 5, 30
Don Edwin " 1925, 10, 1

1809, 8, 19. James [Jacob] rocf Back Creek MM, N. C., dtd 1809,3,25
1908, 2, 8. Earl & Ross recrq
1925, 7, 11. Rose relrq

JAMES
1837, 11, 27. Thomas, s Isaiah, d bur South Fork

1851, 3, 13. Enoch gct Union MM, to m Eunice Ann Wiles

JAY
1809, 11, 22. Lydia m Moses COPPOCK
1811, 7, 3. William, s John, Miami Co., O.; m at public MH in Newton Twp., Mary Pearson FURNAS, dt Joseph, Miami Co., O.
1829, 6, 25. David, s Samuel & Bathsheba, Miami Co., O.; m at West Branch, Sarah JONES, dt Elisha & Susannah, Miami Co.,O.
1829, 11, 26. Denny, s Jesse & Sally, Miami

JAY, continued
Co., O.; m at West Branch, Mary JONES, dt Elisha & Susannah, Miami Co., O.
----, --, --. James & Martha
Ch: James C. b 1832, 8, 16
Furnice " 1834, 2, 18
Isaac " 1836, 10, 10
1832, 8, 23. John, s Denny & Mary, Miami Co., O.; m at West Branch, Rebecca MOTE, dt John & Rachel, Miami Co., O.
1833, 4, 25. Jonathan, s James & Martha, Miami Co., O.; m at West Branch, Ann JONES, dt Elisha & Susanna, Miami Co., O.
1837, 9, 11. Rebecca, w John, d bur West Branch
1838, 11, 22. John, s Denny & Mary, Miami Co., O.; m at West Branch, Mahala HOOVER, dt Noah & Michael, Miami Co., O.
1837, 11, 30. Mary Elizabeth, dt John R., d bur West Branch
1840, 3, 18. Rebecca, dt John, d bur West Branch
1840, 2, 6. John, s Walter D., d bur West Branch
----, --, --. Thomas, s Denny & Mary, b 1813, 11,22 d 1890,4,14 bur West Branch; m Sarah YOUNT, dt Henry & Elizabeth, b 1819,11,15
Ch: A son b 1841, --, --
Elizabeth " 1842, 7, 5
Oliver " 1844, 6, 3
Daniel Webster " 1846, 11, 16
Rebecca Ella " 1849, 5, 10
Mary Macy " 1851, 9, 8 d 1891, 9,24 bur West Branch
Anna Marie b 1854, 4, 1 d 1871,10,23 bur West Branch
Rhoda B. b 1856, 3, 22
Mahala Emma " 1859, 2, 18
Orlistus " 1861, 6, 5
Clara Frances " 1863, 9, 7
A son " 1865, --, 0-
----, --, --. Walter Denny, s Jno., d 1865,7,9 bur West Branch; m Mary MACY, dt Thomas & Anna, d 1868,8,6 bur West Branch
1840, 9, 24. Job P., s Samuel & Bathsheba, Miami Co., O.; m at West Branch, Rachel COMMONS, dt John & Elizabeth, Miami Co.,O.
1841, 3, 7. Mahala, 2nd w John, d
1853, 3, 23. Samuel, s Elijah & Anna, Miami Co., O.; m at West Branch, Sarah HOOVER, dt Jesse & Rebecca, Miami Co., O.
1853, 5, 26. Susannah m James COPPOCK
1856, 8, 20. James, s John & Keturah, Miami Co., O.; m at West Branch, Susannah JONES, dt Elisha & Rebecca, Miami Co., O.
1---, --, --. Eli b 1826,2,19; m Mahala ----- b 1827,12,7

1808, 10, 22. John & s, William & James, rocf Miami MM, dtd 1808,10,8
1808, --, --. Betty & dt, Lyddia & Jane, rocf Miami MM
1809, 8, 19. Layton & s, William, John, James, David & Elijah, rocf Centre MM, dtd 1809, 7,1
1810, 1, 20. Samuel & w, Bathsheba, & ch, Vielinda & David, rocf Miami MM, dtd 1809, 10,14
1810, --, --. Lydia rocf Miami MM, dtd 1809,6, 10
1810, 10, 20. Sarah & ch, John, James, Thomas, Mary, Samuel & Donny, rocf Miami MM, dtd 1810,9,25
1810, 12, 22. Mary con mcd
1811, 5, 23. Cert rec for Walter Denny endorsed to Mill Creek MM
1811, 8, 22. Elizabeth con mcd
1817, 5, 22. William recrq
1817, 5, 22. Guliann, dt Lydia, recrq
1819, 12, 18. Cert rec for James & fam from Bush River MM, S. C., dtd 1819,4,3, endorsed to Caesars Creek MM
1830, 10, 16. James & s, Jesse & Richard, rocf Silver Creek MM, dtd 1830,9,25
1830, 10, 16. Lydia & dt, ----- & Mary, rocf Silver Creek MM, Ind., dtd 1830,9,25
1830, 12, 9. William dis disunity
1831, 1, 15. Sarah & Mary gct Mill Creek MM
1831, 8, 20. Juliann dis disunity
1832, 3, 17. Samuel Jr. rocf Mill Creek MM, dtd 1832,2,25
1833, 10, 17. Elizabeth & ch, Isaac, Martha & Thomas, recrq
1834, 5, 15. Ann gct Mill Creek MM
1834, 12, 18. John Jr. rocf Mill Creek MM, dtd 1834,11,11
1835, 5, 14. James & fam gct Mississiniwa MM
1835, 9, 17. Samuel Jr. & fam gct Mississiniwa MM
1839, 9, 19. Samuel Jones gct Mill Creek MM, to m Anna Jay
1840, 9, 17. Job P. prcf Mill Creek MM, to m Rachel Commons
1841, 4, 15. Thomas & w, Sarah, rocf Mill Creek MM, dtd 1841,4,13
1851, 11, 15. Susannah rocf Back Creek MM, Ind., dtd 1851,10,16
1854, 7, 13. Keturah rocf Back Creek MM, dtd 1854,6,15
1857, 9, 17. Walter D. & w, Mary, rocf Mississiniwa MM, Ind., dtd 1857,8,12
1861, 12, 19. Eli & w, Mahala, gct Spiceland MM, Ind.
1863, 4, 16. Eli & w, Mahala, rocf Spiceland MM, Ind., dtd 1863,3,25
1868, 8, 13. Oliver rpd mcd
1872, 10, 17. Eli & w, Mahala, & dt gct Hopewell MM
1886, 1, 9. Dennis recrq
1900, 2, 10. Dennis relrq
1905, 3, 11. Mertie M. recrq

JENKINS
1808, 2, 4. David, s Isaac & Rebecca, Miami Co., O.; m at home of Enoch Pearson, Ann RUSSELL, dt Samuel & Rosannah
----, --, --. Evans H., s Robert & Jemima, b 1819,9,19; m ----- SHEPHERD
Ch: Silas N. b 1842, 1, 24
David H. " 1844, 4, 23
Mary Elizabeth " 1845, 11, 27
Evans m 2nd Emeline -----
Ch: Chas. M. b 1855, 12, 5
Clement C. " 1856, 9, 14
Robert A. " 1858, 7, 31
1862, 11, 20. Verlinda m Benjamin F. SYMONS
1863, 5, 21. Jemima m Harris HUTCHINS
1866, 4, 23. Robert, s David & Martha, d bur Randolph
1876, 8, 23. Anna, 3rd w Robert, d bur Randolph Gr Yd
1877, 5, 21. Alvine H., s Robert & Ann (Pearson) d bur Earlham Cemetery, Richmond, Ind.

1807, 6, 20. William & s, David, Phinihas, Joseph William & James, rocf Bush River MM, S. C., dtd 1806,7,26
1807, --, --. Mary & ch, Mary, Hannah, Sarah & Elizabeth, rocf Bush River MM, S. C., dtd 1806,7,26 (cert was directed to Miami MM but was rec here)
1808, 12, 17. John rocf Bush River MM, S. C., dtd 1808,10,9
1823, 11, 15. John dis disunity
1866, 5, 17. Amasa M. gct New Garden MM
1866, 12, 13. Mary Ann, w Amasa, rocf New Garden MM, Ind., dtd 1866,10,20
1868, 3, 19. Newton gct White Water MM, Ind.
1870, 1, 13. Cert for Amasa M. & fam sent to New Garden MM, Ind.
1875, 9, 16. Abijah gc
1875, 12, 16. Laura B. & Josie, dt Lucinda J., recrq
1876, 1, 13. Lucinda recrq
1878, 9, 19. Laura B. dis
1880, 12, 16. Charles M. gct White Water MM, Ind.

JENKS
1836, 10, 13. Rebecca rocf Smithfield MM, R. I., dtd 1836,7,26
1856, 11, 13. Rebecca H. rocf Union MM, dtd 1856,11,12
1861, 4, 18. Rebecca H. gct Smithfield MM, R. I.
1861, 9, 19. Cert returned for Rebecca H. from Smithfield MM, R. I. by rq
1862, 6, 19. Rebecca gct Bangor MM, Ia.

JESSOP
1808, 11, 24. Jonathan, s Jacob & Rachel, Dearborn Co., Ind.; m at White Water, Elizabeth HILL, dt Thomas & Anna, Dearborn Co., Ind.

JESTER
1825, 11, 17. Mary, dt Hiram & Elizabeth Pearson, b
1828, 6, 18. Lemuel F., s Wm. & Ann, b

1860, 9, 15. William P. & Martha Ellen rocf Union MM, dtd 1860,9,12

JONES
----, --, --. Samuel, s Francis Sr., b 1755, 3,8 d 1836,12,24 bur West Branch; m Mary MOTE, dt David & Dorcas, b 1760,2,10 d 1847,12,6 bur West Branch
Ch: John b 1781, 1, 19
Jonathan " 1783, 1, 23
Dorcas " 1784, 9, 18
Samuel " 1786, 9, 8
Francis " 1788, 3, 31
Thos. " 1790, 8, 13
Sarah " 1792, 3, 9
Jesse " 1794, 4, 15
Mary " 1796, 10, 12
Asa " 1798, 12, 26
Rachel " 1802, 6, 28
----, --, --. Wallace b 1773,3,6; m Rachel ----- b 1774,12,27
Ch: Philemon b 1794, 11, 21
John " 1797, 11, 21 d 1897, 8, 5
Jesse " 1799, 10, 7
Mary " 1802, 3, 22
Wiley " 1804, 8, 17
Dorcas " 1806, 12, 4
Pearson " 1809, 10, 26
----, --, --. John, s Francis; m Phebe McDANOLD
Ch: Elizabeth b 1803, 12, 30
Leahorn " 1806, 5, 27
Milborn " 1809, 5, 16
Henry " 1812, 9, 30
Sarah " 1815, 1, 19
Mary Ann " 1817, 4, 3
Francis " 1819, 5, 15
Rachel " 1822, 4, 20
Lydia " 1823, 9, 21
----, --, --. Francis, s Francis, b 1778,2,18; m Mary ----- b 1782,4,7
Ch: Rachel b 1806, 1, 29
David " 1809, 8, 22
Allen " 1812, 6, 2
Rebecca " 1814, 11, 24
1806, 5, 15. Elisha, s John & Margaret, Warren Co., O., b 1786,1,19 d 1840,9,7; m at Tadsfork MH, Susannah ----- b 1788,1,9 d 1817,5,22 bur West Branch (Susannah, dt Isaac & Susannah Hollingsworth, Warren Co. O.)
Ch: Sarah b 1807, 5, 31
Mary " 1809, 1, 18 d 1873, 3,--
Ann " 1811, 4, 28 " 1849,10, 9
Charity " 1813, 6, 13 " 1894, 6,22
David " 1815, 10, 4 " 1886,11,19 bur West Branch
Elisha m 2nd Rebecca ----- b 1789,8,31

JONES, Elisha & Rebecca, continued
d 1876,11,--
Ch: Enoch b 1819, 7, 9
Susannah " 1820, 8, 23
Esther " 1823, 3, 19
Zilpah " 1824, 8, 21 d 1842, 9, 9 bur West Branch
Martha b 1826, 2, 10
Rebecca " 1828, 3, 11
Lydia " 1829, 12, 30 d 1831, 8,26 bur West Branch
Elisha Benson b 1831, 8, 18 d 1831,12, 1 bur West Branch
Elijah Benson b 1834, 1, 21 " 1834, 4,16 bur West Branch

----, --, --. John & Sarah
Ch: Amelia b 1808, 11, 9
Mary " 1810, 4, 15
Deborah " 1812, 3, 16
Dorcas " 1814, 2, 24
Samuel " 1815, 11, 10
Sarah " 1817, 10, 27
Susannah " 1819, 10, 10
Prudence " 1822, 1, 14
Eleanor C. " 1823, 12, 14

1811, 6, 18. Henry, s Wallace, d bur West Branch

1812, 1, 19. Hiram b

1818, 1, 1. Philemon, s Wallace & Rachel, Miami Co., O., d 1830,5,2 bur West Branch; m at West Branch, Naomi TUCKER, dt Abraham & Mary, Montgomery Co., O.
Ch: Henry b 1819, 1, 11
Samuel B. " 1820, 12, 13
Anna " 1823, 5, 19
Benjamin " 1825, 1, 31
Elizabeth " 1828, 7, 25
Philemon " 1830, 5, 12 d 1888, 7,-- m Esther COATE

1819, 2, 25. John, s Wallace & Rachel, Miami Co., O., b 1797,11,21; m Sarah TUCKER, dt Abraham & Mary, b 1800,11,27
Ch: Mary b 1820, 1, 23
Rachel " 1822, 1, 9
Jesse " 1823, 10, 27
Wallace " 1825, 10, 17
Naomi " 1827, 6, 19
Jonathan " 1829, 8, 6
Abraham " 1831, 1, 23
Dorcas " 1833, 8, 3
Margaret " 1835, 2, 27
John
Saray Ann
William " 1842, 7, 29

1822, 2, 21. Mary m Isaac ELLEMAN

1824, 2, --. Mary, w Francis Sr. & sister to Joseph McDonald, d

----, --, --. Daniel H. & Amelia
Ch: James Brantson b 1827, 2, 21
C. Rollin " 1829, 10, 1
J. Byron b 1833, 4, 21
I. Newton " 1835, 9, 30
Luvenia " 1840, 4, 27

1828, 5, 16. Rachel, w Wallace, d bur West Branch

1829, 6, 25. Dorcas m Benjamin PEARSON

1829, 6, 25. Sarah m David JAY

1829, 11, 26. Mary m Denny JAY

1830, 6, 24. Wallace, s Wallace & Elisabeth, Miami Co., O.; m at West Branch, Ruth PEARSON, wd John, dt Isaac & Susannah HOLLINGSWORTH

1833, 4, 25. Ann m Jonathan JAY

1834, 4, 24. Dorcas m Daniel HUTCHINS

1834, 4, 24. Deborah m Zeno MOTE

1834, 10, 23. Charity m Luke S. MOTE

1835, 2, 21. Dorcas, dt John, d bur Union

1835, 10, 23. John, s Samuel, d bur West Branch

1837, 10, 26. Jesse, s Samuel & Mary, Miami Co., O.; m at West Branch, Naomi JONES, dt Abraham & Mary TUCKER, Miami Co., O.

1838, 9, 20. Susannah m David W. MILES

----, --, --. Henry, s Philemon; m Susannah ELLEMON, b 1819,12,29
Dt: Rhoda b 1839, 11, 29

----, --, --. Samuel, s John, b 1815,4,10; m Anna JAY, dt Walter D. & Mary, d 1883,2, 24 bur West Branch
Ch: Elizabeth M. b 1840, 11, 7
A son
Rhoda C. " 1843, 9, 7
Sarah Elma " 1845, 7, 11
John " 1847, 10, 19 d 1854, 8,13 bur West Branch
Walter D. b 1850, 2, 18
William " 1852, 10, 16
Mary Eleanor " 1855, 7, 17
Samuel Rufus b 1858, 10, 12
Anna Alice " 1861, 7, 11 d 1890, 7,13. bur West Branch

1841, 9, 23. Prudence m Benjamin MILES

----, --, --. Collin m Alice Ann ---- d 1851, 10,9 bur West Branch
Ch: Amanda M. b 1843, 8, 15

----, --, --. William, s Jesse, b 1825,8,25; m Elizabeth H. HARSHBURGER, dt H. & E., b 1826,1,16

----, --, --. David m Eunice THAYER, dt Davis W. & Elizabeth (Macy), d 1895,4,13 bur West Branch
Ch: Charlotte B. b 1844, 4, 9
Mary Jane " 1846, 3, 30
Enes Thayer" 1849, 2, 12
Lambert Jefferson " 1852, 5, 10 d 1853, 1,21 bur West Branch
Wm. Allen b 1854, 1, 21
Davis W. " 1856, 12, 18
Elisha " 1859, 1, 31

JONES, David & Eunice, continued
Ch: Unnamed b 1861, 10, 13
Dorah
Elizabeth " 1862, 9, 13
Susan E. " 1865, 6, 26 d 1870, 9,11
bur West Branch
Chas. W. b 1868, 2, 3
----, --, --. Enoch m Sarah KAY d 1848,5,3 bur West Branch
Ch: Almeida b 1844, 7, 27
Miriam " 1846, 7, 24 d 1848, 3,21
bur West Branch
Enoch m 2nd Eunice Ann MILES d 1852,3,16 bur Union Bur. Gr.
Dt: Mary b 1852, 2, 26
Enoch m 3rd Lydia Ann GRAVE
Ch: Elisha
Davis b 1856, 9, 5
Eliza Rebecca " 1857, 12, 26
Lambert
Jefferson " 1859, 9, 17
Anna Maria " 1860, 1, 30
Martha Ellen " 1862, 12, 7
Emma Luella " 1864, 10, 3
Sarah Elizabeth b 1866, 9, 15 d 1867,12,21
bur West Branch
Arthur E. b 1868, 12, 4
1844, 11, 18. Sarah, w John, d bur West Branch
1848, 11, 23. Martha m Isaac C. TEAGUE
1852, 10, 15. Rebecca m Joseph C. TEAGUE
1854, 6, 8. Ruth, w Wallace, dt I. Hollingsworth, d bur West Branch
1854, 9, 20. Wallace d bur West Branch
1854, 4, 20. Jesse, s Samuel & Mary, Miami Co., O.; m at West Branch, Betsy DAVIS, dt James & Ann Haworth (now Embree), Miami Co., O.
1856, 8, 20. Susannah m James JAY
1868, 6, 13. Mary Ann,w Eli, dt S. Gregg bur Randolph Gr Yd
----, --, --. Enos, s David & Eunice; m Sadie TACE b 1846,3,14
Ch: Maurice
Motta b 1884, 1, 19
Ruby E. " 1888, 6, 28
----, --, --. William Allen, s D. & Eunice; m S. Lydia ELLIS, dt James & Louisa
Ch: Inez D. b 1888, 3, 7
Carlton
Ellis " 1890, 7, 9 d 1898, 5, 6
1921, 10, 27. Lydia d
1933, 8, 19. Enos P. d

1807, 2, 21. David con mcd
1807, 8, 22. John rocf Wrightsboro MM, Ga., dtd 1805,4,6
1808, 1, 23. Phebe & ch, Elizabeth & Deborah (or Ceborn) recrq
1808, 10, 22. Abijah & s, Obadiah, Daniel & David, rocf Miami MM, dtd 1808,10,8
1808, --, --. Rachel & dt, Rebecca, Jemima & Mary, rocf Miami MM
1808, 10, 22. John con mcd
1810, 1, 20. Francis Jr. & w, Mary, rocf New Garden MM, dtd 1809,11,4
1810, 3, 17. Elizabeth recrq
1811, 1, 19. Wallace & w, Rachel, & ch, Phillamoh, John, Jesse, Mary, Wiley, Dorkis & Henry, recrq
1811, 5, 8. Elisha & w, Susannah, rocf Miami MM, dtd 1811,3,27
1811, 12, 26. Samuel Jr. con mcd
1813, 3, 25. Sarah & ch, Milly, Mary & Deborah, recrq
1813, 10, 28. Francis Jr. con mcd
1814, 6, 28. Mary Hoover (form Jones) con mcd
1814, 7, 28. Jonathan gct Lick Creek MM, Ind.
1814, 12, 22. John, s Wallace, gct Miami MM
1816, 2, 22. Thomas con mcd
1816, 10, 24. Jesse gct Union MM
1817, 12, 25. Asa gct Union MM, to m
1818, 11, 26. John rocf Miami MM, dtd 1818,10, 28
1818, 11, 26. Hester rocf Union MM, dtd 1818, 11,7
1819, 2, 20. Rebecca rocf Mill Creek MM, dtd 1819,1,23
1820, 3, 18. John, s Wallace, & fam gct Miami MM
1820, 12, 16. John & fam rocf Miami MM, dtd 1820,9,27
1821, 11, 17. Mark Patty gct Mill Creek MM, to m Mary Jones
1823, 1, 18. Asa con mcd
1823, 6, 21. Jesse con mcd
1824, 1, 17. Rachel Thomas (form Jones) con mcd
1824, 6, 19. Rachel Mote (form Jones) con mcd
1825, 2, 19. Elizabeth Thomas (form Jones) con mcd
1825, 7, 16. Francis Jr. dis
1825, 10, 19. Wiley dis mcd
1826, 5, 20. Thomas dis disunity
1826, 6, 17. Francis dis disunity
1827, 5, 19. Amelia con mcd
1827, 8, 18. David Jr. dis mcd
1827, 11, 17. John & fam gct Elk MM
1828, 7, 19. Sarah Ann dis mcd
1828, 12, 20. John & s, Jesse & Wallace, rocf Elk MM, dtd 1828,11,6
1829, 1, 17. Sarah & dt, Mary, Rachel & Naomi rocf Elk MM, dtd 1828,12,6
1829, 2, 21. David dis disunity
1829, 6, 11. Asa dis disunity
1829, 6, 20. Elizabeth dis disunity
1829, 8, 15. Jesse dis disunity
1829, 10, 17. Willborn dis mcd
1829, 10, 17. Seborn dis mcd
1829, 12, 10. Charity gct Vermillion MM, Ill.
1830. 8, 12. Allen dis disunity

JONES, continued
1830, 10, 16. Henry dis disunity
1831, 2, 19. John & fam gct Union MM
1831, 10, 15. Rebecca, dt Francis, dis disunity
1832, 9, 13. Sarah Stiner (form Jones) dis mcd
1833, 1, 17. John & s, Jesse, Wallace, Jonathan & Abraham, rocf Union MM, dtd 1832, 11,22
1833, 1, 17. Sarah & dt, Mary, Rachel & Naomi rocf Union MM, dtd 1833,1,16
1833, 7, 16. Jonathan & s, Lindley M., rocf Lick Creek MM, Ind., dtd 1833,5,16
1833, 7, 16. Mary Stubbs (form Jones) dis mcd
1833, 7, 18. Eleaner C., dt Jonathan, rocf Lick Creek MM, Ind., dtd 1833,5,18
1834, 4, 17. Daniel Hutchins prcf Mill Creek MM, dtd 1834,4,15, to m Dorcas Jones
1834, 4, 17. Charity rocf Vermillion MM, Ill., dtd 1834,1,9
1835, 2, 19. Anna (form Mote) dis mcd
1835, 3, 19. John & fam gct Union MM
1835, 8, 13. Elisha dis disunity (decision reversed later by YM)
1835, 10, 15. Rebecca dis disunity (decision reversed later by YM)
1837, 10, 19. Jesse prcf Union MM, dtd 1837,10, 18, to m Naomi Jones
1837, 11, 20. Henry gct Union MM, to m Susannah E. Pemberton
1837, 12, 14. Naomi & ch gct Union MM
1838, 4, 19. Brantson, Rollin, Byron & Newton, ch Amelia, recrq
1838, 5, 17. John & fam gct Mississiniwa MM
1839, 5, 16. Eleanor C. Davis (form Jones) dis mcd
1839, 9, 19. Samuel gct Mill Creek MM, to m Anna Jay
1841, 6, 17. Lindley M. dis mcd
1841, 11, 18. Henry & fam gct Mississiniwa MM, Ind.
1842, 10, 13. Rebecca recrq
1844, 3, 14. David con mcd
1848, 7, 13. Alice recrq
1849, 1, 18. Union MM was given permission to rst Lindley M.
1849, 2, 15. Daniel H. recrq
1849, 3, 15. Amanda, dt Alice, recrq
1849, 6, 14. Daniel H. & w, Amelia, & fam gct White Water MM, Ind.
1853, 1, 13. Jonathan gct Union MM
1855, 9, 13. Enoch gct West Union MM, to m Lydia Ann Grave
1855, 11, 15. Rebecca & Esther gc
1856, 2, 14. Lydia Ann rocf West Union MM, dtd 1856,1,14
1868, 10, 15. Lydia gct Union MM
1869, 3, 18. William & w, Elizabeth, recrq
1869, 4, 15. Hiram recrq
1871, 6, 15. Enoch & fam gct Baltimore MM,Md.
1871, 6, 15. Mary, dt Enoch, gct Baltimore MM, Md.
1875, 12, 16. Norman recrq (colored)
1877, 2, 15. Sinai E. rocf Spiceland MM, Ind.
1882, 3, 16. Hannah, w Hiram, recrq
1882, 3, 16. Mary Emma & s, Victor W., recrq
1883, 5, 17. Samuel C. rocf Van Wert MM, O., dtd 1883,4,28
1887, 5, 14. Sarah Lydia (form Ellis) rocf Back Creek MM, Ind.
1891, 6, 13. Samuel & w gct Columbus MM, O.
1897, 2, 14. Maurice, Mattie & Ruby, ch Enos T., recrq
1903, 2, 14. Rubie recrq
1903, 2, 14. Inez, birthright mbr, recorded mbr by choice
1913, 5, 10. Charles dropped from mbrp
1919, 11, 8. A. Lindley & w, Mary Eliza, & ch, Elma, Marvin Hatcher, Lois Emily, Allen Picketting, Elizabeth Jane Beryl & Iva Roberts, rocf Fairmount MM, Ind.
1919, 12, 13. Elma & Marvin recrq
1928, 6, 13. William A., Enos P., Davis W. & Charles recrq

JUSTICE
1814, 5, 26. Jonathan & s, Benjamin & John, recrq
1814, 5, 26. Elizabeth [Justis] & dt, Mary Sarah & Elizabeth, recrq
1815, 10, 26. Jonathan & fam gct White Water MM

KECK
1876, 2, 17. Christopher & w & ch, George C., recrq
1878, 9, 19. Christopher relrq
1883, 2, 15. Lola recrq
1885, 4, 16. Louisa relrq

KELLY
----, --, --. Moses & Mary [Kelley]

Ch:		
	Samuel	b 1801, 9, 24
	Anna	" 1804, 3, 30
	Rebecca	" 1806, 9, 17
	John	" 1808, 9, 6
	Esther	" 1810, 10, 10
	Joseph Teague	" 1812, 10, 6
	Mary	" 1814, 9, 4

1816, 6, 10. Samuel rocf Smithfield MM, R.I., dtd 1816,4,25
1817, 4, 24. Moses & fam gct Union MM
1817, 4, 24. Mary & dt gct Union MM
1819, 12, 16. Mahala con mcd
1820, 1, 15. Samuel [Kelley] dis mcd
1822, 11, 16. Seth [Kelley] Jr. rocf Smithfield MM, R. I., dtd 1822,9,26
1923, 4, 14. Max rec as associate mbr
1826, 8, 19. Seth [Kelley] dis mcd
1826, 8, 19. Amelia (form Yount) dis mcd
1826, 11, 18. Milly dis
1830, 12, 18. Mahala dis disunity
1852, 2, 19. Sarah dis mcd

KELLY, continued
1863, 8, 13. Robert & ch, Mary Victoria, Martha Ellen, Lucretia Mott, Gulielma, Eva Janet & Laura May, rocf Bloomfield MM,Ind.
1865, 4, 13. Robert & ch, Mary Victoria, Martha Ellen, Lucretia Mott, Gulielma, Eva Jane & Laura May, gct Vermillion MM, Ill.
1911, 2, 11. Joseph, Dewain & Donald recrq
1913, 4, 12. Ella recrq
1923, 6, 9. Charles [Kelley] recrq

KELLOGG
1882, 3, 16. Edward P. & s, George N., Charles W. Arthur & Merton E., recrq
1883, 4, 17. Rhetta recrq
1885, 5, 9. Maria recrq
1892, 2, 13. B. P. & fam relrq
1893, 2, 11. Retta Whitson (form Kellogg) relrq

KENDALL
1890, 12, 23. Eunice, w John, dt Joseph & Rachel MENDENHALL, d bur West Branch
1923, 10, 29. Harry d

1829, 2, 21. Eunice (form Mendenhall) dis mcd
1867, 4, 18. Eunice recrq
1883, 3, 15. Albert & ch, Harold & Orilla, recrq
1913, 3, 8. Marie & Robert recrq
1913, 5, 10. Rebecca recrq

KENWORTHY
1812, 10, 22. Ann [Kinworthy] & ch gct Caesars Creek MM
1932, 4, 13. Margaret recrq

KERNS
1891, 2, 14. Jesse R. recrq

KESSLER
1885, 2, 19. Arden P. recrq
1897, 1, 9. Arden P. gct Union MM

KING
1911, 2, 11. William recrq
1911, 2, 11. _____ recrq
1914, 2, 14. Claudine & Druella, ch William, recrq

KLEPINGER
----, --, --. Harold & Juanita
Ch: Nolan
Wayne b 1923, 1, 1
Eleon Dale " 1926, 5, 14

1922, 5, 13. Harold & Glenna recrq

KOONS
1809, 8, 19. Jasper & s, John, Jasper, Jeremiah, William, Nathan, Henry & Samuel, rocf Back Creek MM, N. C., dtd 1808,7,30
1809, -- --. Abigail [Coons] & dt, Hannah, rocf Back Creek MM, N. C., dtd 1808,7,30

KREITZER
1893, 8, 12. George F. & w, Alice, recrq

LAIR
1913, 5, 10. Rosa dropped from mbrp
1913, 9, 13. Rosa rst

LAMB
1807, 4, 18. Josiah & s, John Evan & Jonathan rocf Miami MM, dtd 1807,3,12
1807, --, --. Naomi & dt, Ruth & Nancy, rocf Miami MM, dtd 1807,3,12

LANCASTER
1807, --, --. Rachel rocf Bush River MM, S.C., dtd 1806,5,31

LEASE
1865, 11, 16. Louisa (form Thomas) dis mcd & jas

LIGHTNER
1891, 2, 14. Harvey recrq
1909, 1, 9. Ella, Charley & Roy, form mbr Chambersburg MM, recrq
1913, 5, 10. Ella, Charles & Roy dropped from mbrp

LINDLEY
1809, 9, 23. William rocf Spring MM, N. C., dtd 1808,8,27

LINN
1890, 1, 19. Wm. Linus, s Alba B. & Jane Elizabeth (French), d bur Milton Cemetery

1887, 3, 12. William recrq

LINSEY
1903, 2, 14. Lottie [Linse] recrq
1907, 5, 11. Lottie dropped from mbrp for lack of interest

LITTLEJOHN
1809, 10, 21. Sarah (form Dunkin) dis mcd

LITTLETON
1923, 2, --. Myra d
1928, 4, 23. Chauncy d

1909, 1, 9. Chauncy, Myrta, Ernest, Orpha & Wayne, form mbr of Chambersburg MM, recrq
1925, 6, 13. Orpha & Wayne dropped from mbrp for jas
1927, 7, 13. Wayne & Raymond dropped from mbrp

LOCHNER
1891, 2, 14. Philip C., Alma C. & Clyde C. [Lachner] recrq
1908, 2, 8. May recrq

LOCHNER, continued
1913, 5, 10. Clyde & May dropped from mbrp

LOCKE
1888, 9, 8. Jesse D. recrq

LOE
1810, 1, 20. Ann & ch, William & Ann, rocf New Garden MM, dtd 1809,11,4
1810, 9, 22. Ann gct Elk MM

LONG
1873, 2, 6. Sarah, 2nd w Joseph, dt John & Katharine CURTIS, d bur Randolph Gr Yd

1885, 3, 19. John & w, Esther, & dt, Ella, recrq

LYONS
1922, 4, 7. Mahala d

1889, 1, 12. Thomas E. recrq

McBRIDE
1886, 2, 13. George recrq
1886, 2, 13. John recrq

McCAINE
1883, 3, 15. Harrison [McCain] & w, Ann, recrq
1886, 5, 8. Harrison & w, Ann, gct Union MM

McCARTY
1913, 4, 12. Estella recrq

McCOOLE
----, --, --. Thos., s John & Mary, (Hanks), b 1814,1,31 d 1879,4,7 bur Union; m Julia Ann MILLER, dt A----- & Christina, b 1820, 8,14

1807, 5, 23. Gabriel & s, Wells & Elisha, rocf Bush River MM, S. C., dtd 1806,8,30
1807, --, --. Betty [McCool] & dt, Betsy & Martha, rocf Bush River MM, S. C., dtd 1806,8,30 (cert was directed to Miami MM but was rec here)
1812, 4, 23. Martha Hanks (form McCoole) con mcd
1813, 7, 22. Cert rec for John from New Garden MM, N. C. dtd 1812,12,26; endorsed to Union MM
1819, 7, 17. James & w, Charity, & ch, Eliza Ann & Rachel, rocf Hopewell MM, Va., dtd 1819,2,4, endorsed by Mill Creek MM, 1819, 6,26
1821, 7, 21. -----, s John, rocf Union MM, dtd 1821,4,18
1823, 11, 15. Charity & ch gct Mill Creek MM
1840, 12, 17. Thomas W. con mcd
1842, 5, 19. Julian recrq
1855, 5, 17. Thomas W. [McCool] & w, Juliann, gct Western Plain MM, Ia.
1877, 11, 15. Thomas W. & w, Julia Ann, rocf Back Creek MM, N. C.

McDANIEL
1831, 8, 20. Temperance rocf Union MM, dtd 1831,8,6

McDARGH
1876, 3, 16. Margaret recrq
1876, 5, 18. Mary Catherine & Nora Frances recrq
1909, 1, 9. Margaret, form mbr Chambersburg MM, recrq
1913, 5, 10. Margaret dropped from mbrp

McDONALD
----, --, --. Joseph [McDanold] m Sarah M. ----- b 1789,11,7
Ch: John b 1807, 9, 6 d 1888,--,--
Mark " 1809, 9, 20
Charles " 1811, 9, 29
1811, 10, 9. Sarah, w Joseph, d bur West Branch
1855, 11, 1. Temperance, 2nd w Joseph, d bur West Branch
1877, 7, 27. Henrietta, w Allen, dt James & Elizabeth THOMAS, d

1807, 2, 21. Joseph con mcd
1807, 3, 21. Sarah con mcd
1813, 5, 27. Joseph dis mcd
1823, 11, 15. William & ch, Mark, John & Charles, gct Union MM
1835, 11, 19. Lydia (form Mendenhall) con mcd
1838, 6, 14. Lydia gct Union MM

1871, 5, 18. William rocf Cottonwood MM, Kans., dtd 1871,4,1
1872, 3, 14. Keron recrq
1874, 8, 13. Keron relrq
1878, 3, 14. William relrq
1880, 5, 13. Allen gct Wabash MM, Ind.
1885, 5, 9. William & w, Keron, recrq
1888, 9, 8. Anna recrq
1893, 2, 11. William & fam gct White River MM, Ind.

McELVANE
1909, 1, 9. Alice, form mbr Chambersburg MM, recrq
1913, 5, 10. Alice dropped from mbrp

McGLOTHER
1901, 9, 14. Anna E. (form Elleman) relrq

McGLOTHIN
1907, 1, 12. Verlin & Marley [McGlothan] recrq
1923, 6, 9. Verlin relrq

McGRIFFEN
1889, 8, 2. Rebecca, w Dr., dt John & Mary (Mattock) HASKET, d bur West Branch

McKINLEY
1904, 3, 12. Mrs. Mamie Coate relrq

McMUNN
1810, --, --. Prudence & dt, Elizabeth & Sarah, rocf Wrightsboro MM, Georgia, dtd 1809,11,4

McPHERSON
1857, 12, 17. Lydia E. rocf Wabash MM, Ind., dtd 1857,10,10

MACY
----, --, --. Thos., s Paul, b 1765,2,25 d 1833,2,--; m Anna SWEET b 1768,9,29 d 1840,3,28 bur Mill Creek
Ch: Mary b 1787, 12, 7
Isaac " 1789, 8, 20
Thomas " 1791, 7, 18
Rhoda " 1793, 5, 5
John " 1795, 8, 6
Paul " 1798, 3, 16
Elizabeth " 1800, 3, 18
Jonathan " 1802, 5, 31
Anne " 1804, 3, 29
Phebe " 1806, 9, 22
Aaron " 1809, 2, 16
Lydia " 1811, 3, 26 [JAY, b
1795, 6, 9. Jane, w Thos., dt John & Betty
----, --, --. Paul, s Paul, b 1780,7,10; m Eunice MACY, dt Matthew, b 1782,5,25
Ch: Phebe b 1802, 1, 17
Thos. " 1804, 9, 30
Lydia " 1806, 12, 19
Anna " 1809, 2, 10
Beulah " 1811, 2, 1
John G. " 1813, 9, 27
Paul " 1816, 2, 8
David S. " 1818, 5, 28
Eunice " 1821, 2, 21
Obed " 1826, 5, 26
1811, 3, 29. Mary Ann Macy, 2nd w Thos., b
1823, 8, 18. James, s Zacheus & Sarah, Union Co., Ind.; m at West Branch, Anna MENDENHALL, dt Joseph & Rachel, Miami Co., O.
----, --, --. Aaron, s Thomas & Anns S., d 1880 11,3 bur West Branch; m Matilda PRILL, dt Michael & Elizabeth, b 1812,3,21 d 1893, 3,26
Ch: Jonathan b 1831, 6, 19
Ann Elizabeth " 1832, 10, 1
Maria " 1835, 8, 21
Sarah Jane " 1837, 3, 6
Wm. " 1839, 3, 29
James Rufus" 1841, 6, 3
Mary Jay " 1843, 1, 28
Calvin " 1845, 4, 26
Elmira " 1847, 9, 20
Thos. Webster " 1850, 5, 7
----, --, --. Thos., s Paul & Eunice, b 1804, 9,30; m (2) Mary Ann ----- b 1811,3,29
----, --, --. David S., s Paul, b 1818,5,28; m Delilah GARDNER, dt Wm., b 1818,9,1
Ch: Amanda b 1839, 1, 12
Laura " 1842, 10, 1
Emily " 1845, 10, 23
Lindley " 1847, 7, 31
Barclay " 1849, 4, 11
Esther " 1851, 8, 25
----, --, --. Eli Oliver, s Stephen & Mary, Jefferson Co., O., b 1844,4,4; m at Center, Anna PEARSON, dt Benjamin H. & Dorcas (Jones), Miami Co., O., b 1845,12,24
Ch: Elbert b 1873, 1, 25

1808, 8, 28. Stephen & s, John, rocf Deep Creek MM, N. C., dtd 1808,3,5
1808, --, --. Rebecca & dt, Anna & Catharine, rocf Deep Creek MM, N. C., dtd 1808,3,5
1808, 11, 19. Robert & w, Elizabeth, & ch, William, Obed, Susannah & Seth, rocf New Garden MM, N. C., dtd 1808,8,27
1809, 9, 23. Robert & fam gct New Garden MM
1810, 11, 17. Thomas & w, Anna, & ch, Thomas, John, Paul, Elizabeth, Jonathan, Anna, Phebe & Aaron, rocf New Hope MM, Tenn., dtd 1810,4,21
1812, 2, 27. Robert & w, Elizabeth, & ch, William, Obed, Susannah, Seth & Elizabeth, rocf New Garden MM, N. C., dtd 1811,9,28
1816, 11, 28. Robert & w, Elizabeth, gct New Garden MM
1824, 8, 21. Anna & dt, Lydia Ann,gct Silver Creek MM, Ind.
1825, 9, 17. Gardner Mendenhall gct Mill Creek MM, to m Phebe Macy
1836, 10, 13. Anna rocf Mill Creek MM, dtd 1836,9,13
1848, 11, 16. Paul & w, Eunice, rocf Mill Creek MM, dtd 1848,11,14
1849, 3, 15. David S. & w, Delilah, & ch, Amanda Laura & Lindley, rocf Mill Creek MM, dtd 1849,3,13
1853, 9, 15. David S. & fam gct Red Cedar MM, Ia.
1853, 10, 13. Paul & w gct Union MM
1861, 1, 17. Matilda M. recrq
1866, 3, 15. Aaron recrq
1872, 3, 14. Eli O. rocf Pleasant Plain MM, Ia., dtd 1872,1,13
1876, 4, 13. Eli O. & fam gct Pleasant Plain MM, Ia.
1903, 2, 14. Pauline recrq
1915, 10, 9. Lenna rocf Union MM

MADDOCK
1818, 4, 23. Dorcas [Mattock] con mcd
1836, 8, 18. Dorcas dis disunity
1840, 4, 18. Riley Davis gct Elk MM, to m Rachel Maddock
1840, 9, 17. John Hasket gct Elk MM, to m Mary Maddock

MALCOM
1916, 10, 29. Newton d

1911, 4, 8. A. N. & w, Lena, recrq

MARKLEY
1915, 11, 2. John Jacob, s John & Opal, b
1923, 12, 27. Joseph d
1924, 1, 12. Martin d

1911, 2, 11. Joseph recrq
1911, 2, 11. Callie recrq
1911, 2, 11. Mrs. Rachel recrq
1913, 3, 8. Martin recrq
1914, 8, 8. Opel recrq
1915, 1, 9. Victoria recrq
1919, 12, 13. Aaron recrq
1919, 12, 13. Elmina recrq
1923, 4, 14. Johnnie rec as associate mbr
1923, 4, 14. Helen recrq

MARTIN
1888, 9, 8. Charles recrq

MARTINDALE
1809, 9, 23. Elizabeth [Martindill] dis mcd

MAST
1813, 1, 11. Susannah, w John M., d bur West Branch
1922, 3, 24. Mary d

1810, 4, 21. Susannah recrq
1887, 3, 12. Hattie recrq
1911, 3, 11. Mrs. Winifred recrq
1913, 3, 8. Herbert recrq
1913, 6, 14. Alta & ch, Richard Eugene, Isabel & Margaret, recrq

MEDLEY
1875, 12, 16. James M. recrq (colored)
1878, 10, 17. Madison dis (colored)

MENDENHALL
----, --, --. Caleb b 1769,12,-- d 1848,--,0-; m Susana ----- b 1771,1,--
Ch: Miriam b 1792, 6, 10 d 1873,10,25
Griffith " 1793, 10, 4 " 1878, 1,13
William " 1795, 8, 1
Caleb " 1797, 5, 29 " 1849,--,--
Susanna " 1799, 3, 5 " 1865,--,--
m Anthony WISENER
Grace b 1801, 1, 31 " 1888, 8,30
Tamar " 1802, 9, 9 " 1896,10, 3
m Isaac THOMAS
Gardner b 1804, 9, 16 " 1875, 2,18
Charity " 1806, 10, 31 " 1879, 6,--
Rhoda " 1808, 8, 15 " 1873, 5, 7
Kirk " 1811, 11, 27 " 1839,--,--
----, --, --. Joseph b 1772,4,18; m Rachel ---- b 1773,3,-- d 1860,2,13 bur West Branch
Ch: Mary b 1795, 9, 27 d 1871,--,--
m ----- BROWN
Abia b 1797, 2, 7
Tamar " 1798, 11, 20 d 1871,12,25
m ----- BROWN
Thaddeus b 1800, 10, 2 d 1846,11,--
Lydia " 1802, 9, 11 " 1848,--,--
m ----- McDONALD
Anna b 1805, 3, 10 " 1891, 8, 8
m ----- MACY
Ruth b 1806, 12, 15 " 1864, 5,20
m ----- BALLINGER
Eunice b 1808, 12, 3 " 1890,12,--
m ----- KENDALL
Joseph b 1814, 2, 14 d 1880, 1,22
bur West Branch
1811, 11, 14. Miriam m David MOTE
1820, 12, 21. Grace m John THOMAS
1823, 8, 18. Anna m James MACY
1826, 8, 24. Rachel m Henry COMPTON
1827, 10, 25. Tamer m Isaac THOMAS
----, --, --. Gardner m Phebe MACY
Ch: Aldus b 1828, 4, 29 d 1833, 5, 8
bur West Branch
Anna b 1830, 9, 17
Linus " 1833, 12, 26
Enos " 1835, 1, 19
Kirk "
Wm.
Susan
Mary
Rhoda
Gardner m 2nd Elizabeth THAYER
Ch: Alice
Thayer b 1864, 12, 8
Cora
Elizabeth " 1866, 10, 24
Adella
Gardner " 1868, 11, 11
David James" 1872, 2, 25
Everetta F." 1875, 3, 10
1833, 5, 5. Anna d bur West Branch
1850, 9, 27. Joseph Sr., s Phineas, d bur West Branch

1819, 5, 15. Ann con mcd
1821, 5, 19. Thaddeus con mcd
1821, 7, 21. Susan Anthony (form Mendenhall) con mcd
1821, 10, 20. William gct Honey Creek MM,Ind.
1823, 9, 20. Tamer Russel (form Mendenhall) dis mcd
1825, 9, 17. Gardner gct Mill Creek MM, to m Phebe Macy
1829, 2, 21. Charity Watts (form Mendenhall) con mcd
1829, 2, 21. Eunice Kendall (form Mendenhall) dis mcd
1829, 6, 11. Phebe rocf Mill Creek MM, dtd 1829,4,25
1829, 6, 20. Caleb dis disunity
1830, 12, 9. Rhoda Dulin (form Mendenhall) con mcd
1831, 4, 16. Gardner dis jH
1831, 5, 21. Thadeus dis disunity

MENDENHALL
1835, 2, 19. Caleb Jr. & fam gct White Water MM
1835, 3, 19. Kirk dis mcd
1835, 7, 16. Phebe & ch gct White Water MM, Ind.
1835, 11, 19. Lydia McDonald (form Mendenhall) con mcd
1842, 3, 17. Ruth Bolinger (form Mendenhall) dis mcd
1865, 4, 13. Elizabeth R. gct White Water MM
1890, 3, 8. Sarah A. recrq

MICHAEL
1811, 12, 26. Elizabeth [Mickle] con mcd
1887, 3, 12. Bertie recrq
1887, 3, 12. Norah recrq

MILES
1812, 10, 14. William, s David & Elizabeth, Miami Co., O.; m at Union, Mary PEARSON, dt Benjamin & Esther, Miami Co., O.
1838, 9, 20. David W., s William & Mary, Miami Co., O.; m at West Branch, Susannah JONES, dt John & Sarah, Miami Co., O.
1841, 9, 23. Benjamin, s William & Mary, Miami Co., O.; m at West Branch, Prudence JONES, dt John & Sarah, Miami Co., O.
1850, 11, 24. William, s William & Mary, Miami Co., O.; m at West Branch, Elizabeth HOOVER, dt Jesse & Rebecca, Miami Co., O.
1853, 8, 23. Enoch P., s David & Jane, Miami Co., O.; m at West Branch, Mary HOOVER, dt Jesse & Rebecca, Miami Co., O.

1807, 3, 21. William & s, William, Samuel & David, rocf Bush River MM, S. C., dtd 1806,7,26
1807, --, --. Mary & dt, Mary, rocf Bush River MM, S. C., dtd 1806,8,26 (cert rec here but was directed to Miami MM)
1807, --, --. Rachel & dt, Anne & Abigail, rocf Bush River MM, S. C., dtd 1806,8,30, endorsed by Miami MM, 1807,3,12
1807, --, --. Sally rocf Bush River MM, S. C., dtd 1807,3,28
1810, 3, 17. William con mcd
1811 5, 23. William, s William, con mcd
1811 7, 25. Jane rocf New Garden MM, N. C., dtd 1810,12,29
1813, 7, 22. Cert rec for William from New Garden MM, N. C., dtd 1812,11,28, endorsed to Union MM
1814, 4, 28. William gc
1838, 10, 18. Samuel M. Abbott gct Union MM, to m Rebecca Miles
1852, 5, 13. William & w, Elizabeth, & dt, Anzinnetta, rocf Cincinnati MM, dtd 1852, 5,12
1854, 1, 19. William & w, Elizabeth, & dt gct Red Cedar MM, Ia.
1861, 3, 14. David W. & w, Susan, & ch, John Webster, Branson J. & Wilkinson, rocf Red Cedar MM, Ia., dtd 1861,2,6
1863, 6, 17. David W. & w, Susan, & ch gct Union MM
1871, 5, 18. Catharine C. rocf Union MM, dtd 1871,5,17
1874, 1, 15. John prcf Milford MM, Ind., to m Dorcas Hutchens
1874, 1, 15. John, s William & Rachel, Wayne Co., Ind.; m Dorcas HUTCHINS, at residence of John Miles

MILLER
1922, 9, 2. Jonas d

1807, 7, 18. Jonathan rocf Bush River MM, S. C., dtd 1806,7,26
1860, 6, 14. William R. rocf New Garden MM, Ind., dtd 1860,4,21
1865, 4, 13. William R. gct Back Creek MM, Ind.
1871, 4, 13. Jane rpd mcd & jas; dropped from mbrp
1885, 3, 19. George recrq
1889, 4, 13. Jane & dt, Sallie, recrq
1891, 4, 11. Mary recrq
1907, 5, 11. George dropped from mbrp for lack of interest
1911, 1, 14. Jonas & w, Mary E., recrq
1932, 4, 13. Freda & Mrs. Mina recrq

MILLS
----, --, --. John, s Alexander, b 1795,12,12; m Anna MACY, dt Paul, b 1809,2,10

Ch:		
	Oliver	b 1828, 12, 28
	Eunice	" 1831, 2, 13
	Mary	" 1833, 8, 9
	David	" 1835, 4, 13
	Alexander	" 1837, 4, 13
	Lydia	" 1840, 8, 8
	Samuel	" 1842, 11, 22
	Aaron	" 1846, 2, 6
	Sarah	" 1848, 3, 3
	Martha	" 1851, 2, 3

1850, 9, 3. Sarah, dt John, d bur West Branch

1829, 12, 19. Philip Farmer gct Cherry Grove MM, Ind., to m Anna Mills
1850, 4, 18. Anna rocf Union MM, dtd 1850,4, 17
1850, 10, 17. Mary, David, Alexander, Lydia, Samuel & Aaron, ch John, recrq
1850, 12, 13. John recrq
1851, 1, 16. Eunice recrq
1853, 1, 13. John & w, Anna, & ch, Eunice, Mary I., David, Alexander, Lydia, Samuel, Aaron & Martha, gct Salem MM, Ia.

MODLIN
1807, 8, 22. Benjamin & s, Samuel, Thomas & John, rocf Back Creek MM, N. C., dtd 1807,2,28

MOON
1875, 8, 19. Aaron & w, Eunice, & ch rocf Caesars Creek MM, O.
1880, 6, 17. Aaron & w, Eunice, & fam gct Caesars Creek MM, O.
1883, 6, 14. Oliver gct Caesars Creek MM, O.

MOORE
1925, 6, 13. Maple dropped from mbrp for jas

MORGAN
1807, 12, 19. Benjamin & s, Micajah, Charles & Isaac, rocf Back Creek MM, N. C., dtd 1807,3,28

MORRIS
1878, 12, 19. Abraham D. & w, Martha, recrq

MORROW
1808, 4, 23. John & s, Andrew & Joseph, rocf Cain Creek MM, N. C., dtd 1807,9,5, endorsed by Miami MM, 1808,3,10
1808, --, --. Mary & dt, Hannah, Mary & Ruth, rocf Cane Creek MM, N. C., dtd 1807,9,5, endorsed by Miami MM, 1808,3,10

MOTE
----, --, --. Jonathan b 1758,8,23; m Ann -----
Ch: Timothy b 1784, 3, 17
Ann " 1785, 8, 22; m ----- JONES
David " 1787, 8, 1
Sarah " 1789, 11, 7
Jonathan " 1791, 5, 1
Wm. " 1793, 4, 27
Elizabeth " 1795, 12, 3; m ----- INMAN
Dorcas " 1798, 11, 7 ; m ----- MADDOCK
Mary " 1800, 9, 2; m ----- HICKMAN
Jeremiah " 1803, 12, 8
Jonathan m 2nd Susannah ----- b 1773,--,-- d 1809,1,3
Ch: Nathan b 1808, 8, 12 d 1809, 2,15 bur West Branch
----, --, --. Jeremiah m Mary Ann BUTLER
Ch: Wm. b 1791, 6, 8
David " 1792, 12, 8
Aaron " 1795, 2, 10
Ann & Dorcas " 1796, 12, 3
Jeremiah " 1798, 3, 17
Isaiah " 1800, 7, 1
Mary " 1803, 9, 6
Susannah " 1805, 10, 15
Sarah " 1808, 3, 1
Miriam " 1809, 3, 13
Hannah " 1812, 7, 14
Enoch " 1814, 3, 11
----, --, --. John, s David, b 1767,4,4 d 1845,12,16 bur West Branch; m Rachel ----- dt Daniel, b 1772,5,12 d 1844,3,19 bur West Branch
Ch: David b 1793, --, --
Elizabeth " 1795, 3, 7
John " 1797, 12, 31
David " 1800, 12, 22
Rachel " 1804, 1, 30
Daniel " 1808, 12, 8
Anna S. " 1811, 4, 7
Rebecca " 1814, 9, 17
Mary " 1818, 7, 19
1811, 11, 14. David [Motte], s Jeremiah & Mary, Montgomery Co., O., b 1792,12,8; m at West Branch, Miriam MENDENHALL, dt Caleb & Susannah, Miami Co., O., b 1792, 6,10 d 1873,10,25 bur West Branch (David d 1862,9,23 bur West Branch)
Ch: Luke Smith b 1812, 8, 21
Zeno " 1814, 5, 5 d 1893,--,--
Marcus " 1817, 6, 19
Linus " 1819, 10, 6 " 1887,--,--
Enos " 1827, 10, 17 " 1856,--,--
1816, 10, 31. Elizabeth m John COMMONS
----, --, --. John m Rhoda TEAGUE, dt Samuel & Lydia, d 1834,11,22 bur Union
Ch: Elizabeth b 1824, 5, 4
Samuel Teague " 1826, 9, 25
Anna " 1828, 9, 30
----, --, --. David Jr., s John & Rachel; m Barbara STEARGEON, dt Wm. & Phebe
Ch: Mary b 1824, 8, 22
Phebe L. " 1826, 10, 28
Joseph " 1828, 10, 18
Rachel " 1830, 11, 24
Rebecca " 1832, 11, 30
Thos. Elwood " 1835, 12, 21
John Webster " 1838, 6, 25
Susan Margaret " 1842, 1, 27
1824, 2, 26. Rachel m David COMMONS
----, --, --. Asa m Charity NORTH
Ch: Elijah b 1827, 1, 27
Nancy V. " 1828, 9, 20
Asa m 2nd Keziah PEARSON
Ch: Margaret L. b 1830, 7, 14
Sarah P. " 1832, 2, 9
Susannah " 1835, 9, 1
Jesse Jordan b 1842, 3, 21
----, --, --. Daniel, s John; m Nancy Waggoner dt John
Ch: Rachel b 1828, 4, 2
Caroline Matilda " 1829, 8, 28
Hannah " 1833, 9, 8 d 1855, 4,14 bur West Branch
John W. b 1836, 1, 3
Rhoda " 1839, 2, 7 " 1855, 6, 5 bur West Branch
1832, 8, 23. Rebecca m John JAY

MOTE, continued
1834, 4, 24. Zeno, s David & Miriam, Miami Co., O.; m at West Branch, Deborah JONES, dt John & Sarah (McKee), Miami Co., O., d 1893,5,17 (Zeno d 1895,4,--)
Ch: Jane b 1835, 3, 17 d 1859, 8,26 bur West Branch
John J. b 1836, 4, 21
Orrin L. " 1837, 8, 30
Ethan A. " 1839, 2, 16
Linnias " 1841, 5, 5
Thos. Clarkson " 1842, 11, 25 d 1872, 6,24 bur West Branch
David b 1844, 10, 23
Daniel H. " 1846, 12, 7 " 1848, 6,26 bur West Branch
Anson b 1849, 7, 19 d 1850, 9,29 bur West Branch
Albert Louis b 1852, 1, 9
1834, 10, 23. Luke Smith [Motte], s David & Miriam (Mendenhall), Miami Co., O., b 1812, --,-- at West Branch; m Charity J. JONES, dt Elisha & Susanna (Hollingsworth), Miami Co., O., b 1813,6,13 d 1894,6,22 bur West Branch
Ch: Elisha J. b 1836, 9, 21
Arena E. " 1838, 8, 24
Wm. Aldin " 1840, 8, 27
Celestia Susan " 1842, 7, 22
Mary Melona" 1844, 11, 17
Arriadne " 1847, 3, 15
Marcus Benson " 1850, 3, 29 d 1891,8, 29 bur West Branch
Cordelia Bayes b 1852, 12, 4
----, --, --. David, Jr. d 1817,3,4 bur West Branch; m Dorcas ----- d 1817,9,17 bur West Branch
1836, 3, 24. John [Motte] Jr., s John & Rachel, Miami Co., O.; m at West Branch, Lydia HASKET, dt Isaac & Rebecca, Miami Co., O.
----, --, --. Marcus m Rhoda STEDDOM
Ch: Kirk Linus b 1840, 1, 28
Samuel Steddom " 1842, 9, 15
1848, --, --. Linus, s David & Miriam, d 1887, 9,12 bur West Branch; m Hannah GRAVES, d 1881,--,-- bur West Branch
Linus m 2nd Rebecca (Reeder) HARVEY, wd Jehu
1849, 2, 22. Mary m Jehu BALLARD
----, --, --. Enos m Martha Ann REED, dt John G. & Sarah, d 1856,4,17 bur West Branch
Ch: Alvale Eugene b 1851, 1, 27
Ledru Rollin " 1853, 6, 22 d 1884, 8,28
Ch: Edwin Enos b 1856, 2, 7
----, --, --. Joseph, s David Jr., b 1828,10, 18; m Martha P. PAINTER, dt Thos. & Mary, b 1832,11,6
Ch: Wm. Oscar b 1852, 3, 24
Mary Ellen " 1854, 1, 3
1853, 11, 24. Margaret S. m Solomon HOOVER
1854, 9, 3. Lydia [Motte], 2nd w John, dt I. HASKETT, d bur West Branch
----, --, --. Samuel T., s John & Rhoda T., b 1826,9,25; m Anna Maria MACY, dt Aaron & Matilda M., b 1835,8,21
Ch: Lydia Chloria b 1855, 7, 14
Rhoda Matilda " 1857, 7, 16
Louis Kossuth " 1859, 5, 15
Mary Elizabeth " 1862, 2, 13
John Franklin " 1863, 8, 5
1856, 8, 14. Enos, s David & Miriam, d bur West Branch
1858, 8, 8. Mary, dt Dr. John, d bur West Branch
1859, 10, 28. John, s Dr. John, d bur West Branch
1863, 4, 23. Elizabeth C. m Joseph J. BUNDY
1864, 3, 24. Arena E. m Samuel KERSEY
----, --, --. Ledru Rollin, s Enos & Mary Ann (Reed), d 1884,8,28; m Mary Olivia DEAN, of Spiceland, Ind.
1931, 2, 22. Lottie d

1807, 5, 23. Timothy con mcd
1811, 1, 19. William Jr. con mcd
1812, 10, 22. William Jr. dis disunity
1813, 6, 24. Jonathan Sr. dis
1813, 10, 28. Jonathan Jr. dis mcd
1813, 10, 28. David, s Jonithan, dis mcd
1813, 12, 23. Timothy dis disunity
1814, 7, 28. William Sr. con mcd
1814, 7, 28. Aaron con mcd
1814, 8, 25. Jeremiah & fam gct Lick Creek MM
1814, 11, 24. Aaron gct Lick Creek MM, Ind.
1816, 10, 24. John Commons prcf White Water MM, dtd 1816,9,28, to m Elizabetn Mote
1816, 10, 24. William Jr. gct Lick Creek MM, b Ind.
1820, 12, 16. David & fam gct Honey Creek MM, Ind.
1821, 4, 21. Jeremiah dis disunity
1821, 10, 20. David & fam gct Honey Creek MM, Ind.
1822, 4, 20. Elizabeth recrq
1822, 6, 17. John Jr. gct Union MM, to m Rhoda Teague
1822, 11, 16. David & s, Luke, Zeno, Marcus & Linus, rocf Honey Creek MM, Ind., dtd 1822,10,12

MOTE, continued
1822, 11, 16. Miriam rocf Honey Creek MM, dtd 1822,10,12
1823, 6, 21. Rhoda rocf Union MM, dtd 1823,6,7
1824, 6, 19. David, Jr. con mcd
1824, 6, 19. Rachel (form Jones) con mcd
1825, 10, 15. Barbara & dt, Mary, recrq
1825, 10, 19. Aaron rocf Honey Creek MM, dtd 1825,6,11
1828, 4, 19. Daniel con mcd
1828, 5, 17. Nancy (form Waggoner) con mcd
1828, 12, 20. Grace rocf Union MM, dtd 1828, 10,7
1829, 10, 17. Daniel dis
1830, 2, 20. Elizabeth dis disunity
1832, 7, 19. Rachel Jr. dis disunity
1833, 4, 16. Aaron dis disunity
1835, 1, 15. Grace gct Union MM
1835, 2, 19. Anna Jones (form Mote) dis mcd
1837, 3, 16. Mary Coppock (form Mote) con mcd
1837, 12, 14. Margaret con mcd
1842, 8, 18. Asa & ch, Elijah, Nancy, Margaret, Sarah, Susannah & Jesse, recrq
1845, 6, 19. Marcus & fam gct Miami MM
1858, 6, 15. Linas gct White Water MM, Ind., to m Hannah L. Grave
1848, 7, 13. Rachel Eller (form Mote) dis mcd
1848, 12, 14. Hannah L. rocf White Water MM, Ind., dtd 1848,11,22
1849, 4, 19. Enos gct White Water MM, Ind., to m Martha Ann Reed
1850, 3, 14. Martha Ann rocf White Water MM, dtd 1850,2,22
1850, 10, 17. Joseph gct Union MM, to m Martha Painter
1851, 3, 13. Martha P. rocf Center MM, dtd 1851,1,15
1853, 6, 16. Elijah con mcd
1854, 10, 19. Samuel T. con mcd
1855, 5, 17. Joseph & w, Martha P., & fam gct Honey Creek MM, Ind.
1855, 11, 15. David Jr. & w, Barbara, & fam gct Honey Creek MM, Ind.
1855, 11, 15. Phebe S., Rachel & Rebecca gc
1857, 8, 13. Asa & w, Keziah, & s, Jesse J., gct Westland MM, Ia.
1859, 6, 16. Elijah dis jas
1860, 5, 17. Zeno dis
1861, 3, 14. Aann M. & ch, Lydia Chloris, Rhoda Matilda & Louis Kossuth, recrq
1865, 6, 15. Samuel T. & w, Annie M., & ch, Lydia Chloris, Rhoda M., Louis K., Mary Elizabeth & John Franklin, gct LeGrand MM, Ia.
1868, 3, 19. Elisha J. gct White Water MM,Ind.
1868, 3, 19. Linneous gct Legrand MM, Ia.
1868, 4, 16. John W. gct Ash Grove MM, Ill.
1868, 12, 17. Ethan A. rpd mcd
1869, 4, 15. Ethan A. gct LeGrand MM, Ia.
1871, 9, 14. Orrin S. gct White Water MM, to m Martha J. Tyler
1873, 5, 15. Linnaeus rocf LeGrand MM, Ia.
1873, 5, 15. Orris S. gct White Water MM, Ind.
1876, 3, 16. Louis Albert gct White Water MM, Ind., to m Anna E. Wallace
1877, 3, 15. Alvah E. dropped from mbrp
1885, 7, 11. Rebecca H. & ch, William R. Harvey & Alice Harvey, rocf Fairmount MM, Ind., dtd 1885,5,13
1886, 3, 13. Anson [Motte] recrq
1888, 5, 12. Rebecca H. & ch, William R., Harvey & Alice Harvey, gct Fairmount MM, Ind.
1890, 3, 8. Roy Dale, Carrie Albertine & Spencer Joyce [Motte] ch M. B., recrq
1890, 3, 8. Mary J. & Sarah Elizabeth [Motte] recrq
1893, 1, 14. Lottie B. gct Miami MM, O.
1903, 3, 14. Anson & w, Mary E., relrq
1907, 5, 11. Raymond & Neva dropped from mbrp; jas
1907, 5, 11. Edwin E. dropped from mbrp for lack of interest
1913, 5, 10. David dropped from mbrp
1913, 5, 10. Kirke & w, Lottie, recrq
1916, 2, 12. Kirk's d rpd
1928, 6, 13. Lottie recrq
1929, 5, 8. Omar & w, Emily, recrq

MULLENER
1819, 12, 16. Elizabeth [Muliner] con mcd
1825, 10, 15. Elizabeth gct Springfield MM, Ind.

NEAL
1807, 3, 21. James rocf New Hope MM, Tenn., dtd 1805,9,21
1809, 7, 22. James con mcd
1810, 3, 17. Anna recrq
1882, 11, 16. Mary O. recrq

NETZLEY
1913, 5, 10. Angie dropped from mbrp
1920, 12, 11. Alice recrq

NEWPORT
1882, 12, 14. James recrq
1886, 1, 9. Jason recrq
1886, 2, 13. William & Jane recrq

NILES
1920, 4, 6. Amanda d

1911, 2, 11. Mrs. William recrq
1913, 3, 8. Emma & Amanda recrq
1915, 6, 12. Sadie relrq

NISHWITZ
1883, 2, 15. Jacob E. recrq
1886, 1, 9. J. E. relrq

OAKS
1836, 8, 18. Susannah dis mcd
1837, 1, 19. Susannah (form Elleman) dis mcd

OAKS, continued
1888, 9, 8. C. [Oackes] recrq
1888, 9, 8. Emily [Oacks] recrq

O'NEAL
1884, 9, 18. Elizabeth recrq

OSBORNE
1888, 9, 8. Sarah recrq

OVERCASH
1912, 7, 13. Mattie B. relrq

OVERHOLSER
1888, 9, 8. Harry recrq

OVERLEACE
1833, 8, 15. Susannah (form Surgeon) rpd mcd (unable to locate her)
1848, 7, 13. Susannah [Overleece] (form Sturgeon) dis mcd

OVERMAN
1807, 6, 20. Ephraim & s, Ephraim, Silas & Reuben, rocf Mt. Pleasant MM, Va., dtd 1807,3,28
1807, --, --. Rachel & dt, Lydda & Rachel, rocf Mt. Pleasant MM, Va., dtd 1807,3,28 (cert directed to Miami MM but rec here)
1807, 10, 17. Jesse rocf Mt. Pleasant MM, Va., dtd 1807,7,25
1807, 10, 17. Eli rocf Mt. Pleasant MM, Va., dtd 1807,7,25

OWEN
----, --, --. Ephraim & Sarah
Ch: Amos b 1805, 12, 23
Samuel " 1807, 4, 21
1807, 10, 28. Sarah Owen d bur Rocky Spring

1808, 1, 23. Benjamin recrq
1815, 9, 28. John gct Lick Creek MM, Ind.
1815, 9, 28. Ephraim & fam gct Lick Creek MM, Ind.
1815, 9, 28. Sarah & dt gct Lick Creek MM
1816, 2, 22. Benjamin gct Lick Creek MM, Ind.
1828, 6, 16. Benjamin & fam gct White Lick MM, Ind.

PAIN
1843, 12, 14. Lydia (form Thomas) dis mcd

PAINTER
1850, 10, 17. Joseph Mote gct Union MM, to m Martha Painter

PARK
1915, 1, 9. Ethel S. relrq
1916, 6, 10. Ethel Coates [Parks] relrq

PATTY
----, --, --. Chas. b 1788,11,21; m Phebe ----- b 1789,8,5
Ch: Mary b 1808, 7, 27
Rebecca " 1810, 2, 3
James " 1812, 3, 19
Enoch " 1814, 11, 8
John " 1817, 4, 15
Anna " 1820, 4, 15
Mark " 1825, 4, 20
Wm. " 1827, 12, 30
Phebe " 1830, 4, 16
1821, 9, 20. Sarah m Thomas COATE

1807, 3, 21. James & s, Mark, rocf Bush River MM, S. C., dtd 1806,8,30, endorsed by Miami MM, 1807,2,12
1807, --, --. Anna & dt, Sarah, rocf Bush River MM, S. C., dtd 1806,8,30, endorsed by Miami MM, 1807,2,12
1807, --, --. Phebe rocf Bush River MM, S.C., dtd 1807,8,30
1808, 8, 28. Charles recrq
1813, 11, 25. James & fam gct Miami MM
1814, 11, 24. James & w, Anne, & ch, Sarah, Mark, Samuel, Nancy & Phebe, rocf Miami MM, dtd 1814,10,26
1815, 1, 26. Charles & fam gct Mill Creek MM
1821, 11, 17. Mark gct Mill Creek MM, to m Mary Jones
1826, 2, 18. Samuel dis disunity
1826, 9, 16. Mary rocf Mill Creek MM, dtd 1826,6,24
1828, 1, 19. James & fam gct Mill Creek MM
1828, 11, 15. Nancy gct Mill Creek MM
1829, 4, 16. Mark & fam gct Mill Creek MM
1835, 8, 13. Hugh rocf Mill Creek MM, dtd 1835,8,11
1835, 11, 19. Lot, minor, rocf White Water MM, Ind., dtd 1835,10,28
1838, 5, 17. Lot gct Mill Creek MM
1861, 12, 19. Lot gct Kansas MM

PAULSGROVE
1889, 9, 14. Anna relrq

PEARSON
1800, 12, 17. Hiram b
----, --, --. John m Ruth HOLLINGSWORTH
Ch: Keziah b 1801, 5, 11
Isaac " 1803, 10, 22
Benjamin " 1806, 6, 26
Margaret " 1809, 5, 7 d 1878, 6, 7 bur West Branch
John b 1811, 12, 26
1804, 3, 29. Nancy b
1812, 10, 14. Mary m William MILES
----, --, --. Joseph, s Benjamin & Elizabeth, b 1792,11,9; m Delphina -----
Ch: Elizabeth b 1821, 5, 23
Benj. " 1824, 12, 8
Jane " 1828, 10, 8
1826, 9, 23. Keziah, w Robert, d bur West Branch
----, --, --. Benjamin, s John P. & Ruth, Miami Co., O., b 1806,6,26 d 1880,2,4 bur

PEARSON, Benjamin, continued
Center; m at West Branch, Dorcas JONES, dt Wallace & Rachel, b 1806,12,4 d 1880,9, 26 bur Center
Ch: Rachel b 1830, 3, 31
John R. " 1831, 12, 6
William L. " 1833, 9, 7
Margaret " 1835, 7, 11
Mary " 1837, 4, 15 d 1856,10,30 bur West Branch
Sydney b 1838, 11, 18
Henry Jones b 1841, 8, 17
Elihu " 1843, 12, 7
Anna Mary " 1845, 12, 24
William Spencer " d 1871, 5,12 bur West Branch
1830, 6, 24. Ruth m Wallace JONES
----, --, --. Robert, s Robert, b 1815,4,22; m Mary ABBOTT, dt John & Sarah, b 1816,7,14
Ch: Alpha b 1839, 12, 15
Daniel " 1841, 12, 17
Keziah H. " 1843, 4, 8
Sarah A. " 1845, 8, 1
Rachel " 1849, 2, 14
1846, 12, 13. Keziah H., dt Robert, d bur West Branch
1850, 9, 26. William, s Benjamin & Esther, Miami Co., O.; m at West Branch, Sarah PEARSON, dt Robert & Keziah, Miami Co.,O.
1850, 9, 8. Robert, s Robert, d bur West Branch
1852, 8, 20. Charity m Lewis WILLETS
1853, 3, 24. Rachel m Isaiah PEMBERTON
----, --, --. Wm. A., s Benj. H. & Dorcas P., b 1833,9,7; m Mahala McDANOLD, dt Jos. & Temperance, b 1838,1,4
Ch: Laura Ellayne b 1854, 9, 26 d 1863, 4, 9 bur West Branch
Horace Melvin b 1857, 8, 11
Jasper Newton " 1859, 8, 16
Adah Jeanette " 1861, 8, 20
Mary Eveline " 1864, 12, 31
Herbert R. " 1868, 3, 16
----, --, --. John R. m Prudence PEMBERTON
Ch: Chas. E. b 1857, 5, 19
Mary Jane " 1858, 12, 26 d 1859, 8, 9 bur West Branch
Alice b 1860, 4, 19
David S. " 1862, 1, 31
Leonidas " 1863, 9, 24
Luvenia " 1864, 4, 5
Unnamed
Henry A. " 1867, 12, 27
Eber " 1869, 11, 12
Adelbert " 1871, 5, 6
Idella " 1873, 2, 20
1862, 3, 20. Sydnie m Joseph PEMBERTON
1862, 3, 20. Sydnie m Joseph PEMBERTON
1864, 7, 3. Mary, w Enoch, dt Robert & Catharine R. PEARSON, d bur West Branch
----, --, --. Elihu, s B. H. & Dorcas, b 1843, 12,7; m Anna FISHER
Ch: Warren b 1867, 8, 16
Edith " 1869, 10, 27
Emily " 1872, 6, 8
Omar " 1874, 1, 2
Mary " 1877, 2, 26
1874, 7, 9. Moses, s Samuel & Esther, d bur Union Gr Yd
1874, 8, 18. Anna J. m Eli O. MACY
1886, 8, 28. Rosanna, w Enoch, dt Robert & Marjorie (Buffington) McCLURE, d bur Old Concord Gr Yd
1888, 6, 11. Ann, w Benjamin, dt Thos. & Anna MACY, d
1894, 11, 26. Rhoda, dt Robert & Keziah H., d
----, --, --. Herbert R., s Wm. & Mahala (McDonald); m Lizzie THOMAS, dt Aaron & Susanna (Patty)
Dt: Lova L. b 1895, 1, 30
1896, 12, 18. Rachel, w Paul, dt Amos & Mary (Long) PERRY, d
1922, 11, 20. Obed d
1923, 8, 8. Robert Lee, s Everett & Eva, b
1923, 1, 23. Elihu d
1925, 2, 28. Eva Brumbaugh d

1807, 8, 22. Joseph & s, Thomas & James, rocf Bush River MM, N. C., dtd 1806,8,30
1807, --, --. Maelea & dt, Mary, Hannah & Elizabeth, rocf Bush River MM, S. C., dtd 1806,8,30 (cert was directed to Miami MM, but was rec here)
1807, 9, 19. Benjamin & s, Joseph, Noah & Benjamin, rocf Bush River, S. C., dtd 1806,4,26
1809, --, --. Keziah rocf Bush River MM, S. C. dtd 1809,7,25
1810, 6, 23. Nathan & s rocf Back Creek MM, N. C., dtd 1808,2,27
1811, 7, 25. Pheba rocf New Garden MM,N. C., dtd 1810,12,29
1812, 4, 23. Isaac, Benjamin & John, ch Ruth, recrq
1812, 4, 23. Keziah & Margaret, ch Ruth, recrq
1813, 4, 22. Robert & fam gct Mill Creek MM
1836, 3, 17. Isaac gct Union MM
1836, 9, 15. John con mcd
1837, 3, 16. John gct Vermillion MM
1847, 8, 19. Daniel, s Mary, recrq
1848, 6, 15. Robert Jr. recrq
1849, 6, 14. Sarah & Rhoda recrq
1850, 4, 18. Charity rocf Mill Creek MM, dtd 1850,4,16
1852, 4, 15. Polly Ann rocf Spring Creek MM, Ia., dtd 1852,2,7
1853, 7, 14. Isom C. Thomas gct Mill Creek MM, to m Zilpha Pearson
1854, 6, 15. William S. con mcd
1856, 3, 13. John R. gct Back Creek MM, Ind.,

PEARSON, continued
1856, 3, 13. John R. gct Back Creek MM, Ind., to m Prudence Pemberton
1856, 7, 17. Enoch K., minor, rocf Mill Creek MM, dtd 1856,7,15
1856, 11, 13. Prudence rocf Back Creek MM, Ind., dtd 1856,10,16
1857, 9, 17. Robert V. rpd mcd; dropped from mbrp
1859, 7, 14. Anna & dt, Rachel, rocf Union MM, dtd 1859,7,13
1860, 1, 19. Enoch K. gct Union MM, O.
1860, 10, 18. Jeremiah rocf Union MM, dtd 1860,9,12
1861, 5, 16. Theresa Yount (form Pearson) dis mcd
1863, 4, 16. Mahala & ch, Laura E., Horace M. Jasper N. & Ada J., recrq
1865, 6, 15. Robert rpd mcd
1867, 6, 13. Hiram gct Union MM
1867, 12, 19. Elihu rpd mcd
1868, 6, 18. Henry J. rpd mcd
1870, 12, 15. Moses & w, Eunice, & ch, Obed, rocf Union MM, dtd 1870,12,14
1870, 12, 15. Thomas gct Onargo MM, Ill.
1872, 2, 15. Benjamin & w, Mary, & ch, Sarah S. & Stephen A., recrq
1872, 2, 15. Kezia, Jr., dt Benjamin, recrq
1873, 5, 15. John R. & w, Prudence, & ch gct Back Creek MM, Ind.
1878, 12, 19. Charley E. & w, Alice J., rocf Back Creek MM, Ind., dtd 1878,10,17
1882, 4, 13. Charles E. & w, & ch gct Back Creek MM, Ind.
1883, 3, 15. Thursey & dt, Delphina, recrq
1884, 1, 17. Charles E. & fam roc
1886, 6, 12. Charles E. & fam gct Liberty MM, Kans.
1890, 6, 14. Rachel recrq
1896, 11, 14. Lizzie, w Dr. H. R., recrq
1897, 5, 14. Valeria recrq
1906, 3, 10. Myron recrq
1906, 3, 10. Lova & Ernest, birthright mbr, recorded mbr by choice
1906, 3, 10. Paul rst
1907, 5, 11. Stephen dropped from mbrp for lack of interest
1908, 6, 30. Robert V. recrq
1915, 1, 9. Clark recrq
1915, 2, 13. Homer & Everett rocf Union MM
1915, 2, 13. Stephen & w & dt rocf Union MM
1917, 7, 14. Arthur & w, Mina, & ch, Arlyn, Virginia & Donna, roc dtd 1917,7,6
1919, 12, 13. Virginia recrq
1923, 4, 14. Jean recrq
1925, 6, 13. Elma recrq
1926, 10, 13. L. A. & s, L. A. Jr. (associate mbr) recrq
1926, 11, 10. Etta Hall recrq
1927, 1, 12. Margaret recrq
1927, 7, 13. Omar dropped from mbrp
1932, 4, 13. May, Elmer, Evelyn & Delbert recrq

PEGGOT
1809, 2, 18. Joshua & s, Benjamin & Joshua, rocf Cain Creek MM, N. C., dtd 1807,9,5

PEIRCE
1808, 11, 19. Samuel rocf Mt. Pleasant MM, Va., dtd 1808,8,27
1809, 11, 16. Gainer [Pierce] & w, Ruth, & ch, John, James, Mary, George, Ruth & Benjamin, rocf Mt. Pleasant MM, dtd 1809, 8,26
1879, 1, 16. M. F. recrq
1879, 3, 13. William R. [Pierce] & w, Rachel, rocf Back Creek MM, Ind.
1882, 10, 19. William R. & w, Rachel, gct Back Creek MM, Ind.
1886, 2, 13. Charles [Pierce] recrq
1886, 4, 10. Alvine & w, Susan, & ch, Bertha, Ermina, Esta, Maurice & Erie Dudley, rocf Union MM
1888, 9, 8. Melinda recrq
1891, 3, 10. Charles gct Lewisburg Mtg, O.
1901, 3, 9. Minnie [Pierce] & ch, Howard & Ethel, rocf Union MM
1913, 5, 10. Howard & Ethel dropped from mbrp
1923, 10, 13. Maggie recrq

PEMBERTON
1794, 2, 4. Drusilla b
1809, 8, 2. Robert, s Isaiah & Esther, Miami Co., O.; m at Ludlow Creek, Eunice COPPOCK dt John & Anne, Miami Co., O.
1810, 11, 7. John, s Isaiah & Esther, Miami Co., O.; m at Union, Drusilla ELLEMAN, dt John & Susannah, Miami Co., O.
1811, 2, 1. Isaiah, s Robert & Eunice, b
1811, 5, 15. Elizabeth m Jesse DUNCAN
1830, 12, 20. John, s Robert & Eunice, Miami Co., O.; m at West Branch, Susannah HOLLINGSWORTH, dt Joel & Anna
----, --, --. Isaac, s Isaiah & Elizabeth, b 1814,2,24; m Mary P. MITCHENER, dt Thos. & Betsy, b 1818,3,14

Ch:		
	Enos	b 1837, 4, 22
	Sarah	" 1839, 12, 29
	David	" 1841, 12, 29
	Ginsey	" 1843, 1, 29
	Henry	" 1846, 7, 17
	Elizabeth	" 1848, 1, 11
	Maryan	" 1850, 3, 1
	Margaret F.	" 1853, 9, 25
	Dorcas M. Arvilla	" 1860, 2, 16

1848, 2, 24. John E., s Isaiah & Elizabeth, Miami Co., O.; m at West Branch, Sarah ALLISON, dt James & Sarah
1853, 3, 24. Isaiah, s Isaiah & Elizabeth, Howard Co., Ind., b 1829,6,28 d 1874,3,2 bur Center; m at West Branch, Rachel PEARSON, dt Benj. & Dorcas, Miami Co., b 1830, 3,31
1862, 3, 20. Joseph, s Isaiah & Elizabeth, Miami Co., O., b 1836,12,26; m at West

PEMBERTON, Joseph, continued
Branch, Sydney PEARSON, dt Benj. & Dorcas, b 1838,11,18
Ch: Amy E. b 1862, 11, 2
Benj. Aldus " 1865, 1, 30
Anna Mary " 1867, 5, 25
Elma J. " 1870, 3, 19
Wm. H. " 1872, 5, 12
----, --, --. Enos, s Isaac & Mary, b 1837,4, 22; m Mary HOOVER, dt John, d 1872,5,2
Ch: Dorsey E. b 1867, 1, 1 d 1877, 2,15
Enos m 2nd Thursey PEARSON, dt Enoch & Rosanna (McClure), b 1838,8,3
Ch: Albert b 1874, 8, 27
Rosa " 1876, 5, 30
1868, 10, 27. Clarence, s David & Mary Ann, d bur Smyrna, Ind.
----, --, --. Wm. A., s Benj. Y. & Dorcas P., b 1833,9,7; m Mahala McDANOLD, dt Jos. & Temperance, b 1838,1,4
1919, 7, 27. Sydney d
1922, 5, 11. Alders d
1924, 1, 9. May d
1924, 1, 21. Enos d

1812, 2, 27. Isaiah Jr. con mcd
1812, 2, 27. Elizabeth con mcd
1812, 5, 28. Mary con mcd
1833, 4, 18. Susannah gct Union MM
1835, 8, 13. David Thomas gct Union MM, to m Esther Pemberton
1849, 4, 19. Benjamin Thomas gct Union MM, to m Rhoda Pemberton
1853, 9, 15. Rachel gct Union MM
1855, 10, 18. Joseph Thomas gct Union MM, to m Elizabeth Pemberton
1856, 3, 13. John R. Pearson gct Back Creek MM, Ind., to m Prudence Pemberton
1864, 11, 17. Joseph rocf Union MM
1867, 1, 17. Enos rpd mcd
1868, 4, 16. Drusilla gct LeGrand MM, Ill.
1870, 12, 15. Mary M. recrq
1874, 12, 17. Theresa, w Enos, recrq
1878, 11, 14. Isaiah rocf Hartland MM, Ia.
1888, 2, 11. Isaiah gct Back Creek MM, Ind.
1889, 8, 10. Isaac & w, Mary, relrq
1889, 12, 14. Anna B. dis disunity
1902, 1, 11. Louie recrq
1906, 8, 8. Joseph, s Luie, recorded a birthright mbr
1915, 3, 13. Charles rec as associate mbr by rq
1915, 3, 13. Helen recrq
1915, 3, 13. Alta recrq
1915, 4, 10. William & w, Louie, & ch, Joseph & Mary, relrq
1923, 4, 14. Charles rec in active mbrp by rq

PEPPER
1881, 4, 14. Elijah S. recrq

PHILLIPS
1875, 12, 16. Frank & w, Hannah, recrq

PICKERING
1906, 6, 9. Alice gct 8th St. Mtg, Richmond, Ind.

PIKE
1807, 7, 18. Sarah con mcd
1809, --, --. Rachel rocf Cain Creek MM, N.C., dtd 1808,4,2
1832, 10, 16. Sarah dis disunity

POLING
1921, 11, 18. Geo. d
1927, 12, 31. Ellen d

1920, 12, 11. George recrq
1925, 6, 13. Ethel dropped from mbrp for jas

POOL
1809, 8, 19. John & s, Charles, rocf Back Creek MM, N. C., dtd 1809,2,25

POWELL
1909, 1, 9. Lula, form mbr Chambersburg MM, recrq
1913, 5, 10. Lula dropped from mbrp

PRAY
1852, 4, 15. Enos & w, Elvira, & fam gct Springfield MM, O.

PRESTON
1879, 1, 16. Robert H. recrq

PRICE
1809, 5, 20. Rice & s, James & Robert, rocf Contentney MM, N. C., dtd 1807,3,12, endorsed by Miami MM, 1809,4,18
1809, --, --. Sarah rocf Contentney MM, N.C., dtd 1807,3,14

PURCELL
1913, 3, 8. Catherine recrq

PUTERBAUGH
1925, 12, 12. Roy, William & Mildred recrq
1932, 4, 13. Alberta recrq
1932, 12, 14. Mildred dropped from mbrp for jas

QUILLING
1907, 1, 12. William Henry recrq
1913, 5, 10. William dropped from mbrp

RANDALL
1887, 7, 19. Eliza Ann, w Jonathan H., Jr., d bur West Milton Cemetery

1875, 12, 16. Eliza, w J. H., & s, Harry, recrq
1878, 11, 14. Emma J. rocf Caesars Creek MM, O.

RANDALL, continued
1880, 1, 15. Harry dis
1887, 3, 12. I. A. & Oscar recrq

RANK
1876, 1, 13. Henry & w, Susan, & ch, Edward, Morris & Lewis W., recrq
1895, 2, 9. Henry & fam dropped from mbrp

RAZOR
1888, 9, 8. Aaron recrq

REECE
1909, 1, 9. Daniel & Willie, form mbr Chambersburg MM, recrq
1913, 5, 10. Daniel & Willie dropped from mbrp

REED
1849, 4, 19. Enos Mote gct White Water MM, Ind., to m Martha Ann Reed
1907, 4, 13. Harvey O. & w, Minnie, recrq
1912, 3, 9. Harvey O. & w, Minnie, relrq
1916, 4, 7. Harry & w, Minnie, & ch, Howard & Margaret, recrq
1919, 12, 13. Margaret rec in active mbrp by rq

REEDER
1885, 9, 12. Frank & Rebecca recrq
1885, 10, 10. Howell recrq
1886, 2, 13. Harley Leroy recrq
1886, 2, 13. Della May recrq

REESER
----, --, --. Clarence A., s A. & Sarah, b 1872,4,23 d 1873,7,1

RHOETTER
1917, 2, 10. Tressie relrq

RICE
1903, 2, 14. Blanch recrq

ROBBINS
1888, 9, 8. Elizabeth recrq

ROBINSON
1909, 1, 9. Alvin, form mbr Chambersburg MM, recrq
1913, 5, 10. Alvin dropped from mbrp

ROCKY
1876, 1, 13. Thomas & Mary J. recrq

ROGERS
1925, 12, 12. David A., Eva M., Agatha, Naomi, Marguerite, Esther & Vernon, recrq
1931, 1, 14. David Norman, Norman Lester & Wesley Earl recrq

ROGGE
1885, 9, 12. Frederick W., Myrtle May & Lula Lenora recrq

ROOKER
1810, 3, 17. Pheba con mcd

RUSSELL
1808, 2, 4. Ann m David JENKINS

1823, 9, 20. Tamer (form Mendenhall) dis mcd
1884, 7, 17. Phebe C. rocf Alum Creek MM, dtd 1884,6,19
1900, 10, 13. Phoebe C. relrq

SABER
1885, 3, 19. William H. [Seaber] recrq
1895, 2, 9. Cora & William dropped from mbrp

SCHWAB
1885, 8, 8. George & w, Grace, recrq

SCOTT
1861, 2, 5. Rebecca, w David, d bur Concord [Bur Gr
1869, 12, 8. John [Scotts] Sr. d bur in fam gr yd on his farm

1819, 4, 17. Rebecca rocf Mill Creek MM, dtd 1819,3,27
1883, 2, 15. Eli J. & w, Ella R., recrq
1883, 2, 15. Luther S., s Eli J. & Ella, & w, Maime C., recrq
1886, 7, 10. Eli J. & w gct Indianapolis MM, [Ind.

SEANCE
1913, 3, 8. Albert recrq

SERVIS
1876, 5, 18. Julia A. recrq

SHAFER
1924, 2, 18. Bobbie Ruth, dt Herbert & May, b

1916, 5, 13. Rebecca Anna [Schaeffer], dt Herbert & Mary, b rpd
1922, 7, 8. Rebecca Ann & Mary Esther, ch May, rec as associate mbr by rq
1922, 9, 9. Herbert recrq

SHATZLEY
1920, 5, 29. Byron Lee, s Ira & Minnie, b
1886, 2, 13. Mattie [Schatzle] recrq
1908, 3, 14. Ira [Schatzley] & w, Minnie, [recrq
1923, 4, 14. Elizabeth & Kyle recrq

SHAW
1823, 2, 15. Mary dis mcd
1901, 2, 9. Dora relrq

SHEARER
1883, 3, 15. Sarah recrq
1913, 6, 14. Eva Beard relrq

SHEETS
1894, 3, 15. Mary, 2nd w Martin, dt Daniel & Hannah (Mast) HOOVER, d bur near W. Milton

1809, 5, 20. Ann (form Zink) con mcd
1810, 10, 20. Jacob & s, Andrew, recrq
1872, 2, 15. Mary, wd Martin, recrq

SHEIK
1923, 7, 13. Edna Hines d

1923, 4, 14. Jacob & Mary recrq
1923, 4, 14. Anna relrq

SHELLY
1915, 9, 19. Herbert A. d

1913, 3, 8. Esta [Shelley] recrq

SHOE
1885, 3, 19. R. L. & w, Anna M., recrq

SHOMO
1852, 3, 18. Hannah H. dis mcd

SHORES
1904, 11, 12. Joseph & w, Jemima, rocf New Garden MM

SHORT
1902, 5, 10. George A. & w, Lulu, recrq
1908, 2, 8. Stella & Mable recrq
1909, 7, 10. George A. & w, Luella, & dt, Mabel & Estella, gct Cleveland MM

SHROYER
1920, 5, 8. Faye Elleman relrq

SIMPSON
1810, 8, 18. John & w, Ann, rocf Falls MM, Pa., dtd 1810,6,5

SINKS
----, --, --. Andrew, s George & R., d 1869, 12,2 bur S. E. Union Town; m Amelia ----- d 1872,1,2 bur C----- Ch Gr Yd

1809, 5, 20. Anna Sheets (form Zink) con mcd
1860, 5, 17. Amelia recrq
1860, 12, 13. Andrew recrq (his father spelled his name Zink)

SLEPPY
1893, 2, 11. Harvey recrq
1902, 9, 13. Della relrq
1902, 10, 11. Harvey relrq
1911, 10, 9. Anna relrq

SLONAKER
1919, 12, 13. Ada recrq
1922, 5, 13. Guy recrq
1923, 4, 14. Ruth recrq

SMALL
1807, 8, 22. Benjamin & s, Aaron, Abner & Jesse rocf Mt. Pleasant MM, Va., dtd 1807,5,30
1807, --, --. Elizabeth & dt, Peninah, Mary, Miriam & Sarah, rocf Mt. Pleasant MM, Va., dtd 1807,5,30 (cert was directed to Miami MM but was rec here)

SMITH
1885, 9, 12. Clara recrq
1888, 9, 8. Sallie recrq
1891, 11, 14. Francis & w, Ellen, recrq
1906, 3, 10. Eva & Velma, birthright mbr, recorded mbr by choice
1913, 2, 7. Mabel relrq
1913, 4, 12. Mary E. & dt, Velma & Lillie, relrq

SNEATHEN
1834, 10, 16. Sarah (form Thomas) dis mcd
1836, 7, 14. Elizabeth (form Thomas) dis mcd
1849, 4, 19. Mary dis mcd

SNYDER
----, --, --. Salathiel & Eleanor C.
Ch: Annie
Amelia b 1856, 1, 8
Cassius
Delmi " 1857, 10, 24
1927, 9, 7. Letha Eloise, dt Raymond & Helen, b

1855, 11, 15. Eleanor C. (form Grisom) dis mcd
1861, 11, 14. Eleaner C. & ch, Anna Amelia & Cassius Delmi, rocf Elk MM, O., dtd 1861, 9,21
1918, 4, 13. Raymond & Lenna rec in mbrp at Center MM
1931, 1, 14. Charles E. recrq

SPEELMAN
1883, 2, 15. Elvira recrq
1883, 3, 15. L. D. & s, Levi Augustus, recrq

SPENCER
1820, 2, 19. William & w, Sarah, rocf Bush River MM, S. C.
1824, 7, 17. William & w, Sarah, gct Springfield MM, N. C.

SPITLER
1923, 4, 14. Ralph rec as associate mbr
1923, 4, 14. Viola recrq

STALEY
1829, 7, 18. Huldah (form Waymire) dis mcd

STANLEY
1903, 1, 10. Francis C. & w, Sarah A., rocf West Grove MM
1910, 5, 14. F. C. gct Marion MM, Ind.

STEDDOM
1811, 2, 27. John, s Henry, Warren Co., O.; m at public mtg place in Newton Twp., Alice TEAGUE, dt Samuel, Miami Co., O.
1862, 3, 20. Henry, s Samuel & Susannah, Warren Co., O.; m at West Branch, Rhoda HASKET, dt Isaac & Rebecca, Miami Co., O.

1811, 2, 23. John [Steadham] prcf Miami MM, to m Alice Teague

STEINBARGER
1886, 2, 13. John G. recrq

STICKLE
----, --, --. Clinton & Callie
Ch: Paul
Markley b 1920, 2, --
Ralph " 1921, 7, 8
1926, 12, 12. Rachel d

1895, 2, 9. Sallie, wd, & ch recrq
1897, 2, 14. Sallie recrq
1899, 3, 11. Sallie relrq
1913, 3, 8. Clinton recrq

STINER
1832, 9, 13. Sarah (form Jones) dis mcd

STOKER
1876, 3, 16. Elizabeth recrq
1876, 5, 18. Cora recrq
1879, 1, 16. Peter John recrq

STOLTZ
1858, 5, 13. John recrq
1872, 12, 19. John [Stolts] Jr. & w, Abigail, & ch, Martha Ellen & Daniel, recrq
1885, 2, 19. David A. recrq

STONEMAN
----, --, --. Henston Floyd b 1843,12,31; m Elizabeth T. THOMAS, dt David & Esther, b 1841,3,12
Ch: John
Watson b 1868, 7, 21
Emma Jane " 1869, 10, 4
David Wm. " 1873, 5, 16

1869, 1, 14. Henston Floyd recrq

STREET
1869, 8, 31. Anna Rachel, dt Margaret P., b

STUBBS
1833, 7, 16. Mary (form Jones) dis mcd
1849, 6, 14. Isaac & w, Charlotte, & ch, Susannah, William, Esther & Lindley, rocf Elk MM, dtd 1849,5,19
1850, 8, 15. Isaac & fam gct Elk MM

STUHLMAN
1924, 5, 10. Eva relrq

STULTS
----, --, --. John, s Jno. S. & Christinia (Ullery), b 1827,8,4; m Abigail (Harshbarger) HICKMAN, wd Jer., b 1832,2,18
Ch: Martha
Ellen b 1863, 8, 8
David " 1865, 9, 13

STURGEON
1820, 9, 16. Phebe [Sturgion] & ch, Levi, George & Susannah, recrq
1826, 5, 20. Levi [Stergion] gct Green Plain MM
1833, 7, 16. George dis disunity
1833, 8, 15. Susannah Overleace (form Surgeon) rpd mcd (unable to locate her)
1848, 7, 13. Susannah Overleece (form Sturgeon) dis mcd

STUTSMAN
1854, 8, 17. Nancy (form Thomas) dis mcd

STYLES
1848, 11, 16. Robert rocf Milford MM, Ind., dtd 1848,10,28
1849, 3, 15. Robert gct Alum Creek MM, to m Rachel Benedict
1849, 11, 15. Robert gct Alum Creek MM

SULLIVAN
1879, 1, 16. Charity recrq

SURFACE
1883, 4, 17. Jacob recrq

SWAIN
1815, 5, 25. Paul & w, Unice, & ch, Hepzibah, Judith, Rebeckah, Mary, Francis & Thomas, rocf Deep Creek MM, N. C., dtd 1814,12,3
1815, 12, 28. Paul & fam gct Caesars Creek MM

SWALLOW
1809, 4, 22. Silvenius rocf Deep Creek MM, N. C., dtd 1808,3,5
1810, --, --. Lydda rocf Deep River MM, N. C., dtd 1810,8,6
1813,* 4, 27. Catharine (form Cox) dis mcd
1853, 10, 13. Sarah (form Thomas) dis mcd
1871, 10, 15. Lula Elizabeth recrq

SWANDER
1900, 5, 12. Charles W. & w rocf Friends Chapel MM, dtd 1900,4,21
1902, 12, 13. Charles & Etta [Swanders] gct Dublin MM, Ind.
1904, 9, 10. Frances V. & Blanche Virginia [Swadner] recrq
1913, 5, 10. Blanche & Frances [Swadner] dropped from mbrp
1923, 1, 13. James & w, Minnie, (Frankie in

SWANDER, continued
Dover) & ch, Elvin, Lester & Elsie, rocf Dover MM, Ind., dtd 1922,10,25
1924, 11, 8. James & w, Frankie, & ch, Elvin, Lester & Elsie, gct West Elkton MM, O.

SYMONS
1862, 11, 20. Benjamin F., s Abram & Achsah, Henry Co., Ind.; m at Randolph, Verlinda JENKINS, dt Robert & Ann

SYPES
1879, 1, 16. John C. recrq

TAYLOR
1854, 11, 18. Martha (form Thomas) dis mcd

TEAGUE
1807, 10, 28. Luranah m James COATE
1809, 8, 30. Esther m John COATE
1811, 2, 27. Alice m John STEDDOM
1848, 11, 23. Isaac C., s Samuel & Prudence, Montgomery Co., O.; m at West Branch, Martha JONES, dt Elisha & Rebecca, Miami Co., O.
1852, 10, 15. Joseph C., s Samuel & Prudence, Wabash Co., Ind.; m at West Branch, Rebecca JONES, dt Elisha & Rebecca, Miami Co., O.
----, --, --. David B., b 1842,1,27; m Arrie L. -----
Ch: Duane
West b 1878, 7, 25 d 1880, 8,20
bur Milton Cem.
Delia
Ethel b 1880, 2, 3
Chester
Wayne " 1883, 1, 19

1811, 2, 23. John Steadham prcf Miami MM, to m Alice Teague
1822, 6, 17. John Mote, Jr. gct Union MM, to m Rhoda Teague
1853, 2, 17. Rebecca gct Wabash MM, Ind.
1879, 8, 14. David B. & s, Duane W., recrq
1885, 11, 14. David B. & w, Arrie L., & ch relrq
1911, 1, 14. Chester recrq
1911, 1, 14. Mrs. Arrie L. recrq
1912, 1, 13. Arria & Chester relrq

TEAS
1885, 3, 19. Cora recrq
1895, 2, 9. Cora dropped from mbrp

TENNEY
1888, 2, 11. Anna F. relrq

THAYER
----, --, --. Davis W., s Ichabod & Eunice, b 1796,2,9 d 1856,10,4 bur West Branch; m Elizabeth MACY, dt Thos. & Anna, b 1800, 3,18 d 1873,2,5 bur West Branch
Ch: Enos b 1824, 1, 4 d 1839, 7, 7
bur West Branch
Eunice b 1826, 2, 27
Anna " 1828, 9, 8 d 1839, 7,10
bur West Branch
Mary J. b 1830, 10, 9 " 1839, 8,11
bur West Branch
Elizabeth b 1832, 5, 29
Jane " 1836, 4, 18 " 1839, 6,28
bur West Branch
Davis
James b 1838, 9, 14 " 1862, 3,30
bur Tenn. (d in the Army)
Erasmus b 1844, 3, 12

1822, 7, 20. Davis recrq
1822, 7, 20. Elizabeth rocf Mill Creek MM, dtd 1822,6,22
1830, 2, 20. Davis dis disunity
1832, 10, 18. Elizabeth dis disunity
1847, 12, 16. Davis James & Erasmus M., ch Elizabeth M., recrq
1848, 3, 16. Davis W. con misconduct (form dis)
1867, 2, 14. Erasmus M. rpd mcd
1874, 1, 15. Erasmus M. dis disunity
1903, 1, 10. Erasmus recrq
1906, 4, 10. Erasmus relrq
1919, 7, 12. John recrq

THOMAS
----, --, --. John b 1765,6,5 d 1847,10,3; m Ann ----- b 1764,3,15 d 1840,7,22
Ch: Elizabeth b 1787, 3, 3
Isaiah " 1791, 7, 30
Ann " 1794, 2, 20
John " 1796, 7, 5
Geo. " 1798, 7, 20 d 1872,1,22
bur South Fork
Wm. b 1801, 8, 14
Sarah " 1810, 12, 5
----, --, --. Abel, Jr. & Ruth
Ch: Wm. b 1798, 5, 28
Isaiah " 1800, 3, 19
Mary " 1802, 5, 30 d 1837, 5, 7
bur South Fork
Phebe b 1804, 9, 16
Sarah Ann " 1807, 3, 25
Ruth " 1809, 5, 10
Susannah " 1811, 6, 14
Abel " 1813, 9, 22
Elizabeth " 1816, 2, 12
----, --, --. Evan, s Isaac & Mary, b 1775,5, 18; m Sarah COX, dt David & Jane, b 1793, 11,29
Ch: Mary b 1809, 12, 23
Sarah " 1812, 5, 15
Evan " 1814, 10, 14
Elizabeth " 1817, 3, 24
John D. " 1820, 5, 22
Joanna Owen" 1823, 2, 25
Nancy " 1826, 1, 18
Jesse " 1833, 1, 7
1809, 9, 27. Phebe m David COX

THOMAS, continued

1813, 9, 29. Isaiah, s John & Ann, Warren Co., O., d 1862,5,8 bur South Fork; m at Rocky Spring MH, Elizabeth COX, dt David & Jane, Montgomery Co., O., b 1795,10,2
Ch: Ann b 1814, 7, 4
David " 1816, 3, 8
James " 1818, 6, 6
Elijah " 1820, 7, 7
Susan " 1825, 3, 30
Isom C. " 1830, 5, 24
Martha " 1832, 6, 9
Joseph " 1835, 3, 4

1813, 9, 1. Sarah m Thomas THORNTON

1819, 1, 21. Wm., s John & Ann, Montgomery Co., O.; m at Rocky Spring, Mary COX, dt David & Jane, Montgomery Co., O., b 1796, 12,30 d 1839,3,28

Ch: Priscilla b 1820, 10, 12
Asenath " 1822, 11, 25
Hannah C. " 1825, 1, 3
Salley " 1827, 4, 16
Levi " 1829, 10, 9
Nancy " 1833, 3, 30
Micajah C. " 1835, 5, 25
Hugh Martin" 1838, 2, 22

1820, 12, 21. John, s John & Ann, Montgomery Co., O., b 1796,7,5; m at West Branch, Grace MENDENHALL, dt Caleb & Susanna, b 1801,1,31
Ch: Miriam b 1821, 11, 3
Elias " 1828, 12, 19
Huldah " 1843, --, --

----, --, --. Nehemiah, Sr. d 1843,3,24 bur South Fork; m Elizabeth PEMBERTON d 1845, 2,1 bur South Fork
Ch: Isaac b 1821, 6, 13 d 1849, 8,12 bur South Fork
Esther b 1823, 7, 1 " 1840, 4, 9 bur South Fork
Mary b 1827, 4, 7
Anna " 1832, 3, 21 " 1849, 7,15 bur South Fork
Daniel b 1831, 10, 19 " 1842, 1, 6 bur South Fork

1822, 11, 21. John, s Isaac & Saray, Montgomery Co., O., b 1793,2,27 d 1853,11,21 bur South Fork; m at Rocky Spring, Hannah FARMER, dt Moses & Sarah, Montgomery Co.,O., d 1828,2,17 bur South Fork
Ch: Benj. b 1824, 6, 21
Sarah " 1826, 8, 22
John m 2nd Miriam -----
Dt: Hannah b 1830, 10, 13

----, --, --. Wm., s Isaac Jr., b 1795,5,4 d 1856,9,30 bur South Fork; m Mary FARMER, dt Moses, b 1793,10,25
Ch: Lydia b 1824, 10, 14
Noah " 1826, 4, 1
Martha " 1827, 10, 10
Rueben " 1829, 4, 20
Abigail " 1831, 3, 12 d 1855, 6,14
Ch: Stephen b 1832, 11, 15
Mary " 1834, 9, 10
Martin " 1836, 5, 9

----, --, --. George m Hannah ELLEMAN, dt John & Susanna, b 1806,12,18 d 1857,11,18 bur South Fork
Ch: Rhoda b 1825, 10, 15
Enos " 1829, 11, 12
Lewis " 1845, 9, 15
George m 2nd Christian -----
Ch of Christian Thomas by a form m
Elva b 1834, 2, 9
Henry P. " 1843, 10, 21
Reuben " 1846, 11, 12

----, --, --. Edward & Rachel
Ch: Jacob W. b 1825, 6, 19
Henry " 1827, 9, 29
Mary P. M. " 1830, 4, 14
Rebecca " 1832, 12, 11
Levina " 1835, 4, 1
Allen J. " 1837, 10, 11
Absolom " 1840, 6, 16
Temperance " 1845, 2, 24
Louisa " 1848, 8, 20
Louiza " 1848, 8, 20

1826, 10, 26. Elizabeth m John FARMER

1827, 10, 25. Isaac, s Isaac & Sarah, Montgomery Co., O., b 1804,2,25; m at West Branch Tamar MENDENHALL, dt Caleb, b 1802, 9,9
Ch: Parmelia P.b 1828, 7, 10
Harriet " 1830, 5, 24
Milo " 1832, 1, 11
Caleb " 1834, 2, 23
Seth " 1836, 1, 6
Irvin " 1838, 1, 29
Susannah " 1838, 1, 29
Elam " 1841, 12, 27

1831, 4, 20. Susannah m Philip FARMER

----, --, --. Nehemiah m Phebe GILBERT
Ch: Thos. Gilbert b 1832, 10, 1 d 1850, 7, 7 bur South Fork
Elias b 1834, 11, 4
John " 1837, 2, 20
Emily " 1839, 7, 25
Gulielma " 1842, 5, 13

1833, 4, 13. Abel Sr. d bur South Fork

1835, 6, 14. Mary, dt Wm. J., d bur South Fork

----, --, --. David, s Isaiah & Elizabeth (Cox), b 1816,3,8; m Esther PEMBERTON, dt Isa & Elizabeth, b 1817,4,6 d 1877,8,5 bur South Fork
Ch: Lewis b 1836, 8, 11 d 1837,12,21
Edward " 1838, 10, 11[bur South
Elizabeth " 1841, 3, 12[Fork
Melissa " 1843, 1, 15
Rhoda J. " 1845, 2, 27
Calvin W. " 1847, 1, 7
Elvira " 1849, 4, 20

THOMAS, David & Esther, continued
Ch: Susanna b 1851, 4, 9
Martha Ann " 1853, 4, 9
Almeidia " 1855, 4, 10
Henry " 1859, 2, 2
Joseph P. " 1861, 2, 10 d 1861, 9,10 bur South Fork
1836, 1, 7. Isaac Sr. d bur South Fork
1842, 9, 21. Nehemiah, Jr., s Isaac, d bur South Fork
1848, 8, 28. Rachel, dt Francis JONES, d bur South Fork
----, --, --. Benj. m Rhoda ELLEMAN, dt Isaiah P. & Elizabeth, b 1824,10,12
Ch: Lindley
Murray b 1850, 4, 7 d 1851, 6, 3 bur South Fork
Elwood C. b 1852, 1, 26
1852, 5, 20. Edward, s Isaac & Sarah, Montgomery Co., O.; m at West Branch, Elizabeth TUCKER, dt Henry & Frances Ellen, Montgomery Co., O.
----, --, --. Isom C. m Zilpah PEARSON
Ch: Catharine
Elizabeth b 1854, 5, 22
Amanda " 1856, 2, 13
Joanna
----, --, --. Joseph, s Isaiah & Elizabeth, b 1835,3,4 d 1905,2,23; m Elizabeth PEMBERTON, dt John E. & Susanna, b 1836,5,15 d 1900,--,--
Ch: John b 1856, 11, 17
Henrietta " 1859, 12, 15
Wm. " 1863, 6, 21
Emma " 1865, 8, 21
Clara " 1868, 7, 8
Francis " 1871, 2, 25
Sarah " 1873, 4, 3
1859, 10, 24. Amanda, dt Isom C. d bur South Fork
----, --, --. Edward Jr. m Elizabeth JÈSTER
Dt: Laura
Elizabeth b 1860, 6, 4
Edward m 2nd Barbara Ann NICOLAS
Ch: Isaiah F. b 1865, 2, 17
Esther A. " 1866, 10, 21
Susannah " 1867, 2, 8
Edward m 3rd Rachel COATE
Ch: David
Johnson b 1872, 4, 15
Lindley C. d 1875, 8,20
1862, 1, 24. Isom C., s Isaiah & Elizabeth, d bur South Fork
1862, 5, 12. Joanna, infant dt I. C. & E., d bur South Fork
----, --, --. Reuben m Louvisa THOMAS, dt Edward & Rachel, b 1848,8,20
Ch: Clarkson b 1870, 11, 20
----, --, --. John, s Joseph & Elizabeth, b 1856,11,17; m Ada J. PEARSON, dt Wm. & Mahala McDonald
Ch: Leona
Chloe
Hazel
Merle
----, --, --. Wm., s Joseph & Elizabeth (Pemberton), b 1863,6,21; m Minerva BELSTON, dt Henry & Susan, d 1900,0-,--
Ch: Clyde
Mary
Lillian
Lucille d 1900,--,--
----, --, --. Francis, s Joseph & Elizabeth, b 1871,2,25; m Anna HUNT, dt Abraham & Eliza, b 1871,2,26
Ch: Eva b 1893, 1, 1
Marie " 1895, 3, 24
1917, 2, 20. Henry d
1930, 1, 21. Anna d
1931, 2, 26. Ada d

1808, 11, 19. Mary & ch, Evin, Nehemiah, Sarah & Phebe, rocf Bush River MM, S. C., dtd 1807,1,31, endorsed by Miami MM 1808,8,11
1813, 8, 26. Thomas Thornton prcf Mill Creek MM, dtd 1813,7,24, to m Sarah Thomas
1813, 9, 23. Isaiah prcf Miami MM, dtd 1813, 8,28, to m Elizabeth Cox
1817, 2, 27. John & w, Ann, & ch, Ann, John, George, William & Sarah, rocf Miami MM, dtd 1816,12,25
1817, 2, 27. Isaiah & w, Elizabeth, & ch, Ann & David, rocf Miami MM, dtd 1816,12, 25
1817, 4, 23. Isaac & s, Isaac & Nehemiah, recrq
1817, 9, 25. John recrq
1819, 8, 20. Nehemiah gct Union MM, to m
1819, 11, 20. Elizabeth rocf Union MM, dtd 1819,11,6
1820, 7, 15. William, s Isaac, recrq
1822, 11, 16. Abel & s, William, Isaiah & Abel, roc dtd 1822,7,27
1822, 11, 16. Ruth & dt, Mary, Phebe, Sarah, Ruth, Susannah & Elizabeth, rocf New Garden MM, N. C., dtd 1822,7,27
1823, 9, 20. William gct Cherry Grove MM, to m Mary Farmer
1824, 1, 17. Rachel (form Jones) con mcd
1824, 4, 17. William dis
1824, 5, 15. Mary rocf Cherry Grove MM, Ind., dtd 1824,2,14
1824, 6, 19. William & s, John, Isaiah & Eli, rocf Mill Creek MM, dtd 1824,4,24
1824, 6, 19. Sarah & dt, Eunice, rocf Mill Creek MM, dtd 1824,4,24
1825, 2, 19. John con mcd
1825, 2, 19. Elizabeth (form Jones) con mcd
1826, 2, 18. Hannah rocf Union MM, dtd 1826, 5,6
1827, 3, 17. Phebe dis jas
1829, 4, 16. Isaiah, s Abel, dis jas
1829, 8, 15. John, s Isaac, gct Arby MM, Ind., to m Miriam Hill
1829, 12, 19. John, s William, dis disunity
1830, 4, 17. Mariam rocf Arba MM, Ind., dtd

THOMAS, continued
1829,11,25
1831, 2, 19. Nehemiah Jr. gct Milford MM, Ind., to m Phebe Gilbert
1831, 5, 21. Mary Graves (form Thomas) dis mcd
1831, 7, 16. Ruth Jr. dis jas
1831, 12, 17. Phebe rocf Milford MM, dtd 1831, 5,28
1831, 12, 17. Sarah Hollingsworth (form Thomas) con mcd
1833, 1, 17. Eli dis disunity
1833, 7, 16. Isaiah, s William, con mcd
1833, 7, 18. Priscilla Brooks (form Thomas) con mcd
1833, 7, 18. Ann Hollingsworth (form Thomas) con mcd
1834, 3, 13. Evan Jr. dis disunity
1834, 5, 15. Elizabeth Jr. dis disunity
1834, 7, 17. William Sr. dis disunity
1834, 8, 14. Sarah Sr. dis disunity
1834, 10, 16. Sarah Sneathen (form Thomas) dis mcd
1835, 1, 15. Evan Sr. dis disunity
1835, 6, 18. Abel dis disunity
1835, 8, 13. David gct Union MM, to m Esther Pemberton
1836, 1, 14. John, s John, & fam gct White Water MM, Ind.
1836, 1, 14. Esther rocf Union MM, dtd 1835, 12,16
1836, 6, 16. Elizabeth Sneathen (form Thomas) dis mcd
1837, 11, 20. Isaiah Jr. gct Mississiniwa MM, Ind.
1838, 6, 14. Ruth & five ch gct Mississiniwa MM, Ind.
1840, 3, 19. John D. dis disunity
1842, 2, 17. Levi, s William, gct West Grove MM, Ind.
1842, 3, 17. Elijah gct Mississiniwa MM,Ind.
1842, 3, 17. Hannah Jr. dis disunity
1842, 6, 16. Jane Owen dis jas
1843, 4, 13. Ira & Asa, ch Elizabeth, rocf Mississiniwa MM, Ind.
1843, 9, 14. Isaiah dis disunity
1843, 12, 14. Lydia Pain (form Thomas) dis mcd
1844, 6, 13. Elizabeth dis jas
1845, 1, 16. Mary dis joining Methodist society
1846, 2, 19. Jacob W. con mcd
1846, 3, 19. Elizabeth dis disunity
1849, 1, 18. Henry con mcd
1849, 4, 19. Benjamin gct Union MM, to m Rhoda Pemberton
1849, 6, 14. Permelia dis jas
1849, 8, 16. Rhoda rocf Union MM, dtd 1849, 8,15
1849, 9, 13. Isaiah rst
1850, 1, 17. Isaac dis disunity
1850, 2, 14. Rueben dis mcd
1850, 7, 18. Noah con mcd
1850, 11, 14. Ira dis mcd
1850, 11, 14. Isaac rst
1850, 11, 14. Enos E. con mcd
1851, 6, 19. Henry gct Union MM
1851, 6, 19. Jacob W. gct Union MM
1851, 6, 19. Reuben gct Honey Creek MM, Ind.
1851, 6, 19. Noah gct Union MM
1851, 7, 17. Nancy rocf White Water MM,Ind., dtd 1851,5,28
1852, 9, 16. Abigail Williamson (form Thomas) dis mcd
1852, 9, 16. Enos dis disunity
1853, 5, 19. Milo dis disunity
1853, 7, 14. Isom C. gct Mill Creek MM, to m Zilpha Pearson
1853, 7, 14. Micajah dis jas
1853, 7, 14. Harriet dis disunity
1853, 10, 13. Sarah Swallow (form Thomas) dis mcd
1854, 2, 16. Benjamin & fam gct Union MM
1854, 3, 16. Zilphah rocf Mill Creek MM, dtd 1854,3,14
1854, 8, 17. Nancy Stutsman (form Thomas) dis mcd
1854, 11, 18. Martha Taylor (form Thomas) dis mcd
1855, 1, 18. Elias dis disunity
1855, 10, 18. Joseph gct Union MM, to m Elizabeth Pemberton
1857, 1, 15. Martin dis disunity
1857, 4, 16. Elizabeth rocf Union MM, dtd 1857,4,15
1857, 8, 13. Stephen rpd mcd; dropped from mbrp
1858, 1, 14. Caleb dis disunity
1858, 12, 16. Esther Ann & dt recrq
1859, 2, 17. Edward rpd mcd
1859, 8, 20. Irvin dis mcd
1859, 10, 13. Absolam dis disunity
1860, 3, 15. Edward Jr. rpd mcd
1860, 3, 15. George gct Mississiniwa MM, Ind., to m Christian Thomas
1860, 8, 16. John dis disunity
1860, 8, 16. Christian P. & s, Henry P. & Ruelien, rocf Mississiniwa MM, Ind.
1860, 8, 16. Elva rocf Mississiniwa MM, Ind.
1863, 4, 16. Zilphah & dt, Catharine E., gct Mississiniwa MM, Ind.
1864, 7, 14. Joseph & w, Elizabeth, & ch, John, Henrietta & William, gct Union MM
1865, 3, 16. Edward Jr. rpd mcd
1865, 11, 16. Lewis con mcd
1865, 11, 16. Louisa Lease (form Thomas) dis mcd & jas
1866, 9, 13. Lewis dis disunity

THOMAS, continued
1868, 7, 16. Mary gct Kokomo MM, Ind.
1871, 8, 17. Edward rpd mcd
1871, 8, 17. Reuben rpd mcd
1872, 3, 14. Laura E., dt Edward, recrq
1873, 4, 17. Edward Sr. & w, Esther Ann, gct New Garden MM, Ind.
1873, 4, 17. Jemima Cox, dt Esther Ann Thomas, gct New Garden MM, Ind.
1874, 6, 18. Reuben & fam gct New Garden MM, Ind.
1875, 1, 14. David relrq
1878, 1, 17. Elwood C. rocf Union MM, O.
1878, 3, 14. David rst (form relrq)
1882, 9, 14. Elwood gct Union MM
1883, 2, 15. Susan M. recrq
1886, 2, 13. Minerva recrq
1889, 1, 12. Rhoda J. relrq
1889, 12, 14. Calvin & ch, Lindley, Minnie & Cora, relrq
1892, 5, 14. Edward & w relrq
1894, 2, 10. Anna recrq
1902, 11, 8. Martha M. rocf Marion MM
1906, 8, 8. Martha M. gct Marion QM
1913, 3, 8. Nora E. recrq
1919, 12, 13. Merle rec in active mbrp by rq
1922, 3, 11. Clyde Henry relrq

THOMPSON
1808, 4, 23. Joseph rocf Bush River MM, S.C., dtd 1806,5,31, endorsed by Miami MM, 1808, 3,10
1810, 2, 17. Isaac [Thomson] Jr. rocf New Garden MM, N. C., dtd 1809,7,29, endorsed by Miami MM, 1809,12,27
1872, 8, 15. Noah A. & w, Martha E., & dt, Ida May, recrq
1907, 5, 11. Noah & Martha dropped from mbrp for lack of interest

THORNBURGH
1810, 3, 17. Joseph Sr. & w, Rebecca, rocf Lost Creek MM, Tenn., dtd 1809,11,25

THORNTON
1813, 9, 1. Thomas, s Thomas & Elizabeth, Montgomery Co., O.; m at Rocky Spring, Sarah THOMAS, dt Isaac & Mary, Montgomery Co., O.

1810, 12, 22. Eli recrq
1813, 8, 26. Thomas prcf Mill Creek MM, dtd 1813,7,24, to m Sarah Thomas
1814, 5, 26. Thomas & ch, Nathan, Eli, Thomas & Mary, rocf Mill Creek MM, dtd 1814,3, 26
1818, 6, 25. Thomas & fam gct Mill Creek MM
1821, 5, 19. Thomas & s, Eli, Thomas, Joshua & Isaac, rocf Mill Creek MM, dtd 1821,4,28
1821, 5, 19. Sarah & dt, Mary, Lydia, Rebecca & Anna, rocf Mill Creek MM, dtd 1821,4, 28
1823, 3, 15. Thomas dis
1824, 3, 20. Nathan rocf Silver Creek MM, dtd 1824,1,19
1826, 2, 18. Isaac & Joshua gct Silver Creek MM
1826, 2, 18. Sarah & dt, Abigail, Rebecca, Anna & Sarah, & step dt, Mary Thornton, gct Silver Creek MM
1826, 3, 18. Thomas con mcd
1827, 1, 20. Thomas gct Silver Creek MM
1827, 2, 17. Eli dis disunity

TITUS
1881, 6, 16. Charles H. & w, Albertine, & ch, Allen Gilbert, Mary Jenet & Martha Esther, recrq

TOWNSEND
1808, 9, 17. John & s, Jonathan, William & John, rocf Miami MM, dtd 1808,3,10
1809, 8, 19. James rocf Miami MM, dtd 1808, 5,12
1857, 11, 19. Elvira rocf West Grove MM, dtd 1857,11,14

TROXWELL
1888, 9, 8. Robert recrq

TUCKER
----, --, --. Abraham m Mary ----- d 1869,5, -- ae 89y
Ch: Nicolas b 1795, 9, 10
Jacob " 1797, 10, 6 d 1877,--,--
Naomi " 1799, 2, 12; m ----- JONES
Sarah " 1800, 11, 27 d 1882, 4, 1 m ----- JONES
Mitchener b 1802, 12, 27
Jonathan " 1804, 11, 30
Mary " 1806, 10, 6 d in infancy
Abraham " 1806, 10, 6 " in 40th yr
Joseph " 1809, 1, 18
1818, 1, 1. Naomi m Philemon JONES
1819, 2, 25. Sarah m John JONES
---- --, --. Jacob m Elizabeth KESSLER
Ch: Mary b 1820, 10, 23
Anna " 1822, 1, 15
Naomi " 1823, 9, 29
Joseph " 1825, 2, 7
Benj. " 1827, 1, 22
Daniel " 1828, 7, 15
Elizabeth " 1830, 7, 31
Deborah " 1833, 1, 10
Rollin " 1834, 9, 3
Erasmus " 1837, 2, 20
Rhoda " 1839, 9, 14
Thos. " 1842, 7, 7
Susannah " 1842, 7, 7
1838, 12, 20. Mary m William COATE
1843, 9, 5. Susanna, dt Jacob, d bur West Branch
1852, 5, 20. Elizabeth m Edward THOMAS

1809, 11, 18. Mary & ch. Nicholas, Jacob,

TUCKER, continued
Michaner, Jonathan, Abraham, Naomy & Sarah, recrq
1812, 4, 23. Pheba gct White Water MM
1814, 6, 23. Mary Brown & ch, Nicolas, Jacob, Naomi, Sarah, Michoes, Jonathan, Abraham & Joseph Tucker, rocf Union MM, dtd 1814,4,6
1817, 4, 23. Nicholas gct Miami MM, to m
1820, 1, 15. Jacob con mcd
1820, 4, 15. Nicholas gct Miami MM
1823, 11, 15. Michener dis mcd
1825, 5, 21. Jonathan dis disunity
1826, 3, 18. Jonathan dis mcd
1826, 12, 16. Joseph dis disunity
1828, 1, 19. Abraham dis mcd
1830, 3, 20. Nancy (form Brown) con mcd
1833, 2, 19. Nancy gct Union MM
1836, 6, 16. Joseph, Benjamin, Daniel & Rollin, ch Jacob, recrq
1836, 6, 16. Elizabeth & ch, Mary, Anne, Naomi, Elizabeth & Deborah, recrq
1847, 9, 16. Naomi Harrington (form Tucker) dis mcd
1849, 1, 18. Benjamin con mcd
1849, 2, 15. Benjamin gct Honey Creek MM, Ind.
1849, 3, 15. Joseph gct Honey Creek MM, Ind.
1849, 3, 18. Jacob & fam gct Honey Creek MM, Ind.
1852, 3, 18. Elizabeth recrq
1870, 1, 13. Jacob & w, Anna, & ch, Jonathan, Harvey, Deborah, Amanda Jane, Margaret & Davis L., recrq
1887, 4, 9. Myrtie, minor, recrq
1891, 2, 14. Frances C. recrq
1899, 1, 14. Allie relrq

TURNER
1875, 12, 16. Nancy recrq

TYLER
1871, 9, 14. Orrin S. Mote gct White Water MM, to m Martha J. Tyler

ULLERY
1922, 5, 13. Virginia recrq
1927, 3, 9. Vera & Virginia relrq

UNDERHILL
1812, 5, 28. Cert rec for John & w, Hannah, from Lost Creek MM, dtd 1811,11,30, endorsed to Mill Creek MM

VAN HORN
1810, 6, 23. Duriah & ch, Mary Sarah & Rebecca, recrq
1833, 6, 13. Betsy rocf Union MM, dtd 1833,6,11

VAUGHN
1887, 4, 9. Charles R. recrq
1895, 2, 9. Charles R. [Vahn] dropped from mbrp

VERNON
1816, 11, 28. Nathaniel d bur West Branch
1818, 6, 8. Samuel, s Nathaniel, d bur West Branch

1807, 7, 18. Nathaniel & s, Thomas & Samuel, rocf Bush River MM, S. C.
1807, --, --. Grace & dt, Margaret, Lydda & Ann, rocf Bush River MM, S. C., dtd 1806, 9,27 (cert was directed to Miami MM but was rec here)
1807, 10, 19. Margaret dis
1809, 7, 22. Lydia dis
1817, 6, 26. Thomas con mcd
1821, 7, 21. Thomas gct Union MM
1823, 10, 18. Grace gct Union MM

VORE
1896, 2, 5. Hannah, dt Abner & Catharine (Siler) d
1921, 11, 29. Judson F. d

1883, 3, 15. W. Wesley recrq
1885, 3, 19. Delbert recrq
1895, 2, 9. Delbert dropped from mbrp
1903, 4, 11. Anna J. recrq
1906, 3, 10. Nelson recrq
1911, 2, 11. Judd recrq
1913, 3, 8. Nelson recrq
1913, 5, 10. Lena dropped from mbrp
1923, 4, 14. Rose, Georgia & Mary recrq
1924, 7, 12. Nelson dropped from mbrp for jas

VOSBURG
1914, 2, 14. Mable Falkner gct Rollin MM, Mich.

WADE
1810, 11, 17. Fereba con mcd

WAGGONER
----, --, --. John [Wagginer] b 1775,1,22; m Mary MAST, dt John, b 1772,3,20
Ch: Jacob b 1802, 7, --
Mary " 1804, 11, 1
Barbara " 1806, 10, 20
Susanna " 1808, 10, 27
Nancy " 1810, 11, 10
Hannah " 1814, 1, 1
1850, 11, 27. Mary [Wagginer], w John, d bur West Branch
1857, 6, 3. John d bur West Branch

1813, 6, 24. John [Wagginer] recrq
1814, 5, 26. Jacob, s John, recrq
1814, 7, 28. Molly & ch, Mary, Barbary, Nancy & Hannah, recrq
1825, 2, 19. Mary Childress (form Waggoner) con mcd
1826, 11, 18. Jacob [Wagginer] dis disunity
1828, 1, 19. Barbara dis disunity
1828, 5, 17. Nancy Mote (form Waggoner) con

WAGGONER, continued
mcd
1829, 6, 20. John dis disunity
1833, 1, 17. Hannah [Wagginer] dis disunity
1851, 7, 17. John rst
1893, 6, 10. Barbara Coppock (form Wagoner) rst (form dis mcd)

WAKEFIELD
1876, 4, 13. Joseph J. & fam rocf Van Wert MM, O.
1876, 11, 16. Joseph J. & fam gct Wilmington MM, O.

WALLACE
1876, 3, 16. Louis Albert Mote gct White Water MM, Ind., to m Anna E. Wallace
1916, 1, 8. Adaline S. recrq

WARD
1875, 12, 16. Daniel recrq
1903, 2, 14. Margaret recrq
1913, 5, 10. Daniel & Margaret dropped from mbrp

WARFIELD
1875, 12, 16. Isaac & w, Mary E., recrq (colored)
1889, 10, 12. Isaac & w, Mary, relrq

WARNER
1823, 6, 21. Elizabeth con mcd
1823, 8, 16. Elizabeth & ch gct Fairfield MM
1913, 3, 8. Mollie & Martha recrq

WARWICK
1903, 2, 14. Raymond & Lillian recrq
1907, 5, 11. Raymond dropped from mbrp for lack of interest
1907, 5, 11. Lillie [Warrick] dropped from mbrp; jas

WATERS
1863, 2, 19. Jane M. rocf Short Creek MM,O., dtd 1862,4,23, returned to Short Creek MM, at her rq

WATTS
1829, 2, 21. Charity (form Mendenhall) con mcd
1832, 12, 13. Charity dis disunity

WAYMIRE
1808, 10, 22. Dorothy con mcd
1808, 11, 19. Frederic rocf Back Creek MM, N. C., dtd 1808,9,24
1818, 10, 22. Frederick Jr. recrq
1822, 4, 19. Huldah, Elizabeth & Rebecca, ch Frederick, recrq
1822, 4, 20. Andrew & John, s Frederick, recrq
1825, 1, 15. Dorothy dis jas
1828, 6, 21. Andrew dis mcd & jas
1828, 8, 16. Elizabeth dis jas
1829, 7, 18. Huldah Staley (form Waymire) dis mcd

WEAVER
1886, 1, 9. Thomas & w, Katharine, & ch, Lucretia, recrq
1913, 5, 10. Kate dropped from mbrp
1923, 4, 14. Rose recrq

WEBSTER
1819, 8, 21. Elizabeth rocf Fairfield MM, dtd 1819,7,31
1821, 8, 18. Taylor, Abner, William & Hugh, ch Elizabeth, recrq

WEEK
1815, 1, 26. Cert rec for Benjamin & fam from New Garden MM, N. C., dtd 1814,8,27, endorsed to Union MM

WELBAUM
1923, 4, 14. Paul & Glenn recrq

WELDY
1909, 4, 10. Fern recrq

WERTS
1885, 3, 19. Charles recrq
1895, 2, 9. Charles dropped from mbrp

WETZLEY
1920, 12, 11. Alice recrq

WHITEHEAD
1909, 1, 9. Roy, form mbr Chambersburg MM, recrq
1913, 5, 10. Roy dropped from mbrp

WHITSON
1811, 7, 25. Solomon con mcd
1814, 4, 28. Solomon gc
1893, 2, 11. Retta (form Kellogg) relrq

WILES
1851, 3, 13. Enoch James gct Union MM, to m Eunice Ann Wilies
1851, 7, 17. Elizabeth H. gct Union MM

WILGUS
1902, 12, 13. Thomas recrq
1907, 3, 9. Thomas & w, Mary, relrq

WILLETS
1852, 8, 20. Lewis, s Ellis & Rachel, Knox Co., O.; m at West Branch, Charity PEARSON dt Robert & Catharine, Miami Co., O.

WILLIAMS
1807, 7, 18. William rocf Lost Creek MM, Tenn. dtd 1807,3,28
1897, 1, 9. J. Edgar & w, Anna W., rocf Tecumseh MM, Mich.
1898, 12, 10. Edgar & w, Anna, gct Marshall-

WILLIAMS, continued
town MM, Ia.

WILLIAMSON
1843, 9, 14. Susan dis mcd
1852, 9, 16. Abigail (form Thomas) dis mcd
1883, 3, 15. Temperance recrq
1913, 5, 10. Kate dropped from mbrp

WILSON
1919, 9, 2. Minnie Wilson d

1886, 2, 13. Reuben recrq
1886, 2, 13. Minnie recrq
1901, 3, 9. Emma relrq
1903, 2, 14. Alta recrq
1907, 5, 11. Alta dropped from mbrp for lack of interest
1913, 5, 10. Grace dropped from mbrp
1922, 5, 13. Grace Coate dropped from mbrp for jas

WINDELL
1888, 9, 8. Maud recrq

WINTROM
1901, 2, 9. Sarah & ch, Ida & Daniel, recrq
1903, 8, 7. Ida, Sarah & Daniel dropped from mbrp; jas

WISENER
1838, 3, 3. Mary, w Jacob, d bur South Fork

1809, 5, 20. Jacob & s, Isaac, rocf Miami MM, dtd 1809,4,8
1824, 4, 17. Isaac dis
1826, 5, 20. Sarah Brodrick (form Wisener) dis mcd
1833, 3, 14. John dis disunity
1835, 11, 19. Susannah (form Anthony) dis mcd
1840, 7, 16. Jacob dis mcd

WISSINGER
1905, 4, 8. Alma Lockner relrq

WOLF
1891, 2, 14. Otto recrq

WOLLOM
1906, 5, 12. Arthur & w, Lea, rocf Bethel MM
1909, 11, 13. Rev. J. Arthur & fam gct Emporia MM, Kans.

WRIGHT
1811, 12, 11. Rebeckah m Jesse BALLENGER
1894, 7, 21. Orilla E., w Warren, dt William & Sarah COMPTON, d
1926, 4, 22. Warren d

1808, 8, 28. Ralph & s, Ralph & David, rocf Springfield MM, N. C., dtd 1807,9,5
1808, --, --. Hannah rocf Springfield MM,N.C., dtd 1807,9,5
1810, 1, 20. Jonathan rocf Springfield MM, dtd 1808,11,5
1810, 6, 23. Elizabeth & ch, Rebeckah, James, Lucy, Susannah, Welmet, William, Betsy & Mahala Ann, rocf Lost Creek MM, Tenn., dtd 1809,8,26
1810, 8, 18. Cert rec for James from Springfield MM, dtd 1808,11,5, endorsed to White Water MM
1810, --, --. Lucy rocf Lost Creek MM, Tenn., dtd 1809,9,30
1819, 4, 17. James gct New Garden MM
1824, 11, 20. Elizabeth & ch, Betsy, William & Mahala, gct Springfield MM, Ind.
1824, 11, 20. Susanna Brewer (form Wright) dis mcd
1885, 3, 19. Owen recrq
1886, 1, 9. Noah recrq
1891, 5, 9. Warren rocf Muncie MM, Ind.
1895, 12, 14. Elizabeth, w Warren, recrq
1913, 5, 10. Alice dropped from mbrp
1925, 6, 13. Glenn dropped from mbrp for jas

YORTY
1854, 4, 12. Nancy, dt John Wagginer, d bur West Branch

YOUNCE
1844, 5, 15. Mary Ann (form Yount) dis mcd

YOUNG
1882, 3, 16. William A. & w, Elizabeth C., & s, James T., recrq
1907, 4, 13. James relrq
1923, 11, 10. Burton & w, Nora, & dt, Dessie, recrq
1925, 10, 10. Burton dropped from mbrp

YOUNT
1793, 9, 4. Elizabeth, w H-----, b
1797, 7, 22. Solomon b
----, --, --. Frederick b 1778,5,4 d 1864,5,3; m Mary ----- b 1779,11,7 d 1859,10,8
Ch: Michael b 1799, 1, 8 d 1872,--,--
w Noah HOOVER
Mahala b 1802, 11, 6 " 1856, 4,15
w Samuel KELLY
Enos b 1805, 8, 17 " 1826,12, 8
Elizabeth " 1808, 2, 18 " 1875, 6, 9
w Henry FOUTZ
Milly b 1810, 4, 8 " 1835, 6, 9
1st w Seth KELLY
John b 1813, 4, 17 " 1865,--,--
Jacob " 1816, 3, 28 " 1895, 8,--
Elam " 1819, 1, 4 " 1889, 4, 8
Mary Ann " 1823, 8, 16 " 1847,10,22
1799, 7, 30. Frederick b
1811, 1, 24. Sarah m Benjamin IDDINGS
1863, 7, 19. Henry, s John & Mary, d bur West Branch
1870, 4, 20. Solomon, s John, d bur Mill

YOUNT, continued
Creek (with his father)
1871, 9, 12. Elizabeth, w Henry, dt John & Sarah HOOVER, d bur West Branch
1880, 8, 14. Frederick, s John & Mary, d bur Mill Creek
1886, 1, 20. William H., s Samuel & Mary Ann (Matthias), d
----, --, --. Harvey m Emma THOMAS, dt Joseph & Elizabeth, b 1865,8,21
Ch: Harold
Tressie d 1927,--,--
Josie
Leroy
Elizabeth
Clifford
----, --, --. Leroy & Goldie
Ch: Dale Eugene b 1924, 9, 4
Merlin Leroy " 1932, 1, 17
1933, 4, 5. Emma d
----, --, --. Katharine, w Frederick, d

1808, 5, 21. Andrew & s, Daniel, rocf Miami MM, dtd 1808,4,14
1808, --, --. Eve rocf Miami MM, O., dtd 1808, 4,14
1808, 5, 21. Henry rocf Miami MM, dtd 1808,4, 14
1808, --, --. Mary & dt, Sarah, rocf Miami MM, O., dtd 1808,4,14
1809, 5, 20. Mary, w John, & ch, Henry, Delilah, Solomon, Frederic, Caroline & Rebecca, recrq
1811, 8, 22. Frederick recrq
1811, 10, 24. Mary & ch, Micah, Mahala, Enos, Elizabeth & Milly, recrq
1816, 1, 25. Elizabeth con mcd
1824, 11, 20. Elizabeth Fouts (form Yount) con mcd
1826, 8, 19. Amelia Kelly (form Yount) dis mcd mcd
1830, 2, 20. Frederick dis joining Separatists
1830, 6, 19. Mary dis joining Separatists
1836, 7, 14. Jacob dis mcd
1837, 6, 15. John dis disunity
1842, 4, 14. Elim dis disunity
1844, 5, 15. Mary Ann Younce (form Yount) dis mcd
1858, 10, 14. Solomon recrq
1859, 10, 13. Frederick Jr. recrq
1861, 5, 16. Theresa (form Pearson) dis mcd
1886, 2, 13. Edgar W. & s, John H., recrq
1886, 2, 13. Harvey recrq
1913, 3, 8. Effie recrq
1915, 2, 13. Herman & Howard, ch Harold & Effie, rec as associate mbr by rq
1915, 6, 12. Juanita, dt Harold & Effie, b rpd
1915, 10, 9. Edgar, Rettie & Harry recf Union MM
1918, 4, 13. Leroy & Elizabeth rec as active mbr
1920, 9, 11. Harold & Effie dropped from mbrp for joining Mennonites
1924, 4, 12. Golda recrq

ZINK (see SINKS)

* * * * * * *

BOLINGER
1842, 3, 17. Ruth (form Mendenhall) dis mcd

BROOKS
----, --, --. Daniel & Priscilla
Ch: Benjamin b 1834, 3, 17
Malinda " 1838, 2, 15

HOOVER
----, --, --. Noah & Michal
Ch: Mahala b 1816, 11, 3
Celia " 1819, 4, 15
Absalom " 1821, 3, 23
Mary " 1823, 8, 9
Frederic " 1826, 3, 30
Enos " 1829, 3, 15
Deborah " 1832, 6, 13
Wm. Jason " 1835, 2, 1
Andrew " 1837, 7, 10

JOHNSON
1871, 10, 10. James, s Achilla, d bur M. Creek
1925, 1, 14. Orpha d
1925, 2, 6. Chas. d
1849, 10, 18. John G. rocf Miami MM, dtd 1849, 9,26
1851, 7, 17. John G. gct Union MM
1861, 3, 14. Sarah (form Furnas) dis
1876, 3, 16. Sarah B. & Nannie Josie recrq
1876, 3, 16. Mary C. recrq
1888, 9, 8. Rosa recrq
1909, 1, 9. Charlie, Orpha, Reah, Priscilla & Hibbard, form mbr Chambersburg MM, recrq
1909, 1, 9. Mary, form mbr Chambersburg MM, recrq
1909, 1, 9. Belle, form mbr Chambersburg MM, recrq
1913, 5, 10. Belle dropped from mbrp
1927, 7, 13. Priscilla & Hibberd [Johnston] dropped from mbrp

KERSEY
1864, 3, 24. Samuel, s John & Anna, Warren Co., O.; m at West Branch, Arena E. MOTE, dt L. Smith & Charity, Miami Co., O.

MENDENHALL
1810, 12, 6. Rachel, dt Joseph & Rachel, b

PEARSON
----, --, --. Wm. A. & Mahala
Ch: Laura
Ellayne b 1854, 9, 26 d 1863, 4, 9
bur West Branch
Horace Mel-
vin b 1857, 8, 11
Jasper New-
ton " 1859, 8, 16
Adah
Jeanette " 1861, 8, 20
Mary Eve-
line " 1864, 12, 31
Herbert R. " 1868, 3, 16

ROBERTS
1808, 8, 28. Sarah (form Adington) dis mcd

TEAGUE
1825, --, --. Samuel m Prudence TEAGUE b 1807, 10,4 d 1895,5,19

THORNBURGH
1810, 3, 17. Thomas rocf Lost Creek MM, Tenn., dtd 1807,4,25, endorsed by Miami MM, 1809,9,9
1810, 8, 18. Rebeckah & ch, Thomas, William & Rebeckah, recrq
1811, 2, 23. Rachel recrq
1814, 11, 24. Thomas & fam gct Caesars Creek MM
1818, 6, 25. Joseph & w, Rebecca, gct New Garden MM

TOWNSEND
1808, --, --. Elvy & dt, Mary Hester Sarah Elizabeth & Barbary, rocf Miami MM, dtd 1808,3,10

MILL CREEK MONTHLY MEETING

Mill Creek Monthly Meeting, Miami County, Ohio, was set off from West Branch Monthly Meeting 2 Mo. 23, 1811. This monthly meeting was discontinued in 1860.

RECORDS

ADDISON
1843, 9, 6. Samuel d bur Concord

ALLISON
1845, 7, 15. Jonathan & fam rocf West Branch MM (s names are James, John, William, Jonathan & Abram)

ANDERSON
1841, 11, 16. Thomas Pearson gct Union MM, to m Abigail Anderson

BARNARD
1821, 8, 2. Catharine m Joseph COMPTON

1823, 5, 24. Wm., Francis & Ann, ch Samuel, recrq
1840, 3, 17. Martha Freeman (form Barnard) dis mou
1840, 4, 14. Wm. C. dis disunity
1840, 9, 15. Samuel dis disunity
1842, 2, 15. Rebecca & ch gct Vermillion MM, Ill.

BARNHARDT
1838, 2, 13. Sarah dis mou

BATTEN
1831, 12, 1. Richard, s Richard & Catharine, Union Co., Ind.; m in Randolph MH, Catharine COMPTON, dt Francis & Catharine BARNARD, Montgomery Co., O.

BEESON
----, --, --. Joseph, s Wm. & Jenne, b 1777,5, 14; m Mary MACY, dt Tristram & Miriam, b 1776,12,24

Ch: William b 1805, 2, 28
Jesse " 1807, 5, 5
Tristram " 1810, 3, 5
Betsy " 1812, 8, 13
Miriam " 1819, 9, 10

1844, 5, 27. Mary d

1828, 3, 22. Benjamin [Beason] dis disunity
1829, 7, 25. Jesse [Beason] dis mou
1829, 9, 26. Tristram [Beason] dis disunity
1832, 4, 28. Elizabeth dis disunity
1836, 6, 14. Mariam Wolf (form Beeson) dis mou
1845, 7, 15. Joseph gct Salem MM, Ind., to m Hepsibah Macy

BELUE
1830, 11, 27. Susannah gct White Lick MM, Ind.

BINKARD
1838, 4, 17. Judith dis mou

BOND
1843, 11, 14. John Hutchins gct Springfield MM, Ind., to m Frances Malinda Bond

BRANDENBURG
1860, 6, 12. Rhoda dis jas

BROOKS
1834, 4, 15. Noah recrq
1838, 4, 17. Noah gct Union MM, to m Melinda Pierce
1839, 4, 16. Noah & fam gct Union MM

BROWN
1830, 9, 2. Elisabeth m Meredith HUTCHINS
1844, 2, 13. Sarah dis

CAMMACK
1853, 12, 13. James & fam rocf Chester MM, Ind.
1856, 7, 15. James & fam gct Red Cedar MM,Ia.

COATE
1839, 5, 2. Abigail (Conaway) d bur Mill Creek
1842, 8, 25. Joshua, s James & Lurena,Miami Co., O.; m in Randolph MH, Adila JENKINS, dt Robert & Jemima, Miami Co., O.
1858, 4, 22. Jonathan, s James & Luranah, Miami Co., O.; m in Randolph MH, Rachel JENKINS, dt Robert & Verlinda, Montgomery Co., O.

1828, 8, 23. Enoch Pearson Jr. gct Union MM, to m Mary Coate
1846, 5, 12. Joshua & fam rocf Union MM
1851, 7, 15. Rosannah (form Pearson) dis mou
1858, 4, 13. Joshua & w, Adila, gct Union MM

COBLE
1832, 11, 13. Sarah dis disunity

COGGESHALL
----, --, --. Deborah, dt Job & Deborah, b 1769,6,7 d 1823,1,1

COMMONS
1840, 8, 11. Job T. Jay gct West Branch MM, to m Rachel Commons

COMPTON
1821, 8, 2. Joseph, s Samuel & Elizabeth, Warren Co., O.; m in Randolph MH, Catharine BARNHARD, dt Francis & Catharine
1831, 12, 1. Catherine m Richard BATTEN

CONAWAY
1824, 4, 24. Eli, s Elizabeth, recrq
1824, 4, 24. Elizabeth [Conoway] & ch gct Union MM
1824, 12, 25. James D., Samuel & Eli, ch Elizabeth, rocf Union MM, dtd 1824,12,4
1829, 2, 28. James dis
1829, 4, 25. Samuel dis disunity
1832, 3, 24. Eli dis mou

CONAWAY, continued
1842, 3, 15. Rebecca Sweet (form Conaway) dis mou

COOK
1859, 1, 20. Clarkson F., s Zimri & Lydia, Hamilton Co., Ind.; m in Randolph MH, Bathsheba JENKINS, dt Robert & Verlinda, Montgomery Co., O.

1835, 12, 15. Samuel Jenkins gct Salem MM, to m Nancy Cook
1859, 3, 15. Bathsheba J. gct Richland MM, Ind.

COOPER
----, --, --. Isaac, s Isaac & Prudence, b 1774,9,15 d 1825,7,17 bur Randolph Graveyard; m Elizabeth CANADA, dt John & Esther, b 1782,9,14 d 1859,2,3 bur Mississinewa Cemetery
Ch: Prudence b 1807, 10, 4
Joseph " 1809, 2, 1 d 1837,10,11
m Lydia EVANS, dt Thos.
Mary b 1811, 7, 11
Rhoda " 1813, 2, 28
Allen " 1815, 3, 27 d 1838, 7,28
Abijah " 1817, 2, 21 " 1838, 9,20

1825, 6, 2. Prudence m Samuel TEAGUE
1830, 12, 30. Rhoda m Isaac JAY
1831, 3, 3. Mary m Webster WELCH
1836, 5, 17. Joseph C. gct Miami MM, to m Lydia Evans

COPPOCK
----, --, --. Moses, s James & Hannah, b 1787,3,8; m Lydia JAY, dt John & Betty, b 1793,3,18
Ch: Elizabeth b 1811, 4, 18
Hannah " 1813, 1, 20
James " 1814, 11, 11
Samuel " 1817, 9, 21
Jane " 1819, 8, 23
Rebeckah " 1821, 8, 19
John J. " 1823, 9, 20 d 1895, 2, 8
Rebeckah " 1826, 2, 27
1820, 4, 11. Hannah d bur Mill Creek
1823, 7, 27. Rebeckah d bur Mill Creek
1830, 3, 20. Lydia d bur Mill Creek
1834, 2, 19. Hannah m Enoch PEARSON
1838, 2, 9. James d bur Mill Creek
1838, 5, 23. Jane m Gainer PIERCE
1854, 7, 21. Samuel, s Joseph & Rachel, Miami Co., O.; m in Randolph MH, Maryann HUTCHINS, dt Isaac & Rebeccah, Montgomery Co., O.

1833, 4, 16. Moses gct Union MM, to m Mary Elleman
1837, 4, 11. James con mou
1840, 3, 17. Moses & fam gct Union MM
1840, 5, 12. Samuel con mou
1846, 3, 11. James & fam gct Union MM
1848, 9, 12. Samuel dis disunity
1850, 9, 17. Isaac C. Pearson gct Union MM, to m Louisa Coppock
1851, 9, 16. John & w, Susannah, & s, Wesley, rocf Union MM

COX
1830, 12, 25. John gct White Lick MM, Ind.

CURTIS
----, --, --. John, s James & Nancy, b 1781,6, 9; m Catharine -----, dt John & Sarah, b 1787,9,25 d 1856,10,19 bur Randolph
Ch: Ithiel b 1807, 10, 23
Mary " 1809, 3, 12
Henry " 1810, 12, 6
Elam " 1812, 1, 25
Rebeckah " 1813, 10, 8
Daniel " 1814, 12, 25
Andrew " 1816, 2, 4
Sarah " 1818, 2, 26
Nancy " 1820, 1, 10
John " 1822, 3, 28
James " 1824, 5, 10
Davis " 1826, 11, 27
Jesse " 1831, 11, 7
1821, 12, 25. Ithiel d bur Randolph Graveyard
1841, 3, 25. Nancy m Samuel C. MILES
1856, 10, 19. Catherine d ae 69y 24d (an elder)

1828, 2, 23. Mary Hoover (form Curtis) dis disunity
1833, 6, 11. Henry dis disunity
1833, 11, 12. Rebecca dis disunity
1835, 12, 15. Elam dis disunity
1836, 10, 11. Daniel dis disunity
1840, 5, 12. Andrew gct West Branch MM, to m Mary Davis
1848, 12, 12. Davis dis disunity
1853, 2, 15. Samuel dis mou
1854, 1, 17. John H. con mou
1854, 2, 14. John H. gct Wabash MM, Ind.
1860, 8, 4. James con mou

DAVIS
1847, 5, 12. Jacob, s Jesse & Alice, Wayne Co., Ind.; m in Concord MH, Rebecca PEARSON, dt Robert & Catharine, Miami Co., O.

1823, 3, 22. Joseph & fam gct Springfield MM, Ind.
1825, 3, 26. Simon & s, Mark, Ezra, Miles & Pleasant, rocf Chester MM, Ind., dtd 1824,10,20
1828, 12, 27. Isaac dis disunity
1833, 6, 11. Mark dis disunity
1833, 7, 16. Simon & fam gct West Branch MM
1835, 7, 14. Simon & fam rocf West Branch MM
1840, 5, 12. Andrew Curtis gct West Branch

DAVIS, continued
MM, to m Mary Davis
1842, 9, 14. Simon fam gct Mississinewa MM, Ind.
1842, 12, 14. Pleasant dis disunity
1846, 1, 13. Nancy dis

DUNKIN
----, --, --. Amos & Elizabeth [Duncan]
Ch: Isaac b 1809, 5, 4
Mary " 1810, 7, 7

1827, 11, 24. Mary dis
1830, 1, 23. Isaac dis mou

EDGAR
1832, 10, 16. Katherine Ann (form Iddings) dis mou

EDWARDS
1826, 9, 23. Jane dis mou

ELLEMAN
1833, 4, 16. Moses Coppock gct Union MM, to m Mary Elleman

ERVIN
1840, 9, 15. Catherine (form Swallow) dis mou

EULESS
1838, 5, 15. Sarah dis mou

EVANS
1812, 7, 2. Robert, s Joseph & Esther, Montgomery Co., O.; m in Mill Creek, Esther JENKINS, dt Thos. & Maria, Miami Co., O., d 1830,5,30
Ch: Thomas J. b 1813, 4, 4
Joseph " 1815, 4, 12 d 1828, 8,31 bur Mill Creek
Eleanor b 1817, 2, 4
Julian M. " 1819, 8, 18 " 1823, 2,19 bur Mill Creek
Esther b 1821, 8, 31 " 1823, 2, 9 bur Mill Creek
William b 1824, 3, 9
Moses " 1826, 6, 17
Maris " 1828, 11, 20
1814, 12, 7. Aaron d bur Mill Creek
1818, 12, 3. Sally m John FURNAS

1830, 10, 23. Esther dis disunity
1835, 7, 14. Joseph dis joining Methodists
1835, 9, 15. Thomas con mou
1836, 5, 17. Joseph C. Cooper gct Miami MM, to m Lydia Evans
1842, 11, 15. Thomas dis disunity
1848, 8, 15. Moses dis mou
1849, 2, 13. Wm. dis disunity
1852, 7, 13. Jane dis mou
1855, 11, 13. Charity dis

FELL
1822, 2, 23. Mahlon recrq

FOX
1839, 8, 10. Elizabeth (form Macy) dis mou

FREEMAN
1840, 3, 17. Martha (form Barnard) dis mou

FRIEND
1841, 8, 17. Elizabeth dis mou

FURNAS
1816, 10, 3. Christopher Jr., s John & Esther, Clinton Co., O., b 1791,10,18; m in Randolph, Sarah JENKINS, dt Wm. & Mary, Miami Co., O., b 1795,2,8
Ch: John b 1817, 7, 9 d 1826, 8,19 bur Salem
William b 1820, 2, 5
Louisa " 1822, 5, 27
Benjamin " 1824, 3, 15 " 1824,11,15 bur Salem
Maryan " 1825, 12, 3
Sarah " 1829, 7, 18 " 1830, 9,24 bur Salem
1818, 12, 3. John, s Joseph & Sally, Miami Co., O.; b 1796,4,12; m in Lower Concord, Sally EVANS, dt Joseph & Esther, Montgomery Co., O., b 1797,5,20
Ch: Mary b 1819, 12, 2
Joseph " 1821, 9, 4
Joseph Evans b 1822, 9, 26
Esther " 1824, 10, 10
Aaron " 1826, 10, 17
Robert " 1828, 8, 24
Samuel " 1830, 5, 17
Sarah P. " 1832, 8, 22
Thomas W. " 1834, 5, 30
Davis " 1836, 8, 17
Jane " 1839, 7, 16
1821, 10, 26. Joseph d bur Mill Creek
1822, 8, 29. Samuel, s Joseph & Sally, Miami Co., O.; m in Concord MH, Mary JENKINS, dt David & Martha, Miami Co., O.
1823, 9, 21. Mary [Furnace] d bur Concord
1824, 9, 29. Benjamin, s Joseph & Sally, Miami Co., O.; m Mary PATTY, dt Chas. & Pheba, Miami Co., O.
1825, 11, 29. Rachel, dt Wm. & Martha, b
1826, 5, 31. Samuel, s Joseph & Sally, Miami Co., O.; m Lydia MACY, dt Paul & Eunice
1828, 7, 30. Wm., s Joseph & Sally, Miami Co., O.; m Beulah MACY, dt Paul & Eunice, Miami Co., O.
1833, 10, 10. Martha d bur Concord Graveyard
1834, 9, 20. Mary [Furnace] d bur Mill Creek

1827, 3, 24. Benjamin rocf Union MM, dtd 1827,3,3
1832, 4, 28. Christopher & s, Wm., rocf Silver Creek MM, dtd 1832,1,28

FURNAS, continued
1834, 11, 11. Wm. & fam gct Union MM
1836, 5, 17. Rachel, minor, recrq
1840, 3, 17. John dis disunity
1842, 5, 17. Benjamin dis disunity
1844, 9, 11. Joseph E. dis mou
1846, 8, 11. Wm. dis mou
1847, 5, 11. Wilkinson dis mou
1849, 6, 12. Charles dis mou
1849, 11, 13. Christopher & fam gct Fairfield MM
1852, 2, 17. Aaron dis mou
1852, 3, 16. Robert dis
1852, 4, 13. Mary dis disunity
1854, 7, 11. Samuel dis mou

GARDNER
1837, 8, 23. Delilah m David T. MACY
1844, 8, 14. Keturah m Isaac JACKSON

1843, 7, 11. Asabel rocf Elk MM, dtd 1843,6,17
1850, 12, 17. Asahel con mou
1851, 4, 15. Asabel & w, Elizabeth, gct Back Creek MM, Ind.

GIBBS
1853, 7, 12. Mary (form Jay) dis mou

GREGG
----, --, --. Smith b 1820,12,20; m Rachel -----
Ch: William E. b 1841, 11, 6

1833, 2, 18. Rachel dis mou

HALL
1834, 10, 14. Anna (form Macy) dis mou

HARLEY
1845, 2, 11. Rebecca dis mou

HILL
1856, 10, 17. Elizabeth, dt Daniel & Dorcas Hutchins, d bur Randolph

1855, 9, --. Samuel C. rmt Elizabeth Z. Hutchins

HOLLINGSWORTH
----, --, --. James, s James & Sarah, b 1799, 1,31; m Lydia SWAIN, dt Sylvanus & Miriam, b 1808,7,31
Ch: Olive b 1829, 4, 3
Miriam " 1831, 6, 7
Stephen " 1832, 11, 22
Valentine " 1834, 8, 26

1833, 2, 18. James rocf Silver Creek MM, Ind., dtd 1832,11,24
1850, 4, 16. James & w, Lydia, gct Walnut Ridge MM

HOOVER
1828, 2, 23. Mary (form Curtis) dis disunity
1832, 10, 16. Elizann (form McCoole) dis mou

HOUGH
1840, 4, 14. Elijah Johnson gct Dover MM, Ind., to m Elizabeth Hough

HUTCHINS

1756, 5, 8. Benjamin Sr. b
----, --, --. James b 1771,1,13; m Sarah ----- b 1770,10,22
Ch: Davis b 1798, 12, 3
Ann " 1804, 2, 3
----, --, --. Benjamin Jr., s Benj. & Judith, b 1789,5,15 d 1855,5,19 bur Randolph; m Hannah VESTEL, dt Thos. & Amy, b 1789,5,23
Ch: Vestel b 1806, 7, 30
Josiah " 1808, 5, 1
Anderson Thompson " 1810, 10, 23
Meredith " 1811, 10, 19
Anderson " 1811, 10, 19
Isaac " 1814, 4, 5
Jesse " 1814, 4, 5
William " 1816, 8, 26
John " 1820, 9, 10
Hannah " 1823, 4, 17
Benjamin Xenia " 1825, 9, 17
Jemima Jane " 1829, 8, 2
----, --, --. Isaac, s Benj. & Judith, b 1787, 6,15; m Rebeckah JONES, dt Abijah & Rachel b 1791,4,22
Ch: Judith b 1810, 4, 5
Daniel " 1812, 4, 14
Tommy " 1814, 5, 30
David " 1816, 4, 11
Zelinda " 1818, 7, 13
Rhoda " 1820, 9, 19
Isaac " 1823, 9, 9
Rachel " 1825, 2, 22
Branston " 1827, 6, 7
Harris " 1830, 11, 1
Mary " 1835, 8, 12
1815, 2, 9. Benj., s Strangeman & Elizabeth, Montgomery Co., O.; m in Concord, Mary JENKINS, wd Wm., Montgomery Co., O.
1817, 11, 27. Lydia m Wm. JENKINS
1820, 2, 22. Daniel b
----, --, --. Jesse & Tamer
Ch: Fidelia b 1822, 11, 6
Irenia " 1825, 4, 18
Decylvia " 1829, 1, 19
Eli " 1832, 1, 4
Mary Jane " 1837, 6, 1
1828, 10, 2. Judith m Jas. SWALLOW
----, --, --. Josiah & Nancy
Ch: Mariann b 1830, 3, 7 d 1830, 3,15 bur Randolph Graveyard
Mahala b 1831, 5, 12

HUTCHINS, Josiah & Nancy, continued
Ch: Harrietann b 1833, 4, 28
Elizabeth " 1835, 11, 29
Jemima Jane" 1838, 1, 28
Andrew J. " 1840, 4, 17 d 1840, 4,17 bur Randolph Graveyard
1830, 9, 2. Meredith, s Benj. & Hannah, Montgomery Co., O.; m Elizabeth BROWN, dt Samuel & Sarah, Montgomery Co., O.
Ch: Matilda Jane b 1831, 5, 28 d 1832,11, 3 bur Randolph
Delilah Ann b 1833, 9, 28
1833, 6, 16. Tommy, s Isaac & Rebecca, Montgomery Co., O.; m in Randolph MH, Anna JONES, dt Stephen & Mary, Montgomery Co., O.
1836, 1, 27. Benj. d bur Randolph Graveyard
1837, 6, 22. Zelinda m John JONES
1840, 11, 26. Fidelia m Wm. D. JONES
1842, 10, 20. Irenia m Daniel JONES
1843, 8, 24. Daniel, s Jesse & Elizabeth, Montgomery Co., O.; m in Randolph MH, Jemima JONES, dt Stephen & Mary, Montgomery Co., O.
1854, 7, 21. Maryann m Samuel COPPOCK
1856, 11, 10. Isaac d bur Randolph
1858, 9, 18. Hannah, dt T. Vestal, d bur Randolph

1822, 7, 27. Jesse con mou
1828, 8, 23. Vestal con mou
1829, 7, 25. Josiah [Hutchens] con mou
1829, 12, 9. Nancy [Hutchens] (form Patty) dis mou
1834, 4, 15. Daniel H. gct West Branch MM, to m Dorcas Jones
1835, 4, 14. Anderson con mou
1835, 8, 11. Wm. con mou
1836, 3, 15. Elizabeth recrq
1836, 3, 15. Auston & Allen, minor s Vestal, recrq
1836, 5, 17. Wm. dis disunity
1837, 9, 12. Meredith & fam gct Mississinewa MM, Ind.
1837, 9, 12. Anderson & fam gct Mississinewa MM, Ind.
1837, 9, 12. Jesse Jr. gct Mississinewa MM, Ind.
1838, 7, 17. Isaac [Hutchens] Jr. con mou
1838, 9, 11. Merideth [Hutchens] & w, Eliza, & two ch rocf Mississinewa MM, Ind., dtd 1838,7,23
1838, 9, 11. Anderson [Hutchens] & w, Mary, & two ch rocf Mississinewa MM, Ind., dtd 1838,8,20
1839, 10, 15. David I. [Hutchens] dis mou
1841, 11, 16. Daniel recrq
1842, 3, 15. Meredith & w, Elizabeth, & ch gct Union MM
1842, 3, 15. Anderson [Hutchens] & w, Mary, & ch gct Union MM
1842, 3, 15. John [Hutchens] gct Mississinewa MM, Ind.
1843, 7, 11. John rocf Mississinewa MM, Ind., dtd 1843,6,16
1843, 11, 14. John gct Springfield MM, Ind., to m Frances Malinda Bond
1844, 3, 12. Meredith & fam rocf Union MM
1845, 2, 11. Daniel & fam gct Mississinewa MM, Ind.
1845, 4, 15. Josiah gct West Branch MM
1845, 6, 17. Jesse & ch gct Mississinewa MM, Ind.
1845, 11, 17. Benjamin H. dis mou
1846, 3, 11. Meredith & fam gct Mississinewa MM, Ind.
1847, 6, 15. John gct Springfield MM, Ind., to m Ann Hutchins
1847, 6, 15. Isaac J. con mou
1847, 9, 14. Vestal & fam gct Mississinewa MM, Ind.
1848, 3, 14. John gct Springfield MM
1848, 6, 13. Tommy & fam gct Mississinewa MM, Ind.
1854, 5, 16. Branson con mou
1855, 2, 13. Darius con mou
1855, 9, --. Elizabeth Z. rmt Samuel C. Hill
1856, 1, 15. Harris dis mou
1857, 12, 15. Harris recrq

IDDINGS
1829, 12, 26. Benjamin dis disunity
1831, 12, 24. Sally dis disunity
1832, 10, 16. Katharine Ann Edgar (form Iddings) dis mou
1842, 12, 14. Henry dis disunity
1844, 9, 11. Daniel dis disunity
1845, 1, 14. Alexander dis mou
1847, 8, 17. Wm. dis

INSCO
1831, 2, 18. Abel d bur Mill Creek
1842, 2, 14. Ann d bur Mill Creek (dt Thomas)

1822, 12, 23. James dis disunity

JACKSON
1844, 8, 14. Isaac, s Isaac & Ann, Crawford Co.; m in Mill Creek, Keturah GARDNER, dt William & Mary, Union Co., Ind.

JAY
----, --, --. John, s Wm. & Mary, b 1752,10,26 d 1829,4,23; m Elizabeth PUGH, dt Thos. & Ann McCoole-Wright, b 1755,9,6 d 1821,4,23
Ch: Jesse b 1773, 12, 8 d 1840, 9,25
Thomas " 1775, 6, 18 " 1815, 7,8
Ann
Mary
John " 1782, 2, 27 " 1814, 9, 1
Samuel " 1784, 1, 13 " 1859,12,14
Walter Denny " 1786, 7, 15 " 1865, 7, 8
William " 1788, 6, 19 " 1843, 8, 9

JAY, John & Elizabeth, continued
Ch: James b 1791, 11, 6 d 1845,10,22
Lydia " 1793, 5, 15 " 1830, 3,20
Jane " 1795, 9, 6 " 1871,12,22
----, --, --. Jesse, s John & Betty, b 1773,12, 8 d 1840,9,25 bur Mill Creek; m Sary BROOKS, dt James & Sary, b 1779,3,17
Ch: John b 1800, 9, 12
James " 1802, 4, 10
Thomas " 1804, 8, 28
Mary " 1806, 4, 2
Samuel " 1807, 9, 20
Jenny " 1809, 4, 24
----, --, --. Thomas & Mary
Ch: Rebeckah b 1806, 5, 15
John " 1809, 5, 8
Thomas " 1811, 8, 8
----, --, --. Samuel, s John & Betty, b 1784, 1,13; m Bathsheba PUGH, dt David & Rachel, b 1788,12,29 d 1850,1,3 bur Mill Creek
Ch: Virlinda b 1807, 6, 13
David " 1809, 1, 25
Rachel " 1811, 6, 15
Elizabeth " 1813, 10, 6
Job Pugh " 1816, 10, 28
Samuel " 1819, 2, 4
William " 1821, 2, 25
Thomas " 1822, 9, 11
Lydia " 1825, 10, 11 d 1849,10,22 bur Mill Creek
----, --, --. Walter D., s John & Betty, b 1786,7,15; m Mary MACY, dt Thos. & Anna, b 1789,12,7
Ch: Isaac b 1810, 11, 19 d 1880, 5,15 bur near Marion, Ind.
John b 1812, 6, 28
Thomas " 1813, 11, 22
Anna " 1816, 1, 3
Macy " 1818, 7, 24 d 1832, 3,31 bur Mill Creek
Elizabeth b 1821, 3, 28
William " 1823, 12, 17
Eli " 1826, 2, 19
Levi " 1828, 6, 16
1811, 8, 27. Mary d bur Mill Creek
1813, 6, 13. Jane m Thos. MACY
1813, 9, 29. James, s John & Betty, Miami Co., O.; m in Mill Creek, Martha COPPOCK, dt James & Hannah, Miami Co., O.
1814, 5, 4. John Jr. d bur Mill Creek
----, --, --. James, s John & Betty, b 1791, 11,6; m Martha COPPOCK, dt Jas. & Hannah, b 1798,6,17
Ch: Jonathan b 1815, 4, 1
William " 1816, 10, 13
Mary " 1818, 2, 28
Moses " 1819, 2, 21
Jesse " 1821, 2, 26
Elizabeth " 1822, 9, 3
Hannah " 1824, 4, 25
Enoch " 1825, 12, 25
Phebe " 1828, 4, 7
John " 1830, 9, 7
1815, 7, 8. Thomas d bur Mill Creek
1820, 8, 23. Susannah, dt Elisha & Rebecca, b
1821, 4, 11. Wm. d bur Mill Creek
1821, 4, 23. Betty d bur Mill Creek
----, --, --. John, s Jesse & Mary, b 1800,9, 12; m Keturah HOLLINGSWORTH, dt Jas. & Sarah, b 1800,8,18
Ch: James b 1822, 11, 22 d 1851, 4,15
Sarah " 1824, 8, 16 " 1848, 5, 3
Henry " 1827, 1, 20 " 1849,--,--
1822, 12, 17. William d bur Mill Creek
1823, 8, 27. Mary m Isaac JENKINS
1824, 3, 31. Verlinda m Robert JENKINS
1824, 5, 26. Rebecca m John MILES
----, --, --. Thomas m Eliza ----- b 1801,2,18
Ch: Joseph b 1825, 1, 22
Mary " 1826, 4, 29
Rebecca " 1827, 9, 15
Denny " 1829, 5, 28
Isaac " 1830, 12, 8
Daniel " 1832, 8, 5
Sarah " 1834, 4, 9
1826, 4, 11. Hannah d bur Mill Creek
1829, 4, 23. John d bur Mill Creek
----, --, --. Denny & Mary
Ch: Susannah b 1830, 10, 9
Cynthia Ann" 1832, 5, 5
Keturah " 1834, 3, 8
Elisha J. " 1835, 12, 4
Elvirah " 1837, 9, 2
Jesse " 1840, 2, 17
Thomas Elwood " 1842, 4, 16 d 1842, 6,17 bur Mill Creek
David Augustus b 1843, 5, 1
Mary " 1846, 1, 25
Denny " 1848, 11, 25
1830, 1, 27. Rachel m Samuel JENKINS
1830, 12, 30. Isaac, s Denny & Mary, Miami Co., O.; m in Randolph MH, Rhoda COOPER, dt Isaac & Elizabeth, Montgomery Co., O.
Ch: Allen b 1831, 10, 11
Milton " 1833, 5, 10
Wm. Denny " 1835, 1, 2
Abijah E. " 1838, 10, 12
Mary Elizabeth " 1842, 9, 23
----, --, --. David, s Samuel & Bathsheba (Pugh); m Sarah JONES, dt Elisha & Susanna (Hollingsworth)
Ch: Orlinda b 1832, 1, 7
Job P. " 1833, 7, 31
Elisha B. " 1835, 5, 8
1833, 9, 2. Sarah d bur Mill Creek
----, --, --. Jonathan & Ann
Ch: Charity b 1834, 8, 18
James " 1836, 4, 25
Elisha
Rebecca
1839, 10, 23. Anna m Samuel JONES
1840, 2, 8. Elizabeth, dt Wm., d bur Mill Creek

JAY, continued
1840, 4, 22. Thomas, s Walter D. & Mary, Miami Co., O.; m in Mill Creek, Sarah YOUNT, dt Henry & Elizabeth, Montgomery Co., O.
----, --, --. Job P., s Samuel & Bathsheba, b 1815,10,28; m Rachel -----
Ch: Mary
Elizabeth b 1841, 7, 26
1843, 4, 12. Lydia d bur Mill Creek
1843, 6, 21. Sarah m Enoch JONES
1847, 10, 12. Elwood, s James & Susannah, b
----, --, --. Enoch d 1848,3,22 bur 1848,3,22 bur Mill Creek
1848, 3, 30. Elwood d bur West Branch
1848, 4, 11. John d bur Mill Creek
1849, 1, 9. Ann d bur Mill Creek

1823, 3, 22. James con mou
1825, 2, 26. Thomas con mou
1826, 12, 23. James Jr. & fam gct Silver Creek MM
1827, 9, 22. Samuel Jr. con mou
1827, 10, 27. Thomas Jr. gct Union MM
1828, 9, 27. John Jr. & fam gct Silver Creek MM, Ind.
1829, 5, 23. David gct West Branch MM, to m Sarah Jones
1830, 3, 27. John & fam rocf Silver Creek MM, dtd 1830,1,23
1832, 2, 25. Samuel gct West Branch MM
1832, 8, 11. John Jr. gct West Branch MM, to m Rebecca Mote
1833, 4, 16. Jonathan gct West Branch MM, to m Anna Jones
1834, 2, 11. Six minor ch of Thos. recrq (s are Joseph, Denny, Isaac & Daniel)
1835, 6, 16. Eliza & dt recrq
1835, 9, 15. Thomas & fam gct Mississinewa MM, Ind.
1836, 8, 16. David & fam gct Mississinewa MM, Ind.
1838, 10, 16. Moses gct Union MM, to m Margaret Pierce
1839, 9, 17. Moses & w gct Union MM
1840, 8, 11. Job T. gct West Branch MM, to m Rachel Commons
1841, 3, 17. Jane & ch rocf Union MM, dtd 1841,2,-- (s named Henry)
1841, 4, 13. Thomas & w gct West Branch MM
1842, 10, 11. Jesse con mou
1844, 9, 11. Jesse con mou
1844, 12, 17. Thomas gct Back Creek MM, Ind.
1845, 1, 14. Samuel Jr. con mou
1846, 3, 11. Samuel & fam gct Back Creek MM, Ind.
1846, 8, 11. James gct West Branch MM, to m Susannah Jones
1847, 2, 16. Samuel Jr. & fam rocf Back Creek MM, Ind.
1847, 7, 13. Wm. con mou
1849, 3, 13. Jane dis disunity
1849, 10, 16. Eli gct Union MM, to m Mahalah Pearson
1849, 12, 11. Denny Jr. & fam gct Back Creek MM
1850, 1, 15. Henry gct Spiceland MM, Ind.
1850, 8, 13. James & w gct Spiceland MM,Ind.
1850, 8, 13. Mahalah rocf Union MM
1850, 9, 17. Isaac & w gct Mississinewa MM, Ind.
1850, 12, 17. Samuel Jr. & fam gct Back Creek MM, Ind.
1851, 2, 11. Jonathan dis mou
1852, 2, 17. Levi dis
1852, 9, --. James C. con mou
1852, 10, 12. Samuel gct Back Creek MM, Ind.
1853, 2, 15. Phebe dis
1853, 12, 13. Mary Gibbs (form Jay) dis mou
1854, 1, 17. Jesse dis mou
1854, 11, 14. Martha & fam gc
1854, 11, 14. Elizabeth gc
1856, 4, 15. Esther dis
1856, 7, 15. Elisha, Rebecca, Martha & Moses gct Wabash MM, Ind.
1856, 11, 11. Denny & w gct Mississinewa MM, Ind.
1857, 3, 17. James C. dis disunity
1857, 8, 11. Wm. dis jas

JENKINS
1755, 8, 17. William b
----, --, --. David & Elizabeth
Ch: David b 1760, 1, 24
Martha " 1766, 5, 19
----, --, --. David & Martha
Ch: Elizabeth b 1790, 12, 30
Rebeckah " 1792, 10, 2
Robert " 1794, 7, 23
Mary " 1796, 11, 7
Sarah " 1795, 7, 7
Martha " 1800, 9, 5
Isaac " 1802, 8, 25
Ann " 1805, 11, 29
----, --, --. Jesse & Hannah
Ch: Elisabeth b 1798, 4, 2
Rosannah " 1799, 12, 30
Phinehas " 1802, 1, 31
Samuel " 1805, 1, 12
Mary " 1808, 9, 14
Jesse " 1811, 8, 2
Hannah " 18--, 3, 27
----, --, --. Amos & Elizabeth
Ch: Samuel b 1801, 10, 13
Rosanna " 1808, 4, 14
Susannah " 1809, 10, 8
Elisha " 1812, 5, 15
Amos " 1815, 11, 9
1805, 11, 7. Samuel d bur Concord
1807, 3, 13. David d bur Concord
----, --, --. David & Ann
Ch: Isaac b 1808, 12, 2
Rebecca " 1810, 6, 2
Samuel R. " 1812, 3, 31
Ruth " 1814, 9, 12
Olive " 1816, 10, 14
David C. " 1832, 6, 30

JENKINS, continued
1812, 7, 2. Esther m Robert EVANS
1813, 11, 28. Wm. d bur Concord Twp. near Enoch Jenkin's
1815, 1, 16. Mary d bur Concord Twp. near Enoch Jenkin's
1815, 1, 24. Thomas d bur Concord Old Graveyard
1815, 2, 3. Enoch d bur Lower Concord
1815, 2, 7. Samuel d bur Lower Concord
1815, 2, 8. Hannah d bur Lower Concord
1815, 2, 9. Mary m Benj. HUTCHINS
1815, 2, 18. Hannah d bur Concord
1816, 3, 21. Amos d bur Concord
1816, 6, 27. Rebecca m Powel PEARSON
1816, 10, 3. Sarah m Christopher FURNAS Jr.
1817, 11, 27. William, s Wm. & Mary, b 1797, 6,4; m Lydia HUTCHINS, dt Benj. & Judith, Montgomery Co., O., b 1798,10,20
Ch: Elisa Ann b 1818, 11, 9
Anderson H." 1820, 2, 23
Dorothy " 1822, 2, 18
Benjamin " 1823, 11, 27
Mary " 1825, 9, 15
Phebann " 1827, 3, 3
Lucinda " 1829, 3, 16
Esther " 1830, 12, 19
Sarah " 1832, 12, 26
1818, 4, 2. Robert, s David & Martha, Miami Co., O.; m in Randolph MH, Jemima JONES, dt Abijah & Rachel, Montgomery Co., O.
Ch: Evan b 1819, 2, 19
Adila " 1821, 1, 13
Robert m 2nd in Mill Creek 1824,3,31, Verlinda JAY, dt Samuel & Bathsheba, Miami Co., O., d 1830,8,27
Ch: Rachel b 1825, 10, 2
Martha " 1827, 6, 24
Bathsheba " 1828, 8, 26
Robert m 3rd Ann -----
Ch: Verlinda b 1835, 2, 3
David Lindley " 1836, 9, 20
Abijah Milton " 1838, 6, 7
Jemima " 1840, 8, 11
Samuel Addison b 1842, 9, 26
1818, 7, 2. Sarah m Robert PEARSON
1819, 5, 29. Lydia, dt David & Ann, d
1821, 8, 21. Jemima d bur Randolph Graveyard
1822, 8, 29. Mary m Samuel FURNAS
1822, 9, 9. Elisa Ann d bur Concord Graveyard
1823, 8, 27. Isaac, s David & Martha, Miami Co., O.; m in Mill Creek, Mary JAY, dt Jesse & Sarah, Miami Co., O.
Ch: Sarah b 1824, 8, 19
David " 1826, 12, 20
Jesse " 1829, 6, 6
Robert " 1831, 6, 30
Ann " 1834, 3, 20
1823, 9, 28. Rebecca, ch David & Ann, d bur Concord
1824, 1, 29. Elizabeth m Hiram PEARSON
1825, 11, 22. Jesse d bur Concord
1826, 8, 19. John, s David & Ann, d bur Concord
1829, 6, 17. Elisha d bur Concord
1830, 1, 27. Samuel, s Amos & Elizabeth, Miami Co., O.; m Rachel JAY, dt Samuel & Bathsheba, Miami Co., O.
Ch: Enoch b 1830, 10, 21
Elizabeth " 1832, 7, 15
1833, 10, 10. Martha d bur Concord
1834, 2, 20. Robert, s David & Martha, Miami Co., O.; m in Concord MH, Ann PEARSON, dt Robert & Charity, Miami Co., O.
1834, 6, 19. Michael d bur Mill Creek
1836, 2, 25. Ann m Samuel PEARSON
1836, 9, 22. Susannah m Wm. PEARSON
1838, 1, 31. Robert Lindley, s Robert & Ann, d bur Concord
1842, 8, 25. Adila m Joshua COATE
1858, 4, 22. Rachel m Jonathan COATE
1859, 1, 20. Bathsheba m Clarkson F. COOK

1822, 4, 27. David Jr. dis disunity
1824, 4, 24. Wm. & fam gct Silver Creek MM,O.
1825, 10, 22. Phinehas dis disunity
1827, 12, 22. Wm. & fam, s Anderson & Benjamin rocf Short Creek MM, dtd 1827,9,22
1828, 1, 26. Amos dis disunity
1829, 5, 23. Isaac dis disunity
1830, 3, 27. Isaac dis disunity
1830, 6, 26. Jesse dis disunity
1830, 7, 24. Mary dis disunity
1830, 9, 25. Issachar dis disunity
1830, 11, 27. Eli & fam gct Vermillion MM,Ill.
1833, 7, 16. Samuel R. dis disunity
1835, 12, 15. Samuel gct Salem MM, to m Nancy Cook
1836, 4, 12. Margaey (form Pearson) dis mou
1838, 6, 12. Olive dis disunity
1839, 12, 17. Wm. & fam gct Springfield MM, Ind.
1840, 9, 15. Samuel gct West Grove MM, Ind., to m Sarah Russell
1841, 2, 16. Isaac & ch gct Mississinewa MM, Ind.
1841, 4, 13. Evans H. gct Center MM, to m Martha Shepherd
1842, 6, 14. David C. dis mou
1848, 8, 15. Evans H. & fam gct Center MM
1851, 6, 17. Evans H. & ch, Silas Newton, David Harry & Mary Elizabeth, rocf Center MM, dtd 1851,1,15
1853, 5, 17. Evans H. gct Hopewell MM, Ind., to m Emaline A. Lewis
1853, 12, 13. Emaline A. rocf Hopewell MM,Ind.
1857, 12, 15. Enoch dis mou & jas
1860, 8, 4. Abijah con mou

JESTER
1850, 12, 26. Lemuel F., s Wm. S. & Ann, Miami Co., O.; m in Concord MH, Mary PEARSON, dt Hiram & Elizabeth, Miami Co., O.

JESTER, continued
1848, 11, 14. Lemuel F. recrq
1852, 5, 11. Lemuel F. & w gct Spiceland MM, Ind.
1855, 1, 16. Lemuel F. & fam rocf Spiceland MM, Ind.
1857, 6, 16. Lemuel F. & fam gct Union MM

JOHNSON
1841, 10, 22. Elijah W. b

1822, 5, 25. James dis
1830, 1, 23. Nicholas dis mou
1832, 2, 25. David dis disunity
1832, 2, 25. William dis disunity
1835, 10, 13. Mary dis disunity
1840, 4, 14. Elijah gct Dover MM, Ind., to m Elizabeth Hough
1840, 7, 14. James con mou
1840, 10, 13. Cecilia dis disunity
1841, 5, 11. Synthia recrq
1843, 1, 17. Elam recrq
1843, 5, 16. Nancy Smith (form Johnson) dis mou
1844, 3, 12. Elam gct Springfield MM, Ind.
1845, 4, 15. James & fam gct White River MM, Ind.
1846, 1, 13. Elijah dis mou
1846, 7, 14. Mary dis jas
1854, 5, 16. Mary Ann & Julian, dt Nancy, recrq
1860, 9, 11. James Sr. recrq

JONES
----, --, --. Abijah, s Richard & Jemima, b 1767,11,15 d 1852,2,25; m Rachel HARRIS, dt Obediah & Rebecca, b 1771,8,5 d 1853, 11,17 both bur Randolph
Ch: Rebecca b 1791, 4, 22
Obadiah " 1793, 9, 30
Daniel H. " 1795, 8, 8
Jemima " 1797, 12, 26
David H. " 1800, 10, 4
Mary " 1804, 3, 2
James H. " 1806, 8, 10
Lydia Ann " 1810, 4, 4
----, --, --. Stephen b 1792,12,1; m Mary ----- b 1788,2,19
Ch: John b 1814, 2, 16
James " 1815, 7, 25
Anna " 1817, 4, 23
William " 1818, 5, 11
Jemima " 1820, 3, 17
Daniel " 1821, 12, 2
Stephen " 1823, 12, 1
Mark " 1826, 2,26
Simpson " 1828, 9, 6
Mary " 1829, 11, 28
1815, 3, 11. David d bur Randolph Graveyard
1818, 4, 2. Jemima m Robert JENKINS
1818, 7, 30. Elisha, s John & Margaret, Miami Co., O.; m in Concord, Rebecca PEARSON, dt Enoch & Ann, Miami Co., O.
----, --, --. Francis b 1797,4,25; m Mary ----- b 1801,2,4
Ch: Eliza b 1819, 2, 14
Richard " 1822, 11, 23
Nancy " 1824. 7, 25
Stephen " 1827, 6, 17
Nathan " 1830, 1, 20
Mary " 1832, 7, 9
Francis " 1835, 5, 4
1820, 8, 3. Obadiah, s Abijah & Rachel, Montgomery Co., O.; m in Concord MH, Ann PEARSON, dt Enoch & Ann, Miami Co., O.
Ch: David Winston b 1821, 7, 11
Abijah F. " 1823, 1, 14
Martha Ann " 1824, 10, 18
Robert B. " 1826, 7, 27
Enoch P. " 1828, 2, 26
Jonathan H." 1830, 1, 28
Jemima Ann " 1831, 9, 22
1821, 11, 29. Mary m Mark PATTY
1824, 6, 27. James d bur Randolph Graveyard
1833, 6, 16. Anna m Tommy HUTCHINS
1837, 6, 22. John, s Stephen & Mary, Montgomery Co., O.; m in Randolph MH, Zelinda HUTCHINS, dt Isaac & Rebecca, Montgomery Co., O.
1839, 10, 23. Samuel, s John & Sarah, Miami Co., O.; m in Mill Creek, Anna JAY, dt Denny & Mary, Miami Co., O.
1840, 11, 26. Wm. D., s Stephen & Mary, Montgomery Co., O.; m in Randolph MH, Fidelia HUTCHINS, dt Jesse & Tamer, Montgomery Co., O.
1842, 10, 20. Daniel, s Stephen & Mary, Montgomery Co., O.; m in Randolph MH, Irenia HUTCHINS, dt Jesse & Tamer, Montgomery Co., O.
1843, 6, 21. Enoch, s Elisha & Rebecca, Miami Co., O.; m in Mill Creek, Sarah JAY, dt John & Keturah, Miami Co., O.
1843, 8, 24. Jemima m Daniel HUTCHINS

1823, 3, 22. Francis & fam rqct Springfield MM, Ind.
1826, 10, 28. Daniel dis mou
1829, 5, 23. David Jay gct West Branch MM, to m Sarah Jones
1829, 5, 23. James dis mou
1829, 10, 24. Maryann dis
1833, 4, 16. Jonathan Jay gct West Branch MM, to m Anna Jones
1834, 4, 15. Daniel H. Hutchins gct West Branch MM, to m Dorcas Jones
1835, 4, 14. Obadiah & fam gct Mississineway MM, Ind.
1838, 1, 16. Francis & fam gct Mississinewa MM, Ind.
1844, 11, 12. Wm. D. & fam gct Mississinewa MM, Ind.
1844, 11, 12. Daniel & fam gct Mississinewa MM, Ind.
1846, 6, 16. Stephen & fam gct Mississinewa

JONES, continued
MM, Ind.
1846, 8, 11. James Jay gct West Branch MM, to m Susannah Jones
1847, 10, 12. John & fam gct Mississinewa MM, Ind.
1848, 11, 14. Lemuel C. Teague gct West Branch MM, to m Martha Jones
1849, 2, 13. Daniel rst at West Branch MM on consent of this mtg
1850, 4, 16. Stephen dis mou

JULIAN
1843, 1, 19. Charlotte d bur Mill Creek

1827, 2, 24. Azariah [Julin] recrq

KATHCART
1842, 2, 15. Priscilla (form Swallow) dis mou

KELLY
1855, 6, 12. Caroline (form Swallow) dis mou

KESLER
1832, 3, 24. Ruth dis mou

KNIGHT
1827, 8, 25. Kerenhappuck dis

LAMBERT
1853, 12, 13. John recrq

LEWIS
1853, 5, 17. Evans H. Jenkins gct Hopewell MM, Ind., to m Emaline A. Lewis

LONGSTRETH
1852, 10, 12. Wm. [Langstreath] & fam roc
1857, 4, 14. Wm. dis disunity

McCALLAM
1845, 4, 15. Mahala dis mou

McCLURE
1830, 9, 11. Robert d bur on Mississinewa

McCOOLE
1841, 6, 5. Charity d bur Mill Creek

1832, 10, 16. Elizann Hoover (form McCoole) dis mou
1835, 10, 13. Rachel & Graceann dis disunity
1844, 9, 11. William recrq
1857, 6, 16. Wm. dis disunity

MACY
----, --, --. Paul, s Joseph & Hannah (Hobbs), b 1740,5,3 d 1832,2,8; m Bethiah COLEMAN, dt John & Eunice, b 1744,8,3 d 1810,9,29
Ch: Eunice b 1764, 11, 30 d 1840, 8,13
m Isaac GARDNER
Thomas b 1765, 2, 28 " 1833, 2, 1
m Anna Sweet
Judith b 1767, 3, 22 " 1854, 8,20
m Hezekiah Starbuck
Matilda b 1770, 3, 6 d 1832, 5, 3
m Silas Worth
Jemima b 1772, 4, 6 " 1823,10,15
m Michael Weesner
Phebe b 1775, 4, 6 " 1775, 12,-
Lydia " 1777, 3, 27 " 1863,--,--
m Shuball Barnard
Paul b 1780, 1, 10 " 1868, 5,30
m Eunice Macy
Obed b 1782, 5, 26 " 1821, 2,21
m Mary Armfield
Hannah b 1784, 8, 11 " 1825,11,30
m John Cook
Phebe b 1789, 3, 10 " 1842, 1,19
m David Swain
----, --, --. Thomas, s Paul & Bethiah, b 1765 2,28; m Anna SWEET, dt John & Mary (Gardner), b 1768,9,29 d 1840,--,--
Ch: Mary b 1787, 12, 7 d 1868, 8, 6
Isaac " 1789, 8, 20 " 1790, 2,19
Thomas " 1791, 7, 18 " 1840, 1,10
Rhoda " 1793, 5, 5 " 1796, 7,--
John " 1795, 8, 8 " 1854, 1,17
Paul " 1798, 3, 6 " 1891,11,20
Elizabeth " 1800, 5, 18 " 1873, 5, 2
[West Grove p. 753
Jonathan " 1802, 9, 31(sic) See
Anna " 1804, 3, 29 " 1888, 6, 11
Phebe " 1806, 9, 22 " 1864, 9,--
Aaron " 1809, 5, 16 " 1886,11, 3
Lydia " 1811, 3, 26 " 1885, 7,31
----, --, --. Paul, s Paul & Bethiah, b 1780, 1,10; m Eunice MACY, dt Matthew & Lydia, b 1782,5,25
Ch: Phebe b 1802, 1, 17
Thomas " 1804, 9, 30
Lydia " 1806, 12, 19
Anna " 1809, 2, 10
Beulah " 1811, 2, 1
John G. " 1813, 9, 27
Daniel " 1818, 5, 28
Eunice " 1821, 2, 21
Obed " 1826, 5, 26
----, --, --. Stephen & Rebeckah
Ch: Anna b 1802, 6, 25
Catharine " 1804, 9, 13
John " 1806, 12, 28
Eli " 1808, 10, 31
Frances " 1810, 9, 18
Stephen " 1813, 2, 18
Nathan " 1818, 8, 27
Eunice " 1822, 7, 13
1813, 6, 13. Thomas, s Thos. & Anna, Miami Co., O.; m in Mill Creek, Jane JAY, dt John & Betty, Miami Co., O., b 1795,9,6
Ch: Jesse b 1814, 1, 15
Anna " 1815, 12, 2
John " 1818, 8, 11
Paul " 1819, 11, 4
Betty " 1821, 9, 4
Samuel " 1823, 9, 24
Enoch " 1825, 11, 22
Moses " 1828, 11, 15

MACY, Thomas & Jane, continued
Ch: Thomas J. b 1833, 3, 10
Phebe " 1835, 10, 4
1818, 10, 31. Nathan d bur Randolph Graveyard
1821, 7, --. Paul, s Thomas, d bur Mill Creek
1823, 1, 1. Deborah d bur Mill Creek
1825, 9, 28. Pheba m Gardner MENDENHALL
1826, 5, 31. Lydia m Samuel FURNACE
1828, 7, 30. Beulah m Wm. FURNAS
1831, 6, 28. Thomas, s Paul & Eunice, Miami Co., O.; m in Mill Creek, Mary PEARSON, dt Samuel & Ann, Miami Co., O.
1834, 6, 13. Jesse, s Thomas, d bur Mill Creek
1837, 8, 23. David T., s Paul & Eunice, Miami Co., O.; m in Mill Creek, Delilah GARDNER, dt Wm. & Mary, b 1818,9,1
Ch: Amanda b 1839, 1, 12
Laura " 1842, 10, 1
Emily " 1845, 10, 23
Lindley " 1847, 7, 31
1845, 4, 23. Eunice m Moses PEARSON
1845, 5, 1. Mary d bur Mill Creek
1846, 5, 20. Thomas, s Paul & Eunice, Miami Co., O.; m in Mill Creek, Maryann SWEET, dt Richard & Ann BATTEN, Miami Co., O., b 1802,10,26
Ch: Lydia b 1834, 4, 23
Eliza " 1835, 8, 25
Phebe " 1837, 7, 13
John " 1840, 1, 28
Paul " 1842, 9, 19
David " 1845, 4, 30
1846, 8, 16. Emily d bur Mill Creek

1824, 2, 20. Jonathan con mou
1825, 6, 25. John dis disunity
1826, 8, 26. Paul 3rd dis disunity
1827, 2, 24. Jonathan dis disunity
1827, 6, 23. Stephen & fam gct White Water MM, Ind.
1827, 2, 24. Jonathan dis disunity
1827, 6, 23. Stephen & fam gct White Water MM, Ind.
1830, 9, 25. Aaron dis mou
1834, 10, 14. Anna Hall (form Macy) dis mou
1836, 6, 14. Thomas dis disunity
1838, 2, 13. John G. dis mou
1839, 2, 12. John dis disunity
1839, 8, 18. Elizabeth Fox (form Macy) dis mou
1845, 7, 15. Joseph Beeson gct Salem MM, Ind., to m Hepsibah Macy
1845, 7, 15. Samuel dis mou
1847, 4, 13. Enoch dis mou
1848, 11, 14. Paul & w gct West Branch MM
1849, 3, 13. David S. & fam gct West Branch MM
1851, 1, 14. Thomas & fam gct Back Creek MM, Ind.
1852, 8, 17. Moses dis mou
1852, 9, --. Obed dis mou
1855, 1, 16. Thomas dis disunity

MENDENHALL
1825, 9, 28. Gardner, s Caleb & Susannah, Miami Co., O.; m in Mill Creek, Pheba MACY, dt Thomas & Anna, Miami Co., O.

1822, 3, 23. Richard dis mou
1822, 11, 23. Benjamin dis military service
1830, 9, 25. Joseph [Mendinghall) dis disunity
1833, 2, 18. Levi dis military service
1833, 9, 17. John dis disunity

MILES
1824, 5, 26. John, s William & Rachel, Miami Co., O.; m Rebecca JAY, dt Thomas & Mary, Miami Co., O.
1841, 3, 25. Samuel, s David & Jane, Miami Co., O.; m in Randolph MH, Nancy CURTIS, dt John & Katharine, Montgomery Co., O.

1829, 3, 28. Samuel & fam rocf Union MM, dtd 1829,3,7
1831, 5, 28. Samuel & fam gct Union MM

MILLER
1833, 10, 18. Nathaniel d bur Concord

1833, 2, 18. Robert rocf Springborough MM, dtd 1833,1,22
1833, 4, 16. Robert gct Springborough MM
1834, 2, 11. Nathan rocf Hector MM, N. Y., dtd 1833,7,10
1837, 7, 11. Sarah recrq

MILLION
1841, 4, 13. Marietta (form Pearson) dis mou

MILLS
1842, 3, 15. Mary (form Pearson) dis mou
1844, 1, 16. Chas. & w, Ann, rocf Miami MM, dtd 1843,11,22
1844, 9, 11. Charles & w, Ann, gct Miami MM

NEAL
----, --, --. James, s Wm., b 1781,1,12 d 1832,7,19; m Anna BALLENGER, dt James & Lydia, b 1771,2,8
Ch: Sarah b 1811, 3, 26
Mary " 1812, 11, 1
Mahlon " 1814, 3, 13
James B. " 1815, 11, 12

1833, 8, 13. James B. dis disunity
1834, 6, 17. Mahlon & fam gct Union MM
1837, 9, 12. Mahlon gct Mississinewa MM,Ind.

PATTY
1821, 11, 29. Mark, s James & Anna, Montgomery Co., O.; m in Randolph MH, Mary JONES, dt Abijah & Rachel, Montgomery Co., O.
1822, 8, 4. Rebecca d
1824, 9, 29. Mary m Benj. FURNAS
1837, 5, 29. Anna d bur Mill Creek

PATTY, continued
1828, 1, 26. James & fam (s, Lot & Hugh) rocf West Branch MM, dtd 1828,1,19
1829, 9, 26. Mark & fam, s Harvy, rocf West Branch MM, dtd 1829,4,18
1829, 12, 9. Nancy Hutchen (form Patty) dis mou
1830, 3, 11. Anna dis disunity
1831, 5, 28. James Jr. dis disunity
1831, 9, 24. Mark dis jH
1832, 3, 24. James dis jH
1832, 11, 13. Chas. dis jH
1833, 4, 16. Phebe dis disunity
1833, 4, 16. Elizabeth dis disunity
1834, 12, 16. Mary & ch gct White Water MM, Ind.
1837, 5, 18. Enoch dis mou
1839, 2, 12. Lot rocf West Branch MM, dtd 1838,5,17
1844, 9, 11. John dis mou
1846, 3, 11. Phebe & fam gct Union MM

PEARSON
----, --, --. Enoch, s Thomas & Ann, b 1761, 9,27; m Ann EVANS, dt Robert & Rebecca, b 1763,8,18
----, --, --. Enoch & Ann
Ch: Robert b 1785, 9, 26
Rebecca " 1789, 8, 30
Ann " 1793, 1, 17
Thomas " 1795, 5, 8
Isaac " 1798, 5, 19
----, --, --. Joseph & Meolia
Ch: Thomas b 1791, 5, 31
Hannah " 1793, 8, 19
James " 1795, 8, 25
Elizabeth " 1804, 11, 17
Amos " 1809, 3, 27
----, --, --. Benjamin & Elizabeth
Ch: Joseph b 1792, 11, 9
Sally " 1796, 6, 9
Noah " 1798, 5, 16
Ann " 1800, 6, 9
Benjamin " 1803, 12, 15
Elizabeth " 1806, 2, 26
Samuel " 1809, 5, 30
Thomas " 1811, 3, 22
William " 1813, 10, 17
----k --, --. Samuel & Mary
Ch: Enoch b 1794, 7, 26
Benjamin " 1796, 8, 27
Mary " 1799, 1, 17
Hiram " 1800, 10, 17 d 1885, 8,19
Rachel " 1803, 9, 25
John " 1806, 7, 25
Samuel " 1808, 10, 10
Sampson " 1810, 12, 27
David " 1813, 1, 27
Esther " 1815, 4, 27
Eli " 1818, 2, 2
----, --, --. Thomas & Olive
Ch: Samuel b 1802, 1, 24
Elijah " 1803, 3, 22
Ch: Elisha b 1804, 8, 14
Maryan " 1808, 10, 17
Josiah " 1811, 8, 30
Amos " 1813, 12, 15
Thomas " 1816, 4, 2
----, --, --. Robert & Charity
Ch: Sarah b 1805, 9, 21
Ann " 1807, 11, 8
John " 1809, 2, 9
Enoch " 1810, 12, 19
1810, 2, 2. Samuel d
1811, 6, 3. Charity d
1812, 8, 23. Mary d bur Mill Creek
1813, 10, 30. William d
1814, 6, 19. Joseph d bur Mill Creek
----, --, --. Robert m Catharine RICE
Ch: Mary b 1816, 6, 8
Charity " 1818, 2, 21
Rebeckah " 1819, 9, 6
Zilpah " 1821, 11, 15
Rice " 1823, 9, 22
Susannah " 1825, 9, 30
Robert " 1827, 10, 18
Thomas " 1830, 4, 11
Elihu " 1832, 4, 9
Catharine " 1834, 5, 31
1816, 6, 27. Powel, s Wm. & Hannah, Miami Co., O.; m in Lower Concord, Rebecca JENKINS, dt David & Martha, Miami Co., O.
----, --, --. Enoch, s Samuel & Mary (Coate), m Rosannah McCLURE, dt Robert & Margery (Pearson,Buffingham) sic
Ch: Margery b 1818, 7, 3
Samuel " 1820, 1, 7
Mary " 1821, 11, 29
Robert " 1823, 9, 25
John " 1825, 12, 23
Mahala " 1827, 12, 28
Benson " 1829, 12, 15
Rachel " 1832, 1, 20
Sampson " 1834, 5, 25
Ruth " 1836, 7, 21
Thurza " 1838, 7, 14
Enoch " 1840, 7, 12
1818, 7, 2. Robert, s William & Hannah, Miami Co., O.; m in Concord, Sarah JENKINS, dt David & Martha, Miami Co., O.
1818, 7, 5. Esther d bur Concord
----, --, --. Robert, s Wm. & Hannah; m Sarah -----
Ch: Nancy b 1819, 4, 30
Susannah " 1820, 9, 25
1818, 7, 30. Rebecca m Elisha JONES
-----, --, --. Benjamin & Ruth
Ch: Sarah b 1820, 11, 21
Esther " 1824, 3, 18
Valentine " 1827, 8, 16
Mary " 1834, 11, 11
1820, 8, 3. Ann m Obadiah JONES
1820, 10, 13. Thomas d bur Mill Creek
1821, 1, 26. Sarah d bur Concord
----, --, --. Thomas & Mary
Ch: Jesse b 1821, 8, 2

PEARSON, Thomas & Mary, continued
Ch: Moses b 1823, 3, 3
Levi " 1824, 12, 13
Ann " 1827, 2, 21
Ezra " 1829, 7, 8
Elizabeth " 1830, 12, 18
Job " 1832, 8, 30
Jane " 1834, 2, 25
William " 1836, 8, 6
Thomas " 1839, 5, 8
1823, 5, 28. Moses, s Benjamin & Esther, Miami Co., O.; m in Mill Creek, Sarah PEARSON, dt Robert & Charity, Miami Co., O.
1823, 9, --. Esther d bur Concord
1824, 1, 29. Hiram, s Samuel & Mary, Miami Co., O.; m in Mill Creek, Elizabeth JENKINS, dt Jesse & Hannah, Miami Co., O.
Ch: Mary b 1825, 11, 17
Jesse " 1827, 11, 7
Rosanna " 1829, 9, 30
Eli " 1831, 11, 26
Isaac " 1833, 9, 30
----, --, --. Isaac & Rachel
Ch: Seth W. b 1824, 9, 25
Esther " 1826, 12, 5
Henry " 1829, 2, 12
Mary Jane " 1831, 5, 11
Sarah Ann " 1833, 11, 16
Enoch S. " 1836, 7, 22
Rebecca C. " 1839, 4, 18
----, --, --. Benjamin & Nancy
Ch: Lydia b 1825, 3, 19
Mary " 1827, 2, 27
Prudence " 1829, 10, 7
Jesse " 1832, 5, 19 d 1833, 1,23
Paul " 1833, 12, 6
Elizabeth " 1836, 3, 12 " 1838,12, 6
Rosanna " 1838, 11, 14 " 1840, 1,12
Anna Jane " 1841, 1, 16
Rachel " 1843, 4, 12
1827, 8, 7. Isaac, s Samuel & Rachel, b
1827, 9, 28. Mary d
1829, 3, 3. Ann d bur Concord
1831, 9, 7. Prudence d bur Mill Creek
1831, 9, 28. Mary m Thos. MACY
1831, 10, 29. Mary d bur Mill Creek
1832, 9, 3. Amos d bur Concord
1834, 2, 19. Enoch, s Robert & Charity, Miami Co., O.; m in Mill Creek, Hannah COPPOCK, dt Moses & Lydia, Miami Co., O.
Ch: Elizabeth b 1834, 12, 12
Jonathan " 1836, 7, 20
Jane " 1839, 2, 25
Samuel " 1841, 3, 19
Jeremiah " 1843, 2, 9
Elmira " 1843, 2, 9
1834, 2, 20. Ann m Robert JENKINS
1834, 10, 1. Isaac R. d bur Concord
1834, 12, 28. Rachel d bur Union
1836, 2, 25. Samuel, s Benj. & Esther, Miami Co., O.; m in Concord MH, Ann JENKINS, dt David & Martha, Miami Co., O.
1836, 5, 28. Ann d bur Concord
1836, 9, 22. Wm., s Benj. & Esther, Miami Co., O.; m in Concord MH, Susannah JENKINS, dt Amos & Elizabeth, Miami Co., O.
1837, 3, 27. Jonathan, s Enoch, d bur Concord
1837, 8, 10. Esther d bur Concord
1842, 1, 17. Katharine d
1843, 1, 16. Anna Jane d bur Mill Creek
1845, 4, 23. Moses, s Benjamin & Esther, Miami Co., O.; m in Mill Creek, Eunice MACY, dt Paul & Eunice, Miami Co., O.
1846, 10, 10. Ann d bur Mill Creek
1847, 5, 12. Rebecca m Jacob DAVIS
1850, 12, 26. Mary m Lemuel F. JESTER
1853, 8, 24. Zilpah m Isom C. THOMAS
1854, 11, 22. Enoch, s Samuel & Ann, Miami Co., O.; m in Mill Creek, Anna PEARSON, dt Thos. & Anna MACY, Miami Co., O.
1822, 7. 27. Noah con mou

1823, 5, 24. Henry con mcd
1823, 12, 27. Isaac con mou
1824, 6, 26. Thomas dis disunity
1825, 3, 26. John gct White Water MM, Ind.
1825, 4, 23. Noah dis disunity
1825, 4, 23. Robert Jr. con mou
1825, 5, 28. Enoch Jr. dis disunity
1825, 5, 28. Benjamin con mou
1825, 10, 22. John rocf White Water MM, Ind., dtd 1825,8,20
1825, 11, 25. Samuel Jr. con mou
1826, 1, 28. John con mou
1826, 6, 24. Hyram & fam gct Union MM
1826, 7, 22. Thomas dis disunity
1826, 10, 28. Samuel Jr. dis disunity
1826, 12, 23. Samuel & fam rocf Union MM, dtd 1826,11,4
1827, 1, 27. John dis disunity
1827, 4, 28. Hiram & fam rocf Union MM, dtd 1827,4,7
1828, 4, 26. Benjamin dis disunity
1828, 8, 23. Enoch Jr. gct Union MM, to m Mary Coate
1828, 8, 23. Elijah dis mou
1830, 3, 27. Amos dis disunity
1830, 6, 26. Sampson dis disunity & military service
1830, 10, 23. Elisha dis disunity
1830, 11, 27. Robert & dt, Nancy, gct Vermillion MM, Ill.
1830, 11, 27. Hannah gct White Lick MM, Ind.
1832, 2, 25. Moses & fam (s, Timothy) rocf Union MM, dtd 1832,2,11
1832, 2, 25. Samuel Y. dis disunity
1832, 5, 15. Joseph Jr. dis disunity
1832, 8, 11. Thomas Jr. dis mou
1832, 9, 11. John dis disunity
1833, 4, 16. Enoch & fam gct Union MM
1833, 5, 14. John gct Duck Creek MM, Ind.
1833, 12, 17. Moses & fam gct Union MM
1834, 12, 16. David dis disunity
1835, 9, 15. Powell & fam gct Mississinewa MM, Ind.
1836, 7, 12. Joshua dis disunity

PEARSON, continued
1839, 1, 15. Eli dis mou
1840, 4, 14. Powell & three minor ch rocf Mississinewa MM, Ind., dtd 1840,2,14
1841, 4, 13. Marietta Million (form Pearson) dis mou
1841, 11, 16. Thomas gct Union MM, to m Abigail Anderson
1842, 3, 15. Mary Mills (form Pearson) dis mou
1843, 4, 11. William dis mou
1843, 5, 16. Powell dis mou
1844, 7, 16. Benjamin J. dis mou
1845, 10, 14. Samuel dis jas
1846, 6, 16. Enoch dis disunity
1846, 9, 15. Sarah dis
1847, 6, 15. Isaac Jr. dis disunity
1848, 8, 15. Robert W. dis mou
1848, 12, 12. Henry S. dis disunity
1849, 8, 14. Thomas Jr. dis disunity
1849, 10, 16. Eli Jay gct Union MM, to m Mahalah Pearson
1850, 3, 12. Seth W. gct Bloomfield MM, to m Nancy C. Stanley
1850, 4, 16. John dis mou
1850, 9, 17. Isaac C. gct Union MM, to m Louisa Coppock
1850, 9, 17. Levi gct Caesars Creek MM, to m Mary Spray
1851, 2, 11. Ruth dis disunity
1851, 3, 11. Jesse gct Union MM, to m Rachel Furnas
1851, 3, 11. Levi gct Union MM
1851, 4, 15. Valentine dis disunity
1851, 5, 13. Nancy C. rocf Bloomfield MM, Ind.
1851, 7, 15. Jesse dis mou
1851, 7, 15. Rosannah Coats (form Pearson) dis mou
1851, 12, 16. Moses W. dis disunity
1852, 2, 17. Rachel rocf Union MM
1852, 3, 16. Seth W. & fam gct Spiceland MM, Ind.
1852, 9, --. Isaac & ch gct Spiceland MM, Ind.
1852, 9, --. Henry C. gct Spiceland MM, Ind.
1853, 12, 13. Jesse & fam gct Union MM
1853, 12, 13. Eli dis mou
1854, 1, 17. Samuel & fam gct Red Cedar MM, Ia.
1854, 7, 11. Jane dis jas
1854, 12, 12. Ezra dis mou
1856, 1, 15. Paul M. dis mou
1856, 7, 15. Elmira, Nathaniel & Mathias gct Union MM
1856, 7, 15. Enoch Keifer gct West Branch MM
1857, 6, 16. Jeremiah gct Union MM

PEIRCE
1838, 5, 23. Gainer, s Samuel & Milly, Miami Co., O.; m in Mill Creek, Jane COPPOCK, dt Moses & Lydia, Miami Co., O.

1838, 4, 17. Noah Brooks gct Union MM, to m Melinda Pierce
1838, 10, 16. Moses Jay gct Union MM, to m Margaret Pierce

PETIT
1830, 7, 24. Elizabeth dis joining Baptists

PRAY
1846, 4, 14. Enos & fam rocf Elk MM, dtd 1846,3,21
1848, 4, 11. Enos & fam gct West Branch MM

RATCLIFF
1823, 5, 24. John rocf Springfield MM, dtd 1822,12,11

RICKET
1835, 11, 17. Thomas, s Abigail, rocf Cincinnati MM, dtd 1835,10,15
1843, 1, 17. Thomas dis disunity

RUSSELL
1815, 1, 12. Elizabeth d bur Concord Township near Enoch Jenkins
1831, 7, 4. Rosanna d bur Concord

1823, 6, 28. Isaac [Russel] dis mou
1840, 9, 15. Samuel Jenkins gct West Grove MM, Ind., to m Sarah Russell
1855, 5, 15. Elizabeth dis

SHEETS
1823, 5, 24. Jacob dis disunity

SHEPHERD
1840, 12, 15. Jesse & w & ch rocf Miami MM (s names Jacob, Amaziah Thomas & Allen)
1841, 4, 13. Evans H. Jenkins gct Center MM to m Martha Shepherd
1841, 6, 15. Jesse & fam gct Center MM
1851, 6, 17. Allen rocf Center MM, dtd 1851, 5,14
1851, 6, 17. Elizabeth & ch, Thomas & Mary Jane, rocf Center MM, dtd 1850,11,13
1851, 6, 17. Hannah rocf Center MM, dtd 1850,12,18
1854, 11, 14. Elizabeth & dt, Hannah & Mary Ann, gc
1857, 6, 16. Allen gct Center MM

SMITH
1843, 5, 16. Nancy (form Johnson) dis mou

SNYDER
1854, 11, 14. Mary gc

SPEAR
1835, 7, 14. Hannah (form Jenkins) dis mou

SPRAY
1850, 9, 17. Levi Pearson gct Cesars Creek MM, to m Mary Spray

STANLEY
1850, 3, 12. Seth W. Pearson gct Bloomfield

STANLEY, continued
MM, to m Nancy C. Stanley

STARBUCK
1830, 10, 23. Judith rocf Dover MM, dtd 1830, 9,16

STEDMAN
1852, 7, 13. Salie rocf Chester MM

SURFACE
1836, 11, 15. Cynthia dis disunity

SWALLOW
1828, 10, 2. James, s Silvanus & Elizabeth, Montgomery Co., O.; m Judith HUTCHINS, dt Isaac & Rebecca, Montgomery Co., O.

1830, 6, 26. James O. dis disunity
1833, 4, 16. John dis disunity
1836, 6, 14. Simpson dis disunity
1840, 9, 15. Catherine Ervin (form Swallow) dis mou
1842, 2, 15. Priscilla Kathcart (form Swallow) dis mou
1844, 10, 15. Judith dis
1847, 11, 16. Judith recrq
1850, 9, 17. Simpson dis mou
1853, 2, 15. Daniel dis mou
1855, 6, 12. Caroline Kelly (form Swallow) dis mou
1857, 3, 17. John dis mou

SWEET
1808, 10, 15. Lydia, dt Aaron & Elizabeth Conaway, b
1822, 8, 18. Anna, dt Solomon & Catharine, b
1846, 5, 20. Maryann m Thos. MACY

1822, 7, 27. Solomon recrq
1827, 7, 28. Solomon & fam gct White Water MM, Ind.
1842, 3, 15. Rebecca (form Conaway) dis mou

TALBERT
1857, 6, 16. Sylvanus & fam gct Salem MM, Ind.

TAYLOR
1827, 5, 26. Jonathan rocf Hopewell MM, dtd 1826,10,5, endorsed by Springborough MM, O., dtd 1827,4,24
1835, 5, 12. Jonathan dis mou

TEAGUE
1825, 6, 2. Samuel, s Samuel & Rebecca, Miami Co., O.; m Prudence COOPER, dt Isaac & Elizabeth, Montgomery Co., O.

1829, 5, 23. Samuel & fam rocf Union MM, dtd 1829,4,4
1833, 3, 12. Samuel & w, Prudence, & ch, gct Milford MM, Ind.
1836, 2, 16. Samuel & fam rocf Union MM, dtd 1836,1,13
1848, 11, 14. Isaac C. gct West Branch MM, to m Martha Jones
1850, 2, 12. Martha J. rocf West Branch MM
1850, 4, 16. Samuel & w, Prudence, & ch gct Mississinewa MM, Ind.
1850, 8, 13. Isaac & fam gct Mississinewa MM, Ind.
1851, 5, 13. Joseph C. gct Wabash MM, Ind.

THAYER
1831, 12, 24. Lydia dis mou

THOMAS
1853, 8, 24. Isom, s Isaiah & Elizabeth, Montgomery Co., O.; m in Mill Creek, Zilpah PEARSON, dt Robert & Katherine, Montgomery Co., O.

1824, 4, 24. Wm. gct West Branch MM
1824, 12, 25. Isaac dis mou
1850, 4, 16. Isaac & s, Stephen, rocf Mississinewa MM, Ind.
1851, 9, 16. Isaac & fam gct Wabash MM, Ind.

THOMPSON
1728, 3, 10. Joseph b
1813, 10, 22. Joseph d bur Concord

WAYMIRE
1838, 7, 17. Melinda dis mou

WEEKS
1836, 8, 16. Benjamin rocf Union MM, dtd 1836,7,13

WELCH
1831, 3, 3. Webster, s Samuel & Chloe, Warren Co., O.; m in Randolph MH, Mary COOPER, dt Isaac & Elizabeth, Warren Co., O., d 1840,6,2

WERTZ
1827, 7, 11. Delilah d

WILLIAMS
1805, 11, 24. Anna, dt Anna Davis, b
1834, 9, 6. Anna Davis d bur Randolph Gr Yd

WOLF
1836, 6, 14. Mariam (form Beason) dis mou

YOUNT
----, --, --. John & Mary
Ch: Henry b 1793, 9, 4
Delilah " 1795, 7, 29
Solomon " 1797, 7, 22
Frederick " 1799, 7, 30
Rebeckah " 1801, 11, 3
----, --, --. Henry & Elizabeth
Ch: Jesse b 1816, 2, 17
John " 1817, 5, 29
Sarah " 1819, 11, 15

YOUNT, Henry & Elizabeth, continued
Ch: Rebeckah b 1821, 3, 29
Davis " 1825, 1, 12
Enos " 1826, 5, 16
Andrew " 1830, 6, 28
1821, 5, 5. Insco, s Solomon & Joanna, b
1822, 10, 7. Mary Ann d bur Randolph Gr Yd
1822, 10, 20. Henry d bur Randolph Gr Yd
1822, 12, 1. John d bur Mill Creek
1824, 6, 12. Joanna d bur Mill Creek
1840, 4, 22. Sarah m Thos. JAY
1842, 7, 22. Mary d bur West Branch

1822, 1, 26. Frederick con mou

* * * * * * *

DAVIS
1764, 6, 21. Anna b

1828, 2, 23. Andrew & fam gct White Lick MM, Ind.
1828, 6, 28. Solomon dis mou
1832, 9, 11. Frederick dis disunity
1837, 11, 14. Jesse dis mou
1838, 1, 16. John dis mou
1842, 11, 15. Ann dis disunity
1845, 12, 16. Davis dis mou
1846, 8, 11. John C. dis mou
1848, 7, 11. Enos dis mou
1853, 2, 15. Andrew dis mou
1858, 10, 19. Solomon rst at West Branch MM on consent of this mtg
1859, 10, 11. Frederick rst at West Branch MM on consent of this mtg

ZIGLER
1840, 5, 12. Elizabeth dis mou

ADDITIONAL RECORDS

These additional records of Mill Creek were found after all other material was prepared for publication and paged. This made it necessary to insert the following extracts with special paging.

BARNARD
1822, 9, 28. Rebecca recrq
1823, 6, 28. Lotty recrq of mother, Rebecca

BEESON
1813, 8, 28. Mary rocf Deep Creek MM, N. C., dtd 1812,12,7
1814, 9, 24. Sarah rocf Deep Creek MM, N. C., dtd 1814,5,7
1814, 12, 24. Sarah Peelle (form Beeson) dis mcd
1818, 3, 28. Betsy & Mariam [Beason] recrq of mother, Mary

BROOKE
1819, 7, 24. Hannah rocf West Branch MM, O., dtd 1819,7,17

BUFFINGTON
1819, 8, 28. Sarah recrq

BUNKER
1812, 5, 23. Welmet & dt, Rebecca, recrq
1815, 6, 24. John & fam gct White Water MM, Ind.

CAMPBEL
1820, 3, 25. Sarah rocf Bush River MM, S. C., dtd 1819,10,2, endorsed by Caesers Creek MM, O.
1820, 12, 23. Isabel [Cambell] con mcd
1821, 9, 22. Rebecca & Sarah recrq of mother, Sarah

CLARK
1819, 3, 27. Hariot (form Jenkins) con mcd

COBLE
1812, 4, 25. Sarah (form McMunn) con mcd

COFFIN
1818, 4, 25. Adam & fam gct White Water MM, Ind.

COOK
1814, 1, 22. John & fam gct White Water MM, Ind.

COOPER
1821, 2, 24. Elizabeth & ch, Prudence, Mary & Rhoda, rocf West Branch MM, O.

COPPOCK
1814, 3, 26. Hannah & dt, Martha, rocf Miami MM, O., dtd 1814,1,26

COX
1816, 4, 27. Charity rocf Miami MM, O., dtd 1815,6,28, endorsed by West Branch MM, 1816,3,28
1819, 9, 25. Jonathan & fam gct New Garden MM, Ind.

DAVIS
1817, 7, 26. Mary (form Johnson) con mcd
1817, 10, 25. Catharine & dt, Mary & Anna, recrq
1817, 10, 25. John & fam gct New Garden MM

DUNCAN
1812, 5, 23. Mary recrq of her father, Amos

EMBREE
1813, 12, 25. Mary rocf Union MM, dtd 1813,12, 4
1817, 3, 22. Mary gct Union MM

FURNACE
1817, 3, 22. Sarah [Furnice] gct Ceasars Creek MM, O.
1823, 11, 22. Martha con mcd

HODGINS
1816, 10, 26. Robert & fam gct Stillwater MM, O.

HOLLINGSWORTH
1816, 11, 23. Elizabeth (form Hutchins) dis mcd

HOOVER
1820, 5, 27. Rebecca con mcd
1822, 1, 26. Rebecca rqct West Branch MM

HUTCHENS
1814, 8, 27. Sarah & dt, Mary & Ann, rocf Deep Creek MM, N. C., dtd 1814,5,7
1815, 2, 25. Clarey [Hutchins] rocf Deep Creek MM, N. C., dtd 1814,5,7, endorsed by White Water MM, Ind.
1816, 11, 23. Elizabeth Hollingsworth (form Hutchins) dis mcd
1817, 11, 22. Hannah Hutchins recrq
1819, 10, 23. Mary Jones (form Hutchens) con mcd

IDDINGS
1814, 5, 28. Sarah & dt, Maryan, rocf West Branch MM, O., dtd 1814,4,23

INGLE
1813, 11, 27. Mary (form Jenkins) dis mcd

JAY
1813, 4, 24. Samuel & fam gct Miami MM, O.
1815, 8, 29. Bersheba & dt, Verlinda, Rachel & Elizabeth, rocf Miami MM, O., dtd 1815, 6,28
1822, 6, 22. Keturah rocf Silver Creek MM,

JAY, continued
dtd 1822,4,22
1824, 1, 24. Lydia & dt, Levina, recrq

JEFFERS
1811, 10, 26. Rebecca con mcd

JENKINS
1811, 8, 24. Esther con attending two mcd
1813, 3, 27. Elizabeth co
1813, 11, 27. Mary Ingle (form Jenkins) dis mcd
1814, 4, 23. Elizabeth Pettit (form Jenkins) con mcd
1818, 5, 23. Elizabeth co
1819, 3, 27. Hariot Clark (form Jenkins) con mcd

JOHNSON
1812, 7, 25. Mary & dt, Mary & Cisley, rocf Fairfield MM, dtd 1812,6,27
1816, 7, 27. Mary & dt, Judith, recrq
1817, 7, 26. Mary Davis (form Johnson) con mcd

JONES
1813, 8, 28. Jemima & dt, Anna & Elizabeth, rocf Deep Creek MM, N. C., dtd 1811,10,5
1816, 11, 23. Jemima rocf Fairfield MM, O., dtd 1816,10,26
1817, 7, 26. Anna Pierce (form Jones) con mcd
1819, 1, 23. Rebecca gct West Branch MM, O.
1819, 10, 23. Mary & dt, Anna, recrq
1819, 10, 23. Mary (form Hutchins) con mcd
1820, 3, 25. Jemima & fam gct Springfield MM, Ind.
1822, 9, 28. Jemima gct Springfield MM, Ind.

JULIAN
1816, 3, 23. Marjery rocf Miami MM, O., dtd 1815,11,22
1820, 12, 23. Charlotte rocf Bush River MM, S. C., dtd 1820,11,4

KINDLEY
1820, 5, 27. Betty & dt, Sarah, Elizabeth & Ruth, rocf Miami MM, O., dtd 1820,4,26
1821, 3, 24. John & fam gct West Grove MM, Ind.

LAMB
1814, 1, 22. Josiah & fam gct White Water MM, Ind.

McCOY
1821, 8, 25. Huldah & ch recrq

McCLURE
1817, 12, 27. Rosanna Pearson (form McClure) con mcd

McCOOL
1823, 11, 22. Charity & dt, Elizann, Rachel & Joaceann, rocf West Branch MM, O., dtd 1822,11,16

McMUNN
1812, 4, 25. Sarah Coble (form McMunn) con mcd

MACY
1820, 10, 20. Eunice & dt, Lydia, Anna & Beulah, rocf New Garden MM, N. C., dtd 1820, 8,26

MENDENHALL
1820, 5, 27. Deida & dt, Jane & Polly, rocf Ceasars Creek MM, O., dtd 1820,4,28

NEAL
1816, 7, 27. Mary rocf New Hope MM, Tenn., dtd 1816,5,20
1823, 11, 22. Rachel rocf Union MM, dtd 1823, 11,1

NEWMAN
1818, 7, 25. Mary rocf White Water MM, Ind., dtd 1818,6,27

PATY
1815, 1, 28. Phebe & dt, Mary & Rebecca, rocf West Branch MM, O., dtd 1816(?)1,26

PEARSON
1811, 8, 24. Mary dis
1812, 5, 23. Milly co
1813, 6, 24. Sarah & Ann, dt Robert, rocf West Branch MM, dtd 1813,4,22
1814, 9, 24. Hannah & dt, Susannah, rocf New Garden MM, N. C., dtd 1814,5,7
1815, 1, 28. Phebe rocf West Branch MM, dtd 1816,1,26
1815, 9, 23. Olive co
1816, 1, 27. Catharine rocf White Water MM, Ind., dtd 1815,12,30
1817, 10, 25. Mary & Amy, ch Samuel, rocf Miami MM, O., dtd 1817,9,24
1817, 12, 27. Rosanna (form McClure) con mcd
1818, 2, 28. Delpha recrq
1820, 8, 26. Ruth rocf New Garden MM, Ind., dtd 1820,7,15
1821, 3, 24. Mary rocf Union MM, dtd 1821,3,3
1824, 1, 24. Rachel con mcd

PEEL
1814, 12, 24. Sarah (form Beeson) dis mcd

PETTIT
1814, 4, 23. Elizabeth (form Jenkins) con mcd

PIERCE
1817, 7, 26. Anna (form Jones) con mcd
1817, 8, 23. John & fam gct Union MM
1820, 5, 27. Elizabeth con mcd
1821, 2, 24. Elizabeth gct Springfield MM, Ind.

RATLIFF
1822, 9, 28. Sisley con mcd

SCOTT
1816, 7, 27. Rebecca recrq

SWALLOW
1815, 8, 29. Lydia gct White Water MM, Ind.
1821, 7, 28. Fanny rqcuc

SWEET
1816, 3, 23. Edith rocf Deep River MM, N. C.
1822, 2, 23. Catharine con mcd

THAYER
1821, 5, 26. Elizabeth con mcd
1822, 6, 22. Elizabeth gct West Branch MM, O.

THOMAS
1819, 11, 27. Sarah & dt, Una, rocf Bush River MM, S. C., dtd 1819,3,6

THORNTON
1813, 6, 26. -----, minor dt recrq of father, Thomas
1818, 6, 27. Sarah & dt, Mary Abby Rebecca & Anna, rocf West Branch MM, O., dtd 1818,6, 25
1821, 3, 24. Thomas & fam rqct West Branch MM, O.

WERTZ
1814, 8, 27. Delilah (form Yount) con mcd

YOUNT
1812, 3, 28. Rosanna recrq
1814, 9, 24. Delilah Wertz (form Yount) con mcd
1820, 2, 26. Joanna con mcd
1821, 8, 25. Elizabeth rocf West Branch MM, O., dtd 1821,8,18
1822, 5, 25. Ann con mcd

UNION MONTHLY MEETING

Union Monthly Meeting was set off from West Branch Monthly Meeting 1 Mo. 2, 1813. John Coate and Esther Pearson were clerks, William Elleman was treasurer, and Benjamin Pearson, recorder. Samuel Teague and Rebecca Teague were elders and Benjamin Coppock, Samuel Coate, Anne Coppock, and Luraneh Coate were overseers. Other names were Hollingsworth, Iddings, Hasket, Miles, Pemberton, Peirce and Embree.

RECORDS

ABBOTT
1838, 11, 21. Samuel M., s John & Sarah, Miami Co., O.; m in Union, Rebecca MILES, dt Wm. & Mary, Miami Co., O.

1817, 7, 5. Sarah [Abbot] rocf West Branch MM, O., dtd 1817,6,26
1821, 3, 3. Mary con mcd
1821, 4, 7. Mary [Abbot] gct West Branch MM, O.
1839, 3, 13. Rebecca gct West Branch MM, O.

ALLISON
1848, 2, 16. John E. Pemberton gct West Branch MM, O., to m Sarah Allison
1849, 7, 18. Anne (form Coppock) con mcd

ANDERSON
1841, 11, 25. Abigail m Thomas PEARSON

1826, 4, 1. Abigail con mcd

ANTHONY
1838, 3, 14. Samuel Coate gct West Branch MM, O., to m Harriet Anthony

BAILEY
----, --, --. James E. b 1810,8,9; m Rebecca PEARSON, dt Benj. & Esther (Furnas), b 1809,10,4 d 1844,3,25

Ch:			
Almedia	b 1831, 1, 28	d 1832, 8, 6
Albert	" 1832, 5, 14	
Eliza	" 1833, 10, 21	
Benjamin	" 1835, 5, 7	
Esther	" 1836, 12, 23	
Josiah	" 1838, 10, 17	
Moses	" 1840, 2, 12	
James	" 1841, 9, 7	
Robert	" 1843, 5, 10	

1831, 4, 2. Rebecca con mcd
1831, 12, 3. James E. rocf Dover MM, O., dtd 1831,6,6
1847, 6, 16. James E. con mcd
1852, 1, 15. Thos. Chalkley & Rebecca Ann, ch James E., recrq
1852, 2, 18. James E. & ch gct New Garden MM

BALLENGER
1826, 4, 1. Benjamin T. dis mcd
1826, 7, 1. Jonathan dis
1831, 5, 7. Jesse dis neglect & deviating from plainness
1831, 7, 2. James W. dis mcd, neglect & deviating from plainness
1833, 6, 12. Iddings dis neglect & deviating from plainness
1838, 7, 18. John dis training with militia
1841, 5, 12. Lydia gct Mississinewa MM, Ind.
1842, 8, 17. Phebe dis departing from plainness
1843, 10, 18. Lydis dis

BARKER
1863, 4, 15. Samuel Coate gct Pleasant Hill MM, Ind., to m Naomi Ann Barker

BARRETT
1841, 5, 12. Mary & Phebe gct Mississinewa MM, Ind.

BINGHAM
1832, 3, 3. Joseph L. Coate gct Dover MM, to m Agnes [Bangham]
1832, 8, 15. Mary rocf Greenplain MM, O., dtd 1832,5,26
1834, 4, 16. Mary & ch gct Dover MM

BLACK
1844, 10, 16. Delila (form Coate) dis mcd

BLACKMORE
1897, 1, 2. Henry, Clifford, Carrie & Forest recrq

BOLDIE
1895, 4, C. Goldic recrq
1897, 1, 2. Thomas, Charity & Sylvia [Bolding] recrq

BOYCE
1895, 4, 6. Wilbur L. recrq
1895, 11, 2. Lulie [Royse] recrq
1896, 11, 7. Wilbur [Royse] relrq to Christian Ch

BOYD
1853, 3, 17. Jonathan D., s Adam & Elizabeth, Boone Co., Ind.; m in Union, Mary B. PEIRCE, dt Samuel & Milly, Miami Co., O.

1823, 11, 1. Ann rocf West Branch MM, O., dtd 1823,10,13
1833, 6, 12. Anna gct West Branch MM, O.
1853, 12, 14. Mary B. gct Sugar Plain MM, Ind.

BROOKS
1838, 2, 21. Noah, s John & Patience, Miami Co., O.; m in Union, Melinda PEIRCE, dt Samuel & Milly (Iddings), Miami Co., O.

Ch:		
Milly P.	b 1839, 2, 2	
Elizabeth J.	" 1841, 12, 14	
Ruth P.	" 1844, 7, 21	
Lemuel	" 1847, 3, 26	d 1847, 3,26
Manson	" 1848, 2, 17	" 1848, 2,17
Elvira	" 1850, 5, 11	" 1851, 7,22
John J.	" 1857, 12, 15	

1842, 3, 23. Martin, s John & Patience, Miami Co., O.; m in Union, Elmira F. PEIRCE, dt Samuel & Milly (Iddings), Miami Co., O.

Ch:		
Thomas Lindley	b 1843, 7, 27	
Mary Jane	" 1845, 4, 2	

BROOKS, Martin & Elmira F., continued

Ch:			
Isaac	b 1847, 3, 10	d 1852,10, 6
Rhoda Thomas	" 1849, 6, 25	
Calvin	" 1851, 5, 22	
Hannah E.	" 1856, 11, 20	d 1871, 2,20
Henry J. (or B.)	" 1861, 12, 17	" 1866, 12,15
Emma R.	" 1865, 3, 23	" 1866,12,25

1838, 5, 16. Malinda gct Mill Creek MM
1839, 4, 17. Noah & w, Malinda, & dt, Milly, rocf Mill Creek MM, dtd 1839,4,16
1842, 1, 12. Martin recrq
1858, 11, 17. Noah & w, Malinda, & ch gct Back Creek MM, Ind.
1897, 1, 2. Dora recrq

BROWN
1814, 3, 5. Samuel, Montgomery Co., O.; m in Union, Mary TUCKER, Miami Co., O.

1814, 6, 4. Mary & ch gct West Branch MM, O.
1816, 5, 4. Samuel Jr. & w, Sarah, & ch, Nancy, Elizabeth & Joshua, rocf West Branch MM, O., dtd 1816,1,25
1818, 3, 7. Samuel & fam gct West Branch MM, O.
1820, 3, 6. Samuel & s, Joshua, rocf Union MM, endorsed from West Branch MM, O.
1820, 6, 3. Sally & dt, Nancy, Elizabeth & Mary, rocf Union MM, dtd 1818,7,3, endorsed by West Branch MM
1820, 10, 7. Samuel dis
1821, 4, 7. Hannah con mcd
1822, 10, 5. Hannah gct West Grove MM
1825, 7, 2. Nancy & Joshua gct West Branch MM, O.
1829, 3, 7. Samuel & fam & Elizabeth Brown gct Mill Creek MM
1832, 2, 5. Joshua rocf West Branch MM, O., dtd 1832,1,24
1839, 7, 17. Joshua dis mcd
1843, 5, 16. Samuel dis mcd
1843, 9, 13. Jane Young (form Brown) dis mcd
1896, 9, 5. Ivah E. recrq

CABLE
1851, 8, 13. Eunice dis

CADWALLADER
1892, 1, 2. Achilles gct Miami MM, O.

CAMPBELL
1897, 1, 2. Fred recrq

CARROLL
1830, 9, 4. Elizabeth rocf Newberry MM, Tenn., dtd 1830,8,7
1838, 6, 13. Elizabeth gct Sugar River MM, Ind.

CAVENDER
1894, 3, 3. Martha recrq

CECIL
1896, 5, 2. Ardella & ch, Russell Teague, Harley J. & Mabel Florence, recrq

CLEGG
1890, 4, 5. Thomas gct West Branch MM, O.

COATE
----, --, --. Marmaduke & Mary

Ch:		
Esther	b 1766, 9, 3	
Moses	" 1768, 9, 5	
Henry	" 1770, 8. 18	d 1848,11,24 bur Union
Samuel	" 1772, 8, 28	
Sarah	" 1774, 12, 11	
James	" 1777, 6, 23	
William	" 1779, 1, 2	
John	" 1785, 7, 19	
Jesse	" 1788, 1, 3	

----, --, --. Henry, s Marmaduke, d 1848,11, 24 ae 78y 3m 6d; m Mary HASKETT, d 1809, 5,28 upward of 38y

Ch:		
Lydia	b 1793, 10, 23	
Isaac	" 1795, 9, 7	
Mary	" 1797, 6, 28	
Samuel	" 1799, 7, 8	d 1850, 6,22 bur Union
Rhoda	" 1801, 7, 24	" 1823, 3,23 bur Union
Rachel	" 1804, 11, 6	
Esther	" 1807, 12, 21	

Henry m 2nd Rebecca WILSON d 1827,12,28 ae 35y bur Union

Ch:		
Robert	b 1816, 10, 2	
Henry W.	" 1818, 2, 16	
Caleb	" 1821, 2, 1	
David M.	" 1823, 7, 9	d 1852, 1,26 bur Union
John H.	" 1825, 9, 24	

----, --, --. Moses & Elizabeth

Ch:	
Jane	b 1795, 7, 19
Mary	" 1797, 11, 15
Thomas	" 1799, 5, 1
Esther	" 1801, 2, 13
Joseph	" 1802, 10, 22
William	" 1805, 5, 6
Margaret	" 1807, 1, 16
Samuel	" 1808, 12, 29
Benjamin	" 1810, 9, 23
Elizabeth	" 1812, 9, 18
Moses	" 1815, 12, 2
Jesse	" 1818, 3, 1

----, --, --. Samuel d 1867,1,26 ae 96y 4m 22d m Margaret COPPOCK, dt Joseph & Jane, b 1781,5,10 d 1847,2,19

Ch:		
James	b 1802, 4, 28	d 1825,12,30 bur Union
Joseph	" 1803, 11, 15	
Sarah	" 1804, 12, 18	
John	" 1807, 10, 29	

COATE, Samuel & Margaret, continued
Ch: Henry b 1809, 2, 9
Jane " 1810, 6, 27
Thomas " 1812, 12, 16
William " 1815, 2, 2
Mary " 1817, 1, 14
----, --, --. William m Elizabeth MILES
Ch: Mary b 1807, 12, 22
Jane " 1811, 2, 21
David " 1814, 2, 20
Sally " 1817, 8, 20
Elizabeth " 1824, 9, 11
----, --, --. John m Esthor TEAGUE, dt Samuel & Rebecca (Furnas) d 1826,2,1
Ch: Joseph T. b 1810, 1, 11
Elijah " 1812, 7, 20
Hiram " 1815, 9, 8
Rebecca " 1817, 6, 21
Martha " 1819, 3, 26
Lindley M. " 1821, 9, 9
1809, 5, 28. Mary d bur Union
1816, 3, 6. Jean m David MILES
----, --, --. Jesse, s Mary & Marmaduke (Coppock) b 1788,1,3 d 1837,8,7; m Mary JOHNSON, dt Benj., b 1790,7,24 d 1865,12,4
Ch: Eleanor b 1811, 5, 5
Benjamin J." 1813, 3, 16
Josias " 1816, 12, 9
Elizabeth " 1819, 2, 22
Thomas C. " 1821, 3, 22
David J. " 1823, 8, 15
Mary " 1826, 2, 24
Sarah " 1828, 9, 7
Juli Ann J." 1831, 8, 9
----, --, --. James d 1839,12,5 ae 62y 5m 10d m Luranah TEAGUE, dt Sam'l & Rebecca, d 1863,2,6 ae 70y 6m 10d
Ch: Jonathan b 1815, 1, 24
Samuel T. " 1818, 4, 13
Joshua " 1821, 2, 8
T. Elwood " 1825, 7, 1
Mary " 1827, 9, 24
Esther " 1829, 2, 9
1819, 1, 6. Isaac, s Henry & Mary (Hasket), Miami Co., O., d 1819,6,14 ae 23y 9m; m in Union, Mary WEEKS, dt Benjamin & Abigail, Miami Co., O.
Ch: Isaac b 1819, 12, 6
1820, 11, 8. Mary m Thomas PEARSON
1820, 12, 6. Mary m Wm. JAY
1822, 9, 25. Marmaduke d bur Union upward of 84y
----, --, --. Joseph & Lydia
Ch: Delila b 1824, 12, 30
Benjamin " 1827, 5, 23
Abiather Davis " 1829, 5, 3
Sarah Jane " 1832, 11, 4 d 1850, 6,17 bur Union
1824, 4, 14. Mary m Samuel KELLY
1824, 6, 9. Samuel, s Henry & Mary, Miami Co., O., d 1847,2,28 ae 47y 7m 20d; m in Union, Mary MILES, dt Jonathan & Mary, Miami Co., O.
Ch: Rhoda b 1825, 12, 25
1825, 5, 11. Esther m David MILES
1826, 5, 10. Rachel m Samuel PEARSON
1826, 2, 1. Esther d
1828, 9, 10. Mary m Enoch PEARSON
1829, 2, 11. Sarah m Wm. MILES
1830, 10, 6. Eleanor m Layton COPPOCK
1830, 12, 8. Henry, s Marmaduke & Mary, Miami Co., O., d 1848,11,24 ae 78 bur Union; m in Union, Eunice COPPOCK, dt Alexander & Hester COTHRAN, Miami Co., O., d 1866, 5,15 ae 72y 3m 2d
1830, 12, 22. John, s Samuel & Margaret (Coppock) d 1871,3,11, Miami Co., O.; m in Union, Phebe MILLS, dt Jonathan & Mary (Pearson), Miami Co., O., d 1838,12,29 bur Union
Ch: Samuel M. b 1831, 9, 12 d 1863, 2,22
Mary Ann " 1833, 7, 12
Abijah " 1835, 9, 7 " 1836,11,26 bur Union
Margaret " 1837, 11, 19
John m 2nd Nancy FINNEY, b 1808,1,23
Ch: Seth b 1843, 1,27 d 1843,10,12
Robert " 1844, 10, 5
Alfred " 1847, 3, 20 d 1847, 8,15 bur Union
Benjamin C." 1850, 2, 12
John " 1856, 7, 7
----, --, --. Benjamin, s Moses; m Phebe HAWORTH, dt James
Ch: Prudence b 1831, 10, 20
Esther " 1834, 7, 20 d 1836,10,15
James " 1836, 6, 27
Ann " 1837, 9, 29
Jane " 1839, 10, 10
Sarah " 1841, 9, 20
Alfred " 1844, 6, 1
Mary " 1847, 4, 18
Sampson " 1849, 5, 18
David H. " 1854, 5, 27
Wade Lorton" 1858, 4, 8
1832, 6, 20. Jane m Thomas JAY
1832, 6, 27. Elijah, s John & Esther, Miami Co., O.; m in Union, Rebecca COPPOCK, dt Benjamin & Susannah, Miami Co., O.
1832, 12, 19. Henry, s Samuel & Margaret, Miami Co., O.; m in Union, Mary KELLY, dt Moses & Mary (Teague) d 1838,1,27
Ch: Alfred b 1835, 2, 4 d 1836, 4,16 bur Union
Harvey " 1836, 9, 9
Henry m 2nd Sally -----
Ch: Rachel b 1842, 2, 3
Sarah " 1843, 3, 30
1833, 1, 27. Mary, w Henry, d bur Union
1833, 9, 25. Margaret m Joseph HOLLINGSWORTH
1834, 8, 20. Mary m Joseph F. JAY
1835, 8, 12. Jonathan C., s James & Lurana (Teague), Miami Co., O., b 1815,1,24 d 1872,5,6; m in Union, Elizabeth JAY, dt Wm. & Mary (Furnas), b 1815,7,29 d 1856,

COATE, Jonathan C. & Elizabeth, continued
5,14
Ch: Mary L. b 1836, 5, 8
John J. " 1837, 9, 20 d 1838,11,28
James " 1839, 10, 29
William J. " 1841, 12, 2 " 1842, 5, 6
Lurana " 1843, 12, 19
Rebecca " 1846, 1, 16
Sarah " 1849, 7, 5
Elizabeth " 1852, 5, 5
Jonathan C. m 2nd 1858,4,22 Rachel JENKINS, dt Robert & Verlinda, b 1825,10,2 d 1858, 10,--
Jonathan C. m 3rd 1860,6,21 Martha COMPTON, dt Henry & Rachel (Mendenhall), b 1828,12, 22 d 1887,3,24
Ch: Rachel Ema b 1861, 4, 13
Elwood " 1864, 10, 29 d 1864,12,12
Esther " 1866, 11, 23
Lydia Alice" 1868, 11, 25
1835, 10, 21. Benjamin Johnson, s Jesse & Mary, d 1870,9,19; m in Union, Mary JONES, dt John & Sarah, Miami Co., O.
Ch: Calvin b 1836,12, 12
Dorcas " 1838, 7, 22 d 1912, 3, 6
m ----- PEMBERTON
Rachel b 1840, 1, 19
John " 1841, 2, 28
Sarah " 1843, 1, 12
Josias " 1845, 2, 16 d 1863,10,17
Elen " 1846, 9, 27
Hyram " 1847, 12, 11
Elizabeth " 1850, 5, 31
Jesse C. " 1851, 10, 11
Mary B. " 1854, 11, 25 d 1863, 6,16
Jonathan " 1856, 2, 24
William " 1862, 4, 26
1836, 4, 1. Elizabeth C. m Isaac COPPOCK
1836, 8, 25. Thomas, s Samuel & Margaret (Coppock), Miami Co., O., b 1812,12,16; m in Lickbranch, Eliza RAGAN, dt Zadock & Sarah, Darke Co., O., b 1819,7,24
Ch: Sarah R. b 1837, 11, 29
Mary " 1839, 11, 27
Emmeline " 1842, 3, 2
John " 1843, 4, 2 d 1845,12,17
bur Union
Nancy " 1846, 3, 3
Alvah " 1849, 5, 31
1836, 10, 15. Esther d bur Union
1836, 9, 27. James d bur Union
1837, 8, 7. Jesse d bur Union
1838, 3, 22. Josias, s Jesse & Mary, Miami Co., O.; m in Lickbranch, Sarah C. TUCKER, dt Nicholas & Charity, Miami Co., O.
Ch: Jesse M. b 1839, 7, 20
Martha F. " 1841, 7, 12
Mary M. " 1843, 7, 14
Thomas J. " 1846, 3, 31
David J. " 1850, 5, 30
Anna Jane " 1854, 2, 23
1838, 9, 20. Henry W., s Henry & Rebecca, Miami Co., O.; m in Lickbranch, Rebecca D. MILES, dt Jonathan & Mary(Pearson), Miami Co., O., b 1819,12,13 d 1840,10,11
Ch: David b 1839, 5, 23 d 1852, 1,26
Samuel " 1840, 9, 3
Henry W. m 2nd Phebe COTHRAN, dt Jesse & Hannah, b 1815,2,23 d 1846,12,24
Ch: Rachel b 1845, 4, 14
Phebe " 1846,12, 1
Henry W. m 3rd Hannah PEIRCE. dt Sam'l & Milly, b 1825,1,26
Ch: William b 1849, 6, 10 d 1850, 7,19
Lindley
Elwood " 1859, 3, 11 " 1859, 4, 9
Clarkson " 1864, 8, 23
----, --, --. William, s Samuel; m Mary -----
Ch: Jane b 1839, 11, 15 d 1864, 5, 3
Elizabeth " 1841, 4, 18
Eliza " 1842, 12, 5
James " 1844, 9, 22
Albert " 1846, 8, 15
Abijah " 1848, 6, 19
Daniel " 1850, 6, 9
Samuel " 1852, 3, 15
Thomas " 1854, 2, 17 d 1857, 4, 7
bur Union
Martha E. " 1856, 1, 4
Clara " 1858, 1, 3
Mary A. " 1860, 7, 4
Ira " 1863, 3, 16
Infant " 1866, 2, 26
1840, 11, 25. Caleb, s Henry & Rebecca (Wilson), Miami Co., O., b 1821,2,1; m in Union, Lydia PEMBERTON, dt John & Drucilla, Miami Co., O.
Caleb m 2nd Catherine -----
Ch: Lydia Jane b 1860, 1, 13
Florence "
Eveline " 1862, 3, 21
1842, 6, 21. Mary m Aaron COPPOCK
1842, 7, 20. Henry W., s Henry & Rebecca, Miami Co., O.; m in Union, Phebe COTHRAN, dt Jesse & Hannah, Miami Co., O.
----, --, --. Joshua, s James & Luranah; m Adila JENKINS, dt Robt. & Jemima (Jones) b 1821,1,13
Ch: Rachel J. b 1843, 7, 4 d 1857, 2, 4
Abijah " 1845, 5, 1
Robt. Harris " 1847, 10, 13
Esther " 1850, 8, 10
Martha Emaline " 1853, 6, 7
Thos. Elwood " 1855, 9, 6
Lindley M. " 1858, 1, 16
Jemima J. " 1861, 3, 29
Celestia " 1863, 8, 10
1843, 9, 20. David M., s Henry & Rebecca, Miami Co., O.; m in Union, Mary TEAGUE, dt Moses & Jane, Miami Co., O.
1843, 10, 26. Rhoda m Samuel B. JONES
----, --, --. Robert, s John & Nancy (Crew) (nee Finney), b 1844,10,5; m Elizabeth

COATE, Robert & Elizabeth, continued
Jones, dt Alex. & Anna, b 1847,1,1
Ch: Walter V. b 1867, 12, 8 d 1870, 5, 8
Warren D. " 1870, 8, 28 " 1871, 8, 6
Tula May " 1873, 6, 14
Robert m 2nd ----, 3,29, Jemima J. COATE, dt Joshua & Adilah (Jenkins) b 1861,3,29
1846, 12,24. Phebe d bur Union
1847, 2, 19. Margaret d ae 65y 9m 9d (an elder)
1847, 11, 8. Moses d bur Union ae 79y 2m 3d
1848, 5, 24. Henry W., s Henry & Rebecca, Miami Co., O.; m in Union, Hannah C. PEIRCE, dt Samuel & Milly, Miami Co., O.
1848, 11, 21. Prudence m Wm. PEMBERTON
1844, 10, 11. Rebecca d bur Union (1844 or 1848)
1849, 8, 26. Elizabeth d bur Union
1850, 3, 20. Esther m Philemon JONES
1850, 5, 22. John H., s Henry & Rebecca (Wilson), Miami Co., O.; m in Union, Jane COPPOCK, dt Joseph & Rachel (Hollingsworth), Miami Co., O.
Ch: Henry b 1851, 2, 18
Warren " 1855, 8, 20
Orlistus " 1857, 3, 25 d 1862, 4, 5
Lorettie " 1862, 4, 5
1850, 7, 9. William d bur Union
1850, 9, 25. Mary m Ephraim COPPOCK
1852, 9, 23. Juliann m Moses K. MILES
1858, 3, 24. Samuel M., s John & Phebe, Miami Co., O.; m in Union, Mary J. COATE, dt Jonathan & Elizabeth, Miami Co., O.
----, --, --. Caleb, s Henry & Rebecca, b 1821, 2,1; m Cathern ----- b 1831,10,23
Ch: Lydia Jane b 1860, 1, 13
Florence
Eveline " 1862, 3, 21
1860, 1, 25. Jesse, s Josiah & Sarah, Miami Co., O.; m in Union, Fannie J. PEMBERTON, dt Elijah & Sarah, Miami Co., O.
----, --, --. Calvin, s Benj. J. & Mary (Jones) m Sarah -----
Ch: J. C. F. b 1862, 6, 30
Ambrose B. " 1864, 6, 26 d 1865, 8,28
Mary
Emily " 1866, 1, 28
----, --, --. Jesse M. & F. J.
Ch: Oscar Elmer b 1862, 11, 6
Charley " 1870, 7, 8
1863, 12, 23. Abijah J., s Joshua & Adila, Miami Co., O.; m in Union, Almeda COPPOCK, dt Benjamin & Esther, Miami Co., O., d 1865,12,27 ae 21y 1m 28d
Ch: Clara Almeda b 1864, 11, 5
David Orland " 1865, 12, 13
----, --, --. Samuel b 1840,9,3; m Naomi ----- b 1843,7,27
Ch: Elvina b 1865, 3, 18 d 1866,11, 6
David Wm. " 1867, 11, 19
Ch: Mary Elma b 1873, 3, 1
----, --, --. Benjamin, s John & Nancy, b 1850,2,12; m Esther COATE, dt Joshua & Adilah
Ch: Infant b 1870, 9, 4 d 1870, 9,13
Loren M. " 1873, 4, 21
----, --, --. R. Harris, s Joshua; m Vashti MILES, dt Wade
Ch: Mary
Mattie A.
1870, 4, 21. Margaret m David J. COPPOCK

1814, 10, 1. Mary recrq
1816, 7, 6. Henry & w, Rebecca, & ch, Isaac, Mary, Samuel, Rhoda, Rachel & Esther, rocf Miami MM, O., dtd 1816,6,26
1821, 9, 1. Thomas gct West Branch MM, O., to m there
1822, 11, 2. Joseph gct West Branch MM, O., to m Lydia Davis
1824, 1, 3. Lydia rocf West Branch MM, O.
1826, 9, 2. Wm. & fam gct Honey Creek MM, Ind.
1828, 7, 5. John gct Dover MM, to m Mary Johnson
1828, 7, 5. Wm. con mcd
1828, 8, 2. Joseph dis neglect
1828, 12, 6. Sarah rocf West MM
1828, 12, 6. Mary B. & s, Lewis Johnson, rocf Dover MM
1830, 6 5. Isaac gct Cincinnati MM, O.
1830, 12, 4. Thomas dis departing from truth
1831, 2, 5. Margaret & ch, Elizabeth & Allen, recrq
1831, 5, 7. Benjamin con mcd
1832, 3, 3. Joseph L. gct Dover MM, to m Agnes Bangham
1832, 10, 17. Agnes rocf Dover MM, dtd 1832, 6,14
1833, 7, 17. Sarah & ch gct West Branch MM, O.
1833, 9, 18. Phebe & dt, Prudence, recrq
1833, 9, 18. Lydia & ch, Delila, Benjamin & Abiather D., rocf Vermillion MM, Ill., dtd 1833,2,2
1834, 11, 12. Abigail rocf Mill Creek MM
1834, 11, 12. John & fam gct Centre MM
1834, 11, 12. John & fam gct Centre MM
1835, 2, 18. Joseph T. & fam gct Centre MM
1835, 9, 16. Elijah & fam gct Center MM
1836, 2, 17. Robert con mcd
1836, 6, 15. Bethany & dt, Rebecca, recrq
1836, 10, 12. Abigail gct Mill Creek MM
1837, 1, 18. Wm. dis mcd
1838, 1, 17. Elijah & w, Rebecca, & ch rocf Ceasars Creek MM, O., dtd 1837,10,26
1838, 3, 14. Samuel gct West Branch MM, O., to m Harriet Anthony
1838, 6, 15. Moses Jr. dis
1838, 8, 15. Harriett rocf West Branch MM, O., dtd 1838,5,17
1838, 12, 12. Wm. gct West Branch MM, O., to

COATE, continued
m Mary Tucker
1839, 4, 17. Samuel, s Moses, dis mcd & neglect
1839, 5, 15. Mary rocf West Branch MM, O., dtd 1839,4,18
1839, 11, 18. Allen & Elizabeth, minors, gct Back Creek MM, Ind.
1839, 11, 13. Esther gct Back Creek MM, Ind.
1839, 12, 18. Robert & fam gct Mississinewa MM, Ind.
1840, 3, 18. Henry gct New Garden MM, to m Sally Fellow
1840, 6, 17. Sally rocf New Garden MM, dtd 1840,5,16
1842, 1, 12. Jesse dis
1842, 3, 16. John gct West Branch MM, O.
1842, 7, 13. Joshua gct Mill Creek MM, to m Adila Jenkins
1842, 12, 14. Nancy rocf West Branch MM, O., dtd 1842,10,13
1843, 1, 18. Adila rocf Mill Creek MM, dtd 1843,1,12
1843, 8, 16. Henry Jr. & fam gct Mill Creek MM, Ind.
1844, 4, 17. Rebecca dis joining Separatists
1844, 4, 17. Elijah dis disunity & neglect
1844, 10, 16. Delila Black (form Coate) dis mcd
1844, 11, 13. Harriet dis jas
1844, 11, 13. Anne Lacey (form Coate) dis mcd
1844, 12, 18. Samuel T. dis neglect
1846, 1, 14. David J. dis jas
1846, 4, 15. Joshua & fam gct Mill Creek MM
1846, 8, 12. Caleb & fam gct Mississinewa MM, Ind.
1847, 7, 14. Thomas Elwood dis mcd & neglect
1848, 6, 14. Thomas E. rst
1849, 6, 13. Sarah Williams (form Coate) dis mcd
1850, 8, 14. Mary, minor, recrq
1852, 6, 16. David M. & w, Mary, & ch gct West Branch MM, O.
1852, 9, 15. Isaac, s Thos., dis mcd
1852, 9, 15. Abiather Davis dis mcd
1852, 9, 15. Benjamin Jr. dis mcd
1853, 12, 14. Elizabeth Green (form Coate) dis mcd & jas
1853, 12, 14. Ellen Green (form Coate) dis mcd & jas
1853, 12, 14. Aldes, Susanna & Ellwood, minors, gct Red Cedar MM, Ia.
1855, 10, 17. Hugh dis
1858, 3, 17. Jonathan C. gct Mill Creek MM, to m Rachel Jenkins
1854, 4, 14. Joshua & fam rocf Mill Creek MM, dtd 1858,4,13
1859, 5, 18. Thomas & w, Eliza, & fam gct West Branch MM, O.
1860, 6, 13. Jonathan C. gct West Branch MM, O. to m Martha Compton
1860, 9, 12. James rpd mcd; retained mbrp
1860, 9, 12. Lydia & ch, Rebecca, Mary & Lydia Jane, rocf Honey Creek MM, Ind., dtd 1860,8,11
1860, 11, 14. John Jr. rpd mcd; dropped from mbrp
1860, 12, 12. Martha C. rocf West Branch MM, O., dtd 1860,11,15
1860, 12, 12. Caleb rocf Honey Creek MM, Ind., dtd 1860,11,10
1861, 9, 18. Calvin W. con mcd
1862, 2, 12. Candas recrq
1862, 9, 17. John J. recrq
1862, 9, 17. Eliza & dt, Laura Alice, recrq
1863, 4, 15. Samuel gct Pleasant Hill MM, Ind., to m Naomi Ann Barker
1867, 7, 17. Robert rpd mcd; retained mbrp
1867, 12, 18. Abijah J. rpd mcd; retained mbrp
1867, 12, 18. Robert W. rpd mcd; retained mbrp
1868, 5, 13. James Jr. rpd mcd; dropped from mbrp
1869, 1, 13. Abijah J. & fam gct West Branch MM, O.
1869, 2, 17. Robert H. & w gct West Branch MM, O.
1870, 2, 16. Abijah rpd mcd; dropped from mbrp
1870, 8, 17. Isaac gct Cottonwood MM, Kans.
1870, 10, 12. Caleb & fam rocf West Branch MM, dtd 1870,9,15
1870, 11, 16. Catherine recrq
1871, 2, 15. Benj. C. rpd mcd; retained mbrp
1872, 1, 17. Jesse M. dis joining Free Masons
1872, 2, 14. Calvin & w, Candace, & ch gct Smyrna MM, Ia.
1872, 12, 18. Thomas J. rpd mcd; dropped from mbrp
1889, 10, 5. Wm. relrq
1889, 10, 5. Mary J. relrq
1890, 11, 1. T. E. rocf West Branch MM, O., dtd 1890,10,11
1891, 9, 5. Abijah & w, Anna, & ch, Leonard J., Bertha M. & Ethel C., rocf New Garden MM, dtd 1891,7,18
1891, 12, 5. Benjamin & w, Esther, & ch gct New Garden MM, Ind.
1893, 10, 7. T. E. Jr. & fam gct Muncie MM, Ind.
1896, 2, 1. Lindley M. & fam gct New London MM, Ind.
1896, 6, 6. L. Maurice rocf New Garden MM, Ind.
1896, 6, 6. Lucy A., w Maurice, rocf New Garden MM, Ind.
1897, 1, 2. Carlton recrq
1898, 4, 2. Benjamin & w, Esther, & ch, Rufus & Ernest, rocf New Garden MM

COMPTON
1866, 6, 13. Rachel gct West Branch MM, O.

CONAWAY
1824, 5, 1. Elizabeth & ch, James, Lydia, Samuel, Eli, Abigail & Rebecca, rocf Mill Creek MM, dtd 1824,4,24

CONAWAY, continued

1824, 11, 6. Elizabeth & ch gct Mill Creek MM

COOPER

1825, 5, 7. Samuel Teague Jr. gct Mill Creek MM, to m Prudence Cooper

COPPOCK

----, --, --. Aaron b 1762,9,20 d 1837,2,22 ae 74y bur Union; m Margaret TUCKER, dt Abe, of Tenn., b 1770,4,4 d 1848,5,6 ae 78 bur Union
(rem from Tenn. after their fam was grown up)

----, --, --. Benjamin d 1850,3,3 ae 70y 4m 3d; m Susannah JAY, dt Wm., d 1859,6,14 ae 80y 6m 25d
Ch: William b 1797, 3, 10
Ephraim " 1798, 9, 8
Margaret " 1800, 9, 18
Jane " 1802, 11, 20
Joseph " 1805, 2, 7
Elizabeth " 1807, 2, 3
Thomas " 1809, 1, 15
Susannah " 1811, 3, 28
Rebecca " 1813, 8, 17
Isaac " 1815, 6, 27
Benjamin " 1817, 7, 18
Aaron " 1819, 6, 26

1809, 11, 22. Moses b 1787,3,8 Newberry Dist., S. C., d 1877,1,9, Miami Co., O.; m Lydia JAY b 1793,3,18 d 1830,3,20

----, --, --. William, s Joseph & Jane, S. C., b 1788,4,14 d 1813,11,28; m Eunice COTHRAN dt Alex. & Hester, b 1793,3,13
Ch: Susannah b 1811, 2, 2 d 1840, 7,14 bur Union
Joseph " 1812, 4, 7
Hester " 1813, 12, 17 d 1821,10,23 bur Union

1813, 11, 28. William, s Joseph, d bur Union

1813, 6, 9. Jesse, s Joseph & Jane, Miami Co., O.; m in Union, Anna COTHRAN, dt Alexander & Hester, Miami Co., O.

1816, 4, 10. Cynthy, dt Samuel & Elizabeth, b

1816, 11, 6. Jane m Isaac HOLLINGSWORTH

1817, 7, 9. William, s Benjamin & Susannah (Jay), Miami Co., O.; m in Union, Charity HOLLINGSWORTH, dt Henry & Sarah (Cook), b 1797,12,25 d 1839,2,18 bur Union
Ch: Henry b 1818, 3, 18 d 1840, 5,13 bur Union
Zimri " 1819, 11, 11
Sally " 1821, 6, 11 d 1840, 2, 3 bur Union
James " 1823, 9, 6
Delilah " 1824, 12, 1 " 1840, 5, 1 bur Union
Eli " 1828, 6, 6
Esther " 1831, 4, 26 d 1844, 6,23 bur Union
Rachel " 1834, 7, 23
Ch: Isaac b 1836, 5, 9 d 1839, 3,19 bur Union
Jane " 1838, 5, 1 " 1840,12,13 bur Union

1821, 4, 9. Anna d ae 55y 11m 14d

1823, 9, 10. Jane d bur Union ae 71y 11m 12d

1824, 8, 11. John, s John & Anny (Jay), Miami Co., O.; m in Union, Rachel HOLLINGSWORTH, dt Joel & Anny (McConnell), Miami Co., O.

1825, 8, 10. Joseph, s Benjamin & Susannah (Jay), d 1862,2,3; m in Union, Rachel HOLLINGSWORTH, dt Henry & Sarah (Cook), Darke Co., O.
Ch: Ephraim b 1826, 7, 10
m Sampson " 1828, 3, 22
Jane " 1829, 10, 1
Eunice " 1831, 8, 12 d 1849, 9,22 bur Union
Mary Ann " 1833, 8, 23
Benjamin C." 1836, 5, 30 " 1841, 9,17 bur Union
Isaac C. " 1839, 3, 21
David " 1841, 6, 27
Elizabeth " 1841, 6, 27
Sarah " 1845, 9, 27

1826, 4, 5. Joseph, s John & Anna, Miami Co., O.; m in Union, Susannah HOLLINGSWORTH, dt Henry & Sarah, Darke Co., O.

1828, 4, 9. Anna, w John, d bur Union

1830, 6, 9. Susannah m John E. PEMBERTON

1830, 10, 6. Layton, s John & Anne, Miami Co., O.; m in Union, Eleanor COATE, dt Jesse & Mary, Miami Co., O.

1830, 12, 8. Eunice m Henry COATE

1832, 6, 27. Rebecca m Elijah COATE

1833, 4, 24. Moses, s James & Hannah, Miami Co., O.; m in Union, Mary ELLEMAN, dt Wm. & Jane, Miami Co., O., d 1852,5,25 ae 50y 9m 4d bur Union

1833, 8, 21. Elizabeth m Isaac ELLEMAN

1834, 9, 24. Joseph, s Wm. & Eunice, Miami Co., O.; m in Union, Sarah F. JAY, dt Wm. & Mary, Miami Co., O.

----, --, --. Elijah, from Tenn. & Ohio, s Aaron; m Mary -----
Ch: William b 1836, 12, 13 d 1861, 6,14
Elizabeth N. " 1840, 3, 1 " 1845, 1,10
Aaron J. " 1843, 3, 12 " 1845,11, 4
Eleanor B. " 1847, 1,20
Elizabeth E. " 1858, 2, 27
Henry H. " 1860, 2, 20

----, --, --. James, s Moses & Lydia J., b 1814,11,11 d ----,3,4 ae 68y 3m 5d; m Eleanor H. EVANS, dt Robert, b 1817,2,4 d 1847,1,20
Ch: Esther b 1837, 8, 17
Samuel " 1839, 10, 7
Lydia " 1841, 9, 30

1836, 4, 1. Isaac, s Benjamin & Susanna, Miami Co., O., b 1815,6,27; m in Lick-branch, Elizabeth C. COATE, dt Jesse &

COPPOCK, Isaac & Elizabeth, continued
Mary (Johnson), Miami Co., O., b 1819,2,22 d 1856,12,12
Ch: Harvey b 1838, 2, 7
Henry " 1840, 8, 24 d 1863, 5,10
Mary C. " 1844, 2, 28
Jesse C. " 1846, 1, 24
Susannah " 1852, 10, 26
Benjamin " 1855, 3, 28 d 1856, 5, 4
1839, 4, 24. Benjamin, s Benjamin & Susannah (Jay), Miami Co., O.; m in Union, Esther MILES, dt William & Mary (Pearson), Miami Co., O.
Ch: Anson b 1840, 2, 1 d 1840,11,12 bur Union
David M. " 1841, 12, 29
Almeda " 1844, 10, 30
Elwood " 1850, 7, 22
1842, 6, 21. Aaron, s Benjamin & Susannah (Jay) b 1819,6,26 d 1870,7,23; m in Lickbranch, Mary COATE, dt Jesse & Mary (Johnson) b 1826,2,24
Ch: Susanna b 1843, 6, 8 d 1843, 7,20 bur Union
Anson " 1844, 10, 16
Amzi " 1847, 3, 31
Allen " 1850, 6, 25
Benjamin " 1852, 6, 23 d 1852, 8,16
Sarah W. " 1853, 12, 3
William C. " 1856, 5, 17
Mary Elizabeth " 1861, 4, 11
----, --, --. James, s Wm. & Charity, b 1823, 9,6; m Moriah McCONNELL, dt John & Elizabeth, b 1828,8,26
Ch: Henry b 1844, 8, 21 d 1846, 8,10
Sarah J. " 1848, 5, 15 " 1863, 8,30
John M. " 1852, 4, 25
Mary E. " 1856, 9, 9
Wm. P. " 1857, 8, 21
Corrilla " 1860, 5, 7
Lorettie " 1863, 9, 7 d 1867, 2, 2
1844, 3, 21. Mary m Zimri COPPOCK
----, --, --. John, s Moses & Lydia (Jay); m Susannah INMAN, dt Eli & Jane, b 1826,6,30
Ch: Eli b 1845, 9, 12 d 1845,12,14 bur Union
Westley " 1847, 10, 31
Moses " 1853, 10, 20
James Ellis" 1858, 10, 30
Mary Elizabeth " 1861, 11, 10 d 1867, 1,26
Alice " 1868, 1, 25
1844, 3, 21. Zimri, s Wm. & Charity (Hollingsworth), Miami Co., O., b 1819,11,11; m in Lickbranch, Mary COPPOCK, dt Moses & Lydia (Jay), Miami Co., O., b 1826,2,27
Ch: Martha b 1847, 7, 18
Eunice " 1851, 5, 30
Lydia J. " 1856, 11, 20
Almeda " 1867, 8, 15
1850, 9, 25. Ephraim, s Joseph & Rachel, Miami Co., O., b 1826,7,10; m in Union, Mary COATE, dt James & Luranah, Miami Co., O., b 1827,9,24
Ch: Alice b 1851, 11, 24
Ellwood C. " 1853, 5, 13
Adela " 1855, 7, 23
1850, 3, 3. Benjamin d ae 77 bur Union
1850, 9, 25. Louisa m Isaac PEARSON
1851, 7, 23. Calvin, s James & Jane, Miami Co., O.; m in Union, Mary Ann COPPOCK, dt Joseph & Rachel, Miami Co., O.
1856, 2, 21. Esther m Wm. ELLEMAN
1859, 6, 14. Susannah d ae 80 bur Union
1860, 3, 21. David M., s Benjamin & Esther, Miami Co., O.; m Jane JAY, dt Joseph F. & Mary, Miami Co., O.
Ch: Anabel b 1861, 3, 21
Horace " 1863, 3, 30
Lambert " 1865, 10, 7
Almeda " 1867, 8, 2
Furnace Jay" 1869, 11, 17
1861, 6, 20. David J., s Layton & Elenor, Howard Co., Ind.; m in Lickbranch, Ann PEMBERTON, dt. John E. & Susannah, Miami Co., O.
1863, 12, 23. Almeda m Abijah J. COATE
----, --, --. Anson, s Aaron & Mary; m Sarah MILES, dt Wade & Mary (Tucker)
Ch: Orley E. b 1867, 4, 1
Aldey L. " 1868, 12, 3
Ahigah W. " 1870, 9, 29
Maudie May " 1874, 2, 6 d 1874,11,13
Herbert " 1872, 9, 2 " 1872,12, 1
1870, 4, 21. David J., s Layton & Elenor, Miami Co., O.; m in Lickbranch, Margaret COATE, dt John & Phebe, Miami Co., O.

1815, 9, 2. Betty & dt, Deborah, recrq
1819, 11, 4. Aaron gct Ceasars Creek MM, O., to m there
1820, 5, 5. Aaron gct Ceasars Creek MM, O.
1823, 4, 5. Jesse dis jas
1824, 5, 1. Isaac dis mcd
1826, 4, 1. John con mcd
1828, 9, 6. John & w, Martha, & ch, Aaron, Dorcas, Rachel, Margaret, Jane & Sarah, rocf Newbery MM, Tenn., dtd 1828,7,5
1829, 2, 7. Aaron & w, Margaret, & ch, Abigail, Elijah, Elisha & Margaret, rocf Newberry MM, Tenn., dtd 1828,11,1
1829, 7, 4. Wright dis
1832, 4, 7. Joseph, s Anne, dis
1832, 5, 16. Mary con mcd
1833, 2, 13. Dianna rocf Newberry MM, Tenn., dtd 1832,12,1
1833, 7, 17. Mary gct Mill Creek MM
1833, 9, 18. Lydia recrq
1833, 10, 16. Wm. dis jas
1833, 11, 13. Jane dis jas
1834, 5, 14. Abraham & ch, Mary, Rebecca, Seth & Bailes recrq with consent of Newberry MM, Tenn.
1834, 11, 12. John & fam gct Duck Creek MM, Ind.

COPPOCK, continued
1835, 6, 17. Elisha dis paying muster
1835, 7, 15. John & fam gct Mississinewa MM, Ind.
1836, 10, 12. Elijah con mcd
1836, 11, 16. Cynthia recrq
1836, 12, 14. Abraham & w, Lydia, & ch gct Duck Creek MM, Ind.
1837, 5, 17. Elijah gct West Branch MM
1838, 5, 16. Abraham dis
1838, 6, 13. Margaret gct Mississinewa MM, Ind.
1838, 6, 15. Elijah & w, Mary, & s, Wm., rocf West Branch MM, O., dtd 1838,5,17
1838, 8, 15. Lydia, minor, recrq of Eunice Coate
1839, 2, 13. Lydia & ch gct Mississinewa MM, Ind.
1839, 4, 17. Cynthy Haworth (form Coppock) con mcd
1839, 11, 18. Joseph C. dis paying military demands
1840, 3, 18. Moses & w, Mary Ann, & ch, John & Mary, rocf Mill Creek MM, dtd 1840,3,17
1840, 12, 16. Elijah dis
1841, 1, 13. Thomas con mcd
1842, 11, 16. Mary gct Lick Creek MM, Ind.
1842, 12, 14. Margaret rocf Spiceland MM, Ind., dtd 1842,10,19
1845, 3, 12. John con mcd
1845, 3, 12. Susannah con mcd
1845, 10, 15. Jane recrq
1845, 11, 12. James Jr. con mcd
1846, 3, 18. James & w, Eleanor Harriet & ch, Esther, Samuel & Lydia, rocf Mill Creek MM, dtd 1846,3,17
1836, 4, 15. Layton & fam gct Mississinewa MM, Ind.
1847, 12, 15. Sarah Fisher (form Coppock) dis mcd
1849, 7, 18. Anna Allison (form Coppock) con mcd
1850, 4, 17. James dis jas (s of Wm.)
1850, 12, 18. Mary dis
1850, 12, 18. Mary H. recrq
1851, 1, 13. Calvin recrq
1851, 8, 13. John & fam gct Mill Creek MM
1852, 8, 18. Wm., s Joseph, dis mcd
1853, 5, 18. James Jr. gct West Branch MM, O., to m Susana Jay
1853, 5, 18. Lucinda & ch, Sarah & Ann, recrq
1853, 12, 14. Susanna I. rocf West Branch MM, O., dtd 1853,11,17
1854, 7, 12. Mary K. Ringer (form Coppock) dis mcd & neglect
1854, 8, 16. Samson gct Mill Creek MM, to m Mary A. Hutchens
1854, 12, 13. Calvin & w, Mary Ann, & ch gct Back Creek MM, Ind.
1854, 12, 13. Mary Ann rocf Mill Creek MM, dtd 1854,11,14
1856, 3, 12. Elijah & Mary rst
1857, 9, 16. Ephraim & w, Mary, & ch gct Westland MM, Ia.
1858, 10, 13. Henry L. Miles gct Honey Creek MM, Ind., to m Elizabeth C. Coppock
1858, 11, 17. James Jr. & w, Susanna, & ch, gct Wabash MM, Ind.
1860, 8, 15. Harvey rpd mcd; retained mbrp
1861, 5, 15. Jane J. gct Wabash MM, Ind.
1861, 9, 18. Henry dis attending mcd & dancing
1861, 11, 13. Ann gct Honey Creek MM, Ind.
1862, 2, 12. Wm. J. gct Cincinnati MM, O.
1862, 4, 16. Eleanor & fam rocf Honey Creek MM, dtd 1862,4,12
1863, 7, 15. Mariah & ch, Sarah J., Mary Elizabeth & Corilla Ann, recrq
1863, 8, 12. James W. & s, John & Wm., recrq
1866, 5, 16. Allen rpd mcd; dropped from mbrp
1866, 6, 13. Westley rpd mcd; dropped from mbrp
1866, 6, 13. Isaac rpd mcd; retained mbrp
1866, 11, 14. Elizabeth, Emily & Henry Harvey, adopted ch Elijah & Mary, recrq
1866, 11, 14. Anson rpd mcd; retained mbrp
1867, 5, 15. Westley gct Newberry MM, O.
1867, 7, 17. Wesley rpd mcd; retained mbrp
1867, 12, 18. Isaac C. gct West Branch MM, O.
1868, 2, 12. Jesse rpd mcd; retained mbrp
1868, 7, 15. June gct West Branch MM, O.
1869, 4, 14. Amzi rpd mcd; retained mbrp
1870, 2, 16. Ellwood rpd mcd; dropped from mbrp
1870, 7, 13. Margaret gct West Branch MM, O.
1871, 4, 12. James W. & fam gct West Branch MM, O.
1871, 6, 14. David rpd mcd; dropped from mbrp
1872, 1, 17. David M. & Harvy dis joining Free Masons
1889, 10, 5. Mary relrq
1894, 3, 3. Joe F. recrq
1894, 3, 3. Addie & ch, Nellie, Eunice & Nora, recrq
1894, 3, 3. Maria E. & ch, Freddie D., Mary Ethel, Jeddie Carlton & Allen Jr. recrq
1897, 1, 2. Frank recrq.
1897, 2, 6. Frank rocf West Branch MM, O., dtd 1897,1,9

CORREY
1897, 1, 2. Leota DeEtta recrq

COTHRAN
----, --, --. Hannah [Cottern] b 1794,3,22 d 1868,7,22
1813, 6, 9. Anna m Jesse COPPOCK
1816, 12, 11. Jane m Jesse JONES
1818, 2, 11. Hester m Asa JONES
1837, 10, 1. Hester d
1842, 7, 20. Phebe m Henry W. COATE

1823, 11, 1. David S. dis
1828, 1, 5. Ch of Hannah recrq
1834, 7, 16. Alexander dis attending a mus-

COTHRAN, continued
ter
1842, 12, 14. James dis

COUNTS
1897, 10, 2. Mary A. rocf Rose Hill MM, Kans., dtd 1897,8,14

COX
1851, 11, 13. Jane m Benj. HOLLINGSWORTH

1814, 9, 3. John & fam gct Miami MM, O.

CRUMINE
1838, 8, 15. Ruth rocf West Branch MM, O., dtd 1838,6,14

CULVER
1896, 2, 1. Martha recrq

CURTIS
1841, 2, 17. Samuel C. Miles gct Mill Creek MM, to m Nancy Curtis

DAVIS
1830, 9, 3. John, s Abiather & Lydia, Miami Co., O.; m in Union, Betsy ELLEMAN, dt James & Ann HAWORTH, Miami Co., O.
----, --, --. Wm. L. (or F.), s Jonathan & Nelly, b 1845,6,24 d 1879,9,3; m Mahala C. ----- b 1846,3,2
Ch: Minnie Luella b 1866, 8, 27
Jennie Mary " 1868, 5, 13
Murray Willis " 1870, 4, 16
Dellie V. " 1872, 8, 21
Anna B. " 1874, 8, 1
Frank " 1876, 12, 6 d 1879, 2,21 in Arkansas

1822, 11, 2. Joseph Coate gct West Branch MM, O., to m Lydia Davis
1830, 2, 6. Mary, minor dt John, rocf West Branch MM, O., dtd 1829,9,19
1830, 1, 2. Isaac, minor s John, rocf West Branch MM, O., dtd 1829,9,19
1831, 1, 1. John & s, Jonathan, rocf West Branch MM, O., dtd 1830,12,18
1834, 1, 15. John dis
1835, 2, 18. Elizabeth gct West Branch MM, O.
1836, 9, 14. Isaac dis neglect
1839, 2, 13. Mary gct West Branch MM, O.
1854, 4, 12. Jesse Jones gct West Branch MM, O., to m Betsy Davis
1867, 6, 12. Aldas & Henry, ch Rachel, recrq
1870, 3, 16. Wm. L. recrq
1889, 10, 5. Eleanor C. relrq

DIBRA
1829, 12, 9. Susannah m David MILES
1841, 6, 17. Elizabeth m Price F. HALL
1824, 1, 3. Susannah recrq
1827, 7, 7. Elizabeth recrq of Samuel & Rebecca Teague

DICKSON
1822, 9, 7. Sarah (form Vanhorn) dis mcd

DIXON
1822, 9, 7. Sarah dis

DIVIND
1872, 9, 18. Deborah recrq
1873, 2, 12. Michael recrq

DORMAN
1825, 10, 1. Elizabeth dis

DUNGAN
----, --, --. Richard P., s Jesse & Elizabeth, b 1822,11,1 d 1844,3,13; m Drusilla PEMBERTON, dt John, d 1846,10,30 ae 20y 8m 2d
Ch: Elizabeth b 1843, 2, 11

1823, 4, 9. Rachel m Malon NEAL
1830, 4, 13. Mary d bur Union ae 80y
1834, 5, 1. Samuel d bur Union ae 79y
1846, 10, 30. Drusilla d bur Union
1844, 3, 13. Richard P. d bur Union

1816, 5, 4. Isaac dis
1818, 6, 6. Anna dis mcd
1824, 7, 3. Jesse dis mcd
1837, 12, 13. Samuel dis mcd
1839, 1, 16. Amos dis neglect & training with militia
1842, 7, 13. Richard con mcd

EHLER
1890, 3, 1. Mary recrq
1891, 1, 3. Sarah recrq

ELLERS
1833, 4, 17. Elizabeth dis mcd

ELLEMAN
1758, 9, 26. Elizabeth, dt Enos & Catherine, b d 1820,6,8
----, --, --. William, s Enos & Catharine, b 1769,7,10 d 1859,2,11; m Jane JAY, dt Joseph & Mary (Cothran), b 1772,1,6 d 1845,11,15
Ch: Enos b 1792, 5, 22 d 1795, 5, 3 bur Bush River, S. C.
David b 1795, 1, 26
Isaac " 1798, 9, 3
Mary " 1801, 8, 21
Elizabeth " 1805, 2, 18 d 1805, 2,19
William " 1806, 8, 28 " 1828, 7,25 bur Union
John " 1810, 2, 23 " 1828, 7,10 bur Union
Jesse " 1813, 4, 7 " 1828, 9, 2

ELLEMAN, continued
bur Union
1800, 2, 19. Elizabeth d bur Bush River, S.C.
----, --, --. David & Elizabeth
Ch: Susannah b 1818, 2, 30(?)
Jane " 1820, 7, 13
James " 1823, 4, 1
William " 1825, 9, 10
----, --, --. David, s Wm. & Jane (Jay), d 1829,1,25 ae 33y 11m 30d; m Betsy HAWORTH, dt James
1822, 4, 25. Hannah d bur Union
1825, 2, 7. Hannah m George THOMAS
----, --, --. Enos, s John & Susannah (Coppock) b 1802,3,31 d 1889,10,13; m Margaret WARD, dt David & Elizabeth, b 1808,1,20
Ch: Elizabeth b 1825, 10, 12 d 1852,10,27; m Samuel PEIRCE, Jr.
John b 1828, 12, 10.
Mary " 1830, 10, 12
David " 1833, 7, 29
William " 1835, 10, 21
Joseph " 1838, 8, 9
Thomas " 1841, 5, 9
Rebecca " 1843, 11, 28
Isam " 1846, 3, 15
1828, 1, 25. -----, s William, d bur Union
1829, 10, 7. Tace m Isaac PEMBERTON
1829, 10, 15. John d
1830, 9, 3. Betsy m John DAVIS
1833, 4, 24. Mary m Moses COPPOCK
1833, 8, 21. Isaac, s Wm. & Jane, Miami Co., O.; m in Union, Elizabeth COPPOCK, dt Benjamin & Susanna (Jay), b 1807,2,3
Ch: Owen b 1823, 5, 3
Dorcas " 1824, 12, 29
Jordan " 1827, 5, 6
William " 1829, 9, 8
Isaac m 2nd ----- -----
Ch: Mary b 1834, 7, 28
Benjamin " 1836, 4, 30
David " 1837, 7, 7 d 1839, 4, 9
Jane " 1839, 4, 21 " 1877, 6,13
Isaac " 1840, 10, 29
Son " 1843, 5, 17 (b dead)
" " 1844, 6, 29 (" ")
Rachel Elleman " 1846, 11, 8
Son " 1849, 7, 28 (b dead)
1839, 4, 9. David d bur Union
1842, 4, 20. Elizabeth m Samuel PEIRCE, Jr.
----, --, --. Owen [Eleman], s Isaac & Mary (Jones), b 1823,5,3; m Rachel McDONALD, dt Joseph & Temperance (Elleman), b 1828, 7,8
Ch: Sarah b 1847, 7, 14 d 1849, 4, 2
Mark " 1848, 9, 9
Caroline " 1850, 9, 5
Jane " 1855, 4, 25 d 1855, 8,17
Minerva " 1859, 8, 26 " 1864, 3,21
Wm. Isaac " 1862, 3, 6 " 1898, 7, 1
Jos. Aaron " 1863, 10, 4
1848, 6, 21. Mary m John PEIRCE
1854, 9, 14. Mary m Lemuel PEMBERTON
1856, 2, 21. William, s Enos & Margaret, Miami Co., O.; m in Lickbranch, Esther COPPOCK, dt James & Eleanor, Miami Co., O.
----, --, --. Thomas, s Enos & Margaret (Ward) b 1841,5,9; m Martha C. JAY, dt Moses & Margaret (Peirce), b 1839,11,15 d 1893,2, 16
Ch: Infant b 1858, 11, 10 d 1858,11,10
Margaret A." 1860, 10, 24 " 1863, 6,16
Infant " 1859, 11, 10 " 1859,11,10
Mary L. Dorea " 1862, 4, 13
Rosetta Ellen " 1864, 3, 2
Lydia Viola " 1866, 4, 1 " 1869, 1,15
Wm. Calvin " 1868, 5, 20
Orris Alder (or Aldes)" 1870, 3, 20
Robert Walter " 1873, 4, 17
Minnie Pearl " 1877, 9, 14 " 1878, 1,14
Thomas m 2nd 1894,6,28 Richmond, Ind., Emeline HAWKINS
Ch: John H. b 1896, 3, 13
----, --, --. Isom [Elamon], s Enos & Margaret, b 1846,3,15; m Phebe COATE, dt Henry & Phebe, b 1846,12,1
Ch: Sarah Elizabeth b 1865, 1, 28
Clara Hannah " 1866, 3, 29
Thomas Alva " 1870, 1, 28
Joseph Alton " 1871, 9, 23
Anna Mary " 1875, 1, 22
Delbert Clarkson " 1876, 8, 10
Enos Clifford " 1880, 4, 27
----, --, --. Robert Walter b 1873,4,17; m Eldena Elda ----- b 1878,2,28
Ch: Lewis H. b 1895, 3, 21
1898, 7, 1. Wm. J. d

1817, 10, 4. David con mcd
1818, 8, 1. Betsy & dt, Susannah, recrq
1822, 2, 2. Isaac gct West Branch MM, O., to m Mary Jones
1822, 10, 5. Susannah Neal (form Elleman) dis mcd
1824, 4, 3. Isaac & s, Owen, gct West Branch MM, O.
1825, 10, 1. Enos dis mcd
1827, 9, 1. Joseph Pemberton & fam & Tace Elleman, gct Honey Creek MM
1833, 12, 18. Elizabeth gct West Branch MM, O.
1834, 1, 15. Enos rst
1837, 4, 12. Isaac & w, Elizabeth, & ch, Owen, Dorcas, Jorden, William, Mary &

ELLEMAN, continued
Benjamin, rocf West Branch MM, O., dtd 1837,2,16
1837, 4, 12. Margaret & ch recrq
1845, 12, 14. Owen con mcd
1850, 12, 18. Owen & fam gct Honey Creek MM
1851, 5, 14. Jorden gct Back Creek MM, to m Sophia Pemberton
1851, 11, 12. Jorden gct Back Creek MM, Ind.
1852, 9, 15. Wm. gct Back Creek MM
1855, 6, 13. David dis mcd & jas & attending a singing school
1855, 6, 13. Esther dis
1859, 1, 12. Benjamin gct Back Creek MM, Ind.
1859, 8, 17. Joseph con mcd
1860, 9, 12. Esther rocf Wabash MM, Ind., dtd 1860,4,14
1861, 3, 13. Joseph & fam gct Westland MM, Ia.
1863, 2, 18. Isaac rpd mcd; dropped from mbrp
1863, 3, 18. Wm. con mcd
1864, 10, 12. Wright gct Pleasant Hill MM, Ind.
1864, 12, 14. Isom rpd mcd; retained mbrp
1865, 9, 10. Owen & fam rocf Back Creek MM, Ind., dtd 1865,7,13
1892, 3, 5. David W. & w, Esther, & minor ch, Horace Melvin & Frances Esty, & adult ch, Mary Rozella Zelora Edgar & Lindley M., rocf West Branch MM, dtd 1892,2,13
1897, 1, 2. Audrey recrq

ELLIS
1830, 9, 4. Ellis rocf Newberry MM, Tenn., dtd 1830,4,3
1831, 7, 2. Ellis dis mcd &o first cousin
1833, 4, 13. Elizabeth dis mcd

ELMORE
1818, 10, 3. Rachel con mcd
1844, 12, 18. Rachel dis jas

EMBREE
----, --, --. Isaac b 1762,6,24 d 1838,6,29; m Hannah ----- d 1824,1,31 upwards 62y
Isaac m 2nd Ann ----- d 1870,9,11 ae 89y 5m 12d
1825, 6, 8. Isaac, Miami Co., O.; m in Union, Sarah HOLLINGSWORTH, Darke Co., O.
1827, 11, 18. Sarah d bur Union ae 61y
1832, 11, 22. Isaac m in Lickbranch, Ann HAYWORTH
1870, 9, 11. Ann [Embry], "nd w Isaac, d ae 89y 5m 12d

1814, 12, 4. James & w gct Mill Creek MM
1817, 5, 4. James & w rocf Mill Creek MM, dtd 1817,4,24
1818, 10, 5. Isaac Jr. dis mcd
1818, 11, 7. Ruth con mcd
1822, 11, 2. Moses con mcd
1825, 1, 1. James con mcd
1828, 7, 5. Moses dis neglect & training with militia
1834, 8, 13. Ruth dis jas

EMRY
1838, 6, 29. Isaac d bur Union

ENGLE
1816, 8, 3. Rachel (form Hanks) dis mcd

FELLOW
1838, 1, 17. Samuel Miles gct New Garden MM, to m Mary Fellow
1840, 3, 18. Henry Coate Jr. gct New Garden MM, to m Sally Fellow

FISHER
1847, 12, 15. Sarah (form Coppock) dis mcd

FOSTER
1899, 1, 7. Ollie recrq

FURNAS
----, --, --. Joseph, s John & Mary (Wilkinson), of England, b 1763,2,20 d 1812,7,25; m Sally PEARSON, dt Samuel & Mary STEDDOM (wd),
Ch: Mary P. b 1791, 7, 6
Henry " 1793, 11, 5 d 1795, 5,10 bur Bush River, S. C.
John b 1796, 4, 12
Samuel " 1798, 10, 1
Joseph " 1801, 1, 27
Benjamin " 1803, 11, 1
William " 1806, 3, 9
Sally " 1808, 12, 1
Henry S. " 1812, 5, 19
1812, 7, 25. Joseph d bur Union
----, --, --. Joseph, s Jos. & Sally (Pearson) b 1801,1,27; m Patience MILLS
Ch: Mary b 1826, 12, 20
Jason " 1828, 10, 25 d 1838, 9,15 bur Union
Rachel " 1830, 10, 1
Sarah Ellen " 1834, 12, 10
Charles M. " 1839, 8, 21
Edith " 1846, 5, 15 d 1847, 5,24 bur Union
Louisa " 1848, 7, 19 d 1848, 9,23 bur Union
1833, 4, 18. Sally m Joseph HOLLINGSWORTH
1845, 10, 22. Mary m Moses MILES
1851, 3, 19. Rachel m Jesse PEARSON
1856, 8, 9. Charles d ae 18y 6m 18d
1868, 2, 20. Patience d ae 60y 6m 6d

1818, 12, 5. John gct Mill Creek MM, to m
1821, 7, 7. John gct Mill Creek MM
1822, 9, 7. Samuel gct Mill Creek MM, to m Mary Jenkins
1824, 9, 4. Benjamin gct Mill Creek MM, to m Mary Patty
1826, 2, 4. Joseph gct Miami MM, O., to m Patience Mills
1826, 6, 6. Samuel gct Mill Creek MM, to m Lydia Macy

FURNAS, continued
1827, 3, 3. Benjamin gct Mill Creek MM
1827, 8, 4. Prudence rocf Miami MM, O.
1828, 6, 7. Wm. gct Mill Creek MM
1834, 12, 17. Henry S. dis paying military demands
1834, 12, 17. Wm. & w, Beulah, & ch, Priscilla, John & Eunice, rocf Mill Creek MM, dtd 1834,11,11
1835, 7, 15. Wm. dis neglect & paying military demands
1842, 12, 14. Beulah dis disunity
1847, 6, 16. Priscilla Hill (form Furnas) dis mcd & jas
1856, 6, 18. Esther dis

GLUNT
1872, 9, 18. David E. recrq

GREEN
1822, 2, 2. Mary dis jas
1853, 12, 14. Elizabeth (form Coate) dis mcd & jas
1853, 12, 14. Ellen (form Coate) dis mcd & jas

GROVE
1897, 1, 2. Ross & Elzie recrq

HALL
1841, 6, 17. Price F., s Joshua & Charity, Rush Co., Ind.; m in Union, Elizabeth Dibra, dt Daniel & Elizabeth, Miami Co.,O.

1840, 4, 15. Sarah D. rocf New Garden MM, dtd 1840,2,15
1841, 8, 18. Elizabeth gct Walnut Ridge MM, Ind.
1842, 4, 13. Sarah D. gct New Garden MM
1845, 7, 16. Drusilla dis mcd

HANKS
1816, 8, 3. Rachel Engle (form Hanks) dis mcd
1822, 4, 6. Thomas dis neglect
1822, 8, 3. Noah dis neglect
1822, 10, 5. James dis neglect
1825, 12, 3. Martha dis
1829, 10, 3. Mary dis
1831, 6, 4. Phebe dis
1838, 10, 17. Keziah Jay (form Hanks) con mcd
1845, 7, 16. Noah dis

HARRIS
1858, 7, 30. Hannah d ae 66y 7m 24d

HARSHBARGER
----, --, --. ----- m Catharine -----, b 1843, 2,12
Ch: Lena May b 1882, 2, 1

1894, 3, 3. Catherine rolf U. B. Church
1894, 4, 6. Bertha & May recrq
1897, 1, 2. Ethel & Gracia recrq

HASKET
1814, 2, 4. Isaac & fam gct West Branch MM,O.

HAWORTH
1832, 11, 22. Ann m Isaac EMEREE
----, --, --. Nathaniel & Cynthia
Ch: David M. b 1839, 9, 29
Betty " 1840, 12, 7 d 1841, 9,17 bur Union
Keziah " 1842, 6, 21
Sarah Jane " 1845, 2, 26
Julian " 1848, 10, 17 d 1850, 9,11
Prudence " 1853, 9, 6
Enos E. " 1856, 4, 30
1842, 2, 17. Mary m Jesse JONES

1819, 1, 2. Ann recrq
1835, 6, 17. Susanna con mcd
1835, 9, 16. Elizabeth con mcd
1839, 4, 17. Cynthy (form Coppock) con mcd
1839, 8, 14. Nathaniel recrq
1841, 10, 13. Susannah dis jas
1841, 12, 15. Mary recrq
1848, 8, 16. Lucinda con mcd
1852, 6, 16. Lucinda dis
1855, 10, 17. Elizabeth dis
1859, 10, 12. Nathaniel & w, Cinthy, & fam gct Westland MM, Ia.
1872, 9, 18. Elisa recrq

HEATHCOE
1854, 10, 18. Susanna dis

HECKMAN
1897, 1, 2. John & Mary recrq

HEISY
1895, 4, 6. Samuel & Isabelle & Aubry recrq

HILDEBRAN
1911, 10, 30. Rachel [Hildbran] d
1848, 10, 18. Rachel con mcd
1873, 2, 12. Anson recrq
1889, 10, 5. Johnrelrq
1889, 10, 5. Anson relrq
1889, 10, 5. Rachel relrq

HILL
1847, 6, 16. Priscilla (form Furnas) dis mcd & jas
1897, 1, 2. Isaac recrq

HINSHAW
1845, 7, 16. Richard rocf Newberry MM, Tenn., dtd 1836,5,3
1848, 9, 15. Richard dis

HOLDEN
1867, 3, 13. George recrq

HOLLINGSWORTH
----, --, --. Joel, s Isaac & Susannah (Wright), b 1778 d 1847; m Anna McCONNELL

HOLLINGSWORTH, continued
d 1863
Ch: Rachel b 1803, 6, 18
Sophia " 1805, 6, 7; m 1833 James Lunday at Center MM, O.
Susannah b 1807, 4, 9
Joseph " 1809, 1, 28
Rhoda " 1811, 1, 1
Absalom " 1812, 12, 6
Cyrus " 1815, 1, 18
Lodica " 1817, 1, 13
Ruth " 1819, 4, 27
Isaac " 1821, 1, 19
Yates " 1823, 6, 12

1816, 11, 6. Isaac, s Henry & Sarah, Miami Co., O.; m in Union, Jane COPPOCK, dt John & Maryann, Miami Co., O.
1817, 7, 9. Charity m Wm. COPPOCK
1824, 8, 11. Rachel m John COPPOCK
1825, 6, 8. Sarah m Isaac EMBREE
1825, 8, 10. Rachel m Joseph COPPOCK
1826, 4, 5. Susannah m Joseph COPPOCK
1833, 4, 18. Joseph, s Abraham & Unice, Warren Co., O.; m in Union, Sally FURNAS, dt Joseph & Sally, Miami Co., O.
1833, 9, 25. Joseph, s Joel & Ann, Miami Co., O.; m in Union, Margaret COATE, dt Moses & Elizabeth, Miami Co., O.
1834, 5, 21. Absolom, s Joel & Ann, Miami Co., O.; m in Union, Anne PEMBERTON, dt Robert & Eunice, Miami Co., O.
1851, 11, 13. Benjamin, s Joseph & Hannah, Tippecanoe Co., Ind.; m in Union, Jane M. COX, dt Caleb & Phebe Miller, Miami Co., O.

1818, 7, 4. Eli dis mcd
1828, 1, 5. Sophia gct Center MM
1829, 5, --. Susannah gct West Branch MM, O.
1830, 12, 4. John Pemberton gct West Branch MM, O., to m Susanna Hollingsworth
1833, 9, 18. Sally gct Miami MM, O.
1837, 2, 15. Absalom & fam gct Mississinewa MM, Ind.
1838, 10, 17. Cyrus dis mcd
1839, 3, 13. Isaac & fam gct Mississinewa MM, Ind.
1839, 3, 13. Nathan & fam gct Mississinewa MM, Ind.
1839, 9, 18. Joel dis
1841, 2, 17. Anna & ch gct Back Creek MM, Ind.
1841, 2, 17. Ruth gct Back Creek MM, Ind.
1841, 2, 17. Joseph & s gct Back Creek MM, Ind.
1851, 12, 17. Jane M. gct Greenfield MM, Ind.
1860, 9, 12. Phebe Ann gct Honey Creek MM, Ind.
1866, 11, 14. Susanna P. gct Miami MM

HOOVER
1833, 7, 16. John C. b
----, --, --. Frederick, s Noah & Michal (Young) b 1826,3,30; m Deborah TUCKER, dt Jacob
Ch: Laura
Mahala b 1852, 1, 20
Jacob T. " 1853, 10, 19
Mary Evaline " 1856, 3, 23
Manerva Jane " 1858, 10, 5
Michael Elizabeth " 1863, 6, 18
Charles Edgar " 1867, 2, 2
Ema Caroline " 1869, 7, 15
Celia Edna " 1874, 11, 17

----, --, --. Jacob, s. F. Y.; m Martha COATS, dt Joshua
Ch: Florence A. b 1877, 6, 29

1850, 8, 14. John C. [Hover] recrq
1850, 11, 13. Wm. Miles Jr. gct West Branch MM, O., to m Elizabeth Hover
1853, 1, 12. Frederick [Hover] & fam rocf West Branch MM, O., dtd 1852,12,16
1853, 8, 17. Enoch P. Miles gct West Branch MM, to m Mary Hoover
1854, 3, 15. Samuel Jay gct West Branch MM, O., to m Sarah Hoover
1856, 1, 16. John C. rpd mcd; dropped from mbrp
1858, 12, 15. Mary J. recrq of parent, Esther
1858, 12, 15. John C. & w, Esther, & ch gct Westland MM, Ia.

HUSSEY
1851, 3, 12. Jane, w Wm., & ch, John Milton, Martha Lydia, Alfred, Rachel, William Henry, Esther N. & Jane, rocf Clear Creek MM
1851, 3, 12. Cyrus, Charles, Alonzo & Adison, ch Thos. & Jane, rocf Clear Creek MM, O.
1854, 9, 13. Cyrus, John M. & Chas. A. dis mcd
1855, 10, 17. Alonzo dis

HUTCHENS
1836, 2, 17. Mary con mcd
1836, 7, 13. Mary gct Mill Creek MM
1842, 3, 16. Meredith & w, Elizabeth, & ch, Delila Ann, Mary Jane & Joshua B., rocf Mill Creek MM, dtd 1842,3,15
1842, 3, 16. Anderson & w, Mary, & ch, Sally, William H. & Ermina, rocf Mill Creek MM, dtd 1842,3,15
1844, 2, 14. Meredith gct Mill Creek MM
1851, 1, 13. Anderson & fam gct Wabash MM, Ind.
1854, 8, 16. Samson Coppock gct Mill Creek MM, to m Mary A. Hutchens

IDDINGS
1822, 12, 11. Benjamin b 1753,6,15 d 1826,6,15; m in Union, Ruth PEIRCE b 1763,5,8 d 1840, 3,18

IDDINGS, continued
1826, 6, 15. Benjamin d ae 73
1840, 3, 18. Ruth d ae 76 bur Union
----, --, --. ----- m Clara ----- b 1869,8,22
Ch: Edith
Maria b 1895, 3, 22

1829, 9, 5. Wm. dis mcd
1836, 1, 14. John dis mcd
1836, 5, 18. Davis dis mcd
1838, 10, 17. Benjamin dis mcd
1839, 10, 16. Ruth gct West Grove MM, Ind.
1846, 6, 17. Sarah dis jas
1894, 3, 3. Clara recrq
1897, 1, 2. Ida, Elsie, Della & Maggie recrq

INMAN
----, --, --. Eli, s Asa, b 1794,10,20; m Jane COPPOCK, dt. Benj.
Ch: Drusilla b 1820, 4, 6
Benjamin " 1822, 9, 26
Susannah " 1826, 6, 30
Eli m 2nd Elizabeth RUDY b 1813,1,21
Ch: Levi b 1832, 3, 31
Asa " 1834, 6, 14
David " 1836, 9, 8
Rebecca " 1838, 10, 8
Samuel " 1841, 8, 31
William " 1843, 12, 30
John " 1846, 3, 1
Fanny " 1848, 1, 27
Aaron " 1853, 3, 6

1813, 4, 3. Amelia rocf Cesars Creek MM
1818, 12, 5. Mary recrq
1819, 5, 1. Jane con mcd
1829, 3, 7. Eli & ch recrq
1830, 5, 1. Eli con mcd
1833, 1, 10. Elizabeth recrq
1846, 9, 16. Benjamin con mcd
1853, 4, 13. Benjamin dis jas
1853, 6, 15. Asa con mcd
1855, 1, 17. Asa dis
1855, 9, 12. Eli & fam gct Western Plain MM, Ia.

JACKSON
1880, 7, --. Gilead d

JAY
1811, 7, 3. William, s John & Elizabeth, b 1788,6,19 d 1843,8,9; m Mary P. FURNAS, dt Joseph & Sally, d 1819,10,10 ae 28y 3m [4d
Ch: Sally b 1812, 5, 28
Joseph F. " 1814, 2, 23
Elizabeth " 1815, 7, 29
John " 1817, 6, 17
William " 1819, 8, 31
1820, 12, 6. William, s John & Elizabeth, Miami Co., O.; m in Union, Mary COATE, dt Henry & Mary (Hasket) d 1821,7,29 ae 24y 1m
1822, 6, 5. Abigail m Richard THOMPSON
1824, 4, 7. William, s John & Betty, Miami m in Union, Rebecca TEAGUE, dt Samuel & Rebecca (Furnas), Miami Co., O.
1828, 12, 10. Elijah, s Layton & Elizabeth (Mills), d 1894,2,22; m in Union, Anne MILES, dt Jonathan & Mary (Pearson), Miami Co., O., d 1841,2,7
Ch: Prudence H.b 1829, 10, 14
Samuel " 1832, 2, 3
David " 1834, 2, 20
Mary " 1836, 6, 10
Jonathan " 1839, 5, 12
Moses " 1845, 10, 18
Joseph " 1847, 11, 9
Alfred " 1849, 4, 16
James " 1851, 1, 9
Anna M. " 1852, 8, 20 d 1852, 8,27
William Elwood " 1854, 10, 10
Enos E. " 1860, 7, 23
Martha Ellen Crull " 1858, 10, 16
1832, 6, 20. Thomas, s Thomas & Mary (Pearson), b 1811 d 1862; m in Union, Jane COATE, dt Samuel & Margaret, Miami Co., O. b 1810 d 1887
Ch: Mary b 1833, 4, 17
John " 1834, 6, 30
Samuel " 1835, 11, 22
1834, 8, 20. Joseph F., s Wm. & Mary, Miami Co., O.; m in Union, Mary COATE, dt Samuel & Margaret, Miami Co., O.
1834, 9, 24. Sarah F. m Joseph COPPOCK
----, --, --. Insco b 1813,5,22; m Mary ----- b 1814,12,10 d 1881,7,29 Dublin, Ind.
Ch: Sarah b 1835, 2, 23
Martha " 1836, 11, 13 d 1839, 1,18 bur Union
Thomas C. " 1839, 7, 29
John " 1841, 12, 6 " 1842, 6, 8 bur Union
Hery(?) " 1843, 5, 30
Wm. Foster " 1846, 2, 8
Mary " 1849, 8, 22
Ann Eliza " 1851, 7, 17
1835, 8, 12. Elizabeth m Jonathan C. COATE
1836, 10, 3. Esther, w Jesse, dt John Pemberton, d bur Union
1838, 10, 24. Moses, s James & Martha (Coppock), Miami Co., O., b 1819,8,21 d 1840, 6,24; m in Union, Margaret PEIRCE, dt Samuel & Milly, Miami Co., O., b 1813,7,29
Ch: Martha b 1839, 11, 13
1840, 6, 24. Moses, s James, d bur Mill Creek O.
1839, 11, 13. Martha Coppock, dt Moses, b
1844, 9, 25. Elijah, s Layton & Elizabeth, Miami Co., O.; m in Union, Margaret JAY, dt Samuel & Amelia Peirce, Miami Co., O.
1849, 10, 24. Eli, s Walter D. & Mary, Miami Co., O.; m in Union, Mahala PEARSON, dt Moses & Sarah, Miami Co., O.
1849, 10, 25. Prudence m Isaiah PEMBERTON
1852, 8, 29. Insco, s Insco & Mary, d bur

JAY, continued
Union
1858, 9, 2. Sarah m Albert MENDENHALL
1858, 10, 1. Martha E. m Thomas ELLEMAN
1860, 1, 25. Jane m David M. COPPOCK
----, --, --. Alford, s Elijah & Margaret, b 1849,4,16; m Cordelia JONES, dt Alex. & Anna, b 1852,1,20
Ch: Frank Preston b 1869, 8, 2
Thomas Alert " 1871, 2, 26
1873, 7, 31. James, s Elijah & Margaret, b 1851,1,9 d 1892,11,2; m Susannah MILES, dt Henry F. & Rebecca (Pemberton), b 1853, 1,7
Ch: Margaret Fidella b 1876, 1, 22
Martha Louella " 1878, 12, 19
Linnie Alice " 1880, 2, 10
Wade F. (or L. or T.) " 1883, 5, 2
Henry Russell " 1885, 3, 15
Sherman Carl " 1887, 2, 28 d 1887, 7,16
Harry M. " 1888, 11, 4

1813, 7, 3. Elizabeth & ch gct Ceasars Creek MM, O.
1817, 7, 5. Elizabeth & ch, Patience, Charlotte, William, James, Abigail, Mary, Elijah & Ann, rocf Ceasars Creek MM, O., dtd 1817,7,26
1818, 9, 5. Wm. & w, Mary, & ch, Sarah, Joseph, Elizabeth & John, rocf Mill Creek MM, dtd 1818,2,28
1819, 1, 2. Elizabeth White (form Jay) dis mcd
1819, 8, 7. Wm. Jr. con mcd
1819, 11, 6. Stacy recrq
1822, 2, 2. Wm. Jr. dis
1822, 4, 6. Patience dis
1823, 6, 7. James, s Layton, con mcd
1824, 1, 3. James gct Cesars Creek MM, O.
1824, 5, 1. John Miles gct Mill Creek MM, to m Rebecca Jay
1827, 12, 1. Thomas Jr. rocf Mill Creek MM, dtd 1827,10,27
1834, 5, 14. Esther con mcd
1838, 10, 17. Keziah (form Hanks) con mcd
1839, 1, 16. Margaret gct Mill Creek MM
1839, 8, 14. Keziah con mcd
1839, 8, 14. Thomas dis
1839, 9, 18. Joseph F. dis paying military demands
1839, 10, 16. Moses & w, Margaret, rocf Mill Creek MM, dtd 1839,9,17
1839, 10, 16. Margaret rocf Mill Creek MM, dtd 1839,9,17
1840, 9, 16. Mary & ch, Sarah & Thomas C., recrq
1841, 2, 17. Jane & ch gct Mill Creek MM
1842, 5, 18. Wm. Jr. rst
1842, 5, 18. Layton con mcd
1842, 9, 14. Insco recrq
1844, 10, 16. Hugh dis neglect
1845, 4, 16. William dis
1845, 6, 18. Esther P., minor, recrq of Drucilla Pemberton

1852, 8. 18. Elijah, David & Solomon dis jas
1852, 8, 18. Stacy dis
1853, 5, 18. James Coppock gct West Branch MM, O., to m Susana Jay
1854, 3, 15. Samuel gct West Branch MM, O., to m Sarah Hoover
1854, 11, 15. Samuel gct Red Cedar MM, Ia.
1854, 11, 15. Mary gct Red Cedar MM, Ia.
1858, 1, 13. Wm. rpd mcd; dropped from mbrp
1858, 5, 12. Mary & four ch gct Milford MM, Ind.
1859, 8, 17. Jonathan rpd mcd; dropped from mbrp
1860, 9, 12. John rpd mcd; dropped from mbrp
1861, 11, 13. Thomas con mcd
1864, 11, 16. Thomas dis jas
1869, 8, 18. Moses C. rpd mcd; retained mbrp
1870, 2, 16. Alfred rpd mcd; retained mbrp
1872, 9, 18. Jonathan M. & w, Mary Ann, & ch Annie E., Elijah A., Rollin C. & John Edwin, recrq
1872, 11, 13. Mary P. recrq
1891, 8, 1. Jonathan relrq
1895, 11, 2. Jonathan M. recrq
1897, 1, 2. Edna recrq
1898, 4, 2. Elijah & Emma rolf U. B. Ch., dtd 1898,3,2
1898, 4, 2. Ethel A., Merlin & Herman recrq
1899, 10, 7. Edwin J. gct University MM, Kans.

JEFFRIES
1833, 6, 12. Rebecca gct Mill Creek MM

JENKINS
1822, 9, 7. Samuel Furnas gct Mill Creek MM, to m Mary Jenkins
1829, 12, 5. Elizabeth dis mcd
1834, 5, 14. Elizabeth rst
1834, 7, 16. James & ch, John, Hepsibah & Isaac, recrq
1836, 7, 13. Wm. Pearson gct Mill Creek MM, to m Susanna Jenkins
1838, 8, 15. Elizabeth dis
1838, 12, 12. Nancy (form Pemberton) dis mcd
1840, 5, 13. Elizabeth rocf Mill Creek MM, dtd 1840,4,14
1841, 5, 12. Minor ch James, gct Mississinewa MM, Ind.
1842, 5, 18. Elizabeth gct Mill Creek MM
1842, 7, 13. Joshua Coate gct Mill Creek MM, to m Adila Jenkins

JENKINS, continued
1842, 9, 14. James dis
1851, 7, 16. John, Hepsibah, Isaac, Susanna & Drusilla, ch James & Susanna, gct Honey Creek MM
1853, 1, 12. Drusila rocf Honey Creek MM, dtd 1852,12,11

JENKS
1840, 2, 13. Rebecca rocf West Branch MM, O., dtd 1840,1,16
1844, 11, 13. Rebecca gct West Branch MM
1849, 8, 15. Rebecca H. rocf West Branch MM, O., dtd 1849,7,18

JESTER
1857, 6, 17. Lemuel F. & w, Mary, & ch, Wm. P. & Martha, rocf Mill Creek MM, dtd 1857, 6,16
1860, 9, 12. Wm. P. & Martha Ellen gct West Branch MM, O.

JOHNSON
1828, 7, 5. John Coate gct Dover MM, to m Mary Johnson
1828, 12, 6. Mary B. Coate & s, Lewis Johnson, rocf Dover MM
1851, 8, 13. John G. rocf West Branch MM, O., dtd 1851,7,17

JONES
1816, 12, 11. Jesse, s Samuel & Mary (Mote), b 1794,4,18 d 1888,7,3; m in Union, Jane COTHREN, dt Alexander & Hester, Miami Co., d 1836,9,19 (Jesse b 1794,--,--)
Jesse m 2nd Naomi JONES, wd Philemon, dt Abraham TUCKER, d 1852,3,31
Jesse m 3rd Betsy DAVIS, wd, dt James & Ann HAWORTH (m 1854,--,--)
----, --, --. Alexander, s Jesse & Jane (Cothran), b 1818,6,29 d 1900,8,9; m Anna JONES, dt Philemon & Naomi (Tucker), b 1828,5,19 d 1900,3,6
Ch: Mark C. b 1841, 5, 2
Amanda Jane " 1843, 1, 28
Enos " 1845, 8, 28 d 1845,10, 2
Elizabeth " 1847, 1, 1
Albert " 1849, 8, 20 d 1851,10,10
Cordelia B." 1852, 1, 20
Philemon P." 1854, 7, 31
Warren " 1857, 1, 17 d 1851, 1,29
1818, 2, 11. Asa, s Samuel & Mary, Miami Co., O.; m in Union, Hester COTHRAN, dt Alexander & Hester, Miami Co., O.
1835, 10, 21. Mary m Benjamin COATE
1837, 12, 20. Henry, s Philemon & Naomi, Miami Co., O.; m in Union, Susannah E. PEMBERTON, dt Isaiah & Elizabeth, Miami Co.,O.
----, --, --. Lindley M., s Jonathan, b 1818, 11,18; m Hester McCOOLE, dt Thomas, b 1821, 5,10
Ch: Deborah L. b 1841, 7, 10
Lydia A. b 1843, 7, 17
Mary M. " 1846, 1, 17
Luke Thomas" 1849, 11, 18
1842, 2, 17. Jesse, s John & Sarah (Tucker), Randolph Co., Ind., b 1823,10,27; m in Lickbranch, Mary HAWORTH, b 1825,1,14 , dt James & Ann, Miami Co., O.
Ch: Phebe Ann b 1843, 5, 22
Rachel H. " 1845, 4, 4
Mary " 1847, 1, 18
Rosanna " 1849, 7, 8
1843, 10, 26. Samuel B., s Philemon & Naomi (Tucker), Miami Co., O.; m in Lickbranch, Rhoda COATE, dt Samuel & Mary (Miles), Miami Co., O., b 1825,12,25
Ch: Henry Warren b 1845, 2, 23
Laban Jenks" 1846, 11, 5
Ephraim M. " 1849, 6, 13
Roswell B. " 1852, 1, 11
Samuel C. " 1854, 1, 21
Barton H. " 1857, 11, 29
Charles F. " 1860, 5, 15 d 1860,10,16
John W. " 1865, 1, 19 " 1865, 1,26
Josephine J" 1867, 9, 15
Lambert M. " 1870, 7, 10
1850, 3, 20. Philemon, s Philemon & Naomi, Miami Co., O.; m in Union, Esther COATE, dt James & Lurana (Teague), Miami Co., O., b 1829,2,9 (Philemon b 1830,5,12)
1851, 4, 24. Enoch, s Elisha & Rebecca, Miami Co., O.; m in Lickbranch, Eunice Ann MILES, dt Wm. & Mary, Miami Co., O.
1852, 3, 3. Naomi d bur West Branch
1852, 3, 16. Eunice Ann d bur Union
, , --. Mark C., s Alexander & Anna, b 1841,5,2; m Mary C. ----- b 1844,2,28
Ch: Nora Solota b 1867, 5, 11
Ora Anna " 1868, 12, 25
Elizabeth Jane " 1870, 11, 25

1818, 10, 3. Hester rqct West Branch MM, O.
1822, 2, 2. Isaac Elleman gct West Branch MM, O., to m Mary Jones
1825, 8, 6. Mary con mcd
1826, 3, 4. Mary gct West Branch MM, O.
1826, 11, 4. Samuel dis mcd
1831, 3, 5. John & w, Sarah, & ch, Mary, Rachel, Jesse, Wallace, Naomi, Jonathan & Abraham, rocf West Branch MM, O., dtd 1831,2,19
1833, 1, 16. John & fam gct West Branch MM,O.
1835, 4, 16. John & w, Sarah, & ch, Mary, Rachel, Jesse, Wallace, Naomi, Jonathan, Abraham, Dorcas & Margaret, rocf West Branch MM, O., dtd 1835,3,19
1837, 10, 18. Jesse gct West Branch MM, O., to m Naomi Jones
1838, 1, 17. Naomi, wd Philemon, & ch, Samuel, Anna, Benjamin, Elizabeth & Philemon, rocf West Branch MM, O., dtd 1837,12,14
1838, 3, 14. Susanna E. gct West Branch MM,O.

JONES, continued
1838, 9, 12. David W. Miles gct West Branch MM, O., to m Susanna Jones
1840, 1, 15. John & fam gct White River MM, Randolph Co., Ind.
1840, 7, 15. Alexander dis mcd
1840, 7, 15. Anna con mcd
1841, 7, 14. Anna gct West Branch MM, O.
1841, 9, 15. Benjamin Miles gct West Branch MM, O., to m Prudence Jones
1845, 5, 17. Harvey con mcd
1846, 5, 13. Wm. R. dis mcd
1847, 7, 14. Benjamin dis mcd
1847, 12, 15. Anna rocf West Branch MM, O., dtd 1847,11,18
1848, 10, 18. Jesse rocf White River MM, Ind., dtd 1848,9,2
1849, 1, 17. Esther & ch, Deborah, Lydia & Mary, recrq
1849, 2, 14. Lindley M. rst on consent of West Branch MM, O.
1852, 5, 12. Alexander rst
1853, 2, 16. Jonathan rocf West Branch MM, O., dtd 1853,1,13
1853, 10, 13. Mark C., Amanda Jane, Elizabeth & Cordelia P., ch Alexander & Anna, recrq
1853, 11, 16. Lindley M. & w, Lydia, & ch gct Wabash MM, Ind.
1854, 4, 12. Jesse gct West Branch MM, O., to m Betsey Davis
1854, 7, 12. Mary gct Honey Creek MM, Ind.
1854, 8, 16. Betsy rocf West Branch MM, O., dtd 1850,7,13
1854, 9, 13. Lindley M. & w, Hester, & ch gct Spring Creek MM, Ia.
1855, 7, 18. Joshua rqct Western Plain MM, Ia.
1855, 12, 12. Alvin rpd mcd; dropped from mbrp
1857, 6, 17. Philemon & w, Esther, & ch gct Westland MM, Ia.
1858, 6, 16. Harvey dis
1860, 3, 14. Jesse & fam gct Honey Creek MM
1866, 11, 14. Mark C. rpd mcd; retained mbrp
1868, 11, 18. Lydia rocf West Branch MM, O., dtd 1868,10,15
1870, 4, 13. Cyrenia recrq
1870, 5, 18. Jonathan rocf Legrand MM, Ia., dtd 1870,4,13
1872, 9, 18. Alvin recrq

KELLY
----, --, --. Moses, s John & Mary (Evans) King Kings Co., Ireland; m Mary TEAGUE, dt Samuel, b 1782,10,2 d 1825,4,18

Ch:				
Samuel	b 1801,	9,	24	
Ann	" 1804,	3,	30	
Rebecca	" 1806,	9,	17	d 1821,10,15 bur Union
John	" 1808,	9,	6	
Esther	" 1810,	10,	10	
Joseph T.	" 1812,	10,	6	
Mary	" 1814,	9,	4	
Moses	" 1816,	10,	9	
Robert	" 1819,	4,	18	
Rhoda	b 1821,	3,	25	

1822, 4, 10. Anna m Samuel MILES
1824, 4, 14. Samuel, s Moses & Mary, Miami Co., O.; m in Union, Mary COATE, dt Wm. & Elizabeth, Miami Co., O.
1825, 4, 18. Mary d
1832, 12, 19. Mary m Henry COATE
1817, 5, 4. Moses & w, Mary, & ch, Samuel, Anna, Rebecca, John, Esther, Joseph Teague, Mary & Moses, rocf West Branch MM, O., dtd 1817,4,24
1826, 4, 1. Samuel & fam gct Honey Creek MM
1827, 7, 7. Moses & fam gct Honey Creek MM
1832, 5, 16. Mary rocf Bloomfield MM, Ind., dtd 1832,3,7
1836, 8, 17. Rachel con mcd

KESSLER
1897, 1, 2. Dr. Arden rocf West Branch MM,O.

LACEY
1844, 11, 13. Anne (form Coate) dis mcd

LITTLEJOHN
1842, 8, 17. Sally dis mcd

LONG
1890, 3, 1. Jennie recrq
1891, 2, 7. Jennie relrq

McCOOL
1813, 8, 9. Wells con mcd
1813, 11, 6. John rocf New Garden MM, N. C., dtd 1812,12,26, endorsed by West Branch MM, O.
1814, 8, 6. John con mcd with first cousin
1814, 9, 3. Esther & Mark, ch John, recrq
1814, 10, 1. Elisha [McCoole] dis
1814, 11, 4. Mary con mcd
1818, 10, 5. Wells [McCoole] dis
1822, 10, 5. Hester Pickering (form McCool) dis mcd
1829, 2, 7. Mark [McCoole] dis

McCOY
1825, 1, 1. Huldah rocf Mill Creek MM
1825, 4, 2. Mary con mcd
1837, 10, 18. Lydia dis mcd
1840, 9, 16. Laodice con mcd
1844, 2, 14. Elizabeth (form Wright) dis mcd
1845, 1, 15. Laodice gct Mississinewa MM,Ind.
1848, 1, 12. Hulda gct Honey Creek MM, Ind.

McDONALD
----, --, --. Enos m Dorcas ----- b 1824,1,6

Ch:			
William	b 1846,	7,	8
Elizabeth	" 1848,	6,	14
Allen	" 1851,	9,	23

1823, 12, 6. Joseph & s, John, Mark & Charles, rocf West Branch MM, O., dtd 1823, 11,15
1827, 6, 2. John dis mcd

McDONALD, continued
1830, 9, 4. Charles & Mark dis training with militia
1831, 8, 6. Temperance gct West Branch MM,O.
1838, 8, 15. Lydia rocf West Branch MM, O., dtd 1838,6,14
1845, 12, 17. ----- con mcd
1846, 12, 16. Enos recrq
1850, 11, 13. Enos & w, Dorcas, gct Honey Creek MM
1852, 6, 16. Enos & ch, Wm., Elizabeth & Allen, rocf Honey Creek MM, dtd 1852,8,13(?)
1852, 12, 15. Enos con mcd

MACY
----, --, --. Paul b 1780,1,10 in N. C. d 1868, 5,30 Troy, O.; m Eunice ----- d 1863,9,5 ae 81y 3m 11d
1826, 6, 6. Samuel Furnas gct Mill Creek MM, to m Lydia Macy
1833, 4, 13. Abigail dis mcd
1845, 2, 12. Moses Pearson gct Mill Creek MM, to m Eunice Macy
1853, 11, 16. Paul & w, Eunice, rocf West Branch MM, dtd 1853,10,13
1858, 10, 13. Phebe rocf Mississinewa MM, Ind.

MAHAFFY
1899, 2, 4. Wesley recrq

MAXWELL
1897, 1, 2. Arthur T. recrq
1897, 1, 2. Flora recrq
1897, 1, 2. Fern recrq
1897, 1, 2. Vernon recrq
1897, 1, 2. Bonnie recrq
1897, 1, 2. Narcellua recrq

MENDENHALL
1858, 9, 2. Albert W., s Stephen & Sarah, Union Co., Ind.; m in Union, Sarah JAY, dt Insco & Mary, Miami Co., O.

MILES
1774, 10, 22. Rebecca, dt Wm. & Margaret (Golden), b d 1841,8,14 ae 66y 9m 22d
1783, 3, 12. Mary, dt Enoch & Phebe Pearson, b
----, --, --. Jonathan, s Wm., b 1778,7,12 d 1868,6,14; m Mary PEARSON, dt Enoch & Phebe, S. C., b 1783,8,12 d 1855,5,9
Ch: Eunice b 1802, 7, 2
Mary " 1804, 12, 4
William " 1807, 11, 7
Anna " 1810, 3, 7
Phebe " 1812, 7, 7
Jane " 1814, 6, 30 d 1838, 8, 3
Wade " 1817, 1, 6
Rebecca " 1819, 12, 13
James " 1822, 3, 11
Young Samuel " 1823, 10, 6
Henry " 1830, 3, 8
1807, 5, 2. William d ae 53y 4m 3d
----, --, --. William, s David & Elizabeth, b 1788,12,14 d 1853,1,1; m Mary PEARSON, dt Benj. & Esther (Furnas)
Ch: David b 1813, 7, 26
Esther " 1815, 1, 8
Elizabeth " 1816, 10, 17 d 1842, 1,31
Rebecca " 1818, 4, 10
Benjamin " 1819, 11, 3
Samuel " 1821, 6, 9
Eunice Ann " 1823, 2, 26
William " 1826, 2, 9
Wilkinson " 1828, 6, 25 d 1848, 6, 8 bur Union
Mary P. " 1830, 2, 15
Sarah Jane " 1834, 1, 28 d 1852,11,10
1814, 2, 9. Jane m Isaac THOMPSON
1816, 3, 6. David, s David & Elizabeth (Chandler), Miami Co., O., b 1795,4,23; m in Union, Jean COATE, dt Moses & Elizabeth, b 1795,7,19 (David d 1833,4,24)
Ch: Moses b 1816, 12, 17
Samuel " 1818, 11, 13 d 1863, 5,19
Jeremiah " 1820, 5, 13
Israel " 1824, 1, 7
Elizabeth " 1836, 5, 9 d 1853,10, 7
Enoch " 1828, 10, 14
Rebecca " 1831, 2, 2 " 1831, 9, 7
1824, 6, 9. Mary m Samuel COATE
1822, 4, 10. Samuel, s Wm. & Rachel (Elmore), Miami Co., O.; m in Union, Anna KELLY, dt Moses & Mary (Teague), Miami Co., O., d 1836,8,5
Samuel m 2nd Mary F. FELLOW d 1839,5,25 ae 43y 8m 15d
Samuel m 3rd Elizabeth NEAL b 1811,11,28
Ch: Rebecca K. b 1824, 3, 30
Mary Ann " 1827, 1, 27 d 1833, 8,17
Moses Kelly" 1829, 7, 29
Melissa E. " 1833, 6, 26
Anne " 1836, 7, 7 " 1836,10, 6
Rachel E. " 1842, 8, 6
1825, 5, 11. David, s Wm. & Rachel, Miami Co., O.; m in Union, Esther COATE, dt Henry & Mary, Miami Co., O.

----, --, -. John, s Wm. & Rachel (Elmore), b 1802,11,23; m Rebecca JAY, dt Thomas & Mary (Pearson), b 1806,5,15
Ch: Thomas F. b 1827, 5, 9 d 1838, 5,21 bur Union
Linley " 1829, 3, 1
Mary " 1831, 4, 11
Rachel " 1833, 4, 30 d 1852, 3,26 bur Union
Joanna " 1835, 2, 14
Rebecca Jane " 1840, 5, 9 d 1841, 8,14 bur Union
1828, 12, 10. Anne m Elijah JAY
1829, 2, 11. William, s Jonathan & Mary (Pearson), Miami Co., O.; m in Union, Sarah COATE, dt Samuel & Margaret (Coppock),

MILES, William & Sarah, continued
Miami Co., O., d 1879, 4,28 ae 74y 4m 10d
Ch: James b 1829, 10, 29
Mary Jane " 1831, 1, 9
Ellwood " 1832, 7, 18
Abijah " 1834, 3, 31
Enoch " 1835, 10, 1 d 1839, 3,20
Wade " 1837, 3, 14 d 1837, 3,22
Samuel " 1838, 10, 5
John C. " 1841, 1, 6 " 1854, 7, 5
Jonathan B." 1842, 4, 25 " 1854, 7, 5
Henry W. " 1844, 3, 12 " 1914, 7,26
Margaret " 1845, 10, 16
Phebe " 1849, 4, 16 " 1852, 8,28
1829, 12, 9. David, s Wm. & Rachel, Miami Co., O.; m in Union, Susannah DIBRA, dt Daniel & Elizabeth, Miami Co., O.
1830, 12, 22. Phebe m John COATE
1833, 4, 24. David, s John & Rebecca, d
1833, 8, 17. Mary Ann, dt Samuel, d bur Union
1836, 10, 6. Anne, dt Samuel, d
1836, 8, 5. Anne, w Samuel, d
1837, 3, 22. Wade d
1837, 8, 24. Wade, s Jonathan & Mary, d 1854, 11,17 ae 37y 10m 11d; m in Lickbranch, Mary B. TUCKER, dt Nicholas & Charity, Miami Co., O., d 1850,6,22 bur Union ae 31y 2m 6d
Ch: Jane b 1838, 8, 31
Abijah " 1839, 11, 27
Allen " 1841, 1, 20 d 1843, 7,20
Naomi " 1842, 7, 3
Charity " 1843, 11, 10
Jacob T. " 1845, 4, 8
Sarah C. " 1846, 12, 24
Vashti " 1848, 10, 1
----, --, --. David, s Wm. & Mary; m Susan JONES, dt J. & Sarah (Mendenhall)
Ch: Lambert J. b 1839, 7, 26 d 1839, 10, 1
----- " 1840, 8, 12
John W. " 1843, 8, 23
Branston J." 1848, 11, 26
1838, 9, 20. Rebecca D. m Henry W. COATE
1838, 11, 21. Rebecca m Samuel M. ABBOTT
1839, 4, 24. Esther m Benjamin COPPOCK
1839, 5, 25. Mary F. d
1840, 7, 22. Samuel, s Wm. & Rachel, Miami Co., O.; m in Union, Elizabeth NEAL, dt Henry & Rebecca, Miami Co., O.
1841, 8, 25. Jeremiah, s David & Jane, Miami Co., O.; m in Union, Rebecca MILES, dt Samuel & Ann (Kelly), Miami Co., O.
Ch: Anne
Jane b 1842, 11, 19
Esther " 1844, 10, 6
Enos P. " 1847, 9, 27
Joseph I. " 1851, 6, 11
Elizabeth " 1854, 6, 4
----, --, --. Samuel C., s D. & Jane (Coate), d 1863,9,15; m Nancy CURTIS, dt John & Catharine (Hoover), b 1820,1,10
Ch: Sarah Ann b 1842, 2, 4
Martha E. " 1843, 7, 26
David E. b 1845, 4, 10
Mary Jane " 1850, 5, 31
Catherine
C. " 1852, 4, 3
John Edgar " 1858, 1, 31
----, --, --. Benjamin, s Wm. & Mary (Pearson) m Prudence JONES, dt J. & Sarah (Mendenhall), b 1822,1,14 d 1856,1,25
Ch: Isaac
Newton b 1842, 4, 11
Laban J. " 1844, 3, 10
Laura Ellen" 1846, 4, 19
1842, 1, 31. Elizabeth, dt Wm., d bur Union
----, --, --. Samuel, s Jonathan & Mary, b 1823,10,6; m Hester ----- b 1823,5,26 d 1870,4,11
Ch: A. C. b 1844, 12, 3
Hannah J. " 1847, 12, 16
Sarah R. " 1851, 7, 1 d 1851,12,14
Mary E. " 1853, 9, 1
Ira E. " 1859, 4, 2
Rolen O. " 1866, 10, 10
1843, 10, 9. Rachel d ae 77y 5m 12d
1845, 10, 22. Moses, s David & Jane (Coate), d 1874,2,16 ae 57y 2m; m in Union, Mary FURNAS, dt Joseph & Patience (Mills), Miami Co., O.
Ch: Joseph F. b 1846, 9, 5
John " 1848, 8, 16
Thomas " 1852, 3, 3
Enoch " 1857, 2, 19 d 1859, 1, 5
1851, 4, 24. Eunice Ann m Enoch JONES
----, --, --. Henry, s Jonathan & Mary, b 1830 3,8; m Rebecca PEMBERTON, dt John E. & Susannah, b 1832,7,13 d 1856,6,14
Ch: Susannah b 1853, 1, 1
Mark P. " 1854, 5, 5
Margaret E." 1856, 2, 28
Henry m 2nd Elizabeth ----- b 1835,5,15 d 1867,6,12
Ch: Cora Allice
b 1864, 9, 14
Linie Jane " 1867, 3, 27
1852, 9, 23. Moses K., s Samuel & Anna (Kelly) Miami Co., O.; m in Lickbranch, Juliann COATE, dt Jesse & Mary (Johnson), Miami Co., O.
Ch: Anna Mary b 1853, 6, 18
Martha S. " 1854, 9, 12
Elizabeth
C. " 1856, 12, 5
Lydia F. " 1860, 1, 31 d 1860, 4, 7
Leroy G. " 1861, 12, 3
1852, 11, 10. Sarah Jane d bur Union
1853, 1, 1. William d bur Union
1853, 1, 13. Joanna m Isaac C. TEAGUE
1853, 10, 7. Elizabeth, dt Isaac & Jane, d
1856, 6, 14. Rebecca d
----, --, --. Israel, s David & Jane (Coate), b 1824,1,7 d 1874,3,18; m Keturah PICKERING, dt Benj. & Hetty (McCoole), b 1828, 11,11
Ch: Charles F. b 1865, 3, 11 d 1865, 8, 9

MILES, Israel & Keturah, continued
ch: Caroline b 1866, 7, 20
----, --, --. Alexander m Eunice ----- d 1871, 3,15
Ch: Francy E. b 1870, 7, 17 d 1871, 2,24
1873, 8, 3. Wm. Franklin b
1875, 12, 6. Charley L. b

1813, 11, 6. William rocf New Garden MM, N.C., dtd 1812,11,26 endorsed by West Branch MM, O.
1814, 5, 7. Wm. rocf West Branch MM, O., dtd 1814,4,28
1817, 8, 2. Rebecca recrq
1820, 2, 5. Wm., s Wm., dec, dis jas
1824, 5, 1. John gct Mill Creek MM, to m Rebecca Jay
1824, 8, 7. David rocf New Garden MM, N. C., dtd 1823,12,27
1825, 8, 6. Rebecca rocf Mill Creek MM
1825, 12, 3. John dis training with militia
1829, 3, 7. Jonathan dis
1829, 3, 7. Samuel & fam & Elizabeth Brown gct Mill Creek MM
1831, 6, 4. Samuel & w, Anna, & ch, Rebecca K., Mary Ann & Moses K., rocf Mill Creek MM, dtd 1831,5,24
1835, 7, 15. Samuel dis mcd & paying muster fines
1838, 1, 17. Samuel gct New Garden MM, to m Mary Fellow
1838, 5, 16. Mary F. rocf New Garden MM, Ind., dtd 1838,3,17
1838, 9, 12. David W. gct West Branch MM, O., to m Susanna Jones
1839, 3, 13. Susanna rocf West Branch MM, O., dtd 1839,2,14
1841, 2, 17. Samuel C. gct Mill Creek MM, to m Nancy Curtis
1841, 9, 15. Benjamin gct West Branch MM, O., to m Prudence Jones
1841, 12, 15. Nancy rocf Mill Creek MM, dtd 1841,12,14
1842, 1, 12. Prudence rocf West Branch MM, O., dtd 1841,12,16
1842, 2, 16. Wm. Jr. dis
1844, 2, 15. Hester con mcd
1847, 9, 15. John gct Spiceland MM, Ind., to m Mary R. Miller
1847, 12, 15. Samuel Y. dis
1849, 6, 13. Samuel Jr. dis mcd & jas
1850, 11, 13. Wm. Jr. gct West Branch MM, O., to m Elizabeth Hover
1851, 2, 12. David & w, Susanna, & ch gct Wabash MM, Ind.
1851, 8, 13. Elizabeth H. rocf West Branch MM, O., dtd 1851,7,17
1852, 4, 14. Lindley gct Alum Creek MM, O., to m Lidia Willets
1852, 5, 12. Wm. Jr. & w, Elizabeth, & ch gct West Branch MM, O.
1852, 5, 12. Wade con mcd
1852, 10, 13. Henry con mcd
1852, 10, 13. Lydia rocf Allum Creek MM, O., dtd 1852,8,26
1852, 11, 17. Malinda W. & dt, Mahala Catherine & Esther Martin, recrq
1853, 7, 13. Elwood dis jas
1853, 7, 13. Jonathan rst
1853, 8, 17. Enoch P. gct West Branch MM, O., to m Mary Hoover
1853, 9, 14. David & w, Susana, & ch gct Red Cedar MM, Ia.
1853, 9, 14. Mary & dt, Mary P., gct Red Cedar MM, Ia.
1853, 11, 16. John & w, Rebecca, & ch gct Wabash MM, Ind.
1853, 12, 14. Enoch P. gct Red Cedar MM, Ia.
1854, 10, 18. James dis mcd & jas
1855, 2, 14. Jeremiah & w, Rebecca K., & ch gct Western Plain MM, Ia.
1857, 2, 18. Benjamin & fam gct Red Cedar MM, Ia.
1858, 10, 13. Henry L. gct Honey Creek MM, Ind., to m Elizabeth C. Coppock
1859, 3, 16. Elizabeth rocf Honey Creek MM, dtd 1859,2,12
1860, 9, 12. Jacob gct Rich Square MM, Ia.
1861, 10, 16. Samuel P. rpd mcd
1863, 7, 15. David W. & fam rocf West Branch MM, O., dtd 1863,6,18
1863, 8, 12. Henry C. rpd mcd
1863, 8, 12. Israel rpd mcd; retained mbrp
1864, 4, 16. Keturah rocf Raysville MM, dtd 1864,2,27
1864, 10, 12. Moses K. & w gct New Garden MM, Ind.
1865, 1, 18. Samuel gct Chester MM, Ind.
1865, 2, 15. Melissa E. & Rachel E. gct Chester MM, Ind.
1867, 3, 13. Samuel T. recrq
1867, 10, 16. Martha F. gct Cottonwood MM, Kans.
1868, 1, 15. David E. rpd mcd; retained mbrp
1868, 9, 16. Jeremiah & fam rocf Bloomfield MM, Ind., dtd 1868,6,17
1872, 1, 17. Henry W. dis joining Free Masons
1873, 1, 15. Samuel P. relrq
1873, 2, 12. John H. rpd mcd; retained mbrp
1897, 1, 2. Wm. recrq
1897, 1, 2. Emeline recrq

MILLER
1847, 9, 15. John Miles gct Spiceland MM, Ind., to m Mary R. Miller
1852, 9, 15. Lydia dis
1872, 9, 18. Thomas & w, Louisa M., & ch, Samuel M., Louisa B. & Parry E., recrq

MILLS
1826, 2, 4. Joseph Furnas gct Miami MM, O., to m Patience Mills
1827, 5, 5. Hepsibah & Sidney dis
1828, 2, 2. Patience rocf Miami MM, O.
1828, 12, 6. Anna & minor heirs, James, Edith, Zilpha & Patience, rocf New Garden

MILLS, continued
MM
1830, 5, 1. Anna & fam gct Arby MM, Ind.
1833, 11, 13. Deborah con mcd
1836, 10, 12. Anna rocf Mill Creek MM
1844, 5, 16. Patience gct Duck Creek MM, Ind.
1850, 12, 18. John rst at West Branch MM, O., on consent of this mtg
1899, 2, 4. Susan rocf West Grove MM, Ind.

MOIST
1894, 3, 3. Emma & Laura recrq

MOTE
1808, 2, 22. Ezekel b
1822, 9, 11. John, s John & Rachel, Miami Co., O.; m in Union, Rhoda TEAGUE, dt Samuel & Rebecca, Miami Co., O.
1834, 11, 22. Rhoda d

1823, 6, 7. Rhoda gct West Branch MM, O.
1828, 6, 7. Grace con mcd
1828, 10, 4. Grace gct West Branch MM
1835, 2, 18. Grace rocf West Branch MM, O., dtd 1835,1,15
1838, 6, 15. Sally C. & David Noah, minors, rocf West Branch MM, O., dtd 1838,5,17
1852, 2, 18. David Noah dis mcd
1865, 11, 15. Ezekiel recrq

MUMMA
1897, 1, 2. E. R. & Elizabeth recrq

MURDOCK
1826, 5, 6. Rachel gct White Water MM, Ind.

NEAL
1815, 6, 14. Henry, s Wm. & Rachel, Miami Co., O.; m in Union, Mary PEMBERTON, dt Samuel & Mary Dunkin, Miami Co., O.
1823, 4, 9. Malon m in Union, Rachel DUNKIN, dt Samuel & Mary, Miami Co., O.
1840, 7, 22. Elizabeth m Samuel MILES

1821, 5, 5. Wm., a minister, rocf Mill Creek MM, dtd 1821,4,28
1822, 10, 5. Susannah (form Elleman) dis mcd
1822, 11, 2. Benjamin dis mcd
1823, 11, 1. Rachel gct Mill Creek MM
1824, 9, 4. Wm. dis mcd
1824, 12, 4. Esther dis jas
1825, 4, 2. Mary gct Newhope MM, Tenn.
1829, 1, 3. Rachel dis jas
1834, 7, 16. Mahlon & w, Rachel, & ch, Wm., Margaret, James, Eli & Lydia, rocf Mill Creek MM, dtd 1834,6,17
1839, 8, 14. Mahlon & w, Rachel, & fam gct Back Creek MM
1839, 10, 16. John dis mcd in 4th mo 1838
1840, 5, 13. Mahlon dis training with militia

OGAN
1850, 11, 13. Catherine rocf Dover MM, dtd 1850,9,19

OLDFATHER
1897, 1, 2. Dolly recrq

PARHAM
1814, 5, 7. Mary con mcd
1814, 6, 4. Mary gct Elk MM
1818, 7, 1. Mary rocf Elk MM, dtd 1818,5,2
1819, 5, 1. Mary gct Elk MM

PATTY
----, --, --. Charles, s James & Margaret (Mote); m Phebe PEARSON, dt Enoch & Phebe, d 1868,7,24 ae 79y 9m 19d
1824, 9, 4. Benjamin Furnas gct Mill Creek MM, to m Mary Patty
1844, 4, 17. Anna recrq
1846, 3, 18. Phebe & ch, Mark, Wm. & Phebe rocf Mill Creek MM, dtd 1846,3,17
1846, 11, 18. Mark dis
1849, 11, 14. Wm. dis mcd
1862, 4, 16. Rebecca rocf Miami MM, O., dtd 1862,3,26
1869, 6, 16. Margery rocf Miami MM, O., dtd 1869,5,26
1895, 2, 2. Maggie relrq to Christian Church

PEACOCK
1864, 7, 30. Jesse, s Elwood & Naomi, b 1843,12,29; m Amanda Jane JONES, dt Alex. & Anna, b 1843,1,28

Ch:		
Rosetta	b 1865, 12, 21	
Arlistes	" 1867, 8, 10	
Mary Eadith	" 1869, 9, 19	d 1872,10,29
Leona Belle	" 1873, 9, 8	
Albert	" 1875, 9, 3	" 1878, 5,16
John Jones	" 1878, 9, 5	
Charles	" 1880, 6, 3	
Osrow Elwood	" 1885, 12, 28	
Harley Loyde	" 1888, 2, 28	

1872, 9, 18. Jesse A. recrq
1897, 6, 3. Jesse A. relrq
1898, 2, 4. Jesse C. recrq

PEARSON
----, --, --. Benjamin, s Samuel & Mary (Rogers), b 1763,2,26 d 1844,3,1 ae 81 bur Union; m Esther FURNAS, dt John & Mary (Wilkinson), b 1770,7,4 d 1835,5,14 ae 64 bur Union

Ch:		
John F.	b 1790, 10, 22	
Mary	" 1792, 8, 12	
Eunice	" 1793, 11, 8	d 1795, 5,30 bur Bush River, S. C.
Samuel	b 1796, 3, 11	
Moses	8 1798, 12, 27	" 1874, 7, 9
Joseph	" 1800, 5, 6	

PEARSON, Benjamin & Esther, continued
Ch: Robert b 1801, 8, 8 d 1852,11,17 bur Union
Wilkinson " 1803, 7, 30
William " 1806, 10, 29
Rebecca " 1809, 10, 4
1805, 9, 21. Sarah, dt Robert & Charity, b
----, --, --. John, s Benj. & Esther (Furnas) d 1861,4,20 ae 70y 5m 28d; m Mary PEGG, d 1878,8,13 ae 84y 9m 23d
Ch: Benjamin b 1817, 12, 14
Margaret " 1820, 4, 29 d 1845, 2,12
Esther " 1823, 5, 28
John " 1825, 12, 8
Joseph A. " 1829, 6, 4 d 1837, 9,23 bur Union
Mary " 1831, 12, 24
1818, 2, 11. Enoch d
1820, 11, 8. Thomas, s Enoch & Ann, Miami Co., O.; m in Union, Mary COATE, dt Moses & Elizabeth, Miami Co., O.
----, --, --. Moses, s Benj. & Esther, b 1798, 12,27 d 1874,7,19; m Sarah PEARSON, dt Robert & Charity (Galbreath), b 1805,9,21
Ch: Rhoda b 1824, 11, 20 d 1845, 2,10 bur Union
Mahala " 1827, 12, 7
Timothy " 1829, 10, 25 d 1878, 9,7
Ann " 1832, 4, 2
Joshua " 1834, 11, 7
Abram " 1837, 7, 15
Nathan " 1840, 6, 7 " 1864, 2,15
Sarepta " 1841, 12, 30 " 1848, 4,21 bur Union
1826, 5, 10. Samuel, s Benjamin & Esther, Miami Co., O.; m in Union, Rachel COATE, dt Henry & Mary, Miami Co., O.
1828, 9, 10. Enoch, s Samuel & Anna, Miami Co., O.; m in Union, Mary COATE, dt Benjamin & Abigail WEEKS, Miami Co., O.
Ch: David b 1830, 10, 24
Martha Ann " 1834, 12, 22
----, --, --. Joseph, s Benj. & Esther (Furnas) b 1800; m Lydia MACY, dt Paul & Eunice, b 1806 d 1846,4,17 ae 39y 3m 19d
Ch: Phebe b 1830, 7, 29
Esther " 1836, 2, 4
Eunice " 1837, 12, 18
Jane " 1840, 3, 20
----, --, --. William, s Benj. & Esther (Furnas) d 1870,9,17 ae 63y 10m 18d; m Susannah JENKINS, dt Amos & Elizabeth, b 1809, 10,8 d 1846,3,19
William m 2nd Sarah PEARSON, dt Robert & Keziah (Hollingsworth), b 1803,10,29 d 1877,6,15
Ch: Ezra b 1838, 5, 7
Hariet " 1841, 3, 13
Lindley " 1843, 1, 28 d 1844, 7,27
Amos J. " 1845, 5, 5
1841, 11, 25. Thomas, s Enoch & Ann, Miami Co., O.; m in Lickbranch, Abigail ANDERSON, dt Wm. & Rachel MILES, Miami Co., O.

1844, 2, 7. Sarah, dt Robert, d bur Union
----, --, --. Moses m Eunice MACY, dt Paul & Eunice, b 1821, 2, 21 d 1887,1,7
Ch: Orlando b 1846, 7, 3 d 1878,10,23
Hosea " 1848, 7, 24 " 1869,10,--
Zimri " 1850, 12, 28 " 1874, 5,--
Obed A. " 1855, 1, 5
1846, 3, 19. Susannah d bur Union
1849, 10, 24. Mahala m Eli JAY
1850, 9, 25. Isaac, s Samuel & Rachel, Miami Co., O.; m in Union, Louisa COPPOCK, dt Josiah & Diannah, Miami Co., O.
1851, 3, 19. Jesse, s Hiram & Elizabeth (Jenkins), Miami Co., O.; m in Union, Rachel FURNAS, dt Joseph & Patience (Mills), Miami Co., O.
Ch: Sarah Elizabeth b 1853, 8, 28
Amanda Rachel " 1857, 7, 25
Amanuel Jesse " 1857, 7, 25
Joseph Hiram " 1861, 8, 22 d 1866,12,18
1852, 8, 8. Mary, dt Benj. & Abigail Weeks, d bur Union
1853, 3, 17. Esther m Samuel T. STEDDOM
1858, 7, 30. Hannah d ae 66

1813, 2, 6. Memorial to be prepared for Margaret, an ancient Friend
1817, 2, 1. John F. gct New Garden MM, to m
1817, 7, 5. Mary rocf New Garden MM, O., dtd 1817,5,24
1820, 7, 1. Sarah con mcd
1821, 3, 3. Mary gct Mill Creek MM
1823, 5, 3. Moses gct Mill Creek MM, to m Sarah Pearson
1824, 8, 7. Sarah rocf Mill Creek MM
1826, 7, 1. Hiram & w, Elizabeth, & dt, Mary, rocf Mill Creek MM, dtd 1826,6,24
1826, 11, 4. Samuel & w, Rachel, gct Mill Creek MM
1827, 4, 7. Hiram & fam gct Mill Creek MM
1827, 5, 5. Robert con mcd
1827, 6, 2. Wilkinson dis mcd
1828, 9, 6. Joseph dis mcd
1829, 3, 7. Mary Jr. gct Mill Creek MM
1829, 6, 9. Lydia rocf Mill Creek MM
1832, 2, 15. Moses & fam gct Mill Creek MM
1833, 4, 13. Enoch Jr. & w, Mary, & s, David, rocf Mill Creek MM, dtd 1833,4,11
1834, 1, 15. Moses & w, Sarah, & ch, Rhoda, Mahala, Timothy & Anna, rocf Mill Creek MM, dtd 1823,12,17
1834, 4, 16. Juliann dis mcd
1836, 4, 13. Isaac rocf West Branch MM, O., dtd 1836,3,17
1836, 7, 13. Wm. gct Mill Creek MM, to m Susanna Jenkins
1837, 5, 17. Susannah rocf Mill Creek MM, dtd 1837,5,16
1841, 2, 17. Isaac dis jas

PEARSON, continued
1842, 5, 18. Abigail gct Mill Creek MM
1843, 12, 13. Benjamin Jr. dis mcd
1844, 10, 16. Mary dis jas
1845, 2, 12. Moses gct Mill Creek MM, to m Eunice Macy
1845, 7, 16. Eunice rocf Mill Creek MM
1845, 10, 15. Phebe, Esther, Eunice & Jane, ch Lydia, recrq
1846, 10, 14. Timothy dis
1848, 2, 16. Mary R. rocf Spiceland MM, Ind.
1850, 9, 18. Wm. gct West Branch MM, O., to m Sarah Pearson
1851, 1, 13. David dis
1851, 2, 12. Sarah rocf West Branch MM, O.
1851, 3, 12. Levi rocf Mill Creek MM
1851, 4, 16. Mary S. rocf Cesars Creek MM, O., dtd 1851,2,20
1851, 8, 13. Elizabeth rocf Mill Creek MM, dtd 1851,8,12
1852, 5, 12. Isaac rst at Spring Creek MM, Ia., on consent of this mtg
1852, 8, 18. Phelig rocf Chester MM, dtd 1852,6,24
1853, 11, 16. Isaac C. & fam rocf Mill Creek MM, dtd 1853,10,12
1853, 12, 14. Jesse & fam rocf Mill Creek MM, dtd 1853,12,13
1854, 2, 15. Levi & w, Mary, & dt, Sarah Jane, gct Wabash MM, Ind.
1854, 10, 18. Enoch J. gct Mill Creek MM, to m Anna Pearson
1855, 1, 17. Anna & ch, Rachel, rocf Mill Creek MM, dtd 1855,1,16
1855, 7, 18. Joshua dis studying the art of singing & attending mcd
1856, 7, 16. Elmira, Nathaniel & Mathias rocf Mill Creek MM, dtd 1856,7,15
1857, 3, 18. John & w, Mary P., & ch gct Red Cedar MM, Ia.
1860, 3, 14. Enoch rocf West Branch MM, O.
1860, 6, 13. Isaac C. dis
1860, 9, 12. Jeremiah gct West Branch MM, O.
1861, 5, 15. Louisa & ch, Rachel & Sarah Ellen, gct Wabash MM, Ind.
1861, 9, 18. Elizabeth gct Cotton Wood MM, Kans.
1862, 3, 12. Joseph Pemberton gct West Branch MM, O., to m Sidney Pearson
1862, 10, 16. Abram rpd mcd; dropped from mbrp
1867, 9, 18. Hiram rocf West Branch MM, O.
1868, 1, 15. Elizabeth rocf Cottonwood MM, Kans., dtd 1867,12,26
1891, 5, 2. Samuel dropped from mbrp
1894, 3, 3. Annie & Mary E. recrq
1897, 1, 2. Susan, Homer & Charles recrq

PEGG
1828, 9, 6. Mary Ann con mcd
1828, 12, 6. Maryann gct Cherry Grove MM, Ind.

PICKERING
1822, 10, 5. Hester (form McCool) dis mcd
1850, 11, 13. Hester rst at Spiceland MM, Ind., on consent of this mtg

PEIRCE
----, --, --. Samuel [Pierce], s Gainor & Ruth, d 1863,9,23; m Milly IDDINGS, dt Benj. & Phebe, d 1867,4,26
Ch: Ruth b 1811, 9, 7
Margaret " 1813, 7, 29
Malinda " 1815, 8, 19
Gainor A. " 1817, 6, 3
William R. " 1819, 3, 2
Elmira F. " 1820, 12, 4
Samuel " 1822, 9, 12
Hannah " 1825, 1, 6
Mary " 1827, 1, 10
John " 1828, 10, 17
Clarkson " 1832, 10, 8
Zenas " 1834, 4, 17
1821, 10, 23. Gainer d ae 66 7m 23d bur Union
1822, 12, 11. Ruth m Benjamin IDDINGS
1833, 4, 24. Ruth m Jesse PEMBERTON
1838, 2, 21. Melinda m Noah BROOKS
1838, 4, 25. Wm. R., s Samuel & Milly, Miami Co., O., b 1819,3,2; m in Union, Prudence PEMBERTON, dt Robert & Eunice (Coppock), Miami Co., O., b 1820,10,10
Ch: Robert b 1839, 4, 3
Samuel Harrison " 1841, 2, 18
Melicia " 1843, 2, 4
Ezra L. " 1845, 2, 16 d 1846,12,11
Eunice " 1848, 7, 8
Albert " 1848, 7, 8 " 1848, 7,18
Fidella " 1850, 12, 17
----, --, --. Gainer, s Samuel; m Jane COPPOCK dt Moses
Ch: Lydia C. b 1839, 7, 15
Manerva " 1841, 9, 9
Noah " 1843, 9, 20
Moses C. " 1845, 11, 6
George W. " 1848, 10, 10
Henry D. " 1851, 1, 9
Oren " 1853, 4, 30
Albert " 1856, 4, 27
Emma J. " 1859, 6, 25
1838, 10, 24. Margaret m Moses JAY
1842, 3, 23. Elmira m Martin BROOKS
1842, 4, 20. Samuel Jr., s Samuel & Milly, Miami Co., O.; m in Union, Elizabeth ELLEMAN, dt Enos & Margaret (Ward), b 1825,10,12 d 1852,10,27 bur Union
Ch: Enos E. b 1843, 6, 7 d 1849, 8,11 bur Union
Hannah " 1845, 10, 9
Martin Elleman " 1847, 2, 28 d 1876,10,10
Alvin " 1849, 1, 21
Ermina " 1851, 10, 3 " 1875,11, 3
Samuel m 2nd Ann JONES, wd Lyman W.
Ch: Esther b 1855, 10, 22
1848, 5, 24. Hannah C. m Henry W. COATE
1848, 6, 21. John, s Samuel & Milly, Miami

PEIRCE, John, continued
Co., O.; m in Union, Mary ELLERMAN, dt Enos & Margaret, Miami Co., O.
Ch: Margaret Ann b 1850, 7, 2 d 1851, 8, 3 bur Union
Delilah " 1851, 11, 25
William E. " 1854, 8, 31
Mary Elizabeth " 1857, 4, 16
Amanda Alice b 1864, 11, 8
Flora Malinda " 1868, 4, 12 d 1876, 8,16
Charles Hamlin b 1860, 4, 28 (1870?)
Walter Clarence " 1872, 10, 26
1853, 3, 17. Mary B. m Jonathan D. BOYD
----, --, --. Clarkson [Pierce], s Samuel & Milly, b 1831,11,8; m Lucy Ann ----- b 1833, 1,6
Ch: Calvin H. b 1855, 4, 20
Amanda J. " 1857, 8, 4 d 1859, 9, 1
Lavina E. " 1859, 6, 9
Carolin " 1861, 4, 7
Rosella T. " 1863, 2, 26
Lucy Ann " 1866, 2, 12 d 1866, 7,28
----, --, --. Zenas, s Samuel & Milly; m Eliza Ann -----
Ch: Hannah M. b 1856, 2, 15 d 1861, 5,19
Clarkson T." 1857, 10, 25
John T. " 1860, 8, 22
Samuel " 1863, 11, 20
Abram L. " 1866, 6, 3
Zenas Cary " 1869, 6, 27
Rolen Nelson " 1871, 10, 24
1872, 11, 7. James M. d ae 81y

1813, 1, 2. John [Pierce] con mcd
1815, 3, 4. John [Pierce] gct Mill Creek MM
1816, 8, 3. George dis
1816, 11, 2. James dis
1817, 12, 6. John [Pierce] & w, Anna, & ch, Jemima, Ruth, Matilda, rocf Mill Creek MM, dtd 1817,8,23
1823, 4, 5. John & fam gct Springfield MM, Ind.
1825, 10, 1. Benjamin D. dis
1838, 9, 12. Jane rocf Mill Creek MM, dtd 1838,9,11
1839, 3, 13. Rachel recrq
1839, 10, 16. Benj. D. [Pierce] & w, Rachel, gct West Grove MM, Ind.
1852, 2, 18. Wm. [Pierce] & w, Prudence, & fam gct Back Creek MM
1854, 4, 12. Clarkson [Pierce] gct Back Creek MM, Ind.
1854, 5, 17. Samuel Jr. gct Dover MM, to m Ann Pemberton
1864, 8, 16. Ann rocf Dover MM, Ind., dtd 1854,7,19
1854, 11, 15. Zenas [Pierce] con mcd
1855, 4, 18. Eliza Ann [Pierce] recrq
1859, 5, 18. Clarkson & fam rocf Back Creek MM, Ind., dtd 1859,4,14
1864, 4, 14. Hannah rocf New Garden MM, dtd 1864,3,19
1866, 12, 12. Moses C. rpd mcd; retained mbrp
1867, 2, 13. James recrq
1867, 6, 12. Clarkson [Pearce] & w, Lacy Ann, relrq
1896, 11, 7. Lois T. [Pierce] rocf Matehuala M MM, Mex.

PEMBERTON
----, --, --. Robert, s Isaiah & Esther, S.C., d 1828,8,30 ae 40y 7m 10d; m Eunice Anna COPPOCK, dt John & Anna (Jay)
Ch: Isaiah b 1811, 2, 1
John " 1812, 3, 22
Jesse " 1814, 2, 27
Anna " 1815, 9, 14
Mary " 1818, 1, 26
Prudence " 1820, 10, 10
Robert " 1823, 9, 24
Lemuel " 1827, 3, 2 d 1828, 4, 9 bur Union
----, --, --. Isaiah, s Isaiah & Esther, b 1790,10,2; m Elizabeth ELLEMAN, dt John & Susannah, b 1795,11,23 d 1861,5,3 bur Union
Ch: John E. b 1811, 10, 15
Isaac " 1814, 2, 26
Esther " 1815, 11, 9
Temperance " 1817, 4, 6
Susannah E." 1819, 12, 29
David " 1822, 1, 29
Rhoda " 1824, 2, 10
Enos " 1827, 7, 20 d 1835, 9,19
Isaiah " 1829, 6, 6 " 1874, 3, 2
Elizabeth " 1831, 3, 4
Luranah " 1833, 3, 14 " 1833, 4, 2 bur Union
Margaret " 1854, 4, 2 " 1846, 1,10
Joseph " 1836, 12, 26
Hannah " 1840, 4, 19 " 1846, 6,15 bur Union
1815, 6, 14. Mary m Henry NEAL
1819, 9, 8. Elizabeth m Nehemiah THOMAS
1828, 3, 30. Robert d bur Bloomfield, Ind.
1829, 10, 7. Isaac, s Robert & Eunice, Miami Co., O.; m in Union, Tace ELLEMAN, dt John & Susannah, Miami Co., O.
1833, 4, 24. Jesse, s Robert & Unice, Miami Co., O.; m in Union, Ruth PEIRCE, dt Samuel & Milly, Miami Co., O.
----, --, --. John, s Isaiah & Esther, b 1789, 4,12; m Drusilla ELLEMAN, dt John & Susannah, b 1794,2,4
Ch: Elizabeth b 1811, 10, 5
Susannah " 1813, 8, 2
Esther " 1815, 3, 11
Elijah " 1817, 1, 18
Nancy " 1818, 10, 24

PEMBERTON, John & Drusilla, continued
Ch: Hannah b 1821, 10, 28
Lydia " 1823, 9, 20
Drusilla " 1826, 2, 28
Lucinda " 1830, 12, 8
Mary E. " 1837, 4, 3 d 1837, 4,17
---- --, --. Isaiah, s Robt. & Eunice (Coppock) m Tace ELLEMAN, dt John & Susannah
Ch: Jane E. b 1830, 7, 11
Eunice " 1832, 4, 15
Zilpah " 1833, 12, 30
Susannah " 1836, 3, 2
1830, 6, 9. John E., s Isaiah & Elizabeth (Elleman), Miami Co., O.; m in Union, Susannah COPPOCK, dt Benjamin & Susannah, Miami Co., O., d 1846,5,23
Ch: William b 1831, 2, 28
Rebecca " 1832, 7, 13
Martha " 1834, 11, 12
Elizabeth " 1836, 5, 15
Isaiah " 1838, •11, 9
Moses " 1841, 4, 6 d 1863, 1,17
Ann " 1843, 6, 26
Susanna " 1846, 5, 2
1831, 2, 28. William b
1834, 5, 21. Anna m Absalom HOLLINGSWORTH
1835, 9, 19. Enos, s Isaiah, d bur Union
1835, 9, 23. Esther m David THOMAS
1837, 12, 20. Susannah E. m Henry JONES
1838, 4, 25. Prudence m Wm. R. PEIRCE
1840, 11, 25. Lydia m Caleb COATE
----, --, --. Elijah, s Jno. & Drusilla; m Sarah HALL, dt Samuel, b 1825,7,18
Ch: Fanna b 1843, 8, 5
Daniel " 1844, 11, 18
Samuel " 1846, 8, 28 d 1846,11,21
Melinda " 1846, 8, 28
Phineas " 1848, 7, 19
John " 1849, 12, 21
Milan " 1852, 10, 17 d 1852,10,26
Leander " 1854, 9, 26
1846, 5, 23. Susannah d bur Union
1846, 11, 21. Samuel d bur Union
1848, 11, 21. Wm., s John E. & Susannah, Miami Co., O.; m in Union, Prudence COATE, dt Benjamin & Phebe, Miami Co., O.
1849, 5, 23. Rhoda m Benj. THOMAS
1849, 10, 25. Isaiah, s Isaiah & Elizabeth (Elleman), Miami Co., O.; m Prudence H. JAY, dt Elijah & Anna, Miami Co., O., d 1850,11,18 ae 21y 1m 14d
Ch: Enos b 1850, 7, 12 d 1850,11, 1
1852, 1, 22. Mary Ann m Jacob TUCKER
1854, 9, 14. Lemuel, s John & Susannah, Grant Co., Ind.; m in Union, Mary ELLEMAN, dt Isaac & Elizabeth, Miami Co., O.
1855, 11, 22. Elizabeth m Joseph THOMAS
----, --, --. Isaiah, s John E. & Susannah (Coppock), b 1838,11,9 d 1914,3,6; m Dorcas COATE, dt Benj. & Mary (Jones), b 1838,7,22 d 1912,3,16
Ch: Mary Elen b 1850, 5, 13
Aaron E. " 1861, 7, 17
Sarah Eda b 1864, 10, 21
1860, 1, 25. Fannie J. m Jesse COATE
1861, 6, 20. Anna m David COPPOCK
1884, 1, 3. Sarah d (2nd w of John E.)

1817, 9, 6. Wm. con mcd
1827, 9, 1. Joseph & fam & Tace Elleman gct Honey Creek MM
1829, 3, 7. Isaiah & w, Elizabeth, & ch, John, Isaac, Esther, David, Susanna, Rhoda & Enos, rocf Bloomfield MM, Ind., dtd 1828,11,1
1830, 12, 4. John gct West Branch MM, O., to m Susanna Hollingsworth
1833, 5, 15. Susannah rocf West Branch MM, O., dtd 1833,4,18
1836, 7, 13. Isaac con mcd
1836, 10, 12. John Jr. & fam gct Mississinewa MM, Ind.
1838, 3, 14. Eunice & s, Robert, gct Mississinewa MM, Ind.
1838, 12, 12. Nancy Jenkins (form Pemberton) dis mcd
1839, 8, 14. Isaiah & fam gct Back Creek MM
1841, 9, 15. Hannah dis jas
1842, 2, 16. Isaac gct Mississinewa MM, Ind.
1842, 7, 13. Elijah con mcd
1842, 9, 14. David con mcd
1844, 4, 17. Jesse dis jas
1845, 6, 18. Ester P. Jay, minor, recrq of Drucilla Pemberton
1848, 2, 16. John E. gct West Branch MM, O., to m Sarah Allison
1848, 7, 12. Sarah rocf West Branch MM, O., dtd 1848,6,15
1849, 8, 15. Jesse rst
1849, 11, 14. Ruth & ch gct Back Creek MM, Ind.
1849, 11, 14. Jesse & fam gct Back Creek MM, Ind.
1849, 11, 14. Ruth & ch rqct Honey Creek MM
185-, 2, 13. Elijah, minor, rocf Honey Creek MM
1850, 4, 17. David rocf Honey Creek MM, dtd 1850,5,11
1850, 12, 18. David & w, Maryann Louisa, & ch, gct Honey Creek MM
1851, 4, 16. Isaiah Jr. gct Honey Creek MM
1851, 7, 16. Jorden Elleman gct Back Creek MM, to m Sophia Elleman
1853, 10, 13. Isaiah Jr. rocf Honey Creek MM, Ind., dtd 1853,8,13
1853, 10, 13. Rachel rocf West Branch MM, O., dtd 1853,9,15
1854, 5, 17. Samuel Peirce Jr. gct Dover MM, to m Ann Pemberton
1854, 11, 15. Mary gct Back Creek MM, Ind.
1856, 8, 13. David & fam rocf Back Creek MM, dtd 1856,7,17
1857, 1, 14. Wm. & fam have been rec at Salem MM, Ia. (no record of cert issued)
1860, 4, 18. Isaiah con mcd
1860, 8, 15. Enos rocf Greenfield MM, Ind., dtd 1860,6,6

PEMBERTON, continued
1860, 8, 15. Mary & ch, David, Jincy, Henry, Elizabeth & Margaret, rocf Greenfield MM, Ind., dtd 1860,6,6
1861, 7, 17. Isaac rocf Greenfield MM, Ind.
1862, 3, 12. Joseph gct West Branch MM, O., to m Sidney Pearson
1863, 9, 16. Elijah & fam gct Legrand MM, Ia.
1864, 11, 16. Joseph gct West Branch MM, O.
1866, 9, 12. Daniel gct Legrand MM, Ia.
1872, 2, 14. Elijah rpd mcd; retained mbrp
1889, 10, 5. Serena relrq
1889, 10, 5. John E. relrq
1889, 10, 5. Dorcas relrq
1890, 7, 5. Elijah & w, Sarah, rocf Legrand MM, Ia., dtd 1890,6,14
1890, 7, 5. Ellis W. rocf Legrand MM, Ia., dtd 1890,6,14

PENNY
1898, 4, 2. Sylvester Henry, Mattie Elizabeth, Bertha Geneva, Nettie Ellen & Lidema recrq

RAGAN
1836, 8, 25. Eliza m Thomas COATE

1836, 5, 18. Eliza [Reagan] recrq
1856, 1, 16. Martha Ann dis

RHODEHAMBLE
1854, 9, 26. Naomi [Rhotehamel] dt Nicholas & Charity Thomas, d
1826, 6, 3. Kerenhappuck dis mcd

RICHARDSON
1848, 11, 15. Jane (form Thompson) dis mcd

RINGER
1854, 7, 12. Mary K. (Coppock) dis mcd

ROLLMAN
1899, 7, 1. Celia relrq to U. B. Church

SHAFFER
1897, 2, 4. Anne relrq by letter to M. E. Ch.

SHELL
1868, 8, 12. Hannah gct New Garden MM

SPENCER
1837, 9, 13. Selina dis mcd

STANFIELD
1837, 6, 14. Margaret con mcd
1837, 12, 13. Margaret gct Mississinewa MM, Ind.

STEDDOM
1815, 11, 8. Samuel, s Henry & Martha, Warren Co., O.; m in Union, Susanna TEAGUE, dt Samuel & Rebecca, Miami Co., O.
1853, 3, 17. Samuel, s John & Alice, Warren Co., O.; m in Union, Esther Pearson, dt John F. & Mary P., Miami Co., O.

1817, 5, 3. Susanna gct Miami MM, O.
1868, 7, 15. Wm. C. & w, Elizabeth, & dt, Carrie C., rocf Miami MM, O., dtd 1868,6,24

STEPHENS
1855, 9, 12. Mary Ann dis

STEWART
1897, 1, 2. Edna recrq
1897, 1, 2. Lemma recrq

STREET
1891, 5, 2. Perry dropped from mbrp

TEAGUE
----, --, --. Samuel b 1759,3,2 d 1841,2,26 ae 81bur Union; m Rebecca FURNAS b 1764,4,19 d 1842,6,27 ae 78 bur Union

Ch:			
Mary	b 1783, 12, 22		
Rebecca	" 1784, 9, 8		
Lurana	" 1786, 9, 1		
Alice	" 1788, 2, 22		
Esther	" 1790, 2, 26		
Joseph	" 1792, 2, 26	d 1809, 3, 5	
Moses	" 1794, 2, 6		
Furnas	" 1796, 7, 26	" 1796, 9,25	
Susanna	" 1798, 6, 13		
Samuel	" 1803, 8, 31		

1815, 11, 8. Susannah m Samuel STEDDOM
----, --, --. Moses b 1794,2,6 d 1871,2,18; m Jane COPPOCK, dt Thomas, b 1799,6,7 d 1874,1,19

Ch:	
Joseph	b 1818, 9, 15
John	" 1822, 12, 29
Mary	" 1825, 6, 22
Thomas	" 1830, 7, 21
Samuel	" 1832, 3, 5
William	" 1838, 11, 26

1822, 9, 11. Rhoda m John MOTE
1824, 4, 7. Rebecca m Wm. JAY
1841, 2, 26. Samuel d ae 81y 11m 24d (an elder)
1843, 9, 20. Mary m David M. COATE
1853, 1, 13. Isaac C., s Samuel & Prudence, Wabash Co., Ind.; m in Union, Joanna MILES, dt John & Rebecca, Miami Co., O.

1817, 6, 7. Moses con mcd
1817, 10, 4. Jane recrq
1825, 5, 7. Samuel Jr. gct Mill Creek MM, to m Prudence Cooper
1827, 7, 7. Dibra recrq of Samuel & Rebecca Teague
1827, 6, 2. Prudence rocf Mill Creek MM

TEAGUE, continued
1829, 4, 4. Samuel Jr. & fam gct Mill Creek MM
1834, 2, 12. Samuel & w, Prudence, & ch, Isaac, Joseph, Abigail & Moses Furnas, rocf Milford MM, Ind., dtd 1834,1,25
1836, 1, 14. Samuel & fam gct Mill Creek MM
1841, 5, 12. Joseph con mcd
1849, 6, 13. Moses & fam gct Mississinewa MM, Ind.
1853, 9, 14. Joanna M. gct Wabash MM, Ind.
1856, 6, 18. Moses & w, Jane, & s, Wm., rocf White Lick MM, dtd 1856,5,14
1859, 1, 12. Samuel & w, Rachel, & ch, James Madison & Sarah Jane, rocf White Lick MM, dtd 1858,12,15
1859, 8, 17. Wm. con mcd
1859, 9, 14. Moses & Jane gct Wabash MM, Ind.
1860, 9, 12. Wm. & w, Mary, gct Wabash MM, Ind.
1861, 5, 15. Rachel & ch, James & Sarah Jane, gct Birch Lake MM, Mich.
1861, 12, 18. Samuel dis
1868, 8, 12. Moses & w, Jane, rocf Wabash MM, Ind., dtd 1868,6,13
1872, 9, 18. Ruth recrq

THOMAS
1813, 5, 27. Margaret b
1819, 9, 8. Nehemiah, s Isaac & Mary, Montgomery Co., O.; m in Union, Elizabeth PEMBERTON, dt Isaiah & Esther, Miami Co., O.
1825, 2, 7. George, s John & Nancy, Miami Co., O.; m in Union, Hannah ELLEMAN, dt John & Susannah, Miami Co., O.
1835, 9, 23. David, s Isaiah & Elizabeth, Montgomery Co., O.; m in Union, Esther PEMBERTON, dt Isaiah & Elizabeth, Miami Co., O.
1849, 5, 23. Benjamin, s John & Hannah, d 1855,10,8 ae 31y 3m 17d; m in Union, Rhoda PEMBERTON, dt Isaiah & Elizabeth, Miami Co., O., b 1824,2,10
Ch: Lindley M. b 1850, 4, 7
Elwood C. " 1852, 1, 26
Branson " 1854, 3, 2
1855, 10, 8. Benjamin d bur Southbank
1855, 11, 22. Joseph, s Isaiah & Elizabeth, Montgomery Co.; m in Lickbranch, Elizabeth PEMBERTON, dt John E. & Susannah, Miami Co., O.
----, --, --. Branson T. m Annie Jane COATE, dt Josias & Sarah
Ch: Mary Elvurta b 1876, 11, 28
Marvin Esta " 1878, 1, 10
Harley C. " 1885, 2, 19

1819, 11, 6. Elizabeth gct West Branch MM, O.
1826, 3, 4. Hannah gct West Branch MM, O.
1835, 12, 16. Esther gct West Branch MM, O.
1849, 8, 15. Rhoda gct West Branch MM, O.
1852, 6, 16. Henry gct Honey Creek MM
1854, 3, 15. Mariam rocf West Branch MM, O., dtd 1854,2,16
1854, 4, 12. Jacob dis
1858, 5, 12. Noah dis
1861, 2, 13. Hannah & ch, Reuben & Angeline, gct Honey Creek MM, Ind.
1864, 8, 17. Joseph & fam rocf West Branch MM, O., dtd 1864,7,14
1897, 1, 2. Norman recrq

THOMPSON
1810, 4, 10. Ann (Jay), w James P., b
1814, 2, 9. Isaac, s Richard, Miami Co., O.; m in Union, Jane MILES, dt Wm., Miami Co., O.
1822, 6, 5. Richard, s Richard & Susannah, Miami Co., O., b 1792,12,8; d 1849,1,6; m in Union, Abigail JAY, dt Layton & Elizabeth, Miami Co., O., b 1802,6,20
Ch: Samuel b 1823, 9, 5 d 1823,10, 5
Oliver " 1824, 12, 27
Elizabeth " 1826, 10, 15 " 1845,11,10
Mary " 1828, 5, 3
Samuel " 1830, 2, 11
Israel " 1831, 11, 16 " 1834,11,10
Anna " 1833, 8, 16
Esther " 1835, 2, 5 " 1845,11,10
Richard " 1837, 3, 25 " 1849, 1, 6 bur Union
Abigail " 1838, 9, 13
Charlotte " 1840, 12, 26
James H. " 1842, 12, 18
Susannah " 1845, 9, 17 d 1846, 6, 3

1818, 7, 3. Charlotte con mcd
1822, 4, 6. Isaac dis
1824, 8, 7. Samuel Israel rocf New Garden MM, N. C., dtd 1823,12,27
1824, 10, 2. Samuel Israel dis mcd
1830, 5, 1. Anna con mcd
1830, 6, 5. Jane & ch, Susanna, William, Quimby, Elizabeth & Isaac, gct Vermillion MM, Ill.
1830, 6, 5. Charlotte & ch, Richard, Layton, John, William & Jane, gct Vermillion MM, Ill.
1830, 6, 5. Richard & w, Abigail, & ch, Oliver, Elizabeth & Mary, gct Vermillion MM, Ill.
1833, 9, 18. Richard & w, Abigail, & ch, Oliver, Elizabeth, Mary & Samuel, rocf Vermillion MM, Ill., dtd 1833,5,4
1842, 6, 15. Samuel recrq
1842, 9, 14. Charlotty rst
1842, 9, 14. Sally C. dis mcd
1843, 5, 16. John & Wm. rocf Bloomfield MM, Ind., dtd 1843,4,5
1843, 5, 17. Jane P. rocf Bloomfield MM, Ind. dtd 1843,4,5
1844, 10, 16. Richard & Layton rocf Bloomfield MM
1845, 11, 12. Layton con mcd

THOMPSON, continued
1846, 1, 14. Samuel dis mcd
1847, 4, 14. Layton dis
1848, 10, 18. Wm. dis mcd
1848, 11, 15. Jane Richardson (form Thompson) dis mcd
1849, 5, 16. Oliver dis mcd
1851, 3, 12. Samuel dis jas
1851, 3, 12. Abigail & dt, Anna, dis
1851, 3, 12. Mary Wintrow (form Tompson) dis
1861, 12, 18. Richard dis
1870, 1, 12. Gustavus & w, Sarah, & ch, Sarah Ann & Elijah Wm., recrq
1870, 2, 16. James rpd mcd; dropped from mbrp

THORNBERRY
1821, 4, 7. Clarissa con mcd
1822, 10, 5. Clarissa gct West Grove MM

THORNBURGH
1826, 6, 3. Sally dis mcd

THORNTON
1813, 9, 8. Eli gct White Water MM, Ind.

TROST
1893, 1, 7. Henry G., Henrietta & Minnie recrq

TUCKER
1814, 3, 5. Mary m Samuel BROWN
----, --, --. Nicholas, s Abraham; m Charity THOMAS, dt Edward, d 1853,10,22
Ch: Mary B. b 1819, 4, 16
Sarah C. " 1820, 6, 10
Abigail G. " 1823, 1, 25
Naomi G. " 1824, 10, 4 d 1854, 9,26 m ----- Rhotehamil
Jacob b 1826, 7, 27
Rachel " 1829, 1, 14
Vashti " 1831, 7, 6 d 1852, 3, 1
1837, 8, 24. Mary B. m Wade MILES
1838, 3, 22. Sarah C. m Josias COATE
1852, 1, 22. Jacob, s Nicholas & Charity, Miami Co., O.; m in Lickbranch, Mary Ann PEMBERTON, dt John E. & Susannah, Miami Co., O.

1836, 5, 18. Nicholas & w, Charity, & ch, Mary B., Sarah C., Naomi J., Jacob, Rachel & Vashti, rocf New Garden MM, dtd 1836,2,20
1838, 12, 12. Wm. Coate gct West Branch MM, O., to m Mary Tucker
1856, 9, 17. Nicholas gct Salem MM, Ia.
1857, 1, 14. Jacob & fam have been rec at Salem MM, Ia. (no record of cert being issued)
1891; 2, 7. Trudie recrq

UPTON
1852, 9, 15. Martha dis

VAN HORN
----, --, --. Robert & Durah
Ch: Sarah b 1799, 3, 23
Benjamin " 1801, 3, 22 d 1801,11,11
Wilkinson " 1804, 1, 20
Rebecca " 1806, 11, 5
James " 1809, 2, 20
Julian " 1814, 7, 14
John " 1817, 6, 6
Betsy " 1820, 3, 21

1822, 9, 7. Sarah Dickson (form Vanhorn) dis mcd
1823, 2, 1. Wilkinson dis jas
1833, 6, 12. Betsy gct West Branch MM, O.

VANSCOYOC
1834, 9, 17. Rhoda con mcd
1835, 5, 13. Rhoda gct Mississinewa MM, Ind.

VARNER
1881, 6, 29. Mahala d ae 21y 9m 23d

VERNON
1817, 6, 7. Jane con mcd
1821, 9, 1. Thomas rocf West Branch MM, O., dtd 1820,7,21
1823, 11, 1. Grace rocf West Branch MM, O., dtd 1823,10,13
1824, 10, 2. Thomas dis
1832, 9, 13. Hannah con mcd
1841, 5, 12. Hannah gct Mississinewa MM, Ind.
1842, 8, 17. Hannah & Sarah dis jas
1842, 9, 14. Pickering dis mcd & jas

VORE
1897, 1, 2. Adelbert recrq

VORTH
1830, 11, 6. Lydia con mcd

WASSON
1891, 4, 9. Sarah recrq
1897, 1, 2. Henry recrq

WEEKS
----, --, --. Benjamin & Abigail
Ch: Susannah b 1797, 5, 16
Mary " 1798, 11, 20
Hannah " 1801, 9, 4
Claricy " 1803, 6, 28
Abigail " 1805, 10, 31
Kerenhappuck " 1807, 6, 16
Elizabeth " 1809, 11, 28
1819, 1, 6. Mary m Isaac COATE

1815, 3, 4. Benjamin & w, Abigail, & ch, Susannah, Mary, Hannah, Claricy, Abigail, Kerenhappuck & Elizabeth, rocf New Garden MM, N. C., dtd 1814,8,27, endorsed by West Branch MM, O.
1816, 2, 3. Benjamin gct White Water MM,

WEEKS, continued
Ind., to m Margaret Thornbrough
1817, 5, 3. Margaret rocf White Water MM, Ind. dtd 1817,3,29

WHITE
1819, 1, 2. Elizabeth (form Jay) dis mcd
1820, 4, 1. Elizabeth recrq
1827, 2, 3. Elizabeth dis
1843, 9, 13. Elizabeth rst

WHITSON
1814, 4, 2. Lydia recrq
1814, 5, 7. Solomon rocf West Branch MM, O., dtd 1814,4,28
1814, 9, 3. John, s Solomon, recrq
1836, 9, 14. Lydia & ch gct Mississinewa MM, Ind.
1837, 1, 18. Solomon dis
1837, 1, 18. John dis
1837, 1, 18. Phebe dis

WILLETS
1852, 4, 14. Lindley Miles gct Alum Creek MM, O., to m Lidia Willets

WILLIAMS
1837, 12, 13. Sarah dis mcd
1849, 6, 13. Sarah (form Coate) dis mcd

* * * * * * *

COATE
1830, 6, 5. Lydia & ch, Delila, Benjamin & Abiather Davis Coate, gct Vermillion MM, Ill.

JONES
-----, --, --. Jesse & Jane
Ch: Alexander b 1818, 6, 29
Samuel " 1820, 9, 5 d 1823,11,16 bur Union
Harvey " 1823, 2, 9
William " 1825, 8, 25
Mark " 1828, 7, 24 d 1835, 9,20 bur Union
Eunice " 1832, 1, 9 " 1834, 8,16

WINTROW
1851, 3, 12. Mary (form Tompson) dis
1891, 5, 2. Elijah dropped from mbrp

WOODS
1893, 1, 7. Elias, Alice & James recrq

WRIGHT
1814, 9, 3. John, s Ann, recrq
1829, 10, 3. Abigail con mcd
1829, 12, 5. John con mcd
1836, 11, 16. Elizabeth & two ch recrq
1838, 6, 13. Abigail gct Mississinewa MM, Ind.
1844, 2, 15. Elizabeth McCoy (form Wright) dis mcd
1848, 7, 12. John gct Honey Creek MM (a minor)
1848, 7, 12. Nancy, Kesiah & Eunice gct Honey Creek MM
1859, 4, 13. Eunice rocf Honey Creek MM, Ind. dtd 1859,3,12

YOUNG
1843, 9, 13. Jane (form Brown) dis mcd
1844, 3, 13. Samuel Miles con mcd
1853, 5, 18. Phebe dis

ZIEGLER
1892, 2, 1. Della relrq

* * * * * * *

Ch: Alvin b 1835, 1, 5 d 1913, 4, 3
----, --, --. Jesse & Naomi
Ch: Jane b 1838, 8, 25
Mary " 1840, 4, 27 d 1861, 6,27

MILES
1833, 2, 1. Anne, dt David & Jean, b

ELK MONTHLY MEETING

Elk Monthly Meeting, at West Elkton, Ohio, was set off from Miami Monthly Meeting 12 Mo. 2, 1809. The monthly meeting divided 11 Mo. 6, 1828. Names of charter members were Brown, Comer, Cook, Evans, Hatfield, Hawkins, Kenworthy, Maddock, Moore, Roberts, Stubbs, Talbert, Whetson and others.

RECORDS

ADAMS
----, --, --. Thomas & Ann
Ch: Ruth b 1814, 10, 6
Thomas " 1817, 6, 6
Elizabeth " 1819, 12, 1
Samuel Cary" 1824, 7, 31
1827, 3, 26. Solomon b
----, --, --. Simon & Agnes
Ch: Cora Ann b 1873, 8, 8
Charles
William " 1875, 4, 27
Blanch " 1877, 7, 1
Ruetty " 1879, 11, 5
1888, 7, 7. Agnes d ae 32y 6m 9d
1891, 11, 19. Cora A. d ae 18y 3m 11d

1819, 8, 7. Thomas & w, Ann, & ch, Ruth & Thomas, rocf Miami MM, dtd 1819,6,30
1821, 2, 3. William & w, Rachel, & ch, Jonathan Jacob William & Matilda, rocf Deep Creek MM, N. C., dtd 1820,8,5
1821, 12, 1. Jedidiah rpd mou; Byberry MM, Pa. was given permission to accept his offering
1822, 12, 7. Jediah rocf Byberry MM, Pa., dtd 1822,3,26
1835, 1, 17. Ruth dis disunity
1839, 11, 16. Elizabeth dis neglecting attendance & jH
1876, 2, 24. Simon & w, Agnes, & ch, Charles W. & Cora Ann, rec in mbrp
1891, 4, 22. Simon gct New School of Baptists Church, Loveland, O.

AIRY
----, --, --. John & Keziah
Ch: Mary Ann b 1825, 9, 9
William " 1827, 3, 8
George " 1829, 5, 11
Lydia " 1831, 10, 12
Elizabeth " 1834, 6, 6

1825, 4, 2. John con mou
1825, 11, 5. Keziah con mou
1826, 3, 4. John rocf White Water MM, dtd 1825,10,15
1830, 12, 14. John & w, Keziah, & ch, Mary Ann, William & George, gct White Water MM, Ind.
1832, 5, 19. John & w, Keziah, & ch, Mary Ann, William, George & Lydia, rocf White Water MM, dtd 1832,2,2
1836, 1, 16. John & w, Keziah, & ch, Mary Ann, William, George, Lydia & Elizabeth, gct White Lick MM, Ind.
1869, 3, 25. Clara M. [Ary] (form Brown) gct Rocksylvania MM, Ia.

ALBERTSON
1884, 7, 24. Melva & s, Myron Charles, gct White Water MM, Ind.
1886, 7, 22. Melva & s, Myron C., gct Kansas City MM, Missouri
1887, 4, 21. Howard Z., s Edgar B. & Melva S., gct Kansas City MM, Missouri

ALLEN
1821, 5, 5. Meribah Pheres (form Allen) rpd mou; Chesterfield MM, N. J. notified
1824, 10, 2. Zacheriah & w, Susannah, & ch, Nancy & Jane, rocf Cane Creek MM, N. C., dtd 1822,4,6, endorsed by White Water MM, 1822,8,17
1825, 5, 7. Zechariah & fam gct Springfield MM, Ind.

ANDY
1888, 9, 20. William rec in mbrp
1892, 5, 26. William dis

ANTHONY
1811, 3, 2. Christopher rocf Goose Creek MM, Va., dtd 1810,10,4

ARMITAGE
1823, 8, 2. Eleanor & dt, Grace, rocf Miami MM, dtd 1823,5,28

ARNOTT
1854, 12, 21. Elizabeth (form Talbert) con mou (living at New Garden MM, Ind.)
1855, 6, 21. Elizabeth T. gct New Garden MM, Ind.

AUGSBARGER
1868, 8, 30. Jane, dt Elijah & Amy Ann Cooper b

1898, 3, 24. Jennie L. [Augspurger] relrq

BAILEY
1834, 6, 11. Nathan rocf Center MM, dtd 1834, 4,17 (H)
1835, 10, 8. Nathan [Baily] gct Westfield MM (H)

BALLARD
1813, 2, 25. Nathan, Clinton Co., O., s David & Mary; m at Elk Mtg, Catherine THORN, dt Isaac & Sarah, both dec
1821, 2, 8. Alice m William KENWORTHY
1838, 7, 26. Sarah m Jonas BROWN
1853, 11, 25. Benajah, Clinton Co., O., s Spencer & Rebecca; m at Elk Mtg, Phebe LANE, dt Jesse & Hannah, dec
1875, 8, 23. Achsah P. d ae 71y 3m 18d

1813, 2, 6. Nathan prcf Miami MM, to m Catherine Thorn
1820, 3, 4. Joseph & w, Elizabeth, & ch, Alice, David, Susannah, Joel, Juliana, Almeida & Asa, rocf Ceasers Creek MM, dtd 1820,1,20
1822, 8, 3. Joseph & fam gct West Grove MM,

BALLARD, continued
Ind.
1827, 6, 1. Lazarus Denney gct Cherry Grove MM, to m Mary Ballard
1827, 11, 3. Israel rocf Cherry Grove MM, dtd 1827,3,10
1832, 2, 4. Mary (form Cooper) dis mou
1832, 9, 15. Israel dis disunity
1834, 10, 18. Hannah (form Cooper) con mou
1835, 11, 21. Elizabeth rocf Dover MM, O., dtd 1835,9,17
1837, 2, 18. Elizabeth gct Dover MM, O.
1846, 7, 18. Hannah gct Westfield MM, Ind.
1848, 1, 15. Samuel & w, Achsah, & ch, Elizabeth Jane, Lydia & Mary Stanley, rocf Dover MM, N. C., dtd 1847,11,25
1854, 1, 26. Phebe gct Center MM, O.

BALLINGER
----, --, --. Isaac, s Samuel & Elizabeth, b 1776,7,29; m Hannah HAINES, dt Abraham & Hannah, b 1781,10,28
Ch: Mary Ann b 1802, 9, 27
Abraham " 1804, 9, 19
Isaac H. " 1810, 8, 22
Hannah " 1812, 9, 13
Samuel " 1817, 8, 30
Sarah " 1819, 9, 4
1821, 8, 29. Hannah d ae 8y 11m 16d bur Westfield Cemetery
----, --, --. Abraham & Beulah
Ch: Samuel b 1826, 8, 16
John " 1828, 5, 9
1826, 1, 1. Samuel d ae 8y 4m 2d bur Westfield Cemetery
1884, 1, 3. Isaac H. d 1884,1,3 ae 73y 4m 11d

1820, 2, 5. Isaac [Balinger] & w, Hannah, & ch, Mary Ann, Abraham, Isaac H., Hannah, Samuel & Sarah, rocf Miami MM, dtd 1820,1, 26
1839, 7, 20. Sarah Brown (form Ballenger) dis mou & jH
1881, 6, 23. Isaac H. & w rocf Raysville MM, Ind., dtd 1881,5,28
1884, 7, 24. Rachel Ann gct White Water MM, Ind.

BARTON
1820, 1, 4. Samuel & w, Mary, & ch, Martha C., Joseph Collings & Rebeccah, rocf Haddonfield MM, N. J., dtd 1819,10,11
1822, 8, 3. Samuel dis
1823, 3, 1. Martha, Joseph Collins & Rebecca, ch Samuel, gct Haddonfield MM, N. J.

BEALL
1854, 7, 4. Mary d ae 27y 1m 7d

1845, 5, 17. Mary (form Stubbs) con mou

BEARD
1861, 4, 26. Jesse A. rst with consent of Deep River MM, N. C.

BEECHLER
----, --, --. Ira m Mahalah Elizabeth LANTIS, dt Samuel & Eliza

1902, 4, 24. Lizzie relrq

BEESON
1835, 9, 24. Seth, Preble Co., O., s William & Hannah, dec; m at Elk Mtg, Elizabeth TALBERT, Preble Co., O., dt Job & Amanda
1839, 4, 25. Elizabeth m Isaac WRIGHT

1820, 8, 5. Mary rocf Center MM, N. C., dtd 1819,11,20
1829, 8, 1. Eunice & Elizabeth [Beason] rocf Springfield MM, dtd 1829,7,7
1832, 6, 16. Eunice dis
1833, 10, 19. Eunice rst
1835, 1, 17. Seth rocf Springfield MM, Ind., dtd 1834,10,18
1836, 8, 20. Seth [Beason] dis
1837, 6, 17. Elizabeth & s, Isaac Newton, gct Westfield MM, Ind.
1840, 1, 18. Eunice Dicks (form Beeson) con mou
1841, 1, 16. Seth rst at Westfield MM with consent of this mtg

BENNETT
----, --, --. Nimrod m Sarah R. ROBERTS, dt John & Rebecca, b 1825,10,30
Ch: John A.
----, --, --. John m Hannah J. GIFFORD b 1847, 3,5
1890, 1, 29. Sarah d ae 69y 4m 2d

1866, 9, 20. Hannah J. (form Gifford) rpd mou
1871, 5, 26. Sarah Jane rocf Center MM, O., dtd 1871,4,12
1871, 8, 24. Belle rec in mbrp
1872, 1, 25. Sarah & s, John Anderson, rec
1908, 9, 24. John dropped from mbrp

BENSON
1835, 5, 16. Deborah gc
1854, 9, 21. Ruth (form Talbert) con mou & deviating from plainness in dress (living at Cherry Grove MM)
1855, 3, 22. Ruth T. gct Cherry Grove MM,Ind.

BERK
1895, 3, 21. Melia A. relrq

BIRAM
----, --, --. Nathan & Jemima
Ch: Jemima
Elliott
Meriam b 1814, 1, 25
Exum Elliott
b 1817, 1, 22

BIRAM, Nathan & Jemima, continued
Ch: Caleb
Parker b 1819, 7, 13
Emmaline
Isabella " 1821, 12, 19
Orpah " 1824, 3, 12
Alfred
Griffin " 1826, 4, 30
Augustus
Franklin " 182-, 6, 10
John Wesley" 1830, 7, 2
Harriet
Eliza " 1832, 11, 19

1832, 3, 3. William [Byrum] Jr. rocf Piney Woods MM, N. C., dtd 1831,10,1
1833, 2, 16. Jemima & ch, Miriam, Exum, Elliott, Caleb Parker, Emaline Isobella, Orpah, Alfred Griffin & John Wesley, rocf Piney Woods MM, N. C.
1835, 11, 21. Miram [Birum] dis jas
1836, 10, 15. Axom E. dis military service
1837, 5, 20. William dis military service
1837, 5, 20. Jemima dis disunity
1839, 1, 19. Emaline Isabella [Birum] dis disunity
1839, 7, 20. Robert rocf Piney Woods MM, N.C.
1839, 7, 20. Eli rocf Piney Woods MM, N. C.
1844, 7, 20. Robert & Eli [Byrum] gct White River MM, Ind.
1845, 8, 16. Cert for Alfred Griffin, Benjamin Franklin, John Wesley, Harriet Elizabeth & Martha Maria [Birum], ch Nathan & Jemima, dis, granted to Sugar River MM, Ind., returned because they did not reside within limits of that mtg
1845, 9, 20. Caleb P. com for mou; Sugar River MM, Ind. rq to deal with him
1849, 8, 18. Benjamin F. [Byrum] dis disunity

BLANCHARD
1839, 8, 22. Helen m Solomon TALBERT
----, --, --. William & Elizabeth
Ch: Martha
Jane b 1847, 10, 9
Albert B. " 1850, 2, 10
William H.
Granville " 1852, 2, 15
Robert
Lewis " 1858, 12, 5
Emma Luella" 1866, 6, 23
Laura Bell " 1868, 6, 3

1832, 11, 17. Elisha Stubbs, h Elizabeth, & ch, Eli, Hiram & Rachel, also Helia Blanchard, a minor under their care, rec in mbrp (w, Elizabeth, was dis by White Water MM; they were to be communicated with as to rec her)
1842, 6, 18. Rebecca rec in mbrp
1844, 2, 17. Elizabeth (form Lee) con mou
1845, 8, 16. Rebecca gct Salem MM
1859, 7, 21. William & ch, Martha Jane, Albert B.; William Henry Granville & Robert Louis, rec in mbrp
1861, 12, 26. Martha Jane Small (form Blanchard) dis mou
1871, 7, 20. William dis (living at Westfield MM, Ind.)
1872, 1, 25. Elizabeth & ch, Robert Lewis, Emma Luella & Laura Bell, gct Westfield MM
1878, 8, 22. Albert B. gct Cincinnatti MM

BLOSSOM
1825, 3, 5. Keziah (form Kellum) dis mou
1884, 7, 24. Clara B. gct Fruitland MM, Kans.

BOGUE
1772, 3, 16. Josiah [Bouge], s Joseph & Mary, b
----, --, --. Josiah m Elizabeth WILLS, dt Joseph & Mary, b 1781,5,--
Ch: Alfred b 1808, 3, 7
Charles " 1810, 8, 11
John " 1814, 7, 22
1812, 8, 6. Dilwyn, Preble Co., O., s Joseph, dec, & Mary; m at Elk Mtg, Anna JONES, Preble Co., O., dt Henry & Prudence
1815, 8, 18. Job, s Joseph dec & Mary, Preble Co., O.;m at Elk Mtg, Sarah SMITH, dt Joseph, b 1797,9,-- (Job b 1785,5,7)
Ch: William b 1816, 12, 15
Peggy " 1818, 11, 7
Joseph " 1821, 1, 28
Jesse " 1823, 8, 9
Amos " 1826, 6, 6
Josiah " 1828, 11, 28
1818, 9, 9. Marium m John SMITH
1819, 1, 22. Mary d ae 3y 5m 16d bur in fam burial ground, Somers Twp.
1820, 4, 6. Mary m George JONES
----, --, --. Stephen & Elvira
Ch: Mary b 1823, 8, 15
Sarah Ann " 1825, 4, 30
Joseph " 1828, 5, 4
Benjamin E." 1828, 5, 4
1824, 3, 7. Jesse d ae 6m 29d bur Westfield, Cem.
1828, 5, 10. Elvira d bur fam burial ground, Somers Twp.
1830, 10, 16. Elizabeth, dt Alfred & Kezia, b

1811, 10, 5. Mary Sarah Elizabeth Miriam Ann & Mary rocf Piney Woods MM, N. C., dtd 1811,3,2
1812, 3, 4. Samuel & ch, Joseph, Benjamin, Newby, Mary & Sarah, rocf Simons Creek MM, N. C., dtd 1811,4,21
1814, 1, 1. Josiah dis
1819, 8, 7. William con paying a military fine
1820, 3, 4. Dilwin & fam gct Silver Creek MM
1821, 1, 6. Samuel dis

BOGUE, continued
1821, 12, 1. Stephen gct White Water MM, to m Elviry Eliot
1834, 10, 18. Stephen & w, Hannah, & ch, Sarah Ann, James Bonign, William, Elizabeth & Sarah, gct Mississinaway MM, Ind. (rem within limits of Michigan Territory)

BONNER
1894, 4, 26. Ella glt Presbyterian Church, Converse, Ind.

BOOKWALTER
1878, 11, 21. Evaline rocf Ceasars Creek MM, O., dtd 1878,9,26
1878, 12, 26. Evaline relrq

BOON
1877, 5, 24. William B. rec in mbrp
1881, 7, 21. William B. gct Long Lake MM, Mich Mich.

BORTON
1820, 11, 14. Mary C. d

BOWERS
1837, 11, 18. Mary Ann (Bowers or Brown) (form Sanders) dis mou

BOWYER
1874, 4, 23. Margaret rocf Dover MM, O., dtd 1874,3,19
1900, 7, 26. Maggie gct Wilmington MM, O.

BOYER
1873, 9, 11. Joseph m Margaret OREN, dt Joseph & Aseneth, b 1846,1,21

BRANSON
1830, 9, 9. David Jr., Butler Co., O., s David & Sarah, dec; m at Elk, Mary KENWORTHY, dt Jesse & Rachel, b 1811,9,1
Ch: Amos b 1831, 9, 9
Thomas " 1834, 5, 19
Mary, above, m (2) D. Moon
1834, 2, 27. David d ae 65y 7m 15d
1834, 9, 12. Sarah d ae 33y 8m 12d
1836, 5, 20. David Jr. d ae 27y 9m 19d
1865, 9, 5. Amos, Preble Co., O., s David & Mary, b 1831,9,6; m Priscilla EVANS, dt Joseph & Mary, both dec, b 1836,4,28 d 1905,3,11
Ch: Mary Lizzie b 1866, 10, 7
William Gurney " 1870, 5, 25
Lydia Emma " 1874, 1, 19

1822, 11, 2. David & s, David, rocf Mount Holly MM, dtd 1822,6,6
1822, 11, 2. Stacy rocf Mount Holly MM, dtd 1822,6,6
1822, 11, 2. Elizabeth & Sarah rocf Mount Holly MM, dtd 1822,6,6
1832, 6, 16. Stacy dis disunity
1845, 4, 19. Daniel H. Moon prcf Newberry MM, to m Mary Branson
1846, 9, 19. Mary Moon & s, Thomas Branson, gct Newberry MM, O.
1926, 2, 25. Naomi Albert rocf Salem MM,Ind.

BRATTIN
1810, 7, 26. Anna [Bratten] gct White Water MM, Ind.
1810, 8, 26. Jonathan [Brattain] & fam gct White Water MM
1816, 12, 7. Robert rocf White Water MM, dtd 1816,10,26
1817, 8, 2. Robert gct White Water MM

BROWER
1896, 5, 21. Viola relrq

BROWN
1751, 3, 13. Virgin, dt Joseph & Grace Gaskill, b
----, --, --. Richard, s Mercer & Sarah, b 1767,10,2; m Mary EMBREE, dt John & Sarah, b 1769,5,27
Ch: Sarah b 1789, 5, 10
Lydia " 1790, 6, 26
Mercer " 1792, 10, 29
John " 1794, 3, 5
William " 1796, 1, 5
Richard " 1798, 5, 3
Jonathan " 1799, 12, 2
Mary " 1802, 8, 15
Rebeccah " 1804, 10, 3
Peggy " 1807, 7, 26
Rachel " 1809, 4, 21
Phebe " 1811, 3, 29
Anna " 1813, 10, 17
----, -- --. John, s John & Virgin, b 1777, 9,21; m Hannah -----
Dt: Elizabeth J. b 1800, 4, 12
John m 2nd Sarah MOORE, dt Nathaniel & Bathsheba, b 1786,6,29
Ch: Nathaniel M. b 1807, 2, 19
Joseph G. " 1809, 5, 5
Bathsheba " 1811, 8, 30
1803, 8, 25. Sarah C., dt Samuel & Phebe, b
1803, 10, 17. Mary d ae 1y 2m 2d
----, --, --. Clayton, s John & Virgin, b 1781,10,13; m Priscilla MARPLE, dt Isaiah & Elizabeth
Ch: Isaiah M. b 1805, 12, 7
John " 1808, 1, 16
Beulah " 1810, 2, 21
Priscilla " 1821, 2, 11
----, --, --. Mercer & Mary
Ch: Sarah b 1810, 1, 7
Hannah " 1811, 9, 22
Joseph " 1813, 6, 22
Mercer " 1815, 12, 22

BROWN, Mercer & Mary, continued
Ch: Margaret b 1818, 1, 4
Richard " 1820, 5, 27
Mary " 1821, 10, 13
Phebe " 1824, 2, 6
Seth " 1826, 5, 25
----, --, --. Joseph & Abigail
Ch: Joseph F. b 1811, 7, 30
William " 1814, 7, 5
Mary Ann " 1817, 8, 18
Abigail " 1819, 12, 12
Thomas
Clarkson " 1827, 4, 7
1814, 4, 7. Lydia m John RANDLE
----, --, --. William, s John & Virgin, b 1792,1,26; m Elizabeth VANSCHUIVER
Ch: Levi b 1815, 2, 15
William V. " 1817, 4, 18
John " 1819, 6, 23
Barclay " 1822, 12, 17
Sarah Ann " 1827, 1, 10
1815, 11, 16. John Brown, Preble Co., O., s Richard & Mary; m at Elk, Mary RANDEL, dt Jonas & Mary (John b 1794,3,3)
Ch: Jonas b 1816, 8, 26
Sarah " 1818, 2, 21
John R. " 1820, 6, 6
Jonathan " 1822, 9, 28
Richard " 1824, 9, 16
Joseph " 1827, 4, 7
Rebecca " 1829, 8, 18
----, --, --. Samuel, s John & Virgin, b 1785, 4,22; m Mary VANSCUYVAR, dt William J. & Elizabeth, b 1792,1,13
Ch: Abraham b 1816, 8, 18
Elizabeth
A. " 1818, 4, 26
----, --, --. Isaac, s Jacob & Mary, b 1797,3, 9; m Mary MENDENHALL, dt Joseph & Rachel, b 1795,9,28
Ch: Tamer b 1816, 9, 27
Moses " 1819, 12, 1
Rachel " 1822, 3, 9
1816, 12, 11. Samuel, Preble Co., O., s Samuel & Mary; m at Paint Creek, Margaret STUBBS, Preble Co., O., dt John & Jean
Ch: Keziah b 1817, 10, 17
Mary " 1819, 4, 2
Eli " 1821, 2, 24
Rachel " 1823, 1, 10
Robert " 1826, 1, 27
Jane " 1828, 5, 26
Israel " 1830, 4, 13
Samuel H. " 1832, 8, 22
----, --, --. William & Ary
Ch: Zimri b 1819, 5, 24
Keziah " 1820, 1, 8
Isaac " 1822, 9, 10
Elisha " 1824, 9, 23
Rhoda " 1826, 3, 6
Mary Ann " 1830, 4, 26
----, --, --. Samuel & Ruth
Ch: Hannah b 1819, 10, 18

1820, 7, 5. Beulah m David NEWBURN
1820, 11, 13. Richard d ae 5m 13d
1821, 7, 11. Abraham, s John & Virgin, b 1777,9,21; m at Westfield Mtg, Deborah WORRELL, Preble Co., O., dt George & Deborah, b 1781,4,28
Ch: George W. b 1823, 4, 9
Phebe W. " 1825, 5, 24
1821, 4, 12. Richard, Preble Co., O., s Richard & Mary; m at Elk Mtg, Martha STUBBS, dt Samuel & Mary, Preble Co., O.
Ch: Newton b 1822, 11, 15
Elizabeth " 1824, 8, 6
Mariah " 1827, 7, 4
Sarah Ann " 1837, 5, 25
1822, 5, 4. Jonathan d ae 22y 4m 7d
----, --, --. Samuel S., s Clayton & Elizabeth, b 1792,1,28; m Sarah E. EDGERTON, dt Samuel J. & Elizabeth, b 1803,2,6
Ch: Clayton E. b 1822, 11, 13
Samuel " 1824, 12, 5
1822, 11, 7. Rebecca m John ROBERDS
1824, 1, 10. Lydia, dt Mahlon & Alice, b
1824, 10, 16. Samuel S. d ae 32y 8m 19d bur Westfield Cemetery
1825, 10, 28. Elizabeth d ae 10m 13d
----, --, --. Benjamin & Mary Ann
Ch: Clayton N. b 1828, 10, 6
Isaac " 1830, 6, 3
Martha " 1832, 8, 20
1828, 3, 7. Nehemiah, s Isaiah & Mary, b
1829, 6, 10. Nathaniel M. m Sarah NIXON (H)
1830, 1, 12. Samuel d ae 72y 10m 26d bur Westfield Cemetery
1830, 6, 19. Ary d ae 28y 3m
1830, 11, 22. John d ae 36y 8m 19d
1832, 1, 5. Virgin d ae 80y 9m 22d bur Westfield Cemetery
1832, 5, 28. Mary, wd Samuel d ae 75y 1m 11d bur Westfield Cemetery
1833, 3, 20. Samuel C. s Clayton & Sarah, b
1834, 3, 19. Sarah E., wd, m Andrew GIFFORD
1838, 7, 26. Jonas P., Preble Co., O., s John & Mary; m at Elk Mtg, Sarah BALLARD, dt David, dec, & Mary
Ch: Mary b 1839, 12, 15
Phebe " 1842, 3, 2
Eli " 1844, 6, 9; m Phebe WILSON
Enoch " 1847, 1, 6; m Hattie DAVIS
Harvey " 1849, 4, 18 d 1851,11,24
Denise " 1851, 11, 4
David " 1854, 5, 26
Anna " 1856, 12, 29
John " 1861, 11, 27
1840, 3, 26. Anna m Stephen W. TEAS
----, --, --. John, s John, dec, & Mary; m Keziah LAMM, dt John & Elizabeth
----, --, --. John R. & Keziah
Ch: Elizabeth b 1842, 8, 30
Phineas " 1845, 5, 8

BROWN, John R. & Keziah, continued
Ch: William b 1848, 4, 7
Henry " 1850, 6, 14
1842, 9, 19. Mary d ae 73y 2m 22d
1848, 7, 20. Elisha, Preble Co., O., s William & Arah, both dec; m Caroline HUTCHENS dt Joel G. & Rachel, Preble Co., O.
Ch: Charles
Oscar b 1849, 7, 27
Mary Ann " 1850, 12, 11
Rachel Airy" 1852, 11, 13
----, --, --. Richard Jr. d ae 24y 10m 25d
1859, 3, 21. Joseph, s John & Mary, b 1827, 4,7; m Elizabeth STANLEY
Joseph m 2nd/Mary HAISLEY, wd Allen, b 1831,7,17 1859,3,21
Ch: Ella G. b 1860, 3, 28; m Ed BONNER
Milo O. " 1862, 10, 22
Joseph m 3rd Mariah STUBBS
Ch: Samuel S. b 1870, 3, 31 d 1870, 9,26 bur in Fairmount Cem., West Elkton,O.
----, --, --. Jonathan & Rhoda
Ch: Zeri H. b 1854, 10, 3
Enos F. " 1856, 11, 2
Valeria Jane " 1858, 11, 23
1856, 4, 17. Elizabeth J. d ae 25y 6m 24d
1863, 4, 6. Richard d ae 64y 11m 3d
1864, 1, 4. Martha d ae 64y
1865, 1, 17. Mary H. d ae 33y 4m
1867, 6, 14. Mary d ae 69y 6m 20d
1870, 5, 27. Jonas P. d ae 53y 8m 27d
1886, 5, 11. Mariah S. d ae 55y 11m 14d
1888, 6, 20. Sarah d ae 71y 4m 11d
----, --, --. Eli & Phebe
Ch: Louise
Sadie

1810, 2, 3. Samuel rocf New Garden, N. C., dtd 1809,11,4
1810, 5, 5. Richard appointed elder
1810, 9, 1. Benjamin Lancaster recrq of guardian, Sarah Brown
1812, 9, 5. Thomas & w, Mary, & ch, William, Gulielma & Ann, rocf Deep Creek MM, N. C., dtd 1809,7,1, endorsed by White Water MM, 1812,8,29
1813, 6, 5. Mary & s, Samuel, rec in mbrp
1815, 2, 4. Jacob & w, Mary, & ch, Mary, Isaac, Margaret & Jonathan, rocf Deep Creek MM, N. C.
1815, 4, 1. Mercer dis mou
1815, 7, 1. Rebecca con mou
1815, 10, 7. Margaret Mendenhall (form Brown) con mou
1817, 1, 7. Isaac con mou
1818, 9, 5. Clayton rocf Miami MM, dtd 1818, 6,24
1819, 5, 1. John & w, Sarah, & ch, Nathaniel, Joseph & Bathsheba, rocf Miami MM, dtd 1819,3,31
1819, 5, 1. William rocf Miami MM, dtd 1819, 3,31
1819, 6, 5. Samuel S. & w, Ruth, rocf Miami MM, dtd 1819,4,20
1819, 8, 7. William con mou
1820, 1, 4. Mahlon & w, Alice, & ch, Clayton, Virgin, Ann, Mary, Mahlon, Alice & Rebeccah, rocf Miami MM, dtd 1820,3,29
1820, 3, 4. Thomas & fam gct Duck Creek MM
1820, 5, 6. Beulah rocf Miami MM, dtd 1820, 3,29
1820, 5, 6. Virgin rocf Miami MM, dtd 1820,3, 29
1820, 6, 3. Benjamin rocf Upper Evesham MM, N. J., dtd 1820,5,6
1820, 8, 5. Abraham rocf Miami MM, O., dtd 1820,6,20
1820, 10, 7. Samuel rocf Miami MM, dtd 1820, 8,30
1820, 10, 7. Elizabeth rocf Miami MM, dtd 1820,8,30
1821, 5, 5. Martha con mou
1826, 8, 5. Arah & ch, Keziah, Isaac & Elisha, rec in mbrp
1827, 9, 1. Mercer & fam gct Vermillion MM, Ill.
1829, 7, --. Sarah N. rqct Westfield MM (H)
1832, 4, 7. William gct Westfield MM, to m Sarah E. Brown
1832, 8, 18. Cert granted to Westfield MM for William to m Sarah E. Brown, returned by her; she declined accomplishing her m with him
1833, 3, 16. William dis mou
1833, 6, 15. Phebe Maddock (form Brown) con mou
1833, 6, 15. Virgin con mou
1833, 10, 9. Hannah gct Westfield MM (H)
1834, 1, 13. Virgin rst
1834, 5, 17. Alice T. dis disunity
1834, 6, 21. Joseph F. dis disunity
1835, 1, 17. Rebecca dis neglecting attendance
1835, 3, 21. Samuel & w, Margaret, & ch, Keziah, Mary, Eli, Rachel, Robert, Jane, Israel & Samuel, gct West Grove MM, Ind.
1835, 3, 21. Sarah (form Jones) dis mou & disunity
1835, 3, 21. Mary dis disunity & jas
1835, 11, 21. Virgin & h & ch gct Milford MM, Ind.
1836, 1, 16. Phebe (form Silver) rpd mou; living at Springborough MM; dis 1836,11, 16)
1836, 10, 15. Benjamin & w, Mary Ann, & ch, Clayton, Isaac, Martha & Jacob, gct White Water MM, Ind.
1837, 7, 15. Elizabeth A. dis disunity
1837, 7, 15. Lydia (form Decamp) dis mou & jH
1837, 7, 15. Mary Ann dis disunity
1837, 8, 19. Ann (form Wiley) dis mou & disunity
1837, 11, 18. Mary Brown (or Bowers) (form Sanders) dis disunity

BROWN, continued
1839, 7, 20. Sarah (form Ballenger) dis mou & jH
1839, 9, 21. Priscilla dis disunity
1839, 11, 16. Hannah dis disunity
1840, 3, 21. Sarah Harris (form Brown) con mou
1840, 9, 19. Kezia, Isaac, Elisha S., Rhoda, Lydia & Jane, ch William & Aria, rocf Milford MM, Ind., dtd 1840,8,22
1841, 8, 21. Keziah Stubbs (form Brown) con mou
1842, 1, 15. John R. & w, Keziah, gct Richland MM, Ind.
1843, 2, 18. John R. & w, Keziah, & dt, Elizabeth, rocf Richland MM, Ind., dtd 1842,11, 9
1843, 9, 16. Isaac dis mou & disunity
1843, 9, 16. Thomson dis disunity
1843, 10, 21. Sarah Ann (form Talbert) dis mou & disunity
1846, 1, 17. Lydia dis
1846, 4, 18. Rhoda Elliott (form Brown) dis mou
1846, 7, 18. Clayton, Jr. gct White Water MM, Ind.
1847, 2, 20. Clayton & w, Sarah, & s, Samuel C., gct Caesars Creek MM
1847, 2, 20. Mahlon & w, Alice, gct Caesars Creek MM
1847, 6, 19. Newton dis neglecting attendance
1847, 8, 21. Maria Loyner (form Brown) dis mou
1848, 1, 15. Mary Ann Stats (form Brown) con mou
1848, 8, 19. Rebecca Snider (form Brown) con mou
1848, 9, 16. Samuel dis mou (living at Pleasant Plain MM)
1848, 9, 16. Susannah (form Lane) con mou (living at Pleasant Plain MM)
1849, 5, 19. Susannah L. gct Pleasant Plain MM, Ia.
1850, 2, 21. Isaac & w, Sarah Ann, rec in mbrp at Salem MM, Ia. by consent of this mtg
1850, 6, 20. Jonathan con mou
1851, 6, 26. Joseph con mou
1851, 6, 26. Elizabeth J. (form Stánly) con mou
1853, 8, 25. Elisha S. & w, Caroline, & ch, Charles Oscar, Mary Ann & Rachel Arah, gct Salem MM, Ia.
1854, 1, 26. John R. & w, Keziah, & ch, Elizabeth, Phineas, William & Henry, gct Salem MM, Ia.
1855, 3, 22. Caroline Patten (form Brown) dis mou; living at Richland MM, Ind.
1856, 4, 24. Valerie Harris rec in mbrp; minor under care of Mary Brown
1856, 4, 24. Sarah Ann dis disunity
1858, 1, 21. Rhoda & ch, Zeri & Enos F. rst (Rhoda had been dis by Springfield MM, Ind.)
1860, 2, 23. Jonathan & Rhoda & ch, Zeri H., Enos F. & Valeria, gct Dover MM, Ind.
1865, 5, 25. Clara M. rec in mbrp
1869, 3, 25. Clara M. Ary (form Brown) gct Rocksylvania MM, Ia.
1870, 1, 20. Eli rpd mou
1870, 3, 24. Phebe W. rocf Caesars Creek MM, dtd 1870,2,24
1871, 3, 23. Eli & fam gct Caesars Creek MM, O.
1882, 5, 25. Eli S. & fam rocf West Grove MM, Ind., dtd 1882,5,13
1882, 7, 20. Enoch gct Salem MM, Ind.
1886, 1, 21. Eva K. S. relrq
1890, 11, 20. Joseph gct New Garden MM, Ind.
1894, 1, 25. Eli & w, Phebe, gct Van Wert MM, O.
1897, 12, 23. Milo gct Fairmount MM, Ind.
1908, 9, 24. David dropped from mbrp
1917, 1, 25. Jessie Robinson jas; dropped from mbrp
1916, 10, 26. John released from mbrp

BUCKINGHAM
1872, 8, 22. Jane rocf Dover MM, N. C.
1873, 8, 21. Jane gct Springfield MM, Ind.

BURNE
1856, 1, 12. John d ae about 56

1850, 8, 22. John rocf Wilmington MM, Del., dtd 1850,8,8
1851, 4, 24. John gct White Water MM, Ind.
1855, 11, 22. John rocf White Water MM, Ind., dtd 1855,9,26

BURR
1883, 6, 21. Orlando relrq
1880, 4, 22. Orlando R. rec in mbrp

BURSON
1830, 9, 2. Jonathan d ae 87y 2m 2d bur Westfield Cem.
1828, 8, 23. Rebecca d ae 77y 5m 9d bur Westfield Cem.

1818, 9, 5. Jonathan & w, Rebekah, rocf Goose Creek MM, Va., dtd 1818,1,1, endorsed by Derby MM
1850, 1, 5. John dis (living at Center MM, O.)

CAREY
1820, 3, 4. Thomas [Cary] & w, Rhoda, & ch, Elizabeth B., Joseph & Rachel D., rocf Caesars Creek MM, dtd 1820,1,25
1822, 6, 1. Thomas & fam gct West Grove MM

CARTER
1815, 7, 1. Mordicai roc dtd 1814,12,28
1883, 11, 22. Mary Susan rec in mbrp

CARTER, continued
1892, 8, 25. Mary S. glt M. E. Church, Pawnee City, Neb.

CASEY
1890, 12, 25. Mary A. relrq

CHANCE
1921, 10, 20. Orville & w, Lola, rocf Friends Chapel MM, Ill.
1926, 5, 26. O. E. glt Adamsville U. B. in Christ, Edwardsburg, Mich.

CHAPENS
1871, 11, 23. Silas rec in mbrp

CHAPPEL
1832, 3, 3. Isaac rocf Piney Woods MM, N.C., dtd 1831,10,1
1832, 11, 17. Isaac gct Piney Woods MM, N. C.

CLARK
1816, 5, 6. Jesse Clark, Wayne Co., Ind., s John & Margaret, dec; m at Paint Creek Mtg, Elizabeth MOORE, Butler Co., O., dt Alexander & Phebe
1822, 8, 8. John, Wayne Co., Ind., s John, dec; m at Elk Mtg, Alida C. HARNED, wd, Butler Co., O., dt Robert & Catherine Miller, dec

1816, 7, 6. Jane [Clerk] rocf White Water MM, dtd 1816,6,3
1831, 7, 2. Jane gct Silver Creek MM, Ind.
1849, 11, 17. Sarah rec in mbrp in White Water MM with consent of this mtg

CLEAR
1928, 2, 2. Maria H. rocf Bethel Church, Hamilton, O.
1928, 2, 2. Warren E. Jr. & Chester G. rec in mbrp
1928, 2, 2. Joetta V. rec in mbrp
1929, 3, 21. Maria H., Joetta R. V., Warren E. Jr. & Chester G. glt Bethel Church, Hamilton, O.

COALES
1829, 9, 5. Cert rec for Elizabeth & ch, Lydiann, Charles Cyrenius, Elizabeth, Sarah M., Margaret & Pierson, from Stillwater MM, dtd 1829,6,27, endorsed to Westfield MM
1829, 9, 5. Cert rec for Mary & Deborah from Stillwater MM, dtd 1829,5,23, endorsed to Westfield MM

COGGESHALL
----, --, --. Lindley & Hannah
Ch: Emily Jane b 1859, 8, 7
William Albert " 1861, 1, 19
Annuel Harvey b 1863, 12, 15

1858, 6, 24. Lindly [Coggshall] & w, Hannah, rocf Dover MM, Ind., dtd 1858,5,19
1861, 11, 21. Lindley & w, Hannah, & ch, Emily Jane & William Albert, gct Dover MM, Ind.
1864, 4, 21. Lindley [Coggshall] & fam rocf Dover MM, Ind.
1866, 9, 20. Hannah & ch, Emily Jane, William V. & Harvey, gct White Water MM, Ind.
1867, 3, 21. Lindley gct White Water MM, Ind.

COLLUM
1893, 8, 24. Luella jas; dropped from mbrp

COLWELL
1823, 11, 11. Joseph & w, Marium, & ch gct Milford MM, Ind.

COMER
1813, 8, 12. Deborah [Comber] m Nathan COOK

1810, 4, 7. Deborah, dt Rebekah, rec in mbrp
1810, 6, 18. Rebekah appointed clerk
1841, 2, 20. Rebecca gct Salem MM, Ia.

COMMONS
1855, 6, 28. Isaac Jr., Wayne Co., Ind., s Isaac & Mary; m at Elk Mtg, Keziah STUBBS, Preble Co., O., dt John & Eleanor

1856, 1, 24. Keziah S. gct Chester MM, Ind.
1917, 9, 21. J. Clinton & w, Cassie, rocf Dover MM, Ind., dtd 1917,8,22
1918, 11, 29. Clinton & w, Cassie, gct Rockford MM, O.
1919, 5, 22. Clinton & w, Cassie, rocf Van Wert MM, O.

COMPTON
1918, 12, 27. Theo Christine, dt Florence (form Crist) rec in mbrp

CONARROE
----, --, --. John m Harriet SWAIN, dt Gabriel & Amy, d 1899,1,20
Ch: Elizabeth b 1835, 10, 26
Gabriel S. " 1837, 11, 26
Clayton T. " 1840, 3, 5
Martha " 1841, 12, 28
Aaron " 1844, 4, 27 d 1845, 6, 1
Amy Ann " 1846, 12, 31; m Elijah COOPER
Mary S. " 1848, 3, 30; m Alden STUBBS
William B. " 1851, 8, 3; m Alice WING
Reading A. " 1854, 9, 21; m ----- BEADLE
Joel Ellis " 1858, 8, 17; m Elizabeth STUBBS

CONARROE, continued
1857, 3, 5. Elizabeth m Nathan MENDENHALL
1862, 10, 19. Elizabeth d ae 78y
----, --, --. Clayton T. b 1840,3,5; m Elanora KNEED, dt Rebecca
Ch: Mary Anna b 1869, 1, 12
----, --, --. Gabriel b 1837,11,26; m Fanny -----
Ch: Katie Jane b 1869, 8, 22
John W. " 1872, 4, 3
Ivea Leona " 1879, 9, 3
1871, 5, 24. John [Conaroe] d ae 57y 11m 6d
----, --, --. William B. b 1851,8,3; m Alice WING
Ch: Elda
Orcilla b 1885, 10, 19
Lawrence
----, --, --. Joel, s John & Harriet; m Elizabeth STUBBS, dt Levi & T.
Ch: William
Leroy
Sarah
Mary
Edgar
Mary Belle
Earl

1830, 8, 7. Elizabeth [Conaroe] (form Warington) con mou
1835, 5, 16. Harriet [Conaroe] (form Swan) con mou
1843, 2, 18. John [Conaroe] & ch, Elizabeth, Gabriel S., Clayton F. & Martha, rec in mbrp
1861, 7, 25. Martha Cox (form Conarroe) con mou
1867, 12, 26. Clayton rpd mou
1868, 9, 24. Gabriel S. [Connaroe] rpd mou
1871, 7, 20. Frances J., Elnora & Julia M. [Connaroe] rec in mbrp
1883, 6, 21. Reading A. relrq
1884, 7, 24. Gabriel S. & w, Frances J., & ch, Katie J., John W. & Ivea L., gct Estacado MM, Tex.
1885, 5, 21. Alice J. rec in mbrp
1898, 2, 24. William & w, Alice, & ch, Elda & Laurence, gct Denver MM, Colo.
1899, 5, 25. Elizabeth A. & ch, William E., Leroy A., Sarah L., Edgar A., Flora M., Mary B. & John E. rec in mbrp
1918, 8, 23. Dora A. granted permission to have her name changed to Harriet D. on mtg records
1919, 6, 26. Willie dropped from mbrp

CONRAD
1835, 5, 16. James Jr. gct Sugar River MM, Ind.

COOK
----, --, --. James, s Eli & Martha, b 1785, 10,3; m Eleanor MADDOCK, dt Samuel & Rachel, b 1787,3,10
Ch: Sarah b 1808, 8, 14
Eli " 1809, 11, 4
Amos " 1813, 12, 11
Isaac " 1815, 5, 7
Rachel " 1817, 8, 7
Martha " 1819, 10, 26
Mary " 1821, 10, 5
James " 1823, 7, 19
Olive " 1826, 4, 16
1811, 10, 10. Mary m William HOLLINGSWORTH
1813, 8, 12. Nathan, Preble Co., O., s Eli & Martha; m at Elk Mtg, Deborah COMBER, dt Rebeccah, Preble Co., O.
Ch: Jonathan b 1815, 4, 24
Martha " 1817, 3, 3
Nathan m 2nd 1818,9,10 at Elk Mtg, Sarah DENNY, dt Lazarus & Susanna
Ch: Elizabeth b 1819, 7, 18
William " 1820, 12, 6
Eli " 1822, 2, 4
Susannah " 1823, 10, 9
Isaac " 1825, 2, 12
Hannah " 1827, 4, 6
Charity " 1828, 10, 18
Amos " 1830, 8, 29
Henry " 1832, 7, 1
Obadiah " 1834, 3, 31
1814, 8, 18. Charity m Jesse GREEN
1817, 4, 5. Deborah d ae 20y 4m 26d
----, 11, 12. Eli, Preble Co., O., s Eli & Martha; m at Elk Mtg, Elizabeth DENNY, Preble Co., O., dt Lazarus & Susanna
Ch: Susannah b 1819, 11, 4
John " 1820, 11, 8
Joel " 1822, 2, 9
Phebe " 1823, 5, 4
Levi " 1825, 4, 14
Nathan " 1827, 1, 4
Jesse " 1828, 7, 13
Jonathan " 1830, 7, 13
Joseph " 1832, 3, 4
Sarah " 1834, 1, 13
1828, 6, 11. Eli d ae 87y
1828, 9, 11. Sarah m John DENNY
1835, 5, 7. Martha d
1837, 10, 26. Martha m Samuel MADDOCK

1828, 3, 1. Eli Jr. dis disunity
1830, 8, 7. Amos dis mou
1831, 12, 3. James dis disunity
1831, 12, 3. Elenor dis disunity
1833, 7, 20. Isaac dis disunity
1835, 10, 17. Jonathan con mou
1836, 8, 20. Susanna rpd mou; living at Springfield MM, Ind.
1836, 11, 19. Martha Jr. dis disunity
1838, 6, 16. Susannah rocf Springfield MM, Ind., dtd 1836,11,19
1839, 3, 16. Eli & w, Elizabeth, & ch, John, Joel, Phebe, Levi, Nathan, Jesse, Jonathan, Joseph, Sarah, Lewis & Delilah, gct Salem MM, Ia.
1839, 3, 16. Susanna gct Salem MM, Ia.

COOK, continued
1839, 6, 15. Nathan & w, Sarah, & ch, William, Eli, Susanna, Isaac, Hannah, Charity, Amos, Henry, Obadiah, Louise & Elihu, gct Salem MM, Ia.
1839, 6, 15. Elizabeth gct Salem MM, Ia.
1839, 7, 20. Mary disunity
1839, 9, 21. Jonathan & w, Susanna, & ch, Mary Ann & Isaac Newton, gct Salem MM,Ia.
1840, 6, 20. Henry Lamm gct Salem MM, Ia., to m Elizabeth Cook
1842, 3, 19. James Jr. dis disunity
1842, 7, 16. Olive dis disunity
1905, 12, 21. Willis P. & w, Ella, rocf Cherry Grove MM, Ind.
1905, 12, 21. Jay Russel, s Willis P. & Ella, rec in mbrp

COOPER
----, --, --. Jonathan & Esther
Ch: Mary b 1807, 2, 13
Ralph " 1818, 2, 5
Esther " 1820, 4, 6
Christiana " 1822, 9, 7
George " 1824, 7, 8
David " 1827, 5, 6
----, --, --. Ralph & Mary
Ch: Lydia b 1811, 1, 25
Mary " 1813, 1, 8
William " 1815, 1, 27
Hannah " 1817, 2, 17
Sarah Ann " 1819, 4, 12
Felix " 1822, 12, 20
Rachel " 1825, 1, 31
Hulda " 1828, 5, 25
1827, 6, 7. Hannah m Ira LANE
1832, 8, 13. Hulda d ae 4y 2m 14d
1832, 9, 20. Lydia m Eli D. GAUSE
1839, 12, 23. Elizabeth m Richard GAUSE
1841, 5, 14. Esther d
----, --, --. Elijah & Amy Ann
Ch: William b 1865, 8, 18
Jane " 1868, 8, 30; m ----- AUSBARGER
John Elias " 1874, 3, 7
1877, 4, 24. Elizabeth d ae 89y 4m 13d
1890, 11, 13. Elizabeth d ae 74y 16d

1811, 4, 6. Jacob con mou
1811, 10, 5. Mary con mou
1811, 12, 7. Ralph con mou
1815, 10, 7. Jonathan rec in mbrp
1822, 8, 3. Jonathan & ch, William, Jonathan, Jacob, Jeremiah & Ralph, rec in mbrp
1824, 1, 3. Ralph dis disunity
1826, 7, 1. Esther & ch, Christina & George, rec in mbrp
1827, 3, 3. Hannah & Sarah rec in mbrp
1827, 10, 6. Lydia rec in mbrp
1830, 11, 6. Sarah dis disunity
1831, 1, 1. William Jr. dis disunity
1831, 2, 5. Jonathan Jr. dis disunity
1831, 4, 2. Lydia Wilsey (form Cooper) dis mou (living at Westfield MM)
1832, 2, 4. Mary Ballard (form Cooper) dis mou
1833, 10, 19 Jacob Jr. dis disunity
1833, 10, 19. Jeremiah dis disunity
1834, 10, 18. William Jr. dis disunity
1834, 10, 18. Hannah Ballard (form Cooper) con mou
1835, 11, 21. Jonathan dis disunity
1837, 4, 15. Ralph dis disunity
1838, 6, 16. Sarah Ann Talbert (form Cooper) con mou
1839, 9, 21. Christena dis disunity
1841, 1, 16. George dis disunity
1842, 9, 17. Mary (form Ozburn) con mou
1842, 12, 17. Felix dis disunity
1843, 4, 15. Rachel Macy (form Cooper) dis mou
1848, 11, 18. Mary gct Spiceland MM, Ind.
1849, 8, 18. Hannah (form Dewees) con mou
1851, 7, 24. Hannah gct Westfield MM, Ind.
1852, 12, 23. Mary rocf Spiceland MM, dtd 1852,11,24
1855, 1, 25. Mary gct Salem MM, Ia.
1857, 7, 23. Mary Kellum (form Cooper) dis mou
1865, 4, 20. Amy Ann con mou
1868, 10, 22. Elizabeth Sr. rec in mbrp
1871, 7, 20. Elizabeth rec in mbrp
1891, 3, 26. William glt M. E. Church, Middletown, O.
1897, 12, 23. John gct White Water MM, Ind.
1897, 12, 23. Amy Ann gct White Water MM,Ind.

COX
1859, 12, 1. Sarah d ae 42y 1m 3d
----, --, --. William J. m Martha CONARROE, b 1841,12,28
Ch: Sarah Elizabeth b 1866, 6, 15; m Grant SCHAUER
Melva Amy " 1868, 1, 19; m Stephen BERK
John Sherman " 1870, 2, 10; m Ada SAMUELS
Fannie Luisa " 1874, 1, 11
Mina m Ed. Hinne

1840, 12, 19. Sarah rocf West Branch MM
1861, 7, 25. Martha (form Conarroe) con mou
1886, 4, 22. Lizzie relrq
1912, 9, 26. John dropped from mbrp

CREGG
1822, 6, 1. Hannah (form Wilson) dis mou

CRIST
----, --, --. Allison B. m Phebe MADDOCK, dt Joseph & Irene, d 1898,1,25
Ch: John b 1861, 6, 19
Sarah Lu-

CRIST, Allison B. & Phebe, continued
Ch: ella b 1863, 1, 24; m Robert COLLUM
Francis M. " 1864, 10, 17; m Elnora MENDENHALL
Elwood " 1866, 7, 5
Loretta " 1868, 7, 10; m Rev. McGINNIS 1891,5,12
Martha b 1870, 4, 10
Emma " 1872, 2, 16
Allison " 1874, 3, 28
Margaret Ann" 1875, 7, 10
Eva " 1878, 12, 8; m Rev. HICKS 1901,1,--
1876, 8, 4. Margaret Ann d ae ly 24d
1886, 12, 23. Francis M., s Allison B. & Phebe, b 1864,10,17; m Elnora MENDENHALL, dt Nathan S. & Elizabeth, b 1866,12,8
Ch: Homer Raymond b 1888, 2, 11
Gracie Irene " 1889, 11, 19

1858, 7, 22. Phebe [Christ] (form Maddock) con mou
1871, 7, 20. Alison B. & three ch rec in mbrp
1872, 6, 20. Elbert M. rec in mbrp
1889, 5, 23. Elbert dropped from mbrp
1890, 12, 25. Elwood O. relrq
1900, 8, 23. John dropped from mbrp
1901, 3, 21. Eva Hicks (form Crist) glt M.E. Church, Allegheny, Pa.
1904, 3, 24. Allison glt M. E. Church, Seven Mile, O.
1908, 12, 24. Emma jas; dropped from mbrp
1912, 11, 21. Homer R. jas; dropped from mbrp
1917, 6, 22. Grace Irene Erwin (form Crist) glt 3rd M. E. Church, Richmond, Ind.
1918, 3, 22. Pearl rolf U. B. Church, West Elkton, O.
1918, 12, 27. Theo Christine Compton, dt Florence Compton (form Crist), rec in mbrp

CROWELL
1886, 1, 21. Milton & fam rocf Fairmount MM, Ind.
1889, 7, 25. Milton & w, Verlinda, & ch, Emma Gertrude, Susan, Cassinda & Agnes, gct Fairmount MM, Ind.

CUSHMAN
1823, 9, 6. Sarah (form Saunders) dis mou

DAVIS
----, --, --. Amos & Sarah
Ch: William b 1811, 1, 16
Abiather " 1812, 9, 30
John " 1814, 1, --
Agnes " 1815, 5, 9
Uriah " 1817, 3, 29
Stephen " 1818, 8, 27
Lydia " 1820, 1, 15
Elihu " 1821, 7, 27
Robert b 1823, 1, 30
Rebecca " 1824, 9, 21
1823, 4, 9. Robert d ae 2m 10d
1840, 4, 20. Riley, Miami Co., O., s Samuel & Dorcas; m at Elk Mtg, Rachel MADDOCK, Preble Co., O., dt Nathan & Sarah, dec
1855, 8, 30. Riley, Miami Co., O., s Samuel & Dorcas; m at Elk Mtg, Charlotte HUNT, dt James & Rosanna TOWNSEND, both dec
----, --, --. Elwood, s Thomas C. & Rebecca B. m Kittie SMITH
Ch: Clarence
1877, 12, 13. William H., s Thomas C. & Rebecca B., b 1853,7,11; m Rebecca TAYLOR

1811, 5, 4. Sarah rocf Stillwater MM, dtd 1810,2,27
1815, 6, 3. Sarah & Lydia [Davice] rocf West Branch MM
1815, 7, 1. Benjamin [Davies] roc dtd 1815, 2,23
1815, 9, 2. Abiather rocf West Branch MM, dtd 1815,8,24
1817, 2, 1. Abiather [Davies] gct West Branch MM
1817, 2, 1. Sarah & Lydia gct West Branch MM
1817, 8, 2. Benjamin [Davies] gct West Branch MM
1831, 8, 6. Sarah dis disunity & jas
1832, 6, 16. Agnes dis disunity
1832, 6, 16. Abiather, John Uriah, Stephen, Lydia, Elihu, Rebecca & Sarah, ch Amos, gct Sugar River MM, Ind.
1833, 3, 16. Amos dis
1841, 12, 18. Rachel gct West Branch MM, O.
1855, 8, 23. Riley prcf West Branch MM, to m
1856, 1, 24. Charlotte F. gct West Branch MM
1863, 5, 27. Martha A. (form Powell) dis mou
1865, 4, 20. Thomas C. & fam rocf Salem MM, Ind., dtd 1865,3,15
1868, 8, 20. Angelina Taylor (form Davis) con mou
1868, 11, 26. Laura Ann Stubbs (form Davis) rpd mou
1870, 3, 24. Thomas C. & w, Rebecca, & ch, William H., Thomas Elwood, Sarah Florence, Albert Franklin & Huldah Ellen, gct Honey Creek MM, Ia.
1889, 2, 21. Thomas C. & Rebecca B. rocf Sterling MM, Kans.
1890, 4, 24. William H. & T. E. rocf Honey Creek MM, Ia., dtd 1890,4,12
1897, 12, 23. Thomas C. & Rebecca B. gct Pleasant Valley MM, Kans.
1898, 2, 24. Clarence rec in mbrp
1918, 7, 26. Elwood relrq
1919, 6, 26. Clarence dropped from mbrp

DECAMP
1823, 8, 2. John M. & w, Hannah D., & ch, Jane, Lydia, Eli & Anna, rocf Hardwick MM, N. J., dtd 1823,4,3
1829, 7, 4. Hannah dis disunity & joining

DECAMP, continued
Separatists
1829, 9, 5. John M. dis joining Separatists
1834, 3, 12. John M. [D'Camp] & w, Hannah, & ch, Lydia, Eli, Anna, John W. & William, rqct Westfield MM (H)
1834, 4, 19. Jane dis jH
1837, 7, 15. Lydia Brown (form Decamp) com for mou & jH

DENNEY
----, --, --. Lazarus & Susana
Ch: Sarah b 1798, 1, --
Azariah " 1800, 1, 19
Elizabeth " 1801, 7, 6
William " 1803, 12, 5
John " 1806, 3, 15
Rebecca " 1808, 2, 17
Shubel " 1810, 1, 8
Jorden " 1812, 2, 3
Michel " 1816, 5, 8
Ruben " 1818, 4, 24
Keziah " 1820, 12, 8
Lazarus m 2nd Mary -----
Ch: Susanna b 1827, 11, 1
David " 1829, 5, 7
Jonathan " 1831, 1, 28
Mahlon " 1832, 4, 10
Huldah Ann " 1834, 4, 2
Esther " 1837, 9, 12
1818, 9, 10. Sarah [Denny] m Nathan COOK
1818, 11, 12. Elizabeth [Denny] m Eli COOK
1823, 1, 9. Azariah, Preble Co., O., s Lazarus & Susanah; m at Elk Mtg, Rebecca TALBERT, wd, Butler Co., O., dt Nathan & Elizabeth STUBBS
Ch: Joel b 1823, 11, 9
Elizabeth " 1826, 8, 20
William " 1829, 4, 1
Susannah " 1832, 9, 20
Eli " 1834, 6, 19
1823, 10, 11. Susanna d ae 45y 4m 25d
1828, 9, 11. John, Preble Co., O., s Lazarus & Susannah; m at Elk, Sarah COOK, Butler Co., O., dt James & Eleanor
Ch: James b 1829, 6, 29
Joseph " 1831, 3, 18
Susannah " 1833, 4, 29
1830, 8, 21. Susanna d ae 2y 9m 20d
1833, 6, 11. Susanna d ae 8m 22d
1835, 8, 21. Huldah Ann d ae 15d
1837, 3, 11. Esther d ae 17y 28d
1837, 10, 8. Rebecca d
1839, 8, 22. Keziah [Denny] m Reuben LAMM
1856, 4, 4. Lazarus d ae 78y 4m 10d
1878, 11, 14. Mary [Deny] d ae 86y 11m 20d

1818, 4, 4. Lazarus [Denny] & w, Susannah, & ch, Sarah, Azariah, Elizabeth, William, John, Rebecca, Shubal, Jordan & Michael, rocf Westfield MM, N. C.; endorsed by White Water MM
1827, 1, 6. Lazarus gct Cherry Grove MM, to m Mary Ballard
1827, 11, 3. Mary [Denny] & ch rocf Cherry Grove MM, dtd 1827,3,10
1828, 6, 7. William dis
1831, 1, 1. Shubeal [Denny] dis mou
1831, 5, 7. Margaret [Denny] con mou
1831, 10, 1. William [Denny] rec in mbrp at Sugar River MM with consent of this mtg
1831, 11, 5. Jordon [Denny] dis
1833, 2, 16. John [Denny] dis disunity
1836, 4, 13. Michael Spray (form Denny) con mou
1839, 6, 15. Reuben [Denny] gct Salem MM, Ia.
1839, 12, 21. Azariah [Denny] & ch, Joel, Elizabeth, William & Eli, gct Westfield MM, Ind.
1845, 8, 16. Martha Jane Eeks rec in mbrp (a minor under care of Mary [Denny])
1847, 5, 15. Sarah [Denny] & ch, Susanna, Henry, Francis & Eli, gct Salem MM, Ia.
1848, 1, 15. James [Denny] con disunity; living at Salem MM, Ia.
1848, 9, 16. Joseph [Denny] gct Salem MM, Ia.
1849, 12, 15. Margaret [Denny] gct Springfield MM, Ind.
1850, 6, 20. David [Denny] con mou; living at Cherry Grove MM
1850, 10, 24. Shubal [Denny] rec in mbrp at Springfield MM, Ind.
1851, 3, 20. David B. [Denny] gct Cherry Grove MM
1853, 6, 23. Mahlon [Denny] dis mou & jas
1859, 3, 24. James [Denny] rec in mbrp at New Garden MM, Ind.; living there

DEWEES
1846, 5, 15. Chesterfield MM rq this mtg to offer David [Deweese] a copy of their testimony of dis
1846, 5, 16. Hannah F. rocf White Water MM, Ind., dtd 1846,4,22
1847, 1, 16. Hannah & Rebecca rocf Chesterfield MM, dtd 1846,10,19
1847, 1, 16. Thomas, Hannah, Isaac, William & Rebecca [Deweese], ch David B., rocf Chesterfield MM, O.
1849, 8, 18. Hannah Cooper (form Dewees) con misconduct & mou
1850, 6, 20. Thomas dis disunity
1852, 4, 22. Hannah & ch gct Westfield MM, Ind.
1852, 5, 20. Isaac [Deweese] dis disunity

DICKEY
1841, 7, 17. Jane [Dicky] rocf Sparrow Creek MM, Ind.
1843, 1, 21. Jane gct Duck Creek MM, Ind.

DICKS
----, --, --. Jonathan & Keziah
Ch: Enock S. b 1827, 10, 4
Jonathan m 2nd Hannah -----
Ch: John G. b 1830, 2, 1

DICKS, Jonathan, continued
Jonathan m 3rd Ann -----
Ch: Samuel S. b 1834, 2, 20
Isaac H. " 1836, 9, 12
1847, 10, 21. Enoch, Preble Co., O., s Jonathan & Keziah, dec; m at Elk Mtg, Ann HUTCHINS, Preble Co., O., dt Joel G. & Rachel H.
1848, 1, 28. Enoch S. d ae 20y 3m 24d
1849, 1, 2. Jonathan d

1826, 4, 1. Testification from White Water MM delivered to Jonathan [Dix]
1829, 12, 5. Hannah [Dix] (form Gifford) dis mou
1840, 1, 18. Eunice (form Beeson) con mou
1840, 8, 15. Jonathan & ch, Enoch, John G., Samuel S. & Isaac H., rec in mbrp (Jonathan had been dis by White Water MM)
1846, 9, 19. Jonathan & w, Eunice, & ch, Samuel S. & Isaac H., gct Mississinawa MM, Ind.
1849, 1, 20. Jonathan & ch, Samuel S. & Isaac H., rocf Honey Camp MM, Ind., dtd 1848,12,9
1850, 3, 21. John G. dis mou
1851, 7, 24. Ann T. Stephens (form Dicks) dis mou
1855, 4, 26. Samuel S. [Dix] dis mou
1857, 9, 24. Isaac H. [Dix] dis disunity

DILL
1820, 5, 6. Anna (form Kellum) dis mou

DUFFIELD
----, --, --. George m Esther Elma STUBBS, dt Milton & Sarah J., b 1860,3,30

1810, 5, 26. Esther E. relrq

ECCLES
1873, 10, 28. John Milton d ae 51y 4m 13d

1850, 1, 24. Rachel rec in mbrp with consent of Deep River MM, N. C.
1860, 11, 22. Rachel gct Milford MM, Ind.; returned
1862, 3, 20. Rachel gct Sugar Plain MM, Ind.
1873, 10, 23. John M.'s d rpd

EDGERTON
----, --, --. Samuel, s William & Tabitha, b 1776,3,13; m Elizabeth WILKINS, dt William J. & Sarah, b 1775,10,8
Ch: William W. b 1801, 9, 18
Hannah " 1804, 9, 26
Prudence " 1807, 2, 14
Rachel " 1808, 10, 20
Tabitha " 1810, 12, 18
Thomas " 1813, 2, 2
Samuel " 1816, 2, 19
Joseph " 1818, 5, 13
1833, 6, 11. Thomas S., s William & Abigail, b
1834, 1, 23. Thomas, Preble Co., O., s Samuel & Elizabeth; m at Elk Mtg, Mary TAYLOR, Fayette Co., Ind., dt George & Elizabeth

1816, 6, 1. Samuel & w, Elizabeth, & ch, William, Sarah, Hannah, Prudence, Rachel, Tabitha, Thomas & Samuel, rocf Stillwater MM, dtd 1815,11,28, endorsed by Miami MM 1816,3,27
1834, 3, 15. Samuel & w, Elizabeth, & s, Samuel & Joseph, gct Duck Creek MM, Ind.
1834, 8, 15. Tabitha gct Duck Creek MM, Ind.
1836, 10, 15. William & w, Abigail, & s, Thomas S., gct White Water MM, Ind.
1836, 11, 19. Thomas & w, Mary, & ch, William T. & Elizabeth Ann, gct Salem MM, Ind.

EEKS
1845, 8, 16. Martha Jane Eeks rec in mbrp (a minor under care of Mary Denny)

ELLIOTT
1815, 6, 3. Hannah [Eliott] rocf Miami MM
1821, 12, 1. Stephen Bogue gct White Water MM, to m Elviry Eliot
1846, 4, 18. Rhoda (form Brown) dis mou & jas
1912, 12, 26. Fannie rocf New Garden MM, Ind., dtd 1912,12,21
1915, 1, 21. Fannie gct Rockford MM, O.

ELLIS
1871, 10, 9. Leon C. d ae 2y 5m 26d

1871, 4, 20. Edwin C. & w, Mary Ann, & ch, Leon Orlando, rocf Newberry MM, O., dtd 1871,3,20
1873, 4, 24. Edwin C. & fam gct Back Creek MM, Ind.

EMBREE
1814, 9, 3. John [Embra] dis
1821, 2, 3. Joseph con mou
1823, 12, 6. Sarah [Embre] & ch, Mary, Samuel, Jesse & William, gct White Lick MM, Ind.
1823, 12, 6. Mercer [Embre] gct White Lick MM, Ind.
1824, 12, 4. Amos gct White Lick MM, Ind.
1824, 12, 4. Joseph gct White Lick MM, Ind.

EMLEY
1822, 12, 7. Margaret recrq
1823, 7, 5. John C. recrq
1828, 11, 1. John C. [Imly] dis disunity

EMRICK
1889, 10, 24. Lilly relrq
1902, 4, 24. Russell R. [Emerick] rec in mbrp
1910, 4, 28. Bernice Lee & Elwood Richard, s Charles & Eva, rec in mbrp
1911, 8, 24. Jessie rolf U. B. Church
1921, 2, 24. Blanche & Eva rec in mbrp

ENGLE
1821, 12, 1. Hope & five ch rec in mbrp
1823, 1, 4. Jacob rec in mbrp
1823, 1, 4. Joshua rec in mbrp
1826, 11, 4. Rebecca con mou
1827, 3, 3. Rebecca rocf White Water MM, dtd 1826,10,5
1827, 11, 3. John [Ingle], s Joshua, rec in mbrp
1828, 3, 1. Elizabeth dis
1829, 5, 2. Jacob gct Silver Creek MM, Ind.
1830, 11, 6. Joshua & w, Hope, & ch, Joshua, Robert, Ann, Lucinda, John & Samuel, gct Vermillion MM, Ill; had rq cert to Silver Creek MM but they afterwards rem to Vermillion MM
1833, 10, 19. Susannah & William, ch Rebecca, rec in mbrp
1840, 1, 18. Rebecca & s, Isaac, gct Westfield MM, Ind.
1846, 11, 21. Susanna gct Dover MM, Ind.
1847, 10, 18. Susannah rocf Dover MM; she returned to Dover MM, the cert was returned
1853, 3, 24. William rpd mou; mbr Westfield MM
1855, 10, 25. William dis by Westfield MM for mou

ERWIN
1917, 6, 22. Grace Irene (form Crist) glt 3rd M. E. Church, Richmond, Ind.

EVANS
1865, 8, 31. Priscilla m Amos BRANSON

1810, 6, 2. Joseph & fam gct West Branch MM
1861, 3, 21. Priscilla rocf Clear Creek MM, O., dtd 1861,2,19

FARIS
1815, 5, 6. Elizabeth (form Sanders) rpd mou

FERST
1892, 4, 21. Lizzie S. glt U. B. Church, West Elkton, O.

FOUTS
1898, 6 --. John Earl, s William & Elizabeth; m Beatrice BYERS

1832, 10, 20. Elizabeth S. dis disunity
1892, 4, 21. John Earl rec in mbrp
1908, 9, 24. John dropped from mbrp

FOX
1822, 6, 1. Jane (form Wilson) dis mou

FRAZIER
1831, 11, 5. Elwood Ozbun gct Cherry Grove MM, to m Lydia Frazier
1871, 11, 23. Reuben, of Colorado Tertitory, rec in mbrp

FROST
1850, 9, 26. Lydia (form Wright) con mou
1854, 8, 24. Lydia gct White Water MM, Ind.

GALLOWAY
1878, 3, 21. David J. [Galoway] rec in mbrp
1885, 4, 23. David glt M. E. Church, Dayton, O.

GARDNER
1811, 11, 5. Eliab & w, Sarah, & ch, William, Richard & Elisabeth, rocf Deep River MM, N. C., dtd 1811,5,--
1812, 5, 2. Richard dis
1814, 8, 6. William gct White Water MM
1814, 8, 6. Eliab & fam gct White Water MM
1838, 4, 21. Henry & Asael, s William, rocf Salem MM, Ind., dtd 1838,3,24
1843, 6, 17. Asahel A. gct Mill Creek MM
1843, 5, 20. Esther rec in mbrp
1846, 1, 17. Henry gct Salem MM, Ia.
1852, 6, 24. Mary W., Theodore & Endoris, ch Joseph, rocf Salem MM, Ia., dtd 1852,5,22
1862, 1, 23. Esther F. gct Milford MM, Ind.

GAUSE
----, --, --. Nathan, s Solomon & Ruth, b 1778,6,17; m Mary AILES, dt Amos & Ann, b 1787,12,2

Ch:		
Eli D.	b	1807, 12, 23
Ann	"	1810, 4, 14
Solomon	"	1813, 3, 10
Ruth	"	1816, 2, 3
Joseph	"	1818, 11, 2
Isaac	"	1821, 4, 21
Nathan	"	1823, 10, 5
Steven	"	1826, 2, 13
Mary	"	1828, 1, 14

----, --, --. Eli, s Solomon & Ruth, b 1786,3,1; m Martha PIERCE, dt James & Merriam, b 1786,1,10

Ch:		
James P.	b	1810, 5, 30
Jesse	"	1811, 12, 31
Ann E.	"	1814, 1, 8
Ruth	"	1816, 3, 23
Richard	"	1818, 3, 13
Nathan	"	1820, 5, 18
Samuel	"	1820, 5, 18
Hannah B.	"	1822, 4, 25
Eli	"	1824, 11, 7
Aaron	"	1828, 11, 25
Charles	"	1830, 11, 26

----, --, --. Isaac & Patience

Ch:		
Israel	b	1812, 4, 13
John	"	1814, 7, 10

1813, 12, 7. Lydia, dt Jacob & Eliza Cooper,

GAUSE, continued
b
1832, 9, 20. Eli D., Preble Co., O., s Nathan & Mary; m at Elk Mtg, Lydia COOPER, Butler Co., O., dt Jacob & Elizabeth
1833, 11, 27. Ann C. m Joseph B. HUNT
1839, 12, 23. Richard, Henry Co., Ind., s Eli & Martha; m at Elk Mtg, Elizabeth COOPER, dt Jonathan & Esther

1816, 3, 2. Isaac & w, Patience, & ch, Israel & John, rocf Red Stone MM, dtd 1815, 9,29; endorsed by Miami MM, 1816,1,31
1817, 12, 6. Nathan & w, Mary, & ch, Eli, Ann, Solomon & Ruth, rocf Redstone MM, dtd 1817,5,21
1818, 1, 3. Eli & w, Martha, & ch, James, Jesse, Anna & Ruth, rocf Miami MM, dtd 1817,10,2
1827, 6, 2. Isaac rqct Redstone MM, to m Sarah Moore
1827, 11, 3. Isaac con mou
1828, 12, 6. Isaac dis disunity
1829, 1, 3. Sarah rpd dis by Redstone MM for mou; living at this mtg
1831, 4, 13. Sarah M. & dt, Bethsheba, rec in mbrp (H)
1832, 9, 15. Eli D. prcf Westfield MM, to m
1832, 12, 15. Lydia gct Westfield MM
1833, 10, 9. Isaac & fam gct Westfield MM(H)
1833, 10, 9. Sarah M. & h gct Westfield MM(H)
1834, 3, 15. Eli & w, Martha, & ch, Ruth, Richard, Nathan, Samuel, Hannah B., Eli, Aaron & Charles, gct Spiceland MM, Ind.
1834, 3, 15. James P. gct Spiceland MM, Ind.
1834, 3, 15. Jesse gct Spiceland MM, Ind.
1836, 2, 20. Nathan & w, Mary, & ch, Joseph, Isaac, Nathan, Stephen A. & Mary, gct Spiceland MM, Ind.
1836, 2, 20. Ann gct Spiceland MM, Ind.
1836, 2, 20. Solomoh gct Spiceland MM, Ind.
1836, 2, 20. Ruth gct Spiceland MM, Ind.
1837, 3, 18. Eli D. & w, Lydia, gct Spiceland MM, Ind.
1839, 8, 17. Israel dis jH
1840, 2, 15. Elizabeth gct Spiceland MM, Ind.

GIBBONS
1853, 12, 22. Lydia Ann rocf Bloomfield MM, Ind., dtd 1853,11,9
1863, 4, 23. Lydia Ann gct White Water MM,Ind.

GIFFORD
1817, 11, 6. Nathan, Prebble Co., O., s William & Keziah; m at Elk Mtg, Rebeccah HART, Butler Co., O., dt Isaac, dec, & Sarah
1827, 7, 12. William, Preble Co., O., s William & Kisiah; m at Elk Mtg, Ann STUBBS, Preble Co., O., dt Samuel & Mary
1834, 3, 19. Andrew, Preble Co., O., s William & Keziah, both dec; m at Westfield Mtg, Sarah E. BROWN, wd, Preble Co., O., dt Samuel & Elizabeth Edgerton
----, --, --. Jesse & Bethena
Ch: Annuel b 1835, 8, 4
Susannah " 1837, 4, 7
Eliza Ann " 1838, 12, 22
Henry R. " 1841, 9, 3
Hannah J. " 1847, 3, 5
Asa Lindly " 1852, 4, 11
1835, 10, 28. Isaac d ae 17y 1m 29d
1839, 3, 24. Nathan d ae 1y 2m 13d
1840, 6, 10. Esther d ae 19y 20d
----, --, --. Andrew & Sarah
Ch: Elizabeth b 1841, 8, 4
Jesse John " 1843, 2, 8
Daniel " 1835, 2, 16
Keziah " 1847, 1, 14
Nathan " 1838, 1, 11
----, --, --. Annuel b 1835,8,4; m Sarah KOONTS
Anuel m 2nd Ellen -----
----, --, --. Henry R. b 1841,9,3; m Debrah Ann GEETING
1872, 10, 29. Asa Lindley b 1852,4,11 d 1881, 2,8; m Sarah Ann ROSS, dt Charles & Mary Ann, b 1851,9,13
Ch: Alva Edwin b 1872, 12, 9; m 1895,9,4 Pearl Francis
Lurton
Andrew b 1876, 7, 8
Mary B. " 1878, 9, 1; m 1903,3, 26 Charles E. KENWORTHY
1881, 9, 9. Bethena d ae 68y 7m 18d
1882, 11, 19. Jesse d ae 69y 6m 12d
----, --, --. Lindley m Mary Elizabeth BRANSON, b 1866,10,7 (dt Amos & Priscilla)
Ch: Edith b 1888, 9, 27
Lucy " 1891, 3, 5
Fred " 1893, 7, 2
1899, 12, 25. Margaret d

1813, 1, 2. Kezia & ch, Nathan, Henry, Andrew & William, rocf Deep River MM, N.C., dtd 1812,9,7
1826, 5, 6. Nathan dis disunity
1827, 3, 3. Andrew G. con mou
1828, 3, 1. Henry dis mou
1829, 5, 2. William dis joining Separatists
1829, 12, 5. Hannah Dix (form Gifford) dis mou
1830, 2, 6. Rebecca dis disunity
1830, 3, 6. Jesse gct White Water MM
1831, 7, 2. Jesse rocf White Water MM, dtd 1831,4,27
1831, 8, 6. Ann dis disunity
1832, 6, 16. Jesse dis
1847, 9, 18. Hannah Stone (form Gifford) dis mou
1847, 9, 18. Lucy Ann dis disunity
1850, 9, 26. Jesse rst
1850, 10, 24. Bethena & ch, Annuel, Susanna, Eliza Ann, Henry & Hannah, rec in mbrp
1853, 5, 26. Andrew & w, Sarah E., & ch, David, Elizabeth, Jesse & Keziah, gct

GIFFORD, continued
White Water MM, Ind.
1857, 2, 26. Annuel dis mou
1857, 2, 26. Susannah Stubbs (form Gifford) dis mou
1858, 1, 21. Eliza Ann Stubbs (form Gifford) dis mou
1863, 2, 26. Edith H. (form Hunt) rpd mou
1863, 4, 23. Edith H. gct White Water MM, Ind.
1865, 4, 20. Edith H. rocf White Water MM, Ind., dtd 1865,3,22
1865, 7, 22. Edith H. & fam gct Rocksylvania MM, Ia.
1866, 6, 21. Sarah rec in mbrp
1866, 9, 20. Hannah J. Bennett (form Gifford) rpd mou; dropped from mbrp
1872, 4, 26. Sarah Ann (form Rop) rpd mou
1872, 8, 22. Lindley rpd mou
1893, 3, 23. Riley W. & w, Margaret, rec in mbrp
1899, 6, 22. Lizzie B. & ch, Edith May, Lucy Marie & Freddie, rec in mbrp
1900, 6, 21. Alva gct Cincinnati MM, O.

GOOD
1812, 7, 4. Mary rec in mbrp

GOODWIN
1822, 9, 19. Joseph, Preble Co., O., s William & Rachel; m at Elk Mtg, Mary HIXSON, Preble Co., O., dt Wm. & Rachel
Ch: William b 1823, 9, 7
Rebecca " 1824, 12, 5
Henry " 1825, 12, 28
John " 1827, 9, 3
Miles " 1829, 10, 30
Richard " 1832, 8, 13
Rachel " 1835, 2, 19
Samuel " 1839, 7, 4
Joseph " 1844, 4, 18
1826, 3, 27. William d ae 80y
1843, 1, 5. Rachel d ae 7y 10m 16d
----, --, --. Clement, s John & Olive

1817, 12, 6. William rec in mbrp
1818, 9, 5. Rachel rec in mbrp
1824, 12, 4. Nathan gct Westfield MM
1827, 9, 1. Stephen & fam gct Vermillion MM, Ill.
1832, 5, 19. Joseph dis
1843, 2, 18. Nathan rocf Bloomfield MM, dtd 1842,12,7
1843, 2, 18. William dis disunity
1843, 4, 15. Rebecca dis disunity
1846, 12, 19. Henry dis mou & disunity
1850, 4, 25. John dis disunity
1851, 7, 24. Miles dis disunity
1853, 1, 20. Richard dis mou & disunity
1857, 7, 23. Mary & ch gct Pleasant Plain MM, Ia.
1899, 7, 20. C. L. rolf Presbyterian Church, Collinsville
1925, 3, 26. C. L. V. glt M. E. Church, Modesto, Calif.

GORDON
1852, 10, 21. Elizabeth (form Grubbs) con mou
1853, 8, 25. Elizabeth gct Spiceland MM, Ind.

GRAVE
1851, 5, 22. Lydia Ann rocf White Water MM, Ind., dtd 1851,3,26
1854, 12, 21. Lydia Ann [Graves] gct West Union MM, Ind.

GREEN
1814, 8, 18. Jesse, Preble Co., O., s Amos & Esther; m at Elk Mtg, Charity COOK, Butler Co., O., dt John & Olive
1817, 5, 8. Amos, Preble Co., O., s Amos, dec, & Hester (Esther); m at Elk Mtg, Sarah JONES, Preble Co., O., dt George & Lydia
Ch: Hannah b 1818, 3, 6
Lydia " 1819, 4, 22
George " 1820, 6, 6
Rebecca " 1821, 7, 22
Esther " 1823, 1, 23
Asenith " 1824, 9, 11
Sarah " 1826, 5, 1
Amos " 1828, 2, 4
Enoch " 1831, 3, 3
Keziah " 1832, 7, 8
Elizabeth " 1834, 3, 7
1822, 7, 28. Rebecca d ae 1y 5d
1825, 5, 11. Joseph d ae 66y 1m 14d

1810, 3, 3. Esther & ch, Jesse, Hannah & Amos, rocf New Garden MM, N. C., dtd 1809,7,29, endorsed by Miami MM
1814, 7, 1. Hannah Jones (form Green) con mou
1833, 2, 16. Jesse dis disunity
1834, 10, 18. Amos & w, Sarah, & ch, Hannah, Lydia, George, Esther, Ascenith, Sarah, Amos, Enoch, Kezia & Elizabeth, gct Mississinaway MM, Ind. (rem within limits of Michigan Territory)
1835, 7, 18. Charity, w Jesse, & ch, Mary, Abigail, Esther, John, Thomas, Olive, Amos, William Jesse & Eli, gct Mississiniwa MM, Ind.

1852, 7, 22. Hannah (form Taylor) dis disunity

GREGG
1829, 2, 7. Amy rocf Redstone MM, dtd 1828, 6,4

GREYSOM
1855, 8, 23. West Branch MM rq this mtg to deal with Eleanor Snyder (form Greysom)

GRUBBS
1852, 10, 21. Elizabeth Gordon (form Grubbs) con mou

GUEST
----, --, --. John & Elizabeth
Ch: Thomas b 1827, 3, 18
Hannah " 1829, 1, 5
David " 1831, 3, 28
Stephen " 1833, 6, 6
1832, 3, 31. Hannah d ae 75y 5m 21d

1823, 3, 1. John con mou
1823, 8, 2. James con mou
1824, 9, 4. Baker con mou
1826, 3, 4. John con mou
1826, 4, 1. Elizabeth con mou
1829, 12, 5. Baker gct White Lick MM, Ind.
1834, 10, 18. John dis

HADLEY
1820, 2, 5. Jeremiah rocf Cane Creek MM, N. C., dtd 1819,9,4, endorsed by White Water MM

HAGERMAN
1834, 8, 13. Henrietta (form Nelson) dis mou (H)

HAINES
1828, 7, 24. Hannah d bur Westfield Cemetery

1908, 9, 24. Mina dropped from mbrp

HAISLEY
1859, 3, 31. Mary m Joseph BROWN

1859, 2, 24. Mary [Haisly] & ch, Eunice, Lavina & Alfred, rocf Oakridge MM, dtd 1859,1,11
1871, 3, 23. Eunice Vinage (form Haisly) rpd mou; dropped from mbrp; Pipe Creek MM to be notified
1872, 11, 23. Lavina gct Pipe Creek MM, Ind.
1882, 3, 23. Alfred gct Pipe Creek MM, Ind.

HALL
1836, 2, 20. Chalkly dis by Spiceland MM, Ind. for disunity & jas

HALSEY
1849, 10, 20. Amy (form Swain) dis mou

HAMILTON
1906, 6, 21. Emma rec in mbrp

HAMMER
1899, 3, 23. Hattie S. rec in mbrp
1904, 6, 23. Hattie S. glt First Baptist Church, Hamilton, O.

HANCOCK
1822, 2, 2. Bethiah rec in mbrp
1827, 6, 2. Elizabeth & Mary, dt Bethiah, rec in mbrp
1829, 8, 1. Bethiah dis joining Separatists
1831, 8, 6. Elizabeth dis joining Separatist
1833, 7, 20. Mary dis jH

HARKLOO
1913, 4, 24. Stella May rec in mbrp

HARNED
1822, 8, 8. Alida C., wd, m John CLARK

1822, 4, 6. Alida C. rocf Rahway MM, N.J., dtd 1822,1,17

HARRIS
----, --, --. Thompson & Sarah
Ch: John
Wilson b 1840, 8, 12
Angelina G." 1842, 8, 18
Valearia " 1844, 6, 28 d 1866, 3, 3 m Jabez H. KENWORTHY
1862, 8, 28. Valeria m Jabez H. KENWORTHY

1827, 11, 3. Thomas [Harres] rec in mbrp
1840, 3, 21. Sarah (form Brown) con mou
1840, 4, 18. Thompson con mou
1844, 2, 17. Thompson dis joining Separatists
1844, 2, 17. Sarah dis jas
1847, 12, 18. Obediah rocf Cherry Grove MM, Ind., dtd 1847,11,13
1848, 10, 21. Obediah gct Cherry Grove MM,Ind.
1856, 4, 24. Valerie rec in mbrp; a minor under care of Mary Brown
1860, 3, 22. John Milton gct Dover MM, Ind.

HART
----, --, --. Isaac & Sarah
Ch: Esther b 1797, 2, 28
Hannah " 1798, 10, 26
Rebecca " 1801, 1, 8
Elizabeth " 1805, 3, 18
Margaret " 1807, 6, 5
Samuel " 1811, 8, 19
Sarah " 1813, 5, 18
1817, 11, 6. Rebeccah m Nathan GIFFORD
1841, 5, 12. Thomas d ae 59y 6m 28d

1810, 3, 3. Phineas rocf New Garden MM, N. C., dtd 1809,7,29, endorsed by Miami MM
1819, 1, 2. Esther Talbert (form Hart) con mou
1820, 1, 4. Jimmy dis mou
1833, 3, 16. Sarah dis disunity
1837, 11, 18. Thomas gct Walnut Ridge MM,Ind.

HARTLEY
1837, 4, 20. Norton D., Preble Co., O., s Thomas & Barbary; m at Elk Mtg, Deborah Ann JONES, dt William & Deborah Ann, both dec, b 1820,1,26
Ch: William

HARTLEY, Norton D. & Deborah Ann, continued
Ch: Jones b 1838, 2, 10
Elizabeth " 1839, 6, 28
Thomas C. " 1840, 10, 21
John " 1842, 3, 13
George " 1844, 4, 12
Lucinda " 1844, 4, 12
Lydia Caroline " 1846, 1, 16

1836, 3, 19. Norton D. rocf Cherry Grove MM, Ind., dtd 1836,1,9
1839, 1, 19. Thomas & w, Barbara, & ch, Elias & James, rocf Cherry Grove MM, Ind., dtd 1838,12,12
1839, 9, 21. Hannah F. [Hartly] rocf White Water MM, Ind., dtd 1839,7,21
1841, 4, 17. Thomas & w, Barbara, & ch, Elias & James, gct Cherry Grove MM, Ind.
1841, 6, 19. Hannah [Hartly] gct White Water MM, Ind.
1844, 9, 21. James rocf Cherry Grove MM, dtd 1844,8,10
1848, 9, 16. James con mou; living at Salem MM, Ia.
1848, 11, 18. Rachel L. com joining Separatists
1848, 11, 18. Norton D. [Hartly] & w, Deborah Ann, & ch, William, Elizabeth, Thomas, John, George, Lydia & Caroline, gct White Lick MM, Ind.
1849, 1, 20. Elizabeth (form Lamm) rpd mou; living at Salem MM, Ia.
1849, 5, 19. James [Hartly] gct Salem MM,Ia.
1849, 8, 18. Elizabeth L. [Hartly] gct Salem MM, Ia.
1911, 11, 23. Edward E. & w, Susie E., rocf Barbers Mills MM, Ind., dtd 1911,11,4
1912, 11, 21. Edward E. & w, Susie E., gct Bethel MM, Ind.

HARTMAN
1922, 3, 23. Margaret rec in mbrp
1925, 1, 22. Margaret glt U. B. Church, West Elkton, O.

HARVEY
1827, 7, 7. Amos rpd mou; White Water MM rq to deal with him

HASKET
1840, 9, 21. John, Miami Co., O., s Isaac & Rebecca; m at Elk Mtg, Mary MADDOCK, Preble Co., O., dt Francis & Phebe
Dt: Rebecca b 1841, 10, 27

1842, 1, 15. John rocf West Branch MM, dtd 1841,4,15
1843, 5, 20. John & w, Mary, & dt, Rebecca, gct West Branch MM, O.

HATFIELD
1810, 4, 7. Thomas con mou
1810, 4, 7. Sarah con mou

1813, 10, 2. Jonas & fam gct White Water MM
1816, 10, 5. Thomas & fam gct White Water MM

HAWKINS
1811, 1, 24. Hannah m Joseph HOLLINGSWORTH
1813, 1, 7. Mary m Walter ROBERDS
1815, 6, 8. Benjamin d ae 68y 29d

1810, 1, 6. Amos co
1810, 5, 5. Olive appointed elder
1810, 11, 3. Joseph Hollingsworth prc to m Hannah Hawkins
1813, 1, 2. Walter Roberts prc to m Mary Hawkins
1813, 7, 3. Nathan & fam gct White Water MM
1813, 11, 6. James dis mou
1813, 11, 6. Levi dis disunity
1817, 3, 1. Henry gct New Garden MM
1817, 10, 4. Amos & fam gct White Water MM
1828, 9, 6. Olive gct White Lick MM, Ind.
1828, 11, 1. Joseph Benjamin, Robert, Esther, Sarah, William & John, ch Levi, gct White Lick MM, Ind.

HAYWARD
1832, 3, 14. William Jr. rocf Indian Spring MM, dtd 1832,1,4 (H)
1832, 10, 10. William Jr. gct Green Plain MM, to m Mildred Keane Willits (H)
1835, 7, 9. William [Hayworth] gct Green Plain MM

HAZLEY
----, --, --. Allen & Mary H.
Ch: Eunice b 1850, 7, 31
Lavina " 1852, 10, 1
Alfred " 1854, 8, 24

HEATON
1904, 10, 20. John C. rocf Smithfield MM, O.
1910, 5, 26. John C. gct Smithfield MM, O.

HENRY
1877, 1, 24. Samuel rec in mbrp

HERRELL
1810, 6, 2. Obediah rocf Piney Woods MM, N. C., dtd 1810,4,7

HIATT
1832, 2, 4. Isaac & w, Shannah D., & ch, Daniel W., Phebe, Lydia, Martha Jane & Rebecca, rocf White Water MM, dtd 1831,11,23
1834, 10, 18. Isaac & w, Shanna D., & ch, Daniel W. Phebe, Lydia, Martha Jane, Rebecca & Joseph, gct White Water MM, Ind.

HIBBERD
1827, 5, 7. James M., Berkley Co., Va., s Aaron & Martha; m at Elk Mtg, Mary NIXON, Preble Co., O., dt William & Martha

HIBBERD, continued
1827, 7, 7. Mary [Hibbard] gct Hopewell MM, Va.

HICKS
1901, 3, 21. Eva (form Crist) glt M. E. Ch., Allegheny, Pa.

HILLMAN
----, --, --. Samuel b 1788,3,21; m Sarah ----- b 1794,4,12
Ch: Elizabeth b 1816, 1, 28
Edmond " 1818, 6, 4
Abigail Mulhollon " 1820, 6, 28
Sarah Brown " 1822, 6, 29
Samuel " 1824, 3, 11
Rachel " 1826, 9, 9

1837, 7, 15. Elizabeth dis disunity

HINSHAW
1841, 4, 17. Susanna (form Ozbun) con mou

HIXON
----, --, --. William & Rachel
Ch: John b 1800, 12, 19
Mary " 1802, 8, 9
William " 1804, 5, 11
Esther " 1808, 12, 12
Samuel " 1810, 11, 19
Rachel " 1814, 5, 21
Rebecca " 1816, 12, 27
1820, 10, 19. John, Preble Co., s Wm. & Rachel; m at Elk Mtg, Phebe RANDAL, Preble Co., O., dt Isaac & Sarah
Ch: Mary b 1821, 10, 16
Nancy " 1822, 12, 7
Rachel " 1824, 2, 7
Isaac " 1825, 7, 21
Sarah " 1826, 12, 15
William " 1828, 2, 10
Elizabeth " 1829, 10, 19
Esther " 1831, 3, 4
Rebecca " 1832, 5, 6
Phebe " 1833, 10, 1
John " 1835, 10, 25
1822, 9, 19. Mary [Hixson] m Joseph GOODWIN
1830, 10, 17. Isaac d ae 5y 2m 26d
1832, 10, 4. Rebecca [Hixson] d ae 4m 28d
1833, 10, 7. William d ae 5y 8m 27d
1854, 11, 26. William [Hixson] d

1814, 12, 3. Rachel & dt, Rachel, rec in mbrp
1829, 6, 6. William, Jr. dis joining Separatists
1830, 6, 5. Rachel dis disunity
1831, 10, 1. Esther dis joining Separatists
1832, 3, 14. William rpd mou (H)
1832, 8, 18. Samuel dis neglecting attendance & disunity
1835, 4, 18. Rachel Jr. dis disunity
1835, 4, 18. Rebecca dis jH

1836, 2, 20. John & w, Phebe, & ch, Mary, Nancy, Rachel, Sarah, Elizabeth, Esther, Phebe & John, gct New Garden MM, Ind.

HOCKETT
1834, 4, 19. Charles Osborne gct Cherry Grove MM, Ind., to m Ann Hockett

HOLLINGSWORTH
1811, 1, 24. Joseph, Indiana Territory, s Joseph & Margaret; m at Elk Mtg, Hannah HAWKINS, Butler Co., O., dt Benjamin & Martha
1811, 6, 6. Isaiah, Franklin Co., O., s Jonathan & Mary; m at Elk Mtg, Patience Smith, Butler Co., O., dt Joseph & Hannah, dec
1811, 10, 10. William, Franklin Co., Ind., s Joseph & Margaret; m at Elk Mtg, Mary COOK, Butler Co., O., dt John, dec, & Olive
Ch: Sarah b 1812, 11, 18
Susannah " 1813, 11, 9
John " 1816, 4, 14
Elihu " 1818, 4, 20
Midian " 1820, 1, 12
Ascenith " 1821, 11, 10
Olive " 1823, 11, 22
1812, 12, 14. Sarah d ae 3w 4d bur Elk Cem.

1810, 11, 3. Joseph prc to m Hannah Hawkins
1811, 6, 1. Isiah prc to m Patience Smith
1811, 10, 5. Hannah gct White Water MM
1811, 10, 5. William prc to m Mary Cook
1811, 11, 2. Patience gct White Water MM
1812, 6, 6. Joseph & w, Hannah, rocf White Water MM, dtd 1812,5,30
1812, 6, 6. William rocf White Water MM. dtd 1812,5,30
1828, 9, 6. William & fam gct White Lick MM
1828, 10, 4. Joseph & fam gct White Lick MM, Ind.

HOLODAY
1875, 12, 30. Elwood, s John & Ruth, b 1853, 10,1; m Maggie TRUMP

1884, 1, 24. Elwood rocf Newberry MM, dtd 1883,11,19
1884, 1, 24. Joseph rocf Newberry MM, dtd 1883,11,19
1888, 12, 22. Joseph M. glt M. E. Church, Lynchburg, O.

HORNADAY
1859, 1, 10. Ruth d ae 81y 7m 15d

1822, 10, 5. Lydia (form Lane) dis mou
1867, 2, 21. Mary (form Jones) rpd mou
1868, 9, 24. Nancy & ch gct Walnut Ridge MM, Ind.

HORNEY
1849, 4, 21. Rebecca rocf Dover MM, N. C., dtd 1849,4,26
1850, 5, 23. Rebecca gct Richland MM, Ind.

HUDDLESTON
1826, 7, 6. William, Union Co., Ind., s Jonathan & Phebe; m Susanna OZBUN, Preble Co., O., dt John & Sarah

1826, 7, 1. William prcf Silver Creek MM, Ind., to m Susanna Osbun
1826, 10, 7. Susannah [Huddleson] gct Salem MM

HUNT
----, --, --. John m Ann BROWN, dt Joseph & Susanna, b 1785,4,13
Ch: Joseph B. b 1807, 3, 3
Susanna B. " 1810, 3, 23
Esther W. " 1812, 4, 18
Clayton " 1815, 6, 27
Benjamin " 1822, 11, 27
1833, 11, 27. Joseph B., Preble Co., O., s John, dec, & Ann; m at Westfield Mtg, Ann C. GAUSE, Preble Co., O., dt Eli & Martha
1855, 8, 30. Charlotte m Riley DAVIS
1860, 8, 2. Nathan, Clinton Co., O., s Robert, dec, & Ruth; m at Elk Mtg, Esther T. STUBBS, Preble Co., O., dt Elisha & Elizabeth
1861, 3, 1. Esther T. d ae 19y 4m 18d

1811, 11, 2. Elizabeth con mou
1834, 10, 18. Joseph B. & w, Ann E., gct Spiceland MM, Ind.
1834, 10, 18. Benjamin gct Spiceland MM, Ind.
1834, 10, 18. Ann gct White Water MM, Ind.
1834, 10, 18. Clayton gct White Water MM,Ind.
1848, 4, 15. Charlotte (form Townsend) con mou; mbr of West Grove MM
1848, 8, 19. Charlotte T. rocf West Grove MM, Ind., dtd 1848,8,19
1855, 11, 22. Enos P. Stubbs gct Springfield MM, O., to m Mary Hunt
1856, 4, 24. Susan (form Roberts) dis mou
1859, 2, 24. Barbary Lane (form Hunt) rpd mou; Dover MM rq this mtg to deal with her
1860, 7, 26. Nathan prcf Springfield MM, O., dtd 1860,7,21, to m Esther Stubbs
1861, 2, 21. Ruth S. & ch, Henry H., George M. & Rachel G. rocf Springfield MM, O., dtd 1861,1,19
1861, 2, 21. Lydia Ann & Edith S. rocf Springfield MM, O., dtd 1861,1,19
1861, 3, 21. Nathan rocf Springfield MM, O., dtd 1861,2,16
1863, 2, 26. Edith H. Gifford (form Hunt) rpd mou
1863, 4, 23. Nathan gct Roxsylvania MM, Ia.
1863, 4, 23. Lydia gct Roxsylvania MM, Ia.
1864, 10, 20. Ruth & dt, Ann & Rachel, gct Rocksylvania MM, Ia.
1865, 1, 26. George M. gct Roxsylvania MM,Ia.
1866, 12, 8. Henry rpd mou; living at Roxilvania MM, Ia.
1867, 6, 20. Henry gct Roxilvania MM, Ia.
1872, 2, 22. Angelina T. (form Taylor) rpd mou
1880, 8, 26. George M. & fam rocf Rocksylvania MM, Ia.
1884, 7, 24. George M. & w, Angeline, & ch, Irvin L., Sylvia Belle, Myrta Elma, Lottie Alma & Alvin G., gct Estacado MM, Tex.

HUTCHIN
----, --, --. Joel & Rachel
Ch: Mary C. b 1822, 2, 7
Isaac " 1823, 12, 8
Henry " 1825, 11, 1
Ann " 1828, 2, 19
Caroline " 1830, 6, 17
Mary " 1833, 4, 25
James " 1835, 4, 2
1847, 10, 21. Ann [Hutchens] m Enoch DICKS
1848, 7, 20. Caroline [Hutchens] m Elisha BROWN
1850, 11, 22. Mary T. m Amos H. TERRIL
1888, --, --. Henry [Hutchens] d
1891, --, --. Isaac [Hutchens] d

1820, 2, 5. Raceel rocf Miami MM, dtd 1820, 1,26
1823, 1, 4. Nancy [Hutchens] rec in mbrp
1823, 7, 5. Joel G. [Hutchon] rec in mbrp
1825, 5, 7. Rachel rec in mbrp
1825, 5, 7. Isaac, s Joel G. & Rachel, rec in mbrp
1829, 2, 7. Rachel dis disunity & joining Separatists
1844, 12, 21. Isaac dis disunity
1846, 8, 15. Henry W. dis disunity
1855, 10, 25. Joel G. & w, Rachel H., gct Richland MM, Ia.
1856, 8, 21. James T. gct Richland MM, Ia.
1871, 11, 23. Isaac & Henry W., of Colorado Territory, rec in mbrp

ISLES
1885, 6, 2. Sarah Ellen d ae 26y 2m 27d

IVERS
1830, 7, 3. Hannah (form Patty) dis mou; living at White Lick MM

JOHNSON
----, --, --. Jonathan, s Jesse & Hannah, b 1781,8,9; m Hannah JONES, dt Henry & Kesiah, b 1787,8,11
Ch: John b 1816, 3, 7
Mary " 1819, 4, 20
Lydia " 1821, 6, 11
Hannah " 1825, 3, 25
Jonathan Hadley " 1829, 10, 30

JOHNSON, continued
1827, 2, 8. Kesiah m Joseph RANDAL
1833, 9, 24. Jonathan Hadley d ae 3y 10m 24d bur Westfield Cemetery
1852, 4, 14. Hannah d ae 64y 8m 7d
----, 1, 16. Jonathan d ae 71y 5m 7d
----, --, --. William Henry H. & Vienna C.
Ch: Elisha S. b 1859, 4, 10

1827, 4, 7. Jonathan & fam gct Westfield MM
1831, 1, 1. Elizabeth Mendenhall (form Jonson) con mou; living at Westfield
1833, 7, 20. Joseph Pray gct White Lick MM, Ind., to m Anna Jane Johnson
1834, 4, 19. John dis disunity
1835, 3, 21. Jonathan & w, Hannah, & ch, Mary, Lydia & Hannah, gct Cherry Grove MM, Ind.
1838, 1, 20. Ann Silvers (form Johnson) com for mou & jH
1838, 4, 21. Jonathan & w, Hannah, & dt, Hannah, rocf Cherry Grove MM, Ind.. dtd 1838, 3,14
1840, 10, 17. Jonathan & w, Hannah, & dt, Hannah, gct Westfield MM, Ind.
1849, 11, 17. Jonathan & w, Hanna, rocf Richland MM, Ind., dtd 1849,10,31
1858, 6, 24. Vienna (form Puckett) con mou; living at Cherry Grove MM
1859, 2, 24. Henry H. rec in mbrp
1860, 3, 22. William Henry H. & w, Vienna, & s, Elisha S., gct Cherry Grove MM, Ind.
1876, 3, 23. Belle gct Dover MM, O.

JOLLY
1827, 5, 5. Elizabeth rocf Stillwater MM

JONES
1812, 8, 6. Anna m Dilwyn BOGUE
1817, 5, 8. Sarah m Amos GREEN
1818, 8, 7. Henry Sr. d
----, --, --. William, s George & Lydia; m Deborah Ann -----
Ch: Deborah Ann
b 1820, 1, 26; m Norton D. HARTLEY
Wm. m 2nd 1822,9,12 at Elk Mtg, Tabitha STUBBS, Preble Co., O., dt Samuel & Mary
Ch: Keziah b 1825, 5, 9; m Eli Stubbs
Susan " 1827, 11, 6; m Hiram Stubbs, d 1899,7,13
1820, 4, 6. Georbe, Butler Co., O., s George & Lydia; m at Elk Mtg, Mary BOGUE, Preble Co., O., dt Joseph & Mary, both dec
1824, 9, 9. Lydia m John KENWORTHY
1827, 3, 8. Martha m John TOWNSEND
1834, 9, 15. William, an elder, d ae 35y 8m 18d
1837, 4, 20. Deborah Ann m Norton D. HARTLEY
1838, 2, 18. Henry d ae 81y 2m 16d
1847, 8, 26. Keziah m Eli STUBBS
1848, 9, 14. Deborah d ae 75y 4m 7d
1855, 3, 29. Susan m Hiram STUBBS
1862, 4, 28. Tabitha d ae 65y 5m
1877, 8, 7. Elenor d ae 26y 3m 25d
1887, 7, 11. Luella d ae 16y 8m 22d

1810, 5, 5. Prudence appointed elder
1812, 11, 7. Lyda & ch, Sarah, William, George, Rozia, Lyda, Patsy & Nathan, rec in mbrp
1814, 7, 1. Hannah (form Green) con mou
1815, 5, 6. Sarah (form Kellum) dis mou
1816, 7, 6. Martha con mou
1820, 1, 1. Prudence gct Silver Creek MM
1820, 10, 7. William con mou
1822, 4, 6. Ann dis
1825, 3, 5. Deborah Ann, dt William, rec in mbrp
1827, 2, 3. Henry Jr. dis mou
1827, 12, 1. John & w, Sarah, & ch, Mary, Rachel Jesse Wallace & Naomy, rocf West Branch MM, dtd 1827,11,17
1828, 12, 6. John & fam gct West Branch MM
1829, 3, 19. Jonathan dis disunity
1830, 10, 2. Hannah dis disunity
1830, 11, 6. John, Joseph & Newton gct White Lick MM, Ind.
1830, 11, 6. Sarah gct White Lick MM, Ind.
1834, 5, 16. John com for mou & disunity
1834, 7, 19. Newton rocf Sugar River MM, Ind., dtd 1834,5,10
1834, 7, 19. John & Joseph rocf Sugar River MM, Ind.
1834, 9, 20. Sarah rocf Sugar River MM, dtd 1834,5,10
1834, 10, 18. Mary & ch, Ann, Stephen, Nathan, Sarah & George D., gct Mississiniway MM, Ind.; rem within the limits of Michigan territory
1834, 10, 18. Anna & Lydia Sr. gct Mississiniwa MM, Ind.; rem within the limits of Michigan Tertitory
1834, 10, 18. John rpd mou; Sugar River MM ordered notified
1834, 12, 20. Sarah (form Thompson) dis mou & disunity
1835, 3, 21. Sarah Brown (form Jones) dis mou, disunity & attending mtgs of Hicksite
1835, 4, 18. Testimonies against John & Joseph rec from Sugar River MM, Ind.
1835, 7, 18. Nathan rpd mou & disunity
1835, 7, 18. Ruth (form Thompson) dis mou
1839, 5, 18. Nathan dis; living at Mississinawa MM
1841, 9, 18. Samuel N. rec in mbrp
1845, 10, 18. Samuel N. con mou
1845, 10, 18. Jane con mou; mbr Cherry Grove MM
1846, 9, 19. Jane rocf Cherry Grove MM, dtd 1846,7,11
1846, 12, 19. Samuel N. & w, Jane, & s, Wiley B., gct Newbury MM, O.
1849, 6, 16. Newton dis mou; living at Salem MM, Ia.
1850, 4, 25. Newton, who was dis, rpd rem from

JONES, continued
Salem MM, Ia. & now living in this territory
1851, 4, 24. Amy (form Swaim) con mou
1864, 12, 22. Samuel N. & w, Jane, & ch, Mary Emaline & Martha A., rocf Honey Creek MM, Ind.
1866, 9, 20. Samuel N. & w, Jane, & ch, Emiline & Martha, gct Duck Creek MM, Ind.
----, --, --. Testification against Wiley B. rec from Honey Creek MM, dtd 1866,12,8, forwarded to Duck Creek MM
1867, 2, 21. Mary Hornaday (form Jones) rpd mou
1874, 3, 26. Milton & ch, James William & Luella, rec in mbrp
1875, 5, 20. Julia rec in mbrp
1889, 8, 22. Milton relrq
1890, 10, 23. James relrq
1890, 10, 23. Julia dis disunity
1890, 12, 25. Mina (form Price) relrq
1910, 6, 23. Louisa A.'s d rpd
1923, 2, 23. Charles & w, Grace, rec in mbrp
1923, 4, 27. Newell P. & w, Cora V. rec in mbrp
1923, 10, 18. Anna gct Mississinaway MM, Ind.
1924, 7, 31. Newell P. & w, Cora V., gct M. E. Church, Camden, O.
1929, 3, 21. Walter Ray & w, Anna Elsie, rec in mbrp
1929, 3, 21. Ruby Virginia & Mary Elizabeth, ch Walter P. & Alice I., rec in mbrp

JORDAN
----, --, --. Joseph m Emeline TALBERT, dt Solomon & Helah, b 1855,2,25

1918, 8, 23. Skinner rolf M. E. Church, West Elkton, O.

KELLER
1900, 3, 22. Carrie E. glt M. E. Church, Oxford, O.

KELLUM
1810, 6, 2. Nathaniel & w, Elizabeth, & four of their ch, Nathaniel, Joseph, Elijah & Susannah, rocf Plimouth MM, dtd 1810,3,17
1810, 6, 2. Sarah rocf Plymouth MM, O., dtd 1810,3,17
1812, 4, 4. Nathaniel dis disunity
1813, 9, 4. William rec in mbrp
1813, 10, 2. Deborah & ch rec in mbrp
1814, 7, 2. Joseph dis taking up arms in a warlike manner
1815, 5, 6. Sarah Jones (form Kellum) dis mou
1817, 1, 7. Elijah dis mou

KENWORTHY
----, --, --. Jesse & Rachel
Ch: William b 1794, 9, 14
John b 1799, 6, 9
Mary " 1811, 9, 1
Sally " 1814, 6, 8
Jesse " 1817, 10, 2
1820, 12, 1. Sally d ae 6y 6m 22d
1821, 2, 8. William, Preble Co., O., s Jesse & Rachel, b 1794,9,14; m at Elk, Alice BALLARD, Preble Co., O., dt Joseph & Elizabeth
Ch: Amos b 1821, 11, 20
Joseph " 1823, 7, 19
Jesse " 1827, 2, 10
Mary " 1830, 6, 22
Elizabeth " 1832, 4, 2
1823, 8, 29. Amos d ae 1y 9m 9d
1824, 9, 9. John, Preble Co., O., s Jesse & Rachel; m at Elk, Lydia JONES, Butler Co., O., dt George & Lydia (John b 1799, 6,9 d 1883,8,20)
Ch: Sally b 1825, 9, 15 d 1835, 5 6
George " 1827, 6, 18 " 1837, 3,13
Isaac " 1829, 4, 15 " 1837, 2,15
Daniel " 1831, 2, 26 m (1) Mary ROBERTS (2) M. J. LANE
Elihu b 1834, 2, 8 d 1837, 2,16
Silas " 1836, 4, 17 " 1837, 2,23
William H. " 1837, 12, 20; m Harriet SWAIN
Mary Ann " 1840, 3, 4; m John LANE
Jesse G. " 1842, 6, 28 d 1863,11,18
Amy Ella " 1844, 12, 19 " 1848, 11,2
1829, 8, 16. Rachel d ae 56y 10m 8d
1833, 9, 6. David, Preble Co., O., s David & Dinah, dec; m at Elk, Martha MADDOCK, Preble Co., O., dt Frances & Phebe
Ch: Eli b 1834, 12, 15; m Rachel PUCKETT
Milton " 1838, 7, 11 d 1839, 3,15
Jabez " 1840, 7, 7; m (1) Valerie HARRIS (2) Rhoda PUCKET
William b 1843, 12, 4
Henry " 1848, 6, 17
Mary H. " 1851, 5, 16; m John W. RALSTON 1892,3,22 d 1895,5,16
Phebe b 1855, 1, 24 d 1887, 9,10
1838, 4, 26. Jesse, Preble Co., O., s Jesse & Rachel, b 1817,2,10 d 1900,--,--; m at Elk Mtg, Mary LANGSTON, dt Luke & Rebecca
Ch: John R. b 1839, 5, 28; m Rebecca J. REYNOLDS
Susan b 1842, 10, 16; m Marmaduke M. STUBBS
Rachel C. " 1845, 7, 14; m John F. STUBBS
Zimri " 1848, 11, 25; m Anna E. LYNN
Alvan Lindley " 1855, 4, 14; m Sarah Ellen REYNOLDS
----, --, --. Daniel, s John & Lydia, b 1831, 2,26; m Mary ROBERTS
Daniel m 2nd Mary Jane LANE, dt Henry & Sarah, b 1841,9,19 d 1901,3,4 (m 1866,1,4)

KENWORTHY, continued
1858, 8, 7. Jesse d ae 90y 4m 19d
1859, 11, 29. David d ae 49y 21d (an elder)
1862, 8, 28. Jabez H., s David, dec, & Martha, Preble Co., O., b 1840,7,7; m at Elk Mtg, Valearia HARRIS, Wayne Co., Ind., b 1844,6,28 d 1866,3,3, dt Thompson & Sarah, dec
Ch: David Milton b 1863, 4, 23
Sarah Elma " 1865, 5, 28 d 1865,12,29
Jabez m 2nd Rhoda E. PUCKET
Ch: Martha A. b 1872, 12, 3
Alpheus " 1874, 10, 26
Lucy Angie " 1876, 10, 11
Daniel " 1878, 8, 13
1864, 9, 7. David Milton d ae 1y 4m 15d
1865, 11, 27. Henry d ae 17y 5m 10d
----, --, --. Eli b 1834,12,15; m Rachel PUCKETT
Ch: Almira b 1867, 9, 26
Robert B. " 1870, 1, 22
1868, 9, 5. Lydia d in 63rd yr.
1876, 1, 16. Zimri, s Jesse & Mary, b 1848,11,25; m Anna E. LYNN, dt John & Anna, b 1850,7,15
Ch: Earnest L. b 1881, 2, 11
Henry I. " 1883, 9, 16
1876, 9, 28. Alvin L. b 1855,4,14 d 1879,12,2; m Sarah Ellen REYNOLDS, dt William & Josinah, b 1854,7,9
Ch: Tamer Lillian b 1879, 6, 8
Jesse " 1879, 6, 8
1903, 3, 26. Charles E. m Mary B. -----, dt Asa L. & Sarah A., b 1878,9,1

1830, 7, 3. David Jr. rocf White Water MM, dtd 1830,2,24
1832, 6, 16. Amos rocf White Water MM, dtd 1832,5,23
1834, 6, 21. Amos dis disunity
1834, 11, 15. Margaret (form Mendenhall) dis mou
1836, 3, 19. William & ch, Joseph, Jesse, Mary & Elizabeth, gct White Water MM, Ind.
1836, 7, 16. William gct White Water MM, Ind.
1843, 8, 19. Ann (form Lane) con mou
1843, 10, 19. Joseph con mou
1846, 8, 18. Jesse J. gct White Water MM,Ind.
1847, 4, 17. Joseph & w, Anne, gct White Water MM, Ind.
1850, 3, 21. Mary gct White Water MM, Ind.
1853, 5, 26. Daniel dis mou
1864, 3, 24. Jabez H. & fam gct Dover MM,Ind.
1865, 5, 25. Jabez H. & w, Velerie, rocf Dover MM, Ind., dtd 1865,4,19
1866, 9, 20. Rebecca J. rpd mou
1867, 4, 25. Susan H. Stubbs (form Kenworthy) rpd mou
1867, 5, 23. Rachel H. Stubbs (form Kenworthy) rpd mou
1868, 6, 25. Anna & ch, Caroline & William, rocf Fairfield MM, Ind., dtd 1866,9,6
1868, 6, 25. Rachel & ch rocf Dover MM, Ind., dtd 1868,5,20
1868, 8, 20. Joseph rocf Fairfield MM, dtd 1868,6,11
1868, 12, 24. John R. & w gct White Water MM, Ind.
1869, 1, 21. Joseph & fam gct Fairview MM,Ill.
1869, 11, 25. Mary Ann Lane (form Kinworthy) rpd mou
1870, 5, 26. Jabez H. gct Dover MM, Ind., to m Rhoda E. Puckett
1871, 8, 24. Mary Jane rec in mbrp
1872, 10, 26. Eli & w, Rachel, & ch, Elmira, Robert, Barclay & Harriet, gct Dover MM, Ind.
1872, 12, 26. Rhoda E. rocf Dover MM, Ind.
1884, 2, 21. John's d rpd
1885, 10, 22. Jabez H. & w, Rhoda, & ch, Martha, Alma, Alpheus, Lucy A., Daniel Linden, Celestia & Alice Gertrude, gct Dover MM, Ind.
1888, 2, 23. Jabez H. & fam rocf Dover MM, Ind., dtd 1888,1,25
1889, 5, 23. William J. dropped from mbrp
1889, 7, 25. Jabez H. & w, Rhoda E., & ch, Alpheus, Lucy Angie, Daniel L. & Gertrude gc
1895, 4, 25. Anna L. & s, Earnest L. & Henry I., rec in mbrp
1900, 1, 25. Ella & Lillian dropped from mbrp
1900, 11, 22. Mary gct White Water MM, Ind.
1902, 4, 24. Rettie H. & Charles E. rec in mbrp
1902, 8, 21. Daniel rec in mbrp
1913, 3, 20. Henry I. glt U. B. Church, West Elkton, O.
1919, 11, 20. Charle E. & w, Mary B., & dt, Cecil A., relrq

KERSEY
1852, 4, 22. Moses rocf Springfield MM, N.C., dtd 1852,3,10
1854, 10, 26. Moses gct Springfield MM, N. C.

KINSEY
1876, 2, 24. Laura M. recrq

KIRK
1918, 8, 23. Maria rolf M. E. Church, West Elkton, O.
1926, 1, 21. Maria relrq

KLINE
1900, 5, 24. Ida dropped from mbrp

KREKLER
1913, 12, 25. Marion rec in mbrp
1919, 7, 24. Marion McCall gct Florence Avenue M. E. Church, Los Angeles, Calif.

KUCH
1923, 5, 24. Henry & w, Alice, rec in mbrp

LAIRD
1894, 1, 25. Sarah R. gct Van Wert MM, O.
1827, 4, 21. Louise Conarroe glt Ohmer Park M. E. Church, Dayton, O.

LAMAR
----, --, --. William [La Mar] m Martha Ann STUBBS, dt Elijah & Beulah, b 1852,10,3
Ch: Leona
Iva

1872, 11, 23. Greenville rec in mbrp
1877, 8, 23. Greenville relrq
1881, 5, 26. Mattie A. relrq
1893, 2, 23. Martha A. & ch, Leona May & Iva C., rec in mbrp
1912, 9, 26. Martha A. & dt, Leona & Ida, glt Presbyterian Church, Camden, O.

LAMM
----, --, --. John & Elizabeth
Ch: Phines b 1814, 1, 23
Lydia " 1815, 5, 18
Keziah " 1816, 11, 18
Rebecca " 1818, 12, 31
Henry " 1820, 10, 16
Elizabeth " 1822, 11, 10
John " 1824, 10, 22
Martha " 1827, 2, 11
George " 1829, 2, 6
Joseph " 1833, 6, 27
1837, 4, 11. George d ae 8y 2m 5d
1839, 8, 22. Reuben, Preble Co., O., s Amajah & Sarah, dec; m at Elk Mtg, Keziah DENNY, Preble Co., O., dt Lazarus & Sarah, dec
Ch: Milton b 1840, 8, 25
Sarah " 1841, 11, 15
Joseph " 1843, 3, 15
Rebecca " 1844, 9, 19
1841, 10, 21. Keziah m John BROWN
----, --, --. Henry & Elizabeth
Ch: Nathan C. b 1841, 9, 21
William C. " 1843, 4, 27
1843, 6, 29. Joseph d ae 3m 14d
1844, 12, 26. Martha m William TAYLOR
----, --, --. John & Keziah
Ch: Joseph Franklin b 1850, 4, 17
----, --, --. John [Lamb] m Anna CONARROE, dt Clayton & Elnora, b 1869,1,12
1871, 10, 27. Lydia d ae 56y 5m 12d
1877, 3, 30. Elizabeth d ae 83y 2m 9d

1813, 3, 6. Thomas [Lamb] gct White Water MM
1813, 5, 1. John [Lamb] con mou
1813, 7, 3. Elizabeth rec in mbrp
1814, 6, 4. John [Lamb] dis disunity
1829, 1, 14. Jacob [Lamb] Jr. rocf Piney Woods MM, N. C., dtd 1828,4,5 (H)
1832, 3, 3. Daniel [Lamb] rocf Piney Woods MM, N. C., dtd 1831,10,1
1832, 3, 3. Reuben [Lamb] rocf Piney Woods MM, N. C., dtd 1831,10,1
1832, 3, 14. Jacob con attending musters for the performance of military duty (H)
1833, 12, 21. Caleb rocf Arba MM, Ind., dtd 1833,11,20
1838, 1, 20. Caleb [Lamb] dis
1839, 7, 20. Kesiah [Lam] (form Moore) con mou
1839, 9, 21. Phineas gct Salem MM, Ia.
1840, 2, 15. Keziah gct Westfield MM, Ind.
1840, 6, 20. Henry gct Salem MM, Ia., to m Elizabeth Cook
1841, 3, 20. Elizabeth rocf Salem MM, Ia.
1844, 4, 20. Henry & w, Elizabeth, & ch, Nathan C. & William, gct Salem MM, Ia.
1848, 1, 15. Reuben & w, Keziah, gct Salem MM, Ia.
1848, 12, 16. John & w, Keziah, rocf White Lick MM, dtd 1848,10,18
1849, 1, 20. Elizabeth Hartley (form Lamm) rpd mou; living at Salem MM, Ia.
1850, 5, 23. John Jr. dis disunity
1853, 11, 24. John R. & w, Keziah, & ch, Joseph F., gct Westfield MM, Ind.
1856, 7, 24. Joseph dis disunity
1878, 3, 21. Emma rec in mbrp
1880, 2, 26. Rebecca glt Presbyterian Ch., Somerville, O.
1887, 4, 21. Emma relrq
1890, 4, 24. Mary [Lamb] glt M. E. Church, Camden, O.
1891, 2, 26. Annie relrq
1928, 2, 2. Jeanette rec in mbrp

LANCASTER
1810, 9, 1. Benjamin Lancaster recrq of guardian, Sarah Brown
1817, 7, 5. Benjamin dis attending musters in order to perform military duty

LANE
----, --, --. Jesse & Hannah
Ch: Phebe b 1806, 11, 19
Levi " 1809, 11, 9
Ann " 1815, 12, 15
Mary " 1817, 10, 22
Elizabeth " 1819, 10, 4
Rachel " 1823, 1, 9
Susannah " 1826, 4, 26
Lydia
Ira
Rhoda
Annuel
----, --, --. Julius & Sarah
Ch: James b 1811, 11, 28
Jesse " 1813, 12, 7
Hiram " 1815, 12, 2
Charles " 1815, 4, 22
Baker " 1821, 12, 11
Sarah " 1824, 7, 26

LANE, Julius & Sarah, continued
Ch: Jonathan b 1826, 6, 16
Isaac " 1829, 11, 14
Henry " 1832, 8, 8
1827, 6, 7. Ira, Preble Co., O., s Jesse & Hannah; m at Elk Mtg, Hannah COOPER, Butler Co., O., dt Jacob & Elizabeth
Ch: Levi b 1828, 5, 9
Lydia " 1830, 7, 19
Martha " 1832, 5, 1
1830, 2, 8. Rhoda m Anthony WAY
----, --, --. Annuel & Lydia
Ch: William b 1833, 9, 8
Hannah " 1834, 12, 26
Sarah Ann " 1836, 11, 19
Francis Mariam " 1839, 2, 2
Clinton " 1848, 11, 28
Phebe " 1843, 6, 30
Esther " 1845, 9, 4
1835, 1, 30. William d ae 1y 4m 22d
1838, 1, 8. Hannah d
1838, 11, 6. Henry m Sarah RANDALL, dt John & Lydia, b 1819,6,23
1842, 1, 19. Baker d ae 20y 1m 2d
1842, 1, 30. Sarah d ae 53y 7m 15d
1843, 4, 20. Julius, Preble Co., O., s Jesse, dec, & Anna; m at Elk Mtg, Elizabeth RANDALL, Preble Co., O., dt Isaac & Sarah
Ch: Mary Ann b 1845, 4, 30
Elvira R. " 1846, 9, 3
Rosanna " 1848, 7, 3
Enos R. " 1852, 8, 14
1844, 3, 21. Rachel m Jonathan STUBBS
1847, 10, 30. Esther d ae 2y 1m 26d
1849, 9, 20. Clinton F. d ae 10m 22d
1850, 9, 23. Rosanna d ae 2y 2m 20d
1852, 7, 24. Jesse d
1853, 11, 25. Phebe m Benajah BALLARD
1854, 2, 6. Julius d
1868, 12, 20. John m Mary Ann KENWORTHY, dt John & Lydia, b 1840,3,4 d 1898,1,18
Ch: George H. b 1870, 10, 23
Albert " 1872, 7, 19
Sarah " 1874, 4, 10

1812, 7, 4. Sarah con mou
1813, 12, 4. Lidia, Ira, Phebe, Levi & Annuel, ch Hannah, rec in mbrp
1818, 9, 5. Julius & ch rec in mbrp
1822, 2, 2. Jesse rec in mbrp
1822, 4, 6. Rhoda, Anna, Mary & Elizabeth, dt Hannah, rec in mbrp
1822, 10, 5. Lydia Hornaday (form Lane) dis mou
1830, 2, 6. Anthony Way prcf Cherry Grove MM, to m Rhoda Lane
1831, 3, 5. James dis disunity
1833, 3, 16. Annuel con mou
1834, 8, 16. Lydia & s, William, rec in mbrp
1835, 1, 17. Hiram dis disunity
1835, 1, 17. Jesse Jr. dis disunity
1835, 5, 16. Annuel dis disunity
1838, 3, 17. Mary Snipes (form Lane) con mou
1838, 6, 16. Ira & w, Hannah, & ch gct West Grove MM, Ind.
1842, 3, 19. Sarah Lincohorn (form Lane) con mou
1843, 8, 19. Ann Kenworthy (form Lane) con mou
1846, 7, 18. Elizabeth Mendenhall (form Lane) con mou
1848, 9, 16. Susannah Brown (form Lane) con mou; living at Pleasant Plain MM
1849, 4, 21. Jonathan dis mou
1856, 2, 21. Henry dis mou
1856, 3, 20. Lydia & ch, Hannah, Sarah Ann & Phebe, gct Dover MM, Ind.
1857, 11, 26. Elizabeth & ch, Mary Ann, Elvira R. & Enos B., gct Mississinawa MM, Ind.
1858, 1, 21. Francis M. dis disunity
1858, 4, 22. Lydia & dt rocf Dover MM, dtd 1858,3,24
1859, 2, 24. Barbary (form Hunt) rpd mou; Dover MM rq this mtg to deal with her
1869, 11, 25. Mary Ann (form Kinworthy) rpd mou
1870, 4, 21. Isaac rpd mou
1871, 7, 20. Sarah rec in mbrp
1878, 5, 23. Henry J. rec in mbrp
1882, 3, 23. Levi gct Plainfield MM, Ind.
1889, 5, 23. Isaac dropped from mbrp
1908, 9, 24. Allie, George & Sadie dropped from mbrp
1913, 4, 24. Estella Elizabeth rec in mbrp

LANGFORD
1855, 5, 7. Isaac E., s Craig & Fanny, b

1878, 3, 31. Walter J., s Craig & Fanny, b 1850,7,6; m Hattie SEBASTIAN
----, --, --. Jesse S., sCraig & Fannie; m Mary POLLY

1874, 4, 23. Walter rec in mbrp
1874, 4, 23. Isaac E. rec in mbrp
1874, 4, 23. Ann Elizabeth rec in mbrp
1874, 5, 21. Stephen R. & Jesse S. rec in mbrp
1888, 9, 20. Mary J. rec in mbrp
1894, 3, 22. Stephen R. glt M. E. Church, Hamilton, O.

LANGSTON
1816, 8, 15. Luke, Preble Co., O., s Luke & Charity; m at Elk Mtg, Rebecca ROBERDS, Butler Co., O., dt Jonathan & Mary
Ch: Jonathan b 1817, 9, 21
Mary " 1819, 10, 21
1838, 4, 26. Mary m Jesse KENWORTHY Jr.
1838, 10, 25. Jonathan, Butler Co., O., s Luke & Rebecca; m at Elk Mtg, Hannah MENDENHALL, Preble Co., O., dt John & Margaret
1885, 8, 23. Rebecca d ae 91y 10m 21d

LANGSTON, continued
1814, 4, 2. Luke rec in mbrp
1820, 6, 3. Luke dis
1842, 7, 16. Johathan & w, Hannah, gct Salem MM, Ia.

LANTIS
----, --, --. William m Eliza Jane ROBERTS, dt John & Rebecca, b 1831,12,22 d 1900,8mo

----, --, --. Samuel, s David & Hannah; m Eliza YOST
Ch: Mahalah
Elizabeth m Ira BEECHLER

1876, 2, 24. Samuel rec in mbrp
1880, 5, 20. Mahalah Elizabeth [Lantas] rec in mbrp
1896, 9, 24. Eliza Jane rec in mbrp

LARSH
1921, 2, 24. Bertha Commons & dt, Elizabeth & Eleanor, rec in mbrp
1921, 2, 24. Emily, dt Bertha Commons, rec in mbrp

LEE
1841, 8, 21. Elizabeth rec in mbrp
1844, 2, 17. Elizabeth Blanchard (form Lee) con mou

LESLIE
1864, 3, 18. Margaret d ae 56y 8m 22d

1827, 11, 3. Margaret [Lesly] con mou

LEVAL
1894, 4, 26. Amos F. & w, Mary, glt Second Congregational Ch., Colorado Springs, Colo.

LEVINGSTON
1825, 10, 1. James rocf New Garden MM, Ind., dtd 1825,4,21
1826, 5, 6. James gct Springborough MM

LINCKHORN
1842, 3, 19. Sarah [Lincohorn] (form Lane) con mou
1861, 7, 25. Sarah dis jas

LINES
1884, 7, 24. Susan gct Goshen MM, O.

LONG
1886, 7, 31. Caroline d ae 27y 5m 28d

LOW
1859, 4, 20. Ann d

1810, 10, 12. Ann & dt, Ann, rocf West Branch MM, dtd 1810,9,22
1813, 5, 1. William rocf Mill Creek MM, dtd 1812,12,26
1814, 1, 1. William dis

LOYNER
1847, 8, 21. Maria (form Brown) dis mou

LUCAS
1921, 3, 23. Mary Elizabeth rec in mbrp

LYNN
----, --, --. John, s William & Sarah, b 1821,10,29; m Ann Eliza HUSSONG

1896, 12, 24. John rec in mbrp

McDANIEL
1815, 6, 3. Sarah rocf Miami MM
1837, 5, 20. Elizabeth (form Maddock) dis mou

McKINLEY
1914, 11, 26. Henry & w, Cleo, & ch, Darrel F., Dolia Maria & Dorothy Cleo, rocf Dayton MM, O.
1916, 11, 23. Henry & w, Cleo, & ch, Darrell F., Dolia Maria & Dorothy Cleo, gct Mt. Airy MM, N. C.

McLELEN
1845, 9, 20. Charlotte (form Osbern) dis mou

McSHANE
1927, 10, 27. Betty Larsh glt M. E. Church, Camden, O.

MACY
----, --, --. Stephen & Mary
Ch: Rhoda b 1804, 3, 17
Sarah " 1806, 3, 30
Irena " 1812, 8, 11
Verlinda " 1815, 1, 2
Eliab G. " 1817, 10, 13
Eliza " 1820, 8, 12
1836, 9, 22. Irena m Joseph MADDOCK

1819, 10, 20. John rpd mou; Marlborough MM rq this mtg to deal with him
1819, 11, 6. Mary rec in mbrp
1826, 7, 1. Eliza, dt Mary, rec in mbrp
1830, 10, 13. John rec in mbrp (H)
1833, 2, 13. John dis disunity (H)
1833, 1, 19. Virlinda dis disunity
1835, 11, 21. Eliah G. dis disunity
1837, 12, 16. Eliza dis disunity
1843, 4, 15. Rachel (form Cooper) dis mou
1886, 5, 20. Taylor & w, Ida C., & s, Clifton G., rec in mbrp
1892, 11, 24. Taylor & fam gct Christian Ch., Blueball, Ind.

MADDOCK
----, --, --. Frances & Phebe
Ch: Samuel b 1808, 3, 8
Joseph " 1811, 1, 20

MADDOCK, Frances & Phebe, continued
Ch: Eli b 1813, 3, 12
Martha " 1816, 7, 15
Sarah " 1818, 1, 30
Rachel " 1820, 2, 20
Mary " 1821, 9, 9
John " 1823, 10, 15
Francis " 1831, 5, 22
----, --, --. Nathan, Preble Co., O., s Samuel, dec, & Rachel; m Sarar -----
Ch: Joseph b 1811, 2, 10
John " 1812, 1, 29
Henry " 1813, 11, 8
Rachel " 1814, 12, 30
Nathan m 2nd 1817,11,10 at Elk Mtg, Martha MENDENHALL, Preble Co., O., wd Elijah, dt William & Ann MILLER
Ch: Samuel b 1818, 8, 8
----, --, --. William & Hannah
Ch: Elijah b 1813, 9, 6
Nathan " 1815, 5, 26
Joseph " 1817, 8, 3
Elizabeth " 1819, 3, 20
Mary Ann " 1822, 4, 10
1820, 6, 3. Rachel d ae 3m 14d
1833, 9, 6. Martha m David KENWORTHY
1834, 3, 20. Joseph, Preble Co., O., s Nathan & Sarah, dec, b 1811,2,10 d 1889,5,27; m at Elk Mtg, Mary STUBBS, Preble Co., O., dt Joseph & Ann, dec
Ch: Nathan b 1834, 12, 31
Martha Ann " 1845, 8, 30
----, --, --. Henry & Phebe
Ch: William P. b 1835, 6, 10
1836, 9, 22. Joseph, Preble Co., O., s Francis & Phebe; m at Elk, Irene MACY, Preble Co., O., dt Stephen & Mary
Ch: Phebe b 1838, 3, 1
Stephen " 1839, 10, 18
Isaac " 1842, 4, 27
Mary H. " 1844, 5, 21
Francis J. " 1846, 11, 15
Lorenzo S. " 1849, 6, 13
Eli C. " 1852, 3, 11
Virlanda " 1855, 12, 1
1837, 10, 26. Samuel, Preble Co., O., s Nathan & Martha; m at Elk Mtg, Martha COOK, Preble Co., O., dt Nathan & Delilah, dec
1838, 9, 20. John, s Nathan & Sarah, dec, b 1812,1,29; m Martha STUBBS, dt William & Delilah, b 1818,10,14
Ch: Alvin S. b 1840, 3, 13 d 1849, 8,23
Theodore W." 1841, 6, 25
William S. " 1844, 6, 19; m Sue BENNETT
Alpheus T. " 1846, 2, 23; m Lydia Ann RANDALL
Mary Elizabeth b 1855, 5, 19; m Ed SHAFER
Calvin H. " 1859, 12, 29 d 1861, 3, 9
1840, 4, 20. Rachel m Riley DAVIS
1840, 9, 21. Mary m John HASKET
1843, 7, 4. Martha d ae 64y 8m 1d
1844, 2, 7. Francis d ae 64y 1m 19d
1848, 8, 24. John, Preble Co., O., s Francis, dec, & Phebe; m at Elk Mtg, Rachel H. STUBBS, Preble Co., O., dt Elisha & Elizabeth
Ch: Hiram S. b 1850, 6, 6
Martha Ellen " 1861, 4, 5
1856, 10, 12. Virlinda d ae 10m 11d
1864, 10, 31. Nathan d ae 86y 2m 21d
----, --, --. Francis & Mary
Ch: Elmina b 1866, 3, 26
----, --, --. Alpheus T. m Lydia Ann RANDALL
Ch: Frederick Le Fevre b 1872, 4, 27
1875, 8, 8. Phebe d ae 85y 7m 22d
1876, 2, 18. Samuel d ae 67y 11m 11d
1878, 9, 30. Mary d ae 66y 6m 12d
1885, 4, 20. Hannah d ae 55y 9m

1812, 11, 7. Sarah & ch, Joseph & John, rec in mbrp
1814, 4, 2. Hannah con mou
1833, 6, 15. Phebe (form Brown) con mou
1833, 7, 20. Henry con mou
1834, 5, 16. Nathan dis mou
1835, 3, 21. Eli gct New Garden MM, Ind., to m Absillit Wood
1835, 7, 18. Absillit rocf New Garden MM, Ind., dtd 1835,6,20
1836, 3, 19. West Branch MM rq this mtg to treat with Dorcas
1837, 5, 20. Joseph dis mou
1837, 5, 20. Elizabeth McDaniel (form Maddock) dis mou
1840, 1, 18. Sarah Stubbs (form Maddock) con mou
1841, 6, 19. Samuel Jr. & fam gct Salem MM, Ia.
1843, 12, 16. Eli dis joining Separatists
1844, 2, 17. Absillit dis jas
1851, 11, 20. David, Jane, Josiah & Sarah, ch Eli & Absolit, gct Chester MM, Ind.
1854, 9, 21. Absillit rec in mbrp at Chester MM by consent of this mtg
1854, 11, 23. Elijah dis jas
1855, 6, 21. Eli rst; living at Chester MM
1856, 4, 24. Henry & w, Phebe, gct Salem MM, Ia.
1856, 6, 26. William P. dis mou
1856, 6, 26. Tamer dis mou
1859, 11, 20. Joseph dis disunity
1860, 2, 23. Joseph Sr. & w, Irena, & ch, Stephen, Mary, Francis, Lorenzo & Eli, gct Vermillion MM, Ill.
1861, 8, 23. Francis con mou
1869, 4, 22. William S. rpd mou
1870, 8, 25. Alpheus rpd mou
1871, 5, 25. Anna Brummet, adopted dt John C. & Rachel H. Maddock, rec in mbrp
1871, 11, 23. Martha S. & Rachel H., of Colorado Territory, rec in mbrp
1872, 11, 23. Francis rpd mou

MADDOCK, continued
1872, 11, 23. Hannah (form Powel) rpd mou
1877, 7, 26. John relrq
1878, 3, 21. Hiram S. gct Cincinnati MM, O.
1881, 5, 26. John C. & Rachel H. gct Duck Creek MM, Ind.
1883, 3, 22. Martha Ellen & Anna B., gct Duck Creek MM, Ind.
1889, 7, 25. Francis gc
1922, 1, 5. Theodore W. rocf Cincinnati MM,O.

MANN
1836, 7, 16. William [Man] & w, Hannah, & ch, Rebecca, Richard, Mary & Lewis, rocf White River MM, Ind., dtd 1835,5,21
1837, 4, 15. William & w, Hannah, & ch, Rebecca, Rachel, Mary & Lewis, gct White River MM, Ind.

MARDOCK
1814, 7, 2. Ann [Mardick] & ch rocf Newberry MM, Tenn., dtd 1814,3,5

MATLOCK
1847, 2, 20. Chester MM, N. J. rq this mtg to furnish Samuel with their testimony of dis for mou

MATTHEWS
1829, 12, 9. Joel & w, Hannah, & ch, Sarah & Samuel N., rocf Springborough MM, dtd 1829,9,22 (H)
1831, 2, 5. Joel [Matthew] presented with a testimony of dis by rq of Springborough MM
1831, 2, 5. Hannah dis by rq of Springborough MM
1832, 9, 15. Sarah & Samuel, ch Joel & Hannah, rocf Springborough MM, dtd 1832,7,24
1833, 12, 11. Joel & w, Hannah, & ch, Sarah, Samuel N., Ann Eliza & Oliver, gct White Water MM (H)

MENDENHALL
----, --, --. Elijah & Martha
Ch: Ann b 1807, 10, 13
Marmaduke " 1810, 6, 2
Elijah Joseph " 1812, 10, 23
1814, 4, 7. Elijah d ae 31y 8m 10d
----, --, --. John & Margaret
Ch: Elijah b 1816, 1, 29
Hannah " 1818, 4, 23
Mary " 1820, 6, 27
Eliza Ann " 1823, 5, 29
Isaac " 1826, 3, 14
1817, 11, 10. Martha m Nathan MADDOCK
----, --, --. James b 1792,12,22; m Mary BROWN, dt Jacob & Mary,b 1791,2,4
Ch: Peggy b 1816, 4, 13
Jacob " 1818, 4, 4
Marmaduke " 1820, 10, 25
Isaac " 1823, 1, 12
John " 1826, 12, 21
1824, 7, 23. Isaac d ae 1y 6m 11d bur Westfield Cem.
1825, 8, 11. Ann m Nathan STUBBS
----, --, --. Marmaduke, s Marmaduke & Alice, b 1797,8,17; m Nancy GRIFFIN, dt John & Mary, b 1803,4,21
Ch: John G. b 1826, 3, 6
Samuel Thompson " 1828, 8, 11
1828, 6, 3. John d ae 38y 1m
1830, 3, 18. Marmaduke, s Elijah & Martha, b 1809,6,2 d 1893,4,29; m Elizabeth JOHNSON, dt Jonathan & Hannah, b 1813,4,10
Ch: Jonathan b 1831, 1, 14
Martha " 1833, 4, 20; m John STAFFORD
Elijah " 1835, 8, 21; m Elizabeth REEVES
Nathan S. b 1837, 12, 11; m Elizabeth CONARROE 1857,5,3
Andrew b 1840, 3, 16
Hannah Ann " 1844, 3, 13; m Walter ROBERTS
Joseph Lindley " 1847, 10, 9; m Delilah ROBERTS 1866,6,26
William Hadley b 1853, 3, 19; m Eva PAYNE 1874,12,13
1838, 10, 25. Hannah m Jonathan LANGSTON
1842, 12, 19. Andrew d
1854, 11, 30. Elijah, Preble Co., O., s Marmaduke & Elizabeth, b 1835,8,21; m at Elk Mtg, Elizabeth REEVES, dt Allen & Esther b 1835,12,24
Ch: Allen Harvey b 1856, 2, 12; m Esther IRISE
Lindley Clarkson " 1858, 4, 27; m 1879,12, 25, Milly GREGG
Martha Elma b 1860, 5 4 d 1899, 1,--
Esther Alma " 1866, 11, 26; m 1886,3,25 Charles PUGH
Elmer b 1874, 4, 21; m Emma WITHROW
1854, 3, 24. Martha m John H. STAFFORD
1857, 3, 5. Nathan S., Preble Co., O., s Marmaduke & Elizabeth, b 1837,12,11; m at Elk Mtg, Elizabeth C. CONARROE, dt John & Harriett, Butler Co., O.
Ch: Mary Louisa b 1858, 7, 4; m 1883,2,15 Pleasant LANE
Hariett Emma b 1862, 10, 26; m 1885,12, 10, William STUBBS d 1894,7,9
Elnora b 1866, 12, 8; m 1886,12, 23 Frank CRIST
Caroline E.b 1870, 4, 27; m George KELLER

MENDENHALL, Nathan S. & Elizabeth, continued
Ch: Edwin C. b 1874, 1, 8; m Iva KELLER
Orion Curtis " 1879, 5, 24; m 1899,10, 12, Hattie ROBERTS
----, --, --. Joseph L., s Marmaduke & Elizabeth, b 1847,10,9; m Delilah ROBERTS, dt Samuel & Mary, b 1849,10,26
Ch: Theodore S.b 1868, 11, 15
Arthur C. " 1874, 2, 15
1874, 12, 13. William Hadley, s Marmaduke & Elizabeth; m Sarah Eva PAYNE, dt Jonathan & Hannah, b 1849,4,7
Dt: Edith b 1875, 10, 9
Sarah Eva, wd William H., m 1895,1,23 Hal PIPER
1888, 8, 3. Elizabeth A. d ae 71y 7m 29d

1810, 3, 3. Elijah & w, Martha, & dt, Ann, rocf New Garden, N. C., dtd 1809,7,29, endorsed by Miami MM
1815, 10, 7. John con mou
1815, 10, 7. Margaret (form Brown) con mou
1819, 3, 6. John & fam gct White Water MM
1819, 8, 7. Marmaduke con mou
1822, 8, 3. John & w, Margaret, & ch, Elijah, Hannah & Mary, rocf White Water MM, dtd 1822,7,20
1831, 1, 1. Elizabeth (form Jonson) con mou; mbr Westfield MM
1831, 4, 2. Marmaduke con mou
1831, 9, 3. Elizabeth rocf Westfield MM, dtd 1831,8,31
1834, 4, 19. Joseph dis mou
1834, 6, 21. Elijah dis mou
1834, 11, 15. Margaret Kenworthy (form Mendenhall) dis mou
1838, 5, 19. Mary Snider (form Mendenhall) dis mou
1842, 3, 19. Eliza Ann Ricks (form Mendenhall) dis mou
1843, 5, 20. Jacob dis mou
1846, 7, 18. Marmaduke Jr. dis mou
1846, 7, 18. Elizabeth (form Lane) con mou
1847, 10, 18. Mary rst
1847, 12, 18. James rec in mbrp
1848, 7, 15. James & w, Mary, gct Springfield MM, Ind.
1849, 5, 19. John dis mou; living at Springfield MM
1849, 10, 20. Isaac dis mou; living at Springfield MM
1851, 8, 21. Elizabeth gct Back Creek MM,Ind.
1866, 2, 22. Hannah Ann Roberts (form Mendenhall) rpd mou
1867, 5, 23. Delilah A. (form Roberts) rpd mou
1867, 10, 24. Joseph L. rpd mou
1868, 5, 21. Elizabeth Ann rec in mbrp
1876, 2, 24. George W. rec in mbrp
1876, 2, 24. Clara rec in mbrp
1882, 1, 26. Maurice rocf White Water MM, dtd 1881,12,22
1882, 4, 20. Allen H. gct White Water MM, Ind.
1882, 9, 21. George W. relrq
1890, 3, 20. Clara relrq
1890, 5, 22. Allen H. & fam rocf New Salem MM, Ind., dtd 1890,5,3
1891, 11, 26. Allen H. & fam gct New Salem MM, Ind.
1891, 11, 26. Harvey & fam gct New Salem MM, Ind.
1893, 2, 23. Eva rec in mbrp
1893, 2, 23. Elmer C. glt M. E. Church, West Elkton, O.
1898, 2, 24. Marmaduke's d rpd
1899, 5, 25. Iva A. rec in mbrp
1902, 4, 24. Camella J. & dt, Ethel M., rec in mbrp
1906, 12, 20. Corella rocf Ogden MM, O.
1915, 3, 25. Joseph L.'s d rpd (an overseer)
1915, 11, 25. Minnie rec in mbrp
1915, 11, 25. Susie Withrow rolf Presbyterian Church, Seven Mile MM, O.
1930, 2, 20. T. S. relrq

MERKLE
1889, 7, 25. Carrie E. go

MILES
1888, 12, 20. Catherine rocf Pilot Grove MM, Ia., dtd 1888,6,2
1900, 5, 24. Catherine dropped from mbrp

MILLER
1826, 4, 1. Cynthia con mou
1826, 12, 2. Cynthia gct Westfield MM
1892, 7, 21. Flora E. relrq

MOFFITT
1851, 5, 22. Eli Stubbs gct White Water MM, to m Anna F. Moffitt
1856, 2, 21. Abijah prcf White Water MM, to m Lydia Townsend
1856, 8, 21. Lydia T. gct White Water MM,Ind.

MOON

1845, 4, 21. Daniel H., Clinton Co., O., s William & Jane, dec; m at Elk Mtg, Mary BRANSON, Preble Co., O., dt Jesse & Rachel KENWORTHY, dec (Mary, wd David Branson) Mary b 1811,9,1

1845, 4, 19. Daniel H. prcf Newberry MM, to m Mary Branson
1846, 9, 19. Mary Moon & s, Thomas Branson, gct Newbury MM, O.
1859, 11, 24. Daniel & w, Mary, & ch, William K. & Rachel Jane, rocf Newberry MM, dtd 1859,6,20
1860, 11, 22. Daniel H. & w, Mary, & ch, William H. & Rachel Jane, gct Mill Creek MM,

MOON, continued
Ind.

MOORE
----, --, --. David, s Nathaniel & Bathsheba, b 1788,1,20; m Mary BROWN, dt John & Virgin, b 1788,7,17
Ch: Samuel
Brown b 1811, 4, 16
David " 1813, 11, 15
Nathaniel " 1819, 8, 17
Mary " 1821, 8, 19
Sarah " 1827, 5, 4
1816, 3, 6. Seaborn, Butler Co., O., s Alexander & Phebe; m at Paint Creek Mtg, Rachel STUBBS, Preble Co., O., dt John & Jane
Ch: John b 1816, 11, 6
Esther " 1818, 8, 2
Benajah " 1820, 8, 17
Evans " 1822, 8, 26
Thomas Elwood " 1825, 1, 1
David M. " 1827, 2, 14
1816, 5, 6. Elizabeth m Jesse CLARK
1816, 11, 14. Mordecai, Preble Co., O., s Alexander & Phebe; m at Elk, Rachel STUBBS Butler Co., O., dt Nathan & Elizabeth
Ch: Joseph b 1817, 8, 27
Keziah " 1819, 8, 19
Rebecca " 1821, 5, 30
Phebe " 1823, 11, 7
Nathan " 1826, 10, 11
Elizabeth " 1826, 10, 12
Barclay " 1829, 11, 14
Elisha " 1832, 3, 23
Anna " 1834, 5, 7
1828, 8, 13. Nathan d ae 22m 2d

1810, 3, 3. Demey rocf New Garden MM, N.C., dtd 1809,7,29, endorsed by Miami MM
1810, 3, 3. Richard rocf New Garden MM, N. C., dtd 1809,7,29, endorsed by Miami MM
1810, 3, 3. Elizabeth rec in mbrp
1810, 6, 2. Richard dis mou
1810, 6, 2. Dinah Creek (form Townsend) dis mou
1811, 3, 2. Mescanorid(?) rocf New Garden MM, N. C., dtd 1810,5,26
1811, 11, 5. Demsy dis mou
1812, 11, 7. Mordecai rec in mbrp
1813, 12, 4. Alice (form Reybold) dis mou
1818, 7, 4. Alexander & fam gct White Water MM
1820, 5, 6. Mary rocf Miami MM, dtd 1820,3, 29
1827, 6, 2. Isaac Gause rqct Redstone MM, to m Sarah Moore
1834, 7, 19. John, Esther, Benajah, Evans, Thomas E. & David, ch Seaborn & Rachel, gct Chester MM, Ind.
1837, 5, 20. David Jr. dis mou
1839, 4, 20. Mordecai & w, Rachel, & ch, Rebecca, Phebe, Elizabeth, Barclay, Elisha & Anna, gct Westfield MM, Ind.
1839, 5, 18. Joseph gct Westfield MM, Ind.
1839, 7, 20. Kesiah Lam (form Moore) con mou

MULLIN
----, --, --. Samuel, s John S. & Lydia, b 1800,9,12; m Mary Ann -----
Ch: Abraham b 1822, 12, 15
Lydia " 1825, 7, 7
Hannah " 1828, 10, 10

1821, 11, 3. Samuel rocf Miami MM, dtd 1821, 8,29

MURPHY
1813, 9, 4. Ruth (form Townsend) dis mou

NEFF
1922, 7, 20. Ersie (form Pingleton) dropped from mbrp for jas

NELSON
1834, 8, 13. Henrietta Hagerman (form Nelson) dis mou (H)

NEWBURN
1820, 7, 5. David, Preble Co., O., s David & Tamar, b 1792,7,27; m at Westfield Mtg, Beulah BROWN, dt John & Virgin, b 1787,2, 17
Ch: Rachel b 1821, 7, 14
John B. " 1823, 7, 22
Virgin B. " 1827, 3, 27
David " 1829, 1, 22
1829, 2, 22. Beulah d ae 42y 5d bur Westfield Bur Gr, Israel Twp.
1821, 11, 28. Rachel d ae 4m 14d bur Westfield Cem.

1820, 1, 4. David rocf Miami MM, dtd 1820,3, 2

NEWBY
1813, 5, 1. William & w, Elisabeth, & ch, Thomas & Cyrus, rocf Springfield MM, dtd 1813,4,3
1814, 8, 6. William & fam gct White Water MM
1827, 6, 2. Henry rocf Stillwater MM, dtd 1826,10,28
1831, 3, 5. Henry dis disunity

NIXON
1827, 5, 7. Mary m James M. HIBBERD
1829, 6, 10. Sarah m Nathaniel M. BROWN (H)

1812, 8, 1. William & ch, John, Mary, William, Esther & Samuel, rec in mbrp
1827, 3, 3. Henrietta & Ann P. rocf Uwchlan MM, Penn., dtd 1823,2,10
1827, 4, 7. William & w, Martha, & ch, Sarah May, Susannah, Peninah, Martha Ann, William & Anna, rocf Miami MM, dtd 1827,3,

NIXON, continued
28
1828, 10, 4. Martha dis
1828, 10, 4. Sarah dis
1828, 10, 4. William dis disunity
1829, 3, 19. Henrietta dis disunity
1829, 4, 4. Samuel com for mou; treated with by rq of Fall Creek MM
1831, 11, 5. Samuel dis Fall Creek MM
1833, 5, 8. William & w, Martha, & ch, Peninah, Martha Ann, William & Anna, gct White Water MM, Ind. (H)
1833, 5, 8. Susannah gct White Water MM (H)
1833, 9, 21. Ann P. com for disunity; living at White Water MM
1833, 11, 16. Ann P. rpd rem from White Water MM
1833, 12, 21. Penina, Martha Ann, William & Rhoda, ch William, gct White Water MM, Ind.
1834, 12, 10. Ann gct White Water MM (H)

OVERHOLTS
1918, 12, 27. Martha Elizabeth, dt L. O. & Mae, rec in mbrp
1919, 2, 21. Benjamin Bruce [Overholtz], s Lee O. & Mae, rec in mbrp
1921, 10, 20. Ruby Mae, dt Lee & Mae, rec in mbrp

OVERMAN
1810, 6, 14. Jesse, Dearburn Co., Ind., s Ephraim & Rachel; m at Elk Mtg, Kezia STUBBS, Butler Co., O., dt Nathan & Elizabeth

1813, 3, 6. Jesse & ch, Henry & Eli, rocf White Water MM, dtd 1813,1,30
1822, 6, 1. Jesse dis
1823, 1, 4. Jesse rst by QM
1823, 7, 5. Jesse & fam gct New Garden MM, Ind.

OWEN
1918, 1, 25. Bessie (form Roberts) gct Poplar Ridge MM, Ind.

OZBUN
----, --, --. Jonathan & Isabella [Ozburn]
Ch: Elwood b 1812, 11, 3
Charles " 1816, 2, 13
Jonathan m 2nd Mary -----
Ch: Polly b 1819, 3, 10
Sarah " 1819, 3, 10
Susanna " 1821, 6, 29
Hulda " 1823, 1, 4
Charlotte " 1824, 11, 11
1826, 7, 6. Susanna m William HUDDLESTON
1830, 4, 23. Jonathan d ae 41y 1m 20d

1825, 11, 5. Susanna rocf White River MM, dtd 1825,10,12
1826, 4, 1. Jonathan [Osbun] & w, Mary, & ch, Elwood, Charles, Polly, Susanna & Charlotty, roc
1826, 7, 1. William Huddleston prcf Silver Creek MM, Ind., to m Susanna [Osbun]
1830, 5, 1. Jonathan's d rpd
1831, 11, 5. Elwood gct Cherry Grove MM, to m Lydia Frazier
1832, 5, 19. Elwood gct Cherry Grove MM, Ind.
1834, 4, 19. Charles [Osborne] gct Cherry Grove MM, Ind., to m Ann Hockett
1834, 9, 20. Charles gct Cherry Grove MM, Ind.
1841, 4, 17. Susanna Hinshaw (form Ozbun) con mou
1842, 9, 17. Mary Cooper (form Ozburn) con mou
1845, 9, 20. Charlotte McLelen (form Osbern) dis mou
1855, 12, 20. Elwood & w, Lydia, & ch, Joseph, James K. & Elisha, rocf Cherry Grove MM, Ind., dtd 1855,12,8
1857, 4, 23. Elvira [Ozburn] rocf Chester MM, Ind., dtd 1857,3,12
1857, 5, 21. Joseph & w, Elvira, gct Salem MM, Ia.
1857, 9, 24. Elwood & w & ch, James H. & Elisha C., gct Salem MM, Ia.

PARHAM
1842, 8, 11. Rachel d ae 85y 7m 18d

1810, 6, 18. Rachel appointed assistant clerk
1814, 7, 2. Zachaus dis mou
1814, 7, 2. Mary rocf Union MM, dtd 1814,6,14
1818, 5, 2. Mary gct Union MM
1819, 1, 5. Mary rocf Union MM, dtd 1818,3,31
1821, 11, 3. Benejah dis mou
1827, 8, 4. Mary rqct Vermillion MM, Ill.
1829, 9, 5. Rachel gct Vermilion MM, Ill; cert lost & duplicate granted 1830,6,5
1834, 6, 21. Rachel rocf Vermillion MM, Ill., dtd 1833,12,7
1842, 1, 15. Zacheus rst at Vermillion MM, Ill. with consent of this mtg

PARKER
1870, 1, 20. Rachel & ch, Leroy Alvanus, Sarah Rebecca, Milly Anna & Jonathan W., rocf Dover MM, dtd 1870,1,19
1884, 7, 24. Rachel & ch, Leroy, Alvanus, Rebecca, Milla A. & Jonathan, gct White Water MM, Ind.
1889, 5, 23. Leroy, Alvanus, Jonathan, Rachel, Rebecca & Milla A. dropped from mbrp
1907, 10, 3. Willis R. & w, Ella, & ch, Jay Russel, rqct Rush Creek MM, Ind.
1907, 11, 21. Ada B. & dt, Margaret Ruth, rocf Greensfork MM, Ind., dtd 1907,10,19
1911, 9, 28. Ida & Margaret gct Scipio MM, Poplar Ridge, N. Y.
1920, 1, 29. Ida T. rocf White Water MM, Ind.
1921, 1, 20. Lillian Frances Ruger, foster

PARKER, continued
dt Ida T. Parker, rec in mbrp
1921, 10, 20. Ida T. Parker & foster dt, Lillian Ruger, gct Carthage MM, Ind.

PATTEN
1855, 3, 22. Caroline (form Brown) dis mou; living at Richland MM, Ia.

PATTERSON
1829, 12, --. Beulah rocf Miami MM (H)

PATTY
1810, 9, 1. James [Paty] rocf Cain Creek MM, N. C., dtd 1807,3,21
1825, 11, 5. Hannah con mou
1828, 3, 1. Mary rec in mbrp
1830, 2, 6. James [Paty] dis disunity
1830, 7, 3. Hannah Ivers (form Patty) dis mou; living at White Lick MM
1832, 8, 8. James rec in mbrp (H)
1841, 12, 18. Mary gct Sugar River MM, Ind.

PEARSON
1872, 8, 22. Rebecca rec in mbrp

PENNINGTON
1839, 8, 17. Spiceland MM rq this mtg to treat with John for mou, but he had rem from here

PEREGOY
1919, 11, 20. Marion Francis rocf Cleveland MM, O.
1921, 1, 20. Miriam Francis gct Spiceland MM, Ind.

PHALEN
1820, 8, 5. Margaret rec in mbrp
1823, 11, 11. Margaret [Phalin] gct Honey Creek MM, Ind.

PHARES
1870, 6, 27. Clayton m Mary Hannah STUBBS, b 1870,6,27 (dt Elihu & Susanah)

1821, 5, 5. Meribah [Pheres] (form Allen) rpd mou; Chesterfield MM, N. J., to be informed
1898, 4, 21. Mary jas; dropped from mbrp
1915, 11, 25. William T. [Phearus] & w, Blanche, & dt, Thelma, rec in mbrp

PHILIPS
----, --, --. Richard [Phillips] m Cynthia PEARSON, dt Elliott & Mary, b 1836,5,1

1897, 11, 25. Cynthia rolf M. E. Church, Macedonia, O.

PICKET
1812, 5, 2. Joseph [Pigot] & fam (ch, Tamer, Anna, Lydia, Mary & Sarah) rocf Miami MM, dtd 1812,2,26
1813, 5, 1. Joseph & fam gct Center MM

PINGLETON
1921, 2, 24. Ersie rec in mbrp
1922, 3, 23. Dorothy rec in mbrp
1922, 7, 20. Ersie Neff (form Pingleton) dropped from mbrp for jas

PIPER
1895, 1, 23. Hal m Sarah Eva MENDENHALL, wd William Hadley Mendenhall, dt Jonathan & Hannah PAYNE, b 1849,4,7

PLACE
1840, 3, 21. William & fam rocf New Garden MM, Ind., dtd 1839,12,21

PLACK
1916, 11, 23. Mary Belle (form Conarroe) gct U. B. Church, Greenbush

PORTIS
1916, 1, 20. Mary (form Talbert) gct Ypsilanti MM, Mich.

POTTINGER
1856, 1, 27. Lydia (form Powell) dis mou
1889, 7, 25. Almina gc

POWELL
----, --, --. Benjamin & Rachel
Ch: Hannah b 1830, 4, 11
Susanna " 1832, 3, 23
Josiah " 1833, 10, 8
Elijah " 1835, 7, 3
Lydia " 1837, 9, 21
Martha Ann " 1839, 12, 7
Isaac Randal b 1843, 3, 8
1872, 4, 12. Benjamin d ae 64y 8d
1885, 4, 10. Rachel d ae 79y 7m 5d

1830, 1, 2. Rachel [Powel] con mou
1834, 10, 18. Benjamin [Powel] & ch rec in mbrp
1856, 1, 27. Lydia Pottinger (form Powell) dis mou
1857, 8, 20. Elijah dis disunity
1857, 9, 24. Josiah dis disunity
1858, 5, 20. Susanna dis disunity
1863, 5, 27. Martha A. Davis (form Powell) dis mou
1872, 7, 25. Isaac R. rpd mou; dropped from mbrp
1872, 11, 23. Hannah Maddock (form Powel) rpd mou

PRAY
1828, 4, 9. Rachel m Henry STUBBS
1833, 10, 24. Enos, Preble Co., O., s Wm., dec, & Mary; m at Elk Mtg, Elvira STUBBS, Butler Co., O., dt Wm. & Esther, dec

PRAY, Enos & Elvira, continued
Ch: Esther b 1834, 8, 30
William S. " 1836, 2, 2
1835, 8, 28. Esther d ae 11m 28d
1837, 1, 26. Mary H. m Elijah TALBERT

1826, 3, 4. Joseph rocf White Water MM, dtd 1825,10,15
1827, 2, 3. Mary rocf White Water MM, dtd 1826,11,26
1829, 5, 2. Mary H. roc dtd 1828,12,21
1830, 4, 3. Joseph con mou
1830, 12, 4. Mary gct White Water MM, Ind.
1833, 7, 20. Joseph gct White Lick MM, Ind., to m Anna Jane Johnson
1834, 6, 21. Anna Jane rocf White Lick MM, Ind., dtd 1834,3,12
1836, 3, 19. Joseph & w, Anna Jane, & ch, William & Samuel M., gct White Lick MM, Ind.
1839, 3, 16. Enos & w, Elvira, & ch, William S. & Elizabeth, gct Westfield MM, Ind.
1839, 4, 20. Mary gct Westfield MM, Ind.
1844, 2, 17. Enos & w, Elisa, & ch, William S., Elizabeth, Martha & Rachel, rocf Westfield MM, Ind., dtd 1844,1,11
1846, 3, 21. Enos & w, Elvira, & ch, William S., Elizabeth, Martha, Rachel & Sibil, gct Mill Creek MM, O.

PRICE
----, --, --. Miles & Mary
Ch: Curtis
Aaron
Wallace
Robert
Julia A. m ----- TERRY
Maggie

1888, 9, 20. Miles & fam rec in mbrp
1888, 9, 20. Mina & Julia rec in mbrp
1888, 11, 22. Maggie rec in mbrp
1890, 12, 25. Mina Jones (form Price) relrq
1900, 5, 24. Maggie dropped from mbrp
1908, 9, 24. Robert dropped from mbrp
1913, 2, 27. Emory dropped from mbrp

PUCKET
1837, 12, 21. Mary m Samuel ROBERTS

1833, 9, 21. Richard[Pucket] & w, Susanna, & ch, Thomas & Daniel, rocf White River MM, Ind., dtd 1833,6,17
1835, 11, 21. Mary & ch, Daniel, Mary & Jane, rocf White River MM, dtd 1835,9,21
1837, 2, 18. Daniel [Pucket] gct Newbury MM
1837, 5, 20. Richard & w, Susannah, & ch, Thomas, Daniel, Enos & Tamar, rocf Newberry MM, dtd 1837,4,17
1838, 3, 17. Mary & dt, Jane, gct White River MM, Ind.
1839, 1, 19. Richard & w, Susannah, & ch gct White River MM, Ind.
1851, 12, 25. Tamar rocf Poplar Run MM, Ind., dtd 1851,11,13
1856, 12, 25. Vianna C. rocf White River MM, Ind., dtd 1856,12,6
1858, 6, 24. Vienna Johnson (form Puckett) con mou; living at Cherry Grove MM
1870, 5, 26. Jabez H. Kenworthy gct Dover MM, Ind., to m Rhoda E. Puckett

PUGH
----, --, --. John m Eliza Ann GIFFORD b 1838, 12,22

1818, 8, 1. Enoch rocf Hopewell MM, dtd 1809,10,2, endorsed by Miami MM
1818, 9, 5. Enoch gct Cincinnati MM
1913, 2, 27. Etta dropped from mbrp

RAGSDALE
1922, 3, 23. Ruby rec in mbrp

RALSTON
1892, 5, 26. John W. rocf Smyrna MM, Ia., dtd 1892,5,7
1893, 11, 23. John W. & w, Mary H., gct Newberry MM, O.

RANDAL
----, --, --. Isaac & Sarah [Randle]
Ch: Martha b 1795, 7, 23
Ann " 1797, 1, 15
Phebe " 1798, 12, 22
Rachel " 1805, 9, 5
Elizabeth " 1809, 5, 26
Hannah " 1813, 8, 12
1814, 4, 7. John, Preble Co., O., s Jonas & Sarah; m at Elk Mtg, Lydia BROWN, Montgomery Co., O., dt Richard & Mary
1815, 11, 16. Mary [Randel] m John BROWN
----, --, --. Jonathan & Sarah [Randle]
Ch: Rebecca b 1820, 9, 26
Joseph " 1822, 4, 10
Ann " 1824, 5, 9
Phebe " 1826, 5, 26
David " 1828, 4, 27
Martha " 1830, 2, 15
Nathan " 1832, 10, 23
1820, 10, 19. Phebe m John HIXON
1827, 2, 8. Joseph [Randle], Preble Co., O., s Jonas & Sarah; m at Elk Mtg, Keziah JOHNSON, Preble Co., O., dt Jonathan & Hannah
Ch: Hannah b 1829, 8, 6
Susanna " 1831, 2, 24
Alfred " 1833, 2, 28
Emily " 1835, 4, 2
Zimri " 1837, 7, 15
Amy " 1839, 11, 23
1830, 5, 24. Hannah d ae 9m 18d
1834, 4, 16. Hannah [Randel] d
1834, 8, 26. Jonathan d ae 42y 6m 3d
1843, 4, 20. Elizabeth [Randall] m Julius LANE

RANDAL, continued
1846, 7, 1. Sarah d
1852, 4, 23. Jonas [Ranall] d ae 85y 4m 19d
1855, 3, 30. Sarah [Randall] d ae 91y 10m 5d
1855, 10, 8. Isaac [Randall] d ae 86y 9m 16d
1890, 9, 16. Elizabeth [Randall] d ae 94y 10m 17d

1812, 11, 7. Isaac [Randle] & fam rec in mbrp
1812, 11, 7. Sarah [Randle] & dt, Martha & Ann, rec in mbrp
1814, 10, 1. John [Randle] con mou
1818, 2, 7. Jonathan con mou
1820, 3, 4. John [Randel] dis
1821, 5, 5. Sarah [Randall] & ch rec in mbrp
1821, 5, 5. Martha [Randall] (form Smith) con mou
1825, 9, 3. Jonas con mou
1828, 8, 2. Jonas Jr. dis disunity
1831, 11, 5. John dis disunity
1831, 11, 5. Lydia [Randle] dis disunity
1833, 4, 20. Rachel rpd mou
1833, 7, 20. Jonas P. dis disunity
1834, 1, 18. Mary dis disunity
1834, 3, 15. Sarah gct New Garden MM, Ind.
1834, 7, 19. Ann Smith (form Randal) con mou
1835, 5, 16. Richard dis disunity
1835, 8, 15. Sarah Jr. dis disunity
1836, 3, 19. Rachel gct Cherry Grove MM, Ind.
1836, 10, 15. Sarah dis
1838, 12, 15. Delilah Teague (form Randal) dis mou
1840, 9, 19. Joseph & w, Keziah, & ch, Susannah, Alfred, Emely, Zimri & Amy, gct Westfield MM, Ind.
1841, 12, 18. Nancy dis disunity
1842, 2, 19. Joseph Jr. dis disunity
1842, 9, 17. William dis military dervice
1848, 6, 17. Margaret [Randel] dis disunity
1857, 8, 20. Mary Jane [Randle] rocf Honey Creek MM, Ind., dtd 1857,7,11
1859, 1, 21. Louisa rocf Richland MM, Ind., dtd 1858,12,18
1861, 10, 24. Louisa [Randall] gct Richland MM, Ind.
1863, 5, 27. Mary Jane [Randall] gct Sugar Plain MM, Ind.
1865, 8, 29. Elizabeth rec in mbrp
1901, 8, 22. Naomi [Randall] relrq
1909, 7, 22. Charles E. [Randall] rolf U. B. Church, West Elkton, O.
1914, 3, 26. Charles E. [Randall] & w & s gct White Water MM, Ind.

REEVES
----, --, --. Allen & Esther
Ch: Elizabeth M. b 1835, 12, 24
Ann H. " 1837, 5, 19 d 1897,11,13
1854, 11, 30. Elizabeth M. m Elijah MENDENHALL
1879, 9, 7. Esther d ae 65y 11m 14d
1882, 9, 15. Allen d ae 75y 2m 8d
1835, 4, 18. Esther [Reaves] con mou
1850, 4, 25. Allen & two dt rec in mbrp

REYNOLDS
----, --, --. William & Josinah
Ch: Rebecca b 1846, 8, 15
Martha Ann " 1850, 5, 3
Lydia L. " 1851, 8, 22
Sarah Ellen" 1854, 7, 9
1879, 12, 20. Josinah d in 60th yr.

1847, 12, 18. William [Runyolds] & w, Josinah, & dt rec in mbrp
1870, 3, 24. Lydia C. Roberts (form Reynolds) rpd mou
1871, 3, 23. Martha Ann Wright (form Reynolds) rpd mou
1883, 1, 25. William rec in mbrp
1883, 5, 24. William gct Richland MM, Ind.

RICKS
1842, 3, 19. Eliza Ann (form Mendenhall) dis mou

RINER
1917, 11, 23. George rec in mbrp
1919, 3, 21. Charles R. rec in mbrp

RITENOUR
1898, 3, 24. Lettie rec in mbrp

ROBERTS
1813, 1, 7. Walter [Roberds], Wayne Co., Ind., s Thomas & Ann; m at Elk Mtg, Mary HAWKINS, Preble Co., O., dt Nathan & Ann, both dec
1816, 8, 15. Rebecca [Roberds] m Luke LANGSTON
1822, 11, 7. John, Butler Co., O., s Jonathan & Mary; m at Elk Mtg, Rebecca BROWN, Preble Co., O., dt Richard, dec, & Mary
Ch: Mary b 1824, 2, 22
Sarah " 1825, 10, 30
Phebe " 1826, 12, 9
Lydia " 1828, 2, 24
Esceneth " 1829, 3,28
Julietta " 1830, 11, 13
Eliza Jane " 1832, 1, 22
1823, 11, 6. Bethula [Robards] m John WHITACRE
1837, 12, 21. Samuel, Butler Co., O., s Jonathan & Mary; m at Elk Mtg, Mary PUCKET, Preble Co., O., dt Thomas & Mary
Ch: Thomas b 1838, 10, 3
Jonathan " 1840, 11, 7
Elihu " 1842, 8, 14
Martha Jane" 1844, 2, 19
James W. " 1847, 6, 11
Delilah " 1849, 10, 26
Zeno Addison " 1857, 5, 20
1841, 6, 22. Thomas d ae 2y 8m 19d
1845, 3, 21. Martha Jane d ae 3m 2d

ROBERTS, continued
1846, 6, 16. Mary d ae 77y 6m 20d
1850, 9, 22. John d
1855, 6, 7. Jonathan d ae 87y 16d
----, --, --. Elihu H., s Samuel & Mary, b 1842,8,14; m Sarah STUBBS, dt John & Margaret
Ch: Mary Alma b 1862, 1, 1; m John CASY
Samuel Otis" 1865, 10, 18
Alonzo " 1866, 1, 12; m Cora FRAZEE
Alpheus " 1869, 6, 27
Charles F. " 1872, 1, 14
Edwin " 1874, 6, 10
Margaret L." 1877, 3, 2
Roscoe
Sadie
Bessie
1865, 11, 3. Walter d ae 62y 5d
----, --, --. Walter, s Walter & Hannah; m Hannah Ann MENDENHALL, dt Marmaduke & Elizabeth
Ch: Alvadore b 1866, 8, 30; m Hannah HORNADAY
Milton S. " 1868, 10, 5; m Luanna STUBBS 1891,5,10
Orlando b 1871, 5, 17; m Cora E. STUBBS
Viretta " 1874, 5, 24; m Gurney BRANSON 1898
Clara
Elsie
William
1870, 11, 24. James W. s Samuel & Mary, b 1847,6,11; m Lucretia M. DAVIS, dt Nathan H. & Mary A., b 1847,7,25
Ch: Frederic C.b 1873, 4, 1; m Verona STUBBS
Curtis S. " 1875, 7, 9
Willis J. " 1878, 11, 8 d 1887, 3,30
1869, 11, 11. Jonathan, s Samuel & Mary, b 1840,11,7; m Jennie HOLODAY, b 1837,12,13
Ch: Alta Bertha b 1878, 3, 5
Curtis Boswell " 1874, 7, 21 d 1874, 8, 2
1873, 3, 12. Juliette d ae 42y 4m 18d
----, --, --. Zeno, s Samuel & Mary, b 1857,5,20; m Elizabeth BORRODAILE, dt Sarah
Ch: Viola
Albert S. b 1880, 2, 19
Chester E. " 1882, 8, 23
Oressa May " 1890, 5, 4 d 1897,10mo
1880, 3, 6. Mary d ae 59y 7d
1889, 5, 23. Alvadore, s Walter & Hannah A., b 1866,8,30; m Hannah HORNADAY, dt Nelson & Margaret
Ch: Ruth b 1890, 7, 23
Charles DeWitt " 1892, 12, 25
Paul E. " 1894, 1, 29
Mary M. " 1895, 8, 14
----, --, --. Fredric Coleman, s James & Lucretia, b 1873,4,1; m Verona STUBBS, dt Thomas & Rachel, b 1873,12,10
Ch: Fredric Lowell b 1897, 7, 24
Robert Willis " 1898, 9, 30
1891, 5, 10. Milton, s Walter & Hannah A., b 1868,10,5; m Luanna STUBBS, dt Marmaduke & Susan, b 1871,5,10
1891, 11, 18. Samuel d ae 80y 8m 16d

1810, 5, 5. Thomas appointed elder
1811, 7, 2. Thomas [Roberds] & fam gct White Water MM
1811, 9, 17. Ann gct White Water MM
1813, 1, 2. Walter prc to m Mary Hawkins
1829, 2, 7. Walter con mou
1832, 1, 7. Rebecca dis disunity
1833, 1, 19. John & ch, Mary Ann, Sarah, Phebe, Lydia, Eseneth, Julietta & Eliza Ann, gct Chester MM, Ind.
1833, 6, 15. John [Robert] & ch returned cert granted to Chester MM, Ind.; they returned to limits of this mtg
1843, 1, 21. Mary Ann dis disunity
1845, 2, 15. Sarah dis disunity
1849, 4, 21. Lydia dis disunity
1849, 5, 19. Phebe dis disunity
1850, 9, 26. Ascenith dis disunity
1850, 9, 26. Juliet dis disunity
1851, 12, 25. Hannah rec in mbrp
1853, 6, 23. Eliza Jane dis disunity

1856, 4, 24. Susan Hunt (form Roberts) dis mou
1858, 3, 25. Rebecca Talbert (form Roberts) dis mou
1861, 7, 22. Elihu rpd mou
1865, 5, 25. Sarah & ch, Mary Alma & Ottis S., rec in mbrp
1866, 2, 22. Hannah Ann (form Mendenhall) rpd mou
1867, 5, 23. Delilah A. Mendenhall (form Roberts) rpd mou
1870, 3, 24. Lydia C. (form Reynolds) rpd mou
1870, 3, 24. Lydia C. gct White Water MM, Ind.
1870, 4, 21. Lyndley L. gct White Water MM, Ind.
1870, 6, 23. Jonathan con mou
1870, 6, 23. Jennie H. rocf Newberry MM, O., dtd 1870,5,23
1871, 4, 20. James W. rpd mou
1871, 5, 26. Lucretia M. rocf Salem MM, Ind. dtd 1871,5,17
1872, 2, 22. Phebe & Juliett rec in mbrp
1876, 7, 20. Lydia C. rocf White Water MM, Ind., dtd 1876,6,28
1878, 5, 23. Elihu H. dis disunity
1882, 8, 4. Elihu H. dis disunity
1883, 7, 26. Lydia gct Cottonwood MM, Kans.
1885, 5, 21. Elizabeth B. & ch, Viola, Albert

ROBERTS, continued
& Chester, rec in mbrp
1890, 11, 20. Ottis & Alpheus gct Richland MM, Ind.
1893, 8, 24. Hannah rolf U. B. Church of Christ, West Elkton, O.
1893, 8, 24. Ruth & C. Dewitt, ch Alvadare & Hannah, rec in mbrp
1894, 4, 26. Alonzo J. gct East Branch MM,Ind.
1895, 3, 21. Charles F. gct Poplar Ridge MM, Ind.
1896, 2, 20. Alpheus rocf Carmel MM, dtd 1895,8,7
1896, 3, 26. William & w, Luvina, rec in mbrp
1899, 5, 25. Clara B. & Elsie rec in mbrp
1900, 9, 20. Alvadore & w, Hannah, & ch, Ruth; Charles Dewitt, Paul Ellis, Mary Margarite & Walter Nelson, glt U. B. Church, Lewisburg MM, O.
1904, 3, 24. Everett Arthur J., ward of Milton S. & w rec in mbrp
1914, 4, 23. Bertha Lee rolf First M. E. Ch., Liberty, Ind.
1915, 10, 28. Lindley S. gct Muncie MM, Ind.
1915, 11, 25. Emma Florence rec in mbrp
1915, 11, 25. Edna rolf U. B. Ch., West Elkton
1917, 1, 25. Joyce joined Presbyterian Ch., Camden, O.; dropped from mbrp
1917, 4, 26. Albert S. & w, Bertha, gct Salem MM, Ind.
1917, 6, 22. Chester gct Salem MM, Ind. (cert failed to arrive & duplicate granted 1918,2,22)
1918, 1, 25. Bessie Owen (form Roberts) gct Poplar Ridge MM, Ind.
1919, 6, 26. Roscoe dropped from mbrp
1920, 1, 29. Retta & Sadie dropped from mbrp
1921, 5, 26. Fred C. & w, Verona S., gct White Water MM, Ind.
1925, 7, 23. Lowell S. glt M. E. Church, Greenwood, Ind.
1925, 10, 22. Robert W. gct 2nd Friends Ch., West Indianapolis, Ind.

ROBINSON
----, --, --. William m Mary E. ROSS, dt Charles & Mary A.
Ch: Clarence A.b 1887, 9, 5
Jessie B. " 1892, 3, 28

1831, 3, 5. Sarah con mou
1835, 7, 18. Sarah gct Mississinawa MM, Ind.
1838, 7, 21. Sarah treated with on rq of Mississinawa MM
1898, 3, 24. Clarence A. & Jessie B., ch Mary E., rec in mbrp
1917, 6, 22. Mary Emily gct White Water MM, Richmond, Ind.
1919, 6, 26. Clarence dropped from mbrp

ROCKHILL
1831, 11, 9. Samuel rocf Springfield MM,N.J., dtd 1831,10,5 (H)

ROP
1871, 6, 22. Sarah Ann rec in mbrp
1872, 4, 26. Sarah Ann Gifford (form Rop) rpd mou

ROSS
1876, 2, 24. John R. rec in mbrp
1876, 2, 24. Mary Emily rec in mbrp

RUGER
1921, 1, 20. Lillian Frances, foster dt Ida T. Parker, rec in mbrp
1921, 10, 20. Ida T. Parker & foster dt, Lillian Ruger, gct Carthage MM, Ind.

SAUNDERS
1820, 8, 9. Margaret m Joseph STUBBS

1815, 5, 6. Elizabeth Faris (form Sanders) rpd mou
1817, 7, 5. Isaac dis mou
1823, 9, 6. Ann Seabolt (form Saunders) dis mou
1823, 9, 6. Sarah Cushman (form Saunders) dis mou
1828, 1, 5. Rebecca [Sanders] dis jas
1837, 11, 18. Mary Ann Brown (or Bowers) (form Sanders) dis mou

SCHAUERS
----, --, --. Grant [Schauer] m Sarah E. COX, dt William & Martha, b 1866,6,15

1922, 2, 22. Vera & Thelma rec in mbrp
1925, 4, 23. Thelma & Vera jas; dropped from mbrp

SCHOOLEY
1811, 12, 7. John & w, Hannah, & ch, Isaac & Asenath, rocf Mount Pleasant MM, Va., dtd 1811,9,2
1812, 6, 6. John [Schooly] & fam gct Center MM

SCHOUTEN
1876, 5, 14. Charles M. b 1839,4,21; m Sarah J. BENNETT, dt Henry & Nancy, b 1848,3,25

SCHUL
1817, 11, 23. Ella rec in mbrp

SCHWARTZTRAUBER
1909, 8, 26. Lois Maurice & Helen Miriam [Schwarstrauber], dt Hattie, rec in mbrp
1913, 4, 24. William F. & Hope Eleanor rec in mbrp
1921, 7, 21. Lois Showalter (form Schwartztrauber) jas; dropped from mbrp

SCOTT
1827, 12, 6. Sarah m Thomas P. SIMMONS
1830, 4, 10. Marabeth Patience d ae 8y 5m 10d

SCOTT, continued
1817, 11, 1. Thomas & w, Mary, & ch, Abner S., Sarah, Daniel, Mary, Abigail Ann & Amos, rocf Springfield MM, N. J., endorsed by Miami MM
1829, 1, 3. Abner dis disunity & joining Separatists
1829, 2, 7. Thomas dis disunity
1829, 3, 19. Mary dis joining Separatists
1831, 7, 2. Daniel dis disunity
1832, 8, 8. Abner gct Westfield MM (H)
1833, 10, 19. Mary Jr. dis jH
1833, 10, 19. Abigail Ann dis jH
1837, 4, 13. Daniel con mou (H)
1837, 8, 10. Daniel gct Westfield MM (H)
1839, 8, 17. Amos dis jH
1845, 4, 19. Samuel dis disunity

SEAMAN
1929, 5, 2. Myrtle C., Francis F. & Anna Marie rec in mbrp

SEYBOLD
1813, 12, 4. Alice Moore (form Seybold) dis mou
1814, 1, 1. John & fam gct Lick Creek MM
1823, 9, 6. Ann [Seabolt] (form Saunders) dis mou

SHAFER
----, --, --. Alice, dt Ed & Mary

1877, 10, 25. Mary E. [Schaffer] relrq
1900, 7, 26. Alice M. rec in mbrp
1917, 4, 26. Ruth glt Reformed Church, Lewisburg, O.

SHARP
1872, 2, 22. Susan rec in mbrp
1884, 11, 20. Susan relrq

SHELDON
1821, 2, 3. Mary rocf Greenstreet MM, Philadelphia, dtd 1820,5,18

SHOUTEN
1899, 7, 20. Charles M. rolf M. E. Church, West Elkton, O.

SHOWALTER
1921, 7, 21. Lois (form Schwartztrauber) jas; dropped from mbrp

SIDWELL
1813, 10, 2. Esther rec in mbrp
1813, 11, 6. David [Sidwel] rec in mbrp
1814, 1, 1. David [Sidwel] & fam gct White Water MM
1831, 5, 7. Esther [Sydwell] dis joining Separatists; White Water MM to be informed

SILVERS
1838, 1, 20. Ann (form Johnson) com for mou & jH
1838, 7, 21. Ann [Silver] rpd dis by Miami MM
1839, 8, 17. Springboro MM rq this mtg to treat with Joseph for disunity
1839, 11, 16. Sarah Ann (form Woolman) dis mou & jH
1836, 1, 16. Phebe Brown (form Silver) rpd mou; Springborough MM to be informed
1840, 1, 18. Joseph rpd dis by Springborough MM

SIMMONS
1827, 12, 6. Thomas P., Preble Co., O., s Thomas, dec, & Rebecca; m at Elk Mtg, Sarah SCOTT, Preble Co., O., dt Thomas & Mary

1823, 9, 6. Rebecca & ch, Everline & Thomas, rocf Miami MM, dtd 1823,6,26
1828, 12, 6. Rebecca dis disunity
1829, 2, 7. Thomas P. dis joining Separatists
1829, 2, 7. Sarah S. dis disunity
1831, 5, 11. Thomas P. & w, Sarah S., gct Westfield MM (H)
1836, 7, 14. Rebecca & dt, Evelina, gct Westfield MM; Rebecca's d rpd 1836,12,8 & a separate cert granted for her dt 1837, 1,12 (H)

SIMPSON
1893, 8, 24. Minnie rec in mbrp
1894, 7, 26. Minnie rpd rem from vicinity; dropped from mbrp
1898, 2, 24. Minnie dropped from mbrp

SLACK
1916, 10, 26. Fannie dropped from mbrp

SLEEPER
1834, 12, 20. Patience rocf Springborough MM, dtd 1834,11,25

SMALL
1861, 12, 26. Martha Jane (form Blanchard) dis mou

SMITH
-----, --,--. Joseph b 1766,6,6; m Elizabeth ----- b 1766,6,6
Ch: Stephen b 1806,6,11
1811, 6, 6. Patience m Isaiah HOLLINGSWORTH
1815, 8, 18. Sarah m Job BOGUE
1818, 9, 9. John, Preble Co., O., s Joseph & Hannah, dec; m at Paint Creek Mtg, Marium BOGUE, Preble Co., O., dt Joseph, dec, & Mary
1820, 10, 22. Joseph d ae 54y 4m 16d bur on his own ground, Somers Twp.
----, --, --. Jesse & Martha

Ch:		
Ephraim	b	1821, 3, 5
Mary	"	1826, 10, 3
Isaac R.	"	1828, 1, 16
William I.	"	1830, 12, 13

SMITH, continued
1835, 9, 24. Job,Preble Co., O., s Jirah & Avis; m at Elk Mtg, Keziah TALBERT, Preble Co., O., dt Job & Amanda
1849, 12, 27. Ellis C., s Job & Anna, b 1818, 4,12; m Mary SWAIN
Ellis C. m 2nd Bethena LAMM 1855,12,20
----, --, --. Anna E., dt Craig & Fannie Langford

1811, 6, 1. Isaiah Hollingsworth prc to m Patience Smith
1821, 5, 5. Martha Randall (form Smith) con mou
1833, 12, 21. Elizabeth rocf Springfield MM, Ind., dtd 1833,10,19
1834, 7, 19. Ann (form Randal) con mou
1834, 12, 20. Elizabeth gct Springfield MM,Ind.
1836, 11, 19. Jesse & ch, Ephraim, Mary, Isaac & William, rec in mbrp
1837, 1, 21. Job & w, Keziah, & s, Isaiah, gct Westfield MM, Ind.
1840, 12, 11. Jesse & w, Martha, & ch, Ephraim, Mary, Isaac R. & William, gct Mississinaway MM, Ind.
1845, 11, 15. James rocf Rochester MM, N. Y., dtd 1845,10,24
1847, 1, 16. Ann gct Mississinawa MM, Ind.
1850, 8, 22. Mary T. dis mou
1850, 10, 24. James gct Balby MM, Eng.
1876, 2, 24. Ellis C. rec in mbrp
1876, 2, 24. Mary E. rec in mbrp
1900, 5, 24. Ann dropped from mbrp

SNIPES
1838, 3, 17. Mary (form Lane) con mou
1851, 9, 25. Mary gct White Water MM, Ind.

SNYDER
1850, 8, 18. Rebecca [Snider] d ae 21y

1838, 5, 19. Mary [Snider] (form Mendenhall) dis mou
1848, 8, 19. Rebecca [Snider] (form Brown) con mou
1855, 8, 23. West Branch MM rq this mtg to deal with Eleanor (form Greysom)
1856, 1, 27. Eleanor rpd dis by West Branch MM
1860, 10, 25. Eleanor C. rst in mbrp with consent of West Branch MM
1860, 10, 25. Anna Imelia & Cassius Delmar, ch Eleanor, rec in mbrp
1861, 9, 26. Eleanor & ch, Anna Amelia & Cassius Delmi, gct West Branch MM
1862, 6, 26. Mary rst in Cherry Grove MM, Ind., with consent of this mtg

SPONSLER
1888, --, --. Lucinda d

1881, 3, 24. Lucinda rocf Pipe Creek MM, Ind., dtd 1881,3,5

SPRAY
1811, 9, 17. Phebe con mou
1811, 10, 5. Phebe gct Miami MM, O.
1829, 4, 4. Enos rocf Milford MM, dtd 1827, 8,25
1836, 4, 13. Michael (form Denny) con mou
1839, 3, 16. Michael gct Salem MM, Ia.

STAATS
1848, 1, 15. Mary Ann[Stats] (form Brown) con mou
1863, 2, 26. Mary Ann gct Dover MM, Ind.

STAFFORD
1854, 3, 24. John H., Hamilton Co., Ind.,s Samuel & Rachel; m at Elk Mtg, Martha MENDENHALL, Preble Co., O., dt Marmaduke & Elizabeth
1873, 12, 4. Mary J. d ae 28y 5m 26d
----, --, --. Marmaduke J., s John & Martha b 1862,10,29; m Caroline SHAFER
Dt: Mabel
Marmaduke's parents were mbr of Richland MM, Ia. at time of his b & he was taken by M. & E. Mendenhall to raise

1854, 10, 26. John H. rocf Richland MM, Ind., dtd 1834,8,2
1855, 12, 20. John H. & w, Martha, gct Richland MM, Ind.
1872, 4, 25. Mary J. rocf Vermillion MM, Ill. dtd 1872,3,2
1874, 1, 22. Mary Jane's d rpd
1899, 6, 22. Callie M. rolf M. E. Church
1899, 6, 22. Mabel, dt M. J. & Callie M., rec in mbrp
1920, 2, 25. Marmaduke J. & w, Caroline M., & dt, Mabel, gct West Richmond MM, Ind.

STALLING
1812, 11, 7. Rebecca con mou

STANLEY
1851, 6, 26. Elizabeth J. Brown (form Stanly) con mou
1853, 5, 26. Lydia L. Taylor (form Stanley) con mou
1854, 4, 20. Mary P. Wheeler (form Stanly) con mou
1881, 1, 20. Adeline S. gct Cottonwood MM, Kans.

STARR
----, --, --. John, s James & Elizabeth, b 1777,7,31; m Mary WILLITS, dt Jesse & Phebe, b 1786,12,18

Ch:		
Elizabeth	b	1814 8, 6
Jesse	"	1816, 3, 24
Joshua	"	1818, 4, 4
Phebe	"	1820, 2, 8
William	"	1822, 10, 24
James	"	1824, 10, 15
Sarah	"	1827, 3, 2

STARR, continued
----, --, --. Nehemiah, s James & Eleanor, b 1793,7,21; m Esther WILLITS, dt Jesse & Phebe, b 1795,1,25
Ch: Henry b 1818, 11, 24
James " 1820, 6, 8
John " 1822, 10, 3
Charles " 1824, 12, 17
Willits " 1827, 1, 23
1829, 12, 11. Nehemkah d ae 36y 4m 21d bur Westfield Cem.

1820, 6, 3. William [Star] & w, Mary, & ch, Elizabeth, Jesse & Joshua, rocf Exeter MM, dtd 1819,8,25, endorsed by Cincinnati MM
1820, 6, 3. Nehemiah [Star] & w, Esther, & s, Henry, rocf Exeter MM, endorsed by Cincinnati MM

STEPHENS
1851, 7, 24. Ann T. (form Dicks) dis mou

STONE
1847, 9, 18. Hannah (form Gifford) dis mou

STOUT
1835, 1, 14. Mary Stubbs (form Stout) com for mou & Centre MM notified (H)
1840, 3, 21. Charlotte Stubb (form Stout) con mou; living at Springfield MM
1840, 9, 19. Cert rec for Elijah, Susanna & Stephen, ch Jesse & Rosanna, dec, from Springfield MM, dtd 1840,6,16, returned to that mtg
1841, 4, 17. Cert rec for Stephen & ch, Isaac, Elijah, Susanna & Stephen, from Springfield MM, O., dtd 1840,6,16; Stephen was not a resident here & cert was returned with that information

STRATTON
----, --, --. Eli, s Jonathan & Sarah, b 1772,12,20; m Eunice DOLLAR (or Dallas), dt William & Rebecca, b 1771,10,7
Ch: Sarah C. b 1801, 5, 24
Jonathan D." 1804, 11, 8
William L. " 1808, 3, 14
Joseph E. " 1811, 9, 2
1830, 7, 8. Melecent Ann [Strattan], dt Jonathan & Prudence, b

1818, 5, 2. Eli & w, Janice, & ch, Sarah, Jonathan, William L. & Joseph E., rocf Miami MM, dtd 1817,11,26
1835, 3, 21. Eli & w, Eunice, gct Duck Creek MM, Ind.
1835, 3, 21. Joseph E. gct Duck Creek MM, Ind.

STROMAN
1874, 4, 23. Scott recrq
1882, 7, 20. Scott relrq

STUBBS
1810, 6, 14. Kezia m Jesse OVERMAN
1814, 8, 18. Amanda m Job TALBERT
1814, 10, 6. Rebekah m William TALBERT
----, --, --. William & Esther
Ch: Elvira b 1815, 12, 29
Isaac " 1817, 7, 3
Elizabeth " 1819, 3, 28
Jonathan " 1823, 1, 8
1816, 3, 6. Rachel m Seaborn MOORE
1816, 11, 14. Rachel m Mordecai MOORE
1816, 12, 11. Margaret m Samuel BROWN
----, --, --. John & Margaret
Ch: Joseph b 1817, 5, 16
Lydia " 1819, 4, 11
----, --, --. William & Delilah
Ch: Martha b 1818, 10, 14
Elizabeth " 1822, 2, 27
Mary " 1827, 5, 28
Daniel " 1829, 7, 7
Elihu " 1831, 11, 6
----, --, --. Joseph & Sarah
Ch: Celia b 1819, 4, 9
Daniel " 1820, 8, 16
Jemima " 1821, 9, 24
Elisha " 1823, 7, 15
Mahlon " 1825, 2, 2
Amy " 1827, 3, 1
Stephen " 1828, 12, 10
Jacob " 1831, 7, 18
1819, 8, 12. Newton, Preble Co., O., s Samuel & Mary; m at Elk Mtg, Mary TALBERT, Preble Co., O., dt Thomas & Elizabeth
1820, 8, 9. Joseph, Preble Co., O., s John & Jane; m at Westfield Mtg; Margaret SAUNDERS, Preble Co., O., dt Joseph & Martha
Ch: John b 1821, 3, 23
Newton " 1823, 3, 6
Martha Ann " 1825, 3, 17
Charles " 1827, 7, 5
William M. " 1830, 4, 3
1821, 4, 12. Martha m Richard BROWN
1822, 9, 12. Tabitha m William JONES
----, --, --. Elisha & Elizabeth
-- Ch: Eli b 1823, 11, 24
Hiram " 1826, 11, 11
Keziah " 1828, 12, 1
Rachel " 1830, 8, 22
Enos " 1834, 9, 30
Isaac C. " 1836, 9, 16
Thomas " 1838, 8, 10
Esther T. " 1841, 10, 8
1824, 4, 30. Elisha d ae 9m 15d
1825, 8, 11. Nathan, Butler Co., O., s Nathan & Elizabeth; m at Elk Mtg, Ann MENDENHALL, dt Elijah, dec, & Martha
Ch: Martha Ann b 1826, 10, 6
Elijah M. " 1828, 9, 26
Elizabeth J.
b 1830, 11, 16
Enoch " 1833, 5, 4
Milton " 1835, 7, 27

STUBBS, Nathan & Ann, continued
Ch: Marmaduke b 1838, 4, 4
Rachel Alma" 1841, 4, 8
----, --, --. John & Eleanor
Ch: Riley b 1827, 9, 9
Mariah " 1830, 5, 27
Allen " 1832, 7, 16
Joseph " 1834, 8, 24
Keziah " 1836, 4, 8
John " 1843, 4, 16
Amy " 1846, 5, 2
Samuel " 1849, 1, 15
Eleanor " 1858, 4, 12
1827, 7, 12. Ann m William GIFFORD
1828, 4, 9. Henry, Butler Co., O., s Nathan & Elizabeth; m at West Union Mtg, Rachel PRAY, Butler Co., O., dt Wm., dec, & Mary
Ch: William b 1828, 12, 22
Joel " 1830, 3, 17
Mary " 1832, 2, 21
Elizabeth " 1833, 11, 16
Enos " 1835, 12, 28
1828, 6, 7. Elizabeth d ae 59y 11m 29d
1829, 5, 5. Keziah d ae 5m 4d
1831, 11, 7. Elihu, s William & Delilah, b d 1904,9,11
1832, 9, 3. Esther d ae 34y 6m 29d
1832, 9, 18. Esther d ae 15d
1833, 10, 24. Elvira m Enos PRAY
1834, 3, 20. Mary m Joseph MADDOCK, Jr.
1834, 7, 28. Enoch d ae 1y 2m 24d
1836, 3, 5. Rachel d ae 25y 4m 3d
1836, 5, 30. Nathan d ae 20y 11m 24d
1838, 9, 20. Martha m John MADDOCK
----, --, --. Isaac & Charlotte
Ch: Susannah S.b 1839, 5, 1
William I. " 1841, 3, 30
Esther " 1843, 10, 6
Rosannah " 1845, 10, 22
Lindley H. " 1847, 10, 13
Elizabeth Ann " 1849, 11, 14
Elvira " 1853, 2, 10
1843, 9, 21. Elizabeth m John WRIGHT
1844, 2, 5. Hannah d ae nearly 27y
1844, 3, 21. Jonathan, Preble Co., O., s Wm. & Esther, dec; m at Elk Mtg, Rachel LANE, Preble Co., O., dt Jesse & Hannah, dec
Ch: Susan L. b 1845, 7, 21
Alvan " 1847, 1, 24
Enoch " 1848, 2, 18
Albert " 1850, 8, 30
Elvira E. " 1853, 3, 8
Mary Emma " 1857, 12, 27
William P. " 1860, 1, 9
Esther A. " 1861, 5, 11
Phebe Lilian " 1863, 9, 10
----, --, --. Lorenzo & Sarah
Ch: Alden b 1845, 11, 19
Mary Elmina " 1848, 5, 4
John Clinton b 1850, 11, 19
1845, 2, 20. Martha Ann m Lewis TAYLOR
1846, 7, 30. Nathan d ae 44y 7m 25d
1847, 4, 22. Elijah, Butler Co., O., s Nathan, dec, & Ann; m at Elk Mtg, Beulah Ann TAYLOR, Preble Co., O., dt David & Martha
Ch: David T. b 1848, 5, 18
Nathan M. " 1851, 1, 5
Martha Ann " 1852, 10, 3
Mary Jane " 1856, 3, 9
Adaline " 1857, 10, 19
Clara " 1860, 5, 7
Vincent " 1862, 9, 22
Calvin " 1864, 10, 6
Alma " 1866, 7, 15
Alvadore " 1869, 2, 1
Elenor C. " 1871, 1, 30
Anna " 1873, 10, 17
Rilda C. " 1877, 1, 5
1847, 8, 26. Eli, Preble Co., O., s Elisha & Elizabeth; m at Elk Mtg, Keziah JONES, dt William, dec, & Tabitha, b 1825,5,9 d 1849,8,13
1848, 8, 21. Amy d ae 2y 3m 19d
1848, 8, 24. Rachel H. m John C. MADDOCK
1848, 11, 16. Zimri, s John & Margaret, b ----, 7, 2; m Elizabeth T. STUBBS, dt Nathan & Ann, b 1830,11,16
Ch: Lydia A. b 1850, 3, 23; m Samuel A. STUBBS
Caroline Elizabeth " 1853, 3, 30; m George MECKEL
Alma " 1856, 11, 28
Melva " 1860, 4, 30; m 1855,3,29 Edger ALBERTSON
1850, 12, 7. Riley d ae 23y 2m 29d
----, --, --. Eli & Anna F.
Ch: Ruth Emma b 1852, 4, 20
Mary Anna " 1854, 7, 27
Charles Moffitt " 1864, 3, 12
----, --, --. Milton & Sarah Jane
Ch: Jonathan Elijah b 1855, 4, 21
Elizabeth Ann " 1857, 4, 7
Esther Alma" 1860, 3, 30
Zimri " 1870, 10, 11
1855, 3, 29. Hiram, Preble Co., O., s Elisha & Elizabeth, b 1826,11,11; m at Elk Mtg, Susan J. JONES, dt William, dec, & Tabitha, Preble Co., O., b 1827,11,6 d 1899, 7,13
Ch: Eva Keziah b 1856, 12, 13; m L. E. BROWN
Tabitha Elizabeth " 1859, 1, 18 d 1876, 8,13
1855, 6, 28. Keziah m Isaac COMMONS, Jr.
----, --, --. Enos P. & Mary H.
Ch: Robert

STUBBS, Enos P. & Mary H., continued
Ch: Edwin b 1856, 11, 17
Isaac Alvadore " 1858, 4, 22
Orlando Clinton " 1860, 4, 19
1857, 7, 16. Isaac C. d ae 20y 10m
1858, 9, 2. Thomas, Preble Co., O., s Elisha & Elizabeth; m at Elk Mtg, Rachel A. STUBBS, dt Nathan, dec, & Ann
Ch: Effa Luella b 1859, 12, 22
Alva Elisha " 1862, 5, 14
Marmaduke Nathan " 1865, 8, 21
Bertha Anna" 1871, 5, 9
Verona " 1873, 12, 10
1859, 1, 24. Alma d ae 2y 1m 26d
1860, 1, 1. William Jr. d ae 64y 11m 16d (an elder)
1860, 8, 2. Esther T. m Nathan HUNT
----, --, --. Elihu m Susannah GIFFORD b 1837, 4,7
Ch: William Riley b 1862, 10, 25
Jesse G. " 1865, 8, 16
Mary Hannah " 1870, 6, 22; m Clayton PHARES
1863, 11, 26. Edith d ae 75y 9m 28d
1864, 11, 4. Charles Moffit d ae 7m 23d
1864, 11, 8. Alva Elisha d ae 2y 5m 24d
----, --, --. Joseph & Esther
Ch: Sarah Elizabeth b 1865, 6, 13
William C. " 1861, 9, 15
1865, 2, 16. John d ae 63y 7m 14d
1866, 8, 30. Marmaduke M., s Nathan & Ann, b 1838,4,4 d 1898,6,23; m Susan KENWORTHY, dt Jesse & Mary, b 1842,10,16 d 1895,10,22
Ch: Zimri Alvin b 1868, 6, 12
Mary Luanna" 1871, 5, 10; m Milton ROBERTS
1866, 9, 27. John F., s John & Eleanor, b 1843,4,16; m Rachel C. KENWORTHY, dt Jesse & Mary, b 1845,7,14
Ch: Naomi T. b 1867, 12, 11; m James W. RANDALL
Charles W. " 1869, 9, 6
1868, 5, 15. Zimri d ae 39y 10m 13d
----, --, --. Enoch & Laura
Ch: Estella b 1869, 2, 1
Edwin " 1871, 4, 11
Charles H. " 1874, 1, 23
----, --, --. Alden, s Lorenzo & Sarah, b 1845,11,19; m Mary CONARROE, dt John & Harriett
Ch: Amy Evalena b 1870, 1, 3
Sarah F. " 1872, 11, 4
Harriet C. " 1874, 1, 24
Ch: Clayton S. b 1876, 4, 12
Alpheus " 1884, 5, 31
Idella M. " 1888, 4, 10
1870, 7, 25. Elvira d ae 16y 11m 22d
----, --, --. David T. & Matilda
Ch: Elijah M. b 1871, 3, 15
Luna E. " 1873, 8, 25
Melissa " 1872, 3, 26
1871, 4, 11. Elizabeth d ae 68y 3m 13d
1872, 6, 9. Jonathan, s William & Esther; m Rue Ann KEPLINGER b 1839,7,10
Ch: George E. b 1878, 1, 2
Sarah Ellen" 1879, 10, 23
1873, 1, 5. Orla L. d ae 1m 29d
----, --, --. John C., s Lorenzo & Sarah, b 1850,11,19; m Alice ARMSTRONG
Ch: Coretta b 1874, 1, 23
Clifford " 1880, 3, 28
Benjamin " 1884, 5, 20
Clarence B." 1889, 1, 27
1876, 6, 20. Anna d ae 68y 8m 7d
1879, 3, 27. Enoch D., s John & Lydia, b 1848, 7, 9; m Melissa J. TALBERT, dt Asa & Sarah, b 1850,2,4
Ch: Frederic Austin b 1882, 10, 1
Arthur T. " 1883, 12, 20
Lydia Elvira " 1886, 11, 23
1880, 6, 4. Elisha d ae 81y 6m 5d
1880, 8, 11. Jonathan d ae 57y 7m 3d
----, --, --. Albert L. & Sarah E.
Ch: Claud B. b 1881, 9, 12
1881, 6, 7. Delila d ae 83y 4m 3d
1882, 9, 26. Claud B. d ae 11m 14d
1882, 10, 19. Albert d ae 32y 1m 19d
1882, 10, 29. William P. d ae 22y 9m 20d
1885, 5, 6. Effa Luella d ae 25y 5m 14d
1887, 3, 31. Sarah F. d ae 14y 4m 27d
1887, 11, 29. Lorenzo d ae 69y 7m 29d
1888, 2, 14. Esther Anna d ae 26y 9m 3d
----, --, --. Calvin, s Elijah M. & Beulah A., b 1864,10,6; m Dedan A. WING, dt Clara
Ch: Lura G.
Etta M.
Oscar M.
Irvin
Treva
Ruth Alma b 1900, 2, --
1891, 12, 24. Jesse G., s Elihu & Susanah, b 1865,8,16; m Bertha PHARES
1892, 1, 8. Eleanor d ae 82y 10m 18d
1899, 8, 30. Samuel A., s John & Eleanor, b 1849,1,15 d 1896,12,7; m Lydia A. STUBBS dt Zimri & Elizabeth, b 1850,2,23
Ch: Mabel b 1875, 3, 25; m Clarence WERNLAND 1899,8,30
Herbert b 1881, 4, 29
Bessie L. " 1884, 3, 21

1810, 1, 6. Samuel co
1810, 3, 3. Mary rocf New Garden MM, N. C.
1811, 6, 1. Joseph gct White Water MM, to m

STUBBS, continued
1811, 10, 5. Ann rocf White Water MM, dtd 1811,9,20
1815, 2, 4. William gct White Water MM, to m
1815, 6, 3. Margaret rocf Miami MM
1815, 7, 1. John & w, Jane, & ch, John, Rachel, Joseph & Keziah, rocf dtd 1814,12,28
1815, 7, 1. John Jr. roc dtd 1814,12,28
1815, 7, 1. Esther rocf White Water MM
1817, 7, 5. John Jr. con mou
1818, 3, 7. Joseph gct White Water MM, to m
1819, 3, 6. Sarah rocf White Water MM, dtd 1819,2,27
1821, 5, 5. Sarah con mou
1822, 2, 3. Samuel dis
1823, 8, 2. Samuel rst
1824, 12, 4. John dis
1825, 2, 5. Joseph Sr. gct Springfield MM, O., to m
1825, 9, 3. Edith rocf Springfield MM, dtd 1825,6,25
1825, 12, 3. Samuel Jr. dis disunity
1826, 7, 1. Margaret dis mou
1828, 3, 1. Mary dis
1828, 8, 2. Nathan Jr. dis disunity
1828, 8, 2. Rachel dis disunity
1828, 11, 1. Mary dis disunity
1828, 12, 6. Samuel dis disunity
1829, 1, 3. Nathan dis disunity & joining Separatists
1829, 2, 7. Elijah dis mou
1829, 4, 4. Henry dis joining Separatists
1829, 5, 2. William Sr. dis joining Separatists
1830, 6, 5. Mary Sr. dis disunity
1830, 6, 5. Joseph Sr. dis disunity
1831, 5, 7. Jesse dis mou
1831, 11, 5. Sarah Jr. dis disunity
1832, 8, 8. Elijah rec in mbrp (H)
1832, 11, 17. Elisha Stubbs, h Elizabeth, & ch, Eli, Hiram & Rachel, also Helia Blanchard, a minor under their care, rec in mbrp; Elizabeth, the w, was dis by White Water MM;they were to be communicated with as to rec her
1833, 2, 16. Elizabeth rst with consent of White Water MM
1833, 12, 21. Westfield MM rpd laid down; books & papers to be placed in hands of Newton
1834, 1, 18. Mary rpd dis by West Branch MM for mou
1834, 9, 20. Joseph [Stubb] & w, Sarah, & ch, Celia, Daniel, Jemima, Mahlon, Amy, Stephen, Jacob & Mary, gct Milford MM,Ind.
1834, 11, 12. William con mou (H)
1835, 1, 14. Mary (form Stout) com mou & Centre MM notified (H)
1836, 2, 11. Mary rocf Centre MM, dtd 1835, 12,17 (H)
1836, 12, 17. Nathan rst
1837, 5, 13. Henry con mou (H)
1837, 8, 19. Lydia dis
1838, 6, 16. Elizabeth Wheeler (form Stubbs) con mou
1838, 6, 16. Isaac con mou
1838, 11, 17. Isaac gct Westfield MM, Ind.
1839, 8, 17. John dis disunity
1839, 10, 19. Salem MM, Ia. rq to deal with Hannah Stubbs (form Stubbs)
1840, 1, 18. Sarah (form Maddock) con mou
1840, 3, 21. Charlotte [Stubb] (form Stout) con mou; mbr Springfield MM
1840, 4, 18. Hannah gct Salem MM, Ind.
1840, 6, 20. Robert dis mou
1840, 6, 20. Isaac rocf Westfield MM, Ind., dtd 1840,4,9
1841, 2, 20. Charlotte rocf Springfield MM
1841, 8, 21. Keziah (form Brown) con mou
1841, 9, 18. Isaac & w, Charlotte, & ch, Susannah & William, gct Salem MM, Ia.
1842, 11, 19. Hannah rocf Salem MM, Ind., dtd 1842,10,22
1844, 4, 20. Joseph H. dis joining Separatists
1844, 4, 20. Mary dis joining Separatists
1844, 7, 20. Keziah dis joining Separatists
1844, 12, 21. Sarah dis joining Separatists
1845, 5, 17. Mary Beall (form Stubbs) con mou
1846, 8, 15. John rst
1846, 9, 19. Eleanor & ch, Riley, Marian, Allen, Joseph, Keziah, John & Amy, rec in mbrp
1848, 10, 11. Isaac & w, Charlotte, & ch, Susannah, William, Esther & Rosanna, rocf Salem MM, Ia., dtd 1848,8,26
1849, 4, 21. Elizabeth con mou
1849, 5, 19. Isaac & w, Charlotte, & ch, Susannah, William, Esther, Rosanna & Lindley, gct West Branch MM, O.
1849, 11, 17. William dis mou
1850, 4, 25. Daniel P. dis disunity
1850, 9, 26. Isaac & w, Charlotte, & ch, Susanna, William, Esther, Rosanna, Lindly & Elizabeth Ann, rocf West Branch MM, dtd 1850,8,15
1851, 5, 22. Eli gct White Water MM, to m Anna F. Moffitt
1851, 9, 25. Joel dis jas
1852, 4, 22. Anna F. rocf White Water MM, Ind., dtd 1852,3,24
1853, 8, 25. Mary rst
1853, 10, 20. Isaac & w, Charlotte, & ch, Susannah, William, Esther, Rosanna, Lindley, Elizabeth Ann & Elvira, gct Chester MM, Ind.
1854, 5, 25. Zimri & ch, Lydia Ann & Caroline, rec in mbrp
1854, 5, 25. Milton con mou
1854, 6, 22. Sarah Jane rec in mbrp
1854, 10, 26. Jonathan & w, Rachel, & ch, Alvin, Enoch, Albert & Elvira Elizabeth gct White Water MM; returned 1855,2,22 with statement that they were not free to accept it

STUBBS, continued
1855, 9, 20. Jonathan dis
1855, 10, 25. Rachel & ch, Alvan, Enoch Albert & Elvira Elizabeth, gct White Water MM, Ind.
1855, 11, 22. Enos P. gct Springfield MM, O., to m Mary Hunt
1856, 1, 27. Elizabeth M. con mou; mbr Springfield MM
1856, 6, 26. Elizabeth M. rocf Springfield MM, O., dtd 1856,5,17
1856, 6, 26. Mary K. rocf Springfield MM, O., dtd 1856,5,17
1856, 7, 24. Jonathan rst by QM
1856, 8, 21. Jonathan gct White Water MM,Ind.
1856, 12, 25. Elihu dis mou
1857, 2, 26. Susannah (form Gifford) dis mou
1858, 1, 21. Eliza Ann (form Gifford) dis mou
1858, 2, 25. Enos P. dis mou
1858, 6, 24. Allen gct Richland MM, Ia.
1859, 4, 21. Sarah rst
1859, 6, 23. Lorenzo & minor ch, Alden, Mary E. & John C., rec in mbrp
1860, 2, 23. Joseph con mou
1860, 7, 26. Nathan Hunt prcf Springfield MM, O., dtd 1860,7,21, to m Esther Stubbs
1863, 4, 23. Enos P. & w, Mary H., & ch, Robert Edwin, Isaac Alvadore & Orando Clinton, gct Roxsylvania MM, Ia.
1864, 10, 20. Elihu & w, Susannah, & s, William R. rec in mbrp
1867, 3, 21. Mary gct White Water MM, Ind.
1867, 4, 25. Susan H. (form Kenworthy) rpd mou
1867, 5, 23. Rachel H. (form Kenworthy) rpd mou
1867, 6, 20. John F. rpd mou
1867, 6, 20. Marmaduke rpd mou
1868, 8, 20. Jonathan & ch, Alvan, Enoch E., Albert, Elvira Elizabeth, Mary Emma, William P. Esther Ann & Phebe Lillian, rocf Chester MM, dtd 1868,7,23
1868, 11, 26. Eli & fam gct White Water MM,Ind.
1868, 11, 26. Laura Ann (form Davis) rpd mou
1869, 4, 22. Enoch rpd mou
1870, 3, 24. Elizabeth M. & ch gct Cottonwood MM, Kans.
1870, 3, 24. Joseph H. rq to be rst; living at Cottonwood MM, Kans.
1870, 8, 25. Alden rpd mou
1870, 12, 22. David F. rpd mou
1871, 11, 23. Robert & Delilah, Colorado Territory, rec in mbrp
1872, 1, 25. Samuel A. rpd mou
1872, 1, 25. EstherA. & s, William C., rec in mbrp
1872, 2, 22. Lydia Ann rpd mou
1872, 3, 21. John C. rpd mou
1872, 6, 20. Mary rec in mbrp
1872, 8, 22. Jonathan rpd mou
1873, 11, 20. Rue Ann rec in mbrp
1874, 10, 22. Alven gct Spiceland MM, Ind.
1875, 5, 20. Matilda rec in mbrp
1876, 2, 2
1876, 2, 24. Alice rec in mbrp
1877, 10, 25. Jonathan E. dis disunity
1878, 3, 21. Enoch D. gct Sugar Plain MM,Ind.
1878, 3, 21. Laura A. & ch, Estella E., Edwin & Charles, gct Honey Creek MM, Ia.
1879, 3, 20. Susannah dis misconduct
1879, 10, 23. Mary Jane dis
1879, 12, 25. Sarah E. rocf Sugar Plain MM, Ind., dtd 1879,12,6
1880, 7, 22. Elijah M. & fam gct Cottonwood MM, Kans.
1880, 7, 22. David T. gct Cottonwood MM,Kans.
1882, 2, 23. Enoch E. relrq
1882, 4, 20. Ira, Jr. rec in mbrp
1882, 12, 21. Sarah E. gct Sugar Plain MM,Ind.
1883, 2, 22. Emma gct Ceasars Creek MM, Ind.
1883, 8, 23. Sylvanus gct Peace MM, Kans.
1884, 5, 22. Sarah Jane & s, Zimri, & grand s, Irvin Talbert, gct Fruitland MM, Kans.
1886, 1, 21. Ira S. glt Baptist Church, Sterling, Kans.
1888, 6, 21. Dedan & dt, Lura C., rec in mbrp
1890, 1, 23. William C. glt U. B. Church, Lewisburg, O.
1892, 12, 22. Calvin rocf Fruitland MM, Kans., dtd 1892,8,20
1893, 12, 21. Hiram relrq
1894, 8, 23. Cora & Flora B. relrq
1896, 12, 24. Thomas J.'s d rpd; treasurer of MM
1899, 11, 23. Lydia A. & ch, Hebert & Bessie L., gct White Water MM, Ind.
1900, 11, 22. John F., Rachel C. & Amy E. gct White Water MM, Ind.
1901, 8, 22. Charles W. relrq
1901, 11, 21. Elihu rec in mbrp
1905, 3, 23. Dukie E.relrq
1907, 4, 25. Bertha A. gct Dale MM, Kans.
1908, 9, 24. Benj. dropped from mbrp
1909, 8, 26. Martha Jane rec in mbrp
1909, 8, 26. Russel & Raymond, ch Clayton & Martha, rec in mbrp
1909, 11, 25. Jesse G. relrq
1913, 1, 23. Rachel gct Glen Elder MM, Kans.
1913, 2, 27. Oscar, Irvin, Tressa & Alma dropped from mbrp
1914, 3, 26. Della M. gct White Water MM,Ind.
1914, 10, 22. Grace dropped from mbrp
1917, 3, 22. Calvin & Dedan glt M. E. Ch., Gratis, O.
1921, 1, 20. Clayton S. & w, Martha J., & s, Russel A. & Raymond K. jas; dropped from mbrp
1921, 2, 24. Irma Fudge rec in mbrp
1921, 4, 21. Clarence B. relrq
1925, 11, 26. Edith & Mary jas; dropped from mbrp

SWAIN
----, --, --. Gabriel & Amy
Ch: Reading W. b 1815, 12, 27
Harriet " 1817, 8, 24
Mary T. " 1819, 12, 2
Antrim R. " 1824, 10, 14
Amy " 1828, 4, 25
Asher " 1831, 5, 11
1832, 8, 15. Asher d ae 1y 3m
----, --, --. Jonathan & Lydia
Ch: Cyrus b 1839, 8, 21
Martha " 1842, 3, 4
Mary " 1844, 5, 29
1840, 2, 6. Antrim d ae 15y 3m 23d
1842, 8, 16. Gabriel [Swaim] d ae 57y 8m 12d
1851, 10, 13. Mary d ae 7y 4m 14d

1827, 6, 2. Gabriel & w, Amy, & ch, Reading W., Harriet, Mary T. & Antrim R., rec in mbrp
1827, 7, 7. Timothy rocf New Garden MM, N.C. dtd 1827,1,27
1831, 7, 2. Jonathan rocf New Garden MM, N. C., dtd 1831,5,28
1834, 11, 15. Timothy gct Mill Creek MM, Ind.
1835, 5, 16. Reading dis disunity
1835, 5, 16. Harriet Conaroe (form Swan) con mou
1838, 11, 17. Jonathan con mou
1839, 8, 17. Lydia rst; dis by Salem MM, Ia.
1843, 7, 15. Lydia & dt, Esther, rec in mbrp
1849, 10, 20. Amy Halsey (form Swain) dis mou
1851, 4, 24. Amy Jones (form Swaim) con mou
1858, 12, 23. Jonathan & w, Lydia, & ch, Cyrus T. & Martha H., gct Milford MM,Ind.

SWANDER
1924, 11, 20. James M. & w, Frankie R., & ch, Elvin W., T. Lester & Elsie B., rocf West Branch MM, O.

SWOPE
1928, 2, 2. Rachel rec in mbrp

TABER
1883, 9, 20. Reuben R. gct Liberty MM, Ia.

TALBERT
1814, 8, 18. Job, Preble Co., O., s Thomas & Elizabeth; m at Elk Mtg, Amanda STUBBS, Preble Co., O., dt Joseph & Keziah, dec
Ch: Keziah b 1815, 10, 11
Elizabeth " 1817, 3, 4
Jesse " 1819, 3, 19
Joseph " 1821, 2, 17
William " 1823, 2, 15
Aaron " 1825, 9, 6
Eunice " 1827, 9, 2
Asa " 1829, 4, 7
Zimri " 1831, 2, 10
Enoch " 1833, 9, 7
1814, 10, 6. William, Preble Co., O., s Thomas & Elizabeth; m at Elk Mtg, Rebecca STUBBS, Butler Co., O., dt Nathan & Elizabeth
Ch: Elijah b 1815, 9, 13
Nathan " 1817, 7, 15
----, --, --. Jonathan & Esther
Ch: Mary b 1818, 7, 3
Thomas " 1819, 9, 26
Rebecca " 1821, 9, 25
Sarah " 1823, 6, 13
John " 1826, 4, 28
Isaac " 1828, 2, 20
----, --, --. Richard & Rhoda
Ch: Solomon b 1819, 2, 25
Lydia " 1821, 1, 11
Asa " 1824, 2, 12
Richard m 2nd Rachel -----
Ch: Maris b 1828, 4, 1
Elizabeth " 1830, 4, 25
Obadiah " 1832, 4, 16
Ruth " 1834, 2, 16
Susanna " 1836, 4, 10
Thomas " 1837, 9, 23
Isaiah " 1839, 11, 29
Mary " 1842, 9, 13
Sarah " 1844, 11, 19
1819, 8, 12. Mary m Newton STUBBS
1823, 1, 9. Rebecca m Azariah DENNY
1835, 9, 24. Elizabeth m Seth BEESON
1835, 9, 24. Keziah m Job SMITH
1837, 1, 26. Elijah, Preble Co., O., s William, dec, & Rebecca; m at Elk Mtg, Mary H. PRAY, Fayette Co., Pa., dt Wm., dec, & Mary
1839, 8, 22. Solomon, Preble Co., O., s Richard & Rhoda, dec; m at Elk Mtg, Helah BLANCHARD, dt Noah & Ruth, both dec
Ch: Elvira b 1840, 6, 15
Rhoda " 1842, 2, 23
Lindley " 1848, 10, 20
Samuel " 1851, 1, 30
William " 1853, 3, 6
Emeline " 1855, 2, 25
Sarah Ellen" 1859, 3, 5
Mary S. " 1860, 12, 28
Enos " 1857, 6, 27
1841, 8, 18. Thomas d ae 71y 8m 20d
1841, 10, 21. Elizabeth d ae 80y 5m 17d
1843, 3, 11. Susannah d ae 7y 1m 1d
1843, 3, 16. Elvira d ae 2y 9m 29d
1843, 3, 20. Rhoda d ae 1y 27d
1846, 2, 19. Maris d ae 17y 10m 18d
1847, 3, 22. Sarah d ae 2y 4m 3d
1847, 9, 23. Asa, Preble Co., O., s Richard & Rhoda, dec, b 1824,2,12; m at Elk Mtg, Sarah TOWNSEND, Wayne Co., Ind., dt Wm. & Elizabeth, dec
Ch: Melissa Jane b 1850, 2, 4; m Enoch STUBBS
Mary Eveline " 1852, 11, 12
1855, 8, 4. Sarah d ae 35y 11d
1858, 11, 3. Enos d ae 1y 4m 6d

TALBERT, continued
1866, 9, 13. Isaiah, s Richard & Rachel, b 1839,11,29; m Durinda -----, dt Caleb & Anna, b 1843,2,6
Ch: Burgess
Dewitt b 1867, 8, 25
Flora
Zella E. " 1869, 7, 14
Charles T. " 1871, 7, 22
Sarah Anna " 1874, 7, 2
Edith
Lee " 1881, 11, 5
Clara
Mary
Margaret
Florazelle
1872, 10, 31. Elvira d ae 50y 4m 26d
----, --, --. William & Elizabeth Ann
Ch: Ervin M. b 1875, 10, 2
1874, 5, 12. Richard d ae 81y 6m 21d
1877, 4, 14. Elizabeth Ann d ae 20y 2m 7d
1884, 4, 17. Solomon d ae 61y 3m 19d
1889, 11, 17. Rachel d ae 88y 3m 3d
1892, 5, 24. Helah d ae 72y 6m 4d

1810, 1, 6. Thomas appointed clerk
1810, 1, 6. William appointed recorder of m cert, b & d
1810, 6, 18. Elizabeth co
1814, 8, 6. William & fam gct White Water MM
1818, 2, 7. Richard gct Silver Creek MM, to m
1818, 12, 5. Richard gct Silver Creek MM
1819, 1, 2. Jonathan con mou
1819, 1, 2. Esther (form Hart) con mou
1824, 12, 4. Thomas [Talbot] & w, Elizabeth, gct Silver Creek MM, Ind.
1825, 10, 1. Thomas & w, Elizabeth, rocf Silver Creek MM, Ind., dtd 1825,9,24
1826, 5, 6. Paris, Anderson & Joseph rocf Center MM, N. C., dtd 1825,12,7
1826, 9, 2. Jesse Jr. rocf Silver Creek MM, dtd 1826,8,26
1828, 2, 2. Jesse & w, Margaret, rocf Silver Creek MM, dtd 1828,1,26
1829, 6, 6. Jesse & w, Margaret, gct Silver Creek MM
1830, 6, 5. Jesse Jr. & fam gct Silver Creek [MM
1830, 6, 5. Richard & w, Rachel, & ch, Solomon, Lydia, Asia, Maris & Elizabeth, rocf Silver Creek MM, dtd 1831,6,25
1833, 2, 16. Anderson dis disunity
1835, 1, 17. Margaret & Charity dis disunity
1836, 1, 16. Jonathan & w, Esther, & ch, Mary, Thomas, Rebecca, Sarah, John, Isaac, Rhoda & Elizabeth, gct Walnut Ridge MM, Ind.
1836, 6, 18. Paris gct Salem MM, Ind.
1836, 7, 16. Rahab & s, Joseph A., gct Walnut Ridge MM, Ind.
1837, 11, 18. Job & w, Amanda, & ch, Jesse, Joseph, William, Aaron, Eunice, Asa, Enoch & Patience, gct Westfield MM, Ind.
1838, 5, 19. Nathan dis disunity
1838, 6, 16. Sarah Ann (form Cooper) con mou
1839, 3, 16. Elijah & w, Mary H., & dt, Rebecca, gct Westfield MM, Ind.
1843, 10, 21. Sarah Ann Brown (form Talbert) dis mou
1844, 2, 17. Helah dis jas
1844, 2, 17. Solomon dis joining Separatists
1844, 8, 17. Lydia dis joining Separatists
1847, 2, 20. Aaron V. com by Westfield MM, Ind. for mou & joining Separatists
1852, 8, 26. Helah rst
1854, 9, 21. Ruth Benson (form Talbert) con mou; living at Cherry Grove MM
1854, 12, 21. Elizabeth Arnott (form Talbert) con mou; living at New Garden MM, Ind.
1857, 8, 20. Asa gct Chester MM, Ind., to m Elvira Townsend
1858, 3, 25. Rebecca (form Roberts) dis mou
1858, 7, 22. Obediah dis mou
1858, 8, 26. Elvira rocf Chester MM, Ind., ddtd 1858,7,22
1863, 11, 26. Solomon & ch, Lindley, Samuel, William, Emmeline, Sarah Ellen & Mary, rst
1864, 5, 26. Rebecca & three ch rec in mbrp
1867, 9, 26. Rebecca & fam gct Pleasant Hill MM, Ind.
1868, 3, 26. Isiah rpd mou
1872, 1, 25. Samuel rpd mou
1874, 11, 26. Rachel & Mary gct New Garden MM, Ind.
1875, 4, 22. William [Tolbert] rpd mou
1876, 2, 24. Lydia Ellen rec in mbrp
1877, 8, 23. Rachel rocf New Garden MM, Ind., dtd 1877,7,21
1878, 3, 21. Lindley gct Indianapolis MM,Ind.
1884, 5, 22. Sarah Jane Stubbs & s, Zimri, & grand s, Irvin Talbert, gct Fruitland MM, Kans.
1884, 7, 24. Samuel & w, Lydia Ellen, & ch, Jesse, Indianora, Melva E. & Earnest L., gct White Water MM, Ind.
1884, 7, 24. Thomas gct Minneapolis MM, Minn.
1889, 5, 23. Thomas dropped from mbrp
1893, 6, 22. Dorinda & s, Lee R., rec in mbrp
1893, 9, 21. Anna & Edith relrq
1894, 4, 26. Zell E. glt M. E. Church, Camden O.
1899, 9, 21. Clara May, Mary Esther & Margaret, ch Isiah & Durinda, rec in mbrp
1899, 9, 21. Z. E. rocf North Denver MM,Colo.
1908, 5, 21. Emma relrq
1913, 4, 24. Chastine rec in mbrp
1921, 2, 24. Catherine Drake rec in mbrp
1922, 7, 20. Corwin, s Lee R. & Catherine, rec in mbrp
1922, 12, 21. Zell E. relrq

TAYLOR
----, --, --. Isaac & Rebecca
Ch: William b 1822, 7, 5
Lewis " 1824, 8, 1
Mary " 1830, 10, 24

TAYLOR, Isaac & Rebecca, continued
Ch: Hannah b 1833, 4, 14
Thomas " 1836, 9, 17
----, --, --. David & Martha
Ch: John C. b 1825, 10, 24
Beulah Ann " 1830, 7, 24
Isaac " 1834, 12, 23
Enoch " 1837, 1, 26
William Stubbs " 1839, 11, 6
----, --, --. Aaron & Margaret
Ch: Joel C. b 1827, 4, 28
Mary Ann " 1829, 10, 10
Caleb W. " 1836, 3, 3
Henry " 1840, 6, 30
Elizabeth " 1845, 4, 19
John A. " 1847, 9, 19
James Albert " 1850, 6, 21
----, --, --. Clayton & Abigail
Ch: Amos b 1836, 9, 16
David " 1838, 11, 14
Isaac " 1841, 9, 1
Hannah J. " 1846, 5, 26
Mary Ellen " 1849, 4, 30
Harriet Eliza " 1854, 8, 4
1834, 1, 23. Mary m Thomas EDGERTON
1838, 5, 19. Isaac d ae 3y 4m 27d
1844, 12, 26. William, Preble Co., O., s Isaac & Rebecca; m at Elk Mtg, Martha LAMM, Preble Co., O., dt John & Elizabeth
Ch: John b 1845, 10, 14
Henry L. " 1847, 8, 2
Silas " 1849, 3, 22
Alpheus " 1852, 10, 20
Lewis " 1854, 9, 17
1845, 2, 20. Lewis, s Isaac & Rebecca, b 1824,8,1; m at Elk Mtg, Martha Ann STUBBS, dt Nathan & Ann, b 1826,10,6
Ch: Nathan S. b 1845, 12, 13; m Lida FRANER
Isaac Lindley " 1847, 6, 13; m Angelina DAVIS
Alvin " 1848, 10, 3; m Laura STAGGS
Angeline " 1850, 8, 26; m George M. HUNT
Rebecca " 1855, 7, 4; m 1877,12, 13 William M. DAVIS
Zimri b 1857, 1, 22; m Jennie GIFFORD
1845, 4, 30. Elizabeth d
1847, 4, 22. Beulah Ann m Elijah M. STUBBS
1856, 6, 24. Aaron d ae 53y 9m
1856, 11, 29. Clayton d ae 49y 1d
----, --, --. John C. & Beulah
Ch: William E. b 1858, 12, 23
Mattie V. " 1862, 4, 10
Mary Annie " 1867, 3, 31
Charles A. " 1873, 2, 16
1860, 8, 2. Enoch R., s David & Martha, b 1837,1,26; m Mary Elizabeth VANSHIVER, dt William & Sarah
Ch: Theodore M. b 1861, 8, 10
Susan V. " 1865, 3, 29; m Charles LINE
Martin " 1872, 1, 12
Clara Bell " 1873, 5, 28
Ida " 1874, 5, 8
Enoch R. m 2nd Carrie A. -----
Ch: David Walton b 1879, 1, 2
Oliver E. " 1882, 1, 6
Alonzo A. " 1883, 9, 24
Wesley Allen b 1885, 10, 10
----, --, --. William S. & Agnes Lorane
Ch: Emma P. b 1861, 12, 28
Mary E. " 1864, 10, 10
Ira S. " 1869, 9, 26
Clara Bell " 1872, 5, 27
Viola M. " 1877, 10, 4
----, --, --. Isaac L. m Angelina DAVIS
Ch: Charles Emmot b 1868, 6, 15
Loretha May " 1870, 2, 4
Milton S. " 1873, 10, 27
Anna B. " 1875, 1, 6
Rebecca E. " 1878, 1, 25
Sarah " 1880, 11, 9
----, --, --. Nathan S., s Lewis & Martha A., b 1845,12,13; m Lida FRANER
Ch: Orpheus b 1870, 9, 30
Flora Ellen b 1871, 11, 1
Olive M. " 1875, 10, 8
1872, 6, 15. Margaret d ae 64y 2m
1872, 8, 24. Lydia d ae 39y 4m 6d
1873, 10, 10. Rebecca d ae 77y 8m
----, --, --. Frank & Belle
Ch: Maude b 1874, 3, 13
Lewis A. " 1876, 4, 13
1874, 1, 18. John A. d ae 26y 3m 29d
1874, 3, 21. David d ae 75y 1d
1876, 2, 6. Mary E. d ae 34y 3m 18d
1881, 4, 23. Mary E. d ae 16y 6m 13d
1884, 8, 16. Sarah d ae 78y 9m 18d
1888, 5, 13. Isaac d ae 90y 11m 26d
1889, 10, 15. Alvan d ae 41y 12d
1891, --, --. Laura A. d
----, --, --. Israel & Lydia
Ch: Susan E. m George W. RIVER
Sarah J. m ----- CLARK

1833, 10, 19. Mary rocf Silver Creek MM, Ind., dtd 1833,9,28
1834, 3, 15. William rocf Salem MM, Ind., dtd 1834,1,25
1835, 2, 21. Susanna rocf Salem MM, dtd 1835,1,24
1835, 5, 16. John rocf Salem MM, dtd 1835,4,25
1835, 5, 16. Sarah con mou
1835, 11, 21. Isaac & w, Rebecca, & ch, Wil-

TAYLOR, continued
liam, Lewis & Hannah, rec in mbrp
1836, 5, 21. Abigail (form Way) con mou
1836, 7, 16. David & w, Martha, & ch, John, Beulah Ann & Isaac, rec in mbrp
1836, 11, 19. Susanna gct Salem MM, Ind.
1841, 6, 19. Aaron & w, Margaret, & ch, Joel, Mary Ann, Caleb & Henry, rec in mbrp
1844, 7, 20. John gct New Garden MM, Ind.
1845, 2, 15. William dis disunity
1850, 2, 21. Joel con mou
1852, 6, 24. Joel C. dis
1852, 7, 22. Hannah Green (form Taylor) dis mou
1852, 10, 21. Clayton & ch, Amos, David, Isaac, Hannah J. & Mary Ellen, rec in mbrp
1853, 5, 26. Lydia L. (form Stanley) con mou
1854, 11, 23. Mary Ann Van Trump (form Taylor) dis mou
1856, 4, 24. William & w, Martha L., & ch, John, Henry L., Silas, Alpheus & Lewis, gct Cedar Creek MM
1858, 7, 22. John C. dis mou
1861, 1, 24. Enoch R. con mou
1861, 1, 24. William S. con mou
1861, 5, 23. Thomas dis disunity
1864, 11, 24. Abigail & dt, Hannah, Mary Ellen & Harriet, gct Salem MM, Ia.
1866, 12, 8. Caleb W. con mou
1868, 8, 20. Angeline (form Davis) con mou
1868, 12, 24. Isaac L. rst
1870, 6, 23. William S. rpd mou
1870, 10, 20. Alvin rpd mou
1870, 11, 24. Isaac L. & w, Angelina D., & fam gct Honey Creek MM, Ia.
1871, 4, 20. Nathan S. rpd mou
1871, 7, 20. John C. & w, Beulah W., & ch, William Elwood, Martha Viretta & Mary Anna, rec in mbrp
1871, 11, 23. Martha Ann, Colorado Territory, rec in mbrp
1872, 2, 22. Angelina T. Hunt (form Taylor) rpd mou
1874, 6, 25. William S. & ch, Ira S. & Clara Bell, gct Indianapolis MM, Ind.; cert failed to arrive
1875, 2, 25. Caleb W. relrq
1875, 7, 22. Agnes L. & step dt, Emmaretta & Mary Eva rec in mbrp
1875, 8, 26. Mary E. & s rec in mbrp
1878, 4, 25. Amos & David gct Lynn Grove MM, Ia.
1878, 4, 25. Calvin W. rec in mbrp
1878, 5, 23. Joel C. rec in mbrp
1878, 7, 25. Isaac L. & fam rocf Rocksylvania MM, Ia., dtd 1878,7,18
1878, 10, 3. Carrie A. rocf Goshen MM, O., dtd 1878,8,24
1881, 8, 25. Mattie V. dis
1882, 3, 23. William S. & fam gct Missisinawa MM, Ind.
1883, 3, 22. John C. & w, Beulah W., & ch, Mary Annie & Charles A., gct White Water MM, Ind.
1883, 5, 24. William E. gct White Water MM Ind.
1884, 11, 20. Calvin H. relrq
1884, 12, 25. Joel C. relrq
1886, 12, 23. Laura M. gct White Water MM,Ind.
1888, 8, 20. Calvin H. & w, Laura M., rocf White Water MM, Ind.
1889, 10, 24. Mary E. relrq
1892, 4, 21. Calvin dis
1893, 4, 20. Lewis A. rec in mbrp
1893, 4, 20. Maud rec in mbrp
1894, 1, 25. Isaac L. & w, Lena D., & ch, Milton S., Anna B., Rebecca E., Sarah F., Laura B., Melva A. & Mary F., gct Long Hollow MM, Mo.
1894, 1, 25. Lauretta M. gct Long Hollow MM, Mo.
1897, 11, 25. Enoch R. & fam gct Goshen MM, O.
1894, 3, 22. Theodore M. & Martin M. glt M. E. Church, Mitchell, Kans.
1898, 8, 25. Lewis A. gct White Water MM,Ind.
1903, 1, 22. Mary Frances rec in mbrp
1903, 9, 24. Maud gct Spiceland MM, Ind.
1906, 6, 21. Maude rocf Spiceland MM
1913, 1, 22. Orpheus dropped from mbrp
1914, 1, 22. Nathan S. relrq
1916, 4, 20. Maud gct West Richmond MM, Ind.

TEAGUE
1838, 12, 15. Delilah (form Randal) dis mou

TEAS
----, --, --. Thomas & Sarah
Ch: John
Carter b 1827, 11, 12
Edward " 1830, 3, 8
1840, 3, 26. Stephen W., Preble Co., Ind., s Charles & Mary, both dec; m at Elk Mtg, Anna BROWN, dt Richard, dec, & Mary
Ch: Phebe
Ann b 1841, 1, 2
Joseph L. " 1849, 11, 14
Stephen W. m 2nd Susannah -----
Ch: William b 1853, 8, 31

1840, 2, 15. Stephen W. rocf Chester MM, Ind., dtd 1839,11,21
1843, 12, 16. Stephen W. dis joining Separatists
1844, 2, 17. Anne dis jas
1852, 6, 24. Stephen W. rst
1852, 8, 26. Stephen W. gct New Garden MM, to m Susannah Huff
1853, 1, 20. Susannah rocf New Garden MM, Ind., dtd 1852,11,20
1853, 5, 26. Joseph L., s Stephen W., rec in mbrp
1854, 10, 26. Stephen & w, Susanna, & ch, Phebe Ann, Joseph L. & William, gct New Garden MM

TELLIS
1922, 3, 23. Ruth rec in mbrp

TERRILL
1850, 11, 22. Amos H. [Terril], Jefferson Co., O., s Matthew & Elizabeth, dec; m at Elk Mtg, Mary T. HUTCHIN, Preble Co., O., dt Joel G. & Rachel H.

1850, 11, 21. Amos H. prcf Short Creek MM, O., dtd 1850,8,20, to m
1851, 12, 25. Amos H. rocf Short Creek MM, O., dtd 1851,9,23
1853, 7, 21. Amos H. [Terrell] & w, Mary, & s, Joel Albert, gct Richland MM, Ind.
1894, 4, 26. Amos H. & Mary T. [Terrell] glt 2nd Congregational Church, Colorado Springs

TERRY
1897, 12, 23. Julia A. gct Cincinnati MM, O.

THOMAS
1812, 2, 1. Lewis rocf Piney Grove MM, N.C., dtd 1811,5,10
1913, 4, 24. Marjorie E. rec in mbrp
1915, 11, 25. Maude rec in mbrp

THOMPSON
----, --, --. Robert b 1782,5,19; m Nancy ----- b 1787,10,--
Ch: Mary b 1809, 10, 8
Samuel " 1811, 6, 13
Sarah " 1813, 10, 26
Ruth " 1816, 1, 12
William " 1820, 7, 7
Edna " 1822, 12, 6
John " 1825, 2, 17

1817, 10, 4. Jonah [Thomson] rec in mbrp
1817, 12, 6. Susannah rec in mbrp
1822, 2, 2. Joseph & fam gct Honey Creek MM, Ind.
1824, 4, 3. Jonah dis mou
1834, 12, 20. Sarah Jones (form Thompson) dis mou
1835, 7, 18. Ruth Jones (form Thompson) dis disunity & mou
1915, 11, 25. Raymond & w, Grace, & ch, Charles & Marie, rec in mbrp

THORN
1813, 2, 25. Catherine m Nathan BALLARD

1813, 2, 6. Nathan prcf Miami MM, to m Catherine Thorn (Nathan Ballard)

THORPE
1923, 1, 25. Margaret Talbert gct Detroit MM, Mich.

TOWNSEND
1827, 3, 8. John, Preble Co., O., s John & Elvira; m at Elk Mtg, Martha JONES, Butler Co., O., dt George & Lydia
1847, 9, 23. Sarah m Asa TALBERT
1856, 2, 28. Lydia Townsend m Abijah MOFFITT
1854, 6, 21. Eliza Ann d ae 26y 5m 13d
1870, 3, 11. Elvira d ae 102y 1d

1810, 6, 2. Dinah Creek Moore (form Townsend) dis mou
1813, 9, 4. Ruth Murphy (form Townsend) dis mou
1813, 9, 4. Mary dis jas
1826, 6, 3. John rocf White Water MM, Ind., dtd 1826,5,20
1834, 10, 18. Martha & ch, William H., James, George J. & Elvira C., gct Mississinaway MM, Ind. (rem within limits of Mich. Territory)
1835, 7, 18. John gct Mississinawa MM, Ind.
1846, 2, 21. Sarah rocf West Grove MM, Ind., dtd 1846,1,10
1848, 4, 15. Charlotte Hunt (form Townsend) con mou; mbr West Grove MM
1849, 8, 18. Lydia & Elisa Ann rocf West Grove MM, Ind., dtd 1849,7,14
1856, 2, 21. Abijah Moffitt prcf White Water MM, to m Lydia Townsend

TRINE
1885, 6, 15. David B. d

1876, 3, 23. David [Tryian] rec in mbrp

VAIL
1824, 11, 11. Aaron [Vaile], Butler Co., O.; m at Elk Mtg, Eleanor ARMITAGE Butler Co., O.

1829, 1, 3. Aaron [Vale] dis disunity
1831, 2, 5. Eleanor dis joining Separatists
1832, 5, 9. Aaron & w, Eleanor, & ch, Mary, Samuel & Aaron, gct Springborough MM

VANSCHUYVER
----, --, --. William, s Walter & Rebecca, b 1758,1,1; m Elizabeth ADAMS, dt Bartholomew & Mary, b 1771,10,15
Ch: Samuel b 1805, 2, 17
Martha " 1808, 10, 26
William " 1814, 4, 5
1828, 3, 11. John B., s Samuel & Eliza, b

1837, 8, 19. William Jr. dis disunity

VAN TRUMP
1854, 11, 23. Mary Ann (form Taylor) dis mou

VICKERS
1830, 6, 5. Isaac M. & w, Abigail, & ch, Edwin, Samuel N., William & Thomas, rocf Fairfield MM, dtd 1827,6,30
1831, 9, 3. Isaac M. dis joining Separatists

VICKERS, continued
1831, 10, 1. Abigail dis joining Separatists
1833, 12, 21. Edwin, Nixon & Thomas, ch Isaac M., gct White Water MM, Ind.
1835, 10, 8. Cert rec for Isaac M. & w, Abigail, & ch, Edwin, Samuel Nixon, William & Thomas, from Fairfield MM, dtd 1827,6,30, endorsed to White Water MM

VINAGE
1871, 3, 23. Eunice (form Haisly) rpd mou; dropped from mbrp; Pipe Creek MM, Ind., to be notified

WALKER
----, --, --. Samuel m Julia Ann BLOSSOM, dt Perry & Keziah, b 1842,10,24

1887, 2, 24. Julia rec in mbrp

WARRINGTON
1822, 11, 2. Elizabeth rocf Mount Holly MM, dtd 1822,6,6
1830, 8, 7. Elizabeth Conaroe (form Warington) con mou

WAY
1830, 2, 8. Anthony, Randolph Co., Ind., s Nathan & Huldah; m at Elk Mtg, Rhoda LANE, Preble Co., O., dt Jesse & Hannah

1830, 2, 6. Anthony prcf Cherry Grove MM, to m Rhoda Lane
1830, 4, 3. Rhoda gct Cherry Grove MM
1834, 1, 18. Abigail rocf Cherry Grove MM, Ind., dtd 1833,12,14
1836, 5, 21. Abigail Taylor (form Way) con mou

WEST
1901, 12, 26. William & w, Mary, rocf White Water MM, Ind., dtd 1901,11,28
1903, 11, 26. William & w, Mary, gct Back Creek MM, Ind.

WHEELER
1851, 6, 21. Elizabeth d ae 32y 2m 24d

1838, 6, 16. Elizabeth (form Stubbs) con mou
1854, 4, 20. Mary P. (form Stanly) con mou
1855, 4, 26. Mary P. gct White Water MM, Ind.
1855, 10, 25. Mary P. rocf White Water MM

WHITACRE
1823, 11, 6. John, Wayne Co., Ind., s Samuel & Mary; m at Elk Mtg, Bethula ROBERDS, Butler Co., O., dt Jonathan & Mary, dec

1826, 3, 4. John rocf White Water MM, dtd 1825,10,15
1826, 12, 2. John & fam gct White Water MM
1828, 11, 1. John & w, Bethuly, & ch, Ephraim & Christopher, rocf White Water MM, dtd 1828,9,24
1829, 11, 7. John & fam gct New Garden MM, Ind.
1843, 10, 19. Cert rec for John, h Bethula, from West Grove MM, Ind., dtd 1843,7,8, endorsed to Salem MM, Ia.
1843, 10, 19. Cert rec for Bethula & ch, Christopher, Susanna, Mary, Martha, Calvin & Rachel, from West Grove MM, Ind., dtd 1843,1,4, endorsed to Salem MM, Ia.
1843, 10, 19. West Grove MM rq this mtg to offer Ephraim a copy of their testimony of dis; returned with information that he was not a resident within our limits

WHITSON
1810, 6, 18. Rebekah co
1811, 7, 2. Willis & fam gct White Water MM
1813, 4, 3. John rpd mou; Caesars Creek MM informed that he did not con misconduct

WICKERSHAM
1814, 1, 1. Caleb & fam rocf Deep Creek MM, N. C., dtd 1813,9,6

WILEY
----, --, --. Isaac [Wily], s Vincent J. & Margaret, b 1785,3,4; m Sarah WORRELL, dt George & Deborah, b 1788,10,2

Ch:				
Deborah	b	1810,	1,	16
Ann Wright	"	1814,	2,	3
Thomas	"	1818,	1,	31
George	"	1820,	4,	16
Hannah	"	1822,	10,	19
Isaac	"	1825,	8,	26
Elizabeth	"	1826,	10,	20

1820, 6, 3. Isaac & w, Sarah, & ch, Deborah, Ann Wright & Thomas, roc
1837, 8, 19. Ann Brown (form Wiley) dis mou

WILLIAMS
1814, 9, 3. Azariah & w, Sarah, & ch, Charles, Jonathan, David, Alexander, Azariah, Deborah & Nancy, rocf Lost Creek MM, Tenn., dtd 1814,3,26
1817, 1, 7. Azariah & fam gct New Garden MM
1884, 7, 24. Emmaretta gct Goshen MM, O.

WILLITS
1821, 10, 6. Phebe rocf Exeter MM, Pa., dtd 1821,7,25
1832, 10, 10. William Hayward, Jr. gct Green Plain MM, to m Mildred Keane Willits (H)

WILSON
1822, 6, 1. John rpd mou
1822, 6, 1. Hannah Cregg (form Wilson) dis mou
1822, 6, 1. Jane Fox (form Wilson) dis mou
1822, 7, 6. Darcon & William Jr. dis disunity
1822, 8, 3. William dis disunity

WILTSE
----, --, --. Simeon b 1763,7,10; m Elizabeth ----- b 1781,4,30
Ch: Henry b 1806, 2, 28
Simeon " 1808, 9, 10
William " 1811, 5, 11
John C. " 1813, 10, 12
Martin " 1816, 2, 2
George " 1818, 6, 26
Elizabeth " 1820, 12, 19

1818, 7, 4. Simeon & w, Elizabeth, & ch, Henry, Simeon, William, John C. & Martin, rocf Evesham MM, N. J., dtd 1817,6,9, endorsed by Miami MM
1828, 6, 7. Henry [Wilsey] rocf Westfield MM, dtd 1828,4,30
1829, 10, 3. Henry [Wilsee] dis joining Separatists
1830, 8, 11. Henry gct Westfield MM (H)
1831, 4, 2. Lydia [Wilsey] (form Cooper) dis mou; living at Westfield MM
1833, 12, 21. Simeon Jr. & w, Rachel, gct Duck Creek MM, Ind.
1834, 4, 18. Simeon [Wiltse] & w, Elizabeth, & ch, John C., Martin, George & Elizabeth, gct Duck Creek MM, Ind.
1834, 7, 19. William gct Duck Creek MM
1837, 6, 17. Ann W. Brown (form Willsey) dis mou
1838, 11, 8. Henry [Wilsey] rocf Westfield MM, dtd 1838,5,30 (H)

WOLLAM
1878, 8, 27. Hiram, s Alfred & Nancy, b 1849, 11,1; m Emma SMITH, dt Andrew J. & Margaret, b 1858,6,28
Ch: Edgar A. b 1879, 9, 22
Arthur James " 1883, 1, 23
Roy Hiram " 1885, 4, 6
Ruby " 1885, 4, 6

1898, 1, 20. Hiram S. & fam rocf Friends Chapel MM, O., dtd 1897,12,25
1902, 2, 20. Hiram S. & w, Emma, & ch, Arthur J., Roy H. & Ruby F., gct Smithfield MM, O.
1904, 10, 20. Edgar A. gct Tecumseh MM, Mich.
1908, 4, 23. Clara M. gct Tecumseh MM, Mich.

WOOD
1835, 3, 21. Eli Maddock gct New Garden MM, Ind., to m Absillit Wood

WOODRUFF
1925, 3, 26. Marvin rec in mbrp
1829, 3, 21. Alice Irene rec in mbrp

WOOLMAN
1839, 11, 16. Sarah Ann Silvers (form Woolman) dis mou & jH

WOOTEN
----, --, --. Lewis & Martha [Wooton]
Ch: Thomas b 1820, 7, 28
Joel " 1822, 7, 6
James " 1824, 3, 22
Andrew " 1826, 3, 18
Mary Jane " 1828, 3, 25
Henry " 1830, 7, 11
Abijah " 1833, 2, 28
William S. " 1835, 5, 12
Isom P. " 1836, 9, 4
Daniel " 1839, 4, 8

1833, 7, 20. Lewis [Oten] & w, Martha, & ch, Thomas, Joel, James, Andrew, Mary Jane, Henry & Abijah, rocf White River MM, Ind. Lewis' cert dtd 1833,6,17; Martha & ch's cert dtd 1833,5,20
1837, 4, 15. Lewis & w, Martha, & ch, Thomas, Joel, James, Andrew, Mary Jane, Henry, Abijah, William & Isham, gct White River MM, Ind.
1838, 11, 17. Lewis [Woten] & w, Martha, & ch, Thomas, Joel, James, Andrew, Mary Jane, Henry, Abijah, William & Isam, rocf White River MM, Ind., dtd 1838,9,8
1842, 2, 19. Lewis & w, Martha, & ch, Andrew, Mary Jane, Henry, Abijah, William, Isham & Daniel, gct Sparrow Creek MM,Ind.
1842, 11, 19. Joel [Woton] gct Sparrow Creek MM, Ind.
1845, 9, 20. Sparrow Creek MM, Ind. informed this mtg that Thomas [Woton] did not make satisfaction for disunity
1846, 5, 15. James [Wooton] dis jas

WORRALL
1821, 7, 11. Deborah m Abraham BROWN

1821, 5, 5. Deborah Jr. rocf Exeter MM, Pa., dtd 1820,11,29

WRIGHT
1839, 4, 25. Isaac, Preble Co., O., s John & Margaret; m at Elk Mtg, Elizabeth BEESON, Preble Co., O., dt William, dec
1843, 9, 21. John, Preble Co., O., s Isaac & Esther, dec; m at Elk Mtg, Elizabeth STUBBS, Preble Co., O., dt William & Delilah
1856, 6, 3. Elizabeth F. d ae 34y 3m 5d
1879, 10, 2. George W. d ae 30y 7m 11d

1840, 1, 18. John, Lydia, William, Thomas, James & Micajah, ch Isaac, rocf White River MM, Ind., dtd 1839,12,14
1843, 12, 16. Isaac dis disunity & joining Separatists
1843, 12, 16. Elizabeth dis disunity & jas
1848, 5, 20. William dis disunity
1849, 4, 21. Thomas dis mou
1850, 6, 20. Isaac rst
1850, 9, 26. Lydia Frost (form Wright) con

WRIGHT, continued
mou
1852, 8, 26. Elizabeth rst
1854, 8, 24. Isaac & w, Elizabeth, gct White Water MM, Ind.
1856, 12, 25. John R. gct Bloomfield MM, Ind.
1858, 4, 22. James dis mou
1858, 4, 22. Micajah dis mou
1861, 8, 22. Isaac & w, Elizabeth, rocf Bangor MM, Ia., dtd 1861,7,20
1862, 4, 24. Isaac & w, Elizabeth, gct White Water MM, Ind.
1871, 3, 23. Martha Ann (form Reynolds) rpd mou
1871, 7, 20. George F. rec in mbrp

* * * * * * *

BRANSON
1845, 4, 21. Mary m Daniel H. MOON

KENWORTHY
1830, 9, 9. Mary m David BRANSON

1883, 11, 22. Martha Ann & ch, Flora Ellen & William, relrq

YARNELL
1810, 11, 3. Hannah rocf Abington MM, Pa., dtd 1810,10,15

YOUNG
1905, 12, 21. Omer rolf U. B. Church, West Elkton, O.
1906, 2, 22. Ruby Frances rocf Hopewell MM, Ind.
1911, 3, 23. Omar H. & w, Ruby F., & s, J. Francis & Roy Dwight, gct Bellefontaine MM, O.

* * * * * * *

MADDOCK
1811, 6, 1. Nathan con mou

TOWNSEND
1857, 8, 20. Asa Talbert gct Chester MM, Ind. to m Elvira Townsend

WESTFIELD MONTHLY MEETING

Westfield Monthly Meeting, located three miles west of Camden, was set off from Elk Monthly Meeting 12 Mo. 26, 1821. This meeting was divided by the Hicksite Separation and was laid down by direction of Westfield Quarterly Meeting 11 Mo. 20, 1833.

The Westfield Monthly Meeting (Hicksite) records begin 12 Mo. 31, 1828. Charter names of Westfield Monthly Meeting were Brown, Bullezer, Starr, Stratton, Stubbs, Gause, Mendenhall, More, Edgerton and Stubbs.

RECORDS

ADAMS
1823, 2, 26. Jedediah rocf Byberry MM, Pa., dtd 1822,3,26 endorsed by Elk MM, 1822, 12,7
1824, 3, 31. William & w, Rachel, & ch, Jonathan, Jacob, Wm., Matilda, Joel & Ann, gct Springfield MM, Ind.
1828, 5, 28. Jedediah gct Green Plain MM
1829, 1, 28. Thomas & Ann dis jH
1841, 11, 24. Elizabeth rmt Israel Gause (H)
1844, 5, 22. Ruth rmt Joseph B. Woolman (H)
1846, 4, 29. Thomas & w, Ann, & s, Solomon W., gct White Water MM, Ind. (H)
1847, 3, 31. Samuel con mou (H)
1847, 10, 6. Samuel C. gct Milford MM, Ind. (H)

ALLEN
1830, 8, 25. Phillip & w, Elizabeth, & ch, Jacob & Samuel, rocf Stillwater MM, O., dtd 1830,4,17 (H)
1833, 1, 30. Philip & w, Elizabeth, & s, Samuel, gct Cincinnati MM (H)
1833, 1, 30. Jacob gct Cincinnati MM (H)

ASHBEY
1861, 7, 31. Ellen recrq (H)
1872, 8, 28. Ellen dropped from mbrp (H)

BAILEY
1835, 11, 25. Nathan rocf Elk MM, dtd 1835, 11,12

BALLINGER
1823, 2, 26. Mary Ann Mullins (form Ballenger) con mcd
1825, 11, 30. Abraham rmt Beulah Brown
1829, 1, 28. Isaac & Hannah dis jH
1829, 3, 18. Abraham & Beulah dis jH
1833, 9, 25. Isaac H. dis jH
1834, 1, 29. Isaac K. rmt Abigail Borton (H)
1838, 12, 17. Sarah H. rmt Wm. V. Brown (H)
1843, 11, 29. Isaac H. dis breech of m contract & mou (H)
1844, 12, 27. Rachel Ann rocf Evesham MM, N.J., dtd 1844,3,5 (H)
1845, 1, 29. Isaac H. con mou (H)
1845, 4, 30. Wm., s Isaac H., recrq (H)
1849, 8, 29. Hannah (form Mullin) dis mou (H)
1852, 8, 25. Isaac H. dis disunity (H)
1852, 11, 24. John con mou (H)
1853, 10, 26. John gct White Water MM, Ind.(H)
1854, 9, 27. Samuel dis mou (now in Maple Grove limits) (H)
1856, 1, 30. Elizabeth Ware (form Ballinger) con mou (H)
1856, 7, 30. Sarah Elma Henninger (form Ballinger) dis mou (H)
1859, 5, 25. Priscilla Kindley (form Ballinger) dis mou (H)
1859, 10, 5. Abraham H. dis mou
1860, 2, 29. Hannah M. Stewart (form Balinger) con mou (H)
1863, 8, 26. Hannah d ae 8y 10m 16d (a minister & mbr of this mtg) (H)
1869, 12, 29. Beulah dis jas (H)
1871, 8, 30. Mary Ann Cary (form Ballinger) dis mou (H)
1872, 2, 23. Wm. Ellis dis jas (H)
1872, 9, 25. Rachel Ann dis jas (H)
1874, 7, 29. Jane Newton (form Ballinger) dis mou (H)
1898, 10, 16. Emma & ch, Mary Olive & John Wm. Kenneth, recrq (H)
1906, 4, 15. Emma & ch, Olive & John, gl (H)

BEALL
1851, 6, 25. Sarah M. (form Moore) con mou (H)
1868, 1, 29. Mary H. con mou (H)
1896, 8, 19. Francis Asbury recrq (H)

BENINE
1831, 1, 20. Stephen Bogue gct White Water MM, Ind., to m Hannah Benine (H)
1831, 9, 28. Hannah Bogue & s, James Benine, rocf White Water MM, Ind., dtd 1831,6,22 (H)

BENSON
1833, 3, 20. Deborah (form Coles) con mcd (H)

BOGUE
1822, 7, 31. Benjamin & Joseph gct West Grove MM, Ind.
1822, 7, 31. Elizabeth & ch, Mary, Newby, Sarah, Elizabeth & Mariam, gct West Grove MM, Ind.
1822, 9, 25. Elvira rocf White Water MM, Ind., dtd 1822,7,13
1822, 11, 27. Josiah rec after being dis by Elk MM
1823, 11, 26. Elizabeth recrq
1823, 11, 26. Alfred, Charles & John, ch Josiah, recrq

1829, 9, 30. Job & w, Sarah, & ch, Margaret, Wm., Joseph, Ann & Josiah, gct Vermillion MM, Ill. (H)
1830, 1, --. Alfred rmt Keziah Stubbs (H)
1831, 1, 20. Stephen gct White Water MM, Ind., to m Hannah Benine (H)
1831, 9, 28. Hannah & s, James Benine, rocf White Water MM, Ind., dtd 1831,6,22 (H)
1831, 9, 28. Charles con mcd (H)
1833, 10, 23. Josiah & w, Elizabeth, & s, John W., gct Spiceland MM, Ind. (H)
1833, 10, 23. Alfred & w, Keziah, & dt gct Spiceland MM, Ind. (H)
1833, 10, 23. Charles gct Spiceland MM, Ind. (H)

BORDEN
1883, 11, 28. Edward gct White Water MM, Ind. (H)

BORDEN, continued
1894, 2, 28. Henrietta recrq (H)
1895, 9, 18. Gideon S. recrq (H)

BORRADAILE
1845, 6, 25. Priscilla (form Brown) rpd mou (H)
1848, 3, 29. Sarah Ann [Borradaike] con mou

BORTON
1833, 11, 27. Abigail rocf Springborough MM, dtd 1833,10,24 (H)
1834, 1, 29. Abigail rmt Isaac K. Ballinger (H)
1835, 10, 28. Jemima rocf Springborough MM, dtd 1835,8,27 (H)
1842, 3, 30. Elton rocf Evesham MM, N. J., dtd 1842,1,4 (H)
1842, 4, 25. Elton rmt Hannah Brown (H)
1843, 3, 29. Rachel rocf Evesham MM, N. J., dtd 1842,12,6 (H)
1844, 11, 27. Elton & w, Hannah, gct White Water MM, Ind. (H)

BOWEN
1860, 1, 25. Mary (form Clay) dis mou (H)

BROWN
1822, 1, 30. Isiah, John, Beulah & Priscilla, ch Clayton, recrq
1822, 2, 27. Samuel rmt Sarah Edgerton
1822, 2, 27. Priscilla & two ch recrq
1822, 8, 23. Abraham, s Samuel, recrq
1822, 9, 25. Mary & dt, Elizabeth, recrq
1823, 4, 30. Levi, Wm., John & Barkley, ch Wm., recrq
1823, 5, 28. Elizabeth recrq
1823, 6, 25. Jonathan dis mou
1824, 3, 31. Isaac & w, Tamer, & ch, Tamer, Moses, Rachel & Jacob, gct Springfield MM, Ind.
1824, 3, 31. Mary rqc for h & fam to Springfield MM, Ind.
1824, 6, 30. Abigail & dt, Mary Ann & Abigail, recrq
1824, 6, 30. Joseph & Wm., ch Joseph, recrq
1824, 10, 27. Joseph recrq on consent of Woodbury MM
1825, 10, 26. Rebecca dis
1825, 11, 30. Beulah rmt Abraham Ballinger
1826, 8, 30. Clayton Jr. gct Caesars Creek MM, O., to m Lidia Compton
1826, 12, 27. Isiah M. rmt Mary Thompson
1827, 6, 27. Elizabeth rmt Samuel Vanschuyner
1827, 6, 27. Jacob & w, Mary, gct Springfield MM, Ind.
1827, 8, 29. Benjamin gct Miami MM, O., to m Mary Ann Craig
1828, 3, 26 Mary Ann rocf Miami MM, O., dtd 1827,11,28
1829, 1, 28. Clayton, Wm., Abraham & Joseph dis jH
1829, 1, 28. Priscilla, Elizabeth, Deborah & Abigail dis jH
1829, 1, 28. John dis jH
1829, 3, 18. Isaiah, Samuel, Sarah, Mary T. & Mary dis jH
1829, 4, 29. Nathaniel M. gct Elk MM, to m Sarah Nixon (H)
1829, 10, 28. Sarah N. rocf Elk MM (H)
1829, 11, 25. Nathaniel & John Jr. dis jH
1830, 5, 26. Bathsheba dis jH
1830, 9, 29. Ann Willets (form Brown) con mcd
1831, 7, 27. Joseph C. dis mcd
1832, 3, 28. Mary U. con mcd
1832, 6, 20. Clayton & w, Sarah, rocf Cesars Creek MM, O., dtd 1832,4,26
1832, 6, 27. Bathsheba rmt Wm. L. Stratton (H)
1833, 3, 27. Isiah M. gct Springborough MM, to m Martha Ann Silver (H)
1833, 4, 24. Virgin con mcd
1833, 7, 31. Martha Ann rocf Springborough MM, dtd 1833,6,27 (H)
1833, 11, 27. Hannah rocf Elk MM, dtd 1833,11, 13 (H)
1835, 12, 30. John con mou (H)
1835, 12, 30. Phebe E. (form Silver) con mou (H)
1835, 12, 30. Joseph F. rmt Lydia D. Camp (H)
1836, 5, 25. Joseph G. rmt Ann W. Wily (H)
1838, 12, 17. Wm. V. rmt Sarah H. Ballinger (H)
1839, 9, 25. Levi con mou (H)
1840, 5, 27. Wm. dis attending places of diversion (H)
1840, 5, 27. Joseph F. dis (H)
1840, 7, 29. Mary Ann Jones (form Brown) con mou (H)
1841, 8, 25. Abigail Jr. dis attending a mou (H)
1842, 4, 25. Hannah rmt Elton Borton (H)
1844, 7, 31. Clayton dec (H)
1845, 6, 25. Priscilla Borradaile (form Brown) rpd mou (H)
1845, 12, 31. George rmt Abigail B. Sharp (H)
1847, 11, 24. Samuel B. Moore gct Miami MM, O. to m Sarah Brown (H)
1848, 12, 27. Isaiah M. & w, Martha Ann, & ch, Nehemiah, Charles & Leatitia L., gct White Water MM, Ind. (H)
1849, 3, 28. Barclay rmt Sarah Mullin (H)
1854, 3, 29. John Jr. & w, Phebe, & ch, Priscilla M., Oliver, Beulah G., Clayton, Martha Ann, Emeline, Mary Elizabeth, Isaiah & Hannah L., gct White Water MM, Ind. (H)
1859, 12, 28. John M. dis joining secret society & attending diversions (H)
1860, 4, 25. Horatio Franklin dis mou (H)
1860, 11, 28. Abigail gct Maple Grove MM, Ind. (H)
1861, 4, 24. Albert Eli gct Maple Grove MM, Ind. (H)
1862, 11, 26. David M. dis mou (H)
1862, 12, 31. Mary E. Cline (form Brown) dis

BROWN, continued
mou (H)
1867, 10, 30. George & w, Abigail, & ch, Wm. Oscar, Jemima E., Abraham & Phebe Ann, gct Maple Grove MM, Ind. (H)
1868, 5, 27. Mary M. (form Stratton) con mou (H)
1868, 8, 24. Isaac H. con mou (H)
1875, 7, 28. Hannah Ann Dillman (form Brown) dis mou (H)
1879, 5, 28. Isaac W. relrq (H)
1888, 2, 29. Sarah dec (H)
1894, 7, 25. Nathaniel M. dec (H)
1899, 8, 13. Abraham H. & Susan S. rocf Benjaminville MM, Ill. (H)
1908, 4, 19. Wilbur recrq (H)
1910, 4, 17. Sarah J. recrq (H)

BURSON
1823, 11, 26. Mary recrq

CALDWELL
1829, 5, 27. James gct Milford MM, Ind.

CAMP
1845, 10, 28. Eli D. dis absenting himself & joining militia (H)

CARY
1871, 8, 30. Mary Ann (form Ballinger) dis mou (H)

CLAY
1860, 1, 25. Mary Bowen (form Clay) dis mou [(H)

CLINE
1862, 12, 31. Mary E. (form Brown) dis mou(H)

COLES
1829, 10, 28. Elizabeth [Cole] & ch, Lydia Ann, Charles, Elizabeth, Sarah M., Ann Margaret & Pearson, rocf Stillwater MM, O., dtd 1829,6,27, endorsed by Elk MM 1829,9,5
1829, 10, 28. Mary & Deborah [Cole] rocf Stillwater MM, O., dtd 1829,5,23, endorsed by Elk MM 1829,9,5
1833, 9, 25. Elizabeth [Cole] & ch gct Bloomfield MM, Ind.
1833, 10, 23. Mary gct Bloomfield MM, Ind.
1833, 3, 20. Deborah Benson (form Coles) con mcd
1830, 3, 31. Charles rocf Stillwater MM, O., dtd 1830,3,31
1836, 3, 30. Charles gct Honey Creek MM

COMPTON
1826, 8, 30. Clayton Brown Jr. gct Caesars Creek MM, O., to m Lidia Compton

CONRAD
1822, 10, 30. Darby Creek MM rq this mtg to treat with James for mou
1823, 9, 24. Esther, Rachel, Ruth & Esther Jr. rocf Darby Creek MM, O., dtd 1823,4,19
1824, 3, 31. James Jr. rocf Darby Creek MM, O., dtd 1823,12,20
1825, 4, 27. Esther, Rachel & Esther Jr. gct White Lick MM, Ind.
1825, 4, 27. Cert rec for Joseph from Darby Creek MM, O., dtd 1824,1,17, endorsed to White Lick MM, Ind.
1827, 9, 26. Ruth gct Whitelick MM, Ind.

COOK
1853, 11, 30. Joseph B. Woolman gct Fall Creek MM, to m Eliza Cook (H)

COOPER
1832, 8, 22. Eli D. Gause gct Elk MM, to m Lydia Cooper

CRAIG
1827, 8, 29. Benjamin Brown gct Miami MM, O., to m Mary Ann Craig

CRESON
1841, 4, 28. Abigail M. (form Hilman) dis mou & attending places of amusement (H)

DARNELL
1857, 2, 25. Mary (form Woolman) con mou (H)

DAVIES
1825, 12, 28. Jane recrq

DAVIS
1831, 11, 30. Jane gct Vermillion MM, Ill.

DECAMP
1834, 5, 28. John M. & w, Hannah, & ch, Lydia, Eliza Ann, John A. & Wm., rocf Elk MM, dtd 1834,4,9 (H) [(H)
1834, 5, 28. Jane rocf Elk MM, dtd 1834,4,9
1835, 12, 30. Lydia rmt Joseph F. Brown (H)
1850, 1, 30. Anna Jenkins (form D'Camp) dis mou; d before served (H)
1856, 12, 31. Wm. dis mou (H)

DILLMAN
1875, 7, 28. Hannah Ann (form Brown) dis mou [(H)

DUEL
1842, 8, 31. Joshua & w, Abigail B., & ch, Rachel, Lydia B., John & Keziah, rocf Piles Grove MM, N. J., Salem Co., dtd 1842,3,29 (H)
1855, 8, 29. Phebe [Dual] gct White Water MM, Ind. (H)
1859, 10, 5. Lydia Pierce (form Duall) dis mou (H)
1866, 1, 31. Sarah [Duell] dis jas (H)

ECKLE
1864, 5, 25. Mary W. gct White Water MM, Ind.

EDGERTON
1822, 2, 27. Sarah rmt Samuel Brown
1827, 1, 21. Hannah rmt David Maxwell
1828, 10, --. Prudence rmt Jonathan D. Stratton
1832, 4, --. Wm. rmt Abigail Stratton
1833, 1, --. Rachel rmt Simeon Wiltse

EDMONDSON
1900, 5, 20. Frank & s, Charles D., rocf Maple Grove MM (H)
1908, 12, 20. Bertha & ch, Earl & Miriam, recrq (H)

ELLIOTT
1833, 3, 20. Hannah gct Duck Creek MM, Ind.(H)
1901, 8, 11. Susan S. glt M. E. Church, Greenville, O. (H)

FLITCRAFT
1849, 8, 29. Isaiah & w, Mary Ann, & ch, Eliza Ann & Pembrook, rocf Piles Grove MM, N. J., dtd 1849,6,26. Isaiah dec between time cert was granted & rec (H)
1850, 9, 25. Mary Ann rmt Arthur Sharp (H)
1858, 7, 28. Arthur Sharp & w, Mary Ann, & her ch, Eliza M. & Pembrook Flitcraft, gct Battle Creek MM, Mich. (H)

FOSTER
1845, 4, 30. Lydia (form Mullin) dis mou (H)
1859, 8, 31. Emily (form Hopkins) dis mou (H)

GABELL
1855, 1, 31. Mary Ann (form Scott) con mou (H)
1856, 1, 30. Mary Ann [Gabel] gct White Water MM, Ind. (H)

GAUSE
1823, 11, 26. Nathan dis
1833, 10, 30. Isaac & w, Sarah, & ch, John, Wm. M. & Bethsheba, rocf Elk MM, dtd 1833, 10,9
1833, 10, 30. Israel rocf Elk MM, dtd 1833,10, 9
1841, 11, 24. Israel rmt Elizabeth Adams
1845, 5, 28. Israel & w, Elizabeth, & s, Thomas, gct White Water MM, Ind.
1846, 3, 25. Isaac & w, Sarah M., & ch, Wm. M., Bathsheba, Elizabeth & Samuel, gct White Water MM, Ind.

GIBSON
1877, 8, 29. Webster rocf Goose Creek MM, Va., dtd 1877,5,17 (H)

GILLINGHAM
1866, 9, 30. Lewis rocf Alexandria MM, to m Esther Scott (H)
1868, 10, 28. Lewis rmt Esther H. Scott (H)
1869, 4, 23. Esther H. gct Woodlawn MM, Va. (H)

GOODIN
1832, 8, 22. Nathan gct Vermillion MM, Ill.

GOODWIN
1825, 8, 31. Nathan rocf Elk MM, dtd 1825,1,1

HAINES
1826, 7, 26. Hannah rocf Miami MM, O., dtd 1826,2,22

HANCOCK
1844, 2, 28. Elizabeth Smith (form Hancock) con mou (H)
1845, 8, 25. Mary Riddick (form Hancock) con mou (H)
1853, 4, 27. Bethiah gct White Water MM, Ind. (H)

HARTLEY
1903, 4, 19. Daniel N. Shoemaker gct Baltimore MM, to m Frances E. Hartley (H)

HAYWARD
1832, 3, 28. Deer Creek MM rq this mtg to treat with Jacob for mou (H)
1832, 7, 25. Thomas rocf Deer Creek MM, dtd 1831,9,15 (H)
1836, 6, 29. Thomas dis mou (H)

HENNINGER
1856, 7, 30. Sarah Elma (form Ballinger) dis mou

HIBBERD
1857, 5, 27. James M. & w, Mary, & ch, Allen, Lydia D., James Edward & Henry H., rocf Hopewell MM, Va. (H)
1860, 9, 26. Mary R. & ch, Allen, Lydia D., James Edward & Henry Homer, gct White Water MM, Ind. (H)
1861, 2, 27. James M. gct White Water MM, Ind. (H)

HIGBEE
1862, 12, 31. Ann Eliza (form Stratton) dis mou (H)

HILMAN
1825, 2, 23. Sarah recrq
1825, 10, 26. Samuel recrq
1826, 4, 26. Edmund & Samuel, ch Samuel, recrq
1826, 4, 26. Elizabeth, Abigail & Sarah, ch Sarah, recrq
1829, 1, 28. Sarah dis jH
1829, 3, 18. Samuel dis jH
1839, 9, 25. Edmond [Hillman] dis mou
1841, 4, 28. Sarah B. [Hillman] dis attending places of vain amusement
1841, 4, 28. Abigail M. Creson (form Hilman) dis mou & attending places of amusement
1841, 4, 28. Hilman, Samuel dis allowing a m in his house contrary to discipline
1841 9, 29. Sarah dis allowing her dt to m

HILMAN, continued
in home contrary to discipline

HIXON
1848, 8, 30. William dis neglect

HOLLINGSHEAD
1840, 8, 26. Amande E. rocf Springborough MM, dtd 1840,7,23 (H)
1840, 8, 26. Rachel F. rocf Springborough MM, dtd 1840,7,23 (H)
1840, 10, 28. Rachel rmt Wm. Troth (H)
1842, 4, 27. George F. rocf Cherry St. MM, Philadelphia, Pa., dtd 1842,1,19 (H)
1842, 11, 30. Andrew & w, Susana, rocf Springboro MM, dtd 1842,10,27 (H)
1848, 8, 30. Rebecca W. rocf Burlington MM, N. J., dtd 1848,7,3 (H)
1849, 7, 25. Morgan E. rocf Chester MM, N. J., dtd 1849,6,7 (H)
1863, 5, 27. Amanda E. dis jas (H)
1870, 2, 23. Franklin R. con mou (H)
1872, 7, 31. George F. & dt, Mary & Deborah, gct Benjaminville MM, Ill. (H)
1872, 7, 31. Franklin R. gct Benjaminsville MM, Ill. (H)

HOPKINS
1837, 2, 22. Mary M. & ch, Jonathan C. & Mary W., rocf Miami MM, O., dtd 1837,1,25 (H)
1840, 6, 24. Mary W. Wily (form Hopkins) con mou (H)
1845, 8, 27. Richard & w, Hannah, & ch, James W., Joseph, Emily, Ann & Horace, rocf Miami MM, O., dtd 1845,6,25 (H)
1845, 12, 30. Richard & ch, Joseph, Emily Ann & Florence gct White Water MM, Ind. (H)
1846, 10, 6. James W. gct White Water MM, Ind. (H)
1850, 4, 24. Jonathan C. gct Miami MM, O.; returned with the statement that while a minor several years ago he had joined the Mormon Society (H)
1850, 8, 28. Jonothan C. con misconduct & rst (H)
1850, 11, 27. Jonothan C. gct Miami MM, O. (H)
1855, 1, 31. Mary W. Eckel (form Hopkins) con mou (H)
1855, 8, 29. Jonothan rocf Miami MM, O., dtd 1855,7,25 (H)
1859, 2, 23. Horace rocf Miami MM, O., dtd 1858,12,22 (H)
1859, 8, 31. Emily Foster (form Hopkins) dis mou (H)
1860, 4, 25. Jonathan C. gct Miami MM, O. (H)
1860, 7, 25. Horace gct Miami MM, O. (H)

HUGHES
1825, 9, 28. James rocf Springborough MM, dtd 1825,6,30
1825, 9, 28. Phebe rocf Springborough MM, dtd 1825,8,23
1829, 10, 28. James & Phebe, ch John, gct White Water MM, Ind. (H)

HUNT
1829, 3, 18. Joseph B. rocf Chesterfield MM, N. J., dtd 1828,4,11, endorsed by Miami MM, O., 1829,2,25
1829, 3, 18. Clayton, minor, rocf Burlington MM, N. J., dtd 1828,3,11, endorsed by Miami MM, O., dtd 1829,2,25
1829, 4, 29. Ann & ch, Esther W. & Benjamin, rocf Chesterfield MM, N. J., dtd 1828,11, 4, endorsed by Miami MM, O., 1829,2,25
1830, 3, 23. Susannah B. rocf Chesterfield MM, N. J., dtd 1830,1,5
1830, 10, 29. Esther W. rocf Chesterfield MM, N. J., dtd 1830,10,3 (H)
1832, 7, 25. Esther W. dis joining Separatist
1832, 12, --. Susanna rmt Richard Pedric
1833, 4, 24. Estner W. rmt Abner S. Scott (H)
1833, 12, --. Joseph B. rmt Ann E. Gauze

HUDDLETON
1838, 2, 28. Jonathan gct Milford MM, Ind. (H)

IRVIN
1868, 12, 30. Augustus dis military service

JENKINS
1850, 1, 30. Ann (form D'Camp) dis mou; d before served (H)

JENNINGS
1867, 3, 27. Margaret C. gct Piles Grove MM, N. J. (H)
1873, 2, 26. Clarkson & w, Margaret C., & ch, Anna S. & Levi, rocf Piles Grove MM, N.J., dtd 1872,12,31 (H)
1873, 2, 26. Rachel E. rocf Piles Grove MM, N. J., dtd 1873,1,28 (H)
1883, 3, 28. Rachel relrq (H)
1902, 1, 19. Anna S. glt Christian Church, Eaton, O. (H)

JOHNSON
1827, 5, 30. Jonathan & w, Hannah, & ch, Elizabeth, John, Mary, Lydia & Hannah, rocf Elk MM, dtd 1827,4,7
1830, 11, 24. Elizabeth Mendenhall (form Johnson) con mcd
1838, 2, 28. Pleasant & w, Sarah, & ch, Silvester, Dorinda, Martha, Elwood, Elvira, Timothy, Milo & Mary Ann, gct Milford MM, Ind. (H)

JONES
1834, 2, 26. Sarah (form Thompson) dis mou (H)
1837, 12, 27. Martha (form Vanschuyver) dis mou (H)
1840, 7, 29. Mary Ann (form Brown) con mou (H)

JONES, continued
1859, 6, 29. Mary Ann gct Maple Grove MM, Ind. (H)

KENDALL
1852, 3, 31. Samuel B. Moore gct Milford MM, Ind., to m Eliza Kendall (H)

KENWORTHY
1835, 1, 28. Margaret (form Mendenhall) con mou (H)
1854, 9, 27. Peggy dis jas (H)

KINDLEY
1852, 9, 6. Margaret d (minister)

1837, 5, 31. Edward & w, Margaret, rocf Miami MM, O., dtd 1837,3,22 (H)
1837, 11, 29. Susan recrq (H)
1838, 9, 26. Enoch con mou (H)
1839, 4, 24. Enoch rocf Miami MM, O., dtd 1838,12,26 (H)
1840, 11, 25. Daniel gct Fall Creek MM, Ind., to m Susan Weeks (H)
1841, 3, 31. Susan E. rocf Fall Creek MM, Ind., dtd 1841,2,11 (H)
1856, 4, 30. Enoch & w, Susanna, & ch, Daniel, Sarah Eliza, Margaret Jane, Emily & Susan, gct Miami MM, O. (H)
1859, 5, 25. Priscilla (form Ballinger) dis mou
1859, 8, 31. Daniel Jr. dis mou by Miami MM, O. (H)
1864, 9, 28. Sarah rmt Abraham Shoemaker (H)
1887, 8, 23. Abraham Shoemaker gct White Water MM, Ind., to m Margaret Kindley (H)

LARGENT
1823, 9, 24. Elizabeth rocf Derby Creek MM, dtd 1823,4,19
1824, 1, 28. Jonathan recrq
1824, 6, 30. Jonah & Elizabeth, ch Jonathan, recrq
1825, 4, 27. Jonathan & fam gct White Lick MM, Ind.

LINTNER
1843, 11, 29. Mary (form Moore) con mou (H)

McDANIEL
1847, 6, 30. Nancy (form Thompson) dis jas (H)

McDARNELL
1858, 3, 31. Mary W. gct Fall Creek MM, Ind. (H)

MADDOCKS
1822, 8, 23. Elizabeth & Mary, dt Wm. & Hannah, recrq
1822, 9, 25. Wm. & s, Elijah, Nathan & Joseph recrq
1825, 7, 27. Wm. [Maddock] dis
1825, 10, 26. Hannah [Maddock] dis
1875, 5, 26. Stacy [Mattock] dis jas

MATLOCK
1842, 12, 28. Samuel G. rocf Chester MM, N.J., dtd 1842,11,10 (H)
1843, 3, 29. Samuel G. rmt Mary Ann Sharp (H)
1863, 8, 26. Mary Ann [Matlach] dis jas (H)
1868, 1, 29. Samuel G. dis jas (H)

MATTHEWS
1832, 11, 21. Sarah & Samuel, minor ch Joel & Hannah, rocf Springborough MM, dtd 1832,7,24, endorsed by Elk MM, 1832,9,15

MAXWELL
1827, 1, 21. David (Silver Creek MM) rmt Hannah Edgerton
1827, 4, 25. Hannah gct Silver Creek MM

MENDENHALL
1825, 12, 28. Nancy recrq
1829, 1, 28. James & Mary dis jH
1830, 11, 24. Elizabeth (form Johnson) con mcd
1831, 8, 31. Elizabeth gct Elk MM
1833, 5, 22. Marmaduke dis jas
1833, 5, 22. Nancy dis jas
1835, 1, 28. Margaret Kenworthy (form Mendenhall) con mou (H)
1839, 4, 24. James dis refusing to settle a case of difference according to discipline (H)
1839, 9, 25. Mary dis (H)
1841, 4, 28. Jacob dis military service (H)
1848, 3, 29. Marmaduke dis mou & neglect (H)
1849, 1, 31. Wm. Armfield dis mou (H)
1853, 1, 26. Sarah dis (H)
1856, 12, 31. John dis neglect (H)

MILLER
1827, 1, 31. Lytha rocf Elk MM, dtd 1826,12,2
1830, 9, 23. Scytha dis jas
1844, 11, 27. Edna (form Thompson) dis mou (H)

MOORE
1822, 2, 27. David & ch, Samuel, David Nathaniel & Mary, recrq
1829, 1, 28. David & Mary dis jH
1829, 3, 18. Seaborn & Rachel [Moor] dis jH
1833, 8, 21. Samuel dis jH
1835, 2, 25. Seaborn & w, Rachel, & ch gct White Water MM, Ind. (H)
1836, 10, 26. David Jr. dis mou (H)
1843, 11, 29. Mary Lintner (form Moore) con mou (H)
1845, 4, 30. Nathaniel dis mou (H)
1846, 10, 6. Samuel rocf White Water MM, Ind. dtd 1846,8,26, to m Elizabeth Wily (H)
1846, 10, 28. Samuel rmt Elizabeth Wily (H)
1847, 11, 24. Samuel B. gct Miami MM, O., to m Sarah Brown (H)
1847, 12, 29. Elizabeth gct White Water MM, O. (H)

MOORE, continued
1848, 4, 26. Samuel B. & ch, Mary & David, gct Miami MM, O. (H)
1848, 12, 27. Sarah W. gct Miami MM, O. (H)
1850, 2, 27. Samuel B. & ch, Sarah W., Mary B. & David C. rocf Miami MM, O., dtd 1849, 11,21 (H)
1851, 6, 25. Sarah M. Beall (form Moore) con mou (H)
1852, 3, 31. Samuel B. gct Milford MM, Ind., to m Eliza Kendall (H)
1852, 10, 27. Eliza K. rocf Milford MM, Ind. (H)
1853, 4, 27. Samuel B. & w, Eliza K., & dt, Sarah W., gct White Water MM, Ind. (H)
1860, 2, 29. James rmt Phebe Woolman (H)
1860, 12, 26. Mary Brown Simonson (form Moore) dis mou (H)
1861, 5, 29. David & Isaac W. gct Clear Creek MM, Ill. (H)
1867, 12, 25. James & ch, Edward A., Mary E. & Albert A., rocf Fall Creek MM, Ind., dtd 1867,11,14 (H)
1883, 11, 28. James & w, Phebe W., & ch, Albert A. & Rosa Alice, gct White Water MM, Ind. (H)
1883, 11, 28. Edward Andrew & Mary Elizabeth, ch James & Phebe, gct White Water MM, Ind. (H)

MOREN
1825, 11, 30. Elizabeth recrq
1829, 3, 18. Elizabeth dis jH

MORRIS
1860, 8, 29. Susanna & ch, Samuel & Elizabeth E., rocf White Water MM, Ind., dtd 1860,6,27 (H)
1860, 8, 29. Henry G. rocf White Water MM, Ind., dtd 1860,6,27 (H)

MORTON
1852, 4, 28. Hannah J. (form Vansciver) dis mou (H)
1896, 7, 15. Hannah J. rst (H)

MULLIN
1823, 2, 26. Mary Ann (form Ballenger) con mcd
1823, 2, 26. Samuel con mou
1829, 3, 18. Samuel & Mary Ann dis jH
1838, 1, 31. Springboro MM rq this mtg to treat with David for mou; dis by Springboro MM 1838,8,27 (H)
1841, 11, 24. Samuel dis (H)
1845, 4, 30. Lydia Foster (form Mullin) dis mou (H)
1849, 3, 28. Sarah rmt Barclay Brown (H)
1849, 7, 25. Abraham dis mou (H)
1849, 8, 29. Hannah Ballinger (form Mullin) dis mou (H)
1855, 2, 28. Mary Ann & ch, Joshua, Rebecca, Isaac & Beulah, gct Clear Creek MM, Ill.(H)
1857, 5, 29. Abigail Studyvin (form Mullin) dis mou (H)

NEWBURN
1829, 11, 25. David dis jH
1830, 8, 25. David con mou (H)
1831, 4, 27. Gulie Elma recrq (H)
1825, 3, 26. David [Newborn] & w, Gulie Elma, & ch, Virgin B., Warner L., Amy, George & Lydia, gct Clear Creek MM, Ill. (H)
1845, 3, 26. John B. [Newborn] gct Clear Creek MM, Ill. (H)
1855, 2, 28. David Jr. dis mou (H)

NEWTON
1874, 7, 29. Jane (form Ballinger) dis mou (H)

NIXON
1829, 4, 29. Nathaniel M. Brown gct Elk MM, to m Sarah Nixon (H)

OWEN
1869, 8, 24. Abigail H. con mou (H)

PEDRIC
1832, 12, --. Richard rmt Susanna Hunt
1833, 2, 20. Susanna gct White Water MM, Ind.

PIERCE
1859, 10, 5. Lydia (form Duall) diw mou (H)

RIDDICK
1845, 8, 25. Mary (form Hancock) con mou (H)

SANDERS
1822, 2, 27. Martha & ch, Elizabeth, Miriam, Hannah, Thomas & Joseph Wills, gct West Grove MM, Ind.
1822, 2, 27. Mary & Nancy gct West Grove MM, Ind.

SCOTT
1832, 8, 29. Abner S. rocf Elk MM, O., dtd 1832,8,8 (H)
1833, 4, 24. Abner S. rmt Esther W. Hunt (H)
1837, 5, 31. Daniel con mou (H)
1837, 8, 30. Daniel rocf Elk MM, O. (H)
1844, 2, 28. Amos rpd mou (H)
1848, 1, 26. Samuel dis neglect & attending mou (H)
1853, 11, 30. Abigail Ann rmt Joseph E. Silver (H)
1855, 1, 31. Mary Ann Gabell (form Scott) con mou (H)
1868, 10, 28. Esther H. rmt Lewis Gillingham (H)
1894, 2, 28. Walter recrq (H)
1894, 4, 25. Howard T. recrq (H)
1899, 12, 17. Lucy Wilson rol (H)

SHARP
1835, 10, 28. Jemima E. rmt Thomas Wiley (H)

SHARP, continued
1836, 2, 24. Haines & w, Jemima, & ch, Mary Ann, Arthur, Abigail B., Jemima C., Elizabeth & Esther Ann, rocf Springboro MM, dtd 1835,12,24 (H)
1843, 1, 25. Arthur rmt Hannah Wily (H)
1843, 3, 29. Mary Ann rmt Samuel G. Matlock (H)
1845, 12, 31. Abigail B. rmt George Sharp (H)
1850, 9, 25. Arthur rmt Mary Ann Flitcraft (H)
1852, 10, 27. Elizabeth rmt Wm. B. Woolman (H)
1858, 7, 28. Arthur & w, Mary Ann, & her ch, Eliza M. & Pembrook Flitcraft, gct Battle Creek MM, Mich. (H)
1868, 1, 29. Esther Ann gct White Water MM, Ind. (H)

SHELDEN
1822, 3, 27. Mary gct Cincinnati MM, O.

SHINN
1837, 8, 30. David & w, Susan, & ch, Hannah Ann, David R. & Israel, rocf Marlborough MM, O., dtd 1837,5,27 (H)
1837, 8, 30. Rachel rocf Marlborough MM, Stark Co., O.; she d since cert was granted & date recorded in record (H)

SHOEMAKER
1864, 8, 31. Abraham rocf Goose Creek MM, Va., dtd 1864,8,11, to m Sarah Kindley (H)
1864, 9, 28. Abraham rmt Sarah Kindley (H)
1887, 8, 23. Abraham gct White Water MM, Ind., to m Margaret Kindley (H)
1887, 11, 30. Margaret rocf White Water MM, Ind. (H)
1897, 7, 21. Levi T. gct Alexandria MM, Va. (H)
1898, 3, 20. Susan E. rocf Alexandria MM, Va. (H)
1901, 12, 5. Margaret K. gct Maple Grove MM (H)
1902, 2, 16. Memorial for Abraham read (H)
1903, 4, 19. Daniel N. gct Baltimore MM, to m Frances E. Hartley (H)

SILVER
1833, 3, 27. Isaiah M. Brown gct Springborough MM, to m Martha Ann Silver (H)
1834, 12, 31. Samuel & w, Tamson, rocf Miami MM, O., dtd 1834,12,24 (H)
1835, 4, 29. Wm. & w, Rebecca, rocf Springborough MM, dtd 1835,3,26 (H)
1835, 4, 29. Phebe rocf Springborough MM, dtd 1835,3,26 (H)
1836, 10, 26. William B. & w, Ann, rocf Miami MM, O., dtd 1836,8,24 (H)
1838, 5, 30. Joseph E. rmt Sarah Ann Woolman (H)
1853, 11, 30. Joseph E. rmt Abigail Ann Scott (H)
1859, 8, 31. Joseph E. & w, Abigail Ann, gct Maple Grove MM, Ind. (H)
1861, 3, 27. Martha Ann dis jas (H)
1861, 5, 29. Joshua J. dis mou & jas (H)
1865, 6, 28. Joseph E. & Abigail Ann, rocf Maple Grove MM, Ind., dtd 1865,6,28 (H)
1866, 4, 25. Joseph E. & w, Abigail Ann, gct Maple Grove MM, Ind. (H)
1867, 1, 30. Samuel & w, Thamason, gct Miami MM, O. (H)
1869, 4, 28. Wm. B. & w, Ann J., & ch, Robert & Rebecca Ann, gct White Water MM, Ind. (H)
1883, 3, 28. Wm. B. & w, Ann, rocf White Water MM, Ind., dtd 1882,12,31 (H)

SIMMONS
1831, 5, 25. Thomas P. & w, Sarah S., rocf Elk MM, O., dtd 1831,5,11 (H)
1837, 1, 25. Everline rocf Elk MM, dtd 1837, 1,12 (H)

SIMONSON
1860, 12, 26. Mary Brown (form Moore) dis mou

SMITH
1823, 9, 24. John dis mou
1824, 9, 29. Stephen dis
1844, 2, 28. Elizabeth H. (form Hancock) con mou
1829, 5, 27. Elizabeth gct Springfield MM, Ind.

STARR
1832, 4, 25. Esther & fam gct White Water MM, Ind.

STEPHENS
1860, 2, 29. Martha (form Brown) ---------- (H)

STEWART
1860, 2, 29. Hannah M. (form Ballinger) con mou (H)

STORA
1832, 4, 25. John & fam gct White Water MM, Ind.

STRATTON
1826, 11, 27. Sarah C. rmt Thomas S. Teas
1829, 8, 26. Abigail recrq
1829, 10, 28. Wm. L. dis jH
1832, 4, --. Abigail rmt Wm. Edgerton
1832, 6, 27. Wm. L. rmt Bathsheba Brown (H)
1832, 7, 25. Wm. L. & w, Bathsheba, gct White Water MM, Ind. (H)
1832, 10, 24. Jonathan D. & fam gct White Water MM, Ind.
1834, 4, 30. Wm. L. [Stratan] & w, Bathsheba, & dt, Sarah, rocf White Water MM, Ind., dte 1834,3,26 (H)
1839, 7, 31. Wm. L. dis keeping his seat when prayer was made (H)

STRATTON, continued
1851, 10, 29. Sarah B. rmt Lewis Underwood (H)
1862, 12, 31. Ann Eliza Higbee (form Stratton) dis mou (H)
1868, 5, 27. Mary M. Brown (form Stratton) con mou (H)

STUBBS
1822, 1, 30. Joseph & Lydia, ch John Jr., recrq
1823, 2, 26. John Jr. con mou
1830, 1, --. Keziah rmt Alfred Bogue
1831, 9, 28. John dis jH
1833, 9, 25. John Sr. & fam gct Spiceland MM, Ind.
1833, 9, 25. Joseph & fam gct Spiceland MM, Ind.
1848, 6, 28. Henry dis disunity
1861, 11, 27. Wm. gct Milford MM, Ind.

STUDYVIN
1857, 5, 29. Abigail (form Mullin) dis mou

TAYLOR
1859, 5, 25. Beulah (form Woolman) dis mou (H)
1861, 10, 30. Mary Elizabeth (form Vanskiver) dis mou (H)

TEAS
1826, 11, 27. Thomas S., Silver Creek MM, rmt Sarah A. Stratton
1827, 2, 28. Sarah C. gct Silver Creek MM
1830, 10, 27. Thomas S. & w, Sarah, & ch, John & Edward, rocf Silver Creek MM, dtd 1830,9, 25
1832, 10, 24. Thomas L. & fam gct White Water MM, Ind.

TEST
1896, 8, 19. Joseph C. & M. Alice recrq (H)

THOMPSON
1823, 7, 30. ----- & w, Nancy, & ch, Mary, Sarah, Samuel, Ruth, Wm. & Edna, recrq
1823, 7, 30. Elizabeth rocf Exeter MM, Pa., dtd 1823,6,25
1824, 4, 28. Susannah, minor, gct Union MM
1825, 10, 26. Elijah recrq
1825, 10, 26. Mary recrq
1827, 1, 21. Mary rmt Isaiah J. Brown
1827, 5, 30. Mary con mcd
1829, 1, 28. Robert & Nancy dis jH
1829, 3, 18. Elijah & Elizabeth dis jH
1830, 3, 31. Samuel dis neglect & training with militia
1830, 4, 28. Samuel dis jas & joining militia (H)
1830, 9, 23. Mary dis jas
1834, 2, 26. Sarah Jones (form Thompson) dis mou (H)
1835, 7, 29. Ruth Jones (form Thompson) dis mou (H)
1844, 2, 28. Wm. dis mou (H)
1844, 11, 27. Edna Miller (form Thompson) dis mou (H)
1847, 6, 30. Nancy McDaniel (form Thompson) dis jas (H)
1847, 8, 25. John dis joining Methodist Society (H)

TROTH
1840, 4, 29. Wm. rocf Everham MM, N. J., dtd 1840,4,7 (H)
1840, 10, 28. Wm. rmt Rachel Hillingshead (H)
1858, 7, 28. Wm. dis neglect (H)
1863, 5, 27. Rachel F. dis jas (H)
1875, 3, 31. Wm. H. dis jas (H)

UNDERWOOD
1851, 10, 29. Lewis rmt Sarah B. Stratton
1851, 8, 27. Lewis rocf Centre MM, O., dtd 1851,8,14
1855, 6, 27. Sarah B. & dt, Mary Frances, gct Fall Creek MM, Ind.

VANSCIVER
1822, 8, 23. Samuel & Wm. [Vansciner], ch Wm., recrq
1822, 8, 23. Elizabeth [Vansciner] & dt, Martha, recrq
1827, 6, --. Samuel [Vanschuyner] rmt Elizabeth Brown
1829, 1, 28. Wm. & Elizabeth [Vanschuyler] dis jH
1829, 3, 18. Samuel & Elizabeth J. [Vanschuyner] dis jH
1830, 5, 26. Martha [Vanschuyver] dis jH
1837, 12, 27. Martha Jones (form Vanschuyver) dis mou (H)
1840, 11, 25. Wm. A. rmt Susanna B. Woolman (H)
1849, 8, 29. Wm. [Vanschuyver] dis neglect & departure from plainness (H)
1852, 4, 28. Hannah J. Morton (form Vansciver) dis mou (H)
1852, 7, 28. John B. dis mou (H)
1855, 3, 28. Joseph [Vanschuyver] dis mou (H)
1855, 11, 28. Sarah B. Whitacre (form Vanskiver) con mou (H)
1861, 10, 30. Mary Elizabeth Taylor (form Vanskiver) dis mou (H)
1885, 2, 4. Uriah [Vanskiver] dropped from mbrp (H)

WARE
1850, 1, 30. Elizabeth (form Ballinger) con mou (H)

WEEKS
1840, 11, 25. Daniel Kindly gct Fall Creek MM, Ind., to m Susan Weeks (H)

WHITACRE
1855, 11, 28. Sarah B. (form Vanskiver) con mou (H)
1872, 9, 25. Sarah B. gct Miami MM, O. (H)

WHITELY
1859, 12, 28. Uriah Woolman Jr. gct Milford MM, Ind., to m Annie Whitely (H)

WILEY
1829, 1, 28. Isaac dis jH
1829, 1, 28. Sarah dis jH
1829, 10, 28. Deborah dis jH
1832, 10, 31. Cert rec for Thomas & w, Ann, & eight ch from Notingham MM, Md., dtd 1832, 9,14, endorsed to White Water MM, Ind. (H)
1832, 10, 31. Mary rocf Notingham MM, Md., dtd 1832,9,14, endorsed to White Water MM, Ind. (H)
1835, 10, 28. Thomas rmt Jemima E. Sharp (H)
1836, 5, 25. Ann W. rmt Joseph G. Brown (H)
1840, 6, 24. Mary W. (form Hopkins) con mou (H)
1843, 1, 25. Hannah [Wily] rmt Arthur Sharp (H)
1845, 1, 29. David & Philip P., minors, rocf White Water MM, Ind., dtd 1844,12,25 (H)
1845, 1, 29. Geo. W. dis mou (H)
1846, 10, 28. Elizabeth [Wily] rmt Samuel Moore (H)
1847, 5, 26. David [Wily] dis neglect & joining militia (H)
1847, 7, 28. Philip P. [Wily] gct White Water MM, Ind. (H)
1848, 10, 25. Isaac [Wily] Jr. dis neglect & departure from plainness in dress and address (H)
1857, 7, 29. Thomas [Wily] dis joining Odd Fellows. (complaint came from Maple Grove MM, Ind.)(H)
1859, 2, 23. Jemima C. [Wily] & dt, Maria Louise Thomas Wily, gct Maple Grove MM, Ind. (H)
1863, 12, 30. Jemima [Wily] & dt, Maria Louisa Thomas Wily, rocf Maple Grove MM, Ind., dtd 1863,10,10 (H)
1869, 11, 24. Jemima [Wily] gct Maple Grove MM, Ind. (H)
1869, 12, 29. Maria Louise Thomas [Wily] gct Maple Grove MM, Ind. (H)

WILLETS
1822, 4, 24. Phebe gct Exeter MM, Pa.
1830, 8, 25. Susan & Deborah rocf Exeter MM, Pa., dtd 1830,6,30
1830, 9, 29. Ann (form Brown) con mcd
1831, 9, 28. Ann gct White Water MM, Ind.
1832, 10, 24. Deborah dis joining Separatists

* * * * * * *

BROWN
1860, 2, 29. Martha Stephens (form Brown) ----- (H)

WILTSE
1838, 2, 28. Henry [Wiltsey] gct Elk MM (H)
1854, 9, 27. Henry [Wiltsee] dis mou (H)

WILTSE
1828, 4, 30. Henry gct Elk MM
1830, 8, 25. Henry rocf Elk MM, O., dtd 1830,8,11 (H)
1831, 8, 31. Henry con mou (H)
1833, 1, --. Simeon rmt Rachel Edgerton

WOOLMAN
1829, 4, 29. Uriah & w, Mary, & ch, Joseph B., Sarah Ann, John A., Susanna, Wm. R. & Phebe, rocf Evesham MM, N. J., dtd 1829, 3,3 (H)
1832, 3, 28. Joseph B., Sarah Ann, John Stavonsin, Susannah, William, Phebe, Mary, ch Uriah & Mary, rocf Evesham MM, N. J., dtd 1831,9,12
1838, 5, 30. Sarah Ann rmt Joseph E. Silver (H)
1840, 11, 25. Susanna B. rmt Wm. A. Vansciner (H)
1844, 5, 22. Joseph B. rmt Ruth Adams (H)
1847, 8, 25. Wm. R. gct Milford MM (H)
1850, 12, 25. Wm. rocf Milford MM, Ind., dtd 1850,12,19 (H)
1851, 4, 30. John C. gct White Water MM, Ind. (H)
1852, 10, 27. Wm. B. rmt Elizabeth Sharp (H)
1853, 8, 31. Wm. B. & w, Elizabeth, gct Cincinnati MM, O. (H)
1853, 11, 30. Joseph B. gct Fall Creek MM, to m Eliza Cook (H)
1854, 4, 26. Eliza rocf Fall Creek MM, Ind., dtd 1854,4,13 (H)
1857, 2, 25. Mary Darnell (form Woolman) con mou (H)
1858, 12, 29. Joseph B. & w, Eliza, & ch, Isaac C., Wm. V. & Julietta, gct Fall Creek MM, Ind. (H)
1859, 5, 25. Beulah Taylor (form Woolman) dis mou (H)
1859, 12, 28. Uriah Jr. gct Milford MM, Ind., to m Annie Whitely (H)
1860, 2, 29. Phebe rmt James Moore (H)
1860, 8, 29. Anna rocf Milford MM, Ind., dtd 1860,7,19 (H)
1864, 5, 25. Uriah Jr. & w, Annie, & ch, Mary Elsa, gct Milford MM, Ind. (H)
1875, 5, 26. Uriah & w, Anna, & ch, Mary, Elsa, Martha Etta & Orien Clayton, rocf Milford MM, Ind., dtd 1875,4,15 (H)
1880, 2, 25. Uriah & fam gct White Water MM, Ind. (H)

* * * * * * *

STRATTON
1828, 10, --. Jonathan D. rmt Prudence Edgerton

CINCINNATI MONTHLY MEETING

The time Friends first came to Cincinnati cannot be ascertained, but as early as 1811, a few Friends held meetings for worship in the private homes of Oliver M. Spencer, Martha Perry, Cyrus Coffin and John F. Stall. In 1811 Christopher Anthony, a minister with credentials from Goose Creek Monthly Meeting, Virginia, visited Cincinnati and was so favorably impressed with the new town and its inhabitants that in 1813 he came with his family to make it his home.

Land for the building of a meeting house was bought of Nicholas Longworth. The first Preparative Meeting was held 3 Mo. 23, 1814, and the names of Benjamin Hopkins, David Holloway, Elias Fisher, Joseph Evans, Jonathan Wright, Christopher Anthony and Tristram Folger are mentioned. On 3 Mo. 16, 1815, the first monthly meeting was held, being set off from Miami Monthly Meeting by Miami Quarterly Meeting.

In 1819 the first Directory of Cincinnati was published. It says, "The monthly meeting of Friends consists of about forty families and one hundred and eighty individuals." In 1825 the Directory states that the Society "is composed of thirty families and twenty parts of families." This meeting was very much affected by the separation which took place in 1828. Friends here interested themselves very much in the abolition movement, in education and philanthropy.

RECORDS

ADAMS
1824, 2, 26. Elizabeth (form Swift) dis mcd
1877, 12, 20. Betty & Sarah K. recrq (H)

ALCOT
1820, 6, 15. Mary (form King) dis mcd

ALDERSON
----, --, --. Harrison & Emma
Ch: William
Chas. b 1837, 11, 5
Agnes " 1839, 11, 2
Anna Mary " 1841, 1, 27
Alice Ann " 1844, 7, 15
Elisabeth
Samuel " 1847, 12, -- d 1848,--,-- bur Miami

1843, 7, 20. Harrison & w, Emma, & ch, Wm. Chas., Agnes & Anna Mary, rocf Preston MM, England, dtd 1843,1,18, endorsed by Westland MM, Pa.
1843, 7, 20. Elizabeth rocf Preston MM, Eng., dtd 1843,1,18, endorsed by Westland MM,Pa.
1852, 9, 16. Harrison & dt, Alice Ann, gct Preston MM, Lancashire, Eng.
1852, 9, 16. Elizabeth gct Marsden MM, Eng.
1861, 4, 18. Wm. Chas. gct Burlington MM, N. J.
1861, 4, 18. Anna Mary & Agnes gct Burlington MM, N. J.

ALEXANDER
1931, 6, 5. Clarence & Florence rocf Anderson MM, Ind.

ALLEN
1853, 8, 6. Elcy H. m Rueben BAKER (H)
----, --, --. C. C. & Lydia M.
Ch: Isaac
William b 1874, 6, 22
Emily " 1878, 2, 14
Alvie Ray " 1880, 5, 17 d 1901, 2, 1 bur Friends Gr. Yd.
Geneva b 1882, 7, 1
Laura Peninah " 1884, 11, 3
Jessie W. " 1887, 6, 26
Warren
Daniel " 1890, 5, 3
Hubert Emerson b 1892, 11, 15
Helen Nancy " 1895, 1, 4
John C. " 1898, 4, 2
1899, 7, 27. Grace Johnson d
----, --, --. Isaac W. m Alice Virginia ----- d 1915,3,4 bur Spring Grove
Ch: William
LeRoy b 1901, 5, 8 d 1901, 2, 1
Lawrence
Ch: Jerome b 1902, 7, 8 d 1903, 7,11
Robert Warren " 1905, 10, 16
----, --, --. Donald Townsend b 1900,3,23 d 1900,8,10 bur Friends Lot
1906, 11, 29. Jessie Westerman m Walter Philip SCHMICK
1926, 3, 15. Lydia M. d

1833, 4, 25. Philip & w, Elizabeth, & s, Samuel, rocf Westfield MM, dtd 1833,1,30 (H)
1833, 4, 25. Jacob H. rocf Westfield MM, dtd 1833,1,30 (H)
1833, 6, 20. Beulah W. rocf Phila. MM, Pa., dtd 1833,4,25 (H)
1836, 1, 21. Jacob H. gct Nine Partners MM, N. Y. (H)
1836, 1, 21. Philip & w, Elizabeth, & ch, Samuel, gct Nine Partners MM, N. Y. (H)
1836, 10, 20. Alice H. rocf Center MM, dtd 1836,6,16 (H)
1837, 3, 23. Beulah Coats (form Allen) dis mcd (H)
1842, 6, 23. Mary Elizabeth (form Vanzant) dis mcd (H)
1842, 11, 24. Francis Hayes recrq (H)
----, --, --. Ann H. rocf New York MM, dtd 1848,4,5 (H)
1848, 8, 26. Ann F. rocf New York MM, N. Y., dtd 1848,4,5 (H)
1853, 8, 25. Francis H. gct Center MM, Pa., to m Malinda Way (H)
1854, 1, 26. Malinda W. rocf Center MM, dtd 1853,11,9 (H)
1872, 2, 15. Joseph P. rocf Sugar Plain MM, dtd 1872,1,24
1884, 9, 18. Joseph P. relrq
1885, 3, 26. Laura Peninah, dt Columbus & L. Margaret, recrq
1887, 11, 17. Jessie M., ch Christopher & Lydia M., recrq
1894, 8, 16. Hubert Emerson, s C. E. & Lydia, recrq
1895, 7, 18. Helen N., dt C. C. & Lydia M., recrq
1896, 8, 20. Emily & Genevie relrq
1898, 6, 10. John Christopher C., s C. C. & Lydia M., recrq
1901, 6, 14. Wm. Leroy, s Isaac W. & Alice Virginia, recrq
1901, 8, 9. Alice Virginia & Geneva recrq
1906, 1, 12. Robert Warren, s Isaac Wm. & Alice V., recrq
1924, 6, 8. Hubert relrq
1926, 5, 9. C. C. recrq
1930, 7, 6. Warren relrq

ALLEY
1831, 7, 28. Richard & w, Ruth, & s, Benjamin R., rocf Troy MM, N. Y., dtd 1831,7,6 (H)
1831, 7, 28. Henry F. rocf Troy MM, N. Y.,

ALLEY, continued
dtd 1831,7,6 (H)
1831, 8, 25. Lydia rocf Troy MM, N. Y., dtd 1831,7,6 (H)
1842, 11, 24. Benj. R. dis jas (H)

AMBACH
1901, 11, 8. Edwin T. recrq
1918, 4, 12. Edwin T. dropped from mbrp

ANDREE
1914, 3, 13. Helen recrq

ANDREWS
1845, 9, 18. Richard H. rocf Gilead MM, dtd 1845,7,22
1847, 8, 19. Richard dis mcd

ANTHONY
1786, 4, 13. Penelope, dt Christopher & Mary J., b
1815, 10, 27. Christopher, husband of Mary, d bur Cincinnati Public Grounds
1818, 5, 29. Edward Clark, s Samuel P. & Narcissa H., b
1820, 3, 23. Charles, s Joseph & Rhoda, Highland Co., O.; m in Cincinnati Mtg, Elizabeth EVANS, dt Joseph & Rachel, Highland Co., O.
1838, --, --. Mary J. d bur New Grave Yd.

1817, 4, 17. Narcissa rocf Caesars Creek MM, dtd 1817,2,21
1817, 6, 19. Samuel rocf Caesars Creek MM, dtd 1817,3,8
1818, 5, 21. Rhoda & ch, Chas., Jane Wood, Joseph, Rhoda, Moreman, Sarah, Rachel, Penelope & Christopher, rocf Clear Creek MM
1820, 9, 21. Rhoda & ch, Jane Wood, Joseph, Rhoda Mourman, Sarah, Rachel, Penelope, Christopher & Elizabeth, gct Clear Creek MM
1821, 6, 28. Chas. & w, Elizabeth, & dt, Susan Evans, gct Miami MM, O.
1865, 7, 20. Samuel P. & Edward Clark dropped from mbrp
1870, 4, 14. Edwin Clark rst
1870, 5, 19. Edwin C. gct White Water MM, Ind.

ARVILLE
1889, 10, 17. John J. recrq
1889, 11, 14. Emma M. rocf Springfield MM, O.

ATKINSON
1815, 5, 9. Joseph H., s Clayton & Margaret, b

1841, 3, 18. Elizabeth P. rocf White Water MM, Ind., dtd 1841,2,24
1842, 8, 18. Joseph Hendrickson rocf ND MM, dtd 1842,5,24
;844, 9, 19. Joseph H. con mcd
1849, 2, 15. Joseph H. dis disunity
1864, 10, 20. Eliza P. rocf Chesterfield MM, N. J.

ATLEE
1829, 8, 27. Margaret rocf Phila. MM, Pa., dtd 1829,7,22 (H)
1829, 11, 26. Margaret S., Charlotte White, Thos. Scattergood, Richard Jordon & Elizabeth Jane, ch Edwin, rocf WD MM, dtd 1829,8,25
1830, 8, 26. Margaret dis jas
1832, 11, 1. Edwin A. recrq (H)
1832, 11, 23. Edwin A. & w, Margaret, gct Phila. MM, Pa. (H)
1834, 6, 19. Thomas Scattergood, Richard Jordon & Elizabeth Jane, ch Edwin A., gct ND MM, Pa.
1839, 1, 17. Richard J., minor, rocf Phila. MM, Pa., dtd 1838,12,25
1839, 4, 25. Margaret Sr. rocf Phila. MM, Pa., dtd 1838,11,21 (H)
1843, 7, 20. Martaret gct Battle Creek MM, Mich. (H)

AUSTIN
1827, 6, 28. Lydia, w James, rocf Phila. MM, Pa.
1830, 8, 26. Lydia dis jH
1831, 5, 26. Lydia dis jas (H)

AXALINE
1879, 3, 20. Rachel A. & ch, Moreton Homer & Clyde, rocf Newberry MM, O., dtd 1879,2,17
1885, 6, 18. Rachel A. relrq

BABBITT
1899, 7, 14. Catharine W. recrq

BAILEY
----, --, --. Ezra, s Emmor & Elizabeth, b 1802,8,18 d 1878,12,24; m Elizabeth ----- dt Hugh & Sarah BYE, b 1802,1,7 d 1890,2,10
Ch: Elmira b 1829, 1, 12
Hezekiah B." 1830, 12, 9 d 1912, 8,16 bur Spring Grove
1855, 1, 25. Susan A. m Joseph J. GEST
----, --, --. Hezekiah B., s Ezra & Elizabeth, b 1830,12,9 d 1912,8,16 bur Spring Grove; m Elizabeth GRIFFITH, dt Aaron & Mary, b 1831,12,25 d 1906,1,25 bur Spring Grove
Ch: Mary Ella b 1857, 9, 1
Caroline Yarnall " 1859, 6, 2 d 1904,11,14 bur Spring Grove
Euphenia F.b 1861, 6, 7
Martha Griffith b 1863, 4, 28 d 1863, 7, 7
Elizabeth Griffith " 1867, 3, 10

BAILEY, Hezekiah B. & Elizabeth, continued
Ch: Harriett
Ellis b 1871, 11, 14
Edith
Griffith " 1876, 4, 20
----, --, --. Micajah d 1876,6,11 bur Spring Grove; m Elizabeth ----- (Micajah, s David & Sylvia, b 1807,6,7)
Ch: Mable
Gertrude b 1858, 6, 2
Ozro
Whitaker " 1864, 2, 22
William
Forster " 1866, 5, 10
Clara
Grace " 1870, 2, 1 d 1870,12,13 bur Spring Grove
1878, 5, 8. Mary Ellen m Wm. Ellis COALE
1897, 5, 25. Euphemia m H. H. LAWRENCE

1826, 5, 25. Eliza Ann rocf South River MM, dtd 1825,10,8, endorsed to Silver Creek MM, Ind.
1831, 7, 28. Ezra & w, Elizabeth, & ch, Elmira S. & Hezekiah B., rocf Smithfield MM, O.
1846, 5, 21. Micajah & ch, David H., Lydia C. & Susannah, rocf Dover MM, dtd 1846, 4,16
1847, 4, 15. Rachel Orynthia Nealy recrq by Ezra & Elizabeth Bailey, with whom she lived
1853, 5, 19. Sylvia Rutherford (form Bailey) con mcd
1855, 8, 11. Elmira Blanchard (form Bailey) dis mcd
1856, 5, 15. Almira S. Blanchard (form Bailey) dis mcd
1856, 9, 18. Micajah dis
1856, 10, 16. Hezekiah B. gct Hopewell MM, Va., to m Elizabeth B. Griffith
1857, 7, 16. Elizabeth B. rocf Hopewell MM, Va.
1865, 8, 17. David H. con mcd
1868, 11, 19. David H. gct Wilmington MM, O.
1874, 7, 16. Micajah & w, Elizabeth, & ch, Mabel Gertrude, Ozra Whitaker & Wm. Foster, recrq
1889, 5, 16. M. Gertrude relrq
1889, 8, 22. Geo. S. rocf Miami MM, O. (H)
1932, 1, 8. Wm. Foster dropped from mbrp

BAKER
1853, 8, 6. Rueben, s Rueben & Martha, Washington Co., N. Y.; m in Cincinnati Mtg, Elcy H. ALLEN, dt Solomon Howland & Fanney, Clairmont Co. (H)

1853, 10, 20. Elsey H. gct Easton MM, N. Y. (H)
1896, 3, 19. Dicia H. rocf New Garden MM, N. C., dtd 1896,2,22
1899, 6, 9. Dicia H. relrq

BALDERSTON
1873, 7, 9. Lydia Ray b

1874, 7, 16. Lydia Ray [Balderson], dt John P. & Rachel S., recrq

BALLARD
1875, 7, 15. Asa M. & w, Mary, rocf Indianapolis MM, Ind.
1876, 6, 15. Asa N. & w, Mary, relrq

BANER
1821, 6, 9. Wm. J., s Isaac & Sarah, b

1837, 12, 21. Wm. J. [Banner] rocf Springborough MM, dtd 1837,10,24
1850, 6, 20. Wm. I. con mcd
1851, 6, 19. Joseph S. rocf Springborough MM, dtd 1851,1,21
1866, 7, 19. Wm. J. dis jH

BARNARD
1822, 9, 5. Ruth d

1819, 5, 20. Lydia rocf Phila. MM, Pa., dtd 1819,2,23
1819, 7, 15. Lydia Clasby (form Barnard) dis mcd

BARRINGER
----, --, --. George L. b 1826,1,2 d 1904,8,23 bur Spring Grove

1869, 1, 21. Geo. L. & w, Susan, recrq

BARTON
1888, 2, 16. Alice E. rocf White Water MM, Ind.

BATCHFORD
1853, 11, 17. Martha C. gct New York MM, N.Y.

BATEMAN
1879, 7, 2. Caroline S. m Alfred BUTLER

1859, 8, 18. John T. & w, Lydia S., & ch, Edward S., Oliver W. & Caroline, rocf Goshen MM, O., dtd 1859,7,16
1862, 8, 21. Mary Ann & Hannah rocf Goshen MM, O., dtd 1862,5,24
1886, 3, 18. Mary Ella relrq
1899, 6, 9. Edward S. & Oliver H. dropped from mbrp

BAUGHMAN
1926, 9, 3. W. J. & w, Elizabeth, & dt, Mabel, rocf Wilmington MM, O.

BAYNES
1861, 7, 25. John H. rocf Baltimore MM, dtd 1861,5,9 (H)
1879, 1, 23. John H. gct Rising Sun MM, Md.; this cert canceled 1879,9,21 (H)

BAYNES, continued
1879, 2, 20. John H. gct Nottingham MM, Md. (H)

BAYS
1878, 12, 19. Rebecca (form Pauley) relrq

BEAL
1832, 9, 20. Grace (form Shreve) dis mcd

BEARD
1892, 4, 14. Elwood & w, Lizzie, & s, Luther H., rocf Newberry MM, O., dtd 1892,3,21
1902, 5, 9. Elwood dropped from mbrp
1902, 5, 9. Luther dropped from mbrp
1902, 5, 9. Lizzie dropped from mbrp

BEESON
1878, 4, 18. Hannibal & w, Elizabeth, & ch, Annie, John, Chas. & Caroline, rocf Fairfield MM, dtd 1878,3,16
1880, 5, 20. Hannabel A. & w, Elizabeth T., & ch, Annie, John, Chas. & Caroline, gct Fairfield MM, O.

BELL
1846, 3, 19. Hannah Christy, w Wm., & ch, Charlotte Wakefield, John, Isabella Wakefield, Wilhelmina & Wm. Edmond, rocf New York, N. Y., dtd 1846,2,4
1846, 3, 19. Hannah Christy Jr. rocf New York MM, N. Y., dtd 1846,2,4
1850, 12, 19. Hannah C. & ch, Isabella Wakefield, Wilhelmina & Edmund, gct White Water MM, Ind.
1850, 12, 19. John gct White Water MM, Ind.
1853, 3, 17. Charlotte Wakefield (form Bell) dis mcd
1858, 6, 17. John rocf White Water MM, Ind., dtd 1858,5,26
1865, 6, 15. John gct White Water MM, Ind.
1900, 5, 11. Elizabeth Agnes Haughton relrq

BENNETT
1858, 3, 19. Ann d bur West Branch at Cumminsville

1845, 2, 20. Elisha & w, Elizabeth, & ch, Margaret C., Wm. C., Henry S., Mary L., Sarah A. & Cephus G., rocf Redstone MM, Pa., dtd 1844,12,25 (H)
1846, 1, 22. Elisha & w, Elizabeth, & ch, Margaret C., Wm. C., Henry L., Mary & Sarah A., gct Redstone MM, Pa. (H)
1848, 10, 19. Ann rocf Salem MM, Ia., dtd 1848,8,26
1881, 3, 24. J. B. recrq (H)

BENTON
1817, 11, 20. Nancy (form Evans) con mcd
1820, 10, 19. Anne gct West Branch MM

BETTERTON
1846, 9, 24. Wm. G. rocf Baltimore MM, Md., dtd 1846,5,7 (H)

BEVAN
1870, 9, 15. James H. (or Lewis, both given) & w, Jane, & ch, Orlando, Franklin & Edward Emmet, rocf Lytles Creek MM, dtd 1870,8,20
1874, 3, 19. Lewis H. & w, Jane, & ch, Orlando, Franklin & Edward Emmett, gct Springfield MM, O.

BEWLEY
----, -- --. George & Ann Mary [Bewly]
Ch: Anna b 1852, 5, 18
Mary " 1854, 6, 10
Edward Carroll " 1856, 9, 3
1875, 1, 3. George Jr., s Geo. & Mary, d
----, --, --. Charles Arthur m Isabella HOSKINS
Ch: Thomas Jr. b 1903, 5, 25
Helen Margaret " 1910, 8, 8

1849, 5, 17. George & Mary Ann rocf Dublin MM, dtd 1849,2,13
1849, 10, 18. Thomas rocf Dublin MM, Ireland, dtd 1849,8,14
1852, 2, 19. Mary Ann (form Carroll) con mcd
1859, 5, 19. Thos. con mcd
1859, 9, 15. Geo. & w, Mary Ann, & ch, Anna Mary & Fanny, gct Driftwood MM, Ind.
1869, 1, 21. Thos. gct Grove MM, Ind.
1872, 1, 18. Mary & ch, Mary & Geo. rocf Grove MM, Ind.
1872, 1, 18. Anna rocf Grove MM, Ind.
1876, 5, 18. Mary E. recrq
1879, 10, 16. Anna & Minnie relrq
1891, 12, 17. Arthur rocf Grove MM, Ind., dtd 1891,11,14
1902, 6, 13. Chas. Arthur gct Fairmount MM, Ind., to m Isabelle Hoskins
1914, 11, 13. C. Arthur & w, Isabelle H., & ch, Thos. Wm., Frederick Winslow & Helen Margaret, gct Lindsey MM

BIGFORD
1819, 6, 17. Sarah (form Hopkins) dis mcd
1819, 7, 15. Sarah dis disunity

BIRDSALL
1827, 2, 22. Martha Malecca rocf Center MM, dtd 1827,1,20
1827, 4, 26. David & w, Lydia, & ch, James Albert, Hannah, Alvira, Sarah, Lydia, Phebe & Priscilla, rocf Centre MM, dtd 1827,1,20
1831, 11, 24. Daniel dis disunity
1834, 11, 20. Zady & ch, Sarah, Lydia, Phebe, Priscilla & Thos., gct Miami MM, O.
1865, 7, 20. James Albert, Hannah, Elmira,

BIRDSALL, continued
Lydia, Phebe & Priscilla, dropped from mbrp

BLACKLEY
1849, 3, 2. Bayard P. rocf New York MM, N.Y. dtd 1849,2,7 (H)
1868, 2, 20. Bayard P. gct Plainfield MM, N. J.; this cert was changed to New York MM, N. Y., 1868,6,25 (H)

BLACKSTON
1846, 8, 20. Ann rocf Smithfield MM, dtd 1848,6,28 (H)

BLAIR
1817, 5, 15. Rebecca rocf Redstone MM, Pa., dtd 1816,11,20
1865, 7, 20. Rebecca dropped from mbrp
1903, 2, 13. Eva E. dropped from mbrp

BLANCHARD
1829, 1, 12. Elmira, dt Ezra & Elizabeth Bailey, b

1855, 8, 11. Elmira (form Bailey) dis mcd
1856, 5, 15. Almira S. (form Bailey) dis mcd
1878, 12, 19. Albert B. rocf Elk MM, O., dtd 1878,8,21
1899, 6, 9. Albert B. dropped from mbrp

BLATCHFORD
1844, 12, 19. Martha (form Crossman) con mcd
1860, 8, 16. Martha S. rocf New York MM, N. Y., dtd 1860,7,4
1870, 2, 17. Martha C. relrq

BODLEY
1827, 12, 27. Rebecca con mcd
1832, 7, 19. Rebecca dis jas
1860, 10, 25. Sarah E. con mcd (H)
1861, 3, 21. Sarah E. Butterworth rocf White Water MM, Ind. (H)
1867, 10, 24. Sarah dis jas (H)

BOND
1830, 5, 27. Elizabeth rocf Indian Spring MM, Md., dtd 1829,8,5 (H)

BONSALL
1819, 6, 28. Joseph, s Isaac & Mercy, Highland Co., O., b 1796,10,29 d 1843,2,25 bur West Fork; m in Cincinnati Mtg, Elisa CHADWICK, dt Thadeus & Hepseba, Highland Co., O., b 1802,3,9 d 1869,2,3
Ch: Thaddeus C.b 1820, 10, 27 d 1821,12,17 bur Cincinnati
Anna b 1824, 7, 3 " 1824, 7,21 bur Cincinnati
Sidney b 1825, 8, 9 " 1830,11, 7 bur Cincinnati
Mary b 1827, 6, 19
Anna " 1829, 9, 24
Isaac b 1833, 12, 19
Jane " 1836, 10, 2
1848, 4, 27. Mary C. [Bonsell] m Isaac C. FALLIS

1819, 10, 21. Joseph [Bonsell] rocf Phila. MM, Pa., dtd 1819,8,25
1829, 11, 26. Samuel Newbold rocf WD MM, dtd 1829,1,21
1832, 2, 23. Samuel Newbold [Bonsal] dis mcd
1855, 5, 17. Anna Gray (form Bonsall) dis mcd
1857, 2, 19. Isaac [Bonsell] dis mcd
1858, 8, 19. Jane dis jas

BORDEN
1818, 10, 12. Archibald d bur Old Grave Yard

1818, 4, 16. Archibald rocf Miami MM, O., dtd 1818,3,25
1833, 3, 21. Jacob & w, Sidney, & dt, Mary, rocf Springborough MM, dtd 1833,1,24 (H)
1835, 2, 26. Jacob [Borton] & w, Sydney, & ch, Mary & Edward, gct Miami MM, O. (H)
1849, 4, 26. Sydney [Borten], w Jacob, & ch, Edward, Elizabeth & William, rocf Miami MM, O., dtd 1849,2,21 (H) (also ch, Mary)
1854, 6, 22. Mary Reynold (form Borton) dis mcd (H)
1856, 1, 24. Elizabeth [Borton] dis (H)

BOWLES
1829, 7, 29. Grace (form Shreve) con mcd (H)
1829, 8, 27. Grace (form Shreve) dis mcd & jH
1844, 6, 20. Grace dis slave-holding (H)

BRACKET
1840, 5, 21. Rueben [Brackett] & ch, Edward, Moses, Gustavus, Geo. & Jane, rocf Salem MM, Mass., dtd 1839,9,12
1841, 3, 18. Jane Fields (form Brackett) dis mcd
1841, 10, 21. Rueben dis mcd
1865, 7, 20. Edward, Moses, Gustavus & Geo. dropped from mbrp
1865, 7, 20. Margaret dropped from mbrp

BRADBURY
1844, 9, 19. Rebecca (form Wright) dis mcd

BRAGG
1848, 8, 24. Margaret m Thos. KITE

1846, 12, 17. Ann & ch, Isaac, Wm. & James, rocf Marlborough MM, N. Y., dtd 1846,9,23
1846, 12, 17. Margaret rocf Marlborough MM, N. Y., dtd 1846,9,23
1850, 7, 18. Ann & s, James, rocf West Branch MM
1852, 3, 18. Isaac Wm. gct West Branch MM

BRAUM
1918, 4, 12. Grace W. dropped from mbrp

BREESE
1870, 1, 20. Marshall E. recrq
1872, 10, 17. E. Marshall gct New York MM, N.Y.
1920, 8, 8. Peninah Kiphart [Breeze] dropped from mbrp

BRICE
1877, 11, 15. James G. & w, Margaretta, & ch, Maggie, rocf White River MM, dtd 1877,7,7, returned since they wished to resign

BROOKE
1829, 6, 25. Lydia rocf WD MM, dtd 1829,3,18
1832, 7, 19. Lydia Carter (form Brooks) dis mcd

BROWER
1877, 8, --. Alice d

BROWN
1828, 2, 28. Eliza (form Foster) con mcd
1830, 8, 26. Eliza dis jas
1845, 2, 13. Alice rocf Springborough MM, dtd 1845,1,21
1882, 10, 19. Daniel N. & w, Bell, gct White Water MM, Ind.
1885, 5, 21. Daniel N. & w, Belle, dropped from mbrp; unable to locate them

BRUFF
1842, 6, 23. Wm. L. rocf Phila. MM, Pa., dtd 1842,2,17 (H)

BRUNO
1932, 2, 5. Helen Mae recrq

BRYANT
----, --, --. David B. b 1792,10,10; m Jane ----- b 1798,1,15
Ch: Martha A. b 1812, 3, 1 d 1837, 3,21 bur New Graveyard
Alexander b 1816, 4, 4 " 1831,10,-- bur Old Graveyard
William b 1818, 6, 26
Thomas " 1820, 4, 10
James " 1822, 1, 30 d 1839, 8, 3 bur New Graveyard
Rebecca b 1823, 12, 14
John " 1826, 2, 13
David H. " 1828, 2, 15
Lydia " 1830, 6, 20
George F. " 1833, 3, 21 d 1837, 9,15 bur New Graveyard
Hannah C. b 1836, 6, 12
----, --, --. William m Elizabeth BRAGG, dt Thos. & Ann, b 1817,4,28
Ch: Ann b 1842, 9, 23
Mary " 1844, 2, 7
Elizabeth " 1846, 2, 4

1819, 1, 21. David recrq
1821, 5, 31. David [Briant] gct Silver Creek MM
1831, 6, 30. David & w, Jane, & ch, Alexander, Wm., Thos., Rebecca, James, David & Lydia, rocf Silver Creek MM, dtd 1831,6,25
1842, 6, 16. Wm. dis mcd
1844, 11, 14. Rebecca Burnett (form Bryant) dis mcd
1846, 11, 19. John dis mcd
1848, 12, 21. Elizabeth rocf Marlborough MM, N. Y., dtd 1848,10,25
1849, 2, 15. Anna, Mary Ann & Elizabeth, ch Elizabeth, recrq
1850, 4, 18. David H. dis mcd
1850, 7, 18. Elizabeth & ch, Ann, Mary Ann & Elizabeth, gct West Branch MM
1857, 1, 15. Lydia Preston (form Bryant) dis mcd
1868, 12, 17. David & Jane dropped from mbrp

BUCKLEY
1904, 6, 1. Albert Coulson, s Wm. C. & Lucy (Davis), Phila., Pa.; m in Cincinnati Mtg, Harriet ELLIS BAILEY, dt Hezekiah B. & Elizabeth B., Covington, Ky.

1907, 5, 10. Harriet Bailey gct Germantown MM, Pa.

BUFFUM
1845, 12, 18. Rebecca rocf New Garden MM, dtd 1843,4,15; returned to New Garden MM with information she has not been known here

BURGE
1899, 2, --. Jonathan D. [Burdge] d

1891, 5, 21. Jonathan S. & w, Martha J., & ch, Chas. C. & Jesse C., rocf Springfield MM, O., dtd 1891,3,21
1899, 3, 10. Chas. C. gct Wilmington MM, O.
1901, 6, 14. Cora recrq
1913, 7, 11. Jesse C. [Burdge] dropped from mbrp

BURGESS
1831, 12, 29. Jesse & w, Elizabeth, & ch, Ephraim Morgan & David Bryant, rocf Springfield MM, O., dtd 1831,11,15
1832, 6, 14. Jesse & w, Elizabeth, & ch, Mary Emily, gct Springfield MM, O.

BURK
1819, 4, 15. Mary (form Rees) dis mcd

BURNETT
1844, 11, 14. Rebecca (form Bryant) dis mcd

BURTES
1818, 4, 16. Jesse rocf New York MM, N. Y., dtd 1817,12,3

BUTLER
1815, 8, 3. Nancy, w Wm., d bur Cincinnati Public Grounds

BUTLER, continued
1828, 10, 2. William, s Stephen & Mary, Highland Co., O.; m in Cincinnati Mtg, Margaret SHREVE, dt Thomas & Ann, Highland Co., O.
1879, 7, 2. Alfred, s Joshua O. & Eveline M., Logan Co., O.; m in Cincinnati Mtg, Caroline S. BATEMAN, dt John F. & Lydia S., Highland Co., O.

1816, 10, 17. Wm. gct South River MM, Va., to m
1820, 1, 20. Deborah & s, Anslem D. Johnson, rocf South River MM, Va., dtd 1819,9,11
1825, 9, 29. Mary rocf South River MM, dtd 1825,9,10
1826, 5, 25. Cert rec for Stephen & w, Mary, & ch from South River MM, Va., endorsed to Silver Creek MM, Ind.
1829, 6, 25. Wm. dis jH
1829, 6, 25. Margaret dis jH
1882, 3, 16. Carrie S. relrq

BUTTERWORTH
1889, 7, 25. Isaac W. rocf Miami MM, O. (H)

BYERLY
1844, 7, 18. James, minor, rocf Frankford MM, Pa., dtd 1844,2,27

CADBURY
1900, 9, 14. Wm. Ellis Shipley gct Frankfort MM, Pa., to m Caroline W. Cadbury

CADWALLADER
1848, 5, 10. Isaac rocf Smithfield MM, dtd 1848,2,21
1881, 10, 20. Pierce J. [Cadwalader] rocf Miami MM, O., dtd 1880,9,21

CALVERT
1832, 12, 20. Hannah rocf Phila. MM, Pa., dtd dtd 1832,10,24 (H)
1834, 7, 24. Hannah gct Phila. MM, Pa. (H)
1839, 1, 24. Hannah rocf Phila. MM, Pa., dtd 1838,10,17 (H)
1840, 4, 23. Hannah gct Phila. MM, Pa. (H)
1849, 4, 26. Hannah rocf Phila. MM, Pa., dtd 1848,10,-- (H)

CAMERON
1893, 3, 29. Rachel d bur Spring Grove

1868, 5, 21. Rachel recrq

CAMP
1893, 7, 24. Mellie, dt Wm. T. & Emily Haydock, b bur St. Louis

CAMPBELL
1899, 12, 19. Modesta Marguerite, dt Wm. T. & Amanda, b
1911, 3, 5. Willard T. d
1899, 4, 14. Amanda K. & Willard T. recrq

CANBY
1816, 7, 18. Samuel rocf Goose Creek MM, Va., dtd 1816,5,2
1817, 9, 18. Samuel & Louisa rocf Fairfax MM, Va., dtd 1817,8,27
1818, 5, 21. Margaret (form Haines) dis mcd

CAREY
1866, 4, 19. Elias & w, Jane, & ch, Martha, Emily, John Henry, Rachel, Annie, Isaac-Milton, Irena & James Walter, rocf Newberry MM, O., dtd 1866,1,22
1866, 6, 14. Elias & w, Catharine, & dt, Sarah Emeline, rocf Driftwood MM, dtd 1866,5,5
1866, 10, 18. Elias & w, Jane, & ch, John Henry, Rachel, Annie, Isaac-Milton, Irena & James Walter, gct Newberry MM, O.
1870, 3, 17. Daniel M. rocf Oak Ridge MM
1872, 7, 18. Daniel M. & fam gct Fairview MM, Ill.

CARPENTER
----, --, --. Calvin b 1807,10,5 d 1846,5,6 bur Spring Grove
----, --, --. Walter b 1811,1,1 d 1910,8,31 bur Earlham Cemetery, Richmond, Ind.
----, --, --. Nathaniel m Zeruiah ----- b 1799,9,9
Ch: Catharine b 1821, 9, 6
Mary T. " 1824, 5, 10
Edwin " 1825, 8, 10
1844, 9, 26. Catharine m David F. JOHNSON
1849, --, --. Clifford H., s Calvin & Maria, d
1872, 9, 11. Horace E., s Horace & Alice, b
1908, 9, 30. Susan, w Walter T., d bur Earlham Cemetery, Richmond, Ind.

1828, 12, 25. Jacob & w, Elizabeth, & ch, Wm. Comstock, rocf Centre MM, O., dtd 1828,12,17
1829, 12, 31. Jacob & w, Elizabeth H. & Wm. Comstock, minor, gct Center MM, O.
1830, 4, 29. Ezra rocf New York MM, N. Y., dtd 1830,2,3
1831, 1, 27. Clinton C. rocf Centre MM, O., dtd 1830,10,13
1833, 12, 19. Ezra dis mcd
1834, 12, 18. Calvin con mcd
1835, 1, 15. Walter T. & w, Susan, rocf Center MM, O., dtd 1834,11,12
1835, 6, 16. Walter & w, Susan, & s, Chas., gct Center MM
1843, 3, 16. Nathaniel & w, Zeruiah, & ch, Catharine, Mary T. & Edwin, rocf Center MM, dtd 1843,2,15
1843, 3, 16. Anna, minister, rocf Centre MM, dtd 1843,2,15
1844, 12, 19. Walter T. & w, Susan M., & ch, Chas. G., rocf Springfield MM, dtd 1844,

CARPENTER, continued
10,15
1846, 6, 18. Clifford H. & Daniel H., ch Calvin & Ann Maria, recrq
1847, 10, 21. Walter T. & w, Susan M., & ch, Chas. Grey & Caroline, gct Springfield MM
1848, 11, 16. Daniel & w, Zeruiah, gct Springfield MM, O.
1848, 11, 16. Edwin gct Springfield MM, O.
1848, 11, 16. Anna gct Springfield MM, O.
1848, 12, 21. Mary gct Springfield MM, O.
1873, 7, 17. Alice (form Malone) con mcd
1877, 2, 15. Daniel H. dis disunity
1892, 6, 10. Alice M. relrq

CARROLL
1851, 7, 15. Foster W. d bur vault of Presbyterian Grounds
1871, 3, 13. Dr. Thomas d ae 77y
1871, 5, 19. Ann Lynch d ae 73y (w of Dr. Thomas)

1841, 11, 25. Thos. & w, Ann, & ch, Foster, Robert W. & Laura A., rocf Plainfield MM, O., dtd 1841,10,14 (H)
1843, 7, 20. Wm. W. & Foster, ch Thos. & Ann, rocf Plainfield MM, O., dtd 1843,4,19
1848, 5, 25. Robert W. gct Green Plain MM,O. (H)
1849, 12, 20. Mary Ann rocf Salem MM, O., dtd 1849,10,24
1850, 8, 15. Wm. rocf Upper Springfield MM, O., dtd 1850,5,25
1850, 11, 21. Edward & Beulah recrq (H)
1851, 10, 23. Edward & w, Beulah, gct Cherry St. MM, Phila., Pa. (H)
1852, 2, 19. Mary Ann Bewley (form Carroll) con mcd
1853, 2, 24. Robert W. rocf Green Plain MM, O. (H)
1855, 9, 20. Robert W. dis mcd & jH
1857, 10, 23. Edward & w, Beulah, gct Phila. MM, Pa. (H)
1860, 11, 15. Wm. con mcd
1861, 5, 16. Wm. gct Driftwood MM, Ind.
1863, 8, 20. Robert W. con mcd (H)

CARTER
1832, 7, 19. Lydia (form Brooks) dis mcd

CAVEN
1855, 11, 22. Ann E. con mcd (H)
1887, 2, 24. Mary E. relrq (H)

CAVENDER
1847, 6, 24. Abraham & w, Rebecca, & ch, Anthony T., Andrew L., Wm., Hannah & Amos, rocf Deerfield MM, O., dtd 1846,9,9 (H)
1853, 1, 20. Abram & w, Rebecca, & ch, Wm. & Harriett (or Hannah) gct White Water MM, Ind. (H)
1859, 10, 20. Anthony con mcd (H)

CHADWICK
1818, 10, 22. Phebe m Wm. PADDOCK
1819, 6, 28. Elisa m Joseph BONSALL

1816, 3, 21. Eunice Nye (form Chadwick) dis mcd

CHAPMAN
1819, 10, 13. Margaret, dt Wm. & Jane Crassman b
----, --, --. Noah H. & Mary Anna
Ch: Charles A. b 1865, 9, 16
Mary W. " 1869, 11, 3
A. Wright " 1872, 10, 13
Howard " 1875, 1, 11
Charlotte H. b 1877, 9, 16
1905, 9, 28. Margaret d

1840, 3, 19. Margaret (form Crossman) con mcd
1860, 3, 22. Noah H. rocf Miami MM, dtd 1860,2,22 (H)
1864, 5, 26. Noah gct Springborough MM (H)
1869, 2, 25. Mary Anna, w Noah, & s, Chas., rocf Springborough MM (H)
1874, 3, 19. Wm. B. & Maggie C., minor, recrq
1880, 11, 25. Noah H. & w, Marianna W., & ch, Chas. H., Mary W., A. Wright, Howard & Charlotte, gct New York MM, N. Y. (H)
1905, 11, 10. Margaret C. relrq
1920, 8, 8. Beatrix Williams dropped from mbrp
1932, 5, 2. Elizabeth rocf Blue River MM, Ind.
1932, 5, 2. Robert M. & Mary Lowry recrq
1933, 4, 7. Mary recrq

CHASBY
1801, 9, 27. Lydia B., dt Chas. & Elizabeth, b

CHASE
1817, 5, 15. Hepzibah (form Smith) con mcd

CHILDS
1848, 8, 26. Rebecca (form Coats) dis mcd (H)

CHIPPENDALE
1873, 5, 15. Sarah recrq
1899, 1, 13. Sarah dropped from mbrp

CLARBY
1819, 1, 21. Lydia R. rocf Phila. MM, Pa., dtd 1818,10,27

CLARK
----, --, --. William m Elizabeth Stanton PADDOCK
Ch: Clara Paddock b 1851, 7, 14
Benjamin F." 1856, 12, 25

CLARK, William & Elizabeth, continued
Ch: Mary W. b 1859, 12, 25

1825, 1, 27. Eliza (form Folger) dis mcd
1833, 2, 14. Mary (form Skyron) dis mcd
1850, 8, 22. Elizabeth (form Paddock) dis mcd (H)
1850, 9, 19. Jane (form Taylor) con mcd
1854, 8, 17. Jane, w Jonathan, gct Miami MM, O.
1861, 4, 25. Jane rocf Fallowfield MM, Pa.(H)
1863, 6, 25. Jane gct Race St. MM, Phila. Pa. (H)
1883, 6, 17. Verona rocf Newberry MM, O.
1899, 1, 13. Verona dropped from mbrp

CLASBY
1819, 7, 15. Lydia (form Barnard) dis mcd
1820, 10, 19. Lydia Folger (form Clasby) con mcd

CLAYTON
1887, 10, 20. Frederick recrq (H)

CLIBBORN
1832, 6, 14. Edward rocf Dublin MM, dtd 1830,11,16

COALE
1820, 4, 20. Phebe [Cole] com mou
1878, 5, 8. Wm. Ellis, s Thos. E. & Cecilia H., Baltimore, Md.; m in Cincinnati MH, Mary Ella BAILY, dt Hezekiah B. & Elizabeth B., Covington, Ky.

1878, 11, 14. Mary Ellen gct Baltimore MM, Md.

COATS
1837, 3, 23. Beulah (form Allen) dis mcd (H)
1846, 6, 25. Deborah [Coates] rocf Allum Creek MM, dtd 1846,4,23 (H)
1847, 9, 23. Rebecca [Coates] rocf Alum Creek MM, O., dtd 1847,1,21 (H)
1848, 8, 26. Rebecca Childs (form Coats) dis mcd (H)

COFFIN
1814, 9, 13. Sarah, dt Solomon, d
1814, 10, 6. Sarah, w Solomon, d
----, --, --. Moses, s Isaiah & Sarah, b 1791,12,13; m Judith SMITH, dt John & Hepsebeth, b 1790,3,20 d 1867,2,20 bur Spring Grove
Ch: Mary b 1815, 2, 1 d 1817,11,23
William G. " 1817, 12, 13
Mary F. " 1818, 12, 23
Nancy B. " 1820, 11, 3
1817, 10, 23. Sarah m Oliver MARTIN
1818, 6, 22. Henry C., s Benjamin Franklin, d
1818, 6, 22. Benjamin Franklin d
----, --, --. Elijah & Naomi
Ch: Miriam b 1821, 1, 8
Charles F. " 1823, 4, 3
William H. b 1825, 9, 26
Caroline E." 1831, 6, 24
1830, 4, 7. Adam, s Benjamin & Elizabeth, Union Co., Ind.; m in Cincinnati Mtg, Margaret FOLGER, dt Daniel & Hepzibeth RUSSELL, Highland Co., O., b 1764,7,3
1869, 5, 11. Sarah Emeline, dt Levi & Catharine, d bur Spring Grove
1877, 9, --. Levi d bur Spring Grove
1881, 5, 22. Catharine d bur Spring Grove

1815, 4, 20. Judith & dt, Mary, recrq
1819, 6, 17. Eliza Vincent (form Coffin) dis mcd
1820, 3, 16. Hepsebah Garner (or Gummery) dis (Hepsebah Garner, form Coffin)
1820, 3, 16. Eliza Foster (form Coffin) con mcd
1828, 8, 28. Sarah Moss (form Coffin) dis mcd
1831, 6, 30. Adam rocf Silver Creek MM, dtd 1831,6,25
1831, 6, 30. Christopher dis mcd
1832, 3, 15. Chas. dis mcd
1833, 8, 15. Elijah & w, Naomi, & ch, Mariam A., Chas. F., Wm. H. & Caroline E., rocf Milford MM, dtd 1833,7,27
1835, 1, 15. Elijah & w, Naomi, & ch, Miriam A., Chas. F., Wm. H., Caroline E. & Mary, gct White Water MM, Ind.
1855, 8, 16. Henry W. & w, Sarah Emeline, & ch, Levi, rocf New Garden MM, dtd 1855,6,16
1858, 10, 21. Mordecai Morris White gct White Water MM, Ind., to m Hannah Amelia Coffin
1858, 9, 16. Henry W. gct Driftwood MM, Ind.
1866, 6, 14. Levi & fam rocf Driftwood MM, dtd 1866,5,5
1867, 3, 21. Henry W. rocf Driftwood MM, dtd 1867,1,5

COLEMAN
----, --, --. Richard, s Sylvanus & Mary, b 1773,4,23; m Sally HUSSEY, dt Christopher & Lydia, b 1775,5,25 d 1807,3,26 bur Nantucket, R. I.
Ch: Lydia H. b 1796, 8, 25
Charles W. " 1798, 5, 24 d 1820, 5,19
Obed " 1800, 7, 19 " 1801,10, 1
George M. " 1802, 4, 17
Mary " 1804, 3, 7 " 1806, 3,16
Obed B. " 1806, 6, 5 " 1807, 2,16
Richard m 2nd Susannah -----, dt Thadeus & Susannah GARDNER, b 1768,1,27

1816, 1, 18. Susanna recrq
1829, 10, 29. Susanna dis jH

COLLINS
----, --, --. ----- & Ellenor
Ch: Maggie L. b 1870, 7, 5 d 1874,10, 9
Murray H. " 1874, 8, 29
Rachel Min-

COLLINS, continued
Ch: nie b 1878, 11, 5

1850, 5, 16. Martha A. (form Judkins) dis mcd
1873, 9, 18. Eleanor & ch, Almasin & Maggie, rocf Fairfield MM, O., dtd 1873,7,19
1885, 9, 17. Cert for Eleanor & ch, Maggie L. Murray H. & Rachel Minnie, to Chicago MM, Ill., returned 1886,3,18, residence not there

COMLY
1829, 12, 31. Mary (form Nisbet) con mcd
1837, 8, 17. Sarah R. (form Judkins) con mcd
1844, 11, 14. Sarah dis jas
1848, 11, 16. Julia recrq
1850, 11, 14. Frances B. (form Pennington) dis mcd
1865, 12, 21. Julia E. [Comley] gct White Water MM, Ind.

COMMONS
1819, 12, 16. Thomas rocf Wilmington MM, dtd 1819,4,30

COMSTOCK
1849, --, --. Matthew d

1828, 12, 25. Jacob Carpenter & w, Elizabeth, & Wm. Comstock, rocf Center MM, O., dtd 1828,12,17
1829, 2, 26. Elizabeth rocf Center MM, O., dtd 1828,12,17
1830, 1, 28. Elizabeth McHammon (form Comstock) dis mcd
1830, 8, 26. Anna & dt, Mary, Susan, Sarah & Emmeline, rocf Hudson MM, N. Y., dtd 1828,5,20, endorsed by Center MM, O., 1830,8,18
1832, 5, 17. Susan, Mary & Sarah dis jH
1836, 8, 18. Wm. rocf Center MM, dtd 1836, 7,13
1837, 4, 20. Emeline dis jas
1842, 6, 16. Wm. dis disunity

CONOVER
1863, 2, 26. Mary S. rocf New York MM, N. Y., dtd 1862,6,4 (H)

COOK
1830, 5, 27. Amos & w, Anna, & ch, Jas. M., Wm. T., Samuel M., Ann Elizabeth, Amos, Sarah, Jane & Jacob, rocf Indian Spring MM, Md., dtd 1829,8,5 (H)
1840, 10, 22. Marcellius, Elizabeth P., Theadore, Jesse, Andrew M. & Joseph, ch Jesse W. & Elizabeth, rocf Birmingham MM, Pa., dtd 1840,6,27 (H)
1841, 3, 25. Jesse W. recrq (H)
1842, 1, 20. Elizabeth & w, Thos. W. recrq (H)
1842, 3, 17. Cert rec for Noah from Windham MM, Me., dtd 1841,11,26, endorsed to Miami MM, O.
1844, 7, 26. Elizabeth Matlock (form Cook) con mcd (H)
1844, 10, 24. Marcellius S. gct Miami MM, O. (H)
1846, 7, 23. Jesse W. & w, Elizabeth, & ch, Theodore M., Jesse W., Andrew M., Joseph K., Thos. W. & Emma, gct Miami MM, O.(H)

COOPER
1847, 5, 29. John W. d bur Spring Grove
1850, 7, 5. Wm. W. d bur Spring Grove

1824, 8, 26. John W. rocf Phila. MM, Pa., dtd 1824,5,25
1836, 10, 20. Mary E. (form Tucker) dis mcd (H)
1837, 12, 21. Wm. W. con mcd
1841, 12, 16. Hannah rocf ND MM, dtd 1841,11, 23
1852, 3, 18. Hannah gct Burlington MM, N. J.
1880, 2, 19. Phebe E. relrq

COPE
1831, 3, 31. Herman rocf WD MM, dtd 1830,10, 20
1836, 8, 18. Herman U. dis jas

COPELAND
----, --, --. Albert Luther, s David & Lydia, b 1874,10,19; m Alice HIATT, dt Josiah & Rhoda Hiatt, b 1871,1,24
Ch: David Josiah b 1904, 8, 14
Joseph John " 1907, 8, 27
Philip " 1910, 4, 19 d 1910, 4,19 bur Bridgeport, Ind.

1908, 1, 10. Albert & w, Alice H., & ch, David Josiah & Joseph John, rocf South Marion MM, Ind., dtd 1907,12,12
1918, 8, 9. Albert L. & w, Alice H., & ch, David J. & Joseph J., gct Paoli MM, Ind.

COPPOCK
1863, 5, 21. Wm. J. rocf Union MM, O., dtd 1862,12,24
1880, 6, 17. Wm. J. dropped from mbrp

CORBIN
1851, 2, 13. Anna (form Taylor) dis mcd

CORNAL
1816, 2, 15. Lydia recrq

CORNEAN
1863, 7, 23. Rebecca H. rocf Mt. Holley MM, dtd 1863,6,8 (H)
1866, 8, 23. Rebecca gct Green St. MM, Phila. Pa. (H)

CORNELL
----, —, --. William, s Wm. & Mary, b 1776,2,28; m Lydia HUSSEY, dt Christopher & Lydia, b 1776,10,2
Ch: William H. b 1804, 11, 12 d 1806, 3,13
George R. " 1806, 12, 27
William Jr." 1808, 12, 7 " 1809, 4, 7
Susan M. " 1813, 5, 27 " 1815, 8,12
William 2nd" 1814, 12, 15 " 1815, 7,28
John " 1814, 12, 15 " 1815, 5,25

COWAN
1869, 7, 15. Sophia recrq

CRAMP
1884, 11, 12. Theodore Wm., s Jacob G. & Emma, Phila., Pa.; m in Cincinnati Mtg, Mary WHITE, dt Mordecai Morris & Hannah Amelia, Highland Co., O.

1892, 4, 14. Alice White relrq

CRANE
1830, 5, 27. Sarah (form Folger) dis mcd
1831, 3, 31. Sarah dis mcd

CRANMER
1825, 5, 26. Eliza (form Gibson) dis mcd

CREAGHEAD
1893, 6, 7. Thos. James, s Samuel & Susan M., Kenton Co., Ky.; m in public mtg in Covington, Ky., Elizabeth Griffith BAILEY, dt Hezekiah & Elizabeth, Covington, Ky.
Ch: Elizabeth
Griffith b 1896, 2, 26
Robert M. " 1901, 9, 25

1901, 5, 10. Elizabeth Griffith [Craighead] recrq (dt Thos. J. & Elizabeth B.)
1902, 3, 14. Robert Murnan [Craighead], s Thos. Jas. & Elizabeth B., recrq
1928, 6, 3. Elizabeth relrq

CREW
1840, 2, 13. Thos. F. rocf Cedar Creek MM, Va., dtd 1839,9,14
1858, 2, 18. James rocf Smithfield MM, dtd 1858,1,18
1865, 7, 20. Thos. F. dropped from mbrp

CRISPIN
1814, 8, 7. Joseph, s Jonathan, d bur Cincinnati Public Graveyard
1815, 8, 28. Jonathan, h Elizabeth, d bur Cincinnati Public Graveyard

1815, 12, 31. Rebecca, Mary Ward & Rowland Owen, ch Jonathan, rocf Miami MM, O.
1817, 10, 16. Elizabeth, gr dt Isaac Ward, gct Miami MM, O.
1858, 4, 22. Elizabeth rocf Miami MM, O., dtd 1858,1,27 (H)
1867, 4, 25. Elizabeth gct Miami MM, O. (H)

CROSSLEY
1844, 6, 20. Simeon, minor, rocf Flushing MM, O., dtd 1844,2,22
1844, 11, 14. Jonathan rocf Flushing MM, O., dtd 1844,7,25
1845, 4, 17. Mary [Crossly], minor, rocf Flushing MM, O., dtd 1844,3,21
1846, 11, 19. Simeon [Crossly] dis disunity
1846, 12, 17. Jonathan dis disunity

CROSSMAN
----, --, --. William, s Peleg & Margaret, b 1788,2,7 d 1863,11,24 bur Spring Grove; m Jane N. VINCENT, dt Daniel & Hannah, b 1788,7,14 d 1874,12,15 bur Spring Grove
Ch: William H. b 1812, 4, 17 d 1813,11, 3 bur Mass.
Hannah S. " 1814, 8, 15
William F. " 1817, 4, 28 " 1822, 8, 3
Margaret " 1819, 10, 13
Elizabeth " 1822, 6, 4
Martha " 1825, 1, 25
Daniel " 1827, 8, 2 " 1829, 7,25 bur Cincinnati MH
Sarah W. b 1830, 4, 20 " 1835, 1,13 bur New Bur. Gr.

1821, 6, 28. Wm. recrq
1823, 11, 27. Jane recrq
1824, 4, 29. Hannah, Margaret & Elizabeth, ch Wm. & Jane, recrq
1838, 1, 18. Hannah Ott (form Crossman) con mcd
1840, 3, 19. Margaret Chapman (form Crossman) con mcd
1843, 8, 16. Elizabeth Marsh (form Crossman) con mcd
1844, 12, 19. Martha Blatchford (form Crossman) con mcd

CUMMINS
1822, 12, 20. Thos. gct West Grove MM, Ind.

CUNNINGHAM
1838, 1, 25. Elizabeth rocf New York MM, N.Y. dtd 1837,4,5; dec (H)
1864, 6, 23. Susie E. (form Evans) con mcd (H)

CURTIS
1899, 2, 3. Ann, w John, bur Spring Grove

1852, 1, 15. John recrq
1857, 6, 18. Ann recrq
1872, 10, 17. John relrq
1878, 4, 18. Mary L. relrq

DARLINGTON
1855, 11, 15. Wm. T. rocf Red Cedar MM, Ia., dtd. 1855,6,6
1899, 1, 13. Wm. T. dropped from mbrp

DAVIS

----, --, --. John, s Samuel & Annis, b 1774,9,24 d 1842,3,7 bur New Bur. Gr.; m Hannah -----, dt C. & Mary ANTHONY, b 1781,10,26 d 1830,8,13 bur Cincinnati MH

Ch: Anna Maria b 1806, 2, 24
Mary Jordan " 1808, 10, 10
Samuel " 1809, 8, 13
Sarah " 1811, 3, 8
Charlotte " 1813, 2, 21 d 1888, 9,16 bur Spring Grove
William b 1815, 3, 21 " 1837, 4,30 bur New Bur. Gr.
John Jr. b 1818, 4, 15 " 1832,10,18 bur Cincinnati MH
Charles Henry b 1820, 7, 11 " 1837, 1, 7 bur Rushville, Ind.
Hannah J. b 1823, 10, 21 " 1908,12, 5 bur St. Louis, Mo.

1830, 1, 1. Mary Jordan m Caleb W. TAYLOR
1832, 8, 23. Anna Maria m Achilles PUGH
1833, 12, 26. Sarah A. m Hugh H. SMITH
----, --, --. James & Sarah

Ch: Caroline b 1846, 4, 4 d 1846, 6,15 bur New Graveyard
William S. b 1847, 6, 20
Sarah Merrit " 1849, 8, 7 " 1815, 9,11 bur New Graveyard
Mary Elizabeth b 1851, 7, 12
Emma Alderson b 1853, 7, 27
James Arthur " 1855, 5, 23 d 1856, 7, 4 bur West Branch Graveyard

1835, 9, 17. Samuel gct Milford MM
1835, 9, 17. Chas. H., minor, gct Milford MM
1843, 4, 20. Hannah Stagg (form Davis) con mcd
1864, 10, 20. Ellen H. recrq
1875, 5, 20. Eleanor H. gct Kendall MM, Eng.

DEAN

1868, 6, 25. George H., s Jonathan & Sarah B., Highland Co., O.; m in Cincinnati Mtg, Elizabeth L. TAYLOR, dt Caleb W. & Mary I., Highland Co.. O., b 1839,1,27 d 1891,1,22

Ch: Mary b 1869, 4, 8
George B. " 1872, 7, 27 d 1881, 9,25
Anna Elliott " 1874, 5, 23
Morris Burgess " 1876, 1, 17
Elizabeth " 1879, 2, 8
Archer Griffin " 1881, 7, 28

1869, 6, 17. Geo. H. recrq
1914, 8, 14. Elizabeth L. relrq
1916, 1, 16. Archer B. gct Wilmington MM, Del.
1916, 2, 11. Morris B. gct West Chester MM, Pa.
1920, 8, 8. Geo. B. dropped from mbrp

DeVOY

1831, 1, 27. Sarah W. (form Ludlum) con mcd

DIBBLE

1831, 8, 25. Eunice rocf Troy MM, N. Y., dtd 1831,7,6 (H)

DICKINSON

1818, 9, 24. Mary m Jesse EMBREE
1823, 11, 6. Lydia m Oliver MARTIN, Jr.
1832, --, --. Susannah d
1835, 7, --. John, s John & Mary, b
1884, 7, 16. Jane d

1818, 4, 16. John & w, Susannah, & ch, Margaret, Eliza Ann, Mary & Lydia, rocf New York MM, N. Y., dtd 1818,3,4
1829, 7, 30. Susannah dis jH
1829, 10, 29. John dis jH
1829, 11, 26. Margaret dis jH
1830, 12, 30. Ann Eliza dis jH
1837, 2, 23. Margaret [Dickasan] gct Phila. MM, Pa. (H)
1837, 2, 23. Ann Eliza gct Phila. MM, Pa. (H)
1853, 1, 20. John, minor, rocf WD MM, dtd 1852,11,17
1853, 9, 15. John gct White Water MM, Ind.
1876, 4, 20. James rocf Carlow MM, Ireland, dtd 1875,12,7
1885, 9, 17. Emily S. recrq
1918, 4, 12. Emily L. dropped from mbrp

DICKS

1815, 5, 25. Agatha m Isaac HARVEY

1815, 9, 21. Nathan rocf South River MM, dtd 1815,4,8
1817, 11, 20. Nathan gct Center MM
1818, 3, 19. Achilles [Dick] gct Center MM

DILWORTH

1840, 10, 15. Rankin, Abigail, Caleb J., Rebecca Ann & Sarah M., ch Martha Evans (form Dilworth) rocf Short Creek MM, O., dtd 1840,7,21
1841, 3, 18. Martha (Dilworth) Evans & ch, Rankin, Abigail R., Caleb J., Rebecca Ann & Sarah Dilworth & Wm. Henry Evans, gct Salem MM, Ind.
1846, 8, 20. Rankin rpd mcd; d before case was settled

DODDS

1855, 12, 20. Anna Louisa (form Hobbs) dis mcd

DODSON
1898, 10, 14. Cert for Clara from Wilmington MM, O.; returned because of her lack of interest in mtg

DOLE
1931, 8, 29. Russel, nm, m Ruth LEWIS

1932, 9, 2. Russel recrq
1932, 12, 2. Robert Lewis recrq

DONALDSON
1839, 11, 21. Elizabeth (form Shreve) con mcd (H)
1846, 3, 19. Mary Ann recrq
1866, 2, 15. Mary Ann relrq

DORLAND
1884, 2, 20. Robert B. Warder gct Minneapolis MM, Minn., to m Gulielma M. Dorland
1884, 7, 17. Gulielma D. Warder & ch, Claudia M. Dorland, rocf Minneapolis MM, Minn., dtd 1884,6,12

DULING
1920, 12, 12. Anna Johnson relrq

DUNNING
1900, 3, 9. Agnes Powers relrq

DURFEE
1870, 6, 23. Elihu & w, Maria, & ch, Julia P., rocf Farmington MM, dtd 1870,5,26 (H)
1878, 8, 22. Elihu & w, Maria, gct Benjaminville MM, Ill. (H)
1878, 10, 25. Elihu & w, Maria, & dt, Julia D. Smith, gct Benjaminville MM, Ill. (H)

DYMOND
1909, 2, 25. Elizabeth d; cremated

1878, 9, 23. Georgina m Chas. F. HOPKINS

1876, 2, 17. Mary Georgian recrq
1891, 8, 20. Elizabeth recrq

EACHUS
1845, 8, 21. Homer Jr. rocf Chester MM, dtd 1845,7,21 (H)

ECKHOFF
1883, 2, 8. Nettie Haisley b

1918, 4, 12. Nettie H. [Eckoff] dropped from mbrp

EDMUNDSON
1819, 3, 18. Edward rocf Murderkill MM, Del., dtd 1819,1,11
1819, 12, 16. Edward con mcd
1832, 7, 19. Edward gct Springborough MM

EDWARDS
1866, 2, 5. Nettie, dt David & Martha J., b
1871, 5, 22. Eliza E., dt David & Martha J., b
1875, 6, 15. Eusis Helen White, dt M. Morris & Hannah Amelia, b
1878, --, --. Hannah d
1899, 9, 27. Jemima d bur West Fork
1912, 10, 25. Anna B. d

1840, 5, 21. Jemima & Nancy, ch Jemima, rocf Caesars Creek MM, O., dtd 1840,4,24
1843, 4, 20. Wm. rocf Caesars Creek MM, O., dtd 1843,1,26
1851, 9, 18. Jemima recrq
1870, 12, 15. David rocf Miami MM, O., dtd 1870,11,23
1874, 12, 17. Martha J. recrq
1875, 9, 16. David & w, Martha J., & ch, Nettie & Eliza E., gct Dover MM, O.
1876, 4, 20. Hannah rocf Clear Creek MM, O., dtd 1876,2,12
1876, 8, 17. Nettie, dt David & Martha, rocf Miami MM, O., dtd 1876,7,26
1899, 1, 13. Nancy dropped from mbrp

ELLANS
----, --, --. Joseph & Rachel
Ch: Martha d 1809, 4, 3
Joseph
Tullon " 1819, 9,23

ELLERMAN
1880, 10, 21. Joseph [Elleman] & w, Eunice, & ch, Angus, Maggie & Enos W., rocf Pipe Creek MM, Ind., dtd 1880,10,9
1882, 4, 20. Joseph & w, Eunice, & ch, Enos, gct Pipe Creek MM, Ind.
1882, 4, 20. Angus & Maggie gct Pipe Creek MM, Ind.

EMBREE
1818, 9, 24. Jesse, s James & Rebecca, Highland Co., O.; m in Cincinnati Mtg, Mary DICKINSON, dt John & Susannah, Highland Co., O.

1820, 4, 20. Elisha rocf Bradford MM, Pa., dtd 1820,3,8
1821, 4, 26. Davis dis disunity
1828, 1, 31. Elisha dis mou
1830, 12, 30. Mary dis jH
1831, 10, 27. Daniel & w, Sarah, & ch, Rachel, Wm. L., Margaretta & Hannah Mary, rocf Alexandria MM, D. C., dtd 1831,7,21 (H)
1832, 9, 20. James rocf Deerfield MM, O., dtd 1832,6,14
1833, 6, 20. Rachel, Wm., Margaret, Hannah & Mary, rocf Baltimore MM, E. & W. Dist., dtd 1833,5,9
1834, 7, 17. James gct Deerfield MM, O.
1837, 2, 23. Mary gct Phila. MM, Pa. (H)
1837, 10, 19. Rachel, Wm., Margaret, Hannah &

EMBREE, continued
Mary, ch Daniel, gct Mississinewa MM, Ind.

EUSTIS
1901, 4, 9. Geo. Dexter, s Geo. & Nancy (Claypoole), Highland Co., O.; m in Cincinnati Mtg, Helen Lawson WHITE, dt Mordecai Morris & Hannah, Amelia, Highland Co., O.

EVANS
----, --, --. Joseph, s Robert & Rebecca, b 1773,1,11; m Rachel McCOOK, dt Gabriel & Elizabeth, b 1774,11,27
Ch: Nancy b 1799, 12, 10; m Oliver BENTON
Elizabeth " 1801, 6, 14; m Chas. ANTHONY
Robert Franklin " 1803, 7, 7; m Nancy FIFER
Rebecca " 1805, 7, 16
Susan " 1807, 12, 27
Martha " 1810, 4, 3 d 1810, 5, 3 bur West Branch
Mary b 1811, 9, 17 d 1813, 9, 7 bur Cincinnati
Sarah b 1815, 4, 7 " 1816, 7,18
Joseph Fulton b 1818, 9, 27 " 1819, 9,19 bur Cincinnati
1820, 3, 23. Elizabeth m Chas. ANTHONY
----, --, --. Jason b 1807,11,25 d 1876,3,11; m Mary ----- b 1815,8,12
Ch: Sarah b 1837, 6, 12
Benjamin F. " 1843, 4, 23
Susan " 1841, 1, 1
1871, 6, 19. Ulysses b
1874, 4, 16. Cyrus b
1889, 4, 24. Mary d (H)

1817, 11, 20. Nancy Benton (form Evans) con mcd
1826, 3, 30. Robert dis mcd
1829, 8, 27. Rachel dis jH
1832, 1, 26. Rebecca gct West Branch MM, O.
1832, 1, 26. Susan gct West Branch MM, O.
1832, 5, 31. Joseph & w, Rachel, & ch, Rebecca & Susannah, gct Miami MM, O. (H)
1832, 9, 20. Joseph dis disunity
1833, 6, 20. Francis W. rocf Phila. MM, Pa., dtd 1831,10,19 (H)
1833, 8, 15. Francis W. rocf Phila. MM. W. Dist., dtd 1833,4,24
1835, 4, 23. Francis W. [Evens] gct Phila. MM, Pa. (H)
1840, 10, 15. Wm. Henry, s Martha, recrq
1840, 11, 19. Martha rst; dis at Short Creek MM, O.
1841, 3, 18. Martha Dilworth & ch, Rankin, Abigail R., Caleb J. & Sarah M. Dilworth, & Wm. Henry Evans, gct Salem MM, Ind.
1844, 2, 22. Jasen [Evens] & w, Mary, & ch, Sarah, Susannah & Benjamin, rocf Miami MM, dtd 1844,2,22
1845, 4, 17. Wm. G. Kinsey gct Miami MM, O., to m Ann C. Evens
1846, 8, 20. John rocf White Water MM, Ind., dtd 1846,5,29 (H)
1855, 6, 20. Benj. rocf Miami MM, O., dtd 1855,4,25 (H)
1863, 1, 22. Benj. con mcd (H)
1864, 6, 23. Susie E. Cunningham (form Evans) con mcd (H)
1871, 12, 21. Benj. con mcd (H)
1885, 5, 21. Reese M. & w, Ellen A., recrq
1892, 5, 19. Reese M. & w, Ellen A., & ch, Ulysses & Cyrus, dropped from mbrp

FALLIS
1848, 4, 27. Isaac, s Amos & Lydia, Highland Co., O.; m in Cincinnati Mtg, Mary C. BONSALL, dt Joseph & Elisa, Highland Co., O.
Ch: Joseph B. b 1849, 3, 1 d 1857, 4, 8
Clara Best " 1851, 5, 21 " 1852,--,-- bur New Graveyard
Ellan Wright b 1853, 6, 30

1844, 7, 18. Isaac C., minor, rocf Centre MM, dtd 1844,6,12
1855, 12, 20. Mary dis jas
1856, 2, 14. Isaac C. dis jas
1877, 10, 18. Ellen McCrea (form Fallis) dis jas

FAETH
1927, 8, 7. Harold m Amy GUSWEILER

1927, 1, 7. Harold recrq
1931, 5, 1. Erma recrq

FARMER
1849, 3, 15. Luzena C. [Farmar] rocf Springfield MM, dtd 1848,11,18
1849, 11, 15. Luzena C. rocf Springfield MM, dtd 1849,11,18
1851, 4, 17. Luzina C. Winter (form Farmer) con mcd

FARQUHAR
----, --, --. Cyrus, s Benj. & Rachel F., b 1777,7,6 d 1844,8,--; m Lydia -----
Ch: R. Henry b 1828, 2, 28
Louisa " 1831, 5, 10
George

1834, 4, 17. Cyrus & w, Lydia, & ch, Richard, Louisa & Henry, rocf Center MM, dtd 1833, 11,13
1846, 3, 19. Louisa, dt Cyrus & Lydia, gct Centre MM
1865, 7, 20. Richard Henry & George dropped from mbrp

FEBIGER
1846, 9, 17. Sarah T. rocf Wilmington MM, dtd 1846,8,6
1849, 3, 15. Sarah S. gct Delaware MM, Del.

FENTON
1883, 6, 17. Cora A. rocf Newberry MM, O.

FIELDS
1841, 3, 18. Jane (form Brackett) dis mcd
1865, 7, 20. Jane Bryant dropped from mbrp

FINKBINE
1824, 12, 30. Lydia (form Swift) dis mcd

FISHER
1817, 8, 3. -----, dt Jonathan d bur Cincinnati Public Grounds
1869, 8, 22. Rachel A. d

1818, 2, 19. Elizabeth & ch, Mary Ann, Lucinda, Thos. Elwood, Sarah, Hannah & Matilda, rocf South River MM, dtd 1817,12, 13
1821, 2, 22. Elias & w, Hannah, gct Springfield MM
1830, 8, 26. Sarah Houser (form Fisher) con mcd
1833, 9, 20. Ellwood dis disunity
1836, 2, 18. Hannah Moore (form Fisher) con mcd
1842, 6, 23. Rachel A. (form Hopkins) con mcd (H)
1857, 2, 19. Cert rec for Thos. from Scipio MM, N. Y., dtd 1855,11,14, returned; dis disunity
1868, 10, 15. Lucinda dis disunity

FLETCHER
1835, 1, 15. Cert rec for Robert from SD MM, Pa., dtd 1833,12,24, returned for mcd
1836, 7, 21. Mary Ann (form Haines) dis mcd (H)
1842, 7, 21. Benj. rocf SD MM, dtd 1842,4,27
1844, 3, 21. Mary Ann rocf Salem MM, N. J., dtd 1844,1,31
1847, 5, 20. Benj. dis mcd
1868, 5, 21. Mary Ann gct Fairfield MM
1882, 5, 18. Mordecai H. rocf White Water MM, Ind., dtd 1882,3,23
1884, 3, 20. Mordecai H. gct White Water MM, Ind., to m Anna E. Perry
1902, 5, 9. Mordecai H. relrq

FOGG
1829, 4, 30. Cert rec for Samuel & w, Elizabeth, & dt, Sarah Ann, rocf ND MM, dtd 1828,10,25, endorsed to White Water MM, Ind.
1830, 3, 25. Samuel & w, Elizabeth, & dt, Sarah, gct Phila. MM, Pa.

FOLGER
----, --, --. Elizabeth, w David, b 1779,5,28 d 1837,6,2 bur New Gr. Yd.
----, --, --. Silvanus, s Solomon & Lydia, b 1762,8,9 d 1822,4,25; m Margaret RUSSELL dt Daniel & Hepsebeth, b 1764,7,3 d 1832, --,--
Ch: Avis b 1788, 4, 17
Hepzibeth " 1790, 5, 15 d 1791, 7,14
Lydia " 1792, 1, 26 " 1793, 9,25
Phebe " 1794, 1, 24
George " 1796, 1, 24 " 1797, 9,18
Elizabeth " 1798, 10, 27
----, --, --. Tristram, s Tristram & Mary, b 1772,10,28 d 1814,10,15; m Mary FOLGER, dt Nathaniel & Mary, b 1773,12,19 d 1823, 3,8
Ch: Tristram C. b 1795, 9, 28
Eunice " 1797, 5, 8 d 1813,10,10 bur Cincinnati
Elizabeth b 1799, 5, 30
Nathaniel " 1801, 5, 7 " 1802, 9,21
Mary " 1803, 4, 19
Edward " 1805, 6, 27 " 1806, 5,13 bur Cincinnati Public Grounds
Sarah b 1808, 7, 11
Jared " 1810, 11, 26
Edward 2nd " 1814, 8, 3
----, --, --. David, s David & Anna, b 1758, 3,22; m Elizabeth FOLGER, dt Solomon & Lydia, b 1768,11,13
Ch: Anna b 1795, 11, 27 d 1796, 6,27
Elizabeth " 1798, 3, 19
Mary " 1800, 1, 24
Rebecca " 1802, 7, 21 " 1802,11,27
Lydia " 1805, 1, 22 " 1806, 6,19
Phebe R. " 1814, 10, 9 " 1815, 1, 5
----, --, --. Elihue b 1763,10,2 d 1837,5,6 bur New Gr. Yd.; m Elizabeth ----- b 1798, 3,19 d 1851,--,-- bur New Gr. Yd.
Ch: Mary Way b 1819, 7, 11
----, --, --. Jethro, s Elihu & Mary, b 1795, 2,10; m Mary MACY, dt Geo. & Elizabeth, b 1901,8,14
Ch: George M. b 1820, 2, 22
Sarah M. " 1821, 11, 8
----, --, --. Seth, s Elihu & Mary, b 1796, 11,13; m Lydia CLASSBY, dt Chas. & Elizabeth, b 1801,9,27 d 1836,9,27
Ch: Charles C. b 1823, 2, 13 d 1823, 6,--
Seth " ----, --, -- " 1837, 5, 3
1830, 4, 7. Margaret m Adam COFFIN

1815, 5, 18. Mary & dt, Sarah & Phebe, rocf Nantucket MM
1815, 8, 17. Elizabeth recrq
1818, 12, 17. Margaret (form Masey) con mcd
1819, 1, 21. Tristram dis mcd
1819, 7, 15. Mary Anne dis disunity
1820, 10, 19. Lydia (form Clasby) con mcd
1822, 1, 31. Eliza Ann Smith (form Folger) con mcd
1825, 1, 27. Eliza Clark (form Folger) dis

FOLGER, continued
mcd
1830, 5, 27. Sarah Crane (form Folger) dis mcd
1830, 7, 29. Mary dis jas
1831, 11, 24. Margaret dis disunity
1839, 10, 17. Mary dis jas

FOSTER
----, --, --. Thomas, s Asa & Sarah, b 1796, 2,13; m Eliza COFFIN, dt Isaiah & Sarah, b 1801,8,28
Ch: Benjamin
Franklin b 1820, 1, 28
Isiah C. " 1821, 9, 12 d 1822,10,25
William E. " 1823, 9, 4

1820, 3, 16. Eliza (form Coffin) con mcd
1828, 2, 28. Eliza Brown (form Foster) con mcd
1905, 11, 10. Edith Bailey relrq

FOULKE
1817, 9, 14. Sidney, dt Judah & Sarah, d
----, --, --. Thomas & Cassandra
Ch: Ann Eliza b 1819, 2, 15
Everad " 1821, 5, 9 d 1822,7, 2

1815, 7, 20. Thomas rocf Richland MM, Pa., dtd 1815,6,2
1817, 10, 16. Thomas D. con mcd
1826, 7, 27. Levi rocf Guynedd MM, dtd 1826, 6,1
1826, 7, 27. Judah & w, Sarah, & ch, Samuel, Margaret, Thomas, Lydia, Sarah & Mary, gct White Water MM, Ind.
1827, 9, 27. Thos. D. con mcd
1828, 1, 31. John M. & w, Ann, rocf Baltimore MM, Md., dtd 1828,1,11
1830, 3, 25. Ann dis jH
1830, 9, 30. John M. dis jH
1839, 12, 26. Levi con mcd (H)
1840, 11, 26. John M. & w, Ann, & ch, Edward & Lydia, gct Baltimore MM, Md. (H)
1865, 7, 20. Ann Eliza & Edward dropped from mbrp

FRANKLAND
1849, 4, 26. Agnes m Samuel HAUGHTON

1847, 6, 17. Benj., Ann, Thos. & Frances Maris, ch Thos. & Sarah, rocf Hardshaw East MM, Manchester, Eng., dtd 1847,4,14
1847, 6, 17. Agnes & Mary rocf Hardshaw East MM, Manchester, England, dtd 1847,4,14
1859, 8, 18. Mary dis jas
1862, 8, 21. Anna & Frances relrq
1863, 10, 15. Thos. dis jas
1865, 11, 17. Benj. con mcd
1871, 12, 21. Benjamin gct Chicago MM, Ill.

FRENCH
1845, 7, 24. Wm. B. rocf Miami MM, O., dtd 1845,6,25 (H)
1845, 9, 25. Wm. B. gct Green Plain MM, O., to m (H)
1861, 4, 25. Wm. B. dis disunity (H)
1918, 4, 12. Laura W. dropped from mbrp

FULLER
1847, 8, 19. Robert Charlton rocf Scipio MM, N. J., dtd 1847,3,17
1847, 10, 21. Cert rec for John Wilkinson from Scipio MM, N. Y., dtd 1847,3,17, returned; mcd

FULLERTON
1826, 2, 26. Eliza (form Wing) dis mcd

FULTON
1838, 2, 22. Hannah B. rocf Springborough MM, dtd 1838,1,25 (H)

GANO
----, --, --. Aaron Goforth m Cornelia HAGAMAN
Ch: Nixon b 1864, 4, 2
Laura " 1874, 3, 9

1872, 3, 21. Aron Goforth & w, Cornelia Hagaman, & s, Nixon, recrq (H)
1884, 11, 20. Aaron & w, Cornelia, & ch, Nixon & Laura, gct White Water MM, Ind. (H)

GARNER
1820, 3, 16. Hepsebah (form Coffin) dis mcd
1820, 12, 21. Phebe (form Hussey) con mcd
1821, 1, 25. Robert & w, Hepzibah, & dt, Lydia, gct Silver Creek MM
1842, 9, 15. Edmund B., minor, rocf Bedford MM, Mass., dtd 1842,5,26
1853, 2, 17. Edmund B. dis

GARRETSON
1870, 2, 17. Mary recrq
1877, 7, 19. Mary gct Friendsville MM, Tenn.

GATCHELL
1851, 3, 20. Alfred rocf Dublin MM, Ireland, dtd 1851,2,11
1857, 8, 20. Alfred dis mcd

GATES
1859, 8, 31. Frances A. White b

1819, 2, 18. Susanna rocf Miami MM, O., dtd 1819,1,27
1865, 7, 20. Susannah dropped from mbrp
1906, 4, 13. Frances A. relrq

GAUNT
1865, 8, 24. Sarah C. rocf Piles Grove MM, N. J. (H)

GEST
----, --, --. Joseph, s Joseph & Deborah,

GEST, Joseph, continued
b 1776,3,4; m Rebecca MOORE, dt James & Jane, b 1791,7,15
Ch: James b 1814, 3, 21 d 1814, 3,22
bur Sadsbury, Pa.
Clarissa b 1815, 8, 16 " 1901, 6,25
bur Spring Grove
Erasmus b 1820, 4, 12 " 1908, 2, 7
Joseph
John " 1830, 1, 9
1855, 1, 25. Joseph J., s Joseph & Rebecca, Highland Co., O.; m in Cincinnati MH, Susan A. BAILEY, dt Micajah & Phebe, Highland Co., O.

1818, 10, 15. Joseph & w, Rebecca, & dt, Clarissa, rocf Sadsbury MM, Pa., dtd 1818,5,5
1829, 10, 29. Joseph dis jH (H)
1834, 6, 19. Clarissa dis jH
1848, 5, 10. Clarissa rst
1893, 9, 14. Erasmus, s Clifford Haworth Gest, recrq
1903, 2, 13. Joseph G. dropped from mbrp
1903, 2, 13. Susan A. dropped from mbrp
1903, 2, 13. Joseph Henry dropped from mbrp
1903, 2, 13. Clifford H. dropped from mbrp

GIBLON
1913, 10, 18. Earl Z. m Anna WILLIAMS

GIBSON
1815, 9, 2. Joshua & w, Lydia, rocf Redstone MM, Pa., dtd 1815,4,28
1815, 10, 19. Eliza rocf Redstone MM, Pa.
1816, 5, 10. Mary rocf Redstone MM, Pa., dtd 1816,4,28
1816, 10, 17. Mary Glenn (form Gibson) dis mcd
1825, 5, 26. Eliza Cranmer (form Gibson) dis mcd
1865, 6, 22. Ruth con mcd (H)

GILLINGHAM
----, --, --. Helen, dt Harper & Eliza, b 1843,1,13 d 1843,6,16

1839, 2, 21. Wm. & w, Jane, & ch, Catharine, Esther Ann & Sarah, rocf Balt. MM, dtd 1839,1,11 (H)
1839, 2, 21. Eliza rocf Balt. MM, dtd 1839, 1,11 (H)
1844, 10, 24. Eliza dis mcd (H)
1846, 10, 22. Hetty Selden (form Gillingham) con mcd (H)

GIRTON
1900, 10, 29. Howard M., s Geo. & Lydia, Washington Co., O.; m in Cincinnati Mtg, Augusta L. WILL, dt Richard & Elsie, Highland Co., O.

1901, 2, 8. Augusta Will relrq

GLENN
1816, 10, 17. Mary (form Gibson) dis mcd

GODARD
1868, 5, 21. Mary H., w Joseph, & ch, Wm. Henry, rocf New Garden MM, dtd 1868,4,18
1869, 1, 21. Mary H. [Goddard] & w, Wm. H., gct New Garden MM, Ind.

GOODIN
1881, 3, 11. Lucy relrq

GOUGH
1848, 7, 20. Mary rocf Dublin MM, dtd 1846,11,8 endorsed by New York MM, N. Y., dtd 1848,6,7
1849, 5, 17. Mary gct White Water MM, Ind.
1850, 12, 19. Mary rocf White Water MM, Ind., dtd 1850,10,23
1855, 4, 19. Mary gct Dublin MM

GRANVILLE
1913, 7, 11. Richard F. dropped from mbrp

GRAY
1855, 5, 17. Anna (form Bonsall) dis mcd

GREEN
1910, 3, 1. Sarah Ann d bur Martinsville,O.

1846, 9, 17. Daniel rocf Salem MM, O., dtd 1846,7,22
1849, 6, 14. Daniel gct Salem MM, O.
1860, 11, 15. Sewel & w, Tamer, & ch, Francis Marion & Maria Alma, rocf Clear Creek MM, O., dtd 1860,10,13
1864, 5, 19. Sewell & ch, Frances Marion, Maria Alma & David Alonzo, gct Clear Creek MM, O.
1864, 6, 16. Jehiel & w, Rachel, & ch, Joel Wm., James Robert, Aseph Leander, Amanda Jane & Lieuemma Catharine, rocf Springfield MM, O.
1868, 3, 19. Joel Wm. gct Bangor MM, Ia.
1868, 3, 19. Jehiel & w, Rachel, & ch, James Robert, Asaph, Leander, Amanda Jane & Susanna Catharine, gct Bangor MM, Ia.
1870, 6, 16. John P. rocf Goshen MM, dtd 1870,4,23
1886, 3, 17. John P. relrq
1900, 10, 12. Sarah Ann rocf Newberry MM, O., dtd 1900,6,14

GRIEST
1867, 7, 25. Jane rocf Springborough MM (H)

GRIFFITH
1845, 3, 26. Margaretta rocf Chester MM, Pa., dtd 1845,1,27
1845, 10, 16. Collins W. rocf White Water MM, Ind., dtd 1845,9,24
1845, 12, 18. Eli & w, Rachel, rocf White Water MM, Ind., dtd 1845,11,26

GRIFFITH, continued
1846, 9, 17. Eli & w, Rachel, gct Springborough MM
1846, 9, 17. Collins W. gct Springborough MM
1852, 5, 20. Margaretta Prackett (form Griffith) con mcd
1856, 10, 16. Hezekiah B. Bailey gct Hopewell MM, Va., to m Elizabeth B. Griffith

GROFF
----, --, --. William & Sarah Elizabeth
Ch: Willie
Nesley b 1854, 5, 4
Florence " 1863, 8, 1

1831, 6, 30. Sarah rocf Piles Grove MM, N. J., dtd 1831,4,26 (H)

GUSWEILER
----, --, --. Joseph G. & Laura U. B.
Ch: Ellen
Elverta b 1904, 2, 10
Ripley
Frank " 1905, 10, 19 d 1908,11, 3
Amy Annetta" 1908, 12, 25
Anna Margaret " 1911, 2, 5
Frederick
Walton " 1912, 11, 5
Joseph
George Jr." 1915, 6, 25
1906, 6, 14. Frank Morton b
1927, 8, 7. Amy m Harold FAETH

1895, 6, 27. Frank R. recrq
1897, 5, 20. Joseph G. & Richard recrq
1905, 6, 9. Laura recrq
1905, 12, 8. Ripley Frank, s Joseph G. & Laura, recrq
1916, 4, 14. Lura B. & ch, Ellen Elverta, Amy Annetta, Anna Margaret, Frederick Walton & Joseph Geo. Jr., relrq
1926, 4, 11. Joseph Geo. & Frederick Walton, ch Joseph G., recrq
1927, 2, 4. Anna Margaret & Amy A., recrq
1928, 1, 6. Lura recrq
1932, 5, 2. Anna Margaret & Frederick Walton, recrq
1932, 4, 1. Joseph Jr. recrq

HADLEY
1846, 8, 20. Joshua D. & w, Rachel, & ch, Wm., Amos L., James & Mary Ann, rocf Newberry MM, dtd 1846,6,18
1847, 5, 20. Cert rec for Jeremiah & w, Esther, & ch, John, Smith, James Wm., Jane Ann & Samuel S., from Center MM, dtd 1847, 3,17, endorsed to White Water MM, Ind.
1848, 8, 17. Joshua D. & w, Rachel, & ch, Amos L. & James D., gct Newberry MM

HAGERMAN
1887, 7, 21. Geo. E. rocf Clear Creek MM, O.
1899, 6, 9. George E. dropped from mbrp

HAINES
1871, 5, 30. Mary m Wm. H. TAYLOR
1887, 11, 10. Josiah d

1817, 7, 17. Margaret gct Miami MM, O.
1818, 5, 21. Margaret Canby (form Haines) dis mcd
1818, 5, 21. Amos dis disunity
1821, 8, 30. Josiah dis disunity
1831, 6, 30. Mary Ann rocf Piles Grove MM, N. J., dtd 1830,4,26 (H)
1836, 7, 21. Mary Ann Fletcher (form Haines) dis mcd (H)
1856, 10, 23. Elnora & ch, Mary Elizabeth, John, Charles & Edward K., rocf White Water MM, Ind., dtd 1856,9,24 (H)
1865, 3, 23. Eleanor & ch, John & Chas., gct White Water MM, Ind. (H)

HAISLEY
----, --, --. Allen m Abigail Emily TOWNSEND, dt Isaac & Peninah, b 1847,12,17
Ch: Clara F. b 1866, 3, 16
Peninah Ann" 1868, 10, 5
Ida May " 1874, 5, 12
----, --, --. Clifford b 1877,8,26 d 1900,8, 24 bur Tien Tsin, China
1881, 1, 6. Howard b
1883, 2, 8. Nettie b

1868, 5, 21. Abigail Emily (form Townsend) con mcd
1872, 10, 17. Allen rocf Oak Ridge MM, Ind., dtd 1869,11,16
1892, 6, 10. Allen & w, Abigail E., & ch, Clara T., Penninnah Ann & Ida May, relrq
1918, 4, 12. Howard dropped from mbrp

HALL
1891, 6, 8. Judith Delphine rocf WD MM
1918, 4, 12. Judith D. dropped from mbrp

HAM
1878, 9, 14. Martha Elizabeth d bur Richmond, Ind.

1874, 12, 17. Martha Elizabeth rocf White Water MM, Ind., dtd 1874,11,25

HAMPTON
1819, 5, 20. Cert rec for Julia & ch, Emily, Oliver & Henry Dennis, from Short Creek MM, O., dtd 1819,--,19, endorsed to Springfield MM

HANCOCK
1853, 6, 28. Jacob, h Isabella (form Brown), d bur Spring Grove
1892, 2, 2. Isabella (Brown), d bur Spring Grove
1899, 1, 31. Thomas, s Jacob & Isabella,

HANCOCK, continued
bur Oak Grove Cemetery, Marietta, O.

1849, 9, 21. Jacob rocf Dublin MM, dtd 1847, 4,13
1851, 7, 17. Joseph con mcd
1853, 4, 14. Thomas, s Jacob & Isabella, recrq
1858, 7, 15. Isabella recrq

HANDLEY
1931, 12, 4. Dr. Daniel E. & w, Margaret Matilda & Daniel Jr., recrq

HANEN
1850, 12, 26. Rebecca H. (form Paddock) con mcd (H)

HANSON
1878, 2, 14. Emily Allen b

HARE
1828, 5, 29. Mary & dt, Jemima, rocf West Branch MM, Va., dtd 1828,3,22
1828, 5, 29. John Jr. rocf West Branch MM, Va., dtd 1828,3,22
1830, 10, 28. John dis mcd
1831, 1, 27. Mary & dt, Jemima, gct Miami MM, O.
1840, 1, 16. Mary & dt, Jemima, gct Fairfield MM

HARKNESS
1873, 1, 16. Robert P. rocf Providence MM, R. I., dtd 1872,12,25
1878, 12, 19. Robert P. dis disunity

HARLAN
----, --, --. George W., s Enoch & Hannah, b 1810,--,-- d 1877,11,25 bur Spring Grove

1838, 5, 17. Geo. W. rocf Fallowfield MM, Pa., dtd 1838,7,25
1843, 12, 21. Hannah rocf London Grove MM, dtd 1843,11,9
1848, 5, 10. Hannah gct Birmingham MM, Pa.
1892, 2, 18. Warren E. rocf Miami MM, O., dtd 1892,1,27
1913, 7, 11. Warren E. dropped from mbrp

HARMAN
1887, 10, 20. Jamima Woolman relrq (H)

HARRISON
1833, 11, 14. Robert rocf Milford MM, Ind., dtd 1833,9,28
1834, 2, 13. Robert gct Milford MM, Ind.

HART
1841, 10, 21. Mary (form Pugh) con mcd
1853, 8, 18. Mary A. dis jas

HARTLEY
1819, 2, 18. Thos. & w, Barbera, & ch, Eliza, Leah, Esther, Sarah Norton & Rachel, rocf Providence MM, R. I., dtd 1818,9,22
1822, 12, 20. Thos. & w, Barbara, & ch, Eliza, Leah, Esther, Sarah, Norton, Rachel, Rebecca, Elias & Hannah, gct Silver Creek MM Ind.

HARTSHORN
----, --, --. John D., s James & Sarah, b 1823,3,6; m Elizabeth H. SCHOOLEY, dt Benj. & Ann, b 1824,8,29 d 1893,7,11
----, --, --. John D. b 1823,6,13 d 1899,3,10 bur Spring Grove

1817, 8, 21. Patterson rocf Baltimore MM, Md., dtd 1817,7,11
1820, 2, 19. Mary rocf Baltimore MM, Md., dtd 1820,1,7
1848, 12, 21. Elizabeth (form Schooley) con mcd
1874, 3, 19. John D. recrq

HARVEY
1815, 5, 25. Isaac, s William & Elizabeth, Columbiana Co., O.; m in Cincinnati Mtg, Agatha DICKS, dt Micajah & Sarah TERROL
1848, 1, 29. Chas. Townsend, s Joshua & Lavina, b

1815, 10, 19. Agatha gct Center MM, O.
----, --, --. Lavinia rocf Little Falls MM, dtd 1845,2,12 (H)
1846, 5, 21. Joshua & s, Henry, rocf White Water MM, Ind., dtd 1846,4,22 (H)
1847, 3, 25. Levina rocf Little Falls MM, Md., dtd 1845,2,12 (H)
1868, 4, 23. Joshua gct Phila. MM, Pa. (H)
1868, 4, 23. Lavinia & ch, Chas. T. & Eugene, gct Phila. MM, Pa. (H)
1868, 4, 23. Henry gct Phila. MM, Pa. (H)
1887, 12, 15. Eli rocf Springfield MM, O., dtd 1887,11,19
1920, 8, 8. Eli dropped from mbrp

HATHAWAY
----, --, --. Wm. E. & Martha
Ch: Grace b 1875, 3, 1
Wm. Baxter " 1877, 5, 20

1874, 11, 19. Wm. E. rocf Chicago MM, Ill., dtd 1874,10,21
1875, 2, 18. Lillie F., dt Wm. S., rocf Chicago MM, Ill.
1876, 12, 21. Martha T. recrq
1879, 5, 15. Wm. E. relrq
1885, 5, 21. Martha J. & ch, Lillie T., Grace & Wm., gct Maryville MM, Tenn.
1887, 11, 17. Lily T. rocf Marvyille MM, Tenn., dtd 1887,10,22
1889, 8, 15. Lillie relrq

HATTON
1815, 6, 15. Geo. rocf Center MM, O., dtd 1815,5,20
1816, 2, 15. Edward rocf Center MM, O., dtd 1815,12,10
1817, 1, 16. Edward gct Miami MM, O.
1821, 3, 29. Geo. & w, Margaret, & s, Robert, gct White Water MM, Ind.
1827, 7, 26. Rachel rocf Springborough MM, dtd 1827,5,29
1830, 12, 30. Rachel dis jH
1845, 3, 20. Geo. & w, Margaret, gct White Water MM, Ind. (H)

HAUGHTON
1849, 4, 26. Samuel, s Benjamin & Anna, Highland Co., O., d 1887,11,10 ae 77; m in Cincinnati Mtg, Agnes FRANKLAND, dt Thos. & Sarah, d 1908,8,17
Ch: Benjamin Frankland b 1850, 3, 31
Anne " 1853, 1, 10 d 1855,11, 5
Thos. Wilfred " 1855, 10, 21 " 1879, 9,24 bur Spring Grove
Sarah Maria b 1858, 8, 19
Agnes Elizabeth " 1861, 3, 25

1821, 7, 26. Mary rocf Phila. MM, Pa., dtd 1821,4,26
1824, 5, 27. Wm. rocf Carlow MM, Ireland, dtd 1823,4,11
1824, 9, 30. Wm. gct Silver Creek MM, Ind.
1824, 10, 28. Maria gct Silver Creek MM, Ind.
1847, 8, 19. Samuel rocf Lurgan MM, Ireland
1848, 5, 10. Malcomb rocf Hardshaw West MM, Liverpool, Eng., dtd 1847,11,25
1858, 7, 15. Cert for Malcom from New York MM, N. Y., returned 1858,12,16; dis disunity
1859, 5, 19. Malcolm dis disunity
1865, 7, 20. Mary dropped from mbrp
1879, 11, 20. Thos. Milford gct Lisburn MM, Ireland
1886, 4, 15. Sarah M. relrq
1920, 8, 8. Benj. dropped from mbrp

HAUS
1881, 10, 20. Cert rec for Adelia from Bloomington MM, Ind., returned, cannot be located
1883, 4, 19. Adelia rocf Bloomington MM, Ind., dtd 1881,9,7
1885, 5, 21. Adelia dropped from mbrp; unable to locate her

HAVEN
----, --, --. James L. m Rebecca PADDOCK
Ch: George Irwin b 1851, 8, 15
Ella Paddock b 1853, 11, 19
Sarah Paddock " 1856, 4, 18
Georgetta Paddock " 1859, 2, 14
Phebe Paddock " 1861, 10, 4
Fannie Belle " 1865, 11, 14
Willie Augustus " 1866, 12, 16

1871, 3, 23. Rebecca dis disunity

HAWLEY
1854, 1, 26. Martha J. (form Jones) con mcd (H)

HAYDOCK
1885, 9, 21. Thomas T. d bur Spring Grove

1868, 10, 15. Cert rec for Thomas from Miami MM, O., dtd 1868,7,22, returned because jas
1873, 1, 16. John & w, Emily, & dt, Millie, rocf Clear Creek MM, O., dtd 1872,12,14
1905, 4, 14. Emily relrq

HEALD
1855, 3, 22. Wm. H., s Wm. & Sarah, Morrow Co., O.; m in Cincinnati Mtg, Susannah NEVILLE, dt Benjamin & Agnes, Highland Co., O.

1855, 5, 17. Susanna Neville gct Gilead MM, O.

HELLERMAN
----, --, --. Wm. rocf Salem MM, dtd 1850,4, 17 (H)

HENDERSON
1836, 9, 15. William Judkins gct Sadsbury MM, Pa., to m Susan Henderson

HENLEY
1922, 10, 6. Robert Barclay d

1889, 6, 20. Robert B. & w, Florence, & ch, Grace & Ruth, rocf Kerr City MM, Fla.

HIBBERD
1836, 7, 21. Samuel P. rocf Springborough MM, dtd 1836,2,25 (H)

HILDEBRANT
1874, 11, 19. Thos. Q. rocf Wilmington MM, O., dtd 1874,10,16
1879, 5, 22. Thos. Q. relrq

HILL
1866, 5, 4. Rowland, s Daniel & Martha A., b

HILL, continued
1864, 12, 15. Daniel rocf New Garden MM, Ind., dtd 1864,11,19
1865, 1, 19. Daniel gct Clear Creek MM, O., to m Martha Ann Hussey
1865, 5, 18. Martha Ann rocf Clear Creek MM, O., dtd 1865,4,18
1867, 5, 16. Daniel & w, Martha Ann, & ch, Chas. R., rocf Clear Creek MM, O.
1901, 5, 10. Elizabeth Josephine & Eugene Manning Jr., ch Eugene M. & Laura Shermen Hill, recrq
1920, 8, 8. Laura Shearman, Elizabeth & Eugene, dropped from mbrp

HILLES
1883, 4, 1. William, s Samuel E. & Eleanor, b
1883, 1, 4. Wm. Tatum, s Samuel F. & Amy G., b
1879, 4, 17. Samuel Eli rocf Wilmington MM, Del., dtd 1879,4,10
1894, 3, 15. Samuel E. & Amy T. relrq
1901, 8, 9. Wm. relrq
1907, 6, 14. Wm. Tatum recrq
1924, 1, 13. Wm. T. relrq

HILLMAN
1850, 8, 22. Wm. rocf Salem MM, dtd 1850,7,17 (H)

HINCHMAN
1845, 8, 21. Allen rocf WD MM, Pa.
1850, 9, 19. Allen dis mcd
1864, 6, 16. Margaretta S. recrq; dis by Buckingham MM, Pa.
1866, 5, 17. Margaretta L. gct Burlington MM, N. J.

HINSON
1901, 8, 9. Joseph recrq
1901, 10, 11. Emily N. recrq
1920, 8, 8. Joseph & Emily dropped from mbrp

HOBBS
1852, 3, 18. Henry [Hibbs] & w, Hannah, rocf Darlington MM, Eng., dtd 1851,12,2
1852, 3, 18. Joseph John rocf Reading & Warborough MM, Eng., dtd 1852,1,20
1852, 3, 18. Ann Louisa rocf Darlington MM, Eng., dtd 1851,12,2
1855, 12, 20. Anna Louisa Dodds (form Hobbs) dis mcd
1869, 1, 21. Joseph John gct Chicago MM,Ill.
1871, 5, 18. Henry & Hannah gct Southwark MM, Eng.

HOCKETT
1881, 12, 19. Sarah E. rocf Newberry MM, O., dtd 1881,6,20
1884, 8, 21. Uriah rocf Newberry MM, O., dtd 1884,7,21
1918, 4, 12. Uriah dropped from mbrp

HOGE
1846, 1, 15. Asa M. rocf Centre MM, dtd 1845,12,17
1846, 7, 16. Asa H. gct Center MM

HOLLOWAY
1814, 7, 27. Sarah, dt David, d bur Cincinnati Public Grounds

1819, 1, 21. Dayton gct Mill Creek MM, O.
1819, 2, 25. Lydia m Samuel PEIRCE
1823, 5, 29. David & w, Hannah, & ch, Hannah, David, Ruth & Jesse, gct White Water MM, Ind.
1823, 5, 29. Margaret & Abigail, gct White Water MM, Ind.
1831, 3, 31. David Jr. rocf White Water MM, Ind., dtd 1828,12,24
1832, 6, 14. Cert for David Jr. to White Water MM, Ind., returned 1832,9,20; dis disunity
1844, 5, 16. David P. dis mcd

HOLLOWELL
1874, 3, 19. James rocf Blue River MM, Ind., dtd 1874,2,14
1879, 1, 16. James S. gct Blue River MM, Ind.

HOLSOYD
1842, 11, 24. Hannah (form Tucker) con mcd (H)

HOPKINS
----, --, --. Benjamin, s Ebenezer & Ann, b 1771,11,29; m Rebecca WARD, dt Isaac & Rebecca, b 1772,4,7 d 1853,5,14 bur Hicksite Bur. Gr.

Ch:		
Ann	b 1796, 1, 6	
David	" 1797, 3, 2	d 1898, 4,27 bur Haddonfield, N. J.
George	b 1798, 9, 12	" 1799,10, 4 bur Haddonfield, N. J.
Rebecca	b 1800, 7, 5	
Mary Cresson	" 1801, 12, 3	
Lydia Roach	" 1803, 1, 24	
Benjamin	" 1805, 3, 19	
Sarah	" 1807, 4, 16	
John Estaugh	" 1808, 12, 1	
Franklin	" 1810, 3, 30	
Alexander	" 1812, 12, 6	d 1812,12, 7 bur Waynesville Graveyard

1853, 5, 15. Rebecca d ae 81y 1m 8d (a minister)
----, --, --. Benjamin E. & -----

Ch:	
Charles A.	b 1856, 12, 7
Mary Eliza	" 1858, 9, 13
Anna Belle	" 1859, 10, 20
Jessie F.	" 1862, 8, 14
Alice	" 1866, 9, 23
William D.	" 1868, 11, 5

HOPKINS, continued
1878, 9, 23. Chas. F., s G. G. & Mary A., Highland Co., O.; m in Cincinnati Mtg, Georgina DYMOND, dt George F. & Jane, England
1882, 8, 23. Miriam b

1819, 6, 17. Sarah Bigford (form Hopkins) dis mcd
1820, 9, 21. Chas. rocf Phila. MM, Pa., dtd 1820,6,28
1824, 11, 25. Chas. gct Miami MM, O.
1829, 6, 25. Benj. dis jH
1829, 10, 29. Lydia R. dis jH (H)
1830, 3, 25. Rebecca Sr. dis jH
1830, 6, 24. Benj. W. con mcd (H)
1830, 8, 26. Sarah & Mary dis jH
1830, 9, 30. Ann dis jH
1830, 9, 30. Benj. Jr. dis mcd
1830, 12, 30. Rachel rocf Woodbury MM, N. J., dtd 1830,11,29 (H)
1833, 12, 26. Sarah Wright (form Hopkins) dis mcd (H)
1834, 2, 13. Rebecca recrq
1835, 8, 20. Lydia Jacobs (form Hopkins) dis mcd (H)
1835, 9, 17. John E. dis jas
1835, 10, 15. Franklin dis jas
1842, 6, 23. Rachel A. Fisher (form Hopkins) con mcd (H)
1856, 7, 24. Benj. E. con mcd (H)
1868, 4, 16. Rebecca dropped from mbrp
1870, 8, 25. Chas. Henderson, Mary Eliza, Anna Belle, Jesse Fremont, Alice H. & Wm. Dunlap, ch Benj. E., recrq (H)
1879, 11, 20. Chas. F. recrq
1892, 6, 10. Chas. H. & Georgina relrq
1903, 2, 13. Edna & Miriam dropped from mbrp

HORNIMAN
1849, 10, 18. Cert rec for Henry from Coggshall MM, Kelvendon, Eng., dtd 1849,7,2; returned because he mcd
1855, 4, 19. Henry rocf Coggshall MM, Halsted, Eng., dtd 1854,5,4
1869, 1, 21. Henry gct Chicago MM, Ill.

HOSKINS
1858, 4, 15. Richard & w, Anne, rocf Phila. MM, Pa., dtd 1858,3,17 (WDMM)
1863, 2, 12. Richard & Ann gct Manchester MM, Eng.
1902, 6, 13. Arthur Bewley gct Fairmount MM, Ind., to m Isabelle Hoskins

HOUSER
1830, 8, 26. Sarah (form Fisher) con mcd

HOWELL
1835, 8, 20. Emeline rocf Phila. MM, Pa.
1836, 6, 16. Emeline rocf WD MM dtd 1835,5,25
1865, 7, 20. Emeline dropped from mbrp

HOWLAND
1873, 12, 17. Chas. S., s Chas. W. & Gulielma, Highland Co., O.; m in Cincinnati Mtg, Mary C. SHIPLEY, dt Murray & Hannah D., Highland Co., O.
Ch: Murray S. b 1874, 11, 22

1872, 12, 19. Chas. S. rocf Wilmington MM, Del., dtd 1872,12,5
1878, 10, 17. Chas. S. & Mary S. relrq

HUESTON
1855, 12, 20. Margaret A. con mcd

HUFF
1870, 2, 17. Christie recrq

HUNT
1844, 11, 14. Albert, minor, rocf White Water MM, Ind., dtd 1844,9,25
1852, 3, 18. Albert dis mcd
1864, 6, 16. Solomon & w, Sarah, & ch, Benj. & Mary, rocf Mill Creek MM
1865, 3, 16. Solomon & w, Sarah, & ch, Benj. & Mary, gct Bloomfield MM, Ind.
1892, 1, 21. Clarkson A. rocf Newberry MM, O., dtd 1891,12,21
1897, 12, 17. Clarkson gct Chicago MM, Ill.
1900, 10, 12. Cert rec for Oliver from Newberry MM, O., dtd 1900,6,4, endorsed back to Newberry MM, O., 1900,12,14 by rq
1901, 9, 13. Ruth Anna rocf White Water MM, Ind., dtd 1901,8,22

HUNTLEY
1877, 9, 11. Elijah d bur Cumminsville Cemetery

1874, 5, 21. Elijah rocf Young MM, Canada, dtd 1874,3,12

HUSSEY
1820, 12, 21. Phebe Gardner (form Hussey) con mcd
1821, 8, 30. Phebe con mcd
1821, 10, 25. Phebe gct Nantucket MM
1831, 10, 27. Obed rocf New York MM, N. Y., dtd 1831,9,7
1839, 11, 14. Obed gct Baltimore MM
1865, 1, 19. Daniel Hill gct Clear Creek MM, O., to m Martha Ann Hussey

IDEN
1832, 6, 28. John & w, Mary, & ch, Hannah, Elizabeth, Wm., Sarah, Samuel & Mary Ellen, rocf Indian Spring MM, Md., dtd 1832, 3,7 (H)

INNES
1896, 3, 19. Elnetta recrq
1899, 6, 9. El Nettie relrq

JACKSON
1820, 12, 21. John & w, Anne, & ch, Amos, Elizabeth, Rebecca, Samuel, Joseph, Thos., Mary & Amanda, rocf Redstone MM, Pa., dtd 1820,9,2
1827, 11, 29. Elizabeth Riddle (form Jackson) dis mcd
1865, 7, 2[illegible]. John & w, Anna, & ch, Enos, Rebecca, Samuel, Joseph, Thos., Mary & Amanda, dropped from mbrp
1902, 5, 9. Caroline rocf Fairview MM, O., dtd 1893,2,4

JACOBS
1835, 8, 20. Lydia (form Hopkins) dis mcd (H)

JANDEN
1824, 8, 26. Susanna (form Lea) dis mcd

JANNEY
1850, 3, 21. Jacob rocf Salem MM, dtd 1850, 2,20 (H)
1850, 3, 21. Ellen rocf Salem MM, dtd 1850,2, 20 (H)
1855, 3, 22. Jacob gct Alexandria MM, Va. (H)
1855, 5, 24. Ellen M. gct Alexandria MM, Va. (H)

JESSUP
----, --, --. Herbert Levi, s L. M. & S. E., b 1870,4,29 d 1872,3,22 bur Richmond, Ind.
1872, 5, 26. Sarah Elma d bur Richmond, Ind.
1870, 7, 21. Lindley M. & w, Sarah Elma, rocf Spring Creek MM, Ia.
1872, 9, 19. Lindley M. gct White Water MM, Ind.

JENKINS
1846, 9, 17. David [Jinkins] rocf Short Creek MM, O., dtd 1846,7,21
1852, 9, 16. David P. dis mcd

JOHNSON
----, --, --. Brooks, s John & Judith, b 1817, 8,3 d 1900,4,2 bur Spring Grove
1844, 9, 26. David F., s John & Judith, Washington Co., O.; m in Cincinnati Mtg, Catharine CARPENTER, dt Nathaniel & Zeruiah, Highland Co., O.
----, --, --. Edwin & Eliza
Ch: Charles
Edward b 1852, 10, 6 d 1853, 1,30
Emily " 1854, 2, 7
----, --, --. Evan L. & Eunice
Ch: Morris
Lewis b 1853, 6, 28
Eva Eunice " 1856, 11, 25
----, --, --. Alfred & Anna M.
Ch: James Brooks d 1905,12,19
Elizabeth b 1864, 1, 23 " 1865, 9,14
Stephen M. " 1866, 1, 20 " 1868, 2,28

1864, 10, 27. Evan Lewis, s James & Elizabeth Wayne Co., Ind., b 1827,10,21 d 1901,5,31; m in Cincinnati Mtg, Anna M. TAYLOR, dt Caleb W. & Mary F., Highland Co., O., b 1841,6,20
Ch: Mary
Taylor b 1865, 9, 24 d 1866, 5, 7
Alice M. " 1867, 3, 30
Gracy Amy " 1869, 7, 11 " 1899, 7,27 bur Spring Grove
Laura E. b 1872, 9, 29
Eleanor B. " 1875, 10, 24
Julia Dean " 1877, 12, 17
Anna L. " 1879, 6, 24
Florence A." 1882, 9, 20
1867, 3, 21. Anne M., dt John & Elizabeth Thorne, d
1891, 9, 15. Alice Morris m Benj. Franklin LYLE
1906, 6, 5. Florency Anthony m Samuel Edward VANCE
1907, 11, 2. Mary V. d bur Leesburg, Fla.
1911, 1, 2. Evan Lewis d bur Spring Grove

1820, 1, 20. Deborah Butler & s, Anslem D. Johnson, rocf South River MM, Va., dtd 1819,9,11
1820, 9, 21. Christopher A. dis disunity
1845, 7, 17. Catharine, w Daniel, gct Miami MM, O.
1847, 3, 18. David F. & w, Catharine C., & s, Albert C., rocf Miami MM, O., dtd 1847, 1,29
1849, 6, 14. Edwin & w, Eliza, rocf Miami MM, dtd 1849,4,29
1852, 8, 19. Ansalon D. dis mcd
1857, 12, 17. Mary S., w Brooks, & ch, John Edward & Lucy B., rocf Miami MM, O., dtd 1857,11,25
1858, 4, 15. Eli & w, Mary C., rocf Miami MM, O., dtd 1858,2,24, endorsed by White Water MM, Ind., 1858,3,24
1863, 3, 19. Anna M. [Johnston] & ch, Isaac Thorne, James Brooks & John Wm., rocf White White Lick MM, endorsed by Wabash MM, Ind. 1863,2,14
1863, 4, 16. Eli & w, Mary C., relrq
1863, 9, 17. Alfred rocf White Lick MM, Ind., dtd 1863,9,9
1864, 6, 16. Thatcher & w, Mary K., & ch, Emma & Nellie, rocf Wabash MM
1864, 12, 15. Evan Lewis & ch, Morris L., & Eva E., rocf White Water MM, Ind., dtd 1864,11,23
1866, 11, 15. Brooks & w, Mary, & ch, Lucy B. & Chas., rocf Miami MM, O., dtd 1866,9,26
1866, 11, 15. John Edward rocf Miami MM, O., dtd 1866,9,26
1867, 3, 21. Alfred & w, Anna M., & ch, Isaac T., James B. & John Wm., gct Honey Creek MM, Ind.
1867, 6, 20. Edwin & w, Eliza S., & dt, Emily H., gct Milford MM, Ind.

JOHNSON, continued
1874, 4, 16. Emily rocf Indianapolis MM, Ind., dtd 1874,3,21
1879, 1, 16. Eliza S. rocf Indianapolis MM, Ind.
1884, 10, 16. Eliza L. gct Minneapolis MM, Minn.
1889, 12, 19. Morris L. dis
1893, 1, 18. Chas. S. C. relrq
1893, 9, 14. Nellie Johnson Watts relrq (dt Thatcher & Mary K. Johnson)
1924, 5, 11. Eleanor relrq
1933, 2, 3. Julia gct Arch St. MM, Phila., Pa.

JONES
1875, 5, 21. Isaac E. d ae 84y
1885, 6, 23. Priscilla d ae 58y

1815, 5, 18. Hannah rocf Gunpowder MM, dtd 1815,1,25
1817, 12, 18. Hannah gct Stillwater MM, O.
1845, 8, 21. Drusilla rocf White Water MM, Ind., dtd 1845,5,28
1845, 7, 24. Mary P. rocf White Water MM, Ind., dtd 1845,5,28 (H)
1845, 10, 23. Aquilla & w, Ann, & ch, Hannah, Margaret Ann, Sarah H., Martha & Elizabeth, rocf White Water MM, Ind., dtd 1825,9,24 (H)
1846, 2, 26. Hannah B. rocf White Water MM, Ind., dtd 1845,10,22 (H)
1846, 2, 26. Priscilla T. rocf White Water MM, Ind., dtd 1845,11,26 (H)
1846, 3, 26. Albert S. rocf White Water MM, Ind., dtd 1845,12,24 (H)
----, --, --. Wm. Bateman rocf White Water MM, Ind., dtd 1847,2,24 (H)
1847, 5, 20. Wm. Bateman rocf White Water MM, Ind., dtd 1847,2,24 (H)
1848, 11, 23. Isaac E. rocf White Water MM, Ind., dtd 1848,10,25 (H)
1848, 12, 21. Israel rocf Miami MM, O., dtd 1848,11,22 (H)
1852, 2, 26. Albert dis disunity (H)
1853, 11, 24. Wm. B. con mcd (H)
1854, 1, 26. Martha J. Hawley (form Jones) con mcd (H)
1865, 12, 21. Aquilla & w, Anna H., & ch, Hannah & Elizabeth Pleasant, gct Milford MM, Ind. (H)
1867, 3, 21. Priscilla dropped from mbrp

JUDKINS
----, --, --. William m Rachel ----- d 1835,3,20 bur New Graveyard
Ch: Sarah R. b 1814, 6, 14
David S. " 1817, 7, 18
Mary Ann " 1819, 4, 15 d 1822, 2, 7 bur Smithfield, O.
Martha Ann b 1822, 2, 8
Mary " 1828, 8, 7 d 1828, 8,25 bur Mt. Pleasant
Rebecca El-
ma b 1833, 9, 27
----, --, --. Dr. Wm. m Mary ----- d 1895,7,12 bur Spring Grove
Ch: Chas. Palmer b 1842, 8, 4
William Jr." 1847, 9, 7 d 1906, 6,23 bur Spring Grove
Edith b 1855, 8, 13 d 1887,10,22
----, --, --. David m Susan P. McGREW, dt Thos. B. & Ann P., b 1820,9,4
Ch: Anna M. b 1844, 6, 12
Helen W. " 1846, 9, 24 d 1854, 5,24 bur New Bur. Gr.
Francis b 1848, 8, 13
1861, 6, 22. Wm. d bur Cumminsville Cemetery

1832, 7, 19. Wm. & w, Rachel, & ch, Sarah, David & Martha Ann, rocf Short Creek MM, O., dtd 1832,5,22
1836, 9, 15. Wm. gct Sadsbury MM, Pa., to m Susan Henderson
1837, 3, 16. Susan rocf Sadsbury MM, Pa., dtd 1837,2,7
1837, 8, 17. Sarah R. Comly (form Judkins) con mcd
1838, 12, 20. Jesse P. rocf Short Creek MM, O., dtd 1838,5,22
1843, 7, 20. David gct Springfield MM, O., to m Susan P. McGrew
1844, 5, 16. Susan P. rocf Springfield MM, O., dtd 1844,4,22
1845, 7, 17. Mary recrq
1846, 4, 16. Chas. Palmer, s Wm. & Mary, recrq
1850, 5, 16. Martha Collins (form Judkins) dis mcd
1854, 8, 17. Wm. & w, Mary, & ch, Chas. P. & Wm., gct Miami MM, O.
1854, 8, 17. Rebecca E. gct Miami MM, O.
1856, 2, 14. Wm. & w, Mary, & ch, Chas. P., Wm. & Edith, rocf Miami MM, O., dtd 1856,1,23
1856, 2, 14. Rebecca E. rocf Miami MM, O., dtd 1856,1,23
1862, 1, 16. David & Susan R. relrq
1866, 6, 14. Anna M. Sheldon (form Judkins) dis mcd & jas
1866, 6, 14. Fanny dis jas
1871, 7, 20. Rebecca E. dis jas
1877, 11, 15. Wm. Tyson relrq
1904, 2, 12. Edith recrq
1909, 12, 10. Wm. recrq

JUSTICE
1844, 7, 25. Henry & w, Sarah Jane, rocf Milford MM, Ind., dtd 1844,6,20 (H)

JUSTIN
1926, 5, 9. Erwin recrq
1927, 1, 7. Ellen recrq

KEELING
1920, 8, 8. Helen Allen dropped from mbrp

KEITH
1869, 2, 18. Henrietta (form Longstaff) dis mcd
1901, 4, 12. Henrietta L. rocf Cleveland MM, O., dtd 1901,3,15
1920, 8, 8. Henrietta dropped from mbrp

KENWORTHY
1852, 11, 25. Wm., s Jesse & Rachel, Wayne Co., Ind.; m in Cincinnati Mtg, Ann TOWNSEND, dt James & Mary French
1932, 1, 1. Carol m Mary LOWES

1853, 8, 18. Ann, w Wm., & ch, Sina & Mary Ann, gct White Water MM, Ind.

KIPHART
1903, 7, 2. Vincent Williams b
----, --, --. Katharine Henrietta b 1908,10, 27 d 1917,7,23 bur Spring Grove

1917, 7, --. Neil [Kephart], s Leslie & Clara, d

1897, 5, 20. Thos. J. & Leslie [Kephart] recrq
1911, 2, 10. Viola Ross recrq
1911, 7, 7. Peninnah recrq

KIMBRO
1870, 4, 14. Jeremiah & w, Rhoda, rocf Springfield MM, O., dtd 1870,3,19
1872, 9, 19. Jeremiah & w, Rhoda, & ch, Willard & Lula L., gct Springfield MM, O.

KING
----, --, --. John b 1770,2,15; m Mary WARD b 1769,12,27
Ch: Phineas L. b 1792, 9, 15; m Clarissa THOMPSON
Thomas W. " 1794, 11, 30; m Sally THOMPSON
Sarah " 1796, 11, 2 " Doras THOMPSON
Levynas " 1799, 3, 8 " Magdalena ANDERSON
Mary b 1801, 2, 18 " William ALCOTT
Eurity " 1803, 3, 30 " Edward Conners
Dean " 1805, 3, 28
Phebe " 1807, 11, 5

1819, 11, 18. John & w, Mary, & ch, Mary, Levina, Dean, Uretta & Phebe, rocf Stanford MM, N. Y., dtd 1818,7,18
1820, 6, 15. Mary Alcot (form King) dis mcd
1823, 5, 29. Dean, s John, gct Miami MM, O.
1824, 6, 24. John & w, Mary, & dt, Phebe, gct White Water MM, Ind.
1824, 12, 30. Uritta O'Conner (form King) dis mcd
1841, 6, 24. Isaac L. con mcd (H)

KINSEY
----, --, --. Nathaniel m Hannah ----- b 1787, 8,16 d 1864,10,27
Ch: Jane G. b 1813, 9, 28
Pearson " 1815, 8, 8
Cyrus " 1817, 3, 16
William G. " 1821, 5, 16
Rachel G. " 1824, 10, 30
Ezra " 1826, 2, 28
Nathaniel " 1829, 9, 27
1844, 11, 21. Jane G. m Wm. MALONE
----, --, --. Samuel B. & Rachel
Ch: Josephine b 1847, 6, 10
Hannah Ann " 1848, 12, 15
Jane M. " 1850, 10, 16
Mary Ann " 1853, 3, 8
Samuel B. " 1855, 10, 26
Wm. H. Malone " 1858, 1, 1
Rachel Ella" 1860, 12, 28
1848, 9, 25. Sarah Griffith, dt Isaac & Mary P., b d in infancy
----, --, --. Thomas W. b 1824,10,30; m Sallie E. ----- b 1836,7,15
Ch: Rachel C. b 1857, 3, 10
1857, 3, 1. Margaret Lloyd, dt Wm. G. & Mercy L., b

1839, 9, 19. Pearson rocf Wilmington MM, dtd 1839,8,3
1839, 10, 17. Cyrus G. rocf ND MM, dtd 1839,9, 24
1841, 3, 18. Hannah & ch, Rachel G., Ezra & Nathaniel, rocf Wilmington MM, Del., dtd 1841,1,30
1841, 3, 18. Jane G. rocf Wilmington MM, Del., dtd 1841,1,30
1841, 7, 15. Wm. G., minor, rocf Frankfort MM, Phila. Co., Pa., dtd 1841,4,27
1845, 4, 17. Wm. G. gct Miami MM, O., to m Ann C. EVENS
1845, 9, 18. Ann E. rocf Miami MM, O., dtd 1845,7,23
1846, 6, 18. Cyrus G. dis
1846, 8, 20. Cert rec for Samuel B. from Short Creek MM, O.; returned for mcd
1846, 8, 20. Piersen dis mcd
1846, 12, 17. Samuel B. rocf Short Creek MM, O., dtd 1846,6,23
1846, 12, 24. Thos. W., Isaac, Abram & Joseph rocf White Water MM, Ind., dtd 1846,9,23 (H)
1847, 1, 21. Rachel G. con mcd
1847, 8, 19. Ezra dis disunity
1847, 10, 21. Oliver rocf White Water MM, Ind., dtd 1847,9,22 (H)
1847, 11, 25. Isaac con mcd (H)
1847, 11, 25. Mary P. con mcd (H)
1848, 1, 20. Cert rec for Thos. W. & Abraham, ch Oliver, from White Water MM, Ind., dtd 1847,12,22, returned because they attended Hicksites
1848, 5, 10. Wm. G. gct Miami MM, O.

KINSEY, continued
1848, 7, 20. Samuel B. rocf Short Creek MM, O., dtd 1848,1,18
1852, 6, 24. Oliver dis (H)
1852, 10, 21. Isaac & w, Mary, gct Milford MM (H)
1853, 4, 14. Wm. G. rocf Miami MM, O., dtd 1853,3,23
1854, 10, 26. Joseph con mcd (H)
1855, 9, 20. Wm. G. gct Short Creek MM, O., to m Mary Loyd
1856, 8, 21. Mary L. rocf Short Creek MM, O., dtd 1856,5,21
1856, 10, 22. Thos. W. con mcd (H)
1859, 1, 20. Nathaniel Jr. con mcd
1861, 1, 18. Wm. G. & w, Mercy L., & ch, Margaret L. & Wm. Irving, gct Short Creek MM, O.
1866, 1, 18. Samuel B. & w, Rachel G., & ch, Hannah Ann, Jane M., Mary A., Samuel B., Wm. H. M. & Rachel Ella, gct Short Creek MM, O.
1868, 12, 17. Nathaniel dropped from mbrp
1870, 12, 22. Thos. rst rq (H)
1877, 12, 20. Rachel C. recrq (H)
1878, 1, 24. Sallie E. recrq (H)
1891, 5, 21. Susan Miles rocf Lawrence MM, Kans., dtd 1891,1,14
1911, 4, 14. Susan Miles relrq

KIRK
1899, 5, 10. Robert d bur Spring Grove

1859, 11, 24. Prior rocf Green St. MM, Phila., Pa., dtd 1859,10,20 (H)
1884, 12, 18. Robert rocf Springfield MM, O., dtd 1884,10,18
1885, 4, 16. Robert recrq

KIRKMAN
1818, 11, 19. Wm. rocf Southwark MM, London, Eng., dtd 1818,6,16
1819, 4, 15. Wm. gct Phila. MM, Pa.

KITE
1848, 8, 24. Thomas, s Thomas & Edith, Highland Co., O., b 1818,2,25 d 1884,2,6; m in Cincinnati Mtg, Margaret BRAGG, dt Thomas & Ann, Springboro, O., b 1826,6,21
Ch: Thomas Jr. b 1849, 8, 2
Anna Elizabeth " 1851, 9, 8
William Henry " 1854, 8, 22
1911, 7, 7. Margarite d
1931, 7, 7. Anna d

1874, 1, 15. Thos. Jr. con mcd
1879, 7, 17. Thos. relrq
1881, 8, 18. Wm. H. relrq

KITTRELL
1931, 8, 7. Cora H. rocf West Milton MM

KLUG
1920, 8, 8. Modesta dropped from mbrp

KNIGHT
----, --, --. Sarah b 1787,6,26 d 1853,2,2
----, --, --. George m Anna WHITE b 1829,9,9
Ch: Arthur Percival b 1864, 10, 11
George Henry " 1867, 9, 18
Mary Estelle " 1869, 10, 2

1844, 6, 20. Geo. Henry rocf Pool & Southampton MM, Pool, Eng., dtd 1844,4,3
1847, 3, 18. Edward Henry rocf Peel MM, London, England, dtd 1846,8,19
1848, 11, 16. Geo. & w, Sarah, rocf Longford MM, Eng., dtd 1848,8,16
1849, 4, 19. Edward H. dis mcd
1851, 5, 15. Geo. H. dis mcd
1853, 7, 21. George gct Goshen MM
1854, 7, 20. Octavius rocf Waterford MM, Ireland, dtd 1854,4,27
1860, 3, 15. Anna K. recrq
1860, 9, 20. Octavius relrq
1889, 2, 14. Anne K. & dt, Mary E., gct New York MM, N. Y.
1889, 2, 14. Geo. Jr. gct New York MM, N. Y.

KNOWLES
1848, 4, 20. David E. rocf Farnam MM, Canada East, dtd 1847,4,19, endorsed by Ferrisburg QM, Vt., 1847,5,5

KNOWLTON
1847, 2, 18. Julia Ann rocf Springfield MM, dtd 1846,12,19
1852, 9, 16. Julia Ann, w Samuel, gct Dover MM

KRAEMER
1903, 3, 13. Geo. E. recrq
1913, 7, 11. Geo. E. dropped from mbrp
1931, 2, 1. Elizabeth & Geo. E. recrq

KRUZEMAN
1933, 4, 9. John Sr., Florence, John Jr. & Alvin, recrq

KUKUK
1931, 3, 1. Mabel Baugham relrq

KYLE
1883, 6, 12. Ann Lucy d bur St. Louis, Mo.

1859, 5, 19. Lucy Ann rst

LADD
----, --, --. Thomas & Hannah
Ch: Walter Jay b 1862, 3, 10
Isaac G. " 1864, 4, 6

LADD, continued
1857, 12, 17. Thomas W. & w, Hannah P., rocf Smithfield MM, O., dtd 1857,11,3
1865, 1, 19. Thos. W. & w, Hannah P., & ch, Walter J. & Grace G., gct New York MM, N. Y.

LAMB
1817, 12, 18. James rocf Providence MM, dtd 1817,9,23
1820, 4, 20. Joshua G. rocf Providence MM, R. I., dtd 1819,11,23
1824, 11, 25. Joshua G. gct Concord MM, O.
1852, 10, 21. James L. dis mcd

LANDERMAN
1903, 5, 8. Rose rocf New Castle MM, Ind.
1918, 4, 12. Rose dropped from mbrp

LANE
1838, 1, 25. Ann T. con mcd (H)

LANGSTAFF
1816, 5, 7. Lydia E., w John, dt Levi & Mary -----, b
----, --, --. Benjamin, s Samuel & Hannah, b 1806,6,5; m Catharine REEVE, dt Joshua & Millicent, b 1807,7,5
Ch: Laban b 1835, 9, 5
---- --, --. Thomas, s Thos. & Rhoda, b 1811,4,26; m Hannah SMITH, dt Thos. & Nancy, b 1814,10,17
Ch: Rhoda b 1836, 12, 30
Elnathen " 1838, 5, 5
William " 1840, 6, 10
Enoch " 1842, 12, 21
Henry Hall " 1844, 12, 19
Ann S. " 1848, 2, 16 d 1849, 9,24 bur New Gr Yd
----, --, --. James, s Samuel & Hannah, b 1808,3,3; m Sarah B. PENNINGTON, dt Levi & Mary, b 1809,2,18
Ch: Henry C. b 1842, 8, 4 d 1846, 3,26 bur New Gr. Yd.
----, --, --. Elizabeth Euphemia b 1847,11,17 d 1853,--,-- bur New Gr Yd
----, --, --. Taylor m Mary Jane ----- d 1864,12,31
Ch: Samuel Willis b 1857, 4, 13 d 1860,12,14
Ida
1869, 4, 14. Jennie Warren b
1870, 12, 7. Gertrude Landon b
1874, 9, 1. Fannie Belle b
1877, 2, 23. Taylor Franklin b

1836, 6, 16. James con mcd
1836, 6, 16. Sarah (form Pennington) con mcd
1841, 8, 19. Benj. & w, Catharine, & ch, Laban, rocf Chesterfield MM, dtd 1841,7,17
1842, 8, 18. Lydia rocf Sandy Spring MM, O., dtd 1842,6,24
1846, 5, 21. Thos. D. & w, Hannah, & ch, Rhoda, Elnathan, Wm., Enoch & Henry H., rocf Chesterfield MM, dtd 1846,3,21
1851, 8, 21. Benjamin P. & w, Catharine, & s, Laban, gct Newberry MM
1852, 11, 18. Thos. D. & w, Hannah, & ch, Rhoda, Elnathan, Wm., Enoch, Henry & Ellen, gct Plymouth MM, Washington Co., O.
1858, 4, 15. Taylor & w, Mary Jane, & ch, Samuel Willis & Ida, rocf Bloomington MM, dtd 1858,3,6
1866, 4, 19. Lydia dis jas
1869, 2, 18. Mary Ann (form Miller) con mcd
1869, 2, 18. Henrietta Keith (form Langstaff) dis mcd
1869, 4, 15. Taylor F. con mcd
1870, 7, 21. James & w, Sarah B., gct Alliance MM, O.
1880, 3, 18. Taylor & Mary A. relrq
1880, 3, 18. Ida M. gct Clear Creek MM, O.
1885, 4, 16. Jennie Warren relrq
1885, 4, 16. Gertrude Landon, Fannie Belle & Taylor Franklin, ch Taylor F. & Mary, recrq

LAPHAM
1834, 8, 21. Nancy L. rocf Center MM, dtd 1834,4,16
1844, 3, 21. Nancy gct Goshen MM

LATTIN
1852, 3, 18. Catharine (form Schooley) con mcd

LARRANCE
1896, 3, --. Isaac d

LAUDERMAN
1880, 2, 17. Rose b

LAWRENCE
1897, 5, 25. Henry Haydock, s Henry & Caroline (Whiteall), Phila., Pa.; m in Covington, Ky., Euphemia BAILEY, dt Hezekiah B. & Elizabeth B., Kento Co., Ky, b 1861,6,7
1897, 7, 9. Elizabeth d

1861, 5, 16. Elizabeth & dt, Phebe, rocf Wills Creek MM, Ind., dtd 1861,1,24
1866, 6, 14. Isaac recrq
1870, 1, 20. Phebe L. Warden (form Lawrence) coh mcd
1909, 4, 9. Euphemia Baily relrq

LEA
1822, 11, 28. James & w, Elizabeth, & s, Henry, rocf Redstone MM, Pa., dtd 1822,7,31
1822, 11, 28. Susannah & Elizabeth, dt James & Elizabeth, rocf Redstone MM, Pa., dtd 1822,7,31
1824, 8, 26. Susanna Janden (form Lea) dis mcd
1829, 8, 27. Elizabeth dis jH
1834, 6, 19. Elizabeth dis disunity

LEA, continued
1865, 7, 20. Henry dropped from mbrp

LEAF
1916, 2, 11. Joseph Tucker, Shearman & Sarah Megrew, ch Anna S., recrq
1920, 8, 8. Anna Shearman, Joseph & Sarah dropped from mbrp

LEAMING
1879, 5, 15. Lydia H. rocf Wilmington MM, O., dtd 1879,4,--
1892, 6, 10. Lydia H. relrq

LEEDOM
----, --, --. Thomas & Hannah
Ch: Charles b 1859, 10, 31
Clara " 1861, 3, 8

1861, 4, 25. Hannah A. & s, Chas., rocf Green St. MM, Phila., Pa. (H)
1866, 2, 22. Hannah & ch, Chas. & Clara gct Green St. MM, Phila., Pa. (H)

LEEK
1878, 4, 28. Catharine d ae 84

1847, 7, 22. Richard & w, Hannah, & ch, James E., Wm. & Henry, rocf Baltimore MM, Md., dtd 1847,4,8 (H)
1850, 2, 21. Catharine rocf Baltimore MM, Md., dtd 1849,12,6 (H)
1871, 2, 23. Wm. M. dropped from mbrp (H)

LeVASER
1846, 7, 16. Louisa (form Taylor) dis mcd

LEWIS
1929, 2, 18. Benjamin d
1931, 8, 29. Ruth m Russel DOLE (nm)

1818, 8, 20. Nathan gct Clear Creek MM, O., to m
1821, 3, 29. Nathan gct Clear Creek MM, O.
1848, 10, 19. Ann L. & ch, Margaret Ann, Joseph P. & Lucy A., rocf Short Creek MM, O., dtd 1848,4,20
1853, 1, 20. Ann L. & ch, Margaret Ann, Joseph T. & Lucy J., gct White Water MM, Ind.
1855, 11, 22. Maria Ann rocf Falls MM, Pa., dtd 1854,12,9 (H)
1892, 1, 21. Albert N. rocf Coloma MM, Ind., dtd 1891,9,---returned, unable to locate him
1928, 12, 2. Benj. & Elizabeth rocf Baltimore MM

LIGHT
1901, 3, 8. John & w, Mary, rocf West Fork MM, Sycamore, O., dtd 1901,2,16
1913, 7, 11. Wm. A. dropped from mbrp

LINDLEY
1843, 11, 16. Jacob Jr. rocf Uwchland MM, Pa., dtd 1843,8,10
1867, 3, 21. Jacob Jr. dropped from mbrp

LINTON
1834, 9, 18. Wm. & w, Hannah, & ch, John, Sarah, Isaiah, Hannah, Rachel & Anna R., rocf Center MM, dtd 1832,6,13
1835, 10, 15. Isaiah dis
1839, 12, 19. Wm. dis disunity
1865, 7, 20. John, Hannah, Rachel, Anna R. dropped from mbrp

LIPPINCOTT
----, --, --. Wm. F. b 1828,11,4; m Sarah EVANS, dt Jason & Mary, b 1837,6,12
Ch: Jason Evans b 1861, 1, 1
Catharine B. " 1863, 8, 15
Mary Evans " 1865, 8, 23
Jesse T. " 1876, 2, 23

1853, 11, 17. Edwin rocf Upper Evesham MM, N. J., dtd 1853,9,10
1860, 8, 23. Sarah E. [Lippencott] con mcd (H)
1877, 5, 17. Edwin [Lippencott] gct Upper Evesham MM, N. J.

LITTLE
1897, 3, 16. Geo. H. & w, Jessie M. G., rocf Cleveland MM, O., dtd 1896,12,17
1898, 5, 13. Geo. Henry & w, Jessie M. G., & s, Edward, gct Manchester MM, Eng.

LITTLER
----, --, --. John b 1771,5,17 d 1848,6,10

1829, 10, 29. John rocf Hopewell MM, dtd 1829,9,10 (H)

LLOYD
1855, 9, 20. Wm. G. Kinsey gct Short Creek MM, O., to m Mary Loyd

LOCKWOOD
1852, 11, 25. Walter rocf New York MM, N. Y. (H)
1853, 3, 24. Mary rocf New York MM, N. Y.(H)

LODGE
1818, 10, 6. Celine, dt Isabel, d bur Old Gr. Yd.

1829, 7, 30. Jazabad dis jH

LONG
1892, 4, 14. Elizabeth Tatum relrq

LOOP
1820, 4, 20. Elizabeth com mou

LOWES
1871, 8, 15. Herbert A., s James A. & Rhoda, b
1932, 1, 1. Mary m Carol KENWORTHY

1916, 9, 8. Herbert rocf Wilmington MM, O.
1916, 12, 8. Martha H. rocf Springfield MM,O.
1924, 1, 13. Mary rocf Wilmington MM, O.
1927, 8, 7. Mary recrq

LUDLUM
1821, 2, 22. Sarah W. rocf New York MM, N.Y., dtd 1820,6,12
1831, 1, 27. Sarah W. deVOY (form Ludlum) con mcd (H)
1865, 7, 20. Sarah W. dropped from mbrp

LUPTON
1840, 1, 16. Anna (form Neve) dis mcd

LUTON
1829, 11, 6. Daniel recrq
1832, 4, 19. Charlotte recrq
1832, 4, 19. Amelia, Martha, Elizabeth Jane, Ann & Thomas, ch Daniel, recrq
1834, 5, 15. Daniel & w, Charlotte, & ch, Amelia, Martha, Elizabeth Ann & Thomas, gct West Lake MM, Upper Canada

LUTRELL
1896, 6, 18. Robert C. & w, Mary, & ch, Otto C., gct Wilmington MM, O.

LYLE
1891, 9, 15. Benjamin Franklin, s John M. & Mary, Highland Co., O.; m in Cincinnati MH, Alice Morris JACKSON, dt Davan Lewis & Anna M., Highland Co., O., b 1867,3,30

1910, 5, 13. Alice Johnson relrq

LYNCH
1804, 10, 30. Charles E., s Edward & Mary, b

1817, 6, 19. Charity gct Miami MM, O.
1839, 8, 15. Edward & w, Mary, rocf Springborough MM, dtd 1839,6,25
1839, 8, 15. Sarah & Mary Jr. rocf Springborough MM, dtd 1839,6,25
1847, 11, 18. Edward & w, Mary, gct Miami MM, O.
1847, 11, 18. Sarah & Mary Jr. gct Miami MM,O.
1850, 8, 15. Chas. E. gct Miami MM

McCORMACK
1933, 4, 9. Doris recrq

McCLURE
1843, 2, 16. Joseph rocf Middleton MM, dtd 1843,9,15(?)
1852, 5, 20. Joseph dis mcd

McCREA
1877, 10, 18. Ellen (form Fallis) dis jas

McDONALD
1915, 5, 14. Mary Dean relrq

McGREW
----, --, --. Thomas B. b 1792,3,11 d 1857,3, 10 bur Cumminsville Cem.; m Ann PRICE, dt Warrick & Susan, b 1800,5,7 d 1884,5,31
Ch: Thomas O. b 1833, 4, 24
Joseph A. " 1827, 6, 9 d 1883, 7,--

1843, 7, 20. David Judkins gct Springfield MM, O., to m Susan P. McGrew
1850, 5, 16. Ann P. & s, Thos., rocf Smithfield MM, dtd 1850,2,18
1854, 1, 19. Joseph A. rocf Smithfield MM, dtd 1853,9,19
1856, 1, 17. Joseph Addison con mcd
1857, 2, 19. Thos. B. rocf Smithfield MM, O., dtd 1857,1,19
1858, 7, 15. Thos. rpd mcd; dropped from mbrp

McHAMMON
1830, 1, 28. Elizabeth (form Comstock) dis mcd

McKAY
1920, 8, 8. Mary Manning dropped from mbrp

McMILLAN
1854, 12, 16. Hannah S. d bur New Gr. Yd.
1853, 9, --. Jonathan d bur New Gr. Yd.

1834, 8, 21. Hannah & dt, Eliza, rocf Center MM, dtd 1834,5,14
1842, 12, 15. Jonathan rst
1863, 11, 19. Eliza gct Miami MM, O.

McNEELAN
1884, 10, 16. Miriam B. rocf Grove MM, Ind., dtd 1884,10,11
1913, 7, 11. Miriam B. dropped from mbrp.

McPHERSON
1840, 6, 18. Cert rec for Ann from Blue River MM, dtd 1840,3,7 returned
1842, 10, 20. Lydia, Sarah, Martha & Hannah rocf Baltimore MM, dtd 1842,7,8 (H)
1847, 8, 26. Rebecca rocf Baltimore MM, Md., dtd 1847,4,8 (H)
1851, 8, 21. Esther rocf Baltimore MM, Md., dtd 1850,4,10 (H)
----, --, --. Esther rocf Baltimore MM, Md., dtd 1857,4,10 (H)
1864, 5, 19. Cert rec for Ruth & dt, Mary

McPHERSON, continued
Margaret from Oak Ridge MM, dtd 1863,4,14, returned on rq
1871, 4, 20. Sarah, Martha, Lydia & Hannah gct Alexandria MM, Md. (H)

MACKINTOSH
1876, 10, 19. Eliza recrq
1877, 2, 15. Eliza relrq

MACY
----, --, --. George, s Geo. & Margaret, b 1771,1,19 d 1815,10,9 bur Old Gr. Yd.; m Elizabeth BARNARD, dt Thos. & Ruth, b 1771,1,4
Ch: Margaret b 1801, 8, 14
Thomas B. " 1803, 10, 10
Sarah " 1809, 4, 20 d 1834,--,--

1818, 12, 17. Margaret Folger (form Masey) con mcd
1830, 9, 30. Elizabeth dis jH
1831, 1, 27. Sarah Swain (form Macy) dis mcd
1831, 3, 31. Sarah Swayne (form Macy) dis mcd (H)
1831, 9, 29. Thos. B. gct Miami MM, O.

MADDOCK
1863, 12, 17. Theodore M. rocf Elk MM, O.
1878, 11, 14. Hiram S. rocf Elk MM, O.
1913, 7, 11. Hiram S. dropped from mbrp
1921, 12, 11. Theodore gct Elk MM, O.

MALONE
1844, 11, 21. Wm. Harrison, s James & Sarah, Highland Co., O., d 1883,11,26; m in Cincinnati Mtg, Jane G. KINSEY, dt Nathaniel & Hannah, Highland Co., O., d 1883,8, 13
Ch: Charles E. b 1846, 1, 14
Alice " 1847, 9, 24
William H. " 1849, 8, 24
Rachel Ella" 1851, 7, 14 d 1851,11,29 bur New Gr. Yd.
Nathaniel Franklin b 1852, 12, 23 " 1859, 1,16 bur New Gr. Yd.
Franklin Bye b 1855, 1, 25 " 1858,12,27 bur Cumminsville
John Howard b 1857, 8, 14 " 1859, 1, 2 bur Cumminsville
Jane G. b 1860, 7, 7

1841, 5, 20. Wm. Harrison rocf Buckingham MM, Pa., dtd 1841,5,3
1846, 2, 19. Hezekiah B., minor, rocf Buckingham MM, Pa., dtd 1846,2,2
1854, 10, 19. Hezekiah B. dis mcd
1873, 5, 15. Chas. A. con mcd
1873, 7, 17. Alice Carpenter (form Malone) con mcd

1883, 11, 15. Chas. E. relrq

MANNING
1898, 10, 5. Sherman Leroy, s Dr. Preston & Mary (Shearman), b
1900, 7, 6. Laura Meeker, dt Dr. Preston & Mary (Shearman), b

MAROT
----, --, --. Joseph & Mary
Ch: Benjamin Johnson b 1836, 4, 17
Samuel " 1838, 6, 15

1833, 5, 16. Henry & Edward Lewis [Marrott] minors, rocf Phila. MM, Pa. W. Dist., dtd 1833,2,19
1834, 11, 20. Mary, w Joseph, & ch, Edward, Lewis, Henry, Jane Johnson, John Richards & Wm., rocf Phila. MM, Pa., dtd 1833,4,18 (H)
1856, 3, 20. Henry [Marrott] con mcd
1857, 4, 16. Henry [Marott] gct Young MM, Canada, West
1860, 8, 23. Mary & dt, Jane J., gct Clear Creek MM, O. (H)

MARR
1898, 1, 20. Louis recrq
1913, 7, 11. Lewis E. dropped from mbrp

MARSH
1822, 6, 4. Elizabeth, dt Wm. & Jane Crossman, b
1915, 11, 15. Elizabeth, dt Wm. & Jane Crossman, d bur Spring Grove

1843, 8, 16. Elizabeth (form Crossman) con mcd

MARSHALL
1821, 10, 25. Leah C. (form Pugh) con mcd

MARTIN
1817, 10, 23. Oliver, s William & Sarah, Highland Co., O.; m in Cincinnati Mtg, Sarah COFFIN, wd Isaiah, dt Christopher & Abigail FOLGER, d 1822,9,14
1843, --, --. Sarah d bur New Grave Yd.
1823, 11, 6. Oliver Jr., s Oliver & Susannah, Highland Co., O.; m in Cincinnati Mtg, Lydia DICKINSON, dt John & Susannah, Highland Co., O.

1816, 9, 19. Sarah & Elizabeth rocf Plainfield MM, dtd 1816,7,24
1816, 9, 19. Sarah M. & Elizabeth rocf Rahway MM, dtd 1816,8,10
1817, 8, 21. Oliver recrq
1819, 1, 21. Oliver Jr. rocf Phila. MM, Pa., dtd 1818,11,24
1825, 3, 21. Oliver dis disunity
1830, 3, 25. Oliver Sr. gct Arch St. MM,

MARTIN, continued
Phila., Pa.
1842, 5, 19. Oliver & dt, Ann, gct ND MM, Pa.
1855, 8, 23. Mary con mcd (H)
1860, 4, 26. Mary con mcd (H)
1871, 5, 25. Mary dis jas (H)

MATHER
----, --, --. Richard, s Bartholemew & Sarah, b 1764,5,31 d 1831,5,8 bur Old Gr. Yd.; m Sarah ----- b 1769,2,15 d 1845,12,16 bur New Gr. Yd.

1819, 8, 19. Bartholmew T. rocf Phila. MM, Pa., dtd 1819,2,25
1820, 10, 19. Bartholomew T. dis mcd
1826, 11, 30. Richard & w, Sarah, & ch, Lydia, Sarah Ann & Thos., rocf Miami MM, O., dtd 1826,8,30
1826, 11, 30. Mary & ch, Rachel C., Lucy R. & Sarah, rocf Miami MM, O., dtd 1826,9,27
1828, 3, 27. Susan [Mathers] rocf Milford MM, Ind., dtd 1827,12,22
1828, 8, 28. Lydia dis disunity
1868, 4, 16. Sarah A. dropped from mbrp

MATLOCK
1844, 7, 26. Elizabeth (form Cook) con mcd (H)
1847, 3, 25. Elizabeth dis jas (H)

MATTHEWS
1829, 11, 26. Susannah dis jH
1832, 5, 31. Susan Rice (form Matthews) dis mcd (H)
1835, 10, 15. Mary [Matthew] & ch, Rachel, Lucy, Sarah & Mary, gct Mill Creek MM
1838, 9, 20. Phebe recrq (H)
1846, 5, 21. Phebe gct Milford MM, Ind. (H)

MAYLEN
1832, 1, 26. Sarah rocf Redstone MM, Pa., dtd 1832,1,4

MENDENHALL
1874, 1, 15. Henry W. d
1877, 2, 11. Cyrus d bur Oskaloosa, Iowa
1910, 6, 11. Walter S. d bur Spring Grove

1867, 11, 14. Cyrus & w, Phebe E., rocf Short Creek MM, O., dtd 1867,10,24
1870, 1, 20. Henry W. rocf White Water MM, Ind.
1874, 1, 15. Henry W. gct Indianapolis MM, Ind.
1885, 9, 17. Walter S. rocf White Water MM, Ind., dtd 1885,5,25

MEREDITH
1858, 9, 23. Jane R. (form Russel) con mcd (H)

MERRIFIELD
1831, 4, 29. Elizabeth, minor, roc
1832, 7, 19. Elizabeth gct ND MM

MESSINGER
----, --, --. ----- & Martha A.
Ch: Frank R. b 1870, 7, 28
Charles F. " 1873, 6, 30
Walter C. " 1874, 8, 10

1879, 2, 20. Frank R., Chas. F. & Walter [Messenger], ch Martha, recrq (H)

MICHENER
1848, 6, 15. Ann rocf Bradford MM, Pa.
1848, 6, 15. Martha rocf Bradford MM, Pa.
1848, 10, 26. Lydia [Michenor] dis disunity (H)
1865, 7, 20. Ann & Martha dropped from mbrp

MICHY
----, --, --. Elmira A. rocf Landan Grove MM, dtd 1852,10,6 (H)

MIDDLETON
1847, 9, 23. Isaac Stephens Jr. gct Chesterfield MM, N. J., to m Lydia Middleton, dt Samuel, Crosswick, N. J. (H)
1859, 8, 25. Geo. A., minor, rocf Green St. MM, Phila., Pa., dtd 1859,2,17 (H)

MILLER
1852, 3, 17. Maria b

1818, 3, 19. Phebe rocf Redstone MM, Pa., dtd 1817,12,24
1819, 10, 21. Phebe gct Miami MM, O.
1847, 11, 18. Maria & ch, Wm. Franklin, Hezekiah, Mary Ann, James Madison, Mordecai, Frances, Sarah & Henrietta, rocf Sandy Spring MM, O., dtd 1847,9,24
1853, 2, 24. Ann con mcd (H)
1856, 1, 17. Wm. rpd mcd; dropped from mbrp
1856, 2, 14. Maria & ch, James Madison, Mordecai, Frances, Austin, Maria & Henry Clay, gct Newberry MM
1866, 8, 23. Ann G. gct Burlington MM, N. J. (H)
1868, 12, 17. Hezekiah dropped from mbrp
1869, 2, 18. Mary Ann Langstaff (form Miller) con mcd
1878, 12, 19. Franklin relrq
1887, 7, 21. Henry rocf Clear Creek MM, O.

MILLS
1876, 9, 14. Lewis M. & w, Catharine, & ch, Mary Alma & Walter T., rocf Newberry MM, dtd 1876,5,22
1888, 3, 15. Lewis M. & w, Catharine B., gct Newberry MM, O.
1894, 4, 19. Lewis & Catharine rocf Newberry MM, O., dtd 1894,1,22
1899, 6, 9. Lewis M. & Catharine gct Newberry MM, O.
1903, 2, 13. Walter dropped from mbrp

MINOR
1829, 2, 26. Sarah (form Patterson) rpd mcd

MITCHENER
----, --, --. Jacob L. & w, Lydia, rocf Alum Creek MM, O., dtd 1847,1,21 (H)
1847, 5, 20. Jacob L. [Mitchner] & w, Lydia Coates, rocf Alum Creek MM, O., dtd 1847, 1,21 (H)

MITCHELL
----, --, --. Mercy, dt Thos. & Myra Greene, b 1785,1,31 d 1859,1,1
----, --, --. Franklin, s Jethro & Mercy, b 1812,7,22; m Sarah F. RITCHIE, dt Robert & Sarah, b 1818,10,19
Ch: Hannah D. b 1842, 7, 24
Robert R. " 1846, 7, 19

1832, 2, 23. Mercy, w Jethro, & ch, Henry, Rachel, Rowland G., Franklin, Sarah, Eliza, Jethro Jr., Walter & Thomas, rocf New York MM, N. Y., dtd 1831,12,17
1833, 5, 16. Rachel dis jas
1834, 5, 15. Sarah dis jas
1837, 3, 16. Eliza dis jas
1839, 2, 14. Jethro dis mcd & jas
1840, 1, 16. Rowland G. dis mcd
1840, 9, 17. Franklin gct ND MM, to m Sarah Richie Jr.
1841, 5, 20. Sarah S. rocf ND MM, Pa., dtd 1841,3,23
1841, 11, 18. Walter dis jas
1844, 9, 19. Thos. dis disunity
1848, 7, 20. Franklin dis mcd
1849, 9, 20. Hannah rocf Middletown MM, Pa., dtd 1849,7,6 (H)
1852, 1, 15. Hannah D. & Robert R., ch Franklin & Sarah, gct ND MM, Pa.

MODE
1866, 4, 19. Priscilla P. rpd mcd & jas; relrq

MOON
1891, 5, 21. John T. rocf Newberry MM, O., dtd 1891,4,20
1894, 4, 19. Gertrude rocf Newberry MM, O., dtd 1894,1,22, returned, unable to locate her
1894, 12, 20. Gertrude rocf Newberry MM, O., again, but she was so far away from mtg that her right remained at Newberry MM,O.
1899, 1, 13. John T. dropped from mbrp

MOORE
1836, 2, 18. Hannah (form Fisher) con mcd
1856, 12, 25. Thos. & w, Phebe Jane, rocf West Branch MM, Pa. (H)
1859, 5, 26. Thos. gc (H)
1894, 4, 19. Emma gct Wilmington MM, O.

MORGAN
----, --, --. Ephraim, s Jacob & Sarah, b 1790,5,18 d 1873,2,13 bur Spring Grove; m Charlotte ANTHONY, dt Christopher & Mary, d 1858,10,24 bur Cumminsville Cem.
Ch: Mary V. b 1815, 7, 18
James T. " 1817, 2, 18 d 1866,10,--
Sarah Ann " 1819, 6, 1 " 1834,10,11 bur New Bur. Gr.
Christopher A. b 1821, 12, 7
Cornelia " 1824, 4, 16
Elizabeth O. " 1827, 3, 16 d 1848,10,10
Samuel J. " 1829, 5, 21
Edward J. " 1831, 8, 25 " 1837, 1, 4 bur New Gr. Yd.
1858, 10, 24. Charlotte A. d ae 65y 3d (an elder)

1823, 6, 26. Ephraim recrq
1826, 7, 27. Nancy, Mary, James, Sarah & Christopher, ch Ephraim & Charlotte, recrq
1834, 10, 16. Mary Wood (form Morgan) con mcd
1840, 4, 16. James T. con mcd
1845, 1, 16. Plato, minor, rocf Fairfield MM, O., dtd 1844,8,17
1845, 12, 18. Cornelia Pendleton (form Morgan) con mcd
1849, 4, 19. Christopher A. dis disunity
1857, 2, 19. Samuel P. dis mcd

MORRELL
1844, 3, 21. John A. L., minor, rocf Phila. MM, Pa., dtd 1844,1,12
1846, 1, 15. Thaddeus C., minor, rocf Berwick MM, Me., dtd 1845,12,26
1848, 7, 20. John A. L. dis mcd

MORRIS
1856, 8, 21. Sarah F. rocf Seabrook MM, held at West Newberry MM, dtd 1856,4,3

MORRISON
1852, 9, 23. Ellen T. rocf Honey Creek MM, dtd 1862,12,6 (H)
1864, 11, 24. Ellen gct Fall Creek MM (H)

MORTON
1898, 3, 11. Elenora recrq
1910, 3, 11. Agnes E. recrq

MOSS
1828, 8, 28. Sarah (form Coffin) dis mcd
1880, 5, 20. Frances recrq (H)

MOTT
1842, 10, 20. Lydia P. rocf Scipio MM, N. Y., dtd 1842,6,22 (H)
1846, 9, 24. Andrew rocf Farmington MM, N.Y., dtd 1843,5,25 (H)
1848, 11, 23. Lydia P. gct Burlington MM, N.J. (H)

MOUCE
1903, 4, 10. Ulysses L. & w, Clara, & ch, Howard J., Irvin & Edward K., rocf Miami MM, O., dtd 1903,3,25
1913, 9, 12. Vivian, Howard & Edwin relrq

MOYCE
1848, 12, 21. Lucy rocf Pool & Southampton MM, Eng., dtd 1848,9,17
1853, 8, 18. Lucy & ch, Lucy Ann & Clara, gct Goshen MM

MUNDY
1829, 2, 26. Esther F. [Munday] (form Ricket) con mcd
1829, 6, 25. Esther [Monday] dis disunity (H)
1833, 10, 17. Esther gct Springborough MM
1840, 1, 16. Esther gct West Branch MM
1840, 6, 18. Cert for Esther returned by West Branch MM & endorsed to Springborough MM
1840, 12, 17. Cert for Ester to Springborough MM, returned & endorsed to Mill Creek MM

NEALE
1876, 9, 20. Mary d

1851, 1, 16. Mary & ch, Wilhelmina, Alfred Wm., Margaret Louisa & James Henry, rocf Mt. Meleck MM, Ire., dtd 1850,10,23
1851, 1, 16. Richard Webb rocf Carlow MM, Ire., dtd 1850,11,12
1851, 11, 20. Emily rocf Waterford MM, Ire., dtd 1851,8,28
1853, 10, 20. Edwin rocf Mt. Mellick MM, Ire., dtd 1853,8,25
1853, 10, 20. Anna Maria rocf Dublin MM, Ire., dtd 1853,8,16
1859, 9, 15. Mary & ch, Edward & James Henry, gct Driftwood MM, Ind.
1859, 9, 15. Anna Maria, Emily, Wilhelmina Louisa & Alfred, gct Driftwood MM, Ind.
1867, 7, 18. Wilhelmina rocf Grove MM, Ind., dtd 1867,7,4
1867, 7, 18. Anna Maria rocf Grove MM, Ind., dtd 1867,7,4
1875, 7, 15. Mary rocf Grove MM
1875, 10, 28. Louisa rocf Grove MM, dtd 1875, 10,9
1876, 10, 19. Anna Maria dis jas
1891, 11, 19. Richard gct Cleveland MM, O.
1918, 5, 10. Louise & Wilhelmina gct Harveyburg, O.

NEALY
1858, 9, 23. Orynthee [Neely] m Chas. W. THOMAS

1847, 4, 15. Rachel Orynthia recrq of Ezra & Elizabeth Bailey with whom she lives

NEAVE
1815, 5, 25. Elizabeth m Thos. PEIRCE
1816, 10, 24. Thompson, s Jeremiah & Elizabeth, Highland Co., O., b 1790,10,22 d 1870,1,1; m in Cincinnati Mtg, Elizabeth MARTIN, dt Oliver & Susannah, Middlesex Co., N. J., b 1797,1,7 d 1873,5,16
Ch: Ann Elizabeth b 1817, 8, 21
Martin " 1819, 9, 30
Alexander " 1822, 2, 18
Charles " 1824, 11, 5 d 1857,12,12
Thos. Jefferson " 1827, 3, 12 " 1828,11,23
Susannah Martin " 1829, 12, 5 " 1832, 4, 2
Mary Susannah " 1832, 8, 28 " 1841, 3, 9
Thompson Jr. " 1835, 2, 24
Frances " 1837, 7, 20
Oliver Martin " 1840, 5, 30 d 1841, 2, 9
Sarah " 1842, 3, 10 " 1843, 4,12
----, --, --. Alexander m Anna PHILLIPS, dt Isaac & Hannah, b 1818,4,12 d 1900,12,27 bur Spring Grove
Ch: Isaac P. b 1844, 9, 28 d 1864,10,30 bur Spring Grove
William b 1846, 3, 11
Elizabeth M. " 1848, 12, 18
Sarah " 1850, 7, 21 d 1855,10,27 bur Spring Grove
Edward P. b 1852, 8, 6 " 1896,12,25 bur Spring Grove
Frank M. b 1854, 9, 23 " 1855, 8,26 bur Spring Grove
Hattie Lupton b 1861, 5, 28 " 1864,10,29 bur Spring Grove

1823, 11, 27. Thompson & w, Elizabeth, & ch, Anna, Elizabeth, Martin & Alexander, gct Miami MM, O.
1824, 7, 29. Thompson & w, Elizabeth, & ch, Anna, Elizabeth, Martin & Alexander, rocf Miami MM, O., dtd 1824,4,28
1824, 11, 25. Chas. gct Concord MM, O.
1827, 2, 22. Hannah Woolsy (form Neave) dis mcd
1833, 2, 14. Sarah dis disunity
1839, 2, 14. Alexander gct Sadsbury MM, Pa.
1840, 1, 16. Anna Lupton (forn Neve) dis mcd
1841, 4, 15. Alexander [Neve] rocf Sadsbury MM, Pa., dtd 1841,2,2
1842, 10, 20. Alexander gct Sadsbury MM, Pa.
1847, 5, 20. Alexander & w, Anna P., & ch, Isaac P. & Wm., rocf Bradford MM, Pa., dtd 1847,2,3
1847, 10, 21. Martin dis mcd
1853, 4, 14. Chas. con mcd
1858, 3, 18. Thompson Jr. dis mcd
1860, 1, 19. Frances dis jas
1861, 5, 16. Alexander dis disunity

NEAVE, continued
1869, 5, 20. Elizabeth J. Jr. relrq
1873, 7, 17. Wm. relrq
1879, 10, 16. Albert relrq
1883, 6, 17. Emma Rutledge (form Neave) relrq

NEFF
1848, 1, 20. Narcissa (form Williams) dis mcd

NESBIT
1818, 4, 16. Mary rocf Phila. MM, Pa., dtd 1818,2,26
1829, 12, 31. Mary Comly (form Nisbet) con mcd

NEVILL
----, --, --. Joseph b 1797,7,16 d 1851,12,16 bur New Bur. Gr.; m Susanna -----, dt Benj. & Agnes GREENWOOD, b 1802,2,21
Ch: Agnes b 1828, 5, 30
James " 1829, 9, 21
Joseph Wattis " 1831, 4, 22
Benjamin Greenwood " 1834, 12, 17
Alfred " 1836, 1, 21 d 1851, 1,19 bur New Gr. Yd.
Elizabeth b 1838, 8, 18 " 1850,10,11 bur New Gr. Yd.
Edward b 1841, 12, 5 " 1843,12,-- bur New Gr. Yd.
1855, 3, 22. Susannah m Wm. W. HEALD

1843, 8, 17. Joseph & w, Susanna, & ch, Agnes, James, Joseph W., Benj. Greenwood, Alfred, Elizabeth & Edward, rocf Hardshaw West MM, Liverpool, Eng., dtd 1842,7,28 endorsed by New York MM, N. Y., 1843,7,5
1859, 2, 17. James [Neville] dis mcd
1860, 2, 16. Benj. G. [Neville] gct Gilead MM
1860, 4, 19. Joseph W. [Neville] gct New York MM, N. Y.
1869, 7, 15. Joseph W. [Neville] dis disunity

NEWKIRK
1910, 10, 25. Charles W. d bur Spring Grove
1915, --, --. Chas. Wesley, s C. Claudius & Jesse B., b
1911, 10, 21. Wm. Buchanan b

1888, 12, 20. Chas. W. & w, Alice, & s, Elias Claudius, recrq
1912, 2, 9. Jesse Buchanan recrq
1917, 7, 13. Jessie B. gct Berkley MM, Calif.

NEWPORT
1815, 10, 19. Joseph rocf Concord MM, Pa.
1815, 12, 21. Jonathan dis mcd

NICHOLSON
1820, 11, 16. Elisha rocf Phila. MM, Pa., dtd 1820,7,27

NIXON
1840, 10, 15. Wm. rocf White Water MM, Ind., dtd 1840,5,2
1867, 3, 21. Wm. dropped from mbrp

NUTLER
1899, 6, 9. Henry dropped from mbrp

NYE
1816, 3, 21. Eunice (form Chadwick) dis mcd

O'BRIAN
1818, 9, 17. Thos. rocf Carlow MM, Ire., dtd 1818,3,6
1821, 10, 25. Thos. gct Center MM, O.

O'CONNER
1824, 12, 30. Uritta (form King) dis mcd

OGBORN
1844, 7, 18. Ellwood rocf Frankford MM, Pa., dtd 1844,6,25
1847, 10, 21. Elwood [Ogburn] con mcd
1851, 12, 18. Martha C. [Ogburn] rocf Frankford MM, Pa., dtd 1849,7,31
1857, 11, 19. Wm. Elwood dis
1858, 5, 20. Martha gct Frankfort MM, Pa.

OSBORN
1889, 7, 18. Eliza & s, Jesse W., rocf Wilmington MM, O.
1902, 11, 14. Ethel W. gct Dunreath MM, Ind.
1903, 3, 13. Cert for Ethel M. to Dunreath MM, Ind. returned; issued by mistake
1906, 3, 9. Ethel Warman relrq

OTT
1838, 1, 18. Hannah (form Crossman) con mcd
1850, 6, 20. Hannah dis jas

OVERMAN
1901, 10, 11. Frank W. gct Clear Creek MM, O.

OYLER
1865, 5, 18. Hannah Maria rocf Springfield MM, O., dtd 1865,4,15
1885, 5, 21. Hannah Maria dropped from mbrp; unable to locate her
1886, 2, 17. Hannah Maria gct Mt. Pleasant MM, Ill.

PADDOCK
----, --, --. Benjamin b 1762,6,13 d 1832,5,7 bur Columbia Township (an elder); m Jemimah ----- b 1759,10,22
----, --, --. Samuel & Deborah
Ch: Benjamin b 1816, 3, 23
Susannah " 1818, 6, 11
Mary C. " 1821, 10, 23
Lucretia
Barclay
Anna
Avis

PADDOCK, continued
1818, 10, 22. William, s Benjamin & Jemimah, Highland Co., O., b 1792,10,17; m in Cincinnati Mtg, Phebe CHADWICK, dt Richard & Rhoda, Highland Co., O., b 1799,11,30
Ch: Lydia F. b 1820, 6, 3
Elizabeth S. " 1822, 6, 25
Sarah S. " 1825, 2, 3 d 1846, 8,15
Rebecca H. " 1827, 12, 21
William C. " 1834, 11, 19 " 1855, 5, 1
Benjamin " 1837, 1, 4

1815, 8, 17. Joseph & w, Amy, & ch, Phebe & Rueben, rocf Nantucket MM, dtd 1814,11,24
1816, 1, 18. Alice Swain (form Paddock) dis disunity
1816, 10, 17. Tristram dis mcd
1817, 4, 17. Lydia Perry (form Paddock) dis mcd
1818, 4, 16. Chas. con mcd
1819, 7, 15. Chas. gct Silver Creek MM
1821, 5, 31. Joseph & w, Amy, & s, Rueben, gct Silver Creek MM
1826, 1, 26. Joseph Jr. gct Nantucket MM
1829, 10, 29. Wm. dis jH (H)
1831, 10, 27. Samuel & w, Deborah, & ch, Lucretia P., Benj. F., Susannah M., Mary, Ann & Avis, gct Silver Creek MM
1834, 9, 18. Phebe dis jH
1845, 9, 25. Lydia Wilson (form Paddock) dis mcd (H)
1850, 8, 22. Elizabeth Clark (form Paddock) dis mcd (H)
1850, 12, 26. Rebecca H. Hanen (form Paddock) con mcd (H)
1867, 3, 21. Lydia F., Elizabeth & Rebecca H. dropped from mbrp

PAGE
1845, 11, 20. Sarah (form Schooley) rpd mcd; dropped from mbrp
1848, 12, 21. Sarah (form Schooley) dis mcd

PALMER
1856, 7, 5. Lydia S. d bur Mill Creek Gr. Yd.
1858, 11, 25. Hannah d bur Cumminsville Cem.

1835, 11, 19. Julietta rocf Baltimore MM, Md.
1853, 4, 14. Moses D. rocf Cedar Creek MM, Va., dtd 1853,2,9
1853, 8, 18. Lydia L. & Hannah rocf Cedar Creek MM, Va., dtd 1853,5,18

PARKER
1881, 12, 22. Emmet N. recrq (H)
1907, 2, 8. Betty M. rocf Indianapolis MM, Ind.
1908, 1, 10. Bettee gct Indianapolis MM,Ind.

PARRY
1847, 1, 21. Geo. rocf White Water MM, Ind., dtd 1846,10,23 (H)

1855, 6, 14. Elizabeth (form Reynolds) dis mcd
1855, 10, 25. Elizabeth dis mcd & jas (H)

1911, 10, 13. Samuel & w, Rhoda rocf Cherry Grove MM, Ind.
1918, 7, 12. Samuel & Rhoda gct White Water MM, Ind.

PATTERSON
1825, 3, 21. Cert rec for Beulah & ch, Samuel N. & Elwood, from Alexandria MM, dtd 1824,11,18, endorsed to Miami MM, O.
1829, 2, 26. Sarah Minor (form Patterson) rpd mcd

PAULEY
1846, 3, 19. Rebecca (form Schooley) con mcd
1878, 12, 19. Rebecca Bays (form Pauley) relrq

PEARSON
1853, 4, 14. Mary, w Geo., & ch, Joseph John, Jane Ann & Geo., rocf Darlington MM, Eng., dtd 1852,12,21
1855, 8, 16. Mary & ch, Joseph, John, Jane & George, gct White Water MM, Ind.
1857, 8, 20. Mary & ch gct White Water MM, Ind.

PEEBLES
1852, 11, 18. Samuel rocf Dover MM, dtd 1852, 9,16
1856, 7, 17. Samuel dis mcd

PEIRCE
1815, 5, 25. Thomas, s Caleb & Priscilla, Highland Co., O.; m in Cincinnati Mtg, Elizabeth NEAVE, dt Jeremiah & Elizabeth, Highland Co., O.
Ch: Samuel N. b 1816, 3, 25
Alexander " 1818, 6, 12
Sydney " 1820, 2, 18
Charles " 1825, 11, 2
Priscilla " 1831, 10, 29
James " 1834, 1, 23
1819, 2, 25. Samuel, s Caleb & Priscilla, Highland Co., O., b 1790,6,3; m in Cincinnati Mtg, Lydia HOLLOWAY, dt David & Hannah, Highland Co., O., b 1796,12,15
Ch: Gideon b 1819, 11, 30
Kersey " 1821, 11, 20

1818, 7, 16. Samuel rocf Kennett MM, Pa., dtd 1818,6,2
1821, 6, 28. Samuel & w, Lydia, gct West Grove MM, Ind.
1821, 10, 25. Samuel & w, Lydia, & s, Gideon returned cert to West Grove MM, Ind.; again residing in limits of this MM
1825, 5, 26. Samuel & w, Lida, & ch, Gideon, Kersey & David, gct Milford MM, Ind.
1827, 6, 28. Thos. dis disunity

PEIRCE, continued
1832, 7, 26. Mary (form Shreve) con mcd (H)
1843, 5, 18. Samuel dis disunity
1862, 1, 16. Alexander dis disunity
1868, 4, 16. James dropped from mbrp
1868, 12, 17. Chas. dropped from mbrp

PENDLETON
1845, 12, 18. Cornelia (form Morgan) con mcd
1851, 11, 20. Cornelia dis jas

PENNINGTON
1824, 11, 12. Francis B. [Penington], s Levi & Mary, b
1841, 8, 16. Hezekiah B. d bur New Gr. Yd.

1827, 7, 26. John & w, Elizabeth, & s, Robert M., rocf Springborough MM, dtd 1827,5,29
1829, 4, 30. John dis jH
1829, 8, 27. Eliza dis jH
1835, 12, 17. Sarah rocf New Garden MM, dtd 1835,6,25
1836, 6, 16. Sarah Langstaff (form Pennington) con mcd
1837, 6, 15. Hezekiah B. rocf Sandy Spring MM, O., dtd 1837,5,3
1841, 9, 16. Frances B., minor, rocf Sandy Spring MM, O., dtd 1841,8,27
1849, 5, 24. Eliza gct White Water MM, Ind. (H)
1850, 11, 14. Frances B. Comly (form Pennington) dis mcd

PENNEL
1825, 7, 28. Jonathan & w, Rosanna, & ch, Louis M. & Mary Ann, rocf Short Creek MM, O., dtd 1825,5,24
1826, 6, 29. Jonathan & w, Rosanna, & ch, Lewis M. & Mary Ann, gct Springborough MM
1828, 2, 27. James M. [Pennell] gct Springborough MM
1842, 8, 25. Jonathan & w, Rosanna, rocf Springborough MM, O., dtd 1842,7,28 (H)

PERRY
1817, 4, 17. Lydia (form Paddock) dis mcd
1844, 9, 26. Elizabeth (form Williams) con mcd (H)[MM, Ind., to m Anna E. Perry
1884, 3, 20. Mordecai H. Fletcher gct White Water

PETTY
1881, 12, 18. Julius rocf Mill Creek MM, Ind., dtd 1881,5,28

PIM
1847, 10, 21. Alfred rocf Bristol MM, Eng., dtd 1847,8,6, endorsed by New York MM, N. Y., dtd 1847,9,1
1852, 1, 15. Alfred [Pimm] dis mcd

PINE
1873, 7, 24. Mary rocf Springborough MM, dtd 1873,6,26 (H)
1873, 7, 24. Wm. rocf Springborough MM, dtd 1873,6,26 (H)

PLEASANT
1824, 11, 25. Cert rec for Israel P. from Phila. MM, Pa., dtd 1821,4,25, returned
1859, 12, 22. Elizabeth J. con mcd (H)

PLUMMER
1820, 12, 21. Lidia recrq
1821, 5, 31. Lydia recrq
1821, 8, 30. John T., Mary M., Joanora & Sarah C., ch Joseph P., rocf Baltimore MM, Md., dtd 1821,5,5
1823, 11, 27. Joseph P. & w, Lydia, & ch, John F., Mary M., Joannah H. & Sarah C., gct White Water MM, Ind.

PORTER
1919, 8, 10. Walter & ch, Cecil & Archie & his mother, Mary Porter, rocf Mountain Home, Ala.
1923, 1, 14. Jennie recrq
1923, 1, 14. Virgil Randolph recrq
1925, 11, 8. Hershal Donavon recrq (s Walter & Jennie)

POWERS
1897, 6, 18. Agnes R. recrq

PRACKETT
1852, 5, 20. Margaretta (form Griffith) con mcd

PRESTON
1857, 1, 15. Lydia (form Bryant) dis mcd

PRETLOW
1843, 10, 19. Elizabeth Ann rocf White Water MM, Ind., dtd 1843,8,23
1858, 1, 21. Betsy Ann dis jas

PRICE
1908, 2, 12. Clarence, s John Wm. & Florence (Ashley), N. Y., N. Y.; m in Cincinnati Mtg, Susan Morris WHITE, dt Mordecai Morris & Hannah Amelia, Highland Co., O.

1914, 4, 10. Susan Morris White relrq

PUCKET
1854, 1, 19. Henry W. rocf New Garden MM, dtd 1853,6,18
1858, 9, 16. Henry W. [Puckett] gct Wabash MM, Ind.

PUGH
1776, 7, 1. Enoch, s Joshua, b
1785, 1, 26. Caleb, s Joshua, b
----, --, --. Lot b 1791,4,13 d 1850,4,2 bur Spring Grove
1815, 3, 26. Hannah, dt Thos. & Esther, d
1815, 12, 28. Christopher, s Lot & Rachel, d
1816, 3, 28. Ann, w Job, d bur Cincinnati

PUGH, continued
Pub. Gr.
1817, 3, 23. David Jr. d
1818, 8, 27. Job, s David & Rachel, Highland Co., O.; m in Cincinnati MH, Sarah M. MARTIN, dt Oliver & Susannah
Ch: William b 1820, 10, 9 d 1821, 4,27
David " ----, --, -- " 1822, 8,12
1819, 11, 5. David Sr. d ae 62y 2m
1832, 8, 23. Achillies, s Thomas & Esther, Highland Co., O., b 1805,3,10 d 1874,10,31 bur Waynesville, O.; m in Cincinnati Mtg, Anna Maria DAVIS, dt John & Hannah, Highland Co., O., b 1800,2,24 d 1877,2,14 bur Waynesville, O.
Ch: Esther b 1834, 8, 31
John D. " 1838, 3, 14
Mary Taylor " 1840, 9, 24
Rachel " 1843, 4, 29
A. Henry " 1846, 11, 24
1908, 3, 29. Esther d bur Waynesville, O.

1815, 10, 19. Job & w, Ann, & ch, David Thos. & Rue, recrq
1816, 2, 15. David & w, Rachel, & ch, Leah & Hannah, rocf Miami MM, O., dtd 1815,12,27
1816, 3, 21. Caleb rocf Nottingham MM, Md., dtd 1816,3,21
1818, 11, 19. Enoch rocf Elk MM, dtd 1818,9,5
1820, 10, 19. Job & w, Sarah, & ch, David, Thos., Rue, Samuel, Rachel & William, gct Miami MM
1821, 10, 25. Leah C. Marshall (form Pugh) con mcd
1821, 12, 27. Hannah Sexton (form Pugh) con mcd
1822, 8, 29. Job & w, Sarah, & ch, Thomas, Rue, Samuel J. & Rachel, rocf Miami MM, O., dtd 1822,6,26
1829, 1, 29. Rue dis mou
1830, 5, 27. Caleb gct Vermillion MM
1831, 6, 30. Rachel Sr. gct Milton MM, Ind.
1832, 2, 23. Achilles rocf Short Creek MM, O., dtd 1831,12,20
1832, 5, 17. Enoch gct Vermillion MM, Ill.
1835, 12, 17. Hannah rocf Short Creek MM, O., dtd 1835,10,20
1841, 10, 21. Mary Hart (form Pugh) con mcd
1843, 1, 19. Jordan A. dis mcd
1847, 0, 10. Geo. E. dis disunity
1854, 12, 21. Achilles & w, Anna, & ch, John D., Mary F. & A. Henry, gct Miami MM, O.
1854, 12, 21. Esther gct Miami MM, O.
1856, 9, 18. Wm. H. dis mcd
1861, 5, 16. Hannah gct Gilead MM, O.
1868, 4, 16. Thos. dropped from mbrp
1875, 5, 20. Achilles & w, Anna M., & ch, Esther, rocf Miami MM, O.
1875, 7, 15. Henry A. rocf Miami MM, O.
1876, 12, 21. John A. rocf Miami MM, O., dtd 1876,5,22
1879, 1, 16. Esther gct New York MM, N. Y.
1884, 1, 17. Esther rocf New York MM, N. Y., dtd 1883,12,5
1903, 2, 13. John D. dropped from mbrp

PURINTON
1840, 3, 19. Palatiah rocf Salem MM, Mass., dtd 1839,9,12

QUICK
1832, 9, 20. Ellen (form Ricket) dis mcd

RAHWAY
1865, 7, 20. Elizabeth M. dropped from mbrp
1868, 12, 17. Elizabeth dropped from mbrp

RAMBO
----, --, --. William A., s Nathan & Elizabeth, b 1811,7,26 d 1858,8,11 bur Spring Grove; m Miriam Allinson COFFIN, dt Elijah & Naomi, b 1821,9,1
Ch: Sarah Sylvanus b 1840, 5, 21
Elijah Coffin " 1844, 2, 29 d 1844, 4,30 bur New Gr. Yd.
Edward Burroughs b 1845, 4, 5
James Parnell " 1847, 12, 6 d 1849, 2,23 bur New Gr. Yd.
Naomi Coffin b 1850, 8, 8
Francis Howgill " 1853, 7, 17

1844, 6, 20. Wm. A. & w, Mariam, & dt, Sarah Sylvania, rocf White Water MM, Ind., dtd 1844,5,22
1856, 7, 17. Wm. A. & w, Mariam, & ch, Sarah S., Edward B., Naomi C. & Francis A., gct White Water MM, Ind.

RATLIFF
1906, 6, 8. Ruth Anne Hunt gct North A. St. (Hicksite) MM, Richmond, Ind.

REES
1817, 11, 20. Samuel rst
1819, 4, 15. Mary Burk (form Rees) dis mcd
1819, 5, 20. Samuel dis mcd
1874, 3, 26. Thomasin M. & dt, Jane Sidwell, rocf Hopewell MM, Va., dtd 1874,5,3 (H)
1874, 3, 26. Jonah L. & w, Annie J., & ch, Mary Alice, Annie Jackson & Samuel David, rocf Hopewell MM, Va., dtd 1874,5,3 (H)
1877, 10, 25. Samuel D. rocf Hopewell MM, Va. (H)
1879, 2, 20. Jonah L. & w, Annie J., & ch, Mary Alice, Annie Jackson & Samuel D., rocf Hopewell MM, dtd 1874,3,5 (H)
1879, 2, 20. Thomasine M. & dt, Jane Sidwell, rocf Hopewell MM, dtd 1874,3,5 (H)
1883, 11, 22. Jonah L. & w, Anna J., & ch,

REES, continued
Mary Alice & Anna Jackson, gct New York MM, N. Y. (H) (Brooklin, N. Y.)

REEVES
----, --, --. Mark E. & Caroline
Ch: Mary
Taylor b 1851, 6, 1
Arthur
Middleton " 1856, 10, 7

1850, 3, 21. Caroline M. rocf Chesterfield MM, N. J., dtd 1850,2,5 (H)
1860, 2, 23. Mary T. & Arthur M., ch Caroline M., recrq (H)
1870, 3, 24. Caroline M., w Mark E., & s, Arthur M., gct White Water MM, Ind. (H)
1870, 3, 24. Mary T. gct White Water MM, Ind. (H)

RILEY
1854, 12, --. Elizabeth d bur Greenup, Ky.

1819, 8, 19. Elizabeth [Reilly]recrq

REYNOLDS
----, --, --. Jabez s Wm., b 1803,1,31; m Hannah GRIZELL, dt Thos. & Martha, b 1808,8,8
1832, 12, 20. William, s Jabez & Mercy, b
----, --, --. Samuel & Hannah R.
Ch: Elizabeth b 1831, 12, 12
Martha " 1833, 4, 11
Franklin " 1836, 8, 8
William " 1838, 2, 10
Margaretta " 1839, 4, 12
Mary Cornelia " 1842, 2, 12
Samuel Clarkson " 1844, 11, 14
Charles Ernest " 1848, 4, 16

1821, 4, 26. Benjamin & w, Anne, & ch, Daniel, Elizabeth, Phebe, Joshua, David, Rueben, Stephen, Hannah, Sarah & Benjamin, rocf Cornwall MM, N. Y., dtd 1820,4,27
1822, 3, 28. Benj. & w, Anna, & ch, Daniel, Elizabeth, Phebe, Josiah, David, Rueben, Stephen, Hannah, Sarah, Benj. C. & Amos B., gct West Grove MM, Ind.
1832, 9, 20. Jabez rocf East Greenwich MM, R. I., dtd 1832,7,30
1835, 10, 15. Wm. K. rocf Greenwich MM, held at Cranston, dtd 1835,6,1
1843, 4, 20. Hannah & ch, Elizabeth, Martha, Franklin, Wm., Margaretta & Cornelia, rocf Salem MM, 1843,1,25
1848, 11, 16. Wm., s Jabez & Mercy, recrq
1854, 6, 22. Mary (form Borton) dis mcd (H)
1855, 6, 14. Elizabeth Parry (form Reynolds) dis mcd
1856, 2, 14. Wm. rpd mcd; dropped from mbrp
1858, 7, 15. Hannah & ch, Wm., Mary, Cornelia, Samuel Clarkson & Chas. Ernst, gct Fairfield MM, Ind.

RICE
1832, 5, 31. Susan (form Matthews) dis mcd (H)

RICHARD
1815, 5, 21. Rowland, h Lydia, d bur Cincinnati Public Gr.

1823, 8, 28. Lydia [Richards] gct White Water MM, Ind.

RICHIE
1840, 9, 17. Franklin Mitchell gct ND MM, Pa., to m Sarah Richie Jr.

RICKET
1820, 4, 20. Thos. [Rickett] & w, Abigail, & ch, Mary, Abigail, Esther, Ellen, Sarah & Thomas, gct Miami MM, O.
1821, 4, 26. Elizabeth Sloan (form Ricket) con mcd
1826, 11, 30. Thos. & w, Abigail, & ch, Ellen, Sarah & Thos. H., rocf Miami MM, O., dtd 1826,9,27
1826, 11, 30. Esther G. rocf Miami MM, O., dtd 1826,9,27
1829, 2, 26. Esther Munday (form Ricket) con mcd
1832, 9, 20. Ellen Quick (form Ricket) dis mcd
1835, 10, 15. Abigail & s, Thos., gct Mill Creek MM
1835, 10, 15. Sarah gct Mill Creek MM

RIDDLE
1827, 11, 29. Elizabeth (form Jackson) dis mcd

RIDER
1837, 7, 20. Ann (form Wood) dis mcd

RING
1865, 7, 20. Levinia dropped from mbrp

RINGGOLD
1883, 8, 22. Emma W. m Warren B. TOWNSEND

ROBERTS
1871, 4, 6. Hannah d bur Richmond, Ind.

1847, 2, 18. Hannah recrq

ROBINSON
1830, 11, 25. John recrq (H)
1844, 11, 14. Wm. R. rocf New York MM, N. Y., dtd 1844,4,3
1868, 12, 17. Wm. R. dropped from mbrp

ROCKHILL
1833, 10, 17. Sarah rocf Phila. MM, Pa., dtd

ROCKHILL, continued
1832,7,26

ROGERS
1863, 2, 12. Ansel rocf Gilead MM, O., dtd 1862,10,14, endorsed by Alum Creek MM, O.

ROTHERMELL
1848, 3, 23. Nancy rocf Milford MM, Ind., dtd 1847,12,16 (H)

RUSK
1878, 2, 19. Maria d

1870, 5, 19. John & w, Maria, recrq

RUSSELL
1835, --, --. Esther d bur New Gr. Yd.

1815, 6, 15. James & w, Esther, rocf Miami MM, O., dtd 1815,4,26
1845, 9, 25. Jesse & w, Elizabeth, & ch, Jane & Wm., rocf White Water MM, Ind., dtd 1845,7,23 (H)
1858, 9, 23. Jane R. Meredith (form Russel) con mcd
1861, 9, 26. Jesse con mcd (H)

RUST
1879, 8, 21. Elizabeth A. L. rocf Miami MM, O., dtd 1879,7,23

RUTHERFORD
1855, 2, 13. Adelaide Bailey, dt John & Sylvia, b

1853, 5, 19. Sylvia (form Bailey) con mcd
1854, 6, 15. John recrq
1857, 5, 21. John P. & w, Sylvia C., & ch, Ada B., gct Dover MM, O.

RUTLEDGE
1883, 6, 17. Emma (form Neave) relrq

SALTER
1861, 2, 21. Sarah P. gct White Water MM, Ind. (H)

SANDERS
1832, 3, --. Henry, s Hezekiah & Mary, b

1817, 8, 21. David rocf Baltimore MM, Md., dtd 1817,7,11
1819, 7, 15. David dis mcd
1828, 3, 27. Hezekiah [Saunders] recrq
1839, 9, 19. Lucy (form Wright) con mcd
1856, 12, 18. Mary [Saunders] gct White Water MM, Ind.
1859, 4, 14. Lucy [Saunders] dis jas
1865, 7, 20. Henry [Saunders] dropped from mbrp

SANDS
1839, 8, 22. Samuel B. rocf Green Plain MM, dtd 1839,7,17 (H)

SCHMICK
1906, 11, 29. Walter Philip, s Geo. & Johanna, Cuyahoga Co., O.; m in Cincinnati Mtg, Jessie Westerman ALLEN, dt Christopher & Lydia M., Highland Co., O.
Ch: Walter
Ringold b 1908, 2, 12
1908, 11, 18. Erwin J. d
1928, 8, 10. Walter P. d

1897, 5, 20. Ermin J. recrq
1900, 7, 13. Walter recrq
1908, 7, 10. Walter Ringold, s Walter P. & Jessie Allen, recrq
1920, 8, 8. Erwin dropped from mbrp
1932, 9, 2. Paul, Angela & Muriel, minors, recrq

SCHOOLEY
----, --, --. Benjamin b 1789,2,14; m Ann K. ----- b 1791,5,19
Ch: Samuel I. b 1816, 2, 17 d 1841, 3,29 bur New Gr. Yd.
James R. b 1818, 1, 22 " 1856, 4, 6 bur Spring Grove
Sarah C. b 1820, 4, 11
Rebecca Ann " 1822, 8, 3
Elizabeth " 1824, 9, 29
Mary " 1827, 3, 21 d 1841,10,15 bur Spring Grove
Catharine N. b 1829, 6, 3
Benjamin " 1832, 8, 7
Robert N. " 1834, 6, 7 d 1842,10, 6 bur Spring Grove

1837, 12, 21. Benj. & w, Ann W., & ch, Samuel J., James R., Sarah C., Rebecca Ann, Elizabeth, Mary, Catharine, Matilda, Benjamin & Robert N., rocf Chesterfield MM, N. J., dtd 1837,4,4
1845, 11, 20. Sarah Page (form Schooley) rpd mcd; dropped from mbrp
1846, 3, 19. Rebecca Pauley (form Schooley) con mcd
1848, 1, 20. James con mcd
1848, 12, 21. Elizabeth Hartshorn (form Schooley) con mcd
1852, 3, 18. Catharine Lattin (form Schooley) con mcd
1857, 8, 20. Benj. & w, Ann, gct White River MM, Ind.

SCHREPPER
1931, 2, 1. August, Louisa, Hertha & Helmuth, recrq

SCHWEITZER
1928, 3, 4. Jennie recrq

SCOTT
1831, 6, 30. Enoch B. rocf Springborough MM, dtd 1830,5,24 (H)
1833, 8, 22. Naomi rocf Springborough MM, dtd 1833,4,25 (H)

SCOTTON
1836, 8, 25. Ann rocf White Water MM, Ind., dtd 1836,1,27 (H)
1854, 8, 24. Ann gct White Water MM, Ind. (H)

SECRIST
1841, 11, 25. Theresa Ann dis mcd (H)

SELDEN
1846, 10, 22. Hetty (form Gillingham) con mcd (H)
1852, 9, 23. Catharine dis (H)

SEXTON
1821, 12, 27. Hannah (form Pugh) con mcd
1822, 1, 31. Hannah gct Miami MM, O.

SHAFFER
----, --, --. Susan, dt Joshua & Lydia Gibson, b 1785,--,-- d 1862,1,10 bur West Fork Gr. Yd.
1908, 5, 25. Arthur, s Arthur & Geneva, b
1910, 3, 14. Russel Eugene, s Arthur & Geneva, b
1908, 11, 18. Arthur [Shafer], Jr. d

1833, 6, 20. Susan recrq
1903, 3, 13. Arthur C. [Shaefer] recrq
1908, 7, 10. Arthur [Shafer], s Arthur C. & Geneva A., recrq
1931, 11, 6. Leslie D. rocf West Richmond MM, Ind.
1931, 11, 6. Alice rocf West Richmond MM, Ind.
1932, 9, 2. Russel E. Harold & Wesley [Shafer], minors, recrq

SHAW
1780, 11, 24. Thos. b
----, --, --. John, s Samuel & Susannah, b 1780,11,24; m Elizabeth WRIGHT, dt Jonathan & Elizabeth, b 1777,12,21
Ch: Edward b 1815, 4, 29 d 1909, 4, 9 bur near Richmond, Ind.
Thos. Wright b 1817, 9, 17
Rebecca " 1821, 9, 28
1829, 11, 3. Margaret b
----, --, --. Margaret, dt Robert & Jessie Morrison Hamilton, b 1829,11,21 d 1890,6,27 bur Spring Grove
1908, 1, 17. Margaret d bur Spring Grove

1825, 8, 24. John & w, Elizabeth, & ch, Edward Thos. & Rebecca, gct Silver Creek MM, Ind.
1827, 1, 25. John & w, Elizabeth, & ch, Edward, Thos. W. & Rebecca, rocf Silver Creek MM, Ind., dtd 1826,12,23
1829, 6, 25. John dis jH
1829, 8, 27. Elizabeth dis jH
1830, 2, 25. Elizabeth dis jH
1835, 12, 24. John & w, Elizabeth, & ch, Edward, Thos. W. & Rebecca L., gct Green Plain MM, O. (H)
1836, 12, 15. Edward gct Green Plain MM, O.
1836, 12, 15. Rebecca & Thos., ch John, gct Green Plain MM, O.
1876, 5, 18. Margaret recrq
1886, 8, 19. Margaret Jr. recrq

SHEARMAN
1882, 12, 20. Joseph T. Jr. d
1903, 11, 28. Emily d (an elder)
1910, 6, 8. Anna M. d

1880, 9, 16. John D. & w, Emma, & ch, Chas., Mabel & John Russell, rocf Indianapolis MM, Ind.
1881, 1, 20. Joseph T. & w, Anna M., & ch, Laura B., Samuel M., Mary K., David S. & Joseph T. Jr., rocf WD MM, Pa., dtd 1880, 12,22
1885, 11, 19. John D. & w, Emma A., & ch, Chas. H., Mabel A. & John Russell, gct Indianapolis MM, Ind.
1889, 7, 18. Joseph T. dis disunity
1902, 5, 9. Samuel M. gct New York MM, N. Y.
1902, 5, 9. David S. gct Wilmington MM, O.
1913, 7, 11. David S. & Abram H. dropped from mbrp

SHELDON
1822, 4, 25. Mary rocf Westfield MM, dtd 1822,3,27
1865, 7, 20. Mary dropped from mbrp
1866, 6, 14. Anna M. (form Judkins) dis mcd & jas

SHERWOOD
1867, 7, 18. Emily rocf Grove MM, Ind., dtd 1867,7,4

SHIPLEY
----, --, --. Ann b 1760,10,10 d 1854,7,29 bur New Gr. Yd.
----, --, --. Thomas C., s Wm. & Phebe, b 1807,5,16 d 1864,1,4 bur West Fork
----, --, --. Mary Emily, dt Jonathan & Hannah, b 1813,5,21 d 1843,6,4 bur New Gr. Yd
----, --, --. Morris, s Maurice & Ann, b 1784, 11,29; m Sarah ----- dt Wm. & ----- Shotwell, b 1788,9,15 d 1854,12,30 bur New Gr. Yd.
Ch: Ann M. b 1824, 6, 24
Murray " 1830, 3, 1 d 1899, 1,20 bur Spring Grove

SHIPLEY, continued
1837, 8, 13. Wm., s Maurice & Ann, d bur New Gr. Yd.
1838, 1, 21. Chas. J., s Thos. & Mary Emily, b
1844, 10, 24. Elizabeth C. m James TAYLOR
1851, 5, 22. Murray, s Morris & Sarah, Highland Co., O.; m in Cincinnati Mtg, Hannah D. TAYLOR, dt Caleb W. & Mary J., b 1831, 9,21

Ch: Hannah Taylor b 1852, 9, 11
Mary Charlote " 1854, 9, 11
Morris Shotwell " 1856, 12, 7
Elizabeth A. " 1859, 7, 21
Caleb Wright " 1861, 8, 9
Murray Jr. " 1865, 2, 24
Catharine M. " 1867, 12, 9
William Ellis " 1870, 5, 21
Walter Tatum " 1871, 11, 18 d 1872, 1,27 bur Spring Grove

1863, 6, 19. Phebe, dt Maurice & Ann, d bur New Bur. Gr.
1871, 11, 19. Hannah D. d ae 40 (an elder)
1873, 12, 17. Mary C. m Chas. S. HOWLAND
1885, 6, 18. Wm. d bur Spring Grove
1899, 2, 2. Murray d ae 72 (a minister)
1922, 12, 25. Catharine d

1834, 8, 21. Ann, minister, rocf Center MM, dtd 1834,5,14
1834, 8, 21. Wm. & w, Phebe, & ch, Elizabeth C., Mary P., Caroline, Henry H. & Wm. Jr., rocf Center MM, dtd 1834,5,14
1834, 8, 21. Thos. C. & w, Mary Emily, rocf Center MM, dtd 1834,5,14
1835, 6, 18. John W. rocf New York MM, N. Y., dtd 1833,7,3, endorsed by Center MM
1836, 10, 20. John W. dis jas
1843, 8, 17. Morris & w, Sarah, & ch, Ann M. & Murray, rocf New York MM, N. Y., dtd 1843,6,7
1850, 1, 17. Henry H. con mcd
1855, 9, 20. Wm. con mcd
1855, 11, 15. Henry dis
1855, 12, 20. Morris gct New York MM, N. Y.
1855, 12, 20. Anna M. gct New York MM, N. Y.
1859, 9, 15. Mary P. dis jas
1866, 5, 17. Caroline gct Burlington MM, N.J.
1875, 6, 17. Murray gct Newport MM, R. I., to m Catharine M. Shipley
1875, 6, 17. Murray Shipley gct Newport MM, R. I., to m Catharine M. Shipley
1876, 9, 14. Catharine M. rocf R. I. MM, held at Portsmouth, dtd 1876,4,27
1898, 5, 13. Caleb M. relrq
1900, 9, 14. Wm. Ellis gct Frankford MM, Pa, to m Caroline W. Cadbury
1903, 3, 13. Wm. E. gct Frankfort MM, Pa.
1912, 5, 10. Elizabeth A. gct Haverford MM, Pa.
1912, 5, 10. Katharine Morris gct Haverford MM, Pa.

SHOEMAKER
----, --, --. Isaac, s Chas. & Margaret, b 1807,8,-- d 1873,9,21 bur Burlington, N.J.

1846, 9, 17. Isaac rocf Abington MM, dtd 1846,8,4
1848, 7, 20. Abraham M. Taylor gct ND MM, Pa., to m Elizabeth R. Shoemaker

SHREVE
1828, 10, 2. Margaret m Wm. Butler

1827, 6, 28. Thos. [Shreive] & dt, Grace & Mary, rocf Chesterfield MM, N. J., dtd 1827,5,8
1829, 4, 30. Thomas dis jH
1829, 7, 29. Grace Bowles (form Shreve) con mcd (H)
1829, 8, 27. Grace Bowles (form Shreve) dis mcd & jH
1829, 8, 27. Elizabeth dis jH
1829, 10, 29. Thos. H. rocf Chesterfield MM, N. J., dtd 1829,4,7 (H)
1830, 9, 30. Mary [Shreeve] dis jas
1830, 10, 28. Thos. [Shreeve] Jr., minor, rocf Chesterfield MM, N. J., dtd 1830,2,2
1832, 7, 26. Mary Peirce (form Shreve) con mcd (H)
1832, 9, 20. Grace Beal (form Shreve) dis mcd
1832, 11, 15. Thos. H. dis jH
1839, 9, 26. Wm. recrq (H)
1839, 11, 21. Elizabeth Donaldson (form Shreve) con mcd (H)
1839, 12, 26. Wm. gct Chesterfield MM, N. J. (H)
1841, 8, 26. Thos. H. con mcd (H)
1860, 10, 25. Albert rocf White Water MM, Ind. (H)
1863, 10, 22. Richard rocf White Water MM, Ind. (H)

SHULTZ
1900, 5, 11. Rebecca Gest relrq

SHUTE
1846, 5, 21. Samuel & w, Sibyl, & ch, Elias H., rocf White Water MM, Ind., dtd 1846, 3,25 (H)
1847, 5, 20. Samuel dis mcd (H)
1852, 5, 20. Elias H. dis mcd (H)

SIMCOCK
1826, 10, 24. James rocf Phila. MM, Pa., dtd 1825,11,16

SIMCOCK, continued
1835, 12, 17. James [Simcox]con mcd

SISSON
----, --, --. Isaac, s Geo. & Mary, b 1762,8,4; m Elizabeth GARDNER, dt Thos. & Ann, b 1763,6,3
Ch: Mary b 1793, 5, 7
Eunice " 1795, 3, 30
Ann " 1798, 11, 8
Elizabeth " 1803, 6, 6 d 1806, 1,--

SKYSON
1829, 5, 28. Ann rocf WD MM, Pa., dtd 1828,11, 19
1828, 5, 28. Elizabeth rocf WD MM, Pa., dtd 1828,11,19
1829, 5, 28. Mary rocf WD MM, Pa., dtd 1828, 11,19
1833, 2, 14. Mary Clark (form Skyron) dis mcd

SLOAN
1821, 4, 26. Elizabeth (form Ricket) con mcd
1822, 2, 28. Elizabeth gct Miami MM, O.

SLOCUM
1850, 4, 18. Emeline rocf Frankfort MM, Pa., dtd 1850,2,26
1880, 3, 18. Emeline M. gct ND MM, Pa.

SLOFFREGER
1930, 8, 3. Ida B., H. Fred Jr., Francis & David rocf Wilmington MM, O.

SMITH
1780, 3, 25. Mahala, dt Benjamin & Sarah Freeman, b
----, --, --. George D. b 1805,--,-- d 1884, 4,10 bur Spring Grove
1819, 4, 5. Cyrus d
----, --, --. William, s Wm. & Mary, b 1786, 2,8; m Eliza Ann FOLGER, dt David & Elizabeth, b 1798,3,19
Ch: William F. b 1822, 11, 10
1833, 12, 26. Hugh H., s Robert & Anna Maria, Highland Co., O.; m in Cincinnati Mtg, Sarah A. DAVIS, dt John & Hannah, Highland Co., O.
1870, 3, 4. Anna Gilpin, dt Howard & Rachel C., b
1883, 4, 15. Hannah P. d (an elder)
1883, 4, 10. Geo. D. d (an elder)
1907, 10, 30. Laura Gilpin, dt Geo. & Hannah, d bur Spring Grove

1815, 10, 19. Hugh & w, Elizabeth, & ch, Senneca, Chas., Rebecca & David H., rocf Sadsbury MM, Pa., dtd 1815,8,8
1815, 10, 19. Hepzabath rocf Nantucket MM, dtd 1815,7,27
1816, 1, 18. Cyrus N. rocf Sadbury MM, Pa., dtd 1815,7,11
1816, 11, 21. Mordecai dis disunity
1817, 5, 15. Hepzibah Chase (form Smith) con mcd
1821, 6, 28. Oliver C. rocf Butternut MM, dtd 1821,3,28
1822, 1, 31. Eliza Ann (form Folger) con mcd
1825, 8, 24. Hugh H. recrq
1833, 2, 14. Hugh H. gct Miami MM, O.
1833, 11, 14. Hugh H. rocf Miami MM, O., dtd 1833,10,23
1834, 12, 18. Hugh H. & w, Sarah, & ch, Hannah Maria & Elizabeth, gct Fairfield MM, Ind.
1842, 10, 20. Mahala rocf Redstone MM, Pa., dtd 1842,8,31
1847, 1, 21. Joseph rocf Redstone MM, Pa., dtd 1846,11,4
1847, 1, 21. Elias rocf Redstone MM, Pa., dtd 1846,11,4
1852, 4, 15. Hannah P., w Geo., & ch, Henry Howard, Laura G., Frances Eliza, Robert Clinton & Alice Anna, rocf ND MM, Pa., dtd 1852,3,23
1865, 7, 20. Seneca, Chas., Rebecca & David H., dropped from mbrp
1868, 5, 21. Geo. D. recrq
1869, 5, 20. H. Howard con mcd
1878, 8, 22. Julia D. (form Durfee) gct Benjaminville MM, Ill. (H)
1884, 6, 19. Robert Clinton gct Darlington MM, Md.
1892, 2, 18. Anna G. relrq

SNIDER
1827, 7, 26. Eliza D. rocf Miami MM, O., dtd 1827,5,30
1834, 7, 17. Eliza [Snyder] gct Newberry MM, O.

SPENCER
1914, 4, 10. Blanche recrq
1920, 8, 8. Blanch dropped from mbrp

STACKHOUSE
1853, 1, 20. Rebecca Ann rocf Green St. MM, Phila., Pa. (H)
1853, 9, 22. Rebecca Ann gct Green St. MM, Phila., Pa. (H)

STAFFORD
1832, 4, 19. Joseph C. & w, Lydia, & ch, Nathan D., Elias B., Phebe M. & Wm. P., rocf Deep River MM, N. C., dtd 1832,4,19
1833, 1, 17. Joseph C. & w, Lydia, & ch, Nathan D., Elias C., Phebe M., Wm. P. & Julius, gct Silver Creek MM, Ind.

STAGG
1823, 10, 21. Hannah Isabella, dt John & Hannah Davis, b

1843, 4, 20. Hannah (form Davis) con mcd
1854, 5, 18. Hannah Isabella dis jas

STANLEY
1847, 8, 19. Milicent rocf Chesterfield MM, dtd 1847,5,15

STANTON
1831, 7, 28. Wm. F. [Staunton] rocf Miami MM, O., dtd 1831,6,29
1832, 7, 19. Robert, minor, rocf Springborough MM, dtd 1832,6,19
1832, 9, 20. Robert Jr. gct Springborough MM

STARR
----, --, --. Wm. C. & Anna M.
Ch: Francis Cist b 1856, 10, 12 d 1862,11,19
William Cooper " 1859, 6, 4 " 1861,--, 8

1820, 5, 18. William [Star] & w, Mary, & ch, Elizabeth, Jesse & Joshua, rocf Exeter MM, dtd 1819,7,25, endorsed to Elk MM
1820, 5, 18. Cert rec for Nehemiah [Star] & w, Esther, & s, Henry, from Exeter MM, dtd 1819,8,25, endorsed to Elk MM, O.
1849, 6, 21. Wm. C. rocf White Water MM, Ind., dtd 1849,6,13 (H)
1851, 4, 24. Anna M., w Wm., & s, Chas. W., recrq (H)
1868, 7, 23. Wm. C. & w, Anna M., & ch, Chas. West & Horace Chipman, gct White Water MM, Ind. (H)

ST. CLAIR
1891, 5, 21. Ada rocf Springfield MM, O., dtd 1891,3,21
1895, 4, 18. Ada relrq

STEDDOM
1870, 4, 14. Joseph recrq
1876, 2, 17. Cornelia A. P. [Steddon] recrq
1891, 10, 15. Cornelia A. gct White Water MM, Ind.

STEER
1754, 12, 26. Joseph, s Joseph & Grace, b
----, --, --. Samuel, s Joseph & Grace, b 1793,8,18; m Harriet -----, dt Enoch & Hannah Harlan, b 1795,8,20 d 1883,3,23 bur New Bur. Gr.
Ch: Elizabeth b 1821, 1, 10 d 1843, 4,20 bur New Gr. Yd.
Sarah b 1822, 3, 19

1833, 9, 20. Samuel & w, Harriet, & ch, Elizabeth & Sarah, rocf Short Creek MM,O., dtd 1833,7,27
1835, 12, 17. Joseph rocf Short Creek MM, O., dtd 1835,10,20
1841, 3, 18. Sarah dis jas

STEPHENS
----, --, --. Judith Gifford [Stevens] b 1815,4,16 d 1906,1,28 bur Providence, R.I.
1836, 11, 24. Isaac & w, Hanáh, rocf Chesterfield MM, N. J., dtd 1836,11,8 (H)
1836, 11, 24. Isaac Jr. rocf Chesterfield MM, N. J., dtd 1836,11,8 (H)
1836, 11, 24. Jacob rocf Chesterfield MM, N.J., dtd 1836,11,8 (H)
1836, 11, 24. Ann rocf Chesterfield MM, N. J., dtd 1836,11,8 (H)
1839, 1, 24. Jacob [Stevens] con mcd (H)
1840, 6, 25. Isaac Jr. con mcd (H)
1847, 9, 23. Isaac Jr. gct Chesterfield MM, N. J., to m Lydia Middleton, dt Samuel, Crosswick, N. J. (H)
1849, 3, 2. Lydia M. rocf Chesterfield MM, N. J., dtd 1849,3,5 (H)
1853, 2, 24. Hannah gct Chesterfield MM, N.J. (H)
1855, 12, 20. Isaac [Stevens] & w, Lydia, gct Chesterfield MM, N. J. (H)
1883, 6, 14. Judith G. & Ida [Stevens] rocf Providence MM, R. I., dtd 1883,5,30
1883, 7, 19. Ida M. [Stevens] relrq
1883, 7, 19. Eva B. [Stevens] recrq

STOKES
1890, 10, 8. Lydia M., w Samuel, d bur Spring Grove

1830, 10, 28. Edward rocf ND MM, Pa., dtd 1829,12,22, endorsed by White Water MM, Ind., 1830,7,28
1870, 4, 14. Lydia recrq

STONE
1880, 5, 20. Mary E. rocf Friendsville MM, Tenn., dtd 1880,1,30, returned because of complaint against her

STORCH
1878, 11, 18. Geo. Anderson, s Gustavus F. & Sarah Elizabeth, Highland Co., O.; m in Cincinnati Mtg, Mary Catharine TOWNSEND, dt Isaac & Peninnah, Highland Co., O., b 1857,10,29
Ch: Charles Raymond b 1880, 3, 30
Robert Chester " 1884, 3, 28
Dayton Townsend " 1886, 1, 18

STORCH, Geo. Anderson & Sarah Elizabeth, cont.
Ch: John Oliver
b 1895, 8, 9
Elleanor " 1882, 8, 3 d 1890, 8,19
bur Spring Grove
1908, 2, 3. Dorotha Laura, dt Robert & Ella, b
1911, 12, 8. Dayton T. m Caroline STOFFER

1895, 9, 19. Oliver, s Geo. A. & Mary C., recrq
1908, 7, 10. Dorothy Laura, dt Robert & Ella G., recrq
1916, 5, 12. Robert C. relrq
1918, 4, 12. Chas. Raymond dropped from mbrp
1921, 11, 13. Dayton relrq
1932, 9, 2. Vergie Lee recrq
1933, 4, 7. Cora recrq

STRATTON
1815, 6, 15. David rocf Centre MM, O., dtd 1815,5,20
1817, 8, 21. David gct Center MM

STREET
1855, 11, 15. Cert rec for Lewis dtd 1855,9,20 returned

STROUD
1870, 5, 4. Susan B., wd Chas., d bur Spring Grove

1869, 12, 16. Susan B. rocf Miami MM, O.

SUFFRINS
1819, 4, 15. John gct White Water MM, Ind.

SUISFELT
1875, 12, 23. Maria recrq (H)

SUMNER
1851, 5, 30. Martha d (an elder)

1838, 11, 15. Martha rocf Fall Creek MM, dtd 1838,7,25
1869, 1, 21. Frances gct Bath MM, Eng.

SUMMERHAYES
1924, 12, 14. Henry Geo. & Jane Emma rocf Glouster & Nailsworth MM, England

SWAIN
1816, 1, 18. Alice (form Paddock) dis disunity
1831, 1, 27. Sarah (form Macy) dis mcd
1831, 3, 31. Sarah [Swayne] (form Macy) dis mcd (H)

SWEETMAN
1820, 12, 21. Wm. [Swetman] & w, Elizabeth, & ch, Wm. & Eliza, rocf Bristol MM, Eng., dtd 1820,7,4
1865, 7, 20. Wm. & w, Eliza, & ch, Wm. Jr. & Eliza Jr. dropped from mbrp
1874, 12, 17. Eliza rst
1875, 2, 18. Eliza gct Cold Creek MM, Canada

SWIFT
----, --, --. Rueben, s Sylvanus & Elizabeth, b 1769,5,12; m Ruth DILLINGHAM, dt Ignatius & Degorah, b 1768,10,3
Ch: William b 1792, 8, 28 d 1820, 3, 1
Silvanus " 1795, 11, 29
Calvin " 1797, 5, 29
Rueben Jr. " 1798, 11, 29 d 1804, 8,21
Deborah " 1800, 10, 15
Elizabeth " 1802, 1, 29
Lydia " 1805, 10, 21
Stephen " 1804, 3, 1 d 1806,10, 8
Abial " 1807, 7, 15

1821, 7, 26. Ruth, w Rueben, & ch, Eliza, Lidia & Abial, rocf Scipio MM, N. Y., dtd 1819,3,18
1824, 2, 26. Elizabeth Adams (form Swift) dis mcd
1824, 12, 30. Lydia Finkbine (form Swift) dis mcd
1827, 9, 27. Abial con mcd

SYKES
1862, 2, 13. Hannah d bur Spring Grove

1861, 6, 20. Hannah rocf Phila. MM, Pa., dtd 1861,3,28

SYNNESSTREDT
----, --, --. George & Maria
Ch: Otho
Christian b 1845, 8, 13
Frank K.
Andrew " 1847, 3, 8
Margaretta
Elizabeth " 1848, 12, 7
Agusta
Louisa " 1852, 10, 10
Georgianna
Maria " 1855, 10, 20
Nancy
Harvey " 1858, 1, 25
Thomas " 1861, 5, 12

1860, 11, 15. Geo. C. [Synnestvedt] & w, Maria, & ch, Otto Christian, Frederick Andrew, Margaretta Elizabeth, Augusta Louisa, Georgianna Maria & Nancy Harvey, recrq
1865, 11, 16. Geo. [Synestodt] & w, Maria, & ch relrq
1878, 7, 25. Thos. I. [Synisvedt] recrq (H)

TABER
1832, 4, 26. Jethro W. rocf Rensselaerville MM, N. Y., dtd 1831,4,27 (H)
1832, 4, 26. Ann rocf Rensselaerville MM, N. Y., dtd 1831,12,22 (H)
1839, 11, 14. Thos. & w, Ann, & ch, Henry Allen, Ellen Elizabeth, Geo. Derwin & Benj. Phillip, rocf Vasselboro MM, Me., dtd 1839,8,14
1842, 7, 21. Thos. dis disunity
1865, 7, 20. Henry Allen, Ellen Elizabeth Geo. Dowin & Benj. Phillips, dropped from mbrp

TALBERT
1830, 7, 29. David dis mcd
1831, 11, 25. David L. dis mcd (H)
1833, 2, 14. Samuel dis disunity
1846, 6, 18. Aaron S. rocf Salem MM, Ind., dtd 1846,3,28
1847, 5, 20. Aaron dis mcd

TALBOTT
----, --, --. Samuel m Rachel LITTLER
Ch: Joseph b 1795, 8, 14
Nathan " 1798, 7, 29
John L. " 1800, 10, 20
Rebecca W. " 1802, 5, 24
Samuel " 1804, 3, 5
David L. " 1810, 6, 20
----, --, --. John L. m Phebe R. CONKLING
Ch: Sarah Elizabeth b 1833, 12, 19
Wallace Pierson " 1838, 6, 20
----, --, --. John & Mary
Ch: Elisha Saunders b 1844, 4, 1
Sarah Jane " 1846, 4, 1
Charles Russel " 1848, 10, 6

1821, 1, 25. Rachel, w Samuel, & ch, Samuel & David, rocf Short Creek MM, O., dtd 1820,10,24
1821, 1, 25. Rebecca rocf Short Creek MM, O., dtd 1820,9,19
1821, 2, 25. Nathan rocf Short Creek MM, O., dtd 1820,10,24
1821, 10, 25. Nathan dis mcd
1821, 12, 27. Samuel rocf Short Creek MM, O.,. dtd 1821,2,28
1824, 9, 30. Samuel Jr. dis disunity
1826, 3, 30. John con mcd
1829, 11, 26. Sam'l C. dis disunity (H)
1831, 8, 25. Rachel dis jH
1844, 9, 26. John & w, Mary, & ch, Ann E., Mary R., Ruth A., Wm. H., John T. & Elisha S., rocf Milford MM, Ind., dtd 1844,7,18 (H)
1880, 4, 22. John T. & Chas. R. dropped from mbrp (H)

TATUM
----, --, --. Samuel C. b 1827,5,13 d 1887,6, 17 bur Spring Grove
----, --, --. Eleanor b 1830,11,24 d 1912,10, 31 bur Spring Grove (an elder)
1887, 11, 8. Samuel C. Jr. d bur Spring Grove, ae 30
1890, 7, 4. Mary C. d bur Spring Grove

1819, 2, 18. Rachel [Tatem] rocf Wilmington MM, dtd 1818,10,7
1829, 7, 30. Rachel [Tatem] dis jH
1868, 5, 21. Samuel [Tatem] & w, Eleanor, & ch, Mary C., Amy, Elizabeth & Samuel C. Jr., recrq

TERRELL
1875, 7, 15. Pleasant M. & w, Alice, & s, Hezekiah M., rocf Clear Creek MM, O.
1876, 12, 21. Pleasant M. & w, Alice, & ch, Hezekiah, gct Clear Creek MM, O.

TERRY
1898, 1, 20. John A. rocf Elk MM, O., dtd 1897,12,23

TEST
1817, 7, 17. Elizabeth gct Silver Creek MM, Ind.
1817, 7, 17. Samuel Jr. gct Miami MM, O.
1817, 10, 16. Samuel & w, Sarah, & ch, John, Rachel, Mary W., Lydia & Sarah, gct Silver Creek MM, Ind.

THAIN
1834, 1, 16. Lydia rocf New York MM, N. Y., dtd 1833,11,6

THATCHER
1815, 6, 15. David rocf Centre MM, O., dtd 1815,5,20

THISTLEWAITE
1846, 5, 21. Thos. rocf White Water MM, Ind., dtd 1846,3,25 (H)

THOMAS
1820, 9, 16. Ellenor, w Joseph, d
1822, 9, 16. Eleanor d
1858, 9, 23. Chas. W., s Abel & Rebecca, Phila., Pa.; m in Cincinnati Mtg, Orynthee Neely, dt Joseph & Asenath, Highland Co., O.

1815, 5, 18. John rocf Phila. MM, Pa., dtd 1815,4,26
1816, 1, 18. John L. dis military operations
1821, 2, 25. Elenor, w Joseph, rocf Abington MM, dtd 1819,12,27
1821, 1, 25. Sarah rocf Abington MM, dtd 1819,12,27
1831, 12, 31. Ann rocf Springborough MM, O., dtd 1831,11,24 (H)

THOMAS, continued
1832, 2, 23. Isaac rocf Springborough MM, dtd 1831,11,29
1834, 2, 13. Isaac gct Springborough MM
1834, 7, 24. Ann gct Springborough MM, O. (H)
1841, 5, 20. Rebecca H. & ch, Elmira, Chas. W., Benj. F., Albert, Isaac H., Howard D., Sarah & Elihu, rocf White Water MM, Ind., dtd 1841,3,24
1842, 8, 18. Rebecca H. & ch, Elmira, Chas. W., Benj. F., Albert, Isaac H., Howard D. & Sarah Ellen, gct Springborough MM
1845, 11, 27. Chas. H. Williams gct Plainfield MM, O., to m Sarah E. Thomas (H)
1846, 3, 26. Phebe rocf Plainfield MM, dtd 1846,2,19 (H)
1846, 3, 26. Susanna rocf Plainfield MM, dtd 1846,2,19 (H)
1858, 12, 23. Sarah W. con mcd (H)
1859, 2, 17. R. Orynthee gct ND MM, Pa.
1865, 7, 20. Sarah dropped from mbrp

THOMPSON
1821, 7, 26. Joseph D. & fam rocf Phila. MM, Pa., dtd 1821,4,26
1824, 9, 30. Joseph D. & w, Lucy, & ch, Alfred Haughton, Edwin, Joshua & Maria, gct Silver Creek MM, Ind.
1826, 12, 28. Abraham rocf Center MM, Pa., dtd 1823,7,19
1826, 12, 28. Thos. rocf Center MM, Pa., dtd 1823,7,19
1827, 11, 29. Cert for Abraham to Chester MM, Pa., returned with information he resided at White Water MM, Ind.

THORNE
1865, 10, 18. Josephine, dt Levi & Anna K., b
----, --, --. Grace Anna b 1869,10,20 d 1870, 10,10 bur West Branch Gr. Yd.

1848, 11, 23. Joseph & w, Edith Ann, & ch, Elwood E. & Joseph Howard, rocf Milford MM, Ind., dtd 1843,10,19 (H)
1851, 8, 21. Joseph dis
1852, 7, 22. Edith A. & s, Joseph, gc
1868, 1, 16. Levi E. & w, Anna Rosella, & ch, Josephine, rocf White Water MM, Ind., dtd 1867,12,25
1878, 5, 16. Anna Rosella, w L. E., & ch, Josephine, James, Frederick & Walter T., rocf New York MM, N. Y.
1879, 2, 13. Levi E. dis
1879, 11, 20. Levi E. gct New York MM, N. Y.

THORNTON
1830, 5, 27. Samuel Y. rocf Indian Spring MM, Md., dtd 1829,8,5 (H)
1830, 5, 27. Elizabeth B. rocf Indian Spring MM, Md., dtd 1829,8,5
1830, 5, 27. Hannah & ch, Wm. & Edward, rocf Indian Spring MM, Md., dtd 1829,8,5

THWAITE
1851, 8, 21. Richard rocf Preston MM, Blackburn, Eng., dtd 1850,7,11, endorsed by Smithfield MM, O., forwarded by this MM to Flushing MM, O.

TILTON
1819, 6, 12. William d bur Friends Ground
1818, 7, 5. Thomas d bur Friends Ground

1817, 11, 20. Wm. & w, Catharine, & ch, Elizabeth B., Sarah & Millis, rocf New York MM, dtd 1817,9,3
1817, 11, 20. Thos. rocf New York MM, dtd 1817,9,3
1819, 11, 18. Catharine & ch, Elizabeth, Sarah & Millis, gct New York MM, N. Y.

TIMBERLAKE
1844, 9, 20. Richard, s John & Molly, Highland Co.; m in Cincinnati Mtg, Mahala SMITH, dt Benjamin & Sarah, Highland Co., O., b 1780,3,25

1845, 7, 17. Mahala gct Clear Creek MM, O.

TODHUNTER
1815, 6, 15. John & w, Rebecca, rocf Fairfield MM, dtd 1815,4,29
1822, 3, 28. Rebecca gct Fairfield MM, O.
1865, 7, 20. John dropped from mbrp
1880, 12, 16. Oscar B. rocf Hopewell MM, O., dtd 1880,12,4
1899, 6, 9. Oscar B. dropped from mbrp

TOMLINSON
1865, 10, 19. Andrew D. & w, Sina, rocf Bloomfield MM, dtd 1865,9,6

TOWNSEND
----, --, --. Francis m Ann -----, dt James & Ann FRENCH, b 1808,12,10
Ch: Emmor b 1827, 11, 5
Lowis " 1829, 8, 30
Joseph " 1831, 6, 13 d 1855, 5,-- bur White Water
Arvine b 1833, 8, 25 " 1842, 5,26 bur New Gr. Yd.
Sina b 1835, 9, 31
Mary Ann " 1838, 1, 12
Rebecca " 1840, 5, 15 " 1840, 6,18 bur New Gr. Yd.
----, --, --. Elmer & Merle
Ch: Hellen Romina b 1905, 5, 26
John Thomas " 1906, 9, 13
Donald Eugene " 1906, 9, 13
Mary Ellen " 1911, 5, 26
Elmer D. Jr. " 1915, 11, 13
1907, 6, --. Isabel B. dt Henry J. & Minnie,

TOWNSEND, continued
b
----, --, --. Isaac m Peninah ----- d 1915,7, 21 bur Spring Grove
Ch: Abigail
Emily b 1847, 12, 17
Josiah
Dayton " 1849, 5, 24
John
Thomas " 1851, 8, 9
Lydia Margaret b 1855, 3, 3
Mary Catharine " 1857, 10, 29
Warren B. " 1860, 11, 25
Robert C. " 1863, 8, 19
1921, 8, 8. Warren B. d
1883, 8, 22. Warren B., s Isaac & Peninnah, Highland Co., O.; m in Cincinnati Mtg, Emma W. RINGGOLD, dt Thomas & Annie E., Highland Co., O.
Ch: Warren
Ringgold b 1884, 9, 10 d 1890, 1,20 bur Spring Grove
1878, 1, 18. Henry Isaac, s John T., b

1824, 7, 29. Thos. & w, Elizabeth, rocf Plainfield MM, dtd 1824,3,25
1824, 7, 29. Harriet rocf Plainfield MM, dtd 1824,4,22
1828, 1, 31. Harriett Taylor (form Townsend) con mcd
1835, 3, 19. Elizabeth gct Springborough MM
1837, 11, 16. Ann & ch, Emor, Lewis, Joseph, Ervine & Sina, rocf Upper Springfield MM, O., dtd 1837,9,23
1853, 8, 18. Lewis dis mcd
1854, 3, 16. Emmor dis mcd
1861, 10, 17. Isaac & w, Peninah, & ch, Abigail, Emily, Josiah Dayton, John Thomas, Lydia Margaret, Mary Catharine & Warren B., rocf Newberry MM, O., dtd 1861,9,23
1868, 5, 21. Abigail Emily Haizley (form Townsend) con mcd
1885, 3, 26. Warren Ringgold, s Warren B. & Emma R., recrq
1886, 8, 19. Lilly H., w Robert, recrq
1892, 5, 19. Ethel G., dt Robert & Lillie, recrq
1897, 5, 20. Elmer D. recrq
1898, 1, 20. Mary Ellen & s, Ray Dayton, recrq
1901, 6, 14. Emma R., w Warren, recrq
1904, 12, 9. Merle K. & Minnie B. recrq
1905, 4, 14. Mary Elizabeth, dt Henry Isaac & Minnie B., recrq
1906, 12, 14. John Thomas & Donald Eugene, ch Elmer D. & Merle K., recrq
1912, 10, 11. Robert C. & w, Lillie H., & ch, Ethel G. & Ruth B., gct San Diago MM, Calif.
1921, 8, 14. Merle K. relrq

TRIMBLE
----, --, --. Joseph M. & Sarah G.
Ch: William b 1847, 3, 22
Eliza V. " 1856, 1, 15
Joseph Gilpin " 1858, 9, 23
Laura M. " 1861, 3, 5

1850, 2, 21. Joseph M. & w, Sarah G., & s, Wm., rocf Concord MM, Pa. (H)
1852, 4, 22. Joseph M. & w, Sarah M., & s, Wm., gct Milford MM, Ind. (H)
1859, 7, 21. Joseph M. & w, Sarah G., & ch, Wm. & Eliza G., rocf White Water MM, Ind., dtd 1859,4,27

TRIMMER
1867, 6, 20. Francis rocf Grove MM, Ind., dtd 1867,5,30
1869, 1, 21. Frances gct South Parade Bath, Somerset, Eng.

TUCKER
----, --, --. Thomas, s Thomas & Mary, b 1778, 7,9; m Ann SYKES, dt Benj. & Anna, b 1787, 12,13 d 1876,9,21
Ch: Mary
Ellis b 1808, 7, 1
Benj. Sykes" 1810, 3, 3
Hannah " 1811, 6, 20
Elizabeth " 1813, 3, 11
George " 1815, 2, 7 d 1817, 1,21 bur in N. Y.
William b 1817, 2, 11
Samuel
Wood " 1819, 9, 21
Walter
Brown " 1821, 12, 15 d 1823,12,13 bur Cincinnati
Walter b 1823, 12, --

1817, 11, 20. Thomas & w, Ann S., & ch, Mary E., Benjamin S., Hannah, Elizabeth & William, rocf New York MM, dtd 1817,9,3
1829, 6, 25. Ann S. dis jH
1829, 9, 24. Thos. dis
1830, 1, 28. Mary dis jH
1834, 4, 17. Benj. dis jH
1834, 7, 17. Hannah gct Newberry MM
1834, 8, 21. Hannah dis jH
1836, 10, 20. Mary E. Cooper (rorm Tucker) dis mcd (H)
1842, 11, 24. Hannah Holsoyd (form Tucker) con mcd (H)
1849, 10, 25. Samuel W. con mcd (H)
1867, 12, 19. Howard W. dis disunity
1867, 12, 19. Samuel W. dis jas

TURPIN
1881, 4, 14. Elizabeth rocf Smithfield MM, O., dtd 1880,12,20

TUTTLE
1931, 12, 4. Ruth G. rocf Wilmington MM, O.

TAYLOR
----, --, --. Edward & Sarah
Ch: Abraham M. b 1799, 11, 24
James " 1801, 8, 9
Hannah " 1808, 3, 21
1810, 3, 1. Joseph W. b
1830, 1, 1. Caleb, s John & Elizabeth, Highland Co., O., b 1801,9,7 d 1843,2,25 bur New Bur. Gr.; m in Cincinnati Mtg, Mary Jordon DAVIS, dt John & Hannah, Highland Co., O., b 1808,10,10 d 1875,5,9
Ch: John b 1830, 12, 7
Hannah Davis " 1831, 9, 21
Christopher A. " 1833, 10, 15 d 1835, 4,17 bur New Gr. Yd.
William Henry b 1836, 12, 25 d 1910, 2, 6 bur Spring Grove
Elizabeth L. b 1839, 1, 27
Hannah Maria " 1841, 6, 20
----, --, --. Dr. Wm. H., s Caleb W. & Mary (Jordon), b 1836,12,25 d 1910,2,6
1844, 10, 24. James, s Edward & Sarah, Highland Co., O.; m in Cincinnati Mtg, Elizabeth C. SHIPLEY, dt Wm. & Phebe, d 1855, 8,1 bur New Gr. Yd.
Ch: Caroline b 1846, 2, 4 d 1846, 6,15
----, --, --. Wm. m Elizabeth R. SHOEMAKER, dt Chas. & Margaret, b 1809,3,5 d 1855,10, 20
Ch: Margaret b 1849, 7, 5 d 1857, 8,18 bur Spring Grove
----, --, --. Abraham & Elizabeth
Ch: Charles S. b 1850, 11, 26
Sarah M. " 1853, 3, 15
1851, 5, 22. Hannah D. m Murray SHIPLEY
1864, 10, 27. Anna M. m Evan Lewis JOHNSON
1868, 6, 25. Elizabeth L. m Geo. H. DEAN
1871, 5, 30. Wm. H., s Caleb W. & Mary I., Highland Co., O.; m in Richmond, Ind, Mary HAYNES, dt Ira & Eliza, Highland Co., O.
Ch: Anna Haines b 1872, 9, 1
Wm. Jordon " 1874, 11, 7
1881, 6, 15. Helen Mary b
----, --, --. George Dean b 1884,11,21 d 1885, 6,14 bur Spring Grove
1923, 1, 13. Wm. J. d

1815, 6, 15. Joel Wright gct Center MM, O., to m Elizabeth Taylor
1823, 7, 31. John & w, Jane, & dt, Mary Jane, rocf Silver Creek MM, Ind., dtd 1823,7,27
1826, 9, 28. John & w, Jane, & ch, Mary Jane Ann & Joseph, gct Miami MM, O.
1826, 10, 24. Abraham M. rocf Phila. MM, Pa., dtd 1826,7,19
1827, 1, 25. Cert rec for John & ch, Caleb, Elizabeth, Hannah, John W., rocf Springfield MM, N. J., dtd 1821,4,4, endorsed to White Lick MM, Ind.
1827, 1, 25. Amos rocf Springfield MM, N. J., dtd 1821,4,4; dec
1827, 1, 25. Cert rec for Mary from Springfield MM, N. J., dtd 1821,4,4, endorsed to White Lick MM, Ind.
1828, 1, 31. Harriett (form Townsend) con mcd
1829, 6, 25. Israel & w, Susan, & ch, Geo. R., Chas. H., Israel W., Lydia S., Edith S. & Jane, rocf Stillwater MM, O., dtd 1829,4,18
1829, 11, 26. John & ch, Caleb, Elizabeth, Hannah & John W., gct Upper Springfield MM, O., dtd 1821,4,4, endorsed by White Lick MM, Ind., 1827,1,25
1830, 6, 24. Geo. R., Chas. M., Walter W., Lydia S., Edith S. & Jane, rocf Stillwater MM, O., dtd 1830,5,22
1835, 9, 17. James rocf Phila. MM, Pa., dtd 1835,8,27
1840, 1, 16. Joseph rocf Chesterfield MM, N. J., dtd 1839,12,3
1840, 1, 16. Hannah rocf Chesterfield MM, N. J., dtd 1839,12,3
1844, 2, 15. John & w, Jane, & ch, Ann, Joseph & Louisa, rocf Miami MM, dtd 1844,1, 24
1845, 4, 24. Chas. M. gct Phila. MM, Pa. (H)
1845, 6, 19. Harriet dis disunity
1845, 8, 21. Geo. con mcd (H)
1845, 12, 25. Israel & w, Susan, & ch, Edith & Jane, gct Phila. MM, Pa. (H)
1846, 7, 16. Louisa LeVaser (form Taylor) dis mcd
1848, 7, 20. Abraham M. gct ND MM, to m Elizabeth R. Shoemaker
1849, 1, 18. Elizabeth R. rocf ND MM, dtd 1848,12,25
1850, 9, 19. Jane Clark (form Taylor) con mcd
1851, 2, 13. Anna Corbin (form Taylor) dis mcd
1852, 3, 18. Joseph W. gct Burlington MM,N.J.
1852, 3, 18. Hannah gct Burlington MM, N. J.
1856, 11, 20. David M. gct Fairfield MM, Ind.
1862, 3, 20. Wm. H. con mcd
1865, 7, 20. George R., Chas. M., Walter W., Lydia S., Edith S. & Jane, dropped from mbrp
1866, 5, 17. Abram M. & ch, Chas. T. & Sarah M., gct Burlington MM, N. J.
1866, 5, 17. James & ch, Wm. Shipley, Mary Elizabeth & Emma Alderson, gct Burlington MM, N. J.
1867, 3, 21. Joseph dropped from mbrp
1878, 1, 17. Mary Haynes recrq
1878, 12, 19. Frank H. recrq

TAYLOR, continued
1881, 1, 20. Rebecca N. rocf WD MM, Pa., dtd 1880,12,22
1883, 6, 17. Frank H. & w, Rebecca, & ch, Wm. N., gct WD MM, Pa.
1923, 3, 10. Helen M. A. relrq

UPDEGRAFF
1817, 5, 15. Susannah rocf Redstone MM, Pa., dtd 1816,11,20
1865, 7, 20. Susan dropped from mbrp

VALENTINE
1819, 5, 20. Geo. & w, Jane, & s, John, rocf Carlow MM, Ireland, dtd 1819,3,6
1823, 6, 26. Geo. & w, Jane, & ch, John, gct Silver Creek MM, Ind.
1846, 5, 21. Phebe (form Walton) dis mcd (H)

VANCE
1906, 6, 5. Samuel Edward, s Edward Alexander & Agnes Grace, Highland Co., O.; m in Cincinnati Mtg, Florence Anthony JOHNSON, dt Evan Lewis & Anna Maria, Highland Co.,O

1914, 12, 11. Florence Johnson'relrq

VAN DEVORT
1897, 10, 22. Maud rocf Wilmington MM, O., dtd 1897,10,9
1904, 6, 10. Maude E. [Vandervoort] relrq

VANSANT
1838, 3, 22. Cornelius & w, Catharine, & ch, Catharine, Tacy Ann, Mary Elizabeth, James E. & Joseph T., rocf Baltimore MM, dtd 1838,2,9 (H)
1842, 6, 23. Mary Elizabeth Allen (form Vanzant) dis mcd (H)
1847, 11, 25. Cornelius & w, Grace, & ch, Sarah P., Samuel & Rebecca P., rocf White Water MM, Ind., dtd 1847,10,27 (H)
1860, 10, 25. Grace P. & ch, Samuel & Richard R., gct White Water MM, Ind.

VANWINKLE
1821, 6, 28. Martha (form Wood) dis mcd

VINCENT
1819, 6, 17. Eliza (form Coffin) dis mcd

VOILES
1898, 10, 5. Laura M., dt Dr. & Mary S. (Manning), b

VORHEES
1866, 11, 15. Elizabeth (form Warder) dis mcd

WAGONER
1932, 6, 3. Clara A. recrq

walk
1853, 3, 17. Charlotte (form Bell) dis mcd

WALLER
1889, 2, 14. Edward Mintor recrq
1918, 4, 12. Edwin dropped from mbrp

WALTERS
1849, 2, 22. Celine recrq (H)

WALTON
1833, 3, 21. Ruth & ch, Phebe, Lydia, James L., Esther C., Joshua P., Sarah M., Elias H. & Albert G., rocf Little Falls MM, Md., dtd 1833,2,5 (H)
1836, 10, 20. Lyd8a dis joining Methodists (H)
1844, 8, 22. James dis disunity & jas (H)
1845, 11, 20. Esther dis jas (H)
1846, 5, 21. Phebe Valentine (form Walton) dis mcd (H)
1858, 7, 22. Elias H. dis disunity (H)

WANTON
1825, 1, 27. Wm. R. rocf Baltimore MM, Md., dtd 1824,7,9
1865, 7, 20. Wm. R. dropped from mbrp

WANZER
1853, 9, 15. Melinda, w John, & ch, Geo. Hussey & Wm. Haviland, rocf Scipio MM, N. Y., dtd 1853,8,17
1854, 11, 16. John rst
1858, 3, 18. John & fam gct Miami MM, O.
1858, 12, 16. John & w, Melinda, & ch, Geo. & Wm. Haviland, rocf Miami MM, O., dtd 1858,11,28
1863, 5, 21. John & w, Melinda, & ch, Geo. Henry & Wm. Haviland, gct Centre MM

WARD
1817, 10, 16. Elizabeth Crispin, gr dt Isaac Ward, gct Miami MM, O.
1818, 5, 21. Joshua rocf Miami MM, O., dtd 1818,4,29
1819, 7, 15. John Jr. rocf Haddonfield MM, N. J., dtd 1819,2,8
1820, 7, 20. Joshua G. dis disunity

WARDEN
1836, 6, 8. Benson J. b d 1912,10,25 bur Spring Grove
1840, 9, 19. Phebe b
1854, 2, 7. Emily, dt Edwin & Eliza Johnson, b
----, --, --. Olive, dt Isaac & Elizabeth Lawrence, b 1869,8,23 d 1892,6,3 bur Spring Grove
1929, 11, --. Phoebe d

1870, 1, 20. Phebe L. (form Lawrence) con mcd
1884, 10, 16. Emily H. gct Minneapolis MM, Minn.
1894, 4, 19. Benson J. recrq

WARDER
----, --, --. John A., s Jeremiah & Ann, b

WARDER, John A., continued
b 1811,1,19 d 1883,7,14; m Elizabeth B.
----- b 1817,11,4 d 1891/92,2,8 bur Spring Grove
Ch: Anna b 1837, 5, 19
Jane B. " 1839, 3, 27 d 1879, 6,12 bur Spring Grove
Elizabeth b 1841, 1, 12 d 1891, 2, 8 bur Spring Grove
Rueben H. b 1843, 2, 10 " 1907,12,26 bur Spring Grove
John A. b 1846, 1, 21
Robert B. " 1848, 3, 28 d 1905, 7,23 bur Spring Grove
William b 1852, 3, 1
1903, 10, 28. Anna Aston d (an elder)

1840, 4, 16. Elizabeth B. rocf Frankford MM, Phila., Pa. dtd 1839,8,27
1840, 5, 21. John A. rocf Green Plain MM, dtd 1840,2,11
1866, 11, 15. Elizabeth Vorhees (form Warder) dis mcd
1875, 5, 20. John H. relrq
1875, 7, 15. Wm. Jr. relrq
1884, 2, 20. Robert B. gct Minneapolis MM, Minn., to m Gulielma M. Dorland
1884, 7, 17. Gulielma D. & ch, Claudia M. Dorland, rocf Minneapolis MM, Minn., dtd 1884,6,12
1888, 12, 20. Robert & w, Gulielma, & ch, Claudia M. Dorland, gct Baltimore MM, Md.
1892, 2, 18. Rueben H. relrq

WATSON
1825, 9, 29. Jonathan L. rocf Fairfield MM, dtd 1825,8,27
1826, 3, 30. Jonathan gct Buckingham MM, Pa.

WATTS
1893, 9, 14. Nellie Johnson, dt Thatcher & Mary K. Johnson, relrq

WAY
1852, 10, 21. Phocion R. rocf Miami MM, O., dtd 1852,9,22 (H)
1853, 8, 25. Francis H. Allen gct Center MM, Pa., to m Malinda Way (H)

WAYNE
1847, 1, 21. Elizabeth rocf Phila. MM, Pa., dtd 1846,12,16 (H)
1847, 1, 21. Joseph W. rocf Phila. MM, Pa., dtd 1846,4,14 (H)
1853, 11, 24. Joseph W. dis mcd (H)
1888, 10, 25. Elizabeth gct Race St. MM, Phila. Pa. (H)

WEHMIER
1931, 2, 1. Frederick & Lottie recrq

WEIKERT
1881, 11, 17. Emma Johnson gct New York MM, N. Y.

WEINTZ
1903, 3, 13. Chas. H. recrq
1918, 4, 12. Chas. dropped from mbrp

WELLS
1830, 9, 30. Thos. rocf Phila. MM, Pa., dtd 1830,2,22
1831, 8, 25. Thos. gct Miami MM, O.

WEST
----, --, --. John & -----
Ch: Sylvia A. b 1870, 4, 21
Orpha L. " 1872, 2, 2

1870, 4, 14. John W. rocf Newberry MM, O., dtd 1870,3,21
1874, 12, 17. John W. & ch, Sylvia C. & Orpha L., rocf Newberry MM, O.

WESTCOMBE
1836, 12, 15. Chas. T. rocf Worcestershire MM, Eng., dtd 1835,7,9 endorsed by Arch St. MM, Pa., 1836,1,28 to Blue River MM, Ind., & by that MM to this mtg 1836,10,18
1844, 11, 14. Chas. T. [Westcomb] gct Milford MM, Ind.

WETHERALD
1829, 5, 28. Joseph & w, Mary, & ch, Sarah, Haworth, Elizabeth, Wm., Jonathan H., Mary & Susan H., rocf Wilmington MM, Del., dtd 1829,4,3 (H)
1830, 6, 24. Joseph & w, Mary, & ch, Sarah, Haworth, Elizabeth, Wm., Jonathan H., Mary & Susannah H., gct Wilmington MM, O. (H)

WHEELER
1816, 9, 19. Aquila rocf Gunpowder MM, dtd 1816,7,24
1821, 6, 28. Gould rocf Westland MM, Pa., dtd 1821,4,28
1824, 12, 30. Gould dis disunity
1830, 6, 24. Aquilla J. con mcd (H)
1832, 2, 23. Aquilla dis mcd

WHITE
1831, 6, 25. Francis T. b d 1907,6,18
----, --, --. Mordecai Morris b 1830,2,3 d 1913,9,30; m Hannah A. -----
Ch: Frances Alice b 1859, 8, 31
Alice Mary " 1863, 5, 23
Susan Morris " 1869, 3, 3
Helen Lawson " 1875, 6, 15
1884, 11, 12. Alice Mary m Theodore Wm. CRAMP
1901, 4, 9. Helen Lawson m Geo. Dexter EUSTIS
1908, 2, 12. Susan Morris m Clarence PRICE

1841, 2, 18. Thos. Jr. rocf Phila. MM, Pa.,

WHITE, continued
dtd 1841,1,28
1854, 6, 15. Mordecai M. rocf Spiceland MM, Ind., dtd 1854,2,22
1854, 2, 18. Francis T. rocf Spiceland MM, Ind., dtd 1854,2,22
1858, 10, 21. Mordecai Morris gct White Water MM, Ind., to m Hannah Amelia Coffin
1859, 1, 20. Hannah Amelia rocf White Water MM, Ind., dtd 1858,12,22
1878, 2, 14. John T. Jr. rocf Raysville MM, dtd 1877,10,27; returned because of his disunity with Friends

WICKERSHAM
1852, 2, 17. Elijah rst
1860, 2, 16. Elijah dis disunity

WILBUR
1874, 5, 23. Anna B. (Dean) b

1918, 5, 10. Anna dropped from mbrp

WILEY
1820, 5, 18. Isaac & Sarah & ch, Deborah Ann Waight & Thomas rocf Center MM, dtd 1819, 8,25
1852, 11, 25. Elmira A. rocf London Grove MM (H)
1865, 7, 20. Isaac & w, Sarah, & ch, Deborah, Ann Wright & Thos., dropped from mbrp

WILL
1893, 12, 10. Eliza d bur Spring Grove
1900, 10, 29. Augusta L. m Howard M. GIRTON

1892, 4, 14. Augusta recrq

WILLE
1884, 1, 17. Richard & w, Eliza, rocf Dover MM, O., dtd 1883,12,23

WILLIAMS
----, --, --. Micajah Terrell, s Jesse & Sarah, b 1792,6,3; m Hannah JONES b 1793,8,4
Ch: Charles
Henry b 1818, 12, 21
Granville
Sharp " 1820, 10, 10
Elizabeth " 1823, 3, 5
Alfred K. " 1826, 9, 26
----, --, --. Clark & Mary
Ch: Cyrus
Milton b 1822, 3, --
William C. " 1828, 3, --
Narcissa " 1826, 1, --
Martha " 182-, 5, --
1913, 10, 18. Anne m Earl Z. GIBLON
1921, 1, 25. Americus V. d

1816, 2, 15. Jesse & w, Sarah, & ch, Anna, Sarah, Robert, Elizabeth & Jesse, rocf Miami MM, O., dtd 1815,12,27
1817, 2, 20. Jesse & w, Sarah, & ch, Anna L., Sarah Elizabeth, Robert & Jesse, gct Miami MM, O.
1818, 1, 15. Micajah T. gct Stillwater MM, O., to m
1818, 10, 15. Hannah rocf Plainfield MM, dtd 1818,5,2
1831, 2, 24. Hannah dis jH
1832, 3, 15. Micajah T. dis disunity
1835, 3, 19. Sarah, w John S., & ch, Robert, Ann, John, Eliza, Joseph, Sarah Jane, Mary, Louisa & Martha Bell, rocf Stillwater MM, O., dtd 1835,1,24
1835, 4, 16. Benjamin & Sarah, ch Hannah, rocf Stillwater MM, O., dtd 1835,1,24
1835, 8, 20. Cyrus M., Narcissa & Martha, ch Clark & Mary, rocf White Water MM, Ind., dtd 1835,4,22
1844, 9, 26. Elizabeth Perry (form Williams) con mcd (H)

1845, 11, 27. Chas. H. gct Plainfield MM, O., to m Sarah E. Thomas (H)
1848, 1, 20. Narcissa Neff (form Williams) dis mcd
1848, 11, 16. Cyrus M. dis mcd
1865, 7, 20. Sarah dropped from mbrp
1865, 7, 20. Robert dropped from mbrp
1865, 7, 20. Ann dropped from mbrp
1865, 7, 20. John dropped from mbrp
1865, 7, 20. Eliza dropped from mbrp
1865, 7, 20. Joseph dropped from mbrp
1865, 7, 20. Sarah Jane dropped from mbrp
1865, 7, 20. Mary Louisa dropped from mbrp
1865, 7, 20. Martha Belle dropped from mbrp
1865, 7, 20. Benjamin dropped from mbrp
1865, 7, 20. Hannah dropped from mbrp
1865, 7, 20. Martha dropped from mbrp
1867, 3, 21. Elizabeth dropped from mbrp
1869, 6, 17. Alfred K. gct White Water MM, Ind.
1887, 1, 20. Americus V. & w, Caroline, & ch, Katie H., Peter T. Jr., Clara & Alice J., recrq
1909, 3, 12. Beatrix recrq

WILLIAMSON
1840, 3, 5. Joseph d bur New Graveyard

1831, 11, 24. Joseph recrq
1843, 6, 22. John & w, Anna C., rocf White Water MM, Ind. (H)
1867, 4, 25. Anna C. gct Plainfield MM, N. J. (H)

WILLIS
1825, 11, 24. Geo. G. rocf Phila. MM, Pa.

WILSON
1813, 6, 29. Joanna, w Jeremiah, d bur Cincinnati Public Ground
----, --, --. Theophilus m Lydia Folger PADDOCK

WILSON, Theophilus & Lydia, continued
Ch: Mary C. b 1844, 9, 2 d 1850, 4, 8
Morris
Herbert " 1857, 10, 28

1841, 1, 21. Joseph T. [Willson] gct Milford MM, Ind. (H)
1844, 3, 21. Isaac dis mcd
1844, 8, 15. Stephen dis jH
1844, 12, 19. James dis jH
1845, 5, 22. Joseph T. rocf Milford MM, Ind., dtd 1845,3,20 (H)
1845, 7, 24. Enoch rocf Springborough MM, dtd 1845,2,20 (H)
1845, 9, 25. Lydia (form Paddock) dis mcd (H)
1849, 6, 21. Hannah P. rocf Green Plain MM, dtd 1849,6,13 (H)
1850, 9, 24. James W. con mcd (H)
1865, 7, 20. Rebecca, Ann & Mary Jane dropped from mbrp
1874, 1, 22. Israel dis disunity (H)
1819, 2, 18. Gabriel, Elizabeth, Edith, Henry, Wm. & Jeremiah, ch Jeremiah Sr., rocf Darby Creek MM, O., dtd 1815,8,19
1819, 3, 18. Gabriel, Elizabeth, Edith, Henry, William, Jeremiah, ch Jeremiah Sr., gct Lick Creek MM
1819, 6, 17. Asa rocf Short Creek MM, O., dtd 1819,3,23
1821, 12, 27. Asa con mcd
1822, 4, 25. Asa gct Springfield MM
1822, 10, 31. Cert rec for Anna from Hardwick & Randolph MM, N. J., dtd 1819,6,3, endorsed to Smithfield MM, O.
1829, 5, 28. Wugh & w, Ann, & ch, Joseph Taylor, Isaac Blackfan, Rebecca, James, Stephen, Mary Jane, Sarah & Ann, rocf Stillwater MM, O., dtd 1829,4,18 (H)
1830, 6, 24. Isaac, James, Stephen, Rebecca, Mary Jane & Ann, rocf Stillwater MM, O., dtd 1830,5,22
1831, 7, 28. Israel rocf Springborough MM, dtd 1831,6,28 (H)
1838, 8, 23. Isaac B. dis mcd (H)

WINDER
1900, 4, 8. John W. d

1861, 6, 20. John W. rocf Goshen MM, O., dtd 1861,4,20
1882, 1, 19. Lewis recrq

WING
----, --, --. Cornelius m Elizabeth ----- b 1781,7,23
Ch: Charles b 1820, 3, 21

1817, 12, 18. Edward, Eliza & Wm., ch Cornelius, rocf Scipio MM, N. Y.
1820, 8, 17. Elizabeth recrq (dis at Fairfield MM for mou)
1825, 5, 26. Edward dis mcd
1826, 1, 26. Eliza Fullerton (form Wing) dis mcd
1827, 4, 26. Chas., s Elizabeth, recrq
1843, 1, 19. Chas. con mcd
1846, 1, 15. Chas. gct Salem MM, Ind.
1846, 1, 15. Elizabeth gct Salem MM, Ind.

WINSTON
1848, 8, 17. Nathaniel rocf South River MM, Va., dtd 1846,4,9, endorsed to Short Creek MM, O.

WINTERS
1852, 4, 7. Luzena d bur New Graveyard

1851, 4, 17. Luzena C. [Winter] (form Farmer) con mcd

WOOD
----, --, --. Thos. & Susanna
Ch: Louisa b 1822, 5, 21
Sarah

1819, 1, 21. Thos. & w, Susanna, & ch, Thos., Anna & Sarah, rocf Radnor MM, Pa., dtd 1818,12,10
1820, 11, 16. John & w, Theodocia, & dt, Martha & Deadicini, rocf Jerico MM, L. I., N. Y., dtd 1817,3,20
1821, 6, 28. Martha Van Winkle (form Wood) dis mcd
1829, 2, 26. Thos. dis disunity
1832, 1, 26. Susannah dis disunity
1834, 10, 16. Mary (form Morgan) con mcd
1837, 7, 20. Ann Rider (form Wood) dis mcd
1839, 11, 14. Sarah dis disunity
1845, 3, 26. Mary V. dis disunity
1865, 7, 20. Thos. dropped from mbrp
1865, 7, 20. John & w, Theodocia & Louisa, dropped from mbrp
1868, 5, 21. Mary recrq (H)

WOODIN
1818, 10, 12. Archibald d bur Friends Bur. Gr., Cincinnati

WOODNUT
----, --, --. Thomas m Hannah MORGAN
Ch: Abbie M. b 1858, 11, 30
William " 1860, 3, 4
Clement A. " 1864, 1, 27

1816, 11, 21. Wm. [Woodnutt] rocf Baltimore MM, Md., dtd 1815,3,8
1833, 12, 19. Wm. dis jH
1859, 4, 21. Hannah [Woodnutt] rocf White Water MM, Ind., dtd 1859,2,23 (H)
1861, 4, 25. Thos. [Woodnutt] rocf Salem MM, N. J. (H)
1868, 2, 20. Thos. [Woodnutt] & w, Hannah, & ch, Abbie M., Wm. & Clement, gct White Water MM, Ind. (H)

WOODROW
1832, 8, 30. Sarah rocf Phila. MM, Pa., dtd 1832,7,23 (H)
1840, 1, 16. David rocf Clear Creek MM, O., dtd 1839,10,22
1880, 4, 14. David T. dis disunity

WOODWARD
1896, 6, 18. Orlando J. & w, Josephine, & ch, Ralph & Donald, rocf Lawrence MM, Kans., dtd 1896,5,30; returned because of their lack of interest in mtg 1897,2,18

WOOLMAN
----, --, --. Wm. R., s Uriah & Mary, b 1824, 10,16 d 1883,4,20; m Elizabeth SHARP, dt Haines & Jemima, b 1831,7,4
Ch: Eva J. b 1854, 4, 15
Mary Ella " 1857, 7, 23
Jemima Elizabeth " 1859, 6, 30
Ruth " 1875, 10, 6

1853, 10, 20. Wm. R. & w, Elizabeth, rocf WFMM, O. (H) (Westfield MM, O.)
1871, 4, 20. Elizabeth recrq
1876, 6, 22. Elizabeth, Eva J. & Mary Ellen relrq (H)
1884, 6, 19. Jemima recrq

WOOLSEY
1827, 2, 22. Hannah (form Neave) dis mcd

WORTH
1818, 5, 21. Mary rocf Creek MM, N. Y.
1821, 9, 27. Mary gct Nantucket MM

WRIGHT
1876, 8, 27. Ann d

1815, 6, 15. Joel gct Center MM, O., to m Elizabeth Taylor
1816, 2, 15. Elizabeth rocf Centre MM, O., dtd 1815,11,18
1819, 11, 18. Jonathan Sr. & Susannah rocf Silver Creek MM
1821, 3, 1. Jonathan Jr. & w, Susan B., & ch, Aquilla, Martha & Thaddeus, gct Silver Creek MM
1821, 10, 25. Joel Jr. & w, Elizabeth, & ch, Jacob, Thos. & Israel, gct Silver Creek MM, Ind.
1822, 4, 25. Susannah gct Silver Creek MM, Ind.
1824, 8, 26. Ann & ch, Lucy, Anna, Rebecca, Sarah Jane & Mariah, rocf Frankfort MM, Pa., dtd 1824,3,26
1833, 12, 26. Sarah (form Hopkins) dis mcd (H)
1835, 8, 20. Aquilla rocf White Water MM, Ind., dtd 1835,4,22
1839, 9, 19. Lucy Sanders (form Wright) con mcd
1843, 11, 23. Justice & w, Betsey, & ch, Ann & Thos., rocf New Garden MM, O., dtd 1843,10,25 (H)
1844, 7, 25. Anna C. rocf Milford MM, Ind., dtd 1844,6,20 (H)
1844, 9, 19. Rebecca Bradbury (form Wright) dis mcd
1845, 9, 25. Wm. S. rocf Albany MM, N. Y., dtd 1845,9,6 (H)
1847, 4, 22. Wm. S. con mcd (H)
1850, 12, 19. Lydia rocf Short Creek MM, O., dtd 1850,4,23
1851, 10, 16. Lydia gct Exeter MM, Pa.; returned 1852,1,15, she did not reside there
1851, 12, 18. Moses rocf White Water MM, Ind., dtd 1851,6,25
1854, 4, 20. Justus & w, Betsy, gct Chesterfield MM, N. J. (H)
1855, 8, 23. Ann gct Chesterfield MM, N. J. (H)
1859, 10, 20. Moses D. con mcd
1860, 2, 16. John & w, Sarah, rocf White Water MM, Ind., dtd 1860,1,25
1860, 3, 15. Moses D. gct Salem MM, Ind.
1860, 3, 22. Amanda rocf Miami MM, O., dtd 1859,12,21 (H)
1863, 1, 15. John gct New York MM, N. Y.
1863, 12, 17. Sarah gct New York MM, N. Y.
1865, 7, 20. Aquilla dropped from mbrp
1866, 12, 20. Amanda gct Miami MM, O. (H)
1868, 4, 16. Lydia S. dropped from mbrp
1871, 6, 15. Maria relrq
1873, 6, 19. Wm. A. relrq

WYMOND
----, --, --. Wm. W. & Laura
Ch: Laura Harding b 1869, 3, 29
Edwin Paul " 1870, 2, 16

1870, 12, 15. Wm. & w, Laura, & ch, Laura & Edwin Paul, recrq
1874, 1, 15. Wm. W. & w, Laura, & ch, Laura H. & Edwin Paul, gct Indianapolis MM, Ind.
1884, 9, 18. Laura F. & ch, Laura H., Edward Paul & Grace A., rocf Indianapolis MM, Ind., dtd 1884,8,12
1892, 4, 14. Ella recrq
1902, 5, 9. E. Paul & w, Ella, & s, Harry, gct Indianapolis MM, Ind.

WYSONG
1891, 5, 21. Elnora rocf Springfield MM, O., dtd 1891,3,21
1913, 7, 11. Eleanor S. dropped from mbrp

YEATS
1857, 6, 18. Eliza rocf White Water MM, Ind., dtd 1857,5,27
1875, 4, 15. Eliza gct WD MM, Pa.

YOUNG
1833, 4, 18. Geo. H., minor, rocf New York MM, N. Y., dtd 1832,12,5
1833, 4, 18. Wm. L. rocf New York MM, N. Y., dtd 1833,12,5
1837, 12, 21. Robert W. & ch, Robert W., Jr., Hiram & Edward Carnegy, rocf Phila. MM, Pa., dtd 1837,11,21
1839, 4, 18. Rebecca recrq; dis by New York MM, N. Y.

* * * * * * *

BAILEY
1893, 6, 7. Elizabeth Griffith m Thos. James CREAGHEAD
1904, 6, 1. Harriet Ellis m Albert Coulson BUCKLEY

CAREY
1866, 10, 18. Martha Emily gct Newberry MM, O.

MARTIN
1816, 10, 24. Elizabeth m Thompson NEAVE
1818, 8, 27. Sarah m Job PUGH

SMITH
1844, 9, 20. Mahala m Richard TIMBERLAKE

STEWART
1869, 11, 20. Alice [Stuart], dt Alexander & Abbe, b
1872, 1, 9. Alexander Stanton [Stuart] b

1839, 1, 17. Joseph W. rocf Phila. MM, Pa., dtd 1839,11,27
1839, 6, 20. Robert W. & w, Rebecca, & ch, Robert W., Hiram & Edward C., gct White Water MM, Ind.
1842, 10, 20. Wm. L. con mcd
1844, 4, 18. Hiram, minor, rocf Walnut Ridge MM, dtd 1844,3,16
1853, 12, 15. Hiram gct Bath More MM
1859, 7, 21. William L. gct Walnut Ridge MM, Ind.

* * * * * * *

1898, 12, 4. Alexander [Stuart] d (Trustee)
1907, 12, 17. Abigail Cameron [Stuart], w Alexander, d bur Spring Grove

1868, 5, 21. Alexander rocf Carthage MM, dtd 1868,5,2
1869, 4, 15. Abbe L. recrq
1869, 5, 20. Alexander H. con mcd
1893, 1, 18. Stanton Alexander [Stuart], s Alexander & Annie L., relrq

TOWNSEND
1852, 11, 25. Ann m Wm. KENWORTHY
1878, 11, 18. Mary Catharine m Geo. Anderson STORCH

GREEN PLAIN MONTHLY MEETING

Green Plain Monthly Meeting, located in Clark County, Ohio, was set off from Caesar's Creek Monthly Meeting 9 Mo. 22, 1821.

Among the charter members were Richard Wright, clerk and overseer, Thomas Ellis, overseer, John Wildman, Joshua Engle, Peter Williams, Benjamin Bond, Charles Paish, Seth Smith, Charles Sleeper, William Ellis, Jeptha Johnson, William Willis. No list of charter members of women is available.

This meeting divided at the time of the Hicksite Separation. The members still belong to Indiana Yearly Meeting.

RECORDS

ALDRICH
1837, 6, 14. Mary E. (form Birdsall) con mou (H)
1838, 4, 18. Mary C. [Aldrick] rocf Goose Creek MM, Va., dtd 1837,9,14 (H)

ALLEN
1821, 12, 22. Rebecca Woolman (form Allen) con mcd
1822, 6, 22. Amy, w Solomon, & ch, Emily & Cyrus, recrq
1822, 9, 21. Solomon rst on consent of Cesers Creek MM
1825, 8, 3. Anna dis jas
1828, 8, 6. Sarah Crites (form Allen) dis mcd
1830, 12, 1. Harmony Bates (form Allen) dis mcd
1842, 9, 14. Jackson & w, Sarah, gct Bloomfield MM

ANDERSON
1827, 9, 12. James, Clark Co., O.; m in Greenplain, Celia VICKERS, Clark Co., O.

1822, 4, 23. Susannah recrq
1823, 9, 20. Reuben, Susannah, Elijah & Mary, ch Elijah & Susannah, recrq
1829, 4, 1. Celah dis jH
1829, 4, 1. Ruth (form Vickers) dis mcd
1829, 6, 3. Susannah Andrew (form Anderson) dis mou
1830, 3, 3. James rocf North West Fork MM, Md., dtd 1828,8,13 (H)
1833, 8, 23. Susannah rocf Center MM, dtd 1833,6,12
1833, 11, 21. Mary Jane dis disunity
1837, 3, 25. Hannah & h gct Sugar River MM, Ind.
1837, 11, 25. Elijah Jr. rpd mou
1838, 9, 29. Elijah gct White Lick MM, Ind.
1840, 11, 11. Ruth dis disunity
1846, 12, 16. Celia dis disunity (H)

ANDREW
1829, 6, 3. Susannah (form Anderson) dis mou

ATKINSON
1800, 4, 12. John, s Joseph, b
----, --, --. Cephis, s Joseph, b 1790,11,2; m Abigail ORIN, dt John, b 1796,4,8
Ch: Isaac b 1816, 9, 16
Levi " 1818, 12, 5
Mills " 1821, 4, 16
Ruth " 1822, 12, 23

1822, 6, 22. Cephus & w, Abigail, & ch, Isaac & Levi, rocf Caesars Creek MM, dtd 1822,4,26
1823, 1, 18. John rocf Centre MM, dtd 1822, 12,21
1825, 3, 2. Lydia recrq
1832, 9, 28. Lydia dis joining M. E. Church
1839, 6, 12. Cephas & w, Abigail, & ch, Levi John Joseph Jane Wm. & Margaret, gct Gotion MM, Goshen
1841, 7, 14. Nancy & ch, Cephas & Levi, recrq
1841, 10, 13. Thos. dis disunity
1851, 1, 15. Levi rocf Gosion MM, dtd 1850, 12,21

BACON
1825, 5, 4. Rebecca Ann, Mary, John G. & David, ch Rebecca, recrq
1825, 12, 7. Rebecca rocf Salem MM, N. J., dtd 1825,11,2
1837, 11, 25. Joseph Y. recrq
1844, 11, 13. John G. dis disunity

BAKER
1822, 6, 22. Sarah & ch, Brenton & Wm., rocf Miami MM, dtd 1822,2,27
1822, 6, 22. Richard, Joshua & Nayl rocf Miami MM, dtd 1822,2,27
1825, 5, 4. Nayl dis mou
1829, 9, 2. Richard dis (H)
1880, 3, 17. Anna H. (form Harrison) con mcd (H)
1880, 3, 17. Florence H.,dt Anna H., recrq (H)
1883, 11, 14. Jessie B., dt Wm. R. & Anna P., recrq (H)

BANGHAM
1830, 11, 25. Humphrey I., s Benjamin & Lucy, Clinton Co., O.; m in Greenplain, Mary DUTTON, dt David & Phebe, Clark Co., O.

BARRETT
1851, 7, 16. Rebecca L. gct Miami MM (H)

BATES
1830, 12, 1. Harmony (form Allen) dis mcd

BATTIN
1874, 7, 15. Samuel R. [Battan] & w, Emely T., & ch, Orlando G., Kersy R. & Martha Alma, rocf Salem MM, O., dtd 1874,6,25 (H)
1875, 4, 14. Ephraim Ann recrq (H)
1887, 3, 16. Charles Sumner recrq (H)
1887, 6, 15. Mary A. rocf West MM, O., dtd 1887,5,25 (H)

BEAL
1829, 11, 9. Hannah rocf Fairfield MM, dtd 1829,7,25
1840, 10, 14. Hannah gct Springborough MM
1842, 10, 12. Hannah rocf Springborough MM

BEAUCHAMP
1824, 6, 23. Anna m Wm. VICKERS

BEAUCHAMP, continued
1832, 11, 14. Asa con mou & military service (H)
1833, 9, 28. Martha (form Williams) dis mou
1838, 6, 13. Asa & w, Martha, & ch, Clark & Mary, gct White Water MM, Ind. (H)
1840, 4, 15. Lovina Thomas (form Beauchamp) dis mou

BEESON
----, --, --. Amizah b 1766,5,23; m Isabel ----- b 1776,2,27

Ch:		
Rachel	b	1793, 2, 22
Igar	"	1794, 11, 12
Darias	"	1797, 1, 22
Roseanne	"	1799, 5, 31
Amiziah	"	1801, 3, 11
Isabell	"	1803, 1, 21
Nancy	"	1804, 11, 14
Zesonos	"	1806, 10, 12
Eli	"	1808, 8, 19
Betsy	"	1810, 11, 21
John	"	1811, 11, 20
Lydia	"	1813, 3, 20
Allen	"	1815, 4, 29
Susanna	"	1817, 3, 17
Julia	"	1820, 1, 1

1820, 9, 4. Amaziah d bur Greenplain

1822, 9, 21. Igal & w, Margaret, & s, Amiziah, rocf New Garden MM, dtd 1822,5,9
1825, 5, 4. Igal [Beason] & w, Margaret, & ch, Amoriah, Elihugh & Ester, gct White River MM
1826, 4, 5. Isabel & ch, Zenis, Lydia, Allen, Susannah & Julia, rqct Springfield MM,Ind.
1826, 5, 3. Amaziah gct Springfield MM,Ind.

BELL
1828, 9, 3. Alexander & w, Rebecca, & ch, Mary Jane, Hannah, Nancy & John, gct Honey Creek MM, Ind.
1868, 1, 15. Abram & w dropped from mbrp (H)

BENNETT
1842, 6, 22. Caroline m Wm. CAIN

1833, 9, 28. Margaret [Bennet] (form Farr) con mou
1835, 8, 12. Jabez & w, Rachel, & ch, James L., Joseph, Mahala, Ann, Mary, Elizabeth & Isabella, rocf Philadelphia MM, Pa., dtd 1835,2,18 (H)
1836, 5, 18. Lea & w, Mary, rocf New Garden MM, dtd 1836,3,24 (H)
1838, 11, 14. Lee dis disunity (H)
1841, 3, 17. Mary F. & ch, Elmira & Ann Eliza, gct New Garden MM, O. (H)
1841, 11, 17. Caroline rocf Phila. MM, Pa., dtd 1841,9,15 (H)
1848, 5, 17. Mahalah Ann Clement (form Bennet) dis mou (H)
1867, 4, 17. James L., Joseph & Lydia dropped from mbrp (H)

BIRDSALL
1836, 10, 12. Mary C. rocf Goose Creek, Va., dtd 1835,10,15; returned because she had mou & her name was now Mary C. Aldrich (H)
1837, 6, 14. Mary C. Aldrich (form Birdsall) con mou (H)
1859, 1, 12. Jane [Birdsal] (form Brown) con mcd (H)
1859, 6, 15. Jane [Birdsal] gct White Water MM, Ind. (H)
1873, 4, 16. Hannah (form Schooley) con mcd (H)
1873, 6, 18. Hannah gct White Water MM, Ind. (H)
1884, 7, 16. Hannah rocf Camden MM, dtd 1884,3,20 (H)

BLAIN
1846, 2, 18. Lucinda N. con mou (H)

BLOXSOM
1830, 8, 11. Sarah [Bloxom] m Chas. SCOTT (H)

1823, 12, 20. Maria [Blocksome] dis jas
1825, 9, 7. Elizabeth King (form Bloxsom) dis mou
1826, 1, 9. Charles dis disunity
1826, 2, 1. Anna dis disunity
1826, 5, 3. James dis disunity
1830, 6, 2. Sarah dis jH
1830, 12, 15. Mary recrq (H)

BOCOCK
1827, 9, 5. Penelope & dt, Mary Sears, rocf Dover MM, dtd 1827,8,4
1839, 10, 16. Penelope [Bowcock] gct Mississinewa MM

BOND
1826, 5, 23. Edward Sr. d ae 85
1831, 4, 14. Mary Sr. d ae 88

1821, 11, 17. Edward & w, Mary, rocf Lees Creek MM, dtd 1821,7,21, endorsed by Cesars Creek MM 1821,10,26
1829, 9, 2. Sarah dis disunity
1830, 1, 6. Mary (form Sears) con mou
1834, 8, 30. Susannah McNary (form Bond) dis mou
1834, 11, 29. Susanna gct Mississinewa MM, Ind.
1834, 11, 29. Mary & h gct Mississinewa MM, Ind.

BORTON
1832, 6, 6. Thomas & w, Elizabeth, & dt, Elizabeth, rocf Springboro MM, dtd 1832, 2,23 (H)
1832, 6, 6. Sarah, w Asa, & ch, Hannah Ann, Beulah, Miriam, Wm. W., Elizabeth & Ira, rocf Springboro MM, dtd 1832,3,22 (H)

BORTON, continued
1832, 7, 4. Job & Aaron rocf Piles Grove MM, N. J., dtd 1832,2,28 (H)
1834, 10, 25. Aaron Job & Elizabeth rocf Salem MM, N. J., dtd 1834,5,28
1837, 9, 13. Hannah Ann Rowan (form Borton) dis mou (H)
1838, 3, 14. Elwood rocf Woodbury MM, N. J., dtd 1837,10,30 (H)
1839, 7, 17. Miriam, Wm., Elizabeth & Ira, ch Asa, gct Goshen MM (H)
1839, 7, 17. Beulah gct Goshen MM (H)
1844, 11, 13. Elizabeth L. dis disunity (H)
1845, 7, 16. Elizabeth Lunbeck (form Borton) dis mou
1848, 2, 16. Maria Merritt & dt, Elizabeth Ann Borton, rocf Springborough MM, dtd 1847,12,23 (H)
1857, 7, 15. Elizabeth Haley (form Borton) dis mcd (H)

BRANSON
1850, 2, 20. Eliza W. m Marcellius S. COOK (H)

1830, 2, 3. Thomas & w, Anna, & dt, Eliza, rocf Concord MM, dtd 1829,11,20 (H)
1854, 4, 12. Thomasin H. rocf Hopewell MM, Va., dtd 1854,3,9 (H)
1859, 5, 18. Anna S. rocf Fall Creek MM, dtd 1859,3,11 (H)

BREVITT
1822, 11, 23. John W. rocf Miami MM, dtd 1822, 7,31
1825, 8, 3. John W. gct Baltimore MM

BROWN
1836, 2, 18. Asa, s Aaron & Anna; m in Greenplain MH, Hannah B. SANDS, dt Thomas & Ruth, Clark Co., O. (H)

1836, 8, 17. Jacob & w, Judith, & ch, Wm., Sarah Jane, Ruth Hannah & Nixon G., rocf Goose Creek MM, Va. (H)
1836, 8, 17. George rocf Goose Creek MM, Va., dtd 1836,3,17 (H)
1836, 8, 17. Thomas rocf Goose Creek MM, Va., dtd 1836,3,17 (H)
1836, 8, 17. Nancy rocf Goose Creek MM, Va., dtd 1836,3,17 (H)
1836, 8, 17. Lucinda rocf Goose Creek MM, Va., dtd 1836,3,17 (H)
1836, 12, 14. Hannah B. gct Goshen MM, (H)
1851, 11, 12. Margaret Johnson (form Brown) rpd mcd (H)
1853, 9, 14. Hannah P. rocf Goose Creek MM, Va., dtd 1853,8,15 (H)
1854, 3, 15. Sarah gct Hopewell MM, Va. (H)
1854, 12, 13. Eliza E. recrq (H)
1854, 3, 14. Caroline Elliott (form Brown) dis mcd (H)
1854, 3, 14. Virginia Carroll (form Brown) dis mcd (H)
1859, 1, 12. Jane Birdsal (form Brown) con mcd (H)
1867, 4, 17. Edwin J., Virginia C. & Margaret W. dropped from mbrp (H)
1867, 4, 17. Asa & w, Hannah, dis jas (H)
1872, 12, 18. Mary T. (form Thomas) con mcd (H)

BUFKIN
1831, 8, 3. Thomas & w, Ruth, & ch, John, Warner, Gulielma, Sarah & Ruth, rocf Cesars Creek MM, dtd 1831,7,28
1831, 8, 3. Bathsheba rocf Cesars Creek MM, dtd 1831,7,28
1831, 12, 7. Thomas & fam gct Marlborough MM
1831, 12, 7. Bathsheba gct Marlborough MM

BUTLER
1848, 8, 16. Anslem B. rocf Springborough MM, dtd 1848,5,23

BYERS
1858, 9, 15. Drucilla (form Crispin) dis mou

CAIN
1842, 6, 22. Wm., s Thomas & Jane; m in Green plain MH, Caroline BENNETT, dt Joseph W. & Mary

1852, 6, 16. Wm. & w, Caroline, & ch, Thornton, Mary Jane & Wm., gct White Water MM, Ind. (H)

CANBY
1837, 2, 15. Samuel F. rocf Baltimore MM, dtd 1836,8,5 (H)

CARROLL
1854, 3, 14. Virginia (form Brown) dis mcd (H)

CARSON
1887, 11, 16. Ruth H. (form Schooley) relrq (H)

CHALFANT
1864, 6, 15. Abel & Hannah rocf Plainfield MM, dtd 1864,6,16 (H)

CHANCE
1831, 2, 2. Tilmon gct Fairfield MM

CLARK
1822, 12, 21. Robert recrq
1828, 7, 2. Mary, dt Robert, rocf Miami MM, dtd 1828,5,28
1832, 12, 23. Mary dis jas
1837, 12, 30. Elizabeth & dt, Rhoda & Esther, gct Goshen MM

CLEMENT
1848, 5, 17. Mahalah Ann (form Bennet) dis mou (H)

COATS
1868, 1, 15. Sarah Ann dropped from mbrp (H)
1868, 1, 15. Mary & three ch dropped from mbrp (H)
1868, 1, 15. Sarah Ann & ch dropped from mbrp (H)
1868, 1, 15. Deborah dropped from mbrp (H)

COLE
1884, 9, 17. Harry B., s.John & Efphama A., recrq (H)

COMBS
1868, 1, 15. Charity & ch dropped from mbrp (H)

COMPTON
1825, 10, 5. Amos rocf Caesars Creek MM, dtd 1825,7,28
1826, 4, 5. Amos dis training in militia

COOK
1850, 2, 20. Marcellius S., s Jesse & Elizabeth, Clark Co., O.; m in Greenplain MH, Eliza W. BRANSON, dt Thomas & Anna, Clark Co., O. (H)

1847, 6, 16. Elizabeth & h & four s rocf Miami MM, dtd 1847,5,26 (H)
1853, 4, 13. Eliza M. gc (H)
1861, 8, 14. Emma J. dis jas (H)
1861, 12, 18. Mary W. gct Miami MM (H)
1863, 6, 17. Jesse W. & w, Susan G., & three s rocf Fall Creek MM, dtd 1863,4,9 (H)
1876, 1, 12. Isaac Warner & w, Sarah Ann, & gr ch, Isaac W., Emma B. & Sarah A. Cook, gct Third Haven MM, Md. (H)

COOPER
1867, 9, 18. Sarah Esther (form Schooley) con mcd (H)
1868, 3, 18. Sarah E. gct White Water MM, Ind. (H)

CRISPIN
----, --, --. Mathias & Sarah
Ch: Abraham b 1826, 11, 8
Hannah " 1828, 2, 10
Isaac " 1830, 6, 21
Drusilla " 1833, 7, 11

1824, 11, 3. Matthias gct Caesars Creek MM, to m Sarah White
1852, 6, 16. Isaac dis mou & jas
1853, 8, 17. Hannah McConaga (form Crispin) dis mou
1858, 9, 15. Drusilla Byers (form Crispin) dis mou

CRITES
1828, 8, 6. Sarah (form Allen) dis mcd

CROSHAW
1834, 10, 15. Thomas S. rocf Burlington MM, N. J., dtd 1834,6,4 (H)
1835, 11, 18. Thomas con mou (H)
1867, 4, 17. Samuel R. [Crashaw] dropped from mbrp (H)

CUMERINE
1867, 12, 18. Susanna B. (form Mosier) dis mcd (H)

CUMINS
1833, 7, 27. Sarah (form Warden) dis mcd

CURL
1867, 4, 17. Amos, Caty & Joseph dis jas (H)

DAKIN
1823, 1, 18. Rockyfeller rocf Centre MM, dtd 1822,12,21
1824, 5, 22. Rockefeller gct Centre MM

DEAN
1872, 3, 13. Susan J. rocf Springborough MM, dtd 1871,12,28 (H)

DIBBLE
1839, 1, 16. Sarah Ostrone & dt, Catherine Dibble, rocf Troy MM, dtd 1837,10,4 (H)

DOWNS
1867, 4, 17. Esther dis jas (H)
1867, 9, 18. Jane G. [Downes] (form Oldham) con mcd (H)
1888, 1, 18. Jane G. gct Fall Creek MM, Ind. (H)

DUGDALE
1835, 11, 18. Joseph A. & w, Ruth, rocf New-Garden MM, dtd 1835,10,22 (H)
1836, 5, 18. John & w, Sarah B., & ch, Thomas G., Charles R., Sarah A., Rachel E., John & Elizabeth, rocf New Garden MM, dtd 1836,4,21 (H)
1839, 7, 17. Thomas G., Charles R., Sarah, Rachel & Elizabeth, ch John, rocf New Garden MM, O., dtd 1839,5,23
1841, 12, 15. Wm. R. & w, Ann, & ch, Eveline & Sarah Elizabeth, gct Camden MM (H)
1845, 1, 15. Sarah B. dis disunity (H)
1880, 3, 17. Mary E. (form Warner) con mcd (H)
1889, 6, 12. Mary E. relrq (H)

DUTTON
1830, 11, 25. Mary m Humphrey I. Bangham

1829, 8, 5. Mary rocf Fairfield MM, dtd 1829,6,27
1835, 11, 28. Lydia rocf Fairfield MM, dtd 1835,7,25
1845, 5, 14. Lydia Smith (form Dutton) dis mou

EDGERTON
1869, 8, 25. Walter, s James & Sarah, Henry Co., Ind.; m in Greenplain, Eliza A. NEGUS dt Abel & Hannah, Chalfant, Clark Co., O.

EDMUNDSON
1836, 9, 21. Esther m Stanton SCOTT (H)

1834, 5, 14. Thomas & w, Elizabeth, & ch, Thomas, Maria, Ann & John, rocf Center MM, dtd 1834,4,17 (H)
1834, 5, 14. Wm. rocf Centre MM, dtd 1834,4,17 (H)
1834, 7, 16. Esther rocf Centre MM (H)
1837, 8, 16. Thomas & w, Elizabeth, & s, John, gct White Water MM, Ind. (H)
1837, 8, 16. Wm. gct White Water MM, Ind. (H)
1837, 8, 16. Thomas Jr. gct White Water MM, Ind. (H)

ELLIOTT
1854, 3, 14. Caroline (form Brown) dis mcd (H)

ELLIS
1823, 11, 22. Thomas & w, Lydia, & ch, Sophia, Margaret Ann, Emely & Elenor, gct West Grove MM, Ind.

EMBREE
1825, 6, 1. Thomas & w, Esther, rocf Goshen MM, dtd 1825,4,6

ENGLE
----, --, --. Joshua, s Robert & Jane, b 1781, 11,10; m Hannah WEATHERBY, dt Wm. & Elizabeth, b 1781,5,15
Ch: Jane b 1803, 8, 13
Elizabeth " 1805, 10, 2
Joshua " 1808, 9, 25
Hannah Ann " 1812, 12, 4
Nathan " 1817, 10, 16

1836, 12, 21. Isaac, s Robert & Jane, Green Co., O.; m in Greenplain MH, Sarah MERRITT dt Thos. & Elizabeth, Clark Co., O. (H)

1836, 12, 14. Isaac rocf Miami MM, dtd 1836, 11,11 (H)
1839, 5, 15. Joshua W. gct Stillwater MM, O., to m Sarah Ann Swayne (H)
1839, 9, 18. Sarah Ann rocf Stillwater MM, dtd 1839,8,17 (H)
1842, 2, 16. Nathan dis jas
1843, 9, 13. Martha Vanmeter (form Engle) dis mou
1858, 12, 15. Sarah M. rocf Miami MM, dtd 1858,11,24 (H)

FALLIS
1836, 10, 29. Esther & John, ch Isaiah & Elizabeth, rocf Springfield MM, dtd 1836, 9,3
1840, 1, 15. Esther & John, ch Isaiah, gct Miami MM

FARR
----, --, --. Cyrus, s Isaac & Mary, b 1775, 6,3; m Elizabeth GIBSON, dt Robert & Mary, b 1779,12,9
Ch: Mariah Theresa b 1804, 6, 23
James Gibson " 1807, 2, 25
Isaiah Musgrove " 1809, 9, 8
Cyrus Franklin b 1811, 8, 10
Angelina " 1814, 5, 7
Mary Jane " 1817, 7, 14
Elizabeth " 1820, 10, 16
1823, 8, 27. Mariah m Andrew P. WILLISS
1825, 4, 17. Elizabeth m Moses FRAZIER
1830, 4, 8. Mary m Frederick KINDLEY (H)

1822, 9, 21. Cyrus & w, Elizabeth, & ch, James, Gibson, Isaac Musgrave, Cyrus Franklin, Angelina, Mary Jane & Elizabeth, recrq
1822, 9, 21. Maria recrq
1825, 1, 5. James rocf Indian Spring MM, Md., dtd 1824,10,6
1825, 1, 5. Isaac rocf Indian Spring MM, Md., dtd 1824,10,6
1828, 10, 1. Elizabeth dis jas
1829, 3, 4. Jane dis jH
1829, 4, 1. Hannah dis jH
1829, 4, 1. Mary dis jH
1829, 4, 1. Mary Jr. dis jH
1831, 4, 6. Tamer dis jH
1831, 7, 6. Asenith dis jH
1833, 9, 28. Margaret Bennet (form Farr) con mou
1835, 7, 25. Angeline & Mary Jane dis jH
1836, 1, 13. Leah rocf Radnor MM, Pa., dtd 1835,9,10 (H)
1837, 9, 13. Isaac gct Milford MM, Ind. (H)
1838, 8, 15. James gct Springborough MM (H)
1838, 8, 15. Jane gct Springborough MM (H)
1838, 8, 15. Angeline gct Springborough MM (H)
1888, 3, 14. Thomas G. relrq (H)

FARRINGTON
1868, 1, 15. Joseph John dropped from mbrp (H)

FAULKNER
1831, 7, 6. Eliza (form Engle) con mcd
1831, 12, 7. Eliza gct Center MM

FAWCETT
1862, 10, 15. Lucetta (form Thomas) con mcd (H)
1867, 4, 17. Wm. G. [Faucett] dis jas (H)
1868, 1, 15. Edward S. dropped from mbrp (H)

FEUSON
1851, 8, 13. Elizabeth M. (form Scott) dis mou (H)

FISHER
1867, 8, 14. Avis & Susannah (form Thomas) dis mcd (H)

FOLK
1846, 3, 16. Frances & h & four s rocf Buckingham MM, Pa., dtd 1846,2,2 (H)

FOX
1822, 9, 25. Margaret m John WILDMAN

FRAME
1825, 1, 5. James [Fraim] & w, Asenath, & ch, Mahlon, Wm., Elizabeth & John, rocf Indian Spring MM, Md., dtd 1824,10,6
1829, 4, 1. Aseneth dis jH
1843, 6, 14. Wm. dis mou
1846, 2, 11. Leah Linton (form Frame) dis mou
1846, 3, 16. Acenath dis disunity (H)

FRAZIER
1825, 4, 17. Moses, s Ezekiel & Rebecca, Clinton Co., O.; m in Greenplain, Elizabeth FARR, dt John & Leah, Clark Co., O.

FRENCH
1845, 10, 16. Wm. B., s Charles C. & Marcy G., Highland Co., O.; m in Greenplain MH, Lydia L. WILSON, dt Stephen & Hannah P., Clark Co., O. (H)

1848, 3, 15. Lydia L. dis disunity (H)

FUDGE
1887, 8, 17. Rachel (form Schooley) con mcd (H)

GARWOOD
1867, 4, 17. Elizabeth dropped from mbrp (H)

GAUSE
1858, 9, 10. Hannah P. gct Miami MM (H)
1870, 3, 16. Ruth gct Miami MM (H)

GILL
1831, 5, 4. John rocf Short Creek MM, dtd 1831,2,24 (H)
1831, 5, 4. Susannah & ch, John, Susannah & Saltkil, rocf Fall Creek MM, dtd 1831, 4,23 (H)

GOVE
1835, 5, 13. Jonathan & w, Hannah, & ch, Lydia D., rocf Peru MM, dtd 1835,2,19 (H)
1839, 1, 16. Lydia D. dis jas (H)
1839, 4, 17. Jonathan & w, Hannah, gct White Water MM, Ind. (H)

GREEN
1807, 8, 23. Ruth, dt Isaac & Hannah, b

GREER
1868, 1, 15. Parthenia dropped from mbrp (H)

GREGG
1835, 12, 16. Esther rocf Goose Creek MM, Va., dtd 1835,7,16 (H)
1836, 3, 16. Abner rocf Goose Creek MM, dtd 1835,8,13 (H)

GRIEST
1882, 10, 18. Salathiel, Peter & Ruben rocf Menallen MM, Pa., dtd 1882,9,21 (H)
1882, 10, 18. Tabitha & Sarah rocf Menallen MM, Adams Co., Pa., dtd 1882,9,21 (H)
1885, 2, 18. Salathiel, Peter & Rueben [Greist] gct Camden MM, Jay Co., Ind. (H)
1885, 2, 18. Tabitha gct Camden MM, Ind. (H)
1887, 7, 13. Cert for Salathiel etc. destroyed by a fire in home of correspondent of that mtg, duplicate issued by this

GRIFFITH
1836, 11, 16. Wm., Susannah, Ruth & John, ch Amos & Mary, rocf Warrington MM, dtd 1836,5,19 (H) Note. The above cert was returned to Warrington MM because the ch joined Orthodox Branch

GUMMERE
1835, 10, 14. Wm. & w, Phebe, & ch, Wm., Hannah, Joshua, Benjamin & Levina, rocf Plainfield MM, dtd 1835,9,17 (H)
1835, 10, 14. Ephraim Parker, gr s Wm. & Phebe Gummere, rocf Plainfield MM, dtd 1835,9,17 (H)
1836, 9, 14. Swithen rocf Plainfield MM, dtd 1836,6,11 (H)

HADLEY
1831, 8, 7. John, s John & Lydia, Clinton Co., O.; m in Greenplain, Ann WILDMAN, dt John & Elizabeth, Clark Co., O.
1851, 1, 29. Samuel H., s Jacob & Mary, Clinton Co., O.; m in Greenplain, Ruth SMITH, dt Seth & Deborah, Clark Co., O.

1832, 1, 4. Ann gct Springfield MM

HAINES
1835, 10, 14. Rachel rocf Springborough MM, dtd 1835,9,24 (H)
1839, 1, 16. Rachel gct Springborough MM (H)

HALEY
1857, 7, 15. Elizabeth (form Borton) dis mcd (H)

HARDESTY
1847, 7, 14. Mary (form Johnson) dis mou

HARRISON
1859, 10, 19. Eliza m Wm. WILDMAN
1865, 9, 20. Rebecca P. m Simeon WARNER
1868, 11, 25. Abbie P. m David A. NICKERSON

1829, 6, 3. Wm. H. & w gct Center MM
1831, 2, 2. Wm. L. & w, Ann, rocf Center MM, dtd 1830,12,15
1834, 11, 29. William H. & w, Ann, & ch, John, Stephen & Martha Ann, gct Dover MM
1836, 12, 14. Joshua & w, Ann, & ch, Elizabeth P., James P., Ann Eliza, Wm., Edward E., Mary & Catharine, rocf Chester MM, Pa. (H)
1837, 3, 25. Elizabeth P., James, Ann Eliza, Wm. & Edward, ch Joshua & Ann, rocf Chester MM, Pa., dtd 1836,12,26
1841, 6, 16. Elizabeth dis disunity
1856, 3, 12. John F. & w, Elizabeth, & ch, Abigail & Rebecca, recrq
1856, 3, 12. Eliza recrq
1858, 5, 12. Abby Ann rocf Darby MM, dtd 1858,4,20 (H)
1875, 2, 17. Agnes P. & s, Ellwood G., rocf Wilmington MM, Del., dtd 1874,11,27 (H)
1875, 6, 16. Edward E. & w, Esther, & ch, Cornelia J., Mary Hannah & Elizabeth P., gct Wapsinonoch MM, Ia. (H)
1876, 12, 13. Ann Eliza gct Wapsinonoch MM,Ia. (H)
1878, 8, 14. Abby A. gct Darby MM, Pa. (H)
1880, 3, 17. Anna H. Baker (form Harrison) con mcd (H)

HATTEN
1863, 5, 13. Robert & w, Susannah E.,& ch, Eliza, Robert Willets, Lorenzo & Edmond E., rocf Miami MM, dtd 1863,4,22 (H)
1863, 5, 13. Elizabeth E., Sarah & Margaret rocf Miami MM, dtd 1863,4,22 (H)
1872, 4, 17. Margaret [Hatton] dis jas (H)
1875, 12, 15. Robert [Hatton] & w, Susannah, & ch, Lorenzo M. & Edmund E., gct Third Haven MM, Md. (H)
1875, 12, 15. Elizabeth E., Sarah, Eliza & Willets gct Third Haven MM, Md. (H)

HAYWARD
1832, 10, 18. Wm., s Wm. & Keziah, Ann Arundel Co., Md.; m in Greenplain MH, Mildred K. WILLIS, dt Wm. & Henrietta, Clark Co., O. (H)

1835, 11, 18. Wm. rocf Elk MM, dtd 1835,8,13 (H)
1835, 12, 16. Wm. & w, Keziah, rocf Baltimore MM (H)
1835, 12, 16. Geo. rocf Baltimore MM (H)
1846, 3, 16. Mary Ann dis disunity (H)

HEISKEL
1840, 9, 16. Mary (form Paist) dis mou

HILL
1873, 9, 23. Daniel, s Henry & Achsah, Randolph Co., Ind.; m in Greenplain, Thamar THORN, dt Wm. & Rachel, Clark Co., O.

1840, 8, 12. Edward Shaw gct White Water MM, Ind., to m Peninah Hill (H)
1844, 10, 16. Hannah rocf White River MM, Ind. dtd 1843,9,2

HIMLES
1867, 4, 17. Arnold B. dropped from mbrp (H)

HIRST
1857, 6, 17. Eli P. & w, Hannah, rocf Goose Creek MM, Va., dtd 1857,4,16 (H)
1857, 6, 17. Cornelia & Cosmelia rocf Goose Creek MM, Va., dtd 1857,4,16 (H)

HOLLINGSWORTH
1870, 9, 26. Israel H., s Asaph & Anne, Clark Co., O.; m in home of Hannah Wildman, Rachel E. WILDMAN, dt Edward & Hannah, Clark Co., O.

1860, 12, 12. Anna Smith & Hariet Holingsworth, a minor in her care, rocf Center MM, dtd 1860,9,12

HORN
1846, 12, 16. Mary & Soloame gct Phila. MM, Pa. (H)

HOUGH
1862, 8, 20. Hiram, s Jonathan & Culielma, Wayne Co., O.; m in Greenplain, Sarah I. JONES, dt Wm. & Rachel THORN, Green Co.,O.

HOWELL
1865, 4, 19. Samuel C., s Samuel & Hannah, Green Co., O.; m in Greenplain, Rachel THORN, dt Thomas & Ruth, Green Co., O.
1837, 2, 22. Cornelia m Wm. D. PEIRCE (H)

1835, 2, 18. Samuel & w, Hannah, & ch, Cosmelia, John, Mary, Wm., Ann, Samuel & Virginia, rocf Hopewell MM, Va., dtd 1834,9,4 (H)
1835, 2, 18. Rebecca Jane rocf Hopewell MM, Va., dtd 1834,9,4 (H)
1839, 10, 16. John gct Springborough MM, to m Martha Wilson (H)
1840, 3, 18. Martha W. rocf Springborough MM, dtd 1840,2,20 (H)
1846, 12, 16. Martha [Howel] dis attending mou (H)

HUNT
1823, 12, 20. Ketura, Patience & Maryann, ch Rebecca, recrq
1840, 9, 16. Keturah Oosley (form Hunt) dis mou
1857, 7, 15. Edward S. & w, Delphina, & s,

HUNT, continued
Charles Albert rocf Springfield MM, Ind., dtd 1857,6,26

HUTTON
1824, 11, 3. John & w, Mary, & s, Epimonondus rocf Fairfield MM, dtd 1824,4,24
1829, 1, 4. Epaminondas dis mcd (H)
1829, 11, 9. Nancy dis disunity
1830, 6, 2. Levi & w, Rebecca, & dt, Betty, rocf Fairfield MM, dtd 1830,4,24
1842, 9, 14. Betty Oosley (form Hutton) dis mou
1847, 1, 13. John dis mou
1850, 7, 17. Jordon dis mou

IFORD
1889, 5, 15. Mary A. (form Oldham) con mcd (H)
1889, 5, 12. Mary A. gct Fall Creek MM, Ind. (H)

INGRAM
1837, 9, 13. Robert & w, Hannah, & ch, Mary, Harlan, Martha Ann, Maria J., Samuel & Robert Jr. rocf Deerfield MM, O., dtd 1837,8,16 (H)
1873, 6, 18. Mary recrq (H)

JANNEY
1836, 1, 13. Aquila rocf Fairfax MM, Va., dtd 1835,8,12 (H)
1837, 8, 16. Aquila gct Fairfax MM, Va. (H)
1838, 8, 15. Mary A. rocf Hopewell MM, dtd 1836,4,7 (H)
1839, 4, 17. Jonas & w, Ruth D., & ch, Eliza & Mary Ellen, rocf Springborough MM, dtd 1839,3,28 (H)
1839, 4, 17. Abel & w, Lydia, rocf Miami MM, dtd 1839,3,27 (H)
1853, 4, 13. Lydia M. gct Springborough MM (H)
1853, 4, 13. Jonas & w, Ruth, & ch, Elouisa D., Mary Ellen, Nancy E. & James, gct Springborough MM (H)
1868, 1, 15. Samuel [Genny] & w, Sarah, & three ch dropped from mbrp (H)

JEFFERSON
1853, 4, 13. Eliza (form Wright) dis mou

JEFFRIES
1868, 1, 15. Caleb & fam dropped from mbrp (H)

JENKINS
1830, 10, 6. Cert rec for Ann W. from Phila. MM, Pa., dtd 1830,4,21, endorsed to Springborough MM (H)

JESSUP
1822, 8, 24. Rosanna dis

1854, 4, 12. Charles [Jessop] & w, Hannah, & ch, Charety, Elizabeth Ann, Isaac Elmer & Sarah T., rocf Fairfield MM

JOHNSON
1837, 8, 31. Emily m Levi SMITH

1829, 9, 2. Ashley M. & fam rocf Fairfield MM, dtd 1829,6,27
1835, 3, 28. Hannah dis jas
1841, 2, 17. Seth S. dis mou
1841, 11, 17. Ashby dis disunity
1845, 4, 16. Harriet Kelso (form Johnson) dis mou
1847, 7, 14. Mary Hardesty (form Johnson) dis mou
1851, 11, 12. Margaret (form Brown) rpd mcd (H)
1852, 10, 13. Martha Jane dis jas
1867, 12, 18. Sarah A. (form Mosier) dis mcd (H)

JONES
1855, 10, 24. Samuel, s Daniel & Elizabeth, Miami Co., O.; m in Greenplain, Sarah THORN, dt Wm. & Rachel, Green Co., O.
1862, 8, 20. Sarah I. m Hiram HOUGH

1857, 5, 13. Sarah T. rocf Miami MM, dtd 1857,3,25

KELLY
1825, 2, 3. Timothy, s Samuel & Hannah, Warren Co., O.; m in Greenplain, Avis SLEEPER, dt Samuel & Patience, Clark Co., O.

1828, 2, 6. Avis & dt, Jane, rocf Miami MM, dtd 1827,12,26
1835, 10, 24. Timothy & w, Avis, & ch, Jane, Alfred & Mary Ann, gct Mississinaway MM, Ind.

KELSO
1845, 4, 16. Harriet (form Johnson) dis mou

KERBY
1829, 8, 5. Sarah dis jH
1840, 7, 15. Sarah gct White Water MM, Ind. (H)

KERTON
1848, 6, 14. Elma con mou (H)

KESTER
1837, 1, 18. David & w, Ann, & dt, Phebe, rocf Stillwater MM, dtd 1836,5,21 (H)
1867, 8, 14. William dropped from mbrp (H)
1867, 8, 14. Margaret dropped from mbrp (H)
1867, 8, 14. Manser dropped from mbrp (H)
1867, 8, 14. Charles dropped from mbrp (H)
1867, 8, 14. Jason dropped from mbrp (H)
1867, 8, 14. Henry dropped from mbrp (H)

KESTER, continued
1867, 8, 14. Alonzo dropped from mbrp (H)
1867, 8, 14. Alvin dropped from mbrp (H)
1867, 8, 14. Stephen D. dropped from mbrp (H)
1867, 8, 14. Jonathan dropped from mbrp (H)
1867, 8, 14. Elizabeth L. dropped from mbrp (H)
1867, 8, 14. Sarah L. dropped from mbrp (H)
1867, 8, 14. Amy Ann dropped from mbrp (H)
1867, 8, 14. Sabina dropped from mbrp (H)
1867, 8, 14. Jason dropped from mbrp (H)
1867, 8, 14. Louisa dropped from mbrp (H)
1868, 1, 15. Mary & Mary Ann dropped from mbrp (H)

KINDLEY
1830, 4, 8. Frederick, s Edward & Margaret, Warren Co., O.; m in Greenplain MH, Mary FARR, dt Edward & Mary, Clark Co., O. (H)

1830, 6, 2. Mary gc (H)

KING
1825, 9, 7. Elizabeth (form Bloxsom) dis mou

KIRK
1868, 1, 15. Roger & w & ten ch dropped from mbrp (H)
1868, 1, 15. John dropped from mbrp (H)

LAPHAM
1867, 4, 17. Wm.dropped from mbrp (H)
1867, 4, 17. Lorana dropped from mbrp (H)
1867, 4, 17. Amelia dropped from mbrp (H)

LARKINS
1850, 6, 12. Mary (form Vickers) dis mou

LAWRENCE
1871, 9, 14. Daniel, s Peter & Sarah, Grant Co., Ind.; m in home of Ruth Thorn, Hannah THORN, dt Thomas & Ruth, Green Co., O.

1849, 10, 17. Abigail M. rocf Short Creek MM, dtd 1849,6,21 (H)

LEE
1867, 10, 16. Sarah J. Purvis (form Lee) dis mcd (H)

LESTER
1874, 9, 16. Mary E. gct East Jordon MM, ILL. (H)

LEVICK
1845, 1, 15. Wm. gct Frankfort MM, Pa.

LEWIS
1830, 11, 10. Elizabeth m Enoch MOON

1825, 9, 7. Thomas & w, Prudence, & dt, Rachel, rocf Silver Creek MM, Ind., dtd 1825,7,23
1825, 11, 2. Caleb & w, Susannah, & ch, Isaac, Elizabeth, Charity, John, William, Eli, Zimri & Martha, rocf Caesars Creek MM, dtd 1825,7,28
1829, 6, 3. Charity Miller (form Lewis) con mou
1829, 11, 9. Hannah & dt, Elizabeth & Cynthia, rocf Silver Creek MM, Ind., dtd 1829,9,26
1832, 4, 28. Thomas & w, Rebecca, & ch, Wm., Isaac, Hannah & Wesley, gct Flint MM, Ind.
1833, 8, 23. Caleb & w, Susannah, & ch, John, Wm., Eli, Zimri & Martha, gct Silver Creek MM, Ind.
1833, 12, 28. Hannah gct Flint Creek MM, Ind.
1833, 12, 28. Isaac gct Flint MM, Ind.
1834, 5, 24. Elizabeth gct Flint Creek MM, Ind.
1834, 5, 24. Cynthia gct Flint MM, Ind.
1835, 12, 26. Cynthia gct Sugar River MM, Ind.
1837, 11, 25. James P. A. con mou
1839, 11, 13. James P. A. gct Vermillion MM, Ill.

LINTON
1846, 2, 11. Leah (form Frame) dis mou

LITTLER
1822, 7, 20. Thomas gct Hopewell MM, Va., to m Mary Ridgeway
1844, 2, 14. Mary dis jas
1844, 4, 17. Thomas dis jas
1856, 2, 12. Mary Ellen (form Schooley) dis mcd (H)

LONG
1858, 12, 15. Mariam (form Schooley) dis mcd (H)

LOTT
1839, 4, 17. Susan (form Paist) dis mou (H)

LUKENS
1852, 10, 13. Louisa, w Salathiel, rocf Miami MM (H)
1867, 5, 15. Louisa gct Miami MM (H)

LUNBECK
1845, 7, 16. Elizabeth (form Borton) dis mou

McCONAGA
1853, 8, 17. Hannah (form Crispin) dis mou

McDONNELL
1838, 3, 14. Sabina T. rocf Redstone MM, Pa., dtd 1838,1,31 (H)

McNARY
1834, 8, 30. Susannah (form Bond) dis mou

MANDAVILLE
1884, 10, 15. Lydia W. recrq (H)

MARSHALL
1834, 11, 29. Hannah & h gct Mississinewa MM, Ind.

MATTHEWS
1852, 7, 14. Esther gct Fall Creek MM (H)

MECHEM
1867, 8, 14. Lydia dropped from mbrp (H)

MENDENHALL
1867, 2, 13. Anna E. gct White Water MM, Ind. (H)

MERRITT
1836, 12, 21. Sarah m Isaac ENGLE (H)
1842, 11, 23. Elizabeth m Simeon WARNER (H)

1832, 4, 4. Thomas & w, Jane, & ch, Josiah, Edward, Elizabeth & Anna, rocf Mt. Holly MM, dtd 1832,3,8 (H)
1829, 7, 17. Elizabeth [Merrit], dt Thomas, rocf Burlington MM, dtd 1839,6,3
1839, 7, 17. Josiah Edward & Elizabeth [Merrit], ch Thos., rocf Burlington MM, N. J., dtd 1839,6,3
1839, 10, 16. Thomas dis disunity; rst 1840, 8,12 by decision of QM (H)
1847, 7, 14. Elizabeth Warner (form Merritt) dis mou
1848, 2, 16. Maria & dt, Elizabeth Ann Borton, rocf Springborough MM, dtd 1847,12,23 (H)
1852, 8, 18. Anna dis (H)
1886, 9, 15. Rueben M. Roberts rocf Chester MM, N. J., dtd 1886,9,9 to m Susan M. Merritt (H)

MERTON
1832, 2, 1. Martha dis jH

MICHENER
1840, 1, 22. Henry, s Benjamin & Abigail, Logan Co., O.; m in Greenplain MH, Lydia WARNER, dt Levi & Mercy, Ross Co., O. (H)

1841, 9, 15. Lydia W. gct Goshen MM (H)
1866, 2, 14. Isaac & w, Martha, & ch gct Miami MM (H)
1867, 4, 17. Henry relrq (H)
1867, 4, 17. Lydia relrq (H)
1867, 4, 17. Woodrow relrq (H)
1867, 4, 17. Elizabeth relrq (H)
1867, 4, 17. Warner relrq (H)

MILES
1838, 1, 17. Rebecca, w Thos., rocf Troy MM, held at Pittstown, dtd 1837,3,8 (H)

MILLER
1829, 6, 3. Charity (form Lewis) con mou
1832, 6, 6. Lydia & ch, Newton, Jesse, Wm., Rueben & Rachel, rocf Miami MM, dtd 1832, 2,29 (H)
1834, 5, 24. Charity gct Flint Creek MM, Ind.

MILLS
1867, 5, 15. Anna P. (form Mires) con mcd (H)

MIRES
1859, 2, 16. Mary C. Shigley (form Mires) dis mcd (H)
1864, 10, 12. Eliza dis jas (H)
1867, 5, 15. Anna P. Mills (form Mires) con mcd (H)

MOODY
1831, 2, 2. Mary & h & fam gct Bloomfield MM, Ind.

MOON
1830, 11, 10. Enoch, s John & Dinah, Clark Co., O.; m in home of John Wildman, Clark Co., O., Elizabeth LEWIS, dt Caleb & Susannah, Clark Co., O.

1834, 5, 24. Enoch & w, Elizabeth, & ch, Susana & Charity, gct Flint Creek MM, Ind.

MOORE
1872, 3, 28. Joseph, s John P. & Martha, Wayne Co., Ind.; m in home of Ruth THORN, Mary THORN, dt Thos. & Ruth, Green Co.,O.

1869, 7, 14. Gerressa E. [More] gct Milton MM, Ind. (H)

MORGAN
1837, 10, 28. Ann gct Massessineway MM, Ind.

MORRIS
1836, 11, 16. Mary E. rocf Warrington MM, dtd 1836,6,22 (H)
1837, 5, 17. Mary C. rocf Warrington MM, dtd 1836,6,24 (H)

MORTON
1825, 7, 6. Alexander & w, Martha, & ch, John, M---- & Joanna, recrq
1846, 10, 14. Manervy Jane dis jas

MOSHER
1865, 7, 12. Susannah C. gct Wapsinonock MM, Ia. (H)
1865, 11, 15. Eunice & Scolista gct Miami MM (H)
1867, 12, 18. Susanna B. Cumerine (form Mosier) dis mcd (H)
1867, 12, 18. Sarah A. Johnson (form Mosier) dis mcd (H)
1868, 1, 15. Stephen dropped from mbrp (H)
1868, 2, 12. Asa & w, Sarah, gct Prairie Grove MM, Ia.
1868, 2, 12. Mary Ann & Asa Obediah, ch Asa, gct Prairie Grove MM, Ia. (H)
1868, 2, 12. John gct Wapsinanoch MM, Ia.(H)

MULLEN
1832, 3, 7. Aaron & w, Bathsheba, & s, Bethuel, rocf Springboro MM (H)
1839, 1, 16. Aaron & w, Bathsheba, & ch, Bethuel, Isaac, Elma R., Jane & Ruth, gct Springborough MM (H)

NEGUS
1869, 8, 25. Eliza A. m Walter EDGERTON

1853, 8, 17. Oliver Smith gct Chester MM, to m Mary B. Negus

NICHOLSON
1839, 7, 17. Valentine & w, Jane, & ch, Ruth, Elizabeth & Mary Ellen, rocf Miami MM, dtd 1839,5,22 (H)

NICKERSON
1868, 11, 25. David A., s Clark & Martha, Warren Co., O.; m in Greenplain, Abbie P. HARRISON, dt John F. & Elizabeth, of Springfield

OLDHAM
1833, 7, 31. John recrq (H)
1833, 9, 18. Ann recrq (H)
1833, 11, 13. Levi W., Jane G. & Margaret W., ch John & Anna, recrq (H)
1854, 11, 15. Lydia Ellen recrq (H)
1858, 11, 17. Anna Williams & ch, Abner W., Joseph & James G. Oldham, gct Fall Creek MM (H)
1859, 10, 12. Margaret W. & Massie W. gct Fall Creek MM, Ind. (H)
1867, 9, 18. Jane G. Downes (form Oldham) con mcd (H)
1889, 5, 15. Mary A. Iford (form Oldham) con mcd (H)

OOSLEY
1840, 9, 16. Keturah (form Hunt) dis mou
1842, 6, 15. Betty (form Hutton) dis mou

OREN
1824, 6, 19. James & w, Margaret, & ch, Joseph, John, Susannah, Elijah & Wm., rocf Caesars Creek MM, dtd 1824,5,27
1839, 2, 23. James & w, Margaret, & ch, Elijah & Wm., gct Dover MM
1839, 2, 23. John gct Dover MM
1839, 2, 23. Joseph gct Dover MM
1839, 2, 23. Susannah gct Dover MM

OSTRONE
1839, 1, 16. Sarah & dt, Catharine Dibble, rocf Troy MM, dtd 1837,10,4 (H)

OUTLAND
1861, 6, 18. Ann dis mcd (H)

OWEN
1829, 7, 1. Benjamin & Esther rocf Cesars Creek MM, dtd 1829,5,28
1830, 4, 7. Benjamin & fam gct Cesars Creek MM

PACKER
1847, 9, 15. Eliza (form Webster) dis mou (H)
1865, 5, 17. Oren & w, Ann, rocf Short Creek MM (H)

PAIST
----, --, --. Charles, s James & Elizabeth, b 1790,10,1; m Abigail PERKINS, dt Isaac & Phemia, b 1792,11,12
Ch: James b 1817, 3, 31 d 1822, 1,22 bur Greenplain
Lydia b 1819, 8, 18 " 1819, 9, 1 bur Greenplain
Mary b 1821, 10, 5
Isaac " 1823, 8, 28

1829, 8, 5. Abigail dis disunity
1837, 10, 18. Susan rocf Chester MM held at Providence, dtd 1836,11,28 (H)
1839, 4, 17. Susan Lott (form Paist) dis mou (H)
1840, 9, 16. Mary Heiskel (form Paist) dis mou
1847, 3, 17. Isaac dis disunity
1853, 1, 12. William dis mou

PALMER
1868, 1, 15. Elizabeth & Prudence dropped from mbrp (H)

PARKER
1835, 10, 14. Ephraim, gr s Wm. & Phebe Gummere, rocf Plainfield MM, dtd 1835,9,17 (H)
1868, 5, 13. Rebecca V. rocf Short Creek MM, dtd 1868,3,10 (H)

PARSINS
1868, 1, 15. Hannah dropped from mbrp (H)

PAWLEN
1850, 6, 12. Ruth (form Vickers) dis mou

PAXTON
1860, 2, 15. Ruth & ch, Mary Ellen, Anna Elizabeth & Florence, rocf Goshen MM, dtd 1860,1,21
1868, 1, 15. Phebe Ann Wood dropped from mbrp (H)

PENNINGTON
1829, 9, 2. Paul gct Centre MM, O. (H)
1847, 10, 13. Margaret W. rocf Plainfield MM, dtd 1847,9,16 (H)

PICKERING
1883, 1, 17. Henry T. rocf Plainfield MM, O., dtd 1882,12,14, to m Ann Thorp (H)
1883, 6, 13. Ann F. gct Plainfield MM, O.(H)

PIERCE
1837, 2, 22. Wm. D. [Peirce], s Jonathan & Hannah D., Clark Co., O.; m in Greenplain MH, Cornelia HOWELL, dt Samuel & Hannah, Clark Co., O. (H)

1835, 10, 14. Wm. A. rocf New Garden MM, dtd 1835,9,22 (H)
1841, 2, 17. Edwin con mou (H)
1868, 1, 15. Ruth T. Wood dropped from mbrp (H)
1880, 3, 17. Emma W. [Peirce] (form Warner) con mcd (H)

PLACE
1830, 7, 21. Maurice, s Isaac & Jane, Clark Co., O.; m in Greenplain MH, Mary WILLIAMS, dt Peter & Nancy, Clark Co., O. (H)

1830, 7, 7. Maurice rocf Centre MM, dtd 1830, 6,19 (H)
1831, 5, 4. Isaac, Eliza & Benjamin E., ch Maurice, rocf Allum Creek MM, dtd 1830,9, 10 (H)
1832, 11, 28. Mary dis jH
1837, 2, 15. Maurice & w, Mary, & ch, Eliza, Isaac, Benjamin, Martha & Elizabeth, gct White Water MM, Ind. (H)

PURVIS
1867, 10, 16. Sarah J. (form Lee) dis mcd (H)
1868, 1, 15. Eunice (form Spencer) dis mcd (H)

RANDEL
1853, 1, 12. Hannah (form Wright) dis mou

REESE
1833, 8, 14. Stephen R. rocf Miami MM, dtd 1833,6,26 (H)
1834, 1, 15. Stephen & w & ch, Jonathan G., Hannah R. & Wm. Gould, recrq (H)
1837, 4, 12. Stephen P. & w, Sarah, & ch, Jonathan, Hannah, William, Elizabeth & Jason, gct White Water MM, Ind. (H)

RICHARDSON
1829, 7, 1. Isaac & w, Ann, & ch, Ruth & Hannah, rocf Dearfield MM, dtd 1829,4,16
1829, 9, 2. Isaac & w, Ann, & ch, Ruth & Hannah, rocf Dearfield MM, dtd 1829,8,15 (H)
1830, 4, 7. Ann dis jH
1882, 11, 16. Caleb J. gct White Water MM, Ind. [(H)

RIDGEWAY
1822, 7, 20. Thomas Littler gct Hopewell MM, Va., to m Mary Ridgeway

ROBERTS
1876, 4, 12. Elizabeth P. gct Short Creek MM (H)
1886, 9, 15. Rueben M. rocf Chester MM, N. J. dtd 1886,9,9, to m Susan M. Merritt (H)
1889, 7, 17. Rueben M. rocf Chester MM, N.J., dtd 1889,7,4 (H)

ROMAIN
1868, 1, 15. Ephraim dropped from mbrp (H)

ROWAN
1837, 9, 13. Hannah Ann (form Borton) dis mou (H)

SANDS
1836, 2, 18. Hannah B. m Asa BROWN (H)

1833, 11, 13. Thomas & w, Ruth, & s, Whitson, rocf Indian Spring MM, Md., dtd 1833,8,7 (H)
1833, 11, 13. Matthew W. rocf Indian Spring MM, Md., dtd 1833,8,7 (H)
1833, 11, 13. Hannah rocf Indian Spring MM, Md., dtd 1833,8,7 (H)
1836, 3, 16. Matthew T. con mou (H)
1836, 10, 12. Samuel rocf Alexandria MM, D.C., dtd 1836,6,23 (H)
1839, 7, 17. Samuel B. gct Cincinnati MM, O. (H)

SAUNDERS
1841, 10, 13. Alice gct Bloomfield MM, Ind.

SCHOOLEY
1821, 10, 21. Elizabeth m Christopher TERRILL

1821, 10, 20. Cisily [Schooly] & ch, Samuel & Mahlon, rocf Miami MM, dtd 1821,9,26
1821, 10, 20. Elizabeth [Schooly] rocf Miami MM, dtd 1821,9,26
1848, 6, 14. Abigail & ch, Mary, Lambert, Rachel, Sarah Abigail, Samuel, Miriam A., Virginia M., Elizabeth & Ruth Alice, rocf Fairfax MM, dtd 1848,3,15 (H)
1848, 6, 14. Sarah rocf Fairfax MM, dtd 1848, 3,15 (H)
1848, 6, 14. Hannah rocf Fairfax MM, dtd 1848,3,15 (H)
1856, 2, 12. Mary Ellen Litler (form Schooley) dis mcd (H)
1857, 6, 17. Lydia Ann Wade (form Schooley) dis mcd (H)
1858, 12, 15. Mariam Long (form Schooley) dis mcd (H)
1860, 2, 15. Sarah Shuke (form Schooley) dis mcd (H)
1867, 9, 18. Emeline Stowe (form Schooley) dis mcd (H)
1867, 9, 18. Sarah Esther Cooper (form Schooley) con mcd (H)
1871, 4, 12. Joel gct White Water MM, Ind.(H)
1872, 4, 16. Hannah Birdsall (form Schooley) con mcd (H)
1877, 6, 13. Anna recrq (H)
1887, 8, 17. Rachel Fudge (form Schooley) con mcd (H)

SCHOOLEY, continued
1887, 11, 16. Ruth H. Carson (form Schooley) relrq (H)

SCOTT
1830, 8, 11. Charles, s Timothy & Hannah, Clark Co., O.; m in Greenplain MH, Sarah BLOXOM, dt Wm. & Mary, Clark Co., O. (H)
1836, 9, 21. Stanton, s Joshua & Elizabeth, Champaign Co., O.; m in Greenplain MH, Esther EDMUNDSON, dt Ehos. & Elizabeth, Clark Co., O. (H)

1830, 8, 4. Charles rocf Center MM, dtd 1830,7,17 (H)
1837, 1, 18. Esther E. gct Goshen MM (H)
1841, 12, 15. Chas. & w, Sarah, & ch, Wm., Timothy, James, Gideon Bloxsom & Alvan, gct Camden MM (H)
1851, 8, 13. Elizabeth M. Feuson (form Scott) dis mcd (H)

SEARS
1827, 9, 5. Penelope Bocock & dt, Mary Sears, rocf Dover MM, dtd 1827,8,4
1830, 1, 6. Mary Bond (form Sears) con mou

SHAW
1836, 2, 17. John, Elizabeth & ch, Edward, Thos. W. & Rebecca T., rocf Cincinnati MM, dtd 1835,12,24 (H)
1837, 3, 25. Rebecca & Thomas, ch John, rocf Cincinnati MM, dtd 1836,12,15
1837, 5, 27. Edward rocf Cincinnati MM, dtd 1836,12,15
1840, 8, 12. Edward gct White Water MM, Ind., to m Peninah Hill (H)
1842, 4, 13. Edward dis mou & joining Separatists
1844, 4, 17. Peninah & s, Robert H., rocf White Water MM, Ind. (H)
1849, 1, 17. Edward & w, Peninah, & ch, Robert Hill, Rebecca & Mary Elizabeth, gct Miami MM (H)
1849, 1, 17. Elizabeth gct Miami MM (H)

SHIGLEY
1859, 2, 16. Mary C. (form Mires) dis mcd (H)

SHINN
1852, 6, 16. Charles & ch, Joseph, Albina & Hannah, rocf Deer Creek MM, dtd 1851,7,26 (H)
1854, 7, 12. Charles & ch, Joseph, Albina & Hannah, gct White Water MM, Ind. (H)

SHUKE
1860, 2, 15. Sarah (form Schooley) dis mcd (H)

SLAUGHTER
1834, 6, 28. Ann rocf Fairfield MM, dtd 1834,3,20

SLEEPER
----, --, --. Samuel, s John & Hannah, b 1763,1,13; m Patience BURROUGH, dt Jacob & Casandra, b 1767,2,17
Ch: Ephraim b 1788, 10, 8
Elizabeth " 1791, 1, 23 d 1792, 2,23
Charles " 1793, 6, 13
Rebecca " 1796, 9, 26
John " 1799, 6, 3 d 1799, 6,11
Keturah " 1801, 2, 17
Avis " 1804, 1, 30
Buddell " 1806, 7, 29
Jacob " 1808, 12, 30
----, --, --. Charles, s Samuel & Patience, b 1793,6,13; m Anna WILLISS, dt Wm. & Henrietta, b 1803,2,27
1825, 2, 3. Avis m Timothy KELLY

1830, 5, 5. Anna dis jH
1830, 6, 22. Charles & w, Anne, & ch, Ephraim Jane Henrietta, William & Amanda, gct Goshen MM; returned 1830,12,15 since they returned to reside within limits of this MM (H)
1831, 1, 5. Sarah rocf Miami MM, dtd 1830, 11,24
1833, 12, 28. Elizabeth H. rocf Miami MM, dtd 1833,11,25
1834, 10, 25. Samuel & w, Patience, gct Springborough MM
1835, 12, 26. Buddell & w, Elizabeth, & dt, Martha, gct Sugar River MM, Ind.
1836, 12, 24. Jacob & w, Sarah, & ch, Isaiah & Chloe Ann, gct Sugar River MM, Ind.
1840, 1, 15. Ephraim, Jane, Wm. & Amanda, ch Chas., gct Mississinewa MM, Ind.

SMITH
1824, 2, 25. Seth, s Seth & Elizabeth, Clark Co., O.; m in Greenplain, Deborah WILDMAN, dt John & Elizabeth, Clark Co.,O.
1837, 5, 3. Hannah W. m Isaac THORN
1837, 8, 31. Levi, s George & Sarah, Green Co., O.; m in Greenplain, Emily JOHNSON, dt Jephtha & Ruth, Clark Co., O.
1851, 1, 29. Ruth m Samuel HADLEY

1829, 10, 7. Elizabeth dis jH
1833, 7, 27. Sarah & ch, Hannah, Wm., Levi & Jonathan, rocf Hopewell MM, dtd 1833,5,6
1839, 1, 26. Jonathan dis disunity

SMITH, continued
1844, 2, 14. Levi dis paying a military demand
1845, 5, 14. Lydia (form Dutton) dis mou
1853, 8, 17. Oliver gct Chester MM, to m Mary B. Negus
1854, 8, 16. Margaret B. rocf Chester MM, dtd 1854,7,20
1856, 12, 17. Ruth dis jas
1860, 12, 12. Anna & Hariet Holingsworth, a minor in her care, rocf Center MM, dtd 1860,9,12

SNOWDEN
1856, 9, 17. Caroline rocf Baltimore MM, W. Dist., Md., dtd 1856,7,8 (H)

SPENCER
1867, 4, 17. John, Elwood & Hannah J. dis jas (H)
1868, 1, 15. Eunice Purvis (form Spencer) dis mcd (H)

STOWE
1867, 9, 18. Emeline (form Schooley) dis mcd (H)

STRETCHER
1835, 10, 14. Mary (form Warner) dis mou (H)

SWAYNE
1837, 8, 16. Isaac B. & w, Maria, & dt, Amanda, rocf Allum Creek MM, dtd 1837,7,20 (H)
1839, 5, 15. Joshua W. Engle gct Stillwater MM, O., to m Sarah Ann Swayne (H)
1839, 5, 15. Thomas & w, Eliza, & ch, Mary Ann, Joshua, Rebecca, Eliza & Thomas Jr. rocf Flushing MM, dtd 1839,3,23 (H)
1839, 9, 18. Samuel F. rocf Stillwater MM, dtd 1839,4,20 (H)
1840, 6, 17. Samuel F. gct White Water MM, Ind. (H)
1846, 3, 16. Eliza dis disunity (H)

TAYLOR
1876, 12, 13. Fanny rocf Salem MM, O. (H)
1887, 1, 12. Jonathan gct Genoa MM, Neb. (H)

TERRILL
1821, 10, 21. Christopher, s David & Mary, Highland Co., O.; m in Greenplain, Elizabeth SCHOOLEY, dt Samuel & Scisly, Clark Co., O.

THATCHER
1836, 3, 16. John rocf Goose Creek MM, dtd 1835,9,17 (H)

THOMAS
1840, 4, 15. Lovina (form Beauchamp) dis mou
1849, 10, 17. Avis rocf Short Creek MM, dtd 1849,6,21 (H)
1867, 8, 14. Avis & Susannah Fisher (form Thomas) dis mcd (H)
1872, 12, 18. Mary T. Brown (form Thomas) con mcd (H)

THOMSON
1867, 4, 17. Ruth dropped from mbrp (H)

THORN
----, --, --. William, s Isaac & Hannah, b 1781,4,30; m Rachel EMBREE, dt Thomas & Esther, b 1786,8,25

Ch: Thomas b 1809, 9, 3
Hannah " 1811, 1, 7
Esther " 1812, 10, 2
Isaac " 1814, 8, 18
Elijah " 1816, 5, 14
Elihu " 1819, 1, 11
Sarah " 1821, 1, 29
William " 1823, 3, 4
Tamer " 1825, 10, 18

1831, 11, 16. Hannah m Edward WILDMAN
----, --, --. Thomas & Ruth

Ch: Isaac G. b 1835, 11, 13
William P. " 1838, 9, 6 d 1839, 3, 4 bur Greenplain
Levi b 1844, 7, 9

1835, 1, 21. Thomas, s Isaac & Hannah, Green Co., O.; m in Greenplain MH, Nancy WILLIS, dt Wm. & Henrietta, Clark Co., O. (H)
1837, 5, 3. Isaac, s Wm. & Rachel, Green Co., O.; m in Greenplain, Hannah W. SMITH, dt Geo. & Sarah, Green Co., O.
1855, 10, 24. Sarah m Samuel JONES
1865, 4, 19. Rachel m Samuel C. HOWELL
1871, 9, 14. Hannah m Daniel LAWRENCE
1872, 3, 28. Mary m Joseph MOORE
1873, 9, 23. Tamer m Daniel HILL

1825, 6, 1. Wm. & w, Rachel, & ch, Thomas, Hannah, Esther, Isaac, Elijah, Elihu, Sarah & Wm., rocf Goshen MM, dtd 1825,4,6
1835, 5, 30. Ruth rocf Fairfield MM, dtd 1835,3,25
1835, 5, 30. Isaac gct Short Creek MM
1837, 3, 25. Isaac rocf Short Creek MM, dtd 1837,2,21
1834, 12, 17. Thos. & ch, John, Wm., Hannah, Isaac, Sarah & Elizabeth, rocf Short Creek MM, dtd 1834,2,20 (H)
1837, 6, 24. Isaac & w, Hannah, gct White Lick MM, Ind.
1838, 1, 17. John dis mou (H)
1839, 11, 13. Isaac & w, Hannah W., rocf White Lick MM, Ind., dtd 1829,1,16
1839, 4, 17. Wm. F. dis mou (H)
1840, 1, 15. Clark & John Williams, ch Nancy Williams Thorn, gct Mississinewa MM, Ind.
1841, 9, 15. Isaac, Sarah & Elizabeth, ch Thos., rocf Short Creek MM, dtd 1841,5,18
1842, 9, 14. Elihu dis training with militia
1846, 6, 17. Elijah dis mou & joining Separatists

THORN, continued
1847, 2, 17. Isaac dis jas
1847, 7, 14. Hannah W. dis jas
1851, 4, 16. Wm. con mou
1852, 6, 16. Nancy Maria & dt, Sarah Emma, recrq
1859, 3, 16. Elizabeth H. rocf Springfield MM, dtd 1859,2,19

THORP
1865, 5, 17. Thomas & w, Maria, rocf Miami MM, dtd 1865,4,26 (H)
1878, 9, 18. Ann F. rocf Deerfield MM, O., dtd 1878,8,7 (H)
1878, 9, 18. Samuel rocf Deerfield MM, O., dtd 1878,8,7 (H)
1883, 1, 17. Henry T. Pickering rocf Plainfield MM, O., dtd 1882,12,14 to m Ann Thorp (H)

TOMLINSON
1868, 8, 12. Lydia Ann recrq (H)

TRENTEN
1867, 8, 14. Elma dropped from mbrp (H)

VANLAW
1868, 1, 15. Samuel dropped from mbrp (H)
1868, 1, 15. Lydia & ch dropped from mbrp (H)

VANMETER
1843, 9, 13. Martha (form Engle) dis mou

VANSYCLE
1868, 1, 15. Mary Ann dropped from mbrp (H)

VICKERS
----, --, --. Richard b 1786,4,15 d 1822,--,6 bur Greenplain; m Celia ----- b 1772,9,23
Ch: Joshua b 1794, 4, 16
William " 1796, 4, 16
John " 1798, 7, 10
Amelia " 1800, 10, 3
Joseph " 1803, 5, 7
Maryann " 1808, 6, 15
Sarah " 1810, 10, 12 d 1811, 4, 5
Ruth " 1812, 12, 11
Elizabeth Emily " 1816, 4, 19
1824, 6, 23. William, s Richard & Celia, Clark Co., O.; m in Greenplain, Ann Beauchamp, dt Wm. & Amelia, Clark Co., O.
1827, 9, 12. Celia m James ANDERSON

1822, 11, 23. William rst on consent of Center MM
1823, 2, 15. Wm. recrq
1829, 4, 1. Ruth Anderson (form Vickers) dis mcd
1833, 12, 28. Emily dis disunity
1850, 6, 12. Mary Larkins (form Vickers) dis mou
1850, 6, 12. Ruth Pawlen (form Vickers) dis mou

WADE
1857, 6, 17. Lydia Ann (form Schooley) dis mcd (H)

WALKER
1833, 4, 27. Abel & w, Hannah, & ch, Joseph Lupton & Mary, rocf Hopewell MM, Va., dtd 1833,3,7 (H)
1871, 7, 12. Edward gct Maple Grove MM, Ia. (H)
1887, 7, 13. Catherine L. recrq (H)
1887, 7, 13. Arthur H. & Ralph, ch Penias L. & Catharine L., recrq (H)

WARDEN
1830, 11, 3. Jeremiah & w, Ann A., & ch, Elizabeth A. & Mary A., rocf Radnor MM, Pa., dtd 1830,5,13
1830, 11, 3. Sarah Aston rocf Radner MM, Pa., dtd 1830,5,13
1833, 7, 27. Sarah Cumins (form Warden) dis mou
1840, 2, 11. John A. [Warder] gct Cincinnati MM
1859, 6, 15. Mary P. [Warder] & ch, Sally Paul & George Ashton, rocf Phila. MM, Pa., dtd 1859,4,27

WARNER
1840, 1, 22. Lydia m Henry MICHENER (H)
1842, 11, 23. Simeon, s Levi & Massy, Ross Co., O.; m in Greenplain MH, Elizabeth MERRITT, dt Thomas & Jane, Clark Co., O. (H)
1865, 9, 20. Simeon, s Isaac & Sarah Ann, Clark Co., O.; m in Greenplain, Rebecca P. HARRISON, dt John F. & Elizabeth, of Springfield

1822, 3, 23. John dis disunity
1824, 1, 24. Isaac rst on consent of Wilmington MM, Del.
1829, 4, 1. Mary dis jH
1830, 7, 7. Levi dis mou (H)
1833, 4, 27. Wm. dis mou (H)
1833, 9, 18. Levi & w, Elizabeth, & ch, Simeon, Lydia, Abner, Joshua W., Levi W., Hugh & William, rocf Fall Creek MM, dtd 1833,7,20 (H)
1836, 9, 24. Levi dis mou
1835, 10, 14. Mary Stretcher (form Warner) dis mou (H)
1845, 8, 13. Margaret S. rocf Plainfield MM, dtd 1845,7,17 (H)
1847, 7, 14. Elizabeth (form Merritt) dis mou
1851, 5, 14. Sarah Ann recrq (H)
1854, 8, 16. Ann Elizabeth, John G., Simeon, Joseph & Amos P., ch Isaac & Sarah Ann, recrq (H)
1854, 9, 13. Lydia recrq (H)

WARNER, continued
1867, 8, 14. Joseph dropped from mbrp (H)
1870, 3, 16. Mary J. M. rocf White Water MM, Ind. (H)
1876, 1, 12. Isaac & w, Sarah Ann, & gr ch, Isaac W., Emma B. & Sarah A. Cook, gct Third Haven MM, Md. (H)
1876, 1, 12. Lydia gct Third Haven MM, Md. (H)
1880, 3, 17. Laura E. Wilson (form Warner) con mcd (H)
1880, 3, 17. Mary E. Dugdale (form Warner) con mcd (H)
1880, 3, 17. Emma W. Peirce (form Warner) con mcd (H)

WAY
1852, 10, 13. Robert & w, Abigail, & s, David L., rocf Miami MM (H)
1858, 11, 17. Robert & w, Abigail, & ch, David L., gct Center MM (H)

WEBSTER
1835, 11, 18. Wm. con mou (H)
1847, 9, 15. Eliza Packer (form Webster) dis mou (H)

WHITE
1824, 11, 3. Matthias Crispin gct Caesars Creek MM, to m Sarah White
1868, 1, 15. Mary dropped from mbrp (H)

WILDMAN
1822, 9, 25. John, s Wm. & Ann, Clark Co., O.; m in Greenplain, Margaret FOX, dt Geo. & Sarah, Clark Co., O.
1824, 2, 25. Deborah m Seth SMITH
1827, 6, 27. Hannah m Thomas WINDERS
1831, 8, 7. Ann m John HADLEY
1831, 11, 16. Edward, s John & Elizabeth, Clark Co., O.; m in Greenplain, Hannah THORN, dt Wm. & Rachel, Green Co., O.
1840, 10, 5. John d ae 62y 6m 20d (an elder)
1859, 10, 19. William, s Edward & Hannah, Clark Co., O.; m in Greenplain, Eliza HARRISON, dt John F. & Elizabeth, Clark Co., O.
1870, 9, 26. Rachel E. m Israel H. HOLLINGSWORTH

1834, 2, 22. Maria L. rocf Cesars Creek MM, dtd 1834,1,23
1836, 10, 29. Benjamin & w, Mariah L., gct White Lick MM, Ind.
1839, 1, 26. Wm. gct Bloomfield MM, Ind.
1841, 2, 17. Benjamin & w, Mariah L., rocf White Lick MM, Ind., dtd 1841,2,17

WILKINS
1824, 9, 1. Rachel recrq
1832, 2, 1. Rachel dis joining M. E. Church
1839, 1, 16. Rachel gct Miami MM (H)

WILLETS
1867, 4, 17. John E. & Martin dropped from mbrp (H)
1867, 4, 17. Eli dis joining another society (H)

WILLIAMS
----, --, --. Peter, s Ennion & Martha, b 1786,6,23; m Nancy WILLIS, dt Wm. & Henrietta, b 1795,10,17
Ch: Mary b 1813, 5, 23
Martha " 1815, 1, 30
William " 1818, 2, 7 d 1822,11,21 bur Greenplain
Clark b 1819, 9, 10
1830, 7, 21. Mary m Maurice PLACE (H)

1826, 3, 1. Seth & w, Ketturah, & ch, Samuel & Avis, rocf Fairfield MM
1829, 4, 1. Nancy dis jH
1833, 9, 28. Martha Beacham (form Williams) dis mou
1835, 12, 16. Seth & w, Keturah, & ch, Samuel, Avis, Charles Havila & Martha, gct Sugar River MM, Ind.
1840, 1, 15. Clark & John, ch Nancy (Williams) Thorn, gct Mississinewa MM, Ind.
1848, 6, 14. Sarah con mou (H)
1858, 11, 17. Anna & ch, Abner W., Joseph & James G. Oldham, gct Fall Creek MM (H)
1867, 4, 17. Asa & w, Elizabeth, & ch, Wm., Asa, Rachel, Mary, Lott, Daniel & Thomas, dropped from mbrp (H)
1868, 1, 15. Susan dropped from mbrp (H)
1868, 1, 15. Isaac & w, Martha, & ch dropped from mbrp (H)

WILSON
1845, 10, 16. Lydia L. m Wm. B. FRENCH

1825, 1, 5. Elijah C. Williss gct Springboro MM, to m Rachel Wilson
1833, 4, 27. Stephen & w, Hannah P., & ch, Martha, Joseph E., Edward S., Lydia L. & Daniel P., rocf Goose Creek MM, dtd 1833, 2,14 (H)
1834, 4, 15. Stephen Jr. rocf Goose Creek MM, dtd 1833,2,15 (H)
1836, 12, 14. Stephen Jr. dis disunity (H)
1837, 12, 13. Stephen & w, Hannah P., & ch, Martha, Joseph Ely, Edward Stabler, Lydia Lovegrove, Daniel Pope & David Pope, gct Springborough MM (H)
1839, 10, 16. John Howell gct Springborough MM, to m Martha Wilson (H)
1840, 6, 17. Stephen B. & w, Hannah P., & ch, Joseph E., Lydia L., Daniel P. & David P., rocf Springborough MM, dtd 1840, 5,28 (H)
1844, 11, 13. Hannah P. & ch, Lydia L., Daniel P. & David P., rocf Springborough MM, dtd 1844,10,24 (H)
1849, 6, 13. Hannah P. gct Cincinnati MM, O.

WILSON, continued
(H)
1867, 4, 17. Willis & Theodore dropped from mbrp (H)
1867, 8, 14. Elisha dropped from mbrp (H)
1867, 8, 14. Huldah dropped from mbrp (H)
1867, 8, 14. Elvira dropped from mbrp (H)
1867, 8, 14. Jehu R. dropped from mbrp (H)
1867, 8, 14. Zachariah dropped from mbrp (H)
1867, 8, 14. Preycella dropped from mbrp (H)
1868, 1, 15. Deborah dropped from mbrp (H)
1880, 3, 17. Laura E. (form Warner) con mcd (H)
1882, 1, 18. Mabel, dt Fred & Laura E., recrq (H)

WILLISS
---, --, --. William, s Thomas & Lina, b 1772,10,20; m Henrietta CHANCE, dt Tilghman & Nancy, b 1774,10,27
Ch: Arcada b 1794, 1, 5 d 1794, 3, 6
Nancy " 1795, 10, 17
Andrew R. " 1798, 2, 17
Elijah C. " 1800, 11, 16
William " 1805, 11, 29
Anna " 1803, 2, 27
Wesley " 1808, 5, 9
Levi " 1810, 6, 22
Mildred " 1813, 5, 12
Eliza " 1817, 7, 18
Amasa " 1819, 7, 17
1823, 8, 27. Andrew R., s Wm. & Henriette, Clark Co., O.; m in Greenplain, Mariah T. FARR, dt Cyrus & Elizabeth, Clark Co., O.
1832, 10, 18. Mildred K. m Wm. HAYWARD (H)
1835, 1, 21. Nancy m Thos. THORN (H)

1824, 9, 1. Wm. & w, Hannah, & ch, Jacob, Elizabeth, Mary, Rebecca, Ellis, Enos, Hannah & John, gct Caesars Creek MM
1825, 1, 5. Elijah C. gct Springboro MM, to m Rachel Wilson
1829, 3, 4. Henrietta & Maria dis jH
1829, 10, 7. Rachel dis
1830, 10, 6. Mildred dis disunity
1833, 10, 16. Maria dis disunity (H)
1833, 12, 28. Eliza dis disunity
1839, 11, 13. John Wesley dis mou (H)
1840, 1, 15. Elizabeth T. & Hornay, ch Andrew, gct Mississinewa MM, Ind.
1840, 1, 15. Amasa, s Wm., gct Mississinewa MM, Ind.
1840, 1, 15. Jesse Wilson, Elizabeth & Emeline, ch Elijah, gct Springborough MM

WINDERS
1827, 6, 27. Thomas, s Abner & Hapy, Ross Co., O.; m in Greenplain, Hannah WILDMAN, dt John & Elizabeth, Clark Co., O.

1828, 11, 5. John & fam gct Honey Creek MM, Ind.
1829, 6, 3. John & fam gct Vermillion MM, Ill.; cert issued to Honey Creek MM, Ind. returned because of Honey Creek being laid down
1832, 4, 28. Thomas & w, Hannah, & ch, John, Edward & Aaron, rocf Fairfield MM, dtd 1831,11,24

WINDHAM
1868, 1, 15. Mercy dropped from mbrp (H)

WOOD
1868, 1, 15. Samuel N. dropped from mbrp (H)
1868, 1, 15. Jonathan dropped from mbrp (H)
1868, 1, 15. David J. dropped from mbrp (H)

WOOLMAN
1821, 12, 22. Rebecca (form Allen) con mcd
1825, 8, 3. Eber & fam gct Centre MM
1830, 5, 5. Ruth dis jH

WRIGHT
1823, 9, 20. John gct Fairfield MM
1823, 10, 18. Joab con mcd
1823, 12, 20. Lydia dis disunity
1824, 5, 22. Joab gct Fairfield MM
1827, 10, 3. James & fam gct Springfield MM
1829, 3, 4. Rachel dis jH
1835, 8, 29. Mary Jane dis jH
1842, 6, 15. Levi dis disunity
1853, 1, 12. Hannah Randel (form Wright) dis mou
1853, 4, 13. Eliza Jefferson (form Wright) dis mou
1868, 1, 15. Ann & ch dropped from mbrp (H)
1868, 2, 12. Rachel & Joseph gct Wapsenonoch MM, Ia.; returned 1868,7,15 (H)

RECORDS

ADAMS
1828, 8, 6. Cert rec for Jedadiah from Westfield MM, O., dtd 1828,5,28, endorsed to Miami MM, O.

ALLEN
1827, 4, 4. Solomon & w, Anna, & ch, Emily, Samuel & Jackson, gct Honey Creek MM, Ind.
1833, 2, 23. Westley dis mcd
1864, 10, 12. Levi Thorn gct Sugarplain MM, to m Ella Allen

ANDERSON
1829, 5, 6. James dis disunity

ARMSTRONG
1885, 3, 18. Gwen S. gct Dover MM

ATKINSON
1827, 11, 7. Thomas rocf Centre MM, O., dtd 1826,9,16
1833, 8, 24. Leuanna rocf Centre MM, O., dtd 1833,6,12
1862, 10, 15. Abigail Rupert (form Atkinson) con mcd
1870, 3, 16. Mary recrq
1870, 8, 17. Jehu F. con mcd
1871, 7, 12. John jas; relrq
1882, 3, 15. Louisa J. recrq
1887, 5, 18. Mary gl
1897, 3, 17. Elgie & Annie recrq

BACON
1857, 3, 11. Joseph Y. gct Salem MM, Iowa

BAKER
1828, 2, 6. Richard rpd mcd; complaint sent to Goshen MM
1828, 12, 3. Joshua dis mcd & joining Freemasons
1835, 9, 20. Brinton dis disunity

BEACHAM
1830, 3, 3. Wm. dis disunity

BEAUCHAMP
1831, 3, 2. Willis dis training with the militia
1833, 8, 24. Asa dis mcd & jH
1834, 9, 27. Noah dis disunity

BELL
1827, 2, 7. Alexander & w, Rebecca, & ch, Mary Jane, Hannah, Nancy & John, rocf Fairfield MM, dtd 1826,11,25

BLOXOM
1826, 6, 7. James dis disunity

BOND
1826, 8, 2. Susannah chosen elder
1829, 5, 6. Benjamin dis disunity
1830, 8, 4. Moses dis mcd & jas

BORSEL
1882, 3, 15. Henry & w, Sallie, recrq

BRIGGS
1826, 12, 6. Maryann (form Vickers) dis mcd

BRYAN
1897, 3, 17. Dennis D., Jane & Pearl, recrq

BUCKLES
1872, 4, 17. Hester recrq (living in Madison, Co.)

BUFFENBARGER
1883, 3, 14. Darius & Mannains(?) recrq
1886, 7, 14. Darius & Annanios(?) dropped from mbrp

BUFFKIN
1831, 12, 7. Thomas & w, Ruth, & ch, John, Warner, Gulielma, Sarah & Ruth, gct Marlborough MM, O.

BUSH
1876, 2, 16. Thomas recrq
1883, 3, 14. Eva L. recrq

BUTCHER
1897, 3, 17. Wm. & Clara recrq
1897, 4, 14. Della rolf M. E. Church, Selma

CALVERT
1875, 2, 19. Reese recrq
1885, 8, 12. Rees G. gct White Water MM, Ind. to m Anna Ethel Kerk
1885, 10, 14. Anna Ethel Kerk rocf White Water MM, Ind., dtd 1885,9,24

CHANCE
1830, 6, 2. Tilmon rocf Fairfield MM, O., dtd 1830,3,27

CHAPMAN
1883, 3, 14. Jefferson J. & Samuel E. recrq
1883, 3, 14. Wesley Milton & w, Sarah Nancy, & ch, Molly Grace, Minnie M. & Walter, recrq
1886, 7, 14. Samuel E. dropped from mbrp
1897, 3, 17. Mahala F. recrq
1897, 10, 13. Escle & Russell recrq

CHARLES
1877, 6, 13. Emma rocf Springfield MM, Kans.

CLARK
1831, 12, 7. Robert dis
1883, 3, 14. Andrew recrq
1886, 7, 14. Andrew J. dropped from mbrp
1897, 3, 17. Ralph recrq

CLINE
1890, 3, 12. Annie B. recrq

CRANTON
1897, 3, 17. Harry & Anna recrq

CRISPEN
1855, 6, 13. Abraham dis

CRITZ
1897, 3, 17. Sallie recrq

CROSS
1875, 10, 13. Martha recrq
1882, 3, 15. Abi & ch, Ada Harris & Daniel Harris, recrq
1886, 7, 14. James & w, Abi, dropped from mbrp

CURL
1897, 3, 17. Frank recrq

DARLINGTON
1863, 3, 18. Memorial read for Amelia E.

DAVIS
1897, 3, 17. Frank, Mamie & Grace recrq

DOAN
1863, 3, 18. Memorial read for Joseph

DORMAN
1882, 3, 15. W. A. & w, Stella, & dt, Floy, recrq

DUGDALE
1874, 3, 18. Mary recrq

EDGERTON
1869, 8, 18. Walter prcf Spiceland MM, Ind., to m
1869, 11, 17. Eliza A. gct Spiceland MM, Ind.

ELDER
1898, 10, 12. Robert rmt Rachel T. Wildman (m 1898,9,14 at 7:30 PM at home of Wm. Wildman)

ELLIOTT
1897, 3, 17. David M., Elda & Josie recrq

ELLIS
1868, 7, 15. Louisa (form Thorn) con mcd
1868, 12, 16. Louisa gc
1883, 3, 14. Richard recrq
1886, 7, 14. Richard dropped from mbrp

ENGLE
1834, 9, 27. Joshua W. dis disunity

FARR
1828, 11, 5. James Gibson jas; dropped from mbrp
1834, 5, 24. Cyrus Franklin dis disunity
1834, 6, 28. Isaac dis jH
1834, 6, 28. Isaac Musgrave dis disunity

FAUDREE
1897, 10, 13. A. John recrq

FLETCHER
1882, 3, 15. Geo. W. & w, Caroline, recrq
1883, 3, 16. Ruliff L., Howard Edward, James Roscoe, Chester Maurice & Wayne Foy, ch Geo. & Caroline, recrq
1886, 4, 14. Caroline & ch, Ruliff Larkin, Howard Edmund, Roscoe James, Chester Morris & Wayne Foy, relrq
1886, 4, 14. George relrq

FREAM
1829, 2, 4. James dis disunity

GAIN
1872, 4, 17. Jesse S. recrq (living in Madison Co.)

GAINER
1886, 7, 14. Jesse dropped from mbrp

GIBSON
1833, 6, 29. Benjamin Wildman rqct Caesar's Creek MM, O., to m Maria L. Gibson

GILBERT
1883, 3, 14. Henry & s, Harvey, recrq
1886, 7, 14. Henry & Harvey dropped from mbrp

HAINES
1836, 2, 27. John Warder (or Warden) gct Frankfort MM, Pa., to m Elizabeth Haines

HAMABERRY
1897, 10, 13. Geo. & Charles recrq
1897, 3, 17. Bertha [Homabery] recrq

HARRIS
1886, 7, 14. Daniel & w, Ada, dropped from mbrp

HARRISON
1826, 12, 6. Wm. [Harrisson] recrq
1827, 3, 7. Wm. H. gct Centre MM, O., to m Anna Stout
1831, 2, 2. Wm. H. & w, Ann, & ch, John A., rocf Centre MM, O., dtd 1830,12,15
1873, 4, 16. Wm. H. recrq
1879, 1, 15. Wm. & w, Nancy, gct Goshen MM, Logan Co., O.

HARVEY
1858, 10, 13. Wm. Thorn rqct Springfield MM, to m Elizabeth Harvey
1874, 2, 18. Isaac & Sarah rocf Springfield MM, dtd 1874,1,17

HARVEY, continued
1874, 5, 13. Rebecca rocf Springfield MM

HATTON
1872, 9, 18. Robert Jr. recrq
1875, 6, 16. Robert Jr. gct Allum Creek MM, O.
1882, 2, 15. Eliza gct Deer Creek MM, Md.
1884, 4, 16. Robert & w, Josephine, & ch, Robert M. & Hugh W., rocf Alum Creek MM,O.

HICKMAN
1895, 1, 16. J. Freemont & Bertha E. Wildman declared intentions of m; permission for m to be performed at her home granted
1898, 2, 16. Bertha E. W. glt First Presbyterian Church, Wooster, O.

HILL
1871, 11, 15. Edmund & dt, Mary, rq mbrp
1872, 1, 17. Francis C. & Robert B. recrq
1872, 1, 17. Sylvester recrq
1872, 4, 17. Robert & s, Elmer, recrq
1873, 9, 17. Daniel prcf Clear Creek MM, to m
1874, 1, 14. Tamar T. gct Clear Creek MM, O.
1879, 1, 15. Edmund & fam gct Springfield MM, Douglas Co., Kans.
1883, 11, 14. Robert B. & s, Elmer, glt M. E. Church, Louisburg, Kans.

HOLLINGSWORTH
1860, 5, 16. Seth Smith gct Centre MM, O., to m Anne Hollingsworth
1875, 6, 16. Enoch & Hester & ch, Ella & Inez, rocf Wilmington MM, O.
1876, 1, 12. James H. rocf Newberry MM, O., dtd 1875,12,20
1877, 1, 17. Pierce & Sarah Jane & ch, Emma, Asaph, James W. & Charles Wilmer, rocf Bangor MM, Ia., dtd 1876,12,16
1880, 4, 14. Emma gct Bangor MM, Ia.
1880, 4, 14. Peirce & w, Sarah Jane, & ch, Asaph E., Jas. W., Charles Wilmer & Harry T., gct Bangor MM, Ia.
1884, 3, 12. Enoch & Hester A. & ch, Inez & Bessie, gct Bangor MM, Iowa

HORNADAY
1886, 7, 14. Samuel dropped from mbrp

HOUGH
1862, 12, 17. Sarah T. gct New Garden MM, Ind.
1874, 9, 16. Hiram & Sarah T. Hough & Wm. & Rosa Lee Watkins, ch in their care, rocf New Garden MM, dtd 1874,8,15
1875, 2, 17. Hiram gct New Garden MM

HOWELL
1865, 10, 18. Samuel C. recrq
1876, 12, 13. Deborah S. rocf White Water MM, Ind., dtd 1876,11,22
1887, 11, 16. Ruth S. gct New York MM, N. Y.

HUNT
1856, 5, 14. Edward S. gct Springfield MM, Ind.
1870, 12, 1. Edward & w, Delphina, jas; dropped from mbrp
1872, 2, 14. Isaiah recrq

HUTTON
1829, 10, 7. Macy dis disunity
1829, 5, 6. John dis disunity
1830, 6, 2. Levi & w, Rebecca, & ch, Elizabeth, John & Jordan, rocf Fairfield MM, O., dtd 1830,4,24
1833, 7, 27. Levi dis

JOHNSON
1829, 9, 2. Johnson, Ashley M. & w, Hannah, & ch, Harriett & Cyrus, rocf Fairfield MM dtd 1829,6,27
1829, 10, 7. Jephthah dis disunity
1830, 4, 7. Jephthah dis disunity; sent to Fall Creek MM, O.
1863, 3, 18. Memorial read for Jonathan

JORDAN
1883, 3, 14. John W. & w, Louisa J., & ch, R. & Eva, recrq
1886, 4, 14. John W. & w, Louisa Jane, & ch, Eva Laura & Ross, glt some other church

KERK
1885, 8, 12. Rees G. gct White Water MM, Ind. to m Anna Ethel Kerk

KING
1875, 11, 17. Anna recrq
1876, 2, 16. Daniel recrq
1877, 7, 18. Mary Ella Lavina recrq of parents, Daniel & Anna

LAKE
1886, 7, 14. Hannah glt some other church, Mt. Union, Iowa

LARKIN
1883, 3, 14. George, Chester & Nancy recrq
1886, 7, 14. Chester dropped from mbrp

LAWRENCE
1871, 9, 13. Daniel rocf Oak Ridge MM, Grant Co., Ind., dtd 1871,8,15
1872, 3, 13. Daniel [Laurence] rocf Oak Ridge MM, Ind., dtd 1872,2,13
1887, 9, 14. Daniel & fam gct Spiceland MM, Ind.

LEACH
1897, 3, 17. Cora Bell, Barbara Maud, Mary Alice & Chas. Grover, recrq

LEWIS
1832, 4, 28. Thomas & w, Prudence, & ch, William, Isaac, Hannah & Westly, gct Flint

LEWIS, continued
MM, Ind.

LINCH
1872, 2, 14. Wm. recrq

LINSON
1872, 10, 16. John recrq

LINTON
1832, 6, 23. Samuel L. dis at Centre MM, O.

LITTLE
1882, 3, 15. Rhoda recrq
1886, 7, 14. Rhoda dropped from mbrp
1897, 10, 13. Wm. recrq

McCOLLUM
1872, 4, 17. Seth O. & w, Rebecca, & ch, Florence, Stella, Wm. R., Mary Elizabeth & Fulu, recrq
1886, 7, 14. Seth O. & w, Rebecca, & ch, Florence, Stella, Wm. R., Mary Elizabeth & Tula, dropped from mbrp

McDONALD
1875, 2, 19. Aaron recrq
1875, 2, 19. Rebecca recrq
1886, 7, 14. Aaron & dt, Rebecca, dropped from mbrp

McFARLAND
1897, 10, 13. Charles & Ella recrq

MATTHEWS
1828, 6, 4. Joel & w rocf Springborough MM, O., dtd 1826,12,26; he did not reside in the verge of this MM
1897, 3, 17. Dr. Alpheus A. recrq
1898, 7, 13. Mary Margaret recrq

MELOY
1889, 11, 13. Lewis L. & w, Alice, gl

MILLER
1889, 10, 16. Anna Smith glt First Presbyterian Church, Wichita, Kans.

MOFFITT
1875, 10, 13. Charles & Lucinda & ch, Oliver E. & Eunice E., rocf Tonganoxie MM
1876, 12, 13. Charles & Lucinda & ch, Oliver C. & Eunice E., gct Sugar River MM, Ind.

MOON
1830, 10, 6. Enoch rocf Centre MM, O., dtd 1830,9,15

MOORE
1872, 3, 13. Joseph prcf White Water MM, to m
1873, 6, 18. Mary T. gct White Water MM, Ind.

MORTON
1829, 10, 7. Alexander dis disunity
1832, 1, 4. Martha dis joining Methodists

MURRAY
1891, 3, 18. James gl

NEGUS
1861, 12, 18. Albert C. rocf Chester MM, Ind.
1861, 12, 18. Joseph & w, Eliza A., & ch, Mary E. & Ruth Ann, rocf Chester MM, Ind.
1871, 7, 12. Albert C. jas; relrq

NICKLES
1897, 10, 13. Mable M. recrq

OWEN
1830, 4, 7. Benjamin & w, Esther, & ch, Samuel Y., gct Cesars Creek MM, O.

PAIST
1830, 7, --. Charles dis

PARKER
1872, 5, 15. Rebecca recrq
1873, 4, 16. Noah recrq
1878, 6, 12. Rebecca & ch, Noah & Eva, gct Goshen MM, Logan Co., O.
1878, 7, 17. Hannah gct Caesars Creek MM,O.

PAXTON
1864, 9, 14. Ruth J. (or G.) & ch, Mary Ellen, Anne Elizabeth, Florence N. & Thomas T., gct Fairfield MM, O.

PEACOCK
1884, 5, 14. Wm. R. rocf Oak Ridge MM, Grant Co., Ind., dtd 1884,4,15
1886, 1, 13. Wm. & Eliza D. glt M. E. Church, Sedgewood, Kansas; their s, Rolland, to remain with Friends in this mtg

PEMBERTON
1878, 2, 13. Melvina recrq
1886, 7, 14. Mebina dropped from mbrp

PENNINGTON
1830, 6, 2. Paul dis joining Separatists at Center MM, O.
1877, 7, 18. Chas. P. rocf Westland MM
1887, 5, 18. Charles & Ann & ch, Laura Mary & Levi Samuel, gct Dover MM, O.

PETERSON
1899, 3, 15. Sarah E. glt Second Presbyterian Church, Springfield, O.

PHIFER
1886, 7, 14. Nancy & Wm. dropped from mbrp

PRICE
1855, 9, 12. Wm. Warder gct Western MM, Pa., to m Mary P. Price

PUGH
1897, 9, 15. Esther rocf Cincinnati MM, O.

RICHARDSON
1830, 3, 3. Isaac dis disunity

RIDER
1872, 4, 17. Francis, John W., Jane & Alice recrq

RINEHART
1883, 3, 14. Wm. & Sabria & ch, Alfred, Elsie, Lulu & Oren, recrq
1886, 7, 14. Wm. [Rhinehart] & w, Sattira, Alfred, Eliza, Lulu Bell & Oren, dropped from mbrp

ROADAMER
1873, 4, 16. Samuel recrq
1874, 5, 13. Minerva [Roadarmer] recrq
1883, 3, 14. Laura & Lillie [Roadaimer] recrq

ROBINSON
1872, 4, 17. Jennie recrq

ROCKWELL
1898, 6, 15. Lydia rocf Centre MM, O., dtd 1898,5,18

RUPERT
1862, 10, 15. Abigail (form Atkinson) con mcd
1868, 10, 14. Abigail jas; dropped from mbrp

SEARS
1862, 8, 5. Abner W. dis by Goshen MM, O.; notice served by this MM

SHANNON
1897, 10, 13. Lacy recrq

SHINN
1876, 2, 16. Hannah recrq

SLEEPER
1830, 3, 3. Charles dis disunity
1830, 8, 4. Jacob gct Miami MM, O., to m Sarah Welch
1831, 11, 2. Jacob dis; appealed to QM but decision of MM upheld
1832, 11, 24. Buddell gct Miami MM, to m Elizabeth Welch

SMITH
1856, 10, 15. Ruth dis jas
1860, 5, 16. Seth gct Centre MM, O., to m Anne Hollingsworth
1870, 2, 16. Samuel con mcd
1871, 3, 15. Esther recrq
1872, 7, 17. James recrq
1873, 3, 12. Seth Jr. rpd mcd; retained mbrp
1877, 11, 14. Hannah Lewis rocf Clear Creek MM, O., dtd 1877,11,10
1877, 12, 12. Hannah Lewis rocf Clear Creek MM, O., dtd 1877,11,10
1878, 3, 13. James relrq
1883, 12, 12. Anna gct Centre MM, O.
1887, 1, 12. Oliver & Margaret B. & ch, Ruth Esther & Walter Clifford, gct Cottonwood MM, Kans.
1887, 1, 12. Olive H. gct Cottonwood MM, Kans.

SPENCER
1882, 3, 15. Jemima & ch, Stella & Pearlie, recrq
1883, 12, 12. Jemima & ch relrq

STEELE
1897, 3, 17. Harry & Estella recrq

STIFF
1883, 3, 14. Laurence recrq
1886, 1, 13. Laurence gct Salem MM, Ill.

STIGLEMAN
1893, 7, 22. Murry S. Wildman gct White Water MM, Ind., to m Olive Stigleman

STOUT
1827, 3, 7. Wm. H./Harrison gct Centre MM, O., to m Anna Stout

STROUP
1872, 4, 17. David & Mary recrq (living in Madison Co.)
1872, 4, 17. Wm. L. & s, Wilbirt, recrq (living in Madison Co.)
1886, 7, 14. Wilbert dropped from mbrp

STURGEON
1830, 7, --. Levi dis at West Branch

TALOR
1876, 7, 12. Elma recrq

THOMPSON
1897, 3, 17. Clara E. recrq
1899, 11, 15. Clara glt M. E. Church, Terre Haute, Ind.

THORN
1829, 3, 4. Wm. dis disunity
1858, 10, 13. Wm. rqct Springfield MM, to m Elizabeth Harvey
1864, 10, 12. Levi gct Sugarplain MM, to m Ella Allen
1864, 12, 14. Wm. G. gc
1865, 6, 14. Elijah & w, Mary, recrq
1865, 11, 15. Isaac G. con mcd
1866, 1, 17. Edwin I. gct White Water MM, Ind.
1866, 1, 17. Isaac G. gc
1866, 11, 14. Levi gct White Water MM, Ind.
1868, 7, 15. Louisa (form Thorn) con mcd
1871, 6, 14. Edwin I. rocf White Water MM, Ind., dtd 1871,5,24
1873, 5, 14. Edwin I. rpd mcd; retained mbrp

THORN, continued
1875, 4, 14. Wm. rqct Sabin MM, Ill., to m
1875, 7, 14. Lizzie L. rocf Saline MM, dtd 1875,7,10
1886, 7, 14. Isaac G. gct Maryville MM, Tenn.
1892, 10, 12. Emma K. rolf M. E. Church
1896, 5, 13. Mary C. relrq

THURSTON
1872, 12, 18. Amelia gct Springboro MM, O.
1892, 1, 13. Amelia recrq

TOLMAN
1886, 7, 14. Mary J. dropped from mbrp

VICKERS
1826, 12, 6. Maryann/(form Vickers) Briggs dis mcd
1834, 12, 27. Wm. dis disunity

WADDLE
1892, 7, 13. Howell & Mary & ch, Curtice H., Angus L., Mary Elizabeth & Howell Jr., gct Indianapolis MM, Ind.

WAKEFIELD
1881, 2, 16. Joseph recrq
1881, 4, 13. Mary A. & dt, Jennie, rocf Gilead MM, dtd 1881,4,19
1885, 12, 16. Joseph A. & fam gct White Water MM, Ind.
1886, 7, 14. Jos. J. & w, Mary A., & dt, Jennie C., rocf White Water MM, Ind.
1886, 11, 17. Almeda rocf Caesars Creek MM, O.
1888, 3, 14. Joseph J. gct Kokomo MM, Ind.

WALTON
1866, 11, 14. Marion Wildman gct Ceasars Creek to m Elizabeth Walton

WARDER
1830, 11, 3. Jeremiah & Ann A., & ch, Elizabeth Aston, George Aston & Mary Aston, & Wm., James T., Benjamin & Edward Warder, rocf Radnor MM, Pa., dtd 1830,5,13
1832, 1, 4. John A. [Warden] rocf Radnor MM, Pa., dtd 1831,10,31
1836, 2, 27. John (or Warden) gct Frankfort MM, Pa., to m Elizabeth Haines
1855, 9, 12. Wm. gct Western MM, Pa., to m Mary P. Price
1870, 2, 16. Benjamin con mcd
1872, 7, 17. Wm. & Benjamin relrq
1878, 3, 13. Mary P. relrq

WARNER
1873, 3, 12. Rebecca P. & s, Fairlanab(?) Harrison, rocf Indianapolis MM, Ind., dtd 1873,2,13
1879, 9, 17. Rebecca P. & ch gct White Water MM, Ind.

WATKINS
1874, 9, 16. Hiram/& w, Sarah T., & Wm. & Hough Rosa Lee Watkins, ch in their care, rocf New Garden MM, dtd 1874,8,15

WEBB
1872, 4, 17. Catharin & ch recrq
1886, 7, 14. Catharine & ch, Frances, John W. Jane & Alice Ryder, dropped from mbrp

WELCH
1830, 8, 4. Jacob gct Miami MM, O., to m Sarah Welch
1832, 11, 24. Buddell gct Miami MM, to m Elizabeth Welch

WHITE
1893, 2, 15. Hannah Howell gct Walnut Ridge MM, Ind.

WILDMAN
1827, 6, 6. Thomas Winder prcf Fairfield MM, to m Hannah Wildman
1833, 6, 29. Benjamin rqct Caesar's Creek MM, O., to m Maria L. Gibson
1833, 8, 24. Seneca gct Springfield MM
1866, 8, 15. Mary T. rocf Miami MM, O.
1866, 11, 14. Marion gct Ceasars Creek to m Elizabeth Walton
1869, 11, 17. Elizabeth rocf Cesars Creek MM, O., dtd 1869,9,23
1887, 9, 14. Walter glt M. E. Church, Denver, Colorado
1890, 3, 12. Walter & w, Cora, rolf M. E. Church, Denver, Colorado
1893, 7, 22. Murry S. gct White Water MM, Ind., to m Olive Stigleman
1894, 7, 18. Murry S. gc
1895, 1, 16. Bertha E. Wildman & J. Freemont Hickman, declared intentions of m; permission for m to be performed at her home granted
1895, 7, 17. Earnest Adkins recrq of parents, Walter & Cora
1897, 3, 17. Myrtle Maddeville rolf Presbyterian Church, Philo, Ill.
1898, 10, 12. Rachel T. rmt Robert Elder (m 1898,9,14 at 7:30 PM at home of Wm. Wildman
1899, 12, 13. Myrtle M. glt Presbyterian Church, Philo, Ill.

WILLIAMS
1829, 3, 4. Peter dis disunity

WILLIS
1827, 5, 2. Andrew dis
1827, 5, 2. Wm. Sr. dis
1827, 8, 1. Wm. Sr. appealed to QM for his right of mbrp
1827, 12, 5. Wm. rst by QM
1828, 9, 3. Wm. Jr. dis
1829, 1, 7. Elijah C. dis
1829, 2, 4. Wm. dis disunity
1830, 12, 1. Levi dis taking active part in

WILLIS, continued
place of diversion & departing from plainness
1831, 5, 4. John W. dis disunity

WILSON
1834, 8, 30. Stephen & Stephen Jr., of Hopewell MM, Va., have joined Hicksites; they have been treated by this MM on rq of Hopewell, but to no success; dis by Hopewell & this MM served the disownment
1898, 12, 14. Maud S. gct Columbus MM, O.

WINDER
1827, 6, 6. Thomas prcf Fairfield MM, to m Hannah Wildman

WISE
1871, 3, 15. Ruth Anna jas; relrq
1877, 9, 12. John & w, Ruth Anna, & ch, Joseph & Eliza M., recrq

WOLFORD
1897, 3, 17. Arthur recrq

WRIGHT
1827, 10, 3. James & w, Catherine, & ch, George, Judith, Allen, Ruth, David, Joel & Jemima, gct Springfield MM
1829, 2, 4. Richard dis disunity
1897, 3, 17. Mary Lane recrq

ASTON
1830, 11, 3. Jeremiah Warder & w, Ann A., & ch, Elizabeth, George & Mary Aston, & William, James T., Benjamin & Edward Warder, rocf Radnor MM, Pa., dtd 1830,5,13

SPRINGBOROUGH MONTHLY MEETING

Springborough Monthly Meeting, located in Warren County, was established by Miami Quarterly Meeting and composed of Springborough and Sugar Creek Preparative Meetings on 9 Mo. 28, 1824. The meeting was seriously divided at the time of the Hicksite Separation. The monthly meeting was discontinued in 1875, and merged with Miami Monthly Meeting. Jonathan Wright and Deborah Bateman were clerks, Mary Kenworthy and Elizabeth Miller, overseers, and Mary Taylor an elder. Other families were Garretson, Webster, Horner, Williams, Way, Chandler, Wilson, Haines, Leeds, O'Neal, Stanton, Kenworthy, Jones, Taylor and Mitler.

RECORDS

ANTRIM
1872, 5, 21. Hannah relrq to jas

BAILEY
1844, 5, 1. Joshua, s Exum & Tabitha, Warren Co., O.; m in Springborough, Lydia GARRETSON, dt John & Rebecca, Warren Co., O.

1827, 7, 24. David & w, Sylvia, & ch, Micajah, Elizabeth, Jonathan & Almedia, rocf Upper MM, Va., dtd 1827,4,24
1827, 10, 30. David & w, Sylvia, & ch, Micajah, Elizabeth, Jonathan & Almedia, gct Dover MM
1828, 6, 24. Deborah rocf Upper MM, Va., dtd 1828,4,19
1828, 12, 30. Joshua rocf South River MM, Va., dtd 1828,5,10
1828, 12, 30. Mary rocf South River MM, Va., dtd 1828,5,10
1830, 8, 24. Mary gct Silver Creek MM, Ind.
1832, 2, 28. Emmer Sr. & Emmer Jr. dis jH
1854, 5, 23. Joshua gct Allum Creek MM, to m Sarah E. Wood
1854, 8, 22. Sarah E. rocf Allum Creek MM, dtd 1854,7,21
1862, 12, 22. Joshua & dt, Rebecca L., gct Plainfield MM

BATEMAN
1836, 12, 28. Rachel m John W. TIMBERLAKE
1847, 4, 28. John T., s John & Hannah, Warren Co., O.; m in Springborough, Lydia B. STROUD, dt Charles & Susan B., Warren Co., O.
1825, 1, 25. Lydia Thompson (form Bateman) dis mou
1829, 2, 24. Rachel dis jH
1829, 3, 24. Rachel Sr. dis jH
1838, 11, 20. Mahlon gct Miami MM
1841, 8, 24. Mary Ann gct Miami MM, O.
1841, 9, 21. Wm. dis disunity
1844, 6, 25. Mary Ann rocf Miami MM, dtd 1844,5,22
1848, 7, 25. John T. & w, Lydia A., & dt, Mary Anna, gct Goshen MM
1855, 5, 22. Mary Ann & Hannah gct Goshen MM

BAUER
1837, 10, 24. Wm. J., s Isaac, gct Cincinnati MM, O.
1838, 8, 21. Jonathan J. dis mou
1842, 5, 24. Lydia Crosby (form Bauer) con mou
1846, 10, 20. Joseph con mou
1851, 1, 21. Joseph gct Cincinnati MM

BAX
1834, 8, 26. Henry rocf Barmen, Germany, dtd 1833,8,27
1835, 8, 25. Henry gct New Garden MM, Ind.

BEAL
1840, 11, 24. Hannah rocf Green Plain MM, O., dtd 1840,10,14
1843, 9, 20. Hannah [Beale] gct Green Plain MM, O.

BEASLEY
1851, 11, 25. Mary F. (form Butler) dis mou

BENEDICT
1860, 8, 21. Amy & s, Cyrus, rocf Driftwood MM, Ind., dtd 1860,8,4
1860, 8, 21. Melissa rocf Driftwood MM, Ind., dtd 1860,8,4
1863, 4, 21. Melissa gct Caesars Creek MM
1863, 4, 21. Amy & s, Cyrus, gct Caesars Creek MM

BINFORD
1826, 9, 26. James & ch, Thomas, Elwood, Richard & Peninah, rocf Upper MM, Va., dtd 1826,3,18, endorsed by Fairfield MM, O., 1826,8,26
1827, 4, 24. James & w, Anne, & ch, Thos. Elwood, Richard & Peninah, gct White Lick MM, Ind.
1827, 9, 25. John rocf Upper MM, Va., dtd 1827,6,16
1831, 10, 25. John gct Sugar River MM, Ind.

BLACKBURN
1833, 11, 19. Wm. & w, Rachel, & ch, John, Thomas, Ann, Rachel & Joseph, rocf Westland MM, dtd 1833,10,23
1833, 11, 19. Isaac rocf Westland MM, dtd 1833,10,23
1834, 3, 25. Wm. & w, Rachel, & ch, John, Thos., Ann, Rachel & Joseph, gct Sugar River MM, Ind.
1834, 3, 25. Isaac gct Sugar River MM, Ind.

BOONE
1847, 11, 3. Anne S. m Isaac EVANS

1847, 9, 21. Anne S. rocf Abington MM, Pa., dtd 1847,8,30

BORTON
1827, 7, 24. Edward & w, Mary, & ch, Emaline, James S., Mary Ann & Edward D., rocf Miami MM, dtd 1827,5,30
1827, 8, 28. Job, s Edward, gct Miami MM, O.
1829, 3, 24. Edward dis jH
1829, 3, 24. James S. dis jH
1829, 3, 24. Mary dis jH
1829, 3, 24. Emeline dis jH
1831, 3, 29. Jane rocf Evesham MM, dtd 1831, 1,7
1834, 7, 22. Maria (form Mullin) dis mou & jH
1837, 4, 25. Mary Ann dis jH

BROOKS
1837, 5, 23. James B. rocf Marlborough MM,

BROOKS, continued
dtd 1837,5,30
1839, 6, 25. James B. gct Center MM

BROWER
1843, 4, 25. Alice (form Welding) con mou
1845, 1, 21. Alice gct Cincinnati MM

BROWN
1829, 1, 27. Asher dis jH
1834, 6, 24. Rebecca rocf Dunnings Creek MM, Pa., dtd 1833,12,26
1834, 6, 24. Sarah, dt Benj. & Rebecca, rocf Dunnings Creek MM, Pa., dtd 1834,1,30
1836, 6, 21. Phebe (form Silver) dis mou
1864, 11, 22. Samuel & w, Elizabeth, & ch, Mary Ann & Evan H. rocf Miami MM, dtd 1864,10,26
1871, 1, 24. Samuel & w, Elizabeth H., & ch, Mary Ann, Evan Henry & John Franklin, gct Miami MM

BUFKIN
1831, 2, 22. Cert rec for Thomas & w, Ruth, & six ch from Flushing MM, dtd 1830,10,21, endorsed to Caesars Creek MM

BURSON
1837, 9, 19. Edward & w, Jemima, & ch, John W. & Lydia, rocf Stroudsburg MM, dtd 1837, 5,25
1838, 5, 22. Edward & w, Jemima, & ch, John N. & Lydia, gct Centre MM

BUTLER
1839, 10, 23. Mary Emily m Vierling KERSEY

1833, 10, 22. Micajah & w, Ann, & ch, Wike H., Wm. E., Mary E. & Anslem B., rocf Western Branch MM, Va., dtd 1833,9,28
1837, 5, 23. Maria, w Robert, & ch, Edward Thos., Gulia Ann, Joshua Asborn & Maria Frances, rocf South River MM, Va., dtd 1837,4,6
1840, 2, 18. Wm. E. gct Miami MM, to m Rhoda Johnson
1840, 6, 23. Edward T. dis disunity
1841, 4, 21. Rhoda J. rocf Miami MM, dtd 1841,3,24
1846, 12, 22. Anselm con mou
1847, 10, 26. Gulian dis disunity
1848, 5, 23. Anslem B. gct Green Plain MM,O.
1850, 2, 17. Joshua O. dis mou
1851, 11, 25. Mary F. Beasley (form Butler) dis mou
1852, 2, 25. Wm. E. gct Miami MM, to m Rhoda A. Moffitt
1852, 9, 26. Rhoda rocf Miami MM
1855, 7, 24. Wm. E. & w, Rhoda Ann, & ch, Mary E., John & Anselem, gct East Grove MM, Ia.

CADWALADER
1833, 7, 23. Wm. rocf South River MM, Va., dtd 1833,6,6
1833, 11, 19. Elizabeth & ch, Jane, Deborah, Judith, John Thos., Achilles, Elizabeth, Mildred & Charles, rocf South River MM, Va., dtd 1833,8,8
1834, 5, 21. Wm. gct Miami MM, O., to m Mary L. Stanton
1835, 4, 21. Wm. gct Miami MM
1837, 2, 21. Jane Stout (form Cadwalader) con mou
1837, 9, 19. Elizabeth & ch, Judith, John, Achilles, Elizabeth, Mildred & Charles, gct Miami MM, O.
1837, 9, 19. Deborah [Cadwallader] gct Miami MM, O.

CALHOUN
1837, 5, 23. Wm. & Elizabeth rocf Caesars Creek MM, dtd 1837,3,23
1849, 1, 23. Mary Gauker (form Calhoun) dis mou
1849, 7, 24. Wm. dis disunity

CARR
1829, 1, 27. Ruth dis jH
1829, 3, 24. Mary Ann dis jH
1829, 3, 24. Hannah W. dis jH
1829, 4, 28. John M. dis jH

CHANDLER
1829, 1, 27. Goldsmith & Phebe dis jH
1830, 2, 23. Mary Elizabeth [Chandlee] dis jH
1837, 3, 21. Eunice Ann Newport (form Chandler) dis mou & jH
1839, 7, 23. John G. [Chandlee] dis jH

CHAPMAN
1874, 6, 3. Charles F., s Joseph B. & Charlotte H., Warren Co., O.; m in home of Joseph STANTON, Elizabeth M. STANTON, dt Joseph & Catharine Ann, Warren Co., O.

CLEAVER
1826, 5, 26. Ezekiel L. & w, Mary, gct Miami MM, O.

CRACHET
1837, 11, 21. Jane (form Mullen) dis mou & jH

COLE
1824, 12, 28. Mary recrq
1829, 6, 23. Mary Willets (form Cole) dis mcd & jH

COOK
1827, 8, 28. John Hughes gct White Water MM, Ind., to m Hannah Cook

COWMAN
1827, 9, 25. Elizabeth & ch, Edward, Eliza-

COWMAN, continued
beth (dec after cert was granted) & James, rocf Pipe Creek MM, dtd 1827,6,16
1829, 3, 24. Elizabeth dis jH
1848, 7, 25. Edward dis mou & jH

COX
1844, 9, 26. John, s Jeremiah & Catherine, Montgomery Co., O.; m in Springborough, Jane MILLER, dt Caleb & Phebe, Warren Co., O.

1845, 7, 22. Jane M. gct Sugar River MM, Ind.

CRAIGG
1830, 5, 25. Isaac dis disunity

CREIGHTON
1833, 12, 24. John Benj., Wm. & Samuel Thos., gr ch Paul Sears, recrq
1843, 4, 25. John B. dis disunity
1844, 11, 19. Samuel dis disunity
1848, 9, 19. Wm. dis disunity
1865, 6, 20. Mary (form Sears) rpd mou

CROSBY
1842, 5, 24. Lydia (form Bauer) con mou

CURL
1834, 3, 25. Thos. Miller gct Center MM, to m Eliza Curl
1836, 2, 23. Lewis N. Miller gct Springfield MM, to m Rebecca Curl
1839, 4, 23. Catharine rocf Centre MM, dtd 1838,12,12
1841, 9, 21. Catharine Oglesby (form Curl) dis mou

DABNEY
1833, 1, 22. Julieta Pretlow, Caroline & Albert [Daboy], ch Edna, dec, recrq
1837, 2, 21. Caroline Hamilton (form Dabney) dis mou
1837, 12, 26. Albert gct Western Branch MM,Va.
1852, 7, 20. Albert dis owning slaves

DARLINGTON
1838, 6, 19. Richard, Benjamin & Sarah rocf Chester MM, Pa., dtd 1838,2,26
1838, 9, 25. Jesse Jr. rocf Chester MM, Pa., dtd 1838,7,30
1848, 2, 22. Richard dis disunity
1853, 2, 22. Benjamin dis mou
1856, 1, 22. Sarah Wade (form Darlington) dis mou

DAVIS
1840, 11, 25. Nathan, s Elisha & Alice, Henry Co., Ind.; m in Springborough, Mary H. STANTON, dt John & Michal, Dinwiddie Co., Va.

1841, 3, 23. Mary H. gct Spiceland MM, Ind.

DAWSON
1831, 3, 29. Isaack gct Caesars Creek MM

ELLIS
1847, 3, 23. Robert & w, Anna, & ch, Susanna, Seth, Jehu, Lydia Ann & Nancy, rocf Newberry MM, dtd 1847,2,15
1851, 1, 21. Seth dis joining Methodists
1851, 10, 21. Anna, w Robert, & ch, Lydia Ann Nancy Jane & Jehu, gct Back Creek MM, Ind.
1851, 10, 21. Susan gct Back Creek MM, Ind.
1854, 4, 25. Robert dis disunity

EVANS
1834, 2, 26. Thomas, s Benjamin & Hannah, Warren Co., O.; m in Springborough, Elizabeth M. ROBINSON, dt Wm. & Ann
1847, 11, 3. Isaac, s Thomas & Hannah, Warren Co., O.; m in Springborough, Anne S. BOONE, dt Arnold & Hannah, Warren Co., O.

1829, 3, 24. Amirah Haines dis jH
1834, 6, 24. Elizabeth M. gct Miami MM, O.
1836, 10, 25. Mary (form Haines) dis mou & jH
1848, 4, 25. Anna L. gct Miami MM

FIE
1854, 5, 23. July Ann (form Johnson) dis mou

FISHER
1826, 4, 25. Charles rocf South River MM, Va. dtd 1825,12,10, endorsed by Miami MM, 1826 3,29

FORRER
1835, 3, 24. Sarah rocf Allum Creek MM, dtd 1834,12,25

FOULKE
1857, 6, 23. Wm. Henry rocf Lower MM, Va., dtd 1857,4,25
1868, 8, 25. Wm. Henry dis mou

FRENCH
1872, 9, 24. Uriah rocf Miami MM, dtd 1872,7 [24

GARDNER
1834, 1, 21. Isaac rocf Hartland MM, N. J., dtd 1833,6,25

GARRETSON
1826, 4, 25. Ruth Anna m Joseph W. GRIEST
1829, 11, 5. Rhoda m James H. STANTON
1839, 9,26. Phebe m Joseph N. TAYLOR
1839, 12, 14. John d ae 70 (an elder)
1844, 5, 1. Lydia m Joshua BAILEY

1831, 4, 26. Rueben T. gct Miami MM, O., to m Sarah Hawkings
1831, 8, 30. Sarah rocf Miami MM, dtd 1831,7, 27
1833, 4, 23. Rueben T. & w, Sarah, gct Miami MM, O.

GAUKER
1849, 1, 23. Mary (form Calhoun) dis mou

GEBHART
1874, 4, 21. George recrq

GRIEST
1824, 12, 28. William m Lydia MILLER
1826, 4, 25. Joseph W. m Ruth Anna GARRETSON
1827, 3, 27. Anne m James BINFORD

1825, 5, 24. Joseph & w, Mary, & ch, Isaac, John, Amy, Mary & Micajah, rocf Center MM, dtd 1825,3,19
1825, 5, 24. Ann rocf Centre MM, dtd 1825,3, 19
1824, 4, 24. Joseph & w, Mary, gct White Lick MM, Ind.
1827, 4, 24. Joseph & w, Mary, & ch, Isaac, Amy, Mary & Micajah, gct White Lick MM, Ind.
1827, 9, 25. Wm. & w, Lydia, & ch, Susan & Edwin, gct White Lick MM, Ind.
1835, 4, 21. Joseph & w, Ruthanna, & ch, Rebecca Ann, Wm. P. & Mary Eliza, gct Sugar River MM, Ind.
1867, 5, 21. Ruth M. rocf Sugar River MM, Ind., dtd 1867,5,11
1872, 10, 22. Ruth M. gct Sugar River MM, Ind.

GRIFFIN
1855, 6, 19. Mary Jane rocf Lower MM, Va., dtd 1855,5,22

GRIFFITH
1846, 10, 20. Eli & w, Rachel, & s, Collins W., rocf Cincinnati MM
1848, 7, 25. Collins W. dis mou
1849, 4, 27. Eli & w, Rachel, gct White Water MM, Ind.

HADLEY
1848, 3, 22. Simon, s John & Lydia, Clinton Co., O.; m in Springborough, Mary O'NEAL, dt Jonathan & Mary INGHAM, Warren Co., O.
1856, 4, 2. John, s John & Lydia, Clinton Co., O.; m in Springborough, Rhoda STANTON, dt John & Rebecca, Warren Co., O.

1848, 12, 26. Mary T. gct Springfield MM
1856, 3, 25. John rocf Springfield MM, dtd 1856,3,15
1856, 5, 20. Rhoda G. & dt, Lydia G. Stanton, gct Springfield MM
1864, 6, 27. John & w, Rhoda G., & s, Seth, rocf Springfield MM, dtd 1864,6,18
1865, 10, 24. Henry rocf Springfield MM, dtd 1865,7,15
1866, 3, 20. Jonathan D. & w, Susannah, rocf Miami MM, dtd 1866,2,21
1866, 4, 24. Evan H. rocf Miami MM, dtd 1866, 3,21
1866, 9, 25. Henry con mou
1866, 9, 25. John F. Stanton gct West Union MM, Ind., to m Emma Hadley
1867, 9, 24. Mahlon C. & w, Emily C., & ch, Walter & Arthur E., rocf Springfield MM, dtd 1867,8,17
1870, 6, 21. Mahlon C. & w, Emily C., & ch, Walter & Arthur E., gct Springfield MM,O.
1871, 3, 21. James, s Evan, recrq
1871, 4, 25. Evan H. & ch, James E. & Cora L., gct Springfield MM
1871, 4, 25. Jonathan D. & w, Susan W., gct Springfield MM

HAINES
1828, 2, 26. Rachel m Isaac HASKET

1827, 8, 27. Rachel recrq
1829, 3, 24. John dis jH
1829, 3, 24. Sarah dis jH
1830, 5, 25. Susannah dis jH
1834, 2, 18. Charles dis jH
1834, 7, 22. Ann (form Mullin) dis mou & jH
1836, 10, 25. Mary Evans (form Haines) dis mou & jH
1840, 2, 18. Clark E. dis jH

HAMILTON
1837, 2, 21. Caroline (form Dabney) dis mou

HAMPTON
1836, 11, 22. Oliver & Eliza C., ch Chas., rocf Springfield MM, dtd 1836,9,13
1843, 2, 21. Eliza dis jas
1843, 3, 21. Oliver dis jas

HARE
1865, 9, 21. David, s Jesse & Marsha, Rush Co., Ind.; m in Springborough, Rhoda MILLER, dt Thomas & Elizabeth, Warren Co., O.

1859, 12, 20. Robert & w, Maria, & ch, David & Joseph, rocf Lower MM, Va., dtd 1859,11, 26
1866, 1, 23. David & w, Rhoda, gct Walnut Ridge MM, Ind.
1873, 4, 22. Christian & ch, Wm. H., Mary E., Elma E., Frances A. & Marcia J., rocf Lower MM, Va. (or Christianna)

HARPER
1831, 5, 24. Mary Ann & Sarah S., ch Daniel & Sarah S., rocf Woodberry MM, N. J., dtd 1831,8,31, endorsed by Miami MM, O., 1831, 4,27

HARRIS
1868, 9, 26. Wm. H. Sr. s William & Eliza, Warren Co., O.; m in Springborough, Mary H. MILLER, dt Joseph H. & Mary K., Warren Co., O.

1868, 2, 18. Wm. Henry rocf Lower MM, Va., dtd 1867,12,28

HARRIS, continued
1875, 3, 23. Wm. H. & w, Mary H., & ch, Anna E. & Edith R., gct Columbus MM, O.

HASKET
1828, 2, 26. Isaac m Rachel HAINES

1829, 12, 29. Isaac & s, Ner, rocf Miami MM, O., dtd 1829,11,25
1850, 5, 21. Ner dis mou
1851, 11, 25. Isaac [Haskett] & w, Rachel, & ch, Joel, Ann, Susannah & Mary, gct Miami MM

HATTON
1827, 5, 29. Rachel gct Cincinnati MM

HAWKINGS
1831, 4, 26. Rueben T. Garretson gct Miami MM, O., to m Sarah Hawkings

HINCHMAN
1843, 3, 21. Barclay [Henchman] rocf Dover MM, dtd 1842,9,15
1854, 8, 22. Barclay con mou
1855, 1, 23. Barclay gct Burlington MM, N.J.

HENRY
1828, 5, 27. Hannah, w Hugh, rocf Rhadnor MM, Pa., dtd 1828,4,10

HIBBERD
1825, 9, 27. Joseph & w, Rachel, & ch, Israel, Wm., Samuel, James, Elizabeth & Joseph, rocf Pipe Creek MM, dtd 1825,7,10
1825, 9, 27. Cert rec for Benjamin & w, Charity, & ch, Jane Sarah & Allice Ann, from Pipe Creek MM, dtd 1825,7,16, endorsed to White Water MM, Ind.
1827, 4, 24. James [Hibard], s Joseph, gct Hopewell MM, Va.
1829, 1, 27. Joseph [Hibbard] dis jH
1829, 2, 24. Rachel [Hibbard] dis jH
1830, 3, 30. Israel [Hibbard] dis jH
1831, 5, 24. Lydia, Mary Ann & Jesse, ch Jacob, rocf Clear Creek MM, dtd 1831,4,9
1839, 12, 24. Wm. dis mou
1850, 5, 21. Jesse dis mou
1850, 11, 19. Mary Ann dis disunity
1850, 11, 19. Lydia Shehan (form Hibbard) dis mou

HOBLET
1834, 3, 25. Lydia (form Sears) con mou

HORNER
1827, 2, 6. Ann d (an elder)

1827, 9, 25. David & w, Sarah, & ch, James, Geo., Anna, Levi, Margery, Henry, Ruth, Jacob & John, gct White Lick MM, Ind.
1827, 12, 25. Lydia & ch, David & Fannie, gct Caesars Creek MM
1829, 2, 24. Elizabeth gct Caesars Creek MM
1830, 8, 24. Thomas gct White Lick MM, Ind.
1834, 10, 21. Joseph & w, Miriam, & ch, Eber, Jeffrey, Newton, Mary, Ann, Eunice & Jonathan, gct Sugar River MM, Ind.
1835, 10, 20. John & w, Elizabeth, & ch, Amos C., gct Spiceland MM, Ind.
1835, 10, 20. Ann, Rebecca, Rachel, Sally & Lydia, dt John & Elizabeth, gct Spiceland MM, Ind.
1835, 10, 20. Samuel gct Spiceland MM, Ind.

HUGHES
1825, 8, 30. James, s John, gct Westfield MM
1825, 8, 30. Phebe gct Westfield MM
1827, 8, 28. John gct White Water MM, Ind., to m Hannah Cook
1830, 4, 27. John dis jH
1832, 2, 28. Eleanor, dt John, gct White Water MM, Ind.
1832, 3, 20. Hannah rocf New Garden MM, dtd 1831,11,24
1832, 3, 20. Gideon rocf New Garden MM, dtd 1831,12,22
1845, 5, 20. Chas. dis mou

HUNNICUTT
1827, 7, 24. Mary rocf Upper MM, Va., dtd 1827,4,24
1827, 9, 25. Cert rec for Elizabeth & fam from Upper MM, Va., dtd 1827,3,17, endorsed to Dover MM
1827, 10, 30. Mary gct Dover MM
1828, 6, 24. James & w, Delitha, rocf Upper MM, Va., dtd 1828,4,19
1828, 6, 24. Joshua B. & w, Eliza, & ch, Delitha Ann & James B., rocf Upper MM, Va., dtd 1828,4,19
1829, 10, 27. Cert rec for Wm. P. & w, Edna, & two ch roc,endorsed to Dover MM, O.
1830, 4, 27. John Peebles gct Dover MM, to m Mary Ann Hunnicutt
1839, 3, 26. James & w, Delitha, gct White Water MM, Ind.
1839, 3, 26. Joshua Bailey & ch, Delitha Ann, James Benj., Wm. Pearson & Mary Elizabeth, gct White Water MM, Ind.

INGHAM
1827, 3, 27. Mary m John Kelly O'NEAL

1826, 12, 26. Mary & niece, Anna Swain, rocf Fairfield MM, O.

JACKSON
1873, 4, 22. Sarah B. recrq

JANNEY
1853, 5, 11 Mary A. (form Johnson) dis mou

JOHNSON
1841, 6, 9. Edwin, s Micajah & Rebecca,

JOHNSON, Edwin, continued
Warren Co., O.; m in Springborough, Eliza D. STROUD, dt Chas. & Susan B., Warren Co., O.
1853, 8, 31. Brooks, s John & Judith, Warren Co., O.; m in Springfield, Mary P. STROUD, dt Charles & Susan B., Warren Co., O.

1828, 3, 25. James B. & w, Rhoda, & ch, Overton, Harriet W. & Martha, rocf Fairfield MM, dtd 1828,1,26
1828, 5, 27. Elijah & w, Elizabeth, rocf Fairfield MM, dtd 1828,1,26
1829, 1, 27. Rhoda dis jH
1829, 4, 28. James B. dis jH
1831, 10, 25. Elizabeth dis jH
1832, 2, 28. Overton, Harriett W. & Martha, ch James B. & Rhoda, gct Sugar Creek MM, Ind.
1838, 1, 23. Abijah & w, Elizabeth, rocf Miami MM, dtd 1837,12,27
1841, 11, 23. Abijah & w, Elizabeth, & ch, Sylvia & John G., gct Goshen MM
1842, 1, 25. Edwin rocf Miami MM, dtd 1841, 11,24
1842, 12, 20. Lydia B. rocf Centre MM, dtd 1842,11,10
1844, 10, 22. Edwin & w, Eliza, gct Miami MM, O.
1844, 10, 22. Larkin Foster, Mary Ann, Thos. Elwood, Wm. Lewis, Samuel Pleasant & Julia Ann, ch Thos. M. & Susannah, rocf Dover MM, dtd 1844,11,12
1849, 11, 20. Samuel rocf Dover MM, dtd 1849, 10,18
1851, 4, 22. Larkin dis mou
1853, 5, 11. Mary A. Janney (form Johnson) dis mou
1853, 7, 26. Thos. E. dis mou
1854, 5, 23. July Ann Fie (rorm Johnson) dis mou
1854, 12, 26. Samuel P. dis disunity
1855, 6, 19. Wm. L. rpd mou
1855, 7, 24. Brooks & w, Mary E., & ch, John Edward & Lucy B., gct Miami MM
1868, 4, 21. Wm. G. rocf Ash Grove MM, Ill.
1871, 8, 22. Wm. G. gct Sugar River MM, Ind.

JONES
1826, 7, 25. Isaac E. & w, Rachel B., & ch, Hannah B. & Bateman, gct White Water MM, Ind.
1836, 9, 20. Mary (form Miller) con mou
1837, 5, 23. Mary gct Sugar River MM, Ind.

KENWORTHY
1835, 10, 20. Amos & w, Mary, & ch, Wm., Robert, Jesse, Joel, Willis, Ann, Amos M. & Isaac F., gct Spiceland MM, Ind.
1865, 6, 25. Rachel rocf Redstone MM, Pa., dtd 1865,6,28
1875, 3, 23. Rachel gct Columbus MM, O.

KERSEY
1839, 10, 23. Vierling, s Wm. & Rachel, Henry Co., Ind.; m in Springborough, Mary Emily BUTLER, dt Micajah & Ann, Warren Co., O.

1840, 1, 21. Emily Butler gct Spiceland MM, Ind.

KING
1825, 1, 25. Dean rocf Miami MM, O., dtd 1824,7,28
1825, 2, 22. Mary E., John T. & Henry D., ch Thos. W. & Sally, recrq
1825, 4, 26. Whomas W. & w, Sally, & ch, Mary E., John T. & Henry D., gct White Water MM, Ind.
1825, 9, 27. Dean gct White Water MM, Ind.

LEEDS
1825, 5, 24. Warner M. & w, Elizabeth B., & ch, Anna, Wm. B. & Noah L., rocf White Water MM, Ind., dtd 1825,4,16
1827, 5, 29. Warner M. & w, Elizabeth B., & ch, Anna, Wm. B. & Noah, gct White Water MM, Ind.
1827, 9, 25. Anne L., w Noah, & ch, Letitia Craig, Vincent Augustus & Ann E., rocf Philadelphia MM, Pa., dtd 1827,7,26
1829, 3, 24. Letitia C. dis jH
1830, 5, 25. Ann dis jH
1832, 2, 28. Vincent Augustus, Ann C. & Wm., ch Noah & Ann, gct White Water MM, Ind.

LEVINGSTONE
1826, 7, 25. James rocf Elk MM, dtd 1826,5,6
1829, 3, 24. James dis jH

LIGHTFOOT
1829, 7, 28. Wm. rocf Short Creek MM, dtd 1829,1,20
1833, 12, 24. Wm. dis mou

LOWNS
1839, 3, 26. Elizabeth Ann, Wm. & Miriam, rocf Baltimore MM for E. & W. Dist.

LUPTON
1835, 1, 29. David W., s Joseph & Esther, Clinton Co., O.; m in Sugar Creek, Ann Miller, dt Solomon & Ruth, Montgomery Co., O.

1834, 7, 22. David W. rocf Hopewell MM, Va., dtd 1834,6,4
1835, 4, 21. Daniel & w, Ann, & Phebe Miller, minor dt Caleb & Phebe, dec, gct Sugar River MM, Ind.

LYNCH
1835, 1, 20. Edward & w, Mary, & ch, Sarah, Mary & Elizabeth Ann, rocf South River MM, Va., dtd 1834,11,6
1839, 6, 25. Edward & w, Mary, gct Cincin-

LYNCH, continued
nati MM
1839, 6, 25. Sarah & Mary Jr. gct Cincinnati MM

McCLELLEN
1829, 4, 28. John dis jH

McMELLEN
1829, 1, 27. Wm. dis jH

MATTHEWS
1826, 3, 29. Joel m Hannah NIXON

1826, 12, 26. Joel & w, Hannah, gct Green Plain MM, O.; returned 1828,4,19 do not reside in limits
1827, 7, 24. Susanna gct Milford MM, Ind.
1828, 4, 23. Joel & w, Hannah, & dt, Sarah, gct Elk MM; cert returned with information they had jH
1830, 11, 23. Joel & w, Hannah, dis jH
1832, 7, 24. Sarah & Samuel, ch Joel, gct Elk MM

MILLARD
1829, 12, 29. Catharine dis jH

MILLER
1824, 12, 28. Lydia m Wm. GRIEST
1835, 1, 29. Ann m David W. LUPTON
1844, 9, 26. Jane m John COX
1861, 4, 4. Susan m Isaac PEEBLE
1861, 8, 1. Ruth A. m Lindley M. ROGERS
1865, 9, 21. Rhoda m David HARE

1826, 10, 24. David & w, Elizabeth, & ch, Mariah, Hannah G., Sabina, Lydia & Rachel Jane, gct Redstone MM, Pa.
1832, 7, 24. Robert con mou
1832, 9, 25. Sarah (form Peebles) dis mou
1833, 1, 22. Robert gct Mill Creek MM
1833, 5, 21. Robert rocf Mill Creek MM, dtd 1833,4,16
1834, 2, 18. Robert gct Sugar River MM, Ind.
1834, 3, 25. Thos. gct Center MM, to m Eliza Curl
1835, 1, 20. Elizabeth rocf Center MM, dtd 1834,11,12
1835, 4, 21. Phebe, minor dt Caleb & Phebe, dec, gct Sugar River MM, Ind.
1836, 2, 23. Lewis N. gct Springfield MM, to m Rebecca Curl
1836, 9, 20. Mary Jones (form Miller) con mou
1836, 9, 20. Rebecca rocf Springfield MM, dtd 1836,8,16
1838, 2, 20. Lewis N. & w, Rebecca, & ch, Elias F., gct Sugar River MM, Ind.
1838, 2, 20. Wm. gct Sugar River MM, Ind.
1838, 2, 20. David gct Sugar River MM, Ind.
1841, 1, 26. Joseph H. gct Sugar River MM, Ind.
1842, 2, 22. Mary H. gct Spiceland MM, Ind.
1845, 1, 21. Dorcas rocf Springfield MM, dtd 1844,11,12
1845, 4, 22. Wm. R. rocf Sugar River MM, Ind., dtd 1845,1,25
1847, 2, 23. David H. & w, Mary W., rocf Sugar River MM, Ind., dtd 1846,12,26
1853, 7, 26. Lewis N. & w, Rebecca, & ch, Elias F., Ruth N., Hannah F., Mary K., Joseph & Thomas, rocf Springfield MM, dtd 1853,7,16
1857, 7, 21. John T. & w, Dorcas, & ch, Laura, Hiram, Horace, Florence & Ida, gct Honey Creek MM, Ia.
1858, 11, 22. Wm. R. gct New Garden MM, Ind.
1861, 5, 21. Elias dis mou
1865, 6, 25. Joseph H. & w, Rebecca, & dt, Mary H., rocf Redstone MM, Pa., dtd 1865, 6,28
1868, 1, 21. Solomon W. con mou
1868, 5, 26. Solomon W. gct Ash Grove MM, Ill
1868, 8, 25. Joseph, s Lewis N., rpd mou
1871, 2, 21. Solomon W. & w, Emma, rocf Ash Grove MM, Ill., dtd 1870,11,30
1874, 5, 26. Joseph H. & w, Rebecca G. gct Columbus MM, O.
1874, 9, 22. Emily & dt, Viola, rocf Miami MM, dtd 1874,8,26

MILLS
1827, 10, 30. Isaac & w, Catherine, & ch, Sarah, Eli, Samuel, Rowland R., Noah, Mary Ann & Joel T., gct Duck Creek MM, Ind.

MOFFITT
1852, 5, 25. Wm. E. Butler gct Miami MM, to m Rhoda A. Moffitt

MOORE
1862, 9, 4. Joseph, s John P. & Martha, Wayne Co., Ind.; m in Springborough, Deborah A. STANTON, dt Joseph & Catherine, Warren Co., O.
1869, 9, 1. Walter, s John P. & Martha, Washington Co., Ind.; m in Springborough, Lydia B. STANTON, dt Joseph & Catherine, Warren Co., O.

1862, 8, 26. Joseph rocf White Water MM, Ind., dtd 1862,7,23
1862, 12, 23. Deborah A. gct White Water MM, Ind.
1869, 8, 24. Walter rocf Blue River MM, Ind., to m Lydia B. Stanton
1869, 11, 13. Lydia B. gct Blue River MM, Ind.

MULLEN
1830, 7, 8. Ann m Jacob TAYLOR
1827, 4, 24. Wm. [Mullin] m Ann PEEBLES

1829, 3, 24. Christian [Mullin] gct Cherry Grove MM, Ind.
1829, 3, 24. Elizabeth & Ruth [Mullin] dis jH

MULLEN, continued
1829, 6, 23. Isaac dis jH
1829, 6, 23. Job dis jH
1830, 3, 30. Noah dis jH
1829, 4, 28. Aaron dis jH
1829, 4, 28. Lydia dis jH
1834, 5, 21. Nathan dis jH
1834, 7, 22. Ann Haines (form Mullin) dis mou & jH
1834, 7, 22. Maria Borton (form Mullin) dis mou & jH
1837, 11, 21. Jane Crachel (form Mullen) dis mou & jH
1839, 6, 25. Mary Ann dis
1840, 5, 26. Seth dis jH
1840, 5, 26. Lydia dis joining Separatists
1850, 7, 23. Jehu [Mullin] dis disunity

MUNDY
1834, 1, 21. Cert rec for Esther from Cincinnati MM, dtd 1833,10,17, endorsed to Mill Creek MM
1834, 5, 21. Cert for Esther returned to Cincinnati MM to which she has returned

NEAL
1825, 3, 29. Mary dis disunity

NEWBURN
1825, 5, 24. Amy recrq
1829, 3, 24. Amy [Newbern] dis jH
1829, 4, 28. John dis jH

NEWPORT
1837, 3, 21. Eunice Ann (form Chandler) dis mou & jH

NIXON
1826, 3, 29. Hannah m Joel MATTHEWS

1825, 5, 24. William & w, Martha, & ch, Mary, Susannah, Peninah, Martha Ann, Wm. & Anne, rocf Uwchlan MM, Pa., dtd 1824,5,6
1825, 5, 24. Hannah rocf Uwchland MM, Pa., dtd 1824,5,6
1825, 5, 24. Sarah rocf Uwchlan MM, Pa., dtd 1824,5,6
1826, 5, 26. Wm. & w, Martha, & ch, Mary, Susannah, Peninah, Martha Ann, Wm. & Anna, gct Miami MM
1826, 10, 24. Sarah gct Miami MM, O.
1826, 10, 24. Samuel rocf Uwchland MM, Pa., dtd 1826,5,4, endorsed to Miami MM, O.
1827, 4, 24. Samuel R. rocf Symons Creek MM, N. C., dtd 1827,3,17
1829, 10, 27. Samuel R. gct White Water MM, Ind.
1830, 9, 28. Samuel R. gct White Lick MM, Ind.

NORDYKE
1840, 5, 26. Stephen Peebles gct Clear Creek MM, to m Hannah Nordyke

OGLEBY
1841, 9, 21. Catharine (form Curl) dis mou

O'NEAL
1848, 3, 22. Mary m Simon HADLEY
1827, 3, 27. John Kelly m Mary INGRAM

1827, 6, 26. Mary & niece, Anna Swain, gct Miami MM, O.
1833, 1, 22. Mary rocf Miami MM, O., dtd 1832,12,26
1836, 5, 24. Matthias gct Springfield MM

PEACOCK
1826, 12, 26. Tacy (form Wilkerson) dis mou

PEDRICK
1833, 3, 26. Philip & w, Judith, rocf Chester MM, Ind., dtd 1832,11,21 [MM, Ind.
1834, 8, 26. Philip & w, Judith, gct Chester

PEEBLES
1830, 9, 2. Wm. S., s Stephen & Sarah, Warren Co., O.; m in Springborough, Mary Ann STANTON, dt James & Ann, Sussex Co., Va.
1827, 4, 24. Ann m Wm. MULLIN
1861, 4, 4. Isaac, s Wm. & Clarissa, Clinton Co., O.; m in Springborough, Susan MILLER, dt Thomas & Elizabeth, Warren Co., O.

1826, 4, 25. Samuel rocf Upper MM, Va., dtd 1825,10,19, endorsed by Short Creek MM, 1826,2,21
1826, 9, 26. Ann & Deborah rocf Upper MM, Va., dtd 1826,7,15
1826, 12, 26. Samuel gct White Water MM, Ind.
1827, 5, 29. Deborah gct White Water MM, Ind.
1827, 7, 24. John & w, Michal, & ch, Caroline & Lucy Ann, rocf Upper MM, Va., dtd 1827,3,17
1827, 7, 24. Elihu, John Jr. & Stephen rocf Upper MM, Va., dtd 1827,4,21
1827, 7, 24. Mary & Sarah Jr. rocf Upper MM, Va., dtd 1827,4,21
1827, 7, 24. Sarah Sr. rocf Upper MM, Va., dtd 1827,3,17
1827, 11, 27. Cert rec for Deborah & fam, Wm., Simmons, Martha & Susannah, from Upper MM, Va., endorsed to Stillwater MM, O.
1827, 12, 25. Wm. S. rocf Upper MM, Va., dtd 1827,9,15
1828, 1, 29. Lucy rocf Upper MM, Va., dtd 1827,10,20
1828, 4, 29. John & w, Michal, & ch, Caroline, Lucy Ann & Henrietta, gct Dover MM
1828, 6, 24. James rocf Upper MM, Va., dtd 1828,4,19
1828, 6, 24. Sarah H. rocf Upper MM, Va., dtd 1828,4,19
1828, 6, 24. Lucy gct White Water MM, Ind.
1828, 12, 30. Mary Reed (form Peebles) dis mou
1830, 4, 27. Sarah rocf White Water MM, Ind.,

PEEBLES, continued
dtd 1829,9,23
1830, 4, 27. John gct Dover MM, to m Mary Ann Hunnicutt
1831, 11, 29. Mary Ann rocf Dover MM, dtd 1831,11,17
1832, 7, 24. James L. gct Centre MM
1832, 9, 25. John & w, Mary Ann, gct Center MM
1832, 9, 25. Sarah Miller (form Peebles) dis mou
1832, 11, 20. Deborah rocf Miami MM, dtd 1832, 10,14
1833, 2, 19. Cert for James H. to Center MM, 7 Mo. 1832, returned as he has returned within limits of this mtg
1835, 2, 17. Sarah & Deborah gct Dover MM
1836, 1, 26. Deborah rocf Dover MM, dtd 1835, 11,19
1837, 10, 24. James H. dis mou
1840, 5, 26. Stephen gct Clear Creek MM, to m Hannah Nordyke
1840, 9, 22. Elihu gct Springfield MM, to m Mary Ann Rawls
1841, 2, 23. Hannah rocf Clear Creek MM, O., dtd 1840,12,22
1842, 5, 24. Elihu gct Springfield MM
1843, 8, 22. Elihu & w, Mary Ann, & ch, Sarah Ann, rocf Springfield MM, dtd 1843,4,11
1855, 11, 26. Elizabeth Ann Thomas (form Peebles) dis mou
1861, 6, 25. Susan M. gct Dover MM, O.
1865, 9, 19. Zalinda Sears (form Peebles) con mou

PENNELL
1826, 9, 26. Jonathan [Pennel] & w, Rosanna, & ch, Lewis M. & Mary Ann, rocf Cincinnati MM, dtd 1826,6,27
1828, 5, 27. James M. [Pennel] rocf Cincinnati MM, dtd 1828,3,27
1829, 1, 27. Eli dis mou & jH
1829, 6, 23. Rosanna dis jH
1832, 7, 24. James M. dis mou & jH

PENNINGTON
1826, 5, 26. Ann gct Milford MM, Ind.
1827, 5, 29. John & w, Eliza, & s, Robert, gct Cincinnati MM

PENROSE
1829, 3, 24. Mary dis jH
1829, 4, 28. Joseph dis jH

PICKEREL
1829, 8, 25. Jacob rocf Goshen MM, dtd 1829, 7,18
1832, 10, 13. Jacob gct Goshen MM

PINE
1825, 7, 26. Simeon rocf Hadonfield MM, dtd 1825,6,29
1829, 4, 28. Simeon dis jH

POTTS
1827, 7, 24. Samuel & w, Mary, & ch, Lindley & John, rocf Plainfield MM, dtd 1827, 5,24, endorsed by Miami MM
1829, 1, 27. Samuel & w, Mary, dis jH
1829, 3, 24. Lindley dis jH
1829, 3, 24. John dis jH

PRETLOW
1839, 1, 22. Elizabeth Ann & Julieta gct White Water MM, Ind.

RATCLIFF
1837, 9, 21. Elwood, s Isaac & Margaret, Jefferson Co., O.; m in Springborough, Martha J. ROBINSON, dt Wm. & Ann

1838, 2, 20. Martha J. gct Short Creek MM,O.

RAWLS
1840, 9, 22. Elihu Peebles gct Springfield MM, to m Mary Ann Rawls
1847, 10, 26. Sarah & ch, Esther, John, Jehu & Sarah Jane, rocf Walnut Ridge MM, dtd 1847,9,18
1850, 5, 21. Esther T., Jesse, John & Sarah Jane, ch Sarah, dec, gct Dover MM

REED
1828, 12, 30. Mary (form Peebles) dis mou

RICKS
1850, 8, 20. Margaret rocf Lower MM, Va., dtd 1850,7,26
1852, 7, 20. Margaret gct Short Creek MM, O.; returned 1853,6,21
1853, 7, 26. Margaret gct Lower MM, Va.

ROBBINS
1830, 3, 30. Bathsheba dis jH

ROBINSON
1834, 2, 26. Elizabeth M. m Thos. EVANS
1837, 9, 21. Martha J. m Elwood RATCLIFF

ROGERS
1861, 8, 1. Lindley, s Nathan & Atlantic, Fayette Co., Pa.; m in Springborough, Ruth A. MILLER, dt Thomas & Eliza, Warren Co., O.

1862, 6, 24. Lindley M. rocf Redstone MM, Pa., dtd 1862,6,4
1869, 11, 13. Mary K. gct Salem MM, O.
1871, 12, 26. Eli H. & w, Mary K., & dt, Charlotte A., rocf Salem MM, O.
1875, 8, 23. Eli H. & w, Mary K., & ch, Lettie A. & Nathan L., gct Rocksylvania MM, Ia.

SCOTT
1834, 5, 21. Ann rocf Western Branch MM, Va., dtd 1834,3,22
1839, 5, 21. Ann gct Center MM
1845, 2, 18. Ann Eliza, Wm. E. & John L., ch Wm. & Ann, gct Center MM

SEARS
1827, 11, 27. Cert rec for Paul & fam Maria, Lydia Ladd & John Gilliam, from Upper MM, Va., dtd 1827,9,15, endorsed to Stillwater MM, O.
1828, 5, 27. Paul & s, John G., rocf Stillwater MM, dtd 1828,4,26
1828, 5, 27. Maria & Lydia Ladd rocf Stillwater MM, dtd 1828,4,26
1833, 12, 24. Benj., Wm. & Samuel Chas. Creighton, gr ch Paul Sears, recrq
1834, 3, 25. Lydia Hoblet (form Sears) con mou
1836, 10, 25. Huldah rocf Somerset MM, O., dtd 1836,8,29
1837, 3, 21. Mary Ann recrq
1837, 5, 23. Samuel recrq
1838, 1, 23. John G. gct Goshen MM, to m Elizabeth L. Winder
1838, 6, 19. Elizabeth L. rocf Goshen MM, dtd 1838,5,18
1841, 10, 24. John G. & w, Elizabeth, & ch, Abner W. & Sarah Jane, gct Goshen MM
1850, 4, 23. David & w, Rachel, & ch, Rebecca Tabitha & Elva, rocf Miami MM, O., dtd 1850,3,27
1855, 9, 23. Rachel & ch, Rebecca, Tabitha, Elvira & Tilman, gct Red Cedar MM, Ia.
1856, 3, 25. David dis disunity
1865, 6, 20. Mary Creighton (form Sears) rpd mou
1865, 9, 19. Chas. con mou
1865, 9, 19. Zalinda (form Peebles) con mou

SHARP
1831, 3, 29. Mary Ann, Arthur, Abigail & Jemima, ch Haines, rocf Evesham MM, dtd 1831,1,7

SHEHAN
1850, 11, 19. Lydia (form Hubbard) dis mou

SILVER
1825, 1, 25. Samuel rocf Pilesgrove MM, N.J., dtd 1824,12,28
1827, 5, 29. Wm. & w, Rebecca, & ch, Wm. B., Joseph E., Horatio D. & Phebe, rocf Piles Grove MM, N. J., dtd 1827,3,27
1827, 5, 29. Martha Ann rocf Piles Grove MM, N. J., dtd 1827,3,27
1828, 1, 29. Samuel con mou
1828, 5, 27. Samuel gct Miami MM, O.
1829, 1, 27. Wm. & Rebecca dis jH
1829, 4, 28. Martha Ann dis jH
1830, 6, 29. Wm. B. dis jH
1836, 6, 21. Phebe Brown (form Silver) dis mou
1839, 8, 20. Horatio dis jH
1839, 12, 24. Joseph dis jH

SLEEPER
1834, 11, 25. Samuel & w, Patience, rocf Green Plain MM, O., dtd 1834,10,25
1836, 8, 23. Samuel & w, Patience, gct Sugar River MM, Ind.

SMITH
1829, 6, 23. Seth dis mou & joining Methodists
1834, 2, 18. Cert rec for Abraham & w, Ruth, & ch, Hannah & Amy, from White Lick MM, Pa., dtd 1833,11,20, endorsed to Sugar River MM, Ind.

SOMERS
1827, 9, 25. Eli rocf Piles Grove MM, N. J., dtd 1827,7,31
1829, 4, 28. Eli dis jH
1873, 4, 22. John & w, Ruth M., & ch, Lewis E., Ida, Ella, Emma & Laura, recrq

STANTON
1829, 11, 5. James H., s John & Michael, Warren Co., O.; m in Springborough MH, Rhoda GARRETSON, dt John & Rebecca, Warren Co., O.
1830, 9, 2. Mary Ann m Wm. S. PEEBLES
1837, 2, 1. Joseph, s John & Lydia, Warren Co., O.; m in Springborough, Catharine Ann STANTON, dt James & Ann, Warren Co.,O.
1840, 11, 25. Mary H. m Nathan DAVIS
1856, 4, 2. Rhoda m John HADLEY
1862, 9, 4. Deborah A. m Joseph MOORE
1869, 9, 1. Lydia B. m Walter MOORE
1874, 6, 3. Elizabeth M. m Chas. F. CHAPMAN

1826, 2, 21. James & w, Ann, & ch, Elizabeth M., Martha, Robinson, Benjamin C., Wm. R. Catharine Ann & Deborah Jane, rocf West Branch MM, Va., dtd 1825,12,31
1826, 2, 21. Mary, James & Robert, orphan ch John, rocf West Branch MM, Va., endorsed by Fairfield MM 1825,12,31
1826, 3, 28. Ann rocf Centre MM, dtd 1826,2,18
1826, 6, 27. Mary gct Miami MM, O.
1828, 6, 24. Jonathan & w, Almedia, & s, John A., rocf Upper MM, Va., dtd 1828,4,19
1828, 6, 24. Eliza, Edna, Deborah & Joseph, sisters & brother of Jonathan, rocf Upper MM, Va., dtd 1828,4,19
1829, 1, 27. Joseph & Mary dis jH
1829, 3, 24. Mary H. rocf Miami MM, O., dtd 1829,1,28
1829, 11, 24. Elwood & w, Mary, rocf Upper MM, Va., dtd 1829,10,17
1829, 11, 24. Chalkley rocf Upper MM, Va., dtd 1829,10,17
1829, 11, 24. Ann & ch, Mary Ann, James Ed-

STANTON, continued
win, Daniel Wm. & Thomas, rocf Upper MM, Va., dtd 1829,10,17
1830, 6, 29. Elwood dis mou
1830, 9, 28. Deborah dis mou
1831, 10, 25. Daniel gct Short Creek MM, to m Angelina Watkins
1832, 3, 20. Ann gct Center MM
1832, 5, 22. James E. gct Sugar River MM, Ind.
1832, 6, 19. Robert gct Cincinnati MM
1832, 11, 20. Angelina rocf Short Creek MM, dtd 1832,10,23
1832, 12, 25. Robert rocf Cincinnati MM, dtd 1832,9,20
1833, 12, 24. Joseph gct Sugar River MM, Ind.; returned 1834,3,25, because he still lived in limits of this mtg
1834, 5, 21. Wm. Cadwalader gct Miami MM, O., to m Mary L. Stanton
1834, 11, 25. Robert dis disunity
1834, 11, 25. Daniel & w, Angelina, & s, Samuel, gct Goshen MM
1836, 7, 26. Wm. R. gct Springfield MM, to m Mary Ruth Thatcher
1837, 2, 21. Ruth rocf Springfield MM, dtd 1837,1,17
1837, 10, 24. Wm. gct Springfield MM, to m Theodocia Thatcher
1838, 8, 21. Theodocia rocf Springfield MM, dtd 1838,6,12
1839, 1, 22. Almeda & ch, Joseph F., Oliver H. & Edna E., gct White Water MM, Ind.
1839, 3, 26. Wm. & w, Theodocia, gct Springfield MM
1841, 4, 20. Fredrick & w, Hannah, & ch, David, John, Edward & Charles F., rocf Miami MM, O., dtd 1841,3,24
1842, 6, 20. Chalkley gct Sugar River MM, Ind.
1842, 12, 20. Chalkley gct Sugar River MM, Ind., to m Ruth Ann Taylor
1843, 6, 20. Chalkley gct Sugar River MM, Ind.
1843, 8, 22. David gct White Water MM, Ind.
1843, 8, 22. Frederick & w, Hannah, & ch, John, Edward & Charles F., gct White Water MM, Ind.
1856, 5, 20. Rebecca M. gct Springfield MM
1856, 5, 20. Rhoda G. Hadley & dt, Lydia G. Stanton, gct Springfield MM
1858, 7, 20. Deborah J. gct Miami MM
1858, 12, 20. Benj. rpd mou
1864, 6, 27. Rebecca M. & Lydia G. rocf Springfield MM, dtd 1864,6,18
1866, 9, 25. John F. gct West Union MM, Ind., to m Emma Hadley
1867, 2, 19. John F. gct West Union MM, Ind.
1867, 8, 20. Wm. R. & w, Ruth, & ch, Virginia, Emeline & Anne D., gct Spring Creek MM. Ia.

STEWART
1833, 3, 26. Patience & ch, Caroline Ann, George W. & Daniel, rocf Allum Creek MM, dtd 1832,10,25

STOUT
1837, 2, 21. Jane (form Cadwalader) con mou
1837, 10, 24. Jane D. gct Springfield MM

STROUD
1841, 6, 9. Eliza D. m Edwin JOHNSON
1846, 4, 22. Sally Ann m Benj. H. WRIGHT
1847, 4, 28. Lydia B. m John T. BATEMAN
1853, 8, 31. Mary P. m Brooks JOHNSON

1835, 8, 25. Chas. & w, Susan B., & ch, Eliza D., Lydia B., Mary Paul, Sally Ann, George M., Eveline, Caroline & Edward B., rocf Stroudsburg MM, dtd 1835,7,2
1852, 9, 26. George M. dis joining Methodists
1854, 4, 25. Charles & w, Susan B., & ch, Evaline & Caroline, gct Goshen MM

SWAIN
1827, 6, 26. Mary O'Neal & niece, Anna Swain, gct Miami MM, O.

TAYLOR
1830, 7, 8. Jacob, s Isaac & Susannah, Clinton Co., O.; m in Springborough MH, Ann MULLIN, dt James & Sarah PREBLES, Sussex Co., Va.
1839, 9, 26. Joseph N., s Abijah & Mary, Tippecanoe Co., Ind.; m in Springborough MH, Phebe GARRETSON, dt John & Reb cca, Warren Co., O.

1825, 7, 26. Benjamin rocf Hopewell MM, Va., dtd 1825,4,7
1826, 10, 24. Mordica Jr. gct Miami MM, O.
1827, 4, 24. Jonathan rocf Hopewell MM, Va., dtd 1826,10,5, endorsed to Mill Creek MM
1829, 1, 27. Mordecai & Frances dis jH
1829, 3, 24. Benjamin dis jH
1829, 3, 24. Ambrose dis jH
1829, 3, 24. Ann dis jH
1829, 3, 24. Frances Jr. dis jH
1830, 8, 24. Ann gct Center MM
1831, 6, 28. Jacob & w, Ann, rocf Center MM, dtd 1831,6,15
1833, 2, 19. Abijah & w, Mary, & ch, Joseph N., Ruth & Abijah, gct Sugar River MM, Ind.
1829, 9, 24. Jacob, s Mordecai, dis disunity
1839, 12, 24. Phebe G. gct Sugar River MM, Ind.
1840, 5, 26. Sidwell dis jH
1840, 5, 26. Lewis dis jH
1840, 8, 25. Gulielma dis joining Separatists
1842, 12, 20. Chalkley Stanton gct Sugar River MM, Ind., to m Ruth Ann Taylor

THOMAS
1825, 11, 29. Hannah & ch, Phebe, Hiram, Abel, Hanson & Caroline, rocf Warrington MM, Pa., dtd 1824,12,22
1826, 6, 27. Jonah D. & w, Elizabeth, & ch, Emely, Alfred, Ira & Hannah, rocf Monal-

THOMAS, continued
len MM, Pa., dtd 1825,11,23
1829, 1, 27. Jonah D., Elizabeth, Hannah & Lydia dis jH
1829, 4, 28. Ann dis jH
1829, 5, 26. Phebe dis jH
1831, 11, 29. Isaac gct Cincinnati MM
1831, 12, 27. Rebecca M. & ch, Elmira, Chas. W. & Benjamin Franklin, rocf Baltimore MM E. & W. Dist., dtd 1831,10,6
1832, 5, 22. Hiram gct White Water MM, Ind.
1834, 3, 25. Isaac rocf Cincinnati MM, dtd 1834,2,13
1835, 11, 24. Rebecca R. rocf Birmingham MM, Pa., dtd 1835,4,1
1836, 5, 24. Rebecca H. & ch, Almira, Chas. W. Benj. Franklin, Albert & Isaac Hays, gct Miami MM, O.
1837, 3, 21. Emily Wright (form Thomas) dis mou & jH
1837, 8, 22. Rebecca H. & ch, Elmira, Chas. W., Benj. Franklin, Albert & Isaac Hays, rocf Miami MM, dtd 1837,7,26
1839, 4, 23. Rebecca H. & ch gct White Water MM, Ind.
1839, 5, 21. Hanson dis disunity
1839, 6, 25. Caroline dis jH
1839, 4, 23. Rebecca H. & ch, Elmira, Chas. W., Benj. F., Albert, Isaac H. & Howard D., gct White Water MM, Ind.
1841, 10, 24. Alfred dis disunity
1842, 3, 22. Hannah dis jH
1843, 9, 20. Rebecca H. & ch, Elmira, Charles W., Benj. F., Albert, Isaac H., Howard D. & Ellen, rocf Cincinnati MM
1849, 2, 20. Abner dis disunity
1855, 11, 26. Elizabeth Ann (form Peebles) dis mou

THOMPSON
1825, 3, 25. Lydia (form Bateman) dis mou
1834, 2, 18. Lydia B. recrq
1846, 8, 25. Lydia B. [Thomason] gct Miami MM
1856, 7, 22. Lydia B. rocf Goshen MM, dtd 1856,6,21

THORN
1839, 7, 23. Cert rec for Isaac & w, Hannah, from White Lick MM, Ind., dtd 1839,1,16, endorsed to Greenplain MM, O.

THORNBURG
1844, 7, 23. Eli [Thornburgh] & w, Sarah, & ch, Naomi P., Jemima & Dinah, rocf Centre MM, dtd 1844,5,15
1850, 1, 22. Eli dis disunity
1857, 6, 23. Sarah & ch, Naomi, Jamimy, Ann & James Brooks, gct West Union MM

THURSTON
1873, 1, 21. Amelia rocf Green Plain MM, O.
1874, 2, 17. Dora recrq

TIMBERLAKE
1836, 12, 28. John W., s Richard & Mary, Highland Co., O.; m in Springborough, Rachel BATEMAN, dt John & Hannah, Warren Co., O.

1837, 3, 21. Rachel B. gct Clear Creek MM

TOWNSEND
1829, 4, 28. Josiah dis jH
1835, 3, 24. Elizabeth rocf Cincinnati MM, dtd 1835,3,19
1850, 5, 21. Elizabeth gct Goshen MM

TROTTER
1833, 1, 22. Joshua & w, Ann B., & ch, Adaline, Eliza & Ann, rocf Western Branch MM, Va., dtd 1832,7,28; Eliza dec before cert rec
1838, 4, 21. Joshua dis disunity

THATCHER
1836, 7, 26. Wm. R. Stanton gct Springfield MM, to m Mary Ruth Thatcher
1837, 10, 24. Wm. Stanton gct Springfield MM, to m Theodocia Thatcher

WADE
1856, 1, 22. Sarah (form Darlington) dis mou

WALTHAL
1829, 11, 24. Francis & w, Sarah, rocf Upper MM, Va., dtd 1829,8,15

WATKINS
1831, 10, 25. Daniel Stanton gct Short Creek MM, to m Angelina Watkins

WAY
1825, 9, 27. Robert & w, Abigail, & dt, Marianne, gct Green Plain MM, O.

WEBSTER
1824, 10, 26. Mary recrq
1830, 9, 28. Mary dis jH

WELDING
1833, 3, 26. Emily rocf WD MM, dtd 1833,2,13
1836, 9, 20. Alice rocf Stroudsburg MM, dtd 1836,6,23
1837, 5, 23. Emily [Welling] gct WD MM
1843, 4, 25. Alice Brower (form Welding) con mou

WILKERSON
1825, 7, 26. Elizabeth [Wilkinson] & ch, Tacy, Aaron & Rachel, rocf Fairfax MM, Va., dtd 1823,10,15, endorsed by Allum Creek MM, to Miami MM 1825,3,31 & by Miami MM to this 1825,6,29
1826, 12, 26. Tacy Peacock (form Wilkerson) dis mou

1832, 1, 24. Rachel dis jH

WILKERSON, continued
1834, 10, 31. Aaron dis mou

WILLETS
1829, 6, 23. Mary (form Cole) dis mcd & jH

WILLIAMS
1825, 9, 27. Clark & w, Mary, & ch, Cyrus M. & Wm., gct White Water MM, Ind.

WILLIS
1825, 1, 26. Elijah m Rachel WILSON

1825, 5, 24. Rachel gct Green Plain MM, O.
1829, 1, 27. Elijah C. dis jH

WILSON
1825, 1, 26. Rachel m Elijah WILLIS

1824, 10, 26. George con mou
1829, 1, 27. Jesse & Elizabeth dis jH
1829, 4, 28. George & Mary dis jH
1830, 1, 26. Israel dis mou
1836, 2, 23. Enoch dis mou & jH
1839, 7, 23. Aaron dis jH

WINDER
1833, 1, 22. James [Windows] rocf Fairfield MM, dtd 1832,11,22
1835, 9, 22. James gct Fairfield MM
1838, 1, 23. John G. Sears gct Goshen MM, to m Elizabeth L. Winder

WOOD
1854, 5, 23. Joshua Bailey gct Allum Creek MM, to m Sarah E. Wood

WRIGHT
1846, 4, 22. Benj. H., s Benjamin & Hannah, Belmont Co., O.; m in Springborough, Sally Ann STROUD, dt Charles & Susan, Warren Co., O.

1829, 2, 24. Ann dis jH
1829, 7, 28. Mary dis jH
1829, 7, 28. Hannah dis jH
1829, 7, 28. Aaron dis jH
1829, 8, 25. Jonathan dis jH
1829, 8, 25. Mahlon dis jH
1831, 8, 30. Josiah dis jH
1837, 3, 21. Emily (form Thomas) dis mou & jH
1846, 7, 21. Sally Ann gct Short Creek MM, O.

* * * * * * *

ANTRAM
----, --, --. James & Hannah
Ch: Edward b 1865, 11, 26
----- after 1868

BAILEY
----, --, --. Joshua & Lydia C.
Ch: Rebecca
Louisa b 1845, 9, 4[bur Springboro
Wm. Reubin" 1850, 9, 28 d 1850,10, 1
1829, 11, 22. Deborah d ae 34y 3m 26d bur Springboro
1850, 10, 3. Lydia C. d ae 37y 6m 19d bur Springboro
1857, 5, 19. Sarah E. d ae 32y 9m 23d bur Springboro (a minister)

BAINES
1869, 2, 26. Isaac d ae 80 bur Springboro
1875, 3, 3. Sarah d ae 85y 9m bur Springboro

BATEMAN
1838, 6, 23. Joel d ac 29y 4m 7d bur Springboro
1845, 9, 15. John d ae 66y 5m 4d bur Springboro (an elder)
----, --, --. John & Lydia
Ch: Mary Ann b 1848, 2, 29 Warren Co.,O.
1854, 10, 22. Deborah d ae 78y 2m 8d bur Springboro (an elder)

BROWN
----, --, --. Samuel & Elizabeth
Ch: Evan H. b 1862, 5, 25
John
Franklin " 1865, 5, 1

BUTLER
1837, 5, 20. Wyke H. d ae 23y 10m 9d bur Springboro
----, --, --. Wm. E. & Rhoda J.
Ch: Mary Emily b 1840, 12, 23
John
Pearson " 1842, 6, 20
Anselm J. " Salem, Henry Co., Iowa
1843, 5, 26. Rhoda J. d ae 22y 8m 14d bur Waynesville, O.
1851, 1, 12. Ann d ae 73y 1m 6d bur Springboro
1854, 3, 17. Micajah d ae 97y 8m 12d bur Springboro
1867, 6, 10. Moriah d ae 77y 7m 13d bur Springboro

CHRIST
----, --, --. Joseph W. & Ruthanna
Ch: William R. b 1827, 5, 13 d 1830, 9, 4 bur Springboro
Rebecca Ann
b 1829, 8, 8
William P. " 1831, 10, 21

CREIGHTON
----, --, --. William & Mary
Ch: Frank C. b 1867, 4, 12
Fanny Z. " 1869, 9, 30
1866, 12, 14. Mary Ann d ae 4m 21d

1866, 2, --. Mary con mou (m first cousin)

GARRETSON
1839, 12, 14. John d ae 69y 7m 17d
1846, 11, 4. Rebecca d ae 72y 8m 27d bur Springboro (an elder)

GRIEST
1872, 10, 22. Ruth M. gct Sugar River MM

HADLEY
----, --, --. Henry & Henrietta
Ch: Teston b 1867, 1, 29
1872, 9, 29. Rhoda G. d ae 61y 20d (d at Sac & Fox Agency, Indian Territory)

HAINES
1837, 6, 15. Susanna d ae 64y 1m 10d bur Sugar Creek

HARE
1872, 6, 14. Robert d ae 60y 11m 3d bur Springboro

HARRIS
----, --, --. William H. & Mary
Ch: Edith R. b 1872, 5, 26
Anna E.

HASKET
----, --, --. Isaac & Rachel
Ch: Ner b 1828, 11, 14
Thomas " 1830, 8, 21
Joel " 1833, 6, 18
Ann " 1836, 2, 6
Susannah " 1838, 6, 13
Mary " 1846, 4, 11

HENRY
1848, 3, 31. Hannah d ae 64y 14d Springboro

HOBLET
1868, 11, 11. Lydia d ae 70y 10m 14d bur Springboro

HORNER
----, --, --. Joseph & Miriam
Ch: Eber b 1818, 2, 21
Everette " 1819, 6, 12 d 1829, 8,25 bur Sugar Creek
Jeffery b 1821, 12, 27
Newton " 1823, 10, 22
Mary " 1825, 11, 22
Ann " 1828, 10, 25

HUNNICUTT
----, --, --. Joshua B. & Eliza
Ch: William P. b 1828, 10, 5
Mary E. " 1833, 6, 19
1836, 3, 19. Eliza d ae 34y 11m 20d bur Springboro

JACKSON
1873, 4, 22. Sarah Bell recrq

JENNINGS
1863, 6, 11. Job d ae 75y bur near Rehobeth (an elder)

JOHNSON
----, --, --. Abijah & Elizabeth B.
Ch: Sylvia B. b 1839, 6, 8
John Kelley" 1841, 8, 22
----, --, --. Brooks & Lydia B.
Ch: John Edward b 1844, 4, 4
Lucy B. " 1850, 12, 28
1850, 12, 28. Lydia B. d ae 28y 7m 11d bur Waynesville
1852, 10, 29. Samuel d ae 91y 8m 12d bur Seneca, Clinton Co., O.

1868, 4, 21. Wm. G., minor, rocf Ash Grove MM, Ill., dtd 1868,2,15
1871, 8, 22. Wm. G. gct Sugar River MM, Ind.

KENWORTHY
----, --, --. Amos & Mary
Ch: William b 1816, 1, 19
Robert " 1819, 2, 5
Jesse " 1822, 8, 6
Joel " 1824, 9, 11
Willis " 1826, 8, 25
Ann " 1828, 9, 4
Amos M. " 1831, 6, 17
Isaac F. " 1834, 1, 28

LYNCH
1848, 3, 11. Charity d ae 68 bur Hamilton, Butler Co., O. "Copied from the Western Friend"

MILLER
----, --, --. Thomas & Eliza
Ch: Ruth b 1835, 1, 23
Susanna " 1838, 3, 30
Solomon " 1839, 12, 13
Rhoda " 1846, 1, 6
Samuel " 1849, 7, 17
----, --, --. Lewis N. & Rebecca
Ch: Elias F. b 1837, 4, 20 Montgomery Co., O.
Eliza " 1854, 11, 7 Warren Co., O.
----, --, --. John & Dorcus
Ch: Laura b 1846, 9, 11
Amanda " 1848, 7, 12 d 1849, 8,19 bur Springboro
Hiram b 1850, 4, 21
Florence " 1851, 6, 21
Horace G. " 1853, 7, 22
Ida " 1856, 6, 1
1863, 7, 24. Ruth d ae 85 bur Springboro
1864, 8, 24. Solomon d ae 85 bur Springboro

1868, 11, 24. Louisa con mcd
1869, 11, 23. Mary K. Rogers (form Miller) con mcd

PEEBLES
----, --, --. William & Mary Ann
Ch: Elizabeth
A. b 1831, 6, 29
Richard " 1834, 7, 25
Marcia L. " 1836, 7, 14 d 1843, 1,26 bur Springboro
William T. b 1840, 5, 12 " 1841, 6,21 bur Springboro
Julia E. b 1842, 9, 13 " 1846, 2,24 bur Springboro
Louisa Ann b 1844, 11, 8
1836, 6, 1. Deborah d ae 42y 11m 13d bur Springboro
----, --, --. Steven & Hannah
Ch: Amanda b 1841, 6, 11 d 1841, 7,25 bur Springboro
Zalinda b 1842, 7, 20
Charity H. " 1844, 3, 1
Adaline " 1846, 5, 18 d 1846, 8, 7 bur Springboro
----, --, --. Elihu & Mary Ann
Ch: Nathaniel b 1843, 6, 21 d 1843, 7,25
Emaline " 1844, 10, 16 " 1849, 2,21 bur Springboro
Micajah b 1848, 1, 2 " 1849, 8, 3 bur Springboro
1847, 1, 29. Hannah d ae 24y 2m 3d
1849, 8, 23. Mary Ann d ae 31y 7m 12d
1855, 1, 18. Sarah Ann d ae 13y 2m 3d bur Springboro
1859, 10, 14. Wm. S. d ae 63y 21d bur Springboro
1865, 5, 9. Richard S. d ae 36y 7m 14d bur Springboro
1869, 3, 7. Elihu d ae 75y 10m 6d bur Springboro
1875, 3, 25. Stephen d

RAWLS
1849, 10, 20. Sarah d ae 57y 4m bur Center

ROGERS
----, --, --. Eli & Mary
Ch: ----- Charlotte b 1872, 5, 26

1869, 11, 23. Mary K. (form Miller) con mcd
1871, 12, 26. Eli H. & w, Mary K., & ch, Charlotte, rocf Salem MM, O.
1875, 8, 24. Eli H. & w, Mary K., & ch, Lottie A. & Nathan H., gct Rocksylvania MM, Ia.

SCOTT
----, --, --. Wm. J. & Ann
Ch: Ann Eliza b 1832, 9, 13
Wm. Exum " 1835, 10, 23
Mary Virginia " 1835, 10, 23 d in infancy
John Lawrence " 1838, 6, 9
Louisa " 1841, 3, 9

SEARS
----, --, --. Samuel & Mary Ann
Ch: William
Penn b 1838, 3, 21 d 1842, 5,13 bur Sugar Creek
Mary Ann b 1840, 2, 20
Charles W. " 1842, 10, 24
Martha " 1844, 10, 7 d 1847, 1,12 bur Sugar Creek
----, --, --. John C. & Elizabeth
Ch: Abner
Winslow b 1839, 10, 15
Sarah Jane " 1841, 7, 17
1839, 4, 4. Hulda d ae 66y 4m 12d bur Springboro
1841, 4, 14. Paul d ae 72y 4m bur Springboro
1841, 12, 21. Mariah d ae 41y 5m 12d bur Springboro
1867, 11, 17. Samuel d ae 71y 4d bur Sugar Creek

SHARP
1845, 7, 25. James d ae 86y 1m 27d bur Sugar Creek

SILVER
1839, 12, 31. Patience d ae 68 bur Springboro

STANTON
----, --, --. Jonathan & Almeda
Ch: John
Oliver b 1827, 12, 26 Dinwiddy Co., Va.
Joseph
Fleming " 1830, 9, 16 Warren Co., O.
Oliver
Henry " 1833, 3, 19
Julia " 1835, 11, 10 d 1836, 6, 7 bur Springboro
Edna E. b 1837, 6, 24
1829, 7, 21. John Oliver d bur Springboro
----, --, --. James H. d 1845,10,2 ae 38y 9m 17d bur Springboro; m Rhoda -----
Ch: Rebecca M. b 1833, 11, 21 d 1875, 7,14 ae 41y 7m 23d bur Springboro
John W. b 1841, 12, 13 d 1842, 5,17 ae 5m 4d bur Springboro
Lydia C. b 1843, 7, 17
1837, 3, 28. Jonathan d ae 36y 4m 12d bur Gravelly Run, Va.
----, --, --. Wm. R. & Ruth
Ch: Benjamin b 1837, 9, 8
David T. " 1839, 6, 9
Alfred " 1841, 7, 27
Virginia
Ann " 1843, 12, 24
Emaline " 1850, 4, --
Ann L. " in Illinois
----, --, --. Joseph & Catharine Ann
Ch: Deborah
Ann b 1837, 10, 8
Lydia B. " 1839, 4, 21

STANTON, Joseph & Catharine Ann, continued
Ch: John Flemming b 1841, 2, 11
James Albert " 1842, 11, 4
Elizabeth M. " 1845, 3, 11
Thomas Elwood " 1847, 2, 5
Martha Ann " 1850, 2, 4 d 1851, 9, 7
Mary E. " 1852, 3, 17
William E. " 1854, 3, 11
Ellen " 1856, 2, 19
Walter " 1859, 7, 3

1837, 7, 2. Edna d ae 29y 5m 2d bur Springborough
1841, 5, 30. Elizabeth d ae 42y 5m 21d bur Springborough
1839, 6, 30. Mary d ae 59y 1m 12d bur Springborough
1843, 6, 17. Elwood d ae 38y 11m 26d bur Springborough
1844, 5, 22. Ann d ae 60y 10m 18d bur Springborough
1849, 4, 7. Thomas N d ae 30y 9m 2d bur Springborough
1849, 12, 9. Benjamin C. d ae 41y 11m 17d bur Madison City, Ill.
1852, 1, 3. James d ae 72y 5m 17d bur Mt. Pleasant, Jefferson Co., O. (an elder)
1854, 9, 17. Ann d ae 76y 6m 14d bur Springboro
1864, 9, 12. James A. d ae 27y bur Springboro

STROUD
1838, 6, 15. Edward B. d ae 3y 2m 16d bur Springboro

* * * * * * *

SEARS
----, --, --. David & Rachel
Ch: Tilman b 1853, 7, 7

TAYLOR
1827, 4, 22. Abijah, s Abijah & Mary, Montgomery Co., O., b
1830, 7, 7. John Ambrose d ae 14y 10m 9d bur Sugar Creek
1848, 9, 15. Ann d ae 67y 8m 1d bur Springboro
1849, 5, 2. Jacob d ae 87y 4m 1d bur Springboro

THORNBURG
----, --, --. Eli & Sarah
Ch: James Brooks b 1845, 1, 22
1844, 9, 10. Dinah P. d ae 1y 1m 9d bur Springboro

THURSTON
1873, 1, 21. Amelia rocf Green Plain MM, O.
1874, 2, 17. Dora recrq

TROTTER
----, --, --. Joshua & Ann B.
Ch: Emily b 1832, 4, 30
William " 1834, 9, 2 d 1835, 9,20 bur Springboro
Wm. Benjamin b 1836, 12, 2
1832, 11, 6. Eliza d ae 4y 11m 23d bur Springboro
1837, 11, 8. Ann B. d ae 11m 6d bur Springboro

WALTHALL
1837, 3, 9. Francis d ae 50y 9m 4d bur Springboro
1851, 3, 31. Sarah d ae 73y 4m 10d bur Springboro

VAN WERT MONTHLY MEETING

Van Wert Monthly Meeting, in Van Wert County, was set off from Union Monthly Meeting and established by West Branch Quarterly Meeting 5 Mo. 25, 1875. It belongs to Indiana Yearly Meeting and is a part of Van Wert Quarterly Meeting. Minutes 1915 to 1924 have been lost by fire.

Among the charter members, William B. Wallace was clerk, and Huldah Gaskel assistant clerk. Nancy Day, Enoch Hogeland, Mary Crank and John Kesler were overseers. The elders were Rachel Brackney, Elizabeth Sears, Jackson Cronk, James Pope, Lucretia Jackson and Richard Masters.

RECORDS

ACHERMAN
1907, 3, 28. Isaiah recrq

ADAMS
1877, 2, 24. Levi, Mary Ann, Elma & Mattie recrq
1877, 10, 27. Hattie relrq
1877, 11, 24. Abner recrq
1878, 3, 30. Alma relrq
1878, 4, 27. Levi relrq
1884, 2, 23. Jessie recrq
1886, 9, 25. Mary Ann dropped from mbrp
1908, 7, 30. Margaret dropped from mbrp

ADDISON
1878, 5, 25. John E. & Rachel M. [Adison] recrq
1879, 3, 29. Mary recrq
1880, 3, 27. Mary relrq
1880, 10, 30. Clyde & Eveline Pearl recrq

AGIE
1879, 1, 25. Maggie recrq
1884, 2, 23. Oliver recrq

ALBRIGHT
1897, 8, 28. M. dropped from mbrp
1909, 1, 28. Lulu recrq

ALDRICK
1897, 8, 28. Chas. dropped from mbrp

ALLEN
1876, 2, 26. Willie recrq
1876, 3, 25. Smith & w, Rebecca, recrq
1886, 2, 27. Chas. L., Laura & Myrtle recrq
1886, 3, 27. Emma recrq
1886, 9, 25. Rebecca dropped from mbrp
1887, 2, 26. Kittie recrq
1890, 9, 27. Chas. dropped from mbrp
1892, 5, 28. Laura relrq
1894, 3, 31. Eva O. recrq
1895, 4, 27. Chas. & Laura E. recrq
1896, 5, 30. Laura relrq
1896, 7, 25. Chas. dis disunity
1899, 7, 27. Myrtie dropped from mbrp
1899, 7, 27. Eva dropped from mbrp
1899, 7, 27. Emma dropped from mbrp
1903, 1, 29. Lora recrq
1905, 2, 23. Dayt recrq
1908, 7, 30. Diyt dropped from mbrp
1926, 2, 25. Chester recrq
1930, 6, 26. Elmer dropped from mbrp

ALLINGHAM
1915, 3, 31. Richard & Sarah recrq

ALTHA
1897, 8, 28. John B. dropped from mbrp
1898, 10, 27. Wm. & Sarah dropped from mbrp
1899, 5, 25. Ada [Atha] recrq

AMBLER
1884, 2, 23. Mahala recrq

AMBROSE
1891, 4, 25. Wm. recrq

ANCHURTZ
1878, 2, 23. Chas. & Ellen recrq
1879, 6, 28. Chas. [Anschurts] dis disunity
1878, 3, 30. Mary [Annshutis] recrq

ANDERSON
1879, 3, 29. Minerva J. & Alexander J. recrq
1879, 4, 26. Elizabeth recrq
1880, 1, 31. Joseph J. recrq
1880, 1, 31. Sue recrq
1882, 4, 29. Joseph J. & Sue recrq
1899, 7, 27. Elizabeth dropped from mbrp
1907, 1, 5. John W. recrq

ANDREWS
1877, 12, 29. Wm., Ann Eliza & Edwin Z. recrq
1880, 1, 31. Rachel A. recrq
1880, 1, 31. John E. recrq
1886, 9, 25. Rachel dropped from mbrp

ANESWORTH
1912, 2, 29. Bell recrq

ANSON
1879, 5, 31. Ellsworth relrq
1890, 11, 29. Icy relrq

ARGO
1880, 1, 31. Eva recrq

ARMSTRONG
1877, 12, 29. George recrq
1878, 2, 23. Geo. relrq
1886, 2, 27. Mary recrq
1887, 2, 26. Frank & Mary recrq
1895, 8, 31. Mary E. relrq
1900, 7, 26. Frank & w, Mary, & ch dropped from mbrp
1902, 2, 21. Mary relrq
1903, 4, 26. Layfiett & Malinda recrq

ARNOLD
1877, 12, 29. John, Lydia Ann & Hannah recrq
1885, 10, 31. John dis disunity
1885, 12, 30. John rst
1901, 1, 31. Francis recrq
1901, 7, 25. J. H., Mary J. & Jennie dropped from mbrp

ASH
1897, 4, 24. Barrett recrq

ATHY
1879, 10, 25. Andrew J. & Jennie recrq
1889, 2, 23. Rosa [Athey] recrq

ATLEY
1908, 7, 30. Ada dropped from mbrp

ATKINSON
1907, 2, 28. Thadeus recrq

BABB
1914, 12, 30. Ralph Gregory recrq
1914, 12, 30. Florence Bell recrq

BACON
1886, 5, 29. Perry C. recrq
1903, 9, 24. Pary dropped from mbrp

BAGLEY
1876, 4, 29. Urilla recrq
1877, 5, 26. Urilla relrq

BAER
1878, 2, 23. John A. [Bear] recrq
1878, 4, 27. John C., Samuel, Eliza & Elijah [Bear] recrq
1878, 4, 27. Jacob & Mary [Bear] recrq
1879, 10, 25. Hettie & Jacob [Bair] recrq
1880, 1, 31. Mary E. [Bear] recrq
1892, 5, 28. Thomas & Jennie relrq
1899, 7, 27. Samuel [Bear] dropped from mbrp
1899, 7, 27. Mary E. & Rachel [Bair] dropped from mbrp
1928, 2, 23. Wesley, Lendal & Lilas recrq
1928, 2, 23. Altey & Minnie May recrq
1928, 2, 23. Mary, Kenneth L., Wm. E. & Martha L. recrq
1928, 2, 23. Richard L. & Ruth Ellen recrq
1929, 12, 26. Reta Jane recrq
1930, 1, 30. Pearl Dean recrq
1932, 3, 31. Paul Harold recrq

BAILEY
1882, 2, 25. Martha recrq
1882, 11, 25. Rhoda recrq
1888, 5, 26. Harrison & Jane recrq
1897, 8, 28. Emma dropped from mbrp

BAKER
1878, 4, 27. Emanuel & Elmira recrq
1878, 4, 27. Maggie recrq
1878, 6, 29. Henry & Ophelia recrq
1878, 12, 28. Riley recrq
1880, 1, 31. Rachel recrq
1880, 1, 31. Andrew D. recrq
1881, 1, 29. Wm. recrq
1881, 1, 29. Samuel recrq
1881, 1, 29. Siddie recrq
1881, 2, 26. Mary & Enoch N. recrq
1890, 3, 26. Wm. dropped from mbrp
1891, 3, 28. Joseph M., May Ollie & Jennie recrq
1896, 2, 29. Martha recrq
1897, 8, 28. Annie dropped from mbrp
1897, 8, 28. John dropped from mbrp
1898, 8, 25. Riley, Ida & Bessie recrq

1898, 4, 27. Maggie recrq
1899, 7, 27. Riley & Leta dropped from mbrp
1899, 7, 27. Mattie dropped from mbrp
1901, 6, 27. Edna & Jesse recrq
1901, 7, 25. Bessie dropped from mbrp
1911, 2, 23. Miriam recrq

BALDWIN
1878, 4, 27. Alva, Elmore & Lennie recrq
1878, 4, 27. David recrq
1886, 5, 29. Richard [Baulden] recrq
1897, 8, 28. Richard [Bauldin] dropped from mbrp

BALL
1881, 2, 26. Jeremiah recrq
1894, 3, 31. W. E. recrq
1901, 1, 31. Albert recrq
1903, 9, 24. W. C. dropped from mbrp
1912, 4, 25. Gertrude, M. E. & Pauline recrq
1914, 4, 29. N. E. dropped from mbrp

BALTZELL
1887, 11, 26. L. A. recrq
1887, 12, 31. Benjamin recrq
1892, 5, 28. Benjamin & Lydia [Ballszell] relrq
1892, 9, 24. Benjamin & Lydia [Ballazell] recrq
1912, 4, 25. Alta & Bessie recrq

BALYEAT
1894, 2, 24. Addie recrq
1897, 2, 27. Ida relrq
1901, 1, 31. Mable & Olive recrq
1907, 2, 28. Mollie recrq
1914, 4, 29. Adie dropped from mbrp

BANKS
1887, 3, 26. John L. & Edward O. recrq

BANNING
1879, 12, 27. Alpheus recrq
1879, 12, 27. Mary J. recrq
1882, 4, 29. Alpheus & Mary recrq

BARBER
1903, 1, 26. Witsey recrq

BARFELL
1894, 2, 24. Thomas & Sadie recrq
1903, 9, 24. Thomas & w, Sarah, & ch dropped from mbrp

BARKER
1907, 3, 28. Ida recrq

BARKER, continued
1909, 7, 30. Ida dropped from mbrp
1928, 2, 23. Ida Ethel recrq

BARR
1907, 3, 28. Mary E. recrq

BARRET
1897, 4, 24. Daisy recrq
1899, 7, 27. Daisie dropped from mbrp

BARTLETT
1881, 3, 26. George recrq
1886, 9, 25. George dropped from mbrp

BARTON
1878, 5, 25. George recrq
1880, 1, 31. Sarah L. recrq
1880, 1, 31. Hannah recrq

BASS
1881, 2, 26. Mary E. recrq
1881, 2, 26. James & Clara recrq

BATES
1891, 4, 25. Jane recrq
1899, 7, 27. Lulu dropped from mbrp
1907, 3, 28. Alfred & Mauda recrq
1928, 2, 23. Alfred recrq
1928, 2, 23. Maudie recrq

BAUGHMAN
1878, 12, 28. Andrew & w, Mariah, relrq

BAXTER
1884, 12, 22. B. F. recrq
1886, 5, 29. Catharine recrq
1894, 6, 30. Nancy C. & dt, Hattie, recrq
1896, 2, 29. Alonzo recrq
1897, 8, 28. B. F. dropped from mbrp
1909, 4, 29. Alonzo Baxter dropped from mbrp
1913, 12, 25. Glen Baxter recrq

BAXTON
1886, 11, 27. Sarah S. dropped from mbrp

BEADLEY
1901, 1, 31. Flora Dell recrq

BEAMER
1884, 11, 29. Geo. & Caroline recrq
1886, 5, 29. Wm. recrq
1886, 12, 25. Wm. relrq
1888, 7, 28. George & Caroline recrq

BEASTON
1897, 8, 28. Frank dropped from mbrp
1897, 8, 28. Amanda dropped from mbrp

BEATY
1898, 3, 31. Levi R. & Kate recrq
1905, 2, 23. Jay recrq
1908, 7, 30. Jay [Beatty] dropped from mbrp

BEAVER
1889, 10, 26. Lucinda recrq
1891, 2, 28. John & A. J. recrq

BEAVO
1886, 4, 24. Joseph, Eliza & Minnie recrq

BECHTOL
1905, 2, 23. John & Lizzy recrq
1905, 2, 23. Israel V. recrq
1908, 7, 30. Lizzie dropped from mbrp
1908, 7, 30. John dropped from mbrp
1908, 7, 30. Israel dropped from mbrp
1912, 4, 25. Stella & Louise recrq
1914, 10, 28. Estella & Louise recrq

BECK
1884, 11, 29. James recrq
1886, 12, 25. James relrq
1891, 4, 25. John D. recrq
1893, 4, 29. John D. relrq
1903, 9, 24. John recrq

BECKNER
1898, 3, 31. Augusta recrq

BEER
1877, 2, 24. Rachel recrq
1878, 2, 23. Charley [Behur] recrq

BELL
1900, 12, 19. Gladys May b
1905, 5, 2. Wilbur Harold b
1906, 10, 16. Harry Gaylord b
1906, 9, 4. Richard Clifford b
1910, 5, 5. LaDoyt Versile b

1884, 2, 23. Richard E. recrq
1890, 3, 26. Samuel recrq
1891, 3, 28. Jennie & Lottie recrq
1899, 4, 27. R. E., Wesley Glen, Lester L. & Ines, recrq
1899, 4, 27. Grace recrq
1903, 1, 29. Sam & Belle recrq
1911, 2, 23. Gladis recrq
1912, 2, 29. Mary recrq
1912, 5, 30. Lura recrq
1914, 4, 29. Glenn dropped from mbrp
1927, 1, 27. Marquis E., Matilda & Virginia recrq
1930, 1, 30. Pearl Dean recrq

BELLIS
1884, 12, 22. Mariah recrq
1899, 7, 27. Mary [Belas] dropped from mbrp

BELTZ
1878, 4, 27. Lewis recrq
1886, 11, 27. Levi dropped from mbrp

BENNETT
1884, 12, 22. Marget M. & Samuel H. [Bennit] recrq

BENNETT, continued
1889, 2, 23. Samuel [Bennet] recrq
1897, 8, 28. Remus E. dropped from mbrp
1898, 10, 27. Christena dropped from mbrp
1905, 2, 23. Mary Etta dropped from mbrp

BERGNER
1890, 3,26. Nettie recrq

BERKSHIRE
1891, 6, 27. Hannah R. recrq

BERRY
1886, 2, 27. Frank & Libbie recrq
1888, 9, 29. Frank & Libby dis disunity

BEVER
1891, 4, 25. John & Lucinda recrq

BEVERHAMMER
1891, 4, 25. A. J. recrq

BICKEL
1888, 6, 30. Anna M. recrq
1891, 8, 29. Denard W. Fassett & w, Eliza, & ch, Annie M. Bickel, gct Amboy MM, Ind.
1897, 8, 28. Annie [Bicker] dropped from mbrp

BICKNER
1899, 7, 27. Augustus dropped from mbrp

BIGHAM
1908, 7, 30. Wm. & Vora dropped from mbrp

BIGLOW
1879, 3, 29. Sarah recrq

BISHON
1878, 4, 27. Margaret recrq

BLACK
1899, 7, 27. Ella dropped from mbrp
1909, 4, 29. Ella dropped from mbrp
1912, 4, 25. Percilla L. recrq
1914, 4, 29. Percilla Lucile dropped from mbrp
1914, 12, 30. Pearl recrq

BLAKE
1909, 4, 29. O. Jary recrq

BLOSSER
1879, 11, 29. Lizzie recrq

BLOSSOM
1881, 2, 26. Electa recrq

BLOWVELT
1880, 1, 31. Rhoda M. recrq
1899, 7, 27. Rhoda M. [Blovit] dropped from mbrp

BOBBETT
1882, 10, 28. Wm. H. & Marinda [Bobbet] recrq
1892, 8, 27. Hattie & Bessie recrq
1899, 7, 27. Hattie & Bessie dropped from mbrp

BOHAM
1896, 1, 25. John & Charity recrq
1899, 7, 27. John & Charity dropped from mbrp
1901, 4, 25. Lewis & Bell recrq
1902, 5, 29. Lewis & Bell dropped from mbrp
1911, 4, 27. Sada recrq
1912, 4, 25. Effie recrq

BOLINGER
1900, 1, 25. Della recrq

BOLLOCK
1911, 4, 27. Josie recrq

BOLTWOOD
1878, 4, 27. Richard recrq

BOND
1909, 12, 30. Parvin rocf Walnut Ridge MM, Ind.
1913, 11, 1. Parvin W. gct Dublin MM, Ind.

BONNELL
1885, 1, 31. Loretta recrq
1886, 5, 29. John recrq
1897, 8, 28. Lona dropped from mbrp
1897, 8, 28. Maggie dropped from mbrp
1897, 8, 28. John, Loretta & Eliza dropped from mbrp

BOOHER
1878, 2, 23. James [Booker] recrq
1882, 1, 28. Ella recrq
1886, 3, 27. Elizabeth recrq
1886, 3, 27. Emma, Elsie & Bessie recrq
1886, 5, 29. Wm. recrq
1886, 10, 30. Robert dropped from mbrp
1888, 10, 27. Bessie & Sarah E. dropped from mbrp
1889, 5, 30. Chas. recrq
1895, 5, 25. Chas. recrq
1897, 8, 28. Albert dropped from mbrp
1897, 8, 28. Chas. dropped from mbrp

BOROFF
1877, 12, 29. Mattie [Boriff] recrq
1894, 3, 31. Allie recrq
1897, 3, 27. Ollie recrq
1897, 6, 26. Viola relrq

BORING
1898, 10, 27. H. H. & Samantha dropped from mbrp

BORLAND
1903, 9, 24. Rachel dropped from mbrp

BOWERS
1886, 2, 27. James & Susan recrq
1887, 6, 25. Precila recrq
1899, 7, 27. Priscilla dropped from mbrp

BOWMAN
1894, 2, 24. Hattie recrq
1899, 7, 27. Hattie dropped from mbrp

BOYD
1897, 4, 24. A. C. recrq
1899, 7, 27. A. C. dropped from mbrp
1900, 1, 25. A. C. rst
1903, 9, 24. A. C. dropped from mbrp
1912, 4, 25. Harold & Lester recrq
1926, 2, 25. Gaylord & Nellie recrq
1927, 3, 30. Robert R., Walter E., Lois E. & Harold J. recrq
1927, 4, 28. Nellie recrq
1927, 4, 28. Cora recrq
1932, 3, 31. Helen recrq

BOYER
1880, 1, 31. Samuel recrq
1880, 1, 31. Jacob recrq
1880, 1, 31. Louisa recrq
1880, 1, 31. Adex recrq
1882, 9, 30. Alexander [Bohyer] relrq
1883, 2, 24. Jesse & Lydia recrq
1885, 4, 25. Samuel & Louisa dropped from mbrp
1885, 4, 25. Jacob dropped from mbrp
1895, 6, 29. Samuel [Buoyer] recrq
1896, 2, 29. Samuel & Phoeba [Buoyer] recrq
1899, 7, 27. Samuel & Phebe dropped from mbrp
1914, 4, 29. Jessie & Mary dropped from mbrp

BRADLEY
1908, 7, 30. Flora D. dropped from mbrp

BRADSHAW
1891, 2, 28. Benjamin & Mary recrq

BRANAM
1884, 11, 29. Wesley, Allice, Montesco, Nancha, John P., Wm. A., Ellsworth, Wesley E., recrq
1897, 8, 28. Monteto dropped from mbrp
1897, 8, 28. Wm. dropped from mbrp
1897, 8, 28. John P. dropped from mbrp
1897, 8, "8. Ellsworth dropped from mbrp
1897, 8, 28. Wesley E. dropped from mbrp

BRANDENBERG
1927, 5 25. Elsie dropped from mbrp

BREEDING
1879, 3, 29. Ida recrq

BRESLER
1877, 12, 29. George [Bressler] recrq
1878, 1, 26. Elizabeth [Brestler] recrq
1879, 12, 27. Geo. dis disunity
1882, 2, 25. Ellen recrq
1884, 2, 23. Flora recrq
1886, 2, 27. Mary, Marion, Emma, Chas. & Annie [Bressler] recrq
1888, 2, 25. Andrew recrq
1891, 10, 31. S. M. & Emma J. relrq
1892, 3, 26. Chas. & Minnie [Bressler] relrq
1899, 7, 27. Andrew dropped from mbrp
1903, 9, 24. Mable dropped from mbrp
1905, 2, 23. Geo. & Nancy recrq
1914, 4, 29. Nancy [Bressler] dropped from mbrp

BRICKENHOOF
1899, 7, 27. Mary dropped from mbrp

BRIGGS
1879, 12, 27. George recrq
1879, 12, 27. Stanton recrq
1883, 10, 27. Callie [Brigs] recrq
1890, 3, 26. Callie [Brigs] dropped from mbrp

BRIGHAM
1893, 3, 25. Wm. recrq

BRIGHTON
1889, 3, 30. Hiram recrq
1892, 4, 30. Hiram relrq

BRODERICK
1894, 5, 26. Mary recrq
1899, 7, 27. Mary dropped from mbrp

BROWN
1878, 4, 27. Otilla recrq
1878, 4, 27. Edward recrq
1882, 1, 28. Bannona recrq
1886, 5, 29. John F. & Sarah E. recrq
1887, 3, 26. Lillie recrq
1894, 2, 24. Eli & Phebe rocf Elk MM, O., dtd 1894,1,25
1897, 8, 28. Martha dropped from mbrp
1903, 9, 24. John & Sarah dropped from mbrp
1933, 11, 30. A. E. & w, Esther, recrq
1933, 11, 30. Alva & Malcolm recrq

BRULING
1894, 2, 24. Zella recrq
1899, 7, 27. Zella dropped from mbrp

BUCHER
1879, 1, 25. Sarah recrq

BUCK
1879, 12, 27. Lottie recrq

BUCKLES
1878, 1, 26. Dora Royce [Buckels] recrq
1886, 2, 27. Caroline recrq
1890, 3, 26. Dora dropped from mbrp
1892, 2, 27. Caroline relrq
1892, 12, 31. Caroline recrq
1897, 1, 30. Nellie recrq
1898, 3, 31. Caroline dropped from mbrp

BUCKMAN
1881, 2, 26. Geo. W. recrq

BUDD
1883, 12, 29. David recrq
1884, 2, 23. Ida [Rudd] recrq
1894, 2, 24. Polly recrq
1905, 2, 23. Orley recrq

BUHER
1882, 2, 25. Robert recrq

BURCAW
1891, 3, 28. W. L. & Lenora recrq
1897, 6, 26. W. L. & w dropped from mbrp
1911, 4, 27. Sarah A. recrq (d before recorded)
1911, 4, 27. Allen A., Eva & Norma recrq

BURDEN
1905, 2, 23. Mary recrq
1908, 7, 30. Mary dropped from mbrp

BURGNER
1881, 2, 26. Caroline recrq
1882, 3, 25. Jacob recrq
1883, 10, 27. Mary M. recrq
1883, 12, 29. Mary [Bergner] recrq
1892, 2, 27. Jacob relrq
1892, 2, 27. Caroline relrq
1892, 2, 27. M---- relrq
1914, 4, 29. Caroline dropped from mbrp
1914, 4, 29. Mary M. dropped from mbrp
1914, 4, 29. Nettie dropped from mbrp

BURGOINE
1878, 4, 27. Susanna recrq

BURK
1890, 3, 26. Mary recrq
1894, 2, 24. Harry recrq
1899, 7, 27. Mary dropped from mbrp
1914, 4, 29. Mary dropped from mbrp
1914, 4, 29. Harry dropped from mbrp

BURRIS
1891, 2, 28. Ollie recrq
1891, 2, 28. Nettie recrq

BUSH
1878, 4, 27. Wm. recrq
1886, 9, 25. Wm. dropped from mbrp

BUSICK
1886, 2, 27. Wm. & Catherine recrq

BUTLER
1882, 9, 30. Levi R. recrq
1890, 3, 26. L. R. dropped from mbrp
1908, 3, 26. Bert & w, Bertha, & ch, Harvey & Lawrence L., recrq
1812, 4, 25. John & w recrq

BUTNER
1886, 12, 25. Ida relrq

BYRON
1879, 12, 27. Enos recrq

CADWALADER
1878, 4, 27. Aaron & Julia recrq

CAHILL
1878, 1, 26. Sarah recrq
1878, 1, 26. Hiram recrq
1886, 11, 27. Hiram [Kahill] dropped from mbrp

CALENDINE
1912, 4, 25. J. H. & w, Sarah, & ch, Edna & Laurence, recrq

CALLFLOWER
1886, 2, 27. Mary J. [Calfbower] recrq
1886, 3, 27. Florence recrq

CAMP
1879, 10, 25. John W. & Martha recrq
1880, 1, 31. Benjamin recrq
1880, 3, 27. Susan recrq
1884, 11, 29. John dis disunity
1891, 4, 25. John Wm. & Emma recrq
1903, 9, 24. Susan & Emma dropped from mbrp

CAMPBELL
1876, 3, 25. Anna [Cambell] recrq
1878, 2, 23. Libbie & John recrq
1888, 2, 25. Wm. recrq
1908, 7, 30. Chas. dropped from mbrp
1909, 4, 29. Roy recrq
1912, 4, 25. Rexford & Maud recrq
1912, 10, 30. Dora Parker relrq
1915, 2, 24. Maud relrq
1927, 5, 25. Fred & Alice dropped from mbrp

CAPANANA
1899, 7, 27. Ema dropped from mbrp

CARBAUGH
1885, 1, 31. Mary recrq

CARLE
1901, 4, 25. Mary Etta recrq

CARPENTER
1885, 3, 28. Samuel recrq
1887, 7, 30. Samuel relrq

CARR
1911, 4, 27. Lenora recrq

CARTER
1876, 4, 29. Sarah & Elizabeth recrq

CARTER, continued
1877, 12, 29. Milton recrq
1880, 2, 28. Allie recrq
1892, 2, 27. Elizabeth relrq
1892, 2, 27. Milton & Allie relrq
1895, 4, 27. Milton & Alice recrq
1897, 4, 24. Wm., Clarence & Blanche recrq
1905, 2, 23. Milten & Allie dropped from mbrp
1905, 2, 23. Harvey dropped from mbrp
1909, 4, 29. Clarence recrq
1912, 4, 25. McKinley recrq

CARY
1903, 1, 29. Harry & Lucinda recrq
1905, 2, 23. Avis recrq

CASHNER
1879, 12, 27. John recrq

CASTLE
1914, 10, 28. Wm. dropped from mbrp

CAVE
1877, 2, 24. John recrq
1878, 2, 23. John relrq
1905, 2, 23. Boyd recrq

CHAMBERLAIN
1894, 2, 24. James D. recrq
1899, 7, 27. James dropped from mbrp

CHAMBERS
1899, 1, 26. Lewis recrq
1903, 9, 24. Lewis dropped from mbrp
1911, 2, 23. Winnie A. recrq
1911, 2, 23. Raymond recrq
1911, 3, 30. Floyd & Earl recrq
1913, 4, 24. Abbie & Fred recrq

CHANDLER
1886, 2, 27. Sue recrq

CHENOWETH
1881, 2, 26. John recrq

CHUBB
1877, 2, 24. Nanna recrq

CLAPPER
1878, 11, 30. Emmanuel recrq
1912, 4, 25. Raymond recrq

CLARK
1878, 4, 27. Anna recrq
1886, 2, 27. C. P. recrq
1912, 4, 25. Geo. & ch, Velma, Mildred, Lucile & Walter, recrq

CLEMENS
1878, 4, 27. Leroy [Clemons] recrq
1880, 10, 30. Claudie & Clarence recrq
1888, 5, 26. John C. [Clements] recrq
1888, 12, 29. L. S. & w rocf Middlepoint MM
1893, 2, 25. Ella Murphy rocf Newberry MM, dtd 1892,11,27
1897, 11, 27. Leroy S. & w, Ellen, & s, Claude, gct Wilmington MM, O.
1899, 7, 27. Thos. & John dropped from mbrp

CLEVENGER
1878, 6, 29. Martha recrq
1878, 8, 31. James N. recrq

CLINGER
1880, 1, 31. Daniel C. recrq
1880, 1, 31. Sarah Ann recrq
1888, 6, 30. Julia recrq
1907, 3, 28. Chas. Frederick & Gertrude recrq

CLUTTER
1878, 4, 27. Mary recrq
1878, 12, 28. John recrq
1878, 12, 28. Andrew J. recrq

COATE
1885, 5, 30. Robert, Jemima & Gula May roc
1887, 3, 26. Robert [Coats] & w, Mima, & Gula, gct West Branch MM, O.

COIL
1894, 3, 31. Jesse recrq
1899, 7, 27. Jessie dropped from mbrp
1915, 2, 24. Joseph relrq

COKNOUR
1884, 1, 26. Mary E. recrq

COLE
1880, 1, 31. Elizabeth recrq

COLEMAN
1896, 11, 28. John Miller recrq
1901, 3, 28. Naomi J. recrq
1903, 9, 24. John dropped from mbrp

COLLERS
1886, 11, 27. Elizabeth dropped from mbrp

COLLETT
1882, 2, 25. Wm. R. recrq

COLLINS
1877, 3, 31. Isaac N., Franklin, Mary E., Annie & Lavine, recrq
1877, 6, 30. Louisa recrq
1877, 11, 24. Louisa recrq
1878, 1, 26. Daniel W. recrq
1879, 1, 25. John & Sophia recrq
1879, 1, 25. Andrew recrq
1880, 1, 31. Willis I. recrq
1881, 2, 26. Jasper recrq
1881, 3, 26. Gibson recrq
1882, 1, 28. Emma recrq
1884, 2, 23. Andrew recrq
1884, 2, 23. Perry recrq

COLLINS, continued
1897, 1, 30. Josie, Etta & Nora recrq
1902, 7, 31. Florence recrq
1903, 1, 29. Ruby recrq
1907, 2, 28. Nellie recrq
1908, 3, 26. Floyd L. & Walter D. recrq
1909, 6, 25. Minda relrq
1911, 4, 27. Agnes & Elmer recrq
1914, 10, 28. Walter dropped from mbrp
1927, 7, 29. Andrew dropped from mbrp
1927, 9, 29. Etta dropped from mbrp

CONWELL
1907, 1, 5. Elmer recrq
1908, 3, 26. Ora Isaac & Clyde Walter recrq

COOK
1889, 5, 30. Levina recrq
1889, 5, 30. James recrq
1897, 8, 28. Lavina dropped from mbrp
1897, 8, 28. James dropped from mbrp
1897, 8, 28. Geo. W. dropped from mbrp
1897, 8, 28. Noah dropped from mbrp
1897, 8, 28. Alice dropped from mbrp

COOKSEY
1895, 5, 25. Obediah & Clara recrq
1897, 8, 28. Obediah dropped from mbrp
1897, 8, 28. Carrie dropped from mbrp

COON
1877, 2, 24. John H. [Coone] recrq
1877, 12, 29. John H. recrq
1878, 1, 26. Harriet recrq
1878, 1, 26. Jesse [Kuhn] recrq
1878, 4, 27. Wm. & Lillie [Cones] recrq
1878, 4, 27. Phebe [Cones] recrq
1880, 3, 27. Austin [Koon] recrq

COOPER
1928, 2, 23. Carl Thadeous recrq

COPEMAN
1888, 2, 25. Emma recrq

CORATHERS
1886, 2, 27. Phillip C. [Carothers] recrq
1890, 11, 29. C. P. [Crothers] dis disunity
1891, 3, 28. John L. [Crothers] recrq
1894, 2, 24. Philip C., Edward & Julia [Crothers] recrq
1894, 2, 24. Orlie [Crothers] recrq
1896, 8, 29. Ellen [Carothers] relrq
1899, 4, 27. J. L. & Mary recrq
1899, 7, 27. Harley & J. L. dropped from mbrp
1899, 7, 27. Hattie dropped from mbrp
1905, 4, 27. Lemuel & w, Mary, recrq
1912, 4, 25. H. W.[Carothers] & w recrq
1912, 4, 25. L. C. [Carothers] & w recrq
1881, 2, 26. Lemuel & Delilah recrq
1881, 2, 26. Philip C. [Charathers] recrq
1888, 5, 26. Wilbert R. & Ellen recrq

CORDELL
1904, 4, 28. Geo. W. recrq

CORK
1897, 8, 28. Isaiah dropped from mbrp

CORNWELL
1896, 5, 30. Walter recrq

CORY
1908, 7, 30. Henry & Lucinda dropped from mbrp

COTTEREILL
1897, 5, 29. Grace recrq

COUNSELOR
1889, 5, 30. Frank recrq
1897, 8, 28. Frank [Counseller] dropped from mbrp

COVERDALE
1880, 1, 31. Mary N. recrq
1880, 1, 31. Nancy recrq
1880, 5, 29. Nannie recrq

COX
1913, 2, 27. Walter recrq
1913, 2, 27. Celia recrq

CRABTREE
1889, 3, 30. Hattie recrq
1894, 3, 31. Jerry recrq
1899, 7, 27. Jerry dropped from mbrp
1907, 3, 28. Howard A. & Alice F. recrq
1910, 5, 27. Lottie recrq

CRAIG
1878, 1, 26. Maggie recrq
1880, 1, 31. Isabelle recrq
1880, 1, 31. Florence recrq
1880, 1, 31. Rome C. recrq
1884, 2, 23. Maggie recrq
1886, 2, 27. Joseph recrq
1888, 2, 25. Florence, Rome & James recrq
1890, 3, 26. Jos. dropped from mbrp
1890, 10, 25. Jerome dropped from mbrp
1891, 4, 25. Florence relrq
1897, 1, 30. Frank recrq
1897, 12, 30. Franklin & Margaret A. gct Friends Chapel MM
1903, 10, 29. Frank & Margaret rocf Friend's Chaepl MM, dtd 1903,9,19
1908, 7, 30. Walter dropped from mbrp
1914, 12, 30. Wm. recrq
1926, 10, 28. Frank & Margaret recrq
1928, 4, 28. Margaret recrq

CRANSTON
1880, 1, 31. Nancy A. recrq

CRATES
1894, 2, 24. Deck recrq

CRATES, continued
1905, 2, 23. Clifford recrq

CRAUSE
1912, 4, 25. Alpha & Mary recrq

CRAVEN
1879, 12, 27. Minnie recrq
1881, 3, 26. Minnie relrq

CRAWFORD
1878, 4, 27. John M. & Amelia M. recrq
1878, 6, 29. Francis recrq

CRIDER
1890, 3, 26. Joseph M., John F. & Mary L. recrq
1890, 3, 26. John dropped from mbrp

CRONE
1880, 1, 31. Eliza recrq
1880, 1, 31. Wm. recrq
1909, 1, 28. Peter recrq

CROUSE
1934, 1, 25. Lola, Alpha & Patricia Ann recrq

CROW
1878, 4, 27. Huldah recrq
1878, 4, 27. James & Sarah recrq
1884, 2, 23. Julia recrq
1886, 9, 25. James dropped from mbrp
1886, 9, 25. Julia dropped from mbrp
1891, 3, 28. Garner & Manirva recrq
1891, 3, 28. Cora recrq
1895, 4, 27. Franklin Pierce & Ellen recrq
1901, 3, 28. Bertha A. recrq
1908, 7, 30. Chester Arthur & w, Enola, recrq
1915, 4, 28. Bertha Morrison relrq

CROWDER
1882, 11, 25. James recrq
1883, 10, 27. John recrq

CUPP
1877, 12, 29. Manda recrq

CURTIS
1879, 12, 27. James recrq
1879, 12, 27. Eliza recrq

CUSTER
1891, 3, 28. Ida recrq
1899, 7, 27. Ida dropped from mbrp

DAGER
1888, 4, 28. Frederick recrq
1897, 8, 28. Frederick & Calisty dropped from mbrp

DAGUE
1877, 3, 31. Samuel recrq
1877, 6, 30. Samuel relrq

DALLON
1886, 2, 27. Thos. recrq

DANHERT
1882, 1, 28. Wm. recrq
1892, 4, 30. Elizabeth E. [Dankert] recrq
1899, 7, 27. Wm. [Danbert] dropped from mbrp

DANNER
1880, 9, 25. Mamie relrq
1912, 4, 25. Rose [Daning] & ch, Frank & Russel, recrq

DANNISON
1811, 4, 27. Sam recrq

DANSEL
1879, 12, 27. Annie recrq

DARING
1878, 2, 23. Martin recrq
1880, 3, 27. Tilman recrq

DAUGLER
1878, 11, 30. James C. recrq

DAUKIRT
1877, 2, 24. Elizabeth & John recrq

DAVIS
1878, 4, 27. Wm. recrq
1878, 5, 25. James recrq
1879, 6, 28. Priscilla recrq
1879, 12, 27. Jacob recrq
1879, 12, 27. Samuel recrq
1880, 1, 31. James recrq
1880, 3, 27. Geo. W. & Wm. H. recrq
1880, 10, 30. Harry C., Wm. E. & Eva Emeline recrq
1880, 12, 25. Chas. & Mary Jane recrq
1881, 1, 29. Ida recrq
1882, 9, 30. James relrq
1885, 4, 25. Ida dropped from mbrp
1886, 3, 27. George recrq
1895, 1, 26. James recrq
1899, 7, 27. Geo. & Ella dropped from mbrp
1900, 1, 25. Franklin recrq
1900, 3, 29. James B. & Lucy A. relrq
1903, 9, 24. Alice dropped from mbrp
1904, 7, 28. Sherman S. & w, Lulu, relrq
1905, 2, 23. Fred recrq
1910, 3, 31. Mrs. Rebecca Hildebrand recrq
1913, 2, 27. May recrq
1913, 2, 27. Floyd recrq
1914, 10, 28. Libbie & Olive dropped from mbrp

DEALEY
1928, 2, 23. Junita & Kermit recrq
1928, 2, 23. Fay Virra recrq
1932, 3, 31. Lenore recrq

DEARTH
1888, 11, 24. Susan recrq

DEARTH, continued
1899, 7, 27. Susan dropped from mbrp

DECAMP
1878, 11, 30. Lissie recrq
1880, 1, 31. Wm. recrq

DECKER
1889, 2, 23. Wm. & Amanda recrq
1891, 2, 28. Henry recrq
1891, 4, 25. Richard C. recrq
1897, 3, 27. Wm. E. & Ida recrq
1897, 8, 28. Willia A. dropped from mbrp

DEERING
1894, 4, 28. Lucius recrq
1899, 7, 27. Celissa dropped from mbrp
1929, 12, 26. Clara S. recrq

DEFFIELD
1907, 4, 25. Wilma recrq

DELONG
1898, 8, 25. Bert recrq
1899, 7, 27. Bert dropped from mbrp

DEMAN
1880, 3, 27. Nancy J. relrq

DEMINT
1877, 2, 24. Jesse & Lydian recrq
1877, 2, 24. Susan recrq
1877, 3, 31. John & Marthie recrq
1880, 3, 27. Emma recrq
1884, 2, 23. Martha recrq
1884, 2, 23. John recrq
1891, 3, 28. Lucy recrq
1894, 2, 24. Frank [DeMint] recrq
1894, 6, 30. Clara recrq
1899, 7, 27. Frank dropped from mbrp
1899, 10, 26. John A. relrq
1901, 3, 28. Sherman recrq
1903, 7, 30. Merlle recrq
1903, 9, 24. Clara & Clarence dropped from mbrp
1907, 2, 28. Golda recrq
1913, 4, 24. Sherman & w, Drusella, recrq
1913, 4, 24. Drusilla J. recrq

DEMMON
1878, 4, 27. Jane recrq
1899, 7, 27. Wm. & Delilah dropped from mbrp

DEMOSS
1880, 2, 28. Wm. W. & Delilah recrq

DEMPSEY
1930, 1, 30. John Wesley recrq

DENISON
1878, 11, 30. Catharine recrq

DENSEL
1882, 3, 25. Cyrus [Densil] recrq
1885, 4, 25. Edward dropped from mbrp
1896, 2, 29. Wesley & Nettie recrq
1909, 4, 29. Wesley & w, Nettie, relrq

DERFLINGER
1897, 8, 28. Anna dropped from mbrp

DEVOE
1882, 1, 28. Mary recrq

DEWEY
1886, 3, 27. Leffie B. recrq

DICKENSHEET
1881, 2, 26. Freeman recrq
1881, 2, 26. Valley recrq
1881, 5, 28. Alonzo & Voley relrq

DIXON
1894, 6, 30. Ina recrq
1897, 1, 30. Joseph [Dickson] recrq
1897, 8, 28. Ina dropped from mbrp
1903, 9, 24. Joseph dropped from mbrp

DILLON
1886, 3, 27. Emily J. recrq
1907, 10, 31. Mrs. Bell [Dillone] recrq

DIPPERY
1877, 12, 29. Louesa [Dipra] recrq
1880, 2, 28. Louesa [Dipery] dis
1881, 2, 26. A. C. recrq
1881, 2, 26. Daniel recrq
1884, 2, 23. Sarah recrq
1899, 7, 27. Daniel, Sarah, Anna & Mary dropped from mbrp
1914, 4, 29. A. C. dropped from mbrp

DISHONG
1878, 5, 25. Emma recrq
1878, 11, 30. Sarah A. recrq

DIX
1879, 10, 25. David recrq
1879, 12, 27. Laurie P. recrq
1888, 2, 25. David dropped from mbrp

DODSON
1886, 3, 27. Tebitha recrq
1890, 3, 26. Tabitha dropped from mbrp

DOMINY
1901, 1, 31. Mary & Mary Margaret recrq

DONEHUE
1880, 5, 29. Pattie relrq
1886, 5, 29. Jane recrq
1903, 9, 24. Jane dropped from mbrp

DONER
1880, 3, 27. Thomas & Belle recrq
1894, 6, 30. Lolie recrq

DONER, continued
1907, 1, 5. Orva Leroy recrq

DOUGAL
1886, 9, 25. Samuel dropped from mbrp
1891, 2, 28. E. B. recrq
1891, 4, 25. Wm. & Nora recrq
1891, 4, 25. Eva recrq
1897, 8, 28. Cora dropped from mbrp
1899, 7, 27. Nora & Eva dropped from mbrp

DOWNHOUR
1908, 3, 26. Carle recrq

DOWNING
1878, 1, 26. Martha recrq
1878, 2, 23. Eli recrq
1878, 2, 23. Gabriel recrq
1878, 2, 23. Eliza J. recrq
1902, 3, 27. Reuben W. & Anna recrq
1902, 3, 27. Edward recrq

DRAKE
1878, 4, 27. Andrew recrq

DRAPER
1882, 2, 25. Susan recrq
1882, 2, 25. Martin recrq
1882, 2, 25. Chas. Henry recrq
1882, 2, 25. Jeremiah & Mary recrq
1886, 11, 27. Chas. H. dropped from mbrp

DUFFIELD
1909, 4, 29. Robert Dewitt recrq
1912, 4, 25. Paul & Helen recrq

DUKE
1879, 10, 25. Amy, Ida, Sarah & David M. recrq
1903, 9, 24. David, Sarah, Anna & Ida dropped from mbrp

DULL
1912, 4, 25. Jerry W. & w, Etta, recrq

DUNAHEW
1880, 3, 27. ----- recrq

DUNLAP
1879, 6, 28. Ina recrq
1899, 7, 27. Anna dropped from mbrp
1899, 7, 27. Anna dropped from mbrp

DUPES
1891, 2, 28. George M. & Sarah M. recrq
1891, 4, 25. Geo. & Sarah recrq
1891, 11, 28. Sarah L. recrq
1901, 7, 25. Alty dropped from mbrp

DURFLINGER
1895, 5, 25. Annie recrq

DUTCHER
1875, 5, 29. Alice recrq
1876, 2, 26. Ralph & w, Drucilla, recrq
1881, 1, 29. Geo. W. recrq
1882, 1, 28. Ertie & Viola recrq
1889, 8, 31. George relrq

DYSERT
1910, 10, 27. Wm. M. recrq
1911, 5, 25. Wm. M. & w relrq
1914, 10, 28. W. N. & w, Mary M. rst

EADS
1907, 6, 27. Wm. recrq

EAGY
1877, 4, 23. George & Lizzie [Eagg] recrq
1877, 5, 26. Sarah recrq
1878, 1, 26. Oliver recrq
1882, 1, 28. Jonathan [Eagie] recrq
1882, 2, 25. Etta recrq
1884, 12, 22. Gertie recrq
1886, 3, 27. Alice M. recrq
1894, 2, 24. Dora recrq
1897, 12, 30. Oliver dis disunity
1911, 4, 27. Oliver recrq

EAGLER
1878, 1, 26. James & Louisa recrq

EARLE
1824, 11, 29. Lenard recrq
1824, 11, 29. Elsina recrq
1824, 11, 29. Granvil W. recrq
1824, 11, 29. Eugene D. recrq
1824, 11, 29. Howard D. recrq
1824, 11, 29. Myrtia recrq
1824, 11, 29. Harvey recrq
1824, 11, 29. Clarence recrq
1892, 4, 30. Leonard F. & w, Margaret, & ch, Granville W., Eugene G., Howard D., Myrtle A., James H., Clarence B., Ethel E. & Hattie C., relrq

EASTMAN
1879, 6, 28. Mrs. Mary recrq
1882, 2, 25. Louie recrq
1885, 1, 31. Mary recrq
1888, 5, 26. Richard recrq

EDDY
1879, 12, 27. Henry & Sarah recrq
1880, 1, 31. Chas. recrq
1880, 1, 31. Chas. Louis recrq
1896, 5, 30. Albert recrq
1891, 4, 25. Catharine recrq
1901, 3, 28. Geo. recrq

EDWARDS
1896, 2, 29. Wm. recrq
1913, 2, 27. John & Sarah recrq

EILEY
1878, 2, 23. Ida recrq
1878, 2, 23. Elizabeth recrq

ELEXANDER
1879, 12, 27. Stephen recrq
1879, 12, 27. Joshua recrq

ELISON
1884, 2, 23. Mrs. D. recrq

ELDER
1895, 5, 25. John & Rosa recrq
1897, 8, 28. Rosa [Eller] dropped from mbrp
1897, 8, 28. John dropped from mbrp
1907, 2, 28. Newton W., Effie A. & Marie recrq
1912, 4, 25. Branson recrq
1913, 7, 30. Gordon Richard, s Newton, recrq
1926, 2, 25. Graden recrq
1932, 3, 31. Helen recrq
1932, 3, 31. Patty recrq

ELLIOTT
1907, 3, 28. Mrs. Iva Tracy relrq

ELZEY
1880, 3, 27. James M. recrq

EMERICK
1888, 2, 25. Wm. recrq
1899, 7, 27. Wm. dropped from mbrp
1914, 4, 29. Sadie P. dropped from mbrp

ENBODY
1889, 5, 30. Chas. recrq

ENGLERIGHT
1878, 2, 23. Amelia recrq
1878, 3, 30. Chas. recrq

ENGLISH
1928, 4, 28. Robert Lee recrq

ENNIS
1903, 1, 29. Clara recrq
1905, 3, 30. Clara [Ennes] dropped from mbrp
1909, 4, 29. Malord recrq
1911, 4, 27. Nonna M. recrq
1912, 4, 25. Mamie & Mary recrq

EPPS
1878, 12, 28. Dolly recrq

ERTON
1878, 3, 29. Mary recrq

ESLY
1878, 2, 23. Wm. recrq
1880, 1, 31. Clarissa [Essly] recrq

EVANS
1889, 5, 30. Phebe recrq
1897, 8, 28. Phebe dropped from mbrp
1897, 8, 28. Lincoln dropped from mbrp
1901, 3, 28. M. recrq
1907, 1, 5. Lottie Violette recrq
1908, 7, 30. Anna dropped from mbrp

EVERETTS
1878, 1, 26. Kansas recrq
1878, 1, 26. Eva recrq
1880, 3, 27. Emma [Everet] recrq
1882, 2, 25. Etta [Evert] recrq
1887, 2, 26. Kansas [Everts] relrq
1887, 5, 28. A. L. & N. J. [Everett] recrq
1891, 4, 25. David, Annie, Effie & Jason [Everts] recrq
1899, 7, 27. David, Annie, Effie & Jason [Evarts] dropped from mbrp
1901, 3, 28. Gladys M. recrq
1904, 3, 31. A. L. [Everts] & fam dropped from mbrp

EVIC
1879, 12, 27. Adam F. recrq

FACKLER
1891, 2, 28. Sarah A. & W. H. recrq
1897, 8, 28. John H. dropped from mbrp

FAGAN
1895, 4, 27. Nora recrq
1905, 2, 23. Chas. recrq

FAIR
1877, 12, 29. Amie recrq
1878, 1, 26. Mattie recrq
1878, 3, 30. Wm. H. recrq
1879, 4, 26. Thomas recrq
1882, 10, 28. Martha Ellen recrq
1882, 11, 25. Sarah recrq
1882, 11, 25. Obadiah recrq
1886, 9, 25. Adie dropped from mbrp
1890, 3, 26. Anie dropped from mbrp
1890, 3, 26. Mattie dropped from mbrp

FALER
1884, 11, 29. Samuel & Martha recrq
1886, 11, 27. Mary dropped from mbrp
1887, 1, 29. Samuel & w relrq

FALKNER
1876, 2, 26. John B. recrq
1884, 11, 29. Ezra N. [Faltner] recrq
1886, 12, 25. Ezra [Faltner] recrq

FANCE
1877, 12, 29. Eliza Jane recrq

FANDREE
1908, 7, 30. Catharine dropped from mbrp

FANCHAIR
1891, 4, 25. Isaac recrq
1891, 4, 25. Emily [Fancair] recrq
1897, 8, 28. Wm. A. [Fancier] dropped from mbrp

FANCISCO
1897, 8, 28. John W. dropped from mbrp

FANDREL
1894, 3, 31. Catharine recrq

FARIS
1879, 12, 27. Thomas recrq

FARLING
1880, 3, 27. Barbara & Sarah recrq
1881, 1, 29. Samuel recrq
1890, 3, 26. Samuel dropped from mbrp
1893, 3, 25. Frank [Farlow] recrq
1897, 3, 27. Frank [Farlow] relrq
1912, 2, 29. Grace recrq
1912, 4, 25. Amos recrq

FARMER
1877, 12, 29. Clerelia A. recrq

FARRINGTON
1878, 3, 30. Abigail recrq

FAULKNER
1878, 12, 28. Isaac recrq

FASSETT
1879, 6, 28. Emma [Fauset] recrq
1886, 3, 27. Denard W. & Eliza rocf Middlepoint MM
1888, 6, 30. Nora B. recrq
1889, 2, 23. Eliza recrq
1891, 4, 25. Albert [Fawcet] & w, Mary C., & ch, Laura A. & Emory A., recrq
1891, 8, 29. Denard W. & w, Eliza, & ch, Annie M. Bickel & Nora B. Fassett, gct Amboy MM, Ind.
1892, 4, 30. Wm. S. recrq
1895, 6, 29. Albert relrq
1896, 4, 24. Wm. dropped from mbrp
1897, 8, 28. Nora dropped from mbrp
1899, 7, 27. John B. & Mary [Fawcett] dropped from mbrp

FAUSHIRE
1891, 2, 28. Isaac & Emily recrq

FAUST
1897, 8, 28. Rena dropped from mbrp

FEASTER
1894, 2, 24. Louvina recrq
1903, 9, 24. Retta [Fearter] dropped from mbrp
1914, 4, 29. Drusella dropped from mbrp

FEIGHNER
1884, 2, 23. Alice recrq
1886, 11, 27. Alice dropped from mbrp
1891, 2, 28. Max [Feightner] recrq

FELTNERER
1894, 3, 31. Albert recrq

FENSTER
1899, 7, 27. Solomon dropped from mbrp

FERIS
1878, 2, 23. Martha recrq
1886, 9, 25. Martha dropped from mbrp

FERUL
1893, 8, 26. Franklin recrq

FIESTER
1879, 10, 25. John recrq
1885, 3, 28. Rella & Cora [Feaster] recrq
1899, 7, 27. Albert [Feister] dropped from mbrp

FILES
1886, 2, 27. C. A. recrq
1895, 3, 30. Mrs. C. A. [Foles] relrq

FINKHOUSE
1912, 4, 25. Mable & Roy recrq

FISH
1877, 2, 24. Rachel recrq
1880, 3, 27. Mariall H. recrq
1882, 10, 28. James & Clarissa recrq
1897, 8, 28. Sarah dropped from mbrp
1899, 7, 27. James & Clarence dropped from mbrp
1899, 7, 27. Manuel dropped from mbrp

FISHBAUGH
1888, 5, 26. Wesley B. & Margaret E. recrq

FISHER
1880, 3, 27. Frank recrq
1884, 11, 29. Frank dis disunity
1885, 1, 31. Frank, Sarah & Harriet recrq
1885, 1, 31. David recrq
1885, 1, 31. Nancy recrq
1885, 2, 28. Benjamin, Ann & Sarah recrq
1894, 3, 31. Sarah recrq
1899, 7, 27. Sarah dropped from mbrp
1899, 7, 27. Harroett & Sarah dropped from mbrp
1909, 1, 28. Thos. Jerome & Maggie recrq

FLEMMING
1906, 2, 28. Lester Dail b
1907, 7, 27. Donald b
1909, 4, 27. Morris b

1877, 3, 31. Thos. J. & Abigail recrq
1886, 9, 25. Thos. & Abigail dropped from

FLEMMING, continued
mbrp
1907, 1, 5. Chas. recrq

FLETCHER
1891, 4, 25. Joseph recrq
1891, 4, 25. Elizabeth recrq

FOCKLER
1878, 4, 27. Susan recrq

FOLEY
1891, 4, 25. Nancy [Folie] recrq
1891, 7, 25. Jasper W., Margaret A. & Martha A. recrq
1896, 2, 29. James C., John H. & W. M. recrq
1896, 5, 30. Geo. W. & Alveretta recrq
1898, 10, 27. Bertha recrq
1899, 7, 27. James dropped from mbrp
1900, 1, 25. Pearl recrq
1909, 4, 29. Ellen dropped from mbrp
1909, 7, 30. Clem dropped from mbrp
1910, 6, 30. Geo. & w relrq
1913, 2, 27. James recrq
1913, 2, 27. Earl recrq
1913, 2, 27. Gretchen recrq
1915, 2, 24. Lillian recrq
1926, 9, 30. Mrs. Henry recrq
1927, 6, 30. Loretta dropped from mbrp

FOLLIS
1879, 12, 27. Erwin recrq

FORD
1879, 1, 25. Martha recrq
1880, 2, 28. Martha relrq
1885, 4, 25. James C., Emmeline & Edward recrq
1893, 10, 28. James C. & Lovisa E. relrq
1894, 4, 28. David recrq
1894, 9, 22. Susan Ann recrq
1897, 3, 27. Frances recrq
1897, 4, 24. Geo. recrq
1899, 7, 27. David dropped from mbrp
1901, 3, 28. Huldah relrq
1901, 7, 25. George dropped from mbrp
1903, 9, 24. Frances dropped from mbrp

FOREST
1877, 5, 26. Rebecca J. recrq
1886, 11, 27. Rebecca dropped from mbrp

FORWALTER
1880, 1, 31. Christiana M. recrq

FOSS
1878, 1, 26. Jennie recrq

FOSTER
1879, 11, 29. Enos recrq
1905, 3, 30. Homer & Grace recrq
1907, 7, 25. Enos dropped from mbrp
1908, 7, 30. Homer dropped from mbrp

FOUST
1884, 12, 22. Sarah recrq
1884, 12, 22. Turen recrq
1886, 12, 25. Sarah & Laura relrq
1889, 5, 30. Lorrin recrq
1895, 5, 25. Kester, Sarah Ann & Evaline recrq
1895, 5, 25. Frank & Mary recrq
1897, 8, 28. Loren dropped from mbrp
1897, 8, 28. Kester dropped from mbrp
1897, 8, 28. Mary dropped from mbrp
1897, 8, 28. Sarah A. dropped from mbrp
1897, 8, 28. Frank dropped from mbrp
1899, 7, 27. Custer & Albancia dropped from mbrp
1900, 3, 29. Perry & Mary recrq
1906, 7, 26. P. C. & w, Mary, relrq
1909, 4, 29. Hazel & Anna recrq
1911, 4, 27. G. W. & Glenn R. recrq
1912, 2, 29. Ethel R. recrq

FOUTZ
1926, 6, 24. Grant & w recrq
1927, 9, 25. Glenn dropped from mbrp
1928, 4, 26. Grant & Mary recrq

FOWLER
1882, 2, 25. Mary recrq
1882, 2, 25. Sarah recrq
1886, 2, 27. Marion & Alice recrq
1886, 9, 25. Sarah dropped from mbrp
1889, 5, 30. Alice relrq
1890, 10, 25. Marion relrq
1894, 2, 24. Jennie recrq
1894, 2, 24. Tena recrq
1899, 7, 27. Nelson, Jennie & Lena dropped from mbrp
1901, 1, 31. Solomon, L. E. & Raymond recrq

FOX
1895, 4, 27. Hiram & Mary A. recrq
1895, 5, 25. Uriah, Emma, Squire H. F. & Huldah recrq
1899, 7, 27. Mary dropped from mbrp
1901, 7, 25. S. H. & Huldah dropped from mbrp
1932, 3, 31. Mildred & Jane recrq

FRANCE
1886, 11, 27. Eliza Jane dropped from mbrp
1890, 3, 26. Eliza dropped from mbrp

FRAZIER
1878, 1, 26. Addie [Frasier] recrq
1885, 2, 28. Elihu & w, Rachel, & ch, Idella M., Huldah V., Clarkson, Edgar & Thomas, rocf White River MM, dtd 1884,10, 10

FREMONT
1899, 7, 27. C. F. dropped from mbrp

FREY
1897, 1, 30. John recrq
1897, 1, 30. Huldah recrq

FRISBY
1879, 3, 29. Debora recrq
1879, 6, 28. Louisa recrq

FRONEFIELD
1877, 11, 24. Wm. recrq
1878, 1, 26. Solomon & Rosa recrq
1879, 3, 29. Ella recrq
1881, 3, 26. B. F. & Mary E. recrq
1881, 3, 26. Christiana recrq
1882, 1, 28. Maggie A. & Alma recrq
1882, 2, 25. Jacob recrq
1888, 2, 25. Evaline recrq
1889, 2, 23. Christina recrq
1890, 6, 28. Wm. relrq
1892, 2, 27. J. H. relrq
1892, 2, 27. Solomon & Rosa relrq
1892, 2, 27. Eva relrq
1892, 5, 28. B. F. relrq
1894, 2, 24. Wm. Sr. recrq
1895, 4, 27. Solomon recrq
1897, 12, 30. Solomon dis disunity
1899, 7, 27. Maggie [Frownfield] dropped from mbrp
1900, 9, 20. Anna dropped from mbrp
1906, 2, 25. Solomon & w, Rose, recrq
1906, 10, 25. Margaret recrq
1907, 2, 28. Bertha recrq
1910, 10, 27. Alice G. recrq

FRY
1903, 9, 24. John dropped from mbrp

FUESTER
1899, 7, 27. John & Louvina dropped from mbrp

FULLERTON
1897, 8, 28. Elizabeth A. dropped from mbrp

FULMER
1882, 10, 28. Lewis & Julia Ann recrq
1888, 1, 27. Louis dropped from mbrp

FURGESON
1880, 1, 31. Mary recrq
1885, 4, 25. Mary dropped from mbrp
1887, 2, 26. Emma [Furgerson] recrq
1889, 5, 30. Maggie recrq
1894, 6, 30. Maggie [Fergerson] recrq
1897, 8, 28. Maggie [Fergerson] dropped from mbrp
1897, 8, 28. Ida dropped from mbrp
1900, 3, 29. Margrit Jane recrq

FUSTER
1899, 7, 27. Cora dropped from mbrp

GALBREATH
1888, 5, 26. Samuel B. & Mary recrq

GALES
1885, 1, 31. Sarah I. recrq
1885, 1, 31. Warren recrq

GALIGER
1878, 2, 23. Mary recrq
1878, 2, 23. Joseph J. recrq
1890, 3, 26. Mary dropped from mbrp

GALIWAY
1880, 3, 27. Elizabeth & Woodford recrq

GALONGHER
1882, 11, 25. Joseph dropped from mbrp

GAMBLE
1877, 2, 24. Alice recrq
1877, 3, 31. R. W. recrq
1878, 2, 23. Martha E. recrq
1881, 1, 29. Emma recrq
1889, 5, 30. Wesley recrq
1890, 3, 26. Emma dropped from mbrp
1901, 1, 31. Clarence recrq
1905, 2, 23. Wesley dropped from mbrp
1905, 2, 23. Sarah dropped from mbrp
1905, 2, 23. Wilber dropped from mbrp
1905, 2, 23. Orly dropped from mbrp
1909, 8, 25. John E. & w, Daisy, recrq
1910, 7, 28. Rolland G. & Neil E., ch John E., recrq

GANEL
1901, 3, 28. Altha recrq

GARDNER
1930, 6, 26. Ralph dropped from mbrp

GARVIN
1875, 3, 7. Jane recrq

GASKILL
1877, 2, 24. Frank recrq
1877, 2, 24. Alonzo H. recrq
1883, 1, 27. Huldah gct Salem MM, O.

GAUSE
1895, 3, 30. Mahlon & w, Alice, recrq
1898, 3, 31. Mahlon S. & w, Alice, gct Bethel MM, Stillwell, Ind.

GIBSON
1880, 1, 31. William recrq
1880, 1, 31. Mary recrq
1885, 4, 25. Wm. & Mary dropped from mbrp

GILBERT
1891, 2, 28. John & Maggie recrq
1897, 1, 30. Bertha recrq
1897, 3, 27. Mary recrq

GILLILAND
1877, 3, 31. Charley & Mary E. recrq
1886, 9, 25. Mary E. dropped from mbrp

GILMORE
1878, 4, 27. Warren recrq

GLANCY
1880, 1, 31. Mary recrq

GLASS
1882, 10, 28. Wm. T. & Ada recrq
1907, 2, 28. Ruby Irene recrq

GLENN
1897, 8, 28. Robert dropped from mbrp
1899, 7, 27. Geo. dropped from mbrp

GLOSET
1878, 2, 23. Lavina recrq
1882, 1, 28. Geo. recrq
1886, 11, 27. George dropped from mbrp

GODDARD
1895, 5, 25. John A. & Martha Belle recrq

GOLLIVER
1882, 1, 28. Martin recrq
1886, 9, 25. Martin dropped from mbrp
1888, 2, 25. Martin recrq

GOOD
1877, 2, 24. Susan & Andrew Jackson recrq
1880, 1, 31. Alzira recrq
1882, 1, 28. Katie & Emma recrq
1882, 2, 25. Willie recrq
1890, 3, 26. Katie & Emma dropped from mbrp
1899, 7, 27. Albert & Mary dropped from mbrp

GOODWIN
1878, 4, 27. Ebenezer & Jane H. recrq
1888, 2, 25. Park [Goowin] recrq
1902, 3, 27. Russel recrq

GORDON
1893, 3, 25. Leroy recrq
1894, 2, 24. W. P. [Gorden] recrq
1894, 2, 24. Bertha [Gorden] recrq
1899, 7, 27. U. P., Bertha & Louisa dropped from mbrp
1912, 12, 26. Anna recrq

GORREL
1900, 1, 25. Emma [Gorral] recrq
1913, 2, 27. Walter recrq
1914, 2, 25. Emma & Alta relrq
1914, 2, 25. Walter dropped from mbrp

GOSS
1905, 2, 23. Clifford recrq
1914, 4, 29. Clifford dropped from mbrp

GRAHAM
1880, 3, 27. George recrq
1880, 3, 27. Sarah J. recrq
1881, 2, 26. George dis disunity
1885, 3, 28. I. P. & Chas. recrq
1886, 12, 25. I. P. relrq
1886, 12, 25. I. P. relrq
1893, 4, 29. Chas. & w, Ellen, recrq
1897, 8, 28. Wm. dropped from mbrp
1905, 2, 23. Leota recrq
1912, 4, 25. Carlis recrq
1912, 4, 25. Jno. D. & w, Lila, recrq

GRANSTAFF
1876, 2, 26. Andrew N. & w, Mary, recrq
1878, 3, 30. Curtis [Grantstaff] recrq
1879, 1, 25. Elizabeth recrq
1881, 1, 29. Martha M. recrq
1881, 2, 26. Lemuel L. & Nola recrq
1882, 1, 28. James recrq
1882, 2, 25. Owen recrq
1882, 7, 29. Catharine recrq
1883, 9, 29. Owen dis disunity
1884, 2, 23. Catharine relrq
1886, 10, 30. James & w rocf S. Wabash MM, Ind.
1887, 12, 31. James & w rocf S. Wabash MM, Ind., dtd 1887,12,17
1888, 2, 25. Frederick, Martha & Maud recrq
1889, 3, 30. Ella recrq
1890, 3, 26. Owen dropped from mbrp
1892, 2, 27. Andrew N. relrq
1892, 2, 27. Curtis N. & Ella relrq
1892, 2, 27. Frederic & Florence (Bresler) relrq
1892, 2, 27. Elizabeth relrq
1892, 12, 31. Curtis W. & Ella recrq
1894, 2, 24. Clarence recrq
1894, 2, 24. Ralph recrq
1894, 2, 24. Fred & Flora recrq
1895, 11, 30. Elizabeth recrq
1896, 9, 26. James recrq
1897, 5, 29. James relrq
1899, 7, 27. Martha dropped from mbrp
1899, 7, 27. Maud dropped from mbrp
1901, 1, 31. Harry & Ethel recrq
1902, 10, 16. C. N. & w, Ella, & dt, Ethel, relrq
1903, 9, 24. Florence dropped from mbrp
1907, 2, 28. Beatrice recrq
1908, 7, 30. Harry dropped from mbrp
1908, 7, 30. Ralf dropped from mbrp
1908, 7, 30. Clarence dropped from mbrp
1908, 7, 30. Mauda dropped from mbrp
1908, 7, 30. Margaret dropped from mbrp
1908, 7, 30. Harrold dropped from mbrp
1909, 1, 28. Nellie J. recrq
1912, 4, 25. Ruby recrq

GRANT
1901, 7, 25. W. J. & Mary dropped from mbrp

GREEN
1912, 4, 25. Harley G. & w, Maud M., recrq
1912, 4, 25. Fred recrq
1914, 10, 28. Fred dropped from mbrp
1927, 3, 30. Fremont R. & w, Pearl A., & dt, Catherine E. & Hilda R., recrq
1928, 4, 26. Robert Elsworth recrq

GREEN, continued
1932, 4, 27. Fremont & w, Pearl A., & ch, Catherine E., Hilda R. & Robert Ellsworth, relrq

GRIFFITH
1877, 2, 24. Sylvester & Mary recrq
1877, 2, 24. Emma recrq
1877, 3, 31. Sarah R. recrq
1877, 10, 27. Sylvester dis disunity
1877, 12, 29. Benjamin recrq
1878, 1, 26. James recrq
1885, 7, 25. James dropped from mbrp
1886, 3, 27. Ida recrq
1892, 2, 27. Mary relrq

GROSCOST
1888, 2, 25. Ollie recrq
1894, 2, 24. J. L. recrq
1897, 3, 27. Louie S. relrq
1899, 7, 27. J. L. & Alice [Groscosk] dropped from mbrp
1901, 12, 26. Lua recrq
1906, 12, 27. Jesse Lewis recrq
1912, 4, 25. Thelma recrq

GROVE
1878, 2, 23. Daniel & Lottie recrq
1891, 4, 25. Daniel, Lottie & Arthur recrq
1905, 2, 23. Wm. recrq
1908, 7, 30. Wm. dropped from mbrp

GUDER
1878, 4, 27. George recrq

GUINN
1878, 3, 30. Asa relrq
1879, 10, 25. Hickman recrq
1879, 10, 25. J. C. Fremont recrq
1880, 1, 31. Mary recrq
1882, 2, 25. Asa recrq
1886, 9, 25. Asa dropped from mbrp
1888, 2, 25. Charles recrq
1894, 3, 31. Vena & Tina recrq
1912, 4, 25. Vena & Russel recrq

GUISELMAN
1878, 1, 26. Sarah recrq
1878, 2, 23. Ezra recrq

GUNDY
1879, 10, 25. Cyrus & Joanna recrq

GURVIS
1877, 3, 31. Sylvester recrq

GUYSELMAN
1893, 4, 30. E. L. relrq

HAAS
1898, 3, 31. Lena recrq

HAGERMAN
1894, 2, 24. Florence recrq
1897, 1, 30. Chas. recrq
1903, 9, 24. Chas. dropped from mbrp
1905, 2, 23. Cliford recrq

HAGERTY
1914, 4, 29. Wm. H., Bessie H., Basil & Donald recrq

HAGGARD
1882, 2, 25. Jemimah recrq

HALL
1878, 11, 30. Isaac recrq
1878, 12, 28. Mary E. recrq
1899, 7, 27. Bertha dropped from mbrp

HAMILTON
1877, 2, 24. Lewis, Margaret, Pleza J. & Lewis M., recrq
1879, 10, 25. Pleasie relrq
1882, 2, 25. Steward & Katie recrq
1882, 2, 25. Annie & James recrq
1882, 2, 25. Amandah recrq
1882, 10, 28. Lewis [Hamlinton] dropped from mbrp
1890, 3, 26. Annie & James dropped from mbrp
1890, 3, 26. Amanda dropped from mbrp
1895, 8, 28. Mary A. dropped from mbrp

HAMMON
1888, 4, 28. Jack & Minnie recrq
1892, 2, 27. A. J. & Minnie relrq

HANDWERT
1890, 3, 26. Mary A. & Harry recrq
1896, 10, 31. Harry [Handwork] & w, Mary A., relrq

HANN
1889, 5, 30. Hannah recrq
1903, 7, 30. Enos recrq
1903, 7, 30. Della recrq
1915, 11, 24. Mrs. L. B. relrq

HARDESTY
1877, 3, 31. Frank recrq
1877, 12, 29. Nancy A. recrq
1878, 1, 26. Charles recrq
1892, 4, 30. Nancy relrq
1899, 7, 27. Chas. Ona, Frank, Ella M. & Nora dropped from mbrp

HARDING
1903, 9, 24. Susan dropped from mbrp

HARMON
1882, 2, 25. Finley & Carrie recrq
1883, 2, 24. Cary relrq
1913, 12, 25. Maude recrq

HARNLEY
1877, 12, 29. John recrq
1890, 3, 26. John dropped from mbrp
1897, 6, 26. John dropped from mbrp

HARPER
1878, 1, 26. Ida recrq
1889, 5, 30. Chas. recrq
1897, 8, 28. Mattie Miller dropped from mbrp

HARRIS
1895, 6, 29. Adaline recrq

HARROD
1877, 2, 24. Mahala recrq
1892, 2, 27. Mary relrq
1912, 4, 25. Calvennetta & Mary recrq
1927, 12, 29. Millie relrq

HARROLL
1878, 1, 26. James & Phebe recrq
1879, 6, 28. James & w relrq

HARSHMAN
1887, 3, 26. James recrq
1887, 3, 26. Angeline S. recrq
1888, 2, 25. James & Angeline dropped from mbrp

HART
1881, 2, 26. Lyman recrq
1881, 7, 30. Harriet C. recrq

HARTER
1879, 11, 29. Wilson M. recrq
1879, 12, 27. Mariah recrq
1879, 12, 27. Elizabeth recrq
1879, 12, 27. Thomas recrq
1880, 1, 31. Julia A. recrq
1880, 11, 27. Wilson H. & w, Elizabeth, relrq
1897, 8, 28. Chas. dropped from mbrp

HARTMAN
1878, 1, 26. Wm. Henry & Mary Melvine recrq
1878, 2, 23. Ella recrq
1882, 2, 25. Reason & Susan & Estella recrq
1886, 2, 27. Elda recrq
1886, 9, 25. Estella dropped from mbrp
1888, 2, 25. Elda recrq
1899, 7, 27. Elda dropped from mbrp

HARVEY
1877, 2, 24. Joanna recrq
1879, 12, 27. Charley recrq
1885, 1, 31. Minnie recrq
1891, 2, 28. Annie recrq
1891, 4, 25. Ann recrq
1894, 6, 30. Ella recrq
1897, 5, 29. Elzina & Rosella recrq
1897, 8, 28. Peter dropped from mbrp
1897, 8, 28. Etta dropped from mbrp
1899, 7, 27. Minnie dropped from mbrp

HASTINGS
1880, 3, 27. Isaac F. recrq
1881, 2, 26. Seth G. recrq
1881, 2, 26. Edith recrq
1881, 2, 26. Atta recrq
1881, 2, 26. Elba recrq

HATCH
1880, 1, 31. Timothy recrq
1880, 1, 31. Julia recrq

HAY
1880, 3, 27. Nancy recrq
1880, 4, 24. Hannah recrq
1883, 9, 29. Allice dis disunity
1899, 7, 27. Mary & Hannah dropped from mbrp

HAYES
1880, 3, 27. Abner recrq
1898, 3, 31. Wm. recrq
1927, 11, 24. Wm., Ruth Esther & Hugh Ellis relrq
1928, 12, 27. Wm., Ruth Esther & Hugh Ellis recrq
1930, 12, 26. Wm. & ch, Ruth & Hugh dropped from mbrp

HEITH
1878, 2, 23. John recrq

HELMINGER
1897, 8, 28. Newton dropped from mbrp

HENNEY
1897, 8, 28. Solomon dropped from mbrp
1897, 8, 28. Chas. dropped from mbrp
1897, 8, 28. Harriet dropped from mbrp

HENRY
1878, 4, 27. John K. recrq
1880, 1, 31. Lavina recrq
1880, 1, 31. Herbert Wilson recrq
1889, 5, 30. Lorrin & James E. recrq
1889, 5, 30. Alexander & dt, Carrie, rocf Goshen MM, dtd 1888,12,8
1890, 10, 25. Alexander dis disunity
1897, 8, 28. Jamed dropped from mbrp

HEPFER
1880, 1, 31. Rebecca recrq

HERRING
1906, 8, 30. Lorenzo M. & Minnie, & ch, Floyd & Lloyd, recrq

HERROD
1888, 2, 25. Callie & Viola recrq
1888, 2, 25. Mary recrq
1892, 1, 30. Callie relrq

HERMAN.
1878, 4, 27. Wm. & Mary recrq

HESTER
1877, 12, 29. Emerson & Ann Maria recrq
1883, 2, 24. Emerson & w, Minerva, relrq

HESSY
1877, 12, 29. Louisa recrq
1888, 5, 26. Peter & Elizabeth recrq

HETZLER
1889, 3, 30. Mary recrq
1891, 4, 25. Mary dropped from mbrp

HEWS
1878, 4, 27. Frances C. & Sarah A. recrq

HICKFIELD
1899, 7, 27. Susan dropped from mbrp

HICKMAN
1899, 7, 27. Gwin dropped from mbrp

HIDY
1893, 6, 24. Israel & Josephine recrq
1906, 4, 26. G. H. & w, Josephine, relrq

HIEFIELD
1879, 10, 25. Susan recrq

HIFFORD
1886, 11, 27. Davis & Margaret E. dropped from mbrp

HIGH
1879, 10, 25. Susan E. & Sadie M. recrq
1879, 12, 27. Sarah recrq
1879, 12, 27. Sarah E. recrq
1880, 1, 31. Henry recrq
1881, 1, 29. James recrq
1881, 1, 29. Flora A. recrq
1885, 4, 25. Josie dropped from mbrp
1891, 4, 25. Marion & Mary E. recrq
1899, 7, 27. Sarah dropped from mbrp

HIGLEY
1878, 1, 26. Frank recrq

HILEMAN
1930, 1, 30. Celina recrq

HILL
1878, 11, 30. Louisa recrq
1879, 10, 25. Jackson J. & Annis recrq
1883, 9, 29. Anna dis disunity
1894, 2, 24. Samuel & Florence recrq
1899, 7, 27. Samuel & Florence dropped from mbrp

HINTON
1882, 11, 25. F. M. & Rebecca recrq
1882, 11, 25. Mary Luella recrq
1882, 11, 25. Francis recrq
1892, 2, 27. Millard recrq
1896, 3, 28. F. M. relrq
1897, 10, 30. Milliard M. & Louvina relrq

HIPSHER
1878, 4, 27. Esther recrq
1882, 3, 25. Daniel [Hipshier] recrq
1886, 9, 25. Esther [Hipshire] dropped from mbrp

HIRE
1910, 10, 16. Ernest Wilbur, s James & Sarah, d ae 20

1877, 12, 29. John recrq
1877, 12, 29. Eliza M. recrq
1878, 5, 25. Wm. G. recrq
1879, 3, 29. Lucy recrq
1879, 6, 28. Thos. recrq
1879, 10, 25. Sarah recrq
1880, 1, 31. Sullivan J. [Hires] recrq
1880, 2, 28. Wilson F. recrq
1881, 3, 26. James W. recrq
1886, 1, 30. Mary recrq
1886, 2, 27. Wm. & w, Maggie, & dt, Bertha, rocf Middlepoint MM, O.
1886, 3, 27. Lula recrq
1886, 9, 25. Flora A. gct Caesars Creek MM,O.
1888, 6, 30. Alice recrq
1890, 8, 30. James W. & Sarah recrq
1891, 4, 25. Alice recrq
1892, 3, 26. Wilson F. relrq
1894, 3, 31. Bertha recrq
1901, 1, 31. Viola recrq
1905, 2, 23. Russell & Fern recrq
1907, 2, 28. Lola recrq
1908, 7, 30. Sarah dropped from mbrp
1912, 4, 25. Josephine & Lola Marjoric recrq
1934, 1, 25. Sadie recrq

HIRST
1893, 6, 24. Smith & Minda recrq

HISTE
1878, 6, 29. Maria recrq

HIVELEY
1882, 11, 25. Martin recrq
1884, 12, 22. Sarah C. recrq

HOAGLON
1897, 8, 28. Mac dropped from mbrp

HODSON
1887, 7, 30. Joshua recrq
1901, 7, 25. Joshua dropped from mbrp

HOELLY
1896, 2, 29. John recrq
1905, 2, 23. Emma [Holy] recrq
1907, 3, 28. Bertha [Hoelle] recrq

HOFFERD
1881, 1, 29. Marshall recrq
1890, 3, 26. David [Hofford] dropped from

HOFFERD, continued
mbrp
1890, 3, 26. Margaret dropped from mbrp

HOLLAND
1877, 3, 31. Sarah Ida [Holand] recrq
1890, 5, 31. Wilma W. relrq
1928, 2, 23. Donald & Oma recrq
1928, 2, 23. Ruby, Doralee & Kenneth recrq

HOLLEY
1882, 9, 30. John & Mary E. recrq
1890, 3, 26. John & Mary [Holly] dropped from mbrp
1915, 10, 27. Sarah E. [Holler] recrq

HOLLINGER
1881, 2, 26. Chas. E. recrq
1884, 12, 22. Adda recrq
1887, 3, 26. Burley recrq
1890, 3, 26. Chas. dropped from mbrp
1899, 7, 27. Burley & C. E. dropped from mbrp

HOLLIWELL
1882, 1, 28. Jennie recrq
1890, 3, 26. Jennie dropped from mbrp

HOLMES
1878, 4, 27. Giles & Bell recrq

HOLTER
1905, 2, 23. Walter recrq
1908, 7, 30. Walter dropped from mbrp

HOLTRY
1889, 5, 30. Maggie recrq
1897, 8, 28. Maggie dropped from mbrp
1897, 8, 28. William dropped from mbrp
1897, 8, 28. Marvin dropped from mbrp
1897, 8, 28. Lettie dropped from mbrp
1897, 8, 28. Mary dropped from mbrp
1897, 8, 28. Lovey dropped from mbrp
1897, 8, 28. Elizabeth dropped from mbrp

HOLWELL
1882, 2, 25. John D. recrq

HOMEL
1885, 4, 25. Mary Nan dropped from mbrp
1885, 4, 25. Sarah dropped from mbrp

HOMER
1901, 1, 31. Maria recrq

HOMEY
1897, 8, 28. Edna dropped from mbrp

HOOK
1877, 3, 31. Nancie Jane recrq
1877, 3, 31. Lewis recrq
1879, 10, 25. Reece recrq
1883, 6, 30. Rease dis disunity
1886, 9, 25. Nancy J. dropped from mbrp

HOPPER
1906, 10, 25. C. H. & w, Mattie, recrq
1914, 4, 29. Chas. & Mattie dropped from mbrp

HOOPAS
1886, 5, 29. Calvin C. recrq

HOOVER
1886, 3, 27. Henry recrq

HORNES
1886, 2, 27. Frank J. & Rebecca recrq

HOSTETTER
1878, 3, 29. Mary recrq

HOUCK
1879, 10, 25. Wm., Harrison & Lavina recrq
1879, 10, 25. Mahlon recrq
1880, 3, 27. Barbra recrq
1886, 5, 29. James recrq
1888, 6, 30. Geo. & Anna recrq
1888, 6, 30. Nona recrq
1891, 1, 31. George recrq
1891, 4, 25. Wm., Barbara, Susan & Nora recrq
1895, 12, 28. Geo. & w, Annie E., relrq
1899, 7, 27. George & Annie dropped from mbrp
1899, 7, 27. James, Barbary, Hamson & Wm. dropped from mbrp
1899, 7, 27. Mahlon & Nancy dropped from mbrp

HOUGH
1887, 8, 27. Harrison rst

HOULTRY
1884, 12, 22. Elizabeth recrq
1887, 7, 30. Elizabeth relrq

HOUSTEAD
1889, 10, 26. Adam & Rebecca relrq
1905, 2, 23. Wm. & Samuel [Housted] recrq
1907, 2, 28. Jennie [Housted] recrq

HOUTS
1905, 2, 23. Titus recrq
1905, 3, 30. Belle recrq
1908, 7, 30. Bell dropped from mbrp

HOUTZER
1881, 1, 29. Ellen & John C. recrq
1884, 4, 26. Ellen relrq
1905, 2, 23. Ellen recrq
1907, 3, 28. Lydia recrq

HOWARD
1878, 4, 27. Edward recrq
1878, 4, 27. James recrq

HOWARD, continued
1878, 4, 27. Sarah recrq
1891, 8, 29. James gct Springfield MM, O.

HOWER
1901, 1, 31. Maria recrq
1903, 1, 29. Joseph recrq

HOYES
1889, 3, 30. Alice E. recrq

HUBBARD
1877, 12, 29. Doris & Margaret E. recrq

HUDSON
1898, 10, 27. Wm. dropped from mbrp

HUDSPETH
1879, 12, 27. Bulah recrq

HUFFINE
1878, 2, 23. Hiram recrq
1886, 9, 25. Hiram dropped from mbrp
1912, 4, 25. Harry recrq

HUGHES
1882, 9, 30. Wm. L., Mary E., Wm., H., Margaret R., Geo. T., Stephen C. & Joseph M. [Hughs] rocf Gilead MM
1886, 9, 25. Wm. L., Mary E., Wm. H., Margaret, George T., Stephon C. & Joseph M. dropped from mbrp

HUIST
1897, 8, 28. Arminda dropped from mbrp

HULL
1894, 3, 31. Bertha recrq

HULLINGER
1886, 5, 29. C. E. recrq
1897, 8, 28. Eli dropped from mbrp
1897, 8, 28. Ada dropped from mbrp

HUMMIEL
1879, 12, 27. Emma recrq
1880, 1, 31. Mary Ann recrq
1880, 1, 31. Sarah recrq

HUMERICKHOUSE
1886, 4, 24. Elias & Sarah recrq
1894, 6, 30. Annie & Lydia [Humerichehouse] recrq
1899, 7, 27. Elias [Humerichouse] dropped from mbrp

HUNSTEAD
1901, 1, 31. Jennie recrq
1903, 9, 24. Jennie dropped from mbrp
1905, 2, 23. Fred & Anna recrq
1907, 2, 28. Mertle & Estella V. recrq

HUNT
1891, 4, 25. Orin recrq
1899, 7, 27. Orien dropped from mbrp

HUNTER
1878, 11, 30. Wm. H. recrq
1880, 7, 31. Elizabeth relrq
1894, 12, 29. Wm. & Jane relrq

HURLINGER
1884, 11,29. Eli recrq

HURSHMAN
1899, 7, 27. James & Angelina dropped from mbrp

HYATT
1875, 3, 7. Noah & Eliza Emily [Hiatt] recrq
1882, 2, 25. Amy recrq
1886, 11, 27. Annie dropped from mbrp
1890, 11, 29. Niah, Eliza & Jennie [Hyat] relrq
1912, 4, 25. Noah H. & w, Elizabeth R., recrq

IMBODY
1897, 8, 28. Chas. & Wm. dropped from mbrp

INGMIRE
1898, 10, 27. Flora recrq

INWOOD
1889, 5, 30. Catharine recrq
1889, 5, 30. Wm. recrq
1897, 8, 28. Catharine dropped from mbrp
1901, 1, 31. Wm. & Catharine recrq

INYARD
1885, 1, 31. Jane recrq
1885, 1, 31. Allen recrq

IRELAND
1878, 4, 27. C. S. recrq
1880, 3, 27. John & Eva recrq
1881, 3, 26. Jerry recrq
1884, 2, 23. Isaac B. recrq
1886, 5, 29. Elizabeth recrq
1886, 9, 25. C. S. dropped from mbrp
1886, 9, 25. Jerry dropped from mbrp
1891, 3, 28. Annie recrq
1894, 3, 31. Christian S. recrq
1899, 4, 27. Wilber recrq
1899, 4, 27. Christian relrq
1901, 3, 28. Birtha & Hertha recrq
1908, 7, 30. Orven dropped from mbrp
1910, 1, 27. Wilbur D. & Bertha relrq

ISHANE
1878, 12, 28. Chas. recrq

JACKMAN
1877, 2, 24. James E. & Harriett recrq
1882, 2, 25. Albert & Florence recrq
1882, 2, 25. Lillie M. recrq
1899, 7, 27. James, Harriet, Albert, Florence & Lillie dropped from mbrp

JACKSON
1875, 3, 7. Lucretia rocf Dover MM
1882, 2, 25. Zelma recrq
1886, 2, 27. Wm. recrq
1890, 3, 26. Wm. dropped from mbrp
1907, 2, 28. Inez Leora recrq
1908, 11, 19. Glenn recrq
1910, 4, 28. Glenn & w, Bertha, & dt, Doris, relrq
1912, 5, 30. Glen & w, Bertha, & dt, Doris, rst in mbrp

JACOBS
1878, 5, 25. Henry & Mary recrq
1879, 5, 31. Nancy & Jenie recrq
1895, 5, 25. Henry recrq

JEISURE
1879, 12, 27. Alice recrq

JENKINS
1879, 12, 27. John recrq
1886, 9, 25. J. T. dropped from mbrp
1897, 8, 28. John dropped from mbrp

JENSON
1877, 3, 31. W. M. recrq

JESSUP
1896, 5, 30. Gulie E. & ch gct Springfield MM, Ind.

JEWELL
1877, 12, 29. I. B. & Lucretia Ann recrq
1881, 9, 24. Samuel & w recrq
1885, 1, 31. Lucretia recrq
1892, 5, 28. Samuel & Lucretia A. relrq

JOB
1879, 1, 25. Minnie recrq
1879, 5, 31. Minnie [Jobs] relrq

JOHNS
1888, 2, 25. Celissa recrq
1893, 8, 26. Anderson recrq
1896, 2, 29. Samuel recrq
1896, 10, 31. Lewis & w, Pheba, recrq
1897, 8, 28. Samuel dropped from mbrp

JOHNSON
1877, 3, 31. Geo. W. recrq
1877, 12, 29. Ella recrq
1878, 2, 23. Henry R. recrq
1878, 2, 23. Nancy A. recrq
1881, 1, 29. Martha A. recrq
1884, 2, 23. Bill recrq
1886, 11, 27. Martha A. dropped from mbrp
1890, 3, 26. Martha H. dropped from mbrp
1890, 3, 26. Henry R. dropped from mbrp
1890, 3, 26. Nancy dropped from mbrp
1893, 2, 25. Wm. & Ellen relrq
1896, 1, 25. Joseph recrq
1898, 3, 31. Sopha recrq
1900, 3, 29. A. J. & Lorinda recrq
1903, 9, 24. Eva Wiles dropped from mbrp
1907, 1, 5. Chas., Frank C. & Maude recrq
1907, 3, 28. Floyd recrq
1909, 4, 29. Floyd dropped from mbrp
1913, 1, 30. Maude relrq
1914, 4, 29. Virgie Wilson dropped from mbrp
1914, 12, 30. Belva recrq
1926, 2, 25. Pauline recrq

JONES
1876, 7, 29. E. M. rocf Union MM
1876, 11, 25. Samuel B. & w, Rhoda, & ch, Barton K., Josephine & Lambert W., rocf Union MM
1877, 5, 26. Laban J. rocf Union MM, O., dtd 1877,4,18
1877, 12, 29. LaVan P. rocf Union MM
1877, 12, 29. Henry W. & Samuel C. rocf Union MM
1877, 12, 29. Mary Ann recrq
1879, 5, 31. Henry W. gct Spiceland MM, Ind.
1880, 3, 27. Carrie S., Allie D. & Clarence E. recrq
1883, 4, 28. S. C. gct West Branch MM, O.
1883, 11, 24. Gulia E. rocf Springfield MM, dtd 1883,11,17
1885, 1, 31. Roda recrq
1887, 5, 28. Henry W. & w, Carrie T., & ch, Anvard Bevan Beathworth & Barton Elwynn, rocf Spiceland MM, Ind., dtd 1887,4,2
1895, 6, 29. Delilah recrq
1899, 10, 26. H. M. & w, Carry T., & ch, A.B. & B. E. relrq

JOSEPH
1897, 1, 30. Rachel recrq
1904, 5, 26. Rachel relrq

JUNKENS
1878, 4, 27. J. recrq

KAUGH
1876, 4, 29. Andrew & w, Maria, recrq

KAUGHMAN
1899, 7, 27. May dropped from mbrp

KEAR
1886, 1, 30. Elsie recrq
1888, 5, 26. John recrq
1890, 3, 26. Laura recrq
1894, 3, 31. Iva recrq
1899, 7, 27. John dropped from mbrp
1908, 7, 30. Elias dropped from mbrp

KEATH
1891, 1, 31. Wm. recrq
1895, 5, 25. Wm. Sr. & Catharine M. recrq

KELLY
1877, 2, 24. Samuel & Margaret recrq
1877, 3, 31. Dollie M. recrq

KELLY, continued

1878, 2, 23. Nancy recrq
1878, 4, 27. Rebecca [Kelley] recrq
1881, 4, 30. Samuel [Kelley] & w relrq
1901, 1, 31. Wm. H. recrq

KELTNER
1877, 11, 24. Jennie recrq
1877, 12, 29. Sarah recrq
1884, 11, 29. Robert & Sarah recrq
1905, 2, 23. Sarah dropped from mbrp

KEOKENHOUR
1892, 5, 28. Rosa relrq

KERKINDOLL
1880, 1, 31. Ella recrq

KERNNEY
1897, 8, 28. Rhoda dropped from mbrp

KESICE
1901, 3, 28. Samuel recrq

KESLER
1878, 11, 30. Luisa recrq
1881, 1, 29. Peter & Martha Ann recrq
1881, 1, 29. John & Hannah recrq

KEUTCH
1903, 9, 24. Viola dropped from mbrp

KIGGINS
1891, 2, 28. Albert recrq

KIND
1878, 4, 27. Robert recrq

KINSEY
----, --, --. Frank E. & Susie E.
Ch: Francis Lowell b 1899, 3, 27
Margaret Elizabeth " 1901, 6, 10
Dwight Hillis " 1903, 10, 21
John Gaylord " 1906, 12, 1
Thos. Theodore " 1908, 8, 2

1885, 4, 25. Anna dropped from mbrp
1910, 4, 28. Frank E. & w, Susie E., & ch, Francis Lowell, Margaret Elizabeth, Dwight Hillis, John Gaylord & Thomas Theodore, recrq
1914, 3, 25. Harry Raymond recrq

KISER
1877, 11, 24. Byron recrq
1884, 11, 29. Mary recrq
1887, 2, 26. R. M. & Sarah J. recrq
1897, 8, 28. Mary [Keysor] dropped from mbrp
1899, 7, 27. Byron [Kizer] dropped from mbrp

KITSON
1881, 1, 29. Sarah recrq
1915, 6, 30. Nelle Collins [Kitchen] relrq

KITZMILLER
1882, 9, 30. Henry recrq
1888, 2, 25. Chas. recrq
1890, 3, 26. Chas. dropped from mbrp
1903, 9, 24. Maggie Gilbert dropped from mbrp

KNITTLE
1881, 2, 26. Wm. recrq

KNOBLOCK
1894, 6, 30. Adam & Minnie recrq

KNOWLTON
1895, 5, 25. Theodore & Jane recrq

KOUTS
1927, 3, 30. Norma recrq

KRAMER
1879, 12, 27. Annie recrq

KRESSON
1896, 2, 29. A. G. & Sarah E. recrq
1896, 5, 30. D. A. recrq
1897, 8, 28. A. G. & Sarah E. dropped from mbrp
1899, 7, 27. D. A. dropped from mbrp

KREIDER
1881, 2, 26. Mary [Krider] recrq
1894, 2, 24. Hattie & Bertha recrq
1899, 4, 27. Harry M. recrq
1912, 4, 25. Bertha recrq
1914, 4, 29. John dropped from mbrp
1914, 4, 29. Mary dropped from mbrp

KRING
1878, 2, 23. Elizabeth recrq
1878, 2, 23. Albert recrq
1878, 2, 23. Wm. & Elizabeth recrq
1879, 3, 29. Wm. & Albert dropped from mbrp

KULSCH
1894, 2, 24. Nella recrq

KUSHMAUL
1893, 6, 24. Samuel & Henry recrq
1897, 8, 28. Samuel & Henry [Kushmane] dropped from mbrp

KUTCH
1886, 2, 27. Maggie recrq
1888, 12, 29. Maggie relrq
1901, 7, 25. Stella dropped from mbrp

LABECK
1898, 10, 27. Jno. dropped from mbrp

LAHMON
1907, 1, 5. James E. recrq

LAHUE
1900, 1, 25. Edward E. & Emma B. recrq
1901, 1, 31. Kitty recrq

LAIRD
1893, 10, 28. Carrie W. rocf West Grove MM, Ind., dtd 1893,10,14
1894, 2, 24. Geo. A. recrq
1894, 2, 24. Chas. F. recrq
1894, 2, 24. Sarah R. rocf Elk MM, O., dtd 1894,1,25
1898, 1, 27. Chas. F. & Carrie W. relrq
1899, 9, 31. M. E. gct White Water MM, Ind.

LAKE
1878, 1, 26. Lewis recrq
1879, 2, 22. Lewis relrq

LAMB
1889, 2, 23. Daniel & Sarah recrq
1897, 8, 28. Sarah & Daniel dropped from mbrp
1897, 8, 28. James H. dropped from mbrp

LAMBERT
1880, 1, 31. Sarah A. recrq
1899, 7, 27. Sarah dropped from mbrp

LAMPSON
1890, 3, 26. Alfred dropped from mbrp

LANGDON
1881, 2, 26. Lucinda & Minna recrq
1881, 2, 26. Washington F. recrq
1882, 7, 29. Nancy recrq
1886, 4, 24. W. L. relrq
1914, 4, 29. W. F. & Minnie Allen dropped from mbrp

LANINGER
1898, 3, 31. Anna recrq

LARUPE
1914, 4, 29. Saddie dropped from mbrp

LAUGHLIN
1893, 2, 25. Franklin & Lillie recrq
1893, 9, 23. Franklin & Lillie dis

LAWHEAD
1876, 3, 25. Eliza Jane recrq
1877, 2, 24. Emma recrq
1884, 2, 23. George recrq
1890, 7, 26. Millie recrq
1892, 5, 28. Millie relrq
1894, 5, 26. Millie recrq

LAWRENCE
1889, 10, 26. Jane [Laurence] recrq
1891, 2, 28. Frank recrq
1891, 4, 25. Frank recrq
1914, 12, 30. Burt [Lieurance] recrq
1914, 12, 30. Mary [Lieurance] recrq

LAWSON
1897, 8, 28. Emma dropped from mbrp

LAYMAN
1901, 7, 25. Alice & Elizabeth dropped from mbrp

LEAVENS
1883, 6, 30. Emuel dis disunity

LEE
1912, 4, 25. Fred & Glenn recrq

LEFFINGWELL
1880, 3, 27. Hanson recrq
1880, 3, 27. Weodocia recrq

LEHEW
1877, 2, 24. Rosa L. recrq
1877, 3, 31. Thos. M. recrq
1886, 9, 25. Thos. M. dropped from mbrp
1911, 4, 27. Edward E. & w, Emma B., relrq

LEICHTY
1914, 10, 28. Van Buren & Matilda recrq

LEISURE
1876, 2, 26. Eliza recrq
1877, 11, 24. Wm. [Leaser] recrq
1879, 12, 27. Addie J. recrq
1886, 3, 27. Ella recrq
1899, 7, 27. James [Leasure] dropped from mbrp
1905, 2, 23. Mary recrq
1905, 2, 23. Joseph recrq

LEMERICK
1890, 11, 29. Nettie relrq

LEONARD
1886, 4, 24. James A. recrq
1899, 7, 27. James A. dropped from mbrp

LESLIE
1896, 3, 28. Wm. J. & w, Elizabeth, relrq
1908, 7, 30. Montana Evans dropped from mbrp

LEWEN
1879, 12, 27. Emil recrq
1880, 3, 27. Clarinda recrq

LEWIS
1880, 3, 27. Jane, Sophia, Eliza J. & Isaac recrq

LEWIS, continued
1899, 1, 26. C. H. rocf Spring Bank MM, Neb., dtd 1898,12,31
1899, 7, 27. Eugene dropped from mbrp
1899, 7, 27. Laura dropped from mbrp
1900, 8, 30. Caleb H. gct New Garden MM, Ind.
1906, 2, 25. Tennyson & w, Alice J., & ch, Dalton H., Mary C. & Evelyn, rocf Wabash MM, Ind., dtd 1906,2,17
1911, 4, 27. Mary C. recrq
1911, 8, 31. Dalton H. gct Dublin MM, Ind.
1913, 11, 1. Tennyson & w, Alice Jay, & dt, Evelyn, gct Portland MM, Ind.

LICHTY
1878, 1, 26. Van Buren & Matilda recrq
1884, 2, 23. Mose recrq

LINDAMAN
1926, 2, 25. Mrs. Elma relrq

LININGER
1893, 4, 29. Lucy recrq
1894, 2, 24. Andrew J. & Amelia recrq
1899, 7, 27. A. J. & Malissa dropped from mbrp

LINDSEY
1877, 2, 24. Malissa [Linsy] recrq
1884, 2, 23. George [Linsley] recrq
1886, 9, 25. George dropped from mbrp
1893, 3, 25. Wm. [Linsey] recrq
1910, 5, 27. Wm. relrq

LINN
1888, 5, 26. George & Addie recrq

LIOUR
1885, 3, 28. Emma recrq

LIST
1914, 12, 30. Raymond recrq
1914, 12, 30. Pearle recrq

LITTLE
1876, 2, 26. Weltha recrq
1876, 2, 26. Ellen recrq
1876, 2, 26. Walter recrq
1876, 2, 26. Jacob recrq
1882, 2, 25. Clara recrq
1886, 2, 27. Anna recrq
1894, 11, 24. Clara relrq
1899, 7, 27. Mattie & Jacob dropped from mbrp
1899, 7, 27. Elden dropped from mbrp

LITZ
1912, 2, 29. Birl & w, Matilda, & dt, Rachel, recrq

LOCKARD
1878, 12, 28. Mary recrq

LONG
1885, 1, 31. G. recrq
1898, 3, 31. Harry C. & Sarah recrq
1903, 9, 24. Harry & Sarah dropped from mbrp

LORD
1881, 2, 26. Jennie recrq

LOSEY
1879, 5, 31. Daniel R. recrq
1881, 2, 26. Chas. & James E. recrq
1886, 9, 25. James E. dropped from mbrp
1890, 3, 26. Chas. [Locy] dropped from mbrp

LOTH
1899, 6, 29. Anthony recrq
1914, 4, 29. Anthony & Sarah E. dropped from mbrp

LOUTY
1907, 1, 5. Maude recrq

LOVET
1888, 5, 26. Pheby recrq

LOVLESS
1928, 2, 23. Doris recrq

LUCAS
1878, 4, 27. Catharine recrq

LUMBLING
1891, 2, 28. Obediah, Nancy & Wm. M. recrq

LUNDY
1899, 7, 27. Cyrus & Joanna dropped from mbrp

LYBARGER
1914, 2, 25. Albert & Nellie B. recrq

LYNCH
1897, 1, 30. John recrq
1897, 3, 27. Jennie recrq
1899, 7, 27. John & Jennie dropped from mbrp

McBRIDE
1891, 1, 31. J. S. & Melissa recrq
1892, 8, 27. Zella & Flora recrq
1896, 4, 24. Melissa relrq

McCHERE
1889, 5, 30. Maggie recrq

McCHRISTIE
1878, 2, 23. Jennie recrq
1886, 9, 25. Jennie [McChristre] dropped from mbrp

McCLEARY
1878, 1, 26. James & Lucy A. recrq
1879, 3, 29. Chas. recrq

McCLEARY, COntinued
1879, 6, 28. James relrq
1911, 3, 30. Alexander recrq

McCLURE
1878, 1, 26. John P. & Diana recrq
1878, 2, 23. Louisa recrq
1880, 3, 27. Wm. H. & Rosella A. recrq
1882, 4, 29. Joseph & Emma recrq
1885, 1, 31. Mary recrq
1886, 5, 29. John, Henneretta & Ella recrq
1886, 9, 25. Lovina dropped from mbrp
1886, 11, 27. John dropped from mbrp
1888, 8, 25. Emma relrq
1893, 6, 24. Wm. & Henrietta recrq
1897, 5, 29. Moses recrq
1897, 8, 28. Wm. J. & Henrietta dropped from mbrp
1897, 8, 28. Maggie dropped from mbrp
1897, 8, 28. Nathan dropped from mbrp
1897, 8, 28. Hannah dropped from mbrp
1899, 7, 27. Moses dropped from mbrp
1903, 9, 24. Rozella dropped from mbrp

McCOLLUM
1905, 2, 23. Chas. & Gertrude recrq
1908, 7, 30. Gertrude dropped from mbrp
1911, 4, 27. H. R. & Gertie recrq
1914, 10, 28. Chas. dropped from mbrp
1927, 5, 25. Hiram & Gertrude dropped from mbrp

McCONAHY
1888, 6, 30. Maud recrq
1905, 2, 23. Clarence recrq
1908, 7, 30. ----- [McConaley] dropped from mbrp

McCOOL
1878, 4, 27. Mary Ann recrq
1878, 4, 27. James J. recrq
1881, 3, 26. Emma relrq

McCOY
1914, 12, 30. Bertha Bell recrq

McCULLOUGH
1878, 1, 26. Matheny recrq
1878, 4, 27. Jane recrq
1899, 7, 27. Matthew & Jane dropped from mbrp

McDARR
1883, 1, 27. John & Catharine recrq
1884, 2, 23. John dropped from mbrp
1894, 3, 31. Blanch recrq
1899, 7, 27. Blanch dropped from mbrp

McDONALD
1881, 4, 30. Thos. recrq
1885, 1, 31. Mordicai recrq
1886, 3, 27. Geo. W. & Grace recrq
1886, 9, 25. Ida Belle dropped from mbrp
1895, 6, 29. Grace relrq
1899, 7, 27. Thos. dropped from mbrp
1903, 9, 24. Geo. & James dropped from mbrp

McGOWIN
1879, 12, 27. Thomas P. recrq

McHENRY
1896, 2, 29. Solomon recrq
1899, 7, 27. Solomon dropped from mbrp

McILVANE
1880, 3, 27. Michael recrq

McINTIRE
1878, 6, 29. Lucinda recrq

McKINNEY
1889, 5, 30. Caroline recrq
1897, 8, 28. Callie dropped from mbrp

McLOEMAR
1894, 3, 31. Mary J. recrq

McMANIS
1880, 1, 31. Wm. recrq
1880, 1, 31. Francis recrq
1880, 1, 31. Cora recrq
1895, 4, 27. Wm. R. & Emma R. [McMannis] recrq

McMICHAEL
1878, 1, 26. Ida Bell recrq
1890, 3, 26. Ida B. dropped from mbrp

McMILLEN
1878, 4, 27. Rebecca & Ephraim M. recrq
1878, 5, 25. Sadie recrq
1878, 12, 28. Rebecca [McMillan] recrq
1888, 5, 26. Leonides, Eliza & Bertha [McMellen] recrq
1907, 2, 28. John & w, Esther, rocf Fairmount MM, Ind., dtd 1907,2,13
1909, 10, 28. John & Esther gct Fairfield MM, O.

McPHERSON
1880, 10, 30. Zebba recrq

McQUOWN
1888, 4, 28. W. M. & Lydia L. recrq
1888, 5, 26. Rachel recrq
1894, 2, 24. Rachel recrq
1901, 7, 25. Viola dropped from mbrp

McWIRICK
1897, 8, 28. Oda dropped from mbrp

MABEN
1915, 3, 31. ----- recrq

MACE
1912, 4, 25. John & Glenn recrq

MACKS
1881, 2, 26. Mary dis disunity

MADDOX
1879, 12, 27. Wm. Edward [Madex] recrq
1882, 4, 29. Malissa recrq
1891, 1, 31. Alice [Maddix] recrq
1892, 5, 28. Henry B. & Melissa relrq

MAIN
1882, 2, 25. Maggie recrq
1886, 9, 25. Maggie dropped from mbrp

MALACHI
1878, 3, 29. Milton recrq

MALESTER
1882, 2, 25. Rebecca recrq

MALOTT
1893, 9, 23. James rocf White Water MM, Ind.

MANIFEE
1899, 7, 27. Chas. & Mary dropped from mbrp

MANN
1895, 3, 30. Luella relrq

MANTER
1879, 12, 27. David recrq
1879, 12, 27. Lavona recrq
1888, 4, 28. Lovana dropped from mbrp
1899, 7, 27. Lavina [Mantor] dropped from mbrp

MAPES
1877, 12, 29. Allice recrq

MARGESON
1880, 1, 31. Darius recrq
1880, 1, 31. John recrq
1880, 1, 31. James recrq

MARK
1891, 4, 25. Chancy recrq
1903, 9, 24. Channcy & Lucy dropped from mbrp

MARLOT
1903, 9, 24. James dropped from mbrp

MARSHALL
1882, 10, 28. Lydia Ann recrq
1882, 11, 25. James recrq
1882, 11, 25. Letitia recrq
1885, 3, 28. Lida relrq
1885, 4, 25. Halford dropped from mbrp
1886, 5, 29. George recrq
1899, 7, 27. James dropped from mbrp

MARTIN
1878, 1, 26. Nettie recrq
1879, 4, 26. Richard & w, Sarah, relrq
1880, 1, 31. Maggie recrq
1880, 5, 29. Maggie relrq
1886, 9, 25. Nettie dropped from mbrp

MARTS
1879, 10, 25. Mary recrq
1893, 4, 29. Chancy recrq
1899, 7, 27. Chaney dropped from mbrp
1899, 7, 27. Mary dropped from mbrp

MARQUET
1880, 1, 31. Catherine recrq

MARQUIST
1880, 1, 31. Marquis S. recrq

MASSTEN
1899, 7, 27. Rebecca dropped from mbrp

MATHENA
1877, 2, 24. Rebecca E., Malissa & Mary recrq

MATTHEWS
1877, 3, 31. John recrq
1877, 12, 29. J. R. recrq
1881, 2, 26. Eli recrq
1894, 2, 24. Etta [Mathews] recrq
1914, 4, 29. Ettie dropped from mbrp
1926, 2, 25. Joy recrq
1927, 3, 30. Myrtle recrq
1928, 11, 28. Melvie recrq
1930, 5, 29. Dale T. recrq
1931, 1, 29. Russel gct Muncie MM, Ind.
1931, 4, 30. Chas., Cora Lee & Paul Gene recrq
1933, 6, 29. Charlette Eileen & ch, Earl & Nellie, recrq
1933, 6, 29. Richard David & ch, Dale & Evelyn, recrq

MAXSON
1914, 9, 4. Margaret Rose, dt Wm. & Bertha, b

1880, 1, 31. David [Mason] recrq
1880, 1, 31. Lizzie [Mason] recrq
1886, 3, 27. Gertie recrq
1892, 3, 26. Adolphus [Maxon] recrq
1894, 2, 24. Elmer [Maxon] recrq
1897, 2, 27. Gertrude [Maxon] relrq
1905, 2, 23. Wm. recrq
1905, 2, 23. Perl recrq
1905, 2, 28. Cora recrq
1910, 7, 28. Horace Sterman, s Bertha, recrq
1915, 1, 27. Margaret Rose recrq
1928, 2, 23. Doris recrq

MAYHEW
1900, 3, 29. John & w, Lou, & ch, Grace & Zora, rocf Friends Chapel MM, O.
1900, 3, 29. Pearle recrq
1903, 9, 24. John, Lou, Grace & Pearl dropped

MAYHEW, continued
from mbrp

MAYWHERE
1883, 4, 28. Sarah Jane recrq
1901, 3, 28. Richard recrq

MEALS
1915, 2, 24. Bertha Richards relrq

MEEK
1879, 10, 25. Mary recrq
1882, 4, 29. Mary [Meeks] recrq

MEELY
1891, 3, 28. Aaron recrq

MELCHIA
1895, 4, 27. Lucy Pearl recrq
1914, 12, 30. Hazel [Melchi] recrq

MENEFEE
1877, 11, 24. Immogene recrq
1878, 1, 26. Mary E. recrq
1878, 8, 31. Immogene recrq
1880, 11, 27. Maud relrq

MERIS
1905, 2, 23. Alma recrq

MESSENGER
1878, 4, 27. Mary E. & Dora recrq

MILLEN
1891, 4, 25. George recrq

MILLER
1878, 4, 27. Wm. H. recrq
1878, 4, 27. Sarah M. recrq
1878, 4, 27. Israel recrq

1878, 9, 28. Geo. W. recrq
1878, 11, 30. Sarah recrq
1878, 12, 28. Darius recrq
1878, 12, 28. Albert F. recrq
1878, 12, 28. Anna recrq
1879, 3, 29. Perry recrq
1879, 3, 29. Jennie recrq
1879, 5, 31. George & w recrq
1879, 6, 28. Geo., Samantha & Emma recrq
1879, 10, 25. Emma & John recrq
1879, 12, 27. John recrq
1879, 12, 27. Louis recrq
1879, 12, 27. Sindula recrq
1880, 1, 31. Moriah recrq
1880, 1, 31. Jacob A. recrq
1880, 3, 27. Fannie recrq
1880, 3, 27. Martha L. recrq
1880, 10, 30. Frank & Charles recrq
1881, 1, 29. E. J. recrq
1881, 3, 26. John dis disunity
1882, 2, 25. J. & Mattie recrq
1882, 10, 28. Thos. & Mary Alice recrq
1882, 11, 25. Samuel recrq
1884, 1, 26. Rebecca A. recrq
1885, 4, 25. Sindella & Jacob dropped from mbrp
1886, 11, 27. Rebecca dropped from mbrp
1887, 3, 26. Alles recrq
1887, 4, 30. Mary recrq
1888, 2, 25. Myrtie V. recrq
1888, 2, 25. Byran recrq
1888, 4, 28. Louis & Fannie dropped from mbrp
1888, 12, 29. Myrtie dropped from mbrp
1889, 5, 30. Mattie recrq
1890, 1, 25. Ollie recrq
1890, 3, 26. Otho recrq
1890, 3, 26. Mattie recrq
1891, 2, 28. Joseph, Catharine & Mary C. recrq
1891, 4, 25. Lewis & Fannie recrq
1891, 4, 25. Alice recrq
1892, 2, 27. Jacob recrq
1892, 5, 28. George, Cynthia & Ollie relrq
1893, 12, 30. George & Cynthia recrq
1894, 2, 24. James, Fay & Nellie recrq
1894, 2, 24. Alice recrq
1894, 3, 31. Chester & Oscar recrq
1894, 3, 31. Leora recrq
1896, 5, 30. Mary recrq
1896, 5, 30. Wm. H., Sarah & Osa B. recrq
1897, 1, 30. Walton recrq
1897, 5, 29. Emett recrq
1897, 8, 28. Mary L. dropped from mbrp
1898, 1, 27. Geo. & Mariah dropped from mbrp
1899, 7, 27. Fay B. dropped from mbrp
1899, 7, 27. Emmet dropped from mbrp
1899, 7, 27. James, Nellie, Allice & Leona dropped from mbrp
1899, 9, 31. Byron dropped from mbrp
1901, 4, 25. James J. recrq
1901, 7, 25. Samuel, Mary, Walter & Otho dropped from mbrp
1904, 4, 28. James recrq
1907, 2, 28. Lydia recrq
1907, 2, 28. Nellie recrq
1912, 4, 25. Israel W. & Minnie recrq
1912, 4, 25. Addie recrq
1926, 2, 25. Elmer recrq
1927, 3, 30. Helen recrq

MINGESTER
188-, 1, 31. Amanda recrq

MITCH
1907, 3, 28. Alfred recrq
1909, 7, 30. Alfred dropped from mbrp
1913, 2, 27. Alfred recrq
1914, 2, 25. Alfred dropped from mbrp
1926, 9, 30. Mrs. Bertha gc

MITCHELL
1882, 11, 25. Rebeccah recrq
1899, 7, 27. Rebecca dropped from mbrp

MITTEN
1891, 2, 28. Sarah & Geo. recrq

MOORE
1877, 2, 24. Louisa J. [More] recrq
1877, 2, 24. Wm. S. & Amanda M. recrq
1877, 3, 31. Chas. J., Amanda M. & Joseph J. recrq
1877, 12, 29. Wm. relrq
1878, 4, 27. Ursley recrq
1878, 11, 30. John recrq
1879, 3, 29. Wm. recrq
1879, 11, 29. Wm. dis disunity
1885, 7, 25. Jenie [More] dropped from mbrp
1886, 9, 25. Amanda M. dropped from mbrp
1886, 10, 30. Joseph dropped from mbrp
1897, 1, 30. Chas. & Drucilla recrq
1897, 3, 27. Bertha recrq
1899, 7, 27. Jane dropped from mbrp
1905, 2, 23. Leander recrq
1908, 7, 30. Leander dropped from mbrp
1912, 2, 29. Mentra recrq
1913, 1, 30. Mary recrq
1913, 1, 30. Verletta Elizabeth recrq
1914, 3, 25. Wm. H. recrq
1914, 4, 29. Chas. & Drucilla dropped from mbrp
1926, 2, 25. Louise recrq

MOORMAN
1912, 4, 25. Ida & Iola recrq

MOREHOUSE
1879, 12, 27. Charles recrq

MORLINE
1879, 12, 27. Clia & Elice recrq
1879, 12, 27. Millie recrq
1879, 12, 27. Solomon recrq

MORRIS
1877, 12, 29. Samuel & Hannah recrq
1899, 7, 27. Ellen dropped from mbrp

MORTIMER
1880, 1, 31. Robert recrq

MOSIER
1878, 1, 26. Sarah recrq
1878, 1, 26. Emily recrq
1878, 1, 26. Etta recrq
1878, 2, 23. Samuel recrq
1882, 2, 25. Viola recrq
1886, 3, 27. George W. [Mosure] recrq
1886, 9, 25. Samuel dropped from mbrp
1887, 2, 26. Laura E. recrq
1887, 8, 27. Ellen dropped from mbrp
1888, 2, 25. Rachel, Henry, Albert & Frederick [Mosure] recrq
1890, 3, 26. Samuel [Mosure] dropped from mbrp
1896, 1, 25. Henry & w, Louisa, relrq
1899, 7, 27. Albert, Freddie & Etta dropped from mbrp
1908, 7, 30. ----- [Moshure] dropped from mbrp

MOYER
1882, 2, 25. Wm. recrq
1886, 3, 27. Mary recrq
1888, 2, 25. Elmer recrq
1890, 3, 26. Wm. dropped from mbrp
1890, 3, 26. Mary dropped from mbrp
1890, 3, 26. Elmer dropped from mbrp

MULLEN
1877, 2, 24. Mary & Elvira recrq
1877, 2, 24. Nancy recrq
1877, 8, 25. Nancy relrq
1878, 1, 26. Polly recrq
1878, 1, 26. Alexander recrq
1878, 1, 26. Nancy Ann recrq
1878, 2, 23. John W. recrq
1879, 3, 29. Mary Frances recrq
1880, 1, 31. Catherine recrq
1884, 1, 26. Mattie recrq
1886, 2, 27. Etta recrq
1886, 3, 27. Chas. W. recrq
1888, 4, 28. A. R. relrq
1890, 3, 26. Pollie dropped from mbrp
1890, 3, 26. Ella dropped from mbrp
1890, 3, 26. Chas. W. dropped from mbrp
1893, 8, 26. Daniel recrq
1894, 3, 31. Daniel recrq
1896, 7, 25. Daniel dis disunity
1897, 1, 30. A. R. recrq
1901, 1, 31. A. R. dropped from mbrp
1903, 9, 24. Cleo dropped from mbrp

MUMAUGH
1878, 1, 26. Alice recrq

MURPHEY
1877, 2, 24. Anna recrq
1877, 2, 24. Frank recrq
1877, 12, 29. Henry recrq
1878, 1, 26. Rosa Ann recrq
1878, 1, 26. Samuel recrq
1878, 2, 23. Jane recrq
1884, 11, 29. Martha I. recrq
1884, 11, 29. Rolla recrq
1890, 3, 26. Jane [Murphy] dropped from mbrp
1897, 8, 28. Martha E. dropped from mbrp
1897, 8, 28. Huldah dropped from mbrp
1897, 8, 28. Blanch dropped from mbrp
1897, 8, 28. Walter dropped from mbrp
1899, 7, 27. Sam [Murphy] dropped from mbrp
1903, 9, 24. Frank, Anna, Neoma, Nella, Ira & Hattie dropped from mbrp
1905, 2, 23. May recrq
1912, 4, 25. Fred recrq
1912, 4, 25. Lillie recrq
1914, 4, 29. Mary dropped from mbrp

MURRAY
1893, 6, 24. James recrq

MURRAY, continued
1897, 8, 28. James dropped from mbrp

MYERS
1880, 1, 31. Nettie recrq
1897, 4, 24. John & Annie recrq
1897, 8, 28. Minnie dropped from mbrp
1900, 1, 25. Hattie recrq
1901, 3, 28. Joseph, Sadie & C. Nolen recrq
1905, 2, 23. Ida recrq
1910, 3, 31. Mrs. Jennie recrq
1913, 2, 27. John recrq
1913, 2, 27. Wm. recrq
1928, 2, 23. Myrtle May, Russel Abram & Albert recrq
1928, 2, 23. Herbert recrq

NACKBAR
1901, 3, 28. Amy D recrq

NAIL
1878, 2, 23. Carrie recrq
1890, 6, 28. J. H. recrq

NANCE
1882, 11, 25. Obadiah, G. W. & Nancy recrq

NEAL
1885, 3, 28. Nathan recrq
1886, 12, 25. Nathan relrq
1897, 8, 28. Nathan dropped from mbrp

NEALY
1878, 1, 26. Stephen A. recrq
1886, 1, 30. Nancy Jane [Neally] recrq
1886, 5, 29. James [Neely] recrq
1888, 4, 28. James relrq
1893, 4, 29. Nancy Jane & Annie relrq

NEAR
1878, 4, 27. Emanuel recrq
1878, 5, 25. Mary A. recrq
1878, 12, 28. James recrq
1880, 1, 31. Wm. recrq
1881, 3, 26. James C. recrq
1895, 4, 27. James & Etta recrq
1895, 4, 27. Mary Ann, Cora D. & Samuel Peter recrq
1896, 3, 29. Edward recrq
1896, 6, 27. Maud recrq
1899, 7, 27. Mary A. & Edward [Neer] dropped from mbrp
1901, 4, 25. Ada recrq
1901, 7, 25. Samuel & James dropped from mbrp
1902, 5, 29. Ada Barber dropped from mbrp
1903, 4, 26. Flow & Maude recrq

NELSON
1879, 10, 25. George dis disunity

NETRO
1878, 11, 30. Samuel recrq
1880, 3, 27. Joseph C. [Nettron] recrq
1880, 3, 27. Abraham [Nitrow] recrq
1881, 2, 26. J. dis disunity

NICHOLS
1891, 3, 28. I. M. recrq
1897, 6, 26. Matthewson dropped from mbrp
1907, 6, 27. John & w, Etta, recrq
1909, 7, 30. John & Ella dropped from mbrp
1911, 3, 30. John & w, Hattie, relrq
1913, 12, 25. Harold recrq

NIXON
1896, 2, 29. Sarah, Sarah A., Wm. & John recrq
1898, 10, 27. Jennie & Nettie recrq
1898, 10, 27. Harry & John dropped from mbrp
1901, 3, 28. Julia recrq
1909, 4, 29. Wm. & Sarah dropped from mbrp
1909, 4, 29. Harry dropped from mbrp
1910, 3, 31. Robert recrq
1911, 3, 30. Sadie F. recrq
1913, 7, 25. Nobert relrq

NOBLE
1889, 3, 30. Jennie recrq
1891, 4, 25. Jennie dropped from mbrp

NOGLE
1901, 7, 25. Hiram & Betsy dropped from mbrp
1914, 12, 30. Henry [Noggle] recrq

NOLTON
1897, 8, 28. Jane dropped from mbrp
1897, 8, 28. Theodore dropped from mbrp

NORMAN
1878, 4, 27. Daniel recrq
1879, 12, 27. Daniel dis disunity

NORRIS
1877, 12, 29. John W., Harriet S., Sytanis Calista J., Emma & Tallie, recrq
1878, 4, 27. Burgoine recrq
1878, 12, 28. John recrq
1878, 12, 28. Hannah recrq
1878, 3, 29. Maggie recrq
1886, 3, 27. George recrq
1886, 3, 27. Hannah relrq
1888, 2, 25. Ellis recrq
1890, 5, 31. Calista dis disunity
1891, 4, 25. Emma dropped from mbrp
1891, 4, 25. Sylvanus, John & Harriett dis disunity
1897, 8, 28. Bert dropped from mbrp
1905, 2, 23. Geo. & Mary recrq
1905, 2, 23. Libie recrq
1907, 1, 5. Lillie recrq
1907, 2, 28. Jesse recrq

NORTH
1877, 3, 31. Ira & Martha Jane recrq
1878, 4, 27. Susanna recrq

NORTH, continued
1878, 4, 27. Thomas recrq
1879, 3, 29. Loretta & Mary E. recrq
1880, 3, 27. Esther recrq
1880, 3, 27. Ellie recrq
1880, 3, 27. Annie recrq
1886, 9, 25. Ira & Martha J. dropped from mbrp
1886, 9, 25. Susanna dropped from mbrp
1886, 9, 25. Loretta dropped from mbrp
1886, 9, 25. Esther dropped from mbrp
1886, 9, 25. May dropped from mbrp
1892, 3, 26. Ada recrq
1893, 3, 25. Irena & Mary recrq
1894, 6, 30. Minnie recrq
1903, 7, 30. Bessie recrq
1903, 9, 24. Pearl & Minnie dropped from mbrp
1907, 1, 5. Isaac recrq

NULL
1880, 1, 31. Joseph F. recrq

NUTT
1878, 4, 27. George recrq
1878, 11, 30. Hannah recrq
1878, 12, 28. George recrq
1880, 7, 31. George & w, Hannah, relrq

ODELL
1899, 7, 27. Daisy dropped from mbrp

ODEY
1877, 2, 24. Maggie recrq
1877, 11, 24. Maggie [Oday] relrq

OGLESBE
1878, 9, 28. Ida Y. recrq
1881, 2, 26. Ida relrq
1903, 4, 26. Anna recrq

OLIVER
1878, 1, 26. Jane recrq

OLSON
1914, 10, 28. Oscar recrq

OWENS
1927, 1, 27. Mrs. Ford relrq

PAINTER
1906, 11, 28. Seth d ae 85 (an elder)

1877, 3, 31. Seth recrq
1878, 4, 27. Annie recrq
1879, 6, 28. Lucy J. recrq
1883, 3, 31. Mary rocf Dover MM, dtd 1883,3, 15
1884, 2, 23. Seth recrq
1908, 12, 31. Florence relrq

PALMER
1878, 12, 28. John & Mary recrq
1880, 9, 25. Sophia J. & Mary C. recrq
1888, 2, 25. Sylvester & w, Sarah, rocf Middlepoint MM, dtd 1888,2,11
1892, 4, 30. Sophia relrq
1907, 2, 28. Fern P. recrq
1910, 10, 27. Josephine Mable recrq
1912, 4, 25. Minnie & Eugene recrq
1913, 12, 25. Frank & Ida recrq
1914, 10, 28. Sylvester dropped from mbrp
1914, 10, 28. Fern dropped from mbrp

PANGLE
1878, 4, 27. Abraham V. & Mary M. recrq
1878, 12, 28. Louisa recrq
1913, 12, 25. Wm. & Jennic recrq

PARENT
1877, 2, 24. Elizabeth [Pairent] recrq
1877, 12, 29. John recrq
1878, 2, 23. Ella recrq
1878, 3, 30. Franklin recrq
1886, 2, 27. Edith recrq
1892, 2, 27. Ella relrq
1905, 4, 27. Samuel & w, Elizabeth, recrq

PARKER
1911, 7, 29. Dora recrq
1931, 1, 29. Ida T. rocf Perry City MM, N.Y.
1933, 8, 31. Ida T. & dt, Ethel Louise, gct Charlottesville MM

PARKINSON
1895, 9, 21. Joseph & w, Fanny, gct Dover MM, O.

PARMENTER
1881, 2, 26. Mary recrq
1890, 3, 26. Mary dropped from mbrp

PARPHAN
1878, 1, 26. Ida recrq
1886, 11, 27. Ida dropped from mbrp
1890, 3, 26. Ida [Parpham] dropped from mbrp

PARR
1877, 11, 24. Nancy recrq
1877, 11, 24. Wm. recrq
1878, 5, 25. Wm. & w, Nancy, dis disunity

PARRISH
1914, 10, 28. Henry M. recrq

PARRUT
1899, 7, 27. Edith dropped from mbrp

PATRICK
1881, 1, 29. John recrq
1881, 2, 26. Sarah E. recrq
1901, 1, 31. Francis & Margaret recrq
1908, 7, 30. Francis & Margaret [Patric] dis disunity

PEARS
1877, 6, 30. Wm. recrq

PEARSON
1900, 3, 29. Sarah recrq

PEER
1877, 10, 27. George Francis & w, Frances, recrq
1879, 6, 28. Frankie rocf Caesars Creek MM,O.

PENCE
1878, 5, 25. Anna recrq
1894, 4, 28. Jocie & Allie recrq
1898, 8, 25. Bertha [Pense] recrq
1901, 4, 25. Daniel, Bertha & Morgan recrq
1903, 4, 26. Clifford B. & Bertha recrq
1910, 11, 29. Anna recrq (form mbr at Middlepoint now laid down)
1911, 2, 23. Clifford recrq
1912, 4, 25. Daniel & Oscar [Pense] recrq

PENNETT
1908, 7, 30. Mable dropped from mbrp

PENTAN
1884, 12, 22. Ida recrq

PERRY
1879, 6, 28. Belle recrq
1879, 10, 25. Joshua recrq
1880, 1, 31. Mary A. recrq
1880, 1, 31. Ezra A. recrq
1882, 2, 25. Wm. recrq
1897, 1, 30. Eva & Cora recrq
1899, 7, 27. Katie & Lavina dropped from mbrp
1903, 1, 29. Hazel A. recrq

PERTS
1879, 10, 25. Joshua recrq

PETTIFORD
1895, 8, 31. Reuben M. & w, Margaret Ann, & ch, Bessie Delany, Wm. Alexander, Frederick, Marianna & Chas. B., rocf New Garden MM, Ind., dtd 1895,7,20
1901, 7, 25. Reuben M., Margaret A., William, Mareanna, Frederick & Chas. [Petiford] dropped from mbrp

PETTY
1906, 12, 27. Sarah recrq

PHILLIPS
1878, 4, 27. George & Mary recrq
1881, 3, 26. Elizabeth, Sarah, Samuel J. & Chas. recrq
1884, 11, 29. Chloe I. & ch, Nellie & Clifford Towey & Charley G., Luna I. & Lucy Eveline Philips, rocf Fairmount MM, dtd 1884,11,12
1884, 12, 22. Josiah & Icy recrq
1894, 4, 28. Chloe relrq
1894, 6, 30. Josiah relrq
1894, 7, 28. Harry & w, Fanny, recrq
1895, 6, 29. Chloe recrq
1896, 1, 25. Chloe relrq
1898, 11, 24. Chas., Elizabeth & Sarah dropped from mbrp
1901, 4, 25. Elizabeth & Sarah recrq
1914, 10, 28. Sadie dropped from mbrp

PICKERING
1912, 4, 25. Vada recrq
1914, 12, 30. Dorothy recrq

PILLOWS
1881, 2, 26. Freeman recrq

PLUMMER
1907, 2, 28. Pearl recrq
1907, 2, 28. Flossie recrq
1907, 2, 28. Clarence recrq

POLING
1893, 6, 24. Ephraim & Gladdie & Nancy recrq
1897, 8, 28. Gladdie dropped from mbrp
1897, 8, 28. Ephraim dropped from mbrp
1897, 8, 28. Nancy dropped from mbrp

POPE
1876, 2, 26. James & w, Ellen, & ch gct Grassy Run MM, O.

POTTS
1878, 12, 28. Ida May recrq
1881, 2, 26. Harriet recrq
1882, 10, 28. Benjamin G. recrq
1883, 1, 27. Y. H. & Jane recrq
1884, 12, 22. Elizabeth recrq
1899, 7, 27. Jennie & Elizabeth dropped from mbrp

PRAWL
1876, 4, 29. Chas. W. & Mary E. recrq

PRESTON
1896, 5, 30. J. H. & Alwilda recrq
1906, 5, 31. Frank & Fred recrq

PRICE
1877, 12, 29. Mauda recrq
1878, 2, 23. Amanda, dt Henry, relrq
1878, 2, 23. Amos & Matilda recrq
1898, 3, 31. Mae recrq
1903, 9, 24. Nellie dropped from mbrp

PRIDDY
1878, 4, 27. Thos. D., Lucinda, Milla J., Lucy A., Fanny M., Chas. F. & John F., recrq
1880, 3, 27. Lucinda, Millie, Fannie, John & Chas. relrq

PRICHARD
1889, 8, 31. Finley & Sarah L. [Pritchard] recrq
1895, 6, 29. Cassie recrq
1895, 11, 30. Finley & fam gct White River

PRICHARD, continued
MM, Ind.

PRIEST
1878, 1, 26. Wm. & Maggie recrq
1886, 9, 25. Levi & Maggie dropped from mbrp

PRIVE
1879, 12, 27. John recrq

PURK
1905, 2, 23. Katie recrq

PUTNAM
1884, 2, 23. Chas. D. recrq
1894, 3, 31. Tillie recrq
1896, 5, 30. Olive recrq
1897, 1, 30. Chas. recrq
1901, 1, 31. Hazel & Clifford recrq
1903, 9, 24. Chas. dropped from mbrp
1934, 1, 25. Elizabeth recrq

QUACKENBUSH
1878, 4, 27. Armirtie recrq
1881, 3, 26. Chrissy recrq
1886, 9, 25. Arminta dropped from mbrp
1886, 9, 25. Chrisie dropped from mbrp

RAIDER
1886, 4, 24. Catharine recrq
1899, 7, 27. Catharine dropped from mbrp

RALSTON
1896, 3, 28. John W. rocf Newberry MM, O.
1897, 2, 27. John W. gct Little Blue River MM, Ind.
1897, 8, 28. Callie May dropped from mbrp

RAMSEY
1881, 1, 29. John C. & Harriet recrq
1885, 11, 29. Roaka recrq
1905, 2, 23. James & Mattie recrq
1905, 2, 23. Murlin & Nansy recrq
1905, 2, 23. Alice recrq
1905, 2, 23. Albert recrq
1908, 7, 30. Walter dropped from mbrp
1908, 7, 30. Marlin dropped from mbrp
1908, 7, 30. Alice dropped from mbrp
1908, 7, 30. Nancy dropped from mbrp
1908, 7, 30. Albert dropped from mbrp
1914, 4, 29. James dropped from mbrp

RANDALL
1886, 2, 27. Melissa recrq
1890, 3, 26. Melissa A. dropped from mbrp

RANDOBAUGH
1878, 3, 30. Levi, Mariah, Tissie & Mary recrq
1879, 12, 27. John [Redenbaugh] recrq

RAUDABAUGH
1907, 4, 25. Jacob R. [Raidabaugh] recrq
1912, 2, 29. Phoeba R. & Clara E. recrq
1912, 4, 25. Eva [Raudabough] recrq
1912, 4, 25. Wm. [Raudabough] recrq
1926, 2, 25. Jessie recrq

RAY
1879, 12, 27. Albert recrq

RAYER
1911, 4, 27. Ida recrq
1914, 6, 24. Ida F. relrq

RAYMOND
1886, 5, 29. Chas. & Hariet recrq
1886, 5, 29. Caroline recrq
1899, 7, 27. Chas., Harriett & Caroline dropped from mbrp

REAMSNYDER
1880, 1, 31. John recrq

REASOR
1899, 7, 27. Cecil dropped from mbrp

REDMAN
1885, 1, 31. Allen & Edith recrq

REDRUP
1880, 2, 28. Thomas recrq

REEDER
1880, 1, 31. Mary recrq

REESE
1891, 3, 28. Isaiah recrq

REGESTER
1912, 4, 25. Hazel recrq

REID
1912, 2, 29. Charles recrq

RENO
1891, 4, 25. Wm., Ella, Maggie & Etta recrq
1899, 7, 27. Wm., Ella, Maggie & Wm. dropped from mbrp

RESLER
1878, 12, 28. John W. recrq

RESOR
1894, 3, 31. Ceicil recrq

RETMAN
1890, 6, 28. Melissa recrq

REYNOLDS
1913, 12, 25. Augustus & dt, Constance, recrq

RHINEHOLT
1889, 5, 30. Lida recrq

RHINESMITH
1878, 11, 30. Wm. recrq

RHODES
1877, 2, 24. Nettie recrq
1878, 2, 23. Mary A. recrq
1881, 4, 30. David & Amanda recrq
1882, 1, 28. Elmer recrq
1882, 2, 25. Estella recrq
1882, 2, 25. George recrq
1886, 3, 27. Mary O. recrq
1890, 3, 26. David & Amanda dropped from mbrp
1890, 3, 26. Elmer dropped from mbrp
1890, 3, 26. George dropped from mbrp
1895, 3, 30. Mary A. relrq
1903, 9, 24. Nettie dropped from mbrp
1903, 9, 24. Bertha dropped from mbrp

RIBLET
1877, 2, 24. Cynthia recrq
1877, 11, 24. James James E. Jr. recrq
1877, 12, 29. Sylvanis & Rebecca recrq
1880, 2, 28. Isaac R. recrq
1880, 3, 27. Hattie recrq
1882, 1, 28. Jennie recrq
1892, 2, 27. Jennie relrq
1892, 5, 28. Oscar & Rebecca relrq
1895, 2, 23. Rebecca recrq

RICHARDS
1878, 4, 27. Wm. recrq
1878, 4, 27. Josiah C. recrq
1882, 2, 25. James recrq
1882, 2, 25. Mary recrq
1882, 2, 25. Elijah C. recrq
1883, 10, 27. James dis disunity
1889, 2, 23. Bartley, Ellen & Cora recrq
1893, 4, 29. Warren recrq
1897, 8, 28. Ella dropped from mbrp

RICHARDSON
1898, 10, 27. Sarah dropped from mbrp

RICKETTS
1893, 10, 28. Warren dis

RIDENOUR
1897, 1, 30. Florence recrq
1900, 7, 26. Florence dropped from mbrp

RIEHLE
1879, 12, 27. John recrq

RIGDON
1879, 12, 27. David recrq
1884, 2, 23. Jeptha recrq
1885, 4, 25. Jeptha relrq

RIGGINS
1887, 8, 27. Wm. recrq
1898, 10, 27. J. W. relrq

RIGHT
1879, 1, 25. James recrq
1879, 6, 28. Emma recrq

RILEY
1879, 1, 25. Carrie A. recrq
1879, 3, 29. Levi S. recrq
1882, 2, 25. Forest recrq
1884, 2, 23. Nettie M. recrq
1886, 2, 27. Nevada & Susan recrq
1888, 2, 25. James recrq
1888, 10, 27. Susie dropped from mbrp
1889, 10, 26. John gct Friends Chapel MM, O.
1890, 1, 25. Jacob recrq
1891, 2, 28. Jacob dis disunity
1894, 3, 31. Andrew recrq
1899, 7, 27. Andrew dropped from mbrp
1901, 7, 25. Levi dropped from mbrp
1903, 9, 24. Wm. dropped from mbrp
1908, 7, 30. James, Laurie, Leah & Clara dropped from mbrp
1911, 4, 27. Levi L. recrq
1911, 4, 27. Clara recrq
1913, 12, 25. Raymond & Lauta recrq
1926, 2, 25. Evolyn & Janette recrq
1928, 4, 28. Ray recrq

RINGWALD
1914, 3, 25. Gertrude Ilane relrq

ROBBINS
1882, 2, 25. Derisa recrq

ROBERTS
1879, 3, 29. Truman recrq
1881, 3, 26. Milton recrq
1887, 5, 28. Lorena recrq
1897, 6, 26. Truman & w dropped from mbrp
1901, 3, 28. Viola recrq
1911, 2, 23. Mrs. Eva A. recrq
1933, 9, 28. Milten M. recrq

ROBY
1877, 12, 29. Alexander recrq
1878, 2, 23. Amanda F. recrq

ROCKHOLD
1880, 12, 25. Ephraim recrq
1885, 1, 31. Mary [Rockolt] recrq

ROGERS
1876, 2, 26. Elizabeth recrq
1876, 2, 26. Charles recrq
1876, 2, 26. Amos recrq
1876, 2, 26. Florence J. recrq
1877, 12, 29. James recrq
1880, 1, 31. Clara recrq
1881, 1, 29. Ida recrq
1881, 1, 29. Amos recrq
1881, 1, 29. Asberry recrq
1881, 2, 26. Elizabeth recrq
1881, 4, 30. Amos gct Friends Church, Jamestown, O.

ROGERS, continued
1890, 3, 26. Ida dropped from mbrp
1890, 3, 26. Asberry dropped from mbrp
1899, 7, 27. Elizabeth, Chas., Florence, Clara & Anna dropped from mbrp

ROICE
1878, 1, 26. Rebecca, Edward C. & Edwin W. recrq
1882, 1, 28. D. L. recrq
1884, 2, 23. Delilah recrq
1890, 3, 26. Delilah dropped from mbrp

ROLLAND
1884, 2, 23. Wm. recrq
1884, 2, 23. Samuel F. recrq
1886, 9, 25. Wm. dropped from mbrp

ROSE
1880, 1, 31. John recrq
1880, 1, 31. Melcema recrq

ROSS
1891, 4, 25. Levi, Rhoda & Chas. recrq
1899, 7, 27. Levi, Rhoda & Chas. dropped from mbrp

ROTH
1909, 7, 30. Kenneth & May dropped from mbrp

ROUTAN
1891, 4, 25. Milton recrq

ROWE
1885, 3, 28. Anna recrq

RUHER
1890, 3, 26. Ella dropped from mbrp

RUMBOLT
1897, 8, 28. Lydia dropped from mbrp

RUNKLE
1880, 11, 31. Bruno W. recrq

RUNNION
1902, 4, 4. Dorothy Bell b

1886, 4, 24. Albert & Jennie M. recrq
1894, 2, 24. Francis recrq
1899, 4, 27. Susie recrq
1907, 1, 5. Rachel recrq
1914, 3, 25. Dorotha Bell recrq

RUPERT
1877, 2, 24. G. W. & Charity recrq
1880, 1, 31. James recrq
1880, 1, 31. John N. recrq
1880, 1, 31. Sidney recrq
1882, 2, 25. Henrietta recrq
1901, 1, 31. Amanda [Rupe] recrq

RUTAN
1896, 2, 29. Milton recrq
1899, 7, 27. Milton dropped from mbrp

SACKET
1880, 1, 31. Mary recrq

SALTERS
1881, 2, 26. Ezra recrq
1890, 3, 26. Ezra [Stalter] dropped from mbrp

SALTZGABER
1879, 1, 25. Ella & Mamie recrq
1879, 4, 26. Elizabeth recrq
1903, 9, 24. Elizabeth dropped from mbrp

SAMPSON
1878, 1, 26. Alfred recrq

SANDERS
1878, 4, 27. Laura & Charley recrq
1879, 1, 25. Albert recrq
1880, 1, 31. Albert relrq
1893, 3, 25. Huldah J. recrq
1903, 7, 30. Florence & Mable recrq

SANDS
1880, 1, 31. George W. recrq

SARGENT
1888, 2, 25. Joseph recrq
1890, 1, 25. Matilda recrq
1892, 3, 26. Wm. & Viola recrq
1894, 1, 27. Mary recrq
1894, 3, 31. Joseph recrq
1895, 12, 28. Annie recrq
1897, 1, 30. Bessie recrq
1899, 7, 27. Wm. dropped from mbrp
1902, 3, 27. Ola gct Winchester MM, Ind.
1904, 11, 24. Joseph & w, Florence, & ch, Florine, Forest & Lucile, gct Farmland MM, Ind.
1905, 2, 23. Walter recrq
1905, 3, 30. Bessie dropped from mbrp

1909, 1, 28. Lura recrq
1912, 4, 25. Ralph & w, Flo, recrq
1933, 3, 30. Walter A. relrq

SCHICKEDANTZ
1897, 8, 28. John dropped from mbrp
1897, 8, 28. Susie dropped from mbrp

SCOTT
1879, 3, 29. Rebecca recrq
1912, 4, 25. Grover & w, Carrie, recrq
1912, 4, 25. Exira recrq

SEARS
1883, 1, 27. Elizabeth gct Salem MM, O.

SEEDS
1880, 1, 31. Thomas recrq

SEEDS, continued
1880, 1, 31. Martha recrq

SELLERS
1878, 3, 30. Alvin recrq
1886, 11, 27. Alvin T. dropped from mbrp

SERMAN
1881, 7, 30. A. J. dropped from mbrp

SEVERNS
1877, 11, 24. Bell recrq
1888, 7, 28. Chas. & Maria recrq

SHAFFER
1878, 2, 23. Martha recrq
1882, 2, 25. F. M. recrq
1882, 10, 28. Chas. D., Jane, Annie & Sarah Ellen recrq
1886, 8, 28. Marion relrq
1886, 11, 27. Martha dropped from mbrp
1899, 7, 27. James dropped from mbrp
1899, 7, 27. Chas. dropped from mbrp
1899, 7, 27. Anna dropped from mbrp
1899, 7, 27. Sarah E. dropped from mbrp
1911, 4, 27. Mary B. recrq
1927, 5, 25. Blanch Fouty dropped from mbrp

SHANER
1878, 2, 23. Lucy Ann recrq
1888, 1, 27. Lucy A. gct Middlepoint MM
1902, 3, 27. John & Amelia recrq

SHANEYFELT
1896, 2, 29. Orra L. recrq
1897, 8, 28. Della dropped from mbrp
1909, 4, 29. Bird dropped from mbrp

SHAW
1880, 1, 31. Emma J. recrq
1881, 9, 24. Otis & Susie recrq
1899, 7, 27. Otis dropped from mbrp

SHECKLER
1878, 4, 27. Delila recrq
1899, 7, 27. Lester [Sheekler] dropped from mbrp

SHEETS
1881, 2, 26. Mirtie dis disunity
1887, 3, 26. Mary E. [Sheats] recrq

SHELTON
1878, 4, 27. Ellen recrq

SHERBURN
1895, 1, 26. Daniel Edwin & Katie L. recrq
1905, 4, 27. D. E. & w, Catharine, relrq

SHERMAN
1875, 3, 7. James & Mary dis
1877, 2, 24. Clara recrq
1877, 12, 29. Joseph M., Mary C. & George recrq
1878, 1, 26. Jackson & Louisa recrq
1886, 9, 25. James dropped from mbrp
1888, 2, 25. Mely recrq
1894, 3, 31. Nellie recrq
1899, 7, 27. Joseph M. dropped from mbrp
1899, 7, 27. Amelia dropped from mbrp
1903, 9, 24. Mary dropped from mbrp
1907, 3, 28. Una recrq
1907, 3, 28. Mrs. ----- recrq
1908, 1, 30. Mrs. ----- relrq
1909, 4, 29. Eunice & Alva dropped from mbrp

SHEROD
1879, 12, 27. Nettie recrq

SHIEKS
1879, 10, 25. Mintie recrq

SHILLING
1878, 2, 23. Nancy Oday relrq

SHINGLEDECKER
1885, 1, 31. Cyrus recrq

SHIP
1876, 2, 26. Mell recrq

SHIRER
1888, 5, 26. Ida May recrq
1899, 7, 27. Ida May [Shire] dropped from mbrp

SHIRTLIFF
1888, 2, 25. Plymouth recrq
1890, 3, 26. Plimmeth dropped from mbrp
1897, 8, 28. Edward dropped from mbrp

SHOBE
1931, 3, 26. Helen & Caroline recrq

SHOOK
1913, 2, 27. Joseph recrq

SHOOP
1891, 4, 25. Joseph & Minnie recrq

SHRECK
1897, 8, 28. Chas. dropped from mbrp

SHROVE
1895, 6, 29. Lucinda recrq

SHUTT
1912, 4, 25. L. E. & w, Ina, recrq

SIDELLS
1881, 2, 26. George recrq
1881, 2, 26. Stella recrq
1914, 4, 29. Stella [Sidles] dropped from mbrp
1914, 4, 29. Geo. [Sidles] dropped from mbrp

SIDERS
1877, 11, 24. Robert, Joseph, Elsworth & Lucy recrq
1888, 2, 25. Joseph recrq
1890, 3, 26. Robert dropped from mbrp
1892, 4, 30. Ellsworth & w, Lucy, dropped from mbrp

SILER
1926, 6, 24. Mrs. Lou recrq

SIMPSON
1903, 1, 29. Mary recrq

SIPLES
1879, 3, 29. Josiah & Clara recrq
1913, 4, 24. Clara relrq

SITES
1886, 5, 29. Ellen recrq
1887, 3, 26. George recrq
1888, 2, 25. Jacob & w dropped from mbrp
1891, 2, 28. George, Ellen & Geo. Jr. recrq
1891, 4, 25. Geo. & Ellen recrq
1897, 8, 28. Jacob dropped from mbrp
1899, 7, 27. George dropped from mbrp
1903, 7, 30. Jonas & Rachel recrq
1903, 9, 24. Ella dropped from mbrp

SKELLY
1899, 1, 26. Norman [Scelly] recrq
1914, 4, 29. Wm. & Amanda dropped from mbrp

SLAIN
1903, 7, 30. Gertrude recrq

SLUTERBECK
1886, 5, 29. Jacob & Mahala recrq
1897, 8, 28. Maggie [Slutebeck] dropped from mbrp

SMALLEY
1899, 7, 27. Albert & Mary dropped from mbrp

SMELTZER
1885, 1, 31. Abraham & Catharine recrq

SMITH
1906, 3, 24. Wm. L. d (an elder & clerk)

1877, 2, 24. Ella recrq
1877, 3, 31. James F. recrq
1878, 1, 26. Levi recrq
1879, 6, 28. Mary C. recrq
1879, 6, 28. John C. & Emeline recrq
1880, 1, 31. Clara recrq
1880, 1, 31. Wm. A. recrq
1884, 1, 26. Francis recrq
1885, 4, 25. John dis disunity
1886, 2, 27. Minnie recrq
1886, 9, 25. James F. dropped from mbrp
1888, 2, 25. Sarah, May & Olie recrq
1890, 3, 26. Ella dropped from mbrp
1890, 3, 26. Emmeline dropped from mbrp
1891, 2, 28. Wm., Mary & Henry recrq
1891, 2, 28. Bert recrq
1891, 2, 28. Isaac recrq
1891, 4, 25. Jacob recrq
1891, 4, 25. Wm., Henry & Mary recrq
1891, 9, 26. John recrq
1894, 2, 24. Lou recrq
1894, 6, 30. Isaac, Geneva & Meriah recrq
1896, 11, 28. Alice Hays gct Greenforks MM, Ind.
1897, 8, 28. Smith dropped from mbrp
1899, 7, 27. Frank dropped from mbrp
1899, 7, 27. Francis dropped from mbrp
1899, 7, 27. Mary dropped from mbrp
1899, 7, 27. Jacob dropped from mbrp
1899, 7, 27. Chas. dropped from mbrp
1903, 9, 24. Minnie dropped from mbrp
1903, 9, 24. Emma dropped from mbrp
1907, 3, 28. Martha E. recrq
1907, 12, 26. Jacob & w, Jennie, recrq
1914, 4, 29. Beatrice Grandstaff dropped from mbrp
1914, 5, 27. Jacob C. relrq
1931, 6, 25. Hannah rocf Central Mission Friends, Van Wert, O.

SMITTZ
1881, 2, 26. Wm. recrq
1914, 4, 29. Wm. dropped from mbrp

SNELL
1889, 3, 30. J. F. & Nancy E. recrq
1899, 7, 27. J. F. & Nancy dropped from mbrp

SNIDER
1824, 11, 29. Samuel recrq
1824, 11, 29. Mary Ann recrq
1824, 11, 29. Minda recrq
1889, 3, 30. Emily recrq
1894, 2, 24. Amanda recrq
1899, 7, 27. ----- dropped from mbrp
1907, 6, 27. Ira recrq
1909, 6, 25. Daniel & w, Mary Ann, relrq
1927, 6, 30. Ray & Etta dropped from mbrp

SNODGRASS
1879, 5, 31. Chas. & Ella recrq
1880, 6, 26. Ella relrq
1880, 7, 31. Chas. dis disunity

SOLARS
1877, 2, 24. Eva [Solers] recrq
1878, 2, 23. Elizabeth recrq
1878, 2, 23. George recrq
1886, 9, 25. George [Sollers] dropped from mbrp

SOWERS
1888, 2, 25. Julie recrq
1892, 2, 27. Thomas relrq
1899, 7, 27. Bell dropped from mbrp

SPAR
1884, 2, 23. John recrq
1890, 3, 26. John recrq
1899, 7, 27. John dropped from mbrp

SPAULDING
1912, 4, 25. C. E. & w, Rosa, & ch, Hazel, Eugene, Ruth & Tradar, recrq

SPELLMAN
1897, 8, 28. James dropped from mbrp

SPHON
1885, 2, 28. Jasper N. recrq

SPRINGER
1877, 11, 24. Abram recrq
1878, 1, 26. Lizzie recrq
1882, 1, 28. Edward recrq
1908, 3, 26. Zelma relrq

SPROLL
1908, 1, 30. Aaron recrq

SPROUL
1909, 3, 11. Evelyn Irene b

SPRY
1928, 2, 23. Wm. Horace & Helen Lutta recrq

STANLEY
1881, 3, 26. Annie recrq
1885, 3, 28. Samuel & Almeda recrq
1886, 2, 27. H. H. & Julia recrq
1888, 7, 28. Hiram & Julia dropped from mbrp
1897, 8, 28. Lemiel & Malinda dropped from mbrp
1898, 4, 28. Francis C. & Sarah A. rocf Stewart MM, Ia., dtd 1898,4,6
1901, 12, 26. F. C. & w, S. A., gct West Grove MM, Ind.

STANTON
1887, 2, 26. Allie recrq
1887, 8, 27. Almeda dropped from mbrp
1894, 3, 31. Jackson E. & Tillie recrq
1899, 7, 27. J. C. dropped from mbrp

STARK
1894, 3, 31. Ora recrq
1901, 7, 25. Ora dropped from mbrp

STATLER
1877, 3, 31. Sarah Jane & Delila recrq
1886, 9, 25. Sarah J. [Stalter] & Delilah dropped from mbrp
1896, 5, 30. Mary recrq
1903, 9, 24. Ola dropped from mbrp

STEEL
1882, 2, 25. Mary recrq

STEMAN
1910, 1, 27. Hertha relrq
1912, 5, 30. Belle & Luca recrq

STEMP
1879, 3, 29. Louisa recrq

STEPHENS
1881, 8, 27. Noah [Stevens] relrq
1895, 5, 25. Cary & Vadie recrq
1896, 5, 30. Earle recrq
1899, 7, 27. Earl [Steven] dropped from mbrp
1905, 2, 23. Noah recrq
1906, 5, 31. Velma & Cloyd recrq
1912, 2, 29. Grant & w, Allie, relrq
1914, 10, 28. Noah dropped from mbrp

STERLING
1879, 11, 29. Sarah Ann recrq
1906, 5, 31. Mabel recrq

STEVENSON
1879, 12, 27. Sadie recrq

STEWARD
1877, 3, 31. Alice recrq
1880, 3, 27. Mary Ann recrq
1886, 9, 25. Alice dropped from mbrp
1899, 7, 27. Hamilton dropped from mbrp

STILLWAGONER
1878, 1, 26. George & Sarah recrq

STIMEMETZ
1878, 4, 27. Mabel recrq

STOUT
1889, 7, 27. Wm. & Melvin recrq
1893, 6, 24. Wm., Walter & Silas recrq
1897, 8, 28. Wm. & Melvin dropped from mbrp
1897, 8, 28. Walter dropped from mbrp
1897, 8, 28. William dropped from mbrp
1897, 8, 28. Silas dropped from mbrp

STRARS
1879, 12, 27. Hester recrq

STRAUB
1893, 6, 24. Mary recrq
1897, 8, 28. John dropped from mbrp
1901, 1, 31. Mary dropped from mbrp

STRINE
1889, 2, 23. Lemuel & Mahala recrq
1897, 8, 28. Lemuel & Mahala dropped from mbrp

STRIPP
1882, 1, 28. Lizzie, Wm. & Charlie recrq

STUCKEY
1880, 3, 27. Seigle recrq
1881, 3, 26. Susanna recrq

STUCKEY, continued
1884, 2, 23. Eli & Elizabeth recrq
1885, 2, 28. Elihu & Ira P. recrq
1899, 7, 27. Elizabeth dropped from mbrp
1899, 7, 27. Susan dropped from mbrp
1899, 7, 27. Ira dropped from mbrp
1899, 7, 27. Segal dropped from mbrp
1899, 7, 27. Thos. dropped from mbrp
1899, 11, 30. Lucy Demint relrq

STUMP
1884, 2, 23. Mary E. recrq
1890, 3, 26. Samuel J. recrq
1894, 2, 24. Ethel recrq
1894, 2, 24. Francis recrq
1899, 4, 27. Orla, Perly, Mag & Icadore recrq
1899, 4, 27. Florence recrq
1901, 6, 27. Grace recrq
1909, 10, 28. Isadore relrq
1910, 1, 27. Isadore rst
1911, 3, 30. Ford L. recrq
1912, 8, 29. Samuel T. & w, Nettie, recrq
1913, 5, 29. Peter & Clara recrq
1914, 4, 29. Samuel dropped from mbrp
1914, 4, 29. Florence dropped from mbrp
1914, 4, 29. Grace & Mary dropped from mbrp
1914, 4, 29. Francis dropped from mbrp
1914, 4, 29. Isadore dropped from mbrp

STUPP
1877, 2, 24. Edward & Catharine A. recrq
1888, 12, 29. Lizzie relrq
1897, 1, 30. G. W. relrq
1903, 1, 29. Josephine recrq
1903, 10, 29. Catharine A. relrq
1908, 7, 30. Chas. & Josephine dropped from mbrp

STUTLEMIRE
1880, 1, 31. Sarah recrq

SUMMERSETT
1878, 4, 27. Wm. & Tish recrq
1878, 12, 28. Mary C. & Rachel E. recrq
1896, 4, 24. Leah dropped from mbrp

SUNDERLAND
1897, 8, 28. Richard dropped from mbrp
1901, 1, 31. Richard recrq
1901, 4, 25. Louisa recrq
1908, 7, 30. Margaret dropped from mbrp

SWAGGARD
1881, 1, 29. William recrq

SWALLOW
1879, 12, 27. James recrq
1895, 5, 25. Mary J., Rosa May & Alberta recrq
1901, 1, 31. Mary Jane & Rosa May recrq

SWEET
1876, 3, 25. Elizabeth recrq
1899, 7, 27. Elizabeth dropped from mbrp

SWICK
1879, 12, 27. Peter E. recrq

SWIHART
1877, 2, 24. Sarah recrq
1877, 12, 29. Frank recrq
1881, 12, 31. Lucinda dropped from mbrp

SWISHER
1878, 11, 30. Enos & w, Louisa, recrq
1879, 12, 27. Enos dropped from mbrp
1880, 3, 27. Amanda recrq

TACKLER
1897, 8, 28. James dropped from mbrp

TAHAMMONT
1914, 3, 25. John Johnson recrq

TAKE
1911, 8, 31. Mary recrq

TEMPLE
1878, 4, 27. Neuten C. recrq
1879, 1, 25. Jane recrq
1879, 1, 25. Wm. recrq
1879, 3, 29. Louisa & Ida recrq
1908, 12, 31. N. C. dropped from mbrp

TENNIS
1891, 4, 25. Laura recrq

THATCHER
1882, 2, 25. Stephen, Mary M., Rufus & Anna recrq
1884, 9, 27. Mary [Thacher] relrq
1899, 7, 27. Rufus & Anna dropped from mbrp
1903, 9, 24. Eva dropped from mbrp
1911, 11, 30. Cassie recrq
1928, 2, 23. Lon & Clyde recrq
1928, 2, 23. Gordon Estell recrq

THOMAS
1884, 11, 29. Alfred dis disunity
1885, 1, 31. Emma relrq
1892, 3, 26. Ellsworth recrq
1896, 2, 29. Robert Elsworth & Irena recrq
1899, 7, 27. R. E. dropped from mbrp
1903, 9, 24. Rosa A. dropped from mbrp
1908, 2, 28. Anna recrq
1913, 2, 27. David H. recrq

THOMPSON
1878, 4, 27. Eliza & R. J. recrq
1878, 4, 27. Richard R. recrq
1879, 10, 25. Alfred & Jacob R. recrq
1879, 12, 27. Martha recrq
1885, 4, 25. Amanda dropped from mbrp
1886, 9, 25. Liza J. & R. J. dropped from mbrp

THORNBURG
1878, 2, 23. Josiah recrq
1886, 5, 29. Josiah recrq
1889, 5, 25. Wm. W. rocf Walnut Ridge MM, Ind., dtd 1889,4,20
1890, 8, 30. W. W. gct Greenwood MM, Ind.

THORNLIN
1895, 6, 29. Wm. A. recrq

TIMMONS
1879, 12, 27. Wm. recrq
1879, 12, 27. Tillie recrq

TINDOL
1888, 5, 26. Miles recrq

TODD
1876, 2, 26. Margaret J. recrq
1876, 2, 26. Willie recrq
1882, 1, 28. Margaret J. recrq

TOLAND
1913, 9, 25. Mrs. Jennie recrq

TOMLINSON
1901, 6, 27. Edward & Birdie recrq
1914, 4, 29. Edward dropped from mbrp
1914, 4, 29. Birdie dropped from mbrp
1914, 6, 24. Fred H. [Tomohlen] & w, Susie, & dt, Ruth & Martha Helen, recrq

TOUNHUSON
1912, 4, 25. Flo, Gertie, Oral & Cale recrq

TOURS
1882, 11, 25. Belle recrq

TOWLEY
1882, 1, 28. Nellie & Chloie recrq
1884, 11, 29. Chloe I. Philips & ch, Nellie & Clifford Towey, & Charley G., Luni I. & Lucy Eveline Philips, rocf Fairmount MM, dtd 1884,11,12
1899, 7, 27. Nellie dropped from mbrp

TRACY
1879, 12, 27. Dora recrq
1885, 4, 25. Frederick dropped from mbrp
1901, 3, 28. Ida recrq

TRADER
1926, 10, 28. Oscar H. & w, Ada N., & dt, Reta Ruth, recrq
1928, 4, 28. Rev. Oscar recrq
1930, 10, 30. Oscar H. & Reta R. gct Fairmount MM, Ind.

TRICKEY
1878, 4, 27. Lewis recrq

TROUP
1878, 1, 26. John & Sarah recrq
1886, 11, 27. John & Sarah dropped from mbrp

TULLIS
1878, 1, 26. Laura recrq
1879, 4, 26. Laura dis

TUMBLESON
1905, 2, 23. Zala recrq
1908, 7, 30. Lola dropped from mbrp

TURNER
1879, 12, 27. James recrq
1879, 12, 27. Hannah recrq
1907, 3, 28. Calvin & Lydia recrq
1912, 2, 29. Lela recrq
1926, 2, 25. Isabell & Arlo recrq
1931, 3, 26. Calvin & w, Lydia, & ch, Arlo & [Isabel, relrq

TUTTLE
1879, 3, 29. Nancy recrq
1880, 3, 27. Nancy E. & Joseph recrq
1880, 3, 27. Martha recrq
1880, 3, 27. Lucy recrq
1880, 3, 27. William recrq
1880, 3, 27. Mary recrq
1886, 9, 25. Nancy E. dropped from mbrp
1886, 9, 25. Martha dropped from mbrp
1886, 9, 25. Mary dropped from mbrp
1889, 10, 26. Priscilla, Eliza Ann & Samuel H. recrq
1891, 3, 28. Dora & Ella recrq
1892, 3, 26. James recrq

TYO
1897, 3, 27. Thomas recrq
1899, 7, 27. Thomas [Tyle] dropped from mbrp

UNCAPHER (See VUCAPHER)
1881, 2, 26. Katie recrq
1886, 2, 27. Dora & Lydia recrq

UNDERWOOD
1880, 1, 31. Esli recrq
1880, 1, 31. Wm. Luther recrq
1880, 1, 31. Elizabeth recrq

UPDEGROVE
1927, 3, 30. Mary Ellen, Richard, Robert & Margaret Ann, recrq
1929, 12, 26. Glenn & Minnie & Sally Ann recrq
1931, 4, 30. Sally Mae recrq

UPP
1879, 3, 29. Samuel & Catharine recrq

URICH
1881, 3, 26. Mary A. recrq
1886, 9, 25. Mary dropped from mbrp
1899, 7, 27. Cyrus dropped from mbrp

URTON
1878, 4, 27. John K. & John K. Jr. recrq
1878, 4, 27. Charles recrq
1878, 4, 27. Alida recrq
1878, 4, 27. John, Flora & Tilla recrq
1878, 5, 25. Wm. recrq
1878, 11, 30. David recrq
1878, 11, 30. Isaac recrq
1878, 11, 30. Manta recrq
1878, 11, 30. Julia A. recrq
1879, 6, 28. Chas. recrq
1884, 2, 23. Wm. recrq
1890, 3, 26. Wm. dropped from mbrp
1914, 12, 30. Stella recrq

UTTER
1877, 2, 24. Sarah recrq
1878, 1, 26. Alice recrq
1884, 2, 23. Vic recrq

VANCLAVE
1878, 4, 27. Luther & Retta recrq
1891, 3, 28. Luther [Van Cleaf] gct Springfield MM

VANDYKE
1898, 10, 27. Jno. Jr. dropped from mbrp
1901, 7, 25. Pleasant & James dropped from mbrp

VANGUNDY
1897, 8, 28. Chas. E. dropped from mbrp
1897, 8, 28. Myrtle dropped from mbrp
1897, 8, 28. Daniel dropped from mbrp

VANVOINS
1908, 7, 30. Naomi dropped from mbrp

VOSE
1893, 6, 24. Harry recrq

VUCAPHER
1914, 4, 29. Catie dropped from mbrp

WADE
1882, 7, 29. Urzilla recrq
1888, 5, 26. Ishum recrq
1889, 1, 26. Jennie recrq
1893, 3, 25. Nora E. recrq
1894, 6, 30. Cora & Maude recrq
1899, 7, 27. Ishum dropped from mbrp
1907, 1, 5. Isom & Susan recrq
1908, 7, 30. Robert dropped from mbrp
1912, 2, 29. Harry & Velma recrq
1912, 4, 25. Chas. recrq
1914, 4, 29. Jennie dropped from mbrp

WAGONER
1878, 4, 27. John A. & Sarah recrq
1880, 1, 31. Mary [Wagner] recrq
1881, 1, 29. Rosa [Wagers] recrq
1885, 4, 25. Rosa [Wagers] dropped from mbrp
1903, 4, 26. Fred & Emma [Wagnor] recrq
1905, 11, 30. Harry & w, Jesse, & ch recrq
1908, 7, 30. Harry & fam dropped from mbrp

WAIL
1892, 5, 28. J. M. relrq

WAKEFIELD
1876, 2, 26. Joseph gct West Branch MM

WALCUTT
1899, 4, 27. E., Hattie, Arthur, Ida & Ethel recrq
1899, 7, 27. Erastus & Arthur dropped from mbrp
1914, 4, 29. Mattie, Ida & Ethel [Walcut] dropped from mbrp
1914, 4, 29. Janet dropped from mbrp

WALKER
1894, 3, 31. Rosa recrq
1899, 5, 25. Alfred recrq
1908, 7, 30. Alfred dropped from mbrp
1914, 4, 29. Rosa dropped from mbrp
1930, 1, 30. Ruth Madona [Welker] & Walter Edwin recrq

WALLACE
1877, 2, 24. Hudson recrq
1877, 3, 31. Albert recrq
1882, 2, 25. Abraham & Mary recrq
1888, 1, 27. Carrie A. & Eva recrq
1888, 2, 25. Elizabeth recrq
1889, 5, 30. Martha J. [Wallack] recrq
1891, 11, 28. Wm. relrq
1897, 1, 30. Geo. recrq
1897, 1, 30. Nellie & Bertha
1897, 8, 28. Martha J. [Wallick] dropped from mbrp
1899, 7, 27. Geo. & Chanic dropped from mbrp
1899, 7, 27. Abraham & Mary dropped from mbrp
1903, 9, 24. Albert dropped from mbrp
1907, 2, 28. Rose Jenett recrq
1908, 2, 29. Mollie & Huldah recrq
1912, 4, 25. Bell D. & dt, Flossie, recrq
1912, 4, 25. Harrison recrq
1912, 4, 25. Mary recrq
1914, 8, 24. Mrs. Belle relrq

WALLER
1879, 12, 27. Phebe E. recrq
1887, 5, 28. Sylvia recrq

WALLING
1898, 10, 27. Geo. & Sarah dropped from mbrp

WALLMAN
1884, 2, 23. Annie recrq

WALLON
1888, 5, 26. Hiram, Emma & Michael recrq

WALLS
1897, 5, 29. Minnie recrq
1926, 2, 25. Dorothy recrq
1927, 3, 30. John recrq

WALTER
1879, 11, 29. Martha recrq
1912, 4, 25. Viola & Mary Luella recrq
1912, 5, 30. Anna recrq

WALTZ
1880, 3, 27. Edward recrq
1880, 3, 27. Henry recrq
1880, 3, 27. Amanuel recrq
1880, 3, 27. Mary A. recrq
1886, 9, 25. Henry dropped from mbrp
1891, 2, 28. Jennie & Mary S. recrq
1891, 4, 25. Emanuel, Naomi & Jennie recrq

WAPPNER
1907, 11, 28. George H. & w recrq

WARD
1881, 2, 26. Susan [Warde] recrq
1881, 2, 26. Robert [Warde] recrq
1886, 3, 27. Geo. W. recrq
1887, 8, 27. Lydia recrq
1894, 2, 24. Ella recrq
1899, 7, 27. Ella & Lydia dropped from mbrp
1927, 3, 30. Edward Eugene, Raymond Richard, Ervin Harold, Margaret Kalbren & Betty Jane, recrq

WARTS
1891, 3, 28. Isaac recrq

WATTS
1879, 12, 27. Wm. Wesley recrq
1880, 1, 31. Thos. W. recrq
1880, 1, 31. Annie C. recrq
1880, 1, 31. Susannah recrq
1880, 10, 30. Minnie & Rhoda A. recrq
1884, 9, 27. Wm. & fam gct Portland MM

WEAGLEY
1886, 4, 24. Hiley recrq

WEAVER
1904, 8, 1. Helen Delilah b
1906, 5, 25. Esther Opal b
----, --, --. Jennie Mercile ----------

1894, 2, 24. Catharine recrq
1914, 4, 29. Catherine dropped from mbrp
1928, 2, 23. Eva, Edna Elnora, Earl Ray & Cecile Inez recrq
1928, 2, 23. Gale & Harold recrq

WEBB
1877, 2, 24. Josephine & Alice recrq
1881, 1, 29. Annie E., Charlotte, Geo., Wm. & Elias, recrq
1885, 4, 25. Wm. dropped from mbrp
1886, 9, 25. Alice dropped from mbrp
1894, 2, 24. Ella recrq
1899, 7, 27. Josephine & Allice dropped from mbrp
1908, 7, 30. Ella dropped from mbrp

WEBSTER
1878, 5, 25. Aurelius & Ellen recrq
1878, 5, 25. Charley recrq
1889, 1, 26. Mira & Joseph rocf Wabash MM, Ind.

WEDGE
1878, 1, 26. John, Hannah & Susan recrq
1891, 4, 25. Chas., Susan, Mary & Sarah recrq
1892, 5, 28. Susan relrq

WEEKS
1888, 2, 25. Mary dropped from mbrp

WEISENBORN
1930, 4, 24. Thos. & w, Clarissa, & ch, Cordelia & Billy, rocf Lynn MM, Ind.
1931, 11, 26. Thos. & w, Clara, & ch, Cordelia & Wm. relrq

WELCH
1878, 1, 26. Sarah recrq
1878, 2, 23. Charles recrq
1879, 11, 29. Frank recrq
1879, 12, 27. Amanda recrq
1880, 1, 31. Mary & Ruth P. recrq
1880, 1, 31. Geo. W. recrq
1880, 1, 31. Elcie recrq
1882, 1, 28. Catharine recrq
1882, 2, 25. Viola recrq
1885, 4, 25. Wm. & Amanda dropped from mbrp
1890, 3, 26. Catharine dropped from mbrp
1894, 3, 31. Alonzo & Elizabeth recrq
1897, 4, 24. Wm. [Welsch] recrq
1897, 8, 28. Wm. dropped from mbrp
1899, 7, 27. Mary, Ruth, Viola, Alonzo & Elizabeth dropped from mbrp

WELEASY
1886, 11, 27. Chas. dropped from mbrp

WELLS
1888, 5, 26. George & Belle recrq

WERTZ
1881, 3, 26. Susanna recrq
1882, 2, 25. Fanny [Wert] recrq
1886, 11, 27. Nancy [Wert] dropped from mbrp
1890, 3,26. Jennie [Wert] dropped from mbrp
1899, 7, 27. Fanny dropped from mbrp

WERTZ , continued
1903, 9, 24. Elmer dropped from mbrp
1908, 7, 30. Lucy & Elmer dropped from mbrp

WEST
1892, 4, 30. Wm. & w, Mary, rocf West Grove MM, Ind., dtd 1892,4,9
1894, 11, 24. Wm. & Mary gct West Grove MM, Ind.

WESTERFIELD
1876, 2, 26. Wm. & Ida recrq
1877, 12, 29. Minesca recrq
1880, 4, 24. Wm. F. & w relrq
1899, 7, 27. Manerva [Westfield] dropped from mbrp

WESTLAKE
1886, 5, 29. Emma recrq

WESTRICK
1897, 8, 28. Willis dropped from mbrp

WHARTON
1888, 5, 26. Jesse & Elizabeth recrq

WHEELER
1879, 5, 31. Thomas & Clara recrq
1880, 12, 25. Mamie recrq

WHETSTONE
1879, 12, 27. Mary C. recrq

WHITACRE
1878, 4, 27. Samuel B., Annie & Eliza recrq
1878, 4, 27. Benjamin F. recrq
1878, 4, 27. Eliza recrq
1878, 4, 27. Nancy recrq
1878, 4, 27. Harlan recrq

WHITCRAFT
1912, 4, 25. Dora recrq
1914, 12, 30. Daisy recrq

WHITE
1889, 11, 30. Ruth recrq
1915, 2, 24. James N. recrq

WIBLE
1876, 2, 26. John J. recrq

WIBURN
1908, 2, 29. Bessie recrq

WICKEL
1880, 4, 24. Rebecca & ch, Arabell, Leurctta & Rosa Ellen, rocf Center MM, dtd 1880,1, 14

WILCKINSON
1878, 4, 27. Sirus & Rebecca recrq

WILE
1894, 3, 31. Wm., Emma & Eva recrq
1899, 7, 27. W. A. & Emma dropped from mbrp

WILL
1891, 1, 31. Israel A. recrq
1903, 9, 24. Mary [Wills] dropped from mbrp
1911, 4, 27. Mary recrq

WILLEY
1892, 3, 26. Samuel & w, Dora, gct Greensfork MM, Ind.

WILLIAMS
1891, 4, 25. Sallie dropped from mbrp
1899, 7, 27. Andrew dropped from mbrp
1904, 7, 28. P. B. & w recrq
1914, 4, 29. Andrew dropped from mbrp

WILLIAMSON
1885, 9, 26. Sarah relrq

WILSON
1877, 2, 24. Laura recrq
1877, 3, 31. Joseph recrq
1880, 1, 31. Cora recrq
1896, 2, 29. Chas. M. recrq
1897, 1, 30. Vergie recrq
1897, 8, 28. Fletcher & Emeline dropped from mbrp
1898, 11, 24. Theodore & Mary recrq
1899, 7, 27. Chas. dropped from mbrp
1906, 7, 26. J. W. & w relrq
1911, 4, 27. Nellie recrq
1911, 4, 27. Anna recrq
1912, 4, 25. Samuel M. & Mack recrq
1928, 2, 23. Ruth recrq
1928, 3, 29. Earl, Oline & John recrq

WINFIELD
1878, 4, 27. John recrq
1878, 4, 27. W. E. recrq

WINKLE
1909, 4, 29. Catharine relrq

WINTERS
1889, 5, 30. Geo. L. recrq
1897, 8, 28. Geo. L. dropped from mbrp

WISE
1878, 1, 26. Susan recrq

WISENBORN
1925, 12, 31. Thos. & Clara & ch, Cordelia & Wm., gct Hemlock MM

WITHERO
1895, 4, 27. Lloyd recrq

WITTIG
1877, 11, 24. Wm. recrq
1882, 4, 29. Emma [Witty] recrq
1894, 4, 28. Wm. H. & w, Emma, relrq

WOLF
1891, 12, 21. Albert dis disunity
1903, 1, 29. Martha Star recrq
1907, 2, 28. Grace recrq
1907, 2, 28. Bertha May recrq
1912, 4, 25. G. Wesley recrq

WOLFORD
1877, 3, 31. W. M. recrq
1886, 9, 25. W. M. dropped from mbrp
1894, 2, 24. Susan recrq

WOLLET
1931, 4, 30. Owen recrq
1931, 4, 30. Robert Owen recrq

WOODS
1928, 2, 23. Melvin & Iva recrq
1928, 2, 23. Princess recrq

WOOLEM
1886, 5, 29. Joseph recrq

WORDON
1881, 1, 29. Anna recrq

WORTH
1892, 3, 26. Nettie recrq

WORTMAN
1828, 11, 28. Lester & Elva recrq

WRIGHT
1878, 3, 30. Wm. B. recrq
1881, 3, 26. J. W. recrq
1886, 9, 25. Wm. B. dropped from mbrp
1886, 9, 25. G. W. dropped from mbrp
1888, 5, 26. Alice J. recrq
1891, 4, 25. John & Inis recrq
1892, 3, 26. Emma relrq
1903, 9, 24. John & Iva dropped from mbrp
1926, 7, 29. Caroline relrq
1926, 9, 30. Rev. John I. & fam gct Portland MM, Ind.

WROTH
1907, 3, 28. Kenneth & Mary recrq

YEISLEY
1879, 12, 27. John P. recrq
1884, 5, 31. John C. relrq

YOCUM
1888, 5, 26. John H. & Martha recrq

YOH
1910, 10, 27. Ruby recrq
1911, 4, 27. Savilla recrq

YOUNG
1876, 2, 26. Jennie & Mary recrq
1879, 3, 29. Harvey recrq
1880, 1, 31. Newton recrq
1886, 5, 29. Geo., C. B. & Scott recrq
1889, 3, 30. Miranda recrq
1891, 4, 25. Lillie & Myra recrq
1894, 5, 26. Mary M. recrq
1895, 9, 21. Mary M. relrq
1897, 8, 28. Chas. B., George & Scott dropped from mbrp
1897, 8, 28. Miranda dropped from mbrp
1900, 3, 29. Mrs. Marian recrq
1901, 7, 25. Matilda dropped from mbrp
1902, 5, 29. Mary A. relrq
1912, 5, 30. Wm., Lowell H. & Margaret M. recrq
1927, 5, 25. Lowell dropped from mbrp
1927, 5, 25. Will dropped from mbrp

ZANER
1880, 1, 31. Anna recrq
1896, 2, 29. Annie recrq
1897, 8, 28. Annie dropped from mbrp

ZEHISTER
1899, 7, 27. Joseph & Jane dropped from mbrp

ZIMMERMAN
1891, 2, 28. R. L. & M. D. recrq
1891, 4, 25. R. L. & Mary D. recrq
1903, 9, 24. Norah dropped from mbrp

ZINNBECK
1904, 6, 30. Dora Collins relrq

* * * * * * * *

WALLS
1901, 3, 28. Emma recrq
1907, 2, 28. Grace M. [Wall] recrq
1911, 4, 27. Ethel recrq
1914, 12, 30. Jessie recrq

Page numbers without parenthesis refer to family groups. Numbers in parenthesis refer to individuals mentioned in places other than their own family groups. Items which contain more than one family name, and for that reason appear in two or more groups, are indexed only once under each name